Contemporary Authors

Contemporary Authors

A BIO-BIBLIOGRAPHICAL GUIDE TO
CURRENT AUTHORS AND THEIR WORKS

CYNTHIA R. FADOOL

Editor

volumes 57-60

GALE RESEARCH COMPANY • BOOK TOWER • DETROIT, MICHIGAN 48226

CONTEMPORARY AUTHORS

Published By
Gale Research Company, Book Tower, Detroit, Michigan 48226
Each Year's Volumes Are Cumulated and Revised About Five Years Later

Frederick G. Ruffner, *Publisher*   James M. Ethridge, *Editorial Director*

Clare D. Kinsman, *General Editor, Contemporary Authors*

Cynthia R. Fadool, *Editor*
Alexander James Roman, *Associate Editor*
Jane Bowden, Robin Farbman, Frances Carol Locher, Christine Nasso,
Nancy M. Rusin, Adele C. Sarkissian, and Frank Michael Soley, *Assistant Editors*

Anne Commire, *Consultant*
Eunice Bergin, *Copy Editor*
Laura Bryant, *Operations Supervisor*
Daphne Cox, *Production Manager*

WRITERS

Linda Cairo, Laurelyn Niebuhr,
Mary Reif Stevenson, Benjamin True

EDITORIAL ASSISTANTS

John Carey, Norma Sawaya, Shirley Seip

CONTEMPORARY AUTHORS

Indicates that a listing has been compiled from secondary sources believed to be reliable, but has not been personally verified for this edition by the author sketched.

AARONS, Edward S(idney) 1916-1975

1916—June 16, 1975; American author of travel, suspense, and adventure novels. Obituaries: *New York Times*, June 20, 1975; *Washington Post*, June 21, 1975.

* * *

ABBAS, Khwaja Ahmad 1914-

PERSONAL: Born July 6, 1914, in Panipat, India; son of Khwaja (a businessman) and Masroora (Khatoon) Ghulam-Us-Sibtain; married Mujtabai Khatoon, December, 1942 (died, 1958); children: Ushi Abbas Jain (daughter). *Education:* Aligarh Muslim University, B.A., 1933, LL.B., 1935. *Politics:* Progressive, liberal. *Religion:* Islam. *Home:* Philomena Lodge, Church Rd., Juhu, Bombay-400 054, India. *Agent:* K. P. Punnoose, B-4/90, Safdarjang Enclave, New Delhi 110016, India. *Office:* Naya Sansar, B-35 North Bombay Society, Church Rd., Juhu, Bombay-400 054, India.

CAREER: Bombay Chronicle, Bombay, India, reporter and sub-editor, 1935-39, editor of Sunday edition and columnist, 1939-47; *Blitz* (weekly newsmagazine), Bombay, India, columnist, 1947—; author and novelist, screenwriter, and film producer and director. Director, National Education & Information Films Ltd., 1948-75. *Member:* Film Writers Association (president, 1962-63), Film Directors Association (president, 1963-64), Film Forum (president, 1974-75). *Awards, honors:* President of India's Gold Medal, 1964, for film, "Shehar Aur Sapna"; recipient of robe of honor from Government of Haryana (India), 1966; Padma Shri from Government of India, 1967; named honorary special magistrate of Bombay, India, 1974.

WRITINGS: Outside India (travelogue), Hali Publishing House (India), 1939; *An Indian Looks at America,* Thacker (Bombay), 1943; *Tomorrow Is Ours* (novel), Popular Book Depot (Bombay), 1943; (translator) Krishan Chandar, *I Cannot Die: A Story of Bengal,* Kutub (India), 1943; *Let India Fight for Freedom,* Sound Magazine (India), 1943; *. . . And One Did Not Come Back! The Story of the Congress Medical Mission to China,* Sound Magazine, 1944; (with N. G. Yog) *Report to Gandhiji,* Hind Kitabs (Bombay), 1944; *Not All Lies!,* Rajkamal, 1945; *Defeat for Death,* Padmaja (India), 1946; *Invitation to Immortality* (one-act play), Padma, 1946; *Blood and Stones* (novella), Hind Kitabs, 1947; *Rice and Other Stories,* Kutub, 1947; *I*

Write as I Feel, Hind Kitabs, 1948; *Kashmir Fights for Freedom,* Kutub (Bombay), 1948; *Cages of Freedom and Other Stories,* Hind Kitabs, 1952; *In the Image of Mao Tse-tung* (travel), People's Publishing House (Bombay), 1953; *Inqilab* (novel), Jaico (Bombay), 1955; *One Thousand Nights on a Bed of Stones and Other Stories,* Jaico, 1957.

Face to Face with Krushchov (biography), Rajpal & Sons (India), 1960; *Till We Reach the Stars: The Story of Yuri Gagarin,* Asia Publishing House, 1961; *Black Sun and Other Stories,* Jaico, 1963; *Indira Gandhi: Return of the Red Rose,* Popular Prakashan (Bombay), 1966; *When Night Falls* (novel), Orient Paperbacks (New Delhi), 1968; *Divided Heart* (novel), New Light Publishers (New Delhi), 1968; *The Most Beautiful Woman in the World,* New Light Publishers, 1968; *Mera Naam Joker,* Hind Pocket Books (India), 1970; *Maria* (novel), Hind Pocket Books, 1971; *That Woman* (biography), Indian Book Company (New Delhi), 1973; *Bobby* (novel), Sterling Publishers (New Delhi), 1973; *Boy Meets Girl* (novel), Sterling Publishers, 1973; *Jawaharlal Nehru* (biography), National Council of Educational Research & Training (New Delhi), 1974; (with R. K. Karanjia) *Face to Face with Indira Gandhi,* Chetana Publications (New Delhi), 1974; *Distant Dream* (novel), Sterling Publishers, 1975; *How Films Are Made,* National Book Trust, 1975.

WORK IN PROGRESS: I Am Not an Island, an autobiography.

SIDELIGHTS: Abbas, who traveled twice round the world, told *CA:* "Highbrow literary critics and film critics have sometimes sneeringly labelled my short stories and novels—and my films—as 'mere journalese.' Obviously, the fact that most of [the stories] owe their inspiration to real-life incidents chronicled in the daily press is sufficient to put them beyond the pale of literary (or artistic) creation.

"I have no quarrel with the critics. Maybe, I am an un-redeemed journalist and reporter, masquerading as a writer of fiction, even as a maker of feature films. But I have always believed that while the inner life of a man undoubtedly is, and should be, the primary concern of literature, this inner personal life impinges upon the life of the community—and of humanity—at every critical point in human experience. A man is not what his destiny has made him, but what the social and economic circumstances of his life have made him.

"'No man is an island . . .,' said John Donne, and one may add that even if he was, no island is free from the inroads of the sea, as no man is free from the impact of the life around him."

* * *

ABBAZIA, Patrick 1937-

PERSONAL: Surname pronounced "uh-bay-zee-uh"; born July 8, 1937, in Brooklyn, N.Y.; son of Joseph (a compositor) and Patricia Margaret (Bianco) Abbazia; married Catherine Eleanor Del Gaudio (a teacher), January 17, 1976. *Education:* Brooklyn College (now Brooklyn College of the City University of New York), B.A., 1959; University of California, Berkeley, M.A., 1960; Columbia University, Ph.D., 1972. *Religion:* Catholic. *Office:* Kingsborough Community College of the City University of New York, Brooklyn, N.Y. 11235.

CAREER: Kingsborough Community College of the City University of New York, Brooklyn, N.Y., associate professor of history, 1968—. *Member:* U.S. Naval Institute.

WRITINGS: Mr. Roosevelt's Navy: The Private War of the U.S. Atlantic Fleet, 1939-1942, Naval Institute Press, 1975. Contributor to *Dictionary of American Biography*, and to *Naval Institute Proceedings* and *Community College Social Science Quarterly*.

WORK IN PROGRESS: Initiating research for a book on the Spanish-American War.

AVOCATIONAL INTERESTS: Reading, professional football, folk and country music, cards, travel.

* * *

ABBOTT, Raymond H(erbert) 1942-

PERSONAL: Born April 21, 1942, in Newburyport, Mass.; son of Myron E. (a ship worker) and Evelyn (Foley) Abbott. *Education:* University of Massachusetts, B.A., 1965; University of Kentucky, graduate study, 1967-68. *Home address:* P.O. Box 91, West Newbury, Mass. 01985. *Office:* Room 5, City Hall, Newburyport, Mass. 01950.

CAREER: Vista volunteer with Rosebud Sioux tribe of Indians, Rosebud, S.D., 1965-66; Community Development director in Transitional Housing Program for Sioux tribe at Rosebud, 1966-67; elementary schoolteacher in Lost Creek, Ky., 1967-68; social worker for city, in Louisville, Ky., 1967-68; Commonwealth of Massachusetts, social worker in Pittsfield, 1969-70, in South End, Boston, 1970-73, in Newburyport, 1973—. *Member:* Author's Guild of Author's League of America.

WRITINGS: Paha Sapa (novel; title means "The Black Hills"), Akwesasne Notes, 1975. Also author of "The Axing of Leo White Hat," and "Black Horse," novels, as yet unpublished. Contributor to *North American Review, Blue Cloud Quarterly*, and *Phoenix*.

WORK IN PROGRESS: Come Back Tomorrow, a humorous novel.

SIDELIGHTS: Abbott writes: "Much of my inspiration . . . for my first three novels came from living for several years on a Sioux reservation in South Dakota. . . . My interest is to become a good story teller." *Avocational interests:* Travel (Latin America), flying (private pilot).

* * *

ABEL, Theodora M(ead) 1899-

PERSONAL: Born September 9, 1899, in Newport, R.I.; daughter of G. Robert (a lawyer) and M. Elsie (Cleveland) Mead; married Theodore Abel (a university professor), November 9, 1923; children: Peter, Caroline (Mrs. Pierre Lalaire), Zita (Mrs. John Emerson). *Education:* Vassar College, A.B., 1921; University of Paris, Diploma in Psychology, 1923; Columbia University, M.A., 1924; Ph.D., 1925. *Politics:* Democrat. *Religion:* Unitarian Universalist. *Home:* 4200 Sunningdale Ave. N.E., Albuquerque, N.M. 87110. *Office:* 7000 Cutler Ave. N.E., Albuquerque, N.M. 87110.

CAREER: University of Illinois, Urbana, instructor in psychology, 1925-26; Sarah Lawrence College, Bronxville, N.Y., instructor in psychology, 1929-35; Manhattan Trade School for Girls, New York, N.Y., director of research, 1936-40; New York State Department of Mental Hygiene, Lethworth Village, N.Y., chief psychologist, 1940-46; Postgraduate Center for Mental Health, New York, N.Y., director of psychology, 1947-71; University of New Mexico, Albuquerque, clinical associate psychiatrist, 1971—. Consultant, Columbia University Office of Naval Reserve, 1947-49, Veterans Administration Hospital, East Orange, N.J., 1963-68; research psychologist, Bellevue Hospital, New York, N.Y., 1949-51; adjunct professor, Long Island University, 1951-54; chief of family therapy service, Child Guidance Center, Albuquerque, N.M., 1971—. *Member:* American Psychological Association (fellow), American Association for the Advancement of Science, American Orthopsychiatric Association (vice-president, 1955-56), American Psychopathological Association (vice-president, 1953-54), New York Society of Clinical Psychologists (president, 1952-53). *Awards, honors:* Psychologist of the year award from New York Society of Clinical Psychologists, 1972.

WRITINGS: (With Elaine F. Kinder) *The Subnormal Adolescent Girl*, Columbia University Press, 1940; (with others) *Facial Deformities and Plastic Surgery*, C. C Thomas, 1954; *Psychological Testing in Cultural Contexts*, College and University Press, 1973; (with Rhoda Metraux) *Culture and Psychotherapy*, College and University Press, 1975; (contributor) Lewis L. Wolberg and Marvin Aronson, editors, *Group Psychotherapy, 1974*, Stratton Intercontinental Medical Book Corp., in press.

WORK IN PROGRESS: Research on multifamily therapy.

* * *

ABER, William M(cKee) 1929-

PERSONAL: Born July 29, 1929, in Pittsburgh, Pa.; son of William Clarence (an engineer) and Jean (a librarian; maiden name, McKee) Aber; married Sarah Sterrett (a daycare center educational director), February 4, 1952; children: Katherine (Mrs. Michael Gaylor), John, James, Ann. *Education:* College of Wooster, B.A., 1951; University of Pittsburgh, M.Ed., 1956; Pittsburgh Theological Seminary, M.Div., 1956. *Politics:* Democratic. *Home:* 211 Walnut St., Greensburg, Pa. 15601. *Office:* Redstone Presbytery, 33 East Pittsburgh St., Greensburg, Pa. 15601.

CAREER: Ordained Presbyterian minister, 1956; pastor in Gibsonia, Pa., 1956-59, in Oil City, Pa., 1959-64, and in Pittsburgh, Pa., 1964-72; Redstone Presbytery, Greensburg, Pa., executive presbyter, 1972—. President of board of directors of Young Men's Christian Association, 1960-64, and North Hills Youth Ministry, 1969; member of board of Passavant Hospital, 1966-72, and United Presbyterian Health Education and Welfare Association, 1973—.

Military service: U.S. Marine Corps Reserve, 1951-53; became captain. U.S. Naval Reserve, Chaplain Corps, 1956—; now lieutenant. *Awards, honors:* D.D., Westminster College, 1967.

WRITINGS—Nonfiction: *The Gap*, C.S.S. Publishing, 1971; *Avenues of Advent*, C.S.S. Publishing, 1972; *A Lenten Zoo*, C.S.S. Publishing, 1973.

* * *

ABRAHAMS, Howard Phineas 1904-

PERSONAL: Born July 12, 1904, in Yonkers, N.Y.; son of Joseph L. and Sarah (Friedman) Abrahams; married Florence Blostein, July 13, 1926; children: Allen, Elinor (Mrs. Thomas Seaman). *Education:* Cornell University, B.S., 1925; attended University of Florida, 1925-26, and Cumberland University, 1926. *Politics:* Republican. *Religion:* Jewish. *Home address:* Lake Shore Dr., Lake Lincolndale, RD #5, Mahopac, N.Y. 10541; and 45 West 54th St., New York, N.Y. 10019.

CAREER: Rothschild's (department store), Ithaca, N.Y., advertising manager, 1928-29; *Bloomingdale's*, New York, N.Y., advertising manager, 1929; Ludwig Baumann (furniture store), New York, N.Y., advertising manager, 1929-42; Office of Price Administration, Washington, D.C., chief of retail home furnishings, 1942-43; employed with *New York Times,* New York, N.Y., 1943-45; I. J. Fox (specialty store), New York, N.Y., advertising director, 1945-46; National Retail Merchants Association, New York, N.Y., manager of sales promotion division, 1946-54; Television Bureau of Advertisers, New York, N.Y., vice-president, 1955-70; Retail TV Advisors, New York, N.Y., owner, 1970—. Lecturer, New York University, 1945, City College of the City University of New York, 1945-50, Tobe Coburn School, 1955. Co-chairman of U.S. Famine Commission, 1946; member of board of directors, 45 West 54th Corp., 1971—, Interamer Research Corp., 1971—. *Member:* Advertisers Club, Radio-TV Society, Ye Hosts, Cornell Society of Hotelmen, Homefurnishings Club, Cornell Club (New York), Phi Delta Pi, Eta Mu Pi.

WRITINGS: Analysis of Publicity Expenses, National Retail Merchants Association, 1946; *Best Retail Advertisements,* National Retail Merchants Association, 1946; *How to Use TV Successfully,* Cox, 1961; *How to Write Retail Advertising Copy,* National Retail Merchants Association, 1961; *The Sandwich Concept,* National Retail Merchants Association, 1966; *More Sales, More Profits: The TV Way,* Cox, 1971; *Increasing Your Sales with Radio,* Cox, 1971; *Making TV Pay Off,* Fairchild, 1975. Also author of *Sales Promotion Calendar,* 1946. Contributor to journals in his field. Editor, *Retail Broadcaster,* 1973—.

* * *

ABRAHAMS, Peter (Henry) 1919-

PERSONAL: Born March 19, 1919 at Vrededorp, near Johannesburg, South Africa; son of James Henry and Angelina (DuPlessis) Abrahams; married Dorothy Pennington, 1942 (marriage dissolved, 1948); married Daphne Elizabeth Miller (an artist), June 1, 1948; children: (second marriage) Anne, Aron, Naomi. *Education:* Attended St. Peter's College and Teachers' Training College. *Home:* Red Hills, St. Andrews, Jamaica, West Indies. *Agent:* Curtis Brown Ltd., 60 East 56th St., New York, N.Y. 10022; and John Farquharson Ltd., 15 Red Lion Sq., London WC1R 4QW, England.

CAREER: Began working, as a tinsmith's helper, at the age of nine; attended schools between periods of working at jobs such as kitchen helper, dishwasher, porter, and clerk; failed in his attempt to start a school near Capetown for poor Africans; for a short time worked as an editor in Durban; in 1939, to reach England, he took work as a stoker, and spent two years at sea; correspondent for the London *Observer* and the *New York Herald Tribune* (New York and Paris), 1952-64; commissioned by British Government in 1955 to write a book on Jamaica; emigrated to Jamaica in 1956; regular radio news commentator in Jamaica, 1957—; editor of the *West Indian Economist,* Jamaica, 1958-62, and radio commentator for the "West Indian News" Program, 1958-62. *Member:* International P.E.N., Society of Authors, Authors League.

WRITINGS—Novels: *Song of the City,* Dorothy Crisp (London), 1945; *Mine Boy,* Dorothy Crisp, 1946, Knopf, 1955, new edition, Collier Books, 1970; *The Path of Thunder,* Harper, 1948; *Wild Conquest,* Harper, 1950, new edition, Anchor Books, 1970; *A Wreath for Udomo,* Knopf, 1956, new edition, Collier Books, 1971; *A Night of Their Own,* Knopf, 1965.

Short Stories: *Dark Testament,* Allen and Unwin, 1942, reprinted, Kraus Reprint, 1970.

Autobiography: *Tell Freedom,* Knopf, 1954, published as *Tell Freedom: Memories of Africa,* Knopf, 1969, new edition, Macmillan, 1970.

Travel: *Jamaica: An Island Mosaic,* H.M.S.O., 1957; *Return to Goli,* Faber, 1953; *This Island Now,* Faber, 1966, Knopf, 1967, new edition with introduction by Austin C. Clarke, Collier Books, 1971; *The Quiet Voice,* Dorrance, 1966.

Poetry: *A Blackman Speaks of Freedom,* Universal Printing Works (Durban), 1941.

Other: (Editor and author of text) *Souvenir Pictorial Review of the West Indies Federation, 1947-57,* Edna Manley (Kingston), c. 1958; (with the staff of *Holiday* Magazine and others), *The World of Mankind,* Golden Press, 1962; (with others) *History of the Pan-African Congress,* Hammersmith Bookshop, 1963; (editor, with Nadine Gordimer) *South African Writing Today,* Penguin, 1967. Wrote radio scripts for British Broadcasting Corp. during 1950's. Contributor to *Holiday.*

SIDELIGHTS: Peter Abrahams' father was Ethiopian, and his mother was South African "Cape Colored," which is to say she was of mixed African and French parentage. In South Africa, Abrahams grew up as part of the Colored, as distinct from the black African, community. He had a hard childhood (described in his autobiographical *Tell Freedom*), and was still illiterate at the age of nine, although he wrote his first story when he was eleven, after he had discovered Shakespeare and poetry.

In 1941 he settled in England. When his *Song of the City* was published in 1945, it was the first novel by a non-white South African to appear since Solomon Plaatje published *Mhudi* in 1930. After living in France, 1948-40, and a brief residence in the British West African colony of the Gold Coast (now Ghana) in the mid-1950's, he emigrated to Jamaica in 1956, where he has lived since.

Abrahams told *CA* he has always been dedicated to Pan-Africanism. He was present at the Fifth Pan-African Congress (described in *A Wreath for Udomo*) held in Manchester, England, in 1945, which was a milestone in the progress of African colonies towards independence; however, he noted that he is critical of some key aspects of tribalism, which he believed inhibited the emergence of modern African societies.

AVOCATIONAL INTERESTS: Gardening, tennis, walking, conversation, reading, travel.

BIOGRAPHICAL/CRITICAL SOURCES: Critique, Volume XI, number 1, 1968; Michael Wade, *Peter Abrahams*, Evans, 1971; Carolyn Riley, editor, *Contemporary Literary Criticism*, Volume IV, Gale, 1975.

* * *

ABRAMS, M(eyer) H(oward) 1912-

PERSONAL: Born July 23, 1912, in Long Branch, N.J.; son of Joseph (a merchant) and Sara (Shanes) Abrams; married Ruth Gaynes, September 1, 1937; children: Jane, Judith. *Education:* Harvard University, A.B., 1934, M.A., 1937, Ph.D., 1940; Cambridge University, graduate study, 1934-35. *Politics:* Independent. *Home:* 512 Highland Rd., Ithaca, N.Y. 14850. *Office:* Department of English, Cornell University, Ithaca, N.Y. 14850.

CAREER: Harvard University, Cambridge, Mass., instructor in English, 1938-42, research associate in Psycho-Acoustic Laboratory, 1942-45; Cornell University, Ithaca, N.Y., assistant professor, 1945-47, associate professor, 1947-53, professor of English, 1953-61, F. J. Whiton Professor, 1961-73, Class of 1916 Professor, 1973—. Roache lecturer at University of Indiana, 1963; Alexander lecturer at University of Toronto, 1964; fellow of Center for Advanced Study in the Behavioral Sciences, 1967-68.

MEMBER: American Academy of Arts and Sciences (fellow), American Philosophical Society (fellow), American Association of University Professors, Modern Language Association of America (member of executive council, 1961-64), English Institute, Sigma Xi, Century Association (New York, N.Y.), Cornell Club of New York. *Awards, honors:* Rockefeller Foundation fellowship, 1946-47; Ford Foundation fellowship, 1953; Fulbright scholar at University of Malta and Cambridge University, 1954; honorary member of faculty of Royal University of Malta, 1954—; Christian Gauss Prize, from Phi Beta Kappa, 1954, for *The Mirror and the Lamp;* Guggenheim fellowships, 1958, 1960-61; James Russell Lowell Prize from Modern Language Association of America, 1972, for *Natural Supernaturalism.*

WRITINGS: The Milk of Paradise: The Effects of Opium Visions on the Works of De Quincey, Crabbe, Francis Thompson, and Coleridge, Harvard University Press, 1934, text edition, Octagon, 1970; *The Mirror and the Lamp: Romantic Theory and the Critical Tradition*, Oxford University Press, 1953; *A Glossary of Literary Terms*, Holt 1957, 3rd edition, 1971; *Natural Supernaturalism: Tradition and Revolution in Romantic Literature*, Norton, 1971; (with others) *In Search of Literary Theory*, edited by Morton W. Bloomfield, Cornell University Press, 1972.

Editor: *The Poetry of Pope*, Holt, 1954; (and contributor) *Literature and Belief*, Columbia University Press, 1958; and contributor) *English Romantic Poets: Modern Essays in Criticism*, Oxford University Press, 1960, 2nd edition, 1975; *The Norton Anthology of English Literature*, Norton, 1962, 3rd edition, 1974; (and contributor) *Wordsworth: A Collection of Critical Essays*, Prentice-Hall, 1972. Advisory editor of Norton; member of editorial board of "Cornell Concordances" and "Cornell Studies in English."

WORK IN PROGRESS: The Philosophy of Literary Criticism; a critical edition of *The Prelude.*

ACKERMAN, Diane 1948-

PERSONAL: Born October 7, 1948, in Waukegan, Ill.; daughter of Sam (a restaurant owner) and Marcia (Tischler) Fink. *Education:* Boston University, student, 1966-67; Pennsylvania State University, B.A., 1970; Cornell University, M.F.A., 1973. *Home:* 343 Spencer Rd., Ithaca, N.Y. 14850. *Office:* Department of English, Goldwin Smith Building, Cornell University, Ithaca, N.Y. 14853.

CAREER: Writer. Social worker in New York, N.Y., 1967; government researcher at Pennsylvania State University, 1968. *Awards, honors:* Academy of American Poets Poetry Prize, 1973; Abbie Copps Poetry Prize from Olivet College, 1974, for "The Other Night"; Rockefeller graduate fellow at Cornell University, 1974-76.

WRITINGS: (With Jody Bolz and Nancy Steele) *Poems: Ackerman, Bolz, and Steele*, Stone Marrow Press, 1973.

Work is anthologized in *Intro Five Anthology*, edited by George Garrett, Doubleday, 1973; *Intro Six Anthology*, edited by Garrett, Doubleday, 1974; *The First Anthology*, edited by A. R. Ammons and others, Society for the Humanities, 1974; *I, That Am Ever Stranger*, edited by Nancy Esther James, Educational Foundation, American Association of University Women, 1974; *Other Worlds*, by Carl Sagan, Bantam, 1975.

Contributor of poems and reviews to literary journals, including *Ambit, Carleton Miscellany, Carolina Quarterly, Chelsea, Chicago Review, Epoch, Event, Massachusetts Review, Paris Review*, and *Prairie Schooner*. Editorial assistant for *Library Journal*, 1970-71; poetry editor, *EPOCH*, 1973.

WORK IN PROGRESS: Fever's Root, an epistolary novel; *Brainstem Sonata: Science and Poetry*, a critical study; *The Planets: A Cosmic Pastoral*, a suite of poems; *Victim of the Molecule*, poems.

SIDELIGHTS: Diane Ackerman writes: "I'm interested in stretching the limits of what poets, by convention, are expected to think and write about." *Avocational interests:* Astronomy, hooking rya-rugs, skindiving.

BIOGRAPHICAL/CRITICAL SOURCES: Ithaca New Times, May 10, 1973; *Cornell Chronicle*, March 20, 1975.

* * *

ACKLAND, Rodney 1908-

PERSONAL: Born May 18, 1908, in Westcliffe-on-Sea, Essex, England; son of Edward and Diana (Lock) Ackland; married Mab Lonsdale, 1951 (died, 1972). *Education:* Attended Central School for Speech Training and Dramatic Art, London. *Agent:* Robin Dalton, 11 Hanover St., London W.1, England. *Office:* c/o Eric Glass Ltd., 28 Berkeley Square, London W1X 6HD, England.

CAREER: Playwright. Worked in department stores and in advertising department of oil company, London, England, 1924-25; appeared as actor in many London stage productions, 1924-36, including title role in "Young Woodley," 1929; also directed plays, including "The Belle of New York," 1942, and his own *The Dark River*, 1943, and the film "Thursday's Child," 1943.

WRITINGS: (With Elspeth Grant) *The Celluloid Mistress: or, the Custard Pie of Dr. Caligari* (autobiography), Wingate, 1954.

Plays: *Improper People* (first produced in London, England, 1929), Heinemann, 1930; *Dance With No Music* (first produced in London, 1930), Baker's Plays, 1933;

Strange Orchestra (three-act; first produced in London, 1931; produced in New York, 1933), Gollancz, 1932; *Birthday* (three-act; first produced in London, 1934), Samuel French, 1935; *The Old Ladies* (three-act; adapted from the novel by Hugh Walpole; first produced in London, 1935; produced as "Night in the House" in New York, 1935), published under first title by Samuel French, 1935; *After October* (three-act; first produced in London, 1936), Gollancz, 1936, Samuel French, 1937; "Remembrance of Things Past" (first produced in London, 1938; produced as *The Dark River*, London, 1941), published under second title by Samuel French, 1942; *The Diary of a Scoundrel* (adapted from play by A. N. Ostrovsky; first produced in London, 1942; produced in New York, 1956), Low, 1948, Samuel French, 1951; *Crime and Punishment* (adapted from the novel by Dostoevsky; first produced in London, 1946; produced in New York, 1947), Holt, 1948; *Before the Party* (two-act; adapted from the short story by Somerset Maugham; first produced in London, 1949), Samuel French, 1950; *A Dead Secret* (first produced in London, 1957), Samuel French, 1958; *Farewell, Farewell Eugene* (three act; adapted from the work by John Vari; first produced in London, 1959; produced on Broadway, 1960), Samuel French, 1960.

Unpublished plays: "Marian-Ella," first produced in London, 1930; "Ballerina" (adapted from the novel by Eleanor Smith), first produced in London, 1933; "The White Guard" (adapted from the play by Michael Bulgakov), first produced in London, 1934; "Plot Twenty-One," first produced in London, 1936; "Yes, My Darling Daughter" (adapted from a work by Mark Reed), first produced in London, 1937; "Sixth Floor" (adapted from the play by Alfred Gheri), first produced in London, 1939; "Blossom Time," first produced in London, 1942; (with Robert G. Newton) "Cupid and Mars" (adapted from a story by Newton), first produced in London, 1947; (with Newton) "A Multitude of Sins," first produced in London, 1951; "The Pink Room; or, The Escapists," first produced in London, 1952; "The Other Palace," first produced in London, 1964.

Screenplays: (With Alfred Hitchcock and Alma Reville) "Number Seventeen," 1931; "Bank Holiday (Three on a Weekend)," 1937; (with Emeric Pressburger) "The Invaders," 1942; "Continental Express," 1942; "Thursday's Child," 1943; "George and Margaret," 1944; "49th Parallel," 1944; "Uncensored," 1944; "Wanted for Murder," 1946; "Hatter's Castle," 1948; "Temptation Harbour," 1949; "The Queen of Spades," 1949; "Bond Street," 1950; "The Seddens," 1956; and "A Dead Secret."

SIDELIGHTS: Enthusiastic reviews of *Strange Orchestra* cost Ackland his job with British International Pictures, because the company saw no advantage in employing a serious writer. Ackland has been highly praised by critics, and for his early work, which was considered too highbrow to become popularly accepted, was referred to as "the English Chekov." Today, however, Ackland is sometimes characterized as a strictly commercial playwright.*

* * *

ACTON, Thomas (Alan) 1948-

PERSONAL: Born July 1, 1948, in Brentwood, Essex, England; son of John George (a civil servant) and Doreen M. (Mason) Acton. *Education:* Trinity College, Oxford, B.A., 1969; Nuffield College, Oxford, M.A. and D.Phil., 1974. *Politics:* Labour. *Religion:* Baptist. *Office:* Thames Polytechnic, 18 Wellington St., London S.E.18, England.

CAREER: Justin De Blank Provisions, London, England, manager of grocery shop, 1973-74; Thames Polytechnic, London, England, research fellow in social policy, 1974—. Member of National Gypsy Education Council; director of sociological research at Romani Institute. *Member:* Institute of Race Relations, National Council for Civil Liberties, Association of Teachers in Technical Colleges, Union of Shop, Distribution, and Allied Workers, Great Britain-United Soviet Socialist Republic Association, British Sociological Association, Association of Sociologists in Polytechnics.

WRITINGS: Materials for the Study of Gypsy Education, Romanestan Publications, 1970, 4th edition, 1973; *Mo Romano Lil* (stories; title means "My Romani Book"), Romanestan Publications, 1971, 2nd edition, 1972; (with Rosy Denaro and Bernard Hurley) *Romano Drom Song Book*, Romanestan Publications, 1972; (with Michael Connors) *Two Gammon Stories*, Romanestan Publications, 1974; *Gypsy Politics and Social Change*, Routledge & Kegan Paul, 1974. Contributor to Gypsy journals and to *New Society*.

WORK IN PROGRESS: Research on social policy, especially planning.

SIDELIGHTS: Acton writes: "I ran the first Gypsy Council caravan school, living with gypsies for three weeks, when I was a student in 1967, and got hooked."

* * *

ADAMS, Sam 1934-

PERSONAL: Born November 26, 1934, in Gilfach Goch, Wales; son of Thomas (an electrician) and Edith (Love) Adams; married Muriel Samuel (a school teacher), October 25, 1958; children: Nicholas, Jonathan. *Education:* University College of Wales, B.A. (honors in English), 1955, M.A., 1958; University College, Cardiff, M.Ed., 1971. *Home:* Llys Meilyr, Heol Ponthir, Caerleon, Gwent, Wales.

CAREER: Teacher of English in Bristol, England, 1958-66; Caerleon College of Education, Caerleon, Wales, lecturer in English, 1966-74; H.M. Inspector of Schools in Wales, 1974—.

WRITINGS: The Boy Inside (poems), Christopher Davies, 1973; (editor with Roland Mathias) *The Shining Pyramid & Other Stories by Welsh Authors*, Gwasg Gomer, 1973; (editor with G. R. Hughers) *Essays on Welsh & Anglo-Welsh Literature*, two volumes, Christopher Davies, 1973; (editor) *Ten Anglo-Welsh Poets*, Carcanet, 1974; *Geraint Goodwin*, University of Wales Press, 1975. Contributor of short stories, poems, and reviews to magazines. Editor, *Poetry Wales*, 1973-75.

WORK IN PROGRESS: Research on the growth of national consciousness in Anglo-Welsh writing.

SIDELIGHTS: Adams writes: "Meeting Meic Stephens, founder-editor of *Poetry Wales*, and joining him and G. R. Hughes on the magazine marked the true beginning of my career as a writer (I took over as editor in 1973). I am deeply interested in Anglo-Welsh writers and writing, and Welsh culture. Many of my poems recall places, characters, incidents from my childhood in a South Wales mining valley."

* * *

ADCOCK, Betty
  See ADCOCK, Elizabeth S(harp)

ADCOCK, Elizabeth S(harp) 1938-
(Betty Adcock)

PERSONAL: Born September 16, 1938, in Fort Worth, Tex.; daughter of Ralph L. (a landowner) and Sylvia (a teacher of Latin and English; maiden name, Hudgins) Sharp; married Donald B. Adcock (an associate director of music, North Carolina State University), June, 1957; children: Sylvia Elizabeth. *Education:* Attended Texas Tech University, 1956-57, North Carolina State University, 1965-66, and Goddard College, 1966-68. *Home:* 817 Runnymede Rd., Raleigh, N.C. 27607.

CAREER: Ralph Johnson Associates, copywriter and producer, 1969-73; free-lance advertising copywriter, 1973—. Has taught in the Poets-in-the-Schools programs in North Carolina and Virginia; has given poetry readings at colleges and universities. *Member:* Cooperative of Small Magazine Editors and Publishers (member of woman's committee). *Awards, honors:* Poetry selected for inclusion in Borestone Mountain Poetry Awards, *Best Poems of 1966,* 1967.

*WRITINGS—*All under name Betty Adcock: *Walking Out* (poems), Louisiana State University Press, 1975. Work is anthologized in *New Southern Poets,* edited by Guy Owen and Mary C. Williams, University of North Carolina Press, 1975, and *I Have Been Hungry All the Years,* edited by Glenna Luschei and Del Rogers, Solo Press, 1975. Contributor of poems and stories to magazines, including *Red Clay Reader, New American Review, Nation, Pebble, Chicago Review, Crazy Horse,* and *Poetry Northwest.* Associate editor of *Southern Poetry Review.*

WORK IN PROGRESS: Other Names, a series of poems; possibly a novel.

SIDELIGHTS: Betty Adcock writes that her motivations include "growing up in rural, small-town south, folk-tales, ancestral hauntings, objects touched by time, the world's myths, the despair of the present, language as possibility." She adds: "I am interested in pointing out relationships . . . And I care about form. The kind you *discover.* I care about people, our failings, our deaths and the real earth. I have no program for salvation."

*   *   *

ADDE, Leo 1927(?)-1975

1927(?)—March 13, 1975; American urban affairs writer, television news director and managing editor, reporter, and author. Obituaries: *Washington Post,* March 15, 1975; *New York Times,* March 15, 1975; *AB Bookman's Weekly,* April 7, 1975.

*   *   *

ADLARD, John 1929-

PERSONAL: Born January 15, 1929, in Birmingham, England; son of Herbert Charles Thomas (a distribution manager) and Florence Nell (Sutton) Adlard. *Education:* Merton College, Oxford, B.A., 1952, M.A., 1956, B.Litt., 1956. *Home:* 146 Holland Rd., London W.14, England.

CAREER: Lecturer in English at University of Novi Sad, Yugoslavia, 1954-56, Catholic University of Lublin, Poland, 1957-58, University of Jyvaskyla, Finland, 1958-59, 1960-61, 1962-63, University of Groningen, Holland, 1963-64, University of Lodz, Poland, 1966-67, University of Antwerp, Belgium, 1969-70, and at various language schools; teacher and writer, 1970—. *Military service:* Royal Army Ordinance Corps, 1947-49. *Member:* Folklore Society of Great Britain, Eighteen-Nineties Society, Black Country Society, Stratford-on-Avon Society.

WRITINGS: Stenbock, Yeats, and the Nineties, Woolf, 1969; (editor) *Blake,* Studio Vista, 1970; *The Sports of Cruelty: Fairies, Folk Songs, Charms, and Other Country Matters in the Work of William Blake,* Woolf, 1972; *The Debt to Pleasure,* Carcanet Press, 1974; *The Fruit of that Forbidden Tree,* Carcanet Press, 1975. Also translator of French, Italian, Dutch, and Serbo-Croatian poetry which has been printed in magazines and in a series of poetry postcards published by Menard Press. Contributor to *Philological Quarterly, Michigan Quarterly Review, Blake Studies, Blake Newsletter, Folklore, Modern Language Review,* and other journals. Editor with Alan Brownjohn, *Departure* (magazine), 1952-54.

WORK IN PROGRESS: Translations of songs by Lorenzo de Medici; short biography and critical study of Owen Seaman.

*   *   *

ADLER, David A. 1947-

PERSONAL: Born April 10, 1947, in New York, N.Y.; son of Sidney G. (a teacher) and Betty (a social worker; maiden name, Straus) Adler; married Renee Hamada (a school psychologist), April 8, 1973. *Education:* Queens College of the City University of New York, B.A., 1968; New York University, M.B.A., 1971. *Religion:* Jewish. *Home:* 84-23 Manton St., Briarwood, N.Y. 11435.

*WRITINGS—*All for children: *3D, 2D, 1D* (mathematics book), Crowell, 1975; *Base Five* (mathematics book), Crowell, 1975; *A Little at a Time* (fiction), Random House, 1975. Contributor of reviews to journals.

WORK IN PROGRESS: An adult novel; mathematics and fiction books for children.

SIDELIGHTS: Adler has been a professional artist with more than two hundred drawings and cartoons published in magazines and newspapers. His artwork has been publicly exhibited in New York and Florida and is contained in private collections in the United States and Europe.

*   *   *

AINSWORTH, Harriet
   See CADELL, (Violet) Elizabeth

*   *   *

AITCHISON, Janet 1962-

PERSONAL: Born October 2, 1962, in Horley, Surrey, England; daughter of Colin Stuart (a physicist) and Margaret (a secretary; maiden name, Downs) Aitchison. *Education:* Currently attending Court Lodge Comprehensive School in Horley, England. *Religion:* None. *Home:* 24 Priory Drive, Reigate, Surrey RH28AF, England.

CAREER: Student.

WRITINGS: The Pirates' Tale (children's book), Harper, 1970.

SIDELIGHTS: Janet Aitchison writes: "I wrote *The Pirates' Tale* when I was five and a half and just beginning to learn to read and write. I am in the *Guinness Book of Records* as the youngest commercially published author."

*   *   *

AKENSON, Donald Harman 1941-

PERSONAL: Born May 22, 1941, in Minneapolis, Minn. *Education:* Yale University, B.A., 1962; Harvard University, Ph.D., 1967. *Home:* 38 Traymoor Ave., Kingston, Ontario, Canada. *Office:* Department of History, Queen's University, Kingston, Ontario, Canada.

CAREER: Harvard University, Cambridge, Mass., assistant in Financial Aid Office, 1963-64, assistant director of Office of Graduate and Career Planning, 1964-65, associate director, 1965-66, assistant to dean of School of Education, 1965-66, director of Office of Graduate & Career Planning, 1966-67, Allston Burr Senior Tutor in Dunston House, 1966-67; Yale University, New Haven, Conn., assistant professor of history and assistant dean of University, 1967-70; Queen's University, Kingston, Ontario, associate professor of history, 1970—. *Member:* American Committee for Irish Studies, Conference on British Studies.

WRITINGS: A Guide to Postgraduate Planning, Yale College Dean's Office, 1968; (with Lawrence F. Stevens) *The Changing Uses of the Liberal Arts College: An Essay in Recent Educational History*, Pageant-Poseidon for Harvard College, 1969; *The Irish Education Experiment: The National System of Education in the Nineteenth Century*, Routledge & Kegan Paul, 1970; *The Church of Ireland: Ecclesiastical Reform and Revolution, 1800-1885*, Yale University Press, 1971; *The United States and Ireland*, Harvard University Press, 1973; *Education and Enmity: The Control of Schooling in Northern Ireland*, Harper, 1973.*

*   *   *

AKMAKJAIN, Hiag   1926-

PERSONAL: Born July 17, 1926, Jersey City, N.J.; son of Ervant (a tailor) and Vartanoush (Mardirosian) Akmakjian; married Pamela Jones, December 16, 1961 (divorced, 1968); children: Nicolas. *Education:* Columbia University, B.A., 1948; Sorbonne, University of Paris, certificate, 1948; Washington Square Institute for Psychotherapy and Mental Health, certificate, 1971; attended National Psychological Association for Psychoanalysis, 1965-66, Institute for Practicing Psychotherapists, 1966-67, Institute for the Study of Psycho-therapy, 1971-72. *Home:* 185 East 85th St., 21F, New York, N.Y. 10028. *Office:* 8 East 10th St., New York, N.Y. 10003.

CAREER: Psychoanalyst in private practice and writer in New York, N.Y., 1965—. Formerly affiliated with Great Neck Consultation Center, Washington Square Institute for Psychotherapy and Mental Health, and New York City Community Guidance Center. Consultant to McGraw-Hill Book Co., 1966—. *Military service:* U.S. Army, 1944-46.

WRITINGS: Treatment Guide for Psychoanalysis and Psychotherapy, Riverrun Press, 1969; *The Natural Way to Raise a Healthy Child*, Praeger, 1975. Contributor to magazines.

WORK IN PROGRESS: Four books on Taoism, haiku, photography, and psychoanalysis; *Bird of Time*, a novel.

SIDELIGHTS: Akmakjian is competent in French, German, Armenian, and Italian. *Avocational interests:* Photography, nutrition and organic gardening, painting.

*   *   *

ALAN, Jack
See GREEN, Alan (Baer)

*   *   *

ALBERTSON, Chris   1931-

PERSONAL: Born October 18, 1931, in Reykjavik, Ice-land; came to United States, 1957; naturalized U.S. citizen, 1963; son of Thordur (an exporter) and Yvonne (Broberg) Albertson; married Hanne Elizabeth Christensen, June 17, 1954 (divorced, 1958). *Education:* Attended Academy of Free & Mercantile Art, Copenhagen, 1949-52. *Politics:* "Liberal-left; gave up voting after Nixon election." *Religion:* "None that is organized." *Home:* 444 Central Park W., New York, N.Y. 10025. *Agent:* Helen Merrill, 337 West 22nd St., New York, N.Y. 10011.

CAREER: Fona Radio (music store), Copenhagen, Denmark, display artist, 1951-54; Storyville Club (jazz cabaret), Copenhagen, general manager, 1952-54; free-lance radio commentator in Copenhagen, 1953-59; U.S. Armed Forces Radio & Television, Keflavik, Iceland, producer, commentator, and writer, 1954-57; Doubleday Book Shop, New York, N.Y. retail clerk, 1957-58; WCAU Radio, Philadelphia, Pa., producer and writer, 1958; WHAT-FM, Philadelphia, jazz disc jockey, 1958-60; Riverside Records, New York, N.Y., jazz record producer, 1960-62; Prestige Records, Bergenfield, N.J., jazz record producer, 1962-63; employed as an autograph signer by Benny Goodman in New York, N.Y., 1963; WNEW Radio, New York, N.Y., continuity director, 1963-64; WBAI-FM Radio, New York, N.Y., general manager, 1964-66; BBC, London, England and New York, N.Y., director of programs for American syndication, 1966-67; free-lance writer and producer of jazz record albums, 1967—. Talent consultant to "Chicago and All That Jazz" Dupont Show of the Week, 1961; consultant to Pacifica Foundation, 1966-69; co-producer and host of weekly television show, "The Jazz Set" for New Jersey State Television, 1972.

MEMBER: National Academy of Recording Arts & Sciences, Authors Guild. *Awards, honors:* Grammy Award for best non-classical album liner notes, 1970; Grand Prix du Disque from Montreux Jazz Festival, 1971; Trendsetter Award from *Billboard* Magazine, 1971, for originating Bessie Smith reissue series; Grammy Trustees Award, 1971, for production of Bessie Smith reissue series.

WRITINGS: Bessie: A Biography of Bessie Smith, Stein & Day, 1972; *Empress of the Blues* (song book), Schirmer/Macmillan, 1975. Also author of screenplay, with Horton Foote, "Bessie," based on his book, 1974. American music correspondent to *Berlingske Tidende* (Copenhagen), 1966-69. Contributor to newspapers and magazines in the United States and Europe. Contributing editor, *Stereo Review*, 1973—.

WORK IN PROGRESS: A biography of Louis Armstrong for Macmillan; a jazz book for young people for Viking; research on exploitation of jazz artists by music industry, managers, record companies, etc.

SIDELIGHTS: Albertson, who speaks Danish, Icelandic, and German, told *CA:* "My jazz interest led me to this country in 1957 and as my writing activities increased, liner notes, articles, etc., I made it my goal to correct the errors and omissions of past jazz literature by doing thorough research and pulling no punches."

*   *   *

ALBINSON, Jack
See ALBINSON, James P.

*   *   *

ALBINSON, James P.   1932-
(Jack Albinson)

PERSONAL: Born January 15, 1932, in Minneapolis,

Minn.; married Marie L. Ingstad, May 30, 1957; children: Paul O., Julia M. *Education:* Wheaton College, Wheaton, Ill., B.A., 1954; University of Minnesota, degree in mortuary science, 1955. *Politics:* Republican. *Religion:* Protestant. *Home:* 115 Meander Rd., Golden Valley, Minn. 55422. *Office:* 2200 Nicollet Ave., Minneapolis, Minn. 55404.

CAREER: Albin Funeral Chapel, Minneapolis, Minn., vice-president; Albinson Racing Films, Minneapolis, Minn., owner, 1964—. *Military service:* U.S. Army, 1956-58; served in Europe; became staff sergeant. *Member:* Minneapolis Athletic Club.

WRITINGS—Under name Jack Albinson; *Only Seconds,* Bethany Fellowship, 1971; *The Oily Grail* (nonfiction), Denison, 1974. Contributor to auto-racing periodicals. Author of scripts for auto-racing films.

WORK IN PROGRESS: A book; two films.

BIOGRAPHICAL/CRITICAL SOURCES: Christian Life, May, 1969.

* * *

ALDRED, Cyril   1914-

PERSONAL: Born February 19, 1914, in London, England; son of Frederick (a civil servant) and Lilian Ethel (Underwood) Aldred; married Jessie Kennedy Morton, 1938; children: one daughter. *Education:* Kings College, London, and Courtauld Institute of Art, London, B.A., 1936. *Home:* 4a Polwarth Terrace, Edinburgh EH11 1NE, Scotland.

CAREER: Royal Scottish Museum, Edinburgh, Scotland, assistant keeper, 1937; Scottish Education Department, Edinburgh, assistant principal, St. Andrew's House, 1939; Metropolitan Museum of Art, Department of Egyptian Art, New York, N.Y., associate curator, 1955-56; Royal Scottish Museum, keeper of Department of Art and Archaeology, 1961—. Committee member, Egyptian Exploration Society, 1959—. *Military Service:* Royal Air Force (Signals), 1942-46. *Member:* Scottish Arts Club (Edinburgh).

WRITINGS: Old Kingdom Art in Ancient Egypt, Transatlantic Arts, 1949; *Middle Kingdom Art in Ancient Egypt, 2300 to 1590 B.C.,* Tiranti, 1950; *New Kingdom Art in Ancient Egypt during the Eighteenth Dynasty, 1590 to 1315 B.C.,* Tiranti, 1951, 2nd edition published as *New Kingdom Art in Ancient Egypt During the Eighteenth Dynasty, 1570 to 1320 B.C.,* 1961; *The Development of Ancient Egyptian Art, from 3200 to 1315 B.C.,* Tiranti, 1952; *The Egyptians,* Praeger, 1961; *Egypt to the End of the Old Kingdom,* Thames & Hudson, 1965; *Akhenaten, Pharaoh of Egypt: A New Study,* Thames & Hudson, 1968, McGraw, 1969; *Jewels of the Pharaohs: Egyptian Jewelry of the Dynastic Period,* Praeger, 1971; *Tutankhamun's Egypt,* British Broadcasting Corp., 1972; *Akhenaten and Nefertiti,* Viking, 1973. Contributor to *The Cambridge Ancient History,* and to *History of Technology.* Author of script, "Tutankhamun's Egypt," British Broadcasting Corp. Contributor to scientific journals.

WORK IN PROGRESS: A Concise History of Ancient Egypt; a biography of Akhenaten; chapters on ancient Egyptian sculpture.

AVOCATIONAL INTERESTS: Silversmithing, composing light verse, and gardening.

ALEXANDER, Anna B(arbara Cooke)   1913-
(Anne ALEXANDER, Barbara Cooke)

PERSONAL: Born October 6, 1913, in Shanghai, China; daughter of Alfred Francis and Edyth Nora (Brightbill) Cooke; married Charles Edward Alexander (a newspaperman), January 2, 1932; children: Barbara Alexander Constanti, Carol Alexander Krueger, Sharon Alexander Wemple. *Education:* College of San Mateo, A.A., 1964; San Francisco State College (now University), B.A., 1969, teaching credential in secondary education, 1971. *Politics:* "Registered Democrat, disillusioned drop-out." *Religion:* Episcopalian. *Home and office:* 1504 Highway Rd., Burlingame, Calif. 94010. *Agent:* Curtis Brown Ltd., 60 East 56th St., New York, N.Y. 10022.

CAREER: Broadway Editor, Burlingame, Calif., feature writer, and columnist, 1946-48; *Advance-Star and Green Sheet,* Burlingame, columnist, 1948-51; *Let's Dance* (magazine), Danville, Calif., assistant editor, 1951-53; *Peninsula Living,* Redwood City, Calif., book reviewer, 1971—. *Member:* Authors Guild, Burlingame Writers (president, 1956-1958).

WRITINGS—All juvenile; all under name Anne Alexander, except as indicated: *ABC of Cars and Trucks,* Doubleday, 1956; *I Want to Whistle,* Abelard, 1958; *The Pink Dress,* Doubleday, 1959; *Noise in the Night,* Rand McNally, 1960; *Boats and Ships from A to Z,* Rand McNally, 1961; (under name Barbara Cooke) *My Daddy and I,* Abelard, 1961; *Linda,* Doubleday, 1964; *Little Foreign Devil,* Atheneum, 1970; *Trouble on Treat Street,* Atheneum, 1974; *To Live a Lie,* Atheneum, 1975.

WORK IN PROGRESS: Two juvenile novels, *Connie,* completion expected in 1975, and *Billi-Mae,* 1976.

* * *

ALEXANDER, Anne
See ALEXANDER, Anna B(arbara Cooke)

* * *

ALIESAN, Jody   1943-

PERSONAL: Surname is pronounced Al-*ee*-es-ahn; born April 22, 1943, in Kansas City, Mo.; daughter of John David and Minerva Anna (Elliss) Armstrong. *Education:* Occidental College, B.A. (magna cum laude), 1965; Brandeis University, M.A., 1966. *Politics:* "Feminist/environmentalist wondering about socialistic anarchism." *Religion:* "Agnostic mystic or pantheist pagan." *Home:* Box 8761, Rte. 8, Bainbridge Island, Wash. 98110. *Agent:* Adrienne Alexander, 217 East 17th Ave., Olympia, Wash. 98501.

CAREER: Miles College, Birmingham, Ala., instructor in humanities, 1968-69; Vietnam Moratorium Committee, Washington, D.C., press representative and researcher in Washington, D.C., and in Chicago, Ill., 1969-70; Associated Students of the University of Washington Women's Commission, Seattle, Wash., researcher and writer, 1970-71; Young Women's Christian Association, University of Washington, Seattle, co-director, 1972; minstrel in Seattle, Wash., 1973; Puget Consumer's Co-Operative, Seattle, Wash., produce manager, 1973-74; University of Washington, Seattle, extension lecturer in poetry writing and literature, 1974-75; free-lance singer and weaver, 1975—. *Member:* Phi Beta Kappa. *Awards, honors:* International fellowship from Occidental College, 1964, for travel to North Frisian Islands; Woodrow Wilson fellowships, 1965-

66, 1968-69; grant from Seattle Arts Commission, 1973, for work as minstrel.

WRITINGS: Thunder in the Sun (songs and poems), Young Women's Christian Association, University of Washington Branch (Seattle), 1971; *To Set Free* (poems), Second Moon, 1972; *Soul Claiming* (poems), Mulch Press, in press. Has arranged and composed lyrics for recordings. Contributor to journals, including *Everywoman, Isthmus, Moving Out, Aphra, Pandora, Rough Times, Women: A Journal of Liberation, Woman Spirit,* and *Northwest Passage.*

SIDELIGHTS: Jody Aliesan writes: "Much of my poetry comes from the experience of being a woman in a patriarchal culture characterized by rape, domination by force. Things that are important to me: self-awareness, self-love, androgyny, bisexuality, spiritual experiencing of wilderness, vegetarianism. Human beings are arrogant and mistaken when we think we are higher or more important than anything else naturally here on the earth, and we are self-destructive when we categorize and stereotype one another." She told *CA* that she had changed her name legally to Aliesan, an old English word meaning "to set free." *Avocational interests:* Organic gardening, foraging, backpacking, printmaking.

* * *

ALIMAYO, Chikuyo
    See FRANKLIN, Harold L(eroy)

* * *

ALLEN, Elisabeth Offutt   1895-

PERSONAL: Born December 8, 1895, in Bloomfield, Ky.; daughter of Frank Bell and Elisabeth (Russell) Offutt; married William Hogue Allen (a pathologist), November 23, 1921; children: William H., Betty (Mrs. Preston Young), Frances (Mrs. Paul Terry). *Education:* Attended Kentucky College for Women; Mount Holyoke College, A.B., 1917. *Religion:* Presbyterian. *Home:* 2519 Glenmary Ave., Louisville, Ky. 40204. *Agent:* Ann Elmo, 52 Vanderbilt Ave., New York, N.Y. 10017.

CAREER: Writer. *Member:* Louisville Woman's Club, Louisville Boat Club, Monday Afternoon Club.

WRITINGS: Fringes of Sky (poetry), Exposition, 1965; *This Tangled Web* (novel), Bouregy, 1965; *Skip to My Loo, My Darling* (novel), Bouregy, 1974; *Hounds of the Moon* (novel), Popular Library, 1974.

* * *

ALLEN, Frederick G(arfield)   1936-
    (Gary Allen)

PERSONAL: Born August 2, 1936, in Glendale, Calif.; son of Harold King (a realtor) and Virginia (Campbell) Allen; married Barbara Jean Powers, June 16, 1959; children: Michael, Scott, Bonnie, Cathleen. *Education:* Stanford University, B.A., 1958; California State University, Long Beach, further study, 1959-60. *Politics:* "Libertarian." *Home:* 2812 Tigertail Dr., Rossmoor, Calif. 90720.

CAREER: High school teacher of English and history in California, 1959; salesman, 1960-63; writer and lecturer, 1963—. *Awards, honors:* Award of merit from American Academy of Public Affairs, 1971; liberty award from Congress of Freedom, 1973.

WRITINGS—All under name Gary Allen: *Communist*

Revolution in the Streets, Western Islands, 1967; *Richard Nixon: The Man Behind the Mask,* Western Islands, 1971; *Nixon's Palace Guard,* Western Islands, 1971; (with Larry Abraham) *None Dare Call It Conspiracy,* Concord Press, 1971; *The Rockefeller File,* Concord Press, in press.

Films and filmstrips: "The Berkeley Revolution, "Constructive Action, 1960; "Civil Rights: The Red Reconstruction," B & K Productions, 1961; "The Great Pretense: How to Finance Communism while Ostensibly Opposing It," John Birch Society, 1968; "Show Biz in the Streets," John Birch Society, 1967; "The United Nations: Peace Dove Unmasked," John Birch Society, 1969; "War on Poverty: Subsidized Revolution, "John Birch Society, 1970.

Contributor to *Review of the News.* Contributing editor of *American Opinion.*

WORK IN PROGRESS: Research on the Council on Foreign Relations.

SIDELIGHTS: Allen writes that he was originally "an ADA-type 'liberal' who was challenged to read several anti-Communist books by a friend," and read them with a view to showing his friend the error of his ways. He became convinced that his friend's views were right, "moved right and became a student of real history and real economics—not the type taught in most classrooms today."

* * *

ALLEN, Gary
    See ALLEN, Frederick G(arfield)

* * *

ALLEN, Jon L(ewis)   1931-

PERSONAL: Born January 15, 1931, in London, England; naturalized U.S. citizen in 1952; son of Lewis (a motion picture director) and Dorothy (Skinner) Allen; married Monique Schumacher (a retail executive), September 29, 1961; children: Christopher, Victoria. *Education:* Yale University, B.A., 1953. *Religion:* Episcopal. *Home:* 114 East 90th St., New York, N.Y. 10028. *Agent:* Writer's House, 303 West 42nd St., New York, N.Y. 10036. *Office:* Gulf Oil Co., 1290 Avenue of the Americas, New York, N.Y. 10019.

CAREER: Assistant picture editor of *Holiday* Magazine, 1958-59; *Banner,* Bennington, Vt., editor, 1959-61; *Providence Journal-Bulletin,* Providence, R.I., reporter, 1961-62; Pan American Airways, New York, N.Y., public relations representative, 1962-65; Johns-Manville Corp., New York, N.Y., manager of press relations, 1965-69; Continental Oil Co., Stamford, Conn., director of news services, 1969-73; PR Associates, New York, N.Y., vice-president, 1973-75; Gulf Oil Co., New York, N.Y., director of public affairs, 1975—. *Military service:* U.S. Air Force, 1953-57. U.S. Air Force Reserve, 1957—; current rank, lieutenant colonel.

MEMBER: International Motor Press Association, Radio and Television News Directors Association, Public Relations Society of America, Chemical Communications Association, American Aviation Historical Society, Aerospace Historical Foundation, Experimental Aircraft Association, National Aeronautic Association, Aviation and Space Writers Association, Association of Petroleum Writers, Air Force Association, Reserve Officers Association of the United States, Yale Club of New York City, Overseas Press Club of New York City.

WRITINGS: The Stamp Collector's Guide to Europe, Arco, 1974; *Aviation and Space Museums of America*, Arco, 1975.

WORK IN PROGRESS: Research for a book on aviation history; two picture books.

* * *

ALLEN, Minerva C(rantz) 1935-

PERSONAL: Born April 24, 1935, in Lodgepole, Mont.; daughter of Robert Ernest (a rancher) and Felectius (Chopwood) Allen; married John W. Allen (a tribal chairman), December 13, 1951; children: John, Mike, Donna, Wanda, Dean, Holly, Connie, Lisa. *Education:* Attended Northern Montana College, 1964-73; Central Michigan University, B.S., 1974; Weber State College, graduate study, 1975—. *Religion:* Indian. *Home address:* Box 38, Star Rte., Dodson, Mont. 59524. *Agent:* Roxy Gordon, 1216 Lomas N.W., Albuquerque, N.M. 87102. *Office:* Ft. Belknap Headstart, Box 68, R.R.1, Harlem, Mont. 59526.

CAREER: Teacher's aide in public school, Lodgepole, Mont., 1964; Project Headstart, Lodgepole, teacher's aide, 1965—, teacher, 1966; Montana Legal Service, Havre, legal aide specialist, 1966-70; Ft. Belknap Headstart, Harlem, Mont., director, 1971—. Consultant on Indian heritage and performance management to schools and colleges, and to public service organizations.

WRITINGS: Like Spirits of the Past: Trying to Break Out and Walk to the West (Indian poetry and prose), Wowapi Productions (Albuquerque, N.M.), 1974; *Come to Power* (poetry anthology), Crossing Press, 1974. Contributor to *Whole Earth Catalog*, 1972 edition.

WORK IN PROGRESS: An article on the Assiniboine tribe (to which Mrs. Allen belongs), for inclusion in *Encyclopedia of Indians of the Americas*.

* * *

ALLEN, Robert S(haron) 1900-

PERSONAL: Born July 14, 1900, in Latonia, Ky.; married Ruth Finney (a newspaper correspondent), March 30, 1929; *Education:* University of Wisconsin, B.A., 1923; graduate study at University of Munich, 1923-24, George Washington University, 1927-28. *Home:* 1525 28th Street N.W., Washington, D.C. 20007. *Office:* National Press Building, Washington, D.C. 20005.

CAREER: Reporter for *Capital Times*, Wisconsin *State Journal*, and Milwaukee *Journal* during early 1920's; European correspondent in Munich, Germany for *Christian Science Monitor*, and reporter for United Press Association, New York, N.Y., during mid-1920's; chief of Washington bureau of *Christian Science Monitor* until 1932. Also worked as reporter for International News Service, and as Washington correspondent for *Philadelphia Record*. United Features Syndicate columnist with Drew Pearson, "Washington Merry-Go-Round," 1932-42; writer with Pearson of comic strip, "Hap Hazard"; broadcaster with Pearson, "News for the Americas," NBC-News. Writer of syndicated column, "Inside Washington," 1949—. *Military service:* U.S. Army, served in cavalry; became second lieutenant; also served in Wisconsin National Guard; became captain; recalled to active duty, U.S. Army, 1942-45, major; became colonel; received Silver Star, Bronze Star, Commendation Ribbon with cluster, Purple Heart, Legion of Merit, French Legion of Honor, Croix de Guerre with palm and gold star. *Member:* White House Correspondents

Association, National Press Club, Washington Press Club, Sigma Delta Chi. *Awards, honors:* Sigma Delta Chi distinguished service award, 1942.

WRITINGS: (With Drew Pearson) *Washington Merry-Go-Round*, Liveright, 1931; (with Pearson) *More Merry-Go-Round*, Liveright, 1932; *Why Hoover Faces Defeat*, Brewer, Warren & Putnam, 1932; (with Pearson) *Nine old Men*, Doubleday, 1936, reprinted, DaCapo Press, 1974; (with Pearson) *Nine Old Men at the Crossroads*, Doubleday, 1937; *Lucky Forward: The History of Patton's Third U.S. Army*, Vanguard, 1947, reprinted, Macfadden-Bartell, 1965; (editor) *Our Fair City*, Vanguard, 1947, reprinted, Arno, 1974; (editor) *Our Sovereign State*, Vanguard, 1949; (with William V. Shannon) *The Truman Merry-Go-Round*, Vanguard, 1950. Regular contributor to *Collier's, Nation*, and *New Republic*.

BIOGRAPHICAL/CRITICAL SOURCES: Time, February 13, 1939; *Collier's*, April 22, 1939, September 6, 1947.

* * *

ALLEN, Shirley Seifried 1921-

PERSONAL: Born May 25, 1921, in Oak Park, Ill.; daughter of John Francis (a civil engineer) and Hazle Adele (Rogers) Seifried; married Archibald William Allen, June 1, 1942 (divorced, 1970); married James Ernest Spinney, June 12, 1971; children: (first marriage) Anne Rogers Allen, John Alexander Allen, Elizabeth Louise Allen. *Education:* Carleton College, B.A., 1942; Bryn Mawr College, M.A., 1944, Ph.D., 1949. *Politics:* Liberal Democrat. *Religion:* Episcopalian. *Home:* 7 Farmstead Lane, Windsor, Conn. 06095. *Office:* Department of English, University of Connecticut, Hartford Branch, Asylum Ave., West Hartford, Conn. 06117.

CAREER: High school English teacher in Oak Park, Ill., 1944; Church of the Holy Trinity, Middletown, Conn., director of education, 1965-69; Middlesex Community College, Middletown, Conn., lecturer in English, 1969; University of Connecticut, Hartford Branch, assistant professor, 1969-72, associate professor of English, 1972—. Member of Waterville (Maine) charter revision committee, 1961-62. *Member:* Modern Language Association of America, American Society for Theatre Research, American Boccaccio Association, American Association of University Professors.

WRITINGS: Samuel Phelps and Sadler's Wells Theatre, Wesleyan University Press, 1971. Contributor to *CLA Journal*.

WORK IN PROGRESS: Research on attitudes toward women during the Renaissance, especially in works by Shakespeare and Boccaccio.

SIDELIGHTS: Shirley Allen writes: "I am primarily concerned with the interaction of literature and popular culture."

* * *

ALLILUYEVA, Svetlana (Iosifovna Stalina) 1926-

PERSONAL: Born February 28, 1926, in Moscow, U.S.S.R.; came to United States in 1967; daughter of Joseph Stalin (Soviet Communist Party and state leader) and Nedezhda (Alliluyeva) Stalin; married Grigory Morozov, 1943 (divorced, 1947); married Yury Zhdanov (divorced); married, in common law, Brijesh Singh, circa 1963 (died, 1966); married James Wesley Peters, 1970 (separated, 1971); children: (first marriage) Joseph Alliluyev; (second marriage) Ekaterina; (fourth marriage) Olga. *Education:* Moscow University, graduate, 1949; graduate study, Academy of Social Sciences, Moscow. *Agent:* c/o Greenbaum, Wolff, and Ernst, 285 Madison Avenue, New York, N.Y., 10017.

CAREER: Moscow University, Moscow, U.S.S.R., occasional teacher of Soviet literature and English language, 1953-65; Progressive Publishing House, Moscow, English translator, 1965-66.

WRITINGS: Dvadsat pisem k drugu, Harper, 1967, translation by Priscilla Johnson McMillan published as *Twenty Letters to a Friend* (Book-of-the-Month Club selection), Harper, 1967; *Tol'ko odin god*, Harper, 1969, translation by Paul Chavchavadze published as *Only One Year*, Harper, 1969. Also author of a pamphlet, *Borisu Leonidovichu Pasternaku*.

SIDELIGHTS: "In the story of her mother's family, the Alliluyevs, [*Twenty Letters to a Friend*] Svetlana has created an allegory of the sufferings of the Soviet people as a whole. She has shown that terrible as it was to be a subject of Stalin it was no less terrible, and very likely more so, to have been a member of his family. One by one, with hideous inevitability, the Alliluyevs . . . vanish without explanation," comments Priscilla Johnson McMillan. "Svetlana has dedicated her book to the mother she recalls only slightly, having lost her before she reached the age of seven. It was not until 1957 that she took her mother's surname, Alliluyeva, having gone by her father's name of Stalina until then. . . . She is possessed of a remarkable integrity, an instinct for preservation of the spirit." Like her mother, Svetlana was "torn by the conflicting imperatives of loyalty and opposition," and in defecting from the Soviet Union "snuffed out her old life in order to salvage the spirit."

On July 1, 1967, Michel Gordey wrote: "A mother and two brothers lost, two broken marriages, the brief hope of happiness that only lasted two years, then the death of her Indian companion and the awareness of a father who had ruined her life just as he had physically destroyed millions of other lives—that is Svetlana's history. She has come to the West in the hope of finding the inner peace denied her during 41 years in the Soviet Union."

Elizabeth Janeway has commented: "[*Twenty Letters*] will be read for many reasons, but whatever brings readers to it, they will profit; most of all, perhaps, by discovering that the ogre had a human child for a daughter, whose nature obeyed the simplest human laws. Anyone who has been touched by affection for Russian culture has felt that there is a kind of noble simplicity and grandeur of feeling possible, indeed characteristic, in that country (along with a great many less attractive qualities, of course). This simplicity and sincerity shines everywhere in Mme. Alliluyeva's book. It is written with candor and breadth of spirit, and an utter lack of artifice."*

* * *

ALLISON, Michael Frederick Lister 1936-
(Mike Allison)

PERSONAL: Born July 4, 1936, in London, England; son of Frederick Walter and Elizabeth (Lister) Allison; married Anne Drake, September 16, 1961; children: David, Jane. *Education:* University College, London, B.Sc., 1958. *Politics:* "Private." *Religion:* "Private." *Home:* 25 Meadow Close, Grove, Wantage, Oxfordshire OX12 7NN, England.

CAREER: British Leyland Motor Corp., England, manager of laboratories, 1965—. *Member:* Institute of Quality Assurance.

WRITINGS: M.G.: The Early Years, Brooklands Books, 1970; *The Magic of M.G.*, D. Watson, 1972. Contributor to motoring magazines. Editor of *Safety Fast* (M.G. Car Club magazine), 1969-71.

AVOCATIONAL INTERESTS: Music (especially music of Ralph Vaughan Williams).

* * *

ALLISON, Mike
See ALLISON, Michael Frederick Lister

* * *

Alta 1942-

PERSONAL: Born May 22, 1942, in Reno, Nev. *Education:* University of California, A.A. *Address:* Box 424, San Lorenzo, Calif. 94580.

CAREER: Shameless Hussy Press, San Lorenzo, Calif., founder and publisher, 1969—. Editor of *Shameless Hussy Review*; editor of "It Ain't Me Babe", 1969-70; instructor in women's poetry at University of California, Berkeley, 1974-75; television producer.

WRITINGS: Freedom's in Sight (poems and collages), Noh Directions Press, 1969; *Letters to Women* (poems), Shameless Hussy Press, 1970; *Poems and Prose by Alta*, Know, Inc., 1970; *Burn This and Memorize Yourself: Poems for Women*, Times Change Press, 1970; *Song of the Wife, Song of the Mistress*, Shameless Hussy Press, 1970; *True Story*, Mama's Press, 1972; *No Visible Means of Support* (poems), Shameless Hussy Press, 1972; *Momma: A State on All the Untold Stories*, Times Change Press, 1974; *I Am Not a Practicing Angel*, Crossing Press, 1975; *Pauline and the Mysterious Pervert*, Wyrd, 1975; *Theme and Variations*, Aldebaran, 1975.

WORK IN PROGRESS: A novel, *The Only Job in Town.*

AVOCATIONAL INTERESTS: Alta commented simply, "I love to do stuff."

* * *

ALTBACH, Edith Hoshino 1941-

PERSONAL: Born July 21, 1941, in San Francisco, Calif.; daughter of Keiji (an art restorer) and Misae (an art restorer; maiden name, Inouye) Hoshino; married Philip G. Altbach (a university professor), June 16, 1962; children: Eric Gustav Sachio. *Education:* University of Chicago, B.A., 1962, M.A.T., 1964; University of Wisconsin, further graduate study, 1969-70. *Home:* 172 Woodward, Buffalo, N.Y.

CAREER: Writer.

WRITINGS: From Feminism to Liberation, Schenkman, 1971; *Women in America*, Heath, 1974. Contributor to *Radical America.*

WORK IN PROGRESS: Research for a book on Asian Americans.

AVOCATIONAL INTERESTS: Autoharp, music of the Appalachians, country music.

* * *

ALTHAUSER, Robert P(ierce) 1939-

PERSONAL: Surname is pronounced *All-tow-zer*; born

December 8, 1939, in Cincinnati, Ohio; son of Lester William (a purchasing agent) and Helen Katherine (Pierce) Althauser. *Education:* Carleton College, B.A., 1961; Duke University, M.A., 1964; University of North Carolina, Ph.D., 1967. *Religion:* Methodist. *Office:* Department of Sociology, Indiana University, Ballantine Hall, Bloomington, Ind. 47401.

CAREER: Princeton University, Princeton, N.J., assistant professor of sociology, 1967-73; Indiana University, Bloomington, associate professor of sociology, 1973—. Consultant to RAND Corp. and International Bank for Reconstruction and Development. *Member:* American Sociological Association, Society for the Scientific Study of Religion, Bloomington Canoe and Kayak Club (president, 1975).

WRITINGS: (With Sydney S. Spivack and Beverly Amsel) *The Unequal Elites*, Wiley, 1975. Contributor to *Social Forces, American Journal of Sociology, Sociological Methods and Research*, and *Sociological Methodology*. Associate editor of *Sociological Methods and Research.*

WORK IN PROGRESS: Research on the relation of social background, sex, educational level, and other job qualifications and characteristics to managerial, professional, and technical employees of several business firms.

SIDELIGHTS: Althauser writes: "I am a lightweight veteran of the early Sixties Civil Rights movement." His efforts in this regard included coordinating a picketing demonstration in Minneapolis and helping to register fifteen hundred black voters in Raleigh, N.C. His book . . . "reflects my interest in structural changes that produce racial equality, my belief that the discipline of sociology can be developed, substantively and methodologically, to such an extent that it can inform public policies that will produce greater equality. . . ." *Avocational interests:* Classical music, whitewater kayaking, skiing, frisbee.

*   *   *

ALTMAN, Edward I(ra)   1941-

PERSONAL: Born June 5, 1941, in New York, N.Y.; son of Sidney (a draftsman) and Florence (a bookkeeper; maiden name, Brown) Altman; married Elaine Karalus, June 24, 1967; children: Gregory Alain. *Education:* City College of the City University of New York, B.A., 1963; University of California at Los Angeles, M.B.A., 1965, Ph.D., 1967. *Home:* 100 Bleecker St., New York, N.Y. 10012. *Office:* Graduate School of Business Administration, New York University, 100 Trinity Pl., New York, N.Y. 10006.

CAREER: University of California, Los Angeles, instructor in finance, 1966-67; New York University, Graduate School of Business Administration, New York, N.Y., assistant professor, 1967-70, associate professor of finance, 1970—, coordinator of International Management Program, 1973-75. Visiting professor at Centre d'Enseignement Superieur des Affaires, Jouy-en-Josas, France, 1971-72. Consultant to U.S. Commission on Bankruptcy Laws, 1971-73, and New York City Council on the Environment, 1974. *Member:* American Economic Association, American Finance Association, Financial Management Association, Western Finance Association, Eastern Finance Association, Beta Gamma Sigma, Omicron Delta Epsilon. *Awards, honors:* Chambre Syndicale des Agents de Change research grant, 1971-72; Federal Home Loan Bank Board research grant, 1974-75.

WRITINGS: (Contributor) Eugene Brigham, editor, *Readings in Managerial Finance*, Holt, 1971; *Corporate Bankruptcy in America*, Heath, 1971; (contributor) Samuel Eilon and Thomas Fowkes, editors, *Applications of Management Science in Banking and Finance*, Gower Press, 1972; (contributor) Françoís Girault and Richard Zisswiller, editors, *Finances Modernes Theorie et Pratique* (title means "Modern Finance, Theory and Practice"), DUNOD, 1973; (contributor) Brigham and Ramon Johnson, editors, *Issues in Managerial Finance*, Dryden, 1975; (editor with Ingo Walter) *Contemporary Studies of Economic and Financial Analysis*, Johnson Associates, 1975—. Contributor to journals in his field. Proceedings editor of *Journal of Finance*, 1968—.

WORK IN PROGRESS: Applications of Statistical Discrimination Techniques in Business and Finance: Readings and Text; with Menachem Brenner, "Utilizing Reported Financial Information for a Short-Sale Investment Strategy: A Capital Market Efficiency Test"; research on risk among savings and loan associations.

*   *   *

ALTMAN, Nathaniel   1948-

PERSONAL: Born January 25, 1948, in New York, N.Y.; son of Morris (an electronics engineer) and Sadie (a weaver; maiden name, Davis) Altman. *Education:* Attended University of Wisconsin, 1966-68, and Universidad de Los Andes, 1968-69; University of Wisconsin, B.A., 1971. *Home address:* R.F.D. 1, Putnam Valley, N.Y. 10579.

CAREER: Theosophical Society in America, Wheaton, Ill., resident staff member, 1971; Krotona Institute of Theosophy, Ojai, Calif., registrar and member of faculty, 1972-74; full-time writer, 1974—. *Member:* World Federation of Young Theosophists, Theosophical Society, American Vegetarians (coordinator, 1973—), American Vegan Society.

WRITINGS: Eating for Life: A Book About Vegetarianism, Quest Books, 1973.

WORK IN PROGRESS: Revising *Eating for Life,* and preparing Spanish and French editions; editing an anthology about ahimsa, or dynamic harmlessness, in philosophy and practical application.

SIDELIGHTS: Altman writes: "The sense of separativeness and a general callousness towards human and animal suffering are the obstacles which humanity needs most desparately to overcome. The practise of Ahimsa and in particular, vegetarianism, might be considered as important first steps to solving these problems."

AVOCATIONAL INTERESTS: Yoga, cycling, healing, hand analysis.

*   *   *

ALVAREZ, Eugene   1932-

PERSONAL: Born June 25, 1932, in Jacksonville, Fla.; son of Frank and Aline (McKinney) Alvarez. *Education:* Jacksonville University, B.A., 1961; University of Mississippi, M.A., 1962; University of Georgia, Ph.D., 1966. *Home:* 3763 North Lyons St., Macon, Ga. 31206. *Office:* Department of History, Macon Junior College, Macon, Ga. 31206.

CAREER: Gainesville Junior College, Gainesville, Ga., associate professor of history, 1966-68, head of Division of

Social Science, 1966-68; Valdosta State College, Valdosta, Ga., associate professor of history, 1968-70; University of Maryland, College Park, lecturer in Asian Division, 1970-71, in European Division, 1971-72, lecturer in history, 1972-73; Macon Junior College, Macon, Ga., associate professor of history, 1973—. *Military service:* U.S. Marine Corps, 1950-54, 1956-59; served in Korea. *Member:* Georgia Association of Historians, American Association of University Professors.

WRITINGS: Travel on Southern Antebellum Railroads: 1828-1860, University of Alabama Press, 1974. Contributor to history journals.

WORK IN PROGRESS: Co-editing a set of Civil War letters, *Letters from the Laurel Brigade; But We Got There Nevertheless*, on the movement of General Longstreet's First Corps from Virginia to Chickamauga in 1863.

AVOCATIONAL INTERESTS: Leisure, playing guitar, motorcycle riding, travel.

*   *   *

AMATO, Joseph Anthony 1938-

PERSONAL: Born August 31, 1938, in Detroit, Mich.; son of Joseph (a United Foundation organizer and union secretary) and Ethel May (Linsdeau) Amato; married Catherine Jeanne Bavolack (a nurse), August 6, 1966; children: Felice, Anthony, Adam, Ethel. *Education:* University of Michigan, B.A., 1960; University of Laval, M.A., 1962; graduate study at Indiana University, summer, 1959, and Wayne State University, 1961; University of Rochester, Ph.D., 1970. *Politics:* "Conservative, radical anarchist with socialist leanings." *Religion:* Roman Catholic ("Conservative in theology and radical in social gospel"). *Home:* 229 Main St., Cottonwood, Minn. 56229. *Office:* Department of History, Southwest Minnesota State College, Marshall, Minn. 56258.

CAREER: Public high school teacher of history and Spanish in Michigan, 1960-62; University of Rochester, Rochester, N.Y., instructor in western civilization and Italian Renaissance, 1963-65; State University of New York at Binghamton, instructor in western civilization and European history, 1965-66; University of California, Riverside, instructor in western civilization and European history, 1966-68; Southwest Minnesota State College, Marshall, assistant professor, 1969-72, associate professor of history, 1972—. *Member:* Italian Historical Association, French Historical Organization. *Awards, honors:* National Endowment for the Humanities grant, 1975-76, for a study of European intellectual life.

WRITINGS: Emanuel Mounier and Jacques Maritain: A French Catholic Understanding of the Modern World, University of Alabama Press, 1975. Contributor of articles and reviews to *Worldview, Minnesota Teacher, Great Lakes Review*, and *Minneapolis Tribune*.

WORK IN PROGRESS: Personal essays on modern life and multinational work on twentieth century intellectual life.

SIDELIGHTS: Amato has traveled in Mexico, studied in Paris, France, and done research at the Sturzo Institute in Rome, Italy, and the Dolci Center for Social Research and Action in Sicily. He does research in French, Italian, Spanish, German, and Russian.

*   *   *

AMBROSE, John W(illiam), Jr. 1931-

PERSONAL: Born January 23, 1931, in Worcester, Mass.; son of John W. (a factory worker) and Vivian (Lavallee) Ambrose; married Frances McKillop (a reading consultant), April 15, 1961; children: John W. III, Matthew R., Peter J. *Education:* Brown University, A.B., 1952, A.M., 1959, Ph.D., 1962. *Home:* 26 Magean St., Brunswick, Maine 04011. *Office:* Department of Classics, Bowdoin College, Brunswick, Maine 04011.

CAREER: Roxbury Latin School, West Roxbury, Mass., instructor in classics, 1956-61; Phillips Academy, Andover, Mass., instructor in classics, 1961-64; Taft School, Watertown, Conn., teacher of classics and chairman of department, 1964-66; Bowdoin College, Brunswick, Maine, associate professor of classics and chairman of department, 1966—. Trustee of North Yarmouth Academy; president of St. Charles Parish Council. *Member:* American Philological Association, Classical Association of New England.

WRITINGS: (With W. J. Buehner) *Preparatory Latin*, two volumes, Independent School Press, Volume I, 1969, Volume II, 1970; (with Nathan Dane II) *Greek Attitudes*, Scribner, 1974. Contributor to classical studies journals.

WORK IN PROGRESS: A book on irony in Horace's *Odes*.

AVOCATIONAL INTERESTS: Travel (Greece, Italy, Germany, England, France).

*   *   *

AMERINGER, Charles D. 1926-

PERSONAL: Born September 19, 1926, in Milwaukee, Wis.; son of Carl (a musician) and Pearl (Nelson) Ameringer; married Jean McNicol, June 24, 1949; children: Carl, William. *Education:* University of Wisconsin, B.A., 1949; Fletcher School of Law and Diplomacy, M.A., 1950, Ph.D., 1958. *Office:* Department of History, Pennsylvania State University, 601 Liberal Arts Tower, University Park, Pa. 16802.

CAREER: Bowling Green State University, Bowling Green, Ohio, assistant professor of Latin American history, 1959-63; Pennsylvania State University, University Park, associate professor, 1963-74, professor of Latin American history, 1974—. *Member:* American Historical Association, Conference on Latin American History, Latin American Studies Association, Phi Beta Kappa.

WRITINGS: The Democratic Left in Exile: The Antidictatorial Struggle in the Caribbean, 1945-1959, University of Miami Press, 1974. Contributor to history journals.

WORK IN PROGRESS: A Political Biography of Jose Figueres of Costa Rica.

*   *   *

AMES, Evelyn 1908-

PERSONAL: Born June 26, 1908, in Hamden, Conn.; daughter of Henry A. (a professor of physics) and Olga (an editor and actress; maiden name, Flinch) Perkins; married Amyas Ames (an arts administrator and chairman of Lincoln Center and the New York Philharmonic Orchestra), June 14, 1930; children: Oakes, Edward, Olivia (Mrs. Harrison Hoblitzelle), Joan (Mrs. John A. Woodcock). *Education:* Attended Vassar College. *Politics:* Liberal Democrat. *Religion:* Nondenominational. *Agent:* Cyrilly Abels, 119 West 57th St., New York, N.Y. 10019.

CAREER: Writer. *Member:* Authors League of America, Academy of American Poets, Poetry Society of America, New York Women Poets, Cosmopolitan Club.

WRITINGS: Only the Loving (novel), Dodd, 1952; *My Brother Bird* (juvenile), Dodd, 1954; *The Hawk from Heaven* (poems), Dodd, 1957; *Daughter of the House* (novel based on memoirs), Houghton, 1962; *A Glimpse of Eden* (story of East Africa), Houghton, 1967; *A Wind from the West: Bernstein and the New York Philharmonic Abroad*, Houghton, 1970; *In Time Like Glass: Reflections on a Journey in Asia*, Houghton, 1974. Contributor of poems to magazines.

WORK IN PROGRESS: A collection of poems.

SIDELIGHTS: Evelyn Ames writes: "With a Danish mother, a father who was often called a Renaissance man, and early traveling experience, Europe has played an important role for me. I speak French fluently, and was bilingual as a child in German . . . Have been three times to Africa . . . to Japan, to Asia." *Avocational interests:* Environmental concerns, natural history, birds.

* * *

AMMERMAN, David L(eon) 1938-

PERSONAL: Born June 25, 1938, in Richmond, Ind.; son of Hershel Elison (a grocer) and Maxine (Dougherty) Ammerman. *Education:* Wabash College, B.A., 1960; Cornell University, Ph.D., 1964; Florida State University, law student, 1970—. *Home:* 2209 Amelia Cir., Tallahassee, Fla. 32304. *Office:* Department of History, Florida State University, Tallahassee, Fla. 32306.

CAREER: Florida State University, Tallahassee, assistant professor, 1964-72, associate professor of history, 1972—, director of American studies, 1966-70. *Member:* American Historical Association, American Studies Association, American Civil Liberties Union, Omicron Delta Kappa.

WRITINGS: In the Common Cause: American Response to the Coercive Acts of 1774, University Press of Virginia, 1974.

WORK IN PROGRESS: Research on pre-Civil War legal history.

* * *

ANDELMAN, Eddie 1936-

PERSONAL: Born December 3, 1936, in Boston, Mass.; son of Maxwell (a real estate agent) and Bessie (Shriberg) Andelman; married Judith Rosenberg, May 3, 1969; children: David, Michael, Daniel. *Education:* Boston University, B.S. and B.A., 1958; Northeastern University, M.B.A., 1962. *Home:* 27 Grey Lane, Lynnfield, Mass. 01940. *Office:* Andelman Insurance Agency, 141 Milk St., Boston, Mass. 02109.

CAREER: Andelman Insurance Agency, Boston, Mass., insurance agent, 1960—; Maxwell Andelman Associates, Boston, real estate agent, 1960—. Commentator on WEEI radio program, "Sports Huddle," 1969—; WNAC-TV (Channel 7), sports commentator, 1972—.

WRITINGS: Sports Fans of the World: Unite!, Dodd, 1973. Contributor to *TV Guide, Boston Magazine*, and journals.

* * *

ANDERSEN, Richard 1931-

PERSONAL: Born August 23, 1931, in Kansas City, Kan.; son of Marius Teodor (a carpenter) and Ellen K. (Christensen) Andersen; married Lois Jeannette Petersen (a music teacher), June 9, 1957; children: Kristyn, Deryk,

Jennifer. *Education:* Dana College, B.A., 1953; Trinity Theological Seminary (now Wartburg Theological Seminary), B.D., 1960; California Graduate School of Theology, Ph.D., 1972. *Home:* 5510 West Beck Lane, Glendale, Ariz. 85306. *Office:* Community Church of Joy, 16635 North 51st Ave., Glendale, Ariz. 85306.

CAREER: Dana College, Blair, Neb., public relations assistant, 1951-53; University of Dubuque, Dubuque, Iowa, public relations assistant, 1957-60; ordained Luthern minister, 1960; associate pastor of Lutheran church in North Hollywood, Calif., 1960-62; founding pastor of Lutheran church in Ojai, Calif., 1962-64; senior pastor of Lutheran churches in Rancho Cordova, Calif., 1964-68, and La Habra, Calif., 1968-73; Community Church of Joy, Glendale, Ariz., founding pastor, 1973—. Executive director of Lutheran schools in Hacienda Heights, Calif., 1973; member of Lutheran campus council at Arizona State University. *Military service:* U.S. Army, 1954-56. *Member:* Glendale Samaritan Hospital Chaplain's Organization.

WRITINGS: Devotions Along the Way, Augsburg, 1972; *Loving in Forgiveness*, Concordia, 1973; *Your Keys to the Executive Suite*, Concordia, 1973; *Flights of Devotion*, Concordia, 1973; *Roads to Recovery*, Concordia, 1974; *For Those Who Mourn*, Concordia, 1974; *Now for the Good Wine*, Concordia, 1974; *The Love Formula: Living in Forgiveness*, Concordia, 1974; *Living Lenten Portraits*, Concordia, 1975. Contributor to religious periodicals.

WORK IN PROGRESS: The Joy of Prayer; a book of devotional love poetry, with illustrations; a book of Lenten sermons.

SIDELIGHTS: Andersen writes: "I have a novel up my sleeve, and hope to continue producing relevant, though not heavy monographs in Christian theology. I would also like doing a more detailed work in Biblical sites frequented by American tourists, which includes the photography . . . I am interested in serving an English-language congregation in Europe, ministering to English-speaking people who are employed or stationed in that foreign city." *Avocational interests:* International travel, photography.

* * *

ANDERSON, Bernhard Word 1916-

PERSONAL: Born September 25, 1916, in Dover, Mo.; son of Arthur Lincoln and Grace (Word) Anderson; married Joyce Griswold, September 22, 1936; children: Carol Joyce, Sylvia Joan, Ronald Bernhard, Ruth Anne. *Education:* University of the Pacific, B.A., 1936; Pacific School of Religion, M.A., 1938, B.D., 1939; Yale University, Ph.D., 1945. *Home:* 89 Mercer St., Princeton, N.J. 08540. *Office:* Princeton Theological Seminary, Princeton, N.J. 08540.

CAREER: Ordained minister of United Methodist Church, 1939; pastor in Pittsburg, Calif., 1936-37, Sunnyvale, Calif., 1937-41, Connecticut, 1942-44, Millbrae, Calif., 1944-46, Columbus, N.Y., 1946-48; Colgate University, Hamilton, N.Y., instructor in religion, 1946-48; University of North Carolina, Chapel Hill, James A. Gray Associate Professor of Bible, 1948-50; Colgate-Rochester Divinity School, Rochester, N.Y., Joseph B. Hoyt Professor of Old Testament Interpretation, 1950-54; Drew University, Theological Seminary, Madison, N.J., Henry Anson Buttz Professor of Biblical Theology, 1954-68, dean, 1954-63; Princeton Theological Seminary, Princeton, N.J., professor of Old Testament theology, 1968—. Chairman of Study Department of United Student Christian Council, 1951-54;

Annual Professor of Archaeology, American School of Oriental Research, Jerusalem, 1963-64; Lund Lecturer, North Park Theological Seminary, 1965; Burns Memorial Lecturer, University of Otago, 1969; Haskel Lecturer, Oberlin College, 1970. Active in Y.M.C.A., Y.W.C.A., and Student Christian Movement. *Member:* Society of Biblical Literature, American Academy of Religion, Biblical Colloquim, Bible Theologians, American Theological Society, Pi Gamma Mu. *Awards, honors:* D.D., Pacific School of Religion, 1960, Colgate University, 1965; S.T.D., University of the Pacific, 1961.

WRITINGS: Rediscovering the Bible, Association Press, 1951; *The Unfolding Drama of the Bible: Eight Studies Introducing the Bible as a Whole*, Association Press, 1953, revised edition, 1971; *Understanding the Old Testament*, Prentice-Hall, 1957, 3rd edition, 1975; *The Living World of the Old Testament*, Longmans, Green, 1958, 2nd edition, 1967; (editor with Walter Harrelson, and contributor) *Israel's Prophetic Heritage: Essays in Honor of James Muilenburg*, Harper, 1962; (editor) *The Old Testament and Christian Faith: A Theological Discussion*, Harper, 1963; *The Beginning of History: Genesis*, Abingdon, 1963; *Creation Versus Chaos: The Reinterpretation of Mythical Symbolism in the Bible*, Association Press, 1967; *Out of the Depths: Studies into the Meaning of the Book of Psalms*, Westminster Press, 1974. Contributor to *Interpreter's Bible* and to journals in his field. Chairman of editorial board, *Christian Scholar*, 1956-58; member of editorial board, *Old Testament Library*, 1974—.

WORK IN PROGRESS: Commentary on the Book of Genesis, for Fortress Press; a book on archaeological parallels to Old Testament literature, for Prentice-Hall; editing *Essays in Biblical Theology*, by Will Herberg, for Westminster Press.

*   *   *

ANDERSON, (Hobson) Dewey   1897-

PERSONAL: Born January 14, 1897, in Grand Forks, N.D.; son of Hans Daniel (a businessman) and Amalia B. (Peterson) Anderson; married Erma Sams, June 30, 1920; children: Harry, June; stepchildren: Isabel Swisher, Alan Nichols. *Education:* Stanford University, A.B. (with great distinction), 1927, M.A., 1928, Ph.D., 1932. *Politics:* Democrat. *Religion:* Methodist. *Home:* 206 Del Mesa, Carmel, Calif. 93921.

CAREER: Young Mens Christian Association, began as physical education director, field staff member of Work and Relief Committee for Prisoners of War of Poland and Baltic States, 1921-24; executive secretary of American section, European Student Relief, 1924-27; Stanford University, Palo Alto, Calif., member of faculty and director of Stanford-Alaska Educational Study, 1930-34; member of California state legislature, 1935-37; John Randolph and Dora Haynes Foundation, Los Angeles, Calif., research director of economic problems, 1936-38; appointed budgeteer of state of California, 1938-39; director of California State Relief Administration, 1939; Temporary National Economic Committee, Washington, D.C., chief of American hemisphere division, 1942; U.S. Department of State, Washington, D.C., chief of supply and transport division of Office of Foreign Relief and Rehabilitation, 1943; War Food Administration, Washington, D.C., member of food advisory commission, 1943; United Nations Relief and Rehabilitation Administration, founding member and chief of field operations, 1944; U.S. Senate, Washington, D.C.,

executive secretary and research director of Small Business Committee, 1945; Public Affairs Institute, Washington, D.C., founder and executive director, beginning in 1947. Co-director of Institute of Occupational Research of Stanford University; member of board of directors and treasurer of Citizens Committee on Natural Resources. *Military service:* U.S. Army, 1943; became lieutenant colonel. *Member:* American Economic Association, American Political Science Association, Phi Beta Kappa, Phi Delta Kappa, National Press Club.

WRITINGS: (With Walter Crosby Eells) *Alaska Natives: A Survey of Their Sociological and Educational Status*, Stanford University Press, 1935, reprinted, Kraus Reprint, 1972; *Our California State Taxes: Facts and Problems*, Stanford University Press, 1937; (with Percy E. Davidson) *Occupational Trends in the United States*, Stanford University Press, 1940; *Taxation, Recovery, and Defense*, U.S. Government Printing Office, 1940; *California State Government*, Stanford University Press, 1942; (with Davidson) *Ballots and the Democratic Class Struggle: A Study in the Background of Political Education*, Stanford University Press, 1943; (with Davidson) *Recent Occupational Trends in American Labor*, Stanford University Press, 1945; (with Michael M. Davis) *Medical Care for the Individual and the Issue of Compulsory Health Insurance*, U.S. Government Printing Office, 1948; (with Stephen Raushenbush) *A Policy and Program for Success*, Public Affairs Institute, 1950; (with Raushenbush) *To Make a Free World: An Exploration of a New Foreign Policy*, Public Affairs Institute, 1955; *Health Service Is a Basic Right of All the People*, Public Affairs Institute, 1956; (with others) *Natural Resources: Their Protection and Development* (booklet), Public Affairs Institute, 1959; (with others) *The People and 1960*, Public Affairs Institute, 1960; *Always to Start Anew: The Making of a Public Activist* (autobiography), Vantage, 1970.*

*   *   *

ANDERSON, Erica   1914-

PERSONAL: Born August 8, 1914, in Vienna, Austria; came to United States in 1940, naturalized in 1945; daughter of Edward and Ilona Kellner; married Larry Collier Anderson, June 20, 1940. *Education:* Attended photography school in Vienna, Austria. *Home:* 7 Hurlburt Rd., Great Barrington, Mass. 01230.

CAREER: Documentary film maker, with films on such people as Henry Moore, Grandma Moses, Albert Schweitzer, and Carl Jung. President, Erica Anderson, Inc.; founder of Albert Schweitzer Friendship House in Great Barrington, Mass. Member of board of directors, Albert Schweitzer Fellowship.

WRITINGS: (Collection of photographs by Anderson: text and captions by Eugene Exman) *The World of Albert Schweitzer*, Harper, 1955; (collection of photographs by Anderson: introduction and explanatory texts by Louis P. Lochner) *New York*, W. Andermann (Munich), 1960; *Albert Schweitzer*, Chilton, 1961; *Albert Schweitzer's Gift of Friendship*, Harper, 1964; *The Schweitzer Album: A Portrait in Words and Pictures* (with additional text by Albert Schweitzer; Book-of-the Month Club selection), Harper, 1965; (with Ann Atwood) *For All That Lives: With the Words of Albert Schweitzer*, Scribner, 1974.

*   *   *

ANDERSON, Jack(son Northman)   1922-

PERSONAL: Born October 19, 1922, in Long Beach,

Calif.; son of Orlando N. (a postal clerk) and Agnes (Mortensen) Anderson; married Olivia Farley, August 10, 1949; children: Cheri, Lance, Lauri, Tina, Kevin, Randy, Tanya, Rodney, Bryan. *Education:* University of Utah, 1940-41; Georgetown University, 1947-48; George Washington University, 1948. *Religion:* Church of Jesus Christ of Latter-day Saints. *Home:* 7300 Burdette Ct., Bethesda, Md. 20034. *Office:* 1612 K St. N.W., Washington, D.C. 20006.

CAREER: Part time reporter for newspapers in Utah beginning at age 12; *Salt Lake City Tribune*, Salt Lake City, Utah, reporter, 1939-41; missionary for Church of Jesus Christ of Latter-day Saints, 1941-44; *Deseret News*, Salt Lake City, war correspondent in China, 1945; "The Washington Merry-Go-Round" (syndicated column), Washington, D.C., reporter, 1947—; partner, 1965—, sole author, 1969—. *Parade*, Washington, D.C., editor, 1954-68, bureau chief, 1968—. Lecturer; radio ("Jack Anderson Radio Report") and television broadcaster; part owner of *Annapolis Evening Capital*. Trustee, Chinese Refugee Relief, 1962—. Staff member of service newspapers and Armed Forces Radio while serving in U.S. Army, 1946-47. *Military service:* U.S. Merchant Marine, 1944-45; Quartermaster Corps, U.S. Army, 1946-47. *Member:* White House Correspondents Association, National Press Club. *Awards, honors:* Recommended (with Drew Pearson) for the Pulitzer Prize for national reporting, 1967, for articles on U.S. Senator Thomas J. Dodd; Pulitzer Prize for national reporting, 1972, for articles on India-Pakistan crisis.

WRITINGS: (With Ronald W. May) *McCarthy: The Man, the Senator, the "ism,"* Beacon Press, 1952; (with Fred Blumenthal) *The Kefauver Story*, Dial, 1956; (with Drew Pearson) *U.S.A.—Second Class Power?*, Simon & Schuster, 1958; *Washington Expose*, Public Affairs Press, 1967; (with Drew Pearson) *The Case Against Congress*, Simon & Schuster, 1968; (with Carl Kalvelage) *American Government . . . Like It Is*, General Learning Press, 1972; (with George Clifford) *The Anderson Papers*, Random House, 1973.

SIDELIGHTS: Discussing *The Anderson Papers*, Benjamin De Mott feels that "at their best these pieces remain indispensable materials for students of the Watergate world that was opened to view this past summer, and they do much to temper skepticism about the essential value of the Anderson enterprise." Said Al Marlens of the same book: "No newspaperman can read this book, punctuated as it is with quotations from the records of Cabinet meetings, F.B.I. files and diplomatic messages, without admiration and an unsuppressed cheer. No citizen should either." Scott Wright agreed: "Anderson's style of journalism provides a very urgently needed counterforce to a government too far removed from the public." Anderson's column is syndicated in 746 newspapers. He was a journalist from the age of 12, but his first job—editor of the Boy Scout page of the *Deseret News*—hardly indicated that he would become one of the most famous investigative reporters in the country.*

*   *   *

ANDERSON, Jennifer 1942-

PERSONAL: Born July 8, 1942, in Sydney, Australia; daughter of Stephen Peter (a metal worker) and Kathleen (a secretary; maiden name, Johanson) Tomlinson; married David Edward Anderson (a professor of geology), September, 1961; children: Sharon, Scott, Allison. *Education:* Attended Sydney Technical College, 1957-59, Ashton School

of Art, 1960-62, and University of Illinois, 1970—. *Home:* 804 West Hill St., Champaign, Ill. 61820.

CAREER: Sydney University, School of Tropical Medicine, Sydney, Australia, laboratory technician, 1958-62; University of Illinois, School of Life Sciences, Champaign, laboratory technician, 1969—; free-lance illustrator. *Member:* National Speleological Society, Cave Research Foundation (Joint venturer), Mid-Illinois Grotto (chairman, 1971-72).

WRITINGS: (Editor) *American Caving Accidents*, National Speleological Society, 1971; *Cave Exploring*, Association Press, 1974. Editor and illustrator of "The Caving Information Series," National Speleological Society, 1974—. Editor of *Mid-Illinois Grotto Newsletter*, 1968-70.

WORK IN PROGRESS: A novel, *Under the Border*.

SIDELIGHTS: "The tragedy of vandalized caves and the large number of cave exploring accidents appalls me," Jennifer Anderson wrote. "Prevention of both these ills is largely a matter of reaching everyone who is lured to the underground, with information on techniques which protect, as far as possible, both explorer and cave."

*   *   *

ANDERSON, Mona 1910-

PERSONAL: Born March 11, 1910, in New Brighton, New Zealand; daughter of William and Alice (Holland) Tarling; married Ronald Edward Anderson (a sheep rancher), June 15, 1940. *Education:* Attended South Malvern School, Canterbury, New Zealand. *Religion:* Anglican. *Home:* 15 McMillan St., Darfield, Canterbury, New Zealand.

CAREER: Operator, with husband, of sheep ranch in Rakaia Gorge, Canterbury, New Zealand. Writer.

WRITINGS—All published by A. H. & A. W. Reed: *A River Rules My Life*, 1963; *Good Logs of Algidus*, 1965; *Over the River*, 1966; *The Wonderful World at My Doorstep*, 1968; *A Letter From James*, 1972; *MaryLou: A High Country Lamb* (children's book), 1975. Contributor to *Family Doctor*, *Weekly Press*, and *New Zealand Herald*. Writer of radio scripts.

WORK IN PROGRESS: Research into the history of threshing mills of Canterbury, for a book to be titled *The Water-Joey*.

*   *   *

ANDREE, Richard Vernon 1919-

PERSONAL: Born December 16, 1919, in Minneapolis, Minn.; son of Richard A. and Marguerite (Eigner) Andree; married Josephine Peet, December 16, 1944; children: David, Peter, Suzanne, Jeanne. *Education:* University of Chicago, B.S., 1942; University of Wisconsin, Ph.M., 1945, Ph.D., 1949. *Home:* 627 East Boyd St., Norman, Okla. 73069, *Office:* Department of Mathematics, University of Oklahoma, Norman, Okla. 73069.

CAREER: University of Oklahoma, Norman, assistant professor, 1949-54, associate professor, 1954-57, professor of mathematics, 1957—, chairman of department, 1961-69, acting director of Computer Laboratory, 1958, director of Mathematical Computer Consultants, 1962—. Visiting associate professor at Haverford College, 1955-56; visiting professor at Oklahoma State University and Montana State University, both 1956-57; distinguished lecturer at Canadian Mathematics Institute of University of Alberta, 1959; principal lecturer at Karnataki University, 1965. Fellow of

National Bureau of Standards, spring, 1959; member of board of governors of Center for Research in College Instruction of Science and Mathematics; director of Computer Systems Engineers; member of advisory panel for computer applications in research, of National Science Foundation; research councilor for Oklahoma University's Research Institute.

MEMBER: American Association for the Advancement of Science (fellow), American Mathematical Society, American Society for Engineering Education, Association for Computing Machinery (sponsor of student chapter), Association of Educational Data Systems, Association of Symbolic Logic, COMMON Computer Users Group, Computer Assisted Instruction in Mathematics (member of national committee), Data Processing Management Association (member of Oklahoma City board of directors), Mathematical Association of America, Society for Industrial and Applied Mathematics (visiting lecturer), National Council of Teachers of Mathematics, Oklahoma Council of Teachers of Mathematics, Oklahoma Computing Consortium, Sigma Xi, Mu Alpha Theta, Pi Mu Epsilon. *Awards, honors:* Carnegie Foundation grant, 1955-56, for research at Haverford College; C. C. MacDuffee Distinguished Service Award, from Pi Mu Epsilon, 1966; named to DeMolay Legion of Honor, 1967; Her Majesty's Mint, 1973, for outstanding contributions to international civic leadership with youth groups (England); outstanding educator award from National Council of Teachers of Mathematics, 1973.

WRITINGS: (With J. C. Brixey) *Fundamentals of College Mathematics*, Holt, 1954, revised edition, 1961; *Matrices and Congruences*, Summer Conference for Mathematics Teachers, 1954; *Survey of Abstract Algebra*, Mathematics Teacher's Institute, 1955; *The Need for Modern Mathematics*, National Science Foundation Institute, 1955; *Programming the IBM 650*, Magnetic Drum Computer Extension Division, University of Oklahoma, 1955; (with Brixey) *Modern Trigonometry*, Holt, 1955; *Boolean Algebra*, Department of Electrical Engineering, Oklahoma State University, 1965; *Calculus for Secondary School Science Teachers*, National Science Foundation Year Institute, 1956; *Modern Mathematics for High School Science Teachers*, National Science Foundation Summer Institute, 1957; *Calculus for Mature Students*, McGraw, 1958; *Selections from Modern Abstract Algebra*, Holt, 1958, revised edition, 1971; *Programming the IBM 650 Computer*, Department of Mathematics, University of Oklahoma, 1958; *Preparing a Questionnaire for Punched Card Analysis*, Computing Center, Oklahoma University, 1959.

A Table of Indices and Power Residues for All Primes and Prime Powers Below 2000, Norton, 1962; *Introductory Calculus with Analytical Geometry*, McGraw, 1963; *Computer Programming and Related Mathematics for the IBM 1620*, Wiley, 1966; *Introduction A L'Algebre*, Gauthier Villars, 1968; *Twentieth Century Algebra in High School*, National Council of Teachers of Mathematics, 1968; (with wife, J. P. Andree, and son, D. D. Andree) *Computer Programming: Techniques, Analysis, and Mathematics*, Prentice-Hall, 1973.

Contributor to *New Catholic Encyclopedia*. Contributor of more than twenty-five articles and reviews to a variety of professional journals. Editor of *Math Log;* founder and former editor of *Oklahoma University Mathematics Letter;* former editor of *Journal of the Mathematical Association of America*.

WORK IN PROGRESS: Problem Solving; Computers Are for You; Numerical Analysis.

* * *

ANDRESEN, Jack
     See ANDRESEN, John H(enry), Jr.

* * *

ANDRESEN, John H(enry), Jr.   1917-
     (Jack Andresen)

PERSONAL: Born January 25, 1917, in Glen Rock, N.J.; son of John H. (an engineer) and Adelaide (Schmidt) Andresen; married Mary M. McLaughlin, December 21, 1954 (divorced, 1961); married Evelyn M. Brolsma, January 21, 1962; children: (first marriage) Peggy C., J. Susan (Mrs. John Hill), J. Kevin. *Education:* Stevens Institute of Technology, M.E., 1937. *Politics:* "No party affiliation." *Religion:* "Nominally Christian." *Address:* P.O. Box 974, Georgetown, Cayman Island, British West Indies.

CAREER: E. I. Dupont, Wilmington, Del., industrial engineer, 1937-39; General Machine Co., Paterson, N.J., design engineer, 1939-40; civilian inspector of naval materials for U.S. Navy, 1940-41; Kollsman Instrument Co., Elmhurst, N.Y., chief engineer, 1941-60; Astek Instrument Corp., Armonk, N.Y., founder and vice-president for engineering, 1960-63; Intercontinental Dynamics Corp., Englewood, N.J., founder and vice-president for engineering, 1960—. Design consultant to E-P Products, 1958—. Councilman in West Milford, N.J., 1969-73; director of Cayman Islands Conservation Committee, 1974—. *Member:* Society of Automotive Engineers, Aeronautical Radio, Inc., American Water Ski Association (president, 1958-59). *Awards, honors:* Carnegie Hero Medal, 1958, for rescuing victims of plane crash in water; Eastern Ice Yacht Association champion in Arrow Class, 1970, 1971, 1972, 1973, and numerous other amateur sports awards.

WRITINGS—All under name Jack Andresen: *Skiing on Water*, Ronald, 1950, 3rd edition, 1960; *Fundamentals of Aircraft Flight and Engine Instruments*, Hayden, 1969; *Sailing on Ice*, A. S. Barnes, 1974.

WORK IN PROGRESS: Underwater nature photography.

AVOCATIONAL INTERESTS: Travel, water skiing, ice boating, flying, photography, playing organ and piano, scuba diving.

* * *

ANDREWS, Ernest E(ugene)   1932-

PERSONAL: Born July 12, 1932, in Holland, Mich.; son of Clair B. (an electronics engineer) and Helen (Nemeth) Andrews; married Janet Grover (an educator), June 18, 1955; children: Kathryn Mary, David Edward. *Education:* University of Michigan, A.B., 1954, M.S.W., 1956. *Home:* 5425 Brillwood Lane, Cincinnati, Ohio 45243. *Agent:* Marie Wilkerson, 230 Park Ave., New York, N.Y. 10017. *Office:* Family Institute, 2600 Euclid Ave., Cincinnati, Ohio 45219.

CAREER: Private practice of psychotherapy in Cincinnati, Ohio, 1970—; Family Institute, Cincinnati, Ohio, program director, 1970—. Visiting professor at Ohio State University, 1971—, and at University of Cincinnati, 1972—. Consultant to U.S. Air Force. *Military service:* U.S. Public Health Service, 1958-60. *Member:* Royal Society of Medicine (affiliate member), American Group Psychotherapy Association (fellow), American Orthopsychiatric Association (fellow).

WRITINGS: (Contributor) Allan Dye, editor, *Group Counseling: Methods and Procedures*, Houghton, 1973; *The Emotionally Disturbed Family: And Some Gratifying Alternatives*, Jason Aronson, 1974; (contributor) Malcolm L. Gardner and Norman A. Brandes, editors, *Group Therapy for the Adolescent*, Jason Aronson, 1974. Contributor to *International Journal of Group Psychotherapy*.

AVOCATIONAL INTERESTS: Hiking, spelunking, painting.

* * *

ANDREWS, John Williams 1898-1975

PERSONAL: Born November 10, 1898, in Bryn Mawr, Pa.; son of Charles McLean and Evangeline (Walker) Andrews; married Elizabeth Robert, July 14, 1934 (divorced, 1953); married Miriam Benton Wise, October 30, 1953; children: (first marriage) John Douglas Walker. *Education:* Yale University, A.B., 1920, J.D., 1926. *Home:* 52 Cranbury Rd., Westport, Conn. 06830.

CAREER: Manager of Chung Mei News Agency, and International News correspondent, Peking, China, 1921-22; *New Haven Journal Carrier*, New Haven, Conn., legislative correspondent, 1922-23. Admitted to the Bar of New York State, 1927; Root, Clark, Buckner & Ballantine (law firm), New York, N.Y., lawyer, 1926-32; Yale University, New Haven, special instructor in history department, and fellow at Timothy Dwight College, 1938-40; assistant to administrator, Connecticut State Defense Council, 1940-42; U.S. Department of Justice, Washington, D.C., chief of Federal State Relations Section, 1942-48, trial attorney in Anti-Trust Division, 1948-50; Washington Institute of Mental Hygiene, Washington, D.C., director, 1951-52; member of public relations council, Hill & Knowlton, Inc., 1952-53; president, Andrews Associates, Inc., 1954-62. Free-lance writer, 1932—. Administrative vice-chairman, National Conference on Prevention and Control of Juvenile Delinquency, 1947-48; Washington Housing Association, vice-president, 1947-52, president, 1952. Vice-chairman and trustee, Lingnan University, Canton, China. Director, Cooper Hill Writers' Conference, East Dover, Vt. *Military service:* U.S. Aviation Service, World War I; became second lieutenant.

MEMBER: Poetry Society of America, Catholic Poetry Society of America, Wolf's Head, Alpha Delta Phi, Aviation Country Club of Long Island, Elizabethan Club, Cosmos Club (Washington, D.C.), Rowfant Club (Cleveland), Yale Club (New York). *Awards, honors:* Co-recipient of Robert Frost Poetry Award, Holt, Rinehart & Winston, 1963.

*WRITINGS—*All poetry: *Prelude to "Icaros,"* Farrar & Rinehart, 1936, reprinted, Branden Press, 1966, portions published as *First Flight: The Story of Orville and Wilbur Wright at Kitty Hawk*, Pavilion Press, 1962, new edition, 1966; *A Ballad of Channel Crossings*, Press of Timothy Dwight College, Yale University, 1941; *Hill Country North*, Branden Press, 1965; *The Story of Flying*, Robert J. Tyndall, 1968; *A.D. Twenty-One Hundred: A Narrative of Space*, with foreword by Walter Cronkite, Branden Press, 1969; *Triptych for the Atomic Age*, Branden Press, 1970. Also author of *Legends of Flight*; author of radio verse play, "Georgia Transport," 1938. Contributor of poetry and articles to journals. Editor, *St. Lawrence Seaway Fact Sheet*, 1958-61; editor-in-chief, *Poet Lore*.

WORK IN PROGRESS: A documentary poem of the twentieth century, with Charles A. Lindbergh as the central figure, "The Round Earth Under."

OBITUARIES: New York Times, March 20, 1975; *Washington Post*, March 26, 1975; *AB Bookmans Weekly*, April 21, 1975.

(Died March 18, 1975)

* * *

ANDRIC, Ivo 1892-1975

February 10, 1892—March 13, 1975; Yugoslav diplomat, translator, and author of novels, short stories, and poetry. Obituaries: *Washington Post*, March 14, 1975; *New York Times*, March 14, 1975; *Newsweek*, March 24, 1975; *AB Bookman's Weekly*, April 7, 1975; *Current Biography*, May, 1975.

* * *

ANGELL, Roger 1920-

PERSONAL: Born September 19, 1920, in New York, N.Y.; son of Ernest and Katharine Shepley (Sergeant) Angell; married Evelyn Ames Baker, October, 1942 (divorced, 1963); married Carol Rogge, October, 1963; children: (first marriage) Caroline S., Alice; (second marriage) John Henry. *Education:* Harvard University, A.B., 1942. *Home:* 1261 Madison Avenue, New York, N.Y. 10028. *Office:* The New Yorker, 25 West 43rd Street, New York, N.Y. 10036.

CAREER: Curtis Publishing Company, New York, N.Y., editor and writer for *Magazine X*, 1946-47; *Holiday Magazine*, New York, N.Y., senior editor, 1947-56; *New Yorker*, New York, N.Y., fiction editor and general contributor, 1956—. Trustee of Sydenham Hospital and Shalom, Inc. *Military service:* U.S. Army Air Forces, 1942-46; served in Pacific Theatre. *Member:* Author's Guild (vice-president, 1975—), National Book Committee, P.E.N., New York Civil Liberties Union, Century Association, Coffee House.

WRITINGS: The Stone Arbor and Other Stories, Little, Brown, 1960, reprinted, Books for Libraries, 1970; *A Day in the Life of Roger Angell* (humorous sketches), Viking, 1970; *The Summer Game*, Viking, 1972.

* * *

ANGLE, Paul M(cClelland) 1900-1975

December 25, 1900—May 11, 1975; American historian, director and secretary of historical society, librarian, and editor or author of books on Abraham Lincoln, the Civil War, and other historical themes. Obituaries: *New York Times*, May 13, 1975; *Washington Post*, May 15, 1975; *Current Biography*, August, 1975. (CA-21/22)

* * *

ANTOINE-DARIAUX, Genevieve 1914-

PERSONAL: Name is listed in some sources as Dariaux; born June 21, 1914, in Paris, France; daughter of Andre Dariaux (a doctor); married Georges Antoine, February 12, 1936. *Education:* Attended schools in France and England. *Religion:* Catholic. *Home:* 34 rue Desbordes Valmore, 75016 Paris, France.

CAREER: House of Nina Ricci (couturier), Paris, France, director, 1959-68. Secretary of French Fashion Group, Paris, 1966-67.

WRITINGS: Les Voies de l'elegance, Hachette, 1964, translation by Marjorie Stoneridge published as *Elegance: A Complete Guide for Every Woman Who Wants to Be*

Well and Properly Dressed on All Occasions, Doubleday, 1964; *Entertaining with Elegance*, Doubleday, 1965; *The Men in Your Life*, Doubleday, 1968; *Accent on Elegance*, Doubleday, 1970; *The Fall Collection* (novel), Doubleday, 1973. Author of a fashion column, "Le Jardin des modes." Contributor of articles to *Family Weekly*.

WORK IN PROGRESS: A book of cooking recipes.

*　　*　　*

ANTON, Michael J(ames) 1940-

PERSONAL: Born December 6, 1940, in Memphis, Tenn.; son of William H. (a mechanic) and Dorothy (Eken) Anton; married Charlotte Ann Kirsch, June 7, 1964; children: Mark, Philip, Matthew. *Education:* St. Paul's College, A.A., 1960; Concordia College, Fort Wayne, Ind., B.A., 1962; Concordia Theological Seminary, B.Div. and M.Div., 1966. *Politics:* Independent. *Home:* 2658 Quakezik, Hastings, Mich. 49058. *Office:* Grace Lutheran Church, 239 East North St., Hastings, Mich. 49058.

CAREER: Ordained Lutheran minister in 1966; pastor in Niagara Falls, Ontario, 1966-67; Niagara College of Applied Arts and Technology, Welland, Ontario, master teacher of English, philosophy, and social science, 1967-69; Grace Lutheran Church, Hastings, Mich., pastor, 1969—. President of Hastings Community Activities Center, 1971-72.

WRITINGS: From Humbug to Heaven (advent dialogue), C.S.S. Publishing, 1972; *What Are We Going to Do with the King?* (juvenile Christmas play), C.S.S. Publishing, 1972; *The Night That Was* (juvenile Christmas play), C.S.S. Publishing, 1972; *Evangelism in 3-D* (chancel drama), C.S.S. Publishing, 1973; *Snoring through Sermons* (collection), C.S.S. Publishing, 1974.

WORK IN PROGRESS: A chancel drama for Lent.

*　　*　　*

ANTROBUS, John 1933-

PERSONAL: Born July 2, 1933, in Aldershot, England; married Margaret McCormick, 1958; children: Daniel, Nicholas, Louise. *Education:* Attended King Edward VII Nautical College and Sandhurst Military Academy. *Home:* 13 Allfarthing Lane, London S.W. 18, England. *Agent:* Blanche Marvin, Elspeth Cochrane Agency, 31a Sloane St., London S.W. 1, England.

CAREER: Playwright, author of scripts for radio, television, and film, 1955—; theatre director and actor, 1963—. Directed and appeared in "You'll Come to Love Your Sperm Test," Hampstead Theatre, London, 1965; directed "The Bed-Sitting Room," with Spike Milligan, Mermaid Theatre, London, 1963; acted in "An Evening with John Antrobus," London, 1969, and in "The Contractor," London, 1970. *Military service:* British Merchant Navy, apprentice deck officer, 1950-52. British Army, East Surrey Regiment, 1952-55. *Awards, honors:* George Devine Award, 1970.

WRITINGS:—Plays: (With Spike Milligan) *The Bed-Sitting Room* (produced in London at Mermaid Theatre, January, 1963; revised version produced, 1966), Jack Hobbs, 1970; "Royal Commission Review," produced in London, 1964; "Cane of Honour," produced in London, 1965; "You'll Come to Love Your Sperm Test" (produced in London at Hampstead Theatre, 1965), published in *Plays and Players,* edited by Peter Roberts, Volumes 12 and 13, Hansom Books (London), 1965; *Trixie and Baba* (produced

in London at Royal Court Theatre, August 21, 1968), Calder & Boyars, 1969; "Captain Oates' Left Sock," produced in London, 1969, produced in London at Royal Court Theatre, 1973; "An Evening with John Antrobus," produced in London, 1969; *Why Bournemouth? And Other Plays* (contains "Why Bournemouth?," produced in London, 1968; "The Missing Links," televised, 1965; "An Apple a Day," televised, 1971), Calder & Boyars, 1970; "Stranger in a Cafeteria," produced in Edinburgh, 1971; "The Looneys," produced in Edinburgh at Edinburgh Traverse, 1971; "Crete and Sergeant Pepper," produced in London at Royal Court Theatre, May 24, 1972; "Mos Gaaborosky Academy," produced at Royal Court Theatre, 1975.

Screenplays: "Idle on Parade," 1960; (with others) "The Wrong Arm of the Law," 1963; "The Big Job," 1965; "The Bed-Sitting Room" (adaptation of play by Antrobus and Milligan), 1970.

Author of television scripts for numerous series, including "The Army Game," "Bootsie and Snudge," "Early to Braden," and for individual shows. Radio scripts include the "Idiot Weekly" and "Goon Show" series.

*　　*　　*

APPLBAUM, Ronald L. 1943-

PERSONAL: Born December 14, 1943, in Charleroi, Pa.; son of Irwin Applbaum; married Susan Stone (a teacher), July 4, 1968; children: Lee David. *Education:* California State University, Long Beach, B.A., 1965, M.A., 1966; Pennsylvania State University, Ph.D., 1969. *Home:* 4181 Avenida Madrid, Cypress, Calif. 90630. *Office:* Department of Speech, California State University, Long Beach, Calif. 90840.

CAREER: California State University, Long Beach, associate professor of speech, 1969—. *Member:* International Communication Association, Speech Communication Association, American Association of University Professors, Phi Cappa Phi (secretary, 1974-75; vice president, 1975-76).

WRITINGS: (With Karl Anatol and others) *Fundamental Concepts of Communication*, Canfield Press, 1973; (with others) *Process of Group Communication*, Science Research Associates, 1974; (with Anatol) *Strategies of Persuasive Communication*, C. E. Merrill, 1974; (edited with others) *Speech Communication: A Basic Anthology*, Macmillan, 1975; *Communication: Process and Behavior in Organizations*, Holt, in press.

WORK IN PROGRESS: Fundamentals of Group Discussion, publication by Science Research Associates expected in 1977.

SIDELIGHTS: Applbaum told *CA:* "My motivation for writing comes from the words of a former colleague who suggested that the value of writing texts lies not in the material presented or the mode of presentation but in its ability to prompt others to conduct research or produce a better textbook." *Avocational interests:* Bridge, sports.

*　　*　　*

ARCHER, Frank
See O'CONNOR, Richard

*　　*　　*

ARCHER, Fred 1915-

PERSONAL: Born April 30, 1915, in Ashton-Underhill,

England; son of Thomas Archer (a farmer); married October 7, 1944; children: Shelagh Janet, June Sylvia. *Education:* Attended schools in England. *Politics:* Conservative. *Religion:* Methodist.

CAREER: Farmer, market gardener, and sheep breeder. *Member:* National Farmers Union, Society of Authors, History Society, Associated Speakers.

WRITINGS—All published by Hodder & Stoughton except as indicated: *The Distant Scene*, 1967; *Under the Parish Lantern*, 1969; *Hawthorn Hedge Country*, 1970; *The Secrets of Bredon Hill: A Country Chronicle of the Year 1900*, 1971; *A Lad of Evesham Vale*, 1972; *Muddy Boots and Sunday Suits: Memories of a Country Childhood*, 1973; (editor) *The Countryman Cottage Life Book*, David & Charles, 1974. Also author of *Goldensheaves and Black Horses*, 1974. Contributor to *A Guide to Pershore and Its Environs*, by Roger Corbet-Milward, published by Committee of Pershore Millennium 972-1972, 1972.

SIDELIGHTS: Archer told *CA*: "[I am] a countryman still living in the same parish after sixty years in a house in the garden where I was born. I am intensely interested in village folk dialect, folklore, old agricultural implements, customs, local history, talking about nineteenth century country life."

*   *   *

ARCHER, W(illiam) G(eorge)   1907-

PERSONAL: Born November 2, 1907, in London, England; son of William (a teacher) and Amy Alice (a teacher; maiden name, Arnold) Archer; married Mildred Bell (an art historian), July 17, 1934; children: Michael, Margaret Gillian (Mrs. Richard Lecomber). *Education:* Emmanuel College, Cambridge, B.A. (first class honors), 1930, M.A., 1934. *Home and office:* 18 Provost Rd., London NW3 4ST, England.

CAREER: Indian Civil Service, Bihar, India, district magistrate and deputy commissioner, 1931-46, provincial census superintendent, 1939-41, special officer, 1945-46, in Assam, India, deputy commissioner, 1946-48; Victoria and Albert Museum, London, England, keeper of Indian section, 1949-59, keeper emeritus, 1959—. *Member:* Royal Asiatic Society (fellow). *Awards, honors:* Member of Order of the British Empire, 1947; D.Litt. from Punjab University, 1968, for exceptional contributions to the study of Indian art, poetry, and culture.

WRITINGS: The Blue Grove: The Poetry of the Uraons, Grove, 1940; *The Vertical Man: A Study of Primitive Indian Sculpture*, Allen & Unwin, 1947; *The Plains of the Sun* (poems), Routledge & Kegan Paul, 1948; (with Robert Melville) *Forty Thousand Years of Modern Art*, Institute of Contemporary Art, 1948; *Indian Painting in the Punjab Hills*, H.M.S.O., 1952; *Kangra Painting*, Pitman, 1952, revised edition, 1957; *Bazaar Paintings of Calcutta*, H.M.S.O., 1953; *Garhwal Painting*, Pitman, 1953, revised edition, 1957; (with wife, Mildred Archer) *Indian Painting for the British*, Oxford University Press, 1955; *The Dove and the Leopard: More Uraon Poetry*, Longmans, 1956; *Indian Painting*, Batsford, 1956; *The Loves of Krishna*, Grove, 1957; *Indian Paintings from Rajasthan*, Arts Council of Great Britain, 1957; *Central Indian Painting*, Pitman, 1957; (with S. Paranavitana) *Ceylon: Paintings from Temple, Shrine and Rock*, New York Graphic Society, 1957; *India and Modern Art*, Allen & Unwin, 1959; *Indian Painting in Bundi and Kotah*, H.M.S.O., 1959.

Indian Miniatures, New York Graphic Society, 1960; *Kalighat Drawings*, Marg, 1962; (author of foreword) Richard Burton and F. F. Arbuthnot, translators, *The Kama Sutra*, Allen & Unwin, 1963; (with D. Bhattacharya) *Love Songs of Vidyapati*, Grove, 1963; (author of foreword) Edward Rehatsek, translator, *The Gulistan of Sadi*, Allen & Unwin, 1964; *Paintings of the Sikhs*, H.M.S.O., 1966; (with Edwin Binney III) *Rajput Miniatures*, Portland Museum, 1968; (contributor) C. Reynolds, editor, *An Anthology of Sinhalese Literature*, Allen & Unwin, 1970; *Kalighat Paintings*, H.M.S.O., 1971; *Indian Paintings from the Punjab Hills*, two volumes, Sotheby Parke Bernet, 1973; *The Hill of Flutes: Life, Love and Poetry in Tribal India, A Portrait of the Santals*, University of Pittsburgh, 1974. Editor, *Man in India*, 1942-48; member of editorial board of *Marg*, 1956—, *Roopa-Lekha*, 1959—.

WORK IN PROGRESS: A Concise History of Pahari Miniatures; *Visions of Courtly India*, completion expected in 1976; *India in British Painting*, 1977; memoirs, *The End of a Raj*; an autobiography, *A Passion for India*; literary criticism, *India in English Poetry*.

*   *   *

ARDOIN, John (Louis)   1935-

PERSONAL: Born January 8, 1935, in Alexandria, La.; son of Louis and Ruth (Herren) Ardoin. *Education:* University of Texas, B.M., 1955; University of Oklahoma, M.M., 1956; Michigan State University, further graduate study, 1958-59. *Politics:* None. *Religion:* None. *Home:* 4318 Abbott Ave., Dallas, Tex. 75205. *Agent:* Helen Merrill, 337 West 22nd St., New York, N.Y. 10011. *Office: Dallas Morning News*, Dallas, Tex. 75222.

CAREER: Musical America (magazine), New York, N.Y., assistant editor, 1959-62, associate editor, 1962-64, editor, 1964; *Saturday Review* (magazine), New York, N.Y., member of music staff, 1965-66; Dallas *Morning News*, Dallas, Tex., music editor and amusements critic, 1966—. Guest lecturer at University of Southern California, 1967, 1968, Indiana University, 1971, 1972, Eastman School of Music, 1973, and American Institute of Music Studies, 1973.

WRITINGS: (With Gerald Fitzgerald) *Callas*, Holt, 1974; (with others) *The Tenors*, Macmillan, 1974; *The Callas Legacy*, Duckworth, in press. Contributor to music journals. New York music critic for *London Times*, 1964-66, and *Opera*, 1965-66; managing editor of *Philharmonic Hall Program*, 1965-66.

WORK IN PROGRESS: Young People's Introduction to Opera, for Viking; *Callas at Juilliard*, for Knopf.

*   *   *

AREHART-TREICHEL, Joan   1942-

PERSONAL: Born May 19, 1942, in Louisville, Ky.; daughter of Oscar M. (an engineer) and Isabelle (a businesswoman; maiden name, Turner) Arehart; married Horst Klaus Triechel (a shipping owner), May 13, 1972. *Education:* Attended Institute of European Studies, Sorbonne, University of Paris, 1962, and Oxford University, summer, 1962, Indiana University, A.B., 1964; graduate study at New York University, 1970, and Georgetown University, 1971. *Politics:* "Conservative on economic issues; liberal on social issues (rights of the individual)." *Religion:* Roman Catholic. *Home:* 906 Ravenshead, Sherwood Forest, Annapolis, Md. 21405. *Office: Science News*, 1719 N St. N.W., Washington, D.C. 20036.

CAREER: McCall's, New York, N.Y., assistant to senior editor, 1965; Ayerst Laboratories, New York, N.Y., editor of magazine, 1966-67; free-lance science writer in New York, N.Y., 1968-70, and in Washington, D.C., 1971—. *Member:* National Press Club, National Association of Science Writers. *Awards, honors:* Third place award in American Medical Association medical journalism awards contest, 1971, for "Coral Unexpected Boon to Pharmaceutical Research."

WRITINGS: Trace Elements: How They Help and Harm Us, Holiday House, 1974; *Immunity and You*, Holiday House, in press. Contributor to *True, Parents' Magazine, Family Circle, Lady's Circle, Modern Maturity, Kiwanis Magazine, Louisville Courier Journal, Human Behavior, Oceans, Sea Frontiers, Young Miss*, and other publications.

WORK IN PROGRESS: A science book for teenagers, for Holiday House; magazine articles.

AVOCATIONAL INTERESTS: Photography, belly dancing, hiking, biking, tennis.

* * *

ARMS, Suzanne 1944-

PERSONAL: Born April 19, 1944, in Camden, N.J.; daughter of Loren Littauer and Eleanore Frances (Brady) Davis; children: Molly Arms. *Education:* University of Rochester, B.A. (with honors), 1965. *Home:* 48 Plymouth Ave., Mill Valley, Calif. 94941. *Agent:* Mrs. Marie Rodell, 141 East 55th St., New York, N.Y. 10022. *Office:* Harcourt, Brace & Jovanovich Films, San Francisco, Calif.

CAREER: Harcourt, Brace & Jovanovich Films, San Francisco, Calif., film script director and producer, 1974—. Member of Jeroboam Photographers Co-Operative, Inc. Free-lance photojournalist.

WRITINGS: A Season to Be Born (nonfiction), Harper, 1973; *Immaculate Deception: A New Look at Women and Childbirth in America* (nonfiction, with photographs by the author), Houghton-San Francisco Book Co., 1975. Contributor of photographs: Jeremy Hewes, *Build Your Own Playground*, Houghton, 1975.

WORK IN PROGRESS: Editing and preparing photographs for a book on child raising, with Holly Brecherman; editing "Bumps," a children's story.

AVOCATIONAL INTERESTS: Travel, gardening, handcrafts, yoga, dance, cooking for friends.

* * *

ARMSTRONG, David M(ichael) 1944-

PERSONAL: Born July 31, 1944, in Louisville, Ky.; son of John D. (a youth leader) and Elizabeth (a teacher; maiden name, Horine) Armstrong; married Ann Beddoes (a horticulturist), June 11, 1966; children: John David, Laura Christine. *Education:* Colorado State University, B.S. (with high distinction), 1966; Harvard University, M.A.T., 1967; University of Kansas, Ph.D., 1971. *Home:* 2415 Juniper Ave., Boulder, Colo. 80302. *Office:* Department of Integrated Studies, University of Colorado, Boulder, Colo. 80302.

CAREER: University of Colorado, Boulder, assistant professor of biological science, 1971—. Member of Nongame Advisory Council, Division of Wildlife, State of Colorado, 1973—. *Member:* Ecological Society of America, American Society of Mammalogists, Society of Systematic Zoology,

Southwestern Association of Naturalists, Sigma Xi, Beta Beta Beta, Phi Kappa Phi.

WRITINGS: Distribution of Mammals in Colorado, Museum of Natural History, University of Kansas, 1972; *Handbook of Mammals of Rocky Mountain National Park*, Rocky Mountain Nature Association, in press. Author of technical articles.

WORK IN PROGRESS: Mammals of Canyonlands National Park; MacLeay, Swainson, and the Quinary System; Readings in the History of Population Biology.

* * *

ARMSTRONG, Henry H.
See ARVAY, Harry

* * *

ARNOLD, Charlotte E(lizabeth) Cramer

PERSONAL: Born in Philadelphia, Pa.; married Milton D. Arnold (a clergyman and representative of Baptist Mid-Missions); children: Glenn, Don. *Education:* Attended Temple University, c. 1923-26. *Religion:* Baptist. *Home:* 1935 Gaston, Winston-Salem, N.C., 27103.

CAREER: Writer.

WRITINGS: Special Programs for the Sunday School, Standard Publishing, 1952; *Missionary Stories and Illustrations*, Baker Book, 1961; *Missionary Programs and Ideas*, Moody, 1962; *Complete Missionary Programs*, Regular Baptist Press, 1968; *Group Readings for the Church*, Baker Book, 1975. Contributor of articles and poems to Christian periodicals, including *Sunday School Times and Gospel Herald, Pastors' Manual*, and *Christian Life.*

WORK IN PROGRESS: More Group Readings for the Church, completion expected in 1977; *Comets and Other Poems*, 1977.

AVOCATIONAL INTERESTS: Painting, poetry.

* * *

ARNOLD, Milo Lawrence 1903-

PERSONAL: Born November 26, 1903, in LeRoy, Kan.; son of Acel Edwin (a farmer) and LeDora Ann (Hall) Arnold; married Eva W. Clark, February 14, 1929; children: Donna Winifred (Mrs. Morris E. Chambers). *Education:* Attended Friends Bible College. *Home:* 411 Lakewood Circle, Colorado Springs, Colo. 80910. *Office:* Nazarene Bible College, P.O. Box 4746, Colorado Springs, Colo. 80930.

CAREER: Ordained minister of Church of the Nazarene, 1928; pastor of churches in Kirkland, Wash., 1928-29, Portland, Ore., 1929-32, Centralia, Wash., 1932-35, Colfax, Wash., 1935-37, Pullman, Wash, 1937-43, Yakima, Wash., 1943-53, Dodge City, Kan., 1953-57, Moses Lake, Wash., 1957-62, Richland, Wash., 1962-67. Writer of radio program, "The Pastor's Call," aired on radio stations in the West and Northwest, 1937-57, 1963-72. Past member of board of regents of Northwest Nazarene College; member of founding board of Nazarene Bible College, and of general board of Church of the Nazarene, 1964-68. *Member:* Kiwanis.

WRITINGS: Parents Can Be Problems, Beacon Hill, 1961; *Life Is Like That*, Beacon Hill, 1962; *This Adventure Called Marriage*, Beacon Hill, 1966; *The Adventure of the Christian Ministry*, Beacon Hill, 1967; *This Christian Adventure*, Beacon Hill, 1974; *Life Is So Great That I Really*

Don't Want to Get Off, Zondervan, 1975. Author of columns in *Herald of Holiness*, 1968-69, and *Gospel Herald*, 1969-70. Contributor to religious publications.

WORK IN PROGRESS: Studying the human quest for personal fulfillment.

*   *   *

ARNOTT, Kathleen 1914-

PERSONAL: Born November 19, 1914, in London, England; daughter of William Thomas and Mabel (a school teacher; maiden name, Horlock) Coulson; married David W. Arnott (a professor), September 1, 1942; children: Margaret, Rosemary (Mrs. Richard Davies). *Education:* Teacher Training College, Saffron, Essex, England, diploma in education, 1935; attended Kingsmead Theological College, 1938-39. *Religion:* Methodist. *Residence:* Kent, England. *Agent:* John Cushman, 25 West 43rd St., New York, N.Y. 10036; Curtis Brown, 1A Craven Hill, London W2 3EP, England.

CAREER: Elementary school teacher in Beckenham, Kent, England, 1935-38; United Missionary Teacher Training College, Ibadan, Nigeria, lecturer in education, 1939-43; teacher and worker in leper settlement in Nigeria, 1943-52; kindergarten teacher in Sevenoaks, Kent, 1956-72.

WRITINGS: Ayo (juvenile fiction), Oxford University Press, 1951; *Titi Goes Fishing* (juvenile picture book), Longmans, 1959; *Titi Goes to a Party* (juvenile picture book), Longmans, 1959; *Catching the Cattle Thief* (juvenile fiction), Longmans, 1960; *African Myths and Legends*, Walck, 1962; *Jane's New Dress* (juvenile reader), Longmans, 1962; *Peter Runs Away* (juvenile reader), Longmans, 1962; *Richard's Lucky Find* (juvenile reader), Longmans, 1962; *The Fire* (juvenile reader), Longmans, 1962; *Bola at School* (juvenile fiction), Oxford University Press, 1965; (contributor) Jacynth Hope-Simpson, editor, *Book of Witches*, Hamish Hamilton, 1966; *Tales of Temba*, Walck, 1967; *African Fairy Tales*, Muller, 1967; *Bola at College* (juvenile fiction), Oxford University Press, 1968; (contributor) Belle Becker Sideman, editor, *World's Best Fairy Tales*, Reader's Digest Services, 1969; *Animal Folk Tales Around the World*, Walck, 1970; *Auta the Giant Killer*, Clarendon Press, 1971; *Dragons, Ogres, and Scary Things*, Garrard, 1974; (contributor) Marguerite Henry, editor, *Stories from Around the World*, Hubbard Press, 1974.

WORK IN PROGRESS: Three books for Garrard; research into African stories, especially saga types; a novel for teen-agers, *Kachi's Quest*.

AVOCATIONAL INTERESTS: Sketching, music, golf, travel.

*   *   *

ARNSTEIN, Helene S(olomon) 1915-

PERSONAL: Name is pronounced Hel-*lane Arn*-steen; born April 23, 1915, in New York, N.Y.; daughter of Meyer (in real estate) and Rose (Bonn) Solomon; married William E. Arnstein (a management consultant), June 16, 1937; children: Nancy (Mrs. Peter G. Wilson), Lawrence. *Education:* Sarah Lawrence College, A.A., 1932. *Home:* 1095 Park Ave., New York, N.Y. 10028. *Agent:* Carl Brandt, Brandt & Brandt, 101 Park Ave., New York, N.Y. 10017.

CAREER: Former piano teacher; free-lance writer on mental health, family relations, and parent-child relations. *Member:* Authors Guild of Authors League of America,

Child Study Association of America (member of board of directors).

WRITINGS: What to Tell Your Child About Birth, Illness, Death, Divorce, and Other Family Crises, Bobbs-Merrill, 1962; *Your Growing Child and Sex*, Bobbs-Merrill, 1965; *Getting Along with Your Grown-Up Children*, M. Evans, 1970; *What Every Woman Needs to Know About Abortion*, Scribner, 1973; *Billy and Our New Baby* (juvenile), Behavioral Publications, 1973; *The Roots of Love: Helping Your Child Learn to Love in the First Three Years of Life*, Bobbs-Merrill, 1975. Contributor to popular magazines, including *Ladies' Home Journal, Parents' Magazine, Today's Health, Girl Talk, Family Circle*, and New York *Times Sunday Magazine*.

SIDELIGHTS: Helene Arnstein takes care of her three grandchildren one day a week. She writes: "They and my children have been my best 'laboratory' for observing children's emotional needs, growth, and development—even though I've spent years in research, backing up my beliefs with data ... I believe the first years are vital in producing caring, lovable, and loving human beings who can make this world a better one." Her books have been published in Spanish, Italian, and Japanese. *Avocational interests:* Cooking, playing piano, travel.

*   *   *

ARON, Robert 1898-1975

May 25, 1898—April 19, 1975; French historian and author of books on French history, religion, and the history of Israel and Jewish thought. Obituaries: *New York Times*, April 20, 1975; *Washington Post*, April 20, 1975; *AB Bookman's Weekly*, June 2, 1975.

*   *   *

ARTES, Dorothy Beecher 1919-

PERSONAL: Born February 9, 1919, in Maryland; daughter of William Beers and Mary (Willett) Beecher; married Carroll Edward Artes, Sr. (in naval ordinance), June 7, 1942; children: Carroll Edward, Jr. *Education:* Attended high school in Indian Head, Md. *Politics:* Republican. *Religion:* Episcopal. *Home:* 22 Indian Head Ave., Indian Head, Md. 20640.

CAREER: Retail Credit Association, Washington, D.C., credit investigator, 1935-45.

WRITINGS: Bits and Pieces about Maryland (children's book), Maryland Historical Press, 1974. Contributor to *Maryland Independent*.

WORK IN PROGRESS: A book series for boys; adult novels; factual articles for children.

*   *   *

ARTHUR, Burt
See SHAPPIRO, Herbert (Arthur)

*   *   *

ARTHUR, Herbert
See SHAPPIRO, Herbert (Arthur)

*   *   *

ARVAY, Harry 1925-
(Henry H. Armstrong).

PERSONAL: Given name Heinz; born December 21, 1925, in Graz, Austria; son of Geza (a traveling salesman)

tional Children, Washington, D.C., research associate, 1966-67; elementary school teacher in Washington, D.C., 1968; U.S. Department of Health, Education and Welfare, Washington, D.C., education program specialist, 1968-69, child care researcher, 1970-71; Far West Laboratory for Educational Research and Development, Berkeley, Calif., intern in childhood development, 1971—. *Member:* Association for Childhood Education International, Council for Exceptional Children, American Personnel and Guidance Association (life member), National Vocational Guidance Association, National Education Association, National Association for Education of Young Children, American Association of University Women.

WRITINGS: (Editor) *Counselor Education: A Progress Report on Standards*, American Personnel and Guidance Association, 1962; (editor) *NVGA Bibliography of Current Occupational Information*, American Personnel and Guidance Association, 1963; (contributor) Pamela Roby, editor, *Child Care: Who Cares?: Foreign and Domestic Infant and Early Childhood Development Policies*, Basic Books, 1973; (contributor) Roy Fairfield, editor, *Humanizing the Workplace*, Prometheus Press, 1974; (under name Stevanne Auerbach Fink) *Parents and Child Care*, Far West Laboratory for Educational Research and Development, 1974; (editor) *Child Care: A Comprehensive Guide*, four volumes, Behavioral Publications, 1975-76. Also author of *Petals* (poems), 1974. Contributor to journals in her field. Editor, *Counselor's Information Service*, 1963-64.

WORK IN PROGRESS: Whole Child Catalog: Choosing Child Care: Parents Guide to Child Care; Making of a Stepmother.

* * *

AUGUSTIN, Ann Sutherland 1934-

PERSONAL: Born August 11, 1934, in Evergreen Park, Ill.; daughter of Donald A. (a real estate broker) and Helen (Dorsey) Sutherland; married Edward J. Augustin, Jr., January 8, 1955 (divorced, 1974); children: Edward J. III, Kathryn, Donald J., Suzanne. *Education:* Iowa State University, student, 1951-53. *Politics:* "Always for the best man—but with a leaning toward Republican candidates." *Religion:* Roman Catholic. *Home:* 2434 Brandenberry Ct., Apt. 1A, Arlington Heights, Ill. 60004.

CAREER: Standard Register Co., Chicago, Ill., executive secretary, 1953-55; Maine Township High School, Park Ridge, Ill., teacher of sewing in adult education program, 1961-68; Fuller Brush Co., Mt. Prospect, Ill., saleswoman, 1969-71; Henrici's O'Hare Inn, Rosemont, Ill., waitress, 1974—; free-lance writer. *Member:* Juvenile Diabetes Association.

WRITINGS: Help! I Want to Remodel My Home: The New Woman's Guide to Home Improvement, Nelson-Hall, 1975. Contributor of articles to *Reader's Digest, True Story, Playboy, Chicago Daily News, Chicago Tribune,* and *Mt. Prospect Herald.*

WORK IN PROGRESS: Two novels, one on college life during the early 1950's, one about an Army wife; articles on "Creeping Momism," on the inequities of the Social Security system, and on the "whys and wherefores of being a waitress."

SIDELIGHTS: Of her book *Help!*, Mrs. Augustin writes: "I felt it was time that the woman of today need not be dependent on either having a male around the house to do major jobs or being compelled to lay out the money necessary to hire a professional . . . Unfortunately, most of us have been raised in a society that promotes the idea of a woman being helpless and 'needing the man's help' around the home. I tried to debunk that theory." *Avocational interests:* Travel, reading "anything and everything."

BIOGRAPHICAL/CRITICAL SOURCES: Chicago Sunday Tribune, July 16, 1961.

* * *

AVERY, Catherine B(arber) 1909-

PERSONAL: Born August 24, 1909, in Groton, Conn.; daughter of Christopher Lester (a judge) and Elizabeth (Brander) Avery. *Education:* Smith College, B.A., 1931; graduate study at University of Wisconsin, summer, 1932, Columbia University, summers, 1934-35, Connecticut College, 1935-36, 1936-37, and Pennsylvania State College, 1943. *Politics:* Democrat. *Religion:* Congregationalist. *Home:* 39 West 70th St., New York, N.Y. 10023.

CAREER: History teacher in New London, Conn., 1931-43; Hamilton Standard Propellers, Hartford, Conn., layout draftsman, 1944-45; Federal Telecommunications Laboratories, Nutley, N.J., layout draftsman, 1945-47; Appleton-Century-Crofts, Inc., New York, N.Y., editor, 1947-73.

WRITINGS: The New Century Classical Handbook, Appleton, 1962; (editor with Antonio Honaiss) *Appleton's New English-Portuguese, Portuguese-English Dictionary*, Appleton, 1964; *The New Appleton Cuyas English-Spanish, Spanish-English Dictionary*, Appleton, 5th edition (Avery was not associated with earlier editions), 1966; *The New Century Italian Renaissance Encyclopedia*, Appleton, 1972; *The New Century Handbook of Greek Mythology and Legend*, Appleton, 1972; *The New Century Handbook of Greek Literature*, Appleton, 1972; *The New Century Handbook of Leaders of the Classical World*, Appleton, 1972; *The New Century Handbook of Classical Geography*, Appleton, 1972; *The New Century Handbook of Greek Art and Architecture*, Appleton, 1972; *Words into Type*, Prentice-Hall, 3rd edition (Avery was not associated with earlier editions), 1974.

WORK IN PROGRESS: Research for *Handbook of American Painters and Painting.*

AVOCATIONAL INTERESTS: Travel.

* * *

AYDELOTTE, William Osgood 1910-

PERSONAL: Born September 1, 1910, in Bloomington, Ind.; son of Frank (a college president) and Marie Jeannette (Osgood) Aydelotte; married Myrtle Elizabeth Kitchell (a nursing executive), April 22, 1956; children: Marie Elizabeth, Jeanette Farley. *Education:* Harvard University, A.B., 1931; Cambridge University, Ph.D., 1934. *Politics:* Democrat. *Religion:* Quaker. *Home:* 330 South Summit St., Iowa City, Iowa 52240. *Office:* Department of History, University of Iowa, Iowa City, Iowa 52242.

CAREER: Federal Home Loan Bank Board, Washington, D.C., assistant, 1934-36; Trinity College, Hartford, Conn., instructor, 1937-39, assistant professor of history, 1939-43; University of Iowa, Iowa City, assistant professor, 1947-48, associate professor, 1948-50, professor of history, 1950—, chairman of department, 1947-59, 1965-68. Visiting professor at Smith College, 1943-45, Princeton University, 1945-47, Harvard University, summer, 1966, and University of Leicester, 1971. Member of Institute for Advanced

Study, 1945-47; member of board of directors of Social Science Research Council, 1964-70. *Member:* American Historical Association, American Association of University Professors (member of executive committee, 1963-66), Social Science History Association, National Academy of Sciences, Royal Historical Society (fellow), Iowa Academy of Science, Phi Beta Kappa, Athenaeum Club, Century Club. *Awards, honors:* Member of Order of the British Empire, 1961.

WRITINGS: Bismarck and British Colonial Policy, University of Pennsylvania Press, 1937, 2nd revised edition, Russell, 1970; (contributor) Philip Appleman, William A. Madden, and Michael Wolff, editors, *1859: Entering an Age of Crisis*, Indiana University Press, 1959; (author of appendix) G. Kitson Clark, *The Making of Victorian England*, Harvard University Press, 1962; (contributor) Louis Gottschalk, editor, *Generalization in the Writing of History*, University of Chicago Press, 1963; *Quantification in History*, Addison-Wesley, 1971; (editor with Robert W. Fogel and Allan G. Bogue, and contributor) *The Dimensions of Quantitative Research in History*, Princeton University Press, 1972; (contributor) Val R. Lorwin and Jacob M. Price, editors, *The Dimensions of the Past: Materials, Problems, and Opportunities for Quantitative Work in History*, Yale University Press, 1972; (editor and contributor) *The History of Parliamentary Behavior*, Princeton University Press, in press. Contributor of articles and book reviews to history journals.

WORK IN PROGRESS: The Issues of Early Victorian Politics.

SIDELIGHTS: Aydelotte has competence in Latin, Greek, German, French, and Italian.

*   *   *

BAARS, Conrad W(alterus) 1919-

PERSONAL: Born January 2, 1919, in the Netherlands; son of Walter F. C. (a lawyer) and Constance (de Groot) Baars; married Virginia Kennedy, April 3, 1948; children: Michael Conrad, Sue Mary, Eleanor Constance. *Education:* University of Amsterdam, M.D., 1945. *Religion:* Roman Catholic. *Home and office:* 255 Hill St., Whitinsville, Mass. 01588.

CAREER: Psychiatric residency training in Chicago, Ill., Minneapolis, Minn., and in California, 1945-52; Rochester State Hospital, Rochester, Minn., director of psychiatric education, 1952-60; private practice of medicine in Rochester, Minn., 1960-73; International Therapeutic Center for Clergy and Religion, Whitinsville, Mass., founder and director, 1973-75; private practice in psychiatry in Whitinsville, Mass., 1975—. Consultant to Human Life Foundation. *Military service:* Royal Dutch Army, 1938-40. Fought with underground in Netherlands, Belgium, and France, 1940-43. U.S. Army Reserve, Medical Corps, 1951-52; became captain; received Croix du Combattant de l'Europe.

MEMBER: World Federation of Doctors Who Respect Human Life (member of board of directors of U.S. section), American Medical Association, American Psychiatric Association, American Society of Clinical Hypnosis, Massachusetts Medical Society, Massachusetts Psychiatric Society.

WRITINGS: The Psychology of Obedience, Herder Book Center, 1965; (with Jordan Aumann and Philip Roets) *Sex, Love, and the Life of the Spirit*, Priory, 1966; *A Priest for*

All Seasons: Masculine and Celibate, Franciscan Herald Press, 1972; *How to Treat and Prevent the Crisis in Priesthood*, Franciscan Herald Press, 1972; (with Anna A. Terruwe) *Loving and Curing the Neurotic*, Arlington House, 1972; (contributor) Ratibor-Ray M. Jurjevich, editor, *Direct Psychotherapy*, University of Miami Press, 1973; *Born Only Once*, Franciscan Herald Press, 1975. Contributor to *New Catholic Encyclopedia*.

SIDELIGHTS: Baars writes that his career is based on "... new discoveries and interpretations of clinical observations based on the Aristotelian-Thomistic understanding of the nature of man. This led to ability to cure obsessive-compulsive neurotics and discovery of new psychiatric syndrome: deprivation neurosis in adults. My two years in Buchenwald Concentration Camp (1943-45) contributed to my disenchantment with utilitarian philosophy in my specialty and the poor clinical results of psychoanalytic therapy. The syndrome of the non-affirmed individual led to the discovery of the non-Freudian deprivation neurosis, requiring affirmation therapy without probing into the unconscious. Its incidence is huge (in the millions) and increases steadily in a non-affirming, denying society...."

*   *   *

BACON, Marion 1901(?)-1975

1901(?)—June 23, 1975; American bookshop manager and author. Obituaries: *Publishers Weekly*, July 21, 1975.

*   *   *

BAER, Earl E. 1928-

PERSONAL: Born February 27, 1928, in Aberdeen, Wash.; son of Earl E., Sr. and Rose (Duncan) Baer; married Helen A. Church; children: Cathy, Molly, Daniel, Craig, Mary Claire, Joan. *Education:* St. Martin's College, B.A., 1950; Univeristy of Washington, Seattle, M.A., 1966. *Religion:* Roman Catholic. *Home:* 615 Northwest 180th St., Seattle, Wash. 98177. *Office:* Department of Marketing, Highline College, Midway, Wash. 98031.

CAREER: Sales representative, distributor representative, and merchandising specialist with Mobil Oil Corp., 1954-61; Highline College, Midway, Wash., program director of marketing, 1966—. *Military service:* U.S. Air Force, 1950-53. Air National Guard, 1956-68; present rank, major.

WRITINGS: Salesmanship, McGraw, 1972; *The Sensitive I: People in Business*, Wiley, 1975; *Marketing: Human Needs Satisfied*, Goodyear Publishing, 1975.

*   *   *

BAGG, Graham (William) 1917-

PERSONAL: Born January 17, 1917, in Cannington, near Bridgwater, Somerset, England; son of William S. (a nurseryman) and Edith E. (a teacher; maiden name, Townsend) Bagg; married Mary Cracknell, August 8, 1953; children: Jeremy, Simon. *Education:* St. Luke's College, Exeter, England, teacher's certificate, 1937; College of Preceptors, A.C.P. [Associate of the College of Preceptors], 1939, L.C.P. [Licentiateship], 1942; City and Guilds of London, teacher's certificate in handicraft, 1949; College of Craft Education, M.C.C.Ed. [Member of the College of Craft Education], 1952. *Home:* 97 Sandyhurst Lane, Ashford, Kent, England. *Office:* Norton Knatchbull School, Ashford, Kent, England.

CAREER: St. Luke's College, Demonstration School, Exeter, Devonshire, England, teacher of general light crafts, 1937-51, instructor at St. Luke's Training College, 1945-51; teacher of pottery, subsidiary woodwork, and art in grammar school in Brighton, Sussex, England, 1951-58; Ashford Grammar School (now Norton Knatchbull School), Ashford, Kent, England, senior teacher of pottery and woodwork, 1958—. *Military service:* Royal Air Force, 1939-45.

WRITINGS: Woodwork Drawings, Wheaton & Co., 1967; *Pottery Techniques: On and Off the Wheel*, Van Nostrand, 1974; *Comparative Craft Techniques*, Van Nostrand, in press.

SIDELIGHTS: Bagg writes: "I am somewhat dismayed by the present outlook in craft education which seems to me to play down the values inherent in craftsmanship for its own sake and to attempt to make practical skills 'respectable' by turning handicraft teaching into a design problem solving activity. In fact, I could well enjoy writing a 'reactionary' paper to combat this outlook! Designing is an integral part of the craft scene, but I am very convinced that the basis must first be laid as a sound training in practical techniques and first-hand experience of the materials used.

"I attach considerable importance to the unity of the crafts and nothing pleases me more than to see a piece of work which demonstrates several differing skills—a coffee table in wrought iron with a ceramic mosaic top or a wooden chair finished in a hand woven fabric which has itself, been woven by the craftsman on his own home-made loom."

AVOCATIONAL INTERESTS: Gardening (hardy flowering plants).

* * *

BAHADUR, K(rishna) P(rakash) 1924-

PERSONAL: Born February 21, 1924, in Allahabad, India; son of Iqbal (in government service) and Chameli Bahadur; married Premlata Saran, May 4, 1946; children: Arti (daughter), Ajai (son), Sanjay (son), Sandhya (daughter). *Education:* Allahabad University, B.A., 1943, M.A., 1945. *Home:* 1 South Ave. Rd., Lucknow, Uttar Pradesh, India 226001. *Office:* Civil Secretariate, Lucknow, Uttar Pradesh, India 226001.

CAREER: Indian Government, magistrate in Jhansi, 1946-48, sub-divisional magistrate in Barabanki, 1949-52, deputy custodian of evacuee property in Lucknow, 1953-56, deputy land reforms commissioner, board of revenue, Lucknow, 1957-58, additional district magistrate in Allahabad, 1959-60, deputy secretary of Uttar Pradesh Government, 1961-63, district magistrate in Pilibhit, 1964-67, district magistrate and administrator of municipal board in Bulandshahr, 1967-70, district magistrate in Muzaffarnagar, 1970-73, joint secretary of Uttar Pradesh Government, 1973—. Managing director of Majhola Sugar Factory, 1964-67; chairman of L. H. Ayurvedic College, 1964-67; administrator of Lakhaoti College, 1967-70. *Awards, honors:* Vidya Visharada from Arogya Asraman (Madras), 1970, for *Poems of Love & Wisdom.*

WRITINGS: The Burning Bush (verse translation of Gita), Indian Press (India), 1961; *The Story of Rama*, Indian Press, 1961; *Apradhi Kaun* (novel; title means "Who Is the Killer?"), Ajai Publications (New Delhi), 1969; *Poems of Love & Wisdom*, Jaico Publishing (Bombay), 1970; *Love in the East*, Jaico Publishing, 1971; *Stories for Children*, two volumes, Sterling Publishers (New Delhi), 1971; *Sone Ki Chori* (novel; title means "Gold Theft"), Vijay Pocket Books (India), 1971; *Husn Aur Hire* (novel;

title means "Youth and Diamonds"), Arvind Pocket Books (India), 1972; *Folk Tales of Uttar Pradesh*, Sterling Publishers, 1972; *Five Verse Upanishads*, New Light Publishers (New Delhi), 1972; *The Rasikpriya of Kehavdasa*, Motilal Banarsidass (India), 1972; *The Wiles of Women*, Hind Pocket Books (India), 1973; *The Case of the Poisoned Cat*, Sterling Publishers, 1974.

All books in press: *Bangala Poems*, Oriental Publishers (India); *Religious Perspectives*, Oriental Publishers; *Rural Songs of India*, Motilal Banarsidass; *Selections from Ramachandrika*, Motilal Banarsidass; *Love Poems of Ghanananda*, U.N.E.S.C.O. (Paris); *Population Crisis in India*, National Publishers (India); *Complete Book of Fun*, Sterling Publishers; *Eve in the East*, Hind Pocket Books; *The Seventh Step*, Sterling Publishers; *Murder in the Delhi Mail*, Sterling Publishers.

SIDELIGHTS: Bahadur writes: "As an Indian I firmly believe that the only values in life are spiritual. That's why the affluent West keeps turning to Indian Culture. I am not interested much in politics, but it is so silly that we have cut ourselves into bits with different systems of governments, different creeds and colours, hemmed in by all kinds of restrictions, when basically we are all the same. I don't believe in permissive sex. Once morality runs wild, the sky's the limit and there won't be husbands, wives, and families as there won't be any virgins. It's ridiculous. In the literary field too we seem to be running amuck. A Hardy or a Dickens were they to suddenly appear would be dumbfounded at our love scenes and Bronte and Austen would die of blushing. Keats would hardly find the quaint disjointed stuff we write to be 'poetry.' I feel, unfortunately, that foreign publishers don't give much chance to Indian writing in English. Even on Indian subjects they prefer British writers or Indians living abroad. Viva nationality!"

BIOGRAPHICAL/CRITICAL SOURCES: Aaj Ki Kheti (New Delhi), August, 1972; *Books Abroad*, January, 1974.

* * *

BAILEY, Hillary G(oodsell) 1894-

PERSONAL: Born June 5, 1894, in Muncie, Ind.; married Beulah Collins. *Education:* DePauw University, graduate, 1916. *Home:* 2377 Dora Dr., Clearwater, Fla. 33515.

CAREER: Founder and editor of trade journal, *Agfa Diamond*, 1943; Coca Cola Co., Atlanta, Ga., former editor of external company publications. *Member:* Royal Photographic Society (fellow), Photographic Society of America (co-founder), Sigma Delta Chi.

WRITINGS: The Story of a Face, Camera Craft Publishing, 1938; *Indoor Photography*, Ziff-Davis, 1940; *So Was Your Old Man* (reminiscences), Branden Press, 1975.

WORK IN PROGRESS: So Was Your Old Lady.

* * *

BAILEY, M(innie Elizabeth) Thomas

PERSONAL: Born in Pulaski, Tenn.; daughter of Robert Jackson (a pullman porter) and Georgia (a teacher; maiden name, Malone) Thomas; married Robert Lawson Bailey (a professor of agriculture and biology), September 30, 1944; *children:* Barbara Thomascine (Mrs. Anthony J. Wilson). *Education:* Tennessee State University, B.S., 1945; Iowa State University, M.S., 1950; Oklahoma State University, Ed.D., 1967. *Religion:* Baptist. *Home:* 201 West Adams Ave., Grambling, La. 71245. *Office:* Department of History and Philosophy, Grambling State University, Grambling, La. 71245.

CAREER: Principal of elementary school in Giles County, Tenn., 1946-48; area coordinator for schools in Greensboro, N.C., 1953-59; Grambling College (now Grambling State University), Grambling, La., instructor, 1959-60, assistant professor, 1960-63, associate professor, 1963-67, professor of history, 1967—, head of department, 1974—. Member of executive board of Louisiana Colleges and Universities, 1968-70; historian for Links, Inc., 1973. *Member:* American Historical Association, Association of Social and Behavioral Sciences (member of executive board, 1973-75), Civil War Roundtable (president of Stillwater chapter, 1965), Alpha Kappa Alpha, Phi Beta Sigma Shadow, Alpha Kappa Mu, Phi Alpha Theta, Phi Gamma Mu.

WRITINGS: Reconstruction in Indian Territory: A Story of Avarice, Discrimination and Opportunism, Kennikat, 1972. Contributor to journals in her field.

WORK IN PROGRESS: Blacks in Indian Territory.

* * *

BAILEY, Patrick 1925-

PERSONAL: Born December 31, 1925, in Ealing, London, England; son of Waldo Mumford (a civil engineer) and Mabel (Allchurch) Bailey; married Peggy Douglas, 1968. *Education:* Corpus Christi College, Cambridge, B.A., 1950, M.A., 1954. *Religion:* Christian Scientist. *Home:* 32 Guilford Rd., Stoneygate, Leicester LE22RB, England. *Office:* School of Education, University of Leicester, Leicester LE17RF, England.

CAREER: Secondary school teacher of geography and head of department in schools in Norfolk, England, 1951-57; Saltley College of Birmingham, Birmingham, England, lecturer in geography and head of department, 1957-66; College of Education, Northumberland, England, principal lecturer in geography, 1966-68; University of Leicester, Leicester, England, senior lecturer in education, 1968—. Associate of Cambridge Institute of Education, 1958; tutor in Tanzania, 1963, 1964, 1965, 1966. *Military service:* Royal Navy, 1944-47. *Member:* Geographical Association, Geographical Field Group, British Educational Administration Society, Institute of British Geographers. *Awards, honors:* Scholarship from Canadian Geographical Society, 1950, for McGill University.

WRITINGS: British Landscapes Through Maps: The Norwich Area, Geographical Association, 1971; (contributor) Michael Davison, editor, *An Illustrated Guide to Britain*, Drive Publications, 1971; (contributor) Wilfrid Flemming, editor, *The Beginnings of Subjects as the Ordering of Experience*, Institute of Education, Beirut, Lebanon, 1972; (contributor) Paul Fordham, editor, *Rural Development in the Kenya Highlands*, Geographical Field Group, University of Nottingham, 1973; *Orkney*, David & Charles, 1973; *Teaching Geography*, David & Charles, 1975; (with H.W.R. Hawes and F. A. Thompson) *Social Studies for the Primary School*, Longmans, 1975. Contributor of about thirty articles to geography and education journals. Honorary editor of *Teaching Geography* (journal), 1975—.

WORK IN PROGRESS: School Organisation and Management, publication by David & Charles expected in 1977; research on organization and management in secondary schools.

SIDELIGHTS: Bailey writes: "As an educationalist I believe that teaching is a whole-time vocation, not just a job, that knowledge is just as important as ideas, and that hard work and good order are positive virtues which should be supported." *Avocational interests:* Hill walking, travel with a purpose, photography, music (pianist), natural history.

* * *

BAIRD, Marie-Terese 1918-

PERSONAL: Born April 16, 1918, in Antwerp, Belgium; daughter of Theo (a company director) and Lucie (Georlette) Verellen; married second husband, Nigel Baird (a business executive); children: five daughters, three sons. *Education:* Attended convent schools in Belgium. *Home:* Home Farm, Upper Woolhampton, Berkshire, England.

CAREER: Author. *Member:* Society of Authors.

*WRITINGS—*All novels: *The Scorpions*, Macmillan (London), 1961; *A Shining Furrow*, Collins, 1973; *A Lesson in Love*, Houghton, 1974. Author of newspaper articles.

WORK IN PROGRESS: A novel.

SIDELIGHTS: "Although speaking French as my maternal tongue, I have always written in English," Marie-Terese Baird told *CA.* "Write as a daily habit and take about a year to complete a book. *Very, very* conscientious about research." *Avocational interests:* Music, playing piano, working tapestries.

* * *

BAKER, Bill
See BAKER, C(harles) William

* * *

BAKER, Bill Russell 1933-

PERSONAL: Born December 14, 1933, in Pontotoc, Miss.; son of William Joseph (a county tax assessor) and Maudye (a county circuit court clerk) Russell; married Madeline Jill Applewhite (a music teacher), May 1, 1962. *Education:* Mississippi State University, B.S., 1955, Ph.D., 1973; New Orleans Baptist Theological Seminary, B.D., 1958; University of Mississippi, M.A., 1967. *Home address:* P.O. Box 72, Clinton, Miss. 39056. *Office:* First Baptist Church, P.O. Box 72, Clinton, Miss. 39056.

CAREER: Ordained Baptist minister, 1954; pastor of Baptist churches in Mantee, Miss., 1960-64, and Calhoun City, Miss., 1964-73; First Baptist Chruch, Clinton, Miss., pastor, 1973—. Professor of Mississippi history at Mississippi College. *Member:* Phi Kappa Phi.

WRITINGS: Catch the Vision: The Life of Henry L. Whitfield of Mississippi, University Press of Mississippi, 1974.

* * *

BAKER, C(harles) William 1919-
(Bill Baker)

PERSONAL: Born July 28, 1919, in Vienna, Austria; name originally Wilhelm C. Baecker; came to United States in 1945; now U.S. citizen; son of Carl W. (a fur fashion designer) and B. Lea Lehmann (Medina) Baecker; married Ruth Blume Devorin (an actor's agent), September 18, 1949 (divorced, 1973); children: Cary, Claudia, Ronald, Wendell, Melanie. *Education:* Attended trade school in Vienna, 1934-38, and Vienna Academy of Art, 1939-38; University of Southern California, B.A., 1953; also studied at University of Buenos Aires, 1942-44. *Home address:* P.O. Box 69708, West Hollywood, Calif. 90069.

CAREER: Journeyman for woodworking firm in Zurich, Switzerland, 1938-39; Sience a Hijos & subsidiary firms, Buenos Aires, Argentina, and La Paz, Bolivia, designer and supervisor, 1939-45; Twentieth Century-Fox, Hollywood, Calif., designer and set-decorating assistant, 1946-52; free-lance designer and feature writer for technical books, 1952-54; writer, 1955—. *Member:* American Arbitration Association. *Awards, honors:* General products design award from Museum of Science and Industry, Chicago, Ill., 1956.

WRITINGS: Furniture You Can Build, Fawcett, 1955; *Children's Furniture You Can Build*, Fawcett, 1956; *Built-Ins and Space Savers*, Popular Science, 1960; (under name Bill Baker) *House of Ideas*, Macmillan, 1974. Author of Times-Mirror Syndicate columns "Bill Baker: Designer to the Stars," 1954-57, and "House of Ideas," 1975. Contributor to *True*.

WORK IN PROGRESS: A book on selected progressive living features; a syndicated television show.

SIDELIGHTS: Baker moved his family into an almost uninhabitable hundred-year-old house in Connecticut. He writes: "I wanted to take the worst and make it look the best. I wanted to solve situations people face . . . in a very old house." The result is ". . . a house of ideas, a museum, that shows utilization of space without sacrifice of beauty." He has also done interior designing for numerous corporations, banks, hotels, homes, and theaters. He designed the War Room of the Pentagon, President Eisenhower's lectern, the Ready Room of Red Stone Missile Base, electronic remote controlled mechanical rear projection walls for Allied Chemical, the projection theater of Hugh Hefner's "Playboy Mansion West," and others.

BIOGRAPHICAL/CRITICAL SOURCES: New York Times, October 24, 1955, December 12, 1965; *New York World Telegram*, March 17, 1966; *Darien Review*, April 14, 1966; *House and Garden*, April, 1966; *American Builder*, June, 1966.

*   *   *

BAKER, Eleanor Z(uckerman)   1932-

PERSONAL: Born February 14, 1932, in New York, N.Y.; daughter of William (a physician) and Sarah (Aranow) Zuckerman; married Roger M. Baker (an educational diagnostician); children: Susan Ellen (Mrs. Paul L. Mitchell), Cindy Ann, Mary Jane, Roger M. II. *Education:* Syracuse University, B.A., 1951; Stephen F. Austin State University, M.A., 1960, now doctoral candidate. *Religion:* Presbyterian. *Home:* 14713 Perthshire, Houston, Tex. 77024. *Office:* Department of English, University of Houston, 1 Main St., Houston, Tex. 77002.

CAREER: University of Houston, Houston, Tex., lecturer in English, 1960-62; Stephen F. Austin State University, Nacogdoches, Tex., assistant professor of English and Asian studies, 1967-72; Firestone Plantations Co., Harbel, Liberia, English and social studies teacher at company school, 1972-74; University of Houston, member of English faculty, 1974—. Junior high school English and social studies teacher in Houston, Tex., 1960-61; Carnegie Foundation consultant and guest lecturer at Stillman College, 1966-67; visiting research fellow at Australian National University, 1967.

MEMBER: Association of Asian Studies, American Association of University Women, American Association of University Professors, Phi Alpha Theta. *Awards, honors:*

Fulbright scholar at University of Hawaii, summer, 1965; United Nations Award from UNESCO, 1969, for *The Australian Aborigines*; Maverick Award from Piney Woods Writers Conference, 1970, for *New Guinea: A Journey into Yesterday*.

WRITINGS: The Australian Aborigines, Steck, 1968; *New Guinea: A Journey into Yesterday*, Steck, 1968; *Australia Today*, Steck, 1969; *New Zealand: Land of the Mighty Maori*, Steck, 1971; *Japanese Counterfeit Trademarks* (classified monograph), U.S. State Department, 1971; *New Zealand Today*, Steck, 1972. Editor of Australian-Japanese documents on diplomatic relations for Australian Department of External Affairs.

WORK IN PROGRESS: Liberia: From Lapas to Latex, a high school reference book; a novel; a collection of short stories; audio-visual materials for teaching English.

SIDELIGHTS: Eleanor Baker has traveled in Europe, Asia, Australia, Africa, and the Pacific Islands, with a strong interest in emerging nations, assimilation practices, and maintaining cultural values of tribal peoples. *Avocational interests:* Reading, travel, knitting, square dancing, collecting primitive art and artifacts.

*   *   *

BAKER, George   1915-1975

May 22, 1915—May 7, 1975; American cartoonist, animator, and creator of comic strip "Sad Sack." Obituaries: *New York Times*, May 9, 1975; *Washington Post*, May 10, 1975; *Newsweek*, May 19, 1975; *Time*, May 19, 1975; *Current Biography*, August, 1975.

*   *   *

BAKER, James Volant   1903-

PERSONAL: Born July 20, 1903, in Reading, England; son of James Vashon (a colonel in the Royal Artillery) and Lily Melissa (a missionary in India; maiden name, Wyckoff) Baker; married Ann Fullerton, August 28, 1947 (divorced); married Dorothy Helen Davis (a librarian), October 28, 1951; children: (first marriage) Michael Erskine. *Education:* Oxford University, B.A., 1924, M.A. (modern history), 1929; graduate study at University of Pennsylvania, 1931-33; University of Michigan, M.A. (English), 1947, Ph.D., 1954. *Politics:* Liberal. *Religion:* Contemporary existentialism. *Home:* 4369 Fiesta Lane, Houston, Tex. 77004. *Office:* Department of English, University of Houston, Houston, Tex. 77004.

CAREER: Edwardes College, Peshawar, India, lecturer in English and Mohammedan civilization, 1924-26; teacher of English in Egyptian secondary schools, 1926-30; Marshall College, Huntington, W. Va., instructor in English, 1930-31; Westminster College, New Wilmington, Pa., associate professor of English, 1933-45; University of Nebraska, Lincoln, instructor in creative writing, 1947-50; University of Huston, Houston, Tex., associate professor, 1950-55, professor of English, 1955-73, professor emeritus, 1973—. *Member:* Modern Language Association of America, National Council of Teachers of English, South-Central Modern Language Association, Phi Theta Kappa. *Awards, honors:* Hopwood Award for Poetry at University of Michigan, 1947, for "Music for the Eye."

WRITINGS: A Book of Songs and Meditations, Authur H. Stockwell, 1924; *The Sacred River: Coleridge's Theory of the Imagination*, Louisiana State University Press, 1957; (contributor) Warren G. French and Walter E. Kidd, editors, *American Winners of the Nobel Literary Prize*, Oklahoma University Press, 1968; (contributor) Kidd, editor, *British Winners of the Nobel Literary Prize*, Oklahoma University Press, 1973. Contributor of poems, articles, and reviews to periodicals, including *Voices, Forum, Prairie Schooner, Descant, Western Humanities Review, Sewanee Review, Trace*, and others.

WORK IN PROGRESS: A study of poetry as a phenomenological art; a volume of poetry.

AVOCATIONAL INTERESTS: Foreign travel, informal expeditions.

*   *   *

BAKER, Janice E(dla)   1941-

PERSONAL: Born June 18, 1941, in Shreveport, La.; daughter of Glenn Jackson (a geophysicist) and Edla (Hill) Baker. *Education:* Southwestern College at Memphis, B.A. (with honors), 1963; Louisiana State University, M.A. (American history), 1967; University of Wisconsin, M.A. (comparative history), and Certificate in African Studies, 1971. *Religion:* Presbyterian. *Home:* 2122 Massachusetts Ave. N.W., Washington, D.C. 20008. *Office:* Congressional Research Service—Environmental Policy Division, Library of Congress, Washington, D.C. 20540.

CAREER: U.S. Peace Corps, Washington, D.C., English teacher in Guinea, West Africa, 1963-65; American Historical Association, Washington, D.C., assistant editor, 1967-69; Library of Congress, Washington, D.C., analyst for Congressional Research Service—Environmental Policy Division, 1972—. Program chairman and board member of Pilgrimage (Presbyterian hostel), 1973-75. *Member:* Library of Congress Professional Association, Educators to Africa Association, National Wildlife Federation, Phi Beta Kappa, Phi Alpha Theta, Phi Kappa Phi.

WRITINGS—"The Enchantment of Africa" series of Children's Press: (with Alan Carpenter) *Enchantment of Africa: Upper Volta*, 1974; *Niger*, 1975; *Central African Republic*, 1975.

WORK IN PROGRESS: Biographical sketches of leading Presbyterians in the American Revolution; biographies of African leaders, for young readers.

SIDELIGHTS: In addition to Peace Corps work in Africa, Janice Baker has spent time in Mexico, Western Europe, and Yugoslavia. She writes that she is "... particularly interested in cross-cultural exchanges throughout history, and in interpreting Third World cultures to American readers."

*   *   *

BAKER, Keith Michael   1938-

PERSONAL: Born August 7, 1938, in Swindon, Wiltshire, England; son of Raymond Eric and Winifred Evelyn (Shepherd) Baker; married Therese Louise Elzas (a sociologist), October 25, 1961; children: Julian, Felix. *Education:* Peterhouse, Cambridge, B.A., 1960, M.A., 1963; University College, London, Ph.D., 1964; also studied at Cornell University, 1960-61. *Home:* 5240 South Greenwood, Chicago, Ill. 60615. *Office:* Department of History, University of Chicago, Chicago, Ill. 60637.

CAREER: Reed College, Portland, Ore., instructor in history and humanities, 1964-65; University of Chicago, Chicago, Ill., assistant professor, 1965-70, associate professor of history, 1970—, master of Social Sciences Collegiate

Division, 1975—. Visiting associate professor at Yale University, 1974. *Member:* American Historical Association, Society for French Historical Studies.

WRITINGS: Condorcet: From Natural Philosophy to Social Mathematics, University of Chicago Press, 1975; (editor and author of introduction) *Condorcet: Selected Writings*, Bobbs-Merrill, in press.

WORK IN PROGRESS: Research on the history of the idea of social science, on the French Enlightenment, and on European intellectual history.

*   *   *

BAKER, Michael H(enry) C(hadwick)   1937-

PERSONAL: Born June 19, 1937, in Croyden, Surrey, England; son of Leonard Chadwick (a chauffeur) and Elsie (a cook; maiden name, Knight) Baker; married Maeve Finucane (a teacher), August 17, 1968; children: William, Daniel. *Education:* Attended Croyden Art School, 1958-61; Chelsea Art School, diploma in design, 1962; Liverpool Art College, art teacher's diploma, 1963. *Politics:* "Socialist (member of Labour Party)." *Religion:* Christian. *Home:* 45 Home Park, Oxted, Surrey RH8 OJS, England. *Office:* Oxted County Comprehensive School, Oxted, Surrey, England.

CAREER: Newspaper reporter and photographer, 1954-55; industrial and commercial photographer, 1955-58; Southport School of Art, Southport, Lancashire, England, lecturer in photography, 1964-66; art teacher in elementary schools in Huyton, England, 1967-68, and Croydon, England, 1968-73; Oxted County Comprehensive School, Oxted, England, art teacher in secondary school, 1973—. *Military service:* Royal Air Force, senior aircraftsman, 1956-58. *Member:* Amnesty International (Oxted branch), Society of Authors, Irish Railway Record Society.

WRITINGS: Irish Railways since 1916, Ian Allen, 1972; *Journey to Katmandu* (travel book), David & Charles, 1974. Author of scripts for English and Irish television programs. Contributor to *Railway World, Railway*, and *Modern Railways*.

WORK IN PROGRESS: The Villages of Sussex; two books on Irish railways; a pictorial history of seaside Sussex; a novel; collecting photographs and drawings of railways around the world for a book.

SIDELIGHTS: Much of Baker's writing is illustrated with his own photographs and drawings. *Avocational interests:* Travel, Ireland, industrial archaeology, children.

*   *   *

BAKER, Russell (Wayne)   1925-

PERSONAL: Born August 14, 1925, in Loudoun County, Va.; son of Benjamin Rex and Lucy Elizabeth (Robinson) Baker; married Miriam Emily Nash, March 11, 1950; children: Kathleen Leland, Allen Nash, Michael Lee. *Education:* Johns Hopkins University, B.A., 1947. *Home:* 442 East 58th St., New York, N.Y. 10022. *Office: New York Times*, 229 West 43rd St., New York, N.Y. 10036.

CAREER: Baltimore Sun, Baltimore, Md., member of staff, 1947-53, London bureau chief, 1953-54; *New York Times*, member of Washington, D.C. bureau, 1954-62, author of column "Observer," 1962—, now based in New York, N.Y. *Military service:* U.S. Naval Reserve, 1943-45. *Awards, honors:* L.H.D. from Hamilton College, Princeton University, and Franklin Pierce College; LL.D., Union College.

WRITINGS: (Author of text) Washington: City on the Potomac, Arts, 1958; An American in Washington (collection of newspaper articles), Knopf, 1961; No Cause for Panic (collection of newspaper articles), Lippincott, 1964; Baker's Dozen (collection of newspaper articles), New York Times Co., 1964; All Things Considered (collection of newspaper articles), Lippincott, 1965; Our Next President: The Incredible Story of What Happened in the 1968 Elections (fiction), Atheneum, 1968; Poor Russell's Almanac (collection of newspaper articles), Doubleday, 1972. Contributor to periodicals, including Saturday Evening Post, New York Times Magazine, Sports Illustrated, Ladies Home Journal, Holiday, Theatre Arts, Mademoiselle, Life, Look, McCalls.

SIDELIGHTS: Russell Baker's column, "Observer," is nationally syndicated by the New York Times. R. Z. Sheppard says: "At his best, Baker fills his allotted space opposite the editorial page with bizarre, often bleak fantasies about human foolishness. At his second best, he holds a funhouse mirror up to the nature of the consumer state.... Baker is a man of range, sensitive intellect and fertile imagination. He is also a fine stylist whose columns frequently unfurl to defend the language against corruption.... He is most effective in his newspaper, where the reader can wade expectantly toward him through bloated accounts of disaster, inhumanity, avarice and hypocrisy. Russell Baker can then best be appreciated doing what a good humorist has always done: writing to preserve his sanity for at least one more day."

In 1971 one of Baker's articles, entitled "How to Hypnotize Yourself into Forgetting the Vietnam War," was dramatized and filmed by Eli Wallach for presentation on the Public Broadcasting System's "The Great American Dream Machine."

*   *   *

BAKKER, Cornelius B(ernardus) 1929-
PERSONAL: Born January 6, 1929, in Rotterdam, Netherlands; naturalized U.S. citizen; son of Willem and Pauline J. (Reiff) Bakker; married Marianne Kathrine Rabdau (a registered nurse), 1955; children: Paul, James, Gabrielle. Education: State University of Utrecht, M.D., 1952. Home address: P.O. Box 3, 610 Front St., Mukilteo, Wash. 98275. Office: Department of Psychiatry and Behavioral Sciences, University of Washington, Seattle, Wash. 98195.

CAREER: Intern at Clinics of Rotterdam, Rotterdam, Netherlands, 1952-53, and Sacred Heart Hospital, Spokane, Wash., 1953-54; resident in psychiatry at Eastern State Hospital, Medical Lake, Wash., 1954-56, and University of Utrecht Psychiatric Clinic, Utrecht, Netherlands, 1956-57; University of Michigan Medical School, Ann Arbor, resident in psychiatry, 1957-59, instructor in psychiatry, 1958-60, research associate of Mental Health Research Institute, 1959-60; University of Washington School of Medicine, Seattle, instructor, 1960-63, assistant professor, 1963-67, associate professor, 1967-72, professor of psychiatry, 1972—, director of adult psychiatric inpatient service, University Hospital, 1961-69, director of adult development program, University Hospital and department of psychiatry, 1969—. Psychiatric consultant to Comprehensive Cardiology Clinic, Seattle, 1960-64, Vocational Rehabilitation Services for the Blind, Seattle, 1961—, and Bureau of Hearings and Appeals, Social Security Administration, 1963—.

MEMBER: American Psychiatric Association (fellow),

American College of Psychiatrists, World Congress of Psychiatry, King County Medical Society. Awards, honors: Fulbright grant and Committee on International Exchange of Persons grant for study in United States, 1953-56.

WRITINGS: (Contributor) Leonard M. Uhr and J. G. Miller, editors, Drugs and Behavior, Wiley, 1961; (with wife, Marianne K. Bakker-Rabdau) No Trespassing: Explorations in Human Territoriality, Chandler & Sharp, 1973. Contributor to Psychosomatic Medicine Journal Articles (collection) and medical journals.

WORK IN PROGRESS: Understanding Human Behavior: An Introduction to Psychopathology.

*   *   *

BALBUS
    See HUXLEY, Julian (Sorell)

*   *   *

BALDWIN, Marshall W(hithed) 1903-1975
March 30, 1903—July 3, 1975; American historian, educator, and editor or author of books on medieval Europe, the medieval Catholic Church, and the Crusades. Obituaries: New York Times, July 4, 1975; AB Bookman's Weekly, August 4, 1975.

*   *   *

BALL, Sylvia Patricia 1936-
    (E Squires England, Eric Squires, Patricia Squires)
PERSONAL: Born September 18, 1936, in Yapton near Arundel, Sussex, England; daughter of George Richard Henry (a maintenance and decorating contractor) and Lillian (Talbot) Deegan; married Eric Ball, December 17, 1955; children: Sandra Patricia, Jacqueline Anne. Politics: "the obviously unattainable." Religion: Church of England. Residence: Sussex, England.

CAREER: Employed on small holding in tasks concerned with fruits and vegetables, 1951-53; worked as a welder of wire products, 1953-55. Writer.

WRITINGS: (Under pseudonym Patricia Squires) The Ghost in the Mirror, Muller, 1972; (under pseudonym Eric Squires) Pit Pony Heroes, David & Charles, 1974. Writer of short stories. Contributor, under pseudonym E Squires England, of articles to Chance, Talent, London Mystery Magazine, West Sussex Gazette, and other periodicals. Also contributor of material to "How," a television series.

WORK IN PROGRESS: Two books, The Eternal Instinctive, about the existence of ghosts; an as yet untitled book concerning life in a Yorkshire coal mining village.

SIDELIGHTS: Mrs. Ball told CA that her first book, The Ghost in the Mirror, grew out of an interest in the occult which she shares with her husband. The Pit Pony Heroes was based on her husband's life as a coal miner, and his love for the ponies he handled in his work. Avocational interests: Gardening, greenhouse culture, decorating, needlework, country walking, local car travel, historic places, cookery, reading, and conversation.

*   *   *

BALLONOFF, Paul A(lan) 1943-
PERSONAL: Born April 3, 1943, in Cleveland, Ohio; son of Robert (an insurance agent) and Eva Iris (Matt) Ballonoff. Education: University of California, Los Angeles, A.B., 1964, M.A., 1969, Ph.D., 1970. Residence: Houston,

Tex. *Office:* University of Texas Health Science Center, Houston, Texas 77025.

CAREER: Southern Illinois University, Carbondale, visiting assistant professor of anthropology, 1970-71; University of Texas Health Science Center, Center for Demographic and Population Genetics, Houston, research associate, 1972, assistant professor of population genetics, 1973—. Visiting professor at University of Illinois, summer, 1972, and at University of Washington, Seattle, 1974-75. Lecturer at Rice University, 1972-75, and adjunct professor, 1975—; adjunct professor, University of Texas, School of Public Health, 1973-74. Peace Corps volunteer in Colombia, 1964-66. *Member:* American Anthropological Association. *Awards, honors:* University of Illinois postdoctoral fellow, 1971-72.

WRITINGS: (Editor and contributor) *Genealogical Mathematics*, Mouton & Co., 1974; (editor) *Genetics and Social Structure*, Dowden, 1974; (editor and contributor) *Mathematical Models of Social and Cognitive Structures*, University of Illinois Press, 1974; (editor with Kenneth Weiss) *Demographic Genetics*, Dowden, 1975; *Mathematical Foundations of Social Anthropology*, Mouton & Co., 1975. Contributor to professional journals.

WORK IN PROGRESS: A monograph, *Jack Batts: Violin Maker and Repairer*, for University of Tennessee Press; a book tentatively titled *Mathematical Theory of Cultural Semantics.*

*   *   *

BALOGH, Thomas 1905-

PERSONAL: Born November 2, 1905, in Budapest, Hungary; son of Emil (a civil servant) and Eva (Levy) Balogh; married Penelope Tower, March 17, 1945 (divorced, 1970); married Catherine Cole Storr (a writer), September 30, 1970; children: (first marriage) Timil, Stephen, Christopher, Tessa; (second marriage) Sophia, Cecilia, Emma, (stepdaughters). *Education:* University of Budapest, Dr.ver.pol., 1927; attended Hungarian College, Berlin, 1928, and Harvard University, 1928-30. *Politics:* Labour. *Home:* The Cottage, Christmas Common, Watlington, Oxfordshire, England. *Agent:* Curtis Brown Ltd., 1 Craven Hill, London, England. *Office:* Queen Elizabeth House, St. Giles, Oxford, England.

CAREER: Economic adviser to various firms in London, England, 1931-39; Oxford University, Oxford, England, lecturer, 1934-45, special lecturer, 1955-60, reader in economics, 1960-73, economist with Institute of Statistics, 1940-55, fellow of Balliol College, 1945—; Her Majesty's Government, London, adviser to Cabinet, 1964-67, consultant to Prime Minister, 1968, member of House of Lords, 1968—, Minister of State for Energy, 1974—. Economic associate to National Institute of Economic Research, 1938-42, Reserve Bank of Australia, 1942-64, United Nations Relief and Rehabilitation Administration's Mission to Hungary, 1946, Government of Malta, 1955-57, 1973-74, Government of Jamaica, 1956, 1961-62, 1974, United Nations Food and Agricultural Organization, 1957-59, 1961-62, United Nations Economic Commission for Latin America, 1960, Government of India Statistical Institute, 1960, 1971, Government of Greece, 1962, Government of Mauritius, 1962-63, United Nations Special Fund, 1964, 1970, 1971, Organization for European Economic Co-operation, 1964, Governments of Turkey and Peru, 1964. Member of Economic and Financial Subcommittee of Labour Party Executive Committee, 1943-64, 1971—. Visiting professor, University of Minnesota, 1951, University of Wisconsin, 1954, University of Delhi, 1955, Harvard University, 1960, and New York University, 1970; fellow of New York University, 1969. *Member:* Fabian Society (vice-chairman, 1969; chairman, 1970), Little French Club, Reform Club. *Awards, honors:* Rockefeller fellowship, 1928-30.

WRITINGS: (With Ernest Doblin) *Investment Trusts and Investment Companies*, United States Government Printing Office, 1939; *Studies in Financial Organization*, Cambridge University Press, 1947; *The Dollar Crisis, Causes and Cure: A Report to the Fabian Society*, Blackwell, 1949; *Germany: An Experiment in 'Planning' by the 'Free' Price Mechanism*, Blackwell, 1950; *Some Aspects of Economic Growth of Under-Developed Areas: Three Lectures*, National Council of Applied Economic Research (New Delhi), 1961, 2nd edition, 1962; *Planning for Progress: A Strategy for Labour* (booklet), Fabian Society, 1963; *Unequal Partners* (essays), two volumes, Blackwell, 1963; *The Economic Impact of Monetary and Commercial Institutions of a European Origin in Africa*, National Bank of Egypt, 1964; *The Economics of Poverty*, Macmillan, 1966, 2nd edition, International Arts & Sciences Press, 1974; (with Howard Thomas and others) *Crisis in the Civil Service*, Anthony Blond, 1968; *Labour and Inflation*, Fabian Society, 1970; *Fact and Fancy in International Economic Relations: An Essay on International Monetary Reform*, Pergamon, 1973.

Contributor to *Economic Journal* and *Bulletin of Oxford Institute of Statistics*, and others.

WORK IN PROGRESS: Economic Theory and Policy Making and *Government and the Expert.*

SIDELIGHTS: In 1968 Balogh was made a life peer, becoming Baron Balogh of Hampstead. *Avocational interests:* Planting trees and conversation.

BIOGRAPHICAL/CRITICAL SOURCES: Paul Streeten, editor, *Unfashionable Economics*, Weidenfeld & Nicolson, 1970.

*   *   *

BANCROFT, Anne 1923-

PERSONAL: Born April 17, 1923, in London, England; daughter of Arthur Lawrence (an author) and Margaret (Aitken) Hayward; married Keith England (divorced); married Hans Lobstein (divorced); married Richard Bancroft (a librarian); children: (first marriage) Julia (Mrs. Bryan Aspden), Roger; (second marriage) Timothy, Deborah. *Education:* Attended Sidney Webb Teacher's Training College, 1961-63. *Politics:* None. *Religion:* "Mystical Atheism." *Home:* Flat 4, 2 Gosfield St., London W1P 7HD, England.

CAREER: Lecturer in English, liberal studies, and comparative religion in London, England, 1965-72. *Member:* Royal Asiatic Society, Buddhist Society, Fellowship of St. Alban and St. Sergius.

WRITINGS: Religions of the East, St. Martin's, 1974; *Twentieth Century Mystics and Sages*, Regnery, 1975. Manuscript reader for Cassell, Heinemann, P. Davies, and M. Joseph. Contributor to Buddhist journals. Editor of *Middle Way*, 1975—.

SIDELIGHTS: Anne Bancroft is attracted to the teachings of the old Chinese Ch'an (Zen) masters and to the European mystics of the Middle Ages.

BANFIELD, Edward C(hristie) 1916-

PERSONAL: Born November 19, 1916, in Bloomfield, Conn.; son of Edward Christie (a machinist and factory foreman) and Helen Moore (Adams) Banfield; married Laura Margaret Fasano, September 24, 1938; children: Laura, Elliott. *Education:* Connecticut State College (now University of Connecticut), A.B., 1938; University of Chicago, Ph.D., 1951. *Home:* 1830 Rittenhouse Square, Philadelphia, Pa. 19103. *Office:* Department of Political Science, University of Pennsylvania, Philadelphia, Pa. 19104.

CAREER: Rockville Journal, Rockville, Conn., reporter and advertising salesman, 1938; U.S. Forest Service, Boston, Mass., junior administrative assistant, 1939-40; New Hampshire Farm Bureau Federation, Concord, secretary, 1940-41; U.S. Farm Security Administration, information specialist in Upper Darby, Pa., Indianapolis, Ind., Washington, D.C., and San Francisco, Calif., 1941-47; University of Chicago, Chicago, Ill., 1948-59, began as instructor, became associate professor of political science; Harvard University, Cambridge, Mass., professor, 1959-61, Henry Lee Shattuck Professor of Urban Government, 1961-72; University of Pennsylvania, Philadelphia, William R. Kenan, Jr. Professor of Public Policy and Political Science, 1973—. Chairman of a pre-inauguration Task Force on Urban Affairs for President-elect Richard M. Nixon, 1968-69; head of a study group appointed by President Nixon to evaluate the Model Cities program, 1969-70; member of the Advisory Commission on Intergovernmental Relations, 1971-73. *Member:* American Political Science Association (former vice-president), Committee for Economic Development (member of the Social Science Advisory Committee).

WRITINGS: Government Project (foreword by Rexford G. Tugwell), Free Press, 1951; (with Martin Meyerson) *Politics, Planning and the Public Interest: The Case of Public Housing in Chicago*, Free Press, 1955; *The Case of the Handcuffed Sheriff: Political Patronage*, American Foundation for Continuing Education, 1957; (with Morton Grodzins) *Government and Housing in Metropolitan Areas*, McGraw, 1958; (with wife, Laura F. Banfield) *The Moral Basis of a Backward Society*, Free Press, 1958, new edition, 1967; *The Case of the Blighted City: Chicago, Ill.*, American Foundation for Continuing Education, 1959; *The Case of the Growing Problem: The Farm Problem*, American Foundation for Continuing Education, 1959.

(Editor with Martha Derthick) *A Report on the Politics of Boston*, [Cambridge], 1960; *Political Influence*, Free Press, 1961; (editor) *Urban Government: A Reader in Politics and Administration*, Free Press, 1961, revised edition, 1968; (with others) *The Future Metropolis*, American Academy of Arts and Sciences, 1961; (with James Q. Wilson) *City Politics*, Harvard University Press, 1963; *American Foreign Aid Doctrines*, American Enterprise Institute for Public Policy Research, 1963; (with others) *The American City*, [Cambridge], 1964; *Big City Politics: A Comparative Guide to the Political Systems of Atlanta, Boston, Detroit, El Paso, Los Angeles, Miami, Philadelphia, St. Louis and Seattle*, Random House, 1965; (with Meyerson) *Boston: The Job Ahead*, Harvard University Press, 1966.

The Unheavenly City: The Nature and Future of Our Urban Crisis, Little, Brown, 1970; (contributor) Allan P. Sindler, editor, *Policy and Politics in America: Six Case Studies*, Little, Brown, 1973; *The Unheavenly City Revisited: A Revision of the Unheavenly City*, Little, Brown, 1974.

AVOCATIONAL INTERESTS: Gardening and walking on his farm in Vermont.*

BANISTER, Gary L. 1948-

PERSONAL: Born February 14, 1948, in Summerville, Ga.; son of Paul K. (a printer) and Virginia (Abrams) Banister; married Trudy Hagan (a teacher), August 20, 1971; children: Paul Russell. *Education:* University of Alabama, B.S., 1972. *Religion:* Baptist. *Home address:* Route 1, Box 199, Coffee Springs, Ala. 36318. *Office:* Geneva Recreation Department, 411 North Iris, Geneva, Ala. 36340.

CAREER: Recreation director for City of Camilla, Ga., 1972-73; Consultant Services Co., Salisbury, N.C., auditor, 1973-74; recreation and parks director in Geneva, Ala., 1974—. *Member:* National Parks and Recreation Association, National Fellowship of Christian Athletes, Alabama Parks and Recreation Society, Geneva County Development Committee, Lions Club, Optimist Club.

WRITINGS: My War with God, Zondervan, 1973.

* * *

BARBEE, David E(dwin) 1936-

PERSONAL: Born February 26, 1936, in San Francisco, Calif.; son of Edwin W. (a civil engineer) and Mary (Davis) Barbee; married Mary Keenum, August 30, 1956; children: Mark E., Michael D., Mary E., John Eric. *Education:* University of Northern Colorado, A.B., 1957, M.A., 1964; Catholic University of America, Ph.D., 1970. *Home and office address:* P.O. Box 788, Aspen, Colo. 81611.

CAREER: Catholic University of America, Washington, D.C., assistant professor of education, 1967-69; International Institutes of Educational Technology, Inc., Aspen, Colo. (and Washington, D.C.), president, 1970-72; Unco, Inc., Aspen Colo., director of Western operations, 1972-74; educational and training consultant in Aspen, Colo., 1974—. Professor of nursing at Federal City College, Washington, D.C., 1971-72; member of governing committee of Colorado Mountain College. Consultant to the military, government, and business. *Military service:* U.S. Coast Guard, 1957-61; became lieutenant. *Member:* National Society of Performance and Instruction, Phi Delta Kappa.

WRITINGS: A Systems Approach to Community College Education, Auerbach, 1972; (with A. J. Bouck) *Accountability in Education*, Mason-Lipscomb, 1974.

WORK IN PROGRESS: Accountability in Social Services, with Janet Martin; *A Professional Curriculum Based in Task Analysis*; research on accountability throughout delivery of human services; research on improvement of instruction; a systems approach to the problems of improving the human condition from within.

AVOCATIONAL INTERESTS: Skiing, hiking, outdoor sports.

* * *

BARBERO, Yves Regis Francois 1943-

PERSONAL: Born October 20, 1943, in Toulouse, France; son of Joseph (a city official) and Monique (LaCastania) Barbero. *Education:* City College of the City University of New York, B.A., 1969; New School for Social Research, graduate study, 1970-72. *Politics:* "Reasonable." *Religion:* "Taoist without formality." *Agent:* WB Agency, 156 East 52nd St., New York, N.Y.

CAREER: Bangor Daily News, Bangor, Maine, reporter, 1972-74; *New York Cultural Review*, New York, N.Y., contributing editor, 1974—. *Military service:* U.S. Army, 1962-65.

WRITINGS: The CTZ Paradigm (novel), Doubleday, 1975.

WORK IN PROGRESS: Conversations: A Story of Murder.

SIDELIGHTS: Barbero writes: "I have an interest in things oriental, but it's hardly scholarly. I dabble in poetry but find it is hard to take seriously (it's fun, though). Being trained as a sociologist, I find myself solving the world's problems. Fortunately, no one's given me any power. I like children and dogs and will listen to anyone tell me his world view. The drunker that individual is, the better. On a more serious side, I have a full beard and wear glasses."

*　　*　　*

BARBOTIN, Edmond 1920-

PERSONAL: Born October 31, 1920, in St. Servan, France; son of Edmond and Blanche (Jacquart) Barbotin. *Education:* Attended Universite Catholique d'Angers, 1939-45; Sorbonne, University of Paris, Doctorat es-Lettres-Philosophie, 1954; University of Strasbourg, Doctorat en Theologie, 1964. *Home:* 10 rue d'Arras, 67.000, Strasbourg, Bas-Rhine, France. *Office:* Faculte de Theologie Catholique, Universite de Strasbourg, Place de l'Universite (Palais Universitaire), 67.000, Strasbourg, France.

CAREER: Ordained Roman Catholic priest, 1943; University of Strasbourg, Strasbourg, France, professor with Faculte de Theologie Catholique, 1954—. *Awards, honors:* Prix de l'Association des Etudes grecques et de l'Academie des Sciences Morales et Politiques, 1955.

WRITINGS: (Editor) Octave Hamelin, *La Theorie de l'intellect d'apres Aristotle et ses commentateurs* (title means "The Theory of Intellect according to Aristotle and His Commentators"), Vrin (Paris), 1953; *La Theorie aristotelicienne de l'intellect d'apres Theophraste* (title means "The Aristotelian Theory of Intellect according to Theophrastus"), Publications universitaires de Louvain, 1954; (with Roger Verneaux and Jean Trouillard) *La Crise de la raison dans la pensee contemporaine* (title means "The Crisis of Reason in Contemporary Thought"), Desclee de Brouwer (Paris), 1960; *Le Temoignage spirituel* (title means "The Spiritual Testimony"), Epi (Paris), 1964; (editor and translator) Aristotle, *De l'ame* (title means "On the Soul"), Belles-Lettres (Paris), 1966; *Humanite de l'homme*, Aubier (Paris), 1970, translation published as *The Humanity of Man*, Orbis, 1975; *Humanite de Dieu: Approche anthropologique du mystere chretien*, Aubier, 1971, translation published as *Humanity of God*, Orbis, 1975; *Croire*, Desclee de Brouwer, 1971, translation by Matthew J. O'Connell published as *Faith for Today*, Orbis, 1974; *Qu'est-ce qu'un texte? Elements pour une hermeneutique* (title means "What Is a Text? Elements for Hermeneutics"), Corti (Paris), 1975. Contributor to *Vocabulaire oecumenique* and to journals in his field. Editor, *Revue des sciences religieuses*, 1956-66.

SIDELIGHTS: Barbotin has traveled to the United States, India, and Africa.

*　　*　　*

BARBOUR, Arthur Joseph 1926-

PERSONAL: Born August 23, 1926, in Paterson, N.J.; son of Peter John (a chiropractor) and Alma Loretta (Fiedler) Barbour; married Margaret Ann Hines, August 6, 1955. *Education:* Attended Newark School of Fine and Industrial

Arts. *Religion:* Roman Catholic. *Home and office:* 29 Voorhis Pl., Ringwood, N.J. 07456.

CAREER: Free-lance artist, painter, and illustrator. *Military service:* U.S. Navy, 1944-46. *Member:* American Water Color Society, Allied Artists of America, National Society of Painters in Casein and Acrylic, New Jersey Water Color Society. *Awards, honors:* More than fifty awards, including those of New Jersey Watercolor Society, National Society of Painters in Casein and Acrylic, New Jersey Painters and Sculptors, and Allied Artists of America; Grumbacher Award, 1964; award of excellence from Mainstreams, 1969, 1970, 1971; purchase award from Marietta College, 1971.

WRITINGS: Painting Buildings in Water Color, Watson-Guptill, 1973; *Painting the Seasons in Water Color*, Watson-Guptill, 1975; (contributor) Sue Davis, editor, *Complete Guide to Acrylic Painting*, Watson-Guptill, 1971; (contributor) *Acrylic Watercolor Painting*, Watson-Guptill, 1971. Contributor to *American Artist.*

*　　*　　*

BARCLAY, Oliver R(ainsford) 1919-
(A. N. Triton)

PERSONAL: Born February 22, 1919, in Kobe, Japan; son of Joseph Gurney (a missionary) and Gwendoline (a missionary; maiden name, Watney) Barclay; married Dorothy Knott, June 30, 1949 (died May 19, 1964); married Daisy Hickey, October 31, 1965; children: (first marriage) Janet (Mrs. Anthony Johnston), Andrew, Stephen, John. *Education:* Attended Cambridge University, 1938-41. *Religion:* Church of England. *Home:* 17, Holly Lodge Gardens, Highgate, London N6 6AA, England. *Office:* Universities & Colleges Christian Fellowship, 39 Bedford Square, London WC1, England.

CAREER: Cambridge University, Cambridge, England, research zoologist and part-time teacher, 1941-45; Inter-Varsity Fellowship of Evangelical Unions, London, England, staff member, 1945—.

*WRITINGS—*All published by Inter-Varsity Press: *Guidance*, 1956; *Christian Approach to University Life*, 1963; *Time to Embrace*, 1964; (under pseudonym A. N. Triton) *Whose World?*, 1970; (under pseudonym A.N. Triton) *Living and Loving*, 1972; *Reasons for Faith*, 1974.

WORK IN PROGRESS: Social Responsibilities of the Christian.

*　　*　　*

BARDARSON, Hjalmar R(oegnvaldur) 1918-

PERSONAL: Born June 8, 1918, in Isafjoerdur, Iceland; son of Bardur Gudmundur (a naval architect) and Filippia (Hjalmarsdottir) Tomasson; married Else Soerensen, June 16, 1946. *Education:* Technical University, Copenhagen, Denmark, M.Sc., 1947. *Home:* Hrauntunga v.Alftanesveg, Gardahreppi, Iceland. *Office address:* P.O. Box 998, Reykjavik, Iceland.

CAREER: Elsinore Shipyard, Elsinore, Denmark, naval architect, 1947; Cook, Welton & Gemmel (trawler yard), Beverley, Yorkshire, England, ship designer, 1947; Stalsmidjan Shipyard, Reykjavik, Iceland, ship designer and manager, 1948-54; Icelandic Government, Reykjavik, state director of shipping, 1954—. President of assembly of Intergovernmental Maritime Consultative Organization, 1969-71; representative of Iceland at several international conferences. *Member:* International Glaciological Society (England), Icelandic Engineers Association Council, Iceland Glaciological Society, Surtsey Research Society, Federation Internationale de l'Art Photographic (honorary member), Photographic Society of Iceland (president, 1950-75). *Awards, honors:* Gold Pen Prize from Menntaskdinn i Reykjavik, 1939, for *Flugmal Islands.*

WRITINGS: Flugmal Islands (title means "Iceland Aviation"), Heimskringla (Reykjavik, Iceland), 1939; *Table Top*, Belgisk Import Co. (Copenhagen), 1945; *Island farsaelda fron*, Lithoprent Hjalmar R. Bardarson (Reykjavik), 1953; (translator and reviser) Goesta Skogluns, *Ljosmyndabokin* (title means "The Book on Photography"), Setberg (Reykjavik), 1961; *Island-Iceland-Islande* (text in six languages), Hjalmar R. Bardarson, 1965, translation by Soelvi Eysteinsson published as *Ice and Fire*, Hjalmar R. Bardarson, 1971. Contributor to magazines.

WORK IN PROGRESS: Research in geology, glaciology, ornithology.

* * *

BARGER, James (David)   1947-

PERSONAL: Born March 26, 1947, in Harrisburg, Ill.; son of W. L. and Mary (Baker) Barger; married Ernestine Smith, June 13, 1971; children: Adrienne. *Education:* Southern Illinois University, B.S.Ed., 1969. *Politics:* Independent. *Religion:* "The arts, friendship, love, and optimism." *Office:* Allendale School, Allendale, Ill. 62410.

CAREER: Allendale School, Allendale, Ill., high school teacher of English and German, 1969—.

WRITINGS—All for high school students: *William Faulkner: Modern American Novelist and Nobel Prize Winner*, Story House, 1973; *James Joyce: Modern Irish Writer*, Story House, 1974; *Ernest Hemingway*, Story House, 1975.

WORK IN PROGRESS: A novel; short stories; poems.

SIDELIGHTS: Barger writes: "My chief interest is contemporary fiction. I do not side with those who are predicting the death of the novel, or who feel that fiction is irrelevant to modern life. Though I see it 'merging' with what we used to call 'non-fiction,' it is still very much alive, and because it allows the writer to use his imagination, will continue to tell us what we need to know."

* * *

BARISH, Matthew   1907-

PERSONAL: Born October 19, 1907, in Jersey City, N.J.; son of Joseph David (a teacher) and Tillie (Ostrow) Barish; separated; children: David, Emily (Mrs. Clark Josephs). *Education:* City College of New York (now City College of the City University of New York), B.S.S., 1930; New York University, M.A., 1932, further graduate study, 1959-61. *Politics:* Democrat. *Religion:* "Beauty." *Home:* 788 Columbus Ave., New York, N.Y. 10025. *Office:* Parsons School of Design, 2 West 13th St., New York, N.Y. 10011.

CAREER: Public school teacher in New York, N.Y., 1932-33; social worker in New York, N.Y., 1933-36; Hebrew Publishing Co., New York, N.Y., general manager of Greeting Card Division and member of board of directors, 1936-71; Parsons School of Design, New York, N.Y., teacher of greeting card art, 1974—. Personnel manager for United Transformer, 1944-45; teacher at New York School of Visual Art, 1970—. Volunteer teacher of remedial reading in public schools; executive member of Committee on Returning Veterans (to the electronic industry), 1945-46.

WRITINGS: A Comparative Study of Nine New York City Schools, New York City Board of Education, 1932; *Kids Book of Cards and Posters* (on making greeting cards for people of all ages), Prentice-Hall, 1973.

WORK IN PROGRESS: A slide presentation from his book for high schools and geriatric groups.

AVOCATIONAL INTERESTS: Playing chess and bridge, and travel.

* * *

BARKAS, Janet   1948-

PERSONAL: Born December 16, 1948, in New York, N.Y.; daughter of William (a dentist) and Gladys (a teacher; maiden name, Hodes) Barkas. *Education:* Hofstra University, B.A., 1970. *Address:* P.O. Box 31, Cooper Station, N.Y. 10003.

CAREER: Macmillan Co., New York, N.Y., editor, 1971-73; Grove Press, New York, N.Y., editor, 1973-74. Lecturer at New School for Social Research, fall, 1973, 1975. *Member:* Author's Guild, Author's League of America, Society of Magazine Writers, Drama Desk.

WRITINGS: The Vegetable Passion: A History of the Vegetarian State of Mind, Scribner, 1975; *Meatless Cooking: Celebrity Style*, Grove, 1975. Contributor to *Harper's, Family Circle, McCall's, New York Times, Family Health, Opera News, Human Behavior*, and *Contemporary Review*. Drama critic for *Backstage*, 1973—.

WORK IN PROGRESS: A nonfiction book on crime, completion expected in 1976; a novel, 1977; a nonfiction book on women, 1978.

AVOCATIONAL INTERESTS: Travel, painting.

BIOGRAPHICAL/CRITICAL SOURCES: Hofstra Report, February, 1975; *Berkshire Eagle*, March 7, 1975; *Long Island Press*, March 30, 1975; *Newsday*, April, 1975; *San Francisco Examiner*, April 2, 1975.

* * *

BARKLEY, Vada Lee   1919-

PERSONAL: Born September 28, 1919, in Union, Ark.; daughter of Robert Lee and Ada (Matheson) Beard; married Arthur E. Barkley (a printer), June 2, 1950. *Education:* Bethany Nazarene College, A.B., 1942; University of Oklahoma, M.A., 1950. *Politics:* Republican. *Religion:* Church of the Nazarene. *Home:* 509 Matthews, El Reno, Okla. 73036. *Office:* Department of Language Arts, El Reno Junior College, 1300 Country Club, El Reno, Okla. 73036.

CAREER: Public school teacher in Carnegie, Okla., 1942-43; high school English teacher in Alden, Okla., 1943-44; Church of the Nazarene, Bethany, Okla., song evangelist, 1944-46; Bethany Nazarene College, Bethany, Okla., instructor in English and French, 1946-50; Church of the Nazarene, Bethany, Okla., song evangelist, 1950-56; high school English teacher in Mustang, Okla., 1956-59; Southwest Oklahoma Girl Scout Council, Hobart, Okla., executive director, 1959-61; high school English teacher in Hobart, Okla., 1962-69; El Reno Junior College, El Reno, Okla., instructor in English and creative writing, 1969—. *Member:* Higher Education Alumni Council of Oklahoma.

WRITINGS: Pioneering with God: Biography of Augusta Guy, Yukon Printing, 1972; *Layman, Please*, CSS Publishing, 1974; *Pastor, Please*, CSS Publishing, 1974. Contributor to English journals.

WORK IN PROGRESS: Biographical and autobiographical material covering three generations of her family.

SIDELIGHTS: Vada Barkley writes: "Although as a child, I had little opportunity to study music, I used the natural ability I had and what meager training I could afford; through the years I have actively participated in the musical program in many churches. I have even taught beginning piano, organ, guitar, and voice lessons. Music is a vital part of my life. But only recently have I begun to write both words and music for sacred songs." She has made a sound recording, "My Blessed Savior," Command Performance Record Co., 1975.

*　　*　　*

BARKSDALE, E(thelbert) C(ourtland) 1944-

PERSONAL: Born April 9, 1944, in Arlington, Tex.; son of E. C., Sr. (a professor of history) and Marjorie (Miller) Barksdale. *Education:* University of Texas, Arlington, B.A., 1965; Ohio State University, M.A. and Ph.D. *Religion:* Christian. *Home:* 1333 South Pecan St., Arlington, Tex. 76010. *Office:* 261 Arts and Sciences Building, University of Florida, Gainesville, Fla. 32611.

CAREER: University of California, Irvine, instructor in Slavic, 1971-72; University of Florida, Gainesville, assistant professor of Slavic, 1972—. *Member:* Sobro Slovo, Phi Kappa Theta, Sigma Tau Delta.

WRITINGS: The Dacha and the Duchess: An Application of Levi-Strauss's Theory of Myth in Human Creativity to Works of Nineteenth-Century Russian Novelists, Philosophical Library, 1974.

WORK IN PROGRESS: A book on Structuralism.

*　　*　　*

BARNES, Joanna 1934-

PERSONAL: Born November 15, 1934, in Boston, Mass.; daughter of John Pindar (an insurance company executive) and Alice Weston (Mutch) Barnes. *Education:* Smith College, B.A., 1956. *Home:* 410 Castle Pl., Beverly Hills, Calif. 90210. *Agent:* William Morris Agency, 1350 Avenue of the Americas, New York, N.Y. 10019. *Office:* c/o David G. Licht, 9171 Wilshire Blvd., Beverly Hills, Calif. 90212.

CAREER: Actress, 1956—; has appeared in motion pictures "P.S., I Love You," "The War Wagon," and "Auntie Mame" and on television programs "What's My Line," "Merv Griffin Show," and "McCloud"; writer. *Member:* Phi Beta Kappa.

WRITINGS: Starting from Scratch: A Guide to Home Decorating, Hawthorn, 1968; *The Deceivers*, Arbor House, 1970; *Who Is Carla Hart?*, Arbor House, 1973. Author of "Touching Home," home design column for *Chicago Tribune-New York News* Syndicate, 1961-65. Book reviewer for *Los Angeles Times*, 1961-65.

WORK IN PROGRESS: Fiction and screenplays.

*　　*　　*

BARNETT, Marva T(uttle) 1913-

PERSONAL: Born April 24, 1913, in Spanish Fork, Utah; daughter of Haswell Andrew and Emily (Miller) Tuttle; married John Barnett (a teacher), April 15, 1944; children: Marva Ann, Karen Sue. *Education:* University of Utah, B.A., 1938; graduate study at Virginia Polytechnic Institute and University, University of Virginia, and St. Louis University. *Politics:* "Vote for people, not a party." *Home:* 2669 Olympus Dr., Salt Lake City, Utah 84117.

CAREER: Teacher of Latin and English in St. Anthony, Idaho, 1938-39; teacher of English in Sandy, Utah, 1939-42; Scott Field Air Force Base, Ill., radio instructor, 1942-45; high school English teacher in Schoolfield, Va., 1945-51; Stratford College, Danville, Va., part-time instructor in history and English, 1957-59; Rowland Hall, Salt Lake City, Utah, instructor in Latin, 1960-63; Institute for Technological Training, Salt Lake City, Utah, instructor in English, 1963—. Part-time instructor at Virginia Polytechnic Institute and University (Danville Branch), 1957-59; instructor at Rowland Hall, 1963-66; part-time instructor at University of Utah, 1966-74. Technical writing consultant, Christensen Diamond Products Co., 1972—. *Member:* National Writers Club.

WRITINGS: Elements of Technical Writing, Delmar, 1974.

WORK IN PROGRESS: Technical Writing for Public Safety Personnel; Understanding English Grammer; research for *Correct Use of Grammar*.

SIDELIGHTS: Marva Barnett writes: "I strongly believe that most of the problems in America today have resulted from training people rather than educating them. This training has occurred in the homes, the churches, and the schools. I would, therefore, like to see today's education, its goals and its purposes, evaluated. My work with young adults shows that they are disillusioned and frustrated. They need new goals, new ideals, and an awareness of personal worth."

AVOCATIONAL INTERESTS: Music, literature, travel, gardening, arts and crafts, ham radio (has operator's license).

*　　*　　*

BARNETT, Michael 1930-

PERSONAL: Also known as Swami Anand Somendra; born June 7, 1930, in London, England; son of Bearon Aaron (a gambler) and Joyce (Simmonds) Barnett; married Pamela Ann McGarry, May 20, 1963 (divorced, 1974); children: Shem Beckett. *Education:* Cambridge University, B.A. (honors), 1953; University of Birmingham, graduate study, 1969-71. *Politics:* "Allowing." *Religion:* "Cosmic." *Home:* Shree Rajneesh Ashram, 17 Koregaon Park, Poona, 1, Maharashtra, India; and 15 Highbury Grange, London N.5, England.

CAREER: Has worked as a department store manager, teacher, financial analyst, journalist, salesman, encounter group leader, and therapist. *Military service:* British Army.

WRITINGS: People not Psychiatry: A Human Alternative to Psycho-therapy, Allen & Unwin, 1973, Regnery, 1975.

WORK IN PROGRESS: Editing some of the discourses of Bhagwan Shree Rajneesh; a novel, *Death in the Head*.

SIDELIGHTS: Barnett writes: "Currently not reading, not writing, but emptying mind slowly & working with Bhagwan Shree Rajneesh in Poona, India—a modern master. Have little interest in anything apart from gaining the awareness to be aware of everything around at once."

*　　*　　*

BARNIE, John 1941-

PERSONAL: Born March 27, 1941, in Abergavenny, Wales; son of Edward Charles (a shopkeeper) and Melva (Fletcher) Barnie. *Education:* University of Birmingham, B.A., 1963, M.A., 1966, Ph.D., 1971. *Politics:* Welsh Nationalist. *Religion:* "Stoic." *Home:* Griffenfeldsgade 3, lejl. 14, Copenhagen, 2200N, Denmark. *Office:* Engelsk Institut, University of Copenhagen, Lille Kirkestraede 1, Copenhagen 1072K, Denmark.

CAREER: University of Copenhagen, Copenhagen, Denmark, lecturer in English literature, 1969—. *Member:* Cymdeithas yr Iaith Gymraeg (Welsh Language Society), Early English Text Society, Mediaeval Academy of America.

WRITINGS: War in Medieval Society, Cornell University Press, 1974. Contributor of poems to Welsh literary journals, including *Poetry Wales* and *Planet*.

WORK IN PROGRESS: Poems.

AVOCATIONAL INTERESTS: Black American country blues (especially 1924-1940), learning Welsh language.

* * *

BARRETT, Eugene F(rancis) 1921-

PERSONAL: Born June 26, 1921, in Sioux City, Iowa; son of Patrick Daniel (a policeman) and Maria (Mullally) Barrett; married Frances B. Tobin (a registered nurse), August 17, 1946; children: David, Donald, Cynthia, Kelli Anne, Richard. *Education:* University of Portland, B.A., 1948, graduate study, 1957-58, 1964-68, M.A., 1971; graduate study at Willamette University, 1951, and Portland State University, 1960-61. *Politics:* Republican. *Religion:* Roman Catholic. *Home:* 2436 Northeast 46th Ave., Portland, Ore. 97213. *Office:* Department of Language Arts, Portland Community College, Portland, Ore. 97219.

CAREER: High school teacher of English and social studies in Mt. Angel, Ore., 1948-53, of social studies in Los Angeles, Calif., 1953-56, in Gresham, Ore., 1956-59, and in Portland, Ore., 1959-65; Portland Community College, Portland, Ore., instructor in English 1961-65 (part-time), 1965-70, coordinator of department of adult basic education, 1970-71, coordinator of Division of Communications at Cascade Center, 1971-73, chairman of department of language arts, 1973-75, of department of mass communications, 1975—. Instructor at Mt. Angel College, 1962-63, Oklahoma State University, summer, 1966, Oregon State System of Higher Education, Division of Continuing Education, 1966-69. Lecturer, Portland State University, 1974. Consultant to Laidlaw Publishing Co., 1969-71. *Military service:* U.S. Navy, 1942-45. *Member:* National Education Association, National Council of Teachers of English, American Business Communication Association, Oregon Education Association, Multnomah County Education Association (secretary, 1959).

WRITINGS: (With Richard H. Lodwig) *The Dictionary and the Language*, Hayden, 1967; (with Lodwig) *Words, Words, Words: Vocabularies and Dictionaries*, Hayden, 1973.

WORK IN PROGRESS: A compact handbook of composition for working policeman.

* * *

BARRY, Joseph (Amber) 1917-

PERSONAL: Born June 13, 1917, in Scranton, Pa.; married Naomi Jolles, 1946 (divorced, 1965); children: Michael Alexander, John Christopher. *Education:* University of Michigan, A.B., 1939, A.B. in L.S., 1940; Sorbonne, University of Paris, graduate study, 1946. *Politics:* "Liberty, equality, fraternity." *Religion:* Humanism. *Home and of-*

fice: 107 rue Lauriston, Paris, France 75116. *Agent:* Robert Lescher, 155 East 71st St., New York, N.Y. 10021.

CAREER: New York Public Library, New York, N.Y., member of professional staff, 1940-41; *Newsweek*, New York, N.Y., manager of Paris edition, 1946-49; *New York Times*, New York, N.Y., Paris Bureau chief of Sunday edition, 1949-52; *House Beautiful*, New York, N.Y., editorial director, 1952-57; *New York Post*, New York, N.Y., Paris columnist, 1958-65; *Village Voice*, New York, N.Y., Paris columnist, 1965—; free-lance writer, 1965—. *Military service:* U.S. Army, 1941-46; became captain; received Bronze Star. *Member:* P.E.N., Author's Guild, Anglo-American Press Association (Paris), Phi Beta Kappa. *Awards, honors: Passions and Politics* was an American Library Association Notable Book in 1974.

WRITINGS: Left Bank, Right Bank, Norton, 1951; (editor) *Architecture as Space*, Horizon Press, 1957; *Contemporary American Architecture*, Hawthorn, 1958; *France*, Macmillan, 1965; *The People of Paris*, Doubleday, 1966; *Passions and Politics: A Biography of Versailles*, Doubleday, 1972. Contributor to *Horizon, New Republic, Smithsonian, Holiday*, and others.

WORK IN PROGRESS: Biography of George Sand; The French Couple.

SIDELIGHTS: Barry writes: "Once you leave your village, you're a world traveler. I left Scranton. Paris, the French, and Gertrude Stein (I was her 'adopted' nephew) were greatest personal influences; Nietzsche, Freud and Marx—psycho-socio-philo-literary influences. May 1968 near revolution in Paris, most stirring event. Two pillars of life, the Freudian pair: *liebe und arbeit*, love and work; love includes the passions of the mind, which are lifelong."

* * *

BARTELS, Susan Ludvigson 1942-

PERSONAL: Born February 13, 1942, in Rice Lake, Wis.; daughter of Howard C. and Mabel (Helgeland) Ludvigson; married David Bartels (an audiologist), February 20, 1961; children: Joel. *Education:* University of Wisconsin, River Falls, B.S., 1965; University of North Carolina, M.A. in Ed., 1973; doctoral study at University of South Carolina, 1973—. *Home address:* Box 88615, University of South Carolina, Columbia, S.C. 29208. *Office:* Department of English, Box 133, Humanities Bldg., University of South Carolina, Columbia, S.C. 29208.

CAREER: Junior high and high school teacher of English in the public schools of River Falls, Wis., 1964-68, and Ann Arbor, Mich., 1968-71; University of North Carolina, Charlotte, associate in Institute for Urban Studies and Community Service, 1972-73. Community Services consultant for Mecklenburg County Area Mental Health team, 1973-74.

WRITINGS: Step Carefully in Night Grass (poems), Blair, 1974. Contributor of poems to journals, including *Southern Poetry Review, Four Quarters, Paris Review, Cold Mountain Review, Panache, Green River Review, Sanskrit, Tangent, Tar River Poets, Mississippi Review*, and others.

WORK IN PROGRESS: A collection of poems.

* * *

BARTER, A(lice) K(nar) 1918-

PERSONAL: Born November 11, 1918, in Sivas, Turkey;

came to United States in 1921, naturalized citizen, 1927; daughter of Harry and Marguerite (Seraderian) Shamlian; married Lloyd W. Barter, August 18, 1940 (divorced August 18, 1958); children: Andrea Marguerite (Mrs. Joseph B. Kopp). *Education:* Eastern Michigan University, B.A., 1939; University of Michigan, M.A., 1944, Ph.D., 1957, postdoctoral study, summers, 1963, 1967. *Politics:* Democrat. *Religon:* Episcopalian. *Home:* 2216 Country Club Dr., Apt. 26, Woodridge, Ill. 60515. *Agent:* Miriam Gilbert, 146-47 29th Ave., Flushing, N.Y. 11354. *Office:* Department of English, Chicago State University, 95th St. and King Dr., Chicago, Ill. 60628.

CAREER: Teacher of English in public schools in Michigan, 1939-55; University of Detroit, Detroit, Mich., assistant professor of education, 1957-60; Miami University, Oxford, Ohio, assistant professor 1960-63, associate professor of English and education, 1963-67; Chicago State University, Chicago, Ill., professor of English, 1967—. *Member:* National Council of Teachers of English, National Society for the Study of Education, Midwest Modern Language Association, Pi Lambda Theta.

WRITINGS: English in the High School (handbook), Audio-Visual Services, Miami University, 1965; *Spelling by Sound and Sequence*, New Voices, 1975. Contributor of articles and reviews to education journals.

WORK IN PROGRESS: Tools for the Prospective Teacher: A Review of Basic Grammar; "Box 8156" and "Reunion '75," both short stories; research on William Saroyan and on evaluation and development of faculty.

AVOCATIONAL INTERESTS: Painting, playing golf and bridge, travel (Russia, Scandinavia, Turkey, Greece, Mexico, Hawaii, England, France, Italy, Switzerland).

*   *   *

BARTON, Byron   1930-

PERSONAL: Born September 8, 1930, in Pawtucket, R.I.; changed name to Barton, 1953; son of Toros and Elizabeth (Krekorian) Vartanian; married Harriett Wyatt, December, 1967 (divorced April, 1973). *Education:* Attended Los Angeles City College, 1948-50, and Chouinard Art Institute, 1953-56. *Home:* 2 Washington Sq. Village, New York, N.Y. 10012. *Agent:* Marilyn Marlow, Curtis Brown Ltd., 60 East 56th St., New York, N.Y. 10022.

CAREER: Studio 7 Los Angeles, Los Angeles, Calif., illustrator, 1956-57; Equitable Life Assurance Co., New York, N.Y., designer, 1957-60; CBS-TV, New York, N.Y., designer, 1960-66; free-lance designer and illustrator, 1966—. *Military service:* U.S. Army, 1950-52.

WRITINGS—All juveniles; all self-illustrated: *Elephant*, Seabury, 1971; *Where's Al?*, Seabury, 1972; *Applebet Story*, Viking, 1973; *Buzz Buzz Buzz*, Macmillan, 1973; *Harry is a Scaredy-Cat*, Macmillan, 1974; *Jack and Fred*, Macmillan, 1974; *Hester*, Morrow, 1975.

*   *   *

BASHIRA, Damali   1951-

PERSONAL: Born January 6, 1951, in Las Vegas, Nev.; daughter of Willie (formerly with U.S. Air Force) and Ann (a teacher; maiden name, Glenn) Alexander; married Jesse Burnett, June 6, 1971 (divorced, 1975). *Education:* Attended Stephens College, 1969-71, Howard University, 1972-73. *Politics:* "That humankind be free." *Religion:* "I Believe in the Creator of the Universe." *Agent:* Rich Bartee, P.O. Box 1404, New York, N.Y. 10027.

CAREER: Howard University, Institute on Drug Abuse and Addiction, Washington, D.C., administrative secretary, 1971-72; RAP, Inc., Washington, D.C., assistant director of education, 1973; *Blackstage* (magazine), Washington, D.C., associate editor, 1973-74; *Focus* (newspaper), Greenville, S.C., editor, 1974-75; *CORE Magazine*, New York, N.Y., assistant editor, and writer, 1975—. Tape editor, Mutual Black Radio Network, winter, 1974; assistant editor, *Third Press Review of Books*, spring, 1975. Member of Poettential Unlimited Theatre, New York. *Member:* Congress of Racial Equality.

WRITINGS: I Am That We May Be (poetry), Third World Press, 1974. Also author of poems, "Goodnight," Broadside Press, 1970, and "Four Women," Broadside Press, 1973, and play, "Just Like His Mama," 1975. Author of column, "What's Going On," in *Blackstage*, 1974. Contributor of articles to *Encore, Blackstage*, and book reviews to *A Current Bibliography on African Affairs*, and *Third Press Review of Books*.

WORK IN PROGRESS: A second volume of poetry, *I Like You*, for Liberated Libra; a play, "Why in Hell Is Martin Sostre in Jail"; research for a play on Zora Neale Hurston.

SIDELIGHTS: Damali Bashira told *CA:* "My ultimate goal is to be able to write plays to my heart's content. . . . Because I am black I write out of my experience and towards those who wish to share with me. I have no cause other than the cause of justice and freedom."

*   *   *

BASS, Henry B(enjamin)   1897-1975

1897—February 12, 1975; American historian, construction executive, and author of books on American history. Obituaries: *AB Bookman's Weekly*, March 17, 1975.

*   *   *

BASTEN, Fred E(rnest)

PERSONAL: Born in Chicago, Ill.; son of Alfred H. (a salesman) and Jeanne (Bryan) Basten. *Education:* University of California, Los Angeles, B.A. *Home and office:* 3740 Malibu Vista Dr., Malibu, Calif. 90265. *Agent:* Faustina Orner, 7046 Hollywood Blvd., Los Angeles, Calif. 90028.

CAREER: Foote, Cone & Belding (advertising), Los Angeles, Calif., copywriter, 1955-57; Lennen & Newell (advertising), Los Angeles, senior copywriter, 1958-59; A & W International, Inc., Santa Monica, Calif., director of art and publications, 1960-74; full-time writer, 1974—.

WRITINGS: Santa Monica Bay: The First One Hundred Years, Douglas-West, 1974; *Beverly Hills: Portrait of a Fabled City*, Douglas-West, 1975. Contributor to journals.

WORK IN PROGRESS: The Flowers of Paradise, a historical novel; history of color in motion pictures, *Color by Technicolor*.

*   *   *

BATES, Arthenia J.   1920-

PERSONAL: Born June 1, 1920, in Sumter, S.C.; daughter of Calvin Sheperd and Susan Emma (a practical nurse; maiden name, David) Jackson; married Noah Bates, June 11, 1950 (divorced, 1956); married Wilbert Millican, August 14, 1969; children: (second marriage) Wilbert James (stepson). *Education:* Morris College, B.A., 1941; Atlanta

University, M.A., 1948; graduate study at North Carolina Central University, 1953, University of Michigan, 1955, 1958; Louisiana State University, Ph.D., 1972. *Politics:* Democrat. *Religion:* Roman Catholic. *Home address:* Route 2, Box 284, Baker, La. 70714. *Office:* Box 2824, Norfolk State College, Norfolk, Va. 23504.

CAREER: High school teacher of English and civics in Kershaw, S.C., 1942-45, and Hartsville, S.C., 1945-46; Morris College, Sumter, S.C., chairman of department of English, 1947-49; high school teacher of English and history in Halifax, Va., 1949-55; Mississippi Valley State College, Itta Bena, instructor in English, 1955-56; Southern University, Baton Rouge, La., instructor, 1956-59, assistant professor, 1959-63, associate professor, 1963-72, professor of English, 1972-74; Norfolk State College, Norfolk, Va., professor of English, 1974—. Instructor in creative writing, Camp Miniwanca, Stony Lake, Mich., summer, 1962, 1963; official scholarship recruiter, American Youth Foundation, 1964—. *Member:* International Black Writer's Club, College Language Association (life member), National Council of Teachers of English, Conference on College Composition and Communication, Louisiana Folklore Society, Delta Sigma Theta, Gamma Sigma Sigma. *Awards, honors:* Bronze Medal from American Youth Foundation, 1962; various awards for poetry and prose writings.

WRITINGS: Seeds Beneath the Snow (short stories), Greenwich Book, 1969; *The Deity Nodded* (novel), Harlo, 1973; *The Bottoms and Hills* (folk tales), Amuru Press, in press. Contributor of poems to anthologies and of poems and articles to newspapers and journals. Contributing and advisory editor, *Obsidian*, 1974—.

WORK IN PROGRESS: Bayou Twigs, a short story collection.

SIDELIGHTS: Arthenia Bates told *CA:* "The problem of human suffering has always drawn my attention, but to plagarize myself, it is best not 'to beat your sorrow thin.' I suffer most from the inability to write because I must work, but my stolen moments have yielded results. As a teacher, I am interested in Black American literature. I like to write, especially fiction, collect picture post cards, read, and plant vegetables."

BIOGRAPHICAL/CRITICAL SOURCES: Washington Post, July 11, 1970; *College Language Assocation Journal*, December, 1973.

* * *

BATHKE, Edwin A(lbert) 1936-

PERSONAL: Surname is pronounced *Bot*-kee; born April 9, 1936, in Milwaukee, Wis.; son of Edwin J. (a retail grocer) and Lorena (a retail grocer; maiden name, Liehe) Bathke; married Nancy Bittner (an educator), June 8, 1960. *Education:* University of Wisconsin, Madison, B.S., 1957, M.S., 1959; University of Colorado, M.S., 1965. *Home:* 112 Palisade Circle, Manitou Springs, Colo. 80829. *Office:* Kaman Sciences Corp., 1500 Garden of the Gods Rd., Colorado Springs, Colo. 80907.

CAREER: U.S. Army, Signal Research & Development Laboratories, Fort Monmouth, N.J., mathematician, 1957-60; Martin-Marietta Corp., Denver, Colo., engineer, 1960-67; Kaman Sciences Corp., Colorado Springs, Colo., research scientist, 1967—. *Member:* American Philatelic Society, Mensa, New Mexico Philatelic Association, Ghost Town Club of Colorado (president, 1966), Pikes Peak Historical Society (vice-president, 1972, 1975), Denver Posse

of the Westerners (sheriff, 1972), Palmer Lake Historical Society, Colorado Springs Stamp Club, Phi Eta Sigma, Pi Mu Epsilon.

WRITINGS: (Contributor) Francis B. Rizzari, editor, *Denver Westerners Brand Book*, Volume XX, Johnson Publishing Co., 1965; (contributor) Jackson C. Thode, editor, *Denver Westerners Brand Book*, Volume XXVI, Johnson Publishing Co., 1971; (editor and contributor) *Denver Westerners Brand Book*, Volume XXVIII, Johnson Publishing Co., 1973; (with wife, Nancy E. Bathke) *The West in Postage Stamps*, Filter Press, 1973.

WORK IN PROGRESS: Souvenir Spoons of Colorado, with wife, Nancy E. Bathke; research on Colorado history.

AVOCATIONAL INTERESTS: Western history, collecting postage stamps and old Colorado photographs and books.

* * *

BATHKE, Nancy E(dna) 1938-

PERSONAL: Surname is pronounced *Bot*-kee; born June 17, 1938, in Dodgeville, Wis.; daughter of Fred E. (a musician and musician's union official) and Jean (a nurse; maiden name, Pinkerton) Bittner; married Edwin A. Bathke (a research scientist), June 8, 1960. *Education:* University of Wisconsin, Madison, B.S.Ed., 1960; University of Colorado, M.A., 1965. *Home:* 112 Palisade Circle, Manitou Springs, Colo. 80829. *Office:* Pine Valley Elementary School, U.S. Air Force Academy, Colorado Springs, Colo. 80840.

CAREER: Elementary school teacher in Jefferson County, Colo., 1960-67; Pine Valley Elementary School, U.S. Air Force Academy, Colorado Springs, Colo., teacher, 1967—. *Member:* National Education Association, Colorado State Historical Society, Ghost Town Club of Colorado, Historical Society of the Pikes Peak Region, Palmer Lake Historical Society (member of board of directors, 1974), Ghost Town Club of Colorado Springs, Friends of the Pioneers Museum, Pi Lambda Theta, Kappa Delta Pi.

WRITINGS: (Contributor) Jackson C. Thode, editor, *Denver Westerners Brand Book*, Volume XXVI, Johnson Publishing Co., 1971; (contributor) Edwin A. Bathke, editor, *Denver Westerners Brand Book*, Volume XXVIII, Johnson Publishing Co., 1973; (with husband, Edwin A. Bathke) *The West in Postage Stamps*, Filter Press, 1973.

WORK IN PROGRESS: Souvenir Spoons of Colorado, with husband, Edwin A. Bathke.

AVOCATIONAL INTERESTS: Collecting souvenir spoons of Colorado, photography, western history.

* * *

BATSON, Larry 1930-

PERSONAL: Born February 17, 1930, in Colorado; son of Ernest (a farmer) and Myrtle (Diskin) Batson; married Laurel Larson (a medical secretary); children: Ernest, William, James. *Education:* Attended University of Nebraska, 1947-49. *Politics:* Independent. *Religion:* Unitarian-Universalist. *Home:* 3501 Buchanan St. N.E., Minneapolis, Minn. 55418. *Office: Minneapolis Tribune*, 425 Portland Ave., Minneapolis, Minn. 55415.

CAREER: Newspaper reporter and editor. *Member:* Sigma Delta Chi.

WRITINGS—Children's books; all published by Childrens Press: *Frank Robinson*, 1974; *Gordie Howe*, 1974; *Walt*

Frazier, 1974; *Alan Page*, 1974; *Bill Walton*, 1974; *Larry Csonka*, 1974. Sports consultant, writer, columnist for *Insports* Magazine.

*   *   *

BATTLE, Gerald N(ichols) 1914-

PERSONAL: Born September 21, 1914, in St. Louis, Mo.; son of Clifton Hull (a salesman) and Edith Kent (Childs) Battle; married Mary Irmina Krulac, November 28, 1942. *Education:* Attended Cumberland University, 1934-36, and Capitol Radio Engineering Institute, 1942. *Home:* 6417 Brownlee Dr., Nashville, Tenn. 37205. *Office:* Cokesbury Book Stores, 201 Eighth Ave. S., Nashville, Tenn. 37202.

CAREER: Wailuku Sugar Co., Wailuku, Hawaii, agriculturist, 1937-39; Santa Fe Sugar Co., Dominican Republic, assistant superintendent, 1939-42; Cokesbury Book Stores, Nashville, Tenn., sales promotion manager, 1945-50, retail stores marketing manager, 1950—. *Military service:* U.S. Army, 1942-45; became staff sergeant; served in North Africa and Europe; received seven battle Stars. *Member:* American Booksellers Association (member of board of directors, 1970—).

WRITINGS—Juveniles: (With Theo Dunn) *Littlest Fiddler at the Opry*, Word, Inc., 1970; *Peter the Boy Who Became a Fisherman*, Word, Inc., 1970; *Gideon the Boy Who Learned to Lead*, Word, Inc., 1971; *Luke the Boy Who Wanted to Make People Well*, Word, Inc., 1972; *Armed with Love*, Abingdon, 1973.

Other: *The Last Bouquet* (poetry), Norman S. Berg, 1973; (contributor) Charles Anderson and Royce Smith, editors, *A Manual of Bookselling*, Crown, 1974.

WORK IN PROGRESS: Armed with Fire: Armed with Faith; Sam of the Alamo, completion expected in 1976; *Young Readers' Life of Jesus*, 1977.

AVOCATIONAL INTERESTS: Travel.

*   *   *

BATTO, Bernard Frank 1941-

PERSONAL: Born January 16, 1941, in Bandera, Tex.; son of Raymond Howard, Sr. and Agatha (Mazurek) Batto; married Teresa Ann Becker, August 19, 1967; Children: Rachel, Nathan, Amos. *Education:* Maryknoll College, B.A., 1963; Maryknoll Seminary, graduate study, 1963-66; Johns Hopkins University, Ph.D., 1972. *Religion:* Roman Catholic. *Office:* Department of Religion, Willamette University, Salem, Ore. 97301.

CAREER: Mount St. Mary's Seminary, Emmitsburg, Md., assistant professor of theology, 1971-75; Willamette University, Salem, Ore., assistant professor of religion, 1975—. *Member:* Society of Biblical Literature, Catholic Biblical Association, American Oriental Society, American Schools of Oriental Research.

WRITINGS: Studies on Women at Mari, Johns Hopkins Press, 1974. Contributor to theology journals.

WORK IN PROGRESS: Continuing research on the position of women at Mari and on Old Testament subjects.

SIDELIGHTS: Batto says his primary interests are in the field of Biblical scholarship (Hebrew Bible), particularly as part of the broader Ancient Near Eastern culture. He is especially interested in investigating "aspects of ancient Mesopotamian culture for the light they can shed on similar Biblical institutions."

BATY, Gordon B(ruce) 1938-

PERSONAL: Born December 15, 1938, in Tillamook, Ore.; son of Forrest S. and Margaret M. Baty; married Cathryn Pollock, December 21, 1964; children: Janna Margaret, Peter Sloan. *Education:* Massachusetts Institute of Technology, B.S., 1961, M.S., 1963, Ph.D., 1967. *Home:* 11 Castle Rd., Lexington, Mass. 02173. *Office:* Taplin Business Machines, Inc., 4 Ray Ave., Burlington, Mass. 01803.

CAREER: Grumman Aircraft, Bethpage, N.Y., manufacturing engineer, 1961; Massachusetts Institute of Technology, Cambridge, Mass., project administrator, 1961-64; Icon Corp., Cambridge, Mass., founder and president, 1964-73; Taplin Business Machines, Inc., Burlington, Mass., president, 1974—. Lecturer at Northeastern University, 1972—; member of board of directors of small companies and organizations, including Clinical Data, Inc., Girard Trust, and Technology Building Corp. *Member:* Society for Entrepreneurship Research.

WRITINGS: (Contributor) *System Designer's Handbook*, Benwill, 1966; *Entrepreneurship: Playing to Win*, Prentice-Hall, 1974. Contributor to *McGraw-Hill Encyclopedia of Instrumentation and Control*. Contributor of more than fifteen articles to technical and management journals, including *Automation, Metalworking, Tooling and Production, Instruments and Control Systems, Modern Machine Shop, Hydraulics and Pneumatics*, and *Administrative Science Quarterly*.

SIDELIGHTS: Baty writes: "Although trained in the academic aspects of business and management, I have confined my writing and lecturing almost entirely to the non-academic audience—to those people to whom the work might prove useful. I feel most at home in making the results of academic research available to those who can apply them."

*   *   *

BAUER, (Jo)Hanna R(uth Goldsmith) 1918-

PERSONAL: Born September 30, 1918, in Vienna, Austria; daughter of Max (a banker) and Lisi (Karpeles) Goldsmith; married Herbert Bauer (a physician), February 28, 1939; children: Timothy G., Christopher G. *Education:* Attended University of Vienna, 1936-38, and University of London, 1938-39; University of California, Berkeley, M.A., 1942; University of Southern California, further graduate study, 1948-49; University of the Pacific, Ed.D., 1974. *Politics:* "Liberal (either party)." *Religion:* Unitarian-Universalist. *Home:* 831 Oeste Dr., Davis, Calif. 95616.

CAREER: Private practice of psychology, 1958—. Member of local mental health advisory board. *Member:* United World Federalists, American Psychological Association, American Orthopsychiatric Association, California Psychological Association, Davis Psychological Association.

WRITINGS: I Came to My Island (essays and poetry), B. Straub, 1973; *Learning to Be*, Special Child Publications, 1974.

WORK IN PROGRESS: Home School Communication in Early Childhood Education; Hidden Agenda, on issues of mental health practice for the profession.

*   *   *

BAUM, Richard (Dennis) 1940-

PERSONAL: Born July 8, 1940, in Los Angeles, Calif.;

son of Lester A. (a technician) and Nelda (a counselor; maiden name, Lasky) Baum; married Carolyn Paller (a social worker), July 21, 1962; children: Matthew, Kristen. *Education:* University of California at Los Angeles, B.A., 1962; University of California, Berkeley, M.A., 1963, Ph.D., 1970. *Politics:* "Independent radic-lib." *Office:* Department of Political Science, University of California, Los Angeles, Calif. 90024.

CAREER: University of California at Los Angeles, assistant professor, 1968-71, associate professor of political science, 1971—. Visiting professor at University of California, Berkeley, 1971. Consultant to RAND Corp., 1968—; chairman of board of directors of China Trade and Development Services, Inc., Los Angeles, Calif., 1973—; director of National Committee on United States-China Relations, 1974—. *Member:* Association for Asian Studies, American Political Science Association, Social Science Research Council. *Awards, honors:* University Consortium for World Order Studies Award, 1974.

WRITINGS: Bibliographic Guide to Kwangtung Communes: 1959-1967, Union Research Institute, 1969; *Ssu-Ch'ing: The Socialist Education Movement of 1962-1966*, Center for Chinese Studies, University of California, Berkeley, 1968; (editor) *China in Ferment: Perspectives on the Cultural Revolution*, Prentice-Hall, 1971; (with T. W. Robinson) *The Cultural Revolution in China*, University of California Press, 1971; *Prelude to Revolution: Mao, the Party, and the Peasant Question*, Columbia University Press, 1975. Contributor to *Collier's Encyclopedia*; contributor to journals in his field.

WORK IN PROGRESS: Maoism and Modernization: Industrial Development and Social Change in Post-Revolutionary China, completion expected in 1976.

AVOCATIONAL INTERESTS: Northern Chinese cooking and folk and flamenco guitar.

* * *

BAUMBACK, Clifford M(ason) 1915-

PERSONAL: Born January 10, 1915, in Dover, N.J.; son of Harry Louis (a stove molder) and Alice (Mason) Baumback; married Janice Sheldon (a psychiatric social worker), December 21, 1945; children: Rex, Mark, Carol (Mrs. Steven R. Spangler). *Education:* Springfield College, Springfield, Mass., B.S., 1938; Northwestern University, M.B.A., 1945; University of Iowa, Ph.D., 1953. *Politics:* Republican. *Religion:* Episcopalian. *Home:* 705 Diana Ct., Iowa City, Iowa 52240. *Office:* 571 Phillips Hall, University of Iowa, Iowa City, Iowa 52242.

CAREER: Liberty Vulcanizing Works, Troy, N.Y., proprietor, 1938-43; General Electric Co., Erie, Pa., production aide, 1943-44; University of Oklahoma, Norman, assistant professor, 1945-51, associate professor of business management, 1951-55; University of Iowa, Iowa City, research associate, 1955-62, associate professor, 1962-68, professor of management, 1968—. Visiting professor at Miami University, Oxford, Ohio, summers, 1948, 1949, Roosevelt University, summer, 1969, and Northern Illinois University, 1971-72. Consultant to Iowa Development Commission, 1962-66, and U.S. Small Business Administration, 1973—.

MEMBER: National Council for Small Business Management Development (member of advisory board, 1974—), American Production and Inventory Control Society (director of research, 1963-66), Academy of Management,

Society for Entrepreneurship Research, Midwest Economic Association, Midwest Business Administration Association, Pi Gamma Mu, Beta Gamma Sigma, Omicron Delta Epsilon, Sigma Iota Epsilon, Masons, Iowa City Rotary Club. *Awards, honors:* American Production and Inventory Control Society citations for outstanding contributions, 1961, 1965.

WRITINGS: (Contributor) Huxley Madehein and others, editors, *Readings in Organization and Management*, Holt, 1964; (with Kenneth Lawyer and Pearce C. Kelley) *How to Organize and Operate a Small Business*, 4th edition (Baumback was not associated with earlier editions), Prentice-Hall, 1968, 5th edition, 1973; (contributor) James H. Greene, editor, *Production and Inventory Control Handbook*, McGraw, 1970; *Structural Wage Issues in Collective Bargaining*, Heath, 1971; (with Joseph Mancuso) *Entrepreneurship and Venture Management*, Prentice-Hall, 1975.

Monographs: *Arbitration of Job Evaluation Disputes*, 1954, *Merit and Seniority as Factors in Promotion and In-Grade Progression*, 1956, and *Incentive-Wage Problems in Collective Bargaining and Arbitration*, 1956, all published by Center for Labor and Management, University of Iowa; *Patterns of Production Planning and Control*, 1957, and *Systematic Work Simplification*, 1960, both published by Bureau of Business Research, University of Oklahoma; *An Analysis of Environmental and Managerial Factors in the Success or Failure of Small Manufacturing Enterprise*, Bureau of Business and Economic Research, University of Iowa, 1963.

Contributor to Van Nostrand *Encyclopedia of Management*. Contributor of more than thirty articles to business, management, and labor journals. Founding editor, *Journal of Small Business Management*, 1962-68; member of editorial board, *Production and Inventory Management*, 1967—.

WORK IN PROGRESS: Mind Your Own Business, for Prentice-Hall; a sixth edition of *How to Organize and Operate a Small Business*, Prentice-Hall; *Planning the New Business*, completion expected in 1977.

* * *

BAXTER, Charles 1947-

PERSONAL: Born May 13, 1947, in Minneapolis, Minn.; son of John T. and Mary (Eaton) Baxter. *Education:* Macalester College, B.A., 1969; State University of New York at Buffalo, Ph.D., 1974. *Home:* 2248 Glencoe Hills Dr., Ann Arbor, Mich. 48104. *Office:* Department of English, Wayne State University, Detroit, Mich.

CAREER: High school teacher in Pinconning, Mich., 1969-70; Wayne State University, Detroit, Mich., assistant professor of English, 1974—.

WRITINGS: Chameleon (poems), New Rivers Press, 1970; *The South Dakota Guidebook*, New Rivers Press, 1974.

Poems have been anthologized in *The Fifth Annual Best Science Fiction*, edited by Harry Harrison and Brian Aldiss, Putnam, 1972; *Toward Winter*, edited by Robert Bonazzi, New Rivers Press, 1972. Contributor to literary journals, including *Minnesota Review, Kayak, Prairie Schooner*, and *Journal of Modern Literature*. Associate editor of *Minnesota Review*, 1967-69; editor of *Audit/Poetry*, 1973-74.

WORK IN PROGRESS: Ground Zero, a novel; a collection of short stories; a book of poems.

SIDELIGHTS: Baxter writes: "My poetry deals in a general way with the unconscious and three of its primary activities: camouflage, the formation of counterfeit identities, and the articulations of need. I tend to use banal and realistic imagery from small-town America to describe these conscious or unconscious states. The mind, in other words, is as remote and strange as South Dakota. My criticism usually concerns modern fiction, and my fiction usually concerns threatened identities."

*   *   *

BAXTER, James P(hinney) III   1893-1975

February 15, 1893—June 17, 1975; American historian, college president, educator, and author. Obituaries: *New York Times*, June 19, 1975; *Washington Post*, June 19, 1975; *Newsweek*, June 30, 1975; *Time*, June 30, 1975; *Current Biography*, August, 1975.

*   *   *

BEACH, Bert Beverly   1928-

PERSONAL: Born June 15, 1928, in Gland, Switzerland; son of Walter R. (a minister and missionary) and Gladys (a missionary; maiden name, Corley) Beach; married Eliane Palange, April 8, 1954; children: Danielle, Michele. *Education:* Pacific Union College, B.A., 1948; Stanford University, graduate study, 1948-49, 1951; Sorbonne, University of Paris, Ph.D. (magna cum laude), 1958; American University, postdoctoral study, 1960. *Religion:* Seventh-day Adventists. *Home:* 39 Cunningham Hill Rd., St. Albans AL1 5BX, Hertfordshire, England. *Office:* 119 St. Peter's St., St. Albans AL1 3EY, Hertfordshire, England; and 6840 Eastern Ave., Takoma Park, Md. 20012.

CAREER: West Liberty Union School, Gridley, Calif., principal, 1949-50; Instituto Avventista, Florence, Italy, principal, 1952-58; Columbia Union College, Takoma Park, Md., assistant professor of history and chairman of department, 1958-60; General Conference of Seventh-day Adventists, Northern Europe-West Africa Division, St. Albans, England, secretary of education, 1960—, general secretary, 1973—. Lecturer at Newbold College, 1960—. *Member:* American Historical Association, Sons of the American Revolution, College of Preceptors, Conference of Secretaries of World Confessional Families (secretary, 1970—), Phi Alpha Theta.

WRITINGS: Vaticanum II Most Nad Przepascia Znaki Czasu (Warsaw), 1967, translation published as *Vatican II Bridging the Abyss*, Review & Herald Publishing, 1968; (editor with Lukas Vischer) *So Much in Common*, World Council of Churches, 1973; *Ecumenism: Boon or Bane?*, Review & Herald Publishing, 1974. Contributor to encyclopedias and of over 150 articles to journals. Consulting editor of *Liberty*, 1970—; member of editorial board of *Conscience et Liberte*, 1971—; contributing editor of *These Times*, 1973—.

AVOCATIONAL INTERESTS: Prestidigitation.

*   *   *

BEAR, Joan   1918-
(Elizabeth Mayhew)

PERSONAL: Born March 10, 1918, in Shanghai, China; daughter of Frederick Henry (a customs official) and Vera (Fowler) Maas; married Alan Bear, October 7, 1939 (died, 1973); children: Jeremy, Nicholas, Stephen, Richard. *Religion:* None. *Home:* Firs Cottage, Hellingly, Hailsham,

Sussex, England. *Agent:* Bolt & Watson Ltd., 8 Storeys Gate, London S.W.1, England. *Office:* Marlow Ropes Ltd., South Rd., Hailsham, Sussex, England.

CAREER: Marlow Ropes Ltd., Hailsham, England, export sales assistant, 1973—. Governor, Hailsham Comprehensive School, 1946-72.

WRITINGS—Under pseudonym Elizabeth Mayhew, except as noted: *In the Path of Eagles* (historical novel), R. Hale, 1970; *The Queen of Naples* (historical novel), R. Hale, 1971; (under name Joan Bear) *Caroline Murat*, Collins, 1972; *My Son Charles* (historical novel), R. Hale, 1973; *Felicia* (historical novel), Pocket Books, 1974. Translator of French memoirs of J. de Norvins, as yet unpublished.

WORK IN PROGRESS: A historical novel set in Napoleonic times; researching the age of Richelieu and Louis XIII for a future novel.

*   *   *

BEATTY, John (Louis)   1922-1975

January 24, 1922—March 23, 1975; American educator, historian, and editor or author of biographies, historical novels for young people, and other historical works. Obituaries: *Publishers Weekly*, April 28, 1975. (*CA-7/8*)

*   *   *

BEAUFRE, Andre   1902-1975

January 23, 1902—February 13, 1975; French army officer, military historian, analyst, theoretician, and commentator, magazine publisher, newspaper columnist, and author of books on military topics. Obituaries: *New York Times*, February 14, 1975; *Washington Post*, February 14, 1975; *AB Bookman's Weekly*, March 3, 1975.

*   *   *

BEAUSANG, Michael F(rancis), Jr.   1936-

PERSONAL: Born June 9, 1936, in Philadelphia, Pa.; son of Michael F. and Betty-Jane (Barnum) Beausang; married June 14, 1958; children: Michael F. III, Susanne Alice, Elizabeth Jane. *Education:* University of Pennsylvania, B.S. in Mech. Eng., 1958; Georgetown University, LL.B., 1964; New York University, LL.M., 1967. *Home:* 786 Laurel Lane, Wayne, Pa. 19087. *Office:* Butera & Detwiler, 700 Valley Forge Plaza, King of Prussia, Pa. 19406.

CAREER: Admitted to Bar of State of Pennsylvania, 1965; Beale & Jones, Washington, D.C. patent agent, 1962-64; MacCoy, Evans & Lewis, Philadelphia, Pa., attorney, 1964-67; Butera & Detwiler (law firm), King of Prussia, Pa., partner, 1968—; Gilfillan, Gilpin & Brehman (law firm), Philadelphia, Pa., partner, 1968—.

WRITINGS: How to Use Your Home as a Tax Savings Goldmine, Enterprise Publishing, 1974. Contributor to *Criminal Law Bulletin, Tax Management, Dickenson Law Review*, and other tax and law journals.

*   *   *

BECK, Thomas D(avis)   1943-

PERSONAL: Born June 4, 1943, in Los Angeles, Calif.; son of Duane Wesley (an engineer) and Marceline (Davis) Beck; married Martha Wakefield, February 1, 1964; children: John, Kelly, Stacy, Eric. *Education:* University of California, Berkeley, B.A., 1965, M.A., 1966, Ph.D., 1972. *Home:* 810 Lancaster St., Albany, N.Y. 12203. *Office:*

Department of History, State University of New York, Albany, N.Y. 12222.

CAREER: State University of New York, Albany, assistant professor of history, 1973—. *Member:* American Historical Association, Society for French Historical Studies. *Awards, honors:* Summer stipend from National Endowment for the Humanities, 1975.

WRITINGS: French Legislators, 1800-1834: A Study in Quantitative History, University of California Press, 1974.

WORK IN PROGRESS: The One Hundred Days of Napoleon: A National Trauma, publication expected in 1980.

* * *

BECK, Toni 1925-

PERSONAL: Born October 4, 1925, in New York, N.Y.; daughter of Samuel (a merchant) and Margaret (Wise) Beck; married Bob Glatter, 1952 (divorced, 1965); married Paul Bosner (in television industry), December, 1969; children: (first marriage) Lesli Glatter. *Education:* Oberlin College, B.S., 1946; Columbia University, M.A., 1949; also studied at Colorado College, Connecticut College, London School of Contemporary Dance, and Harvard University; private studies in dance and acting in New York. *Home:* 2911 Oxford Ter., Apt. 3207, Dallas, Tex. 75275. *Agent:* Julian Bach, Jr., 3 East 48th St., New York, N.Y. 10017. *Office:* Dance Division, Meadows School of the Arts, Southern Methodist University, Dallas, Tex. 75275.

CAREER: Washington University, St. Louis, Mo., assistant professor of dance, 1949-51; Southern Methodist University, Dallas, Tex., lecturer, 1959-60, assistant professor, 1960-63, associate professor, 1963-65, professor of dance and theater, 1965—, chairman of Dance Division, 1965—. Teacher at Modern Ballet Studio, Dallas, 1954-68; guest teacher and choreographer for Rubin Academy of Music, 1972, Bat Dor Co. and Studio, 1972, Irish Ballet, 1973, 1974, and Utah Repertory Dance Theater, 1974. Has appeared on national television programs, and has danced on "Armstrong Theatre of the Air" and "Studio One"; has performed in New York shows, including "Make Mine Manhattan" and "Wonderful Town"; original member of Cherry Lane Theatre (Off-Broadway); has done choreography for television and theaters, including CBS-Television, national church conferences, and Brunswick Music Theatre, Maine; has performed in concert, 1955—; exercise consultant for the Greenhouse, Arlington, Tex., 1965—, and Neiman-Marcus and Charles of the Ritz, both 1966—.

MEMBER: Actor's Equity, American Federation of Television and Radio Artists, American Association of University Professors, American Association for Health, Physical Education and Recreation, National Dance Teachers Guild. *Awards, honors:* Ford Foundation grant, 1951-52.

WRITINGS: Fashion Your Figure, Houghton, 1971; *Focus Your Figure*, Houghton, 1973. Contributor to *Family Health, Harper's Bazaar, Glamour, Vogue, McCall's, Idea, Cosmopolitan, New York Post*, and *Women's Wear Daily*. Dance correspondent for the Southwest for *Dance*, 1955-69.

SIDELIGHTS: Toni Beck believes in dancing as a profession. Nearly ninety percent of her graduates are now dancing professionally. Feeling that it takes ten years to build a dancer's body, she is a strong proponent of dance in the public schools, especially in high schools. She would like to see more emphasis on ballet as the basic background for all dance—whether it is jazz, rock, or modern. *Avocational interests:* Reading, music (symphony, opera), tennis.

BECKER, Bruce

PERSONAL: Born in New York, N.Y. *Education:* New York University, LL.B., 1961. *Agent:* W. B. Agency, Inc., 156 East 52nd St., New York, N.Y. 10017. *Office:* 160 East 48th St., New York, N.Y. 10017.

CAREER: Attorney and film producer.

WRITINGS: Backgammon for Blood, Dutton, 1974.

* * *

BECKHART, Benjamin Haggott 1897-1975

November 9, 1897—March 21, 1975; American educator, economist, economic consultant, and author of books on economics and banking. Obituaries: *New York Times*, March 22, 1975; *AB Bookman's Weekly*, April 7, 1975.

* * *

BEDFORD, Charles Harold 1929-

PERSONAL: Born October 31, 1929, in Toronto, Ontario, Canada; son of Victor E. (a superintendent) and Winnifred (Farmer) Bedford; married Aune Hannele Malmio, August 12, 1961; children: Kristina, Melanie. *Education:* University of Toronto, B.A., 1951, M.A., 1952; University of London, Ph.D., 1956. *Religion:* Anglican. *Home:* 3264 Havenwood Dr., Mississauga, Ontario L4X 2M1, Canada. *Office:* Department of Slavic Languages and Literatures, University of Toronto, Toronto, Ontario, Canada.

CAREER: University of Toronto, Toronto, Ontario, lecturer, 1955-59, assistant professor, 1959-64, associate professor, 1964-75, professor of Slavic languages and literatures, 1975—, chairman of department, 1971—. *Member:* Canadian Association of Slavists, American Association for the Advancement of Slavic Studies.

WRITINGS: The Seeker: D. S. Merezhkovskiy, University Press of Kansas, 1975. Contributor to Slavic studies journals.

WORK IN PROGRESS: Studying Russian symbolist poet and theoretician, Valery Bryusov.

AVOCATIONAL INTERESTS: Travel (Europe, Finland).

* * *

BEDINGER, Margery 1891-

PERSONAL: "G" in surname is soft; born April 9, 1891, in Salem, Mass.; daughter of Henry (an Episcopal priest) and Ada (Doughty) Bedinger. *Education:* Attended Smith College, 1908-10; Radcliffe College, A.B. (cum laude), 1913; graduate study at New York State Library School, 1917-18, and University of Denver, 1952-55. *Religion:* Episcopalian. *Home:* 45090 Namoku St., Apt. 1302, Kaneohe, Hawaii 96744.

CAREER: Detroit Public Library, Detroit, Mich., trainee, 1916-17; New York City Public Library, New York, N.Y., assistant in technology department, 1918-19; Dupont de Nemours & Co., Wilmington, Del., organizer and head of technical library, 1919-21; United States Military Academy, West Point, N.Y., head librarian, 1921-26; New Mexico State College, State College, head librarian, 1926-27; Seattle Public Library, Seattle, Wash., organizer and head of adult education department, 1928-30; Montana State School of Mines (now Montana College of Mineral Science and Technology), Butte, head librarian, 1930-37; Denver Public Library, Denver, Colo., head of science and engineering department, 1937-56. Exchange librarian to Johannesburg, South Africa, 1947-48; organized library for Institute of Business Management of University of Istanbul, 1956.

WRITINGS: Indian Silver: Navajo and Pueblo Jewelers, University of New Mexico Press, 1973. Columnist, *Engineers' Bulletin*, 1937-53. Contributor to journals in her field, and to general periodicals.

WORK IN PROGRESS: Research and writing for a companion volume to *Indian Silver*; editing diary and letters for travel memoirs.

SIDELIGHTS: Margery Bedinger, who has traveled extensively in North and Central America, Asia, Africa, and the South Sea Islands, told *CA*: "I have always wanted everyone to have a chance to develop fully and to give to society whatever he or she had to contribute. One purpose I hoped to accomplish in my book was to show what gifted people our North American Indians are. I tell how they, a stone age group, taught themselves to work an altogether different material, metal, one quite new to them. They performed a remarkable feat, and one which gave scope to the expression of their very great artistic endowment."

AVOCATIONAL INTERESTS: Outdoor activities, music, art, anthropology, conservation, reading, collecting jade, bridge.

BIOGRAPHICAL/CRITICAL SOURCES: Honolulu Advertiser, September 11, 1973; *American Libraries*, July-August, 1974; *Earth Science*, November/December, 1974.

* * *

BEE, Jay
    See BRAINERD, John W(hiting)

* * *

BEER, Ethel S.   1897-1975

May 14, 1897—March 7, 1975; American social worker and author of books on child care and travel. Obituaries: *New York Times*, March 8, 1975; *AB Bookman's Weekly*, March 24, 1975. (*CA*-25/28)

* * *

BEHLMER, Rudy   1926-

PERSONAL: Born October 13, 1926, in San Francisco, Calif.; son of Rudy H. (a brewer) and Helen (McDonough) Behlmer; married Sandra Lee Wightman, 1959 (divorced, 1966); children: Curt. *Education:* Attended Pasadena Playhouse College, 1946-49, and Los Angeles City College, 1949-50. *Residence:* Studio City, Calif. *Office:* Leo Burnett Co., Inc., 6255 Sunset Blvd., Hollywood, Calif. 90028.

CAREER: KLAC-Television, Hollywood, Calif., television director, 1952-56; free-lance television director for networks based in Hollywood, Calif., 1956-59; Grant Advertising, Hollywood, Calif., director of television and radio, 1959-60; KCOP-Television, Hollywood, Calif., executive producer, 1960-63; Leo Burnett Co., Inc. (advertising firm), Los Angeles, Calif., producer, 1963—. Lecturer at Art Center College of Design, 1967—. *Military service:* U.S. Navy, Air Corps, aviation radioman, 1944-46. *Member:* Directors Guild of America.

WRITINGS: (With Tony Thomas and Clifford McCarty) *The Films of Errol Flynn*, Citadel, 1969; *Memo from David O. Selznick*, Viking, 1972; (with Thomas) *Hollywood's Hollywood*, Citadel, 1975.

Author, (also producer, and director) of "Movies' Golden Age," a television special production, for syndication, 1961. Author of notes for record series, "Classic Film Scores," and of "Warner Brothers: Fifty Years of Film Music," a booklet accompanying a record album, 1973. Contributor to film journals.

AVOCATIONAL INTERESTS: Photographing and editing personal movies, travel (trips down the Colorado River; camera safaris in Africa).

* * *

BEHME, Robert Lee   1924-

PERSONAL: Born May 15, 1924, in Seattle, Wash., son of Boyden (a postal clerk) and Mildred (Ogle) Behme; married Madonna Edwards (divorced); married Margaret Kathryn Anderson, July 17, 1958. *Education:* Art Center School, B.A., 1948. *Home and office address:* Skyway, Maglalia, Calif. 95954. *Agent:* Helen Wilson, 36 Heritage Hill Road, New Canaan, Conn. 06840.

CAREER: Motor Life (magazine), Los Angeles, Calif., managing editor, 1954-55; *Trailer Life* (magazine), Los Angeles, Calif., editorial director, 1957-58; currently editor and publisher of trade magazine in the pet field. Writer and photographer. *Military service:* U.S. Navy, 1943-46. *Member:* Outdoor Writers of America.

WRITINGS: Custom Cars, Peterson, 1954; *Plastic Cars*, Peterson, 1955; *Karting*, Fawcett, 1964; *Bonsai, Boneki and Seikei: Japanese Dwarf Trees and Tray Landscapes*, Morrow, 1969; (with Malcolm Jaderquist) *1970 Motorcycle and Trail Biking Handbook*, Pyramid, 1970; (with Jaderquist) *The Motorcycle and Trail Bike Handbook*, Pyramid, 1971; *1971 Book of Snowmobiling*, Pyramid, 1971; *Outdoor How-to-Build-It Book*, Hawthorn, 1971; *Shasta and the Rogue*, Simon & Schuster, 1974.

WORK IN PROGRESS: A book on Japanese Koi.

* * *

BEL GEDDES, Joan
    See GEDDES, Joan Bel

* * *

BELL, Joyce   1920-
    (Jean Colin)

PERSONAL: Born November 12, 1920, in Nuneaton, Warwickshire, England; daughter of William Henry (a craftsman potter) and Elizabeth (Randle) Bell; married J. Ziemba, 1943 (divorced, 1962); children: Michael, Julie, Anthony. *Education:* Attended local council school in Nuneaton, England, 1925-34, and evening classes at University of Warwick. *Politics:* "I belong to no political party." *Religion:* None. *Home:* 11 Winfield Rd., Nuneaton, Warwickshire, England. *Agent:* Laurence Pollinger, Ltd., 18 Maddox St., Mayfair, London WIR OEU, England.

CAREER: Worked in factory office in Nuneaton, England, 1934-36; employed in hosiery factory in Hinckley, Leicestershire, England, 1936-40; Dunlop Aircraft Factory, Coventry, England, shorthand typist, 1940-44; has worked at various jobs including supervising a typing pool and newspaper reporting, 1962—; free-lance writer in Nuneaton, Warwickshire, England. *Member:* PEN International, Society of Authors, Society of Women Writers and Journalists. *Awards, honors:* Two Nuneaton Festival of Arts short story prizes, both 1955.

WRITINGS: *Garden of the Sun* (mystery), R. Hale, 1971; *Farmhouse By the Sea* (mystery), R. Hale, 1972; (under pseudonym Jean Colin) *Never Had It So Good* (autobiographical), Gollancz, 1974. Contributor to *Birmingham Post* and other newspapers, and to magazines.

WORK IN PROGRESS: A nonfiction book describing the lives, education, and welfare of the working classes starting with her parents, World War II with the Coventry bombings, and the changes of the post-war period; a novel set in a Midland town about ordinary people and attitudes.

AVOCATIONAL INTERESTS: Travel, country and wild life.

* * *

BELL, Quentin (Claudian Stephen) 1910-

PERSONAL: Born August 19, 1910, in London, England; son of Clive (an art critic) and Vanessa (Stephen) Bell; married Anne Olivier Popham, February 16, 1952; children: Julian, Virginia, Cressida. *Education:* Attended Leighton Park School. *Home:* Cobbe Place, Beddingham, Sussex, England. *Office:* University of Sussex, Falmer, Brighton, Sussex, England.

CAREER: Painter, sculptor, potter, author, and art critic. University of Newcastle, King's College, Newcastle, England, lecturer in art education, 1952-57, senior lecturer, 1957-59; University of Leeds, Leeds, England, senior lecturer, 1959-61, professor of fine art, 1961-67, head of department of fine art, 1959-67; University of Sussex, Brighton, England, professor of history and theory of art, 1967—. Slade Professor of Fine Art, Oxford University 1964-65; Ferens Professor of Fine Art, University of Hull, 1965-66. Chairman of Lewes Divisional Labour Party, 1948-52; panel member, National Council for Diplomas in Art and Design, 1962; member of National Advisory Committee on Art Education, 1967. *Member:* Royal Society of Arts (fellow), Reform Club. *Awards, honors:* M.A., University of Durham, 1954.

WRITINGS: (Editor) Julian H. Bell, *Essays, Poems, and Letters*, Hogarth Press, 1938; *On Human Finery*, Hogarth Press, 1947; (with Alison Gernsheim and Helmut Gernsheim) *Those Impossible English*, Crown, 1952; *The Political Notions of the Member for Lewes*, Firle, 1952; (translator of commentaries with J. H. Bell) Stephane Mallarme, *Poems*, Vision Press, 1952; *The True Story of Cinderella*, Faber, 1957, Barnes, 1960; *The Schools of Design*, Routledge & Kegan Paul, 1963; *Ruskin*, Oliver & Boyd, 1963; *Victorian Artists*, Harvard University Press, 1967; *Bloomsbury*, Weidenfeld & Nicolson, 1968, Basic Books, 1969; *Virginia Woolf: A Biography*, Harcourt, 1972. Regular contributor to *Listener*, 1951—. Contributor of articles to magazines and journals.

SIDELIGHTS: Leonard Woolf, a founding member of the group Quentin Bell described in *Bloomsbury*, called the book an account of "sound intelligence," both "judicious and entertaining." Angus Wilson stated that Bell, nephew of Virginia Woolf, "has taken on the difficult task of writing about the cultural aristocracy of which his parents were such eminent members. It is a remarkable juggling feat, in which reasoned criticism is modified with inner light and natural personal prejudice with a fine if markedly academic objectivity."*

* * *

BENAGH, Jim 1937-

PERSONAL: Surname is pronounced *Benn*-aw; born October 10, 1937, in Flint, Mich.; son of William E., Sr. and Christine (Hoiland) Benagh; children: Jeffrey, Jason. *Education:* Attended University of Michigan, 1955-56, 1957-60. *Politics:* "Yes." *Religion:* "No." *Office address:* P.O. Box 1113, Englewood Cliffs, N.J. 07632.

CAREER: *Cheboygan Daily Tribune*, Cheboygan, Mich., sports editor and head photographer, 1953-55; *Ann Arbor News*, Ann Arbor, Mich., sports writer, 1960-61; *Sport* (magazine), New York, N.Y., associate editor, 1962-64; *Newsweek* (magazine), New York, N.Y., assistant sports editor, 1964-68, acting sports editor, 1968; free-lance writer and editor, 1968—. Public relations specialist for Mexican Olympic Committee, 1968; part-time sports editor, Random House, 1969; public relations writer for Fight of Champions, Inc., 1971. *Military service:* U.S. Army Reserve, sports editor of newspaper at Fort Knox, Ky., 1960-66. *Member:* Football Writers Association of America, Metropolitan Track and Field Writers Association (New York).

WRITINGS: *Tom Harmon's Book of Sports Information* (Teen-Age Book Club selection), J. Lowell Pratt, 1963, revised edition, 1965; *The Official Encyclopedia of Sports*, F. Watts, 1964; *1967 Pictorial Sports Annual*, Hammond, Inc., 1967; *Incredible Athletic Feats*, Hart Publishing, 1969; (with Marv Albert) *Krazy about the Knicks*, Hawthorn, 1971, revised edition, 1973; *Watch It!: How to Watch Sports on T.V.*, Benjamin Co., 1971; *Official Ali-Frazier Fight Program*, Fight of the Century, Inc., 1971; *The Great Olympians*, StadiaSports, 1972; *ABC's Wide World of Sports Encyclopedia*, StadiaSports, 1973; *Walt Frazier: Superguard of Pro Basketball*, Scholastic Book Services, 1973; *Incredible Football Feats*, Tempo Books, 1974; *Incredible Basketball Feats*, Tempo Books, 1974; *Incredible Baseball Feats*, Tempo Books, 1975.

Contributor to *Encyclopedia Americana*. Contributor of more than three hundred articles and photographs to magazines, including *True, Argosy, Money, Boys' Life, Life*, and *Tennis*, and to newspapers, including *Washington Star* and *New York Times*. Co-founder and first editor of *Gridiron*; former sports editor of *Michigan Daily*.

WORK IN PROGRESS: A book on college sports recruiting for Dodd; a book on the Olympic games; a novel about college sports.

SIDELIGHTS: Benagh writes: "Writing has allowed me to combine my two favorite pastimes—sports and travel—into a full-time profession. I've been to three summer Olympics, the Soviet Union, most major American cities and many intriguing smaller ones . . . and each time have managed to combine the trip with a sportswriting tie-in. But I also enjoy delving into the depths of sports and sports personalities and not just treat the fun and games of sports as a vacation vehicle. I think that sports have a wide social impact in the nation and that needs to be studied beyond the day-to-day scores . . . ."

* * *

BEN-AVRAHAM, Chofetz Chaim
See PICKERING, Stephen

* * *

BENDINER, Elmer 1916-

PERSONAL: Born February 11, 1916, in Pittsburgh, Pa.; son of William (a businessman) and Lillian (Schwartz) Bendiner; married Esther Shapiro (an editorial assistant), October 4, 1941; children: Winnie (Mrs. Paul G. Viani), Jessica. *Education:* Attended College of the City of New York (now City College of the City University of New York), 1932-35. *Politics:* "Defies neat categorizing." *Religion:* "Defies neat categorizing." *Home:* 2 Hasbrouck Lane, Woodstock, N.Y. 12498. *Agent:* Theron Raines, 244 Madison Ave., New York, N.Y. 10016.

CAREER: Newark Ledger, Newark, N.J., reporter, 1938-39; *Brooklyn Daily Eagle*, Brooklyn, N.Y., reporter, 1939-40; *Flying Age*, New York, N.Y., managing editor, 1945-46; *Esquire*, New York, N.Y., non-fiction editor, 1946-48; *National Guardian*, New York, N.Y., associate editor, 1948-58; Science and Medicine Publishing Co., New York, N.Y., editor, 1958-68; World Wide Medical News Service, New York, N.Y., editor, 1969-72; *Hospital Practice*, New York, N.Y., contributing editor, 1972—. *Military service:* U.S. Army Air Forces, navigator on B-17 bomber, 1941-45; served in Europe; became first lieutenant; received Distinguished Flying Cross, Air Medal with three oak leaf clusters, and Purple Heart Medal. *Member:* Authors Guild of Authors League of America.

WRITINGS: The Bowery Man, Nelson, 1962; *A Time for Angels: The Tragicomic History of the League of Nations*, Knopf, 1975.

Work is anthologized in *Man Alone*, edited by Eric Josephson and Mary Josephson, Dell, 1962. Author of documentary film script "Uptown." Contributor to *Esquire, New York Times Magazine, Nation*, and *Strand*. Editor of *Log of Navigation*, 1944-45.

WORK IN PROGRESS: A history of early American diplomacy, for Knopf; a study of the Golden Age of Spain.

SIDELIGHTS: Bendiner writes: "I look upon my work as journalism, uninhibited by an exclusive preoccupation with the contemporary. If a story provides a clue to the grandeur and/or absurdity of our lives it seems newsworthy to me even though it occurred a thousand years ago. Hence, I see a certain consistency in exploring the lives of homelss men on the Bowery, the performance of diplomats between the world wars, the efforts of 18th century Americans to seduce the rulers of Europe, the strange splendors of Spain five hundred years ago, or the work of doctors and nurses in the Artic, in India, Japan or Tanzania. . . ."

Bendiner's work has taken him to Europe, Central and South America, East Africa, India, Bangladesh, Thailand, New Guinea, the Philippines, Israel, Japan and Canada.

* * *

BENET, Mary Kathleen 1943-

PERSONAL: Born October 25, 1943, in New York, N.Y.; daughter of James Walker (a journalist) and Mary Elizabeth (Liles) Benet; married Julian Anthony Stuart Hale (a writer), June 28, 1971; children: Laura Mary. *Education:* Reed College, B.A., 1965; Indiana University, graduate study, 1965. *Politics:* "Levelling." *Religion:* "Elevating." *Home:* 9 Warwick Ave., London W9, England. *Agent:* John Wolfers, 3 Regent Sq., London WC1, England.

CAREER: Chicago Sun-Times, Chicago, Ill., feature writer and copyreader, 1965-67; Grey Advertising, London, England, typist and copywriter, 1967-69; Observer Books, London, writer, 1969-70; free-lance writer, 1970—. *Member:* London Library.

WRITINGS: The Secretarial Ghetto, McGraw, 1972 (published in England as *Secretary*, Sidgwick & Jackson, 1972); *The Politics of Adoption*, Praeger, 1975.

WORK IN PROGRESS: Men Behind Women (tentative title), a study of Colette, George Eliot, and Katherine Mansfield, for Macmillan; *The Old Left*, a book of reminiscences from the American Old Left of 1920-1945, a personal as well as a political account.

SIDELIGHTS: Mary Benet writes: "Feminism and left-wing politics seem to have provided much of the impetus behind my books; but to me they are simply two aspects of the effort to make sense of human experience, which is the only reason for writing anything at all. I have never wanted to do anything but write; I have no interests that do not feed my work. . . . I am not attracted by the egotism of the artist nor by artificial formal experiment; the humility and seriousness of George Eliot and Christina Stead are my models. Writers these days seem to be pushed towards nonfiction; I am trying to push gradually towards fiction.

Mary Benet and her husband "live part of the year in a deserted part of Normandy. You could call our life the impoverished socialist's Henry James." *Avocational interests:* Gardening, cooking, talking, drinking wine, travel.

* * *

BENGE, Eugene J(ackson) 1896-

PERSONAL: Born May 3, 1896, in Philadelphia, Pa.; son of Elmer (an accountant) and Ella Frances (Logan) Benge; married Grace Griffith, July 22, 1953; children: Janet (Mrs. Vincent J. Danielenko). *Education:* Teachers' College, Philadelphia, B.S., 1917; Carnegie Institute of Technology (now Carnegie-Mellon University), student, 1919-20. *Politics:* Republican. *Religion:* Protestant. *Home and office:* 550 South Ocean Blvd., Apt. 1206, Boca Raton, Fla. 33432.

CAREER: Atlantic Refining Co., Philadelphia, Pa., industrial relations manager, 1920-25; Philadelphia Rapid Transit Co., Philadelphia, chief statistician, 1926-29; American Oil Co., Baltimore, Md., personnel manager, 1930-35; Firestone Tire Co., training director, 1936-38; management consultant and director of self-developed management seminars in eleven foreign countries, 1939—. Former director of Sorg Paper Co.; director and member of executive committee of Council for International Progress in Management. *Military service:* U.S. Army, Psychological Examining Corps, 1917-18; became sergeant first class. *Member:* Society for the Advancement of Management (fellow; life member; international vice-president). *Awards, honors:* Honor key from Society for the Advancement of Management, 1953, for a paper on industrial incentives.

WRITINGS: Standard Practice in Personnel Work, H. W. Wilson, 1920; *Cutting Clerical Costs*, McGraw, 1931; *Office Economies*, Ronald, 1937; (with S. L. H. Burk and E. N. Hay) *Manual of Job Evaluation*, Harper, 1941; *Manpower in Marketing*, Harper, 1945; *You, Triumphant!*, Harper, 1946; (with Jean Benge) *Win Your Man and Keep Him*, Windsor Books, 1948; *The Right Career for You*, Funk, 1950; *Finding and Using Your Magic Emotion Power*, Prentice-Hall, 1958; *Salesmanship*, Alexander Hamilton Institute, 1958; *How to Become a Successful Executive*, Fell, 1960; *The Office: Nerve Center of Management*, Alexander Hamilton Institute, 1963; *How to Manage for Tomorrow*, Dow Jones-Irwin, 1975.

Author of numerous manuals, including *Compensating Employees*, published by Prentice-Hall, 1965, and of booklets, including *How to Motivate Your Employees* and *How to Motivate Your Sales Prospect*, both published by Dartnell, 1960. Author of monthly column in *American Bottler*, seven years, and other columns in newspapers and periodicals. Contributor of several hundred articles on business topics to magazines.

SIDELIGHTS: Benge writes: "I am particularly interested in the factors of success, have written and lectured on the subject. I believe, with the futurists, that we have already entered the post-industrial era, which will greatly alter our lives.

"I wrote a novel-length story, 'The Le Brun Cave Murders,' for one of the pulps which went out of business the next month; I have always hoped there was no connection!" Benge's books have been published in Japanese, Italian, Spanish, and Portuguese.

* * *

BENGELSDORF, Irving S. 1922-

PERSONAL: Born October 23, 1922, in Chicago, Ill.; son of Jacob (a salesman) and Frieda (Wiener) Bengelsdorf; married Beverly Knapp (a proprietress of a needlepoint shop), June 12, 1949; children: Ruth Ann, Lea Beth, Judith Eve. *Education:* University of Illinois, B.S. (with highest honors), 1943; Cornell University, graduate study, 1943-44; University of Chicago, M.S., 1948, Ph.D., 1951; California Institute of Technology, postdoctoral research fellow, 1951-52. *Home:* 256 South Arden Blvd., Los Angeles, Calif. 90004. *Office:* California Institute of Technology, Pasadena, Calif. 91109.

CAREER: University of California, Los Angeles, instructor in chemistry, 1952-54; General Electric Research Laboratory, Schenectady, N.Y., research chemist, 1954-59; Texaco-U.S. Rubber Research Center, Parsippany, N.J., research group leader, 1959-60; U.S. Borax Research Corp., Anaheim, Calif., senior scientist, 1960-63; *Los Angeles Times*, Los Angeles, Calif., science editor, 1963-70; California Institute of Technology, Pasadena, lecturer in science communication and director of science communication, 1971—. Teacher of scientific Russian on WRGB-Television, 1958; Galileo Lecturer at Harvey Mudd College, 1965; senior lecturer at University of Southern California, 1966, 1968, 1971, 1973; senior lecturer at University of California (Los Angeles), 1967, 1968, 1971; Faraday Lecturer at Pasadena City College, 1968; distinguished visiting professor at Whittier College, spring, 1974. Environmental editor for KABC-Radio, 1971; member of Los Angeles mayor's energy policy committee; member of U.S. attorney general's Los Angeles environmental task force, 1971—. *Military service:* U.S. Navy, 1944-46; served in Pacific theater.

MEMBER: American Association for the Advancement of Science, American Chemical Society (member of executive committee of Southern California section, 1974-77), National Association of Science Writers, Chemical Society (London), New York Academy of Sciences, Sigma Xi. *Awards, honors:* First place journalism awards from Consulting Engineers Association of California, 1963, 1965; first place award from American Trucking Associations, Inc., 1963, for safety story; Thomas L. Stokes Awards, 1963, 1964; Jean M. Kline Memorial Award from American Cancer Society, 1965; humanitarian award from Southern Pacific Coast region of Hadassah, 1967; James T. Grady Award from American Chemical Society, 1967; Westinghouse writing awards from American Association for the Advancement of Science, 1967, 1969; Claude Bernard Science Journalism Award from National Society for Medical Research, 1968.

WRITINGS: Space Ship Earth: People and Pollution, Fox-Mathis, 1969; (contributor) *The Information Utility and Social Choice*, AFIPS Press, 1970; (contributor) *Environmental Problems*, W. C. Brown, 1973; (contributor) *Applied Nutrition in Clinical Practice*, Intercontinental Medical Book, 1973. Author of "Of Atoms and Men," a science news column in *Enterprise Science News*, 1971—. Contributor of articles, translations, and reviews to scientific journals.

AVOCATIONAL INTERESTS: International travel (Great Britain, France, Italy, Belgium, Switzerland, Denmark, Finland, Soviet Union, Israel, Puerto Rico, Virgin Islands, Martinique, Haiti, Jamaica, Curacao, Aruba, Venezuela, Costa Rica).

* * *

BENICHOU, Paul 1908-

PERSONAL: Born September 19, 1908, in Tlemcen, Algeria; son of Samuel (a tradesman) and Rachel (Sarfati) Benichou; married Gina Labin (a lawyer and writer), December 26, 1929; children: Sylvia. *Education:* Sorbonne, University of Paris, Licence-es-Lettres, 1927, Agregation-des-Lettres, 1930, Doctorat-es-Lettres, 1971. *Religion:* Free Thinker. *Office:* Boylston Hall, Harvard University, Cambridge, Mass. 02138.

CAREER: Professor of French literature and classics at Ecole Alsacienne, Paris, 1930-34, Lycee de Beauvais, 1934-37, and Lycee Janson de Sailly, Paris, 1937-39; Institut francais d'Etudes Superieures, Buenos Aires, Argentina, professor, 1942-49; professor at Lycee Condorcet, Paris, and attache de recherches at Centre National de la Recherche Scientifique, Paris, 1949-58; Harvard University, Cambridge, Mass., professor of French literature, 1959—. *Military service:* French Army, 1929-30, 1939-40. *Member:* Societe d'Historie litteraire de la France.

WRITINGS: Morales du grand siecle, Gallimard, 1948, translation published as *Man and Ethios*, Doubleday, 1971; *L'Ecrivain et ses travaux* (title means "The Writer and His Works"), Corti, 1967; *Creacion poetica en el Romancero Tradicional* (title means "Poetic Creation in the Traditional Romancers"), Gredos, 1968; *Romancero judes-espanol de Marruecos* (title means "Judco-Spanish Romancero of Morocco"), Castalia, 1968; *Nerval et la chanson folklorique* (title means "Nerval and French Ballads"), Corti, 1971; *Le sacre de l'ecrivain, 1750-1830* (title means "The Consecration of the Writer, 1750-1830"), Corti, 1973. Contributor to literary and academic magazines.

WORK IN PROGRESS: A book, *Les doctrines de l'age romantique* (title means "Doctrines of the Romantic Era").

* * *

BENJAMIN, Alice
See BROOKE, Avery (Rogers)

* * *

BENJAMIN, Joseph 1921-

PERSONAL: Born September 10, 1921, in London, England; son of Samuel (a taxi driver) and Jessie (Wein) Benjamin; married Rivka Black, August 19, 1951 (died May, 1967); married Pauline Clothilde Henriques (a social worker), October 26, 1969; children: (first marriage) Mark, Simon, Adam; (second marriage) Biff (stepson). *Education:* Polytechnic of North London, certificate in child care, 1951. *Politics:* "Vaguely left, a liberal with a small '1'." *Religion:* "All or none." *Home:* 27 Elgin Court, Elgin

Ave., London W9 2NU, England. *Office:* North East London Polytechnic, Holbrook Rd., London E15, England.

CAREER: Worked as a buyer and sales manager in London, 1946-49; Oxfordshire County Council, Oxford, England, warden of children's home, 1951-53; Dulwich College Mission, London, England, manager of a project for delinquents, 1953-54; Grimsby Adventure Playground, Grimsby, England, project leader and secretary, 1955-59; Young Women's Christian Association, London, England, detached youth worker, 1961-62; London Borough of Camden, London, England, organizer of Community Play Centre and section head for day care centres, 1962-71; North East London Polytechnic, London, England, associate lecturer in social work, 1972—, administrative adviser in community work, 1973—. Founder and secretary of Camden Play Centres Association, 1964-73; tutor, Polytechnic of Northern London, 1966-73; member of executive committee and governing council of Newham Community Relations Council, 1973—; member of board of trustees, Playspace, 1973—; visiting lecturer, Goldsmiths' College of University of London, 1960, London School of Economics, 1960, Southwark College of Further Education, 1960, Thurrock Technical College, 1970, Kennington College of Further Education. *Military service:* Royal Artillery, 1941-46; became sergeant.

MEMBER: Community and Youth Service Association (executive member), National Children's Bureau (member of council, 1972—), Institute of Playleadership (executive member), Organization for Student Community Action (member of council, 1973—), Council for Children's Welfare (executive member), Camden Council of Social Service (member of executive committee, 1966-70), Newham Education Concern (executive member). *Awards, honors:* Nuffield Research grant, 1960-61.

WRITINGS: In Search of Adventure, National Council of Social Service, 1961, 3rd edition, 1968; *Grounds for Play*, Bedford Square Press, 1974. Contributor to education and social service journals. Member of editorial board, *Youth Review*, 1962-68.

WORK IN PROGRESS: Research in grass roots community projects.

* * *

BENSON, Carmen 1921-

PERSONAL: Born March 5, 1921, in Fort Sumner, N.M.; daughter of James P. and Mary (Zweifel) Chapman; married Everett Jack Benson (a market owner), March 12, 1939; children: Bonnie Diane (Mrs. Vincent Paul Concialdi). *Education:* Attended Los Angeles City College. *Religion:* Evangelical Christian. *Residence:* Downey, Calif. *Office:* Benson's Market, Downey, Calif.

CAREER: Benson's Market, Downey, Calif., co-owner, 1961—.

WRITINGS: (With Ray Charles Jarman) *The Grace and the Glory of God*, Logos International, 1968; *Supernatural Dreams and Visions*, Logos International, 1970, abridged editions published as *Jesus and Israel* and *This Earth's End*, both Charisma Books, 1971; *Seven Splendid Moments*, Whitaker House, 1974; *What About Us Who Are Not Healed?*, Logos International, 1975.

SIDELIGHTS: Carmen Benson writes: "In 1965 God directly intervened in my life by giving me a remarkable dream. This not only drastically altered the course of my religious life, but was the motivation for my writing career.

My interests are strictly spiritual, with emphasis on evangelical Bible teaching and vital Christian experience for the 'average' person—of whom I am one.''

* * *

BENSON, Ginny
See BENSON, Virginia

* * *

BENSON, Virginia 1923-
(Ginny Benson)

PERSONAL: Born March 31, 1923, in White Plains, N.Y.; daughter of Alexander William (an assessor) and Jessie (Brown) Dodge; married Robert F. Child, Jr., August 29, 1942 (divorced December, 1950); married John A. Benson, December 30, 1954 (divorced December, 1957); children: Kathryn Child (Mrs. John M. Zieran), Robert F. Child III. *Education:* Wayne State University, B.A., 1963; also attended Pasadena Junior College, Sawyer's School of Business, and University of California, Berkeley; studied portrait painting and modern art in Rio de Janeiro, Brazil. *Religion:* "Protestant Stonehenge Druid." *Home and office:* 518 South Madison Ave., Pasadena, Calif. 91101. *Agent:* Maximillian Becker, 115 East 82nd St., New York, N.Y. 10028.

CAREER: Licensed to sell insurance and real estate in Florida. *Brazil Herald* (American colony newspaper), Rio de Janeiro, Brazil, reporter for Associated Press and feature writer, 1948-49; free-lance writer of children's stories in Darien, Conn., 1949-50; Delta Airlines, Miami Beach, Fla., public relations trainee, 1950-52; Auditorium Group, Miami Beach, Fla., executive director of six convention hotels, 1952; self-employed public relations consultant in Coral Gables, Fla., 1953; U.S. House of Representatives, Washington, D.C., secretary to Representative Jeffrey P. Hillelson, 1954; John McShain, Inc., Arlington, Va., administrative assistant to chief supervisor for construction, 1954-57; Pope & Blake Architects and Pope Realty, Inc., Delray Beach, Fla., executive assistant and press agent, 1957-59; *Delray Beach News-Journal*, Delray Beach, Fla., advertising manager, 1959-60; GallenKamp Stores Co. (shoe store chain), Los Angeles, Calif., assistant director of advertising, 1960-61; General Electric Co., Metallurgical Products Department, Detroit, Mich., administrative assistant to manager of advertising, sales promotion, and marketing administration, 1961-62; KCET-Television (of National Educational Television), Hollywood, Calif., publications coordinator, 1963-65; Ben N. Cossart & Associates, (public relations firm), Los Angeles, Calif., account executive and vice-president of Consumer Products Division, 1965; B. D. Howes & Son (jewelry store chain), Pasadena, Calif., director of public relations and advertising, 1965-66; Madison Avenue West, Pasadena, Calif., president of advertising and public relations firm, 1967—.

MEMBER: American Women in Radio and Television, California Writers Guild, Southern California Council on Literature for Children and Young People, Sales Promotion Executives (Los Angeles), George Sherman Writers Workshop, Bamboo Writers.

WRITINGS—Under name Ginny Benson: *Mark Twain: In His Footsteps*, Creative Education Press, 1974. Author of a hundred eighty-five stories for audio visual and remedial reading programs for schools, 1972-73, and of six audio visual programs for Doubleday Multimedia, 1973. Author of "Chukker Chatter," a column in *Delray Beach News-*

Journal, 1959-60, "The Carriage Trade," a column in *Pasadena Star News*, 1974, and "From the Porcupine's Qull," a series of stories in *Pasadena Guardian*. Contributor of poem to *Early Years* and articles to *Pasadena Now*. Editor of *Crest* (for B. D. Howes & Son), *Footprint* (for GallenKamp Stores Co), *H.T.L.-Horizon* (for H.T.L. Industries, Inc.), and *Breakthrough* (of American Cancer Society).

WORK IN PROGRESS—For children: *Paul and Me*, a novel about Paul of Tarsus; *The Private World of Truffles*, a picture book; *The Leather Jacket*, a novel; *The Magic of Wik*, a fantasy.

SIDELIGHTS: Ginny Benson writes: "The only type of writing I have not done is sky writing, only because I can't fly a plane. Once I discover a truth, I must write about it to save others all the bother I went to in order to arrive at that truth. My first poem was published when I was nine years old, and I've been writing ever since. If I have my way, Heaven has typewriters."

BIOGRAPHICAL/CRITICAL SOURCES: Pasadena Now, May, 1970.

*   *   *

BENTLEY, Virginia W(illiams)   1908-

PERSONAL: Born February 17, 1908, in Newton Centre, Mass.; daughter of George Horace (a leather dealer) and Angie (Parker) Williams; married Percy Jardine Bentley, October 31, 1930 (died May 8, 1962); married John Stephen Latta, Jr. (in school supply business), July 24, 1974; children: (first marriage) David West. *Education:* Skidmore College, B.A., 1929. *Politics:* Independent. *Religion:* Presbyterian. *Home address:* R.F.D. 1, Danville, Vt. 05828.

CAREER: Writer. Hosted radio program "Kingdom Kitchen," on WTWN-Radio, 1967-69. *Member:* Chilton Club (Boston).

WRITINGS: A History of the Y.W.C.A. of Easton, Pa., privately printed, 1959; *A Sesquicentennial History of the First Presbyterian Church of Easton, Pa.*, privately printed, 1961; *Rhyming Outline of the Bible for Sunday School Use*, privately printed, 1965; *Let Herbs Do It*, Houghton, 1973; *Bentley Farm Cookbook*, Houghton, 1975.

WORK IN PROGRESS: Gathering material for another cookbook.

SIDELIGHTS: Virginia Bentley writes: "A zeal for making order out of chaos is what really lies behind cooking, homemaking, gardening, decorating and even my writing—especially the writing." *Avocational interests:* Interior decorating, gardening, homemaking.

*   *   *

BENTON, Dorothy Gilchrist   1919-

PERSONAL: Born March 26, 1919, in Westfield, Mass.; daughter of Harry Elmer (a clergyman, lecturer, and writer) and Stella (an accountant; maiden name, Rising) Gilchrist; married Stanley Howard Benton, Sr. (a supervisory accountant for U.S. Immigration Service), August 13, 1939; children: Stanley, Jr., Diane Banister (Mrs. Leland Russell). *Education:* Northampton Junior College, A.A., 1937. *Politics:* "Usually Republican, not always." *Religion:* Methodist. *Home:* 9 Calo Ct., St. Albans, Vt. 05478.

CAREER: Federal Land Bank, Springfield, Mass., secretary, 1937-39; *St. Albans Daily Messenger*, St. Albans, Vt.,

proofreader, 1951-53, general reporter, 1953-56, woman's editor, 1956-58; Vermont Department of Social Welfare, St. Albans, office manager, 1958-71; writer, 1971—. Part-time secretary, Retail Credit Corp., 1972, Buck & Pierce Civil Engineers, 1974. *Member:* Daughters of the American Revolution, United Methodist Women, Daughters of Founders and Patriots of America, Rising Family Association, Genealogical Society of New England, Genealogical Society of Vermont, Poetry Society of Vermont (past historian), St. Albans Writers Workshop, Phi Alpha (vice-president, 1955; president, 1956).

WRITINGS: Mountain Harvest (poems), Windy Row Press, 1973. Contributor of poems to magazines, including *Ideals* and *Mountain Troubadour*, and to newspapers. Editor, *Rising Newsletter*.

WORK IN PROGRESS: A genealogy; poems.

SIDELIGHTS: Dorothy Gilchrist writes: "I think the reason our country is in such a mess today is that people have gotten too far away from religious principles . . . and think only of themselves—nations, as well as individuals. I . . . think parents have become lax in not expecting enough from their children in responsibility and character; and I still believe that mothers of small children belong home with them." *Avocational interests:* Travel (Europe), music (singing and playing the piano), oil painting, swimming, boating, fishing, ice fishing, snowmobiling.

*   *   *

BERARDO, Felix M(ario)   1934-

PERSONAL: Born February 7, 1934, in Waterbury, Conn.; son of Rocco and Maria (Gurrera) Berardo; divorced; children: Marcellino Antonio, Benito Antonio (sons). *Education:* University of Connecticut, B.A., 1961; Florida State University, Ph.D., 1965. *Religion:* Roman Catholic. *Home:* 2035 Northwest 36th Dr., Gainesville, Fla. 32605. *Office:* Department of Sociology, University of Florida, Gainesville, Fla. 32611.

CAREER: Washington State University, Pullman, assistant professor of sociology and assistant rural sociologist, 1965-69; University of Florida, Gainesville, associate professor, 1969-73, professor of sociology, 1973—. *Military service:* U.S. Air Force, 1952-56. *Member:* American Sociological Association, Rural Sociological Society, National Council on Family Relations, Gerontological Society, Southeastern Council on Family Relations, Southern Sociological Society (chairman of program committee, 1974-75), Phi Beta Kappa, Phi Kappa Phi, Alpha Kappa Delta.

WRITINGS: (Editor with F. Ivan Nye and contributor) *Emerging Conceptual Frameworks in Family Analysis*, Macmillan, 1966; (with Nye) *The Family: Its Structure and Interaction*, Macmillan, 1973.

Contributor: Benjamin Schlessinger, editor, *The One-Parent Family*, University of Toronto Press, 1969; Jeffrey K. Hadden and Marie L. Borgatta, editors, *Marriage and the Family: A Comprehensive Reader*, F. E. Peacock, 1969; Howard Bahr, editor, *Disaffiliated Man: Essays and Bibliography on Skid Row, Vagrancy, and Outsiders*, University of Toronto Press, 1970; Jacquelin P. Wiseman, editor, *People as Partners: Individual and Family Relationships in Today's World*, Canfield Press, 1971; Marcia E. Lassell and Thomas E. Lassell, editors, *Love-Marriage-Family: A Developmental Approach*, Scott, Foresman, 1973; *La Familia como Unidad de Estudio Demografico*, Centro Latinoamericano de Demografia, in press.

Contributor of articles and reviews to journals in United States and Brazil. Associate editor, *International Journal of Sociology of the Family*, 1970—, and *Family Coordinator*, 1972-75; associate editor, *Journal of Marriage and the Family*, 1972-75, editor, 1976—; guest editor for special issues, *Journal of Marriage and the Family*, November, 1971, and *Family Coordinator*, January, 1972.

WORK IN PROGRESS: With F. Ivan Nye, a revision of *The Family: Its Structure and Interaction.*

*   *   *

BERGEN, Polly   1930-

PERSONAL: Real name, Nellie Paulina Burgin; born July 14, 1930, in Knoxville, Tenn.; daughter of William Hugh (a construction engineer) and Lucy (Lawhorn) Burgin; married Jerome Courtland (an actor), 1949 (divorced, 1955); married Freddie Fields, February 13, 1956; children: Pamela K. Fields, Peter Fields; stepchildren: Kathy Fields. *Education:* Attended schools in many states as family moved about the country; student at Compton Junior College, Compton, Calif., after graduation from high school in Compton. *Residence:* Malibu, Calif. *Office:* Polly Bergen Co., 1345 Avenue of the Americas, New York, N.Y. 10019.

CAREER: Singer, motion picture and stage actress, and television personality; president of Polly Bergen Co. (cosmetic firm; now a subsidiary of Faberge), 1965—. Sang hillbilly and folk songs with her father as a child, but switched to popular music in her teens and appeared with small bands in vicinity of Los Angeles; recording artist for Columbia Records. Began film career in "At War With the Army," followed by "That's My Boy," "The Stooge," "Warpath," "Arena," "Cry of the Hunted," "Half a Hero," "Move Over Darling," "Kisses for My President," and half a dozen other motion pictures. Featured in title role on Playhouse 90 "Helen Morgan Story," 1957; star of "Polly Bergen Show," National Broadcasting Co., 1958-59; regular panel member of "To Tell the Truth"; guest on "Perry Como Show," "Bell Telephone Hour," and other network programs. On stage made Broadway debut in "Almanac," 1953; later played several dramatic roles. National Chairwoman for U.S. Savings Bond Campaign, 1970; national spokeswoman for Children's Asthmatic Research Institute and Hospital, Denver. Executive vice-president of Women's Guild, Cedars-Sinai Medical Center, Los Angeles.

MEMBER: Screen Actors Guild, American Federation of Television and Radio Artists, American Guild of Variety Artists. *Awards, honors:* Emmy Award as best television actress, National Academy of Television Arts and Sciences, 1957, for "Helen Morgan Story"; Polly Bergen Cardio-Pulmonary Laboratory was dedicated in her honor at Children's Asthmatic Research Institute and Hospital (CARIH), 1970; Humanitarian Award of CARIH, 1971.

WRITINGS: The Polly Bergen Book of Beauty, Fashion and Charm, Prentice-Hall, 1962; *Polly's Principles*, Peter H. Wyden, 1974.

Albums—Issued by Columbia Records, except as noted: "Little Girl Blue," Kem Records, 1951; "Bergen Sings Morgan," 1957; "The Party's Over," 1958; "Polly Bergen Sings the Hit Songs From 'Do Re Mi' and 'Annie Get Your Gun,'" 1958; "All Alone by the Telephone," 1959; "My Heart Sings," 1959; "Polly Bergen's Four Seasons of Love," 1960; "Act One, Sing Two," Phillips Records, 1963.

BERGER, Hilbert J.   1920-

PERSONAL: Born April 9, 1920, in Edgerton, Ohio; son of Hilbert S. (a minister) and Ada (Kleitz) Berger; married Geneva Wagener (a musician), August 13, 1944; children: Daniel, Rebecca (Mrs. Terrence Zarnik). *Education:* North Central College, B.A., 1943; Evangelical Theological Seminary, M.Div., 1946; Mansfield College, Oxford, further study, 1966. *Office:* 2417 Getz Rd., Fort Wayne, Ind. 46804.

CAREER: Ordained minister of United Methodist Church, 1947; assistant general secretary of Division of Stewardship and Finance of United Methodist Church, 1967-72; pastor in Hammond, Ind., 1959-67, West Lafayette, Ind., 1972-74, Fort Wayne, Ind., 1974—. Guest lecturer, Union Theological Seminary, Philippines, 1969; guest professor at five United Methodist Seminaries, 1971-72. *Member:* Alpha Psi Omega.

WRITINGS: (With Jack Reeve) *Mirror for the Chief Oikonomos*, 1966; *Time to Negotiate*, Friendship, 1973. Contributor to *Stewardship Facts*, National Council of Churches, 1967-68, 1973; also contributor to national church publications.

WORK IN PROGRESS: A Theology for Today's Stewards, a series of illustrated and diagrammed addresses on Christian stewardship.

AVOCATIONAL INTERESTS: Travel.

*   *   *

BERGMAN, (Shmuel) Hugo   1883-1975

December 25, 1883—June 18, 1975; Czechoslovakian-born Israeli philosopher, educator, university rector and library director, and author of works on philosophy, logic, mathematics, and religion. Obituaries: *New York Times*, June 20, 1975; *Washington Post*, June 21, 1975.

*   *   *

BERGSTEN, Staffan   1932-

PERSONAL: Born November 12, 1932, in Sweden; son of Nils (a headmaster) and Clara (Wangel) Bergsten; married Gunilla Ulander (a university lecturer), July 30, 1957; children: Cecilia, Andreas, Katja. *Education:* University of Uppsala, Ph.D., 1960. *Home:* Malma Ringvaeg 8, S-752 45 Uppsala, Sweden. *Office:* Department of Literary History, Uppsala University, S-751 03 Uppsala, Sweden.

CAREER: Cambridge University, Cambridge, England, deputy lecturer in Swedish, 1957-58; Uppsala University, Uppsala, Sweden, docent in literary history, 1960—, head of department, 1973—. Has talked on literary subjects for Swedish Broadcasting Co., 1965—. *Military service:* Swedish Army, 1954-55. *Member:* International P.E.N. (Stockholm).

WRITINGS: Time and Eternity: A Study in the Structure and Symbolism of T. S. Eliot's Four Quartets, Svenska Bokfoerlaget, 1960; *Stagnelius Bacchanterna* (critical edition), Gebers Foerlag, 1962; *En Stagneliusbibliografi* (title means "A Stagnelius Bibliography"), Svenska Litteratursaellskapet, 1965; *Erotikern Stagnelius* (title means "Stagnelius, the Erotic Poet"), Svenska Bokfoerlaget, 1966; *Jaget och vaerlden: Kosmiska analogier i svensk 1900-tal-slyrik* (title means "The Self and the World: Cosmic Analogies in Twentieth Century Swedish Poetry"), Uppsala University, 1971; (editor with G. Bergsten and contributor) *Lyrik i tid och otid* (essays in poetry criticism), Gleerups,

1971; (contributor) *Litteraturens världshistoria* (title means "History of World Literature"), Volume IX, Norstedts, 1973; *Oesten Sjoestrand* (biography), Twayne, 1974. Contributor to *Encyclopaedia Britannica, Samlaren* (a yearbook of Swedish literary history), *Orbis Litterarum* (Copenhagen), *Bonniers Litteraera Magasin*, and *Svensk Litteraturtidskrift*.

* * *

BERKE, Joseph H(erman) 1939-

PERSONAL: Born January 17, 1939, in Newark, N.J.; married Roberta Elzey (a writer), 1968; children: Joshua Demian. *Education:* Attended Columbia University, 1957-60; Albert Einstein College of Medicine, M.D., 1964. *Religion:* Jewish. *Home:* 29 Oval Rd., London NW1 7EA, England. *Agent:* A. D. Peters & Co., 10 Buckingham St., London W.C.2, England.

CAREER: Private practice of psychotherapy and family therapy, 1965—. Research fellow in psychiatry and the social sciences at Philadelphia Association (London), 1965-68. Founding member, Institute of Phenomenological Studies, 1966—. *Member:* Royal Society of Medicine (fellow), Arbours Housing Association (founding member; director of Crisis Centre, 1973—).

WRITINGS: Counter Culture: The Creation of an Alternative Society, P. Owen, 1969; (with Mary Barnes, and contributor) *Mary Barnes: Two Accounts of a Journey Through Madness*, Harcourt, 1972; (with Calvin Hernton) *The Cannabis Experience: An Interpretive Study of the Effects of Marijuana and Hashish*, P. Owen, 1974. Contributor of articles, essays, book reviews, plays, and poetry to journals. Editor and publisher, *Fire* magazine, 1967-74.

WORK IN PROGRESS: The Butterfly People (tentative title), for Harper; a study of therapeutic communities like the Arbours Association, and other innovations in psychiatry, contrasted with a critique of current treatment modes.

* * *

BERKOVITZ, Irving H(erbert) 1924-

PERSONAL: Born July 12, 1924, in Boston, Mass.; son of Morris (in retail business) and Frances (Fuxon) Berkovitz; married Anne M. Stern (in public relations), October 25, 1953; children: Karen, Glenn, Joel. *Education:* Harvard University, A.B., 1945; Boston University, M.D., 1950; postdoctoral study at Southern California Psychoanalytic Institute, 1952-60, and Center for Training in Community Psychiatry, 1967-70. *Politics:* Democrat. *Religion:* "Non-practicing." *Office:* 9400 Brighton Way, Beverly Hills, Calif. 90210.

CAREER: Certified by American Board of Psychiatry and Neurology; licensed to practice in California; Wadsworth Veterans Administration General Medical and Surgical Hospital, Los Angeles, Calif., intern, 1950-51; Brentwood Veterans Administration Hospital, Los Angeles, Calif., psychiatric resident, 1951-54; private practice in psychoanalysis and psychotherapy for children and adults in Beverly Hills, Calif., 1954—. Member of staff at Cedars-Sinai Medical Center and Thalian's Children's Clinic, 1958—; instructor at Southern California Psychoanalytic Institute, 1958—; clinical professor at University of California, Los Angeles, 1967—; member of faculty of Los Angeles Group Psychotherapy Association Institute, 1971—. Senior consulting psychiatrist for schools, Los Angeles County Department of Health Services, 1964—. Volunteer therapist at Reiss-Davis Child Guidance Clinic, 1954-58. *Military service:* U.S. Army, Medical Corps, 1943-44.

MEMBER: American Psychiatric Association, American Psychoanalytic Association, American Society for Adolescent Psychiatry, American Medical Association, American Group Psychotherapy Association, American Orthopsychiatric Association, American Psychosomatic Society, California Medical Association, Southern California Psychiatric Society, Southern California Psychoanalytic Society (president-elect, 1975-76), Los Angeles County Medical Association, Los Angeles Group Psychotherapy Association (past president), Los Angeles Society for Child Psychiatry. *Awards, honors:* Second prize from Los Angeles County Medical Association art exhibit, 1974, for photography.

WRITINGS: (Editor) *Adolescents Grow in Groups: Experiences in Adolescent Group Psychotherapy*, Brunner, 1972; (with Muriel Thomson) *Mental Health Consultation and Assistance to School Personnel of Los Angeles County* (monograph), Los Angeles County Superintendent of Schools, 1973; (editor) *When Schools Care: Creative Use of Groups in Secondary Schools*, Brunner, 1975; (contributor) Max Sugar, editor, *The Adolescent in Group and Family Therapy*, Brunner, 1975. Contributor to education and medical journals.

WORK IN PROGRESS: A book on county mental health consultation to school personnel; a book of photographs, possibly with poetry by another author; research on types of anger in adolescents in therapy.

SIDELIGHTS: Berkovitz writes: "A central tenet to my having chosen psychiatry and psychoanalysis as a profession is my belief that open, honest, empathic communication between people is a desirable condition in life . . . constructive and sensitively conducted group experiences for adolescents (and adults) are a necessary part of a healthy growth and maturation, and further the possibility of open, honest, empathic, communicating by young people. . . . In future publications I hope to write more exclusively my own views of human experience, as well as of my profession . . . I hope also someday to have the opportunity to publish a volume featuring color photographs which I have taken over the years. Some of these capture a sense of beauty in a non-verbal, visual mode. Photography provides for me one of the welcome changes from the verbal world in which I live most of the time, as well as being a means of closeness to beauty in nature." *Avocational interests:* Tennis, playing clarinet, camping.

* * *

BERLIN, Normand 1931-

PERSONAL: Born December 6, 1931, in New York, N.Y.; son of Benjamin and Anna (Berefere) Berlin; married Barbara Schoenberg (a teacher), August 25, 1956; children: Adam, David. *Education:* New York University, B.A., 1953; Columbia University, M.A., 1956; University of California, Berkeley, Ph.D., 1964. *Religion:* Jewish. *Home:* 152 Chestnut St., Amherst, Mass. 01002. *Office:* Department of English, University of Massachusetts, Amherst, Mass. 01002.

CAREER: McGill University, Montreal, Quebec, assistant professor of English, 1961-64; University of Massachusetts, Amherst, assistant professor, 1965-68 associate professor, 1968-74, professor of English, 1974—. Visiting professor at University of the Negev, 1971; exchange professor at University of Hawaii, 1974. *Military service:* U.S. Army, Infantry, 1953-55. *Member:* Phi Beta Kappa. *Awards, honors:* Woodrow Wilson fellow, 1955.

WRITINGS: The Base String: The Underworld in Elizabethan Drama, Fairleigh Dickinson University Press, 1968; *Thomas Sackville*, Twayne, 1974. Contributor to professional journals. Member of the editorial board of *English Literary Renaissance*, 1971—.

WORK IN PROGRESS: The Secret Cause: A Discussion of Tragedy.

* * *

BERMANGE, Barry 1933-

PERSONAL: Born November 7, 1933, in London, England; son of David (a tailor) and Gertrude (Rosenthal) Bermange; married Maurine Jewel Lufkin Bright (a writer, under pseudonym Maggie Ross), March, 1961. *Education:* Studied art in England. *Religion:* Jewish. *Residence:* London, England. *Address:* % Eyre Methuen Ltd., 11 New Fetter Lane, London EC4, England.

CAREER: Assistant designer for Perth Repertory Co., 1955; actor and assistant stage manager at Swansea Repertory Co., 1956; playwright. *Military service:* In National Service, 1952-54. *Awards, honors:* British Arts Council drama bursary, 1964; Ohio State University award, 1967, for "Amor Dei"; German Critics Prize, 1969, for television play, "Tramp."

WRITINGS—Plays produced: "No Quarter," broadcast, 1962, first produced in London, 1964; "Nathan and Tabileth" (one-act), broadcast, 1962, first produced at Edinburgh Festival, 1967; "The Cloud" (full-length), first produced in London, 1964; "Four Inventions" (includes "The Dreams," "The Evening of Certain Lives," "Amor Dei," "The After Life"), broadcast, 1964-65, first produced as "Darkness Theatre" in London, 1969; "Oldenburg" (one-act), first produced at Edinburgh Festival, 1967; "The Interview," televised, 1968, first produced in London, 1969; "Invasion," televised, 1969; "Scenes from Family Life," televised, 1969; "Oh Starlings," first produced in London, 1971.

Other plays: "The Voice of the Peanut," 1960; "Never Forget a Face," 1961; "The Imposters," 1962; "The Mortification," 1964; "The Detour," 1964; "Paths of Glory," 1965; "Letters of a Portuguese Nun," 1966; "As a Man Grows Older," 1967; "Tramp," 1968; "Neus vom Krieg," 1969; "International," 1970. Also author of "The Situation" and "Bones."

Collected works: *Nathan and Tabileth. Oldenburg*, Methuen, 1967; *No Quarter and The Interview* (also includes "Invasion"), Methuen, 1969. Work also included in *Collection: Literature for the Seventies*, Heath, 1972.

SIDELIGHTS: Although his early plays were written for the stage, they were first produced on radio or television. Bermange himself did the television film of "Nathan and Tabileth," in Holland. In both the theatre and television he has worked as his own director.

"International," a controversial work on football violence, was ultimately banned by the BBC.

* * *

BERMANT, Chaim 1929-

PERSONAL: Born February 26, 1929, in Breslev, Poland; son of Azriel (a rabbi) and Feiga Tzirl (Daets) Bermant; married Judith Weil, December 17, 1962; children: Alisa,

Eve, Azriel, Daniel. *Education:* Attended Rabbinical College, Glasgow, Scotland, 1948-50; University of Glasgow, M.A., 1955, M.Litt., 1960; London School of Economics and Political Science, M.Sc., 1957. *Politics:* Liberal conservative. *Religion:* Jewish. *Home:* 18 Hill Rise, London N.W.11., England. *Agent:* A. P. Watt, 26 Bedford Row, London W.C.1., England.

CAREER: Teacher in London, England, 1955-56; economist in London, 1956-58; television scriptwriter in Glasgow, Scotland, 1958-59, and in London, 1959-61; features editor, *London Jewish Chronicle*, 1961-66; free-lance writer, 1966—.

WRITINGS: Jericho Sleep Alone (novel), Holt, 1963; *Berl Make Tea* (novel), Holt, 1964; *Ben Preserve Us* (novel), Holt, 1964; *Diary of an Old Man* (novel), Holt, 1966; *Swinging in the Rain* (novel), Hodder & Stoughton, 1967; *Israel*, Walker & Co., 1967; (editor with Murray Mindlin) *Explorations: An Annual on Jewish Themes*, Barrie & Rockliff, 1967; *Troubled Eden: The Anatomy of Anglo-Jewry*, Basic Books, 1969; *Here Endeth the Lesson* (novel), Eyre & Spottiswoode, 1969.

Now Dowager (novel), Eyre & Spottiswoode, 1971; *The Cousinhood*, Macmillan, 1971; *Roses Are Blooming in Picardy* (novel), Eyre & Spottiswoode, 1972; *The Last Supper*, St. Martin's, 1973; *The Walled Garden*, Macmillan, 1975; *Point of Arrival*, Macmillan, 1975; *Next Year in Jerusalem* (autobiographical sketches), Allen & Unwin, in press.

WORK IN PROGRESS: A novel for St. Martins.

* * *

BERNAL, Judith F. 1939-
 (Judith F. Dunn)

PERSONAL: Born June 6, 1939, in England; daughter of James (a biochemist) and Jean (a translator; maiden name, Stewart) Pace; married Martin Bernal, June 18, 1960 (divorced January, 1971); married John Montfort Dunn (a political theorist), June 26, 1973; children: (first marriage) Sophia, William, Paul. *Education:* Cambridge University, B.A. (first class honors), 1961, M.A., 1963. *Religion:* None. *Home:* 3 Tenison Ave., Cambridge, England. *Office:* Medical Research Council Unit, Sub-Department of Animal Behaviour, Madingley, Cambridge, England.

CAREER: Cambridge University, Cambridge, England, researcher on medical applications of psychology, 1968-74; Sub-Department of Animal Behaviour, Medical Research Council Unit, Madingley, Cambridge, scientific officer in developmental psychology, 1974—.

WRITINGS: (Contributor) N. Blurton-Jones, editor, *Ethological Studies of Child Development*, Cambridge University Press, 1972; (contributor) A. S. Barnett, editor, *Ethology and Development*, Heinemann, 1973; (contributor) M. P. M. Richards, editor, *The Integration of a Child into the Social World*, Cambridge University Press, 1974; (under name Judith F. Dunn) *Comfort and Distress*, Harvard University Press, in press.

* * *

BERNARD, Thelma Rene 1940-

PERSONAL: Born May 2, 1940, in Philadelphia, Pa.; daughter of Michael John (a writer, inventor, and sheetmetal worker) and Louise Thelma (a landscape artist; maiden name, Hoffman) Campione; married Gene Bernard (a composer, producer, and audio mixer), February 17,

1962. *Education:* Attended public schools in Philadelphia, Pa. *Politics:* "Non-partisan but against socialism." *Religion:* Christian Mysticism. *Home:* 1929 Bonita Ave., Las Vegas, Nev. 89104. *Office:* N.W.S. Construction Corp., 1532 Western Ave., Las Vegas, Nev. 89102.

CAREER: Secretary, Penn Mutual Life Insurance Co., Philadelphia, Pa., 1958-64, Suffolk Franklin Savings Bank, Boston, Mass., 1964-66, Holmes & Narver, Inc., Las Vegas, Nev., 1968-71; Miles R. Nay, Inc. (mechanical contractors), Las Vegas, site office manager, 1972-74; N.W.S. Construction Corp., Las Vegas, Nev., administrative assistant to president, 1974—. *Member:* National League of American Pen Women (vice-president of Red Rock Canyon branch, 1974-76), Humanitarian Society of Quakertown.

WRITINGS—Gothic novels: *Blue Marsh*, Pinnacle, 1972; *Winds of Wakefield*, Pinnacle, 1972; *Moonshadow Mansion*, Pinnacle, 1973. Editor of Red Rock Canyon branch of National League of American Pen Women newsletter, *Chips Off the Ole Rock*, 1974—. Writer of song lyrics and commercial jingles.

WORK IN PROGRESS: A screenplay, "Top Out"; a screenplay and novel, *Marlana*; with Joseph I. Leveque, a book on pet care, completion expected in 1975.

SIDELIGHTS: Thelma Bernard told *CA*: "I love words.... I write solely to please myself: to channel a fantasy or capture an experience. I know nothing about technique.... My true love affair with words lies in poetry. Most of the poems are far too personal to even consider publishing attempts. A good portion on them are written to friends on special occasions....

"Life's purpose to me is to advance the soul through tests and experience. To sum up: I love people, animals, and the sun—in that order. I believe in forgiving others so that we too may be forgiven. I think that love is the only thing that matters. I believe that being busy is the only salvation and cure-all for troubles."

AVOCATIONAL INTERESTS: Reading, playing piano, sewing, making and collecting greeting cards and miniatures, cats, roses, embroidering, oil painting, poetry, cooking, antiques, music.

BIOGRAPHICAL/CRITICAL SOURCES: Nevadan, October 6, 1974.

* * *

BERNSTEIN, Joseph M(ilton) 1908(?)-1975

1908(?)—July 11, 1975; American editor and translator of books and articles. Obituaries: *AB Bookman's Weekly*, July 28, 1975.

* * *

BERNSTEIN, Margery 1933-

PERSONAL: Born April 18, 1933, in New York, N.Y.; daughter of Henry and Sylvia (Bernstein) Weiss; married Edgar Bernstein (a teacher), December 16, 1955; children: Amy Beth, Hal Barnard. *Education:* University of California, Los Angeles, B.A., 1954. *Politics:* "Rational." *Religion:* Jewish. *Home:* 1344 East 48th St., Chicago, Ill. 60615. *Office:* Laboratory School, University of Chicago, Chicago, Ill. 60637.

CAREER: Company of the Four, Chicago, Ill., stage manager, 1961-65; University of Chicago, Laboratory School, Chicago, Ill., teacher, 1966—. Stage manager and member of board of directors, Last Stage, 1965-72. *Member:* International Reading Association.

WRITINGS—Juveniles: *Coyote Goes Hunting for Fire*, Scribner, 1974; *Earth Namer*, Scribner, 1974; *How the Sun Made a Promise*, Scribner, 1974.

WORK IN PROGRESS: Research for a social studies curriculum for the primary grades.

* * *

BERRIDGE, Elizabeth 1921-

PERSONAL: Born December 3, 1921, in London, England; daughter of Albert (an estate manager) and Phyllis Cecilia (Drew) Berridge; married Reginald Moore (an author and publisher), October 14, 1940; children: Lawrence Gaunt, Karen Veronica (Mrs. Philip Craven). *Education:* Attended Regent Street Polytechnic in London, England; also studied French and German privately in Geneva, Switzerland. *Politics:* Liberal. *Home:* 19 Broad Lane, Hampton-on-Thames, Middlesex, England. *Agent:* David Higham Associates, 5-8 Lower John St., Golden Sq., London W1R 4HA, England.

CAREER: Held early positions as secretary and journalist, later as publisher's editor, 1956-60, all in London, England; novelist, short story writer; book critic for *Daily Telegraph, Books and Bookmen*, and *Country Life*. Appeared on radio program "Woman's Hour," 1964-71. Local press officer for Liberal Party, 1963-64. *Member:* National Book League, Society of Authors, Browning Society. *Awards, honors:* Yorkshire Post award for best novel of the year, 1964, for *Across the Common*.

WRITINGS—Novels, except as indicated: *House of Defence*, Falcon, 1945; *The Story of Stanley Brent*, Falcon, 1945; *Selected Short Stories*, Maurice Fridberg, 1949; *It Won't Be Flowers*, Simon & Schuster, 1949 (published as *Be Clean, Be Tidy*, Heinemann, 1949); *Rose under Glass*, Heinemann, 1962; *Across the Common*, Heinemann, 1964, Coward, 1965; *Sing Me Who You Are*, Heinemann, 1967; (editor and author of introduction) *The Barretts at Hope End: The Early Diary of Elizabeth Barrett Browning*, J. Murray, 1974. Author of plays for television. Contributor of poetry and stories to literary magazines; also contributor to *Cornhill Magazine, London Magazine, Winter's Tales, Punch*, and *Harper's Bazaar*.

WORK IN PROGRESS: A novel; research into the archives of the Welsh squirarchy for a biography of a nineteenth-century ancestor on the Pre-Raphaelite fringe; further research into the poetry and life of Elizabeth Barrett Browning.

AVOCATIONAL INTERESTS: Reading (especially Victorian biographies and books on the position of women in the eighteenth and nineteenth centuries), exploring out-of-the-way places in the country, gliding, watching cricket, research into the possibility of life-after-death and allied ESP phenomena, making patchwork quilts in the winter time.

* * *

BERRY, Adrian M(ichael) 1937-

PERSONAL: Born June 15, 1937, in London, England; married Marina Beatrice Sulzberger, January, 1967; children: two. *Education:* Christ Church, Oxford, graduate with honors in modern history, 1959. *Home:* 11 Cottesmore Gardens, London W.8, England. *Office: Sunday Telegraph*, 135 Fleet St., London EC4P 4BL, England.

CAREER: Reporter on *Walsall Observer*, 1960-61; sub-editor on *Birmingham Post*, 1961-62; financial analyst with *Investor's Chronicle*, 1962-63; *New York Herald Tribune*, New York, N.Y., reporter, 1964-65; *Time*, New York, N.Y., correspondent in Los Angeles and Washington, D.C., and writer in New York, 1965-67; *Daily Telegraph*, London, England, member of science staff, 1968-70; *Sunday Telegraph*, London, England, assistant news editor, 1972—. *Member:* Royal Astronomical Society (fellow), British Interplanetary Society (fellow and senior member).

WRITINGS: The Next Ten Thousand Years: A Vision of Man's Future in the Universe, Saturday Review Press, 1974. Contributor to U.S. magazines.

SIDELIGHTS: Berry covered the first moon landing in 1969 and Apollo 13 in 1970; his book has had editions in England, Germany, Brazil, Spain, Finland, Holland, Turkey, and Japan. *Avocational interests:* Skiing, chess.

* * *

BERRY, Edward I. 1940-

PERSONAL: Born November 30, 1940, in Camden, N.J.; son of Edward Irwin (a lawyer) and Abigail (Steadman) Berry; married Margaret Eisenhardt (an artist), August 26, 1961; children: David, Michelle. *Education:* Wesleyan University, A.B., 1962; University of California, Berkeley, M.A. and Ph.D. *Office:* Department of English, University of Victoria, Victoria, British Columbia, Canada.

CAREER: University of Connecticut, Storrs, assistant professor of English, 1969-70; University of Virginia, Charlottesville, assistant professor of English, 1970-75; University of Victoria, Victoria, British Columbia, member of English department faculty, 1975—. *Awards, honors:* Fulbright fellowship, 1968-69; National Endowment for the Humanities summer fellowship, 1973.

WRITINGS: Patterns of Decay: Shakespeare's Early Histories, University of Virginia Press, 1975.

WORK IN PROGRESS: Research on Shakespeare and on Francis Bacon.

* * *

BESSOM, Malcolm E(ugene) 1940-

PERSONAL: Born September 27, 1940, in Boston, Mass.; son of Harold Eugene (an editor and advertising executive) and Mina (a fashion artist; maiden name, Townley) Bessom. *Education:* Boston University, B.Mus., 1962, graduate study, 1962-63. *Politics:* Conservative Republican. *Religion:* Protestant. *Home:* 4114 Davis Pl. N.W., Washington, D.C. 20007. *Office:* Music Educators National Conference, 1902 Association Dr., Reston, Va. 22091.

CAREER: Public school teacher and director of vocal music in Chelmsford, Mass., 1963-67; Allyn & Bacon, Inc., Boston, Mass., assistant editor, 1967-68, associate editor, 1968-70; Music Educators National Conference, Reston, Va., assistant editor of *Music Educators Journal*, 1970-71, editor, 1971—. *Member:* Washington Edpress. *Awards, honors:* Distinguished achievement awards for excellence in journalism from Educational Press Association of America, 1973, for column "Overtones" in *Music Educators Journal*, 1974, for editing "Sounds of America" and "Arts Impact," and 1975, for "Special Publications."

WRITINGS: Supervising the Successful School Music Program, Parker Publishing, 1969; (contributor) William R. Sur, William R. Fisher, Mary R. Tolbert, and Charlotte DuBois, editors, *This Is Music for Today*, Books VI, VII, and VIII, Allyn & Bacon, 1970-71; (editor) *Music in Special Education*, Music Educators National Conference, 1972; (with Alphonse M. Tatarunis and Samuel L. Forcucci) *Teaching Music in Today's Secondary Schools*, Holt, 1974. Author of "Jazz Session," a column in *National Student Musician*, 1965-66, and "Overtones," in *Music Educators Journal*, 1970—. Contributor of more than a hundred articles and reviews to music journals.

WORK IN PROGRESS: The Jazz Experience, a historical text.

SIDELIGHTS: Bessom writes: "Whether writing about education or music, I believe in thoroughly researched and documented work that is presented without the stuffy, pedantic, tangled jargon common to much of the writing from the education community. My specialty has always been black American music. ... Unfortunately, most music scholars have neglected the native product, especially the popular art-forms."

* * *

BHANA, Surendra 1939-

PERSONAL: Born May 16, 1939, in India; emigrated to South Africa in 1948; son of Magan (a businessman) and Amba (Gopal) Bhana; married Kastoor Jeena (a lecturer), June 20, 1966; children: Hershini, Hemant. *Education:* University of the Witwatersrand, B.A., 1962; University of South Africa, B.A. (honors), 1966; University of Kansas, M.A., 1968, Ph.D., 1971. *Home:* 56 Prince Edward St., Flat 5, Durban 4001, South Africa. *Office:* Department of History, University of Durban-Westville, Private Bag X54001, Durban 4000, South Africa.

CAREER: High school history teacher in Lenasia, South Africa, 1963-66; University of Durban-Westville, Durban, South Africa, lecturer, 1972-75, senior lecturer in history, 1975—. *Member:* South African Historical Society, American Historical Association, Organization of American Historians, Caribbean Studies Association.

WRITINGS: The United States and the Development of the Puerto Rican Status Question: 1936-1968, University Press of Kansas, 1975.

WORK IN PROGRESS: Research on the development of political autonomy within the territories of the United States' Colonial empire since 1898.

SIDELIGHTS: Bhana writes: "History must be written in a detached and dispassionate way, although never without sympathy for the past. I imagine I was able to bring a measure of detachment to my Puerto Rican study largely because I wrote about a sensitive issue as an outsider. Of course an outsider's perspective may have its limitations, but imagine how 'national' histories might benefit from an examination by persons who geographically, politically, culturally, and even racially stand on the outside looking in."

* * *

BIDDLE, Perry H(arvey), Jr. 1932-

PERSONAL: Born July 1, 1932, in Meridian, Miss.; son of Perry Harvey (a minister) and Daisy (an artist; maiden name, Yandell) Biddle; married Mary Sue Sherman (director of a day care home), May 31, 1958; children: Lindsay Louise, Perry Harvey III. *Education:* Davidson College, B.A., 1954; Union Theological Seminary, Richmond, Va., M.Div., 1958, Th.M., 1960; University of Ed-

& Co. Ltd., 40/42 William IV Street, London WC2 N4DD, England.

CAREER: Author.

WRITINGS: The Making of a King: The Early Years of James VI and I, Collins, 1968, Doubleday, 1969; *James V, King of Scots*, Collins, 1971; (contributor) Gordon Menzies, editor, *The Scottish Nation*, BBC Publications, 1972; *The Life and Times of Edward II*, Weidenfeld & Nicolson, 1973; *The Stewart Kingdom of Scotland, 1371-1603*, Weidenfeld & Nicolson, 1974, St. Martin's, 1975; *Kings and Queens of Scotland*, Weidenfeld & Nicolson, in press. Author of commissioned script, "King James VI of Scotland and I of England: An Evocation of the King and His Reigns in Both Kingdoms," for 1975 Edinburgh Festival. Contributor to *Journal of Inter-Disciplinary History, Scottish Field, In Britain*, and *Royal Stuart Viewpoint*.

WORK IN PROGRESS: A new biography of King James VI and I; an anthology of poems on Scottish history.

SIDELIGHTS: Caroline Bingham writes: "I am of Anglo-Scottish ancestry, and am a descendant of Duncan I, the Scottish King who was slain by Macbeth—a remote event made familiar by Shakespeare's tragedy of *Macbeth*. I think it is probable that the Scottish side of my heredity explains my predominant interest in Scottish history. In less personal terms, I feel that the history of the Scots (like that of the Welsh and Irish) is still profoundly unfamiliar to the English, and that the future relations of the different peoples who inhabit the British Isles could be rendered happier and more fruitful by greater mutual understanding, fostered by knowledge of the past. I should like to contribute to it if I could."

BIOGRAPHICAL/CRITICAL SOURCES: Weekend Scotsman, November 6, 1971.

* * *

BIRKENHEAD, Lord
See SMITH, Frederick Winston Furneaux

* * *

BIRO, Charlotte Slovak 1904-

PERSONAL: Born March 19, 1904, in Budapest, Hungary; daughter of Maurice and Aranka (Fenvesy) Slovak; married Zoltan Biro, June 24, 1925; children: Agnes Katalin Biro Rothblatt, Ann Marie Biro Rubendall. *Education:* Educated in Budapest, Hungary. *Address:* c/o 101 Productions, 834 Mission St., San Francisco, Calif. 94110.

CAREER: Has taught cooking at Wellesley University Club, Los Altos, and San Francisco Y.W.C.A.

WRITINGS: Flavors of Hungary: Memoirs and Recipes (with autobiographical introduction), 101 Productions, 1973.

SIDELIGHTS: Charlotte Biro, who speaks German and French in addition to her native Hungarian, writes: "My whole heart is in my life story—every word is true and so much more yet in me; millions of episodes of my—helas!—very eventful life. In spite of that I was not sure who would be really interested in stories of my jail experiences or world wars, revolutions and after all that to be a beginner and to adjust in a new world, until I got to write my book."

* * *

BJORN, Thyra Ferre 1905-1975

September 12, 1905—February 14, 1975; Swedish-born

American educator, lecturer, novelist. Obituaries: *New York Times*, February 20, 1975; *Publishers Weekly*, March 3, 1975; *AB Bookman's Weekly*, March 17, 1975. (*CA-5/6*)

* * *

BLACHLY, Frederick (Frank) 1881(?)-1975

1881(?)—March 13, 1975; American educator, political scientist, and author of works on government, administration, and law. Obituaries: *Washington Post*, March 17, 1975.

* * *

BLACK, David
See WAY, Robert E(dward)

* * *

BLACKBURN, Laurence Henry 1897-

PERSONAL: Born June 30, 1897, in Cleveland, Ohio; son of Edward (a salesman) and Ora Estelle (McMillan) Blackburn; married Ida Lea, June 30, 1922; children: Laurence Henry, Jr. *Education:* Baldwin-Wallace College, A.B., 1921; Boston University, S.T.B., 1924; further graduate study at Episcopal Theological School, 1937-38, and Harvard University, 1947-48. *Politics:* Republican. *Home:* 59 Taft Circle, Watertown, Conn. 06795.

CAREER: Minister of Methodist Episcopal churches in Boston, Mass., Ashland, Mass., and Barre, Vt., 1921-37; rector of Protestant Episcopal churches in Boston, Mass., Lowell, Mass., Cleveland, Ohio, and Akron, Ohio, 1938-64. Lecturer on spiritual healing in twenty states, Canada, and Europe. Trustee of Lowell Institution for Savings, 1939-52; president of Goodwill Industries, Lowell, 1939-52. *Military service:* U.S. Army, Medical Corps, 1917-19; became sergeant first class. *Member:* Institutes of Religion and Health, Newcomen Society, Guild of Health (England), Rotary International, International Order of St. Luke the Physician (president of board of directors, 1974—), Masons, Lambda Chi Alpha. *Awards, honors:* D.D. from Baldwin-Wallace College, 1946.

WRITINGS: God Wants You to Be Well, Morehouse-Barlow, 1974. Contributor to *Zion's Herald, Witness, Churchman, Living Church, Burrswood Herald*, and *Sharing*.

WORK IN PROGRESS: I Am Barabbas, a religious novel.

SIDELIGHTS: In 1960, Blackburn conducted a spiritual healing pilgrimage on a seven-week tour of Europe; he traveled in Europe and the Holy Land again in 1961.

* * *

BLACKER, C(arlos) P(aton) 1895-1975

December 8, 1895—1975; British psychiatrist and author of books on eugenics and population problems. Obituaries: *AB Bookman's Weekly*, May 26, 1975.

* * *

BLACKIE, Bruce L(othian) 1936-

PERSONAL: Born September 25, 1936, in Evanston, Ill.; son of William (a businessman) and Florence (Hewens) Blackie; married Lynn Smith, June 27, 1959; children: Heather Lynn, Holly Ann, Heidi Rebecca. *Education:* Attended California Institute of Technology, 1954-56; Wheaton College, Wheaton, Ill., B.A., 1958; Pittsburgh Theological Seminary, M.Div., 1961; Princeton Theological Seminary, Th.M., 1964. *Residence:* Akron, Ohio. *Office:* First Presbyterian Church, 647 East Market St., Akron, Ohio 44304.

CAREER: Ordained United Presbyterian minister, 1961; assistant pastor in Narberth, Pa., 1961-64; pastor in Plainfield, N.J., 1964-71; First Presbyterian Church, Akron, Ohio, pastor, 1971—. Member of Plainfield Human Relations Commission, 1966-70.

WRITINGS: Gods of Goodness: The Sophisticated Idolatry of the Main Line Churches, Westminster Press, 1975.

*   *   *

BLAIR, Jane N(emec)   1911-

PERSONAL: Born September 22, 1911, in Chicago, Ill.; daughter of Joseph (in advertising) and Josephine (Kral) Nemec; married John P. Blair (a zoologist), August 9, 1949. *Education:* Northwestern University, B.S., 1931, M.A., 1932; further graduate study at Chicago Teacher's College and New York University. *Home:* 10 Country Rd., Westport, Conn. 06880.

CAREER: Engaged in research, ghost writing, and book reviews, 1932-38; teacher of mathematics and English, and guidance counselor in public schools in Chicago, Ill., 1938-57; involved in travel and research of individual cases of child guidance, 1957-60; public school teacher in New York, N.Y., 1960-62; did research on nutrition and older adults, 1962-67; public school teacher in New York, N.Y., 1967-70; "enjoying company of senior citizens and writing," 1970—. *Member:* American Association of University Women, Women's City Club of New York.

WRITINGS: (With W. W. Hatfield and E. E. Lewis) *Senior English Activities*, American Book Co., 1938; (with Lewis) *Practice Activities in Senior English*, American Book Co., 1941; *Gourmet's Bland Diet Cookbook*, Pyramid, 1974; *After the Salad Days Cookbook: For the Older Cook*, Pyramid Press, in press. Contributor of articles, stories, and reviews to education journals and local publications.

WORK IN PROGRESS: A history of mathematics for the young student; *Meaningful Meals for the Happy Family*.

SIDELIGHTS: Jane Blair writes: "The vulnerability of the young and the old always has affected me and influenced my work in education and writing. In the past few years, noting the importance of diet to the well being of the elderly, I studied nutrition, combined my hobbies of cooking and writing, and came up with specialized cookbooks ... Kids and old duffers need all the help they can get. So do other defenseless species—that's why I'm a conservationist!"

*   *   *

BLAKE, Kathleen   1944-

PERSONAL: Born October 4, 1944, in Vernon, Tex.; daughter of Charles C. (a community college administrator) and Anne (a librarian; maiden name, Holthaus) Collins; married Jon W. Blake (a librarian), March 5, 1967. *Education:* California State University, San Diego, A.B., 1966; University of California, Los Angeles, M.A., 1967; University of California, San Diego, Ph.D., 1971. *Office:* Department of English, University of Washington, Seattle, Wash. 98195.

CAREER: San Diego Ballet Co., San Diego, Calif., dancer, 1962-65; University of Washington, Seattle, now

member of faculty of English. *Member:* Modern Language Association of America.

WRITINGS: Play, Games, and Sport: The Literary Works of Lewis Carroll, Cornell University Press, 1974. Contributor to journals.

*   *   *

BLAKE, Reed H(arris)   1933-

PERSONAL: Born January 31, 1933, in St. George, Utah; son of Reed E. (a teacher and coach) and Ethyl Andrea (Harris) Blake; married Katie Dean Hall (a teacher), September 8, 1959; children: R. Murray, Spencer H., Steven E., Kristin D., Laura K. *Education:* Dixie Junior College, A.S., 1953; Brigham Young University, B.S., 1957, M.S., 1959; Utah State University, Ph.D., 1969. *Politics:* Republican. *Religion:* Church of Jesus Christ of Latter-day Saints. *Home:* 2883 Indian Hills Dr., Provo, Utah 84601. *Office:* Department of Sociology, Brigham Young University, Provo, Utah 84602.

CAREER: Dixie Junior College, St. George, Utah, director of public relations, 1959-61; *Improvement Era*, Salt Lake City, Utah, editorial associate, 1961-63; Weber State College, Ogden, Utah, director of journalism, 1963-65; Utah State University, Logan, instructor in communications, 1965-66, instructor in sociology, 1966-67; Brigham Young University, Provo, Utah, associate professor of sociology, 1967—. Visiting professor at Mount Union College, 1973-74. Consultant to Utah State Hospital, 1968-70, Environment West, Inc., 1968—, and Communications Workshop, Inc., 1968—; member of board of directors of Utah Valley Environment Council, 1970—. *Military service:* U.S. Army, Engineers, 1953-55.

MEMBER: International Communication Association, National Council of College Publications (regional director, 1961-63), American Sociological Association, American Association of University Professors, Rocky Mountain Social Science Association (member of executive council, 1969-72), Western Social Science Association, Utah Journalism Association (member of executive council, 1959-60), Utah State Historical Society, Utah Academy of Science, Arts, and Letters, Utah Sociological Association, Kiwanis International (member of regional council, 1959-61), Kappa Tau Alpha, Sigma Xi, Blue Key, Dixie College Alumni Association.

WRITINGS: (Editor and author of introduction) *Wilford Woodruff*, Bookcraft, 1964; *Dictionary of Common Terms for the Behavioral Scientist*, Brigham Young University Continuing Education Press, 1968; (editor) *Studies in Communication: A Reader*, Brigham Young University Continuing Education Press, 1968; *Applied Sociology*, Brigham Young University Continuing Education Press, 1969; *Twenty-four Hours to Martyrdom*, Bookcraft, 1973; (with John R. Christiansen and W. Keith Warner) *Field Testing the Feasibility of Using Residential Shelters as Group Shelters. Appendix A: Colorado Field Test Communication Package*, Department of Sociology, Brigham Young University, 1974; (with Edwin O. Haroldsen) *A Taxonomy of Concepts in Communication*, Hastings House, 1975; (with John S. Harris) *Technical Writing for Social Scientists*, Nelson-Hall, 1975. Contributor to magazines and to journals in his field. Member of editorial board of *Family Perspective*, 1970—, and *Rocky Mountain Social Science Journal*, 1972—; executive editor, *Mountainwest Magazine*, 1975—.

BLANCE, Ellen 1931-

PERSONAL: Born June 26, 1931, in Newcastle, England; daughter of James Cooke (a career soldier) and Kate (Glover) Marshall; married Ian Blance (an architect), December 28, 1953; children: Andrew, Carl. *Education:* University of Durham, B.A., 1952; University of London, diploma in child development, 1969. *Home:* 299 Riverside Dr., New York, N.Y. 10025.

CAREER: British Infants' School, London, England, teacher, 1953-70; New York University, New York, N.Y., educational advisor, 1970-73; Bank Street College of Education, New York, N.Y., educational adviser, 1973—. Has worked as an educational consultant and workshop leader in New York, N.Y., Chicago, Ill., Los Angeles, Calif., and Philadelphia, Pa.

WRITINGS—Author, with Ann Cooke, of "Monster" series, published by Bowmar; all in 1972: *Monster Comes to the City; . . . Looks for a House; . . . Cleans His House; . . . Looks for a Friend; . . . on the Bus; . . . Meets Lady Monster; . . . Goes to the Museum; . . . Goes to School; . . . at School; . . . and the Magic Umbrella; . . . Has a Party; . . . Goes to the Zoo.* Also author of companion filmstrips and teacher's guide, 1975.

(With Ann Cooke) *Reading in the Open Classroom,* C.R.I., 1972; (with Ann Cooke) *Cooking in the Open Classroom,* C.R.I., 1972.

WORK IN PROGRESS: Language, Reading & Writing in Young Children; 12 additional books in the "Monster" series, with Ann Cooke.

*   *   *

BLANCHET, Eileen 1924-

PERSONAL: Born May 30, 1924, in Regina, Saskatchewan, Canada; daughter of Harry C. (a druggist) and Alma (Olson) Grose; married P. H. Tate Blanchet (a geological engineer), September 11, 1942; children: Darrall, Sherry (Mrs. Kirk Henderson), Lianne (Mrs. John Dudley), Bonnie (Mrs. Dana Johnston), Michael, Denise, Eric, Richard, Lori, Krista, Nona, Timothy, Jodi. *Education:* Attended business school in Saskatchewan and British Columbia. *Politics:* "I vote for the man not the party." *Religion:* "Basically Unitarian." *Home:* 22091 26th Ave., Langley, British Columbia V3A 4P4, Canada.

CAREER: Writer. *Member:* Association for Children with Learning Disabilities.

WRITINGS: When Your Child Can't Read: A Do-It-Yourself Program, Academic Therapy Publications, 1972. Author of weekly column, "Knowing Your Child," in *Fraser Valley News Herald,* 1973-75. Contributor to Features Syndicate, 1973-75; contributor of short stories and articles to CBC-Radio, and to small publications and religious magazines.

WORK IN PROGRESS: The Learning Disabled Child and *Who Made Peter?,* both with Peter Martin; *The Pink Palace,* a fictional biography of the eighteenth-century Peruvian actress La Perricholi, Michaela Villegas; three novelettes, *The Pot of Tea, Miss Mouse Will You Marry Me,* and *The Purloined Cash Box;* a novel about young Indian people, *Nothingness Is the Cloak You Wear;* a novel based partially on the pre-recorded history of man; a book on the occult, tentatively entitled *Ghosts, Quinkydinks and Tarot; This House of Never Mind.*

SIDELIGHTS: Eileen Blanchet told *CA* that she puts "much effort and time into understanding children with learning disabilities" because one of her children has a learning disability. She added: "Most of my published writing has been to enlighten the uninformed about children with problems and sometimes to suggest possible solutions. Awareness is itself a solution in many circumstances. Motivation? Shall we call it compulsion. I have been writing for some time around demands for attention and peanut butter sandwiches. I am unable to write frivolously so it is difficult to write merely for money. I cannot write what I cannot read."

*   *   *

BLANCO, Richard L(idio) 1926-

PERSONAL: Born May 12, 1926, in New York, N.Y.; son of Lidio F. (an advertising manager) and Eleanor (Boehm) Blanco; married Irene E. Edry, June 10, 1961; children: Richard L., Jr. *Education:* University of Maryland, B.S., 1950; Western Reserve University (now Case Western Reserve University), M.A., 1956, Ph.D., 1960. *Politics:* Democrat. *Religion:* "No preference." *Home:* 31 Lancet Way, Brockport, N.Y. 14420. *Office:* Department of History, State University of New York College at Brockport, Brockport, N.Y. 14420.

CAREER: Duquesne University, Pittsburgh, Pa., instructor in history, 1959-60; Marietta College, Marietta, Ohio, assistant professor, 1960-63, associate professor of history, 1963-65; Frostburg State College, Frostburg, Md., associate professor of history, 1965-67, head of department, 1965-67; Rollins College, Winter Park, Fla., associate professor of history, 1967-68; State University of New York College at Brockport, associate professor, 1968-71, professor of history, 1971—, director of Overseas Study Program at University of Aberdeen, 1970—. Visiting lecturer at Western Reserve University (now Case Western Reserve University), summer, 1963, and University of Southwestern Louisiana, summer, 1965. *Military service:* U.S. Army Air Forces, 1944-46. *Member:* American Historical Association, Society for Social History of Medicine. *Awards, honors:* Research grants from American Philosophical Society, 1967 and 1972, State University of New York Research Foundation, 1969, 1970, and 1974, and National Library of Medicine, 1974.

WRITINGS: (Contributor) Raymond F. Locke, editor, *Great Military Campaigns,* Mankind Publishing Co., 1970; *Wellington's Surgeon-General: Sir James McGrigor,* Duke University Press, 1974; (contributor) Joseph O. Baylen and Norbert J. Gossman, editors, *Biographical Dictionary of British Radicalism,* Harvester House, 1975. Contributor of articles and book reviews to professional journals including *History of Education Quarterly, Military Affairs,* and *Medical History.*

WORK IN PROGRESS: Dr. Jonathan Potts: Physician of the American Revolution.

*   *   *

BLAND, Hester Beth 1906-

PERSONAL: Born June 22, 1906, in Sullivan, Ind.; daughter of Hudson Anderson and Destine (Denney) Bland. *Education:* Indiana State University, B.S., 1942; Butler University, M.S., 1949; Indiana University, H.S.D., 1956. *Religion:* United Methodist. *Home:* 2511 Parkwood Drive, Apt. B, Indianapolis, Ind. 46224.

CAREER: Teacher in Sullivan County Public Schools,

1930-43, and Speedway Public Schools, 1945-47, both in Ind.; Indiana University School of Medicine, Division of Allied Health, Indianapolis, lecturer in health, 1950-71; Indiana University, Bloomington, lecturer in health, physical education, and education, and recreation, 1958-71, director of, or consultant to seminars and workshops on alcohol and health education, 1950-71; Indiana State University, Terre Haute, adjunct professor of health education, 1972—; Kent State University, Kent, Ohio, adjunct professor of health sciences, 1972—. Consultant to Indiana State Board of Health, 1947-71, and Glick & Lorwin, Inc., 1967—; coordinator of program on drug education, American Health Sciences Association and American Pharmaceutical Manufacturers Association, 1969-72. Visiting professor, Utah State University, Madison College, Harrison, Va., and Union College, Barbourville, Ky. *Member:* American School Health Association (fellow; member of governing council, 1967-71; president, 1972-73), American Public Health Association (fellow), American Association for Health, Physical Education, and Recreation (fellow; member of board of directors, 1957-60; president, Midwest Division, 1957), American Association of University Professors, American Association for the Advancement of Science, Society for State Directors, Indiana Association for Health, Physical Education, and Recreation (fellow; life member; president, 1963), Indiana Public Health Association (secretary, 1948-58; vice-president, 1958; president, 1960), Indiana Heart Association, Indiana Association of Health Educators, Indianapolis Social Health Association (member of board of directors, 1964-68), Eta Sigma Gamma, Delta Psi Kappa. *Awards, honors:* Honor awards, 1957, from Indiana Association for Health, Physical Education, and Recreation, and 1967, from national group; distinguished service awards, 1965, from Indiana Public Health Association, and 1970, from American School Health Association; LL.D. from Indiana State University, 1973.

WRITINGS: (Contributor) W. E. Weber, editor, *Health and the School Child*, C. C Thomas, 1964; (with Elizabeth Neilson and Austin Hill) *Healthful Living in Your Environment*, Laidlaw Brothers, 1972; (contributor) Glenn R. Knotts and J. P. McGovern, editors, *School Health Problems*, C. C Thomas, 1974.

Co-author of filmstrip series for Society for Visual Education (Chicago): "Critical Areas in Health Education" (six), "Physical Education Activities" (four), "Be Healthy—Go Safely" (fifteen). Writer of pamphlets and curriculum guides published by Indiana Department of Public Instruction, and Indiana State Board of Health. Contributor to *Journal of Health, Physical Education, and Recreation, Journal of School Health, Physical Educator, Teachers College Journal*, and other education and health journals. Member of editorial board, American Association for Health, Physical Education, and Recreation, 1957-60; consulting editor, *Journal of School Health*, 1975—.

WORK IN PROGRESS: Filmstrips in health education.

BIOGRAPHICAL/CRITICAL SOURCES: Indianapolis Sunday Star Magazine, April 25, 1971; *Indianapolis News*, January 6, 1972.

*   *   *

BLASER, Robin (Francis) 1925-

PERSONAL: Born May 18, 1925, in Denver, Colo.; naturalized Canadian citizen, 1972; son of Robert Augustus (a trucker) and Ina May Celestine (McCready) Blaser. *Education:* Attended Northwestern University, 1943, and College of Idaho, 1943-44; University of California, Berkeley, B.A., 1952, M.A., 1954, M.L.S., 1955. *Politics:* Socialist. *Religion:* "Imagination." *Home:* 2247 Bellevue Ave., West Vancouver, British Columbia V7V 1C5, Canada. *Office:* Department of English, Simon Fraser University, Burnaby, British Columbia, Canada.

CAREER: Harvard University, Library, Cambridge, Mass., librarian, 1955-59; California Historical Society, San Francisco, librarian, 1960; San Francisco State College (now University), Library, San Francisco, Calif., librarian, 1961-65; Simon Fraser University, Burnaby, British Columbia, professor of English, 1970—. Reader for Canada Council. *Awards, honors:* New York Poetry Society Award, 1962; Canada Council Arts Award, 1970-71.

WRITINGS—Poetry: *The Moth Poem*, Open Sapce, 1964, 2nd edition, 1964; *Les Chimeres* (versions of Gerard de Nerval), Open Space, 1965; *Cups*, Four Seasons Foundation, 1968; *The Holy Forest Section*, Caterpiller, 1970; *Image-Nations 1-12 & The Stadium of the Mirror*, Ferry Press, 1974; *Image-Nations 13-14*, Cobblestone, 1975; (editor and author of essay) *The Collected Books of Jack Spicer*, Black Sparrow Press, 1975; (editor and author of essay) *Troilus: A Play by Jack Spicer*, Black Sparrow Press, 1975. Work represented in anthologies, including *New Writing in the U.S.A.*, edited by Donald M. Allen and Robert Creeley, Penguin, 1967; *The Poetics of the New American Poetry*, edited by D. M. Allen and Warren Tallman, Grove, 1973. Also author of poems recorded on video-tape. Editor, *Pacific Nation*, 1967-69.

WORK IN PROGRESS: Editing the last lectures and early poems (1945-56) of Jack Spicer.

SIDELIGHTS: Blaser writes: "With *Image-Nation 12*, my own poetry has turned a corner where I work blindly and uneasily—toward an entangling that is the world and the beloved. Recently, with a few friends and poets, I've begun a book called *Astonishments*. It is taped in order to have a prose which is direct speech. This is really about the poets I've known—Spicer, Duncan, Wieners, Olson, Creeley, and I mix them with Dante or whatever astonishment."

*   *   *

BLAU, Sheldon Paul 1935-

PERSONAL: Born September 18, 1935, in New York, N.Y.; son of Saul (a writer) and Rose (Fleisler) Blau; married Bette Feingold (a movement therapist), September 2, 1957; children: Steven, Debra. *Education:* City College of the City University of New York, B.A., 1957; Albert Einstein College of Medicine, M.D., 1961, postdoctoral study, 1964-65. *Home:* 1825 James St., Merrick, N.Y. 11566. *Agent:* Dodi Schultz, 1939 Broadway, New York, N.Y. *Office:* 566 Broadway, Massapequa, N.Y. 11758.

CAREER: Montefiore Hospital and Medical Center, Bronx, N.Y., intern, 1961-62, resident in internal medicine, 1962-64; private practice of medicine in Long Island, N.Y., 1964-69; Nassau County Medical Center, Long Island, N.Y., chief of Arthritis Clinic, 1969—, director of rheumatic disease, 1973—, associate attending physician, 1970-73, attending physician, 1974—, member of executive committee of medical staff, 1972-74, vice-president of medical staff, 1975. Certified by National Board of Medical Examiners, 1961, and American Board of Internal Medicine, 1969, with subspecialty in rheumatology, 1972. Consultant in internal medicine at Massapequa General Hospital, 1967. Assistant clinical professor at Albert Einstein College of Medicine, 1970-75; associate professor of clinical medicine at State University of New York at Stonybrook, 1973—, member of admissions committee, 1975—. Attending physician at Albert Einstein College of Medicine, 1970—; visiting attending physician at Bronx Municipal Hospital, 1970—. Member of professorial advisory committee of National Arthritis Foundation, 1969—, governing member-at-large, 1973—.

MEMBER: American College of Physicians (fellow), American Medical Association, American Rheumatism Association, Harvey Society, New York Rheumatism Association, New York State Society of Internal Medicine, Nassau County Medical Society, Phi Beta Kappa. *Awards, honors:* National Institutes of Health fellowship in rheumatology, 1964-65; American Medical Association recognition awards, 1969, 1972.

WRITINGS: (With Dodi Schultz) *Arthritis: Complete Up-to-Date Facts for Patients and Their Families,* Doubleday, 1974; (with Schultz) *Lupus: The Body Against Itself,* Doubleday, 1975; (editor with Jerome Simson, and contributor) *Review Book in Internal Medicine,* Westbrook Medical Books, 1973. Co-author of subspecialty examination series; contributor to medical journals.

* * *

BLETTER, Rosemarie Haag 1939-

PERSONAL: Born February 27, 1939, in Heilbronn, Germany; daughter of Karl (a painter) and Johanna (Bischoff) Haag; married Robert Bletter (a director of a university press), 1965; children: Nathaniel. *Education:* Columbia University, B.S., 1962, Ph.D., 1973. *Office:* Department of Art History, Columbia University, New York, N.Y. 10027.

CAREER: Columbia University, New York, N.Y., assistant professor of architectural history, 1974—. *Member:* Society of Architectural Historians.

WRITINGS: (With Cervin Robinson) *Skyscraper Style: Art Deco New York,* Oxford University Press, 1975. Contributor to *Progressive Architecture* and *Society of Architectural Historians Journal.*

WORK IN PROGRESS: A monograph on Bruno Taut, completion expected in 1977; a monograph on Gottfried Semper, 1978.

* * *

BLEVINS, Leon W(ilford) 1937-

PERSONAL: Born October 2, 1937, in Brownfield, Tex.; son of Bernice Wilford Blevins (an automobile worker) and Virgie (Bevers) Blevins Dobkins; married Shannah Kathryne Pharr (a pre-school teacher of the deaf), August 28, 1960; children: Timothy Allan, Michael Keith, Shaleah Xan. *Education:* Texas Technological College (now Texas Tech University), student, 1956-57; Wayland Baptist College, B.A., 1961; Southwestern Baptist Theological Seminary, graduate student, 1961-63; University of Texas, El Paso, M.A., 1967; Universidad Anahuac, further graduate study, summer, 1973. *Home:* 10305 Ashwood, El Paso, Tex. 79925. *Office:* Department of Political Science, El Paso Community College, El Paso, Tex. 79904.

CAREER: Ordained minister in Southern Baptist Convention, 1957; Philadelphia Girls' Home, Fort Worth, Tex., director, 1961; high school English and history teacher in Deming, N.M., 1963-64, and Holtville, Calif., 1964-65; Texas Tech University, Lubbock, instructor in government, 1967-70; West Texas State University, Canyon, instructor in government, 1970-72; El Paso Community College, El Paso, Tex., instructor in political science, 1972—. Pastor of Southern Baptist churches in Texas, New Mexico, and California, 1962-70; chaplain of Interfaith Chapel at Texas State Technological Institute, 1971-72. Acted in "Texas," outdoor musical drama at Palo Duro Canyon State Park, summers, 1971-72, and many college productions. Delegate to Texas State Democratic Convention, 1972, 1974; member of El Paso Citizens Advisory Committee on Constitutional Revision, 1973-74; Member of El Paso Bicentennial Steering Committee, 1975-76; chairman of issues committee of Progressive Democrats of El Paso, 1975. *Member:* Alpha Chi, Alpha Psi Omega, Alpha Mu Gamma, Phi Alpha Theta, Pi Sigma Alpha, Pi Gamma Mu.

WRITINGS: The Young Voter's Manual: A Topical Dictionary of American Government and Politics, Littlefield, 1973. Author and producer of one-act play, "Backstage," first performed in Deming, N.H., 1964. Contributor to *Baptist Standard.*

WORK IN PROGRESS: Revising *The Young Voter's Manual*; *The Texas Voter's Manual: A Topical Dictionary of Texas Government and Politics,* with Lyle Brown and Eugene Jones; *The Topical Dictionary of American History,* with John R. Harley; "And Jesus Said . . .," a church drama, with wife, Shannah Blevins.

BIOGRAPHICAL/CRITICAL SOURCES: Amarillo Daily News, July 7, 1971.

* * *

BLISH, James (Benjamin) 1921-1975

May 23, 1921—July 30, 1975; American-born newspaper editor and author of science fiction novels, short stories, poetry, plays, and criticism. Obituaries: *New York Times,* July 31, 1975; *Washington Post,* August 1, 1975; *AB Bookman's Weekly,* September 8, 1975. (CA-3)

* * *

BLOCK, Walter (Edward) 1941-

PERSONAL: Born August 21, 1941, in New York, N.Y.; son of Abraham (an accountant) and Ruth (Peps) Block. *Education:* Brooklyn College of the City University of New York, B.A., 1964; Columbia University, Ph.D., 1972. *Politics:* "Libertarian." *Religion:* None. *Residence:* New York, N.Y.

CAREER: National Bureau of Economic Research, Washington, D.C., research analyst, 1967; Bronx Community College of the City University of New York, Bronx, N.Y., instructor in economics, 1967-68; State University of New York at Stony Brook, instructor in economics, 1968; Rutgers University, New Brunswick, N.J., assistant professor of economics, 1968-71; Bernard M. Baruch College of the City University of New York, New York, N.Y., assistant professor of economics, 1971-74; *Business Week* (magazine), New York, N.Y., assistant editor, 1974-75; freelance writer, 1975—. Instructor at New York University, 1970, and City College of the City University of New York, 1972. *Member:* American Economic Association.

WRITINGS: Defending the Undefendable: Pimps, Prostitutes, Libelers, Slanderers, Blackmailers, and Other Heroes in the Rogues Gallery of American Society, Fleet Press, 1975. Contributor to business, tax, and real estate journals.

BLODGETT, Beverley 1926-

PERSONAL: Born September 7, 1926, in Oregon City, Ore.; daughter of George Homer (a businessman) and Bertha Louise (Hartke) Buchholz; married Forrest Blodgett (a college professor), December 21, 1946; children: Cherine (Mrs. Jon R. Klein), Candis (Mrs. Mark Schaeffer), Clinton. *Education:* Attended Linfield College, 1943, 1944. *Politics:* Republican. *Religion:* Episcopal. *Residence:* Dayton, Ore.

CAREER: Oregon City Enterprise, Oregon City, Ore., society reporter and feature writer, 1941-42; Blodgett Enterprises, Inc., McMinnville, Ore., vice-president, 1972—. *Member:* Federation of Republican Women, McMinnville Duplicate Bridge Club, Michelbook Country Club, Reserve Officer's Association Ladies Club, McMinnville Association of the Arts.

WRITINGS: A Picture or Two: The Story of Ray Eyerly, Oakwood Press, 1974. Contributor of articles to newspapers.

WORK IN PROGRESS: Morning Gold.

AVOCATIONAL INTERESTS: Travel, oil painting (has exhibited in national and international shows), china painting, sculpture.

* * *

BLOOM, Erick Franklin 1944-

PERSONAL: Born September 3, 1944, in Philadelphia, Pa.; son of Jack (a food broker) and Meye (Levin) Bloom; *Education:* Attended Pennsylvania State University, 1962-63; Moravian College, B.A., 1966; graduate study at Syracuse University, 1966, Washington State University, 1967, and Indiana State University, 1967-68; West Chester State College, M.Ed., 1974. *Residence:* Merion, Pa. *Address:* P.O. Box 18831, Philadelphia, Pa. 19119.

CAREER: National Teacher Corps, Gary, Ind., teacher of experimental English, and program director, 1966-67; Logan School, Philadelphia, Pa., teacher of content skills to handicapped retarded children, 1967; Welsh Valley Junior High, Narberth, Pa., teacher of English and math to underachievers, and director of drama department, 1967-68; Upsal Day School, Philadelphia, musical therapist, 1968-69; Philadelphia Board of Education, teacher of experimental English, 1969—. Member of Big Brothers of America, 1968—; program director of North Light Boy's Club, 1969. *Member:* American Personnel and Guidance Association, Phil Delta Kappa, Phi Sigma Tau (former vice-president).

WRITINGS: Bloomism (poetry), Windy Row Press, 1972. Writer of column, "Franklin Makes Waves," and associate editor, *Suburbia Weekly*, 1971-72.

WORK IN PROGRESS: Creative English Handbooks for Macmillan; editing *Big City Survival Handbook*; a documentary film showing society's affect on children; several children's plays complete with musical scores; a serial cartoon designed for the inner city child; a movie script, "Shipwreck Nine."

SIDELIGHTS: Bloom told *CA:* "I have been influenced by many writers/poets/philosophers: from John Fowles' *The Magus* and Stephen Crane's poetry to Carl Rogers' soft approach to understanding people—to the heavier works of Hesse, and Gurjieff, and Ouspensky. . . . I have found contentment within myself—and I seek to express my programs for educational reforms, my poetry, my to-be novel, as one might look at a painting one has done. I can appreciate reading back on a part of my growth: hopefully, others might grow or learn as well."

* * *

BLOOMFIELD, Harold H. 1944-

PERSONAL: Born October 8, 1944, in New York, N.Y.; son of Max (an accountant) and Fridl (Waldman) Bloomfield. *Education:* University of Pittsburgh, B.S. (cum laude), 1965; State University of New York, Downstate Medical Center, M.D. (honors in public health and psychiatry), 1969. *Religion:* Jewish. *Office:* Institute of Psychophysiological Medicine, 1662 East Main St., El Cajon, Calif. 92021.

CAREER: Kaiser Foundations Hospital, San Francisco, Calif., intern, 1969-70; Yale University School of Medicine, New Haven, Conn., psychiatric resident, 1970-73; Institute of Psychophysiological Medicine, El Cajon, Calif., director of psychiatry, 1974—; Maharishi International University, Fairfield, Iowa, professor of psychiatry, 1974—. Mental health consultant to West Haven Board of Education, West Haven, Conn., 1972-73. *Member:* American Psychiatric Association, Association for the Advancement of Behavior Therapy.

WRITINGS: (Contributor) J. White, editor, *What is Meditation?*, Anchor, 1974; (contributor) D. W. Orme-Johnson, and J. Farrow, editors, *Scientific Research on the Transcendental Meditation Program: Collected Papers*, Maharishi International University Press, Volume I, 1975; (with M. P. Cain, D. T. Jaffee, and R. B. Kory) *TM: Discovering Inner Energy and Overcoming Stress*, introduction by R. Buckminster Fuller, Delacorte, 1975. Contributor to *Behavior Therapy, Psychotherapy, Medical Dimensions*, and other journals.

WORK IN PROGRESS: A book, *Why Not Happiness?*, expected in 1976; a report on his clinical experience using Transcendental Meditation as therapy.

SIDELIGHTS: Bloomfield studied with Maharishi Mahesh Yogi, the proponent of Transcendental Meditation, in 1973 and 1974. Bloomfield told *CA* that in 1973 he became the first American psychiatrist to be made a teacher of Transcendental Meditation, and that he is currently involved with using Transcendental Meditation in conjunction with medical and psychiatric techniques with his parents.

Bloomfield has lectured throughout the U.S., Canada, and Europe. He is competent in German and Hebrew. *Avocational interests:* Tennis, swimming, basketball, and travel.

* * *

BLUMBERG, Robert S(tephen) 1945-

PERSONAL: Born August 23, 1945, in San Francisco, Calif.; son of Harry and Mary (Abrams) Blumberg; married Marion Allen Koerper (a physician), August 19, 1973. *Education:* Attended University of Bordeaux, 1965-66; University of California, Davis, B.A., 1967; University of California, San Francisco, M.D., 1971. *Residence:* San Francisco, Calif. *Office:* U.S. Public Health Service, San Francisco, Calif.

CAREER: U.S. Public Health Service, San Francisco, Calif., physician with rank of lieutenant commander, 1971—. Extension instructor in wine appreciation, University of California, San Francisco, 1970-73; wine consultant and lecturer at San Francisco Wine Co., 1973—. *Member:* American Board of Internal Medicine, Commissioned Officers Association of United States Public Health Service, Delta Upsilon.

WRITINGS: (With Hurst Hannum) *The Fine Wines of California*, Doubleday, 1971, revised edition, 1973; (with Hannum) *Brandies and Liqueurs of the World*, Doubleday, in press.

* * *

BLUNSDEN, John (Beresford) 1930-

PERSONAL: Born February 5, 1930, in Bristol, England; son of Archibald Beresford (an engineer) and Adeline (Hillier) Blunsden; married Pauline Richardson, April 1, 1961; children: Nicholas. *Education:* Educated in private schools in England. *Home and office:* 56 Fitzjames Ave., Croydon, Surrey, England.

CAREER: Saunders Abbott Ltd., Beckenham, Kent, England, sales manager, 1951-56; editor for National Trade Press Ltd., and *Motoring News*, both London, England, 1957-61; *Motor News and Features*, Croydon, Surrey, England, editor and writer, 1961-69; Motor Racing Publications Ltd., Croydon, managing director, 1969—. Managing director of *Connoisseur Carbooks*, Chiswick, London, 1974—. Free-lance broadcaster on motoring and motor racing subjects. *Military service:* British Army, Royal Engineers, 1948-50; became sergeant. *Member:* International Racing Press Association, Guild of Motoring Writers (member of committee, 1967—; chairman, 1973), Steering Wheel Club. *Awards, honors:* Motor sport driving awards.

WRITINGS: Formula Junior, Motor Racing Publications, 1961; (with David Phipps) *Such Sweet Thunder*, Motor Racing Publications, 1971; (with Peter Browning) *The Jensen Healey Stories*, Motor Racing Publications, 1974. Motor racing correspondent for *Times*. Editor of *Motoring News*, 1959-61, *Motor Racing Year* annual publications, 1961-69, and *Motor Racing and Sportscar*, 1961-70; European editor of *Sports Car Graphic*, 1966-71.

WORK IN PROGRESS: Research on automotive history and contemporary and historical motor sports subjects.

SIDELIGHTS: Blunsden is deeply involved in motoring. In the early 1960's he carried through a series of racing car track tests on more than a hundred cars.

* * *

BOALT, (Hans) Gunnar 1910-

PERSONAL: Born August 26, 1910, in Stockholm, Sweden; son of Anton (a civil servant) and Ruda (Brodin) Boalt; married Carin Akerman, June 1, 1935 (divorced, 1957); married Pian Halden, August 8, 1957 (divorced, 1973); married Berit Petterson, April 27, 1974; children: (first marriage) Siv (Mrs. Jorgen Boethius), Birgitta (Mrs. Erik Alexius), Kaj (Mrs. Thomas Fischer), Ake, Arne; (second marriage) Margareta. *Education:* University of Stockholm, Ph.D., 1947. *Religion:* Lutheran. *Home:* Bredangsvagen 208, 127 32 Stockholm, Sweden. *Office:* Department of Sociology, University of Stockholm, 104 05 Stockholm, Sweden.

CAREER: High school teacher of biology in public schools in Stockholm, Sweden, 1939-47; University of Stockholm, Stockholm, Sweden, assistant professor, 1948-54, professor of sociology, 1954—, dean of social science faculty, 1952-60, 1966-72. Adjunct professor at Southern Illinois University, 1967. Chairman of Central Union for Social Work, 1956-72; representative of Sweden to Scandinavian Board for Studies in Alcohol, 1957-65; Royal Social Board, member of science council, 1963—.

WRITINGS: Family and Marriage, McKay, 1965; (with Torsten Husen) *Educational Research*, Wiley, 1968; *The Sociology of Research*, Southern Illinois University Press, 1969; (with Robert Erikson) *European Orders of Chivalry*, Southern Illinois University, 1971; (with Herman Lantz) *Resources and Production of University Departments*, Wiley, 1971; (with Lantz and Helena Herlin) *The Academic Pattern*, Almqvist & Wiksell, 1972; (with Lantz, Torgny Segerstedt and Paul Lindblom) *Communication and Communication Barriers in Sociology*, Almqvist & Wiksell, 1975.

WORK IN PROGRESS: Research on the social role of researchers, and on the sociology of academic career patterns.

* * *

BOARD, C(hester) Stephen 1942-

PERSONAL: Born April 4, 1942, in Charleston, W.Va.; son of Chester Charles and Edith (Russell) Board; married Nancy Davis, June 13, 1964; children: Mary, Perry. *Education:* Philadelphia College of Bible, B.S., 1965; Wheaton College, Wheaton, Ill., M.A., 1966; Chicago Theological Seminary, B.D., 1968. *Politics:* Republican. *Home:* 205 MacIntosh Rd., Cherry Hill, N.J. 08003. *Office: Eternity Magazine*, 1816 Spruce St., Philadelphia, Pa. 19103.

CAREER: Inter-Varsity Christian Fellowship, Chicago, Ill., campus staff member, 1968-71; *His*, Downers Grove, Ill., editor, 1971-75; *Eternity Magazine*, Philadelphia, Pa., executive editor, 1975—.

WRITINGS: Doubt, Inter-Varsity Press, 1972; (editor) *HIS Guide to Life on Campus*, Inter-Varsity Press, 1973; *HIS Guide to Sex, Singleness, and Marriage*, Inter-Varsity Press, 1974. Contributor to religious periodicals.

AVOCATIONAL INTERESTS: Photography.

* * *

BOBBE, Dorothie de Bear 1905-1975

March 1, 1905—March 19, 1975; American newspaper and publishing editor and author of biographies of American historical figures. Obituaries: *New York Times*, March 20, 1975; *AB Bookman's Weekly*, April 21, 1975. (*CA*-25/28)

* * *

BOBROW, Davis Bernard 1936-

PERSONAL: Born September 2, 1936, in Boston, Mass.; son of Robert (an accountant) and Elizabeth (Gelfand) Bobrow. *Education:* University of Chicago, B.A. (general education), 1955, B.A. (communication), 1956; Queen's College, Oxford, B.A. (philosophy-politics-economics), 1958; Massachusetts Institute of Technology, Ph.D., 1962. *Home:* 256 Eighth St. S.E., Washington, D.C. 20003. *Office:* Department of Government and Politics, University of Maryland, College Park, Md. 20742.

CAREER: Princeton University, Princeton, N.J., lecturer, 1961-62, assistant professor of politics and research associate of Center of International Studies, 1962-64; Oak Ridge National Laboratory, Oak Ridge, Tenn., senior social scientist, 1964-68; Advanced Research Projects Agency, Washington, D.C., acting director of behavorial sciences office, 1968-70; Office of Director of Defense Research and Engineering, Washington, D.C., special assistant for behavioral and social sciences, 1968-70; University of Minnesota, Minneapolis, professor of political science and public affairs and director of Quigley Center of International Studies, 1970-74; University of Maryland, College Park, professor and chairman of department of government and politics, 1974—. Professorial lecturer at School for Advanced International Studies, Johns Hopkins University, 1970. Member of U.S. Air Force Scientific Advisory Board, 1971—, Defense Science Board, 1972—, international advisory board, Korean Institute of International Studies, 1972—, and National Academy of Sciences-National Research Council Committee on Energy and the Environment, 1974—.

MEMBER: American Political Science Association, American Association for the Advancement of Science, Peace Science Society (councillor, 1972—), International Studies Association (chairman of research commission, 1971-73). *Awards, honors:* Rhodes scholar, 1956-58.

WRITINGS: (Editor and contributor) *Components of Defense Policy*, Rand McNally, 1965; (editor with J. L. Schwartz and contributor) *Computers and the Policy-Making Community: Applications to International Relations*, Prentice-Hall, 1968; (editor and contributor) *Weapons System Decisions: Political and Psychological Perspectives on Continental Defense*, Praeger, 1969; *International Relations: New Approaches*, Free Press, 1972.

Contributor: Tang Tsou, editor, *China, the United States, and Asia*, Volume II, University of Chicago Press, 1968; M. R. Van Gils, editor, *The Perceived Role of the Military*, Rotterdam University Press, 1971; Richard L. Morritt, editor, *Communication in International Politics*, University of Illinois Press, 1972; Raymond Tanter and Richard H. Ullman, editors, *Theory and Policy in International Relations*, Princeton University Press, 1972; Kenneth F. Gordon and Walter A. Hahn, editors, *Assessing the Future and Policy Planning*, Gordon & Breach, 1973; John P. Lovell and Phillip S. Kroneberg, editors, *The New Civil-Military Relations*, Transaction Books, 1974; W. Phillips Davison and F.T.C. Yu, editors, *New Directions in Mass Communications Research*, Praeger, 1974; Peter A. Toma, Andrew Gyorgy, and Robert S. Jordan, editors, *Basic Issues in International Relations*, 2nd edition (Bobrow did not contribute to earlier edition), Allyn & Bacon, 1974; Nazil Choucri and Thomas W. Robinson, editors, *Forecasting in International Relations*, W. H. Freeman, in press; Louis R. Beres and Harry R. Targ, editors, *Planning for Global Design: Essays on the Study of Alternative World Futures*, Praeger, in press.

Contributor of more than thirty articles and reviews to *Papers* of Peace Research Society, *World Politics, American Behavioral Scientist*, and other journals. Editorial associate, *Public Opinion Quarterly*, 1963-64; member of advisory board, *Policy Sciences*, 1969—; member of editorial board, *Journal of Conflict Resolutions*, 1972—; associate editor, *International Interactions: A Transnational Multidisciplinary Journal*, 1972.

WORK IN PROGRESS: Writing on anticipation and management of international crises, on policies for resource cartels, and on governing a steady state society.

* * *

BOCK, Joanne 1940-

PERSONAL: Born August 29, 1940, in New Haven, Conn.; daughter of William Lawrence (a salesman) and Anne (a secretary; maiden name, Mauro) Bock. *Education:* College of New Rochelle, B.A., 1962; Catholic University of America, M.A., 1968; State University of New York at Oneonta, M.A., 1970; University of Michigan, M.A., 1975, working toward doctoral degree. *Religion:* Roman Catholic. *Home:* 15021 James St., Oak Park, Mich. 48237. *Office:* 71 East Ferry St., Detroit, Mich. 48202.

CAREER: Aaron Carter Museum of Western Art, Fort Worth, Tex., photo archivist, 1969-70; Smithsonian Institution, Washington, D.C., coordinator in National Portrait Gallery, 1970-71, museum specialist in Division of Ethnic and Western Cultural History, 1971-73; South East Michigan Regional Ethnic Heritage Studies Center, Detroit, cultural developer, 1974—. Cataloger at New Haven Colony Historical Society, 1967-68 docent at Yale University Art Gallery, 1968. *Member:* International Institute, American Association of Museums, College Art Association, American Folklore Society, American Studies Association, American Association for State and Local History. *Awards, honors:* Seminar for Historical Administrators grant, summer, 1968; Andrew Mellon Foundation grant, 1973, for publication of color plates in *Pop Wiener: Naive Painter*.

WRITINGS: Pop Wiener: Naive Painter, University of Massachusetts Press, 1974. Contributor to *Connoisseur* and *Antiques.*

WORK IN PROGRESS: A book on Romanian-American folk art, completion expected in 1976.

AVOCATIONAL INTERESTS: Woodcarving, woodburning, watercolor painting.

BIOGRAPHICAL/CRITICAL SOURCES: Fort Worth Star Telegram, October 26, 1969; *New Haven Register*, March 24, 1974; *Detroit News*, January 2, 1975.

* * *

BODO, Murray 1937-

PERSONAL: Born June 10, 1937, in Gallup, N.M.; son of Louis John (a politician) and Pauline (Bonan) Bodo. *Education:* Duns Scotus College, B.A., 1960; Xavier University, Cincinnati, Ohio, M.A., 1967. *Politics:* Democrat. *Home and office:* 10290 Mill Rd., Cincinnati, Ohio 45231.

CAREER: Ordained Roman Catholic priest of Franciscan Order (O.F.M.), 1964; St. Francis Seminary, Cincinnati, Ohio, teacher of English, 1965—, spiritual director, 1966—, head of department of English, 1970—, vice-rector, 1972.

WRITINGS: Francis: The Journey and the Dream, St. Anthony Messenger Press, 1972; *Walk in Beauty: Meditations from the Desert*, St. Anthony Messenger Press, 1974. Contributor of poems to *St. Anthony Messenger.*

WORK IN PROGRESS: Song of the Sparrow, a spiritual journal; *Four Loves*, a book of poems, completion expected in 1978.

SIDELIGHTS: Bodo grew up in Gallup, N.M., the closest town to the Navajo Reservation. As a Franciscan he spent summers working at St. Michaels, central mission for the Navajo apostolate. His second book describes, with the aid of photographs, the Navajo country and the people who live there.

* * *

BOHN, Frank 1878-1975

1878—July 29, 1975; American journalist, lecturer, and author of works on economics and international relations. Obituaries: *Washington Post*, August 1, 1975.

BOISSEVAIN, Jeremy 1928-

PERSONAL: Born August 5, 1928, in London, England; son of Cornelis Alfred (a businessman) and Mildred (Goerwitz) Boissevain; married Inga Otterstrand, March 29, 1952; children: Ieneke, Liet, Maria, Anna. *Education:* Sorbonne, University of Paris, Diplome, 1951; Haverford College, B.A., 1952; London School of Economics and Political Science, Ph.D., 1962. *Home:* Koningslaan 45, Bussum, Holland. *Office:* Department of Social Anthropology, University of Amsterdam, Keizersgracht 397, Amsterdam, Holland.

CAREER: CARE (Cooperative for American Relief Everywhere), New York, N.Y., chief of mission in the Philippines, Japan, India, and Malta, 1953-58; Centro Regionale per lo Sviluppo di Comunita, Sicily, research director, 1962-63; University of Montreal, Montreal, Quebec, assistant professor of social anthropology, 1963-65; University of Sussex, Brighton, England, lecturer in sociology, 1965-66; University of Amsterdam, Amsterdam, Holland, professor of social anthropology, 1966—. *Military service:* U.S. Army, 1946-48.

MEMBER: American Anthropological Association, Royal Anthropological Institute of Great Britain, Commonwealth Association of Social Anthropologists, Association of Sociologists and Anthropologists of the Netherlands, Malta Union Club. *Awards, honors:* Research grants from Colonial Social Research Council, 1960-61, American Philosophical Society, 1963—, Canadian Social Science Research Council, 1964—, U.S. Social Science Research Council, 1965—, Wenner-Gren Foundation for Anthropological Research, 1967—, and Netherlands Association for Pure Scientific Research, 1968—; University of Amsterdam research fellowship, 1973-74.

WRITINGS: Saints and Fireworks: Religion and Politics in Rural Malta, Humanities Press, 1965, revised edition, 1969; *Hal-Farrug: A Village in Malta*, Holt, 1969; *The Italians of Montreal: Social Adjustment in a Plural Society*, Information Canada, 1970; (editor with J. Clyde Mitchell) *Network Analysis: Studies in Human Interaction*, Mouton & Co., 1973; *Friends of Friends: Networks, Manipulators, and Coalitions*, St. Martin's, 1974. Contributor to *Journal of Commonwealth Political Studies, New Society, American Anthropologist, Man*, and other anthropological journals.

WORK IN PROGRESS: Beyond the Community: Studies in European Society, a collection of thirteen essays on European social processes and trends; a book on social developments in Malta based on research and personal experiences over the past eighteen years in Malta.

AVOCATIONAL INTERESTS: Dinghy sailing, wine making, hiking.

* * *

BOLCH, Ben W(ilsman) 1938-

PERSONAL: Born August 22, 1938, in Danville, Ill.; son of Carl E. (a businessman) and Juanita (Newton) Bolch; married Anne Whisnant (a teacher), August 26, 1961; children: Suzanne E. *Education:* Emory University, B.B.A., 1960, M.A., 1962; University of North Carolina, Chapel Hill, Ph.D., 1966. *Home:* 1619 East Main St., Murfreesboro, Tenn. 37130. *Office:* Department of Economics, Vanderbilt University, Nashville, Tenn. 37235.

CAREER: Vanderbilt University, Nashville, Tenn., assistant professor, 1966-70, associate professor of economics,

1970—. Member of board of directors, Bolch Enterprises, Inc. *Military service:* U.S. Army Reserve, 1960-61. *Member:* American Economic Association, American Statistical Association (president, Middle Tennessee chapter, 1969-70), Beta Gamma Sigma, Sigma Alpha Epsilon. *Awards, honors:* Ford Foundation fellowship, 1965-66.

WRITINGS: (With F. E. Croxton and D. J. Cowden) *Practical Business Statistics*, Prentice-Hall, 1969; (with C. J. Huang) *Multivariate Statistical Methods for Business and Economics*, Prentice-Hall, 1974. Contributor to journals in his field.

* * *

BOLGER, Philip C(unningham) 1927-
(Corporal Trim)

PERSONAL: Born December 3, 1927, in Gloucester, Mass. *Education:* Educated in public schools in Gloucester, Mass., and private school in North Andover, Mass. *Politics:* "Libertarian." *Religion:* "Olympian." *Home and office:* 250 Washington St., Gloucester, Mass. 01930.

CAREER: Self-employed boat designer. *Military service:* U.S. Army, 1946-47.

WRITINGS: Small Boats, International Marine Publishing, 1973. Contributor, sometimes under pseudonym Corporal Trim, of about fifty articles on boats and boating to magazines.

WORK IN PROGRESS: Simple Boats, for International Marine Publishing: *Admiral of Aragon*, a biography of Roger de Lauria; "Artemesia," a screenplay about the Lady of Salamis.

* * *

BOLING, Katharine (Singleton) 1933-

PERSONAL: Born July 8, 1933, in Florence, S.C.; daughter of Burt Newman (an army officer) and Katherine (Atkinson) Singleton; married William D. Boling, Jr. (a planter), August 31, 1957; children: William III, Michelle, Christopher, Stephanie, Jonathan, Rebecca, Celeste. *Education:* Attended University of Wisconsin, 1951-52, and University of Alaska, 1953; Coker College, A.B., 1955; University of North Carolina, M.A., 1957. *Home address:* Box #456, Pamplico, S.C. 29583.

CAREER: KFRB-Radio, Fairbanks, Alaska, continuity writer and broadcaster, 1953-54; Francis Marion College, Florence, S.C., lecturer in English literature and composition, 1974—; Florence Darlington Technical College, Florence, S.C., lecturer in English literature and composition, 1974—. Professional raconteur of Sea Island stories in Gullah dialect; member of board of visitors, Coker College, 1974—. *Member:* Florence County Historical Society (life member), Long Bluff Historical and Recreational Society (member of board of directors, 1973—).

WRITINGS: A Piece of the Fox's Hide, Sandlapper Press, 1972; (author of introduction) *The Last of the Bighams*, State Printing Co., 1973; *Country Bunnies*, State Printing Co., 1973; "Miss Carrie" (one-act play), first produced at University of North Carolina, 1956. Contributor to Banner Publications.

WORK IN PROGRESS: Swan's Nest, a novel; *Under an Old Camelia Bush*, a book of verse.

SIDELIGHTS: Katherine Boling writes: "Southern literature has, hopefully, found a new dimension. I hope to be part of that expression." *Avocational interests:* Sailing.

BIOGRAPHICAL/CRITICAL SOURCES: Palmetto Bookshelf, September, 1975.

* * *

BOLTON, Isabel
   See MILLER, Mary Britton

* * *

BOND, Brian 1936-

PERSONAL: Born April 17, 1936, in Marlow, Buckinghamshire, England. *Education:* Worcester College, Oxford, B.A. (honors), 1959; King's College, University of London, M.A., 1962. *Office:* Department of War Studies, King's College, University of London, Strand, London WC2R 2LS, England.

CAREER: University of Exeter, Exeter, England, lecturer in history, 1961-62; University of Liverpool, Liverpool, England, lecturer in history, 1962-66; University of London, King's College, London, England, lecturer in war studies, 1966—. Visiting professor at University of Western Ontario, 1972-73; visiting lecturer at U.S. Naval War College, 1972-74. *Military service:* British Army, Royal Artillery, 1952-54; became second lieutenant. *Member:* International Institute for Strategic Studies, Royal United Services Institute (member of council), United Oxford and Cambridge Club.

WRITINGS: (Editor) *Victorian Military Campaigns*, Hutchinson, 1967; *The Victorian Army and the Staff College*, Eyre Methuen, 1972; (editor) *Chief of Staff*, Leo Cooper, Volume I, 1973, Volume II, 1974; *France and Belgium: 1939-1960*, David-Poynter, 1975.

Author of television film "The Conduct of War in the Twentieth Century," for Open University. Editor of *War and Society Yearbook*, 1975—.

WORK IN PROGRESS: The Military Thought and Influence of Sir Basil Liddell Hart.

* * *

BONE, Edith 1889(?)-1975

1889(?)—February 14, 1975; Physician, translator, interpreter, and author. Obituaries: *AB Bookman's Weekly*, March 17, 1975.

* * *

BONE, Jesse F. 1916-

PERSONAL: Born June 15, 1916, in Tacoma, Wash.; son of Homer Truett (a U.S. Senator and federal judge) and Eva (a secretary; maiden name, Wildt) Bone; married Jayne M. Clark, January 20, 1942 (divorced October, 1946); married Felizitas Margarete Endter (a teacher), June 15, 1950; children: (first marriage) Janice Lee (Mrs. Michael Vaughan), (second marriage) Brigitta Marianne (Mrs. Ronald Fernandez), Michael Jay, David F. *Education:* Washington State University, B.A., 1937, B.S., 1949, D.V.M., 1950; Oregon State University, M.S., 1953. *Politics:* "Undecided." *Religion:* Agnostic. *Home:* 3329 Southwest Cascade Ave., Corvallis, Ore. 97330. *Agent:* Scott Meredith Literary Agency, Inc., 580 Fifth Ave., New York, N.Y. 10036. *Office:* Department of Veterinary Medicine, Oregon State University, Corvallis, Ore. 97331.

CAREER: Oregon State University, Corvallis, Ore., instructor, 1950-52, assistant professor, 1953-57, associate professor, 1958-65, professor of veterinary medicine,

1965—. *Military service:* U.S. Army, 1937-46; served in Pacific and Asiatic campaigns; became lieutenant colonel. U.S. Army Reserve, 1946-66. *Member:* American Veterinary Medical Association, American Association for Laboratory Animal Science, Royal Society of Health, Science Fiction Writers of America, American College of Veterinary Toxicologists, Oregon Veterinary Medical Association, Sigma Xi, Phi Kappa Phi, Triad, Corvallis Chamber of Commerce. *Awards, honors:* Veterinarian of the Year Award from Washington State University, 1959; Fulbright lecturer in Egypt, 1965-66; postdoctoral award from U.S. Department of Health, Education and Welfare, 1969-70.

WRITINGS: (Editor) *Canine Medicine*, American Veterinary Publications, 1959, 2nd edition, 1962; *Animal Anatomy and Physiology*, Oregon State University Bookstore, 1961, 4th edition, 1975; (editor with others) *Equine Medicine and Surgery*, American Veterinary Publications, 1963.

Science fiction: *The Lani People*, Bantam, 1962; *Legacy*, Harlequin, in press; *The Meddler*, Harlequin, in press.

Author of "Diagnostic Quiz," a column in *Modern Veterinary Practice*, 1957-66; editor of *Modern Veterinary Practice*, 1957-59, associate editor, 1959-70. Chairman of board of governors, Oregon State University Press, 1971—.

WORK IN PROGRESS: Two science fiction novels: *Frontiersman* and *The Maculate Conception*; short stories.

AVOCATIONAL INTERESTS: Travel (Central America, Australia, India, Egypt, Middle East, Turkey, Greece, Europe), sailing, skiing.

* * *

BONTLY, Thomas (John) 1939-

PERSONAL: Born August 25, 1939, in Madison, Wis.; son of Thomas Leon (a machine accountant) and Mary (Hackett) Bontly; married Marilyn Mackie, August 25, 1962; children: Thomas David. *Education:* University of Wisconsin, B.A. (with honors), 1961; Cambridge University, graduate study, 1961-62; Stanford University, Ph.D., 1966. *Residence:* Milwaukee, Wis. *Agent:* Curtis Brown Ltd., 60 East 56th St., New York, N.Y. 10022. *Office:* Department of English, University of Wisconsin, Milwaukee, Wis. 53201.

CAREER: University of Wisconsin-Milwaukee, assistant professor, 1966-71, associate professor of English, 1971—, co-ordinator of creative writing, 1975—. *Member:* Modern Language Association of America. *Awards, honors:* Maxwell Perkins Commemorative Novel award from Scribner, 1966, for *The Competitor.*

WRITINGS: (Author of introduction) William Allen White, *Stratagems and Spoils*, Johnson Reprint, 1969; *The Competitor* (novel), Scribner, 1966; (contributor) Gordon Lish, editor, *The Secret Life of Our Times*, Doubleday, 1973; (contributor) David Madden, editor, *Creative Responses*, Scott, Foresman, 1974; *The Adventures of a Young Outlaw* (novel), Putnam, 1974. Contributor of short stories and reviews to *Queen's Quarterly*, *Falmouth Review*, *Boy's Life*, *Esquire*, *McCall's*, *Fiction Midwest*, *Studies in English Literature*, and *Wisconsin Studies in Literature.*

WORK IN PROGRESS: A novel, *Ducks on the Pond*, for Putnam.

AVOCATIONAL INTERESTS: Gardening, fishing, racquet ball, model trains, music, sketching, travel.

BOORER, Wendy 1931-

PERSONAL: Born November 14, 1931, in St. Albans, England; daughter of William (a clerk) and Winifred (Brookson) Rowan; married Michael Keith Boorer (a zoologist), March 27, 1953; children: James, Matthew, Samantha. *Education:* Attended University College of Leicester (now University of Leicester), 1949-52; University of London, B.A. (honors in English literature), 1952. *Home:* 34 Milton Park, London N6 5QA, England.

CAREER: Has worked as an aerodynamics technician, teacher, library indexer, market researcher, and magazine editor; now author, dog breeder and exhibitor. *Member:* Avicultural Society, Bearded Collie Club of Great Britain (secretary, 1969-73), Griffon Club, Newfoundland Club.

WRITINGS: The World of Dogs, Hamlyn, 1969; *Dogs*, Hamlyn, 1970, published as *Dogs: Selection, Care, Training*, Grosset, 1971; *Dog Care*, Hamlyn, 1970; *Puppies*, Hamlyn, 1970; *The Book of the Dog*, Hamlyn, 1970; (with others) *The Treasury of Dogs*, Octopus, 1972; (with others) *The Love of Dogs*, Octopus, 1974; *The All Colour Book of Dogs*, Octopus, 1975. Adviser on dogs to Elsevier, 1973—. Contributor to *Avicultural Magazine, Dog's Life, Animal World*, and others.

SIDELIGHTS: Wendy Boorer writes: "I am fascinated by the pet/owner relationship, dog psychology, dog training and the historical background to the development of different breeds."

*   *   *

BORDIN, Edward S. 1913-

PERSONAL: Born November 7, 1913, in Philadelphia, Pa.; son of Morris (a jobber) and Jennie (Zarovsky) Bordin; married Ruth Birgitta Anderson (an historian), June 20, 1941; children: Martha Christine, Charlotte Anna. *Education:* Temple University, B.S.C., 1935, M.S., 1937; Ohio State University, Ph.D., 1942. *Politics:* Democrat. *Religion:* None. *Home:* 1000 Aberdeen, Ann Arbor, Mich. 48104. *Office:* Department of Psychology, University of Michigan, Ann Arbor, Mich. 48104.

CAREER: University of Minnesota, Minneapolis, assistant to coordinator, and counselor of university testing bureau, 1939-42, acting director, 1945; War Department, Washington, D.C., personnel technician, 1942-45; Washington State University, Pullman, associate professor of psychology and director of counseling center, 1946-48; University of Michigan, Ann Arbor, 1948—, became professor of psychology, 1955. Consultant to Veteran's Administration, and National Institute of Mental Health. *Member:* American Psychological Association, American Association for the Advancement of Science.

WRITINGS: Psychological Counseling, Appleton, 1955, 2nd edition, 1968; *Research Strategies in Psychotherapy*, Wiley, 1974. Contributor to journals in his field. Editor, *Journal of Consulting Psychology*, 1959-64.

WORK IN PROGRESS: Research and theory in psychotherapy, personality, vocational choice, and work.

BIOGRAPHICAL/CRITICAL SOURCES: C. H. Patterson, *Theories of Counseling and Psychotherapy*, Harper, 1966.

*   *   *

BORNSTEIN, Diane (Dorothy) 1942-

PERSONAL: Born April 22, 1942, in New York, N.Y.; daughter of Irving (a teacher) and Ruth (Vogel) Fox; married Barry Bornstein (a lithographer), April 2, 1960. *Education:* Hunter College of the City University of New York, B.A. (summa cum laude), 1966; New York University, M.A., 1967, Ph.D. (with distinction), 1970. *Home:* 56-56 220th St., Bayside, N.Y. 11364. *Office:* Department of English, Queens College of the City University of New York, Flushing, N.Y. 11367.

CAREER: Hunter College of the City University of New York, New York, N.Y., lecturer in English, 1970-71; Queens College of the City University of New York, Flushing, N.Y., instructor, 1971-73, assistant professor of English, 1973—. *Member:* Modern Language Association of America, Mediaeval Academy of America, Linguistic Society of America, Early English Text Society, Medieval Club of New York, Phi Beta Kappa. *Awards, honors:* Grant from American Council of Learned Societies, 1973-74.

WRITINGS: (With John F. Fisher) *In Forme of Speche Is Chaunge*, Prentice-Hall, 1974; *Mirrors of Courtesy* (nonfiction) Shoe String, 1975; (editor) *Readings in the Theory of Grammar*, Winthrop, 1975; (editor) *Sir William Segar's Book of Honor and Armes and Honor, Military and Civil*, Scholars Facsimiles & Reprints, 1975. Contributor to literature journals, including *Mediaeval Studies, English Studies, Shakespeare Studies, Comparative Literature Studies*, and *Studies in Scottish Literature*.

WORK IN PROGRESS: The Lady in the Tower, a study of medieval and Renaissance courtesy, completion expected in 1977; *An Introduction to Transformational Grammar*, 1977; editing *The Book of the Body of Polycye*, by Christine de Pisan.

SIDELIGHTS: Diane Bornstein wrote the script and liner notes for "A History of the English Language," a sound recording for Caedmon Records.

*   *   *

BOSERUP, Ester 1910-

PERSONAL: Born May 18, 1910, in Frederiksberg, Denmark, daughter of Holger (a director of a textile company) and Talke (Hansen) Boergesen; married Mogens Boserup (a professor at University of Copenhagen), September 5, 1931; children: Birte (Mrs. Efrem Beretta), Anders, Ivan. *Education:* University of Copenhagen, Cand. Polit., 1935. *Home:* Raadhusvej 19, 2920 Charlottenlund, Denmark.

CAREER: Government of Denmark, Copenhagen, civil servant, 1935-47; United Nations, Geneva, Switzerland, researcher, 1947-57; free-lance writer and researcher, 1957—. Member of United Nations Committee of Development Planning, 1972—, and Danish Council of Research Planning, 1973—. *Awards, honors:* Rosenkaer Prize from Danish Broadcasting Company, 1970, for *Woman's Role in Economic Development*.

WRITINGS: The Conditions of Agricultural Growth, Aldine, 1965; *Woman's Role in Economic Development*, St. Martin's, 1970; *Fra Boplads til Storstad* (title means "From the Shelter to the City"), Mellenfolkeligt Samvirke (Copenhagen), 1970; (editor with Ignacy Sachs) *Foreign Aid to Newly Independent Countries*, Mouton & Co., 1971.

WORK IN PROGRESS: Research on population and technology.

BIOGRAPHICAL/CRITICAL SOURCES: Brian Spooner, editor, *Population Growth: Anthropological Implications*, M.I.T. Press, 1972; *Peasant Studies Newsletter*, April, 1972.

BOSLEY, Keith   1937-

PERSONAL: Born September 16, 1937, in Bourne End, Buckinghamshire, England; son of William Edward and Grace Emily (Bushnell) Bosley; married Helen Sava (a singer), October 13, 1962; children: Benjamin. *Education:* University of Reading, B.A. (with honors), 1960; also attended University of Caen and Institut Britannique, Paris. *Home:* 108 Upton Rd., Slough SL1 2AW, England.

CAREER: Poet, translator.

WRITINGS: Tales from the Long Lakes: Finnish Legends from the Kalevala, Gollancz, 1966, published in America as *The Devil's Horse: Tales from the Kalevala*, Pantheon, 1971; *Russia's Other Poets*, Longmans, Green, 1968, published in America as *Russia's Underground Poets*, Praeger, 1969; *An Idiom of Night* (translations from Pierre Jean Jouve), Rapp & Whiting, 1968; *The Possibility of Angels*, Macmillan, 1969; *And I Dance: Poems Original and Translated* (for children), Angus & Robertson, 1972; *The War Wife: Vietnamese Poetry*, Allison & Busby, 1972; *The Song of Aino*, Moonbird Publications, 1973; *Finnish Folk Poetry*, SKS (Helsinki), in press; *The Song of Songs*, Whittington Press, in press; *The Poems of Stephane Mallarme*, Penguin, in press; *Dark Summer*, Menard Press, in press.

Work is represented in anthologies, including *The Young British Poets*, edited by Jeremy Robson, Chatto & Windus, 1971; and *New Poetry 1*, edited by Charles Osborne and Peter Porter, Arts Council of Great Britain, 1975. Contributor of poems, articles, and reviews to periodicals, including *Agenda, Encounter, Listener, Peace News, Poetry Reivew, Tribune, Child Education*, and *New Statesman*.

*   *   *

BOSS, Judy   1935-

PERSONAL: Born November 26, 1935, in Minneapolis, Minn; daughter of David Robert (a produce broker) and Florence (Weisner) Alford; married James Manley McCarthy, April 21, 1956 (died, 1969); married Wallace Andrew Boss (a banker), July 9, 1970; children: (first marriage) Kevin, Kathleen, Michael, Mary, James. *Education:* University of Minnesota, B.S., 1961; Institute of Psychorientology, graduate study, 1974. *Religion:* Christian. *Home:* 1510 Edgcumbe Rd., St. Paul, Minn. 55116. *Office:* 2239 Carter, St. Paul, Minn. 55108.

CAREER: Lecturer and writer on human psyche, 1969—. *Member:* Academy of Parapsychology and Medicine, Spiritual Frontiers Fellowship, Gamma Phi Beta.

WRITINGS: In Silence They Return (nonfiction), Llewellyn, 1972; *A Garden of Joy* (nonfiction), Llewellyn, 1974.

WORK IN PROGRESS: Dying to Live! A Glimpse of the Life after Death, completion expected in 1976; research for a book about a psychic search for a missing person.

SIDELIGHTS: Judy Boss told *CA:* "My husband's fatal accident left me a young widow with a large family and many questions about death. For many years I had been interested in psychic phenomena and the survival of the soul and so I decided to attempt to psychically communicate with him. What followed was revealing and astonishing to me! I made the commitment to share my experiences with others so they could be comforted and helped as I had been."

*   *   *

BOTKIN, B(enjamin) A(lbert)   1901-1975

February 7, 1901—July 30, 1975; American folklorist, archivist, educator, and editor or author of works in his field. Obituaries: *New York Times*, July 31, 1975; *Publishers Weekly*, August 18, 1975. (*CA*-15/16)

*   *   *

BOTTERILL, Cal(vin Bruce)   1947-

PERSONAL: Born October 17, 1947, in Portage, Manitoba, Canada; son of Stanley (a farmer) and Ilene (McDonald) Botterill; married Doreen McCannell (a teacher), August 21, 1970. *Education:* University of Manitoba, B.P.E. (honors), 1968; University of Alberta, M.A., 1972, Ph.D., 1976. *Home:* 14504 78th Ave., Edmonton, Alberta T5R 3C5, Canada. *Office:* Department of Physical Education, University of Alberta, Edmonton, Alberta, Canada.

CAREER: Government of Manitoba, Winnipeg, recreation director in department of tourism and recreation, 1966; Young Men's Christian Association (YMCA), Winnipeg, Manitoba, associate physical director and director of boys and youth department, 1969; physical education teacher and director of sports program at private school in Winnipeg, Manitoba, 1970-74, coach of hockey teams, 1972-74, manager of Dutton Arena, 1972-74; University of Alberta, Edmonton, lecturer in physical education, 1971-72, 1974-76. Hockey instructor and recreation director at Harris-Keon Hockey School, 1971; hockey instructor at University of Alberta's Hockey School, 1972, and at Hockey Canada Certification Clinics, 1974-75. *Member:* Coaching Association of Canada, Canadian Association of Health, Physical Education, and Recreation.

WRITINGS: (With Terry Orlick) *Every Kid Can Win*, Nelson-Hall, 1975.

WORK IN PROGRESS: Research on the psychology of sport and education; periodical research on sociology of sport and education.

SIDELIGHTS: Botterill has been a hockey player since 1965; he attended Canadian National Hockey Team Training Camps and Boston Bruins Professional Hockey Club Training Camp; he was a member of Canada's National Hockey Team, 1967-68, and of University of Alberta's Golden Bears Varsity Hockey Club, 1971-72.

*   *   *

BOURNE, Peter Geoffrey   1939-

PERSONAL: Born August 6, 1939, in Oxford, England; naturalized U.S. citizen; son of Geoffrey Howard (a scientist) and Gwen (a psychologist; maiden name, Jones) Bourne; married Judith Pence, December 12, 1964 (divorced, 1972); married Mary King (a corporation president), November 9, 1974. *Education:* Attended primary and secondary schools in England; Emory University, M.D., 1962, fellow, 1962-63; Stanford University, M.A., 1969. *Politics:* Democrat. *Religion:* None. *Home:* 130 E St. S.E., Washington, D.C. 20003. *Office:* Drug Abuse Council, 1828 L St. N.W., Washington, D.C. 20036.

CAREER: King County Hospital, Seattle, Wash., intern, 1963-64; Stanford University Medical Center, Stanford, Calif., resident in psychiatry, 1967-69; Southside Comprehensive Health Center, Atlanta, Ga., director of mental health unit, 1969-71; Atlanta South Central Community Mental Health Center, Atlanta, Ga., founder and director, 1970-71; Office of Drug Abuse (originally Georgia Narcotics Treatment Program), Atlanta, Ga., director, 1971-72; White House Special Action Office for Drug Abuse Prevention, Washington, D.C., assistant director, 1972-74, consultant, 1974—; Drug Abuse Council, Washington, D.C., consultant, 1974—. Assistant professor in department of psychiatry and in department of preventive medicine and community health at Emory University, 1969-72; visiting lecturer in department of psychiatry at Harvard University, 1974—; president, Foundation for International Resources, 1975—. Consultant to World Health Organization. *Military service:* U.S. Army, psychiatrist with Walter Reed Army Institute of Research, 1964-67; served in Vietnam, 1965-66; became captain; received Bronze Star and Air Medal.

MEMBER: American Psychiatric Association (chairman of Task Force on Drugs and Drug Abuse Education, 1969—), National Coordinating Council on Drug Abuse Education (vice-president, 1971-72), American Association for the Advancement of Science, Royal Society of Medicine (England), American Medical Society on Alcoholism, American Anthropological Association, World Federation for Mental Health, Institute for Southern Studies (member of board, 1968—), Medical Association of Georgia, Georgia Psychiatric Association, Washington Psychiatric Society. *Awards, honors:* William C. Menninger Award of Central Neuropsychiatric Association, 1967; named one of five outstanding young men in Georgia by Georgia Jaycees, 1972; Public Service Award of National Association of State Drug Abuse Program Coordinators, 1974; Aspen Institute for Humanistic Studies fellow, 1975.

WRITINGS: (Editor and contributor) *Psychology and Physiology of Stress*, Academic Press, 1969; *Men, Stress, and Viet Nam*, Little, Brown, 1970; (editor with Ruth Fox and contributor) *Alcoholism: Progress in Research and Treatment*, Academic Press, 1973; (editor and contributor) *Addiction*, Academic Press, 1973.

Contributor: David N. Daniels and others, editors, *Violence and the Struggle for Existence*, Little, Brown, 1970; Harry S. Abrams, editor, *The Psychological Aspects of Stress*, C. C Thomas, 1970; James Finn, editor, *Conscience and Command: Justice and Discipline in the Military*, Random House, 1970; Basil E. Eleftheriou and J. M. Scott, editors, *The Physiology of Aggression and Defeat*, Plenum, 1971; Richard R. Falk and others, editors, *Crimes of War*, Random House, 1971; James F. Adams, editor, *Human Behavior in a Changing Society*, Holbrook, 1973. Contributor to *International Encyclopedia of Psychiatry, Psychoanalysis and Psychology* and of more than forty articles to journals. Member of editorial board, *Psychiatry*, 1968—.

WORK IN PROGRESS: A *Treatment Manual for Drug Abuse Emergencies*, for National Clearing House for Drug Abuse Information.

AVOCATIONAL INTERESTS: Flying (holds private pilot's license).

* * *

BOWEN, Peter 1939-

PERSONAL: Born November 28, 1939, in Edmonton, Alberta, Canada; son of John A. (a civil servant) and Elizabeth (Campbell) Bowen. *Education:* Carleton University, B.A., 1961; Oxford University, D.Phil., 1969. *Home:* Flat 5, Rootes Hall, University of Warwick, Coventry CV4 7AL, England. *Agent:* John Perry, 12A Goodwin's Court, St. Martin's Lane, London WC2, England. *Office:* Audio-Visual Centre, University of Warwick, Coventry, CV4 7AL, England.

CAREER: University of London, London, England, producer, 1970-74; University of Warwick, Coventry, director of Audio-Visual Centre, 1974—. *Member:* Writer's Guild of Great Britain, Canadian Association of Anatomists, Writer's Action Group, Society of Film and Television Arts.

WRITINGS: Screen Test (nonfiction), Penguin, 1975; *Creatures of the Sea*, Marshall Cavendish, 1975; *Creatures of the Land*, Marshall Cavendish, 1975; *Creatures of the Air*, Marshall Cavendish, 1975. Contributor of articles on film, television, and education to journals.

WORK IN PROGRESS: A book on the state of the film industry in Britain, with a specific reference to one director's career.

* * *

BOWES, Anne LaBastille
See LaBASTILLE, Anne

* * *

BOWLER, R(eginald) Arthur 1930-

PERSONAL: Born August 7, 1930, in Ottawa, Ontario, Canada; son of John R. (a lawyer) and Winnifred (Brownlee) Bowler; married Sheila M. MacKay, August 13, 1955; children: John, Patricia, Winnifred, Kathleen. *Education:* Queen's University, Kingston, Ontario, B.A., 1963, M.A., 1965; University of London, Ph.D., 1970. *Home:* 115 Crescent Ave., Buffalo, N.Y. 14214. *Office:* Department of History, State University of New York at Buffalo, Buffalo, N.Y. 14261.

CAREER: Royal Canadian Air Force, enlisted technician, serving in Canada and in Germany, 1949-59; State University of New York at Buffalo, assistant professor, 1966-71, associate professor of history, 1971—. *Member:* Canadian Historical Association, Institute of Early American History. *Awards, honors:* Canada Council and McLaughlin fellowships at University of London, 1964-66.

WRITINGS: The War of 1812, Holt, 1973; *Logistics and the Failure of the British Army in America: 1775-1783*, Princeton University Press, 1975. Contributor to history journals and to newspapers.

WORK IN PROGRESS: The Social and Economic Composition of the American Loyalists.

SIDELIGHTS: Bowler writes: "Wars have probably taken up more of society's time than any other single endeavor. They deserve more consideration than social scientists have so far given them."

* * *

BOWLES, Ella Shannon 1886-1975

1886—March 28, 1975; American editor of journals and university publications and author. Obituaries: *New York Times*, April 3, 1975; *Washington Post*, April 5, 1975; *AB Bookman's Weekly*, April 28, 1975.

* * *

BOWLES, Frank H(amilton) 1907-1975

November 20, 1907—May 15, 1975; American educator, administrator, and author of books on education. Obituaries: *New York Times*, May 17, 1975; *AB Bookman's Weekly*, July 7, 1975. (*CA-15/16*)

BOYD, R(obert) L(ewis) F(ullarton) 1922-

PERSONAL: Born October 19, 1922, in Saltcoats, Scotland; son of William John (a scientist) and Dorothy Jane (Sibthorpe) Boyd; married Mary Higgins, September 6, 1949; children: Hazel Mary (Mrs. Paul Anthony Lamb), Robert Paul Fullarton, Stephen John Fullarton. *Education:* Imperial College of Science and Technology, London, B.Sc., 1943; University College, London, Ph.D., 1949. *Politics:* None. *Religion:* Christian. *Home:* Ariel House, Holmbury St. Mary, Dorking RH5 6NS, Surrey, England. *Office:* Mullard Space Science Laboratory, University College, University of London, London, England; Holmbury House, Holmbury St. Mary, Dorking RH5 6NS, Surrey, England.

CAREER: British Admiralty Mining Establishment, West Leigh House, Havant, England, temporary experimental officer, 1943-46; University of London, University College, London, England, Imperial Chemical Industries Research Fellow, 1949-52, lecturer, 1952-58, reader in physics, 1959-62, director of Mullard Space Science Laboratory, 1965—. Professor of astronomy at Royal Institution, 1961-64. Governor of Croydon College of Technology and Design, 1964—, St. Lawrence College, Ramsgate, 1964—, and London Bible College, 1974—. *Member:* Royal Society (fellow), Institution of Electrical Engineers (fellow), Institute of Physics (fellow), Royal Astronomical Society (vice-president, 1964-66), Victoria Institute (president, 1965—. *Awards, honors:* Created Commander of the Order of the British Empire, 1972.

WRITINGS: (Editor with M. J. Seaton and H.S.W. Massey) *Rocket Exploration of the Upper Atmosphere*, Pergamon, 1954; (with Massey) *The Upper Atmosphere*, Hutchinson, 1958; *Space Research by Rocket and Satellite*, Hutchinson, 1960; *Can God Be Known?*, Inter-Varsity Press, 1967; *Space Physics*, Oxford University Press, 1975. Editor of astronomical texts to "Oxford Physics Series." Contributor of more than one hundred scientific papers to proceedings.

WORK IN PROGRESS: Broadcasting.

AVOCATIONAL INTERESTS: Preserving old Rolls Royce motor cars.

*   *   *

BOZE, Arthur Phillip 1945-

PERSONAL: Surname rhymes with "nose"; born July 23, 1945, in Washington, D.C.; son of Lewis and Margaret (Monk) Boze; married Linda Rusin, November 27, 1970. *Education:* George Washington University, B.A., 1967. *Residence:* Los Angeles, Calif. *Office:* Poetry Co., P.O. Box 74622, Los Angeles, Calif. 90004.

CAREER: Los Angeles County Public Social Services, Compton, Calif., social worker, 1968-72; Los Angeles City Personnel Department, Los Angeles, Calif., junior administrative assistant, 1975—. Publisher, Poetry Co., Los Angeles, Calif. *Member:* Chaparral Federation of California Poets, Beyond Baroque Poetry Workshop. *Awards, honors:* Gold medal literary award from International Poetry Shrine, 1973, for *Loving You*.

WRITINGS—Poems: *Black Words*, Broadside Press, 1972; *Loving You*, Hallmark, Inc., 1973; *In Love with You*, Poetry Co., 1973. Contributor of poems to literary journals, including *Beyond Baroque*, *Journal of Black Poetry*, *Archer*, and *International Poetry Review*.

WORK IN PROGRESS: To a Midnight Stranger, a book of poems.

SIDELIGHTS: Boze wrote: "I . . . write because I want to leave something behind to show that I was here, that I existed. People are treated so much like faceless nonentities today that I decided poetry would be my way of rebelling against such a fate."

*   *   *

BRACEWELL, Ronald N(ewbold) 1921-

PERSONAL: Born July 22, 1921, in Sydney, Australia; son of Cecil Charles and Valerie Zilla (McGowan) Bracewell; married Helen Mary Lester Elliott; children: Catherine Wendy, Mark Cecil. *Education:* University of Sydney, B.Sc., 1941, B.E. (first class honors), 1943, M.E. (first class honors), 1948; Cambridge University, Ph.D., 1950. *Home:* 836 Santa Fe Ave., Stanford, Calif. 94305. *Office:* Department of Electrical Engineering, Stanford University, Stanford, Calif. 94305.

CAREER: Commonwealth Scientific and Industrial Research Organization, Sydney, Australia, designer of microwave radar equipment in Radiophysics Laboratory, 1942-45; Cavendish Laboratory, Cambridge, England, engaged in ionospheric research, 1946-49; Commonwealth Scientific and Industrial Research Organization, senior research officer in long wave propagation and radio astronomy at Radiophysics Laboratory, 1949-54; University of California, Berkeley, lecturer in radio astronomy, 1954-55; Stanford University, Stanford, Calif., associate professor, 1955-60, professor of electrical engineering, 1960—, Lewis M. Termin Professor, 1974—. Director of Sidney Sussex Foundation. Past chairman of astronomy advisory panel of National Science Foundation, member of panel on large radio telescopes; member of astronomy panel of National Academy of Science, National Radio Astronomy Observatory; chairman of Arecibo Evaluation Panel of Advanced Research Projects Agency; chairman of National Astronomy and Ionospheric Center advisory board at Cornell University.

MEMBER: International Astronomical Union, International Scientific Radio Union, Institute of Electrical and Electronic Engineers (fellow), American Astronomical Society (past councilor), American Institute of Physics, Institute of Radio Engineers (fellow), Royal Astronomical Society (fellow), Astronomical Society of the Pacific (life member). *Awards, honors:* Duddell Premium, from Institution of Electrical Engineers (London, England), 1952, for experimental contributions to the study of the ionosphere by means of very low-frequency waves.

WRITINGS: (With W. C. Bain, T. W. Straker, and C. H. Westcott) *The Ionospheric Propagation of Radio Waves of Frenquency 16 kc/s Over Distances of About 540 km* (monograph), Institution of Electrical Engineers, 1952; *The Ionospheric Propagation of Radio Waves of Frequency 16 kc/s Over Distances of About 200 km* (monograph), Institution of Electrical Engineers, 1952; (with Straker and John Harwood) *The Ionospheric Propagation of Radio Waves of Frequency 30-65 kc/s Over Short Distances* (monograph), Institution of Electrical Engineers, 1953; (with J. L. Pawsey) *Radio Astronomy*, Clarendon Press, 1955; (editor) *Paris Symposium on Radio Astronomy*, Stanford University Press, 1959; *Proposal Leading to Future Large Radio Telescopes*, Radio Astronomy Institute, Stanford University, 1961: *Interferometry of Centaurus "A"*, Radio Astronomy Institute, Stanford University, 1961; (translator) J. L. Steinberg and Jean Lequeux, *Radio Astronomy*, McGraw, 1963; *The Fourier Transform and Its Applications*,

McGraw, 1965; *The Galactic Club: Intelligent Life in Outer Space*, Stanford University Alumni Association, 1974.

Contributor) E. G. Brown, editor, *Textbook of Radar*, Angus & Robertson, 1946, 2nd edition, Cambridge University Press, 1954; Horace Jacobs, editor, *Advances in Astronautical Sciences*, Volume IV, American Astronomical Society, 1959; D. H. Menzel, editor, *The Radio Noise Spectrum*, Harvard University Press, 1960; L. N. Ridenour and Walter Nierenberg, editors, *Modern Physics for the Engineer*, McGraw, 1960; H. E. Landsberg, editor, *Advances in Geophysics*, Volume VIII, Academic Press, 1961; Siegfried Fluegge, editor, *Handbuch der Physik*, Springer-Verlag, 1952; Thornton L. Page, editor, *Stars and Galaxies*, Prentice-Hall, 1962; Samuel Silver, editor, *Radio Waves and Circuits*, Elsevier, 1963; S. T. Butler and Harry Messel, editors, *Light and Life in the Universe*, Shakespeare Head Press, 1964; David L. Arm, editor, *Vistas in Science*, University of New Mexico Press, 1968; Messel and Butler, editors, *Man in Inner and Outer Space*, Shakespeare Head Press, 1968.

Contributor to *Encyclopedia of Electronics* and *Encyclopaedia Britannica*. Contributor of about a hundred articles to scientific journals. Member of editorial advisory board of *Planetary and Space Science*; co-founder and member of review board of *Astronomy and Astrophysics*, 1961-68.

WORK IN PROGRESS: Trees on the Stanford Campus.

SIDELIGHTS: At Stanford University, Bracewell constructed a microwave spectroheliograph, a large and complex radio telescope which produced daily temperature maps of the sun reliably for eleven years, the duration of a solar cycle. The first radiotelescope to give output automatically in printed form, and therefore capable of worldwide dissemination by teleprinter, its weather maps received acknowledgment from the National Aeronautics and Space Administration for support of the first manned landing on the moon. A second major radiotelescope employing advanced concepts was constructed and applied to both solar and galactic studies.

With the advent of the space age, Bracewell became interested in celestial mechanics, made observations of the radio emission from Sputnik I, and supplied the press with accurate charts predicting the path of Soviet satellites, which were perfectly visible, but only if one knew when and where to look.

* * *

BRADLEY, Marion Zimmer 1930-

PERSONAL: Born June 3, 1930, in Albany, N.Y.; daughter of Leslie (a carpenter) and Evelyn (a historian; maiden name, Conklin) Zimmer; married Robert A. Bradley, October, 1949 (divorced, 1963); married Walter Henry Breen (a numismatist), February, 1964; children: (first marriage) David Robert; (second marriage) Patrick Russell, Dorothy Evelyn. *Education:* Attended New York State College for Teachers, 1946-48; Hardin-Simmons College, B.A., 1964; University of California, Berkeley, graduate study. *Politics:* None. *Residence:* Berkeley, Calif. *Agent:* Scott Meredith Literary Agency, Inc., 580 Fifth Ave., New York, N.Y. 10036. *Office address:* P.O. Box 352, Berkeley, Calif. 94701.

CAREER: Musician (sings at folk music concerts and for professional choirs) and writer. *Member:* Mystery writers of America, Science Fiction Writers of America, Alpha Chi.

WRITINGS—Science fiction novels: The Door Through Space, Ace Books, 1961; *Seven from the Stars*, Ace Books, 1962; *The Colors of Space*, Monarch Books, 1963; *Falcons of Narabedla* and *Dark Intruder and Others* (published in one volume), Ace Books, 1964; *The Brass Dragon*, Ace Books, 1969; *Hunters of the Red Moon*, DAW Books, 1973; *The Endless Voyage*, Ace Books, 1975.

Gothic novels: *Castle Terror*, Lancer Books, 1965; *Souvenir of Monique*, Ace Books, 1967: *Bluebeard's Daughter*, Lancer Books, 1968; *Dark Satanic*, Berkley Publishing, 1972; *In the Steps of the Master*, Grosset, 1973; *Can Ellen Be Saved?*, Tempo Books, 1975.

Science fiction novels of "The Darkover Series": *Sword of Aldones* and *The Planet Savers* (published in one volume), Ace Books, 1962; *The Bloody Sun*, Ace Books, 1964; *Star of Danger*, Ace Books, 1965; *Winds of Darkover*, Ace Books, 1970; *The World Wreckers*, Ace Books, 1971; *Darkover Landfall*, DAW Books, 1973; *The Spell Sword*, DAW Books, 1974; *Heritage of Hastur*, DAW Books, 1975; *Free Amazons of Darkover*, DAW Books, in press.

Criticism: *Men, Halflings, and Hero-Worship*, T-K Graphics, 1973; *The Necessity of Beauty: Robert W. Chambers and the Romantic Tradition*, T-K Graphics, 1974; *The Jewel of Arwen*, T-K Graphics, 1974; *The Parting of Arwen*, T-K Graphics, 1975.

Translator: Lope di Vega, *El Villano in su Rincon*, privately printed, 1971.

Songs: *Songs from Rivendell* (taken from *The Hobbit* and *The Lord of the Rings* by J.R.R. Tolkien), privately printed, 1959.

Contributor to science fiction magazines.

WORK IN PROGRESS: A book on the history of the Italian opera; a booklength poem; research on autism and mental retardation in children; translating libretto for opera, *Norma*, by Vincenzo Bellini, a libretto for children's operetta.

SIDELIGHTS: Marion Bradley writes: "I consider myself basically a musician, and my writings of science fiction and fantasy are largely an extension of my original interest in folklore and folk music. I have also done serious work in parapsychology, believe in it, and almost all of my serious writings embody a deep and basic belief in the paranormal powers of the human mind, and in forces which transcend humanity as such."

* * *

BRADNER, Enos 1892-

PERSONAL: Born October 7, 1892, in Powers, Mich.; son of Charles Edward (a storekeeper) and Antonia (Dofek) Bradner, *Education:* University of Michigan, B.A., 1915. *Home:* 1729 12th St., Seattle, Wash. 98122.

CAREER: Worked as manager of general store in Powers, Mich.; owned and operated book store in Seattle, Wash., 1930-40; *Seattle Times*, Seattle, Wash., outdoor editor, 1943-69. *Military service:* U.S. Army, Artillery, 1917-18. *Member:* Federation of Fly Fisherman (vice-president, 1966-68), Washington Duck Hunters, Washington Fly Fishing Club (president, 1939-40).

WRITINGS: North West Angling, A. S. Barnes, 1950; *Fish On*, Superior, 1971; *Inside on Outdoors*, Superior, 1973. Contributor to *Field and Stream* and *Outdoor Life*.

BRADT, A(cken) Gordon 1896-

PERSONAL: Born September 22, 1896, in Wichita, Kans.; son of Charles Edwin and Nellie (Acken) Bradt; married Aliff Bosier, June 18, 1918; children: Elizabeth Margaret (Mrs. Leonard Parsons), Virginia Helen (Mrs. W. Bruce Fullerton), Gordon Edwin. *Education:* Northwestern University, A.B., 1920, M.B.A., 1941; *Religion:* Presbyterian. *Home:* 606 Michigan Ave., Evanston, Ill. 60202. *Office:* University Bldg., 1604 Chicago Ave., Evanston, Ill. 60201.

CAREER: Assistant secretary of Board of Foreign Missions, Presbyterian Church of United States of America, 1920-28; Continental Illinois National Bank and Trust Co., Chicago, 1928-61, served as second vice-president, 1943-49, as vice-president, 1959-61; management and personnel consultant, 1961—. Member of faculty and lecturer, Northwestern University, 1944—, University of Wisconsin, 1949-63, University of Washington, 1950-63, and Southern Methodist University, 1958-63; guest lecturer, Louisiana State University and Princeton University; member of board of trustees, Evanston Civic and Arts Foundation, and Evanston Public Library; president, Evanston United Community Services; member of advisory board, Illinois Department of Personnel, chairman of business education advisory council, Board of Education of Chicago Public Schools; vice-chairman, Chicago Community Fund-Red Cross Joint Appeal Campaign, 1958; McCormick Theological Seminary, secretary, member of executive committee, and member of board of directors; member of board of directors, Evanston Chamber of Commerce; member of executive committee of Evanston Council of Churches; vice-president and member of board of directors, Evanston Y.M.C.A. *Member:* American Institute of Banking (former chairman of board of regents), Financial Public Relations Association (former treasurer), Illinois Bankers Association, Chicago Association of Commerce and Industry, Evanston Historical Society, Sigma Alpha Epsilon (life member), Kiwanis (former member of board of directors), Union League Club (Chicago), University Club (Evanston), Wilmette Golf Club.

WRITINGS: A Boy's Experiences Around the World, Missionary Press, 1914; *How to Triple Your Talents and Multiply Your Earning Power,* Prentice-Hall, 1963; *The Secrets of Getting Results Through People,* Parker Publishing, 1967; *Five Keys to Productivity and Profits,* Parker Publishing, 1973. Contributor to management journals.

*   *   *

BRAGDON, Clifford R(ichardson) 1940-

PERSONAL: Born June 30, 1940, in St. Louis, Mo.; married Sarah Vaughn, August 21, 1965; children: Katherine, Rachel, Elizabeth. *Education:* Westminster College, Fulton, Mo., B.A., 1962; Michigan State University, M.U.P., 1965; University of Pennsylvania, Ph.D., 1970. *Religion:* Episcopalian. *Home:* 4270 Autumn Hill Dr., Stone Mountain, Ga. 30083. *Office:* College of Architecture, Georgia Institute of Technology, Atlanta, Ga. 30332.

CAREER: Layton & Associates (city planners and landscape architects), St. Louis, Mo., city planner, 1961-65; University of Pennsylvania, Philadelphia, research associate, Institute for Environmental Studies, 1966-68, urban environmental planner, West Philadelphia Community Mental Health Consortium, 1967-69; U.S. Army Environmental Hygiene Agency, Edgewood Arsenal, Md., environmental noise specialist, 1969-72; Georgia Institute of Technology, Atlanta, associate professor of city planning,

1972—. Member of land use planning-airports panel, U.S. Department of Transportation, and of Georgia Coastal Zone Management Group, Department of Natural Resources, and Department of Human Resources; consultant to U.S. Environmental Protection Agency, United Nations, and to other governmental bodies and industries.

MEMBER: Acoustical Society of America, American Industrial Hygiene Association, American Society of Planning Officials, American Institute of Planners, Environmental Design Research Association, Friends of the Earth, National Trust for Historic Preservation, Georgia Conservancy, Sigma Xi, Omicron Delta Kappa. *Awards, honors:* U.S. Army Commendation Medal (for civilian service), 1972.

WRITINGS: (Contributor) Roy L. Meek and J. A. Straayer, editors, *The Politics of Neglect: The Environmental Crisis,* Houghton, 1971; *Noise Pollution: The Unquiet Crisis,* University of Pennsylvania Press, 1972; (contributor) P. Walton Purdom, editor, *Environmental Health,* 2nd edition (Bragdon did not contribute to earlier edition), Academic Press, 1976; (editor) *Noise Pollution: A Guide to Information Sources,* Gale, in press. Contributor to *Planning Comment, Scientist and Citizen,* and other journals. Contributing editor, *Sound and Vibration,* 1973-76.

*   *   *

BRAGG, Melvyn 1939-

PERSONAL: Born October 6, 1939, in Carlisle, England; son of Stanley (a shopkeeper) and Ethel (Parks) Bragg; married Elisabeth Roche, June 26, 1961 (died, September 1, 1971); married Catherine Mary Haste (a writer), December 18, 1974; children: (first Marriage) Marie-Elsa. *Education:* Wadham College, Oxford, M.A., 1961. *Home:* 9 Gayton Rd., London NW3 1TX, England. *Agent:* Richard Scott Simon, 32 CollEge Cross, London W1, England.

CAREER: British Broadcasting Corp., London, England, producer, 1961-67; novelist and broadcaster, 1967—. *Member:* Royal Society of Literature (fellow), Association of Cinematograph, Television & Allied Technicians, P.E.N., Garrick Club.

WRITINGS–Novels; all published by Knopf: *For Want of a Nail,* 1965; *The Second Inheritance,* 1966; *Without a City Wall,* 1968; *The Hired Man,* 1970; *A Place in England,* 1971; *The Nerve,* 1972; *Josh Lawton,* 1973; *The Silken Net,* 1974. Author of film scripts, "Isadora," 1969, "Music Lovers" 1970, "Jesus Christ Superstar," 1973. Contributor to *Listener* and *New Review.*

WORK IN PROGRESS: Speak for England, nonfiction.

*   *   *

BRAHS, Stuart J(ohn) 1940-

PERSONAL: Born June 29, 1940, in Akron, Ohio; son of Lawrence Rayner (a U.S. Government official) and Violet Jane (Miller) Brahs; married Ruth Ellen Smith (a teacher), August 15, 1962; children: Lynda Marie, Victoria Louise. *Education:* Attended Georgetown University, 1958-60, 1961-62, and University of Madrid, 1960-61; George Washington University, B.A., 1968, M.A., 1973. *Politics:* Liberal Democrat. *Religion:* Protestant. *Home:* 803 Brice Rd., Rockville, Md. 20852. *Office:* U.S. House of Representatives, 1228 Longworth, Washington, D.C. 20515.

CAREER: Special assistant to U.S. Congressman Richard Ottinger, 1965-70, to Congressman Herman Badillo, 1970-75; legislative assistant to Congressman Stephen J. Solarz,

1975—. *Member:* American Academy of Political and Social Science, Runners Club of America (national director of public relations/information, 1975—), Potomac Valley Amateur Athletic Union (athletes representative to executive board, 1975—).

WRITINGS: An Album of Puerto Ricans in the U.S., F. Watts, 1973.

WORK IN PROGRESS: A novel on some phase of amateur athletics.

* * *

BRAINERD, John W(hiting) 1918-
(Jay Bee)

PERSONAL: Born February 14, 1918, in Dover, Mass.; son of Henry Boies (a businessman) and Eleanor (Shepard) Brainerd; married Barbara Hale, June 25, 1941; children: Jill (Mrs. Robert A. Root), Roger W., Allen H. *Education:* Harvard University, A.B., 1940, M.A., 1941, Ph.D., 1949. *Religion:* Society of Friends. *Home:* 836 Wilbraham Rd., Springfield, Mass. 01109. *Office:* Department of Biology, Springfield College, Springfield, Mass. 01109.

CAREER: Springfield College, Springfield, Mass., 1949—, currently professor of biology and conservation. Former chairman of Springfield Conservation Commission. Civilian public service, 1942-46. *Member:* American Institute of Biological Sciences, National Association of Biology Teachers, American Nature Study Society (past president), Association of Interpretive Naturalists (fellow), Ecological Society of America, The Nature Conservancy (former state representative), National Audubon Society.

WRITINGS: Nature Study for Conservation: A Handbook for Environmental Education, Macmillan, 1971; *Working with Nature: A Practical Guide,* Oxford University Press, 1973. Also author of poems under pseudonym Jay Bee. Writer of filmstrip series, "Forest of the Northeast," and "Shores: The Edges of Things."

WORK IN PROGRESS: Research in sensitivity to nature in different environments; educational methods for training community leaders.

AVOCATIONAL INTERESTS: Adaptation of people to landscapes and landscapes to people; the ecology of words as they find their niches in sentences, paragraphs, and essays; pictorial education through photographs, drawings, and paintings.

* * *

BRAMWELL, Dana G. 1948-

PERSONAL: Born September 21, 1948, in Kansas City, Mo.; son of G. P. (a mortgage banker) and Dorothy (Stands) Bramwell; re-married former wife, Kay, April 2, 1970; children: Heather Elizabeth. *Education:* Colorado College, B.A., 1970. *Politics:* "Variable." *Home:* 1940 South Cedar, Colorado Springs, Colo.

CAREER: Western Agricultural Chemical Co., Colorado Springs, Colo., truck loader, 1972; Dave's Pizza, Colorado Springs, Colo., manager, 1973; science teaching assistant in high school in Cripple Creek, Colo., 1974; Four Seasons Motor Inn, Colorado Springs, Colo., security officer, 1975.

WRITINGS: The Tragedy of King Richard (play), Survey Press, 1974.

WORK IN PROGRESS: The Book of Judas; a series of short stories; poems.

SIDELIGHTS: Bramwell wrote his play "... to exercise my mind ... the idea came from a Doonesbury cartoon, where Nixon was comparing himself to Lincoln. I felt that he could more aptly compare himself to some of Shakespeare's villains. When I finished it friends urged me to publish it ..."

* * *

BRANDES, Norman Scott 1923-

PERSONAL: Born December 19, 1923, in New York, N.Y.; son of Frederick Emile and Claire (Grodin) Brandes; married Patsy Ruth Greenwood, December 16, 1950; children: Roger Neil, Fred Emile, Deborah Ann. *Education:* New York University, B.A., 1947; University of Tennessee, M.D., 1950. *Home:* 2718 Mount Holyoke Rd., Columbus, Ohio 43221. *Office:* 3620 North High St., Columbus, Ohio 43214.

CAREER: Physician and psychiatrist in private practice, 1957—. New York Polyclinic Postgraduate Medical School and Hospital, New York, N.Y., intern, 1950-51; public health physician in maternal and child care, State of Tennessee, 1951-52; Brooke Army Hospital, San Antonio, Tex., neuropsychiatric resident, 1952-53; Fort Campbell Army Hospital, Fort Campbell, Ky., neuropsychiatric resident, 1953-54; resident, Bridgeport General Hospital, Bridgeport, Conn., 1954-55, Ohio State University, 1955-57; Columbus Child's Psychiatric Hospital, Columbus, Ohio, assistant director, 1957-58, director, 1958-60; Ohio State University, Columbus, teaching consultant in adolescent psychiatry, 1961-66, assistant clinical professor, 1966-69, associate clinical professor of adolescent psychiatry, 1969—. Diplomate of American Board of Psychiatry and Neurology, 1959. *Military service:* U.S. Army Reserve, Medical Corps, 1951-58; active duty, 1952-54; became captain.

MEMBER: American Group Psychotherapy Association (fellow), American Association of Psychoanalytic Physicians (fellow), American Psychiatric Association (fellow), American Medical Association, Association of Medical Group Psychoanalysts, Art Association of the American Psychiatric Association, Ohio Medical Association, Ohio Psychiatric Association, Columbus Academy of Medicine. *Awards, honors:* Recognized by American Medical Association, 1969, 1972, and Tri-State Group Psychotherapy Society, 1972; teaching award from American Group Psychotherapy Association, 1971.

WRITINGS: Group Therapy for the Adolescent, Jason Aronson, 1974. Author of cassette book, "Para-analytic Treatment Approaches in Adolescent Group Psychotherapy," Behavioral Sciences Tape Library, 1975. Contributor to medical journals.

WORK IN PROGRESS: Search for Erick Dell, M.D., a novel; *How to Program Your Cerebral Computer,* a booklet, with drawings; contribution to a book on group therapy.

SIDELIGHTS: Brandes writes: "I am a psychiatrist who likes to write. My background of training has emphasized psychoanalysis and analytic group psychotherapy and, therefore, I am very much involved in the study of human behavior on a daily basis. The two practical areas of communication available to humans are verbal and non-verbal. I am devoted to improving both—in my practice, writing, painting, and home life."

BRANDYS, Marian 1912-

PERSONAL: Born January 25, 1912, in Wiesbaden, Germany; son of Henry (a tradesman) and Eugenia (Landau) Brandys; married Halina Mikolajska (an actress), July 20, 1953. *Education:* University of Warsaw, M.A., 1934. *Home:* Marszatkowska 10/16, Warsaw 00-590, Poland. *Agent:* Authors' Agency, Hipoteczna 2, Warsaw 00-092, Poland.

CAREER: Has held positions as journalist, including foreign correspondent, and as editor of a literary weekly. *Military service:* Served in Polish Army during World War II; became major in Army Reserve; received Braves' Cross. *Member:* Union of Polish Writers, Polish P.E.N. *Awards, honors:* Literary Prize from the government of Poland, 1974, for historical essays.

*WRITINGS—*Nonfiction: *Spotkania wloskie* (title means "Italian Encounters"), Czytelnik, 1949, revised and enlarged edition, Nasza Ksiegarnia, 1953; *Poczatek opowiesci* (title means "The Beginning of a Saga"), Pantstwowy Instytut Wydayniczy, 1952; *Wyprawa do oflagu* (title means "A Visit to the Camp of War Prisoners"), Pantstwowy Instytut Wydawniczy, 1955; *Od Kairu do Addis Abeby* (title means "From Cairo to Addis Ababa"), Wydawnictwo Ministerstwa Obrony Narodowej, 1957; *O Krolach i kapuscie* (title means "Of Cabbages and Kings"), Panstwowy Instytut Wydawniczy, 1959, 2nd edition, enlarged, Iskry, 1964; *Nieznany Ksiaze Poniatowski* (title means "The Unknown Prince Poniatowski"), Iskry, 1960; *Officer najwiekszych nadziei* (title means "An Officer of the Greatest Promise"), Iskry, 1964; *Kozietulski i inni* (title means "Kozietulski and Others"), Iskry, 1967; *Klopoty z pania Walewska* (title means "The Troubles with Madame Walewska"), Iskry, 1969; *Koniec swiata szwolezerow* (title means "The End of the Chevau-Legers, Polish Lancers"), five volumes, Iskry, 1972-75; *Poland* (translated from the Polish), Doubleday, 1974.

Books for children: *Wyprawa do Arteku* (title means "A Visit to Artek"), Nasza Ksiegarnia, 1953; *Dom odzyskanego dziecinstwa* (title means "Childhood Regained"), Nasza Ksiegarnia, 1953; *Honorowy lobuz* (title means "A Rogue of Honor"), Nasza Ksiegarnia, 1957; *Sladami Stasia i Nel* (title means "In the Footsteps of Stas and Nel"), Nasza Ksiegarnia, 1961; *Z Panem Biegankiem w Abisynii* (title means "With Mr. Bieganek in Ethiopia"; sequel to *Sladami Stasia i Nel*), Nasza Ksiegarnia, 1962.

*   *   *

BRASCH, Ila Wales 1945-

PERSONAL: Born May 26, 1945, in Oskaloosa, Iowa; daughter of Raymond and Mabel (Edinger) Wales; married Walter Milton Brasch (a journalist), September 30, 1970. *Education:* University of Northern Iowa, B.A., 1970; Ohio University, M.A., 1974; Temple University, doctoral study, 1974—. *Politics:* Independent Democrat. *Residence:* c/o 1707 South Pleasant Ave., Ontario, Calif. 91671.

CAREER: Bussey Telephone Co., Bussey, Iowa, telephone operator, 1960-62; *Northern Iowan*, Cedar Falls, Iowa, member of editorial staff, 1964-67, editor, 1967-68; *Cedar Falls Daily Record*, Cedar Falls, Iowa, staff writer, 1968-69; *Waterloo Daily Courier*, Waterloo, Iowa, staff writer, 1969-71; MID Productions, Athens, Ohio, assistant producer, 1971-74. Member of Iowa Governor's Committee for the Employment of the Handicapped, 1971-72. *Member:* American Dialect Society, American Name Society, Alpha Phi Gamma.

WRITINGS: (With husband, Walter Milton Brasch) *A Comprehensive Annotated Bibliography of American Black English*, Louisiana State University Press, 1974. Contributor to popular magazines and linguistic journals. Member of Ohio Governor's committee for preparing *Dictionary of American Regional English*, 1973.

WORK IN PROGRESS: A study of pidginization in immigrant speech; a study of English loanwords in several West African languages; continuing research on American language and dialect; a study of creolization of language.

SIDELIGHTS: Ila Brasch writes: "Research must have as its end a contribution to the enrichment of the world we live in. My research, which combines ethnolinguistics and mass communications, will hopefully bring a greater awareness to the potential of the communicative skills." She has been associate producer for MID Productions multimedia programs "In the Beginning . . . (the Indian)," "Songs of the Battle," and "The Firemark: A Language and Culture Study," 1972-74. *Avocational interests:* American crafts, folk music, "people's lib."

*   *   *

BRASCH, Walter Milton 1945-

PERSONAL: Born March 2, 1945, in San Diego, Calif.; son of Milton and Helen (Haskin) Brasch; married Ila Wales (a journalist-linguist), September 30, 1970. *Education:* Attended University of California, 1962-64, LaVerne College, 1964; San Diego State College (now University), A.B., 1966; Ball State University, M.A., 1969; Ohio University, Ph.D., 1974. *Politics:* Independent Democrat. *Religion:* Jewish. *Home:* c/o 1707 South Pleasant Ave., Ontario, Calif. 91761.

CAREER: Was sports editor, city editor, features writer, and investigative reporter for daily newspapers in California, Indiana, Iowa, and Ohio, 1965-71; MID Productions, Athens, Ohio, executive director, 1971-74; Temple University, Philadelphia, Pa., assistant professor of journalism and mass communications, 1974—. Free-lance advertising-publicity writer and consultant, 1964—; member of Iowa Governor's Committee for the Employment of the Handicapped, 1971-73; member of Ohio Governor's Committee for the Dictionary of American Regional English, 1973-74; member of U.S. Coast Guard Auxiliary. *Member:* American Dialect Society, Association for Education in Journalism, Popular Culture Association, Society of Professional Journalists, Phi Kappa Phi, Kappa Tau Alpha, Pi Gamma Mu, Alpha Kappa Delta. *Awards, honors:* Certificate of Outstanding Service from Alpha Phi Omega, 1966; Certificate of Appreciation from U.S. Department of Commerce, 1970; Certificate of Merit from Gordon Wiseman Conference on Interpersonal Communication, 1973.

WRITINGS: (With wife, Ila Wales Brasch) *A Comprehensive Annotated Bibliography of American Black English*, Louisiana State University Press, 1974.

Also author of plays, "Answer Me Not in Mournful Numbers," first produced in Waterloo, Iowa at Theatre Seventies, 1969; "Sand Creek," first produced at Theatre Seventies, 1972. Author of television script, "The Royal Symbols of the Kom," 1973; and, with Ila Wales Brasch, a radio script, "The Day Santa Claus Forgot . . .," 1974.

Multimedia shows: "In the Beginning . . . (the Indian)," 1972; "A Language and Culture Happening," 1972; "Songs of the Battle," 1972; "Songs of the Civil War," 1973; (with Edward J. Duffy) "The Firemark: A Language and Culture Study," 1975.

Contributor to general interest magazines and to academic journals.

WORK IN PROGRESS: Black English and the Mass Media; Benjy; a book on West African folklore, with Gilbert D. Schneider; a book on the animation industry; a series of short stories, *The Tainted Quill.*

SIDELIGHTS: Brasch writes: "I'm a journalist, a writer who looks at society and tries to understand, then analyze and explain its many complex parts as they relate to an organic whole. For that reason, my writings—both popular as well as academic—can't really be pigeon-holed; the writings are, in reality, about man and his world, the process is journalism." *Avocational interests:* First aid instruction, working with the special person (gifted, handicapped, retarded), music (especially country, bluegrass, dixieland, jazz), theatre, popular culture, "and just about anything that happens to tickle my fancy at the moment."

* * *

BRATHWAITE, Errol (Freeman) 1924-

PERSONAL: Born April 3, 1924, in Clive, Hawkes Bay, New Zealand; son of Jack Lister (a garage proprietor) and Dorothea (Anstis) Brathwaite; married Alison Irene Whyte (a clerk), March 20, 1948; children: Michael John, Pamela Ann. *Education:* Attended high school in Timaru, New Zealand. *Religion:* Church of England. *Home:* 12 Fulton Ave., Christchurch 1, New Zealand.

CAREER: New Zealand Army, 1942-43; Royal New Zealand Air Force, 1943-45, 1947-55, became flight sergeant; New Zealand Corps of Signals, 1955-58; New Zealand Broadcasting Corp., Christchurch, copywriter, 1960-61; Dobbs, Wiggins, McCann, & Ericson, Christchurch, New Zealand, creative director, 1962-67; Carlton-Carruthers du Chateau Ltd., Christchurch, creative director, 1968-70, manager, 1969-70; writer. *Awards, honors*—Military: Pacific Star, Empire War Medal, New Zealand War Medal. Civilian: *Otago Daily Times Centennial* Novel Contest first prize, 1961, and New Zealand Government Literary Fund award for merit, 1962, both for *An Affair of Men.*

WRITINGS—Novels: *Fear in the Night,* Caxton Press, 1959; *An Affair of Men,* Collins, 1961, St. Martin's, 1962; *Long Way Home,* Caxton Press, 1963; *The Flying Fish,* Collins, 1963; *The Needle's Eye,* Collins, 1966; *The Evil Day,* Collins, 1967.

Nonfiction: *The Companion Guide to the North Island of New Zealand,* Collins, 1970; *The Companion Guide to the South Island of New Zealand,* Collins, 1972; *New Zealand and Its People,* New Zealand Government Printer, 1974; *The Beauty of New Zealand,* Lloyd O'Neil, 1974.

Author of radio plays for New Zealand Broadcasting Corp.: "An Affair of Men," 1961; "Long Way Home," 1964; "The Needle's Eye."

WORK IN PROGRESS: A history of British Petroleum New Zealand Ltd.; a novel-length fairy tale, a history of the Royal New Zealand Air Force; a fictionalized New Zealand family saga.

BIOGRAPHICAL/CRITICAL SOURCES: J. C. Reid, *New Zealanders at War in Fiction,* New Zealand Publishing Society, 1966.

* * *

BRATTSTROM, Bayard H(olmes) 1929-

PERSONAL: Born July 3, 1929, in Chicago, Ill.; son of Wilbur LeRoy (a banker) and Violet (in real estate; maiden name, Holmes) Brattstrom; married Cecile D. Funk, June 15, 1952 (divorced May, 1975); children: Theodore, David. *Education:* San Diego State College (now University), B.S., 1951; University of California, Los Angeles, M.A., 1953, Ph.D., 1959; California Institute of Technology, research fellow, 1955; California State University, Fullerton, study toward degree in clinical psychology, 1970—. *Residence:* Fullerton, Calif. *Office:* Department of Biology, California State University, Fullerton, Calif. 92634.

CAREER: Natural History Museum, San Diego, Calif., assistant curator of herpetology, 1948-51, director of education, 1949-51; Los Angeles County Museum, Los Angeles, Calif., assistant in paleontology, summer, 1956; Adelphi College, Garden City, N.Y., instructor in biology, 1956-60; California State University, Fullerton, assistant professor, 1960-61, associate professor, 1961-66, professor of zoology, 1966—. Associate professor of zoology, University of California, Los Angeles, summers, 1962-63. Past president and member of board of directors, Fullerton Youth Museum and Orange County Zoological Society; member of board of trustees, Mexican-American Scholarship Association; member of Orange County Board of Supervisors, Orange County Natural Lands and Parks Committee. Consultant on environmental impact studies.

MEMBER: American Association for the Advancement of Science (fellow; member of council, 1965-66, 1969-75), American Institute of Biological Science, American Society of Zoologists, Ecological Society of America, Society for the Study of Evolution, American Society of Ichthyologists and Herpetologists (past member of board of governors; past Western vice-president), Herpetologists League (fellow), Society of Systematic Zoology, Southern California Academy of Sciences (past member of advisory board and board of governors), Society of Vertebrate Paleontology, American Society of Mammalogists, American Ornithological Union, Cooper Ornithological Society, San Diego Society of Natural History, Sigma Xi. *Awards, honors:* American Philosophical Society grants, 1958, 1959; National Science Foundation grants, 1959-60, 1964-66, senior postdoctoral fellowship, 1966-67; named honorary research associate, Los Angeles County Museum of Natural History, 1964; California State University, Fullerton, research grants, 1969, 1972.

WRITINGS: The Talon Digs Deeply into My Heart (collected poems, 1958-1971), Windy Row Press, 1974.

Contributor: Paul F. Brandwein, editor, *Research Problems in Biology,* Doubleday-Anchor, 1963; J. L. Grissitt, editor, *Pacific Basin Biogeography: A Symposium,* Bishop Museum Press (Honolulu), 1963; W. W. Milstead, editor, *Lizard Ecology: A Symposium,* University of Missouri Press, 1967; G. C. Whitlow, editor, *The Comparative Physiology of Temperature Regulation,* Academic Press, 1970; E. O. Price and A. W. Stokes, editors, *Animal Behavior in Laboratory and Field,* 2nd edition, W. H. Freeman, 1975.

Contributor to proceedings and transactions, to *Encyclopedia of Science and Technology,* published by McGraw, and to scientific journals. Manuscript reviewer for *Tulane Studies in Zoology, Animal Behavior, Copeia, Ecology, Herpetologica,* and other publications. Member of board of editors, American Society of Ichthyologists and Herpetologists, 1971.

WORK IN PROGRESS: Changes: In Me, in My Teaching, and in Student Self Esteem; What to Do in Big Lecture

Halls, Other than Lecturing; two books of poetry, *I Pulled the Talon Out Myself* and *Images or Views from a Window*; an adventure story, "Letters from Ingrid"; continued research on ecology, temperature regulation, social behavior, and the repopulation of a Mexican volcanic island.

AVOCATIONAL INTERESTS: Metal sculpture (using rusty found objects), wood-leather hangings, abstract water-color painting, yoga and Zen meditation, travel.

* * *

BREAULT, William 1926-

PERSONAL: Born September 17, 1926, in Saratoga Spa, N.Y.; son of Cyril Felix and Ruth (La Bonte) Breault. *Education:* Gonzaga University, Ph.L., 1956; University of Santa Clara, M.S.T., 1963; Collegium Almanum a Sancto Joseph (Los Gatos, Calif., since moved to Berkeley), S.T.L., 1963; San Francisco State College (now University), M.A. (drama), 1965; College of Notre Dame, Belmont, Calif., B.A. (art), 1969. *Politics:* Democrat. *Home and office:* Jesuit High School, P.O. Box 4647, Sacramento, Calif. 95825.

CAREER: Loyola High School, Los Angeles, Calif., teacher of English and Latin, 1956-59; St. Ignatius High School, San Francisco, Calif., teacher of religion and drama, 1964-69; concurrently head of religious education at St. Ignatius parish, and artist-in-residence and part-time teacher of theology and art at Jesuit High School, both in Sacramento, 1969—. Independent producer of television shows for station KXTV, Sacramento, 1969—. *Military service:* U.S. Army Air Forces, 1945-47; served in South Pacific. *Awards, honors:* First prize in St. John's Lutheran annual religious art show, 1969, and second prize. Sacramento Valley Art Academy, 1970, both for metal sculpture.

WRITINGS: Power and Weakness, Daughters of St. Paul, 1973; *The Lord's Way*, Daughters of St. Paul, 1974. Author of unpublished boys' novel, *Rio del Oro*, and of media show, *The Man* (a life of Christ), published by Ave Maria Press, 1975. Writer of about two dozen television productions, including "Mission," "Damien: Leper-Priest," "The Man," and "Islands in the Sun," and about ninety-five one-minute spots on prayer, life, and scripture.

WORK IN PROGRESS: The Sea-Wind; part II of *The Man*, to be issued as a media show; a book of poetry and prayer, with pictures; a media show on Damien (the leper priest of Molokai), for publication.

SIDELIGHTS: Breault told *CA*: "As a priest, whose first duty is to proclaim the good news, or, the Gospel of Christ, I am constantly challenged to see how I can (utilizing all that is most worthwhile in media and life), convey in convincing terms to the modern mentality just what the good news is! For me it includes entertainment, poetry, beauty and adventure—above all, art, without which man cannot function." Breault specializes in watercolors, metal sculpture, and print-work, for which he has had numerous one-man shows and commissions, and writes that he is entirely self-supporting through the sale of his paintings and books.

* * *

BREIT, Marquita E(laine) 1942-

PERSONAL: Surname is pronounced "bright;" born January 19, 1942, in Louisville, Ky.; daughter of Louis Frederick, Sr. (a contractor) and Ruth (Brightman) Breit. *Education:* Ursuline College, Louisville, Ky., B.A., 1964;

Spalding College, M.A.L.S., 1970. *Religion:* Roman Catholic. *Home:* 2534 West Main St., Louisville, Ky. 40212. *Office:* Library, Bellarmine College, 2000 Norris Pl., Louisville, Ky. 40205.

CAREER: Louisville Free Public Library, Louisville, Ky., assistant librarian, 1964-67; Bellarmine College, Louisville, Ky., assistant circulation librarian, 1967-69, circulation librarian, 1969—, catalog librarian, 1975—. *Member:* American Library Association, American Association of University Professors, Kentucky Library Association, Louisville Library Club.

WRITINGS: Thomas Merton: A Bibliography, 1957-1973, Scarecrow, 1974.

WORK IN PROGRESS: A bibliography of Thomas Merton, up to 1957.

AVOCATIONAL INTERESTS: Reading, travel, sewing, needlecrafts, furniture refinishing.

* * *

BREITNER, I. Emery 1929-

PERSONAL: Born September 14, 1929, in Budapest, Hungary; son of Eugene and Margaret Breitner; married to wife Edith, June, 1955. *Education:* University of Budapest, M.D., 1955. *Home and office:* 22 Pine Dr. N., Roslyn, N.Y. 11576.

CAREER: Psychiatrist in private practice in Roslyn, N.Y., 1967—. Liason consultant in psychiatry to Hillside Medical Center, 1965—; psychiatric consultant, St. Francis Hospital, Roslyn, N.Y., 1970—; director of Institute for Marriage and Family Counselling, 1972—; visiting lecturer, Hofstra University, 1975. *Member:* American Psychiatric Association, American Group Psychotherapy Association, New York State Medical Association, Nassau County Psychiatric Society.

WRITINGS: Philotherapy: A New Approach to Psychotherapy, Institute of Human Relations, 1974. Author of column, "Dialogue" in *Newsday* (Long Island), 19—. Contributor to journals in his field. Associate editor, *Nassau County Psychiatric Society Newsletter*, and *Forum*.

WORK IN PROGRESS: A nonfiction book, *Love Addicts*; research on personalty and intrapsychic conflicts.

* * *

BRESSLER, Leo A(lbert) 1911-

PERSONAL: Born April 20, 1911; son of Lloyd Homer (a teacher) and Annie (Stutzman) Bressler; married Marion Ann Waters (a teacher), June 12, 1948; children: William Lloyd, Ann Lee. *Education:* Ursinus College, B.A., 1932; Pennsylvania State University, M.A., 1943; University of Pennsylvania, Ph.D., 1951. *Politics:* Republican. *Religion:* Protestant. *Home:* 505 East Waring Ave., State College, Pa. 16801.

CAREER: High school teacher of English in public schools in Higgins, Pa., 1934-37; Pennsylvania State University, University Park, assistant professor, 1943-48, associate professor of English, 1948-70. Member of Volunteer Service for Senior Citizens, 1974—. *Military service:* U.S. Navy, 1942-46; became petty officer. *Member:* Art Alliance, Order of Masons.

WRITINGS: (with wife, Marion A. Bressler) *Country, Conscience and Conscription*, Prentice-Hall, 1970; (with M.A. Bressler) *Youth in American Life*, Houghton, 1972; (with M.A. Bressler) *War or Peace: Does Humanity Have a Choice?*, Prentice-Hall, 1975. Contributor to *American-German Review, College English, Pennsylvania Magazine of History and Biography. Pennsylvania Angler*, and other magazines and journals.

WORK IN PROGRESS: Research for a book on euthanasia for use in educational institutions; a novel dealing with disillusionment of youth.

AVOCATIONAL INTERESTS: Fishing, American culture, art.

* * *

BRESSLER, Marion Ann   1921-

PERSONAL: Born July 20, 1921, in Nanticoke, Pa.; daughter of William Watkin (a physician and surgeon) and Anna (Owens) Waters; married Leo Albert Bressler (a professor of English), June 12, 1948; children: William Lloyd, Ann Lee. *Education:* Bucknell University, B.A., 1943, M.A., 1943; University of Pennsylvania, further study, 1946-48. *Politics:* Republican. *Religion:* Protestant. *Home:* 505 East Waring Ave., State College, Pa. 16801. *Office:* State College Area High School, State College, Pa.

CAREER: Teacher of history in public high school in Haddon Heights, N.J., 1943-47; Pennsylvania State University, Swarthmore, instructor in history, 1947-48; State College Area High School, State College, Pa., teacher of history, 1959—. Instructor at Pennsylvania State University, 1951-59, 1965—. Member of humanities committee of Pennsylvania Department of Public Instruction, 1963-66. *Member:* National Education Association, Pennsylvania State Education Association, State College Area Education Association (president, 1965-66), Phi Alpha Theta, Phi Gamma Mu, Kappa Delta Epsilon.

WRITINGS: (With husband, Leo A. Bressler) *Country, Conscience, and Conscription*, Prentice-Hall, 1970; (with L. A. Bressler) *Youth in American Life*, Houghton, 1972; (contributor) *Contemporary Soviet Society: Episodes in Social Inquiry*, Allyn & Bacon, 1973; (with L. A. Bressler) *War or Peace: Does Humanity Have a Choice?*, Prentice-Hall, 1975. Contributor to *Pennsylvania News and Views*.

* * *

BRIDGMAN, Sarah Atherton   1889(?)-1975
  (Sarah Atherton)

1889(?)—February 12, 1975; American author of novels. Obituaries: *AB Bookman's Weekly*, March 17, 1975.

* * *

BRIGGS, L(loyd) Cabot   1909-1975

June 27, 1909—May 14, 1975; American anthropologist, educator, and author of books in his field. Obituaries: *New York Times*, May 19, 1975; *AB Bookman's Weekly*, July 7, 1975. (*CA-5/6*)

* * *

BRIGGS, Peter   1921-1975

April 15, 1921—July 18, 1975; American magazine editor, advertising and promotion manager for publishers, and author of books on oceanography. Obituaries: *New York Times*, July 19, 1975; *AB Bookman's Weekly*, August 4, 1975. (*CA-25/28*)

* * *

BRIGHTON, Howard   1925-

PERSONAL: Born August 22, 1925, in Jackson, Mich.; son of Howard W. and Eva E. (Campbell) Brighton; married Patricia Ann Larson, April 17, 1948; children: Cheryl Lee, Susan Kay, Lori Jo, Todd Alan. *Education:* Central Michigan University, B.S., 1954; University of Michigan, M.S., 1955; Michigan State University, graduate study, 1960; University of Oklahoma, Ph.D., 1964. *Home:* 2231 Riverwood Dr., Okemos, Mich. 48864. *Office:* South-Central Regional Center, Michigan State University, East Lansing, Mich.

CAREER: Teacher of social science in junior high and high schools in Ovid, Mich., 1954-55, and East Jordan, Mich., 1955-60; Northern Illinois University, Laboratory School, DeKalb, guidance director and administrative assistant, 1961; Office of Economic Opportunity, Camp Quachita, Ark., deputy director of education, 1964-65; Custer Job Corps Experimental Reception Center, Battle Creek, Mich., director of group life, 1965; Olivet College, Olivet, Mich., chairman of education department and director of teacher education, 1966; Michigan State University, East Lansing, associate professor of education and director of South-Central Regional Center, 1967—. Consultant on education and poverty to Radio Corp. of America and University of Wisconsin. *Military service:* U.S. Navy, 1943-46, 1951-52; served in Pacific and Asiatic theatres, respectively. U.S. Naval Reserve, 1946-51. *Member:* National University Extension Association, Adult Education Association of Michigan.

WRITINGS: Handbook for Teacher Aides, Pendell, 1972; *Utilizing Teacher Aides in Differentiated Staffing*, Pendell, 1972. Also author of eight training guides.

* * *

BRIGHTON, Wesley, Jr.
  See LOVIN, Roger Robert

* * *

BRIGNANO, Russell C(arl)   1935-

PERSONAL: Born June 26, 1935, in Hartford, Conn.; son of Joseph Francis and Adelina (a clerk; maiden name, Accomasso) Brignano; married Mary Louise Germann (a writer and editor), January 24, 1969. *Education:* Dartmouth College, B.A., 1957; University of Wisconsin, M.S., 1963, Ph.D., 1966. *Home:* 2265 Buena Vista Rd., McKeesport, Pa. 15135. *Office:* Department of English, Carnegie-Mellon University, Pittsburgh, Pa. 15213.

CAREER: Carnegie-Mellon University, Pittsburgh, Pa.; assistant professor, 1966-70, associate professor of English, 1970—. Visiting professor at University of Pittsburgh, summer, 1970. Literature consultant to McCullough Communications, 1973—; member of board of directors of Mendelssohn Choir of Pittsburgh, 1974—. *Military service:* U.S. Army, 1957-59. *Member:* Modern Language Association of America, American Association of University Professors, Pennsylvania English Association. *Awards, honors:* Younger Humanist fellowship from National Endowment for the Humanities, 1970-71.

WRITINGS: Richard Wright: An Introduction to the Man and His Works, University of Pittsburgh Press, 1970; *Black Americans in Autobiography: An Annotated Bibliography of Autobiographies and Autobiographical Books Written Since the Civil War*, Duke University Press, 1974. Contributor to *Studies in Black Literature, Negro American Literature Forum, Three Rivers Poetry Journal*, and *CEA Forum*.

WORK IN PROGRESS: Research for a book-length study of twentieth-century American first-person novels.

* * *

BRINGHURST, Robert 1946-

PERSONAL: Born October 16, 1946, in Los Angeles, Calif.; son of George H. and Marion (Large) Bringhurst; married Miki Cannon Sheffield, June 3, 1975. *Education:* Attended Massachusetts Institute of Technology, 1963-64, 1970-71, and University of Utah, 1964-65; Indiana University, B.A., 1973; University of British Columbia, M.F.A., 1975. *Home:* 1752 Ottawa Pl., West Vancouver, British Columbia V7V 2T7, Canada.

CAREER: Worked as journalist in Beirut, Lebanon, 1965-66, and in Boston, Mass., 1970-71; dragoman for U.S. Army in Israel and Palestine, 1967-68; law clerk in Panama Canal Zone, 1968-69; University of British Columbia, Vancouver, British Columbia, fellow of creative writing department, 1973-75. *Awards, honors:* Macmillan Prize for Poetry, 1975.

WRITINGS: The Shipwright's Log (poems), Kanchenjunga Press, 1972; *Cadastre* (poems), Kanchenjunga Press, 1973; *Deuteronomy* (chapbook), Sono Nis Press, 1974; *Eight Objects* (chapbook), Kanchenjunga Press, 1975; *Bergschrund* (poems), Sono Nis Press, 1975. Contributor of essays, poems, translations, and articles to literary magazines, including *Poetry, Malahat Review, Kayak, Ontario Review, Fiddlehead, Ohio Review, Prism International, The Canadian Fiction Magazine,* and *West Coast Poetry Review.* Review editor of *The Canadian Fiction Magazine,* 1974-75; member of editorial board, 1973—, and guest editor of Arabic literature and Greek issues of *Contemporary Literature in Translation.*

WORK IN PROGRESS: Translating with H. G. Edinger, Aeschylus' *Persians; The Oral Performance of Poetry: A Polemical History; The Presidential Poems* (tentative title).

SIDELIGHTS: Of *Deuteronomy,* Dennis Lee has written: "This poem compels the recognition of excellence—among other things, because it works beyond having to compel such recognition—in a way almost nothing I've seen by peers, here or elsewhere, does. It is a beautifully sure-footed poem, tough, with real content, easy in its own skin. It moves like somebody stalking, and some of those terse throwaways go for the jugular." Guy Davenport said of *Eight Objects* that "the man who doesn't like these poems doesn't like poetry, and doesn't know what it is."

Bringhurst translates from Arabic, Greek, Italian, and French, and has given poetry readings on Canadian Broadcasting Corp. network radio and at universities and other institutions in the United States and Canada. His poems have appeared in Polish and Portuguese translations.

* * *

BROCK, Gerald Wayne 1948-

PERSONNAL: Born March 31, 1948, in Hanford, Calif.; son of Aston A. and Leila (McAtee) Brock; married Ruth Reisner, June 27, 1971; children: Jane Ruth. *Education:* Harvard University, B.A. (magna cum laude), 1970, M.A., 1973, Ph.D., 1973. *Politics:* Democrat. *Religion:* Christian. *Home:* 2419 Blacklidge, Tucson, Ariz. 85719. *Office:* Department of Economics, University of Arizona, Tucson, Ariz. 85721.

CAREER: Potter-Brock Associates (computer software and consulting firm), Cambridge, Mass., manager and partner, 1970-73; University of Arizona, Tucson, assistant professor of economics, 1973—. Consultant to U.S. Senate Subcommittee on Antitrust and Monopoly. *Member:* American Economic Association.

WRITINGS: The United States Computer Industry: A Study of Market Power, Ballinger, 1975; (contributor) Richard Caves and Marc Roberts, editors, *Regulating the Product: Quality and Variety,* Ballinger, 1975.

WORK IN PROGRESS: Research for a book on the economics of the telecommunications industry, focusing on the effect of regulation on technological progress.

SIDELIGHTS: Brock writes: "My goal is to apply the tools of formal economic analysis to areas of significant public concern in an attempt to improve the political decisions that are made. I have chosen the computer and communications industries as research subjects because of the likelihood of their being affected by antitrust, regulatory, and legislative decisions." *Avocational interests:* Gardening, building.

* * *

BROCK, Stanley E(dmunde) 1936-

PERSONAL: Born April 21, 1936, in Preston, England; son of William Frederick Stanley (a government employee) and Irene (Mandley) Brock. *Education:* Attended schools in England. *Agent:* Oliver Swan, Julian Bach, Inc., 18 East 48th St., New York, N.Y. 10017. *Address:* Stan Brock Enterprises, Inc., P.O. Box 2530, Sanford, Fla. 32771.

CAREER: General manager of Dadanawa Ranch in Guyana, 1953-68; co-host of Mutual of Omaha's "Wild Kingdom" television series, 1967-72; free-lance writer, actor, and producer in England and United States, 1968—; Stan Brock Enterprises, Inc., Sanford, Fla., president, 1972—; Stan Brock Wilderness Adventures, Inc., Knoxville, Tenn., president, 1973—. Federal Aviation Administration certified flight instructor, 1974—; collector of mammals for scientific study for Royal Ontario Museum and United States National Museum, 1960—. *Member:* Zoological Society of London (fellow), Royal Life Saving Society Lifeguard Corps, Royal Ontario Museum (research associate), Central Florida Zoological Society (member of board of trustees, 1975—), Explorers Club of New York, Adventurers Club of Chicago.

WRITINGS—All nonfiction: *Hunting in the Wilderness,* R. Hale, 1962; *Leemo: The Story of a Mountain Lion,* Taplinger, 1966; *More About Leemo,* Taplinger, 1967; *Jungle Cowboy,* Taplinger, 1972. Contributor to *Reader's Digest, Outdoor Life, Geographical Magazine* and other magazines. Writer of motion picture scripts, "Beyond Kaieteur," "Lasso," and "Forgotten Wilderness."

WORK IN PROGRESS: Women and Exploration of the Nile, completion expected in 1976; a humorous account of the formation of the Central Florida Zoo, 1976.

SIDELIGHTS: When Brock was seventeen he travelled to South America with his father, and the lure of the unspoiled wilderness of Guyana prompted him to stay there for the next sixteen years. During the years he spent there he discovered a new species of bat in the remote Kuitaro River Rain Forest which is now known as *Vampyressa brockii.* His travels have been extensive and he speaks Portuguese and Wapishana, a language used by one of the tribes in the Amazon Basin. He holds a Black Belt in Tae Kwon Do.

Brock stars in the motion picture "The Forgotten Wilderness," released in the fall of 1975, and in the Japanese television series, "Adventures."

BIOGRAPHICAL/CRITICAL SOURCES: Argosy, August, 1972.

* * *

BRODATZ, Philip 1915-

PERSONAL: Born May 12, 1915, in New York, N.Y.; son of Barnett and Sophia (Tobin) Brodatz; married Lillian Schwarcz, June 19, 1938; children: Judith (Mrs. Gerald Wolfsohn). *Education:* Fordham University, Ph.G., 1936, B.S., 1938; Brooklyn Polytechnical Institute, graduate study, 1938-39. *Home:* 100 Edgewater Dr., Coral Gables, Fla. 33133.

CAREER: Estates Camera Shop, Jamaica, N.Y., owner and manager, 1940-55; Time-Life, Inc. Photo Lab, New York, N.Y., photographer, 1956-57; professional photographer for advertising, public relations, industry, and book publishing. Lecturer at School of Visual Arts, New York, N.Y., 1966, Germain School of Photography, 1956-57, New York City Community College, 1967-68, University of Miami, 1969-74, and Fairchild Tropical Gardens, 1969—; associate of Suffolk Museum, Stony Brook, N.Y., 1958-68; has had many one-man shows and exhibits of his photography; director of Photo Center of University of Miami, 1969-74. *Military service:* U.S. Army Medical Corps, 1945. *Member:* Professional Photographers Guild of Florida. *Awards, honors:* Awards from New York World's Fair and Philadelphia Art Directors Club, 1965, and from Center for the Arts, Boca Raton, Fla., 1975.

WRITINGS: (With Dori Watson) *The Human Form in Action and Repose,* Van Nostrand, 1966; *Textures: A Photographic Album for Artists and Designers,* Dover, 1966; (with Watson) *The Elements of Landscape,* Van Nostrand, 1967; *Wood and Wood Grains,* Dover, 1971; *Earth, Air, Fire, Water,* Dover, 1974. A limited edition of his photographs, *Gulls in Flight,* was published in 1973.

WORK IN PROGRESS: Poland: People and Places; Plant and Flower Photography.

SIDELIGHTS: Brodatz writes: "People keep accusing me of producing works of art, but this I vigorously deny. Art is a word with many ancient connotations. It presents an image of an earlier age and its tortuous handicraft—the chipping of marble, the meticulous daubing of canvas or ivory with pigment—and bears no relation whatever to a visual experience produced by the elements of light, time and space in simultaneous reaction. When these elements combine in their most felicitous relationship, the result is what I call a 'light work.'"

BIOGRAPHICAL/CRITICAL SOURCES: Photographic Product News, March, 1967.

* * *

BRODE, Douglas 1943-

PERSONAL: Born August 4, 1943, in Patchogue, N.Y.; son of Joseph (an antique dealer and artist) and Irma (Lichenstein) Brode; married Sue Anne Johnson (a teacher), July 22, 1967; children: Shane. *Education:* State University of New York College at Genesco, B.S., 1965; Syracuse University, M.A., 1969. *Politics:* Liberal Democrat. *Religion:* "Jewish, thinking about becoming a Quaker." *Home:* 104 Longdale Dr., Liverpool, N.Y. 13088. *Office:* English Department, Onondaga Community College, Syracuse, N.Y. 13215.

CAREER: Teacher of high school English, Long Island, N.Y., 1965-66; Onondaga Community College, Syracuse, N.Y., professor of English, 1970—. Part-time teacher of film, Syracuse University, 1970—. Theatre and film critic, WHEN-Radio, Syracuse, 1972—. Host of public television shows on cultural affairs and film festivals, 1970-73. *Member:* University Film Association, Young New York Film Critics.

WRITINGS: Crossroads to the Cinema, Holbrook, 1975; *Films of the Fifties,* Citadel, 1976. Entertainment editor, and author of weekly column, "Film Rap," in *Syracuse New Times,* 1970—. Contributor of articles to numerous magazines, including *Show, Cineaste, Rolling Stone, Sepia,* and *Event.*

WORK IN PROGRESS: Two books, *The Blondes: A History of the Blonde Mystique in Movies,* and *Writing about Film,* completion of both expected in 1976.

* * *

BRODER, Patricia Janis 1935-

PERSONAL: Born November 22, 1935, in New York, N.Y.; daughter of Milton W. and Rheba (Mantell) Janis; married Stanley H. Broder (an attorney), January 22, 1959; children: Clifford James, Peter Howard, Helen Anna. *Education:* Attended Smith College, 1953-54; Barnard College and Columbia University, joint B.A., 1957; Rutgers University, graduate study, 1962-64. *Home and office:* 488 Long Hill Dr., Short Hills, N.J. 07078.

CAREER: A. M. Kidder (stock broker), New York, N.Y., trainee, 1958-59; Thomson & McKinnon (stock broker), New York, N.Y., customer's broker, 1962-64; art historian and writer, 1964—. Independent investment adviser, 1962-64. Member of Speaker's Bureau of New York Stock Exchange. *Member:* American Association of University Women, Western History Association, Smith Club, Barnard Club. *Awards, honors:* Herbert Adams Memorial Medal from National Sculpture Society, 1975, and Gold Medal from National Academy of Western Art, 1975, both for *Bronzes of the American West.*

WRITINGS: Bronzes of the American West, Abrams, 1974. Contributor to *Southwest Art, American Art Review, Arizona Highways,* and *Antiques.*

SIDELIGHTS: Patricia Broder has traveled in Europe and in the United States, especially Colorado, Arizona, New Mexico, and Oklahoma. She writes: "Bronze sculpture of the West glorifies the cowboy and the Indian, the explorer and the hunter, wild life and cattle.... This history is meaningful in the light of our present day concern with the preservation of our natural resources and our interest in our past and present relationship with the American Indian. I am concerned with bronze sculpture of both the past and the present. I include the vision of pioneer, cowboy, and Indian artists, traditionalist and abstractionist." *Avocational interests:* Fox hunting, painting (ink, acrylic, and oil combinations), skiing, and tennis.

* * *

BRODY, Polly 1919-

PERSONAL: Born November 23, 1919, in Chicago, Ill.; daughter of Harry J. (a building contractor) and Ida (Altman) Brody; married Alex Temkin, August 29, 1942 (divorced, 1966); children: Joan (Mrs. John Lambdin), Frances, Ruth. *Education:* University of Wisconsin, Madison, B.A., 1940. *Home:* 1707 North Prospect Ave. #9E, Milwaukee, Wis. 53202.

CAREER: Spanish language secretary to exporter in Fort Wayne, Ind., 1940-41, and in Chicago, Ill., 1941-42; University of Wisconsin, Madison, instructor in Spanish, 1942-44; Mohawk Building Corp., Madison, Wis., secretary and treasurer, 1945-65. Chairman of Madison Red Cross campaign, 1956, Madison Cancer Crusade, 1959, and of Shorewood League Combined Health Fund Campaign, 1963. *Member:* National League of American Pen Women, National Writers Club, Council of Wisconsin Writers.

WRITINGS: Discovering Wisconsin, Wisconsin House, 1973. Contributor to periodicals.

WORK IN PROGRESS: A book concerning personal experience in growth using Gestalt, bioenergetics, and creative fantasy techniques, titled *Nowhere to Go But Inside.*

* * *

BROEKMAN, Marcel 1922-

PERSONAL: Born September 14, 1922, in Amsterdam, Netherlands; married Minnie Goudeket (a motion picture editor), December 25, 1945; children: Jack Donald, Renee Theresa. *Education:* Educated in Amsterdam, Netherlands and Paris, France. *Office:* Professional Films, Inc., 1600 Broadway, New York, N.Y. 10019.

CAREER: Motion picture producer, 1945-54; Professional Films, Inc., New York, N.Y., cameraman and producer, 1954—. Teacher of vocational courses in private schools in New York, N.Y., 1951-62.

WRITINGS: The Complete Encyclopedia of Practical Palmistry, Prentice-Hall, 1973.

WORK IN PROGRESS: Research on palmistry.

AVOCATIONAL INTERESTS: Palmistry (student since 1937; palmist since 1950), astronomy, ham radio.

* * *

BROESAMLE, John J(oseph) 1941-

PERSONAL: Born February 10, 1941, in Long Beach, Calif.; son of Otto Albert (a teacher) and Josephine (Young) Broesamle; married Katharine Warne (a teacher), June 12, 1963; children: Carolyn Jo, Robert Alan. *Education:* University of the Pacific, B.A., 1964; Columbia University, M.A., 1965, Ph.D., 1970. *Politics:* Democrat. *Home:* 895 Valley High Ave., Thousand Oaks, Calif. 91360. *Office:* Department of History, California State University, 18111 Nordhoff St., Northridge, Calif. 91324.

CAREER: California State University, Northridge, assistant professor, 1968-72, associate professor, 1972-75, professor of history, 1975—, associate dean of School of Social and Behavioral Sciences, 1973—. *Member:* American Association of University Professors, American Historical Association, Organization of American Historians. *Awards, honors:* Woodrow Wilson fellowships, 1964-65, 1966-67.

WRITINGS: William Gibbs McAdoo: A Passion for Change, 1863-1917, Kennikat, 1973; (contributor) Lewis L. Gould, editor, *The Progressive Era*, Syracuse University Press, 1974. Contributor to journals.

WORK IN PROGRESS: Research on twentieth-century American liberalism, with publication expected to result; research for a second volume on McAdoo.

SIDELIGHTS: Broesamle writes: "My primary interest as a scholar is in twentieth-century political processes in the United States—the party system, liberal and conservative ideologies, and the uses of governmental power."

BROKHIN, Yuri 1934-

PERSONAL: Born October 4, 1934, in Dnepropetrovsk, U.S.S.R.; came to United States, 1972; son of Abe and Rachel (Bogopolskaja) Brokhin; married Tania Dobrjanskaja (an actress), August 22, 1970. *Education:* Mining Engineering Institute, Dnepropetrovsk, diploma in engineering, 1958; All-Union Institute of Cinematography, M.F.A. equivalent, 1967. *Home:* 585 West 214th St., Apt. 4B New York, N.Y. 10034.

CAREER: Worked as a mining engineer in Donbass, U.S.S.R., 1958-61; editor, director, and writer for Lugansk Television Studio and Central U.S.S.R. TV Broadcasting Studio, Moscow, 1961-67; director and scriptwriter for Studio of the Central TV Broadcasting Studio, Central Studio of Scientific Films, and Central Studio of Documentary Films, Moscow, 1967-72; Berlitz School, New York, N.Y., instructor in Russian, 1973; State University of New York at Albany, instructor in Russian, 1973-74. Instructor at Moscow Institute of Cinematography, 1970-72. *Awards, honors:* Award from VIII International Film Festival in Krakow, Poland, 1971, for film, "The Day of Doctor Berezov."

WRITINGS: Hustling on Gorky Street: Sex and Crime in Russia, translated from the Russian by E. B. Kane, Dial, 1975. Author of twenty screenplays for Soviet films and television. Also author and narrator of industrial show for Reithion, Inc. and Federal Aviation Administration. Contributor to *Dissent, Russian Language Journal, Jewish Digest*, and *New York Times.*

WORK IN PROGRESS: A book, *How Soviet Jews Discover America.*

* * *

BROOKE, Avery (Rogers) 1923-
(Alice Benjamin)

PERSONAL: Born May 28, 1923, in Providence, R.I.; daughter of Morgan Witter and Lucy (Benjamin) Rogers; married Joel Brooke (a sociologist), September 14, 1946; children: Witter, Lucy, Sarah. *Education:* Rhode Island School of Design, B.F.A., 1945; Union Theological Seminary, graduate study, 1968-71. *Politics:* Democrat. *Religion:* Episcopalian. *Home:* 129 Nearwater Lane, Noroton, Conn. 06820.

CAREER: Teacher of art in Pomfret, Conn., 1945-46; teacher of prayer and meditation in Noroton, Conn., 1961-71; Vineyard Books, Inc., Noroton, Conn., president, 1972—. Founder and director of St. Luke's School for Laymen. *Member:* United World Federalists, League of Women Voters, Darien Democratic Town Committee, Darien-Mercara India Committee (co-founder).

WRITINGS: Youth Talks with God, Scribner, 1959; *Doorway to Meditation*, Vineyard Books (Noroton, Conn.), 1973; *Plain Prayers for a Complicated World*, Reader's Digest Press, 1975; (editor) *Roots of Spring*, Vineyard Books (Noroton, Conn.), 1975; *How to Meditate without Leaving the World*, Vineyard Books (Noroton, Conn.), 1975.

(Under pseudonym Alice Benjamin, with Harriett Corrigan) *Cooking with Conscience*, Vineyard Books (Noroton, Conn.), 1975. Founder and editor of *St. Luke's Quarterly.*

SIDELIGHTS: Avery Brooke writes: "I like to write simply, but not carelessly. I love to think, but I am not a scholar. I lean to practicality, but not if it's dull."

BROOKS, Karen 1949-

PERSONAL: Born May 28, 1949, in St. Louis, Mo.; daughter of Alan Herbert (president of Champion Marketing) and Ethel Marion (Berk) Fleishman. *Education:* Attended University of Missouri. *Politics:* Independent. *Religion:* "Zen Judaism." *Residence:* Creve Coeur, Mo. *Agent:* Oscar Collier, 280 Madison Ave., New York, N.Y. 10016.

CAREER: Creator of candlecraft and beadwork in the western United States, 1969-75. Classical pianist and piano teacher, 1969-71; manager and cook for Barnetts Restaurant, Columbia, Mo., 1970; volunteer worker in occupational therapy department of Renard Hospital, 1975, teaching breadmaking.

WRITINGS: The Forget About Meat Cookbook, Rodale Books, 1974. Author of weekly column, "Natural Foods," for *St. Louis Post Dispatch*, 1974—. Contributor to *National Observer* and *Leisure Living*.

WORK IN PROGRESS: The Age of Vegetarius (tentative title), a cookbook; *Eye of the Tornado*, a novel.

SIDELIGHTS: Karen Brooks writes: "In 1970 I lived at Rainbow Ridge, a one hundred-twenty-acre farm in Easley, Missouri. We grew almost all of our food, did our own canning, and even tapped the maple trees for syrup. Creativity in cooking became a real challenge. To help preserve the 'old school' of cooking simon-pure, I managed and cooked for the first health food restaurant off the University of Missouri campus. We made everything that was feasible ourselves—the bread, mayonnaise, granola, yogurt, applesauce, etc. Our objective was to see cooking return to what it was, an art, to be done with originality, skill, and love. Our restaurant was a gastronomical success and a financial disaster . . . I began my book in Silverado Canyon in Southern California. Then I moved to Sedona, Arizona, where I studied medicinal herbs with a Hopi medicine man while I completed the book." *Avocational interests:* Athletics, gardening, poetry, drama, folk-rock guitar, backpacking, camping out.

* * *

BROOKS, Pat 1931-

PERSONAL: Born February 27, 1931, in Greensboro, N.C.; daughter of Wilbur W. and Helen (Caspari) O'Donovan; married Richard F. Brooks (an engineer), June 23, 1953; children: Charles, John, Beth Ann, William. *Education:* Attended Duke University, 1948-50; Tufts University, B.A., 1952; graduate study at University of California, Berkeley, 1956, Newark State College, 1957-59, Columbia Bible College, 1960, and at Syracuse University, 1973. *Politics:* Conservative: Republican. *Religion:* Christian and Missionary Alliance. *Home and office:* 163 Wood Dale Dr., Ballston Lake, N.Y. 12019.

CAREER: Missionary and free-lance writer. *Awards, honors:* Logos Writers' Workshop prize, 1973; Guideposts' Workshop prize, 1973.

WRITINGS: Out! In the Name of Jesus (autobiography), Creation House, 1973; *Using Your Spiritual Authority*, Whitaker House, 1973; *Climb Mount Moriah*, Whitaker House, 1974; *Daughters of the King*, Creation House, 1975. Contributor to *Christian Life, Human Events, Christian Reader, New Wine*, and *Christian Teacher*.

* * *

BROOKS, Robert Emanuel 1941-

PERSONAL: Born September 11, 1941, in Detroit, Mich.; son of Rubin Brown (a foreman) and Alva (Young) Brooks; married Louella Ellis, August 1, 1964 (divorced, 1968); married Anna Louise Blackwell (employed with IBM), February 2, 1969; children: Troy Emanuel, Kent, Dawn. *Education:* Attended high school in Detroit, Mich. *Religion:* Protestant. *Residence:* East Elmhurst, N.Y. *Agent:* Miriam Gilbert, 146-47 29th Ave., Flushing, N.Y. 11354. *Office:* 96-05 Horace Harding Expressway, Flushing, N.Y. 11369.

CAREER: U.S. Army, 1958-68; served in Far East and Europe. Currently employed in clerical work. *Awards, honors:* High Quality Award for Outstanding Service in Social Security Administration, 1974.

WRITINGS: Utopian Universe, R.J.R. Press, 1973. Contributor to *Long Island Press* and *Oasis*.

WORK IN PROGRESS: Three books: *Poetic Reflections of a Utopian*; *Black GIs in the Military Bag*; *Sex Via Telepathy*.

* * *

BROOKS, W. Hal 1933-

PERSONAL: Born June 11, 1933, in Silverton, Tex.; son of Wilford Houston (a farmer and manager of an oil field supply company) and Madge Brooks; married Paula Preston Griffin (a drama teacher), June 7, 1957; children: Kriss Renee, Mark David. *Education:* Attended Oklahoma State University, 1952-54; Oklahoma Baptist University, B.A., 1957; Southwestern Baptist Theological Seminary, B.D., 1961. *Home:* 4820 Reynolds Rd., Fort Worth, Tex. 76118. *Office:* North Richland Hills Baptist Church, 4001 Vance Rd., Fort Worth, Tex. 76118.

CAREER: Ordained Southern Baptist minister, 1953; pastor of Southern Baptist churches in Sumner, Okla., 1953-54, and Irving, Tex., 1957-59; North Richland Hills Baptist Church, Fort Worth, Tex., pastor, 1959—, director of Christian Counseling Center, 1973—. President of board of directors of Sowers of Seed Publishing Co. Has conducted more than five hundred revivals and Bible conferences; speaker at State Evangelism Conferences in Texas and Colorado; Bible teacher at Glorieta Assembly; cofounder of Texas Falls Creek Youth Camp. Member of board of directors of Haltom-Richland Area Chamber of Commerce.

WRITINGS: Your Life in Christ, Broadman, 1971; *Follow-Up Evangelism*, Broadman, 1972; *Daily Light for Daily Living*, Broadman, 1975. Author of Sunday school lessons for the Baptist Sunday School Board, 1971-72.

WORK IN PROGRESS: Life of Christ; Life of Peter; Pictorial Bible Survey; Role and Relationship: Husband and Wife; Life's Basic Problems as Seen in Temptation of Christ.

AVOCATIONAL INTERESTS: Travel (Europe and the Holy Land), sculpture, architectural designing, building of stained glass windows.

* * *

BROUGH, R(obert) Clayton 1950-

PERSONAL: Surname rhymes with "rough"; born May 29, 1950, in Los Angeles, Calif.; son of Robert Marshall (a businessman) and Utahna Peterson; married Ethel Mickelson, August 22, 1973; children: Alison Utahna. *Education:* Santa Monica City College, student, 1969; Brigham Young University, B.S., 1974, M.S., 1975. *Politics:* Republican.

Religion: Church of Jesus Christ of Latter-day Saints (Mormon). *Home:* 445 East 200th N., Springville, Utah 84663. *Office:* Springville Junior High School, Springville, Utah 84663.

CAREER: Springville Junior High School, Springville, Utah, science teacher, 1975—; executive vice-president of American Geographical Research Corp., 1975—. *Member:* Gamma Theta Upsilon.

WRITINGS: Mosida, Utah: Past, Present, and Future, Press Publishers, 1974; *His Servants Speak,* Horizon, 1975. Contributor to magazines and newspapers.

WORK IN PROGRESS: Utah History and Geographical Atlas; Mormonism in Contemporary Society.

SIDELIGHTS: Brough writes: "Throughout grammar school and junior high school I was continually told by many of my teachers that I was a 'failure' in 'reading and writing,' and that it would be a 'miracle if I ever graduated from high school.' By the time I finished the eighth grade I was nearly convinced that they were right.

"However, in the ninth grade one social-studies teacher 'believed' in me, and through positive approaches convinced me that I was 'not a failure.' From that moment on I determined to fight to succeed . . . I am convinced of the power a teacher possesses to encourage others to achieve and develop a confident and happy image of themselves."

* * *

BROUGHTON, Panthea Reid   1940-

PERSONAL: Born September 11, 1940, in Birmingham, Ala.; daughter of John and Nell (a teacher of mathematics; maiden name, Marshall) Reid; married George Broughton, September 8, 1962 (divorced, 1975); children: Reid. *Education:* Attended Randolph-Macon Woman's College, 1958-59; University of Alabama, B.A., 1962, M.A., 1963; University of North Carolina, Ph.D., 1971. *Home:* 1262 Aberdeen Ave., Baton Rouge, La. 70808. *Office:* Department of English, Louisiana State University, Baton Rouge, La. 70803.

CAREER: University of Alabama, Birmingham, instructor in English, 1964-65; Virginia Polytechnic Institute and State University, Blacksburg, instructor, 1967-71, assistant professor of English, 1971-75; Louisiana State University, Baton Rouge, associate professor of English, 1975—. *Member:* Modern Language Association of America, American Association of University Professors.

WRITINGS: William Faulkner: The Abstract and the Actual, Louisiana State University Press, 1974; (editor and contributor) *Essays on Walker Percy,* Louisiana State University Press, in press; (editor with Joseph K. Davis and Michael Wood) *Literature: Craft and Content,* Scott, Foresman, in press. Contributor of about twenty articles and reviews to magazines and newspapers, including *Mississippi Quarterly, Southern Humanities Review, Southern Review, Wordsworth Circle, Twentieth Century Literature, Magill's Literary Annual, Saturday Review-World,* and *New Republic.*

WORK IN PROGRESS: Dismantling the Idea: A Study of Early Modern Art and Literature.

* * *

BROWER, Reuben Arthur   1908-1975

May 5, 1908—March 27, 1975; American educator, literary critic, and editor or author of books on literature and criti-

cism. Obituaries: *New York Times,* March 29, 1975; *AB Bookman's Weekly,* April 21, 1975. (*CA*-4)

* * *

BROWN, David (Clifford)   1929-

PERSONAL: Born July 8, 1929, in Gravesend, Kent, England; son of Bertram Critchley (an industrial manager) and Constance (Nicholls) Brown; married Elizabeth Valentine (a university lecturer), 1953; children: Gabrielle Elizabeth, Hilary Ann. *Education:* University of Sheffield, B.A., 1950, B.Mus., 1951, M.A., 1960; University of Southampton, Ph.D., 1971. *Home:* 56 Pentire Ave., Southampton, Hampshire SO1 2RS, England. *Office:* Department of Music, University of Southampton, Southampton, Hampshire SO9 5NH, England.

CAREER: Private school teacher of music in Kent, England, 1954-59; University of London, London, England, music librarian, 1959-62; University of Southampton, Southampton, England, lecturer, 1962-71, senior lecturer in music, 1971—. *Military service:* Royal Air Force, 1952-54; became pilot officer. *Member:* Royal Musical Association, Incorporated Society of Professional Musicians.

WRITINGS: Thomas Weelkes: A Biographical and Critical Study, Faber, 1969; *Mikhail Glinka: A Biographical and Critical Study,* Oxford University Press, 1974; *John Wilbye,* Oxford University Press, 1974. Contributor to *Grove Dictionary of Music and Musicians, Encyclopaedia Britannica,* and *Die Musik in Geschichte und Geganwart* and to professional journals.

WORK IN PROGRESS: A book on the life and works of Tchaikovsky, and one on the English madrigal; editions of English Renaissance music.

* * *

BROWN, Harry G(unnison)   1880-1975

1880—March 18, 1975; American economist, educator, university dean, and author of books on public finance, tax reform, and economic principles. Obituaries: *New York Times,* March 20, 1975; *AB Bookman's Weekly,* April 21, 1975.

* * *

BROWN, Hazel E(lizabeth)   1893-

PERSONAL: Born August 30, 1893, in Lowell, Mass.; daughter of Frederick Stanley (a retailer) and Elizabeth (Mitchell) Brown. *Education:* Coe College, B.A., 1915; University of Illinois, M.A., 1918. *Politics:* Democrat. *Religion:* Unitarian. *Home:* 225 29th St. Drive S.E., Cedar Rapids, Iowa 52403.

CAREER: High school teacher of English in Burley, Idaho, 1916-17; Western Union, Chicago, Ill., worked in welfare department, 1918; Penick and Ford Corn Products Co., Cedar Rapids, Iowa, head of department of welfare, 1924; owner of a gift and china shop in Cedar Rapids, Iowa, 1924-56. *Member:* Cedar Rapids Art Association, Beethoven Club, Chi Omega, Zeta Phi Eta.

WRITINGS: Grant Wood and Marvin Cone, Iowa State University Press, 1971. Writer of song lyrics.

WORK IN PROGRESS: Pottery to Porcelain; The Savage Breast; Tales from the Red Hen; Gift Show.

* * *

BROWN, Richard Howard   1929-

PERSONAL: Born January 7, 1929, in New York, N.Y.;

son of Lester Howard and Katherine Elizabeth (Read) Brown; married Violet Agnes Barsa, September 19, 1953; children: Pamela, Christopher, Trevor. *Education:* Attended Iona College, 1946-48, and Oxford University, 1949; Syracuse University, B.A., 1950. *Politics:* Democrat. *Religion:* Roman Catholic. *Home:* 1009 Washington Ave., Pelham, N.Y. 10803. *Agent:* John Cushman Associates, 25 West 43rd St., New York, N.Y. 10036. *Office:* R. R. Bowker Co., 1180 Avenue of the Americas, New York, N.Y. 10036.

CAREER: Daily Argus, Mount Vernon, N.Y., sports writer and cartoonist, 1953-55; General Features, New York, N.Y., promotion manager, 1955-57; Fleet Publishing, New York, general manager, 1957-59; sales manager, Pennington Press, 1959-60; *Foreign Affairs*, New York, N.Y., advertising sales manager, 1960-64; *New York Herald Tribune*, New York, N.Y., business manager of *Bookweek*, 1964-66; *Foreign Affairs*, business manager, 1966-70; partner, Visi-Med, 1970; *Phoenix*, Cambridge, Mass., advertising manager, 1970-72; publisher's consultant, 1973; R. R. Bowker Co., New York, N.Y., advertising sales manager, 1974—. *Military service:* U.S. Army, 1951-53. *Member:* Publishers Advertising Club (president, 1965-67).

WRITINGS: I Am of Ireland (nonfiction), Harper, 1974. Contributor to children's magazines, and to newspapers, including *Washington Post, Phoenix*, and *Real Paper*.

WORK IN PROGRESS: A novella, based on the escape of British agent Kenneth Littlejohn from a Dublin prison in 1974; a creative study of Michael Collins and the Irish Rebellion of 1916-1923, completion expected in 1977.

SIDELIGHTS: Brown writes: "I am a romantic; I am very Catholic, though I left the Church; I greatly value my past and the idea that the past is of value; I probably have a madonna complex; I like to think I'm a rebel and I am interested in rebellion—but essentially in an existentialist sense. Ireland is my metaphor for the human condition." *Avocational interests:* Playing the guitar, singing folksongs, drawing cartoons and portraits.

* * *

BROWN, Thomas H. 1930-

PERSONAL: Born July 23, 1930, in Copperton, Utah; son of Harold King (a mine foreman) and Emma (Featherstone) Brown; married Sheila Ann Dorius, June 30, 1955; children, Emma Rebecca, John Bradley, Alison Leigh, Thomas Christopher, Elizabeth Ann, Michael Harold. *Education:* Brigham Young University, B.A., 1955; University of Illinois, M.A., 1957, Ph.D., 1960. *Home:* 1635 North 1550 E., Provo, Utah 84601. *Office:* Department of French and Italian, Brigham Young University, Provo, Utah 84601.

CAREER: Brigham Young University, Provo, Utah, member of faculty in department of French, 1959—. Director of summer Brigham Young University French Studies at Laval University, 1961, and Sorbonne, University of Paris, 1962; visiting professor at University of Arizona, 1963 (summer), University of Colorado, 1967 (summer), and University of LaLaguna. Fulbright lecturer in Spain, 1965-66. Mission president for Church of Jesus Christ of Latter-Day Saints in France and Belgium, 1969-72. *Member:* American Association of Teachers of French, American Council on Learning of Foreign Languages.

WRITINGS: French: Listening, Speaking, Reading, Writ-

ing, McGraw, 1965, 2nd edition, 1971; *Writing Exercises for French*, McGraw, 1965, 2nd edition, 1971; *Langue et Litterature* (title means "Language and Literature"), with workbook, McGraw, 1967, 2nd edition, 1974; (author of preface) Jacques Morel, *La Tragedie*, McGraw, 1967; *La Fontaine and Cupid and Psyche Tradition*, Brigham Young University Press, 1968; (with Karl Sandberg) *Conversational English*, Xerox College Publishing, 1969. Contributor to journals in his field, including *Modern Language Journal* and *French Review*.

WORK IN PROGRESS: A study of La Fontaine's style in writing *Les Amours de Psyche et de Cupidon*.

AVOCATIONAL INTERESTS: Travel.

* * *

BROWN, W(illiam) Norman 1892-1975

June 24, 1892—April 22, 1975; American scholar on India, educator, museum curator, and editor or author of books on India, Pakistan, and Ceylon. Obituaries: *New York Times*, April 26, 1975.

* * *

BROWN, William Campbell 1928-

PERSONAL: Born May 25, 1928, in Los Angeles, Calif.; son of Marland Emery (a salesman) and Willie (Campbell) Brown; married Marie Harriet Thorson, June 8, 1956; children: William, Melinda, Karen, Paul. *Education:* Attended Multnomah School of Bible, 1953-55, Biola School of Missionary Medicine, 1955-56, and Summer Institute of Linguistics, 1955, 1956. *Politics:* Conservative. *Religion:* "Follower of the Messiah of Israel." *Home:* 1118 Refugio Rd., Santa Ynez, Calif. 93460. *Address:* Box 618, Solvang, Calif. 93463.

CAREER: Self-employed in California as landlord, 1947-50, shipping agent, 1957-60, general handyman and landlord, 1959—; Summer Institute of Linguistics, Mexico, field worker in descriptive linguistics, 1956-59; Christian Supply Center, Glendale, Calif., owner and bookkeeper, 1963-73; *Member:* John Birch Society (president of local chapter). *Military service:* U.S. Army, 1950-52.

WRITINGS: (With Brandon Rimmer) *The Unpredictable Wind*, Aragorn, 1972. Writer of KLOM radio programs, "The Bible Truths," 1959-74, and "Five Minutes with the Bible," 1967—.

* * *

BROWNING, Elizabeth 1924-

PERSONAL: Born March 19, 1924, in Yorkshire, England; daughter of Frank Brindley (a wool merchant and farmer) and Amy (Megson) Hirsch; married Christopher George Browning (a military historian and bookseller), April 9, 1946; children: Sarah (Mrs. James Gould), Hazel (Mrs. Peter Docherty), Jarvis. *Education:* Educated in England. *Politics:* "Have never belonged to any political party." *Religion:* Christian. *Home:* Forge House, Kemble, near Cirencester, Gloucester GL7 6AD, England. *Agent:* Richard Simon, 32 College Cross, London N1 1PR, England. *Office:* Association For All Speech Impaired Children, Toynbee Hall, 28 Commercial St., London E1 6LS, England.

CAREER: Writer. Member of management committee of Cheltenham Literary Festival, 1956-66; member of committee of Swindon District Council for Community Relations, 1967-70. *Member:* Association For All Speech Impaired Children (chairman), Writers Guild of Great Britain, Writers Action Group, Great Britain and East Europe Centre, National Star Centre for Disabled Youth.

WRITINGS: I Can't See What You're Saying, Elek, 1972, Coward, 1973. Contributor to *New Society, Social Services, Good Housekeeping, Lady, Woman,* and *Lion.*

WORK IN PROGRESS: Let's Face It, with Mary Charnock; a novel about defectors from a Communist-invaded country; a play about "responsible anarchy" and human relationships; a story of a young man who got involved helping non-communicating children; various magazine articles.

SIDELIGHTS: Elizabeth Browning writes: "We totally fail to communicate. We are all in isolation.... After the experience of my own son being born aphasic [she realized] seeing truth about oneself and facing it is the only way to growth. I abhore prevalent attitudes to young in schools and present day values held by most educational establishments. People are constantly de-valuing people. My cry is to value what is in each person."

*   *   *

BROWNING, Preston M(ercer), Jr.   1929-

PERSONAL: Born June 26, 1929, in Culpeper, Va.; son of Preston Mercer (a farmer and real estate broker) and Gertrude (Stephenson) Browning; married Ann Virginia Hutt (a director of education), June 14, 1959; children: Katharine, Sarah, Rachel, Preston III. *Education:* Washington and Lee University, B.A., 1951; University of North Carolina, Chapel Hill, M.A., 1957; University of Chicago, Ph.D., 1966. *Politics:* "Kennedy Democrat." *Religion:* Christian (Episcopalian). *Home:* 4921 South Dorchester Ave., Chicago, Ill. 60615. *Office:* University of Illinois at Chicago Circle, Chicago, Ill. 60680.

CAREER: University of Missouri, Columbia, instructor in English, 1957-59; Berea College, Berea, Ky., instructor in English, 1959-60; University of Illinois at Chicago Circle, Chicago, instructor, 1966-69, assistant professor, 1969-75, associate professor of English, 1975—, chairman of board of United Campus Ministry, 1973-74. *Military service:* U.S. Army, 1951-53; became corporal. *Member:* Modern Language Association of America, American Academy of Religion, Society for Religion in Higher Education, Hawthorne Society.

WRITINGS: Flannery O'Connor, Southern Illinois University Press, 1975. Contributor of articles to journals in his field, including *Midwest Quarterly, Modern Fiction Studies, Forum,* and *Southern Humanities Review.*

WORK IN PROGRESS: The grotesque in American fiction, especially that of Sherwood Anderson; love and sexuality in contemporary American fiction; religion in the literature of the South.

SIDELIGHTS: Preston Browning told *CA:* "My book on Flannery O'Connor grew out of a longstanding interest in southern culture and the effect of southern Protestant religiosity upon the development of character and personality. I am convinced that influence is, on the whole, a negative one, although I am attracted to O'Connor's sympathetic treatment of fanatical sectarian Christians."

About his own background, Browning comments that "while my formal education was principally in theology and literature, I find myself increasingly drawn to psychological analysis and expect someday to do a study of religion in

southern literature, with the chief emphasis being the psychic structures various kinds of religious backgrounds tend to produce." He adds, "I have lived in France (academic year 1970-71) and read, write and speak French. Foreign travel includes Great Britain, Italy, Greece, and Yugoslavia."

*   *   *

BROWNING, Reed   1938-

PERSONAL: Born August 26, 1938, in New York, N.Y.; son of Arthur M. (an insurance executive) and Martha (Reed) Browning; married Susan Lampley (a musician), January 8, 1963; children: Stephen Drew. *Education:* Dartmouth College, B.A., 1960; Yale University, M.A., 1962, Ph.D., 1965; graduate study at University of Vienna, 1962-63. *Home address:* Box 382, Gambier, Ohio 43022. *Office:* Department of History, Kenyon College, Gambier, Ohio 43022.

CAREER: Amherst College, Amherst, Mass., instructor, 1964-65, assistant professor of history, 1965-67; Kenyon College, Gambier, Ohio, associate professor of history, 1967—. *Member:* American Historical Association, Conference on British Studies. *Awards, honors:* Fulbright fellowship, 1962-63.

WRITINGS: The Duke of Newcastle, Yale University Press, 1975.

WORK IN PROGRESS: Court Whig thought in the reigns of George I and George II.

*   *   *

BROWNLEE, Walter   1930-

PERSONAL: Born September 9, 1930, Hartlepool, England; son of Mark (an engineer) and Elizabeth Jane Brownlee; married Joyce Cynthia Harrison (a teacher), July 30, 1960; children: Neville. *Education:* South Shields Nautical College, Second Officer's Cert., 1952, Chief Officer's Cert., 1955, Master Mariner, 1958; Sunderland College of Education, teaching certificate, 1961. *Home:* 23 Valley Gardens, Eaglescliffe, Cleveland TS16 OLY, England.

CAREER: Served in British Merchantile Marine, 1948-58; became master mariner. Teacher at various primary schools in North of England, 1961-66; Thornaby Church of England Primary School, Cleveland, England, deputy headmaster, 1964-66; Ragworth Primary School, Stockton, Cleveland, headmaster, 1969-74; Stockton Teachers Center, Cleveland, principal, 1974—.

WRITINGS: The White Dove (novel), Evans Brothers, 1966, Houghton, 1968; *The First Ships Round the World,* Cambridge University Press, 1974. Contributor to *Teachers World.*

WORK IN PROGRESS: A book on Napoleonic naval warfare for Cambridge University Press.

SIDELIGHTS: Brownlee has held an International Glider Pilots "A" License since 1948. *Avocational interests:* Photography, archaeology, historical research, wargames.

*   *   *

BRUENING, William H(arry)   1943-

PERSONAL: Born August 16, 1943, in Cincinnati, Ohio; son of Carl Bernard and Winifred (a clerk and typist; maiden name, Weunemann) Bruening; married Sheila McGarry (a teacher), June 9, 1969; children: Jennifer, William, Sean. *Education:* Thomas More College, B.A., 1965; University of Notre Dame, M.A., 1968, Ph.D., 1969. *Politics:* Independent. *Religion:* Roman Catholic. *Home:* 2317 Leroy, Fort Wayne, Ind. 46805. *Office:* Purdue University at Fort Wayne, 2101 U.S. 30 Bypass E., Fort Wayne, Ind. 46805.

CAREER: Purdue University at Fort Wayne, assistant professor, 1969-74, associate professor of philosophy, 1974—. Lecturer in philosophy at Thomas More College, summer, 1967; lecturer in philosophy at Indiana University at Fort Wayne, summer, 1974. *Member:* American Philosophical Association, American Catholic Philosophical Association, Institute for Ethics, Society, and the Life Sciences (of Hastings Center), Indiana Philosophical Association.

WRITINGS: (Contributor) George McLean, editor, *The Role of Reason in Belief*, Concord, 1974; (editor and contributor) *Self, Society, and the Search for Transcendence*, National Press Books, 1974; (editor with William Durland) *Ethical Issues: A Search for Patterns in the Contemporary Conscience*, National Press Books, 1975; *Ludwig Wittgenstein*, Twayne, in press; (with wife, Sheila Bruening) *Jean-Paul Sartre*, Twayne, in press.

Contributor of articles and reviews to *Ethical Issues, Archiv fuer Rechtsund Sozialphilosophie, Journal of Black Studies, Proceedings of the American Catholic Philosophical Association, Ethics,* and *New Scholasticism.*

WORK IN PROGRESS: Types of Religious Believers; Introduction to Ethics: A Critical Approach; Consciousness and Freedom: The Writings of Jean-Paul Sartre, with wife, Sheila M. Bruening; *The Writings of Albert Camus*, with J. Spencer Churchill; *The Is-Ought Problem: Its History, Analysis, and Dissolution; War and Peace: A Theological, Philosophical, and Psychological Investigation of Pacifism and Its Opponents*; research on two dogmas of liberalism, on prayer in a post-Christian era, on values, teaching, and education, on two dogmas of emotivism, on the good in Aristotle and Austin, on nonsense, nothingness, and personal identity, on the doctrine of analogy in Aristotle, Aquinas, and Austin, on ethics and analyticity, and on the analytic and synthetic.

*   *   *

BRUSH, Douglas Peirce   1930-

PERSONAL: Born March 1, 1930, in Cleveland, Ohio; son of Fred W. (a banker) and Doris I. (a real estate agent; maiden name, Peirce) Brush; married second wife, Judith M. Swulius (a communications consultant and writer), October 23, 1970; children: (first marriage) Stephanie E., Jennifer L., Meredith A. *Education:* Miami University, Oxford, Ohio, B.S., 1952. *Politics:* Democrat. *Home:* 1 David Lane, Yonkers, N.Y. 10701. *Office:* Mobil Oil Corp., 150 East 42nd St., New York, N.Y. 10017.

CAREER: Cleveland Electric Illumination Co., Cleveland, Ohio, public relations executive, 1954-57; Ferro Corp., Cleveland, Ohio, public relations manager, 1957-62; Burson-Marsteller Associates, New York, N.Y., account executive, 1962-63; BBD&O Advertising Co., New York, account supervisor, 1963-66; N.W. Ayer & Sons, Inc., New York, N.Y., account group director, 1966-71; Kalmus Corp., New York, N.Y., senior vice-president, 1971-72; D/J Brush Associates, Yonkers, N.Y., partner and communications consultant, 1972-74; Mobil Oil Corp., New York, N.Y., manager of media relations, 1974—. *Military service:* U.S. Navy, 1952-54. U.S. Naval Reserve, 1954-66;

became lieutenant commander. *Member:* International Industrial Television Society, Radio Television News Directors Association, Public Relations Society of America.

WRITINGS: (With wife, Judith M. Brush) *Private Television Communications: A Report to Management*, Knowledge Industry Publications, 1974.

WORK IN PROGRESS: Research into the use and effect of the media within corporate organizations; a management guide to the use of private television communications.

SIDELIGHTS: Brush is a semi-professional photographer.

*   *   *

BRUSH, Judith M(arie)   1938-

PERSONAL: Born August 27, 1938, in Chicago, Ill.; daughter of Aloysius F. (a bus driver) and Marie (Paczkowski) Swulius; married Douglas Peirce Brush (a corporate communications manager and writer), October 23, 1970. *Education:* Northwestern University, B.S.J., 1960. *Home:* 1 David Lane, Yonkers, N.Y. 10701. *Office:* D/J Brush Associates, 1 David Lane, Yonkers, N.Y. 10701.

CAREER: Market Facts, Inc., Chicago, Ill., director of public relations, 1960-62; Cook County Board of Commissioners, Chicago, Ill., assistant director of public relations, 1962-63; WBBM-TV, Chicago, Ill., assistant director of public and community relations, 1963-66; Black Star (international photojournalists), director of public relations in Chicago, Ill., 1967-69, and in New York, N.Y., 1969; Judith Swulius Associates (creative services), New York, N.Y., proprietor, 1969-70; Dudley-Anderson-Yutzy Public Relations, New York, N.Y., account executive, 1970-71; freelance public relations and communications consultant in New York, N.Y., 1971-73; D/J Brush Associates, (communications consultants), New York, N.Y., managing partner, 1973—. Director of public relations of Young Democrats of Illinois and Cook County, 1961-65. *Member:* International Industrial Television Association.

WRITINGS: (Contributor) Lawrence Senesh, editor, *Our Working World: Cities at Work*, Science Research Associates, 1967; (with husband, Douglas P. Brush) *Private Television Communications: A Report to Management*, Knowledge Industry Publications, 1974. Contributor to audio-visual journals. Member of national editorial board of Young Democratic Clubs of America, 1962-66.

WORK IN PROGRESS: Research on the use and effect of the media within U.S. corporations; a book on the older mother, focusing on professional women who choose to have their first child at thirty-five years of age or over.

AVOCATIONAL INTERESTS: Gourmet cooking, sewing, crewel embroidery, gardening.

*   *   *

BRUSILOFF, Phyllis   1935-

PERSONAL: Born June 6, 1935, in New York, N.Y.; daughter of Benjamin and Belle (Simon) Haber; married Eugene Brusiloff (a musician), April 11, 1963; children: Paul, Amy. *Education:* Brooklyn College (now of the City University of New York), B.S., 1959; Yeshiva University, M.S., 1962. *Office:* Child Development Center, 120 West 57th St., New York, N.Y. 10019.

CAREER: League School for Seriously Disturbed Children, Brooklyn, N.Y., member of staff, working with schizophrenic children, 1959-64, director of Nursery School

Division, 1962-64; Hudson Guild, New York, N.Y., group therapist, working with children, 1968-71; Jewish Board of Guardians, Child Development Center, New York, N.Y., project director, 1971—. Lecturer at City College of the City University of New York, 1972—. *Member:* American Orthopsychiatric Association. *Awards, honors:* National Institute of Mental Health grant, 1974-77, to train four nursery school teachers for therapeutic intervention and the delivery of service to twenty disturbed pre-schoolers, on-site in day care centers.

WRITINGS: (With Mary Jane Witenberg) *The Emerging Child*, Jason Aronson, 1973. Contributor to psychology journals.

SIDELIGHTS: Phyllis Brusiloff writes: "I consider intervention in the earliest years with children who come from families with generations of problems, crucial to resolving many problems especially in urban settings." *Avocational interests:* National and international travel, music, playing cello, ecology, swimming.

* * *

BRUTEAU, Beatrice 1930-

PERSONAL: Born July 25, 1930, in Carbondale, Ill.; daughter of Fred Bruto (an agronomist) and Ruth (a technical secretary; maiden name, Leebrick) Bruteau. *Education:* University of Missouri at Kansas City, B.A., 1950; University of Pittsburgh, M.Litt., 1951; Fordham University, Ph.D., 1969. *Address:* Philosophers' Exchange, Box 11144 Bethabara, Winston-Salem, N.C.

CAREER: International Philosophical Quarterly, New York, N.Y., managing editor, 1959-67; Teilhard Research Institute, New York, N.Y., coordinator, 1964-67; Bea Institute of Spirituality, New York, N.Y., assistant director, 1966-67; Foundation for Integrative Education, New York, N.Y., executive director, 1967-68; Philosophers' Exchange, Winston-Salem, N.C., director, 1972—. Consultant to Winston-Salem Model City Commission, 1970-71, and to Mandala Center, 1972-74. *Member:* American Academy of Religion, Society for Religion in Higher Education, American Teilhard Association for the Future of Man (vice-president, 1965-69; member of board of directors, 1965—), Committee on Cosmic Humanism (chairman, 1974—), International Wizard of Oz Club.

WRITINGS: Worthy Is the World: The Hindu Philosophy of Sri Aurobindo, Fairleigh Dickinson University Press, 1972; *Evolution toward Divinity: Teilhard de Chardin and the Hindu Traditions*, Theological Publishing, 1974; (contributor) Judith Plaskow and Joan A. Romero, editors, *Women and Religion*, Scholars Press, 1974. Contributor to journals.

WORK IN PROGRESS: A series in feminist philosophy: *The Psychic Grid: Epistemology*, completion expected in 1975, *The Intercommunicating Universe: Cosmology*, 1976, *The Virgin-Mother: Metaphysics and Natural Theology*, 1977, *Matristic Ethics*, and *Wisdom at Play: Esthetics; In the Temple of Athene: A Spiritual Odyssey*, 1975; an Oz book.

* * *

BUBB, Mel
See WHITCOMB, Ian

* * *

BUCHAN, Stuart 1942-
PERSONAL: Born August 30, 1942, in Sydney, Australia;

son of Reginald S. and Elizabeth (Denholm) Buchan. *Education:* University of British Columbia, B.A., 1965, M.Ed., 1969. *Home:* 1386 Nicola St., Apt. 1, Vancouver, B.C., Canada. *Agent:* Paul R. Reynolds Inc., 12 East 41st St., New York, N.Y. 10017.

CAREER: Capilano College, Vancouver, British Columbia, lecturer in early childhood education, 1969-71; Jewish Community Center, Vancouver, British Columbia, director of nursery schools, 1972; free-lance writer, 1973—. *Awards, honors:* Short story award from Macmillan of Canada, 1965, for "The Dead Sea Shell."

WRITINGS: Fleeced, Putnam, 1975.

* * *

BUCHANAN, (Eric) David 1933-
PERSONAL: Born July 2, 1933, in Edinburgh, Scotland; son of Eric Paton (a lawyer) and Kathleen (Porter) Buchanan. *Education:* University of Edinburgh, M.A., 1953, LL.B. (with distinction), 1955. *Office:* 6 Alva St., Edinburgh, Scotland.

CAREER: Steedman Ramage & Co. (law firm), Edinburgh, Scotland, partner, 1959—. *Military service:* British Army, Royal Scots, 1956-58; became lieutenant. *Member:* Law Society of Scotland.

WRITINGS: The Treasure of Auchinleck: The Story of the Boswell Papers, McGraw, 1974.

WORK IN PROGRESS: Continuing research on Boswell.

* * *

BUCHDAHL, Gerd 1914-
PERSONAL: Born August 12, 1914, in Mainz, Germany; son of Moritz (a businessman) and Emmy (Bendix) Buchdahl; married Nancy Miriam Wann, December 6, 1947; children: Roger M., Christopher M., Joseph M. *Education:* University of Melbourne, B.A. (honors), 1945, M.A., 1953. *Religion:* Church of England. *Home:* 11 Brookside, Cambridge CB2 1JE, England. *Office:* Department of History and Philosophy of Science, Cambridge University, Free School Lane, Cambridge CB2 3RH, England.

CAREER: University of Cambridge, Cambridge, England, fellow of Darwin College, 1964—, reader in history and philosophy of science, 1966—. *Member:* British Society for the Philosophy of Science, British Society for the History of Science, Aristotelian Society, Centro Superiore di Logica e Scienze Comparate, Academie Internationale de Philosophie des Sciences.

WRITINGS: The Image of Newton and Locke in the Age of Reason, Sheed & Ward, 1961; *Aristotle, Induction, and Necessity*, Aquinas Society, 1963; *Metaphysics and the Philosophy of Science. The Classical Origins: Descartes to Kant*, M.I.T. Press, 1969. Co-editor of *Studies in History and Philosophy of Science*, 1970—.

WORK IN PROGRESS: Science and Rational Structures, publication by Blackwell expected in 1976; research in the philosophy of science, the history of philosophy, and Kant.

AVOCATIONAL INTERESTS: Modern painting, modern music.

* * *

BUCHELE, William Martin 1895-
PERSONAL: Born July 15, 1895, in Louisville, Ky.; son of Otto and Mary (Kirchner) Buchele; married Wilma Sancta

Rower; children: Donald, Jeanne, Ruth, Elvin. *Education:* "I finished the seventh grade only, I only wanted to be an artist." *Politics:* "I vote for either party, probably most for Dem." *Religion:* "Now agnostic. Originally Catholic." *Home:* 2832 Sagamore Rd., Toledo, Ohio 43606.

CAREER: Sign painter for 26 years; worked making precision prisms during World War II, and, later, made optical elements for study of wind flow in air tunnels; considered tops by NACA in making the long-gun (muzzle-loader). *Military service:* U.S. Army, World War I. *Awards, honors:* Recipient of numerous trophys for marksmanship.

WRITINGS: (With George Shumway) *Kentucky Long Rifle*, George Shumway, 1973.

SIDELIGHTS: Buchele holds two and one-half optical patents. Interested in astronomy, he built a 20″ aperture reflector telescope, weighing 2,200 lbs. He was the Ohio amateur bicycle racing champion in 1915.

* * *

BUCHER, Glenn R(ichard) 1940-

PERSONAL: Born May 20, 1940, in Mechanicsburg, Pa.; son of K. Ezra (a businessman) and Esther (a teacher; maiden name, Markley) Bucher; married Mary K. Gladfelter (a musician), June 9, 1963; children: Christina Hope, Timothy Jon. *Education:* Elizabethtown College, A.B., 1962; Union Theological Seminary, New York, M.Div. (cum laude), 1965; Boston University, Ph.D., 1968. *Politics:* Independent. *Home:* 437 Pearl St., Wooster, Ohio 44691. *Office address:* Box 3185, College of Wooster, Wooster, Ohio 44691.

CAREER: Emerson College, Boston, Mass., part-time instructor in philosophy, 1967-68; Howard University, School of Religion, Washington, D.C., assistant professor of ethics and society and chairman of department, 1968-70; College of Wooster, Wooster, Ohio, assistant professor, 1970-74, associate professor of religion, 1975—, academic dean, Clergy Academy of Religion, 1972-73. Trustee of Elizabethtown College, 1968-74. *Member:* American Academy of Religion, American Society of Christian Ethics, American Association of University Professors, Omicron Delta Kappa. *Awards, honors:* National Endowment for the Humanities fellowship, 1971.

WRITINGS: (Contributor) R. T. Long and R. T. Handy, editors, *Theology and Church in Times of Change: Essays in Honor of John Coleman Bennett*, Westminster, 1974; (editor with Patricia R. Hill) *Confusion and Hope: Clergy, Laity, and the Church in Transition*, Fortress, 1974; (editor and contributor) *Liberation: White and Male and Straight*, Fortress, in press; (contributor) John Carey, editor, *White Responses to Black Theology*, Seabury Press, in press.

WORK IN PROGRESS: With Richard H. Bell, *Community As Christian Presence*; sole author, *A Liberation Ethic: Oppressor Praxis*; continuing research in the theological origins and solutions of white racism, in white Anglo-Saxon consciousness, in liberation theology, in theology for the oppressor, and in social gospel christianity and racism.

* * *

BUELER, Lois E(aton) 1940-

PERSONAL: Born July 16, 1940, in Ithaca, N.Y.; daughter of Theodore H., Jr. (a professor) and Grace (a physical therapist; maiden name, Janoschek) Eaton; married William M. Bueler (a journalist), June 7, 1962; chil-

dren: Katherine, Edward. *Education:* Attended Colorado State University, 1957-59, and University of Paris, 1959-60; University of Kansas, B.A., 1961; Cornell University, M.A., 1962; College of William and Mary, graduate study, 1962-63; University of Colorado, doctoral candidate, 1970—. *Address:* c/o Mrs. Gladys Bueler, 2111 East Van Buren, Apt. 2, Colorado Springs, Colo. 80909. *Agent:* Theron Raines, 244 Madison Ave., New York, N.Y. 10016.

CAREER: Louisiana State University, Baton Rouge, instructor in English, 1972-75. *Awards, honors:* Woodrow Wilson fellow, 1961.

WRITINGS: Wild Dogs of the World (nonfiction), Stein & Day, 1973.

* * *

BULLIET, Richard W(illiams) 1940-
(Clarence J.-L. Jackson)

PERSONAL: Born October 30, 1940, in Rockford, Ill.; son of Leander Jackson (an engineer) and Mildred (a physicist, maiden name Williams) Bulliet; married Lucianne Cherry (a Sanskritist), June 24, 1962. *Education:* Harvard University, B.A., 1962, M.A., 1964, Ph.D., 1967. *Home:* 10 Swan Street, Arlington, Mass. 02174.

CAREER: Harvard University, Cambridge, Mass., instructor, 1967-69, assistant professor of Middle Eastern history, 1969-73; University of California, Berkeley, lecturer in Middle Eastern history, 1973-75. *Member:* Middle East Studies Association, Mediaeval Academy of America, Iranian Studies Association. *Awards, honors:* Guggenheim fellowship, 1975.

WRITINGS: The Patricians of Nishapur, Harvard University Press, 1972; (under pseudonym Clarence J.-L. Jackson) *Kicked to Death by a Camel*, Harper, 1973; *The Camel and the Wheel*, Harvard University Press, 1975. Contributor of articles to scholarly journals.

WORK IN PROGRESS: Research on the history of the conversion of the Middle East to Islam; a murder mystery set in the Galapagos Islands, tentatively titled *The Purloined Egg*.

SIDELIGHTS: Bulliet has studied and traveled extensively in the Middle East. *Avocational interests:* Mystery writing, painting.

* * *

BURCH, Pat 1944-

PERSONAL: Born November 21, 1944; daughter of Clinton B. (a pilot) and Patricia (a stenographer; maiden name, Gareau) Clifton; married Charles Burch (a writer), 1968. *Education:* Pennsylvania State University, B.A., 1965; New York University, graduate study, 1966-67. *Politics:* "I'm a lazy feminist leftist." *Religion:* "Literature." *Home:* 100 West 57th St., New York, N.Y. 10019.

CAREER: Worked as typist in ribbon factory in Philadelphia, Pa., and as a custard vendor in Ocean City, N.J.; Temple University Library, Philadelphia, cataloger, 1966; New York Life Insurance Co., New York, N.Y., correspondent, 1966; American Management Associations, New York, N.Y., creative group supervisor in marketing department, 1968—. *Member:* New York Koto Club (director; secretary-treasurer).

WRITINGS: Early Losses (novel), Daughters, Inc., 1973.

WORK IN PROGRESS: Discipline (novel); *The Consultant* (novel); and a third novel, as yet untitled.

SIDELIGHTS: Pat Burch told *CA*, "My obsession is to write scenes and create characters that ring true. . . . In pursuit of realism, I raid my own experience (first and second and third hand) for props and scenery. At the same time, I make things up like crazy, with all the enthusiasm of a compulsive liar, so I don't consider myself an autobiographical writer." *Avocational interests:* Camping in Vermont, studying koto (an ancient Japanese stringed instrument).

* * *

BURCHWOOD, Katharine T(yler)

PERSONAL: Born in Portland, Ore.; daughter of Lewis Morris (a businessman) and Ellen A. (Richmond) Tyler; married Louis Frederick Burchwood (an official of First National Bank of Chicago), November 24, 1943 (deceased). *Education:* Art Institute of Chicago, B.A.Ed., 1916; University of Chicago, Ph.B., 1927, A.M., 1931. *Politics:* Republican. *Religion:* Episcopalian. *Home:* 1305 Lincoln St., Evanston, Ill. 60201.

CAREER: Assistant supervisor of art in public schools of Evanston, Ill., 1922-23; teacher of art, art history, and English in public schools in Chicago, Ill., 1923-56. Head of department of art at State Teachers College, Valley City, N.D., summer, 1932; lecturer in art at Syracuse University, summer, 1933. *Member:* Daughters of Colonists, Colonial Dames of the Seventeenth Century, Daughters of the American Revolution, Mayflower Descendants in Illinois, Evanston Colony New England Women.

WRITINGS: (With Kathryn D. Lee) *Art Then and Now*, Appleton, 1948; (self-illustrated) *The History and Legacy of Mexican Art*, A. S. Barnes, 1973. Contributor to *Art Education Topics*, *School Arts*, and *Design*.

WORK IN PROGRESS: *New Orleans Saga*, with own illustrations.

* * *

BURDICK, Loraine 1929-

PERSONAL: Born May 20, 1929, in Seattle, Wash.; daughter of Walter H. (a farmer and engineer) and Clerice (Canfield) Weber; married George L. Burdick (a teacher), March 19, 1948; children: Frances (Mrs. Charles Noll), Gloria. *Education:* University of Washington, Seattle, B.S., 1960. *Politics:* Conservative. *Religion:* Evangelical Christian. *Home:* 5 Court Pl., Puyallup, Wash. 98371. *Agent:* Jack Scagnetti, 4634 Kraft Ave., North Hollywood, Calif. 91602.

CAREER: Writer and editorial consultant; owner of Quest-Eridon Books (formerly Quest Books). *Member:* National Writers Club.

WRITINGS—For children, except as noted: *Janice and Bob at Family Worship*, Moody, 1961; *Conquistador*, American Southern, 1965; *Shirley Dolls and Related Delights*, Quest, 1966; *Alaskettes: Alaskan Lore and Crafts for Children*, Quest, 1967; *In Reference to Silents*, two volumes, Quest, 1968; *Child Star Dolls and Toys*, Quest, 1968; *Folio of Shirley's Dolls*, Quest, 1970; *A Doll for Christmas or Anytime*, Quest, 1971; *Adult Star Dolls and Toys*, Book One, Quest-Eridon, 1973; *Shirley's Christmas Book*, Quest-Eridon, 1973; *Shirley's Christmas Toys*, Quest-Eridon, 1973; *Shirley's Dolls*, Quest-Eridon, 1973; *Shirley's Toys*, Quest-Eridon, 1973; *Celebrity Paper Dolls to Color*, Quest-Eridon, 1973; *Shirley Temple Scrapbook*, Jonathan David, 1975; *The Ezra Meeker Picture Album*, Quest-Eridon, 1975.

Teaching guides: "Alaskan Skin Clothes," Quest, 1967; "Alaskan Indian Copper Money," Quest, 1967; "Alaskan Homes," Quest, 1967.

Author of "Arctic Alaska Adventure," photographic slides with text, for Quest and Wolfe Worldwide Films. Author of "Alaskettes," a weekly column in *Anchorage Daily Times*, 1966-67. Also author of *Out of Alaska's Arctic* (poems), 1955. Contributor of more than a thousand photographs, poems, stories, drawings, and articles to magazines, including *Alaska Sportsman*, *Parents' Magazine*, *Grade Teacher*, *Instructor*, *Coin World*, *Jack and Jill*, *American Collector*, *Antique Trader*, and *West Coast Peddler*, and to church publications. Editor and publisher of *Celebrity Doll Journal*, 1966—. Consultant to Time-Life Books.

SIDELIGHTS: Loraine Burdick writes: "My writing covers areas of Bible teaching and study, research for hobbyists and collectors in movies, dolls, toys, paper dolls, coins, stamps, and many other fields. . . . Because I now have a considerable following among collectors, my own publishing company issues my books in those fields so that I can give my readers the thorough research and accuracy they've come to expect and appreciate but I always emphasize the service of it rather than some fancy presentation."

* * *

BURGER, George V(anderkarr) 1927-

PERSONAL: Born January 22, 1927, in Woodstock, Ill.; son of Irwin Louis (a landscaper) and Nettie (Vanderkarr) Burger; married Jeannine Willis, June 23, 1949; children: Suzanne Linda, Christine Melissa, Nancy Willis. *Education:* Beloit College, B.S., 1950; University of California, Berkeley, M.A., 1952; University of Wisconsin, Madison, Ph.D., 1958. *Religion:* Congregational. *Home:* 1766 Country Knolls Lane, Elgin, Ill. 60120. *Address:* McGraw Wildlife Foundation, P.O. Box 194, Dundee, Ill. 60118.

CAREER: Contra Costa Junior College, Richmond, Calif., instructor in life sciences, 1952-54; Sportsmen's Service Bureau, La Crosse, Wis., field representative, 1958-62; Remington Arms Co., Chestertown, Md., in charge of wildlife management, 1962-66; McGraw Wildlife Foundation, Dundee, Ill., general manager, 1966—. Member of Kane County Regional Planning Commission, 1974—. *Military service:* U.S. Army, 1945-47; became sergeant. *Member:* Wildlife Society (president of Illinois chapter, 1972), American Fisheries Society, National Audubon Society, Outdoor Writers Association of America, Izaak Walton League, Illinois Shooting Preserve Association (president, 1970-72), Association of Great Lakes Outdoor Writers (member of board of directors, 1961-62), Illinois Audubon Society, Kiwanis. *Awards, honors:* Nature Conservancy award, 1954.

WRITINGS: *Practical Wildlife Management*, Winchester Press, 1973. Contributor of more than one hundred articles to journals. Writer of monthly column on conservation, 1967—, and contributing editor of *Shooting Times*, 1968—; editor of *Wildlife Society Bulletin*, 1973—.

WORK IN PROGRESS: Research on waterfowl, on upland game, and on songbird management.

AVOCATIONAL INTERESTS: Gardening, fishing, travel.

* * *

BURKE, John
See O'CONNOR, Richard

BURNE, Glen
   See GREEN, Alan (Baer)

* * *

BURNETT, John 1925-
PERSONAL: Born December 20, 1925, in Nottingham, England. *Education:* Emmanuel College, Cambridge, B.A. (honors), 1946, M.A., 1950, LL.B., 1951; University of London, Ph.D., 1958. *Office:* Department of Government Studies and Law, School of Social Sciences, Brunel University, Kingston Lane, Uxbridge, Middlesex UB8 3PH, England.

CAREER: Primary school teacher, 1946-48; Guildford Technical College, Surrey, England, lecturer in history and law, 1948-59; Borough Polytechnic (now Polytechnic of the South Bank), London, England, head of division of liberal studies, 1959-62; Brunel College, London, England, head of department of general studies, 1962-66; Brunel University, Uxbridge, England, reader in social and economic history, 1966-72, professor of social history, 1972—. Lecturer at University of London, 1952-72, visiting reader, 1966—.

WRITINGS: Plenty and Want: A Social History of Diet in England from 1815 to the Present Day, Thomas Nelson, 1966; *A History of the Cost of Living*, Pelican, 1969; *The Challenge of the Nineteenth Century*, Hamlyn, 1970; *The Annals of Labour*, Indiana University Press, 1974 (published in England as *Useful Toil: Autobiographies of Working People from the 1820's to the 1920's*, Allen Lane, 1974).

WORK IN PROGRESS: A Social History of Housing from 1815 to the Present Day, for David & Charles.

* * *

BURROWS, Fredrika Alexander 1908-
PERSONAL: Born August 22, 1908, in Montpelier, Vt.; daughter of Fred Wilmer and Lula (Keir) Alexander; married Ronald Powell Burrows, July 12, 1930; children: Martha Jane (Mrs. James Curtis), Roberta Ann (Mrs. Paul Gray). *Education:* Middlebury College, A.B., 1929. *Home address:* Box 447, West Hyannisport, Mass. 02672.

CAREER: High school teacher in Princeton, Mass., 1929-33, in St. Johnsbury, Vt., 1934-36, and substitute teacher in Scituate, Mass., 1948-60; *The Children's Shop*, Cohasset, Mass., co-owner, 1962-65. *Member:* Craigville Writers' Conference, Twelve O'Clock Scholars, Centerville Historical Society, Green Thumb Garden Club, St. Johnsbury Womans Club (president, 1945-46), North Church Women's Society (president, 1946-47), Scituate Garden Club (president, 1956-57), St. Johnsbury College Club (secretary, 1943-44).

WRITINGS: (With others) *The Cape Cod Sampler*, William Sullwold Publishers, 1971; *The Yankee Scrimshanders*, William Sullwold Publishers, 1973; (with others) *The Seven Villages of Barnstable*, Town of Barnstable, in press. Contributor to magazines. Antiques editor, *Cape Cod Illustrated Magazine*, 1974—.

WORK IN PROGRESS: Women in Medicine for Dillon Press; *Heroines in the American Revolution*; *Iron Bogs and Cranberries* for William Sullwold Publishers; *Early Salt Making on Cape Cod*.

SIDELIGHTS: Fredrika Burrows has travelled throughout the U.S., Canada, Europe, and the Caribbean and is a collector of scrimshaw and antique dolls and books.

BIOGRAPHICAL/CRITICAL SOURCES: National Antiques Review, December, 1973.

* * *

BURTON, Nelson, Jr. 1942-
PERSONAL: Born June 5, 1942, in St. Louis, Mo.; son of Nelson and June (Curran) Burton; married Louise C. Hanson, December 1, 1967; children: Catrina, Nicolette. *Education:* Attended St. Louis University, 1961-63. *Religion:* Roman Catholic. *Home:* 17767 Honeygrove Ct., Creve Coeur, Mo. 63141. *Office:* Burton Lanes, 9520 Olive, Olivette, Mo. 63132.

CAREER: Professional bowler, 1960—. Professional Bowlers Association of America Tour sportscaster with ABC-TV, 1975. *Military service:* U.S. Army, 1959-67. *Member:* Professional Bowlers Association of America (president, 1975-76). *Awards, honors: Sporting News* Bowler of the Year, 1970.

WRITINGS: Bowling, Atheneum, 1975.

* * *

BUSCH, Julia 1940-
PERSONAL: Born March 27, 1940, in Teaneck, N.J.; daughter of William H. and Julia (Gergo) Busch. *Education:* Attended Juilliard School of Music, 1957-59, and Dade Community College, 1965; University of Miami, Coral Gables, B.A., 1967, graduate study; Columbia University, graduate study. *Residence:* Coconut Grove, Fla. *Agent:* McIntosh & Otis, Inc., 18 East 41st St., New York, N.Y. 10017. *Office:* 3891 Little Ave., Coconut Grove, Fla. 33133.

CAREER: Artist, painting portraits and sculpting portraits in gold; jeweler, teacher, and writer. Instructor in art history at Miami Dade Community College, 1967, and University of Miami, Coral Gables, Fla., 1968; gives private lessons in drawing, painting, and sculpture. Assistant to Eugene Massin in plastics experimentation research, 1970-74.

WRITINGS: (Contributor) Thelma Newman, *Plastic as Design Form*, Chilton, 1972; *A Decade of Sculpture: Sculpture of the Sixties*, Art Alliance Press, 1974; (contributor) Newman, *Plastics as Sculpture*, Chilton, 1974. Contributor to art journals.

WORK IN PROGRESS: How Many Ways, a series for art and sensitivity training of children; *Drawing Your Way*; a biography of painter and sculptor, Eugene Massin.

SIDELIGHTS: Julia Busch writes: "For me 'life is art' as opposed to art being my life. There are many facets to that coin: writing, drawing, singing, loving, breathing—it's a consuming-expanding totality." *Avocational interests:* Breeding Burmese and Himalayan cats, travel (Europe, Hungary).

* * *

BUSH, Jim 1926-
PERSONAL: Born September 15, 1926, in Cleveland, Ohio; son of Walter (an insurance agent) and Edith (Stanley) Bush; married Peggy Babcock, June, 1947 (divorced, 1965); married Therese Baldwin, August 27, 1975; children: Jean, Don. *Education:* University of California, Berkeley, A.B., 1951, graduate study, 1951-52. *Residence:* Marina Del Rey, Calif. 90291. *Office:* Department of Physical Education, University of California, Los Angeles, 405 Hilgard Ave., Los Angeles, Calif. 90024.

CAREER: Fullerton High School, Fullerton, Calif., assistant varsity football coach and head track and cross country coach, 1952-59, chairman of department of physical education and athletic director, 1956-58; Fullerton Junior College, Fullerton, Calif., head track and cross country coach, 1959-61; Occidental College, Los Angeles, Calif., head track and cross country coach, 1961-64; University of California, Los Angeles, cross country coach, 1964-72, head track coach, 1964—. Head track coach of U.S. National Team, 1967-73. Physical fitness consultant for Los Angeles Rams, Los Angeles Lakers, and Los Angeles Kings. *Military service:* U.S. Navy, Air Corps, 1944-46; became petty officer third class. *Member:* U.S. Track Coaches Association (president, 1972-73). *Awards, honors:* Named Coach of the Year by U.S. Track Coaches Association, 1971-73.

WRITINGS: (With Tom Valentine) *Inside Track*, Regnery, 1974; (with Don Weiskopf) *Track and Field*, Bert Nelson, in press.

* * *

BUTCHER, (Anne) Judith 1927-

PERSONAL: Born September 18, 1927, in Alverstoke, Hampshire, England; daughter of Reginald (a naval officer) and Ethel King (Brock) Butcher. *Education:* Bedford College, London, B.A. (honors), 1949. *Home:* 97 Milton Rd., Cambridge CB4 1XD, England. *Office:* Cambridge University Press, Trumpington St., Cambridge CB2 1RP, England.

CAREER: Edward Arnold Publishers, London, England, secretary to senior partner, 1951-53; Penguin Books, Harmondsworth, England, editorial assistant, 1956-63; Cambridge University Press, Cambridge, England, subeditor, 1963-66, chief subeditor, 1966—, associate director, 1974—.

WRITINGS: Copy-Editing: The Cambridge Handbook, Cambridge University Press, 1975.

WORK IN PROGRESS: A booklet for authors, on preparing books for the publisher and printer.

* * *

BUTLER, Bill
See BUTLER, William Huxford

* * *

BUTLER, Hal 1913-

PERSONAL: Born January 3, 1913, in St. Louis, Mo.; son of Charles (an accountant) and Estelle (Gieselman) Butler; married Eleanor Davis, August 20, 1938; children: Beverly, Joyce (Mrs. J. Norbert Musto). *Education:* Educated in public schools in Detroit, Mich. *Politics:* Independent. *Religion:* Protestant. *Home:* 25160 Waycross Rd., Southfield, Mich. 48075. *Agent:* Blanche C. Gregory, Inc., 2 Tudor City Pl., New York, N.Y. 10017.

CAREER: Michigan Consolidated Gas Co., Detroit, Mich., correspondence writer, 1936-42; Ford Motor Co., Dearborn, Mich., office clerk, 1942-47, reporter for *Rouge News*, 1947-53, editor of *Ford Dealer* (magazine), 1953-63, associate editor of *Ford Times* (magazine), 1963-66, managing editor of *Ford Times*, 1966-74; free-lance writer, 1974—. *Member:* Society of American Travel Writers. *Awards, honors:* First place in *Writer's Digest* Contest, 1964, for article "Niagara's Most Hair-Raising Stunt."

WRITINGS—For young people; all published by Messner: *The Harmon Killebrew Story*, 1966; *The Bob Allison Story*, 1967; *There's Nothing New in Sports: The Story of How Sports Began*, 1967; *Baseball's All Star Game Thrills*, 1968; *Stormin' Norman Cash*, 1968; *Roar of the Road*, 1969; *Underdogs of Sport*, 1969; *The Willie Horton Story*, 1970; *Millions of Cars*, 1972; *Sports Heroes Who Wouldn't Quit*, 1973; *Baseball's Champion Pitchers*, 1974.

For adults: *Al Kaline and the Detroit Tigers*, Regnery, 1973; *Abandon Ship!*, Regnery, 1974; *Inferno!*, Regnery, 1975. Contributor of articles on sports and travel to periodicals.

WORK IN PROGRESS: A book on natural disasters, *Nature at War*, for Regnery; research for a book on Polynesia.

* * *

BUTLER, Richard 1925-

PERSONAL: Born April 29, 1925, in Liverpool, England; son of Arthur Odessa (an insurance salesman) and Elizabeth (Buck) Butler; married Patricia Lee Holden (a bank officer), January 28, 1956; children: Miles John, Charles Richard. *Education:* Attended Chester College, 1948-50. *Residence:* Victoria, Australia.

CAREER: Teacher of English and French in schools in England, Tasmania, and Australia, 1950-73; professional television actor. *Military service:* Royal Air Force, 1943-48; became flight lieutenant. *Member:* Fellowship of Australian Writers.

WRITINGS—Novels: *Fingernail Beach*, Long, 1964; *More Dangerous Than the Moon*, Walker & Co. (published in England as *South of Hell's Gates*, Long, 1967), *Sharkbait*, Long, 1970; *The Buffalo Hook*, Hutchinson, 1974; *The Men That God Forgot*, Hutchinson (Melbourne), 1975. Author of "The Doll," a play for television, produced by Crawford Productions, Melbourne, Australia, 1970.

WORK IN PROGRESS: Researching little-known aspects of Australian colonial history.

* * *

BUTLER, Robert Lee 1918-

PERSONAL: Born February 12, 1918, in Kansas City, Kan.; son of Coleman Prentis (a restauranteur) and Laura Selma Butler; married Faye Arlene Evans, July 21, 1943; children: Christopher C., Cynthia L., Samuel R. *Education:* Park College, B.A., 1941; University of Minnesota, B.S., 1947, M.S., 1950, Ph.D., 1962. *Office:* 328 Life Science Bldg., Cooperative Fishery Unit, Pennsylvania State University, University Park, Pa. 16802.

CAREER: Teacher of biology and general science in Mount Berry, Ga., 1941-42; University of Minnesota, Minneapolis, assistant at Red Lake Commercial Fishery, 1949-52, rodent and insect contamination, research assistant, 1952-54; California State Department of Fish and Game, Sacramento, Calif., fisheries biologist, 1954-62; University of California, Berkeley, research zoologist, 1962-63; Pennsylvania State University, University Park, assistant professor, 1964-69, associate professor of zoology, 1969-72; professor of biology, 1972—, unit leader, Cooperative Fishery Unit, 1964—. Captain of Division II, Middle Atlantic Task Force of International Biological Program, subcommittee on Fresh-Water Productivity, 1966, 1967, 1970, 1971; teacher of woodcarving.

MILITARY SERVICE: U.S. Naval Air Corps, 1942-45,

became lieutenant; received Distinguished Flying Cross and Air Medal with two gold stars. *Member:* International Association of Theoretical and Applied Limnology, American Society of Limnology and Oceanography, Ecological Society of America, American Fisheries Society, American Institute of Fisheries Research Biologists, Animal Behavior Society, Sigma Xi. *Awards, honors:* U.S. Bureau of Sport Fisheries and Wildlife grant, 1966-67; Federal Water Pollution Control grant, 1968-70; Rockefeller Environmental Funds, 1973.

WRITINGS: Wood for Wood-Carvers and Craftsmen: The Selection, Cutting and Treatment of Flitches, A. S. Barnes, 1974; (contributor) Bruce Rosenberg, editor, *Pennsylvania 1776*, Pennsylvania State University Press, 1975. Writer of television series, "Chips of Time," for Public Broadcasting Service. Also writer of papers and reports for U.S. Environmental Protection Agency and U.S. Department of the Interior. Contributor of articles and reviews to *Pennsylvania Farmer, Transactions of the American Fisheries Society, Progressive Fish Culturist, Trout, California Fish and Game*, and other professional periodicals.

WORK IN PROGRESS: A summary paper on the effects of pollutants on cover-seeking behavior in freshwater fish, completion expected in 1977; *Fishpond Management for the Homeowner*, completion expected in 1978.

* * *

BUTLER, Stanley 1914-

PERSONAL: Born March 6, 1914, in Jones, Mich.; son of Loren Butler (a farmer) and Leone (Poe) Butler Born; married Celia Perry, June 14, 1943; children: Faye (Mrs. Charles Q. North, Jr.), Victoria (Mrs. Steven N. Ailes). *Education:* Michigan State University, B. Mus., 1936, graduate study, 1937-38; Harvard University, M.A., 1941. *Politics:* Republican. *Religion:* Protestant. *Home:* 245 Hansen Ave. S., Salem, Ore. 97302. *Office:* Division of Music, Willamette University, Salem, Ore. 97301.

CAREER: Longy School of Music, Cambridge, Mass., teacher, 1939-41; Western Reserve University (now Case Western Reserve University), Cleveland, Ohio, member of faculty of music, 1941-48; Willamette University, Salem, Ore., professor of music, and division head, 1950—. *Member:* American Association of University Professors, Oregon Music Teachers Association (president, 1954-56).

WRITINGS: Guide to the Best in Contemporary Piano Music, two volumes, Scarecrow, 1973. Contributor to *American Music Teacher* and *Clavier*.

* * *

BUTLER, William Huxford 1934-
(Bill Butler, Hassan i Sabbah)

PERSONAL: Born November 3, 1934, in Spokane, Wash. *Education:* Attended University of Montana, University of Washington, University of California at San Francisco, San Francisco State College (now University), San Francisco City College, and San Francisco Conservatory. *Politics:* None. *Religion:* None. *Home and office:* Llanfynydd, Carmarthenshire SA32 7TT, Wales, United Kingdom.

CAREER: U.S. Forest Service, Missoula, Mont. and Redding, Calif., fire fighter, 1951, 1955; KBTK (radio), Missoula, Mont., announcer, 1958; poet, 1958—; KRIZ (radio), Phoenix, Ariz., announcer, 1960; Unicorn Bookshop, Brighton, Sussex, England, proprietor, 1967-73. Poet-in-residence at Aegean School of Fine Arts, Paros, Greece,

1971. *Military service:* U.S. Marine Corps, 1953. *Awards, honors:* Young Writer's grant from National Foundation for the Arts, 1971.

WRITINGS—All poetry, under name Bill Butler, except as noted: *In Progress: Alder Gulch and Other Poems*, Haunted Bookshop, 1961; *Capricorn*, privately printed, 1963; *Discovery of America and Other Poems*, Writers' Forum, 1966; *Discovery of America*, Interim Books, 1967; *A Long Slow Waltz*, Prensa de Lagar, 1968; *Gertrude Stein Cookbook*, Unicorn Bookshop, 1969; *Byrne's Atlas*, Wallrich Books, 1969; *My One Leaf Head*, Unicorn Bookshop, 1969; *Country Decadence and Other Tender Ballads of Young Lust*, Unicorn Bookshop, 1971; (under pseudonym Hassan i Sabbah) *Leaves of Grass* (nonfiction), Unicorn Bookshop, 1971; *Savanarola's Drum*, Claude Rains Books, 1971; *Angel Dancing*, privately printed, 1971; *Seattle Everybody Died*, Aloes Books, 1971; *Unicorn*, Unicorn Bookshop, 1972; *Home Movies*, Unicorn Bookshop, 1972; *Cheyenne Legend*, Turret Books, 1972; *The Definitive Tarot* (nonfiction), Rider Books, 1975; *The Dictionary of the Tarot* (nonfiction), Schocken, 1975; (advisory editor) Alexander Eliot, *The World of Myth*, McGraw, in press; *Dictionary of Mythology*, Schocken, in press. Contributor of poetry, reviews, and interviews to *International Times, Friends, Spectator, Guardian*, and *Scotsman*.

WORK IN PROGRESS: Dictionary of Symbols from Folklore and Mythology.

SIDELIGHTS: Butler regards himself as "an American author in exile with hopes but no plans to return."

* * *

BUTT, (Howard) Edward, Jr. 1927-

PERSONAL: Born September 8, 1927, in Kerrville, Tex.; son of Howard Edward (a groceryman) and Mary Elizabeth (Holdsworth) Butt; married Barbara Dan Gerber, March 21, 1949; children: Howard E. III, Stephen William, Deborah Dan. *Education:* Baylor University, B.A., 1947; Southwestern Baptist Theological Seminary, graduate study, 1947-48. *Home:* 33 Hewit Dr., Corpus Christi, Tex. 78404. *Office:* H. E. Butt Grocery Co., P.O. Box 9216, Corpus Christi, Tex. 78408.

CAREER: H. E. Butt Grocery Co., Corpus Christi, Tex., store manager, 1948-51, vice-president, 1951-67, vice-chairman of board of directors, 1967—. Established Christian Men, Inc. (public foundation for development of laity), 1959, now chairman of board of directors; established Laity Lodge Foundation (public foundation for lay education), 1963, now chairman of board of directors; organizer of Layman's Leadership Institutes, 1956—; member of H. E. Butt Foundation (for family philanthropies), 1953—. *Member:* Corpus Christi Country Club, Corpus Christi Yacht Club.

WRITINGS: The Velvet Covered Brick, Harper, 1973.

WORK IN PROGRESS: Authority and Submission: Sex and the Family, and *Authority and Submission: The Church and Society.*

* * *

BUTTERFIELD, Stephen T(homas) 1942-

PERSONAL: Born March 17, 1942, in Boston, Mass.; son of Charles A. (a machinist) and Emily (Fisher) Butterfield; married Constance Rickert, December 25, 1960; children: Stephen Scott, Nathan Douglass, Alison Emily. *Education:* Boston University, B.S., 1963; Tufts University, M.A.,

1965; University of Massachusetts, Ph.D., 1972. *Office:* Department of English, Castleton State College, Castleton, Vt. 05735.

CAREER: University of Cincinnati, Cincinnati, Ohio, instructor in English, 1965-67; Rhode Island College, Providence, instructor in English, 1969-70; Castleton State College, Castleton, Vt., assistant professor, 1970-74, associate professor of English, 1974—. *Member:* American Federation of Teachers (chairman of local chapter, 1973-75).

WRITINGS: Black Autobiography in America, University of Massachusetts Press, 1974. Also author of radio script, "Rivers of the Skull," for Corporation for Public Broadcasting. Contributor to *Nimrod, Beyond Baroque, University Review, Negro American Literature Forum*, and other periodicals.

WORK IN PROGRESS: American Revolutionary War narratives; a volume of poetry; a novel.

SIDELIGHTS: Butterfield writes: "[My] sense of history is obsessive: I am haunted by ghosts. My first direct-line American ancestor (Benjamin Butterfield) came to New England in 1635." *Avocational interests:* Folk music, guitar, chess.

* * *

BUXTON, Thomas H(amilton) 1940-

PERSONAL: Born January 18, 1940, in Blowing Rock, N.C.; son of Augustin Kennard (a salesman) and Carrie (Miller) Buxton; married Elizabeth Fleming, August 19, 1960; children: W. Gregory, Thomas H., Jr., Kennard Prichard. *Education:* Wake Forest University, B.A., 1962; Indiana University, M.S., 1963; University of Nebraska, Ed.D., 1970. *Religion:* Episcopalian. *Home:* 2819 Celtic Rd., Columbia, S.C. 29210. *Office:* College of Education, University of South Carolina, Columbia, S.C. 29208.

CAREER: Public high school and junior high school teacher of Latin in Huntersville, N.C., 1963-65; junior high school principal in Darlington, S.C., 1966-68; Adult Education Program, Darlington, S.C., director, 1966-68; University of South Carolina, Columbia, assistant professor, 1970-72, associate professor of social foundations, 1973—. *Member:* Society for the Advancement of Education, Phi Delta Kappa.

WRITINGS: (With Keith Prichard) *Concepts and Theories in Sociology of Education*, Professional Educators Publications, 1973; (editor with Prichard, and contributor) *Excellence in University Teaching: New Essays*, University of South Carolina Press, 1975. Contributor to professional journals. Executive editor of *National Directory of Sociology of Education and Educational Sociology*, 1974—.

WORK IN PROGRESS: Editing a book of essays on education.

* * *

BYRD, Richard E(dward) 1931-

PERSONAL: Born January 23, 1931, in St. Petersburg, Fla.; son of Edward Melvin Parker and Louise Parker Byrd; married Helen Penn, August 31, 1950; children: Jackie Louise, Richard Edward, Jr. *Education:* University of Florida, B.A., 1952; Protestant Episcopal Theological Seminary in Virginia, M.S.T., 1956; New York University, Ph.D., 1970. *Home and office:* 4626 Bruce Ave. S., Minneapolis, Minn. 55424.

CAREER: Episcopal Diocese of Florida, vicar of Episcopal missions, 1956-58; vicar, then rector of Episcopal church in West Palm Beach, Fla., 1957-61; Episcopal Church, Executive Council, New York, N.Y., consultant and trainer, 1961-63; St. Martin's-by-the-Lake, Minnetonka Beach, Minn., consultant on training for Action Program, 1964-66; independent management and professional development consultant in Minneapolis, Minn., 1966—, under name, Richard E. Byrd & Associates, 1966-67, Jones & Byrd, Inc., 1967-70, Richard E. Byrd, Inc., 1970—, and REB Associates, Inc., 1974—. Licensed clergyman, Episcopal Diocese of Minnesota; vice-president and provost, Constance Bultman Wilson Center for Education and Psychiatry, Minnesota; member of adjunct faculty, Antioch College, 1973. Consulting psychologist for organization development to corporations, and to U.S. Department of State, U.S. Department of Health, Education and Welfare, and other agencies.

MEMBER: American Association for the Advancement of Science, American Psychological Association, International Association of Applied Social Scientists (charter member), NTL Organization Development Network, Association for Creative Change in Religious and Other Social Systems (founding member and first president), Minnesota Psychological Association.

WRITINGS: Crises in Faith, privately printed, 1964; *Creative Risk Taking Laboratory: Book of Basic Readings*, privately printed, 1967, 2nd edition, 1968; (with David G. Jones) *Communication*, privately printed, 1970; (editor) *Seize the Times*, privately printed, 1971; (contributor) Thomas H. Patten, editor, *O.D.: Emerging Dimensions and Concepts*, American Society for Training and Development, 1972; (contributor) David W. Johnson, editor, *Contemporary Social Psychology*, Lippincott, 1973; *A Guide to Personal Risk Taking*, American Management Association, 1974. Writer of guide on organizational problems for American Institute of Architects, and other training and management materials. Contributor to journals, including *Adult Leadership* and *Management Review*.

WORK IN PROGRESS: The Organizational Life Cycle, for American Management Association, completion expected in 1977.

* * *

CADELL, (Violet) Elizabeth 1903-
(Harriet Ainsworth)

PERSONAL: Born November 10, 1903, in Calcutta, India; daughter of Frederick Reginald (a colonial officer) and Elizabeth (Lynch) Vandyke; married Henry Dunlop Raymond Mallock Cadell (a banker), 1928 (deceased); children: one son, one daughter. *Politics:* Conservative. *Religion:* Church of England. *Residence:* Portugal.

CAREER: Novelist.

WRITINGS—All novels: *My Dear Aunt Flora*, R. Hale, 1946; *Last Straw for Harriet*, Morrow, 1947 (published in England as *Fishy, Said the Admiral*, R. Hale, 1948); *River Lodge*, R. Hale, 1948; *Gay Pursuit*, Morrow, 1948; *Iris in Winter*, Morrow, 1949.

Brimstone in the Garden, Morrow, 1950; *Sun in the Morning* (for young readers; Catholic Children's Book Club selection), Morrow, 1950, abridged edition, University of London Press, 1963; *The Greenwood Shady*, Hodder & Stoughton, 1951; *Enter Mrs. Belchamber*, Morrow, 1951 (published in England as *The Frenchman and the*

Lady, Hodder & Stoughton, 1952); *Men and Angels*, Hodder & Stoughton, 1952; *Crystal Clear*, Morrow, 1953 (published in England as *Journey's Eve*, Hodder & Stoughton, 1953); *Spring Green*, Hodder & Stoughton, 1953; *The Cuckoo in Spring*, Morrow, 1954; *Money to Burn*, Hodder & Stoughton, 1954, Morrow, 1955; *Around the Rugged Rock*, Morrow, 1954 (published in England as *The Gentlemen Go By*, Hodder & Stoughton, 1964); *The Lark Shall Sing*, Morrow, 1955; (under pseudonym Harriet Ainsworth) *Consider the Lilies*, Hodder & Stoughton, 1955, published under name Elizabeth Cadell, White Lion, 1974; *The Blue Sky of Spring*, Hodder & Stoughton, 1956; *I Love a Lass*, Morrow, 1956; *Bridal Array*, Hodder & Stoughton, 1957; *Shadows on the Water*, Morrow, 1958; *The Green Empress*, Hodder & Stoughton, 1958; *Sugar Candy Cottage*, Hodder & Stoughton, 1958; *Alice, Where art Thou?*, Hodder & Stoughton, 1959.

The Yellow Brick Road, Morrow, 1960; *Honey for Tea*, Hodder & Stoughton, 1961, Morrow, 1962; *Six Impossible Things*, Morrow, 1961; *The Toy Sword*, Morrow, 1962 (published in England as *Language of the Heart*, Hodder & Stoughton, 1962); *Letter to My Love*, Hodder & Stoughton, 1963; *Mixed Marriage, The Diary of a Portuguese Bride*, Hodder & Stoughton, 1963; (under pseudonym Harriet Ainsworth) *Death Among Friends*, Hodder & Stoughton, 1964; *Come Be My Guest*, Morrow, 1964 (published in England as *Be My Guest*, Hodder & Stoughton, 1964); *Canary Yellow*, Morrow, 1965; *The Corner Shop*, Hodder & Stoughton, 1966, Morrow, 1967; *The Fox from his Lair*, Morrow, 1966; *The Stratton Story*, Hodder & Stoughton, 1967; *Mrs. Westerby Changes Course*, Morrow, 1968; *The Golden Collar*, Morrow, 1969.

The Friendly Air, Hodder & Stoughton, 1970, Morrow, 1971; *The Past Tense of Love*, Morrow, 1970; *Home for the Wedding*, Morrow, 1971; *Royal Summons*, Morrow, 1973; *Deck with Flowers*, Morrow, 1974; *The Haymaker*, Hodder & Stoughton, 1974; *The Fledgling*, Morrow, 1975.

SIDELIGHTS: Raised in India, Elizabeth Cadell was educated in England and traveled often to Ireland. As a widow she discovered her pleasure and talent for writing, and has since produced a prodigious number of light, romantic novels.*

*   *   *

CADIEUX, Charles L.   1919-

PERSONAL: Born September 5, 1919; son of Kenneth B. and Amy E. (Simmons) Cadieux; married Elida M. Brady, July 9, 1945; children: Daniel C., Marie (Mrs. Charlie Hodges). *Education:* North Dakota State University, B.S. *Religion:* Roman Catholic. *Home and office:* 4611 Chase Ave., Bethesda, Md. 20014.

CAREER: North Dakota Game and Fish Department, Bismarck, assistant director, 1953-54; U.S. Fish and Wildlife Service, 1954-72, employed in Sioux City, Iowa, Mitchell, S.D., San Antonio, Tex., and in Albuquerque, N.M.; U.S. Department of Interior, Washington, D.C., staff member, 1972—. *Military service:* U.S. Naval Reserve, 1943-46; became lieutenant senior grade; served in South Pacific; received four battle stars. *Member:* Outdoor Writers Association of America (president, 1973-74; chairman of board, 1974—), Society of Magazine Writers. *Awards, honors:* Recreational Vehicle Institute grand award, 1970, magazine award, 1972.

WRITINGS: Introduction to Ocean Fishing, Stackpole, 1972; *The Ways of Game Fish*, Doubleday, 1972; *Introduc-

tion to Motorboat Cruising, J. Philip O'Hara, 1975. Former contributor of monthly column to *Trailer Travel Magazine*. Contributor of more than six hundred articles to periodicals. Editor of *North Dakota Outdoors*, 1951-53.

WORK IN PROGRESS: A chapter for a book, for J. G. Ferguson; *Goose-hunting Spoken Here* and *Recreational Vehicle Bible*, plus a book chapter, "These are the Endangered."

AVOCATIONAL INTERESTS: Mexican travel.

*   *   *

CAIRNCROSS, Frances (Anne)   1944-

PERSONAL: Born August 30, 1944, in Otley, England; daughter of Sir Alec (an economist) and Mary (Glynn) Cairncross; married Hamish McRae (a journalist), September 10, 1971. *Education:* St. Anne's College, Oxford, M.A. (history; first class honors), 1965; Brown University, M.A. (economics), 1966. *Home:* 6 Canonbury Lane, London N.1, England. *Office:* Guardian, Grays Inn Rd., London W.C.1, England.

CAREER: Times, London, England, reporter, 1967-69; *Banker* (financial magazine), London, England, editorial assistant, 1969; *Observer* (weekly newspaper), London, England, economics writer, 1969-73; *Guardian* (known in United States as *Manchester Guardian*; national daily newspaper), London, England, economic correspondent, 1973—.

WRITINGS: (With husband, Hamish McRae) *Capital City: London as a Financial Centre*, Methuen, 1973; (with Hamish McRae) *The Second Great Crash*, Prentice-Hall, 1975.

SIDELIGHTS: Frances Cairncross writes: "I want to convey some of the excitement I felt about the changing world economic situation to people who otherwise would shy away from the subject—even though it is a subject that intimately affects everybody's life."

*   *   *

CALDERWOOD, Ivan E.   1899-

PERSONAL: Born December 9, 1899, in Vinalhaven, Me.; son of Frank L. (a carpenter and painter) and Josephine (Ewell) Calderwood; married Isabel B. Fraser (a school teacher), June 24, 1939. *Education:* Attended public schools of Vinalhaven, Me. *Religion:* Protestant. *Home:* Vinalhaven, Me.

CAREER: Has worked as a gardener, paving cutter, road commissioner, lobster fisherman, and caretaker of summer estates in Vinalhaven, Me. *Member:* Masons, Lions Club.

WRITINGS—All published by Courier-Gazette, Inc.: *Days of Uncle Dave's Fish House*, 1969; *Sequel to Days of Uncle Dave's Fish House*, 1972; *Saga of Hod*, 1972; *Vinalhaven: The Isle of Happiness*, 1974; *Ditto*, 1974.

WORK IN PROGRESS: A novel about life on Vinalhaven.

SIDELIGHTS: The high school library on Vinalhaven Island was named in Calderwood's honor.

*   *   *

CALHOON, Richard P(ercival)   1909-

PERSONAL: Born February 3, 1909, in Sewickley, Pa.; son of Richard Percival (a professor) and Elizabeth (a secretary; maiden name, Sigman) Calhoon; married Frances

Abercrombie, July 2, 1940; children: Kathryn F., Susan Elizabeth (Mrs. Joseph P. Straley, Jr.), Carol Clark (Mrs. Michael P. Earey), Bruce A. *Education:* University of Pittsburgh, A.B., 1930, M.A., 1932. *Politics:* Democrat. *Home:* 104 Pine Lane, Chapel Hill, N.C. 27514. *Office:* School of Business Administration, University of North Carolina, Chapel Hill, N.C. 27514.

CAREER: National Industrial Recovery Administration (NIRA), Pittsburgh, Pa., labor adjuster, 1934-36; Ansco Co., Binghamton, N.Y., assistant to factory manager, 1936-37; U.S. Rubber Co., Naugatuck, Conn., public relations and executive development director, 1937-41; Kendall Mills, Charlotte, N.C., personnel director, 1941-46; University of North Carolina, Chapel Hill, professor of personnel administration, 1946—. Arbitrator for American Arbitration Association, Federal Mediation and Conciliation Service, and the Labor Department of the State of North Carolina. *Member:* Academy of Management, National Academy of Arbitrators, Industrial Relations Research Association, American Association of University Professors, National Historical Society, Southeastern Personnel Conference (member of the board of directors, 1943—), Beta Gamma Sigma, Delta Sigma Pi, Phi Alpha Theta.

WRITINGS: Moving Ahead on Your Job, McGraw, 1946; *Problems in Personnel Administration*, Harper, 1949; *Relationships Between Wages, Wage Payment Methods, and Personnel Efficiency in the Furniture Industry* (monograph), Bureau of Business Services and Research, University of North Carolina, 1951; (with C. A. Kirkpatrick) *Influencing Employee Behavior*, McGraw, 1956; (with E. W. Noland and A. M. Whitehill) *Cases on Human Relations in Management*, McGraw, 1958; *The Competitive Factor in Employee Performance* (monograph), School of Business Administration, University of North Carolina, 1959; (with L. Frederick Van Eck) *An Analytical Study of Requirements for Top Positions in Personnel Administration* (monograph), School of Business Administration, University of North Carolina, 1963; *Managing Personnel*, Harper, 1963; *Personnel Management and Supervision*, Appleton, 1967; *Cases in Personnel Management and Supervision*, Appleton, 1968, 2nd edition, 1971. Contributor to professional journals.

WORK IN PROGRESS: Dirty Practices in Management; Public Personnel Management; First Level Supervisory Training Needs and Organizational Development; Training Needs of First Level Supervisors in North Carolina State and Local Government, for Institute of Government, University of North Carolina.

* * *

CALLENBACH, Ernest 1929-

PERSONAL: Born April 3, 1929, in Williamsport, Pa. *Education:* University of Chicago, Ph.B., 1949, M.A., 1953. *Home:* 1517 Francisco St., Berkeley, Calif. 94703. *Office:* University of California Press, 2223 Fulton St., Berkeley, Calif. 94720.

CAREER: University of California Press, Berkeley, Calif., publicity writer and assistant editor, 1955-58, editor of *Film Quarterly*, 1958—, film book editor, 1960—.

WRITINGS: Our Modern Art: The Movies, Center for the Study of Education for Adults, University of Chicago, 1955; *Living Poor with Style*, Bantam, 1972; *Ecotopia*, Banyan Tree Books, 1975.

WORK IN PROGRESS: Screenplays.

CALVEZ, Jean-Yves 1927-

PERSONAL: Born February 3, 1927, in Saint Brieuc, France; son of Jean-Marie and Claire (LeMaire) Calvez. *Education:* Attended University of Paris, 1945-53; School of Divinity, Lyon-Fourviere, France, Licence, 1958. *Home:* Borgo S. Spirito 5, Rome, Italy 00193.

CAREER: Entered Roman Catholic order of Society of Jesus (Jesuits), 1943, ordained priest, 1957; instructor in social philosophy in Chantilly, France, 1953-54; Catholic University of Paris, Institut d'Etudes Sociales, Paris, France, professor of political philosophy, and president, 1960-70; University of Paris, Institut d'Etudes Politiques, Paris, France, professor of political science, 1963-69; provincial superior of Society of Jesus in France, 1967-71, assistant general to superior general of the Society, headquartered in Rome, 1971—. Visiting professor at Loyola University, Chicago, 1958, 1959, University of Montreal, 1959, University of Laval, 1959, University of Rio de Janeiro, 1964, University of Belo Horizonte, 1964, and University of Porto Alegre, 1964. *Member:* Association Francaise de Science Politique, Association Francaise de Science Economique. *Awards, honors:* Prize of Academie d'Education et d'Entr'aide Sociale, 1963, for *Eglise et Societe Economique.*

WRITINGS: Droit international et souverainete en URSS (title means "The Concept of Sovereignty in Soviet International Law"), Colin, 1953; (with Jean-Louis Fyot) *Politique economique regionale en Grande Bretagne* (title means "Regional Economic Organization in Great Britain"), Colin, 1956; *Revenu national en URSS* (title means "National Income in the USSR"), Editions SEDES, 1956; *La Pensee de Karl Marx* (title means "The Thought of Karl Marx"), Le Seuil, 1956; *Eglise et Societe Economique*, Aubier, Volume I, 1959, Volume II, 1963, translation of Volume I by J. R. Kirwan published as *The Church and Social Justice*, Burns and Oates, 1961, Regnery, 1962, translation of Volume II by George J. M. McKenzie published as *The Social Thought of John XXIII*, Regnery, 1965; *Introduction a la vie politique* (title means "An Introduction to Politics"), Aubier, 1967; *Aspects politiques et sociaux des pays en voie de developpement*, Dalloz, 1971, translation by M. J. O'Connell published as *Politics and Society in the Third World*, Orbis Books, 1973. Contributor to journals in his field.

WORK IN PROGRESS: A sociological analysis of religious orders in the Roman Catholic church.

* * *

CAMPBELL, Howard E(rnest) 1925-

PERSONAL: Born September 20, 1925, in Detroit, Mich.; son of Howard Ernest (an engineer) and Marie (a teacher; maiden name, Brown) Campbell; married second wife, Ramona Ann Anderson, July 30, 1972; children: Tanaquil R. (Mrs. James Sampson), Howard B., Thane G., Lowell L. *Education:* Attended Stevens Institute of Technology, 1943-44; University of Wisconsin, B.S., 1946, M.S., 1947, Ph.D., 1949. *Office:* Department of Mathematics, University of Idaho, Moscow, Idaho 83843.

CAREER: University of Pennsylvania, Philadelphia, instructor in mathematics, 1949-51; Emory University, Atlanta, Ga., assistant professor of mathematics, 1951-56; Michigan State University, East Lansing, assistant professor, 1956-59, associate professor of mathematics, 1959-63; University of Idaho, Moscow, professor of mathematics, 1963—, head of department, 1963—. Chairman of committee of examiners of general examination in mathematics of College-Level Examination Program for Educational Testing Service and College Entrance Examination Board, 1971-74; member of accreditation team of Commission on Higher Schools of the Northwest Association, 1968. *Military service:* U.S. Navy, 1943-46; became lieutenant, junior grade. *Member:* Mathematical Association of America, American Mathematical Society, Idaho Academy of Science, Sigma Xi, Pi Mu Epsilon. *Awards, honors:* Air Force Office of Scientific Research grant, 1952, 1957-58; National Science Foundation research grant, 1958-60.

WRITINGS: The Structure of Arithmetic, Appleton, 1970; (with Paul F. Dierker) *Calculus*, Prindle, 1975. Contributor to proceedings and to *Pacific Journal of Mathematics*.

WORK IN PROGRESS: Research on snakes in N-dimensional cubes.

*   *   *

CAMPBELL, James   1920-

PERSONAL: Born April 19, 1920, in Inverness, Scotland; son of Henry Gordon and Elizabeth Ann (Mackay) Campbell; married Irene Innes (a secretary), April 3, 1952; children: Douglas, Lorene Ann. *Education:* Attended Inverness Royal Academy. *Religion:* Protestant. *Office:* Press Gallery, House of Commons, London, England.

CAREER: Kemsley Newspapers, London, England, crime reporter, 1949-51, parliamentary correspondent, 1951-60; *Scottish Daily Record*, political correspondent from House of Commons in London, 1960-75; *Glasgow Daily Record*, Glasgow, Scotland, political correspondent from London. *Military service:* British Army, 1939-41. Royal Air Force, Bomber Command, 1941-45; became flight lieutenant; flew thirty-eight missions over Western Europe.

WRITINGS: Maximum Effort (novel), Muller, 1953, new edition, Allison & Busby, 1974; *The Man Who Kissed Babies* (political novel about British Parliament), Muller, 1955; *The Bombing of Nuremberg* (nonfiction; Military Book Club selection), Allison & Busby, 1973, Doubleday, 1974.

WORK IN PROGRESS: The Bombers, a novel about British and German air crews.

*   *   *

CAMPBELL, Luke
See MADISON, Thomas A(lvin)

*   *   *

CAMPBELL, Malcolm J(ames)   1930-

PERSONAL: Born April 11, 1930, in Portsmouth, England; son of Francis James (a ship's fitter) and Dorothy (Hellier) Campbell; married Margaret Heather, June 29, 1957; children: Colin, Sarah. *Education:* Associate of Library Association, 1965. *Religion:* Church of England. *Home:* 98 Agar Grove, London NW1 9TC, England. *Office:* City Business Library, 55 Basinghall St., London EC2V 5BX, England.

CAREER: Holborn Public Library, London, England, assistant librarian, 1946-59; British Employers' Confederation, London, England, librarian, 1959-64; Confederation of British Industry, London, England, librarian, 1964-68; City Business Library, London, England, librarian, 1968—. Lecturer at City University (London). *Military service:* British Army, 1952-54; became sergeant. *Member:* Library Association, Aslib (member of council, 1975—).

WRITINGS: Business Information Services, Shoe String, 1974; (editor) *Manual of Business and Library Practice*, Bingley, 1975. Contributor to library journals.

WORK IN PROGRESS: Directory of Financial Directories.

SIDELIGHTS: "I believe the public (free) provision of information to business to be important," Campbell wrote, "but in the United Kingdom, United States, and elsewhere inadequate, with a few exceptions. Insufficient stress is laid upon this area in education of librarians."

*   *   *

CAMPBELL, R(obert) Wright   1927-

PERSONAL: Born June 9, 1927, in Newark, N.J.; son of William James and Florence (Clinton) Campbell. *Education:* Attended Pratt Institute, 1944-47. *Home:* 21371 Pacific Coast Highway, Malibu, Calif. 90265. *Agent:* Elizabeth Trupin, Box 276, Hastings-on-Hudson, N.Y. 10706.

CAREER: Artist, novelist, screenwriter. *Military service:* U.S. Army, 1950-52. *Member:* Alcoholics Anonymous.

WRITINGS: The Spy Who Sat and Waited (novel), Putnam, 1975.

Screenplays: "Five Guns West"; "Quantez"; "Gun for a Coward"; "Man of a Thousand Faces"; "Machine Gun Kelly"; "Masque of the Red Death"; "Young Racers"; "Secret Invasion," and others.

Also author of scripts for television.

WORK IN PROGRESS: A novel, *Circus Couronne or the Shadow Assassin*; "Grotius," a play; *Pepe, Coco, Mistinquette and Claude*, a novella; *In the Name of the Juggler*, a novella; *The Marchland*, a novel.

*   *   *

CAMPBELL, (John) Ramsey   1946-
(Montgomery Comfort)

PERSONAL: Born January 4, 1946, in Liverpool, England; son of Alexander Ramsey and Nora (Walker) Campbell; married Jenny Chandler (a teacher), January 1, 1971. *Education:* Educated in Liverpool, England. *Politics:* "Leftist: But I become progressively more cynical about political generalizations!" *Religion:* Agnostic. *Home and office:* 54 Buckingham Rd., Liverpool, Lancashire L13 8AZ, England. *Agent:* Kirby McCauley, 220 East 26th St., New York, N.Y. 10010.

CAREER: Inland Revenue, Liverpool, England, tax officer, 1962-66; Liverpool Public Libraries, Liverpool, library assistant, 1966-73, acting librarian in charge, 1971-73; writer, 1973—. Lecturer on films and horror fiction; film critic, BBC Radio Merseyside, 1969—. *Member:* British Film Institute, Science Fiction Writers of America, British Fantasy Society (president, 1971-72).

WRITINGS—Horror fiction: The Inhabitant of the Lake, Arkham, 1964; *Demons by Daylight*, Arkham, 1973; *The Height of the Scream*, Arkham, 1975; *The Doll Who Ate His Mother*, Bobbs-Merrill, in press; (editor and contributor) *Superhorror*, Star Books, in press.

Short stories represented in anthologies, including: *Dark Things*, edited by August Derleth, Arkham, 1971; *Year's Best Horror Stories*, edited by Richard Davis, Daw Books, 1971, 1974, 1975; *The Spawn of Cthulhu*, edited by Lin Carter, Ballantine, 1971; *The Devil's Kisses*, edited by Michel Parry, Orbit Books, 1974; *Taste of Fear*, edited by

Hugh Lamb, W. H. Allen, 1975; *The Satyr's Head*, edited by David Sutton, Corgi Books, 1975. Author of column, "Layouts," for *Bulletin* of the British Fantasy Society, 1974—. Contributor to science fiction magazines, sometimes under pseudonym Montgomery Comfort.

WORK IN PROGRESS: A collection of short stories: *Little Horrors*, a collection of horror stories; *Horror Erotica*; two novels, *From the Hole* and *The Swordsman and the Ghost-Girl*.

SIDELIGHTS: Campbell writes: "I write horror fiction because it's what I do best—and I reckon one should spend as much time as possible doing what one does best.... Whenever I become depressed by the disrepute into which horror fiction has been brought by the gore-and-entrail-purveying hack writers, I recall ... the dozens of damn good people who are still working to write horror fiction as well and as carefully as they possibly can." *Avocational interests:* Cinema, music.

*   *   *

CAMPBELL, Rita Ricardo 1920-

PERSONAL: Born March 16, 1920, in Boston, Mass.; daughter of David and Elizabeth (Jones) Ricardo; married Wesley Glenn Campbell, September 15, 1946; children: Barbara Lee, Diane Rita, Nancy Elizabeth. *Education:* Simmons College, B.A., 1941; Harvard University-Radcliffe College, M.A., 1945, Ph.D., 1946. *Home:* 26915 Alejandro Dr., Los Altos Hills, Calif. 94022. *Office:* Hoover Institution, Stanford University, Stanford, Calif. 94305.

CAREER: Harvard University, Cambridge, Mass., instructor, 1947-48; Tufts University, Medford, Mass., assistant professor, 1948-51; Wage Stabilization Board, Washington, D.C., labor economist, 1951-53; U.S. House of Representatives, Ways and Means Committee, Washington, D.C., economist, 1953; consulting economist, 1957-60; Stanford University, Hoover Institution, Stanford, Calif., archivist and research associate, 1961-68, senior fellow, 1968—, lecturer in health services at Stanford Medical School, 1973—. Visiting professor at San Jose State University, 1960-61. Member of board of directors of Independent Colleges of Northern California, 1971—, Watkins-Johnson Co., 1974—, and Simmons College, 1975—. *Member:* American Economic Association, Mont Pelerin Society, Phi Beta Kappa. *Awards, honors:* National Endowment for the Humanities senior fellowship, 1975.

WRITINGS: (Co-author) *Economics of Mobilization and War*, Irwin, 1952; *Economics of Health and Public Policy*, American Enterprise Institute for Public Research, 1971; (contributor) *Food Safety Regulation: Uses and Limitations of Cost-Benefit Analysis*, American Enterprise Institute—Hoover Institution Joint Study, 1974. Contributor of articles and reviews to journals.

*   *   *

CANARY
See CONN, Canary Denise

*   *   *

CANCIAN, Francesca M(icaela) 1937-

PERSONAL: Born October 31, 1937, in New York, N.Y.; daughter of Pierre Rudolf (an engineer) and Natascha (an author; maiden name, Hirschberg) Wendel; married Frank Cancian (an anthropologist and professor), 1959; children: Maria Michele, Steven Alexander. *Education:* Reed College, B.A., 1958; Harvard University, Ph.D., 1963. *Home:* 1055 Vernier Pl., Stanford, Calif. 94305. *Office:* Department of Sociology, Stanford University, Stanford, Calif. 94305.

CAREER: Harvard University, Cambridge, Mass., lecturer in social relations, 1963-64; Cornell University, Ithaca, N.Y., assistant professor of child development and family relationships, 1966-69; Stanford University, Stanford, Calif., assistant professor of sociology, 1969—. Consultant to Stanford Research Institute, 1970-71.

MEMBER: American Sociological Association, Sociologists for Women in Society, Social Science Research Council, Joint Committee on Latin American Studies, Pacific Sociological Association, Phi Beta Kappa. *Awards, honors:* National Institute of Mental Health fellow at Stanford University, 1965-66; National Science Foundation research grant in Mexico, 1966-70; Stanford Committee on Latin American Studies research grant, 1970-71; Center for Advanced Studies in Behavioral Sciences fellow, 1970-71.

WRITINGS: What Are Norms? A Study of Beliefs and Action in a Maya Community, Cambridge University Press, 1975. Contributor to *Explorations in General Theory in the Social Sciences*, edited by Jan Loubser and Andrew Effrat, Free Press. Contributor to encyclopedias and professional journals.

WORK IN PROGRESS: A study of the effects of the women's liberation movement in the United States, and of the importance of ideology or consciousness versus material forces or power in changing society.

*   *   *

CANHAM, Kingsley 1945-

PERSONAL: Born February 18, 1945, in Port Elizabeth, South Africa; married Jean Fairclough, February 7, 1970; children: Caroline. *Education:* Attended St. Andrew's College, South Africa, 1958-62. *Home:* 11a Blashford St., Hither Green, London SE13 6VA, England. *Office:* c/o Tantivy Press, 108 New Bond St., London W1Y O QX, England.

CAREER: Jack Swifts, London, England, bookmaker clerk, 1963-65; *Observer*, London, assistant subscription manager, 1966-70; University of London, London, clerical officer, 1970-74.

WRITINGS: (Contributor) David Will and Peter Wollen, editors, *Samuel Fuller*, Edinburgh Film Festival, 1969; (contributor) Peter Cowie, editor, *A Concise History of the Cinema*, Tantivy Press, Volume II, 1971; *The Hollywood Professionals*, A. S. Barnes, Volume I, 1973, Volume II, with Clive Denton and Tony Thomas, 1974, Volume V, with Denton, 1975. Contributor to film journals. Contributing editor, *Screen*, 1969-70.

WORK IN PROGRESS: Film Directors Guide: Western Europe; a novel, *Broken Down Angel* (tentative title); *A Dictionary of Cinema*.

SIDELIGHTS: Canham speaks Dutch and reads French and German.

*   *   *

CANNAN, Denis 1919-

PERSONAL: Original name Dennis Pullein-Thompson; name legally changed in 1964; born May 14, 1919, in Oxford, England; son of H. J. (a captain in the British Army Medical Corps) and Joanna (Cannan) Pullein-Thompson;

married Joan Ross, 1946; married Rose Evansky, 1965; children: two sons, one daughter. *Education:* Attended Eton College. *Home:* Godley's, Rudgwick, Horsham, Sussex RH12 3AJ, England.

CAREER: Actor in repertory theater groups in England and Scotland, 1936-39 and 1946-51; performed in plays by George Bernard Shaw and others; appeared in television plays, 1948 and 1949; playwright, 1949—. *Military service:* British Army, Queen's Royal Regiment, 1939-45; mentioned in dispatches.

WRITINGS:—Plays: *Captain Carvallo* (three-act comedy; first produced in London at St. James Theatre, 1950), Hart-Davis, 1951, acting edition, Samuel French, 1951; *Colombe* (adaptation of the play by Anouilh; first produced in London at the New Theatre, 1951), Methuen, 1952; *Misery Me: A Comedy of Woe* (three-act comedy; first produced in London at the Duchess Theatre, 1955), Samuel French, 1956; *You and Your Wife* (three-act comedy; first produced in Bristol at the Old Vic Theatre, 1955), Samuel French, 1956; (with Pierre Bost) *The Power and the Glory* (three-act drama; adaptation of the novel by Graham Greene; first produced in London at the Phoenix Theatre, 1956, and in New York at the Phoenix Theatre, December 10, 1958), Samuel French, 1959; *Who's Your Father?* (three-act comedy; first produced in London at the Cambridge Theatre, 1958), Samuel French, 1959; (with others) "US" (three-act drama; first produced in London at the Aldwych Theatre, 1966), published as *Tell Me Lies: The Book of the Royal Shakespeare Production US/Vietnam/US/Experiment/Politics* ..., Bobbs-Merrill, 1968 (published in England as *US: The Book of the Royal Shakespeare Production US/Vietnam/US/Experiment/Politics* ..., Calder & Boyars, 1968).

Unpublished plays: "Max" (three-act drama), first produced at the Malvern Festival, Malvern, England, 1949; "Ghosts" (adaptation of the play by Ibsen), first produced in London at the Aldwych Theatre, 1967; "One at Night" (three-act drama), first performed in London at the Royal Court Theatre, April 13, 1971.

Screenplays: "The Beggar's Opera," 1953; "Why Bother to Knock," 1965; "A Boy Ten Feet Tall," 1965; "The Amorous Adventures of Moll Flanders," 1965; "Sammy Going South," 1965; (with others) "A High Wind in Jamaica," 1965.

Radio plays: "Headlong Hall," 1950; "The Moth and the Star," 1950; "The Greeting," 1964.

AVOCATIONAL INTERESTS: Manual labor.*

* * *

CANTWELL, Dennis P(atrick) 1940-

PERSONAL: Born February 28, 1940, in East St. Louis, Ill.; son of John (vice-president of Granite City Steel) and Rose (Brzostowski) Cantwell; married Susan McKenna, June 12, 1965; children: Susan, Dennis, Colleen, Erin. *Education:* University of Notre Dame, B.S. (maxima cum laude), 1961; Washington University, St. Louis, Mo., M.D., 1965. *Home:* 4490 Poe Ave., Woodland Hills, Calif. *Office:* Department of Psychiatry, School of Medicine, University of California, Los Angeles, Calif. 90024.

CAREER: University of California Hospitals, San Francisco, intern, 1965-66; Washington University, St. Louis, Mo., resident in psychiatry, 1966-67; University of California, Los Angeles, resident in psychiatry, 1969-71, fellow in child psychiatry, 1970-72, assistant professor of psychiatry,

1972—, director of residency training in child psychiatry, 1972—. Licensed to practice medicine in Missouri, 1965, and California, 1968; psychiatric resident at Los Angeles Neuropsychiatric Institute, 1969-71, fellow in child psychiatry, 1970-72; fellow in child psychiatry at University of London's Institute of Psychiatry, 1971-72; research clinic psychiatrist at Hyperkinetic Children's Clinic of Gateways Hospital, 1967-71, research child psychiatrist, 1972—; consultant to California Angels, Los Angeles Rams, California Sun, CIBA Pharmaceutical, Merck, Sharp & Dohme Pharmaceutical, Bristol Laboratories, NBC-Television, and American Youth Soccer Organization. *Military service:* U.S. Navy, Medical Corps, chief psychiatrist at El Toro Marine Corps Air Station, 1967-69; became lieutenant commander.

MEMBER: American Medical Association, American Psychiatric Association, American Board of Child Psychiatry, American Academy of Child Psychiatry, American Association on Mental Deficiency, Association of University Affiliated Facilities, American Professional Practice Association, Association for Child Psychology and Psychiatry, Society for Research in Child Psychiatry, Southern California Psychiatric Association, Sigma Xi, Phi Beta Pi, Alpha Omega Alpha. *Awards, honors:* U.S. Public Health Service grants, 1962, 1963, 1964; National Institute of Mental Health grants, 1969-72, 1971-72, 1972-73, 1973-77, 1973-74, 1974-75; Falk fellow of American Psychiatric Association, 1970-71; California State Department of Mental Hygiene grant, 1973; Easter Seal Foundation grant, 1973-76; J. Franklin Robinson Memorial Award, from American Academy of Child Psychiatry, 1974.

WRITINGS: (Contributor) Allan Beigel and Alan Levenson, editors, *The Community Mental Health Center: Strategies and Programs*, Community Mental Health Centers Support Branch, National Institute of Mental Health, 1972; (contributor) Stella Chess and Alexander Thomas, editors, *Annual Progress in Child Psychiatry and Child Development: 1972*, Brunner, 1973; (contributor) E. J. Anthony, editor, *The Child Psychiatrist as Clinical Investigator*, Plenum, 1975; (editor and contributor) *The Hyperactive Child: Diagnosis, Management, and Current Research*, Spectrum, 1975; (contributor) D. V. Siva Sankar, editor, *Studies on Childhood Psychiatric and Psychological Problems*, PJD Publications, in press; (with P. E. Tanguay) *Basic Clinical Child Psychiatry: A Textbook for Medical Students and Students in Allied Disciplines*, Spectrum, in press. Editor of Spectrum's "Child Behavior and Development" series.

Writer of abstracts; contributor to *Psychology Encyclopedia*; contributor of more than forty articles and reviews to medical and psychiatric journals in the United States and abroad. Co-editor of *Child Psychiatry Newsletter*, 1972-73; member of editorial board of *Manual on Terminology and Classification in Mental Retardation*; referee for *American Journal of Psychiatry, Archives of General Psychiatry*, and *Diseases of the Nervous System*, all 1973—; book reviewer for *American Journal of Psychiatry*, 1974—, *Psychiatric Annals*, 1974—, and *U.A.F. Bibliography in Mental Retardation*.

WORK IN PROGRESS: A contribution to *The Basic Handbook of Child Psychiatry*, edited by Joseph Noshpitz; research on parental adequacy in the families of autistic and aphasic children, educational retardation in hyperactive children, language styles of mothers, and related topics; a contribution to *Psycho-Pharmacology for Non-Psychiatric Physicians and Psychologists*, edited by M. E. Jarvik.

CAPLIN, Alfred Gerald 1909-
  (Al Capp)

PERSONAL: Born September 28, 1909, in New Haven, Conn.; son of Otto Philip and Matilda (Davidson) Caplin; married Catherine Wingate Cameron, 1929; children: Julie Ann (Mrs. Julian Cairol), Catherine Jane (Mrs. Michael Pierce), Colin C. *Education:* Studied at Pennsylvania Academy of the Fine Arts, Designer's Art School, Boston Museum of Fine Arts, Boston University, Harvard University. *Office:* Capp Enterprises, 122 Beacon St., Boston, Mass. 02116.

CAREER: Began career as cartoonist working for Associated Press on the comic strip "Colonel Gilfeather" in 1932; worked as an illustrator for the *Sunday Post*, Boston, Mass., 1933; ghost artist for several major comic strips including Ham Fisher's "Joe Palooka"; creator and developer of comic strip "Li'l Abner," 1934—; creator and author of comic strip "Abbie an' Slats"; author of comic strips "Private Li'l Abner, Infantry" for the *Infantry Journal* and "Small Change" for the Treasury Department during World War II. Columnist, New York Daily News Syndicate, 1960-72; daily syndicated radio and television commentator, 1970-73; teacher of cartooning workshop course at New York University; has lectured at Harvard University.

WRITINGS: The Life and Times of the Shmoo, Simon & Schuster, 1948; *The World of Li'l Abner*, introduction by John Steinbeck and foreword by Charles Chaplin, Farrar, Straus, 1953; *Bald Iggle: The Life It Ruins May Be Your Own*, Simon & Schuster, 1956; *Fearless Fosdick*, Simon & Schuster, 1956; *The Return of the Shmoo*, Simon & Schuster, 1959; (with David Manning White) *From Dogpatch to Slobbovia: The Gasp!! World of Li'l Abner, As Seen by David Manning White, with Certain Illuminating Remarks by Al Capp*, Beacon Press, 1964; *The Hardhat's Bedtime Story Book*, Harper, 1971. Author of script for motion picture, "Li'l Abner," produced by RKO, 1940. Contributor to *Encyclopaedia Britannica.*

SIDELIGHTS: Capp lost his right leg when he was nine years of age. He is, however, an active man who believes strongly in independence and self-reliance. His comic strip, "Li'l Abner," represents a form of true social satire. In the strip Capp has commented on social and political issues of the day in the United States, criticizing the conservative political climate of the 1950s and the radical liberals of the 1960s and 1970s.

The strip has been popular since its first appearance in eight newspapers in 1934; it was published in 500 newspapers by the late 1940's. Capp's books center about the characters that appear in "Li'l Abner." He also collaborated on the play, "Li'l Abner," and on the movie of the same name produced in the late 1950s.

BIOGRAPHICAL/CRITICAL SOURCES: Newsweek, June 22, 1970.

* * *

CAPP, Al
  See CAPLIN, Alfred Gerald

* * *

CARDUS, Neville 1889-1975

April 2, 1889—February 28, 1975; British journalist, music critic, sports writer, and author of books on music and cricket. Obituaries: *New York Times*, March 1, 1975; *Washington Post*, March 1, 1975; *AB Bookman's Weekly*, March 17, 1975.

* * *

CAREY, Gary 1938-

PERSONAL: Born February 19, 1938, in Chester, Pa.; son of Paul James and Ruth (Fawcett) Carey; married Carol Koshinskie, July 5, 1969; children: Sean. *Education:* Columbia University, B.A., 1960, M.F.A., 1963. *Home:* 20 St. Paul's Ct., Brooklyn, N.Y. 11226. *Agent:* Ray Pierre Corsini, 12 Beekman Pl., New York, N.Y. 10022. *Office:* School of Visual Arts, New York, N.Y.

CAREER: Seventh Art (magazine), New York, N.Y., editor and publisher, 1963-65; Museum of Modern Art, New York, N.Y., assistant curator of film, 1966-69; MCA-Universal, New York, N.Y., member of story department, 1970; School of Visual Arts, New York, N.Y., instructor in film and theatre, 1971—.

WRITINGS: Lost Films, Museum of Modern Art, 1970; *Cukor & Co.: The Films of George Cukor and His Collaborators*, Museum of Modern Art, 1971; (with Joseph L. Mankiewicz) *More About "All About Eve"*, Random House, 1972; *Brando!*, Pocket Books, 1973; *Lenny, Janis, and Jimi*, Pocket Books, 1975; *Katharine Hepburn*, Pocket Books, 1975. Contributor of articles and reviews to *Film Quarterly*, *Film Comment*, and *Library Journal.*

SIDELIGHTS: Publishers Weekly explained that in *Lenny, Janis and Jimi* Carey "goes beyond the usual hyperbole of both the straights and the counter-culture to put some perspective on the tangled slinky-toy lives of these three turned-on folk heroes and what led them unavoidable, inevitably, to their tragic early deaths. Carey keeps a distance; throughout he's objective, non-judgmental yet sympathetic." *Avocational interests:* Popular music, television.

* * *

CAREY, John 1934-

PERSONAL: Born April 5, 1934, in London, England; son of Charles William and Winifred Ethel (Cook) Carey; married Gillian Mary Florence Booth, 1960; children: Leo Jonathan. *Education:* Oxford University, B.A. (first honors), 1957, M.A., 1960, D.Phil., 1960. *Home:* 38 St. John St., Oxford, England.

CAREER: Oxford University, Oxford, England, lecturer at Christ Church, 1958, Andrew Bradley Research Fellow at Balliol College, 1959, fellow of Keble College, 1960-64, lecturer in English literature and fellow of St. John's College, 1964—.

WRITINGS: (Editor with Alastair Fowler) *The Poems of John Milton*, Longmans, Green, 1968, Norton, 1972; (editor) James Hogg, *The Private Memoirs and Confessions of a Justified Sinner*, Oxford University Press, 1969; *Milton*, Evans Brothers, 1969, Arco, 1970; (compiler) *Andrew Marvell: A Critical Anthology*, Penguin, 1969; (contributor) Christopher Ricks, editor, *Sphere History of Literature*, Volume II, Sphere Books Ltd., 1970; (editor) John Milton, *Complete Shorter Poems*, Longmans, 1971; *The Violent Effigy: A Study of Dickens' Imagination*, Faber, 1973; (translator) Milton, *Christian Doctrine*, Yale University Press, 1973. Contributor to *Encyclopaedia Britannica*; also contributor of articles to *Modern Language Review* and *Review of English Studies.*

CARGO, David N(iels) 1932-

PERSONAL: Born June 27, 1932, in Grand Rapids, Mich.; son of Hugh William (an engineer) and Helen (Hansen) Cargo; married Demetria Ann Kelly (a teacher), June 27, 1959; children: Karen, Mary Ann, Ross, John. *Education:* University of Nebraska, B.S.Ed., 1953; University of New Mexico, M.S., 1959; University of Utah, Ph.D., 1966. *Politics:* "Democrat, usually." *Home:* 222 West Second St., Maryville, Mo. 64468. *Office:* Department of Earth Science, Northwest Missouri State University, Maryville, Mo. 64468.

CAREER: Northwest Missouri State University, Maryville, assistant professor, 1966-71, associate professor, 1971-75, professor of geology, 1975—. *Member:* American Association of Petroleum Geologists, American Association for the Advancement of Science, Association of Missouri Geologists, Missouri Academy of Science.

WRITING: (With Bob F. Mallory) *Man and His Geologic Environment*, Addison-Wesley, 1974.

WORK IN PROGRESS: A physical geology textbook, publication by McGraw expected in 1978; an earth science textbook, Houghton, 1978.

* * *

CARLSON, Richard Stocks 1942-

PERSONAL: Born April 23, 1942, in New Britain, Conn.; son of Halvard and Jane (Stocks) Carlson. *Education:* Boston University, B.S. (summa cum laude), 1970, M.S., 1971; Michigan State University, Ph.D., 1973. *Home:* 300 Tremont St., Newton, Mass. 02158. *Office:* Suffolk University, 45 Mt. Vernon St., Boston, Mass.

CAREER: Suffolk University, Boston, Mass., assistant professor of communications and language, 1973—. *Member:* Phi Beta Kappa.

WRITINGS: Earth Images (poems), Boston University, 1973; *The Benign Humorists*, Shoe String Press, 1975. Also author of *Pinch, The Crab*, a children's book, and filmscript, "The Suicides." Contributor to journals and magazines.

WORK IN PROGRESS: The New Communicators; *Rule Holmes*, a novel; *Oxford*.

* * *

CARMAN, Robert A(rchibald) 1931-

PERSONAL: Born May 14, 1931, in Homestead, Pa.; son of Alexander A. and Nellie (Krupinski) Carman; married Marilyn Porter (a teacher), June 11, 1955; children: Patricia, Laurie, Mary, Eric. *Education:* Carnegie Institute of Technology (now Carnegie-Mellon University), B.S., 1953; University of Pittsburgh, M.S., 1960; University of California, Los Angeles, Ed.D., 1975. *Residence:* Santa Barbara, Calif. 93111. *Office:* Santa Barbara City College, Santa Barbara, Calif. 93105.

CAREER: Carnegie Institute of Technology (now Carnegie-Mellon University), lecturer, 1956-57; University of Pittsburgh, Pittsburgh, Pa., lecturer in physics, 1957-58; University of Wyoming, Laramie, instructor, 1961; San Bernardino Valley College, San Bernardino, Calif., professor of physics, 1961-69; Santa Barbara City College, Santa Barbara, Calif., professor of physics and math, 1969—, director of Learning Resources Center. *Member:* American Physical Society, American Association of Physics Teachers, National Science Teachers Association, Society for History of Technology, History of Science Society, National Council of Teachers of Mathematics, Omicron Delta Kappa, Psi Chi, Alpha Tau Omega. *Awards, honors:* National Science Foundation fellow.

WRITINGS—All published by Wiley: *A Programmed Introduction to Vectors*, 1963; *Numbers and Units for Physics*, 1969; (with W. R. Adams) *Study Skills: A Student's Guide for Survival*, 1972; (with wife, Marilyn J. Carman) *Quick Arithmetic*, 1974; (with Marilyn J. Carman) *Basic Mathematical Skills*, 1975. Contributor to journals in his field.

WORK IN PROGRESS: Basic algebra text; a work on mathematics for non-mathematicians.

* * *

CARMICHAEL, Stokely 1941-

PERSONAL: Born June 29, 1941, Port-of-Spain, Trinidad, B.W.I.; came to United States, 1952; son of Adolphus (a carpenter) and Mabel F. (also known as May Charles) Carmichael; married Miriam Makeba (a professional singer), April, 1968. *Education:* Howard University, B.A., 1964.

CAREER: Student Non-Violent Coordinating Committee (SNCC; now Student National Coordinating Committee), Atlanta, Ga., organizer, 1964-66, chairman, 1966-67; Black Panthers, Oakland, Calif., prime minister, 1967-69.

WRITINGS: (With Charles V. Hamilton) *Black Power: The Politics of Liberation in America*, Random House, 1967; *Stokely Speaks: Black Power Back to Pan-Africanism*, Random House, 1971.

SIDELIGHTS: Stokely Carmichael first became involved in the civil rights struggle through the Freedom Rides that were designed to end the segregation of Blacks on public buses in the South, in 1960. His influence as a leader grew steadily after he organized the Lowndes County Freedom Organization, an independent political party, in Mississippi in the early 1960s and adopted the black panther as its symbol. During the height of the integrationist movement, Carmichael shocked civil rights leaders and drew the allegiance of thousands of Blacks through his cry for "Black Power" and his reluctance to work with white liberals. By 1969 Carmichael had become disillusioned with the civil rights movement in the United States and interested in Pan Africanism. He has lived in self-imposed exile in Guinea since May of that year.

BIOGRAPHICAL/CRITICAL SOURCES: Life, May 19, 1967; *New York Review of Books*, February 29, 1968; *Antioch Review*, Spring, 1968.*

* * *

CARPENTER, Clarence Ray 1905-1975

November 28, 1905—March 1, 1975; American educator, animal behaviorist, psychologist, anthropologist, editor, and author. Obituaries: *New York Times*, March 4, 1975.

* * *

CARPENTER, Rhys 1889-

PERSONAL: Born August 5, 1889, in Cotuit, Mass.; son of William Henry and Anna Morgan (Douglass) Carpenter; married Eleanor Houston Hill, April 23, 1918. *Education:* Columbia University, A.B., 1908, Ph.D., 1916; Balliol College, Oxford, B.A., 1911, M.A., 1914; studied at American School of Classical Studies, Athens, 1912-13. *Home:* Goose Walk, R.D.1, Chester Springs, Pa. 19425.

CAREER: Bryn Mawr College, Bryn Mawr, Pa., instructor, 1913-15, assistant professor, 1915-16, associate professor, 1916-18, professor of classical archaeology, 1918-55, professor emeritus, 1955—. American Academy, Rome, annual professor, 1926-27, professor-in-charge of Classical School, 1939-40; American School for Classical Studies, Athens, director, 1927-32, 1946-48, visiting professor, 1956-57; University of California, Sather Professor of Classical Literature, 1944-45. Member of American Commission to Negotiate Peace, 1919. Military service: U.S. Army, 1918-19, Military intelligence; served as first lieutenant.

MEMBER: American Philosophical Society, Archaeological Institute of America, American Philological Association, Linguistic Society of America, Hispanic Society of America (honorary member), Greek Archaeological Society (honorary member), German Archaeological Institute (honorary member), Austrian Archaeological Institute (honorary member), Pontifical Roman Academy of Archaeology (corresponding member), Philadelphia Oriental Club, Phi Beta Kappa. Awards, honors: Gold medal of American Institute of Archaeology, 1969; Litt.D., Rutgers University, 1941.

WRITINGS: The Tragedy of Etarre: A Poem, Sturgis & Walton, 1912; The Sun-Thief and Other Poems, Oxford University Press, 1914; The Ethics of Euripides, Columbia University Press, 1916; The Land Beyond Mexico, R. G. Badger, 1920; The Plainsman and Other Poems, Oxford University Press, 1920; The Esthetic Basis of Greek Art of the Fifth and Fourth Centuries B.C., Longmans, Green, 1921, revised edition, Indiana University Press, 1959; The Greeks in Spain, Longmans, Green, 1925, reprinted, AMS Press, 1971; The Sculpture of the Nike Temple Parapet, Harvard University Press, 1929, reprinted, McGrath Publishing, 1971.

The Lost Statues of the East Pediment of the Parthenon, Harvard University Press, 1933; The Humanistic Value of Archaeology, Harvard University Press, 1933, reprinted, Greenwood Press, 1971; (with Antoine Bon and A. W. Parsons) The Defenses of Acrocorinth and the Lower Town, Harvard University Press, 1936; (with Richard Bernheimer, K. Koffka, and Milton C. Nahm) ART: A Bryn Mawr Symposium, Bryn Mawr College, 1940, reprinted, Oriole Editions, 1972; (with Carl Blegen and others) Studies in the Arts and Architecture, University of Pennsylvania Press, 1941, reprinted, Kennikat, 1969; Observations on Familiar Statuary in Rome, American Academy in Rome, 1941; (with Maxwell Anderson and Roy Harris) The Bases of Artistic Creation (essays), Rutgers University Press, 1942; Folk Tale, Fiction and Saga in the Homeric Epics, University of California Press, 1946.

Greek Sculpture: A Critical Review, University of Chicago Press, 1960; Everyday Life in Ancient Times, National Geographical Society, 1961; Greek Art: A Study of the Formal Evolution of Style, University of Pennsylvania Press, 1962; (with James S. Ackerman) Art and Archaeology, Prentice-Hall, 1963; Beyond the Pillars of Heracles: The Classical World Seen Through the Eyes of its Discoverers, Delacorte Press, 1966; Discontinuity in Greek Civilization, Cambridge University Press, 1966, Norton, 1968; The Architects of the Parthenon, Penguin, 1970.

Contributor to Encyclopaedia Britannica and professional journals, including American Journal of Archaeology.

AVOCATIONAL INTERESTS: Mountain-climbing, archaeological exploration.*

CARR, Arthur Japheth 1914-

PERSONAL: Born April 21, 1914, in Bad Axe, Mich.; son of Arthur Wellesley and Margaret (McAuslan) Carr; married Penelope Gall, February 1, 1964; children: (previous marriage) Jennifer (Mrs. John McGee), Adam Fyfe, Daniel Arthur, Alice (Mrs. Jan A. Van den Brock III). Education: University of Michigan, A.B., 1935; Syracuse University, A.M., 1937; University of Illinois, Ph.D., 1947. Home address: Green River Rd., Williamstown, Mass. 01267. Office: Department of English, Williams College, Williamstown, Mass. 01267.

CAREER: Instructor in English at Syracuse University, Syracuse, N.Y., 1937-40, and University of Illinois, Urbana, 1947-49; University of Michigan, Ann Arbor, assistant professor, 1949-54, associate professor, 1955-61, professor of English, 1961-67; Williams College, Williamstown, Mass., professor of English, 1967-70, Edward Dorr Griffin Professor, 1970—, chairman of department, 1967—. Director, University of Michigan National Defense Education Act Institute, 1965; consultant to U.S. Office of Education, 1965-69; member of College Entrance Examination Board, Educational Testing Service, 1966-71. Military service: U.S. Naval Reserve, 1943-45; served in Pacific Theatre. Member: Modern Language Association of America, National Council of Teachers of English, American Association of University Professors, Phi Beta Kappa, Phi Eta Sigma, Phi Kappa Phi.

WRITINGS: (Editor with Alexander Ward Allison and Arthur M. Eastman) Masterpieces of Drama, Macmillan, 1957, 2nd edition, 1966; (editor and author of introduction and notes) Victorian Poetry: Clough to Kipling, Rinehart, 1959, 2nd edition, Holt, 1972; (editor with William Steinhoff) Points of Departure: Essays and Stories for College English, Harper, 1960, reprinted, Books for Libraries, 1971; (co-editor) The Norton Anthology of Poetry, Norton, 1970.*

* * *

CARR, Stephen L(amoni)

HOME: 2180 East 4500 S., Holladay, Utah 84117.

CAREER: Physician. Writer. Awards, honors: Certificate of commendation from American Association for State and Local History, 1974.

WRITINGS: The Historical Guide to Utah Ghost Towns, Western Epics Publishing, 1972.

* * *

CARRANCO, Lynwood 1922-

PERSONAL: Born April 2, 1922, in Eureka, Calif.; son of Filberto (a millworker) and Cecilia (Ysais) Carranco; married Ruth Cannam (a teacher), June 12, 1947; children: Robert, Donald. Education: Humboldt State University, A.B., 1949; Columbia University, M.A., 1951; University of Southern California, graduate study, 1959-60, and Ball State University, 1967-68; University of Sarasota, Ph.D., 1973. Politics: Democrat. Religion: Roman Catholic. Home: 2778 Buttermilk Lane, Arcata, Calif. 95521. Office: Department of English, College of the Redwoods, Eureka, Calif. 95501.

CAREER: Public high school teacher of languages in Arcata, Calif., 1951-56; Humboldt State University, Arcata, Calif., assistant professor, 1956-59, associate professor of English, 1959-64; College of the Redwoods, Eureka, Calif., associate professor, 1964-68, professor of English, 1968—.

Military service: U.S. Navy, Air Corps, 1942-45. *Member:* Humboldt County Historical Society (president, 1975), Redwood Council of English Teachers (president, 1964).

WRITINGS: Fundamentals of Modern English, Kendall/Hunt, 1963; *The Redwood Country: History, Language, Folklore,* Kendall/Hunt, 1971; (with John Labbe) *Logging the Redwoods,* Caxton, 1975. Contributor of twenty articles to journals.

WORK IN PROGRESS: A dictionary of words and expressions used in logging, for Caxton; a history of Mendocino and Trinity counties, the Yolla Bolly country; *Charles Barnum and the Redwood Lumber Industry,* completion expected in 1976.

SIDELIGHTS: Carranco played two years of professional baseball. *Avocational interests:* Travel, gardening.

* * *

CARRINGTON, Frank G(amble, Jr.) 1936-

PERSONAL: Born May 11, 1936, in Paris, France; son of Frank Gamble (an engineer) and Edith (Rule) Carrington; married Susan Gilhooley, September 7, 1959 (marriage ended, May 30, 1967); married Mary Nymoen Olson, May 11, 1968; children: (first marriage) Christine Margaret, Claire Lynn. *Education:* Hampden-Sydney College, B.A., 1956; University of Michigan, LL.B., 1960; Northwestern University, LL.M., 1970. *Politics:* Republican. *Religion:* Episcopal. *Home:* 1341 Chestnut St., Wilmette, Ill. 60091. *Office:* Americans for Effective Law Enforcement, Inc., 960 State National Bank Plaza, Evanston, Ill. 60201.

CAREER: Admitted to practice in Ohio, 1966, Colorado, 1969, and Illinois, 1974, and before the U.S. Supreme Court; U.S. Treasury Department, Cincinnati, Ohio, special agent and criminal investigator, 1960-67; Chicago Police Department, Chicago, Ill., legal adviser, 1967-68; Denver Police Department, Denver, Colo., legal adviser, 1968-70; Americans for Effective Law Enforcement, Inc., Evanston, Ill., executive director, 1970—. Guest lecturer in law at University of Michigan and Northwestern University. Member of board of advisers of Young Americans for Freedom. *Military service:* U.S. Marine Corps, 1957. U.S. Marine Corps Reserve, 1957-63. *Member:* International Association of Chiefs of Police, National Sheriff's Association, Colorado Association of Chiefs of Police, University Club (Evanston).

WRITINGS: (With Fred E. Inbau and Marvin Aspen) *Evidence Law for the Police,* Chilton, 1972; *The Victims* (nonfiction), Arlington House, 1975.

WORK IN PROGRESS: A novel on the criminal justice system and the victims of crime.

* * *

CARROLL, John 1944-

PERSONAL: Born May 22, 1944, in Manchester, England; son of Bernard (a businessman) and Margot (a teacher; maiden name, Bolland) Carroll. *Education:* Melbourne University, B.A., 1965; Pembroke College, Cambridge, B.A., 1968, M.A., 1972, Ph.D., 1972. *Politics:* Radical conservative. *Home:* 618 Canning St., Carlton, Melbourne, Australia. *Office:* Department of Sociology, LaTrobe University, Bundoora, Melbourne, Australia.

CAREER: LaTrobe University, Melbourne, Australia, tutor and lecturer in sociology, 1972—.

WRITINGS: (Editor and author of introduction) *Max*

Stirner: The Ego and His Own, Harper, 1971; *Break-Out from the Crystal Palace,* Routledge & Kegan Paul, 1974. Consultant, *Meanjin Quarterly.*

WORK IN PROGRESS: Puritanism, Paranoia, and the Remissive: A Cultural Sociology.

* * *

CARROLL, Vern 1933-

PERSONAL: Born September 2, 1933, in Brooklyn, N.Y.; son of Verny (a naval officer) and Virginia Margaret (Yelvington) Carroll; married second wife, Mireille Raymonde Cohen (a university professor), March 7, 1975; children: Tama. *Education:* Yale University, B.A., 1959, M.A., 1962; Cambridge University, B.A. (honors), 1961, M.A., 1966; University of Chicago, Ph.D., 1966; University of Hawaii, postdoctoral study, 1970-71. *Home:* 560 South First, Ann Arbor, Mich. 48103. *Office:* Department of Anthropology, 221 Angell Hall, University of Michigan, Ann Arbor, Mich. 48104.

CAREER: University of Washington, Seattle, assistant professor, 1966-69, associate professor of anthropology, 1969-72; University of Michigan, Ann Arbor, associate professor, 1972-75, professor of anthropology, 1975—, associate at Center for South and Southeast Asian Studies, 1974—. Visiting assistant researcher at Pacific and Asian Linguistic Institute of University of Hawaii, 1967-68, senior fellow at East-West Center (Honolulu), 1972-73. Conducted research on Nukuoro Atoll, 1963-66, and in Hawaii, 1967-69. *Military service:* U.S. Navy, 1951-53. U.S. Naval Reserve, 1953-55. U.S. Marine Corps Reserve, 1955-62; became captain.

MEMBER: Association Internationale de Semiotique, American Anthropological Association (fellow), American Association for the Advancement of Science (fellow), Current Anthropology (associate), Association for Anthropology in Micronesia (member of executive committee, 1970-74), Association for Social Anthropology in Oceania (fellow; member of executive committee, 1967-73; chairman of executive committee, 1969-72), Friends of Micronesia, Polynesian Society, Royal Anthropological Institute of Great Britain and Ireland (fellow), Linguistic Society of New Zealand. *Awards, honors:* American Council of Learned Societies fellowship, 1967-68; National Science Foundation grant, 1967-69; American Philosophical Society grant, 1969; National Institute of Mental Health fellowship, 1970-71.

WRITINGS: An Outline of the Structure of the Language of Nukuoro (monograph), Polynesian Society, 1965; (editor and contributor) *Adoption in Eastern Oceania* (monograph), University of Hawaii Press, 1970; (contributor) Gregory Bateson, editor, *Steps to an Ecology of Mind,* Chandler Publishing, 1971; (with Tobias Soulik) *Nukuoro Lexicon,* University Press of Hawaii, 1973; (editor and contributor) *Pacific Atoll Populations* (monograph), University Press of Hawaii, 1975; (editor and contributor) *Incest Prohibitions in Micronesia and Polynesia* (monograph), University Press of Hawaii, in press; *Field Notes on Nukuoro Ethnocentrism,* Human Relations Area Files Press, in press; (contributor) Michael D. Lieber, editor, *Exiles and Migrants in the Pacific,* University Press of Hawaii, in press.

Editor of monograph series of Association for Social Anthropology in Oceania. Contributor to *Chambers Encyclopedia.* Contributor of articles and reviews to anthropology and linguistics journals.

WORK IN PROGRESS: Nukuoro Texts, with Tobias Soulik and Raymonde Carroll; *Nukuoro Ethnography: 1878-1912; Essays in Nukuoro Sociology; The Communicational Analysis of Culture;* research on comparative cultural and social anthropology of Micronesia and Polynesia, especially atoll societies; research on Nukuoro ethnography and linguistics, and on the American national character.

* * *

CARRUTH, Gorton Veeder 1925-

PERSONAL: Born April 9, 1925, in Woodbury, Conn.; son of Gorton Veeder and Margery Tracy Barrow (Dibb) Carruth; married Gisele Leliet, December 28, 1955; children: Gorton Veeder III, Hayden III, Christopher Leliet. *Education:* University of Chicago, Ph.B., 1948; Columbia University, B.A., 1950, M.A., 1954. *Address:* Box 168, Pleasantville, N.Y. 10570.

CAREER: Thomas Y. Crowell Co., New York, N.Y., reference book editor, 1954-63; McGraw-Hill Book Co., New York, executive editor, 1963-68; Funk & Wagnalls, New York, editor-in-chief, 1968-71; Morningside Associates, Pleasantville, N.Y., president, 1971—. *Member:* Linnaean Society, Phi Beta Kappa.

WRITINGS: (Editor in association with others) *Encyclopedia of American Facts and Dates,* Crowell, 1956, 6th edition, with supplement, 1972. Has edited and contributed to numerous publications. Developed series, *Our Living World of Nature,* McGraw, fourteen volumes, 1966-72.

AVOCATIONAL INTERESTS: Natural history, particularly ornithology; nature education.

* * *

CARSON, Kit
See CARSON, Xanthus

* * *

CARSON, Robert B. 1934-

PERSONAL: Born July 6, 1934, in Greensburg, Pa.; son of Harry Robert and Catherine (Postlewaite) Carson; married Marjorie Ruth Gale (an artist), May 31, 1958; children: James Andrew, Sarah Elizabeth. *Education:* Hamilton College, A.B., 1956; Syracuse University, M.A., 1960, Ph.D., 1967. *Home:* 109 East Street, Oneonta, N.Y. 13820. *Office:* Department of Economics, State University of New York, College at Oneonta, Oneonta, N.Y. 13820.

CAREER: Cazenovia College, Cazenovia, N.Y., instructor in economics, 1961-62; Millersville State College, Millersville, Pa., assistant professor of economics, 1962-63; State University of New York College at New Paltz, assistant professor of economics, 1963-66; State University of New York College at Oneonta, professor of economics, 1966—, director of Center for Economic Education and Research, 1967-70. Consultant to Hudson Valley Council on Economic Education, 1963-66, Project PROBE, 1968-71, and Institute for Policy Studies, 1975; member of board of directors, New York State Council on Economic Education, 1968-70. *Military service:* U.S. Army, 1957-59. *Member:* Association for Evolutionary Economics, Union of Radical Political Economists, United University Professors. *Awards, honors:* State University of New York research grants, 1968, 1971.

WRITINGS: (Compiler and contributor) *The American Economy in Conflict: A Book of Readings,* Heath, 1971; *Main Line to Oblivion: The Disintegration of New York Railroads in the Twentieth Century,* Kennikat, 1971; (contributor) David H. DeGrood, Dale M. Reipe, and John Sommerville, editors, *Radical Currents in Contemporary Philosophy,* Warren H. Green, 1971; (contributor) Edward D'Angelo, Reipe, and DeGrood, editors, *Reflections on Revolution,* Spartacus Press, 1971; (with Jerry Ingles and Douglas McLaud) *Government in the American Economy: Conventional and Radical Studies on the Growth of State Economic Power,* Heath, 1973. Writer of independent study courses, student workbook, and teacher guide. Contributor of articles to *Socialist Revolution, The Historian, Journal of Economic Issues, Social Studies, Telos, Monthly Review, Executive Quarterly,* and other professional periodicals.

WORK IN PROGRESS: A social and economic history of the United States since the 1890's; a short study of American higher education.

* * *

CARSON, Xanthus 1910-
(Kit Carson, Kit Wade)

PERSONAL: Given name is pronounced *Zan*-thus; born July 6, 1910, in Mt. Vernon, Tex.; son of Xystus (a farmer and merchant) and Minnie (Davis) Carson; married Loyas Hendon, June 16, 1957. *Education:* Educated in high school in Mt. Vernon, Tex. *Politics:* Republican. *Religion:* Baptist. *Home:* 3120 Ortiz N.E., Albuquerque, N.M. 87110.

CAREER: Writer. Has worked as newspaper reporter, farmer, oilfield and construction worker. *Military service:* U.S. Army, Corps of Engineers, 1942-43. *Member:* American Legion, Albuquerque Corral of Westerners.

WRITINGS: (Under pseudonym Kit Carson) *New Mexico's Inscription Rock,* Vantage, 1967; *Treasure!: Bonanzas Worth a Billion Bucks,* Naylor, 1974. Contributor of more than five hundred articles to magazines, sometimes under pseudonym Kit Wade.

WORK IN PROGRESS: Saga of the Incredible Victoria Peak Treasure; The Naked Truth About the Lady Be Good Situation!

SIDELIGHTS: Carson is most interested in the American West and the great deserts of the Middle East. He writes: "Digging up lost treasure clues is of primary interest. Like to do hair-line investigation. I consider my extensive world travels highly educational. Enjoyed the careful study of the Saudi Arabian people and their religion, Libyan Sahara desert, et cetera. Found travel in Old Mexico very exciting!"

* * *

CARSWELL, Evelyn M(edicus) 1919-

PERSONAL: Born February 1, 1919, in Baltimore, Md.; daughter of Harry M. and Daisy (Ingley) Medicus; married David F. Carswell (a biology teacher), March 24, 1946; children: David A., Wron B. *Education:* Northern Arizona University, B.S.Ed., 1953, M.A., 1962; University of Arizona, Ed.D., 1968. *Politics:* Republican. *Home:* 3708 Hills of Gold Dr., Tucson, Ariz. 85705. *Office:* College of Education, University of Arizona, Tucson, Ariz. 85721.

CAREER: Elementary teacher in Oxon Hill, Md., 1939-43, in Tucson, Ariz., 1952-60; elementary school principal in Tucson, Ariz., 1960-67; consultant to schools in forty-six states, 1968-70; University of Arizona, Tucson, associate professor of elementary education and director of open education block program, 1970—. Program specialist for

National Education Association, 1967-68; member of executive committee of Southern Arizona Environmental Council, 1974-75; member of board of directors of Tucson Young Women's Christian Association (YWCA), 1971-76, vice-president, 1974-76. *Military service:* U.S. Naval Reserve, 1943-46; became lieutenant junior grade.

MEMBER: American Association of Elementary-Kindergarten-Nursery Educators, National Council of Administrative Women in Education (member of national board, 1969-71), American Association of School Administrators, National Association of Elementary School Principals, Association for Supervision and Curriculum Development, National Education Association (life member), American Association of University Professors, Arizona Council of Administrative Women in Education (president, 1972-75), Arizona School Administrators, Arizona Association for Supervision and Curriculum Development, Arizona Education Association, Kappa Delta Pi, Pi Lambda Theta (faculty adviser, 1975-78), Phi Delta Kappa (vice-president, 1975-76).

WRITINGS: (With Carroll Lane) *Wild Folk in the Desert*, John Day, 1958; (contributor) Lou Blachly, editor, *Mammals, Snakes, and Lizards of the Southwest*, [Tucson, Ariz.], 1964; (contributor) Malcolm Provus, editor, *Innovations for Time to Teach*, National Education Association, 1966; (contributor) James Bozarth, editor, *Evaluation of Elementary Schools*, Arizona Association of Elementary School Administrators, 1966; (contributor) *Elementary Education*, Prentice-Hall, 1966; (contributor) Richard I. Miller, editor, *Perspectives on Educational Change*, Appleton, 1967; (contributor) *The Non-Graded Elementary School*, Department of Elementary School Principals, National Education Association, 1968; (with Darrell Roubinek) *Open Sesame: Text on Open Education*, Goodyear Publishing, 1974. Contributor to education journals.

WORK IN PROGRESS: Webbing: A New Curriculum Approach.

*   *   *

CARTER, James E(dward) 1935-

PERSONAL: Born January 19, 1935, in New Edinburg, Ark.; son of E. F. and Sue (a clerk; maiden name, Reaves) Carter; married Carole Ann Hunter (a teacher), September 4, 1955; children: Craig, Edward Keith, Chyrisse Ann. *Education:* Louisiana College, B.A., 1957; Southwestern Baptist Theological Seminary, Fort Worth, Tex., M.Div., 1960, Ph.D., 1964. *Politics:* Democrat. *Home:* 220 Williams, Natchitoches, La. 71457. *Office:* First Baptist Church, 508 Second, Natchitoches, La. 71457.

CAREER: Ordained minister of the Baptist Church, 1955; pastor in Lena, La., 1955-57, Fort Worth, Tex., 1958-61, Gainesville, Tex., 1961-64, and Natchitoches, La., 1964—. Louisiana Baptist Convention, member of executive board, 1968—, vice-president, 1971, president, 1973; member of board of directors, Southwestern Baptist Theological Seminary, 1973—; member of Natchitoches Parish Committee on Drug Abuse Control, 1973-74. *Member:* American Society of Church History, Southern Baptist Historical Society, Rotary Club. *Awards, honors:* Freedoms Foundation award, 1971, for "An Appreciation and Dedication for Independence Day."

WRITINGS: A Source Book for Stewardship Sermons, Baker Book, 1972; *People Parables*, Baker Book, 1973; *The Mission of the Church*, Broadman, 1974. Contributor to *Bible Teacher's Commentary, Encyclopedia of Southern*

Baptists, and *Zondervan's Pastor's Annual*; contributor to *Context, Proclaim, Home Life*, and *Royal Service*. Member of board of directors, *Baptist Message*, 1969-72.

AVOCATIONAL INTERESTS: Hunting, fishing, jogging, paddle ball, travel.

*   *   *

CARTER, John (Waynflete) 1905-1975

May 10, 1905—March 18, 1975; British bibliographer, antiquarian, journalist, editor, and author of works on book collecting and publishing. Obituaries: *New York Times*, March 28, 1975; *AB Bookman's Weekly*, April 7, 1975; *Publishers Weekly*, May 12, 1975; *Current Biography*, May, 1975. (*CA*-7/8)

*   *   *

CARTER, Lief Hastings 1940-

PERSONAL: Born October 9, 1940, in New York, N.Y.; son of Robert Spencer and Cynthia (Root) Carter; married Nancy Saunders Batson, December 22, 1962; children: Stephen, Robert, Laura. *Education:* Harvard University, A.B., 1962, J.D., 1965; University of California, Berkeley, Ph.D., 1972. *Politics:* "Discerning." *Religion:* "Also discerning." *Home:* 475 Forest Rd., Athens, Ga. 30601. *Office:* Department of Political Science, University of Georgia, Athens, Ga. 30602.

CAREER: University of Tennessee, Chattanooga, assistant professor of political science, law, and government, 1971-73; University of Georgia, Athens, assistant professor of political science, law, and justice administration, 1973—. *Member:* American Political Science Association, Bar of the District of Columbia. *Awards, honors:* Edward Corwin Award from American Political Science Association, 1973, for *The Limits of Order.*

WRITINGS: The Limits of Order, Heath, 1974.

WORK IN PROGRESS: Extended research on perception of fairness or unfairness in decision-specific interpersonal authoritative settings.

SIDELIGHTS: Carter writes: "I originally researched *The Limits of Order* to fill a gap in the literature on the operation and management of prosecuting attorneys' offices. The research experience convinced me of a broader conclusion: that many forms of political and social behavior can be understood as a method of coping with technological and environmental uncertainty." *Avocational interests:* Playing the piano, growing vegetables, playing squash.

*   *   *

CARTER, Luther J(ordan) 1927-

PERSONAL: Born October 21, 1927, in Charlotte, N.C.; son of Luther Jordan (a businessman) and Isabel (Pinnix) Carter; married Marsha Knott, April 27, 1957; children: Amy, Marsha. *Education:* Duke University, B.A., 1951; attended Graduate Institute of International Studies, Geneva, Switzerland, 1951-52. *Home:* 4522 Lowell St. N.W., Washington, D.C. 20016. *Office: Science Magazine*, 1515 Massachusetts Ave. N.W., Washington, D.C. 20005.

CAREER: Le Maroc Presse, Casablanca, Morocco, reporter for English-language edition, 1952; employed by PUSOM (engineering firm) at U.S. Air Force base near Casablanca, 1952-53; reporter, *Concord Tribune*, Concord, N.C., 1954, and *Sanford Herald*, Sanford, N.C., 1955; *Virginian-Pilot*, Norfolk, Va., race relations and city hall reporter, 1956-50, Washington correspondent, 1961-65; *Science* Magazine, Washington, D.C., reporter, 1965-70; research associate, Resources for the Future, 1970-72; *Science* Magazine, reporter, 1973—. *Military service:* U.S. Marine Corps, 1946-48; became sergeant. *Awards, honors:* Congressional fellow, 1960-61.

WRITINGS: The Florida Experience: Land and Water Policy in a Growth State, Johns Hopkins Press, 1975.

*   *   *

CARTER, Samuel III 1904-

PERSONAL: Born October 6, 1904, in New York, N.Y.; son of Samuel Thomson, Jr. (a lawyer) and Annie (Burnham) Carter; married Justine Smith, September 5, 1929 (died, 1940); married Alison Nott (a writer), March 2, 1940; children: (first marriage) Peter Burnham, Dorothy de Longpre; (second marriage) Margo Alison. *Education:* Princeton University, B.A., 1927; Oxford University, B.A., 1929; Sorbonne, University of Paris, diploma, 1931. *Politics:* "No party affiliation." *Religion:* Presbyterian. *Residence:* Ridgefield, Conn. *Agent:* Paul R. Reynolds, Inc., 12 East 41st St., New York, N.Y. 10017.

CAREER: J. Walter Thompson Co. (advertising firm), New York, N.Y., radio commercial writer, 1931-40, radio scriptwriter in Hollywood, Calif., 1940-48; National Broadcasting Company, New York, N.Y., editor of television scripts, 1950-55; radio and television scriptwriter and author, 1955—. *Member:* Authors Guild, Princeton Club (New York).

WRITINGS: How to Sail, Leisure League of America, 1936, revised edition, Sentinel Books, 1967; *Kingdom of the Tides*, Hawthorn, 1966; *Cyrus Field: Man of Two Worlds*, Putnam, 1968; *Lightning Beneath the Sea: The Story of the Atlantic Cable*, Putnam, 1969; *The Boat Builders of Bristol*, Doubleday, 1970; *The Incredible Great White Fleet*, Crowell-Collier, 1970; *The Gulf Stream Story*, Doubleday, 1970; *The Happy Dolphins*, Putnam, 1971; *Blaze of Glory: The Fight for New Orleans, 1814-1815*, St. Martin's, 1971; *Vikings Bold: Their Voyages and Adventures*, Crowell, 1972; *The Siege of Atlanta, 1864*, St. Martin's, 1973; *Cowboy Capital of the World: Dodge City*, Doubleday, 1973; *The Riddle of Dr. Mudd*, Putnam, 1974; *The Cherokees*, Doubleday, 1975.

Author of screenplay, "I Love You Truly," for 20th Century-Fox. Also author of television scripts for "Philco Television Playhouse," "Chevrolet on Broadway," "NBC Masterpiece Theatre," "Believe It or Not," and "Celanese Theatre." Author of radio scripts for "Lux Radio Theatre," "The Tommy Dorsey Show," "Duffy's Tavern," and "The Gracie Fields Show."

Contributor of short stories to *Colliers, Woman's Home Companion*, and others.

*   *   *

CARTER, Worrall Reed 1885(?)-1975

1885(?)—July 21, 1975; American naval officer, and author of books on naval history. Obituaries: *New York Times*, July 23, 1975.

*   *   *

CARY, Diana Serra
   See CARY, Peggy-Jean Montgomery

CARY, Peggy-Jean Montgomery 1918-
   (Diana Serra Cary, Diana Serra)

PERSONAL: Born October 29, 1918, in San Diego, Calif.; daughter of Jack Travers (a rancher and rider) and Marian (Baxter) Montgomery; married Gordon D. Ayers, December 12, 1938 (divorced, 1948); married Robert Edward Cary (an artist and illustrator), May 15, 1954; children: (second marriage) Mark Francis. *Education:* Educated privately and at Lawlor's Professional School, Hollywood, Calif.; "my education after graduating from high school is entirely self-taught through use of libraries and extensive research, reading, and field work." *Politics:* Liberal. *Religion:* Catholic (convert, 1946). *Residence:* Encinatas, Calif. *Agent:* Ann Elmo, 52 Vanderbilt Ave., New York, N.Y. 10017. *Office:* University Bookstore, University of California at San Diego, La Jolla, Calif. 92093.

CAREER: Public relations writer for canonization cause of Padre Junipero Serra, in California, 1948-54; owner/operator of nationwide greeting card line, 1954-57; free-lance writer, in Mexico, 1957-67; Bell Book Stores, Houston, Tex., assistant to the president, 1969-71; University of California at San Diego, University Bookstore, La Jolla, Calif., book buyer for general book department, 1971—. *Member:* Western Writers of America, National Organization for Women. *Awards, honors:* Rosemary Award as outstanding silent screen star, 1975.

WRITINGS: (Under pseudonym Diana Serra Cary) *The Hollywood Posse: The Story of a Gallant Band of Horsemen*, Houghton, 1975. Contributor, under pseudonyms Diana Serra Cary and Diana Serra, of nearly 300 articles to periodicals including *Marianist Magazine, Catholic Digest, Extension, Reader's Digest, Catholic Family*, and others.

WORK IN PROGRESS: Four books on Mexican social history over four centuries; a biography of a little-known nineteenth century Indian warrior; several juvenile novels; and a major work dealing with biographical and sociological aspects of early Hollywood.

SIDELIGHTS: Mrs. Cary spent her childhood as the star "Baby Peggy," and her years in Hollywood, she said, provided her with a tremendous amount of eyewitness but unwritten history as it was happening. *Avocational interests:* Art history, ancient architecture, reading, traveling, and collecting Mexican colonial art objects.

*   *   *

CASE, Marshal T(aylor) 1941-

PERSONAL: Born February 21, 1941, in Buffalo, N.Y.; son of Melville (an engineer) and Helen (Taylor) Case; married Nancy Whiting, June 15, 1964; children: Laura Jean, Jennifer Lynn. *Education:* Cornell University, B.S., 1964. *Politics:* Republican. *Religion:* Episcopalian. *Home:* 2325 Burr St., Fairfield, Conn. 06430.

CAREER: Cape Cod Museum of Natural History, Brewster, Mass., director, 1964-69; Cape Cod Community College, Hyannis, Mass., associate professor, 1967-69; Connecticut Audubon Society, Fairfield, executive director, 1969—; University of Bridgeport, Bridgeport, Conn., assistant professor of biology, 1972—. Research associate, Tufts University, 1968—. *Member:* Association of Interpretive Naturalists, American Nature Study Society (member of board of directors, 1972—), American Ornithologists' Union, American Society of Mammologists, American Society of Ichthyologists and Herpetologists, Connecticut Association for Environmental Education (president,

1971—), Eastern Bird Banding Association, Connecticut Botanical Society. *Awards, honors:* Award of Merit of Federated Garden Clubs of Connecticut, 1973, for "exceptional work with youth and conservation" and for *Look What I Found.*

WRITINGS: Look What I Found (juvenile), Chatham Press, 1971. Editor, *Connecticut Audubon Bulletin*, 1970—, and *Nutmeg Naturalist* (annual magazine), 1974—; associate editor, *Journal of Nature Study* (quarterly publication of American Nature Study Society), 1974—.

WORK IN PROGRESS: Feeder Birds of Connecticut, completion expected in 1976; a research paper on the birds of Exuma Cays, Bahamas.

SIDELIGHTS: Case wrote: "Subjects that will result in a benefit to conservation in general, nature appreciation and habitat preservation specifically, motivate me to write. Time is the factor that prevents me from doing more writing about what I think is necessary and of interest."

* * *

CASEY, Daniel J(oseph) 1937-
(Donal O'Cathasaigh)

PERSONAL: Born February 11, 1937, in Brooklyn, N.Y.; son of John L. (a salesman) and Frances E. (McNerney) Casey; married Linda M. Brown, April 9, 1958; children: Daniel B., Thomas J., Michael P. *Education:* St. John's University, Jamaica, N.Y., B.A., 1958, M.S., 1960, M.A., 1963; University of Helsinki, Ph.D., 1968. *Religion:* Roman Catholic. *Home address:* R.D. 1, Wilber Lake Rd., Oneonta, N.Y. 13820. *Office:* Department of English, State University of New York College at Oneonta, Oneonta, N.Y. 13820.

CAREER: Universita degli Studi di Cagliari, Cagliari, Italy, Fulbright lecturer in English, 1963-64; University of Delaware, Newark, instructor in English, 1964-66; State University of New York College at Oneonta, associate professor, 1968-72, professor of English, 1972—. *Member:* International Association for the Study of Anglo-Irish Literature, Modern Language Association of America, American Conference on Irish Studies. *Awards, honors:* Fulbright grants, 1963, 1967, 1968; American Philosophical Society grant, 1974; order of merit from Ancient Order of Hibernians, 1974.

WRITINGS: Benedict Kiely, Bucknell University Press, 1974. Editor of *Delaware English Journal,* 1965, *Carleton Newsletter,* 1970-73, and *English Record,* 1970-74.

WORK IN PROGRESS: Editing *The Irish Peasant: 1800-1916,* with Robert Rhodes, for Gill and Macmillan; *Irish-American Fiction,* a study of the major authors; poetry and fiction for Irish periodicals, to be published under pseudonym Donal O'Cathasaigh.

* * *

CASEY, William Van Etten 1914-

PERSONAL: Born January 7, 1914, in Boston, Mass.; son of Thomas Francis and Mary Agnes (Van Etten) Casey. *Education:* Boston College, A.B., 1938, M.A., 1940; Weston College, Ph.L., 1939, S.T.L., 1945. *Office:* Department of Religious Studies, College of the Holy Cross, Worcester, Mass. 01610.

CAREER: Entered Order of the Society of Jesus (Jesuit; S.J.), 1932; ordained Roman Catholic priest, 1944; College of the Holy Cross, Worcester, Mass., instructor in English,

1940-41; Boston College, Chestnut Hill, Mass., instructor, 1946-48, associate professor of theology, 1948-60, chairman of department, 1948-57, dean of College of Arts and Sciences, 1956-60, trustee and academic vice-president, 1958-60; College of the Holy Cross, professor of theology, 1960—. Biblical archaeologist in Jerusalem, 1962-63; director of American School of Oriental Research, Jerusalem, 1967-68. *Member:* Society of Biblical Literature, Catholic Biblical Association, Catholic Theological Society, Religious Education Association.

WRITINGS: (Editor with Philip Nobile and author of introduction) *The Berrigans,* Praeger, 1971. Editor, *Holy Cross Quarterly,* 1969—; Catholic editorial advisor, Oxford University Press.

* * *

CASO, Adolph 1934-

PERSONAL: Born January 7, 1934, in Passo Eclano, Italy; U.S. citizen from birth; son of Ralph and Prisca (De Luca) Caso; married Amelia Maruffa (a pianist), June 6, 1959; children: Richard A., Robert R., Liana C. *Education:* Northeastern University, B.A., 1957; Harvard University, M.A., 1964. *Home:* 654 Wellesley St., Weston, Mass. 02193. *Office:* Waltham Public Schools, 205 Bacon St., Waltham, Mass. 02154.

CAREER: Waltham Public Schools, Waltham, Mass., teacher of Italian, French, and Spanish, 1964-67, director of bilingual department, 1967—. Chairman of Waltham Overseas Study, 1965-67, Culture Commission for Massachusetts, 1968—, and of Italian section of "Boston 200" Bicentennial, 1975—; president of Dante University Cultural Center, 1975. *Military service:* U.S. Army, Signal Corps, 1957-63; became captain. U.S. Army Reserve, 1964—; current rank, lieutenant colonel. *Member:* Dante Society of America, American Association of Teachers of Italian, Reserve Officers Association of the United States. *Awards, honors:* Fulbright award, 1965.

WRITINGS: The Straw Obelisk (novel), Branden Press, 1973; *America's Italian Founding Fathers* (nonfiction), Branden Press, 1975. Contributor to professional journals.

WORK IN PROGRESS: A book of poems, *Water and Life;* research on linguistics, especially language reduction and computer programming, completion expected in 1977.

SIDELIGHTS: Caso told *CA:* "I am interested in the field of applied linguistics hoping to invent the Dictawriter, a machine that will automatically transcribe sounds to printed symbols. I am the inventor of an underwater fishing gun with patent being awarded shortly."

* * *

CASSO, Evans J(oseph) 1914-

PERSONAL: Surname is pronounced Koss-o; born June 1, 1914, in Donaldsonville, La.; son of Joseph Christian and Laura Aloysia (Babin) Casso; married Madeleine Noto, January 17, 1938; children: Markey Cathereine (Mrs. Bert Hugh Swails), Mary Madeleine; Douglas H. de Priest and Dwight A. de Priest, adopted sons. *Education:* Studied at Louisiana State University and La Salle Extension University. *Politics:* Democrat. *Religion:* Roman Catholic. *Home:* 7835 South Claiborne Ave., New Orleans, La. 70125. *Office:* Avondale Shipyards, Inc., P.O. Box 50280, New Orleans, La. 70150.

CAREER: Star Rice Mills Inc., New Orleans, La., manager and buyer, 1945-54; C. T. Smith Co., New Orleans, superintendent and buyer, 1955-59; Dickey Foods, New Orleans, production superintendent, 1956-59; Elmer's Fine Foods, Inc., New Orleans, production superintendent, 1960-72; Avondale Shipyards, Inc., New Orleans, cost control engineer, 1973—. Efficiency expert with own consulting firm, 1945-65. Lecturer on civil war and Napoleonic history; member of Orleans Parish Civil War Centennial Commission, 1961-65. *Member:* Confederate Historical Society (England), Central Bonaparte Committee (France; honorary member), New Orleans Civil War Round Table (member of executive board, 1958—; president, 1961-62).

WRITINGS: Lorenzo: A History of the Casso Family in Louisiana, Pelican, 1972; *Salvatore: A Brief History of the Noto Family*, privately printed, 1974. Former regular contributor to *Delta Shipbuilder* and to *Stanocolan* (Standard Oil Co. of La.); presently feature writer for *Donaldsonville Chief* and *Italian-American Digest.*

WORK IN PROGRESS: Louisiana Legacy: A History of the Louisiana National Guard; Francis T. Nicholls: A Biography; A History of Italian Immigration in Louisiana.

* * *

CASTLE, Coralie 1924-

PERSONAL: Given name is accented on first syllable; born July 9, 1924, in Evanston, Ill.; daughter of Marshall and Gretchen (Bilharz) Davies; married Robert J. Strasenburgh, March 31, 1946 (divorced, 1957); married Alfred E. Castle (a businessman), March 22, 1958; children: (first marriage) John, Peter, Coralie. *Education:* Attended Smith College, 1942-44, and Northwestern University, 1944-45. *Politics:* "Either/or." *Religion:* Protestant. *Home and office:* 283 Summit Ave., San Rafael, Calif. 94901.

CAREER: Writer. European representative for Schiller College and director of admissions for summer high school sessions, 1971—. Volunteer worker for Marin Community Workshop for Retarded and Handicapped Adults. *Member:* Symphony Foundation, World Affairs Council, KQED.

WRITINGS—All published by 101 Productions: *Soup*, 1971; (with Margaret Gin) *Peasant Cooking of Many Lands*, 1972, revised edition published as *Country Cookery of Many Lands*, 1975; (with Barbara Lawrence) *Hors d'- Oeuvre, Etc.*, 1973; (with John Bryan) *The Edible Ornamental Garden*, 1974; (with Astrid Newton) *Cooking for Two*, in press.

SIDELIGHTS: Coralie Castle writes that she began writing in order to make money for the Marin Community Workshop for Retarded and Handicapped Adults.

* * *

CATALANO, Donald B(ernard) 1920-

PERSONAL: Born October 2, 1920, in New York, N.Y.; son of Frank (a tailor) and Mary (Higgins) Catalano; married Mary Elizabeth Curtis, August 15, 1947; children: Mary Danielle. *Education:* Attended Fenn College. *Home:* 11801 Lake Ave., Apt. #304, Lakewood, Ohio 44107. *Agent:* Scott Meredith Literary Agency, Inc., 580 Fifth Ave., New York, N.Y. 10036. *Office:* 5417 Fleet Ave., Cleveland, Ohio 44105.

CAREER: Writer. Has worked as bulldozer operator on a city dump, boxer (Golden Gloves), Judo instructor, house painter, cotton picker, linoleum layer, radio announcer, newspaperman, and dump truck driver; police officer in Cleveland, Ohio, 1949, plainclothes officer in vice squad, 1951; longshoreman in Cleveland, Ohio, 1960. Democratic

candidate for Ohio State Senate, 1954. *Military service:* U.S. Marine Corps, 1940-45; served in Solomon Islands, Tarawa, Saipan, and Tinian; received Silver Star. *Member:* American Society of Composers, Authors, and Publishers.

WRITINGS: Hit the Beach! (humorous stories of military service), High Twelve, 1948; *The Seduction of the Cantaloupe from Venus* (short stories), Crown, 1952; *If Hearts Could Talk and Other Things* (poems), Hilton House, 1973.

Songs: "The United States Marine," 1964; "That Makes a Man a Man," 1969; "Danielle," 1969; "I Don't Miss You Very Much," 1969; "Si Couri Poi Palari (If Hearts Could Talk)," 1969; "Life's Golden Years," 1969; "It's Christmas Time Again," 1971; "Now and Then," 1971; "A Teen-Age Request," 1971; "To Be a Kid Again," 1971; "Sugar, I'm Sweet on You," 1971; "I Don't Intend," 1972; "I Live the Life of Riley," 1972; "I'm a Cop!," 1972, and 342 others.

Author of "The Inside," a column in *Cleveland News*, 1954. Contributor of poems and articles to national magazines, including *Reader's Digest, Atlantic Monthly*, and *Saturday Evening Post*. Editor of *Guide*, 1953.

WORK IN PROGRESS: The Other War, a novel.

SIDELIGHTS: Catalano writes: "A voracious reader, I wrote my first story at seven—sold it eleven years later. Can't remember when I didn't want to write, although for a time, wanted to be world welterweight champion. A beloved English teacher ... told me that with a little effort I'd be another Charles Dickens!"

* * *

CATLEDGE, Turner 1901-

PERSONAL: Born March 17, 1901, in Ackerman, Miss.; son of Lee Johnson and Willie Anna (Turner) Catledge; married second wife, Abby Ray Izard, 1958; children: (first marriage) Mildren Lee (Mrs. Robert Sampson), Ellen Douglas. *Education:* Mississippi State University, B.Sc., 1922. *Home:* 2316 Prytania St., New Orleans, La. 70130. *Office:* 229 W. 43rd St., New York, N.Y. 10036.

CAREER: Neshoba Democrat, Neshoba, Miss., staff member, 1921; *Tunica Times*, Tunica, Miss., editor, 1922-23; *Tupelo Journal*, Tupelo, Miss., managing editor, 1923; reporter, *Memphis Commercial Appeal*, Memphis, Tenn., 1923-27, *Baltimore Sun*, Baltimore, Md., 1927-29; *New York Times*, New York, N.Y., member of city staff, 1929, Washington bureau correspondent, 1930-36, chief Washington news correspondent, 1936-41; *Chicago Sun*, Chicago, Ill., chief correspondent, 1941-42, editor-in-chief, 1942-43; *New York Times*, national correspondent, 1943-44, managing editor, 1951-64, executive editor, 1964-68, vice president, 1968-70, director, 1968-73. Member of Pulitzer Prizes Advisory Committee, 1955-67; chairman of Greater New Orleans Educational TV Foundation; trustee of New Orleans Art Museum.

MEMBER: American Press Institute (member of advisory board, 1946-70), American Society of Newspaper Editors (director and president, 1961), Sigma Delta Chi, National Press Club, Gridiron Club (Washington), Century Association (New York), International House (New Orleans). *Awards, honors:* Litt.D., Washington and Lee University; D.H.L., Southwestern University (Memphis); LL.D., University of Kentucky, Tulane University.

WRITINGS: (With Joseph W. Alsop, Jr.) *The 168 Days*, Doubleday, 1938, reprinted, DaCapo Press, 1973; *My Life and The Times* (autobiography), Harper, 1971. Contributor of articles to magazines.

SIDELIGHTS: Covering a Mississippi flood in the late 1920s, Catledge met then Secretary of State Herbert Hoover, who recommended him to Adolph Ochs of the New York Times. Several years later, Ochs acted on that recommendation and hired him away from the *Baltimore Sun*.

Catledge's career with the *Times* coincided with events of great social change and significance. As Washington correspondent he reported on the events of Franklin D. Roosevelt's New Deal and during his years as an administrator he sought to keep the newspaper abreast with the political and social movements of the post-World War II era.*

*   *   *

CAVAIANI, Mabel   1919-

PERSONAL: Born September 12, 1919, in Manley, Iowa; daughter of Bert G. and Ida (Hall) Sniffin; married Charles C. Cavaiani, April 14, 1950. *Education:* Iowa State University, B.Sci., 1940; St. Xavier's College, Chicago, Ill., graduate study. *Religion:* United Methodist. *Home address:* P.O. Box 66, Wadena, Iowa 52169. *Agent:* Dominick Abel Literary Services, 612 North Michigan Ave., Chicago, Ill. 60611.

CAREER: Registered dietitian; in restaurant management in Chicago, Ill., 1940-61; U.S. Army Research Center, Chicago, Ill., dietitian, 1961-63; U.S. Food Service Center, Menu Planning Division, Chicago, Ill., dietitian, 1963-67, Army representative on Armed Forces Recipe Service Committee, 1967-71. Member of board of trustees of Oak Lawn Public Library, 1968-72. Consultant to nursing homes and programs for the elderly. Reporter for Webster City, Iowa, newspaper, 1943. *Member:* American Dietetic Association, American Home Economic Association, American Association of University Women, Iowa State Home Economics Alumni Association, Chicago Restaurant Women's Club, United Methodist Women.

WRITINGS: *The Low Cholesterol Cookbook*, Regnery, 1972; (with Audrey Ellis) *Farmhouse Kitchen*, Regnery, 1973; (with Muriel Urbashich) *Simplified Quantity Recipes: Nursing-Convalescent Homes and Hospitals*, National Restaurant Association, 1974. Contributor to government publications.

WORK IN PROGRESS: *The Senior Citizen's Cookbook* (tentative title); *Simplified Quantity Recipes: American Regional and Ethnic*.

SIDELIGHTS: Mabel Cavaiani writes: "My husband and I both retired in 1971 when our government installations moved to different locations. We bought a ninety-four acre farm in Northeast Iowa with some huge walnut trees, several springs, one of which is in the yard, sixty-four acres of timber, and about thirty acres of tillable land. My husband has a fabulous garden in what used to be the barnyard and except for the garden, one dog which came with the farm, and five cats, we don't pretend to farm . . . We attend a church with stained glass windows, old fashioned pews, and the friendliest group of people I ever knew. Our friends feel sorry for us out here so far from the city but we love it and intend to stay here as long as we are physically able to do so."

*   *   *

CEMACH, Harry P(aul)   1917-

PERSONAL: Born November 1, 1917, in Vienna, Austria; son of Isaac Alexander (a physician) and Franziska (Epstein) Cemach; married Ruth Stein (a circulation manager), February 9, 1944; children: Anne (Mrs. Ian J. Starkey), Barbara. *Education:* Educated in Vienna; later undertook evening courses and independent study. *Home:* 27 Clarence Ter., Regent's Park, London NW1 4RD, England. *Office address:* P.O. Box 23, Wembley HA9 8DJ, England.

CAREER: Chartered accountant, 1942; Anglo-Indonesian Plantations, Subang, Indonesia, finance officer, 1948-55; Urwick Orr & Partners Ltd., London, England, management consultant, 1956-72; Anbar Publications Ltd., Wembley, England, part-time managing editor, 1961-72, full-time managing editor, 1972—. *Military service:* British Army, 1940-46; became staff captain. *Member:* Institute of Chartered Accountants in England and Wales, Institute of Linguists, Institute of Practitioners in Work Study, Organization and Methods, Institute of Management Consultants.

WRITINGS: (Author of adaptation for English-speaking students) S van der Molen, *Bahasa Indonesia: A Textbook of Elementary Indonesian Malay*, W. van Hoeve (The Hague), 1949, 3rd edition, revised and enlarged, 1959; *The Elements of Punched Card Accounting*, Pitman, 1951; *Work Study in the Office*, Current Affairs, 1958, 4th edition, Maclaren, 1969; *The Reduction of Correspondence Costs* (booklet), Anbar, 1964; *Guilty Men in the Office* (booklet), Anbar, 1965; *A Farewell to Typists*, International Publications Service, 1974.

Editor of yearbook, *The Compleat Anbar*, 1972—. Editor of professional abstracting journals, *Accounting + Data Processing Abstracts, Marketing + Distribution Abstracts, Personnel + Training Abstracts, Top Management Abstracts, Work Study + O and M Abstracts*.

WORK IN PROGRESS: A fifth edition of *Work Study in the Office*, completion expected about 1976.

SIDELIGHTS: Cemach told *CA*: "I took my final accountancy exams in uniform and found in my first responsible job that it was systems that interested me rather than figures. So my next move was into management consulting, specializing in administrative procedures, with the objective of making office work more efficient and, at the same time, 'better' from the worker's viewpoint. Writing, editing and publishing were consultant's hobbies which took over in the end." Cemach is trilingual in English, German, and Dutch, and "too shy to mention the other languages in which he can only just manage."

*   *   *

CHALK, John Allen   1937-

PERSONAL: Born January 16, 1937, in Lexington, Tenn.; son of Bonnie S. (an engineer) and Mary Nell (Brumley) Chalk; married Martha Sue Traughber (a teacher), August 6, 1957; children: Mary Elizabeth, John Allen, Jr. *Education:* Freed-Hardeman College, A.A., 1956; attended Miami University, Oxford, Ohio, 1956-57, University of Dayton, 1957-58; Tennessee Technological University, B.S., 1962, M.A., 1967; graduate study in religion, Harding College, 1962-63, Abilene Christian College, 1963; University of Texas, J.D., 1973. *Religion:* Church of Christ. *Home:* 15 Dutton Circle, Abilene, Tex, 79601. *Office:* 104 Citizens Bank Bldg., Abilene, Tex. 79601.

CAREER: Ordained to Church of Christ ministry, 1956; minister in Prince George, British Columbia, Canada, 1956, Dayton, Ohio, 1956-60, and Cookeville, Tenn., 1960-66;

Herald of Truth Radio and Television, Abilene, Tex., radio-television writer and speaker, 1966-69; Highland Church of Christ, Abilene, minister, 1969-71; Sweet Publishing Co., Austin, Tex., executive editor, 1971-73, executive editor of *Christian Woman* and *Christian Chronicle*, 1971-72; admitted to Texas Bar, 1973; Rhodes, Doscher, Chalk & Heatherly (law firm), Abilene, attorney-at-law, 1973—. Instructor in campus evangelism, Abilene Christian College, 1969-70; instructor in American history, Tennessee Technological University, 1963-65. Speaker on weekly program, WONE-Radio, Dayton, 1960-62, on daily program, WHUB-Radio, Cookeville, 1960-66; host for talk show, "Campus Call-In," KRBC-Radio and KACC-Radio, Abilene, 1969-70. Special lecturer on religious subjects at more than twenty colleges, workshops, and seminars, 1961—; campaign and youth rally speaker in United States, Canada, and Africa, 1964-71; leader of more than one hundred evangelistic meetings in fifteen states and three foreign countries. Member, Texas Governor's Committee on Human Relations, 1969-73, Abilene Bicentennial Committee, 1974—, Abilene Chamber of Commerce, Abilene Business and Estate Planning Council; member of board of trustees, Hendrick Memorial Hospital Foundation, Abilene; member of advisory board, Midwestern Children's Home, Cincinnati.

MEMBER: American, Texas, and Abilene Bar Associations; Association of Trial Lawyers of America, Texas Trial Lawyers' Association, Texas Criminal Defense Lawyers' Association, Phi Delta Phi, Phi Alpha Theta, Rotary, Optimist Club (Cookeville; charter president, 1962-63).

WRITINGS—All published by Sweet Publishing, except as indicated: *The Praying Christ and Other Sermons*, Christian Publishing, 1964; (with others) *Jesus Christ: The Answer*, 1967; (with others) *Voices of Action*, Christian Publishing, 1967; *Great Sermons*, 1967; *Their God Is Real*, 1968; *Jesus' Church*, Biblical Research Press, 1970; *Three American Revolutions*, Carlton, 1970; (with others) *Missions for the Seventies*, Oklahoma Christian College, 1970; (with others) *The Minister and His Work*, 1970; *The Christian Family*, 1971; *Great Biblical Doctrines*, 1973; (with Ron Durham, Joe Schubert, Michael Weed, and Libby Weed) *The Devil, You Say?*, 1974. Author of numerous tracts; also author of more than 120 radio scripts and 20 television scripts, 1966-69. Staff writer, *Gospel Advocate*, 1961-72, *Action*, 1966—, and *Twentieth Century Christian*, 1968—. Contributor of more than 125 articles to religion journals.

*   *   *

CHAMBERLAIN, John (Rensselaer) 1903-

PERSONAL: Born October 28, 1903, in New Haven, Conn.; son of Robert Rensselaer and Emily (Davis) Chamberlain; married Margaret Sterling, April 22, 1926 (deceased); married Ernestine Stodelle, June 29, 1956; children: (first marriage) Elizabeth, Margaret; (second marriage) John. *Education:* Attended Loomis Institute, Windsor, Conn.; Yale University, Ph.B., 1925. *Home:* 840 North Brooksvale Rd., Cheshire, Conn. 06410. *Office:* King Features Syndicate, 235 East 45th St., New York, N.Y. 10017.

CAREER: Writer with Thomas F. Logan advertising agency, 1925; *New York Times*, New York, N.Y., reporter from Washington bureau, 1926-28, assistant editor of *New York Times Book Review*, 1928-33, daily book columnist, 1933-36, 1942-44; *Saturday Review of Literature*, New

York, associate editor, 1933; *Scribner's Magazine*, New York, book editor, 1936-38; *Fortune*, New York, editor, 1936-41; *Harper's Magazine*, New York, book editor and reviewer, 1939-47; *Life*, New York, editor, 1945-50; *The Freeman*, New York, editor, 1950-52; *Barron's*, New York, associate editor, 1953-55; *Wall Street Journal*, New York, staff writer, beginning in 1955; King Features Syndicate, New York, N.Y., now daily columnist. Columbia University, lecturer, 1934-35, summer lecturer, 1937, associate professor of journalism, 1941-44; lecturer at New School for Social Research, 1935; dean of journalism program, Troy State University, 1972—.

WRITINGS: *Farewell to Reform, Being a History of the Rise, Life and Decay of the Progressive Mind in America*, Liveright, 1932, 2nd edition, John Day, 1933, reprinted, Peter Smith, 1958; *John Dos Passos: A Biographical and Critical Essay*, Harcourt, 1939; *The American Stakes*, Carrick & Evans, 1940; (editor with Benfield Pressey and Reginald E. Watters) *Living, Reading and Thinking: 56 Essays in Exposition*, Scribner, 1948; (with Charles A. Willoughby) *MacArthur, 1941-51*, McGraw, 1954; (editor and author of introduction) *The National Review Reader*, Bookmailer, 1957; *The Roots of Capitalism*, Van Nostrand, 1959, revised edition, 1965; *The Enterprising Americans: A Business History of the United States*, Harper, 1963, new edition, 1974.

Contributor: C. H. Grattan, editor, *Critique of Humanism*, Harcourt, 1930; A. M. Bingham and Selden Rodman, editors, *Challenge to the New Deal*, McGraw, 1934; Malcolm Cowley, editor, *After the Genteel Tradition*, Norton, 1937; Cowley and Bernard Smith, editors, *Books that Changed Our Minds*, Doubleday, 1939. Contributor to *America Now*, and to other publications.*

*   *   *

CHAMBLISS, William C. 1908(?)-1975

1908(?)—February 3, 1975; American naval officer, and author of books on sea and sailing. Obituaries: *New York Times*, February 11, 1975.

*   *   *

CHAN, Loren Briggs 1943-

PERSONAL: Born September 10, 1943, in Palo Alto, Calif.; son of S. Wing (a professor) and Anna Mae (Chin) Chan; married Frances A. Chow (a dietitian), April 19, 1975. *Education:* Stanford University, A.B., 1965, A.M., 1966; University of California, Los Angeles, M.A., 1967, C.Phil., 1969, Ph.D., 1971. *Office:* Department of History, San Jose State University, San Jose, Calif. 95192.

CAREER: San Fernando Valley State College (now California State University), Northridge, lecturer in history, 1970-71; San Jose State University, San Jose, Calif., lecturer, 1971-72, assistant professor of history, 1972—. *Member:* American Historical Association, Organization of American Historians, Chinese Historical Society of America (member of executive committee, 1972-75), Mormon History Association, Western History Association, Nevada State Historical Society. *Awards, honors:* D.D., Universal Life Church of Arizona, 1969.

WRITINGS: *Sagebrush Statesman: Tasker L. Oddie of Nevada*, University of Nevada Press, 1973. Contributor of articles and reviews to journals.

WORK IN PROGRESS: Research on twentieth century Nevada history, and on Chinese-Vietnamese comparative linguistics.

CHANAN, Gabriel   1942-

PERSONAL: Born August 27, 1942, in Twickenham, England. *Education:* Magdalen College, Oxford, B.A., 1973, M.A., 1967. *Office:* National Foundation for Educational Research in England and Wales, The Mere, Upton Park, Slough, Berkshire SL1 2DQ, England.

CAREER: Lecturer in English, literature, language, and drama in British colleges, 1964-69; National Foundation for Educational Research in England and Wales, Slough, Berkshire, England, editor, 1969—.

WRITINGS: Longstephen (novel), Anthony Blond, 1964; (with Linda Gilchrist) *What School Is For*, Praeger, 1974. Contributor to British literature and education journals.

WORK IN PROGRESS: Stories; plays; research on relations between literature and politics, and between literature, politics, and education.

SIDELIGHTS: Chanan writes that his motivations are "(a) to reform educational system and practice (b) as a mode of prayer (c) to give emotional reality a domain among public affairs (d) so as not to forget (e) so as to be able to forget."

* * *

CHANCELLOR, Paul   1900-1975

1900—February 16, 1975; American educator, and author of works on local history. Obituaries: *New York Times*, February 21, 1975.

* * *

CHANDLER, Frank
   See HARKNETT, Terry

* * *

CHANG, Dae H(ong)   1928-

PERSONAL: Born January 9, 1928, in Nara, Japan; naturalized U.S. citizen; son of Chun B. (a scholar) and Kim I. (Kim) Chang; married Seung Hi Cho, August 20, 1964; children: Morris B., Richard J. *Education:* Michigan State University, B.A., 1957, M.A., 1958, Ph.D., 1962. *Office:* Department of the Administration of Justice, Wichita State University, Wichita, Kan. 67208.

CAREER: National Police Headquarters, Seoul, Korea, lieutenant of police, 1951-56, secretary for director of national police, 1954-55, liaison officer for United Nations Command Force in Korea, 1952-56; Michigan Secretary of State, Lansing, statistical analyst for Driver and Vehicle Service, 1958-61; Olivet College, Olivet, Mich., assistant professor, 1962-63, associate professor of sociology and chairman of department, 1963-66; Northern Illinois University, DeKalb, assistant professor, 1966-69, associate professor of sociology, 1969; University of Wisconsin, Whitewater, professor of sociology and anthropology, 1969-75, chairman of department, 1969-74; Wichita State University, Wichita, Kan., professor of the administration of justice and chairman of department, 1975—. President of American Corp. for Penal Research and Reform, 1971—. Host of "Around the World in Thirty Minutes," on WMMR-Radio, 1965-66, and "International Interlude," WNIU-Radio, 1968; appeared on "Milwaukee Reports," CBS-Television, 1971. Professor and researcher at University of Wisconsin—Copenhagen, Denmark, 1972-73. Member of Wisconsin Task Force for Higher Education, 1972-73; member of steering committee for Wisconsin Criminal Justice Institute, 1973—.

MEMBER: American Sociological Association, American Society of Criminology, Midwest Sociological Society, Wisconsin Sociological Association, Michigan Academy of Science, Arts, and Letters (vice-chairman of Asian section, 1968, chairman, 1969). *Awards, honors:* Smith-Mundt fellowship, 1954-55, to study American law enforcement agencies; National Science Foundation grant, 1970-75, to study crime control on and near Lake Michigan; received United Nations Service Medal, Korean War Service Medal, and Wharang War Merit Medal.

WRITINGS: (Contributor) Eugene Kim and Ch'angboh Chee, editors, *Aspects of Social Change in Korea*, Western Michigan University, 1969; *Sociology: A Syllabus and Workbook*, Kendall/Hunt, 1970; (with Warren Armstrong) *The Prison: Voices from the Inside*, Schenkman, 1972; *Sociology: An Applied Approach*, Paladin House, 1973; (contributor) Man Singh Das, editor, *The Asian Family: Past, Present, and the Future*, Lucknow Publishing House, in press; *Criminology: A Cross-Cultural Approach*, Vikas Publishing House, in press; *Crime and Delinquency Prevention: A Universalistic Approach*, Schenkman, in press. Contributor to sociology, criminology, and Asian studies journals. Associate editor of *International Review of Sociology* and *International Journal of Sociology of the Family*, both 1969—.

WORK IN PROGRESS: Research on inmates' and security guards' perceptions of themselves and of each other; studying aquatic crime; research on police evaluative perceptions of themselves, the general public, and selected occupational groups, on occupational values and attitudes toward modernization of Korea among Korean youths, and on Korean high school students' occupational prestige ranking with special reference to structuralist and culturalist positions.

* * *

CHANG, Parris (Hsu-Cheng)   1936-

PERSONAL: Born December 30, 1936, in Chiayi, Taiwan; son of Chao (a farmer) and Liu (Ch'en) Chang; married Shirley Lin (a librarian), August 3, 1963; children: Yvette, Elaine. *Education:* National Taiwan University, B.A., 1959; University of Washington, Seattle, M.A., 1963; Pennsylvania State University, further graduate study, 1963-64; Columbia University, Ph.D., 1969. *Home:* 1221 Edward St., State College, Pa. 16801. *Office:* Department of Political Science, Pennsylvania State University, University Park, Pa. 16802.

CAREER: University of Michigan, Ann Arbor, research political scientist at Center for Chinese Studies, 1969-70; Pennsylvania State University, University Park, assistant professor, 1970-72, associate professor of political science, 1972—. Consultant to RAND Corp., 1974—. *Member:* American Political Science Association, Association for Asian Studies, International Studies Association. *Awards, honors:* Fulbright scholar, 1961-62; Social Science Research Council grant for work in Tokyo, Hong Kong, and Taipei, 1972-73.

WRITINGS: Radicals and Radical Ideology in China's Cultural Revolution, School of International Affairs, Columbia University, 1973; *Power and Policy in China*, Pennsylvania State University Press, 1975.

Contributor: Robert A. Scalapino, editor, *Elites in Communist China*, University of Washington Press, 1972; William Whitson, editor, *The Role of the Military in China*, Praeger, 1972; Paul Sih, editor, *Taiwan in Modern Times*,

St. John's University Press (New York), 1973; Jan Pry-byla, editor, *The Pentagon of Power: U.S.A., U.S.S.R., Western Europe, Japan, China*, Center for Continuing Liberal Education and Slavic and Soviet Languages and Area Center, Pennsylvania State University, 1973; Frank Horton and others, editors, *Comparative Defense Policy*, Johns Hopkins Press, 1974. Contributor of about thirty articles to Asian affairs and other journals.

WORK IN PROGRESS: Studies on military intervention in Chinese politics since the 1960's and on China's military-industrial complex and its impact on Chinese foreign policy.

SIDELIGHTS: Chang says that his writings are intended "to demonstrate and explicate the plot and acting of the political drama in China." In 1972 he had a meeting with Premier Chou En-lai.

* * *

CHANKIN, Donald O(liver) 1934-

PERSONAL: Born February 18, 1934, in New York, N.Y.; son of Dannis D. and Evelyn (Rosenberg) Chan-kin.*Education*: Queens College of the City University of New York, B.S., 1955; New York University, J.D., 1958, M.A., 1962, Ph.D., 1973.*Home*: 30 Charlton St., New York, N.Y. 10014.*Office*: Department of English, Queens-borough Community College, Bayside, N.Y. 11364.

CAREER: Admitted to Bar of State of New York, 1959; private practice of law in New York, N.Y., 1958-62; Queens College of the City University of New York, Flushing, N.Y., lecturer in English, 1962-64, 1966-68; Skidmore College, Saratoga Springs, N.Y., lecturer in English, 1964-66; Queensborough Community College, Bayside, N.Y., assistant professor of English, 1968—. New York County Democratic committeeman, 1973—. *Member:* Modern Language Association of America.

WRITINGS: Anonymity and Death: The Fiction of B. Traven, Pennsylvania State University Press, 1975.

WORK IN PROGRESS: Research on applying the insights of Freud and the post-Freudians to literature, and on Claude Levi-Strauss and primitive art.

AVOCATIONAL INTERESTS: Travel, especially to Mayan and other pre-Columbian sites in Mexico, Central and South America; photography.

* * *

CHANTILES, Vilma Liacouras 1925-

PERSONAL: Surname is pronounced Shan-*till*-eez; born August 11, 1925, in Philadelphia, Pa.; daughter of James Peter and Stella (Lagakos) Liacouras; married Nicholas G. Chantiles (a vice-president of International Book Publishers), March 2, 1952; children: Dean, James, Maria Nicole. *Education:* Drexel University, B.S., 1947; New York University, M.A., 1970; private study of music (voice), art, weaving, and foreign languages. *Religion:* Greek Orthodox. *Residence:* Scarsdale, N.Y.

CAREER: Rosenau Brothers, Philadelphia, Pa., designer of "Cinderella Frocks," 1948-50; free-lance reporter for trade newspapers and for Fairchild Publications, all 1950-53; *Women's Wear Daily*, New York, N.Y., reporter from Germany on leather products, 1954; substitute teacher of home economics and art in public schools in Radnor, Pa., 1965-66, and Westchester County, N.Y., 1967-68; home economics teacher in junior high school in Scarsdale, N.Y.,

1969; Herbert H. Lehman College of the City University of New York, Bronx, N.Y., lecturer, 1970, instructor in home economics, 1971; writer and researcher, 1972-73; New York University, New York, N.Y., part-time lecturer in home economics, 1973-74; writer and researcher, 1974—. Sings with Westchester Philharmonic Choral Society. *Member:* American Home Economics Association, Scarsdale Women's Club, Overhill Association, Omicron Nu.

WRITINGS: The Food of Greece, Atheneum, 1975; *Folk Art and Embroideries of Greece*, C. N. Potter, in press. Contributor to journals and to women's and children's magazines.

WORK IN PROGRESS: Cultural Foods; *Chinese Embroideries*; an interdisciplinary study of food and cooking.

SIDELIGHTS: Vilma Chantiles writes: "My American education and Greek cultural heritage have stimulated interdisciplinary research in food and arts ... especially ... correlation between food habits and individual cultures; cultural use of the arts applied to daily life; language and communications; applied science in food studies; aesthetic link between fine and applied arts." *Avocational interests:* Painting, watercolor, batik on silk, pen and ink drawing, charcoal drawing, textiles, interiors, stained glass, wildflowers, plants, shells, birds, embroidery, crochet, weaving, clothing design and sewing, home sewing and crafts, bicycling, swimming, walking, folk dancing, international travel.

BIOGRAPHICAL/CRITICAL SOURCES: Washington Post, April 10, 1975.

* * *

CHAPELLE, Howard I(rving) 1901-1975

February 1, 1901—June 30, 1975; American historian, marine writer, naval architect, museum curator, editor, and author. Obituaries: *New York Times*, July 2, 1975; *Washington Post*, July 3, 1975; *AB Bookman's Weekly*, July 28, 1975. (*CA-25/28*)

* * *

CHAPMAN, Dorothy Hilton 1934-

PERSONAL: Born September 4, 1934, in Victoria, Tex.; daughter of Rosker Henry and Irene (Burnett) Hilton; married Warren Adlee Chapman, June 18, 1960 (divorced November 10, 1971); children: Dessalyn Renee, Karen Adele. *Education:* Tuskegee Institute, B.S., 1958; Carnegie Institute of Technology, M.L.S., 1960. *Politics:* Democrat. *Religion:* Baptist. *Home:* 6913 Burgess St., Houston, Tex. 77021.

CAREER: Richard B. Harrison Public Library, Raleigh, N.C., library cataloger, 1960-61; St. Augustine's College, Raleigh, N.C., cataloger in library, 1961-69; Texas Southern University, Houston, curator of special collections in library, 1969—. *Member:* American Library Association, Texas Library Association, Texas Association of College Teachers.

WRITINGS: Index to Black Poetry, G. K. Hall, 1974.

* * *

CHAPMAN, Victoria L(ynn) 1944-

PERSONAL: Born April 28, 1944, in Vancouver, Wash.; daughter of William Paul (a traveling salesman) and Betty Bonny (Bool) Chapman. *Education:* Hamline University, B.A., 1966. *Home:* 320 Central Park W., New York, N.Y.

10025. *Office:* Scholastic Magazines, Inc., 50 West 44th St., New York, N.Y. 10036.
CAREER: Scholastic Magazines, Inc., New York, N.Y., associate editor of *Junior Scholastic*, 1970-72, managing editor of "Headline Focus Wall Maps," 1972-75, editor of *Sprint*, 1975—.
WRITINGS—All for children: *Let's Go to a Supermarket*, Putnam, 1972; *Let's Go to a Garage*, Putnam, 1974. Contributor to education journals.
AVOCATIONAL INTERESTS: Wilderness canoeing, ceramics, textiles, hand crafts.

* * *

CHAPPELL, Gordon (Stelling) 1939-

PERSONAL: Born February 10, 1939, in Sacramento, Calif.; son of Bertram George (a high school principal) and Helen (a teacher; maiden name, Bullard) Chappell. *Education:* University of California, Berkeley, B.A., 1961; University of Arizona, M.A., 1965. *Politics:* Independent. *Religion:* Presbyterian. *Residence:* San Francisco, Calif. *Office:* National Park Service, 450 Golden Gate Ave., San Francisco, Calif. 94102.
CAREER: Colorado Railroad Museum, Golden, Colo., assistant to executive director, 1966-71; State Historical Society of Colorado, Denver, Colo., project historian, 1972-73; U.S. Department of the Army, Carlisle, Pa., curator of museums, 1973-74; National Park Service, San Francisco, Calif., regional historian, 1974—. Park ranger in Fort Laramie, Wyo. and Washington, D.C., summers, 1960-71; consultant to Western Interpretive Services, 1972-73. *Military service:* U.S. Army, 1962-64. *Member:* Company of Military Historians (fellow; curator, 1974), Council on Abandoned Military Posts (director, 1974—), Western History Association, California Historical Society.
WRITINGS: Brass Spikes and Horsehair Plumes: A Study of U.S. Army Dress Helmets, 1872-1903, Arizona Pioneers' Historical Society, 1966; *Logging Along the Denver and Rio Grande: Narrow Gauge Logging Railroads of Southwestern Colorado and Northern New Mexico*, Colorado Railroad Museum, 1971; *The Search for the Well-Dressed Soldier*, Arizona Historical Society, 1972; *Rails to Carry Copper: A History of the Magma Arizona Railroad*, Pruett, 1973. Editor of print series "Military Uniforms in America," Company of Military Historians, 1974. Contributor to military and Western history magazines. Associate editor of *Colorado Rail Annual*, 1969-74, editor, 1975—.
WORK IN PROGRESS: Narrow Gauge to the San Juan, about Denver and Rio Grande narrow gauge rail lines in the San Juan region of Colorado and northern New Mexico, completion expected in 1977; *Indians in the U.S. Army, 1850-1900*; research on military and railroad history.
SIDELIGHTS: Chappell writes: "Perhaps as a result of ancestors being involved in Gold Rushes to California in 1849 and 1852 and Alaska in 1898, having then settled in the West, I have developed a great interest in the history of the American West, with especial focus on the Indian wars (from both military and Indian viewpoints), mining (a family interest), and railroads. I have traveled widely in the United States ... and in Canada, Mexico, and Central America, and am interested in the same areas of history in these geographical areas."

* * *

CHAR, Tin-Yuke 1905-

PERSONAL: Born July 4, 1905, in Honolulu, Hawaii; son of See Yick (a utility man) and Fo (Chong) Char; married Wat Jane Chun, January 30, 1934; children: David, Judith (Mrs. John Flagg), Peter, Janice (Mrs. Arthur A. Chung). *Education:* Yenching University, B.A., 1928; University of Hawaii, M.A., 1932; Columbia University, graduate study, 1934-35. *Politics:* Democrat. *Religion:* Christian. *Home:* 3898 Diamond Head Rd., Honolulu, Hawaii 96816. *Office:* Hawaii Chinese History Center, 111 North King St., Honolulu, Hawaii.
CAREER: University of Hawaii, Honolulu, instructor in Chinese, 1930-36; Lingnan University, Canton, China, registrar and director of admissions, 1936-38; Continental Insurance Agency of Hawaii, Honolulu, president, 1952-69; Chinese University of Hong Kong, student counselor, 1969-70; Hawaii Chinese History Center, Honolulu, historical researcher, 1970—. *Member:* Hawaiian Historical Society.
WRITINGS: (With C. H. Kwock) *The Hakka Chinese: Their Origin and Folk Songs*, Jade Mountain Press, 1969; *Chinese Proverbs*, with bilingual text, Jade Mountain Press, 1970; (editor) *The Sandlewood Mountains: Readings and Stories of the Early Chinese in Hawaii*, University Press of Hawaii, 1975. Contributor to journals.
WORK IN PROGRESS: Research in Hawaiian Chinese history.
SIDELIGHTS: Char has traveled to the South Pacific, Southeast Asia, Europe, Canada, and South America, studying the overseas Chinese.

* * *

CHARNY, Israel W(olf) 1931-

PERSONAL: Born July 18, 1931, in New York, N.Y.; son of Bernard (a rabbi) and Anna (Aichenbaum) Charny; married Phyllis B. Ellen (a music teacher), April 14, 1957; children: Adam Shalom, Rena S., Anna L. *Education:* Temple University, A.B. (with distinction), 1952; University of Rochester, Ph.D., 1957. *Home and office:* Hamaapilim 26, Herzliya Pituach, Israel.
CAREER: Board of Education, Rochester, N.Y., clinical psychologist, 1956-58; Oakbourne Hospital, West Chester, Pa., chief psychologist, 1958-62; private practice as clinical psychologist in Paoli, Pa., 1962-73, in Herzliya Pituach, Israel, 1973—; Tel-Aviv University, Tel-Aviv, Israel, associate professor of psychology, 1974—. Professor of psychology and counseling consultant at Reconstructionist Rabbinical College, Philadelphia, Pa., 1971-73; senior researcher at Szold National Institute for Research in Behavioral Sciences, Jerusalem, 1973—; senior consultant to Ribbutz Family Clinic, Ramat Aviv, 1973—. Diplomate in clinical psychology, American Board of Examiners in Professional Psychology. *Member:* American Orthopsychiatric Association (fellow), American Psychological Association, American Academy of Psychotherapists, International Peace Research Association.
WRITINGS: Individual and Family Developmental Review (manual), Western Psychological Services, 1969; *Marital Love and Hate*, Macmillan, 1972; (author of introduction) Luther Lee Bernard, *War and Its Causes*, new edition (Charny was not associated with original edition), Garland Publishing, 1972; *The Courage of Real Family Experiencing*, Simon & Schuster, in press. Contributor to several collections and about thirty articles to professional and popular periodicals.
WORK IN PROGRESS: Editing *Design for Nonviolent*

Change: Demonstrating Transitions from Social Science Theory to Social Action; writing *The Cancer of Human Experiencing: A New Search for the Essence of Man's Genocidal Destructiveness*, for Grossman and Institute for World Order.

* * *

CHAUDHURI, Sukanta 1950-

PERSONAL: Born June 23, 1950, in Calcutta, India; son of Kanti Prosad (a professor) and Sujata (a professor; maiden name, Roy) Chaudhuri. *Education:* Presidency College, B.A., 1970; University College, Oxford, B.A., 1972. *Religion:* Hindu. *Home:* DA 211 Salt Lake, Calcutta-64, India 700064. *Office:* Department of English, Presidency College, College St., Calcutta-12, India 700012.

CAREER: Presidency College, Calcutta, India, professor of English, 1973—. *Member:* Writers Workshop.

WRITINGS: Poems, Writers Workshop, 1967; *The Glass King and Other Poems*, Writers Workshop, 1970. Poetry represented in anthology *Modern Indian Poetry in English*, edited by P. Lal, Writers Workshop, 1969.

WORK IN PROGRESS: Research on European literature of the Renaissance; editing Bacon's *Essays*.

BIOGRAPHICAL/CRITICAL SOURCES: P. Lal, editor, *Modern Indian Poetry in English*, Writers Workshop, 1969.

* * *

CHEAVENS, Martha Louis (Schuck) 1898-1975

1898—March 26, 1975; American novelist, short story writer, and poet. Obituaries: *New York Times*, March 28, 1975; *AB Bookman's Weekly*, April 21, 1975.

* * *

CHERNOW, Carol 1934-

PERSONAL: Born May 16, 1934, in Brooklyn, N.Y.; daughter of Jack and Anne (Grossman) Grossman; married Fred B. Chernow (a school principal), April 10, 1954; children: Barbara Diane, Lynne Tracey. *Education:* Brooklyn College of the City University of New York, B.A. (cum laude), 1967. *Religion:* Jewish. *Home and office:* 60 Vassar St., Staten Island, N.Y. 10314.

CAREER: Teacher in Anne Arundel County, Md., 1955-56, and for Welfare Education Plan in New York, N.Y., 1972-74. Legislative aid to member of New York State Assembly; Regular Democratic Committee, Staten Island, N.Y., committeewoman and zone leader, 1973—.

WRITINGS—With husband, Fred B. Chernow: *Reading Exercises in Black History*, Continental Press, Volume I, 1968, Volume II, 1972; *Reading Exercises in Spanish American History*, Continental Press, 1973; *Teaching the Culturally Disadvantaged Child*, Prentice-Hall, 1973.

WORK IN PROGRESS: The School Administrator's Guide to Managing People, with husband, Fred B. Chernow, for Parker Publishing.

* * *

CHERNOW, Fred B. 1932-

PERSONAL: Born November 2, 1932; son of Barnet (a salesman) and Mabel (Rosenthal) Chernow; married Carol Grossman (a legislative aide), April 10, 1954; children: Barbara Diane, Lynne Tracey. *Education:* Brooklyn College (now Brooklyn College of the City University of New

York), B.A., 1953, M.A., 1954; New York University, Ed.D., 1961. *Politics:* Democrat. *Religion:* Jewish. *Home:* 60 Vassar St., Staten Island, N.Y. 10314. *Office:* John Tyler School, West Brighton, Staten Island, N.Y. 10310.

CAREER: Guidance counselor at junior high schools in Brooklyn, N.Y., 1961-66; assistant principal and principal at grammar schools in Brooklyn, 1966-68; supervisor of guidance for high schools in New York, N.Y., 1968-73; John Tyler School, Staten Island, N.Y., principal, 1973—. Trustee of Sailors' Snug Harbor Cultural Center; chairman of North Richmond Community Mental Health Center; assistant examiner on New York City Board of Examiners; member of Staten Island Community Planning Board; delegate to New York City Council of Supervisors and Administrators. *Military service:* U.S. Army, 1954-56.

WRITINGS: (With wife, Carol Chernow) *Reading Exercises in Black History*, Continental Press, Volume I, 1968, Volume II, 1972; (with C. Chernow) *Reading Exercises in Spanish-American History*, Continental Press, 1972; (with C. Chernow) *Teaching the Culturally Disadvantaged Child*, Prentice-Hall, 1973; *Administering the High School Alternative Education Program*, Parker Publishing, 1975.

WORK IN PROGRESS: The School Administrator's Guide to Managing People, with wife, Carol Chernow, for Parker Publishing.

SIDELIGHTS: Chernow writes that he ". . .prepared high interest level, easy reading level materials for ghetto pupils depicting the lives of famous black and Hispanic leaders. The pupils and their parents found these extremely readable and asked for more."

* * *

CHERRY, Caroline L(ockett) 1942-

PERSONAL: Born June 16, 1942, in Washington, D.C.; daughter of Walter M., Jr. (a clergyman) and Helen (Booth) Lockett; married Charles L. Cherry (an associate professor), May 4, 1968; children: Helen Gaylord. *Education:* Randolph-Macon Woman's College, A.B., 1964; University of North Carolina, M.A., 1965, Ph.D., 1968. *Home:* 229 East Beechtree Lane, Wayne, Pa. 19087. *Office:* Department of English, Eastern College, St. Davids, Pa. 19087.

CAREER: Eastern College, St. Davids, Pa., associate professor of English, 1968—. *Member:* Modern Language Association of America, Phi Beta Kappa. *Awards, honors:* Woodrow Wilson fellowship, 1968.

WRITINGS: (With husband, Charles L. Cherry) *Contemporary Composition*, Prentice-Hall, 1970; *The Most Unvaluedst Purchase: Women in the Plays of Thomas Middleton*, Universitat Salzburg Institut fur Englische Sprache und Literatur, 1973.

WORK IN PROGRESS: Research on Elizabethan and Jacobean drama.

* * *

CHERRY, Charles L(ester) 1942-

PERSONAL: Born July 30, 1942, in Baltimore, Md.; son of Lester W. and Mary (Murphy) Cherry; married Caroline Lockett (a teacher), May 4, 1968; children: Helen Gaylord. *Education:* Loyola College, B.A., 1964; University of North Carolina, M.A., 1966, Ph.D., 1968. *Home:* 229 East Beechtree Lane, Wayne, Pa. 19087. *Office:* English Department, Villanova University, Villanova, Pa. 19085.

CAREER: Villanova University, Villanova, Pa., assistant professor, 1968-74, associate professor of English, 1975—, director of Honors Program, 1972—. Communications consultant to government and business. *Member:* Modern Language Association of America, American Association of University Professors, American Business Communication Association, National Council of Teachers of English, Alpha Sigma Nu, Lambda Iota Tau.

WRITINGS: (With wife, Caroline L. Cherry) *Contemporary Composition*, Prentice-Hall, 1970; (with George Murphy) *Write Up the Ladder: A Common Sense Guide to Better Business Communication*, Goodyear Publishing, in press. Contributor to journals in his field.

WORK IN PROGRESS: A book about the history of insanity, *Madness and Imagination* (tentative title).

AVOCATIONAL INTERESTS: Swimming, tennis, squash.

* * *

CHERVIN, Ronda 1937-

PERSONAL: Born April 24, 1937, in Los Angeles, Calif.; daughter of Ralph and Helen (Winner) DeSola; married Martin Chervin (a writer), July 9, 1962; children: Carla, Diana, Charles. *Education:* University of Rochester, B.A., 1957; Fordham University, M.A., 1959, Ph.D., 1967. *Religion:* Roman Catholic. *Home:* 7612 Cowan Ave., Los Angeles, Calif. 90045. *Office:* Department of Philosophy, Loyola Marymount University, Los Angeles, Calif. 90045.

CAREER: Lecturer at Fordham University Extension, University of California, Irvine Extension, Chapman College, and St. Joseph's College, 1967-69; Loyola Marymount University, Los Angeles, Calif., assistant professor, 1969-73, associate professor of philosophy, 1973—.

WRITINGS: Church of Love, Liguorian Books, 1973; *The Art of Choosing*, Liguorian Books, 1975.

WORK IN PROGRESS: Day by Day with the Holy Spirit; two novels based on religious subjects.

SIDELIGHTS: Ronda Chervin writes that she is a convert from atheism to the Roman Catholic Church.

* * *

CHEVIGNY, Bell Gale 1936-

PERSONAL: Born March 17, 1936, in Mount Vernon, N.Y.; daughter of Marland (an attorney) and Virginia (Caldwell) Gale; married Paul Chevigny (an attorney), July 25, 1964; children: Katherine Gale, Gale Blue. *Education:* Wellesley College, B.A., 1957; Yale University, M.A., 1959, Ph.D., 1963. *Home:* 112 West 81st St., New York, N.Y. 10024. *Office:* Department of English, State University of New York-Purchase, Purchase, N.Y. 10577.

CAREER: City University of New York, Queens College, Flushing, N.Y., instructor in English literature, 1961-66; Cooperative College Center, Mount Vernon, N.Y., instructor in English literature, 1969-71; Sarah Lawrence College, Bronxville, N.Y., instructor in English literature, 1966-68, 1971-72; State University of New York at Purchase, associate professor of English literature, 1972—. Free-lance reviewer and essayist. *Member:* Phi Beta Kappa. *Awards, honors:* Danforth Foundation fellow, 1960-61; National Endowment for the Humanities stipend, 1973.

WRITINGS: Twentieth Century Interpretations of Beckett's "Endgame", Prentice-Hall, 1969. Contributor to *Village Voice*.

WORK IN PROGRESS: An introduction and anthology of writings by and about Margaret Fuller; exploring Latin American literature.

* * *

CHEW, Peter 1924-

PERSONAL: Born April 5, 1924, in New Rochelle, N.Y.; son of John A. (a chemical merchant) and Octavia (Thomson) Chew; married Virginia Gaillard (a real estate broker), June 21, 1952; children: Elizabeth, Peter, Jr., Benjamin. *Education:* Princeton University, A.B., 1946. *Politics:* Independent. *Religion:* Episcopalian. *Home and office:* 4664 Garfield St. N.W., Washington, D.C. 20007. *Agent:* Arthur Pine Associates, Inc., 1780 Broadway, New York, N.Y. 10019.

CAREER: Newark Evening News, Newark, N.J., reporter, 1947-48; Associated Press, New York, N.Y., reporter, 1949-52; *Look* (magazine), New York, N.Y., staff writer, 1952-54; free-lance writer, 1954-62; *National Observer*, Silver Spring, Md., staff writer, 1962-74; free-lance writer, 1974—. *Wartime service:* American Field Service, attached to British Eighth Army, 1943-44; served in the Middle East and Italy. *Member:* Authors Guild of Authors League of America, Metropolitan Club (Washington, D.C.), Chevy Chase Club, University Cottage Club (Princeton, N.J.). *Awards, honors:* Award from Florida Thoroughbred Breeders, 1965, for best magazine article on horse racing and breeding; award from Thoroughbred Racing Associations, 1969, for best magazine article on horse racing; award from National Steeplechase and Hunt Association, 1970, for best magazine article on steeplechasing.

WRITINGS: The Kentucky Derby: The First One Hundred Years, Houghton, 1974. Contributor to national magazines, including *American Heritage, Travel and Leisure, Smithsonian, Army, Reader's Digest, Coronet*, and *Pageant*.

WORK IN PROGRESS: A book on psychological and physiological problems of middle-aged American men, for Macmillan.

SIDELIGHTS: Chew writes that he has loved horses since childhood, when he exercised race horses and schooled jumpers. But at the same time, he wanted to be a general assignment newspaperman and war correspondent; he covered the Vietnam War in 1966 and 1969, the Dominican Republic revolution, 1965, and the Arab-Israeli War, 1967.

* * *

CHILSON, Richard William 1943-

PERSONAL: Born April 20, 1943, in Grosse Pointe Farms, Mich.; son of Julius Wells (a store manager) and Jean (Bell) Chilson. *Education:* Wayne State University, B.A. (with honors), 1965; University of Illinois, M.A., 1966; St. Paul's College, Washington, D.C., M.A., 1969; Episcopal Theological School, graduate study, 1970-71. *Home and office:* St. Thomas Aquinas Chapel, 46 North Eagleville Rd., Storrs, Conn. 06268.

CAREER: Entered Paulist Community, 1967, ordained Roman Catholic priest of Paulist Order (C.S.P.), 1972; University of Connecticut, Storrs, chaplain, 1972—.

WRITINGS: The Faith of Catholics, Paulist/Newman, 1972, revised edition, 1975; *A Believing People*, Paulist/Newman, 1974. Contributor to *Thought*.

WORK IN PROGRESS: A book on the expansion of consciousness and Christianity.

SIDELIGHTS: Chilson wrote: "My long range interests at present point to work in transpersonal psychology, specializing in Eastern spiritualities especially Yoga and Zen, in order to find a way to make these disciplines at home in our life." *Avocational interests:* Classical music, opera, films, literature.

* * *

CHINOY, Ely 1921-1975

September 5, 1921—April 21, 1975; American educator, editor, and author of books on sociology. Obituaries: *New York Times*, April 22, 1975. (*CA*-3)

* * *

CHRISTENSEN, Jo Ippolito
  See CHRISTENSEN, Yolanda Maria Ippolito

* * *

CHRISTENSEN, Yolanda Maria Ippolito 1943-
  (Jo Ippolito Christensen)

PERSONAL: Born October 12, 1943, in Raleigh, N.C.; daughter of Luciano (an artist and a lieutenant colonel in the U.S. Army) and Ruth (a teacher; maiden name, Mason) Ippolito; married John Jacob Christensen (an electrical engineer and a major in the U.S. Air Force), November 27, 1965; children: Elizabeth Kirsten (deceased), Peter John. *Education:* Attended University of North Carolina, Greensboro, 1961-63; University of Maryland, B.S., 1965. *Politics:* Conservative. *Home:* 20 Evergreen Trail, Severna Park, Md. 21146; (temporary address) 30-391-G Cherry Dr., APO Seattle, Wash. 98742.

CAREER: U.S. Department of Defense, Fort Meade, Md., computer programmer, 1965-66; University of Maryland, Extension Service, Annapolis, extension agent in home economics, 1966-67; substitute teacher in public schools in Dayton, Ohio, 1967-69; University of Missouri, Extension Service, Independence, instructor in clothing construction, 1970-72; U.S. Air Force, Special Services, Elmendorf Air Force Base, Alaska, instructor in needlepoint, 1973-74; writer, 1974—. Sewing teacher in high school in Dayton, Ohio, 1968-69; instructor at Morningside Knit Shop and Virginia's Cut 'n Sew (both in Missouri), 1970-72; instructor at University of Alaska, 1973-75.

MEMBER: Embroiderer's Guild of America, Needle Art Guild, Officer's Wives Club, Needlepoint Club, Alpha Gamma Delta. *Awards, honors:* Nominated for Air Force wife of the year, 1972.

*WRITINGS—*All under name Jo Ippolito Christensen: (With Sonie Ashner) *Needlepoint Sampler*, Sterling, 1971; *Trapunto*, Sterling, 1972; (with Ashner) *Bargello Stitchery*, Sterling, 1972; (with Ashner) *Needlepoint Cross Stitches*, Sterling, 1973; (with Ashner) *Applique*, Sterling, 1974; *The Needlepoint Book*, Prentice-Hall, 1976.

Wrote and presented radio scripts on home economics, 1966-67. Author of column, "Homemaker's Corner," in *Maryland Gazette*, 1966-67, and *Anchorage Daily Times*, 1972. Contributor to needlework journals.

WORK IN PROGRESS: Research on three-dimensional needlepoint.

SIDELIGHTS: Jo Christensen writes: "In 1970 I was introduced to the so-called fancy stitches of needlepoint and. . .I. . .found what I had spent ten years looking for! From that day to this I have lived, slept, and eaten needlepoint in all its aspects. I've done research and research and research. I've made so many things in needlepoint that my house looks like a shop." *Avocational interests:* Danish modern furniture, popular music, jazz, dancing, bicycle riding, sewing (makes her family's clothing and clothing patterns), crocheting, knitting, playing bridge, cats, singing, collecting art (especially oil paintings), travel (all over Europe).

BIOGRAPHICAL/CRITICAL SOURCES: Annapolis Evening Capital, June, 1966; *Maryland Gazette*, December 2, 1971.

* * *

CHRISTENSON, Larry 1928-

PERSONAL: Born March 10, 1928, in Northfield, Minn.; son of Ade Leonard (a coach) and Mimi (Donhowe) Christenson; married Nordis Evenson, December 18, 1951; children: Timothy, Laurie, Stephen, Arne. *Education:* St. Olaf College, B.A. (magna cum laude), 1952; Luther Theological Seminary, B.D. (honors), 1959; Institute for Ecumenical and Cultural Research, graduate study, 1971-72. *Office:* 1450 West Seventh St., San Pedro, Calif. 90732.

CAREER: Ordained minister of American Lutheran Church, 1960; Pacific Finance Corp., Los Angeles, Calif., technical writer, 1953-55; Augsburg Publishing House, Minneapolis, Minn., advertising writer, 1955-59; Trinity Lutheran Church, San Pedro, Calif., pastor, 1960—. *Military service:* U.S. Army, Airborne Division, 1946-48. *Member:* Phi Beta Kappa.

WRITINGS: The Heartless Troll (libretto), Denison, 1960; *Speaking in Tongues and Its Significance for the Church*, Bethany Fellowship, 1968; *The Christian Family*, Bethany Fellowship, 1968; *The Trinity Bible Series*, Bethany Fellowship, 1971; *A Message to the Charismatic Movement*, Bethany Fellowship, 1972; *A Charismatic Approach to Social Action*, Bethany Fellowship, 1974; *The Renewed Mind*, Bethany Fellowship, 1974; (translator from the German) Basilea Schlink, *Realities*, Zondervan, 1966; (translator from the German) Schlink, *None Would Believe It*, Zondervan, 1967; (translator from the German) Schlink, *For Those Who Love Him*, Zondervan, 1969; *Husbands, Love Your Wives*, Bethany Fellowship, in press. Author of booklets and cassettes.

* * *

CHRISTIAN, James L(ee) 1927-

PERSONAL: Born March 13, 1927, in Phoenix, Ariz.; son of Herman Lee (an architect) and Annie Laurie (Lambeth) Christian; married Wilma Peterson, August 25, 1950 (divorced, 1963); married Barbara Jean Taylor (an educator), August 30, 1967; *children:* Cathy, Dane, Carla, Marcia, Sherrie, Reinar, Shawna, Shannon, Linda, Laurie. *Education:* Arizona State University, A.B., 1947; Boston University, S.T.B., 1953, Ph.D., 1957. *Politics:* Non-partisan. *Home:* 27031 Calle Juanita, Capistrano Beach, Calif. 92624. *Office:* Department of Philosophy, Santa Ana College, Santa Ana, Calif. 92706.

CAREER: The Methodist Church, Elisabethsville (now Shaba), Democratic Republic of the Congo, secretary to the bishop, 1948-50; Hartzell's Training School (secondary), Umtali, Rhodesia, science teacher, 1950-51; St. John's Methodist Church, Medford, Mass., pastor, 1952-

55; Boston University, Boston, Mass., lecturer in biblical literature, 1954-57; Simpson College, Indianola, Iowa, assistant professor of philosophy and religion, 1957-59; Chapman College, Orange, Calif., associate professor of religion, and chairman of religion department, 1959-64; Santa Ana College, Santa Ana, Calif., professor of philosophy, 1964—, chairman of department, 1970—. *Member:* American Academy of Religion (treasurer and secretary, 1961-63), American Philosophical Association, Western Society of Malacologists. *Awards, honors:* Annual Book Award, University of California Friends of the Library, Irvine, 1974, for *Philosophy: An Introduction to the Art of Wondering.*

WRITINGS: Philosophy: An Introduction to the Art of Wondering, Rinehart Press, 1973; (editor) *Extraterrestrial Intelligence: First Encounter,* Prometheus Books, 1975.

WORK IN PROGRESS: The Western Philosphers; The Art of Wondering: Readings in Synoptic Philosophy, for Holt.

SIDELIGHTS: Christian told *CA*: "My professional concern is to humanize philosophy and to re-focus it upon its original goal: the search for wisdom. When I ask today, "Where are the professors of wisdom?" I find I can't say, "Listen to us philosophers." Too many of us have given in to specialization and lost the wisdom that comes from synoptic thinking, and from seeking insights and metaphors which would illuminate life." *Avocational interests:* Astronomy, skin diving, shell collecting, ornithology.

*   *   *

CHRISTOPHERSEN, Paul (Hans)   1911-

PERSONAL: Surname is accented on second syllable; born November 18, 1911, in Copenhagen, Denmark; son of Anders Frederik (an engineer) and Marie (Jensen) Christophersen; married Margaret Travers, August 1, 1950; children: David. *Education:* University of Copenhagen, M.A., 1937, Dr.Phil., 1939; Corpus Christi College, Cambridge, Ph.D., 1943. *Religion:* Anglican. *Home:* 70 Mullaghinch Rd., Aghadowey, Coleraine BT51 4AT, Northern Ireland. *Agent:* A. P. Watt & Son, 26/28 Bedford Row, London WC1R 4HL, England. *Office:* Department of English, New University of Ulster, Coleraine BT52 1SA, Northern Ireland.

CAREER: British Broadcasting Corporation European Service, London, England, announcer and translator, 1942-44; Royal Institute of International Affairs, London, England, research assistant, 1944-46; University of Copenhagen, Copenhagen, Denmark, professor of English language and literature, 1946-48; University College (now University of Ibadan), Ibadan, Nigeria, professor of English, 1948-54; University of Oslo, Oslo, Norway, professor of English philology, 1954-68; New University of Ulster, Coleraine, Northern Ireland, reader, 1969-74, professor of English, 1974—. External staff examiner in Danish at University of London, 1941-45; lecturer at Cambridge University, 1942-45; visiting professor at Emory University, 1965-66. Danish representative to UNESCO constituent conference in London, fall, 1945, and to Preparatory Commission, 1945-46.

MEMBER: Philological Society, Linguistic Association of Great Britain, Royal Anthropolical Institute (fellow), Norwegian Academy of Sciences (member by invitation), Modern Humanities Research Association, United Oxford and Cambridge Club, Arts Theatre Club. *Awards, honors:* King Christian X's Freedom Medal, 1946, for work in the

Danish cause during World War II; Fellow Commoner of Cambridge University, 1968.

WRITINGS: The Articles: A Study of Their Theory and Use in English, Oxford University Press, 1939; (with Otto Jespersen) *A Modern English Grammar,* Volume VI, Munksgaard, 1942; (with Henning Krabbe) *To Start You Talking,* Schultz, 1948; *Bilingualism* (pamphlet), Methuen, 1949; *The Ballad of Sir Aldingar,* Clarendon Press, 1952; *An English Phonetics Course,* Longmans, 1956; *Some Thoughts on the Study of English as a Foreign Language* (pamphlet), Olaf Norlis Forlag (Oslo), 1957; (contributor) Hallgjerd Brattset, editor, *Spraakforskning og Spraakopplaering* (title means "Linguistic Research and Language Teaching"), Oslo University, 1964; (contributor) C. I. Duthie, editor, *English Studies Today,* Edinburgh University Press, 1964; (contributor) W. R. Lee, editor, *ELT Selections,* Oxford University Press, 1967; (with A. O. Sandved) *An Advanced English Grammar,* Macmillan, 1969, 5th edition, 1974; (contributor) B. Benedikz, editor, *On the Novel,* Dent, 1971; *Second-Language Learning: Myth and Reality,* Penguin, 1973. Contributor of more than twenty articles and reviews to journals.

WORK IN PROGRESS: Research on varieties of English, especially pidgin English.

*   *   *

CHRISTY, Betty   1924-

PERSONAL: Born January 28, 1924, in Chicago, Ill.; daughter of Lawrence J. and Helen (Hummel) Lindsay; married William L. Christy, January 2, 1942 (divorced, 1968); children: Larry, Bill, Lynn (Mrs. Edward Hennessy), Janet Lee. *Education:* Attended Stephens College. *Religion:* Protestant. *Home:* 15W, 728 59th St., Hinsdale, Ill. 60521. *Office Address:* Box 492, Hinsdale, Ill. 60521.

CAREER: Craft Shop, Hinsdale, Ill., partner, 1966-69; receptionist for pediatrician in Hinsdale, Ill., 1968—; partner in quilling mail-order business in Hinsdale, Ill., 1971—.

WRITINGS: (With Doris Tracy) *Quilling: Paper Art for Everyone,* Regnery, 1974.

*   *   *

CHUNG, Hyung C(han)   1931-

PERSONAL: Born August 6, 1931, in Seoul, Korea; son of Sung-chai and Soo-Myun (Chung) Chung; married Jongsoon Park (an artist), August 27, 1960; children: Junehee, Kee Young, Jeanhee. *Education:* Keystone Junior College, A.A., 1956; Yale University, B.Arch., 1960, M.C.P., 1962; Columbia University, Ph.D., 1970. *Home:* 397 Fairlea Rd., Orange, Conn. 06477. *Office:* College of Business Administration, University of Bridgeport, Park Ave., Bridgeport, Conn. 06902.

CAREER: Greater Bridgeport Regional Planning Agency, Trumbull, Conn., assistant planner, 1961-62, regional planner, 1962-63, planning director, 1963-67; Columbia University, Institute of Urban Environment, New York, N.Y., staff associate, 1967-70, consultant, 1970-71; University of Bridgeport, Bridgeport, Conn., associate professor of economics and urban-suburban studies, 1970—, director of Urban Management Program, 1971—, director of Long-term Job Market-Monitoring and Information Center, 1972—. Member of board of directors of Greater Bridgeport Mental Health Planning Association, 1965-67; planning consultant for federal, state, and municipal agencies, including the United Nations and U.S. General Accounting Office. *Military service:* Republic of Korea Army, 1950-54; became first lieutenant. *Member:* American Institute of Planners, American Society of Planning Officials. *Awards, honors:* First prize award in oil painting from Scranton Art Museum, 1955; William Kinne post-doctoral travelling fellowship from Columbia University, 1970.

WRITINGS: The Economics of Residential Rehabilitation: The Social Life of Housing in Harlem, Praeger, 1973; *The Connecticut Manpower Market in the 1970's*, Connecticut Manpower Executives Association, 1973; *Projection Methodology for Manpower Planning in Local Labor Market Areas*, Connecticut Manpower Executives Association, 1973.

WORK IN PROGRESS: Capital Cities of China: Principles of City Planning; Economics of Housing, a housing textbook.

AVOCATIONAL INTERESTS: Music, painting.

*   *   *

CIMBOLLEK, Robert (Carl)   1937-

PERSONAL: Born September 14, 1937, in Hampden, Maine; son of William C. and Hilda (Wood) Cimbollek; married Judith Murphy (a teacher), August 31, 1959; children: Kimberly Anne, Robert Murphy. *Education:* Husson College, B.S., 1959; University of Maine, graduate study, 1959-65. *Politics:* Republican. *Religion:* Methodist. *Home:* 188 Howard St., Bangor, Maine 04401. *Office:* Abraham Lincoln School, Forest Ave., Bangor, Maine 04401.

CAREER: Junior high school physical education teacher and athletic coach in Bangor, Maine, 1960-61; high school physical education teacher and coach in Fort Fairfield, Maine, 1961-62, and Orono, Maine, 1962-69; Abraham Lincoln School (high school), Bangor, Maine, physical education and health teacher and boys' varsity basketball coach, 1969—. Has played basketball since 1952; has a college scoring average of 27.5 per game; member of Eastern Maine Board of Approved Basketball Officials, vice-president of board, 1972, president, 1972; member of State Basketball Commission; 1972-76; Young Men's Christian Association (YMCA) athletic director, 1955-70, 1969-75; summer basketball director for Bangor Parks and Recreation Department, 1969-75. *Member:* Maine State Coaches Association (member of executive board, 1969-74).

WRITINGS: Basketball's Percentage Offense, Parker Publishing, 1972. Contributor to basketball magazines.

*   *   *

CLAGHORN, Charles Eugene   1911-

PERSONAL: Born December 12, 1911, in Narberth, Pa.; son of William C. (a real estate broker) and May R. (Clarke) Claghorn; married Eileen Armstrong (a secretary), December 12, 1941; children: Charles Eugene, Thomas Stuart. *Education:* Pierce Junior College, A.A., 1931; attended University of Pennsylvania, 1939-41. *Politics:* Independent-Republican. *Religion:* Congregationalist. *Home:* 38 Crawford Terrace, Riverside, Conn. 06878. *Office:* Interpublic, 1271 Avenue of the Americas, New York, N.Y. 10020.

CAREER: Was an accountant with various firms, 1932-66; Interpublic (advertising firm), New York, N.Y., manager, 1966—. *Military service:* U.S. Army, 1943-46. *Member:* Connecticut Society of the Cincinnati (historian, 1952-62), Pennsylvania Society of the Sons of the Revolution, Colonial Society of Pennsylvania.

WRITINGS: The Mocking Bird: The Life & Diary of Its Author, Septimus Winner, Magee Press, 1937; *Biographical Dictionary of American Music*, Prentice-Hall, 1973; *Battle Hymn: The Story Behind the Battle Hymn of the Republic*, Hymn Society of America, 1974.

WORK IN PROGRESS: Yellow Rose: The Story Behind the Yellow Rose of Texas; Whispering Hope: The Story Behind the Song; Best Loved Hymns: Stories About American Composers; a musical directory.

SIDELIGHTS: Claghorn writes: "My interest in musical research stemmed from the fact that my great-grandfather, Septimus Winner, wrote 'Listen to the Mocking Bird' in 1855, 'Where Has My Little Dog Gone?' in 1864, 'Ten Little Indians' in 1868 and 'Whispering Hope' in 1868, and my great grand uncle, Joe Winner, wrote 'Little Brown Jug' in 1869. Sep. Winner died before I was born, but my father told me many stories about him. I knew Mrs. Joseph Winner who died in 1939. I remember Mrs. Sep. Winner who died in 1918. She fell down a flight of steps and broke her back at age 91."

*   *   *

CLAIRE, William Francis   1935-

PERSONAL: Born October 4, 1935, in Northampton, Mass.; son of William Cahil and Vena Marie (Lasonde) Claire; married Sedgley Mellon Schmidt (a manager of concert tours), November 22, 1973; children: Mark Andrew William. *Education:* Columbia University, B.A., 1958; Georgetown University, graduate study. *Home:* 2101 Connecticut Ave. N.W., Washington, D.C. 20008. *Office:* Washington Office, State University of New York, 1730 Rhode Island Ave. N.W., Washington, D.C. 20008.

CAREER: Legislative assistant and press assistant to U.S. Representative Silvio O. Conte, Washington, D.C., 1960-62; American Paper Institute, Washington, D.C., director of government relations, 1962-69; World Federalists of the United States of America, Washington, D.C., executive director, 1970-71; State University of New York, Washington Office, Washington, D.C., director, 1971—. Member of board of directors of Coalition on National Priorities, 1968-69; trustee of International Development Corp., 1968-69. Judge of District of Columbia Commission on the Arts; member of board of directors of Washington Poetry Center. State coordinator of Humphrey-Muskie presidential campaign, 1968. *Military service:* U.S. Army, 1959-60; served in Korea.

MEMBER: International Club, National Press Club, Friends of the Folger Shakespeare Library, Cosmos Club (Washington, D.C.), Rolling Rock Club (Ligonier, Pa.). *Awards, honors:* Ernie Pyle Award from *Pacific Stars and Stripes*, 1959; editors award from National Endowment for the Arts, 1970; Yaddo fellowship, 1975.

WRITINGS: Strange Coherence of Our Dreams (poems), Magic Circle Press, 1973; *From a Southern France Notebook* (poems), Ragnarok Press, 1974; (editor and author of introduction) *Publishing in the West: Alan Swallow*, Lighting Tree Press, 1975. Contributor of articles and reviews to popular magazines and literary publications, including *American Scholar, New Republic, Nation, New York Quarterly, Smithsonian, West Coast Review, California Review, Columbia Forum*, and *Antioch Review*. Editor and publisher of *Voyages*, 1967-74.

WORK IN PROGRESS: The American Essays of Mark Van Doren; editing *An Anthology of Painting and Poetry;*

editing *An Anthology of Voyages: 1967-1974*; a collection of poems, *Separating from Silence*.

SIDELIGHTS: Claire has recorded his own poems on tape for the Library of Congress, and on videotape for U.S.I.A. film, "American Poetry Now."

* * *

CLANTON, Gordon 1942-

PERSONAL: Born March 25, 1942, in Bayonne, N.J.; son of Robert G. (an owner of a machine shop) and Vivian (Singletary) Clanton; married Jan Dyer (a psychotherapist), April 18, 1963. *Education:* Louisiana State University, B.A., 1964; Austin Seminary, B.D., 1967; Graduate Theological Union, further graduate study; University of California, Berkeley, Ph.D., 1973. *Home:* 2817 Camino del Mar, Del Mar, Calif. 92014. *Office:* Department of Sociology, San Diego State University, San Diego, Calif. 92182.

CAREER: Rutgers University, New Brunswick, N.J., lecturer in religion, 1970-73; Trenton State College, Trenton, N.J., assistant professor of sociology, 1973-74; San Diego State University, San Diego, Calif., lecturer in sociology, 1975—. Has led encounter groups at colleges and growth centers. *Member:* American Sociological Association, American Academy of Religion, Society for the Scientific Study of Religion, Society for Religion in Higher Education, Groves Conference on Marriage and the Family.

WRITINGS: (Editor with Chris Downing) *Face to Face to Face*, Dutton, 1975.

WORK IN PROGRESS: Editing *Sexual Jealousy: An Anthology of Research, Reflection, and Opinion*, with Lynn G. Smith.

* * *

CLARK, Carol (Lois) 1948-

PERSONAL: Born May 23, 1948, in Salt Lake City, Utah; daughter of Norman W. (a management consultant) and Lois (Colt) Clark. *Education:* University of Utah, B.A., 1970, M.Ed., 1972. *Religion:* Church of Jesus Christ of Latter-Day Saints (Mormons). *Home:* 1861 Herbert Ave., Salt Lake City, Utah 84108. *Office:* Jordan High School, 9351 South State, Sandy, Utah 84070.

CAREER: Teacher of English, Jordan High School, Sandy, Utah. *Member:* National Education Association, Utah Education Association.

WRITINGS: *A Singular Life* (nonfiction), Deseret, 1974. Contributor to *Folklore Forum, New Era, Nevermind, Commentary, Pencilings, Woods of Wisdom, Salt Lake Tribune*, and Utah Council of Teachers of English *Journal*.

WORK IN PROGRESS: A novel; research on early Mormon pioneer women who were involved in Relief Society.

* * *

CLARK, Don(ald Rowlee) 1925-

PERSONAL: Born July 3, 1925, in Seattle, Wash.; son of Donald H. (a writer and professor) and Mildred (Taylor) Clark; married Joyce Douglass (in public affairs for KOMO-Television), December 21, 1947; children: Kimberly (Mrs. George Erickson), Jennifer (Mrs. George Lambert), Lorinda (Mrs. Leonard Francoeur). *Education:* University of Washington, Seattle, B.A. *Home:* 1520 Northeast 62nd, Seattle, Wash. 98115. *Office:* Business News Bureau, 747 Logan Bldg., Seattle, Wash. 98101.

CAREER: Employed with *Daily Alaska Empire*, Juneau, 1949-50, *Bellingham Herald*, Bellingham, Wash., 1951-52, Taskett Advertising Agency, Seattle, Wash., 1952-53, *Seattle Times*, 1953-55; *Northgate Journal*, Seattle, manager, 1955-59; self-employed, Don Clark & Associates, Seattle, 1959-60; Clark & Gropp (advertising agency), Seattle, president, 1960-67; Lennen & Newell Advertising Agency, Seattle, vice-president, 1967-72; Smyth Greyhound, director of public relations, 1972-75; Business News Bureau, Seattle, owner, 1975—. Currently public relations director for McCann-Erickson, and director of International Explosive Services. *Military service:* U.S. Navy. *Member:* CEDAM (Conservation, Exploration, Diving, Archaeology, Museums; member of Mexican and American chapters; past president of Mexican chapter), CHAOS (Cannon Hunters Association of Seattle; head hunter), CHAOS in Depth (president), Seattle Seafair, Rotary International, Chamber of Commerce. *Awards, honors:* Order of the Purple Lanyard and Ch.D., both from Cannon Hunting Association of Seattle.

WRITINGS: *Wild Blue Yonder*, Superior, 1972. Contributor of several hundred articles to magazines.

WORK IN PROGRESS: Brother XII, completion expected in 1975; *Adventures of Peter and Polly*, a children's book, to be privately printed; two films.

SIDELIGHTS: Clark writes: "CHAOS is prime activity—serious plus tongue-in-cheek organization with nine hundred fifty members in thirty nations. Have recovered more than three thousand muzzle loading cannon since 1949." He is an archaeological diver, licensed as commercial diver in state of Washington.

* * *

CLARK, Mary Jane 1915-

PERSONAL: Born July 28, 1915, in Belmont, Mass.; daughter of Percy (in wool industry) and Jenny G. (Swift) Dewey; married John Alexander, May 22, 1937; children: Peter H., Gentry II, Penelope (Mrs. Robert Sampson). *Education:* Amy Sackers School of Design, graduate, 1936; attended Cambridge Art School, 1936-37. *Politics:* Republican. *Religion:* Protestant. *Home and office:* 2 Wildcat Lane, Scrabble Arts, Norwell, Mass. 02061.

CAREER: Writer. Teacher of antique decoration, demonstrator, and lecturer. *Member:* Norwell Art Association, Historical Society of Early American Decoration (master craftsman; master teacher).

WRITINGS: Illustrated Glossary of Decorated Antiques, Tuttle, 1972.

WORK IN PROGRESS: Research on early American decoration and decorated antiques of any kind, and on reverse painting on glass, goldleaf work, and freehand bronze techniques from 1700 to 1900.

* * *

CLARK, Mavis Thorpe
(Mavis Latham)

PERSONAL: Born in Melbourne, Victoria, Australia; daughter of John Thorpe (a contractor) and Rose Matilda (Stanborough) Clark; married Harold Latham; children: Beverley Jeanne (Mrs. Ralph Henderson Lewis), Ronda Faye (Mrs. Peter Hall). *Education:* Attended Methodist Ladies' College, Melbourne. *Home:* 2 Crest Ave., Melbourne, Victoria 3103, Australia.

CAREER: Writer since her school days. *Member:* International P.E.N. (Australia Centre; vice-president of Melbourne branch, 1968, 1971, 1973, 1974; president of Melbourne branch, 1969), Australian Society of Authors (member of management committee), Fellowship of Australian Writers. *Awards, honors:* Commendation by Children's Book Council of Australia for *The Brown Land Was Green*, 1956, and *Blue Above the Trees*, 1968, and Book of the Year Award for *The Min-Min*, 1967; Deutscher Jugendbuchpreis (German Children's Book Award) for German editions of *Spark of Opal*, 1971, and *Iron Mountain*, 1973.

WRITINGS—Novels for young teens, except as noted: *Dark Pool Island*, Oxford University Press, 1949; *The Twins from Timber Creek*, Oxford University Press, 1949.

Home Again from Timber Creek, Oxford University Press, 1950; *Jingaroo*, Oxford University Press, 1951; *Missing Gold*, Hutchinson, 1951; *The Brown Land Was Green*, Heinemann, 1956, special school edition, Heinemann, 1957, reissued with new illustrations, Lansdowne Press, 1967; *Gully of Gold*, Heinemann, 1958, reissued with new illustrations, Lansdowne Press, 1969; *Pony from Tarella*, Heinemann, 1959, reissued with new illustrations, Lansdowne Press, 1969.

(Under name Mavis Latham) *John Batman* (short biography), Oxford University Press, 1962; *They Came South*, Heinemann, 1963, reissued with new illustrations, Lansdowne Press, 1971; *Fishing* (textbook), Oxford University Press, 1963; *The Min-Min*, Lansdowne Press, 1966, Macmillan (New York), 1969; *Blue Above the Trees*, Lansdowne Press, 1967, Meredith, 1969; *Spark of Opal*, Lansdowne Press, 1968, Macmillan (New York), 1973; *The Pack-tracker* (textbook), Oxford University Press, 1968; *The Opal Miner* (textbook), Oxford University Press, 1969; *Nowhere to Hide*, Lansdowne Press, 1969.

Iron Mountain, Lansdowne Press, 1970, Macmillan (New York), 1971; *Iron Ore Mining* (textbook), Oxford University Press, 1971; *New Golden Mountain*, Lansdowne Press, 1973; *Wildfire*, Hodder & Stoughton, 1973, Macmillan (New York), 1974.

Adult biographies: *Pastor Doug*, Lansdowne Press, 1965, revised edition, 1972; *Strolling Players*, Lansdowne Press, 1972.

Formerly contributor of short stories and articles to adult magazines and author and adapter of scripts for children's radio programs.

WORK IN PROGRESS: A children's novel set in the Australian opal fields at Coober Pedy.

SIDELIGHTS: "I started to write while still at school and, at fourteen, wrote a full-length children's book which was published in serial form by the *Australasian*, a weekly newspaper of the time.... Many of my novels are set against some particular Australian background.... I have travelled thousands of miles in search of material, crisscrossing this vast country from east to west and north to south. I've travelled to Europe and Asia, too, but the spell of my own wide red land lures me continually and set me on the lonely dusty Outback track. Here again is the tremendous reward of friends in out-of-the-way places and glimpses of lives that are lived so simply yet so richly with the earth of the world's oldest continent. These intangible joys are the real reward of the writer."

Pastor Doug was updated when Pastor Doug Nicholls was created a Knight of the British Empire in 1972 and became Sir Douglas Ralph Nicholls, the first aboriginal to receive such an honor. *Pastor Doug* and two youth books, *Blue Above the Trees* and *The Min-Min* have been transcribed into Braille. In addition to Australian and American editions of *Min-Min*, the book has been published in German and Japanese and in paperback in England under the title, *Armada Lions*.

* * *

CLARK, Sydney A(ylmer) 1890-1975

August 18, 1890—April 20, 1975; American travel writer, real estate broker, and lecturer on travel. Obituaries: *New York Times*, April 21, 1975. (*CA*-7/8)

* * *

CLARKE, William Thomas 1932-

PERSONAL: Born July 20, 1932, in Toronto, Ontario, Canada; son of Louis Ivan (a railway porter) and Jessie (Blanc) Clarke. *Education:* University of Toronto, B.Sc., 1956; Gonzaga University, B.A. (with honors), 1962, M.S., 1962; Saint Mary's University, Halifax, Nova Scotia, M.A., 1967; Catholic Institute, Paris, graduate study, 1968-70. *Home and office:* Regis College, 3425 Bayview Ave., Willowdale, Ontario M2M 3S5, Canada.

CAREER: Entered Order of Society of Jesus (Jesuits; S.J.), 1956, ordained Roman Catholic priest, 1966; St. Mary's University, Halifax, Nova Scotia, lecturer in mathematics, 1962-63; Regis College, Willowdale, Ontario, spiritual director, 1971-72, vice-rector, 1973—.

WRITINGS: Enough Room for Joy, Paulist/Newman, 1974.

WORK IN PROGRESS: Meeting God in Daily Experience.

SIDELIGHTS: Clarke told *CA* that his "first book is the fruit of a three year association with l'Arche, a community founded by Jean Vanier to share life with the mentally handicapped."

* * *

CLARY, Jack 1932-

PERSONAL: Born September 7, 1932, in Atlantic City, N.J.; son of John Thomas (an engineer) and Eleanor (Connors) Clary; married Patricia Looby (a teacher), August 8, 1970. *Education:* Fordham University, B.S., 1954; Columbia University, M.S., 1955. *Politics:* Independent. *Religion:* Roman Catholic. *Home and office:* 5 Fletcher St., Maynard, Mass. 01754.

CAREER: Associated Press, New York, N.Y., newsman and editor, 1957-63; *New York World Telegram and Sun*, New York, N.Y., newsman and editor, 1964-66; *Boston Herald-Traveler*, Boston, Mass., newsman and sports columnist, 1967-72; writer, 1972—. *Member:* Professional Football Writers Association of America, Overseas Press Club.

WRITINGS: Army versus Navy, Ronald, 1965; *Great Teams: Cleveland Browns*, Macmillan, 1973; *Great Teams: Washington Redskins*, Macmillan, 1974; *Main Men of the Seventies: Quarterbacks*, NFL Creative Services, 1975. Contributor to *Pro!*, *Sports World*, *Pro Quarterback*, and *Christian Science Monitor*.

BIOGRAPHICAL/CRITICAL SOURCES: Jimmy Cannon, *Who Struck John?*, Dial, 1955.

CLAYTON, Thompson B(owker) 1904-

PERSONAL: Born June 8, 1904, in Washington, D.C.; son of Richard Bard (an air force officer and government official) and Grace (Thompson) Clayton; married Lois Althea Mills (a nurse and librarian), October 6, 1937; children: Anne (Mrs. Robert B. Straton), Persis (Mrs. Robert Radcliff), Sally (Mrs. Stephen Mixer). *Education:* Attended George Washington University, 1925; University of Maryland, B.A., 1927, graduate study, 1928-29; graduate study at Colby College, 1958-59, Farmington State Teachers College (now University of Maine at Farmington), summer, 1961, and Gallaudet College, 1964; University of Maine at Orono, M.Ed., 1966. *Politics:* "Registered Democrat, vote Independent." *Religion:* Christian. *Home and office address:* Box 93, Deer Isle, Me. 04627.

CAREER: Teacher and/or coach in Washington, D.C., 1932-42, in Bethesda, Md., 1942-44, in Fort Fairfield, Me., 1944-45, Bethesda, 1945-47; Gallaudet College, Washington, D.C., athletic director, 1947-56; teacher and/or coach in Maine, 1957-62; Gallaudet College, dean of men, 1962-71. Served as coach or director of Y.M.C.A. and Washington Boys Club, 1933-39. *Member:* American Wrestling Coaches Association.

WRITINGS: Living and Understanding, International Paper Co., 1963; *A Handbook of Wrestling Terms and Holds*, A. S. Barnes, 1968, revised edition, 1974; *An Introduction to Wrestling*, A. S. Barnes, 1970; *What It Takes*, Fearon, 1972; *Wrestling for Fun*, A. S. Barnes, 1973. Contributor of articles to journals in his field and short stories to magazines.

WORK IN PROGRESS: Supplementary reading material for the slow and reluctant reader.

SIDELIGHTS: Clayton writes: "Although I am now writing for pay, I occasionally contribute to newspapers to say, principally, that the world does not owe any of us a living. In the final analysis, we are responsible for ourselves and our actions."

* * *

CLEMMONS, William (Preston) 1932-

PERSONAL: Born December 7, 1932, in Nashville, Tenn.; son of James Preston (a salesman) and Sallie Celeste (Baker) Clemmons; married Bettie Louise Owens (a teacher), May 30, 1953; children: Jane Louise, William Preston, Jr. *Education:* Vanderbilt University, student, 1950; University of South Carolina, B.A., 1956; Southern Baptist Theological Seminary, B.D., 1959, M.R.E., 1965, Ed.D., 1971; graduate study at Universita degli Stranieri, 1961, and Universita degli Studi di Roma, 1961-62; postdoctoral study at George Peabody College for Teachers, 1972. *Home:* 417 Iola Rd., Louisville, Ky. 40207. *Office:* 3105 Lexington Rd., Louisville, Ky. 40206.

CAREER: Ordained Southern Baptist clergyman, 1956; associate pastor of Baptist church in Columbia, S.C., 1954-56; pastor of Baptist church in Nashville, Tenn., 1956-59; Southern Baptist Convention, Nashville, Tenn., missionary to Italy, 1959-69, director of program of vocational guidance, 1969-72, director of program of family ministry, 1971-72; Vineyard Retreat and Conference Center, Louisville, Ky., director, 1973—. Visiting professor at Istituto Linguistico and Istituto Filadelfia (both Rivoli, Italy), 1965-66; Garret fellow at Southern Baptist Theological Seminary, 1966-67; instructor at Jefferson Community College, 1968-69. Minister of education at Baptist churches in Louisville,

Ky., 1964-65, 1966-69. *Military service:* U.S. Air Force, 1951-52.

MEMBER: North American Association of Retreat Center Directors (chairman, 1975-76), Religious Education Association, Association of Creative Change, Association for Humanistic Psychology, Southern Baptist Religious Education Association, Southern Baptist Historical Society.

WRITINGS: (With Harvey A. Hester) *Growth Through Groups* (Faith at Work Book Club selection), Broadman, 1974; *Discovering the Depths: Dimensions of a Christian Lifestyle*, Broadman, in press. Contributor to religious magazines.

* * *

CLEVENGER, Ernest Allen, Jr. 1929-
(Ben Rovin)

PERSONAL: Born October 30, 1929, in Chattanooga, Tenn.; son of Ernest Allen, Sr. (a company president) and Mary Ellen (Fridell) Clevenger; married Glenda Willoughby (a high school registrar), December 17, 1950; children: Ernest Allen III, Elisabeth Anne. *Education:* David Lipscomb College, B.A., 1951; McKensie College, graduate study, 1953; Harding Graduate School of Bible and Religion, M.A., 1967; Alabama Christian School of Religion, B.Th., 1971; Alabama Christian College of Biblical Studies, M.R.E., 1974, M.Th., 1975. *Home:* 1569 Berry Rd., Birmingham, Ala. 35226. *Office:* West End Church of Christ, 420 Seventh St. S.W., Birmingham, Ala. 35211.

CAREER: Became minister of Church of Christ, 1949; minister in Athens, Tenn., 1951-53, Murray, Ky., 1953-57, Russellville, Ala., 1957-63, Birmingham, Ala., 1963—. Teacher of general and physical science in Russellville, Ala., 1959-63; Alabama Christian School of Religion, Montgomery, professor of Bible, 1968-73; Alabama Christian College of Biblical Studies, Birmingham, president, 1973—. Member of board of trustees and director, Central Alabama Christian Youth Camp, 1958—; member of board of trustees, Childhaven Orphan Home, 1961-66; owner and manager of Parchment Press, 1963—; member of board of directors, Alabama Christian School of Religion, Birmingham, 1969-73; executive vice-president, Bible Learning Materials, Inc., 1974—; director of annual Christian Campers Workshop at David Lipscomb College, 1975—; guest lecturer, David Lipscomb College, Alabama Christian College, Abilene Christian College. Has conducted teacher and leadership training courses, 1952—. *Member:* American Schools of Oriental Research, Creation Research Society, Bible-Science Association, American Scientific Affiliation, Southern Association of Marriage Counselors (life member), Sons of the American Revolution, Franklin County Conservation Club (founder and president, 1957—). *Awards, honors:* American Chemical Society research grant, 1962; S.L.D. from Berean Christian College and Seminary, 1972.

WRITINGS—All published by Parchment Press: *The Bible*, 1960; *Lesson Commentary Index*, 1963, 3rd edition, 1973; *The History of God's People*, 1963; *Leadership Training Course*, 1964; *A Condensed Harmony of the Gospels*, 1964; *Bible Geography*, 1965; *Pocket Bible Ready Reference*, 1965; *Jesus of the Bible*, 1965, 2nd edition, 1972; *Wisdom Books of the Bible*, 1966; *Bible Doctrine*, 1967; *The Church Usher's Guide*, 1967, 2nd edition published as *The Art of Greeting and Seating*, 1970; *Bible Evidences*, 1968, revised edition, 1973; (editor) *Bible Survey*, 1969; *Bible Characters*, 1970; *History of the Bible*

Church, 1971; *Psychology of Jesus*, 1975; *Men's Leadership Training Course*, 1975.

Weekly columnist, *Ledger and Times* (Murray, Ky.), 1954-59, and under pseudonym Ben Rovin, *Franklin County Times*, 1958-63. Contributor to religious publications. *Christian Bible Teacher Magazine*, contributing editor, 1964-70, high school editor, 1970—.

WORK IN PROGRESS: Directory of Churches of Christ in Alabama; *Bible Geography Handbook*; *How to Publish an Effective Church Bulletin*; *Christian Youth Camp Handbook*.

AVOCATIONAL INTERESTS: Photography, archaeology, fishing, hunting, archery.

* * *

CLEVER, (Warren) Glenn 1918-

PERSONAL: Born February 10, 1918, in Champion, Alberta, Canada; son of George (a farmer) and Florence (Anderson) Clever; married Elizabeth Hall, June, 1942; children: Christine. *Education:* Attended Canadian Army Staff College, 1951-52, and Baylor University, 1960-61; University of Ottawa, B.A., 1964, M.A., 1966, Ph.D., 1969. *Home:* 9 Ashburn Dr., Ottawa, Ontario K2E 6N4, Canada. *Office:* Department of English, University of Ottawa, Ottawa, Ontario K1N 6N5, Canada.

CAREER: Canadian Army, Medical Corps, 1939-66, retiring as major; Canadian Army Reserve, 1966—; University of Ottawa, Ottawa, Ontario, lecturer, 1967-69, assistant professor, 1970-71, associate professor of English, 1972—, chairman of department, 1972—. President of Borealis Press, 1971—, and Tecumseh Press, 1973—; director of Canadian Writers' Foundation. *Member:* Association of Canadian University Teachers of English, Association for Canadian and Quebec Literatures, American Association of Eighteenth Century Studies.

WRITINGS: Go Gentle (poems), Bytown Press, 1971; *Age of the Astronauts* (poems), Bytown Press, 1971; *O Can* (verse satire), Borealis Press, 1972; (editor) *Selected Stories of Duncan Campbell Scott*, University of Ottawa Press, 1972; *Count Down* (poems), Borealis Press, 1974; *Alberta Days* (poems), Borealis Press, 1974; (editor) *Selected Poetry of Duncan Campbell Scott*, Tecumseh Press, 1974; (editor) *Index to Canadian Literature*, Golden Dog Press, 1975. General editor, "The Canadian Short Story Library," University of Ottawa Press, 1971—. Contributor to literary journals, including *Canadian Fiction, Inscape, Golden Dog*, and *Journal of Narrative Technique*.

WORK IN PROGRESS: A Study of the Canadian Novel.

* * *

CLEW, Jeffrey Robert 1928-

PERSONAL: Born January 26, 1928, in London, England; son of Christopher Bertram and Edith Mary (Barnes) Clew; married Audrey Claire Kendrick, May 9, 1953; children: Alison Jane, Philippa Anne. *Education:* Educated in England. *Politics:* None. *Religion:* Church of England. *Home:* Sulby, 10 Mildmay Dr., Queen Camel, near Yeovil, Somerset, England. *Office:* J. H. Haynes & Co. Ltd., Sparkford, near Yeovil, Somerset, England.

CAREER: Distillers Plastics Group, London, England, group information officer, 1955-65; Chevron Oil Europe Ltd., London, information/market research officer, 1966-68; Electricity Council, London, industrial information en-

gineer, 1969-70; Gulton Europe Ltd., Brighton, England, publicity and advertising manager, 1970-72; J. H. Haynes & Co., Sparkford, England, motor cycle book editor, 1972—. Motorcycle book editor for G. T. Foulis & Co., 1972—. Has appeared on British television and radio programs. *Member:* Institute of Information Scientists.

WRITINGS: (With Bob Burgess) *Always in the Picture: A History of the Velocette Motorcycle*, Goose & Son, 1972; *The Best Twin: A History of the Douglas Motorcycle*, Goose & Son, 1974; *The Scott Motorcycle: The Yowling Two-Stroke*, G. T. Foulis, 1975.

Workshop manuals: "BSA A7 and A10 Twin Cylinder Models," "BSA Bantam," "Honda 50 Motor Cycles," "Honda XL250/350 Trail Bikes," "Honda 65, 70, and 90 Motor Cycles," "Honda 750 Fours," "Norton Commando," "Puch Maxi Mopeds," "Suzuki 250 and 350 Twins," "Triumph 650 and 750 Unit-Construction Twins," "Triumph 500 and 650 Pre-Unit Twins," "Velocette Singles," "Vespa Scooters," and "Yamaha 250 and 350 Twins."

Contributor to magazines, including *Motor Cycle, Motor Cycle Sport, Cycle* (United States), and *Motor Cycle Mechanics*.

WORK IN PROGRESS: A biography of trails rider Sammy Miller; *British Racing Motorcycles*; the restoration of vintage and thoroughbred motor cycles; a book on motor cycle care.

* * *

CLICK, J(ohn) W(illiam) 1936-

PERSONAL: Born April 22, 1936, in Huntington, Ind.; son of Eric Alger (a lumber company manager) and Ethel (a high school art teacher; maiden name, McKenzie) Click; married Dixie Darlene Brown (a registered nurse), November 27, 1960; children: Reid William, Kevin Leon. *Education:* Ball State University, A.B., 1958; Ohio University, M.S., 1959; summer graduate study at University of Missouri, 1961; Ohio State University, Ph.D. candidate. *Religion:* United Methodist. *Home:* 135 Lamar Dr., Athens, Ohio 45701. *Office:* School of Journalism, Lasher Hall, Ohio University, Athens, Ohio 45701.

CAREER: Findlay College, Findlay, Ohio, instructor in English and journalism, and director of public relations, 1959-60; Central Michigan University, Mount Pleasant, instructor in journalism, 1960-65; Ohio University, Athens, assistant professor, 1965-71, associate professor of journalism, 1971—. *Member:* National Council of College Publications Advisers (president, 1971-75), Society of Professional Journalists, Society for Collegiate Journalists (vice-president, 1975-77), Blue Key, Sigma Tau Delta, Sigma Zeta, Kappa Tau Alpha. *Awards, honors:* Gold Key award from Columbia Scholastic Press Association, 1972; special honor award from National School Yearbook Association, 1972.

WRITINGS: (With R. N. Baird) *Magazine Editing and Production*, W. C. Brown, 1974. Contributor to journalism journals.

WORK IN PROGRESS: Articles for professional journals.

* * *

CLOUTIER, David 1951-

PERSONAL: Surname is pronounced Clou-*tyay*; born April 20, 1951, in Providence, R.I.; son of Maurice Roger and Adeleine Alice (Abbott) Cloutier; married Anne Greene (a painter), June 11, 1972. *Education:* Brown University, A.B. and M.A., 1974. *Residence:* Providence, R.I. *Office:* Rhode Island State Council on the Arts, East Greenwich, R.I.

CAREER: Rhode Island State Council on the Arts, East Greenwich, poetry specialist, 1970—. Founder and editor of Bonewhistle Press; poetry instructor for Rhode Island Governor's School for Youth in the Arts, 1971-73, coordinator of training program for poets, 1974-75.

WRITINGS: Spirit Spirit: Shaman Songs, Incantations, Copper Beech Press, 1973; *Northwest Coast Songs* (pamphlet), Blue Cloud Quarterly, 1974; (editor with Stephen Coon) *The Ear of the Bull: Nine French Poets,* Bonewhistle Press, 1974. Contributor of poems to literary magazines, including *Chelsea, Cincinnati Poetry Review, Nimrod, Prism International, Shaman, Stinktree, Ironwood, Blacksmith,* and *Akwesasne Notes.*

WORK IN PROGRESS: Homing, poems; *Ghost Call,* poetry; *Elf-Struck: Charms, Spels;* studying Mongol texts of shaman songs.

* * *

COATES, Ruth Allison 1915-

PERSONAL: Born May 18, 1915, in Mt. Carmel, Ill.; daughter of Earl L. (an editor) and Esther (Ross) Allison; married Robert E. Coates (a lawyer), December 24, 1939; children: Margaret Ann (Mrs. Richard Polese), Nancy Lynn Coates Loker, David Allison, Steve Wendell. *Education:* Bethel College, Hopkinsville, Ky., A.A., 1936; Indiana University, A.B., 1938. *Home and office:* 4340 Knollton Rd., Indianapolis, Ind. 46208. *Agent:* Ruth Cantor, 156 Fifth Ave., Room 1005, New York, N.Y. 10010.

CAREER: Commercial artist in department stores in Indianapolis, Ind., 1938-41, and in San Antonio, Tex., 1942. Former portrait artist, now working in silk screen and collage; work has been shown in exhibits and in a one-man show in Indianapolis. *Member:* Graphics Society, Authors Guild, Hoosier Salon, Spiritual Frontiers, Astara. *Awards, honors:* Robert Martin Award from New York Poetry Forum contest, 1970, for poem, "The Loaf."

WRITINGS: Great American Naturalists (juvenile), Lerner, 1974. Short fiction has been anthologized in *The Real Book of First Stories,* edited by Dorothy Haas, Rand McNally, 1973. Contributor of short stories, poems, and articles to *Teen, Minnesota Review, Parents' Magazine, Phylon, Guideposts,* and other periodicals.

WORK IN PROGRESS: Three novels, one a juvenile, requiring research into Greek history, the early Christian era, and eighteenth-century England.

SIDELIGHTS: "Working on biographies is a delight," Ruth Coates wrote, "especially doing those people who should be known, but aren't. . . . I am a great believer in people's lives crossing because there's a plan unfolding, a plan often beyond the grasp of our limited intuition. Hence all word-building is an awesome responsibility to me. . . . The spirit world, the historical world, the world not yet discovered—all these have more solidity to me than the apparent, touchable world. I am a writer dealing in and forever investigating clues, or keys, to the meaning of the constantly shifting illusion that lies about us. It's a spirited adventure. . . . My mother is Swedish. She has seen angels and auras—which must account for my fascination with the mystical."

AVOCATIONAL INTERESTS: World religions, reading, travel.

* * *

COCHARD, Thomas S(ylvester) 1893-

PERSONAL: Born November 30, 1893, in Anderson, Ind.; son of August (a millworker) and Annie (Kirchner) Cochard; married Helen Blanche Burkhart, July 21, 1921. *Education:* Muskingum College, B.A., 1921; Pittsburgh-Xenia Theological Seminary (now Pittsburgh Theological Seminary), B.Th., 1924; Yale University, M.Rel.Ed., 1932. *Politics:* Republican. *Home and office:* 1073 Elm Ave., Beaumont, Calif. 92223.

CAREER: Ordained United Presbyterian clergyman, 1924; pastor of United Presbyterian churches in Dubois, Pa., 1924-26, Reedurban, Ohio, 1926-29; pastor of United Church of Christ in Prospect, Conn., 1929-41; member of office and sales staff, Chase Brass and Copper Co., Waterbury, Conn., and a Los Angeles, Calif. mill, 1949-51; employed in office sales, Pacific Metals Co., Los Angeles, 1951-56; owner and operator of fruit ranch in Beaumont, Calif., c. 1956—. Has also worked as census supervisor, businessman, and employment interviewer. *Military service:* U.S. Army, 1918-19; became sergeant.

WRITINGS: The Beloved Community: America!, Branden Press, 1974.

* * *

COCHRAN, Charles L(eo) 1940-

PERSONAL: Born May 3, 1940, in Salisbury, Md.; married Mary Anne Ratke, 1966; children: Christine, Colleen, Cathleen, Kevin. *Education:* Mount St. Mary's College, Emmitsburg, Md., B.S., 1962; Niagara University, M.A., 1963; Tufts University, Ph.D., 1969. *Home address:* Route 3, Box 127, Annapolis, Md. 21403. *Office:* Department of Political Science, U.S. Naval Academy, Annapolis, Md. 21402.

CAREER: U.S. Naval Academy, Annapolis, Md., assistant professor, 1966-69, associate professor of political science, 1969—. U.S. representative to United Nations International Law Seminar, 1973.

WRITINGS: Civil-Military Relations: Changing Concepts in the Seventies, Free Press, 1974. Contributor to political science journals. Associate editor of *Journal of Political and Military Sociology.*

* * *

CODY, D(ouglas) Thane R(omney) 1932-

PERSONAL: Born June 23, 1932, in St. John, New Brunswick, Canada; son of Douglas and Eleanore (Romney) Cody; married Joanne Gerow, April 6, 1963; children: Douglas Thane Romney, Romney Joanne. *Education:* Dalhousie University, M.D. and C.M., both 1957; Mayo Graduate School of Medicine, postdoctoral study, 1958-63; University of Minnesota, Ph.D.. 1966. *Home:* 1506 Weatherhill Ct., Rochester, Minn. 55901. *Office:* 200 First St. S.W., Rochester, Minn. 55901.

CAREER: St. John General Hospital, St. John, New Brunswick, intern, 1956-57; Provincial Laboratories, St. John, New Brunswick, resident, 1957-58; physician, 1958—. University of Minnesota, Mayo Foundation for Medical Education and Research, Rochester, Minn., Mayo Graduate School of Medicine, consultant in otorhinolaryngology, 1963-68, instructor, 1963-66, assistant professor, 1966-70, associate professor of otorhinolaryngology, 1970-73, chairman of department, 1968—, Mayo Medical School, associate professor, 1973-74, professor of otolaryngology, 1974—.

MEMBER: International Society of Audiology, American Medical Association, American Academy of Ophthalmology and Otolaryngology (representative to Council of Medical Specialty Societies), American College of Surgeons, American Triological Society, American Otological Society, Barany Society, Association for Research in Otolaryngology, American Physiological Society, American Council of Otolaryngologists, Society of University Otolaryngologists, American Audiology Society, Society of Academic Chairmen of Otolaryngology, Mayo Foundation for Medical Education and Research, Pacific Coast Oto-Ophthalmological Society (honorary member), Minnesota Academy of Ophthalmologists and Otolaryngologists, Illinois Society of Ophthalmologists and Otolaryngologists (honorary member), New York Academy of Sciences, Zumbro Valley Medical Society, Sigma Xi, Centurion Club (of Deafness Research Foundation). *Awards, honors:* Award for research from American Academy of Ophthalmology and Otolaryngology, 1961; Edward John Noble Award for foreign travel from Mayo Foundation, 1961; Dr. John Black Award for Surgery from Dalhousie University, 1965; award of merit from American Academy of Ophthalmology and Otolaryngology, 1972.

WRITINGS: Your Child's Ears, Nose and Throat: A Parent's Medical Guide, Macmillan, 1974. Contributor of more than a hundred articles to medical journals. Associate editor for otolaryngology, *Transactions of the American Academy of Ophthalmology and Otolaryngology*; member of board of editors of *Otorhinolaryngology Digest*; collaborant for *Acta Oto-Laryngologica*; member of review board of *Annals of Otolaryngology*; consulting editor of *Minnesota Medicine*.

*   *   *

COFFIN, Joseph (John)   1899-

PERSONAL: Born August 9, 1899, in Whitestone, N.Y.; son of Benjamin (an engineer) and Catherine (Sheridan) Coffin. *Education:* Attended LaSalle Academy, New York, N.Y., two years. *Religion:* Roman Catholic. *Home:* 32-42 33rd St., Long Island City, N.Y. 11106. *Office:* 1170 Broadway, Floor 13, New York, N.Y. 10001.

CAREER: Worked as a telegraph clerk, a printer, and passenger rate man for the Pennsylvania Railroad, 1923-59. Rare coin collector and dealer; writer.

WRITINGS: Coin Collecting, Coward, 1938; *Our American Money*, Coward, 1940; *Coins of the Popes*, Coward, 1945; *The Complete Book of Coin Collecting*, Coward, 1945, 5th edition, 1973. Contributor to *Numismatic Scrapbook, Leisure*, and other periodicals.

WORK IN PROGRESS: 100 Railroad Medals and Coins; a revision of *Coins of the Popes*.

AVOCATIONAL INTERESTS: Deep sea fishing.

*   *   *

COHART, Mary   1911-

PERSONAL: Born June 27, 1911, in New York, N.Y.; daughter of Jacob and Sarah Schleifer; married Edward M. Cohart (a professor of public health at Yale University), October 23, 1933; children: Paul Edward, Diana Mary

Cohart Reisen. *Education:* Hunter College of the City University of New York, B.A., 1931; Columbia University, M.A., 1933; City College (now of the City University of New York), further graduate study, 1937-38; Yale University, M.A., 1950, Ph.D., 1953.

CAREER: Businesswoman, 1931-36; high school teacher in New York, N.Y., 1938-42, 1947-48; Connecticut Commission on Alcoholism (now Department of Mental Health), Hartford, clinical psychologist, 1954-61; Yale University, New Haven, Conn., researcher, 1973.

WRITINGS: Unsung Champions of Women, University of New Mexico Press, 1975.

WORK IN PROGRESS: Harbingers of Feminism in the Drama; Women in Opera.

*   *   *

COHEN, Anne Billings   1937-

PERSONAL: Born April 2, 1937, in Berkeley, Calif.; daughter of Robert Samuel and Melba (Roat) Billings; married Norman Cohen (a physical chemist), July 11, 1959; children: Alexa and Carson (twins). *Education:* Reed College, B.A., 1958; University of California, Los Angeles, M.A., 1968. *Home:* 626 Haverford Ave., Pacific Palisades, Calif. 90272. *Office:* Folklore-Mythology Center, University of California, Los Angeles, Calif. 90024.

CAREER: University of California, Los Angeles, Extension Division, instructor in folklore and mythology, and supervisor of John Edwards Memorial Foundation (folk music archive). *Member:* American Folklore Society, California Folklore Society.

WRITINGS: Poor Pearl, Poor Girl: The Murdered Girl Sterotype in Ballad and Newspapers, University of Texas Press, 1974. Contributor to folklore and music publications.

WORK IN PROGRESS: Research on political uses of folklore, Biblical folklore, narrative techniques in ballads and tales, and American balladry, especially attempts to distinguish genres.

AVOCATIONAL INTERESTS: Gardening (emphasizing tracking down and acquiring seeds, clones, or seedlings of unusual fruits, nuts, herbs, and rare roses).

*   *   *

COHEN, Edmund D(avid)   1943-

PERSONAL: Born January 26, 1943, in Washington, D.C.; son of Samuel Erwin and Gertrude (Barr) Cohen. *Education:* George Washington University, A.B., 1965, law studies, 1974—; Case Western Reserve University, M.S., 1967, Ph.D., 1968; C. G. Jung Institute, postdoctoral study, 1970-71. *Home:* 315 North George Mason Dr., #3, Arlington, Va. 22203. *Office:* Department of Psychology, George Mason University, 4400 University Dr., Fairfax, Va. 22030.

CAREER: George Mason University, Fairfax, Va., assistant professor, 1968-74, lecturer in psychology, 1974—. *Member:* American Psychological Association, Society for the Scientific Study of Religion.

WRITINGS: C. G. Jung and the Scientific Attitude, Philosophical Library, 1975.

AVOCATIONAL INTERESTS: Flying (holds private pilot's license).

COHEN, Gary G. 1934-

PERSONAL: Born August 18, 1934, in Philadelphia, Pa.; son of Abraham (a grocer) and Mary (Sagel) Cohen; married Marion Isobel Vandermey, December 18, 1959; children: Sharon, Caralee, Steven. *Education:* Temple University, B.S., 1956; Faith Theological Seminary, M.Div., 1961, S.T.M., 1964; Grace Theological Seminary, Th.D., 1966. *Home:* 792 Boxwood Dr., Warminster, Pa. 18974. *Office:* Biblical School of Theology, 200 North Main, Hatfield, Pa. 19440.

CAREER: Ordained minister of Presbyterian Church, 1959; high school teacher of chemistry and biology in the public schools of Germantown, Pa., 1956-58; Shelton College, Cape May, N.J., instructor in physics, Bible, sociology, and church history, 1961-63, dean of students, 1962-63; Faith Theological Seminary, instructor, 1965-66, professor of New Testament, 1966-71; Biblical School of Theology, Hatfield, Pa., professor of New Testament, 1971—, director of postgraduate studies, 1973—. Pastor in Chester, Pa., 1968-71. Member of board of directors and vice-president of Shofar, Inc. (mission board), 1963—. *Military service:* U.S. Army, Artillery, 1957-66. U.S. Army Reserve, chaplain, 1963—; current rank, major.

WRITINGS: Biblical Separation Defended, Presbyterian & Reformed, 1964; (editor) *Encyclopedia of Christianity,* Foundation for Christian Education, 1968; *Pilgrim's Progress in the Twentieth Century,* Christian Beacon, 1968; *Understanding Revelation,* Christian Beacon, 1968; (with Salem Kirban) *Revelation Visualized,* Salem Kirban, 1971, Moody, 1972; *Israel: Land of Promise,* Salem Kirban, 1974; *Civilization's Last Hurrah,* Moody, 1974. Contributor to religion journals.

WORK IN PROGRESS: To Save the Temple: 66-70 A.D. (historical novel); contributing to *Theological Word Book of the Old Testament.*

SIDELIGHTS: Cohen led tours of the Holy Land in 1968 and 1973, and has constructed an eight-by-twelve foot model of Jerusalem as it appeared in 66 A.D. *Avocational interests:* Flying (licensed pilot).

* * *

COHEN, Robert Carl 1930-

PERSONAL: Born September 24, 1930, in Philadelphia, Pa.; son of Isadore Wolf and Ida (Gabriel) Cohen; married Helene Konidare (a motion picture producer), June 21, 1961; children: Dianna, Julia. *Education:* University of California, Los Angeles, B.A., 1952, M.A., 1954, further study, 1959-61; also did graduate work at Sorbonne, University of Paris, 1956-57, and University of Southern California, 1961-62. *Politics:* Registered Democrat. *Religion:* "Optimist." *Residence:* Los Angeles, Calif. *Address:* c/o Random House, 201 East 50th St., New York, N.Y. 10022.

CAREER: Columbia Broadcasting System-Television, New York, N.Y., writer for "Adventure Show," 1954; Jean Image Films, Paris France, writer-designer in cartoon production, 1956; National Broadcasting Co.-Television, New York, N.Y., special correspondent in China, 1957; public lecturer for "The World Around Us," 1959-65; National Educational Television (WNEW-TV), Chicago, Ill., producer of "Three Faces of Cuba," 1964-65; Metro-Goldwyn-Mayer Studios, Culver City, Calif., supervisor of minority training program, 1972-73. *Military service:* U.S. Army, 1954-56. *Member:* Writers Guild of America, West. *Awards, honors: The Color of Man* was an American Library Association Notable Book of 1968.

WRITINGS: The Color of Man, Random House, 1968, revised edition, 1973; *Black Crusader: A Biography of Robert Franklin Williams,* Lyle Stuart, 1972.

Television specials; produced by Robert Carl Cohen Productions, Inc.: "Inside East Germany," 1959; "Inside Red China," 1961; "Committee on Un-American Activities," 1962; "Three Cubans," 1965.

Motion picture scripts: "Cudjoe, the Maroon," 1974.

WORK IN PROGRESS: Screen treatment of Harry Rhodes' *A Chosen Few,* for H and R Productions; "Inner Trip," a documentary film about the Reiyakai Buddhist sect.

SIDELIGHTS: "My motivation is to attempt to understand the nature of life through dealing with the primary problems which torment humanity: racism, ideology, etc., and to then share whatever insights I may have reached through the media of books, films, TV, and other means of communication. I do this because I have found that the most satisfactory means for solving problems is to study the factors causing them, and to then try to either adjust those factors or otherwise manipulate the situation so as to eliminate or alleviate the effects of the contradictions. My profession is, therefore, education, but always tempered by concern with esthetics because I believe that important subjects require effective presentation."

FOR MORE INFORMATION SEE: Young Readers' Review, September, 1968; *Horn Book,* August, 1969.

* * *

COHN, Norman 1915-

PERSONAL: Born January 12, 1915, in London, England; son of August Sylvester (a barrister) and Daisy (Reimer) Cohn; married Vera Broido (an author), September 3, 1941; children: Nik. *Education:* Christ Church, Oxford, B.A. (first class honors), 1936, M.A., 1947; University of Glasgow, D.Litt., 1957. *Home:* 61 New End, London NW3 1HY, England. *Agent:* A. D. Peters, 10 Buckingham St., London WC2N 6DD, England. *Office:* University of Sussex, Falmer, near Brighton, England.

CAREER: University of Durham, Durham, England, professor of French, 1963-66; University of Sussex, Falmer, England, professorial fellow and director of Columbus Centre, 1966-73, Astor-Wolfson Professor of History, 1973—. Hugh Le May fellow, Rhodes University, 1950; fellow, Center for Advanced Study in Behavioral Sciences, Stanford University, 1965-66, Center for Humanities, Wesleyan University, 1971, and Netherlands Institute for Advanced Study, 1975-76. *Military service:* British Army, 1940-46; became captain. *Member:* Royal Historical Society (fellow), Athenaeum. *Awards, honors:* Anisfield-Wolf Award in Race Relations, 1967, for *Warrant for Genocide.*

WRITINGS: Gold Khan and Other Siberian Legends, Secker & Warburg, 1946; *The Pursuit of the Millennium: Revolutionary Millennarians and Mystical Anarchists of the Middle Ages,* Oxford University Press, 1957, 3rd revised edition, 1970; (contributor) Sylvia S. Thrupp, editor, *Millennial Dreams in Action,* Mouton & Co., 1962; (contributor) Anthony A. de Reuck and Julie J. Knight, editors, *Caste and Race,* Little, Brown, 1967; *Warrant for Genocide: The Myth of the Jewish World-Conspiracy and the Protocols of the Elders of Zion,* Eyre & Spottiswoode, 1966, Harper, 1967, revised edition, Harper, 1970; *Europe's Inner Demons,* Basic Books, 1975. Editor of Columbus Centre's "Studies in the Dynamics of Persecution and Extermination," 1966—. Contributor to *Horizon, Twentieth Century, Commentary*, and *Encounter*.

WORK IN PROGRESS: Research on changing ideas about the future held in the course of Western history.

SIDELIGHTS: Pursuit of the Millennium has had editions in French, German, Italian, and Spanish; *Warrant for Genocide* has been translated into French, German, Italian, Spanish, Portuguese, and Hebrew. Cohn has travelled in Europe, North America, and South Africa. He reads Dutch, Spanish, Italian, Medieval Latin, Medieval French, and Medieval German. *Avocational interests:* Walking, looking at pictures, travel.

* * *

COHN, Rubin (Goodman) 1911-

PERSONAL: Born February 16, 1911, in Chicago, Ill.; son of Morris (a businessman) and Anna (Goodman) Cohn; married Lillian Ruttenberg, July 7, 1935; children: Reina Marilyn (Mrs. Loren Pollack), Stuart. *Education:* University of Illinois, B.A., 1932, J.D., 1934. *Religion:* Jewish. *Home:* 6 O'Connor Ct., Champaign, Ill. 61820. *Office:* College of Law, University of Illinois, Champaign, Ill. 61820.

CAREER: State of Illinois, Springfield, legislative draftsman, 1935-44; private practice of law in Chicago, Ill., 1945-49; University of Illinois, Champaign, associate professor, 1949-51, professor of law, 1951—. Legal counsel for State Universities Retirement System, 1953-73; staff counsel and member of judiciary committee of Sixth Illinois Constitutional Convention, 1970. Member of Illinois Intergovernmental Cooperation Commission, 1943-45; member of Illinois Public Employees Pension Laws Commission, 1949—; member of Illinois unit of National Conference of Commissioners on Uniform State Laws, 1968-69. Member of law faculty at Lincoln Academy of Illinois.

MEMBER: American Bar Association, American Judicature Society, American Association of University Professors (vice-president of University of Illinois chapter, 1973-74), Illinois State Bar Association, Chicago Bar Association, B'nai B'rith (president of Champaign-Urbana chapter, 1960-62), Order of the Coif, Phi Kappa Phi.

WRITINGS: (With George D. Braden) *The Illinois Constitution: An Annotated and Comparative Analysis*, Institute of Government and Public Affairs, University of Illinois, 1969; *To Judge with Justice: History and Politics of Illinois Judicial Reform*, University of Illinois Press, 1973. Contributor to law journals.

WORK IN PROGRESS: A book analyzing strengths and weaknesses of legal education; an autobiography, with special emphasis on Jewish influences which shaped his development.

SIDELIGHTS: Cohn writes that he was motivated toward the study of law by the Loeb-Leopold trial in 1923. He feels that, since then, "... service in numerous public bodies in research or advisory capacities sharpened perceptions of gaps between pretensions and realities of political and professional principles and values." He is active in civil libertarian causes, and has a strong commitment to the preservation of Israel; he was a member of the Conference on Human Needs in Israel in 1969. *Avocational interests:* European travel, reading history, philosophy, and biography.

COLBERT, Douglas A(lbert) 1933-

PERSONAL: Born October 13, 1933, in Mount Airy, N.C. *Education:* Attended College of Marin, California State College, Sonoma, and San Francisco State University. *Home:* 331 Nova Albion Way, San Rafael, Calif. 94903.

CAREER: Senior systems designer for City of San Francisco.

WRITINGS: Data Processing Concepts, McGraw, 1968; *Computers and Management for Business*, Petrocelli, 1974.

* * *

COLEMAN, Thomas R. 1942-

PERSONAL: Born October 6, 1942, in Wellsville, N.Y.; son of Myles Bowman (a mechanical engineer) and Emma (Schoenfeld) Coleman; married Jaynie Edna Ponge (a special education teacher), June, 1973. *Education:* Concordia Junior College, A.A., 1963; Washington Square College, B.A., 1965; New School for Social Research, M.A., 1970; Nova University, Ed.D., 1975. *Religion:* Protestant. *Home:* 33 Branch Brook Pl., Newark, N.J. 07104. *Agent:* A. L. Fierst, Box 155, Old Northern Blvd., Roslyn, N.Y. 11576. *Office:* Essex County College, 31 Clinton St., Newark, N.J.

CAREER: Essex County Hospital Center, Cedar Grove, N.J., attendant, 1965-68; Upsala College, East Orange, N.J., instructor in psychology, 1968—; Essex County College, Newark, N.J., assistant professor of psychology, 1968—. Consultant and therapist, Integrity House (drug rehabilitation center), Newark, N.J.

WRITINGS: The Angle of Vision (novel), Vantage, 1970; *Abnormal Psychology*, MSS Information Corp., 1974. Contributor of poems and articles to magazines and of articles to journals in his field.

WORK IN PROGRESS: Three novels, *Journey into Today, The Forest of Madness*, and *The Legend of Silver Wolf*; a psychology book on demonology; a novel concerning drug addiction.

AVOCATIONAL INTERESTS: Traveling, skiing, bicycling, jogging, camping, and hiking.

* * *

COLEMAN, William V(incent) 1932-

PERSONAL: Born January 27, 1932, in Waterbury, Conn.; son of William V. and Ethel (Brennan) Coleman; married Patricia Register (a writer), November 27, 1975. *Education:* Saint Bernard College, Rochester, N.Y., B.A., 1953; Saint Bernard Seminary, B.D., 1955, M.Div., 1957; Fairfield University, M.A., 1965; Florida State University, Ph.D., 1976. *Home and office address:* P.O. Box 20126, Tallahassee, Fla. 32304.

CAREER: Ordained Roman Catholic priest, 1957; Catholic Diocese of Savannah, Ga., rector of St. John's Seminary, 1958-68, director of education, 1968-74; left priesthood, 1974. *Member:* American Education Association, National Association for the Advancement of Colored People, National Association of Public Continuing Adult Education.

WRITINGS: Mine Is the Morning, six volumes, XXIII Publications, 1974-75; *God Believes in Me*, Ave Maria Press, 1975; *The Way of the Cross*, XXIII Publications, 1975; *Teach Us How to Pray*, XXIII Publications, in press.

Author of scripts for XXIII Publications filmstrip series "Sin and Reconciliation," 1974, and "The Mass," 1975. Author of "Update," a column in *Today's Parish*, 1974—. Publisher of *Southern Cross*; section editor, *Today's Parish*.

WORK IN PROGRESS: Three additional volumes of *Mine Is the Morning*; a program for young people about to marry, including book, guide, and filmstrip series; a popular commentary on the gospels; research on popular parables.

SIDELIGHTS: Coleman writes: "I am searching for language in which to communicate religious truth. This springs from the conviction that the traditional language no longer means what it did. I am also convinced that mere reading without some interaction with other people leads the ordinary person into shallow, usually useless knowledge."

* * *

COLES, Flournoy (Arthur), Jr. 1915-

PERSONAL: Born April 25, 1915, in Trenton, N.J.; son of Flournoy Arthur (a coal miner) and Susie (Poole) Coles; married Pauline Johnson, August 23, 1943 (divorced, 1966); children: Flournoy Arthur III. *Education:* Xavier University of Louisiana, B.A., 1941; University of Pennsylvania, M.A., 1942, Ph.D., 1949. *Politics:* Independent. *Religion:* None. *Home:* 4810 Old Hickory Blvd., Hermitage, Tenn. 37076. *Office:* Graduate School of Management, Vanderbilt University, 2505 West End Ave., Nashville, Tenn. 37203.

CAREER: Professor of economics at Florida A & M University and at Texas Southern University, 1949-51; Agency for International Development, Washington, D.C., program officer, 1951-63; System Development Corp., Santa Monica, Calif., technical assistant to management, and economist, 1963-66; Fisk University, Nashville, Tenn., professor of economics and chairman of department, 1966-69; Vanderbilt University, Nashville, Tenn., professor of management, 1969—. External examiner for School of Administration at University of Ghana; member of long-term goals subcommittee on Minority Business Education Curriculum Committee; chairman of small business development subcommittee of Nashville Mayor's Goals Committee of Two Thousand; member of Washington, D.C. National Business League; member of Full Employment Action Council. *Military service:* U.S. Army, 1942-46; served in European theater, in Italian campaign; became first lieutenant.

MEMBER: American Economic Association, American Academy of Political and Social Science, American Association of University Professors, African Association for Public Administration and Management, Southern Economic Association.

WRITINGS: Black Economic Development, Nelson-Hall, 1975. Contributor to management and black studies journals.

WORK IN PROGRESS: Management of Economic Development in Africa; Commodity Demand and Supply Changes and the Less-Developed Countries; The Economic Study of the Nation of Islam.

SIDELIGHTS: Coles writes: "My interest in economic development . . . was motivated by a deep concern about inequalities in income and wealth distribution and factors related thereto. This I consider the major threat to national and international peace." *Avocational interests:* African art, music, golf, fishing, cooking.

COLIN, Jean
See BELL, Joyce

* * *

COLLIER, Boyd D(ean) 1938-

PERSONAL: Born January 16, 1938, in Waco, Tex.; son of Denis Lee (an antique dealer) and Anne Alice (a special education teacher; maiden name, Berry) Collier; married Barbara Nell Joseph (an interior designer), June 21, 1966; children: Deidra Michelle. *Education:* Baylor University, B.B.A., 1963, M.S., 1965; University of Texas at Austin, Ph.D., 1970. *Religion:* "Universal Christian." *Home:* 9602 Newfoundland Cir., Austin, Tex. 78758. *Office:* Center of Business Administration, St. Edward's University, South Congress, Austin, Tex. 78704.

CAREER: Certified public accountant in Texas, 1965; University of North Carolina, Greensboro, assistant professor of business and economics, 1969-72, assistant to dean of School of Business and Economics, 1970-72; University of Houston, Houston, Tex., associate professor of business administration, 1972-73; Glastron Boat Co., Austin, Tex., chief internal auditor, 1973; St. Edward's University, Austin, Tex., associate professor of business administration, 1974—; private practice as certified public accountant in Austin, Tex., 1974—. Auditor at Marwick, Mitchell, and Co., summer, 1964; instructor at Michigan Technological University, winter and spring, 1965; financial consultant to Pohl, Inc., 1974; member of board of directors of Execucom, Inc., 1974-75, and Accounting Information Systems, 1975. Precinct chairman of Democratic Party, 1968. *Military service:* U.S. Navy, radioman, 1955-59. U.S. Naval Reserve, 1959-63.

MEMBER: American Institute of Certified Public Accountants, American Accounting Association, National Accounting Association, Association for Evolutionary Economics, University of Texas at Austin Ex-Students Association (life member), Phi Kappa Phi, Alpha Chi, Beta Gamma Sigma, Beta Alpha Psi (president of Alpha Rho chapter, 1963), Omicron Delta Epsilon (president of Beta chapter, 1968-69).

WRITINGS: Measurement and Environmental Deterioration (monograph), Bureau of Business Research, University of Texas, 1971. Contributor of articles and poems to *Journal of Environmental Planning and Pollution Control* and *Balloonist*.

WORK IN PROGRESS: A monograph, *Value Formation in Society and Organization*; research for a book entitled *Humanistic Capitalism*.

AVOCATIONAL INTERESTS: Rock climbing, tennis, chess, hiking, solitude in woods.

* * *

COLLINS, Barbara J. 1929-

PERSONAL: Born April 29, 1929, in Passaic, N.J.; daughter of Cornelius F. (an engineer) and Gladys (Holt) Schenck; married Lorence G. Collins (a professor), February 26, 1955; children: Glenn, Elizabeth, Gregory, Kevin, Rachel. *Education:* Bates College, B.S., 1951; Smith College, M.S., 1953; University of Illinois, Ph.D., 1955, M.S., 1959. *Religion:* Methodist. *Home:* 139 Prentiss St., Thousand Oaks, Calif. 91360. *Office:* California Lutheran College, Thousand Oaks, Calif. 91360.

CAREER: California Lutheran College, Thousand Oaks, professor of biology, 1963—. *Member:* American Society for Microbiology, Phi Beta Kappa, Sigma Xi, Phi Kappa Phi, Sigma Delta Epsilon.

WRITINGS: The Story of Our Earth, Franklin Publications, 1965; *California Plant and Animal Communities*, Franklin Publications, 1966; *Exploring and Understanding Insects*, Benefic Press, 1970; (with husband, Lorence G. Collins) *Exploring and Understanding Beyond the Solar System*, Benefic Press, 1970; *Wildflowers, Trees and Shrubs of Holden Village*, Matador Press, 1970; *Exploring and Understanding the Human Body*, Benefic Press, 1971; *Key to Coastal and Chaparral Flowering Plants of Southern California*, California State University Foundation, 1972; *Key to Trees and Wildflowers of the Mountains of Southern California*, California State University Foundation, 1974.

WORK IN PROGRESS: Winter Key to Desert Trees and Shrubs of California, completion expected in 1977; *Key to Wildflowers of the Deserts of California*, 1979.

AVOCATIONAL INTERESTS: Playing flute and piano, painting, drawing, arts and crafts, tennis, swimming, bicycling, and mountain climbing.

* * *

COLLINS, Gary (Ross) 1934-

PERSONAL: Born October 22, 1934, in Hamilton, Ontario, Canada; son of H. A. (a businessman) and Vera (Stanger) Collins; married Julie Heinz, July 18, 1964; children: Marilynn, Janice Carolyn. *Education:* McMaster University, B.A., 1956; University of Toronto, M.A., 1958; University of London, graduate study, 1958-59; Purdue University, Ph.D., 1963; Western Baptist Seminary, postdoctoral study, 1963-64. *Religion:* Evangelical Free Church of America. *Home:* 524 South Prairie Ave., Mundelein, Ill. 60060. *Office:* Division of Psychology, Trinity Evangelical Divinity School, Bannockburn, Deerfield, Ill. 60015.

CAREER: Portland State College, Portland, Ore., counselor, 1963-64; Bethel College, St. Paul, Minn., assistant professor, 1964-66, associate professor of psychology, 1966-68, chairman of department, 1966-68; Conwell School of Theology, Philadelphia, Pa., professor of psychology, 1968-69; Trinity Evangelical Divinity School, Deerfield, Ill., professor of psychology, and chairman of Division of Pastoral Psychology and Counseling, 1969—. *Military service:* Royal Canadian Navy Reserve, 1953-63. *Member:* Canadian Psychological Association, American Psychological Association, Christian Association for Psychological Studies, American Scientific Affiliation (fellow; president, 1974).

WRITINGS: Search for Reality, Vision House, 1969; *Living in Peace*, Vision House, 1970; *Overcoming Anxiety*, Vision House, 1971; (editor) *Our Society in Turmoil*, Creation House, 1971; *Man in Transition*, Creation House, 1972; *Effective Counseling*, Creation House, 1972; *Fractured Personalities*, Creation House, 1973; *Man in Motion*, Creation House, 1973; *The Christian Psychology of Paul Tournier*, Baker Book, 1973; *Coping with Christmas*, Bethany Fellowship, 1975. Contributor of more than fifty articles on religion and psychology to journals.

WORK IN PROGRESS: A book on stress, and one on counseling; editing a book on the family.

* * *

COLLINS, Lorraine (Hill) 1931-

PERSONAL: Born September 24, 1931, in Rapid City, S.D.; daughter of Elmer Roy (a real estate broker) and Marion (Morrill) Hill; married R. Keith Collins (a mining engineer), February 8, 1958; children: Laura, Robert, Marian. *Education:* Cornell College, Mt. Vernon, Iowa, B.A., 1953; graduate study at Black Hills State College, 1955, and at University of Denver, 1957. *Politics:* Registered as Republican. *Religion:* Congregational. *Home:* 1828 7th Ave., Belle Fourche, S.D. 57717.

CAREER: Time, New York, N.Y., editorial researcher, 1953-55; teacher of high school English in public school in Deadwood, S.D., 1956-57; free-lance writer and humorist in Belle Fourche, S.D., 1969—. Belle Fourche Independent School District, member of board, 1969-74, president, 1972-74; press secretary for South Dakota U.S. Senate candidate, spring, 1974; chairperson of South Dakota Commission on the Status of Women, 1975—. *Member:* South Dakota Press Women Association.

WRITINGS: What's a Place Like This Doing to a Nice Girl Like Me?, Abbey Press, 1973. Contributor of articles and reviews to *Good Housekeeping, PTA Magazine, MS, American School Board Journal, Education Digest, Denver Post, Rapid City Journal*, and other publications. Contributor of regular humor column, "Marriage Go Round," to *Marriage and Family Living*, 1974—.

WORK IN PROGRESS: A short satirical novel, *The Clean Water Caper*; with Marilynn Sawin, editing letters from women covering the years 1953-74, tentatively titled *Letters from a Generation*.

SIDELIGHTS: Lorraine Collins told *CA*: "The full flowering of the feminist movement has caught me, and a lot of my friends, on the far side of forty. We find the movement articulating some of the things we've thought and experienced for a long time, but there's a generation gap here, too. If there is any coherence and unity to my life and career (a presumption it isn't safe to make) I'd have to say that by spending years alternating my time and attention between the laundry room, the boardroom, and the typewriter, I'm personally and professionally well prepared to do something definitive and creative in the cause of American womanhood. It's what I want to do. Maybe, I tell myself, it's all going to make sense at last."

* * *

COLMAN, E(rnest) A(drian) M(ackenzie) 1930-

PERSONAL: Born December 8, 1930, in Glasgow, Scotland; son of Ernest (a company secretary) and Rhoda Mackenzie (Corbett) Colman; married Maureen Mary Caldwell (an educational administrator), March 21, 1954; children: Juliet (Mrs. Zigurds P. Richters), David, Randal. *Education:* University of Glasgow, M.A. (honors), 1952; University of New South Wales, Ph.D., 1970. *Religion:* Agnostic. *Office:* Department of English, University of Sydney, Sydney, Australia 2006.

CAREER: Fibre Building Board Development Organization, London, England, industrial journalist, 1954-62; University of New South Wales, Sydney, Australia, lecturer in English, 1962-71; University of Sydney, Sydney, Australia, senior lecturer, 1971-74, associate professor of English literature, 1975—. Chairman of board of Australian Theatre for Young People, 1974-75. *Military service:* British Army, 1952-57; became first lieutenant. *Member:* Australasian Universities' Language and Literature Association. *Awards, honors:* Australian Academy of Humanities grant-in-aid, 1970.

WRITINGS: The Structure of Shakespeare's "Antony and Cleopatra", English Association, (Sydney), 1971; The Dramatic Use of Bawdy in Shakespeare, Longman, 1974. Author of plays: "Julius Caesar in Rehearsal" (two-act), first produced in Sydney, Australia at Independent Theatre, 1965; and "The Shylock Affair" (one-act), first produced in Perth, Western Australia at New Fortune Theatre, 1968. Contributor to professional journals. Co-editor of Poetry (Australia; now titled New Poetry), 1965-68. Adaptor of works of Shakespeare and other Elizabethan dramatists for Australian Broadcasting Commission.

WORK IN PROGRESS: Editing anthology, Residing Myth: A Collection of Poems Based on Shakespeare.

SIDELIGHTS: "Julius Caesar in Rehearsal" was adapted as a four-part television series for Australian Broadcasting Commission, 1965. Avocational interests: Indonesian theatre, German opera (particularly Wagner), carpentry.

* * *

COLTON, Helen 1918-

PERSONAL: Born January 4, 1918, in Newark, N.J.; daughter of Sander (a truck driver) and Rose (Colton) Grossman; married Martin Field, November 19, 1942 (divorced, March, 1965); married Irvin E. Good (a designer of metal art work), October 9, 1969; children: (first marriage) Mona, Corey. Education: Attended University of California, Los Angeles, c.1954, Los Angeles City College, 1964. Politics: Liberal Democrat. Religion: Jewish. Home and office: 1539 North Courtney Ave., Los Angeles, Calif. 90046.

CAREER: California State Department of Education teaching credential in family relations, 1969; Family Forum, Los Angeles, Calif., founder and director, 1964—, therapist, 1970—; Teacher at Institute for Comprehensive Medicine, 1974-75. Member of Western Regional Conference on the Ombudsman, 1968—, Los Angeles City Commission on Human Relations, 1968—, and of Los Angeles Citizen's Advisory Committee on Education, 1968—. Lecturer at University of California at Los Angeles Experimental College, San Diego, University of Washington, Seattle, University of Redlands, International University in San Diego, Fort Wright College, Los Angeles City College, Pepperdine University, San Diego City College, Western Arizona College, University of Nevada at Las Vegas, Eastern Washington State University, Mt. Angel College, Institute for Science of Living, Everywoman's Village, and Westwood Temple. Consultant to Family Communication Skills Center.

MEMBER: International Academy of Forensic Psychology, International Transactional Analysis Association, National Conference on Family Relations, Society for Humane Abortion (honorary member of board of directors, 1969—), Association for Humanistic Psychology, American Association of Sex Educators and Counselors, Society for Psychosomatic Medicine and Dentistry, Society for Scientific Study of Sex, American Federation of Radio and Television Artists, Los Angeles Transactional Analysis Association. Awards, honors: Sc.D., National Christian University, 1974.

WRITINGS: What's on Woman's Future Agenda?, Family Forum, 1967, revised edition, 1970; Adults Need Sex Education Too, Family Forum, 1970; Our Sexual Evolution, F. Watts, 1972; Sex after the Sexual Revolution, Association Press, 1973. Sex education columnist for Coronet. Contributor of more than two hundred articles and reviews to Forum, New York Times, Variety, Harper's Bazaar, McCall's, Reader's Digest, Good Housekeeping, Mademoiselle, Coronet, Redbook, and other periodicals. Editor of Hollywood Press-Times, 1950.

WORK IN PROGRESS: With Dina Mellon, Transactional Analysis.

SIDELIGHTS: Helen Colton is the host on her nationally syndicated television show, "Joys of Living." Avocational interests: Folk dancing, travel, architecture.

* * *

COLVIN, Ian G. 1912-1975

November 23, 1912—April 20, 1975; British journalist and author of works on contemporary world affairs. Obituaries: AB Bookman's Weekly, June 2, 1975. (CA-19/20)

* * *

COMFORT, Montgomery
See CAMPBELL, (John) Ramsey

* * *

COMPLO, Sister Jannita Marie 1935-

PERSONAL: Born July 22, 1935, in Monroe, Mich.; daughter of Daniel John (a laborer) and Mary Lena Complo. Education: Marygrove College, B.A., 1957; Wayne State University, M.Ed., 1968, Ed.D., 1971. Office: Department of Education, Marygrove College, Detroit, Mich.

CAREER: Roman Catholic nun of Immaculate Heart of Mary (I.H.M.), 1953—. School teacher in Michigan, 1957-67, supervising teacher, 1962-67; Marygrove College, Detroit, Mich., instructor, 1967-71, assistant professor, 1971-75, associate professor of education, 1975—, director of Creative Arts Summer Workshop, 1968-69, director of elementary student teaching, 1968-75; coordinator of elementary education, 1975—. Director of education and drug abuse workshops in Michigan. Member: American Association of University Professors, National Council of Teachers of English, Association of Teacher Educators, Immaculate Heart of Mary Educational Association, Michigan Association for Student Teaching, International Reading Association (Monroe County, Mich.).

WRITINGS: Creative Writing for the Primary Teachers, Archdiocesan Publications, 1967; Dramakinetics in the Primary Classroom, Wayne State University Press, 1971; Dramakinetics in the Classroom; A Handbook of Creative Dramatics and Improvised Movement, Plays, 1974. Contributor to Arithmetic Teacher, Instructor, Elementary English, Drama for Young Readers, and Teacher.

WORK IN PROGRESS: The Sunflower Grows, for children; researching a creative movement for in-service teachers; a comparison of two methods for creative writing in the first grade; an evaluative study in the use of creative dramatics toward the total personality development of the child; a creative arts workshop for elementary school children; research on the design and validation of a curriculum which would provide the classroom teacher with content and specific methods for the basic teaching of dramatic movement.

SIDELIGHTS: Sister Jannita Complo writes that she has "... given many demonstrations in-state and out-of-state to teachers, administrators, parents of the normal child, emotionally impaired, mentally impaired, pre-school child, and children in religious education programs. There is a desperate need to develop the affective domain and psychomotor domain as well as the cognitive domain for children. Through Dramakinetics Workshops I hope to inspire many in this way of thinking.

"Dramakinetics is a method of teaching which helps all children to creatively express themselves. All children have one basic channel of expression—their bodies. It is through the use of their bodies that feelings, emotions, and thoughts can be expressed."

*   *   *

CONDE, Jesse C(lay) 1912-

PERSONAL: Born May 25, 1912, in Everett, Mass.; son of Jesse C., Sr. and Cecelia (Stock) Conde; married Isadore G. Rymer, October 28, 1939. *Education:* Massachusetts Maritime School, graduate, 1932; Sperry Gyroscope School, graduate, 1932; attended Boeing School of Aeronautics, 1937, and several aviation technical schools, 1947-50. *Home:* 156 Starlite Dr., San Mateo, Calif. 94402. *Office:* Glenwood Publishers, P.O. Box 194, Felton, Calif. 95018.

CAREER: Worked for several steamship companies in various capacities, including seaman, quartermaster, carpenter, and third mate, 1932-36; worked as an aircraft instrument man, systems instructor, and flight engineer for various aircraft companies, 1943-72. Employed as civilian flight engineer by U.S. Army Air Forces, 1943-47; later involved in Korean Airlift, 1950-51, and Saigon support, 1967-68. *Member:* National Model Railroad Association, Railway & Locomotive Historical Society, National Railroad Historical Society, Hawaiian Historical Society, Lahaina Foundation Group.

WRITINGS—All published by Glenwood: *Narrow Gauge in a Kingdom: The Hawaiian Railroad Company, 1878-1897*, 1971; *Sugar Trains Narrow Gauge Rails of Hawaii*, 1973; *Sugar Trains Pictorial*, 1975.

WORK IN PROGRESS: Cadet Daze.

*   *   *

CONE, William F. 1919-

PERSONAL: Born August 23, 1919, in Caruthersville, Mo.; son of William Louis (a farm worker) and Anna (Jones) Cone; married Norma Smith (a library technician), April 16, 1944; children: Carolyn (Mrs. Mark A. Brown), Barbara, Jeffrey. *Education:* University of California, Los Angeles, M.A., 1954. *Politics:* "Democrat: Wilsonian; Rooseveltian; Trumanian." *Religion:* American Lutheran. *Home:* 537 North Stanford Ave., Fullerton, Calif. 92631.

CAREER: Hughes Aircraft Co., Fullerton, Calif., head of professional resources and development, 1959—. Professor at Fullerton Community College, 1972—; adviser to Los Angeles Technical College and Orange Coast College. Director of community affairs for Fullerton Chamber of Commerce, 1969-70; member of board of directors of local Young Men's Christian Association (YMCA), 1968-71. *Military service:* U.S. Coast Guard Reserve, active duty, 1942-45; became chief petty officer; received Philippine Liberation Medal. *Member:* Southern California Technical Personnel Committee (chairman, 1968-69), University of California, Los Angeles Orange County Alumni Association, Phi Beta Kappa.

WRITINGS: Supervising Employees Effectively, Addison-Wesley, 1974. Contributor to engineering, education, and management journals.

WORK IN PROGRESS: Improving Communication at Work.

SIDELIGHTS: Cone writes: "Productivity in any organization measures the leadership capacity of first line supervision. To improve productivity, the organization must gain the commitment of first-line supervisors, and then provide them with the tools and training to accomplish the production goals. My own commitment is toward improving productivity through improved leadership at all levels."

*   *   *

CONFUCIUS
See LUND, Philip R(eginald)

*   *   *

CONGREVE, Willard J(ohn) 1921-

PERSONAL: Born August 16, 1921, in Chicago, Ill.; son of Willard (a manufacturer) and Anna Marie (Johannsen) Congreve; married Beth Olsen, June 6, 1950; children: Judith Ann, Linda Sue. *Education:* Chicago Teachers College, B.Ed., 1942; Northwestern University, M. Music, 1947; Eastman School of Music, further study, summers, 1948, 1949; University of Chicago, Ph.D., 1957. *Religion:* Protestant. *Residence:* Hammond, Ind. *Office:* Hammond School City, 5935 Hohman, Hammond, Ind. 46320.

CAREER: Midland Lutheran College, Fremont, Neb., assistant professor of music, 1947-49; Chicago public schools, Chicago, Ill., high school teacher of music and department head, 1949-58, principal of elementary schools, 1958-60; University of Chicago, Chicago, Ill., principal of University High School and assistant director of Laboratory Schools, 1960-67, associate professor of education, Graduate School of Education, 1960-69; Newton Community School District, Newton, Iowa, superintendent, 1969-72; Washington Township School District, Gloucester County, N.J., superintendent, 1972-75; Hammond School District, Hammond, Ind., superintendent, 1975—. Part-time lecturer at Chicago Teachers College, 1958-65, and Illinois Teachers College, 1965-68. Church organist or organist and choirmaster, 1946-49, 1952-72; ruling elder, United Presbyterian Church of America. *Military service:* U.S. Army Air Forces, 1942-46; received Bronze Star. U.S. Army, 1951-52; became second lieutenant.

MEMBER: American Association of School Administrators, National Society for the Study of Education, American Educational Research Association, Phi Delta Kappa, Pi Kappa Lambda, Phi Mu Alpha, Rotary International, Optimists Club.

WRITINGS: (With George J. Rinehart) *Flexibility in School Programs*, Wadsworth, 1972.

Contributor: David W. Beggs III and Edward G. Buffie, editors, *Independent Study: Bold New Venture*, Indiana University Press, 1965; Leslie W. Kindred, editor, *The Intermediate Schools*, Prentice-Hall, 1968; Roald F. Campbell, L. A. Marx, and R. L. Nystrand, *Education and Urban Renaissance*, Wiley, 1968; Madan Mogan and Ronald E. Hull, editors, *Individualized Instruction and Learning*, Nelson-Hall, 1974. Contributor to *Education and Urban Society* and other journals.

WORK IN PROGRESS: Developing a series of "how to" booklets to enable parents to deal with school issues and problems.

SIDELIGHTS: Congreve has studied Russian schools in Moscow, Leningrad, and elsewhere, and primary schools in

England. *Avocational interests:* Working on cars, gardening, canoe trips, playing the piano and organ "to maintain equilibrium."

* * *

CONN, Canary Denise 1949-
(Canary)

PERSONAL: Born August 24, 1949, in Boise, Idaho. *Agent:* Dick Irving Hyland, 8961 Sunset Blvd., Los Angeles, Calif. 90069. *Office address:* P.O. Box 69902, Los Angeles, Calif. 90069.

CAREER: Author, singer, songwriter, lecturer, musician, and sound impressionist.

WRITINGS: Canary: The Story of a Transsexual, Nash Publishing, 1974. Author of "The Hollywood Cage," a column for *Hollywood Citizen News*, 1972-74.

WORK IN PROGRESS: Love Song 1864 and *The Black Hole of Calcutta*, historical novels; *Mirror-Mirror*, a thriller novel.

* * *

CONN, Charles Paul 1945-

PERSONAL: Born December 23, 1945, in Leadwood, Mo.; son of Charles W. (an educator) and Edna (Minor) Conn; married Darlia McLuhan, August 15, 1967; children: Vanessa, Heather, Brian. *Education:* Lee College, B.A., 1967; Emory University, M.A., 1970, Ph.D., 1974. *Politics:* Democrat. *Religion:* Pentecostal. *Home:* 450 Apache Tr., Cleveland, Tenn. 37311. *Office:* Department of Psychology, Lee College, Cleveland, Tenn. 37311.

CAREER: Lee College, Cleveland, Tenn., assistant professor of psychology, 1971—.

WRITINGS: The Music Makers, Pathway Press,·1971; (with Sammy Hall) *Hooked on a Good Thing*, Revell, 1972; *The New Johnny Cash*, Revell, 1973; (with Terry Bradshaw) *No Easy Game*, Revell, 1973.

* * *

CONROW, Robert 1942-

PERSONAL: Born February 24, 1942, in Pasadena, Calif.; son of Willard and Eleanor Francis (McFedries) Conrow; married Virginia J. Paley (a potter), June 23, 1975; children: Aaron. *Education:* Macalester College, B.A., 1964; University of Michigan, M.A., 1968, Ph.D., 1972. *Home:* 354 Richard Ter., Grand Rapids, Mich. 49506. *Office:* William James College, Grand Valley State Colleges, Allendale, Mich. 49401.

CAREER: Grand Valley State Colleges, William James College, Allendale, Mich., professor of literature, history, and video, 1972—.

WRITINGS: Field Days: The Life, Times and Reputation of Eugene Field, Scribner, 1974.

* * *

CONSILVIO, Thomas 1947-

PERSONAL: Born December 22, 1947, in Boston, Mass.; son of Felix J. (a teacher) and Nancy (Gulino) Consilvio; married Jenethen G. Pearl, April 26, 1970; children: Amos, Eli. *Education:* Attended Boston University, 1965-67. *Home:* 4 Camelot Court, Boston, Mass. 02135.

CAREER: Free-lance commercial photographer in Boston, Mass., 1968—. Teacher of photography at Massachusetts College of Art, summer, 1975.

WRITINGS: Snapshooters, Mouse Press, 1973; *Creative Camera* (portfolio), Coo Press Ltd., 1974.

WORK IN PROGRESS: Photographing people in leisure activities; photographing movie directors.

SIDELIGHTS: Consilvio traveled and photographed throughout the United States from 1967-68, Italy in 1972, and Canada and England in 1973. He had a one-man exhibit at the Orson Welles Gallery in Cambridge, Mass., in 1974.

* * *

COOK, Chris(topher) 1945-

PERSONAL: Born June 20, 1945, in Leicester, England; son of William and Kathleen (Chatterton) Cook. *Education:* St. Catharine's College, Cambridge, B.A., 1967, M.A., 1970; Oriel College and Nuffield College, Oxford, D.Phil., 1970. *Politics:* Labor. *Religion:* Anglican. *Residence:* Surrey, England. *Agent:* Hilary Rubinstein, A. P. Watt and Co., 26-28 Bedford Row, London, England. *Office:* London School of Economics and Political Science, University of London, Houghton St., London W.C.2, England.

CAREER: Oxford University, Magdalen College, Oxford, England, lecturer in politics, 1969-70; London School of Economics and Political Science, London, England, senior research officer, 1970—.

WRITINGS: (Editor with David McKie) *The Decade of Disillusion*, Macmillan, 1972; (editor with John Ramsden) *By-Elections in British Politics*, Macmillan, 1973; (with John Paxton) *European Political Facts: 1918-1973*, Macmillan, 1975; (editor with Gillian Peele) *The Politics of Reappraisal: 1918-1939*, Macmillan, 1975; (with Brendan Keith) *British Historical Facts: 1830-1900*, Macmillan, 1975; (with Philip Jones) *Sources in British Political History*, three volumes, Macmillan, 1975—; *The Age of Alignment: Electoral Politics in Britain, 1922-1929*, Macmillan, 1975; *The Liberal Party: 1900-1975*, Macmillan, 1975; (with John Stevenson) *Atlas of Modern British History*, Longmans, Green, 1976. Co-editor of *Pears Cyclopaedia*, 1974—.

WORK IN PROGRESS: The Slump: Society and Politics during the Depression; *British Historical Facts, 1714-1830*, with John Stevenson; *English Historical Facts, 1485-1603*, with Ken Powell.

* * *

COOK, David C(harles) III 1912-

PERSONAL: Born June 11, 1912, in Elgin, Ill.; son of David Charles, Jr. (a publisher) and Frances Lois (in publishing business; maiden name, Kerr) Cook; married Betty Mae Crume; children: Martha Lynn Cook Beattie, Margaret Anne Cook Canary, Bruce Lawrence, Gregory Douglas, Rebecca Jane. *Education:* Occidental College, student, 1930-32; University of Chicago, Ph.B., 1934. *Religion:* Methodist. *Home:* 32 River Bluff Rd., Elgin, Ill. 60120. *Office:* David C. Cook Publishing Co., 850 North Grove Ave., Elgin, Ill. 60120.

CAREER: David C. Cook Publishing Co., Elgin, Ill., editor, 1934, president and editor-in-chief of publications, 1935—. President of David C. Cook Foundation, 1945—. Director of Youth Study Tour Cultural Travel Foundation, 1935; trustee of Judson College. *Member:* Phi Kappa Psi. *Awards, honors:* Litt.D. from Judson College, 1965.

WRITINGS: Walk the High Places, David Cook, 1964; *Invisible Halos*, David Cook, 1975. Contributor to Sunday school and church publications.

SIDELIGHTS: For the David C. Cook Foundation, Cook has traveled to Europe, the Middle East and Far East, Latin America, Africa, Australasia, and Indonesia. He writes: "The Foundation's program functions primarily among Third World nations emphasizing indigenous development in Christian literature, literacy and leadership training. The present Foundation program reaches people in every continent and in over a hundred languages." The publishing company Cook heads was founded by his grandfather in 1875.

* * *

COOK, Hugh C(hristopher) B(ult) 1910-

PERSONAL: Born March 24, 1910, in Nuneaton, Warwickshire, England; son of Frederick Charles and May (Bult) Cook; married Elspeth Ballard, March 9, 1934 (divorced August, 1953); married Maxine Payne, November 7, 1953; children: (first marriage) Timothy C. B., Martin R. B., Simon H. B. *Education:* Educated in England. *Politics:* "Independent, with conservative sympathies." *Religion:* Church of England. *Home:* Radhurst Grange, Barton under Needwood, Staffordshire, England. *Office:* R.H.Q. Staffordshire Regiment, Whittington Barracks, Lichfield, Staffordshire, England.

CAREER: British Army, South Staffordshire Regiment, career officer, 1932-61; served in India, 1933-39, in United Kingdom, Western Europe, and Norway, 1939-45; instructor at Army Staff College, 1943-44, and R.A.F. Staff College, 1943; served in Austria, Palestine, Hong Kong, Japan, and Korea, 1945-52; military attache in Saigon, 1959-61; retired as colonel. Employed as Staffordshire Regimental secretary and curator of Regimental Museum, Staffordshire, England, 1961-75. *Member:* Society of Army Historical Research, Military Historical Society. *Awards, honors:* Liberty Cross of Norway, 1945; Officer of the Order of the British Empire, 1955.

WRITINGS: The North Staffordshire Regiment, Leo Cooper Ltd., 1970; *The Sikh Wars,* Leo Cooper Ltd., 1975. Contributor to military history journals. Editor, *Stafford Knot,* 1966-75.

WORK IN PROGRESS: The Battle Honours of the 1914-1918 War, for Leo Cooper Ltd.

* * *

COOK, Joan Marble 1920-

PERSONAL: Born April 8, 1920, in Boston, Mass.; daughter of Henry O. (a surgeon) and Alice (Ingram) Marble; married Robert H. Cook, Jr. (a sculptor), March 10, 1951; children: Jennifer, Henry Marble. *Education:* Smith College, B.A., 1941. *Politics:* Democrat. *Religion:* "Quaker—by birth." *Home:* Piazza Borghese 91, Rome, Italy. *Agent:* McIntosh & Otis, Inc., 18 East 41st St., New York, N.Y. 10017.

CAREER: Journalist; has worked for United Press International. *Member:* Foreign Press Club (Rome).

WRITINGS: In Defense of Homo Sapiens, Farrar, Straus, 1975. Contributor to magazines and newspapers, including *Op Ed* and *New York Times Sunday.*

WORK IN PROGRESS: The View from 99, a utopia; research on primate behavior.

* * *

COOKE, (Alfred) Alistair 1908-

PERSONAL: Born November 20, 1908, in Manchester, England; came to United States in 1938; naturalized in 1941; son of Samuel (a Wesleyan preacher) and Mary Elizabeth (Byrne) Cooke; married Ruth Emerson, August 24, 1934; married Jane White Hawkes, April 30, 1946; children: (first marriage) John Byrne; (second marriage) Susan Byrne. *Education:* Jesus College, Cambridge, B.A. (summa cum laude), 1930, Diploma in Education, 1931; graduate study at Yale University, 1932-33, and Harvard University, 1933-34. *Home:* Nassau Point, Cutchogue, N.Y. 11935; and 1150 Fifth Ave., New York, N.Y. 10028.

CAREER: British Broadcasting Corp. (BBC), London, England, film critic, 1934-37, commentator on American affairs, 1938—, broadcaster of "Letters from America," 1947—. London correspondent for National Broadcasting Co., 1936-37; special correspondent for *London Times,* 1938-40; American feature writer for *London Daily Herald,* 1941-43; *Manchester Guardian* (now *Guardian*), United Nations correspondent, 1945-48, chief U.S. correspondent, 1948-72. Master of ceremonies for Ford Foundation weekly television series, "Omnibus," 1952-61; host for United Nations television series, "International Zone," 1961-67, and for television series "Masterpiece Theatre," 1971—; writer and narrator of television series "America: A Personal History of the United States," 1972-73.

MEMBER: National Press Club (Washington), Savile Club and Athenaeum Club (both London), Royal and Ancient Golf Club (St. Andrews). *Awards, honors:* Commonwealth Fund fellow, 1932-33, and 1933-34; Peabody award, 1952, for international news reporting; "Emmy" award, 1958; four "Emmy" awards, 1973, for "America"; Benjamin Franklin medal of the Royal Society of Arts, 1973; LL.D. from University of Edinburgh, 1969, and University of Manchester, 1973; Knight Commander, Order of the British Empire.

WRITINGS: (Compiler and editor) *Garbo and the Night Watchmen: A Selection from the Writings of British and American Film Critics,* J. Cape, 1937, new edition, Secker & Warburg, 1971, published as *Garbo and the Night Watchmen: A Selection Made in 1937 from the Writings of British and American Film Critics,* McGraw-Hill, 1971; *Douglas Fairbanks: The Making of a Screen Character,* Museum of Modern Art, 1940; *A Generation on Trial: U.S.A. v. Alger Hiss,* Knopf, 1950, 2nd edition, 1952, enlarged 2nd edition, Penguin, 1968; (contributor) John Gehlmann, editor, *Challenge of Ideas,* Odyssey, 1950; *Letters from America* (radio essays), Hart-Davis, 1951; *One Man's America* (radio essays), Knopf, 1952; *Christmas Eve* (short stories), Knopf, 1952; *A Commencement Address,* Knopf, 1954; (compiler) *The Vintage Mencken,* Vintage, 1955; *Around the World in Fifty Years: A Political Travelogue,* limited edition, Field Enterprises, 1966; *Talk about America* (radio essays), Knopf, 1968; *General Eisenhower on the Military Churchill: A Conversation with Alistair Cooke,* edited by James Nelson, Norton, 1970; *America,* Knopf, 1973. Author of weekly column in *Listener.* Contributor of articles to *Theatre Arts Monthly, New Republic, Encore, Fortnightly Review,* and *Spectator.*

SIDELIGHTS: Said Gerald Johnson: "Alistair Cooke is technically an essayist, or in modern parlance, a commentator, but in non-technical fact he is a translator. He speaks American like a native and British is, of course, his mother tongue. Thus he has been able to weld these two dialects of English into a medium of communication as smooth as optical glass and usually as clear." Basil Boothroyd states: "He has other qualities, all admirable. The journalist's observing eye and questing mind, the literate man's insistence on the only word that will do, an objectivity touched with the compassion for human follies that redeems it from the icy Olympian, no discernible egotism, and an almost theatrical instinct for the dramatic stroke of presentation.''

Wanting originally to be an actor, Cooke helped found the Cambridge University Mummers (a dramatic society) in 1928, and spent part of his Commonwealth Fund study on dramatic research. Instead, he became the premier journalistic liaison for two continents. Broadcasting from Britain and Europe, Cooke told Americans about the abdication of King Edward VIII, the Munich Conference, and the Wimbledon tennis matches. Broadcasting from America, he described to the British how the average American was being affected by World War II. In 1942, he took a 20,000 mile, six month automobile tour through the United States to gather information for his radio broadcasts. In 1944, he helped start the BBC program ''Transatlantic Quiz,'' which further stimulated cross-cultural exchange.

Asked about his reading habits, Cooke once stated; ''I'm one of those people who loves reading dictionaries. The *Official Airline Guide* is one of my favorites, too. . . . I'm a rampant and compulsive reader. . . . If you're a newspaper writer, you've got to read. Just to rinse the newspaper jargon out of your mind; otherwise you're going to be a poor writer. I read books as a sort of literary Water-Pic. And I tell you quite on the level, I get more pleasure out of the Old Testament than most current fare, because in spite of the fact that it's 17th century and quite often ornate, it can be marvelously simple.''

AVOCATIONAL INTERESTS: Golf, photography, music, motion pictures, beachcombing, the American West, travel, chess.*

* * *

COOKE, Barbara
See ALEXANDER, Anna B(arbara Cooke)

* * *

COON, Stephen 1948-

PERSONAL: Born November 5, 1948, in Great Lakes, Ill.; son of William D., Jr. (formerly in U.S. Marine Corps) and Elve (Kaski) Coon. *Education:* University of California, Irvine, B.A. (summa cum laude), 1970; Brown University, Ph.D., 1975. *Home:* 135 Transit St., Providence, R.I. 02906.

CAREER: Writer. *Member:* Modern Language Association of America, American Comparative Literature Association. *Awards, honors:* Woodrow Wilson fellowship, 1970.

WRITINGS: (Editor with David Cloutier, and contributor of translations) *The Ear of the Bull: Nine French Poets*, Bonewhistle Press, 1974. Contributor to *Incarnations* and *Kumanitu*.

WORK IN PROGRESS: Research on a poetics of visionary writing, with special attention to Blake, Rimbaud, Lautreamont, Michaux, and Burroughs.

* * *

COOPER, Joseph D(avid) 1917-1975

May 25, 1917—March 25, 1975; American educator, civil servant, technical expert in photography, and author. Obituaries: *Washington Post*, March 28, 1975. (*CA*-5/6)

COOVER, James B(urrell) 1925-
(C. B. James)

PERSONAL: Born June 3, 1925, in Jacksonville, Ill.; son of James V. (a printer) and F. Elizabeth (Burrell) Coover; married Georgena Walker (a childhood specialist), September 28, 1945; children: Christopher, Mauri, Regan. *Education:* Northern Colorado University, B.A., 1949, M.A., 1950; University of Denver, M.A., 1953. *Home:* 111 Marjann Ter., Tonawanda, N.Y. 14223. *Office:* Music Department, State University of New York, Buffalo, N.Y. 14214.

CAREER: Bibliographical Center for Research, Denver, Colo., assistant director, 1950-53; Vassar College, George Sherman Dickinson Library, director, 1953-67; State University of New York at Buffalo, professor of music, 1967—. Manager and player with Hudson Valley Philharmonic Orchestra, 1959-67. Member of New York State Council on the Arts, 1964-65, consultant, 1965-68; member of Mayor's Commission on the Arts, Poughkeepsie, N.Y., 1965-67. *Military service:* U.S. Army, 1943-45; served in European theater. *Member:* Association Internationale des bibliotheques musicales, American Association of University Professors, Music Library Association (president, 1959-60).

WRITINGS: Photoduplication Services: A Survey, 1951, Bibliographical Center for Research, 1951; *A Bibliography of Music Dictionaries*, Bibliographical Center for Research, 1952, 3rd edition published as *Music Lexicography*, Carlisle Books, 1971; *Provisional Checklist of Medieval and Renaissance Music on Long-Playing Records* (pamphlet), Vassar College, 1957; (compiler) *'Festschriften': A Provisional Checklist of Those Proposed for Indexing* (pamphlet), Vassar College, 1958; *Music Lexicography Including a Study of Lacunae: 1500-1700*, Bibliographical Center for Research, 1958; (editor) *The 'Rainbeau' Catalog*, Distant Press, 1962; (author of appendix) Johannes Tinctoris, *Terminorum musicae diffinitorium* (title means ''Dictionary of Musical Terms''), Free Press, 1963; (with Richard Colvig) *Medieval and Renaissance Music on Long-Playing Records*, Information Service, 1964; (contributor) C. J. Bradley, editor, *Manual of Music Librarianship*, Music Library Association, 1966; *Gesamtausgaben: A Checklist*, Distant Press, 1970; (with Colvig) *Medieval and Renaissance Music on Long-Playing Records: Supplement, 1962-1971*, Information Coordinators, 1973; (contributor) Bradley, editor, *Reader in Music Librarianship*, Microcard Editions, 1974; (author of preface) Guy A. Marco, *Information on Music*, Kent State University Press, 1974; *Guide to Basic Information Sources in Music*, Holt, 1975; (contributor) *Grove's Dictionary of Music and Musicians*, 6th edition, Macmillan, in press. Contributor of articles and reviews to music and library journals. Under pseudonym C. B. James, author of ''The Hardcore Index.''

* * *

COPE, Myron 1929-

PERSONAL: Born January 23, 1929, in Pittsburgh, Pa.; son of Ellis A. (in insurance) and Elizabeth (Schaeffer) Kopelman; married Mildred Lindberg, December 28, 1964; children: Martha Anne (deceased), Daniel Lawrence, Elizabeth Ann. *Education:* University of Pittsburgh, B.A., 1951. *Residence:* Upper St. Clair Twp., Pa. *Agent:* Sterling Lord Agency, 660 Madison Ave., New York, N.Y. 10021. *Office:* WTAE-Radio and Television, 400 Ardmore Blvd., Pittsburgh, Pa. 15230.

CAREER: Reporter, Erie Times, Erie, Pa., 1951, and Pittsburgh Post-Gazette, Pittsburgh, Pa., 1951-61; free-lance writer, 1961—, contributing regularly to Saturday Evening Post, 1963, and to Sports Illustrated, 1965; sports commentator, WTAE-Radio and Television, Pittsburgh, 1968—. Member: American Federation of Television and Radio Artists, Football Writers Association of America, Pittsburgh Radio-Television Club, Pittsburgh Press Club. Awards, honors: E. P. Dutton Prize, 1962, for sports magazine writing; award for outstanding sportscaster in Pittsburgh, from American Federation of Television and Radio Artists, 1971.

WRITINGS: (With Jim Brown) Off My Chest, Doubleday, 1964; Broken Cigars, Prentice-Hall, 1968; The Game That Was, World Publishing, 1970, revised edition, Crowell, 1974; Myron Cope's Super Steeler Year, privately printed, 1975. Contributor to sports magazines.

* * *

COPELAND, Melvin T. 1884-1975

July 17, 1884—March 27, 1975; American educator, and author of works on business topics. Obituaries: New York Times, March 29, 1975; AB Bookman's Weekly, April 28, 1975. (CA-21/22)

* * *

COPMAN, Louis 1934-

PERSONAL: Born January 17, 1934, in Philadelphia, Pa.; son of Jacob (a clothing cutter) and Eve (Snyder) Copman; married Avera Schuster, June 8, 1958; children: Mark, Linda. Education: University of Pennsylvania, B.A., 1955, M.D., 1959. Religion: Jewish. Home: 50 Sunshine Rd., Southampton, Pa. 18966. Office: Naval Regional Medical Center, Philadelphia, Pa. 19145.

CAREER: Licensed to practice medicine in Pennsylvania, New Jersey, Maryland, and California; U.S. Navy, Medical Corps, 1958-69, radiologist at U.S. Naval Hospital, Pensacola, Fla., 1966-69, leaving service as commander; Doctors Hospital, Philadelphia, Pa., radiologist, 1969-73; Mercer Medical Center, Trenton, N.J., radiologist, 1973-75; U.S. Navy, Medical Corps, radiologist at Naval Regional Medical Center, Philadelphia, Pa., 1975—; current rank, captain. Diplomate of American Board of Radiology, 1967. Member: American College of Radiology, Radiological Society of North America, American Medical Association, Phi Beta Kappa, Alpha Omega Alpha.

WRITINGS: (Contributor) James D. Hardy, editor, Temperature in Biology and Medicine, Reinhold, 1963; The Cuckold (novel), Ashley Books, 1975. Contributor to medical journals.

WORK IN PROGRESS: A humorous science fiction novel, The Schnook.

* * *

CORINA, Maurice 1936-

PERSONAL: Born June 10, 1936, in London, England; son of John (a company director) and Kathleen Corina; married Mavis Jean Franklin, November 14, 1955; children: Judith, Susan Diane. Education: Attended University of London. Religion: Church of England. Home: Orchard Piece, Blackmore Village, Blackmore, Essex, England. Agent: Murray Pollinger, Laurence Pollinger Ltd., 11 Long Acre, London WC2E 9LH, England. Office: Times, New Printing House Sq., Grays Inn Rd., London, England.

CAREER: London night editor of Liverpool Daily Post, Liverpool, England, and commercial correspondent for Financial Times, London, England; presently industrial editor for Times, London. Secretary for Fleet Street Industrial Correspondents Group. Radio and television broadcaster. Military service: British Army, Royal Service Corps. Awards, honors: National Proficiency Award from Council for Journalists.

WRITINGS: Pile It High: Sell It Cheap, Wiedenfeld & Nicolson, 1972; Trust in Tobacco, St. Martin's, 1975. Contributor to popular magazines.

WORK IN PROGRESS: Politics of Prices; a biography of Wedgewood Benn, British cabinet minister.

* * *

CORNWALL, E(spie) Judson 1924-

PERSONAL: Born August 15, 1924, in San Jose, Calif.; son of Espie James (a clergyman) and Beulah V. (Stiles) Cornwall; married Eleanor L. Eaton, June 20, 1943; children: Dorothy Darlene Cornwall Cook, Eleanor Jean (Mrs. Robert Miller), Justine (Mrs. Nobert Senftleben). Education: Attended Southern California College, 1942-44. Home and office: 223 Yorktown Rd., Tabb, Va. 23602.

CAREER: Ordained Assembly of God minister, 1948; associate pastor in Bell Gardens, Calif., 1943-44; pastor in Stirling City, Calif., 1945, Kennewick, Wash., 1946-52, Yakima, Wash., 1952-57, and Eugene, Ore., 1957-72; Charles Church, Tabb, Va., minister, 1973—. Instructor at School of the Bible, 1954-57.

WRITINGS: Let Us Praise, Logos International, 1973. Contributor to periodicals.

WORK IN PROGRESS: Let Us Abide and Let Us Draw Nigh, completion of both expected in 1976; So You Want to Minister Overseas.

SIDELIGHTS: Cornwall has traveled to twenty-two countries in the last six years. He has a private pilot's license and owned his own plane when he was on the West coast. He built the house he lived in in Eugene, Oregon, and totally rebuilt the house he lives in in Virginia. Let Us Praise has had editions in Indonesian and Spanish. Avocational interests: Gardening.

* * *

CORPORAL TRIM
See BOLGER, Philip C(unningham)

* * *

CORRIGAN, Barbara 1922-

PERSONAL: Born April 30, 1922, in Attleboro, Mass.; daughter of Owen H. (a jewelry manufacturer) and Florence (Hasler) Corrigan. Education: Massachusetts College of Art, Certificate in Design, 1944. Politics: Independent ("lean toward liberal Democrat"). Home: 18 Hayward St., Attleboro, Mass. 02703.

CAREER: Bresnick & Solomont (advertising agency), Boston, Mass., staff artist, 1944-45; free-lance designer and illustrator with own studio in Boston, Mass., 1945-61; self-employed at home in Attleboro, Mass., 1961—, first as artist, later as sewing teacher and custom dressmaker. Awards, honors: Work included in Book Jacket Designers' Guild annual exhibit, 1950, 1951, 1952.

WRITINGS—Self-illustrated: Of Course You Can Sew: Basics of Sewing for the Young Beginner, Doubleday, 1971; I Love to Sew, Doubleday, 1974.

Illustrator: Virginia Pasley, *The Christmas Cookie Book*, Atlantic-Little, Brown, 1949; Ogden Nash, *Parents Keep Out*, Little, Brown, 1951; Wilma Lord Perkins, reviser, *The Boston Cooking School Cook Book*, Little, Brown, 1951; Pasley, *The Holiday Candy Book*, Atlantic-Little, Brown, 1952; Joan Lowell, *Promised Land*, Duell, Sloan & Pearce, 1952; Ruth Wakefield, *The Toll House Cook Book*, Little, Brown, 1953; Heloise Frost, *Early American Recipes*, Phillips Publishers, 1953; L. Belle Pollard, *Experiences in Homemaking*, Ginn, 1954; Laura Sootin, *Let's Go to a Bank*, Putnam, 1957; Naomi Buchheimer, *Let's Go to the Telephone Company*, Putnam, 1958; Helen Boyd Higgins, *Old Trails and New*, Friendship, 1960; H. Allen Smith, *Waikiki Beachnik*, Little, Brown, 1960; Pollard, *Experiences with Clothing*, Ginn, 1961; Ruth Stempel, *Hello, Joe*, Whitman Publishing, 1961; Tirsa Saavedra Scott, *Como se Dice?*, Ginn, 1963; Margil Vanderhoff, *Clothes: Part of Your World*, Ginn, 1968. Also illustrator of spelling books and a sewing program published by Ginn.

WORK IN PROGRESS: How to Make Something Out of Practically Nothing, for Doubleday; research for an ecological history of a river near her home.

SIDELIGHTS: Barbara Corrigan writes: "I live with my elderly mother and two pampered cats in the gingerbready Victorian house where I was born. That may not sound very exciting, but there never seems to be enough time for all the things I would enjoy doing. I love working in the garden—even the grubby, dirty part of it. The house is on the bank of a small river, and the surroundings turn into a jungle if I don't keep at it.... I love to read (and must confess to a weakness for detective stories), do double crostics, take color photographs, listen to classical music and jazz."

* * *

CORTRIGHT, David 1946-

PERSONAL: Born November 15, 1946, in East Stroudsburg, Pa.; son of Vernon (a plumber) and Margaret (Blaney) Cortright; married Monica Heilbrunn, September, 1970 (divorced, 1973); married Tricia Cameron (a social worker), June, 1974; children: (second marriage) one. *Education:* University of Notre Dame, B.A., 1968; New York University, M.A., 1970; Union Graduate School, Ph.D., 1975. *Politics:* "Resist militarism and build democratic socialism." *Religion:* "Catholic, sort of." *Home:* 1930 Biltmore St. N.W., Apt. 4, Washington, D.C. 20009. *Office:* Center for National Security Studies, 122 Maryland Ave. N.E., Washington, D.C. 20002.

CAREER: Institute for Policy Studies, Washington, D.C., researcher and student, 1972-74; Center for National Security Studies, Washington, D.C., associate, 1974—. Military policy adviser to Pennsylvania Senatorial Campaign of Herbert Denenberg, 1974. Organized and served as chairman of GI's for Peace, at Fort Bliss, 1971; organized environmental action groups in Pennsylvania, 1972-74. *Military service:* U.S. Army, 1968-71.

WRITINGS: Soldiers in Revolt, Doubleday, 1975. Contributor to *Nation, Progressive, Society-Transaction, Working Papers for a New Society*, and *Liberation*.

WORK IN PROGRESS: Research on the military in post-industrial society and on the emergence of an international soldiers movement.

SIDELIGHTS: Cortright writes: "I'm committed to scholar-activism, to the merging of theory and practice.

Social science should be critical and should consciously strive to end injustice and oppression. I hope my work can identify and support those forces which can liberate society."

* * *

CORY, Jean-Jacques 1947-

PERSONAL: Born August 1, 1947, in Westport, Conn.; son of Jacques and Ethel (Gerber) Cory. *Politics:* "Decentralist." *Religion:* "Rationalist." *Residence:* Westport, Conn.

CAREER: Writer.

WRITINGS: Lists, Assembling Press, 1974. Work is represented in anthologies, including: *Assembling*, 1970, *Second Assembling*, 1971, *Third Assembling*, 1972, *Fourth Assembling*, 1973, and *Fifth Assembling*, 1974, all published by Assembling Press; *Future's Fictions*, Panache, 1971; *Breakthrough Fictioneers*, edited by Richard Kostelanetz, Something Else Press, 1973; *Essaying Essays*, edited by Kostelanetz, Oolp, 1975. Work is included in traveling exhibition, "Language and Structure," 1975. Contributor to *Fault, Beyond Baroque*, and *Out of Sight*.

WORK IN PROGRESS: More Lists; Particulars.

SIDELIGHTS: Cory considers himself the most rigorously experimental writer in the world, in that his work appears in only one highly restrictive form, the enumerated list.

* * *

COSGROVE, Maynard G(iles) 1895-

PERSONAL: Born June 5, 1895, in Sylvania, Ohio; son of Thomas Taylor (a physician) and Delia (Comstock) Cosgrove; married Leota May Holt, June 11, 1921; children: Margaret L., Suzanne Giles (Mrs. William R. Conrad). *Education:* University of Michigan, B.S.E.E., 1917. *Politics:* "Republican—ever after the Wilson debacle." *Religion:* Congregationalist. *Home:* 52 Covered Bridge Rd., Cherry Hill, N.J. 08034.

CAREER: Employed by electric and gas utility companies, 1918-22; valuation engineer for railroad companies, 1922-32; engineer employed in appraisal for electric and gas utility companies, 1932-39; Federal Power Commission, Washington, D.C., senior valuation engineer, 1939-65. Member of Sylvania Library Board, 1928-35.

WRITINGS: A History of Sylvania for the First Hundred Years: 1833-1933, Sentinel Publishing, 1933; *A History of the Sylvania Community Church (Congregational): 1834-1934*, Sentinel Publishing, 1934; *The Enamels of China and Japan: Champleve and Cloisonne*, Dodd, 1974.

WORK IN PROGRESS: Further research on enamels, for a revision of *The Enamels of China and Japan: Champleve and Cloisonne*.

SIDELIGHTS: Cosgrove writes: "I am a great-grandson of the first of a line of doctors who lived and practiced in Sylvania, Ohio. There is no better source of information regarding life in a small town than the background offered by a century of physicians in the family. The difficulty: to be sure to know what *not* to say . . .."

Of his third book, he writes: "Enameling is a valuable and unique form of art, especially as developed by the Chinese and the Japanese. Although this so-called 'handicraft' dates back (in China) to the fourteenth century, available literature on the subject, both native and foreign, is extremely scarce.... As early as 1926 ... the outstanding combination of artist and artisan exhibited in oriental champleve and cloisonne work fascinated me. It was not until the 1950's that I could pursue my studies." *Avocational interests:* Wood carving (sculpting in walnut, butternut, and mahogany).

*   *   *

COSSEBOOM, Kathy Groehn
  See EL-MESSIDI, Kathy Groehn

*   *   *

COUNSELL, John William   1905-

PERSONAL: Born April 24, 1905, in Beckenham, Kent, England; son of Claude Christopher (a school master) and Evelyn (Fleming) Counsell; married Mary Kerridge (an actress), July 29, 1939; children: Jennifer Mary, Elizabeth Antoinette. *Education:* Exeter College, Oxford, B.A. (second class honors), 1926. *Religion:* Church of England. *Home:* 3 Queen's Ter., Windsor, Berkshire, England. *Office:* Theatre Royal, Thames St., Windsor, Berkshire, England.

CAREER: Tutor to son of British Minister in Belgrade, Yugoslavia, 1926-27; actor with Oxford Playhouse, 1928, Shavian Repertory, 1928-29, and Northampton and Folkestone repertory companies, 1929-30; New Theatre, London, England, stage manager for "Richard III," 1930; Oxford Repertory Company, Oxford, England, stage director, designer, and director, 1930-33; Windsor Repertory Company, Windsor, England, joint managing director and producer, 1933-34; Vaudeville Theatre, London, England, stage manager for "Lover's Leap," 1934; actor in motion pictures, radio, and early television, 1935-36; touring actor, 1936-37; Theatre Royal, Windsor, England, founder and director of Windsor Theatre Company, 1938—. Director of a dozen plays in London, 1947-59. Has toured as actor, director, and producer in South Africa, Canada, United States, and Hong Kong, including a U.S. coast-to-coast tour in 1968, traveling twenty-two thousand miles and playing forty-six theaters in sixteen weeks. Governor of East Berkshire College of Further Education. *Military service:* British Army, 1940-45; became lieutenant colonel; served in North Africa, France, and Germany; received Bronze Star (U.S.). *Member:* Green Room Club. *Awards, honors:* Officer of the Order of the British Empire, 1975.

WRITINGS: Counsell's Opinion (autobiography), Barrie & Rockliff, 1963; *Play Direction,* St. Martin's, 1973.

SIDELIGHTS: As chief of post-hostilities planning section of the Operations Division of Supreme Headquarters, Allied Expeditionary Force, Counsell was responsible for advising the procedure for accepting the surrender of Germany at Rheims on May 7, 1945, and drafted the document which was used. *Avocational interests:* Photography, gardening.

*   *   *

COURTER, Gay   1944-

PERSONAL: Born October 1, 1944, in Pittsburgh, Pa.; daughter of Leonard M. (an international businessman) and Elsie (Spector) Weisman; married Philip Courter (a film director), August 18, 1968; children: Blake Zachary. *Education:* Antioch College, B.A., 1966. *Address:* Rural Delivery 1, Box 355B, Columbia, N.J. 07832. *Agent:* Julian Bach, 3 East 48th St., New York, N.Y. 10017.

CAREER: Free-lance film writer and producer (the Courters have produced more than sixty films), 1969—. Childbirth and Parent Education of New Jersey, member of board of directors, 1973, vice-president, 1975. *Member:* International Childbirth Education Association, Society of Motion Picture and Television Engineers. *Awards, honors:* American Film Festival first prize, 1974, for animation film, "Handy-Dandy Do-It-Yourself."

WRITINGS: The Beansprout Book (nonfiction), Simon & Schuster, 1973; (with husband, Philip Courter) *The Filmmaker's Craft* (textbook), Van Nostrand, 1976. Contributor to periodicals.

WORK IN PROGRESS: Surviving Motherhood, completion expected in 1977; another book on women.

SIDELIGHTS: Gay Courter and her husband have been trying to capture, on film, "the lifestyles of individuals and families with unusual vocations: a cidermaker, a gristmiller, and quiltmakers. We are also concerned with films on childbirth and parent education subjects such as postpartum, fathering, family-centered maternity care, and nutrition."

*   *   *

COVER, Robert M.   1943-

PERSONAL: Born July 30, 1943, in Boston, Mass.; son of Jacob L. (a retail salesman) and Martha (a secretary; maiden name, White) Cover; married Diane Bornstein (an artist), October 29, 1967; children: Avidan. *Education:* Princeton University, A.B., 1965; Columbia University, LL.B., 1968. *Residence:* New Haven, Conn. *Office:* School of Law, Yale University, New Haven, Conn. 06520.

CAREER: Columbia University, New York, N.Y., assistant professor of law, 1968-71; Hebrew University of Jerusalem, Jerusalem, Israel, visiting senior lecturer in law, 1971-72; Yale University, New Haven, Conn., associate professor, 1972-75, professor of law, 1975—.

WRITINGS: Justice Accused: Antislavery and the Judicial Process, Yale University Press, 1975. Contributor to *Columbia Law Review, Nation, Yale Law Journal,* and *Clearinghouse Review.*

WORK IN PROGRESS: A book on the legal history of immigration in the United States.

*   *   *

COVIN, Theron Michael   1947-

PERSONAL: Born February 27, 1947, in Repton, Ala.; son of Fisher Bert (a contractor) and Doris Covin Knight; married June Nolin (a counselor and college instructor), August 21, 1971. *Education:* Jefferson Davis Junior College, A.A., 1968; Troy State University, B.S., 1969, M.S., 1971; further graduate study at University of Alabama and Troy State University, 1972-73, and University of Utah, 1974; University of Sarasota, Ed.D., 1975. *Home address:* Route 6, Box 6048, Troy, Ala. 36081. *Office:* Department of Psychology, Troy State University, 114 McCartha Hall, Troy, Ala. 36081; and Box 439, Troy, Ala. 36081.

CAREER: Certified psychologist and psychometrist by State of Alabama Board of Education; certified humanist counselor by the American Humanist Association. Glorieta Baptist Assembly, Glorieta, N.M., assistant manager of dining hall, 1967, manager, 1968; Alabama Baptist Children's Home, Troy, assistant to director of activities, 1969-71, director of remedial education, 1970-71; Troy State University, Troy, Ala., instructor in psychology, 1971—.

Baptist minister in Skinnerton, Ala., 1969-71. Co-director of Help-a-Crisis Center, 1973—; consulting psychologist and private therapist; member of board of trustees of University of Sarasota, 1974-75.

MEMBER: International Council on Education for Teaching, National Education Association, National Collegiate Honors Council, American Association of University Professors, Association for Transpersonal Psychology, American Association on Higher Education, Institute of Society, Ethics, and the Life Sciences, National Rehabilitation Association, American Humanistic Association, Bass Anglers Sportsman Society of America, Alabama Education Association, Alabama Association on Teacher Education, Alabama Rehabilitation Association, Pike County Mental Health Association, Troy State University Education Association (vice-president, 1973-74; president, 1974-75), Kappa Delta Pi (vice-president of Zeta Gamma chapter, 1970-71), Phi Delta Kappa, Psi Lambda Psychology Club (president, 1969-71).

WRITINGS: Basic Statistics for Teachers, Troy State University Press, 1973; *Basic Statistics for Educators*, Troy State University Press, 1973; *The Psychological Case Study*, Troy State University Press, 1974; (editor) *Classroom Test Construction: A Sourcebook for Teachers*, MSS Educational Publishing, 1974; (editor) *Readings in Human Development: A Humanistic Approach*, MSS Educational Publishing, 1974; (editor) *Readings in the Psychology of Early Childhood*, MSS Educational Publishing, 1975. Managing editor of *Education Echoes* (of Troy State University).

WORK IN PROGRESS: A book, *Jesus Christ, a Communist???? and Other Essays*; a comparison of the Otis-Lennon Elementary I Level and II Level with the Wechsler Intelligence Scale for Children; a comparison of the Wide Range Achievement Test and the Wechsler Intelligence Scale for Children; a comparison of the Peabody Picture Vocabulary Test and the Wechsler Adult Intelligence Scale; a study of the stability of the PPVT-Form A among kindergarten five year olds; research on the effects of institutionalization on development of I.Q.; a comparison of the Wechsler Intelligence Scale for Children with the revised Wechsler Intelligence Scale for Children.

SIDELIGHTS: Covin writes: "Today we know enough psychology, religion, and technology to solve most of the existential and historical problems from which human beings the world over suffer. To utilize the vast amount of knowledge correctly, we must be cooperative and replace such goals as power and wealth with goals of developing and using the maximum potential of each human being, regardless of the cost.

"In a democratic society, there is no place for the marginal man—e.g., the poor, the retarded, the ugly. However, in the American capitalistic society, the poor are needed so a few can be rich, the retarded are necessary to reassure some that they themselves are smart, and the ugly are required so there can be those who are beautiful."

AVOCATIONAL INTERESTS: Bass fishing, coin collecting.

* * *

COVINO, Frank 1931-

PERSONAL: Born October 16, 1931, in New York, N.Y.; son of Frank George (a postal employee) and Katherine (Mazzeo) Covino; married Diane Bayles, November, 1966

(divorced, July, 1967); married Virginia Goodlett, November, 1968 (divorced, August, 1972); married Marge Hlinka, June 24, 1973; children: (second marriage) Cameron Connor. *Education:* Attended New York School of Visual Arts, 1949-50; Pratt Institute, B.S., 1958, M.S. (summa cum laude), 1959. *Politics:* "Conservative Isolationism." *Religion:* Roman Catholic. *Home:* Glen Ellen Mountain, Waitsfield, Vt. 05673. *Office:* Academy of Art, Fairfield Young Men's Christian Association, Fairfield, Conn. 06430.

CAREER: Famous Artists School, Westport, Conn., instructor in art, 1959-62; New England Academy of Art, Bridgeport, Conn., teacher of portraiture in oils or bronze, and director, 1962-72; Academy of Art, Fairfield, Conn., teacher and director, 1972—. Professional ski instructor in Vermont, 1956-72; portrait artist in oils, acrylics, bronze, and stone, 1959—. *Military service:* U.S. Air Force, 1950-54; served in Korea; became sergeant; received Syngman Rhee Presidential Unit Citation, 1953. *Awards, honors:* Connecticut Classic Arts first place in painting and first place in sculpture, both 1966.

WRITINGS: The Fine Art of Portraiture, Van Nostrand, 1970; *Skiing Made Easy*, Lancer Books, 1971; *Discover Acrylics with Frank Covino*, Watson-Guptill, 1974; *Diary of a Ski Instructor* (autobiography), Tower, 1975; (editor) *Skier's Digest*, Digest Books, in press. Contributor of reviews to *Leonardo*, 1973—. Contributor of syndicated column, "Ski School," to newspapers nationwide, 1965-69. Editor of *Skier's Digest*, 1975—.

WORK IN PROGRESS: The Science of Painting, completion expected in 1976; *Sculpture and Modern Casting Techniques*, 1977.

SIDELIGHTS: Covino told *CA*: "I follow Leonardo Da Vinci's prescription that 'as a well-spent day brings happy sleep, so a well-spent life brings happy death.' I curse money and people who worship it and abhor the necessity of attaching prices to my paintings. My catharsis is writing. . . . I consider the entire modern art movement to be an incredible hoax perpetrated by frauds to cover up their technical inadequacy. When my head gets crowded, I split for the mountains and ski."

* * *

COWLES, Frank, Jr. 1918-

PERSONAL: Born January 2, 1918, in Jacksonville, Fla.; son of Frank L. (a certified public accountant) and Emarine (Burnett) Cowles. *Education:* University of Florida, Gainesville, B.A.J., 1940. *Religion:* Methodist. *Home:* 3301 McKay Ave., Tampa, Fla. 33609.

CAREER: Tampa Tribune, Tampa, Fla., real estate editor, 1945-47; *Florida Builder*, Tampa, publisher, 1946-48. *Military service:* U.S. Army, 1941-45; became sergeant. *Member:* Sigma Delta Chi, Sigma Nu.

WRITINGS: What to Look for in Florida, Trend Publications, 1967. news editor of *Florida Trend*, 1967-69.

AVOCATIONAL INTERESTS: Organic vegetable gardening.

* * *

COWLES, Ginny 1924-

PERSONAL: Born October 29, 1924, in New York; daughter of Wilton (a lawyer) and Marjorie (Fleming) Lloyd-Smith; married William S. Cowles, Jr. (a farmer),

May 27, 1944; children: Cedar, Tim, Robert, Tory, Nick, Evan. *Education:* Educated in New York, N.Y. *Politics:* None. *Religion:* None. *Home address:* Shelburne Orchard, Shelburne, Vt. 05482. *Agent:* Marilyn Marlow, Curtis Brown, Ltd., 60 East 56th St., New York, N.Y. 10022.

CAREER: Writer. *Awards, honors:* National pilot's award from National Pilots' Association, 1971, for one thousand safe flying hours.

WRITINGS: Nicholas (juvenile), Seabury, 1975.

WORK IN PROGRESS: Darling Starling; Folly, juvenile.

AVOCATIONAL INTERESTS: Photography, flying (has flown single engine airplanes all over the world).

* * *

COXE, George Harmon 1901-

PERSONAL: Born April 23, 1901, in Olean, N.Y.; son of George H. and Harriet C. (Cowens) Coxe; married Elizabeth Fowler, May 18, 1929; children: Janet, George III. *Education:* Attended Purdue University, 1919-20, and Cornell University, 1920-21. *Politics:* Republican. *Home:* Deepledge, Old Lyme, Conn. 06371. *Agent:* Brandt & Brandt, 101 Park Ave., New York, N.Y. 10017.

CAREER: Worked as a reporter, 1922-27, with *Santa Monica Outlook,* Santa Monica, Calif., *Los Angeles Express,* Los Angeles, Calif., *Utica Observer Dispatch,* Utica, N.Y., *Commercial & Financial Chronicle,* New York, N.Y., and *Elmira Star-Gazette,* Elmira, N.Y.; Barta Press, Cambridge, Mass., advertising salesman, 1927-32; Metro-Goldwyn-Mayer, Hollywood, Calif., writer, 1936-38, 1944; novelist. *Member:* Mystery Writers of America (member of board of directors, 1946-48, 1969-70; president, 1952), Authors Guild, Sigma Nu, Phi Zeta, Old Lyme Country Club, Cornell Club (New York), Plantation Club, Sea Pines Golf Club. *Awards, honors:* Grand Masters Award from Mystery Writers of America, 1964.

WRITINGS—Novels; all published by Knopf, except as noted: *Murder with Pictures,* 1935; *The Barotique Mystery,* 1936; *The Camera Clue,* 1937; *Four Frightened Women,* 1939; *Murder for the Asking,* 1939; *The Glass Triangle* (also see below), 1940; *The Lady Is Afraid,* 1940; *Mrs. Murdock Takes a Case,* 1941; *No Time to Kill,* 1941; *Assignment in Guiana,* 1942; *Silent Are the Dead,* 1942; *The Charred Witness,* 1942; *Alias the Dead,* 1943; *Murder for Two,* 1943; *Murder in Havana,* 1943; *The Groom Lay Dead,* 1944; *The Jade Venus* (also see below), 1945; *Woman at Bay,* 1945; *Dangerous Legacy,* 1946; *Flash Casey: Detective,* Avon, 1946; *Fashioned for Murder,* 1947; *The Fifth Key* (first published in *American Magazine,* 1945; also see below), 1947; *The Hollow Needle,* 1948; *Venturous Lady,* 1948; *Inland Passage,* 1949; *Lady Killer,* 1949.

Eye Witness, 1950; *The Frightened Fiances,* 1950; *The Man Who Died Twice,* 1951; *The Widow Had a Gun,* 1951; *Never Bet Your Life,* 1952; *The Crimson Clue,* 1953; *Uninvited Guest* (first published in *Chicago Tribune* as "Nobody Wants Julia"), 1953; *Death at the Isthmus,* 1954; *Focus on Murder,* 1954; *Top Assignment,* Knopf, 1955; *Suddenly a Widow,* 1956; *Murder on Their Minds,* 1957; *One Minute Past Eight,* 1957; *The Impetuous Mistress,* 1958; *Man on a Rope,* 1958; *The Big Gamble,* 1958; *Slack Tide* (condensed version published in *American Magazine* as "The Captive-Bride Murders"), 1959; *Triple Exposure* (includes *The Glass Triangle, The Jade Venus, The Fifth Key),* 1959; *The Last Commandment,* 1960; *One Way Out,*

1960; *Error of Judgment,* 1961; *Moment of Violence,* 1961; *Mission of Fear,* 1962; *The Man Who Died Too Soon,* 1962; *One Hour to Kill,* 1963; *The Hidden Key,* 1963; *Deadly Image,* 1964; *The Reluctant Heiress,* 1965; *With Intent to Kill,* 1965; *The Ring of Truth,* 1966; *The Candid Imposter,* 1968; *An Easy Way to Go,* 1969; *Double Identity,* 1970; *Fenner,* 1971; *Woman with a Gun,* 1972; *The Silent Witness,* 1973; *The Inside Man,* 1974.

Creator of television and radio series, "Crime Photographer," 1943-52. Contributor of short stories, novellas, and serials to magazines.

WORK IN PROGRESS: No Flare for Murder.

* * *

CRAMPTON, Georgia Ronan 1925-
(Georgia Ronan)

PERSONAL: Born May 22, 1925, in Minnesota; daughter of Thomas Bernard (a farmer) and Mary (Daley) Ronan; married John A. Crampton (a teacher), September 6, 1949. *Education:* College of St. Teresa, B.A., 1949; University of Oregon, M.A., 1963, Ph.D., 1967; also studied at University of California, Santa Barbara, Colorado College, and University of Washington, Seattle. *Politics:* "Democrat; leftish." *Religion:* Roman Catholic. *Residence:* Lake Oswego, Ore. *Office:* Department of English, Portland State University, Portland, Ore. 97207.

CAREER: Marylhurst College, Marylhurst, Ore., lecturer in English, 1960-69; University of Portland, Portland, Ore., assistant professor of English, 1969-72; Portland State University, Portland, Ore., assistant professor, 1972-74, associate professor of English, 1974—. *Member:* Modern Language Association of America, Mediaeval Academy of America, Medieval Association of the Pacific, American Association of University Professors. *Awards, honors:* Folger Shakespeare Library fellowship, 1967; Southeastern Institute of Medieval and Renaissance Studies fellowship, 1975.

WRITINGS: The Condition of Creatures: Suffering and Action in Chaucer and Spenser, Yale University Press, 1974. Contributor of articles and poems, sometimes under name Georgia Ronan, to magazines.

WORK IN PROGRESS: Research on the medieval lyric and on the Bronte novels.

SIDELIGHTS: Georgia Crampton writes: "Having been a member of a large, close family . . . and having been reared on a farm remain central to my sense of what life is. Close things remain close; my parents, my husband, a quiet life with more time spent reading than doing anything else . . . I am a propagandist of sorts for the humanities—and for women's liberation (though I regret abortion has become the kind of symbolic issue it seems to be for mainstream feminism) . . . I am a pacifist, though, my husband tells me, unconscionably argumentative." *Avocational interests:* Theater, gardening, European travel, studying classical Greek.

* * *

CRANDALL, Joy
See MARTIN, Joy

* * *

CRAWFORD, Char 1935-
(Charlene Johnson)

PERSONAL: Born April 29, 1935, in Minneapolis, Minn.;

daughter of Charles H. (an efficiency expert) and Margaret (Larson) Gardner; married second husband, Jack V. Crawford (a family counselor), August 14, 1969; children: Raymond, Richard, Reesie; (stepchildren) Jacqueline, Christina, Joel, Douglas, Karen. *Education:* Attended Augsburg College, 1952-53. *Religion:* Methodist. *Residence:* Seattle, Wash.

CAREER: Instructor, Estelle Compton Modeling Agency, Minneapolis, Minn., 1952-54; instructor of YWCA charm courses in Davenport, Iowa, and Moline, Ill., 1958-59; author.

WRITINGS—Under name Charlene Johnson: *Altogether Lovely*, Fortress, 1960; *Beautiful Homemaking*, Fortress, 1961; *Letters on Loveliness*, Zondervan, 1969.

Under name Char Crawford: *Luvly You: Luvable You*, Zondervan, 1973; (contributor) *For Women Only*, Tyndale, 1974. Author of "Dear Charlene" column in *Youth for Christ*, 1962-69.

WORK IN PROGRESS: Hang in There, Mom!, completion expected in 1976.

* * *

CRAWFORD, Clan, Jr. 1927-

PERSONAL: Born January 25, 1927, in Cleveland, Ohio; son of Clan (an attorney) and Caroline (Herrmann) Crawford; married Alice Bishop Berle (an artist), June 18, 1949; children: Peter, Lloyd, David. *Education:* Oberlin College, A.B., 1948; University of Michigan, J.D., 1952. *Politics:* Republican. *Home:* 2024 Geddes Ave., Ann Arbor, Mich. 48104. *Office:* 304 Wolverine Bldg., Ann Arbor, Mich. 48104.

CAREER: Admitted to Bar of State of Michigan and U.S. District Court in eastern Michigan, 1953, and to U.S. Sixth Circuit Court of Appeals, 1954; Dun & Bradstreet, Inc., Cleveland, Ohio, credit reporter, 1948-50; practiced law with Roscoe O. Bonisteel in Ann Arbor, Mich., 1953-57; private practice of law in Ann Arbor, Mich., 1957—. First Assistant Prosecuting Attorney of Washtenaw County, 1955-57. Lecturer at Institute of Continuing Legal Education, Michigan State University, University of Michigan, Central Michigan University, Western Michigan University, Detroit Real Estate Board, ENACT Ecology Center, Inc., Michigan Society of Planning Officials, Citizens Council for Land Use Research and Education, Michigan Student Environmental Confederation, and West Michigan Environmental Council. President of Ann Arbor Civic Theater, 1956-57; Ann Arbor city councilman, 1957-58; chairman of Ann Arbor Civic Art Committee, 1962-65. *Military service:* U.S. Naval Reserve, 1944-46. *Member:* American Bar Association, State Bar of Michigan, Washtenaw County Bar Association, Michigan Society of Planning Officials, Tri-County Sportsmen's League, Trout Unlimited, Sierra Club.

WRITINGS: Michigan Zoning and Planning, Matthew Bender, 1965; *Strategy and Tactics in Municipal Zoning*, Prentice-Hall, 1969; *Handbook of Zoning and Land Use Control Ordinances, with Forms*, Prentice-Hall, 1974.

WORK IN PROGRESS: Research on zoning administration.

* * *

CRAWFORD, Richard (Arthur) 1935-

PERSONAL: Born May 12, 1935, in Detroit, Mich.; son of Arthur Richard (a foundryman) and Mary Elizabeth (Forshar) Crawford; married Sophie Shambes, December 27, 1958 (divorced, 1965); married Penelope Ball (a musician), April 26, 1967; children: (first marriage) Lynn E., William J.; (second marriage) Amy E., Anne L. *Education:* University of Michigan, B.Mus., 1958, M.Mus., 1959, Ph.D., 1965. *Religion:* Protestant. *Home:* 1158 Baldwin, Ann Arbor, Mich. 48104. *Office:* School of Music, University of Michigan, Ann Arbor, Mich. 48105.

CAREER: University of Michigan, Ann Arbor, instructor, 1962-66, assistant professor, 1966-69, associate professor, 1969-75, professor of music history and musicology, 1975—. Visiting professor and senior research fellow at Brooklyn College of the City University of New York, 1973-74; consultant to National Endowment for the Humanities and Rockefeller Foundation. *Member:* American Musicological Society, Society for Ethnomusicology, Music Library Association, American Antiquarian Society.

WRITINGS: Andrew Law: American Psalmodist, Northwestern University Press, 1968; (with David P. McKay) *William Billings of Boston: Eighteenth-Century Composer*, Princeton University Press, 1975; *American Studies and American Musicology*, Institute for Studies in American Music, Brooklyn College of the City University of New York, 1975; *Parlor Music of the Civil War*, Dover, 1975. Contributor to biographical dictionaries and of articles and reviews to music journals.

WORK IN PROGRESS: A Bibliography of Sacred American Music: 1698-1810; The Core Repertory of Early American Psalmody.

AVOCATIONAL INTERESTS: Camping.

* * *

CRECINE, John Patrick 1939-

PERSONAL: Born August 22, 1939, in Detroit, Mich.; son of H. Jess (an engineer) and Janet K. (an office manager; maiden name, Hull) Crecine; married Barbara Lea Paltnavich, August 17, 1968; children: Robert Patrick. *Education:* Carnegie-Mellon University, B.S., 1961, M.S., 1963, Ph.D., 1966; graduate study at Stanford University, 1961-62. *Home:* 911 Robin Rd., Ann Arbor, Mich. 48103. *Office:* Institute of Public Policy Studies, University of Michigan, Ann Arbor, Mich. 48104.

CAREER: University of Michigan, Ann Arbor, assistant professor of political science and sociology, 1965-67; RAND Corp., Santa Monica, Calif., economist, 1967-68; University of Michigan, Institute of Public Policy Studies, Ann Arbor, professor of political science and sociology, 1968-73, director, 1968—. Fellow, Center for Advanced Study in the Behavioral Sciences, Stanford, Calif., 1973-75. Secretary of Ann Arbor Planning Commission, 1969-72; member of Governor's Commission on Local Government, 1970-71; president, B.P.T., Inc., 1963—; consultant to U.S. Department of Commerce, U.S. Department of Transportation, U.S. Bureau of the Budget, and Commission on the Organization of the Government for the Conduct of Foreign Policy; member of National Board on Graduate Education, 1972-75.

MEMBER: National Association of Schools of Public Affairs and Administration (member of executive committee, 1969-72), American Economics Association, American Society of Public Administration, American Political Science Association, American Sociological Association, Institute of Management Sciences, American Institute of Planners.

Awards, honors: L. D. White Award from American Political Science Association, 1968.

WRITINGS: Governmental Problem Solving: Computer Simulation of Municipal Budgeting, Rand McNally, 1969; *Defense Budgeting*, RAND Corp., 1970; (editor) *Financing the Metropolis*, Sage Publications, 1970. Associate editor of *Management Science*, 1969—; member of editorial advisory board, *Urban Affairs Quarterly*, 1970-74, *Urban Analysis*, 1972—, and *Policy Analysis*, 1974—.

WORK IN PROGRESS: Research on U.S. budgeting and fiscal policy processes, national security decision processes, and urban spatial location.

* * *

CRENSHAW, Mary Ann

PERSONAL: Born in Montgomery, Ala.; daughter of Jack (an attorney) and Catherine (Westcott) Crenshaw. *Education:* Vanderbilt University, B.A., 1951; also studied at University of Havana (Cuba), and Parsons School of Design. *Politics:* Democrat. *Religion:* Episcopalian. *Residence:* New York, N.Y., and Montgomery, Ala. *Agent:* Roberta Pryor, 40 West 57th St., New York, N.Y. 10019. *Office: New York Times*, 229 West 43rd St., New York, N.Y. 10036.

CAREER: Assistant to couturier Charles James, New York, N.Y., 1958; member of staff, merchandising department, *Vogue Magazine*, New York, 1959-62; boutique manager for designer "Tiger" Morse, and publicist for Adolfo, both in New York, 1962; fashion coordinator for Ohrbach's, New York, 1962-65; *New York Times*, New York, N.Y., fashion and beauty reporter, 1965—.

WRITINGS: The Natural Way to Super Beauty, McKay, 1974. Contributor to *Cosmopolitan, Harper's Bazaar, Family Circle*, and *Rags* (now defunct).

WORK IN PROGRESS: A book for Delacorte, publication expected in 1976.

AVOCATIONAL INTERESTS: Antiques, primitive paintings, collecting quilts, needlepoint, gymnastics, dance, travel.

* * *

CROW, Mark (Alan) 1948-

PERSONAL: Born April 21, 1948, in Wichita, Kan.; son of Joseph Jason (an accountant) and Lila Mae (McArthur) Crow. *Education:* Kansas Wesleyan University, B.A. (magna cum laude), 1969; Kansas State University, M.A., 1973. *Religion:* Presbyterian. *Home:* 212 East Jewell, Salina, Kan. 67401.

CAREER: Salina High School, Salina, Kan., teacher of government, 1969-72; Kansas Vocational Rehabilitation Center, Salina, vocational counselor, 1973-74. *Military service:* Kansas National Guard, 1969-73. *Member:* National Education Association, Professional Guidance and Counseling Association, Kansas Education Association.

WRITINGS: Windchimes (prose and poetry), Celestial Arts, 1974.

WORK IN PROGRESS: A novel dealing with teaching experiences; a supplement to *Windchimes*.

SIDELIGHTS: Crow writes: "I am very much concerned with the fact that Americans take themselves entirely too seriously. Everything seems to be a struggle to reach some unobtainable goal.... We ... seem to have forgotten how to relax and especially how to laugh at ourselves. The thing that concerns me most is how this has affected our youth ... it is disheartening to me to see how much sadness, loneliness, and feeling of being lost are found within this generation."

* * *

CROWELL, Joan 1921-

PERSONAL: Born June 6, 1921, in New York, N.Y.; daughter of Sam A. (an art collector and businessman) and Margaret (Seligman) Lewisohn; married Sidney Simon, May 24, 1944 (divorced, August 6, 1962); married David G. Crowell, December 17, 1972; children: (first marriage) Mark, Teru (Mrs. T. Farren Bratton), Rachel, Nora, Juno. *Education:* Bennington College, B.A., 1942; New York University, M.A., 1943. *Politics:* Socialist. *Religion:* None. *Home and office:* 226½ East 62nd St., New York, N.Y. 10021. *Agent:* Virginia Barber, 44 Greenwich Ave., New York, N.Y.

CAREER: New York University, New York, N.Y., assistant professor of English, 1942-44. Executive director of Friends of Danilo Dolci, 1972—. *Member:* P.E.N., James Joyce Society, Modern Language Association of America, Authors Guild.

WRITINGS: Portrait of a Father (novel), Atheneum, 1960; *Fort Dix Stockade: Our Prison Camp Next Door* (nonfiction), Links, 1974. Contributor of articles and poems to *Ramparts, Life, Commonweal, Nation, New York Times*, and *New York Quarterly*. Writer and translator of librettos.

WORK IN PROGRESS: A trilogy of novels on New York City: *The Gardens, Three Sisters Revisited*, and *The Heights*.

SIDELIGHTS: Joan Crowell has travelled throughout Europe, Egypt, and Peru, and lived in France for a year.

* * *

CROWELL, Muriel Beyea 1916-

PERSONAL: Born September 4, 1916, in New York, N.Y.; daughter of George M. and Elsie (Hughes) Beyea; married William B. Hutchinson, September 24, 1938 (died December, 1965); married Robert L. Crowell (a publisher), December 19, 1967; children: (first marriage) Ann H. (Mrs. Edward P. Sutherland), William B., Priscilla. *Education:* Attended Connecticut College for Women (now Connecticut College), 1934-38; graduate study at Silvermine College of Art, 1960, and at University of Bridgeport, 1961. *Address:* Box 92, West St., Newfane, Vt. 05345.

CAREER: Museum of Art, Science, and Industry, Bridgeport, Conn., assistant exhibits director, 1965-67; In-Stitches Needlepoint, New York, N.Y., shop owner, 1969-74; In-Stitches Vermont, Newfane, Vt., designer, 1975—. Vice-president of board of directors of Minneapolis Northwestern Hospital, 1950-52; director of State of Connecticut League for Planned Parenthood, 1955-56; corresponding secretary of Bridgeport Junior League, 1963-64. *Member:* League of Women Voters (vice-president of Easton, Conn. chapter, 1960-61).

WRITINGS: The Fine Art of Needlepoint, Crowell, 1973.

WORK IN PROGRESS: A cook book with the tentative title, *Zucchini Coming Out of My Ears*.

* * *

CRUMP, Galbraith Miller 1929-

PERSONAL: Born November 2, 1929, in Elizabeth, N.J.;

son of William Leslie (an artist) and Alice (an artist; maiden name, Miller) Crump; married Joan Lee, February 22, 1952; children: Andrew, Ian, Patrick, Timothy, Nicholas. *Education:* Hamilton College, A.B., 1951; Reading University, M.A., 1955; St. John's College, Oxford, D.Phil., 1959. *Religion:* Episcopalian. *Home address:* Box 586, Gambier, Ohio 43022. *Office:* Department of English, Kenyon College, Gambier, Ohio 43022.

CAREER: Yale University, New Haven, Conn., instructor, 1958-61, assistant professor of English, 1962-65; Kenyon College, Gambier, Ohio, associate professor, 1965-66, professor of English, 1966—, chairman of department, 1973—. *Military service:* U.S. Army, 1951-53; worked in psychological warfare. *Member:* Modern Language Association of America. *Awards, honors:* Morse Fellowship from Yale University, 1961-62.

WRITINGS: (Editor) *Poems and Translations of Thomas Stanley*, Clarendon Press (of Oxford University), 1962; (editor) *Poems on Affairs of State, 1685-88*, Volume IV: *Augustan Satirical Verse*, Yale University Press, 1968; (editor) *Twentieth Century Interpretations: Samson Agonistes*, Prentice-Hall, 1968; *The Mystical Design of Paradise Lost*, Bucknell University Press, 1975. Contributor to journals in his field.

WORK IN PROGRESS: Research on Shakespeare and the Elizabethan stage.

AVOCATIONAL INTERESTS: Painting, theatre.

* * *

CUEVAS, Clara 1933-
(Isa de Rivel)

PERSONAL: Born October 30, 1933, in Rio Piedras, P.R.; daughter of Javier (a civil engineer) and Clara (Silva) Cuevas. *Education:* University of Puerto Rico, B.A., 1966, graduate study, 1972—. *Religion:* "Liberal Roman Catholic." *Address:* Box 11821, San Juan, P.R. 00922.

CAREER: El Mundo (newspaper), Hato Rey, P.R., reporter, critic, feature writer, translator, columnist, 1965-75; free-lance writer, 1975—. Lecturer, University of Puerto Rico, 1969. Assistant editor, Libreria Internacional, Inc., Rio Piedras, P.R., 1972; assistant editor of literary review, Inter-American University of Puerto Rico, Hato Rey, 1972; feature writer, *Revista Bohemia*, 1972; translator, *Pro Tempo*, Santurce, P.R., 1972—. *Member:* Society of Puerto Rican Authors, Society of Women Journalists, Catholic Daughters of America, Mu Alpha Phi. *Awards, honors:* Aguey Dana de Oro from National Council of Art, 1974, for feature writing for *El Mundo*.

WRITINGS: (Under pseudonym Isa de Rivel) *Canto al amor profundo* (title means "Song to Profound Love"), Imprenta Irizarry, 1956; *Triptico del amor, del dolor y de la muerte* (poetry; title means "Triptych of Love, Death and Sorrow"), Imprenta Irizarry, 1969; *Kaleidoscopio del amor* (poetry; title means "Kaleidoscope of Love"), Publishers Group (San Juan), 1970; *La Carcel del tiempo* (short stories; title means "The Prison of Time"), Editorial Cordillera, 1970; *Maremagnum* (novel), Editorial Cultural, 1975; *Driftwood* (poetry), Editorial Cultural, 1975; *Los Buitres del alma* (play; title means "The Vultures of the Soul"), Editorial Cultural, 1975; *Amor ultraterrestre* (poetry; title means "Ultra-terrestrial Love"), Editorial Cultural, 1975; *Poemas de un robot que llora* (title means "Poems of a Crying Robot"), Editorial Cultural, 1975; *Puente entre dos mundos* (title means "Bridge between Two Worlds"; contains one-act plays: "House of Mirrors," "The Aquarium," "Sun and Mink," and "Marriage a la Carte"), Editorial Cultural, 1975.

Author of play, "The Jigsaw Puzzle," first produced in San Juan at Ateneo Theatre, 1970. Author of radio script, "Los muertos de tedio," broadcast by W.I.P.R., 1970, and of a series of television documentaries for Public Broadcasting System.

Translator from Spanish into English, *Problema de la desigualdad social en Puerto Rico*, Editorial Libreria Internacional, 1972. Also translator, from English into Spanish, *Man and Woman* (poetry), by James Weber.

WORK IN PROGRESS: A novel, to be titled *God's Country* or *The Land of God*; an autobiography.

SIDELIGHTS: Clara Cuevas, who told *CA* that she has been writing since the age of ten, has founded a Creative Writing Workshop for young people. The workshop has been approved by the governor of Puerto Rico and is scheduled for sponsorship by the Puerto Rican Government.

* * *

CULP, Paula 1941-

PERSONAL: Born April 9, 1941, in Fort Smith, Ark. *Education:* Oberlin College, B.Mus., 1963; Mozarteum, Salzburg, Austria, graduate study; Indiana University, M.Mus., 1965. *Home:* 3820 East 26th St., Minneapolis, Minn. 55406.

CAREER: Metropolitan Opera National Co., principal timpanist with touring company, 1965-67; Indianapolis Symphony, Indianapolis, Ind., principal percussionist, 1967-68; Minnesota Orchestra, Minneapolis, percussionist and associate timpanist, 1968—. Percussion instructor at University of Minnesota, 1968—. *Member:* Percussive Arts Society. *Awards, honors:* Music awards.

WRITINGS: A Thousand Portholes (poetry), Pacul, 1973.

AVOCATIONAL INTERESTS: Writing lyrics for songs.

* * *

CUMMINGS, Violet M(ay) 1905-

PERSONAL: Born May 8, 1905, in Allegan, Mich.; daughter of Fred R. and Ida Marie (Haenke) Essex; married Eryl A. Cummings (a realtor), April 27, 1928; children: Marilyn Joy (Mrs. Don Wallace), Phyllis Edora (Mrs. Albert Watson). *Education:* Attended Hinsdale Sanitarium and Hospital, 1924, and Emmanuel Missionary College (now Andrews University), 1925-26. *Religion:* Seventh-day Adventist. *Home:* 401 North Auburn, Farmington, N.M. 87401. *Address:* P.O. Box 797, Farmington, N.M. 87401.

CAREER: Battle Creek Sanitarium, Battle Creek, Mich., hydrotherapist, 1923-25, receptionist, 1925; secretary with husband's real estate business, Farmington, N.M., 1946-47, 1956-75. *Member:* Farmington Writer's Association (charter member; member of board of directors, 1972-75).

WRITINGS: Along Navajo Trails (nonfiction), Review & Herald, 1965; *Noah's Ark: Fact or Fable?* (nonfiction), Creation Science Research Center, 1972. Contributor to *Youth's Instructor, Junior Guide, Woman's Day, Navajo Newsletter, Union Reaper, Science and Scripture, Facts for Faith*, and *Christian Standard*.

WORK IN PROGRESS: A book to contain additional facts learned from persons claiming first or second-hand knowledge about the existence of the Ark, *Update on*

Noah's Ark: Fact of Fable?; research on facts about a gigantic April Fool's joke in Germany during World War II.

* * *

CUNNINGHAM, Aline

PERSONAL: Married James L. Cunningham; children: five. *Education:* Washington University, St. Louis, Mo., B.F.A. *Home:* 225 Highland, St. Louis, Mo. 63122.

CAREER: Self-employed commercial artist.

WRITINGS—Self-illustrated juveniles; all published by Concordia: *Gifts*, 1973; *My Counting Book*, 1973; *My House*, 1973; *Who Am I*, 1973; *Getting Ready*, 1973; *Friends*, 1974.

WORK IN PROGRESS: Six more preschool books for Concordia.

* * *

CURLEY, Charles 1949-

PERSONAL: Born May 18, 1949, in Bridgeport, Conn.; son of William (a surgeon) and Nadine (Barlow) Curley. *Education:* University of Connecticut, B.A., 1972. *Politics:* Libertarian. *Agent:* Oscar Collier, 280 Madison Ave., New York, N.Y. 10016.

CAREER: Self-employed auto mechanic, 1970-73; Bead Chain Corp., Bridgeport, Conn., machinist, 1973-74. Chairperson of Connecticut Libertarian Party, 1972. *Member:* Young Americans for Freedom.

WRITINGS: The Coming Profit in Gold, Bantam, 1974. Contributor to *Reason, New Guard, Freeman, New Libertarian Notes*, and others. Editor of *Charles Curley Letter*, 1974—.

* * *

CURRAN, Dolores 1932-

PERSONAL: Surname is pronounced Kern; born February 11, 1932, in Edgerton, Wis.; daughter of William Edward (a farmer) and Lillian (Spohn) Fox; married James Curran (an educator), June 28, 1958; children: Teresa, Patrick, Daniel. *Education:* University of Wisconsin, Whitewater, B.Ed., 1953. *Religion:* Roman Catholic. *Home:* 336 West Peakview, Littleton, Colo. 80120. *Agent:* James Alt, 300 Dauphin, Green Bay, Wis.

CAREER: English teacher in public schools in Beloit, Wis., 1953-55, and Englewood, Colo., 1955-61; free-lance writer, 1961-70; Arapahoe Community College, Littleton, Colo., lecturer in writing, 1970; full-time author and lecturer, 1970—. *Member:* Catholic Press Association, Colorado Author's League. *Awards, honors:* Awards from Colorado Author's League, 1974, for best philosophical article and best humor, and 1975, for best short-short story.

WRITINGS: Who, Me Teach My Child Religion?, Winston Press, 1970, revised edition, 1974; *Do Not Fold, Staple, or Mutilate*, Ave Maria Press, 1970; *Today's Catholic Woman*, Ave Maria Press, 1971; *What Are Parents For, Anyway?*, Abbey Press, 1974. Author of columns: "From One End of the Log," in *Colorado Education Association Journal*, 1967-69; "Showcase," in *Parent Educator*, 1967-72; "On the Other Hand," syndicated by *National Catholic News Service*, 1967-74; "Teacher Talking," in *Today's Catholic Teacher*, 1969-71; "Between Parish and Parent," in *Religion Teacher's Journal*, 1972-73; "Talks with Parents," distributed by Alt-Curran Associates, 1974—. Con-

tributor to more than fifty magazines. Editor-at-large of *Parent Educator*, 1967-72.

WORK IN PROGRESS: In the Beginning (tentative title), a book for Christian parents; a book on home-school relationships.

SIDELIGHTS: Dolores Curran writes: "I have three goals: to touch the forgotten reader's needs; to inject humor in lives, and to write a novel like *To Kill a Mockingbird*."

* * *

CURRIER, Richard L(eon) 1940-

PERSONAL: Born March 3, 1940, in New York, N.Y.; son of Robert Elson (a violinist, salesman, grocer, and mechanic) and Jeanette (Goldstein) Currier; married Devera Ehrenberg, September, 1959 (divorced); married Susan Kaiser (a clinical psychologist), June 12, 1963; children: (second marriage) Chad Joseph, Guy Michael. *Education:* University of California, Berkeley, A.B. (with honors), 1963, Ph.D., 1974. *Home:* 618 Seventh Ave. S.E., Minneapolis, Minn. 55414. *Agent:* Rhoda A. Weyr, William Morris Agency, 1350 Avenue of the Americas, New York, N.Y. 10019. *Office:* Department of Anthropology, University of Minnesota, 210 Ford Hall, Minneapolis, Minn. 55455.

CAREER: University of California, Berkeley, acting instructor in anthropology, 1969; University of Minnesota, Minneapolis, assistant professor of anthropology, 1969-71, research fellow in anthropology, 1972—; free-lance writer, 1971—. *Member:* American Anthropological Association, American Association for the Advancement of Science. *Awards, honors:* First prize from Prose Writer's Contest at New York University, 1957, for "Miracle at the Falls."

WRITINGS—All published by Lerner: (With Michael Avi-Yonah) *Search for the Past: An Introduction to Archaeology*, 1973; (with Rivka Gonen) *Pottery in Ancient Times*, 1973; (with Avi-Yonah) *Ancient Scrolls*, 1973; (with Avi-Yonah) *The Art of Mosaics*, 1974; (with Ya'akov Meshorer) *Coins of the Ancient World*, 1974; (with Renate Rosenthal) *Jewelry of the Ancient World*, 1974; (with Elisha Linder) *Underwater Archaeology*, in press; (with Gonen) *Weapons and Warfare in Ancient Times*, in press; (with Arthur Segal) *City Planning in Ancient Times*, in press. Member of editorial board, *Spider*, 1964-65.

WORK IN PROGRESS: Homo Sapiens and the Planet Earth: An Introduction to Anthropology, for Wiley; *Grownups in Diapers: Childishness in Sexual and Social Behavior*, for Knopf.

SIDELIGHTS: Currier writes: "My general orientation is toward using the data and theory of modern anthropology—ethnography, archaeology, and primate behavior studies—to shed light on the workings of society in general and of modern society in particular. I have done field research in rural Mexico (1963, 1964) and the Greek Islands (1966-68) . . . I am an adherent and devotee of the 'immersion' school of anthropological research, believing that it is vital to participate in the life of an alien society in order to comprehend it fully."

* * *

CURRY, Andrew 1931-

PERSONAL: Born July 1, 1931, in Cleveland, Ohio; son of Fletcher (a laborer) and Jannie (Rhodes) Curry; married Georgia Baker; children: Kevin Laird. *Education:* Cleveland State University, B.A., 1955; Case Western Reserve

University, M.S., 1957; private graduate study in psychology and psychotherapy. *Politics:* "Humanist." *Religion:* Buddhist. *Office:* Department of Humanities-Arts, California School of Professional Psychology, San Francisco, Calif.; and Temenos Seminars, 5536 Carlton St., Oakland, Calif. 94618.

CAREER: Mendocino State Hospital, Mendocino, Calif., psychiatric social worker, 1958-61; California State Bureau of Social Work, San Francisco, psychiatric social worker, 1961; Langley Porter Neuropsychiatric Institute, San Francisco, Calif., psychiatric social worker, 1967-71; University of California, San Francisco, instructor in Family Therapy Center, 1966—, lecturer in psychiatry, School of Social Welfare, 1967—. Lecturer at University of California, Berkeley, 1968—; professor and head of department of humanities-arts at California School of Professional Psychology, 1971—. Director of Temenos Seminars and Study Center, 1974—. Member of board of directors of Institute for the Study of Social and Health Issues. *Military service:* U.S. Army Reserve, 1957-63.

MEMBER: National Association of Social Workers, American Group Psychotherapy Association, American Orthopsychiatric Association, Association of Family Therapy, General Systems Society, Golden Gate Group Psychotherapy Society.

WRITINGS: Seventeenth Tractatus on Words, Dustbooks, Inc., 1969; *Bringing Forth Forms*, Dustbooks, Inc., 1973; *Shadow Quaternity*, Dustbooks, Inc., in press. Contributor of more than a hundred articles to professional journals. Editor of *Journal of Clinical Phenomenology*; contributing editor of *Small Press Review*.

WORK IN PROGRESS: Phenomenology of "No": Negation and Denial; The Psychological and Literary Aspects of the Fool; director and choreographer for Tantra Feets Ensemble, a resident dance group at California School of Professional Psychology.

AVOCATIONAL INTERESTS: Painter, poet, musician, literary critic; raising Bonzai trees, clerical work (ordained minister in Universal Life Church).

BIOGRAPHICAL/CRITICAL SOURCES: Bill Henderson, editor, *Publish It Yourself Handbook*, Pushcart Book Press, 1973.

* * *

CURTIN, Mary Ellen 1922-

PERSONAL: Born February 6, 1922, in Carthage, Ill.; daughter of Arlo W. (a farmer) and Ellis (Ellwood) Kunkel; married Robert E. Curtin (in finance), February 10, 1946; children: Barbara Ellen (Mrs. John C. Glasgow), Jane Ellwood (Mrs. Carl R. Vertuca, Jr.). *Education:* Methodist Hospital School of Nursing, Peoria, Ill., R.N., 1944; University of Kentucky, B.S., 1956, M.S., 1959, Ph.D., 1965. *Office:* Department of Justice, 209 St. Clair, Frankfort, Ky. 40601.

CAREER: U.S. Department of State, Washington, D.C., clerk, 1946; Filene's Department Store, Boston, Mass., comparison shopper, 1947; registered nurse in private duty, Georgetown and Lexington, Ky., 1947-56; Veterans Administration Hospital, Lexington, Ky., experimental trainee, 1963-65; Eastern Kentucky University, Richmond, assistant professor of psychology, 1965-68; Veterans Administration Hospital, Lexington, Ky., clinical research psychologist, 1967-74; Kentucky Department of Justice, Frankfort, supervisor of evaluation section, 1975—. Presi-

dent of Richard M. Griffith Memorial Fund, 1969—; member of merit board of Fayette County Police and Fireman, 1970-73; President of advisory board of Lexington Volunteers of America, 1972-74; lecturer to community groups on alcoholism. *Military service:* U.S. Army, Nurse Corps, 1945-46.

MEMBER: American Psychological Association (fellow), Midwestern Psychological Association, Southeastern Psychological Association, Southern Society for Philosophy and Psychology (member of council, 1972-75), Kentucky Psychological Association (past president), Kentucky Academy of Science (past chairman), Kentucky Gerontological Society (member of board of directors, 1974), Central Kentucky Psychological Association (past president), Lexington Montessori Society (past director), Phi Beta Kappa, Sigma Xi, Psi Chi.

WRITINGS: (Editor) *Symposium on Love*, Behavioral Publications, 1973. Contributor to psychology and social science journals.

WORK IN PROGRESS: Alcoholism; Criminal Justice.

SIDELIGHTS: Mary Ellen Curtin writes: "In our society, is romantic love overemphasized such that persons for whom this kind of interpersonal relation is out of the question are made to feel as if they are incomplete persons? When romantic love is not possible, is there an acceptable substitute/alternative?" *Avocational interests:* Water skiing, collecting old things.

* * *

CUTHBERTSON, Gilbert Morris 1937-

PERSONAL: Born November 20, 1937, in Warrensburg, Mo.; son of Gilbert and Marion D. (Morris) Cuthbertson. *Education:* University of Kansas, A.B. (highest distinction), 1959; Harvard University, Ph.D., 1963. *Politics:* Democrat. *Religion:* Presbyterian. *Home:* 2214 Bellefontaine, Houston, Tex. *Office:* Rice University, 484 Sewell Hall, Houston, Tex. 77001.

CAREER: Rice University, Houston, Tex., assistant professor, 1963-69, associate professor of political science, 1970—, resident associate of Will Rice College, 1964—. *Member:* American Political Science Association, Phi Beta Kappa, Pi Sigma Alpha, Delta Phi Alpha. *Awards, honors:* Woodrow Wilson fellowship, 1959-60; Woodrow Wilson dissertation fellowship, 1962-63.

WRITINGS: Political Power, Rice University, 1968; *Political Myth and Epic*, Michigan State University Press, 1975. Contributor to journals.

WORK IN PROGRESS: The Issue Is Politics!, an introduction to political theory; *Inlaws and Outlaws*, a history of Texas politics; a new translation and critical edition of Marx's poetry.

SIDELIGHTS: Bridge (life master).

* * *

CUTTER, Fred 1924-

PERSONAL: Born November 18, 1924, in Boston, Mass.; son of Leo and Mary (Siders) Cutter; married Dorothy Kantor (a professional artist), July 12, 1951; children: David L., Amelia R. *Education:* Boston University, B.A., 1949, M.A., 1950; Catholic University of America, Ph.D., 1955; also studied at Washington School of Psychiatry, 1951-55. *Home:* 290 Cypress Ave., Morro Bay, Calif. 93442. *Office:* 2615 East Clinton St., Fresno, Calif. 93703.

CAREER: Psychologist at Medfield State Hospital, Medfield, Mass., 1950-51, and Spring Grove State Hospital, Catonsville, Md., 1951-52; Howard University, Medical School, Washington, D.C., fellow at Freedmen's Hospital, 1953-55; Atascadero State Hospital, Atascadero, Calif., clinical psychologist, 1955-63; California Rehabilitation Center, Corona, clinical psychologist, 1963-65; Veterans Administration Center, Los Angeles, Calif., research psychologist, Central Research Unit for the Study of Unpredicted Death, 1966-72; Veterans Administration Hospital, Fresno, Calif., chief psychologist, 1972—. Consultant to Los Angeles County Health Department, 1964-74, Los Angeles Suicide Prevention Center, 1967-72, Help in Emotional Trouble (hot line), Fresno, Calif., 1972—, and Al Vets Corp. *Military service:* U.S. Army, 1943-46. *Member:* American Psychological Association, International Association for Suicide Prevention, American Association of Suicidology, Western Psychological Association, California State Psychological Association, Central California Psychological Association.

WRITINGS: (Contributor) Bruno Klopfer and others, editors, *New Developments in the Rorschach*, Volume III, Harcourt, 1970; *Coming to Terms with Death*, Nelson-Hall, 1974. Author with N. L. Farberow of discussion guide for sound movie, "Suicide in the Hospital," 1968. Contributor to scientific journals; contributor of public information articles to *Private Pilot, Sport Flying, Popular Medicine, Sexology*, and other magazines.

Editor, *Dear Friends* (periodic newsletter circulated among his professional colleagues), 1964—; contributing editor, *Popular Medicine*, 1964-65, and *Real Life Guide*, 1964-66; associate editor, *VITA* (newsletter of International Association for Suicide Prevention), 1965-70; member of editorial board, *Omega*, 1971—. Guest editor, *Journal of Clinical Psychology*, January, 1967, January, 1970; guest reviewer, *Quarterly Journal of Studies on Alcohol*, 1970—.

WORK IN PROGRESS: Books on the self-injury theme in visual art, and on management of the public inebriate and severe alcoholism.

*   *   *

CUTTER, Robert Arthur   1930-

PERSONAL: Born July 4, 1930, in New York, N.Y.; son of Arthur J. and Letitia A. (Pray) Cutter. *Education:* St. John's University, B.A., 1952; graduate study at New York University, 1956-58, and New School for Social Research, 1969. *Home and office:* 607 South Benson Rd., Fairfield, Conn. 06430.

CAREER: Weider Publications (publishers of *Mr. America, T.V. Boxing, Boxing & Wrestling, Inside Baseball*), Jersey City, N.J., associate editor, 1952-54; St. John's University, Brooklyn, N.Y., assistant to director of public relations, 1954-56; U.S. Rubber Co., New York, N.Y., public relations manager, 1956-60; D'Arcy Advertising Co., New York, N.Y., public relations account executive, 1960-64; General Dynamics Corp., New York, N.Y., public relations executive, 1964-68; Hudson River Valley Commission, Tarrytown, N.Y., director of public relations and publications, 1968-69; public relations consultant to business and industry, 1970—.

MEMBER: International Motor Press Association (vice-president, 1972; member of board of directors, 1970-71, 1973—), Federation Internationale des Associations de Journalistes de l'Automobile, American Auto Racing Writers and Broadcasters Association, American Aviation

Historical Society, Society of World War One Aero Historians, U.S. Naval Institute, New York Historical Society (life member), New York State Historical Association (life member).

WRITINGS: (Editor and contributor) *Sherlockian Studies*, privately printed, 1948; *The Rocky Marciano Story*, William Allen Publishing, 1954; (with Robert Fendell) *Encyclopedia of Auto Racing Greats*, Prentice-Hall, 1973; *The New Guide to Motorcycling*, Arco, 1974; (with Jas Patterson) *How to Go Single-Seater Racing*, Sports Car Press, 1975.

Author of "The Steering Column" in *Long Island Sunday Press*, 1958—, and "MotoSports" in *Saga*, 1972—. Contributor to *True's Baseball Yearbook*, and to *True's Boxing Yearbook*; contributor of more than eighty articles to sports and men's magazines, including *Saga, Baseball Illustrated, On the Sound, Sport, Americana, Competition Car, Sports Car, National Speed Sport News*, and *Impact*. Editor of *Redman* (of St. John's University), 1954-56; associate editor of *U.S.* (of U.S. Rubber Co.), 1956-60, and *Dynamis* (of General Dynamics Corp.), 1964. Automotive editor of *Saga*, 1973—; U.S. editor of *Competition Car International*, 1973—.

WORK IN PROGRESS: The Islands Called Wake (tentative title); *Fort Jefferson* (tentative title), about the south-of-Florida National Historic Site.

AVOCATIONAL INTERESTS: Collecting (books, political memorabilia, scale model cars, stamps), travel (Europe, Caribbean, England), cars, motion pictures, sports, aviation, ships and naval matters, history, biography.

*   *   *

CUTTLE, Evelyn Roeding

PERSONAL: Daughter of George C. (a horticulturist) and Elizabeth T. (Thorne) Roeding; married Tracy D. Cuttle, August 12, 1933; children: Alexa (Mrs. Edward L. Cottingham), Lynn (Mrs. Henry Davis), Cynthia (Mrs. Roy T. Jackson). *Education:* Alliance Francaise, Paris, France, Diplome D'Etudes Francaises, 1926; University of California, Berkeley, A.B., 1930. *Politics:* Conservative. *Religion:* Protestant Christian. *Home:* 4330 Opal Cliff Drive, Santa Cruz, Calif. 95062.

CAREER: Author; missionary-traveler, currently associated with Grace Mission, Inc., Grand Rapids, Mich. Radio broadcaster, Bible reading program aired in California and the Philippines.

WRITINGS: God Gave Us Roeding Park, privately printed, 1971; *Be a Star Witness*, Christian Literature Crusade, 1972. Author of religious pamphlets. Contributor to periodicals including *Natural History Magazine, Homelife, Voice, Truth, She, Power for Living, Outreach*, and others.

WORK IN PROGRESS: Two books, *No Bars to Heaven* and *Lord, What Am I Doing Here?*

*   *   *

CZAJA, Michael   1911-

PERSONAL: Surname sounds like "high-ya"; born October 22, 1911, in Adams, Mass.; son of Antoni and Mary (Mendes) Czaja; married Helen Manley (a teacher), October 21, 1938; children: Viki (Mrs. Dennis Wong), Toni (Mrs. Robert G. Crane). *Education:* Rensselaer Polytechnic Institute, B.Arch., 1934, M.Arch., 1936. *Home:* 1440 Maria Lane, Walnut Creek, Calif. 94596. *Office:* Department of Architecture, University of California, Berkeley, Calif. 94720.

CAREER: Architect in the United States and abroad, 1936-44; Bennington College, Bennington, Vt., director of curriculum in architecture, 1944-47; Washington State College, Pullman, associate professor of architecture, 1947-48; University of California, Berkeley, lecturer, 1948-50, associate professor, 1950-58, professor of architecture, 1958—. Visiting professor, Stanford University, 1948; lecturer at Waseda University, Keio University, Hiroshima University, and Kyoto University, all 1962. Has had thirty-six one-man exhibitions of his paintings in galleries and museums, including Denver Art Museum, Santa Barbara Art Museum, California Palace of the Legion of Honor in San Francisco, San Francisco Museum of Art, Albany Institute of History and Art, Phoenix Art Museum, and in many group shows; his fifty rubbings of sacred Japanese roadside carvings from sculptures found in Nagano Prefecture in 1961-62 have been exhibited. Chairman of Walnut Creek planning commission, 1951, member of board of directors of Valley Art Center, 1952-70, president, 1956; member of California Board of Architectural Examiners. Appeared on NHK-Radio in Japan, 1962. Exhibition chairman of Japanese Modern Print Show at several California schools, 1963-64.

WRITINGS: (With wife, Helen Czaja) *The Bountiful Cow* (juvenile), Holt, 1944; *Gods of Myth and Stone*, Weatherhill, 1974. Contributor to *Architectural Association Journal* (London).

WORK IN PROGRESS: Roadside Gods: Sacred Stone Carvings of Japan; *Horses of the Gods: Shamanism in Japanese Folk Religion.*

SIDELIGHTS: Czaja writes that his book is ". . . the result of ten years probing of a folk art tradition characterized by stone sculptures found along the roadsides of remote areas of Japan. These sculptures portray a view of human sexuality that is direct, simple, and affectionate. They are the visual expression of religious beliefs held by the common people, and the gods carved in stone represent people from all walks of life—but always as man and wife. In this direct way these sculptures symbolize the fundamental concept that the making of life is the ultimate weapon against the finality of death." *Avocational interests:* Horseback riding.

* * *

D'AGOSTINO, Giovanna P. 1914-

PERSONAL: Born June 23, 1914, in Minneapolis, Minn.; daughter of John and Marie (Guiseppe) Iaquinto; husband deceased; children: Saverio, John, Eugene. *Politics:* "Best Party." *Religion:* Catholic. *Home:* 701 Buchanan St. N.E., Minneapolis, Minn. 55413. *Office:* Sammy D's, 1301-4th St. S.E., Minneapolis, Minn. 55414.

CAREER: Writer; lecturer; appears on ABC television show, "A.M. Chicago," and on television shows in Boston, Duluth, Minneapolis, and St. Paul. Member of board, University of Minnesota, Y.M.C.A., and Children's Theatre. *Awards, honors:* Voted woman of the year for City of Hope Foundation.

WRITINGS: Mama D's Homestyle Italian Cookbook, Western Publishing, 1974.

WORK IN PROGRESS: A book in menu form, *Mama D's Vegetarian Cookbook.*

DALRYMPLE, Byron W(illiam) 1910-

PERSONAL: Born August 7, 1910, in Fostoria, Mich.; son of Charles E. (a teacher) and Hattie (Church) Dalrymple; married Ellen F. Christoffers (a secretary), April 30, 1949; children: Michael C., Terence A. *Education:* University of Michigan, B.A., 1932. *Home address:* P.O. Box 709, Kerrville, Tex. 78028. *Agent:* August Lenniger, 437 Fifth Ave., New York, N.Y. 10016.

CAREER: Free-lance magazine writer, 1940—; War-Dal Productions (outdoor television filming), Kerrville, Tex., producer, scriptwriter, and actor, 1962—. *Awards, honors:* Sunset Travel Film Festival Award, 1971, for "Wildlife Cameraman"; citation of merit from National Outdoor Travel Film Festival, 1971, for "Discovering Wildlife Refuges," and 1975, for "What Is a Living Stream Worth"; Texas Tourist Development Award, 1973, for magazine writings.

WRITINGS: Light Tackle Fishing, McGraw, 1947; *Ice Fishing for Everybody*, Lantern Press, 1948; *Doves and Dove Shooting*, Putnam, 1949; *Fishing, Hunting, Camping*, Pocket Books, 1950, revised edition published as *Fundamentals of Fishing and Hunting*, 1959; *Sportsman's Guide to Game Fish*, Outdoor Life Book Club and World Publishing, 1968; *Hunting Across North America*, Outdoor Life Book Club and Harper, 1970; *Modern Book of the Black Bass*, Winchester Publishers, 1972; *Survival in the Outdoors*, Outdoor Life Book Club and Dutton, 1972; *Complete Book of Deer Hunting*, Winchester Publishers, 1973; *North American Big Game Hunting*, Winchester Publishers, 1974; *How To Call Wildlife*, Outdoor Life Book Club, 1975; *Fishing for Fun with Byron Dalrymple*, Winchester Publishers, 1975.

Contributor: Brian Vesey-Fitzgerald and Francesca La-Monte, editors, *Game Fish of the World*, Harper, 1949; Bill Bueno, editor, *American Fisherman's Guide*, Prentice-Hall, 1952; Chet Fish, editor, *The Outdoor Life Deer Hunting Book*, Outdoor Life Book Club, 1974; Robert Elman, editor, *Hunting America's Game Birds and Animals*, Winchester Press, 1975.

Contributor to *Encyclopaedia Britannica, Outdoor Encyclopedia*, and *American Oxford Encyclopedia*. Contributor of over two thousand-five hundred articles to popular magazines, including *Field & Stream, True, Cosmopolitan, Holiday*, and *Better Homes and Gardens*. Writer and producer of twenty-four television film scripts. Columnist for *Sports Afield, Argosy*, and *Outdoor Life.*

WORK IN PROGRESS: Game Animals of North America for Outdoor Life Book Club.

* * *

DALTON, Richard 1930-

PERSONAL: Born October 1, 1930, in Philadelphia, Pa.; son of John F. and Marie (Sangmeister) Dalton; married Mary Gebhard (a secretary), May 25, 1963; children: Lisa Marie, Jennifer Ann, Christina Louise. *Education:* Williams College, B.A., 1952. *Politics:* Independent. *Religion:* Roman Catholic. *Home:* 5002 Barto St., Midland, Mich. 48640. *Office:* Dow Chemical Co., 2020 Dow Center, Midland, Mich. 48640.

CAREER: Procter & Gamble Co., Cincinnati, Ohio, field advisor and crew manager, 1955-58; Formica Corp., Cincinnati, manager of displays and exhibits, 1958-62; Dow Chemical Co., Midland, Mich., building production advertising manager, 1962-65, chemicals advertising manager,

1965-69, industrial advertising manager, 1969-72, manager of special projects, 1972—. *Military service:* U.S. Marine Corps, 1952-54; became first lieutenant. *Awards, honors:* Advertising Club of New York Andy Award of Excellence, 1972, for corporate advertising campaign, and award of merit, 1974, for *All about Energy;* Esquire Corp. social responsibility in advertising award, 1973.

WRITINGS: All about Energy (children's book), Third Press, 1975.

WORK IN PROGRESS: An expanded series of educational children's books on business, environment, health, and nutrition.

* * *

DALY, Saralyn R(uth) 1924-

PERSONAL: Born May 11, 1924, in Huntington, W.Va.; daughter of John R. and Ruth (Kaufman) Daly. *Education:* Ohio State University, B.A. (with high distinction), 1944, M.A., 1945, Ph.D., 1950; graduate study at Yale University, 1945-46; summer postdoctoral student at Indiana University, 1952. *Office:* Department of English, California State University, Los Angeles, Calif. 90032.

CAREER: College of Emporia, Emporia, Kan., professor of English and chairman of department, 1949-50; Midwestern University, Wichita Falls, Tex., professor of English, 1950-61; Texas Christian University, Fort Worth, associate professor of English, 1961-62; California State University, Los Angeles, assistant professor, 1962-66, associate professor, 1966-72, professor of English, 1972—. Fulbright professor at American University at Beirut, 1964-65, Tokyo Gakugei University and Tsuda College, 1967-68, and University of Bujumbura, Burundi, 1970-71. *Member:* Mediaeval Academy of America, Modern Language Association of America, Phi Beta Kappa. *Awards, honors:* American Council of Learned Societies grant to study at Indiana University, 1952.

WRITINGS: Katherine Mansfield, Twayne, 1965; (translator with A. N. Zahareas) Juan Ruiz, *Book of True Love,* New York University Press, in press. Contributor of articles and short stories to English journals, including *Descant* and *Notes and Queries.*

WORK IN PROGRESS: Two novels, *Biyumbura* and *In the Net.*

SIDELIGHTS: Saralyn Daly has competence in French, German, Greek, Russian, Italian, Spanish, Turkish, Latin, and Japanese.

* * *

DAM, Hari N(arayan) 1921-

PERSONAL: Born October 1, 1921, in Sylhet, India; son of Hem Chandra (a landlord) and Nihar (Sengupta) Dam. *Education:* University of Calcutta, B.A., 1944, M.A. (ancient Indian history and culture), 1947; University of Minnesota, M.A. (journalism), 1961, Ph.D., 1968. *Politics:* Democrat. *Religion:* Hindu. *Home:* 622 West Ella, #4, Kingsville, Tex. 78363. *Office:* Department of Journalism, Texas A & I University, Kingsville, Tex. 78363.

CAREER: University of Minnesota, Minneapolis, instructor in communications, 1962-64; Montana State University, Bozeman, assistant professor, 1964-68, associate professor of journalism, 1968-70; Texas Agricultural and Industrial University, Kingsville, associate professor of journalism, 1970—, acting chairman of department, 1974—.

Member: Association for Education in Journalism, Texas Association of College Teachers, Sigma Delta Chi, Kappa Tau Alpha.

WRITINGS: The Intellectual Odyssey of Walter Lippmann: A Study of His Protean Thought, Gordon Press, 1973. Contributor to journals.

WORK IN PROGRESS: No Easy Answers: Problems in Mass Communication; a historiography.

SIDELIGHTS: Dam writes: "My major interest now centers around the problem of alienation in mass society and its relation to the ever-increasing demand for entertainment peddled by the mass media. I'm also interested in the rationality of technology and its imperatives and its dehumanizing effects on modern man."

Dam was actively engaged in India's freedom movement. Following independence in 1947, he was a member of the Indian National Congress until 1956.

* * *

DAMIANI, Bruno Mario 1942-

PERSONAL: Born April 15, 1942, in Trieste, Italy; naturalized U.S. citizen; son of Vito and Maria Damiani; married. *Education:* Received early schooling in Bergamo, Italy; Ohio State University, B.A., 1963, M.A., 1964; Johns Hopkins University, Ph.D., 1967. *Home:* 6700 Belcrest Rd., Apt. 610, Hyattsville, Md. 20782. *Office:* Catholic University of America, Washington, D.C. 20017.

CAREER: Catholic University of America, Washington, D.C., instructor in Italian, summer, 1966, assistant professor, 1967-69, associate professor of Romance languages and literature, 1969—. Visiting lecturer or lecturer in Spanish at Goucher College, 1966-67, Johns Hopkins University, spring, 1967, American University, 1967-68, and University of Maryland, 1969-70. Specialist with Institute of International Studies, U.S. Office of Education, 1970-71.

MEMBER: Modern Language Association of America, Asociacion Internacional de Hispanistas, American Association of Teachers of Spanish and Portuguese, Italian Professionals of America (member of executive board, 1973-74), American Association of University Professors, South Atlantic Modern Language Association (chairman of Spanish I Section, 1971-72), Italian Cultural Society of Washington (vice-president, 1972-73), Sigma Delta Pi. *Awards, honors:* American Philosophical Society research grant, 1974; American Council of Learned Societies travel grant, 1974.

WRITINGS: (Author of introduction and notes) *La Lozana Andaluza,* Clasicos Castalia (Madrid), 1969; (co-editor) *Estudios literarios de hispanistas norteamericanos dedicados a Helmut Hatzfeld con motivo de su 80 aniversario,* Catholic University of America Press, 1973; (author of introduction and notes) *La Celestina,* Catedra (Madrid), 1974; (author of introduction and notes) *La Picara Justina,* two volumes, Castalia, 1974; *The Life and Works of Francisco Delicado,* Twayne, 1974. Contributor of articles and reviews to language journals.

WORK IN PROGRESS: Jorde de Montemayor and *F. Lopez de Ubeda,* both critical-analytical studies, for Twayne; a critical edition of *La Lozana Andaluza,* with Giovanni Allegra.

* * *

DAMTOFT, Walter A(tkinson) 1922-

PERSONAL: Born June 1, 1922, in Asheville, N.C.; son of

Walter J. (a forester and paper company executive) and Dorothy Damtoft; married Janet Russell (a journalist and public information specialist), March 31, 1951; children: Russell Walter, Lisa. *Education:* Attended Yale University, 1940-41; University of North Carolina, B.S., 1944. *Home:* 11013 Montrose Ave., Garrett Park, Md. 20766. *Office: National Observer*, 11501 Columbia Pike, Silver Spring, Md. 20910.

CAREER: WKIX-Radio, Columbia, S.C., time salesman, 1947; *Arkansas Gazette*, Little Rock, reporter, 1947-50; *Asheville Citizen*, Asheville, N.C., reporter, 1950-54, city editor, 1954-55; *Charlotte Observer*, Charlotte, N.C., reporter, 1955-56, city editor, 1956-58, North Carolina editor, 1958-60, Carolinas editor, 1960-62; *National Observer*, Silver Spring, Md., staff writer, 1962-69, government and politics reporter, 1963-65, Washington columnist (author of "This Week in Washington"), 1963-65, news editor, 1969-72, senior editor in charge of consumer affairs and travel departments, 1972—. Member of Garrett Park Town Council, 1972—. *Military service:* U.S. Navy, deck officer on sub tender, 1943-46; served in Pacific theater; became lieutenant junior grade. U.S. Naval Reserve, 1946—; present rank, lieutenant. *Member:* American Society of Travel Writers (first vice-chairman of Mid-Atlantic chapter), Society of Professional Journalists, Garrett Park Citizens Association (president, 1969-71), Sigma Delta Chi.

WRITINGS: (Editor) *Consumer's Handbook II*, Dow Jones, 1971; (editor) *Here's Help!*, Dow Jones, 1974.

SIDELIGHTS: In 1971, Damtoft was the fifteenth U.S. citizen to fly (as a passenger) over the Bernese Alps from Switzerland to Italy in a gas balloon.

*   *   *

DANIEL, Glyn (Edmund) 1914-
(Dilwyn Rees)

PERSONAL: Born April 23, 1914, in Lampeter Velfrey, Pembrokeshire, England; son of John and Mary Jane (Edmunds) Daniel; married Ruth Langhorne, 1946. *Education:* University College, University of Wales, student, 1931-32; St. John's College, Cambridge, B.A., 1935; Cambridge University, Ph.D., 1938, M.A., 1939. *Home:* The Flying Stag, 70 Bridge St., Cambridge, England; and La Marniere, Zouafques-par-Tournehem, 62890 France. *Office:* St. John's College, Cambridge University, Cambridge, England.

CAREER: Cambridge University, Cambridge, England, fellow of St. John's College, 1938-45, faculty assistant lecturer, 1945-48, university lecturer in archaeology, 1948-74; Disney Professor of Archaeology, 1974—. Steward of St. John's College, 1946-55. Munro Lecturer, University of Edinburgh, 1954; Rhys Lecturer, British Academy, 1954; O'Donnell Lecturer, University of Edinburgh, 1956; Josiah Mason Lecturer, University of Birmingham, 1956; Gregynog Lecturer, University College, Cardiff, 1968; Ballard-Matthews Lecturer, University College of North Wales, 1968; visiting professor, University of Aarhus, 1968; Ferrens Professor, University of Hull, 1969; George Grant MacCurdy Lecturer, Harvard University, 1971. Director of Anglia Television Ltd., Antiquity Publications Ltd., and Cambridge Arts Theatre. Trustee, Cambridge Arts Theatre. *Military service:* Royal Air Force, intelligence officer, 1940-45; became wing commander.

MEMBER: Society of Antiquaries (fellow), Instituto Italiano di Preistoria e Protostoria (honorary member), German Archaeological Institute (corresponding fellow), Jutland Archaeological Society (corresponding member), South Eastern Union of Scientific Societies (president, 1955), Bristol and Gloucestershire Archaeological Society (president, 1962-63), United Oxford and Cambridge University Club. *Awards, honors:* Knight (First Class) of the Dannebrog, 1961; Litt.D., Cambridge University, 1962.

WRITINGS: The Three Ages: An Essay on Archaeological Method, Cambridge University Press, 1943; (under pseudonym Dilwyn Rees) *The Cambridge Murders* (novel), Gollancz, 1945.

A Hundred Years of Archaeology, Duckworth, 1950; *The Prehistoric Chamber Tombs of England and Wales*, Cambridge University Press, 1950; (with Stuart Piggott) *A Picture Book of Ancient British Art*, Cambridge University Press, 1951; *Welcome Death* (novel), Gollancz, 1954, Dodd, 1955; *Lascaux and Carnac*, Lutterworth Press, 1955, revised and enlarged edition published as *The Hungry Archaeologist in France: A Travelling Guide to Caves, Graves, and Good Living in the Dordogne and Brittany*, Faber, 1963; (with others) *Myth or Legend?* (broadcasts), Macmillan, 1955; (with Thomas George Eyre Powell) *Barclodiad y Gawres: The Excavation of a Megalithic Chamber Tomb in Anglesey, 1952-53*, Liverpool University Press, 1956; *The Megalith Builders of Western Europe*, Hutchinson, 1958, Praeger, 1959.

(Translation editor) Raymond Block, *Die Etrusker*, M. DuMont Schauberg, 1960; *The Prehistoric Chamber Tombs of France: A Geographical, Morphological, and Chronological Survey*, Thames & Hudson, 1960; *The Idea of Prehistory*, C. A. Watts, 1962, World Publishing, 1963; *The Pen of My Aunt*, Merry Boys (Cambridge), 1962; (with Sean P. O'Riordain) *New Grange and the Bend of the Boyne*, Praeger, 1964; (editor with Idris Llewelyn Foster), *Prehistoric and Early Wales*, Routledge & Kegan Paul, 1965; *Oxford Chicken Pie*, Merry Boys, 1966; *Man Discovers His Past*, Duckworth, 1966, Crowell, 1968; *The Origins and Growth of Archaeology*, Penguin, 1967, Crowell, 1968; (with J. D. Evans) *The Western Mediterranean*, Cambridge University Press, 1967; *The First Civilizations: The Archaeology of Their Origins*, Crowell, 1968.

Archaeology and the History of Art, University of Hull, 1970; *Megaliths in History*, Thames & Hudson, 1972. General editor of series, "Ancient Peoples and Places," Thames & Hudson, 1958—. Contributor to *Nation, Natural History*, and archaeological journals. Editor, *Antiquity*, 1958—.

SIDELIGHTS: According to the *Times Literary Supplement*, "[Daniel's] reputation as an archaeologist of great experience and breadth of knowledge ensures that both what he cites and what he writes is well worthy of careful study." Discussing *The Origins and Growth of Archaeology*, P. C. Hammond states: "Daniel's contributions in this volume, as both historian and archaeologist, make it a professional presentation of major significance.... In particular, the emergence of Daniel's current anthropological outlook in this volume is far broader (and more specific) than in the past and will become a matter of professional concern in future discussions regarding the definition and origins of 'civilizations' ('culture')."

AVOCATIONAL INTERESTS: Travel, walking, swimming, food, wine, writing detective novels.

*   *   *

DANIEL, Norman (Alexander) 1919-
PERSONAL: Born May 8, 1919, in Manchester, England;

son of Frederick George (a building inspector) and Winifred (a writer; maiden name, Jones) Daniel; married Marion Ruth Pethybridge (a teacher at time of marriage), August 23, 1941; children: David Richard Gerald Patrick (deceased). *Education:* Oxford University, B.A., 1940; University of Edinburgh, Ph.D., 1956. *Politics:* "Uncommitted." *Religion:* Roman Catholic. *Home:* Landmark, Flimwell, Wadhurst TN5 7PA, England. *Office:* British Embassy, Cairo, Egypt.

CAREER: Civil Defence, St. Pancras, London, England, light rescue worker, 1941-44; Save the Children Fund, relief worker in Greece, 1944-45; British Council, London, England, assistant representative in Basra, Iraq, 1947-48, Baghdad, 1948-52, 1957-60, Beirut, Lebanon, 1952-53, Edinburgh, Scotland, 1953-57, 1960-62, and representative in Khartoum, Sudan, 1962-69; Cambridge University, University College, Cambridge, England, visiting fellow, 1969-70; British Council representative counselor and cultural attache at British Embassy in Cairo, Egypt, 1971—. *Awards, honors:* Commander of Order of the British Empire.

WRITINGS: Islam and the West: The Making of an Image, Aldine, 1960, revised edition, 1966; *Islam, Europe, and Empire*, Aldine, 1966; *The Arabs and Mediaeval Europe*, Longmans, Green, 1975; *The Cultural Barrier*, University of Edinburgh Press, 1975. Contributor to learned journals.

WORK IN PROGRESS: Research on medieval European attitudes toward the Arab and Islamic world; studying modern problems of intercultural relations, especially cultural imperialism.

SIDELIGHTS: Daniel writes that he is primarily a medievalist, also interested in the application of remoter history to modern imperialist and post-imperialist history. He maintains a strong belief in the need for cultures to retain their differences. *Avocational interests:* Gardening.

*   *   *

DANIELLS, Roy 1902-

PERSONAL: Born April 6, 1902, in London, England; emigrated to Canada in 1910; son of James (a builder) and Constance Daniells; married Laurenda Francis, 1948; children: Susan, Sara. *Education:* University of British Columbia, B.A., 1930; University of Toronto, M.A., 1931, Ph.D., 1936. *Home:* 1741 Allison Rd., Vancouver V6T 1S7, British Columbia, Canada.

CAREER: Victoria College, Toronto, Ontario, lecturer, 1934-37; University of Manitoba, Winnipeg, head of the department of English, 1937-46; University of British Columbia, Vancouver, head of the department of English, 1948-65, professor, 1965-74. *Member:* Royal Society of Canada (fellow; president, 1970-71). *Awards, honors:* LL.D., University of Toronto, 1964, Queen's University, Kingston, Ontario; Lorne Pierce medal, 1970; named Companion of the Order of Canada, 1972; also holds honorary degrees from McMaster University and the Universities of New Brunswick, Windsor, and British Columbia.

WRITINGS: (Editor) Thomas Traherne, *A Serious and Pathetical Contemplation of the Mercies of God, in Several Most Devout and Sublime Thanksgivings for the Same* ... (poetry), University of Toronto Press, 1941; *Deeper into the Forest* (poetry), McClelland & Stewart, 1948; (contributor) J. Park, editor, *The Culture of Contemporary Canada*, Cornell University Press, 1957; *The Chequered Shade* (poetry), McClelland & Stewart, 1963; *Milton,*

Mannerism, and Baroque, University of Toronto Press, 1963; (contributor and associate editor) S. F. Klinck, editor, *Literary History of Canada*, University of Toronto Press, 1965; *Alexander Mackenzie and the North West*, Barnes & Noble, 1969.

Represented in anthologies, including: *Canadian Poetry in English*, edited by B. Carman and others, Ryerson Press, 1954; *Blasted Pine*, edited by F. R. Scott and A. J. M. Smith, Macmillan (Toronto), 1957; *Oxford Book of Canadian Verse in English and French*, selected and introduced by A. J. M. Smith, Oxford University Press, 1960; *Penguin Book of Canadian Verse*, compiled by Ralph Gustafson, Penguin (Harmondsworth), 1967. Contributor of poetry to periodicals, including *Fiddlehead, Canadian Literature, University of Toronto Quarterly, Dalhousie Review*; contributor of scholarly articles and reviews to learned journals in Canada and the United States.

SIDELIGHTS: Daniells writes mostly in sonnet form using contemporary language. A major subject of his poetry is religion.

BIOGRAPHICAL/CRITICAL SOURCES: British Columbia Library Quarterly, Number 24, July, 1960.

*   *   *

DANIELSON, J. D.
See JAMES, M. R.

*   *   *

DANISH, Barbara 1948-

PERSONAL: Born December 7, 1948, in Washington, D.C.; daughter of Abraham Wolfe (a physician) and Sophie (an artist; maiden name, Levinson) Danish. *Education:* Goucher College, B.A., 1970; Johns Hopkins University, M.A., 1973. *Home:* 3602 Sequoia Ave., Baltimore, Md. 21215.

CAREER: Teacher of writing and modern dance for gifted and talented children in the public schools of Baltimore, Md., 1974—; poet.

WRITINGS: The Dragon and the Doctor, Feminist Press, 1972. Contributor of poems to *Far Point, Interstate, New Voices, Stonecloud, Aleph*, and *Green Horse for Poetry*.

WORK IN PROGRESS: A sequel to *The Dragon and the Doctor*; poetry.

*   *   *

DARK, Harris Edward 1922-

PERSONAL: Born November 23, 1922, in Springfield, Mo.; son of Melville Evan (an insurance salesman) and Katherine (O'Dowd) Dark; married Phyllis Betty Dolan, October 29, 1949; children: Katherine Ann. Michael Philip, Joan Amelia, Christine Marie, Diana Sue, Beverly Jean, Emily Jane. *Education:* University of Missouri, Drury College Extension, diploma in electronics engineering, 1943; Southwest Missouri State University, A.B. (journalism), 1947, B.S. (speech), 1948. *Politics:* Independent. *Religion:* Roman Catholic. *Home and office:* 1057 South Roanoke Ave., Springfield, Mo. 65807.

CAREER: KGBX-Radio, Springfield, Mo., announcer, 1947-48; WCLO-Radio, Janesville, Wis., announcer, 1948; WGEZ-Radio, Beloit, Wis., news editor, 1948-49; Sun Electric Corp., Chicago, Ill., export manager, 1950-57; free-lance magazine writer and editor, 1957—. Public relations consultant, 1971—. *Military service:* U.S. Army Air

Forces, Air Transport Command, manager of radio stations in China and editor of *Kiangwan Raven* in Shanghai, 1943-46; served in China-Burma-India theater.

MEMBER: Society of American Travel Writers, Missouri Writers Guild (president, 1958), Chicago Press Club, Chicago Headline Club, Sigma Delta Chi. *Awards, honors:* Public safety award from National Safety Council, 1964; medical journalism award from American Medical Association, 1966.

WRITINGS: The Wankel Rotary Engine: Introduction and Guide, Indiana University Press, 1974; *Auto Engines of Tomorrow: Power Alternatives for Cars to Come,* Indiana University Press, 1975. Contributing editor of *Changing Times,* 1963—; editor of *Family Safety,* 1965-71; editor of *Direction* (of C.N.A. Financial Corp.), 1970-72.

WORK IN PROGRESS: Continuing research on alternative automobile engines, on new sources of energy, antipollution measures, recycling of paper, metal, and combustibles.

* * *

DARR, Ann 1920-

PERSONAL: Born March 13, 1920; married; children: three daughters. *Education:* University of Iowa, B.A., 1941. *Home:* 4902 Falstone Ave., Chevy Chase, Md. 20015.

CAREER: Radio writer and actress for National Broadcasting Company (NBC) and American Broadcasting Company (ABC), both New York, N.Y.; writer. Recorder for the blind for Library of Congress. Member of election board, Somerset Town. *Military service:* Women's Air Force Service Pilots, World War II. *Member:* Poetry Society of America, Academy of American Poets, Phi Beta Kappa, Zeta Phi Eta. *Awards, honors:* Annapolis Arts Festival award, Discovery 70 award from New York Poetry Center, Hollins Critic award, and Georgia Review award, all 1970.

WRITINGS: St. Ann's Gut (poetry), Morrow, 1971; *The Myth of a Woman's Fist,* Morrow, 1973. Also author of plays and short stories. Contributor to periodicals including *New Republic Quarterly, New York Times, Poetry Northwest, New Mexico Quarterly, Voyages, New Orleans Review, Dryad, Southern Poetry Review, Saturday Evening Post, Buffalo Stamps, Red Clay Reader, Quartet, Hollins Critic, Mill Mountain Review,* and *Charles Street Journal.*

SIDELIGHTS: Ms. Darr holds a commercial multi-engine pilot's license and an Army instrument instructor's rating.*

* * *

DARRAH, William C(ulp) 1909-

PERSONAL: Born January 12, 1909, in Reading, Pa.; son of William Henry (an engineer) and Dorothy (Culp) Darrah; married Helen Marie Hinsman (a college professor), December 28, 1934; children: Barbara Anne (Mrs. Mason Philip Smith), Elsie Louise (Mrs. Philip R. Morey). *Education:* University of Pittsburgh, B.S., 1931, graduate study, 1931-33. *Home:* R.D. 1, Gettysburg, Pa. 17325.

CAREER: Harvard University, Cambridge, Mass., instructor in botany and paleobotany, and research curator, 1934-42; Raytheon Manufacturing Co., Waltham, Mass., research and development engineer, 1942-51; Gettysburg College, Gettysburg, Pa., professor of biology, 1952-74, professor emeritus, 1974—. Research associate in paleobo-

tany, West Virginia Geological Survey, 1974—. Advisory editor, Chronica Botanica Co., 1939-57. Director, Adams County Public Library, 1952-55. *Member:* Botanical Society of America, Society for the History of Technology, Adams County Historical Society (director, 1954; curator, 1959-64).

WRITINGS: Principles of Paleobotany, Chronica Botanica, 1939, 2nd edition, Ronald, 1960; *Textbook of Paleobotany,* Appleton, 1939; *An Introduction to the Plant Sciences,* Wiley, 1942; *Powell of the Colorado,* Princeton University Press, 1951; *Stereo Views: A History of Stereographs in America,* privately printed, 1964; *A Critical Review of the Pennsylvanian Floras of Eastern North America,* privately printed, 1970; *Pithole: The Vanished City,* privately printed, 1972; *Engineering at Gettysburg College,* Gettysburg College, 1973. Contributor of more than 125 articles to science and history journals.

WORK IN PROGRESS: Two books, *The World of Stereographs,* and *The Tradition of Science in America;* a history of the natural vegetation of Pennsylvania, tentatively entitled *Penn's Woods.*

SIDELIGHTS: Darrah has traveled throughout France, Belgium, the Netherlands, and in the eastern United States doing geological fieldwork. He maintains a large cross-indexed research collection of stereographs.

* * *

DARVILL, Fred T(homas), Jr. 1927-

PERSONAL: Born August 16, 1927, in Salt Lake City, Utah; son of Fred Thomas and Ruth (Schols) Darvill; married Eunice Waterbury, December 30, 1953; children: Fred Thomas III, Kari Duna. *Education:* University of Washington, Seattle, B.S. (magna cum laude), 1948, M.D. (with honors), 1951. *Office:* 809 South 15th, Mount Vernon, Wash. 98273.

CAREER: King County Hospital, Seattle, Wash., intern, 1951-52; Herman Kiefer Hospital, Detroit, Mich., resident, 1953; Veterans Administration Hospital, Seattle, Wash., resident, 1954-55, chief resident, 1955-56; physician in private practice in internal medicine in Mount Vernon, Wash., 1956—. Licensed to practice medicine in states of Washington, 1952, and California, 1965; diplomate of American Board of Internal Medicine, 1959. Member of hospital staff at Veterans Administration Hospital (Seattle), Northern State Hospital, Skagit Valley Hospital (chief of staff, 1968), Swedish Hospital, and University Hospital (Seattle). Assistant in medicine at University of Washington (Seattle), 1954-56, associate, 1956-60, clinical instructor, 1960-69, clinical assistant professor, 1969—. Member of board of directors of North Cascade Conservation Council, 1961-67, Skagit Mountain Rescue Unit, 1964-66 (president, 1967), and Washington Environmental Council, 1972-74; president of Skagit Environmental Council, 1974.

MEMBER: American College of Physicians (fellow), American Society of Internal Medicine, American Federation for Clinical Research, Federation of Western Outdoor Clubs (Washington vice-president, 1964-66), Northwest Society for Clinical Research, Washington State Society of Internal Medicine (fellow), Washington State Heart Association, Washington Wilderness Society (president, 1969-70), Skagit County Medical Society, Skagit Alpine Club (founder and first president; vice-president, 1969), Phi Beta Kappa, Alpha Omega Alpha.

WRITINGS: (Contributor) James Wilkerson, editor, *Medi-*

cine for Mountaineering, Seattle Mountaineers, 1967; Forty by Fred (poems), privately printed, 1968; A Pocket Guide to Selected Trails of the North Cascades National Park and Associated Recreational Complex, privately printed, 1968; (with Louise B. Marshall) Winter Hikes: A Pocket Guide to the Lowland Trails in Northwestern Washington, privately printed, 1970; A Pocket Guide to the North Cascades National Park and Associated Recreational Complex, privately printed, 1970; (with Marshall) Winter Walks: A Pocket Guide to Lowland Trails in Whatcom, Skagit, San Juan, and Island Counties, Signpost Publications, 1970; Mountaineering Medicine (booklet), Skagit Mountain Rescue Unit, 1965, 6th edition, 1972; Darvill's Guide to the North Cascades National Park and Associated Areas, Part I: Western Section, Part II: Eastern Section, privately printed, 1973; North Cascades Highway Guide, privately printed, 1973. Contributor to medical journals and mountaineering publications.

WORK IN PROGRESS: A seventh edition of Mountaineering Medicine; research in internal medicine.

SIDELIGHTS: From 1956 to 1958, Darvill coached his local Young Men's Christian Association (YMCA) swimming team. Avocational interests: Color photography, mountain climbing, travel.

*   *   *

DAS, Jagannath Prasad   1931-

PERSONAL: Born January 20, 1931, in Puri, Orissa, India; son of Biswanath (in postal service) and Nilomoni (Mohanty) Das; married Gita Dasmohapatra (a psychologist), 1955; children: Satya, Sheela. Education: Utkal University, B.A. (honors), 1951; Patna University, M.A., 1953; University of London, Ph.D., 1957. Religion: Hindu. Home: 11724—38A Ave., Edmonton, Alberta, Canada. Office: Centre for the Study of Mental Retardation, University of Alberta, Edmonton, Alberta T6G 2E1, Canada.

CAREER: Utkal University, Rhubaneswar, India, lecturer, 1953-55, reader in psychology, 1958-63; George Peabody College for Teachers, Nashville, Tenn., Kennedy Foundation Professor of Psychology, 1963-64; University of California at Los Angeles, associate professor of psychology, 1964-65; Utkal University, reader in psychology, 1965-67; University of Alberta, Centre for the Study of Mental Retardation, Edmonton, Alberta, research professor, 1968-71, director, 1972—. Member: International Association for Cross-Cultural Psychology, Canadian Psychological Association (fellow), American Psychological Association, American Association for the Advancement of Science. Awards, honors: Nuffield Foundation fellow at Institute of Psychiatry, University of London, 1972.

WRITINGS: Verbal Conditioning and Behavior, Pergamon, 1969; (contributor) N. R. Ellis, editor, International Review of Research in Mental Retardation, Volume VI, Academic Press, 1973; Asustha Mana (title means "Mental Illness"), Orissa Textbook Bureau, 1974. Contributor of over seventy articles to Journal of Experimental Psychology, British Journal of Psychology, and other professional journals. Editor of Indian Journal of Mental Retardation, 1967-68.

WORK IN PROGRESS: A book with David Baine, Mental Retardation for Special Educators, for C. C Thomas; research on attention in children, and on cognitive processes across cultures.

DATHORNE, O(scar) R(onald)   1934-

PERSONAL: Born November 19, 1934, in Georgetown, British Guiana (now Guyana); son of Oscar Robertson and Rosalie Belona (Peazer) Dathorne; married Hildegard Ostermaier, 1959; children: Shade Cecily and Alexander Franz Keith. Education: University of Sheffield, B.A. (honors), 1958, M.A., 1960, Ph.D., 1966; University of London, Grad. Cert. in Ed., 1959, Diploma in Ed., 1967. Home: 8904 Friedberg bei Augsburg, Luberstrasse 2, Germany.

CAREER: Ahmadu Bello University, Zaria, Nigeria, lecturer in English, 1959-63; University of Ibadan, Ibadan, Nigeria, lecturer in English, 1963-66; U.N.E.S.C.O., Paris, France, adviser to Government of Sierra Leone, 1967-68; University of Sierra Leone, Njala University College, Freetown, professor of English and chairman of department, 1968-70; professor of Afro-American studies at Howard University, Washington, D.C. and University of Wisconsin, 1970-71; Ohio State University, Columbus, professor of English and black studies, 1971—; visiting professor of literature, Florida International University, 1974—. Has given radio lectures and poetry readings for Nigerian Broadcasting Corp., B.B.C. (London), and several university-owned radio stations. Part-time teacher at Western Nigerian Training College, 1963-66, University of Sierra Leone, 1967-68; visiting professor at Yale University, 1970.

WRITINGS: Dumplings in the Soup (novel), Cassell, 1963; The Scholar-Man (novel), Cassell, 1964; (editor and author of introduction) Caribbean Narrative: An Anthology of West Indian Writing, Heinemann, 1966; (author of introduction) Donald St. John-Parsons, compiler, Our Poets Speak, University of London Press, 1966; (editor and author of introduction) Caribbean Verse: An Anthology, Heinemann, 1967; (editor with Willfried Feuser) Africa in Prose, Penguin, 1969; (editor and author of introduction) African Poetry for Schools and Colleges, Macmillan, 1969; (contributor) D. R. Dudley and D. M. Lang, editors, Penguin Companion to Literature: Part IV, Penguin, 1969; (contributor) Bruce King, editor, Introduction to Nigerian Literature, Evans Brothers, 1971; (author of introduction) Mongo Beti, King Lazarus, Collier-Macmillan, 1971; (contributor) David Lowenthal and Lambros Comitas, editors, West Indian Societies, Doubleday, 1973; The Black Mind: A History of African Literature, University of Minnesota Press, 1974; (editor with others) Four Way Dictionary, Cassell, in press; (author of introduction) Samuel Selvon, Ways of Sunlight, Heinemann, in press.

Represented in anthologies, including Young Commonwealth Poets '65, edited by P. L. Brent, Heinemann, 1965; Commonwealth Poems of Today, edited by Howard Sergeant, J. Murray, 1967; New Voices of the Commonwealth, edited by Sergeant, Evans Brothers, 1968. Contributor of verse to Black Orpheus, Transition, Outposts, and Presence Africaine; contributor of critical articles to Journal of Commonwealth Literature, Times Literary Supplement, New African, Phylon, London Magazine, and others.

WORK IN PROGRESS: A-Z of African Literature; Dark Ancestor: The Fourth World in Literature; writing introduction and notes to Selected Poems by Derek Walcott; translating Aime-Cesaire's Et les chiens se taissaient; a novel, Granman (tentative title).

*   *   *

DAVEY, John
See RICHEY, David

DAVIDOW, Mike 1913-

PERSONAL: Born February 15, 1913, in Russia; came to U.S., 1917; naturalized U.S. citizen, 1928; son of Joseph (a photographer and artist) and Maria (Hertzman) Davidow; married Ruth Gordon (a bookkeeper), November 26, 1947; children: Anthony, Michael, Joseph. *Education:* Attended Brooklyn College (now Brooklyn College of the City University of New York), 1930-34. *Religion:* "None. I'm Jewish, but I don't identify with any religion." *Home:* 1207 De Haro St., San Francisco, Calif. 94107. *Agent:* Leah Siegel, Am Rus Literary Agency, 25 West 43rd St., New York, N.Y. 10036.

CAREER: Has worked as a garment presser, and as a warehouse, department store, and hotel worker; *Daily World* (formerly *Daily Worker*), New York, N.Y., political writer and drama critic, 1961-68, Moscow correspondent, 1969-72; free-lance writer, 1972—. Organizer of Unemployed Councils and Workers Alliance, 1933-40. *Military service:* U.S. Army, 1942-45; served in Pacific Theatre. *Awards, honors:* First prize in nation-wide play contest sponsored by New Haven Jewish Community Center, 1964, for "The Long Life."

WRITINGS: Life Without Landlords, New Outlook, 1973; *Cities Without Crisis*, International Publishers, in press. Author of plays, "The Long Life," 1964; "Eagle-Doves," 1966; "The Closest Battlefield," 1969. Also author of pamphlet series, "The Soviet Union Through the Eyes of an American," 1974-76.

Contributor to newspapers in the Soviet Union, German Democratic Republic, and Bulgaria.

WORK IN PROGRESS: Peoples' Theatre: From the Box Office to the Stage; a book on U.S. and Soviet schools; a play about the Depression years.

SIDELIGHTS: Davidow writes: "My writing covers the journalistic and literary fields. I see them as complementing rather than competing with each other. In both, my pen is a weapon in the struggle for a more human world which can only be based on the most human society. My six years of life in the Soviet Union has confirmed my conviction that such a society is socialism. I was the first U.S. correspondent to go from Hanoi to the Demilitarized Zone (17th Parallel) in North Vietnam."

* * *

DAVIDSON, David 1908-

PERSONAL: Born May 11, 1908, in New York, N.Y.; son of Hyman N. (a cigar manufacturer) and Jeanette (Godnick) Davidson; married Hilda Abel (a novelist); children: Carla Abel. *Education:* City College (now of the City University of New York), B.A., 1928; Columbia University, B.Lit., 1930; London School of Economics and Political Science, further graduate study, 1931. *Home:* 114 East 90th St., New York, N.Y. 10028. *Agent:* Ann Elmo Agency, Inc., 52 Vanderbilt Ave., New York, N.Y. 10017.

CAREER: Newspaper reporter and foreign correspondent for *Brooklyn Eagle, New York World, New York Post, Baltimore News Post*, and for Universal Service in London, at various times, 1928-39; free-lance writer of novels, and of scripts for radio, television, and record albums, 1939—. Visiting professor of creative writing, University of Montana, 1952; writer-in-residence at Yale University School of Drama, 1965-66; instructor in film writing at New York University, 1966-67; writer-in-residence at University of Iowa, 1972. *Wartime service:* U.S. Military Government, civilian specialist in Germany, 1945-46.

MEMBER: International P.E.N., National Association of Television Arts and Sciences (governor and trustee), Writers Guild of America (past national chairman; past president of Eastern branch). *Awards, honors:* Pulitzer traveling fellowship, 1931; Christopher Award, 1954, for television drama, "POW"; Silver Gavel Award of American Bar Association, 1967, for television drama, "The Iron Man"; International Film Festival Award, 1968, for documentary, "The Sun Never Sets"; Gabriel Award, 1969, for documentary film, "Hook Down, Wheels Down"; Writers Guild of America Award, 1969, for documentary film, "The Ship that Wouldn't Die."

WRITINGS—Novels: The Steeper Cliff, Random House, 1947; *The Hour of Truth*, Random House, 1949; *In Another Country*, Random House, 1950; *The Quest of Juror Nineteen*, Doubleday, 1971; *We Few, We Happy Few*, Crown, 1974.

Author of over 100 television plays for programs, including "Playhouse 90," "Studio One," "U.S. Steel Hour," "Kraft Theatre," and "Armstrong Circle Theatre." Has written more than forty documentary films, for NBC Special Projects, U.S. Navy, U.S. Department of Defense, U.S. Information Agency, National Endowment for the Humanities, Muscular Dystrophy Association, the AFL-CIO, and other organizations.

SIDELIGHTS: Davidson writes: "I have never wanted to be anything but a writer, perhaps as a result of growing up in a New York jungle where the acknowledged leaders were boys who became world champion boxers and/or gangsters, and I lost too many bouts. After forty-seven years as a writer I still wake up in the morning disbelieving I managed it. An obsessive subject with me is physical and moral courage." He has made two record albums, "To the Moon," for Time-Life Records, and "The Nixon Tapes," for Warner Records.

AVOCATIONAL INTERESTS: Gardening, fishing, travel (has lived in England, France, Germany, and Ecuador), former tennis player and skier.

* * *

DAVIE, Michael 1924-

PERSONAL: Born January 15, 1924, in Cranleigh, Surrey, England; son of Russell (a stock broker) and Harriet (Browne) Davie; married Mollie Robin Atherton, November 8, 1954 (divorced, 1975); children: Annabel, Simon, Emma. *Education:* Merton College, Oxford, B.A., 1949. *Home:* 136 Fellows Rd., London N.W. 3, England. *Office: Observer*, 160 Queen Victoria St., London E.C.4, England.

CAREER: Observer, London, England, associate editor, 1969—. *Military service:* Royal Navy, 1942-46. *Awards, honors: Yorkshire Post* literary award, 1973.

WRITINGS: LBJ: A Foreign Observer's Viewpoint, Duell, Sloan & Pearce, 1966; *California: The Vanishing Dream*, Dodd, 1972; (editor) *The Diaries of Evelyn Waugh*, Little, Brown, in press.

* * *

DAVIES, Hunter 1936-

PERSONAL: Born January 7, 1936, in Renfrew, Scotland; son of John Hunter and Marion (Brechin) Davies; married Margaret Forster (an author), June 11, 1960; children: Caitlin, Jake. *Education:* University of Durham, B.A., 1957. *Home:* 11 Boscastle Rd., London NW5, England.

CAREER: Manchester *Evening Chronicle*, Manchester, England, reporter, 1958-60; *Sunday Times*, London, England, reporter, 1960, columnist ("Atticus"), 1961—; writer.

WRITINGS: Here We Go, Round the Mulberry Bush (novel), Heinemann, 1965, Little, Brown, 1966; (editor) *The New 'London Spy': A Discreet Guide to the City's Pleasures* (nonfiction), Blond, 1966, David White, 1967; *The Other Half* (nonfiction), Heinemann, 1966, published as *The Other Halves*, Stein & Day, 1968; *The Beatles: The Authorized Biography*, McGraw-Hill, 1968; (editor and contributor with seventeen others) *I Knew Daisy Smuten* (communal novel), Coward, 1970; *The Rise and Fall of Jake Sullivan* (novel), Little, Brown, 1970; *A Very Loving Couple* (novel), Weidenfeld & Nicolson, 1971; *The Glory Game*, Weidenfeld & Nicolson, 1972, St. Martin's, 1973; *Body Charge*, Sphere, 1974.

Film scripts: "The Rise and Fall of Jake Sullivan."

SIDELIGHTS: Here We Go, Round the Mulberry Bush and *The Rise and Fall of Jake Sullivan* have been made into movies.*

*   *   *

DAVIES, J. Kenneth 1925-

PERSONAL: Born April 30, 1925, in Los Angeles, Calif.; married; children: one. *Education:* Attended Denison University, 1943-44; Marquette University, B.N.S., 1945; Brigham Young University, M.S., 1950; University of Southern California, Ph.D., 1960. *Politics:* Republican. *Religion:* Church of Jesus Christ of Latter-day Saints. *Home:* 877 North 700 St. W., Provo, Utah 84601. *Office:* Brigham Young University, Provo, Utah 84602.

CAREER: Brigham Young University, Provo, Utah, instructor, 1953-57, assistant professor, 1957-59 and 1960-61, associate professor, 1961-64, professor of economics, 1964—, acting chairman of economics department, 1957-58. Visiting assistant professor, Duke University, 1959-60; visiting summer professor, University of Maryland, 1965. Director, Office of Education and Publication of Federal Deposit Insurance Corp., 1966-67; chairman, Mountain States Regional Manpower Advisory Committee, 1970-74; associate member, National Manpower Advisory Committee, 1970-74; associate vice-chairman, Mountainlands Manpower Advisory Committee, 1971—. Consultant, Olympus Research Corp., 1970—, Howard & Lewis (attorneys), 1970—, and to state and local education committees and school systems. Labor arbitrator. *Military service:* U.S. Naval Reserve; active duty, 1942-46. *Member:* American Economics Association, Industrial Relations Research Association (president of Utah chapter, 1969-71), American Association of University Professors (former vice-president of Utah council; former president of Brigham Young University chapter), Western Economics Association (section chairman, 1963), Utah Academy of Sciences, Arts, and Letters (chairman of economics section, 1962-63), Utah Council on Economic Education, Omicron Delta Epsilon. *Awards, honors:* Ford Foundation fellowship, 1960.

WRITINGS: (With Glen F. Ovard) *Economics and the American System* (text with teachers' edition and tests), Lippincott, 1970; *Deseret's Sons of Toil*, Olympus, 1975; (co-author) *Micro Manpower Planning in the Public Sector*, Olympus, 1975; *Artist With a Camera*, Brigham Young University Press, in press. Also co-author of Olympus Research Corp. papers. Contributor of articles to *Junior College Journal, Review of Religious Research, Utah Historical Quarterly, Dialogue*, and journals in his field.

DAVIES, Laurence 1926-

PERSONAL: Born in 1926, in Merthyr Tydfil, Glamorganshire, Wales; married Menna Morgan. *Education:* Studied at University of Wales and University of London; studied piano with Mark Hambourg, 1943-44. *Home:* 103 Minehead Ave., Sully, Glamorganshire, Wales.

CAREER: Monmouthshire, Wales, education officer, 1957-59; University of Wales, Cardiff, senior lecturer in psychology, 1966—; free-lance music critic. *Military service:* Royal Air Force, 1945.

WRITINGS: Liberal Studies and Higher Technology, University of Wales Press, 1965; *The Gallic Muse*, Dent, 1967, A. S. Barnes, 1969; *Cesar Franck and His Circle*, Houghton, 1970; *Ravel Orchestral Music*, British Broadcasting Corp., 1970, University of Washington Press, 1971; *Paths to Modern Music: Aspects of Music from Wagner to the Present Day*, Scribner, 1971; *Franck*, Octagon Books, 1973. Contributor of articles to *Music and Letters, Music, Opera, Music and Musicians, Journal of Liberal Education, Cambridge Review*.*

*   *   *

DAVIES, Thomas M(ockett), Jr. 1940-

PERSONAL: Born May 25, 1940, in Lincoln, Neb.; son of Thomas Mockett (a lawyer) and Faith (Arnold) Davies; married Eloisa Carmela Monzon, June 10, 1968; children: Jennifer Elena. *Education:* University of Nebraska, B.A., 1962, M.A., 1964; University of New Mexico, Ph.D., 1970; also attended Universidad Nacional Autonoma de Mexico, 1961. *Home:* 4617 Edenvale Ave., La Mesa, Calif. 92041. *Office:* Department of History, San Diego State University, San Diego, Calif. 92182.

CAREER: University of New Mexico, Albuquerque, lecturer in Latin American history at Peace Corps Center, 1964-66; San Diego State University, San Diego, Calif., assistant professor, 1968-72, associate professor, 1972-75, professor of Latin American, Andean, and American history, 1975—. Conducted research in U.S. National Archives, and in Peru and Bolivia.

MEMBER: Latin American Studies Association, Organization of American Historians, American Historical Association (conference on Latin American History), Organization of Andean Historians, Pacific Coast Council on Latin American Studies. *Awards, honors:* Fellowship from Henry L. and Grace Doherty Foundation, 1966-68, for research in Peru; postdoctoral fellowship from University of Texas, 1969-70; Hubert Herring Memorial Award from Pacific Coast Council on Latin American Studies, 1973, for a manuscript on Latin America.

WRITINGS: Indian Integration in Peru: A Half Century of Experience, 1900-1948, University of Nebraska Press, 1974; (contributor) John J. TePaske, editor, *Field Research Guide to the Andean Area*, Duke University Press, 1975. Contributor of articles and reviews to historical journals. Editorial consultant for *Hispanic American Historical Review, Societas, New Scholar, Journal of Developing Areas*.

WORK IN PROGRESS: The Politics of Anti-Politics: A Reader on the Military in Latin America, with Brian Loveman; *The Decade of Violence: A Socio-Political History of Peru in the 1930's*, completion expected in 1978; editing an annotated bibliography of books on Peru published in English between 1820 and 1970, with Howard Karno; *El Indigenismo Historico del Partido Aprista Peruana: Un Analisis Nuevo* (title means "The Indigenismo of the Peruvian Aprista Party: A Reinterpretation"), for Instituto de Estudios Peruanos; *La Integracion Legal de los Indios en el Peru, 1820-1948: Un Estudio Panoramico* (title means "Indian Integration in Peru, 1820-1948: An Overview"), Instituto de Estudios Peruanos.

AVOCATIONAL INTERESTS: Latin American travel, playing stringed instruments, American folk music.

* * *

DAVIS, Angela (Yvonne) 1944-

PERSONAL: Born January 26, 1944, in Birmingham, Ala.; daughter of B. Frank (a teacher and businessman) and Sallye E. (a teacher) Davis. *Education:* Sorbonne, University of Paris, student, 1963-64; Brandeis University, B.A. (magna cum laude), 1965; University of Frankfurt, graduate study, 1965-67; University of California, San Diego, M.A., 1968, graduate study, 1968-69. *Politics:* Communist. *Address:* c/o Communist Party U.S.A., 23 West 26th St., New York, N.Y. 10001.

CAREER: University of California, Los Angeles, acting assistant professor of philosophy, 1969-70; currently works with National Alliance Against Racist and Political Repression. *Awards, honors:* Ph.D. (honorary), Lenin University.

WRITINGS: (With Ruchell Magee, the Soledad Brothers, and others) *If They Come in the Morning: Voices of Resistance*, foreword by Julian Bond, Third Press, 1971; *Angela Davis: An Autobiography*, Random House, 1974. Contributor of articles to *Ebony* and other periodicals.

SIDELIGHTS: Angela Davis took part in civil rights demonstrations and helped form interracial study groups while a teen-ager in Birmingham. She attended the Elizabeth Irwin High School in New York on a scholarship from the American Friends Service Committee. In college, she studied under the political philosopher Herbert Marcuse, who considered her the best student he had ever had. While at the University of California, San Diego, she helped form the Black Students Council, worked with the San Diego Black Conference and the Student Nonviolent Coordinating Committee, and joined the Communist party on June 22, 1968.

In 1969, Ms. Davis was dismissed from the University of California faculty by the Board of Regents but was reinstated shortly thereafter by court order. The University of California, Los Angeles failed to renew her contract in 1970 and was censured by the American Association of University Professors for its decision. While on the faculty at the University of California, she was judged an "excellent" teacher and reasonably unbiased by the administration. Her reinstatement was unsuccessfully requested by the philosophy department in September, 1972. As the result of a trial in 1972 that aroused worldwide interest, Ms. Davis was acquitted of charges of kidnapping, murder, and conspiracy in connection with the 1970 escape attempt of George Jackson and other prisoners from the courthouse in Marin County, California.

The author may be heard on the record "Angela Davis Speaks," Folkways, 1971, and seen in the documentary "Portrait of a Revolutionary," prepared by one of her students.

BIOGRAPHICAL/CRITICAL SOURCES: Charles R. Ashman, *The People vs. Angela Davis*, Pinnacle Books, 1972.

DAVIS, Creath 1939-

PERSONAL: Born November 13, 1939, in Comanche, Tex.; son of Vernon (a telephone lineman) and Treva (Johnston) Davis; married Verdell Watson (a substitute teacher), February 26, 1960; children: David Creath, Shawna Lee, Stephen Mark. *Education:* Howard Payne University, B.A., 1962, graduate study, 1962-65; Southwestern Baptist Theological Seminary, M.Div., 1968. *Residence:* Dallas, Tex. *Address:* Christian Concern Foundation, P.O. Box 8049, Dallas, Tex. 75205.

CAREER: Ordained Baptist minister, 1958; minister in Gorman, Tex., 1958-61, and Deleon, Tex., 1961-66; Christian Concern Foundation, Dallas, Tex., founder, 1965, executive director, 1965—. Chaplain of Slaughter Industries, 1973—. Teacher of Psycho Cybernetics, 1971-73. *Member:* American Association of Marriage and Family Counselors (associate member).

WRITINGS: Beyond This God Cannot Go, Zondervan, 1971; *Sent to Be Vulnerable*, Zondervan, 1973.

WORK IN PROGRESS: How to Win in a Crisis, completion expected in 1976.

SIDELIGHTS: Davis led a World Civilization study tour of Western Europe, the Middle East and Far East during the summer of 1968. *Avocational interests:* Ranching, raising wheat.

* * *

DAVIS, George L(ittleton), Sr. 1921-

PERSONAL: Born November 21, 1921, in Knoxville, Tenn.; son of Fred Russell (a custodian) and Anna A. (Lowe) Davis; married Anna Novella Lawson (a school librarian), December 19, 1954; children: George L., Jr., Vernessa Lynn. *Education:* Knoxville College, A.B., 1940; University of Pittsburgh, M.A., 1948, Ph.D., 1951. *Politics:* Independent. *Religion:* Presbyterian. *Home:* 1431 15th Ave. S., Nashville, Tenn. 37212. *Office address:* Tennessee State University, 3500 Centennial Blvd., Nashville, Tenn. 37203.

CAREER: High school teacher of English in the public schools of Charlottesville, Va., 1941-42, and Clifton Forge, Va., 1942-43; State Teachers College, Elizabeth City, N.C., professor of history, 1951-58, head of department, 1952-58, acting dean of faculty, 1953-54, dean of faculty, 1954-58; Tennessee State University, Nashville, professor of history, 1958—, head of department of political science, 1958-70. *Military service:* US. Army Air Forces, 1943-46; served in European theater; became staff sergeant. *Member:* Southern Slavic Studies Association, Southern Historical Association, Southern Political Science Association, Tennessee Political Science Association (vice-president, 1973-74), North Carolina College Conference (secretary, 1954-58), Tennessee Historical Association, Association of College Deans and Registrars, Phi Alpha Theta, Alpha Phi Alpha.

WRITINGS: (With Amrit Lal and Samuel H. Shannon) *American National Government*, Volume I, W. C. Brown, 1967; (with Shannon and Anthony O. Edmonds) *Institutions of American Government*, MSS Information Corp., 1973; (contributor) Paul Mohr and Adelbert Jones, editors, *The Law and the Unitary System of Higher Education*, University of Nebraska Printing and Duplicating Service, 1975. Contributor to journals in his field.

WORK IN PROGRESS: Two books, *Readings in American History* and *Black Minorities in the Soviet Union*, completion expected in 1977.

AVOCATIONAL INTERESTS: Travel and bowling.

* * *

DAVIS, Harold S(eaton)   1919-

PERSONAL: Born September 5, 1919, in Detroit, Mich.; son of Maurice and Henriette (Seaton) Davis; married Jean V. Lee, November, 1946; children: Janice Lee. *Education:* Wayne State University, B.A., 1942, M.A., 1947, Ed.D., 1963; graduate study at Oxford University, 1945, and University of Paris, 1945. *Politics:* Independent. *Religion:* Protestant. *Home:* 15 Hallmark Dr., Wallingford, Conn. 06492. *Office:* Department of Administration and Supervision, Southern Connecticut State College, New Haven, Conn. 06515.

CAREER: Detroit Board of Education, Detroit, Mich., teacher, 1947-57, school administrator, 1957-63; Educational Research Council of America, Cleveland, Ohio, director of in-service education and staff utilization, 1963-69; Southern Connecticut State College, New Haven, professor of education, 1969—, chairman of department of administration and supervision, 1969—. Moderator of twenty half-hour educational panel programs for NBC-TV, 1966-67, and ten for WKYC-TV, Cleveland, 1966. *Military service:* U.S. Army, Artillery, 1941-46; became colonel; received Bronze Star Medal and European Theater Ribbon with four battle stars. *Member:* National Association of Secondary School Principals, National Association of Elementary School Principals, National Society for Study of Education, Connecticut Professors of Educational Administration (president, 1971-72), Phi Delta Kappa.

WRITINGS: The Effect of Team Teaching on Teachers, Wayne State University Press, 1963; *How To Organize an Effective Team Teaching Program,* Prentice-Hall, 1966; (contributor) Marion Pope Franklin, editor, *School Organization: Theory and Practice,* Rand McNally, 1967; (editor) *Innovative Teaching* (booklet), Area Cooperative Educational Services, 1970; (editor) *New Schools in Connecticut* (booklet), Area Cooperative Educational Services, 1970; (contributor) Robert H. Anderson, editor, *Current Trends in Education,* [Tokyo, Japan], 1971; *Instructional Media Center: Bold New Venture,* Indiana University Press, 1971; (contributor) Marjorie M. Cann, editor, *An Introduction to Education,* Crowell, 1972; *Modern Approaches to School Organization,* MSS Educational Publishing, 1974; (contributor) *Handbook of Successful School Administration,* Prentice-Hall, 1974; *Centros Audiovisuales,* Editorial Pax-Mexico, 1975.

Author of about twenty booklets, published by Educational Research Council of America. Contributor to Macmillan *Encyclopedia of Education,* and to education journals.

WORK IN PROGRESS: Wit and Wisdom; Supervision by Objectives.

* * *

DAVIS, Joseph S(tancliffe)   1885-1975

November 5, 1885—April 23, 1975; American economist, educator, statistician, editor, and author. Obituaries: *New York Times,* April 24, 1975; *Current Biography,* June, 1975.

* * *

DAVIS, Lanny J(esse)   1945-

PERSONAL: Born December 12, 1945, in Jersey City, N.J.; son of Mortimer (a dentist) and Frances (Goldberg) Davis; married Elaine Joyce Charney, December 18, 1966; children: Marlo, Seth. *Education:* Yale University, B.A., 1967, LL.B., 1970. *Home:* 11812 Selfridge Rd., Silver Spring, Md. 20906. *Agent:* Timothy Seldes, Russell & Volkening, 551 Fifth Ave., New York, N.Y. 10017. *Office:* 1200 17th St., Washington, D.C. 20036.

CAREER: Admitted to Bar of Connecticut, 1970, and District of Columbia, 1972; member of staff of Senator Abraham Ribicoff, 1968, and of Senator Edmund Muskie, Washington, D.C., 1970-72; Patton, Boggs & Blow, Washington, D.C., attorney, 1975—. Democratic candidate for U.S. House of Representatives from Eighth District of Maryland, 1974. *Member:* District of Columbia Bar Association.

WRITINGS: The Emerging Democratic Majority, Stein & Day, 1974. Contributor to *Washington Post* and *Washington Monthly.* Contributing editor of *Democratic Review.*

* * *

DAVIS, R. G.   1933-

PERSONAL: Born July 9, 1933, in Brooklyn, N.Y.; son of Herman B. (a manufacturer) and Shirley (Gerst) Davis; children: Matthew Aaron Davis-Raffael, Robert Bryan Davis-Raffael. *Education:* Attended Ohio University, 1951-53, University of New Mexico, 1953-55. *Politics:* "Left-Left." *Address:* c/o Ramparts Press, Box 10128, Palo Alto, Calif. 94303.

CAREER: Member of Actors Workshop, San Francisco, Calif., 1959-63; director, producer, actor, teacher, San Francisco Mime Troupe, San Francisco, 1960-70. Member of Artists Liberation Front, 1965-66. *Member:* Actors Equity Association, Portrero Hill League of Active Neighbors. *Awards, honors:* Fulbright grant to Paris, 1957.

WRITINGS: God Forbid, Exposition, 1974; *The San Francisco Mime Troupe: The First Ten Years,* Ramparts, 1975.

Contributor: Massimo Teodori, editor, *New Left: A Documentary History,* Bobbs-Merrill, 1971; Erika Monk, editor, *Brecht,* Bantam, 1972. Contributor to *Film Quarterly, Ramparts, Jump/Cut, Take One, City, Tulane Drama Review, Performance.*

WORK IN PROGRESS: Method Mime Mar, completion expected in 1976; *Commedia dell'Arte in Practice,* completion expected in 1977.

* * *

DAWLEY, Powel Mills   1907-

PERSONAL: Born March 1, 1907, in Newport, R.I.; son of William James and Mabel Cleveland (Wilson) Dawley; married Dorothy Wainwright Knapp, December 1, 1941; children: Victoria Wainwright, Pamela Wilson, Dorothy Maris. *Education:* Brown University, Ph.B., 1929, A.M., 1931; Episcopal Theological School, B.D., 1936; Corpus Christi College, Cambridge, Ph.D., 1938; General Theological Seminary, S.T.D., 1955. *Home:* 6 Sparwell Lane, Brunswick, Me. 04011.

CAREER: Ordained dean of Protestant Episcopal Church, 1935, priest, 1936; St. David's Church, Baltimore, Md., associate rector, 1938-42; St. Luke's Cathedral, Portland, Me., dean, 1942-45; General Theological Seminary, New York, N.Y., professor of ecclesiastical history, 1945-71, sub-dean and professor emeritus, 1971—. *Member:* American Society of Church History, Lambda Sigma Nu, Masons. *Awards, honors:* Phillips Brook fellow, 1936; D.D., Episcopal Theological School, 1961, Brown University, 1965.

WRITINGS: (With Walden Pell) *The Religion of the Prayer Book*, Morehouse, 1943, 2nd edition, 1950; *Highlights of Church History, The Reformation*, Church Historical Society, 1949; (with authors' committee of the Department of Christian Education) *Chapters in Church History*, National Council, Protestant Episcopal Church, 1950, revised edition, Seabury, 1963; *The Words of Life: Addresses for Good Friday on the Words of Christ on the Cross*, Oxford University Press, 1950; *Brazilian Destiny*, National Council, Protestant Episcopal Church, 1951; *John Whitgift and the English Reformation*, Scribner, 1954; (with James Thayer Addison and authors' committee of the Department of Christian Education) *The Episcopal Church and Its Work*, Seabury, 1955, revised edition, 1961; *Our Christian Heritage: Church History and the Episcopal Church*, Morehouse, 1959, 2nd edition, 1965; *The Story of the General Theological Seminary: A Sesquicentennial History, 1817-1967*, Oxford University Press, 1969. Author of booklets about the Episcopal Church.*

* * *

DAWSON, Jennifer

EDUCATION: St. Anne's College, Oxford, B.A., 1952.

CAREER: Social worker in a mental hospital; staff member at Clarendon Press, Oxford, England; novelist and short story writer. *Awards, honors:* Black Memorial prize, 1962.

WRITINGS: The Ha-Ha (novel), Little, Brown, 1961; *Fowler's Snare* (novel), Anthony Blond, 1962; *The Cold Country* (novel), Anthony Blond, 1965; (contributor) E. J. Burnley, editor, *Penguin Modern Stories 10*, Penguin, 1972.

SIDELIGHTS: According to the *Times Literary Supplement:* "Off-putting as the description may sound, Miss Dawson must now take her place, along with George Eliot and many other distinguished predecessors, as a novelist with a mission. Society—'free society' as she ironically refers to it—may not need quite so much of a shock now to make readers uncomfortably aware of its ills, but casualties remain; it is even possible that Miss Dawson wants us to share with her the conviction that these are more shocking, more hopelessly irredeemable, under the welfare state than ever they were in workhouse and gallows days ... her intense and rare vision of worlds it is conventional to shun has now established her as one of the most necessary, as well as most skilled, of all the defiant originals in the fictional field."

The Ha-Ha was adapted for the stage, produced in London in 1968, and shown on television in 1969.*

* * *

DAYTON, Irene 1922-

PERSONAL: Born August 6, 1922, in Lake Ariel, Pa.; daughter of F. B. and Effie (Wargo) Glossenger; married Benjamin B. Dayton (a physicist), October 16, 1943; children: David B., Glenn C. *Education:* Roberts Wesleyan College, A.A., 1942. *Politics:* Republican. *Religion:* Protestant. *Home:* 209 South Hillandale Dr., East Flat Rock, N.C. 28726.

CAREER: Poet. Poet-in-residence in high schools and colleges. *Member:* International Platform Association, International Poetry Society, Poetry Society of America, North Carolina Poetry Society, Rochester Poetry Society (president, 1960-62, 1970-72). *Awards, honors:* Poetry Guinness Award in the Cheltenham, England Festival of Literature, 1963.

WRITINGS: The Sixth Sense Quivers (poems), Windy Row, 1970; *The Panther's Eye* (poems), Windy Row, 1974.

Poems anthologized in *Golden Year Anthology*, edited by Melville Care, John Farrar, and Louise Nicholl, Poetry Society of America, 1960; *Editions Moderne Review*, edited by Jacques Cardonnet, [Paris], 1962, 1964; *The Various Light*, edited by Leah B. Drake and Charles Muses, [Switzerland], 1964; *The Diamond Anthology*, edited by Charles Angoff and others, Poetry Society of America, 1971; *Adam Among the Television Trees*, edited by Virginia Mollenkot, Word Books, 1971. Contributor to poetry journals and literary magazines in the United States, Europe, and Japan, including *Poet Lore, Kansas Quarterly, Malahat Review, Roanoke Review, Midwest Quarterly, Modern Age, Black Mountain Review, Poetry-Australia, Quixote, Literary Review*, and *Chicago Sunday Magazine*. Editor of *Rochester Poetry Society Anthology*, 1958-69 and 1969-70.

WORK IN PROGRESS: The Rain Forest (poems), completion expected in 1977 or 1978; *Tale of the Vercors*, an epic poetic drama of the French Resistance in novel form, 1977.

SIDELIGHTS: Mrs. Dayton told *CA:* "I am a working poet writing in free verse cadence who truly believes a poet must stay in the stream of life trying to understand the joys and sufferings of mankind. The poet sees the world with heightened awareness that is both the penalty and glory of poets—and he follows unmarked paths in imagery, rhythm, meaning through disciplines of the creative faculty where memory is a winged angel. The poet needs energy and great reserves to draw upon."

* * *

DEAGON, Ann (Fleming) 1930-

PERSONAL: Born January 19, 1930, in Birmingham, Ala.; daughter of Robert Fulton (a grocer) and Alice (Webb) Fleming; married Donald David Deagon (a drama professor), June 29, 1951; children: Andrea Webb, Ellen Lathrop. *Education:* Birmingham-Southern College, B.A., 1950; University of North Carolina, M.A., 1951, Ph.D., 1954. *Politics:* Democratic Party. *Religion:* Society of Friends (Quaker). *Home:* 802 Woodbrook Dr., Greensboro, N.C. 27410. *Office:* Department of Classics, Guilford College, Greensboro, N.C. 27410.

CAREER: Furman University, Greenville, S.C., assistant professor of classics, 1954-56; Guilford College, Greensboro, N.C., professor of classics, 1956—. *Member:* Academy of American Poets, American Philological Association, American Classical Association, Vergilian Society, North Carolina Poetry Society (president, 1974-75), North Carolina Writers Conference (secretary, 1974-75), Alabama State Poetry Society, Alabama Writers Conclave, Greensboro Writers Club, Phi Beta Kappa. *Awards, honors:* Recipient of thirty-five prizes for poetry in state and national contests, 1970-75.

WRITINGS—Poetry: *Poetics South*, Blair, 1974; *Carbon 14*, University of Massachusetts Press, 1974; *Indian Summer*, Unicorn Press, 1975; *There Is No Balm in Birmingham*, Godine Press, 1976. Contributor of one hundred and fifty poems to forty-five magazines.

WORK IN PROGRESS: The Polo Poems, completion expected in 1977.

* * *

DEAN, Roy 1925-

PERSONAL: Born August 2, 1925, in London, England; son of Henry Charles (a signwriter) and Alice (Hopkins) Dean. *Education:* Privately educated in Reading, England. *Religion:* Christian. *Residence:* Los Angeles, Calif. *Office:* Rho-Delta Press, 807 Hillsdale Ave., Los Angeles, Calif. 90069.

CAREER: Actor and photographer.

WRITINGS—All published by Rho-Delta Press: *A Time in Eden*, 1969; *Before the Hand of Man*, 1972; *The Naked Image*, 1974; *A World of Nudes*, 1975; *The Ecstasy of Eden*, 1975; *The Orison*, 1975; *In Search of Adam*, 1975. Also author of scripts for documentary films, "The Virgin Islands" and "The October Trees."

WORK IN PROGRESS: Outside of Eden.

SIDELIGHTS: Dean was British Hurdling Champion for two years.

* * *

deBARY, William Theodore 1919-

PERSONAL: Born August 9, 1919, in Bronx, N.Y.; son of William Emil and Mildred (Marquette) deBary; married Fanny Brett, June 16, 1942; children: Mary Brett, Paul Ambrose, Catherine Anne, Mary Beatrice. *Education:* Columbia University, A.B., 1941, A.M., 1948, Ph.D., 1953. *Home:* 98 Hickory Hill Rd., Tappan, N.Y. 10983. *Office:* 205 Low, Columbia University, New York, N.Y. 10027.

CAREER: Columbia University, New York, N.Y., 1949—, professor of Chinese and Japanese, 1959-66, Horace Walpole Carpenter Professor of Oriental Studies, 1966—, chairman of department of East Asian languages and cultures, 1960-66, director of East Asian Language and Area Center, 1960—, executive vice-president for academic affairs and provost, 1971—. Director of Catholic Commission on Intellectual and Cultural Affairs, 1960—. *Military service:* U.S. Naval Reserve, 1942-46; became lieutenant commander. *Member:* Association of Asian Studies (member of board of directors, 1961-64; president, 1969-70), American Council of Learned Societies (fellow, 1947-48), China Society, Japan Society of New York (member of board of directors, 1964-66). *Awards, honors:* Fulbright scholarship to China, 1948-49; Watumull Prize from American Historical Association, 1958; Fishburn Prize of Educational Press Association, 1964; D.Litt., St. Lawrence University, 1968; L.H.D., Loyola University, Chicago, 1970.

WRITINGS—All published by Columbia University Press, except as noted: (Editor) *Sources of Indian Tradition*, 1958; (editor) *Sources of Japanese Tradition*, 1958; (editor) *Approaches to Oriental Classics*, 1959; (editor) *Approaches to Chinese Tradition*, 1960; (editor) *Approaches to Asian Civilizations*, 1964; *A Guide to Oriental Classics*, 1964; (editor) *The Buddhist Tradition*, 1968; (compiler) *The Buddhist Tradition in India, China and Japan*, Modern Library, 1969; (editor) *Self and Society in Ming Thought*, 1970; *The Unfolding of Neo-Confucianism*, 1975. Oriental records editor, *Records of Civilization*, 1952—.

DEBERDT-MALAQUAIS, Elisabeth 1937-

PERSONAL: Born September 12, 1937, in Neuf-Brisach, France; daughter of Charles H. and Helene (Ancel) Deberdt; married Jean Paul Malaquais (a writer), March 22, 1963; children: Dominique (daughter). *Education:* University of Paris, Licence-es-lettres, 1959; Columbia University, Ph.D., 1965. *Home:* 6 Norfolk Terrace, Wellesley, Mass. 02181; and 18 rue Visconti, Paris 6e, France 75006. *Agent:* William Aspenwall Bradley, 18 Quai de Bethune, Paris 4e, France.

CAREER: Columbia University and Barnard College, New York, N.Y., assistant professor of French literature, 1958-63; Wellesley College, Wellesley, Mass., assistant professor of French literature, 1963-65; Monash University, Clayton, Victoria, Australia, lecturer in French literature, 1966-67; Wellesley College, Wellesley, Mass., 1968—, began as assistant professor, now associate professor of French literature. *Member:* Modern Language Association, American Association of University Professors. *Awards, honors:* Fulbright scholar, 1958-59; American Council of Learned Societies fellow, 1971-72.

WRITINGS: La Quete de l'identite dans le theatre de Ghelderode, Editions Universitaires (Paris), 1967; (contributor of translation) Alain Bosquet, *Selected Poems*, Ohio University Press, 1972.

Translator from the English: Alice Fleming, *Educatrices a l'oeuvre*, Nouveaux Horizons, 1965; Frederick M. Watkins, *L'Ere des Ideologies*, Nouveaux Horizons, 1966; Ronald Gross, editor, *Moderniser l'enseignement*, Nouveaux Horizons, 1972; Herbert Gold, *Le Boum a l'americaine*, Calmann-Levy (Paris), 1972; Lawrence A. Cremin, *L'Ecole en marche*, Nouveaux Horizons, 1975.

WORK IN PROGRESS: An Anthology of Contemporary French Literature in English Translation; A Study of the French Intellectual Emigration to the Americas During the Second World War.

SIDELIGHTS: Ms. Deberdt-Malaquais has a thorough knowledge of French and English and a good knowledge of Spanish and Italian. *Avocational interests:* Travels to the Far East, Australia, and extensively throughout Europe.

* * *

DE CANIO, Stephen J(ohn) 1942-

PERSONAL: Born July 9, 1942, at Crow Agency, Mont.; son of John (a physician) and Alice (a hospital administrator; maiden name, Hamernik) DeCanio; married Carol Beatrice Hoffman (a poet), August 6, 1972. *Education:* University of Oklahoma, student, 1960-62; University of California, Berkeley, B.A., 1964; Massachusetts Institute of Technology, Ph.D., 1972. *Residence:* New Haven, Conn. *Office:* Department of Economics, Yale University, New Haven, Conn. 06520.

CAREER: Yale University, New Haven, Conn., assistant professor of economics, 1972—. *Member:* American Economic Association, Economic History Association, University Seminar in Economic History (at Columbia University).

WRITINGS: Architecture in the Postbellum South: The Economics of Production and Supply, M.I.T. Press, 1974. Contributor to *Journal of Economic History* and *Reviews in American History*.

WORK IN PROGRESS: Research on the economic consequences of the American Civil War, on a history of

American agriculture from 1866 to 1975, and on economics and the political history of the United States.

* * *

de CRESPIGNY, (Richard) Rafe (Champion) 1936-

PERSONAL: Surname is pronounced *Krep*-ny; born March 16, 1936, in Adelaide, South Australia; son of Richard Geoffrey and Kathleen Cavenagh (Cudmore) Champion de Crespigny; married Christa Charlotte Boltz (a researcher); children: Christine Anne, Richard Mark. *Education:* Cambridge University, B.A. (history; honors), 1957, M.A., 1961; University of Melbourne, B.A., 1961; Australian National University, B.A. (Chinese; honors), 1962, M.A. (honors), 1964, Ph.D., 1967. *Religion:* Anglican. *Home:* 3 Arnhem Pl., Red Hill, Australian Capital Territory 2603, Australia. *Office:* Department of Chinese, Australian National University, Camberra, Australian Capital Territory, Australia.

CAREER: Australian National University, Canberra, lecturer, 1965-70, senior lecturer, 1970-74, reader in Chinese, 1974—, sub-dean of faculty of Oriental Studies, 1965-67, member of tour to People's Republic of China, 1973. Visiting lecturer at University of Melbourne, 1966. Senior research fellow on Han Project at University of Washington, Seattle, 1971; visiting fellow at Clare Hall, Cambridge, 1971-72; academic exchange visitor of Federal Republic of Germany, 1972. Secretary general of Twenty-Eighth International Congress of Orientalists; member of third Sino-American Conference on Mainland China, 1973.

MEMBER: Royal Geographical Society of Australasia (South Australian branch), Australian Institute of International Affairs (president of Canberra branch and member of national executive committee, 1973—; acting director, 1974), Oriental Society of Australia (councillor), Asian Society of Canberra.

WRITINGS: The Biography of Sun Chien, Centre of Oriental Studies, Australian National University, 1966; (with H. H. Dubs) *Official Titles of the Former Han Dynasty* (monograph), Australian National University, 1967; *The Last of the Han* (monograph), Australian National University, 1969; *The Records of the Three Kingdoms,* Centre of Oriental Studies, Australian National University, 1970; *China: The Land and Its People,* St. Martin's, 1971; *China This Century: A History of Modern China,* Thomas Nelson, 1975. Contributor to Asian studies and education journals.

WORK IN PROGRESS: The Geography of Han China; The Fall of the Later Han Dynasty and the Politics of the Second Century A.D. in China; translating, with Liu Ts'un-yan, *Nieh hai hua,* a novel by Tseng P'u.

SIDELIGHTS: de Crespigny writes: "I started with an interest in China: academically it is an enormous, rich, and fascinating field. I now find that I am interested primarily in the history of states in decline—and from that point of view the collapse of the great Han empire in the second century is a tragedy as impressive and moving as the tragedy of China in the first part of this century."

* * *

DELANEY, Bud
See DELANEY, Francis, Jr.

DELANEY, Francis, Jr. 1931-
(Bud Delaney)

PERSONAL: Born August 26, 1931, in Morris, N.Y.; son of Francis J. and Helen (Fullington) Delaney; married Lolo Reed (a writer), March 2, 1957; children: Kris, Ron, Terri, Kyle. *Education:* State University Teachers College (now State University of New York College at Oneonta), B.S., 1957, M.S., 1960. *Home and office:* 608 Curry Rd., Schenectady, N.Y. 12306.

CAREER: Has been employed as a bartender, and as construction worker; teacher in central schools of New Berlin, N.Y., 1957-59, West Winfield, N.Y., 1959-62, and Rotterdam, N.Y., 1962-71; presently manager of Polish National Alliance (fraternal group), also baseball and basketball official, and songwriter. Basketball coach, 1957-58. Presently summer teacher of driver education in Colonie, N.Y., schools, and substitute teacher in Schenectady, N.Y. area schools. *Military service:* U.S. Navy, 1950-54.

WRITINGS:–Under name Bud Delaney; with wife, Lolo Delaney: *The Daily Laugh,* Scholastic Book Services, 1973; *The Laugh Journal,* Scholastic Book Services, 1974.

WORK IN PROGRESS: Four collections of humorous stories for Scholastic Book Services: *It Only Hurts When I Laugh, Photo-Fun, Awful Lawful Laughs,* and one involving animals, all with Lolo Delaney.

* * *

DELANEY, Lolo M(ae) 1937-

PERSONAL: Born March 2, 1937, in Oneonta, N.Y.; daughter of Clifford (a trailer park owner) and Phyrn (Pettus) Reed; married Francis Delaney, Jr. (a writer and teacher), March 2, 1957; children: Kris, Ron, Terri, Kyle. *Education:* Attended New York State Agricultural and Technical Institute at Delhi (now Agricultural and Technical College at Delhi), 1955-57. *Home and office:* 608 Curry Rd., Schenectady, N.Y. 12306.

CAREER: Writer.

WRITINGS—All with husband, Bud Delaney: *The Daily Laugh,* Scholastic Book Services, 1973; *The Laugh Journal,* Scholastic Book Services, 1974.

WORK IN PROGRESS—All with husband, Bud Delaney: A collection of humorous stories involving animals, for Scholastic Book Services; three additional humorous collections, *It Only Hurts When I Laugh, Photo-Fun,* and *Awful Lawful Laughs.*

* * *

DELANO, Kenneth J(oseph) 1934-

PERSONAL: Born April 12, 1934, in Taunton, Mass.; son of Kenneth E. (an engineer) and Isabelle (Tatro) Delano. *Education:* St. Mary's Seminary and University, Baltimore, Md., B.A., 1956, graduate study, 1956-60. *Politics:* Independent. *Home:* 22 Ingell St., Taunton, Mass. 02780. *Office:* St. Patrick's Rectory, 1598 South Main St., Fall River, Mass. 02724.

CAREER: Ordained Roman Catholic priest by Diocese of Fall River, Mass., 1960; assistant pastor of Roman Catholic churches in Fall River, Mass., 1960-61, Wareham, Mass., 1961-62, and New Bedford, Mass., 1962-67; St. Patrick's Parish, Fall River, Mass., assistant pastor, 1971—. *Member:* Astronomical League (chairman of Northeast region, 1968-70), Association of Lunar and Planetary Observers (member of staff, 1964—), American Association of Variable Star Observers, British Astronomical Association.

WRITINGS: Astrology: Fact Or Fiction?, Our Sunday Visitor Press, 1973. Contributor to astronomy and theology journals.

WORK IN PROGRESS: A book about the possibility of intelligent life in space and its religious implications.

SIDELIGHTS: Delano writes: "Except for a correspondence course provided by the University of California, I learned astronomy on my own, through reading and experience. I have made several telescopes over the years, the largest being a reflector telescope with a twelve and a half inch mirror. The sight of a 'shooting star' when I was only seven years old first aroused my interest in astronomy.... During the International Geophysical Year (1957-58), I participated in the Visual Meteor Program, observing and reporting over two thousand meteors to the National Research Council of Canada.... During the Apollo Program, I was a member of the Smithsonian Astrophysical Observatory's Lunar International Observers' Network submitting observations of glows on the moon that might be of a volcanic nature ... I received invitations from NASA to watch from the VIP viewing stands the launches of Apollo 15 and Apollo 17. I have also had the pleasure of observing four total eclipses of the sun, by journeying to Maine, Virginia, Nova Scotia, and most recently, to Akjoujt, Mauritania...." *Avocational interests:* Nature, photography.

*   *   *

D'ELIA, Donald John   1933-

PERSONAL: Born June 16, 1933, in Jersey City, N.J.; son of Anthony (an architect and officer in the U.S. Army) and Frances (Santello) D'Elia; married Margaret P. Cingle, May 25, 1957; children: Keith Christopher, Gregory Stephen, Nancy Marie, Anthony Francis. *Education:* Citadel, student, 1952-53; Rutgers University, B.A., 1956, M.A., 1957; Pennsylvania State University, Ph.D., 1965. *Religion:* Roman Catholic. *Home:* 14 Mohonk Ave., New Paltz, N.Y. 12561. *Office:* Department of History, State University of New York College at New Paltz, New Paltz, N.Y. 12561.

CAREER: Bloomsburg State College, Bloomsburg, Pa., assistant professor, 1961-63, associate professor of social studies, 1963-65; State University of New York College at New Paltz, associate professor, 1965-71, professor of history, 1971—. Boyd Lee Spahr Lecturer at Dickinson College, 1966; lecturer at Marist College (Poughkeepsie, N.Y.), 1967. Faculty adviser, University of Dijon, 1972. Volunteer worker for Hungarian Relief Program (Operation Mercy, Camp Kilmer, N.J.), 1956-57. *Military service:* U.S. Army, 1956-57; became first lieutenant. U.S. Army Reserve, 1957-64. *Member:* Friends of the Dickinson College Library.

WRITINGS: (Contributor) Charles C. Sellers, editor, *Boyd Lee Spahr Lectures in Americana*, Dickinson College, 1970; *Benjamin Rush: Philosopher of the American Revolution*, American Philosophical Society, 1974. Contributor to Harper *Encyclopedia of American Biography*; contributor to professional journals.

WORK IN PROGRESS: The American Revolution in the Perspective of Western Civilization; historical and philosophical studies of the eighteenth and nineteenth centuries.

*   *   *

DE LIMA, Clara Rosa   1922-
   (Penelope Driftwood)

PERSONAL: Born July 27, 1922, in Trinidad, West Indies; daughter of Yldefonso (a merchant) and Rosario (Hernandez) De Lima. *Education:* Attended Long Island University, 1945-48. *Politics:* "Left of center." *Religion:* "None though christened Catholic." *Home:* Aldegonda Flats, 7 St. Anns Rd., Port of Spain, Trinidad, West Indies. *Agent:* Anita Diamant, 51 East 42nd St., New York, N.Y., 10017.

CAREER: Clara De Lima Holdings, Port of Spain, Trinidad, director, 1952-54; during the years 1954-68 was private executive secretary to a bank vice-president who later became Venezuelan ambassador to Brazil, an economic advisor in the Dominican Republic, and lastly, a vice-president of General Electric in England; Yldefonso De Lima and Co., Port of Spain, Trinidad, director, 1968—. Writer. Volunteer social worker, 1970—.

WRITINGS: Tomorrow Will Always Come (novel), Obolensky, 1965; *Thoughts and Dreams* (poems), Stockwell, 1973; *Dreams Non Stop* (poems), Stockwell, 1974; *Reminiscing* (poems), Stockwell, in press; *Not Bad: Just a Little Mad* (novel), Stockwell, in press. Contributor of short stories and articles to periodicals. Author of poems, occasionally under pseudonym Penelope Driftwood.

WORK IN PROGRESS: A novel about carnival in Brazil; research on the background of the De Lima family, Sephardics who came to the New World three hundred years ago.

SIDELIGHTS: Clara Rosa De Lima has travelled extensively and has lived in the Caribbean, North and South America, and Europe.

*   *   *

DeLOACH, Clarence, Jr.   1936-

PERSONAL: Born March 20, 1936, in Dickson, Tenn.; son of Clarence T. (a farmer) and Ella (Batey) DeLoach; married Eddie A. Lowe, June 10, 1956; children: Angela, Rhonda, Darrell, Craig. *Education:* Freed Hardeman College, A.A., 1965; attended David Lipscomb College, 1956-58. *Home:* 505 Schultz St., Parkersburg, W.Va. 26101. *Office:* Church of Christ, 2900 Camden Ave., Parkersburg, W.Va. 26101.

CAREER: Ordained Church of Christ minister; minister in Rossville, Ga., 1958-63, and in Marietta, Ohio, 1963-68; Church of Christ, Parkersburg, W.Va., minister, 1968—. Instructor in homilectics at Ohio Valley College, 1969-75.

WRITINGS: Christ, America, and the New Morality, Christian Publications, 1968; *Bound to Abound*, Parchment Press, 1969. Contributor to *Bible Herald*. Member of staff of *Gospel Advocate*, 1971—.

WORK IN PROGRESS: Research on Armstrongism.

*   *   *

DELTON, Judy   1931-

PERSONAL: Born May 6, 1931, in St. Paul, Minn.; daughter of A. F. (a plant engineer) and Alice (Walsdorf) Jaschke; married Jeff J. Delton (a school psychologist), June 14, 1958; children: Julie, Jina, Jennifer, Jamie. *Education:* Attended School of Associated Arts, 1950, and College of St. Catherine, 1954-57. *Home:* 511 Sixth St., Hudson, Wis. 54016.

CAREER: Dental assistant, bank teller, bookkeeper; elementary school teacher in parochial or private schools of St. Paul, Minn., 1957-64; free-lance writer. Lecturer at University of Wisconsin, 1973, and at Lakewood Community College, Minnesota Metropolitan State College, and Minneapolis schools, all 1974—. *Awards, honors: Two Good Friends* was named an American Library Association Notable Book, 1975.

WRITINGS: Two Good Friends (Junior Literary Guild selection), Crown, 1974; *Rabbit Finds a Way*, Crown, 1975. Contributor of about two hundred essays, articles, poems, and short stories to popular magazines including *Wall Street Journal, Saturday Review, Humpty Dumpty, Instructor*, and *Highlights for Children*.

WORK IN PROGRESS: A children's book series for Crown.

BIOGRAPHICAL/CRITICAL SOURCES: Junior Literary Guild, March, 1974; *Hudson Star-Observer*, June 20, 1974; *St. Paul Sunday Pioneer Press*, August 11, 1974.

* * *

DE MARINIS, Rick   1934-

PERSONAL: Born May 3, 1934, in New York, N.Y.; son of Alphonse and Ruth (Siik) De Marinis; married Carole Joyce Bubash (an artist and writer); children: Richard Michael, Suzanne Louise, Naomi Anna. *Education:* Attended San Diego State College (now University), 1952-54; and University of Montana, B.A., 1961, M.A., 1967. *Politics:* Independent. *Home:* 10142 Aquilla Dr., Lakeside, Calif. 92040. *Agent:* Jane Schwenger, Box 5295, Grand Central Station, N.Y. 10017. *Office:* Department of English, San Diego State University, San Diego, Calif. 92115.

CAREER: University of Montana, Missoula, instructor in English, 1967-69; San Diego State University, San Diego, Calif., assistant professor of English, 1969—. *Military service:* U.S. Air Force, 1954-58.

WRITINGS: A Lovely Monster (novel), Simon & Schuster, 1976. Contributor of short stories to *Esquire, Atlantic Monthly, Iowa Review, Malahat Review, Cavalier, Colorado State Review*, and other publications.

WORK IN PROGRESS: Scimitar, a novel.

* * *

De MILLE, Nelson   1943-

PERSONAL: Born August 23, 1943, in New York, N.Y.; son of Huron (a builder) and Antonia (Panzera) De Mille; married Ellen Wasserman (a medical technologist), July 17, 1971. *Education:* Hofstra University, B.A., 1970. *Politics:* "Dead center." *Religion:* Roman Catholic. *Home and office:* 4 Sixth Pl., Garden City, N.Y. 11530. *Agent:* Robert P. Mills Ltd., 156 East 52nd St., New York, N.Y. 10022.

CAREER: Carpenter, electrician's apprentice, lumber yard worker, house painter, men's clothing salesman, art dealer, stable boy, deck hand on a sloop, and insurance investigator; National Learning Corp., Plainview, N.Y., editorial assistant, 1972-73; novelist. *Military service:* U.S. Army, Infantry, 1966-69; became first lieutenant; received Bronze Star Medal, Air Medal, combat infantryman's badge, Vietnamese Cross of Gallantry. *Member:* Mensa.

WRITINGS:—All police novels: *The Sniper*, Leisure Books, 1974; *The Hammer of God*, Leisure Books, 1974; *The Agent of Death*, Leisure Books, 1974; *The Smack Man*, Manor Books, 1975; *The Cannibal*, Manor Books, 1975; *The Night of the Phoenix*, Manor Books, 1975.

WORK IN PROGRESS: Three novels, one tentatively titled *Death Squad*.

SIDELIGHTS: "A rather unstructured life of college, Army, and drifting has provided me with numerous anecdotes and stories," De Mille wrote. "My first books were in the contemporary New York City police genre because the vehicle provided by that type of book was useful in commenting on the establishment and anti-establishment sub-cultures in modern urban America. I plan eventually to look at contemporary American society through the eyes of members of other cultures and sub-cultures; lawyers, politicians, doctors, businessmen, farmers, etc. . . . I feel . . . all the definitive statements on the world in which we live have been and can best be handled more effectively by the novelist."

* * *

DeMIRJIAN, Arto, Jr.   1931-

PERSONAL: Born January 9, 1931, in New York, N.Y.; son of Arto DeMirjian. *Education:* Attended high school in New York, N.Y. *Home:* 23 Leroy St., New York, N.Y. 10014.

CAREER: Holt, Rinehart & Winston, New York, N.Y., in college advertising, 1961-65; Free Press/Macmillan, New York, N.Y., marketing manager, 1965-67; Bantam Books, New York, N.Y., promotion manager in education, 1967-71.

WRITINGS: Not a Clue, Popular Library, 1974. Contributor of short stories to *Ararat*. Contributing editor, *Publisher's Weekly*.

AVOCATIONAL INTERESTS: Photography, the graphic arts.

* * *

DENBIE, Roger
See GREEN, Alan (Baer)

* * *

DENNIS-JONES, H(arold)   1915-
(Paul Hamilton, Dennis Hessing)

PERSONAL: Born December 2, 1915, in Mauritius; son of Harold Richard (a master mariner) and Helen Marjory (a piano teacher; maiden name, Small) Jones; married Kathleen Jean Nelson (a health visitor), March 18, 1953; children: Esther Caroline, Helen Clare. *Education:* St. John's College, Oxford, M.A., 1938. *Politics:* None. *Religion:* None. *Residence:* Kent, England. *Office:* Tourplan Ltd., NEM House (2nd floor), 24 Worple Rd., London SW19 4BA, England.

CAREER: Kemsley Newspapers, London, England, member of news staff, 1945-48; free-lance journalist and photographer, 1948-53; senior classics master in various high schools in England, 1953-60; *Guide Kleber*, Paris, France, United Kingdom editorial representative, 1964-72; Tourplan Ltd. (travel and editorial consultants), London, England, managing director, 1974—. Chairman of board of trustees, Children's Relief International, 1962-69. *Military service:* Served with Civil Defence in London, Royal Air Force, and Royal Artillery, 1939-45. *Member:* Society of Authors, Guild of Travel Writers.

WRITINGS: (Contributor of translations under pseudonym Dennis Hessing) Fred Marnau, editor, *New Roads*, Grey Walls Press, 1955; (translator under pseudonym Dennis Hessing with Reginald Snell) Alois Jalkotzy, *School for Parents*, Galley Press, 1963; *Your Guide to the Dalmatian Coast (of Yugoslavia)*, International Publication Service, 1963; *Your Guide to Denmark*, International Publication Service, 1963; *Your Guide to Brittany (in France)*, Redman, 1964, International Publication Service, 1965; *Your Guide to Morocco*, International Publication Service, 1965; *Romania*, Horizon Press, 1969; *Bulgaria*, Horizon Press, 1969; *Israel*, McGraw, 1970, 3rd edition, 1975; *Portugal*, Letts, 1974; *Costa Del Sol (of Spain)*, Letts, 1974; *Majorca and the Balearics (of Spain)*, Letts, 1974; *Costa Brava (of Spain)*, Letts, 1974; *Morocco & Tunisia*, Letts, 1974; *Holland*, Letts, 1975; *Denmark*, Letts, 1975; *France*, Letts, 1975.

Contributor to "Fodor's Modern Guides" series sometimes under pseudonym Paul Hamilton: *Italy*; *Yugoslavia*; *Morocco*; *Scandinavia*; *Europe*; *Budget Guide to Europe*; *Youth Guide to Europe*. Contributor to *Times* (London), *Guardian*, *Daily Telegraph* (London), *Times Educational Supplement*, and others. Regional editor for Fodor for Yugoslavia, Romania, Bulgaria, 1971—.

WORK IN PROGRESS: Travel books on Northern Spain, a road book of Spain, railway travel in Europe, Romania, and others; a foreign language learning system employing printed material and tape cassettes.

SIDELIGHTS: Dennis-Jones told *CA*: "I was born into travel-addicted families (both mother's and father's) who, till recently, had members in every continent of the world. I myself was born in Mauritius, my sister in what was British India and later became first Pakistan and now Bangladesh, and my brother in Ceylon (now Sri Lanka), etc., etc. Though very highly qualified academically I am far more interested in communicating with ordinary people than with remoter academics. If my relatively simple travel books, guides, and articles help people of one country to learn about another nation's ways I am very happy."

*   *   *

DENNISON, A(lfred) Dudley, Jr.   1914-

PERSONAL: Born January 6, 1914, in Johnstown, N.Y.; son of Alfred Dudley and Marguerite (France) Dennison; married Virginia Beers, October 24, 1940; children: Wayne, Norman, Melanie. *Education:* Hamilton College, B.A., 1935; Cornell University Medical College, M.D., 1939. *Home:* Lake Panorama, Panora, Iowa 50216. *Agent:* (Speaking) Redpath Bureau, 343 South Dearborn St., Chicago, Ill. 60604. *Office:* Dallas County Hospital, Perry, Iowa 50220.

CAREER: Diplomate, American Board of Internal Medicine, 1950, Subspecialty Board of Cardiovascular Diseases, 1951; consulting cardiologist. Veterans Administration Hospital, Des Moines, Iowa, chief of cardiology and assistant chief of medicine, 1970-72. Member of faculty, New York University Postgraduate Medical School, 1948-52; associate in medicine, Indiana University Medical School. *Military service:* U.S. Naval Reserve, 1942-45; became lieutenant commander. *Member:* American College of Physicians (fellow), American College of Chest Physicians (fellow; member of board of governors, 1957—), American College of Cardiology (fellow, member of board of governors, 1957-60), American College of Angiology (fellow), Council on Clinical Cardiology of American Heart Association (fellow), American Scientific Affiliation, Polk County Heart Association (member of board of directors, 1971-73), Essex County Heart Association (president, 1950-51), Nu Sigma Nu, Alpha Phi Omega, Theta Delta Chi, Masons, Blue Lodge, Scottish Rite, Shrine, York Rite.

WRITINGS: (With James Hefley) *Biblical World*, Baker Publishing, 1966; *Shock It to Me, Doctor*, Zondervan,

1970; *Give It to Me Straight, Doctor*, Zondervan, 1972; (contributor) J. Allen Peterson, editor, *For Men Only*, Zondervan, 1973; *Prescription for Life*, Zondervan, 1975. Member of editorial advisory board, *Emergency Medicine*, 1969—; health editor, *Christian Life*, 1970—. Contributor to *Emergency Medicine*, and other publications.

WORK IN PROGRESS: Windows, Ladders and Bridges: A Book of Illustrations for Public Speakers.

*   *   *

de REYNA, Rudy   1914-

PERSONAL: Born September 8, 1914, in San Fernando, Spain; came to U.S., 1924; naturalized U.S. citizen, 1945; son of Julian (a merchant) and Maria (Rodriguez) de Reyna; married Marjorie Rickard, December 11, 1945 (divorced, 1962); married Marylin Hafner (an artist), August 17, 1970. *Education:* Educated in Spain, England, Mexico, and U.S. *Politics:* "Democrat, but open to persuasion." *Religion:* "The Chap upstairs and I have always been on good terms but I belong to no denomination." *Home:* 98 Woodland Rd., New Canaan, Conn. 06840; and Route 6A, East Sandwich, Mass. 02537. *Office:* Famous Artists Schools, 54 Wilton Rd., Westport, Conn. 06880.

CAREER: Southern Poster Studios, Los Angeles, Calif., movie poster artist, 1933-39; General Exhibits & Displays, Chicago, Ill., exhibit and display artist, 1939-56; Illustrators' Group, New York, N.Y., free-lance illustrator, 1956-59; Famous Artists Schools, Westport, Conn., instructor and supervisor, 1959-70; artist. *Military service:* U.S. Navy, 1942-45; served in Pacific. *Member:* Silvermine Guild of Artists (member of board of trustees, 1972-74), Rowayton Arts Centre, Connecticut Watercolor Society. *Awards, honors:* Recipient of numerous art awards, including the Douglas Grimshaw Prize, 1975.

WRITINGS—All published by Watson-Guptill: *Painting in Opaque Watercolor*, 1969; *How to Draw What You See*, 1971; *Magic Realist Painting Techniques*, 1973; *Creative Painting from Photographs*, 1975.

WORK IN PROGRESS: Magic Realist Landscape Painting.

SIDELIGHTS: de Reyna writes: "Mine is the well-blazed trail of the lad who defied parental expostulations to become an artist. Only fools, according to my father, embarked on any other career but the Law, the Military, or the Church. And although I considered him the wisest of men, I couldn't help disagreeing with this particular attitude.... And [now] I paint as I paint, not for plaudits to tickle my ego or for silver to line my purse but because the die was cast when I was six, and at sixty I cannot do otherwise." *Avocational interests:* Reading, travel.

BIOGRAPHICAL/CRITICAL SOURCES: American Artist, August, 1973.

*   *   *

DERN, Karl L(udwig)   1894-

PERSONAL: Born December 24, 1894, in Stanton, Neb.; son of John Louis (a businessman) and Emma (Bucholz) Dern; married Gretchen Pilger, June 22, 1925; children: Philip. *Education:* Attended Illinois Institute of Technology, 1914-15; University of Illinois, B.S., 1918. *Politics:* Democrat. *Religion:* Presbyterian. *Home:* 2105 Roosevelt Ave., Burlingame, Calif. 94010.

CAREER: Johns-Manville Corp., chemical engineer in

Lompoc, Calif., 1920-22, Cleveland, Ohio, 1922-25, Chicago, Ill., 1925-30, and in San Francisco, Calif., 1930-60. *Military service:* U.S. Army, Chemical Warfare Service, 1918-1919. *Member:* American Chemical Society, American Scientific Affiliation.

WRITINGS: Pioneers! Pioneers! (nonfiction), Monocacy, 1972.

*   *   *

DERVIN, Daniel A(rthur) 1935-

PERSONAL: Born April 8, 1935, in Omaha, Neb.; son of Arthur Thomas (a repairman) and Mamie (Hudson) Dervin; married Katherine Chaplin (a psychiatric social worker), June 28, 1964; children: Douglas, Hilary. *Education:* Creighton University, B.A., 1959; Columbia University, M.A., 1963, Ph.D., 1970. *Politics:* Democrat. *Religion:* "Unaffiliated." *Home:* 905 Monument Ave., Fredericksburg, Va. 22401. *Office:* Department of English, Mary Washington College, Fredericksburg, Va. 22401.

CAREER: Mary Washington College, Fredericksburg, Va., associate professor of English. *Awards, honors:* First prize in Irene Leache short story contest, 1973.

WRITINGS: Bernard Shaw: A Psychological Study, Bucknell University Press, 1974.

WORK IN PROGRESS: Collection of short stories; psychoanalytic study of D. H. Lawrence; psychoanalytic study of film.

*   *   *

de SCHWEINITZ, Karl 1887-1975

1887—April 20, 1975; American consultant on social affairs, educator, administrator, reporter, and author of book on social security. Obituaries: *New York Times,* April 21, 1975; *Washington Post,* April 23, 1975.

*   *   *

DESHEN, Shlomo 1935-

PERSONAL: Born in 1935; married; children: five. *Education:* Hebrew University of Jerusalem, B.A., 1960, graduate study, 1960-62; University of Manchester, Ph.D., 1968. *Office:* Department of Sociology and Anthropology, Tel-Aviv University, Ramat-Aviv, Tel-Aviv, Israel.

CAREER: Land Settlement Department, Lachish Region, Israel, rural sociologist, 1961-64; Tel-Aviv University, Tel-Aviv, Israel, lecturer, 1968-71, senior lecturer, 1971-75, associate professor of social anthropology, 1975—. *Awards, honors:* Literary prize from American Friends of Alliance Israelite Universelle, 1971, for *Immigrant Voters in Israel: Parties and Congregations in a Local Election Campaign.*

WRITINGS: Immigrant Voters in Israel: Parties and Congregations in a Local Election Campaign, Manchester University Press, 1970; (with M. Shokeid) *The Predicament of Homecoming: Cultural and Social Life of North African Immigrants in Israel,* Cornell University Press, 1974; (with D. Handelman) *The Social Anthropology of Israel: A Bibliographical Essay with Primary Reference to Loci of Social Stress,* Institute for Social Research, Tel-Aviv University, 1975; (editor with Shokeid and E. Marx) *Mikra'a be'antropologia Levratit* (title means "Readings in Social Anthropology"), two volumes, Schocken, in press.

Contributor: O. Shapira, editor, *Inhabited Rural Centers,* National and University Institute for Agriculture, 1968; S. N. Eisenstadt, editor, *Integration and Development in Is-*

rael, Israel Universities Press, 1970; Shapira, editor, *Rural Settlements of New Immigrants in Israel,* Rehovot Settlement Study Centre, 1971; A. Arian, editor, *The Elections in Israel: 1969,* Academic Press (Jerusalem), 1972; A. Cohen, editor, *Urban Ethnicity* (monograph), Tavistock Publications, 1974; C. Caldarola, editor, *Oriental Religions,* Mouton & Co., in press. Contributor of more than a dozen articles and reviews to journals of the social sciences in the United States and Israel.

*   *   *

de VINCK, Catherine 1922-

PERSONAL: Born February 20, 1922, in Brussels, Belgium; came to United States in 1948; daughter of Joseph (a general in Belgian Army) and Julie Prudence (Oeyen) Kestens; married Jose de Vinck (a writer, publisher, and editor), February 1, 1945; children: Bruno, Oliver, Anne-Catherine (Mrs. John B. Ochs), Christopher, Jose, Jr., Maria-Gloria. *Education:* Attended schools in Brussels. *Religion:* Roman Catholic. *Home:* 672 Franklin Turnpike, Allendale, N.J. 07401; and Domus Aurea, Combermere, Ontario K0J 1L0, Canada. *Office address:* Box 103, Allendale, N.J. 07401.

CAREER: Writer. *Awards, honors:* Keats Society (London) prize, 1975, for poem, "Mothering."

WRITINGS: A Time to Gather: Selected Poems, Alleluia Press, 1967; *Ikon,* Alleluia Press, 1972; *A Liturgy,* Cross Currents, 1974; (contributor) Michele Murray, editor, *A House of Good Proportion: Women in Literature,* Simon & Schuster, 1974; *A Passion Play,* Alleluia Press, in press; *A Book of Uncommon Prayers,* Weston Priory, in press.

WORK IN PROGRESS: The Book of Eve; The Prodigal Son; a book of selected poems.

*   *   *

De VRIES, Simon J(ohn) 1921-

PERSONAL: Born December 20, 1921, in Denver, Colo.; son of Peter H. (an electrician) and Katherine (Tamminga) De Vries; married Betty Marie Schouten (a secretary), August 28, 1943; children: Judith Kathleen (Mrs. Peter S. Kammeraad), Garry Peter. *Education:* Calvin College, A.B., 1943; Calvin Theological Seminary, Th.B., 1949; Union Theological Seminary, New York, N.Y., S.T.M., 1950, Th.D., 1958; further study at Leiden University, 1956-57, and Tuebingen University, 1965-66. *Home:* 35 Darlington Rd., Delaware, Ohio 43015. *Office:* Methodist Theological School in Ohio, Delaware, Ohio 43015.

CAREER: Ordained minister of United Presbyterian Church, 1950; pastor of churches in Iowa, New Jersey, and Michigan, 1950-57, 1959-61; Drew University, Theological School, Madison, N.J., instructor in Old Testament, 1957-58; Hope College, Holland, Mich., associate professor of religion, 1961-62; Western Theological Seminary, Holland, Mich., instructor in Hebrew, 1961-62; Methodist Theological School in Ohio, Delaware, associate professor, 1962-68, professor of Old Testament, 1968—. Member of Delaware County (Ohio) Democratic Central Committee, 1972—. *Military service:* U.S. Marine Corps Reserve, active duty, 1943-46; became first lieutenant. *Member:* American Academy of Religion, Society of Biblical Literature (president of Eastern Great Lakes Region, 1973-74), American Association of University Professors, Ohio Theological Colloquium (president, 1968-69). *Awards, honors:* Fulbright fellowship, 1956-57; Lilly Foundation fellowship,

1965-66; Ecumenical Institute for Advanced Theological Studies fellowship, 1973.

WRITINGS: Bible and Theology in the Netherlands, Veenman (Wageningen, Netherlands), 1968; *Yesterday, Today and Tomorrow: Time and History in the Old Testament*, Eerdmans, 1975. Contributor to *Interpreter's Dictionary of the Bible* and to journals in his field.

WORK IN PROGRESS: Two books, *Prophet Against Prophet: The Role of the Micaiah Narrative in the Development of Biblical Theology* and *Tales Told by the Prophets.*

* * *

DICKERSON, John 1939-

PERSONAL: Born October 11, 1939, in Norfolk, England; son of Frederick E. (a game dealer) and Beulah (a nurse; maiden name, Bellham) Dickerson; married Teresa Mary Brigid, August 3, 1963; children: Evan Michael. *Education:* Goldsmiths' College, London, diploma in history of art, 1965; attended Art Students League of New York, 1967; Pratt Institute, M.F.A., 1968; Royal College of Art, Dr.R.C.A., 1973. *Home:* 86 Tudor Rd., Hampton, Middlesex, England. *Office:* Department of Fine Arts, Borough Road College, Isleworth, Middlesex, England.

CAREER: Borough Road College, Isleworth, Middlesex, England, lecturer in fine arts, 1969—. Visiting lecturer at Victoria and Albert Museum, Royal College of Art, Camberwell School of Art, Cardiff College of Art, Wimbledon School of Art, Colleges of London University Institute of Education. *Member:* Oriental Ceramic Society of London, Japan Society of London. *Awards, honors:* Winston Churchill memorial fellowship, 1970, for study in Japan.

WRITINGS: Raku Handbook, Van Nostrand, 1972; *Pottery Making: A Complete Guide*, Viking, 1974. Contributor to magazines and journals dealing with ceramics and Japanese studies.

WORK IN PROGRESS: A book for beginners in ceramics; research on a history of the Raku family of Kyoto, and the life and art of Sen-No-Rikyu.

SIDELIGHTS: Dickerson's painting and pottery are represented in collections and have been exhibited in England, United States, Japan, Australia, Sweden, and Yugoslavia. *Avocational interests:* Photography, particularly non-camera photography.

* * *

DICKINSON, Susan 1931-

PERSONAL: Born December 26, 1931, in Surrey, England; daughter of William Croft (a university professor) and Margery (Tomlinson) Dickinson; married Arnold Gibson (an insurance consultant), February 11, 1961; children: Sophie Elizabeth, Emily Jane. *Education:* Attended St. Margaret's School, Edinburgh; University of Edinburgh, M.A., 1953. *Politics:* Liberal. *Religion:* Presbyterian. *Home:* 2 Westmoreland Rd., London S.W.13, England. *Office:* William Collins, Sons & Co. Ltd., 14 St. James's Pl., London S.W.1, England.

CAREER: Thomas Nelson & Sons Ltd., editorial assistant in educational books, Edinburgh, Scotland, 1954-56, assistant editor of children's books, London, England, 1956-59; William Collins, Sons & Co. Ltd., London, children's books editor, 1960—.

WRITINGS: (Compiler) *The Restless Ghost and Other*

Encounters and Experiences, Collins, 1970, published as *The Usurping Ghost and Other Encounters and Experiences*, Dutton, 1971; (compiler) *The Case of the Vanishing Spinster and Other Mystery Stories*, Collins, 1972, published in America as *The Drugged Cornet and Other Mystery Stories*, Dutton, 1973; (editor) *Mother's Help: For Busy Mothers and Playground Leaders*, Collins, 1972.

WORK IN PROGRESS: Editing a collection of original stories for children under five; abridging *Vanity Fair* for Collins "Classics for Today" series.

SIDELIGHTS: Susan Dickinson writes: "Main interest is old children's books, but generally lack the money to buy them! As an editor of new children's books, find the changes in the last hundred years fascinating. Love exploring old castles and churches, possibly partly due to the fact that my father was a professor of mediaeval history, so we were brought up on ancient monuments of which Scotland has plenty."

* * *

DILES, Dave 1931-

PERSONAL: Born October 14, 1931, in Middleport, Ohio; son of Lisle Desmond (a railroader) and Lucille (Bowman) Diles; married Jean Schoseiger, May 22, 1954 (divorced, 1970); children: Beverly Susan, David Lisle. *Education:* Ohio University, A.A., 1951. *Religion:* Protestant. *Residence:* West Bloomfield, Mich.

CAREER: Gallipolis Tribune and Gallia Times, Gallipolis, Ohio, news and sports reporter, 1947-49; *Pomeroy Daily Sentinel*, Pomeroy, Ohio, sports editor, 1948-49; *Athens Messenger*, Athens, Ohio, reporter, 1949-51; Associated Press, correspondent in Columbus, Ohio, 1949-51, writer-reporter in Louisville, Ky., 1951, writer-editor, Columbus, Ohio, 1951-56, sports editor, Detroit, Mich., 1956-61; WXYZ, Inc., Detroit, Mich., radio and television sports director, 1961-72; American Broadcasting Corp., network sportscaster and commentator on "ABC Wide World of Sports," 1963-75; WJR, Detroit, Mich., sports commentator, 1973-75; WDEE, Detroit, Mich., sports commentator, 1975. Commentator for Detroit Lions' football on radio, 1973-74, Detroit Pistons' basketball on television, 1973-75.

WRITINGS: Duffy, Doubleday, 1974; *Nobody's Perfect*, Dial, 1975.

WORK IN PROGRESS: Two books.

* * *

DILLARD, Emil L(ee) 1921-

PERSONAL: Surname sometimes spelled Dilliard; born March 14, 1921, in Langdon, Kan.; son of Oscar W. (a farmer) and Mabel (Brooks) Dilliard; married Leona Sneed (a financial analyst), September 12, 1942. *Education:* Kansas State Teachers College, B.A., 1946; Columbia University, M.A., 1948, M.Ph., 1974. *Politics:* Independent. *Religion:* Unitarian Universalist. *Home:* 74 Rutland Rd., Hempstead, N.Y. 11550. *Office:* Department of English, Adelphi University, South Ave., Garden City, N.Y. 11530.

CAREER: High school English teacher in Kansas, 1946-47; University of Oregon, Eugene, instructor in English, 1948-50; Hunter College (now Hunter College of the City University of New York), New York, N.Y., instructor in English, 1953; Adelphi University, Garden City, N.Y., instructor, 1954-59, assistant professor, 1959-68, associate professor, 1968-74, professor of English, 1974—. *Military service:* U.S. Army, 1942-43. U.S. Army Air Forces, 1943-46; served in South Pacific; became first lieutenant.

MEMBER: Modern Language Association of America, National Council of Teachers of English, American Association of Higher Education, American Studies Association, American Association of University Professors (vice-president of local chapter, 1966-67; president, 1967-70, 1972-74; president of state conference, 1974-76), New York State English Council, New York Civil Liberties Union, Common Cause.

WRITINGS: Nouns and Pronouns: I and Others (poems), Windy Row Press, 1974.

Work is anthologized in *The Golden Quill Anthology*, Golden Quill, edited by Paul S. Mowrer and Clarence E. Farrar, 1966-69, 1971 (1971 edition edited by Farrar).

Contributor of poems to literary magazines.

WORK IN PROGRESS: A second book of poems.

AVOCATIONAL INTERESTS: Travel (England, Europe), theater, reading fiction, working for faculty and civil rights.

* * *

DIMONT, Penelope
See MORTIMER, Penelope (Ruth)

* * *

DINNEEN, Betty 1929-

PERSONAL: Born August 28, 1929, in London, England; naturalized U.S. citizen in 1975; daughter of Albert Ernest and Edith Louise (Taylor) Newark; married Barry Dinneen, March 2, 1957 (divorced, 1971); children: Penelope Jane, Hugh Martin. *Education:* Educated at Tiffin Girls School. *Home:* 1430 30th Ave., San Francisco, Calif. 94122. *Office:* 300 Montgomery St., Suite 700, San Francisco, Calif. 94104.

CAREER: Times Book Club, London, England, assistant librarian, 1945-47; South African Embassy, London, secretary, 1947-54; Government of Sarawak, Kuching, secretary, 1954-56; Government of Tanganyika, Department of Lands and Surveys, Dar es Salaam, secretary, 1956-58; Government of Kenya, Ministry of Defence, Nairobi, secretary, 1958-63; African Medical and Research Foundation (Flying Doctor Service), Nairobi, secretary, 1963-64; Thacher, Jones, Casey & Ratcliff, San Francisco, Calif., legal secretary, 1970—.

WRITINGS—Juvenile: Lions and Karen, Dent, 1965; *A Lurk of Leopards,* Walck, 1972; *Lion Yellow,* Walck, 1975. Contributor to *Golden Magazine for Boys and Girls.*

AVOCATIONAL INTERESTS: Conservation.

* * *

DIONE, Robert L(ester) 1922-

PERSONAL: Born February 23, 1922, in South Portland, Me.; son of Lester Elmer (a fisherman) and Elwilda (Harvey) Dione; married second wife, Ruth Dinnen (a tax preparer), August 7, 1965; children: (first marriage) Robert A., Steven J.; (second marriage) Donald P., Michelle L., Janine G. *Education:* Attended Purdue University, 1945; University of Maine, B.S.Ed., 1949; Columbia University, M.A.Ed., 1951. *Politics:* "Not affiliated." *Religion:* "Non-practicing Catholic." *Residence:* Clinton, Conn. *Office:* Board of Education, Sheffield, Old Saybrook, Conn.

CAREER: Casco Bay Lines, Portland, Me., truck driver, 1940-42; high school art teacher in Cheshire, Conn., 1952-62; Variety Homes, Newington, Conn., salesman, 1963-65; Old Saybrook Junior High School, Old Saybrook, Conn., art teacher, 1965—. *Military service:* U.S. Army, Parachute Infantry, 1943-46; served in European theater. *Member:* Writers Exchange (Madison, Conn.).

WRITINGS: God Drives a Flying Saucer, Bantam, 1973.

WORK IN PROGRESS: Exegesis, a technological explanation of the scriptures; *The Wisdom and the Word,* a novel.

SIDELIGHTS: Dione writes: "Even as a child in a practicing Catholic family, I found the mysticism of Christian dogma incompatible with common sense. Then, as an adult student of the Bible, I discovered that the abhorred mysticism was not an ingredient of Christian doctrine, but rather an outgrowth of primitive misinterpretation." *Avocational interests:* Chess, sports (former Golden Glove champion in Maine).

BIOGRAPHICAL/CRITICAL SOURCES: New Era, December 4, 1969; *Hartford Courant,* December 11, 1969; *Middletown Press,* February 7, 1970.

* * *

DiORIO, Al 1950-

PERSONAL: Born June 20, 1950, in Philadelphia, Pa.; son of Albert J. (a tailor) and Martha (Breve) DiOrio. *Education:* Glassboro State College, student, 1969-71. *Religion:* Roman Catholic. *Home:* 21 Station Ave., Somerdale, N.J. 08083. *Office:* N.W. Ayer ABH International, 1345 Avenue of the Americas, New York, N.Y. 10017.

CAREER: N.W. Ayer ABH International, New York, N.Y., budget-cost control administrator/contract specialist, 1971—. *Member:* Authors League of America.

WRITINGS: Little Girl Lost: The Life and Hard Times of Judy Garland, Arlington House, 1974.

WORK IN PROGRESS: Research for *Sammy Davis* and *Talent: The Common Denominator.*

* * *

DiPASQUALE, Dominic 1932-

PERSONAL: Born February 21, 1932, in Buffalo, N.Y.; son of Sebastian (in business management) and Carmela (St. George) DiPasquale; married Susan E. Anderson, January 11, 1957 (divorced, October, 1973); children: Mark Douglas, Rory Steven. *Education:* State University of New York College at Buffalo, B.S., 1960; Rochester Institute of Technology, M.F.A., 1963. *Home:* 24 West Fifth St., Oswego, N.Y. 13126. *Office:* Department of Art, State University of New York College at Oswego, Tyler Hall, Oswego, N.Y. 13126.

CAREER: Elementary school teacher in Buffalo, N.Y., 1958-60; junior high school art teacher in Arcade, N.Y., 1960-61; high school art teacher in Rochester, N.Y., 1961-62; State University of New York College at Oswego, instructor, 1963-66, assistant professor, 1966-70, associate professor, 1970-75, professor of art, silver, and goldsmithing, 1975—, chairman of department of art, 1974—. Visiting professor at Penland School of Crafts, summer, 1965, and International Studies, Inc. (Rome), summer, 1969. Built, owned, and operated Pickwick Alley Gallery, 1970-71; jewelry designer for Finelt Manufacturing Co., 1970-71. Art work has been exhibited across the United

States, at galleries, festivals, colleges, and by professional organizations. Juror for North Country Art Association, 1967, and New York State Fair, 1974. Member of board of trustees of One Patent Family Council, 1975.

MEMBER: College Art Association, American Crafts Council, New York State Craftsmen, Buffalo Craftsmen's Association. *Awards, honors:* Art awards include jury award from Southern Tier National Art Exhibition, 1966; four awards to the Court of Honor at New York State Crafts Fair, 1966; first prize for metals from Westchester National Art Exhibition, 1968; jury award from Southern Tier National Art Exhibition, 1969; first prize from Las Vegas National Art Round Up, 1969; first prize for holloware from New York State Fair, 1971; second prize for holloware and first prize for jewelry from New York State Fair, 1973; named to Court of Honor at Southern Tier National Exhibition, 1973; honorable mention from National Art Slide Competition, 1975.

WRITINGS: Jewelry Making: An Illustrated Guide to Technique, Prentice-Hall, 1975.

WORK IN PROGRESS: A reference book on contemporary American silversmiths, publication expected in 1977.

SIDELIGHTS: DiPasquale is an American of Italian descent, who worked for his father from age twelve to age sixteen as a shoe repairman. Before deciding to attend college, he worked at more than twenty different types of employment, including billiard parlor operator, punchpress operator, private detective, chauffeur, clothing model, carpenter, painter, and advertising executive.

*   *   *

Di PESO, Charles C(orradino)   1920-

PERSONAL: Surname is pronounced De *Pay*-so; born October 20, 1920, in St. Louis, Mo.; son of Charles Corradino and Emma (Klein) Di Peso; married Frances Teague, June 13, 1942; children: Charles Corradino, David Conner. *Education:* Beloit College, B.A. and B.S., 1942; American Institute for Foreign Trade, B.F.T., 1947; University of Arizona, M.A., 1950, Ph.D., 1952. *Office address:* Amerind Foundation, Inc., P.O. Box 248, Dragoon, Ariz. 85609.

CAREER: City archaeologist, Phoenix, Ariz., 1946-47; Amerind Foundation, Inc., Dragoon, Ariz., archaeologist-in-charge, 1948-52, foundation director, 1952—, member of board of directors, 1953—. Member of board of governors, Cochise College, 1962—, chairman, 1966-68. Member of Arizona Committee for State Parks, 1966—, and Arizona Historical Advisory Commission, 1967—; chairman of Arizona Landmarks Committee, 1971-75; consultant to International Center for Arid and Semi-Arid Land Studies, Texas Technological University, 1968—. Member of board of directors, Tucson Museum of Art, 1972. *Military service:* U.S. Army Air Forces, pilot, 1942-45; became first lieutenant.

MEMBER: American Anthropoligical Association (fellow), Society for American Archaeology (fellow; member of executive committee, 1970-71; president, 1972-73), American Association for the Advancement of Science (fellow), Society for Historical Archaeology (fellow), American Society for Ethnohistory, American Association of Museums, Latin American Studies Association, International Congress of Americanists, Institute of Andean Research (honorary member), Southwestern Anthropological Association (fellow), Western History Association, South-

western Archaeological Research Group, Arizona Academy of Science (fellow), Cochise County Historical and Archaeological Society, Pimeria Alta Historical Society, Sulphur Springs Valley Historical Society, Cochise Trail Visitors Association, Sigma Xi, Explorers Club (New York; fellow), Westerners (Tucson Corral). *Awards, honors:* Alfred Vincent Kidder Award for achievement in American archaeology, American Anthropological Association, 1959; D.Sc., Beloit College, 1970.

WRITINGS: The Babocomari Village Site on the Babocomari River, Southeastern Arizona, Amerind Foundation, 1951; *The Sobaipuri Indians of the Upper San Pedro Valley, Southeastern Arizona,* Amerind Foundation, 1953; *The Upper Pima of San Cayetano del Tumacacori,* Amerind Foundation, 1956; *The Reeve Ruin of Southeastern Arizona,* Amerind Foundation, 1958; (with John B. Rinaldo and Gloria J. Fenner) *Casas Grandes: A Fallen Trading Center of the Gran Chichimeca,* eight volumes, Northland Press, for Amerind Foundation, 1974.

Contributor: Raul Noriega and others, editors, *Esplendor del Mexico Antiguo,* Volume II, [Mexico City], 1959; Betty J. Meggers and Clifford Evans, editors, *Aboriginal Cultural Development in Latin America: An Interpretative Review,* Smithsonian Institution Press, 1963; Gordon F. Ekholm and Gordon R. Willey, editors, *Handbook of Middle American Indians,* Volume IV, University of Texas Press, 1966.

Documentary and educational film scripts; all for Harmon Foundation, except as noted: "Point of Pines," 1948; "Betatakin," 1949; "Los Ninos," 1950; "The Sierra Madre," 1951; "Casas Grandes and the Gran Chichimeca," Reading Laboratory, Inc., 1974.

Contributor to *Encyclopaedia Britannica, Conspectus and Chronology: Encyclopedia of Indians of the Americas,* and to journals, including *American Antiquity* and *Arizona and the West.* Member of advisory council, *American Indian Reference Book,* 1971—; member of editorial advisory board, *American Indian Quarterly,* 1974—.

WORK IN PROGRESS: Continuing studies of the American Southwest and northern Mexico's prehistory in relationship with donor and recipient cultures and the mechanisms of urbanization in arid lands.

*   *   *

DIRINGER, David   1900-1975

June 16, 1900—February 13, 1975; Ukrainian-born educator, and author of works on history of writing and book arts. Obituaries: *New York Times,* February 15, 1975; *AB Bookman's Weekly,* March 3, 1975. (*CA*-4)

*   *   *

DITZION, Sidney   1908-1975

November 23, 1908—June 28, 1975; American educator, librarian, and author of books on history. Obituaries: *New York Times,* June 30, 1975. (*CA*-41/44)

*   *   *

DOAK, Wade Thomas   1940-

PERSONAL: Born February 23, 1940, in North Canterbury, New Zealand; son of Deryck Steads and Lorna Evelyn Doak; married Janet Mary Turpin, December 15, 1962; children: Brady, Karla. *Education:* Canterbury University, B.A., 1962. *Home address:* Box 20, Whangarei, New Zealand.

CAREER: Taught French and English in secondary schools in New Zealand, 1963-69; full-time author. Publisher of *Dive South Pacific Magazine*.

WRITINGS: The Elingamite and Its Treasure, Hodder & Stoughton, 1969; *Beneath New Zealand Seas*, A. H. Reed, 1971; *Fishes of the New Zealand Region*, Hodder & Stoughton, 1972, British Book Centre, 1974. Contributor to *Mondo Sommerso, American Skindiver, New Zealand Listener*, and *New Zealand Weekly News*.

WORK IN PROGRESS: Sharks & Other Ancestors; *I Am a Fish*; *The Unknown Polynesians*.

AVOCATIONAL INTERESTS: Skindiving, underwater photography, marine biology, European literature, and anthropology.

* * *

DOBBINS, Austin C(harles) 1919-

PERSONAL: Born October 14, 1919, in Nashville, Tenn.; son of Gaines Stanley (a teacher) and May (Riley) Dobbins; married Mary Denmead Willis, June 21, 1947; children: Mary Virginia, Elizabeth Anne. *Education:* Mississippi College, B.A., 1941; University of North Carolina, M.A., 1948, Ph.D., 1950; also studied at University of Tulsa, University of Louisville, and University of California, Los Angeles. *Politics:* Independent. *Religion:* Southern Baptist. *Home:* 1113 South Shadesview Ter., Birmingham, Ala. 35209. *Office:* Department of English and Journalism, Samford University, Birmingham, Ala. 35209.

CAREER: Samford University, Birmingham, Ala., assistant professor, 1950-51, associate professor, 1951-52, professor of English, 1952—, head of department of English and journalism, 1957—, chairman of Division of Humanities, 1962-64, 1969-72. Distinguished visiting scholar at University of California, Los Angeles, 1964. *Military service:* U.S. Army, 1943-45; served in China-Burma-India theater; became sergeant.

MEMBER: American Education Association, National Council of Teachers of English, American Educational Theatre Association, Renaissance Society of America, South Atlantic Modern Language Association, Sigma Tau Delta, Kappa Phi Kappa, Alpha Phi Omega, Omicron Delta Kappa. *Awards, honors:* Folger Library fellowship, 1956; Foundation for Economic Education fellowship, 1957; Duke University library fellowship, 1963.

WRITINGS: Milton and the Book of Revelation: The Heavenly Cycle, University of Alabama Press, 1975. Contributor to literature journals, including *Modern Language Review, College English*, and *Shakespeare Studies*.

WORK IN PROGRESS: A study of Shakespeare's major plays.

* * *

DOBIE, Edith 1894-1975

February 10, 1894—April 24, 1975; American educator, and author of books on history. Obituaries: *New York Times*, April 25, 1975. (*CA*-23/24)

* * *

DOBKIN, Alexander 1908-1975

May 1, 1908—March 21, 1975; American painter, graphic artist, illustrator, lecturer, and author of books on art. Obituaries: *New York Times*, March 27, 1975; *AB Bookman's Weekly*, April 28, 1975.

DODD, Arthur Herbert 1893(?)-1975

1893(?)—1975; Welsh historian, educator, and author of books on British history. Obituaries: *AB Bookman's Weekly*, July 7, 1975.

* * *

DODD, Donald B(radford) 1940-

PERSONAL: Born February 6, 1940, in Manchester, Ala.; son of Ben G. (a businessman and local politician) and Alta (Weaver) Dodd; married Sandra Whitten, June 18, 1961; children: Donna Ellen, Donald Bradford, Jr. *Education:* University of North Alabama, B.S., 1961; Auburn University, M.A., 1966; University of Georgia, Ph.D., 1969. *Religion:* Applied Christianity. *Home:* 6012 Pinebrook Dr., Montgomery, Ala. 36109. *Office:* Department of History, Auburn University, Montgomery, Ala. 36109.

CAREER: Troy State University, Troy, Ala., assistant professor of history, 1968-69; Auburn University, Montgomery, Ala., assistant professor, 1969-72, associate professor of history, 1972—. *Military service:* U.S. Army, 1963-65. U.S. Air Force Reserve, 1972—; now major. *Member:* Organization of American Historians (life member), Southern Historical Association (life member).

WRITINGS: (With Wynelle Dodd) *Winston*, Annals of Northwest Alabama, 1972; (with Dodd) *Historical Statistics of the South*, University of Alabama Press, 1973; *Historical Atlas of Alabama*, University of Alabama Press, 1974. Contributor to *American History Illustrated*.

WORK IN PROGRESS: Continuing the regional "Historical Statistics" series with the University of Alabama Press; research on American participation in twentieth-century wars, Unionism in the Confederacy, and classroom use of simulation games.

* * *

DOHERTY, Edward J. 1890-1975

October 30, 1890—May 4, 1975; American newsman, clergyman, and author of biographies and other works. Obituaries: *New York Times*, May 5, 1975; *Washington Post*, May 8, 1975.

* * *

DOLAN, Winthrop W(iggin) 1909-

PERSONAL: Born March 13, 1909, in Agawam, Mass.; son of Edwin Bailey (a clergyman) and Marion (Wiggin) Dolan; married Thelma Miller, November 21, 1933; children: Kathleen (Mrs. John C. Huneke), Edwin, John. *Education:* Denison University, B.A., 1930; Harvard University, M.A., 1937; University of Oklahoma, Ph.D., 1947. *Politics:* Independent. *Religion:* American Baptist. *Home:* 935 Cozine Lane, McMinnville, Ore. 97128.

CAREER: Bacone Junior College, Bacone, Okla., dean, 1931-42; Denison University, Granville, Ohio, assistant professor of mathematics, 1943-45; University of Oklahoma, Norman, assistant professor of mathematics, 1947-48; Linfield College, McMinnville, Ore., professor of mathematics, 1948-74, dean of faculty, 1949-54, 1959-65, 1968-69, acting president, 1968, vice-president, 1968-74. Assistant director of Linfield Research Institute, 1956-59, trustee, 1963—.

MEMBER: Mathematical Association of America, American Commons Club, Oregon Academy of Science (president, 1963-64), Phi Beta Kappa, Sigma Xi, Pi Mu Epsilon,

Sigma Pi Sigma. *Awards, honors:* Distinguished scientist award from Oregon Academy of Science, 1975.

WRITINGS: (Contributor) L. Marton, editor, *Advances in Electronics and Electron Physics*, Volume VIII, Academic Press, 1956; *A Choice of Sundials*, Stephen Greene Press, 1975. Contributor to mathematics and physics journals.

AVOCATIONAL INTERESTS: Bird study, canoeing, gardening, travel.

*   *   *

DOLCE, Philip C(harles) 1941-

PERSONAL: Born November 23, 1941, in New York, N.Y.; son of Joseph Philip (a barber) and Emma (Gallo) Dolce; married Patricia Pasciuto (a teacher), July 16, 1966; children: Susan Elizabeth. *Education:* St. John's University, Jamaica, N.Y., B.A., 1963; Fordham University, M.A., 1966, Ph.D., 1971. *Residence:* Brooklyn, N.Y. *Office:* Department of History, Bergen Community College, 400 Paramus Rd., Paramus, N.J. 07652.

CAREER: Private school teacher of social studies in New York, N.Y., 1963-66; St. John's University, New York, N.Y., assistant professor of history, 1966-72; Bergen Community College, Paramus, N.J., associate professor of history and coordinator of media programming, 1972—. Coordinator/director of documentaries: CBS television series, "The American Presidency: The Men and the Office" and "Science and Society: A Humanistic View"; NBC television series, "The American Suburbs: Myth and Reality"; and WPAT radio series "Race to the Suburbs: The American Dream and Dilemma," "The Impact of Science on the Modern World," and "Pinnacle of Power: The United States Presidency."

MEMBER: Organization of American Historians, Oral History Association, American Historical Association, Committee on Sociological History, Center for the Study of the Presidency, Columbia University Seminar on the City (associate). *Awards, honors:* St. John's University grant, 1969, for research on presidential policies; Harry S. Truman Library Institute grant, 1972.

WRITINGS: (Editor with Frank J. Coppa) *Cities in Transition: From the Ancient World to Urban America*, Nelson-Hall, 1974; (editor with George H. Skau) *The American Presidency: The Men, the Policies and the Office*, Scribner, in press; (editor) *Suburbia: The American Dream and Dilemma*, Doubleday, in press; (contributor) Frank J. Coppa and Thomas Curran, editors, *The Immigrant in American Life*, Twayne, in press. Contributor to journals. Business manager, 1970-72, *Journal of Social History*; member of editorial board, 1972-73.

WORK IN PROGRESS: Coordinating and directing series, "Higher Education in America," for WPAT-Radio, and "The Transformation of American Society," for CBS-Television.

*   *   *

DOLINSKY, Meyer 1923-
(Mike Dolinsky)

PERSONAL: Born October 13, 1923, in Chicago, Ill.; son of Hyman (a housepainter) and Lillian (a milliner; maiden name, Milchman) Dolinsky. *Education:* Attended Roosevelt College, 1940-41; University of California, Los Angeles, B.A., 1949; University of Southern California, secondary teaching credential, 1950. *Religion:* Jewish. *Home:* 10529 Valparaiso St., Los Angeles, Calif. 90034. *Agent:*

Theron Raines, 244 Madison Ave., New York, N.Y. 10016; and Frank Cooper Agency, 9000 Sunset Blvd., Los Angeles, Calif.

CAREER: Screen and television writer, 1947—. Instructor. Writers Round Table, West Los Angeles College, 1973—. *Member:* TV Academy, Writers Guild of America.

WRITINGS: (Under name Meyer Dolinsky) *There Is No Silence*, R. Hale, 1959; (under name Mike Dolinsky) *Mind One*, Dell, 1972; (under name Mike Dolinsky) *The Big Gate*, Dell, 1976. Author of 80 scripts for television series, "Startrek," "Outer Limits," and "Science Fiction Theatre."

WORK IN PROGRESS: A novel about school teachers; a pilot for Playboy Productions.

AVOCATIONAL INTERESTS: Photography, psychology, chess, sailing, poker, and the commodities market.

*   *   *

DOLINSKY, Mike
See DOLINSKY, Meyer

*   *   *

DONCHESS, Barbara (Briggs) 1922-

PERSONAL: Born September 26, 1922, in New Bedford, Mass.; daughter of Carleton (an electrician) and Alice (Dale) Briggs; married Kalman Donchess (a commercial artist), April 19, 1947; children: Ann, Carleton, Christine. *Education:* Attended Kinyon's Business School, 1942. *Politics:* "Independent veering toward Republican." *Religion:* Roman Catholic. *Home:* 5 South St., Canton, Mass. 02021. *Office:* Perky Publications, 5 South St., Canton, Mass. 02021.

CAREER: Brayton Photo Studio, New Bedford, Mass., manager, 1941-47; Horn Book, Boston, Mass., secretary, 1950-51; Perky Publications, Canton, Mass., owner and publisher, 1974—.

WRITINGS: *How to Cope with His Horoscope*, Perky, 1975; *A Book for Stringers*, Perky, in press. Contributor of humorous weekly column to *Canton Journal*, 1973-75. Contributor to *Horoscope* and *Writer's Digest*.

*   *   *

DONNE, Maxim
See DUKE, Madelaine

*   *   *

DONOHUE, Mark 1937-

PERSONAL: Born March 18, 1937, in Orange, N.J.; son of Mark N. (a lawyer) and Hazel (Wright) Donohue; married Eden White (an interior designer), December 14, 1974; children: (first marriage) Michael, David. *Education:* Brown University, Sc.B., 1959; New York University, graduate study, 1959-61. *Politics:* Republican. *Religion:* Roman Catholic. *Home:* 28 Wimboine Rd., Gables 6, Bournemouth, Dorset, England. *Agent:* International Literary Management, General Motors Building, New York, N.Y. *Office:* Penske Racing, Creekmore Estate, Poole, Dorset, England.

CAREER: Penske Racing, Reading, Pa., race car driver, 1966—. President of Racemark; vice-president of B & B Auto Sport. *Member:* Road Racing Drivers Club (president), Grand Prix Drivers Association, Society for Automotive Engineering, American Society of Mechanical Engineers, National Highway Safety Advisory Council. *Awards, honors:* Won Trans American racing title, 1968, 1969, Daytona Twenty-Four Hour Race, 1969, Indianapolis Five Hundred race, 1972, and Canadian American racing title, 1973.

WRITINGS: The Unfair Advantage (autobiography), Dodd, 1975.

*　　*　　*

DOOLEY, William G(ermain)   1905(?)-1975

1905(?)—February 16, 1975; American critic, public relations man, editor, and author. Obituaries: *New York Times*, February 18, 1975.

*　　*　　*

DOORNKAMP, John Charles   1938-

PERSONAL: Surname is pronounced *Dawn*-camp; born April 1, 1938, in Drenthe, Holland; son of Hendrik (a minister) and Mable (a teacher; maiden name, Welsford) Doornkamp; married Margaret Wragg (a teacher), August 8, 1964; children: Sarah, Elizabeth. *Education:* University of Sheffield, B.Sc., 1959, M.Sc., 1962; University of Nottingham, Ph.D., 1967. *Religion:* Christian. *Agent:* Curtis Brown Academic, 13 King St., London WC2, England. *Office:* Department of Geography, University of Nottingham, Nottingham, England.

CAREER: University of Nottingham, Nottingham, England, senior lecturer in geography, 1964—. Consultant engineering geomorphologist to Rendel, Palmer and Tritton, 1973—; consultant geomorphologist to Ministry of Development and Engineering Services, Government of Bahrain, 1974—. *Member:* British Geomorphological Research Group (honorary secretary, 1968-71), African Studies Association of the United Kingdom (council member, 1972—), Geological Society of London (fellow).

WRITINGS: (Editor with R. H. Osborne and F. A. Barnes) *Geographical Essays in Honour of K. C. Edwards*, University of Nottingham Press, 1970; *The Geomorphology of the Mbarara Area* (monograph), Geological Survey and Mines Department (Uganda), 1970; (with C. A. M. King) *Numerical Analysis in Geomorphology*, Edward Arnold, 1971; (contributor) R. J. Chorley, editor, *Spatial Analysis in Geomorphology*, Methuen, 1971; (contributor) S. H. Ominde, editor, *Studies in East African Geography and Development*, Heinemann, 1971; *Plausible Reasoning in Geomorphology: An Application to the Study of Bornhardt Formation*, Environmental Studies, University of Witwatersrand, 1972; (editor with J. A. Dawson) *Evaluating the Human Environment*, Edward Arnold, 1973; (with D. H. Krinsley) *Atlas of Quartz Sand Surface Textures*, Cambridge University Press, 1973; (with R. U. Cooke) *Geomorphology in Environmental Management*, Oxford University Press, 1974; (editor with Denys Brunsden) *The Unquiet Landscape*, David & Charles, 1974. Contributor to geology journals. Editor of *East Midlands Geographer*, 1966—.

WORK IN PROGRESS: Research in engineering geomorphology; a natural resource survey of Bahrain.

AVOCATIONAL INTERESTS: Water skiing, driving, photography, swimming.

*　　*　　*

DOTTS, M. Franklin   1929-

PERSONAL: Born May 26, 1929, in South Williamsport,

Pa.; son of Merrill M. and Helen (Holt) Dotts; married Maryann J. Dreese (a free-lance writer), August 9, 1958; children: Ruthann C. *Education:* University of Pittsburgh, B.A., 1951, M.Ed., 1954; Garrett-Evangelical Theological Seminary, M.Div., 1961; Columbia University, D.Ed., 1969. *Home:* 2514 Blair Blvd., Nashville, Tenn. 38212. *Office:* Section on Curriculum Resources, United Methodist Board of Discipleship, 201 Eighth Ave. S., Nashville, Tenn. 37202.

CAREER: Ordained United Methodist minister, 1961; affiliated with churches in Arlington Heights, Ill., 1958-61, Omaha, Neb., 1961-65; United Methodist Board of Discipleship, Nashville, Tenn., children's curriculum editor, 1967-73, coordinator of curriculum planning, 1973—. *Member:* Association for Supervision and Curriculum Development, Association of Church Teachers, Religious Education Association, Association of Professors and Researchers in Religious Education, Christian Educators Fellowship, Phi Delta Kappa.

WRITINGS: (With wife, Maryann J. Dotts) *Clue to Creativity*, Friendship, Volume I, 1974, Volumes II and III, 1975.

BIOGRAPHICAL/CRITICAL SOURCES: Spectrum/International Journal of Religious Education, summer, 1975.

*　　*　　*

DOUGLASS, Robert W.   1934-

PERSONAL: Born March 18, 1934, in Philadelphia, Pa.; son of Joseph W. and Katherine (Klaus) Douglass; married Joe Ann Hoffer, November 23, 1955; children: Steven, Scott, Glenn, Grant. *Education:* Pennsylvania State University, B.S., 1956, M.S., 1961; University of Minnesota, Ph.D., 1972. *Office:* Lockheed Electronics Corp., 16811 El Camino Real, Houston, Tex. 77058.

CAREER: U.S. Forest Service, Upper Darby, Pa., forester, 1960-63; Pennsylvania State University, Mont Alto, assistant professor, 1963-71, associate professor of forestry, 1971-75; Lockheed Electronics Corp., Houston, Tex., staff scientist, 1975—. *Military service:* U.S. Army, 1956-58. *Member:* American Society of Photogrammetry, Society of American Foresters, National Management Association.

WRITINGS: Forest Recreation, Pergamon, 1969, 2nd edition, 1975; *Evaluation of High Altitude Photography for Recreation Planning in the Upper Allegheny River Basin*, U.S. Department of the Interior, 1974.

WORK IN PROGRESS: A fiction adventure; research on remote sensing and its applications to forestry.

SIDELIGHTS: Douglass writes: "The motivating drive behind my interests has been a search for the experience. It is the experience for which we invest time and money." *Avocational interests:* Hunting, outdoor recreation, deep sea fishing, any outdoor activity requiring exercise and providing excitement.

*　　*　　*

DOWELL, Jack (Larder)   1908-

PERSONAL: Born April 29, 1908, in Halifax, Nova Scotia, Canada; son of William James (a businessman) and Muriel (Larder) Dowell; married Mary Webber, April 29, 1939 (divorced, 1969); children: Jack Webber. *Education:* Commercial College, Truro, Nova Scotia, graduate in bookkeeping, 1927. *Politics:* Conservative. *Religion:* Protestant. *Home address:* Waverley, Nova Scotia BON 2S0,

Canada. *Office address:* Downtown Halifax Business Association, P.O. Box 761, Halifax, Nova Scotia, Canada.

CAREER: Manufacturers' agent and business administrator at various periods; president of W. J. Dowell & Son, 1942-50; founder and managing director of savings corporation, 1963-68; Downtown Halifax Business Association, Halifax, Nova Scotia, executive manager, 1969—. Former member of Halifax Board of Trade.

MEMBER: Canadian Association in Support of Native People (past vice-president), Halifax Wildlife Association (member of board of directors), Halifax City Club, Kiwanis Club (director of Halifax chapter), Masons (past master).

WRITINGS: The Look-Off Bear: Stories of the Outdoors, McGraw, 1974. Contributor to *Atlantic Advocate* and to Halifax newspapers.

WORK IN PROGRESS: Research on Chapel Island, ancient seat of the Grand Council of Micmac Indians, for a magazine article; a second book.

SIDELIGHTS: Jack Dowell said: "I guess I am a rebel, in a sense, particularly against some of the 'profound' thoughts of the past that I do not find profound. I would dearly love to research the origins of our eastern Indian tribes, most of whom are Semitic in appearance, not Asiatic, but do not have the financial resources to pursue such research. Have unearthed faint evidence that the Meegumaag Indians may have roots in ancient Akkad."

* * *

DOWNING, Chris(tine)   1931-

PERSONAL: Born March 21, 1931, in Leipzig, Germany; daughter of Edgar Fritz (an executive) and Herta (a poet; maiden name, Fischer) Rosenblatt; married George Downing (a chemist), June 9, 1951; children: Peter, Eric, Scott, Christopher, Sandra. *Education:* Swarthmore College, B.A., 1952; Drew University, Ph.D., 1966. *Home:* 2805 Camino del Mar, #37, Delmar, Calif. 92014. *Agent:* Albert Zuckerman, 303 West 42nd St., New York, N.Y. 10036. *Office:* Department of Religion, San Diego State University, San Diego, Calif. 92182.

CAREER: Rutgers University, New Brunswick, N.J., instructor, 1963-66, assistant professor, 1966-70, associate professor of religion, 1970—. Adjunct professor at Temple University, 1973-74; visiting professor at San Diego State University, 1974-75; member of faculty at California School of Professional Psychology, 1974—. Chairman of board of directors of Pendle Hill Graduate Center; member of board of directors of Beard-Morristown School, Oakwood School, and Earlham School of Religion.

MEMBER: American Academy of Religion (president, 1973-74), Society for Religion in Higher Education (member of board of directors, 1966—), Society for the Scientific Study of Religion, C. G. Jung Institute, American Association of University Professors, Friends Conference on Religion and Psychology. *Awards, honors:* Cross-disciplinary fellowship from Society for Religion in Higher Education, 1967-68.

WRITINGS: (With Gordon Clanton) *Face to Face to Face*, Dutton, 1975. Contributor to *Journal of the American Academy of Religion, Journal of Religion, Judaism, Religion in Life, Theology Today, Inward Light*, and *Quaker Religious Thought.* Editor of *Quaker Religious Thought*, 1969-74.

WORK IN PROGRESS: Studying Freud's and Jung's writings on mythology.

SIDELIGHTS: Chris Downing writes: "My teaching, writing, and research all focus on human symbolic activity and on the cultural world created by that activity. Thus I am interested in the history of religion, in-depth psychology, imaginative literature, and in social experimentation, especially in relation to sexuality and lifestyle."

* * *

DOXIADIS, Constantinos Apostolos   1913-1975

May 14, 1913—June 28, 1975; Greek architect, city planner, developer of concept of ekistics, educator, and author of books on city planning and urban renewal. Obituaries: *Washington Post*, June 30, 1975; *Newsweek*, July 14, 1975; *Time*, July 14, 1975; *Current Biography*, September, 1975. (*CA*-41/44)

* * *

DRAPKIN, Israel   1906-

PERSONAL: Born July 17, 1906, in Rosario, Argentina; son of Isaac Hafkin (a pharmacist) and Louise (Senderey) Drapkin; married Rebeca Gidekel (a pianist), September 6, 1936; children: Luisa (Mrs. Leon Zeldis), Allan George. *Education:* University of Chile, B.A., 1923, M.A., 1925, M.D., 1929; postdoctoral study at Sorbonne, University of Paris, 1935, and University of London, 1945-46. *Home:* 48 Harlap St., Jerusalem, Israel. *Office:* Institute of Criminology, Hebrew University, Jerusalem, Israel.

CAREER: Saint Louis Hospital, Santiago, Chile, head of pathological laboratory, 1929-35; Ministry of Justice, Institute of Criminology, Santiago, Chile, director, 1936-59; University of Chile, Santiago, assistant professor, 1938-42, associate professor, 1943-50, Extraordinary Professor, 1950—, professor of social pathology, 1950-59, professor of mental hygiene, 1953-59, professor of criminology, 1958-59; Hebrew University, Jerusalem, Israel, professor of criminology, 1959-74, director of Institute of Criminology, 1959-74. Visiting professor at Central University of Venezuela, 1968, 1970, Haile Selassie I University, 1968, American University, 1972, and University of Pennsylvania, 1972; visiting lecturer at major universities in Europe, the United States, and Latin America. Chilean correspondent to U.N. Social Defense Section, 1950-74; U.N. Technical Assistance Administration expert in Israel for Criminological Studies and Services, 1957; visiting expert, U.N. Asia and Far East Institute for Prevention of Crime and Treatment of Offenders, Tokyo, 1965, 1968.

MEMBER: International Society of Criminology (vice-president, 1966-71), American Society of Criminology (fellow), Israel Society of Criminology, Chilean Society of Criminalistics, Forensic Medicine and Criminology (founding member), Society of Forensic Medicine of Chile (founding member); corresponding member of Australian Academy of Forensic Sciences, and other association. *Honorary member:* Inter-American Association of Criminological Studies, Argentinian Society of Criminology, Institute of Criminology of the Republic of Argentina, Brasilian Society of Criminology and Penitentiary Science, Venezuelan Society of Criminal Law and Criminology, Criminological Circle of Peru, Society of Penal Law and Criminology of the Province of Buenos Aires.

AWARDS, HONORS: British Council fellow, 1945-46; received citations from Costa Rican legislative assembly, 1956, Japanese Association of Criminology, 1965, Oscar Freire Institute (Brazil), 1968, and American Society of Criminology, 1972.

WRITINGS: Manual de Criminologia (title means "Handbook on Criminology"), Chilean Governmental Press, 1949; *Prensa y Criminalidad* (title means "Press and Criminality"), University of Chile Press, 1958; (editor) *The Prevention of Crime and the Treatment of Offenders in Israel*, Israel Government Press, 1965; (editor) *Studies in Criminology*, Magness Press, 1969; (editor with Emilio C. Viano) *Victimology: A New Focus*, Lexington Books, Volume I: *Theoretical Issues in Victimology*, 1974, Volume II: *Society's Reaction to Victimization*, 1974, Volume III: *Crimes, Victims, and Justice*, 1975, Volume IV: *Violence and Its Victims*, 1975, Volume V: *Exploiters and Exploited*, 1975. Contributor of one hundred papers to criminological journals in the United States, Europe, and Latin America.

WORK IN PROGRESS: The First International Symposium on Victimology; Historical Criminology, publication expected in 1976; *Clinical Criminology*, 1977; *Selected Problems in Criminology*, 1977; *Selected Criminological Problems*, 1978; *Crime and Punishment in Pre-Columbian America*, 1980.

SIDELIGHTS: "I thought that medicine could be of use to understand man," Drapkin wrote. "When I realized it does not, I started to study anthropology (physical and cultural), then switched to criminology in 1935, and I have not changed my interest. The basic mistake in this field is to consider that 'criminal' and 'non-criminal' are different types of human beings."

* * *

DREW, Donald J. 1920-

PERSONAL: Born September 13, 1920, in Lincoln, England; son of John Thomas (a company president) and Elsie (Spacey) Drew. *Education:* Cambridge University, M.A., 1954, B.A., 1960. *Home:* 7 Hartfield Close, Tonbridge, Kent, England.

CAREER: St. Lawrence College, Ramsgate, England, housemaster and head of English department, 1949-69; lecturer and counsellor at L'Abri Fellowship in Switzerland, 1969-73; The Skinners' School, England, senior lecturer in English, 1975—. Visiting professor, Geneva College, Beaver Falls, Pa., 1974. Lecturer in England and United States in alpine climbing, Biblical psychology, literary figures, and cinema. *Member:* Alpine Club. *Awards, honors:* D.Litt., Geneva College, 1974.

WRITINGS: An English Literature Notebook, St. Lawrence College Press, 1962; *Images of Man: A Critique of the Contemporary Cinema*, Inter-Varsity Press, 1974.

WORK IN PROGRESS: Research into Biblical basis for psychology; studies on men and women who altered the nature and purpose of twentieth-century writing.

* * *

DRIFTWOOD, Penelope
See DE LIMA, Clara Rosa

* * *

DRIVER, Christopher (Prout) 1932-

PERSONAL: Born December 1, 1932, in Ranipet, South India; son of Arthur Herbert (a doctor) and Kathleen (a teacher; maiden name, Shepherd) Driver; married Margaret Perfect (a social worker), May 3, 1958; children: Catherine, Penelope, Beatrice. *Education:* Christ Church, Oxford, M.A., 1956. *Politics:* Liberal. *Religion:* United Reformed Church. *Home:* 6 Church Rd., London N6 4QT, England.

Agent: A. D. Peters, 10 Buckingham St., London W.C.2, England.

CAREER: Liverpool Daily Post, Liverpool, England, reporter and sub-editor, 1958-60; *Guardian*, London, England, reporter, 1960-62, political reporter, 1962-64, features editor, 1964-68; The Book in Hand (antiquarian), Shaftesbury, Dorset, England, proprietor, 1968—. Member of board of directors of Christian Aid, 1973—. Member of Friends Ambulance Unit International Service, 1955-58.

WRITINGS: A Future for the Free Churches?, SCM Press, 1962; *The Disarmers: A Study in Protest*, Hodder & Stoughton, 1964; (editor) *The Good Food Guide*, Consumers Association, 1968—; *The Exploding University*, Hodder & Stoughton, 1970, Bobbs-Merrill, 1971. Contributor to *London Times, Guardian, Listener, New Statesman, New Society, Encounter*, and *Frontier*.

WORK IN PROGRESS: Researching the human and musical relationships of professional and amateur string quartet ensembles, and the history and sociology of restaurants in Britain; editing *The Good Food Guide*.

AVOCATIONAL INTERESTS: Playing the violin, cooking, mountaineering, visiting secondhand bookshops.

* * *

DRIVER, Godfrey Rolles 1892-1975

August 20, 1892—April 22, 1975; British scholar, educator, and author of books on Hebrew and Semitic studies. Obituaries: *Time*, May 12, 1975; *AB Bookman's Weekly*, July 7, 1975. (*CA*-21/22)

* * *

DRURY, Allen Stuart 1918-

PERSONAL: Born September 2, 1918, in Houston, Tex.; son of Alden Monteith and Flora (Allen) Drury. *Education:* Stanford University, B.A., 1939. *Office:* Drukill Co., Box 378, Rutherford, Calif. 94920.

CAREER: Tulare Bee, Tulare, Calif., editor, 1940-41; *Bakersfield Californian*, Bakersfield, Calif., county editor, 1941-42; United Press International, Washington, D.C., U.S. Senate staff, 1943-45; free-lance correspondent, 1946; *Pathfinder* magazine, Washington, D.C., national editor, 1947-53; *Washington Evening Star*, Washington, D.C., national staff, 1953-54; *New York Times*, Washington, D.C., U.S. Senate staff, 1954-59; *Reader's Digest*, Pleasantville, N.Y., political contributor, 1959-62. *Military service:* U.S. Army, 1942-43. *Member:* National Press Club, Sigma Delta Chi, Alpha Kappa Lambda, Cosmos Club and University Club (Washington), Bohemian Club (San Francisco). *Awards, honors:* Sigma Delta Chi award for editorial writing, 1942; Pulitzer Prize in fiction, 1960, for *Advise and Consent*; Litt.D. from Rollins College, 1961.

WRITINGS: Advise and Consent (novel; Book-of-the-Month Club selection), Doubleday, 1959; *A Shade of Difference* (novel), Doubleday, 1962; *A Senate Journal, 1943-1945* (a personal diary), McGraw, 1963, reprinted, DaCapo Press, 1972; *That Summer* (novel), M. Joseph, 1965, Coward, 1966; *Three Kids in a Cart: A Visit to Ike and Other Diversions* (selected newspaper articles), Doubleday, 1965; *Capable of Honor* (novel), Doubleday, 1966; *"A Very Strange Society": A Journey to the Heart of South Africa*, Trident, 1967; *Preserve and Protect* (novel), Doubleday, 1968; (author of notes; with photographer Fred Maroon) *Courage and Hesitation: Notes and Photographs of the Nixon Administration*, Doubleday, 1971; *The Throne of*

Saturn: A Novel of Space and Politics, Doubleday, 1971; *Come Nineveh, Come Tyre: The Presidency of Edward M. Jason* (novel), Doubleday, 1973; *The Promise of Joy: The Presidency of Orrin Knox* (novel), Doubleday, 1975.

SIDELIGHTS: Drury is one of the foremost political novelists in the United States. His books have grown increasingly more outspoken in their criticism of the "liberal press" and the "liberal establishment." George Snow says that Drury's premise in each of his novels has been the same: "the struggle between the forces of a God-fearing Americanism and hordes of journalistic, acronym-inventing, intellectual, peace-at-any-price liberals."

M. Stanton Evans says: "Drury is very much a writer with a cause, and his cause is to expose the confusions of the liberal mind in American politics. To this endeavor he brings a remarkable instinct for issues and an intimate knowledge of the political and journalistic world of Washington. These qualities have produced a series of novels that our future historian would be wise to consult if he wants to know something about the feel and shape of mid-twentieth century politics."

Advise and Consent was produced as a film.

BIOGRAPHICAL/CRITICAL SOURCES: Gordon Milne, *The American Political Novel*, University of Oklahoma Press, 1966.

* * *

DRVOTA, Mojmir 1923-

PERSONAL: Given name is pronounced Moy-*meer*; born January 13, 1923, in Prague, Czechoslovakia; son of Jan (a dentist) and Zdenka (Krejcikova) Drvota; married Jana Kratochvilova, May 18, 1957; children: Monica. *Education:* Charles University, student, 1945-48; Palacky University, Ph.D., 1953; Columbia University, M.S., 1961. *Home:* 3559 Chowning Ct., Columbus, Ohio 43220. *Office:* Department of Photography and Cinema, Ohio State University, 156 West 19th Ave., Columbus, Ohio 43210.

CAREER: Czechoslovak State Film, Prague, script writer, 1948-52; stage director for state theaters in Czechoslovakia, 1952-56; "The Magic Lantern" (multi-media program at Brussels World's Fair), Prague, and Brussels, Belgium, writer, 1956-57; Brooklyn Public Library, Brooklyn, N.Y., librarian, 1958-62; Columbia University, New York, N.Y., assistant professor of dramatic arts, 1962-69; New York University, New York, N.Y., associate professor of cinema, 1969-72; Ohio State University, Columbus, associate professor of cinema, 1972—. Stage director in Czechoslovakia, 1950-52. *Member:* Phi Kappa Phi.

WRITINGS: Povidky (title means "Short Stories"), Melantrich, 1946; *Pension pro umelce* (novel; title means "Boarding House for Artists"), Melantrich, 1947; *The Constituents of Film Theory*, Department of Cinema, Ohio State University, 1973; *Solitaire* (novel), Ohio State University Press, 1974.

Author of plays "Ostrov Real" ("The Island Real"), 1947, and "Nasr-ed-Din," 1951. Writer and assistant director of, and actor in, film "Daleka Cesta" ("The Distant Journey"), 1950. Also writer of eight scripts for Czechoslovak State Film, 1948-52. Author of "Theory of Film: Part One," a film script, Department of Cinema, Ohio State University, 1973.

WORK IN PROGRESS: Mirage, a novel; *A Report on the Second Sun*, a philosophical treatise; *Human Planetarium*, a multi-media project for Batelle Memorial Institute.

SIDELIGHTS: Drvota writes: "My career in Czechoslovakia culminated in my participation in the "Magic Lantern," a multimedia program for the Czechoslovak Pavillion in the 1958 Brussels World's Fair. This program eventually won first prize among the contributions of more than forty countries.

"As a professor, I have been concentrating on the theoretical aspect of film, and of arts in general. Lately, deepening and broadening my approach, I finally opened myself to the two ultimate questions; namely, the ontological quest for reality and the epistemological problem of human knowledge and action.

"I was not interested in these problems for intellectual or academic reasons. I was, and still am, motivated by an attempt to feel and articulate some essential paths which lead to a new region where human beings may find their roots, not as things subordinated to psychophysical or social order, but as free creatures constituting a different sphere by genuine self-realization, by immanent communication."

BIOGRAPHICAL/CRITICAL SOURCES: New York Herald Tribune, August 28, 1950; *New York Times*, August 28, 1950, September 10, 1950; *News in Engineering*, September, 1974; *Choice*, February, 1975; *Literary Tabloid*, February, 1975.

* * *

DUARTE, Joseph S(imon) 1913-

PERSONAL: Born March 16, 1913, in Portugal; son of Jose Simoes (a businessman) and Olinda (Felix) Duarte; married Leota Lambert, September 5, 1945; children: Philip, Linda (Mrs. Chris Loumakis), Lourdes. *Education:* Attended Long Beach Junior College, 1941. *Home:* 11024 Telechron Ave., Whittier, Calif. 90605. *Office:* 13215 East Penn St., Suite 500, Whittier, Calif. 90602.

CAREER: General Motors Corp., Southgate, Calif., production planner, 1936-40; California Shipbuilding, Wilmington, Calif., draftsman, 1940-42; Badgers Sales Co., Los Angeles, Calif., export manager, 1947-57; Duarte International Sales, Los Angeles, Calif., president, 1957-67; Delta Leisure Products Corp., Los Angeles, Calif., president, 1968-72; business consultant, 1972—. *Military service:* U.S. Army, Corps of Engineers, 1942-46; served in Pacific theater; became captain. *Member:* Hamiltonian Society (director).

WRITINGS: The Income Tax Is Obsolete, Arlington House, 1974.

WORK IN PROGRESS: Hamilton and American Taxation (tentative title), a historical analysis of federal tax policy; a book on the media.

* * *

DUBROVIN, Vivian 1931-

PERSONAL: Born March 24, 1931, in Chicago, Ill.; daughter of Ross (a school superintendent) and Emilie (a teacher; maiden name, Robert) Herr; married Kenneth P. Dubrovin (a director of agricultural research), September 5, 1954; children: Kenneth R., Darryl, Diana, Laura, Barbara. *Education:* University of Illinois, B.S., 1953. *Religion:* Episcopalian. *Home:* 1901 Arapahoe Dr., Longmont, Colo. 80501.

CAREER: Cuneo Press, Chicago, Ill., editor of "Cuneo Topics," 1953; U.S. Savings & Loan League, Chicago, Ill., staff writer for *News*, 1954; University of Wisconsin Press, Madison, editor, 1955-56; free-lance writer, 1971—. *Member:* National League of American Penwomen, American Association of University Women.

WRITINGS—For children: *Baseball Just for Fun*, EMC Corp., 1974; *The Magic Bowling Ball*, EMC Corp., 1974; *The Track Trophy*, EMC Corp., 1974; *Rescue on Skis*, EMC Corp., 1974. Contributor to *Wee Wisdom*, *Crusader*, *Adventure*, and *Humpty Dumpty*.

WORK IN PROGRESS—For children: A series of four horse stories; a skiing novel; a mystery story.

BIOGRAPHICAL/CRITICAL SOURCES: Longmont Times-Call, October 31, 1974; *Boulder Town and Country*, December 25, 1974; *Loveland Reporter-Herald*, April 19, 1975.

* * *

DUEKER, Christopher W(ayne) 1939-

PERSONAL: Born December 21, 1939, in Fresno, Calif.; son of Kenneth Earnest (an electrical engineer) and Ruth (Learned) Dueker; married Joyce Sutherlin (an editor and writer), June 27, 1964; children: Kenneth, Donna. *Education:* Dartmouth College, student, 1957-59; Pomona College, B.A., 1961; University of Southern California, M.D., 1965. *Religion:* Christian. *Home:* 37 Ringwood, Atherton, Calif. 94025. *Office:* School of Medicine, Stanford University, Stanford, Calif. 94305.

CAREER: Anesthesiologist in California, 1965—. Assistant professor at Stanford University, 1973—. Diplomate of American Board of Anesthesiology. *Military service:* U.S. Navy, Medical Corps, submarine and diving medical officer, 1965-70; became lieutenant commander. *Member:* American Society of Anesthesiologists, Undersea Medical Society, California Society of Anesthesiologists.

WRITINGS: Medical Aspects of Sport Diving, A. S. Barnes, 1970; (with wife, Joyce Dueker) *Old Fashioned Homemade Ice-Cream Cookbook*, Bobbs-Merrill, 1974.

WORK IN PROGRESS: A cookbook; a novel.

* * *

DUEKER, Joyce S(utherlin) 1942-

PERSONAL: Born February 5, 1942, in Takoma Park, Md.; daughter of Howard (a used car dealer) and Myrtle (a teacher; maiden name, Davidson) Sutherlin; married Christopher W. Dueker (an anesthsiologist), June 27, 1964; children: Kenneth, Donna. *Education:* University of California, Santa Barbara, B.A., 1963, Los Angeles, M.A., 1965. *Religion:* Christian. *Residence:* Atherton, Calif. *Agent:* Gloria R. Mosesson, Thomas Nelson, Inc., 30 East 42nd St., New York, N.Y. 10017.

CAREER: University of Hawaii, Honolulu, instructor in English, 1967-68; free-lance writer. *Member:* Toyon Poets (vice-president, 1965).

WRITINGS: (With husband, Christopher Dueker) *Old Fashioned Homemade Ice Cream Cookbook*, Bobbs-Merrill, 1974, Author of booklet, *Writing Better Bluebooks*, Fearon, 1968. Contributor of articles to medical and military periodicals.

WORK IN PROGRESS: Another cookbook; a nonfiction religious book.

SIDELIGHTS: Regarding the idea for an ice cream cookbook, Joyce Dueker told *CA:* "Looking through all kinds of cookbooks we found that as of that year there was no really authoritative book on homemade ice cream. The recipes were elaborate. So we decided to make up our own recipes and keep them as simple and easy as possible."

* * *

DUFFY, John J(oseph) 1934-

PERSONAL: Born November 17, 1934, in Trenton, N.J.; son of John J. (a fire-protection equipment retailer) and Agnes J. (Veldof) Duffy; married Barbara M. Kelly (a registered nurse), August 26, 1961; children: Arline, Sarah. *Education:* Georgetown University, B.S., 1957; University of Vermont, M.A., 1958; Syracuse University, Ph.D., 1964. *Home:* Allen's Pt., South Hero, Vt. 05986. *Office:* Office of the Dean, Johnson State College, Johnson, Vt. 05656.

CAREER: University of Maryland, College Park, assistant professor of English literature, 1965-68; Rensselaer Polytechnic Institute, Troy, N.Y., assistant professor of English literature, 1968-69; University of New Hampshire, Durham, assistant professor of American literature, 1969-71; University of Vermont, Burlington, adjunct professor of American literature, 1971-72; Johnson State College, Johnson, Vt., professor of humanities, and dean, 1972—. *Member:* Vermont Historical Society (executive director, 1971-72).

WRITINGS: (Editor) *Coleridge's American Disciples: Selected Correspondence of James Marsh*, University of Massachusetts Press, 1973; (editor) *Early Vermont Broadsides: 1776-1820*, University Press of New England, 1975. Contributor of articles to journals.

WORK IN PROGRESS: With H. N. Muller, *Aspects of the American 1830's*, completion expected in 1976.

* * *

DUKE, Madelaine
(Maxim Donne, Alex Duncan)

PERSONAL: Born in Geneva, Switzerland; married Alexander Macfarlane (a physician), 1949. *Education:* University of St. Andrews, B.Sc., 1945; University of Edinburgh, M.B., 1949; University of Vienna, Ch.B., 1955. *Address:* c/o Mondial Books Ltd., Norman Alexander & Co., 13 Bolton St., Piccadilly, London W1Y 8HD, England.

CAREER: Author, novelist, and part-time medical psychotherapist. *Member:* P.E.N., Society of Authors, Royal Society of Medicine. *Awards, honors:* Huntington Hartford Foundation fellow, 1962.

WRITINGS: Top Secret Mission, Evans Brothers, 1954, Criterion, 1955; *Slipstream: The Story of Anthony Duke*, Evans Brothers, 1955; *No Passport: The Story of Jan Felix*, Evans Brothers, 1957; *Beyond the Pillars of Hercules: A Spanish Journey*, Evans Brothers, 1957; *Azael and the Children*, J. Cape, 1958; *No Margin for Error*, J. Cape, 1959, Walker & Co., 1963.

A City Built to Music, J. Cape, 1960; *Ride the Brooding Wind*, Walker & Co., 1961; (under pseudonym Alex Duncan) *It's A Vet's Life*, M. Joseph, 1961; *The Vet Has Nine Lives*, M. Joseph, 1962, large print edition, Ulverscroft, 1969; *Thirty Pieces of Nickel*, J. Cape, 1962; *The Sovereign Lords*, J. Cape, 1963; *Vets in the Belfry*, M. Joseph, 1964; (under pseudonym Maxim Donne) *Claret, Sandwiches, and Sin: A Cartoon*, Heinemann, 1964, Doubleday, 1966; *Sobaka*, Heinemann, 1965; *This Business of Bomfog: A Cartoon*, Heinemann, 1967, Doubleday, 1969; *The Secret People*, Brockhampton Press, 1967, Doubleday,

1969; *The Lethal Innocents*, M. Joseph, 1968; *The Sugar-cube Trap* (for young adults), Brockhampton Press, 1969.

Death of a Holy Murderer, M. Joseph, 1974; *Death at the Wedding* (sequel to *Death of a Holy Murderer*), M. Joseph, in press.

Short fiction is represented in anthologies, including: *Pick of Today's Short Stories*, edited by John Pudney, Putnam, Volume XI, 1958, Volume XII, 1960.

Contributor to medical journals and to literary periodicals, including *Books and Bookmen*.

SIDELIGHTS: Top Secret Mission was adapted for television by Irving G. Neiman and broadcast on U.S. Steel Hour, 1958. Miss Duke, who holds the title Baroness de Hartog, is competent in German and knows Spanish and Italian. She is a registered silversmith. *Avocational interests:* Geology, travel.

* * *

DUKE, Richard DeLaBarre 1930-

PERSONAL: Born December 19, 1930, in Washington, D.C.; son of James Paul and Florence Hilda (a teacher; maiden name, DeLaBarre) Duke; married Marie Alice Myers, August 27, 1955; children: Kathryn, Paul, Michelle, Lynda, Lorraine, Richard, Jr. *Education:* University of Maryland, B.S., 1952; Michigan State College (now Michigan State University), B.S., 1954, M.U.P., 1956; University of Michigan, Ph.D., 1964. *Home:* 321 Park Lake Ave., Ann Arbor, Mich. 48103. *Office:* 2036 Dana, S.N.R., University of Michigan, Ann Arbor, Mich. 48104.

CAREER: Maryland National Capital Park and Planning Commission, Washington, D.C., planner, 1952-55; Detroit City Planning Commission, Detroit, Mich., planner, 1955-57; Tri-County Regional Planning Commission, Akron, Ohio, planner, 1957-58; Michigan State University, East Lansing, assistant professor, 1958-62, associate professor, 1962-65, professor of urban planning, 1965—, director of Urban-Regional Research Institute, 1963-67; University of Michigan, Ann Arbor, professor of urban and regional planning, 1967—, associate director of Institute of Public Policy Studies, 1967-71, and director of Environmental Simulation Laboratory, 1967-74. Fellow of Netherlands Institute for Advanced Study, 1973-74; visiting professor at University of Hawaii, 1973. Lecturer at more than thirty American universities, 1962-71. Member of advisory committee of National Research Council's Commission on Natural Resources. Member of board of directors of Community Systems Foundation, 1962-71, and HDI, Inc. (housing renovation firm), 1969-72. Consultant to United Nations, Governments of France and Germany, and U.S. Department of State. *Military service:* U.S. Army, Corps of Engineers, 1956-66; became first lieutenant.

MEMBER: International Simulation and Gaming Association (member of secretariat, 1967—), American Institute of Planners (president of Michigan chapter, 1961-62; member of executive board, 1959-63), American Society of Planning Officials, North American Simulation and Gaming Association (member of board of directors, 1967—), Sister Lake Conservation Association (member of board of directors, 1970-72), Phi Kappa Phi. *Awards, honors:* Samuel Trask Dana Award, 1964; Fulbright scholarship to Germany, 1969.

WRITINGS: (Contributor), *New Concepts and Municipal Governments,* National League of Cities, 1968; (contributor) *Simulation in the Study of Politics,* Markham, 1968;

Gaming: The Future's Language, Sage Publications, 1974; (with Cathy Greenblat) *Gaming-Simulation: Rationale, Design, Use,* Sage Publications, 1974; *The Metropolis Game,* two volumes, Gamed Simulations, Inc., 1975; (editor with Greenblatt) *Game Generating Games for Community and Classroom,* Little, Brown, 1975.

Creator of simulation games: "Metropolis," Michigan State University, 1964; "Cosmexopolis," Michigan State University, 1965; "METRO," Michigan State University, 1967; "APEX," University of Michigan, 1969; "AEPS," University of Michigan, 1972; "Impasse?," University of Michigan, 1972; "At-Issue!," University of Michigan, 1973; "Conceptual Mapping," University of Michigan, 1973; "Upper Limit," University of Michigan, 1973; "F.A.O. Game," University of Michigan, 1975.

Contributor of more than fifty articles to professional journals. Member of editorial board of *Journal of Simulation and Games,* 1971, and of *Simulation Gaming News,* 1975—.

* * *

DUNCAN, Alex
See DUKE, Madelaine

* * *

DUNCANSON, Michael E(dward) 1948-

PERSONAL: Born January 15, 1948, in Mondovi, Wis.; son of Franklin C. (a postal employee) and Patricia A. (a crafts teacher; maiden name, Werrell) Duncanson; married Kathleen R. Pheifer (an editor), June 7, 1975. *Education:* Wisconsin State University, Eau Claire, B.S., 1970. *Home:* 1813 Golf Dr., Eau Claire, Wis. 54701.

CAREER: U.S. Peace Corps volunteer in India, 1970-71; *Wisconsin Sportsman,* Oshkosh, Wis., contributor, 1973-75; University of Wisconsin Extension, Eau Claire, outdoor recreation instructor, 1974-75; free-lance outdoor writer. Consultant to Cartographic Institute, Eau Claire, Wis., 1972-75; executive secretary of Eau Claire Area Ecology Action, 1973-74. *Member:* Ice Age Park and Trail Foundation, Gamma Theta Upsilon.

WRITINGS: Canoe Trails of Southern Wisconsin, Wisconsin Trails, 1974; *A Guide to the Apostle Islands and the Bayfield Peninsula,* Cartographic Institute, 1975.

WORK IN PROGRESS: Indianhead Rivers: A Canoeing Guide to West Central Wisconsin; A Paddler's Guide to the Boundary Waters Canoe Area; Wisconsin Hiking and Backpacking Guide.

AVOCATIONAL INTERESTS: Travel, camping, hiking, canoeing, kayaking, snowshoeing, cross-country skiing.

* * *

DUNLEAVY, Janet Egleson 1928-
(Janet F. Egleson, Janet Frank)

PERSONAL: Born December 16, 1928, in New York, N.Y.; married second husband, Gareth W. Dunleavy (a professor). *Education:* Hunter College (now Hunter College of the City University of New York), B.A., 1951; New York University, M.A., 1962, Ph.D., 1966. *Home:* 2723 East Bradford, Milwaukee, Wis. 53211. *Office:* Department of English, University of Wisconsin, Milwaukee, Wis. 53201.

CAREER: Hunter College of the City University of New York, New York, N.Y., lecturer in English, 1964-66; State

University of New York at Stony Brook, assistant professor of English, 1966-70; University of Wisconsin—Milwaukee, assistant professor, 1970-71, associate professor of English, 1971—. *Member:* International Association for the Study of Anglo-Irish Literature (member of executive committee, 1970-76), Modern Language Association of America, American Committee for Irish Studies (secretary, 1972-75), American Association of University Professors, Wisconsin Academy of Science, Arts, and Letters, Wisconsin Coordinating Council of Women in Higher Education, English Graduate Association of New York University. *Awards, honors:* State University of New York summer research grant, 1967, 1969, Graduate School faculty summer research grant, 1968; American Council of Learned Societies grant, 1971; American Irish Foundation grant, 1973, 1974.

WRITINGS: (Under name Janet F. Egleson; with Jim Egleson) *Parents Without Partners*, Dutton, 1961; (under name Janet F. Egleson) *Design for Writing*, Glencoe Press, 1970; *George Moore: The Artist's Vision, the Storyteller's Art*, Bucknell University Press, 1973; (contributor) Huffman, Canary, and Kozicki, editors, *The Uses of Historical Criticism: Essays in Honor of Irving Ribner*, University of Pittsburgh Press, 1974.

Children's books; under name Janet Frank: *Daddies*, Simon & Schuster, 1954; *Davy Crockett and the Indians*, J. C. Winston, 1955; *Happy Days: What Children Do the Whole Day Through*, Simon & Schuster, 1955. Author of two additional books for children.

Translator and editor, *Simone Weil*, by Jacques Cabaud. Contributor to journals in her field, including *An Feinisc, Victorian Studies, Irish University Review*. Editorial consultant to encyclopedia firms and to Bucknell University Press. Editor, *American Committee for Irish Studies Newsletter*, 1971—.

WORK IN PROGRESS: With husband, Gareth Dunleavy, working on a catalog of the O'Conor Papers and a collection of Jeremiah Curtin's Irish folktales; a critical study of works of Mary Lavin; research on the Irish question in the political novels of Trollope; research on Samuel Lover.

* * *

DUNLOP, John B(arrett) 1942-

PERSONAL: Born September 10, 1942, in Boston, Mass.; son of John Thomas (a professor) and Dorothy (Webb) Dunlop; married Olga Verhovskoy, September 12, 1965; children: Maria, John, Olga. *Education:* Harvard University, B.A., 1964; St. Vladimir's Orthodox Seminary, graduate study, 1965-67; Yale University, M.A., 1965, Ph.D., 1973. *Religion:* Eastern Orthodox. *Home:* 21 South Cedar St., Oberlin, Ohio 44074. *Office:* Department of German and Russian, Oberlin College, Oberlin, Ohio 44074.

CAREER: Oberlin College, Oberlin, Ohio, instructor, 1970-73, assistant professor, 1973-75, professor of Russian, 1975—. *Member:* Association of Russian-American Scholars in the United States of America. *Awards, honors:* Woodrow Wilson fellowship, 1964-65; Younger Humanist Fellowship from National Endowment for the Humanities, 1974-75; academic visitor at London School of Economics and Political Science, 1974-75.

WRITINGS: Staretz Amvrosy (biography), Nordland, 1972; (editor with Richard Haugh and Alexis Klimoff) *Aleksandr Solzhenitsyn: Critical Essays and Documentary Materials*, Nordland, 1973, expanded edition, Collier-Macmillan, 1975; *The New Russian Revolutionaries*, Nordland, 1975. Contributor to *Times Literary Supplement, Russian Review, Frontier, Oberlin Alumni, Survey*, and *Transactions of the Association of Russian-American Scholars*.

WORK IN PROGRESS: Research on contemporary Russian nationalism and Solzhenitsyn.

* * *

DUNN, (Henry) Hampton 1916-

PERSONAL: Born December 14, 1916, in Floral City, Fla.; son of William Harvey (a phosphate miner) and Nannie L. (Hemrick) Dunn; married Charlotte Rawls (a registered nurse and school teacher), August 16, 1941; children: Janice (Mrs. Clark Oldroyd), Henry Hampton, Jr., Dennis Harvey. *Education:* Attended Mercer University, 1934-35, and University of Tampa, 1935-36. *Politics:* Republican. *Religion:* Baptist. *Home:* 10610 Carrollwood Dr., Tampa, Fla. 33618. *Office:* Peninsula Motor Club (AAA), P.O. Box 22087, Tampa, Fla. 33622.

CAREER: Tampa Daily Times, Tampa, Fla., reporter, 1936-46, city editor, 1947-49, managing editor, 1949-58, author of column "Palm Tree Politics," 1950-58; WCKT-Television, Miami, Fla., news analyst, political commentator, and feature editor, 1958-59; Peninsula Motor Club (AAA), Tampa, Fla., vice-president, 1967—, public relations director, 1959—. Personal assistant to Attorney General of Florida, 1964; press director for Democratic candidates for governor and state cabinet, 1960. *Military service:* U.S. Army Air Forces, 1942-46; served in Mediterranean theater; became major; received Bronze Star Medal and five battle stars.

MEMBER: International Platform Association, Associated Press Association of Florida (past president), Tampa Historical Society (past president), Visiting Nurses Association (past president), Tampa Mental Health Association, Salvation Army (past chairman of local unit), United Cerebral Palsy Association (past local and state president), Tampa Old Timers Association (vice-president), Masons, Eastern Star, Rotary International (past president; past district governor), Sigma Delta Chi. *Awards, honors:* Associated Press award for best spot news story of 1946 in Florida, 1947; Florida Historical Society award for excellence in presentation of Florida history in media, 1970; Jefferson Davis Medal, United Daughters of Confederacy, 1972; Florida Award for outstanding contribution to Florida history, from Peace River Valley Historical Society, 1974.

WRITINGS: Re-Discover Florida, Hurricane House, 1969, 2nd edition, Trend House, 1973; *Florida: Treasureland in the Sun*, Beach Products, 1971; *WDAE: Florida's Pioneer Radio Station*, WDAE-Radio, 1972; *Yesterday's Tampa*, E. A. Seemann, 1972; *Yesterday's St. Petersburg*, E. A. Seemann, 1973; *Yesterday's Clearwater*, E. A. Seemann, 1973; *Yesterday's Tallahassee*, E. A. Seemann, 1974; *Florida Sketches*, E. A. Seemann, 1974; *Accent Florida*, Tribune Co., 1975. Author of "Florida's Past," in *Florida Trend*, 1961-72, "Photouring Florida," in about fifty Florida newspapers, 1966—, and "Accent Florida," in *Sunday Tampa Tribune-Times*.

WORK IN PROGRESS: A History of Citrus County, Florida.

AVOCATIONAL INTERESTS: Reading biography and history.

DUNN, Judith F.
See BERNAL, Judith F.

* * *

DUNN, Lloyd W. 1906-

PERSONAL: Born September 29, 1906, in Brooklyn, N.Y.; son of Ernest Linwood and Florence (Bennet) Dunn; married Priscilla White; children: Jeffrey L., Stephen W., Jonathan L. *Education:* Attended Art Students League. *Politics:* None. *Religion:* None. *Home:* 17437 Rancho St., Encino, Calif. 91316.

CAREER: Rickard Advertising Agency, New York, N.Y., executive vice-president for four years; spent ten years with McGraw-Hill Publishing Co. as sales promotion manager; Dunn-Fenwick Advertising Agency, Los Angeles, Calif., president, 1947-50; Capitol Records, Hollywood, Calif., 1950-73, vice-president at various times of merchandising and sales, of artists and repertoire, and of the international office. *Member:* National Academy of Recording Arts and Sciences (a founder), California Yacht Club.

WRITINGS: Hit the Road, Associated Business Papers, 1945; *On the Flipside* (autobiography), Billboard Publishing, 1975. Contributor of articles and short stories to various magazines.

* * *

DUNN, Stuart 1900-

PERSONAL: Born August 12, 1900, in Amboy, Minn.; son of Sherman James (a farm implement dealer) and Lelia (Nourse) Dunn; married Mildred Specker, September 10, 1941; children: David S., Judith S. (Mrs. Bryant Puffer). *Education:* University of Minnesota, B.S., 1923, Ph.D., 1931; Iowa State College (now University), M.S., 1926. *Politics:* Republican. *Religion:* Protestant. *Residence:* Durham, N.H. *Office:* Department of Botany and Plant Pathology, University of New Hampshire, Durham, N.H. 03824.

CAREER: Iowa State College (now University), Ames, instructor in plant physiology, 1924-26; University of New Hampshire, Durham, instructor, 1926-37, assistant professor, 1937-47, associate professor, 1947-60, professor of plant physiology, 1960-70, professor emeritus, 1970—. Visiting professor at Louisiana State University, summer, 1950; research fellow at California Institute of Technology, 1952-53. *Member:* American Association for the Advancement of Science, American Society of Plant Physiologists, Weed Science Society of America, American Association of University Professors, Sigma Xi, Gamma Alpha, Phi Kappa Phi, Phi Sigma. *Awards, honors:* Award of merit from Northeast Weed Science Society, 1972, for service to weed science and to the society.

WRITINGS: Elementary Plant Physiology, Addison-Wesley, 1949; (with E. D. Bickford) *Lighting for Plant Growth*, Kent State University Press, 1972. Contributor to scientific journals.

WORK IN PROGRESS: Research on light and soil factors affecting plant growth.

SIDELIGHTS: Dunn is a pioneer in the use of mercury vapor and fluorescent lamps in horticultural research. His studies at University of New Hampshire led to the building of the school's Phytotron. His first book has been published in Korean.

DUPUY, R(ichard) Ernest 1887-1975

March 24, 1887—April 25, 1975; American army officer, newspaperman, military historian, editor, and author. Obituaries: *New York Times*, April 26, 1975; *Washington Post*, April 27, 1975. (*CA*-4)

* * *

DURAND, Robert 1944-

PERSONAL: Born August 10, 1944, in St. Louis, Mo.; son of Robert Louis (a physician) and Florence (Snyder) Durand; children: Christian James. *Education:* University of Portland, B.A., 1966; San Francisco State College (now University), M.A., 1969. *Residence:* Lake Oswego, Ore. *Office address:* P.O. Box 587, Lake Oswego, Ore. 97034.

CAREER: Richard Abel & Co., inventory control manager, 1967-71; Capra Press, Santa Barbara, Calif., editor of "Capra Chapbook Series," 1972—. Publisher and editor of Yes! Press, 1970-72, of Lost Pleiade Press, 1974—. Poetry and drama book buyer, Cody's Books, Berkeley, Calif., 1973-74.

WRITING: The Book of Months (poetry), Capricorn Press, 1971; *J.* (poetry), Christopher Books, 1971; *The Old Man and the Monkey-King*, Capricorn Press, 1972; (editor) *The Yes! Press Anthology*, Christopher Books, 1972; *The Ages of J.* (poetry), Christopher Books, 1973; *Landscape for Two Figures* ("prosepoems"), Mudra Press, 1975. Author of songs produced by Autumn and Warner Bros.

WORK IN PROGRESS: A science fiction novel; a pornographic novel; a murder novel; three books of poems about women in murder.

SIDELIGHTS: Durand writes: "My influences are friends, fellow writers—the werewolf poet madman Walter Hall, the beautiful kabbalist-surrealist poet Jack Hirschman, the printer Noel Young, the composer Ron Elliott, the bookman Aaron Saady, the great conversationalists G. E. Flanagan and Ed Fischer, Diane di Prima and Faye Kicknosway, two of the strongest poetic voices in America. Jack Kerouac was the mentor." Durand notes that he is currently employed as a garbageman, "the best job I've ever had for multitudinous reasons."

* * *

DURHAM, Mae
See ROGER, Mae Durham

* * *

DURLAND, William R(eginald) 1931-

PERSONAL: Born March 28, 1931, in New York, N.Y.; son of William Reginald and Lillian (Seymour) Durland; married Leona Mary Ann Semenas, July 24, 1954; children: Patrick, Michael, Jenifer. *Education:* Bucknell University, A.B., 1953; Georgetown University, LL.B., 1959, J.D., 1967; University of Notre Dame, M.A., 1975. *Politics:* Independent. *Religion:* Christian Catholic. *Home:* 3525 Elwood Dr., Fort Wayne, Ind. 46805. *Office:* Department of Philosophy, Purdue University, Fort Wayne, Ind. 46805.

CAREER: U.S. Commission on International Rules of Judicial Procedure, Washington, D.C., assistant to director, 1959-60; U.S. Department of Health, Education & Welfare, Washington, D.C., trial attorney, 1960-61; private practice in law in Fairfax, Va. and Washington, D.C., 1961-73; Purdue University, Fort Wayne, Ind., associate professor of philosophy, 1973—, chairman of department, 1975—.

Admitted to Bar of Washington, D.C. and Wisconsin, 1961, U.S. Supreme Court, 1963, Virginia, 1965, and Indiana, 1973; advance coordinator of Democratic national presidential campaigns, 1964, 1968, delegate to Democratic National Convention, 1968; Democratic candidate for U.S. Congress from Virginia, 1972. Member of Virginia State Legislature, 1966-70. Vice-president and director of Virginia Citizens Consumer Council, 1968-72. *Military service:* U.S. Army, Medical Service Corps, 1954-57. U.S. Army Reserve, Judge Advocate's General Corps, 1966-67; became captain.

MEMBER: American Bar Association (vice-chairman of international judicial cooperation committee, 1962-63), Virginia Rehabilitation Association (director, 1967), Virginia Association for Retarded Children (director, 1968-70).

WRITINGS: *No King But Caesar*, Herald Press, 1975; (editor with William H. Bruening) *Ethical Issues: A Search for the Contemporary Conscience*, Mayfield, 1975. Contributor to *Quaker Religious Quarterly, Georgetown Law Journal*, and *Law Review Digest*.

WORK IN PROGRESS: A novel about pacifism; editing an anthology on non-violence.

* * *

DYCK, J. William 1918-

PERSONAL: Born in 1918; married, wife's name Sarah. *Education:* Bethel College, North Newton, Kan., B.A., 1951; University of Missouri, M.A., 1953; University of Michigan, Ph.D., 1956. *Office:* University of Waterloo, Waterloo, Ontario, Canada.

CAREER: Professor at University of Waterloo, Waterloo, Ontario. *Member:* Modern Language Association of America. *Awards, honors:* Canadian Council Nuffield Award.

WRITINGS: *Mozart*, Ginn, 1963; (with H. E. Huelsbergen) *Alexander von Humboldt*, Blaisdell, 1965; (with Huelsbergen) *Wagner*, Blaisdell, 1965; *Nietzsche*, Blaisdell, 1967; (with W. J. Schwarz) *Mensch und Welt: An Elementary Science Reader*, Blaisdell, 1970; *Pasternak*, Twayne, 1972. Contributor to journals in his field.

WORK IN PROGRESS: A book on the German dramatist Kleist; a comparative study of Goethe, Shelley, and Pasternak.

* * *

DYSON, A(nthony) E(dward) 1928-

PERSONAL: Born November 28, 1928, in London, England; son of Sidney Herbert (a civil servant) and Lilian (Drake) Dyson. *Education:* Pembroke College, Cambridge, M.Litt. (first class honors), 1952. *Politics:* "Floating." *Religion:* Anglican. *Residence:* London, England. *Office:* School of English and American Studies, University of East Anglia, Norwich NOR 88C, England.

CAREER: University College of North Wales, Bangor, lecturer in English, 1955-63; University of East Anglia, Norwich, England, senior lecturer in English and American studies, 1963—. Visiting professor at Sir George Williams University, summers, 1967-69. *Member:* Critical Quarterly Society (co-founder).

WRITINGS: (With C. B. Cox) *Modern Poetry*, Edward Arnold, 1963; *The Crazy Fabric: Essays in Irony*, St. Martin's, 1965; *The Practical Criticism of Poetry*, Edward Arnold, 1965; (editor) *Modern Judgments on Dickens*, Macmillan, 1968; (editor with Cox) *Word in the Desert*, Oxford University Press, 1968; (editor) *Casebook on "Bleak House"*, Macmillan, 1969; (editor with Cox) *Black Papers on Education*, three volumes, Critical Quarterly Society, 1969-70.

The Inimitable Dickens, Macmillan, 1970; (with others) *Down with the Poor*, Churchill Press, 1971; *Between Two Worlds: Aspects of Literary Form*, Macmillan, 1972; (editor with Cox) *Twentieth Century Mind*, three volumes, Oxford University Press, 1972; (editor) *English Poetry: Select Bibliographical Guides*, Oxford University Press, 1973; (editor) *English Novel: Select Bibliographical Guides*, Oxford University Press, 1974; (editor with Julian Lovelock) *Casebook on "Paradise Lost"*, Macmillan, 1974; *Freedom in Love*, S.P.C.K., 1975; (with Lovelock) *Masterful Images: Metaphysicals to Romantics*, Macmillan, 1975; (editor with Lovelock) *Education and Democracy*, Routledge & Kegan Paul, 1975.

General editor of "Casebooks on Literature," Macmillan, 1965—. Contributor to British publications, including *Spectator, Daily Telegraph*, and *Listener*. Co-editor of *Critical Quarterly*, 1959—, and *Christian*, 1973—.

WORK IN PROGRESS: A book on Yeats and T. S. Eliot, for Macmillan; research on his own return to Christianity, with publication expected to result.

SIDELIGHTS: Dyson writes: "People have called me 'left-wing' and 'right-wing' in turn, but I prefer the word 'Christian.' For a time, I thought of myself as a 'liberal humanist,' but looking back, this was clearly a mistake. Literature is celebration; teaching is celebration, of oneself and others. I suppose I am a traditionalist because I believe in the present. What is worse than provincialism? Almost everything that makes life rich was said or written or created by people who are now no longer living; almost all the colour and joy came from religious men. . . . The great need for the times, as I see it, is a Christian critique of our civilisation, to challenge secularism, and restore confidence in love, and hope, in a darkening world. The 1970's challenge everyone to rethink their assumptions and discover what rings true for them; I'm glad I was shaken out of the wrong tradition—wrong for me, certainly—in time."

BIOGRAPHICAL/CRITICAL SOURCES: *Times Literary Supplement*, July 25, 1968; *London*, November, 1968; *Listener*, May 28, 1970.

* * *

EAGLE, Chester (Arthur) 1933-

PERSONAL: Born October 10, 1933, in Bendigo, Victoria, Australia; son of Norman Percy (a farmer) and Alice Myra (Duncan) Eagle; married Mary Elizabeth Hutchings, June 19, 1965; children: Aston Arthur, Miriam Joan. *Education:* University of Melbourne, B.A., 1955. *Politics:* Australian Labour Party. *Home:* 23 Langs Rd., Ivanhoe 3079, Australia.

CAREER: Teacher of English at Preston Institute of Technology, Preston, Victoria, Australia.

WRITINGS: *Hail and Farewell: An Evocation of Gippsland* (nonfiction), Heinemann, 1971; *Who Could Love the Nightingale?* (novel), Wren, 1974; *Four Faces, Wobbly Mirror* (novel), Wren, 1976.

SIDELIGHTS: Eagle writes: "I admire those writers who make me most conscious of language, of the art of writing: Shakespeare, Lampedusa, . . . Frederick Manning, . . . Turgenev, . . . Hal Porter, . . . James Gould Cozzens, . . .

James Thurber.... My aim—to make my art as rich and varied as life itself."

* * *

EAGLETON, Terence (Francis) 1943-
(Terry Eagleton)

PERSONAL: Born in 1943, in Salford, England; married Elizabeth Rosemary Galpin. *Education:* Trinity College, Cambridge, M.A. and Ph.D. *Home:* 6 Coppock Close, Headington Quarry, Oxford, England. *Office:* Wadham College, Oxford University, Oxford, England.

CAREER: Cambridge University, Jesus College, Cambridge, England, fellow, 1964-69; Oxford University, Wadham College, Oxford, England, fellow and tutor in poetry, 1969—. Selector for Poetry Book Society, 1969-71.

WRITINGS: The New Left Church (essays), Helicon, 1966; *Shakespeare and Society: Critical Studies in Shakespearean Drama*, Schocken, 1967.

Under name Terry Eagleton: (Editor) *Directions: Pointers for the Post-Conciliar Church* (essays), Sheed & Ward, 1968; (editor with Brian Wicker) *From Culture to Revolution* (essays), Sheed & Ward, 1968; *The Body as Language: Outline of a "New Left" Theology*, Sheed & Ward, 1970; *Exiles and Émigrés: Studies In Modern Literature*, Schocken, 1970. Contributor to *Slant, Times Literary Supplement, Stand*, and *Commonweal*. Poetry reviewer, *Slant*.

AVOCATIONAL INTERESTS: Poetry, theatre.

* * *

EAGLETON, Terry
See EAGLETON, Terence (Francis)

* * *

EAMES, S(amuel) Morris 1916-

PERSONAL: Born June 5, 1916, in Silex, Mo.; son of Jesse S. and Velma (Morris) Eames; married Elizabeth Ramsden (a professor), August 21, 1952; children: Ivan Lee, Anne. *Education:* Culver-Stockton College, A.B., 1939; University of Missouri, M.A. (philosophy), 1941, M.A. (sociology), 1952; University of Chicago, Ph.D., 1958. *Home:* 205 Gray Drive, Carbondale, Ill. 62901. *Office:* Department of Philosophy, Southern Illinois University, Carbondale, Ill. 62901.

CAREER: Member of faculty at Culver-Stockton College, Canton, Mo., 1942-44, University of Missouri, Columbia, Mo., 1944-50, Washington University, St. Louis, Mo., 1951-63; Southern Illinois University, Carbondale, Ill., 1963—, became professor of philosophy, 1968. Oreon Scott lecturer, Bethany College, 1965. *Member:* American Philosophical Association, Missouri Philosophical Association (president, 1961-62), John Dewey Society, C. S. Peirce Society, Metaphysical Society of America, Mind Association, Disciples of Christ Historical Society. *Awards, honors:* Litt.D. from Bethany College, 1968.

WRITINGS: (With wife, Elizabeth Ramsden Eames) *The Leading Principles of Pragmatic Naturalism*, [Bruges], c. 1962; (with Claude E. Spencer) *The Philosophy of Alexander Campbell*, Bethany College, 1966; (with E. R. Eames) *Logical Methods: A Workbook for a General Education Course in Logic*, Stipes, 1966, revised edition, 1971; (co-editor and contributor) *Guide to the Works of John Dewey*, Southern Illinois University Press, 1972. Also author of *John Dewey: The Early Works, 1882-1898*. Contrib-

utor of articles, poems, and reviews to professional journals and magazines. Member of editorial board, Cooperative Research Project for Dewey Publications, 1963—.*

* * *

EARDLEY, George C(harles) 1926-

PERSONAL: Born February 19, 1926, in Chicago, Ill.; son of John K. (a career soldier) and Janet (Gallagher) Eardley. *Education:* Attended Gregg College of Commerce, 1946-47. *Politics:* Democrat. *Religion:* Episcopalian. *Home and office:* 2529 La Veta Dr. N.E., Albuquerque, N.M. 87110.

CAREER: Reynolds Aluminum Co., Phoenix, Ariz., machine tool operator, 1951-53; Lively Equipment Co., Albuquerque, N.M., clerk, 1956-60; writer. Importer of African carvings, 1960—. *Military service:* U.S. Navy, 1943-44. *Member:* American Legion.

WRITINGS: The Holy Man, Branden Press, 1974; *A Letter for Josephine*, Branden Press, in press.

WORK IN PROGRESS: My Spiritual Record, a record of psychic experiences.

SIDELIGHTS: Eardley writes: "My writing is what is called automatic writing. Therefore, my research material comes from within. Naturally my scope is broadened through wide scope reading."

* * *

EARL, Donald (Charles) 1931-

PERSONAL: Born in 1931; married; children: three daughters, two sons. *Education:* Cambridge University, B.A., 1953, M.A., Ph.D., 1958. *Office:* Department of Latin, University of Leeds, Leeds LS2 9JT England.

CAREER: University of Leeds, Leeds, England, assistant lecturer in classics, 1955-58, lecturer, 1958-67, senior lecturer, 1967-70, reader in Roman politics, 1970—. Visiting associate professor, Northwestern University, 1965; Vanier lecturer, Ottawa University, 1971. Governor, Trinity and All Saints' College of Education, Leeds, England, 1967—. *Member:* Society for the Promotion of Roman Studies (member of council, 1962-65, 1968-71).

WRITINGS: The Political Thought of Sallust, Cambridge University Press, 1961; *Tiberius Gracchus, a Study in Politics*, [Brussels], 1963; *The Moral and Political Tradition of Rome*, Cornell University Press, 1967; *The Age of Augustus*, Crown, 1968. Contributor to *Athenaeum (Pavia), Historia, Journal of Roman Studies*, and *Latomus*.

SIDELIGHTS: The Age of Augustus has been translated into French and German.*

* * *

EARNEY, Fillmore C(hristy) F(idelis) 1931-

PERSONAL: Born October 25, 1931, in Butts, Mo.; son of Patrick Timmins and Grace Vivian (Wilderman) Earney; married Winnie Jo Beasley, April 16, 1955; children: Christopher Patrick, Peggy Jo, Luanne Sue. *Education:* California State University, San Jose, A.B., 1957, M.A., 1958; Michigan State University, Ph.D., 1965. *Home:* 63 Elder Dr., Marquette, Mich. 49855. *Office:* Department of Geography, Northern Michigan University, Marquette, Mich. 49855.

CAREER: High school teacher of social studies in Chester, Calif., 1958-60; Castleton State College, Castleton, Vt., instructor, 1961-63, assistant professor of geography, 1961-63; Slippery Rock State College, Slippery Rock, Pa., associate professor of geography, 1965-66; Northern Michigan University, Marquette, assistant professor, 1966-69, associate professor, 1969-75, professor of geography, 1975—. Member of Citizens to Save the Superior Shoreline.

MEMBER: American Association of University Professors (president of local chapter, 1962-65), American Geographical Society, Association of American Geographers, National Council for Geographic Education, American Association for the Advancement of Science, Cousteau Society (charter member), American Forestry Association, Smithsonian Institution, Michigan Council for Geographic Education, Michigan Academy of Science, Arts and Letters, Chester Community Ski Club (president, 1959-60).

WRITINGS: (Contributor) James O'Hern, editor, *This Is Our World: Problem Solving Booklet*, Silver Burdett, 1972, 2nd edition, 1975; (contributor) Gilbert F. White, editor, *Natural Hazards: Local, National, Global*, Oxford University Press, 1974; *Researchers' Guide to Iron Ore: An Annotated Bibliography on the Economic Geography of Iron Ore*, Libraries Unlimited, 1974. Contributor to proceedings and to professional journals. Consulting editor to *Journal of Environmental Education*.

WORK IN PROGRESS: An annotated bibliography, *Mining, Planning and the Urban Environment* for Council of Planning Librarians *The Geography of the Mineral Industries*.

AVOCATIONAL INTERESTS: Travel.

*　　*　　*

EBAN, Abba (Solomon) 1915-
(Aubrey Eban)

PERSONAL: Surname originally Solomon; later adopted stepfather's name, Eban; born February 2, 1915, in Cape Town, South Africa; emigrated to England, 1915; son of Abraham Meir Solomon and Alida (Sachs) Solomon Eban; married Susan Ambache, March 18, 1945; children: Eli, Gila. *Education:* Queen's College, Cambridge, B.A., 1931, M.A. (triple first class honors), 1938. *Religion:* Jewish.

CAREER: Cambridge University, Pembroke College, Cambridge, England, research fellow and tutor in Oriental languages, 1939; Jewish Agency for Palestine, Political Department, Jerusalem, member of staff, 1946-47, liaison officer to United Nations, 1947; appointed representative of provisional government of Israel to United Nations, 1948; head of Israeli mission to United Nations, 1948-53, also serving as vice-president of U.N. General Assembly, 1953; Israeli ambassador to United States, 1950-59; elected to Israel's Knesset, 1959, serving as Minister without Portfolio, 1959-60, and Minister of Education and Culture, 1960-63; Deputy Prime Minister of Israel, 1963-66, Minister of Foreign Affairs, 1966-74; member of foreign affairs and security commission of Knesset, 1974—. Head of Israeli delegation to United Nations General Assembly, 1964. Visiting professor, Columbia University, 1974. *Military service:* British Army, 1939-46; became major; served in Middle East. *Member:* World Academy of Arts and Sciences (fellow), American Academy of Arts and Sciences (foreign member), Weizmann Institute of Science (president, 1958-66; honorary fellow). *Awards, honors:* Honorary degrees from New York University, Boston University, University of Maryland, University of Cincinnati, Lehigh University, Brandeis University, Dropsie College, Yeshiva University, Temple University, Chicago Institute of Jewish Studies, Hebrew Union College, Jewish Theological Seminary, Tel Aviv University.

WRITINGS—Under name Aubrey Eban: (Translator and editor) Leo Pinsker, *Auto-Emancipation*, Federation of Zionist Youth (London), 1939; (translator from the Arabic) Tawfiq al-Hakim, *The Maze of Justice* (novel), Harvill Press, 1947.

Under name Abba Eban: *The Modern Literary Movement in Egypt*, [London], 1946; *Social and Cultural Problems in the Middle East*, [London], 1947; *The Toynbee Heresy*, Israel Office of Information (New York), 1955; *Voice of Israel*, Horizon Press, 1957, revised edition, 1969; *The Tide of Nationalism*, Horizon Press, 1959; *Chaim Weizman: A Collective Biography*, Weidenfeld & Nicolson, 1962; *My People: The Story of the Jews*, Behrman House, 1968; (author of foreword) Avigdor Dagan, *Moscow and Jerusalem*, Abelard, 1971; *My Country: The Story of Modern Israel*, Random House, 1972. Contributor to learned journals in English, French, Hebrew, and Arabic.

SIDELIGHTS: A *New Yorker* critic notes that *My People: The Story of the Jews* cannot be called history, in the strict sense of the word—"Mr. Eban is too passionately involved with his people and their past, and too committed to their future—but it is still a magnificent piece of work." Nelson Glueck calls it "a fascinating book, written with knowledge, perception, lucidity, eloquence and passion ... a deeply personal and moving psalm of glorious quality on the theme of miraculous rebirth, indomitable vitality and enduring significance of Israel."

Eban is fluent in English, Hebrew, Arabic, Persian, French, and German.

*　　*　　*

EBAN, Aubrey
See EBAN, Abba (Solomon)

*　　*　　*

ECHERUO, Michael J(oseph) C(hukwudalu) 1937-

PERSONAL: Born 1937, in Okigwe, Owerri Province, Nigeria; son of J. M. (a tribal chieftain) and Martha N. Echeruo; married Rose N. Ikwueke, 1968; children: Ikechukwu, Okechukwu, Ijeoma, Chinedu, and Ugonna. *Education:* Attended Stella Maris College; University College of Ibadan (now University of Ibadan), B.A., 1960; Cornell University, M.A., 1963, Ph.D., 1965. *Office:* Department of English, University of Ibadan, Ibadan, Nigeria.

CAREER: Lecturer in English at the University of Nigeria (now University of Ibadan), Nsukka, until the outbreak of the Biafran civil war in 1967; returned to his post after the fighting ended in 1970; now professor of English and head of department.

WRITINGS: Mortality: Poems, Longmans, 1968; (editor) *Igbo Traditional Life, Culture, and Literature,* Conch Magazine Ltd., 1971; *Joyce Cary and the Novel of Africa,* Africana Publishing, 1973. Represented in anthologies, including *Modern Poetry from Africa,* edited by Gerald Moore and Ulli Beier, Penguin, 1963; *West African Verse: An Anthology,* edited by Donatus I Nwoga, Longmans Green, 1967; *New African Literature and the Arts,* edited by Joseph Okpaku, Crowell, 1970. Contributor of poems to *Black Orpheus*.

SIDELIGHTS: Echeruo directed the first production of John Pepper Clark's "Song of a Goat" at Enugu, Nigeria, in 1962.

ECKHOLM, Erik P(eter) 1949-

PERSONAL: Born May 23, 1949, in Tucson, Ariz.; son of Wendell (a public school administrator) and Margaret (Head) Eckholm; married Kathleen Courrier (a college teacher), September 5, 1972. *Education:* Occidental College, B.A., 1971; Johns Hopkins University, M.A., 1974. *Office:* Worldwatch Institute, 1776 Massachusetts Ave. N.W., Washington, D.C. 20036.

CAREER: Associate fellow, Overseas Development Council, 1973-74; Worldwatch Institute, Washington, D.C., senior researcher, 1975—. Instructor at Occidental College, summers, 1972-74.

WRITINGS: (With Lester R. Brown) *By Bread Alone*, Praeger, 1974. Contributor to professional journals, magazines, and newspapers.

WORK IN PROGRESS: Losing Ground: The Ecological Undermining of World Food Systems.

*   *   *

ECKSTEIN, Gustav 1890-

PERSONAL: Born October 26, 1890, in Cincinnati, Ohio; son of Gustav and Emma (Imig) Eckstein; married Francesca Bendeke, April 19, 1919 (marriage dissolved). *Education:* Cincinnati College of Dental Surgery, D.D.S., 1911; University of Cincinnati, M.D., 1924; also attended Harvard University. *Residence:* Cincinnati, Ohio. *Address:* c/o College of Medicine, University of Cincinnati, Cincinnati, Ohio 45221.

CAREER: Practiced dentistry, 1911-18; Cincinnati College of Dental Surgery, Cincinnati, Ohio, professor of chemistry, 1911-15; University of Cincinnati, College of Medicine, Cincinnati, Ohio, began as instructor, 1922, assistant professor, 1933-36, associate professor, 1936-51, professor of physiology, 1951-60, professor emeritus, 1960—. *Awards, honors:* L.H.D., Hamilton College, 1939.

WRITINGS—All published by Harper, unless otherwise noted: *Noguchi* (biography), 1931; *Lives* (animal biographies), 1932 [also see below]; *Kettle* (novel), 1933; *Hokusai* (play in fourteen scenes), 1935; *Canary: The History of a Family*, 1936 [also see below]; *Christmas Eve* (three-act play; produced on Broadway), 1940; *Friends of Mine* (contains *Lives* and *Canary: The History of a Family*), foreword by Alexander Woollcott, Press of the Readers Club, 1942; *In Peace Japan Breeds War* (nonfiction), 1943; *The Pet Shop* (play), 1944; *Everyday Miracle* (essays), 1948, reissued with illustrations by Kevin McIntyre, 1965; *The Body Has a Head* (nonfiction; Book-of-the-Month Club selection), 1970. Contributor of articles to *Harper's, Atlantic Monthly*, and other periodicals.

WORK IN PROGRESS: A study of Russian scientist, Ivan Pavlov; a play.

AVOCATIONAL INTERESTS: Music, travel.

BIOGRAPHICAL/CRITICAL SOURCES: American Magazine, September, 1937; *Science Illustrated*, March, 1949; *Time*, July 26, 1948; Joseph Wood Krutch, editor, *Great American Nature Writing*, Sloane, 1950; *Coronet*, April, 1954; *Washington Post*, September 12, 1970.

*   *   *

EDEY, Maitland A(rmstrong) 1910-

PERSONAL: Born February 13, 1910, in New York, N.Y.; son of Alfred (a stockbroker) and Marion (a writer; maiden name, Armstrong) Edey; married Helen Winthrop Kellogg (a physician), April 24, 1934; children: Maitland A., Jr., Winthrop K., Beatrice Edey Hicks, Marion Edey Browder. *Education:* Princeton University, A.B., 1932. *Politics:* Independent. *Religion:* None. *Home:* 1199 Park Ave., New York, N.Y. 10028.

CAREER: Messenger on Wall Street, 1932-33; clerk for book publishers in New York, 1933-41; *Life*, New York, N.Y., 1941-55, began as editor of "Speaking of Pictures" section, became assistant managing editor; free-lance writer, 1955-60; Time-Life Books, New York, N.Y., 1960-70, began as series editor, became editor-in-chief; free-lance writer, 1972—. Trustee, 1946-62, and mayor, 1958-62, of Incorporated Village of Upper Brookville, N.Y.; director of New York Philharmonic Symphony Society, 1950—; trustee of Putney School, 1958-74; chairman of advisory council of Old Westbury College, 1967-72; member of corporation of Woods Hole Oceanographic Institution, 1968-73; director of Conservation Foundation, Washington, D.C., 1969—; trustee of Scudder Special Fund (mutual fund), 1961—, and Felix Neck Wildlife Trust, 1973—. *Military service:* U.S. Army Air Forces, Intelligence, 1942-46; became major; received Legion of Merit and presidential citation. *Member:* Century Club (New York), Coffee House Club (New York).

WRITINGS: American Songbirds, Random House, 1940; *American Waterbirds*, Random House, 1941; (with F. Clark Howell) *Early Man*, Time-Life, 1965; *The Cats of Africa*, Time-Life, 1968; *The Northeast Coast*, Time-Life, 1972; *The Missing Link*, Time-Life, 1973; *The Sea Traders*, Time-Life, 1974; *The Lost World of the Aegean*, Time-Life, 1975.

WORK IN PROGRESS: Two novels.

AVOCATIONAL INTERESTS: Ornithology, photography, collecting stones on the beaches of Martha's Vineyard, and tumbling and polishing rocks and making them into jewelry.

*   *   *

EDGAR, David 1948-

PERSONAL: Born February 26, 1948, in Birmingham, England; son of Barrie (a TV producer) and Joan (Burman) Edgar. *Education:* Manchester University, B.A. (honors), 1969. *Politics:* Socialist. *Religion:* None. *Agent:* Michael Imison, 81 Shaftesbury Ave., London W.1, England.

CAREER: Leeds Polytechnic, Leeds, England, fellow in creative writing, 1972-74; Birmingham Repertory Theatre, Birmingham, England, resident playwright, 1974-75. *Member:* Association of Cinematograph, Television and Allied Technicians.

WRITINGS—Plays: "Two Kinds of Angel" (one-act), first produced in Bradford, England at University of Bradford, 1970; "Still Life: Man in Bed" (one-act), first produced in Edinburgh, Scotland at Pool Theatre, 1971; "The National Interest" (one-act), first produced in Edinburgh, Scotland at Edinburgh Festival, 1971; "Tedderella" (one-act), first produced at Pool Theatre, 1971; "The Rupert Show" (one-act), first produced at University of Bradford; "Excuses Excuses" (two-act), first produced in Coventry, England at Belgrade Theatre, 1972; "State of Emergency" (one-act), first produced at Edinburgh Festival; "Death Story" (two-act), first produced at Birmingham, England in Birmingham Repertory Theatre, 1972, produced in New York, N.Y. at Manhattan Theatre Club, 1975; (with Howard Brenton) "A Fart for Europe" (one-act), first produced in London at Royal Court Theatre Upstairs, 1973; "Baby Love" (one-act), first produced in Leeds, England at Leeds Playhouse, 1973; "The Case of the Workers' Plane" (two-act), first produced in Bristol, England at Bristol New Vic Theatre, 1973, shortened version produced in Bristol at Bristol Arts Centre, by Avon Touring Co., 1975; "Operation Iskra" (three-act), first produced in London at King's Head Theatre Club, 1973; "The Dunkirk Spirit" (two-act), first produced in Birmingham, England, at Arts Laboratory, 1974; *Dick Deterred* (two-act; first produced in London at Bush and Terrace Theatres, 1974), Monthly Review Press, 1974; "O Fair Jerusalem" (three-act), first produced in Birmingham, England at Birmingham Repertory Theatre, 1975.

Television plays: "The Eagle Has Landed," telecast by Granada Television, 1973; "I Know What I Meant," telecast by Granada Television, 1974; "Baby Love," telecast by BBC, 1974; "Concorde Cabaret," telecast by Harlech Television, 1975.

WORK IN PROGRESS: "Destiny," a play about fascism in England.

SIDELIGHTS: Edgar writes: "The purpose of all my work is political in the widest sense.... I am, as a socialist, keen to show people as society has made them, but to reject a mechanical approach: To show the possibility of people breaking out of their roles, as Brecht says, 'people should never be treated as if they can only act one way.' There is a stream of European 20th century drama best summed up in the line from *Waiting for Godot*: 'Nothing to be done.' I aspire to the contrary school, believing that there is a great deal to be done, and that it is high time we set about doing it." *Avocational interests:* Competitive games (not involving physical exertion or money) and the preparation and consumption of food.

* * *

EDGLEY, Charles K(enneth) 1943-

PERSONAL: Born March 10, 1943, in Beaumont, Tex.; son of Hugh (an electronics engineer) and Hilda Lou Edgley; married Betty Marie Scott, August 22, 1964; children: Erin Elizabeth, Aimee Allison. *Education:* Wayland Baptist College, B.A., 1965; Texas Technological University, M.A., 1966; State University of New York at Buffalo, Ph.D., 1970. *Home:* 4615 North Britton Dr., Stillwater, Okla. 74074. *Office:* Department of Sociology, Oklahoma State University, Stillwater, Okla. 74653.

CAREER: Oklahoma Baptist University, Shawnee, assistant professor, 1969-73, associate professor of sociology, 1973-75; Oklahoma State University, Stillwater, visiting assistant professor, 1972-73, associate professor of sociology, 1974—. *Member:* American Association of University Professors, Society for the Study of Symbolic Interaction, Southwestern Sociological Association, Oklahoma Sociological Association.

WRITINGS: (Contributor) Mhyra S. Minnis and Walter J. Cartwright, editors, *Sociological Perspectives: Readings in Deviant Behavior and Social Problems*, W. C. Brown, 1968; (with Dennis Brissett) *Life as Theater: A Dramaturgical Sourcebook*, Aldine, 1975. Contributor to academic journals. Member of editorial board, *Free Inquiry*, 1974.

WORK IN PROGRESS: A textbook in the sociology of death and dying.

AVOCATIONAL INTERESTS: Piloting planes.

EDMONDSON, G. C.

PERSONAL: Born in the United States; married. *Agent:* Robert P. Mills, Ltd., 156 East 52nd St., New York, N.Y. 10022.

CAREER: Science fiction writer. *Military service:* U.S. Marine Corps, 1942-46. *Member:* Science Fiction Writers of America.

WRITINGS—Novels: *The Ship That Sailed the Time Stream*, Ace Books, 1965; *Stranger Than You Think*, Ace Books, 1965; *Chapayeca*, Doubleday, 1971, published as *Blue Face*, Daw Books, 1972; *T.H.E.M.*, Doubleday, 1974; *The Aluminum Man*, Berkley, 1975; *Dil Dies Hard*, Doubleday, 1975; *The Laird of Baja*, Doubleday, in press.

WORK IN PROGRESS: A western novel, a science fiction novel, and a historical novel set in Ireland, Iceland, Finland ca. 1000 A.D.

SIDELIGHTS: "Speaks Spanish, Portuguese, Italian, French, German in descending scale of fluency."

* * *

EDWARDES, Michael (F. H.) 1923-

PERSONAL: Born in 1923, in Liverpool, England; married Margery Reay Tannahill. *Education:* Studied at Sorbonne, University of Paris. *Address:* c/o Campbell Thomson & McLaughlin Ltd., 79-80 Chancery Lane, London WC2A 1DD, England.

CAREER: Writer, 1958—.

WRITINGS: (Compiler) *The Reverend Mr. Punch: Pictorial Record of a Sixty Years' Ministry*, Mowbray, 1956, revised edition published as *The Reverend Mr. Punch: A Pictorial Record of His Ministry*, 1968; *The Necessary Hell: John and Henry Lawrence and the Indian Empire*, Cassell, 1958.

The Orchid House: Splendours and Miseries of the Kingdom of Oudh, 1827-1857, Cassell, 1960; *A History of India, from the Earliest Times to the Present Day*, Farrar, Straus, 1961, revised edition, New English Library, 1967, published as *The History of India, from the Earliest Times to the End of Colonialism*, Grossett, 1970; *Asia in the European Age: 1498-1955*, Thames & Hudson, 1961, Praeger, 1962; *Nehru: A Pictorial Biography*, Viking, 1962; *Asia in the Balance*, Penguin, 1962; *The Battle of Plassey and the Conquest of Bengal*, Macmillan, 1963; *The Last Years of British India*, Cassell, 1963, World Publishing, 1964; *Battles of the Indian Mutiny*, Macmillan, 1963; *High Noon of Empire: India under Curzon*, Eyre & Spottiswoode, 1965; *The West in Asia, 1850-1914*, Putnam, 1967; *British India, 1772-1947: A Survey of the Nature and Effects of Alien Rule*, Sidgwick & Jackson, 1967, Taplinger, 1968, published as *Raj: The Story of British India*, Pan Books, 1969; *Glorious Sahibs: The Romantic as Empire-builder, 1799-1838*, Eyre & Spottiswoode, 1968, Taplinger, 1969; *Indian Temples and Palaces*, Hamlyn, 1969; *Everyday Life in Early India* (juvenile), Putnam, 1969; *Bound to Exile: The Victorians in India*, Sidgwick & Jackson, 1969, Praeger, 1970; *Plassey: The Founding of an Empire*, Hamish Hamilton, 1969, Taplinger, 1970.

King of the World: The Life and Times of Shah Alam, Emperor of Hindustan, Secker & Warburg, 1970, Taplinger, 1971; *Nehru: A Political Biography*, Allen Lane, 1971, Praeger, 1972; *East-West Passage: The Travel of Ideas, Arts, and Inventions Between Asia and the Western World*, Taplinger, 1971; *Ralph Fitch: Elizabethan in the Indies*,

Faber, 1972, Barnes & Noble, 1973; *Red Year: The Indian Rebellion of 1857*, Hamish Hamilton, 1973; *A Season in Hell: The Defense of the Lucknow Residency*, Taplinger, 1973.

Editor: (And contributor) William Howard Russell, *My Indian Mutiny Diary*, Cassell, 1957, reprinted, Kraus, 1970; Niccolo Manucci, *Memoirs of the Mogul Court*, Folio Society, 1957; (and contributor) Hans Keusen, *South Asia*, Praeger, 1958; Keusen, *Picturesque India and the East*, D. B. Taraporevala (Bombay), 1958; Maria V. Germon, *Journal of the Siege of Lucknow: An Episode of the Indian Mutiny*, Constable, 1958; *A Life of the Buddha from a Burmese Manuscript*, Folio Society, 1959; (and author of introduction) William Forbes-Mitchell, *The Relief of Lucknow*, Folio Society, 1962; Ibn Hisham, 'Abd al-Malik, *The Life of Muhammad, Apostle of Allah*, Folio Society, 1964; John Corneille, *Journal of My Service in India*, Folio Society, 1966.

Other: (Adapter from the French) Van Tung Tran, *Vietnam*, Thames & Hudson, 1958. Contributor of articles to *The Times, International Affairs, Encounter*, and other journals and magazines.*

*   *   *

EDWARDS, Carl N(ormand)   1943-

PERSONAL: Born January 22, 1943, in Norwood, Mass.; son of Wilfred Carl (in textile business) and Cecile (an author; maiden name, Pepin) Edwards; married Elizabeth Anne Pyper, 1964. *Education:* Attended Bridgewater State College, 1960-63; Suffolk University, M.Ed., 1969; Harvard University, graduate study, 1964-68. *Office:* P.O. Box 86, Village Station, Medway, Mass. 02053.

CAREER: Harvard University, Cambridge, Mass., lecturer in social relations, 1971-72; Goddard College, Plainfield, Vt., member of field faculty, 1972—. Consulting social scientist in private practice in Medway, Mass., 1967—. Research social psychologist for Tufts-New England Medical Center Hospitals, 1969—; assistant clinical professor of psychiatry at Tufts University School of Medicine, 1971—; senior associate for policy planning and research at Boston's Justice Resource Institute, 1972—.

MEMBER: Peace Research Society, American Psychological Association, Society for the Psychological Study of Social Issues, National Trust for Historic Preservation, American Civil Liberties Union, National Pilots Association, Sierra Club, Appalachian Mountain Club, Massachusetts Psychological Association, Harvard Club of Boston.

WRITINGS: Drug Dependence: Social Regulation and Treatment Alternatives, Jason Aronson, 1974; *All the Tomorrows: A Longitudinal Study of Educated American Women*, Heath, in press. Contributor of about twenty articles and reviews to psychology and education journals.

WORK IN PROGRESS: Human Dynamics of Change and Challenge: A Handbook for Public Policy and Social Change, for Holt; *Flag City, USA*.

*   *   *

EDWARDS, Marie Babare

PERSONAL: Born in Tacoma, Wash.; daughter of Nick and Mary (Mardesich) Babare; married Tilden Hampton Edwards (divorced); children: Tilden Hampton, Jr. *Education:* Stanford University, B.A., 1948, M.A., 1949; University of California, Los Angeles, graduate study. *Home:* 6100 Buckingham Parkway, Culver City, Calif. 90230.

Agent: Theron Raines, 244 Madison Ave., New York, N.Y. 10016.

CAREER: University of Southern California, Los Angeles, counselor at guidance center, 1950-52; Southern California Society for Mental Hygiene, Los Angeles, project coordinator, 1952-54; Welfare Federation of Los Angeles, Los Angeles, Calif., public speaker, 1953-57; Los Angeles County Association for Mental Health, Los Angeles, field representative, 1957-58; University of California, Los Angeles, intern in psychology, 1958-60; private practice in human relations counseling and counselor training, 1960—. Originator and conductor of "Challenge of Being Single" workshops in continuing education divisions at University of Southern California, 1971—, University of California at San Diego and at Irvine, both 1971—, University of British Columbia, 1974—, York University, Toronto, 1975, and other schools; has appeared on television and radio programs in the United States and Canada.

MEMBER: International Platform Association, American Psychological Association, Society for Humanistic Psychology, American Association for the Advancement of Science, National Academy of Religion and Mental Health, Society for the Advancement of Management, Western Psychological Association, California State Psychological Association, Southern California Society for Clinical Hypnosis, Group Psychotherapy Association of Southern California, Los Angeles County Psychological Association.

WRITINGS: (With Eleanor Hoover) *The Challenge of Being Single*, Tarcher-Hawthorn, 1974.

SIDELIGHTS: Marie Edwards writes: "Perhaps my most significant contribution as a psychologist·... has been my advocacy of equal status for the single person ... especially for the single woman.... Working with both single and married people over a period of years, I noted that many singles felt guilty because they were not married; that there were many myths and much misinformation about singles that needed correcting; that singles needed someone to speak for them to formulate a new way of looking at singlehood.... Individuals and institutions are beginning to appreciate singlehood as an alternate and viable life-style, which can and should be equal in status to marriage.... This all results in a lessening of defenses between the sexes and a greater appreciation of each person as an individual, both male and female."

*   *   *

EDWARDS, Owen Dudley   1938-

PERSONAL: Born in 1938, in Dublin, Ireland; married Barbara Balbirnie Lee; children: one son, two daughters. *Education:* Studied at National University of Ireland and Johns Hopkins University. *Office:* Department of History, University of Edinburgh, 50 George Square, Edinburgh EH8 9YL, Scotland.

CAREER: University of Oregon, Eugene, Oregon, visiting lecturer in history, 1963-65; University of Aberdeen, Aberdeen, Scotland, assistant lecturer in history, 1966-68; University of Edinburgh, Edinburgh, Scotland, lecturer in history, 1968—. Correspondent on American and Scottish affairs, *Irish Times*, 1959—; consultant on Irish history, Radio-Telefis Eireann, 1966—. *Member:* Organization of American Historians, American Historical Association (life member).

WRITINGS: (With Gwynfor Evans, Ioan Rhys, and Hugh MacDiarmid) *Celtic Nationalism*, Barnes & Noble, 1968;

(editor with Fergus Pyle) *1916: The Easter Rising*, Mac-Gibbon & Kee, 1968; (editor) *Conor Cruise O'Brien Introduces Ireland*, Deutsch, 1969, McGraw-Hill, 1970; *The Sins of Our Fathers: Roots of Conflict in Northern Ireland*, Gill & Macmillan, 1970; *The Mind of an Activist—James Connolly: The Centenary Lecture Delivered on 10 May 1968 Under the Auspices of the Irish Congress of Trade Unions, in Liberty Hall*, Gill & Macmillan, 1971. Contributor to the *London Tribune, Journal of American Studies, New York Times*.*

* * *

EDWARDS, Paul Geoffrey 1926-

PERSONAL: Born July 31, 1926, in Birmingham, England; son of Albert and Frances Edwards; married Maj Ing-Britt Nilsson, July 31, 1954; children: two daughters. *Education:* University of Durham, B.A., 1952; Emmanuel College, Cambridge, M.A., 1954. *Home:* 82 Kirk Brae, Edinburgh 9, Scotland. *Office:* Department of English, University of Edinburgh, Edinburgh EH8 9YL, Scotland.

CAREER: Teacher in Ghana and Sierra Leone, 1954-63; University of Edinburgh, Edinburgh, Scotland, lecturer in English, 1963-68, senior lecturer, 1968—, reader, 1971. *Military service:* Royal Air Force, 1944-48.

WRITINGS: (Compiler) *West African Narrative: An Anthology for Schools*, Nelson, 1963; (compiler) *Modern African Narrative: An Anthology*, Nelson, 1966; (compiler) *Through African Eyes*, two volumes, Cambridge University Press, 1966; (editor) Olaudah Equiano, *Equiano's Travels*, Heinemann, 1967; (editor and compiler) *A Ballad Book for Africa*, Faber, 1968; (translator with Hermann Palsson) *Gautrek's Saga, and other Medieval Tales*, New York University Press, 1968; (translator with Palsson) *Arrow-Odd; A Medieval Novel*, New York University Press, 1970; *Legendary Fiction in Medieval Iceland*, University of Iceland, 1971; (translator with Palsson) *Hrolf Gautreksson, a Viking Romance*, University of Toronto Press, 1972; (translator with Palsson) *The Book of Settlements*, University of Manitoba Press, 1972; (translator with Palsson) *Eyrbyggja Saga*, University of Toronto Press, 1973. Contributor of articles to the *Durham University Journal, Journal of Commonwealth Literature, Studia Islandica, Phylon*, and other literary and scholarly journals.

* * *

EGGER, M(aurice) David 1936-

PERSONAL: Born June 21, 1936, in Bakersfield, Calif.; married; children: three. *Education:* Stanford University, B.A. (with honors), 1958; University of Hamburg, graduate study, 1958-59; Yale University, Ph.D., 1962, postdoctoral study, 1962-65. *Home address:* R.D.1, Box 80, Cranbury, N.J. 08512. *Office:* Department of Anatomy, Medical School, Rutgers University, Piscataway, N.J.

CAREER: Yale University, New Haven, Conn., instructor, 1965-66, assistant professor, 1966-69, associate professor of anatomy, 1970-74; Rutgers University, Medical School, Piscataway, N.J., associate professor of anatomy, 1974—. Visiting research scientist at University of London, 1969-70; lecturer at colleges and universities in the United States and England. Executive secretary of Institute of Renaissance Studies, Ashland, Ore., 1958. *Member:* American Association of Anatomists, American Physiological Society, American Psychological Association, Animal Behavior Society, Society for Neuroscience, Eastern Psychological Association, Phi Beta Kappa, Sigma Xi.

Awards, honors: Fulbright grant, University of Hamburg, 1958-59; research scientist development award from National Institute of Mental Health, 1969-74.

WRITINGS: (Contributor) G. H. Glaser, editor, *EEG and Behavior*, Basic Books, 1963; (contributor) E. L. Wike, editor, *Secondary Reinforcement: Selected Experiments*, Harper, 1966; (contributor) W. R. Adey and Toshihiko Tokizane, editors, *Progress in Brain Research*, Volume XXVII: *Structure and Function of the Limbic System*, Elsevier Publishing, 1967; (contributor) B. E. Eleftheriou, editor, *Behavior and Brain Function: The Neurobiology of the Amygdala*, Plenum, 1972; *Poems: The First Fifteen Years*, published in one volume with *Reflections on the Pond and Elsewhere*, by son, L. Daniel Egger, L'Rakia, 1974. Contributor of about forty articles on science and the social sciences to professional journals, and to popular magazines, including *Nature* and *Science*.

WORK IN PROGRESS: Further scientific research.

* * *

EGLESON, Janet F.
See DUNLEAVY, Janet Egleson

* * *

EICHENBERG, Fritz 1901-

PERSONAL: Born October 24, 1901, in Cologne, Germany; came to United States in 1933, naturalized in 1940; son of Siegfried and Ida (Marcus) Eichenberg; married Mary Altmann, 1926 (died, 1937); married Margaret Ladenburg, 1941 (divorced, 1965); married Antonie Ida Schulze-Forster (a graphic designer), January 7, 1975; children: (first marriage) Suzanne Eichenberg Jensen; (second marriage) Timothy. *Education:* School of Applied Arts, Cologne, student, 1916-20; State Academy of Graphic Arts, Leipzig, M.F.A., 1923. *Religion:* Society of Friends (Quakers). *Home and studio:* 142 Oakwood Dr., Peace Dale, R.I. 02879.

CAREER: Graphic artist and illustrator of classics and other books. Started as newspaper artist in Germany, 1923, and worked as artist and traveling correspondent for Ullstein Publications, Berlin, before settling in United States; New School for Social Research, New York, N.Y., member of art faculty, 1935-45; Pratt Institute, Brooklyn, N.Y., professor of art, 1947-72, chairman of department of graphic arts, 1956-63, founder-director of Graphic Arts Center, 1956-72; University of Rhode Island, Kingston, professor of art, 1966-71, chairman of department, 1966-69; Albertus Magnus College, New Haven, Conn., professor of art, 1972-73. Had one-man shows at New School for Social Research, 1939, 1949, Associated American Artists Gallery, 1967, Pratt Manhattan Center Gallery, 1972, and Klingspor Museum (Offenbach, Germany), 1974; work has been shown in Xylon international exhibitions in Switzerland, Yugoslavia, and other countries, in U.S. Information Agency traveling exhibits, and Society of American Graphic Artists shows; represented in collections of National Gallery of Art, Hermitage Museum (Moscow), Metropolitan Museum of Art, Philadelphia Museum of Art, and other museums. Member of Pennell Committee, Library of Congress, 1959-65.

MEMBER: National Academy of Design, Royal Society of Arts (London; fellow), Society of American Graphic Artists, Xylon International, Bund Deutscher Buchkuenstler. *Awards, honors:* Joseph Pennell Medal of Pennsylvania Academy of Fine Arts, 1944; first prize for print, National

Academy of Design, 1946; Silver Medal of Limited Editions Club, 1954; grant from John D. Rockefeller III Fund, 1968; D.F.A., Southeastern Massachusetts University, 1972; S.F.B. Morse Medal of National Academy of Design, 1973; D.F.A., University of Rhode Island, 1974.

WRITINGS: (Self-illustrated) Ape in a Cape: An Alphabet of Odd Animals (juvenile), Harcourt, 1952; (self-illustrated) Art and Faith (booklet), Pendle Hill, 1952; (self-illustrated) Dancing in the Moon: Counting Rhymes (juvenile), Harcourt, 1955; (translator with William Hubben) Helmut A. P. Grieshaber, H. A. P. Grieshaber, Arts, 1965; (author of text) Naoko Matsubara, Nantucket Woodcuts, Barre Publishers, 1967; (editor) Artist's Proof: A Collector's Edition of the First Eight Issues of the Distinguished Journal of Print and Printmaking, New York Graphic Society, 1971; (translator and illustrator) Desiderius Erasmus, In Praise of Folly, Aquarius, 1972; The Print: Art, History and Techniques, Abrams, 1975.

Illustrator: Puss in Boots, Holiday House, 1936; Moritz A. Jagendorf, Tyll Ulenspiegel's Merry Pranks, Vanguard, 1938; Therese Lenotre, Mystery of Dog Flip, translated from the French by Simone Chamoud, Stokes, 1939; Robert Davis, Padre: The Gentlemanly Pig, Holiday House, 1939, enlarged edition, 1948; Rosalys Hall, Animals to Africa, Holiday House, 1939.

Stewart Schackne, Rowena, the Skating Cow, Scribner, 1940; Eula Griffin Duncan, Big Road Walker, Stokes, 1940; Babette Deutsch, Heroes of the Kalevala: Finland's Saga, Messner, 1940; Jonathan Swift, Gulliver's Travels, Heritage Press, 1940, junior text edition, 1947, new edition, 1961; Richard A. W. Hughes, Don't Blame Me (short stories), Harper, 1940; Joel Chandler Harris, Uncle Remus Stories, limited edition, Peter Pauper Press, 1937; William Shakespeare, Tragedy of Richard the Third, Limited Editions Club, 1940; Henry Beston, The Tree That Ran Away, Macmillan, 1941; Marjorie Fischer, All on a Summer's Day, Random House, 1941; Irmengarde Eberle, Phoebe-Bell, Greystone Press, 1941; Ivan S. Turgenev, Fathers and Sons, translated from the Russian by Constance Garnett, Heritage Press, 1941; Mabel Leigh Hunt, "Have You Seen Tom Thumb?," Stokes, 1942; Charlotte Bronte, Jane Eyre [and] Emily Bronte, Wuthering Heights (companion volumes), Random House, 1943; Hendrik Ibsen, Story of Peer Gynt, retold by E. V. Sandys, Crowell, 1943; Irmengarde Eberle, Wide Fields: The Story of Henry Fabre, Crowell, 1943; Eleanor Hoffmann, Mischief in Fez, Holiday House, 1943; Lev N. Tolstoi, Anna Karenina, translated from the Russian by Constance Garnett, two volumes, Doubleday, 1944, two volumes in one, 1946, deluxe edition, Garden City Publishing, 1948; Stephen Vincent Benet, The Devil and Daniel Webster, Kingsport, 1945; Edgar Allen Poe, Tales, Random House, 1944; Mark Keats, Sancho and His Stubborn Mule, W. R. Scott, 1944; Rose Dobbs, No Room: An Old Story Retold, Coward, 1944; Feodor M. Dostoevski, Crime and Punishment, translated from the Russian by Constance Garnett, Heritage Press, 1944; Glanville W. Smith, Adventures of Sir Ignatius Tippitolio, Harper, 1945; Anna Sewell, Black Beauty, Grosset, 1945; Terence H. White, Mistress Masham's Repose, Putnam, 1946; Emily Bronte, Wuthering Heights, Random House, 1946; Maurice Dolbier, The Magic Shop, Random House, 1946; Felix Salten, compiler, Favorite Animal Stories, Messner, 1948; Feodor M. Dostoevski, The Grand Inquisitor, Haddam House, 1945; Dostoevski, The Brothers Karamazov, translation from the Russian by Constance Garnett revised, with introduction

by Avrahm Yarmolinsky, Limited Editions Club, 1949; Ruth Stiles Gannett, Wonderful House-Boat-Train, Random House, 1949.

Rudyard Kipling, Jungle Book, Grosset, 1950; Mark van Doren, The Witch of Ramoth, Maple Press, 1950; Wilkie Collins, Short Stories, Rodale Books, 1950; Nathaniel Hawthorne, Tale of King Midas and the Golden Touch, Limited Editions Club, 1952; (with Vassily Verestchagin) Lev N. Tolstoi, War and Peace, translated from the Russian by Louise and Aylmer Maude, two volumes in one, Heritage Press, 1951; Margaret Cousins, Ben Franklin of Old Philadelphia, Random House, 1952; Dorothy Day, Long Loneliness (autobiography), Harper, 1952; Johann Wolfgang von Goethe, Story of Reynard the Fox, translated by Thomas J. Arnold from original German poem, Heritage Press, 1954; Feodor M. Dostoevski, The Idiot, translation from the Russian by Constance Garnett revised, with introduction by Avrahm Yarmolinsky, Heritage Press, 1956; Elizabeth J. Coatsworth, The Peaceable Kingdom and Other Poems, Pantheon, 1958; Edna Johnson and others, compilers, Anthology of Children's Literature, 3rd edition (Eichenberg did not illustrate earlier editions), Houghton, 1959, 4th edition, 1970.

Feodor M. Dostoevski, The Possessed, translated from the Russian by Constance Garnett, Heritage Press, 1960; Lev N. Tolstoi, Resurrection, translation by Leo Wiener revised and edited by F. D. Reeve, Heritage Press, 1963; Jean Charlot, Posada's Dance of Death, Graphic Arts Center, Pratt Institute, 1965; Etienne Decroux, Mime: The Art of Etienne Decroux, Pratt Adlib Press, 1965; Dylan Thomas, A Child's Christmas in Wales, limited edition, New Directions, 1969.

Lev N. Tolstoi, Childhood, Boyhood, Youth, translation by Wiener, Press of A. Colish, 1972; John M. Langstaff, The Two Magicians, Atheneum, 1973; Dostoevski, A Raw Youth, Limited Editions Club, 1974.

Founder and chief editor, Artist's Proof: An Annual of Prints and Printmaking, Pratt Institute, 1960-72. Contributor to American Artist and other journals.

WORK IN PROGRESS: Monograph, text, and illustrations, The Wood and the Graver, for C. N. Potter; Fables with a Twist; illustrating J. C. Grimmelshausen's The Adventurous Simplicissimus.

SIDELIGHTS: Eichenberg's favorite mediums are lithographs, wood engravings, and woodcuts. Many of the classics he illustrated have been reissued several times and there have been British and Japanese editions of some of the classics and children's books.

BIOGRAPHICAL/CRITICAL SOURCES: American Artist, December, 1944, May, 1964, October, 1975; Graphis, Volume XIII, number 43, 1952; Library of Congress Quarterly, April, 1965; Rhode Islander, August 12, 1973; Idea (Tokyo), January, 1974.

*   *   *

EISENBERG, Daniel Bruce   1946-

PERSONAL: Born October 4, 1946, in Long Island City, N.Y.; son of Louis (a physician) and Marcia (a librarian; maiden name, Jesiek) Eisenberg; married Lynn Rimmer, May 31, 1968 (divorced, 1974); married Irene Ferreira de Sousa, June 15, 1974. Education: University of Madrid, Diploma de estudios hispanicos, 1966; Johns Hopkins University, B.A., 1967; Brown University, M.A., 1968, Ph.D., 1971. Religion: "Jewish Atheist." Residence: Tallahassee,

Fla. *Office:* Department of Modern Languages, Florida State University, Tallahassee, Fla. 32306.

CAREER: University of North Carolina, Chapel Hill, assistant professor of Spanish, 1970-73; City College of the City University of New York, assistant professor of Spanish, 1973-74; Florida State University, Tallahassee, associate professor of Spanish, 1974—. *Member:* Modern Language Association of America, Asociacion Internacional de Hispanistas, Renaissance Society of America. *Awards, honors:* National Endowment for the Humanities fellowship, 1972; research award from American Philosophical Society, 1975.

WRITINGS: Textos y documentos lorquianos (title means "Lorca Texts and Documents"), privately printed, 1975; (editor) Diego Ortunez de Calahorra, *Espejo de principes y caballeros* (title means "The Mirror of Princely Deeds and Knighthood"), six volumes, Espasa-Calpe (Madrid), 1975; (editor) Federico Garcia Lorca, *Songs*, translated by Philip Cummings, Duquesne University Press, 1975; *The Textual Tradition of "Poeta en Nueva York"*, North Carolina Studies in the Romance Languages and Literature, in press; *Hacia "Poeta en Nueva York"* (title means "Toward 'Poet in New York'"), Ariel (Barcelona), in press. Contributor to journals in his field. Founder and editor, *Journal of Hispanic Philology*, 1975—.

WORK IN PROGRESS: Editing a critical edition of Feliciano de Silva's *Amadis de Grecia*; monograph on romances of chivalry, *Los libros de caballerias en el Siglo de Oro.*

SIDELIGHTS: Eisenberg writes: "My research has been in several quite diverse areas within the field of Spanish literature; my work on Lorca, for example, began as a hobby and has turned into a major interest. Much of my work has been focused on correcting errors of perspective held by many writers on Spanish literature; I think of myself more as a literary historian, biographer, and textual critic than as a literary critic."

*   *   *

ELDER, Leon
See YOUNG, Noel

*   *   *

ELIOT HURST, M(ichael) E(liot)   1938-
PERSONAL: Born May 7, 1938, in London, England; Canadian citizen; son of Harry Clifton (a heating engineer) and Emily (Davis) Hurst; married Wendy Pullin, October 19, 1963 (divorced December, 1974); children: Nicholas Ivan. *Education:* University of Durham, B.Sc. (first class honors), 1962, Ph.D., 1966. *Politics:* Socialist. *Home:* 2256 Chapman Way, North Vancouver, British Columbia, Canada. *Office:* Department of Geography, Simon Fraser University, Burnaby, British Columbia, Canada.

CAREER: Simon Fraser University, Burnaby, British Columbia, lecturer, 1965-66, assistant professor, 1966-69, associate professor of geography, 1969—, chairman of department, 1971-75. Visiting lecturer at California State University, Northridge, 1969-70. Member of Board of Variance, District of North Vancouver. *Member:* Association of American Geographers, Canadian Association of Geographers. *Awards, honors:* Royal Geographical Society award, 1957; University of Durham open scholar, 1958-62; Department of Science and Industrial Research fellowship, 1962-65.

WRITINGS: (With R. McDaniel) *A Systems Analytic Approach to Economic Geography* (monograph), Association of American Geographers, 1968; *A Geography of Economic Behavior*, Duxbury, 1972; (editor) *Transportation Geography: Comments and Readings*, McGraw, 1974; (editor) *I Came to the City: Essays on the Urban Scene*, Houghton, 1975; (contributor) J. Weford Watson and T. O'Riordan, editors, *The American Environment*, Wiley, 1975; *Transport Geography*, Penguin, in press. Contributor of articles to journals in his field, including *Urban Studies, Transportation Research, Annals of the Association of American Geographers*, and *Economic Geography.*

WORK IN PROGRESS: The Geography of Poverty, publication by Clarendon Press expected in 1977; editing, with Colm Regan, *The Geography and Society*, Houghton, 1977; editing *The Sixth Transformation*, Houghton, 1978.

SIDELIGHTS: Michael Eliot Hurst told *CA* he is "particularly interested now in community work and a Marxist approach to geography and social science."

*   *   *

ELISCU, Frank   1912-
PERSONAL: Born July 13, 1912, in New York, N.Y.; son of Charles Henry and Florence (Kane) Eliscu; married Mildred Norman, May 3, 1942; children: Norma Banas. *Education:* Attended Pratt Institute Art School, Brooklyn, N.Y., 1931-34. *Home:* 440 Rock House Rd., Easton, Conn. 06612.

CAREER: Sculptor; National Academy of Design, New York, N.Y., instructor in art, 1972-75; has had exhibitions at National Academy of Design, Pennsylvania Academy of Fine Arts, Cleveland Museum of Art, Detroit Institute of Art, Connecticut Academy of Fine Art, Springfield Museum of Art, and a one-man show in Mexico sponsored by the U.S. government. *Member:* National Sculpture Society (past president), Sculpture Center of New York (trustee). *Awards, honors:* Moore prize, 1950; Bennet prize for sculpture, 1953.

WRITINGS—All published by Chilton: *Three Techniques: Wax, Clay, Slate*, 1957; *Direct Wax Sculpture*, 1969; *Slate and Soft Stone Sculpture*, 1972.

SIDELIGHTS: Eliscu's commissioned work includes busts for Aeronautical Hall of Fame, fountains at Brookgreen Gardens, S.C., and in New York, N.Y., a war memorial for Cornell Medical College, and heroic horses in slate for Banker's Trust Building, New York, N.Y.

*   *   *

ELKON, Juliette
See ELKON-HAMELECOURT, Juliette

*   *   *

ELKON-HAMELECOURT, Juliette   1912-
(Juliette Elkon)
PERSONAL: Surname is pronounced *Ham*-le-court; born July 17, 1912, in Brussels, Belgium; daughter of Jacques Marie-Madeleine (Vermeiren) Hamelecourt de Hemricourt; married Abraham Elkon, 1942 (divorced, 1958); children: Jacqueline Elkon Dunham, Claire Elkon Phillips, Peter. *Education:* Educated in England, China, and Belgium; Louvain University, M.A., 1934. *Religion:* Roman Catholic. *Home:* Hotel Chelsea, 222 West 23rd St., New York, N.Y. 10011.

CAREER: Designer for the needlework trade and the Swiss embroidery industry; artist and tapestry maker. Industrial Embroidery Designers, Inc., New York, N.Y., president, 1973—. Has had about twenty group and solo exhibitions in the United States and Haiti. *Member:* Gourmet Society, Taste Vin, American Crafts Council, Embroiderers Guild of America, Artists Equity Association of New York, New York State Crafts Council, Gourmet Club of Port au Prince (president, 1962-63). *Awards, honors:* Citation for technical ability from Pen and Brush Club, 1973; honor award for "satirycal crafts of today," from Hands of Man Gallery, 1974.

WRITINGS: (Under name Juliette Elkon) *The Belgian War Relief Cookbook*, Moretus Press, 1943; *The Honey Cookbook*, Knopf, 1953; *Edith Cavell: Heroic Nurse* (juvenile), Messner, 1956; *A Belgian Cookbook*, Farrar, Straus, 1958; (with Elaine Ross) *Menus for Entertaining*, Hastings House, 1960; *The Chocolate Cookbook*, Bobbs-Merrill, 1974. Contributor to *Gourmet*. Editor of *Needle Arts*, 1973—.

WORK IN PROGRESS: Biographical notes on the education of a gourmet, *A Cookbook Meant to be Read*; *Afro-Caribbean Cookery of the French Antilles*; *Rituals of the King's Table*, ethnological research on the eating habits of theocratic rulers; *How to Design for Embroidery*, for Van Nostrand.

SIDELIGHTS: Self-taught in design, Juliette Elkon-Hamelecourt's work reflects the profound impact of ethnic art in countries where textile art is traditional. To early twelfth century techniques, she has added a strong individual contemporary accent. She lived for ten years in Haiti, where she took up ethnology as a pastime which led to teaching Haitian women to use their own folkloric designs, and marketing their work in a boutique. In 1970, she returned to the United States and founded a workshop in the Chelsea Hotel. She teaches, produces embroidered tapestries on commission, and designs embroidery patterns and rug charts for commercial purposes.

BIOGRAPHICAL/CRITICAL SOURCES: Embroiderer's Journal, Volume I, number 3, 1972; Maida Sylvan, *Step by Step Stitchery*, Western Publishing, in press.

* * *

ELLENS, J(ay) Harold 1932-

PERSONAL: Born July 16, 1932, in McBain, Mich.; son of John S. (a mechanical engineer) and Grace (Kortman) Ellens; married Mary Jo Lewis (a school administrator), September 7, 1954; children: Deborah, Jacqueline, Daniel, Rebecca, Harold, Brenda. *Education:* Calvin College, A.B., 1953; Calvin Seminary, B.D., 1956; Princeton University, Th.M., 1965; Wayne State University, Ph.D., 1970; also studied at Cranbrook Institute for Advanced Pastoral Studies, 1965, and Educational Sciences Institute, 1972. *Politics:* Independent. *Home:* 25762 Kilreigh Dr., Farmington, Mich. 48024. *Office:* University Hills Christian Center, 27000 Farmington Rd., Farmington, Mich. 48024.

CAREER: Ordained Christian Reformed minister, 1956; private practice in pastoral counseling, 1956—. Pastor of Newton Christian Reformed Church in Newton, N.J., 1961-65; pastor at University Hills Christian Center, 1965—. Member of faculty at U.S. Army Staff College, 1964-70, 1973; part-time instructor at Calvin College and Calvin Seminary, 1967-70; part-time associate professor at Oakland Community College, 1970—; lecturer at Wayne County Community College, 1968-72, and Wayne State University, 1972—; professor at Oakland University, 1973—. Staff therapist and member of board of directors of Midwest Mental Health Clinic; member of board of directors of Farmington Community Arts Council. Host of "Dialogue," a weekly program on WXYZ-Radio, 1971-73, and "Let's See," a weekly program on WJBK-Television, 1973; has appeared on "Church of the Crossroads" and "Church World News," both on WWJ-Television, 1968-72. *Military service:* U.S. Army, chaplain, 1956-61. U.S. Army Reserve, chaplain, 1955-56, 1961—; present rank, lieutenant colonel.

MEMBER: World Association of Christian Communication, Society of Biblical Literature and Exegesis, Archaeological Institute of America, Speech Communication Association of America, Christian Association for Psychological Studies (executive secretary), American Classical League, Reserve Officers Association (life member), Military Chaplains Association (life member), Oriental Institute. *Awards, honors:* Awarded Maltese Cross as Knight of Grace by Queen Juliana of the Netherlands, 1974.

WRITINGS: Models of Religious Broadcasting, Eerdmans, 1974. Contributor of more than fifteen articles to professional religious publications, including *Orb: Religious Affairs, Federation Messenger, Reformed Journal, Journal of Psychology and Theology, Banner*, and *Proceedings of the Christian Association for Psychological Studies.*

WORK IN PROGRESS: Worship and the Christian Way; translating Ganoczy's *Ecclesia Ministrans: Diende Kirche und kirchlicher Dienst bei Calvin* (title means "The Ministry of the Church"); translating Zimmerman's *Neutestamentliche Methodenlehre* (title means "New Testament Methodology"), with John Timmer.

SIDELIGHTS: Ellens is proficient in German and Dutch, Swedish, Danish, Latin, Greek, Hebrew, and Chaldean. He has traveled widely in Asia, lived four years in Europe, and traveled around the world in 1971. He writes: "I am vigorously commited to the notion that an urgent quest for idealism in life is the motivational genius which enables persons and cultures to transcend the erosive tendencies of life toward the deadly, divisive, and demeaning in all spheres of experience. I am furthermore convinced that the epitome of human idealism is the quest for the aesthetic ideal. In the final analysis, it seems to me, that is the real issue of moral concern and the true standard of all morality." *Avocational interests:* Studying the development of human linguistics, archaeology, art history, general history.

* * *

ELLENSON, Gene 1921-

PERSONAL: Born March 24, 1921, in Chippewa Falls, Wis.; son of Eugene Argard (a professional golfer) and Catherine (Flinn) Ellenson; married Jeanne Center, January 24, 1951; children: Donna Susan, Eugene Mark. *Education:* University of Georgia, B.A., 1943; University of Miami, Coral Gables, Fla., M.A.Ed., 1946. *Religion:* Roman Catholic. *Home:* 3525 Northwest 8th Ave., Gainesville, Fla. 32605. *Address:* Gator Boosters, Inc., Box 13796, Gainesville, Fla. 32604.

CAREER: University of Miami, Coral Gables, Fla., assistant football coach, 1950-59; University of Florida, Gainesville, assistant head football coach, 1960-69, assistant athletic director, 1970-73, director of Gator Boosters, 1974—. Director of Ray Graves Sports Camp, and of National Football Foundation and Hall of Fame. *Military service:*

U.S. Army, 1943-46, 1951-52; became captain; received four European theater campaign stars, Silver Star, Bronze Star, Purple Heart. *Member:* National Football Coaches Association, National Athletic Directors Association, Florida Blue Key, University of Miami Iron Arrow, Sigma Delta Chi, Omicron Delta Chi.

WRITINGS: ABC's of Offensive Line Play, University of Florida Press, 1962; *Ray Graves Guide to Modern Football Defense*, Parker Publishing, 1965; *Coaching Line Backers and Perimeter Defense*, Parker Publishing, 1972; *One Ghost Job*, Parker Publishing, 1973. Contributor to professional journals.

* * *

ELLIS, Jody 1925-

PERSONAL: Born September 29, 1925, in Sterling, Colo.; daughter of W. H. Ellis (an accountant) and Gladys (a legal stenographer; maiden name, Reynolds) Ellis McMahon. *Education:* Attended MacMurry Women's College, 1943-45; St. Francis School of Nursing, R.N., 1946. *Religion:* Jewish. *Address:* Sunstone Press, P.O. Box 2321, Santa Fe, N.M. 87501. *Agent:* Aaron Priest Literary Agency, 15 East 40th St., New York, N.Y. 10016.

CAREER: Placita Bon Bon Shop, Sante Fe, N.M., owner, 1953-56; Ellis Research Associates, Sante Fe, N.M., owner and president, 1970; Sunstone Press, Santa Fe, N.M., president and editor-in-chief of *Sunstone Review*, 1972—; Century 21, Santa Fe, N.M., president, 1974—; Sleeping Fox Enterprises (publishing consultants), Santa Fe, N.M., president, 1974—. Member of board of directors of Historic Santa Fe Foundation, 1973—. *Military service:* U.S. Air Force, nurse, 1950-53. *Member:* Chamber of Commerce of the United States, Altrusa, Southwestern Association on Indian Affairs, Santa Fe Press Club.

WRITINGS: ABC's of Successful Living, Sunstone Press, 1974.

* * *

ELLISON, Craig W(illiam) 1944-

PERSONAL: Born August 21, 1944, in Springfield, Mass.; son of William C. (a school district administrator) and Marilyn (Otto) Ellison; married Sharon Andre (a registered nurse), September 20, 1969; children: Scott, Timothy. *Education:* King's College, Briarcliff Manor, N.Y., B.A. (magna cum laude), 1966; Wayne State University, M.A., 1969, Ph.D., 1972. *Religion:* Protestant. *Office:* Department of Psychology, Westmont College, 955 La Paz Rd., Santa Barbara, Calif. 93108.

CAREER: Westmont College, Santa Barbara, Calif., assistant professor of psychology, 1971—. Community organizer for Metropolitan Action Center (Detroit, Mich.), summer, 1968; visiting professor at State University of New York at Binghamton, summer, 1973; director of International Conference on Human Engineering and the Future of Man, 1975. Director of Central City Conference of Evangelicals (Detroit), 1969-71. *Member:* American Psychology-Law Society, American Psychological Association, American Scientific Affiliation, Christian Association for Psychological Studies (member of board of directors, 1974-77), Society for the Psychological Study of Social Issues, World Future Society, Western Psychological Association, Western Association of Christians for Psychological Studies (executive director), Psi Chi.

WRITINGS: (Editor) *The Urban Mission*, Eerdmans, 1974. Contributor to psychology and religion journals.

WORK IN PROGRESS: Editing *Modifying Man: Implications and Ethics*; *Alienation and Celebration*, completion expected in 1978; *Trusting: Toward a Psycho-Theology of Trust*, 1980.

* * *

ELLISON, Max 1914-

PERSONAL: Born March 21, 1914, in Bellaire, Mich.; son of Roy (a farmer) and Maggie (Fuller) Ellison; married Florence Norton, September 17, 1943 (divorced November 8, 1974); children: Edith (Mrs. Donald Williams), Margaret (Mrs. James Redmond), John, Roy, Andrew. *Education:* Educated in public schools in Michigan. *Home:* Bellaire, Mich. 49615.

CAREER: Has worked as a farmer, stablehand, night watchman, and janitor in Michigan. Has lectured and read his poetry in elementary and high schools and in colleges and universities in the United States. *Military service:* U.S. Army, 1943-45; received Purple Heart with two oak leaf clusters.

WRITINGS—Poetry: The Underbark, Conway House, 1969; *The Happenstance*, Conway House, 1972; (with Lynn Berry) *Double Take*, Conway House, 1974.

WORK IN PROGRESS: Clean Livers of Antrim County and Other Myths.

* * *

ELMENDORF, Mary Lindsay 1917-

PERSONAL: Born April 13, 1917, in Ruby, S.C.; daughter of James Calvin (a farmer) and Jean (MacGregor) Lindsay; married John Elmendorf (an educator), December 27, 1937; children: Calvin Lindsay, Susan (Mrs. Jeffrey Roberts). *Education:* Queens College, Charlotte, N.C., student, 1933-35; University of North Carolina, B.A., 1937; Union Graduate School, Ph.D., 1973. *Politics:* Democrat. *Religion:* Quaker. *Home and office:* 535 Blvd. of the Presidents, Sarasota, Fla. 33577.

CAREER: Cooperative for American Relief Everywhere (CARE), Mexico City, Mexico, chief of mission, 1952-60; Hampshire College, Amherst, Mass., assoicate professor of anthropology, 1973; Chapman College, Orange, Calif., professor of anthropology, 1974-75; writer, 1975—. Chief of refugee section of American Friends Service Committee (Paris, France), 1945-46; consultant to Peace Corps, Agency for International Development, and Department of State Overseas Education Fund. *Member:* American Anthropological Association (fellow), Society for International Development, Society for Applied Anthropology, Latin American Studies Association. *Awards, honors:* Gold medal from the Goverment of Mexico, for youth work.

WRITINGS: The Mayan Woman and Change, Centro Intercultural de Documentacion, 1972; *Nine Mayan Women: A Village Faces Change*, Schenkman, 1975. Contributor of articles to government publications.

WORK IN PROGRESS: A film about women of Yucatan; continuing research on the changing roles of women in Latin America; studying women's roles in development.

SIDELIGHTS: Mary Elmendorf writes that she vacillates " . . . between scholarship and action, with art always in the background," adding that she is a " . . . late bloomer who is excited by ideas and deeply concerned about people, particularly peasants and women." *Avocational interests:* International travel (more than fifty countries in last few years), painting, sculpture, teaching making of pottery.

EL-MESSIDI, Kathy(anne) Groehn 1946-
(Kathy Groehn Cosseboom)

PERSONAL: Surname is pronounced L Mess-*ee*-dee; born January 23, 1946; in Detroit, Mich.; daughter of Thomas Emil (a General Motors executive) and Helen Margaret (Schreck) Groehn; married Raymond Eugene Cosseboom, August 20, 1967 (divorced, 1969); married Adel El Sayed El-Messidi (a petroleum engineer), September 14, 1974. *Education:* University of Michigan, B.A., 1967; Southern Oregon College, M.A., 1970; University of Oklahoma, Ph.D., 1975. *Religion:* Christian Science. *Home:* Barcelona Apts., #133, Big Spring, Tex. 79720; or, 716 Lochmoor Blvd., Grosse Pointe Woods, Mich. 48236.

CAREER: Grosse Pointe News, Grosse Pointe, Mich., reporter, 1966; *Christian Science Monitor*, Boston, Mass., staff member, free-lance writer and research librarian, 1967, 1968-69; in public relations for Jackson & Perkins Flower Co., and Harry & David Gift Foods, both Medford, Ore., 1970-71; WNAD radio, Norman, Okla., advertising and feature writer, 1973. Teaching assistant in history, University of Oklahoma, 1972-75. *Member:* American Pen Women, American Historical Association, Women in Communications, Phi Alpha Theta, Kappa Kappa Gamma. *Awards, honors:* Informational book first prize from American Pen Women Biennial Contest, 1974, for *Grosse Pointe, Michigan: Race Against Race.*

WRITINGS: (Under name Kathy Groehn Cosseboom) *Grosse Pointe, Michigan: Race Against Race* (nonfiction), Michigan State University Press, 1972. Contributor of articles and short stories to *Christian Science Monitor* and *Boulder Express.*

BIOGRAPHICAL/CRITICAL SOURCES: Detroit Free Press, November 27, 1972.

* * *

ELWELL, Jerry MacElroy 1922-

PERSONAL: Born April 9, 1922, in Patten, Maine; daughter of Frank Nevers (a Maine guide) and Eva (Noonan) MacElroy; married John E. Elwell (a woodworker), July 17, 1959. *Politics:* "A disillusioned Republican!" *Religion:* "Member of no church . . . just a Bible-believing Fundamentalist." *Home address:* Star Route, Box 1, Stafford Hill, Sharman Station, Maine 04777.

CAREER: Atlas Plywood, Patten, Maine, bookkeeper, 1940-41; Katahdin Trust Co., Patten, Maine, bank clerk, 1945-55; Cameron Ford Sales, Patten, Maine, secretary, 1955-59; writer, 1964—.

WRITINGS: Cuddles: The True Story of a Befuddled Maine Woodchuck, Rockland Courier-Gazette, 1972. Author of nature columns in *Bangor Daily News*, 1964—, *Maine Life*, 1973-74, and *Purple Martin News*, 1974—. Contributor of articles and photographs to *Grit.*

WORK IN PROGRESS: Squirrels, Nuts 'n' Nonsense, nonfiction.

SIDELIGHTS: Jerry Elwell writes: "We're all 'kids-at-heart' and long to escape today's dark headlines . . . so my writings are in the simple . . ., mostly humorous . . . language which allows adults to 'escape into childhood and fantasy' and for children to enjoy as only children do.

"I write partly for 'financial survival' and because of reader response . . . and because I'm at my happiest when writing. . . Subjects vital to me are ecology, the un-balancing of nature by man, pollution, cruelty to animals, the questionable 'fruits' of our so-called civilization, the wearing away of our natural environment, etc."

Mrs. Elwell comes from a family of game and fire wardens, guides, sporting camp operators, game biologists, surveyors, and woodsmen. She maintains a non-profit, time-consuming, patience-taxing sanctuary for orphaned and injured birds and beasts who are given their freedom in the Maine woods when they are able to fend for themselves.

AVOCATIONAL INTERESTS: Photography, art (former sign painter), decorating woodenware created by her husband, hiking, snowshoeing, the woods and out-of-doors, gardening, listening to music, travel on country and woodland roads.

* * *

ELWOOD, Roger 1943-

PERSONAL: Born January 13, 1943, in Atlantic City, N.J.; son of Raymond C. (an accountant) and Dorothy F. Elwood. *Education:* Attended high school in New Jersey. *Home and office:* 1700 Somerset Blvd., Linwood, N.J. 08221.

CAREER: Free-lance writer and editor.

WRITINGS: Alien Worlds, Paperback Library, 1964; *Strange Things Are Happening: Satanism, Witchcraft, and God*, David Cook, 1973; *Anita Bryant, Dale Evans Rogers: Two Stars for God*, Paperback Library, 1974.

Editor: *Great Spy Novels and Stories*, Pyramid Books, 1965; (with Samuel Moskowitz) *Strange Signposts*, Holt, 1966; (with Moskowitz) *The Time Curve*, Tower, 1968; (with Vic Ghidalia) *Beware the Beasts*, Manor Books, 1970; *Horror Hunters*, Manor Books, 1971; *Little Monsters: Children of Wonder and Dread*, Manor Books, 1971; *And Walk Now Gently Through the Fire, and Other Stories*, Chilton, 1972; *Signs and Wonders*, Revell, 1972; (with Ghidalia) *Androids, Time Machines, and Blue Giraffes: A Panorama of Science Fiction*, Follett, 1973; *Children of Infinity: Original Science Fiction Stories for Young Readers*, F. Watts, 1973; *Flame Tree Planet: An Anthology of Religious Science Fantasy*, Concordia, 1973; *Future City*, Trident, 1973; *Monster Tales: Vampires, Werewolves, and Things*, Rand McNally, 1973; (with Virginia Kidd) *Saving Worlds: A Collection of Original Science Fiction Stories*, Doubleday, 1973; *Science Fiction Tales: Invaders, Creatures, and Alien Worlds*, Rand McNally, 1973; *Showcase*, Harper, 1973; *The Other Side of Tomorrow: Original Science Fiction Stories About Young People of the Future*, Random, 1973; *Children of Eden*, Pyramid Publications, 1973; *The Far Side of Time*, Dodd, 1973; *Omega: A Collection of Original Science Fiction Stories*, Walker & Co., 1973; *Future Quest*, Avon, 1973; *The New Mend*, Macmillan, Volume II, 1973; *Ten Tomorrows*, Fawcett, 1973; *Tomorrow's Alternatives*, Macmillan, 1973; *More Little Monsters*, Manor Books, 1973; *Continuum One*, Putnam, 1974; *Continuum Two*, Putnam, 1974; *Continuum Three*, Putnam, 1974; *The Beeseekers*, Trident, 1974; *Prince of Darkness*, Gibbon, 1974; *Science Fiction Creatures*, Rand McNally, 1974; *Strange Gods*, Pocket Books, 1974.

You Can Win Over "Innocent" Sins, Victor Books, 1974; (with Virginia Kidd) *The Wounded Planet*, Bantam, 1974; *Vampires, Werewolves and Other Monsters*, Curtis, 1974; *Survival from Infinity: Original Science Fiction Stories for Young Readers*, F. Watts, 1974; *Night of the Sphinx and Other Stories*, Lerner, 1974; *The Many Worlds of Andre*

Norton, Chilton, 1974; *The Learning Maze and Other Science Fiction*, Messner, 1974; *Horror Tales*, Rand McNally, 1974; *Future Kin: Eight Science Fiction Stories*, Doubleday, 1974; *The Extraterrestrials*, Macrae, 1974; *Crisis: Ten Original Stories of Science Fiction*, Nelson, 1974; *Chronicles of a Comer and Other Religious Science Fiction Stories*, John Knox, 1974; *The Berserkers*, Pocket Books, 1974; Poul Anderson, *The Many Worlds of Poul Anderson*, Chilton, 1974; *Missing Worlds and Other Stories*, Lerner, 1974; *Killer Plants and Other Stories*, Lerner, 1974; *Graduated Robot and Other Stories*, Lerner, 1974; *Tunnel and Other Stories*, Lerner, 1974; *Long Night of Waiting and Other Stories*, Aurora Publications, 1974; (with Samuel Moskowitz) *Other Worlds Other Times*, 2nd edition, Manor Books, 1974; *Mind Angel and Other Stories*, Lerner, 1974; *Adrift in Space and Other Stories*, Lerner, 1974; *Journey to Another Star and Other Stories*, Lerner, 1974; *Corruption*, Paperback Library, 1975.

* * *

EMMERSON, John K(enneth) 1908-

PERSONAL: Born March 17, 1908, in Canon City, Colo.; son of John Woods and Margaretta (Hitchcock) Emmerson; married Dorothy McLaughlin, August 18, 1934; children: Dorothy Louise, Donald Kenneth. *Education:* Colorado College, A.B., 1929; New York University, A.M., 1930; graduate study at Sorbonne, University of Paris, 1927-28, and Georgetown University, 1932-33. *Home:* 24899 Olive Tree Lane, Los Altos Hills, Calif. 94022. *Office:* Hoover Institution, Stanford University, Stanford, Calif. 93405.

CAREER: University of Nebraska, Lincoln, instructor in history and government; Berlitz School of Languages, Chicago, Ill., assistant director, 1933-35; U.S. Foreign Service, Washington, D.C., Japanese language officer in Tokyo, Japan, 1936-38, vice-consul in Taiwan, 1938-40, third secretary of embassy in Tokyo, 1940-42, officer in Washington, D.C. and Peru, both 1942, political adviser to the U.S. military in China, 1943-45, officer in Washington, D.C. and Tokyo, both 1945, assistant chairman of Division of Japanese Affairs in the Department of State in Washington, D.C., 1946-47, first secretary of embassy in Russia, 1947-49, planning adviser to Bureau of Far Eastern Affairs, 1950-52, counselor and deputy chief of mission at embassy in Karachi, Pakistan, 1952-55, and Beirut, Lebanon, 1955-57, political counselor in Paris, France, 1957, consul general in Lagos, Nigeria, 1958-60, and Salisbury, Rhodesia and Nyasaland, 1960-62, consul general (minister) in Tokyo, 1962-67; Stanford University, Stanford, Calif., diplomat in residence, 1967, senior research fellow at Hoover Institution on War, Revolution, and Peace, 1968—, lecturer in history, 1973. Senior adviser to U.S. delegation of United Nations General Assembly, 1956-57; research associate of Center for Strategic and International Studies at Georgetown University; consultant to U.S. State Department and Institute for Defense Analyses.

MEMBER: Association for Asian Studies, Asiatic Society of Japan (life member), World Affairs Council of Northern California, Japan Society of San Francisco, Phi Beta Kappa. *Awards, honors:* Meritorious service award from U.S. Department of State, 1954; LL.D. from Colorado College, 1968.

WRITINGS: Arms, Yen, and Power: The Japanese Dilemma, Dunellen, 1971; (with Leonard A. Humphreys) *Will Japan Rearm?*, American Enterprise Institute and Hoover Institution, Stanford University, 1973. Contributor to *Yearbook on International Communist Affairs*. Contributor to foreign affairs journals and to *Reader's Digest*.

WORK IN PROGRESS: A book on his personal experiences in the foreign service.

* * *

EMMETT, Bruce 1949-

PERSONAL: Born October 7, 1949, in Greenwich, Conn.; son of Robert A. (a Cities Service executive) and Jean (Bertram) Emmett; married Lisa Smith (a fashion illustrator), June 9, 1973. *Education:* Syracuse University, B.F.A., 1973. *Home and office:* 200 East 16th St., New York, N.Y. 10003.

CAREER: Free-lance illustrator.

WRITINGS: A Storybook with Magic Tricks: Rooftop Wizard (juvenile), Prentice-Hall, 1974.

BIOGRAPHICAL/CRITICAL SOURCES: Art Direction, October, 1973; *Swank*, May, 1975.

* * *

ENGEBRECHT, P(atricia) A(nn) 1935-

PERSONAL: Born December 19, 1935, in Los Angeles, Calif.; daughter of D. W. (in merchant marine) and Aloha (Stoddard) Davis; married Ronald H. Engebrecht (a research chemist), December 19, 1954; children: Jeffrey, Laura Jo, Kurt. *Education:* Attended Oregon State University. *Politics:* Republican. *Religion:* Agnostic. *Home:* 20 Lodgepole Rd., Pittsford, N.Y. 14534. *Agent:* McIntosh & Otis, 18 East 41st St., New York, N.Y. 10017.

CAREER: Writer.

WRITINGS: Under the Haystack (fiction), Thomas Nelson, 1973. Contributor of short stories, articles, and poems to national magazines, including *Columbia*, *Girl Talk*, and *Yankee*.

WORK IN PROGRESS: The Promise of Moonstone, young adult fiction.

SIDELIGHTS: Pat Engebrecht writes: "Having had the good fortune to be married to a man who has always treated me as an equal, I often fail to understand the complaints of most women libbers. Equalization being a state of mind, I think 'society' is used as a crutch for personal failings. I hope my children will enter freely into a world of no closed doors for we have endeavored to teach them that success is in the believing and the struggle. Because young people are continually seeking, I find them a rewarding audience."

* * *

ENGLAND, E Squires
See BALL, Sylvia Patricia

* * *

ENGLE, John D(avid), Jr. 1922-
(David Johnn)

PERSONAL: Born September 29, 1922, in Yocum, Ky.; son of John David (a grocer and farmer) and Mary A. (Combs) Engle; married Anita M. Jacobs, August 20, 1948 (divorced, 1972); children: Mariamne A., Brent Elwin. *Education:* University of Kentucky, B.A., 1950, M.A., 1953. *Politics:* Independent. *Religion:* Independent. *Home:* 1311-B Chesterwood Ct., Cincinnati, Ohio 45246. *Office:* Princeton High School, 11080 Chester Rd., Cincinnati, Ohio 45246.

CAREER: Teacher of English and creative writing at high schools in Belfry, Ky., 1950, Jenkins, Ky., 1950-51, Athens, Ky., 1951-53, and Lexington, Ky., 1953-56; Princeton High school, Cincinnati, Ohio, teacher of English and creative writing, 1956—. Poet; has given poetry readings and lectures at high schools, colleges, and writers conferences; formerly conducted poetry reading-music program on WLEX, Lexington, Ky. Literary adviser to Ohio Arts Council; member of Ohio Poets in the Schools program. *Military service:* U.S. Army Air Forces, 1942-45.

MEMBER: Poetry Society of America, National Education Association, Ohio Education Association, Verse Writers' Guild of Ohio, Kentucky State Poetry Society. *Awards, honors:* Awards from Kentucky State Poetry Society; four awards at Ohio Poetry Day Awards, 1970; Selden Rodman Award for poetry, Indiana University Writers' Conference, 1970.

WRITINGS—Poems: *Modern Odyssey*, Golden Quill, 1971; *Laugh Lightly*, Golden Quill, 1974.

Plays: "The Opening Door" (three-act), first produced in Louisville, Ky., at Kentucky Education Association Centennial Conference, 1957; *The Charm* (one-act; produced by amateur and college groups), Eldridge Publishing, 1958.

Poems have been included in *To Each His Song, A Treasury of Unity Poems, The Best of the Daily Word, Poets of the Midwest*, and other anthologies. More than 1,000 poems have been published in magazines and newspapers, including *Saturday Evening Post, Good Housekeeping, Christian Science Monitor, Ladies' Home Journal*, and *Kansas City Star*; contributor of articles, essays, and short stories for young people to other journals. Former monthly columnist, *Student Writer*; conductor of poetry column, "Engle's Angle," in two community newspapers. Associate editor, *Writer's Digest*, 1960—.

WORK IN PROGRESS: Sea Songs; a collection of poetry of Appalachia, *With Appalachian Love*; and a collection of poems about trees, *Treed*.

SIDELIGHTS: "I grew up in the hills of Kentucky where I was able to spend much time alone with nature," Engle writes. "When but a child, I was fortunate to find some of the world's greatest literature in a deserted shack. I read it all.... [Besides writing] I also do stone sculpture, decoupage poetry, and photography. My latest venture is photos, biographical sketch, and an original poem for the cover of a record album done by Susan Rose, a local entertainer."

AVOCATIONAL INTERESTS: Gardening, nature study, people-watching.

* * *

ENGLEBERT, Victor 1933-

PERSONAL: Surname is pronounced Engla-berre; born February 5, 1933, in Brussels, Belgium; son of Joseph (a musician) and Rosa (Leberzorg) Englebert; married Lucienne Girard, April, 1955 (divorced, 1972); married Martha Jaramillo, September 21, 1972; children: (first marriage) Barbara, Eric. *Education:* Self-educated. *Religion:* None. *Home:* Apartado aereo 8221, Cali, Colombia.

CAREER: Professional photographer. *Military service:* Belgian Army, 1952-54. *Member:* American Society of Magazine Photographers, American Society of Picture Professionals.

WRITINGS—Books for children illustrated with own photographs: *Camera on Africa: The World of an Ethiopian Boy*, Harcourt, 1970; *Camera on Ghana: The World of a Young Fisherman*, Harcourt, 1971; *Camera on the Sahara: The World of Three Young Nomads*, Harcourt, 1971; *The Goats of Agadez*, Harcourt, 1973.

Contributor of chapters and illustrations to National Geographic Society publications, including *Nomads of the World*, 1971, and *Primitive Worlds*, 1973. Writer and illustrator of *National Geographic* features; contributor of articles to *International Wildlife, Venture, Clipper*, and *Diversions*.

WORK IN PROGRESS: Books on the Tuareg nomads of the Sahara and on Colombia.

SIDELIGHTS: Englebert writes: "Became photographer to help satisfy an urge to travel and explore. Started to write to help sell my pictures. But now take pictures and write for sheer pleasure. Have studied a dozen or more primitive tribes in Africa, Asia, South America, mostly to write *National Geographic* articles, and so am interested in anthropology. I speak fluently French, English, Spanish, and less well, Dutch, German, and Portuguese." Englebert lived in the Belgian Congo (now Zaire), 1955-57, Canada, 1960-61, the United States, 1961-73, and has been a resident of Colombia since 1974.

* * *

ENGSTROM, W(infred) A(ndrew) 1925-

PERSONAL: Born May 26, 1925, in Willmar, Minn.; son of Edvin L. (a farmer) and Agnes (Anderson) Engstrom; married Barbara Jarvis (a teacher), June 16, 1953; children: Philip, David, Daniel, Ruth. *Education:* Macalester College, B.A., 1949; Austin Presbyterian Seminary, M.Div., 1953; University of Texas, M.A., 1972. *Home:* 1421 South Congress, Austin, Tex. 78704. *Office:* Christian Communication Consultants, 1421 South Congress, Austin, Tex. 78704.

CAREER: Ordained to Presbyterian ministry, 1953; minister in Natalia, Tex., 1953-56, Pleasanton, Tex., 1956-59, Burnet, Tex., 1959-65, Seguin, Tex., 1965-68, and Austin, Tex., 1968-74; Christian Communication Consultants, Austin, owner and audio visual consultant, 1971—. Relief newscaster, KLRN-TV, Austin, 1969-70; administrator, Extend-A-Care, Inc., 1970-71. *Awards, honors:* Named Rural Minister of the Year, State of Texas, 1963.

WRITINGS: Multi-Media in the Church: A Beginner's Guide for Putting It All Together, John Knox, 1973.

AVOCATIONAL INTERESTS: Photography, fishing, camping, golf, and woodworking.

* * *

ENIS, Ben M(elvin) 1942-

PERSONAL: Born January 5, 1942, in Baton Rouge, La.; son of Ben Melvin (a football coach) and Marjorie (a realtor; maiden name, Wood) Enis; married Randy Kay Fetty, September 1, 1962; children: Ben M. III. *Education:* Louisiana State University, B.S., 1963, M.B.A., 1965, Ph.D., 1967. *Politics:* Libertarian. *Religion:* None. *Home:* 1438 Scenic Ridge, Houston, Tex. 77043. *Office:* Department of Business Administration, University of Houston, Cullen Blvd., Houston, Tex. 77004.

CAREER: University of Houston, Houston, Tex., assistant professor, 1967-69, associate professor, 1969-73, professor of marketing, 1973—. Consultant to firms in publishing, retailing, real estate, transportation, and banking.

Member: American Marketing Association, American Institute of Decision Sciences, Southwestern Federation of Administrative Disciplines, Southern Marketing Association, University of Houston College of Business Administration Alumni Association.

WRITINGS: (Contributor) Leon C. Megginson, editor, *Human Resources: Cases and Concepts,* Harcourt, 1968; (editor with Keith K. Cox) *Marketing Classics: A Selection of Influential Articles,* Allyn & Bacon, 1969, revised edition, 1973; (with Cox) *Experimentation for Marketing Decisions,* International Textbook Co., 1969; (with Charles L. Broome) *Marketing Decisions: A Bayesian Approach,* International Textbook Co., 1971; (with Cox) *The Marketing Research Process,* Goodyear Publishing, 1972; (editor with Cox) *Readings in 'The Marketing Research Process,'* Goodyear Publishing, 1973; (editor with Betsy D. Gelb) *Marketing Is Everybody's Business,* Goodyear Publishing, 1974; *Marketing Principles: The Management Process,* Goodyear Publishing, 1974; (contributor) O. C. Ferrell and Raymond A. LaGarce, editors, *New Issues in Public Policy in Marketing,* Heath, 1975; (contributor) *Fundamentals of Marketing: Additional Dimensions,* McGraw, 2nd edition (Enis was not involved in 1st edition), 1975; (contributor) *Selected Academic Readings: Marketing,* Simon & Schuster, 1975; (contributor) *Annual Editions: Readings in Marketing, 1974-75,* Dushkin Publishing Group, 1975. Contributor to proceedings and to business journals.

* * *

EPLER, Percy H. 1872-1975

July 19, 1872—March 13, 1975; American author. Obituaries: *New York Times,* March 21, 1975; *AB Bookman's Weekly,* April 28, 1975.

* * *

EPSTEIN, Jason 1928-

PERSONAL: Born August 25, 1928, in Cambridge, Mass.; son of Robert and Gladys (Shapiro) Epstein; married Barbara Zimmerman (an editor), December 30, 1953; children: Jacob, Helen. *Education:* Columbia University, B.A., 1949, M.A., 1950. *Home:* 33 West 67th St., New York, N.Y. 10023. *Office:* Random House, Inc., 201 East 50th St., New York, N.Y. 10022.

CAREER: Doubleday & Co., New York, N.Y., editor, 1951-58; Random House, Inc., New York, N.Y., vice president, 1958—. Director, New York Review of Books, Inc.; consultant, Children's Television Workshop. *Member:* Phi Beta Kappa.

WRITINGS: The Great Conspiracy Trial: An Essay on Law, Liberty, and the Constitution, Random House, 1970.

* * *

EPSTEIN, Julius 1901-1975

1901—July 3, 1975; Austrian-born journalist, educator, and author. Obituaries: *New York Times,* July 5, 1975; *AB Bookman's Weekly,* July 28, 1975.

* * *

ESAU, Helmut 1941-

PERSONAL: Born October 22, 1941, in Danzig, Germany; naturalized U.S. citizen in 1970; son of Heinrich and Kaete (Heidebrecht) Esau; married Naomi Rivera, June 13, 1964; children: Kenny, Penny. *Education:* Eastern Mennonite College, B.A., 1965; University of Virginia, M.A., 1967; University of California, Los Angeles, Ph.D., 1971. *Home:* 1409 Lawyer St., College Station, Tex. 77840. *Office:* Department of English, Texas A & M University, College Station, Tex. 77843.

CAREER: University of California, Los Angeles, assistant professor of Germanic philology, 1971-72; Texas A & M University, College Station, associate professor of linguistics, 1972—. *Member:* Linguistic Society of America, Modern Language Association of America, Conference of College Teachers of English.

WRITINGS: Nominalization and Complementation in Modern German, North Holland Publishing, 1973. Contributor to professional journals.

WORK IN PROGRESS: An interdisciplinary book, an introduction to language and communication; investigating the structure of the lexicon (i.e., the internal dictionary) of speakers of human languages.

* * *

ESCRIVA, Josemaria
See ESCRIVA de BALAGUER, Josemaria

* * *

ESCRIVA de BALAGUER, Josemaria 1902-1975

January 9, 1902—June 26, 1975; Spanish priest, founder of Opus Dei secular order, and author. Obituaries: *New York Times,* June 28, 1975.

* * *

ESTES, John E(dward) 1939-

PERSONAL: Born July 21, 1939, in Holton, Kan.; son of Donald Hamilton and Maysel (Replogle) Estes; married Claire Marie Mosson, July 20, 1963; children: John Edward, Thomas Robert Albert. *Education:* San Diego Junior College, A.A., 1959; San Diego State College (now University), A.B., 1963, M.A., 1964; University of California, Los Angeles, Ph.D., 1969. *Office:* Department of Geography, University of California, Santa Barbara, Calif. 93106.

CAREER: Texas Instruments Inc., Dallas, Tex., geographer, 1964-65; University of California, Santa Barbara, lecturer, spring, 1969, assistant professor of geography, 1969—. Consultant to Santa Barbara District Attorney. *Member:* International Geographical Union, American Association for the Advancement of Science, American Society of Photogrammetry, Association of American Geographers, National Council for Geographic Education, Association of Pacific Coast Geographers, Gamma Theta Upsilon, Sigma Xi.

WRITINGS: (Editor with L. W. Senger, and contributor) *Remote Sensing: Techniques for Environmental Analysis,* Hamilton Publishing, 1974; (contributor) Leonard W. Bowden and Evelyn Pruitt, editors, *Manual of Remote Sensing,* American Society of Photogrammetry, 1975; (contributor) A. N. Strahler, editor, *Physical Geography,* 4th edition (Estes was not associated with earlier editions), Wiley, 1975. Contributor of articles and reviews to proceedings and professional journals.

* * *

EVAIN, Elaine 1931-

PERSONAL: Born January 14, 1931, in Indianapolis, Ind.; daughter of James Orville (a purchasing agent) and Winifred (Whitehead) Newell; married second husband, Jean Andre Evain (an electronic engineer), September 14, 1957; children: (first marriage) Peggy Ann, Leslye Carole; (second marriage) Michael Gerard, Eric James. *Education:* Attended Butler University. *Politics:* "Honesty—so it's been awhile since I've voted." *Religion:* "God." *Residence:* Brockton, Mass.

CAREER: Writer, 1971—. Dancer with United Service Organizations (U.S.O.), 1945-47, and with road company; has appeared in little theatre and summer stock. *Member:* Authors Guild, Authors League of America.

WRITINGS: Return Trip (novel), Pyramid Publications, 1974. Contributor to *Good Housekeeping* and *Coronet.*

WORK IN PROGRESS: The Musician, a novel about a man who overcomes hatred; a television script for a pilot program; a play; a book of humor.

SIDELIGHTS: Elaine Evain writes: "I think I'm interested in everything except mathematics and people who do nothing with the time the Good Lord has given them.... My husband is French. We have lived in Paris (my favorite city of the world) and travel as much as possible. Otherwise our lives are quiet, and pretty typical." *Avocational interests:* Theater, books, reading, acting, dancing, cooking, gardening, skiing, sailing, travel.

* * *

EVANS, Abbie Huston 1881-

PERSONAL: Born December 20, 1881, in Lee, N.H.; daughter of Lewis Darenydd and Hester Annette (Huston) Evans. *Education:* Radcliffe College, B.A., 1913, M.A., 1918. *Home:* 400 North Walnut St., West Chester, Pa. 19380.

CAREER: Settlement Music School, Philadelphia, Pa., staff member, 1923-53; College Settlement Farm-Camp, Horsham, Pa., staff member, 1953-57. Member of jury for Shelley Memorial Award, 1940, United States Award for Poetry, 1967, and International Poetry Forum, 1967. *Member:* Americans for Democratic Action, American Civil Liberties Union, Phi Beta Kappa. *Awards, honors:* Guarantor's Prize from *Poetry,* 1931; Loines Memorial Award from National Institute of Arts and Letters, 1960; Golden Rose Award of New England Poetry Club, 1965; citation from Maine Commission on Arts and Humanities, 1970; citation from Pennsylvania Council on Arts and International Poetry Forum, 1970; Litt.D., Bowdoin College, 1961.

WRITINGS—All poetry: *Outcrop* (with foreword by Edna St. Vincent Millay) Harper, 1928; *The Bright North,* Macmillan, 1938; *Fact of Crystal,* Harcourt, 1961; *Collected Poems,* University of Pittsburgh Press, 1970. Represented in several anthologies, including *A Little Treasury of Modern Poetry,* edited by Oscar Williams, Scribner, 1946; *Poems and Poetry,* edited by Elisabeth Wintersteen Schneider, American Book, 1964. Contributor of poetry to periodicals, including *Nation* and *New Yorker.* Member of advisory board, *Contemporary Poetry,* 1940—.

SIDELIGHTS: Miss Evans' poetry was recorded for the Library of Congress in 1964.

* * *

EVANS, Donald P(aul) 1930-

PERSONAL: Born December 11, 1930, in Rome, N.Y.; son of Richard and Gladys (Ryder) Evans; married Jane E.

Davis (a library assistant), June 9, 1956; children: Marta F. *Education:* Sophia University, student, 1952-53; Vallejo Junior College, A.A., 1954; Bowling Green State University, further study, 1954-55; San Francisco State College (now University), B.A., 1957. *Politics:* Independent. *Religion:* None. *Home:* 606 North Madison St., Rome, N.Y. 13440. *Office:* Vernon Downs, Vernon, N.Y. 13476.

CAREER: Rome Daily Sentinel, Rome, N.Y., reporter and sports editor, 1959-66; Vernon Downs (race track), Vernon, N.Y., publicity and public relations director, 1966—. *Military service:* U.S. Army, 1949-50. U.S. Air Force, 1950-53; became sergeant. *Member:* North American Harness Publicists Association (past president; past member of board of directors), U.S. Harness Writers Association. *Awards, honors:* John Hervey Grand Prize for Harness Racing Feature Writing, from Harness Racing Institute, 1965, for "The Byline Stable: Rags to Riches."

WRITINGS: Hooked on Harness Racing, Prospect Books, 1965; *Big Bum: The Story of Bret Hanover,* A. S. Barnes, 1969; *Nevele Pride: Speed 'n' Spirit,* A. S. Barnes, 1972; *Super Bird: The Story of Albatross,* A. S. Barnes, 1975. Contributor to magazines, including *Hoof Beats,* and newspapers.

WORK IN PROGRESS: A book about Hanover Shoe Farms, for A. S. Barnes; research on harness racing for a ninety-minute television script.

SIDELIGHTS: Evans writes: "I love harness racing and I love writing, so what more could I want? Of course, I'd like to vary my schedule a bit—like to get back to humor and perhaps do a book about my family's experiences with animals. We've had some awful weird pets."

BIOGRAPHICAL/CRITICAL SOURCES: Hoof Beats, February, 1975.

* * *

EVANS, J(ohn) Robert 1942-

PERSONAL: Born November 6, 1942, in DeKalb, Ill.; son of George "Chick" (athletic director at Northern Illinois University) and Venus (a teacher; maiden name, Johnson) Evans; married Roberta Ann Shelhamer, January 25, 1965; children: Julianne, Thomas, Kristin. *Education:* Northern Illinois University, B.S. in Ed., 1964, M.S. in Ed., 1965; University of New Mexico, Ed.D., 1970. *Home:* 650 Tarento Dr., San Diego, Calif. 92106. *Office:* 1030 Pearl St., Suite 6, LaJolla, Calif. 92037.

CAREER: High school teacher of physical education and coach in the public schools of Hinsdale, Ill., 1965-68; United States International University, San Diego, Calif., associate dean, 1970-74; Personal Health Management Systems, Inc. (development and presentation of biofeedback training and programs), LaJolla, Calif., president and director of educational services, 1974—. *Member:* National Collegiate Physical Education Association for Men, Biofeedback Research Society, California Teachers Association.

WRITINGS: Blowing the Whistle on Intercollegiate Sports, Nelson-Hall, 1974. Contributor to *Scholastic Coach, Marriage,* and *San Diego Magazine.*

WORK IN PROGRESS: So You Want to Be a Coach?, a book on teaching sports to youngsters; co-authoring a book on biofeedback; articles on biofeedback; research in stress and sports and in perceptual motor learning; short stories.

EVANS, Travers Moncure 1938-

PERSONAL: Born February 6, 1938, in Fredericksburg, Va.; daughter of Robert Travers (a business executive) and Frances (Stephens) Moncure; married Charles Edward Evans (a partner in an executive recruiting firm), September 5, 1964. *Education:* University of Virginia, B.A., 1960. *Politics:* Liberal. *Home:* 40 East 88th St., Manhattan, N.Y. 10028.

CAREER: J. Walter Thompson Co. (advertising agency), New York, N.Y., copywriter, 1960-63; D'arcy Advertising Agency, New York, N.Y., copywriter, 1963; Taitham-Laird & Kudner, New York, N.Y., copywriter, 1963-66; Grey Advertising Agency, New York, N.Y., copywriter, 1966-67; free-lance writer, 1967—. Member of executive committee of Alliance for a Safer New York, 1974-75. *Member:* Junior League of the City of New York (member of board of managers, 1972-74).

WRITINGS: (With David Greene) *The Meat Book*, Scribner, 1973; (with others) *New York Entertains: The New York Junior League Cookbook*, Doubleday, 1974; (contributor) *Pennywise, Party Perfect Dinners*, Ferguson, 1975; *The Good Cooking School Guide to Simple, Exotic, Unusual, and Extraordinary Dinner Parties on a Tight Budget*, Doubleday, 1975.

WORK IN PROGRESS: With Frank C. Baker, *A Silver Spoon*, a biographical recipe book spanning seventy-five years of cooking and eating experience.

AVOCATIONAL INTERESTS: Serious cooking, sailing on a sloop, deep sea diving (especially in the Caribbean and Mexico).

* * *

EVERMAN, Welch D(uane) 1946-

PERSONAL: Born September 24, 1946, in Allentown, Pa.; son of Welch C. (an upholsterer) and Ruth (Sacher) Everman. *Education:* Northwestern University, B.A., 1968. *Home:* 422 South 45th Street, Apt. 1-B, Philadelphia, Pa. 19104.

CAREER: Writer. Has lectured and given readings in high schools and colleges. *Member:* Poets and Writers, Inc., Associated Writing Programs, Phi Beta Kappa.

WRITINGS: Orion (novel), Ithaca House, 1975. Regular reviewer for *Small Press Review*.

WORK IN PROGRESS: Markings, a novel; *The Act*, a novel; a third novel; studies of Karl Jaspers, Martin Heidegger, and Paul Tillich.

SIDELIGHTS: Everman writes: "I would prefer to live as a total man who is *engaged in writing* rather than to accept the limited role of simply *being a writer*. The task of writing is isolating and challenging, but it is perhaps a more challenging task to be a man within the world, for a man is not an image, a role, or a fact, but a free and continuing becoming. My thoughts and my novels move toward an explication not of the fact of human life but of the process of human living."

* * *

EVSLIN, Dorothy 1923-

PERSONAL: Born April 6, 1923, in Brooklyn, N.Y.; daughter of Nathan D. (a lawyer) and Bess (Nemerov) Shapiro; married Bernard Evslin (a writer), April 18, 1942; children: Tom, Lee, Pamela Evslin Zino, Janet Evslin Burbank. *Education:* Hunter College of the City University of New York, B.A., 1965, M.A., 1967. *Politics:* Honest independent. *Religion:* Jewish. *Home:* 158 Sutton Manor, New Rochelle, N.Y. 10805. *Agent:* Knox Burger, 37½ Washington Sq. S., New York, N.Y. 10012. *Office:* Department of English, Westchester Community College, Valhalla, N.Y. 10595.

CAREER: Rockland Community College, Suffern, N.Y., instructor in English, 1967-68; Hofstra University, New College, Hempstead, N.Y., instructor in English, 1968-69; Westchester Community College, Valhalla, N.Y., assistant professor, 1969-74, associate professor of English, 1974—.

WRITINGS: The Fortunate Sex, Saturday Review Press, 1971. Contributor to *New York Times, New York Sunday News*, and *Family Circle*.

WORK IN PROGRESS: Stony Point, a novel; an autobiography; articles and fiction.

SIDELIGHTS: "I'm quite old: 52, chock full of memories, hopes, stories that have happened and are happening to me," Dorothy Evslin wrote. "I've always written, always read, have that reader's double vision so that I can see flowers with D. H. Lawrence, walk corridors with Kafka. What has not yet been written I feel I must do.... So I came professionally to the world when the anti-feminism of the woman's movement sent me into a book-provoking rage. I wrote *The Fortunate Sex* in memory of the wonderful meaningful years when I was free, raising human beings, mistress of my arena."

* * *

EWING, Sherman 1901-1975

May 26, 1901—May 15, 1975; American philanthropist, lawyer, and playwright. Obituaries: *New York Times*, May 16, 1975.

* * *

FABRI, Ralph 1894-1975

April 23, 1894—February 12, 1975; Hungarian-born American artist, educator, editor, and author of instructional books on art. Obituaries: *New York Times*, February 14, 1975; *AB Bookman's Weekly*, March 3, 1975. (*CA*-19/20)

* * *

FAGERSTROM, Stan 1923-
(Stanley Scott)

PERSONAL: Born June 4, 1923, in Shaeffer, N.D.; son of Gustav and Ruth (Judkins) Fagerstrom; married Anita Mae Lolcoma, October 10, 1943; children: Daniel Gustav, Stanley Scott. *Education:* Attended Lower Columbia College, 1942-43. *Religion:* Protestant. *Home address:* P.O. Box 27, Silver Lake, Wash. 98645. *Office address: Daily News*, P.O. Box 189, Longview, Wash. 98632.

CAREER: Daily News, Longview, Wash., outdoor editor, 1946—, advertising director, 1960—; *Vancouver Columbian*, Vancouver, Wash., outdoor writer, under pseudonym Stanley Scott, 1965—. *Military service:* U.S. Army, Infantry, 1943-46; became sergeant; received Bronze Star with oak leaf cluster. *Member:* Outdoor Writers of America, Berkley Outdoor Council, Braniff Outdoor Council, Elks. *Awards, honors:* Three first place awards from Allied Dailies of Washington, 1957, 1958, and 1959, for excellence in sports writing.

WRITINGS: Catch More Bass, Caxton, 1973. Contributor to *Garcia Annual*, and to sports magazines including *Field*

& *Stream*, *Bass Master*, *Outdoor Life*, and *Angler*. Member of editorial board of *Angler*, 1974—.

WORK IN PROGRESS: Catch More Steelhead; *Me 'n Cousin Art*.

*   *   *

FAITHFULL, Gail 1936-
(Gail Faithfull Keller)

PERSONAL: Born November 20, 1936, in New York, N.Y.; daughter of George Edward (a lawyer) and Lucia (Turner) Faithfull; divorced; children: Bayard Faithfull Keller, Elizabeth Coburn Keller. *Education:* Rosemary Hall, student, 1951-54; Vassar College, A.B., 1958; Union Theological Seminary and Columbia University, M.A. (joint degree), 1960, currently graduate student. *Politics:* Democrat. *Home:* 1 Delsmere Ave., Delmar, N.Y. 12054. *Office:* Albany Academy for Girls, 140 Academy Rd., Albany, N.Y. 12208.

CAREER: Assistant to minister of Presbyterian church in Yonkers, N.Y., 1958-59; Rosemary Hall, Greenwich, Conn., instructor in ancient and biblical history, 1960-61; *Columbia Encyclopedia*, New York, N.Y., researcher for religious entries, 1963; Albany Academy for Girls, Albany, N.Y., assistant to headmaster, director of guidance, and teacher of English and history, 1969—. Ordained elder of Westminster Presbyterian Church, Albany, 1974; chairperson of executive council, FOCUS (an interdenominational coalition of churches), Albany.

WRITINGS: (Under name Gail Faithfull Keller) *Jane Addams* (juvenile), Crowell, 1971.

WORK IN PROGRESS: Research on educational trends and on ancient history, especially the ancient Near East.

SIDELIGHTS: Gail Faithfull writes: "I am still seriously considering going into the ministry, but my present occupation and preoccupation is girl's education, K-12."

*   *   *

FARABEE, Barbara 1944-

PERSONAL: Born December 24, 1944, in Moberly, Mo.; daughter of Fred Cleo and Wand Lee (Gipson) Haley; married Michael O. Farabee (an electrician, welder, and drag racer), April 14, 1963; children: Michael O., Jr., Stephen James. *Education:* Attends Indiana University, South Bend. *Politics:* "Feel that old, out-of-date laws should be revised, instead of making new useless ones." *Religion:* "Do not believe in organized religion." *Home and office:* 3231 Essex Dr., South Bend, Ind. 46615.

CAREER: Formerly factory worker; instructor, Slenderform Universal Health Spa, 1968; free-lance writer, 1968—. Organized and participated in poetry and music program for nursing homes, sponsored by South Bend Creative Arts Association. *Member:* Clover International Poetry Association, Creative Artists Guild (president, 1974), Fine Arts Society, Writers Correspondence Club, New Writers Club, South Bend Writers Club.

WRITINGS: A Young Woman's Secret Book of Erotic Love Poems, Celestial Arts, 1974. Work is anthologized in *Clover Collection of Verse*, and *No Longer Blank Book*, Altoan Press, 1974. Contributor to *Poet*, *Creative Arts Review*, and *International Brotherhood of Electrical Workers Journal*, and to newspapers. Associate editor of *Poet*, 1975—.

WORK IN PROGRESS: Chains Are Heavy to Carry,

poems; *And the Sun Does Shine Even on Rainy Days*, poems; *The Essence of Love*, poems; *Silk Nights and Satin Dreams*, poems; *I Do, and Other Vows of Love*, poems; *The Best Thing That Could Happen to (Some) Parents, Is Not to Have Kids*, non-fiction; *Biff McBreed, Where Were You When I Needed You?*, a novel; *The Split in the Middle*, a novel, perhaps in poem form.

SIDELIGHTS: Barbara Farabee writes: "It is difficult to determine exactly what motivated me to write. Probably Rod McKuen was the beginning force and influence. I do know, I wanted some purpose in my life and writing has given this to me. My perspective of life has broadened and I have a deeper insight of the values that are important to me. It has forced me to think in positive terms and clarified things I was unsure of. It's a personal challenge that promotes growth and is richly satisfying being able to relate to those I share my work with. Communication is far more important to me, with my readers, than writing a sophisticated piece of work that can take hours to find the underlying message, or meaning."

BIOGRAPHICAL/CRITICAL SOURCES: South Bend Tribune, August 22, 1974.

*   *   *

FARBER, Seymour M(organ) 1912-

PERSONAL: Born June 3, 1912, in Buffalo, N.Y.; son of Simon and Matilda (Goldstein) Farber; married Geraldine Ossman; children: Burt, Margaret, Roy. *Education:* University of Buffalo, B.A., 1931; Harvard University, M.D., 1939. *Residence:* San Francisco, Calif. *Office:* University of California, San Francisco, Calif. 94143.

CAREER: Newton Hospital, Newton, Mass., intern, 1939-40; Gaylord Hospital, Wallingford, Conn., resident, 1940-42; University of California, San Francisco, instructor in medical department (now School of Medicine), 1942-47, assistant professor, 1947-53, associate professor, 1953-61, clinical professor of medicine, 1961—, special assistant for academic affairs to the president, 1964—, dean of educational services, 1963-70, dean of continuing education in health sciences, 1970-73, vice-chancellor for public programs and continuing education, 1973—. Private practice as physician specializing in chest diseases, San Francisco, 1946—; chief of University of California Tuberculosis and Chest Service, San Francisco General Hospital, 1945-65, senior consultant, 1965—. Lecturer at School of Public Health, University of California, Berkeley, 1948—; lecturer at university medical schools and medical societies in Japan, 1958, and in United States and other countries. Special consultant, National Institutes of Health, 1958-60; national consultant emeritus to surgeon general, U.S. Air Force; member of President's Commission on the Status of Women, 1962-63. Member of board of directors, Sun Valley Center for the Arts and Humanities; academic member of international board of governors, Technion Institute of Haifa (Israel); executive director and vice-president, Howard Florey Medical Foundation.

MEMBER: American College of Chest Physicians (president, 1959-60), American Medical Association, American Society of Internal Medicine, American Federation for Clinical Research, American Society of Cytology, American Cytologic Association, American College of Cardiology, International Academy of Pathology, International Association of Medical Museums, Association of American Medical Colleges, American Geriatrics Society, American Association for the Advancement of Science, Pan American Medical Association, New York Academy of Sciences (regional adviser), California Medical Association, American Physicians Fellowship for Israel Medical Association, Commonwealth Club.

AWARDS, HONORS: D.H.L., St. Mary's College of California, 1964; First Honor Award for Creativity from Division of Conferences and Institutes, National University Extension Association, 1969, for development of multidisciplinary symposia in the health sciences and humanities.

WRITINGS: (With others) *Cytologic Diagnosis of Lung Cancer*, C. C Thomas, 1950; *Lung Cancer*, C. C Thomas, 1954.

Editor: (With Roger H. L. Wilson) *The Air We Breathe: A Study of Man and His Environment*, C. C Thomas, 1961; (with Wilson) *Man and Civilization: Control of the Mind*, McGraw, 1962; (with Wilson) *Man and Civilization: Conflict and Creativity*, McGraw, 1963; (with Wilson) *Man and Civilization: The Potential of Woman*, McGraw, 1963; (with Wilson and Piero Mustacchi) *California and the Challenge of Growth: Man Under Stress*, University of California Press, 1964; (with Wilson and Mustacchi) *Man and Civilization: The Family's Search for Survival*, McGraw, 1965; (with Wilson) *The Challenge to Women: The Biologic Avalanche*, Basic Books, 1966; (with Wilson) *Food and Civilization*, C. C Thomas, 1967; (with Wilson) *Sex Education and the Teen-Ager*, Diablo, 1967; (with Wilson) *Teen-Age Marriage and Divorce*, Diablo, 1967; (with Geraldine O. Browning and J. A. Alioto) *Teilhard de Chardin: In Quest of the Perfection of Man*, Fairleigh Dickinson University Press, 1973.

Contributor: Burgess L. Gordon, editor, *Clinical Cardiopulmonary Physiology*, Grune, 1957, 2nd edition, 1960; Boris M. Fried, editor, *Tumors of the Lung and Mediastinum*, Lea & Febiger, 1958; David M. Greenberg and H. A. Harper, editors, *Enzymes in Health and Disease*, C. C Thomas, 1960; David M. Spain, *Diagnosis of Bronchogenic Cardinoma: Medical and Cytologic*, Grune, 1960; Andrew L. Banyai and E. R. Levine, editors, *Dyspnea: Diagnosis and Treatment*, F. A. Davis, 1963; Nancy L. Wilson, editor, *Obesity*, F. A. Davis, 1969.

Contributor of about ninety papers and articles to medical journals. Member of editorial board, *Diseases of the Chest*, 1948-61; consulting editor, *General Practice*, 1958; member of board of consultants, *Pre-Med Journal*, 1965—.

AVOCATIONAL INTERESTS: Mountaineering and reading.

*   *   *

FARLEY, Miriam Southwell   1907(?)-1975

1907(?)—March 4, 1975; American editor and writer. Obituaries: *Publishers Weekly*, April 7, 1975.

*   *   *

FARMER, Charles J(oseph)   1943-

PERSONAL: Born November 12, 1943, in New York, N.Y.; son of Charles A. (an accountant) and Viola (Dauria) Farmer; married Kathleen Usher (a free-lance writer), June 6, 1972. *Education:* Kansas State University, B.A., 1966. *Politics:* Independent. *Religion:* Roman Catholic. *Home and office address:* P.O. Box 1227, Jackson Hole, Wyo. 83001.

CAREER: Free-lance outdoor writer and photographer. Advertising manager for Squire Publications, 1966-67;

writer and photographer for Wyoming Game and Fish Department, 1967-69. *Military service:* U.S. Army National Guard, 1966-72. *Member:* Outdoor Writers Association of America, Sigma Delta Chi.

WRITINGS: Creative Fishing, Stackpole, 1973; (editor with wife, Kathleen Farmer) *Campground Cooking*, Digest Books, 1974; *Backpack Fishing*, J. Philip O'Hara, 1975.

*   *   *

FARMER, Gary R(ay)   1923-

PERSONAL: Born December 4, 1923, in Broken Bow, Neb.; son of Arthur (a farmer) and Louise Farmer; married Margaret Cecelia Simmons (an economist), July 2, 1949; children: Bruce Arthur. *Education:* Attended University of Nebraska, 1940-42; Colorado State University, D.V.M., 1945; Reed College, postdoctoral study, 1958. *Politics:* American Conservative Union. *Religion:* Protestant. *Home and office:* 7315 Northwest Kaiser Rd., Portland, Ore. 97229.

CAREER: U.S. Army, Veterinarian, career officer, 1946-66; retiring as lieutenant colonel; Oregon State Board of Health, Portland, director of radiation section, 1966-69; Chem-Nuclear Systems, Inc., Portland, Ore., manager, and vice-president of Western Division, 1969-72; Gary Farmer Consulting Group, Portland, Ore., consultant in nuclear radiation and ecological sciences, 1972—. *Member:* International Radiation Protection Association, Society of Nuclear Medicine, American Nuclear Society, Health Physics Society, American Veterinary Medical Association, American College of Veterinary Toxicologists. *Awards, honors*—Military: Humane Action Medal, El Condor de los Andes from Bolivia, Hoskins Award from Walter Reed Army Institute of Research. Civilian: Commendation from Atomic Energy Commission.

WRITINGS: Unready Kilowatts: The High-Tension Politics of Ecology, Open Court, 1975. Contributor to *Science*.

WORK IN PROGRESS: Research on global aspects of food and agriculture production and resource potentials, on energy resources, on exploitation, on economics, and on environmental extremism.

AVOCATIONAL INTERESTS: Travel, hunting, fishing, skiing, photography, mechanics, farming.

*   *   *

FARQUHAR, Francis P(eloubet)   1887-1975

December 31, 1887—1975; American conservationist, certified public accountant, lecturer, mountaineer, book collector, bibliographer, and author. Obituaries: *AB Bookman's Weekly*, March 3, 1975. (*CA*-19/20)

*   *   *

FAUCHER, W. Thomas   1945-

PERSONAL: Born October 4, 1945, in Boise, Idaho; son of Bernard A. (a businessman) and Florence (Kern) Faucher. *Education:* Attended Mt. Angel Seminary, 1963-65; St. Thomas Seminary, Kenmore, Wash., B.A., 1967; Catholic University of America, S.T.B., 1970, M.A., 1971. *Home:* 811 South Latah, Boise, Idaho.

CAREER: Ordained Roman Catholic priest; associate pastor, St. Anthony Parish, Pocatello, Idaho, 1971-72, Sacred Heart Parish, Boise, Idaho, 1972—. Visiting professor of practical liturgy, Mt. Angel Seminary, 1975—. Chairman, Idaho Catholic Liturgical Commission. Federation of

Diocesian Liturgical Commissions, member of board of directors, president of Region XII.

WRITINGS: (With Ione C. Neiland) *Touching God*, Ave Maria Press, 1975.

WORK IN PROGRESS: Liturgy for the elderly, for junior and senior high school students, and for rural America.

* * *

FAUST, Clarence H(enry) 1901-1975

March 11, 1901—May 20, 1975; American educator, clergyman, and author. Obituaries: *New York Times*, May 22, 1975; *Current Biography*, August, 1975.

* * *

FAY, John 1921-

PERSONAL: Born September 12, 1921, in Sao Paulo, Brazil; son of Samuel Ernest (a railway officer) and Mabel Mary (Foulger) Fay; married Catherine Elizabeth Hutchinson (a hotel proprietress), November 4, 1961. *Education:* Attended Bradfield College, 1935-40. *Politics:* Conservative. *Religion:* Agnostic. *Home and office:* Pickett Witch House Hotel, 100 Ilchester Rd., Yeovil, Somerset, England.

CAREER: British European Airways, Peterborough and Liverpool, England, pilot in helicopter unit, 1947-52; Westland Aircraft Ltd., Yeovil, England, test pilot, 1952-68; Pickett Witch House Hotel, Yeovil, England, proprietor, 1968—. *Military service:* Royal Navy, 1940-46; became lieutenant. *Member:* Royal Aeronautical Society (associate fellow). *Awards, honors:* Queen's Commendation award, 1967, for services to British helicopters.

WRITINGS: *The Helicopter and How It Flies*, Pitman, 1954, 3rd edition, Beekman Publishers, 1975. Contributor to *Flight, Aeroplane, American Helicopter*.

AVOCATIONAL INTERESTS: Music, gardening, photography.

* * *

FAY, Peter Ward 1924-

PERSONAL: Born December 3, 1924, in Paris, France; son of Willis and Joan (Peters) Fay; married Phyllis Ford, September, 1950 (divorced, 1955); married Mariette Robertson, December 21, 1957; children: (first marriage) Jennifer; (second marriage) Todor, Lisa, Jonathan, Benjamin. *Education:* Harvard University, B.A. (summa cum laude), 1947, Ph.D., 1954; Balliol College, Oxford, B.A., 1949. *Home:* 400 Churchill Rd., Sierra Madre, Calif. 91024. *Office:* Humanities Division, California Institute of Technology, Pasadena, Calif. 91125.

CAREER: Williams College, Williamstown, Mass., instructor in history, 1951-55; California Institute of Technology, Pasadena, assistant professor, 1955-60, associate professor, 1960-70, professor of history, 1970—. Visiting professor at Indian Institute of Technology, Kanpur, 1964-66. *Military service:* U.S. Army, Field Artillery, 1943-46; served in Italy; became first lieutenant. *Member:* American Historical Association, Association of Asian Studies, Signet Society. *Awards, honors:* Rhodes scholarship, 1947-49, for study at Oxford University.

WRITINGS: *The Opium War: 1840-1842*, University of North Carolina Press, 1975. Contributor to scholarly journals.

WORK IN PROGRESS: A short biography of Prem Sahgal and Lakshmi Swaminathan, participants in the Free India movement of Subhas Chandra Bose; a biography of Robert Morrison, Protestant missionary to China; a narrative survey of Westerners in China, 1840-1950.

SIDELIGHTS: Fay writes: "Though I have lived a fair amount in western Europe, both as a child and adult, and feel most at home (as an historian) in nineteenth-century Europe, I am more and more interested in Europeans in Asia, particularly in the nineteenth century. . . ."

* * *

FEAGANS, Raymond (John) 1953-

PERSONAL: Born May 25, 1953, in Bremerton, Wash. *Education:* University of Washington, Seattle, student, 1971-73; Washington State University, B.S., 1975; Iowa State University, doctoral study, 1975—. *Office:* Department of Computer Science, Iowa State University, Ames, Iowa 50010.

CAREER: Iowa State University, Ames, teaching assistant in computer science, 1975—.

WRITINGS: *Railroad that Ran by the Tide*, Howell-North, 1972. Author of column in *Chinook Observer*, 1973-74. Contributor to *Sou'wester* and to regional newspapers.

WORK IN PROGRESS: *Puget Sound Ferryboats*, nonfiction.

SIDELIGHTS: Feagans writes: "Though my primary interest is computer science, I enjoy writing as a hobby because it complements my other interest in photography. In words and pictures I hope to preserve details of life that might otherwise be lost to the future."

* * *

FEEGEL, John R(ichard) 1932-

PERSONAL: Born November 16, 1932, in Middletown, Conn.; son of Fred B. (a member of the state police) and Eva (Lillian) Feegel; married Elaine Blanchet, February, 1959 (divorced, 1973); children: John, Jr., Mark Robert, Catherine, Elizabeth, Tom. *Education:* College of the Holy Cross, B.S., 1954; University of Ottawa, M.D., 1960; University of Denver, J.D., 1964. *Politics:* Republican. *Religion:* Roman Catholic. *Home:* 429 Champagne Lane, Brandon, Fla. 33511. *Office:* Feegel and Howard Laboratories, 3407 Bay to Bay Blvd., Tampa, Fla. 33609.

CAREER: Admitted to the Bar of Florida, 1967; certified pathologist by the American Board of Pathology, 1966; South Florida Baptist Hospital, Plant City, chief pathologist, 1969—, chief of staff, 1974—; chief medical examiner of Hillsborough County, Tampa, Fla., 1973—. Assistant clinical professor at University of South Florida Medical School, 1973. *Military service:* U.S. Public Health Service, 1965-67; became commander. *Member:* American Medical Association, American College of Clinical Pathologists, College of American Pathologists, American Academy of Forensic Sciences, Florida Medical Association, Florida Bar Association.

WRITINGS: *Legal Aspects of Laboratory Medicine*, Little, Brown, 1973; (contributor) Cyril Wecht, editor, *Legal Medicine Annual*, Appleton, 1973; *Autopsy* (novel), Avon, 1975. Contributor to *Yankee* and to scientific journals. Author of a monthly column, "Medical-Legal Notes," in *Hillsborough County Medical Bulletin*, 1972—.

WORK IN PROGRESS: A sequel to *Autopsy*; a detective novel.

AVOCATIONAL INTERESTS: Sailing, Mayan architecture, pistol shooting, fishing.

* * *

FEINBERG, Walter 1937-

PERSONAL: Born August 22, 1937, in Boston, Mass.; son of Nathan and Adeline (a clerical worker; maiden name, Weisberger) Feinberg; married Eleanor Kemler (a counselling psychologist), June 21, 1964; children: Deborah, Jill. *Education:* Boston University, A.B., 1960, A.M., 1962, Ph.D., 1966. *Home:* 1704 Henry St., Champaign, Ill. *Office:* Education Bldg., University of Illinois, Urbana, Ill. 61801.

CAREER: Boston State College, Boston, Mass., part-time assistant professor of educational philosophy, 1963-65; Oakland University, Rochester, Mich., assistant professor of educational philosophy, 1965-67; University of Illinois, Urbana, 1967—, began as assistant professor, now professor of educational philosophy, 1975—. Visiting lecturer at Interuniversity Post Graduate Center, Dubrovnik, Yugoslavia, 1974. Co-founder and co-director of Pontiac-Oakland Educational Assistance Team, 1965-67. *Member:* Philosophy of Education Society, Educational Studies Association, American Philosophical Association, Society for the Advancement of American Philosophy (member of executive council, 1972-74).

WRITINGS: Reason and Rhetoric: The Intellectual Foundations of Twentieth-Century Liberal Educational Policy, Wiley, 1975; (editor with Henry Rosemont, Jr.) *Work, Technology, and Education,* University of Illinois Press, in press. Associate editor of *Educational Theory,* 1967-75.

WORK IN PROGRESS: Research on the growth and distribution of knowledge.

* * *

FEINSTEIN, Sherman C. 1923-

PERSONAL: Born September 20, 1923, in New Haven, Conn.; son of Joseph and Bessie (Cohen) Feinstein; married, June 22, 1948; children: Joel Michael, Paul Louis. *Education:* Attended New York University, 1942-44; Chicago Medical School, M.B., 1948, M.D., 1949. *Address:* 741 St. Johns, Highland Park, Ill.

CAREER: Licensed to practice medicine in Illinois; certified by American Board of Psychiatry, 1958, and by American Board of Child Psychiatry, 1965. Intern at University of Arkansas Hospital, Little Rock, 1948, and at St. Peter's General Hospital, New Brunswick, N.J., 1948-49; University of Michigan, Neuropsychiatric Institute, Ann Arbor, resident, 1949-51; private practice in child psychiatry in Highland Park, Ill., 1953—. Institute for Juvenile Research, Chicago, Ill., staff psychiatrist, 1953-55; William Healy School, Chicago, clinical director, 1954-55; Michael Reese Hospital, Psychosomatic and Psychiatric Institute, Chicago, attending psychiatrist, 1955—, director of child and adolescent psychiatry training program, 1968—. Instructor in psychiatry at University of Illinois Medical School, 1953-56, and clinical associate professor of child psychiatry at University of Chicago, Pritzker School of Medicine, 1970—. Kathryn S. Hill Visiting Professor at University of Michigan, School of Medicine, 1972. Member of staff at Highland Park Hospital. Consultant to St. Charles Training School for Boys, 1953-55, Jewish Children's Bureau, 1960-69, Highland Park Community Nursery School, 1965—, New Trier High School, 1966-67,

Highland Park High School, 1967—, Lake Forest Elementary School District, 1967-73, Illinois State Psychiatric Institute, 1970-73, and North Suburban Special Education District, 1971—. Fellow of Institute for Juvenile Research, 1952-54. *Military service:* U.S. Army, Medical Corps, 1951-52; became captain.

MEMBER: International Association of Child Psychiatry and Allied Professions, American Academy of Child Psychiatry (fellow), American Psychiatric Association (fellow), American Orthopsychiatric Association (fellow), American Medical Association, American Society for Adolescent Psychiatry (president, 1969-70), American Association for the Advancement of Science, Illinois Psychiatric Association, Chicago Medical Association, Chicago Society of Adolescent Psychiatry (president, 1964-66), Chicago Council of Child Psychiatry. *Awards, honors:* World Health Organization travel and study fellowship, 1973.

WRITINGS: (With Peter C. Giovacchini and A. A. Miller) *Adolescent Psychiatry: Developmental and Clinical Studies,* Basic Books, Volume I, 1971, (with Giovacchini) Volume II, 1973, Volume III, 1974; (with E. Kalina, M. Knobel, and B. Slaff) *Psicopatologia y Psiquiatria del Adolescente* (title means "Adolescent Psychiatry and Psychopathology") Paidos, 1973. Contributor to professional journals. Managing editor of *Annals of the American Society for Adolescent Psychiatry,* 1969—.

* * *

FELKENES, George T(heodore) 1930-

PERSONAL: Born November 19, 1930, in Dayton, Ohio, son of Theodore (a barber) Felkenes; married Sandra Weeks Hartness (a professor), March 24, 1961. *Education:* University of Maryland, B.S., and J.D., 1961; California State University, Long Beach, M.A., 1968; University of California, Berkeley, D.Crim., 1970. *Home:* 1832 Highway 150, Birmingham, Ala. 35216. *Office:* Department of Criminal Justice, University of Alabama, University Station, Birmingham, Ala. 35294.

CAREER: Federal Trade Commission, Washington, D.C., attorney and investigator, 1961; Olmsted Air Force Base, Middletown, Pa., deputy chief of security and law enforcement, 1961-64; California State University, Long Beach, assistant professor, 1964-68, associate professor, 1968-69, professor of criminology, 1969-71, chairman of department, 1964-71; University of Alabama in Birmingham, professor of criminology, 1971—. Consultant to private and governmental agencies on criminal justice. *Military service:* U.S. Army, served in counterintelligence and law enforcement, 1951-57; became first lieutenant. *Member:* International Association of Chiefs of Police, American Society of Criminology, Academy of Criminal Justice Sciences (president, 1975-76), California Peace Officers Association, Phi Alpha Delta.

WRITINGS: (With Paul Whisenand and Harold Becker) *New Dimensions in Criminal Justice,* Scarecrow, 1968; (with Becker) *Law Enforcement: A Selected Bibliography,* Scarecrow, 1968; (with Whisenand) *Police Patrol Operations,* McCutchan, 1972; (with Whisenand and James Cline) *Police-Community Relations,* Goodyear Publishing, 1974; *Rules of Evidence,* Delmar Publishers, 1975; *The Criminal Justice System: Its Functions and Personnel,* Prentice-Hall, 1975; *Criminal Law and Procedure: Text and Cases,* Prentice-Hall, in press. Case decisions editor of *Journal of California Law Enforcement,* 1967-71.

WORK IN PROGRESS: A book on constitutional law for

Prentice-Hall; revising *Law Enforcement: A Selected Bibliography*, for Scarecrow; *Police Supervision: A Behavioral Approach*, for Justice Systems Development, Inc.

AVOCATIONAL INTERESTS: Travel, reading.

*   *   *

FELKER, Evelyn H. 1933-

PERSONAL: Born November 29, 1933, in Otsego County, Mich.; daughter of Hugh Theodore (a teacher) and Olive (a teacher; maiden name, Morrow) Harrington; married Donald W. Felker (a college professor), May 7, 1954; children: Donald, Linda, Ruth, Shirley, Jeffrey. *Education:* Geneva College, B.S., 1954; Purdue University, graduate study, 1973—. *Religion:* Reformed Presbyterian. *Home:* 822 North Salisbury St., West Lafayette, Ind. 47906.

CAREER: National Union Insurance Co., Pittsburgh, Pa., secretary, 1954-56; Indiana University, Bloomington, examination clerk, 1960-62. *Member:* Foster Parents Association. *Awards, honors:* Girl Scout Council special service award, 1972.

WRITINGS: Foster Parenting Young Children: Guidelines from a Foster Parent, Child Welfare League of America, 1974. Editor of *Foster Parents Association Newsletter*, 1975—.

WORK IN PROGRESS: Recruiting and Training Foster Parents; "Materials for In-service Agency Training of Foster Caseworkers."

*   *   *

FENDELL, Bob 1925-
(Dell Roberts)

PERSONAL: Born August 14, 1925, in Bayonne, N.J.; son of Stanton J. D. (a teacher) and Athie (Tucker) Fendell; married Elaine Tetelman, September 5, 1955; children: Susan Debra. *Education:* Rutgers University, B.L., 1946; graduate study at New York University. *Home and office:* 9 Hickory Ave., Oradell, N.J. 07649.

CAREER: Southeastern regional sports editor, International News Service, 1947-49; reporter, and editor of sports extra, *Journal of Commerce*, 1949-53; auto columnist, sports writer, and desk man, *World Telegram & Sun*, 1953-66; reporter, *New York World Journal Tribune*, New York, N.Y., 1966-67; editor, *Automotive News*, New York, N.Y., 1967; public relations account executive with Morrison-Gottlieb, Inc., New York, 1967. Coordinator of Society of Automotive Engineers' International Symposium on the Automobile. *Member:* International Motor Press Association (past president).

WRITINGS: Encyclopedia of Auto Racing Greats, Prentice-Hall, 1973; *The New Era Car Book and Auto Survival Guide*, Holt, in press. Writer and co-host for television program, "Wheels," New York, N.Y., 1957-58; writer for radio shows. Contributor to *Encyclopaedia Britannica Yearbook*; contributor to sport, automotive, and general periodicals (under pseudonym Dell Roberts from 1954-60), including *Sports Illustrated, Car & Driver, Road & Track, Family Weekly, True, New York Times, Gentleman's Quarterly*, and *Science and Mechanics*.

SIDELIGHTS: Fendell writes: "I think the world has come to the point where average people like me can do only two things—try to cope as best they can or laugh about things as often as possible. Anything I write will be directed to those areas. That is, anything I write that I care about."

FENNIMORE, Keith John 1917-

PERSONAL: Born November 20, 1917, in Parma, Mich.; son of Frank Hugh (a storekeeper) and Beatrice (Robinson) Fennimore; married Jean Joy Livingston, March 29, 1941; children: James Livingston, Robert Keith. *Education:* Albion College, B.A., 1939; University of Michigan, M.A., 1940; Michigan State University, Ph.D., 1956. *Politics:* Independent. *Religion:* Methodist. *Home:* 511 Perry, Albion, Mich. 49224. *Office:* Department of English, Albion College, Albion, Mich. 49224.

CAREER: Starr Commonwealth for Boys, Albion, Mich., director of education, 1941-42; Kemper Junior College, Boonville, Mo., instructor in English, 1942-44; University of Illinois, Urbana, instructor in English, 1944-46; Albion College, Albion, Mich., assistant professor, 1946-58, associate professor, 1959-73, professor of English, 1974—. Dean and registrar of Bay View Summer College of Liberal Arts, 1964-69. *Member:* National Council of Teachers of English, American Association of University Professors, Michigan College English Association (past president), Phi Gamma, Phi Mu Alpha, Sinfonia.

WRITINGS: Booth Tarkington: Man and Novelist, Twayne, 1974; *The Heritage of Bay View*, Eerdmans, 1975.

WORK IN PROGRESS: Early Fugitive American Fiction; Emerson at Kalamazoo; Selected Writings of Bronson Alcott; The Quest for American Literary Identity; Foundations of American Literature.

SIDELIGHTS: Fennimore writes: "More and more I see literature as a natural emanation from its times, hence my growing interest in matters historical and my increasing concern for preserving our literary identity."

*   *   *

FERGUSON, Chris(topher Wilson) 1944-

PERSONAL: Born March 5, 1944, in Danville, Va.; son of Eugene Wesley and Pauline (Wilson) Ferguson; married Jennifer Ann Adams, June 8, 1968 (separated); children: Melissa Erin. *Education:* Attended Pembroke State College (now University), 1962-63, North Carolina State University, 1963-64; University of North Carolina, B.A. from Chapel Hill branch, 1970, M.F.A. from Greensboro branch, 1973. *Residence:* Houston, Tex. *Agent:* Wendy Weil, Julian Bach Literary Agency, Inc., 3 East 48th St., New York, N.Y. 10017. *Office:* Department of English, University of Houston, Houston, Tex. 77004.

CAREER: Quantico High School, Quantico, Va., teacher of English, 1970-71; Janus House (home for delinquents), Chapel Hill, N.C., teacher, 1971-73; Heartwood Realty, Carrboro, N.C., salesman, 1973-74; University of North Carolina, Chapel Hill, lecturer, 1973-75; University of Houston, Houston, Tex., assistant professor of fiction writing, 1975—. *Military service:* U.S. Marine Corps, 1964-68; served in Vietnam.

WRITINGS: The Molting Season, Harper, 1974. Contributor of short stories and poems to *Greensboro Review* and other "little" magazines.

WORK IN PROGRESS: A novel.

*   *   *

FERGUSON, Suzanne 1939-

PERSONAL: Born August 13, 1939, in Pennsylvania; daughter of Edwin R. (a printer) and Enda (a teacher; maiden name, Reeves) Butts; married James H. Ferguson (a connoisseur), June 1, 1960; children: Cynthia. *Education:* Virginia Intermont Junior College, A.A., 1958; Converse College, B.A., 1960; Vanderbilt University, M.A., 1961; Stanford University, Ph.D., 1966. *Home:* 33 Erie Rd., Columbus, Ohio 43214. *Office:* 164 West 17th Ave., Columbus, Ohio 43210.

CAREER: University of California, Santa Barbara, assistant professor of modern literature, 1966-71; Ohio State University, Columbus, associate professor of modern literature, 1971—. *Member:* Modern Language Association of America, Midwest Modern Language Association, Society for the Study of Southern Literature. *Awards, honors:* Woodrow Wilson fellowship, 1960.

WRITINGS: The Poetry of Randall Jarrell, Louisiana State University Press, 1971. Author of essays and reviews on modern and Victorian literature.

WORK IN PROGRESS: A history of formal change in the English short story in the nineteenth and early twentieth centuries.

* * *

FETROS, John G. 1932-

PERSONAL: Born August 19, 1932, in Billings, Mont.; son of Gust (a chef) and Angelina (Pappastamatakis) Fetros. *Education:* University of California, Berkeley, B.S., 1954; University of Southern California, M.L.S., 1964. *Politics:* Republican. *Home:* 3220 24th St., Sacramento, Calif. 95818. *Office:* San Francisco Public Library, Civic Center, San Francisco, Calif. 94102.

CAREER: U.S. Air Force, Sacramento and San Bernardino, Calif., supply and requirements officer, 1957-63; San Francisco Public Library, San Francisco, Calif., reference librarian, 1964-72, head of General Reference Department, 1972-74, head of acquisitions, 1974—. Chief editorial adviser to Newton K. Gregg (publisher), 1971-72. *Military service:* U.S. Navy, 1955-57. *Member:* American Library Association, Western Association of Map Libraries, Phi Beta Kappa, Beta Phi Mu, Beta Gamma Sigma.

WRITINGS: (Compiler and contributor) *Maps in the Local Historical Society*, Conference of California Historical Societies, 1973; *This Day in Sports*, Newton K. Gregg, 1974. Contributor to library journals.

WORK IN PROGRESS: Famous People and Their Horses; This Day at the Movies, completion expected in 1976.

AVOCATIONAL INTERESTS: Popular culture, serious American music, movies, thoroughbred racing as a sport.

* * *

FIE, Jacquelyn Joyce 1937-

PERSONAL: Born July 11, 1937, in Chicago, Ill.; daughter of Peter Carl and Dorothy (Berndt) Klein; married John J. Uphues, June 18, 1960 (divorced, 1970); married Larry Eugene Fie (sports equipment manufacturing executive), July 24, 1971; children: (first marriage) Jeffrey, Christopher. *Education:* Northwestern University, B.S. in Ed. (magna cum laude), 1959. *Religion:* Roman Catholic. *Home:* 1205 Southfield Dr., Jefferson, Iowa 50129. *Office address:* United States Gymnastic Federation, Box 312, Jefferson, Iowa 50129.

CAREER: High school teacher of physical education in Evanston, Ill., 1959-62; Northwestern University, Evanston, Ill., teacher of physical education, 1962; Evanston

Parks & Recreation, Evanston, Ill., teacher of physical education, 1963-68; high school teacher of physical education in Niles, Ill., 1970-71. Licensed international gymnastics judge, participating in Olympic Games at Mexico City, 1968, and Munich, 1972, and at World Games in Ljubljana, Yugoslavia, 1970; chairman of Citizens Savings Hall of Fame for Women's Gymnastics, 1972—; member of Greene County (Ill.) Republican Committee, 1974—; international affairs chairman of St. Joseph's Guild, 1974-75. *Member:* American Association for Health, Physical Education and Recreation, United States Gymnastic Federation, America Turners, National Association of Women's Gymnastic Judges, Midwest Olympians (secretary, 1957-65; vice-president, 1966-72), Alpha Lambda Delta, Pi Lambda Theta. *Awards, honors:* Achievement & contribution award from Athletic Institute, 1968.

WRITINGS: Rules & Policies of USGF Women's Gymnastics, United States Gymnastic Federation, 1968; (with others) *Judging and Coaching Women's Gymnastics*, Mayfield Publishing, 1972; *Judging Guide 1972*, United States Gymnastic Federation, 1972. Advisor and contributor to *Gymnastic Guide* of National Association of Girl's and Women's Sports, 1967—.

WORK IN PROGRESS: Revising *Judging and Coaching Women's Gymnastics.*

SIDELIGHTS: Jacquelyn Fie was a member of the U.S. Olympic gymnastic team in 1956. She is competent in French and German.

* * *

FIELD, Dawn Stewart 1940-

PERSONAL: Born November 23, 1940, in Fairmont, W.Va.; daughter of George Harrap and Louise (Thorn) Stewart; married H. Robert Field (an attorney), October 1, 1966; children: Robert Stuart, Mary-Louise Elizabeth Jennings. *Education:* Marietta College, student, 1958-59; University of Kentucky, A.B., 1962; Harvard University, A.M., 1964. *Home:* 7818 Ridgecrest Dr., Alexandria, Va. 22308.

CAREER: Library of Congress, Washington, D.C., supervisor of a Russian translating unit working with material in the fields of biology and medicine, 1964-69; writer, 1969—. *Member:* Phi Beta Kappa. *Awards, honors:* Woodrow Wilson fellowship, 1962-63, Ford Foundation fellowship, 1963-64.

WRITINGS: Luise (first volume of a series of historical novels), Putnam, 1974.

WORK IN PROGRESS: Corotoman Creek, a historical romance and suspense novel continuing the series begun with *Luise.*

AVOCATIONAL INTERESTS: International travel, books, music, animals, flowers, painting, old houses, cooking, country life, ballet, genealogy, archaeology, domestic architecture, collecting miniature period furniture and costume paper dolls, gardening, interior decoration, crewel embroidery, walking, social history, British history, English literature.

* * *

FIELD, Dick 1912-

PERSONAL: Born October 18, 1912, in Winson, Gloucestershire, England; son of Walter W. (a carpenter and wheelwright) and Elizabeth Lily (Davis) Field; married Molly

Clapham (an embroidery artist), July 25, 1939; children: Jenny Elisabeth (Mrs. Ulrich Hofer). *Education:* Attended College of Art, Cheltenham, Gloucestershire, 1931-33; Royal College of Art, art teacher's diploma, 1937. *Religion:* Deist. *Home:* 77 Vicarage Rd., Marsworth, Tring, Hertfordshire HP23 4LU, England.

CAREER: Teacher of art and craft in the secondary schools of Hertford, England, 1937-41, 1946-47, and London, England, 1947; School of Art and Craft, Dewsbury, England, teacher of fine art, 1947-49; West Riding, Yorkshire, England, art adviser, 1949-53; College of Art and Design, Birmingham, England, head of department of teacher-training, 1953-62; University of London, Institute of Education, London, England, head of department of art, 1962-73. Governor of Shoreditch College, 1965-71, and Middlesex Polytechnic, 1971-73. *Military service:* Royal Air Force, 1941-46.

WRITINGS: (Contributor) James Britton, editor, *Studies in Education: The Arts*, Evans Brothers, 1963; *Change in Art Education*, Routledge & Kegan Paul, 1970; (contributor) Richard Whitfield, editor, *Disciplines of the Curriculum*, McGraw, 1971; (editor with John Newick) *The Study of Education and Art*, Routledge & Kegan Paul, 1973; (editor) *The Middle Ground: Theory and Practice in Art Education*, Routledge & Kegan Paul, 1975. Contributor to art education journals.

WORK IN PROGRESS: Research in theory and practice in art education.

AVOCATIONAL INTERESTS: Archaeology of British canals, canal-boating.

* * *

FIGUEROA, Loida
See FIGUEROA-MERCADO, Loida

* * *

FIGUEROA-MERCADO, Loida 1917-
(Loida Figueroa)

PERSONAL: Born October 6, 1917, in Yauco, Puerto Rico; daughter of Agustin (a cane cutter) and Emeteria (Mercado) Figueroa; married third husband, Jose Nelson Castro, November 14, 1953 (divorced, 1957); children: Eunice, Maria Antonia, Rebeca, Avaris (daughter). *Education:* Polytechnic Institute, San German, P.R., B.A. (magna cum laude), 1941; Columbia University, M.A., 1952; Universidad Central de Madrid, Ph.D., 1963. *Politics:* Independentist. *Religion:* Protestant. *Home:* A-17 Reparto Feliciana, Mayaguez, Puerto Rico 00708. *Office:* Department of Puerto Rican Studies, Brooklyn College of the City University of New York, Brooklyn, N.Y. 11210.

CAREER: Teacher in elementary and high schools, 1942-57; Guanica High School, Guanica, P.R., acting principal, 1947-55; University of Puerto Rico, Mayaguez, professor of Puerto Rican history, 1957-74; Brooklyn College of the City University of New York, Brooklyn, N.Y., professor of Puerto Rican history, 1974—. *Member:* Ateneo Puertorriqueno, Sociedad de Autores Puertorriquenos, Latin American Studies Association, Phi Alpha Theta.

WRITINGS: Acridulces (poems), Rodriquez Lugo, 1947; *Arenales* (novel), Ediciones Rumbos, 1961; *Breve Historia de Puerto Rico*, Editorial Edil, Volume I: *Desde sus comienzos hasta 1800*, 1968, Volume II: *Desde 1800 a 1892*, 1969, 4th edition, published in one volume, 1971, translation published in one volume as *History of Puerto Rico*

from the Beginning to 1892, Anaya Book Co., 1972; *Tres puntos claves: Lares, idioma, soberania*, Editorial Edil, 1972. Editor of *Atenea* (journal).

WORK IN PROGRESS: Third volume of the *History of Puerto Rico*; *Una Isla en el Mar de los Caribes y otros ensayos*, a book of essays; *La Historiografia en Puerto Rico.*

* * *

FINCH, Robert (Duer Claydon) 1900-

PERSONAL: Born May 14, 1900, in Freeport, Long Island, N.Y.; son of Edward and Ada Finch. *Education:* University of Toronto, B.A., 1925; attended University of Paris, 1928. *Home:* 4 Devonshire Place, Toronto M5S E21, Ontario, Canada. *Office:* Massey College, University of Toronto, Toronto 181, Ontario, Canada.

CAREER: University of Toronto, University College, Toronto, Ontario, lecturer, 1928-30, assistant professor, 1931-42, associate professor, 1942-51, professor of French, 1952-68, professor emeritus, 1970—, writer-in-residence, 1970-71. Poet, literary critic, painter. Member of board of trustees, Massey College, University of Toronto, and Leonard Foundation. *Member:* Royal Society of Canada (fellow). *Awards, honors:* Jardine Memorial Prize, 1924, for poetry; Governor General's Awards, 1946, for *Poems*, and 1961, for *Acis in Oxford*; Lorne Pierce Gold Medal, 1968; received LL.D., 1973.

WRITINGS: Poems, Oxford University Press, 1946; *The Strength of the Hills* (poems), McClelland & Stewart, 1948; *A Century Has Roots* (masque), University of Toronto Press, 1953; *Acis in Oxford, and Other Poems*, privately printed, 1959, University of Toronto Press, 1961; *Dover Beach Revisited, and Other Poems*, Macmillan, 1961; *Silverthorn Bush, and Other Poems*, Macmillan, 1966; *The Sixth Sense: Individualism in French Poetry, 1686-1760*, University of Toronto Press, 1966; (compiler with Eugene Joliat) *French Individualist Poetry, 1686-1760: An Anthology*, University of Toronto Press, 1971. Contributor to periodicals.

BIOGRAPHICAL/CRITICAL SOURCES: Canadian Literature, Volume XIII, 1962.

* * *

FINCKE, Gary (William) 1945-

PERSONAL: Born July 7, 1945, in Pittsburgh, Pa.; son of William A. (a janitor) and Ruth (Lang) Fincke; married Elizabeth Locker (an elementary teacher), August 17, 1968; children: Derek, Shannon. *Education:* Thiel College, B.A., 1967; Miami University, Oxford, Ohio, M.A., 1969; Kent State University, Ph.D., 1974. *Politics:* "Cynical." *Religion:* "Despairing." *Office:* Department of English, LeRoy Central School, LeRoy, N.Y.

CAREER: High school teacher in public schools in Freedom, Pa., 1968-69; Pennsylvania State University, Beaver Campus, Monaca, instructor in English, 1969-75; LeRoy Central School, LeRoy, N.Y., chairman of English department, 1975—. Tennis instructor, 1970—.

WRITINGS: Victims (poetry), Windy Row Press, 1974; *Emptied* (poetry), Branden Press, 1974; *Permanent Season* (poetry), Branden Press, 1975. Contributor of short stories, articles, and poems to *Twigs, Houston Forum, Chowder Review, Stone Country, Green's, Wisconsin Review, Bitterroot, Wind, Lake Superior Review*, and other journals.

WORK IN PROGRESS: The Fitzgerald Polka, a novel; poetry collections: *Eating a Late Dinner and Other Atrocities*, *Translating the Present*, and *Since I Have Not Yet Been Destroyed*; and a short story collection, *The Final Words of a Variety of People*.

SIDELIGHTS: Fincke, who says he would be a full-time tennis pro if someone would hire him, wrote: "I identify more with the perceptive student than the educated one, and this causes me great difficulty in maintaining an incentive for formal teaching. The recent change of job and location has brought a freshening, with luck, sustainable. As for my writing, I was isolated in a heavily-industrialized, tradition-oriented neighborhood, which allowed me to be left alone but also brought problems. I write in a variety of styles about a variety of subjects, but my attitude is generally dark. . . . I think I have just recently discovered how to write well, and this has brought a deluge of fresh material."

* * *

FINE, Benjamin 1905-1975

September 1, 1905—May 16, 1975; American educator, newspaper editor, and author of books on education. Obituaries: *New York Times*, May 17, 1975; *Washington Post*, May 18, 1975; *AB Bookman's Weekly*, July 7, 1975. (CA-5/6)

* * *

FINK, Joseph 1915-

PERSONAL: Born June 24, 1915, in New York, N.Y.; son of Louis M. (a businessman) and Augusta (Schuman) Fink; married Sylvia Klarfeld (a guidance counselor), September 8, 1940; children: Kenneth P. *Education:* John Jay College of Criminal Justice of the City University of New York, B.S., 1966, M.P.A., 1971. *Home:* 2751 Palm-Aire Dr. S., Pompano Beach, Fla. 33060.

CAREER: New York Police Department, New York, N.Y., patrolman, 1942-52, sergeant, 1952-56, lieutenant, 1956-63, captain, 1963-67, deputy inspector, 1967-71; John Jay College of Criminal Justice of City University of New York, New York, N.Y., assistant professor of police science, 1970—. Has lectured in New York, Boston, St. Louis, Indianapolis, and Dayton, Ohio; consultant on police community relations, police administrative and personnel problems, and security. *Member:* American Academy for Professional Law Enforcement, B'nai B'rith. *Awards, honors:* New York public service award for professional achievement, 1969.

WRITINGS: (Author of preface) *Reform in the Administration of Justice*, AMS Press, 1972; (with Lloyd Sealy) *The Community and the Police: Conflict or Cooperation*, Wiley, 1974. Contributor to criminology and psychiatry journals.

SIDELIGHTS: As a police commander, Fink's beat was the bohemian quarter of Manhattan's Lower East Side. He called his job preventive enforcement. There, using "community empathy," he gained a reputation for handling discontented young people.

BIOGRAPHICAL/CRITICAL SOURCES: Village Voice, June 8, 1967; *New York Daily News*, September 2, 1968; *Time*, November 8, 1968; *New York Times*, August 24, 1969; *El Tiempo*, November 23, 1969; *Reader's Digest*, November, 1969; Arthur Niederhoffer and Alexander B. Smith, *New Directions in Police Community Relations*, Rinehart Press, 1974.

FINK, Stevanne Auerbach
See AUERBACH, Stevanne

* * *

FISHMAN, Charles 1942-

PERSONAL: Born July 10, 1942, in Freeport, N.Y.; son of Murray (a color chemist) and Naomi (Ades) Fishman; married Ellen Marcie Haselkorn (a teacher), June 25, 1967; children: Jillana, Tamara. *Education:* Hofstra University, B.A., 1964, M.A., 1965. *Politics:* "Pro-life: people, animals, plants, earth." *Home:* 1704 Auburn Rd., Wantagh, N.Y. 11793. *Office:* Department of English, State University of New York at Farmingdale, Route 110, Farmingdale, N.Y. 11735.

CAREER: High school teacher of American, English, and world literature, 1965-70; State University of New York at Farmingdale, assistant professor of creative writing, 1970—. Poet-in-residence at Veterans Administration hospitals; member of Poets-in-the-Schools Program; co-founder and member of board of directors of Long Island Poetry Collective. *Member:* Poets and Writers, Wantagh Chess Club (founder and first president). *Awards, honors:* Third prize in Stephen Vincent Benet Narrative Poetry Awards from *Poet Lore*, 1969, for "Dust for Beetles"; first prize in creative writing contest from *Writer's Digest*, 1972, for "The Tallyers"; grant from America the Beautiful Fund, 1973.

WRITINGS: Aurora (poems), Tree Press, 1974. Contributor to more than fifty magazines, including *New York Quarterly*, *Epoch*, *New York Times*, *Dimensions in American Judaism*, *Mississippi Review*, and *Kansas Quarterly*. Co-editor of poetry magazine, *Xanadu*.

WORK IN PROGRESS: Portrait Without a Face, a book-length poem on the American Communist underground in the 1930's and on the murder of Jacob Fishman by the American Bund; *Hiding Out from the Saviors*, a collection of poems; poems based on nursery rhymes.

SIDELIGHTS: Fishman writes: "I gripe about much but grieve for the destruction of the natural environment/The surreal beauty and quietude of night is important to me/Human losses are my starting point for poetry." He has hitch-hiked twice across the United States in the early 1960's, and once across Europe, in 1966. *Avocational interests:* Organic gardening, photography, nature study.

* * *

FISK, Samuel 1907-

PERSONAL: Born March 24, 1907, in Oakland, Calif.; son of Henry A. (an educator) and Clotilde (Grunsky) Fish; married Hilda Riffel, June 12, 1955. *Education:* College of Idaho, B.A., 1929; graduate study at Biola College, 1930-32, and Gordon College of Theology and Missions, 1934-35; University of Arlington, M.A., 1937. *Home and office:* 6620 Cutting Blvd., El Cerrito, Calif. 94530.

CAREER: John Brown University, Siloam Springs, Ark., professor of Bible, head of department, and college pastor, 1934-37; Manila Evangelistic Institute, Manila, Philippines, director, 1937-39; pastor, First Baptist Church, Manila, 1939-41; pastor of Congregational church in Los Angeles, Calif., 1941-43; field representative, Association of Baptists for World Evangelism, 1943-46; missionary in Philippines, 1946-50; Los Angeles Baptist College and Seminary, Los Angeles, Calif., professor of missions and comparative religions, 1950-59; pastor of Baptist church in Long Beach,

Calif., 1959-61; Western Baptist Bible College, El Cerrito, Calif., associate professor of missions and New Testament, 1961-69; lecturer and author, 1969—. U.S. defense foreign expert, 1943-46. *Member:* General Association of Regular Baptist Churches.

WRITINGS: Divine Sovereignty and Human Freedom, Loizeaux Brothers, 1973; *Letters to Teresa,* Biblical Evangelism Press, 1973; *Confronting "Jehovah's Witnesses,"* Biblical Evangelism Press, 1975. Contributor to religious periodicals.

WORK IN PROGRESS: Divine Healing in the Light of Scripture; The Question of Calvinism among Baptists.

AVOCATIONAL INTERESTS: International travel.

* * *

FLACK, Dora D(utson) 1919-

PERSONAL: Born July 9, 1919, in Kimberly, Idaho; daughter of Alonzo Edmund and Iona (James) Dutson; married A. LeGrand Flack (an accountant), January 7, 1946; children: Marc Douglas, Lane LeGrand, Kent Dutson, Marlane (Mrs. Alan T. Smith), Karen, Marie. *Education:* Attended University of Utah, Brigham Young University, Utah State University, Latter-day Saints Business College. *Religion:* Church of Jesus Christ of Latter-day Saints. *Home and office:* 448 East 775 N., Bountiful, Utah 84010.

CAREER: Secretary to bank executive, Salt Lake City, Utah, 1938-46. Writer; lecturer on the drying, preservation, and storage of food. Professional entertainer and singer. Member of Governor's Committee for Employment of the Handicapped. *Member:* National League of American Pen Women, Soroptimists International, League of Utah Writers (board member; chapter president, 1972-74). *Awards, honors:* Awards from Utah State Institute of Fine Arts, League of Utah Writers, National League of American Pen Women.

WRITINGS: (With Vernice G. Rosenvall and Mabel H. Miller) *Wheat for Man: Why and How,* Bookcraft, 1952, 3rd edition, Woodbridge Press, 1975; (with Ida Watt Stringham) *England's First Mormon Convert,* Utah Printing, 1956; (with Louise Nielsen) *The Dutson Family History,* Utah Printing, 1957; *What About Christmas?,* Horizon, 1971; (contributor) Duane S. Crowther and Jean D. Crowther, editors, *The Joy of Being a Woman,* Horizon, 1972; *Fun with Fruit Preservation,* Horizon, 1973; (with Lula Parker Betenson) *Butch Cassidy, My Brother,* Brigham Young University Press, 1975. Contributor of articles and short stories to *Utah Historical Quarterly, American West, Organic Gardening and Farming, Guideposts, Friend, New Era, Ensign,* and other periodicals.

WORK IN PROGRESS: A biography of a blind youth; a biography set in England, and a book on Butch Cassidy, both for young people; a book on food drying, and a book on grains, both with accompanying recipes; several articles and stories.

SIDELIGHTS: Dora Flack told *CA:* "Since the publication of *Wheat for Man* in 1952, constant continuing questions have highlighted the need for specifics in the field of food storage and use of whole grain flour. In a world which faces shortages, homemakers must learn about mixing whole grains and the resulting high nutritional value and low cost....Drying is the economical route for economy of food value and space, hence my efforts in this direction."

FLAMHOLTZ, Eric 1943-

PERSONAL: Born February 2, 1943, in New York, N.Y.; son of Alexander (a salesman) and Pearl (Rossien) Flamholtz; married Diana Troik (a professor), June 20, 1964; children: Laurie. *Education:* Hunter College of the City University of New York, B.A., 1964; Washington University, St. Louis, Mo., M.B.A., 1966; attended University of Michigan, 1969. *Office:* Graduate School of Management, University of California, Los Angeles, Calif. 90049.

CAREER: University of Michigan, Ann Arbor, assistant project director at Institute for Social Research, 1967-69; University of California, Los Angeles, assistant professor of accounting, 1969-71; Columbia University, New York, N.Y., assistant professor of accounting, 1971-73; University of California, Los Angeles, associate professor of accounting, 1973—. *Member:* American Accounting Association, Academy of Management, Beta Gamma Sigma. *Awards, honors:* Post-doctoral fellowship from McKinsey Foundation for Management Research, 1969.

WRITINGS: Human Resource Accounting, Dickenson, 1974. Consulting editor for Dickenson.

WORK IN PROGRESS: Human Resource Management, publication by Wiley expected in 1977; *Principles of Accounting,* with wife, Diana Flamholtz, Wiley, 1981.

* * *

FLANDERS, Michael (Henry) 1922-1975

March 1, 1922—April 14, 1975; British lyricist, humorist, actor, radio and television commentator, and author. Obituaries: *New York Times,* April 16, 1975; *Current Biography,* June, 1975. (*CA*-7/8)

* * *

FLANNERY, Harry W. 1900-1975

March 13, 1900—March 11, 1975; American author and correspondent. Obituaries: *AB Bookman's Weekly,* March 24, 1975.

* * *

FLYNN, Charles F(rederick) 1949-

PERSONAL: Born October 7, 1949, in Boston, Mass.; son of Frederick Charles (a travel agent) and Margaret (an insurance adjuster; maiden name, Cushing) Flynn. *Education:* University of Chicago, B.A., 1971. *Politics:* "Goldwater conservative." *Office:* Post, Keyes, Gardner, Inc., 875 North Michigan Ave., Chicago, Ill. 60611.

CAREER: Post, Keyes, Gardner, Inc. (advertising agency), Chicago, Ill., copywriter, 1972—. *Member:* Chicago Film Festival.

WRITINGS: (With Todd McCarthy) *Kings of the Bs: Working within the Hollywood System,* Dutton, 1975. Contributor to *Chicago Sun-Times, Chicago Daily News, Journal of Popular Culture, Midwest,* and *Reader.* Writer of educational films.

WORK IN PROGRESS: Several feature-length film scripts.

BIOGRAPHICAL/CRITICAL SOURCES: Publishers' Weekly, January 27, 1975; *Kirkus Reviews,* April 1, 1975.

* * *

FOGLIO, Frank 1921-

PERSONAL: Born May 21, 1921, in Burgettstown, Pa.;

son of James Vincent and Angelina (Credo-Dio) Foglio; married Julia Clemence Cujas; children: Marilyn Joyce Foglio Crudo, Frank Anthony, Jr. *Education:* Attended Robert F. Sharpe Institute, Skadron School of Business, and Anthony Schools. *Politics:* Democrat. *Religion:* Assembly of God. *Home:* 3553 Syracuse Ave., San Diego, Calif. 92122. *Office:* Youth Crusades of America, Tustin, Calif. 92680.

CAREER: Pennsylvania Railroad, Pittsburgh, Pa., train control electrician, 1942-43; owner of a trucking company in Burgettstown, Pa., 1943-44; Weirton Steel Co., Weirton, W.Va., floating expediter, 1948-52; Swift & Co., Fontana, Calif., member of engineering staff, 1952-55; realtor in Fallbrook, Calif., 1956—. Regent of Oral Roberts University. President of council of Southern California Bible College; member of council of Evangel College. *Member:* Full Gospel Businessmen (international director), Light House for the Blind, Southern California Democratic Association, San Bernardino Cancer Society, Colton Chamber of Commerce.

WRITINGS: He God, Logos International, 1972.

WORK IN PROGRESS: The Little God Father, religious book; *Answers to Hey God; He Mom*, sequel to *He God*.

*   *   *

FOLEY, Doug 1942-

PERSONAL: Born August 17, 1942, in Providence, R.I.; son of Thomas Henry (an insurance agent) and Eleanor (Johnson) Foley; married Barbara Carol Sylvester (a secretary, writer, and singer), August 28, 1965; children: Dawn Celeste. *Education:* Wentworth Institue, A.S.E.E., 1963; Lowell Technological Institute, graduate study, 1965; Williams College, B.A., 1972. *Residence:* Southington, Conn.

CAREER: Consulting design engineer, 1965-67; administrator, clergyman, teacher, and cvangclist, 1970—. Founder and president of Trumpeteers Evangelistic Association.

WRITINGS: How Great I Was!, Whitaker House, 1974.

SIDELIGHTS: Foley writes that he was drawn into Christian work after being healed of multiple sclerosis, considered to be an incurable disease.

*   *   *

FOLEY, Vincent D. 1933-

PERSONAL: Born July 21, 1933, in New York, N.Y.; son of Arthur E. and Anna M. (Faulkner) Foley; married Ann M. Harrington (a reading specialist), August 16, 1974. *Education:* Cathedral College, A.B., 1955; Catholic University of America, S.T.B., 1959; Iona College, M.S., 1967; Boston University, Ph.D., 1970. *Home:* 85-50 169th St., Jamaica, N.Y. 11432. *Office:* Department of Counseling Education, St. John's University, Jamaica, N.Y. 11439.

CAREER: Catholic Charities, New York, N.Y., marriage counselor, 1964-66; Metropolitan Consultation Center, New York, N.Y., marriage and family counselor, 1966-67; Menninger Foundation, Topeka, Kan., fellow and member of counseling staff, 1967-68; Dr. White Community Center, Brooklyn, N.Y., director of marriage and family therapy, 1970—; St. John's University, Jamaica, N.Y., associate professor of counseling education, 1970—. Consultant on family therapy to North Shore University Hospital. *Member:* American Psychological Association, American Orthopsychiatric Association (fellow), American Group Psychotherapy Association, American Association of Mar-

riage and Family Counselors, American Association of Pastoral Counselors, Society for Family Therapy and Research, Eastern Group Psychotherapy Society.

WRITINGS: An Introduction to Family Therapy (American Association of Marriage and Family Counselors Book Club selection, 1975), Grune, 1974; (contributor) R. del Castillo and G. Goldman, editors, *In Counseling and Psychotherapy with Minority Groups*, C. C Thomas, 1975; (contributor) B. Ard and C. Callahan, editors, *Handbook of Marriage Counseling*, Science & Behavior Books, 1975. Contributor to journals. Consultant to Grune.

WORK IN PROGRESS: Research on cultural dimensions in family therapy; a book that will be a popularization of some basic concepts in family therapy, *A New Angle on an Old Triangle*.

AVOCATIONAL INTERESTS: Travel.

*   *   *

FOLSOM, Marvin Hugh 1929-

PERSONAL: Born March 12, 1929, in Vancouver, British Columbia, Canada; son of Donald Whitakter (a postal clerk) and Ellen Rose (Binns) Folsom; married Ruth Ellen Weinheimer, September 12, 1956; children: Susan, Cindy, Richard Lee, Cheryl, Robert Alan. *Education:* Brigham Young University, B.A., 1956, M.A., 1957; Cornell University, Ph.D., 1961. *Religion:* Church of Jesus Christ of Latter-day Saints. *Home:* 12 East 2050 N., Provo, Utah 84601. *Office:* Department of Germanic Languages, 322 McKay Building, Brigham Young University, Provo, Utah 84602.

CAREER: Brigham Young University, Provo, Utah, assistant professor, 1961-64, associate professor, 1965-68, professor of German and linguistics, 1969—. *Military service:* U.S. Army, Military Intelligence, 1952-54. *Member:* Linguistic Society of America, Modern Language Association of America, American Association of Teachers of German, Rocky Mountain Modern Language Association. *Awards, honors:* Alexander von Humboldt Foundation grant for research at Institut fuer deutsche Sprache, Mannheim, Germany, 1967-68 and 1974-75.

WRITINGS: The Syntax of Substantive and Non-Finite Satellites to the Finite Verb in German (based on doctoral thesis), Mouton & Co., 1966; (with Hans-Wilhelm Kelling) *Deutsche Aufsatzhilfe*, Brigham Young University Press, 1967; (with Kelling) *Wie man's sagt und schreibt*, Holt, 1972. Author or co-author of several workbooks in German. Contributor of articles and reviews to language journals. Associate editor of *Unterrichts praxis*.

WORK IN PROGRESS: Modern Biblical German.

*   *   *

FOOTE, Wilder 1905-1975

August 30, 1905—February 14, 1975; American journalist, U.N. press officer, and author. Obituaries: *New York Times*, February 17, 1975.

*   *   *

FORD, Arthur L(ewis) 1937-

PERSONAL: Born May 6, 1937, in Columbia, Pa.; son of Arthur Lewis (a painter) and Nellie (Logan) Ford; married Mary Ellen Keiser, August 30, 1958; children: Penny Louise, Peggy Marie, Jean. *Education:* Lebanon Valley College, B.A., 1959; Bowling Green State University,

M.A., 1960, Ph.D., 1964. *Politics:* Democrat. *Home:* 618 East Queen St., Annville, Pa. 17003. *Office:* Department of English, Lebanon Valley College, Annville, Pa. 17003.

CAREER: Heidelberg College, Tiffin, Ohio, assistant professor of English, 1964-65; Lebanon Valley College, Annville, Pa., assistant professor, 1965-70, associate professor, 1970-73, professor of English, 1973—. *Member:* Modern Language Association of America, American Association of University Professors.

WRITINGS: The Poetry of Henry David Thoreau, Transcendental Press, 1970; (editor with William K. Bottoroff) *The Works of Joel Barlow*, Scholars Facsimiles and Reprints, 1970; *Joel Barlow*, Twayne, 1971.

WORK IN PROGRESS: A critical study of Robert Creeley.

* * *

FORD, David
see HARKNETT, Terry

* * *

FORDIN, Hugh 1935-

PERSONAL: Born December 17, 1935, in New York, N.Y.; son of Lee (in luggage manufacturing) and Annette (Bernstein) Fordin. *Education:* Syracuse University, B.S., 1957. *Home:* 404 East 55th St., New York, N.Y. 10022. *Agent:* Curtis Brown Ltd., 60 East 56th St., New York, N.Y. 10022.

CAREER: Publisher and editor-in-chief of *Film-TV Daily*, 1968-70; writer. *Member:* Writers Guild of America. *Awards, honors:* All American Press Award, 1968, for work on *Film-TV Daily*.

WRITINGS: Yearbook of Motion Pictures and Television, Film-TV Daily, 1970; *Vocal Selections for "That's Entertainment,"* Big Three Music, 1974; *Jerome Kern: The Man and His Music*, T. B. Harms, 1974; *The World of Entertainment*, Doubleday, 1975; *Getting to Know Him: The Authorized Biography of Oscar Hammerstein II*, Random House, 1975.

WORK IN PROGRESS: All in the Family/The Fields Family: Lew, Herbert, Joseph, and Dorothy.

* * *

FORMAN, Marc A(llan) 1935-

PERSONAL: Born January 23, 1935, in Philadelphia, Pa.; son of David and Ida (Lubart) Forman; married Phyllis Taylor, September 5, 1959; children: Robert, Victoria, William, Alyssa. *Education:* Haverford College, A.B., 1955; University of Pennsylvania, M.D., 1959. *Home:* 312 Winding Way, Merion Station, Pa. 19066. *Office:* 2603 North Fifth St., Philadelphia, Pa. 19133.

CAREER: Licensed to practice medicine in Pennsylvania; certified by American Board of Psychiatry and Neurology, 1969; certified in child psychiatry, 1970. St. Christopher's Hospital for Children, Philadelphia, Pa., director of Child Psychiatry Center, 1970—; Temple University, Philadelphia, Pa., associate professor, 1971-74, professor of psychiatry, 1974—. *Military service:* U.S. Air Force, 1962-64; received Air Force Commendation Medal. *Member:* American Psychiatric Association, American Orthopsychiatric Association, Phi Beta Kappa, Alpha Omega Alpha.

WRITINGS: (With William Hetznecker) *On Behalf of Children*, Grune, 1974. Contributor to journals.

FORREST, Richard S(tockton) 1932-

PERSONAL: Born May 8, 1932, in Orange, N.J.; son of Williams Kraemer and Georgia (Muller) Forrest; married Frances Anne Reese, December 20, 1952 (divorced May, 1955); married Mary Brumby (an office manager), May 11, 1955; children: (first marriage) Richard; (second marriage) Christopher, Remley, Katherine, Mongin. *Education:* Attended New York Dramatic Workshop, 1950, and University of South Carolina, 1953-55. *Politics:* Democrat. *Religion:* Unitarian-Universalist. *Home address:* Cox Rd., Portland, Conn. *Agent:* Flora Roberts, Inc., 116 East 59th St., New York, N.Y. 10022.

CAREER: Playwright, 1955-58; Lawyers Title Insurance Corp., Richmond, Va., state manager, 1958-68; Chicago Title Insurance Co., Chicago, Ill., vice-president, 1969-72; free-lance writer, 1972—. Vice-president of Connecticut Board of Title Underwriters. *Military service:* U.S. Army, Rangers, 1951-53; served in Korea; became staff sergeant. *Member:* New England Land Title Association (vice-president). *Awards, honors:* Nominated for Edgar Award from Mystery Writers of America, 1975.

WRITINGS—Mystery novels: *Who Killed Mr. Garland's Mistress*, Pinnacle Books, 1974; *A Child's Garden of Death*, Bobbs-Merrill, 1975.

Plays: "Cry for the Spring"; "The Meek Cry Loud"; "The Sandhouse."

WORK IN PROGRESS: Death Wind, a suspense novel.

SIDELIGHTS: Forrest writes that he "spent early years as a playwright until growing family made business a necessity. Resigned position as vice president of major insurance company on fortieth birthday to write full time—why not?"

* * *

FOSTER, Charles William 1939-

PERSONAL: Born January 1, 1939, in Chattanooga, Tenn.; son of James William (a trucker) and Miriam (Crick) Foster; married Anne Brandon (a teacher), March 24, 1962; children: Melissa Ann, William Carl. *Education:* University of Chattanooga, B.S., 1961; East Tennessee State University, M.A., 1962; University of Alabama, Ph.D., 1968. *Politics:* "Agrarian with Jacksonian Democrat leanings." *Religion:* Methodist. *Home:* 820 Olive, Florence, Ala. 35630. *Office:* Department of English, University of North Alabama, Florence, Ala. 35630.

CAREER: University of North Alabama, Florence, assistant professor, 1968-70, associate professor, 1970-73, professor of English, 1973—. Member of Alabama Committee for Humanities and Public Policy. *Military service:* U.S. Army, Infantry, 1961; became second lieutenant. *Member:* American Dialect Society (chairman of Southeast section, 1974-75), National Council of Teachers of English, Tennessee Folklore Society, Tennessee Valley Old-Time Fiddler's Association, Phi Kappa Phi. *Awards, honors:* National Council of Teachers of English research grant, 1973—, for dialect study; named Tennessee Valley champion folksinger, 1972 and 1973; mid-South champion old-time banjo picker, bluegrass banjo picker, and folksinger, and champion folksinger of Yellow Daisy Festival, 1973; North Alabama champion of five-string banjo and folksinger, 1974; folksinging and banjo-picking champion of the Upper Cumberlands, 1975.

WRITINGS: (With Lee Pederson, Raven McDavid, and Charles Billiard) *A Manual for Dialect Research in the*

Southern States, University of Georgia Press, 1973, 2nd edition, University of Alabama Press, 1975; *The Phonology of the Conjure Tales of C. W. Chesnutt*, American Dialect Society, 1971. Contributor to *Devil's Box* and to folklore journals.

WORK IN PROGRESS: A dialect study of North Alabama; a script about Alabama's Bicentennial celebration, and "Doctor Foster and Friends," a script for a festival of music, both for public television; research on Medieval English, folklore, and traditional music; folklore projects in the greater Tennessee Valley.

SIDELIGHTS: Foster's interest in the Appalachian mountains and the insulated and independent mountaineer (or hill-man) is responsible for his work combining dialectology and folklore. He is currently attempting to fight the myth of cultural deprivation as applied to the folk of the Appalachians. He feels that his background—he was born and reared in the mountains in a near-microscopic community—enables him to move freely in the world of the folk, while his training gives him the necessary academic credentials to bring to the public the rich background of the hill people.

As credentials (or door-openers) for his work in rural Appalachia, Foster has his semi-professional status as a five-string banjo picker, and a singer. He has appeared on national television, and is well-known on the bluegrass festival circuit from Kentucky to Florida.

*   *   *

FOSTER, Earl M(asters)   1940-

PERSONAL: Born May 28, 1940, in Boston, Mass.; son of John J. (an insurance agent) and Etta (Masters) Foster; married Nancy R. Hall (a nurse), September 20, 1964; children: Tamar, Elana, Dara. *Education:* Tufts University, A.B., 1962; Boston University, M.B.A., 1964; New York University, Ph.D., 1969. *Home:* 14522 Southwest 75th St., Miami, Fla. 33143. *Office:* Southeast First National Bank of Miami, 100 South Biscayne Blvd., Miami, Fla.

CAREER: Boston University, Boston, Mass., assistant professor of finance, 1968-72; Southeast First National Bank of Miami, Miami, Fla., analyst, 1972, director of research, 1973, director of trust investments, 1974—.

WRITINGS: Common Stock Investments, Lexington Books, 1974. Contributor to *Financial Analyst Journal*, *Quarterly Review of Economics and Business*, and *Journal of Finance*.

WORK IN PROGRESS: Common Stock Valuation Models.

*   *   *

FOSTER, Herbert L(awrence)   1928-

PERSONAL: Born January 31, 1928, in Bronx, N.Y.; married Anita Greenberg (a teacher), December, 1952; children: Donna Fern, Andre Kim. *Education:* New York University, B.S., 1950, M.A., 1952; Columbia University, Ed.D., 1969. *Politics:* Democrat. *Religion:* Hebrew. *Home:* 100 Sedgemoor Ct., Williamsville, N.Y. 14221. *Office:* Department of Instruction, State University of New York at Buffalo, Buffalo, N.Y. 14214.

CAREER: Teacher of industrial arts and chairman of department, 1951-64, curriculum consultant, 1964-65, and assistant principal and dean, 1965-67, in the public schools of New York, N.Y.; State University of New York at Buf-

falo, lecturer, 1967-69, associate professor, 1969-75, professor of education, 1975—, director of Teacher Education Centers in Buffalo public schools, 1967-75. Director of Woodlawn Teacher Education Center, 1967-75; member of the board of directors of National Committee to Abolish Corporal Punishment in Schools, 1973—, and of Camp Fire Girls of Buffalo and Erie County, 1974—. *Member:* American Orthopsychiatric Association, Council for Exceptional Children (president of New York State federation, 1974-75), Council for Children with Behavioral Disorders, Association of New York State Educators for the Emotionally Disturbed, New York State Outdoor Education Association, Citizens Committee for Children of Western New York, Boy Scouts of America. *Awards, honors:* Research grants from Office of Urban Teacher Corps, New York State Education Department, 1969-71, and National Outward Bound, 1971.

WRITINGS: An Analytical Study of the Experienced Teacher Fellowship Proposals: 1966-67 Award Year (report), U.S. Office of Education, 1967; *Plans for Progress: Vocational Guidance Institute* (report), Niagara Falls Plans for Progress Council, 1968; (with others) *Development Team Report: DeVeaux School*, Deveaux School (Niagara Falls, N.Y.), 1973; *Ribbin', Jivin', and Playin' the Dozens: The Unrecognized Dilemma of Inner-City Schools*, Ballinger, 1974. Contributor to proceedings and papers; contributor to *Encyclopedia of Education*; contributor to education journals, including *Colleague* and *Phi Delta Kappan*.

WORK IN PROGRESS: Developing and gathering data for Jive Test IIA.

AVOCATIONAL INTERESTS: Outdoor education.

*   *   *

FOSTER, James C(aldwell)   1943-

PERSONAL: Born April 10, 1943, in Madison, Wis.; son of Mark A. (a physician) and Ruth C. (a physician) Foster; married Diane Mohn, September 2, 1966; children: Jeffrey, Justin. *Education:* University of Wisconsin, B.S., 1967; Cornell University, Ph.D., 1972. *Home:* 2012 East Duke Dr., Tempe, Ariz. 85283. *Office:* Department of History, Arizona State University, Tempe, Ariz. 85281.

CAREER: University of Alaska, Fairbanks, assistant professor of history and co-director of Labor Education Program, 1971-74; Arizona State University, Tempe, assistant professor of history, 1974—. Visiting assistant professor at University of New Mexico, summer, 1972. *Member:* American Historical Association, Pacific Northwest Labor Historians.

WRITINGS: The Union Politic: The C.I.O.'s Political Action Committee, University of Missouri Press, 1975. Contributor to *Labor History*, *Pacific Northwest Quarterly*, *Alaska Journal*, and *Arizona and the West*.

WORK IN PROGRESS: Since the War: The U.S., 1945-1975, a textbook; *The Other Federation: The Western Federation of Miners* (tentative title).

SIDELIGHTS: Foster writes: "I am an old fashioned labor historian trying to combine some of the interest and romance of the great American union movement with the demands of modern scholarship."

*   *   *

FOSTER, M(ichael) A(nthony)   1939-

PERSONAL: Born July 2, 1939, in Greensboro, N.C.; son

of Maurice G. and Helen Anthony (Voltz) Foster; married Judith Ann Forsythe, May 29, 1965; children: Matthew, Eugene. *Education:* Studied at Syracuse University, 1957-60, and University of Maryland in Europe, Karamursel, Turkey, 1961-62; University of Oregon, B.A., 1964. *Politics:* "Republican; economic conservative, civil rights liberal." *Religion:* Eastern Orthodox. *Home and office:* 209 Polifka Dr., Ellsworth Air Force Base, S.D. 57706.

CAREER: U.S. Air Force, 1957-62, 1965—; present rank, captain; holding positions as Russian linguist, 1957-62, intelligence officer, 1965-71, missile launch officer, 1971-75, weapons director, 1975—. *Member:* Sierra Club.

WRITINGS: The Warriors of Dawn (science fiction novel), DAW Books, 1975.

WORK IN PROGRESS: The Tessaract, a science fiction novel about a character from *The Warriors of Dawn*; *The Sky Is the Teacher of Form*, collected short stories.

SIDELIGHTS: Foster writes: "I have been a science-fiction reader since about age twelve. . . . I would now like to see a greater emphasis in SF be placed on more tradition . . . such as characterization, motivation, depth of back-grounds, subtle emotional effects. SF seems to be headed toward wooden characters and high-technology backgrounds. Since I worked in that kind of environment for fifteen years, I am well acquainted with its limitations, and do not consider the general run of modern SF either inspiring or instructive."

*   *   *

FOUT, John C(alvin) 1937-

PERSONAL: Born November 11, 1937, in Omaha, Neb.; son of Carl F. and Fannie E. (Mitchell) Fout; married Mary Jane Eaton, 1960 (divorced, 1972); children: Justine, Elizabeth, John. *Education:* University of Nebraska at Omaha, B.A., 1963, M.A., 1964; University of Minnesota, Ph.D., 1969. *Politics:* Democrat. *Religion:* Methodist. *Office:* Department of History, Bard College, Annandale-on-Hudson, N.Y. 12504.

CAREER: University of Nebraska, Omaha, instructor in history, 1967-68; University of Minnesota, Minneapolis, part-time instructor in history, 1968-69; Bard College, Annandale-on-Hudson, N.Y., assistant professor, 1969-72, associate professor of history, 1973—, chairman of department, 1974—. *Military service:* U.S. Army, Security Agency, 1959-62. *Member:* American Historical Association, Conference Group for Central European History, American Society of Church History. *Awards, honors:* Fulbright scholarship, 1964-65, for study in Heidelberg.

WRITINGS: (Editor) *German History and Civilization, 1806-1914: A Bibliography of Scholarly Periodical Literature*, Scarecrow, 1974. Contributor to *Journal of Church and State, Church History*, and *American Historical Review*.

WORK IN PROGRESS: Protestant Christian Socialism in Germany; A Collection of Documents on German Anti-Semitism; a second bibliography, on twentieth-century Germany.

AVOCATIONAL INTERESTS: European travel.

*   *   *

FOWLER, Charles B(runer) 1931-

PERSONAL: Born May 12, 1931, in Peekskill, N.Y.; son of Charles B. (a conductor) and Mabel (Ackerman) Fowler.

Education: State University of New York College at Potsdam, B.S.Mus.Ed., 1952; Northwestern University, M.M., 1957; Boston University, D.M.A., 1964. *Home and office:* 320 Second St. S.E., Washington, D.C. 20003.

CAREER: Vocal music supervisor in elementary schools in Rochester, N.Y., 1952-56; Mansfield State College, Mansfield, Pa., assistant professor of music, 1957-62; Northern Illinois University, DeKalb, associate professor of music, 1964-65; Music Educators National Conference, Washington, D.C., editor of *Music Educators Journal*, 1965-71, director of publications, 1970-71; journalist and consultant in the arts, 1971—. Vocal music supervisor in junior and senior high schools in Mansfield, Pa., 1957-62; guest professor at Indiana University, Ball State University, Mansfield State College, and Virginia Commonwealth University. Member of District of Columbia Commission on the Arts and Humanities, 1975, 1976.

MEMBER: Music Educators National Conference (life member), Music Critics Association, Society for Ethnomusicology, Educational Press Association of America (member of board of directors of District of Columbia chapter, 1969-71), Friends of the Kennedy Center, Kappa Delta Pi, Pi Kappa Lambda, Phi Mu Alpha Sinfonia (honorary life member). *Awards, honors:* Danforth grants, 1962-63, 1963-64; certificate for excellence in educational journalism, from Educational Press Association of America, 1970, for editorial "Facing the Music in Urban Education."

WRITINGS: (With Robert W. Buggert) *The Search for Musical Understanding*, Wadsworth, 1973; *The Arts Process*, Pennsylvania State Department of Education, 1973. Author of education column in *Musical America*, 1974—. Contributor to *Encyclopedia of Education*. Contributor of about thirty articles to music and education journals. Editor-in-chief, *Parks and Recreation*, and manager of publications for National Recreation and Parks Association, 1973-75.

SIDELIGHTS: Fowler writes: "I don't think I ever received more than a 'C' in any course in English in high school or college. . . . A person can't write until there is a viewpoint, something to be said, and a compunction to communicate it. Specialism can only go so far in establishing a unique viewpoint. This is a time for synthesis. We need the generalist to coordinate the specialists. . . . Basically I believe in a democratic art . . . I believe the arts are for all people and that the schools should provide opportunities for all students to study all the arts. . . . Education, by and large, is too cerebrally oriented with intellect too narrowly defined. We need to educate the feelings and sensibilities—the aesthetic mind—the affective as well as the cognitive domain." *Avocational interests:* Painting, theater, gardening, exercise, travel abroad.

*   *   *

FOWLER, Douglas 1940-

PERSONAL: Born October 12, 1940, in Springfield, Ill.; son of Russel Henry (a college professor) and Nadina (Boardman) Fowler; married Marilyn Stachenfeld, February 27, 1965; children: Nicholas Russel. *Education:* Cornell University, A.B., 1962, M.F.A., 1970, Ph.D., 1972. *Religion:* None. *Home:* 706 Lothian Dr., Tallahassee, Fla. 32303. *Office:* Department of English, Florida State University, Tallahassee, Fla. 32306.

CAREER: Florida State University, Tallahassee, assistant professor, 1972-75; associate professor of English, 1975—. *Military service:* U.S. Army, 1966-68; became sergeant.

Member: Modern Language Association of America. *Awards, honors:* Corson-Morisson Poetry Prize from Cornell University, 1962; Arthur Lynn Andrews short story prize from Cornell University, 1970; Forbes-Heermans Playwriting Prize from Cornell University, 1971.

WRITINGS: Reading Nabokov, Cornell University Press, 1974.

WORK IN PROGRESS: A critical book on Thomas Pynchon.

SIDELIGHTS: Fowler writes: "My interest is in demonstrating that certain imaginations always create the same story, no matter how they vary the surface."

* * *

FOX, H(enry) B(enjamin) 1910-

PERSONAL: Born October 19, 1910, in Granger, Tex.; son of J. S. (a banker) and Fannie (West) Fox; married Marie Price, January 14, 1937; children: Carol (Mrs. Larry Schmucker), John. *Education:* Southwestern University, B.A., 1932. *Address:* Route 3, Box 460, Taylor, Tex. 76574. *Agent:* Mrs. William W. Johnson, Box 37, Warner Springs, Calif. 92086.

CAREER: Madisonville Meteor, Madisonville, Tex., publisher, 1937-44; rancher in Taylor, Tex., 1945—. *Military service:* U.S. Army, 1943-44. *Awards, honors:* Crowell-Collier Award, 1939, for best U.S. weekly newspaper writer.

WRITINGS: The Two Thousand Mile Turtle and Other Episodes from Editor Harold Smith's Private Journal, Madrona, 1975. Contributor to *Saturday Evening Post, Collier's, Harper's, Reader's Digest*, and other periodicals. Contributor of syndicated humor column to weekly newspapers, 1950—.

* * *

FRANK, Janet
See DUNLEAVY, Janet Egleson

* * *

FRANKENBERG, Lloyd 1907-1975

September 3, 1907—March 12, 1975; American poet, critic, anthologist, and author. Obituaries: *New York Times*, March 14, 1975; *AB Bookman's Weekly*, April 21, 1975. (*CA*-2)

* * *

FRANKLIN, Alfred White 1905-

PERSONAL: Born June 2, 1905, in London, England; son of Philip (a surgeon) and Ethel (White) Franklin; married Ann Grizel Vaisey (a medical social worker), January 30, 1943; children: Juliet (Mrs. David Trotter), Victoria (Mrs. Timothy Bale), Thomas, Philip. *Education:* Cambridge University, Epsom College, M.A., 1933, Clare College, M.B., 1933, B.Ch., 1933; fellow of Royal College of Physicians, 1942. *Religion:* Anglican. *Office:* 149 Harley St., London W1N 2DE, England.

CAREER: Pediatrician in private practice in London, 1936—; St. Bartholomew's Hospital, London, intern, 1928-31, junior demonstrator of pathology, 1931-33, registrar in pediatrics department, 1933-37, assistant physician, 1937-39, physician in charge of Sector III Pediatric Department, Emergency Medical Service, 1939-46, physician, 1946-70, consulting pediatrician, 1970—. M.R.C. Research Fellow

in Pediatrics, Johns Hopkins Hospital, 1934-35. Chairman, Invalid Children's Aid Association, 1952-65; medical director, Word Blind Centre for Dyslexic Children, 1963-70; councillor, Royal College of Physicians, 1966-69, Osler Orator, 1971; member of attendance allowance board of Department of Health and Social Security, 1970—; convener, Tunbridge Wells Study Group on Child Abuse, 1972—. *Member:* British Paediatric Association (president, 1968-69), Royal Society of Medicine (president of pediatric section, 1970—), British Society for the History of Medicine (president, 1974-76), British Dyslexia Association, Osler Club (London; co-founder, 1928).

WRITINGS—Editor: *Selected Writings of Sir D'Arcy Power*, Clarendon Press (of Oxford University), 1931; *Selected Writings of Sir William Osler*, Oxford University Press, 1951, published as *A Way of Life*, Dover, 1953; *The Care of Invalid and Crippled Children*, Oxford University Press, 1960; *Geoffrey Keynes on His Seventieth Birthday*, Hart-Davis, 1960; *Word Blindness or Specific Developmental Dyslexia*, Pitman, 1962; *Saint Batholomew's Hospital Cancer Report, 1945-1952*, E. & S. Livingstone, 1963; *Children with Communication Problems*, Pitman, 1965; *Selected Writings of Lord Moynihan*, Pitman, 1967; *Concerning Child Abuse*, Churchill-Livingstone, 1975. Contributor to journals in his field.

WORK IN PROGRESS: Child Health Needs in England and Wales; Bio-Bibliography of Dr. Thomas Sydenham (1624-1689); Nicolas Lanier and Parmigianino.

* * *

FRANKLIN, Harold L(eroy) 1934-
(Chikuyo Alimayo)

PERSONAL: Born March 14, 1934, in Mobile, Ala.; son of Harold (a postman) and Julia (a sales clerk; maiden name, Nicholson) Franklin. *Education:* Philadelphia College of Art, graduate (honors), 1958. *Politics:* Black Nationalist. *Home:* 1315 South 53rd St., Philadelphia, Pa. 19143.

CAREER: Commercial artist; City of Philadelphia, Philadelphia, Pa., art director, 1961—. Free-lance art agent, Mulvey-Crump Associates, New York, N.Y., 1963—. *Military service:* U.S. Army, 1958-60.

WRITINGS: (Self-illustrated) *Which Way to Go*, EKO Publications, 1969; (under pseudonym Chikuyo Alimayo) *A Garden on Cement*, EKO Publications, 1973; (under pseudonym Chikyuo Alimayo; self-illustrated) *Once Around the Track*, EKO Publications, 1974.

WORK IN PROGRESS: A book on the juvenile gang situation in Philadelphia.

SIDELIGHTS: Franklin told *CA*: "My basic philosophy is that of separation. This is not a philosophy of hatred, but one of necessity. Blacks need a place (land) to correct values within us and values surrounding us that are causing all kinds of problems. This culture, which is primarily European, is much too racist and selfish for us to remain here. It puts undue pressure on black people, generating subconscious self-hatred that causes resentment and disrespect for everybody who looks like us.... The only medicine that will help us, is nature—living in the proper black environment for a long, long time. Blacks can then learn to relate to themselves again.

"My goal is to use my talents as an artist and writer to awaken those true integrationists, and those who wear various political disguises, to the urgency for black people to return to Africa to help restore us and our culture."

FRASER, Allan   1900-

PERSONAL: Born September 13, 1900, in Strathpeffer, Ross and Cromarty, Scotland; son of George and Wilhelmine (duta) Fraser; married Wilhelmine Shaw, August, 1929 (deceased); children: Derek, Robert, Peter. *Education:* University of Aberdeen, M.D. (honours), 1929. *Religion:* Scottish Episcopal. *Home:* 10 Kings Cross Ter., Aberdeen, Scotland.

CAREER: Rowett Research Institute, Aberdeen, Scotland, research worker, 1929-39; University of Aberdeen, Aberdeen, senior lecturer in agriculture, 1946-68. *Military service:* British Army, 1917-18; Royal Army Medical Corps, 1939-44, Arab Legion, 1944-45; became major. *Awards, honors:* George Hedley Memorial Award for outstanding service to the sheep industry, 1968; D.Sc., University of Aberdeen, 1950.

WRITINGS—Technical works; all published by Crosby Lockwood, except as indicated: *Sheep Farming*, 1937, 7th edition, 1965; *Growing Scotland's Food: The Farmers' Plight*, Oliver & Boyd, 1939; *Sheep Production*, Thomas Nelson, 1947; *Cobalt in Animal Nutrition*, Mond Nickel Co. (London), 1948; *Sheep Husbandry*, 1949, 3rd edition (with John T. Stamp) published as *Sheep Husbandry and Diseases*, 1957, 5th edition, 1969; *Farming for Beef*, 1950; *Beef Cattle Husbandry*, 1953, 2nd edition, 1959; *Animal Husbandry Heresies*, 1960, Philosophical Library, 1961; *Breeder and Boffin*, 1962; (editor) Arend Lourens Hagedoorn, *Animal Breeding*, 6th edition (Fraser was not associated with earlier editions), 1962; (with Tom Dodsworth and others) *In Search of Beef*, 1970; *The Bull*, Osprey, 1972, Scribner, 1974.

Novels; all published by W. & R. Chambers: *Herd of the Hills*, 1934; *Hansel Craig*, 1937; *Fiddler's Doom*, 1939; *Second Crop*, 1945.

Other: *Saighdear gu Chul* (title means "Every Inch a Soldier"; biography of Sir Hector MacDonald), Gaelic Book Council, 1975.

Contributor of articles to journals in his field, including *Farmers Weekly* and *Farmer and Stock-Breeder*.

AVOCATIONAL INTERESTS: Birds, Gaelic language and literature.

*   *   *

FRASER, Jane
   See PILCHER, Rosamunde

*   *   *

FRASER, Janet Hobhouse
   See HOBHOUSE, Janet

*   *   *

FRASSANITO, William A(llen)   1946-

PERSONAL: Born September 28, 1946, in New York, N.Y.; son of Americo Anthony (a jeweler) and Edythe (Totten) Frassanito. *Education:* Gettysburg College, B.A., 1968; State University of New York at Oneonta, M.A., 1969. *Politics:* Independent. *Religion:* Protestant. *Home:* 7 Broadway, Garden City Park, N.Y. 11040. *Office:* 333 Baltimore St., Gettysburg, Pa. 17325.

CAREER: National Park Service, licensed guide at Gettysburg (Pa.), Battlefield, 1966-68; Frassanito Bros., Huntington, N.Y., jeweler, 1973-75. *Military service:* U.S. Army Intelligence, 1969-71; became first lieutenant; received

Bronze Star. *Member:* National Stereoscopic Association, Animal Protection Institute of America, Friends of Animals, Committee for Humane Legislation, Photographic Historical Society of New York. *Awards, honors:* Pennsylvania Commandery and War Library and Museum Award, 1968, for research in military history.

WRITINGS: Gettysburg: A Journey in Time, Scribner, 1975.

WORK IN PROGRESS: A companion volume to *Gettysburg* which focuses on early war photography, *Antietam: The War Comes Home.*

SIDELIGHTS: Frassanito told *CA:* "I am interested in the early photograph as an historical document: a moment captured, preserved and transported through time. As a document the historical photograph provides a unique means for making the past 'come alive' and thereby enhances the relevancy of the past to the present."

BIOGRAPHICAL/CRITICAL SOURCES: Publishers' Weekly, April 28, 1975; *Newsday*, May 2, 1975.

*   *   *

FRAYDAS, Stan   1918-

PERSONAL: Born September 4, 1918, in Betecom, Belgium; came to United States in 1940; son of Maurice (a dentist) and Helen (Gerson) Fraydas; married Miriam Schloss, 1936; children: May Fraydas Giesen. *Education:* Academie Royale des Beaux Arts de Bruxelles, graduate. *Home:* 34 East Stanton Ave., Baldwin, N.Y. 11510.

CAREER: Free-lance cartoon illustrator for leading advertising agencies, magazines, and newspapers, 1940—. Instructor at New York University, 1961—; designer and consulting art director for book publishers. *Military service:* U.S. Army, 1943. *Member:* American Institute of Graphic Artists, Art Directors Club (New York).

WRITINGS: Graphic Humor: A Complete Course in Cartooning, Reinhold, 1963; *Professional Cartooning*, Krieger, 1972; *Find It* (juvenile), Golden Books, 1974. Illustrator of children's books. Contributor of articles and editorial cartoons to magazines, including *Better Editing, Life, Look, Cosmopolitan, Ladies' Home Journal*, and *Seventeen*, and to newspapers. Contributor of Christmas card designs to American Artists Group, Inc.

WORK IN PROGRESS: Self-illustrated children's books, for Western Publishing.

SIDELIGHTS: Fraydas writes: "As an artist and author, I think I have a predilection for sharing my experience with younger and less experienced people. I consider all my books as primarily educational. The same applies to my painting and political cartoons (1942-1950)."

*   *   *

FREEMAN, Margaret C(ooper)   1913-

PERSONAL: Born August 9, 1913, in San Francisco, Calif.; daughter of Joseph Welles (a rancher) and Marguerite (Horr) Cooper; married· William H. Freeman (a textbook publisher), September 23, 1961. *Education:* University of California, Berkeley, A.B., 1935. *Politics:* "Republican but not always." *Religion:* Episcopalian. *Home:* 1730 Kearny St., San Francisco, Calif. 94133. *Office:* Freeman, Cooper & Co., 1736 Stockton St., San Francisco, Calif. 94133.

CAREER: Freeman, Cooper & Co., San Francisco, Calif., editor, 1964—. Partner in Silver Ridge Ranch, Oroville, Calif., 1959—.

WRITINGS: (With Charles F. Park, Jr.) *Affluence in Jeopardy*, Freeman, Cooper, 1968; (with Park) *Earthbound* (nonfiction), Freeman, Cooper, 1975. Contributor to *Science Journal*.

SIDELIGHTS: Margaret Freeman owns with her brother a ranch on which they "grow olives and run a few head of cattle.

* * *

FREGLY, Bert 1922-

PERSONAL: Born August 19, 1922, in Patton, Pa.; son of Alphonse Francis (a merchant) and Mary (Vaccario) Fregly; married Violet Elizabeth Milovich, April 26, 1952 (died October 7, 1957). *Education:* San Diego City College, A.A., 1966; San Diego State University, B.S., 1970. *Politics:* Democrat. *Religion:* Roman Catholic. *Home:* 4344 Campus Ave., San Diego, Calif. 92103.

CAREER: WFAH-Radio, Alliance, Ohio, broadcast engineer, 1948-51; WFMT-Radio, Chicago, Ill., broadcast engineer, 1951-52; Packard Bell Electronics, San Diego, Calif., television bench technician, 1952-54; U.S. Naval Air Station, North Island, Calif., electronic technician in guided missile program, 1955-56; Electro Instruments, Inc., San Diego, packaging designer and research and development technician, 1956-63; real estate salesman in residential property and raw land, at various times, 1959—; Kiddie Town Toy Giant, San Diego, owner and manager, 1963-66; White Front (residential interiors), San Diego, branch manager, 1971-72; San Diego Community Colleges, San Diego, instructor in vocational guidance training, 1973—. Free-lance writer and lecturer. Vocational guidance counselor; business and management consultant. President, Allied Gardens Merchants Association, 1963-64. Volunteer police reserve officer and probation officer in San Diego. *Military service:* U.S. Navy, 1942-45; served in European, Atlantic, and South Pacific theaters. *Member:* San Diego Square Dance Callers Association.

WRITINGS: *How to Get a Job*, Education Technology Communications Publications (Homewood, Ill.), 1974; *How to Do Your Own Horoscope Casting*, Ashley Books, 1975; *How to Be Self Employed*, Volume I, Education Technology Communications Publications, 1975. Contributor of more than twenty-five articles on electronics, astrology, business, biology, and social science to magazines.

WORK IN PROGRESS: *How to Delineate Your Horoscope*; *How to Be Self Employed*, Volume II; *How to Pass All Employment and Civil Service Tests*.

SIDELIGHTS: Fregly writes: "My whole concept centers on employment and business. To this end I have devoted my energies to help solve the problems of the unemployed, the under-employed, the unsuccessful businessman, and the test taker trying to compete in the world of mental discrimination.

"I have but one desire in life, to bring about an equality in employment and business. I want everyone to have an equal chance at success. For those who lack the necessary skills and techniques I hope to create an equality through the medium of my class rooms and my books." *Avocational interests:* Ham radio operator, square dance caller, organic gardener.

* * *

FREILICH, Joan S(herman) 1941-

PERSONAL: Born November 3, 1941, in Albany, N.Y.; daughter of Julius (a lawyer) and Bessie (Bergner) Sherman; married Sanford Freilich, January 24, 1965. *Education:* Barnard College, A.B., 1963; Columbia University, M.A., 1964, Ph.D., 1971; also studied at Hamilton College, 1961-62. *Office:* Office of the Academic Dean, College of New Rochelle, New Rochelle, N.Y. 10801.

CAREER: French teacher in private school in New York, N.Y., 1970-74; College of New Rochelle, New Rochelle, N.Y., assistant to the dean, 1974—. Instructor at Columbia University, 1973-75. *Member:* American Association of Teachers of French (member of board of directors of Metropolitan chapter), Modern Language Association of America, American Council on the Teaching of Foreign Languages, Paul Claudel Society (vice-president, 1975), Societe Paul Claudel (Paris), New York State Association of Foreign Language Teachers, Phi Beta Kappa. *Awards, honors:* Grant from Humanities Research Council of Canada, 1972.

WRITINGS: *Paul Claudel's "Le Soulier de satin": A Stylistic, Structuralist, and Psychonalytic Interpretation*, University of Toronto Press, 1973. Contributor to language journals. Associate editor of *Claudel Studies*.

WORK IN PROGRESS: Research on language teaching methods, and on college administration.

* * *

FRENCH, Scott Robert 1948-

PERSONAL: Born July 17, 1948, in Ohio; son of Robert Dean (an editor) and Shirely (a librarian; maiden name, Kiely) French; children: Jason Fox. *Education:* Attended University of Colorado, 1966-69; O'Connell School of Radio/Television Technology, diploma, 1974. *Residence:* San Francisco, Calif. *Office:* Gnu Publishing, Box 6820, San Francisco, Calif. 94101.

CAREER: Radio engineer/announcer; writer and editor, now affiliated with Gnu Publishing, San Francisco, Calif. President of Sound Security, Inc.

WRITINGS: *New Earth Catalog*, Gnu Publishing, 1971; *New Earth Catalog: Living Here and Now*, Putnam Berkley, 1973; *Peoples Yellow Pages of America*, Heller, 1974; *Complete Guide to the Street Drug Game*, Lyle Stuart, 1975; *Big Brother Game*, Gnu Publishing, 1975.

WORK IN PROGRESS: Co-authoring *Catalog of Challenge and Adventure*, with Richard Heller.

SIDELIGHTS: French, a federally-licensed electronics engineer, says that with his last book he "got quite involved with surveillance, bugging, private and public spying, etc....got quite good at bugging, de-bugging, lock picking, tailing, etc." *Avocational interests:* Martial arts.

* * *

FRIED, William 1945-

PERSONAL: Born June 13, 1945, in New York, N.Y.; son of Walter and Frances (Ruderman) Fried; married Marlene Gerber (a professor of philosophy), June 28, 1970. *Education:* University of Pittsburgh, B.A., 1967; Brown University, M.A., 1969. *Home:* 9 South Balch St., Hanover, N.H. 03755.

CAREER: Brown University, Providence, R.I., lecturer in ecology, 1968-69; University of Connecticut, Storrs, instructor in philosophy, 1969-70; Dartmouth College, Hanover, N.H., visiting lecturer in philosophy, 1972-73.

WRITINGS: (With Joan Smith) *The Uses of the American Prison*, Heath, 1974.

WORK IN PROGRESS: Second Generation Ecology, completion expected in 1977; research on Vermont's penal reform.

SIDELIGHTS: Fried writes: "My basic interest is formulating an analysis of our main social and environmental problems in such a way as to preclude the traditionally flawed avenues of reform. I would also like to grow a twenty-five-pound tomato. But not in that order."

* * *

FRIEDLAND, Ronald Lloyd 1937-1975

July 6, 1937—July 27, 1975; American educator, editor, and author. Obituaries: *New York Times*, July 30, 1975. (*CA*-33/36)

* * *

FRIEDMAN, Marcia 1925-

PERSONAL: Born August 26, 1925, in New York, N.Y.; daughter of Henry (a designer and sculptor) and Bess (a musician; maiden name, Rosenbloom) Goodman; married Leib Leon Friedman (an aerospace administrator), August 6, 1950; children: Joshua Paul (deceased), Simon Asa. *Education:* California State University, Northridge, B.A. (cum laude), 1968, graduate study, 1969-70. *Politics:* Independent Democrat. *Religion:* "Jewish non-believer." *Home:* 3675 Longview Valley Rd., Sherman Oaks, Calif. 91423. *Agent:* Paul R. Reynolds, Inc., 12 East 41st St., New York, N.Y. 10017.

CAREER: Worked for defense effort in an airplane factory, 1943-44; held various jobs, 1946-48; United Jewish Welfare Fund, Los Angeles, Calif., director of speakers' bureau and member of women's division fund-raising staff, 1948-50; writer. *Military service:* U.S. Army, Women's Army Corps, 1945.

WRITINGS: The Story of Josh (nonfiction), Praeger, 1974.

WORK IN PROGRESS: A book about unemployment among aerospace engineers and professionals, *Nobody Gave a Damn*; research on the welfare program, and on crime and punishment.

* * *

FRIEDMAN, Murray 1926-

PERSONAL: Born September 15, 1926; married, 1949; children: three. *Education:* Brooklyn College (now Brooklyn College of the City University of New York), B.A., 1948; New York University, M.A., 1949; Georgetown University, Ph.D., 1958. *Home:* 610 Boyer Rd., Cheltenham, Pa. 19012. *Office:* American Jewish Committee, 1612 Market St., Philadelphia, Pa. 19103.

CAREER: Historian, Office of the Chief of Military History, 1949-51; Washington Housing Association (WHA), Washington, D.C., assistant to director, 1952-53; B'nai B'rith, Richmond, Va., regional director and intergroup relations official of Anti-Defamation League, 1954-59; American Jewish Committee, Philadelphia, Pa., regional director, 1959—. Adjunct professor of urban sociology, La Salle College, Philadelphia, 1967—. Lecturer, University of Pennsylvania, 1968-69; guest lecturer of U.S. Information Agency in Republic of South Africa, Kenya, Ethiopia, and India, 1974; lecturer, Temple University, University of Massachusetts. *Military service:* U.S. Marine Corps, 1945. *Member:* National Association of Human Rights Workers

(member of board), American Historical Association, Association of Jewish Agency Executives of Philadelphia (president).

WRITINGS: (Contributor) Alan F. Westin, editor, *Freedom Now!: The Civil-Rights Struggle in America*, Basic Books, 1964; (editor) *Overcoming Middle Class Rage*, Westminster Press, 1971; (contributor) Peter Isaac Rose and others, editors, *Through Different Eyes: Black and White Perspectives on American Race Relations*, Oxford University Press, 1973; (contributor) Leonard Dinnerstein and M. D. Pallson, editors, *Jews in the South*, Louisiana State University Press, 1973. Contributing columnist, *Evening Bulletin* (Philadelphia), 1972—; contributor of essays to *American Jewish Yearbook*, 1972, 1973; contributor of articles and book reviews to journals, including *Commentary, New Republic, Progressive* and *New Leader*.

* * *

FRIEDMAN, Myles I(van) 1924-

PERSONAL: Born April 5, 1924, in Chicago, Ill.; son of Max and Ethel Friedman. University of Chicago, M.A., 1957, Ph.D., 1959. *Office:* College of Education, University of South Carolina, Columbia, S.C. 29208.

CAREER: Corporate executive, 1946-57; Northwestern University, Evanston, Ill., assistant professor, 1958-60, associate professor of education, 1960-63; University of South Carolina, Columbia, professor of education, 1964—, named E. Smythe Gambrell Distinguished Professor, 1975. Director of Head Start Evaluation and Research Center, 1966-70; director of research at Regional Education Laboratory for the Carolinas and Virginia, 1966-70; professor at University of California, Berkeley, summer, 1968. *Military service:* U.S. Army Air Forces, meteorologist, 1942-46. *Member:* American Psychological Association, American Educational Research Association.

WRITINGS: Rational Behavior, University of South Carolina Press, 1975. Author of "Pre-Primary Profile," a test, Science Research Associates, 1963.

WORK IN PROGRESS: Introduction to Educational Evaluation.

* * *

FRIEDMAN, Saul S. 1937-

PERSONAL: Born March 8, 1937, in Uniontown, Pa.; son of Albert Elias (a stonecutter) and Rebecca (Landau) Friedman; married Nancy Evans, October 25, 1964; children: Jonathan, Molly. *Education:* Kent State University, B.A. (summa cum laude), 1959; graduate study at Harvard University, 1959-60, and Dropsie College, 1962; Ohio State University, M.A., 1962, Ph.D., 1969. *Politics:* "Harry Truman Democrat." *Religion:* Jewish. *Home:* 3650 Sandburg Dr., Youngstown, Ohio 44511. *Office:* Department of History, Youngstown State University, Youngstown, Ohio 44555.

CAREER: Franklin County Welfare Department, Columbus, Ohio, caseworker, 1962-64; Community Action for Youth, Cleveland, Ohio, social worker, 1964-66; Otterbein College, Westerville, Ohio, instructor in history, 1966-68; Ohio Dominican College, Columbus, instructor in history, 1968-69; Youngstown State University, Youngstown, Ohio, assistant professor, 1969-74, associate professor of history, 1974—. President of Youngstown Zionist District, 1971—; member of Kentucky-Ohio regional board of Anti-Defamation League, 1973—; member of Youngstown Jewish

Community Relations Council, 1975—; member of Middle East task force of Youngstown Jewish Community Center, 1975. *Member:* American Professors for Peace in the Middle East, Phi Alpha Theta, Phi Kappa Phi, Phi Kappa Sigma, Blue Key.

WRITINGS: No Haven for the Oppressed: Official American Policy Toward European Jewish Refugees, 1938-1945, Wayne State University Press, 1973; *Pogromschik: The Assassination of Simon Petlura*, Hart Publishing, in press. Contributor to Jewish magazines and national publications, including *Jewish Frontier* and *Midstream*.

WORK IN PROGRESS: Incident at Massena: The Blood Libel in America; *Amcha: Voices of Holocaust*, based on interviews with survivors; *The Red Cross and the Jews*, completion expected in 1977.

SIDELIGHTS: Friedman writes: "My experience as a Jew in the Galut has formed my outlook, shaped my writings. I am indebted to my people for having given to me a sense of tzedokah, social justice; rachmones, compassion; naches, joy; tachlis, purpose; and hadar, pride."

*   *   *

FROOKS, Dorothy 1899-

PERSONAL: Born February 12, 1899, in Saugerties, N.Y.; daughter of Reginald and Rosita (Siberez) Frooks. *Education:* Hamilton College, LL.B., 1918, LL.M., 1919; National Institute of Psychology, Ps.D., 1946; student at Industrial College of the Armed Forces, 1953; also attended special courses at Harvard University, New York University, St. Lawrence University, University of North Carolina, Tulane University, and Duquesne University. *Residence:* Peekskill, N.Y. *Office:* 237 Madison Ave., New York, N.Y. 10016; and Lake Mohegan, Peekskill, N.Y. 10547.

CAREER: Lawyer, 1920—; author. Admitted to the bar in New York, 1920, Puerto Rico, 1925, California, 1926, Louisiana, 1929, Alaska, 1935, Hawaii, 1958, to the Bar of the U.S. Supreme Court, 1934, Bar of U.S. Court of Appeals, 1943, and to the Bar of the U.S. Court of Military Appeals, 1954. Publisher of *Oyster Bay News* (weekly), 1916-19; owner and editor of *Public Service Record*, New York City, 1920-21; currently publisher of the *Murray Hill News* and of House of Ideas Publishing Co. Lecturer; delegate to numerous international and regional legal conferences, and to American Legion conventions; former national commander of Women World War Veterans; former commander of Women Veterans American Legion local post. *Wartime service:* Served as chief yeoman in U.S. Navy during World War I, in charge of women's enrollments and recruiting; received medal for patriotic services from President Woodrow Wilson. Served in Judge Advocate's Office, U.S. Army, during World War II.

MEMBER: International Law Association, Inter-American Bar Association, International Bar Association, American Bar Association, American Judicature Association, National Association of Women Lawyers, National Aeronautic Association, Order of the Eastern Star, New York State Bar Association, Wisconsin Archeological Society, Westchester County Bar Association, Women of Greater New York (past president), Iota Tau Tau, Epsilon Eta Phi, Westchester Junior League, Peekskill Country Club (former member of board of directors).

WRITINGS—Nonfiction: The American Heart, Burton Publishing, 1919; *Love's Law* (foreword by Cornelius Van-

derbilt, Jr.), Avondale Press, 1928; *All in Love*, Macauley, 1932; *Over the Heads of Congress*, Nelson, 1935; *The Olympic Torch*, House of Ideas, 1946; (with brother, Richard Frooks) *Are You a Happy American?*, House of Ideas, 1970; (with Cay Dorney) *Lady Lawyer*, Speller, 1974. Columnist for *New York Evening World*, 1920-32.

SIDELIGHTS: Miss Frooks was the first woman attorney for the national Salvation Army.

*   *   *

FRUCHT, Phyllis 1936-

PERSONAL: Born January 16, 1936, in Brooklyn, N.Y.; daughter of Herman and Anna (Bogitch) Leber; married Samuel Frucht (in insurance), September 2, 1962; children: Robin, Madeline, Michael, Sarah. *Education:* Brooklyn College (now Brooklyn College of the City University of New York), B.A., 1957. *Religion:* Jewish. *Home:* 7805 Mary Cassatt Dr., Potomac, Md. 20854.

CAREER: Mathematics teacher in Brooklyn, N.Y., 1958-62; cooking instructor.

WRITINGS: (Editor with Gertrude Katz and Joy Rothschild) *The Best of Jewish Cooking*, Dial, 1974.

WORK IN PROGRESS: Jewish Creative Cooks, Festival Foods of the World's Great Religions, and *How to Cater Your Own Simcha*.

BIOGRAPHICAL/CRITICAL SOURCES: New York Times, March 23, 1972; *Washington Post*, February 21, 1974, September 12, 1974.

*   *   *

FRY, Ronald W(illiam) 1949-

PERSONAL: Born October 21, 1949, in Bethlehem, Pa.; son of William James (a financier) and Gloria (a teacher; maiden name, Boyko) Fry. *Education:* Princeton University, B.A., 1972. *Politics:* Independent. *Religion:* Nichiren Shoshu (Buddhist). *Home:* 632 Ocean Parkway, #D-3, Brooklyn, N.Y. 11230. *Agent:* Jay Garon-Brooke Associates, Inc., 415 Central Park W., #17-D, New York, N.Y. 10025.

CAREER: FM Affiliated Insurance Co., Providence, R.I., underwriter, 1969; Oxford Personnel Agency, New York, N.Y., employment counselor, 1972; Simmons-Boardman Publishing Co., New York, N.Y., associate editor of *Railway Age*, 1973; full-time writer, 1975—. *Member:* Authors Guild of Authors League of America, Magazine Writers of America, Mensa, Princeton Club.

WRITINGS: (With Alan LeMond) *No Place to Hide: A Guide to Bugs, Wiretaps, Surveillance, and Other Privacy Invasions*, St. Martin's, 1975. Author of consumer affairs column in *Swank*, 1973-74, and column on campus film in *Film International*, 1975. Contributor of articles, stories, and reviews to national magazines, including *True, Argosy, Cosmopolitan, Saga, Worldview, Photo News Features, Film International, Cavalier, Nostalgia Illustrated*, and *Gallery*.

WORK IN PROGRESS: A nonfiction work on the ethics of dying, publication by Prentice-Hall expected in 1976; a novel on computer warfare; "Crystal Hydra," a science fiction screenplay; research on nonfiction books about psychic phenomena and nuclear reactor safety.

SIDELIGHTS: Ronald Fry told *CA* he planned to become an engineer until ". . . I realized the laziest engineer put in three times as much time as the hardest working Liberal

Arts candidate ... I quickly switched to English ... [I] failed Creative Writing and was told 'never, never NEVER to consider a career in writing.' Thankfully, I didn't listen to the troll's advice.

"I am, more than anything, interested in humanity, not so much in man's inhumanity to man as in man's common bond, common feeling, common desires. . . . I hope, through my future work, to accelerate man's return to a basic humanistic concern for his fellow man. I also ... want to write 'everything there is to write.' I might not make it, but getting there should be quite interesting!"

* * *

FRYATT, Norma R.

Office address: P.O. Box 546, Princeton, N.J. 08540.

CAREER: Horn Book, Inc., Boston, Mass., managing editor, 1956-59, editor of juvenile books, 1961—.

WRITINGS: A Horn Book Sampler, Horn Book, 1959; *Faneuil Hall: Cradle of Liberty*, World Publishing, 1970; *Boston and the Tea "Riots,"* Mason-Charter, 1974; *Sarah Josepha Hale: The Life and Times of a Nineteenth-Century Career Woman*, Hawthorn, 1975. Contributor to *Newberry and Caldecott Medal Books, 1956-1965*.

* * *

FUCHS, Estelle

PERSONAL: Born in New York; daughter of Joseph and Ida Sillen; married William Fuchs; children: Jonathan, Andrew. *Education:* Brooklyn College (now of the City University of New York), B.A., 1944; Columbia University, Ph.D., 1964. *Office:* Department of Educational Foundations, Hunter College of the City University of New York, 695 Park Ave., New York, N.Y. 10021.

CAREER: Hunter College of the City University of New York, New York, N.Y., associate professor, 1966-70, professor of education, 1971—. Professor of education at Graduate Center of City University of New York, 1972—. *Member:* American Association for the Advancement of Science (fellow), American Anthropological Association (fellow), Society for Applied Anthropology (fellow).

WRITINGS: Pickets at the Gates, Free Press, 1966; *Teachers Talk*, Doubleday, 1969; (with Robert J. Hanghurst) *To Live on This Earth: American Indian Education*, Doubleday, 1972.

* * *

FUENTES, Roberto 1934-

PERSONAL: Born December 4, 1934, in Miami, Fla.; son of Roberto (a lawyer) and Margot (Planas) Fuentes; married Grace Jorge, April 7, 1962; children: Roberto. *Education:* Attended University of Havana, 1954-60. *Politics:* "Extremely anti-communist—between Goldwater and George Wallace." *Religion:* Roman Catholic. *Home:* 470 Jefferson Ave., Apt. 5-A, Elizabeth, N.J. 07201. *Agent:* Lurton Blassingame, 60 East 42nd St., New York, N.Y. 10017.

CAREER: Has worked as a toll collector, dishwasher, busboy, waiter, and factory worker; judo instructor at University of Havana, Catholic University of Villanova, Spanish Club, St. Thomas Military Academy, all in Havana, Cuba, 1954-60; Carter, Ledyard & Milburn (law firm), New York, N.Y., statistical typist, 1969—. Judo instructor at Cranford Judo & Karate Center and Samurai

Judo Club of Elizabeth, N.J. *Member:* Science Fiction Writers of America, United States Judo Federation, United States Judo Association, Cuban College of Black Belts (vice-president, 1950-58). *Awards, honors:* Twice Black Belt Judo grand champion of Cuba.

*WRITINGS—*All novels; all published by Berkley Publishing: (With Pier Anthony) *Klal*, 1974; (with Anthony) *Mistress of Death*, 1974; (with Anthony) *Bamboo Bloodbath*, 1975; *Ninja's Revenge*, 1975.

Regular reviewer and contributor to *Judo Times*.

WORK IN PROGRESS: Two novels, *Dead Morn* and *Biography of a Terrorist*; *Judo*, nonfiction; *Black Castle of the Amazon*.

SIDELIGHTS: Fuentes writes: "Was student of law at University of Havana (4th year) when Castro came to power. I actively fought him. Was arrested in 1960 and sent to Cabanas Prison. Freed in my trial, I went underground till the Bay of Pigs Invasion made it impossible to remain in Cuba and I sought asylum in the Mexican Embassy. I have been action and sabotage chief of the largest anti-Castro organization, the MRR (Movement for Recuperating the Revolution). Continued the fight from exile returning to Cuba in 1962 till I was caught in Havana during the missile crisis and had to seek refuge in the Uruguayan Embassy. I then continued as an MRR commando from Nicaragua."

* * *

FULMER, Robert M(arion) 1939-

PERSONAL: Born October 6, 1939, in Florence, Ala.; son of Robert and Reba (Smith) Fulmer; married Arlene Hogan, March 12, 1960; children: Robert Jeffrey, James Burton. *Education:* David Lipscomb College, B.A., 1961; University of Florida, M.B.A., 1962; University of California, Los Angeles, Ph.D., 1965. *Politics:* Republican. *Religion:* Protestant. *Home:* 227 Treasure Way, San Antonio, Tex. 78209. *Office:* School of Business, Trinity University, San Antonio, Tex. 78284.

CAREER: Proctor & Gamble, Cincinnati, Ohio, member of marketing staff in brand management, 1962-63; National Industrial Conference Board, New York, N.Y., research associate, 1965; Pepperdine University, Malibu, Calif., chairman of department of business, 1965-66; Florida State University, Tallahassee, associate professor of business, 1966-68; Georgia State University, Atlanta, professor of management, 1968-73; Trinity University, San Antonio, Tex., George R. Brown Professor of Business, 1973—. Executive director of Certified Professional Managers; director of Executive Council, Inc. (consultants); faculty associate of Danforth Foundation, 1968—; consultant to about fifty organizations. *Member:* American Marketing Association (director of Atlanta chapter, 1969), Academy of Management (member of board of governors, 1969), World Futures Society, Southern Management Association (president, 1970).

WRITINGS: (Editor) *Organizing for New Product Development*, National Industrial Conference Board, 1966; *Managing Associations of the 1890's*, Foundation of the American Society of Association Executives, 1972; *The New Management*, Macmillan, 1974; (with Harold Koontz) *A Practical Introduction to Business*, Irwin, 1975; *The Management of Associations*, American Society of Association Executives, 1975; *Supervision: Essentials of Professional Practice*, Glencoe Press, 1975; *The New Marketing*, Macmillan, in press; *Practical Human Relations*, Irwin, in press. Contributor of about eighty articles to scholarly journals, including *Business Horizons*.

* * *

FULTON, Len 1934-

PERSONAL: Born May 15, 1934, in Lowell, Mass.; son of Claude E. and Louise (Vaillant) Fulton; children: Timothy. *Education:* University of Maine, A.A., 1957; University of Wyoming, B.A., 1961; University of California, Berkeley, graduate study, 1961-63. *Religion:* None. *Home and office:* 5218 Scottwood Rd., Paradise, Calif. 95969.

CAREER: Freeport Press and *Weekly News*, Freeport, Me., publisher, 1957-59; *Tourist Topic*, Kennebunkport, Me., publisher, 1963—; Dustbooks, Paradise, Calif., publisher, 1963, publishing and editing *International Directory of Little Magazines and Small Presses* and *Small Press Record of Books in Print*, and literary magazine, *Dust*. Biostatistician in Berkeley, Calif., 1962-68. Consultant to American Library Association. *Military service:* U.S. Army, Corps of Engineers, 1953-55. *Member:* Committee of Small Magazine Editors and Publishers (co-founder; chairman, 1968-71, 1973). *Awards, honors:* Grants from Coordinating Council of Literary Magazines, 1970, 1971, 1972, 1973; National Endowment for the Arts grant, 1975.

WRITINGS: Two Short Stories, Dustbooks, 1969; *The Grassman* (novel), Thorp Springs, 1974; *American Odyssey* (travelogue), Dustbooks, 1975; *Dark Other Adam Dreaming* (novel), Dustbooks, 1975. Contributor of more than a hundred fifty articles to literary magazines and newspapers. Editor of *Small Press Review*.

WORK IN PROGRESS: A definitive book on small presses; a novel.

SIDELIGHTS: Fulton was reared in the mill towns and farms of northern New England. After his newspaper publishing companies "went broke" in 1959, in what he calls "the adamantine wastes" of New England, he "dog-legged west by hitching on with several newspapers" until reaching Wyoming. It wasn't until 1963 that he became a publisher again.

Of his books, Fulton writes that *The Grassman* "... replays the Oresteia in Western American terms, and searches for a kind of root American morality based on a literary sense of place." His third book describes his travels in order to sell his second book: "Writers cannot *only* write anymore. They have to spend a certain percentage of their time on the business of their book. They have to get out and humanize the marketplace." Of his fourth book he writes that his "... vision of the nexus between morality and place is the thread of this work ... but the whole is more condensed and ... a lot less classically American." *Avocational interests:* Horsemanship, gardening.

* * *

FURNISS, W(arren) Todd 1921-

PERSONAL: Born June 5, 1921, in Pelham, N.Y.; son of Henry Dawson (a surgeon) and Ruth (maiden name, Pine; a novelist and short story writer) Furniss; married Barbara Ann Ripley (an educational counselor), June 11, 1949; children: Patricia Kellogg, Abigail Anne (deceased). *Education:* Yale University, B.A., 1942, M.A., 1948, Ph.D., 1952. *Home:* 3422 Dent Place N.W., Washington, D.C. 20007. *Office:* American Council on Education, One Dupont Circle, Washington, D.C. 20036.

CAREER: Mount Holyoke College, South Hadley, Mass., instructor, 1949-51; Ohio State University, Columbus, instructor, 1952-55, assistant professor, 1955-59, associate professor of English, 1959-64, assistant dean, 1957-60, associate dean, 1960-64; University of Hawaii, Honolulu, professor of English and dean of College of Arts and Sciences, 1964-69; American Council on Education, Washington, D.C., director of office of academic affairs, 1969—. Council of Colleges of Arts and Sciences, president, 1967, member of board of directors, 1968; member of Commission on Non-Traditional Study, 1970-72. *Military service:* U.S. Air Force, 1942-46; became captain. *Member:* Modern Language Association of America, American Association of University Professors, American Ornithologists Union, Wilson Ornithological Society, Cosmos Club (Washington, D.C.), Elizabethan Club (Yale University). *Awards, honors:* Carnegie travel grant, 1962-63.

WRITINGS: (With Richard B. Young and William G. Madsen) *Three Studies in the Renaissance*, Yale University Press, 1958; (editor and contributor) *Higher Education for Everybody?*, American Council on Education, 1971; *Steady-State Staffing in Tenure Granting Institutions*, American Council on Education, 1973; (editor) *American Universities and Colleges*, 11th edition, American Council on Education, 1973; (editor with Patricia Albjerg Graham) *Women in Higher Education*, American Council on Education, 1974. Regular contributor to *Educational Record* and contributor to other education journals.

WORK IN PROGRESS: A book on academic tenure.

* * *

GADD, David 1912-

PERSONAL: Born July 10, 1912, in Dover, England; son of Charles Alfred (in railway industry) and Fanny (Lord) Gadd; married Gwenrudd Edwards, 1936 (died, 1965); married Margaret Meijering-Koehler, August 4, 1965; children: (first marriage) Simon C. L. and Jennifer F. (twins). *Education:* Peterhouse College, Cambridge, B.A., 1931, M.A., 1936. *Home:* Greenleaze, Long Sutton, Somerset, England.

CAREER: Language teacher in England, 1934-40; British Army, career officer, 1940-65, in intelligence, 1940-45, in education, 1945-65, director of Education Service, 1962-65, retiring as major general; London Chamber of Commerce, London, England, linguistic director, 1968—. *Awards, honors*—Military: Named Commander of Order of the British Empire.

WRITINGS: Georgian Summer: The Story of Eighteenth-Century Bath, Adams & Dart, 1972; *The Loving Friends: A Portrait of Bloomsbury*, Hogarth, 1974. Compiler of daily crossword puzzles for London *Times*.

* * *

GADDIS, J. Wilson 1910(?)-1975

1910(?)—July 9, 1975; American newspaperman, radio commentator, publicity consultant, and author of books on Korea. Obituaries: *New York Times*, July 12, 1975.

* * *

GAFFNEY, James 1931-

PERSONAL: Born February 21, 1931, in New York, N.Y.; son of James George (a banker and lawyer) and Lucille (a secretary; maiden name, Lynch) Gaffney; married Kathleen McGovern (a teacher), June 30, 1970; children: Elizabeth, Margaret. *Education:* Spring Hill College,

B.S., 1956; Fordham University, M.A., 1965; Gregorian University of Rome, Ph.D., 1968; Texas Southern University, M.Ed., 1971. *Politics:* "More socialist than otherwise." *Religion:* Christian. *Home:* 916 Lacey Ave., Lisle, Ill. 60532. *Office:* Department of Religious Studies, Illinois Benedictine College, Lisle, Ill. 60532.

CAREER: High school teacher of languages in New York, N.Y., 1956-59; University of Gonzaga, Florence, Italy, assistant professor of philosophy and theology, 1968-70; University of Liberia, Monrovia, lecturer in foreign languages, 1970-72; Illinois Benedictine College, Lisle, associate professor of religious studies and chairman of department, 1973—. *Member:* American Academy of Religion, American Society of Christian Ethics, American Society for Religion in Public Education, Catholic Theological Society of America, College Theology Society, Dante Society.

WRITINGS: (Contributor) A. D. Lee, editor, *Vatican II: The Theological Dimension,* Thomist Press, 1963; *Focus on Doctrine,* Paulist Press, 1975; *Moral Questions,* Paulist Press, 1975; (contributor) Thomas McFadden, editor, *Revolution, Liberation, and Freedom,* Seabury, 1975. Contributor to theological journals and to *Commonweal, America,* and *Chicago Studies.*

WORK IN PROGRESS: A study of relationships, both constructive and destructive, between religion and ethics in the great religious traditions of East and West.

* * *

GAHERTY, Sherry 1951-

PERSONAL: Born April 2, 1951, in Pittsfield, Mass.; daughter of William T. (a newspaper engraver) and Elizabeth (a salesperson; maiden name, Wheeler) Gaherty. *Education:* Bridgewater State College, B.A., 1973; State University of New York at Albany, M.L.S., 1975. *Home:* 247 Pleasant St., Dalton, Mass. 01226.

CAREER: Writer. *Member:* Phi Alpha Theta.

WRITINGS: (Editor with Bill Katz) *Library Literature Four: The Best of 1973,* Scarecrow, 1974.

WORK IN PROGRESS: Social and Economic Life in Berkshire County as Reflected by Advertisements in the Pittsfield Sun, 1808-1810/1819-1820.

* * *

GALLAGHER, J(ames) Roswell 1903-

PERSONAL: Born May 7, 1903, in New Haven, Conn.; son of John Currier (a lawyer) and Bessie K. (a nurse; maiden name, Radigan) Gallagher; married Constance R. Dann, July 12, 1926; children: John Currier. *Education:* Yale University, B.A., 1925, M.D., 1930. *Home:* 67 Mill Rock Rd., New Haven, Conn. 06511.

CAREER: Hill School, Pottstown, Pa., school physician, 1932-34; Phillips Academy, Andover, Mass., school physician, 1935-50; Wesleyan University, Middletown, Conn., college physician, 1950-51; Childrens' Hospital Medical Center, Boston, Mass., chief of adolescents' unit, 1951-67, chief emeritus, 1967—. Clinical professor of pediatrics at Harvard Medical School, 1965-67; Yale University School of Medicine, clinical professor of pediatrics, 1967-72, professor emeritus, 1972—. Overseer of Boys' Clubs of Boston, 1956-68. *Member:* American Medical Association, American Academy of Pediatrics, American College of Physicians, American Public Health Association, American Pediatric Society, National Safety Council, Boy Scouts for America. *Awards, honors:* Foneme Award from Foneme Institution for Studies and Research in Human Development, 1970; Aldrich Award from American Academy of Pediatrics, 1972.

WRITINGS: Understanding Your Son's Adolescence, Atlantic-Little Brown, 1951; (with H. I. Harris) *Emotional Problems of Adolescents,* Oxford University Press, 1958, 3rd edition, 1975; (with I. S. Goldberger and G. M. Hallock), *Health for Life,* Ginn, 1961; *Medical Care of the Adolescent,* Appleton, 1960, revised 3rd edition (with F. P. Heald and D. C. Garell), 1975. Contributor to *Reader's Digest, Atlantic Monthly, Seventeen,* and medical journals.

* * *

GALLON, Arthur J(ames) 1915-

PERSONAL: Born July 15, 1915, in Portland, Ore.; son of Arthur Hudson (a boilermaker) and Elizabeth (Bader) Gallon; married June M. Aasheim, 1940; children: Cheryl, Kristi, Tracey. *Education:* Willamette University, A.B., 1939, M.A., 1940; further graduate study at Stanford University and University of Hawaii; University of California, Berkeley, Ed.D., 1954. *Politics:* Republican. *Religion:* "Unity." *Home:* 2864 Glendessary Lane, Santa Barbara, Calif. 93105. *Office:* Department of Physical Activities, 1014 Robertson Gymnasium, University of California, Santa Barbara, Calif. 93106.

CAREER: High school science teacher and athletic coach in Honolulu, Hawaii, 1940-45; junior high school teacher in Palo Alto, Calif., 1945-46; Mid-Pacific Institute, Honolulu, Hawaii, science teacher, head of department, athletic director and coach, 1946-47; University of Hawaii, Honolulu, assistant professor of health, physical education and recreation and head basketball coach, 1947-51; University of California, Berkeley, assistant basketball coach, 1951-56; assistant athletic director, 1954-56, assistant supervisor of mens' physical education, 1956-57; University of California, Santa Barbara, assistant professor, 1957-60, associate professor of physical education, 1960-65, head basketball coach, 1957-64, supervisor of physical education, 1965—, chairman of department of physical activities, 1965-71. Member of college division rating board for basketball of Associated Press, 1963-64.

MEMBER: National College Physical Education Association for Men (member of executive council), American Association of Health, Physical Education, and Recreation, National Association of Basketball Coaches (associate member), Western College Men's Physical Education Society (member of central committee), California Association of Health, Physical Education, and Recreation, Southern California Administrator's Club.

WRITINGS: Coaching: Ideas and Ideals, Houghton, 1974. Contributor to research and physical education journals.

* * *

GALTON, Lawrence 1913-

PERSONAL: Born October 30, 1913, in Bayonne, N.J.; son of Arthur (a businessman) and Frieda (Globe) Galton; married Barbara Brandt, 1945; children: Christopher, Gillian, Jeremy. *Education:* Columbia University, student, 1930-32; Rutgers University, B.S., 1936. *Home and office:* 1140 Fifth Ave., New York, N.Y. 10028.

CAREER: Automatic Electric Co., New York, N.Y.,

sales promotion manager, 1937-42; free-lance writer, 1946—. Visiting professor and consultant to dean of engineering, Purdue University, 1961-72. *Military service:* U.S. Army, Signal Corps, 1943-46; became first lieutenant. *Member:* American Association for the Advancement of Science, National Association of Science Writers, American Medical Writers Association, Society of Magazine Writers. *Awards, honors:* Cecil award of Arthritis Foundation, 1956, 1965; American Dental Association Science Writers' Award, 1970.

WRITINGS: The Family Book of Preventive Medicine, Simon & Schuster, 1972; *Freedom from Heart Attacks,* Simon & Schuster, 1973; *The Silent Disease: Hypertension,* Crown, 1974; *Your Inner Conflicts,* Simon & Schuster, 1975; *Don't Give Up on an Aging Parent,* Crown, 1975; *The Disguised Disease: Anemia,* Crown, 1975. Columnist for Washington Star Syndicate; contributor to *New York Times Magazine* and *Reader's Digest.* Contributing medical editor for *Family Circle.*

WORK IN PROGRESS: Non-fiction books.

* * *

GAMMAGE, William Leonard 1942-

PERSONAL: Surname rhymes with "damage"; born November 3, 1942, in Orange, New South Wales, Australia; son of John William (a lecturer) and Hazel Jean (a therapist; maiden name, Tosh) Gammage; married Janet Elizabeth Knox (a clerk), February 18, 1972. *Education:* Australian National University, B.A., 1965, Ph.D., 1970. *Religion:* Church of England. *Office:* Department of History, University of Papua New Guinea, P.O. Box 4820, University, Papua New Guinea.

CAREER: University of Papua New Guinea, Port Moresby, lecturer in history, 1972—.

WRITINGS: The Broken Years: Australian Soldiers in the Great War, Australian National University Press, 1974. Contributor to professional journals.

WORK IN PROGRESS: A book about New Zealand soldiers in World War One; research on the history of Papua New Guinea.

* * *

GANT, Phyllis 1922-

PERSONAL: Original surname Hill; name legally changed in 1970; born May 16, 1922, in Nhill, Victoria, Australia; daughter of Joseph Thomas (a laborer) and May Bernice (Stone) Hill; married Howard Cyril Richard Ferrabee, July 14, 1940 (divorced, 1955); children: Janet (Mrs. John Jarvis), Graeme, Brian. *Education:* Attended schools in Victoria, Australia. *Politics:* Labour. *Religion:* "Deep—but not specific." *Home and office:* 11 Howden Rd., Hamilton, New Zealand.

CAREER: Writer, 1953—. Worked in book order department of publishers, Paul's Book Arcade, Hamilton, New Zealand, and Blackwood & Janet Paul, Auckland, New Zealand, 1955-65; senior proofreader, librarian, and columnist for *The Waikato Times,* Waikato, New Zealand, 1966-68; senior filing clerk for Waikato Hospital Board Office, Waikato, 1969-73. *Member:* International P.E.N. (New Zealand section), Australian Society of Authors, Friends of the Waikato Art Museum, Waikato Society of Arts, Hamilton Chamber Music Society, 221 Yoga Club. *Awards, honors:* Mary Elgin Memorial Prize for gifted new writers of fiction, 1973, for *Islands.*

WRITINGS: Islands (autobiographical novel), Hodder & Stoughton, 1973. Also author of a novel, *The Fifth Season.* Author of column, "Action Line," for *The Waikato Times,* 1966-68. Contributor of short story to *The English Journal.* Also contributor of articles to education journals, and short stories to literary magazines, including *Landfall, Arena, Thursday,* and *New Zealand Listener.*

WORK IN PROGRESS: The Unguarded Interval, a novel; short stories.

SIDELIGHTS: Phyllis Gant has been published under that name since 1966. She told *CA:* "The name 'Gant'—comes from Thomas Wolfe's fictional family in *Look Homeward, Angel* ... because a poet friend said, ... 'Why not call yourself Helen Gant?—you're enough like her.' But I wasn't *that* much like her...so I changed only my surname.

"To achieve any degree of perception one must first look inwards, get to know oneself at deepest possible levels. The relationship of inner and outer life fascinates me and is an essential part of my work...I believe a writer cannot be divorced from life and to this end involve myself in most of the major issues of our time—even if in a minor way. I believe the biggest discoveries of the future will be within our psychological and spiritual aspects. My religious belief leans to Eastern mysticism. I practice the various branches of yoga, and regard it as an indispensable part of my life." *Avocational interests:* Gardening (grows most of her own vegetables on the compost and companion plants method), reading, and walking.

* * *

GARBER, Eugene K. 1932-

PERSONAL: Born October 5, 1932, in Birmingham, Ala.; son of Eugene Keenan (in real estate) and Margaret (Reid) Garber; married Barbara Morrow, November 27, 1954; children: Anne Morrow, William Keenan. *Education:* Tulane University, B.A., 1954; University of Iowa, M.A., Ph.D. *Politics:* Democrat. *Religion:* Episcopalian. *Home:* 1486 Chuckanut Dr., Bellingham, Wash. 98225. *Office:* Department of English, Western Washington State College, Bellingham, Wash. 98225.

CAREER: University of Iowa, Iowa City, instructor, 1958-61, assistant professor of English, 1962-68; Western Washington State College, Bellingham, associate professor, 1968-74, professor of English, 1974—. *Military service:* U.S. Navy, 1954-57; became lieutenant. *Member:* Modern Language Association of America, National Council of Teachers of English, American Association of University Professors, Phi Beta Kappa, Eta Sigma Phi.

WRITINGS: (With Walter Blair and John Gerber) *Better Reading I,* Scott, Foresman, 1963; (with Blair and Gerber) *Better Reading II,* Scott, Foresman, 1966; (with John Crossett) *Liberal and Conservative,* Scott, Foresman, 1968. Contributor of short stories to journals.

WORK IN PROGRESS: A collection of tales; a novel; an introductory literature anthology.

SIDELIGHTS: Garber told *CA:* "I am interested in my writing in the tale (as opposed to the realistic short story) and in the romance (as opposed to the realistic novel)." *Avocational interests:* Fly-fishing.

* * *

GARFIELD, Evelyn Picon 1940-

PERSONAL: Born August 23, 1940, in Newark, N.J.;

daughter of Sol and Edith (Haskell) Picon; married Louis Garfield (a businessman), November 3, 1961; children: Gene Douglas, Audrey Suzanne. *Education:* University of Michigan, A.B., 1963; Washington University, St. Louis, Mo., M.A., 1967; Rutgers University, Ph.D., 1972. *Residence:* Newton, Mass. *Office:* Office of the Vice-Chancellor for Academic Affairs, University of Massachusetts, Boston, Mass.

CAREER: Montclair State College, Upper Montclair, N.J., assistant professor of Spanish language and literature, 1970-74; University of Massachusetts, Boston, co-director of Affirmative Action, in the office of the vice-chancellor for academic affairs, 1974—. *Member:* Modern Language Association of America, American Association of University Professors, National Organization for Women, Women's Equity Action League, Phi Sigma Iota, Sigma Delta Pi. *Awards, honors:* Grant from American Philosophical Society, 1973, for travel to France; National Endowment for the Humanities grant, 1973.

WRITINGS: (Contributor) Helmy Giacoman, editor, *Homenaje a Enrique Anderson Imbert* (title means "In Homage to Enrique Anderson Imbert"), Las Americas-Anaya Press, 1974; *Julio Cortazar*, Ungar, 1975; *Es Julio Cortazar un surrealista?* (title means "Is Julio Cortazar a Surrealist?"), Editorial Gredos (Madrid), 1975. Contributor to supplement to *Encyclopedia of World Literature in the Twentieth Century*. Also contributor to *Revista de estudios hispanicos*, and to *Review* of Center for Inter-American Relations (New York).

WORK IN PROGRESS: Cortazar sobre Cortazar: Charlas desde Saignon (title means "Cortazar Talks About Himself: Conversations from Saignon"), a book of personal interviews with Julio Cortazar.

* * *

GARRETT, Franklin M(iller) 1906-

PERSONAL: Born September 25, 1906, in Milwaukee, Wis.; son of Clarence R. and Ada (Kirkwood) Garrett; divorced; children: Patricia Abbott, Franklin Miller, Jr. *Education:* Woodrow Wilson College of Law, LL.B., 1941. *Politics:* Independent. *Religion:* Presbyterian. *Home:* 3433 Roxboro Rd. N.E., Atlanta, Ga. 30326. *Address:* Atlanta Historical Society, P.O. Box 12423, Atlanta, Ga. 30305.

CAREER: Western Union Telegraph Co., Atlanta, Ga., branch manager, 1924-38; real estate salesman in Atlanta, Ga., 1939-40; Coca-Cola Co., Atlanta, Ga., member of advertising department and company historian, 1940-63, executive, 1964-68; Atlanta Historical Society, Atlanta, Ga., director, 1968-74, historian, 1974—. Chairman of board of Fulton County Personnel Board, 1955-72; member of board of directors of Children's Center of Metropolitan Atlanta, Inc., 1955-70; president of Grand Jurors Association of Fulton County, 1965; member of Atlanta Civic Design Commission, 1969-73. *Military service:* U.S. Army, 1941-45.

MEMBER: American Legion, National Railway Historical Society, Symposium, Newcomen Society in North America, Georgia Genealogical Society, Virginia Historical Society, Georgia Historical Society, South Carolina Historical Society, DeKalb Historical Society, Atlanta Historical Society (president, 1942; member of board of directors, 1932—), Atlanta Civil War Round Table, Atlanta Art Association, Piedmont Driving Club, Commerce Club, Rotary, Kappa Phi Kappa, Sigma Delta Kappa, Omicron Delta Kappa. *Awards, honors:* D.H.L., Oglethorpe College,

1970; official historian of the City of Atlanta by resolution of the Atlanta Board of Aldermen, 1973.

WRITINGS: Atlanta and Environs: A Chronicle of Its People and Events, two volumes, Lewis Historical Publishing Co., 1954, new edition, University of Georgia Press, 1969; *Yesterday's Atlanta*, E. A. Seeman Publishing Co., 1974. Contributor to journals.

WORK IN PROGRESS: A necrology of Fulton and DeKalb Counties in Georgia.

* * *

GARTENBERG, Egon 1911-

PERSONAL: Born April 17, 1911, in Vienna, Austria; came to United States in 1940; son of Victor (a hardware wholesaler) and Valerie (Wasservogel) Gartenberg; married Belle Berman, February 11, 1945; children: Valerie (Mrs. Patrick Martin), Vicki (Mrs. David Ginsburg), Andrew. *Education:* Academy of Commerce, Vienna, Austria, B.A., 1931; Austrian State Academy for Music, M.Mus., 1933. *Politics:* "Liberal with conservative leanings." *Religion:* Jewish. *Home:* 641 South Coldbrook Ave., Chambersburg, Pa. 17201. *Office:* Department of Music, College of Arts & Architecture, Pennsylvania State University, Commonwealth Campus, Mont Alto, Pa. 17237.

CAREER: Worked in wholesale firms in Vienna, Austria, 1933-38; Standard Oil of New Jersey, Aruba, Netherlands West Indies, in purchasing and inventory control, 1938-40; laborer and inventory control worker for automotive parts companies in New York and Pennsylvania, 1940-46; owned and operated a jewelry store in Chambersburg, Pa., 1946-71; Pennsylvania State University, Commonwealth Campus, Mont Alto, instructor, 1966-70, assistant professor, 1970-73, associate professor of music history, 1974—. Part-time instructor in music appreciation at Pennsylvania Department of Adult Education, 1951, and Hagerstown Junior College, 1952; conductor of Cumberland Valley Symphony, 1948-57; lecturer at Penn Hall Junior College and Wilson College, 1958-68; producer and narrator of "Immortal Music," on WCHA-Radio; director of Gilmore-Hoerner Art Endowment Fund.

WRITINGS: Vienna: Its Musical Heritage, Pennsylvania State University Press, 1968; *Johann Strauss: The End of an Era*, Pennsylvania State University Press, 1974. Music critic for *Public Opinion* (newspaper).

WORK IN PROGRESS: Daumier and Music; research for *Gustav Mahler: The Last Great Romantic*.

SIDELIGHTS: Gartenberg writes that he was always involved with music, that even on the island of Aruba he lectured on music and gave recitals, in solo performance or with Anne Weinberg of the Berlin-Charlottenburg opera. He spoke mainly on Viennese music. Upon reading that Rachmaninoff had created some of his greatest music after having undergone hypnotic treatment, Gartenberg sought the same treatment, then began writing books. *Avocational interests:* Collecting stamps and prints (medieval prints and manuscripts and Daumier lithographs on music and musicians).

* * *

GARVIN, Charles D. 1929-

PERSONAL: Born June 17, 1929, in Chicago, Ill.; son of Hyman and Etta (Raphaelson) Garvin; married Janet Tuft (a social worker), January 27, 1957; children: David, Amy, Anthony. *Education:* Attended Wright Junior College,

1946-48; University of Chicago, A.M., 1951, Ph.D., 1968. *Religion:* Jewish. *Home:* 2925 Park Ridge, Ann Arbor, Mich. 48103. *Office:* Department of Social Work, Frieze Building, University of Michigan, Ann Arbor, Mich. 48104.

CAREER: Henry Booth House, Chicago, Ill., director of social service, 1954-56; Jewish Community Centers of Chicago, program director, 1957-64; University of Michigan, Ann Arbor, professor of social work, 1965—. Consultant to Chapin Hall for Children (Chicago), and to Family Group Homes of Ann Arbor. *Military service:* U.S. Army, 1952-54. *Member:* National Association of Social Workers, American Sociological Association, American Orthopsychiatric Association, Academy of Certified Social Workers, Council on Social Work Education, British Association of Social Workers.

WRITINGS: (With Harvey Bertcher) *Staff Development in Social Welfare Agencies*, Campus Publishers, 1968; (contributor) *Social Work Practice*, Columbia University Press, 1969; (contributor) Fred M. Cox and others, editors, *Strategies of Community Organization*, Peacock Press, 1970, 2nd edition, 1974; (contributor) Paul Glasser, Rosemary Sarri and Robert Vinter, editors, *Individual Change Through Small Groups*, Free Press, 1974; (editor and contributor) *Incentives and Disincentives to Participation in the Work Incentive Program*, School of Social Work, University of Michigan, 1974; (editor with William Reid and Audrey Smith) *Experiences With Workfare*, University of Michigan Press, in press. Writer of social science training materials for Michigan Department of Social Services, 1967-69. Contributor to *Social Work Encyclopedia*. Also contributor of articles to *Social Welfare Forum, Journal of Jewish Communal Service, Social Service Review, Public Welfare* and other professional publications.

WORK IN PROGRESS: Social Work Treatment Text, completion expected in 1977; research on child abuse and family stress.

*   *   *

GASKILL, Harold V.   1905-1975

February 3, 1905—April 19, 1975; American banker, scientist, educator, and author. Obituaries: *Washington Post*, April 24, 1975.

*   *   *

GATES, J(eannette) M(cPherson)   1924-

PERSONAL: Born July 6, 1924, in New Orleans, La.; daughter of James Gordon (a minister) and Dolly (Taylor) McPherson; married Osly James Gates (an administrator), June 12, 1943; children: Sylvia Jeanne. *Education:* West Virginia State College, B.S. (summa cum laude), 1948; New York University, M.B.A., 1949; Portland State University, further graduate study, 1972-74. *Politics:* Democrat. *Religion:* Episcopal. *Home:* 4215 Southeast Bybee Blvd., Portland Ore. 97206.

CAREER: Texas Southern University, Houston, instructor in accounting, 1949-51; Far East Command, Central Purchasing Office, Tokyo, Japan, accountant and auditor, 1952-54; City of Portland, Portland, Ore., accountant, 1957-62. Instructor at Portland Community College, 1967-68. Member of board of directors of Portland Young Women's Christian Association, 1962-65, and of Jane Jefferson Democratic Women of Multnomah County, 1966-67, and 1970-71; associate chairman of Southeast Portland Neighborhoods Division Campaign of United Good Neighbors,

1965-66; chairman of Citizens for Interracial Understanding, 1967-70; member of Industrial Resources Study Committee of Multnomah County, 1968-69; evaluation consultant to Seattle regional office of U.S. Department of Health, Education and Welfare, 1974—.

MEMBER: American Accounting Association, National Association for the Advancement of Colored People, Oregon Historical Society, Oregon State Poetry Association, Alpha Kappa Mu, Alpha Kappa Alpha, Iota Phi Lambda. *Awards, honors:* National Science Foundation grant, 1971, for "Science, Society and Our World Conference" for non-scientists; *Oregon Journal* award, 1971, in recognition of *Reflections* and of "Human Understanding." L.H.D., West Virginia State College, 1973.

WRITINGS: Reflections (poems), Press 22, 1971; *Silhouettes* (poems), St. Paul's Press, 1972; *Relevance and Reality* (poems), St. Paul's Press, 1973. Contributor of monthly column, "The Agenda," to *Portland Observer*, 1975. Editor of *Circle*, 1973—.

WORK IN PROGRESS: A documentary book on civil rights, *Preface to Protest*; Americana in narrative poetry, *Mirrors of Living*; two-directional reversible poetry, *Poetry in Panorama*; *A Bibliography of Unconscious Reversible Poetry*; a video-tape, "Poetry Checkers."

SIDELIGHTS: J. M. Gates was a delegate to the Fourteenth Japan-United States Student Conference and an observer at the Sixth World Evangelical Congress in Tokyo, Japan, in 1953. She was the originator of reversible poetry as a contemporary poetry form and has developed a video-tape, "A Thumbnail Sketch of Reversible Poetry by J. M. Gates."

*   *   *

GAUCH, Patricia Lee   1934-

PERSONAL: Born January 3, 1934, in Detroit, Mich.; daughter of William Melbourne (an investor) and Muriel (Streng) Lee; married Ronald Raymond Gauch (a biostatistics director), August 21, 1955; children: Sarah, Christine, John. *Education:* Miama University, Oxford, Ohio, B.A., 1956; Manhattanville College, M.A.T., 1970. *Residence:* Basking Ridge, N.J. *Agent:* Dorothy Markinko, McIntosh & Otis, Inc., 18 East 41st St., New York, N.Y. 10017.

CAREER: Reporter for *Louisville Courier-Journal*, Louisville, Ky.; former teacher; Coward-McCann & Geoghegan, New York, N.Y., publisher-writer, 1969—.

WRITINGS—All published by Coward: *A Secret House*, 1970; *Christina Katerina and the Box*, 1971; *Aaron and the Green Mountain Boys*, 1972; *Christina Katerina and the First Annual Grand Ballet*, 1973; *Grandpa and Me*, 1973; *This Time, Tempe Wick?*, 1974.

WORK IN PROGRESS: Thunder at Gettysburg.

*   *   *

GAUQUELIN, Michel (Roland)   1928-

PERSONAL: Born November 13, 1928, in Paris, France; son of Roland (a dental surgeon) and Madeleine (Lenoir) Gauquelin; married Francoise Schneider (a science writer and psychologist), November 4, 1954; children: Daniel. *Education:* Sorbonne, University of Paris, Ph.D., 1954. *Home:* 8 rue Amyot, Paris, France 75005. *Agent:* Georges Borchardt, 145 East 52nd St., New York, N.Y. 10022. *Office:* Bibliotheque RETZ, 114 Champs Elysees, Paris, France 75008.

CAREER: Psychologist and writer in Paris, France, 1956-66; Bibliotheque RETZ (publishers), Paris, editor of psychology book series, 1967—; Latoratoire d'etudes des relations entre rythmes cosmiques et psychophysiologiques, Paris, director, 1969—. *Military service:* French Military Reserve, active duty, 1953-54; became lieutenant. *Member:* International Society of Chronobiology, International Society of Sport Psychology, International Society of Biometeorology, International Society of Chacterology, International Committee for the Study of Ambient Factors (member of board of directors). *Awards, honors:* Medal for psychological writings from 16th Congress of Health, Ferrara, Italy, 1969.

WRITINGS: L'Influence des astres: Etude critique et experimentale (title means "The Influence of Stars: A Critical and Experimental Study"), Le Dauphin, 1955; (with wife, Francoise Gauquelin) *Methodes pour etudier la repartition des astres dans le mouvement diurne* (title means "Methods for the Study of the Stars' Distribution in the Diurnal Movement"), privately printed, 1957.

Les Hommes et les astres (title means "Men and Stars"), Denoel, 1960; (with Francoise Gauquelin) *L'Epanouissement de la personnalite dans la famille et la societe moderne* (title means "Personality Development in Modern Family and Modern Society"), Editions Sociales Francaises, 1963, 2nd edition, 1969; *L'Astrologie devant la science*, Planete, 1965, translation by James Hughes published as *The Scientific Basis of Astrology: Myth or Reality?*, Stein & Day, 1969 (published in England as *Astrology and Science*, P. Davies, 1970); (with Francoise Gauquelin and Francois Richaudeau) *Methode de lecture rapide* (title means "Method of Speed Reading"), Centre d'etude et de promotion de la lecture, 1966; *L'Heredite Planetaire* (title means "Planetary Heredity"), Planete, 1966; *The Cosmic Clocks: From Astrology to a Modern Science*, Regnery, 1967; *Le Sante et les Conditions Atmospheriques*, Hatchette, 1967, translation by Joyce E. Clemow published as *How Atmospheric Conditions Affect Your Health*, Stein & Day, 1971; *Songes et Mensonges de l'Astrologie* (title means "Dreams and Fallacies of Astrologie"), Hatchett, 1969.

Connaitre les autres (title means "To Know the Others"), Centre d'etude et de promotion de la lecture, 1970; (editor) *La Psychologie moderne de A a Z* (title means "Modern Psychology from A to Z"), Centre d'etude et de promotion de la lecture, 1971; (with Jacques Sadoul) *L'Astrologie* (title means "Astrology"), Denoel, 1972; (with Francoise Gauquelin) *20 tests pour se connaitre* (title means "Twenty Tests to Know Oneself"), Denoel, 1972; *Cosmic Influences on Human Behavior*, Stein & Day, 1973; *Rythmes biologiques, Rythmes Cosmiques* (title means "Biological Rhythms, Cosmic Rhythms"), Gerard, 1973; *La Cosmo-Psychology* (title means "Cosmo-Psychology"), Retz, 1975.

Contributor to over twenty publications of Laboratoire D'Etudes des Relations entre Rythmes Cosmiques et Psychophysiologiques. Contributor to *Psychology Today, Figaro litteraire*, and other periodicals. Writer of television programs on psychology and cosmic influences. Scientific editor of *Psychologie* (Paris), 1970—; psychology publications editor, Centre d'etude et de promotion de la lecture (Paris), 1972—.

WORK IN PROGRESS: The Cosmo-Psychology, a study of the psychology of personality with relation to cosmic influences; a study of the behavior and life story of renowned persons on the basis of planetary patterns at the time of their birth.

SIDELIGHTS: Gauquelin told *CA*: "Until the beginning of this century, science believed that man was in isolation on earth, separated from the rest of the universe. Now we know that the biological clocks of our brain and our body are attuned to the movement of the cosmic forces. . . . This new conception should have not only scientific but also philosophical and even poetical implications for modern thought." *Avocational interests:* Tennis.

BIOGRAPHICAL/CRITICAL SOURCES: New Behavior, May 29, 1975.

* * *

GAZIS, Denos C(onstantinos) 1930-

PERSONAL: Born September 15, 1930, in Salonica, Greece; naturalized U.S. citizen in 1960; son of Evangelos (an army officer) and Lila (Veniamin) Gazis; married Diana Beckwith, February 3, 1955 (divorced, 1974); married Jean Ryniker, September 15, 1974; children: (first marriage) Paul, Jean, Lynn, Andrew, Carey, Jessie, Alexander. *Education:* Technical University, Athens, Greece, B.A. and M.S., 1952; Stanford University, M.S., 1954; Columbia University, Ph.D., 1957. *Address:* Lake Rd., R.D. 2, Katonah, N.Y. 10536. *Office address:* International Business Machines Research Center, Box 218, Yorktown Heights, N.Y. 10598.

CAREER: Tippetts and Associates, New York, N.Y., design engineer, 1955-57; General Motors Corp. Research Center, Warren, Mich., senior research scientist, 1957-61; International Business Machines Research Center, Yorktown Heights, N.Y., research staff member, 1961-71, director of department of general sciences, 1971-74, consultant to director of research, 1974—. Visiting professor at Yale University, 1969-70. *Member:* American Physical Society, Operations Research Society of America, Transportation Research Board, Society for Natural Philosophy. *Awards, honors:* Lanchester prize from Operations Research Society of America, 1969, for outstanding operations research paper.

WRITINGS: (With A. E. Armenakas and George Herrmann) *Free Vibrations of Circular Cylindrical Shells*, Pergamon, 1969; (editor and contributor) *Traffic Science*, Wiley, 1974. Contributor of more than seventy-five articles on physics and mathematical modeling of societal problems to journals. Associate editor of *Computing*, 1966—, of *Transportation Science*, 1970—, of *Networks*, 1971—, and of *IEEE Transactions of Automatic Control*, 1971-74.

WORK IN PROGRESS: Research on optimization of transportation systems, and on systems of production and distribution of electric power.

SIDELIGHTS: Gazis speaks French, Italian, and Spanish, as well as English and his native Greek; he reads German and Russian.

* * *

GEARHART, Sally Miller 1931-

PERSONAL: Born April 15, 1931, in Pearisburg, Va.; daughter of Kyle M. and Sarah Gearhart. *Education:* Sweet Briar College, B.A., 1952; Bowling Green State University, M.A., 1953; University of Illinois, Ph.D., 1956. *Politics:* "Lesbian-Feminist." *Religion:* "Philogyny." *Home:* 1167 Rhode Island, San Francisco, Calif. 94107. *Office:* Department of Speech, San Francisco State University, 1600 Holloway, San Francisco, Calif. 94132.

CAREER: Stephen F. Austin State University, Nacogdoches, Tex., assistant professor of speech, 1956-59; Texas Lutheran College, Seguin, associate professor of speech and drama and head of department, 1960-70; San Francisco State University, San Francisco, Calif., assistant professor of speech, 1972—. Member of board of directors of San Francisco Family Service Agency; co-chairperson of Council on Religion and the Homosexual; member of San Francisco Women's Centers; lecturer and consultant for National Sex Forum. *Member:* Speech Communication Association of America, Western Speech Association, San Francisco Mental Health Association.

WRITINGS: (With William R. Johnson) *Loving Women/Loving Men: Gay Liberation and the Church*, Glide, 1974.

WORK IN PROGRESS: Women and Words: Toward a Feminist Rhetoric; *Sex Roles and Communication*, with Alana Silver; science fiction stories.

SIDELIGHTS: Sally Gearhart writes: "My love of myself as a woman and my love of other women motivates all my writing (and my creative existence). In a society that hates women and the womanly, woman-love is a miracle and therefore a hefty motivation."

* * *

GEDDES, Joan Bel 1916-

PERSONAL: Born December 2, 1916, in Los Angeles, Calif.; daughter of Norman Bel (an artist) and Helen Bel (Sneider) Geddes; married Barry Ulanov, December 16, 1939 (divorced, 1968); children: Anne, Nicholas, Katherine. *Education:* Barnard College, B.A., 1937. *Politics:* Independent. *Religion:* Roman Catholic. *Home:* 60 East Eighth St., New York, N.Y. 10003. *Agent:* Holub Associates, 432 Park Ave. S., New York, N.Y. 10016. *Office:* UNICEF, United Nations Plaza, New York, N.Y. 10016.

CAREER: Norman Bel Geddes, Inc., New York, N.Y., office assistant, researcher, and publicist, 1937-41; Compton Advertising, Inc., New York, N.Y., member of staff, 1941-47, as publicity director one year and new program manager, four years; Birch Wathen School, New York, N.Y., drama teacher, 1950; Shaw Publications, New York, N.Y., editor, 1952-56, editor-in-chief of *My Baby* and *Congratulations* (magazine), 1954-56; United Nations Children's Fund (UNICEF), New York, N.Y., public information officer, 1970—. Member of faculty, Institute on Man and Science, Rensellaerville, N.Y., summer, 1969, and of Christian Family Movement National Conference at Monmouth College, 1970. Interviewer-hostess on weekly radio show, "Religion and the Arts," National Broadcasting Co. Network, 1968. *Member:* National Society of Literature and the Arts, Authors League of America, American Teilhard de Chardin Association, National Citizens Committee for Public Broadcasting.

WRITINGS: (Editor) Norman Bel Geddes, *Magic Motorways*, Random House, 1940; (translator from the French with Barry Ulanov) *Last Essays of Georges Bernanos*, Regnery, 1955; *Small World: A History of Baby Care from the Stone Age to the Spock Age*, Macmillan, 1964; *How to Parent Alone: A Guide for Single Parents*, Seabury, 1974; (editor) Isaac Asimov, *Earth: Our Crowded Spaceship* (juvenile), John Day, 1974; *To Barbara with Love: Prayers and Reflections by a Believer for a Skeptic*, Doubleday, 1974.

Contributor: (Author of introduction) Jeanne De Good, *The Long Weight*, State Publishing Co. (St. Louis), 1955;

John M. Oesterreicher, editor, *The Bridge*, Volume III, Pantheon, 1958; Clayton C. Barbeau, editor, *Art, Obscenity and Your Children*, Abbey Press, 1969; Thomas E. Quigley, editor, *American Catholics and Vietnam*, Eerdmans, 1970; Barbeau, editor, *The Future of the Family*, Bruce, 1971; Alfred R. Joyce and E. Mark Stern, editors, *Holiness and Mental Health*, Paulist-Newman, 1972.

Designer, author, or editor of six booklets for adults and six for children on the United Nations, published by UNICEF, and of five booklets on health for Equitable Life Assurance Co. Contributor to magazines and newspapers in United States, Canada, Australia, India, Kenya, Pakistan, and the Philippines, including *Redbook, Family Digest, Better Homes and Gardens, Popular Gardening, Way, New Era* (Kenya), *Pakistan Times*, and *Australian Student*.

Editorial associate and reviewer, *Listen* (monthly music and record magazine), 1940-43; associate editor (nonfiction), *Today's Woman*, 1951; consulting editor, *Journal of Pastoral Counseling*, 1971—; editor, *UNICEF Information Bulletin*, 1973—, and Syndicated Feature Service, published by UNICEF, 1974—.

SIDELIGHTS: "There is a problem about my name," Joan Bel Geddes points out. "My last name is Geddes, but since my father Norman (a well-known artist), and my sister, Barbara (an equally well-known actress), and I all adopted my mother's middle name, Bel, many people have concluded that our last name was 'Bel Geddes.' In my publishers' catalogues and the UN phone directory I am listed as 'Bel Geddes, Joan and nothing I say will make them change it!

"I am interested in almost everything and everyone! My major interests are: (1) religion, (2) people, (3) internationalism, (4) the arts. . . . I have traveled widely, both on personal and official trips. The regions I love most are New England (I have a summer home in Vermont but also get to the seacoast as often as possible), the Southwest and California, Asia (especially India and Sri Lanka), and Europe (especially England, Scotland and the Netherlands; I lived in London for a full year, in 1961).

"In addition to writing and editing mentioned elsewhere, I write and research many speeches, statements and reports about children and family life in many countries. I also do quite a lot of lecturing—to school children, college seminars, women's clubs and church groups. . . .

"I have also been a professional playreader (for Norman Bel Geddes and for Metro-Goldwyn-Mayer) and a production assistant in the theatre (including the first ice show produced by Sonja Henie, the Ringling Brothers Barnum & Bailey Circus, and several Broadway plays), on radio (interview programs, variety shows, situation comedies and daytime serials) and on television (variety specials)."

AVOCATIONAL INTERESTS: Reading, especially in history, biography, religion, philosophy, and psychology; reading and writing poetry, going to the theatre, jigsaw and crossword puzzles, yoga, travel.

* * *

GEIS, Florence L(indauer) 1933-

PERSONAL: Born April 3, 1933, in Oakland, Calif.; daughter of Earl S. (a farm owner) and Alma (Dahm) Lindauer; married H. Jon Geis (divorced, 1960). *Education:* University of Arizona, B.A., 1956; Columbia University, M.A., 1961, Ph.D., 1964. *Residence:* Landenberg, Pa. *Of-*

fice: Department of Psychology, University of Delaware, Newark, Del. 19711.

CAREER: New York University, New York, N.Y., assistant professor of psychology, 1964-67; University of Delaware, Newark, assistant professor, 1967-71, associate professor of psychology, 1971—. *Member:* American Psychological Association, Association for Women in Psychology, Eastern Psychological Association, Delaware Psychological Association.

WRITINGS: (With Richard Christie) *Studies in Machiavellianism*, Academic Press, 1970.

WORK IN PROGRESS: A student workbook, *Personality Research Manual*; research on psychology of women.

* * *

GELL, Frank
See KOWET, Don

* * *

GEORGE, Malcom F(arris) 1930-

PERSONAL: Born July 10, 1930, in Michie, Tenn.; son of James Robert and Arbie (Farris) George; married Verlin Horton, July 26, 1951; children: George David, Rose Ann. *Education:* Attended Freed-Hardeman College, 1950-52; David Lipscomb College, B.A., 1954; Harding Graduate School, M.A., 1962. *Home:* Market Ave., Bolivar, Tenn. 38008. *Agent:* Ernest Clevenger, Jr., Box 3909, Birmingham, Ala. *Office address:* P.O. Box 255, Bolivar, Tenn. 38008.

CAREER: Became minister of Church of Christ, 1950; minister in Ripley, Miss., 1964-68; Middle East Bible Training College, Beirut, Lebanon, director, 1969-71; minister in Bolivar, Tenn., 1973—. *Member:* Bolivar Civitan Club (president, 1975—).

WRITINGS: *The Role of the Preacher as a Counselor*, Williams Printing Co., 1967, revised edition published as *Introduction to Christian Counseling*, 1975.

WORK IN PROGRESS: Editing *My Experiences in the Middle East*, by wife, Verlin George.

* * *

GERHARD, Happy 1920-

PERSONAL: Born October 13, 1920, in New York, N.Y.; daughter of F. Wilham L. (a president of an import-export firm) and Harriett (Briggs) Dreckmeier; married William H. Gerhard (an executive), October 30, 1941 (divorced, 1969); children: Pamela K. (Mrs. Stephen G. Phillips), Lang H., Bruce H. *Education:* Attended French Fashion Academy, New York, N.Y. *Politics:* Republican. *Religion:* Protestant. *Home:* 551 Park St., Montclair, N.J. 07043. *Office:* 241 East 76th St., New York, N.Y. 10021.

CAREER: Asiatic Petroleum Co., New York, N.Y., executive secretary, 1939-42; Happy Gerhard Interior Design, West Chester, Pa., interior decorator, 1959-70; French Fashion Academy, New York, N.Y., teacher, 1971-73; medical secretary for a surgeon in New York, N.Y., 1974—. Gave private classes in dress designing, 1972-74.

WRITINGS: (With Ruth Amiel) *Finally It Fits*, New York Times Book Co., 1973.

* * *

GERHART, Genevra 1930-

PERSONAL: Born January 3, 1930, in Seattle, Wash.; daughter of Stanley and R. Elizabeth (Baker) Thomesen; married James B. Gerhart (a professor of physics), June 21, 1958; children: Ned, Sara. *Education:* University of Washington, Seattle, B.A., 1950, graduate study, 1957-64; School of Oriental Languages, Paris, graduate study, 1951-52. *Home:* 2134 East Interlaken Blvd., Seattle, Wash. 98112.

CAREER: Part-time university instructor, 1965-67; substitute teacher in public schools, 1971-74; author. *Member:* American Association for the Advancement of Slavic Studies, American Association of Teachers of Slavic and East European Languages, American Council of Teachers of Russian, American Council on the Teaching of Foreign Languages, Washington Association of Foreign Language Teachers.

WRITINGS: *The Russian's World: Life and Language*, Harcourt, 1974.

WORK IN PROGRESS: A sequel to *The Russian's World* that will include food, communications, work, medicine, plants, ceremonies, and proprieties.

* * *

GERIG, Reginald R(oth) 1919-

PERSONAL: Born April 20, 1919, in Grabill, Ind.; son of Safara Samuel (an accountant) and Sarah (Roth) Gerig; married Irene Conrad (a piano teacher), June 17, 1944; children: Sarah Elizabeth (Mrs. Bruce A. Campbell), Reginald, Jr. *Education:* Wheaton College, Wheaton, Ill., B.Mus., (with highest honors), 1942; Juilliard School of Music, B.S., 1948, M.S., 1949. *Religion:* Undenominational. *Home:* 1328 Naperville Rd., Wheaton, Ill. 60187. *Office:* Conservatory of Music, Wheaton College, Wheaton, Ill. 60187.

CAREER: Nyack College, Nyack, N.Y., member of piano faculty, 1946-50; University of Rochester, Rochester, N.Y., member of piano faculty at Eastman School of Music, 1950-52; Wheaton College, Wheaton, Ill., assistant professor, 1952-57, associate professor, 1957-62, professor of piano, 1962—, chairman of department of piano, 1969—, organist at College Church in Wheaton, 1953—. *Military service:* U.S. Naval Reserve, welfare specialist, 1942-45. *Member:* National Guild of Piano Teachers, Music Teachers National Association, Society of American Musicians, National Society of Literature and the Arts, Illinois State Music Teachers Association, Wheaton College Scholastic Honor Society (president, 1974-75).

WRITINGS: (Compiler) *Piano Preludes on Hymns and Chorales*, Hope, 1959; *Famous Pianists and Their Technique*, Luce, 1974.

* * *

GERMAN, Donald R(obert) 1931-

PERSONAL: Born February 11, 1931, in Philadelphia, Pa.; son of S. Edward and Reba (Trimble) German; married Joan Wolfe (a writer), September 4, 1954; children: D. Robert, Jr. *Education:* Temple University, B.S., 1955. *Politics:* Independent. *Religion:* Unitarian Universalist. *Home and office:* Lanesboro Mountain Rd., Cheshire, Mass. 01225. *Agent:* Toni Mendez, 140 East 56th St., New York, N.Y. 10022.

CAREER: Industrial Valley Bank, Philadelphia, Pa., business development director, 1960-61; publicity director, Savings Banks Association of Massachusetts, 1963-64; Warren, Gorham & Lamont, Inc., Boston, Mass. and New York, N.Y., editor, 1964—; free-lance writer and editor. *Military service:* U.S. Army, 1954-56; became first lieutenant. *Member:* Society of Magazine Writers, Berkshire Poet's Workshop (founding member).

WRITINGS: Banker's Complete Guide to Advertising, Warren, 1966; (with wife, Joan German) *Bank Teller's Handbook,* Warren, 1970; *Bank Employee's Security Handbook,* Warren, 1972; (with J. German) *Successful Job Hunting for Executives,* Regnery, 1974; (with J. German) *Bank Employee's Marketing Handbook,* Warren, 1975. Contributor to *Berkshire Sampler* and poetry journals. Co-editor of *Branch Bankers Report,* 1968—, *Bank Teller's Report,* 1969—, *Teller's Marketing Bulletin,* 1974—.

WORK IN PROGRESS: A novel; a book on writing nonfiction for Sol III Press.

AVOCATIONAL INTERESTS: Organic gardening, gourmet cooking.

* * *

GERMAN, Joan W(olfe) 1933-

PERSONAL: Born February 9, 1933, in Philadelphia, Pa.; daughter of Merrill P. Wolfe (a salesman) and Jeanette (Anderson) Wolfe Evans; married Donald R. German (a writer), September 4, 1954; children: D. Robert, Jr. *Education:* Attended Temple University, 1951-54. *Politics:* Independent. *Religion:* Unitarian Universalist. *Home and office:* Lanesboro Mountain Rd., Cheshire, Mass. 01225. *Agent:* Toni Mendez, 140 East 56th St., New York, N.Y. 10022.

CAREER: Warren, Gorham & Lamont, Inc., New York, N.Y. and Boston, Mass., editor, 1966—; free-lance writer and editor. *Member:* National League of American Pen Women (president of Berkshire Branch, 1974-75), Berkshire Poet's Workshop (founding member).

WRITINGS—With husband, Donald R. German: *The Bank Teller's Handbook,* Warren, 1970; *Successful Job Hunting for Executives,* Regnery, 1974; *Bank Employee's Marketing Handbook,* Warren, 1975. Contributor to *Berkshire Sampler* and poetry journals. Co-editor of *Branch Banker's Report,* 1968—, *Bank Teller's Report,* 1969—, *Teller's Marketing Bulletin,* 1974—.

AVOCATIONAL INTERESTS: Painting, art needlework.

* * *

GERSHOY, Leo 1897-1975

September 27, 1897—March 12, 1975; Russian-born American educator, historian, editor, and author of books on French history. Obituaries: *New York Times,* March 14, 1975; *AB Bookman's Weekly,* April 21, 1975. (CA-13/14)

* * *

GERSTER, Patrick G(eorge) 1942-

PERSONAL: Born January 5, 1942, in St. Paul, Minn.; son of Bradley John (in wholesale lumber business) and Catherine (Morrisey) Gerster; married Carole Jean Young, September 30, 1967; children: Mark, Jennifer, Jason. *Education:* College of St. Thomas, B.A., 1964; University of Minnesota, M.A., 1965, Ph.D., 1970. *Politics:* Democrat. *Home:* 47 Grove St., Mahtomedi, Minn. 55115. *Office:* Department of History, Lakewood Community College, 3401 Century Ave., White Bear Lake, Minn. 55110.

CAREER: Lakewood Community College, White Bear Lake, Minn., professor of history, 1970—. Lecturer at College of St. Thomas (St. Paul, Minn.), 1975—. *Member:*

American Historical Association, Organization of American Historians, Southern Historical Association, Lakewood Faculty Association (president, 1974—). *Awards, honors:* Fellowships from National Endowment for the Humanities, summers, 1973-74, for research on myth, symbolic modes, and ideology.

WRITINGS: (Editor) *Myth and the American Experience,* Glencoe, 1973; (editor) *Myth and Southern History,* Rand McNally, 1974; *Myth America,* Glencoe, in press. Contributor to social science journals.

WORK IN PROGRESS: Myth and History, a monograph; research on northern origins of southern mythology, and on mythology old and new.

SIDELIGHTS: Gerster writes that his interest is the relationship between national ideology and national mythology.

* * *

GETTY, Gerald W(inkler) 1913-

PERSONAL: Born June 17, 1913, in Chicago, Ill.; son of Oliver P. (in railroad business) and Pearl (Winkler) Getty; married Helen M. Brennan, October 2, 1937 (died, April 15, 1955); married Gracia Gibbs, June 3, 1957; children: (first marriage) L. Michael, Muriel Getty Ranochowski, H. Leo, Marie Terese Getty Goldberg, H. John. *Education:* DePaul University, J.D., 1937. *Politics:* Democrat. *Religion:* Roman Catholic. *Home:* 15531 University, Dolton, Ill. 60419. *Office:* 14150 Chicago Rd., Dolton, Ill. 60419.

CAREER: Attorney for Federal Government Price Administration, 1937-42; assistant public defender, Cook County, Ill., 1942-54, public defender, 1954-71; private practice of law in Dolton, Ill., 1971—. Part-time lecturer in real estate law, Roosevelt University, Chicago, 1940-46.

WRITINGS: Public Defender, Grosset, 1974. Contributor to law journals.

* * *

GHOSH, Jyotis Chandra 1904(?)-1975

1904(?)—May 28, 1975; Educator, scholar, and author. Obituaries: *AB Bookman's Weekly,* July 28, 1975.

* * *

GIBBS, Esther 1904-

PERSONAL: Born August 1, 1904, in Hinton, Okla.; daughter of Thomas E. and Ida E. Nail; married James M. Welch, 1921 (deceased); married Cecil F. Gibbs, 1950; children: (first marriage) two sons, one daughter (all deceased); son (adopted grandchild). *Education:* High school (correspondence). *Home:* Route 1, Spooner, Wis. 54801.

CAREER: Professional cook, beginning, 1940; writer.

WRITINGS: We Went a Loggin', North Star Press, 1974.

SIDELIGHTS: Because of the varied experience of her seventy years, Esther Gibbs feels she has lived several lives. Marrying very young, it wasn't until her retirement that she found time to write, something she had always wanted to do. Mrs. Gibbs and her husband built the log house in which they live.

* * *

GIBBS, Joanifer 1947-

PERSONAL: Born January 3, 1947, in Baltimore, Md.; daughter of Charles Raymond Gibbs and Elizabeth (Calvert) Steuart Gibbs. *Education:* Maryland Institute of Art,

B.F.A., 1969. *Home:* 4214 North Charles St., Baltimore, Md. 21218.

CAREER: Free-lance illustrator and craftswoman.

WRITINGS: Batik Unlimited, Watson-Guptill, 1974.

WORK IN PROGRESS: A "how-to" book on making jewelry, for Chilton.

SIDELIGHTS: Joanifer Gibbs writes: "I am researching meditation . . . may travel to India soon . . . am deeply involved in all aspects of mysticism, yoga, and meditation practices."

* * *

GIFFORD, James Fergus, Jr. 1940-

PERSONAL: Born March 3, 1940, in Lynn, Mass.; son of James Fergus (manager of a car dealership) and Joyce (Scannell) Gifford; married Clarice Mason, August 31, 1963. *Education:* Dartmouth College, B.A., 1961; Andover Newton Theological School, B.D., 1964, S.T.M., 1965; Duke University, Ph.D., 1969. *Religion:* American Baptist Convention. *Home:* 2621 David Caldwell Dr., Greensboro, N.C. 27408. *Office:* Department of History, Guilford College, 5800 Friendly Ave., Greensboro, N.C. 27410.

CAREER: Guilford College, Greensboro, N.C., assistant professor of history, 1969—. *Member:* American Historical Association, Organization of American Historians, American Association of University Professors, Phi Beta Kappa, Phi Alpha Theta. *Awards, honors:* Josiah Macy, Jr. Foundation fellow, 1967-69.

WRITINGS: The Evolution of a Medical Center: A History of Medicine at Duke University to 1941, Duke University Press, 1972. Contributor of articles to *Journal of College Science Teaching* and *North Carolina Journal of Mental Health*.

WORK IN PROGRESS: Second volume of *The Evolution of a Medical Center*, publication expected in 1978; editing *Experiences with the Duke Medical Curriculum*, completion expected in 1976.

* * *

GILBERT, Anne 1927-

PERSONAL: Born May 1, 1927, in Chicago, Ill.; daughter of David and Joy (Arnold) Wieland; married George Gale Gilbert III (an actor), April 7, 1953; children: Douglas, Christopher. *Education:* Northwestern University, B.S., 1949. *Politics:* Republican. *Religion:* Presbyterian. *Home and office:* 932 15th St., Wilmette, Ill. 60091. *Agent:* Toni Mendez, Inc., 140 East 56th St., New York, N.Y. 10022.

CAREER: Ruder-Finn, Chicago, Ill., fashion copywriter for Marshall Fields department store, 1949; free-lance writer for motion pictures, slide films, and public relations, 1950-70; Accent International, public relations director, 1952; Grant Advertising, public relations director, 1965-66; public relations account executive, 1970. Producer of "Collector's World" on WLTD-Radio, 1973—, and on television; public relations consultant to Chicago Community Music Foundation. Guest editor for NBC-TV programs on Chicago and on antiques. *Member:* Chicago Press Club.

WRITINGS: Antique Hunting: A Guide for Freaks and Fanciers, Grosset, 1975; *Knickknacks, Keepsakes, and other Nostalgic Collectibles*, C. R. Gibson, 1975. Author of "Antiques & Stuff," a syndicated column appearing in newspapers, including *New York Daily News, San Fran-*

cisco *Chronicle*, and *Chicago Daily News*. Contributor to *Hobbies* and *Sphere*.

WORK IN PROGRESS: Antique Detective; a television series about how to be an "antique detective."

AVOCATIONAL INTERESTS: Travel.

* * *

GILBERT, Harriett 1948-

PERSONAL: Born August 25, 1948, in London, England; daughter of Michael (a lawyer and novelist) and Roberta (a creche supervisor; maiden name, Marsden) Gilbert. *Education:* Attended Rose Bruford College of Speech and Drama. *Politics:* "Yes." *Religion:* "No." *Residence:* London, England. *Agent:* Richard Scott Simon, 32 College Cross, London N1 1PR, England.

CAREER: Writer. Has worked as an actress, nanny, artist's model, and teacher of French.

WRITINGS—Novels: *I Know Where I've Been*, Harper, 1972; *Hotels with Empty Rooms*, Harper, 1973; *An Offence against the Persons*, Hodder & Stoughton, 1974, Harper, 1975. Contributor of articles and stories to *Girl about Town* and *Flair*.

WORK IN PROGRESS: A novel.

* * *

GILBERT, Sara (Dulaney) 1943-

PERSONAL: Born October 5, 1943, in Washington, D.C.; daughter of Ben Bane (a journalist) and Jean (an editor; maiden name, Brownell) Dulaney; married Ian R. Gilbert (a lawyer), August 31, 1963; children: Sean Dulaney. *Education:* Attended Brown University, 1961-63; Barnard College, B.A. (with honors), 1966. *Residence:* New York, N.Y. *Agent:* Marilyn Marlowe, Curtis Brown Ltd., 60 East 56th St., New York, N.Y. 10022.

CAREER: Cowles Communications, New York, N.Y., editor and writer, 1966-68. *Awards, honors:* Mr. Freedom Award from Religious Liberty Association, 1972, for articles.

WRITINGS: Three Years to Grow: Guidance for Your Child's First Three Years, Parents' Magazine Press, 1972; *What's a Father For?*, Parents' Magazine Press, 1975; *Fat Free*, Macmillan, 1975. Contributor to *Baby Care, Ms, Good Housekeeping, Travel, Campfire Girl, Negro Digest, Liberty, Metrolines*, and *National Businesswoman*.

WORK IN PROGRESS: Research on domestic violence, and on parent-teenager relations; juvenile fiction; adult mysteries.

AVOCATIONAL INTERESTS: Gardening.

* * *

GILFILLAN, Edward S(mith), Jr. 1906-

PERSONAL: Born March 3, 1906, in Washington, D.C.; son of Edward S. and Caroline (Whitman) Gilfillan; married Ruth Chudderdon, August 20, 1929 (divorced, May, 1959); married Elinor Anderson (an administrator), June 19, 1959; children: (first marriage) Ellen May, Edward Smith. *Education:* Kalamazoo College, B.A., 1928; Harvard University, M.A., 1929, Ph.D., 1932. *Home and office:* 34 Tappan St., Manchester, Mass. 01944.

CAREER: Arthur D. Little, Inc. (research and development firm), Cambridge, Mass., consulting chemist, 1935-38; Westinghouse Electric & Manufacturing Co., Pittsburgh,

Pa., consulting engineer, 1938-40; consulting engineer, 1947-58; Lowell Technological Institute, Lowell, Mass., professor of nuclear engineering, 1958-69, head of department of mechanical engineering, 1958-69, head of department of nuclear engineering, 1958-59, head of department of textile engineering, 1959-69; Chinese University of Hong Kong, Hong Kong, visiting professor of engineering, 1969-71. Civilian employee of U.S. Air Force, Office of Army Operations Research, Office of the Secretary of Defense, Committee for Amphibious Operations, and National Research Council. *Military service:* U.S. Naval Reserve, 1934—; active duty, 1940-47; retiring as commander. *Member:* American Chemical Society, Cosmos Club. *Awards, honors:* Sheldon traveling fellowship from Harvard University, 1932-33, for study in France, Germany, and Spain; National Research fellowship from Massachusetts Institute of Technology, 1933-35.

WRITINGS: Migration to the Stars, Luce, 1975. Contributor to *Effects of Atomic Weapons*, Atomic Energy Commission. Contributor of scientific articles, travel articles, and book reviews to magazines.

WORK IN PROGRESS: The Coastal Dialects of China.

*   *   *

GILLES, Albert S(imeon), Sr. 1888-
(Oklahoma Peddler)

PERSONAL: Born January 18, 1888, near Marysville, Kan.; son of Simeon J. (a farmer and trader) and Martha Ellen (Bevens) Gilles; married Tennie Clair Blackburn, April, 1911 (deceased); children: Albert Simeon, Lois (Mrs. Harry A. Mentzel), Pauline (Mrs. Charles L. Rogers; deceased), Willard C. *Education:* Attended Epworth University (now Oklahoma City University), 1907-11, and University of Oklahoma, part-time, 1961-74. *Politics:* Conservative Republican. *Religion:* Methodist. *Home and office:* 310 West Apache St., Norman, Okla. 73069.

CAREER: Admitted to the Bar of Oklahoma, 1913; private practice of law in Oklahoma City, Okla., 1913-43, in Norman, Okla., 1943-53; free-lance writer, 1963—. Served as steam construction foreman during both World Wars.

WRITINGS: Comanche Days, Southern Methodist University Press, 1974. Contributor to *Southwestern Review*; under name Oklahoma Peddler, contributor of poems to journals.

WORK IN PROGRESS: A western novel.

SIDELIGHTS: "It is fun writing fiction...," Gilles wrote, "but as I'm eighty-seven years old, feel my main effort should be spent on near history ... for I was there. Sort of have it on my conscience to put it on paper.... never had to invent a cliff-hanger. Saw things beyond the LSD dreams of Hollywood script writers. Just interested in putting down what my eyes saw and ears heard."

*   *   *

GILLETTE, Virginia M(ary) 1920-
(J. Sloan McLean; joint pseudonym with Josephine Wunsch)

PERSONAL: Born January 27, 1920, in Detroit, Mich.; daughter of Philip William (an engineer) and Mable (Wheelock) Sloan; married William R. Gillette (a staff engineer), May 3, 1941; children: Susan (Mrs. Carl Ranno), William, Sarah (Mrs. Robert Hughes), Mary Virginia, Philip. *Education:* Attended Elmira College, 1937-38, and University of Michigan, 1938-39. *Religion:* Roman Catholic. *Home and office:* 47 Surrey Lane, Pontiac, Mich. 48055. *Agent:* Park Avenue Literary Agency, 230 Park Ave., New York, N.Y. 10017.

CAREER: Writer.

WRITINGS: (Under joint pseudonym J. Sloan McLean, with Josephine Wunsch) *The Aerie* (novel), Nash Publishing, 1974. Contributor of more than two hundred short stories to national magazines, including *Good Housekeeping, Woman's Day, Home Life, Marriage, Together, Catholic Miss, Writer, Family Digest, Modern Woodmen of America*, and to confession magazines, religious periodicals, and newspapers.

WORK IN PROGRESS: The Villa, a suspense novel, with Josephine Wunsch, under joint pseudonym J. Sloan McLean.

SIDELIGHTS: "Life did not begin at forty," Virginia Gillette wrote, "but rather some freedom to pursue other loves. I am enthusiastic about writing. I like the results. I like the people I meet. I like seeing my name and my work in print. The only thing I do not like is sitting in front of the typewriter." *Avocational interests:* Knitting, sewing, swimming, travel in a travel-trailer, working on building the family's cottage.

*   *   *

GILLIGAN, Sonja Carl 1936-

PERSONAL: Born January 12, 1936, in Phoenix, Ariz.; daughter of Hugo August (a mining and chemical engineer) and Irmgard (Martin) Carl; married Michael G. Gilligan (a film maker), June 24, 1961; children: Patrick. *Education:* Attended Kuenst Akademie, 1955-57; Art Institute of Chicago, B.F.A., 1959. *Politics:* Democrat. *Religion:* "Protestant (not practicing)." *Office address:* Hardtimes Movie Co., Indian Brook Rd., Garrison, N.Y. 10524.

CAREER: Graphic designer for Scott, Foresman & Co. (publishers), Chicago, Ill., 1959, and Scholastic Book Services, New York, N.Y., 1959-62; free-lance book designer in New York, N.Y., 1962-65. Group leader in encounter therapy for Fusion Groups and Dr. Dan Casriel, in New York, N.Y., 1967-72. Film maker for U.S. Department of Health, Education and Welfare documentary productions, 1971-73; film producer, writer, director for Hardtimes Movie Co., 1971—.

WRITINGS: The Heterosexuals Are Coming, Fusion Groups, Inc., 1971.

Author and director of television films, from Hardtimes Movie Co.: "The Anatomy of Success," 1972; "Christina's World," 1973; "Women: The Way We Were," 1974. Author of short stories and film narrations.

WORK IN PROGRESS: Directing "The Murder of Edith Stein," a feature film, for Hardtimes Movie Co.

SIDELIGHTS: Several years ago, six couples were in an encounter group together, sharing one another's thoughts and feelings. Now all these people live in the same community and share one another's lives. They are not members of a commune, nor do they feel they have bohemian life styles. Sonja Gilligan and her husband were the pioneers of this encounter group, Fusion, which was a "couple-oriented" endeavor.

Most of the members of this group formed Hardtimes Movie Co., and continue to work together. They feel it is not just the relationships between individuals and couples that count, but that among the families as well.

BIOGRAPHICAL/CRITICAL SOURCES: New York Times, July 30, 1973; *American Cinematographer*, November, 1973.

*   *   *

GILLMER, Thomas C(harles)   1911-
(Tom Gillmer)

PERSONAL: Born July 17, 1911, in Warren, Ohio; son of Derr Oscar (an investment broker) and Hazel (Voit) Gillmer; married Anna May Derge, June 5, 1937; children: Christina (Mrs. Richard Erdmann), Charles Voit. *Education:* Western Reserve University (now Case Western Reserve University), student, 1930-31; U.S. Naval Academy, B.S., 1935; Johns Hopkins University, graduate study, 1947. *Home:* 1 Shipwright Harbor, Annapolis, Md. 21401. *Office:* Thomas Gillmer Naval Architects, 300 State St., Annapolis, Md. 21403.

CAREER: U.S. Navy, career officer, 1935-45, leaving service as lieutenant commander; U.S. Naval Academy, Annapolis, Md., assistant professor, 1946-49, associate professor, 1949-63, professor of marine engineering, 1963-67, director of Model Towing Basin, 1955-67, director of Ship Hydrodynamics Laboratory, 1956-67, chairman of department of naval architecture, 1961-67, chairman of department of naval engineering, 1964-67; Thomas Gillmer Naval Architects, Annapolis, Md., owner, 1967—. Member of board of directors of Historic Annapolis, Inc., 1968-72; member of panel of experts for fishing craft of Food and Agriculture Organization of United Nations. During military service, served in Atlantic and Mediterranean theaters on cruisers and destroyers. *Member:* Society of Naval Architects and Marine Engineers, American Society of Naval Engineers, Annapolis Yacht Club, Club de Voile (Villefranche, France).

WRITINGS: (With Eric Neitch) *Clouds, Weather, and Flight*, Van Nostrand, 1945; *Construction and Stability of Naval Ships*, U.S. Naval Institute, 1956, revised edition, 1959; *Modern Ship Design*, U.S. Naval Institute, 1970, revised edition, 1975; *Working Watercraft: A Survey of Surviving Local Boats of America* (with own photographs), International Marine Publishing, 1972; *Ships of the American Revolution*, Admiralty Publishing, 1973; *Brigs and Sloops of the American Navy*, Admiralty Publishing, 1973. Contributor, occasionally under name Tom Gillmer, to boating magazines, including *American Neptune, Yachting, Rudder*, and *Sail*. Member of board of advisers of Admiralty Publishing.

WORK IN PROGRESS: Ancient Watercraft: Ships of Bronze Age Aegeans; research on yacht design.

SIDELIGHTS: Gillmer has concerned himself mainly with the design of small vessels and yachts. Among his designs of off-shore sailing auxiliaries is the ketch "Apogee," the first fiberglass boat to circumnavigate the world.

*   *   *

GILLMER, Tom
See GILLMER, Thomas C(harles)

*   *   *

GILMAN, George G.
See HARKNETT, Terry

*   *   *

GILMORE, Al-Tony   1946-

PERSONAL: Born June 29, 1946, in Spartanburg, S.C.;

son of Margaret Gilmore; married, wife's name Beryl. *Education:* North Carolina Central University, B.A., 1968, M.A., 1969; University of Toledo, Ph.D., 1972. *Home:* 18624 Shady View Lane, Brookeville, Md. 20729. *Office:* Department of History, Howard University, Washington, D.C. 20059.

CAREER: University of Toledo, Toledo, Ohio, lecturer in Afro-American history, 1970-72; Howard University, Washington, D.C., assistant professor of history, 1972—. *Member:* Association for the Study of Afro-American Life and History, American Historical Association, Organization of American Historians, Phi Alpha Theta.

WRITINGS: Bad Nigger!: The National Impact of Jack Johnson, Kennikat, 1975; *The Life and Times of Amos n' Andy*, Oxford University Press, in press. Contributor of articles and reviews to *Directory of Black Historians, Essays, and Commentaries* and *Dictionary of American Negro Biography*, and to professional journals. Consultant on minority treatment to McGraw.

WORK IN PROGRESS: Research on the internationally famous case of Willie McGee, a black Mississippian who was sentenced to death on the charge of rape during the years 1945 to 1951.

*   *   *

GIMMESTAD, Victor E(dward)   1912-

PERSONAL: Born August 13, 1912, in Galesville, Wis.; son of Lars Monsen (a minister) and Amalie (Anderson) Gimmestad; married Lucille Gray (a teacher and research assistant), August 26, 1937; children: Carole Kay (Mrs. Larry Johnson), Vickie Gail (Mrs. Milford Hofius), Gary Gene. *Education:* St. Olaf College, B.A., 1934; University of Wisconsin, M.A., 1940, Ph.D., 1950; University of Southern California, graduate study, summer, 1940. *Religion:* Lutheran. *Home:* 204 West Summit, Normal, Ill. 61761. *Office:* Department of English, Illinois State University, Normal, Ill. 61761.

CAREER: High school teacher of English in public schools in Minnesota, 1934-39, in New London, Wis., 1939-41, and in Panama Canal Zone, 1941-42; St. Olaf College, Madison, Wis., assistant professor of English, 1947-48; Illinois State University, Normal, assistant professor, 1948-51, associate professor, 1951-57, professor of literature, 1957—, chairman of department, 1960-67. Visiting professor and chairman of English department at California Lutheran College, 1968-69. Member of advisory committee of Illinois Governor's Commission on Higher Education, 1957-58. *Member:* International Platform Association, Norwegian-American Historical Association, Modern Language Association of America, Melville Society, National Education Association, Midwest Modern Language Association (president, 1963-64), Illinois Association of Higher Education.

WRITINGS: John Trumbull, Twayne, 1974. Contributor to *Yale University Liberty Gazette* and *American Literature*.

WORK IN PROGRESS: Joseph Hergesheimer, publication by Twayne expected in 1977; research on Ole Roelvaag.

AVOCATIONAL INTERESTS: Travel, sports, physical science.

*   *   *

GINTIS, Herbert   1940-

PERSONAL: Born February 11, 1940, in Philadelphia,

Pa.; son of Gerson (in retail furniture) and Shirley (Malena) Gintis; married Marci Susan Greisler (an artist), August 26, 1961; children: Daniel Moses. *Education:* University of Pennsylvania, B.A., 1961; Harvard University, M.A., 1962, Ph.D., 1969. *Office:* Department of Economics, Thompson Hall, University of Massachusetts, Amherst, Mass. 01002.

CAREER: University of Massachusetts, Amherst, associate professor of economics, 1974—. *Member:* Union for Radical Political Economics, Phi Beta Kappa. *Awards, honors:* Pitrim Sorokin award from American Sociological Association, 1974, for *Inequality.*

WRITINGS: (With Christopher Jencks and others) *Inequality*, Basic Books, 1972; (with Samuel Bowles) *Schooling in Capitalist America: Educational Reform and the Contradictions of Economic Life*, Basic Books, 1975. Contributor to journals in his field. Member of editorial board of *Union for Radical Political Economics Journal*, 1974-76.

WORK IN PROGRESS: Work on a Marxist theory of organizational structure, and the Marxist economic theory.

* * *

GIORDAN, Alma Roberts 1917-

PERSONAL: Born February 19, 1917, in Watertown, Conn.; married Robert Giordan (an artist), November 29, 1939; children: Nancy. *Education:* Educated in Watertown, Conn. *Home:* 70 Edward Ave., Watertown, Conn. 06795.

CAREER: Writer. *Awards, honors:* First place prizes from Connecticut's Federation of Women's Clubs, 1971, for poetry, and 1972, for essay.

WRITINGS: Torch Bearer and Other Poems, Golden Quill Press, 1972. Contributor of stories, poems, and articles to national magazines, including *America, Commonweal, McCall's, Saturday Evening Post, Ladies' Home Journal, Saturday Review, Yankee, Modern Maturity*, and *Christian Science Monitor.*

WORK IN PROGRESS: A collection of short essays and poems.

* * *

GLATZER, Hal 1946-

PERSONAL: Born January 31, 1946, in New York, N.Y.; son of Harold (an attorney) and Glenna (a teacher; maiden name, Beaber) Glatzer. *Education:* Syracuse University, B.A., 1968; Hilo College, graduate study. *Politics:* Democrat. *Home address:* P.O. Box 361, Pepeekeo, Hawaii 96783.

CAREER: Honolulu Advertiser, Hilo, Hawaii, bureau chief, 1971; *Orchid Isle* (magazine), Hilo, Hawaii, editor, 1972-74; KITV-Television, Honolulu, Hawaii, Big Island Bureau chief, 1974—. Member of Big Island Committee on Crime Prevention. *Member:* Hawaii Newspaper Guild, Big Island Press Club.

WRITINGS: Kamehameha County (journalistic novel), Friendly World Enterprises, 1974. Contributor to local magazines and to *Christian Science Monitor.*

WORK IN PROGRESS: A sequel to *Kamehameha County*; television documentary scripts on Big Island life; research on the life of Sergeant John D. Provoo, tried for treason in the 1950's.

SIDELIGHTS: Glatzer writes: "I am an eclectic radical thinker . . . I believe in God and Mankind. I do not believe in owning land. I believe in beating swords into ploughshares and spears into pruning hooks. I do not study war." *Avocational interests:* Playing banjo, guitar, fiddle, mandolin, autoharp, and dulcimer in the style of traditional mountain music and Bluegrass; reading, watching television, gardening.

* * *

GLAVIN, John P(atrick) 1933-

PERSONAL: Born June 28, 1933, in Chicago, Ill.; son of Patrick and Mary Glavin. *Education:* Attended University of Redlands, 1951-52, and Wilson Junior College, 1952-53; University of Chicago, B.A., 1958, M.A., 1965; Chicago Teachers College, M.A., 1960; George Peabody College, Ed.D., 1966. *Office:* Department of Special Education, Temple University, Philadelphia, Pa. 19122.

CAREER: Elementary school teacher of the mentally retarded and emotionally disturbed in the private and public schools of Chicago, Ill., 1961-64; University of British Columbia, Vancouver, assistant professor of special education, 1966-67; University of Illinois, Champaign, assistant professor of special education, 1967-68, research assistant professor at Children's Research Center, 1967-68; Temple University, Philadelphia, Pa., associate professor of special education, 1968—. *Member:* American Council on Exceptional Children, Society for Research in Child Development, American Educational Research Association, Association of Child Psychology and Psychiatry, Pennsylvania Council on Exceptional Children.

WRITINGS: (Contributor) Harry Dupont, editor, *Educating Emotionally Disturbed Children: Readings*, 2nd edition (Glavin was not associated with earlier edition), Holt, 1975; *Major Issues in Special Education*, M.S.S. Information Corp., 1973; *Behavioral Strategies for Classroom Management*, C. E. Merrill, 1974; *Ferment in Special Education*, M.S.S. Information Corp., 1974; *Perceptual Motor Training for Handicapped Children*, M.S.S. Information Corp., 1975. Contributor to abstracts and to journals in his field.

* * *

GLENDAY, Alice 1920-

PERSONAL: Born June 26, 1920, in Canada; daughter of Robert (a teacher) and Alice (Innes) Darling; married Archibald Glenday, October 10, 1942 (deceased); children: April, David. *Education:* Educated in Stratford, Ontario, Canada. *Home:* 412 Albert St., Palmerston North, New Zealand. *Agent:* Carl Brandt, Brandt & Brandt, 101 Park Ave., New York, N.Y. 10017.

CAREER: Actress and secretary. *Member:* International P.E.N. (New Zealand chapter), Women Writers' Society (New Zealand). *Awards, honors:* Katherine Mansfield Memorial Award from Bank of New Zealand, 1969, for short story "One Fine Day"; award from Auckland Centennial Fiction Contest, 1972, for *Follow, Follow.*

WRITINGS: Follow, Follow (novel), Collins, 1973. Contributor of short stories to magazines.

WORK IN PROGRESS: A novel, *Past Imperfect.*

* * *

GLES, Margaret Breitmaier 1940-

PERSONAL: Born December 7, 1940, in New York, N.Y.; daughter of Gottlob (a contractor) and Elisabeth

(Linder) Breitmaier; married Carlos R. Gles (an architect), November 26, 1969. *Education:* Cazenovia College, A.A.S., 1960; attended Hunter College of the City University of New York, 1969-70; George Mason University, B.S., 1973. *Home:* 3336 Jones Bridge Ct., Chevy Chase, Md. 20015.

CAREER: B. Altman & Co., New York, N.Y., assistant buyer, 1960-63; Wallachs, New York, N.Y., assistant to men's clothing manager and buyer, 1963-64; Roaman's Mail Order, Inc., New York, N.Y., administrative assistant to general manager, 1964-65; *Chemical Week*, New York, N.Y., advertising service manager, 1965-69; substitute teacher of kindergarten and elementary school in Virginia, 1973-74; full-time elementary school teacher in Sterling, Va., 1974—.

WRITINGS: Come and Play Hide and Seek, Garrard, 1975. Correspondent, *Commentary*, 1969-70.

SIDELIGHTS: Margaret Gles writes: "Feel it is extremely important for children to be exposed to varied literature which is easy and enjoyable for them to read. This not only helps them to read better but increases their literary interest as they mature."

*   *   *

GLUCKMAN, Max   1911-1975

January 26, 1911—April 14, 1975; South African-born anthropologist, educator, and author. Obituaries: *New York Times*, April 30, 1975. (*CA*-9/10)

*   *   *

GLYNN, James A.   1941-

PERSONAL: Born September 10, 1941, in Brooklyn, N.Y.; son of James A. and Muriel (Lewis) Glynn; married Marie Janet Gates (an occupational therapist), December 17, 1966; children: David Sean. *Education:* Foothill College, A.A., 1961; California State University, San Jose (now San Jose State University), A.B., 1964, M.A., 1966; graduate study at University of California, Santa Barbara, California State College, Bakersfield, and California State University, Fresno. *Politics:* Democrat. *Religion:* None. *Home:* 1712 Country Club Dr., Bakersfield, Calif. 93306. *Office:* Bakersfield College, 1801 Panorama Dr., Bakersfield, Calif. 93305.

CAREER: Bakersfield College, Bakersfield, Calif., associate professor of sociology, 1966—, president of academic senate, 1975-76. Adjunct assistant professor of sociology, California State University, Fresno, 1968-70, Chapman College, Orange, Calif., 1972; founder of Kern College Federation of Teachers, 1973. Book reviewer for Little, Brown & Co., 1969—. *Member:* American Sociological Association, Faculty Association of California Community Colleges, California Federation of Teachers, Kiwanis Club.

WRITINGS: (With Elbert W. Stewart) *Introduction to Sociology*, McGraw, 1971, 2nd edition, 1975.

WORK IN PROGRESS: Manuscript for a text in social problems.

*   *   *

GODFREY, Vincent H.   1895(?)-1975

1895(?)—July 15, 1975; American naval officer, and author of books on sea and sailing. Obituaries: *Washington Post*, July 24, 1975.

GOLANN, Stuart E(ugene)   1936-

PERSONAL: Born March 26, 1936, in New York, N.Y.; son of Harold and Rose (Zuss) Golann; married Dorothy Blitzer, August 24, 1958; children: Evan. *Education:* Queens College (now of the City University of New York), Flushing, N.Y., B.A., 1957; University of North Carolina, M.A., 1959, Ph.D., 1961. *Home:* 65 Mount Pleasant, Amherst, Mass. 01002. *Office:* Department of Psychology, University of Massachusetts, Amherst, Mass. 01002.

CAREER: Duke University, Durham, N.C., National Institute of Mental Health psychology intern, 1959-60, instructor in department of psychiatry at Medical Center, 1961-62; U.S. Veterans Administration Hospital, Durham, N.C., supervisory clinical psychologist, 1961-62; University of Maryland, College Park, chief investigator of mental health project at Counseling Center, 1962-65, assistant professor of psychology, 1965-67, lecturer, 1967-68; American Psychological Association, Washington, D.C., associate administrative officer for professional affairs, 1967-70; University of Massachusetts, Amherst, associate professor, 1970-73, professor of psychology, 1973—. Lecturer in community psychology at Catholic University of America, 1968-70. Consultant to Maryland Department of Mental Health, 1966-67; member of professional advisory council, National Parent-Teacher Project on Children's Emotional Health, 1969-71.

MEMBER: American Psychological Association (member of board of professional affairs, 1970-73), American Association for the Advancement of Science, Eastern Psychological Association, Massachusetts Psychological Association, Sigma Xi, Psi Chi.

WRITINGS: Coordinate Index Reference Guide to Community Mental Health, Behavioral Publications, 1969; (with Thomas Magoon and R. W. Freeman) *Mental Health Counselors at Work*, Pergamon, 1969; (editor with Carl Eisdorfer and contributor) *Handbook of Community Mental Health*, Appleton, 1972; (editor with Milton Shore and contributor) *Current Ethical Issues in Mental Health*, U.S. Government Printing Office, 1973; (editor with Jeffery Baker) *Current and Future Trends in Community Psychology*, Behavioral Publications, 1974; (editor with Jay Pomerantz and Jeffery Baker) *The Bethlehem Diaries*, Canfield Press, 1974; (editor with William Fremouw, and contributor) *Perspectives on the Right to Treatment: The Amherst Conference on the Right to Treatment*, Federal Legal Publications, in press.

Contributor: Ira Iscoe and Charles D. Spielberger, editors, *Community Psychology*, Appleton, 1970; Morton Bloomberg, editor, *Creativity: Theory and Research*, College & University Press, 1973; Alan C. Kamil and Norman R. Simonson, *Patterns of Psychology: Issues and Prospects*, Little, Brown, 1973. Contributor to books of readings and to psychology, counseling, and public health journals.

Member of editorial board, *Psychotherapy: Theory, Research and Practice*, 1967-71; consulting editor, *American Psychologist*, 1969-73, Journal Supplement Abstract Service, National Information System in Psychology, 1971—, and *American Journal of Community Psychology*, 1973—; manuscript consultant, John Wiley & Sons, 1973—.

*   *   *

GOLD, Phyllis
    See GOLDBERG, Phyllis

GOLDBERG, Phyllis 1941-
   (Phyllis Gold)

PERSONAL: Born May 26, 1941, in Long Island, N.Y.; daughter of James J. (a lawyer) and Blanche (Levenbron) Weissman; married Paul Goldberg (a mortgage banker); children: Mitchell, Lizbeth. *Education:* Attended Syracuse University; Hofstra University, B.A. *Home and office:* 2 Forestdale Dr., Huntington, N.Y. 11743.

CAREER: Has held positions as Family Court probation officer, photographer's fashion model in New York, N.Y., and agent for advertising photographers in New York; Photography Unlimited, New York, N.Y., owner of agency representing professional photographers, 1975—. *Member:* National Society for Autistic Children (founding president of New York chapter; past national vice-president).

WRITINGS: (Under name Phyllis Gold) *Please Don't Say Hello* (on infantile autism; for children; with photographs), Human Sciences Press, 1975.

"Please Don't Say Hello," a television script. Author and photographer for filmstrips "Shoplifter" and "Deserted," both for Activity Records.

WORK IN PROGRESS: *Long Distance* (tentative title), a novel; audio-visual material aimed at teaching high school students about establishing ego strength and achieving genuine intimacy through real communication minus traditional courtship role-playing; adapting "Please Don't Say Hello" into a filmstrip.

SIDELIGHTS: Phyllis Gold writes: "Being the mother of an autistic boy, *Please Don't Say Hello* was a labor of love . . . I believe when one lives through difficult experiences which may be outside the rounds of the average person, one also gains in perspective and understanding. I think I should attempt to transmit some of the things I feel fortunate enough to have learned through my personal experiences and observations." *Avocational interests:* Music, writing poetry, tennis, anything related to the ocean, gourmet cooking, photography, transcendental meditation.

*   *   *

GOLDHABER, Gerald Martin 1944-

PERSONAL: Born January 23, 1944, in Brookline, Mass.; son of Robert (a restaurateur) and Ruth (a realtor; maiden name, Steinman) Goldhaber; married Marylynn Blaustein (a clinical social worker), August 17, 1969; children: Michelle Beth. *Education:* University of Massachusetts, B.A., 1965; University of Maryland, M.A., 1966; Purdue University, Ph.D., 1970. *Politics:* Democrat. *Religion:* Jewish. *Home:* 48 Jamstead Ct., Williamsville, N.Y. 14221. *Office:* Department of Communication, State University of New York at Buffalo, 4226 Ridge Lea Rd., Buffalo, N.Y. 14226.

CAREER: University of New Mexico, Albuquerque, assistant professor in department of speech communication, 1970-74; State University of New York at Buffalo, associate professor of communication, 1974—, associate chairman of department, 1974—. *Member:* International Communication Association (vice-president, 1974-76), International Transactional Analysis Association (teaching member), International Sociological Research Association (life fellow), American Association of University Professors, Industrial Communication Council, Speech Communication Association of America, Academy of Management, Western Speech Communication Association. *Awards, honors:* Grant from Office of Economic Opportunity, 1973-74.

WRITINGS: Organizational Communication, W. C. Brown, 1974; (with Brent Peterson and R. Wayne Pace) *Communication Probes,* Science Research Associates, 1974; (with Lawrence Rosenfeld and Val Smith) *Experiments in Human Communication,* Holt, 1975; (with wife, Marylynn Goldhaber) *Readings and Principles in Transactional Analysis,* Allyn & Bacon, 1975. Contributor to *Speech Monographs, Speech Teacher, Journal of Communication, Western Speech, Law and Order,* and *College and University Teaching.*

WORK IN PROGRESS: Communication Audit; Gay Talk, interviews giving descriptions of male homosexual courtship communication behavior.

AVOCATIONAL INTERESTS: Sunshine, good exercise, proper diet, water skiing, paddleball.

*   *   *

GOLDHURST, Richard 1927-

PERSONAL: Born January 4, 1927, in Larchmont, N.Y.; son of Harry L. (a writer) and Genevieve (Gallagher) Golden (surname originally Goldhurst); married Doris Warren (a writer-editor), September 19, 1953; children: John. *Education:* Kenyon College, B.A., 1950; Princeton University, M.A., 1951; New York University, Ph.D., 1955. *Politics:* Democrat. *Home:* 3 Lehn Farm Rd., Westport, Conn. 06880. *Agent:* P. Knowlton, Curtis Brown, 60 East 56th St., New York, N.Y. 10022.

CAREER: New York University, New York, N.Y., instructor in classics, 1952-55; story analyst for Columbia Broadcasting System, 1955; editor of journal for motion picture and television engineers, 1955-56; stage manager (New York, N.Y.), 1957; Hartford Jewish Community Center, Hartford, Conn., director of the arts, 1957-59; *Carolina Israelite,* Charlotte, N.C., assistant editor, 1959-68; *County Magazine,* Westport, Conn., assistant editor, 1970—. *Military service:* U.S. Army, 1944-46; served in Japan.

WRITINGS: In the Center, New American Library, 1959; *The Deceivers,* New American Library, 1960; (with Yale David Koskoff) *The Dark Side of the House,* Dial, 1968; *The Chances We Take,* Baron, 1970; *America Is Also Jewish,* Putnam, 1972; (with father, Harry L. Golden) *Travels Through Jewish America,* Doubleday, 1973; *Many Are the Hearts,* Reader's Digest Press, 1975; *Pipe Clay and Drill: John J. Pershing and the American Military Mind,* Reader's Digest Press, 1975. Author of television script "Mr. Lincoln Goes to Gettysburg," for American Heritage television series, 1960.

*   *   *

GOLDMAN, A(ndrew) E. O. 1947-

PERSONAL: Born June 21, 1947; son of Harry (a physician) and Ida (an artist; maiden name, Gurman) Goldman. *Education:* Amherst College, B.A., 1968; Columbia University, graduate study, 1969; Harvard University, M.Arch., 1973. *Home:* 30 East Hartsdale Ave., Hartsdale, N.Y. 10530. *Office:* Maitland/Strauss, Architects, 80 Mason St., Greenwich, Conn.

CAREER: Perkins & Will, New York, N.Y., designer, 1973; Maitland/Strauss, Architects, Greenwich, Conn., architect, 1973—. *Awards, honors:* Carpenter Center/Harvard University Award, 1972, for *Notebook of Leonardo.*

WRITINGS: "Trapshod" (play), first produced in New

York, N.Y. by Actor's Voyage East, 1971; "She's Bad Today" (play), first produced in Waterford, Conn., at National Playwrights Conference, 1974. Also author of play, "Your Basic Shelter," 1975, and self-illustrated children's books, *Lsle Makes It Up*, 1970, *Notebook of Leonardo*, 1972, and *Murray & Elizabeth*, 1975, all as yet unpublished.

WORK IN PROGRESS: Two novels, *The Animals of the Forest* and *A Final Rest*; two plays, "NetherNetherland," a comedy about occupied Europe, ca. 1943, and "Picture of the People," about the Nazi film industry.

* * *

GOLDNER, Nancy 1943-

PERSONAL: Born March 19, 1943, in New York, N.Y.; daughter of Sigmund and Rose (Trilling) Goldner. *Education:* University of Michigan, B.A., 1964. *Residence:* New York, N.Y.

CAREER: Macmillan Publishing Co., New York, N.Y., editor, 1966-67; T. Y. Crowell Co., New York, N.Y., editor, 1968-74; dance critic, 1969—. Teacher at New School for Social Research and at critic's institutes at Mills College and in New London, Conn.

WRITINGS: *The Stravinsky Festival of the New York City Ballet*, Eakins, 1974. Dance critic for *Christian Science Monitor, Nation*, and *Dance News*.

* * *

GOLDSMITH, Jack 1931-

PERSONAL: Born April 18, 1931, in San Francisco, Calif.; son of Lawrence Goldsmith and Clare (Greenberg) Goldsmith Berger; married Sharon Sweeney, March 27, 1970. *Education:* University of California, Berkeley, B.A., 1955, M.A., 1958; University of California, Los Angeles, Ph.D., 1970; postdoctoral study at State University of New York at Albany, 1971-72; Institute for Court Management, certification, 1972. *Home:* 4201 Massachusetts Ave. N.W., Washington, D.C. 20016. *Office:* Center for the Administration of Justice, American University, Washington, D.C. 20016.

CAREER: Lassen College, Susanville, Calif., instructor in political science, 1959-61; University of California, Los Angeles, research analyst for Institute of Government and Public Affairs, 1962-63; California State University, Northridge, assistant professor of political science, 1965-70; California Lutheran College, Thousand Oaks, assistant professor of criminal justice and political science, 1970-71; State University of New York at Albany, lecturer in criminal justice, 1971-72; American University, Washington, D.C., associate professor of criminal justice, 1972—, chairman of National Conference on Crime Against the Elderly, 1975. Director, Institute for Law Enforcement Management, 1975—; principal counselor, Superior Court of Los Angeles County, 1975—.

MEMBER: Academy of Criminal Justice Science, American Society for Public Administration, American Society of Criminology, American PoliticaL Science Association, National Council on Crime and Delinquency, Gerontological Society. *Awards, honors:* Public administration fellow at the Administration on Aging, 1973-74.

WRITINGS: (With Winston Crouch) *Agricultural Cities: Paradox in Politics of Metropolis*, University of California, Los Angeles, 1964; (editor with Gil Gunderson, and contributor) *Comparative Local Politics: A Systems-Function Approach*, Holbrook, 1973; (editor with Sharon S. Goldsmith, and contributor) *The Police Community: Dimensions of an Occupational Subculture*, Palisades Publishers, 1974. Contributor to *Gerontologist, Aging, Crime Prevention Review*, and *Perspectives on Aging*.

WORK IN PROGRESS: Editing and contributing to *Crime Against the Elderly: Selected Papers*, with Sharon S. Goldsmith; *Report of the National Conference on Crime Against the Elderly*; *Police and the Political System*, for Palisades Publishers.

* * *

GOLDSMITH, Sharon S(weeney) 1948-

PERSONAL: Born June 11, 1948, in Geneva, Ill.; daughter of Arthur F. (an engineer) and Alice B. (Johnson) Sweeney; married Jack Goldsmith, March 27, 1970. *Education:* University of California, Los Angeles, B.A. (with honors), 1970, M.A., 1974. *Home:* 4201 Massachusetts Ave. N.W., Washington, D.C. 20016. *Office:* College of Public Affairs, American University, Washington, D.C. 20016.

CAREER: American University, Washington, D.C., program coordinator of National Conference on Crime Against the Elderly, 1974—, guest lecturer at Center for the Administration of Justice, 1975. *Member:* American Political Science Association, American Society for Public Administration, Gerontological Society.

WRITINGS: (Editor with Jack Goldsmith) *The Police Community: Dimensions of an Occupational Subculture*, Palisades Publishers, 1974. Contributor to *Perspectives on Aging*.

WORK IN PROGRESS: Editing, with Jack Goldsmith, and contributing to *Crimes Against the Elderly: Selected Papers*.

* * *

GOLDSTEIN, Bernard R. 1938-

PERSONAL: Born January 29, 1938, in New York, N.Y.; son of Harry (a teacher) and Ernestine (a teacher; maiden name, Trachtenberg) Goldstein; married Pauline Walters (a librarian), May 4, 1961; children: Hanina, Rachel. *Education:* Columbia University, A.B., 1958, M.A., 1961; Brown University, Ph.D., 1963. *Home:* 2122 Beechwood Blvd., Pittsburgh, Pa. 15217. *Office:* Jewish Studies Program, University of Pittsburgh, Pittsburgh, Pa. 15260.

CAREER: Yale University, New Haven, Conn., assistant professor, 1965-69, associate professor of history of science and medicine, 1969-72; University of Pittsburgh, Pittsburgh, Pa., associate professor of Jewish studies and history and philosophy of science, 1973—. Fellow of St. Edmund's House, Cambridge University, 1971—. *Member:* International Academy of the History of Science, American Oriental Society, History of Science Society, Association for Jewish Studies (member of board of directors, 1974—), Phi Beta Kappa. *Awards, honors:* National Science Foundation postdoctoral fellowship, 1963-65; Guggenheim fellowship, 1975.

WRITINGS: *The Astronomical Tables of Levi ben Gerson*, Connecticut Academy of Arts and Sciences, 1974.

Editor and translator: *Ibn al-Muthanna's Commentary on Astronomy*, Yale University Press, 1967; *The Arabic Version of Ptolemy's Planetary Hypotheses*, American Philosophical Society, 1967; *Al Bitruji: On the Principle of Astronomy*, two volumes, Yale University Press, 1971. Advisory editor, *Journal for History of Astronomy*, 1970—.

WORK IN PROGRESS: *Medieval Hebrew and Arabic Astronomy*, *Ptolemy in the Middle Ages*, and *Ancient Mathematics and Astronomy*.

*   *   *

GOLDSTEIN, Rhoda L(ois) 1926-

PERSONAL: Born February 3, 1926, in Brooklyn, N.Y.; divorced; children: Mary Sheryl, Meyer Harold, Helena Jo. *Education:* Brooklyn College (now Brooklyn College of the City University of New York), B.A., 1946; New School for Social Research, M.A., 1948; Fisk University, further graduate study, 1948-49; University of Chicago, Ph.D., 1954. *Residence:* Highland Park, N.J. *Office:* Department of Sociology, Douglass College, Rutgers University, New Brunswick, N.J. 08903.

CAREER: Part-time teacher in Chicago, Ill., 1947-48, and Brooklyn, N.Y., 1948-56; consultant on the Negro in medicine at University of Chicago, Chicago, Ill., for Rockefeller Foundation, 1956; Rutgers University, New Brunswick, N.J., instructor in sociology, spring, 1957, autumn, 1959; Somerset Hospital School of Nursing, Somerset, N.J., instructor in sociology, 1960-61; Rutgers University, lecturer, 1962-68, assistant professor at Douglass College, 1968-71, associate professor of sociology, 1971—. Chairman of Franklin Township Civil Rights Commission, 1961-62. Member of executive board of Committee to End Discrimination in Chicago Medical Institutions, 1953-55, Central Jersey Civil Rights Council, 1960-62, Parents' League for Educational Advancement, 1963-65, Highland Park Fair Housing Committee, 1965-66, Special Emergency Legal Force, 1970-72, and Greater New Brunswick Urban League, 1972-74. Organizer and first president of Pine Grove Manor Cooperative Nursery School, 1957-59. Consultant to Heritage Foundation.

MEMBER: American Sociological Association, Society for the Study of Social Problems, Association of Social and Behavioral Sciences, Sociologists for Women in Society, Eastern Sociological Association. *Awards, honors:* Fulbright-Hays scholarship, 1966-67.

WRITINGS: (Contributor) Clifton O. Dummett, editor, *The Growth and Development of the Negro in Dentistry in the United States*, National Dental Association, 1952; (contributor) Arthur B. Shostak, editor, *Sociology in Action*, Dorsey, 1966; (with Bernard Goldstein) *Doctors and Nurses in Industry: Social Aspects of In-Plant Medical Programs* (monograph), Institute of Management and Labor Relations, Rutgers University, 1967; (contributor) F. Baker, P. J. M. McEwan, and A. Sheldon, editors, *Industrial Organizations and Health*, Volume I: *Selected Readings*, Tavistock Publications, 1969; (editor and author of introduction) *Life and Culture of Black People in the United States*, Crowell, 1971; *Indian Women in Transition: A Bangalore Case Study*, Scarecrow, 1972; (with June T. Albert) *Black Studies Programs at American Colleges and Universities: A Preliminary Report* (pamphlet), Rutgers University, 1973; (contributor) J. V. Gordon and J. M. Rosser, editors, *The Black Studies Debate*, University Press of Kansas, 1974; (contributor) Dhirendra Narain, editor, *Explorations in the Family and Other Essays: Professor K. M. Kapadia Commemoration Volume*, Thacker & Co., 1975.

Contributor of more than fifteen articles and reviews to sociology journals. Book review editor of *Journal of Asian and African Studies*, 1969-71.

WORK IN PROGRESS: Editing *Interracial Bonds*, with W. J. Roye; *White Women and Racial Justice*, and interview study of white women civil rights activists.

*   *   *

GOLENBOCK, Peter 1946-

PERSONAL: Born July 19, 1946, in New York, N.Y.; son of Jerome (an attorney and art dealer) and Annette (Sklarin) Golenbock. *Education:* Dartmouth College, B.A. (with honors), 1967; New York University, J.D., 1970. *Agent:* Joan Raines, Theron Raines, Inc., 244 Madison Ave., New York, N.Y. 10016.

CAREER: Sport columnist on newspapers in Stamford, Conn., 1968-70, and in New York, N.Y., 1970; Washington Business Institute, New York, N.Y., professor of law, 1969-70; private practice of law in New York, N.Y., 1971-72; Prentice-Hall, Englewood Cliffs, N.J., editor, 1972; *North Bergen Surburbanite*, Englewood, N.J., political reporter, 1975—.

WRITINGS: *Dynasty: The New York Yankees, 1949-1964*, Prentice-Hall, 1975.

WORK IN PROGRESS: *Amarillo: The Erotic Adventures of a Baseball Team*, completion expected in 1976.

SIDELIGHTS: Golenbock told *CA:* "Since I was a kid, I have been a Yankee fan. I had been a fan of the men about whom I wrote: Mickey Mantle, Yogi Berra, Whitey Ford, Casey Stengel, etc. I wanted to be the author of the definitive work on this era, because I wanted the story to be an honest one, not press agentry or puffery. No man is all good or all bad. So it was with these men. I spent three full years writing *Dynasty*, traveling twenty-seven thousand miles after researching through two hundred fifty thousand newspaper clippings. I interviewed over eighty ex-players and officials." *Avocational interests:* Land sports, travel ("a favorite adventure was a tour of the National Parks in 1969").

*   *   *

GOOD, Thomas L(indall) 1943-

PERSONAL: Born October 4, 1943, in Owensboro, Ky.; son of Thomas Edison (a store owner) and Bessie (Howard) Good; married Suzanne R. Fischer, June 24, 1967; children: Heather Lynn, Jeffrey Thomas. *Education:* University of Illinois, A.B., 1965; University of Michigan, graduate study, 1966; Indiana University, M.S., 1967, Ph.D., 1968. *Home:* 112 Parkhill, Columbia, Mo. 65201. *Office:* Department of Curriculum and Instruction, University of Missouri, Columbia, Mo. 65202.

CAREER: University of Texas, Austin, assistant professor of educational psychology, and project director of Research and Development Center for Teacher Education, 1968-71; University of Missouri, Columbia, associate professor, 1971-73, professor of curriculum and instruction, 1974—, and research scientist at Center for Research in Social Behavior, 1971—. Assistant director at Southeastern Educational Service Center, 1967-68; staff development coordinator for Early Childhood Education Program at Southwest Educational Development Laboratory, 1970-71. Consultant to State of Texas Education Agency, 1970, and to U.S. Office of Child Development, National Child Development Associate Program, 1972.

MEMBER: American Educational Research Association, American Association of University Professors, American Psychological Association. *Awards, honors:* National Institute of Mental Health grants, 1969, 1970; Hogg Foundation grant, 1970; National Academy of Education Spencer fellow, 1972; Spencer Foundation grant, 1972; National Institute of Education grant, 1973.

WRITINGS: (With Gordon Greenwood and B. Siegel) *Problem Situations in Teaching*, Harper, 1971; (with J. E. Brophy) *Looking in Classrooms*, Harper, 1973; (with Brophy) *Teacher-Student Relationships: Causes and Consequences*, Holt, 1974; (with Brophy and S. E. Nedler) *Early Education: Teaching and Program Implications*, Harper, 1974; (with B. J. Biddle and Brophy) *Teachers Make a Difference*, Holt, 1975.

Contributor: A. Simon and E. G. Boyer, editors, *Mirrors for Behavior: An Anthology of Observation Instruments Continued, 1970 Supplement*, Volumes A and B, Research for Better Schools, 1970; H. C. Lindgren and F. Lindgren, editors, *Current Readings in Educational Psychology*, 2nd edition (Good was not associated with earlier edition), Wiley, 1971; J. F. Rosenblith, W. Allensmith, and J. P. Williams, editors, *The Causes of Behavior*, 3rd edition (Good was not associated with earlier editions), Allyn & Bacon, 1972; U. Bronfenbrenner, editor, *Influence on Human Development*, Dryden, 1972; R. Coop and K. White, editors, *Psychological Concepts in the Classroom*, Harper, 1973; R. A. Magoon, editor, *Educational Psychology: Past, Present, and Future*, C. E. Merrill, 1973; J. M. Palardy, editor, *Teaching Today*, Macmillan, 1973; P. C. Stetson, editor, *Educational Psychology Reader*, MSS Educational Publishing, 1975; M. D. Gall, editor, *Educational Psychology Reader*, Little, Brown, 1975; H. Stub, editor, *The Sociology of Education*, Dorsey, 1975. Contributor of more than thirty articles and reviews to journals.

* * *

GOODE, Stephen Ray 1943-

PERSONAL: Born March 5, 1943, in Elkins, W.Va.; son of Ersel R. (a lumberman) and Dorothy (a practical nurse; maiden name, Vanscoy) Goode. *Education:* Davidson College, B.A., 1965; University of Virginia, M.A., 1968; Rutgers University, Ph.D., 1975. *Home:* 331 13th St. S.E., Washington, D.C. 20003.

CAREER: Rutgers University, New Brunswick, N.J., lecturer in history, 1971-72. *Member:* American Historical Association, American Association for the Advancement of Hungarian History.

WRITINGS: Affluent Revolutionaries: A Portrait of the New Left, F. Watts, 1974; *The Prophet and the Revolutionary*, F. Watts, 1975; *National Defense*, F. Watts, in press.

WORK IN PROGRESS: Militant Revolutionaries: A Portrait of Terrorism and Guerilla Warfare.

AVOCATIONAL INTERESTS: Gourmet cooking, plants.

* * *

GOODERS, John 1937-

PERSONAL: Born January 10, 1937, in London, England; son of Edwin and Winifred Alice Gooders; married Su Highfield (a photographic agent), April 4, 1962; children: Timothy, Sophie. *Education:* Southampton University, B.Sc.; London University Institute of Education, postgraduate certificate of education, and diploma in philosophy of education. *Home:* 35 Brodrick Rd., London S.W.17, England. *Agent:* Julian Bach Literary Agency, 3 East 48th St., New York, N.Y. 10017.

CAREER: Teacher at a London comprehensive school, 1959-65, at Avery Hill College of Education, 1967-69; International Publishing Co., London, editor of "Birds of the World" series, 1969-71; founded monthly magazine, *World of Birds*, 1971, leaving shortly thereafter to write scripts and commentaries for "Survival," a television wildlife series; now full-time writer. *Member:* British Ornithologists Union, British Trust for Ornithology. *Awards, honors:* Churchill fellowship, 1970, for study and travel in North Africa.

WRITINGS: Where to Watch Birds, Deutsch, 1967, revised edition, 1974; (editor) *Birds of the World*, nine volumes, International Publishing, 1969-71; (with Jeremy Brock) *Where to Watch Birds in Britain and Europe*, Deutsch, 1970, British Book Centre, 1971, revised edition, Deutsch, 1974; (with Eric Hosking) *Wildlife Photography*, Hutchinson, 1973, Praeger, 1974; (editor) *The Bird-Watcher's Book*, David & Charles, 1974; *The Second Bird-Watcher's Book*, David & Charles, 1975; *Birds: A Survey of the Bird Families of the World*, Dial, 1975; *Wildlife Paradises*, Praeger, 1975; *How to Watch Birds*, Deutsch, 1975.

Children's books: *How and Why Book of Birds*, Transworld, 1972; *How and Why Book of the Spoilt Earth*, Transworld, 1973.

Author of scripts for film series, "Wild, Wild World of Animals," Time-Life, 1974-75, and for "The World about Us," B.B.C., 1975. Contributor to Reader's Digest *Book of the British Countryside*, and to periodicals, including *Country Life, Animals, Observer, Teachers World*, and *Birds*.

WORK IN PROGRESS: World Guide to Birds, completion expected in 1975; *World Guide to Mammals*, 1976.

SIDELIGHTS: Gooders told *CA*: "Travel to see wildlife particularly in India and Nepal, in which a keen interest is conservation, [is] now a primary aim in any articles that I write. The effects of wildlife conservation on the people that live alongside animals is a key in my approach." Gooders and his wife have traveled widely in pursuit of pictures and birds.

* * *

GOODMAN, A(dolph) W(inkler) 1915-

PERSONAL: Born July 20, 1915, in San Antonio, Tex.; son of William Wolf (a laborer) and Hannah (Winkler) Goodman; married Betty Posman, December 6, 1947; children: William Louis, Sheila Lynn, Glenn David. *Education:* University of Cincinnati, B.Sc., 1939, M.A., 1941; Columbia University, Ph.D., 1947. *Politics:* "Yes." *Religion:* Jewish. *Home:* 11321 Carrollwood Dr., Tampa, Fla. 33618. *Office:* Department of Mathematics, University of South Florida, Tampa, Fla. 33620.

CAREER: U.S. Navy Yard, Philadelphia, Pa., engineering draftsman, 1941-43; Syracuse University, Syracuse, N.Y., instructor in mathematics, 1943-44; Republic Aviation Corp., Farmingdale, N.Y., stress analyst, 1943-45; Rutgers University, New Brunswick, N.J., instructor in mathematics, 1947-49; University of Kentucky, Lexington, associate professor, 1949-58, professor of mathematics, 1958-64; University of South Florida, Tampa, professor of mathematics, 1964—, distinguished professor, 1966—. Member of Institute for Advanced Study, Princeton, N.J., 1956-57.

MEMBER: American Mathematical Society, Mathematical Association of America (member of board of governors,

1961-64), Indian Mathematical Society, Societe Mathematique de France, Sigma Xi, Sigma Pi Sigma, Pi Mu Epsilon. *Awards, honors:* University of Kentucky Alumni Award for outstanding research, 1958; National Science Foundation grants, 1965-66, 1966-67, 1968-70, and 1970-72.

WRITINGS: Plane Trigonometry, Wiley, 1959; *Analytic Geometry and the Calculus*, Macmillan, 1962, 3rd edition, 1974; *The Pleasures of Math*, Macmillan, 1964; *Modern Calculus with Analytic Geometry*, Macmillan, Volume I, 1967, Volume II, 1968; (with J. S. Ratti) *Finite Mathematics with Applications*, Macmillan, 1971, 2nd edition, 1975; *The Mainstream of Algebra and Trigonometry*, Houghton, 1972. Contributor of more than forty research articles to mathematical journals in United States and abroad. Reviewer, *Mathematical Review*, 1948—; associate editor, *Proceedings* of American Mathematical Society, 1951-53; referee for six mathematics journals.

WORK IN PROGRESS: An introduction to the theory of univalent functions; research on calculus for the social sciences.

* * *

GOODWIN, Harold 1919-

PERSONAL: Born June 10, 1919, in New York, N.Y.; son of Abraham (a businessman) and Edith (Blacker) Goodwin; married Barbara Eckhardt (a painter), October 25, 1941; children: Georgiana. *Education:* Attended Art Students League, New York, N.Y., 1937-39, and New York University, 1949-50. *Residence:* Lyme, Conn. 06371.

CAREER: Artist and writer (painted a mural in a post office, designed greeting cards, painted portraits from photographs, made film strips). Member of board of education in Lyme, Conn., 1967-71. *Military service:* Royal Canadian Air Force, 1942-45. *Member:* Authors Guild of Authors League of America.

WRITINGS: Magic Number (juvenile), Bradbury, 1969; *Top Secret: Alligators* (juvenile), Bradbury, 1975.

WORK IN PROGRESS: The Bridge; *Cargo*; *Garbage Island*.

SIDELIGHTS: Goodwin writes that he came to children's literature after illustrating books for children. "After illustrating half a dozen books I couldn't resist writing one—now, I am reluctantly weighing abandoning illustration in favor of writing."

* * *

GOODWIN, Stephen 1943-

PERSONAL: Born October 20, 1943, in Pennsylvania; son of Claudius Lee and Jeannette (Levy) Goodwin; married Lucia Stanton, June 16, 1964; children: Eliza. *Education:* Harvard University, A.B., 1965; University of Virginia, M.A., 1969. *Home:* 202 Woodside Ave., Narberth, Pa. 19072. *Agent:* Russell & Volkening, 551 Fifth Ave., New York, N.Y. 10017.

CAREER: Washington and Lee University, Lexington, Va., instructor in English, 1969-73; Bryn Mawr College, Bryn Mawr, Pa., assistant professor of English, 1973—. *Military service:* U.S. Army, 1966-68. *Awards, honors:* National Endowment for the Arts literary fellowship, 1973.

WRITINGS: Kin (novel), Harper, 1975. Contributor to journals. Fiction editor of *Shenandoah*, 1972-73, and *Southern Voices*, 1974.

WORK IN PROGRESS: A novel.

SIDELIGHTS: "Having been raised in Alabama," Goodwin wrote, "I consider myself a Southerner. Though I now work in Pennsylvania, I spend much of every year in the mountains of Virginia, where I have built a small cabin."

* * *

GORDON, Antoinette K. 1892(?)-1975

1892(?)—March 24, 1975; American educator, museum curator, and author of books on Tibetan art, literature, and religion. Obituaries: *New York Times*, March 26, 1975; *AB Bookman's Weekly*, April 28, 1975.

* * *

GORDON, John Steele 1944-

PERSONAL: Born May 7, 1944, in New York, N.Y.; son of Richard Haden, Jr. (an executive) and Mary (Steele) Gordon. *Education:* Vanderbilt University, B.A., 1966. *Politics:* Liberal. *Religion:* None. *Home:* 706 South Pascack Rd., Spring Valley, N.Y. 10977.

CAREER: Harper & Row Publishers, Inc., New York, N.Y., production editor, 1966-72; free-lance writer, 1972. *Member:* Union Club.

WRITINGS: Overlanding (nonfiction), Harper, 1975.

WORK IN PROGRESS: A book on the adaptation of animals to the urban environment, *Urban Animals*, completion expected in 1976.

SIDELIGHTS: Gordon has been on overland expeditions from England to India and back, in East Africa, in Mexico, and from New York to Tierra del Fuego; he has sailed in the Caribbean Sea and to the Galapagos Islands. *Avocational interests:* Photography, history, politics, cooking, zoology.

* * *

GORECKI, Jan 1926-

PERSONAL: Born April 10, 1926, in Warsaw, Poland; son of Jozef Hilary (a businessman) and Jadwiga (Frendzel) Kraushar; married Danuta Wojnar (a library instructor), December 26, 1954; children: Piotr, Marie. *Education:* University of Cracow, M.J., 1947, D.S.J., 1958; University of Wroclaw, D.J., 1949. *Home:* 510 West Washington St., Urbana, Ill. 61801. *Office:* Department of Sociology, University of Illinois, Urbana, Ill. 61801.

CAREER: University of Cracow, Cracow, Poland, assistant, 1947-51, adjunct, 1951-59, associate professor of law, 1959-68; Center for Advanced Study in the Behavioral Sciences, Stanford, Calif., fellow, 1969-70; University of Illinois, Urbana, professor of sociology, 1970—, member of executive committee of Russian and East European Center. Research associate at Stanford University, 1970. *Member:* International Sociological Association, International Family Law Association, American Sociological Association, American Association for the Advancement of Slavic Studies. *Awards, honors:* British Council scholar at London School of Economics and Political Science, 1959-60.

WRITINGS: Przeniesienie Wlasnosci (title means "Transfer of Property"), Wroclaw Society of Arts and Sciences, 1950; *Uniewaznienie Malzenstwa* (title means "Annullment of Marriage"), Cracow University Press, 1958; *Rozwod* (title means "Divorce"), Polish Scientific Publishers, 1965; *Divorce in Poland*, Mouton & Co., 1970; (editor and contributor) *Sociology and Jurisprudence of Leon Petrazycki*, University of Illinois Press, 1975. Contributor to English, German, Polish, and American journals of law and sociology.

WORK IN PROGRESS: Research on criminology and criminal justice, on sociology of law, and on family law and family sociology.

* * *

GOREY, Hays

PERSONAL: Born in Salt Lake City, Utah; son of Andrew William (a banker) and Lou (Hays) Gorey; married Nonie Hammond (an interior designer); children: Hays, Jr., DeAnn (Mrs. Larry Barrigar), Thomas H., Susan. *Education:* University of Utah, B.A.; Harvard University, graduate study, 1950. *Home:* 4606 Tournay Rd., Washington, D.C. 20016. *Agent:* David Obst, 36 East 10th St., New York, N.Y. *Office:* Time, Inc., 888 16th St. N.W., Washington, D.C. 20006.

CAREER: Salt Lake Tribune, Salt Lake City, Utah, reporter, 1948-49, night city editor, 1949-50, city editor, 1950-58, news editor, 1958-65; Time, Inc., Washington, D.C., correspondent, 1965-75. *Member:* Washington Press Club, Sigma Chi, Sigma Delta Chi, Nieman Fellows.

WRITINGS: Ralph Nader and the Power of Everyman, Grosset, 1975; (with Maureen Dean) *Mo: A Woman's View of Watergate*, Simon & Schuster, 1975. Contributor to *Fortune, Life, People, Sports Illustrated, Harper's*, and *Nieman Reports*.

SIDELIGHTS: Gorey writes: "I was motivated to write a book with Maureen Dean because I felt it important to understand how limited and insignificant is the role of wives of high government officials, and with what disastrous results." *Avocational interests:* Travel, tennis, reading.

* * *

GORTON, Richard A. 1932-

PERSONAL: Born July 11, 1932, in Cedar Rapids, Iowa; son of Lester R. and Marie (Aller) Gorton; married Patricia Bittle (a media specialist), February 5, 1960; children: John, James. *Education:* State University of Iowa, B.A., 1958, M.A., 1959; Stanford University, Ed.D., 1965. *Home:* 3720 North Farwell, Milwaukee, Wis. 53211. *Office:* School of Education, University of Wisconsin—Milwaukee, Milwaukee, Wis. 53201.

CAREER: High school teacher of social studies and counselor in Monticello, Iowa, 1959-61; high school director of guidance and assistant principal in Pleasant Valley, Iowa, 1961-63; intern principal of high schools in Palo Alto, Calif., 1963-64, and Fremont, Calif., 1964-65; principal of junior-senior high school in Madison, Wis., 1965-69; University of Wisconsin—Madison, instructor in education, summer, 1969; University of Wisconsin—Milwaukee, assistant professor, 1969-71, associate professor, 1971-75, professor of administrative leadership, 1975—, chairman of department of educational leadership, 1972—. Member of National Committee to Develop Recommendations for Fostering Greater Understanding of the Role of the School Counselor, 1969; member of Wisconsin State Department of Public Instruction Committee to Revise State Certification Standards for Administrators, 1973—. *Military service:* U.S. Marine Corps, 1952-55.

MEMBER: National Association of Secondary School Principals (member of publications committee, 1972—;

chairman of committee, 1974-75), American Educational Research Association, Wisconsin Secondary School Administrators Association, Wisconsin Association of Secondary School Principals (member of board of directors, 1970-73). *Awards, honors:* Outstanding service award from Wisconsin Secondary School Administrators Association, 1973.

WRITINGS: (Contributor) Jean Grambs, editor, *The World Today*, Addison-Wesley, 1971; *Conflict, Controversy, and Crisis in School Administration and Supervision: Issues, Cases, and Concepts*, W. C. Brown, 1972; *School Administration: Challenge and Opportunity for Leadership*, W. C. Brown, in press. Contributor of about twenty-five articles to education journals. Editor of *Bulletin of the Wisconsin Association of Secondary School Principals*, 1969-73, contributing editor, 1973—; contributing editor of *National Association of Secondary School Principals Bulletin*, 1970-74.

WORK IN PROGRESS: A study of administrators' reactions to federal legislation on student records and on regulations against sex discrimination.

* * *

GOSS, Clay 1946-

PERSONAL: Born May 26, 1946, in Philadelphia, Pa.; son of Douglas P. (a counselor) and Alfreda (a teacher; maiden name, Ivey) Jackson; married Linda McNear (a teacher and performer), March 25, 1969; children: Aisha, Uhuru (daughters). *Education:* Howard University, B.F.A., 1972. *Agent:* Dorothea Oppenheimer, 866 United Nations Plaza, New York, N.Y. 10017. *Office:* Institute for the Arts & Humanities, Howard University, P.O. Box 723, Washington, D.C. 20001.

CAREER: Department of Recreation, Washington, D.C., drama specialist, 1969; Howard University, Washington, D.C., playwright-in-residence in drama department, 1970-73, in Institute for the Arts & Humanities, 1973-75. Instructor in poetry and development of Afro-American theater, Antioch College, Washington and Baltimore campuses, 1971-73. *Member:* Theatre Black, Kappa Alpha Psi.

WRITINGS—Plays: *Homecookin': Five Plays* (contains "Homecookin'," "Oursides," "Andrew," "Of Being Hit," and "Mars: Monument to the Last Black Eunuch"; see below for production information), Howard University Press, 1974.

"Hip Rumpelstiltskin," first produced in Washington, D.C., by Department of Recreation, 1969; "Oursides," first produced in New York, N.Y., at New Federal Theatre, 1972; "Mars: Monument to the Last Black Eunuch," first produced in Washington, D.C., at Howard University, 1972; "Andrew," first produced in New York, N.Y., at New York Shakespeare Festival Theatre, 1972; "Of Being Hit," first produced in Brooklyn, N.Y., at Billie Holiday Theater, 1973; "Spaces in Time," first produced in Washington, D.C., by D. C. Black Repertory Co., 1973; "Ornette," first produced in Amherst at University of Massachusetts, 1974; "Keys to the Kingdom," as yet unproduced.

Juvenile novel: *Bill Pickett: Black Bulldogger*, Hill & Wang, 1970.

Contributor: *We Speak as Liberators: Young Black Poets*, edited by Orde Coombs, Dodd, 1970; *The Drama of Nommo*, edited by Paul Carter Harrison, Grove, 1972; *The Sheet*, edited by Carol Kirkendall, Compared to What, Inc. (Washington, D.C.), 1974.

Plays are represented in anthologies: *Transition*, Department of Afro-American Studies, Howard University, 1972; *Kuntu Drama*, edited by Paul Carter Harrison, Grove, 1974; *The New Lafayette Theatre Presents: Six Black Playwrights*, edited by Ed Bullins, Anchor Press, 1974.

Author of television play, "Billy McGhee," for "The Place," broadcast by WRC-TV, Washington, D.C., 1974. Contributor of short fiction, articles, and reviews to periodicals, including *Liberator*, *Reflect*, *Black Books Bulletin*, *Blackstage*, and *Black World*.

WORK IN PROGRESS: A novel, *Throne of the Third Heaven*; two screenplays; revision of "Keys to the Kingdom."

SIDELIGHTS: Goss commented to *CA*: "What we must first do is to make our goals become our models instead of models becoming our goals. Then build from there."

BIOGRAPHICAL/CRITICAL SOURCES: Jet, October 15, 1970; *Washington Post*, March 21, 1971, March 1, 1973; *Encore*, June, 1973; *Washington Star-News*, October 20, 1974; James Hatch and Omanii Abdullah, *An Annotated Bibliography of Black Drama (1823-1975)*, Drama Book Specialists, in press.

* * *

GOTTLIEB, Naomi R(uth) 1925-

PERSONAL: Born May 8, 1925, in New York, N.Y.; daughter of Harry Lionel (a salesperson) and Anna (Goldstone) Gottlieb; married Ted Streshinsky, March 13, 1948 (divorced, 1966); children: David Alan. *Education:* Hunter College (now Hunter College of the City University of New York), A.B., 1944; University of California, Berkeley, M.S.W., 1949, D.S.W., 1970. *Home:* 6206 50th Ave. N.E., Seattle, Wash. 98115. *Office:* School of Social Work, University of Washington, Seattle, Wash. 98105.

CAREER: Family Service Agency, San Francisco, Calif., advanced caseworker, 1949-59; University of Washington, Seattle, assistant professor, 1970-71, associate professor of social work, 1971—, assistant dean, 1974. Co-director, Women's Institute of the Northwest, Seattle, 1973—. *Member:* National Association of Social Workers, Friends of Welfare Rights Organization, Council of Social Work Education.

WRITINGS: The Welfare Bind, Columbia University Press, 1974. Contributor to social work journals. Member of editorial board of *Journal of Public Social Services*, 1969-70.

WORK IN PROGRESS: A study on appropriate therapeutic approaches to women based on non-stereotyped roles for both women and men.

* * *

GOTTSCHALK, Louis (Reichenthal) 1899-1975

February 21, 1899—June 24, 1975; American educator, historian, and author of books on French history. Obituaries: *AB Bookman's Weekly*, August 4, 1975. (*CA*-15/16)

* * *

GOULART, Frances Sheridan 1938-
(C. F. Johnson)

PERSONAL: Born March 3, 1938, in Detroit, Mich.; daughter of Earl J. and Helen (Lennon) Sheridan; married Ron Goulart (a writer), June 13, 1964; children: Sean Lucien, Steffan Eamon. *Education:* Attended Wayne State

University, 1959-60. *Home and office:* 72 Stonebridge Rd., Wilton, Conn. 06897.

CAREER: Fashion copywriter for Macys, Bendel's, and Lord & Taylors stores in New York, N.Y., 1958-59; Dorothy Ross Associates, New York, N.Y., assistant to Dorothy Ross, 1959-60; Dell'Arte Publicity Agency, Detroit, Mich., founder, 1960-62; Guild, Bascom Bonfigli Advertising Agency, San Francisco, Calif., food consultant and copywriter, 1962-63; Dancer-Fitzgerald-Sample Advertising, San Francisco, Calif., food consultant and copywriter, 1963-64; Potsanjammer School of Natural Cooking, Westport, Conn., co-founder, director, and instructor, 1973—. Lecturer on health and natural foodmaking at Norwalk Community College and Westport (Conn.) Board of Education Adult Education Program, 1974, 1975; consultant to Wilton Family Day Camp, 1973. *Member:* Environmental Health Association (Northeast chapter), Huxley Institute for Biosocial Research, North American Vegetarian Society, Americans Against Famine, National Health Federation, Homemakers of America Federation, Natural Food Associates, Road Runners Club of America, American Athletic Association, American Physical Fitness Institute, Consumers Institute for Food Research. *Awards, honors:* Recipient of numerous awards for long-distance running.

WRITINGS: The Mother Goose Cookbook, Price, Stern, 1969; *The Ecological Eclair*, Macmillan, 1975; *Bum Steers*, Chatham Press, 1975; *Wonder Breads*, Scribner, in press. Contributor to magazines, sometimes under pseudonym C. F. Johnson. Nutrition consultant, *Road Runner Club Newsletter*, 1974-75.

WORK IN PROGRESS: With Nothing But a Pack of Cards, children's nonfiction; *Without Power*, adult nonfiction; *Baggie*, a cookbook.

* * *

GOULD, John A(llen) 1944-

PERSONAL: Born February 3, 1944, in Miami, Fla.; son of Gardner S. (a civil engineer) and Martha (Howell) Gould; married Springli B. Johnson, August 4, 1973. *Education:* Williams College, B.A., 1966; Indiana University, M.A., 1969. *Home:* 19 Chamberlain St., Brewer, Me. 04412.

CAREER: High school teacher of English in public schools in Evansville, Ind., 1966-70, and in Brunswick, Me., 1971-73; now full-time writer.

WRITINGS: The Great Little Hot Dog Cookbook, Doubleday, 1973; *The Brown Bag Cookbook*, Doubleday, 1974.

WORK IN PROGRESS: A novel set in Maine, *The Greenleaf Fires*, completion expected in 1975.

AVOCATIONAL INTERESTS: Travel in Mexico.

* * *

GRAHAM, Ilse 1914-

PERSONAL: Born July 4, 1914, in Berlin, Germany; daughter of Paul (a businessman) and Else Martha (Henschel) Appelbaum; married Gerald Graham (a consulting physician), July 9, 1951; children: Nina, Martin. *Education:* Bedford College, London, B.A. (first class honors), 1939, Ph.D., 1951. *Home:* 60, Northway, London N.W.11, England. *Office:* Department of German, King's College, University of London, Strand, London W.C.2, England.

CAREER: University of London, London, England, assistant lecturer in German at Queen Mary College, 1942-46, assistant lecturer at University College, 1946-49, lecturer in German, 1949-51, part-time lecturer at King's College, 1954-57, lecturer, 1957-65, reader in German, 1965-75, professor of German, 1975—. *Member:* International Goethe Society, English Goethe Society, Modern Humanities Research Association. *Awards, honors:* Modern Humanities Research Association prize, 1972, for *Schiller: A Master of the Tragic Form.*

WRITINGS: Goethe and Lessing: The Wellsprings of Creation, Elek, 1973; *Schiller's Drama: Talent and Integrity,* Barnes & Noble, 1974; *Schiller: Ein Meister der Tragischen Form,* Wissenschaftliche Buchgesellschaft, 1974, translation by Klaus Boerner and Graham published as *Schiller: A Master of the Tragic Form,* Dusquesne University Press, 1975; *Goethe: Portrait of the Artist,* Methuen, in press. Contributor to journals in her field.

WORK IN PROGRESS: Kleist: Word into Flesh: A Poet's Quest for the Symbol.

SIDELIGHTS: Ilse Graham writes: "Most of my work is motivated by the combination of artistic, critical and philosophical preoccupations which is mine. Hence they move on the borderline between literary criticism and aesthetics. My study of Kleist will draw heavily on my philosophical, psychological, and theological training and reading, but will remain firmly within the orbit of literary criticism."

*   *   *

GRANT, Brian 1939-

PERSONAL: Born November 13, 1939, in Kansas City, Mo.; son of Fred W. and Winifred R. Grant; married Claudia Ewing (a minister), June 3, 1972; children: Donna, Mary, Helen. *Education:* College of the Bible (now Lexington Theological Seminary), B.D. (honors), 1964; University of Chicago, M.A., 1966, Ph.D., 1969. *Politics:* Left-liberal. *Home:* 5168 North Kenwood, Indianapolis, Ind. 46208. *Office:* Continuing Education Program in Mental Health, Christian Theological Seminary, 1000 West 42nd St., Indianapolis, Ind. 46208.

CAREER: Ordained Disciples of Christ minister, 1966; licensed psychologist in Indiana; minister in Chicago, Ill., 1964-68; University of Chicago, Chicago, Ill., chaplain, 1966-68, instructor in religion and personality, 1968-69; Christian Theological Seminary, Indianapolis, Ind., affiliate professor of culture and personality, 1969—, associate director of continuing education program in mental health, 1969—; diplomate from American Association of Pastoral Education; Marriage and Family Life Institute, Indianapolis, Ind., founding partner, 1974—. Consultant to Indiana Counseling and Pastoral Care Center; assistant supervisor of Association for Clinical Pastoral Education. *Member:* Society for Scientific Study of Religion, American Association of Pastoral Counselors, American Association of Marriage and Family Counselors.

WRITINGS: Schizophrenia: A Source of Social Insight, Westminster, 1975; *A Process View of Schizophrenia as Revelatory,* Westminster, 1975.

WORK IN PROGRESS: Research on Gestalt and on family therapy.

*   *   *

GRANT, Ellsworth Strong 1917-

PERSONAL: Born October 8, 1917, in Wethersfield, Conn.; son of Horace R. (a manufacturer) and Mabel (deBarthe) Grant; married Marion Hepburn (a writer), June 12, 1939; children: John Barnard, Katharine Houghton, Ellsworth Strong, Jr. *Education:* Harvard University, A.B. (cum laude), 1939. *Religion:* Congregationalist. *Home and office:* 134 Steele Rd., West Hartford, Conn. 06119.

CAREER: Hartford Newsdaily, Hartford, Conn., writer, 1939-40; Allen Manufacturing Co., Hartford, Conn., vice-president of industrial relations, 1940-58; Connecticut Manifold Forms, West Hartford, president, 1958-64; Children's Museum, Hartford, president, 1965-69; town councilman of West Hartford, Conn., 1967—, mayor, 1969-73. Founder of Fenwick Productions (makers and distributors of educational films), 1972—. Executive director of Combined Health Appeal, 1967-71; director of Bay State Film Productions, Connecticut Water Co., and Hitchcock Chair Co. *Member:* Association for the Study of Connecticut History, Connecticut Historical Society.

WRITINGS: (With wife, Marion Grant) *Passbook to a Proud Past and a Promising Future,* Society for Savings, 1968; *Yankee Dreamers and Doers,* Pequot Press, 1974.

Also author of scripts for documentary films: "Long Tidal River," "Quiet, Please!," "Yankee Calling," "Hands," "Resolved to be Free" (official Connecticut Bicentennial Commission film), "We the Enemy," and "If Elected, I Promise." Contributor to magazines, including *American Heritage.*

*   *   *

GRANT, J(ohn) B(arnard) 1940-

PERSONAL: Born March 23, 1940, in Hartford, Conn.; son of Ellsworth S. (a historical writer and maker of documentary films) and Marion (a historical writer; maiden name, Hepburn) Grant; married Ann Halterman, May 28, 1965; children: Jason, Schuyler. *Education:* University of California, Berkeley, B.A., 1965. *Residence:* Freestone, Calif.

CAREER: High school teacher during 1960's; skipper of a charter sailing boat in Florida waters, for a private school located in Florida, 1968-70; writer and editor, 1970—. *Military service:* U.S. Marine Corps, 1960-64.

WRITINGS: The Geocentric Experience (bulletin), Lamplighters Roadway Press, 1972; (with Stanley Keleman) *The Body Speaks Its Mind,* Simon & Schuster, 1975; (with Katharine Houghton) *Two Beastly Tales,* Lamplighters Roadway Press, 1975. Contributing editor of *San Francisco Review of Books.*

WORK IN PROGRESS: The Living Art of Writing, poems, parables, and essays centering on the psychology and physiology of the creative experience; *No & Yes,* six stories and a short novel about women and men opening to new levels of love.

SIDELIGHTS: Grant writes: "I used to treat my writing as a means for unloading, or as a weapon. Now it's my principal means for exploring and celebrating. I am interested in anything whose whole is greater than the sum of its parts: from sonnets to atoms to apple trees to marriages. I am an evolutionary rather than a revolutionary, prefer the creating that gives more, to that which gets rid of." *Avocational interests:* Playing the piano (blues, rhythm and blues, Irish dance music), playing soccer, pruning and preening fruit trees, building his house.

*   *   *

GRAVES, Richard L(atshaw) 1928-

PERSONAL: Born November 27, 1928, in Philadelphia,

Pa.; son of Russell Briggs (a manufacturer) and Melicent (Latshaw) Graves; married Teru Nakano, June 30, 1951; children: Richard N., Sarah T. *Education:* University of Pennsylvania, B.A., 1952. *Home:* 70 Beacon Hill Rd., Port Washington, N.Y. 11050. *Office:* Colt Industries, 430 Park Ave., New York, N.Y. 10022.

CAREER: Writer for Associated Press in Harrisburg, Pa., 1952-64, and in New York, N.Y., 1964-66; General Telephone and Electronics Corp., New York, N.Y., project manager, 1966-69; Colt Industries, Inc., New York, N.Y., director of public information, 1969—. *Military service:* U.S. Army, 1946-47.

WRITINGS—Novels: *The Black Gold of Malaverde*, Stein & Day, 1973; *The Platinum Bullet*, Stein & Day, 1974; *Cobalt 60*, Stein & Day, 1975. Contributor to journals.

WORK IN PROGRESS: Several novels.

* * *

GRAY, Bradford H(itch)   1942-

PERSONAL: Born December 31, 1942, in Greenwich, Conn.; son of John Bradford (a businessman) and Joyce (Hitch) Gray; married Anne Morgan (a weaver and spinner), August 6, 1966; children: Carrie Elizabeth, Joshua Bradford. *Education:* Oklahoma State University, B.S., 1964, M.S., 1966; Yale University, Ph.D., 1973. *Home:* 8506 Wilkesboro Dr., Potomac, Md. 20854. *Office:* National Commission for the Protection of Human Subjects in Biomedical and Behavioral Research, 125 Westwood Building, 5333 Westbard Ave., Bethesda, Md. 20016.

CAREER: University of North Carolina, Chapel Hill, assistant professor of sociology, 1971-74, research associate at Health Services Research Center, 1971-73; Columbia University, Barnard College, New York, N.Y., research associate in sociology, autumn, 1974; National Commission for the Protection of Human Subjects in Biomedical and Behavioral Research, Bethesda, Md., director of social research, 1975—. *Member:* American Sociological Association, American Association for the Advancement of Science, Southern Sociological Association.

WRITINGS: Human Subjects in Medical Experimentation: A Sociological Study of the Conduct and Regulation of Clinical Research, Wiley, 1975. Contributor of articles and reviews to *Medical Care, Journal of Health and Social Behavior, Social Science Quarterly*, and *Social Forces.* Associate editor of *Social Forces.*

WORK IN PROGRESS: Designing empirical studies of human experimentation, for National Commission for the Protection of Human Subjects; research on ethical issues in social research.

SIDELIGHTS: Gray writes: "An initial interest and training in the sociology of medicine has led to a heavy involvement in the study of many questions related to the links between science and society. The most immediate, but not sole, link is in the use of human subjects in research. That such work can be of both sociological and social policy relevance is very important to me." *Avocational interests:* Jazz, collecting first editions and signed copies of early American sociological works.

* * *

GRAYBAR, Lloyd J(oseph)   1938-

PERSONAL: Born November 29, 1938, in New York, N.Y.; son of Bennett (a blue-collar worker) and Maude (Osher) Graybar. *Education:* Middlebury College, A.B., 1960; Columbia University, M.A., 1961, Ph.D., 1966. *Politics:* Republican. *Religion:* Protestant. *Office:* Department of History, Eastern Kentucky University, Richmond, Ky. 40475.

CAREER: Eastern Kentucky University, Richmond, assistant professor, 1966-70, associate professor of history, 1971—. Summer visiting instructor at University of North Dakota, 1967, and Bowling Green State University, 1968; summer visiting professor at Syracuse University, 1969. *Member:* United States Naval Institute, American Historical Association, Organization of American Historians, American Association of University Professors, Immigration History Society, Southern Historical Association, Kentucky Civil War Round Table.

WRITINGS: Albert Shaw of the Review of Reviews: An Intellectual Biography, University Press of Kentucky, 1974.

WORK IN PROGRESS: Research on Admiral Ernest King and the U.S. Navy in World War II.

AVOCATIONAL INTERESTS: Traveling, playing golf and tennis.

* * *

GREEN, Alan (Baer)   1906-1975
(Jack Alan; Glen Burne, Roger Denbie, joint pseudonyms)

October 30, 1906—March 10, 1975; American author and advertising executive. Obituaries: *New York Times*, March 11, 1975; *AB Bookman's Weekly*, March 24, 1975; *Publishers Weekly*, April 21, 1975. (*CA*-53/56)

* * *

GREEN, Ernestene L(everne)   1939-

PERSONAL: Born December 28, 1939, in Cameron, Tex.; daughter of Joseph Nelson and LeVerne (Calhoun) Green. *Education:* University of Arizona, B.A., 1961, M.A., 1963; graduate study at University of Hawaii, 1963-65; University of Pennsylvania, Ph.D., 1970. *Home:* 610 McCourtie, Kalamazoo, Mich. 49008. *Office:* Department of Anthropology, Western Michigan University, Kalamazoo, Mich. 49008.

CAREER: Western Michigan University, Kalamazoo, assistant professor, 1968-73, associate professor of archaeology and anthropology, 1973—. *Member:* Society for American Archaeology, American Anthropological Association, Southwestern Archaeological Research Group, Central States Anthropological Association, Council on Michigan Archaeology, Sigma Xi.

WRITINGS: In Search of Man, Little, Brown, 1972.

* * *

GREEN, Galen   1949-

PERSONAL: Born April 30, 1949, in Kansas City, Mo.; adoptive son of Harry Pearl (a toolmaker) and Margaret (McCall) Green; married Kate Schulte (a paralegal assistant), June 19, 1971. *Education:* Wichita State University, B.A., 1972; University of Utah, M.A., 1974. *Home:* 1214 East Whittier, Apt. C., Columbus, Ohio 43206.

CAREER: Keystone Funds, Boston, Mass., research correspondent, 1972-73; private tutor, 1974; South Side Settlement, Columbus, Ohio, teacher, writer, and community worker, 1974-75; instructor, variously, in creative writing, literature appreciation, poetry workshop, drama at Ohio State University, YMCA, and Ohio Dominican College, all Columbus, all 1975. VISTA worker, 1974-75; volunteer instructor at poetry workshop, United Christian Center of Ohio State University, 1975.

WRITINGS: Apple Grunt (poems), Hamburger Press, 1971. Contributor of poems, short stories and essays to *New York Quarterly, Epoch, Western Humanities Review, Dragonfly, Center, West Coast Review*, and other periodicals and little magazines. Guest editor, *Out of Sight*, 1972, 1974; founder and editor, with wife, Kate Green, *Fireweed* (underground magazine of the arts), 1975—.

WORK IN PROGRESS: Consolation of Breathing, a book of poems; *The Settlement House*, a novel.

SIDELIGHTS: Green wrote: "The central image which keeps me going at this point is that of a sleeping person who is trying to awaken from a nightmare but cannot. That person is all of us together. Poets and writers are integral to the process of our awakening. Certainly they can make our nightmare less horrifying in the meantime."

*   *   *

GREEN, Landis K(night)   1940-

PERSONAL: Born June 15, 1940, in Blackfoot, Idaho; son of Ronald Adrian (a grocer) and Verrell (Jarvis) Green; married Iride Biba Ravaioli, November 2, 1962. *Education:* Attended Palomar College, 1961-63, Merritt College, 1964-65, University of California, Berkeley, 1966-67. *Home:* 499 Ridge Rd., Novato, Calif. 94947.

CAREER: Grocery clerk in California, 1961-64. Self-employed astrologer, 1967—; artist; scriptographer; writer. *Military service:* U.S. Navy, 1959-61; became petty officer. *Member:* National Geographic Society.

WRITINGS: (Self-illustrated) *The Astrologer's Manual*, Arco, 1975.

WORK IN PROGRESS: A Guide to Astrological Types, for popular audiences, *The Visitors*, an illustrated science-fantasy tale, and *Famous Horoscopes*, on notable persons in history, expected completion of all in 1976.

SIDELIGHTS: Green told *CA*: "I am a serious student of the 'I Ching' (a Confucian text) and certain ideas related to the philosophy of the ancient Greeks; astrology serves me as a vehicle to the realm of higher ideas. I am interested in those things that enhance mankind's spiritual and intellectual development." *Avocational interests:* Music, hiking, collecting minerals, cooking.

*   *   *

GREEN, Martyn   1899-1975

April 22, 1899—February 8, 1975; American singer, actor, and author. Obituaries: *New York Times*, February 9, 1975; *Washington Post*, February 9, 1975; *Current Biography*, April, 1975.

*   *   *

GREEN, Morton   1937-

PERSONAL: Born May 18, 1937, in Los Angeles, Calif.; son of Sidney (owner of a small business) and Ruth (Tenner) Green. *Education:* University of California, Los Angeles, B.A. and Secondary School Teaching Credential, 1960; University of Southern California, School of Librarianship Credential and M.S.L.S., 1964. *Politics:* Independent. *Religion:* Religious Science. *Home:* 1829 Westholme Ave., Los Angeles, Calif. 90025.

CAREER: Los Angeles city schools, Los Angeles, Calif., junior high school teacher, 1960-61; West Los Angeles Regional Library, Los Angeles, Calif., librarian trainee, 1962-64; Arcadia Public Library, Arcadia, Calif., reference librarian and young adult librarian, 1964-70; Los Angeles City Public Library, Los Angeles, Calif., adult librarian at Robertson Branch, 1970-73, substitute librarian, 1973—. Substitute librarian, Los Angeles Community College District, 1974—. *Member:* Society of Children's Book Writers, Southern California Council on Literature for Children and Young People, Young Adult Reviewers of Southern California (member of executive board, 1965-70).

WRITINGS: Garden of Mystery (easy-reading adaptation of Nathaniel Hawthorne's "Rappaccini's Daughter"), Leswing Press, 1973; *Blue Skies Magic* (picture book), Ginn, 1974. Stories included in textbooks published by Noble, Globe Book, Science Research Associates, and other publishers. Contributor of stories, articles, poems, and plays to education journals, Scholastic Magazines, *Photoplay, Los Angeles*, and others.

WORK IN PROGRESS: An easy-reading biography of Henry Kissinger, combined with a simplified survey of contemporary U.S. foreign relations; more picture books and beginning to read books.

SIDELIGHTS: Green writes: "Since 1973 I have worked in about twenty-five branches and the Central Children's Room of LAPL, as a substitute librarian. This has given me an invaluable insight into the reading interests of children in different environments. Non-writers always want to know where writers get their 'ideas.' I can only say that the writer learns to set his mind in a certain way, and then relaxes, knowing that ideas will come to him. The writer learns to become attuned to the Universal Mind, in which all ideas already exist in their complete forms. Knowing the craft and mechanics of writing is important, but achieving this mental 'set' is critical for success."

*   *   *

GREEN, Thomas F.   1927-

PERSONAL: Born February 8, 1927, in Lincoln, Neb.; son of Roy M. and Norma (Kidd) Green; married Rosemary Louise Gass, March 24, 1948; children: Charles Hilton, Sara Elizabeth, Priscilla Louise, James Frederick. *Education:* University of Nebraska, B.A., 1948, M.A., 1949; Cornell University, Ph.D., 1952. *Home address:* Box 24, Pompey, N.Y. 13138. *Office:* 305 Comstock Ave., Syracuse, N.Y. 13210.

CAREER: School of Mines and Technology, Rapid City, S.D., instructor in English and social science, 1952-55; Michigan State University, East Lansing, assistant professor of humanities, 1955-58, assistant professor of education, 1958-59, associate professor of education, 1959-64; Syracuse University, Syracuse, N.Y., associate professor, 1964-66, professor of education, 1966—, Educational Policy Research Center, director, 1967-69, co-director, 1970-73, Division of Education and Social Policy, acting director, 1974—. Associate member, East-West Philosophers Conference, University of Hawaii, summer, 1959; U.S. delegate to World Conference on Teaching and Theology, University of Strasbourg, 1960. Senior research fellow, Princeton Theological Seminary, 1962-63; visiting professor of philosophy, Colorado College, summer, 1963; Robert Jones lecturer in Education, Austin Theological Seminary,

1965; J. Richard Street lecturer, Syracuse University, 1966; guest lecturer at various other universities. Consultant, Organisation for Economic Co-operation and Development, Paris, France, 1970-71, Wayne Management Inc., Rochester, N.Y., 1972; trustee and treasurer, Center for a Human Future, Inc., Syracuse, N.Y., 1973—.

MEMBER: American Philosophical Association, American Educational Research Association, Philosophy of Education Society (president, 1975-76). *Awards, honors:* Guggenheim fellowship and Alfred North Whitehead fellowship, 1969-70.

WRITINGS: Education and Pluralism: Ideal and Reality, Syracuse University Press, 1966; *Work, Leisure and the American Schools,* Random House, 1968; *Educational Planning in Perspective,* IPC Science and Technology Press, 1971; *The Activities of Teaching,* McGraw, 1971.

Contributor: Marjorie Reeves, editor, *Essays in Education and Theology,* World Student Christian Federation, 1965; *Problems and Issues in Contemporary Education: A Collection of the Best from the "Harvard Educational Review" and "Teacher's College Record,"* Scott, Foresman, 1966; Israel Scheffler, editor, *Philosophy and Education,* Allyn & Bacon, 1966; Paul Komisar and C. J. B. Macmillan, editors, *Psychological Concepts of Education,* Rand McNally, 1967; M. L. Wax, Diamond, and Gearing, editors, *Anthropological Perspectives on Education,* Basic Books, 1971; Sylvan J. Kaplan and Evelyn Kivy-Rosenberg, editors, *Ecology and the Quality of Life,* C. C Thomas, 1973; Akper and Sandow, editors, *The Politics of Education: Challenges to State Board Leadership,* PDK Press, 1975; Robert Bundy, editor, *Images of the Future: The Twenty-first Century and Beyond,* Prometheus Books, 1975.

Contributor to Macmillan *Encyclopedia of Education,* and to *New Directions for Higher Education, Liberal Education, Futures, Colloquy Magazine, Harvard Educational Review, Educational Forum, Journal of Engineering Education,* and other educational periodicals.

WORK IN PROGRESS: Images of Education in Kyklios Paideia; Letters to Larry, a set of fifteen to twenty informal and personal explorations of theological and biblical topics; contributing an essay to *Contemporary Alienation,* edited by Roy S. Bryce-Laporte.

* * *

GREENBERG, Kenneth R(ay) 1930-

PERSONAL: Born January 14, 1930, in Steubenville, Ohio; son of Samuel T. and Leah M. Greenberg; married Cynthia Towsner, June 22, 1963; children: Scott D. *Education:* Ohio State University, B.Sc., 1951, M.A., 1952; Case Western Reserve University, Ph.D., 1960. *Home:* 9814 Hill St., Kensington, Md. 20795. *Office:* Department of Counseling and Personnel Services, University of Maryland, College Park, Md. 20742.

CAREER: College of Steubenville, Steubenville, Ohio, assistant professor of psychology, 1954-60; District of Columbia Department of Public Health, Washington, D.C., psychologist, 1961-62; private practice in psychology, 1962—; University of Maryland, College Park, associate professor of education, 1963—. Chairman of governor's committee to hire handicapped; president of medical board of United Cerebral Palsy; consultant to Council of Cooperative Nursery Schools, Ohio Bureau of Vocational Rehabilitation, and Society for Crippled Children and Adults. *Mili-*

tary service: U.S. Army, 1952-54. *Member:* American Psychological Association, American Personnel and Guidance Association, Society of Clinical and Experimental Hypnosis, Association of Counseling Education and Supervision, Maryland Psychological Association, District of Columbia Psychological Association, District of Columbia Society of Clinical Psychologists, Kiwanis.

WRITINGS: (Editor) *Personality: A Book of Readings,* Academic Press, 1968; *A Tiger by the Tail: Parenting in a Troubled Society,* Nelson Hall, 1974.

WORK IN PROGRESS: Child Counseling and Psychotherapy.

SIDELIGHTS: Greenberg writes: "Because I call myself a realist, I am not always pleased with what I observe in our society today. My book, *A Tiger by the Tail,* reflects my concern in the direction our society is moving. I view myself as an educator. Both as an academician and clinician I am convinced that our only hope lies in our success in educating future parents and to expose children to the values which a society must have if the welfare and protection of its members are given a high priority. A passive, wait-and-see attitude will add problems to our already troubled society. Parents must become more aware of the tremendous responsibility they have assumed and the impact their parenting has on both present and future generations."

* * *

GREENBLATT, Augusta 1912-

PERSONAL: Born August 13, 1912, in New York; daughter of Raful and Rissi (Hendelman) Pecker; married I. J. Greenblatt (director of clinical laboratories at Brookdale Hospital Medical Center), March 28, 1940; children: Richard, Laurence. *Education:* Cornell University, B.A., 1933; graduate study at Brooklyn College (now Brooklyn College of the City University of New York), 1938-40; Hofstra University, M.S., 1956. *Religion:* Jewish. *Home:* 511 Allen Rd., Woodmere, N.Y. 11598.

CAREER: New York City Department of Hospitals, New York, N.Y., supervisor of clinical chemistry and microbiology, 1935-42; U.S. Army Medical Department, Camp Stoneman, Calif., civilian supervisor of clinical laboratories, 1942-45; Clinical Diagnostic Laboratory, Woodmere, N.Y., director, 1950-64; Hewlett-Woodmere Continuing Education, Hewlett, N.Y., lecturer, 1964-74; writer and lecturer on science and health topics for the general public, 1964—. Lecturer at New York University School of Continuing Education, 1965, 1967. *Member:* National Association of Science Writers, American Medical Writers Association, American Public Health Association, Authors Guild. *Awards, honors:* Certificate of Commendation from Army Service Forces, 1944.

WRITINGS: Teenage Medicine: Questions Young People Ask About Their Health, Cowles, 1970, published as *Why Do I Feel This Way,* Pyramid, 1974; *Heredity and You: How You Can Protect Your Family's Future,* Coward, 1974. Contributor to *Grolier's Encyclopedia;* contributor to professional journals, including *Journal of Biochemistry* and *American Journal of Medical Sciences,* and popular magazines, including *Family Circle, Woman's Day,* and *McCall's.* Writer and editor for U.S. Public Health Service, 1968.

SIDELIGHTS: Augusta Greenblatt wrote: "Since 1964 when I switched careers from the laboratory to the typewriter and lectern, I am constantly reinforced in my early belief (and hope) that there are women who would rather talk DNA than diapers; teenagers who are willing to open their minds on touchy subjects when they are not preached at or talked down to; and persons of all ages who welcome the translation of the technical jargon of the scientist to everyday language.''

*   *   *

GREENE, Bert 1923-

PERSONAL: Born October 16, 1923, in Flushing, N.Y.; son of Samuel Michael (an electrical contractor) and Paula (a pianist; maiden name, Cohn) Greene. Education: Attended College of William and Mary, Richmond Professional Institute, Pratt Institute, and Yale University. Politics: "Independent, with Democrat bias." Religion: None. Home: 240 West 12th St., New York, N.Y. 10014. Agent: Emil, Kobrin, Klein & Garbus, 540 Madison Ave., New York, N.Y. 10022. Office: Esquire, 488 Madison Ave., New York, N.Y. 10022.

CAREER: Helena Rubenstein, Inc. (beauty preparations), New York, N.Y., art director, 1950-53; I. Miller & Sons (shoe firm), New York, N.Y., art director, 1954-60; Esquire (magazine), New York, N.Y., art director in promotion, 1970—. Co-owner of The Store in Amagansett, 1967—.

WRITINGS: The Store Cookbook, Regnery, 1974; The Poor, Poor Rich, Regnery, in press.

Plays: (Author of adaptation, with Aaron Fine) Franz Kafka, "The Trial" (two-act), first performed in New York at Provincetown Playhouse, June 19, 1955; (author of adaptation) Frank Wedekind, "Springs Awakening" (three-act), first produced at Provincetown Playhouse, November 1, 1956; "The Summer of Daisy Miller" (two-act), first performed in New York at Phoenix Theatre, May 17, 1964; (author of adaptation) Colette, "My Mother's House" (television play in three acts), first performed in New York, N.Y., on WNET-Television, 1969.

Contributor of stories to Harper's Bazaar and Mademoiselle.

WORK IN PROGRESS: Research on food idiosyncracies.

SIDELIGHTS: Greene writes: "I began to write early on (but the conflict of a double talent waylaid me into graphics where I have strayed too long). My greatest single influences have always been women writers. I love Elizabeth Bowen, Rosamond Lehman, and Colette dearly—and have an active ongoing friendship with M. F. F. Fisher who inducted me into the mysteries of taste and smell. I am a gourmand who loves to cook and eat well and takes enormous pleasure in reading and writing about food. I have travelled fairly extensively, mostly to France and England—and Haiti, and would consider any one of the three my spiritual home.''

*   *   *

GREENE, Harry J(oseph) 1906-

PERSONAL: Born June 19, 1906, in Rockyford, Colo.; son of Harry J. (a dry cleaner) and Alice (Irwin) Greene; married Leota Williams (an accountant), June 25, 1940; children: Arla Jo (Mrs. Eric Roles). Education: Attended University of Kansas, 1924-26. Politics: Independent. Religion: Protestant. Home: C-121, 4139 East McDowell Rd., Phoenix, Ariz. 85008.

CAREER: Employed in dry cleaning business in Tonganoxie, Kan., 1926-38; Kansas State Employment Office, clerk and interviewer in Topeka and Ottawa offices, 1938-41; self-employed, 1944-51; worked as quality control inspector for General Motors Corp., Remington Arms Co., and Ford Motor Co., 1951-55; Lockheed Aircraft, Burbank, Calif., quality control inspector, 1955-57; self-employed in Phoenix, Arizona, 1957-67; Talley Industries, Mesa, Ariz., quality control inspector, 1967-72; full-time writer, 1972—. Military service: U.S. Army Air Forces, 1941-44; became first lieutenant.

WRITINGS: How to Make High Profits in Apartment Investments, Prentice-Hall, 1974.

WORK IN PROGRESS: The Sell or Hold Dilemma.

*   *   *

GREENWALD, Jerry 1923-

PERSONAL: Born August 26, 1923, in Cincinnati, Ohio; son of Isador Leonard and Fanny (Saloshin) Greenwald; divorced. Education: University of California, Los Angeles, A.B., 1950, Ph.D., 1955. Office: 1029 Second St., Santa Monica, Calif. 90403.

CAREER: Psychotherapist in private practice in Santa Monica, Calif., 1955—. Military service: U.S. Army, 1942-46.

WRITINGS: Be the Person You Were Meant to Be, Simon & Schuster, 1973; Creative Intimacy, Simon & Schuster, 1975.

*   *   *

GREER, Georgeanna H(errmann) 1922-

PERSONAL: Born March 5, 1922, in Ann Arbor, Mich.; daughter of George R. (a physician) and Anna (Williams) Herrmann; married Sam J. Greer (a surgeon), August 5, 1943; children: Cassandra (Mrs. Mark P. Gainey), Walter M., Margret S. Education: University of Texas, Austin, B.A., 1940; University of Texas, Galveston, M.D., 1943; San Antonio Art Institute, postdoctoral study, 1958-65. Religion: Episcopalian. Home and office: 213 Black Hawk, San Antonio, Tex. 78232.

CAREER: University of Michigan Hospital, Ann Arbor, intern, 1943-44, assistant resident, 1944-45, resident in pediatrics, 1946; Texas State Health Department, Austin, pediatric clinician, 1946; private practice of medicine in Ann Arbor, 1947-51; San Antonio City Health Department, San Antonio, Tex., part-time physician, 1954—. Consultant to Texas State Historical Commission, 1972-75; volunteer assistant at Witte Museum. Member: Historic Site Archeology Conference.

WRITINGS: (With Harding Black) The Meyer Family, Trinity University Press, 1971. Contributor to Historic Site Archeology Forum Paper and Ceramics Monthly.

WORK IN PROGRESS: A history of pottery in Texas and in the southern United States.

SIDELIGHTS: Georgeanna Greer writes: "I have always had an interest in ceramics and after we had lived in San Antonio a few years, I found that excellent classes were given here in making of stoneware on the potter's wheel and glazing and firing. After about eight years of this study I found by accident that much utilitarian pottery had been made in Texas, but that no history or material was available on the subject. This started me on an investigation of early potteries and collecting of early wares which has not waned. It is entirely an avocation, but quite consuming in the past few years.''

*   *   *

GREGOR, A(nthony) James 1929-

PERSONAL: Born April 2, 1929, in New York, N.Y.; son of Antonio (a factory worker) and Mary (Gazzini) Gimigliano. *Education:* Columbia University, B.A., 1952, M.A., 1959, Ph.D., 1961. *Home:* 75 Parnassus Rd., Berkeley, Calif. 94708. *Office:* Department of Political Science, University of California, Berkeley, Calif. 94720.

CAREER: University of Hawaii, Honolulu, assistant professor of philosophy, 1961-63; University of Kentucky, Lexington, associate professor of philosophy, 1964-66; University of Texas, Austin, associate professor of philosophy, 1966-67; University of California, Berkeley, professor of political science, 1967—. Adjunct professor at U.S. Department of State, School of Professional Studies, 1968—. *Military service:* U.S. Army, 1946-48. *Member:* Institut International de Sociologie, American Philosophical Association, American Political Science Association, American Sociological Association. *Awards, honors:* Guggenheim fellow, 1974.

WRITINGS: A Survey of Marxism, Random House, 1965; *Contemporary Radical Ideologies*, Random House, 1968; *The Ideology of Fascism*, Free Press, 1969; *An Introduction to Metapolitics*, Free Press, 1971; *The Interpretations of Fascism*, General Learning Press, 1974; *The Fascist Persuasion in Radical Politics*, Princeton University Press, 1974; *The Young Mussolini and the Origins of Fascism*, University of Michigan Press, in press. Author of monographs. Contributor to journals.

WORK IN PROGRESS: The Ideologues of Fascism, for University of Chicago Press.

SIDELIGHTS: Gregor has directed field research in Central Australia, South West Africa and East Germany.

*   *   *

GREGORY, R(ichard) L(angton) 1923-

PERSONAL: Born July 24, 1923, in London, England; son of Christopher Clive Langton (an astronomer) and Helen Patricia (Gibson) Gregory; married Margaret Hope Pattison Muir, 1953 (divorced, 1966); married Freja Mary Balchin (in antique business), 1966; children: (first marriage) Mark, Romilly Caroline. *Education:* Downing College, Cambridge, B.A., 1949, M.A., 1954. *Politics:* "Pale Blue." *Religion:* Agnostic. *Home:* 7 Canynge Sq., Clifton, Bristol, England. *Office:* Brain and Perception Laboratory, Department of Anatomy, University of Bristol, Bristol BS8 1TH, England.

CAREER: Medical Research Council Applied Psychology Research Unit, Cambridge, England, researcher, 1950-53; Cambridge University, Cambridge, England, university demonstrator, 1953-58; lecturer in psychology, 1959-67; fellow of Corpus Christi College, 1962-67; University of Edinburgh, Edinburgh, Scotland, professor of bionics, 1967-70, chairman of department of machine intelligence and perception, 1968-70; University of Bristol, Bristol, England, professor of neuropsychology and director of Brain and Perception Laboratory, 1970—. Visiting professor at University of California, Los Angeles, 1963, Massachusetts Institute of Technology, 1964, and New York University, 1966. Creator and host of "Windows on the Brain," a television series, for BBC-2, 1971, and has appeared on other

television and radio programs. Consultant to Cambridge Instrument Co. and British Aircraft Corp. *Military service:* Royal Air Force, Signals, 1941-46.

MEMBER: Royal Microscopical Society (fellow), Royal Society of Arts (fellow), Zoological Society (fellow), Royal Institution (manager, 1972-75), Biological Engineering Society, Experimental Psychological Society, Royal Society of Edinburgh (fellow). *Awards, honors:* Senior International Prize for Research Ageing from CIBA Foundation, 1956; Craik Prize for Physiological Psychology, 1958, from St. John's College, Cambridge; Waverly gold medal and prize, 1960, from *Discovery*.

WRITINGS: (With Jean Wallace) *Recovery from Early Blindness*, Heffer, 1963; *Eye and Brain*, Weidenfeld & Nicolson, 1966, 2nd edition, 1972; *The Intelligent Eye*, Weidenfeld & Nicolson, 1970; (editor with E. H. Gombrich) *Illusion in Nature and Art*, Duckworth, 1973; *Concepts and Mechanisms of Perception*, Duckworth, 1974. Contributor to scientific publications. Founder and editor of *Perception*.

WORK IN PROGRESS: A book on the history and philosophy of empiricism; scientific research on human perception.

SIDELIGHTS: Gregory writes: "I believe in solving human problems without reference to theological presuppositions. In this sense I am a humanist. Science may in principle provide adequate working models for politics and economics—but at present I believe we should live with ad hoc trial-and-error solutions. These may not be efficient but are less dangerous than inadequate theory applied blindly. I feel we should learn to live with—and enjoy—questions. Humour is underestimated. It serves as a uniquely important bridge between people and creeds. Until we can joke with our enemies we will fail to turn those we fear into friends.''

Gregory's field research includes investigating a unique deep-sea creature (Copepod copelia quadrata) in the Bay of Naples, and testing a new kind of camera on telescopes in New Mexico and Arizona. He holds several patents for optical and recording instruments.

AVOCATIONAL INTERESTS: Punning and pondering.

*   *   *

GREGORY, Violet L(efler) 1907-

PERSONAL: Born January 19, 1907, in Ontario, Canada; daughter of Lewis (a farmer) and Alice (a music teacher; maiden name, Hughes) Lefler; married Allen Shelby Pruett, August 2, 1927 (divorced March 1, 1933); married Walter B. Gregory, August 9, 1947 (died July 18, 1963); children: (first marriage) Gerald Allen Pruett. *Education:* University of California, San Diego, student, 1961-66; San Diego City College, A.A., 1967; San Diego State College (now University), B.A., 1972. *Religion:* Protestant. *Home:* 1649 Pennsylvania Ave., San Diego, Calif. 92103.

CAREER: Western Union Telegraph Co., Detroit, Mich., file clerk, 1925-27; Harper Hospital, Detroit, Mich., nurse's aide, 1931-38; Lady Madison Hosiery Co., Detroit, store manager, 1938-40; Palmer House Restaurant, Detroit, receptionist, 1940-41; Jewel Tea Co., Detroit, Mich., route manager, 1941-46; Grace Holmes Club Plan, Newark, N.J., correspondent, 1949-53; owner, Little Corner Store, Lyndhurst, N.J., 1953-55, Star Market, San Diego, Calif., 1956-59, Gregory Distributors, San Diego, 1961-64; freelance writer, and tutor in literature interpretation, 1972—.

MEMBER: World Poetry Society (India), International Poetry Society (fellow), National League of American Pen Women (vice-president of San Diego branch, 1966-68; president, 1970-72), California Federation of Chaparral Poets, California State Poetry Society, Pennsylvania Poetry Society, San Diego Poets Association. *Awards, honors:* Sweepstake prize from Forest Lawn Foundation and California Federation of Chaparral Poets, 1966, for "No Questions Asked," 1967, for "In Myriad Containers"; also received about forty additional awards for poetry (ranging from first prizes to honorable mentions), 1961—.

*WRITINGS—*Poems: *Mixed Bouquet*, Centro Studi E Scambi Internazionale, 1966; *The Silver Link*, Dorrance, 1969; *Full Circle*, Branden Press, 1974.

Poetry is represented in anthologies, including: *The Minds Create*, edited by Lilith Lorraine, Different Press, 1961; *Poetry Parade*, edited by Lincoln B. Young, Young Publications, 1963; *Rhymetime for the Very Young*, edited by Young, Young Publications, 1964; *Spring Anthology*, edited by B. K. Shaw, Mitre Press, 1968; *Clover Collection of Verse*, edited by Evelyn Petry, Clover Publishing, 1972; *International Who's Who in Poetry Anthology*, edited by Ernest Kay, Melrose Press, 1973; *Ipso Facto: An I.P.S. Anthology*, edited by Robin Gregory, Hub Publications, 1975. Contributor of about two hundred articles and poems to magazines and newspapers.

WORK IN PROGRESS: Two books of poetry; prose mood pieces; research on modern poetry and poets' works and techniques.

* * *

GRIFFIN, Gerald G(ehrig) 1933-

PERSONAL: Born April 13, 1933, in Flint, Mich.; son of Jasper C. (a tool and dye setter) and Lillian (O'Toole) Griffin; married Sally Atkinson, August 10, 1951 (divorced, 1959); married Patricia A. Wilbur (a marriage and family counselor), July 23, 1965; children: (first marriage) Gregory, John, Diane (stepdaughter). *Education:* General Motors Institute, B.B.A., 1956; Flint Junior College, A.S., 1959; Michigan State University, M.A., 1963, Ph.D., 1966. *Office:* Suite 220, One Perimeter Way N.W., Atlanta, Ga. 30339.

CAREER: Fuller Brush Co., Saginaw, Mich., field manager, 1960-61; Ionia State Hospital, Ionia, Mich., clinical psychologist, 1963-65; private practice as consulting psychologist in Atlanta, Ga., 1967-75. Consultant to Bobby Dodd Workshop, 1967-72, and Walden University, 1972—. Member of board of directors of Pro Data, Inc., 1955-56. *Member:* American Psychological Association, American Association of Marriage and Family Counselors, American Psychologists in Private Practice, Georgia Psychological Association, Georgia Psychologists in Private Practice, Alabama Psychological Association.

WRITINGS: The Silent Misery: Why Marriages Fail, C. C Thomas, 1974; (contributor) Richard Hardy and John Cull, editors, *Deciding on Divorce*, C. C Thomas, 1974. Contributor to *Detroit Free Press, American Personnel and Guidance Journal*, and *Highway Magazine*.

WORK IN PROGRESS: Comin' To: And Making Your Next Marriage a Success, completion expected in 1975; a novel, *The Conversation Piece*.

SIDELIGHTS: Griffin wrote a novel in ninth grade that has not been published, *Sir Griffin and the Fair Princess Velva.*

GRIFFIN, Keith B(roadwell) 1938-

PERSONAL: Born November 6, 1938, in Panama; son of Marcus S. (an army officer) and Elaine (Broadwell) Griffin; married Dixie Beth Griffin, April 2, 1956; children: Janice Marie, Kimberley Moffatt. *Education:* Williams College, B.A., 1960; Balliol College, Oxford, B.Phil., 1962, D.Phil., 1965. *Home:* Wodetun, 31 Blenheim Rd., Horspath, Oxford, England. *Office:* Department of Economics, Magdalen College, University of Oxford, Oxford, England.

CAREER: University of Oxford, Magdalen College, Oxford, England, fellow in economics, 1965—. *Member:* American Economic Association, Royal Economic Society.

WRITINGS: Underdevelopment in Spanish America, Allen & Unwin, 1969; (with John Enos) *Planning Development*, Addison-Wesley, 1970; (editor) *Financing Development in Latin America*, Macmillan, 1971; (editor with A. R. Khan) *Growth and Inequality in Pakistan*, Macmillan, 1972; *The Political Economy of Agrarian Change*, Macmillan, 1974; *Land Concentration and Rural Poverty*, Macmillan, in press.

* * *

GROENHOFF, Edwin L. 1924-

PERSONAL: Born August 11, 1924, in Alden, Iowa; son of Fred (a farmer) and Edith (Nicolet) Groenhoff; married Viola Rittel, June 25, 1948. *Education:* Northwestern College, B.A., 1955; Macalester College, M.Ed., 1957; University of Colorado, Ed.D., 1968. *Religion:* Evangelical Free Church. *Home address:* Box 3142, Mankato, Minn. 56001. *Office:* Department of Geography, Mankato State University, Mankato, Minn. 56001.

CAREER: Pastor. 1949-53; high school teacher in Robbinsdale, Minn., 1957-59; Macalester College, St. Paul, Minn., instructor in geography and education, 1959-68; Bethel College, St. Paul, professor of social science, 1968-70; Mankato State University, Mankato, Minn., associate professor of geography, 1970—. *Member:* National Council for Geographic Education, National Writers Club.

WRITINGS: (Illustrated with photographs by the author) *Psalms for Cloudy Days*, Free Church Publications, 1962; *So You're Going to College*, Beacon Publications, 1965; *The Quiet Prince*, His International, 1974; *It's Your Choice*, His International, 1975; *Joey's Summer* (novel), David Cook, in press. Contributor of short stories to religious magazines.

AVOCATIONAL INTERESTS: Photography.

* * *

GROOCOCK, J(ohn) M(ichael) 1929-

PERSONAL: Born April 29, 1929, in England; son of Frederick John (a shopkeeper) and Flora (Mitchell) Groocock; married Sheila Mary Larman (a teacher), December 28, 1952; children: Jonathan Charles, Nicola Mary. *Education:* University of London, A.R.C.S., 1949, B.Sc. (honours), 1950, Ph.D., 1953, D.I.C., 1953. *Home:* 187 Dreve Richelle, 1410 Waterloo, Belgium. *Office:* ITT Europe Inc., 480 Avenue Louise, B-1050 Brussels, Belgium.

CAREER: United Kingdom Ministry of Supply, Sevenoaks, England, research chemist, 1951-58; Standard Telephones and Cables (United Kingdom subsidiary of International Telephone & Telegraph), London, England, quality manager, of semiconductor division, 1958-66, company quality manager, 1966-69; International Telephone & Telegraph—Europe, Brussels, Belgium, vice president and director of quality, 1969—. *Member:* International Academy of Quality, Chemical Society (fellow), Institute of Electrical Engineers (London), Institute of Quality Assurance, American Society of Quality Control.

WRITINGS: The Cost of Quality, Pitman, 1974. Contributor to journals.

WORK IN PROGRESS: Research on quality control in service industry and on quality control of computer software.

* * *

GROSS, James A. 1933-

PERSONAL: Born June 29, 1933, in Philadelphia, Pa.; son of James A. (a pianist) and Ella (Costello) Gross; married Linda LaForte, October 15, 1960; children: James Joseph, John Scott Fitzgerald, Justin Michael, Caitlin Alexandra. *Education:* LaSalle College, B.S., 1956; Temple University, M.B.A., 1957; University of Wisconsin, Ph.D., 1962. *Politics:* Independent. *Religion:* Roman Catholic. *Home:* 119 Simsbury Dr., Ithaca, N.Y. 14850. *Office:* Department of Labor and Industrial Relations, Cornell University, 267 Ives Hall, Ithaca, N.Y. 14850.

CAREER: Cornell University, Ithaca, N.Y., professor in department of labor and industrial relations, 1966—. Labor arbitrator. *Military service:* U.S. Army Reserve, active duty, 1957-59; became captain. *Member:* Industrial Relations Research Association, American Arbitration Association, Federal Mediation and Conciliation Service, American Association of University Professors, American Academy of Political and Social Science. *Awards, honors:* American Philosophical Society grants, 1965, 1968; National Endowment for the Humanities grant, 1970.

WRITINGS: The Making of the National Labor Relations Board: A Study in Economics, Politics, and the Law, Volume I: *1933-1937*, State University of New York Press, 1974. Contributor to labor relations, law, and history journals.

WORK IN PROGRESS: The Making of the National Labor Relations Board: A Study in Economics, Politics, and the Law, Volume II: *1938-1947*, for State University of New York Press, completion expected in 1977; *A History of the Black Worker*, completion expected about 1979.

* * *

GROSS, Stuart D. 1914-

PERSONAL: Born February 2, 1914, in Vincennes, Ind.; son of Charles A. (in Chamber of Commerce activities) and Winifred (MacGillvary) Gross; married Vernice M. Lee, August 5, 1939; children: Amy (Mrs. Edward Grezisiak), Mary (Mrs. Gerald Daenzer). *Education:* Hope College, B.A., 1936. *Politics:* Independent. *Religion:* Protestant. *Home:* 315 Kennely Rd., Saginaw, Mich. 48603. *Office:* Saginaw Valley State College, 2250 Pierce Rd., University Center, Mich. 48710.

CAREER: Saginaw News, Saginaw, Mich., reporter, 1936-65, city editor, 1965-67; Saginaw Valley State College, University Center, Mich., director of community affairs, 1967—. Chairman of Saginaw County Red Cross; past director of Youth for Understanding; past director of International Cultural Exchange; past member of Michigan Coalition for Financing Equitable Education; member of Michigan School Finance Study. *Member:* American

Association of State Colleges and Universities. *Awards, honors:* Photography award from *Inland Daily Press*, 1938; Michigan School Bell Award, from Michigan Education Association, 1960, and award from Education Writers of America, 1962, both for education reporting.

WRITINGS: Indians, Jacks, and Pines: Saginaw History, Saginaw Board of Education, 1962; *Trouble at the Grass Roots*, Pendell, 1973.

WORK IN PROGRESS: The Schemers, a novel concerning the appointment of a college president; research for a historical novel on Saginaw's lumbering era.

SIDELIGHTS: Gross writes: "As a reporter for the *Saginaw News*, I was sent to Europe in 1962 to do a series on former exchange students in the Youth for Understanding Program. The articles pointed out what lasting effects there are for teen-agers to spend six months to a year living as the son or daughter of a family in the United States. Since then I have traveled extensively in Europe and South America.

"I find I am a serious writer, as opposed to a person who can write comedy. My subjects for novels are quite contemporary. I have in mind a book on the problems of the K-12 school district, and the political ramifications of a district in the throes of organizing itself or annexing to a large city district. In Michigan, at least, this can be a traumatic experience.

"I will do, regardless, however, the historical novel on Saginaw. I have some excellent material, including one court transcript that describes Saginaw as a very wild city during its reign as Lumber Capital of the World from 1865 to 1890. The great lumber years in Michigan's white pine forests never have been done very well . . . and I hope to rectify that."

* * *

GROSSMAN, Frances Kaplan 1939-

PERSONAL: Born May 28, 1939, in Newport News, Va.; daughter of Rubin H. (a physician) and Beatrice (Fischlowitz) Kaplan; married Henry Grossman (in computer planning), July 26, 1970; children: Jennifer, Benjamin. *Education:* Oberlin College, A.B., 1961; Yale University, M.S., 1963, Ph.D., 1965. *Religion:* Jewish. *Home:* 61 Huntington Rd., Newton, Mass. 02158. *Office:* Department of Psychology, Boston University, 64 Cummington St., Boston, Mass. 02215.

CAREER: Yale University, New Haven, Conn., assistant professor of psychology, 1965-69; Boston University, Boston, Mass., assistant professor, 1969-70, associate professor of psychology, 1970—. *Member:* American Psychological Association, American Association of University Professors, National Organization for Women, Massachusetts Psychological Association.

WRITINGS: (Editor with S. B. Sarason) *The Psychoeducational Clinic: Papers and Research Studies*, Massachusetts Department of Mental Health, 1969; (contributor) S. E. Golann and Carl Eisdorfer, editors, *Handbook of Community Psychology and Mental Health*, Appleton, 1972; *Brothers and Sisters of Retarded Children*, Syracuse University Press, 1972; (with Sarason and G. Zitney) *The Creation of Settings*, Division of Special Education and Rehabilitation, Syracuse University, 1973. Contributor to psychology journals.

WORK IN PROGRESS: Adaptation to Pregnancy, Birth, and Early Parenting.

SIDELIGHTS: Frances Grossman writes: "My professional and personal interests have always been closely related. My roles as mother of two small children, teacher of graduate and undergraduate students, wife, therapist, researcher, all are kept compatible in part by my selecting topics to teach and research about that also relate to my personal life. I find myself becoming more of a feminist, almost despite myself."

*   *   *

GROSSMAN, Shelly 1928(?)-1975

1928(?)—July 30, 1975; American photographer, conservationist, and author of books and filmscripts. Obituaries: *New York Times*, August 6, 1975.

*   *   *

GROSSU, Sergiu 1920-

PERSONAL: Born November 14, 1920, in Cubolta, Rumania; son of Ion and Maria (Cudalbu) Grossu; married Nicole-Valerie Bruteanu, April 24, 1957. *Education:* Bucharest University, B.A., 1947. *Religion:* Orthodox. *Office:* Catacombes, B.P. 79, 92405 Courbevoie, France.

CAREER: Journalist in Rumanian Ministry of Propaganda, 1941-43; employed as civil servant, 1950-58, 1962-69; *Catacombes*, Paris, France, editor, 1971—. Preacher on Rumanian religious broadcast in Paris, 1971—. *Military service:* Rumanian Army Reserve, 1943-45; became lieutenant. *Member:* Arts et Lettres de France, La Chaine, Presence de Gabriel Marcel.

WRITINGS: Nous attendons une nouvelle terre (title means "We Look for a New Earth"), La Pensee Universelle, 1971; *La Chaine* (poems; title means "The Chain"), Les Paragraphes litteraires de Paris, 1971, 2nd edition, 1973; *Un rayon de soleil* (poems; title means "A Beam of Sunshine"), Debresse-Poesie, 1971; (editor) *The Church in Today's Catacombs*, Arlington House, 1975; *Derriere le rideau de Bambou* (title means "Behind the Bamboo Curtain"), Editions des Catacombes, 1975. Also editor of *Les Camps de travail en U.R.S.S.* (title means "U.S.S.R. Labor Camps"). Contributor to French periodicals.

WORK IN PROGRESS: Au fond de l'abime; *La Lituanie heroique et martyre*; *Le Jeune martyr de Volontirovka*; *Lettres d'U.R.S.S.*

SIDELIGHTS: Grossu writes that he wishes "to defend Jesus' cause in the free world, after 3 years of prison in communist Rumania, solely for my religious fight, as leader of the 'unlawful' orthodox organization, 'The Army of the Lord.' To inform against the persecution of the Christians behind the iron and bamboo curtain."

*   *   *

GRUNDT, Leonard 1936-

PERSONAL: Born September 5, 1936, in Brooklyn, N.Y.; son of Louis (a salesman) and Augusta (Machlis) Grundt; married Barbara Joyce Schwartz, June 17, 1967; children: Adam Matthew, Amy Diahann. *Education:* Brooklyn College (now of the City University of New York), B.A., 1958; Columbia University, M.S., 1960; Rutgers University, Ph.D., 1965. *Politics:* Democrat. *Religion:* Jewish. *Home:* 12 Commander Vic Lane, Nesconset, N.Y. 11767. *Office:* Nassau Community College, Stewart Ave., Garden City, N.Y. 11530.

CAREER: Brooklyn College Library, Brooklyn, N.Y., fellow, 1958-60, assistant to librarian, 1960-61; Free Public Library, Linden, N.J., senior librarian, 1961-62; Boston Public Library, Boston, Mass., research librarian, 1962-63; Rutgers University, Graduate School of Library Service, New Brunswick, N.J., assistant research specialist, 1964-65; Nassau Community College, Library, Garden City, N.Y., assistant professor, 1965-66, deputy director, 1966-67, director, 1967-75, professor of library science and head of department, 1975—. Reference librarian, Library/USA, New York World's Fair, 1965; visiting professor at State University College at Geneseo, 1966; adjunct professor at Queens College of the City University of New York, 1973. Long Island Library Resources Council, member of board of directors, 1972—, president, 1974.

MEMBER: American Civil Liberties Union, American Association of University Professors, American Library Association, Association for Educational Communications and Technology, Freedom to Read Foundation, New York Library Association, Nassau County Library Association, Phi Beta Kappa, Beta Phi Mu.

WRITINGS: (Contributor) Ralph W. Conant, editor, *The Public Library and the City*, M.I.T. Press, 1965; (editor with Ralph Blasingame) *Research on Library Service in Metropolitan Areas*, Graduate School of Library Service, Rutgers University, 1967; *Efficient Patterns for Adequate Library Service in a Large City: A Study of Boston*, Graduate School of Library Science, University of Illinois, 1968; (contributor) Conant and Kathleen Molz, editors, *The Metropolitan Library*, M.I.T. Press, 1972; (contributor) Norman D. Stevens, editor, *Essays for Ralph Shaw*; Scarecrow, in press. Contributor to *American Reference Books Annual, 1975* and to library journals.

WORK IN PROGRESS: Compiling *Academic Libraries: A Guide to Information Sources*, for Information Guide Series "Books, Publishing, and Libraries," for Gale; contributing to *American Reference Books Annual, 1976*.

*   *   *

GUNN, Drewey Wayne 1939-

PERSONAL: Born August 9, 1939, in North Carolina; son of Bruce E. (a nurseryman) and Josephine (a nurserywoman; maiden name, Smith) Gunn. *Education:* Wake Forest University, B.A., 1961; University of North Carolina, M.A., 1962, Ph.D., 1968; graduate study at University of Texas, 1964, Center for Intercultural Documentation, 1970, and French Alliance, 1973, 1975. *Politics:* Democrat. *Address:* c/o Postmaster, Wentworth, N.C. 27375.

CAREER: Presbyterian College, Clinton, S.C., instructor in English, 1962-64; Texas A & I University, Kingsville, assistant professor, 1968-72, associate professor of English, 1972-73; Fulbright teacher in normal schools and high schools in Denmark, 1972-73; Reine Institute, Versailles, France, TEFL (Teaching English as a Foreign Language) teacher, 1973-74; University of Mětz, Metz, France, maitre de conferences associe, 1974—.

WRITINGS: Gunn: A Genealogy, privately printed, 1972; *Mexico in American and British Letters: A Bibliography*, Scarecrow, 1974; *American and British Writers in Mexico: 1556-1973*, University of Texas Press, 1974. Contributor to *Southwest Review* and several newspapers.

WORK IN PROGRESS: Writing on American and British expatriates in France.

GUNN, Giles B(uckingham) 1938-

PERSONAL: Born January 9, 1938, in Evanston, Ill.; son of Buckingham Willcox (in radio and television advertising) and Jane (Fargo) Gunn; married Janet Varner (an English professor), December 29, 1961; children: Adam Buckingham. *Education:* Amherst College, B.A., 1959; graduate study at Episcopal Theological Seminary, 1959-60; University of Chicago Divinity School, M.A., 1963, Ph.D., 1967. *Politics:* Independent. *Religion:* Episcopalian. *Home:* 315 Burris Pl., Chapel Hill, N.C. *Office:* 101 Saunders Hall, University of North Carolina, Chapel Hill, N.C. 27514.

CAREER: Florida Presbyterian College (now Eckerd College), St. Petersburg, Fla., assistant professor of literature, 1965-66; University of Chicago Divinity School, Chicago, Ill., instructor, 1966-68, assistant professor of theology and literature, 1968-73, chairman of the department, 1971-73; University of Chicago, Chicago, Ill., assistant professor of English, 1972-73, associate professor of religion and literature and of English, 1973-74; University of North Carolina, Chapel Hill, associate professor of religious and American studies, 1974—. Amherst-Doshisha fellow and lecturer in English at Doshisha University, Kyoto, Japan, 1960-61; visiting assistant professor of religious studies at Stanford University, summer, 1973. *Member:* Modern Language Association of America, American Studies Association, American Academy of Religion (chairman of Art, Literature and Religion section, 1972-74; chairman of research and publication committee, 1974—; member of executive committee and board of directors, 1974—), Society for Art, Religion and Contemporary Culture (lifetime fellow), Society for Religion in Higher Education, Smithsonian Institution.

WRITINGS: (Contributor) Nathan A. Scott, editor, *Adversity and Grace: Studies in Recent American Fiction*, University of Chicago Press, 1968; (editor) *Literature and Religion*, Harper, 1971; (editor) *Henry James, Senior: A Selection of His Writings*, American Library Association, 1974; *F. O. Mathiessen: The Critical Achievement*, University of Washington Press, 1975; (contributor) James B. Wiggins, *Religion as Story: Reflections and Explorations*, Harper, 1975. Contributor of articles and reviews to periodicals and journals in his field, including *Amherst Review, Criterion, American Quarterly*, and *New Republic*. Member of board of consultants, *Journal of the American Academy of Religion*, 1970—, and *Journal of Religion*, 1974—; member of editorial board, *Soundings*, 1974—; member of board of directors, Scholars Press, 1974—.

WORK IN PROGRESS: Critical study of shifts in ethical and religious orientation in the American literary tradition from the Puritans to the present; theoretical study of various aspects of the relationship between literature and religion; further works on what R. P. Blackmur termed the "irregular metaphysics" of both the American and Modern traditions.

SIDELIGHTS: Giles Gunn writes: "Most of my work has been devoted in one way or another to a repossession of what Van Wyck Brooks referred to as the usable past."

* * *

GUPTA, Marie (Jacqueline) 1946-

PERSONAL: Born January 24, 1946, in Suffern, N.Y.; daughter of Horace N. (a research scientist) and Lee (Hechtman) Goldie; married Vijander Kumar Gupta (an accountant), June 28, 1967; children: Ravi Kumar, Lorena Cathie. *Education:* Student at Goucher College, 1963-65,

and Mississippi State College for Women, 1966-67. *Home:* 90-09 Northern Blvd., Jackson Heights, N.Y. 11372.

CAREER: Free-lance writer. Member of parents' advisory council for Lexington School for the Deaf; has worked for Baltimore Tutorial Project and McKim Community Center.

WRITINGS: (With Frances Brandon) *A Treasury of Witchcraft and Devilry*, J. David, 1975. Editor of *Sounds of Lexington* (publication of Lexington School for the Deaf).

WORK IN PROGRESS: Turning the Wheel, a suspense novel dealing with reincarnation; a series of short stories.

* * *

GUPTA, S(ushil) (Kumar) 1927-
(Morris N. Placere)

PERSONAL: Born April 15, 1927, in India; married Alicja Ursula (a physician); children: Sheila, Leila, Maureen, Steven. *Education:* Lucknow University, M.D., 1949; postdoctoral study at American Trudeau Society, 1956, and at State University of New York Downstate Medical Center, 1957. *Office:* Quincy City Hospital, Quincy, Mass.

CAREER: Licensed to practice medicine in New York and Massachusetts; certified by American Board of Surgery, 1959, and by American Board of Thoracic Surgery, 1960. University Hospital, Lucknow, India, intern, 1949-50; South East London and Kent Group Hospitals, London, England, house surgeon, 1951-52; Beth Israel Hospital, Boston, Mass., resident in general surgery, 1952-55; State University of New York Downstate Medical Center and Kings County Hospital, Brooklyn, N.Y., resident in thoracic surgery, 1955-57; City Hospital, Elmhurst, N.Y., senior resident in surgery, 1957-58; St. Francis Hospital, Roslyn, N.Y., chief resident in cardiovascular surgery, 1958-59, research assistant in cardiac surgery and resident coordinator, 1959; Peter Bent Brigham Hospital, Boston, Mass., director of cardiac research laboratory, and assistant in surgery, 1959-60; has served as director of cardiopulmonary laboratory and thoracic surgeon at Brockton Hospital, Brockton, Mass.; now chief thoracic surgeon at Quincy City Hospital, Quincy, Mass. Staff thoracic surgeon and thoracic consultant to various hospitals.

MEMBER: Society of Thoracic Surgeons, American College of Surgeons (fellow), American College of Chest Physicians (fellow), American Heart Association, American Medical Association, American Cancer Society, Massachusetts Medical Society.

WRITINGS: (Contributor) K. A. Merendino, editor, *Prosthetic Valves in Cardiac Surgery*, C. C Thomas, 1961; (under pseudonym Morris N. Placere) *How You Can Get Better Medical Care for Less Money*, Walker, 1973. Contributor to medical journals.

WORK IN PROGRESS: Under pseudonym Morris N. Placere, *Ship of Life*.

* * *

GUPTA, Shiv K(umar) 1930-

PERSONAL: Born April 16, 1930, in Simla, Punjab, India; son of Jai (a government officer) and Leela (Aggarwal) Narayan; married Elizabeth Coilparampil (in accounting), November, 1953; children: Nirmal, Vinita, Vimal, Kamal, Rita, Anita. *Education:* University of Punjab, B.A., 1950; University of Dayton, M.B.A., 1967. *Religion:* Hindu. *Home:* 1026 North Cory St., Findlay, Ohio 45840. *Office:* Department of Business and Economics, Findlay College, Main St., Findlay, Ohio 45840.

CAREER: Government of India, New Delhi, chief purchasing officer, 1963-65; University of Dayton, Dayton, Ohio, instructor in economics, 1967-69; Findlay College, Findlay, Ohio, assistant professor of business administration, 1969-73, associate professor of marketing, 1973—.

WRITINGS: Starting a Small Business: A Simulation Game, Prentice-Hall, 1974.

WORK IN PROGRESS: Franchise Management: A Simulation Game; Consumer Behavior in Market Place.

BIOGRAPHICAL/CRITICAL SOURCES: Ohio Business Teacher, March, 1973, March, 1974.

* * *

GUSTAFSON, W(illiam) Eric 1933-

PERSONAL: Born November 18, 1933, in Pittsfield, Mass.; son of Alton Herman (a biologist) and Maude (Bosworth) Gustafson; married Elizabeth Boardman (a gerontologist), June 17, 1961; children: Richard, Rustom, Nicholas, Sylvia. *Education:* Williams College, B.A. (summa cum laude), 1955; Harvard University, A.M., 1957, Ph.D., 1959. *Religion:* Society of Friends (Quaker). *Home:* 1808 Drexel Dr., Davis, Calif. 95616. *Office:* Department of Economics, University of California, Davis, Calif. 95616.

CAREER: New York Metropolitan Region Study, New York, N.Y., economist, 1957-58; Harvard University, Cambridge, Mass., instructor in economics and research associate in public administration, both 1959-63; Pakistan Institute of Development Economics, Karachi, research adviser under auspices of Stanford University, 1963-65; University of California, Davis, assistant professor, 1965-72, lecturer in economics, 1972—. Faculty fellow at American Institute of Indian Studies (New Delhi), 1968-69; visiting research economist at University of Karachi, 1974; guest lecturer at National Institute of Public Administration (Lahore, Pakistan). Member of California selection committee for Woodrow Wilson fellowships. Trustee of John Woolman School, 1969-73. Consultant to RAND Corp. and Arthur D. Little.

MEMBER: American Economic Association, Association for Comparative Economics, Association for Asian Studies, Research Committee on the Punjab (vice-chairman), Royal Society for India, Pakistan, and Ceylon, Pakistan Economic Association, Phi Beta Kappa.

WRITINGS: (Contributor) Max Hall, editor, *Made in New York: Case Studies in Metropolitan Manufacturing*, Harvard University Press, 1959; (editor) Milton Mayer, *What Can a Man Do?*, University of Chicago Press, 1964; (contributor) Anwar Tahmasp Khan, editor, *Cost-Benefit Analysis*, National Institute of Public Administration (Lahore, Pakistan), 1965; (contributor) J. Henry Korson, editor, *Contemporary Problems of Pakistan*, E. J. Brill, 1974; (editor with Kenneth W. Jones) *Sources on Punjab History*, Manohar, 1975; (editor and contributor) *Pakistan and Bangladesh: Bibliographic Essays in Social Science*, University of Islamabad Press, 1975; (editor) Milton Mayer, *The Nature of the Beast*, University of Massachusetts Press, 1975. Co-author of *Workbook in Economics*, 1966, and *Instructor's Manual*, 1968, both to accompany Prentice-Hall series, "Foundations of Modern Economics."

Contributor of articles and reviews to economics and education journals. Editor for Research Committee on the Punjab. Manuscript referee for Irwin, Little, Brown, and *Journal of Asian Studies*.

WORK IN PROGRESS: Research on the economic history of irrigation in India and Pakistan.

* * *

GUSTIN, Lawrence Robert 1937-

PERSONAL: Born May 26, 1937, in Flint, Mich.; son of Robert Stuart and Doris Mary (Irving) Gustin; married Rose Mary Murphy, July 10, 1965; children: Robert Lawrence, David Martin. *Education:* Michigan State University, B.A., 1959. *Religion:* Presbyterian. *Home:* 1438 Country View Lane, Flint, Mich. 48504. *Office: Flint Journal*, 200 East First St., Flint, Mich. 48502.

CAREER: United Press International, New York, N.Y., capitol correspondent in Lansing, Mich., 1959, Michigan sports editor in Detroit, 1960; *Flint Journal*, Flint, Mich., 1960—, automotive editor, 1969—. Member of acquisitions committee of Sloan Museum. *Military service:* U.S. Army, 1960. U.S. Air Force Reserve, active duty, 1963-66. *Member:* Mensa, Detroit Press Club. *Awards, honors:* For *Billy Durant: Creator of General Motors*, received award of merit from Michigan Historical Society, 1974, certificate of commendation from American Association for State and Local History, 1974, and Thomas McKean Memorial Cup from Antique Automobile Club of America, 1975.

WRITINGS: Billy Durant: Creator of General Motors, Eerdmans, 1973.

WORK IN PROGRESS: A pictorial history of Flint, for centennial celebrations; research on the careers of W. C. Durant and other automobile pioneers, including Louis Chevrolet.

SIDELIGHTS: Gustin writes: "Durant was not only one of the two or three major pioneers of the modern U.S. auto industry but also the most important man in Flint history—yet he had been almost forgotten in Flint."

* * *

GUSTKEY, Earl 1940-

PERSONAL: Surname is pronounced *Gus*-key; born February 20, 1940, in Washington, Pa.; son of Harry Earl and Delphine (Arehart) Gustkey; married Cathey W. Fowler, April 5, 1968 (divorced, 1972). *Education:* Orange Coast College, A.A., 1960; California State University, San Jose (now San Jose State University), B.A., 1962. *Politics:* Democrat. *Religion:* None. *Office: Los Angeles Times*, 1375 Sunflower, Costa Mesa, Calif. 92626.

CAREER: Reporter on newspapers in Oceanside, Calif., 1963-65, and in Costa Mesa, Calif., 1965-69; *Los Angeles Times*, Costa Mesa, Calif., reporter, 1969—.

WRITINGS: Roman Gabriel, Putnam, 1974.

* * *

GUTHMAN, William H(arold) 1924-

PERSONAL: Born October 22, 1924, in Chicago, Ill.; son of Harold Sol (a photographer) and Ethel (Goodman) Guthman; married Patricia Rosenäu (an antiquarian), September 11, 1948; children: Pamela, William Scott. *Education:* Northwestern University, B.A., 1951. *Politics:* Republican. *Home and office address:* P.O. Box 737, Westport, Conn. 06880.

CAREER: Society photographer, 1946-52; purchasing agent, 1952-66; antiquarian, 1966—. *Military service:* U.S. Army Air Forces, 1942-45; served in China theater; received two bronze battle stars. *Member:* American Society of Arms Collectors (director), Company of Military Historians (fellow), American Colonial Arms Collectors Society (president), Kentucky Rifle Association (director), Antique Arms Collectors Association of Connecticut.

WRITINGS: (With John Curtis) *New England Militia Uniforms and Accoutrements*, Old Sturbridge Village, 1971; *March to Massacre*, McGraw, 1975; *U.S. Army Weapons: 1784-1791*, American Society of Arms Collectors, 1975. Contributor to *Antiques*.

WORK IN PROGRESS: Research on eighteenth- and nineteenth-century warfare between American Indians and the white man; studying the Wayne Campaign of 1794.

* * *

GUTHRIE, A(lfred) B(ertram), Jr. 1901-

PERSONAL: Born January 13, 1901, in Bedford, Ind.; son of Alfred Bertram (an educator) and June (Thomas) Guthrie; married Harriet Larson, June 25, 1931 (divorced, 1963); married Carol Bischman, April 3, 1969; children: Alfred Bertram III, Helen Guthrie Atwood. *Education:* Attended University of Washington, Seattle, 1919-20; University of Montana, A.B., 1923; Harvard University, graduate study, 1944-45. *Home:* 2600 Queen St., Missoula, Mont. 59801. *Agent:* Brandt & Brandt, 101 Park Ave., New York, N.Y. 10017.

CAREER: Lexington Leader, Lexington, Ky., reporter, 1926-29, city editor and editorial writer, 1929-45, executive editor, 1945-47; University of Kentucky, Lexington, teacher of creative writing, 1947-52. Writer. *Awards, honors:* Litt.D., University of Montana, 1949; Pulitzer Prize for fiction, 1950, for *The Way West*; Western Heritage Wrangler Award, 1970, for *Arfive*; Distinguished Achievement Award of the Western Literature Association, 1972; Dr. of Humane Letters, Indiana State University, 1975.

WRITINGS: The Big Sky, Sloane, 1947; *The Way West*, Sloane, 1949; *These Thousand Hills*, Houghton, 1956; *The Big It*, Houghton, 1960; *The Blue Hen's Chick*, McGraw, 1965; *Arfive*, Houghton, 1970; *Wild Pitch*, Houghton, 1973; *Once Upon a Pond*, Mountain Press, 1973; *The Last Valley*, Houghton, 1975.

Writer of screenplays, "Shane" (Paramount, 1953), and "The Kentuckian" (United Artists, 1955). Contributor of articles and stories to *Esquire, Holiday*, and other periodicals.

SIDELIGHTS: Three of Guthrie's novels have been adapted for film; *The Big Sky*, produced by RKO, 1952, *These Thousand Hills*, produced by 20th Century-Fox, 1959, and his Pulitzer prizewinning novel, *The Way West*, produced by United Artists, 1967.

* * *

GUTTENTAG, Marcia 1932-

PERSONAL: Born November 9, 1932, in Brooklyn, N.Y.; married Paul Secord (a professor of urban studies), 1955; children: Lisa, Michael. *Education:* University of Michigan, B.A. (with honors), 1953; further study at University of Freiburg, 1953-54, and Harvard University, 1954-55; Adelphi University, Ph.D., 1960. *Office:* Graduate School of Education, Harvard University, Cambridge, Mass. 02138.

CAREER: Queens College of the City University of New York, Flushing, N.Y., instructor in psychology, 1960-64;

State University of New York at Stony Brook, assistant professor of psychology, 1964-65; Yale University, New Haven, Conn., visiting fellow at Social Interaction Laboratories, 1965-66; Queens College of the City University of New York, Flushing; assistant professor of social psychology, 1966-70; City University of New York, Graduate Center, New York, N.Y., associate professor, then professor of psychology, 1970-73, director of Harlem Research Center, 1970-72; Harvard University, Cambridge, Mass., Richard Clarke Cabot Visiting Professor of Social Ethics, 1972-73, developmental social psychologist at Graduate School of Education, 1973—. Member of social sciences research review panel, National Institute of Mental Health, 1971-75; evaluation consultant to UNESCO, Office of Child Development, National Institute of Mental Health, and other federal agencies. Visiting lecturer at Hebrew University of Jerusalem, Ohio State University, University of Southern California, Cornell University, and other universities.

MEMBER: American Psychological Association (fellow; president of Division 9, 1971-72; president of Division 8, 1974—), Society for the Psychological Study of Social Issues (fellow; member of council, 1968; president, 1971-72), American Sociological Association (fellow), American Association for the Advancement of Science (fellow), Association for the Advancement of Psychology (member of board of trustees, 1973—; chairman of committee on policy and planning, 1974—), Association for Women Psychologists, Psychonomic Society, Bayesian Society, New York Academy of Sciences.

AWARDS, HONORS: Fulbright scholar at University of Freiburg, 1953-54; Certificate of Merit, New York State Psychological Association, 1970; Distinguished Alumna Award, Adelphi University, 1974; grants from U.S. Office of Education, 1965-66, National Institute of Mental Health, 1965-66, 1969-71, 1973, 1974, 1975, National Science Foundation, 1968-70, Carnegie Foundation, 1970-71, Carnegie Corp. and Rockefeller Foundation, 1971, Ford Foundation, 1973, and National Academy of Sciences, 1974.

WRITINGS: (Translator from the German) *Farbpyramiden Test Manual*, Hans Huber, 1955; (with F. Denmark and R. Riley) *Communication Patterns in Integrated Classrooms and Pre-Integration Subject Variables as They Affect the Academic Achievement and Self-Concept of Previously Segregated Children* (monograph), U.S. Office of Education, 1967; (with Marilyn Gittell and others) *Local Control of Education*, Praeger, 1972; (with T. Kiresuk and M. Oglesby) *The Evaluation of Training in Mental Health*, Behavioral Publications, 1974; (editor with E. L. Struening and contributor) *Handbook of Evaluation Research*, Sage Publications, Volume I, in press, Volume II, in press.

Contributor: Harry Rivlin and V. Robinson, editors, *The Preparation of Urban Teachers*, National Defense Education Act National Institute, 1968; Nathaniel N. Wagner and M. J. Haug, editors, *Chicanos: Social and Psychological Perspectives*, Mosby, 1971; Marvin Leiner, editor, *Children of the Cities: Education of the Powerless*, New American Library, 1974; Ronald Krate, editor, *Social Issues in Human Development*, Praeger, 1974.

Author of a number of research reports. Contributor of articles and reviews to psychology and sociology journals. Editor, *Newsletter* of Division of Personality and Social Psychology, American Psychological Association, 1972—; member of editorial board, *Journal for the Theory of Social Behavior*, 1970—, *Basic Readings in Social Psychology*,

1972—, and *Journal of Homosexuality*, 1974—; member of publications committee, *Personality and Social Psychology Bulletin*, 1974—. Editorial reviewer, *Journal of Personality and Social Psychology*.

WORK IN PROGRESS: Evaluating Social, Health and Educational Programs: The United Nations Handbook; a national evaluation study of women and mental health.

* * *

GWYN, Julian   1937-

PERSONAL: Born March 30, 1937, in Birmingham, England; son of Quintin Jermy (the Grand Chancellor of the Order of Malta) and Barbara (Mitchell) Gwyn; married Clare Devlin (a community development teacher), April 10, 1961; children: Frances, Anya, Elin, Christopher, Joseph (deceased). *Education:* Loyola College, Montreal, B.A., 1956; McGill University, M.A., 1958; Oxford University, B.Litt., 1961, D.Phil., 1971. *Politics:* Socialist. *Home:* 484 Highland Ave., Ottawa, Ontario K2A 2J6, Canada. *Office:* Department of History, University of Ottawa, Ottawa, Ontario K1N 6N5, Canada.

CAREER: University of Ottawa, Ottawa, Ontario, lecturer, 1961-63, assistant professor, 1963-69, associate professor of history, 1969—. Sessional lecturer, Carleton University, 1971-72. *Military service:* Canadian Army Reserves, 1954-59; became captain. *Member:* Society for Nautical Research. *Awards, honors:* Canada Council fellow, 1971-73.

WRITINGS: (Editor) *Reference Works for Historians*, University of Ottawa, 1971; (editor) *The American Manuscripts in the Gage Papers*, British Association for American Study, 1972; *The Enterprising Admiral: The Personal Fortune of Admiral Sir Peter Warren*, McGill-Queens University Press, 1974. Contributing editor, *Collections* of Navy Records Society; member of editorial board, *Canadian Historical Papers*, 1972-73; assistant editor, *Histoire Sociale—Social History*, 1972—. Contributor to historical journals.

WORK IN PROGRESS: La Chute de Louisbourg, 1745; Le journal du siege de Louisbourg par Girard Lacroix.

* * *

HAAS, Kenneth B(rooks), Sr.   1898-

PERSONAL: Surname is pronounced Haws; born January 24, 1898, in Pennsylvania; son of John Louis (a businessman) and Mary (a seamstress; maiden name, Brooks) Haas; married Verna Hoffman, December 24, 1921; children: Kenneth B., Jr., Noel L. *Education:* University of Pittsburgh, B.S., 1924, M.A., 1931; New York University, Ed.D., 1935. *Politics:* Republican. *Religion:* Protestant. *Home:* 3737 Atlantic Ave., Long Beach, Calif. 90807.

CAREER: Proprietor of small wholesale business in Pittsburgh, Pa., 1924-28; high school teacher of commerce in the public schools of Pennsylvania and New Jersey, 1928-35; College of Commerce, Bowling Green, Ky., professor of marketing, 1935-38; U.S. Office of Education, Washington, D.C., specialist in business education, 1938-46; Montgomery Ward, Chicago, Ill., national retail training director, 1946-48; training consultant in Chicago, Ill., and New York, N.Y., 1948-58; Hofstra University, Hempstead, N.Y., professor of marketing, 1958-63; University of Washington, Seattle, lecturer in marketing, 1963-67. *Military service:* U.S. Navy, 1915-19. U.S. Naval Fleet Reserve, 1919-23. U.S. Army, Chemical Warfare Service, 1942-43; be-

came major. *Member:* Veterans of World War I, California Genealogical Society, Historical Society of Western Pennsylvania, Masons.

WRITINGS: Studies in Problems of the Consumer, College of Commerce, 1936; *Adventure in Buymanship*, College of Commerce, 1937; *Distributive Education*, Gregg, 1941; *Better Retailing*, National Cash Register, 1941; *Military Instructor's Manual*, U.S. Army, Washington, D.C., 1942; *How to Coordinate School-Work Experience*, Gregg, 1944; (with O. P. Robinson) *How to Establish and Operate a Retail Store*, Prentice-Hall, 1946; (with H. Q. Packard) *Preparation and Use of Audio-Visual Aids*, Prentice-Hall, 1946; (with C. H. Ewing) *Tested Training Techniques*, Prentice-Hall, 1949; (with W. H. Wilson) *The Film Book*, Prentice-Hall, 1949; (author and editor) *Handbook of Sales Training*, Prentice-Hall, 1949.

Creative Salesmanship, Prentice-Hall, 1950; (with son, Kenneth B. Haas, Jr.) *Business Practices in Veterinary Medicine*, Veterinary Medicine Publishing, 1953; (with E. C. Perry) *Sales Horizons*, Prentice-Hall, 1957, 3rd edition, 1968; *How to Develop Successful Salesmen*, McGraw, 1959; *Opportunities in Selling*, Vocational Guidance Manuals, 1960; *Professional Salesmanship*, Holt, 1962; (with John W. Ernest) *Creative Salesmanship*, Glencoe Press, 1969, 2nd edition, 1974. Author of more than two hundred manuals, monographs, and magazine articles for professional and scientific publications. Author of film scripts and scenarios for sales training purposes.

WORK IN PROGRESS: Our Scotch-Irish Heritage and *History of the Haas Family of Erie County, Pa.*, both to be privately printed.

SIDELIGHTS: "I was a grade school dropout and never attended secondary school...." Haas wrote. "I worked on farms, drove a team of horses, worked in retail stores, served in the U.S. Navy. My absence from formal schooling gained me an enormous advantage.... I taught myself during those years ... and what I learned was practical and thorough, even if sketchy. Thus I got into my bones the essentials of a secondary education and more, which enabled me to pass college entrance exams with ease. One principle I learned was 'never, never, never give in; never, never, never yield to adversity.' That rage to succeed is the quality which carried me through my low points ... for fortune never smiled on me except when I applied this principle."

* * *

HABERMAN, Martin   1932-

PERSONAL: Born June 8, 1932, in Brooklyn, N.Y.; son of Joseph (a carpenter) and Rebecca (Herberman) Haberman; married Florence Rita Taplin (an art teacher), February 1, 1953; children: David Phillip, Jill Beth. *Education:* Brooklyn College (now of the City University of New York), B.A., 1953; New York University, M.A. (sociology), 1955; Columbia University, M.A. (elementary education), 1956, Ed.D., 1962. *Politics:* Independent. *Religion:* Jewish. *Home:* 1301 East Lake Bluff, Shorewood, Wis. 53211. *Office:* School of Education, University of Wisconsin—Milwaukee, Milwaukee, Wis. 53211.

CAREER: Columbia University, Teacher's College, New York, N.Y., instructor in education, 1959-62; University of Wisconsin—Milwaukee, 1962-66, began as assistant professor, became associate professor of education; Central Atlantic Regional Educational Laboratory, Washington, D.C., director of teacher education, 1967; Rutgers University, New Brunswick, N.J., professor of education and director of teacher education, 1968; University of Wisconsin—Milwaukee, professor of education, 1969—. Appeared for six years on "Schoolmanship," on WVWM-FM Radio; has appeared on fifteen television programs, discussing cultural pluralism. *Member:* American Association of Colleges for Teacher Education, A.T.E.

WRITINGS: The Art of Schoolmanship, Warren, Greene & Co., 1970; (with Tobie Meisel) *Dance: An Art in Academe,* Teachers College Press, 1973; (with T. M. Stinnet) *Teacher Education and the New Profession of Teaching,* McCutchan, 1973; *Cultural Pluralism and Human Relations in the American School,* University of Wisconsin Extension, 1974. Member of editorial board of *Journal of Teacher Education.*

WORK IN PROGRESS: A Bus Ride Away: Catholic, Protestant, and Jewish Students in the Urban University, a study of students at University of Wisconsin—Milwaukee.

* * *

HAGEN, John Milton 1902-
(Sterling Sherwin)

PERSONAL: Born December 3, 1902, in Omaha, Neb.; son of Sanford (a businessman) and Clara (Parmenter) Hagen; married Constance Manning (deceased). *Education:* Stanford University, B.A., 1920. *Politics:* "Republican—Independent." *Religion:* Metaphysics. *Home and office address:* Route 19, P.O. Box, Mill Valley, Calif. 94941.

CAREER: Edwin T. Grandy Book Review Syndicate, Mill Valley, Calif., book reviewer, 1960-75. Has also worked as advertising copywriter, public relations director, editor, Hollywood columnist, stage magazine writer, and correspondent. *Military service:* U.S. Army, Infantry, World War I. U.S. Coast Guard, Security Forces, 1944. *Member:* American Society of Composers, Authors and Publishers, Sigma Delta Chi (founder of Stanford University Chapter), Bohemian Club (San Francisco).

WRITINGS: (With Dane Rush) *The Radio Mystery,* Longmans, Green, 1929; *The Shrewd Nude, and Other Light Verse—and Dark,* A. S. Barnes, 1961; *I Am in Iambics* (biblical verses), A. S. Barnes, 1965; *Lecherous, Licentious, Lascivious Lyrics Is Not the Title of This Book: The Violent Violet Is the Actual Title,* foreword by Erskine Caldwell, A. S. Barnes, 1969; *Holly-Would!* (nonfiction), Arlington House, 1975.

Plays: "Band Box Follies," first produced on Broadway at Daly's Theatre, 1927; "Bare Facts of 1927," first produced in New York, N.Y. at Triangle Theatre, 1927; (with Dane Rush) "The Rabic Mystery," first produced Off-Broadway, 1927.

Under pseudonym Sterling Sherwin: *Songwriting and Selling Secrets: A Manual of Popular Songwriting,* A. D. Freese, 1935; (with Harry K. McClintock) *Railroad Songs of Yesterday,* Shapiro, Bernstein, 1943; *Singin' in the Saddle: A New Collection of Original and Standard Cowboy Songs,* Boston Music Co., 1944; *Saddle Songs,* Francis, Day & Hunter (London), 1948. Also author of *Songs of the Round-Up, Western College Songs, Songs of San Francisco, Bad Man Songs, American Cowboy Songs, Songs of the Saddle, Mac's Songs of the Road and Range, Fifty Years from Now.*

Author of songs for films produced in the United States and England. Contributor to magazines and newspapers.

WORK IN PROGRESS: Hollywood to Broadway; "The Honkey and the Nigger," a play.

* * *

HALKETT, John G(eorge) 1933-

PERSONAL: Born May 3, 1933, in Chicago, Ill.; son of John G. and Mabel (Barth) Halkett. *Education:* Loyola University, Chicago, Ill., B.A., 1955; Northwestern University, M.A., 1957, Ph.D., 1964. *Office:* Department of English, Syracuse University, Syracuse, N.Y. 13210.

CAREER: Marycrest College, Davenport, Iowa, instructor in English, 1957-59; Yale University, New Haven, Conn., instructor, 1962-65, assistant professor of English, 1965-69; Syracuse University, Syracuse, N.Y., associate professor of English, 1969—. Member of board of directors of Opera Theater of Syracuse. *Member:* Modern Language Association of America.

WRITINGS: Milton and the Idea of Matrimony: A Study of the Divorce Tracts and "Paradise Lost," Yale University Press, 1970; (editor with Robert E. Kuehn) *This Powerful Rime: An Anthology of Ten Poets,* Prentice-Hall, 1970.

* * *

HALL, B(axter) C(larence) 1936-

PERSONAL: Born June 9, 1936, in Buckhorn, Ark.; son of B. C. and Hattie (Younger) Hall; married Daphna Haviland Knight (a singer and teacher), June 6, 1959; children: B. C. III, Joseph Nathan. *Education:* Henderson State University, B.A., 1959; University of Iowa, M.F.A., 1961. *Religion:* "Apostasy." *Home:* 1971 West Brichta Dr., Tucson, Ariz. 85705. *Agent:* Charles Neighbors, Inc., 240 Waverly Pl., New York, N.Y. 10014. *Office:* Department of English, University of Arizona, Tucson, Ariz. 85703.

CAREER: Log Cabin Democrat, Conway, Ark., reporter and editor, 1958-59; Arkansas Polytechnic College, Russellville, professor of English, 1961-74; University of Arizona, Tucson, professor of English, 1974—. Reporter for *Arkansas Gazette,* 1963-67.

WRITINGS: (Editor) *Writings from the Lower Sonoran Region* (anthology), Aware Press, 1972; *The Burning Season* (novel), Putnam, 1974; *Bluebells and the King of Pain* (novel), Putnam, in press.

SIDELIGHTS: Hall writes: "I once served on a censorship-of-film board during which time no films whatsoever were censored. I was later impeached." He adds: "I consider hardly anything vital except for wife, my sons, my dogs, and some bourbon. I learned vocabulary from listening to Harry Caray broadcast St. Louis Cardinal baseball games; I learned something about life from watching my brother ride horses and shoot pool."

BIOGRAPHICAL/CRITICAL SOURCES: Iowa Review, February, 1975.

* * *

HALL, Georgette Brockman 1915-

PERSONAL: Born November 24, 1915, in New Orleans, La.; daughter of Thomas Harry (an engineer) and Gertrude (a teacher; maiden name, Ott) Brockman; married Norman Bernard Hall (a professor), December 28, 1938; children: Lynne Gertrude (Mrs. Ralph Wood Pringle). *Education:* Tulane University, B.A., 1937; George Peabody College for Teachers, M.L.S., 1966. *Residence:* Diamondhead,

Miss. 39520. *Office:* St. Bernard Parish Community College, Chalmette, La. 70043.

CAREER: English teacher in public schools in Bay St. Louis, Miss., 1948-62; St. Bernard Parish School Board, Chalmette, La., librarian, 1962—. *Member:* American Association of University Women, Greater New Orleans Library Club, Diamondhead Yacht and Country Club, Delta Kappa Gamma (president of Beta Delta, 1969-70), Theta Nu, Beta Phi Alpha.

WRITINGS: House on Rampart Street, Vantage, 1954; *The Sicilian* (on the assassination of Chief of Police David C. Hennessy by the Mafia), Pelican, 1975.

WORK IN PROGRESS: A novel about cruises in the Caribbean.

AVOCATIONAL INTERESTS: Travel.

* * *

HALL, Jay C.
  See HALL, John C.

* * *

HALL, John C. 1915-
  (Jay C. Hall)

PERSONAL: Born October 5, 1915, in Pasadena, Calif.; son of Harlan Wolcott (a journalist) and Edith (Smith) Hall; married Marian E. Miller, June 23, 1936 (divorced, 1970); married Sibyl Elizabeth Stewart (a writer), May 15, 1970; children: (first marriage) John, Jr., Harlan W., Robert Page, Deborah Ann (Mrs. Brian Giles). *Education:* Pasadena City College, A.A., 1935. *Home:* 239 Los Banos, Walnut Creek, Calif. 94598. *Agent:* Jay Garon-Brooke Associates, Inc., 415 Central Park W., #17D, New York, N.Y. 10025.

CAREER: Pasadena Police Department, Pasadena, Calif., administrative clerk and assistant to police chief, 1936-53; regional director for National Safety Council, 1953-72; general manager of programs for California Traffic Safety Foundation, 1972-74. Host of television program, "Traffic Quiz." *Military service:* California National Guard, 1923-25.

WRITINGS—Under name Jay C. Hall: *Inside the Crime Lab*, Prentice-Hall, 1974. Contributor to technical journals. Editor of house organs, and magazine publisher.

WORK IN PROGRESS: "Knit One Pearl," a musical drama; research for *My Sons, My Daughters: Understanding and Accepting the Homosexual in Your Life.*

SIDELIGHTS: Hall writes: "My grandfather was a major publisher in St. Paul, Minn., and my father a working journalist all his life. My first rejection slip at age six commenced my writing activity which has never abated."

* * *

HALL, Nancy Lee 1923-

PERSONAL: Born June 6, 1923, in Rochester, N.Y.; daughter of Milton Galloway (an editor and writer) and Zelda (Conklin) Hall; children: Ricky Huber, Roxanne Huber, Randy Huber, Rory Huber, Rex Huber, Ramona Huber, Rusti Lee Huber. *Education:* Attended University of California, 1965. *Politics:* Humanism. *Religion:* "Love." *Home:* 1933 Hornblend St. #14, San Diego, Calif. 92109. *Office:* Marine Engineering, San Diego, Calif.

CAREER: Marine Engineering, San Diego, Calif., design

draftsperson, 1964—. Drama teacher at San Diego Unified Public Schools, 1968; social worker at Alcoholism Counseling and Education Center, 1972. Member of Community Women's Liberation Consciousness Raising Rap Group, 1968-75. *Member:* Alcoholics Anonymous, Narcotics Anonymous. *Awards, honors:* Grossmont College One-Act Play Contest first prize, 1968, for "Lost," 1969, for "Smith."

WRITINGS: A True Story of a Drunken Mother, Daughters, Inc., 1974.

Plays: "The Freezer" (one-act), first produced in San Diego, Calif., at Scripteasers, February, 1963; "Hut 64" (one-act), first produced at Scripteasers, September, 1963; "The Room" (one-act), first produced at Scripteasers, October, 1963; "Babes in Evil" (one-act), first produced in San Diego at Midway Drama Workshop, November, 1963; "Bosom of Fools" (three-act), first produced at Scripteasers, September, 1964; "What Shall It Profit?" (three-act), first produced at Scripteasers, November, 1965; "Gabrielle" (three-act), first produced at Scripteasers, October, 1966; "Lost" (one-act), first produced in San Diego at Grossmont College, March, 1968; "Smith" (one-act), first produced at Grossmont College, March, 1969.

WORK IN PROGRESS: A novel dealing with contemporary social adjustment problems of the lone mother, with the tentative title, *A True Story of a Sober Mother*, completion expected in 1976; poems; short stories; several three-act plays; a script for puppet show.

SIDELIGHTS: Nancy Lee Hall has held rap sessions with women in jails and psychiatric wards. She writes, "I come from a long line of strong 'feminist thinking' women and two of my male ancestors signed the Declaration of Independence . . . I'm sure they're all uneasy in their graves. The extremes to which our country has carried the master-slave relationship is not what my ancestors had in mind! I will continue to write and work for equality of the sexes, the races, and all human beings in the world." *Avocational interests:* Figure skating, oil painting.

* * *

HALL, Robert Benjamin 1918-

PERSONAL: Born July 9, 1918, in Marshalltown, Iowa; son of Ross Benjamin (an automobile dealer) and Rita (Lewis) Hall; married Marjorie Bruce Wilson (a speaker and bookstore owner), September 4, 1944; children: Alex Gash, Ross Benjamin. *Education:* University of Arkansas, B.A., 1948; University of the South, M.Div., 1949. *Home and office:* P.O. Box 920, Live Oak, Fla. 32060.

CAREER: Ordained Episcopal priest, 1949; rector of churches in Arkansas, South Dakota, Louisiana, and Florida. Executive director of Episcopal Center for Evangelism, 1972—.

WRITINGS: Receiving the Holy Spirit, Episcopal Center for Evangelism, 1964; *Sharing .Your Faith*, Episcopal Center for Evangelism, 1971; *There's More*, Logos International, 1973.

WORK IN PROGRESS: Anyone Can Prophesy; Lenten Meditations.

* * *

HALL, Susan 1940-

PERSONAL: Born March 4, 1940, in New York, N.Y. *Home:* 923 Fifth Ave., New York, N.Y. 10021.

WRITINGS: (With Robert Adelman) *On and Off the Street*, Viking, 1970; *Benjie Beats the Mark*, Western Publishing, 1970; (with Adelman) *Street Smart*, McGraw, 1972; (with Adelman) *Down Home*, McGraw, 1972; (with Adelman) *Gentleman of Leisure*, New American Library, 1973; *Ladies of the Night*, Trident, 1974.

* * *

HALLETT, Kathryn J(osephine) 1937-

PERSONAL: Born May 9, 1937, in Cleveland, Ohio; daughter of Charles and Josephine (Sotosanti) Stella; children: Regan, Hilary-Anne, Kaitlin; Rebecca Sammons. *Education:* Southern Illinois University, M.S., 1969. *Home:* 34 Calverton Rd., Florissant, Mo. 63135. *Office:* 1005 Dunn Rd., Florissant, Mo. 63031.

CAREER: International Transactional Analysis Association, Berkeley, Calif., teacher and director of St. Louis office, 1973—. *Member:* Association for Humanistic Psychology, American Psychological Association, American Association of Marriage and Family Counselors, American Personnel and Guidance Association.

WRITINGS: *A Guide for Single Parents: People in Crisis*, Celestial Arts, 1974. Also author of booklet, "Keeping Yourself Together," published by Transactional Analysts in St. Louis.

WORK IN PROGRESS: *The Persecuted Parent.*

* * *

HALLGARTEN, George W(olfgang) F(elix) 1901-1975

January 3, 1901—May 22, 1975; German-born historian, university instructor and lecturer, author of books on the history of European politics, unity, and German industry, writing in German, French, and English. Obituaries: *Washington Post*, May 26, 1975.

* * *

HALPERIN, Don A(kiba) 1925-

PERSONAL: Born January 22, 1925, in Cleveland, Ohio; son of Moses Philips (an architect) and Sara (Allen) Halperin; married Elsa Paul (a teacher), June 18, 1949; children: Philip Max, Kenneth Martin. *Education:* Case School of Applied Science (now Case Western Reserve University), B.S.C.E., 1945; University of Illinois, B.S.Arch.E., 1948; Virginia Polytechnic Institute and State University, M.S.Arch.Ed., 1959, Ph.D., 1964. *Religion:* Jewish. *Home:* 745 Northwest 18th St., Gainesville, Fla. 32603. *Office:* Department of Building Construction, University of Florida, Gainesville, Fla. 32611.

CAREER: U.S. Navy, Bureau of Yards and Docks, Washington, D.C., civil engineer, 1945-46; Braverman and Halperin (architects), Cleveland, Ohio, architect, 1948-53; University of Florida, Gainesville, assistant professor, 1953-60, associate professor, 1960-65, professor of building construction, 1965—, chairman of department, 1973—. Chairman of Florida Governor's Committee on Architectural Accessibility, 1969-72; member of President's Committee on Employing the Handicapped, 1970—. *Military service:* U.S. Army, 1948-49. *Member:* American Institute of Constructors, American Council on Construction Education (member of board of trustees, 1974—), Association of Schools of Construction (regional director, 1973—), B'nai B'rith (president of Gainesville chapter, 1969), Sigma Lambda Chi.

WRITINGS: *Building with Steel*, American Technical Society, 1960, revised edition, 1966; *Ancient Synagogues of Iberia*, University of Florida Press, 1967; *Construction Funding*, Wiley, 1974; *Statics and Strength for Technology*, Wiley, in press.

WORK IN PROGRESS: *Structural Design for Technology*, completion expected in 1976.

* * *

HALPERN, Paul J(oseph) 1942-

PERSONAL: Born April 30, 1942, in Cambridge, Mass.; son of Julius (a physicist) and Phyllis Emily (Melnick) Halpern. *Education:* Cornell University, A.B., 1964; Harvard University, M.A., 1968, Ph.D., 1972. *Home:* 1345 South Beverly Glen Blvd., No. 11, Los Angeles, Calif. 90024. *Office:* Department of Political Science, Bunche 4289, University of California, Los Angeles, Calif. 90024.

CAREER: University of California, Los Angeles, assistant professor of political science, 1970—. *Awards, honors:* National Endowment for the Humanities Younger Humanist fellowship, 1974-75.

WRITINGS: *Why Watergate?*, Palisades, 1974.

* * *

HALPERN, Stephen Mark 1940-

PERSONAL: Born January 24, 1940, in New York, N.Y.; son of Louis and Sonia (Handelsman) Halpern; married Sheila Louise Handelman, October 25, 1968; children: Benjamin, Kate. *Education:* University of Rochester, B.A., 1961; Columbia University, M.A., 1963, Ph.D., 1969. *Home:* 43 Sutton Pl., Pleasantville, N.Y. 10570. *Office:* Social Science Department, Borough of Manhattan Community College, City University of New York, New York, N.Y. 10019.

CAREER: Rutgers University, Newark, N.J., instructor in history, 1966-68; City University of New York, Borough of Manhattan Community College, New York, N.Y., instructor, 1968-70, assistant professor, 1970-72, associate professor of history, 1972—. *Member:* American Historical Association, American Studies Association. *Awards, honors:* Woodrow Wilson fellowship, 1961.

WRITINGS: *Looking Back: Modern America in Historical Perspective*, Rand McNally, 1975. Assistant editor, *Manhattan Mind*, 1971-74.

WORK IN PROGRESS: A biography, possibly on major American feminist.

AVOCATIONAL INTERESTS: Classical music (piano, oboe), woodcraft.

* * *

HAMILTON, Paul
See DENNIS-JONES, H(arold)

* * *

HAMLEY, Dennis 1935-

PERSONAL: Born October 14, 1935, in Crockham Hill, Kent, England; son of Charles Richard (a post office engineer) and Doris May (Payne) Hamley; married Agnes Moylan (a nurse), August 6, 1965; children: Peter Richard John, Mary Elizabeth Carmel. *Education:* Jesus College, Cambridge, M.A., 1959; further study at University of Bristol, 1959-60, University of Manchester, 1962-65; and

University of Leicester, 1973—. *Politics:* "Sort of social democrat—supporter but not member of British Labour Party." *Religion:* Anglican. *Home:* 114 Whalley Dr., Bletchley, Milton Keynes MK3 6HV, England. *Office:* Milton Keynes College of Education, Stratford Rd., Wolverton Mill, Milton Keynes MK12 6NS, England.

CAREER: English master at grammar schools in England, 1960-67; Milton Keynes College of Education, Bletchley, Milton Keynes, England, lecturer, 1967-69, senior lecturer in English, 1969—. Counselor and tutor for Open University, 1971—. *Military service:* Royal Air Force, 1954-56. *Member:* Society of Authors, Association of Teachers in Colleges and Departments of Education.

WRITINGS: Three Towneley Plays (adapted into modern English), Heinemann, 1963; *Pageants of Despair* (novel for children), S. G. Phillips, 1974; (with Colin Field) *Fiction in the Middle School*, Batsford, 1975; *Very Far From Here* (novel for juveniles), Deutsch, in press. Reviewer for *School Librarian.*

WORK IN PROGRESS: More adaptations of medieval plays; *Language Activities in the First School* (tentative title), with Colin Field; research on fiction teaching in schools.

AVOCATIONAL INTERESTS: Drama, railways.

* * *

HAMMING, Richard W. 1915-

PERSONAL: Born February 11, 1915, in Chicago, Ill.; son of Richard J. H. and Mabel (Redfield) Hamming; married Wanda Little. *Education:* University of Chicago, B.S., 1937; University of Nebraska, M.A., 1939; University of Illinois, Ph.D., 1942. *Office:* Bell Laboratories, Mountain Ave., Murray Hill, N.J. 07974.

CAREER: Bell Laboratories, Murray Hill, N.J., head of computing science research. Professor, Stevens Institute. *Member:* Institute of Electrical and Electronics Engineers (fellow), Mathematical Association of America, American Association for the Advancement of Science, Association for Computing Machinery, Society for Industrial and Applied Mathematics. *Awards, honors:* Association for Computing Machinery Turing fellow, 1968.

WRITINGS: Numerical Methods for Scientists and Engineers, McGraw, 1962, 2nd edition, 1973; *Introduction to Applied Numerical Analysis*, McGraw, 1971; *Computers and Society*, McGraw, 1972.

* * *

HAMMOND, Paul 1947-

PERSONAL: Born July 19, 1947, in Derby, England; son of William Frederick (a factory worker) and Hannah May (a factory worker; maiden name, Hinchliffe) Hammond; married Christine Dunn (a teacher), September 6, 1969. *Education:* Leeds College of Art, diploma in art and design (first class honours), 1969; Slade School of Fine Art, diploma in fine art, 1971, diploma in film studies, 1973. *Politics:* "Libertarian Marxist." *Religion:* Atheist. *Home:* 28 Auden Pl., Manley St., London NW1, England. *Agent:* Hilary Rubenstein, A. P. Watt & Son, 26-28 Bedford Row, London WC1R 4HL, England.

CAREER: Bookseller; writer.

WRITINGS: Marvellous Melies, Gordon Fraser, 1974, St. Martin's, 1975; *French Undressing* (on erotic postcards), Gentry Books, 1975. Contributor of stories, articles, and

translations to *Adventures in Poetry, Roy Rogers, Juillard,* and other little literary magazines, and to *Art and Artists, Cinema,* and *Photon.*

WORK IN PROGRESS: Upon the Pun: Dual Meaning in Words and Pictures, with Patrick Hughes.

* * *

HAMSHER, J. Herbert 1938-

PERSONAL: Born June 16, 1938, in Davenport, Iowa; son of John H. and Ruth (Higgins) Hamsher. *Education:* Northwestern University, Ph.B., 1961; Northern Illinois University, M.A., 1966; University of Connecticut, Ph.D., 1968. *Home and office:* 1801 John F. Kennedy Blvd., Philadelphia, Pa. 19103.

CAREER: Temple University, Philadelphia, Pa., associate professor of psychology, 1971—. *Military service:* U.S. Naval Air Reserve. *Member:* American Psychological Association, American Group Psychotherapy Association, International Transactional Analysis Association (chairman of research committee), American Association of University Professors, Eastern Psychological Association.

WRITINGS: Psychology and Social Issues, Macmillan, 1973. Consulting editor, *Transactional Analysis Journal.*

WORK IN PROGRESS: Handbook of Political Psychology; or, How to Avoid Impeachment Before the Election.

* * *

HANBURY-TENISON, (Airling) Robin 1936-

PERSONAL: Born May 7, 1936, in London, England; son of Gerald Evan Farquhar and Ruth (Hanbury) Tenison; married Marika Hopkinson (an author), January 14, 1959; children: Lucy Antonia, Rupert Thomas Treveddoe. *Education:* Magdalen College, Oxford, B.A., 1957, M.A. *Religion:* Church of England. *Home:* Maidenwell, Cardinham, Bodmin, Cornwall, England. *Agent:* A. M. Heath & Co., 40-42 William IV St., London WC2N 4DD, England. *Office:* Survival International, 36 Craven St., London WC2N 5NG, England.

CAREER: Explorer, farmer, and author. Survival International, London, England, chairman, 1969—. *Member:* Royal Geographical Society (fellow; member of council), Linnean Society (fellow).

WRITINGS: The Rough and the Smooth, R. Hale, 1969; *A Question of Survival*, Scribner, 1973; *A Pattern of Peoples*, Scribner, 1975. Contributor of articles and reviews to *Geographical Magazine, The Times* (London), *Geographical Journal, Expedition, Vogue,* and other periodicals.

SIDELIGHTS: As chairman of Survival International, an organization attempting to prevent the extinction of primitive tribal groups, Hanbury-Tenison visits remote sections of the globe gathering information for his books.

* * *

HAND, J(oan) C(arole) 1943-

PERSONAL: Born September 8, 1943, in Brooklyn, N.Y.; daughter of Frank (a teacher) and Betty (a teacher and artist; maiden name, Cohen) Hand; married David B. Axelrod (a writer and teacher), May 29, 1966; children: Jessica Ellen, Emily Elizabeth. *Education:* Bard College, A.B., 1965; Johns Hopkins University, M.A., 1966; University of Iowa, M.F.A., 1968, graduate study, 1968-69; State University of New York, Stony Brook, graduate study, 1969-

72. *Home:* 194 Soundview Dr., R.R. #3, Box 147-A, Rocky Point, N.Y. 11778. *Agent:* Otte Agency, 9 Park St., Boston, Mass. 02108. *Office:* Department of English, Suffolk County Community College, 533 College Rd., Selden, N.Y. 11784.

CAREER: Pennsylvania State University, University Park, teaching assistant in English, 1966-67; Southampton College, Southampton, N.Y., instructor in English, 1970-71; Suffolk County Community College, Selden, N.Y., assistant professor of English, 1972—. Teacher at Skidmore College, summer, 1968; co-founder of Writers Unlimited Agency, 1971; visiting writer for New York Poet-in-School Program, 1972—; mentor, Empire State College, 1975—. *Awards, honors:* New York Council of the Arts performing arts grant, 1971—.

WRITINGS: Your Witch (novella), Despa Press, 1973. Contributor of poems and short stories to magazines and journals, including *Nimrod, Epos, Descant, Poetry Newsletter,* and others.

WORK IN PROGRESS: Two novels, *A Photo of Emily Singer* and *US* (tentative titles); *Poems: 1969–.*

BIOGRAPHICAL/CRITICAL SOURCES: North Shore Record (Port Jefferson, N.Y.), June 7, 1973; *Street Magazine,* September, 1975.

* * *

HANDELMAN, Howard 1943-

PERSONAL: Born April 29, 1943, in Brooklyn, N.Y.; son of Victor (a professional fund-raiser and businessman) and Ruth (an artist and businesswoman; maiden name, Goodman) Handelman; married Nancy Rae Forster (a high school teacher), September 22, 1967; children: Michael Jesse. *Education:* Attended London School of Economics and Political Science, 1963-64; University of Pennsylvania, B.A. (cum laude), 1965; University of Wisconsin, M.A., 1967, Ph.D., 1971. *Politics:* Democratic Socialist. *Home:* 2915 North Stowell Ave., Milwaukee, Wis. 53211. *Office:* Department of Political Science, University of Wisconsin, Milwaukee, Wis. 53201.

CAREER: University of Wisconsin, Milwaukee, assistant professor of political science, 1970—. Member of Wisconsin Alliance, 1973—. *Member:* American Political Science Association, Latin American Studies Association. *Awards, honors:* Ford Foundation field research fellowship, 1968-69, for research in Peru; American Philosophical Society fellowship, 1973, for research in Mexico.

WRITINGS: Struggle in the Andes: Peasant Political Mobilization in Peru, University of Texas Press, 1974. Contributor to *Latin American Research Review.*

WORK IN PROGRESS: Research on politics in Uruguay; writing on the politics of the Mexican working class.

AVOCATIONAL INTERESTS: Travel, music, sports, films.

* * *

HANEY, David 1938-

PERSONAL: Born January 11, 1938, in Dayton, Ohio; son of George G. (a clergyman) and Lucille (Bales) Haney; married Aileen Faulkner (a teacher), November 9, 1957; children: Karen, Steven, Philip. *Education:* Harrison-Chilhouse Baptist Academy, student, 1955-57; Georgetown College, B.A., 1961; Southeastern Baptist Theological Seminary, graduate study, 1961-62; Earlham School of Reli-

gion, M.A., 1966; Luther Rice Seminary, Th.D., 1969. *Office:* Baptist Brotherhood, 1548 Poplar, Memphis, Tenn. 38104.

CAREER: Ordained to Baptist ministry, 1958; pastor of Baptist churches in Sadieville, Ky., 1958-61, New Lebanon, Ohio, 1961-67, and Annapolis, Md., 1967-74; Southern Baptist Convention, Memphis, Tenn., director of lay ministries, 1974—.

WRITINGS: Renew My Church, Zondervan, 1972; *The Idea of the Laity,* Zondervan, 1973; *Breakthrough into Renewal,* Broadman, 1974; *Journey into Life,* Brotherhood Commission, 1974.

* * *

HANLON, John J(oseph) 1912-

PERSONAL: Born May 7, 1912, in Boston, Mass.; son of John Joseph and Florence (Livingston) Hanlon; married Frances Pizzo, June 24, 1939; children: Jon J., Donald L. *Education:* Massachusetts Institute of Technology, B.S., 1933, M.S., 1934; Harvard University, graduate study, 1934; Wayne State University, M.B., 1940, M.D., 1941; Johns Hopkins University, M.P.H., 1942. *Home:* 9805 Canal Rd., Gaithersburg, Md. 20760. *Office:* 5600 Fishers La., Rockville, Md. 20852.

CAREER: Assistant sanitary engineer in Eaton County, Mich., 1934; Detroit Department of Health, Detroit, Mich., assistant epidemiologist and statistician, 1935-40; licensed to practice medicine in Michigan; Harper Hospital, Detroit, Mich., intern, 1940-41; Tennessee Department of Health, Nashville, director of nutrition, 1941-43; health officer in Bradley County, Tenn., 1942; University of North Carolina, Chapel Hill, associate professor of public health administration, 1943-44; Duke University, Durham, N.C., lecturer in preventive medicine, 1943-44; University of Michigan, Ann Arbor, associate professor of public health, 1944-49; Institute of Inter-American Affairs, Bolivia, chief of health mission, 1949-51; City of Detroit, Detroit, Mich., special assistant to Commissioner of Health, 1951-52; University of Michigan, professor of public health, 1951-52; U.S. Public Health Service, Washington, D.C., medical director, 1952-57; U.S. Department of State, Washington, D.C., chief of foreign aid program in Public Health Division, 1952-57; City of Philadelphia, Community Health Service, Philadelphia, Pa., director, 1957-64; Temple University, Philadelphia, Pa., professor of public health and chairman of department, 1957-64; City of Detroit, Commissioner of Health, 1964-68; public health director in Wayne County, Mich., 1964-68; Wayne State University, Detroit, Mich., professor of community medicine and chairman of department, 1964-68; Department of Health, Education and Welfare, Public Health Service, Washington, D.C., assistant surgeon general, 1968-71; Health Services Administration, coordinator for public health programs, 1972—. Diplomate of American Board of Preventive Medicine and Public Health, Adjunct professor of health administration at University of Michigan, 1964-68. Member of Expert Panel on Public Health Administration of World Health Organization, 1952—; member of executive committee and counsellor of International Union for Health Education, 1960-66. Member of U.S. delegation to World Health Assembly, 1953, 1954, 1956.

MEMBER: Sociedad Boliviana de Salud Publica (life member), Pan American Medical Association (honorary fellow), Royal Society of Health (honorary fellow), Hellenic Public Health Society (honorary life member), American Public Health Association (fellow; president, 1967-68), American Medical Association, National Association of Sanitarians (honorary life member), American College of Preventive Medicine and Public Health (fellow), American Academy of Political and Social Science (fellow), Association of Professors of Preventive Medicine, Philadelphia College of Medicine (honorary fellow), Delta Omega, Alpha Omega Alpha, Sigma Xi. *Awards, honors:* Order of the Cordor of the Andes from Republic of Bolivia, 1951; Michigan State Medical Soceity distinguished professional service award, and flag award, 1968; Michigan Public Health Association distinguished service award, 1969.

WRITINGS: (With Adelia Beeuwkes) *Nutrition and the Public Health*, Overbeck, 1945, 2nd edition, 1947; *Principles of Public Health Administration*, Mosby, 1950, 6th edition, 1974; (contributor) I. T. Sanders, editor, *Interprofessional Training for Technical Assistance Personnel Abroad*, Council on Social Work Education, 1959; (with Elizabeth McHose) *Design for Health*, Lea & Febiger, 1963, 2nd edition, 1971; (contributor) C. E. Bruess and J. T. Fisher, editors, *Selected Readings in Health*, Macmillan, 1970; (contributor) J. H. Bailey, editor, *The Nation's Environment: Problems and Action*, East Tennessee State University Press, 1971; (contributor) *Collective Bargaining Today*, Bureau of National Affairs, 1971; (contributor) John LaPlace, editor, *Perspectives in Health*, Appleton, 1971; (contributor) *Contributions of the Biological Sciences to Human Welfare*, Federation of American Societies for Experimental Biology, 1971; (contributor) Kenneth D. Fisher and Ann Nixon, editors, *The Science of Life*, Plenum, 1972; (contributor) E. Fuller Torrey, editor, *Community Health and Mental Health Care Delivery for North American Indians*, MSS Information, 1974; (contributor) C. D. Ray, editor, *Medical Engineering*, Year Book Medical Publishers, 1974. Contributor of more than one hundred articles to professional journals. Member of editorial board of *American Journal of Public Health*, 1956-62, and *Public Health Reports*, 1966-70.

WORK IN PROGRESS: With Carmen G. Warner, *Challenges in a Changing Society*; a novel set in Central America.

SIDELIGHTS: Hanlon has travelled widely and has visited many notable archaeological sites.

* * *

HANNA, David   1917-

PERSONAL: Born September 11, 1917, in Philadelphia, Pa.; son of Hugh J. (a writer) and Lenore (an actress; maiden name, Torriani) Hanna. *Education:* Attended Pepperdine College. *Home:* 49 West 44th St., New York, N.Y. *Office:* 185 Madison Ave., New York, N.Y. 10016.

CAREER: Los Angeles Daily News, Los Angeles, Calif., feature writer, 1940-46; *Hollywood Reporter*, Los Angeles, Calif., feature writer, 1947-52; free-lance journalist in Europe and the United States, 1952-62; editor of *Confidential* and *Whisper*, 1963-65; editor of *Uncensored* and *Inside Story*, 1965-72; writer.

WRITINGS: Ava: Portrait of a Star, Putnam, 1960; *Virginia Hill: Queen of the Underworld*, Belmont Tower Books, 1974; *Murder, Inc.*, Leisure Books, 1974; *Frank Costello: The Gangster with a Thousand Faces*, Belmont Tower Books, 1974; *Vito Genovese*, Belmont Tower Books, 1974; *Bugsy Siegel: The Man Who Invented Murder, Inc.*, Belmont Tower Books, 1974; *Harvest of Horror: Mass Murder in Houston*, Belmont Tower Books, 1974;

King of the Mafia: Carlo Gambino, Belmont Tower Books, 1975; *Henry Kissinger: His Rise and ?*, Manor Books, 1975; *The Lucky Luciano Connection*, Belmont Tower Books, 1975; *Robert Redford: The Superstar Nobody Knows*, Belmont Tower Books, 1975; *The World of Jacqueline Susann*, Manor Books, 1975; *Mafia Over Hollywood*, Belmont Tower Books, 1975.

SIDELIGHTS: Hanna is competent in French, Italian, and German.

* * *

HANSEN, Alvin H(arvey)   1887-1975

August 23, 1887—June 6, 1975; American economist, governmental advisor and consultant on economic policy, university professor, author of books on economics. Obituaries: *Washington Post*, June 7, 1975; *New York Times*, June 7, 1975; *Time*, June 16, 1975; *AB Bookman's Weekly*, June 23, 1975; *Current Biography*, August, 1975. (*CA*-15/16)

* * *

HARAP, Louis   1904-

PERSONAL: Born September 16, 1904, in New York, N.Y.; son of Moses (a sewing machine operator) and Yetta (Karp) Harap; married Evelyn Mann, August 17, 1957. *Education:* Antioch College, student, 1922-25; Harvard University, A.B., 1928, M.A., 1930, Ph.D., 1932. *Politics:* "Left-wing." *Religion:* None. *Residence:* Belmont, Vt. 05730.

CAREER: Harvard University, Library of Philosophy and Psychology, Cambridge, Mass., librarian, 1934-39; *Jewish Survey*, New York, N.Y., managing editor, 1941-42; *Jewish Life*, New York, N.Y., managing editor, 1948-57; New Lincoln School, New York, N.Y., librarian, 1959-69; independent scholar, 1969—. *Military service:* U.S. Army, 1942-45; became technical sergeant.

WRITINGS: Social Roots of the Arts, International Publishers, 1949; *The Image of the Jew in American Literature: From Early Republic to Mass Immigration*, Jewish Publication Society, 1974. Contributor of articles and reviews to magazines, including *Journal of Philosophy*, *Musical Quarterly*, *Nation*, and *Masses and Mainstream*. Member of editorial board of *Jewish Currents* (formerly *Jewish Life*), 1957—.

* * *

HARBESON, John Willis   1938-

PERSONAL: Born September 14, 1938, in New Brunswick, N.J.; son of Robert Willis and Gladys (Evans) Harbeson; married Ann Elizabeth Warmoth (a teacher), August 25, 1963; children: Eric John, Kristen Lynne. *Education:* Swarthmore College, B.A. (cum laude), 1960; University of Chicago, M.A., 1962; University of Wisconsin, Ph.D., 1970. *Politics:* Democrat. *Religion:* Congregationalist. *Home:* 1020 Park Ave., Racine, Wis. 53403. *Office:* Department of Political Science, University of Wisconsin–Parkside, Kenosha, Wis. 53140.

CAREER: University of Wisconsin–Parkside, Kenosha, assistant professor, 1967-72, associate professor of political science, 1972—. Visiting associate professor at National University of Ethiopia, 1973-75; member of board of directors of Racine Urban League, 1971-72. *Member:* International African Studies Association, American Political Science Association, African Studies Association, Wisconsin Civil Liberties Union (member of board of directors).

WRITINGS: Nation Building in Kenya: The Role of Land Reform, Northwestern University Press, 1973. Associate editor, *Ethiopian Journal of Development Studies*, 1973-75.

WORK IN PROGRESS: Politics of Rural Change in Ethiopia; Land Reform and Political Development in Ethiopia; The Ethiopian Revolution.

SIDELIGHTS: Harbeson has made research tours in Kenya, 1965-67, and Ethiopia, 1973-75; he speaks French, German, and Swahili. *Avocational interests:* Music (organ, piano, voice, theory, composition), sports (tennis, swimming).

* * *

HARDESTY, Nancy A(nn) 1941-

PERSONAL: Born August 22, 1941, in Lima, Ohio; daughter of Byron Tapscott (a tool and die maker) and Ruth Lucille (a bank clerk; maiden name, Parr) Hardesty. *Education:* Wheaton College, Wheaton, Ill., A.B., 1963; Northwestern University, M.S.J., 1964; University of Chicago, doctoral study, 1973-76. *Politics:* Democrat. *Religion:* Episcopalian. *Home:* 1215 East Hyde Park Blvd., Chicago, Ill. 60615.

CAREER: Lima News, Lima, Ohio, reporter, 1961-63; *Christian Century*, Chicago, Ill., editorial assistant, 1964-65; *Eternity*, Philadelphia, Pa., assistant editor, 1966-69; Trinity College, Deerfield, Ill., assistant professor of English, and sports information director, 1969-73. Member of executive committee of Evangelicals for Social Action.

WRITINGS: (Contributor) Robert G. Clouse and other editors, *The Cross and the Flag*, Creation House, 1972; (with Letha Scanzoni) *All We're Meant To Be: A Biblical Approach to Women's Liberation*, Word Books, 1974. Contributor to religious publications.

WORK IN PROGRESS: Collecting a series originally published in *Eternity* in book form; a book on the problems of single Christian adults; research on two types of biblical hermeneutics seen in the nineteenth-century American woman's movement.

SIDELIGHTS: Nancy Hardesty writes: "I have been reared, educated and employed within a conservative, 'evangelical' Christian context. There I have seen first-hand the discrimination practiced against women and have felt the frustration when such oppression is buttressed with biblical and religious arguments. My co-author and I decided to fight back.... My goal is to learn more about Christian women of the past, their work and their beliefs, and then to communicate their inspiring stories to people today."

* * *

HARGER, William Henderson 1936-

PERSONAL: Born February 6, 1936, in Los Angeles, Calif.; son of Stillwell Russell (an engineer) and Valentina (Nalivaiko) Harger; married Sandra Cummings, May 5, 1956 (divorced, 1975); children: William Patrick, Lorn Scot. *Education:* Northrop Institute of Technology (now Northrop University), B.S., 1963. *Politics:* Democrat. *Address:* Box 34, Douglas City, Calif. 96024.

CAREER: Nor-Air, Hawthorne, Calif., wind tunnel engineer, 1955-61; Contour, Inc., Rosemead, Calif., general manager, 1961-63; FMC Corp., San Jose, Calif., engineer, 1963-67; International Business Machines Corp., San Jose, Calif., inventor, 1967-69. Teacher of creative writing at Shasta Junior College, 1973—.

WRITINGS: Somebody (poems), privately printed, 1969; *Of a Poet* (poems), Celestial Arts, 1973; *To My Beloved Earth* (poems), Celestial Arts, 1973; *It's Easy to Be Loved* (poems), Celestial Arts, 1974. Also author of an as yet untitled anthology of poems to be published by Celestial Arts.

WORK IN PROGRESS: A volume of philosophy.

SIDELIGHTS: Harger told *CA*: "My poetry often has a wry twist at the conclusion to effect the reader's identification with the story told. I live in the wilderness, seeking self-sufficiency, generating own electricity, food, heat, etc., to aid in my self-identification."

* * *

HARKEY, Ira B(rown), Jr. 1918-

PERSONAL: Born January 15, 1918, in New Orleans, La.; son of Ira Brown and Flora B. (Lewis) Harkey; married, Marie E. Gore, 1939 (divorced, 1963); married Marion Marks, December 10, 1963; children: Ira Brown III, Marie Ella (Mrs. Loran E. Bosarge), Erik G., Lewis, Amelie (Mrs. Rex Foster), William Millsaps. *Education:* Tulane University, A.B., 1941; Ohio State University, M.A., graduate study; graduate study at New Mexico Military Institute, and University of Florida, 1960-61. *Agent:* Lurton Blassingame, 60 East 42nd St., New York, N.Y. 10017.

CAREER: New Orleans Times-Picayune, New Orleans, La., reporter and magazine writer, 1940-42, 1946-49; *Chronicle*, Pascagoula, Miss., editor, president, and publisher, 1949-63; Ohio State University, Columbus, member of journalism faculty, 1965-66; Carnegie visiting professor at University of Alaska, 1968-69; Dean Stone lecturer at University of Montana, 1970; Eric Allen lecturer at University of Oregon, 1972. Vice-president and member of board of directors of Oklahoma Coca-Cola Bottling Co. *Military service:* U.S. Navy, 1942-46; became lieutenant; served in Pacific.

MEMBER: American Association of University Professors, Association for Education in Journalism, American Political Science Association, Phi Beta Kappa, Kappa Tau Alpha, Sigma Delta Chi, Delta Kappa Epsilon. *Awards, honors:* Pulitzer Prize, 1963, for editorial writing; Sigma Delta Chi national award, 1963, for distinguished public service in newspaper journalism; National Conference of Christian and Jews award, 1963.

WRITINGS: The Smell of Burning Crosses, Harris-Wolfe, 1967; (contributor) *Places to Fly*, Aircraft Owners and Pilots Association, Volume II, 1967, Volume III, 1969; (contributor) *Toward a Better America*, Macmillan, 1968; *Pioneer Bush Pilot: The Story of Noel Wien*, University of Washington, 1974. Contributor to *Pageant, Christian Herald, Negro Digest, Venture, Pilot, True*, and other journals and newspapers.

WORK IN PROGRESS: Work on correlates among socio-economic status variables and role self-perception variables in state legislative political communications of the print mass media.

AVOCATIONAL INTERESTS: Flying own plane (holds single and multi-engine ratings).

HARKNETT, Terry 1936-
(Frank Chandler, David Ford, George G. Gilman, Jane Harman, Joseph Hedges, Charles R. Pike, William Pine, James Russell, Thomas H. Stone, William Terry; William M. James, a joint pseudonym)

PERSONAL: Born December 14, 1936, in Rainham, Essex, England; son of Frederick Thomas (a truck driver) and Louisa (a waitress; maiden name, Jaggs) Harknett; married Jane Harman (secretary to husband), January 16, 1960. *Education:* Attended secondary school in England. *Politics:* "Depends, but Rightism." *Religion:* Church of England. *Home:* 16 Old Fold, Chestfield, Whitstable, Kent CP5 3NL, England.

CAREER: Reuters News Agency, London, England, copy boy, 1951-52; Newspapers Features Ltd., London, feature writer, 1952-55; Twentieth Century-Fox, London, exploitation assistant, 1957-58; *National Newsagent* (trade magazine), London, features editor, 1958-71; professional writer and novelist, 1971—. *Military service:* Royal Air Force, 1955-57.

WRITINGS—All novels, except as noted: *The Benevolent Blackmailer*, R. Hale, 1962; *The Scratch on the Surface*, R. Hale, 1962; *Invitation to a Funeral*, R. Hale, 1963; *Dead Little Rich Girl*, R. Hale, 1963; *The Evil Money*, R. Hale, 1964; *The Man Who Did Not Die*, R. Hale, 1964; *Death of an Aunt*, Hammond, Hammond, 1967; *The Softcover Kill*, R. Hale, 1971; *The Caribbean* (guide book), New English Library, 1972; *Promotion Tour*, New English Library, 1972; *The Upmarket Affair*, R. Hale, 1973; *Sweet and Sour Kill*, Futura, 1974; *Macao Mayhem*, Futura, 1974; *Bamboo Shoot-Out*, Futura, 1975.

Under pseudonym Frank Chandler: *A Fistful of Dollars*, Tandem Books, 1972.

Under pseudonym David Ford: *Cyprus* (guide book), New English Library, 1973.

Under pseudonym George G. Gilman; all published by New English Library: *The Loner*, 1972; *Ten Thousand Dollars American*, 1972; *Apache Death*, 1972; *Killer's Breed*, 1972; *Blood on Silver*, 1972; *The Blue the Grey and the Red*, 1973; *California Killing*, 1973; *Seven Out of Hell*, 1973; *Bloody Summer*, 1973; *Vengeance Is Black*, 1973; *The Violent Peace*, 1974; *The Bounty Hunter*, 1974; *Hell's Junction*, 1974; *Sioux Uprising*, 1974; *The Biggest Bounty*, 1974; *A Town Called Hate*, 1974; *The Big Gold*, 1974; *Blood Run*, 1975; *The Final Shot*, 1975; *Ten Tombstones to Texas*, 1975; *Valley of Blood*, 1975; *Gun Run*, 1975.

Under pseudonym Jane Harman: *W.I.T.C.H.*, New English Library, 1971.

Under pseudonym Joseph Hedges; all published by Sphere Books: *Funeral Rites*, 1973; *Arms for Oblivion*, 1973; *The Chinese Coffin*, 1974; *The Gold-Plated Hearse*, 1974; *The Rainbow-Coloured Shroud*, 1974; *Corpse on Ice*, 1975; *The Mile-Deep Grave*, 1975.

Under pseudonym Charles R. Pike: *The Killing Trail*, Mayflower Books, 1974; *Double-Cross*, Mayflower Books, 1974; *The Hungry Gun*, Mayflower Books, 1975.

Under pseudonym William Pine: *The Protectors*, Constable, 1967.

Under pseudonym James Russell: *The Balearics* (guide book), New English Library, 1972.

Under pseudonym Thomas H. Stone; all published by New English Library: *Dead Set*, 1972; *One Horse Race*, 1972;

Stopover for Murder, 1973; *Black Death*, 1973; *Squeeze Play*, 1973.

Under pseudonym William Terry; *Once a Copper*, Hammond, Hammond, 1965; *A Town Called Bastard*, New English Library, 1971; *Hannie Caulder*, New English Library, 1971; *The Weekend Game*, New English Library, 1971; *Red Sun*, New English Library, 1972.

With Laurence James under pseudonym William M. James: *The First Death*, Pinnacle Books, 1974; *Knife in the Night*, Pinnacle Books, 1974; *Duel to the Death*, Pinnacle Books, 1975.

WORK IN PROGRESS: "One new book each month."

* * *

HARLOW, Francis H(arvey) 1928-
PERSONAL: Born January 22, 1928, in Seattle, Wash.; son of Francis H., Sr. and Florence (Melvin) Harlow; married Patricia Nystuen, June 21, 1952; children: Catherine, Carol, Celia, Keith. *Education:* University of Washington, Seattle, B.S., 1949, Ph.D., 1953. *Home:* 1407 11th, Los Alamos, N.M. 87544. *Art agents:* Jamison Galleries, 111 San Francisco St., Santa Fe, N.M. 87501; and Cliff Dwellers Gallery, Los Alamos, N.M. 87544. *Office:* Los Alamos Scientific Laboratory, Los Alamos, N.M. 87544.

CAREER: Los Alamos Scientific Laboratory, Los Alamos, N.M., member of staff in theoretical physics, 1953—. Artist; has about two hundred fifty paintings in private and public collections in the United States and abroad; has had four one-man shows in New Mexico, 1971—. Appraiser of Southwestern Indian pottery. *Military service:* U.S. Army, 1945-46. U.S. Army Reserve, 1946-54; became first lieutenant. *Member:* Museum of New Mexico (research associate).

WRITINGS: (Contributor) Berni Adler, Sidney Fernbach, and Manuel Rotenberg, editors, *Methods in Computational Physics*, Volumes III and IV, Academic Press, 1964; (with John V. Young) *Contemporary Pueblo Indian Pottery* (booklet), Museum of New Mexico Press, 1965; *Historic Pueblo Indian Pottery* (booklet), Monitor Press, 1967; (contributor of supplementary material) K. M. Chapman, *The Pottery of San Ildefonso Pueblo*, School of American Research, 1969; (with A. A. Amsden) *Fluid Dynamics: An Introductory Text*, Los Alamos Scientific Laboratory, 1969, 2nd edition, 1971.

(Contributor) Sidney Fernbach and A. H. Taub, editors, *Computers and Their Role in the Physical Sciences*, Gordon & Breach, 1970; (contributor) C. K. Chu, editor, *Computational Fluid Dynamics*, American Institute of Aeronautics and Astronautics, 1971; (with P. K. Sutherland) *Pennsylvania Brachiopods and Biostratigraphy in Southern Sangre de Cristo Mountains, New Mexico*, New Mexico Bureau of Mines and Mineral Resources, 1973; *Matte Paint Pottery of the Tewa, Keres, and Zuni Pueblos*, Museum of New Mexico Press, 1973; (editor) *Turbulence Transport Modeling*, American Institute of Aeronautics and Astronautics, 1973; (editor) *Computer Fluid Dynamics: Recent Advances*, American Institute of Aeronautics and Astronautics, 1973; (with Larry Frank) *Historic Pottery of the Pueblo Indians: 1600-1880*, New York Graphic Society, 1974; *Modern Pottery of the Pueblo Indians*, Northland Press, in press. Contributor to scientific journals. Associate editor of *Journal of Computational Physics*; advisory editor of *Computer Methods in Applied Mechanics and Engineering*.

WORK IN PROGRESS: Short stories; philosophical essays; continuing research in mathematics and physics.

SIDELIGHTS: Harlow writes: "Since 1968, I have been painting, mainly in acrylics, and exhibiting my paintings in art galleries. . . . My painting and writing are closely coordinated in spirit. Both refer to the strength, dignity, and feelings of people, especially those who are artists, craftsmen, philosophers, or just ordinary folks who love the beauty of nature, human talents, and life." *Avocational interests:* Paleontology (especially Paleozoic brachiopods), anthropology (especially Pueblo Indian).

BIOGRAPHICAL/CRITICAL SOURCES: Science Digest, July, 1975; Jeanne Hassenzahl, *Harlow* (booklet), Vergara Press (Santa Fe, N.M.), 1975.

*   *   *

HARMAN, Jane
See HARKNETT, Terry

*   *   *

HARMON, Susanna M(arie)   1940-

PERSONAL: Born April 10, 1940, in Lansing, Mich.; daughter of James Russell (a minister) and Shirley E. (a teacher; maiden name, Blewfield) Pollock; married Gary L. Harmon (a professor of languages and literature), December 27, 1960; children: Thomas Thorburn, James Matthias, Nathan Martin. *Education:* University of Michigan, A.B., 1961, M.A., 1964; University of Geneva, further graduate study, 1966. *Religion:* Protestant. *Home and office:* 3419 Beauclerc Rd., Jacksonville, Fla. 32217.

CAREER: High school teacher of English, speech, and debate in Flint, Mich., 1961-64, chairman of department, 1962-64; high school teacher of literature and composition in Bloomington, Ind., 1964-66; Morehead State University, Morehead, Ky., instructor in composition and literature, 1966-67; researcher and editor, 1967—. Coordinator of Welcome League, Inc.; member of Women of Jacksonville Art Museum. *Member:* Modern Language Association of America, American Association of University Women, Society for the Study of Midwestern Literature.

WRITINGS: (Contributor) R. F. Dickinson and Gary L. Harmon, *Write Now! Substance, Strategy, Style*, Holt, 1972; (with G. L. Harmon) *Scholar's Market: An International Directory of Periodicals Publishing Literary Scholarship*, Ohio State University Libraries, 1974.

WORK IN PROGRESS: Editing an anthology, *Image of the Aging in Short Fiction.*

AVOCATIONAL INTERESTS: Discussion of films, environmental conditions, philately, gourmet groups (founded two groups), international travel (especially Switzerland).

*   *   *

HARRIMAN, Sarah   1942-

PERSONAL: Born February 6, 1942, in Pittsburgh, Pa.; daughter of William Allen (a business executive) and Catherine (Porter) Brobston; married Anthony Harriman, August 22, 1964 (divorced, 1972). *Education:* Connecticut College, B.S., 1963. *Politics:* "Humane." *Religion:* "Pantheist." *Home address:* Reading, Vt. 05062. *Agent:* Jerome Meyers, P.O. Box 76, Reading, Vt. 05062. *Office: Connecticut*, Fairfield, Conn.

CAREER: American Management Association, New York, N.Y., assistant editor, 1963-67; *Encyclopaedia Britannica*, New York, N.Y., senior editor of life sciences, 1967-70; free-lance editor and writer, 1970—.

WRITINGS: The Book of Ginseng, Pyramid Publications, 1973. Contributing consumer affairs editor for *New York*, 1972-74; science editor for *Connecticut*, 1975—.

WORK IN PROGRESS: An adventure novel; two health books; research on consumer affairs, science, and local history.

SIDELIGHTS: Sarah Harriman writes that her aim is ". . . to stimulate curiosity by using lay language to discuss complex issues in areas of science and technology, health, consumer affairs, and bizzare phenomena." *Avocational interests:* Vegetable gardening, star gazing, bird watching.

*   *   *

HARRINGTON, Geri

PERSONAL: Born in New Haven, Conn.; daughter of Frederick A. and Evelyn (Richey) Spolane; married Don Harrington (in advertising); children: Peter Tyrus, John Jeffrey. *Education:* Smith College, B.A. *Home address:* Merwin Lane, Wilton, Conn. 06897.

CAREER: Good Housekeeping Magazine, New York, N.Y., market research analyst, 1949-50; U.S. Department of Commerce, Washington, D.C., writer/analyst, 1950-52; Columbia University, Bureau of Applied Social Research, New York, writer and analyst, 1953-55; Ted Bates, Inc., New York, copywriter, 1955-57; Grey Advertising, New York, copywriter, 1957-59; Don Harrington Associates (advertising firm), Wilton, Conn., partner, 1960—. *Member:* Northeast Archeological Researchers.

WRITINGS: The College Cookbook, Scribner, 1973; *The Edible Root*, Atheneum, in press. Contributor of articles and poems to magazines.

*   *   *

HARRINGTON, Jack   1918-

PERSONAL: Born May 1, 1918, in Bennington, Okla.; son of E. M. (a cowboy, farmer, and lawman) and Grace (Bell) Harrington; married Sylvia Collier, December 19, 1941; children: Mary Ann. *Education:* Southeastern State University, B.S., 1939; East Texas State University, M.S., 1946; University of Houston, Ed.D., 1954; also studied at University of Oklahoma and Arizona State University. *Politics:* Liberal Democrat. *Religion:* Baptist. *Home:* 215 South Park, San Angelo, Tex. 76901. *Office:* Department of Education, Angelo State University, San Angelo, Tex. 76901.

CAREER: Teacher of biology, chemistry, and physics in public schools in Oklahoma and Arizona, 1939-48; Blinn College, Brenham, Tex., teacher of biology, chemistry, and physics, 1948-51; Lee College, Baytown, Tex., teacher of biology, chemistry, and physics, 1951-54; Northeast Louisiana University, Monroe, professor of education, 1954-61; Angelo State University, San Angelo, Tex., professor of education and head of department, 1962—. *Military service:* U.S. Navy, 1942-45; served in Africa, Sicily, Sardinia, and Europe. *Member:* John Dewey Society, Kappa Delta Pi (counselor), Phi Delta Kappa.

WRITINGS: Aims of Education: Early Twentieth Century, MSS Information Corp., 1974. Contributor of philosophical articles to academic journals.

WORK IN PROGRESS: Researching the potential of existentialism for contemporary education and the dehumanization of man in emerging bureautechnocracy.

SIDELIGHTS: Harrington writes: "Ends and means can not be separated in education, but I am more interested in the outcomes of educational practice than in its methodology. The unconscious shapings of American youth for life in an anti-man culture are too serious to be ignored." *Avocational interests:* Reading, music, nature lore.

* * *

HARRIS, Ben Charles 1907-

PERSONAL: Born November 17, 1907, in Boston, Mass.; son of Samuel William (a musician) and Minna (a dressmaker; maiden name, Pollack) Harris; married Fannie Snyder (a secretary), February 5, 1939; children: Irwin M., Saul S., Herbert R., Alan W. *Education:* Massachusetts College of Pharmacy, Ph.G., 1930; graduate study at Clark University, 1954-55, and at Worcester State College, 1973-74. *Politics:* "Left of center Socialist." *Home and office:* 237 May St., Worcester, Mass. 01602. *Agent:* David Otte, 9 Park St., Boston, Mass.

CAREER: Webster Square Pharmacy, Worcester, Mass., owner, 1933-65; Liggett's Drug, Worcester, Mass., pharmacist, 1965-72. Herbalist and curator of economic botany at Worcester Museum of Science, 1940-62. Lecturer at Worcester County Extension Service and at Worcester State College. Writer of "Herbs for Health" feature of WTAG radio program, "Nature in New England," and of WORC radio program, "Yours for Better Health." *Member:* Society of Economic Botany, American Society of Pharmacognosy, American Natural Hygiene Society (past president of Boston chapter), Natural Foods Associates (vice-president of Massachusetts chapter, 1969-72), Massachusetts Citizens Rights Association, Boston Nutrition Society (past president). *Awards, honors:* Worcester County Horticultural Flower Show awards for outstanding herb displays.

WRITINGS: Better Health with Culinary Herbs, Christopher, 1952, new edition, Barre-Westover, 1971; *Kitchen Medicines*, Natura Publications, 1955; *Eat the Weeds*, Natura Publications, 1955; *The Compleat Herbal*, Barre-Westover, 1972; *Kitchen Tricks*, Crown, 1975. Contributor of "Herbs for Health" column to *Herald of Health*, and to *Green Revolution.*

WORK IN PROGRESS: Health Begins in the Kitchen or Ends There; *Health Rules of the Bible*; *Make Use of Your Garden Plants*, completion expected in 1976; *The Four Humors*, 1976.

SIDELIGHTS: Harris is a member of the Worcester State College Orchestra in which he plays the viola. He gives lectures and demonstrations on the use of herbs, and conducts field trips in nearby areas to identify plants and their everyday applications.

* * *

HARRIS, Frederick John 1943-

PERSONAL: Born July 29, 1943, in New York, N.Y.; son of Frederick and Anna (Guttmann) Harris. *Education:* Attended Sorbonne, University of Paris, 1963-64; Fordham University, B.A., 1965; Columbia University, M.A., 1966, Ph.D., 1969; language study at University of Grenoble, Universita Cattolica del Sacro Cuore, and University of Vienna. *Residence:* New York, N.Y. *Office:* Department of French, Fordham University, Lincoln Center, New York, N.Y. 10023.

CAREER: Columbia University, Barnard College, New York, N.Y., instructor in French, 1970; Fordham University at Lincoln Center, New York, N.Y., assistant professor of French and German, 1970—. *Member:* Modern Language Association of America, American Association of Teachers of French, Association des Amis d'Andre Gide, Phi Beta Kappa.

WRITINGS: Andre Gide and Romain Rolland: Two Men Divided, Rutgers University Press, 1973. Contributor to journals.

WORK IN PROGRESS: Research studies in French and comparative literature.

SIDELIGHTS: Harris has competence in German, Italian, Spanish, Latin, and ancient Greek.

* * *

HARRIS, Gertrude (Margaret) 1916-

PERSONAL: Born August 19, 1916, in New York, N.Y.; daughter of Louis and Sonia (Rabinowitch) Anshen; married Daniel A. Harris (a sculptor and painter), November 27, 1941. *Education:* Cornell University, student, 1936; New York University, B.A., 1938. *Home:* 763 Ocean Ave., Point Richmond, Calif. 94801. *Agent:* Hope Leresche, Hope Leresche & Steele, 11 Jubilee Pl., London SW3 3TE, England.

CAREER: Director of modern art galleries in New York, N.Y., Monterey, Calif., and Rome, Italy. Consultant to 101 Productions.

*WRITINGS—*All published by 101 Productions: (Editor) *Picnic-in-the-Point-Park Cookbook*, 1970; *Pots and Pans Etc.*, 1971, 2nd edition, 1975; *Manna: Foods of the Frontier*, 1972.

WORK IN PROGRESS: Two cookbooks on the art of creativity or invention in cooking.

SIDELIGHTS: Gertrude Harris writes: "Having lived in Europe for over twelve years—and traveling widely during that time—I realize all too well that local activities are now so widespread that a dish or a costume once (and not too long ago) known only in a small locale, is now a part of the world knowledge."

* * *

HARRIS, Michael H(ope) 1941-

PERSONAL: Born February 24, 1941, in Yankton, S.D.; son of Andrew Hope (an insurance adjustor) and Frances (Fleeger) Harris; married Linda Hexom, March 3, 1962; children: Andrew, Aimee. *Education:* Wahpeton State School of Science, A.A., 1961; University of North Dakota, B.S., 1963; University of Illinois, M.S.L.S., 1964; Indiana University, Ph.D., 1971. *Home:* 912 Lily Dr., Lexington, Ky. 40504. *Office:* College of Library Science, University of Kentucky, Lexington, Ky. 40506.

CAREER: Florida Atlantic University, Boca Raton, social sciences librarian, 1964-65; Northern Illinois University, DeKalb, assistant reference librarian, 1965-66; Indiana University, Bloomington, visiting lecturer in library science, 1967; University of Kentucky, Lexington, associate professor of library science, 1969—.

MEMBER: American Library Association, Association of American Library Schools, Intellectual Freedom Foundation, Kentucky Library Association (president, 1973), Beta Phi Mu. *Awards, honors:* Traveling fellowship from *Journal of Library History*, 1971-72; grants from Kentucky Research Foundation, 1971, from U.S. Office Education's

Right to Read Institute, 1971-72; fellowship from American Antiquarian Society, 1972; Herbert Putnam Honor Fund Award, from American Library Association, 1972.

WRITINGS: (Compiler) *Reader in American Library History*, NCR Microcard Editions Press, 1971; (compiler) *Florida History: A Bibliography*, Scarecrow, 1972; *A Guide to Research in American Library History*, Scarecrow, 1968, 2nd edition, 1974; *The Role of the Public Library in American Life: A Speculative Essay*, Graduate Library School, University of Illinois, 1975; *The Age of Jewett: Charles Coffin Jewett and American Librarianship, 1841-1868*, Libraries Unlimited, 1975.

General editor of "The Heritage of Librarianship" series, Libraries Unlimited, 1974—. Contributor of about thirty articles to library science journals. Assistant editor of *Information Storage and Retrieval*, 1968-69; member of editorial board of *College and Research Libraries*, 1972-74, and *Dictionary of American Library Biography*, 1974—; co-editor of *Advances in Librarianship*, 1974—.

WORK IN PROGRESS: Books on the Frontier: The Availability of Books and the Nature of Bookownership in the Ohio Valley, 1800-1865; The Impact of Print on American History; a book demonstrating the impact of print on behavior; preparing *The Checklist of American Imprints for 1860-1870*, with wife, Linda Harris; preparing third edition of *History of Libraries in the Western World*, by Elmer D. Johnson; *A Social History of the American Public Library*.

SIDELIGHTS: Harris writes: "My work has two main focuses . . . I am very interested in the ways in which reading influences human behavior . . . these studies cover . . . the nature and extent of book ownership on the American frontier; the impact of the printed work on major social and political movements in nineteenth century America; the construction of a series of case studies. . . . The second focus of my work is upon the history of the library in America."

* * *

HARRIS, Patricia

PERSONAL: Born in Bartlesville, Okla.; daughter of Warren Eugene (a newspaper editor) and Victoria (a county court reporter; maiden name, Fournier) Milligan; married Richard Willard Harris (a newspaper copy editor), October, 1957; children: Barbara Anne. *Education:* Attended high school in Bartlesville, Okla. *Politics:* Independent. *Religion:* Roman Catholic. *Office:* State Department of Education, Cordell Hull Building, Nashville, Tenn. 37219.

CAREER: International News Service, Springfield, Ill., reporter, 1945-46, manager of Springfield Bureau, 1946-52; State Department of Education, News Bureau, Nashville, Tenn., assistant editor, 1965—.

WRITINGS: Adlai: The Springfield Years, Aurora, 1975. Contributor to newspapers.

WORK IN PROGRESS: Trapped: The Saga of Floyd Collins, with husband, Richard Willard Harris, and daughter, Barbara Anne Harris.

SIDELIGHTS: Patricia Harris writes: "I was graduated from high school at the age of sixteen and immediately left for Chicago with an eighteen-year-old sister and a twelve-year-old sister. We had careers in mind—radio script writing, news reporting and singing. After a year of grim struggle which produced hilarious results on occasion, we returned to our home town of Bartlesville, Oklahoma, to seek another way out of the dead-end jobs for which we had been ticketed by an implacable educational system.

"I worked variously as a stenographer, typist, receptionist, errand girl, advertising copywriter, public relations director, presidential campaign aide, news reporter and all-round workhorse in Chicago, Dallas, Tulsa, Oklahoma City, Memphis, Wichita Falls (Texas), Carthage (Missouri), Denver, Greenville (Texas), Muskogee (Oklahoma) and Nashville (Tennessee)."

* * *

HARRISON, Allan E(ugene) 1925-

PERSONAL: Born September 13, 1925, in Tucson, Ariz.; son of Frank and Evelyn (Gower) Harrison; married Marjorie Sultzbaugh (a bank teller), June 22, 1945; children: Dian, Frank, Allan A., James. *Education:* San Jose State College (now San Jose State University), B.A., 1949; graduate study at University of Santa Clara, 1950. *Religion:* Protestant. *Home:* 21863 Brill Rd., Riverside, Calif. 92508.

CAREER: Elementary school teacher in Moreno Valley Unified School District, 1959-74. *Military service:* U.S. Air Force, 1943; became captain. U.S. Air Force Reserve, 1959.

WRITINGS: How to Teach Children Twice As Much, Arlington House, 1973.

WORK IN PROGRESS: How to Raise Children for a Profit at Home.

SIDELIGHTS: Harrison writes: "I want to instill self-reliance in children. This is sadly lacking today and really apparent. When its achievement can be so easy it's almost a crime to ignore the simple tools available to every parent and teacher."

* * *

HARRISON, Cynthia Ellen 1946-

PERSONAL: Born October 29, 1946, in Brooklyn, N.Y.; daughter of Herbert (a salesman) and Jean (a secretary; maiden name, Hacken) Harrison; married Richard J. Peppin (an engineer), August 9, 1970. *Education:* Brooklyn College of the City University of New York, B.A., 1966; Columbia University, M.S.L.S., 1967, doctoral study, 1973—. *Religion:* Jewish. *Home:* 1711 West Wind Way, McLean, Va. 22101.

CAREER: Brooklyn Public Library, Brooklyn, N.Y., librarian, 1967-70; McMaster University, Hamilton, Ontario, librarian, 1970-72; writer, 1972—. *Member:* American Historical Association, Organization of American Historians, National Organization for Women.

WRITINGS: (Compiler) *A Subject Guide to Indexes to Periodicals Held by McMaster University Libraries* (pamphlet), McMaster University Library Press, 1971; *Women in Canada, 1965-1972: A Bibliography* (booklet), McMaster University Library Press, 1972; (editor) *Women's Movement Media: A Source Guide*, Bowker, 1975. Contributor to feminist periodicals.

WORK IN PROGRESS: Research on John F. Kennedy's public policy toward women.

SIDELIGHTS: Cynthia Harrison writes: "My writing has been motivated by my interest in feminism. Since I am now studying for a doctorate in twentieth-century American history, I expect future writings to be devoted to women in American history."

* * *

HARRISS, Joseph 1936-

PERSONAL: Born March 19, 1936, in Galveston, Tex.;

son of Joseph B. (an electronics engineer) and Bivian (Arnold) Harriss; married Claudie Meunier, December 24, 1970; children: Christopher. *Education:* University of Notre Dame, A.B. (cum laude), 1958; Sorbonne, University of Paris, certificat de langue francaise, 1959; also studied at Institut d'Etudes Politiques, 1962. *Politics:* None. *Religion:* None. *Home:* 52 Avenue Bosquet, Paris 75007, France. *Agent:* Philip Spitzer, 111-25 76th Ave., Forest Hills, N.Y. 11375. *Office: Reader's Digest,* 216 Blvd. St.-Germain, Paris 75007, France.

CAREER: Time (magazine), New York, N.Y., correspondent from Paris, Algiers, and Brussels, 1963-69; *Reader's Digest,* Pleasantville, N.Y., associate editor in European office in Paris, France, 1969—. *Military service:* U.S. Air Force, information officer, 1959-62; became first lieutenant. *Member:* Anglo-American Press Association (Paris).

WRITINGS: The Tallest Tower: Eiffel and the Belle Epoque, Houghton, 1975. Contributor to *Time, New Republic,* and *New York Times.*

* * *

HARTMAN, Chester W(arren) 1936-

PERSONAL: Born April 12, 1936, in New York, N.Y.; son of Irving L. (an importer) and Dorothy (Friedman) Hartman. *Education:* Harvard University, A.B., 1957, Ph.D., 1967. *Home:* 360 Elizabeth St., San Francisco, Calif. 94114.

CAREER: Special Commission on Low Income Housing, Commonwealth of Massachusetts, director, 1964-65; Institute for Policy Studies, Washington, D.C., associate fellow, 1966-67; Harvard University, Cambridge, Mass., assistant professor of urban planning, 1966-70, member of Massachusetts Institute of Technology-Harvard Joint Center for Urban Studies, 1966-69; University of California, Berkeley, senior planning associate, 1970-74, lecturer in urban planning, 1970-74. Visiting lecturer at Yale University, 1967-68. Consultant to Office of Economic Opportunity, Department of Housing and Urban Development, Institute of Public Administration, New England Regional Commission, Urban Coalition, U.S. Civil Rights Commission, Joint Economic Committee of the U.S. Congress, Puerto Rican Urban Renewal and Housing Administration, and Stanford Research Institute. Co-chairman of Massachusetts Committee on Discrimination in Housing, 1965-67; member of board of directors of Urban Planning Aid, 1966-70, Citizens Housing and Planning Association of Metropolitan Boston, 1968-70, and Boston Architectural Center, 1969-70; member of advisory committee of Massachusetts Housing Finance Agency, 1969-70; member of San Francisco Housing Planning Committee, 1973. *Military service:* U.S. Army, 1960.

WRITINGS: (Editor with Jon Pynoos and Robert Schafer) *Housing Urban America,* Aldine-Atherton, 1973; (with Marc Fried and others) *The World of the Urban Working Class,* Harvard University Press, 1973; *Yerba Buena: Land Grab and Community Resistance in San Francisco,* Glide, 1974; *Housing and Social Policy,* Prentice-Hall, 1975. Contributor to *Boston Globe, Dissent, Reporter,* and to legal and planning journals.

WORK IN PROGRESS: Research on the Bay Area Rapid Transit (BART) system.

* * *

HARTMAN, Shirley 1929-

PERSONAL: Born November 15, 1929, in Cincinnati,

Ohio; daughter of Albert Hugo (a sales executive) and Eleanor (Smith) Hartman. *Education:* Attended University of Cincinnati. *Religion:* Presbyterian. *Residence:* North Hollywood, Calif. *Agent:* William Morris Agency, 1350 Avenue of the Americas, New York, N.Y. 10019.

CAREER: Ad-Vance Advertising Agency, Cincinnati, Ohio, publicity and copy writer, 1943-47; *Your Host* (weekly entertainment magazine), Cincinnati, founder and editor, 1948-55; Walt Disney Productions, Burbank, Calif., member of staff, 1958-61; Parthenon Pictures, Los Angeles, Calif., associate producer, 1961-65; assistant to producer Ross Hunter, 1965-73; full-time author, 1973—.

WRITINGS: (With Walter Ellerbeck) *The Surgeons* (novel), McKay, 1975.

WORK IN PROGRESS: Two novels.

SIDELIGHTS: Shirley Hartman, commenting on *The Surgeons,* once told a *Writer* interviewer: "I feel very strongly that even in fiction, if the author presents an idea as a fact, the reader has a right to take it as gospel. I was intrigued with what *really* happened under a certain set of medical circumstances, what the inside scoop was about rumors I'd heard [Ms. Hartman had been hospitalized for a surgical illness], about the power plays, the conflicts and the personal problems of the dedicated men in green.... Then I discovered that physicians are conditioned to be reticent about the 'in' happenings concerning their profession and colleagues, so it took questioning, badgering and cajoling to get the good doctor to open up. Not a single scene or word of dialogue can be labeled anything but authentic in *The Surgeons.*" Research was often necessary, continued Ms. Hartman, "even when you have a living, walking research source as your co-writer" (Walter Ellerback is a surgeon).

AVOCATIONAL INTERESTS: Animals, country and western music, movies, travel, poker.

BIOGRAPHICAL/CRITICAL SOURCES: Writer, November 23, 1974.

* * *

HARTSUCH, Paul Jackson 1902-

PERSONAL: Born September 17, 1902, in Kendallville, Ind.; son of George Wesley (an accountant) and Agnes (Ritter) Hartsuch; married Lucile Grover, July 2, 1925; children: Grover, George. *Education:* Michigan Agricultural College (now Michigan State University), B.S., 1924; University of Chicago, M.S., 1930, Ph.D., 1935. *Religion:* Protestant. *Home:* 334 South Kensington Ave., La Grange, Ill. 60525. *Office: Graphic Arts Monthly,* 222 South Riverside Plaza, Chicago, Ill. 60606.

CAREER: Case School of Applied Science (now Case Western Reserve University), Cleveland, Ohio, instructor in chemical engineering, 1927-33; St. Lukes Hospital, Chicago, Ill., Seymour Coman fellow in medical research, 1934-38; Central YMCA Community College, Chicago, Ill., associate professor of chemistry, 1938-45, chairman of department, 1944-45; Graphic Arts Technical Foundation, Chicago, Ill., assistant to research director, 1945-50; Inmont Corp., Chicago, Ill., lithographic consultant in Printing Ink Division, 1950-59; Graphic Arts Technical Foundation, assistant to research director, 1959-65; *Graphic Arts Monthly,* Chicago, Ill., editor, 1965—. *Member:* International Association of Printing House Craftsmen, Technical Association of the Graphic Arts (president, 1955-56), Graphic Arts Technical Foundation (fellow), Lithographers Club of Chicago.

WRITINGS: Chemistry of Lithography, Graphic Arts Technical Foundation, 1952, 2nd edition, 1960; *Think Metric Now!*, Follett, 1974.

AVOCATIONAL INTERESTS: Travel (Europe, Australia, Thailand, Hong Kong, Taiwan, Japan).

* * *

HARVARD, Stephen 1948-

PERSONAL: Born March 16, 1948, in Rochester, Minn.; son of B. Marvin (a physician) and Anne Carson (Kilpatrick) Harvard; married Paula McLain (a weaver), April 22, 1972; children: Shelagh. *Education:* Dartmouth College, B.A. (cum laude), 1970. *Home address:* Lost Nation Rd., Lancaster, N.H.

CAREER: Stone cutter in Newport, R.I., 1970-72; book designer, calligrapher, and illustrator, 1972—. *Member:* Phi Beta Kappa. *Awards, honors:* Three book designs named to American Institute of Graphic Arts "Fifty best books of the year," 1974.

WRITINGS: Ornamental Initials, Godine, 1975.

* * *

HARVEY, Virginia I(sham) 1917-

PERSONAL: Born July 5, 1917, in Hot Springs, S.D.; daughter of Russell R. (a veterinarian) and Goldie (a nurse; maiden name, Coles) Isham; married William A. Harvey, August 27, 1937; children: William A., Jr., Russell W. *Education:* Attended Mills College, and University of Washington, Seattle. *Address:* P.O. Box 468, Freeland, Wash. 98249.

CAREER: University of Washington, School of Home Economics, Seattle, curator of costume and textile study collection, 1958—; H.T.H. Publishers, Santa Ana, Calif., vice-president and editor, 1973—. *Member:* Handweavers Guild of America, Pacific Northwest Needle Arts Association, Northwest Designer Craftsmen (secretary, 1962), Seattle Weavers' Guild (president, 1956-57), Lambda Rho.

WRITINGS: Macrame: The Art of Creative Knotting, Van Nostrand, 1967; (with Harriet Tidball) *Weft Twining*, Shuttlecraft Guild, 1968; *Color and Design in Macrame*, Van Nostrand, 1970; *The Techniques of Basketry*, Van Nostrand, 1974. Contributor to periodicals. Editor of *Threads in Action*, 1968-74.

WORK IN PROGRESS: Two monographs, *Split-Ply Twining* and *Porcupine Quill Embroidery*; a series of monographs for Shuttlecraft Guild, *The Bateman Weaves*.

* * *

HARWELL, Ann (Manning) J(ohnson) 1936-

PERSONAL: Born December 25, 1936, in Delphi, Ind.; daughter of Myron J. (a newspaper publisher) and Eileen (Rahilly) Johnson; married Rolly M. Harwell, December 23, 1959 (divorced, February, 1972); children: Sarah Coleman, Mary Vincent, Ross Marks. *Education:* DePauw University, B.A., 1958; Vanderbilt University, M.A.T., 1959, graduate study, 1962-63. *Home:* 2875 South High St., Denver, Colo. 80210. *Office:* Libraries Unlimited, Inc., 6931 South Yosemite, Englewood, Colo.

CAREER: Teacher of French, Punahou Schools, Honolulu, Hawaii, 1959-60; Vanderbilt University Press, Nashville, Tenn., assistant to director, 1960-61; self-employed, 1961-62; University of Alabama, University, instructor in French, 1963-68; self-employed, 1968-71; Libraries Unlim-

ited, Inc., Englewood, Colo., editor, 1971—. *Member:* Phi Beta Kappa.

WRITINGS: (Editor) *Guide to Living High in Colorado*, United Banks of Colorado, 1973; (with Rolly M. Harwell) *Crafts for Today*, Libraries Unlimited, 1974.

* * *

HATCH, Alden 1898-1975

September 26, 1898—February 1, 1975; American biographer, journalist, historian, and author. Obituaries: *Washington Post*, February 2, 1975; *AB Bookman's Weekly*, February 17, 1975; *Publishers Weekly*, March 3, 1975.

* * *

HAUERWAS, Stanley Martin 1940-

PERSONAL: Born July 24, 1940, in Dallas, Tex.; son of Coffee Martin (a bricklayer) and Gertrude (Berry) Hauerwas; married Anne Harley (in crafts), December 29, 1962; children: Adam John. *Education:* Southwestern University, B.A., 1962; Yale University, B.D., 1965, M.A., M.Phil., Ph.D. *Politics:* Radical. *Religion:* Christian. *Home:* 210 East Pokagon, South Bend, Ind. *Office:* Department of Theology, University of Notre Dame, Notre Dame, Ind. 46556.

CAREER: Augustana College, Rock Island, Ill., assistant professor of theology, 1968-70; University of Notre Dame, Notre Dame, Ind., associate professor of theology, 1970—. Member of board of directors of St. Joseph County Council for the Retarded, 1973-76. *Member:* American Association of Religion, American Society of Christian Ethics, Society for Religion and Higher Education.

WRITINGS: Vision and Virtue: Essays in Theological Ethics, Fides, 1974; *Character and the Christian Life: A Study in Theological Ethics*, University of Trinity Press, 1975. Associate editor of *Encyclopedia of Bioethics*, 1973-76.

WORK IN PROGRESS: Research on the ethics of marriage.

* * *

HAUGH, Richard 1942-

PERSONAL: Born May 4, 1942, in Boston, Mass.; son of Victor Stanley (a businessman) and Marion Haugh; married Vera Verhovskoy (a translator), June 26, 1965; children: Alexandra, Andrew, Peter. *Education:* University of Massachusetts, B.A., 1965; Andover Newton Theological School, M.A., 1968; Fordham University, Ph.D., 1973. *Religion:* Greek Orthodox. *Home:* 74 President St., New Rochelle, N.Y. 10801. *Agent:* Robert Nilson, 48 Elizabeth Jean Drive, Falmouth, Mass. 02536. *Office:* Department of Humanities, Iona College, New Rochelle, N.Y.

CAREER: High school teacher of German and English in Boston, Mass., 1966, Brookline, Mass., 1966-68; Academy of Aeronautics, Flushing, N.Y., assistant professor of literature, 1968-71; Iona College, New Rochelle, N.Y., assistant professor of religious studies, 1971-75, visiting professor of humanities, 1975—. *Member:* Mediaeval Academy of America, Society for the Scientific Study of Religion, Society of American Orthodox Theologians, Association of Russian-American Scholars (member of board of directors, 1970—), Norwegian-American Historical Association.

WRITINGS: (Editor with John B. Dunlop and Alexis

Klimoff, and contributor) *Aleksandr Solzhenitsyn: Critical Essays and Documentary Material*, Volume I, Nordland, 1973, enlarged edition, Macmillan, 1975; *Photius and the Carolingians: The Trinitarian Controversy*, Nordland, 1975; (co-translator) George P. Fedotov, *St. Filipp: Metropolitan of Moscow*, Nordland, 1975. Contributor to journals in his field. Editor, *Transactions*, 1970—.

WORK IN PROGRESS: John Cassian and Augustine; *Augustine and Eastern Christianity*; *The "Libri Carolini"*; *Dostoevsky: A Critique of Criticism*; editing *The Collected Works of George Florovsky*; co-editing a second volume of Solzhenitsyn criticism.

* * *

HAWKINS, Odie 1937-

PERSONAL: Born July 6, 1937, in Chicago, Ill.; son of Odie and Lillian (Trice) Hawkins; children: Erika. *Education:* Attended Wilson Junior College, 1956-57. *Home:* 5159 Clinton Street, Los Angeles, Calif. 90004. *Agent:* Robinson-Weintraub, 554 South San Vincente, Los Angeles, Calif. 90048.

CAREER: U.S. Post Office, Chicago, Ill., mail clerk, 1958-66; Veterans Administration, Los Angeles, Calif., mail clerk and messenger, 1966-67; Beverly Hilton Hotel, Beverly Hills, Calif., busboy, 1967-68; Century City, Beverly Hills, Calif., stockboy, 1968-69; full-time writer. Teacher at Watts Writer's Workshops in Southern Calif. *Military service:* U.S. Army, 1962-64. *Member:* Writers Guild (West).

WRITINGS: Ghetto Sketches, Holloway House, 1972. Contributor of script to the "Sanford and Son," television series. Contributor to *Presence Africain*.

WORK IN PROGRESS: The Avon Journal I & II, a surrealistic exercise in world understanding; three novels, *The Whirl of Willie O. Jenkins*, *A Brother Named Wright*, and *The Ghetto Jet Set*.

SIDELIGHTS: Hawkins told *CA*: "Being able to write has given me, an Afro-American with little formal education, or anything else, a chance to imagine myself beyond the white man's overwhelming odds."

* * *

HAWLEY, Isabel Lockwood 1935-

PERSONAL: Born February 8, 1935, in Wilmington, Del.; daughter of William Howard and Elizabeth Allen Lockwood; married Robert C. Hawley, August 22, 1964; children: two. *Education:* Randolph-Macon Woman's College, B.A., 1956; University of North Carolina, M.A., 1962, Ph.D., 1970. *Home:* 4 Amherst Rd., R.R. #2, Amherst, Mass. 01002. *Office:* Education Research Associates Press, Amherst, Mass. 01002.

CAREER: High school teacher of English in the public and private schools of Wynnewood, Pa., 1956-58, Honolulu, Hawaii, 1958-60, and Waterbury, Conn., 1964-70; University of Massachusetts, Cooperative School Service Center, Amherst, instructor in English, 1971; Education Research Associates, Amherst, Mass., associate director, 1972—, and executive editor of ERS Press, 1972—. Member of board of trustees of Amherst Montessori School, 1973—, and The Common School, 1974—. *Member:* League of Women Voters.

WRITINGS—All with husband, Robert C. Hawley: *A Handbook of Personal Growth Activities for Classroom Use*, Education Research Associates Press, 1972; *Writing for the Fun of It*, Education Research Associates Press, 1974; *Human Values in the Classroom: A Handbook for Teachers*, Hart Publishing, 1975; *Developing Human Potential: A Handbook of Activities for Personal and Social Growth*, Education Research Associates Press, 1975. Contributor to education journals.

WORK IN PROGRESS: Common Sense Composition, a teacher's handbook on helping students improve their written communication.

* * *

HAWLEY, Robert Coit 1933-

PERSONAL: Born September 18, 1933, in Nevada, Iowa; married Isabel Allen Lockwood; children: two. *Education:* Bowdoin College, A.B., 1955; Wesleyan University, M.A.L.S., 1968; University of Massachusetts, Ed.D., 1972. *Office:* Education Research Associates, 4 Amherst Rd., Amherst, Mass. 01002.

CAREER: English teacher in elementary school in Washington, Conn., 1957-61 (chairman of department, 1959-61), and Waterbury, Conn., 1961-70 (head of department, 1961-70; assistant headmaster, 1964-70); University of Massachusetts, Amherst, part-time instructor in education, 1970-72; Education Research Associates, Amherst, Mass., director, 1972—. Member of adjunct faculty at Goddard College, 1974—.

WRITINGS: (With wife, Isabel L. Hawley) *A Handbook of Personal Growth Activities for Classroom Use*, ERA Press, 1972; *Human Values in the Classroom: Teaching for Personal and Social Growth*, ERA Press, 1973; (with S. B. Simon and D. D. Britton) *Composition for Personal Growth: Values Clarification through Writing*, Hart Publishing, 1973; (with Isabel L. Hawley) *Writing for the Fun of It*, ERA Press, 1974; *Value Exploration through Role Playing: Practical Strategies for Use in the Classroom*, Hart Publishing, 1975; (with Isabel L. Hawley) *Human Values in the Classroom: A Handbook for Teachers*, Hart Publishing, 1975. Contributor of more than ten articles and reviews to education journals, including *Instructor, School Counselor, Independent School Bulletin, Teacher, Teacher Paper, Goddard Journal*, and *Classical World*.

* * *

HAYES, Alden C(ary) 1916-

PERSONAL: Born January 11, 1916, in Englewood, N.J.; son of Cary Walker (a sociologist) and Joy (Mauck) Hayes; married Gretchen Greenamyer, February 6, 1941; children: Eric, Marc. *Education:* University of New Mexico, B.A., 1939. *Address:* S.S. Box 203A, Corrales, N.M. 87048. *Address:* Box 26176, Chaco Center, National Park Service, Albuquerque, N.M. 87125.

CAREER: Archaeologist for Texas and Tennessee State Surveys, 1939-41; self-employed rancher in Cochise Co., Ariz., 1941-57; National Park Service, archaeologist in Arizona, 1957—. Member of Albuquerque Historic Landmark Survey. *Military service:* U.S. Army, 1942-45, 1950-52; served in European Theatre. *Member:* Society for American Archaeology, Archaeological Society of New Mexico (member of board of trustees, 1973—).

WRITINGS: Archaeological Survey of Wetherill Mesa, National Park Service, 1964; *The Four Churches of Pecos*, University of New Mexico Press, 1974; (with James A. Lancaster) *Badger House Community: Mesa Verde Na-*

tional Park, National Park Service, in press; *The Excavation of Mound 7: Gran Quivira*, National Park Service, in press. Contributor of archaeological articles to journals.

SIDELIGHTS: Hayes writes that he is "a regionalist, interested in all aspects of life and land, flora and fauna, history and folklore of the Southwest."

* * *

HAYES, Paul J(ames) 1922-

PERSONAL: Born September 26, 1922, in West Orange, N.J.; son of James Edward (a plumber) and Teresa (Meyers) Hayes. *Education:* Seton Hall University, A.B., 1944; Immaculate Conception Seminary, graduate study, 1944-48. *Home:* 111 South St., New Providence, N.J. 07974.

CAREER: Ordained Roman Catholic priest, 1948; named monsignor in 1965. Assistant pastor of Roman Catholic church in Newark, N.J., 1948-51; National Catholic Office for Motion Pictures, New York, N.Y., assistant executive secretary, 1953-57; Archdiocese of Newark, Newark, N.J., assistant director of Communications Office, 1957-65, director, 1965—; pastor of Roman Catholic church in Jersey City, N.J., 1969-75, and New Providence, N.J., 1975—. Chaplain of Roman Catholic high school in East Orange, N.J., 1959—.

WRITINGS: (With brother, Edward J. Hayes) *Three Keys to Happiness*, Society of Saint Paul, 1952; (with E. J. Hayes) *The Catholic Church and Race Relations* (pamphlet), America Press, 1953; (with E. J. Hayes) *Love for a Lifetime*, Society of Saint Paul, 1955; (with E. J. Hayes and Dorothy E. Kelly) *Moral Handbook of Nursing*, Macmillan, 1956; (with E. J. Hayes and Kelly) *Moral Principles of Nursing*, Macmillan, 1964; (with E. J. Hayes) *Catholicism and Reason*, Our Sunday Visitor Press, 1973; *Catholicism and Society*, Our Sunday Visitor Press, 1975.

Author of pamphlets published by Paulist Press, Catholic Information Society, and Catechetical Guild Educational Society. Writer of films produced by United World Films, 1950: "The Holy Sacrifice of the Mass," "Gateway to the Faith," and "The King's Highway." Contributor to religious magazines. Editor, *Comment: Media Today.*

WORK IN PROGRESS: Catholicsm and Life, for Our Sunday Visitor Press.

* * *

HAYNES, Betsy 1937-

PERSONAL: Born October 20, 1937, in Benton, Ill.; daughter of Paul DeWitte (a musician) and Marounah Lee (a secretary; maiden name, Phillips) Shadle; married James Monroe Haynes (a manager for General Telephone and Electronics Corp.), October 8, 1960; children: Craig Johnasen, Stephanie Jo. *Education:* Attended University of Illinois, 1955-57; Southern Illinois University, B.Journalism, 1962. *Home:* 116 Hunter Rd., Fairfield, Conn. 06430.

CAREER: Writer. Has worked as clerk, switchboard operator, insurance claims examiner, classified advertising manager for a newspaper, and secretary. *Member:* Authors Guild of Authors League of America, Society of Children's Book Writers.

WRITINGS: Cowslip (juvenile), Nelson, 1973, published in paperback form as *Slave Girl*, Scholastic Book Services, 1973; *Spies on the Devil's Belt* (juvenile), Nelson, 1974.

WORK IN PROGRESS: A novel set in Okefenokee Swamp.

SIDELIGHTS: Betsy Haynes writes: "As a writer of historical fiction for young people in these days of rapid advance and transition, I believe that it is important to help children see themselves as a part of the whole historical perspective, not just the future but the past as well."

* * *

HAYNES, Sybille 1926-

PERSONAL: Born July 3, 1926, in Leverkusen, Germany; daughter of Julius (an author) and Edith (an orientalist; maiden name, Kloeppel) Overhoff; married Denys Haynes (a keeper of antiquities at British Museum), January 18, 1951. *Education:* Attended University of Munich, 1950; University of Frankfurt, B.A. (honors), 1951, Ph.D. (summa cum laude), 1951. *Home:* 24 Hereford Sq., London SW7 4TS, London, England; and Merle Cottage, Dean near Charlbury, Oxfordshire, England. *Office:* British Museum, London W.C.1, England.

CAREER: British Museum, London, England, classical archaeologist specializing in Etruscology in Greek and Roman Department, 1951—. *Member:* Institute of Etruscan and Italic Studies (foreign member).

WRITINGS: Etruscan Bronze Utensils, British Museum, 1965; *Etruscan Sculpture*, British Museum, 1970; *Land of the Chimaera: An Archaeological Excursion in Southwest Turkey*, Chatto & Windus, 1974. Contributor to scholarly journals in Europe and America.

WORK IN PROGRESS: Research on Etruscan and general archaeology.

AVOCATIONAL INTERESTS: Travel, languages.

* * *

HAYSTEAD, Wesley 1942-

PERSONAL: Born April 11, 1942, in New York, N.Y.; son of Kenneth Mark (a minister) and Gladys (Brown) Haystead; married Judy DeVries, July 24, 1964 (divorced, 1973); children: Karen. *Education:* Cascade College, B.A., 1964; University of Southern California, M.S.Ed., 1974. *Religion:* Christian. *Home:* 119 South California, #23, San Gabriel, Calif. 91776. *Office:* Gospel Light Publications, 110 West Broadway, Glendale, Calif. 91204.

CAREER: Truck driver in Portland, Ore., 1960-62, elevator operator, 1962-63; minister of education for Assembly of God churches in Portland, Ore., 1964-65, and Alhambra, Calif., 1965-72; Gospel Light Publications, Glendale, Calif., writer and editor, 1973—. Early childhood coordinator for International Center for Learning, 1970—.

WRITINGS: Ways to Plan and Organize Your Sunday School: Early Childhood, Gospel Light Publications, 1971; *You Can't Begin Too Soon*, Gospel Light Publications, 1974. Contributor to education and religious magazines.

SIDELIGHTS: Haystead writes: "The major concern of my work is to help upgrade the quality of Christian education, particularly as it is conducted within the structure of local congregations. This work includes writing and conducting seminars for lay teachers...." *Avocational interests:* Bicycling, motorcycling.

* * *

HAYTON, Richard Neil 1916-
(Thomas Starling)

PERSONAL: Born November 25, 1916, in Pine Bluff, Ark.; son of Richard Raymond (a carpenter) and Ruth

Naomi (Owens) Hayton; married Virginia Ann Ridenour (an administration specialist), April 18, 1943; children: Richard Neil, Jr., Stephen Brian. *Education:* Attended Louisiana State University, Northeast Center, 1935; University of Maryland, B.S., 1955; George Washington University, M.A., 1956. *Politics:* "Marxist-Leninist." *Religion:* "Humanist." *Residence:* Baltimore, Md. *Office address:* P.O. Box 3252, Catonsville, Md. 21228.

CAREER: U.S. Air Force, career officer, 1940-60, retiring as major; free-lance writer, 1960—. During military career served in European theater, 1943-45, Anchorage, Alaska, 1950-52, and Tokyo, Japan and Honolulu, Hawaii, 1956-58. *Member:* Committee of Small Magazine Editors and Publishers.

WRITINGS: The King and the Cat (satirical novel), Spindrift Press, 1975. Contributor of military histories, articles, and stories to little magazines; contributor of essays, under pseudonym Thomas Starling, to *Churchman, Progressive World,* and *John Milton Magazine.*

WORK IN PROGRESS: Ringling Hall, a satirical novel based on personal experiences and observations before and during World War II; a futuristic novel, *The South Will Rise Again;* a collection of essays, *An Intellectual Safari.*

SIDELIGHTS: Hayton writes: "During military career edited publications and did historical research, while thinking subversive thoughts about the idiocy of it all. Goal as a writer is to create social satire of the first rank, in the hope of helping to illuminate our way of life as others have done for their times and places." He believes ". . . with Voltaire that exposing the follies and foibles of nations is the essence of true comedy." *Avocational interests:* Studying German and French, jogging, gardening, chess, observing the "human tragicomedy."

* * *

HAYWARD, Jack 1931-

PERSONAL: Born August 18, 1931, in Shanghai, China; son of Menahem (a businessman) and Stella (Isaac) Hayward; married Margaret Glenn, December 14, 1965; children: Clare, Alan. *Education:* London School of Economics and Political Science, B.Sc., 1952, Ph.D., 1958; graduate study at Institute of Political Studies, Paris, 1952-53, and Sorbonne, University of Paris, 1955-56. *Politics:* Liberal socialist. *Religion:* Agnostic. *Home:* "Hurstwood," Church Lane, Kirkella, Humberside, England. *Agent:* A. P. Watt & Sons, 26-28 Bedford Row, London W.C.1, England. *Office:* Department of Politics, University of Hull, Cottingham Rd., Hull HU6 7RX, England.

CAREER: University of Sheffield, Sheffield, England, lecturer in politics, 1959-63; University of Keele, Staffordshire, England, lecturer, 1963-68, senior lecturer in politics, 1969-73; University of Hull, Hull, England, professor of politics, 1973—. Senior research fellow at Nuffield College, Oxford, 1968-69. *Military service:* Royal Air Force, 1956-58; became flying officer. *Member:* Association for Franco-British Political Studies (chairman, 1974—), Political Studies Association of the United Kingdom (chairman, 1975—).

WRITINGS: Private Interests and Public Policy, Longmans, Green, 1966; *The One and Indivisible French Republic,* Weidenfeld & Nicolson, 1973; (editor with Michael Watson) *Planning Politics and Public Policy: The British, French, and Italian Experience,* Cambridge University Press, 1975. Contributor to *Parliamentary Affairs, Political*

Studies, Government and Opposition, and *Comparative Politics.*

WORK IN PROGRESS: A study of employee association-government relations in Britain and France.

AVOCATIONAL INTERESTS: Listening to classical and pre-classical music, gardening, walking.

* * *

HEALEY, James Stewart 1931-

PERSONAL: Born July 14, 1931, in Chicago, Ill.; son of James Alfred (a hotel manager) and Bernice Nellie Healey; married Evelyn Jewel Murphy (a school librarian), August 10, 1958; children: James, Siobhan, Kathleen. *Education:* Stonehill College, B.A., 1955; Simmons College, M.S.L.S., 1958; Columbia University, D.L.S., 1973. *Politics:* Democrat. *Religion:* Roman Catholic. *Home:* 30 Carriage Hill Rd., North Kingston, R.I. 02852. *Office:* Graduate Library School, University of Rhode Island, 74 Lower College Rd., Kingston, R.I. 02881.

CAREER: Free Public Library, New Bedford, Mass., city librarian, 1961-68; University of Rhode Island, Kingston, assistant professor, 1968-74, associate professor of library science, 1974—. Chief of Division of Library Extension Services of Rhode Island Department of State Library Services, 1967-68; chairman of Committee on Standards for Rhode Island Public Libraries, 1973. *Member:* American Library Association, New England Library Association, Rhode Island Library Association.

WRITINGS: John E. Fogarty: Political Leadership for Library Development, Scarecrow, 1974. Contributor to *Wilson Library Bulletin, Library Journal, Journal for the Education for Librarianship, Bay State Librarian, Journal of the American Society of Information Science,* and *College and Research Libraries.*

WORK IN PROGRESS: Library Administration: A Guide to the Real World, a textbook; a chapter for centennial anniversary volume of American Library Association; two biographical sketches for *Dictionary of American Library Biography.*

* * *

HEATER, Derek (Benjamin) 1931-

PERSONAL: Born November 28, 1931, in London, England; son of Benjamin Lawrence (a shop manager) and Enid (Nunn) Heater; married Joyce Dean (a teacher), March 31, 1956; children: Jane Elizabeth, Michael John Benjamin. *Education:* University of London, B.A. (honors), 1953, postgraduate certificate in education, 1954. *Home:* 16 Cornwall Gardens, Brighton, Sussex BN1 6RJ, England. *Office:* Department of History, Brighton College of Education, Falmer, Brighton BN1 9PH, England.

CAREER: Assistant teacher in boys' schools in Leyton, England, 1957-59, and Buckhurst Hill, England, 1959-62; Brighton College of Education, Brighton, England, lecturer in history, 1962—, head of department, 1966—. *Military service:* Royal Air Force, education officer at Joint Air Reconnaissance Intelligence Center, 1954-57; became flight lieutenant. *Member:* Historical Association, Politics Association (founder and chairman, 1969-73).

WRITINGS: Political Ideas in the Modern World, Barnes & Noble, 1960, 4th edition, 1971; *Order and Rebellion: A History of Europe in the Eighteenth Century,* Harrap, 1964; *The Cold War,* Oxford University Press, 1965, 2nd edition, 1969; (editor and contributor) *The Teaching of Politics*, Barnes & Noble, 1969; (with Gwyneth Owen) *World Affairs*, Harrap, 1972, 2nd edition, two volumes, 1975; *Contemporary Political Ideas*, Longman, 1974; *History Teaching and Political Education* (pamphlet), Politics Association, 1974; *Britain and the Outside World*, Longman, in press.

Contributor: J. L. Henderson, editor, *Since 1945*, Methuen, 1966, 2nd edition, 1971; Martin Ballard, editor, *New Movements in the Study and Teaching of History*, University of Indiana Press, 1970; Michael Raggett and Malcolm Clarkson, editors, *The Middle Years Curriculum*, Ward, Lock, 1974; Tom Brennan and Jonathan Brown, editors, *Teaching Politics: Problems and Perspectives*, British Broadcasting Corp., 1974; T. Brennan, editor, *Schools Council General Studies Report Collection: Politics*, Longman, 1974.

General editor, with Bernard Crick, of "Political Realities," a series, Longman, 1974—. Contributor to history and education journals, including *Teaching History, History, Political Quarterly, Education for Teaching, Teaching Politics, Trends in Education, Timely Issues in Education*, and *Royal Air Force Quarterly*. Editor of *Teaching Politics* (journal of the Politics Association), 1973—.

WORK IN PROGRESS: A book on teaching world studies, completion expected in 1977; a survey of British research in teaching international studies.

* * *

HEDGES, Elaine R(yan) 1927-

PERSONAL: Born August 18, 1927, in Yonkers, N.Y.; daughter of John A. (an auditor) and Catherine (Ryan) Ryan; married William L. Hedges (a college professor), June, 1956; children: Marietta, James. *Education:* Barnard College, B.A., 1948; Radcliffe College, M.A., 1950; Harvard University, Ph.D., 1970. *Home:* 317 Hawthorne Rd., Baltimore, Md. 21210. *Office:* Department of English, Towson State College, Baltimore, Md. 21204.

CAREER: Wellesley College, Wellesley, Mass., instructor in English, 1954-56; University of California, Berkeley, lecturer in English, 1957-58; Towson State College, Baltimore, Md., assistant professor, 1967-70, associate professor, 1970-72, professor of English, 1972—, co-director of women's studies, 1972—. Trustee of Park School, Brooklandville, Md., 1974—. *Member:* Modern Language Association of America, Women's Caucus for the Modern Languages. *Awards, honors:* American Association of University Women fellowship, 1953-54; Outstanding educator of America, 1974.

WRITINGS: (Editor) Louis Sullivan, *Democracy: A Man-Search*, Wayne State University Press, 1961; (author of afterword) Charlotte Perkins Gilman, *The Yellow Wallpaper*, Feminist Press, 1973. Contributor to journals in her field; contributor of reviews to *Baltimore Sunday Sun*.

WORK IN PROGRESS: Editing *The Rural Dream: Myths of the Land* (anthology), for Hayden; a book on William Dean Howells.

* * *

HEDGES, Joseph
    See HARKNETT, Terry

HEGEL, Richard 1927-

PERSONAL: Born April 26, 1927, in Philadelphia, Pa.; son of Henry John and Clara (Lehr) Hegel; married Linda Pratt, June 29, 1968. *Education:* U.S. Merchant Marine Academy, graduate, 1948; Yale University, B.S., 1950; Southern Connecticut State College, M.L.S., 1969, M.A., 1972. *Home:* 29 Loomis Pl., New Haven, Conn. 06511. *Office:* Library, Southern Connecticut State College, 501 Crescent St., New Haven, Conn. 06515.

CAREER: Industrial power engineer, Connecticut Light and Power Co., 1953-67; New Haven Colony Historical Society, New Haven, Conn., executive director, 1968-70; Southern Connecticut State College, New Haven, assistant director of library services, 1971—. Member of New Haven Historic District Commission, 1970—; director of New Haven Scholarship Fund, 1970—; member of executive committee of New Haven Bicentennial Commission, 1973—; former vice-president of New Haven Festival of Arts. *Military service:* U.S. Naval Reserve, active duty; served in Korea; became lieutenant junior grade.

MEMBER: New Haven Colony Historical Society (member of board of directors, 1974—), New Haven Preservation Trust (secretary, 1970—), Ronan-Edgehill Neighborhood Association (vice-president and secretary, 1971—), Friends of the New Haven Free Public Library (co-chairman, 1973—), Woman's Seaman's Friend Society (member of board of managers, 1969—), Yale Club (New Haven; member of board of directors, 1974—), Graduates Club, Mory's, New Haven Lawn Club, Quinnipiack Club.

WRITINGS: Nineteenth Century Historians of New Haven, Archon, 1972; *Carriages from New Haven: A History of New Haven's Nineteenth Century Carriage Industry*, Archon, 1974.

* * *

HEGSTAD, Roland R(ex) 1926-

PERSONAL: Born April 7, 1926, in Stayton, Ore.; son of Philip Roland (a businessman) and Lydia Bertha (Prospal) Hegstad; married Stella Marie Radke, August 22, 1949; children: Douglas Roland, Sheryl Marie (Mrs. Jack Clarke III), Kimberly Marie. *Education:* Walla Walla College, B.Th., 1949; Seventh-day Adventist Theological Seminary, M.A., 1955. *Politics:* Independent. *Home:* 2121 Sondra Ct., Silver Spring, Md. 20904. *Office:* General Conference of Seventh-day Adventists, 6840 Eastern Ave. N.W., Washington, D.C. 20012.

CAREER: Ordained Seventh-day Adventist minister, 1955; pastor for Seventh-day Adventists in state of Washington, 1949-54; Southern Publishing Association, Nashville, Tenn., assistant editor, 1955-57, associate editor of *These Times*, 1957-58, book editor, 1958-59; General Conference of Seventh-day Adventists, Washington, D.C., editor of *Liberty*, 1959—. Specialist in East European religious liberties affairs; has appeared before Congressional committees; member of executive council of General Conference of Seventh-day Adventists; member of Associated Church Press. Directed and narrated documentary films: "One Day Criminal," on "blue laws," "A Matter of Conscience," on the "right-to-work" controversy, "Crusader for Freedom," a biography of W. Jean Nussbaum, and "Grand Delusion," on threats to religious rights guaranteed by the U.S. Constitution. *Member:* International Religious Liberty Association (associate director), National Historic Society (founding member), Smithsonian Associates, Maryland Suburban Fair Housing Association.

WRITINGS: Rattling the Gates, Review & Herald, 1973; *The Mind Manipulators*, Review & Herald, 1974; *Tall in the Saddle*, Freedom House, 1975. Acting editor of *Insight*, for Seventh-day Adventist youth, 1971-72.

* * *

HEIDEN, Carol A. 1939-

PERSONAL: Born February 4, 1939, in La Porte, Ind.; daughter of Earl Linder (a machinist) and Dorothy (Gardner) Wilhelm; married Frederick Allen Heiden (a shipping and receiving supervisor), April 2, 1960; children: Judy Kathleen. *Education:* Attended high school in La Porte, Ind. *Religion:* "Charismatic Free Methodist." *Home:* 3014 West 450 N., La Porte, Ind. 46350.

CAREER: Writer. Worked as a secretary in La Porte, Ind., 1957-64.

WRITINGS: Why Speak in Tongues and Prophesy?, Whitaker House, 1974.

WORK IN PROGRESS: Reigning with Christ.

SIDELIGHTS: Carol Heiden writes that she herself "speaks in tongues" and has complete control of this process. She adds that she was an adult when she became aware of her ability to do this, and that it came after a severe illness and much prayer.

* * *

HEIFETZ, Milton D. 1921-

PERSONAL: Born February 7, 1921, in Hartford, Conn.; son of Oscar and Molly (Fuchsman) Heifetz; married Betsy Baron, December 26, 1943; children: Lawrence, Daniel, Ronnie, Deborah. *Education:* University of Illinois, B.S., 1940, M.D., 1945. *Politics:* Democrat. *Religion:* Hebrew. *Home:* 704 North Bedford Dr., Beverly Hills, Calif. 90210. *Office:* 9735 Wilshire Blvd., Beverly Hills, Calif. 90212.

CAREER: Loma Linda University, Loma Linda, Calif., assistant professor of neurosurgery, 1955—; Los Angeles County Hospital, Los Angeles, Calif., senior attending surgeon, 1956—. Chief of Mt. Sinai Division department of neurosurgery at Cedars of Lebanon-Mt. Sinai Medical Center, 1968-75; associate clinical professor, University of Southern California at Los Angeles. *Military service:* U.S. Army Medical Corps, 1947-48; became captain. *Member:* American Academy of Neurology, American Association of Neurosurgeons, Explorers Club of America, Ethnic Art Council of Los Angeles (founder).

WRITINGS: The Right to Die: A Neurosurgeon Speaks of Death with Candor, Putnam, 1975. Contributor of articles to professional journals.

WORK IN PROGRESS: A textbook for neurosurgery and *The Foundation of Aesthetics.*

* * *

HEILMAN, Joan Rattner

PERSONAL: Daughter of Louis (a salesman) and Erna (Schneider) Rattner; married Morton Heilman (an engineer), August 12, 1956; children: Katherine, Julia, David. *Education:* Smith College, B.A., 1944. *Home and office:* 812 Stuart Ave., Mamaroneck, N.Y. 10543. *Agent:* Julian Bach Literary Agency, Inc., 3 East 48th St., New York, N.Y. 10017.

CAREER: This Week Magazine, New York, N.Y., women's editor, 1954-69; free-lance writer, 1969—. *Member:* Society of Magazine Writers.

WRITINGS: (With Joan Nidetch) *The Story of Weight Watchers*, World Publications, 1970; *Large-Type Knitting Book of Babies and Children's Clothes*, Crowell, 1971; (editor) *Kenneth's Complete Book on Hair*, Doubleday, 1972; (with Alvin Eden) *Growing Up Thin*, McKay, 1975. Contributor of articles to magazines.

* * *

HEINE, Carl 1936-

PERSONAL: Born May 28, 1936, in the Marshall Islands; son of Bourn (a minister) and Kathy (Juda) Heine; married Susan Eliu, July 29, 1961; children: Francis, Thomas, Eric, Kenneth, Robert. *Education:* Pacific University, B.A., 1965; University of Hawaii, M.A., 1974, Ph.D. candidate. *Politics:* "Liberal-Micronesian." *Religion:* Christian United Church. *Home address:* Majuro, Marshall Islands 96960. *Office:* Department of Public Affairs, Headquarters, Saipan, Mariana Islands 96950.

CAREER: Teacher of social studies in Marshall Islands Intermediate Schools, 1958-60; clerk of courts, 1961-63, and assistant education administrator, 1966-68, in Marshall Islands District; Congress of Micronesia, House of Representatives, Saipan, Mariana Islands, chief clerk, 1968-69; YAP District, Saipan, deputy district administrator, 1969-71, staff director, Joint Committee on Future Status, 1971-73; Trust Territory Government, Department of Public Affairs, Saipan, deputy director, 1974—. Member of Marshall Islands Congress, 1960-62; member of Marshall Islands delegation to Constitutional Convention, 1975; member of Marshall Islands Scholarship Committee, 1966-68; member of board of directors of Marshall Islands Seafood Enterprise, 1973. *Member:* American Political Science Association.

WRITINGS: Micronesia at the Crossroads: A Reappraisal of the Micronesian Political Dilemma, University Press of Hawaii, 1974. Contributor to publications of Australian National University: *Politics of Melanesia*, edited by Marion Ward, 1970; and *Priorities in Melanesian Development*, edited by Ronald J. May, 1973. Contributor to *Pacific Islands Monthly*, *Journal of Pacific History*, and *Micronesian Reporter.*

WORK IN PROGRESS: Two books, *Micronesia: Land and Politics*, and *Micronesia in Transition*; writing on Micronesian unity and the territorial sea.

SIDELIGHTS: "I am a Micronesian, the first author of a book in this area," Heine wrote. "I am a minority in a way; I hate U.S. military colonialism, and paternalism ... I'd like to see the Micronesian people govern themselves, show some of their own pride, develop a sense of independence, and not be so dependent on the United States for everything. I am working toward the goal of national government and a united Micronesia in the near future."

BIOGRAPHICAL/CRITICAL SOURCES: Pacific Islands Monthly, April, 1969.

* * *

HEINTZE, Carl 1922-

PERSONAL: Born June 18, 1922, in Sacramento, Calif.; son of Carl Feodor (an engineer) and Bertha (a legal secretary) Heintze; married Marguerite Hindle (a social worker), June 13, 1953; children: Mary, Jane, Richard. *Education:* Stanford University, B.A., 1947; Columbia University, M.S., 1948, further graduate study, 1961-62. *Politics:* Democrat. *Religion:* United Church of Christ. *Home:* 1077

Woodbine Way, San Jose, Calif. 95117. *Agent:* Marilyn Marlow, Curtis Brown Ltd., 60 East 56th St., New York, N.Y. 10022. *Office:* 751 South Bascom Ave., San Jose, Calif. 95128.

CAREER: San Jose Mercury-News, San Jose, Calif., reporter, 1948-59, science writer, 1959-69; public information officer, San Jose, Calif., 1969—. *Military service:* U.S. Army, Infantry, 1943-46; served in Belgium and Germany; became sergeant; received Purple Heart Medal. *Member:* National Science Writers Association, Magazine Writers Association, Sierra Club, Hospital Public Relations Association of Northern California, Stanford Alumni Association (life member), San Jose Public Relations Roundtable, San Jose Newspaper Guild (past president).

WRITINGS: Search Among the Stars, Van Nostrand, 1964; *The Circle of Fire*, Meredith, 1968; *A Million Locks and Keys*, Hawthorn, 1970; *The Priceless Pump: The Human Heart*, Nelson, 1973; *Genetic Engineering*, Nelson, 1974; *The Bottom of the Sea and Beyond*, Nelson, in press; *Summit Lake*, Nelson, in press. Consulting editor of *Medical Alert Communications* (malpractice bulletin).

WORK IN PROGRESS: Endmark, a novel about a newspaper strike; a book on the biosphere, for children; research on California and the Sierra Nevada.

AVOCATIONAL INTERESTS: Backpacking, photography, travel.

*　*　*

HEISE, Kenan 1933-

PERSONAL: Born December 17, 1933, in Ferndale, Mich.; son of Claude A. and Evelyn (Scheiblich) Heise; married Carol Rose Eck, April 16, 1966; children: Tiger, DanDan, Benjy. *Education:* Duns Scotus College, B.A., 1956. *Religion:* "Agnostic Catholic." *Home:* 929 Elmwood, Evanston, Ill. 60202. *Office:* "Action Line," *Chicago Tribune*, 435 North Michigan, Chicago, Ill. 60611.

CAREER: Free-lance writer, reporter, and editor, 1955-65; *Chicago's American*, Chicago, Ill., editor of "Action Line," 1965-68; *Chicago Today*, Chicago, Ill., editor of "Action Line," 1968-74; *Chicago Tribune*, Chicago, Ill., editor of "Action Line," 1974—.

WRITINGS: They Speak for Themselves: Interviews with the Destitute of Chicago, Young Christian Workers (Chicago), 1965; *The Death of Christmas*, Follett, 1971; *Is There Only One Chicago?*, Westover, 1973; *How to Survive in Chicago and Enjoy It*, Crown, 1975. Author of "Chicago's Personal Post," a column in *Chicago*, 1974—.

*　*　*

HEISEY, Alan Milliken 1928-

PERSONAL: Born May 20, 1928, in Toronto, Ontario, Canada; son of Karl Brooks (an engineer) and Alice Isabel (a secretary; maiden name, Smith) Heisey; married Barbara Muriel Cornes Sweet (a social worker), June 13, 1953; children: Alan, Jr., Peter, Rob. *Education:* University of Toronto, B.A.Sc., 1951; Harvard University, M.B.A., 1953. *Politics:* Progressive Conservative. *Religion:* Presbyterian. *Home:* 19 Tanbark Cres., Don Mills, Ontario, Canada. *Office: Daily Commercial News*, 34 St. Patrick St., Toronto, Ontario M5T 1V2, Canada.

CAREER: Held editorial and managerial posts with magazine division of Southam Press Ltd. of Canada, eighteen years; now with *Daily Commercial News*, Toronto, On-

tario. Candidate for Progressive Conservative Party in parliamentary election of 1968.

WRITINGS: The Great Canadian Stampede: The Rush to Economic Nationalism, Griffin House, 1973. Editor of *P. C. Metro Times*.

WORK IN PROGRESS: Canadian Leadership in the North American Community, completion expected in 1976.

SIDELIGHTS: Heisey told *CA*: "Education in the United States and Britain, ancient American ancestry, and immense admiration of the American accomplishment have helped to cast me in a minor but real role as critic of the 'new nationalist' mood which is the Canadian vogue. I see it as the denial of great open-ness in our tradition which we now stand fair to lose."

*　*　*

HELLER, Abraham M. 1898-1975

March 25, 1898—February 27, 1975; Lithuanian-born American rabbi, author of books on Judaism, Zionism, and Jewish civilization. Obituaries: *New York Times*, March 1, 1975; *AB Bookman's Weekly*, March 24, 1975.

*　*　*

HENDRICKS, Glenn Leonard 1928-

PERSONAL: Born March 16, 1928, in Pendleton, Ore.; son of Freeman O. (a clerk) and Leona (Lorenzen) Hendricks. *Education:* University of Oregon, B.S., 1949, M.A., 1960; Columbia University, Ed.D., 1972. *Home:* 4346 Fourth Ave. S., Minneapolis, Minn. 55409. *Office:* Student Life Studies, University of Minnesota, 327 Walter Library, Minneapolis, Minn. 55455.

CAREER: High school social studies teacher in Oregon, 1949-54; U.S. Army Dependent Schools Section, elementary school teacher in Germany, 1954-55, and high school teacher, 1955-60; junior and senior high school guidance counselor in Frankfurt, Germany, 1960-61, and Bremerhaven, Germany, 1961-62; assistant principal of elementary school in Geissen, Germany, 1962-63; principal of junior high school in Stuttgart, Germany, 1963-65; University of Minnesota, Minneapolis, assistant professor, 1970-75, associate professor of student life studies, 1975—, adjunct professor of anthropology, 1970—. Lecturer at University of Maryland, Overseas Branch (Heidelberg), 1962-64; adjunct lecturer at City College of the City University of New York, 1970—. Conducted field research in the Dominican Republic, 1967-69. U.S. Delegate to World Confederation of Organizations for the Teaching Professions, 1960, 1962.

MEMBER: American Anthropological Association (fellow), American Ethnological Association, Society for Applied Anthropology (fellow), National Education Association, Council on Anthropology and Education (associate; secretary-treasurer), Phi Delta Kappa. *Awards, honors:* National Science Foundation anthropology grant, 1965, at University of Arizona.

WRITINGS: The West Indian Experience in Puerto Plata, Teachers College, University Consortium for Caribbean Research, Columbia University, 1967; *The Dominican Diaspora: From the Dominican Republic to New York City—Villagers in Transition*, Teachers College Press, 1974; (contributor) Donald A. Biggs, editor, *Counseling and Values Book of Readings*, American Personnel and Guidance Association Press, 1975. Contributor to anthropology and education journals. Member of board of editors of *Anthropology and Education Quarterly*, 1973—.

WORK IN PROGRESS: A cross-cultural view of illegal migration; studying socialization of professional school students.

*   *   *

HENIG, Gerald S(heldon)   1942-

PERSONAL: Born October 9, 1942, in New York, N.Y.; son of Joseph (a pharmacist) and Sarah (Grabina) Henig; married Lorraine Lipsky (a teacher), September 3, 1972; children: Jennifer. *Education:* Brooklyn College of the City University of New York, B.A., 1964; University of Wisconsin, Madison, M.A., 1965; City University of New York, Ph.D., 1971. *Office:* Department of History, California State University, Hayward, Calif. 94542.

CAREER: California State University, Hayward, assistant professor, 1970-75, associate professor of history, 1975—. *Member:* American Historical Association, Organization of American Historians.

WRITINGS: Henry Winter Davis: Antebellum and Civil War Congressman from Maryland, Twayne, 1974. Contributor to history journals.

WORK IN PROGRESS: Studying the history of pre-Civil War America, with particular emphasis on the politics of the 1850's.

*   *   *

HENKELS, Robert M(acAllister), Jr.   1939-

PERSONAL: Born September 20, 1939, in Philadelphia, Pa.; son of Robert M. and Jane (Kaiser) Henkels; married Wickham Taylor (a college loan counselor); children: Karin; two stepsons. *Education:* Princeton University, A.B. (cum laude), 1962; Brown University, M.A., 1965, Ph.D., 1967. *Home:* 1260 Glen Forest Way, Decatur, Ga. 30032. *Office:* Department of Romance Languages, Emory University, Atlanta, Ga. 30322.

CAREER: Instructor in English and French at Noble and Greenough School, 1962-63; Phillips Academy, Andover, Mass., instructor in French, 1966-67; Williams College, Williamstown, Mass., assistant professor of Romance languages, 1968-73, director of program in Belgium, 1972; Emory University, Atlanta, Ga., assistant professor of Romance languages and coordinator of French language program, 1973—, director of summer program in Paris, 1975. Evaluation panelist for National Foundation for the Humanities. *Member:* Modern Language Association of America, American Association of Teachers of French, National Cum Laude Society, Nouveau Roman Newsletter, Southeast Modern Language Association.

WRITINGS: Robert Pinget: The Novel as Quest, University of Alabama Press, 1975. Contributor of about fifteen articles and reviews to literature journals, including *L'-Inquisitoire, Presence Francophone, Studies in the Twentieth Century, South Carolina Studies in French Literature, Novel,* and *French Review.*

WORK IN PROGRESS: Research on graphic symbols in explicating the French new novel; studying stylistic repetition and alternation in Pinget's *Fable*; an article for a festschrift honoring Albert Savan.

AVOCATIONAL INTERESTS: Hiking, skiing.

*   *   *

HENRY, Kenneth   1920-

PERSONAL: Born May 13, 1920, in Brockton, Mass.; son

of Walter J. and Josephine R. (Bedore) Henry. *Education:* Attended Harvard University, 1940-42; New School for Social Research, A.B., 1949; New York University, M.A., 1964, Ph.D., 1969; University of Oslo, postdoctoral study, summer, 1970. *Home:* 321 East 43rd St., New York, N.Y. 10017. *Office:* Department of Sociology, Fairleigh Dickinson University, 1000 River Rd., Teaneck, N.J. 07666.

CAREER: Dun's Review and Modern Industry, New York, N.Y., senior editor, 1956-57; National Association of Credit Management, New York, N.Y., director of public relations, 1959-64, administrative assistant to executive vice-president, 1964-68; Fairleigh Dickinson University, Teaneck, N.J., associate professor of sociology, 1968—, chairman of department, 1972-74. *Member:* International House of Japan, Japan Society, Society for the Study of Social Problems, American Association for the Advancement of Science, American Association of University Professors, American Sociological Association, Authors League of America.

WRITINGS: Defenders and Shapers of the Corporate Image, College & University Press, 1972. Contributor of about thirty articles to *Harvard Business Review* and *Dun's Review and Modern Industry.*

SIDELIGHTS: Henry was a member of the International Council of Educational Exchange-Japan Society study tours of Japan in the summer of 1972 and 1975.

*   *   *

HENSHEL, Richard L(ee)   1939-

PERSONAL: Born January 27, 1939, in Dallas, Tex.; son of Walter (an executive) and Beatrice (Bach) Henshel; married Anne-Marie Dermine (a professor), June 16, 1967 (divorced). *Education:* University of Texas, B.A., 1962; Cornell University, Ph.D., 1969. *Home:* 115 Cherryhill Blvd., Apt. 803, London, Ontario, Canada. *Office:* Department of Sociology, University of Western Ontario, London, Ontario, Canada.

CAREER: University of Texas, Austin, assistant professor of sociology, 1968-70; University of Western Ontario, London, assistant professor of sociology, 1970—. Visiting assistant professor at Columbia University, summer, 1972. *Military service:* U.S. Army, 1962-64. *Member:* American Sociological Association, American Society of Criminology, World Future Society, American Academy of Political and Social Science, Canadian Sociology and Anthropology Association. *Awards, honors:* Hogg Foundation grant, University of Texas, 1969-70; Canada Council research grant, 1972-73.

WRITINGS: (With Anne-Marie Henshel) *Perspectives on Social Problems,* Longmans Canada, 1973; (editor with Robert Silverman) *Perception in Criminology,* Columbia University Press, 1975; *On the Future of Social Prediction,* Bobbs-Merrill, 1975. Contributor to *American Sociologist* and *American Journal of Sociology.*

WORK IN PROGRESS: Reacting to Social Problems, for Longmans Canada; preparing a collection on the self-fulfilling prophecy; a collection on the context of discovery in social research (strategies for the creation of social theory).

SIDELIGHTS: Henshel writes: "My personal interests these days are in the problems of social prediction, especially the problems posed by the self-fulfilling prophecy, in the perception of people, especially insofar as this labeling tends to perpetuate individual deviance, and in the political and policy aspects of social problems. I am developing a taste for what might be called social engineering—the designing of sophisticated alternatives to contemporary social arrangements."

* * *

HEPBURN, Andrew H.   1899(?)-1975

1899(?)—July 18, 1975; American magazine travel editor, and author of travel books. Obituaries: *AB Bookman's Weekly*, August 4, 1975.

* * *

HEPNER, James O(rville)   1933-

PERSONAL: Born April 24, 1933, in Cedar Rapids, Iowa; son of Thomas O. (owner of a carpet and rug service) and Alma (Koski) Hepner; married Donna M. Rondabush, August 30, 1960 (divorced, 1974). *Education:* University of Iowa, B.A., 1955, Ph.D., 1964; Washington University, St. Louis, Mo., M.Hospital Administration, 1959. *Home:* The Frontenac, #3-B, 40 North Kingshighway, St. Louis, Mo. 63108. *Office:* School of Medicine, Washington University, 724 South Euclid Ave., St. Louis, Mo. 63110.

CAREER: Jewish Hospital of St. Louis, St. Louis, Mo., assistant director and administrative resident in hospital administration, 1958-62, assistant director, 1964; Washington University, St. Louis, Mo., lecturer, 1965-66, assistant professor of hospital administration, 1966-72, associate professor of health care administration, 1972—, director of graduate program in health care administration, 1967—, associate professor of hospital administration at School of Nursing, 1966-67, research associate at Social Science Institute and project director at Medical Care Research Center, both 1965-72. Hospital orderly in Cedar Rapids, Iowa, 1950-51; program director at Young Men's Christian Association (YMCA) Boy's Camp in Cedar Rapids, 1950-55, 1957. Member of health care financing task force of Alliance for Regional Community Health, 1971-72; member of panel on administration and hospital productivity of National Commission on Productivity, 1973. Member of health manpower committee of Bi-State Regional Medical Program, 1968-71; member of board of directors of Cooperative Information Center Hospital Management Studies, of University of Michigan, 1968-71. Chairman of nursing advisory committee of Junior College District of St. Louis, 1968-73; associate medical staff member at Jewish Hospital of St. Louis, 1964—; member of advisory committee for social service departments of Barnes Hospital and St. Louis Children's Hospital, 1971-74; member of board of directors of Maryville College (St. Louis), 1972-74. Consultant to governmental agencies. *Military service:* U.S. Marine Corps, Infantry, 1955-57; became captain.

MEMBER: American College of Hospital Administrators (fellow), American Public Health Association (fellow), American Academy of Medical Administrators (honorary fellow), American Hospital Association, Association of American Medical Colleges, American Management Association, Association of Schools of Allied Health Professions, Royal College of Health (fellow), Missouri Hospital Association, Missouri Public Health Association, Washington University Health Care Administration Alumni Association. *Awards, honors:* Grants from Department of Health, Education and Welfare, National Institutes of Health, Public Health Service, and Health Services Research, 1969-74.

WRITINGS: (Contributor) *Tulsa Child Health Study* (monograph), Tulsa Council of Social Agencies, 1966; (contributor) *Homemaker-Home Health Aide Service in Home Care Programs*, National Council for Homemaker Services, 1967; (with John M. Boyer and Carl L. Westerhaus) *Personnel Administration and Labor Relations in Health Care Facilities*, Mosby, 1969; (contributor) Rodney M. Coe, editor, *Organizational Innovation: Studies of Planned Change in the Hospital*, Praeger, 1970; (with Donna M. Hepner) *The Health Strategy Game: A Challenge for Reorganization and Management*, Mosby, 1973. Contributor to medical and hospital administration journals. Editorial consultant to Mosby, 1974—.

WORK IN PROGRESS: Case Studies in Hospital Administration.

* * *

HERBERT, Arthur
See SHAPPIRO, Herbert (Arthur)

* * *

HERDT, Sheryll (Enette) Patterson   1941-

PERSONAL: Born January 3, 1941, in Scottsbluff, Neb.; daughter of Lannon Samuel (a farmer) and Marian (Mohrlang) Patterson; married Ronald Charles Herdt, January 19, 1958 (divorced, 1974); children: Timothy Andrew, Julie Ann, Gregory Charles. *Education:* Attended Nebraska Western College. *Politics:* "Decentralist." *Religion:* "Yes." *Home address:* P.O. Drawer 112, Crawford, Neb. 69339.

CAREER: Western Interstate Commission for Higher Education, Boulder, Colo., library researcher and editor of scholarly publications, 1967-71; University of Colorado, Boulder, member of faculty, 1972—. Helped establish local Community Free School; member of board of Institute for Research and Dissemination of Human Knowledge. *Member:* Authors Guild of Authors League of America.

WRITINGS: Nitty Gritty Foods, Keysign Press, 1971; *Nitty Gritty Foodbook*, Praeger, 1975; *The Homestead Way of Life*, Praeger, in press; (contributor) *Our Working World* (for children), Science Research Associates, revised edition (Herdt was not included in original edition), in press.

WORK IN PROGRESS: The American Windmill, with Gary Emerson and John Graham; *Life During the Great Depression*; *The Women Homesteaders*; a biography of Willa Cather; historical and mystery novels for children; poems; a novel; research on Mari Sandoz and other women homesteaders, and on Agatha Christie and Dorothy Sayers.

SIDELIGHTS: Sheryll Herdt writes: "My writings are primarily concerned with love of the land, development of self-reliance and methods of self-reliance in recent history, and the search for quality in life. I believe that simple technology and decentralized lifestyles should be re-examined for future application in maintaining balance in our increasingly complex, dehumanizing, polluted, and vulnerable society. I am a coordinator of the Eco-Energy Farming Cooperative, which is experimenting with the potential of the small family farm, using non-polluting energy sources, such as wind, sun, and methane gas. Its goal is to develop an organic lifestyle, to use technology with discretion, and to share the resulting information." She adds that she is a "student of Sufi ideas."

BIOGRAPHICAL/CRITICAL SOURCES: Colorado Daily, May 16, 1975; *Boulder Daily Camera*, June 8, 1975.

HERTZLER, Lois Shank 1927-

PERSONAL: Born November 25, 1927 in Linville, Va.; daughter of Samuel Aaron and Mary Kate (Geil) Shank; married Elam K. Hertzler (an educator), December 13, 1947; children: Ann (Mrs. Gene Stutsman), Carol (Mrs. Charles Tisdale), Kevin. *Education:* Attended American University, 1963-64, and North Virginia Community College, 1974-75. *Politics:* Independent. *Religion:* Methodist. *Home:* 7004 Elizabeth Dr., McLean, Va. 22101. *Office:* Bauman Bible Telecasts, 3436 Lee Highway, Arlington, Va. 22207.

CAREER: Arlington County Medical Society, Arlington, Va., assistant to the administrative assistant, 1970-72; E. F. Shelley (consultants), Washington, D.C., research assistant, 1972-74; Bauman Bible Telecasts, Arlington, Va., graphic artist and assistant director of audio visual placements, 1974—.

WRITINGS: Leaning Into Life, Abingdon, 1974.

WORK IN PROGRESS: Touch the Joy, a book of open verse poetry.

AVOCATIONAL INTERESTS: Oil painting, boating, hiking, bicycling.

* * *

HERZSTEIN, Robert Edwin 1940-

PERSONAL: Born September 26, 1940, in New York, N.Y.; son of Harold Leon (an attorney) and Jean (Lewis) Herzstein. *Education:* New York University, B.A., 1961, M.A., 1963, Ph.D., 1964. *Religion:* Jewish. *Home:* Quail Run 2008, Columbia, S.C. 29206. *Agent:* Susan A. Protter, 320 Central Park W., New York, N.Y. 10025. *Office:* Department of History, University of South Carolina, Columbia, S.C. 29208.

CAREER: Served as special aide to governor of Connecticut, 1965-66; Massachusetts Institute of Technology, Cambridge, Mass., assistant professor of history, 1966-72; University of South Carolina, Columbia, associate professor of history, 1972—. *Member:* American Committee on the History of the Second World War.

WRITINGS: (Editor) *The Holy Roman Empire in the Middle Ages: Universal State or German Catastrophe?*, Heath, 1966; (translator) Hajo Holborn, *Germany and Europe: Historical Essays*, Doubleday, 1970; (editor) *Adolf Hitler and the Third Reich*, Houghton, 1971; (editor with Leon Apt) *Sources of the Western Heritage*, three volumes, Dryden, 1974—; *Adolf Hitler and the German Trauma, 1913-1945: An Interpretation of the Nazi Phenomenon*, Putnam, 1974; *Western Civilization*, Houghton, 1975. Contributor to history journals. Member of editorial board, *Red River Valley Historian*, 1975—.

WORK IN PROGRESS: Victory or Death (tentative title) for Putnam; *Europe in the Modern World* (tentative title) for Harper; a monograph, *Adolf Hitler at War: Strategy, Occupation Policy, and Personality in the New Order, 1939-1945*.

* * *

HESS, Eckhard H(einrich) 1916-

PERSONAL: Born September 27, 1916, in Bochum, Germany; son of Heinrich Peter (an artist) and Wilhelmina (Salewski) Hess; married Dorothea Burghard-Nawiasky (an artist), September 29, 1942. *Education:* Blue Ridge College, A.B., 1941; Johns Hopkins University, M.A., 1947,

Ph.D., 1948. *Home:* 1151 East 56th St., Chicago, Ill. 60637. *Office:* Department of Behavioral Sciences, University of Chicago, 5848 South University Ave., Chicago, Ill. 60637.

CAREER: University of Chicago, Chicago, Ill., assistant professor, 1950-53, associate professor, 1953-59, professor of psychology, 1959—, head of department, 1963-68, director of W. C. Allee Laboratory for Animal Behavior, 1961-72. Fellow of Center for Advanced Studies in the Behavioral Sciences, Stanford, Calif., 1955-56; visiting professor at Swarthmore College, 1957, and University of California, Berkeley, 1958. Consultant and director of Perception Laboratory of Interpublic, New York, 1960-67. *Military service:* U.S. Army, 1943-44. *Member:* American Psychological Association (fellow), American Association for the Advancement of Science (fellow), Society of Experimental Psychologists, Animal Behavior Society, Behavior Genetics Association.

WRITINGS: (With Roger W. Brown, Eugene Galanter, and George Mandler) *New Directions in Psychology*, Holt, 1962; (editor with H. W. Stevenson and H. L. Rheingold) *Early Behavior: Comparative and Developmental Approaches*, Wiley, 1967; *Imprinting: Early Experience and the Developmental Psychobiology of Attachment*, Van Nostrand, 1973; *The Tell-Tale Eye: How Your Eyes Reveal Hidden Thoughts and Emotions*, Van Nostrand, 1975. Associate editor of *Animal Learning and Behavior*.

WORK IN PROGRESS: A study of imprinting in waterfowl, Japanese quail, and domestic chickens in laboratory and natural situations; study of eye pupil size changes in nonverbal communication, mental, emotional, and sensory processes.

* * *

HESS, Margaret Johnston 1915-

PERSONAL: Born February 22, 1915, in Ames, Iowa; daughter of Howard Wright (a clergyman) and Jane (Stevenson) Johnston; married Bartlett Leonard Hess (senior pastor of a Presbyterian Church), July 31, 1937; children: Daniel Bartlett, Deborah (Mrs. Hans Morsink), John Howard and Janet Elizabeth (twins). *Education:* Coe College, B.A., 1937. *Religion:* Presbyterian. *Home:* 16845 Riverside Dr., Livonia, Mich. 48154.

CAREER: Writer. Appears on WEXL-Radio, Royal Oak, Mich., and WYFC-Radio, Ypsilanti, Mich.

WRITINGS: (With husband, Bartlett Leonard Hess) *How to Have a Giving Church*, Abingdon, 1974. Contributor to church publications.

WORK IN PROGRESS: Books on the growing church and on marriage.

SIDELIGHTS: Margaret Hess has taught Bible classes in the Philippines and in India, 1961. She has made two trips to the Far East, conducted four trips to the Bible Lands, and conducted a tour of Scandinavia. She has traveled around the world, and spent time in Europe.

* * *

HESSING, Dennis
     See DENNIS-JONES, H(arold)

* * *

HEWITT, James 1928-

PERSONAL: Born April 9, 1928, in Belfast, Northern Ireland; married Kathleen Ellen Casselden, September 13, 1969; children: Bryan James. *Education:* Educated in Belfast. *Politics:* "Away with all labelling!" *Religion:* "Away with all labelling!" *Home:* 11 Howard Rd., Dorking, Surrey, England.

CAREER: Daily Express, London, England, reporter in Belfast, 1946-52; free-lance reporter and writer in Belfast, 1953-62; employed with Thorsons Publishers Ltd., London, 1963; British Foreign Office, London, member of staff in research department, 1964-68; Royal National Institute for the Blind, London, joint-warden of residential hostel in Bayswater, 1969-72; free-lance writer and photographer, 1972—.

WRITINGS: Relax and Be Successful, Thorsons, 1951; *The Art of Relaxed Living*, Thorsons, 1955; *Teach Yourself Yoga*, English Universities Press, 1960; *About Sea Foods*, Thorsons, 1964; *Yoga and You*, Anthony Gibbs, 1966; *New Faces*, Books for You, 1966; *Isometrics and You*, Books for You, 1967; *Techniques of Sex Fitness*, Universal Publishing, 1969; *A Practical Guide to Yoga*, Funk, 1969; *Eye-Witness to Nelson's Battles*, Osprey, 1972; *Eye-Witnesses to the Indian Mutiny*, Osprey, 1972; *Eye-Witnesses to Wagon Trains West*, Scribner, 1973; *Eye-Witnesses to Ireland in Revolt*, Osprey, 1974; *Yoga of Vitality, Yoga of Posture, Yoga of Meditation*, Osprey, 1975; *Exploration of North America*, Osprey, 1975. Contributor of features on historical events and short stories to British Broadcasting Corp. radio.

*   *   *

HEYDUCK-HUTH, Hilde   1929-

PERSONAL: Born March 18, 1929, in Niederweisel, Germany; daughter of Reinhard (a clergyman) and Irmgard (Eick) Huth; married Christof Heyduck (a stage designer), 1956; children: Nikolaus. *Education:* Studied at Hochschule fuer bildende Kuenste (Academy of Art), Kassel, Germany, 1949-53. *Home:* Waldstrasse 36, 6113 Babenhausen, West Germany.

CAREER: Art teacher in Frankfurt am Main, Germany, 1953-57; free-lance artist exhibiting in one-woman and group shows in Essen, Kassel, Frankfurt am Main, and elsewhere in Germany, 1958—; author and illustrator of children's books, 1961—. *Awards, honors:* Premio Grafico-Preis (first prize for illustration) at International Children's Book Show in Bologna, Italy, 1967, for *Drei Voegel (Three Birds)*; *The Three Birds, In the Forest, In the Village*, and *When the Sun Shines* were included among the Child Study Association of America Children's Books of the Year, 1971.

WRITINGS—All self-illustrated; all published in Germany by Otto Maier, except as noted: *Wenn die Sonne scheint*, 1961, translation published as *When the Sun Shines*, Harcourt, 1971; *Im Kinderland* (title means "In Nurseryland"), 1962; *Kommt in den Wald*, 1963, translation published as *In the Forest*, Harcourt, 1971; *Drei Voegel*, 1966, translation published as *The Three Birds*, Harcourt, 1971; *Thomas im Dorf*, 1967, translation published as *In the Village*, Harcourt, 1971; *Jahreszeiten-Bilderbuch* (title means "Seasons of the Year Picture Book"), 1968; *Fahrzeuge* (title means "Vehicles"), 1968; *Kinderspiele* (title means "Children's Games"), 1969; *Malen und Zeichnen* (title means "Paint and Draw"), two books, 1969; *Weihnachten* (title means "Christmas"), 1971; *14 Bilder zum Weitermalen* (title means "Fourteen Pictures to Paint"), 1971; *Schau, was ich gefunden hab* (title means "Look What I

Have Found"), 1973; *3 Malmappen Religion* (title means "Three Painting Files for Religion"), Benziger, 1973.

WORK IN PROGRESS: A book on animals for children six to ten years old.

SIDELIGHTS: Hilde Heyduck-Huth writes: "I studied painting and pedagogy. In addition I am interested in psychology. I think that it is very important for one's later life, what kind of pictures one has seen in their early years. When my son was small, I made the first children's book. I observed him and learned what was particularly interesting or gave pleasure to him. All my later books and workbooks were a result of direct contact with children."

*   *   *

HEYMAN, Abigail   1942-

PERSONAL: Born in August, 1942, in Danbury, Conn.; daughter of Lazarus S. (a lawyer) and Annette (Siverman) Heyman; divorced. *Education:* Sarah Lawrence College, B.A., 1964. *Politics:* "Feminist." *Office:* Magnum Photos, Inc., 15 West 46th St., New York, N.Y. 10036.

CAREER: Magnum Photos, Inc., New York, N.Y., "name photographer," 1974—. Member of faculty at New School for Social Research, Center for Concerned Photography, Country Photography Workshop, Woman's School, International Center of Photography, and Aperion Photography Workshops. Has had group and solo photographic shows in Montreal, New York, Washington, D.C., San Francisco, and other American cities.

WRITINGS: Growing Up Female: A Personal Photo-Journal (with own photographs), Holt, 1974; (contributor of photographs) Margery Mann and Ann Noggle, editors, *Women of Photography: An Historical Survey*, San Francisco Museum of Art, 1975. Contributor to *Time, Life, New York Times, Ms., Popular Photography*, and *Modern Photography*.

SIDELIGHTS: Abigail Heyman took photographs for a UNICEF study on population and the needs of the child in India and Nepal, 1973, and in Morocco, 1974. She writes: "I have been a girl child and, in my expectations, a mother. I have tried to be prettier than I am. I have been treated as a sex object, and at times I have encouraged that. I have been married and have seen my husband's work as more important than my own, his decisions sounder than my own. And I have been divorced. I have been a premedical student and did not go on to medical school because I could not take my education seriously.... And so, instead, I have been a salesgirl, and a receptionist, and a full-time housewife. I have thought housewives and mothers did nothing of importance. I have disrespected all women but the rare woman who did what men did. I have disregarded women, as I disregarded myself. And I have changed. I have faced the conflicts inherent in growing up female, as I am now facing the conflicts in trying to change...."

BIOGRAPHICAL/CRITICAL SOURCES: Mann and Noggle, editors, *Women in Photography: An Historical Study*, San Francisco Museum of Art, 1975.

*   *   *

HIDORE, John J.   1932-

PERSONAL: Born July 6, 1932, in Cedar Falls, Iowa; son of John Henry (a factory foreman) and Vearle (Thomas) Hidore; married Ruth Norton (a teacher), June 6, 1954; children: Jill Helen, John Warren. *Education:* Iowa State Teachers College, B.A., 1954; State University of Iowa,

M.A., 1958, Ph.D., 1960. *Home:* 1310 Prairie Dr., Bloomington, Ind. 47401. *Office:* Department of Geography, Indiana University, Bloomington, Ind. 47401.

CAREER: Illinois Central Railroad, Waterloo, Iowa, rodman and member of field survey crew, summers, 1952-54; mathematics teacher in public schools in Esterville, Iowa, spring, 1957; University of Wisconsin, Madison, instructor in geography, 1960-62; Oklahoma State University, Stillwater, assistant professor, 1962-64, associate professor of geography, 1964-66; Indiana University, Bloomington, associate professor, 1966-72, professor of geography, 1972—. Visiting professor at State College of Iowa, summers, 1960-61, Wisconsin State University (Eau Claire), summer, 1965, University of Ife, 1971-72, and University of Khartoum, 1974-75. Member of conference on water resources at New Mexico State University, summers, 1963, 1969; director of National Defense Education Act (NDEA) Institute in Geography at Oklahoma State University, summer, 1966. *Military service:* U.S. Army, topographic computor, 1955-56; served in France.

MEMBER: American Geographical Society, American Meteorological Society, American Water Resources Association, Association of American Geographers, National Council for Geographic Education.

WRITINGS: The Undergraduate Curriculum in Geography, Iowa Department of Public Instruction, 1966; *Introduction to Physical Geography: Laboratory Exercises,* W. C. Brown, 1967; *A Workbook of Weather Maps,* W. C. Brown, 1968, 2nd edition, 1971; *A Geography of the Atmosphere,* W. C. Brown, 1969, 2nd edition, 1972; (with Michael C. Roberts) *Physical Geography: A Laboratory Manual,* Burgess, 1974; *Physical Geography: Earth Systems,* Scott, Foresman, 1974.

Contributor: *Reading Wisconsin's Landscape,* State of Wisconsin Department of Public Instruction, 1962; John W. Alexander, editor, *Economic Geography,* Prentice-Hall, 1963; Peter Haggett, editor, *Locational Analysis in Human Geography,* Edward Arnold, 1965; Robert E. Gabler, editor, *Handbook for Secondary Teachers,* National Council for Geographic Education, 1966; Howard G. Roepke, editor, *Readings in Economic Geography,* Wiley, 1967; Maurice H. Yeates, editor, *An Introduction to Quantitative Analysis in Economic Geography,* McGraw, 1968; G. J. Fielding, R. E. Hure, and K. W. Rumage, editors, *Computer Assisted Instruction in Geography,* Commission on College Geography, Association of American Geographers, 1969; Peter E. Lloyd and Peter Dicken, editors, *Location in Space: A Theoretical Approach to Economic Geography,* Harper, 1972; L. Lloyd Haring and Marilyn Haring, editors, *Problem Solving in World Geography,* Education Associates, 1973. Contributor to professional journals.

*   *   *

HIERNAUX, Jean   1921-

PERSONAL: Born May 9, 1921, in Huy, Belgium; son of Aime (a bank manager) and Victorine (Rosenboom) Hiernaux; children: Anne-Michele, Yves. *Education:* University of Brussels, M.D., 1945; Institute of Tropical Medicine, degree in tropical medicine, 1946; University of Paris, Sc.D., 1967. *Politics:* "Against any oppression and inequality of rights." *Religion:* Free-thinker. *Home:* 14, Square de Port-Royal, Paris 13, France. *Office:* Labo d'-Anthropologie, 2 Place Jussieu, Paris 5, France.

CAREER: Institute of Scientific Research in Central Af-

rica, Astrida, Rwanda, researcher, 1949-56; State University of the Congo (now State University of Zaire), Lubumbashi, Zaire, professor of biology, 1956-57, rector, 1957-60; University of Paris, Paris, France, associate professor of biology, 1962-64; National Center for Scientific Research, Paris, France, director of research, 1964—. *Member:* International Association of Human Biologists (secretary general, 1967-73), Society for the Study of Human Biology, Slovak Anthropological Society, Polish Anthropological Society, Societe d'Anthropologie de Paris, Current Anthropology. *Awards, honors:* Edouard Toulouse Prize from Societe de Biometrie Humaine, 1964, and, Broca Prize from Societe d'Anthropologie de Paris, 1974, both for the whole of his work.

WRITINGS: L'Avenir biologique de l'homme (title means "The Biological Future of Man"), Cercle d'Education Populaire (Brussels), 1964; *Decouvertes recentes sur l'-origine de l'homme* (title means "Recent Discoveries on the Origin of Man"), Cercle d'Education Populaire, 1968; *Egalite ou inegalite des reces?* (title means "Equality or Inequality of Races?"), Hachette (Paris), 1969; *The People of Africa,* Scribner, 1974. Contributor of over 100 articles to journals in his field.

WORK IN PROGRESS: Research in human ecology.

SIDELIGHTS: Hiernaux writes: "All my scientific career has been devoted to one object: the pattern of biological diversity of mankind, past and present: which features does it concern? is it random or orderly? to which factors does it respond? what are its possible futures? The last question is partly under our control; it is vital to know what is biologically 'good' for mankind and to understand what 'progress' may mean in biology at a time when man changes his environment so fast and when eugenics and genetic engineering expand their technical power."

*   *   *

HILDEBRAND, Grant   1934-

PERSONAL: Born September 16, 1934, in Battle Creek, Mich.; son of Gustave Matthew (a sculptor) and Frances (a graphic artist; maiden name, Walter), Hildebrand; married Judith Pennington Way (a graphic artist), June 21, 1958; children: Matthew, Peter. *Education:* University of Michigan, B.Arch., 1957, M.Arch., 1964. *Home:* 3314 43rd Ave. N.E., Seattle, Wash. 98105. *Office:* Gould Hall, University of Washington, Seattle, Wash. 98195.

CAREER: Albert Kahn Associates, Inc., Detroit, Mich., designer-architect, 1959-61; Minoru Yamasaki & Associates, Birmingham, Mich., designer-architect, 1961-64; University of Washington, Seattle, 1964—, now professor of architectural history. *Military service:* U.S. Army Reserve, 1958-64; became sergeant. *Member:* Society of Architectural Historians.

WRITINGS: Designing for Industry: The Architecture of Albert Kahn, M.I.T. Press, 1974. Author of "Architecture and Yankee Ingenuity," a ten-program telecourse.

WORK IN PROGRESS: Rewriting "Architecture and Yankee Ingenuity" as a book for the lay audience; a book on the American house, its practical history; a college text on a general history of architecture.

*   *   *

HILL, Helen M(orey)   1915-

PERSONAL: Born March 26, 1915, in Brooklyn, N.Y.; daughter of Arthur H. (in insurance) and Sophie (Baker)

Williams; married Donald L. Hill (a professor), June 8, 1941; children: Rebecca (Mrs. Ross L. Finney, Jr.), Anthony, Richard, Alan. *Education:* Wheaton College, Norton, Mass., A.B., 1936; Brown University, A.M., 1937. *Politics:* Democrat. *Religion:* Unitarian Universalist. *Home:* 928 Olivia Ave., Ann Arbor, Mich. 48104. *Agent:* John Schaffner, 425 East 51st St., New York, N.Y. 10022. *Office:* 612E Pray-Harrold Bldg., East Michigan University, Ypsilanti, Mich. 48197.

CAREER: University of Michigan, Ann Arbor, editorial assistant on *Smithsonian Institution: Ars Orientalis*, 1959-63; Eastern Michigan University, Ypsilanti, assistant professor of English, 1963—. *Member:* American Association of University Professors, Midwest Modern Language Association, Children's Literature Association, National Council of Teachers of English, Women's Research Club (University of Michigan).

WRITINGS: (With Agnes Perkins) *New Coasts and Strange Harbors: Discovering Poems*, Crowell, 1974; (contributor with Perkins) Jared Lobdell, editor, *A Tolkien Compass*, Open Court, 1974.

WORK IN PROGRESS: The Journals of Edward Baker: 1848-1860, completion expected in 1976; with Agnes Perkins and Alethea Helbig *Hunting Dragonflies* (tentative title), anthology of poems for children, for Crowell; and two other anthologies of poems for children.

* * *

HILL, Mary Raymond 1923-
(Lee Raymond)

PERSONAL: Born September 2, 1923, in Great Falls, Mont.; daughter of Raymond Ernest Hill (a salesman) and Mary Caroline (a teacher; maiden name, Brantly) Hill; divorced. *Education:* University of Colorado, A.B., 1944; graduate study, 1946-48; graduate study at University of Illinois, 1945-46; San Francisco State University, M.A., 1970. *Home:* 6069 Contra Costa Rd., Oakland, Calif. 94618. *Office:* California Division of Mines and Geology, 1416 Ninth St., Rm. 1341, Sacramento, Calif. 95814.

CAREER: Phillips Petroleum Co., Bartlesville, Okla., geologist, 1944-45; Illinois Geological Survey, Urbana, Ill., geologist, 1945-46; State of California, Division of Mines and Geology, Sacramento, Calif., geologist, 1949—; editor of *California Geology* (formerly *Mineral Information Service*), State of California, 1952-73, publications coordinator, 1973—. *Member:* Geological Society of America, Earth Science Editors Association (founding member; president, 1973-74), Sierra Club, Audubon Society.

WRITINGS: (With Ann Rice, under pseudonym, Lee Raymond) *Marin Indians* (monograph), Pages of History, 1957; *Guide to Virginia City, Nevada, and the Comstock Lode Area, including Book and Map Which Locate and Describe Points of Interest in the History of Mining the Lode: A Self-Guided Tour for the Serious Tourist*, Pages of History, 1959; *Diamonds in California*, Pages of History, 1959, revised edition issued as *Hunting Diamonds in California*, Naturegraph, 1972; *Diving and Digging for Gold*, Pages of History, 1960, 2nd edition, Naturegraph, 1974; *California Public Outdoor Recreation Plan*, Parts I and II, State of California, 1960; *The Mojave of the Colorado* (monograph), Pages of History, 1960; *Jade in California* (monograph), Pages of History, 1965; (with others) *The Status of California's Heritage: A Report to the Governor and Legislature of California*, State of California, 1973; (editor with Wendell Cochran and Peter Fenner) *Geo-*

writing: A Guide to Writing, Editing, and Printing in Earth Science, American Geological Institute, 1973, 2nd edition, 1974; *Geology of the Sierra Nevada*, University of California Press, 1975; (with Cochran) *Into Print: A Key to Publication for Scientists and Other Writers of Nonfiction*, Staples Press, in press; *Geologic Guide to the Sierran Gold Country*, California Division of Mines and Geology, in press. Contributor to *California Almanac*; contributor to geology journals. Editor of *Sausalito Pictorial Quarterly*, 1960-62. Author and photographer of "Barrier Beach," a 16mm film distributed by ACI Films, New York.

WORK IN PROGRESS: Pacific Coast Rocks, for Sierra Club; *Landforms and Landscape*, for University of California Press; a study of dune and beach sand that makes noises; *Rocks and Mountains*; *Mountains of the World*; co-authoring *Sacred Mountains*, and *California Wildlife: A History*; "The Disposal of Nuclear Waste," a 16mm film.

AVOCATIONAL INTERESTS: Hiking, music.

BIOGRAPHICAL/CRITICAL SOURCES: Independent Journal (San Rafael, Calif.), July 30, 1969; *California Geology*, September, 1974.

* * *

HILL, Wilhelmina 1902-

PERSONAL: Born August 29, 1902, in Fishers Island, N.Y.; daughter of William E. (a hotel owner) and Ida R. (a teacher; maiden name, Seabury) Hill. *Education:* University of Kansas, B.S., 1930; Columbia University Teachers College, M.A., 1933, Ed.D., 1939. *Politics:* Democrat. *Home and office:* 4000 Cathedral Ave., Washington, D.C. 20016.

CAREER: Teacher in elementary and secondary schools in Kansas City, Kan., 1923-37; *Scholastic Magazine*, New York, N.Y., associate editor, 1938-39; University of Denver, Denver, Colo., professor of education, 1939-49; U.S. Office of Education, Washington, D.C., specialist for social studies, 1949-72. Lecturer in geography at Shippensburg State College, Shippensburg, Pa., 1975; consultant to Longview Social Science Foundation for International Understanding, 1975. *Member:* National League of American Penwomen, National Council of Administrative Women in Education (president of Washington, D.C. branch, 1964), Soroptimist Club of Washington, D.C., English-Speaking Union. *Awards, honors:* Citation from President's Office of Emergency Preparedness, 1971; Educational Pacesetter award from President's National Advisory Council on Supplementary Centers and Services, 1972.

WRITINGS: (With Effie Bathurst) *Conservation Experiences for Children*, U.S. Government Printing Office, 1957; *Social Studies in the Elementary School Program*, U.S. Government Printing Office, 1960; *Unit Planning and Teaching in Elementary Social Studies*, U.S. Government Printing Office, 1963; *Curriculum Guide for Geographic Education*, National Council for Geographic Education, 1964. Author, with Alta M. McIntire, of social studies textbook series, Follett, thirty volumes, 1945-73. Member of advisory editorial boards, *Ranger Rick's Nature Magazine*, *Journal of Environmental Education*, *Social Education*.

WORK IN PROGRESS: Currently engaged in research on geographic and world affairs, environmental education.

SIDELIGHTS: Wilhelmina Hill told *CA:* "Major life interest [is] education—with special attention to social science, geography, environmental studies. Have visited Asia,

Europe, and Latin America many times to collect geographic data for my writing, lecturing, and educational positions."

* * *

HILLIS, Dave 1945-

PERSONAL: Born November 13, 1945, in Chicago, Ill.; son of Don W. (an author) and Doris (Schluntz) Hillis; married Mary Nell, June 30, 1967; children: Stephen Todd, Daniel Scott, Mary Andrew. Education: Columbia Bible College, student, 1964-65; LeTourneau College, B.A., 1968; graduate study at Wheaton College and Trinity College. Politics: Independent. Religion: Protestant. Office: Word of Life, P.O. Box 205, Ryde, New South Wales 2112, Australia.

CAREER: Word of Life International, Schroon Lake, N.Y., director of Australian branch, 1968—. Youth evangelist and preacher.

WRITINGS: How Big Is God (juvenile), Tyndale House, 1974. Contributor to Christian magazines.

WORK IN PROGRESS: Another book for teen-agers, depicting Biblical truth, with cartoon illustrations.

* * *

HILTON, Lewis B. 1920-

PERSONAL: Born November 21, 1920, in Saskatchewan, Canada; son of George W. (a farmer) and Myra (Bozarth) Hilton; married Mary Jean O'Banion, March 22, 1943. Education: Attended University of Nancy, 1939; Iowa State Teachers College, B.A., 1942; Columbia University, M.A., 1946, Ed.D., 1951. Politics: Independent. Home: 1335 Purdue Ave., University City, Mo. 63130. Office: Department of Music, Washington University, St. Louis, Mo. 63130.

CAREER: Elementary school teacher in the public and private schools of Belleville, N.J., 1945-46, and Des Moines, Iowa, 1946-48; Drake University, Des Moines, Iowa, member of faculty, 1946-49; professional clarinetist and oboist in New York, Des Moines, and St. Louis, 1945-46, 1949-51; Washington University, St. Louis, Mo., assistant professor, 1951-53, associate professor, 1953-59, professor of music, 1959—. Editor, Roger Dean Co., Macomb, Ill. Chairman of board of directors of Young Audiences, St. Louis, Mo., 1971-73; member of board of directors of Community Music School, St. Louis, 1970-72, and Community Association of Schools for the Arts, St. Louis, 1972—. Military service: U.S. Coast Guard, 1942-45. Member: International Society for the Study of Music Education, Music Educators National Conference, Missouri Music Education Association, Council for Research in Music Education, Phi Mu Alpha Sinfonia.

WRITINGS: Learning to Teach through Playing: The Woodwinds, Addison-Wesley, 1971. Contributor of articles and papers to music and education journals. Editor of Missouri Journal of Research in Music Education, 1962—; member of editorial board of Journal of Research in Music Education, 1972—.

WORK IN PROGRESS: A bassoon method book, for Roger Dean; editions of early clarinet concerti and arrangements of Beethoven wind ensemble music, for Roger Dean; a study of pre-Cortesian Mexican music; various musical arrangements.

AVOCATIONAL INTERESTS: Travel.

HINCKLEY, Barbara 1937-

PERSONAL: Born August 12, 1937, in Boston, Mass.; children: Sandra, Karen. Education: Mount Holyoke College, A.B. (magna cum laude), 1959; Cornell University, Ph.D., 1968. Office: Department of Political Science, University of Wisconsin, Madison, Wis. 53706.

CAREER: University of Massachusettts, Amherst, assistant professor of political science, 1968-70; Cornell University, Ithaca, N.Y., assistant professor of political science, 1970-72; University of Wisconsin, Madison, associate professor, 1972-75, professor of political science, 1975—. Member: American Political Science Association, Phi Beta Kappa. Awards, honors: Received Guggenheim fellowship.

WRITINGS: The Seniority System in Congress, Indiana University Press, 1971; Stability and Change in Congress, Harper, 1971; (editor and contributor) Coalitions and Time, Saga Publications, 1975. Contributor to professional journals.

WORK IN PROGRESS: Coalitions and Politics; continuing study of coalitions.

* * *

HINCKLEY, Ted C(harles) 1925-

PERSONAL: Born October 4, 1925, in New York, N.Y.; son of Theodore C. and Eunice (Platt) Hinckley; married Caryl Chesmore (a teacher), June 17, 1948. Education: Claremont Men's College, B.A., 1950; Northwest Missouri State College, B.S., 1951; University of Kansas City, M.A., 1953; Indiana University, Ph.D., 1961. Politics: Independent. Religion: Presbyterian. Home address: P.O. Box 456, Saratoga, Calif. 95070. Office: Department of History, San Jose State University, San Jose, Calif. 95192.

CAREER: Secondary teacher of history in Kansas City, Mo., 1951-53; Claremont Men's College, Claremont, Calif., assistant to president, 1953-55; headmaster of private school in Davenport, Iowa, 1955-57; San Jose State University, San Jose, Calif., assistant professor, 1959-63, associate professor, 1963-67, professor of history, 1967—, director of Sourisseau Academy, 1970-73, co-director of American Revolution Bi-Centennial Series, 1971-76. Director of Pacific Basin History Conference, 1965, 1967; member of board of directors of American West Publishing Co., 1971—. Military service: U.S. Navy, 1943-46; U.S. Army Reserve, 1950-52, U.S. Navy Reserve, Air Intelligence, 1953-59; became ensign; received three air medals. Member: American Association of University Professors, Organization of American Historians, American Historical Association (Pacific Coast Branch), Presbyterian Historical Society, Western History Association. Awards, honors: American Philosophical Society grants, 1962, 1966; Danforth associate; Huntington Library summer fellowship, 1971.

WRITINGS: (Editor) Proceedings: The Westward Movement and Historical Involvement of the Americas in the Pacific Basin, San Jose State College Press, 1965; (editor with Tom Wendel) Student Manual for U.S. History, 17a, San Jose State College Press, 1967; The Americanization of Alaska, 1867-1897, Pacific Books, 1972; (contributor) Tsuguo Arai, editor, Alaska and Japan: Perspectives of Past and Present, Alaska Methodist University Press, 1972. Contributor of about forty articles to historical journals. Member of editorial board of Pacific Northwest Quarterly, 1974—.

WORK IN PROGRESS: Biographies of John Green

Brady and Sheldon Jackson; a history of the assimilation of Alaska's southeastern natives into American culture.

AVOCATIONAL INTERESTS: Carpentry, skiing, sailing.

* * *

HINSHAW, Robert E(ugene) 1933-

PERSONAL: Born December 2, 1933, in Wichita, Kan.; son of Cecil E. (a teacher) and Pauline (Smith) Hinshaw; married Ardith Tjossem, August 28, 1953; children: Julia Ellen (Mrs. Mats Ryberg), Kenneth Robert, Christopher Lawrence. *Education:* Haverford College, B.A., 1955; University of Chicago, M.A., 1963, Ph.D., 1966. *Politics:* Independent. *Religion:* Society of Friends (Quakers). *Office:* Beloit College, Beloit, Wis. 53511.

CAREER: Olney Friends School (secondary boarding school), Barnesville, Ohio, instructor in English, Spanish, and Quakerism, 1955-58, assistant headmaster, 1956-58, headmaster, 1958-61; University of Kansas, Lawrence, assistant professor, 1966-70, associate professor of anthropology, 1970; Wilmington College, Wilmington, Ohio, president, 1971-75; Beloit College, Beloit, Wis., associate professor of anthropology and chairman of department, 1975—. Instructor at Colorado Rocky Mountain School, summer, 1962; visiting professor at University de San Carlos de Guatemala, 1968-69, Illinois State University, 1975-76. Did anthropological field work with Guatemalan Indians, 1963-65, 1968-69, 1970.

MEMBER: American Anthropological Association (fellow), Society for Applied Anthropology, American Association for Higher Education. *Awards, honors:* National Institute of Mental Health grant for restudy of Guatemalan Indian community, 1963-65; Ford Foundation and University of Kansas grant for research in Guatemala, 1968-69.

WRITINGS: (Contributor) Flavio Rojas Lima, editor, *Los Pueblos del Lago de Atitlan*, El Seminario de Integracion Guatemalteca (Guatemala City), 1968; (contributor) Robert Wauchope, general editor, *Handbook of Middle American Indians*, Volume VII, University of Texas Press, 1969; (contributor) Walter Goldschmidt and Harry Hoijer, editors, *The Social Anthropology of Latin America: Essays in Honor of Ralph Leon Beals*, Center for Latin American Studies, University of California, Los Angeles, 1970; *Panajachel: A Guatemalan Town in Thirty-year Perspective*, University of Pittsburgh Press, 1975.

WORK IN PROGRESS: Editing and writing a section for a festschrift in honor of Sol Tax, for Peter de Ridder (Netherlands).

* * *

HIPPLER, Arthur E(dwin) 1935-

PERSONAL: Born August 25, 1935, in St. Louis, Mo.; son of Arthur M. (a firefighter) and Marie D. (Malawey) Hippler; married Joan Talarski, September 4, 1956 (divorced, June, 1970); married Loni Brewis (a secretary), October 20, 1973; children: Arthur M., Laura A. *Education:* Attended St. Mary's College, Moraga, Calif., 1953-55; University of California, Berkeley, B.A. (honors), 1963, Ph.D., 1968. *Home:* 3241 West 69th St., Anchorage, Alaska 99502. *Office:* Institute of Social Economics and Government Research, University of Alaska, Fairbanks, Alaska 99701.

CAREER: University of Alaska, Institute of Social Economics and Government Research, Fairbanks, assistant professor, 1967-69, associate professor of anthropology,

1969—. *Military service:* U.S. Army, 1958-60. *Member:* American Anthropological Society, American Association for the Advancement of Science, Alaska Civil Liberties Union (founder; president, 1968), Phi Beta Kappa.

WRITINGS: Alaska and Other Eskimos, University of Alaska Press, 1969; (with Stephen Conn) *Athabascan Law Ways*, University of Alaska Press, 1972; (with Conn) *Eskimo Law Ways*, University of Alaska Press, 1973; *The Sub-arctic Athabascans*, University of Alaska Press, 1973; *Hunter's Point: A Black Ghetto*, Basic Books, 1973. Contributor of more than fifty articles to professional journals, including *American Anthropologist* and *Transcultural Psychiatric Research*. Contributing editor to *History of Childhood Quarterly*, 1974—.

WORK IN PROGRESS: Monographs on Uppertanana Indians, Tanaina Indians, and Yukon Eskimos; research on Australian aboriginals.

* * *

HIRSCHHORN, Clive 1940-

PERSONAL: Born February 20, 1940, in Johannesburg, South Africa; son of Colin and Pearl (Rabinowitz) Hirschhorn. *Education:* University of the Witwatersrand, B.A., 1960. *Politics:* Conservative. *Religion:* Jewish. *Home:* 42d South Audley St., Mayfair, London W.1, England. *Agent:* Roslyn Targ, 250 West 57th St., New York, N.Y. 10022. *Office: Sunday Express*, Fleet St., London E.C.4, England.

CAREER: Empire Films, Johannesburg, South Africa, publicist, 1960-62; American Broadcasting Co. Television, Teddington, England, story editor, 1962-63; *Sunday Express*, London, England, feature writer and theater critic, 1964—.

WRITINGS: Gene Kelly, W. H. Allen, 1974, Regnery, 1975; *The Films of James Mason*, L.S.P. Books, 1975.

* * *

HOBHOUSE, Janet 1948-

PERSONAL: Born March 27, 1948, in New York, N.Y.; daughter of Henry and Frances (Liedloff) Hobhouse; married Nicholas Fraser (a journalist). *Education:* Lady Margaret Hall, Oxford, B.A. (with honors), 1969. *Home and office:* 18 East 81st St., New York, N.Y. 10028.

CAREER: Arts Magazine, New York, N.Y., art reviewer, 1970-72; Barrie & Jenkins (publishers), London, England, editor, 1972; *Studio International* (magazine), London, art reviewer, 1972-73; Secker & Warburg Ltd. (publishers), London, editor, 1973.

WRITINGS: Everybody Who Was Anybody: A Biography of Gertrude Stein, Putnam, 1975. Contributor of articles to *Arts Magazine* and *Studio International*.

WORK IN PROGRESS: A book on Roger Fry.

* * *

HOCHSCHILD, Arlie Russell 1940-

PERSONAL: Born January 15, 1940, in Boston, Mass.; daughter of Francis Henry (a diplomat) and Ruth (Libbey) Russell; married Adam Marquand Hochschild (a magazine editor), June 26, 1965; children: David Russell. *Education:* Swarthmore College, B.A., 1972; University of California, Berkeley, M.A., 1965, Ph.D., 1969. *Politics:* Socialist. *Religion:* Agnostic. *Home:* 2711 Virginia St., Apt. 4, Berkeley, Calif. 94709. *Office:* Department of Sociology, University of California, Berkeley, Calif. 94720.

CAREER: University of California at Santa Cruz, assistant professor of sociology, 1969-71; University of California, Berkeley, assistant professor, 1971-75, associate professor of sociology, 1975—. *Member:* American Sociological Association, Sociologists for Women in Society, American Gerontological Society, American Federation of Teachers.

WRITINGS: The Unexpected Community, Prentice-Hall, 1973; *Coleen, the Question Girl* (children's story), Feminist Press, 1973. Contributor to professional journals.

* * *

HODGETTS, Richard M(ichael) 1942-

PERSONAL: Born March 10, 1942, in Bronx, N.Y.; son of Harold Thomas (a postal employee) and Regina (McDermott) Hodgetts; married Sara J. Fontana, August 1, 1970; children: Steven Michael, Jennifer Anne. *Education:* New York University, B.S., 1963; Indiana University, M.B.A., 1964; University of Oklahoma, Ph.D., 1968. *Home:* 7721 North Hazelwood, Lincoln, Neb. 68510. *Office:* College of Business, University of Nebraska, Lincoln, Neb. 68508.

CAREER: University of Nebraska, Lincoln, assistant professor, 1968-70, associate professor, 1970-73, professor of management, 1973—. *Member:* Academy of Management, Midwest Business Administration Association.

WRITINGS: Top Management Simulation, D. H. Mark, 1970; (with Fred Luthans) *Social Issues in Business*, Macmillan, 1972, 2nd edition, in press; (editor with Luthans) *Readings on the Current Social Issues in Business: Poverty, Civil Rights, Ecology, and Consumerism*, Macmillan, 1972; (with Henry Albers) *Cases and Incidents on the Basic Concepts of Management*, Wiley, 1972; (with Luthans) *Study Guide with Cases to Accompany Organization Behavior*, McGraw, 1973; *Management: Theory, Process and Practice*, Saunders, 1975; (editor with A. Thomas Hollingsworth) *Readings in Basic Management*, Saunders, 1975; (with Richard L. Howe) *Study Guide to Accompany Management: Theory, Process and Practice*, Saunders, 1975; (with Max Wortman) *Administrative Policy: Text and Cases in the Policy Sciences*, Wiley, 1975.

WORK IN PROGRESS: American Business: Social Challenge, Social Response, for Saunders; a text, *Introduction to Business*, for Addison-Wesley.

* * *

HODGSON, Martha (Keeling) 1906-

PERSONAL: Born February 16, 1906, in Berlin, Germany; daughter of Henry Hawkins Dougher (a stockbroker) and Florence Alice Darling; married Edward Herbert Keeling (a member of British Parliament), April 6, 1930 (died, 1954); married Patrick Harold Hodgson (a lawyer), December 24, 1962; children: (first marriage) Christopher Anthony Gedge Keeling. *Education:* Educated in England, France, Germany, and Italy. *Politics:* Conservative. *Religion:* Church of England. *Home:* Flat 2, 51 Onslow Sq., London S.W.7, England. *Agent:* Carl Brandt, Brandt & Brandt, 101 Park Ave., New York, N.Y. 10017; Jacintha Alexander, A. M. Heath & Co., 48 King William IV St., London, England. *Studio:* 43A Onslow Sq., London S.W.7, England.

CAREER: Mayor of City of Westminster, 1946; University of London, Courtauld Institute of Art, London, England, restorer and conservator of oil paintings for department of technology, 1947-51; National Trust, London, England,

member of staff, 1955-62. Member of council and executive committee of British School of Archaeology (Iraq); member of Committee of Friends of St. George's Hospital, 1947-67. *Military service:* Women's Royal Naval Service, 1940. *Member:* National Trust (life member), Georgian Group (life member), College of Psychic Studies (fellow), Conchological Society of Great Britain and Northern Ireland, National Arts Collection Fund, Friends of the Royal Opera House. *Awards, honors:* Honorary guide at Westminster Abbey.

WRITINGS: The Spell of the Shell, Hawthorn, 1975.

WORK IN PROGRESS: Beware the Bright Angel, a psychological thriller; *A Trio of Traumas*, short fiction.

AVOCATIONAL INTERESTS: Travel.

* * *

HODGSON, Pat 1928-

PERSONAL: Born June 23, 1928, in London, England; daughter of Arthur Weston (an electrical engineer) and Margaret (Michael) Reed; married James Hodgson (in telecommunications), March 26, 1951. *Education:* Girton College, Cambridge, Honours Degree in History, 1950. *Home address:* Rohan, Hatherley Road, Kew, Richmond, Surrey, England.

CAREER: British Broadcasting Corporation, Radio Times Hulton Picture Library, London, England, researcher, 1958-63; Council of Industrial Design, London, England, photo and slide librarian, 1964-67; Picture Research Agency, Richmond, Surrey, England, founder and proprietor, 1968—. *Member:* Society of Authors, Richmond Film Society (member of committee), Richmond and Twickenham Photographic Society, Richmond Squash Rackets Club, Richmond Lawn Tennis Club (member of committee).

WRITINGS: Early War Photographs, Osprey, 1974; (contributor) Ann Hoffmann, editor, *Research: A Handbook for Writers and Journalists, 1975/6*, Midas Books, 1975; *The War Illustrators*, Osprey, in press. Reviewer, *Film* magazine, 1969.

WORK IN PROGRESS: Research projects in early photography, Victorian history and periodicals; free-lance picture research.

* * *

HOFF, Ebbe Curtis 1906-

PERSONAL: Born August 12, 1906, in Rexford, Kan.; son of Hans Jacob (a professor of modern languages) and May (Knudson) Hoff; married Phebe Margaret Flather (an ecumenist with Episcopal Diocese of Virginia), June 2, 1934; children: Phebe May (Mrs. Leigh Van Valen), David Christiansen. *Education:* University of Washington, B.S. (summa cum laude), 1928; Oxford University, B.A. (with honors), 1930, Ph.D., 1932, M.A., 1936, B.M. and B.Ch., 1941, M.D., 1953. *Politics:* Democrat. *Religion:* Episcopalian. *Home:* 117 Gaymont Rd., Richmond, Va. 23229. *Agent:* Robert Gilday, 815 Second Ave., New York, N.Y. 10017. *Office:* Medical College of Virginia Hospitals, Virginia Commonwealth University, Richmond, Va. 23298.

CAREER: Yale University, School of Medicine, New Haven, Conn., Sterling Research Fellow in Physiology, 1932-33, Alexander Browne Coxe Research Fellow in Neurophysiology, 1933-34, instructor in physiology, 1934-36, research assistant in aviation medicine for National Research Council, 1940-43; clinical training at London Hospital Medical College, University of London, 1936-40; Sarah Lawrence College, Bronxville, N.Y., professor of physiology, 1941-43; Medical College of Virginia (now Virginia Commonwealth University), Richmond, associate professor, 1943-50, professor of neurological science, 1950-62, professor of physiology and psychiatry, 1962, chairman of department of neurological science, 1946-62, chairman of Division of Psychiatric Research, 1962-68, dean of School of Graduate Studies, 1956-66; Virginia State Department of Health, Richmond, medical director of Bureau of Alcohol Studies and Rehabilitation unit at Medical College of Virginia Hospital, Virginia Commonwealth University, 1948—. *Military service:* U.S. Naval Reserve, Medical Corps, 1943-46; became commander.

MEMBER: American Physiological Society, American Medical Association (fellow), American Psychiatric Association (associate), American Academy of Neurology (associate), American College of Neuropsychopharmacology, Royal Society of Medicine (fellow), British Medical Association, Association of Military Surgeons of the U.S., Aerospace Medical Association, History of Science Society, Society for Experimental Biology and Medicine, New York Academy of Science (fellow), Virginia State Medical Society, Virginia Neuropsychiatric Association, Phi Beta Kappa, Sigma Xi, Alpha Omega Alpha.

WRITINGS: Decisions about Alcohol, Seabury, 1961; (author of introduction) *Aspects of Alcoholism*, Lippincott, 1963; (author of introduction) Henrik Wallgren and Herbert Barry III, *Action of Alcohol*, Elsevier, 1970; *Alcoholism: The Hidden Addiction*, Seabury, 1974.

Editor: (With John F. Fulton) *A Bibliography of Aviation Medicine*, C. C Thomas, 1942, supplement (with Fulton and wife, Phebe M. Hoff), Division of Medical Sciences, National Research Council, 1944; *A Bibliographical Sourcebook of Compressed Air, Diving and Submarine Medicine*, U.S. Government Printing Office, Volume I, 1948, Volume II (with L. J. Greenbaum), 1954, Volume III (with Greenbaum), 1966; (editor with Phebe M. Hoff) *History of Preventive Medicine: U.S. Army, World War II*, U.S. Government Printing Office, eight volumes, 1955-69.

Contributor: John F. Fulton, editor, *Howell's Textbook of Physiology*, 15th edition (Hoff was not associated with earlier editions), W. B. Saunders, 1946; Fulton, editor, *Textbook of Physiology*, W. B. Saunders, 1955; *Origins of Resistance to Toxic Agents*, Academic Press, 1955; D. J. Pittman, editor, *Alcoholism: An Interdisciplinary Approach*, C. C Thomas, 1959; Roger P. Maickel, editor, *Biochemical Factors in Alcoholism*, Pergamon, 1966; Alfred M. Freedman and Harold I. Kaplan, editors, *Comprehensive Textbook of Psychiatry*, Williams & Wilkins, 1967; Ronald J. Catanzaro, editor, *Alcoholism: The Total Treatment Approach*, C. C Thomas, 1967; Thomas F. A. Plaut, *Alcohol Problems: A Report to the Nation*, Oxford University Press, 1967; Yedy Israel, editor, *Biological Basis of Alcoholism*, Wiley, 1971; *Limbic System Influences on Autonomic Function*, C. C Thomas, 1971; Elizabeth D. Whitney, editor, *World Dialogue on Alcohol and Drug Dependence*, Beacon Press, 1970.

Contributor to *Cyclopedia of Medicine, Surgery and Specialties*, and *Encyclopedia of Mental Health*; contributor to transactions, proceedings, and to journals in his field.

WORK IN PROGRESS: Special Faces of Alcoholism, for Seabury, completion expected in 1976 or 1977; research on physiology, neurology, and the psychiatric aspects of alcoholism; *Mechanism of Anxiety*; research on the neurophysiology of autonomic regulation by the cerebral cortex.

AVOCATIONAL INTERESTS: Astronomy, amateur radio operation, camping, travel.

* * *

HOFFMAN, Donald S(tone) 1936-

PERSONAL: Born December 10, 1936, in Albany, N.Y.; son of Benjamin G. (a physician) and Dollie (Stone) Hoffman; married Carolyn Benn (a real estate saleswoman), June 16, 1963; children: Amy Elizabeth, Nathaniel S. *Education:* Syracuse University, A.B., 1958; attended University of Bonn, 1960-61; University of Delaware, Ph.D., 1969. *Home address:* P.O. Box 641, Edinboro, Pa. 16412. *Office:* Department of History, Edinboro State College, Edinboro, Pa. 16444.

CAREER: University of Western Ontario, London, 1965-71, began as lecturer, became assistant professor of history; Edinboro State College, Edinboro, Pa., associate professor of history, 1971—, coordinator of academic research, 1973—. Member of board of directors of Edinboro Foundation; chairman of Edinboro Housing Review Board, 1973—, and Edinboro Historical Commission, 1974; member of executive committee of Save Our Lake Edinboro (for water quality of Lake Edinboro) and New Democratic Coalition.

MEMBER: American Historical Association, Conference Group on Central European History, New York State Association of European Historians, Association of Edinboro Historians (member of executive committee), Phi Alpha Theta (vice-president of Tau Nu chapter). *Awards, honors:* Boden fellowship from University of Delaware, 1963; Canada Council fellowship, summer, 1969; Edinboro Foundation grant, 1974.

WRITINGS: (Editor with James Young) *Readings in the History of Civilization*, Edinboro State College, 1972; (contributor) R. P. Stonesifer, Jr. and others, editors, *The American Fabric*, Edinboro Foundation, 1973; (contributor) L. P. Meyer, editor, *Regional Public Affairs*, Edinboro State College, 1975. Coordinator of "Faculty Forum," a column in *Spectator*, 1974—. Author of *ESC Research Newsletter*, a monthly newsletter, Edinboro State College, 1973—. Contributor to *Erie Daily Times*.

WORK IN PROGRESS: Dream of Disunity, on nineteenth-century German railways; research on Prussian particularism or anti-nationalism.

SIDELIGHTS: Hoffman writes that the "study of the past has not only proved challenging and enjoyable but has also made the present more comprehensible. As time passes and my own research continues, I become more convinced that individual will and action remain critical components in a society's development, even when the individual is easily manipulated and shaped by forces outside of his or her control.

"I cannot say that I view the present or future too optimistically as the level and success of manipulation seems to outpace all attempts to prepare our youth to meet or understand the ways they are used." *Avocational interests:* Reading historical studies, novels, mysteries, contemporary economic literature, political analyses, and popular writings, international travel, study of alternative sources of energy.

HOFFMAN, William M(oses) 1939-

PERSONAL: Born April 12, 1939, in New York, N.Y.; son of Morton and Johanna (Papiermeister) Hoffman. *Education:* City College (now City College of the City University of New York), B.A. (cum laude), 1960. *Home:* 199 Prince St., New York, N.Y. 10012. *Agent:* Helen Merrill, 337 West 22nd St., New York, N.Y. 10011.

CAREER: Barnes & Noble (book publishers), New York, N.Y., editorial assistant, 1960-61; Hill & Wang (book publishers), New York, N.Y., assistant editor, 1961-67, associate editor and drama editor, 1967-68, editor of "New American Plays Series," 1968—. Founder and director, Wolf Company, 1968—; lecturer, Eugene O'Neill Foundation, 1971; artist-in-residence, Lincoln Center Student Program, 1971-72, Changing Scene, 1972; drama adviser, Cable Arts Foundation, 1973; visiting lecturer, University of Massachusetts, 1973; member of board of directors, Orion Repertory Company, 1975—. *Member:* American Society of Composers, Authors, and Publishers (ASCAP), New York Theatre Strategy (founding member), Phi Beta Kappa. *Awards, honors:* MacDowell fellowship, 1971; Carnegie Fund for Authors grant, 1972; P.E.N. American Center grant, 1972; Guggenheim fellowship, 1974-75; National Endowment for the Arts, librettist's grant, 1975-76.

WRITINGS—Plays: "Thank You, Miss Victoria" (one-act), first produced Off-Broadway at Martinique Theatre, 1965; "Saturday Night at the Movies" (one-act), first produced Off-Broadway at Cafe Cino, 1965; *Good Night, I Love You* (one-act; first produced at Cafe Cino, 1966), Breakthrough Press, 1974; "Spring Play" (two-act), first produced Off-Broadway at La Mama Theatre, 1967; "Incantation" (one-act), first produced at La Mama Theatre, 1967; "Three Masked Dances" (two-act), first produced at La Mama Theatre, 1967; "Uptight" (musical; three-act), first produced Off-Off-Broadway at Old Reliable Theatre, 1968; XXXXX (long one-act), first produced at La Mama Theatre, 1969, produced in London, England as "Nativity Play," 1970; "Luna" (one-act), first produced at Old Reliable Theatre, 1970; "A Quick Nut Bread to Make Your Mouth Water" (long one-act), first produced at Old Reliable Theatre, 1970; "From Fool to Hanged Man" (dance play), first produced in New York, N.Y. at Clark Center, 1972; "The Children's Crusade" (dance play), first produced at Clark Center, 1972; "I Love Ya, Ya Big Ape" (one-act), first produced at University of Massachusetts, 1973.

Other writings: *The Cloisters* (song cycle; music by John Corigliano), G. Schirmer, 1968; (editor) *New American Plays*, Hill & Wang, Volume II, 1968, Volume III, 1970, Volume IV, 1971, Volume V, in press; (editor) *31 New American Poets*, Hill & Wang, 1970; *Fine Frenzy* (poems), McGraw, 1972.

Plays represented in anthologies, including *M.E.A.L.*, edited by Peter Fusco, Hunter College of the City University of New York, 1970; *Now: Theater der Erfahrung*, edited by Jens Heilmeyer and Pia Frolich, M. Dumont Schauberg (Cologne), 1971; *More Plays from Off-Off-Broadway*, edited by Michael Smith, Bobbs-Merrill, 1973; *Spontaneous Combustion*, edited by Rochelle Owens, Winter House, 1973; *The Off-Off-Broadway Book*, edited by Albert Poland and Bruce Mailman, Bobbs-Merrill, 1973.

Literary adviser, *Scripts*, 1971—.

WORK IN PROGRESS: "Gilles de Rais," a three-act play with music.

SIDELIGHTS: Hoffman told *CA:* "I prefer to let my work speak for itself."

BIOGRAPHICAL/CRITICAL SOURCES: Changes, March, 1971.

* * *

HOFFMANN, Felix 1911-1975

April 11, 1911—June 16, 1975; Swiss illustrator of children's books, artist and painter, also illustrator of bibliophile books for German and American publishers. Obituaries: *Publishers Weekly*, August 18, 1975; *AB Bookman's Weekly*, September 8, 1975. (*CA*-29/32)

* * *

HOHIMER, Frank 1928-

PERSONAL: Born September 14, 1928, in Pekin, Ill.; son of Wikle William (a laborer) and Dolly (Vaughn) Hohimer; married Josephine Regean (a restaurant manager), September 6, 1966; children: April, Johnny, Jr. *Education:* Attended Dartmouth College, 1971-72; Southeastern Community College, A.A., 1975. *Religion:* Roman Catholic. *Residence:* New York, N.Y. *Address:* Box B, Iowa State Prison, Anamosa, Iowa.

CAREER: Barber shop owner, 1962-65; night club owner, 1964-66; used car lot employee, 1964-66; employed with International House of Pancakes, Greenwich, Conn., 1967-69; professional jewel thief; professional artist.

WRITINGS: The Home Invaders, Chicago Review Press, 1975; *The Stolen Years*, Chicago Review Press, in press.

WORK IN PROGRESS: Windsor State Prison; *From Ghetto to the Chair*; *Sons of Satan*.

SIDELIGHTS: Hohimer will soon complete a ten-year prison term for a two-hundred-thousand-dollar jewel theft. He told *CA:* "I have spent nearly twenty years in prisons. . . . Crime is a total waste of life, even though you steal millions of dollars. . . . Maybe one of my books will keep some other person from this same road. . . . Whatever the outcome I will never be back in prison."

* * *

HOLDEN, Matthew, Jr. 1931-

PERSONAL: Born September 12, 1931, in Mound Bayou, Miss.; son of Matthew (a factory worker) and Estelle (Welch) Holden; married Dorothy Amanda Howard (an educational researcher), 1963; children: two. *Education:* Attended University of Chicago, 1946-50; Roosevelt University, B.A., 1952; Northwestern University, M.A., 1955, Ph.D., 1961. *Politics:* Democrat. *Religion:* Episcopalian. *Home:* 4134 Manitou Way, Madison, Wis. 53711. *Office:* Department of Political Science, University of Wisconsin, Madison, Wis. 53706.

CAREER: University of Illinois, Urbana, research associate of Institute of Government and Public Affairs, 1959-61; Northwestern University, Chicago, Ill., part-time lecturer in political science in Evening Division, 1961; Wayne State University, Detroit, Mich., instructor, 1961-62, assistant professor of political science, 1962-63; University of Pittsburgh, Pittsburgh, Pa., assistant professor of political science, 1963-66; Wayne State University, associate professor, 1966-68, professor of political science, 1968-69; University of Wisconsin, Madison, professor of political science, 1969—; Wisconsin Public Service Commission, Madison, commissioner, 1975—. Research associate, Ohio

Legislative Service Commission, summers, 1954, 1955; visiting assistant professor at University of Vermont, summer, 1963. Member of Air Quality Advisory Board, 1971—. Consultant to Ford Foundation, U.S. Public Health Service, National Council of Churches, Urban Institute, and other public and private agencies. *Military service:* U.S. Army, 1955-57; served in Korea.

MEMBER: American Political Science Association (member of council, 1972—), Institute for Policy Studies (member of council, 1973—), Inter-University Consortium for Political Research (member of council, 1974—), Social Science Research Council (member of board of directors, 1969-72), American Society for Public Administration (member of advisory council, Wisconsin Capital chapter, 1973), American Association for the Advancement of Science, American Association of University Professors, Midwest Political Science Association (member of council, 1972—).

WRITINGS: Pollution Control as a Bargaining Process (monograph), Water Resources Center, Cornell University, 1966; *The Divisible Republic*, Abelard, 1973; *The Politics of Poor Relief: A Study in Ambiguities*, Sage Publications, 1973; *The Politics of the Black "Nation,"* Intext, 1974; *The White Man's Burden*, Intext, 1974.

Contributor: Clyde J. Wingfield, editor, *Political Science: Some New Perspectives*, Texas Western Press, 1967; Scott A. Greer and others, editors, *The New Urbanization*, St. Martin's, 1968; Henry J. Schmandt, editor, *The Quality of Urban Life*, Sage Publications, 1969; James R. Klonoski and Robert I. Mendelsohn, editors, *The Politics of Local Justice*, Little, Brown, 1970; Harvey S. Perloff, editor, *The Future of the U.S. Government: Toward the Year 2000*, Braziller, 1971; W. R. D. Sewell and others, *Modifying the Weather*, University of Victoria, 1973. Contributor to other symposia, to *Urban Affairs Annual Review*, and to journals. Editor, *Yearbook of Politics and Public Policy*, 1974. Member of editorial board or editorial advisory board, *American Behavioral Scientist, American Politics Quarterly, Ethnicity*, and *Policy Analysis*; special issue editor, *American Behavioral Scientist* and *American Politics Quarterly*.

WORK IN PROGRESS: Environmental Regulation as a Bargaining Process, a revision of *Pollution Control as a Bargaining Process*; *Congress and the Social Services*, a companion to *The Politics of Poor Relief*; a volume of reflections and empirical studies, *The Conduct of Government*; and *Ethnicity in the Urban Political Order*.

*   *   *

HOLL, Jack M. 1937-

PERSONAL: Born November 18, 1937, in Oregon City, Ore.; son of Herbert M. (a newspaper circulator) and Eunice Lorraine (Kellington) Holl; married Jacqueline I. Olsen, August 15, 1959; children: Inga Ione, Mark Monroe, Kerstin Kellington. *Education:* Pacific Lutheran University, B.A., 1959; University of Maine, M.A., 1961; Cornell University, Ph.D., 1969. *Office:* Historian's Office, U.S. Energy Research and Development Administration, Washington, D.C. 20545.

CAREER: Williams College, Williamstown, Mass., assistant professor of history, 1965-70; University of Washington, Seattle, assistant professor of history, 1970-74; U.S. Energy Research and Development Administration, Washington, D.C., associate historian, 1974—. Visiting fellow at U.S. Department of Justice, 1970-71. *Member:* Organiza-

tion of American Historians, American Studies Association, American Correctional Association.

WRITINGS: Juvenile Reform in the Progressive Era: William R. George and the Junior Republic Movement, Cornell University Press, 1971. Contributor to history journals.

WORK IN PROGRESS: A History of the U.S. Atomic Energy Commission in the Eisenhower Years; *A History of Anglo-American Penal Reform*.

*   *   *

HOLLADAY, Sylvia A(gnes) 1936-

PERSONAL: Born January 14, 1936, in Lanett, Ala.; daughter of Edward David and Florence (Hunnicutt) Holladay. *Education:* Attended Stetson University, 1954-56; Auburn University, B.S., 1958, M.A., 1961; graduate study at University of West Florida, summer, 1971, University of South Florida, summer, 1973, and University of Mississippi, summer, 1974. *Politics:* "Democrat, most of the time." *Home:* 5909 Gulfport Blvd. S., Gulfport, Fla. 33707. *Office:* Department of English, St. Petersburg Junior College, St. Petersburg, Fla. 33733.

CAREER: Auburn University, Auburn, Ala., instructor in English, 1960-61; public high school teacher of English in Land O'Lakes, Fla., 1962; St. Petersburg Junior College, St. Petersburg, Fla., instructor, 1962-65, assistant professor, 1965-73, associate professor of English, 1973—. *Member:* Modern Language Association of America, National Council of Teachers of English, College Composition and Communications Conference, National Junior College Committee (member of executive committee, 1974—), College English Association, American Association of University Professors, South Atlantic Modern Language Association, Southeastern Conference on English in the Two-Year College (member of executive committee, 1968-70), Florida Council of Teachers of English, Florida College English Association (executive secretary, 1971-74), Florida Association of Community Colleges, Pinellas County Council of Teachers of English, Common Cause, Public Citizen, Delta Kappa Gamma, Phi Mu, Kappa Delta Pi, Phi Kappa Phi.

WRITINGS: (Editor with Lloyd A. Flanigan) *Developing Style: An Extension of Personality*, Holbrook, 1972, 2nd edition, in press. Contributor of articles, reviews, and poems to professional journals. Editor of *Newsletter of the Southeastern Conference on English in the Two-Year College*, 1968-70, of *Newsletter of the Florida College English Association*, 1971-74, and of *Newsletter of the National Junior College Committee*, 1974—. Editorial consultant to Human Research and Development Services, Inc.

WORK IN PROGRESS: Research on individualized and self-pacing instruction in college composition, on William Faulkner, and on Ernest Hemingway.

*   *   *

HOLLAND, Barbara A(dams) 1925-

PERSONAL: Born July 12, 1925, in Portland, Me.; daughter of Leicester B. and Louise (Adams) Holland. *Education:* University of Pennsylvania, A.B., 1948, M.A., 1951. *Home:* 14 Morton St., Apt. 9, New York, N.Y. 10014.

CAREER: G. & C. Merriam Co., New York, N.Y., lexicographer, 1953-55; John C. Winston, New York, N.Y., lexicographer, 1957-60; Funk & Wagnalls, New York, N.Y., lexicographer, 1961-62; free-lance writer and researcher, 1962—. *Awards, honors:* Creative Artists Public Service fellowship, 1974-75.

WRITINGS: Return in Sagittarius, Eventorium, 1965; *A Game of Scraps*, Prairie Press, 1967; *Autumn Wizard*, Poets Press, 1973; *Crises of Rejuvenation*, Grim Reaper Books, Volume I, 1974, Volume II, 1975. Contributor to literary journals. Guest editor of *Samskaras*, summer, 1969, and *Stone Soup Poetry*, 1975; consulting editor of *Hyn Poetry*, winter, 1970.

SIDELIGHTS: Barbara Holland writes that she considers performing as a poet as important as publishing poetry. She tours extensively and conducts workshops, particularly in the northeast states.

* * *

HOLLAND, Deborah Katherine   1947-

PERSONAL: Born March 26, 1947, in Perth Amboy, N.J.; daughter of William Dean (a chemical engineer) and Katherine (Schenck) Holland. *Education:* Attended Dean Junior College, 1965-67, and Parsons School of Design, 1967-70. *Office:* Gorilla Graphics, 1153 Guereno, San Francisco, Calif. 94110.

CAREER: Free-lance artist in New York, N.Y., 1970-72; Gorilla Graphics, San Francisco, Calif., partner, 1972—. Chairperson of board of directors of Artists in Print of San Francisco Graphics Guild, 1975—; secretary of Institute for Aesthetic Development, 1975—. *Member:* United Cartoon Workers of the World, Friends of Books and Comics.

WRITINGS: Optricks, Troubador, 1973; *Optricks Two*, Troubador, 1974.

WORK IN PROGRESS: Orange Crate Art: People's Art of California, 1910-1940, with museum show to accompany publication of book.

SIDELIGHTS: Deborah Holland writes: "Having had the name Guerrilla Graphics for two years before changing it to Gorilla Graphics, I was painfully aware of the movements of the SLA [Symbionese Liberation Army] and other underground agencies that are currently in the public's eye and mind. Consequently feeling the guilt for the capitalist I felt it necessary to establish contact with the community of San Francisco on a socialist level, hence founding Artists in Print, an organization of professional writers, graphic artists, photographers, etc., all working toward the betterment of commercial art and offering services to the community."

* * *

HOLLAND, Hilda   1901(?)-1975

1901(?)—February 18, 1975; American advertising manager, editor, author and compiler of symposium. Obituaries: *New York Times*, February 20, 1975.

* * *

HOLLAND, Tim   1931-

PERSONAL: Born March 3, 1931; son of Simeon Harold and Inez (Robinson) Holland; married Lona Crawford, September 19, 1970. *Education:* Attended Miami University, Oxford, Ohio. *Home:* 53 East 66th St., New York, N.Y. 10021.

MEMBER: Deep Dale Golf Club, Regency Whist Club.

WRITINGS: Beginning Backgammon, McKay, 1973; *Better Backgammon*, McKay, 1974.

SIDELIGHTS: Holland is an amateur golfer who has won

several tournaments, and also a winner of backgammon tournaments.

* * *

HOLLICK, Ann L(orraine)   1941-

PERSONAL: Born October 2, 1941; daughter of Robert and Geraldine (Monroe) Hollick. *Education:* Attended University of Vienna, 1961, and Freiburg University, 1962; University of California at Berkeley, B.A., 1963; Johns Hopkins University, M.A., 1966, Ph.D., 1971; United States Department of Agriculture Graduate School, graduate study, 1966-67. *Home:* 1611 31st St. N.W., Washington, D.C. 20007. *Office:* School of Advanced International Studies, Johns Hopkins University, Baltimore, Md.

CAREER: U.S. Senate, Washington, D.C., member of staff of Committee on Foreign Relations, 1971-72; Johns Hopkins University, School of Advanced International Studies, Baltimore, Md., assistant professor of American foreign policy, 1972-75, associate professor of international law and organization, 1975—, executive director of Ocean Policy Project, 1972—. Educational adviser, U.S. Information Service, 1964-65; social insurance research analyst, U.S. Department of Health, Education, and Welfare, 1966; Latin American research analyst, Atlantic Research Corporation, 1966-67; research assistant, National Planning Association, 1968-69; research fellow, Brookings Institution, 1970-71; consultant on foreign relations to various private and governmental agencies; bibliographer, Law of Sea Institute, 1970-73, and member of board of directors, 1974—. *Member:* International Studies Association, Council on Foreign Relations, American Society of International Law, Marine Technology Society, American Political Science Association, Phi Beta Kappa. *Awards, honors:* Carnegie Endowment for International Peace grant, 1973.

WRITINGS: Marine Policy, Law and Economics: Annotated Bibliography, Law of the Sea Institute, University of Rhode Island, 1970, supplement, 1973; (contributor) Richard N. Cooper, editor, *A Reordered World*, Potomac Associates, 1973; (with Robert E. Osgood) *New Era of Ocean Politics*, Johns Hopkins Press, 1974; (contributor) Ryan Amacrer, editor, *Law of the Sea: U.S. Interests and Alternatives*, American Enterprise Institute, in press; (contributor) Joseph S. Nye and Robert Keohane, editors, *Organizing for Global Environmental and Resource Interdependence*, Commission on the Organization of Government for the Conduct of Foreign Policy, in press. Contributor to journals in her field. Associate editor, *Ocean Development and International Law*, 1974—.

WORK IN PROGRESS: Ocean Resources as an International Management Problem: Evolution and Outcome of the Law of the Sea Policy Process (tentative title).

SIDELIGHTS: Miss Hollick is competent in Spanish, German, French, and Latin.

* * *

HOLLIS, Harry Newcombe, Jr.   1938-

PERSONAL: Born July 19, 1938, in Memphis, Tenn.; son of Harry Newcombe (a real estate broker) and Evelyn Dixie (Hess) Hollis; married Mary Fern Caudill (a music teacher), December 25, 1962; children: Mary Melissa, Harry Newcombe IV. *Education:* Attended Carson-Newman College, 1956-57; University of Tennessee, A.B., 1960; Southern Baptist Theological Seminary, M.Div., 1964, Ph.D., 1968. *Home:* 736 Richfield Dr., Nashville,

Tenn. 37205. *Office:* Christian Life Commission, Southern Baptist Convention, 460 James Robertson Parkway, Nashville, Tenn. 37219.

CAREER: Ordained Baptist minister, 1960; pastor of Baptist church in Finchville, Ky., 1961-69; Christian Life Commission of the Southern Baptist Convention, Nashville, Tenn., director of family and special moral concerns, 1969—. Instructor at Southern Baptist Theological Seminary, 1968-69, visiting professor, 1975; visiting professor at Vanderbilt University, 1974. *Member:* American Society of Christian Ethics, National Association of Sex Educators and Counselors, National Council of Family Relations, Southeastern Council of Family Relations, Tennessee Council of Family Relations, World Future Society.

WRITINGS: (Editor with B. A. Clendining, and contributor) *Christian Sex Education: A Resource Packet*, Broadman, 1970; (editor and contributor) *Helping People with Drug Problems: A Resource Packet*, Seminary Extension Department, Southern Baptist Seminaries, 1971; *The Shoot-'em-up Society*, Broadman, 1974; (editor and contributor) *Christian Freedom for Women and Other Human Beings*, Broadman, 1975; *Thank God for Sex: A Christian Model for Sexual Understanding and Behavior*, Broadman, 1975.

* * *

HOLMES, C. Raymond 1929-

PERSONAL: Born May 14, 1929, in Waukegan, Ill.; son of Carl L. Holmes; married Shirley S. Jarvinen, June 25, 1955; children: Carl David, Rhoda Ann. *Education:* Northern Michigan University, B.A. (with distinction), 1958; Lutheran School of Theology, Chicago, Ill., M.Div., 1961; Andrews University, M.Th. (magna cum laude), 1972, D.Min., 1975. *Home address:* Berrien Springs, Mich. 49103.

CAREER: Clergyman of Lutheran Church in America, 1961-71; clergyman of Seventh-Day Adventist Church, 1971—.

WRITINGS: Stranger in My Home, Southern Publishing, 1974. Contributor to *These Times, Signs of the Times*, and *Review and Herald*.

WORK IN PROGRESS: Listen to Him, on the theology of preaching, completion expected in 1978; *By Faith We Enter*, on theology of worship, 1980.

AVOCATIONAL INTERESTS: Horticulture, history, travel.

* * *

HOLMES, Robert A(lexander) 1943-

PERSONAL: Born July 13, 1943, in Shepherdstown, W.Va.; son of Clarence Arthur (a laborer) and Priscilla Lee (a maid; maiden name, Washington) Holmes; married Jean Ann Patterson (a registered nurse), February 2, 1963; children: Donna Lee, Darlene Marie, Robert A., Jr. *Education:* Shepherd College, B.S., 1964; Columbia University, M.A., 1966, Ph.D., 1969; post-doctoral study at Georgia State University, 1973-74. *Politics:* Democrat. *Religion:* Baptist. *Home:* 2421 Poole Rd. S.W., Atlanta, Ga. 30311. *Office:* Department of Political Science, Atlanta University, 223 Chesnut St. S.W., Atlanta, Ga. 30314.

CAREER: United Nations Development Program, New York, N.Y., intern-researcher, 1967; Hunter College of the City University of New York, New York, N.Y., instructor in political science, 1967-68; Upward Bound Program, Project Double Discovery, New York, N.Y., teacher, 1967-68; Harvard-Yale-Columbia Intensive summer study program, New York, N.Y., coordinator, 1968-69; Southern University, Baton Rouge, La., associate professor of political science, 1969-70; Bernard Baruch College of the City University of New York, New York, N.Y., director of "Search of Elevation, Education, and Knowledge Project," 1970-71; Atlanta University, Atlanta, Ga., associate professor, 1971-75, professor of political science, 1975—. Fellow at Center for African and Afro-American Studies, 1973. Senior research associate of Urban Affairs and Urban Transportation Project, Atlanta, Ga., 1972—; state representative in the Georgia General Assembly, 1974—. Member of advisory council on governmental services to Atlanta Regional Commission, 1973-74.

MEMBER: American Political Science Association, National Conference of Black Political Scientists (president, 1973-74), Association of Social and Behavioral Scientists (president-elect, 1975-76), Committee of Concerned Asian Scholars, Southern Council on International and Public Affairs, Atlanta Forum on National and International Affairs, University Center in Georgia Interdepartmental Political Science Group (president, 1973-74).

WRITINGS: (Contributor) David S. Smith, editor, *The Next Asia*, Columbia University Press, 1969; (contributor) Hanes Walton, Jr., editor, *The Study and Analysis of Black Politics*, Scarecrow, 1973; (with Sidney Davis) *A Study Design for the Westside Transportation Evaluation Study*, Georgia Department of Transportation, 1973; (with Davis, George Napper, and Robert Kronley) *Urban Transportation and Impact Analysis: A Bibliography*, U.S. Department of Transportation, 1973; (with Norman J. Powell) *Black Politics and Public Policy*, Emerson-Hall, 1975. Contributor to journals in his field. Member of editorial board of *Phylon*, 1972—; associate editor of *Journal of Social and Behavioral Sciences*, 1973—; contributing editor of *Black Collegian*, 1973—.

WORK IN PROGRESS: The Political Career of Andrew Young, and *Urban Transportation and Impact Analysis*, completion of both books expected in 1976.

SIDELIGHTS: "As a black political scientist," Holmes wrote, "I believe it is my responsibility to analyze the origins of black political powerlessness and to suggest strategies, ideas, and solutions for ameliorating the black situation. . . . Black scholars must not only point out the options available, but also participate in the mobilization and organization of the masses, because if theoreticians don't try to put their ideas into practice, most of their ideas will be stillborn."

AVOCATIONAL INTERESTS: Swimming, tennis, karate (third place in Georgia state championships, 1974).

* * *

HOLMES, Tommy 1903-1975

1903—March 25, 1975; American sports writer, and author of books about baseball. Obituaries: *New York Times*, March 26, 1975; *AB Bookman's Weekly*, April 21, 1975.

* * *

HOLT, Rochelle L(ynn) 1946-

PERSONAL: Born March 17, 1946, in Chicago, Ill.; daughter of Russell Thomas and Olga (Kochick) Holt. *Education:* University of Illinois, Chicago Circle, B.A.,

1967; University of Iowa, M.F.A., 1970. *Residence:* Birmingham, Ala. *Office:* Department of English and Fine Arts, Daniel Payne College, Birmingham, Ala. 35212.

CAREER: Morningside College, Sioux City, Iowa, instructor in English, 1970-73; Rust College, Holly Springs, Miss., instructor in Spanish, 1973-74; Mississippi Industrial College, Holly Springs, assistant professor of fine arts, 1974-75; Daniel Payne College, Birmingham, Ala., assistant professor of fine arts, 1975—. Co-owner of Ragnarok Press, 1970—. *Member:* Committee of Small Magazine Editors and Publishers. *Awards, honors:* National Endowment for the Arts grant, 1975, for Ragnarok Press; play production grant from Office of Advanced Drama of University of Minnesota, summer, 1975, for production, "Celebration of Woman."

WRITINGS—All published by Ragnarok, except as indicated—Books of poems: *To Make a Bear Dance*, 1970; *The Human Omelette*, 1971; *A Seismograph of Feeling*, 1972; *The Bare Tissue of Her Soul*, 1972; *Wing Span of an Albatross*, 1972; *A Ballet of Oscillations*, 1973; *A Peaceful Intent*, 1973; *Holly Springs: A Letter*, 1974; (with Margaret Taylor) *Landscapes*, 1974; *Poems for Amaefula*, 1974; *The Sun and the Moon*, 1974; *Yellow Pears: Smooth as Silk*, 1975; (with D. H. Stefanson) *Water, Light, Woman*, 1974; *Love in Spring*, 1975; (with Stefanson) *Gold Fantasy*, 1975; (with Srdjan Maljkovic) *Passports Out of Loneliness*, 1975; *Raks Rochelle* (Middle Eastern poems), 1975; *The Song of the Robin* (children's book), 1976.

Editor: *Eidolons*, 1972; *Children of the Moon*, 1973; (with Sharon Spencer) *Sprays of Rubies*, 1975; Leonora Carrington, *The Oval Lady* (short story translations), Capra, 1975; James Hearst, *Dry Leaves*, 1975.

Contributor: Bill Henderson, editor, *The Publish-It-Yourself Handbook*, Pushcart Book Press, 1975, reissued as *NOW Women Writers Conference Book*, United Sisters, 1975.

Author of multi-media play, "Celebration of Woman," first performed in Omaha, Neb., at Magic Theatre, November 7, 1975.

WORK IN PROGRESS: "Birmingham: A Moving Drama," a multi-media play; a multiple identity play for Black people to incorporate her libretto for the first part of "Cane" by Jean Toomer; a novel, *Figures*, with D. H. Stefanson, to be issued under joint pseudonym, Holt Stefanson.

SIDELIGHTS: Rochelle Holt writes: "I have been encouraged and inspired by my friends Anais Nin, Sharon Spencer, Megan Terry, Valerie Harms to continue my interest in a multi-media type writing involving poetry, plays, stories, novellas to explain my sense of poetic reality to a new innovative world of fiction."

*　　*　　*

HOLTROP, William Frans 1908-

PERSONAL: Born June 14, 1908, in Holland; son of John (a railroad engineer) and Geertruida (Bootsman) Holtrop; married Pauline Monette Black, June 6, 1938; children: John W., Barbara Jo (Mrs. Steve Erden), Marsha Jean (Mrs. Robert McBain). *Education:* Kearney State Teachers College, B.Sc., 1935; University of Missouri, M.Ed., 1938; University of California at Los Angeles, Ed.D., 1948. *Politics:* Democrat. *Religion:* Episcopalian. *Home:* Copco Lake, Montague, Calif. 96064.

CAREER: High school teacher of industrial and vocational

education in Lee's Summit, Mo., 1937-40, Corcoran, Calif., 1940-45, and Los Angeles, Calif., 1945-49; University of California, Santa Barbara, assistant professor, 1949-55, associate professor, 1955-64, lecturer in German and Dutch, 1964-73, professor emeritus, 1973—. Guest professor at Technical School, Port Harcourt, Nigeria, 1961-63. *Member:* Phi Delta Kappa.

WRITINGS: (With A. C. Newell) *Coloring, Finishing, and Painting Wood*, Charles A. Bennett, 1930, revised edition, 1972; (with Herman Hjorth) *Modern Machine Woodworking*, Bruce, 1937, revised edition, 1960; *Vocational Education in the Netherlands*, University of California Press, 1951; (with B. M. Cunningham) *Woodshop Tool Maintenance*, Charles A. Bennett, 1956; (with Hjorth) *Operation of Modern Woodworking Machines*, Bruce, 1958, revised edition, 1966; (with Hjorth) *Principles of Woodworking*, Bruce, 1961; *Building a Vacation Home Step By Step*, Sams, 1975.

WORK IN PROGRESS: *Wood Technology*, a major revision of the above woodworking books.

AVOCATIONAL INTERESTS: Travel (United States, Europe, Africa), swimming, fishing, sailing, bowling, and golf.

*　　*　　*

HOLWAY, John 1929-

PERSONAL: Born November 12, 1929, in Glen Ridge, N.J.; son of Edward J. (an engineer) and Frances (Rimbach) Holway; married Motoko Mori, October 15, 1954; children: James, John, Diane, Mona. *Education:* University of Iowa, B.A., 1950; Georgetown University, graduate study, 1956-57. *Home:* 7805 Chase Court, Manassas, Va. 22110. *Office:* U.S. Information Agency, 1776 Pennsylvania Ave. N.W., Washington, D.C. 20547.

CAREER: Employed with U.S. Information Agency, Washington, D.C., 1956—. *Military service:* U.S. Army, 1951-56; became first lieutenant.

WRITINGS: Japan Is Big League in Thrills, Tokyo News Service, 1955; *Sumo*, Tokyo News Service, 1956; *Voices of the Great Black Baseball Leagues*, Dodd, 1975. Contributor to national magazines and newspapers including *Look* and *American Heritage*.

WORK IN PROGRESS: Parapsychology in Sports; *A History of Presidential Elections*.

*　　*　　*

HONEYCUTT, Benjamin L(awrence) 1938-

PERSONAL: Born August 30, 1938, in Cliffside, N.C.; son of Jesse William (a superintendent of a water department) and Eloise (Sorgee) Honeycutt; married Joan Angle (a high school teacher), June 12, 1965; children: Mark Weldon, Kevin Forrest. *Education:* Wake Forest University, B.A. (magna cum laude), 1960; Ohio State University, M.A., 1962, Ph.D., 1969. *Home:* 1962 Jackson St., Columbia, Mo. 65201. *Office:* Department of Romance Languages, University of Missouri, Columbia, Mo. 65201.

CAREER: Ohio State University, Columbus, instructor, 1965-69, assistant professor of French, 1969-70; University of Missouri, Columbia, assistant professor, 1970-74, associate professor of French, 1974—. *Member:* Modern Language Association of America, American Association of Teachers of French, Mediaeval Academy of America, Midwest Modern Language Association, Phi Beta Kappa.

WRITINGS: (Contributor) John R. Allen, editor, *The Study of French Literature with Computers*, University of Manitoba, 1973; (editor with Thomas D. Cooke, and contributor) *The Humor of the Fabliaux: A Collection of Critical Essays*, University of Missouri Press, 1974. Contributor to language journals.

WORK IN PROGRESS: The Old French Fabliaux: Plots, Analogues, Manuscripts, and Editions, with Thomas D. Cooke; *A Concordance to the Lais of Marie de France*; research on the tenth-century bilingual alba; research on names of saints in the fabliaux.

SIDELIGHTS: Honeycutt writes: "I am particularly interested in the application of the computer to literary research, especially in my own area of medieval French language and literature."

* * *

HOOKER, Craig Michael 1951-

PERSONAL: Born November 2, 1951, in New Britain, Conn.; son of William James (a minister) and Doris (a saleswoman; maiden name, Walker) Hooker. *Education:* Attended Newbury Junior College, 1970-71, and Tunxis Community College, 1971. *Religion:* Methodist. *Home and office:* 496 Allen St., New Britain, Conn. 06051.

CAREER: Mail clerk, Fafnir Bearing, New Britain, Conn.; poet. *Member:* Young Men's Christian Association, National Association for the Advancement of Colored People, Organization of Black Social Unity.

WRITINGS: Honor Awakens Again for We All Are Gifted and Real (poems), Oyez Holmes Book Co., 1973.

WORK IN PROGRESS: A book of poetry, *The Real Me.*

SIDELIGHTS: Hooker told *CA*, "I consider writing of vital importance because this is how I talk with people."

* * *

HOOVER, Kenneth H(arding) 1920-

PERSONAL: Born December 11, 1920, in Cherry Hill, Ark.; son of Henry Ancil (a farmer) and Myrtle Virginia (Barber) Hoover; married Helene Mae Perry (a college professor), June 8, 1946; children: Annette Renee (Mrs. Thomas Riskas, Jr.), Rana Suzanne, Michelle Ann. *Education:* Louisiana State University, B.S., 1948, M.A., 1951; University of Washington, Seattle, Ed.D., 1955; summer postdoctoral study at Oklahoma State University, 1961. *Politics:* Independent. *Religion:* Church of Jesus Christ of Latter Day Saints. *Home:* 8525 South Newberry Lane, Tempe, Ariz. 85284. *Office:* College of Education, Arizona State University, Tempe, Ariz. 85281.

CAREER: High school teacher of science in the public schools of Sedro Woolley, Wash., 1950-53; University of Montana, Missoula, assistant professor of education, 1954-55; San Francisco State College (now University), San Francisco, Calif., assistant professor of education, 1955-56; Arizona State University, Tempe, professor of education, 1956—. Visiting lecturer at Washington State College, 1964, and Utah State University, 1965. *Military service:* U.S. Army Air Forces, 1941-45. *Member:* American Psychological Association, American Educational Research Association, National Association for Research in Science Teaching, Association for Student Teaching, National Education Association, Phi Kappa Phi, Kappa Delta Pi. *Awards, honors:* Certificate from National Conference of Christians and Jews, 1960, for outstanding leadership and service in the area of human relations.

WRITINGS: (With others) *Psychological Foundations of Education*, W. C. Brown, 1963; *Scientific Foundations of Education*, W. C. Brown, 1960, 2nd edition (with T. M. Weiss), 1964; *Learning and Teaching in the Secondary School*, Allyn & Bacon, 1964, 4th edition, 1975; *Readings on Learning and Teaching in the Secondary School*, Allyn & Bacon, 1968, 2nd edition, 1971; *A Handbook for High School Teachers*, Allyn & Bacon, 1970; (with P. M. Hollingsworth) *Learning and Teaching in the Elementary School*, Allyn & Bacon, 1970; (with Hollingsworth) *A Handbook for Elementary Teachers*, Allyn & Bacon, 1973, 2nd edition, 1974; *The Professional Teacher's Handbook*, Allyn & Bacon, 1973. Contributor to educational journals.

WORK IN PROGRESS: An Instructional Program for Secondary Methods; *A Learning Program for New Teachers*, completion expected in 1976.

* * *

HOPKINS, Lee (Wallace) 1934-

PERSONAL: Born June 30, 1934, in Los Angeles, Calif.; son of Leon Wallace (a publisher) and Eva (Bong) Hopkins; married Carol Porter (a dietitian), November 12, 1970. *Education:* University of California, Los Angeles, B.A., 1956. *Politics:* Populist. *Religion:* Anglican. *Home:* 855 Union St., San Francisco, Calif. 94133.

CAREER: Los Angeles Examiner, Los Angeles, Calif., member of advertising department, 1954-57; California Blue Shield, San Francisco, Calif., public relations and advertising director, 1959-66; Doremus & Co. (advertising agency), San Francisco, account executive, 1966-70; public relations consultant, San Francisco, 1970—; writer. *Military service:* U.S. Army, Infantry, 1957-59; became sergeant. *Member:* Audubon Society, San Francisco Bay Area Publicity Club.

WRITINGS: After They Learn to Dance, Capra, 1974. Contributor of reviews to *San Rafael Independent Journal* and *Peninsula Living.*

WORK IN PROGRESS: A collection of interlocking short fiction, *The Deceiving Mirror*, completion expected in 1975; a novel, *A Garden Full of Snow*, 1976.

SIDELIGHTS: Lee Hopkins told *CA*: "The politicalization of literature is its debasement. . . . Style today is best maintained by William Gaddis, Thomas Pynchon, J. P. Donleavy and few others." He described his work as "satiric in intent" and added that his personal outlook "is tempered by Anglophilia and distrust of certainties."

* * *

HORNGREN, Charles T(homas) 1926-

PERSONAL: Born October 28, 1926, in Milwaukee, Wis.; son of William E. and Grace K. (Manning) Horngren; married Joan E. Knickelbine, September 6, 1952; children: Scott W., Mary, Susan E., Catherine E. *Education:* Marquette University, B.S., 1949; Harvard University, M.B.A., 1952; University of Chicago, Ph.D., 1955. *Home:* 757 Tolman Dr., Stanford, Calif. 94305. *Office:* School of Business, Stanford University, Stanford, Calif. 94305.

CAREER: Certified public accountant in Wisconsin, 1953; Peat, Marwick, Mitchell & Co., Milwaukee, Wis., auditor, 1949-50; University of Chicago, Chicago, Ill., instructor, 1952-54, assistant professor, 1954-55, associate professor, 1959-62, professor of accounting, 1962-66; Marquette University, Milwaukee, Wis., assistant professor of accounting, and assistant to director of department, 1955-56; University of Wisconsin, Milwaukee, associate professor of accounting, 1956-59; Stanford University, Stanford, Calif., Edmund W. Littlefield Professor of Accounting, 1966—. Independent consultant in accounting, 1953—. Management services work at Touche, Ross, Baily & Smart, summer, 1963; member of board of directors of American Building Maintenance Industries, 1973—. *Military service:* U.S. Army, 1944-46. *Member:* American Accounting Association (president-elect, 1975-76), American Institute of Certified Public Accountants, National Association of Accountants, Institute of Management Sciences.

WRITINGS: (With J. A. Leer) *CPA Problems and Approaches to Solutions*, two volumes, Prentice-Hall, 1959, 4th edition, 1974; (editor with S. Davidson, D. O. Green, and G. H. Sorter) *Readings in Accounting Theory*, Prentice-Hall, 1964; *Cost Accounting: A Managerial Emphasis*, Prentice-Hall, 1962, 3rd edition, 1972; *Accounting for Management Control: An Introduction*, Prentice-Hall, 1965, 3rd edition, 1974; (contributor) Robert R. Sterling, editor, *Institutional Issues in Public Accounting*, Scholars Book Co., 1974. Contributor of more than thirty articles and reviews to journals. Member of board of consulting editors of *Management Services*, 1964—.

* * *

HORTON, Stanley M(onroe) 1916-

PERSONAL: Born May 6, 1916, in Huntington Park, Calif.; son of Harry Samuel (a minister) and Myrle May (a librarian; maiden name, Fisher) Horton; married Evelyn Gertrude Parsons (an organist), September 11, 1945; children: Stanley, Jr., Edward, Faith. *Education:* University of California, Berkeley, B.S., 1937; Gordon-Conwell Theological Seminary, M.Div., 1944; Harvard University, S.T.M., 1945; Central Baptist Theological Seminary, Th.D., 1959. *Politics:* Republican. *Home:* 615 West Williams St., Springfield, Mo. 65803. *Office:* Central Bible College, 3000 North Grant Ave., Springfield, Mo. 65802.

CAREER: Ordained minister of Assemblies of God Church, 1946; Metropolitan Bible Institute, North Bergen, N.J. instructor in Bible, 1945-48; Central Bible College, Springfield, Mo., assistant professor, 1948-56, associate professor, 1956-60, professor of Bible, 1960-75; Assemblies of God Graduate School, Springfield, Mo., associate professor of Bible, 1973—. Guest professor at Near East School of Bible and Archaeology, Jerusalem, 1962. *Member:* Society of Biblical Literature, Evangelical Theological Society, American Scientific Affiliation, Society for Pentecostal Studies, American Association of Professors of Hebrew, National Association of Evangelicals, Phi Alpha Chi.

WRITINGS—All published by Gospel Publishing: *Into All Truth*, 1955; *Panorama of the Bible* (manual), 1961; *Great Psalms* (teacher's and student's manuals), 1962; *Bible Prophecy* (manual), 1963; *Gospel of John* (manual), 1965; *The Promise of His Coming*, 1967; *Ready Always*, 1974; *It's Getting Late*, 1975; *Welcome Back Jesus*, 1975. Also author of *Adult Teacher*, an annual, 1952—. Contributor to *Encyclopedia Americana*; also contributor to *Pentecostal Evangel* and *Advance*. Consulting editor to *Paraclete*, 1967-75.

WORK IN PROGRESS: Prophets in Profile; a biblical theology of the Holy Spirit; 1976 edition of *Adult Teacher*; Greek and Hebrew word studies.

SIDELIGHTS: Horton has reading competence in French, German, Hebrew, Aramaic, and New Testament Greek.

HOSFORD, Philip L(ewis) 1926-

PERSONAL: Born May 7, 1926, in Lincoln, Neb.; son of Lisle R. (a professor) and Jessie (an author; maiden name, Wiegand) Hosford; married Mary Valentine, December 27, 1947; children: Hollis, Matthew, Shannon, Michael, Philip. *Education:* New Mexico Highlands University, B.A., 1949, M.A., 1953; University of Northern Colorado, Ed.D., 1963. *Home:* 2110 Gladys Dr., Las Cruces, N.M. 88001. *Office:* Department of Elementary and Secondary Education, New Mexico State University, Las Cruces, N.M. 88001.

CAREER: Roswell (N.M.) City Schools, teacher, principal, and director of instruction, 1950-63; New Mexico State University, Las Cruces, associate professor, 1963-69, professor of education and mathematics, 1969—, head of department of elementary and secondary education, 1967-69. *Member:* Association for Supervision and Curriculum Development (president, 1976-77).

WRITINGS: A Unit of Instruction on the PTA (booklet), New Mexico PTA, 1960; *Algebra for Elementary Teachers*, Harcourt, 1968; *An Instructional Theory: A Beginning*, Prentice-Hall, 1973. Contributor of articles and reviews to education journals. Editor of *New Mexico ASCD Newsletter*, 1969-75.

WORK IN PROGRESS: Researching the validity and reliability of objectively gained judgments of teacher-effectiveness.

AVOCATIONAL INTERESTS: Tennis, music.

* * *

HOSKEN, Fran(ziska) P(orges) 1919-

PERSONAL; Born July 12, 1919, in Vienna, Austria; came to United States, 1938, naturalized, 1944; daughter of Otto (a physician and educator) and Mary (an artist; maiden name, Low) Porges; married James C. Hosken (an engineer), 1947 (divorced, 1962); children: John, Caroline, Andrew. *Education:* Attended University of Vienna and University of Zurich, 1937-38; Smith College, B.A., 1940; Harvard University, M.Arch., 1944; Massachusetts Institute of Technology, special studies in urban planning, 1964-67. *Politics:* "My own/feminist." *Religion:* None. *Home and Office:* 187 Grant St., Lexington, Mass. 02173.

CAREER: Skidmore, Owings & Merrill, Chicago, Ill., architectural designer, 1946-47; Hosken, Inc. (design and manufacture of contemporary furniture), Boston, Mass., owner, manager, and designer-in-chief, 1948-54; Architectural Color Slides (educational slides and slide programs with text, by mail order), owner and photographer, 1948—; teacher of interior design, Garland College, Boston, and Cambridge Adult Education Center, Cambridge, 1958-61; interior design consultant with M. Brown, Boston, 1959-61; Bertram Goldberg & Associates, Chicago, technical editor for study based at State University of New York at Stony Brook, 1968-69; Tufts University, Experimental College, Boston, professor of urban design, 1970; teacher and developer of urban teaching programs, Education for Urban Living project of Harvard University and Community Projects Laboratory of Massachusetts Institute of Technology, both in Boston area, 1970-71; University Without Walls, Boston, associate professor of urban studies, 1971-74. Has developed multi-media presentations on architecture and urban affairs; has shown photography at Lexington Library, 1969-70, and paintings at Boston City Hall Concourse Gallery, 1973, 1974. Member of board, University

Without Walls. Consultant in housing. *Military service:* U.S. Coast Guard Women's Reserve, Communication Intelligence, 1944-45.

MEMBER: National Urban League, American Institute of Architecture, American Society of Planning Officials, American Institute of Planners (associate), National Housing Conference, Society for International Development, Boston Society of Architects (associate), National Organization for Women, Women's Equity Action League, National Women's Political Caucus, Federation of Professional Women's Organizations. *Awards, honors:* Awards from Museum of Modern Art, New York, 1948, 1949, for furniture design; Alpha Prize, Smith College, 1940.

WRITINGS: The Language of Cities, Macmillan, 1968, 2nd edition, Schenckman, 1972; (self-illustrated with photographs) *The Functions of Cities*, Schenckman, 1972; *The Kathmandu Valley Towns*, John Weatherhill, 1974.

Designer of media packages, including "The Changing Form and Functions of Cities" (twenty-one tapes), McGraw, 1970, and "The Visual City" (filmstrip and text), Warren Schloat Productions, 1972. Developed twelve newsletters for National Urban League, 1968-70. Weekly columnist on urban affairs, *Boston Globe*, 1964-65. Contributor to professional journals, and to *Christian Science Monitor, St. Louis Post, Boston Herald*, and other newspapers and magazines. Correspondent-at-large, *Architectural Forum*, 1972-74; founder and editor, *WIN News* (of Women's International Network), 1975—.

WORK IN PROGRESS: Women and the Urban Environment; a cross-cultural study, *Commitment for Change: The Status of Women around the World*; preparing an international directory of women's organizations, under auspices of the U.S. Agency for International Development; organizing the Women's International Network.

SIDELIGHTS: Fran Hosken has made urban study and photography trips to Europe, the Near East, Africa (East, West, and South), South and Central America, Japan, India, and Asia, and has visited Australia, New Zealand, and the U.S.S.R. She is bilingual in German and English, fluent in French, and knows Latin and some Spanish and Italian.

*   *   *

HOWALD, Reed Anderson   1930-

PERSONAL: Surname is pronounced *How*-ald; born November 23, 1930, in Pittsburgh, Pa.; son of Arthur Mark (a chemist) and Katharine (Anderson) Howald; married Elaine Sheperd, December 29, 1962; children: Glenn, Shere, Craig. *Education:* Oberlin College, B.A., 1952; University of Wisconsin, Ph.D., 1955. *Politics:* Independent or Democrat. *Religion:* Protestant. *Home address:* R. R. #2, Box 91, Bozeman, Mont. 59715. *Office:* Department of Chemistry, Montana State University, Bozeman, Mont. 59715.

CAREER: University of California at Los Angeles, instructor in chemistry, 1955-56; Harvard University, Cambridge, Mass., instructor in chemistry, 1956-59; Oberlin College, Oberlin, Ohio, assistant professor of chemistry, 1959-60; St. John's University, Jamaica, N.Y., assistant professor of chemistry, 1960-63; Montana State University, Bozeman, assistant professor, 1963-65, associate professor, 1965-69, professor of chemistry, 1969—. *Member:* American Chemical Society, Sigma Xi.

WRITINGS: (With Walter A. Manch) *The Science of Chemistry*, Macmillan, 1971.

WORK IN PROGRESS: Matrix Chemistry, an introduction to quantum mechanics; a novel, *A Pair of Kings*.

AVOCATIONAL INTERESTS: Fly fishing.

*   *   *

HOWE, Helen   1905-1975

January 11, 1905—February 1, 1975; American novelist, biographer, monologuist. Obituaries: *New York Times*, February 2, 1975; *Washington Post*, February 3, 1975; *AB Bookman's Weekly*, February 17, 1975; *Current Biography*, March, 1975. (*CA*-23/24)

*   *   *

HOWE, Hubert S(hattuck), Jr.   1942-

PERSONAL: Born December 21, 1942, in Portland, Ore.; son of Hubert S. (a salesman) and Anna (a teacher; maiden name, Moody) Howe; married Nancy Garland, February, 1965 (divorced, 1969); married Susan Frank (a psychologist), February 21, 1970. *Education:* Princeton University, A.B. (magna cum laude), 1964, M.F.A., 1967, Ph.D., 1972. *Politics:* Democrat. *Religion:* None. *Home:* 309 West 104th St., Apt. 3A, New York, N.Y. 10025. *Office:* Department of Music, Queens College of the City University of New York, Flushing, N.Y. 11367.

CAREER: Queens College of the City University of New York, Flushing, N.Y., instructor, 1967-68, assistant professor, 1969-73, associate professor of music, 1974—. Member of literature and materials faculty of Juilliard School, 1974—. *Member:* International Society for Contemporary Music (president of U.S. section of League of Composers), American Society of University Composers (past chairman), American Composers Alliance, American Music Center, College Music Society. *Awards, honors:* Grant from National Endowment for the Humanities, 1972; grant from City University of New York Research Foundation, 1973.

WRITINGS: Electronic Music Synthesis, Norton, 1975. Composer of "Computer Variations," "Kaleidoscope," "Interchanges," "Macro-Structure," "Freeze," "Three Studies in Timbre," and "Canons," all electronic music. Contributor to music journals. Associate editor of *Perspectives of New Music*.

WORK IN PROGRESS: A book on the theory of tonal music, for advanced students of harmony; a workbook for *Electronic Music Synthesis*; musical compositions; computer research in music.

*   *   *

HOWELL, Helen (Jane)   1934-

PERSONAL: Born January 28, 1934, in Ottawa, Kan.; daughter of John Merl (a Union Pacific railroad man) and Maurine (Gregg) Howell. *Education:* University of Omaha, B.S., 1955, M.S., 1962; University of Colorado, Ed.D., 1969. *Politics:* Republican. *Religion:* Methodist. *Home:* 4410 North 53rd St., Omaha, Neb. 68104. *Address:* Department of Education, University of Nebraska at Omaha, Box 688, Omaha, Neb. 68101.

CAREER: Omaha Public Schools, Omaha, Neb., elementary school teacher, 1955-62, supervisor of intermediate grades, 1962-64; University of Nebraska at Omaha, instructor, 1964-67, assistant professor, 1967-70, associate professor, 1970-72, professor of education, 1972—. *Member:* International Reading Association, National Council of

Teachers of English, Association for Supervision and Curriculum Development, Nebraska Association for the Gifted, Metropolitan Reading Council, P.E.O., Delta Kappa Gamma, Kappa Delta Pi, Alpha Xi Delta, Kappa Kappa Iota.

WRITINGS: (With Donald C. Cushenbery) *Reading and the Gifted Child: A Guide for Teachers*, C. C Thomas, 1974.

WORK IN PROGRESS: Research in the individualization of instruction in the elementary school.

AVOCATIONAL INTERESTS: Reading, travel.

* * *

HOWELL, Richard W(esley) 1926-

PERSONAL: Born September 6, 1926, in Berkeley, Calif; son of Lyle Wesley and Velma Pauline (Callender) Howell; married Jacqueline DelaMater, September 16, 1948; children: Paul Martin, Benjamin Alexander, David Luke, Andrew Philip. *Education:* University of California, Berkeley, A.B., 1949, Ph.D., 1967; University of Hawaii, M.A., 1951. *Home:* 162 Hoonanea St., Hawaii 96720. *Address:* Department of Anthropology, Hilo College, University of Hawaii, Box 1357, Hilo, Hawaii 96720.

CAREER: Intelligence analyst with National Security Agency in Washington, D.C., and in Japan, 1953-58; cryptolinguist with Army Security Agency in Japan, 1958-62; Richmond College of the City University of New York, Staten Island, N.Y., assistant professor of anthropology, 1967-69; University of Saskatchewan, Saskatoon, associate professor of anthropology, 1969-70; University of Hawaii, Hilo College, Hilo, associate professor of anthropology, 1970—, visiting professor of East Asian languages at Honolulu, 1975-76. *Military service:* U. S. Army, 1945-46; became staff sergeant. *Member:* American Anthropological Association, Asian Studies Association, Southern Anthropological Association. *Awards, honors:* U.S. Office of Education grant, 1968-69.

WRITINGS: (With H. J. Vetter) *Language in Behavior*, Behavioral Publications, 1975. Contributor to professional journals.

WORK IN PROGRESS: A book on Japanese emotional life.

* * *

HOY, James F(ranklin) 1939-

PERSONAL: Born December 15, 1939, in Wichita, Kan.; son of Kenneth L. (a farmer and stockman) and Marteil (a teacher; maiden name, Rice) Hoy; married Catherine June Thompson, March 13, 1965; children: Farrell Alysoun, Joshua Thompson. *Education:* Attended University of Kansas; Kansas State University, B.S., 1961; Emporia Kansas State College, M.A., 1965; University of Missouri, Ph.D., 1970. *Home:* 901 Rural, Emporia, Kan. 66801. *Office:* Department of English, Emporia Kansas State College, Emporia, Kan. 66801.

CAREER: Emporia Kansas State College, Emporia, assistant professor of English, 1970—. Visiting professor at Idaho State University, summer, 1975. *Member:* Modern Language Association of America, Mediaeval Academy of America, Central Renaissance Society, Rocky Mountain Modern Language Association, Western Literature Association, Kansas Folklore Society (president).

WRITINGS: (Editor with John Somer) *The Language*

Experience, Delta, 1974. Contributor to *Modern Philology, Milton Quarterly, Cattleman, Sixteenth Century Journal, Western American Literature, Heritage of Kansas*, and *Emporia State Research Studies*. Editor of *Newsletter* (of Kansas Folklore Society).

WORK IN PROGRESS: The Life and Times of the Texas and Southwestern Cattleman, an anthology from *Cattleman*; research on medieval drama in York.

AVOCATIONAL INTERESTS: Ranching, rodeoing, camping.

* * *

HOYER, Mildred N(aeher)

PERSONAL: Born in Brooklyn, N.Y.; daughter of Herman and Cora Ella (Merritt) Naeher; married Nils Gunther Hoyer, June 1, 1930. *Education:* Attended New York public schools. *Politics:* Republican. *Home:* 352 85th St., Brooklyn, N.Y. 11209.

CAREER: Poet and free-lance writer, 1935—. Associate editor, *Our Message*, 1937—; director of poetry workshop for National League of American Pen Women, 1961—; poets consultant and critic, 1965—. *Member:* Poetry Society of America, National League of American Pen Women, Haiku Society of America, Women Poets of New York (president, 1973—), Brooklyn Poetry Circle (president, 1968-72). *Awards, honors:* Various Brooklyn Poetry Circle awards (sponsored by Countess Ethelyn d'Esternaux), 1955, 1956, 1957, 1958, 1959, 1960, 1961, 1964, as well as their annual book award, 1963, and gold medal, 1968; awards from National League of American Pen Women, 1959, 1965, 1968, 1969, 1970, 1971; World Poetry Day award from *Imprints Quarterly*, 1969; *Haiku Highlights* book award, 1970; Anne Lloyd award from Women Poets of New York, 1971.

WRITINGS: The Master Key (poetry), Golden Quill, 1965; *Leaves of Laughs* (light verse), Peacock Press, 1974. Contributor to poetry journals, newspapers, and magazines including *Christian Science Monitor, Saturday Evening Post, Poetry Personalities*, and *Educational Forum*.

WORK IN PROGRESS: This Is the Day, a book of inspirational poetry; *Ever the Evergreen*, a book of traditional and modern poetry.

* * *

HUBER, Leonard Victor 1903-

PERSONAL: Born May 25, 1903, in New Orleans, La.; son of Victor (a contractor) and Eleonora (Reisig) Huber; married Audrey Wells, September 27, 1928; children: Leonard V., Jr., Lloyd Wells. *Education:* Attended Tulane University, 1926-35. *Politics:* "Democrat who generally votes Republican." *Religion:* Presbyterian. *Home:* 204 Fairway Dr., New Orleans, La. 70124. *Office:* 4841 Canal St., New Orleans, La. 70119.

CAREER: Victor Huber & Sons, Inc. (contractors), New Orleans, La., president, 1938—, President of St. John Cemetery Association, Inc., 1941—, and of Orleans Parish Landmarks Commission, 1956—; member of Vieux Carre Commission, 1957-61; chairman of board of trustees of Keyes Foundation, 1961—. *Member:* Louisiana Historical Association (past board member), Friends of the Cabildo (president, 1972-73), Orleans Philharmonic Symphony Society. *Awards, honors:* M.H.L. from Tulane University, 1974.

WRITINGS: (With Clarence A. Wagner) *The Great Mail: A Postal History of New Orleans*, American Philatelic Society, 1949; *Impressions of Girod Street Cemetery and a Plan to Rescue Some of Its Monuments* (booklet), Louisiana Landmarks Society, 1951; (with Samuel Wilson, Jr. and Garland F. Taylor) *Louisiana Purchase* (booklet), Louisiana Landmarks Society, 1953; (with Ray Samuel and Warren C. Ogden) *Tales of the Mississippi*, Hastings House, 1955; (with Albert R. Huber) *The New Orleans Tomb*, Design Hints, 1956; *Advertisements of Lower Mississippi River Steamboats: 1812-1920*, Steamship Historical Society, 1959; *Beginnings of Steamboat Mail on Lower Mississippi* (booklet), American Philatelic Society, 1960; (with Guy F. Bernard) *To Glorious Immortality: The Rise and Fall of the Girod Street Cemetery*, Alblen Books, 1961; (with Wilson and Abbye A. Gorin) *The St. Louis Cemeteries of New Orleans* (booklet), St. Louis Cathedral, 1963; (with Wilson) *Baroness Pontalba's Buildings*, Louisiana Landmarks Society, 1964; (with John C. Chase, Hermann B. Deutsch, and Charles L. Dufour) *Citoyens, Progres et Politique de la Nouvelle Orleans: 1889-1964* (title means "Citizens, Progress, and Politics of New Orleans"), E. S. Upton, 1964; (with Wilson) *The Basilica on Jackson Square and Its Predecessors: 1727-1965*, Basilica of St. Louis, 1965; *New Orleans as It Was in 1814-1815* (booklet), Battle of New Orleans One Hundred and Fiftieth Anniversary Committee, 1965.

(With Wilson) *The Cabildo on Jackson Square*, Friends of the Cabildo, 1970; (with Dufour) *If Ever I Cease to Love: One Hundred Years of Rex, 1872-1971*, School of Design, Rex Organization, 1971; *New Orleans: A Pictorial History from the Earliest Times to the Present Day*, Crown, 1971; *Lakeview Lore* (booklet), First National Bank of Commerce, 1972; *Mardi Gras Invitations of the Gilded Age*, Upton Printing, 1972; (with Peggy McDowell and Mary Lou Christovich) *New Orleans Architecture: The Cemeteries*, Friends of the Cabildo, 1974; *Notable New Orleans Landmarks*, Orleans Parish Landmarks Commission, 1974; *Louisiana: A Pictorial History*, Scribner, 1975.

Contributor to magazines, including *Waterways Journal*, *New Orleans Magazine*, *American Heritage*, and *Civil War History*.

WORK IN PROGRESS: *A History of New Orleans Carnival and Mardi Gras*; a monograph or small book on the history of Mortuary Chapel, to be called *The Church Which Wouldn't Die*.

SIDELIGHTS: Huber spent forty years assembling a collection of more than ten thousand pictures, prints, and other items chronicling the history of New Orleans and Louisiana. His archives were recently acquired by the Kemper and Leila Williams Foundation for inclusion in the Historic New Orleans Collection, housed in the Vieux Carre.

BIOGRAPHICAL/CRITICAL SOURCES: *New Orleans Times-Picayune*, May 19, 1974.

*		*		*

HUDDLE, David 1942-

PERSONAL: Born July 11, 1942, in Ivanhoe, Va.; son of Charles R., Jr. (an industrial manager) and Mary F. (Akers) Huddle; married Lindsey Massie (a recreation director), August 31, 1968; children: Elizabeth Ross. *Education:* University of Virginia, B.A., 1968; Hollins College, M.A., 1969; Columbia University, M.F.A., 1971. *Home address:* P.O. Box 172, Essex Center, Vt. 05451. *Agent:*

Ellen Levine, Curtis Brown Ltd., 60 East 56th St., New York, N.Y. 10022. *Office:* Department of English, University of Vermont, Burlington, Vt. 05401.

CAREER: University of Vermont, Burlington, assistant professor of English, 1971—. *Military service:* U.S. Army, parachutist, 1964-67; became sergeant; received Bronze Star Medal.

WRITINGS: *A Dream with No Stump Roots in It* (stories), University of Missouri Press, 1975. Contributor of stories, poems, and reviews to literary magazines, including *Texas Quarterly*, *Georgia Review*, and *Carleton Miscellany*, and to *Esquire*.

*		*		*

HUFFORD, Susan 1940-

PERSONAL: Born December 15, 1940, in Cincinnati, Ohio; daughter of William, Jr. and Helen (Berger) Hufford. *Education:* DePauw University, B.A., 1960; Temple University, M.A., 1961; also studied in Austria. *Agent:* Jane Jordan Browne, 9507 Santa Monica, Beverly Hills, Calif.

CAREER: Actress and singer; appeared in Broadway production of "Fiddler on the Roof," 1970-72, in Broadway musical production "Billy," on television, and with theatrical touring companies.

WRITINGS—Gothic novels: *Midnight Sailing*, Popular Library, 1975; *Devil's Sonata*, Popular Library, 1975; *A Delicate Deceit*, Popular Library, in press.

WORK IN PROGRESS: *Trial of Innocence*, a novel, for Popular Library; a motion picture screenplay about contemporary relationships.

SIDELIGHTS: Susan Hufford writes: "... As a form I've become quite intrigued with the gothic novel ... its history and its potential for modern women. I reject the notion that the gothic revolves around a weak, ineffectual female. In the past, many of these books have been written by men, using women's names but as elsewhere in our lives, women are demanding more for themselves. As a feminist, I was at first in conflict over the fact that I was writing gothic novels—a traditionally unliberated form. But now I feel quite differently."

*		*		*

HUG, Bernal D(ean) 1896-

PERSONAL: Born August 4, 1896, in Elgin, Ore.; son of Walter F. (a farmer) and Beatrice (a teacher; maiden name, McKinnis) Hug; married Carmi E. Holbrook, February 3, 1920; children: Bernal, Jr., Betty (Mrs. Gifford Hulse), Anna Louise (Mrs. James Carlson), Caryl (Mrs. Robert Dawes), Edwin, Elwyn. *Education:* Attended Oregon Agricultural College (now Oregon State University), 1914-15. *Politics:* "Vote for the man not party. Think most of government should be in small community." *Religion:* "Christian principles are vital to save our culture." *Home and office address:* Rt. 1, Box 10, Elgin, Ore. 97827.

CAREER: Farmer. Member of advisory council for county agricultural agent, member of school board and Chamber of Commerce, and justice of the peace, all in Elgin, Ore.; Union County (Ore.) commisioner, 1962-70. *Member:* Farmers Union, Farm Bureau, Grange, Grain Growers (member of board), Blue Mountain Seed Growers, Oregon Seed Growers League (co-organizer, 1942; president, 1945—). *Awards, honors:* Forester of the Year award from Union County Chamber of Commerce, 1958, Conservation Man of the Year award, 1966.

WRITINGS: *100 Years of Hugs*, Elgin Recorder Publishing Co., 1960; (editor) *History of Union County, Oregon*, Historical Society of Union County, Oregon, 1961; *Salt of the Earth*, Elgin Recorder Publishing Co., 1964; *Our Space Ship*, East Oregonian, 1973.

WORK IN PROGRESS: Research on indians and outstanding individuals and their accomplishments; poetry.

AVOCATIONAL INTERESTS: Photography.

* * *

HUGHES, Graham 1928-

PERSONAL: Born July 20, 1928, in Wales; son of William John (an engineer) and Elizabeth (James) Hughes; married Catherine Dolan, 1949 (divorced, 1958); married Helene Feldman, January 21, 1959; children: (first marriage) Geraint; (second marriage) Dafydd. *Education:* Cambridge University, B.A., 1948, M.A., 1950; University of Wales, LL.B., 1952; New York University, LL.M., 1961. *Politics:* Socialist. *Religion:* None. *Home:* 5 Woodcock Rd., West Nyack, N.Y. 10994. *Office:* School of Law, New York University, Washington Sq., New York, N.Y. 10012.

CAREER: University of Hull, Hull, England, lecturer in law, 1952-56; Yale University, New Haven, Conn., assistant professor of law, 1956-59; University of Wales, Aberystwyth, senior lecturer in law, 1959-63; New York University, New York, N.Y., professor of law, 1963—. Attorney in private practice; director of Public Studies Corp.; member of court of governors of University of Wales. *Member:* New York Bar, American Society for Political and Legal Philosophy (president, 1972-74). *Awards, honors:* Journal Fund Award for learned writing, 1959.

WRITINGS: *Law, Reason, and Justice*, New York University Press, 1969; *The Conscience of the Courts*, Doubleday, 1975. Contributor to *Encyclopaedia Britannica*. Contributor to legal journals and to *New Republic*, *Village Voice*, and *Antioch Review*.

WORK IN PROGRESS: Continuing research on legal philosophy, criminal law, and procedure.

AVOCATIONAL INTERESTS: Romance and Celtic languages and literature, folk-music, particularly Portuguese fados.

* * *

HUGHES, John Jay 1928-

PERSONAL: Born May 14, 1928, in New York, N.Y.; son of William Dudley Foulke (an Anglican priest) and Marguerite Montgomery (Jay) Hughes. *Education:* Harvard University, A.B., 1948; graduate study at Kelham Theological College, 1948-51, and University of Innsbruck, 1960-61; General Theological Seminary, S.T.B., 1953; University of Muenster, D.Th., 1969. *Politics:* Independent. *Home:* 6825 Natural Bridge, St. Louis, Mo. 63121. *Office:* Department of History, St. Louis University, St. Louis, Mo. 63103.

CAREER: Ordained Anglican priest, 1954; Grace Episcopal Church, Newark, N.J., curate, 1953-55; St. John's Episcopal Church, Bisbee, Ariz., rector, 1956-59; Collegium Augustinianum, Gaesdonck bei Goch, Germany, housemaster, 1962-65; conditionally ordained Roman Catholic priest, 1968; St. Thomas More Church, Muenster, Germany, curate and choirmaster, 1968-69; St. Louis University, St. Louis, Mo., associate professor, 1970-74, adjunct professor of history, 1974—. Visiting professor at University of Louvain, 1969. *Member:* Conference on British Studies, American Association of University Professors (vice-president of local chapter, 1973-74), American Historical Association, American Catholic Historical Association (member of executive council), American Society of Church History, Sixteenth Century Studies Conference, Common Cause, Harvard Club of St. Louis. *Awards, honors:* Silver medal from German Cruising Club, 1964; American Philosophical Society research grant, 1974.

WRITINGS: *Absolutely Null and Utterly Void*, Corpus Publications, 1968; *Stewards of the Lord*, Sheed, 1970; *Man for Others*, Sheed (London), 1970, Our Sunday Visitor, 1971; *Zur Frage der Anglikanischen Weihen* (title means "On the Question of Anglican Orders"), Herder Verlag, 1973. Contributor of more than seventy articles and reveiws to periodicals.

WORK IN PROGRESS: A biography of Gilbert Burnet (1643-1715), the historian and Bishop of Salisbury.

SIDELIGHTS: Hughes is an enthusiastic and experienced salt-water sailor, having sailed almost ten thousand miles in northern European waters.

BIOGRAPHICAL/CRITICAL SOURCES: *Catholic Bookseller and Librarian*, January/February, 1969.

* * *

HULT, Ruby El 1912-

PERSONAL: Born August 14, 1912, in Belgrove, Idaho; daughter of John A. (a blacksmith) and Carolina (Pearson) Hult; married Sven J. Sether, August 14, 1953 (died June, 1959); married Raymond L. McAndrew, May 29, 1961. *Education:* Attended University of Washington, Seattle, 1945-47. *Home:* 540 East Santa Clara St., Apt. 105, Ventura, Calif. 93001.

CAREER: *Washington State Journal of Nursing*, Seattle, assistant editor, 1949-52; *Port Angeles Evening News*, Port Angeles, Wash., proofreader, 1952-53; *CHANGE* (publication of Center for the Study of Democratic Institutions), Santa Barbara, Calif., 1965-66; author; has also worked as a secretary.

WRITINGS: *Steamboats in the Timber*, Caxton, 1952, 2nd edition, Binfords, 1968; *The Untamed Olympics: The Story of a Peninsula*, Binfords, 1954, 2nd edition, 1971; *Lost Mines and Treasures of the Pacific Northwest*, Binfords, 1957; *Northwest Disaster: Avalanche and Fire*, Binfords, 1960; *Guns of the Lewis and Clark Expedition* (pamphlet), Washington State Historical Society, 1960; (contributor) Ellis Lucia, editor, *This Land Is Our Land* (anthology), Doubleday, 1969; *Treasure Hunting Northwest*, Binfords, 1971. Contributor of one hundred articles to magazines, including *Negro Digest*.

WORK IN PROGRESS: *An Olympic Mountain Enchantment*; *Through the Sausage Grinder at the Think Factory: A Working Girl's Experiences at the Center for the Study of Democratic Institutions*.

* * *

HUME, Kathryn 1945-

PERSONAL: Born December 10, 1945, in Boston, Mass.; daughter of John W. (a professor of chemistry) and Fedna (Tweedt) Irvine; married Robert D. Hume (a professor of English), June 18, 1966. *Education:* Radcliffe College, A.B., 1967; University of Pennsylvania, M.A., 1968, Ph.D., 1971. *Office:* Department of English, Cornell University, Ithaca, N.Y. 14853.

CAREER: Cornell University, Ithaca, N.Y., assistant professor of English, 1973—. *Member:* Modern Language Association of America, Society for the Advancement of Scandinavian Study, Viking Society for Northern Research, Mediaeval Academy of America, Modern Language Society (Helsinki, Finland).

WRITINGS: The Owl and the Nightingale: The Poem and Its Critics, University of Toronto Press, 1975. Contributor to scholarly journals.

WORK IN PROGRESS: A book on the non-mimetic, fantasy component of Western literature.

* * *

HUMPHREY, Robert L. 1923-

PERSONAL: Born February 12, 1923, in Emporia, Kan.; son of Robert B. (a salesman) and Sue (an educator; maiden name, Rawlings) Humphrey; married wife, Margaret, November 24, 1949; children: Robert, Bradford, Galen, Susan, Jess. *Education:* University of Wisconsin, B.B.A., 1947; Harvard University, J.D., 1950; Fletcher School of Law and Diplomacy, M.A., 1952. *Politics:* Independent. *Home:* 820 Avenue F, Coronado, Calif. 92118. *Office:* American Institutes for Research, WCMTT MCRD MCB, San Diego, Calif. 92140.

CAREER: Cross-cultural educator in Italy, Turkey, Korea, Thailand, Vietnam, and Latin America; U.S. Cross Cultural Center, Izmir, Turkey, director, 1958-60; executive and public affairs director, U.S.A.F.T.A., 1960-62; American Institutes for Research, San Diego, Calif., executive scientist, 1962—; Cross-cultural Studies Center, La Jolla, Calif., president, 1974—. *Military service:* U.S. Marine Corps, 1943-45.

WRITINGS: Handbook for Overseas Orientation Officers, American Institutes for Research, 1966; *Scientific Ethic: Dual Life Value*, Grossmont Press, 1974. Contributor to political science journals.

WORK IN PROGRESS: With Aliton M. Fairchild, *Values Identification*, an adult education human relations programmed text.

BIOGRAPHICAL/CRITICAL SOURCES: Bridge and Bay, winter, 1974.

* * *

HUNKINS, Francis P(eter) 1938-

PERSONAL: Born May 22, 1938, in Cambridge, Mass.; son of Franklin P. (a businessman) and Marguerite (a teacher; maiden name, Sullivan) Hunkins; married Doreen B. Field (an artist), December, 1964; children: Leah Denese, Francis P., Jr. *Education:* Salem State College, B.A.Ed. (magna cum laude), 1960; Boston University, M.Ed., 1963; Kent State University, Ph.D., 1966. *Politics:* Independent. *Religion:* Roman Catholic. *Office:* College of Education, 111 Miller Hall, University of Washington, Seattle, Wash. 98195.

CAREER: Elementary school teacher in Gloucester, Mass., 1960-63; University of Washington, Seattle, assistant professor, 1966-69, associate professor, 1969-73, professor of education, 1973—. Former field reader for U.S. Office of Education; former field evaluator for Educational Media Selection Centers project. Member of National Council for the Social Studies' task force for the study of international education, 1970-72. Consultant to Bureau of Indian Affairs and Coronet Films. *Member:* American

Educational Research Association, Association for Supervision and Curriculum Development, National Council for the Social Studies, National Society for the Study of Education, Professors of Curriculum, World Future Society, Phi Delta Kappa.

WRITINGS: The Influence of Analysis and Evaluation Questions on Achievement and Critical Thinking in Sixth Grade Social Studies, University of Washington Press, 1968; (with O. L. Davis, Jr.) *Asking About the U.S.A. and Its Neighbors*, with teacher's guide, American Book Co., 1971, revised edition, 1975; (editor with Davis and others, and contributor) *Seeing Near and Far*, American Book Co., 1971, revised edition, 1975; (editor with Davis and others, and contributor) *Observing People and Places*, American Book Co., 1971, revised edition, 1975; (editor with Davis and others, and contributor) *Comparing Ways and Means*, American Book Co., 1971, revised edition, 1975; (editor with Davis and others, and contributor) *Investigating Communities and Cultures*, American Book Co., 1971, revised edition, 1975; (editor with Davis and others, and contributor) *Learning About Countries and Societies*, American Book Co., 1971, revised edition, 1975; *Questioning Strategies and Techniques*, Allyn & Bacon, 1972; (with Patricia F. Spears) *Social Studies for the Evolving Individual*, Association for Supervision and Curriculum Development, 1973; *Involving Students in Questioning*, Allyn & Bacon, in press.

Contributor: John Jarolimek and Huebner Walsh, editors, *Readings for Social Studies in Elementary Education*, 2nd edition (Hunkins did not contribute to first edition), Macmillan, 1969; Wayne L. Herman, editor, *Current Research in Elementary School Social Studies*, Macmillan, 1969; Ralph Jones, editor, *Social Studies Education for Young Americans*, Kendall-Hunt, 1970; *Washington State's Alternative Education*, Washington State Board of Education, 1972; Allan O. Kownslar, editor, *Teaching American History: The Quest for Relevancy*, National Council for the Social Studies, 1974.

Contributor of more than forty articles to education journals. Member of advisory board of *Social Education*, 1972, 1973; former consultant to *Educational Leadership*.

WORK IN PROGRESS: Research on cognitive responses of children to specific types of questions; a book dealing with curriculum.

AVOCATIONAL INTERESTS: Travel (New Zealand, Australia, India, England, and Ireland), dance, skiing.

* * *

HUNT, Dave
See HUNT, David C(harles Hadden)

* * *

HUNT, David C(harles Hadden) 1926-
(Dave Hunt)

PERSONAL: Born September 30, 1926, in Riverside, Calif.; son of Albert E. (a chiropractor) and Lillian M. (Wilkins) Hunt; married Ruth E. Klassen (a teacher), June 24, 1950; children: David, Janna, Karen, Jon. *Education:* Oregon State University, student, 1947-48; University of California, Los Angeles, B.A., 1951. *Politics:* Conservative. *Religion:* Christian. *Residence:* Northridge, Calif.

CAREER: Thomas & Moore (certified public accountants), Los Angeles, Calif., staff accountant, 1951-54; David C. Hunt, Beverly Hills, Calif., certified public accountant,

1954-56; United Properties of America, Beverly Hills, Calif., vice-president and general manager, 1956-66; Amerige Convalescent Hospital, Fullerton, Calif., owner and administrator, 1967-72; writer, 1972—. *Military service:* U.S. Naval Reserve, 1944-45; served in South Pacific. U.S. Army, 1946-47; served in Japan.

WRITINGS—All under name Dave Hunt: (Editor) William Law, *The Power of the Spirit*, Christian Literature Crusade, 1970; *Confessions of a Heretic* (autobiography), Logos International, 1972, published in paperback as *On the Brink*, 1975; (with Hershel Smith) *The Devil and Mr. Smith* (biography), Revell, 1974; (with Hans Kristian) *Mission: Possible* (biography), Revell, 1975.

WORK IN PROGRESS: Death of a Guru, biography of a young Hindu, the son of a famous yogi; *Beyond Charisma*, autobiographical sequel to *Confessions of a Heretic; Death Where Is Your Sting?*, a novel based on Hunt's original story from which was made the film "A Time to Run"; *Passport to Immortality*, nonfiction.

SIDELIGHTS: Hunt writes: "... My interest is in presenting the validity of Christian experience to the contemporary public ... I have a series of books in mind involving the return of Christ and the end of the world, almost science-fiction but more realistic because not projected so far into the future ... I am also interested in writing a definitive dramatic-history of the persecution of believers in the Soviet Union, and have visited there twice and interviewed a number of people and accumulated a great deal of source material. I believe that current events prove the failure of the psychological-sociological-political methods to cure the ills of society, and want to present man's return to God as the only solution." *Avocational interests:* International travel, skiing, backpacking, tennis, fishing.

* * *

HURST, M(ichael) E(liot) Eliot
See ELIOT HURST, M(ichael) E(liot)

* * *

HUSSEY, David Edward 1934-

PERSONAL: Born June 28, 1934, in London, England; son of Walter and Alma (Pearl) Hussey; married Evelyn Dorothy Wilson, April 23, 1960; children: Dorothy Anne, Susan Catherine. *Education:* Chartered Institute of Secretaries, A.C.I.S., 1957; University of South Africa, B.Com., 1966. *Religion:* Methodist. *Residence:* Horsham, Sussex, England. *Office:* Otis Elevator Co. Ltd., St. Clare House, 30-33 Minories, London E.C.3, England.

CAREER: Employed by Government of Rhodesia and Nyasaland, 1951-64; Union Carbide, London, England, project analyst, 1964-67; Fyffs Group (United Fruit), London, England, planning manager, 1967-69; Wander Ltd. and Sandoz Ltd., planning manager, 1969-72; Otis Elevator Co. Ltd., London, England, planning manager, 1972—. *Military service:* Rhodesian Territorials, 1952-64. *Member:* Society for Long Range Planning (past vice-chairman; member of executive committee, 1967—). *Awards, honors:* Co-winner, John Player Management Author of the Year award, 1974, for *Corporate Planning: Theory and Practice*.

WRITINGS: Introducing Corporate Planning, Pergamon, 1971; *Corporate Planning: Theory and Practice*, Pergamon, 1974; (editor) *Corporate Planner's Yearbook*, Pergamon, 1974, 2nd edition, in press; *Inflation and Business Policy*, Longman, in press.

Contributor: Martin Christopher and Gordon Wills, editors, *Marketing Logistics and Distribution Planning*, Allen & Unwin, 1972; Philip Sadler and Alan Robson, editors, *Corporate Planning*, Institute of Cost and Management Accountants, 1973; Peter Baynes, editor, *Case Studies in Corporate Planning*, Pitman, 1973; Subhash Jain and Surendra Singhvi, editors, *Essentials of Corporate Planning*, Planning Executives Institute, 1973; Stanley Oliver, editor, *Accountant's Guide to Management Techniques*, Gower Press, 1975; Bernard Taylor and David Farmer, editors, *Corporate Planning and Procurement*, Longman, in press. Contributor of more than twenty-five articles to scholarly journals, including *Accountant, Long Range Planning, Director, Financial Times, International Journal of Physical Distribution*, and *Works Management*.

WORK IN PROGRESS: The Magic Sandcastle, fiction for children; research on corporate planning in local government and on smuggling in the eighteenth century.

SIDELIGHTS: Hussey is turning his attention to corporate strategy and business policy under conditions of high inflation, which he sees as one of the major problems of management and society today.

When the Rhodesian Federation broke up it dissolved what was to Hussey a worthwhile experiment in racial partnership, and he went to England to live. He has traveled in Australia, New Zealand, Jamaica, to Singapore, and to much of Africa and Europe. *Avocational interests:* His family, the countryside, gardening, antique maps, reading, history.

BIOGRAPHICAL/CRITICAL SOURCES: Financial Times, February 19, 1971; *International Management*, March, 1971, April, 1972; *Bulaway Chronicle*, May, 1971.

* * *

HUSTE, Annemarie 1943-

PERSONAL: Born May 30, 1943, in Ulm, Donau, Germany; daughter of Karl (a furrier) and Anna (a furrier; maiden name, Bass) Huste; children: Beatrice Tara. *Education:* Attended schools in Germany. *Office:* 164 Lexington Ave., New York, N.Y. 10016.

CAREER: Chef for Billy Rose in New York, N.Y., 1965-66, for Jacqueline Kennedy Onassis in New York, N.Y., 1966-68; Annemarie Enterprises, Inc., New York, N.Y., president, 1969—. *Awards, honors:* R. T. French Tastemaker Award, 1968.

WRITINGS: Annemarie's Personal Cookbook, Bartholomew House, 1968; *Annemarie's Cookingschool Cookbook*, Houghton, 1974. Contributor to *Saturday Evening Post* and *Cosmopolitan*.

WORK IN PROGRESS: A book on good food and good nutrition.

* * *

HUTCHISON, (Dorothy) Dwight 1890(?)-1975

1890(?)—February 22, 1975; American artist, and author of short stories, articles, and books. Obituaries: *New York Times*, February 26, 1975; *AB Bookman's Weekly*, March 24, 1975.

* * *

HUTT, Max L. 1908-

PERSONAL: Born September 13, 1908, in New York, N.Y.; son of Israel (a builder) and Pauline Hutt; married

Anne Gromet, February 4, 1933. *Education:* City College (now City College of the City University of New York), A.B., 1928, M.S., 1930; graduate study at Columbia University, 1929-33. *Religion:* Jewish. *Home:* 21 Regent Dr., Ann Arbor, Mich. 48104. *Office:* 512 First National Bldg., Ann Arbor, Mich. 48108.

CAREER: City College (now City College of the City University of New York), New York, N.Y., instructor in psychology, 1928-41, head of Educational Clinic, 1939-41; Child Consultation Center, New York, N.Y., director, 1941-43; private practice as consulting psychologist, 1947—. University of Michigan, Ann Arbor, professor of psychology, 1947-60, consultant to University Hospital, 1947-50; University of Detroit, Detroit, Mich., professor of psychology, 1968-73, director of Psychology Clinic, 1968-73. Diplomate in clinical psychology from American Board of Examiners in Professional Psychology. *Military service:* U.S. Army, 1943-47; became lieutenant. *Member:* American Psychological Association (council member), American Association of University Professors, Society for the Study of Social Issues, Society for the Study of Projective Techniques, Midwestern Psychological Association, Michigan Society of Consulting Psychologists, Michigan Psychological Association, Michigan Society of Projective Techniques, Psi Chi.

WRITINGS: Patterns of Abnormal Behavior, Allyn & Bacon, 1957; *The Mentally Retarded Child*, Allyn and Bacon, 1958, 3rd edition, 1975; *The Child: Development and Adjustment*, Allyn & Bacon, 1959; *The Hutt Adaptation of the Bender-Gestalt Test*, Grune, 1960, 2nd edition, 1969; *Psychology: The Science of Behavior*, Harper, 1965, 2nd edition, 1971; *Psychology: The Science of Interpersonal Behavior*, Harper, 1966; *An Atlas for the Hutt Adaptation of the Bender-Gestalt Test*, Grune, 1970. Author of thirty-five research papers.

WORK IN PROGRESS: Psychosynthesis: The Genuine Therapist; three research studies.

* * *

HUTT, W(illiam) H(arold) 1899-

PERSONAL: Born August 3, 1899, in London, England; son of William and Louisa (Fricker) Hutt; married Margaretha L. Schonken, December 14, 1946. *Education:* London School of Economics and Political Science, B.Com., 1924. *Politics:* None. *Religion:* None. *Address:* Department of Economics, University of Dallas, Irving, Tex. 75061.

CAREER: Employed by Benn Brothers Ltd., London, England, 1924-26, and by Individualist Bookshop Ltd., London, 1926-28; University of Cape Town, Cape Town, South Africa, senior lecturer, 1928-31, professor of commerce, 1931-65, professor emeritus, 1965—, dean of Faculty of Commerce, 1931-64, director of Postgraduate School of Business Administration, 1962-64; University of Dallas, Irving, Tex., Distinguished Professor of Economics, 1971—, chairman of department, 1972—. Visiting professor at University of Virginia, 1966, Rockford College, 1967, 1968, Wabash College, 1967, Texas A & M University, 1968-69, California State University (Hayward), 1970-71. Visiting research fellow at Hoover Institution on War, Revolution, and Peace (of Stanford University), 1969-71. *Military service:* Royal Air Force, 1917-19. *Member:* Mont Pelerin Society, Philadelphia Society.

WRITINGS: The Theory of Collective Bargaining, Staples Press, 1930, 2nd edition, in press; *Economists and the Public*, J. Cape, 1936; *The Theory of Idle Resources*, J.

Cape, 1939; *Plan for Reconstruction*, Routledge & Kegan Paul, 1943; *Keynesianism: Retrospect and Prospect*, Regnery, 1963; *The Economics of the Colour Bar*, Institute of Economic Affairs (London), 1964; *Politically Impossible ...?*, Institute of Economic Affairs, 1971; *The Strike-Threat System*, Arlington House, 1973; *A Rehabilitation of Say's Law*, Ohio University Press, 1975. Contributor to economic journals.

SIDELIGHTS: Hutt writes: "In economics I have swum against the tide. I have spent a long academic life exposing the error of blaming the market economy for the consequences of 'controls' and tolerated duress-imposed prices. In 1936 I forecast that Keynes' *General Theory* would have an unprecedented influence by reason of its demerits."

* * *

HUXLEY, Julian (Sorell) 1887-1975
(Balbus)

June 22, 1887—February 14, 1975; British biologist, philosopher, educator, editor, and author. Obituaries: *Detroit News*, February 16, 1975; *Washington Post*, February 16, 1975; *New York Times*, February 16, 1975; *Time*, February 24, 1975; *Newsweek*, February 24, 1975; *Current Biography*, April, 1975. (*CA*-11/12)

* * *

HYBELS, Saundra 1938-

PERSONAL: Born December 18, 1938, in Kalamazoo, Mich.; daughter of Elbertus and Adrienne (Roelof) Hybels. *Education:* Western Michigan University, B.A., 1961; University of Pennsylvania, M.A. in Comm. 1962; University of Michigan, Ph.D., 1971. *Religion:* Unitarian Universalist. *Home:* F106 University Park, Ithaca, N.Y. 14850. *Office:* Department of Radio and Television, Ithaca College, Ithaca, N.Y. 14850.

CAREER: Schnader, Harrison, Segal & Lewis, Philadelphia, Pa., consultant, 1962-63; Northwest Missouri State University, Maryville, assistant professor of communications, 1965-66; teacher of journalism and English in secondary and post-secondary schools in Tanzania and Swaziland, 1966-69; Jackson State College, Jackson, Miss., assistant professor of communications, 1969-73; Ithaca College, Ithaca, N.Y., assistant professor of radio and television, 1973—. *Member:* Speech Communication Association of America, National Organization for Women.

WRITINGS: (With Richard Weaver) *Speech: Communication*, Van Nostrand, 1974. Author of television documentaries.

WORK IN PROGRESS: With Dana Ulloth, *Broadcasting in the United States*.

AVOCATIONAL INTERESTS: Travel.

* * *

HYMAN, David N(eil) 1943-

PERSONAL: Born September 5, 1943, in Brooklyn, N.Y.; son of Irving and Tillie (a school aide; maiden name, Rosner) Hyman; married Amy Eldridge (a social worker), July 24, 1971. *Education:* Brooklyn College of the City University of New York, B.A., 1965; Princeton University, M.A., 1967, Ph.D., 1969. *Home:* 2105 Saint Mary's St., Raleigh, N.C. 27608. *Office:* Department of Economics, North Carolina State University, Raleigh, N.C. 27607.

CAREER: North Carolina State University, Raleigh, assistant professor, 1969-73, associate professor of economics, 1973—. Program analyst at U.S. Bureau of Budget, summer, 1966; economist at U.S. Comptroller of the Currency, summer, 1967, and at Board of Governors of Federal Reserve System, summer, 1968. *Member:* American Economic Association, American Agricultural Economic Association, Public Choice Society, Southern Economic Association. *Awards, honors:* Woodrow Wilson fellow, 1965; Earhart Foundation fellow, 1966; Ford Foundation fellow, 1967.

WRITINGS: The Economics of Governmental Activity, Holt, 1973. Contributor to *Southern Economic Journal, National Tax Journal,* and *Economic and Business Bulletin.*

WORK IN PROGRESS: Research on fiscal structure and population distribution.

* * *

HYMANS, Jacques Louis 1937-

PERSONAL: Born October 20, 1937, in Rotterdam, Netherlands; son of Jacques Herman (a businessman) and Hanna (a librarian; maiden name, Citroen) Hymans; married Myrna Kelley (in economic research), March 28, 1970; children: Jacques Edson Citroen. *Education:* Stanford University, B.A., 1958; University of Aix-Marseille, diplome d'etudes politiques, 1960; Sorbonne, University of Paris, doctorat de troisieme cycle, 1964. *Politics:* "New Left." *Religion:* Jewish. *Office:* Department of History, San Francisco State University, San Francisco, Calif. 94132.

CAREER: Stanford University, Stanford, Calif., instructor in history, 1962-63; Northwestern University, Evanston, Ill., assistant professor of history, 1965; Lovanium University, Kinshasa, Zaire, visiting professor of history, 1966-68; San Francisco State University, San Francisco, Calif., associate professor of history, 1968—. *Member:* African Studies Association (fellow), Phi Beta Kappa. *Awards, honors:* Fulbright fellowships, 1958-60, 1966-68.

WRITINGS: Leopold Sedar Senghor: An Intellectual Biography, Edinburgh University Press, 1971. Contributor to *American Historical Review, African Historical Studies, Race, Geneve-Afrique, Africana Newsletter, Research in African Literatures,* and *Acta Africana.*

WORK IN PROGRESS: A biography of Mbope Mabinchi Makene, former sovereign of the Ba-Kuba people of the Kasai Province of Zaire.

SIDELIGHTS: Hymans has traveled extensively in Africa, in Western Europe and Mexico. He speaks French, Dutch, Spanish, and Afrikaans. He writes: "I am a divided being, torn between admiration for, and distrust of, the industrial world of the West and the 'underdeveloped' cultures of Africa. My biography of Senghor describes the same kind of buffeted being."

BIOGRAPHICAL/CRITICAL SOURCES: Nigrizia, May-June, 1968.

* * *

HYNDMAN, Donald W(illiam) 1936-

PERSONAL: Born April 15, 1936, in Vancouver, British Columbia, Canada; son of Andrew William (a high school principal) and Joan (MacDonald) Hyndman; married Shirley Boyes, August 25, 1960; children: Karen, David. *Education:* University of British Columbia, B.A.Sc., 1959;

University of California, Berkeley, Ph.D., 1964. *Home:* 615 Hastings, Missoula, Mont. 59801. *Office:* Department of Geology, University of Montana, Missoula, Mont. 59801.

CAREER: University of Montana, Missoula, assistant professor, 1964-68, associate professor, 1968-72, professor of geology, 1972—. Technical officer of Geological Survey of Canada in British Columbia, summers, 1959-62. *Member:* Mineralogical Association of Canada, Geological Association of Canada (fellow), Geological Society of America (fellow), Mineralogical Society of America, Sigma Xi.

WRITINGS: Petrology and Structure of Nakusp Map-area, British Columbia, Geological Survey of Canada, 1969; *Petrology of Igneous and Metamorphic Rocks,* McGraw, 1972; (with D. D. Alt) *Roadside Geology of Northern Rockies,* Mountain Press, 1972; (with Alt) *Rocks, Ice, and Water: Geology of Watertow Glacier Park,* Mountain Press, 1973; (with Alt) *Roadside Geology of Northern California,* Mountain Press, 1975. Contributor to journals.

WORK IN PROGRESS: With D. D. Alt, *Roadside Geology of Oregon,* completion expected in 1976.

* * *

INCE, Basil A(ndre) 1933-

PERSONAL: Surname rhymes with "prince"; born May 1, 1933, in Trinidad, West Indies; son of Arthur Johnson (a newspaper editor) and Leonora (Williams) Ince; married Laurel Barnwell (lecturer at a teacher's college), August, 1961; children: Avery, Stirling. *Education:* Tufts University, B.A., 1959; New York University, M.A., 1961, Ph.D., 1965. *Home:* 27 Realspring Ave., Valsayn, Trinidad, West Indies. *Office:* Institute of International Relations, University of the West Indies, St. Augustine, Trinidad, West Indies.

CAREER: Government of Trinidad and Tobago, Port of Spain, second secretary to United Nations, 1963-66; City University of New York, New York, N.Y., assistant professor of political science, 1966-68; University of Puerto Rico, Mayaguez, associate professor of political science, 1968-70; State University of New York at Binghamton, associate professor of international relations, 1970-73; University of the West Indies, St. Augustine, Trinidad, senior lecturer in international relations, 1973—. Member of Caribbean task force on political and economic integration in the Caribbean, 1972-74. *Member:* International Studies Association (president of Caribbean section, 1970-71), Caribbean Studies Association (vice-president, 1974-75).

WRITINGS: (Editor) *Race, Economics, and Politics in the Caribbean,* University of Puerto Rico Press, 1972; *Decolonization and Conflict in the United Nations: Guyana's Struggle for Independence,* Schenkman, 1974; (editor) *Linkages in the Black World: Africa, Afro-America, and the Caribbean,* two volumes, Emerson Hall, 1975. Associate editor of *Caribbean Review.*

WORK IN PROGRESS: Editing *Contemporary International Relations in the Caribbean, New States in the World of Diplomacy,* and *A Small State in International Politics.*

SIDELIGHTS: Ince has traveled in the Caribbean, Latin and North America, and Europe.

* * *

ISAACS, Jacob
See KRANZLER, George G(ershon)

ISENHOUR, Thomas Lee 1939-

PERSONAL: Born January 29, 1939, in Statesville, N.C.; son of Harold B. (a businessman) and Ruth (Peacock) Isenhour; married Linda A. Aikins, June 11, 1960; children: Anastasia, Joseph Bradley. *Education:* University of North Carolina, B.S., 1961; Cornell University, Ph.D., 1965. *Home:* 311 Reade Rd., Chapel Hill, N.C. 27514. *Office:* Department of Chemistry, University of North Carolina, Chapel Hill, N.C. 27514.

CAREER: University of Washington, Seattle, assistant professor of chemistry, 1965-69; University of North Carolina, Chapel Hill, associate professor, 1969-74, professor of chemistry, 1975—, chairman of department, 1975. *Member:* American Chemical Society, Pattern Recognition Society, Phi Beta Kappa, Alpha Chi Sigma, Sigma Xi. *Awards, honors:* Venable Medal, 1961; Gulf Research fellow, 1964; Alfred P. Sloan fellow, 1971.

WRITINGS—All published by Allyn & Bacon, except as indicated: (With Norman J. Rose) *Introduction to Quantitative Experimental Chemistry*, 1971; (with Charles L. Wilkins, Charles Klopfenstein, and Peter C. Jurs) *Introduction to Computer Programming for Chemists*, 1972, 2nd edition (with Jurs), 1975; (with Howard Orr, J. C. Marshall, and Jurs) *Introduction to Computer Programming for Biological Scientists*, 1973; (with Peter B. Harkins and Jurs) *Introduction to Computer Programming for the Social Sciences*, 1973; (with Gary Kockenberger, Bruce A. McCarl, and Jurs) *Computer Programming in Business*, Holbrook, 1974; (with Jurs) *Chemical Applications to Pattern Recognition*, Wiley, 1975. Contributor of more than seventy-five articles to science journals.

WORK IN PROGRESS: Scientific research.

AVOCATIONAL INTERESTS: International travel, motorcycle touring.

*   *   *

ISER, Wolfgang 1926-

PERSONAL: Born July 22, 1926, in Marienberg, Germany; son of Paul (a businessman) and Else (Steinbach) Iser; married Lore Reichert (a translator), May 24, 1952. *Education:* Attended University of Leipzig, 1946, and University of Tuebingen, 1946-47; University of Heidelberg, Ph.D., 1950. *Home:* 21 Gallus Zembrothstrasse, Allenbach, Germany D 7753. *Office:* University of Constance, Constance, Germany D 775.

CAREER: University of Heidelberg, Heidelberg, Germany, instructor in English, 1951-52; University of Glasgow, Glasgow, Scotland, assistant lecturer in German, 1952-55; University of Heidelberg, assistant professor, 1955-57, associate professor of English, 1957-60; University of Wuerzburg, Wuerzburg, Germany, professor of English and comparative literature, 1960-63; University of Cologne, Cologne, Germany, professor of English and comparative literature, 1963-67; University of Constance, Constance, Germany, professor of English and comparative literature, 1967—.

WRITINGS: Die Weltanschauung Henry Fieldings (title means "The World View of Henry Fielding"), Max Niemeyer, 1952; *Walter Pater. Die Autonomie des Aesthetischen* (title means "Walter Pater: The Concept of Autonomous Art"), Max Niemeyer, 1960; *Die Appellstruktur der Texte*, Konstanzer Universitaet Verlag, 1970, translation by the author, published in *Aspects of Narrative*, edited by J. Hillis Miller, Columbia University Press, 1971; *Spensers Arkadien. Fiktion und Geschichte* (title means "Spenser's Pastoral Poetry: The Interrelation Between Fiction and History in the 16th Century"), Scherpe, 1970; (editor) *Dargestellte Geschichte in der europaeischen Literatur des 19. Jahrhunderts* (title means "The Representation of History in 19th Century European Fiction"), Klostermann Verlag, 1970; *Der Implizite Leser*, Fink, 1972, translation by the author and David H. Wilson published as *The Implied Reader*, Johns Hopkins Press, 1974. Contributor to German, British, Japanese, and American journals.

WORK IN PROGRESS: Der Akt des Lesens. Theorie literarischer Wirkung (title means "The Hermeneutics of Reading: A Theory of the Aesthetic Response").

*   *   *

IYER, Baghavan Narashimhan 1930-

PERSONAL: Born March 10, 1930, in Madras, India; son of Lakshmi Narasimhan (an accountant) and Laxmi (Aiyer) Iyer; married Nandini Mehta (a professor of philosophy), November 17, 1955; children: Siddharth Pico. *Education:* University of Bombay, B.A., 1948, M.A., 1950; Magdalen College, Oxford, B.A., 1953; Nuffield College, Oxford, D.Phil., 1962. *Politics:* "Beyond isms." *Religion:* "Theosophist (beyond isms)." *Home:* 1975 Old San Marcos Rd., Santa Barbara, Calif. 93111. *Office:* Department of Political Science, University of California, Santa Barbara, Calif. 93106.

CAREER: Indian Institute of World Culture, Bangalore, India, director, 1954-55; Government of India, New Delhi, chief research officer of Planning Commission, 1955-56; Oxford University, St. Antony's College, Oxford, England, lecturer in politics, and fellow, 1956-63; University of Chicago, Chicago, Ill., visiting professor, 1963; University of Ghana, Legon, visiting professor, 1964; University of California, Santa Barbara, professor of political science, 1966—. President, Institute of World Culture, Santa Barbara, 1974—. Visiting professor, Oslo University, 1958. Consultant to Fund for the Republic, 1966-69. *Member:* World Association of World Federalists, United Nations Association, American Society for Legal and Political Philosophy, American Political Science Association, Club of Rome, Oxford University Socratic Club. *Awards, honors:* Rhodes scholar at Oxford University, 1950-53; grants from Ford Foundation, 1960, Humanities Institute, 1967.

WRITINGS: (Editor and contributor) *South Asian Affairs*, Chatto & Windus, 1960; (editor and contributor) *The Glass Curtain*, Oxford University Press, 1965; *Looking Forward: The Abundant Society*, Fund for the Republic, 1966; (contributor) Thomas C. Greening, editor, *Existential Humanist Psychology*, Brooks-Cole, 1971; *The Future Is Tomorrow*, Mouton & Co., 1972; *The Moral and Political Thought of Gandhi*, Oxford University Press, 1973. Associate editor of *Aryan Path*, 1954-55; editor of *Hermes*, 1975—.

SIDELIGHTS: Iyer has traveled in Norway, Sweden, the Netherlands, France, Germany, Switzerland, Italy, Greece, Egypt, and Japan. He writes that he is a practitioner of Einstein's rule "fulfillment equals work plus relaxation plus silence'" and Unamuno's motto "if you wish to achieve the impossible, attempt the absurd," and Lamartine's axiom "the ideal is only truth at a distance."

*   *   *

JACK, Ian 1923-

PERSONAL: Born December 5, 1923, in Edinburgh, Scotland; son of John McGregor Bruce and Helena Cockburn (Buchanan) Jack; married Jane Henderson McDonald, 1948 (divorced, 1970); married Margaret Elizabeth Crone, 1972; children: (first marriage) Humphry, Walter, Belinda; (second marriage) Rowland. *Education:* University of Edinburgh, first class honors in English literature, 1946; Merton College, Oxford, D.Phil., 1949. *Office:* Department of English, Pembroke College, Cambridge University, Cambridge, England.

CAREER: Cambridge University, Pembroke College, Cambridge, England, fellow, 1961—, reader in English poetry, 1973-76, professor of English literature, 1976—. De-Carle lecturer at University of Otago, Dunedin, New Zealand, 1964; Warton lecturer at British Academy, 1967; visiting professor at University of Chicago, 1968-69, and University of California, Berkeley, 1969. Traveling lecturer in India, Pakistan, Egypt, Thailand, Australia, New Zealand, Canada, France, Germany, Italy, Finland, and Denmark. *Awards, honors:* Litt.D. from Cambridge University, 1973.

WRITINGS—All published by Clarendon Press: *Augustan Satire: Intention and Idiom in English Poetry, 1660-1750*, 1952; *English Literature: 1815-1832*, 1963; *Keats and the Mirror of Art*, 1967; *Browning's Major Poetry*, 1973.

WORK IN PROGRESS: A book, *The Poet and His Audience*; editing the poems of Browning, for Clarendon Press; editing the Clarendon edition of the novels of the Brontes.

*   *   *

JACKSON, Basil   1920-

PERSONAL: Born April 3, 1920, in Swansea, Wales; emigrated to Canada, 1948; son of Harry and Pauline (Zeltzer) Jackson; married, wife's name Eileen; children: Pauline, David. *Education:* Educated in Great Britain; attended evening courses in science and mechanical engineering at Merchant Venturers' Technical College, University of Bristol. *Home:* 442 St. Clements Ave., Toronto M5N 1M1, Ontario, Canada. *Agent:* John Cushman Associates, Inc., 25 West 43rd St., New York, N.Y. 10036. *Office:* The *Financial Post*, 481 University Ave., Toronto, Ontario, Canada.

CAREER: Bristol Aeroplane Co. (now British Aircraft Corp.), Bristol, England, plant errand boy, rivet sorter, and airframe assembler, 1937-39; Fairey Aviation Co., London, draftsman, 1939-46; Airspeed Ltd. (aircraft engineering firm), London, senior design draftsman, 1946-48; technical writer, compiling flight instruction and ground maintenance manuals, employed by de Havilland Aircraft Co., and A. V. Roe of Canada Ltd., 1948-61; *Financial Post*, Toronto, Ontario, science editor, 1961—. *Member:* Authors League (New York), Royal Aeronautical Society (London; associate member).

WRITINGS: *Epicenter*, Norton, 1971; *Rage under the Arctic*, Norton, 1974; *Supersonic*, Norton, 1975.

WORK IN PROGRESS: Another aviation novel.

SIDELIGHTS: Jackson told *CA:* "All three of my novels (which are *not* science fiction) are based on the philosophy that however cleverly a high-technology product is made and tested, the human element often leads to disaster, e.g., Apollo 13 didn't make it to the moon because someone on the ground, during a routine test, plugged in a 56 volt input instead of 28 volts. As a result Apollo's oxygen tank leaked and set off a chain of events that nearly caused the deaths of the three astronauts."

JACKSON, Blyden   1910-

PERSONAL: Born October 12, 1910, in Paducah, Ky.; son of George Washington (a teacher) and Julia Estelle (Reid) Jackson; married Roberta Bowles Hodges (a university teacher), August 2, 1958. *Education:* Wilberforce University, A.B., 1930; University of Michigan, A.M., 1938, Ph.D., 1952. *Home:* 102 Laurel Hill Rd., Chapel Hill, N.C. 27514. *Office:* Department of English, 216 Greenlaw Hall, University of North Carolina, Chapel Hill, N.C. 27514.

CAREER: High school English teacher in Louisville, Ky., 1934-45; Fisk University, Nashville, Tenn., assistant professor, 1945-53, associate professor of English, 1953-54; Southern University, Baton Rouge, La., professor of English, 1954-64, head of department, 1954-63, dean of Graduate School, 1963-64; University of North Carolina, Chapel Hill, professor of English, 1969—, associate dean of Graduate School, 1973—.

MEMBER: College Language Association (vice-president, 1955-57; president, 1957-59), National Council of Teachers of English (distinguished lecturer, 1970-71; trustee of research foundation, 1974-77), Modern Language Association of America, College English Association, North Carolina Council of Teachers of English, Louisville Association of Teachers in Colored Schools (vice-president, 1940-42; president, 1942-44), Alpha Phi Alpha.

WRITINGS: (With Louis Rubin) *Black Poetry in America*, Louisiana State University Press, 1974. Contributor to professional journals. Associate editor of College Language Association's bulletin; advisory editor of *Southern Literary Journal*.

*   *   *

JACKSON, Clarence J.-L.
See BULLIET, Richard W(illiams)

*   *   *

JACKSON, Katherine Gauss   1904-1975

May 20, 1904—May 28, 1975; American journalist, columnist, editor. Obituaries: *New York Times*, May 29, 1975; *Publishers Weekly*, June 9, 1975.

*   *   *

JACOBS, David Michael   1942-

PERSONAL: Born August 10, 1942, in Los Angeles, Calif.; son of Jack and Ethel (Raskin) Jacobs; married Irene Schultz (an editor), November 9, 1963. *Education:* University of California, Los Angeles, B.A., 1966; University of Wisconsin-Madison, M.A., 1968, Ph.D., 1973. *Office:* Department of History, Temple University, Philadelphia, Pa. 19122.

CAREER: University of Wisconsin-Madison, lecturer in history, 1973; University of Nebraska, Lincoln, assistant professor of history, 1974-75; Temple University, Philadelphia, Pa., assistant professor of history, 1975—. Consultant to Aerial Phenomena Research Organization, 1971—; historical consultant on syndicated television show "UFO's, Past, Present and Future," 1974. *Member:* American Historical Association, Organization of American Historians, Aerial Phenomena Research Organization, National Investigations Committee on Aerial Phenomena, Center for UFO Studies.

WRITINGS: *The UFO Controversy in America*, Indiana University Press, 1975.

JACOBS, William Jay 1933-

PERSONAL: Born August 23, 1933, in Cincinnati, Ohio; son of Louis (a merchant in fine wines and gourmet foods) and Fannie (Kletter) Jacobs; married Phoebe Lloyd (an art historian), November 27, 1959; children: Catherine Elizabeth, Adam Eleazar. *Education:* University of Cincinnati, B.A. (with high honors in history), and B.S. (education), both 1955, M.A., 1956; Columbia University, Ed.D., 1963. *Politics:* Independent. *Religion:* "Ethical Humanist within the Judaeo-Christian tradition." *Home and office:* William Jay Jacobs Associates, Inc., 61 Addison Ave., Rutherford, N.J. 07070.

CAREER: History teacher in secondary schools in Hamilton County, Ohio, 1956-58, New York, N.Y., 1959-60, and Oradell N.J., 1961-64 (chairman of department in Oradell, 1960-64); Hofstra University, Hempstead, N.Y., assistant professor of education, 1964-65; Rutgers University, New Brunswick, N.J., assistant professor of social studies education, 1965-68; Hunter College of the City University of New York, New York, N.Y., associate professor of social studies education, 1968-70; Ramapo College of New Jersey, Mahwah, professor of education and director of Division of Teacher Education, 1970-73, distinguished visiting professor, 1973-74; William Jay Jacobs Associates, Inc. (educational consultants), Rutherford, N.J., president, 1974—. Special assistant to chief of Job Corps Plans and Programs, Office of Economic Opportunity, 1967-68. Adjunct or summer teacher at University of Cincinnati, Brooklyn College of the City University of New York, Columbia University, and Harvard University.

MEMBER: American Historical Association, National Council for the Social Studies, Authors Guild of Authors League of America, Council for Basic Education (New Jersey state chairman, 1965-67), Reading Reform Foundation, Phi Beta Kappa, Phi Alpha Theta, Kappa Delta Pi, Phi Delta Kappa. *Awards, honors:* Ford Foundation fellowship, 1967-68.

*WRITINGS—*For children: *Search for Freedom: America and Its People*, Benziger, Bruce & Glencoe, 1973; *Prince Henry the Navigator*, F. Watts, 1973; *Hannibal: An African Hero*, McGraw, 1973; *Hernando Cortes*, F. Watts, 1974; *Samuel de Champlain*, F. Watts, 1974; *William Bradford of Plymouth Colony*, F. Watts, 1974; *Roger Williams*, F. Watts, 1975; *Robert Cavelier de La Salle*, F. Watts, 1975; *Edgar Allan Poe*, McGraw, 1975; *Created Equal!: The Story of American Women*, Benziger, Bruce & Glencoe, 1975; *Hitler*, Benziger, Bruce & Glencoe, in press; *Churchill*, Benziger, Bruce & Glencoe, in press; *Stalin*, Benziger, Bruce & Glencoe, in press; (editor) *Land of Promise: American History through Literature and Art* (anthology), Benziger, Bruce & Glencoe, in press.

Contributor of more than forty articles and reviews to education journals and other magazines, including *Teachers College Record*, *Audiovisual Instruction*, *Urban Review*, *New Jersey Education Association Review*, *Elementary Education*, and *Horn Book*. Children's book review editor of *Teachers College Record*, 1966-69; consultant to McGraw's Junior Book Division, 1965—.

WORK IN PROGRESS: A world history textbook for readers from age eleven to adult, from the perspectives of biography and history of art; fifteen books for "Our Violent Century," a juvenile series for Benziger, Bruce & Glencoe.

JACOBSON, Helen Saltz 1921-

PERSONAL: Born November 30, 1921, in New York, N.Y.; daughter of Arthur (a businessman) and Minnie (Blumenkrantz) Saltz; married Eugene Jacobson (a professor of physics), June 25, 1943; children: Peter, Janet. *Education:* Brooklyn College (now of the City University of New York), B.A., 1943; graduate study at University of Chicago and University of Wisconsin; New York University, M.A., 1966. *Home and office:* 55 Thompson Hay Path, Setauket, N.Y. 11733.

CAREER: State University of New York, Agricultural and Technical Institute, Alfred, instructor in Russian, 1959-60; high school Russian teacher in Lincoln, Neb., 1960-61; Suffolk College, Selden, N.Y., instructor in Russian, 1961-64; Adelphi College—Suffolk (now Dowling College), Oakdale, N.Y., instructor in Russian, 1964-65; State University of New York at Stonybrook, instructor in Russian, 1967-70; free-lance translator from Russian to English, 1970—. *Military service:* Women's Army Corps, psychiatric social worker, 1944-45.

MEMBER: American Translators Association, Guild of Professional Translators, Association of Teachers of Slavic and East European Languages, Dobro Slovo. *Awards, honors:* SUNY grant, 1969, to speak at an international conference in Moscow.

WRITINGS: (Translator) Robert Magidoff, editor, *Russian Science Fiction, 1968*, New York University Press, 1968; (editor and translator) *Diary of a Russian Censor: Aleksandr Nikitenko*, University of Massachusetts Press, 1975. Author of Russian textbooks for correspondence courses at University of Nebraska.

WORK IN PROGRESS: Translating from Russian a juvenile science fiction novel and an adult science fiction anthology.

AVOCATIONAL INTERESTS: Hiking, bicycling, cross-country skiing, tennis.

* * *

JACOBY, Stephen M(ichael) 1940-

PERSONAL: Born November 10, 1940, in New York, N.Y.; son of Gustav (a lawyer) and Eva (Michaelis) Jacoby; married Jordy Bell (a historian and teacher), December 17, 1967; children: Raphael. *Education:* Harvard University, B.A., 1962; Columbia University, LL.B., 1965; New York University, LL.M., 1972. *Home:* 208 Eighth Ave., Brooklyn, N.Y. 11215. *Office:* American Jewish Congress, 15 East 84th St., New York, N.Y. 10028.

CAREER: Szold, Brandwen, Meyers & Altman (general practice law firm), New York, N.Y., associate, 1969-71; American Jewish Congress, New York, N.Y., staff counsel to Metropolitan Council, 1971—. Member of board of directors of Selfhelp Community Services, Inc. *Military service:* U.S. Coast Guard Reserve, active duty, 1966-69; became lieutenant junior grade.

WRITINGS: *The Right to Worship and to Work*, American Jewish Congress, 1974; *Architectural Sculpture in New York City*, Dover, 1975. Contributor to journals.

WORK IN PROGRESS: *Subway Poems*, a photographic collection; verse with drawings; research on secrecy and the law.

SIDELIGHTS: Jacoby writes: "*Architectural Sculpture* was a natural outgrowth of my collecting 'portraits' of sculpture for my own reference. In the beginning, I hoped to catalogue an overlooked genre. By the time I had finished the book, I was more interested in conveying the vitality of individual works and the enthusiasm of their makers. I attended drawing classes at the National Academy of Design and sculpt in wood, clay, and stone."

* * *

JACOPETTI, Alexandra 1939-

PERSONAL: Born August 1, 1939, in Preston, Idaho; daughter of Newell Scheib (a musician, carpenter, and writer) and Ruth (a store manager; maiden name, Cutler) Hart; married Gregory L. Williams, May, 1957 (divorced November, 1958); married Roland Jacopetti (a radio producer), October 8, 1960; children: Hobert, Lucas, Natalia. *Education:* Attended University of Utah, 1956-57. *Politics:* Feminist. *Religion:* Subud. *Home and office:* Sunshine Camp, Forestville, Calif. 95436.

CAREER: Atelier Alexandra Jacopetti (weaving), Forestville, Calif., fibre artist, 1967—. Member of board of directors and gallery director of Berkeley Experimental Arts Foundation, 1965-66; director of apprentices in weaving for Baulines Craftsman's Guild, Marin Co., Calif., 1972—, member of board of directors, 1972-74.

WRITINGS: (With collaborator and photographer, Jerry Wainwright) *Native Funk and Flash: An Emerging Folk Art*, Scrimshaw Press (California), 1974.

WORK IN PROGRESS: Research in ethnic clothing fashions; paper patterns for ethnic clothing for current use, including a book of information and instruction.

SIDELIGHTS: "I am mainly a visual artist and craftswoman working in textile fibres," Alexandra Jacopetti wrote. "I . . . have found that those who are most productive and satisfied with their lives . . . are people who are actively involved with making inner states material through an art or craft." An exhibit of material from *Native Funk and Flash* is touring several western states under arrangements made by Western Association of Art Museums.

BIOGRAPHICAL/CRITICAL SOURCES: Saturday Review of Education, May, 1973; *Sunset*, June, 1974; *Art Week*, September 28, 1974; Ben Van Meter, "The Saga of Macrame Park" (film), Eccentric Circle Films, 1973.

* * *

JAEGER, Lorenz Cardinal 1892-1975

1892—April 1, 1975; German priest and archbishop, author of books on the church and Christendom. Obituaries: *New York Times*, April 12, 1975.

* * *

JAFFE, William 1898-

PERSONAL: Born June 16, 1898, in New York, N.Y.; son of Morris (a shopkeeper) and Mary (Pomerantz) Jaffe; married Grace Mary Spurway, January, 1922 (divorced, 1948); married Olive Caroline Weaver, October 4, 1948; children: (first marriage) Ghita Elizabeth, David Spurway, Peter Langdon (twins). *Education:* City College of New York (now City College of the City University of New York), B.A. (summa cum laude), 1918; Columbia University, M.A., 1919; University of Paris, Dr. en Droit (honors), 1924. *Home:* 10 Pratt Circle, Unionville, Ontario L3R 1Y2, Canada. *Office:* Department of Economics, York University, 4700 Keele St. Downsview, Ontario M3J 1P3, Canada.

CAREER: Research assistant with United States Government Inquiry, 1918; City College of New York (now City College of the City University of New York), New York, N.Y., tutor in economics and French, 1924-25; Columbia University, Social Science Research Council, New York, N.Y., associate in Paris, France, 1926-28; Northwestern University, Evanston, Ill., assistant professor, 1928-38, associate professor, 1938-56, professor of economics, 1956-66, professor emeritus, 1966—; York University, Downsview, Ontario, professor of economics, 1970—. Visiting professor at University of Algiers, 1956; Fulbright lecturer at University of Genoa, 1956-57; visiting professor at University of California at Riverside, 1965, Harvard University, 1967-69, and University of British Columbia, 1969-70.

MEMBER: American Association for the Advancement of Science (fellow), American Economic Association, Econometric Society (fellow), Royal Economic Association, Canadian Economic Association, Royal Netherlands Academy of Science and Letters (foreign member), History of Economics Society (member of executive committee, 1972-75), Phi Beta Kappa. *Awards, honors:* Fulbright research grant to France, 1951-53; Guggenheim fellow in Switzerland, 1958-59; Rockefeller Foundation grant to Switzerland, 1958-59; Ford Foundation faculty research fellowship, 1963-64; National Science Foundation research grant, 1965-69, 1971; LL.D., York University, 1974.

WRITINGS: Les theories economiques et sociales de Thorstein Veblen (title means "The Economic and Social Theories of Thorstein Veblen"), Giard & Briere, 1924; (with W. F. Ogburn) *The Economic Development of Post-War France*, Columbia University Press, 1929; (contributor) Oscar Lange and others, editors, *Studies in Mathematical Economics and Econometrics*, University of Chicago Press, 1942; (translator) Leon Walras, *Elements of Pure Economics*, Irwin, 1954; *Histoire des doctrines walrasiennes* (title means "History of the Walrasonian Doctrines"), University of Algiers, 1956; (editor) *Correspondence of Leon Walras and Related Papers*, three volumes, North Holland Publishing, 1965; (contributor) Arnold Heertje and others, editors, *Schaarste en Welvaart* (title means "Scarcity and Welfare"), Stenfert Kroese, 1971; (contributor) R. D. Collison Black and others, editors, *The Marginal Revolution: Interpretation and Evaluation*, Duke University Press, 1973. Contributor to economic journals. Member of editorial advisory board of *History of Political Economy*, 1969—.

WORK IN PROGRESS: A book, *Life and Writings of Leon Walras*; studies in the history of general equilibrium economics to 1934.

* * *

JAFFEE, Dwight M. 1943-

PERSONAL: Born February 7, 1943, in Chicago, Ill.; married Annette Williams (a writer), August 16, 1964; children: Jonathan, Elizabeth. *Education:* Attended Oberlin College, 1960-61; Northwestern University, B.A. (with highest distinction), 1964; Massachusetts Institute of Technology, Ph.D., 1968. *Office:* Department of Economics, Princeton University, Princeton, N.J. 08540.

CAREER: Massachusetts Institute of Technology, Cambridge, instructor in economics, 1967-68; Princeton University, assistant professor, 1968-72, associate professor of economics, 1972—. Visiting summer professor at Massachusetts Institute of Technology, 1974. Consultant to U.S. Treasury Department, Federal Home Loan Bank Board, and U.S. Department of Housing and Urban Development. *Member:* Phi Beta Kappa.

AWARDS, HONORS: Woodrow Wilson fellowship; Social Science Research Council grants, 1968, 1972; Federal Reserve Bank of Philadelphia research fellowship, 1969; North Atlantic Treaty Organization-National Science Foundation postdoctoral fellowship in science at University of Essex, 1970-71; National Science Foundation grant, 1973; Life Insurance Association of American research grant, 1973; Institute for International Economic Studies research associate, 1973-74.

WRITINGS: Credit Rationing and the Commercial Loan Market, Wiley, 1971; (editor with E. Gramlich) *Savings Deposits, Mortgages, and Residential Construction,* Heath, 1972; (with M. Flannery) *Economic Implications of an Electronic Monetary Transfer System,* Heath, 1973. Contributor to proceedings, and to *American Economic Review, Journal of Finance,* and other journals of economics, business, and finance. Associate editor, *Journal of Money, Credit, and Banking,* 1973—, *Journal of Finance,* 1974—.

WORK IN PROGRESS: The Economics of a Monetary Economy, for Wiley.

* * *

JAKES, John W(illiam) 1932-
(Alan Payne, Jay Scotland)

PERSONAL: Born March 31, 1932, in Chicago, Ill.; son of John A. (a Railway Express general manager) and Bertha (Retz) Jakes; married Rachel Ann Payne (a teacher), June 15, 1951; children: Andrea, Ellen, John Michael, Victoria. *Education:* DePauw University, A.B., 1953; Ohio State University, M.A., 1954. *Politics:* Independent. *Religion:* Protestant. *Residence:* Dayton, Ohio.

CAREER: Abbott Laboratories, North Chicago, Ill., 1954-60, began as copywriter, became product promotion manager; Rumrill Co. (advertising agency), Rochester, N.Y., copywriter, 1960-61; free-lance writer, 1961-65; Kircher, Helton & Collett, Inc. (advertising agency), Dayton, Ohio, senior copywriter, 1965-68; Oppenheim, Herminghausen, Clarke, Inc. (advertising agency), Dayton, 1968-70, began as copy chief, became vice-president; Dancer-Fitzgerald-Sample, Inc. (advertising agency), Dayton, creative director, 1970-71; free-lance writer, 1971—. *Member:* Authors Guild, Dramatists Guild, Science Fiction Writers of America.

WRITINGS: The Texans Ride North: The Story of the Cattle Trails, John C. Winston, 1952; *Wear a Fast Gun,* Arcadia House, 1956; *A Night for Treason,* Bouregy & Curl, 1956; (under pseudonym Alan Payne) *Murder, He Says,* Ace Books, 1958; *The Devil Has Four Faces,* Bouregy, 1958; *The Seventh Man,* Bouregy, 1958; *The Imposter,* Bouregy, 1959.

Johnny Havoc, Belmont Books, 1960; *Johnny Havoc Meets Zelda,* Belmont Books, 1962; *Johnny Havoc and the Doll Who Had "It",* Belmont Books, 1963; *G.I. Girls,* Monarch Books, 1963; *Tiros: Weather Eye in Space,* Messner, 1966; *When the Star Kings Die,* Ace Books, 1967; *Great War Correspondents,* Putnam, 1967; *Famous Firsts in Sports,* Putnam, 1967; *Making It Big,* Belmont Books, 1968; *Brak the Barbarian,* Avon, 1968; *Great Women Reporters,* Putnam, 1969; (with Laurence M. Janifer and S. J. Treibich) *Tonight We Steal the Stars [and] The Wagered World* (the first by Jakes; the second by Janifer and Trei-

bich), Ace Books, 1969; *Brak the Barbarian Versus the Sorceress,* Paperback Library, 1969; *Brak the Barbarian Versus the Mark of the Demons,* Paperback Library, 1969; *The Hybrid,* Paperback Library, 1969; *The Last Magicians,* Signet, 1969; *Secrets of Stardeep,* Westminster Press, 1969; *The Planet Wizard,* Ace Books, 1969; *The Asylum World,* Paperback Library, 1969; *Mohawak: The Life of Joseph Brant,* Macmillan, 1969.

Black in Time, Paperback Library, 1970; *Six Gun Planet* (originally published as *The Legend of Buffalo Yung*), Paperback Library, 1970; (with Barrington J. Bayler) *Mask of Chaos [and] The Star Virus* (the first by Jakes; the second by Bayler), Ace Books, 1970; *Monte Cristo,* Modern Library, 1970; *Master of the Dark Gate,* Lancer Books, 1970; *Conquest of the Planet of the Apes,* Award Books, 1972; *Time Gate,* Westminster Press, 1972; *Witch of the Dark Gate,* Lancer Books, 1972; *Mention My Name in Atlantis,* Daw Books, 1972; *On Wheels,* Paperback Library, 1973.

Plays: *A Spell of Evil* (three-act melodrama), Performance Publishing, 1972; *Violence* (two one-act plays), Performance Publishing, 1972; *Stranger with Roses* (one-act), Dramatic Publishing, 1972.

All musicals; author of book and lyrics, except as indicated: (Author of lyrics) *Dracula, Baby* (comedy), Dramatic Publishing, 1970; *Wind in the Willows* (comedy), Performance Publishing, 1972; *Gaslight Girl,* Dramatic Publishing, 1973; *Pardon Me, Is this Planet Taken?,* Dramatic Publishing, 1973; *Doctor, Doctor!,* McAfee Music Corp., 1973; *Shepherd Song,* McAfee Music Corp., 1974.

Also author of "American Bicentennial" series, published by Pyramid: Volume I: *The Bastard,* 1974, Volume II: *The Rebels,* 1975, Volume III: *The Seekers,* 1975.

Under pseudonym Jay Scotland: *I, Barbarian,* Avon, 1959; *Strike the Black Flag,* Ace Books, 1961; *Sir Scoundrel,* Ace Books, 1962; *Veils of Salome,* Avon, 1962; *Arena,* Ace Books, 1963; *Traitors' Legion,* Ace Books, 1963.

WORK IN PROGRESS: The remaining three volumes in the "American Bicentennial" series.

* * *

JAKUBAUSKAS, Edward B(enedict) 1930-

PERSONAL: Born April 14, 1930, in Waterbury, Conn.; son of Constantine and Barbara Jakubauskas; married Ruth Friz, August 29, 1959; children: Carol, Marilyn, Mark, Eric. *Education:* University of Connecticut, B.A. (with honors), 1952, M.A., 1954; University of Wisconsin, Ph.D., 1961. *Home:* 1055 Duna Dr., Laramie, Wyo. 82070. *Office address:* University of Wyoming, University Station Box 3275, Laramie, Wyo. 82071.

CAREER: U.S. Federal Power Commission, Washington, D.C., economist, 1956; U.S. Department of Labor, Washington, D.C., economist, 1956-58; University of Wisconsin, Madison, instructor, 1958-61, assistant professor of economics, 1961-63; Iowa State University, Ames, assistant professor, 1963-65, associate professor, 1965-66, professor of economics, 1966-71, director of Industrial Relations Center, 1966-71; University of Wyoming, Laramie, professor of economics, 1971—, dean, 1971—. Director of Iowa State Manpower Development Council, Office of the Governor of Iowa, 1965-66; member of Iowa Governor's Commission on the Aging, 1967-71, Wyoming Governor's Council on Administration of Justice, 1971—, and Wyoming State Sciences Advisory Council, 1972—; appointed by U.S. Secretary of Commerce to Regional Expansion Council, 1974—. *Military service:* U.S. Army, 1954-56.

WRITINGS: (Editor with C. Philip Baumel) *Human Resources Development*, Iowa State University Press, 1967; (editor with Neil A. Palomba) *Manpower Economics*, Addison-Wesley, 1973.

* * *

JAMES, C. B.
See COOVER, James B(urrell)

* * *

JAMES, M. R. 1940-
(J. D. Danielson)

PERSONAL: Born December 6, 1940; son of Francis Miller (an oil producer) and Lorraine (Wylie) James; married Janet Sue Tennis (a bookkeeper), June 16, 1960; children: Jeffrey Glenn, David Ray, Daniel Scott, Cheryl Lynne. *Education:* Oakland City College, B.S., 1964. *Home:* 9713 Saratoga Rd., Fort Wayne, Ind. 46804. *Office:* Magnavox Co., 1700 Magnavox Way, Fort Wayne, Ind. 46804.

CAREER: Princeton Daily Clarion, Princeton, Ind., sports and city editor, 1963-65; high school English teacher in Osgood, Ind., 1965-66; Whirlpool Corp., Evansville, Ind., industrial editor, 1966-68; Magnavox Co., Fort Wayne, Ind., industrial editor, 1968—. Founder and president of Blue-J Publishing Co., 1971—; coach of Police Athletic League basketball team. *Member:* International Association of Buisness Communicators, Professional Bowhunters Society, Magnavox Industrial Toastmasters Club (president, 1973), Pope and Young Club, Fort Wayne Association of Business Editors (vice-president, 1974-75; president-elect).

WRITINGS: Bowhunting for Whitetail and Mule Deer, J. Philip O'Hara, 1975; (editor) *Bowhunting Big Game Records of North America*, Pope and Young Club, 1975. Author of column in *Bowhunter*. Contributor of both nonfiction and short stories to national magazines. Editor and publisher of *Bowhunter*.

SIDELIGHTS: James writes: "I am a writer with a special interest in the role of the hunter-sportsman in today's modern world. I founded *Bowhunter Magazine* . . . to educate both hunters and serious-minded outdoorsmen, encouraging them to practice good sportsmanship at all times and be efficient, responsible conservationists. Contrary to popular belief, hunting and game management go hand in hand."

* * *

JAMES, Marlise Ann 1945-
(Wabun)

PERSONAL: Born April 5, 1945, in Newark, N.J.; daughter of Bernard E. and Anne (Roberts) James; married Sun Bear (an editor and medicine man), January 23, 1972; *Education:* George Washington University, A.B., 1967; Columbia University, M.S., 1968. *Politics:* Traditional Indian. *Religion:* Traditional Indian. *Home and office address:* P.O. Box 1961, Klamath Falls, Ore. 97601.

CAREER: Single, New York, N.Y., managing editor, 1969; *Move*, New York, editor, 1970. Manager of press relations for American Society of Travel Agents, 1968—. *Member:* Bear Tribe.

WRITINGS: (Under name Wabun; with husband, Sun Bear) *Walk in Balance*, Many Smokes Publishing, 1972;

The People's Lawyers, Holt, 1973. Member of editorial board of *Many Smokes*, 1972—.

WORK IN PROGRESS: With Sun Bear, *Retribalizing*, the first years of the Bear Tribe; *Behold, a Nation is Coming*, the story of the termination and resurrection of the Klamath Tribe of Oregon.

SIDELIGHTS: Marlise Ann James' Indian name is Wabun, meaning East Wind.

* * *

JAMES, Peter N. 1940-

PERSONAL: Born September 19, 1940, in Jamestown, N.Y.; son of Basil Argir (a tailor) and Constance (Baye) James; married Diane Millman (a research assistant), February 22, 1964. *Education:* Case Institute of Technology (now Case Western Reserve University), B.S., 1962. *Religion:* Albanian Orthodox. *Residence:* Palm Beach Shores, Fla. 33404. *Office address:* P.O. Box 9661, Riviera Beach, Fla. 33404.

CAREER: Pratt & Whitney Aircraft, Research & Development Center, Palm Beach County, Fla., 1962-71, worked as assistant project engineer and as program manager of foreign (Russian) technology; writer and lecturer, 1971—. Informant on Soviet space and military technology for Central Intelligence Agency (CIA), 1965-72. *Member:* American Institute of Aeronautics and Astronautics, Air Force Association.

WRITINGS: Soviet Conquest from Space, Arlington House, 1974; *The Air Force Mafia*, Arlington House, 1975.

WORK IN PROGRESS: Anatomy of a Kidnapping, describing events leading to the kidnapping and brutal murder of the child of a prominent radiologist; *The Air Force Mafia, Part Two; The House That John Built*, the life and accomplishments of multibillionaire John D. MacArthur.

SIDELIGHTS: James writes: "I have been quite concerned over the public's lack of knowledge on matters concerning both the national defense of the United States and the individual rights of all Americans. My writings in both fields reflect my attempt to crack the Government's monopoly of information that has been unjustifiably witheld from the American people because of political reasons. My travels abroad and involvement with the C.I.A., Air Force Intelligence, the Defense Department and other agencies greatly contributed to my awareness that a serious problem existed."

BIOGRAPHICAL/CRITICAL SOURCES: Washington Post, March 14, 1974; *Pittsburgh Press*, February 23, 1975.

* * *

JAMES, Theodore E(arle) 1913-

PERSONAL: Born November 14, 1913, in Baltimore, Md.; son of William B. (a photo engraver) and Mary Leah (Eder) James; married Faith Sabella, September 6, 1941; children: Theodore E., Jr., Nicholas D., William B., Francis J., John P., Faith D. *Education:* University of Montreal, A.B. (magna cum laude), 1939; Fordham University, M.A., 1940; Columbia University, Ph.D., 1968. *Politics:* Independent. *Religion:* Roman Catholic. *Home:* 5 Ridgeview Ave., White Plains, N.Y. 10606. *Office:* Department of Philosophy, Manhattan College, Bronx, N.Y. 10471.

CAREER: Manhattan College, Bronx, N.Y., assistant professor, 1949-54, associate professor, 1954-68, professor of philosophy, 1968—. *Military service:* U.S. Naval Reserve,

1942-46; became lieutenant. *Member:* American Catholic Philosophical Association.

WRITINGS: (Author of introduction) J. Kiernan, editor, *Aristotle Dictionary*, Philosophical Library, 1962; (author of introduction) Ibn Gabirol, *The Fountain of Life*, Philosophical Library, 1962; (author of introduction) Morris Stockhammer, editor, *Plato Dictionary*, Philosophical Library, 1963; (author of introduction) Stockhammer, editor, *Aquinas Dictionary*, Philosophical Library, 1965; (with Stockhammer) *Kant Dictionary*, Philosophical Library, 1971; (contributor) *Humanism and Philosphy: Renaissance Studies in Honor of Paul Oskar Kristeller*, Columbia University Press, 1975. Contributor to *Encyclopedia of Philosophy* and to *Journal of the History of Philosophy.* Editorial associate of *New Scholasticism*, 1965—.

WORK IN PROGRESS: Handbook of Logic; writing on Plato's "Euthyphro"; *Peter Alborini of Mantua, De Primo et ultimo Instanti: Science and Philosophy in the Fourteenth Century.*

*   *   *

JAMES, Thomas N.
  See NEAL, James T(homas)

*   *   *

JAMES, William M.
  See HARKNETT, Terry

*   *   *

JARRETT, (John) Derek   1928-
PERSONAL: Born March 18, 1928, in Surrey, England; son of John Edgar (a draper) and Madge (a draper) Jarrett; married Elizabeth Ann Mayne (a drama teacher), July 27, 1965; children: Wendy Jane, Caroline Ann. *Education:* Keble College, Oxford, B.A. (first class honors), 1951, B. Litt, and M.A., 1955. *Home:* 58 Beaconsfield Rd., London SE3 7LG, England. *Agent:* Curtis Brown Ltd., 1 Craven Hill, London W2, England.

CAREER: Senior history master at Sherborne School, Dorset, England, 1956-64; University of London, Goldsmith's College, London, England, lecturer, 1964-65, senior lecturer, 1965-71, principal lecturer in history, 1971—.

WRITINGS: Britain: 1688-1815, St. Martin's, 1965; *Begetters of Revolution*, Rowman & Littlefield, 1973; *Pitt the Younger*, Scribner, 1974; *England in the Age of Hogarth*, Hart-Davis, 1974, Viking, 1975. Contributor to *English Historical Review.*

WORK IN PROGRESS: Research on eighteenth-century history and on biographies.

AVOCATIONAL INTERESTS: Walking, beachcombing, painting, metal sculpture and collage.

*   *   *

JEFFERY, William P., Jr.   1919-
PERSONAL: Born September 17, 1919, in Brooklyn, N.Y.; son of William P. (a lawyer) and Idelle (Scott) Jeffery; married Elizabeth Meek (a teacher), March 6, 1948; children: Priscilla Jeffery Adkins, William Jeremy, John MacKnight, Charles Robert, Patrick Gillespie. *Education:* Yale University, graduate, 1941. *Office:* 25 Woodland Ave., Westwood, N.J. 07675.

CAREER: Cos-Chem Corporation, Westwood, N.J., president, 1962—. Trustee, Greenwich (Conn.) Country Day

School. *Military service:* U.S. Naval Reserve, pilot during World War II; became lieutenant. *Member:* Field Club of Greenwich (former president; governor).

WRITINGS: Unless..., Dodd, 1975.

SIDELIGHTS: Jeffery told *CA:* "In the course of my business I have travelled to over 100 countries. As a result of such travel, I found poverty and lack of education abhorrent. After studying reasons for this, I decided it was due to overpopulation. This is what prompted me to write *Unless....*"

*   *   *

JEFFREY, David Lyle   1941-
PERSONAL: Born June 28, 1941, in Ottawa, Ontario, Canada; son of Lyle Elmo (a farmer) and Florence (Brown) Jeffrey; married Wilberta Johnson, June 17, 1961; children: Bruce, Kirstin, Adrienne. *Education:* Wheaton College, Wheaton, Ill., B.A., 1965; Princeton University, M.A., 1967, Ph.D., 1968. *Home:* 182 Barkley Ter., Victoria, British Columbia, Canada. *Office:* Department of English, University of Victoria, Victoria, British Columbia V8W 2Y2, Canada.

CAREER: Jef-flite of Canada (luggage manufacturers), Arn Prior, Ontario, sales manager, 1960-61, general manager, 1961-63; University of Victoria, Victoria, British Columbia, assistant professor of English, 1968-69; University of Rochester, Rochester, N.Y., assistant professor, 1969-72, associate professor of Medieval English, 1972-73; University of Victoria, associate professor of Medieval English and chairman of department of English, 1973—. Visiting professor at University of British Columbia, summers, 1970, 1973, and University of Hull, 1971-72. Director of Bishop Cridge Centre for the Family.

MEMBER: International Society for Arthurian Literature, Modern Language Association of America, Early English Text Society, Mediaeval Academy of America, Conference on Christianity and Literature, Amerian Academy of Religion, Association of Canadian University Teachers of English, Medieval Association of the Pacific, Ontario Federation of Farmers, Lambda Iota Tau. *Awards, honors:* Awards from *Atlantic Monthly*, 1964, for short story "The Transfer," and 1965, for short stories "In Common Bond" and "New Hay," and for poems "To Marcel Proust" and "Nomad"; Woodrow Wilson fellowships, 1965, 1967-68; Canada Council humanities award, 1969, for research in Florence, Italy.

WRITINGS: (Contributor) C. A. Huttar, editor, *Imagination and the Spirit*, Eerdmans, 1971; (contributor) Neville Denny, editor. *Medieval English Drama*, Edward Arnold, 1973; *Modern Fictions and the Rebirth of Theology* (monograph), State University of New York Press, 1973; *Franciscan Spirituality and the Early English Lyric*, University of Nebraska Press, 1975. Contributor of articles and stories to professional journals, including *Journal of the American Academy of Religion, Mosaic, Viator, English Quarterly, Shakespeare Studies, Journal of English and Germanic Philology, American Benedictine Review*, and *Kodon.*

WORK IN PROGRESS: Editing *By Things Seen: The Ordering of Experience in Medieval Culture*, with R. A. Peck and R. W. Kaeuper; a book on medieval romance; editing and translating Anglo-Norman lyrics, with Brian Levy.

JEFFRIES, Derwin J(ames) 1915-

PERSONAL: Born September 20, 1915, in South Dakota; son of Waldo and Annette Jeffries; married Edith Herron, 1940; children: Joan (Mrs. Denis Berman), LeAnn (Mrs. Jack Morin). *Education:* Southern State College, Springfield, S.D., Elementary Diploma, 1936; University of Montana, B.A., 1948, M.A. 1951. *Religion:* Christian. *Office:* Department of Education, Trenton State College, Trenton, N.J. 08625.

CAREER: Elementary and high school teacher in South Dakota and Montana, 1939-42; elementary and high school principal in Montana, 1944-49; superintendent of schools in Willsall and Townsend, Mont., 1949-56; New York University, New York, N.Y., in administration, 1956-58; Trenton State College, Trenton, N.J., associate professor of education, 1958—. Editor and publisher, Home and School Press.

WRITINGS: To Hell with the PTA!, Home & School, 1965; *Lesson Planning and Lesson Teaching*, Home & School, 1966; *Your Child Is Crying!*, Home & School, 1970.

WORK IN PROGRESS: A Communication Theory of Teaching; Tomorrow's Teacher Training; Educational Evaluation: Sham, Fraud, and Atrocity!; We Must Get Technical about Teaching; a novel, *The Motivation Mountains.*

SIDELIGHTS: Jefferies told *CA* that he looks forward to Christian writings in the future, and that in his current work he stresses "communications as the very basis of the educative complex (not 'education process'); the fundamental role of cultural analysis throughout education (one day it may be realized that the understanding of culture has as much, or more, to do with quality teaching than does psychology); the need for closer parent-teacher communication that faces up to significant issues, controversial or not."

* * *

JENKINS, Alan 1914-

PERSONAL: Born September 5, 1914, in London, England; son of Donald James (an insurance underwriter) and Mabel (Witcomb) Jenkins; married Margaret Elizabeth Hoskin (a teacher), December 15, 1956; children: Annabel. *Education:* St. Edmund Hall, Oxford, B.A. (honors), 1935, M.A., 1948. *Politics:* "Vaguely Conservative." *Religion:* "Vaguely Church of England." *Home:* Stars Wood, High Barn Lane, Effingham, Surrey, England. *Agent:* David Higham, 5, Lower John St., London W.1, England.

CAREER: Nash's Magazine, London, England, fiction editor, 1936-37; *Argosy*, London, assistant editor, 1938-39; Hulton Press Ltd., London, assistant editor of *World Review* and *Lilliput*, 1940, 1946-51; *John Bull*, London, fiction editor, 1952-54; Ogilvy, Benson & Mather, London, public relations director, 1954-70; full-time writer, 1970—. *Military service:* British Army, Intelligence Corps, 1941-46; became major. *Member:* Reform Club.

WRITINGS: Castle Avalon (novel), Cassell, 1941; *Absent Without Leave* (novel), Heinemann, 1949; *The Swimming Pool* (novel), 1951; *The Young Mozart* (children's book), Parrish, 1961; *Drinka Pinta*, Heinemann, 1970; *On Site*, Heinemann, 1971; *The Stock Exchange Story*, Heinemann, 1973; *London's City*, Heinemann, 1973; *The Twenties*, Universe Books, 1974; *The Thirties*, Heinemann, in press. Also author of radio and television plays. Contributor to popular magazines.

WORK IN PROGRESS: The Forties: Society and the Writer; research on eighteenth-century Venice.

SIDELIGHTS: Jenkins writes: "I regard myself as an entertainer rather than as an artist. I am not unhappy enough to be a true artist. I regard my background of journalism as my most valuable equipment, and would never be ashamed of having been a newspaperman. I speak French and German with fair fluency, and can muddle along in Italian. I have visited eight oriental countries, most European ones, and America (Hollywood mainly)."

* * *

JENKINS, Ferrell 1936-

PERSONAL: Born January 3, 1936, in Huntsville, Ala.; son of B. M. (a grocer) and Vera (Mann) Jenkins; married Elizabeth A. Williams (with business faculty at Florida College), December 16, 1954; children: Ferrell, Jr., Stanley. *Education:* Florida College, A.A., 1957; Harding Graduate School of Religion, M.A., 1971. *Home:* 513 Carolyne St., Temple Terrace, Fla. 33617. *Office:* Department of Religion, Florida College, Temple Terrace, Fla. 33617.

CAREER: Minister at Spring & Blaine Church of Christ, St. Louis, Mo., 1958-62, West End Church of Christ, Bowling Green, Ky., 1962-64, Emerson Church of Christ, Indianapolis, Ind., 1965-66, and at Brown St. Church of Christ, Akron, Ohio, 1966-67; Florida College, Temple Terrace, Fla., professor of Bible, 1969—. Cogdill Foundation (publishing company), Marion, Ind., editor, 1968—, member of board of directors. *Member:* Evangelical Theological Society, American Schools of Oriental Research, Near East Archaeological Society.

WRITINGS: (Contributor) W. Smith, editor, *The New Smith's Bible Dictionary*, Doubleday, 1966; *The Theme of the Bible*, Cogdill Foundation, 1969; *The Old Testament in the Book of Revelation*, Cogdill Foundation, 1973; (contributor) *Resurrection*, C.E.I. Publishing, 1974. Editor, *Evidence Quarterly*, 1960-62; associate editor, *Truth in Life* (Bible class series), 1969—.

WORK IN PROGRESS: A book on Christian apologetics.

SIDELIGHTS: Leading study groups, Jenkins has made eight trips to the Middle East since 1967. *Avocational interests:* Photography (several of his photos have been published in *Truth in Life* literature).

* * *

JENKINS, Will(iam) F(itzgerald) 1896-1975 (Murray Leinster)

June 16, 1896—June 8, 1975; American author of science fiction and other novels, television scripts, radio plays, screenplays, and short stories. Obituaries: *New York Times*, June 10, 1975. (*CA*-9/10)

* * *

JENNINGS, S.M. See MEYER, Jerome Sydney

* * *

JENSEN, Andrew F(rederick), Jr. 1929-

PERSONAL: Born January 12, 1929, in Selma, Calif.; son of Andrew F. (in agriculture) and Hazel (Whitney) Jensen; married Kathleen Anna Van Caneghen, December 18, 1954; children: Andrew F. III, David Whitney. *Education:* University of Redlands, B.A., 1951; Eastern Baptist Theological Seminary, M.Div., 1954; Princeton University, Th.M., 1973; Antioch College, M.Ed., 1974. *Residence:* Marlton, N.J. 08053. *Agent:* Julian Bach, 3 East 48th St., New York, N.Y. 10017. *Office:* Naval Hospital, Philadelphia, Pa. 19145.

CAREER: Pastor of Baptist church in Philadelphia, Pa., 1952-55; U.S. Navy, 1955—; serving as chaplain; present rank, commander; presently stationed at Naval Hospital, Philadelphia, Pa. *Member:* American Association of Family and Marriage Counselors, College of Chaplains, California Association of Family and Marriage Counselors.

WRITINGS: The Trial of Chaplain Jensen, Arbor House, 1974.

SIDELIGHTS: Jensen told *CA* that he is "the first chaplain in the military to be court martialed, according to records, and the only case tried in a general court martial on the charges of adultery only." The government's case, contends Jensen, "was based upon false testimony and a perjured witness, a fact that the Navy attorneys knew before the trial but refused to reveal." Jensen was acquitted of misconduct charges by a six-officer jury at Cecil Field Naval Station in Jacksonville, Florida.

* * *

JENSEN, Frede 1926-

PERSONAL: Born February 17, 1926, in Auning, Denmark; son of Hans and Jenny (Martinussen) Jensen; married Marguerite Lorre, October 20, 1968. *Education:* University of Grenoble, Certificat de grammaire et philologie francaises, 1950; University of Copenhagen, M.A., 1953; University of Salamanca, Diplomado de filologia hispanica, 1955; University of California, Los Angeles, Ph.D., 1961. *Home:* 2805 Colby Dr., Boulder, Colo. 80303. *Office:* Department of French, University of Colorado, Boulder, Colo. 80302.

CAREER: University of Alberta, Calgary, assistant professor of French, 1961-64; University of California, Los Angeles, assistant professor of French, 1964-67; University of Colorado, Boulder, associate professor, 1967-73, professor of French and linguistics, 1973—. *Military service:* Danish Army, 1953-55. *Awards, honors:* Fulbright award.

WRITINGS: The Italian Verb: A Morphological Study, University of North Carolina Press, 1971; *From Vulgar Latin to Old Provencal*, University of North Carolina Press, 1972; (with Thomas Λ. Lathrop) *The Syntax of the Old Spanish Subjunctive*, Mouton, 1973; *The Syntax of the Old French Subjunctive*, Mouton, 1974. Contributor of articles to professional journals. Member of editorial board, *Semasia*.

WORK IN PROGRESS: Three books, *Introduction to Indo-European Phonology, Old Provencal Morphology*, and *The Poetry of the Troubadours*.

AVOCATIONAL INTERESTS: Mountaineering, travel.

* * *

JENSEN, Gwendolyn Evans 1936-

PERSONAL: Born February 5, 1936, in Upper Darby, Pa.; daughter of John Temple (a businessman) and Mary Elizabeth (Hicks) Evans; married Gordon Maurice Jensen (a professor of history), 1967; children: Elizabeth, Donald, Alice. *Education:* Attended Connecticut College, 1953-55, and Cedar Crest College, 1955-56; University of Hartford, B.A., 1962; Trinity College, Hartford, Conn., M.A., 1963;

University of Connecticut, Ph.D., 1971. *Home:* 168 South Main St., Wallingford, Conn. 06492. *Office:* Department of History, University of New Haven, New Haven, Conn.

CAREER: Central Connecticut State College, New Britain, instructor in history, 1967-68; University of New Haven, New Haven, Conn., assistant professor, 1968-73, associate professor of history, 1973—. *Member:* American Historical Association, Conference Group for Central European History, Economic History Association, Berkshire Conference (secretary-treasurer, 1974—), New England Historical Association (member of executive committee, 1973—), New Haven Opera Society (member of board of governors, 1974—; vice-president, 1975). *Award, honors:* American Philosophical Society grant, 1973, for research in the social history of the Prussian church; Lilly fellowship, Yale University, 1975.

WRITINGS: (Contributor) Douglas Robillard, editor, *Essays in Arts and Science*, University of New Haven, 1971; (with Thomas Katsaros) *The Western Tradition to 1660*, MSS Information, 1972. Contributor of articles and reviews to *Connecticut Historical Society Bulletin, Central European History*, and *Reprint Bulletin*. Editor of *New England Historical Association News*, 1974—.

WORK IN PROGRESS: A comparative study of ecclesiastical reform in the Prussian and Anglican churches in the first half of the nineteenth century.

* * *

JENSEN, Rosalie (Seymour) 1938-

PERSONAL: Born February 25, 1938, in Elberton, Ga.; daughter of William Lloyd (an electrician) and Bertha (Lucille) Seymour; married Richard Alan Jensen, December 22, 1963; children: Karen Irene. *Education:* Shorter College, B.A., 1960; University of Georgia, M.A., 1962; Florida State University, Ph.D., 1966. *Religion:* Unity. *Home:* 1369 Emory Rd. N.E., Atlanta, Ga. 30306. *Office:* Department of Mathematics, Georgia State University, Atlanta, Ga. 30303.

CAREER: West Georgia College, Carrollton, instructor in mathematics, 1961-63; Shorter College, Rome, Ga., assistant professor of mathematics and chairman of department, 1966-68; Georgia State University, Atlanta, assistant professor, 1968-71, associate professor, 1971-74, professor of mathematics education, 1974—. Director of day camp for Atlanta Girl's Club, 1961. *Member:* National Council of Teachers of Mathematics, Mathematics Association of America, Georgia Association of Educators (president of local chapter, 1970-71), Georgia Council of Teachers of Mathematics, Georgia Education Association (president of local chapter, 1970-71), Metropolitan Atlanta Mathematics Club (president 1972-74), Georgia State University Women's Club, Pi Mu Epsilon, Pi Sigma Alpha.

WRITINGS: Developing Mathematical Concepts and Skills for the Young Child, Georgia State University, 1970; *Developing Mathematical Concepts and Skills for Children*, Georgia State University, 1972; (contributor) Peter Martorella, editor, *Concept Learning: Designs for Instruction*, Intext, 1972; *Exploring Mathematical Concepts and Skills in the Elementary School*, C. E. Merrill, 1973; (editor) *Metres for Millions* (collection of articles), Georgia State University, 1975. Publications editor of Georgia Council of Teachers of Mathematics, 1975-77.

JOHN, Dane
See MAJOR, Alan P(ercival)

* * *

JOHNN, David
See ENGLE, John D(avid), Jr.

* * *

JOHNS, June 1925-

PERSONAL: Born June 1, 1925, in Salford, England; married Jack Smith (a cameraman); children: one son. *Education:* Attended high school in Pendleton, Salford, England. *Home:* 10 Neston Dr., Upton Park, Chester, England. *Agent:* Bolt & Watson, 8 Storey's Gate, London, England.

CAREER: Manchester Evening News, Manchester, England, reporter, 1942-44; *Manchester Daily Mirror*, Manchester and London, England, reporter, 1944-50; free-lance feature writer for newspapers and magazines. Teacher for Workers' Educational Association, 1970—(part-time). *Member:* National Union of Journalists, Society of Authors, Workers' Educational Association, North of England Zoological Society, Mensa.

WRITINGS—Nonfiction: The Grasshopper Boy, Epworth, 1967; *Zoo without Bars*, Gollancz, 1969; *King of the Witches*, P. Davies, 1969, Coward, 1970; *Little Brother*, Gollancz, 1970; *The Mating Game*, P. Davies, 1970, St. Martin's, 1971; *Black Magic Today*, New English Library, 1971; *Practical Yoga*, David & Charles, 1974.

* * *

JOHNS, Whitey
See WHITE, John I(rwin)

* * *

JOHNSON, Bradford 1937-

PERSONAL: Born July 30, 1937, in Boston, Mass.; son of Richard J. (a businessman) and Ruth E. (Judkins) Johnson; married Susan Phillips, September 9, 1961; children: Martha, Katherine. *Education:* Amherst College, B.A., 1959. *Office:* Thorndike, Doran, Paine & Lewis, 28 State St., Boston, Mass. 02109.

CAREER: First National Bank of Boston, Boston, Mass., assistant vice-president, 1959-68; Thorndike, Doran, Paine & Lewis, Boston, Mass., senior vice-president, 1968—. Member of Boston Trust and Estate Planning Council, 1962-68, and New England Tax Institute, 1965—; Washingtonian Hospital, director, 1965-68, treasurer, 1966-68; member of Greater Boston Hospital Council, 1966-68; director of Winchester Savings Bank, 1971—; commissioner of Wildwood Cemetery, 1974—. *Member:* Financial Analysts Federation (fellow), Boston Society of Security Analysts, Amherst Club (Boston), Somerset Club.

WRITINGS: Pulpits to the North (poems), Mosher Press, 1974. Contributor to *Analyse Financiere, Fund Guide International*, and *Winding Roads.*

WORK IN PROGRESS: Verse for a new book tentatively titled *Roasted in Rosemary* or *Eastern Oysters.*

AVOCATIONAL INTERESTS: Vocal music, lumbering, cabinetmaking, gardening.

* * *

JOHNSON, C.F.
See GOULART, Frances Sheridan

JOHNSON, Charlene
See CRAWFORD, Char

* * *

JOHNSON, Crockett
See LEISK, David Johnson

* * *

JOHNSON, Douglas W(ayne) 1934-

PERSONAL: Born August 21, 1934, in Clinton County, Ill.; son of Noel Douglas and Laura Margaret (Crocker) Johnson; married Phyllis A. Heinzmann, June 8, 1956; children: Kirk Wayne, Heather Renee, Kirsten Joy, Tara Carlynne. *Education:* McKendree College, B.A., 1956; Boston University, S.T.B., 1959, M.A., 1963; Northwestern University, Ph.D., 1968. *Home:* 420 Cambridge Rd., Ridgewood, N.J. 07450. *Office:* 475 Riverside Drive, New York, N.Y., 10027.

CAREER: Ordained Methodist minister, 1959; pastor in Chicago, Ill., 1960-64; Rock River Conference of the Methodist Church, Chicago, director of research of Chicago Home Missionary and Church Extension Society, 1964-66; Garrett Theological Seminary, Evanston, Ill., research assistant in Bureau of Social and Religious Research, 1966-68, teaching fellow, 1967-68; National Council of Churches, New York, N.Y., director of research services in Office of Planning and Program, 1968-73, associate in Office of Research, Evaluation and Planning, 1973—. Teacher at Western Connecticut State College, 1969-73. *Member:* American Sociological Association, Religious Research Association (member of board of directors, 1970—), Society for the Scientific Study of Religion, Rural Sociological Society, Religious Education Association.

WRITINGS: (Editor) *Information and Research Needs of the Churches in the 1970s*, National Council of Churches, 1970; (with Paul Picard and Bernard Quinn) *Churches and Church Membership in the United States: 1971*, Glenmary Research Center, 1971; (with George W. Cornell) *Punctured Preconceptions: What North American Christians Think About the Church*, Friendship Press, 1972; *Managing Change in the Church*, Friendship Press, 1974. Contributor to religious journals.

WORK IN PROGRESS: Facing the Future Within Us; The Destiny, a novel; papers.

* * *

JOHNSON, Gertrude F(alk) 1929-

PERSONAL: Born August 20, 1929, in Poland; came to United States, 1956; daughter of Ewald (a farmer) and Emilie (Jetz) Fenske; married Arthur James Johnson (a chemist), May 7, 1955; children: Boyd Arthur, Ralph Herbert, Kenneth Harold. *Education:* Attended schools in Poland and Germany. *Residence:* Corpus Christi, Tex.

WRITINGS: A Gathering of Lambs, Concordia Publishing, 1975.

SIDELIGHTS: Mrs. Johnson commented on her early life during World War II: "In November 1940 we were moved to a farm in the Polish corridor. There my father continued his fight against the Nazis and was almost caught. Even I, as a fifteen year old, managed to disrupt the local Hitler Jugend.... Immediately after the war we again had to flee—this time from the Poles. In our flight we went through many harrowing experiences. Finally we arrived half starved in Berlin and settled on a farm near Hanover. We went through periods of starvation and typhoid fever and I lost my memory of all that happened to me. . . . In the late 1960's I watched the upheaval on the American campuses on television. I was frightened. Then my memory of my own youth in Poland started to flood back. I immediately started writing and finally my whole childhood was clear before me.''

AVOCATIONAL INTERESTS: Painting, sewing, tennis, reading, swimming.

* * *

JOHNSON, Joe Donald 1943-

PERSONAL: Born April 21, 1943, in Norfolk, Va.; adopted son of George Thomas Johnson and Winnie (Reed) Johnson; married Darlene Tankersley, October 7, 1966 (divorced, 1974); children: Shauna Enid, Sherrild Maeve. *Education:* State University of New York at Albany, A.A., 1975. *Address:* P.O. Box 73, Cutten, Calif. 95534.

CAREER: Agnews State Hosp., San Jose, Calif., psychiatric technician, 1966-75. *Military service:* U.S. Army, 1960-61. *Member:* Recreation Equipment.

WRITINGS: Silent for Long Silent Forever (poems), Windy Row Press, 1969; *Poems for V.J.A.*, privately printed, 1971; *The Garbage Rat, Wilson, and Poems of Painstaken*, privately printed, 1971; *Herenow Poems*, privately printed, 1972; *Warp Oems*, privately printed, 1974; *Peeple Poems*, privately printed, 1975; *You Cry for Worse than Nothing and Other Poems*, privately printed, 1975.

WORK IN PROGRESS: Several compilations of narrative poems; more *Peeple Poems*.

AVOCATIONAL INTERESTS: Rafting, mountaineering, athletics.

* * *

JOHNSON, Kristi Planck 1944-

PERSONAL: Born July 8, 1944, in Omaha, Neb.; daughter of Edmund Lawrence and Esther (Hansen) Planck; married John E. Johnson (a computer consultant), November 22, 1974. *Education:* Dana College, B.A., 1966; University of Minnesota, M.A., 1971; also studied at University of Copenhagen, 1965. *Religion:* Lutheran. *Home:* 4501 Edgefield Rd., Kensington, Md. 20795.

CAREER: History and German teacher in public schools in Omaha, Neb., 1966-69; White House, Washington, D.C., member of speech writing staff, 1972-73; Prince Georges Public Schools, Hyattsville, Md., teacher of history and geography, 1973—. Organist, 1959—. Volunteer worker for American Red Cross, 1959—. *Member:* National Education Association, American Scandinavian Foundation (Washington chapter vice-president, 1973—), American Guild of Organists, Maryland State Education Association, Prince Georges County Education Association.

WRITINGS: (Translator from the Danish) H. C. Branner, *The Story of Boerge*, Twayne, 1973.

WORK IN PROGRESS: Translating *Eve Serves Her Term as a Child*, by Kjeld Abell.

* * *

JOHNSON, Lois Walfrid 1936-

PERSONAL: Born November 23, 1936, in Starbuck, Minn.; daughter of A. B. (a clergyman) and Lydia (Chris-

tiansen) Walfrid; married Roy A. Johnson (an elementary school teacher), June 26, 1959; children: Gail, Jeffrey, Kevin. *Education:* Gustavus Adolphus College, B.A. (magna cum laude), 1958; University of Oklahoma, graduate study, 1968-72. *Politics:* Independent. *Religion:* Lutheran. *Home:* 8117 35th Ave. N., Minneapolis, Minn. 55427.

CAREER: High school English teacher in Wayzata, Minn., 1958-59, and lay reader in Edina, Minn., 1962-63, 1964-65; free-lance writer, 1971—. Has taught at *Decision* Magazine School of Christian Writing, 1973-75, and Midwest Writer's Conference, 1974-75; editorial associate, *Writer's Digest* School (correspondence school), 1974—. *Member:* Society of Children's Book Writers, Minnesota Guild of Christian Writers (vice-president, 1970-71; president, 1971-72), Iota Delta Gamma. *Awards, honors:* Dwight L. Moody Award for excellence in Christian literature, from *Decision* Magazine School of Christian Writing, 1969, for short story "Spaces in the Heart."

WRITINGS—Juvenile: Just a Minute, Lord (prayers for girls), Augsburg, 1973; *Aaron's Christmas Donkey* (picture book), Augsburg, 1974; *Hello, God! Prayers for Small Children* (picture book), Augsburg, 1975.

Work has been anthologized in *Complete Christmas Programs*, Volume IV, edited by Grace Ramquist, Zondervan, 1972, and *Children of Light* (juvenile), edited by Wilson G. Egbert, Augsburg, 1973; a short story was included as part of a chapter in *Jesus Stood by Us*, by Helen Reagan Smith, Broadman, 1970.

Lyrics for hymns: "Father, Lead Us to Your Table," Augsburg, 1974; "Come to Us, Living Spirit," Augsburg, 1975.

Contributor of about thirty articles, poems, stories, and reviews to religious and general magazines, including *Decision, Scope, Clarion, Moody Monthly, A.D., Teach, Lutheran Standard*, and *Grit*.

WORK IN PROGRESS: A picture book for children; two adult books, one to be published by Augsburg in 1976; short stories.

SIDELIGHTS: Lois Johnson writes: "I take special delight in the writing I do for juveniles, and the children themselves make it that way. . . . My husband has taught in inner-city elementary schools since 1958 and is my favorite resource person when I wonder about age-level characteristics, likes and dislikes of children. . . . I hope that my writing reflects two things—my religious faith, which means a great deal to me, and the way I feel about people. I like the curiosity and wide-eyed honesty often present in children. With adults I tend to seek out the individuals who seem real. . . . If my work captures the spontaneity of these individuals and the love of the God in whom I believe, then I am happy."

AVOCATIONAL INTERESTS: Biking, swimming, water skiing, music, playing piano, gardening, photography, reading.

* * *

JOHNSON, Richard
See RICHEY, David

* * *

JOHNSTON, Brenda A(rlivia) 1944-

PERSONAL: Born December 5, 1944, in Welch, W.Va.;

daughter of William H. (a machine operator) and Lucille M. (Graves) Thomas; divorced; children: Dana W. *Education:* Attended Case Western Reserve University, 1972-76. *Politics:* Democrat. *Religion:* Christian. *Home:* 14515 Savannah, East Cleveland, Ohio 44112. *Office:* Cuyahoga County Board of Mental Retardation, Cleveland, Ohio 44113.

CAREER: Navy Finance Center, Cleveland, Ohio, department secretary, 1964-65; Neighborhood Youth Corps, Cleveland, administrative secretary, 1966-68; Legal Aid Society, Cleveland, administrative secretary, 1968-69; Equitable Life Insurance Co., Cleveland, office manager, 1969-70; Erie Lackawanna Railroad, Cleveland, medical secretary, 1970-72; Case Western Reserve University, Cleveland, administrative secretary, 1972-73; Cuyahoga County Board of Mental Retardation, Cleveland, Ohio, staff writer, 1973—. *Awards, Honors:* Honorable mention from Council of Interracial Books, for *Between the Devil and the Sea.*

WRITINGS: Big Bill (juvenile mystery), Scholastic Book Services, 1974; *Between the Devil and the Sea* (children's historical novel), Harcourt, 1974; *Office Deskbook of Model Letters for Every Occasion,* Parker Publishing, 1975. Also author of *Michael and the Ebony Knight* and *The Train Ride,* both 1975, for Scholastic "Sprint" series, edited by Ray Shepard.

WORK IN PROGRESS: A novel, *Internal Revolution;* a collection of short stories for adults, *Chains of Darkness;* a research project on developmental learning in the retarded, *Early Intervention for Retarded Children;* a book of children's stories of Black heroes, *Come out the Wilderness.*

* * *

JOHNSTON, Johanna

PERSONAL: Born in Chicago, Ill.; daughter of John F. (a lawyer) and Florence (Bell) Voigt; divorced; children: Abigail. *Education:* Attended University of Chicago, 1934-36, and Art Institute of Chicago, 1936-38. *Residence:* New York, N.Y.

CAREER: CBS Television and Radio, New York, N.Y., staff writer, 1951-60. *Awards, honors:* Thomas Alva Edison Award, 1962, for *Thomas Jefferson: His Many Talents.*

WRITINGS—Adult biographies: *Runaway to Heaven: The Story of Harriet Beecher Stowe and Her Era,* Doubleday, 1964; *Mrs. Satan: The Incredible Saga of Victoria Woodhull,* Putnam, 1967; *The Heart That Would Not Hold: The Life of Washington Irving,* M. Evans, 1971.

Juvenile books: *Sugarplum* (novel), Knopf, 1956; *Stories of the Norsemen,* Doubleday, 1961; *Hannibal,* Doubleday, 1962; *Sugarplum and Snowball* (fiction), Knopf, 1963; *Thomas Jefferson: His Many Talents,* Dodd, 1962; *Joan of Arc,* Doubleday, 1963; *Edie Changes Her Mind* (novel), Putnam, 1964; *The Challenge and the Answer* (history), Dodd, 1964; *Together in America* (history), Dodd, 1967; *A Special Bravery* (biographies), Dodd, 1967; *That's Right, Edie* (novel), Putnam, 1967; *The Eagle in Fact and Fiction,* Crown, 1967; *The Connecticut Colony* (history), Macmillan, 1969.

(With Murry Karmiller) *All Kinds of Kings in Fact and Legend: From Hammurabi to Louis XIV,* Norton, 1970; *Paul Cuffee: America's First Black Captain,* Dodd, 1970; *Speak Up, Edie* (novel), Putnam, 1970; *The Indians and the Strangers* (history), Dodd, 1972; *Women Themselves* (biographies), Dodd, 1973; *Who Found America?* (history),

Golden Gate, 1974; *Frederick Law Olmstead: Partner with Nature* (biography), Dodd, 1975.

* * *

JONES, Ezra Earl   1939-

PERSONAL: Born December 30, 1939, in Birmingham, Ala.; son of Ezra Elith (a sheet metal mechanic) and Eunice (Minor) Jones; married Mary Elizabeth Slaughter, September 11, 1960; children: Robert Drew, Camilla Diane. *Education:* Birmingham-Southern College, B.A., 1960; Duke University, B.D., 1963, Th.M., 1964; Drew University, further graduate study, 1966-68; Northwestern University, Ph.D., 1971. *Politics:* Democrat. *Home:* 4 Franklin Ave., Cranford, N.J. 07016. *Office:* United Methodist Church, 475 Riverside Dr., New York, N.Y. 10027.

CAREER: Ordained United Methodist minister in 1964; pastor of Methodist churches in Alabama, 1958-60, 1964-66, North Carolina, 1960-64, and New Jersey, 1966-68; Garrett Theological Seminary, Evanston, Ill., instructor in sociology of religion, 1969-70; United Methodist Board of Global Ministries, New York, N.Y., associate director of research, 1970—. Piano and choral music instructor, 1956-60. *Member:* American Sociological Association, American Religious Research Association.

WRITINGS: The Church and Extremism, National Division of the Board of Missions, United Methodist Church, 1970; *Where United Methodists Stand on Extremism,* Women's Division of Board of Missions, United Methodist Church, 1971; *You Are the Target (pamphlet),* Board of Missions, United Methodist Church, 1971; (with Robert L. Wilson) *What's Ahead for Old First Church,* Harper, 1974; *New Churches for New Communities,* Harper, 1976. Author of research reports. Contributor to *Drew University, Response, Adult Leader, Virginia Advocate,* and *Review of Religious Research.*

WORK IN PROGRESS: The Management of Ministry, with James Anderson, completion expected in 1977.

* * *

JONES, Gwilym Peredur   1892-1975

April 24, 1892—February 12, 1975; British educator, author of works on modern industrial development and other topics. Obituaries: *AB Bookman's Weekly,* March 17, 1975.

* * *

JONES, Kenneth E(ffner)   1920-

PERSONAL: Born March 17, 1920, in Enid, Okla.; son of Thomas A. (a minister) and Ruby (a minister; maiden name, Dayton) Jones; married Elizabeth Miller, September 15, 1940; children: Lorelei Jones Atteberry, DonDeena Jones Duvall. *Education:* Anderson College, B.Th., 1943; Oberlin College, B.D., 1947; Winona Lake School of Theology, Th.M., 1965. *Residence:* Houston, Tex. *Office:* 911 West 11th St., Houston, Tex. 77008.

CAREER: Ordained minister of the Church of God, 1943; pastor in Ohio, Kentucky, and Illinois, 1943-50, 1951-62; Alberta Bible Institute, Camrose, Alberta, dean, 1950-51; missionary in Kingston, Jamaica, West Indies, 1962-63; Gulf-Coast Bible College, Houston, Tex., professor of Bible, 1963-65; Warner Pacific College, Portland, Ore., professor of theology, 1965-74; Gulf-Coast Bible College, professor of Bible, 1974—. *Member:* Society of Biblical Literature, American Scientific Affiliation, Wesleyan Theological Society. *Awards, honors:* D.D., Warner Pacific College, 1974.

WRITINGS: Strange New Faiths, Warner Press, 1954; (editor with F. G. Smith) *What the Bible Teaches*, Warner Press, 1955; *What About the Gift of Tongues?*, Warner Press, 1962; *Let's Study the Bible*, Warner Press, 1962; *Isaiah*, Eerdmans, 1969; *Numbers: A Study Guide*, Baker Book, 1972. Contributing editor to *Vital Christianity*, 1955-69.

WORK IN PROGRESS: The first of a series of books on Christian theology for the layman; *Beliefs That Make a Difference*, for Warner Press.

* * *

JOPP, Hal
See JOPP, Harold Dowling, Jr.

* * *

JOPP, Harold Dowling, Jr. 1946-
(Hal Jopp)

PERSONAL: Born October 20, 1946, in Baltimore, Md.; son of Harold Dowling (a salesman) and Violet (Karpinski) Jopp; married Margaret Carole Wallace (a nurse), December 20, 1967; children: Harold Dowling III, Devin Alexander. *Education:* St. Charles College, A.A., 1966; Catholic University of America, student, 1966-67; Washington College, Chestertown, Md., B.A., 1968; University of Delaware, M.A., 1970; University of Maryland, J.D., 1967; also attended Ecumenical Institute of Theology, Baltimore. *Religion:* Roman Catholic. *Home address:* R.F.D.1, Box 438-A, Greensboro, Md. 21639. *Office:* Chesapeake College, Wye Mills, Md. 21679.

CAREER: Chesapeake College, Wye Mills, Md., instructor in English, 1969-72, assistant dean of students and registrar, 1972-74, assistant to president of college, 1974-75, interim president of college, 1975—. Legal assistant to an attorney in Denton, Md., 1974-75. Director of athletics and recreation at Benedictine School for Exceptional Children, 1968-70. Vice-chairman of Caroline County Health Planning Council. *Member:* American Bar Association (Law Student Division), National Organization on Legal Problems of Education, American Council on Education, Maryland Council of Community College Presidents. *Awards, honors:* Academy of the Arts prizes in poetry, 1970, short story, 1971, and nonfiction, 1971.

WRITINGS: (Editor with Robert H. Ingersoll) *Shoremen: An Anthology of Eastern Shore Prose and Verse*, Tidewater, 1974.

Work is anthologized in *Pegasus, 1964-68*, edited by Dennis Hartman, National Poetry Press, 1968; *America Sings*, edited by Hartman, National Poetry Press, 1968. Poetry and newspaper writing published under name Hal Jopp. Feature writer for *Dorchester News*, 1970. Contributor to *Heartland*.

WORK IN PROGRESS: The Inheritance, a novel; editing *Eastern Shore Sampler*, nonfiction selections; *The Immigrants*, poems.

SIDELIGHTS: Jopp writes: "I am deeply troubled by the ethical and moral bankruptcy in which many Americans find themselves. Until we, as a nation, have clarified and reaffirmed our values we will be ineffective in solving our national problems.

"I am in hopes of a literary renaissance in America. Style and language have suffered too long at the hands of facile plots, stereotyped characters, and the Beulah land of motion picture and television rights. Good writing is still at a premium."

As interim president of Chesapeake College, Jopp is one of the youngest college presidents in the country. *Avocational interests:* European travel, gardening, reading, theology.

* * *

JORDAN, David P(aul) 1939-

PERSONAL: Born January 5, 1939, in Detroit, Mich.; son of Joseph Jay (an electrical engineer) and Florence (a librarian; maiden name, Fraiberg) Jordan; married Virginia Bell, March 10, 1973. *Education:* University of Michigan, B.A., 1961; Yale University, M.A., 1962, Ph.D., 1966. *Home:* 852 West Aldine, Chicago, Ill. 60657. *Office:* Department of History, University of Illinois at Chicago Circle, Chicago, Ill. 60680.

CAREER: Brooklyn College of the City University of New York, New York, N.Y., instructor, 1966-67, assistant professor of history, 1967-68; University of Illinois at Chicago Circle, Chicago, assistant professor, 1968-71, associate professor of history, 1971—. *Awards, honors:* Woodrow Wilson fellowship, 1961, 1965-66; American Philosophical Society grant, 1971.

WRITINGS: Gibbon and His Roman Empire, University of Illinois Press, 1971. Contributor of articles and reviews to *Church History, History and Theory*, and *Journal of Modern History*.

WORK IN PROGRESS: The King's Two Trials, a narrative history of the trial and death of Louis XVI; research on the life and character of Edward Gibbon.

* * *

JORDAN, Lois B(reedlove) 1912-

PERSONAL: Born May 2, 1912, in Decatur, Tex.; daughter of Hugh Taylor (a lumberman) and Grace Ruth (Lindley) Breedlove; married Howard J. Jordan (a retired law officer), June 3, 1933; children: Cherry Lynn (Mrs. Al Mayer), Virginia Kay. *Education:* Decatur Baptist College (now Dallas Baptist College), graduated (with honors), 1930; attended North Texas State Teachers College (now North Texas State University), 1930; Texas Woman's University, B.S., 1963, M.L.S., 1966. *Politics:* Democrat. *Religion:* Protestant. *Home:* 2402 College Park Dr., Denton, Tex. 76201. *Office:* School of Library Science, Texas Woman's University, P.O. Box 22905, TWU Station, Denton, Tex. 76204.

CAREER: Public elementary and high school music teacher and private piano teacher in Texas, 1930-32; Bridgeport (Tex.) Public Schools, high school librarian and supervisor of elementary and junior high school, 1963-66; Texas Woman's University, School of Library Science, Denton, librarian and instructor, 1966—. Bridgeport Library board member, 1963-66. *Member:* American Library Association, Daughters of the American Revolution, Southwest Library Association, Texas Library Association, Texas State Teachers Association.

WRITINGS: Mexican Americans: Resources to Build Cultural Understanding, Libraries Unlimited, 1973.

WORK IN PROGRESS: Genealogical research.

* * *

JORDAN, Ruth 1926-

PERSONAL: Born in 1926; married N.J. Kivity (a journalist and television commentator), 1955; children: one daughter, one son. *Education:* Graduated from Hebrew

University, Jerusalem, and University of London. *Residence:* London, England.

CAREER: Worked for British Broadcasting Corp., London, England, as scriptwriter, drama producer, newsreader, interviewer, and current affairs commentator.

WRITINGS: Sophie Dorothea (biography), Constable, 1971, Braziller, 1972; *Berenice* (biography), Barnes & Noble, 1974. Regular contributor on current affairs to leading Hebrew-language dailies in Israel. Wrote scripts for "Royal Romances," a radio series of six half-hour plays; "As Cooks Go," a television dramatization of an autobiography by Elizabeth Jordan; and "The Meddlers," a television dramatization of a novel by Claire Rayner.

SIDELIGHTS: For the past several years Ruth Jordan has been a voluntary tutor for adult illiterates. *Avocational interests:* Theatre, music, and education.

* * *

JOURNET, Charles Cardinal 1891(?)-1975

1891(?)—April 15, 1975; Swiss cardinal, educator, author of texts on theology. Obituaries: *New York Times*, April 16, 1975.

* * *

JOYNSON, R(obert) B(illington) 1922-

PERSONAL: Born September 5, 1922, in Norwich, England; son of John and Grace (Blackburn) Joynson; married Eileen Mary Smith, August 31, 1961; children: Sarah, Roger. *Education:* Oriel College, Oxford, M.A., 1948, B.Litt., 1949, Ph.D., 1959. *Religion:* Church of England. *Home:* 17 Westgate, Southwell, Nottinghamshire, England. *Office:* Department of Psychology, University of Nottingham, Nottingham, England.

CAREER: University of Nottingham, Nottingham, England, lecturer, 1949-59, senior lecturer in psychology, 1959—. *Military service:* Royal Air Force, 1942-45; served as flight lieutenant. *Member:* British Psychological Society.

WRITINGS: Psychology and Common Sense, Kegan Paul, 1974.

WORK IN PROGRESS: Research on the historical development of modern psychology.

* * *

KADESCH, Robert R(udstone) 1922-

PERSONAL: Surname is pronounced *Kay*-desh; born May 14, 1922, in Cedar Falls, Iowa; son of William H. (a professor) and Mary (a teacher; maiden name, Barnum) Kadesch; married Arlene Tow, August 15, 1943; children: Joan Lea, Ann Marie (Mrs. Thomas Carter), Thomas Robert. *Education:* University of Northern Iowa, B.S., 1943; University of Rochester, M.S., 1949; University of Wisconsin, Ph.D., 1955. *Home:* 3050 South Grace St., Salt Lake City, Utah 84109. *Office:* Department of Physics, University of Utah, Salt Lake City, Utah 84112.

CAREER: University of Utah, Salt Lake City, assistant professor, 1956-61, associate professor, 1961-65, professor of physics, 1965—, associate dean for science, 1966-68, Visiting professor at University of Minnesota, 1963-64; visiting research physicist at University of California, Berkeley, 1973-74. Writer for School Mathematics Study Group, Stanford University, summer, 1963; program manager for National Science Foundation, 1968-69; member of board of directors of Utah Common Cause, 1973, 1975-76. *Military*

service: U.S. Naval Reserve, 1943-46; became lieutenant junior grade. *Member:* Sigma Xi, Phi Kappa Phi. *Awards, honors:* Notable book of the year award from U.S. Library Association, 1970, for *Math Menagerie*.

WRITINGS: The Crazy Cantilever and Other Science Experiments, Harper, 1961; *Math Menagerie*, Harper, 1970. Contributor to *Salt Lake Tribune*.

WORK IN PROGRESS: A text in elementary physics for non-science majors, publication by Holt expected in 1977; a monograph on mathematical foundations of plausible reasoning; a book of astronomy activities (juvenile).

* * *

KAESE, Harold 1909(?)-1975

1909(?)—May 10, 1975; American newspaper sports columnist and editor, author of books on sports. Obituaries: *New York Times*, May 12, 1975; *AB Bookman's Weekly*, August 4, 1975.

* * *

KAGAN, Richard (Lauren) 1943-

PERSONAL: Born September 18, 1943, in Newark, N.J.; son of George M. (an attorney) and Sylvia (an artist; maiden name, Gurkin) Kagan. *Education:* Columbia University, B.A., 1965; Cambridge University, Ph.D., 1968. *Office:* Department of History, Johns Hopkins University, Baltimore, Md. 21218.

CAREER: Indiana University, Bloomington, assistant professor of history, 1968-72; Johns Hopkins University, Baltimore, Md., assistant professor, 1972-74, associate professor of history, 1974—. *Member:* American Historical Association, Society for Spanish and Portuguese History.

WRITINGS: Students and Society in Early Modern Spain, Johns Hopkins Press, 1974. Contributor to history journals, including *Past and Present* and *Revista Storica Italiana*.

WORK IN PROGRESS: Research on the social history of law in Spain between 1500 and 1780.

* * *

KAISER, Bill
    See SUMNER, David (W. K.)

* * *

KAISER, Frances E(lkan) 1922-

PERSONAL: Born September 13, 1922, in Atlanta, Ga.; daughter of Herbert (a real estate developer) and May (Johnson) Kaiser. *Education:* Agnes Scott College, B.A. (with honors), 1943; Emory University, M.A., 1950. *Politics:* Republican. *Religion:* Roman Catholic. *Home:* 2965 Pharr Ct. N.W., Apt. 402, Atlanta, Ga. 30305. *Office:* Price Gilbert Memorial Library, Georgia Institute of Technology, Atlanta, Ga. 30332.

CAREER: Emory University, Atlanta, Ga., secretary to dean of School of Law, 1943-48; Georgia Institute of Technology, Price Gilbert Memorial Library, Atlanta, instructor, 1950-65, assistant professor, 1966-69, associate professor of library science, 1970—, reference librarian, 1950-55, 1964-70, interlibrary loan librarian, 1955-64, head of department of library instruction, 1971—.

MEMBER: Special Libraries Association, Southeastern Library Association, Georgia Library Association, Council of Planning Librarians, Phi Beta Kappa, Beta Phi Mu,

Mortar Board. *Awards, honors:* Dogwood Award from South Atlantic chapter of Special Libraries Association, 1959, for editing *Translators and Translations: Services and Sources.*

WRITINGS: (Editor) *Translators and Translations: Services and Sources,* Special Libraries Association, 1959; (editor) *Translators and Translations: Services and Sources in Science and Technology,* Special Libraries Association, 1965; (editor) *Handling Special Materials in Libraries,* Special Libraries Association, 1974.

WORK IN PROGRESS: Editing a third edition of *A Guide to the Literature of Science, Engineering, and Management in the Georgia Tech Library,* with Edward Graham Roberts (author of original publication).

* * *

KAKONIS, Thomas E. 1930-
(Tom E. Kakonis)

PERSONAL: Born November 13, 1930, in Long Beach, Calif.; son of Gus Peter and Olive (Woodward) Kakonis; married Judith J. Whitlock (a reading consultant), May 29, 1971; children: Tom D., Daniel J. *Education:* University of Minnesota, B.A., 1952; South Dakota State University, M.S., 1958; University of Iowa, Ph.D., 1965. *Politics:* None. *Religion:* None. *Home:* 630 Clark St., Big Rapids, Mich. 49307. *Office:* Department of Languages and Literature, Ferris State College, Big Rapids, Mich. 49307.

CAREER: Northern Illinois University, DeKalb, English instructor, 1964-66; University of Wisconsin, Whitewater, associate professor, 1966-68; South Dakota State University, Brookings, associate professor, 1968-69; University of Wisconsin, Whitewater, associate professor, 1969-72; Ferris State College, Big Rapids, Mich., head of department of languages and literature, 1972—. Education consultant, Film Counselors, Inc., 1970—; editorial consultant, Brevet International, Inc., 1970—. *Military service:* U.S. Army, 1953-55; became first lieutenant. *Member:* Modern Language Association of America, Popular Culture Association. *Awards, honors:* National Endowment for the Humanities grant, 1974-75.

WRITINGS—Editor; all under name Tom E. Kakonis: (With Louis E. Glorfeld) *The Short Story: Ideas and Backgrounds,* C. E. Merrill, 1967; (with Glorfeld) *Language, Rhetoric, and Idea,* C. E. Merrill, 1967; (with others) *Plays by Four Tragedians,* C. E. Merrill, 1968; (with Barbara Demarais) *The Literary Artist as Social Critic,* Glencoe Press, 1969; (with James C. Wilcox) *Forms of Rhetoric,* McGraw, 1969; (with others) *Strategies in Rhetoric from Thought to Symbol,* Harper, 1971; (with David A. Evans) *Statement and Craft,* Prentice-Hall, 1971; (with Evans) *From Language to Idea: An Integrated Rhetoric,* Holt, 1971; (with Wilcox) *Now and Tomorrow,* Heath, 1971; (with Ralph Desmarais) *America: Involvement of Escape,* Cummings, 1971; (with Richard Shereikis) *Scene Seventy: Nonfiction Prose,* Houghton, 1972; (with Wilcox) *Crossroads: Quality of Life Through Rhetorical Modes,* Heath, 1972; (with John Scally) *We Have But Faith,* Brevet Press, 1975; *Writing In an Age of Technology,* Macmillan, in press. Contributor of reviews to *Minneapolis Tribune* book section.

* * *

KAKONIS, Tom E.
See KAKONIS, Thomas E.

KAMIL, Jill 1930-

PERSONAL: Surname is pronounced "camel"; born July 22, 1930, in Nairobi, Kenya; daughter of Victor Maurice (an opthalmic optician) and Stella (Wescob) Browse; married Nabeeh Kamil, 1954 (divorced, 1973); children: Tamara Katrina, Wahib. *Education:* Educated in Johannesburg, South Africa. *Home:* Road 213, #14, Digla, Maadi, Cairo, Egypt. *Agent:* Curtis Brown Ltd., 1 Craven Hill, London W.2, England.

CAREER: Writer. Member of permanent staff of *Arab Observer* (official organ at that time of Egyptian Information Bureau), 1960-64; linguistic adviser to *Lotus* (magazine of Afro-Asian writing) of Permanent Bureau of Afro-Asian Writers in Cairo, 1970-72.

WRITINGS: Luxor: A Guide to Ancient Thebes, Longman, 1973, 2nd edition, in press; *The Ancient Egyptians: How They Lived and Worked,* David & Charles, in press.

WORK IN PROGRESS: Sakkara: A Guide to the Necropolis of Sakkara and the Site of Memphis.

SIDELIGHTS: Jill Kamil writes: "I have a special interest in monotheism in ancient Egypt; evidence that the earliest dwellers in the Nile Valley recognized and worshipped one eternal God, and that the development of local cults (part of the political development of the country which led to the manifestation of a symbolic polytheism) did not alter their basic beliefs . . . To the best of my knowledge no effort has been made to trace the religious beliefs of ancient Egypt and its accompanying mythology alongside the political development of the country. I have endeavoured to do this in my . . . study of the Old Kingdom civilization. . . ."

* * *

KANE, E. B., pseudonym 1944-

PERSONAL: Born March 17, 1944, in Brooklyn, N.Y.; married in 1970; children: Abraham. *Education:* Hunter College of the City University of New York, B.A., 1963; Columbia University, M.A., 1966, Ph.D., 1972. *Address:* Box 105, Cadman Plaza Station, Brooklyn, N.Y. 11202.

CAREER: Teacher of Russian and German in the New Jersey state college system, 1970-72; associate editor with Macmillan, Inc., 1972-74; professional translator of Russian, German, French, and Arabic, 1974—.

WRITINGS: (Translator) Yuri Brokhin, *Hustling on Gorky Street,* Dial, 1975.

WORK IN PROGRESS: The Earliest Dostoevskij, a monograph for Mouton & Co.; a tetralogy of novellas spanning America, Russia, and the Middle East.

* * *

KANTOR, Herman I. 1909-

PERSONAL: Born December 7, 1909, in New York, N.Y.; son of Sam (a manufacturer) and Gussie Kantor; married Ruth Zlabovsky (an artist), September 20, 1936; children: Paula (Mrs. Harvey Deutsch), Robert, Carol. *Education:* University of Alabama, A.B., 1932; New York University, M.D., 1934. *Politics:* Uncommitted. *Religion:* Jewish. *Home:* 6531 Lupton Dr., Dallas, Tex. 75225. *Agent:* Evelyn Oppenheimer, Dallas, Tex. *Office:* Obstetrics-Gynecology Association, 8210 Walnut Hill, Dallas, Tex. 75231.

CAREER: Completed residency at Mt. Sinai Hospital, New York, N.Y.; was chief of St. Paul Hospital in Dallas, Tex.; University of Texas, Southwest Medical Branch,

Dallas, assistant professor, 1950-60, associate professor, 1960-64, professor of obstetrics and gynecology, 1964—. *Military service:* U.S. Army, Medical Corps, 1943-46. *Member:* Dallas-Fort Worth Obstetrics-Gynecology Society (president, 1964).

WRITINGS: Doctors Must Invest, Warren H. Green, 1974. Contributor to medical journals.

WORK IN PROGRESS: Mother Goose Revised; books for children.

* * *

KAPLAN, Jack A(rnold) 1947-

PERSONAL: Born October 29, 1947, in Brooklyn, N.Y.; son of Joseph (a glazier) and Jeanette (Schoenberg) Kaplan. *Education:* Brooklyn College of the City University of New York, B.A., 1969; Pace College, graduate study, 1971; further study at Indiana University, 1971, and New School for Social Research, 1972. *Religion:* Judaism. *Home:* 1909 East 17th St., Brooklyn, N.Y. 11229.

CAREER: Junior high school English teacher in New York, N.Y., 1969; U.S. Bureau of the Census, Brooklyn, N.Y., clerk, 1970; Pace College, New York, N.Y., clerk in Library, 1971; *Show Business*, New York, N.Y., editor, 1972; Dell Publishing Co., New York, N.Y., proofreader, 1972-73; free-lance proofreader and copyeditor, 1973—. *Member:* Dramatists Guild.

WRITINGS: "The Revenge of the Chipmunks, or, The Chipmunks' Revenge" (one-act play), reading production on Off-Off-Broadway at St. Clement's Church, 1970; "Alligator Man" (one-act play), first produced on Off-Off-Broadway at Cubiculo Theatre, July, 1972. Work included in anthology, *The Best Short Plays of 1976*, edited by Stanley Richards, Chilton, in press. Also author of five-act play, "Queen Karen" and "Prelude to 'Albernact,'" an orchestral overture, 1969. Theatre reviewer for *Show Business*, 1972.

WORK IN PROGRESS: "Nothing But Punks," a full-length play; "Roll Over, Jehovah," one-act play; "Without a Paddle," one-act play; a play, "Rocky Mountain Rip-off"; a play concerning Emma Goldman and/or William McKinley.

SIDELIGHTS: Kaplan plays the guitar and cello and writes songs.

* * *

KARNOW, Stanley 1925-

PERSONAL: Born February 4, 1925, in New York, N.Y.; son of Harry (a businessman) and Henriette (Koeppel) Karnow; married Claude Sarraute, July 15, 1948 (divorced, 1955); married Annette Kline, April 21, 1959; children: Curtis Edward, Catherine Anne, Michael Franklin. *Education:* Harvard University, A.B., 1947; graduate study at Sorbonne, University of Paris, 1947-48, and Ecole des Sciences politiques, 1948-49. *Home:* 10850 Springknoll Dr., Potomac, Md. 20854. *Agent:* David Obst, 26 East 10th St., New York, N.Y. 10007. *Office:* German Marshall Fund, 11 Dupont Circle, Washington, D.C. 20036.

CAREER: Time (magazine), New York, N.Y., correspondent from Paris, 1950-57; Time-Life, New York, N.Y., bureau chief in North Africa, 1958-59, and Hong Kong, 1959-62; Time, Inc., New York, N.Y., special correspondent, 1962-63; *Saturday Evening Post*, Philadelphia Pa., Far East correspondent, 1963-65; *Washington Post*, Washington, D.C., Far East correspondent, 1965-71, diplomatic correspondent, 1971-72; National Broadcasting Corp. (NBC) News, Washington, D.C., special correspondent, 1972-73; *New Republic*, Washington, D.C., associate editor, 1973-75; now affiliated with German Marshall Fund. Correspondent for *London Observer*, 1961-65; fellow of Institute of Politics at John F. Kennedy School of Government and East Asian Research Center at Harvard University, both 1970-71. *Military service:* U.S. Army Air Forces, 1943-46.

MEMBER: Signet Society, Harvard Club, Foreign Correspondents Club, Shek-O Club (Hong Kong). *Awards, honors:* Citation from Overseas Press Club, 1966, and annual award for best newspaper interpretation of foreign affairs, 1968.

WRITINGS: Southeast Asia, Time-Life Books, 1963; *Mao and China: From Revolution to Revolution*, Viking, 1972. Contributor to magazines.

* * *

KASS, Jerome 1937-

PERSONAL: Born April 21, 1937, in Chicago, Ill.; son of Sidney J. and Ceil (Gorman) Kass; married Artha Schwartz, August 6, 1961; children: Julie. *Education:* New York University, A.B., 1958, A.M., 1959; Brandeis University, graduate study, 1960-61. *Residence:* Los Angeles, Calif. *Agent:* International Creative Management, 9255 Sunset Blvd., Los Angeles, Calif. 90069.

CAREER: Taught literature at Brandeis University, Waltham, Mass., Queens College of the City University of New York, and at Suffolk County Community College, Lake Ronkonkoma, N.Y., 1961-67; playwright and screenwriter. *Member:* Phi Beta Kappa.

WRITINGS—Plays: "In Glass Houses" (one-act), first produced in New York, N.Y. at Les Deux Megots, 1962; "Monopoly" (four one-act plays), first produced Off-Broadway at Stage 73, March 5, 1966, published as *Four Short Plays by Jerome Kass*, Dramatists Play Service, 1967; *Saturday Night: A Play* (two-act; first produced in New York, N.Y., at Sheridan Square Playhouse, 1968), Dramatists Play Service, 1968.

Screenplays; all adaptations, except as noted: "Going, Going, Going, Going, Going . . ." (original), 1966; "Shady Baby," Warner Bros., 1968; "Wise Blood" (from the novel by Flannery O'Connor), 1968; "Cellini," 1969; "The Delinquents" (from the novel by Crienna Rohan), 1970; "The Headshrinker's Test" (from the novel by Sue Kaufman), 1970; "Yentl, the Yeshiva Boy" (from a story by Isaac Bashevis Singer), First Artists, 1971.

Author of screenplay, "A Brand New Life," an ABC "Movie of the Week," 1973; also author of television drama, "Queen of the Stardust Ballroom," produced by CBS, February 13, 1975.

WORK IN PROGRESS: A dramatic special, "A Romance," for CBS-TV; a screenplay, "Love and Death in Las Vegas," loosely based on *Camille*, for ABC.

SIDELIGHTS: Kass writes: "In 1962, my first play, a one-acter called 'In Glass Houses,' was produced in an East Village coffee shop (Les Deux Megots, now extinct) for $180. During its two-week run, about 50 people came to see it. I was so appalled by the failure that I sat down and wrote an article about the state of the American theatre. I sent the article to Eric Bentley, whom I did not know, and he sent it to Gordon Rogoff who, at the time, was editing

Theatre Arts Magazine. Rogoff published it in the August, 1962 issue under the title, 'Letter from a Young Playwright.' One month later, the magazine folded.

"Herbert Berghof read the article and called me. He invited me to join a playwriting seminar in his acting studio on Bank Street in Manhattan. I became Berghof's protege, I suppose. What is certain is that he was instrumental in freeing my playwriting talent and in encouraging me in a writing career. He got me an agent, who got me a director, Daniel Petrie, who got me my first commercial production in 1966. The Establishment Theatre Company produced four of my short plays under the omnibus title, 'Monopoly.' Dan Petrie directed. Estelle Parsons was but one of the eight fine actors. The reviews were most enthusiastic, and I was launched."

*   *   *

KASTL, Albert J(oseph) 1939-

PERSONAL: Born June 25, 1939, in New York, N.Y.; son of Albert and Emmy (Kannengeiser) Kastl; married Lena Hahn, June 8, 1963 (divorced, March 20, 1974). *Education:* City College of the City University of New York, B.A., 1961; Yale University, M.S., 1964, Ph.D., 1965. *Residence:* Santa Rosa, Calif. *Office:* California School of Professional Psychology, 2450 17th St., San Francisco, Calif. 94110.

CAREER: San Joaquin General Hospital, Children's Services, Stockton, Calif., consultant, 1969—; California School of Professional Psychology, San Francisco, faculty member, 1972—; Center for Human Development, Santa Rosa, Calif., professional staff member, 1972—. *Military service:* U.S. Army, 1965-67; became captain. *Member:* American Psychological Association, Western Psychological Association, Redwood Psychological Association. *Awards, honors:* National Institute of Mental Health postdoctoral fellow, 1968.

WRITINGS: (With Lena Kastl) *Journey Back: Escaping the Drug Trip.* Nelson-Hall, 1975. Contributor to journals in his field.

WORK IN PROGRESS: Research on biofeedback and on new systems of psychotherapy.

*   *   *

KATSAROS, Thomas 1926-

PERSONAL: Born February 21, 1926, in New York, N.Y.; son of John and Helen (Drivas) Katsaros; married Nancy Massa (a teacher), June 26, 1971. *Education:* New York University, B.A., 1953, M.A., 1955, M.B.A., 1958, Ph.D., 1963, A.P.C., 1975. *Politics:* Independent. *Home:* 11 Carriage Dr., North Haven, Conn. 06573. *Office:* Department of History, University of New Haven, West Haven, Conn. 06505.

CAREER: State University of New York College at Potsdam, assistant professor of social science, 1963-65; University of New Haven, West Haven, Conn., assistant professor, 1965-67, associate professor, 1968-70, professor of economic history, 1970—, chairman of department, 1969—. *Military service:* U.S. Army, Airborne, 1943-47; received Bronze Star Medal. *Member:* American Historical Association, American Management Association, American Economic Association, Hellenic Association.

WRITINGS: (With Nathaniel Kaplan) *The Western Mystical Tradition: An Intellectual History of Western Civilization,* College & University Press, 1969; (with Kaplan) *The*

Origins of American Transcendentalism in Philosophy and Mysticism, College & University Press, 1975. Contributor to journals in his field. Co-editor of *Essays in Arts and Sciences,* 1971—.

WORK IN PROGRESS: Research on the cultural effects of multinational business.

*   *   *

KATZMAN, Anita 1920-

PERSONAL: Born February 6, 1920, in Manhattan, N.Y.; daughter of Louis and Saralee (Fox) Butensky; married Nathan Katzman, March 29, 1942 (died, 1965); children: Mark, Drew, Bruce, Mindi. *Education:* New York University, B.A., 1940. *Politics:* Democrat. *Religion:* Jewish. *Home:* 39 Sandy Cove Rd., Sarasota, Fla. 33581.

CAREER: Writer.

WRITINGS: My Name Is Mary . . . (novel), Harper, 1975.

WORK IN PROGRESS: Queen Pomare of Tahiti, a biography.

*   *   *

KAUFFMAN, James M(ilton) 1940-

PERSONAL: Born December 7, 1940, in Hannibal, Mo.; son of Nelson Edward (a clergyman) and Christmas Carol (a novelist; maiden name, Miller) Kauffman; married Myrna Miller (a registered nurse), April 9, 1960; children: Tim, Melissa. *Education:* Goshen College, B.S., 1962; Washburn University, M.Ed., 1966; University of Kansas, Ed.D., 1969. *Office:* School of Education, University of Virginia, Charlottesville, Va. 22903.

CAREER: Menninger Clinic, Topeka, Kan., teacher of emotionally disturbed elementary school children, 1962-64; teacher of emotionally disturbed and normal children in elementary school in Tecumseh, Kan., 1964-67; Illinois State University, Normal, assistant professor of special education, 1969-70; University of Virginia, Charlottesville, assistant professor, 1970-73, associate professor of education, 1973—. Member of Illinois State Committee on the Emotionally Disturbed and Social Maladjusted, 1969-70. Field reader for Bureau of Education for the Handicapped, 1973—. *Member:* National Council for Exceptional Children, Association for the Advancement of Behavior Therapy, Society for Research in Child Development, Virginia Council for Exceptional Children, Charlottesville Council for Exceptional Children, Phi Delta Kappa.

WRITINGS: (With Gerald Wallace) *Teaching Children with Learning Problems,* C. E. Merrill, 1973; (editor with C. D. Lewis) *Teaching Children with Behavior Disorders: Personal Perspectives,* C. E. Merrill, 1974; (contributor) N. G. Haring, editor, *Behavior of Exceptional Children: An Introduction to Special Education,* C. E. Merrill, 1974; (with J. S. Payne, G. B. Brown, and R. M. DeMott) *Exceptional Children in Focus: Incidents, Concepts, and Issues in Special Education,* C. E. Merrill, 1974; (contributor) W. M. Cruickshank and D. P. Hallahan, editors, *Perceptual and Learning Disabilities in Children,* Volume I: *Psychoeducational Practices,* Volume II: *Research and Theory,* Syracuse University Press, 1975; (editor with Payne) *Mental Retardation: Introduction and Personal Perspectives,* C. E. Merrill, 1975; (with Payne, Edward Polloway, and T. R. Scranton) *Living in the Classroom: The Currency-Based Token Economy,* Behavioral Publications, 1975; (with Hallahan) *Introduction to Learning Disabilities,* Prentice-Hall, in press; (editor with Hallahan)

Teaching Children with Learning Disabilities: Personal Perspectives, C. E. Merrill, in press; *Development of Behavioral Disorders in Children*, C. E. Merrill, in press.

Special editor of "Personal Perspectives in Special Education," a series of books, C. E. Merrill, 1974—. Contributor of about thirty articles and reviews to education and psychology journals. Associate editor of *Exceptional Children*, 1973—.

WORK IN PROGRESS: Research on education and psychology.

* * *

KAVALER, Lucy 1930-

PERSONAL: Born August 29, 1930, in New York, N.Y.; daughter of L. I. (a banker) and Helen (Vishniac) Estrin; married Arthur R. Kavaler (a publisher), November 9, 1949; children: Roger, Andrea. *Education:* Oberlin College, B.A. (magna cum laude), 1949. *Residence:* New York, N.Y. *Agent:* Marie Rodell, 141 East 55th St., New York, N.Y. 10022.

CAREER: Maher-Wade Publishing Co., New York, N.Y., senior editor of medical publications, 1970—; author. *Member:* P.E.N. American Center (member of executive board, 1972—), Society of Magazine Writers (member of executive council, 1971-72), National Association of Science Writers, Authors Guild. *Awards, honors:* Advanced science writing fellowship from Columbia University Graduate School of Journalism, 1969-70.

WRITINGS: The Private World of High Society, McKay, 1960; *Mushrooms, Molds, and Miracles*, John Day, 1965; *The Astors*, Dodd, 1966; *Freezing Point*, John Day, 1970; *Noise: The New Menace*, John Day, 1975.

Juvenile: *The Wonders of Algae*, John Day, 1961; *The Artificial World Around Us*, John Day, 1963; *The Wonders of Fungi*, John Day, 1964; *Dangerous Air*, John Day, 1967; *The Astors*, Dodd, 1968; *Cold Against Disease*, John Day, 1971; *Life Battles Cold*, John Day, 1973. Contributor of articles to magazines including *Redbook, Natural History, Woman's Day, Smithsonian, McCall's*, and *Family Circle*.

* * *

KAY, Donald 1939-

PERSONAL: Born August 30, 1939; son of John Wayne (a farmer) and Louise (Norris) Kay; married Carol McGinnis (an English professor), June 8, 1968. *Education:* Presbyterian College, A.B., 1961; University of Tennessee, M.A., 1963, Ph.D., 1967. *Home:* 81 Woodland Hills, Tuscaloosa, Ala. 35401. *Office:* Drawer AL, Department of English, University of Alabama, University, Ala. 35486.

CAREER: University of Alabama, University, assistant professor, 1967-72, associate professor of English, 1972—. *Member:* Modern Language Association of America, English Institute, Southern Humanities Conference (secretary-treasurer, 1971-73; member of executive committee, 1973-77), South Atlantic Modern Language Association, Southeastern American Society for Eighteenth-Century Studies, Auchinleck Boswell Society, Phi Kappa Phi.

WRITINGS: Short Fiction in 'The Spectator,' University of Alabama Press, 1975. Contributor of about twenty-five articles to English journals.

WORK IN PROGRESS: Essays on Boswell's *London Journal*; an edition of essays on Restoration and 18th century fiction and drama, for University of Alabama Press.

KAYAL, Joseph M(itchell) 1942-

PERSONAL: Born January 24, 1942, in Brooklyn, N.Y.; son of Mitchell B. (a garment worker) and Alice (Kassar) Kayal; married Patricia A. Jehle (a teacher), June 20, 1964; children: Michele, Matthew, Justin. *Education:* Fordham University, B.S., 1963, M.A., 1964. *Home:* 30 Pioneer Blvd., Huntington, N.Y. 11746. *Office:* Room 770, 10 Columbus Circle, New York, N.Y. 10019.

CAREER: New York Telephone, New York, N.Y., sales manager, 1965-74, supervisor of community relations and educational services, 1974—. Instructor at Herbert H. Lehman College of the City University of New York, and Hofstra University. Member, South Huntington Board of Education. *Member:* American Association for the Advancement of Science, American Sociological Association, American Civil Liberties Union, Center for the Study of Democratic Institutions, Wilderness Society, New York State School Boards Association, South Huntington Youth Development Association.

WRITINGS: (With brother, Philip M. Kayal) *The Syrian-Lebanese in America: A Study in Religion and Assimilation*, Twayne, 1975.

* * *

KAYAL, Philip M(itchell) 1943-

PERSONAL: Born November 18, 1943, in Brooklyn, N.Y.; son of Mitchell (a garment worker) and Alice (Kassar) Kayal. *Education:* Fordham University, B.S., 1965, M.A., 1966, Ph.D., 1970. *Religion:* Roman Catholic—Melkite Rite. *Home:* 186 Glenwood Ave., #6, East Orange, N.J. *Office:* Department of Sociology, Seton Hall University, South Orange, N.J. 07079.

CAREER: Notre Dame College of Staten Island, New York, N.Y., instructor of sociology, 1968-70; Seton Hall University, South Orange, N.J., assistant professor, 1970-75, associate professor of sociology, 1975—, chairman of department, 1970-74. *Member:* Melkite Association of North America, American Sociological Association, Association of Arab American University Graduates, Center for the Study of Democratic Institutions, American Civil Liberties Union, Haddad Foundation (member of board of directors), Arabic Cultural Institute of New Jersey (director).

WRITINGS: (With brother, Joseph M. Kayal) *The Syrian-Lebanese in America: A Study in Religion and Assimilation*, Twayne, 1975. Editor of *International Migration Review*.

WORK IN PROGRESS: Research on sexism and homosexuality.

SIDELIGHTS: Kayal writes: "I was born a Roman Catholic of the Byzantine-Melkite from parents from Syria. My book is a search for personal and social origins."

* * *

KAYE, Evelyn 1937-

PERSONAL: Born October 1, 1937, in London, England; married Christopher Sarson (a TV producer), March 25, 1963; children: Katrina, David. *Education:* Educated in England. *Home:* 162 Waverly Ave., Newton, Mass. 02158.

CAREER: Elek Books Ltd., London, England, secretary and publicity assistant, 1957-58; general reporter in England for *Southend Times, Willesden Citizen*, and East London News Agency, 1958-61; worked as an economist's editorial assistant in Jerusalem, Israel, 1959-60; Reuters News Agency, Paris, France, staff reporter, 1961-62; *Guardian*, Manchester, England, reporter and feature writer, 1962-63; free-lance writer in Boston, Mass., 1963-68; Action for Children's Television, Newtonville, Mass., co-founder and president, 1969-71, executive director, 1971-73, publications director, 1973-74; free-lance author and journalist, 1974—. Speaker and media consultant on children's television.

WRITINGS: (Editor) *Action for Children's Television*, Avon, 1971; *Family Guide to Children's Television*, Pantheon, 1974; (with Bernice Chesler) *A Guide to Cape Cod: What to Do When You Don't Want to Do What Everyone Else Is Doing*, Crown, in press. Contributor to *Boston Globe*.

SIDELIGHTS: Evelyn Kaye, who is competent in Spanish, French, Hebrew, and German, writes: "There is almost no serious coverage of broadcasting and television in the media—newspapers, magazines or television itself. TV today is one of the most pervasive forces in our daily lives and yet few writers examine or comprehend its impact. There is a need for regular coverage of broadcasting issues, *not* just gossip and reviews."

* * *

KAYE, Myrna 1930-

PERSONAL: Born October 18, 1930, in Brooklyn, N.Y.; daughter of Max J. (a government appraiser) and Zelda R. (Caspe) Hechel; married Murray Kaye (an electronics engineer), June 8, 1952; children: Sharon, David, Stephen. *Education:* Brooklyn College (now Brooklyn College of the City University of New York), A.B. (cum laude), 1952. *Religion:* Jewish. *Residence:* Lexington, Mass. 02173. *Office:* Department of Art, Mount Ida Junior College, Newton Centre, Mass. 02159.

CAREER: Elementary school teacher in public school in Aberdeen, Md., 1952-53; Mount Ida Junior College, Newton Centre, Mass., instructor in decorative arts history, 1972—. Adjunct lecturer at Boston Museum of Fine Arts, 1973—.

WRITINGS: (Contributor) Walter Muir Whitehill, editor, *Boston Furniture of the Eighteenth Century*, University Press of Virginia, 1974; *Yankee Weathervanes*, Dutton, 1975. Contributor of monthly column, "Antiques to look for. . .," to *Yankee*, 1966-69.

WORK IN PROGRESS: Research for a book on a social history of American interior design.

SIDELIGHTS: Myrna Kaye told *CA:* "I wrote *Yankee Weathervanes* because the ubiquitous vanes atop all types of buildings reflected the interests of the entire society. The varied subjects of vanes showed the interests of all the people, rich and poor, urban and rural, commercial and religious. Furniture too allows us to look at history, not merely as battles fought or laws passed, but as lived by people every day."

* * *

KEARLEY, F(loyd) Furman 1932-

PERSONAL: Surname sounds like "curly"; born November 7, 1932, in Montgomery, Ala.; son of J.A. (a farmer) and Zelma (Suggs) Kearley; married Helen Bowman (a secretary), June 18, 1951; children: Janice Gail, Amelia Lynn. *Education:* Alabama Christian College, B.A., 1954; Harding Graduate School, M.A., 1956, M.R.E. and M.Th., both 1965; Auburn University, M.Ed.,

1960; Hebrew Union College, Ph.D., 1971. *Politics:* Independent. *Home:* 728 Diamond Lake Dr., Abilene, Tex. 79601. *Office:* Department of Bible, Abilene Christian College, Campus Court at 16th St., Abilene, Tex. 79601.

CAREER: Ordained minister of Church of Christ, 1952; Alabama Christian College, Montgomery, professor of Bible and chairman of department, 1956-69; Lubbock Christian College, Lubbock, Tex., professor of Biblical studies and chairman of Division of Biblical Studies, 1970-75; Abilene Christian College, Abilene, Tex., professor of Bible, 1975—. *Member:* Society of Biblical Literature, American Association of Hebrew Professors, Rotary International, Phi Delta Kappa. *Awards, honors:* F. W. Mattox Distinguished Professor award from Lubbock Christian College, 1974.

WRITINGS: *The Significance of the Genesis Flood*, World Mission Publishing, 1974; *The Effect of Evolution of Modern Society*, World Mission Publishing, 1974; *God's Indwelling Spirit*, Parchment Press, 1975. Contributor to theology journals.

* * *

KEARNS, Martha 1945-

PERSONAL: Born March 23, 1945, in Flint, Mich.; daughter of Lewis Gamble and Mary Lucille (Williamson) Kearns. *Education:* Attended Alma College, 1963-65; Beaver College, B.A., 1967. *Politics:* Revolutionary. *Home:* 515 Carpenter Lane, Philadelphia, Pa. 19119. *Office:* Durham Child Development Center, 16th and Lombard Sts., Philadelphia, Pa. 19036.

CAREER: Writer for underground newspapers, San Francisco (Calif.) *Express Times*, 1968-69, and *International Times*, London, England, 1969; Marcel Dekker, Inc. (publisher), New York, N.Y., promotion assistant, 1969; Bread and Puppet Theatre, Cate Farm, Goddard College, Vt., puppeteer, 1970-71; Philadelphia Actors' Theatre, Philadelphia, Pa., company member, 1973—; Durham Child Development Center, Philadelphia, Pa., art teacher, 1972—.

WRITINGS: *Kaethe Kollwitz: Woman and Artist*, Feminist Press, 1975. Work included in *Campfires of the Resistance: Poetry from the Movement*, edited by Todd Gitlin, Bobbs-Merrill, 1971.

WORK IN PROGRESS: Co-authoring a book of poetry; an autobiographical book of short stories tentatively entitled *Nonfiction*; a study of witchcraft in America during the Colonial and Revolutionary Periods.

AVOCATIONAL INTERESTS: Making woodcuts and silk-screen posters; painting.

BIOGRAPHICAL/CRITICAL SOURCES: The City, August-September, 1973.

* * *

KEEFE, Carolyn 1928-

PERSONAL: Born October 2, 1928, in Grand Rapids, Mich.; daughter of Martin and Sigrid (Walstrom) Berglund; married Frederick L. Keefe (a clergyman), June 11, 1949; children: Cheryl, Larry. *Education:* Oberlin College, A.B., 1950; Temple University, M.A., 1968; Villanova University, M.A., 1975. *Politics:* Republican. *Religion:* United Presbyterian. *Home:* 12 South Pennock Ave., Upper Darby, Pa. 19082. *Office:* Department of Speech Communication and Theatre, West Chester State College, West Chester, Pa. 19380.

CAREER: Elementary school teacher in East Millstone, N.J., 1951-53; Rutgers University, Camden, N.J., lecturer, 1965-68, instructor in speech, acting chairman of department, and director of forensics, all 1968-69; West Chester State College, West Chester, Pa., assistant professor of speech, 1969—, director of forensics, 1971—. Member: Speech Communication Association of America, American Forensic Association, Collegiate Forensic Association (vice-president, 1971), Religious Speech Communication Association, Speech Communication Association of Pennsylvania, Pennsylvania State Colleges Forensic Association (president, 1970-71), Debating Association of Pennsylvania Colleges (executive secretary, 1973—), Pi Kappa Delta (member of national council, 1975—). Awards, honors: First prize, poetry division, from Evangelical Press Association, 1972, for "Two Lovers and Twenty-Two More," and 2nd prize, poetry division, 1973, for "Incarnation."

WRITINGS: (Editor and contributor) C. S. Lewis: Speaker and Teacher, Zondervan, 1971. Editor of Forensic, of Pi Kappa Delta, 1975—.

WORK IN PROGRESS: Freedom for Females and Other Human Creatures (tentative title), for Word, Inc.; poems; other short writings.

*   *   *

KEEGAN, Warren J(oseph) 1936-

PERSONAL: Born October 19, 1936, in Junction City, Kan.; son of Donald R. and Edia S. Keegan; married, 1961; children, three. Education: Kansas State University, B.S., 1958, M.S., 1959; Harvard University, M.B.A., 1961, D.B.A., 1967. Office: Department of Marketing, Bernard Baruch College of the City University of New York, 17 Lexington Ave., New York, N.Y. 10010.

CAREER: Columbia University, New York, N.Y., assistant professor, 1967-70, associate professor of business, 1970-74; Baruch College of the City University of New York, New York, N.Y., professor of international business policy, 1974—. Visiting professor at European Institute of Business Administration, 1972-74, International Marketing Programme at Emmanuel College, Cambridge University, 1973, and Stockholm School of Economics, 1974; Massachusetts Institute of Technology fellow in Africa, 1962-64. Assistant secretary in the Ministry of Development Planning, Dar es Salaam, Tanzania, 1962-64. Military service: U.S. Army, 1959. U.S. Army Reserve, 1959-67; became first lieutenant. Member: American Marketing Association, Academy of Management, Academy of International Business. Awards, honors: Grant from Marketing Science Institute, 1969.

WRITINGS: Case Studies in Public Administration, Volume I, Institute of Public Administration, University College (Dar es Salaam), 1964; Case Studies in the Management of Economic Development, Volume I, Oxford University Press, 1968; Multinational Marketing Management, Prentice-Hall, 1974. Contributor to professional journals.

*   *   *

KEFFERSTAN, Jean
    See PEDRICK, Jean

*   *   *

KEHOE, Patrick E(mmett) 1941-

PERSONAL: Born November 12, 1941, in Olympia,

Wash.; son of Adlore R. (an attorney) and Elise (Brophy) Kehoe; married Carole J. Fitzgerald (a professor of nursing), August 16, 1969; children: Elisabeth C., Robert P. Education: Seattle University, B.C.S., 1963; University of Washington, Seattle, J.D., 1966, M.L.Libr., 1968. Politics: Republican. Religion: Roman Catholic. Home: 22 Keystone Dr., Gaithersburg, Md. 20760. Office: Washington College of Law, American University, Washington, D.C. 20016.

CAREER: Admitted to Bar of State of Washington, 1966; University of Houston, Law Library, Houston, Tex., assistant professor of library science and assistant law librarian, 1968-71, lecturer in legal bibliography at Law School, 1969-71; Yale Law School Library, New Haven, Conn., assistant librarian, 1971-73; American University, Washington College of Law, Washington, D.C., law librarian and assistant professor of law, 1973—. Member of Gaithersberg West Riding Citizens Association, 1974—, president, 1975-76. Consultant to Social Law Library, Boston, spring, 1974, Law Reprints, Inc., spring, 1974, and Redgrave Information Resources Corp, 1974—. Member: American Association of Law Libraries, American Trial Lawyers Association, Washington State Bar Association, Delta Theta Phi.

WRITINGS: Cooperatives and Condominiums, Oceana, 1974. Contributor Ervin Pollack's Fundamentals of Legal Research, 4th edition, Supplements and Assignments, by J. Myron Jacobstein and Roy M. Mersky, Foundation Press, 1974, 5th edition, in press. Contributor to Texas Bar Journal and Law Library Journal. Editor of book appraisals column, Texas Bar Journal, 1970-71; editor, Law Library Lights, 1974—.

*   *   *

KEITH, Noel L. 1903-

PERSONAL: Born February 1, 1903, in Cassville, Mo.; son of Otis Parker and Vesta Pearl (Kelly) Keith; married Beulah Irene Dorsey, August 27, 1927: children: Marvin Russell. Education: Attended Phillips University; Texas Christian University, A.B., 1938, B.D., 1940, M.A., 1950; Iliff School of Theology, Th.D., 1953. Politics: Democrat. Home and office: 3882 South Hills Cir., Fort Worth, Tex. 76109.

CAREER: Ordained minister of the Disciples of Christ Church, 1927; pastor in Galena, Kan., 1928-29, Wetumka, Okla., 1930-31, Sulphur, Okla., 1932-37, Arlington, Tex., 1937-41, Marfa, Tex., 1941-43, and Temple, Tex., 1943-46; Texas Christian University, Fort Worth, special assistant to the president, 1946-50, part-time instructor, 1946-50, professor of church history, 1950-73, head of department, 1953-73, professor emeritus of religion, 1973—.

WRITINGS: (With S. W. Hutton) Worship Highways, Bethany Press, 1943; A Presentation of the Church, Amos Myers, 1946; The Brites of Capote (biography), Texas Christian University Press, 1950; The Green Horse (fable), Stafford-Lowden, 1949; Toward a Constructive Christian Faith (monograph), University Christian Church, 1952; D. S. Burnet: Undeserved Obscurity, Bethany Press, 1954; The Human Rift, Bethany Press, 1963; Religion: An Introduction and Guide to Study, W. C. Brown, 1967; Paul's Message for Today, Texas Christian University Press, 1970. Also editor of J. O. Jones: A Cowman's Memoirs, published by Texas Christian University Press. Contributor to Christian-Evangelist, Iliff Review, and Texas College and Career Guide; contributor to Intermediate Sunday School quarterlies. Former columnist for Sulphur Daily News, Sulphur, Okla.

WORK IN PROGRESS: Whirlwind South of Wounded Knee; *Mirth in the Ministry*, an autobiography.

SIDELIGHTS: Keith has competence in Greek, German, Spanish, Latin, and French. *Avocational interests:* Rocky Mountain trout fishing, deep-sea fishing, traveling, searching out historical places in western United States.

*   *   *

KELLER, Gail Faithfull
See FAITHFULL, Gail

*   *   *

KELLER, Karl   1933-

PERSONAL: Born May 29, 1933, in Manti, Utah; son of Calvin T. and Lillie B. Keller; married Ruth Anderson, July 27, 1956; children: Kristin, Michael, Chad, James, Mather. *Education:* University of Utah, B.A., 1958, M.A., 1959; University of Minnesota, Ph.D., 1964. *Politics:* Left. *Religion:* "Gone." *Home:* 4174 South Tropico Dr., La-Mesa, Calif. 92041. *Office:* School of Literature, San Diego State University, San Diego, Calif. 92182.

CAREER: University of Minnesota, Minneapolis, instructor in English, 1959-64; State University of New York College at Cortland, assistant professor of English, 1964-66; San Diego State University, San Diego, Calif., assistant professor, 1966-69, associate professor, 1969-72, professor of English, 1972—. *Member:* Modern Language Association of America. *Awards, honors:* Fulbright scholar in France, 1973; American Council of Learned Societies grant, 1974; Huntington Library fellowship, 1975.

WRITINGS: (Contributor) Robert A. Rees, editor, *Twelve American Authors: A Review of Research and Criticism*, University of Wisconsin Press, 1969; (with Clifton Fadiman) *American Literature, Post, 1945: Future Resources and Development*, Famous Writers, 1970; (contributor) Gene Russell, editor, *A Concordance to the Poems of Edward Taylor*, National Cash Register Co., 1972. Contributor to *Early American Literature.* Member of board of editors of *Dialogue*, 1964-74; member of bibliography staff of *American Literature*, 1967-72.

WORK IN PROGRESS: The Only Kangaroo among the Beauty: Emily Dickinson and America; *Solomon Stoddard and a Puritan Left*; *Stairway to Surprise: The Metaphysical Strain in Nineteenth-Century Poetry*, for Mouton & Co.

*   *   *

KELLING, George W(alton)   1944-

PERSONAL: Born April 7, 1944, in Philadelphia, Pa.; son of Harold D. (an English professor) and Dora (Walton) Kelling; married second wife, Rosemarie (a teacher), December, 1972; children: (stepchildren) Annette, Michael, Kenneth. *Education:* University of Colorado, B.A., 1965, M.A., 1971, Ph.D., 1972. *Politics:* "I do not vote." *Religion:* Society of Friends (Quaker). *Home:* 46 Prospect St., Midland Park, N.J. 07432. *Office:* Department of Psychology, Barnard College, New York, N.Y. 10027.

CAREER: Barnard College of Columbia University, New York, N.Y., assistant professor of psychology, 1972—.

WRITINGS: Language: Mirror, Tool, and Weapon, Nelson-Hall, 1975; (contributor) Desmond S. Cartwright, Barbara Tomson, and Hershey Schwartz, editors, *Gang Delinquency*, Brooks-Cole, 1975; *Relations between People*, Nelson-Hall, in press. Contributor to *Crime and Delin-*

quency, *Psychoanalytic Review*, and *Psychological Reports*.

WORK IN PROGRESS: A book on the perception of people.

*   *   *

KENDALL, Dorothy Steinbomer   1912-

PERSONAL: Born May 27, 1912, in Bayonne, N.J.; daughter of Frank II (a petroleum engineer) and Mary E. (Hart) Hovell; married Henry J. Steinbomer, December 26, 1933 (died, 1964); married James I. Kendall (a professor), August 29, 1972; children: (first marriage) Shirley (Mrs. Jerome C. Parker), Richard H., Robert A. *Education:* Our Lady of the Lake College, B.A., 1933, M.S.L.S., 1968; San Antonio Art Institute, graduate study, 1952-53, 1958; University of the Americas, M.L.A.S., 1972. *Politics:* Independent. *Home and office:* 1515 Nouanu Ave., Queen Tower 79, Honolulu, Hawaii 96817.

CAREER: Henry Steinbomer (architect), San Antonio, Tex., executive secretary, 1939-41, 1954-59; San Antonio Public Library, San Antonio, Tex., art librarian and director of public relations, 1959-61, head of department of fine arts, 1961-66; St. Mary's University, San Antonio, Tex., fine arts librarian, 1967-72, instructor, 1967-70, assistant professor, 1970-72, chairman of department of urban studies, 1970-72. Staff artist for Orco Studios, 1956; accepted stained glass and fused glass commissions from Henry Steinbomer's architectural firm, 1959-63. Work has been exhibited in group shows in Texas and throughout the Southwest; has organized national and international exhibitions; executive director of religious arts program for Hemisfair, 1968. Co-founder of Mexican-American Institute for Cultural Exchange, 1963; member of fine arts advisory council at University of Texas, 1958-65; member of advisory board of San Antonio Art Institute and Witte Museum, both 1956-61; member of advisory board of Southwest Crafts Center.

MEMBER: College Art Association, National Society of Literature and the Arts, Hawaii Council for Culture and the Arts, San Antonio Craft Guild (honorary life member), Honolulu Academy of Art. *Awards, honors:* Dana Award from American Library Association and Wilson Library Bulletin, 1960, for library publicity work; regional historic preservation award from San Antonio Conservation Society, and humanities award from Our Lady of the Lake College, both 1975, for *Gentilz: Artist of the Old Southwest*.

WRITINGS: Gentilz: Artist of the Old Southwest, University of Texas Press, 1974. Contributor of articles and reviews to local and regional publications.

WORK IN PROGRESS: Research for a book on Maya town planning; research for a juvenile book on the French-Alsatian colony of Castroville, Tex., in the nineteenth century; research on stylistic relationships of Oriental and Pre-Columbian arts.

*   *   *

KENNEDY, Bruce M.   1929-

PERSONAL: Born March 13, 1929, in Basin, Wyo.; son of Gilbert V. (an insurance man) and Leila (a librarian; maiden name, McKenzie) Kennedy; married Betty Green (a journalist), March 18, 1951; children: Brian, Ann, Robert. *Education:* University of Nebraska, Lincoln, A.B., 1951. *Religion:* Presbyterian. *Home and office address:* Box 1032, Greybull, Wyo. 82426.

CAREER: Greybull Standard (weekly newspaper), Greybull, Wyo., editor and publisher, 1959-74; co-publisher of newspapers, *Wyoming State Journal* (weekly), Lander, 1967—, *News-Record* (daily), Gillette, Wyo., 1970—, *Cody Enterprise* (weekly), Cody, Wyo., 1971—, and *Green River Star* (weekly), Green River, Wyo., 1975—. *Military service:* U.S. Army, 1951-53. *Member:* Sigma Delta Chi.

WRITINGS: Community Journalism: A Way of Life, Iowa State University Press, 1974.

SIDELIGHTS: Bruce Kennedy told *CA* that his "book was an outgrowth of my experience as a newspaperman and also my desire to see more young people in the profession, and those in the profession to achieve higher standards of journalism. The weekly newspaper or small daily are enjoying more success now than ever before. Such a paper can be a source of personal satisfaction; as an independent newspaperman you can accomplish a great deal of good, you can excel in the profession, you can have a great life. That's what the book was about and what it attempted to give to the reader."

* * *

KENNEDY, John J(oseph)   1914-

PERSONAL: Born September 13, 1914, in Cortland, N.Y.; son of John Austin (a merchant) and Anna (a teacher; maiden name, Ryan) Kennedy; married Elizabeth Carol Riordan, August 19, 1942; children: John Christian, Kathryn (Mrs. Miguel Bueno). *Education:* University of New Mexico, B.A. (with distinction), 1936; Columbia University, A.M., 1938, Ph.D., 1954. *Politics:* Registered Democrat. *Religion:* Roman Catholic. *Home:* 1937 Inglewood Pl., South Bend, Ind. 46616. *Office:* University of Notre Dame, Box 201, Notre Dame, Ind. 46556.

CAREER: Latin American Public Administration Clearing House, Chicago, Ill., liason officer, 1938-42; regional specialist on Latin America to U.S. Department of State, 1946-48; University of Puerto Rico, Rio Pedras, visiting professor of political science, 1949-50; University of Notre Dame, Notre Dame, Ind., associate professor, 1951-59; University of Virginia, Charlottesville, professor of foreign affairs, 1959-64; University of Notre Dame, professor of government and international studies, 1964—. Ford Foundation consultant in Peru and Chile, 1964; Rockefeller Foundation visiting professor at Universidad del Valle, Cali, Colombia, 1968-71. *Military service:* U.S. Naval Reserve, 1942-46; became lieutenant commander. *Member:* American Political Science Association, Council on Religion in Higher Education. *Awards, honors:* Council on Foreign Relations (N.Y.) research fellow, 1957-58.

WRITINGS: Catholicism, Nationalism and Democracy in Argentina, University of Notre Dame Press, 1958; (translator) Alberto Conil Paz and Gustavo Ferrari, *Argentine Foreign Policy, 1930-62*, University of Notre Dame Press, 1966; (editor with Mario Zanartu) *Overall Development in Chile*, University of Notre Dame Press, 1969. Contributor of articles to *Foreign Affairs* and *Annals of the American Academy.* Associate editor and contributor, *Review of Politics*, 1955-59.

WORK IN PROGRESS: Two works on Colombia, one dealing with contemporary politics, the other personal reflections on Kennedy's experience as a teacher in a principal Colombian university for three years.

SIDELIGHTS: John Kennedy told *CA*: "My work centers in the study of Latin America, its people and its institutions. My early working years were spent in various South American countries.... I have traveled or lived in Latin America extensively since 1938. Current concentration is on Colombia."

* * *

KENNEDY, Kathleen   1947(?)-1975

1947(?)—July 26, 1975; American publicist, author of dramatic adaptation and book on theatrical history. Obituaries: *Washington Post*, July 28, 1975.

* * *

KENNEDY, (Jerome) Richard   1932-

PERSONAL: Born December 23, 1932, in Jefferson City, Mo.; son of Donald and Mary Louise (O'Keefe) Kennedy; married Lillian Nance, 1960; children: Joseph Troy, Matthew Cook. *Education:* Portland State University, B.S., 1958; Oregon State University, graduate study, 1964-65. *Home:* 504 Northwest Brook, Newport, Ore. 97365.

CAREER: Author. Odd-jobs include selling out-of-print books and working for an out-of-print search service, working with archives at University of Oregon, Cabdriver, and woodcutter. Currently working as a janitor. *Military service:* U.S. Air Force, 1951-54.

WRITINGS: The Parrot and the Thief, Atlantic-Little, Brown, 1974; *The Contests at Cowlick*, Atlantic-Little, Brown, 1975. Contributor of poems to little magazines.

WORK IN PROGRESS: Four books, for Harper, Sierra Club/Scribner, and two for Atlantic-Little, Brown.

* * *

KENNEDY, Robert L(ee)   1930-

PERSONAL: Born January 6, 1930, in Compton, Calif.; son of Harold W. and Nora (Christian) Kennedy. *Education:* University of Denver, B.A., 1956, M.A., 1971. *Politics:* Independent. *Home:* 107 West Cheyenne Rd., Colorado Springs, Colo. 80906. *Office:* Air Force Academy Foundation, Colorado Springs, Colo. 80906.

CAREER: Colorado Tuberculosis Association, Denver, director of public information, 1956-58; University of Denver, Denver, Colo., editor of *University of Denver* and assistant director of public relations, 1958-59; American School Food Service Association, Denver, Colo., editor of *School Food Service Journal* and director of communication, 1959-66; University of Denver, assistant director of public relations, 1966-71; Air Force Academy Foundation, Colorado Springs, Colo., director of communication, 1971—. Communication consultant to National Association of Environmental Health, Association of School Business Officials of the United States and Canada, Robert McCollum Associates, CVD Studios, and Rockmont College. *Military service:* U.S. Air Force, 1949-53; became staff sergeant. *Member:* Associated Business Writers of America.

WRITINGS: (With Geraline Hardwick) *Fundamentals of Quantity Food Preparation*, Cahners, Volume I, 1975, Volume II, in press. Also author of one-act play, "Take It to Tennessee," first produced in Denver at University of Denver, August 18, 1971. Author of film scripts for CVD Studios. Contributor and editorial consultant, *Journal of Environmental Health*.

WORK IN PROGRESS: With Geraline Hardwick, Volumes III and IV of *Fundamentals of Quantity Food Prepara-*

ration; a novel, *Compound*; with Gerald Ramsey, *Quantity Food with Flair*; with John N. Perryman, *Fine Art of Business Entertaining*.

AVOCATIONAL INTERESTS: Contemporary literature, opera, theatre, communications research.

* * *

KERES, Paul (Petrovich) 1916-1975

January 7, 1916—June 5, 1975; Estonian chess champion, author of books in his field. Obituaries: *New York Times*, June 6, 1975.

* * *

KERMAN, Cynthia Earl 1923-

PERSONAL: Born July 16, 1923, in Srinagar, Kashmir; daughter of Edwin Charles (a Young Men's Christian Association secretary) and Barbara (Thurtell) Earl; married Ralph O. Kerman (an executive secretary), March 22, 1944; children: Caroline Wildflower, Edwin, Jody-Loren, Nancy. *Education:* Kalamazoo College, B.A., 1944; University of Illinois, graduate study, 1949-51; University of Michigan, M.A., 1967, Ph.D., 1971. *Politics:* "More often Democratic than Republican." *Religion:* Society of Friends (Quaker). *Home:* 4200 Elsrode Ave., Baltimore, Md. 21214. *Office:* Department of English, Villa Julie College, Greenspring Valley Rd., Stevenson, Md. 21153.

CAREER: American Friends Service Committee, Ann Arbor, Mich., secretary, 1962-64; University of Michigan, Ann Arbor, secretary, 1964-66; Eastern Michigan University, Ypsilanti, lecturer in English, 1970-71; Villa Julie College, Stevenson, Md., instructor, 1971-72, assistant professor of English, 1972—. *Member:* American Studies Association, College English Association, National Council of Teachers of English, Edgar Allan Poe Society, Phi Kappa Phi.

WRITINGS: (Editor with Carol Murphy) *The Mayer-Boulding Dialogue on Peace Research*, Pendle Hill, 1967; (contributor) Charles Chatfield, editor, *Peace Movements in America*, Schocken, 1973; *Creative Tension: The Life and Thought of Kenneth Boulding*, University of Michigan Press, 1974. Contributor to *American Friend, Friends World News, Kalamazoo College Alumnus, Friends Journal*, and *Michigan Daily*.

WORK IN PROGRESS: Research on the biography and interpretation of Jean Toomer, author of *Cane*; poems and short stories.

AVOCATIONAL INTERESTS: Travel, hiking, photography.

* * *

KESSLER, Diane Cooksey 1947-

PERSONAL: Born January 8, 1947, in New Bern, N.C.; daughter of Dan Harrison (a director of industrial relations) and Martha (Holfelder) Cooksey; married Charles W. Kessler, Jr. (a hospital chaplain), June 3, 1969; children: Peter Nathan. *Education:* Oberlin College, B.A., 1969; Andover Newton Theological School, M.A., 1971. *Politics:* Democrat. *Religion:* Protestant. *Home:* 73 Glen Ave., Newton Centre, Mass. 02159.

CAREER: Civil Liberties Union of Massachusetts, Boston, Mass., lobbyist, 1972; *Valley Reporter*, Waitsfield, Vt., reporter, 1973-74. Member of Vermont Governor's Commission on the Status of Women, 1974—. *Member:*

American Civil Liberties Union (Vermont chapter, member of board of directors, 1973-75, treasurer, 1974-75).

WRITINGS: Parents and the Experts, Judson, 1974.

WORK IN PROGRESS: Research on educational literature, focusing on the question of discipline in the classroom that could evolve into a book tentatively titled, *Teachers and the Experts*.

AVOCATIONAL INTERESTS: Music, reading, travel.

* * *

KESSLER, Sheila

PERSONAL: Born in Seattle, Wash.; daughter of Chester M. (a sales executive) and Elouise (Rogers) Kessler; married Rudy Kohnle, June 11, 1968 (divorced, July, 1972); married Barry Halsted (a regional sales manager of aircraft manufacturing firm), June 1, 1973. *Education:* University of Washington, Seattle, B.A., 1966, M.Ed., 1969, Ph.D., 1971. *Home:* 843 Artwood Rd. N.E., Atlanta, Ga. 30307. *Office:* Counseling Center, Georgia State University, Atlanta, Ga. 30303.

CAREER: University of Puget Sound, Tacoma, Wash., assistant professor of psychology and associate director of counseling center, both 1971-72; University of Nevada, Reno, assistant professor of psychology and counselor, both 1972-73; Georgia State University, Atlanta, assistant professor of psychology and counselor, both 1973—. Executive director for training and research at Atlanta's Family Mediation Center, 1974—; has conducted psychology workshops; has appeared on local television and radio programs. Consultant to governmental agencies. *Member:* American Psychological Association, American Personnel and Guidance Association, Western Psychological Association, Southeastern Psychological Association, Georgia College Personnel Association, Phi Lambda Theta.

WRITINGS: The American Way of Divorce: Prescriptions for Change, Nelson-Hall, 1975. Contributor to *Journal of Counselor Education and Supervision, Journal of Counseling Psychology, Gerontologist*, and *Personnel and Guidance Journal*.

WORK IN PROGRESS: Research on divorce adjustment and counseling.

SIDELIGHTS: Sheila Kessler writes that her "... current interest in divorce stemmed from working in Reno, Nevada with a divorcing population and realizing how totally remiss our society was in not keeping up with the changes in the institution of marriage and divorce. The book was an attempt to update attitudes, coping mechanisms of the individuals, and societal provisions for divorce." *Avocational interests:* Flying (pilot), guitar, skiing, scuba diving, tennis, painting, travel (Europe, South America, Far East).

* * *

KEYES, Margaret Frings 1929-

PERSONAL: Born August 8, 1929, in Butte, Mont.; daughter of John Matthew (a longshoreman) and Mary (Dyer) Frings; married Vincent Ettoire Keyes (an attorney), April 11, 1969. *Education:* University of California, Berkeley, B.A., 1951; Catholic University of America, M.S.W., 1953; University of Chicago, further graduate study, 1961-62; also studied with Eric Berne, 1957-61, and Fritz Perls, 1965-68. *Religion:* Roman Catholic. *Office:* 850 Bay St., San Francisco, Calif. 94109.

CAREER: University of California, Medical Center, San

Francisco, therapist, researcher, and teacher, 1956-61; Catholic Social Service of Marin, San Rafael, Calif., director of professional programs, 1962-69; private practice in psychiatric social work in San Francisco, Calif., 1965-75; Berkeley Center for Human Interaction, Berkeley, Calif., associate, 1972-74, member of board of directors, 1974—. Has taught at Lone Mountain College; director of workshops at Western Institute for Group and Family Therapy and Lloyd Center. *Member:* Society of Clinical Social Workers (fellow).

WRITINGS: The Inward Journey, Celestial Arts Publishing, 1974; (contributor) Paul T. Olsen, editor, *New Directions in Psychotherapy*, National Institute for the Psychotherapies and Behavioral Publications, 1975; *Staying Married*, Celestial Arts Publishing, 1975; (contributor) Hilarion Petzold, editor, *Gestalt Therapy in Practice*, Fritz Perls Institute (Dusseldorf), in press. Contributor to professional journals.

WORK IN PROGRESS: Turning Point, biographies of contemporary women.

* * *

KICKNOSWAY, Faye 1936-

PERSONAL: Surname is pronounced Kick-*nos*-way; born December 16, 1936, in Detroit, Mich.; daughter of Walter (an inventor) and Louise (Standish) Blair; married Leonard Kicknosway, December 11, 1959 (divorced, September 15, 1968); children: Kevin Leo, Lauren Beth. *Education:* Attended Society of Arts and Crafts, 1957-58, and University of Michigan, 1958-59; Wayne State University, B.A., 1967; San Francisco State College (now University), M.A., 1969. *Politics:* "Shamanism." *Religion:* "Poetry." *Residence:* Detroit, Mich. *Office:* Department of English, Wayne State University, Room 400, State Hall, Detroit, Mich. 48201.

CAREER: Macomb County Community College, Warren, Mich., instructor in English, 1967-68; Michigan Lutheran College, Detroit, Mich., instructor in English, 1968; Wayne State University, Detroit, Mich., instructor in English, 1970—. Model for commercial artists, 1958-69. Member of Poet-in-the-School Program of Michigan Council for the Arts, 1973-74; chairperson of Miles Poetry Committee, 1974—. Gives poetry readings at high schools, universities, and on radio and television. *Member:* Authors Guild of America. *Awards, honors:* Woodrow Wilson fellowship, 1968-69; American Academy of Poets Award, 1969.

WRITINGS—Poetry: *O, You Can Walk on the Sky?: Good*, Capra Press, 1972; *Poem Tree*, Red Hanrahan Press, 1973; *A Man Is a Hook: Trouble*, Capra Press, 1974; *Second Chance Man: The Cigarette Poems*, Alternative Press, 1975; *Capricorn: That Old Hillbilly Tune Called My Heart*, Red Hanrahan Press, in press; *The Cat Approaches*, Capra Press, in press.

Work is anthologized in *Ten Wayne Poets*, edited by John Sinclair, Artists' Workshop Press, 1965; *Under 30: Fiction, Poetry, and Criticism of the New American Writers*, edited by Charles Newman and William Henkin, Jr., Indiana University Press, 1969; *Anthology of Women Poets*, edited by Pamela Victorine, Dremen Press, 1971; *No More Masks!*, edited by Ellen Bass and Florence Howe, Doubleday, 1973.

Contributor of poetry to *Paris Review, Prairie Schooner, Chicago Review, New York Quarterly, Kayak, Isthmus*, and other journals.

WORK IN PROGRESS: Two novels, *Janie (Or Unlove):*

A Diary, and *Conversations with Beethoven*; a book of poetry, *Bearwalk*.

SIDELIGHTS: Faye Kicknosway writes: "Poetry has changed my life. It is a process of revelation, of inner and outer communication. There is only honesty in it."

* * *

KIM, Hyung-chan 1938-

PERSONAL: Born November 4, 1938; married to Seung-joo, (a registered nurse); children: Kim, Kathryn. *Education:* Hankuk University of Foreign Studies, Seoul, Korea, B.A., 1961; George Peabody College for Teachers, B.A., 1964, M.A., 1965, Ed.D., 1969. *Home:* 2210 St. Clair St., Bellingham, Wash. 98225. *Office:* College of Ethnic Studies, Western Washington State College, Bellingham, Wash. 98225.

CAREER: Western Washington State College, Bellingham, associate professor of ethnic studies, 1968—.

WRITINGS: North Korean Education and Society, Institute of Education, University of London, 1973; (with Wayne Patterson) *The Koreans in America: 1882-1974*, Oceana, 1974; *The Filipinos in America: 1898-1975*, Oceana, 1975. Contributor to *Journal of Ethnic Studies* and *Korea Journal*.

* * *

KIM, Yong Choon 1935-

PERSONAL: Born January 1, 1935, in Kyongju, Korea; naturalized U.S. citizen in 1972; son of Chang Ho and Chung Ja Kim; married Joyce Chung Ja (a nurse), December 18, 1965. *Education:* Belhaven College, B.A., 1960; Westminster Theological Seminary, B.D., 1963, Th.M., 1964; Temple University, Ph.D., 1969. *Home:* 58 Parkwood Dr., Kingston, R.I. *Office:* Department of Philosophy, University of Rhode Island, Kingston, R.I. 02881.

CAREER: Frederick College, Portsmouth, Va., assistant professor of philosophy and religion, 1966-67; York College of Pennsylvania, York, assistant professor of Asian studies, 1969-70; Cleveland State University, Cleveland, Ohio, assistant professor of philosophy and religion, 1970-71; University of Rhode Island, Kingston, assistant professor, 1971-73, associate professor of philosophy, 1974—. Teacher of Korean Bible Club of Rhode Island, 1971-75. *Member:* Royal Asiatic Society, Society of Korean Philosophy, Society for Asian and Comparative Philosophy, Association for Asian Studies, American Academy of Religion.

WRITINGS: Oriental Thought: An Introduction to the Philosophical and Religious Thought of Asia, C. C Thomas, 1973.

WORK IN PROGRESS: Korean Thought: Ch'ondogyo Concept of Man; Ch'ondogyo Kyongjon.

* * *

KIMPEL, Ben D(rew) 1915-

PERSONAL: Born November 6, 1915, in Fort Smith, Ark.; son of Ben Drew (a lawyer) and Gladys (Crane) Kimpel. *Education:* Harvard University, B.A., c. 1937, M.A., 1939; University of Northern Carolina, Ph.D., 1942. *Politics:* Democrat ("liberal branch"). *Religion:* "None." *Home address:* Box 2321, Fayetteville, Ark. 72701. *Office:* Department of English, University of Arkansas, Fayetteville, Ark. 72701.

CAREER: University of Arkansas, Fayetteville, 1952—,

now professor of English. *Military service:* U.S. Army, 1942-46; became second lieutenant. *Member:* Modern Language Association, American Association of University Professors.

WRITINGS: (With T. C. Duncan Eaves) *Samuel Richardson: A Biography*, Oxford University Press, 1972.

WORK IN PROGRESS: A companion to Ezra Pound's *Cantos*.

* * *

KING, Ben F(rank) 1937-

PERSONAL: Born September 9, 1937, in Prairie du Chien, Wis.; son of Ben Frank (a civil engineer) and Marguerite (Lawless) King. *Education:* Loyola University, Los Angeles, Calif., B.Sc., 1959; Yale University, M.Sc., 1970. *Politics:* Independent. *Address:* Ornithology Department, American Museum of Natural History, Central Park West at 79th St., New York, N.Y. 10024.

CAREER: South East Asia Treaty Organization, Medical Research Laboratory, Bangkok, Thailand, field biologist, 1964-66; Bird Bonanzas, Miami, Fla., Asian tour leader, 1971—; Quester's Tour and Travel, New York, N.Y., Asian and Alaskan tour leader, 1975. *Military service:* U.S. Navy, 1959-62; became lieutenant. *Member:* Royal Naval Bird Watchers Society, Hong Kong Bird-Watchers Society, Bombay Natural History Society, American Ornithologists Union.

WRITINGS: A Field Guide to the Birds of South-East Asia, Houghton, 1975.

WORK IN PROGRESS: A Field Guide to the Birds of the Indian Region, completion expected in 1977; *A Field Guide to the Birds of Japan, Korea, Taiwan, and Micronesia*, 1978.

SIDELIGHTS: King has lived six years in Asia, including Korea, Thailand, and India.

* * *

KING, Charles (Lester) 1922-

PERSONAL: Born February 15, 1922, in Gosford, Calif.; son of Clarence Wilbur (a rancher) and Velva Dona (Hadlock) King; married Helen Eileen White, December 20, 1949; children: Gail Elena, Carol Beverly, Laura Linda. *Education:* University of New Mexico, B.A., 1948; University of Southern California, Los Angeles, M.A., 1950, Ph.D., 1953. *Home:* 2870 Duke Cir., Boulder, Colo. 80303. *Office:* Department of Spanish, University of Colorado, Boulder, Colo. 80302.

CAREER: Binational Center grantee with U.S. Information Agency in La Paz, Bolivia, 1954-56, in Montevideo, Uruguay, 1956-57, in Bucaramanga, Colombia, 1957-58, and in Tehran, Iran, 1959-60; U.S. Office of Education, Washington, D.C., specialist for Language Institutes, 1960-64; University of Colorado, Boulder, Colo., assistant professor, 1964-68, associate professor, 1968-74, professor of Spanish, 1974—. *Military service:* U.S. Army, 1942-46. *Member:* American Association of Teachers of Spanish and Portuguese (vice-presidential nominee, 1975), Modern Language Association of America, Colorado Congress of Foreign Language Teachers.

WRITINGS: Ramon J. Sender (literary criticism), Twayne, 1974. Editor of *Modern Language Journal*, 1971-76.

WORK IN PROGRESS: An Annotated Bibliography of

Ramon J. Sender: 1928-1974, for Scarecrow, completion expected in 1975; *Francisco Garcia Pavon*, for Twayne, 1976.

BIOGRAPHICAL/CRITICAL SOURCES: Modern Language Journal, Volume 54, number 8, December, 1970.

* * *

KING, Florence 1936-

PERSONAL: Born January 5, 1936, in Washington, D.C.; daughter of Herbert Frederick (a musician) and Louise (Ruding) King. *Education:* American University, B.A., 1957; University of Mississippi, graduate study, 1958-59. *Politics:* "Royalist (I'm serious)." *Religion:* Episcopalian. *Agent:* Mel Berger, William Morris Agency, 1350 Avenue of the Americas, New York, N.Y. 10019.

CAREER: News and Observer, Raleigh, N.C., woman's page reporter, 1964-67. *Member:* Phi Alpha Theta. *Awards, honors:* North Carolina Press Women award, 1965, for reporting.

WRITINGS: Southern Ladies and Gentlemen, Stein & Day, 1975. Contributor to *Redbook, Playgirl, Viva, Penthouse, Ms., Cosmopolitan*, and *Harper's Magazine*.

AVOCATIONAL INTERESTS: Gay Nineties and turn-of-the-century popular songs, horseback riding.

* * *

KING, Harold 1945-

PERSONAL: Born February 27, 1945, in Grand Rapids, Mich.; son of Harold R. and Anne (Whitten) King; married Elaine Tucker (a news reporter), September 9, 1972. *Education:* Attended Pennsylvania State University, 1963-65; West Texas State University, B.S., 1970; University of Oklahoma, M.A., 1974. *Home:* 4101 Parkway, Bossier City, La. 71010. *Agent:* Josephine Rogers, Collins-Knowlton-Wing, 60 East 56th St., New York, N.Y. 10022. *Office: Shreveport Times*, 222 Lake, Shreveport, La. 71102.

CAREER: Amarillo Globe-News, Amarillo, Tex., reporter, 1970-72; *Shreveport Times*, Shreveport, La., reporter, 1972-73, 1974—. *Military service:* U.S. Marine Corps, 1965-67; served in Vietnam. *Member:* Sigma Delta Chi. *Awards, honors:* Frank C. Allen Award for excellence in journalism from Associated Press, 1974.

WRITINGS: Paradigm Red (novel), Bobbs-Merrill, 1975.

WORK IN PROGRESS: A novel, *Four Days*, for Bobbs-Merrill; a novel of espionage, political intrigue, and military confrontation set in the 1950's.

* * *

KING, Thomas M(ulvihill) 1929-

PERSONAL: Born May 9, 1929, in Pittsburgh, Pa.; son of William M. (a real estate agent) and Catherine (Mulvihill) King. *Education:* University of Pittsburgh, B.A., 1951; Fordham University, M.P.E., 1958; Woodstock College, M.Th., 1965; University of Strasbourg, Doctorat es Sciences Relieuses, 1968. *Politics:* Independent. *Home:* Jesuit Community, Georgetown University, Washington, D.C. 20057. *Office:* Department of Theology, Georgetown University, Washington, D.C. 20057.

CAREER: Entered Order of Society of Jesus (Jesuits), 1951, ordained Roman Catholic priest, 1964; Georgetown University, Washington, D.C., assistant professor, 1968-74, associate professor of theology, 1974—.

WRITINGS: Sartre and the Sacred, University of Chicago Press, 1974.

WORK IN PROGRESS: A book tentatively titled, *Teilhard de Chardin and the Mysticism of Knowledge.*

* * *

KING, William Donald Aelian
  See LESLIE KING, William (Donald Aelian)

* * *

KINGSLEY-SMITH, Terence 1940-

PERSONAL: Born March 15, 1940; son of Maurice O. Smith (a developer of shopping centers) and Dorothy (Kingsley) Smith Durney. *Education:* Attended William and Mary College, Santa Monica City College, and San Fernando Valley State College (now California State University, Northridge); University of California, Los Angeles, B.A., 1963. *Religion:* "Fallen away Catholic." *Home:* 333 West Channel Rd., Santa Monica, Calif. 90402. *Agent:* Charles Hunt, Bret Adams Agency, 36 East 61st St., New York, N.Y. 10021.

CAREER: Actor and writer. Has appeared in plays, including "Summer and Smoke," at Huntington Hartford Theater in Los Angeles, Calif., and "Desire Under the Elms," at Kennedy Center in Washington, D.C., and feature films, including "Marianne," "The Other Side of the Wind." *Military service:* U.S. Army, 1963-65; served in Korea. *Member:* Actors Equity, American Society of Composers, Authors and Publishers, Screen Actors Guild, Writers Guild.

WRITINGS: The Forsaken (novel), Simon & Schuster, 1975. Author of original screenplay "Molly and Lawless John," and "De Martians Is Comin'," a feature film, for Twentieth Century Fox. Staff writer for television series "Daniel Boone."

WORK IN PROGRESS: The James Dean Generation, a novel; "The Late Rose of Summer," a musical play; "The Barker," a musical adaptation of "The Brother's Keepers," by J. Kenyon Nicholson; a novel.

AVOCATIONAL INTERESTS: Jazz dancing, tap dancing, figure skating, Tai-Chi, guitar, studying Romance languages.

* * *

KINTON, Jack F(ranklin) 1939-

PERSONAL: Born December 6, 1939, in Ottawa, Ill.; son of Howard Earl (a printer) and Dorothy Evelyn (a teacher; maiden name, Condon) Kinton; married Evelyn Ruth Holmes (an executive secretary), August 26, 1961; children: Daryl Allan, Keith Banks. *Education:* Illinois Wesleyan University, B.S., 1961; Ohio State University, M.A., 1963; University of Colorado, graduate study, 1969. *Home:* 435 Jackson St., Aurora, Ill. 60505. *Office:* Milton College, Milton, Wis. 53563.

CAREER: Carthage College, Kenosha, Wis., assistant professor of sociology, 1965-67; Loras College, Dubuque, Iowa, assistant professor of sociology, 1967-69; Iowa Wesleyan College, Mount Pleasant, assistant professor of sociology, 1969-73; Social Science Services and Resources, Aurora, Ill., executive director, 1974—; Milton College, Milton, Wis., visiting professor of sociology and psychology, 1975. Consultant to numerous planning and community service councils. *Member:* American Association for the Advancement of Science (fellow), American Sociological Association, American Anthropological Association (fellow), World Future Society, American Academy of Political and Social Sciences, Midwest Sociological Society, Southern Sociological Society, Alpha Kappa Delta, Gamma Upsilon, Blue Key Club.

WRITINGS—All published by Social Science & Sociological Resources, except as indicated: *Leaders in Anthropology: The Men and Women of the Science of Man*, 1972; *American Ethnic Groups and the Revival of Cultural Pluralism*, 1972, 4th edition published as *American Ethnic Groups: A Source Book*, 1974; *American National Character: A Multidisciplinary Evaluative Bibliography of Key Books and Special Periodical Issues*, 1972; *Higher Education as a Social Problem*, 1973, 2nd edition published as *Higher Education: Its Response to the Social and Political Issues of the 1970's*, 1975; (editor) *Criminology, Law Enforcement and Offender Treatment: A Sourcebook for the 1970's*, 1974; (editor) *The American Community: A Multidisciplinary Perspective*, C.P.L., 1974; *Criminology Tomorrow*, 1974; *America's Ethnic Groups: A Revival Reader*, 1975; (editor) *The American Police in the Seventies*, 1975; *The American Community: Creation and Revival*, 1975. Consulting editor, Social Science & Sociological Resources, 1972—.

WORK IN PROGRESS: Research on higher educational institutions in transition, the future of the liberal arts college, anthropology of the future, the sociology of human services and social welfare, and the future of postindustrial societies.

* * *

KINZER, H(arless) M(ahlon) 1923(?)-1975

1923(?)—March 19, 1975; American photographer, editor, and author. Obituaries: *New York Times*, March 21, 1975; *AB Bookman's Weekly*, April 28, 1975.

* * *

KIPLINGER, Austin H(untington) 1918-

PERSONAL: Born September 19, 1918, in Washington, D.C.; son of Willard Monroe (an editor and writer) and Irene (Austin) Kiplinger; married Mary Louise Cobb, December 11, 1944; children: Todd Lawrence, Knight Austin. *Education:* Cornell University, A.B., 1939; Harvard University, graduate study, 1939-40. *Home:* 16801 River Rd., Poolesville, Md. 20837. *Office:* Kiplinger Washington Editors, 1729 H St. N.W., Washington, D.C. 20006.

CAREER: San Francisco Chronicle, San Francisco, Calif., reporter, 1940-41; *Changing Times*, Washington, D.C., executive editor, 1945-48; *Chicago Journal of Commerce*, Chicago, Ill., columnist, 1948-50; news commentator in Chicago for American Broadcasting Corp., 1951-55, and National Broadcasting Corp., 1955-56; Kiplinger Washington Editors, Inc., Washington, D.C., executive vice-president, 1956-59; president, 1959—, chairman, 1967—. President of Chicago Juvenile Protective Association, 1955-56; chairman, Chicago Mayor's Advisory Committee on Youth Welfare, 1956, Cornell University Council, 1965-68, Montgomery County (Md.) Community Action Committee, 1967-70; vice-chairman of National Capital Health and Welfare Council, 1960-67; trustee, Landon School, 1960-63, Cornell University, 1960—, Washington, D.C. Federal City Council, 1968—, Washington Journalism Center, 1968—. *Military service:* U.S. Navy, aviator, 1942-45. *Member:* Association of Radio and Television News Analysts, National Press Club, Overseas Writers Club, Metropolitan Club, Commonwealth Club, Cornell Club, Potomac Hunt Club, Chevy Chase Club, Sigma Delta Chi, Phi Beta Kappa, Delta Upsilon. *Awards, honors:* Television Digest award, 1953, for best Chicago newscaster.

WRITINGS: (With father, Willard Monroe Kiplinger) *Boom and Inflation Ahead*, Simon & Schuster, 1958; (with son, Knight A. Kiplinger) *Washington Now*, Harper, 1975. Wrote column, "The Round Table," for *Chicago Journal of Commerce*, 1948-50. Executive editor, *Changing Times*, 1945-48; editor, *Kiplinger Washington Letter*, 1961—.

*   *   *

KIRK, Donald R.   1935-

PERSONAL: Born April 19, 1935, in Canon City, Colo.; married to Janice E., (an artist); children: Ned, Amy. *Education:* Shasta College, A.A.; University of Oregon, B.S. and M.S. *Politics:* Democrat. *Religion:* "Process theology." *Home address:* Box 190, Palo Cedro, Calif. 96073. *Office:* Department of Biology, Shasta College, Redding, Calif. 96001.

CAREER: Boise Junior College (now Boise State College), Boise, Idaho, assistant professor of biology, 1963-65; Shasta College, Redding, Calif., professor of biology, 1965—. *Member:* American Nature Study Society, Natural Wildlife Federation, Audubon Society, Sierra Club.

WRITINGS: Wild Edible Plants of the Western United States, Naturegraph, 1970.

WORK IN PROGRESS: A field guide to western insects, for Naturegraph.

*   *   *

KIRK, John Esben   1905-1975

November 8, 1905—April 7, 1975; American gerontologist, university research director, and author of science and medical books. Obituaries: *Washington Post*, April 9, 1975; *New York Times*, April 9, 1975.

*   *   *

KIRK, Mary Wallace   1889-

PERSONAL: Born July 26, 1889, in Tuscumbia, Ala.; daughter of James T. (a lawyer) and Ella Pearsall (Rather) Kirk. *Education:* Agnes Scott College, A.B., 1911. *Politics:* Democrat. *Religion:* Presbyterian. *Home:* Locust Hill, Tuscumbia, Ala. 35674.

CAREER: Artist and etcher. *Member:* Garden Club of America, Agnes Scott College Alumnae Association (president, 1921-24), Phi Beta Kappa. *Awards, honors:* Silver Loving Cup from Poetry Society of Alabama, 1937, for poem, "The Sum of Living."

WRITINGS: Cabins and Characters, Southern University Press, 1969; *The Sum of Living: A Collection of Poems*, privately printed, 1973; *Locust Hill: This House Was Full of People*, University of Alabama Press, 1975.

*   *   *

KIRKPATRICK, Evron M(aurice)   1911-

PERSONAL: Born August 15, 1911, near Raub, Ind.; son of Omer and Lenna Mae (Haines) Kirkpatrick; married Jeane Jordan (a professor of political science and author), February 20, 1955; children: Douglas, John, Stuart. *Education:* University of Illinois, B.A. (with high honors), 1932, A.M., 1933; Yale University, Ph.D., 1939. *Politics:* Demo-

crat. *Home:* 6812 Granby St., Bethesda, Md. 20034. *Office:* American Political Science Association, 1527 New Hampshire Ave. N.W., Washington, D.C. 20036.

CAREER: University of Minnesota, Minneapolis, instructor, 1935-39, assistant professor, 1939-43, associate professor, 1943-48, professor of political science, 1948, head of Social Science Division, 1944-48; U.S. Department of State, Washington, D.C., chief of External Research Staff, 1948-52, chief of Psychological Intelligence and Research Staff, 1952-54, deputy director of Office of Intelligence Research, 1954; American Political Science Association, Washington, D.C., executive director, 1954—. Assistant research director of Research and Analysis, Office of Strategic Services, 1945; assistant research director and projects control officer of research and intelligence, U.S. Department of State, 1946; Intelligence Program adviser, U.S. Department of State, 1947; lecturer at Howard University, 1957-61; professorial lecturer at Georgetown University, 1959—. Member of Advisory Committee on Foreign Affairs, Southern Regional Education Board, 1952-56; director of Governmental Affairs Institute, 1954-64; chairman of the board of trustees of Operations and Policy Research, 1955—; trustee of Citizenship Clearing House, 1956-62; chairman of the board of trustees of Institute of American Universities, Aix En Provence, France, and Canterbury, England, 1958—; trustee of Helen Dwight Reid Foundation, 1960—, president, 1972—; trustee of National Center for Education in Politics, 1962-67; member of Commission on Presidential Campaign Debates, 1963-64; member of President Kennedy's Commission on Registration and Voting Participation, 1963-64; member of National Research Council, National Academy of Sciences, Division of Behavioral Sciences, 1963-66, and Committee on International Relations in the Behavioral Sciences, 1966-70; member of President Johnson's Task Force on Career Advancement in the Federal Service, 1966.

MEMBER: International Political Science Association (member of executive council, 1955-67; member of executive committee, 1958-64), National Arbitration Association (member of board of arbitrators, 1943-47), American Peace Society (president, 1969—), Pi Sigma Alpha (president, 1973), Phi Beta Kappa.

WRITINGS: (Contributor) *Man and Society*, Prentice-Hall, 1938; *The People, Politics, and the Politician*, Holt, 1941, 3rd revised edition (with A. N. Christensen), 1953; (with Christensen) *Running the Country*, Holt, 1946; *Target, The World: Communist Propaganda Activities in 1955*, Macmillan, 1956; (with Jeane Kirkpatrick) *Elections: U.S.A.*, Holt, 1956; *Year of Crisis: An Analysis of Communist Propaganda Activities in 1956*, Macmillan, 1957; (contributor) *Essays on the Behavioral Study of Politics*, University of Illinois Press, 1962; (contributor) *Perspectives*, Houghton, 1963; (contributor) Donald Freeman, editor, *Political Science: History, Scope and Methods*, Free Press, 1975. Contributor to *Encyclopaedia Britannica* and *Encyclopedia Americana*; contributor to *American Political Science Review*. Editorial adviser in political science to Henry Holt & Co., 1952-60, and Holt, Rinehart & Winston, 1960-68.

*   *   *

KLAREN, Peter F(lindell)   1938-

PERSONAL: Born October 18, 1938, in Summit, N.J.; son of Karl O. (in advertising) and Leonora (Flindell) Klaren; married Sara Castro (a professor), September 3, 1963. *Edu-*

cation: Dartmouth College, A.B., 1960; University of California at Los Angeles, M.A., 1964, Ph.D., 1968. *Home:* 3 Hilltop Dr., Hanover, N.H. 03755; 2121 Columbia Pike, Arlington, Va. *Office:* Department of History, George Washington University, Washington, D.C. 20052.

CAREER: Washington State University, Pullman, assistant professor of history, 1968-70; Dartmouth College, Hanover, N.H., adjunct assistant professor of history, 1971-72; George Washington University, Washington, D.C., assistant professor, 1972-75, associate professor of history, 1975—. Visiting professor at Dartmouth College, 1973 (summer). *Member:* Latin American Studies Association, American Historical Association. *Awards, honors:* Social Science Research Council post-doctoral fellowship to Peru, 1973-74; Mellon Foundation fellowship, 1975-76.

WRITINGS: La formacion de las haciendas azucareras y los origenes del Apra (title means "Formation of the Sugar Plantations and the Origins of Apra"), Instituto de Estudios Peruanos, 1970; *Modernization, Dislocation, and Aprismo: Origins of the Peruvian Aprista Party, 1870-1932*, University of Texas Press, 1973; (contributor) Kenneth Duncan, editor, *Landlord and Peasant in Latin America and the Caribbean*, Cambridge University Press, 1975; (contributor) John J. Te Paske, editor, *Field Research Guide to the Andean Area*, Duke University Press, 1975. Contributor of reviews to *Hispanic American Historical Review* and *Los Angeles Times*. Assistant editor of *Papers of Daniel Webster*, 1971-72.

WORK IN PROGRESS: Rural Proletarians in the Andes; research on rural labor systems in Latin America, 1850-1950.

* * *

KLEIN, Alan F(redric) 1911-

PERSONAL: Born May 14, 1911, in New York, N.Y.; son of Frederick (a locksmith) and Sallie (Greene) Klein; married Jacqueline Spivak, June 13, 1938; children: Peter. *Education:* Brooklyn College (now Brooklyn College of the City University of New York), B.S. in S.S., 1934; Brooklyn Law School, LL.B., 1938, J.D., 1967; Columbia University, M.S.W., 1942. *Politics:* Liberal Democrat. *Home:* 39 Patroon Pl., Albany, N.Y. 12211. *Office:* School of Social Work, State University of New York at Albany, 1400 Washington Ave., Albany, N.Y. 12203.

CAREER: Admitted to the Bar of New York State, 1938; American Red Cross, Washington, D.C., field representative, 1942-47; University of Toronto, Toronto, Ontario, associate professor of social work education, 1948-55; University of Pittsburgh, Pittsburgh, Pa., professor of social work education, 1955-68; State University of New York, Albany, professor of social work education, 1968—. Consultant to Albany Home for Children, 1970—, and Veteran's Administration Hospital, 1971—. *Member:* Council of Social Work Education.

WRITINGS: Society, Democracy, and the Group, Woman's Press, 1953; *Role Playing in Leadership Training and Problem Solving*, Association Press, 1956; *How to Use Role Playing Effectively*, Association Press, 1959; *Social Work through Group Process*, State University of New York Press, 1970; *Effective Groupwork*, Association Press, 1972; *The Professional Child Care Worker*, Association Press, 1975. Author of "Comprehensive Correspondence Course in Municipal Recreation" for Department of Education of Ontario, 1953.

AVOCATIONAL INTERESTS: Travel, scuba diving, leather carving, square dance.

* * *

KLEIN, Isaac 1905-

PERSONAL: Born September 5, 1905, in Hungary; son of Samuel (a laborer) and Ilka (Hershkowitz) Klein; married Henrietta Levine (a teacher), June 26, 1932; children: Hannah (Mrs. Paul Katz), Miriam (Mrs. Saul Shapiro), Rivke (Mrs. Gerald Berkowitz). *Education:* City College (now City College of the City University of New York), B.A., 1930; Jewish Theological Seminary of America, Rabbi, 1934, M.H.L., 1935; University of Massachusetts, M.A., 1937; Harvard University, Ph.D., 1947. *Home:* 40 Hardt Lane, Buffalo, N.Y. 14226. *Office:* Temple Saarey Zedeck, 621 Getzville Rd., Buffalo, N.Y. 14226.

CAREER: Ordained rabbi, 1934; rabbi in Buffalo, N.Y., 1953-74. Lecturer at University of Buffalo, 1954-59, University of Judaism, 1959-73; associate professor at Jewish Theological Seminary of America, 1963. Advisor on Jewish affairs to occupation government in Germany, 1949-50; president of rabbinical assembly of World Organization of Conservative Rabbis, 1958-60. *Military service:* U.S. Army, chaplain, 1942-46; received six battle stars. *Awards, honors:* D.D., Jewish Theological Seminary of America, 1960.

WRITINGS: The Ten Commandments in a Changing World, Bloch & Co., 1945; (translator) *The Book of Acquisition of Maimonides*, Yale University Press, 1951; (translator and author of notes) *The Book of Women*, Yale University Press, 1972; *The Anguish and the Ecstacy of a Jewish Chaplain*, Vantage, 1973. Contributor of papers to professional journals.

WORK IN PROGRESS: A Guide to Traditional Jewish Practice; The Book of Agriculture of Maimonides; Responsa on Questions of Jewish Law.

* * *

KLEIN, Stanley 1930-

PERSONAL: Born November 7, 1930, in Brooklyn, N.Y.; son of Joseph (a businessman) and Jennie (Rosen) Klein; married Leila Dibner (a teacher), June 29, 1952; children: Nancy, Jamie Ann. *Education:* New York University, B.A., 1952; Southern Connecticut State College, M.S., 1957; University of Connecticut, graduate study, 1960-62. *Home:* 42 Fawn Dr., Stamford, Conn. 06905. *Agent:* Barthold Fles, 507 Fifth Ave., New York, N.Y. 10017. *Office:* Department of Education, Western Connecticut State College, 181 White St., Danbury, Conn.

CAREER: American Education Publications, Middletown, Conn., editor, 1959-64; Holt, Rinehart & Winston, Inc., New York, N.Y., senior editor of school department, 1964-69; General Learning Corp., New York, N.Y., director of corporation planning, 1969-71; Western Connecticut State College, Danbury, assistant professor of education, 1971—. President of Stanley Klein Associates, Inc., 1971—. *Member:* National Education Association, Connecticut Education Association, North Stamford Exchange Club, Phi Delta Kappa. *Awards, honors: The Final Mystery* was selected as one of the outstanding science books for children by American Book Council and American Association of Science Teachers, 1974.

WRITINGS—For children: *The World of a Tree*, Doubleday, 1969; *A World of Differences*, Doubleday, 1971; *The Final Mystery*, Doubleday, 1974.

WORK IN PROGRESS: Research on childrens' attitudes and understanding of death; an adult book on the nature of sleep.

* * *

KLEIN, Suzanne Marie 1940-

PERSONAL: Born December 10, 1940, in Chicago, Ill.; daughter of James Francis (a businessman) and Anna (a secretary; maiden name, Hansen) Seguin; married William Peter Klein (an electrical engineer), October 27, 1962; children: Kelly, Peter. Education: University of Arizona, B.A., 1962. Home: 1430 South Perlman Ave., Tucson, Ariz. 85710.

CAREER: Elementary school teacher in Phoenix, Ariz., 1967-70.

WRITINGS: An Elephant in My Bed (juvenile), Follett, 1974.

WORK IN PROGRESS: Picture and beginning-to-read books for children.

* * *

KLEMM, Edward G., Jr. 1910-

PERSONAL: Born June 6, 1910, in Louisville, Ky.; son of Edward G. (an attorney) and Roberta (a teacher and poet; maiden name, Kohnhorst) Klemm. Education: University of Chicago, Ph.B., 1932, graduate study, 1933; University of Louisville, further graduate study. Home: 2034 Eastern Parkway, Louisville, Ky. 40204. Office: 138 Breckinridge Lane, Louisville, Ky. 40207.

CAREER: Police reporter, 1931-33; junior high and high school teacher in Louisville, Ky., 1933-36; owner of a real estate and insurance office in Louisville, Ky., 1936—. Member: National Association of American Composers and Conductors (life member), American Society of Composers, Authors, and Publishers, Pendennis Club (Louisville), Filson Club (Louisville; life member), J. B. Speed Art Museum (life member), Kentucky Colonels.

WRITINGS: Precious Heritage, Echo Publishers, 1974. Composer, with mother, Roberta K. Klemm, of "Holiday in Napoli" and "Shadows," Whitney Blake, 1945, "They Never Told Me," Edition Bristol (Vienna), 1945, and "Desert Dance," Composers Press, 1945.

AVOCATIONAL INTERESTS: International travel (Mexico, Europe, Egypt).

* * *

KLEYMAN, Paul (Fred) 1945-

PERSONAL: Born June 17, 1945, in Minneapolis, Minn.; son of Maurice (a card dealer) and Sue (Supak) Kleyman; married Pamela Wilson; children: Shana Bethea. Education: University of Minnesota, B.A., 1967. Home: 757½ Guerrero St., San Francisco, Calif. 94110. Office: 165 Grove St., San Francisco, Calif. 94102.

CAREER: Intersection Newsletter, San Francisco, Calif., editor and designer, 1969—. Editor and writer, night clerk, and office aid for Glide United Methodist Church's Urban Center (period included in civilian public service, 1967-71, after having refused induction into military service and been sentenced to three years probation); public information director of San Francisco Art Commission's Neighborhood Arts Program, 1971—; member of board of directors of Intersection Art Center, 1971—; publicist for San Francisco Annual Art Festival, 1972—.

WRITINGS: Senior Power: Growing Old Rebelliously, Glide Publications, 1974. Editor of San Francisco Flyer, 1971-72.

WORK IN PROGRESS: Research on the arts and their place in the daily lives of Americans, socially, politically, economically, and "energetically."

SIDELIGHTS: Kleyman writes: "In 1899 my grandmother, Sophie Katz Supak, was working for a dressmaker in the Jewish ghetto of her Ukrainian town. She was nine years old and became a socialist organizer of local house girls who were terribly exploited. Her story and that of my grandfather, who is now dead, are vital to me. I have taped interviews with her, which may or may not supply material for a book some day."

* * *

KLINE, Nancy Meadors 1946-

PERSONAL: Born May 1, 1946, in Clovis, N.M.; daughter of Max Irby (in finance and investments) and Edelweiss (Corbin) Meadors; married Peter Kline (a teacher and writer), June 17, 1972. Education: Scripps College, B.A., 1968. Residence: Sandy Spring, Md. Office: Sandy Spring Friends School, Sandy Spring, Md. 20860.

CAREER: High school teacher of English in Sandy Spring, Md., 1968-70, and Greenway, Va., 1970-72; Sandy Spring Friends School, Sandy Spring, Md., director of Interlocking Curriculum, 1973—. Teacher of re-evaluation counseling; consultant to Mankind Research Unlimited, 1972—.

WRITINGS: (With husband Peter Kline) Physical Movement for the Theater, Richards Rosen Group, 1971; Enjoying the Arts/Dance, Richards Rosen Group, 1975. Author of three teaching models for Croft Publications, 1974.

WORK IN PROGRESS: The Filled Aperture in Keats' "Ode to a Nightingale."

SIDELIGHTS: Nancy Kline writes: "I believe that with sufficient emotional discharge full human functioning intellectually and physically can be reclaimed. I believe that disease is a result of inappropriate nutrition and emotional distress. I believe that the nature of the human being is zestful, loving, creative, and enormously intelligent. I plan to live a hundred fifty years or so and in that time to contribute significantly to changing the educational system in this country to one of a fully human, intellectually invigorating, dynamic experience. The Interlocking Curriculum is one step in that direction.

"I know that poetry can be better appreciated and understood if it is first experienced through body movement."

BIOGRAPHICAL/CRITICAL SOURCES: Washington Post, March 23, 1974.

* * *

KLISE, Thomas S. 1928-

PERSONAL: Surname rhymes with "ice"; born March 15, 1928, in Chicago, Ill.; son of David D. (a businessman) and Mary (Shaw) Klise; married Marjorie Costello; children: Elizabeth, Molly, Sarah, Catherine, Julia, James. Education: St. Ambrose College, B.A., 1948; University of Notre Dame, graduate study, 1948-50. Politics: Democrat. Religion: Roman Catholic. Home: 1322 West Moss, Peoria, Ill. 61606. Office: 203 Perry, Peoria, Ill. 61601.

CAREER: Thomas S. Klise Co. (producers of educational films), Peoria, Ill., owner, 1965—. Military service: U.S. Navy, 1952-56.

WRITINGS: The Last Western (novel), Argus, 1974.

KNAUTH, Percy 1914-

PERSONAL: "K" in surname is pronounced; born June 17, 1914, in New York, N.Y.; son of Theodore W. and Gabriele (Roediger) Knauth; married Gisele Gries, July 7, 1941 (divorced, August, 1952); married Behri Pratt (a layout artist), December 6, 1953; children: (second marriage) Timothy Pratt, Elisabeth Anne, Geoffrey (adopted). Education: Petri-Gymnasium, Leipzig, Germany, Arbitur, 1934; Bowdoin College, student, 1935-36. Politics: Liberal Democrat. Religion: Episcopalian. Home and office address: Box 64, 8 Trumbull St., Stonington, Conn. 06378. Agent: Pat Berens, Sterling Lord Agency, 600 Madison Ave., New York, N.Y. 10022.

CAREER: Chicago Tribune, correspondent in Berlin, Germany, 1937-38; New York Times, correspondent in Berlin, 1939-41, writer for Sunday Department in New York, N.Y., 1941-42; Time, New York, N.Y., writer in foreign news department, 1942-44, war correspondent, 1944-45, Paris Bureau chief, 1945-46, correspondent in Berlin, 1946-48; Life, New York, N.Y., assistant text editor, 1948-50, correspondent in Germany, 1950-51; Sports Illustrated, New York, N.Y., text editor, 1953-62; Time-Life Books, New York, N.Y., senior editor, 1962-66, European editor in Paris, 1966-70; free-lance editor and writer, 1970—. National chairman, National Association for Mental Health, 1975. Member: Authors Guild. Awards, honors: Special Award from National Association for Mental Health, 1972, for a Life article on mental depression.

WRITINGS: Germany in Defeat, Knopf, 1946; Wind on My Wings, Doubleday, 1960; (editor) An Illustrated Encyclopedia of Animal Life, Grolier, 1971; The North Woods, Time-Life, 1972; The Metalsmiths, Time-Life, 1973; A Season in Hell, Harper, 1975.

WORK IN PROGRESS: White Squall, a novel; a reminiscent social history about Berlin between wars.

SIDELIGHTS: Knauth writes: "I am interested in almost any subject that lends itself to interesting writing. I have written (ghosted) textbooks for the Life Nature Library, articles for Life on subjects ranging from war reports to Marlene Dietrich at 50 and the man who invented the Toni home permanent back in 1948. I wrote a book on learning to fly (Wind on My Wings) and numerous articles on my experiences as a private pilot. I love to write about aviation and the sea, about nature subjects, about people. But people are really my abiding interest, with all their troubles, problems, joys, delusions, illusions, their various ways of coping with the incredible problems life poses. I am still fascinated with the formative period of my life, Germany before and under Hitler. I am fluent in German and French. My political viewpoint is that of a fascinated (often frustrated or outraged) liberal idealist. Not much room for that anymore."

BIOGRAPHICAL/CRITICAL SOURCES: Mental Health Magazine, winter, 1974-1975; People, April 21, 1975.

*   *   *

KNIGHT, David Marcus 1936-

PERSONAL: Born November 30, 1936, in Exeter, England; son of Marcus (a clergyman) and Claire (Hewett) Knight; married Sarah Prideaux (a college tutor), July 21, 1962; children: Marcus, Teresa, Susannah, Jacob. Education: Keble College, Oxford, B.A., 1960, M.A. and D.Phil., both 1964. Politics: Labour. Religion: Church of England. Home: 61 Hallgarth St., Durham DHI 3AY, England. Agent: A. D. Peters, 10 Buckingham St., London WC2N 6BU, England. Office: Department of Philosophy, University of Durham, Durham DHI 3HN, England.

CAREER: University of Durham, Durham, England, lecturer in the history of science, 1964—. Military service: British Army, Royal Artillery, 1955-57. Member: British Society for the History of Science, Chemical Society, Royal Institution, Society for the Study of Early Chemistry, Hakluyt Society, Navy Records Society, Society for Bibliography of Natural History.

WRITINGS: Atoms and Elements, Hutchinson, 1967, 2nd edition, 1970; (editor) Classical Scientific Papers: Chemistry, Mills & Boon, 1968, 2nd series, 1970; Natural Science Books in English, Praeger, 1972; Sources for History of Science, Cornell University Press, 1975. Contributor to Ambix, Isis, and Studies in Romanticism. Member of editorial board of Annals of Science.

WORK IN PROGRESS: On Understanding Nature, for Deutsch; a book on zoological illustration; research on materialism and early nineteenth century science.

SIDELIGHTS: Knight writes: "I suffer from mild bibliomania, and enjoy old books on science; and firmly believe that the history of science is an important part of general history. I've done work-camps in the American South-West, in Greece, Uganda, and Madagascar; and I've been to conferences in the U.S.A., U.S.S.R., Czechoslovakia, France, Poland, and Japan."

*   *   *

KNIGHT, Glee 1947-

PERSONAL: Born November 15, 1947, in Bay City, Mich.; daughter of John Alfred and Lavina (Carrier) Marquardt; married Arthur Knight (a writer and professor), September 27, 1966. Education: Attended Delta College, 1965-66. Residence: California, Pa. Agent: Ray Peekner, 2625 North 36th St., Milwaukee, Wis. 53210. Office address: TUVOTI, P.O. Box 439, California, Pa. 15419.

CAREER: Poet and free-lance writer, 1966—; TUVOTI Books, California, Pa., editor and publisher, 1971—. Poet for Pennsylvania Council on the Arts, 1974—. Member: Committee of Small Magazine Editors and Publishers, Coordinating Council of Literary Magazines.

WRITINGS—All poetry: The Big Apple, Sceptre, 1974; In Lower Michigan, New York Culture Review, 1975; Until the Lights in Us Come On, Cider Press, 1975; Timetables (broadside), Bellevue Press, 1975. Poetry represented in anthologies, including Peace and Pieces: An Anthology of Contemporary American Poetry, Peace and Pieces Press, 1973. Contributor of poems to Panache, Poetry View, Maine Review, New York Culture Review, Wisconsin Review, Coe Review, Poetry Newsletter, and Firelands Arts Review.

Author of "Cornucopia," a column for Wild Fennel, 1975—. Editor with husband, Arthur Knight, The Beat Book, 1974.

WORK IN PROGRESS: Co-editing The Beat Diary with Arthur Knight.

*   *   *

KNOTT, John R(ay), Jr. 1937-

PERSONAL: Born July 9, 1937, in Memphis, Tenn.; son

of John Ray and Wilma (Henshaw) Knott; married Anne Percy, 1959; children: Catherine, Ellen, Walker, Anne. *Education:* Yale University, A.B., 1959; Harvard University, Ph.D., 1965. *Residence:* Ann Arbor, Mich. *Office:* Department of English, University of Michigan, Ann Arbor, Mich. 48104.

CAREER: Harvard University, Cambridge, Mass., instructor in English, 1965-67; University of Michigan, Ann Arbor, assistant professor, 1967-72, associate professor of English, 1972—, director of Undergraduate Studies in English, 1974—. *Member:* Modern Language Association of America, Milton Society. *Awards, honors:* Carnegie Foundation fellowship, 1959; Woodrow Wilson fellowship, 1960; Rackham fellowship, University of Michigan, 1969; Junior Humanist fellowship from National Endowment for the Humanities, 1974.

WRITINGS: (Editor) *Let's Go,* Harvard Student Agencies, 1963; (editor) *The Triumph of Style,* Houghton, 1969; *Milton's Pastoral Vision,* University of Chicago Press, 1971; (editor) *Mirrors: An Introduction to Literature,* Canfield Press, 1972. Contributor to *PMLA, English Literary Renaissance,* and *PQ.*

WORK IN PROGRESS: A study of English Puritan writers, including Milton and Bunyan.

*　*　*

KNOWLTON, Derrick 1921-

PERSONAL: Born April 4, 1921, in Hampshire, England; son of James (a master baker) and Laura Letitia (Snook) Knowlton; married Gladys May Shelley (a writer), May 2, 1945; children: Heather. *Education:* Attended school in Hampshire, England. *Religion:* Methodist. *Home and office:* 66 Stoke Common Rd., Eastleigh, Hampshire, England.

CAREER: Apprentice joiner in building industry in Hampshire, England, 1935-39; clerk in Hampshire, 1940-41, fireman, 1941-46, administrative assistant in local government, 1946-49; free-lance writer, 1969—. *Member:* Royal Society for the Protection of Birds, British Naturalists Association, Scottish Ornithologists Club, Hampshire Naturalists Trust, Southampton Natural History Society (chairman, 1965).

WRITINGS: The Naturalist in Central Southern England, David & Charles, 1973; *The Naturalist in Scotland,* David & Charles, 1974. Contributor to country life magazines, including *Hampshire* and *Scottish Gardener.*

WORK IN PROGRESS: The Naturalist in the Hebrides; Discovering Walks in the New Forest, for Shire Publications.

SIDELIGHTS: Knowlton writes that, "...experiencing frustration in local government career and believing physical and mental health coupled with job satisfaction more important than money [I] gave up pensionable post for full-time writing on countryside subjects." *Avocational interests:* Preaching and church work, observing nature, gardening, walking.

*　*　*

KOBER, Arthur 1900-1975

August 25, 1900—June 12, 1975; Ukranian-born American humorist, journalist, columnist, screenwriter, and playwright. Obituaries: *New York Times,* June 13, 1975; *Washington Post,* June 15, 1975; *Time,* June 23, 1975; *Newsweek,* June 23, 1975; *AB Bookman's Weekly,* August 4, 1975. (CA-13/14)

KOBRIN, Janet 1942-

PERSONAL: Surname is pronounced *Koe*-brin; born July 10, 1942, in Chicago, Ill.; daughter of Solomon (a sociologist) and Charlotte (a psychiatric social worker; maiden name, Adland) Kobrin. *Education:* Brandeis University, B.A., 1964; University of Chicago, M.S.T., 1965. *Home:* 5550 South Dorchester, Chicago, Ill. 60637. *Office:* Laboratory School, University of Chicago, 1362 East 59th St., Chicago, Ill. 60637.

CAREER: University of Chicago, Laboratory School, Chicago, Ill., elementary school teacher, 1965—. *Member:* Society of Children's Book Writers.

WRITINGS—For children, all with Margery Bernstein: *Coyote Goes Hunting for Fire,* Scribner, 1974; *Earthnamer,* Scribner, 1974; *How the Sun Made a Promise and Kept It,* Scribner, 1974.

WORK IN PROGRESS: Research on myths for more children's stories.

*　*　*

KOCHER, Eric 1912-

PERSONAL: Born June 29, 1912, in Trinidad, British West Indies; came to United States, 1919, naturalized, 1925; son of Paul William and Frieda Marie (Schwabe) Kocher; married Margaret Helburn, April 26, 1947; children: Eric Glenn, Terry, Christopher, Debra. *Education:* Princeton University, A.B., 1932; Harvard University, M.B.A., 1934; studied at Yale Drama School, 1940-41, and at New School for Social Research. *Home:* 102 Shore Rd., Douglaston, N.Y. 11363. *Office:* School of International Affairs, Columbia University, New York, N.Y.

CAREER: U.S. Government, Washington, D.C., assistant economist with Federal Housing Administration, 1934-36, associate social science analyst with Social Security Board, 1936-40; director of displaced persons camps in Austria, for United Nations Relief and Rehabilitation Administration, 1945-46; New England organizer for Citizens Committee on Displaced Persons, 1947; U.S. Department of State, labor attache, American Embassy in Brussels, 1947-52, member of staff, National War College, 1952-53, consul-general in Kuala Lumpur, Malaya, 1953-55, deputy director of Office of Southeast Asian Affairs, Washington, D.C., 1956-58, director, 1958-59, deputy chief of mission and counselor in American Embassy in Amman, Jordan, 1959-61, and in Belgrade, Yugoslavia, 1962-65; University of Texas, Austin, diplomat-in-residence, 1965-66; U.S. Department of State, Washington, D.C., chief of professional placement service, 1966-68, Job Corps representative, 1968-69; Columbia University, School of International Affairs, New York, N.Y., associate dean, 1969—. Playwright; member of Playwrights Unit, Actors Studio, 1971-73. *Military service:* U.S. Army, 1942-45; received Bronze Star. *Member:* Diplomatic and Consular Officers Retired, Princeton Alumni Association. *Awards, honors:* Awards for best original play from American Theatre Wing, 1958, for "Five Bags of Rice," and from Baton Rouge Little Theatre, 1959, for "The Voting Booth on Elephant Hill."

WRITINGS—Plays: *Apocalypse* (radio play), Expression Co., 1940; "Shadow of the Cathedral" (one-act), published in *Best One Act Plays of 1951-52,* edited by Margaret Mayorga, Dodd, 1952; "Karma" (drama with dance), published in *Best Short Plays of 1953-54,* edited by Mayorga, Dodd, 1954; "A Medal for Julien," published in *Best Short Plays of 1954-55,* edited by Mayorga, Dodd, 1955; "Five Bags of

Rice,'' produced in Cape Cod, Mass., at Dennis Playhouse, 1958; ''The Voting Booth on Elephant Hill,'' produced in Baton Rouge, La., at Baton Rouge Little Theatre, 1959; ''Night Wound,'' first produced Off-Off-Broadway at New York Theatre Ensemble, 1975. Also author of radio plays produced in the 1940's, ''Two Sisters'' and ''Dearly Beloved.''

* * *

KOFSKY, Frank (Joseph) 1935-

PERSONAL: Born November 18, 1935, in Los Angeles, Calif.; son of Philip (in sales) and Charlotte (a teacher; maiden name, Carash) Kofsky. *Education:* California Institute of Technology, B.S., 1957; graduate study at University of California, Berkeley, 1957-61; California State University, Los Angeles, M.A., 1964; University of Pittsburgh, Ph.D., 1973. *Politics:* ''Suspect.'' *Office:* Department of History, California State University, 6000 J St., Sacramento, Calif. 95819.

CAREER: Free-lance writer, journalist, and critic, 1959—; California State University, Long Beach, instructor in physics and astronomy, summer, 1963; free-lance photographer, 1966-68; Carnegie-Mellon University, Pittsburgh, Pa., instructor in history, 1966-67; University of Pittsburgh, Greensburg, Pa., instructor in history, 1966-67; Immaculate Heart College, Los Angeles, Calif., assistant professor of history and political science, 1968-69; California State University, Los Angeles, instructor in history and political science, 1968-69; California State University, Sacramento, associate professor of black history and music, 1969—. Producer-narrator for a series of programs on ''New Black Music,'' KPFA-KPFB (FM radio), Berkeley, Calif., 1973—. *Member:* Organization of American Historians, American Historical Association. *Awards, honors:* Research grant from Louis A. Rabinowitz Foundation, 1966, to write *Black Nationalism and the Revolution in Music.*

WRITINGS: (Contributor) Frances Kelley, editor, *Review One*, Modern Reader, 1965; (contributor) Jonathan Eisen, editor, *The Age of Rock*, Volume I, Random House, 1969; (contributor) Robert Levin and Paul Rivelli, editors, *Black Giants*, World Publishers, 1970; *Black Nationalism and the Revolution in Music*, Pathfinder, 1970, 2nd revised edition, 1975; *Lenny Bruce: The Comedian as Social Critic and Secular Moralist*, Monad Press, 1974; *Lying About War: From McKinley to Nixon*, Harper, in press. Contributor to music and history journals, including *Journal of Black Studies, Commonweal, Renaissance 2, Black Lines*, and *Monthly Review*, and to San Francisco *Chronicle*, and other papers. Associate editor of *Jazz*, 1967-69.

WORK IN PROGRESS: Researching the history of black art music, jazz, 1945-1962, to discover causes of the stylistic changes that took place in those years and perceptions of black musicians regarding such changes, particularly in Philadelphia and Detroit; *Black Music/White Business: Control of Media and Minds.*

* * *

KOHL, James (Virgil) 1942-

PERSONAL: Born March 6, 1942, in Duluth, Minn.; son of Virgil J. (an employment supervisor) and Maryon T. (a registered nurse) Kohl; married Mary Sharon Hunnicutt, August 28, 1965 (divorced June, 1973). *Education:* University of California, Berkeley, B.A., 1964; University of New Mexico, M.A., 1966, Ph.D., 1969. *Politics:* ''Anti-totalitarian.'' *Religion:* None. *Home address:* P.O. Box 297, Burlington, Mass. 01803.

CAREER: Massachusetts Institute of Technology, Cambridge, assistant professor of humanities, 1969-73; freelance journalist, 1973-74; lecturer at Cambridge Center for Adult Education, Cambridge, Mass., 1975—, and instructor in sociology, Newbury Junior College, Boston, Mass., 1975—. Conducted field research in Bolivia, 1967-72. *Member:* American Historical Association, American Anthropological Association, Conference on Latin American History. *Awards, honors:* Ford Foundation fellowships, 1966-69, 1971; National Endowment for the Humanities fellowship, 1970; Old Dominion fellowship from Massachusetts Institute of Technology, 1971-72.

WRITINGS: (With John Litt) *Urban Guerrilla Warfare in Latin America*, M.I.T. Press, 1974. Author of ''Political Repression in Latin America,'' a script for WGBH-Television, 1973. Contributor to *Nation, New Politics, Real Paper, Ramparts*, and *Boston Globe*.

WORK IN PROGRESS: Peasant and Revolution in Bolivia; a novel.

AVOCATIONAL INTERESTS: Archaeology, film, contemporary culture, tennis.

* * *

KOO, Anthony Y(ing) C(hang) 1918-

PERSONAL: Born November 22, 1918, in Shanghai, China; naturalized U.S. citizen; son of Vee Sing and Mayling (So) Koo; married Delia Z. F. Wei (a professor), June 6, 1943; children: Victoria M. (Mrs. Anthony Hitchins), Margery E. (Mrs. James Bussy), Emily D. *Education:* St. John's University (China), B.A. (with honors), 1940; University of Illinois, M.S., 1941; Harvard University, A.M., 1943, Ph.D., 1946. *Politics:* Independent. *Religion:* Episcopalian. *Residence:* Okemos, Mich. *Office:* Department of Economics, Michigan State University, East Lansing, Mich. 48824.

CAREER: Michigan State University, East Lansing, assistant professor, 1950-55, associate professor, 1955-58, professor of economics, 1958-64; University of Michigan, Ann Arbor, professor of economics, 1964-67; Michigan State University, professor of economics, 1967—. *Member:* American Economic Association, Econometric Society. *Awards, honors:* Social Science Research Council grants, summers, 1953, 1957, 1964, 1968; Ford Foundation fellowships, 1956-57, 1961-62; National Science Foundation research grants, 1965-67, 1967; senior fellow of East-West Center, Honolulu, Hawaii, 1973.

WRITINGS: (Contributor) Martin Shubik, editor, *Essays in Mathematical Economics in Honor of Oskar Morgenstern*, Princeton University Press, 1966; *Land Reform and Economic Development: A Case Study of Taiwan*, Praeger, 1968; (contributor) Marvin J. Sternberg, editor, *Agrarian Reform and Employment*, International Labor Office, 1971; (contributor) Paul K. T. Sih, editor, *Taiwan: From Prehistory to Modern Times*, St. John's University Press (Jamaica, N.Y.), 1973; (contributor) Willy Sellekaerts, editor, *International Trade and Finance: Essays in Honor of Jan Tinbergen*, Macmillan, in press. Contributor to economics journals in the United States and abroad.

* * *

KORENBAUM, Myrtle 1915-

PERSONAL: Born March 24, 1915, in Central Falls, R.I.; daughter of Bernard (a merchant) and Rose (Rosen) Korenbaum. *Education:* Brown University, A.B., 1953, M.A.,

1955; attended Sorbonne, University of Paris and Ecole Pratique des Hautes Etudes, 1955-57; University of Minnesota, Ph.D., 1966. *Home:* 531 Belmont Park N., Dayton, Ohio 45405. *Office:* Department of Sociology, Wright State University, Dayton, Ohio 45431.

CAREER: Allegheny College, Meadville, Pa., instructor in sociology, 1957-59; University of Wisconsin, River Falls, assistant professor, 1961-63; Northern Illinois University, DeKalb, assistant professor, 1964-65; Illinois Teachers College Chicago-North (now Northeastern Illinois University), Chicago, assistant professor, 1965-67; University of Bridgeport, Bridgeport, Conn., associate professor, 1967-70; Wright State University, Dayton, Ohio, associate professor of sociology, 1970—. *Member:* American Association for the Advancement of Science, American Sociological Association, North Central Sociological Society.

WRITINGS: (Translator with Philip Bosserman and editor) Georges Gurvitch, *The Spectrum of Social Time*, D. Reidel (Dordrecht, Netherlands), 1964. Editor of *The Annals of Phenomenological Society*, 1975-76.

* * *

KOTOWSKI, Joanne 1930-

PERSONAL: Born May 8, 1930, in Springfield, Mass.; daughter of Carl (an author and antiquarian) and Lois (Spengler) Jacobs; married Frank Kotowski, September 24, 1955 (divorced, 1973); children: Suzanne Cain, Jan Shay, Sandra, Kim, Elaine, Mary. *Education:* Attended Boston University, 1949, and Julius Hart School of Music, 1965, 1966. *Address:* Box 24, Suffield, Conn. 06078.

CAREER: Puppeteer and entertainer on WHNC-TV program, "Come Little Children," in Hartford, Conn., 1971; free-lance puppeteer and writer for WWLP-TV bilingual children's series, "Coqui," in Springfield, Mass., 1974—. *Member:* Puppeteers of America, Connecticut Puppetry Fellowship.

WRITINGS: Say It with Puppets, Pflaum, 1975.

WORK IN PROGRESS: A collection of stories in Spanish and English, *Coqui Stories*, completion expected in 1976.

AVOCATIONAL INTERESTS: Writing music and poetry, cross-country skiing, snowshoeing, hiking, biking, reading, storytelling.

* * *

KOUBOURLIS, Demetrius J(ohn) 1938-

PERSONAL: Born June 18, 1938, in Rion-Patras, Greece; naturalized U.S. citizen, 1972; son of John (a businessman) and Sophia (a businesswoman; maiden name, Iliopoulou) Koubourlis; married Olympia Karaiskou, December 28, 1957 (divorced December 28, 1967); married Toni Jean Hall, December 29, 1967; children: (first marriage) Sophia Carletona Margarita; (second marriage) Yana Divina Hilda, Koren Thalia Daphne. *Education:* California State University, Sacramento, B.A., 1963; University of Washington, Seattle, Ph.D., 1967; postdoctoral study at University of Illinois, summer, 1968, and at Leningrad State University, summer, 1970. *Home:* 210 North Van Buren, Moscow, Idaho 83843. *Office:* Department of Foreign Languages, University of Idaho, Moscow, Idaho 83843.

CAREER: Greek-American Cultural Institute, Patras, Greece, teacher of English, 1958-59; University of Colorado, Boulder, instructor in Slavic languages, 1966-67; Tulane University, New Orleans, La., assistant professor of Slavic languages and literatures, 1967-68; University of North Carolina, Chapel Hill, assistant professor of Slavic languages and literatures, 1968-71; University of Idaho, Moscow, assistant professor, 1971-73, associate professor of foreign languages and literatures, 1973—.

MEMBER: International Linguistic Association, American Association for the Advancement of Slavic Studies, American Association of Teachers of Slavic and East European Languages (president of Carolinas chapter, 1969-70, 1970-71), American Institute for Foreign Studies, Association for Computational Linguistics, Association for Computing Machinery, Association for Literary and Linguistic Computing, Modern Language Association of America, Southeastern Conference on Linguistics, Western Slavic Association. *Awards, honors:* International Research and Exchanges Board summer exchange participant at Moscow State University, 1973, grantee, 1974, for first United States-Union of Soviet Socialist Republics cooperative concording project; scholarship for Third International Institute on Mathematical and Computational Linguistics at International Business Machines Research Center, Pisa, Italy, 1974.

WRITINGS: Soviet Academy Grammar: Phonology and Morphology, A Computer Index, Idaho Research Foundation, University of Idaho, 1972; *A Concordance to the Poems of Osip Mandelstam*, Cornell University Press, 1974; (editor and contributor) *Topics in Slavic Phonology*, Slavica, 1974; (contributor) L. Mitchell, editor, *Computers in the Humanities*, University of Edinburgh Press, 1974; (with Kenneth E. Naylor) *Studies in Slavic Morphology*, Slavica, in press. Contributor to *Papers in Linguistics* and *Computers and the Humanities*. Editor of "Language Series" at Idaho Research Foundation, 1972—; member of editorial board of *Folia Slavica*, 1975—.

WORK IN PROGRESS: A Concordance to the Poems of Alexander Blok; with Georgia Shurr, *A Concordance to 'Les Tapisseries'*; *A Concordance to the Poetry of Nikolai Gumilev*; *Russian Motivational Reader*; with V. P. Grigor'ev, *A Concordance to the Works of V. Khlebnikov*; with G. Bessette, *A Concordance to the Poems of Corippus*; *Computerrationed Stress in Russian Language Materials*.

* * *

KOUPERNIK, Cyrille 1917-

PERSONAL: Born March 13, 1917, in Petrograd, Russia; son of Nahum B. Glasberg (a lawyer) and Anna L. Koupernik (a physician); married Micheline Phankim, September 9, 1961 (divorced July, 1973). *Education:* Paris Medical School, M.D., 1948. *Politics:* "Mild left." *Religion:* None. *Home:* Ave. Marceau 74, Paris, France 75008. *Office: Le Concours Medical*, 37 rue de Bellefond, Paris 75441, France 09.

CAREER: Psychiatrist in private practice in Paris, France, 1950—; American Hospital in Paris, Neuilly, France, member of active staff, 1970—. *Military service:* French Army, 1939-40, 1944-45; became lieutenant. *Member:* International Association for Child Psychiatry (vice-president, 1966-70), French Society for Child Psychiatry (secretary general, 1960-72), Evolution Psychiatrique.

WRITINGS: (Editor) *Psychiatrie sociale de l'enfant* (title means "Social Psychiatry of the Child"), International Children's Centre (Paris), 1951; *Developpement psychomotour du nourrisson* (title means "Psycho-motor Development of the Infant"), Presses Universitaires de France,

1954; *L'Equilibre mental* (title means "The Balance of the Mind"), A. Fayard, 1959, 2nd edition, 1968; *Les Medications du psychisme* (title means "Biological and Chemical Therapies of Mental Illnesses"), Hachette (Paris), 1964; (with Robert Dailly) *Developpement neuro-psychique du nourrisson* (title means "Neurological and Psychological Development of the Infant"), Presses Universitaires de France, 1968, 3rd edition, 1975; *Regards sur la psychiatrie* (title means "Outlooks upon Psychiatry"), L'Expansion Scientifique Francaise, 1970; (editor with E. J. Anthony) *The Child in His Family*, Wiley-Interscience, Volume I, 1970, Volume II, 1973, Volume III, 1974; (with F. H. Stone) *Child Psychiatry*, Churchill & Livingstone, 1975. Editor-in-chief and columnist, *Le Concours Medical*, 1965—.

WORK IN PROGRESS: Psychologie Medicale.

SIDELIGHTS: Koupernik is competent in French, Russian, and English. *Avocational interests:* Literature and history.

* * *

KOUSSER, J(oseph) Morgan 1943-

PERSONAL: Born October 7, 1943, in Lewisburg, Tenn.; son of Joseph Maximillian and Alice (a teacher and television coordinator; maiden name, Morgan) Kousser; married Sally Ward, June 1, 1968; children: Rachel Meredith, Thaddeus Benjamin. *Education:* Princeton University, A.B. (summa cum laude), 1965; Yale University, M.Phil., 1968, Ph.D., 1971. *Politics:* "Left." *Religion:* "Puritan-Atheist." *Home:* 1320 Daveric Dr., Pasadena, Calif. 91107. *Office:* Department of Humanities and Social Sciences, California Institute of Technology, Pasadena, Calif. 91125.

CAREER: California Institute of Technology, Pasadena, instructor, 1969-71, assistant professor, 1971-74, associate professor of history, 1974—. *Member:* American Historical Association, Organization of American Historians, Social Science History Association, ACT, F.D.R. Democratic Club (Pasadena; past president), Phi Beta Kappa. *Awards, honors:* Woodrow Wilson fellowship, 1965-66; National Endowment for the Humanities research grant, 1974-75.

WRITINGS: The Shaping of Southern Politics, Yale University Press, 1974. Contributor to *Encyclopedia of Southern History*, and to *Journal of Interdisciplinary History, Political Science Quarterly, Mississippi Quarterly, Journal of the American Statistical Association, Arkansas Historical Quarterly*, and other journals.

WORK IN PROGRESS: The Politics of Education in the South, 1880-1910.

* * *

KOWET, Don 1937-
(Frank Gell)

PERSONAL: Born March 29, 1937, in Boston, Mass.; son of Jack (an executive) and Anne (Saltzman) Kowet; married Begona Reparaz, October 27, 1962; children: Jack. *Education:* Brandeis University, B.A., 1961; London School of Economics and Political Science, M.A., 1964. *Home address:* Box 164A, Zena Rd., Kingston, N.Y. 12401. *Agent:* Ellen Levine, Curtis Brown Ltd., 60 East 56th St., New York, N.Y. 10022

CAREER: Has worked as a social worker in New York, N.Y. and as an English teacher; *Sport* (magazine), New York, N.Y., managing editor, 1970-75.

WRITINGS: (Under pseudonym Frank Gell) *The Black Badge: Confessions of a Case Worker*, Harper, 1969; *Golden Toes* (nonfiction), St. Martin's, 1973; *Vida Blue: Coming Up Again*, Putnam, 1974. Author of "The Mag Bag," an instructional kit on reading magazines, Random House, 1974. Contributor to magazines, including *Today's Health* and *Sport*.

* * *

KOYAMA, Kosuke 1929-

PERSONAL: Born December 10, 1929, in Tokyo, Japan; son of Zentaro and Tama Koyama; married Lois Eleanor Rozendaal, November 22, 1958; children: James, Elizabeth, Mark. *Education:* Attended Tokyo Union Theological Seminary, 1946-52; Drew University, B.D., 1954; Princeton Theological Seminary, Th.M., 1955, Ph.D., 1959. *Home:* 108 Evans St., Dunedin, New Zealand. *Office:* Department of Religion, University of Otago, Box 56, Dunedin, New Zealand.

CAREER: Ordained minister of United Church of Christ in Japan, 1952; Thailand Theological Seminary, Chiengmai, Thailand, lecturer in systematic theology and Christian ethics, 1960-68; South East Asia Graduate School of Theology, Singapore, dean, 1968-74; University of Otago, Dunedin, New Zealand, senior lecturer in phenomenology of religion, 1974—. Executive director, Association of Theological Schools in South East Asia, 1968-74; member of Faith and Order Commission of World Council of Churches, 1970—.

WRITINGS: Water Buffalo Theology, S.C.M. Press, 1974; *Theology in Contact*, Christian Literature Society of India, 1974. Author of booklets on theology, in Thai, 1965-68. Editor of *South East Asia Journal of Theology*, 1968-74.

BIOGRAPHICAL/CRITICAL SOURCES: Gerald H. Anderson and others, *The Future of the Christian World*, Eerdmans, 1971.

* * *

KOZLENKO, William 1917-

PERSONAL: Born October 1, 1917, in Philadelphia, Pa.; son of Jacob and Sarah (Feinstein) Kozlenko; married Leonore Moore, 1939; children: Richard. *Education:* Attended University of Pennsylvania. *Home and office:* 1236 South Camden Drive, Los Angeles, Calif. 90035. *Agent:* Mike Zimring, William Morris Agency, 151 El Camino Drive, Beverly Hills, Calif. 90212.

CAREER: Founder and editor, *One-Act Play Magazine*, 1937-40; program consultant to Diamond Jubilee of Light for General Electric, 1941; Metro-Goldwyn-Mayer, Culver City, Calif., director of programming, 1957; Screen Gems, Hollywood, Calif., producer, 1958; Columbia Pictures Corp., Hollywood, Calif., producer, 1958; Southern Illinois University, Carbondale, professor of drama, 1971-73; University of Southern California, Los Angeles, professor of drama, 1974—. Member of board of directors, Beverly Hills Symphony Orchestra, 1964. *Member:* Writers Guild of America, West (charter member). *Awards, honors: Players Magazine* Thespian Award for best one-act play, 1941, for "Jacob Comes Home."

WRITINGS: (Editor) *Contemporary One-Act Plays*, Scribner, 1938; (editor) *The One-Act Play Today*, Harcourt, 1938; (editor) *The Best Short Plays of the Social Theatre*, Random House, 1939; (editor) *One Hundred*

Non-Royalty One Act Plays, Greenberg, 1940; (editor) *100 Non-Royalty Radio Plays*, Greenberg, 1941; (editor) *American Scenes*, John Day, 1941; (editor with Ernest Hemingway) *Men at War*, Crown, 1942; *25 Non-Royalty One Act American Comedies*, Greenberg, 1943; (editor) *Men & Women* (short stories), Lion Books, 1953; (editor) *A Treasury of Non-Royalty One Act Plays*, Doubleday, 1959; (editor) *Acts of Violence* (short stories), Pyramid Publications, 1959; *Disputed Plays of William Shakespeare*, Hawthorn, 1974; (editor with Charles Leonard) Michael Chekhov, *To the Director and Playwright*, Harper, 1975.

Plays: "This Earth Is Ours," first produced in New York, N.Y., by Allied Theatre Group, January 15, 1937; "The Devil Is a Good Man," first produced on Off-Broadway at Provincetown Playhouse, 1939; "Trumpets of Wrath," first produced on Broadway at Belasco Theatre, 1940; "The Street Attends a Funeral," first produced in Pasadena, Calif. at Pasadena Playhouse, 1940; "Jacob Comes Home," first produced in 1940; "Not for Glory," first produced in Boston, Mass., 1941. Also author of "A Fearful Madness."

Screenplays: "Holiday in Mexico," 1945; "Wassaja," 1974.

Also author of radio play, "My Mothers Never Weep," produced on N.B.C., 1944, and television scripts for "Pulitzer Prize Playhouse," "Lux Video Theatre," "Climax," "Playhouse 90," "Front Row Center," "Philco Playhouse," "Studio One," "Madison Productions," "Repertoire Workshop," and "Alcoa House." Work included in anthology, *Free World Theatre*, edited by Arch Oboler and Stephen Longstreet, Random House, 1944.

WORK IN PROGRESS: "Journey to No End," a screenplay.

BIOGRAPHICAL/CRITICAL SOURCES: Kenneth Rowe, *Write That Play*, Funk, 1939; John Gassner, *Masters of Drama*, Random House, 1940; *Enciclopedia dello Spettacolo*, La Maschere (Rome), 1956; Gassner, *Dramatic Soundings*, Crown, 1968.

* * *

KRAFT, Hy(man Solomon) 1899-1975

April 30, 1899—July 29, 1975; American journalist, playwright, screenplay writer, author. Obituaries: *New York Times*, July 30, 1975; *Washington Post*, July 31, 1975. (CA-41/44)

* * *

KRANZLER, George G(ershon) 1916-
(Jacob Isaacs, Gershon Kranzler)

PERSONAL: Born January 27, 1916, in Stuttgart, Germany; son of Meyer L. and Hanna (Adler) Kranzler; married Trude Neuman, December 4, 1944; children: Harvey, Chani, Elliot M., Shari. *Education*: Columbia Univeristy, M.A., 1943, Ph.D., 1954; University of Wuerzburg, Ph.D., 1948. *Religion*: Jewish. *Home*: 3509 Devonshire Dr., Baltimore, Md. 21214.

CAREER: High school principal in New York, N.Y., and Baltimore, Md., 1945-65; Towson State College, Baltimore, Md., professor of sociology, 1966—. Part-time professor at Johns Hopkins University, Evening College, 1967—. *Member*: American Sociological Association, National Education Association, National Association of Secondary-School Principals, Society of Education, American Association of University Professors. *Awards, honors*: Seltzer-Brodsky Prize, 1967, for *The Face of Faith*.

WRITINGS: *Williamsburg, U.S.A.*, Volume I: *Williamsburg, a Jewish Community in Transition: A Study of the Factors and Patterns of Change in the Organization and Structure of a Community in Transition*, Feldheim, 1961, Volume II: *The Face of Faith*, Baltimore Hebrew College Press, 1972; *The Broken Bracelet: A Historical Novel for Young Jews*, Merkos L'Inyonei Chinuch, 1967; *Yoshko the Dumbbell and Other Stories*, Feldheim, 1969; *The Secret Code and Other Stories for Boys*, Merkos L'Inyonei Chinuch, 1971; *Seder in Herlin and Other Stories for Girls*, Merkos L'Inyonei Chinuch, 1971.

Under name Gershon Kranzler: (Compiler) *Jewish Youth Companion: Stories, Games, and Adages for the Jewish Year*, Merkos L'Inyonei Chinuch, 1957; *Galuth Melodies: Stories for Young and Old*, three volumes, Merkos L'-Inyonei Chinuch, 1957; (with Nissan Mindel) *Who, What, When, Where: Interesting Facts from Jewish History, Law, and Lore*, Merkos L'Inyonei Chinuch, 1959; *The Golden Shoes and Other Stories*, Feldheim, 1960.

Also author, under pseudonym Jacob Isaacs, of *Our People*, four volumes, published by Merkos L'Inyonei Chinuch.

WORK IN PROGRESS: Volume III of *Williamsburg, U.S.A.*, *The Spirit of a Jewish Community*; a textbook, *The Sociology of the Contemporary Jewish Community*; Volume V of *Our People*.

* * *

KRANZLER, Gershon
See KRANZLER, George G(ershon)

* * *

KREH, Bernard 1925-

PERSONAL: Born February 26, 1925, in Frederick, Md.; son of Theodore Christian and Helen May (Purdy) Kreh; married Evelyn Louise Mask, July 13, 1947; children: Victoria Ann Robinson, Larry Victor. *Education*: Attended public schools in Frederick, Maryland. *Politics*: Republican. *Home*: 210 Wickersham Way, Cockeysville, Md. 21030. *Office*: Baltimore Sun Papers, Baltimore, Md. 21203.

CAREER: Outdoor editor for *Morning Sun*, Baltimore, Md. *Military service*: Served during World War II. *Member*: Outdoor Writers of America, Federation of Fly Fisherman and Salt Water Fly Rodders of America (member of advisory board), Mason-Dixon Outdoor Writers. *Awards, honors*: Inducted into Fishing Hall of Fame.

WRITINGS: *Fly Casting with Lefty Kreh*, Lippincott, 1974; *Fly Fishing in Salt Water*, Crown, 1974. Also author, with Mark Sosin, of *Practical Fishing Knots*, published by Crown. Contributor of regular column to *Fishing World*. Associate editor of *Florida Sportsman*.

* * *

KREMEN, Bennett 1936-

PERSONAL: Born August 12, 1936, in Chicago, Ill.; son of Boris (a merchant) and Rera (Appelbaum) Kremen; married Viana Muller, July 7, 1962 (divorced, 1967); married Jeanette Arnone (an actress). *Education*: Antioch College, B.A., 1960; New School for Social Research, M.A., 1962. *Politics*: "Free thinker." *Religion*: "Free thinker." *Home and office*: 151 East 26th St., New York, N.Y. 10010. *Agent*: Owen Laster, William Morris Agency, 1350 Avenue of the Americas, New York, N.Y. 10019.

CAREER: Holiday (magazine), New York, N.Y., associate editor, 1966-68; Friends World College, Huntington, N.Y., associate professor, 1968-69; Odessey House, New York, N.Y., psychologist, 1969-70; U.S. Steel Co., Chicago, Ill., laborer, 1970—. Member: Authors League of America. Awards, honors: Breadloaf Writers Conference scholarship.

WRITINGS: Dateline: America, Dial, 1974. Work is represented in anthologies. Contributor to Nation, Dissent, Village Voice, New York Times and other periodicals.

WORK IN PROGRESS: A novel.

*   *   *

KRENEK, Ernst 1900-

PERSONAL: Born August 23, 1900, in Vienna, Austria; came to United States, 1937; naturalized U.S. citizen, 1945; son of Ernst (an army officer) and Emanuela (Cizek) Krenek; married Anna Mahler, 1924 (divorced, 1925); married Berta Hermann, 1927 (divorced, 1949); married Gladys Nordenstrom (a composer), August 8, 1950. Education: Attended Vienna Academy of Music, 1916-21, University of Vienna, 1919-21, and Berlin Academy of Music, 1921-23. Home: 623 Chino Canyon Rd., Palm Springs, Calif. 92262.

CAREER: State Opera House, Kassel, Germany, adviser, 1925-27; Malkin Conservatory, Boston, Mass., guest lecturer, 1937; Vassar College, Poughkeepsie, N.Y., professor of music, 1939-42; Hamline University, St. Paul, Minn., professor of music and dean of School of Fine Arts, 1942-47; composer. Visiting professor at University of Michigan, 1939, 1940, University of Wisconsin, 1941, 1942, 1943, University of New Mexico, 1947-49, 1951, and University of Hawaii; guest lecturer at Chicago Music College, 1949, Brandeis University, 1965, and Peabody Institute, 1967. Military service: Austrian Army, 1918. Member: International Society for Contemporary Music (honorary member), National Institute of Arts and Letters, P.E.N. (Austria), Austrian Senate for Arts, German Society for Performing Rights, Berlin Academy of Arts, Vienna Academy of Music (honorary member), Salzburg Academy of Music (honorary member), Graz Academy of Music (honorary member), Stuttgart Academy of Music (honorary senator), Hamburg Opera House (honorary member). Awards, honors: D.Mus. from Hamline University, 1947, Chapman College, 1952, University of New Mexico, 1965; Cross of Merit from Republic of Austria, 1960, from Federal Republic of Germany, 1965; Gold Medal from City of Vienna, 1960, from City of Hamburg, 1966; named honorary citizen of Minnesota, 1965; honorary fellow of University of California, San Diego, 1967; honorary ring, City of Vienna, 1970.

WRITINGS: Ueber neue Musik, Ringbuchhandlung (Vienna), 1937, translation by Barthold Fles published as Music Here and Now, Norton, 1939, reprinted, Atheneum, 1967; Studies in Counterpoint (Twelve-Tone), G. Schirmer, 1940; (editor) Hamline Studies in Musicology, Hamline University, Volume I, 1945, Volume II, 1947; Selbstdarstellung (title means "Self-Analysis"), Atlantis (Zurich), 1948; Musik im goldenen Westen (title means "Music in the Golden West"), Hollinek (Vienna), 1949; Johannes Ockeghem, Sheed, 1953; De rebus prius factis (title means "About Things Previously Made"), W. Hansen (Copenhagen), 1956; Tonal Counterpoint, Boosey & Hawkes, 1958; Zur Sprache gebracht (title means "Given Word"), Langen-Mueller (Munich), 1958; Modal Counterpoint, Boosey & Hawkes, 1959; Gedanken unterwegs (title means "Thoughts along the Way"), Langen-Mueller, 1959; Prosa, Dramen, Verse, Langen-Mueller, 1965; Exploring Music, Calder & Boyars, 1966; Horizons Circled, University of California Press, 1974; Briefwechsel T. W. Adorno und Ernst Kernek (title means "The Letters of T. W. Adorno and Ernst Krenek"), Suhrkamp (Frankfurt), 1974.

Operas: "Die Zwingburg" (title means "The Tyrant's Castle"), produced in Berlin, 1924; "Der Sprung uber den Schalten" (title means "Leap Over the Shadow"), first produced in Frankfurt, 1924; "Orpheus and Eurydike," first produced in Kassel, 1926; "Jonny Spielt auf" (title means "Jonny Strikes Up the Band"), first produced in Leipzig, 1927; "Der Diktator" (title means "The Dictator"), produced in Wiesbaden, 1928; "Das Geheime Koenigreich" (title means "The Secret Kingdom"), produced in Wiesbaden, 1928; "Schwergewicht" (title means "Heavyweight"), produced in Wiesbaden, 1928; "Leben des Orest" (title means "Life of Orestes"), produced in Leipzig, 1930; "Karl V," first produced in Prague, 1938; "Dark Waters" (translation of "Dunkle Wasser"), produced in Los Angeles, 1950; "Pallas Athene weint" (title means "Pallas Athene Weeps"), produced in Hamburg, 1955; "The Bell Tower" (translation of "Der Glockenturm"), produced in Urbana, Ill., 1957; "What Price Confidence?" (translation of "Vertrauenssache"), produced in Saarbruecken, 1962; "Ausgerechnet und verspielt" (title means "Computed and Confounded"), produced in Vienna, 1962; "Der goldene Bock" (title means "The Golden Ram"), produced in Hamburg, 1964; "Der Zauberspiegel" (title means "The Magic Mirror"), produced in Munich, 1966; "Sarda Kai," produced in Hamburg, 1970.

*   *   *

KRIENSKY, Morris (Edward) 1917-

PERSONAL: Surname is pronounced Kree-en-ski; born July 27, 1917, in Glascow, Scotland; came to United States in 1922, naturalized in 1927; son of Barney (a cabinet maker) and Jeannie (Kanopate) Kriensky; married Bertha Bochner, 1946 (divorced, 1951); married Beatriz Tapia, 1951 (divorced, 1955); children: (first marriage) Reva Susan. Education: Attended Boston Museum of Fine Arts, 1936-40, Art Students League of New York, 1948-49, and Escuela de Technica Mexicana, 1950-51. Politics: Independent (Democratic). Home and office: 463 West St., New York, N.Y. 10014.

CAREER: Poet and painter; exhibited one-man shows at Knoedler Gallery, Chicago Art Institute, Frick Art Library, U.S. White House, University of Connecticut, Wilmington Society of Fine Arts, Hackley Art Gallery, Currier Gallery of Art, Dartmouth College, Indiana University of Fine Arts, George School, George Walter Vincent Smith Art Gallery, Carus Gallery, Revel Gallery, Castagno Gallery, Shreve, Crump & Low, and other public galleries in Mexico and China; paintings exhibited in Pushkin Museum, Alfred Khouri Memorial Collection, and Lincoln Ellsworth Collection; owner and painter of "Cards for All Seasons" (peace cards). Military service: U.S. Army Air Forces, 1941-45; became technical sergeant; served in China; received Bronze Star and President's Medal. Member: National Society of Literature and the Arts, International Platform Association, American Association of Retired Persons, Flying Tigers Association, Common Cause, and museum societies. Awards, honors: Many first prizes for painting in the United States, Mexico, and China, including first prize from Institute of Mexican and North American Cultural Relations, 1950.

WRITINGS: The Way is Peace ... The Road Is Love (drawings, paintings, and poems), C. R. Gibson, 1973; *Visions of Art and Life* (paintings and poems), C. R. Gibson, 1976.

* * *

KROEBER, Karl 1926-

PERSONAL: Born November 24, 1926, in Oakland, Calif.; son of Alfred L. (a teacher) and Theodora (a writer; maiden name, Kracaw) Kroeber; married Jean Taylor, March 21, 1953; children: Paul, Arthur, Katharine. *Education:* University of California, Berkeley, B.A., 1947; Columbia University, M.A., 1951, Ph.D., 1956. *Office:* Department of English and Comparative Literature, Columbia University, New York, N.Y. 10027.

CAREER: University of Wisconsin, Madison, assistant professor, 1956-61, associate professor, 1961-63, professor of English, 1963-70, associate dean of Graduate School, 1963-65; Columbia University, New York, N.Y., professor of English and comparative literature, 1970—, head of department, 1973—. *Military service:* U.S. Navy, 1944-46. *Member:* International Association of University Professors of English, Modern Language Association of America, Modern Humanities Research Association.

WRITINGS: Romantic Narrative Art, University of Wisconsin Press, 1960; *The Artifice of Reality*, University of Wisconsin Press, 1964; (with John L. Lyons) *Studying Poetry*, Harper, 1965; *Styles of Fictional Structure*, Princeton University Press, 1970; *Romantic Landscape Visions*, University of Wisconsin Press, 1974.

BIOGRAPHICAL/CRITICAL SOURCES: Wordsworth Circle, Volume 4, number 3, summer, 1973.

* * *

KROOSS, Herman E. 1912-1975

July 12, 1912—March 21, 1975; American educator, author of books on economics. Obituaries: *New York Times*, March 22, 1975; *AB Bookman's Weekly*, April 7, 1975. (*CA*-17/18)

* * *

KRUEGER, Robert B(lair) 1928-

PERSONAL: Born December 9, 1928, in Minot, N.D.; son of Paul Otto and Lila (Morse) Krueger; married Virginia Ruth Carmichael, June 3, 1956; children: Lisa, Paula Leah, Robert Blair. *Education:* University of Kansas, A.B., 1949; University of Michigan, J.D., 1952; University of Southern California, graduate study, 1960-65. *Politics:* Republican. *Home:* 501 Vallombrose Dr., Pasadena, Calif. 91107. *Office:* Nossaman, Waters, Krueger, Marsh & Riordan, 445 South Figueroa St., Los Angeles, Calif. 90017.

CAREER: Admitted to Kansas bar, 1952, California bar, 1955; O'Melveny & Myers, Los Angeles, Calif., associate, 1955-59; Blair & Krueger, Los Angeles, Calif., partner, 1959-61; Nossaman, Waters, Krueger, Marsh & Riordan, Los Angeles, Calif., partner, 1961—, senior partner in natural resources section, 1961—. Adjunct professor at University of Southern California, 1973-74; lecturer at colleges and universities. Member of California Governor's Advisory Commission on Ocean Resources, 1966-68, chairman, 1970-73; member of California Advisory Commission on Marine and Coastal Resources, 1968-73; member of National Security Council's Advisory Committee on the Law of the Sea, 1972—; member of U.S. Delegation to U.N.

Seabeds Committee, 1973. Member of committee of visitors of University of Michigan's School of Law, 1967-71; member of board of councillors of University of Southern California's Law Center, 1972—. *Military service:* U.S. Marine Corps Reserve, 1952-54; became first lieutenant.

MEMBER: International Bar Association, International Law Association, World Association of Lawyers, Inter-American Bar Association, American Bar Association, American Bar Foundation (fellow), American Society for International Law, British Institute for International and Comparative Law, Los Angeles County Bar Association, California Club, University Club, Chancery Club, Town Hall of Los Angeles, Valley Hunt Club (Pasadena), Tau Kappa Epsilon, Phi Alpha Theta.

WRITINGS: The Outer Continental Shelf Lands of the United States, Public Land Law Review Commission, 1968; *The United States and International Oil*, Praeger, 1975. Contributor to law journals and to *Natural Resources Journal*. Assistant editor of *Michigan Law Review*, 1951-52; editor of *Los Angeles Bar Bulletin*, 1961-63; member of editorial board of *California State Bar Journal*, 1963-66, 1969-74.

WORK IN PROGRESS: Research on the establishment of multilateral negotiations between oil producing and oil consuming countries, analyzing conditions which will need to be present if progress is to occur; research on the law of the sea.

* * *

KUBO, Sakae 1926-

PERSONAL: Born May 8, 1926, in Honolulu, Hawaii; son of Kumashichi (a farmer) and Teki (Shimoda) Kubo; married Hatsumi Sakai (a teacher), June 27, 1948; children: Wesley, Charlene, Calvin. *Education:* Andrews University, B.A., 1947, M.A., 1954, B.D., 1955; University of Chicago, Ph.D., 1964; Western Michigan University, M.L.S., 1968. *Politics:* Independent. *Religion:* Seventh-Day Adventist. *Home address:* Box 148, University Station, Berrien Springs, Mich. 49104. *Office:* James White Library, Andrews University, Berrien Springs, Mich. 49104.

CAREER: English teacher at Seventh-day Adventist school in Honolulu, Hawaii, 1947-48; minister of Seventh-day Adventist churches in Hawaii, 1948-50, and California, 1950-52; Andrews University, Berrien Springs, Mich., instructor in Biblical languages, 1955-57, assistant professor, 1957-65, associate professor, 1965-68, professor of New Testament, 1968—, seminary librarian, 1968—. *Member:* Society of Biblical Literature, American Theological Library Association, Chicago Society of Biblical Research, Chicago Area Theological Librarians.

WRITINGS: P[72] *and Codex Vaticanus*, University of Utah Press, 1965; (editor with Jim Walters and Charles Sandefur) *Theological Bibliography*, Seminary Student Forum, Andrews University, 1970; *A Reader's Greek-English Lexicon of the New Testament*, Andrews University Press, 1971; *Calculated Goodness?*, Southern Publishing, 1974; (with Walter Specht) *So Many Versions?*, Zondervan, 1975. Contributor to theology journals. Book review editor of *Andrews University Seminary Studies*.

WORK IN PROGRESS: Acquitted: Message from the Cross, for Pacific Press; *Your Summons to Court*, Southern Publishing; *Meaning of the Sabbath*, Review & Herald.

KUCHAREK, Casimir (Anthony) 1928-

PERSONAL: Born March 1, 1928, in Elmira, Mich.; son of John A. (a farmer) and Mary (Skowronski) Kucharek. *Education:* Attended Maryknoll College, 1947-49; St. Mary's of the Lake Seminary, Norwalk, Conn., B.A., 1951; graduate study at St. Joseph's Seminary, Edmonton, Alberta, 1951-53, and Propaganda Fide University, 1953-56. *Home address:* P.O. Box 23, Rama, Saskatchewan S0A 3H0, Canada. *Office:* Church of Saints Peter and Paul, Rama, Saskatchewan S0A 3H0, Canada.

CAREER: Ordained Byzantine Ukrainian Catholic priest, 1956; Ukrainian Catholic Matrimonial Court, Rama, Saskatchewan, judge, 1969—. Member of academic advisory council of Fordham University's John XXIII Institute for Eastern Christian Studies. *Member:* Ukrainian Catholic Theological Society of Canada (secretary, 1968—).

WRITINGS: The Byzantine-Slav Liturgy of St. John Chrysostom, Alleluia Press, 1971; *To Settle Your Conscience*, Our Sunday Visitor Press, 1974; *Byzantine Sacramental Mysteries*, Alleluia Press, 1975. Contributor to *Holos Khrysta Chelovikoljubtsia, Svitlo, Our Family*, and *Holos Spasyletelja.*

WORK IN PROGRESS: Byzantine Mysteries of Initiation.

SIDELIGHTS: Kucharek speaks Polish, Ukrainian, Russian, Slovak, Latin, classical Greek, Spanish, Italian, French, and Old Slavonic.

* * *

KUHLMAN, Kathryn

PERSONAL: Born in Concordia, Mo.; daughter of Joe and Emma (Walkenhorst) Kuhlman. *Residence:* Pittsburgh, Pa. *Address:* c/o Bethany Fellowship, Inc., 6820 Auto Club Rd., Minneapolis, Minn. 55438.

CAREER: Kathryn Kuhlman Foundation (religious organization), Pittsburgh, Pa., and Los Angeles, Calif., president, 1954—. Originator of daily radio broadcasts throughout the United States and overseas, and of weekly television shows broadcast in United States and Canada, 1966—; twenty-two missions have been established by Kathryn Kuhlman Foundation overseas, including missions in Nicaragua, India, Hong Kong, Republic of South Africa, and Viet Nam. Has held public services in United States, and in Sweden and Israel. Honorary Kentucky Colonel. *Awards, honors:* Medal of Honor from Vietnamese military, 1970; D.H.L. from Oral Roberts University, 1972; presented with keys to cities of Pittsburgh and Los Angeles.

WRITINGS: I Believe in Miracles, Prentice-Hall, 1962; (compiler) *God Can Do It Again*, Prentice-Hall, 1969; *Captain LeVrier Believes in Miracles*, Bethany Fellowship, 1973; *Nothing Is Impossible with God*, Prentice-Hall, 1974; *10,000 Miles for a Miracle*, Bethany Fellowship, 1974; *How Big Is God?* (juvenile), Bethany Fellowship, 1974; *Standing Tall*, Bethany Fellowship, 1975.

SIDELIGHTS: Kathryn Kuhlman's works have been translated into over a dozen languages, including Korean and Vietnamese; *I Believe In Miracles* is available in Braille.

* * *

KUNTZLEMAN, Charles T(homas) 1940-

PERSONAL: Born November 4, 1940, in Bloomsburg, Pa.; son of Walter Allen (a minister) and Phyllis (Lehman) Kuntzleman; married Carol Lee Ermhardt, June 9, 1962 (died September, 1973); married second wife, Beth Ann McDonald (a professor of health and physical education), October 27, 1974; children: Deborah Ann, John Walter, Thomas Scott, Rebecca Ann, Lisa Kristen (stepdaughter). *Education:* Muhlenberg College, A.B., 1962; Temple University, M.Ed., 1965, currently Ed.D. candidate. *Politics:* Independent. *Religion:* Lutheran. *Home and office:* 178 East Harmony, Spring Arbor, Mich. 49238.

CAREER: Muhlenberg College, Allentown, Pa., instructor, 1962-66, assistant professor of physical education, 1966-67, assistant football and track coach, 1962-67, head lacrosse and wrestling coach, 1962-67; New Life Boy's Ranch, Harleysville, Pa., principal, and teacher of health and physical education, 1967-68; Lehigh County Community College, Schnecksville, Pa., assistant professor of physical education, and lecturer in anatomy and physiology, 1968-70; Rodale Press, Emmaus, Pa., consultant, 1970-75; Fitness Finders Program, Spring Arbor, Mich., owner, and national program director, 1975—. Exercise physiologist, La Crest Aerobic Clinic, 1974-75. Director, Good Shepherd Rehabilitation Hospital Human Performance Laboratory, 1970-74; national program director, YMCA-Fitness Finders, 1971—; conductor of physical fitness workshops in the United States, Canada, and Sweden, 1970—. Co-host of television show "Fun and Fitness," 1973—. *Member:* American Association for Health, Physical Education and Recreation, Society for Public Health Education, American College of Sports Medicine, National College Physical Education Association, Pennsylvania Association for Health, Physical Education and Recreation. *Awards, honors:* Jaycees-Metropolitan Life Insurance Physical Fitness Leadership Award for Pennsylvania, 1969.

WRITINGS: (Editor) *Physical Fitness Encyclopedia*, Rodale Press, 1970; *Activetics: Fitness Finders Way to Weight Control*, Peter H. Wyden, 1975. Also author of physical fitness manuals. Recorded "Fitness Finders Home Exercise Program" (with manual), and "Sounds of Fitness," Fitness Finders, Inc. Contributor of more than twenty-five articles to journals in his field, including *Fitness for Living, Organic Gardening and Farming, Pennsylvania Journal of Health and Physical Education*, and *Journal of Physical Education*. Consulting editor, *Fitness for Living*, 1967-74; research director, *Executive Fitness Newsletter*, 1970-74.

WORK IN PROGRESS: Developing an integrated health and physical education program for upper elementary and junior high school students, "Feelin' Good Program," and two national programs for the YMCA.

* * *

KUYKENDALL, Jack L(awrence) 1940-

PERSONAL: Surname is pronounced *Kur*-ken-dall; born April 25, 1940, in Pampa, Tex.; son of James Newton and Clara Jane (Hopkins) Kuykendall; married Mary Margaret Schmidt (a teacher), July 19, 1969. *Education:* West Texas State University, B.S. (with honors), 1967; Washington State University, M.A., 1968. *Politics:* Independent. *Religion:* None. *Home:* 391 Maplewood Ave., San Jose, Calif. 95117. *Office:* Department of Criminal Justice Administration, San Jose State University, San Jose, Calif. 95127.

CAREER: Police officer in Amarillo, Tex., 1963-65; University of Alaska, Fairbanks, assistant professor of police administration, 1968-69; San Jose State University, San Jose, Calif., assistant professor, 1970-74, associate professor of criminal justice administration, 1974—, director of Administration of Justice Bureau. *Military service:* U.S. Army, 1960-63. *Member:* American Society of Criminology, Academy of Criminal Justice Sciences, California Administration of Justice Educators.

WRITINGS: (Editor with Charles Reasons) *Race, Crime, and Justice*, Goodyear Publishing, 1972; (with Peter Unsinger) *Community Police Administration*, Nelson-Hall, 1975.

Contributor: William J. Bopp, editor, *Police-Community Relationships: An Introductory Undergraduate Reader*, C. C Thomas, 1972; P. F. Cromwell, Jr., and George Keefer, editors, *Police-Community Relations*, West Publishing, 1973; R. E. Blanchard, editor, *Introduction to the Administration of Justice*, Wiley, 1975; H. W. More, editor, *Principles and Procedures in the Administration of Justice*, Wiley, 1975. Contributor to law enforcement and criminology journals.

WORK IN PROGRESS: A book on criminal justice education, with Armand P. Hernandez; a book on a theory of community policing.

* * *

KUZNETSOV, (Edward) 1939-

PERSONAL: Born January 29, 1939; son of Samuel Kuznetsov; married Sylva Zalmanson (a lecturer), 1970. *Education:* Attended University of Moscow, 1960-61. *Religion:* Jewish. *Address:* c/o Editorial Director, Vallentine, Mitchell & Co. Ltd., 67 Great Russell St., London WC1B 3BT, England.

CAREER: Translator. Arrested as dissident for co-editing poetry anthology, *Phoenix*, 1961, interned in Mordovian prison camp, 1961-68, returned to Mordovia, 1970, for fifteen-year commuted death sentence. *Awards, honors:* Globus Literary Prize, 1975, for French edition of *Prison Diaries*.

WRITINGS: Prison Diaries, Stein & Day, 1975.*

* * *

LaBASTILLE, Anne 1938-
(Anne LaBastille Bowes)

PERSONAL: Born November 20, 1938, in New York, N.Y.; daughter of Ferdinand Meyer (a professor) and Irma (a pianist and writer; maiden name, Goebel) LaBastille; divorced. *Education:* University of Miami, Coral Gables, Fla., student, 1951-53, secondary teaching certificate, 1961; Cornell University, B.S., 1955, Ph.D., 1969; Colorado State University, M.S., 1958. *Home and office:* West of the Wind Publications, Inc., Big Moose, N.Y. 13331. *Agent:* John Cushman, John Cushman Associates, Inc., 25 West 43rd St., New York, N.Y. 10036.

CAREER: National Audubon Society, wildlife tour leader, Palm Beach, Fla., 1955-56; Caribbean Wildlife Tours, Miami, Fla., organizer and co-leader, winters, 1956-63; Covewood Lodge, Big Moose, N.Y., owner, co-manager, and naturalist, summers, 1956-64; Everglades National Park, Fla., ranger-naturalist, 1964; Cornell University, Ithaca, N.Y., assistant professor in department of natural resources and department of science and environmental education, 1969-71, research associate, Laboratory of Ornithology, 1971-73; free-lance wildlife ecologist, consultant, writer, and photographer, 1971—. Owner of West of the Wind Publications, Big Moose, N.Y. Field director and biologist in campaign to save endangered Atitlan grebe,

Guatemala, between 1964-68; biologist and writer on National Geographic Society expedition in Guatemala, 1968; conducted wildlife studies on Atlantic Coast for Smithsonian Institution, 1972-74, and made other surveys for World Wildlife Fund, Defenders of Wildlife, and Environmental Protection Agency. Lecturer at Harvard University, Cornell University, State University of New York at Albany, and Philadelphia Academy of Natural Sciences. Member and consultant, Survival Services Commission, International Union for Conservation of Nature and Natural Resources; member of scientific advisory board, Island Resources Foundation, U.S. Virgin Islands. Registered Adirondack guide.

MEMBER: Society of Women Geographers, American Women in Science, American Ornithologists' Union, Association for Tropical Biology, American Institute of Biological Sciences, Wildlife Society, National Audubon Society. *Awards, honors:* World Wildlife Fund Gold Medal for conservation, 1974; research grants from International Union for Conservation of Nature and Natural Resources, Caribbean Research Institute, World Wildlife Fund, Smithsonian Institution, and other agencies.

WRITINGS: (Author and illustrator under name Anne LaBastille Bowes) *Birds of the Mayas* (folk tales and guide to birds of Yucatan and Guatemala), West of the Wind Publications, 1964; (under name Anne LaBastille Bowes) *Bird Kingdom of the Mayas* (folklore of birds), Van Nostrand, 1967; (author of appendix material) *Life of the Jungle*, McGraw, 1970; *Ecology and Management of the Atitlan Grebe, Guatemala* (monograph), Wildlife Society, 1974.

"Ranger Rick's Best Friends" series for young people, published by National Wildlife Federation: *White-Tailed Deer*, 1973; *The Seal Family*, 1974; *Wild Bobcats*, 1974; *The Opposums*, 1974.

Contributor to journals, juvenile magazines, and newspapers, including *Nature, Travel, Reader's Digest, Historia Natural y Pro Natura, Outdoor Life, Audubon, National Geographic, New York Times, Fauna, Northeastern Logger, Auk*, and *Biological Conservation*. Weekly columnist, writing on wildlife and travel, in Florida and rural New York newspapers under name Anne LaBastille Bowes, 1958-65. Contributing editor in ecology, *Today's Girl*, 1971-72.

WORK IN PROGRESS: A book on the Adirondack Mountains and her life there in a log cabin, for Dutton.

* * *

LA BRIE, Henry George III 1946-

PERSONAL: Born August 28, 1946, in Brooklyn, N.Y.; son of Henry George, Jr. (an accountant) and Blanche Mildred (Smythe) La Brie; married Vicki Louise Gwynn (a learning disabilities consultant), July 14, 1969. *Education:* Bethany College, Bethany, W.Va., B.A., 1968; West Virginia University, M.S., 1970; University of Iowa, Ph.D., 1972; Harvard University, postdoctoral study, 1972-73. *Politics:* Independent. *Home and office address:* Clover Leaf Farm, R.F.D. 1, Biddeford, Maine 04005.

CAREER: University of Maine, Portland, lecturer in communications, 1973; consultant in Southern Maine, 1973—. *Member:* Sigma Delta Chi, Pi Delta Epsilon, Beta Theta Pi.

WRITINGS: Intermedia: An Experience-Based Approach to Journalism Education, University Associates, 1973; *The*

Black Press: A Bibliography, Mercer House, 1973; *The Black Newspaper in America: A Guide*, Mercer House, 1973; (editor) *Perspectives of the Black Press*, Mercer House, 1974. Contributor to journalism and Black studies journals, and to *Christian Science Monitor*.

WORK IN PROGRESS: Why Teach?: An Inquiry into Sharing Knowledge; The Dilemma of Human Communication.

* * *

LABUTA, Joseph A(nthony) 1931-

PERSONAL: Born October 7, 1931, in St. Louis, Mo.; son of Joseph Frank (a mechanic) and Marie (Hribal) Labuta; married Beverly Briggs (a piano accompanist for Michigan Opera Theatre), May 28, 1953; children: Karen, Joseph Wayne, Steven. *Education:* Central College (now Central Methodist College), B.M.E. (cum laude), 1953; University of Missouri, M.E., 1957; University of Illinois, Ed.D., 1965. *Home:* 3472 South Boulevard, Bloomfield Hills, Mich. 48013. *Office:* 105 Music Bldg., Wayne State University, Detroit, Mich. 48202.

CAREER: Elementary, junior high school, and high school director of band, orchestra, and chorus in the public schools of Huntsville, Mo., 1953-54, Willow Springs, Mo., 1956-59, and Lexington, Mo., 1959-61; Shepherd College, Shepherdstown, W.Va., assistant professor of music, 1962-66; Central Methodist College, Fayette, Mo., associate professor of music, 1966-67, director of bands, 1966-67; Wayne State University, Detroit, Mich., associate professor of music, 1967—. Visiting professor at Glenville State College, 1965; visiting lecturer at Oakland University, 1973. Member of Advisory Council to the Fine Arts, Michigan Department of Education, 1970-72. *Military service:* U.S. Army, Band, 1954-56. *Member:* Music Educators National Conference, Michigan Music Educators Association (member of executive board, 1971—), Michigan School Band and Orchestra Association, Phi Kappa Phi, Sigma Tau Epsilon, Phi Mu Alpha.

WRITINGS: Teaching Musicianship in the High School Band, Parker Publishing, 1972; *Guide to Accountability in Music Instruction*, Parker Publishing, 1974. Contributor to *Music Educators Journal, Michigan Music Educator, Instrumentalist, Missouri Journal of Research in Music Education*, and other music journals. Editor of research column, *Michigan Music Educator*, 1971—; member of editorial committee of *Journal of Research in Music Education*, 1972-78.

* * *

LAFFERTY, R(aphael) A(loysius) 1914-

PERSONAL: Born November 7, 1914, in Neola, Iowa; son of Hugh David (an oil-lease broker) and Julia Mary (a teacher; maiden name, Burke) Lafferty. *Education:* Attended University of Tulsa, 1932-33; further study at International Correspondence School, 1939-42. *Politics:* Independent. *Religion:* Roman Catholic. *Home:* 1715 South Trenton, Tulsa, Okla. 74120. *Agent:* Virginia Kidd, Box 278, Milford, Pa. 18337.

CAREER: Clark Electrical Supply Co., Tulsa, Okla, buyer, 1935-42, 1946-71; writer. *Military service:* U.S. Army, 1942-46; became staff sergeant; received New Guinea Campaign Star. *Member:* Authors Guild, Science Fiction Writers of America. *Awards, honors:* Phoenix award at Deep South Convention, New Orleans, La., 1971,

for contributions in the writing field; Hugo award at World Science Fiction Convention, Toronto, Ontario, 1973, for the year's best short story, "Eurema's Dam".

WRITINGS—Novels, except as indicated: *Past Master*, Ace Books, 1968; *The Reefs of Earth*, Berkley Publishing, 1968; *Space Chantey*, Ace Books, 1968; *Fourth Mansions*, Ace Books, 1969; *Nine Hundred Grandmothers* (short stories), Ace Books, 1970; *The Devil Is Dead*, Avon, 1971; *Arrive at Easterwine*, Scribner, 1971; *The Fall of Rome*, Doubleday, 1971; *The Flame Is Green*, Walker, 1971; *Okla Hannali*, Doubleday, 1972; *Strange Doings* (short stories), Scribner, 1972; *Does Anyone Else Have Something Further to Add?* (short stories), Scribner, 1974. Contributor of about one hundred and fifty short stories to magazines and other publications.

WORK IN PROGRESS: Research for a series of American-set historical novels entitled "Chapters of the American Novel"; *Esteban*, a novel for this series.

AVOCATIONAL INTERESTS: Travel, eschatology, geology, politics, the Church.

* * *

LaFONTAINE, Charles Vivian 1936-

PERSONAL: Born May 1, 1936, in Plattsburgh, N.Y.; son of Raphael Charles (a teacher) and May (Tecklenburg) LaFontaine. *Education:* State University of New York, Albany, B.A., 1958; University of Wisconsin, A.M., 1959; attended St. Pius X Seminary, 1960-62, Atonement Seminary, 1962-66, Catholic University of America, summers, 1962-64, and 1968-69; University of Chicago, A.M., 1971, currently Ph.D. candidate; also studied at Centre Cultural Francais and Instituto Dante Alighieri (Rome). *Religion:* Roman Catholic. *Home:* 44 Bouck St., Dannemora, N.Y. 12929. *Office:* Graymoor, Garrison, N.Y. 10524.

CAREER: Ordained Roman Catholic priest, 1966; supply pastor of churches in Connecticut, New York, and in Italy, 1966-68; St. Pius X Seminary, Garrison, N.Y., assistant professor in classic studies, 1966-67; Graymoor Ecumenical Institute, Garrison, N.Y., associate director and associate editor of ecumenical publications, 1973—. Society of the Atonement, delegate to general chapter, 1970 and 1973, member of commission on human resources, 1970—. *Member:* American Historical Association, American Society of Church History, American Catholic Historical Association, Associated Church Press, Phi Kappa Phi, Pi Gamma Mu, Signum Laudis. *Awards, honors:* Woodrow Wilson fellowship, 1958; American Humismatics Society fellowship, 1959.

WRITINGS: (With Charles Angell) *Prophet of Reunion: The Life of Paul of Graymoor*, Seabury, 1975. Editor, *At-One-Ment*, 1965; assistant editor, *The Lamp*, 1969-73; associate editor, *Ecumenical Trends*, 1973—; contributing editor, *Nova et Vetera*, 1974—; ecumenical events editor, *Journal of Ecumenical Studies*.

WORK IN PROGRESS: A book, *Architects of Christian Unity: The Americans, 1800-1950*; American Roman Catholics and war, 1895-99 and ecumenical dialogues (especially Anglican-Roman Catholic), both research interests.

* * *

LaFORTE, Robert Sherman 1933-

PERSONAL: Born September 8, 1933, in Frontenac, Kan.; son of Modesto N. (a laborer) and Josephine (Slapshach) LaForte; married Margaret Ann Colegrove, November 21,

1954 (divorced, 1957); married Frances Ann Crain (a librarian), December 19, 1959; children: (first marriage) Mark; (second marriage) Geoffrey, Russell. *Education:* Kansas State College, B.S.E., 1959, M.S., 1959; University of Kansas, Ph.D., 1966; University of Texas, M.L.S., 1968. *Politics:* Republican. *Religion:* Episcopal. *Home:* 1401 Sherman Dr., Denton, Tex. 76201. *Office address:* Box 13752, North Texas State University, Denton, Tex. 76203.

CAREER: East Texas State University, Commerce, assistant professor of history, 1964-67; North Texas State University, Denton, assistant professor, 1968-73, associate professor of history, 1973—, university archivist, 1974—. *Military service:* U.S. Army, 1955-57. *Member:* Organization of American Historians, American Historical Association, Society of American Archivists, American Library Association, Society of Southwest Archivists.

WRITINGS: Leaders of Reform, University Press of Kansas, 1974. Contributor to journals in his field.

WORK IN PROGRESS: A biography, *Cyrus Leland, Jr.: Republican Boss.*

* * *

La FOUNTAINE, George 1934-

PERSONAL: Born November 10, 1934, in Attleboro, Mass.; son of George Alfred and Amalia Milly (Verna) La Fountaine; married Rita Mauch, December 23, 1955; children: Richard, George, Gabie, Christian. *Education:* Attended high school in Seattle, Wash.; studied at Pasadena Playhouse, 1955-57. *Politics:* Democrat. *Religion:* Roman Catholic. *Home and office:* 10620 Samoa Ave., Tujunga, Calif. 91042. *Agent:* Eisenbach-Greene, Inc., 760 North La Cienega, Los Angeles, Calif. 90069.

CAREER: KCET-TV (educational station), Hollywood, Calif., lighting director, 1964-65; Hollywood Video Center, Hollywood, Calif., lighting director, 1965-68; Academy Lighting Consultants, Hollywood, Calif., partner, 1968-72. *Military service:* U.S. Marine Corps, 1952-55; became sergeant.

WRITINGS: Two Minute Warning (novel), Coward, 1974.

WORK IN PROGRESS: A mystery based on the immigration service, completion expected in 1975; research on love among the elderly, and on the American immigrant.

* * *

LAMBRO, Donald 1940-

PERSONAL: Born July 24, 1940, in Wellesley, Mass.; son of Pascal (a barber) and Mary (Lapery) Lambro; married Jacquelyn Mae Killmon, October 6, 1968; children: Jason. *Education:* Boston University, B.A., 1963. *Politics:* Conservative. *Religion:* Albanian Orthodox. *Residence:* Alexandria, Va. *Office:* United Press International, National Press Building, Washington, D.C.

CAREER: Young Americans for Freedom, Washington, D.C., editor, 1963-64; Republican National Committee, Washington, D.C., writer, 1964; Richard A. Viguerie Co., Inc. (direct mail political consultants), Falls Church, Va., vice-president, 1965; free-lance political writer in Washington, D.C., 1966-67; United Press International, Washington, D.C., reporter, 1967—.

WRITINGS: The Federal Rathole, Arlington House, 1975. Contributor to *Parade* and *Human Events*.

AVOCATIONAL INTERESTS: Tennis, music (especially classical), cooking, the outdoors, collecting stamps.

LAMM, Joyce 1933-

PERSONAL: January 17, 1933, in Bunker Hill, Ill.; daughter of Ernest Levi (a heavy oils supervisor for Standard Oil Co.) and Ellen Ruth (Reed) Allen; married Kenneth M. Lamm (a design draftsman), October 30, 1954; children: Rebecca, Thomas, William, Tricia. *Education:* Southern Illinois University, B.S., 1953; also studied at Colorado Agricultural and Metallurgical College and University of Illinois. *Politics:* Independent. *Residence:* Decatur, Ill. *Office:* Department of Social Science, Richland Community College, 100 North Water, Decatur, Ill. 62523.

CAREER: Special education teacher in public schools in Decatur, Ill., 1968-73; Richland Community College, Decatur, Ill., instructor in geography, 1974—.

WRITINGS: Let's Talk About the Metric System, Jonathan David, 1975. Contributor to *Lady's Circle, Flowers and Garden*, and *Down River.*

WORK IN PROGRESS: B'tween Time, a novel of a Missouri farm family; research for a book on volcanism and the Mid-Atlantic Ridge, for young people; research on the history of canoeing.

AVOCATIONAL INTERESTS: Gardening, travel, camping, hiking, canoeing.

* * *

LAMONT, Marianne
See RUNDLE, Anne

* * *

LANDAU, Sidney I(van) 1933-

PERSONAL: Born April 11, 1933, in New York, N.Y.; son of Emanuel and Sadie M. (Halpern) Landau; married Sarah Bradford (an architectural historian), June 19, 1959; children: Paul Stuart, Amy Bradford. *Education:* Queens College (now of the City University of New York), B.A., 1954; State University of Iowa, M.F.A., 1959. *Home:* 50 West 96th St., New York, N.Y. 10025. *Office:* J. G. Ferguson Publishing Co., 100 Park Ave., New York, N.Y. 10017.

CAREER: Miami University, Oxford, Ohio, instructor in English, 1959-61; Funk & Wagnalls, New York, N.Y., definer, 1961-63, managing editor of dictionary department, 1963-66, editor-in-chief of Funk & Wagnalls dictionaries, 1966-70; J. G. Ferguson Publishing Co., New York, N.Y., executive editor, 1970—, editor-in-chief of *The Doubleday Dictionary*, 1970—. *Military service:* U.S. Army, 1954-56. *Member:* New York Academy of Sciences, New York Road Runners Club.

WRITINGS: (Editor) *Funk and Wagnalls Standard College Dictionary*, Funk, 1965—; (editor) *Funk and Wagnalls Standard Dictionary*, International Edition, Funk, 1965— (Landau was not associated with earlier editions); (editor) *Funk and Wagnalls Standard Desk Dictionary*, Funk, 1965; (editor) *The Doubleday Dictionary*, Doubleday, 1975. Contributor to journals in his field.

SIDELIGHTS: "Of course, dictionaries are not written by any one person," Landau wrote. "My job has been to organize the writing and editing, to see that out of the thousands of galley proofs and pages, pieces of art, etc., assembled, read and reread, corrected, lost and found, copied and recopied, sent and received, a dictionary somehow emerges of approximately the right number of pages, more or less on schedule and not outrageously over budget, and that it is—it better be—a good dictionary and preferably with several notable 'features' that will be more marketable than the subtleties of lexicographic excellence."

* * *

LANDSBURG, Sally (Breit) 1933-

PERSONAL: Born August 19, 1923, in Binghamton, N.Y.; daughter of Hugo (a physician) and Nellie (Schwab) Breit; married Alan Landsburg, February 10, 1957 (separated, 1975); children: Valerie Ann, Michael Lee. *Education:* Ithaca College, B.S., 1955; California State University, Los Angeles, M.A., 1966; graduate study at City College of the City University of New York, 1958-62, and Azusa Pacific College, 1975. *Politics:* None. *Religion:* Jewish. *Home:* 512 North Bedford Dr., Beverly Hills, Calif. 90210. *Agent:* Julian Bach, Jr., 3 East 48th St., New York, N.Y. 10017. *Office:* Department of Public Service, Rio Hondo College, Workman Mill Rd., Whittier, Calif. 90608.

CAREER: National Broadcasting Corp. (NBC), New York, N.Y., tour guide in guest relations, 1955-56; Rio Hondo College, Whittier, Calif., instructor in English, 1968—. Instructor at Berlitz School of Languages, 1967-69; instructor at Rio Hondo Police Academy. *Member:* American Federation of Teachers, Association of Humanistic Psychology.

WRITINGS: In Search of Ancient Mysteries, Bantam, 1974; *The Outer Space Connection*, Bantam, 1975. Story consultant for feature-length documentary film "The Outer Space Connection."

WORK IN PROGRESS: The Academy (tentative title), nonfiction about police officers.

* * *

LANGLEY, Wright 1935-

PERSONAL: Born January 10, 1935, in Tarboro, N.C.; son of William Wright (a watchmaker) and Ruth (Harrison) Langley; married Joan Knowles (a free-lance writer and photographer), June 1, 1958; children: Mark, Lisa. *Education:* Rochester Institute of Technology, B.F.A., 1957; Boston University, M.S., 1964. *Politics:* Democrat. *Religion:* United Church of Christ. *Home:* 821 Georgia St., Key West, Fla. 33040. *Office: Miami Herald*, 1201 Duval St., Key West, Fla. 33040.

CAREER: Rochester Institute of Technology, Rochester, N.Y., instructor in photography, 1961-62; *Raleigh Times*, Raleigh, N.C., writer, 1962-63; Health Careers for North Carolina, Raleigh, N.C., director of public relations, 1963-65; *Key West Citizen*, Key West, Fla., writer and photographer, 1965-68; *Miami Herald*, Key West, Fla., bureau chief, 1968—. *Military service:* U.S. Army, 1957-59. *Member:* Historical Association of Southern Florida, Western North Carolina Historical Association, Key West Art and Historical Society.

WRITINGS: (With Stan Windhorn) *Yesterday's Key West*, E. A. Seemann, 1973; (with Windhorn) *Yesterday's Florida Keys*, E. A. Seemann, 1974; (with wife, Joan Langley) *Yesterday's Asheville*, E. A. Seemann, 1975.

SIDELIGHTS: Langley spent the summer of 1960 aboard the turtle schooner, *A.M. Adams*, in the Caribbean.

* * *

LANGWORTHY, Harry W(ells III) 1939-

PERSONAL: Born October 23, 1939, in Utica, N.Y.; son of Harry Wells (an educator) and Esther Edith (an educator; maiden name, Johnson) Langworthy. *Education:* Colgate University, B.A., 1961; Boston University, M.A., 1963, Ph.D., 1969. *Politics:* Democrat in the United States. *Religion:* Unitarian-Universalist. *Home:* 15602 Oakhill Rd., East Cleveland, Ohio 44112. *Office:* Department of History, Cleveland State University, Cleveland, Ohio 44115.

CAREER: University of Zambia, Lusaka, lecturer in history, 1966-70; Cleveland State University, Cleveland, Ohio, assistant professor, 1971-73, associate professor of history, 1973—. *Member:* International Africa Institute, African Studies Association, American Association of University Professors, British Institute in Eastern Africa, Society of Malawi, Historical Association of Zambia, Historical Society of Tanzania.

WRITINGS: (Contributor) B. Pachai, editor, *Early History of Malawi*, Longman, 1971; *Zambia before 1890: Aspects of Precolonial History*, Longman, 1972. Contributor to *African Historical Studies* and *Transafrican Journal of History*.

WORK IN PROGRESS: Studies of aspects of precolonial history of Chewa and other peoples of eastern Zambia and central Malawi, of Senga origins and establishment, and of politics, trade, and religion in Mkanda's kingdom to 1850; translation of and commentary on exploration journals of Karl Weise in central Africa.

* * *

LANKFORD, Philip Marlin 1945-

PERSONAL: Born December 29, 1945, in St. Louis, Mo.; son of Philip O. (a writer) and Vona (Ochterbeck) Lankford; married Donna Marie Rice, June 25, 1967; children: Lori Ellen, Danielle Aurelia. *Education:* University of Chicago, A.B., 1967, A.M., 1968, Ph.D., 1971. *Politics:* Left. *Religion:* None. *Home:* 2011 Parker, Berkeley, Calif. 94704. *Office:* Association of Bay Area Governments, Hotel Claremont, Berkeley, Calif. 94705.

CAREER: University of California, Los Angeles, assistant professor, 1970-75; Association of Bay Area Governments, Berkeley, Calif., research planner, 1975—. Consultant to California State Highway Division, Southern California Association of Governments, and Venice Community Planning Group. *Member:* Association of American Geographers, Classification Society, Urban Regional Information Systems Association, Regional Science Association, Sigma Xi.

WRITINGS: (With Brian J. L. Berry) *Commodity Flows and Spatial Structure*, Department of Geography Research Series, University of Chicago, 1966; *Regional Incomes in the United States, 1929-1967: Level, Distribution, Stability, and Growth*, Department of Geography Research, University of Chicago, 1972; *An Introduction to Spatial Systems*, Dickenson, in press. Contributor to proceedings; contributor of articles and reviews to professional journals. Reviewer for Duxbury Press.

* * *

LAPPIN, Peter 1911-

PERSONAL: Born April 29, 1911, in Ireland; son of John (a railroad employee) and Sarah (Barrett) Lappin. *Education:* Fordham University, M.A., 1953; also attended Salesian Studentate, Hong Kong, International School of Theology, Shanghai, Belfast School of Technology, Salesian

College, Cowley, Oxford, England, and Columbia School of Writing. *Home and office:* Marian Shrine, Filors Lane, West Haverstraw, N.Y. 10993. *Agent:* William Holub Associates, 432 Park Ave. S., New York, N.Y. 10016.

CAREER: Ordained Roman Catholic priest; Marian Shrine, West Haverstraw, N.Y., public relations agent. Lecturer on the Far East, South America, and other topics. *Member:* Catholic Press Association, Ancient Order of Hibernians, International Order of the Alhambra, Knights of Columbus. *Awards, honors:* Received Venice Festival awards, Catholic Family Club award, and two Catholic Literary Foundation awards.

WRITINGS: General Mickey: A True Story, Salesiana Publishers (New Rochelle, N.Y.), 1952; *Dominic Savio: Teenage Saint*, Bruce, 1955; *Conquistador!*, Salesiana Publishers, 1957; *Stories of Don Bosco*, Irish Press, 1958; *Land of Cain*, Doubleday, 1958; *Mighty Samson* (juvenile), [Garden City, N.Y.], 1961; *Bury Me Deep*, Our Sunday Visitor, 1974. Member of editorial board, "Biographic Memoirs of St. John Bosco." Editor of U.S. edition, *Salesian Bulletin.*

WORK IN PROGRESS: A biography of St. John Bosco; *The Boy Who Discovered America*, story of a Puerto Rican boy, for the U.S. Bicentennial; *City of Sorrow*, a story of Belfast, Ireland.

AVOCATIONAL INTERESTS: Travel.

* * *

LARRISON, Earl J(unior)   1919-

PERSONAL: Born May 11, 1919; in Mabton, Wash.; son of Earl (an accountant) and Anna Marie (an educator; maiden name, Kuble) Larrison. *Education:* University of Washington, Seattle, B.S., 1941, M.S., 1946; further graduate study at University of Michigan, 1946-49. *Politics:* Independent. *Religion:* Unitarian. *Home:* 803 Residence St., Moscow, Idaho 83843. *Office:* Department of Biological Sciences, University of Idaho, Moscow, Idaho 83843.

CAREER: Metallurgical chemist for Washington Iron Works, 1942-46; University of Idaho, Moscow, 1949—, now professor of bird and mammal ecology. *Member:* American Association for the Advancement of Science (fellow), American Society of Mammalogists, Wildlife Society, National Audubon Society, Ecological Society of America, Cooper Ornithological Society, American Ornithologists Union, American Association of University Professors, American Federation of Teachers, Northwest Scientific Association, Idaho Academy of Science (founder), Palouse Audubon Society (founder; president, 1971-73), Phi Beta Kappa, Phi Delta Kappa, Sigma Xi, Phi Sigma.

WRITINGS: (With Harry W. Higman) *Pilchuck: The Life of a Mountain*, Superior, 1949; (with Higman) *Union Bay: The Life of a City Marsh*, University of Washington Press, 1951; *Field Guide to the Birds of Puget Sound*, Seattle Audubon, 1952; *Owyhee: The Life of a Northern Desert*, Caxton, 1957; *Wildlife of the Northern Rocky Mountains*, Naturegraph, 1961; (with Edward M. Francq) *Field Guide to the Birds of Washington State*, Seattle Audubon, 1962; (with Jerry L. Tucker and Malcomb Jollie) *Guide to Idaho Birds*, Idaho Academy of Science, 1967; *Guide to Idaho Mammals*, Idaho Academy of Science, 1967; (with Klaus G. Sonnenberg) *Washington Birds: Their Location and Identification*, Seattle Audubon, 1968; *Washington Mammals: Their Habits, Identification and Distribution*, Seattle Audubon, 1970; (editor, with others) *Washington Wildflow-*

ers, Seattle Audubon, 1974. Editor of *Idaho Academy of Science Bulletin*, 1965-70.

WORK IN PROGRESS: Northwest Animals, publication by Seattle Audubon expected in 1977; *The Mammals of Idaho*; an autobiography, *Trails of a Mouse Trapper*; research on chipmunk behavior, bird and mammal faunistics, and winter animal behavior.

AVOCATIONAL INTERESTS: Photography, camping, expeditions, organ playing, music, travel (Canada, Alaska, Africa, Central America).

* * *

LARSON, Bruce   1925-

PERSONAL: Born in 1925, in Chicago, Ill.; married; children: three. *Education:* Lake Forest College, B.A. (with honors), 1949; Princeton Theological Seminary, B.D., 1952; Boston University, M.A., 1956. *Home:* 1525 San Carlos Bay Dr., Sanibel, Fla. 33957.

CAREER: Ordained Presbyterian minister in 1952; assistant minister of Presbyterian church in Binghamton, N.Y., 1952-55; minister of Presbyterian church in Pana, Ill., 1956-59; Faith at Work, Inc., Columbia, Md., field representative, 1959-62, executive director, 1962-68, president, 1968-73; founder and director of independent research project, Group Research and Individual Learning (GRAIL), 1973—. Visiting fellow, Princeton Theological Seminary, Princeton, N.J., 1975. Host of "Search," a national television series, distributed by Communications Foundations, Inc., 1972—. *Awards, honors:* Lilly Endowment research grant, 1973-75.

WRITINGS: Dare to Live Now, Zondervan, 1965; *Setting Men Free*, Zondervan, 1967; *Living on the Growing Edge*, Zondervan, 1968; (with Ralph Osborne) *The Emerging Church*, Word, Inc., 1970; *No Longer Strangers*, Word, Inc., 1971; *Ask Me to Dance*, Word, Inc., 1972; *The One and Only You*, Word, Inc., 1974; (with Keith Miller) *The Edge of Adventure*, Word, Inc., 1974; *Thirty Days to a New You*, Zondervan, 1974.

SIDELIGHTS: Larson's books have been published in German, Chinese, Swedish, Afrikaans, and Spanish.

* * *

LARSON, Clinton F(oster)   1919-

PERSONAL: Born September 22, 1919, in American Fork, Utah; son of Clinton and Lillian (Foster) Larson; married Naomi Barlow, June 24, 1942; children: Susan (Mrs. John Paxman), Diane (Mrs. Vard Porter). *Education:* University of Utah, B.A., 1943, M.A., 1947; University of Denver, Ph.D., 1956. *Religion:* Church of Jesus Christ of Latter Day Saints. *Home:* 569 Sagewood Ave., Provo, Utah. 84602. *Office:* Department of English, Brigham Young University, Provo, Utah 84602.

CAREER: Brigham Young University, Provo, Utah, assistant professor, 1950-56, associate professor, 1956-63, professor of English, 1963—, poet-in-residence, 1974—. Chairman of Provo City Cultural Development Committee, 1974—. *Military service:* U.S. Army Air Forces, 1942-45. *Member:* National Federation of State Poetry Societies (president, 1961-62). *Awards, honors:* Creative arts award from Karl G. Maeser Associates, 1966; awards from Utah State Institute of Fine Arts.

WRITINGS: Coriantumr and Moroni (two three-act plays), Brigham Young University Press, 1962; *The Mantle of the Prophet and Other Plays*, Deseret, 1966; *The Lord of Experience* (poems), Promised Land Publications, 1968; *Counterpoint* (poems), Brigham Young University Press, 1973; *Modern Poetry of Western America*, Brigham Young University Press, 1975. Editor of *Illustrated Stories from the Book of Mormon*, sixteen volumes, 1965-72.

WORK IN PROGRESS: A book of poems, *The Western World*; *Centennial Poems*.

* * *

LARSON, Donald (Norman) 1925-

PERSONAL: Born November 1, 1925, in Chicago, Ill.; son of Norman (a builder) and Ferne (Sellstrom) Larson; married Llewellyn M. Johnson (a teacher), July 14, 1949; children: Jeffrey, Rebecca, Brett. *Education:* Wheaton College, Wheaton, Ill., B.A., 1949; University of Chicago, M.A., 1957, Ph.D., 1965. *Religion:* Protestant. *Home:* 3570 North Rice St., St. Paul, Minn. 55112. *Office:* Department of Linguistics and Anthropology, Bethel College, St. Paul, Minn. 55112.

CAREER: Trinity College, Chicago, Ill., associate professor of Greek and linguistics, 1949-61; Interchurch Language School, Manila, Philippines, director, 1961-63; American Bible Society, New York, N.Y., special secretary for translations, 1963-66; Bethel College, St. Paul, Minn., professor of linguistics and anthropology, 1966—. Principal, Toronto Institute of Linguistics, 1963—. Linguist-in-residence, Union Language School, Bangkok, Thailand, 1972-73. Consultant to Foreign Mission Board of Southern Baptist Convention, 1967—. *Military service:* U.S. Naval Reserve, 1944-46. *Member:* Linguistic Society of America, American Anthropological Association, American Scientific Affiliation, Pi Gamma Mu.

WRITINGS: Philippine Language Scene, Interchurch Language School, 1963; *Structural Approach to Greek*, Lincoln College Press, 1970; (with William A. Smalley) *Becoming Bilingual*, William Carey Press, 1974. Contributor of about fifty articles and reviews to linguistic, religious, and anthropological journals.

WORK IN PROGRESS: Deschooling Language Study; *Making Sense When Worlds Collide*; *First Lessons in Pidgin*; *Encounters for Witness*; *A Single New Humanity*.

* * *

LARSON, Jeanne 1920-

PERSONAL: Born November 17, 1920, in Eveleth, Minn.; daughter of Joe (a fisherman) and Freda (Mystrom) Riederer; married Ralph Larson (a clergyman), June 15, 1943; children: David, Thom, Karen. *Education:* Walla Walla College, B.A., 1942; Andrews University, M.A., 1968; further graduate study at Pacific Union College and Atlantic Union College. *Religion:* Seventh-day Adventist. *Office:* Arizona Conference of Seventh-day Adventists, P.O. Box 21147, Phoenix, Ariz. 85016.

CAREER: Seventh-day Adventist missionary in Hawaii, 1946-58; free-lance writer, 1958-60; junior high school teacher of English in Pleasant Hill, Calif., 1960-62; teacher in a preparatory school in Angwin, Calif., 1962-66; public school teacher in Michigan, 1967-68; Atlantic Union College, South Lancaster, Mass., instructor in English, 1970-71, director of media communications, 1971-72; free-lance writer, 1973—.

WRITINGS: (With Ruth McLin) *Fifty-Two Sabbath Menus*, Southern Publishing, 1969; (with McLin) *Creative*

Ideas for Child Raising, Review & Herald, 1971; (with McLin) *The Vegetable Protein and Vegetarian Cookbook*, Arco, 1974; *Valao of the South Seas* (biography), Southern Publishing, 1975. Contributor to religious publications.

WORK IN PROGRESS: Creative Ideas for Marriage, with Ruth McLin; a book of devotions for young people, with McLin; an autobiography of her Alaskan childhood; Bible study lessons for early teens, for international use by the Seventh-day Adventist Church; research on biographies of New England women.

* * *

LASATER, Alice E(lizabeth) 1936-

PERSONAL: Born August 18, 1936, in Chattanooga, Tenn.; daughter of Joseph Howard (an ironmaker) and Eleanor (Bradley) Lasater. *Education:* University of Chattanooga, B.A., 1967; University of Tennessee, M.A., 1968, Ph.D., 1971. *Politics:* None. *Home:* Lamar Hills Apartment #1406, Hattiesburg, Miss. 39401. *Office:* Department of English, University of Southern Mississippi, Hattiesburg, Miss. 39401.

CAREER: Secretary for U.S. Civil Service in Huntsville, Ala., 1954-55, and in Aberdeen, Md., 1955-60, in American Embassies in Tripoli, 1961, and in Benghazi, Libya, 1961-64; University of Southern Mississippi, Hattiesburg, assistant professor, 1971-75, associate professor of English, 1975—. *Member:* Modern Language Association of America, South Atlantic Modern Language Association, South Central Modern Language Association, Phi Kappa Phi, Pi Delta Phi. *Awards, honors:* Woodrow Wilson fellow at University of Tennessee, 1970-71.

WRITINGS: Spain to England: A Comparative Study of Arabic, European, and English Literature of the Middle Ages, University Press of Mississippi, 1974. Contributor to *Southern Quarterly*.

WORK IN PROGRESS: A collection of medieval romances.

AVOCATIONAL INTERESTS: Travel, playing viola in community orchestras.

* * *

LATHAM, Mavis
See CLARK, Mavis Thorpe

* * *

LAURITSEN, John (Phillip) 1939-
(Red Butterfly)

PERSONAL: Born March 5, 1939, in Grand Island, Neb.; son of Walter P. (a lawyer) and S. Marie (Grosshans) Lauritsen. *Education:* Harvard University, B.A., 1963. *Politics:* "Unaffiliated Marxist." *Religion:* None. *Home:* 26 St. Mark's Pl., Apt. 3-FE, New York, N.Y. 10003.

CAREER: Marketscope Research Co., New York, N.Y., project director and analyst, 1966-69; free-lance writer, 1969—; Source Data Automation Information Sciences, New York, N.Y., operations manager and analyst, 1970-73.

WRITINGS: (With David Thorstad) *The Early Homosexual Rights Movement (1864-1935)*, Times Change Press, 1974; *Religious Roots of the Taboo on Homosexuality* (pamphlet), Come Unity Press, 1974; (with Thorstad) *Sexual Morality in Historical Materialist Perspective* (pamphlet), privately printed, 1975.

Under pseudonym Red Butterfly: (Translator) Kurt Hiller, *Appeal to the Second International Congress for Sexual Reform* (pamphlet), privately printed, 1970; (contributor) Karla Jay and Allen Young, editors, *Out of the Closets: Voices of Gay Liberation*, Douglas Books, 1972.

Contributor of articles and photographs to magazines, including *Gay Liberator, Advocate, Freethinker*, and *Militant*. Editor of *Come Out!*, newspaper of the Gay Liberation Front, 1969.

WORK IN PROGRESS: Editing an anthology of materials from the early homosexual rights movement, with David Thorstad; collecting material on modern instances of clerically-inspired intolerance directed against homosexuals.

SIDELIGHTS: Lauritsen writes: "I first became aware of the early homosexual rights movement in 1970, when I found Kurt Hiller's 1928 speech. I was amazed to discover, bit by bit, that a radical and influential ... movement had flourished in the late nineteenth- and early twentieth centuries, and my co-author and I determined that the gay liberation movement should learn about it ... We hope that learning about the pioneer activists for gay rights will be an inspiration for those in the movement now."

* * *

LAVAN, Spencer 1937-

PERSONAL: Born December 31, 1937, in New York, N.Y.; son of Peter I. B. (an attorney) and Fay (maiden name, Collen; a writer) Lavan; married Susan Anthony Kohlberg, December 22, 1961; children: Johnathan Peter, Daniel Horton, Timothy Spencer, Joanna Be. *Education:* Tufts University, A.B. (cum laude), 1959; Harvard University, S.T.B., 1962; McGill University, M.A., 1966, Ph.D., 1970. *Religion:* Unitarian Universalist. *Home:* 52 Hancock St., Lexington, Mass. 02173. *Office:* Dean of Liberal Arts, Tufts University, Medford, Mass. 02155.

CAREER: Minister in Charleston, S.C., 1962-64, in Montreal, Quebec, 1965-67; Tufts University, Medford, Mass., assistant professor of religion, 1969—, associate dean of liberal arts, 1973—. Founder of Collegium: Liberal Religious Studies; trustee of Research Committee on Punjab. Town meeting member, town of Lexington, Mass., 1973-77. *Member:* American Academy of Religion, Association of Asian Studies, Unitarian Historical Society (trustee), Bengal Studies Association, Middle East Studies Association, American Oriental Society.

WRITINGS: (Editor with Barbara Thomas) *West Bengal and Bangladesh: Perspectives from 1972*, Michigan State University, 1973; *The Ahmadiyah Movement: A History and Perspective*, South Asia Books, 1974; (contributor) Jones and Gustafson, editors, *Sources on Punjab History*, [Delhi], 1975. Contributor to journals in his field.

WORK IN PROGRESS: Unitarians and India: A Study in Encounter and Acculturation.

* * *

LAVER, James 1899-1975
(Jacques Reval)

March 14, 1899—June 3, 1975; British fashion historian, art historian, poet, novelist, playwright, biographer, translator, and author. Obituaries: *New York Times*, June 4, 1975; *Washington Post*, June 5, 1975; *Time*, June 16, 1975; *AB Bookman's Weekly*, June 23, 1975. (CA-2)

LAWLER, James R. 1929-

PERSONAL: Born August 15, 1929, in Melbourne, Australia; son of James and Kathleen (Mahony) Lawler; married Christiane Labossiere, July 7, 1954; children: Ariane, Jerome. *Education:* University of Melbourne, B.A. (with honors), 1950, M.A., 1952; University of Paris, D.U.P., 1954. *Office:* Department of French, Dalhousie University, Halifax, Nova Scotia, Canada.

CAREER: University of Queensland, Brisbane, Australia, lecturer in French, 1955-56; University of Melbourne, Parkville, Australia, senior lecturer in French, 1957-62; University of Western Australia, Nedlands, Australia, professor of French and head of department, 1963-71; University of California, Los Angeles, professor of French, 1971—, chairman of department, 1971-74. McCulloch Professor and chairman of department of French, Dalhousie University, 1974—. Australian Academy of the Humanities Foundation fellow, 1969—. *Member:* Association Internationale des Etudes Francaises (vice-president, 1974). *Awards, honors:* Carnegie fellow, 1961-62; Commonwealth Interchange Scholar, 1967; Officier, Palmes Academiques, 1970; Guggenheim fellow, 1974.

WRITINGS: Form and Meaning in Valery's "Le Cimetiere marin," Melbourne University Press, 1959; (compiler) *An Anthology of French Poetry*, Oxford University Press, 1960, 3rd edition, 1968; *Lecture de Valery: Une etude de "Charmes,"* Presses Universitaires de France, 1963; *The Language of French Symbolism*, Princeton University Press, 1969; *Tableau de la France*, McGraw, 1969; (translator and compiler) Paul Valery, *Poems* [and] *On Poets and Poetry*, the former translated by David Paul, Princeton University Press, 1971; (translator with Malcolm Cowley) Valery, *Poe, Mallarme*, Princeton University Press, 1972; *The Poet as Analyst: Essays on Paul Valery*, University of California Press, 1974; (compiler) *A Valery Anthology*, Princeton University Press, in press. Founding editor, *Essays in French Literature*, 1964—; assistant editor, *French Review*, 1974—; member of advisory board, *Mosaic*, 1975—.

WORK IN PROGRESS: Research on Rene Char, Paul Claudel, and Paul Valery.

* * *

LAWRENCE, Daniel 1940-

PERSONAL: Born December 28, 1940, in North Shields, England; son of Daniel (a shipyard wireman) and Ellen (Smith) Lawrence; married Helen Madeline Wilson (a former teacher of physics), August 2, 1966; children: John Daniel, David James. *Education:* University of Hull, B.A., 1964; University of Nottingham, Ph.D., 1974. *Home:* 40 Holkham Ave., Chilwell, Beeston, Nottingham NG9 5EQ, England. *Office:* Department of Sociology, University of Nottingham, Nottingham NG7 2RD, England.

CAREER: Swan Hunters and Wigham Richardson Shipyard, Wallsend, England, personnel assistant, 1960-61; University of Nottingham, Nottingham, England, lecturer in sociology, 1965—. Consultant to Young Volunteer Force Foundation, 1970—. *Member:* British Sociological Association.

WRITINGS: Black Migrants, White Natives: A Study of Race Relations in Nottingham, Cambridge University Press, 1974; (contributor) Ivor Crewe, editor, *1975 British Political Sociology Yearbook*, Croom Helm, 1975. Contributor of articles and reviews on race relations and sociology to journals.

WORK IN PROGRESS: A study of the effects of urban renewal and housing markets on race relations in Nottingham.

* * *

LAWSON, David 1927-

PERSONAL: Born October 11, 1927, in London, England; son of Albert (a builder) and Marjorie (Turner) Lawson; married Sondra Ewing, November, 1954 (divorced, 1958). *Education:* City College (now City College of the City University of New York), B.S.S., 1950; Columbia University, M.A., 1952, Ed.D., 1959. *Politics:* Independent. *Religion:* Existential Humanist. *Residence:* Montreal, Quebec, Canada. *Address:* c/o New Voices Publishing Co., 146-47 29th Ave., Flushing, N.Y. 11354.

CAREER: University of British Columbia, Vancouver, assistant professor of education, 1960-63; Hunter College of the City University of New York, New York, N.Y., assistant professor of education, 1964-66; Western Washington State College, Bellingham, associate professor of education, 1966-68; McGill University, Montreal, Quebec, associate professor of education, 1968-70; Boston University, Boston, Mass., visiting professor of education, 1971-72; poet, 1972—. *Military service:* U.S. Army, 1946.

WRITINGS: Alcestis: A Narrative Poem, Ganis & Harris, 1967; *Peregrines* (poems), privately printed, 1970; *The Teaching of Values: From Ethical Idealism to Social Psychology,* privately printed, 1970; *Patches: A Montage* (novel), New Voices Publishing, 1975. Contributor to *Aspen Leaves, Aspen, Magazine, ETC., New Voices, Personalist, Twigs, Journal of Thought, Ethical Outlook, Journal of Education, Educational Forum,* and other periodicals.

WORK IN PROGRESS: Mount Royal and Other Poems.

AVOCATIONAL INTERESTS: Art, philosophy, education, magic, music, travel (Mexico, Guatemala, Peru, Ecuador, Galapagos Islands).

* * *

LAWSON, Evelyn 1917-

PERSONAL: Born November 15, 1917, in Crisfield, Md.; daughter of William Price (a banker) and Edmonia Polk Ridgeway Lawson; married William Henry Wells (divorced); married Heaton White Vorse (divorced, 1949). *Education:* Attended Wellesley College and Columbia University. *Politics:* Independent Republican. *Religion:* Episcopalian. *Home:* 20 Woodland Ave., Hyannis, Mass. 02601. *Agent:* Glenn Shaw, 8440 West Sunset Blvd., Los Angeles, Calif. 90069. *Office address:* P.O. Box 254, Hyannis, Mass. 02601.

CAREER: Public relations director for United Feature Syndicate, 1948-52; *Los Angeles Examiner,* Los Angeles, Calif., writer, 1954-56; *Variety,* Hollywood, Calif., writer, 1956-57; *New York American,* New York, N.Y., reporter, 1957-66; *Cape Cod News,* Hyannis, Mass., columnist, 1966-67; *Cape Cod Register,* Yarmouth Port, Mass., columnist, 1967-69; *Boston Herald Advertiser,* Boston, Mass., writer, 1970-71; *Cape Cod Standard Times,* Hyannis, Mass., theatre critic, 1970—; *Santuit Caper,* Santuit, Mass., columnist, 1974—. Public relations director of Ethnic Dance Arts, 1969-75; member of board of directors of Cape Cod Ballet, 1973—. *Member:* Screen Writers Guild of America, Academy of Motion Picture Arts and Sciences. *Awards, honors: Variety* Best of the Year Award for "Death of a

Neighbor" and "Bankhead in Dennis," both 1965; outstanding Cape news coverage award from Massachusetts Elks, 1966.

WRITINGS: Theatre on Cape Cod, Parnassus, 1969; *Yesterday's Cape Cod,* E. A. Seeman, 1975. Author of half-hour television scripts for "I Led Three Lives," "The Millionaire," "Sky King," and "Death Valley Days"; author of feature film, "Snowfire" and a documentary for American Optometric Association, "The Eyes Have It." Author of films and filmstrips for elementary and high schools in New York State. Contributor to *New Bedford Standard Times.*

WORK IN PROGRESS: Deadly Charm, a novel about mass murderer Tony Costa; a book of humorous poetry, *Cape Cats and Dogeral.*

AVOCATIONAL INTERESTS: Cats, chess, sailing.

* * *

LAWSON, S. Alexander 1912-

PERSONAL: Born December 26, 1912, in Glasgow, Scotland; son of Oswald S. (an engineer) and Margaret (Robertson) Lawson; married Evelyn Tipping, September 1, 1947; children: Douglas, Kenneth. *Education:* Rochester Institute of Technology, diploma, 1947. *Home:* 49 East Park Rd., Pittsford, N.Y. 14534. *Office:* Department of Graphic Arts and Photography, Rochester Institute of Technology, Rochester, N.Y. 14623.

CAREER: Rochester Institute of Technology, Rochester, N.Y., began as instructor, 1947, professor, 1959-69, Melbert B. Cary, Jr. Professor of Graphic Arts, 1969—. *Military service:* U.S. Navy, 1941-45; became chief quartermaster. *Member:* Association Typographique International, American Institute of Graphic Arts, American Printing History Association, Typophiles, Goudy Society, Printing Historical Society (London, England). *Awards, honors:* Golden Key Award for writing from International Club of Printing House Craftsmen, 1972; typographic industry distinguished service award, from Printing Industries of America, 1973.

WRITINGS: A Printer's Almanac, North American Publishing, 1966; *Printing Types: An Introduction,* Beacon Press, 1971. Editor of composing room department of *Inland Printer/American Lithographer,* 1954-65; editor of *Typographer's Digest,* 1959-68; editor of column, "Typographically Speaking," in *Printing Impressions,* 1966—.

WORK IN PROGRESS: History of Printing Technology.

SIDELIGHTS: Lawson writes: "I have attempted in my books and articles on typography to restore a balance between the esthetic interest of fine printing and the present technological factors which tend to diminish interest in printing as an historic craft."

* * *

LAZARUS, Simon 1941-

PERSONAL: Born March 30, 1941, in Cincinnati, Ohio. *Education:* Harvard University, B.A., 1963; Yale University, LL.B., 1967. *Office:* Arnold & Porter, 1229 19th St. N.W., Washington, D.C. 20036.

CAREER: Admitted to the Bar of Washington, D.C.; Federal Communications Commission, Washington, D.C., legal assistant to Nicholas Johnson, 1967-68; Department of Consumer Affairs, New York, N.Y., general counsel, 1969-70; Harvard University, Institute of Politics, Cambridge, Mass., fellow, 1970-71; Arnold & Porter, Washington, D.C., attorney, 1972—.

WRITINGS: The Genteel Populists, Holt, 1974. Contributor to journals in his field.

* * *

LEAF, VaDonna Jean 1929-

PERSONAL: Born April 12, 1929, in Hamilton Co., Iowa; daughter of Leon (a farmer) and Leona (Christianson) Hughes; married Paul A. Leaf (a farmer and in the sorghum business), March 2, 1951; children: Paul Arnold, Suzanne Jean, Christopher Mark, Melissa Jane. *Education:* Attended high school in Stanhope, Iowa. *Politics:* "Republican sometimes." *Religion:* Lutheran. *Home and office address:* Route #1, Stratford, Iowa 50249.

CAREER: Writer.

WRITINGS: (Contributor) A. L. Furman, editor, *Everygirl's Sports Stories*, Lantern Press, 1956; *Willie Wilson's Wonderful Watermelon*, Carolrhoda Books, 1974. Contributor of over 270 short stories to popular magazines, including *Jack and Jill* and *Parent's Magazine*.

WORK IN PROGRESS: Three children's books; an adult novelette.

AVOCATIONAL INTERESTS: Reading, gardening, hiking, crocheting.

* * *

LEAHY, Syrell Rogovin 1935-

PERSONAL: Given and middle names are accented on second syllable; surname is pronounced *Lay*-he; born January 4, 1935, in Brooklyn, N.Y.; daughter of Samuel (an optometrist) and Dora (a teacher; maiden name, Cedar) Rogovin; married Daniel J. Leahy (a lecturer in mathematics), August 25, 1963; children: Joshua, Melinda. *Education:* Cornell University, B.A., 1956; Phillipps Universitat, graduate study, 1956-57; Columbia University, M.A., 1959, further graduate study, 1959-61. *Politics:* "Frequently Democrat." *Religion:* Jewish. *Residence:* New Jersey. *Agent:* Claire Smith, Harold Ober Associates, Inc., 40 East 49th St., New York, N.Y. 10017. *Office:* American Telephone & Telegraph Co., 100 Church St., New York, N.Y.

CAREER: Textbook writer in New York, N.Y., 1961-62; International Business Machines, Yorktown Heights, N.Y., linguistic researcher, 1962-65; teacher of remedial courses for adults in New York, N.Y., 1966-69; American Telephone & Telegraph Co., New York, N.Y., writer of training materials, 1970—. *Member:* Linguistic Society of America, Authors Guild of Authors League of America.

WRITINGS: Modern English Sentence Structure, Random House, 1964; *Baby Care*, McGraw, 1966; (with Harry Huffman) *Programmed College English*, McGraw, 1968; *A Book of Ruth* (novel), Simon & Schuster, 1975.

WORK IN PROGRESS: A novel.

* * *

LEBO, Dell 1922-

PERSONAL: Surname is pronounced *Lee*-bow; born August 6, 1922, in New York, N.Y.; son of Dell Roy (in steel construction) and Marguerite (Bruneel) Lebo; married Elaine Pauline Larsen (an artist, macrame instructor, and museum docent), July 1, 1949; children: Lea. *Education:* New York Institute, B.A. (cum laude), 1949; Florida State University, M.A., 1951, Ph.D., 1956. *Politics:* Democrat.

Religion: Unitarian-Universalist. *Home:* 5340 Weller Ave., Jacksonville, Fla. 32211. *Office:* Child Guidance Clinic, 1635 St. Paul Ave., Jacksonville, Fla. 32207.

CAREER: College of William and Mary, Richmond, Va., assistant professor, 1955-56, associate professor of psychology, 1957-59; private practice of psychology in Virginia and Florida, 1956—; Child Guidance Clinic of Duval County, Jacksonville, Fla., clinical psychologist, 1959-62, chief psychologist, 1962—. Lecturer at Jacksonville University, 1959-66, and 1975—; senior psychologist of Gender Identity Association, Jacksonville, Fla., 1967—; consultant to professional advisory committee of Florida Foundation for the Handicapped, Jacksonville, Fla., 1973—; field representative for Personnel Data Systems, New York, N.Y., 1967—; member of board of directors of Small Business Security Service, 1972—; community staff member of *Jacksonville Magazine*, 1972—. *Military service:* U.S. Army Air Forces, 1942-46; served in European, African, and Mid-Eastern theaters.

MEMBER: American Psychological Association, Psychonomic Society (charter member), Florida Psychological Association (member of executive council, 1959-69), Northeast Florida Psychological Association (president, 1962, 1966, and 1967), Torch Club, Arcane Order. *Awards, honors:* Diploma di Benemerenza, 1967, silver medal of honor, 1967, and gold medal of honor, 1969, from Centro Studi e Scambi Internazionali; Diplome di Benemerenza for poetry from Accademia Leonardo da Vinci, 1967, for "The Arcane Way"; World Poet Award, 1970, for "Guardian of the Road"; distinguished service citation, 1973, from World Poetry Society.

WRITINGS: (Contributor) H. B. McDaniel, J. E. Lallas, J. E. Saum, and J. L. Gilmore, editors, *Readings in Guidance*, Holt, 1959; (contributor) L. Gorlow and W. Katkovsky, editors, *Readings in the Psychology of Adjustment*, McGraw, 1959; (contributor) M. R. Haworth, editor, *Child Psychotherapy*, Basic Books, 1964; *Poems and Verse by Dell Lebo*, Bitterroot Press, Book I: *The Metaphysical Poetry*, 1966, Book: *The Three Cornered Habit*, 1966; (contributor) C. Rogers, editor, *The Complete Works of Dr. Carl Rogers*, Iwaski Gakujutsu Syuppan, 1967; (contributor) M. Gold and E. Douvan, editors, *Adolescent Development: Readings in Research and Theory*, Allyn & Bacon, 1969, 2nd edition, 1973; (contributor) C. Schaefer, editor, *The Therapeutic Use of Child's Play*, Jason Aronson, 1975; *Intimations of Precariousness* (poems), HUB Publications, 1975.

Poetry represented in many anthologies including *The Spring Anthology*, Mitre Press, 1967.

Author of television production "Psychologist's Notebook," presented on WJCT-TV, 1959. Author and recorder of several "Sound Seminars" for McGraw. Author with Elaine and Lea Lebo, his wife and daughter, of three-act play, "Southern Comfort," presented by Jacksonville Role Players, 1973. Contributor of about two hundred articles and poems to scientific and professional magazines, newspapers, and journals. *Florida Psychologist*, editor, 1959-69, book review editor, 1969-72; editor, *Jacksonville Poetry Quarterly*, 1974—.

WORK IN PROGRESS: Poetry; a three-act play, "I'm Sensitive, You're Sensitive."

AVOCATIONAL INTERESTS: Collecting the works of local contemporary artists, travel.

BIOGRAPHICAL/CRITICAL SOURCES: Florida Times

Union, December 5, 1965; *Compass*, spring, 1969; *Industry Week*, January 3, 1972.

* * *

LEE, A. R.
See ASH, Rene Lee

* * *

LEE, Francis Nigel 1934-
(Nik)

PERSONAL: Born December 5, 1934, in Kendal, England; son of William Sydney (a company director) and Alice Maud (Smith) Lee; married Nellie Vanderwesthuizen, December 7, 1963; children: Johanna, Annamarie. *Education:* University of Capetown, B.A., 1957, LL.B., 1960, M.A., 1966; Reformed Theological Seminary, Cand. Litt., 1959, Dip. Theol., 1962; University of Stellenbosch, B.D., 1962, L.Th., 1963, Th.M., 1964, Th.D., 1966; Orange Free State University, Ph.D., 1972. *Politics:* Conservative. *Home:* 3651 Spottswood, Memphis, Tenn. 38111. *Office:* Christian Studies Center, 314 South Goodlett, Memphis, Tenn. 38117.

CAREER: Licensed Presbyterian minister, 1963; Shelton College, Cape May, N.J., professor of philosophy, 1967-69; minister in Winterton, South Africa, 1969-73; Fairfax Christian Junior College, Fairfax, Va., professor of theology, 1973-74; Christian Studies Center, Memphis, Tenn., scholar-in-residence, 1974—. Member of National Board for Anti-Communism, 1969-73; chairman of Natal State Board for Advancement of Protestantism, Natal, South Africa, 1971-73; Staley Distinguished Lecturer at Covenant Theological Seminary, 1974. *Member:* International Association for Calvinistic Philosophy, Association for Christian Higher Education, Calvinistic Students Association (chairman, 1962-63), South African Association for the Advancement of Christian Scholarship. *Awards, honors:* Ernest Oppenheimer Postgraduate Memorial scholarships, 1967, 1968, 1969.

WRITINGS: The Sabbath in the Bible, Lord's Day Observance Society (London), 1966; *Culture: Its Origin and Development*, Shelton College Press, 1967; *Nationality and the Bible*, Shelton College Press, 1967; *Philosophy and the Bible*, Shelton College Press, 1967; *The Biblical Theory of Christian Education*, Shelton College Press, 1967; *Calvin on the Sciences*, Sovereign Grace Union (England), 1969; *Communism Versus Creation*, Craig Press, 1969.

(Under pseudonym Nik) *Christian Philosophy in 20th Century North America*, SAVBCW-Potchestroom (South Africa), 1970; (under pseudonym Nik) *Die Mens se Verantwoordelikheid Teenoor sy Gees* (title means "Man's Responsibility for His Soul"), Akos (South Africa), 1970; *A Christian Introduction to the History of Philosophy*, Craig Press, 1970; (under pseudonym Nik) *Die Grondgedagtes van die Kommunisme en Hoedat Dit Gepropageer Word* (title means "The Basic Ideas of Communism and How They Are Propagated"), SAVBCW-Potchestroom, 1971; (under pseudonym Nik) *Ras en Nasie—Wat se die Bybel?* (title means "Race and Nation: What Does the Bible Teach?"), Wever (South Africa), 1971; (under pseudonym Nik) *Die Saligheid van Vroegsterwende Kindertjies* (title means "The Salvation of Those Dying during Infancy"), N. G. Uitgewers (South Africa), 1971; (under pseudonym Nik) *Die Sendingtaak as Hart van die Kerk se Roeping* (title means "The Missionary Task as the Heart of the Church's Calling"), N. G. Uitgewers, 1971.

The Westminster Confession and Modern Society, Scottish Reformed Fellowship (Edinburgh, Scotland), 1972; *The Covenantal Sabbath*, Lord's Day Observance Society, 1972; (under pseudonym Nik) *Julle Doop Mos Verkeerd!* (title means "Ye Baptise Incorrectly!"), N. G. Vitgewers, 1973; *Communist Eschatology: A Christian Philosophical Analysis of the Post-Capitalistic Views of Marx, Engels and Lenin*, Craig Press, 1974; *Are the Ten Commandments Relevant Today?*, Blue Banner, 1974; *The Origin and Destiny of Man*, Presbyterian and Reformed Publishing Co., 1974; *Effective Evangelism*, Renewal, 1975; *The Central Significance of Culture*, Craig Press, in press; *Were Ye Baptized?*, Scottish Reformed Fellowship, in press; (under pseudonym Nik) *Sondag die Sabbat* (title means "Sunday the Sabbath"), N. G. Uitgewers, in press; *Toward a Biblical Theology*, Craig Press, in press; *Toward a Biblical Philosophy*, Craig Press, in press; *Abraham Kuyper and the Rebirth of True Knowledge*, Great Commission Publications, in press; *John Calvin: True Presbyterian*, Presbyterian Church in America Publications, in press.

WORK IN PROGRESS: Onward, Christian Soldiers; Our Life in This World; In God We Trust.

SIDELIGHTS: Lee has traveled to 69 countries of the world and is competent in seven languages. He writes that the important circumstances of his life are "my conversion to Christ, my marriage, my overall viewpoint—the total Lordship of Jesus Christ over every atom of His universe and over everyone and everything in it."

BIOGRAPHICAL/CRITICAL SOURCES: H. J. Hegger, editor, *Jesus Arrested Me*, Velp (Netherlands), 1960.

* * *

LEE, John R(obert) 1923-

PERSONAL: Born December 26, 1923, in Petoskey, Mich.; son of Chester T. (a game warden) and Beryl (a social worker; maiden name, Niles) Lee; married second wife, Susan Dye (a writer), January 11, 1968; children: (first marriage) Elizabeth (Mrs. Keith Simon), Jennifer (Mrs. Damon Huffman), Leslie Ann. *Education:* Central Michigan University, B.A., 1948; University of Michigan, M.A., 1952; Stanford University, Ed.D., 1957. *Home:* 2300 Sherman, Evanston, Ill. 60201.

CAREER: Northwestern University, Evanston, Ill., assistant professor, 1957-61, associate professor, 1961-65, professor of social science education, 1965—. Consultant to Law in American Society Foundation, 1966-75. *Military service:* U.S. Army, Infantry, 1942-46; became first lieutenant; received Bronze Star Medal and Purple Heart. *Member:* National Council for the Social Studies, Phi Delta Kappa. *Awards, honors:* Silver medal from Venice Film Festival, 1970, for "Helen Keller"; first prize from New York International Animated Film Festival, 1974, for "The Munchers"; about thirty other awards, ribbons, and cups for films and filmstrips.

WRITINGS: (With Jonathon C. McLendon) *Prologue to Change*, Allyn & Bacon, 1965; (with McLendon and William W. Joyce) *Readings on Elementary Social Studies: Emerging Changes*, Allyn & Bacon, 1970; (with Stephan E. Ellenwood and Timothy H. Little) *Teaching Social Studies in the Secondary School*, Free Press, 1973; *Teaching Social Studies in the Elementary School*, Free Press, 1974.

Children's book series; all with wife, Susan Lee; all published by Childrens Press: "Heroes of the Revolution," *Benjamin Franklin*, 1974, *Thomas Jefferson*, 1974, *John*

Hancock, 1974, *George Washington*, 1974, *Sam and John Adams*, 1974, *John Paul Jones*, 1974; "Cities of the Revolution," *Charles Town*, 1975, *New York*, 1975; "Events of the Revolution," *The Battle for Long Island and New York*, 1975, *The Fall of the Quaker City*, 1975.

Author of about one hundred films and two hundred filmstrips for children, for McGraw-Hill Films. Contributor to professional journals.

WORK IN PROGRESS: Additional books for "Events of the Revolution" series, and for "Cities of the Revolution" series, including books on Boston, Philadelphia, and Williamsburg; filmstrip series on U.S. history, on economics, on science fiction, and on law-focused education.

* * *

LEE, Mary Price 1934-

PERSONAL: Born July 10, 1934, in Philadelphia, Pa.; daughter of Llewellyn and Elise (Mirkil) Price; married Richard Lee (a copywriter), May 12, 1956; children: Richard, Barbara, Monica. *Education:* University of Pennsylvania, B.A., 1956, M.S. in Ed., 1967. *Residence:* Flourtown, Pa.

CAREER: Teacher for short period; employed in public relations department at Westminster Press, Philadelphia, Pa., 1973-74. Has tutored foreign students in English. *Member:* Women in Communications, Children's Reading Roundtable, Phi Beta Kappa, Philadelphia Athenaeum.

WRITINGS: Money and Kids: How to Earn It, Save It, and Spend It (juvenile), Westminster Press, 1973. Columnist, *Chestnut Hill Local*, 1970-72. Contributing editor, *Today's Girl*, 1972-73. Contributor to *Philadelphia Magazine*.

WORK IN PROGRESS: A book on the veterinarian career.

SIDELIGHTS: Mrs. Lee writes: "My children provide great incentive to write for their teen age group and serve both as guinea pigs and critics. I am a travel enthusiast and particularly a Francophile."

* * *

LEE, Stewart M(unro) 1925-

PERSONAL: Born August 7, 1925, in Beaver Falls, Pa.; son of Charles Marston (a college president) and Alice (Stewart) Lee; married Ann Gilchrist, June 11, 1947; children: Kathryn Ann. *Education:* Geneva College, B.A., 1949; University of Pittsburgh, M.A., 1950, Ph.D., 1956. *Politics:* Republican. *Religion:* Reformed Presbyterian Church. *Home:* 3227 Fourth Ave., Beaver Falls, Pa. 15010. *Office:* Department of Economics and Business Administration, Geneva College, Beaver Falls, Pa. 15010.

CAREER: Geneva College, Beaver Falls, Pa., lecturer, 1949-50, instructor, 1950-51, assistant professor, 1951-57, professor of economics and business administration, 1958—, head of department, 1956—. Summer visiting professor at University of Wisconsin, 1963, 1965, New York University, 1964, and Kansas State University, 1964-1975; visiting professor at University of Missouri, 1967. Consultant to Federal Trade Commission, 1966; member of board of directors and executive committee of Consumers Union, 1970-73; member of President's Consumer Advisory Council, 1970—, chairman, 1974—; vice-president of Consumer Interest Foundation, 1971-72; member of National Consumer Energy Advisory Committee to Federal Energy Office, 1974; delegate of American Council on Consumer In-

terests to biennial congresses of the International Organization of Consumers Unions in Norway, Israel, Austria, and Sweden. *Military service:* U.S. Naval Reserve, 1943-46.

MEMBER: American Council on Consumer Interests (president, 1962-63), American Marketing Association, American Economic Association.

WRITINGS: (With Leland J. Gordon) *Economics for Consumers*, 5th edition (Lee was not associated with earlier editions), American Book Co., 1967, 6th edition, Van Nostrand, 1972. Editor of *American Council of Consumer Interests Newsletter*, 1959—.

WORK IN PROGRESS: Seventh edition of *Economics for Consumers*.

SIDELIGHTS: Lee has testified in the consumer's interest before House and Senate committees, and government agencies.

* * *

LEEPER, Sarah H(ammond) 1912-

PERSONAL: Born February 22, 1912, in Bonifay, Fla.; daughter of William Bryant and Anna (Green) Hammond; married Robert R. Leeper (an educational editor), December 27, 1963. *Education:* Florida State College for Women, A.B., 1932; Florida State University, M.A., 1947, Ed.D., 1953. *Home:* 1239 Noyes Dr., Silver Spring, Md. 20910. *Office:* Department of Early Childhood-Elementary Education, College of Education, University of Maryland, College Park, Md. 20742.

CAREER: Teacher in public school in Pensacola, Fla., 1932-37; teacher in private school in Miami, Fla., 1937-45; Florida State University, Tallahassee, teacher and director of kindergarten, 1949-50, instructor, 1950-52, assistant professor, 1953-55, associate professor, 1955-57, professor of education, 1957-63, head of department of early childhood education, 1963-63, head of department of elementary education, 1963; University of Maryland, College Park, visiting professor of education, 1964-65, acting head of kindergarten nursery school, 1965, professor of education, 1965—. Elementary school teacher at demonstration school of Florida State University, 1942-43; teacher at Southeastern Jurisdictional Leadership School of the Methodist Church, 1964, 1967; Florida delegate to Golden Anniversary White House Conference, 1962, and Mid-Century White House Conference, 1965.

MEMBER: Association for Childhood Education International (vice-president, 1954-56; president, 1957-59), National Association for the Education of Young Children, National Education Association, Association for Supervision and Curriculum Development, American Association of Elementary, Kindergarten, and Nursery Educators, Maryland State Teachers Association, Maryland Association for Supervision and Curriculum Development, Maryland Association for Childhood Education, Kappa Delta Pi, Phi Kappa Phi, Phi Alpha Theta.

WRITINGS: (Editor) *A Guide to Child Development Through the Beginning School Years* (bulletin), Florida State Department of Education, 1946; (editor) *A Guide for Organizing and Developing Kindergartens in Florida* (bulletin) Florida State Department of Education, 1948; (with Ruth Dales, Dora Skipper, and Ralph Witherspoon) *Good Schools for Young Children: Teaching the Three, Four, and Five-Year-Old*, Macmillan, 1963, 3rd edition, 1974; *What Research Says to the Teacher: Nursery School and Kindergarten*, National Education Association, 1968. Contributor of about twenty articles and reviews to education journals.

* * *

LEES, John G(arfield) 1931-

PERSONAL: Born September 7, 1931, in New Waterford, Cape Breton, Nova Scotia, Canada; son of William Edward (a coal miner) and Velma (Murray) Lees; married Katherine Lorraine McGill, August 1, 1955 (died, 1961); married Alice Ruth Lennox, June 26, 1966; children: (first marriage) Elizabeth, Alan; (second marriage) Ross, Julie, Brenda. Education: Acadia University, B.A., 1952, B.Ed., 1953, M.Ed., 1959. Religion: Baptist. Home address: R.R.3, Merrigomish, Pictou County, Nova Scotia B0K 1G0, Canada. Office: Department of Education, P.O. Box 277, New Glasgow, Nova Scotia, B2H 5E3, Canada.

CAREER: Department of National Defense, R.C.A.F. Station, Greenwood, Nova Scotia, school administrator, 1959-66; Nova Scotia Department of Education, New Glasgow, inspector of schools, 1966—. Member: Canadian Education Association, Canadian Association of School Administrators, School Administrators Association (executive director), Home and School Association (president), Nova Scotia Association of School Administrators (member of board of directors, 1970-73; vice-president, 1975).

WRITINGS—Western novels: Six Gun Law, Arcadia House, 1957; Rider of Wilderness Valley, Arcadia House, 1958; Conestoga Trail, Arcadia House, 1960; Nash, Lenox-Hill, 1973; Trail Hardened, Lenox-Hill, 1974. Editor of Nova Scotiana, 1951, and Canadian Association of School Administrators' Yearbook, 1969.

WORK IN PROGRESS: Dynamics of Educational Administration; a western novel; research for a textbook on English grammar.

SIDELIGHTS: Lees lost his left leg as a small child, but has led an active athletic life since then. He has worked as a lifeguard, forest warden, swimming coach, recreational director, has won swimming contests as a university student, and is a farmer by hobby.

* * *

LEFEBURE, Molly

PERSONAL: Born in London, England; daughter of Charles Hector and Elizabeth (Cox) Lefebure; married John Edward Gerrish (an oil company executive), November 23, 1925; children: Nicholas, Hilary John. Education: Attended King's College, London, 1939-40.

CAREER: Newspaper reporter in Plymouth and London, England, 1939-41; private secretary in London, 1941-45; free-lance writer in London, 1945—. Counsellor of Local Education Authority, 1950—. Wartime service: Air Raid Precautions warden, 1939-45. Member: Society of Authors, Cumberland and Westmorland Antiquarian and Archaeological Society.

WRITINGS: Evidence for the Crown (autobiography), Heinemann, 1954, Lippincott, 1955; Murder with a Difference (nonfiction), Heinemann, 1957; The Lake District (travel), Batsford, 1963, Hastings House, 1964; Scratch and Company (juvenile), Gollancz, 1969, Meredith, 1970; The Hunting of Wilberforce Pike (juvenile), Gollancz, 1971, Tap Toe, 1972; Cumberland Heritage (nonfiction), Gollancz, 1972; Samuel Taylor Coleridge: A Bondage of Opium (biography), Stein & Day, 1974; The Loona Bal-

loona (juvenile), Thomas Nelson, 1974. Contributor to journals.

SIDELIGHTS: Molly Lefebure told CA: "I live half of my life in London or travelling: the rest of the time in the Lake Country. Conservationist: anti-all pollution, particularly television (my pet hate) and the motor-car. If possible, I travel on foot, but I also adore flying, in small airplanes if possible. Suffer from mild claustrophobia. Do not believe in the modern mania for questionnaires. I also climb mountains, cook, and at times act Neolithic."

* * *

LE FEVRE, Robert 1911-

PERSONAL: Surname is pronounced "luh-fave"; born October 13, 1911, in Gooding, Idaho; son of Daniel G. (a teacher and salesman) and Ethel (Thomas) LeFevre; married Lois K. Reuling, April 9, 1944; children: Robert, Jr., David T., Thomas R. Education: Attended Hamline University, 1931-32. Politics: "Analyst-teacher; non-participant." Address: Box 2353, Orange, Calif. 92669.

CAREER: Gazette Telegraph, Colorado Springs, Colo., editorial writer, 1955-65, editor, 1960-65; Rampart College, Santa Ana, Calif., founder, 1957, president, 1957-72; independent lecturer, 1973—. Military service: U.S. Army Air Forces, 1942-45; served in European Theatre of Operations; became captain. Member: Fictionaires. Awards, honors: LL.D., Burton College, 1959.

WRITINGS: The Nature of Man and His Government, Caxton, 1959; This Bread is Mine, ALP Publications, 1960; Constitutional Government Today in Soviet Russia, Exposition, 1962; Philosophy of Ownership, Pinetree Press, 1966; The Libertarian (pamphlet), Bramble Minibooks, 1973. Regular contributor to Colorado Springs Gazette Telegraph. Publisher of Rampart College Newsletter, 1964-72, Rampart Journal, 1965-68, and LeFevre's Journal, 1973—.

WORK IN PROGRESS: Novels; short stories.

BIOGRAPHICAL/CRITICAL SOURCES: California Sun, July, 1971; The Lady and the Tycoon, Caxton, 1973; Franklin Auditor, August, 1974.

* * *

LEHMAN, David 1948-

PERSONAL: Born June 11, 1948, in New York, N.Y.; son of Joseph and Anne (Lusthaus) Lehman; married Bethany Ladimer (a college teacher of French), January 26, 1975. Education: Columbia University, B.A. (magna cum laude), 1970, M.Phil., 1974; Cambridge University, B.A., 1972. Politics: "As legislators poets are doomed to go unacknowledged." Religion: Jewish. Home: 301 West 105th St., New York, N.Y. 10025. Office: Department of English and Comparative Literature, Columbia University, 501 Hamilton Hall, New York, N.Y. 10025.

CAREER: Columbia University, New York, N.Y., preceptor in English, 1974—. Instructor at Brooklyn College of the City University of New York, 1975—. Co-producer and host of "The Only Poetry Show," on WKCR-FM Radio, 1972-73. Member: Phi Beta Kappa. Awards, honors: Bennett A. Cerf Prize for Poetry from Columbia University, 1973, for "Baby Bunning"; prize from Academy of American Poets, 1974, for "Threatening Weather."

WRITINGS: Breakfast (poetry broadsheet), Sycamore Press, 1968; Some Nerve (poems), Columbia Review

Press, 1973. Contributor of poems and reviews to *Poetry, Paris Review, Times Literary Supplement*, and *Newsday.* Editor of *Columbia Review*, 1969-70.

WORK IN PROGRESS: The Presidential Years and Other Poems; The Marriage of Poetry and Prose.

SIDELIGHTS: Lehman writes: "My French is so-so, my German even worse, but that doesn't prevent me from reading or, as Harold Bloom would say, mis-reading Henri Michaux ... and Rilke.... Also of importance was the year I spent as Lionel Trilling's research assistant, 1973-74—it was the academic equivalent of clerking for the kind of Supreme Court justice who turns out to display a greatness commensurate with that of his reputation.... The fact that my father was a Talmudic scholar may help to explain my love for mental gymnastics." *Avocational interests:* Baseball.

* * *

LEHMANN, Peter 1938-

PERSONAL: Born December 11, 1938, in Hamburg, Germany; son of Carl Lehmann (a technician); children: Susan, Christine. *Education:* Attended Rackow School of Business, 1957, and University of Hamburg, 1958. *Politics:* "Past republican; lately democrat." *Religion:* Protestant. *Home:* 30 Sierra Vista Lane, Valley Cottage, N.Y. 10989.

CAREER: Production manager and consultant in the baking industry. *Military service:* U.S. Army, 1961-63. *Member:* Bakery Production Club.

WRITINGS: Masks, Celestial Arts, 1974.

WORK IN PROGRESS: You: Yesterday, Today, and Life; The Mountain of Life; The Fool, the Image, and Me; Our Good Earth. Songs, "The Hidden Wishing Well," "Have You Ever Known?," "Hip-Hop-Susan!," and "I'll Catch Your Heart This Spring".

* * *

LEHMANN, Robert A(rthur) 1932-

PERSONAL: Born October 13, 1932, in Pierce, Neb.; son of Arthur H. and Mildred (Pilger) Lehmann; married Judith E. Wandel, June 23, 1962; children: David, Rachel, Jason. *Education:* Concordia Teachers College, Seward, Neb., B.S.Ed., 1959; University of Michigan, M.A., 1963. *Religion:* Lutheran. *Home:* 335 East Roberts, Seward, Neb. 68434. *Office:* Department of Speech and Drama, Concordia Teachers College, Seward, Neb, 68434.

CAREER: High school teacher of speech and drama in private school in Detroit, Mich., 1959-61, of Christian education in private school in Birmingham, Mich., 1961-64; Concordia Lutheran College, Ann Arbor, Mich., assistant professor of speech and drama, 1964-67; Texas Lutheran College, Seguin, Tex., assistant professor of speech and drama, and chairman of department, 1967-70; Faith Lutheran Church, Topeka, Kan., director of Christian education, 1970-73; Concordia Teachers College, Seward, Neb., assistant professor of speech and drama, and chairman of department, 1973—. *Military service:* U.S. Army, Military Police, 1953-55; became sergeant. *Member:* Speech Communication Association of America, Christian Drama Society of America, American Legion (adjutant of local post, 1955-56).

WRITINGS: Action and Reaction (one-act play; first produced in Ann Arbor, Mich. at Concordia College, 1967, C.S.S. Publishing, 1974; *Vehicles and Vessels* (one-act play), C.S.S. Publishing, 1974.

WORK IN PROGRESS: Expanded Parables: For Dramatization in the Church; research on Readers Theatre in the church, and on teaching speech and drama in teacher education.

* * *

LEHNUS, Donald James 1934-

PERSONAL: Born November 7, 1934, in Lyons, Kan.; son of Carl Henry (a machinist) and Maude (Proffitt) Lehnus. *Education:* University of Kansas, B.A., 1956; University of California, Berkeley, M.L.S., 1957; Case Western Reserve University, Ph.D., 1973. *Religion:* Protestant. *Address:* P.O. Box 21563, San Juan, P.R. 00931. *Office:* Graduate School of Library Science, University of Puerto Rico, Rio Piedras, P.R. 00931.

CAREER: Queens Borough Public Library, Jamaica, N.Y., assistant librarian, 1957-58; Franklin Square Public Library, Franklin Square, N.Y., assistant director, 1958-62; San Leandro Community Library Center, San Leandro, Calif., librarian, 1962-63; University of Antioquia, Medellin, Colombia, professor of cataloging, 1964-66; Western Michigan University, Kalamazoo, assistant professor of cataloging, 1967-70; University of Puerto Rico, Graduate School of Library Science, Rio Piedras, associate professor of cataloging, 1973—. Visiting professor at University of Washington, Seattle, 1969. *Member:* Sociedad de Bibliotecarios de Puerto Rico, American Library Association (life member), Association of American Library Schools, American Association of University Professors, American Society for Information Science.

WRITINGS—Monographs: *Principios de catalogacion y clasificacion para bibliotecas pequenas* (title means "Fundamentals of Cataloging and Classification for Small Libraries"), Editorial Universidad de Antioquia, 1966; *How to Determine Author and Title Entries According to Anglo-American Cataloging Rules: An Interpretive Guide with Card Examples*, Oceana, 1971; *Catalogacao descritiva: manual pratico contendo 225 modelos de fichas exemplificativas das Regras de Catalogacao Descritiva* (title means "Descriptive Cataloging: A Practical Manual Containing 225 Examples of Cards Illustrating the Rules of Descriptive Cataloging"), Editora e Distribuidora VIPA, 1971; *A Comparison of Panizzi's Ninety-One Rules and the Anglo-American Cataloging Rules of 1967*, Graduate School of Library Science, University of Illinois, 1972; *Milestones in Cataloging: Famous Catalogers and Their Writings, 1835-1969*, Libraries Unlimited, 1974; *Entrada principal* (title means "Main Entries"), Editora e Distribuidora VIPA, in press. Contributor to *Journal of the American Society for Information Science, Journal of Education for Librarianship, Wilson Library Bulletin*, and *Library Journal.*

WORK IN PROGRESS: An anthology of cataloging articles; a manual of descriptive cataloging which explains and illustrates the International Standard Bibliographic Description (ISBD).

AVOCATIONAL INTERESTS: Travel.

* * *

LEIDER, Frida 1888-1975

April 18, 1888—June 4, 1975; German opera soprano, and author of autobiography. Obituaries: *Washington Post*, June 5, 1975.

LEIGH, Egbert Giles, Jr.   1940-

PERSONAL: Born July 27, 1940, in Richmond, Va.; son of Egbert Giles and Lucinda (Kinsolving) Leigh; married Elizabeth Hodgson, March 21, 1968. *Education:* Princeton University, A.B., 1962; Yale University, Ph.D., 1966. *Religion:* Christian. *Office:* Smithsonian Tropical Research Institute, Box 2072, Balboa, Canal Zone.

CAREER: Princeton University, Princeton, N.J., assistant professor of biology, 1966-72; Smithsonian Tropical Research Institute, Balboa, Canal Zone, biologist, 1969—. *Member:* American Society of Naturalists.

WRITINGS: Adaptation and Diversity: Natural History and the Mathematics of Evolution, Freeman, Cooper, 1971. Contributor of articles to *American Naturalist, Science*, and other periodicals.

WORK IN PROGRESS: Research on tropical rain forests and on the ecology of population and genetics.

SIDELIGHTS: Leigh told *CA:* "In my book, I wished to recall some sense of the shapes of animals and the feel of landscapes to a subject too much occupied with the numbers of different kinds of organisms or genotypes. I also wanted to show something of the beauty of mathematical theory."

* * *

LEIMBACH, Patricia Penton   1927-

PERSONAL: Surname is pronounced *Lime*-bock; born October 25, 1927, in Amherst, Ohio; daughter of Harold Ryall (a farmer) and Nina (a farmer and teacher; maiden name, Musselman) Penton; married Paul Richard Leimbach (a farmer), December 21, 1950; children: Dane Penton, P. Theodore, Orrin Alfred. *Education:* Western Reserve University (now Case Western Reserve University), B.A., 1949; McGill University, summer graduate study, 1950. *Religion:* United Church of Christ. *Home:* The End O' Way, R.D. #2 Bank Rd., Vermilion, Ohio 44089.

CAREER: Partner in Farm Enterprise, Vermilion, Ohio; teacher of English and French in schools in Henrietta, Ohio, 1949-51; substitute teacher at secondary level in schools in Lorain County, Ohio, 1951-73; public speaker. Member of boards of directors of Lorain County Cancer Society, 1969-75, and of Lorain County Farm Bureau, 1972-75.

WRITINGS: A Thread of Blue Denim (essays), Prentice-Hall, 1974. Writer of column, "The Country Wife," for *Chronicle Telegram*, Elyria, Ohio, 1965—, and *Co-op Country News*, 1974—. Contributor to *A. D., Trail Bike, Cycle News, East*, and *Farm Journal*.

AVOCATIONAL INTERESTS: Motorcycling, skiing, sewing, traveling, and yoga.

* * *

LEINSTER, Murray
See JENKINS, Will(iam) F(itzgerald)

* * *

LEISK, David Johnson   1906-1975
(Crockett Johnson)

October 20, 1906—July 11, 1975; American cartoonist (creator of "Barnaby" strip), artist, author and illustrator of juvenile novels. Obituaries: *New York Times*, July 13, 1975; *Newsweek*, July 28, 1975. (CA-9/10)

LEITCH, D(avid) B(ruce)   1940-

PERSONAL: Born October 30, 1940, in Feilding, New Zealand; son of Stanley David (a newspaper director) and Gwladys (a registered nurse; maiden name, Bealing) Leitch; married Prudence Anne Williams (an artist), January 4, 1964; children: Deborah, Timothy, Peter. *Education:* Victoria University of Wellington, LL.B., 1963. *Politics:* "Middle of road." *Religion:* "Nominal Presbyterian." *Home:* 27 Essex St., Masterton, New Zealand. *Office:* Burridge, Jaine, Leitch & Garstang, Bannister St., Masterton, New Zealand.

CAREER: Burridge, Jaine, Leitch & Garstang (law firm), Masterson, New Zealand, partner, 1965-73, senior partner, 1973—. President of Wairarapa Samaritan Service, 1969-72; president of Wairarapa College Education Trust, 1969—; member of executive board of Wairarapa Chamber of Commerce, 1972—; president of Wairarapa Arts Foundation, 1973—; district coroner, 1973—. *Member:* New Zealand Railway and Locomotive Society (honorary legal counsel, 1970—), Wairarapa Law Society (secretary, 1969-72), Wairarapa College Old Students Association, Masterton Jaycees.

WRITINGS: A Century of Worship, Knox Church Masterton, 1967; *Engine Pass: New Zealand Railways*, A. H. & A. W. Reed, 1967; *Railroads of New Zealand*, Drake, 1972 (published in England as *Railways of New Zealand*, David & Charles, 1972); (contributor) G. S. Troup, editor, *Steel Roads of New Zealand*, A. H. & A. W. Reed, 1973. Contributor to *Rails, New Zealand Railway Observer, Trains, Railway Magazine*, and *Australian Model Railroad Magazine*. New Zealand correspondent for *Railway Transportation*, 1970—.

WORK IN PROGRESS: Research on the final years of steam locomotives on New Zealand railways, and general railway history.

SIDELIGHTS: Since 1974 Leitch has been the holder of a steam locomotive driver's certificate. He writes: "Concerned at ever-increasing invasions of everyday activities by government bureaucracies and the hydra-like growth of bureaucracies. Kept sane by operating one-third-scale steam locomotive on 15-gauge track. Unashamed sentimentalist for steam railway locomotives. Believe World War II hindered steam technology and diesel gained unfair advantage. Electric traction was logical steam successor . . . future for rail traffic unlimited, even if society unready to recognize this yet."

* * *

LEITER, Sharon   1942-

PERSONAL: Surname is pronounced *Light*-er; born August 12, 1942, in Brooklyn, N.Y.; daughter of Albert (a salesman) and Selma (a secretary; maiden name, Weiss) Sherman; married Darryl Jay Leiter (a physicist), June 3, 1962; children: Robin Jennifer. *Education:* Brandeis University, B.A. (magna cum laude), 1963; Boston College, M.S.W., 1967; University of Michigan, M.A., 1973, doctoral candidate, 1976—. *Religion:* Jewish. *Home:* 2439 Stone Dr., Ann Arbor, Mich. 48105.

CAREER: Poet. *Member:* Phi Beta Kappa.

WRITINGS: The Lady and the Bailiff of Time (poems), Ardis, 1974. Contributor of translations of contemporary Russian poetry to academic journals.

WORK IN PROGRESS: Research on the Petersberg imagery in the poetry of Osip Mandelstam.

LEITH, J(ames) Clark   1937-

PERSONAL: Born December 9, 1937, in Brandon, Manitoba, Canada; son of James Scott and Bertha (Clark) Leith; married Carole Ann R. Mason, 1964; children: James Douglas, Deborah Ann, Jonathan Gregory. *Education:* University of Toronto, B.A. (honors), 1959; University of Wisconsin, M.S., 1960, Ph.D., 1967. *Home:* 80 Friar's Way, London, Ontario, Canada. *Office:* Department of Economics, University of Western Ontario, London, Ontario, Canada.

CAREER: Canadian Foreign Service, Santo Domingo, officer, 1961-63, charge d' affaires, 1963-64; University of Western Ontario, London, assistant professor, 1967-71, associate professor of economics, 1971—, chairman of department, 1972—. Lecturer at University of Wisconsin, summer, 1966; consultant to Canadian International Development Agency, 1968-69; member of University of Western Ontario team at University of Ghana, 1969-71.

WRITINGS: (With P. T. Ellsworth) *The International Economy*, 4th edition (Leith was not associated with earlier editions), Macmillan, 1969, 5th edition, 1975; (contributor) H. G. Grubel, editor, *Effective Tariff Protection*, Graduate Institute of International Studies (Geneva), 1971; *Foreign Trade Regimes and Economic Development: Ghana*, National Bureau of Economic Research, 1974. Contributor to economics journals in the United States and abroad.

*   *   *

LENGYEL, Jozsef   1896-1975

1896—July 14, 1975; Hungarian novelist, author of autobiographical works. Obituaries: *New York Times*, July 16, 1975; *Washington Post*, July 18, 1975.

*   *   *

LENNENBERG, Eric H.   1921-1975

September 19, 1921—June 2, 1975; German-born American educator, psychologist, author of books on language. Obituaries: *New York Times*, June 7, 1975; *AB Bookman's Weekly*, June 23, 1975. (*CA*-53/56)

*   *   *

LENNIG, Arthur   1933-

PERSONAL: Born February 22, 1933, in East Williston, N.Y.; son of Arthur O. G. and Katherine (Gardiner) Lennig; married Hannelore Wilfert (a college teacher), June 14, 1955; children: Kurt. *Education:* State University of New York at Albany, B.A., 1955, M.A., 1956; University of Wisconsin, Ph.D., 1961. *Home:* 169 Second St., Troy, N.Y. 12180. *Office:* Department of Art, State University of New York at Albany, Albany, N.Y. 12203.

CAREER: Russell Sage College, Troy, N.Y., assistant professor of English, 1962-66; State University of New York at Albany, associate professor of cinema, 1966—. President of Washington Park Association, 1965-68. *Member:* Society of Cinema Studies.

WRITINGS: (Editor and contributor) *Film Notes*, Film Society, University of Wisconsin, 1960; (editor and contributor) *Classics of the Film*, Wisconsin Film Press, 1965; *The Silent Voice*, Faculty-Student Association, State University of New York at Albany, 1966; *The Silent Voice: A Sequel*, Walter Snyder, 1967; *The Silent Voice: A Text*, Walter Snyder, 1969; (editor) *The Sound Film: An Introduction*, Walter Snyder, 1969; *The Count: The Life and Films of Bela "Dracula" Lugosi*, Putnam, 1974. Contributing editor of *Film Journal*.

WORK IN PROGRESS: The Sound Film: From the Talkies to Today; an analysis of D. W. Griffith's film *Intolerance*; a revised version of *The Silent Voice*; a biography of D. W. Griffith.

*   *   *

LENTZ, Harold H(erbert)   1910-

PERSONAL: Born June 11, 1910, in Nevada, Iowa; son of John Nelson (a clergyman) and Ida Vera (Bowes) Lentz; married Mary Eleanor Selby, June 15, 1935; children: Julia Edythe (Mrs. Charles R. Streich), Thomas William. *Education:* Wittenberg University, A.B., 1932; Hamma School of Theology, B.D., 1935; Oberlin College, A.M., 1939; Yale University, Ph.D., 1943. *Home:* 623 17th Pl., Kenosha, Wis. 53140. *Office:* 2001 Alford Dr., Kenosha, Wis. 53140.

CAREER: Ordained Lutheran clergyman, 1935; pastor of Lutheran church in Ashland, Ohio, 1935-51; Carthage College, Kenosha, Wis., president, 1951—. Lecturer at International Lutheran Academy (Germany) and University of Goettingen. President of College Conference of Illinois and Wisconsin, 1965—; director of Wittenberg College, 1944-51, Johnson Foundation, and Fritsch Charitable Foundation. President of Lutheran national board of social missions, 1950-52, chairman of national commission on evangelism, 1965-69; member of U.S. advisory board to Lutheran World Federation, 1967—. Member of Wisconsin Chamber of Commerce (director, 1965-69); director of local Young Men's Christian Association, Salvation Army, and Red Cross.

MEMBER: Tau Kappa Alpha, Pi Delta Epsilon, Pi Kappa Alpha (national chaplain, 1966-69), Blue Key, Kiwanis, University Club (Chicago), Racine Country Club, Lakeshore Club (Chicago). *Awards, honors:* LL.D. from Wittenberg University, 1952; L.H.D. from Carroll College, Waukesha, Wis., 1974.

WRITINGS: A History of Wittenberg College: 1845-1945, Wittenberg Press, 1945; *Reformation Crossroads*, Augsburg, 1953; *The Miracle of Carthage*, CSS Publishing, 1974.

WORK IN PROGRESS: Research on participation by the Lutheran church in the social gospel.

AVOCATIONAL INTERESTS: International travel.

*   *   *

LEONARD, Jonathan Norton   1903-1975

May 25, 1903—May 15, 1975; American author, magazine writer and editor, author of short stories, biographies, and books on historical and scientific subjects. Obituaries: *New York Times*, May 16, 1975; *Time*, May 26, 1975; *Publishers Weekly*, June 2, 1975.

*   *   *

LERNER, Janet W(eiss)   1926-

PERSONAL: Born June 27, 1926, in Milwaukee, Wis.; daughter of Alex and Nellie (Rubin) Weiss; married Eugene Lerner (an economist), July 1, 1951; children: Susan, Laura, Dean. *Education:* University of Wisconsin, Milwaukee, B.A., 1947; National College of Education, M.Ed., 1958; New York University, Ph.D., 1965. *Home:* 823 Ingleside Pl., Evanston, Ill. 60201. *Office:* Department of Special Education, Northeastern Illinois University, Bryn Mawr and St. Louis Avenues, Chicago, Ill. 60625.

CAREER: Elementary teacher of special education in the public schools of Villa Park, Ill., 1952-54, Skokie, Ill., 1958-59, and Lynbrook, N.Y., 1959-65; City College of the City University of New York, New York, N.Y., assistant professor of education, 1965-66; National College of Education, Evanston, Ill., instructor in education, 1966-67; Northeastern Illinois University, Chicago, assistant professor of special education, 1967-69; Northwestern University, Evanston, Ill., associate professor of learning disabilities, 1969-73; Northeastern Illinois University, Chicago, professor of special education, 1974—. *Member:* International Reading Association, Council for Exceptional Children, Association for Children with Learning Disabilities, National Council of Teachers of English, Kappa Delta Pi. *Awards, honors:* Award from Pi Lambda Theta, 1971-72, for outstanding book in education.

WRITINGS: A Foniks Kwiz, Northeastern Illinois State College Press, 1968; (with Estelle Bradley) *Linguistics for the Teacher of Language Arts,* Illinois Department of Public Instruction, 1968; *Children with Learning Disabilities: Theories, Diagnosis, Teaching Strategies,* Houghton, 1971. Contributor to *Journal of Learning Disabilities, Reading Teacher, Journal of Special Education, Elementary English,* and other journals in her field.

*   *   *

LESLIE KING, William (Donald Aelian) 1910-

PERSONAL: Born June 23, 1910, in Farnborough, Hampshire, England; son of William Albert de Courcy (a British Army colonel) and Georgina (McKenzie) King; married Anita Leslie (an author), January 12, 1949; children: Richard, Leonie Rose. *Education:* Attended Royal Naval Cadet Training College, 1924-27. *Politics:* "Middle of the road." *Religion:* "Tolerant." *Home:* Oranmore Castle, Oranmore, Galway, Eire. *Agent:* E. Holtzmann, Holtzmann & Holtzmann, Bar Building, 36 West 44th St., New York, N.Y. 10036.

CAREER: Royal Navy, submarine specialist; commanded operational submarines, 1939-45; present rank commander. *Member:* Royal Naval Sailing Association.

WRITINGS: The Stick and the Stars (nonfiction), Norton, 1958; *Capsize* (nonfiction), Nautical Publishing, 1969; *Adventure in Depth* (nonfiction), Putnam, 1975.

AVOCATIONAL INTERESTS: Farming, yachting, and skiing.

*   *   *

LESOWITZ, Robert I(rwin) 1939-

PERSONAL: Born August 31, 1939, in Akron, Ohio; son of Moe (a grocer) and Sally (Shapiro) Lesowitz; married Daryl Schwartz, June 17, 1961; children: Toni, Abby. *Education:* University of Akron, B.S., 1961; Ohio State University, M.D., 1965. *Religion:* Jewish. *Office:* Robert I. Lesowitz, M.D., Inc., 100 30th St. N.W., Canton, Ohio 44709.

CAREER: Akron City Hospital, Akron, Ohio, intern, 1965-66; University of Michigan Medical Center, Ann Arbor, residency in adult and child psychiatry, 1966-69; private practice in adult and child psychiatry in Canton, Ohio, 1972—. Adjunct assistant professor at University of Akron, 1974—. Consultant to Stark County Mental Health Center, 1974—. *Military service:* U.S. Army, 1969-72; served in Germany; became major. *Member:* Ohio State Medical Society, Northeast Ohio Psychiatric Association,

Stark County Medical Society, Phi Delta Epsilon (treasurer of graduate club, 1975).

WRITINGS: Rules for Raising Kids, C. C Thomas, 1974.

AVOCATIONAL INTERESTS: Owning and raising walking horses, riding, handball.

*   *   *

LESTER, William

PERSONAL: Born in New Orleans, La.; son of John Sidney and Clara (Dofing) Lester. *Education:* Attended Loyola University, Los Angeles, Santa Clara University, Gonzaga University, Alma College (Pontifical). *Politics:* "Individual freedom modified by social responsibilities. (Adenauer's Christian Democrat?)." *Address:* c/o Arlington House, 81 Centre Ave., New Rochelle, N.Y. 10801.

CAREER: Entered Roman Catholic order of Society of Jesus (Jesuits), ordained priest. Author of nationally syndicated column, "The Moral Angle," 1965—.

WRITINGS: Basic Principles of Saul D. Alinsky (booklet), St. Dismas Publishers, 1969; *Morality, Anyone?,* Arlington House, 1975.

WORK IN PROGRESS: A book, *Recognizing Love.*

SIDELIGHTS: Lester writes: "My work in general consists in the application of Aristotle and Aquinas to contemporaneous problems. The principles are those which founded Western Civilization but which for the last few generations have been quite overlooked. Both men were geniuses and their interpretation of reality simply has no equal and their principles are as cogent today as they ever were."

*   *   *

LEVENSON, Jordan 1936-

PERSONAL: Born 1936, in Los Angeles, Calif.; son of Max (a woodturner) and Hilda (a librarian; maiden name, Rothstein) Levenson. *Education:* California State College (now University), Los Angeles, B.S., 1966; University of Southern California, M.B.A., 1970. *Politics:* "Middle of the road." *Office address:* Levenson Press, P.O. Box 19606, Los Angeles, Calif. 90019.

CAREER: Has worked as salesman, manufacturer's representative, decorator, and motion picture construction laborer; works as professional musician in Los Angeles, Calif., 1951—; Los Angeles County Department of Public Social Services, Los Angeles, Calif., eligibility worker, 1972—. Instructor, University of Southern California Experimental College, 1971—. *Military service:* U.S. Army Reserve, 1959-65.

WRITINGS—All published by Levenson Press: *Retail Fruit Species: Your Shopper's Guide to Their Best Varieties,* 1972; *The Back Lot: Motion Picture Studio Laborer's Craft Described by a Hollywood Laborer,* 1972; *Abilities of Refracting Telescope Optics: A "Non-Mathematical" Understanding for Buyers and Users,* 1973; *Vitamins: A Systems Analysis Solution to the Doctor vs. Health Faddist Controversy,* 1974; *Underlying Concepts of Room Lighting for the Intelligent Layman,* 1974. Contributor to *Journal of Irreproducible Results.*

WORK IN PROGRESS: Books on acoustics, the stock market, and mathematics.

AVOCATIONAL INTERESTS: Trade shows of various industries, preventing aging using a systems approach, body building, social life and dancing, and money markets.

LEVER, Tresham (Joseph Philip) 1900-1975

September 3, 1900—April 30, 1975; British biographer, and author of books on literature and political history. Obituaries: *AB Bookman's Weekly*, June 16, 1975. (*CA*-13/16)

* * *

LEVINE, Daniel Urey 1935-

PERSONAL: Surname rhymes with "divine"; born March 11, 1935, in Chicago, Ill.; son of Nathan H. Levine and Rachel Levine Margolis (an office accountant); married Rayna Freeman (a teacher), December 20, 1958; children: Jennifer, Bruce. *Education:* University of Chicago, B.A., 1954, M.A., 1959, Ph.D., 1963. *Home:* 433 West .68th Terr., Kansas City, Mo. 64113. *Office:* Department of Education, University of Missouri, 5100 Rockhill Rd., Kansas City, Mo. 64110.

CAREER: High school teacher of social studies in Chicago, Ill., 1962-64; Chicago Board of Education, Chicago, Ill., survey associate with Chicago schools survey, 1964; University of Missouri, Kansas City, assistant professor, 1964-67, associate professor, 1967-70, professor of educational administration, 1970—. Consultant-evaluator to North Central Association. Member of Fulbright Screening Committee in Education, 1972-74. *Military service:* U.S. Army, 1954-56. *Member:* American Educational Research Association, American Association of School Administrators, National Society for the Study of Education, American Educational Studies Association, Phi Beta Kappa.

WRITINGS: (With Robert J. Havighurst) *Education in Metropolitan Areas*, Allyn & Bacon, 1971; (with Allan Ornstein and Doxey Wilkerson) *Reforming Metropolitan Education*, Goodyear Publishing, 1974. Editorial advisor of *Phi Delta Kappan*, 1969—.

WORK IN PROGRESS: Study of relationships between census data and school achievement.

* * *

LEVINSON, Irene
See ZAHAVA, Irene

* * *

LEVY, Hyman 1889-1975

March 7, 1889—March 27, 1975; British mathematician, educator, and author of books on mathematics, philosophy, science, and other topics. Obituaries: *AB Bookman's Weekly*, April 7, 1975.

* * *

LEVY, Sue 1936-

PERSONAL: Born December 20, 1936, in Washington, D.C.; daughter of Julius (a U.S. Air Force officer) and Amy (Behrend) Goldstein; married Mayer Levy (a dentist), August 30, 1959 (divorced March 11, 1975); children: Lon, Guy. *Education:* American University, B.A. Fine Arts, 1959. *Politics:* Independent. *Religion:* Animist. *Home and office:* 4615 North Park Ave., Chevy Chase, Md. 20015.

CAREER: Has worked in public relations. Ms. Levy adds that she has "done some deadly PR work for the Jewish Funeral Directors of America." *Member:* "I have just resigned from all societies with committees. All societies have committees."

WRITINGS: The Daisy Book (poetry, prose, and illustrations), Acropolis Books, 1975.

WORK IN PROGRESS: "I write every day about me, my environment and the absurd—which may all be synonymous."

SIDELIGHTS: Sue Levy writes that *The Daisy Book* describes how she "went from Dependent Wife to Independent Person. Included are divorce, leaving my boys (whom I still see) with their father, living alone (for the first time), getting jobs (without a resume), overcoming credit discrimination, learning how to have fun (also first time)." Her book, Ms. Levy continues, "was originally designed as a poster, but ended up being a book jacket with the book written to go with it. . . . *The Daisy Book* seems to be something for everyone—a lovely bonus—because I had only intended it to be everything to me. I am most proud of the foreword that my children asked to write. . . ." *Avocational interests:* Dancing, "analyzing rocks and bringing them to life with a few lines of a black marker."

* * *

LEVY, Wilbert J. 1917-

PERSONAL: Born March 20, 1917, in Brooklyn, N.Y., son of Benjamin (a fire chief) and Minnie (Wolfe) Levy; married Jeanne Hassberg, March 20, 1941; children: Nora Elizabeth (Mrs. William Johnston), Jonathan Benjamin. *Education:* City College (now City College of the City University of New York), B.S., 1936; Columbia University, M.A., 1938; Brooklyn College (now Brooklyn College of the City University of New York), graduate study, 1941-42; New York University, graduate study, 1944, 1949. *Home:* 123-60 83rd Avenue, Kew Gardens, N.Y. 11415. *Office:* AMSCO School Publications, Inc., 315 Hudson St., New York, N.Y. 10013.

CAREER: New York City Civil Service Commission, New York, N.Y., examiner, 1942-45; Midwood High School, Brooklyn, N.Y., teacher of English, 1945-54; Newton High School, Queens, N.Y., chairman of department of English, 1954-74. Consultant, AMSCO School Publications, Inc., 1968—. Member, East Norwich-Oyster Bay Board of Education, 1962-66. *Military service:* U.S. Navy, 1945. *Member:* National Council of Teachers of English.

WRITINGS—All published by AMSCO School Publications: *Patterns of Meaning: A Program Towards More Powerful Reading*, 1969; (with Samuel F. Zimbal) *Reading Comprehension*, 1972; *Man Studies Himself*, 1973; *Man Studies His Past*, 1973; *Man Studies the World Around him*, 1973; *Reading and Growing*, 1975; *Sense of Sentences*, 1975. General editor, "AMSCO Literature Program" series, twenty-one volumes, 1971-75.

AVOCATIONAL INTERESTS: "Reading, ceramics and glasswork, reading, alpine gardening, reading, European travel, reading, golf, reading."

* * *

LeWARNE, Charles P(ierce) 1930-

PERSONAL: Born August 16, 1930, in Kirkland, Wash.; son of Charles T. (a store owner and surveyor) and Angie (a teacher; maiden name, Pierce) LeWarne; married Pauline Nelson, June 10, 1956; children: Charles Nelson, Anne Jennifer, David Joel. *Education:* Western Washington State College, B.A.Ed. and B.A., 1955; University of California, Berkeley, M.A., 1958; University of Washington, Seattle, Ph.D., 1969. *Religion:* Congregationalist. *Home:* 20829 Hillcrest Pl., Edmonds, Wash. 98020.

CAREER: Public school teacher of history in Battle Ground, Wash., 1955-57, and Edmonds, Wash., 1958—. Part-time instructor at Everett Community College, 1962-65, and Edmonds Community College, 1967. *Member:* Organization of American Historians, National Education Association, Pacific Northwest Labor History Conference, Western History Association, Washington State Historical Society. *Awards, honors:* Charles M. Gates Award from Washington State Historical Society, 1969, for article in *Pacific Northwest Quarterly.*

WRITINGS: Utopias on Puget Sound: 1885-1915, University of Washington Press, 1975. Contributor to *Pacific Northwest Quarterly, Labor History*, and *Arizona and the West.*

WORK IN PROGRESS: Research on early twentieth-century radicalism in the Pacific Northwest; studying communitarian experiments of the late nineteenth and early twentieth centuries.

SIDELIGHTS: LeWarne writes: "I tend toward more conservative political and social views personally than those which were held by these individuals and groups whom I admire and write about. The task of the regional historian must be to find what is unique about his area and to relate it to the wider national scene while avoiding provincialism as much as possible. The Pacific Northwest is young enough that historians are only recently exploring seriously the facts and characteristics which I find of importance and interest."

* * *

LEWIS, Horacio D(elano) 1944-

PERSONAL: Born January 17, 1944, in Republic of Panama; son of Clarence E. Lewis (a professor) and Daisy (Campbell) Lewis Blake; married Marsha Russ, 1970 (divorced, 1975); children: Sheena L. *Education:* Attended Universidad Nacional de Panama, 1963; Canal Zone College, A.A., 1965; Morningside College, B.S., 1967; Northeastern Illinois University, M.A., 1972. *Residence:* Bloomington, Ind. *Office:* Indiana University (Maxwell 104), Bloomington, Ind. 47401.

CAREER: Teacher in Republic of Panama, 1963; Young Men's Christian Association (YMCA), Chicago, Ill., teacher and group worker on jobs project, 1967-68, guidance director and teacher at Central Y.M.C.A. High School, 1968-72, instructor at Central Y.M.C.A. Community College, 1972-73; University of Indiana, Bloomington, assistant dean and director of Latino Affairs, 1973—. Has lectured on Latin-American related subjects in Iowa and Chicago, Ill.; caseworker in Chicago, Ill., summer, 1968; advisor, Aspira of Ill., Inc., 1972—, Foundation for Multilingualism and Polyculturalism, 1973—. *Awards, honors:* Decorated by president of Republic of Panama, 1963.

WRITINGS: I Might as Well Move to the Moon, Latino Affairs Publication, 1974; *Latino Affairs Working Papers*, Latino Affairs Publication, 1974; (general editor) *Pueblo Latino*, Latino Affairs Publication, Volume I: *The Chicanos*, 1974, Volume II: *The Puerto Ricans*, 1975, Volume III: *The Cubans*, in press. Also author of scripts for video tape productions for Office of Latino Affairs, Indiana University, including "Latinos: The Second Largest Minority in Higher Education," "The Latino Woman," "Chicano Spanish."

WORK IN PROGRESS: La Situacion Racial en Panama; The U.S. in Panama: A Study of Culture Conflicts; La Jerarquia Racialen Panama.

LEWIS, John E(arl) 1931-

PERSONAL: Born December 23, 1931, in Provo, Utah; son of Walter E. and Marie (Burt) Lewis; married Carolyn Coles, September 24, 1953; children: LynnAnne, John R., Jeannine. *Education:* Brigham Young University, B.S., 1953; graduate work at Brigham Young University, 1957-59, and at University of Utah, 1960-61. *Religion:* Church of Jesus Christ of Latter-Day Saints (Mormon). *Home:* 682 West 40 North, Orem, Utah 84057. *Office:* Utah State Department of Employment Security, 174 Social Hall Ave., Salt Lake City, Utah 84111.

CAREER: Utah State Department of Employment Security, Salt Lake City, assistant personnel director, 1954—. *Military service:* U.S. Army Reserve, 1950—; currently lieutenant colonel. *Member:* International Association of Personnel in Employment Security (vice-president of Utah chapter, 1965), Reserve Officers Association (president of central Utah chapter, 1975—). *Awards, honors:* Freedoms Foundation essay awards, 1970, 1972.

WRITINGS: Vengence Is Mine (novel), Lenox Hill Press, 1975; *The Man Called Sam* (novel), Lenox Hill Press, 1975. Contributor of more than fifty articles to *National Guardsman, Christian Science Monitor, Family Weekly*, and *Supervision.*

WORK IN PROGRESS: A western novel relating to silver mining in Utah in the 1870's, *The Silver Wagons.*

AVOCATIONAL INTERESTS: Travel, skiing, tennis, reading.

* * *

LEWIS, Richard S. 1916-

PERSONAL: Born January 8, 1916, in Pittsburgh, Pa.; son of S. Morton (a dentist) and Mary (a building contractor; maiden name, Lefstein) Lewis; married Louise Silberstein (a teacher), June 8, 1938; children: Jonathan, David. *Education:* Pennsylvania State University, B.A., 1937. *Politics:* Independent. *Home and office:* 3114 Isabella St., Evanston, Ill. 60201.

CAREER: Cleveland Press, Cleveland, Ohio, reporter, 1937-43; *Indianapolis Times*, Indianapolis, Ind., reporter, critic, and city editor, 1946-49; *St. Louis Star-Times*, St. Louis, Mo., investigator-reporter, 1949-51; *Chicago Sun-Times*, Chicago, Ill., reporter, assistant city editor, and science editor, 1951-68; editor of *Science and Public Affairs, Bulletin of the Atomic Scientists*, 1968-74. Member, Illinois Board of Mental Health Commissioners. *Military service:* U.S. Army, 1943-46; served in European theater. *Member:* National Press Club, National Association of Science Writers, Quadrangle Club.

WRITINGS: The Other Child, Grune, 1951, revised edition, 1960; *A Continent for Science*, Viking, 1965; *Appointment on the Moon*, Viking, 1968, revised edition, 1969; (editor with Eugene I. Rabinowitch) *Man on the Moon: The Impact on Science, Technology, and International Cooperation*, Basic Books, 1969 (published in England as *Men in Space: . . .*, Chiltern, 1970); (editor with Jane Wilson and Rabinowitch) *Alamogordo Plus Twenty-Five Years*, Viking, 1970; *The Nuclear Power Rebellion: Citizens vs the Atomic Power Establishment*, Viking, 1972; (editor with P. M. Smith) *Frozen Future: A Prophetic Report from Antarctica*, Quadrangle, 1972; *The Voyages of Apollo*, Quadrangle, 1974.

WORK IN PROGRESS: Continuing the history of the U.S. space program with a third book, to update the program to 1976.

LEY, Sandra 1944-

PERSONAL: Born March 11, 1944, in New York, N.Y.; daughter of Willy (a scientist-writer) and Olga (Feldman) Ley. *Education:* "Self-educated," after attending public schools of New York City. *Politics:* "Radical Stevensonian Liberal." *Religion:* "Lapsed atheist." *Home and office:* 50 West 72nd St., New York, N.Y. 10023. *Agent:* Barthold Fles, 507 5th Ave., New York, N.Y. 10017.

CAREER: Free-lance fashion designer, 1967-75; free-lance writer, 1971—. Member for two years of drama and literature department at WBAI-Radio.

WRITINGS: America's Sewing Book, Scribner, 1972; *Fashion for Everyone,* Scribner, 1975; (contributor) *Beyond Time,* Simon & Schuster, in press. Contributor to *Dictionary of American Culture.*

WORK IN PROGRESS: Two books of embroidery designs, Slavic and Chinese; a book about designing clothes for men.

SIDELIGHTS: Sandra Ley ran on the Liberal Party ticket for the state assembly in New York in 1965 (unsuccessfully). She writes: "I feel the most important thing in life is to develop my full potential as a human being and individual. I hope this does not sound pompous, I really do feel that it is essential. It is not selfish, as if one does not develop one's own potential, one has little or nothing to offer anyone else." *Avocational interests:* History and music.

* * *

LIBERMAN, M(yron) M(andell) 1921-

PERSONAL: Born October 3, 1921, in New York, N.Y.; son of Morton J. and Jane (Schatz) Liberman; married Mathilda Nahra (a college professor), 1958; children: Noah, Alexander. *Education:* Lafayette College, B.A., 1943; New York University, M.A., 1946. *Home:* 1315 Broad St., Grinnell, Iowa 50112. *Agent:* Richmond Agency, P.O. Box 57, Staten Island, N.Y. 10307. *Office:* Carnegie Hall, Grinnell College, Park St., Grinnell, Iowa 50112.

CAREER: Batavia Metal Trades Vocational School, Batavia, N.Y., instructor in English, 1946-55; State University of New York at Buffalo, instructor in English, 1956-57; Wayne State University, Detroit, Mich., instructor in English, 1958-60; Grinnell College, Grinnell, Iowa, assistant professor, 1960-62, associate professor, 1963-67, professor of English, 1967-70, Oakes Ames Professor of English Literature, 1970—.

WRITINGS: (With James Kissane and S. P. Zitner) *A Preface to Literary Analysis,* Scott, Foresman, 1964; *The Practice of Criticism,* Scott, Foresman, 1966; (with Edward E. Foster) *A Modern Lexicon of Literary Terms,* Scott, Foresman, 1968; *Maggot and Worm and Eight Other Stories,* Cummington Press, 1969; *Katherine Anne Porter's Fiction,* Wayne State University Press, 1971.

Work represented in many anthologies, including *Prize Stories, 1957: The O. Henry Awards,* edited by Paul Engle and Constance Urdang, Doubleday, 1957; *Fiction as Process,* edited by Carl Harman and Hazard Adams, Dodd, 1968; *Accent Anthology,* edited by Daniel Curley, University of Illinois Press, 1975.

WORK IN PROGRESS: An expanded edition of *Maggot and Worm and Eight Other Stories.*

LIEBERMAN, R(obert Howard) 1941-

PERSONAL: Born February 4, 1941, in New York, N.Y.; son of Oscar and Gertrude (Riegelhaupt) Lieberman; married Anna Gunilla Rosen (a dance teacher), April 10, 1965; children: Zorba B. O., Boris R. Z. *Education:* Polytechnic Institute of Brooklyn, B.S. in E.E., 1962; Cornell University, M.S., 1965; graduate study at Stockholm, 1965-66. *Politics:* "Against all politicians regardless of race, creed, or color." *Religion:* "Against all religions regardless of race, creed, or color." *Home:* 1612 Coddington Rd., Brooktondale, N.Y. 14817. *Agent:* Raines & Raines, 244 Madison Ave., New York, N.Y. 10016.

CAREER: Lieberman noted that he was "professor of math and physics on the university level while pursuing his writing, diligently stealing time, pens, and paperclips from his academic posts. He taught in a wide variety of institutions for well over ten years ranging from 'predominently black colleges' in the South to a technical university in the arctic north of Sweden to a chairmanship of a math department in Hong Kong"; now full-time writer. *Member:* Eta Kappa Nu.

WRITINGS: Paradise Rezoned (novel), Berkley Books, 1974. Contributor of about one hundred articles and short stories to magazines.

WORK IN PROGRESS: Two novels, one entitled *Goobersville Breakdown*; an original screenplay.

SIDELIGHTS: Lieberman, who has now written nine novels, calls himself "an incessant writer . . . who has found that writing can become an obsessive matter." He began his education by studying veterinary medicine, switched to engineering, physics, mathematics, and then biophysics" (in that order) before realizing that [I] had been born a writer, not a scientist—which meant that [I] had only wasted fifteen years. . . . I want to be read because I think I have something to say. Money is secondary. If that was my interest I would have stayed in science with all of my now-wealthy friends." He speaks Swedish, German, French, Spanish, and Cantonese, and has resided at least once on every continent.

BIOGRAPHICAL/CRITICAL SOURCES: Syracuse Herald-American, January 12, 1975.

* * *

LIEBMAN, Arthur 1926-

PERSONAL: Born September 22, 1926, in Brooklyn, N.Y.; son of Louis (a furrier) and Yetta (Schneider) Liebman; married Joyce Ann Braufman (a concert pianist and teacher) December 19, 1954; children: Robert. *Education:* Brooklyn College (now Brooklyn College of the City University of New York), B.A., 1959, M.A., 1954; New York University, Ph.D. (with honors), 1971. *Politics:* Democrat. *Religion:* Jewish. *Home:* 18 Meadow Lane, Roslyn Heights, N.Y. 11577.

CAREER: High school English teacher in Roslyn, N.Y., 1965—; Hofstra University, Hempstead, N.Y., lecturer in English, 1969-74; State University of New York at Stony Brook, adjunct assistant professor of English, 1975—. Consultant to Human Resources School. *Military service:* U.S. Navy, radioman, 1944-46. *Member:* Broadcast Music Incorporated, Song Writers Association.

WRITINGS: Macbeth: A Student's Workbook, Educator's Publishing, 1970; *Thirteen Classic Detective Stories: A Critical History of Detective Fiction,* Rosen Press, 1973; (editor) *Tales of Horror and the Supernatural,* Rosen

Press, 1974; (editor) *Classic Crimes*, Rosen Press, 1974; (editor) *The Book of Quickie Thrillers*, Simon & Schuster, 1975; (editor) *Book of Ms. Mysteries*, Simon & Schuster, in press.

WORK IN PROGRESS: A college textbook, with readings in the literature of the occult and supernatural; a study of the supernatural in British and American fiction.

SIDELIGHTS: Liebman has devised a dramatics program for the handicapped students at the Human Resources School. *Avocational interests:* Chamber music.

* * *

LIEM, Nguyen Dang 1936-

PERSONAL: Born February 6, 1936, in Cho-Lon, South Vietnam; son of Nguyen Dang Tu and Hua Thi Bon; married Linda Tran Huynh Diep (a university instructor in Vietnamese); children: two. *Education:* University of Paris, Baccalaureat, 1956; University of Michigan, M.A. (English language and literature), 1961, M.A. (linguistics), 1961; University of Saigon, Licence-es-Lettres d'enseignement de francais, 1962; Australian National University, Ph.D., 1966; University of Paris, Doctorat-es-Lettres candidate. *Home:* 7081 Kamilo St., Honolulu, Hawaii 96825. *Office:* Department of Indo-Pacific Languages, University of Hawaii, 2528 The Mall, Honolulu, Hawaii 96822.

CAREER: University of Michigan, Ann Arbor, member of research staff of South-East Asian Regional English Project, United States Operations Missions Contract, Saigon, 1961-63; University of Saigon, Saigon, South Vietnam, lecturer in English and linguistics, 1962-64, chief of University Affairs Bureau, 1962-64; National Institute of Administration, Saigon, South Vietnam, lecturer in English, 1962-64; Australian National University, Canberra, Australia, post-doctoral research scholar in linguistics, 1966-67, part-time lecturer in linguistics, 1966-67; University of Hawaii, Honolulu, linguist and assistant coordinator for Language and Culture at Asia Training Center, 1967-68, became assistant professor, 1968, now associate professor in department of Indo-Pacific Languages. *Awards, honors:* U.S. Department of Health, Education, and Welfare awards, 1970, for preparing a Vietnamese intermediate reader, and 1971, for preparing a Vietnamese advanced reader.

WRITINGS: English Pronunciation for Vietnamese, South-East Asian Regional English Project, University of Michigan, 1962; *English Grammar for Vietnamese*, South-East Asian Regional English Project, University of Michigan, 1963; *English Pattern Practice for Vietnamese*, two volumes, South-East Regional English Project, University of Michigan, 1963; *English Grammar: A Combined Tagmemic and Transformational Approach*, Linguistic Circle of Canberra, Australian National University, 1966; *A Contrastive Grammatical Analysis of English and Vietnamese*, Linguistic Circle of Canberra, Australian National University, 1967; *Four-Syllable Idiomatic Expressions in Vietnamese* (monograph), Institute of Advanced Projects, East-West Center, 1969; *Vietnamese Grammar: A Combined Tagmemic and Transformational Approach*, Pacific Linguistics, Australian National University, 1969; *A Contrastive Phonological Analysis of English and Vietnamese*, Pacific Linguistics, Australian National University, 1970; *Vietnamese Pronunciation*, University of Hawaii Press, 1970; *Intermediate Vietnamese*, Volumes I and II, Seton Hall University Press, 1971; *Advanced Vietnamese: A Culture Reader*, Seton Hall University Press, in press; (editor

and contributor) *Studies in Southeast Asian Linguistics*, Pacific Linguistics, Australian National University, in press. Contributor to proceedings and papers; contributor to professional journals.

* * *

LIGGETT, John 1923-

PERSONAL: Born June 18, 1923, in Manchester, England; son of John William (a schoolmaster) and Ethel (Gale) Liggett; married Arline Payne (a television writer), 1946; children: John Spencer. *Education:* University of London, B.S., 1951. *Home:* Plwcca Lodge, Pendoylan, Cowbridge, Glamorgan, Wales. *Office:* Department of Psychology, University College, University of Wales, Cardiff, Wales.

CAREER: University of Newcastle, Medical School, Newcastle upon Tyne, England, lecturer in applied psychology, 1951-62; University of Wales, University College, Cardiff, senior lecturer in psychology, 1962—. *Military service:* Royal Navy, 1943-48; became lieutenant; received Atlantic Star. *Member:* British Psychological Society (secretary of Northeast England branch, 1956-62), Royal Anthropological Institute (fellow), Society of Authors, Naval Club of London.

WRITINGS: Faces Test, Bealls, 1957; *Exercises in Social Science*, Constable, 1968; *The Human Face*, Stein & Day, 1974. Contributor of articles and reviews to journals.

WORK IN PROGRESS: A reference text on the human face, completion expected in 1975; a compilation of one thousand cases tested with *Faces Test* to provide validity and reliability data.

AVOCATIONAL INTERESTS: Travel, long sea voyages on yacht.

* * *

LIMAN, Claude Gilbert 1943-

PERSONAL: Born May 7, 1943, in Mt. Kisco, N.Y.; son of Edwin (a printer) and Louella (Kluck) Liman; married Ann Elizabeth Holland (an art teacher), September 11, 1965; children: Ben, Sarah. *Education:* Dartmouth College, B.A., 1965; New York University, M.A., 1968; University of Colorado, Ph.D., 1973. *Politics:* "Indifferent: Apathetic." *Religion:* Transcendentalism. *Home:* 407 Pineview Bay, Thunder Bay, Ontario P7C 1Y4, Canada. *Office:* Department of English, Lakehead University, Thunder Bay, Ontario, Canada.

CAREER: High school teacher of English in private school in Andover, N.H., 1966-69; Lakehead University, Thunder Bay, Ontario, assistant professor of English, 1973—. *Member:* League of Canadian Poets, Poets and Writers. *Awards, honors:* Ontario Arts Council award, 1974.

WRITINGS: Landing (poems), Sesame Press, 1975. Contributor of poems to journals. Editor of *Lake Superior Journal*, 1974-75; poetry editor of *Lakehead University Review*, 1974-75.

WORK IN PROGRESS: A new collection of poems giving Whitmanesque recipes and menus for health, *Keeping Fit*; a novel about teaching an adult education course, *Continuing Ed.*

AVOCATIONAL INTERESTS: Baseball, tennis, squash, golf, running.

* * *

LINCOLN, George Arthur 1907-1975

July 20, 1907—May 24, 1975; American military officer,

educator, and author of books on economics, foreign policy, and national security. Obituaries: *New York Times*, May 26, 1975; *Washington Post*, May 27, 1975. (CA-3)

* * *

LINDER, Darwyn E(llsworth) 1939-

PERSONAL: Born September 23, 1939, in Minneapolis, Minn.; son of Ellsworth M. and Ferne (Carlson) Linder; married Marie Johnson (a psychologist), August 21, 1965. *Education:* Macalester College, B.A., 1961; University of Minnesota, Ph.D., 1965. *Home:* 11436 North Sundown Dr., Scottsdale, Ariz. 85260. *Office:* Department of Psychology, Arizona State University, Tempe, Ariz. 85281.

CAREER: Duke University, Durham, N.C., assistant professor, 1965-69, associate professor of psychology, 1969-72; Arizona State University, Tempe, professor of psychology, 1972—. Visiting professor at Stanford University, 1971-72. *Member:* American Psychological Association, American Association of University Professors, American Association for the Advancement of Science, Society for Experimental Social Psychology, Sigma Xi.

WRITINGS: (Editor) *Social Interaction in Contemporary Society: Readings and Perspectives*, Addison-Wesley, 1973; (with wife, Marie J. Linder) *Experience and Personality Change: A Psychometric Assessment of the Impact of Outward Bound Courses*, Outward Bound, 1973; *Personal Space*, General Learning Press, 1974. Contributor to psychological journals. Member of board of consulting editors, *Journal of Experimental Social Psychology*, 1971—, and *Journal of Personality*, 1972—.

WORK IN PROGRESS: Experimental research on nonverbal behavior and social communication.

AVOCATIONAL INTERESTS: Tennis, golf, skiing, mountaineering, wilderness expeditions.

* * *

LINDNER, Edgar T(heodore) 1911-

PERSONAL: Born June 5, 1911, in San Francisco, Calif.; married Maude Rennie; children: Eric R., Edgar T., Jr., Jane, Maude. *Education:* University of California, Berkeley, B.A., 1932. *Religion:* Protestant. *Home:* 15 Blue Ridge Rd., Kentfield, Calif. 94904. *Office:* Medi-Fund Corp., 525 Spruce St., San Francisco, Calif. 94118.

CAREER: Fireboard Products, Stockton, Calif., worked in sales promotion, 1932-40; financial consultant to medical-dental groups, 1950-58; worked as manager of brokerage firm in San Rafael, Calif., 1958-61; president of properties investment firm in San Rafael, 1961-68; Medi-Fund Corp., San Francisco, Calif., president and chief executive officer, 1968—. Member of Marin County Grand Jury. *Military service:* U.S. Army, Infantry, Transportation Corps, 1940-45; became major. *Member:* Northern California Golf Association (member of board of directors), Meadow Club (member of board of directors, 1951-58; president, 1959-63).

WRITINGS: (With Richard S. Isaacs) *A Layman's Guide to Investment Alternatives* (Business Book-of-the-Month Club selection), Chronicle Books, 1974. Contributor to financial columns in newspapers and magazines.

WORK IN PROGRESS: The Best Is Yet to Come, on unemployment and remedies.

* * *

LING, H(sien) C(hang) 1910-

PERSONAL: Born July 25, 1910, in Tsingtao, China; naturalized U.S. citizen, 1961; son of Yun-ke and Shih (Wang) Ling; married Te-fong Sun (in business), 1932; children: James C., Betty Ling Lin. *Education:* University of Illinois, B.S., 1931; Northwestern University, M.B.A., 1933; University of Michigan, graduate study, 1933-34. *Home:* 3384 South Court, Palo Alto, Calif. 94306. *Office:* Lou Henry Hoover Bldg., Rm. 228, Stanford University, Stanford, Calif. 94305.

CAREER: Government of China, Nanking, specialist with Ministry of Railways, 1934-37, secretary general and planning commissioner of War Mobilization Board of Ministry of Railways, 1936-37, director of Chang-sha office of Ministry of Communications, 1937-38, research commissioner with Ministry of Communications in Chungking, 1938-40; Joint Board of Four National Banks, Chungking, China, chief auditor and supervisor of Industrial Loan Division, 1940-43; Farmers' Bank of China, vice and acting manager of Cheng-tu branch, 1943-46; Chi-Chi-Ha-Erh Railway Administration, Mukden, Manchuria, vice-president, 1946-47; Northeastern Production Administration, Mukden, vice and acting president, 1947-48; Central Bank of China, Shanghai, research commissioner, 1948-49; Stanford University, Hoover Institution, Stanford, Calif., research associate with China Research Project, 1955—, and research associate with Arms Control Projects, 1960—.

WRITINGS—All published by Hoover Institution, except as noted: (With others) *Regional Handbooks of Communist China*, Human Relations Area Files Project, Stanford University, 1956; (with Yuan-li Wu) *Economic Development and the Use of Energy Resources in Communist China*, 1963; (contributor) Wu, editor, *The Economic Potential of Communist China*, SRI Publication, Volumes I & II, 1963, Volume III, 1964; (contributor) Wu, *Steel: A Study on the Industrialization of Communist China*, 1965; (with Wu) *The Spatial Economy of Communist China*, 1967; (contributor) Wu, editor, *Arms Control Arrangements for the Far East*, 1967; (contributor) Wu, editor, *Communist China and Arms Control*, 1968; (with Wu) *As Peking Sees U.S.*, 1969; *The Petroleum Industry of the Peoples' Republic of China*, 1975.

WORK IN PROGRESS: With Yuan-li Wu, *The Energy Problem of Japan* (tentative title).

* * *

LINGS, Martin 1909-

PERSONAL: Born January 24, 1909, in Burnage, England; son of George Herbert (a cotton merchant) and Gladys Mary (Greenhalgh) Lings; married Lesley Smalley, August 14, 1944. *Education:* Magdalen College, Oxford, B.A. (English), 1932, M.A., 1937; University of London, B.A. (Arabic), 1954, Ph.D., 1959. *Politics:* Conservative. *Home:* 3 French St., Westerham, Kent, England.

CAREER: University of Kaunas, Kaunas, Lithuania, lecturer in Anglo-Saxon and Middle English, 1935-39; University of Cairo, Cairo, Egypt, lecturer in Shakespeare, 1940-52; British Museum, London, England, assistant keeper in charge of Arabic books and manuscripts, 1955-70, keeper of Oriental manuscripts and printed books, 1970-73; British Library, London, England, keeper of Oriental manuscripts and printed books, 1973-74. Consultant to World of Islam Festival Trust, 1974—. *Member:* British Museum Society, Royal Asiatic Society (fellow; member of council, 1971—).

WRITINGS: The Book of Certainty: The Sufi Doctrine of Faith, Vision, and Gnosis, Rider & Co., 1952, 2nd edition, Samuel Weiser, 1970; *A Moslem Saint of the Twentieth*

Century: Shaikh Ahmad al-Alawi, Macmillan, 1961, 2nd edition published as *A Sufi Saint of the Twentieth Century*, University of California Press, 1971; *Ancient Beliefs and Modern Superstitions*, Perennial Books, 1965; *Shakespeare in the Light of Sacred Art*, Allen & Unwin, 1966; *The Elements and Other Poems*, Perennial Books, 1967; *The Heralds and Other Poems*, Perennial Books, 1970, 3rd edition, 1975; (contributor) J. Needleman, compiler, *The Sword of Gnosis: Metaphysics, Cosmology, Tradition, Symbolism*, Penguin, 1974; *What is Sufism?*, University of California Press, 1975; *The Quranic Art of Calligraphy and Illumination*, World of Islam Festival Trust, 1976.

Contributor to *Encyclopaedia Britannica, New Encyclopedia of Islam*, and to journals in his field.

WORK IN PROGRESS: The Life of Muhammad.

* * *

LIPTON, Lawrence 1898-1975

1898—July 9, 1975; Polish-born American poet, novelist, lecturer, educator, and author of books on the "beat" generation. Obituaries: *New York Times*, July 11, 1975.

* * *

LITTLE, Elbert L(uther), Jr. 1907-

PERSONAL: Born October 15, 1907, in Fort Smith, Ark.; son of Elbert Luther (a railroad tax agent) and Josephine (Conner) Little; married Ruby Rema Rice, August 14, 1943; children: Gordon Rice, Melvin Weaver, Alice Conner (Mrs. Ronald E. Mannan). *Education:* University of Oklahoma, B.A., 1927, B.S., 1932; graduate study, University of Michigan, 1927, Utah State University, 1928; University of Chicago, M.S., Ph.D., 1929. *Home:* 924 20th St. S., Arlington, Va. 22202. *Office:* Forest Service, United States Department of Agriculture, Washington, D.C. 20250.

CAREER: Oklahoma Forest Commission, Broken Bow, Okla., botanist, 1930; Southwestern State College, Weatherford, Okla., assistant professor of biology, 1930-33; U.S. Department of Agriculture, Forest Service, in Tucson, Ariz., assistant forest ecologist, 1934-39, associate forest ecologist, 1939-42, in Washington, D.C., dendrologist, 1942-67, chief dendrologist, 1967-75, consultant, 1975—. Dendrologist in Ecuador and Costa Rica, 1943; botanist, Foreign Economic Administration, Bogota, Colombia, 1943-45; production specialist, U.S. Commercial Co., Mexico, 1945; professor of dendrology, Universidad de Los Andes, 1953-54, 1960; botanist, University of Maryland, Guyana, 1955; consultant and professor, Inter-American Institute of Agricultural Sciences, 1964-65, 1967, 1974; visiting professor, Virginia Polytechnic Institute and State University, 1966-67; consultant, United Nations Food and Agriculture Organization, Ecuador, 1965, 1975, Nicaragua, 1971; member, International Commission for the Nomenclature of Cultivated Plants, 1956—; collaborator, U.S. National Museum of Natural History, 1965—.

MEMBER: American Association for the Advancement of Science (fellow), American Institute of Biological Sciences (member of governing board, 1956-60), Society of American Foresters, Botanical Society of America, Ecological Society of America, Society for Economic Botany, American Society of Plant Taxonomists, International Association for Plant Taxonomy, Association for Tropical Biology, Sociedad Botanica de Mexico, American Fern Society, American Bryological and Lichenological Society, Washington

(D.C.) Academy of Sciences (fellow), Oklahoma Academy of Science (fellow), Phi Beta Kappa, Sigma Xi, Phi Sigma, Beta Beta Beta. *Awards, honors:* U.S. Department of Agriculture, Superior Service award, 1960, Distinguished Service award, 1973, Forty Years Federal Service award, 1974.

WRITINGS—All published by U.S. Government Printing Office, except as indicated: (With L. R. Holdridge and others) *The Forests of Western and Central Ecuador*, U.S. Forest Service, 1947; *Important Trees of the United States*, 1949; (with Raymond F. Taylor) *Pocket Guide to Alaska Trees*, 1950; *Southwestern Trees: A Guide to the Native Species of New Mexico and Arizona*, 1950; *Check List of Native and Naturalized Trees of the United States*, 1953.

(With Roy O. Woodbury and Frank H. Wadsworth) *Trees of Puerto Rico and the Virgin Islands*, Volume I, 1964, Volume II, 1974, Spanish-language edition of Volume I, with Wadsworth and Jose Marrero, published as *Arboles comunes de Puerto Rico y las Islas Virgenes*, Editorial Universidad de Puerto Rico, 1967; (with William B. Critchfield) *Geographic Distribution of the Pines of the World*, 1966; (with Critchfield) *Subdivisions of the Genus Pinus (Pines)*, 1969; (with Robert G. Dixon) *Arboles comunes de la Provincia de Esmeraldas, Ecuador*, Food and Agriculture Organization of the United Nations, 1969.

Atlas of United States Trees, Volume I: *Conifers and Important Hardwoods*, 1971, Volume II (with Leslie A. Viereck): *Alaska Trees and Common Shrubs*, 1975, Volume III: *Minor Western Hardwoods*, 1975, Volume IV: *Minor Eastern Hardwoods*, in press; (with Viereck) *Alaska Trees and Shrubs*, 1972; (with Viereck) *Guide to Alaska Trees*, 1974; *Arboles Comunes de Venezuela* (title means "Common Trees of Venezuela"), Universidad de Los Andes, in press.

Contributor of more than one hundred articles to scientific journals and encyclopedias.

WORK IN PROGRESS: Books and articles on trees and tree identification in the United States and tropical America.

SIDELIGHTS: Little is competent in Spanish. He has lived and worked in eight countries in tropical America and Puerto Rico.

* * *

LITTLE, William Alfred
See LITTLE, Wm. A.

* * *

LITTLE, Wm. A. 1929-
(William Alfred Little)

PERSONAL: Born July 29, 1929, in Boston, Mass.; son of William A. and Myrle (Holmes) Little; married Mary Schimmel (a silversmith), June 3, 1961. *Education:* Tufts College (now University), B.A. (magna cum laude), 1951; Trinity College of Music, L.T.C.L., 1952; Harvard University, M.A., 1953; University of Michigan, Ph.D., 1961. *Religion:* Episcopalian. *Home:* Kirklea, Ivy, Va. 22945. *Office:* Department of Germanic Languages and Literature, Cocke Hall, University of Virginia, Charlottesville, Va. 22903.

CAREER: Williams College, Williamstown, Mass., assistant professor of German, 1957-63; Tufts University, Medford, Mass., associate professor of German, and chairman of department, 1963-66; University of Virginia, Charlottesville, professor of German, 1966—, chairman of department, 1966-72, sesquicentennial fellow, 1972-73. Guest professor for research, Nationale Forschungs- und Gedenkstaetten der klassischen deutschen Literatur in Weimar, fall, 1972. Member of committee on preparation of advanced achievement examination in German, Educational Testing Service, 1968-70. Consultant on development of foreign language program, Virginia Union University. *Military service:* U.S. Army, Intelligence, 1953-55; served in Germany.

MEMBER: American Association of Teachers of German (member of national executive council, 1968—), Modern Language Association of America (chairman of comparative literature section, 1969-70), National Society for Literature and the Arts, American Lessing Society, Internationale Goethe-Gesellschaft, Internationale Grillparzer-Gesellschaft, American Guild of Organists, American Musicological Society, South Atlantic Modern Language Association, Virginia Education Association, Delta Phi Alpha.

WRITINGS: (Contributor) *Fritz Heitmann Gedenkschrift,* Merseburg Verlag, 1963; *Gottfried August Buerger,* Twayne, 1974; (contributor) *Festschrift for W. A. Reichart,* University of Michigan Press, 1975; *Die Orgelwerke Felix Mendelssohn Bartholdys* (title means "The Organ Works of Mendelssohn"), two volumes, VEB Deutscher Verlag fuer Musik, 1975; *A Bibliography of Biedermeier,* Bibliographical Society of America, in press. Contributor of articles to professional journals. Member of editorial board, *Historisch-kritische Ausgabe Felix Mendelssohn Bartholdys Saemmtliche Werke* (title means "An Historical and Critical Edition of the Complete Works of Felix Mendelssohn Bartholdy"), for VEB Deutscher Verlag fuer Musik. Editor, *German Quarterly,* 1970—.

WORK IN PROGRESS: Der Briefwechsel Gottfried August Buergers: Eine historisch-kritische Ausgabe, for Walter De Gruyter Verlag; *The Windows of the Soul: A Study in Grillparzer's Use of Non-Verbal Language; The "Gemalde": A Forgotten Literary Genre.*

AVOCATIONAL INTERESTS: Music, European travel, gastronomy, tennis, antiques.

*   *   *

LITVAG, Irving 1928-

PERSONAL: Surname rhymes with "wit-bag"; born September 5, 1928, in St. Louis, Mo.; son of Joseph (a movie theater owner) and Ida (Rosenberg) Litvag; married Ilene Gallop, June 3, 1962; children: Julie, Joseph. *Education:* Washington University, St. Louis, Mo., A.B., 1950. *Politics:* Independent. *Religion:* Jewish. *Home:* 655 Fairways Circle, St. Louis, Mo. 63141. *Agent:* Curtis Brown, Ltd., 60 East 56th St., New York, N.Y. 10022. *Office:* Washington University School of Dental Medicine, 4559 Scott Ave., St. Louis, Mo. 63110.

CAREER: Columbia Broadcasting System, St. Louis, Mo., radio news writer, 1951-58; Jewish Federation of St. Louis, Mo., director of public relations, 1958-61; Washington University, St. Louis, Mo., director of special events, 1961-72, director of special projects, School of Dental Medicine, 1972—. *Member:* Authors Guild, Society of Professional Journalists, Sigma Delta Chi. *Awards, honors:* First prize, National Playwriting Contest, Webster Groves Theater Guild, 1956, for "The Hitter."

WRITINGS: Singer in the Shadows: The Strange Story of Patience Worth, Macmillan, 1972.

Plays: "Spike" (one-act), first produced in St. Louis, Mo., 1950; "Keep It Clean" (one-act; musical comedy), first produced in St. Louis, Mo., 1950. Also author of "To Make Room for the Factory," a one-act play, and "The Distant Drummer," a three-act play, both as yet neither published nor produced.

Author of newspaper and magazine feature articles, and of radio scripts.

WORK IN PROGRESS: The Collie Man, a biography of author Albert Payson Terhune.

SIDELIGHTS: Litvag told *CA:* "My literary political affiliation is Populist: I believe fervently in clear, direct, readable writing; in other words, the kind that does not win literary prizes or awards. I have received little encouragement (except from Isaac Bashevis Singer, blessed be his name, who called my book a 'masterpiece,') but I shall persevere, fight the good fight, and hopefully last the course." *Avocational interests:* His family, his dog, writing, reading, watching professional football, observing and studying Judaism.

*   *   *

LITZEL, Otto 1901-

PERSONAL: Born June 8, 1901, in Neustadt, Germany; naturalized U.S. citizen in 1938; son of Heinrich (a metal worker) and Mary (Lallman) Litzel; married Alyse Wenzel, March 18, 1962. *Education:* Educated at schools in Germany; attended The New School, 1950, and Museum of Modern Art, 1952. *Home:* 49 Elizabeth St., River Edge, N.J. 07661.

CAREER: Map Draft Co., New York, N.Y., cartographer, 1929-36; free-lance artist, 1936-50; worked as photography teacher, 1950-54; New York University, New York, N.Y., teacher of photography, 1954-66. *Member:* Royal Photographic Society of Great Britain (associate member), Photographic Society of America (fellow), Metropolitan Camera Club Council (fellow), Park West Camera Club (president, 1948-56). *Awards, honors:* Photographic Society of America fellowship, 1966; New Jersey Federation of Camera Clubs citation, 1967; Delaware Valley Council associate, 1974.

WRITINGS: Darkroom Magic, Amphoto, 1967; *Photographic Composition,* Amphoto, 1974.

WORK IN PROGRESS: Fundamental Photography.

SIDELIGHTS: Litzel told *CA:* "My art training in Europe as well as in this country had a great influence on my photography. Because of it I put great emphasis on strong composition. I started to submit photographs to international salons. These competitions are very difficult and the prints submitted must have high quality and universal appeal." He has also judged international salons.

*   *   *

LLEWELLYN, D(avid) W(illiam) Alun 1903-
(Taffy)

PERSONAL: Born April 17, 1903, in London, England; son of David William and Elizabeth Jane (Lewis) Llewellyn; married Lesley Deane (an actress and producer, Royal Academy of Dramatic Art), January 17, 1953. *Education:* St. John's College, Cambridge, B.A. (honors in history and literature), 1924, LL.B. (honors), 1925, M.A.,

1928; Lincolns Inn of Court, called to bar, 1927. *Politics:* Liberal. *Religion:* Christian. *Home:* 52 Silchester Park, Glenageary, Dan Laoghire, County Dublin, Ireland.

CAREER: Liberal Parliamentary candidate from South Croydon, 1931, 1935; League of Nations, Geneva Secretariat, Geneva, Switzerland, engaged in legal translation and treaty revision, 1936-39; also represented Egyptian Government at Montreaux Capitulation Conference, 1937, and at Egypt's admission to the League of Nations; British Central Valuation Board, secretary, and member of Coal Nationalisation Panel of Arbitrators, 1947-49; counsel to Camberwell Borough, 1951-53. Public speaker for British Ministry of Information, Southern Division, 1940-42, for Commonwealth Industries Association, 1955—. *Military service:* British Army, served in Intelligence Corps, World War II. *Member:* International Commission of Jurists (Justice), Union Society of London (president, 1935), Hardwicke Society (president, 1953), Poetry Society of Great Britain (treasurer and counsellor, 1949-63), Bladon Galleries, Confederation of Craft Societies (member of committee). *Awards, honors:* Chancellor's Gold Medal for English Poetry, St. John's College, Cambridge, 1923; College Literature Prize, St. John's College, 1925.

WRITINGS—Listed in some bibliographic sources under name Alun Llewellyn: *Ballads and Songs*, Stockwell, 1921; *Confound Their Politics*, G. Bell, 1934; *The Deacon* (novel), G. Bell, 1934; *The Strange Invaders*, G. Bell, 1934; reprint, New English Library, in press; (with Kenneth Ingram) *History of the Union Society of London*, Union Society, 1935; *The Soul of Cezar Azan*, Arthur Barker, 1938; *The Emperor of Britain*, Montgomeryshire Society, 1939; *Jubilee John: Being the Record of a Pilgrim's Progress Through an Arabian Night*, Arthur Barker, 1939; *The Tyrant from Below: An Essay in Political Revaluation*, Macdonald & Evans, 1957; *Ways to Love* (one-act comedy), Samuel French, 1958; *The World and the Commonwealth*, British Commonwealth Union, 1968; (with Wynford V. Thomas) *The Shell Guide to Wales*, edited by John Betjeman and John Piper, International Publications Service, 1969.

Contributor: *Public School Verse*, Heinemann, 1921; *Prolusiones Academicae*, Cambridge University Press, 1923; *Icarus, Poetry of Flight*, Macmillan, 1937; *Pick of Punch*, Chatto & Windus, 1953; *Oxford Book of Spoken Verse*, Oxford University Press, 1957; *Modern Lyrical Verse*, Thomas Nelson, 1958; *Penguin Comic Verse III*, Penguin, 1959; *Borestone Mountain Best Poems of Year*, 1961; *Pattern of Poetry*, Burke Publishing Co., 1963.

Author of play, "Shelley Plain," produced by Proscenium Club, 1959. Contributor to *Granta* and *New Cambridge*, under pseudonym Taffy; regular contributor to *Punch*, 1949-53; political commentator, *Truth*, 1958-60; contributor to other periodicals, including *Time and Tide, Country Life, Poetry Review, Chambers Journal, Anglo-Welsh Review, Aryan Path*, and *Contemporary Review*.

WORK IN PROGRESS: A first translation of the ancient Arthurian poems in early medieval Welsh; a study of the idea of "natural justice" from early classic to modern scientific philosophy; plays and novels; a collected edition of poems, lyrics, and stories.

SIDELIGHTS: Llewellyn has spent almost four years in research into the conditions of thought in western Europe in the immediate sub-Roman period as background for translating the early Welsh scripts of Taliesin, Aneirin, and other Arthurian poets. These poems are a series of scientific essays on the formation of the universe in accordance with the stoic philosophy of late classical times, Llewellyn's poems were recorded and distributed by the Library of Congress in 1968.

The Shell Guide to Wales was written for the Installation of the Prince of Wales, a copy being presented for his acceptance. Besides Welsh, Llewellyn speaks French, Spanish, Italian, knows Latin and Greek, and has some knowledge of Portuguese and German.

AVOCATIONAL INTERESTS: Walking (he is chief guide of the Sunday Tramps, an organization for broad philosophical discussion during country walks, founded by Sir Leslie Stephen in 1879), riding, swimming, and archeology.

* * *

LLOYD, G(eoffrey) E(rnest) R(ichard) 1933-

PERSONAL: Born January 25, 1933, in London, England; son of William Ernest (a medical practitioner) and Olive Irene Neville (Solomon) Lloyd; married Janet Elizabeth Lloyd (a translator), September 14, 1956; children: Adam John Peregrine, Matthew David Nathaneal, Gwilym Nicholas Edward. *Education:* King's College, Cambridge, B.A., 1954, M.A., 1958, Ph.D., 1958. *Office:* King's College, University of Cambridge, Cambridge CB2 1ST, England.

CAREER: University of Cambridge, Cambridge, England, fellow of King's College, 1957—, senior tutor, King's College, 1969-73, assistant university lecturer, 1965-67, lecturer in classics, 1967-74, reader in ancient philosophy and science, 1974—. *Military service:* British Army, Intelligence Corps, 1958-60; became captain. *Member:* Hellenic Society, Royal Anthropological Institute.

WRITINGS: Polarity and Analogy: Two Types of Argumentation in Early Greek Thought, Cambridge University Press, 1966; *Aristotle: The Growth and Structure of His Thought*, Cambridge University Press, 1968; *Early Greek Science: Thales to Aristotle*, Chatto & Windus, 1973; *Greek Science after Aristotle*, Chatto & Windus, 1973; (editor) *Hippocratic Writings*, Penguin, in press. Contributor to proceedings; contributor to classical journals and (London) *Times Literary Supplement*.

WORK IN PROGRESS: Research on ancient philosophy and science.

SIDELIGHTS: Lloyd has competence in French, Spanish, Italian, Greek, and German. *Avocational interests:* Travel.

* * *

LO, Irving Yucheng 1922-

PERSONAL: Born September 19, 1922, in Foochow, China; son of M. H. (a banker) and H. C. (Wu) Lo; married Lena Dunn (an editor), August 11, 1945; children: Adrian Hsiang-yun. *Education:* St. John's University, Shanghai, China, B.A., 1945; Harvard University, M.A., 1949; University of Wisconsin, Ph.D., 1954. *Home:* 2219 Sussex Dr., Bloomington, Ind. 47401. *Office:* Department of East Asian Languages and Literatures, Indiana University, 248 Goodbody Hall, Bloomington, Ind. 47401.

CAREER: Stillman College, Tuscaloosa, Ala. instructor, 1952-53, professor of English and chairman of department, 1953-57; Western Michigan University, Kalamazoo, assistant professor, 1957-60, associate professor of English, 1960-64; University of Iowa, Iowa City, associate professor of Orientatl studies, 1964-67; Indiana University, Bloomington, associate professor, 1967-72, professor of Chinese, 1972—, head of department, 1974—.

WRITINGS: *Hsin Ch'i-chi* (a Sung poet, 1140-1207), Twayne, 1971; (editor with Wu-chi Liu) *Sunflower Splendor: Three Thousand Years of Chinese Poetry*, Doubleday, 1975. Contributor to *Literature East and West*.

* * *

LODGE, Orlan Robert 1917-1975

1917—June 27, 1975; American military officer, computer systems analyst, and author of book on military history. Obituaries: *Washington Post*, June 29, 1975.

* * *

LOESER, Herta 1921-

PERSONAL: Born March 23, 1921, in Berlin, Germany; daughter of Hans and Henny (Elkan) Lewent; married Hans F. Loeser (a lawyer); children: Helen, Harris, H. Thomas. *Education:* Educated in Germany and England. *Office:* Civic Center and Clearing House, Inc., 14 Beacon St., Boston, Mass. 02108.

CAREER: Civic Center and Clearing House, Inc., Boston, Mass., co-director and vocational advisor, 1967—; Radcliffe Institute, Cambridge, Mass., visiting research scholar, 1972-74; Cambridge Center for Adult Education, Cambridge, Mass., instructor of courses on creative leisure and career choice, 1974—, member of board of trustees, 1969-76. Member of board of trustees, Franconia College, 1972—. *Member:* Association of Voluntary Action Scholars, Society of Fellows, Radcliffe Institute.

WRITINGS: *Women, Work, and Volunteering*, Beacon Press, 1974.

SIDELIGHTS: Herta Loeser came to this country from England after World War II, a refugee from Hitler's Germany. For two years she worked with displaced persons and was involved in setting up a search service for survivors from concentration camps. In addition to having counseled and placed hundreds of volunteer workers, she now devotes time to advising clients on vocational and career choices, and suggesting unorthodox methods of work entry.

* * *

LOGAN, Terence P(atrick) 1936-

PERSONAL: Born November 6, 1936, in Boston, Mass.; son of Francis D. and Caroline J. (Swan) Logan; married Kathlyn Guyther, 1965; children: Deirdre E. *Education:* Boston College, A.B., 1959; Dartmouth College, graduate study, 1959-60; University of Wisconsin-Madison, M.A., 1961; Harvard University, Ph.D., 1966. *Home:* 2 Moharinet Way, Durham, N.H. 03824. *Office:* Department of English, University of New Hampshire, Durham, N.C. 03824.

CAREER: University of Maryland, College Park, assistant professor of English, 1965-68; University of New Hampshire, Durham, assistant professor, 1968-71, associate professor of English, 1971—, assistant vice-president of research, 1972-73. Visiting professor at University of Wisconsin-Milwaukee, 1967. *Awards, honors:* Dante Prize from Dante Society, 1964, for "The Characterization of Ulysses in Homer, Dante, and Virgil"; Southeastern Institute of Medieval and Renaissance Studies fellow, summer, 1966.

WRITINGS: (Editor with Denzell S. Smith) *The Predecessors of Shakespeare*, University of Nebraska Press, 1973; (editor with Smith) *The Popular School*, University of Nebraska Press, 1975. Editing with Smith "Recent Studies in English Renaissance Drama" series, for University of Nebraska Press. Contributor to *Annual Report of the Dante Society, Kentucky Romance Quarterly, Notes and Queries, Library, Papers of the Bibliographical Society of America, Comparative Literature Studies*, and *Modern Language Journal*. Editor of *Shakespeare Newsletter*, 1970—, and of *English Literary Renaissance*, 1971—.

WORK IN PROGRESS: Editing two books with Densell S. Smith in the "Recent Studies in Engish Renaissance Drama" series, for publication by University of Nebraska Press, *The New Intellectuals*, 1977, and *The Later Jacobean and Caroline Dramatists*, 1979.

* * *

LOGSDON, Thomas S(tanley) 1937-
(Tom Logsdon)

PERSONAL: Born September 27, 1937, in Springfield, Ky.; son of George Stanley (a miller) and Margaret (a nurse; maiden name, Buckman) Logsdon; married Fae Shobe (a teacher), August 21, 1960; children: Donna Lorraine. *Education:* Eastern Kentucky University, B.S., 1959; University of Kentucky, M.S., 1961; University of California, Los Angeles, further graduate study, 1961-75. *Home:* 235 Clipper Way, Seal Beach, Calif. 90740. *Office:* Rockwell International, Bay Blvd., Seal Beach, Calif. 90740.

CAREER: Naval Ordnance Laboratory, Silver Spring, Md., student trainee, 1958; Douglas Aircraft, Santa Monica, Calif., senior engineer, 1959-61; Rockwell International, Seal Beach, Calif., flight mechanics engineer, 1961—. *Member:* North American Mathematical and Statistical Community, American Institute of Aeronautics and Astronautics, American Astronautical Society, American Mathematical Society, National Aerospace Education Council, Thursday Exchange Club. *Awards, honors:* Radio Corp. of America science scholarship, 1957-58.

WRITINGS: *The Rush toward the Stars*, W. C. Brown, 1969; *An Introduction to Computer Science and Technology*, Franklin Publishing (Palisade, N.J.), 1970; *The Computers in Our Society*, Anaheim Publishing, 1974, workbook, 1975. Author of "Grouches by Groucho" and "The Spice of Life," columns appearing in *Eastern Progress*.

WORK IN PROGRESS: *Programming in Basic*, for Anaheim Publishing; *The Sex Life of American Blurbles*, a joke book; *Project Skyhook*, on the ultimate solution to the energy crisis; *A Search along the Thumb Circuit*, a novel.

* * *

LOGSDON, Tom
See LOGSDON, Thomas S(tanley)

* * *

LONDON, Carolyn 1918-

PERSONAL: Born October 24, 1918, in Denver, Colo.; daughter of Thomas B. and Lillie Dale (Gunby) McCormick; married Paul A. London (a missionary), July 20, 1945. *Education:* Attended Biola College, 1940-42. *Religion:* Protestant. *Home:* 201 West 89th St., New York, N.Y. 10024. *Agent:* Marilyn Marlowe, Curtis Brown Ltd., 60 East 56th St., New York, N.Y. 10022. *Office:* Sudan Interior Mission, Cedar Grove, N.J. 07009.

CAREER: Missionary with Sudan Interior Mission in West Africa, Lebanon, and New York, N.Y., 1942—; author of children's books. *Member:* Society of Children's Book Writers, Puppeteers of America.

WRITINGS—Children's books: *Adventures of Mr. Jeeponary*, Scripture Press, c. 1961; *Adventures of Mr. Bicycle*, Scripture Press, c. 1961; *Further Adventures of Mr. Jeeponary*, Scripture Press, c. 1961; *Littlest Airplane*, Scripture Press, c. 1961; *Zarga's Shadow*, Duell, Sloan & Pearce, 1966, reissued as *Shadow of the Spear*, Moody, 1971; *Yaro of Africa*, Christian Publications, 1969; *Cat-a-log*, Moody, 1971; *Ratcatcher's Son and other Stories*, Moody, 1971; *Dugout Canoe*, Sudan Interior Mission, 1971; *Olu's Lions*, Moody, 1971; *You Can Be a Puppeteer*, Moody, 1972; *Mystery of the Stolen Curse*, Moody, 1973; *Doctors, Nurses, and Hospital Mystery Workers*, McGraw, 1975; *Twins Solve the Fire Mystery*, Moody, 1975. Also author of radio scripts in connection with missionary work.

WORK IN PROGRESS: A new puppet book and a book for very young children.

SIDELIGHTS: Mrs. London and her husband were "bush" missionaries in Nigeria from 1945 to 1958. Of their work there, she writes: "We lived in a city of over ten thousand Nigerians, and we kept many little African boys in our compound. We fed them, clothed them and taught them to read, and came to know and love them. Much of my writing then was done between mending torn pants, settling childish arguments or dishing up grain for their meals."

* * *

LONESOME COWBOY
   See WHITE, John I(rwin)

* * *

LONE STAR RANGER
   See WHITE, John I(rwin)

* * *

LONGEAUX y VASQUEZ, Enriqueta 1930-

PERSONAL: Born May 30, 1930, in Cheraw, Colo.; daughter of Abundio Cortez (a laborer) and Faustina (a laborer; maiden name, Perez) Vasquez; married Herman Tafoya, 1952 (divorced, 1955); married Yermo Longeaux y Vasquez (an artist and sculptor), July 7, 1967; children: (first marriage) Ruben, Ramona. *Education:* Attended Peublo College, 1958, and University of New Mexico, 1974—. *Address:* P.O. Box 43, San Cristobal, N.M. 87564.

CAREER: Weinberg's Furniture Store, Denver, Colo., office worker, 1950-53; Bellinger & Faricy, Pueblo, Colo., legal secretary, 1957-60; Hughes Aircraft, Los Angeles, executive secretary, 1960-63; U.S. District Court, Denver, secretary to U.S. Attorney, 1964-66; Operation Service, Denver, Colo., director of skills bank, 1966-67. *Awards, honors:* G.I. Forum outstanding member, 1967.

WRITINGS: (With Elizabeth Southerland Martinez) *Viva la Raza* (title means "Long Live the Race"), Doubleday, 1974. Work is represented in *Sisterhood is Powerful*, edited by Robin Morgan, Random House, 1970, and in Chicano anthologies. Contributor of "Despierten Hermanos" column to *El Grito del Norte*, 1968-73 (also appeared in other Chicano newspapers).

WORK IN PROGRESS: Cultural research in parapsychology in relation to pre-Columbian information seen in the contemporary world; a book concerned with the god-

dess myth relating its four hundred year history to the Americas, *Book of Chal.*

* * *

LOOK, Al 1893-

PERSONAL: Born August 15, 1893, in Lincoln, Neb.; son of Albert L. and Marie (Sturm) Look; married Margaret L. Langen, June 30, 1921; children: A. T., Jean (Mrs. Albert Comiskey), Anne (Mrs. Lester Beauvais). *Education:* Attended University of Nebraska, 1915-17. *Home and office:* 1248 Ouray Ave., Grand Junction, Colo. 81501.

CAREER: Homesteaded in Dove Creek, Colo., 1919; worked as mail order manager for mercantile store in Durango, Colo., 1919-20; worked for *Durango Herald*, 1919-20, and *Daily News*, 1921-27; *Daily Sentinel*, Grand Junction, Colo., advertising director, 1927-60; U.S. Bank of Grand Junction, advertising manager, 1960-75. Taught retail advertising and conducted advertising clinics. *Military service:* U.S. Navy, 1917-19; became ordinance officer. U.S. Naval Reserve, 1919-30. *Member:* International Newspaper Advertising Executives (life member; member of board of directors, 1960-65), Society of Vertebrate Paleontologists, Bank Marketing Association, Rocky Mountain Advertising Men's Association (president, 1942-43), Colorado Archaeological Society, American Cancer Society (Colorado Division, board member, 1965-70, honorary member), Lions Club, American Legion, Ancient Free and Accepted Masons.

WRITINGS: In My Back Yard, University of Denver Press, 1951; *John Otto*, Sandstone Press, 1952; *1000 Million Years on the Colorado Plateau*, Golden Bell, 1955; *Advertising at Retail*, Golden Bell, 1955; *U-Boom*, Golden Bell, 1956; *Harold Bryant: Colorado's Maverick With a Paint Brush*, Golden Bell, 1962; *S'Fact*, Sandstone Press, 1963; *No Advertising*, Golden Bell, 1963; *Unforgettable Characters of Western Colorado*, Pruett, 1966; *Sidelights on Colorado History*, Golden Bell, 1967; *Utes Last Stand*, Golden Bell, 1972; *Bits of Colorado History*, Golden Bell, 1975. Author of booklets, "Ute Indians: Meeker Massacre," "Hopi Indian Snake Dance," "Grand Junction 1881," and "Western Colorado." Contributor to Denver Westerners Brand Book and to newspapers and magazines.

WORK IN PROGRESS: Hopi Snake Dance; *How and Why I Quit Smoking.*

SIDELIGHTS: Look is credited with discovering *Spractolambda looki*, an archaic mammal that lived 50 million years ago and, also, two prehistoric human cultures named the Turner-Look site and the Taylor-Look site. *Avocational interests:* Archaeology, paleontology, geology, travel, and oil painting.

* * *

LOOMBA, N(arendra) Paul 1927-

PERSONAL: Born December 22, 1927, in Dhilwan, Panjab, India; came to United States in 1949, naturalized in 1961; married Mary Adams, August, 1957; children: Sonya Kumari, Sheela Kumari, Lalit Kumar. *Education:* University of Panjab, B.S., 1947; University of Nebraska, B.S. (mechanical engineering), 1952, B.S. (electrical engineering; with distinction), 1952; Massachusetts Institute of Technology, M.S., 1954; University of Wisconsin, Ph.D., 1957. *Home:* 24 Taunton Rd., Scarsdale, N.Y. 10583. *Office:* 315 Park Ave. S., New York, N.Y. 10010.

CAREER: Loomba & Co. (marketing firm), Panjab, India,

vice-president, 1947-49; University of Wichita, Wichita, Kan., assistant professor of management science, 1957-59; University of Iowa, Iowa City, assistant professor, 1959-62, associate professor of management science, 1962; Lehigh University, Bethlehem, Pa., associate professor, 1962-63, professor of management science, 1963-66, head of department, 1966; Ogden Corp., New York, N.Y., vice-president of operations research and planning, 1966-69; Bernard M. Baruch College of the City University of New York, New York, N.Y., professor of management, 1968—, head of department, 1972—; Lalit Corp. (management planning and financial consulting), New York, N.Y., consultant, 1969—. Consultant to Beech Aircraft Co., 1957-58, Frontier Chemcial Co., 1959-61, U.S. Army Management Engineering Training Agency, Rock Island, Ill., 1961-63, Air Product and Chemicals, Inc., 1965, Pennsylvania Power and Light Co., 1965, Bethlehem Steel Corp., 1965-66, chancellor of Board of Trustees of State Colleges of Rhode Island, 1968-70, City of New York, 1971, White Plains Hospital, 1972—, and the Government of Mauritius. President of Fund for the Advancement of Education in India, Inc., 1963—.

MEMBER: Academy of Management, American Economic Association, Institute of Management Science, Operations Research Society of America, National Society for Corporate Planning, American Institute for Decision Sciences, Omicron Delta Kappa, Beta Gamma Sigma, Order of Artus, Sigma Xi, Pi Mu Epsilon, Eta Kappa Nu.

WRITINGS: Engineering Economics for Decision-Making, U.S. Army Management Engineering Training Agency, 1962; *Application of O. R. to Small Business Administration* (monograph), Bureau of Business and Economic Research, University of Iowa, 1963; *An Analysis of Environmental and Managerial Factors in the Success or Failure of Small Manufacturing Enterprises* (monograph), Bureau of Business and Economic Research, University of Iowa, 1963; *Linear Programming: An Introductory Analysis*, McGraw, 1964, 2nd edition, Macmillan, in press; (with Samuel Levey) *Health Care Administration: A Managerial Perspective*, Lippincott, 1973; (with Levey) *Health Care Administration: A Selected Bibliography*, Lippincott, 1973; (with Efraim Turban) *Applied Programming for Management*, Holt, 1974; (with Turban) *Readings in Operations Research and Management Science*, Business Publications, in press. Contributor to proceedings; contributor to journals in his field. Associate editor of *Journal of the Society of Management Science and Applied Cybernetics*, 1973—; management science editor of *Planning Review Journal*, 1974—.

WORK IN PROGRESS: Quantitative Management, publication by Macmillan expected in 1977.

*   *   *

LOOTS, Barbara Kunz   1946-

PERSONAL: Surname rhymes with "notes"; born September 30, 1946, in Kansas City, Mo.; daughter of William Ellis (a U.S. Air Force lieutenant colonel) and Doris (Schuerman) Kunz; married Larry Rolfe Loots (a Hallmark Cards senior planner), July 20, 1969. *Education:* Winthrop College, B.A., 1967. *Politics:* Conservative. *Religion:* Christian. *Home:* 7943 Charlotte, Kansas City, Mo. 64131. *Office:* Hallmark Cards, Inc., 25th and McGee, Kansas City, Mo. 64141.

CAREER: Hallmark Cards, Inc., Kansas City, Mo., children's editor of Hallmark Editions, 1967—.

WRITINGS: Season of Love (poems), Hallmark Editions, 1974; *The Fifth Season* (nonfiction), Hallmark Editions, 1975; *A Horse, Of Course* (juvenile verse story), Hallmark Editions, 1975; *Debbie's Dollhouse* (juvenile story), Hallmark Editions, 1975. Contributor to *Ladies' Home Journal* and other periodicals.

WORK IN PROGRESS: A collection of verse.

*   *   *

LOPES, Michael   1943-

PERSONAL: Born April 29, 1943, in Watsonville, Calif.; son of Allen Miller and Maxine (McElroy) Lopes; married Katherine Hale (a teacher), July 24, 1964; children: David, Nathaniel. *Education:* University of California, Santa Barbara, student, 1961-62; University of California, Berkeley, B.A., 1966; State University of New York at Stonybrook, M.A., 1971. *Home:* 682 East Sixth St., Chico, Calif. 95926.

CAREER: Variously employed during his early years as machine operator, truck driver, house painter, and camp counselor; Ohlone College, San Jose, Calif., instructor in English, 1971-72; California State University, Chico, assistant professor of English, 1972—. *Member:* Modern Language Association of America.

WRITINGS: Mr. and Mrs. Mephistopheles and Son, Dustbooks, 1975. Work is anthologized in *Hard Six*, edited by Phillip Hemenway, Kopy Kat Press, 1973; *Eating the Menu*, edited by Bruce Edward Taylor, Kendall/Hunt, 1974; *Poets West*, edited by Lawrence Spingarn and Harold Norse, Perivale Press, 1975; *A Tumult for John Berryman*, edited by Marguerite Harris, Corinth, 1975. Contributor to literary journals, including *Apple, Poetry Now, Hanging Loose, Cape Rock Journal, Cutbank, Big Moon*, and *College Composition and Communication*.

WORK IN PROGRESS: Botanists of the Heart and *The People on My Street*, both poetry.

SIDELIGHTS: Lopes writes: "What am I trying to do in my writing? Each new poem seems—in retrospect—to say some slightly new thing, which I would have been unable to articulate beforehand. And this new articulation, I suppose, is what motivates me to continue writing. That, plus the sheer joy of the process. My subject is almost always myself (taken broadly) and my immediate surroundings. I shed selves periodically and travel as much as possible."

*   *   *

LORIMER, Lawrence T(heodore)   1941-

PERSONAL: Born March 26, 1941, in Denver, Colo.; son of Robert L. and Norma Gustafson) Lorimer; married Janice McClintic, June 5, 1964; children: Paul, Judith. *Education:* Attended University of St. Andrews, 1962-63; Augustana College, Rock Island, Ill., B.A., 1964; Columbia University, M.A., 1967. *Politics:* Democrat. *Religion:* Lutheran. *Residence:* New York, N.Y. *Office:* Random House, Inc., 201 East 50th St., New York, N.Y. 10022.

CAREER: Prentice-Hall, Inc., New York, N.Y., assistant editor of professional books, 1964-65; Random House, Inc., New York, N.Y., assistant editor of juvenile books, 1965-66; Cowles Book Co., New York, N.Y., associate editor of reference books, 1968; Random House, Inc., associate editor of juvenile books, 1970-75, senior editor of adult trade books, 1970—.

WRITINGS: (Editor and compiler) *Breaking In: Nine*

First-Person Accounts about Becoming an Athlete, Random House, 1974.

WORK IN PROGRESS: An autobiographical book.

AVOCATIONAL INTERESTS: Music, books.

* * *

LORTZ, Richard 1930-

PERSONAL: Born January 13, 1930, in New York, N.Y.; divorced; children: one. *Education:* Attended Columbia University, 1949-52. *Home:* 545 Beach 133rd St., Belle Harbor, Long Island, N.Y. 11694. *Office:* 322 West 88th St., New York, N.Y. 10024.

CAREER: Hoffman Publications, New York, N.Y., successively managing editor and editor of various business magazines, 1954-65; *Industrial Photography* and *Audio-Visual Communications*, New York, managing editor, 1965-71. Novelist, playwright, artist, 1954—. *Military service:* U.S. Army, 1952-53; became sergeant. *Awards, honors:* St. Gaudens Medal for fine draftsmanship, 1948; Hallmark International Art Award for painting, 1952; Stanley Drama Award, 1970, for play "Three Sons."

WRITINGS—Novels: *A Crowd of Voices*, Bobbs-Merrill, 1958; *A Summer in Spain*, P. Davies, 1961; *Children of the Night*, Dell, 1974; *The Betrothed*, Dell, 1975.

Plays: "A Journey with Strangers" (three-act), first produced Off-Broadway at Greenwich Mews Theatre, 1958; "The Others" (two-act) first produced in Leatherhead, England, 1967, produced in West End at Strand Theatre, 1968, produced as "Voices" on Broadway at Ethel Barrymore Theatre, 1972 (also see below); "Three Sons" (two-act; later titled "Prodigal"), first produced in Staten Island, N.Y., at Wagner College, 1970; produced in New York by Circle Theatre Repertory Company, 1974; "The Juniper Tree" (two-act), first produced Off-Off-Broadway by the Splinters Company, 1972; *Voices* [and] *The Widow* (both one-act), Performance Publishing, 1974.

Author of television plays, all produced in the late 1950's: "Mr. Nobody," "The Kiss-Off," "The Bet," "The Others," "Vacancy for Death," "M Is for Murder," "The Key," "Circle of Doom," and other dramas for series, including "Studio One," "Suspense," "The Web," and "Danger." Writer of radio dramas. Contributor of stories to magazines, including *Esquire, Story, New Story* (Paris), *Virginia Quarterly Review of Literature, Tiger's Eye on Arts and Letters, Liberty,* and *Scholastic Voice.*

WORK IN PROGRESS: Three novels, *Bereavements, Strangers in Cameroon,* and *Ramon.*

SIDELIGHTS: Adaptations of Lortz's play, "The Others," were televised by Thames-TV, London, and CBC-TV, Toronto, 1967, 1970; the original stage play was also adapted as a film, under the title "Voices," 1974.

Lortz, who has been publishing his writings since the age of seventeen, is also an accomplished artist whose paintings have been exhibited in one-man shows and in several group shows.

* * *

LOTTMAN, Eileen 1927-
(Maud Willis)

PERSONAL: Born August 15, 1927, in Minneapolis, Minn.; daughter of Myer (a certified public accountant) and Goldye (Cohn) Shubb; married Evan Lottman (a motion picture film editor), August 25, 1956; children: Jessica.

Education: Attended University of Iowa, 1950. *Home:* 890 West End Ave., New York N.Y. 10025. *Agent:* Phoebe Larmore, 44 Greenwich Ave., New York, N.Y. 10011.

CAREER: Held numerous odd jobs, 1950-53; Arthur P. Jacobs Co., New York, N.Y., film press agent, 1953-57; Allan, Foster, Ingersoll & Weber, New York, N.Y., film press agent, 1957-65; G. P. Putnam's Sons, New York, N.Y., publicity director, 1965-68; Dell Publishing Co., New York, N.Y., publicity director, 1968-69; Bantam Books, New York, N.Y., copy chief, 1969-70, editor, 1970-71; writer, 1971—. *Member:* National Book Critics Circle.

WRITINGS: *The Hemlock Tree* (gothic novel), Popular Library, 1975; *Summersea*, Coward, 1975; (under pseudonym Maud Willis) *The Devil's Rain* (novelization of own filmscript), Dell, 1975; (under pseudonym Maud Willis) *Doctors' Hospital* (novelization of own filmscript), Pocket Books, 1975. Author of filmscripts, under name Eileen Lottman, "The Devil's Rain" and "Doctors' Hospital." Author of study guides on the making of films, for Universal Pictures. Author of "Under Covers," a column in *Village Voice.*

WORK IN PROGRESS: Two novels, one of them set in Madrid.

SIDELIGHTS: Eileen Lottman writes: "I write for fun and money. I wrote my first book in order to pay for a flute, which I took up when I began free-lancing and found I had time to practice. My husband's work allows us to travel the best way—three to six months in each new place. I feel extraordinarily lucky, may never try to write for art's sake."

* * *

LOUIS, Tobi 1940-

PERSONAL: Born April 14, 1940, in Madison, Wis. *Education:* American Academy of Dramatic Arts, teaching certificate, 1958; New York University, A.B., 1960, M.A., 1963; University of Wisconsin, B.A., 1962; also studied dance at Martha Graham and Katherine Dunham schools of the dance. *Residence:* New York, N.Y.

MEMBER: Dramatists Guild, Actors Equity, Association, Eugene O'Neill Memorial Theatre Center (co-chairperson, O'Neill Playwrights, 1975-76), American National Theatre and Academy, Museum of Modern Art, American Museum of Natural History, National Trust for Historic Preservation, Smithsonian Associates. *Awards, honors:* John Golden Playwriting Fellowship of Hunter College of the City University of New York, 1968, for "The Insides of Orchid Price."

WRITINGS—Plays: "Sounds of Laughter," first produced in New York at Actors Playhouse, 1965; "Cry of a Summer Night," first produced at Actors Playhouse, 1965; "Time Is a Thief," first produced in Waterford, Conn., at O'Neill Theatre Center, 1967; "The Insides of Orchid Price," first produced at Hunter College of the City University of New York, 1968; "Fantasy," first produced at O'Neill Theatre Center, 1969, produced in New York at Playbox Theatre, 1970; "Solitude, Frenzy, and the Revolution," first produced at New York Cultural Center, 1974; produced in New York at Manhattan Theatre Club, 1974. Also author of filmscript, "The Witty and the Dumb," Joseph Wienner Productions, 1974. Contributor to medical journals, and other publications.

WORK IN PROGRESS: A nonfiction book on business dynamics; two plays, "Sing to Me of Far Away Places" and "Tears Are for a Very Young Man"; a musical play, "Take a Chance"; a bicentennial play.

SIDELIGHTS: Tobi Louis told *CA:* "My love of animals is exceeded only by my love of people. I hope that what I write and how I live does justice to both and exemplifies the only philosophy I have which is to judge a fellow being not by what is on his back but rather by what is in his soul"

*   *   *

LOVELESS, E(dward) E.   1919-

PERSONAL: Born July 29, 1919, in Lafayette, Ind.; son of M. Benjamin (a farmer) and Belva (Bowles) Loveless; married Jean Skinner, May 18, 1941; children: Linda (Mrs. Karl Johnson), Kathleen (Mrs. Tom Bodine), Stephen, Melissa (Mrs. Rollo Campbell), Benjamin. *Education:* Purdue University, B.S., 1940, M.S., 1941; Stanford University, Ed.D., 1960. *Politics:* Democrat. *Religion:* Presbyterian. *Home:* 2895 Moana Lane, Reno, Nev. 89502. *Office:* Department of Educational Administration and Higher Education, University of Nevada, Reno, Nev. 89507.

CAREER: Teacher and principal of public school in Tippecanoe County, Ind., 1941-50; superintendent of schools in Indiana, 1951-57; University of Nevada, Reno, professor of education, 1965—. Visiting professor at San Francisco State College (now University), 1961, San Jose State College (now California State University, San Jose), 1964, Purdue University, 1965, 1968, 1975. *Member:* International Society for General Semantics, National Education Association, Nevada Education Association, Indiana Schoolmen's Club, Northwest Indiana Superintendents Association, Phi Delta Kappa.

WRITINGS: (With Frank R. Krajewski) *The Teacher and School Law: Cases and Materials in the Legal Foundations of Education*, Interstate Printers & Publishers, 1974; (editor) *Who's Who in Nevada Education*, University of Nevada Printers, in press. Contributor of more than thirty articles to education journals.

AVOCATIONAL INTERESTS: Chess, golf, swimming.

*   *   *

LOVIN, Roger Robert   1941-
(Wesley Brighton, Jr.)

PERSONAL: Surname rhymes with "oven"; born May 11, 1941, in Knoxville, Tenn.; son of Chet E. (an engineer) and Molly (Rogers) Lovin; married Sandra Dale Trahan (a philosopher), November 7, 1963 (divorced). *Education:* Louisiana State University, student, 1964. *Politics:* "Intense dislike of politicians." *Religion:* None. *Agent:* Virginia Kidd, Box 278, Milford, Pa. 18337.

CAREER: The Ungarbled Word (weekly newspaper), New Orleans, La., publisher, 1968, 1969; *Los Angeles Free Press*, Los Angeles, Calif., ecology editor, 1972-73; writer, 1973—. *Military service:* U.S. Navy, 1959-63. *Member:* Science Fiction Writers of America.

WRITINGS: The Complete Motorcycle Nomad, Little, Brown, 1974. Author of columns in *Road Rider* and *Drive*. Contributor of articles, essays, short fiction, and book reviews to periodicals under pseudonym.

WORK IN PROGRESS: M'Kabba, a novel; for Harper; *The Happy Seamster*, nonfiction, for Little, Brown; *Truckin'!*, nonfiction, Little, Brown; *White Rabbit*, a novel, Little, Brown.

SIDELIGHTS: Lovin writes: "I am a nomad, physically

and philosophically. My interests are eclectic, my viewpoint humanistic, and my approach scientific. My intellectual thrust is directed toward correlations—how it all fits together. I am concerned with social and environmental overviews, and with the veracities of sexual structures in the law and in application."

*   *   *

LOWANCE, Mason I(ra), Jr.   1938-

PERSONAL: Born June 2, 1938, in Atlanta, Ga.; son of Mason Ira and Kathleen (Bowden) Lowance; married Susan Coltrane, July 19, 1963; children: Susan Radcliffe and Margaret Elizabeth. *Education:* Princeton University, A.B. (cum laude), 1960; Columbia University, graduate study, 1961; Oxford University, B.A. (second class honors), 1964, M.A., 1966; Emory University, Ph.D., 1967. *Home:* 18 Echo Hill Rd., Amherst, Mass. 01002. *Office:* Department of English, University of Massachusetts, Amherst, Mass. 01002.

CAREER: Punahou School, Honolulu, Hawaii, instructor in English and religion, 1960-61; Morehouse College, Atlanta, Ga., instructor in English and assistant to director of Upward Bound Program, 1964-67; University of Massachusetts, Amherst, assistant professor, 1967-71, associate professor of English, 1971—. Visiting professor at Tufts University, 1971. Instructor and director of teaching at Northampton Prison, 1972-73. Consultant to Educational Services, Inc., 1965-67, Educational Projects, Inc., 1966-68, U.S. Office of Economic Opportunity, 1967-69, and U.S. Office of Education, 1967—. *Member:* Modern Language Association of America, American Studies Association, American Association of University Professors, American Antiquarian Society. *Awards, honors:* American Antiquarian Society research fellowship, 1972; Huntington Library and Art Gallery research fellowships, 1973, 1975.

WRITINGS: (Contributor) Sacvan Bercovitch, editor, *Typology and Early American Literature*, University of Massachusetts Press, 1972; *Increase Mather: A Critical Biography*, G. K. Hall, 1974; (with Georgia Bumgardner) *Massachusetts Broadsides of the American Revolution: 1765-1790*, University of Massachusetts Press, 1975; (author of introduction) John Duffy, editor, *Vermont Broadsides of the Revolution and Early Federal Period*, New England University Press, 1975; (contributor) Earl Miner, editor, *Typology and Literature: Religious Figuralism from Medieval to Modern Times*, Princeton University Press, in press. Contributor of articles and reviews to journals. Managing editor of *Early American Literature*, 1969-73.

WORK IN PROGRESS: The Language of Canaan: Metaphor in American Thought from 1620 to 1776, with Jesper Rosenmeier; *Seeing Is Believing: The Symbolic Imagination in American Literature from the Puritans to the Civil War*; a contribution to *The Works of Jonathan Edwards*, edited by John E. Smith, for Yale University Press.

*   *   *

LOWREY, Kathleen   1943-

PERSONAL: Born April 28, 1943, in Bristol, Conn.; daughter of Robert Lewis (a factory worker) and Germaine (Tousignant) Lowrey. *Education:* Mount Sacred Heart College, A.A., 1964; attended Normandy College, 1964-65, Loyola University, Chicago, Ill., and Rosary College, 1965-66. *Politics:* Independent. *Religion:* Non-sectarian. *Residence:* West Hartford, Conn.

CAREER: Roman Catholic nun of the Congregation of the Apostolic Sisters of the Sacred Heart, 1963-67; elementary school teacher in St. Louis, 1963-65, Melrose Park, Ill., 1965-66, and junior high school teacher in Hamden, Conn., 1966-67; St. Francis Hospital, Hartford, Conn., isotope technician, 1967-68; executive secretary for insurance agencies, a wholesale/import company, and a real estate firm in Florida, 1968-74; Aetna Life & Casualty, Hartford, now executive secretary. *Member:* Religious Science Alumni.

WRITINGS: Up Among the Stars (autobiography), Ashley Books, 1974. Contributor to *Science of Mind* and *Religious Science Alumni Newsletter.*

WORK IN PROGRESS: A sequel to her autobiography.

* * *

LOWTHER, George F.   1913-1975

1913—April 28, 1975: American radio and television writer, director, producer, and author of juvenile novels and science-fiction television plays. Obituaries: *New York Times*, April 30, 1975.

* * *

LUBANS, John, Jr.   1941-

PERSONAL: Born June 15, 1941, in Riga, Latvia; son of John A. (a contractor) and Irene S. Lubans; married Judith M. Abbe (a legal secretary), September 9, 1960; children: Stephanie V., Dace A., John A. *Education:* Lebanon Valley College, B.A., 1964; University of Michigan, M.A.L.S., 1966; State University of New York at Albany, further graduate study, 1968. *Home:* 1031 Waite Dr., Boulder, Colo. 80303. *Office:* Library, University of Colorado, Boulder, Colo. 80302.

CAREER: Rensselaer Polytechnic Institute, Troy, N.Y., head of circulation department of library, 1966-68, head of Reader Services Division, 1968-70; University of Colorado Libraries, Boulder, assistant director for public services, 1970—.

WRITINGS: (With Edward A. Chapman and Paul L. St. Pierre) *Library Systems Analysis Guidelines*, Wiley, 1970; (editor) *Educating the Library User*, Bowker, 1974; (with Chapman) *Reader in Library Systems Analysis*, Microcard Editions, 1975. Contributor to library journals.

WORK IN PROGRESS: Public service programs for educating library users; studies to understand the needs of library users; research on the effectiveness of public service programs in libraries, with reference to implementation and evaluation.

* * *

LUCAS, Joyce   1927-

PERSONAL: Born December 21, 1927, in Plymouth, England; daughter of William Charles and Caroline (Cobbledick) Brinham; married Noel Thomas Lucas (a lecturer and electrical engineer), April 9, 1955; children: Caroline Rebecca, Deborah Mary, Benjamin Brinham. *Education:* Gipsy Hill Training College, teacher's certificate, 1947; London School of Economics and Political Science, child care officer's diploma, 1954. *Politics:* Socialist. *Religion:* Society of Friends (Quaker). *Home:* 40 Thornbury Ave., Southampton SO1 5DA, England. *Office:* Education Department, La Sainte Union College of Education, Southampton SO9 5HB, England.

CAREER: Teacher in schools in England, 1947-53; child care officer in Southampton, England, 1954-57; La Sainte Union College of Education, Southampton, England, lecturer in education, 1970—. Area organizer for Southampton Playgroups, 1966-70; tutor of playgroup worker and parent groups, 1968—; manager and governor of various Southampton schools, 1970—. Justice of the Peace in Southampton, 1964—. *Member:* Southampton Pre-School Playgroup Association (founder/chairman).

WRITINGS: (With Vivienne McKennel) *The Penguin Book of Playgroups*, Penguin, 1974.

WORK IN PROGRESS: A new approach to nursery education; curricula development in pre-school education.

SIDELIGHTS: Joyce Lucas writes: "My great interest in life is people, their relationship one with another, and with their surroundings. I have a particular concern for disadvantaged children and the sad way our modern way of living has of crippling their potential." *Avocational interests:* Listening to music, surfing, gardening.

* * *

LUCAS, Noah   1927-

PERSONAL: Born June 30, 1927, in Glasgow, Scotland; married Beatrice Sarah Taylor (a nurse), November 4, 1965; children: Sonia, Tamara. *Education:* University of Glasgow, M.A. (honors), 1951; Washington University, St. Louis, Mo., Ph.D., 1961. *Office:* Department of Political Theory and Institutions, University of Sheffield, Sheffield S10 2TN, England.

CAREER: Histadrut Executive, Tel Aviv, Israel, international secretary, 1953-57; Southern Illinois University, Edwardsville, assistant professor of government, 1961-63; Hebrew University of Jerusalem, Jerusalem, Israel, research fellow, 1963-66; University of Glasgow, Glasgow, Scotland, visiting lecturer in politics, 1966-67; University of Sheffield, Sheffield, England, lecturer in American government and politics, 1967—. Visiting associate professor, Southern Illinois University, 1965; senior associate member, St. Antony's College, Oxford University, 1975-76; visiting fellow, Oxford Centre for Postgraduate Hebrew Studies, 1975-76. *Military service:* British Army, 1945-48. *Awards, honors:* Research fellowship in social science from Nuffield Foundation, 1975-76.

WRITINGS: The Modern History of Israel, Weidenfeld & Nicolson, 1974, Praeger, 1975.

* * *

LUND, Philip R(eginald)   1938-
(Confucius)

PERSONAL: Born July 28, 1938, in Christchurch, New Zealand; son of Reginald G. (a businessman) and Melva Isabel (Haigh) Lund. *Education:* Harvard University, A.B., (magna cum laude), 1962; London Business School, graduate study, 1971. *Office:* 714 Willoughby House, Barbican, London EC2Y 8BN, England.

CAREER: Chemstrand Co., New York, N.Y., international market analyst, 1962-64; Viyella International, London, England, economist, 1964-65; Rank Xerox, London, England, salesman, 1965-67; Ultrasonic Machines, Slough, Buckinghamshire, England, sales manger, 1967-69; Philip Lund Ltd. (consultants), London, England, sales and marketing troubleshooter, 1969—. *Military service:* Royal Navy, 1957-59.

WRITINGS: Sales Reports Records and Systems, Gower

Press, 1972; *Compelling Selling: A Framework for Persuasion*, Macmillan, 1974; (under pseudonym Confucius) *Confucius and Company: Thoughts of the Chairman*, Business Books, 1974. Contributor to business journals.

WORK IN PROGRESS: A novel; a script.

AVOCATIONAL INTERESTS: Travel, golf, theatre, creative solutions to problems.

* * *

LURIE, Ranan R(aymond) 1932-

PERSONAL: Born May 26, 1932, in Egypt; son of Joseph (a certified public accountant) and Rose (a teacher; maiden name, Same) Lurie; married Tamar Fletcher, February 25, 1959; children: Rod, Barry, Daphne. *Education:* Attended Herzelia College, until 1950, Universal College, 1951, and Saligsberg Art School, 1952; also studied art in Paris, 1954. *Religion:* Jewish. *Home and office:* Baldwin Farms North, Greenwich, Conn. 06830.

CAREER: Editor, writer, and cartoonist with *Yedioth-Aharonot, Ma'Ariv*, and *Hador*, daily newspapers in Israel, 1950-66; *Life* (magazine), New York, N.Y., political cartoonist, 1968-73; syndicated political cartoonist, 1970—; *Newsweek International* (magazine), New York, N.Y., contributing editor and political cartoonist, 1974—; chief editorial cartoonist for *Vision* magazine, South American and Spanish editions, 1975—. Has had 22 fine art exhibits. *Military service:* Israeli Army Reserve, Infantry, 1948-67; became major. *Member:* Overseas Press Club, National Cartoonists' Society of America, Association of Editorial Cartoonists. *Awards, honors:* Voted one of the three best editorial cartoonists in America by National Cartoonists' Society of America, 1971, 1972, 1973, 1974; Front Page Award from Newspaper Guild of New York, 1971; Montreal Cartoon Salon Award, 1971; Headliners' Award from National Headliners Club, 1972; Publication Designers Award, 1975; numerous fine arts awards.

WRITINGS: Among the Suns, Het Alef (Israel), 1953; *Lurie's Best Cartoons*, Tversky (Israel), 1960; *Nixon Rated Cartoons*, Quadrangle, 1973, 2nd edition, 1974; *Pardon Me, Mr. President!*, Quadrangle, 1975.

SIDELIGHTS: Lurie writes: "I believe that a sincere, dedicated political analyst and cartoonist must be nonpartisan. He is an instant historian, treating every event according to its own merit. It is impossible that one person, one state, one regime, will always by right or will always be wrong. Therefore, any political analyst or cartoonist who assumes that President Ford, for instance can only do bad, can't be a professional analyst. The same goes for the cartoonist who thinks that President Ford can only do good. You cannot play tennis with the forehand only."

WORK IN PROGRESS: Henry Kissinger on the Unemployment Line, in cartoons, for Quadrangle.

* * *

LUSSIER, (Joseph) Ernest 1911-

PERSONAL: Born February 21, 1911, in Fall River, Mass.; son of Louis (an operative) and Victoria (Labonte) Lussier. *Education:* Angelicum, S.T.L., 1938; Ecole Biblique and Pontifical Biblical Commission, S.S.L., 1952. *Home:* Eymard Seminary, Hyde Park, N.Y. 12538.

CAREER: Roman Catholic priest of Congregation of Blessed Sacrament Fathers (S.S.S.), ordained 1938; Blessed Sacrament Seminary, Cleveland, Ohio, professor of biblical literature, languages, and archeology, 1938-67; St. Mary of the Lake Seminary, Mundelein, Ill., professor of New Testament, 1968-74; Eymard Seminary, Hyde Park, N.Y., research professor, 1974—. *Member:* Catholic Biblical Association of America, American Schools for Oriental Research, Society for Biblical Literature and Exegesis, Catholic Biblical Association of England.

WRITINGS: Commentary on Proverbs and Sirach, Liturgical Press, 1965; *Getting to Know the Eucharist*, Alba House, 1974; *Christ's Priesthood According to the Epistle to the Hebrews*, Liturgical Press, 1975; *Living the Eucharistic Mystery*, Alba House, 1975. Contributor to *New Catholic Encyclopedia* and to religion journals. Book review editor for *Emmanuel*, 1965—.

WORK IN PROGRESS: Priestly Living; Christian Living; Biblical Prayer.

* * *

LYNN, David B(randon) 1925-

PERSONAL: Born February 25, 1925, in Dallas, Tex.; son of Moore (a certified public accountant) and Griffie (Watson) Lynn; married Rosalie Clifton (a clinical psychologist), January 18, 1946. *Education:* State University of Iowa, B.A., 1949; Purdue University, M.S., 1951, Ph.D., 1955. *Politics:* Democrat. *Home:* 222 Baja Ave., Davis, Calif. 95616. *Office:* Department of Applied Behavioral Sciences, University of California, Davis, Calif. 95616.

CAREER: Indiana University, Bloomington, supervisor of psychological services at Riley Child Guidance Clinic, 1953-54; Institute for Social Research, Oslo, Norway, research project director, 1955-56; Indiana University, supervisor of psychological services at Riley Child Guidance Clinic, 1956-57; University of Colorado, Boulder, assistant professor of clinical psychology, 1957-61; College of San Mateo, San Mateo, Calif., member of psychology faculty, 1961-68; University of California, Davis, professor of human development, 1968—. *Military service:* U.S. Army, 1943-45. *Member:* American Psychological Association, Society for Research in Child Development, Western Psychological Association, Phi Beta Kappa, Sigma Xi.

WRITINGS: Parental and Sex-Role Identification: A Theoretical Formulation, McCutchan, 1969; *The Father: His Role in Child Development*, Brooks-Cole, 1974. Contributor to psychology journals.

WORK IN PROGRESS: Parents and Daughters: Parental Influence in the Development of Daughters.

SIDELIGHTS: Lynn writes: "I was influenced very much by a year spent doing research on the effects of father absence in Norwegian sailor families in 1955-56 ... My later works on the theory of the development of masculinity and femininity and the book on the father stem from thinking that began twenty years ago in Norway ..." *Avocational interests:* Hiking, the city of San Francisco.

* * *

LYNN, Edward S(hird) 1919-

PERSONAL: Born November 27, 1919, in McGregor, Tex.; son of Doley Houston (a carpenter) and Mary (Lindsey) Lynn; married Marcille Umland, May 10, 1942; children: Edward S., Jr., Sarah Ellen (Mrs. Richard C. Festger), Robert Bruce. *Education:* Baylor University, B.B.A., 1941; University of Texas at Austin, Ph.D., 1955. *Residence:* Tucson, Ariz. *Office:* Department of Accounting, BPA, University of Arizona, Tucson, Ariz. 85721.

CAREER: Lybrand, Ross Brothers, and Montgomery (accountants and auditors), Dallas, Tex., staff member, 1945-47; certified public accountant, 1947; Baylor University, Waco, Tex., assistant professor of accounting, 1947-48, acting head of department, 1947-48; Texas Economy Commission, Austin, Tex., research analyst, 1951-52; University of Texas, Austin, assistant professor of accounting, 1952-55; University of Tennessee, Knoxville, associate professor of accounting, 1955-56; University of Wisconsin, Madison, associate professor of accounting, 1956-60; private accounting practice in Madison, Wis., 1957-60; American Institute of Certified Public Accountants, New York, N.Y., director of education, 1960-65; University of Arizona, Tucson, professor of accounting, 1965—, head of department, 1966-69. Secretary of Commission to Study the Common Body of Knowledge for Certified Public Accountants, 1963-66; lecturer at School for Bank Administration, Bank Administration Institute, University of Wisconsin, summer, 1971-73. Military service: U.S. Army Air Forces, pilot, 1941-45; became captain.

MEMBER: American Accounting Association (vice-president, 1968-69), American Institute of Certified Public Accountants, Arizona Society of Certified Public Accountants, Beta Alpha Psi, Beta Gamma Sigma, Delta Sigma Pi, Sigma Iota Epsilon.

WRITINGS: Special Funds and the Dedication of Revenues of the State of Texas, Texas Economy Commission, 1952; Auditing Wisconsin School Districts, Bureau of Business Research and Service, School of Commerce, University of Wisconsin, 1959; Municipal and Governmental Accounting, fourth edition (Lynn was not associated with earlier editions), Prentice-Hall, 1960; Unofficial Answers to the Uniform CPA Examinations of the American Institute of Certified Public Accountants: May 1960 to November 1962, American Institute of Certified Public Accountants, 1963; (with William C. Bruschi) Unofficial Answers to the Uniform CPA Examinations of the American Institute of Certified Public Accountants: May 1963 to November 1965, American Institute of Certified Public Accountants, 1966; (contributor) Herbert E. Miller, editor, CPA Review Manual, 3rd edition, Prentice-Hall, 1966; Miller and George C. Mead, editors, 4th edition, 1972; (contributor) James A. Cashin, editor, Handbook for Auditors, McGraw, 1971; (with Robert J. Freeman) Fund Accounting, Prentice-Hall, 1974; (with Joan W. Thompson) Introduction to Fund Accounting, Reston Publishing, 1974. Contributor to proceedings; contributor to journals in his field. Editor of "Education and Professional Training," Journal of Accountancy, 1962-65.

*　*　*

MAAS, Audrey Gellen 1936-1975

December 7, 1936—July 2, 1975; American film producer, adapter of plays and books for television, and novelist. Obituaries: New York Times, July 3, 1975. (CA-23/24)

*　*　*

MacCLINTOCK, Dorcas 1932-

PERSONAL: Born July 16, 1932, in New York, N.Y.; daughter of James T. (a businessman) and Helen (Kay) Eason; married Copeland MacClintock (an invertebrate paleontologist), June 30, 1956; children: Margaret, Pamela. Education: Smith College, A.B., 1954; University of Wyoming, A.M., 1957. Politics: Independent. Religion: Episcopalian. Home: 33 Rogers Rd., Hamden, Conn. 06517.

CAREER: American Museum of Natural History, New York, N.Y., student assistant, 1947-53; Yale University, Peabody Museum of Natural History, New Haven, Conn., curator of osteology collection, 1965-67. Research associate, California Academy of Sciences, San Francisco, 1958—. Member: American Society of Mammalogists, Society of Vertebrate Paleontology, Ecological Society of America, Sigma Xi. Awards, honors: New York Academy of Sciences Award for outstanding 1973 science book in the older category (ages 7-14), for A Natural History of Giraffes; the same book was selected by Children's Book Council as one of the outstanding books of the year.

WRITINGS: Squirrels of North America, Van Nostrand, 1970; (with Ugo Mochi) A Natural History of Giraffes (juvenile), Scribner, 1973. Contributor of articles to Audubon Magazine, Pacific Discovery, and other journals.

WORK IN PROGRESS: A book on zebras, for Scribner; research for a book on raccoons.

SIDELIGHTS: Mrs. MacClintock writes: "Interest in natural history, especially mammals, stems from childhood. Traveled to East Africa in 1970."

*　*　*

MacDONALD, Craig 1949-

PERSONAL: Born September 26, 1949, in Oakland, Calif.; son of Franklin (an English professor) and Jane (Curry) MacDonald. Education: San Jose State College (now University), B.A. (with distinction), 1971. Address: P.O. Box 191, San Diego, Calif. 92112.

CAREER: San Diego Union, San Diego, Calif., reporter, 1972—. Guest lecturer at San Jose State University, 1971—. Military service: U.S. Army Reserve, 1972—. Member: California Writers Club, San Diego Historical Society, San Jose State University Alumni Association, San Diego Press Club, Phi Alpha Theta, Sigma Delta Chi, Phi Kappa Phi. Awards, honors: McCormick journalism scholarship, 1972, for feature articles in Spartan; Copley newspaper editorial fellowship, 1972; second place in J. C. Penny-University of Missouri Newspaper Journalism Awards and Pulitzer Prize nomination, both 1974, for six-part series on energy crisis.

WRITINGS: Cockeyed Charley Parkhurst: The West's Most Unusual Stagewhip (biography), Filter Press, 1973. Contributor to Ebony, Quill, Desert Magazine, Friends (Chevrolet magazine), California Highway Patrolman, and California Today.

WORK IN PROGRESS: Books on western transportation, on western mining camps, and on the western migration of relatives.

SIDELIGHTS: MacDonald crossed the Sierra Nevada range in a covered wagon and in a stage coach. He also swam the American River rapids in an effort to capture the flavor of early pioneers who ventured west.

*　*　*

MACE, David Robert 1907-

PERSONAL: Born June 21, 1907, in Montrose, Scotland; came to United States in 1949; retains British citizenship; son of Joseph (a minister) and Josephine (Reid) Mace; married Vera Chapman, July 26, 1933; children: Sheila Mace Runge, Fiona Mace Patterson. Education: University of London, B.Sc., 1927; Cambridge University, B.A., 1930, M.A., 1932; University of Manchester, Ph.D., 1942. Reli-

gion: Society of Friends. *Home:* Route #1, Black Mountain, N.C. 28711. *Office:* Behavioral Sciences Center, Bowman Gray School of Medicine, Wake Forest University, Winston-Salem, N.C. 27103.

CAREER: Methodist minister in England, 1930-40; National Marriage Guidance Council of Great Britain, Rugby, England, executive director, 1942-49, honorary vice-president, 1949—; Drew University, Madison, N.J., professor of human relations, 1949-59; University of Pennsylvania School of Medicine, Philadelphia, associate professor of family study, 1959-60; American Association of Marriage Counselors, Claremont, Calif., executive director, 1960-67; Wake Forest University, Bowman Gray School of Medicine, Winston-Salem, N.C., professor of family sociology, 1967—. Visiting professor, University of the Witwatersrand, 1954. Vice-president, International Union of Family Organizations, 1963-70; president, Sex Information and Education Council of the U.S., 1966-68. Consultant to Parents Without Partners, Inc., 1946—, World Council of Churches, 1957-71, Marriage Council of Philadelphia, 1959-60, North Carolina Family Life Council, 1970—. *Member:* American Association of Marriage Counselors, National Council on Family Relations (president, 1961-62), Association of Couples for Marriage Enrichment (president, 1973—), American Association of Sex Educators, and Counselors, Society for the Scientific Study of Sex (charter member), Groves Conference on Marriage and the Family.

WRITINGS: Does Sex Morality Matter?, Rich & Cowan, 1943; *Marriage Counseling,* J. & A. Churchill, 1948; *Marriage Crisis,* Delisle, 1948; *Marriage: The Art of Lasting Love,* Doubleday, 1952 (published in England as *Marriage: The Art of Lasting Happiness,* Hodder & Stoughton, 1952); *Hebrew Marriage: A Sociological Study,* Philosophical Library, 1953; *Whom God Hath Joined: A Book of Christian Marriage,* Westminster, 1953, revised edition, 1973; *Success in Marriage,* Abingdon, 1958; *The Christian Family in East Asia,* World Council of Churches, 1958; *Youth Looks Toward Marriage,* Finlayson, 1958.

(With wife, Vera Mace) *Marriage: East and West,* Doubleday, 1960; (with Vera Mace) *The Soviet Family,* Doubleday, 1963; (with Evelyn Duval and Paul Popenoe) *The Churches Look at Family Life,* Broadman, 1964; (translator) Robert Grimm, *Love and Sexuality,* Association Press, 1964; *Sex, Love, and Marriage in the Caribbean,* World Council of Churches, 1965; *Youth Considers Marriage,* Thomas Nelson, 1966; (contributor) Jules Saltman, compiler, *Love, Sex, and Marriage,* Grosset, 1968; *Sex, Marriage, and the Family in the Pacific,* World Council of Churches, 1969.

The Christian Response to the Sexual Revolution, Abingdon, 1970; *Getting Ready for Marriage,* Abingdon, 1972; *Abortion: The Agonizing Decision,* Abingdon, 1972; *Sexual Difficulties in Marriage,* Fortress Press, 1972; (with Vera Mace) *We Can Have Better Marriages–If We Really Want Them,* Abingdon, 1974; *Men, Women, and God,* John Knox, 1975. Contributor of numerous articles to periodicals. Member of editorial board, *Journal of Marriage and the Family,* 1962-69.

SIDELIGHTS: Mace has traveled extensively throughout the world, serving as a marriage and family consultant in Africa, South America, Australia, Europe, Asia, and the Pacific Islands. Translations of his books and articles have appeared in Chinese, Finnish, Japanese, Russian, Urdu, as well as in the major European languages.

MACHT, Joel 1938-

PERSONAL: Born June 20, 1938, in Baltimore, Md.; son of Emanuel (a realtor) and Eunice Hoffberger (Rosen) Macht; married Jeanne Soltz (divorced); married Carole Eisele; children: Randy, Jobi, Kim, David. *Education:* University of Miami, Coral Gables, Fla., B.S., 1963; Colorado State University, M.S., 1965; Arizona State University, Ph.D., 1969. *Residence:* Littleton, Colo. *Office:* Department of Educational Psychology, University of Denver, 2040 South Race, Denver, Colo. 80210.

CAREER: University of South Florida, Tampa, assistant professor of educational psychology, 1969-70; University of Denver, Denver, Colo., associate professor of educational psychology, 1970—. *Military service:* U.S. Army Reserve, Medical Unit, 1957-63. *Member:* American Psychological Association.

WRITINGS: Teaching Our Children, Wiley, 1975; *TeacHER/TeacHIM: The Toughest Game in Town,* Wiley, 1975. Contributor to *Journal of Applied Behavioral Analysis* and *Journal of Experimental Child Psychology.*

WORK IN PROGRESS: The Slaying of the Dragon Within, a modern look at psychology and psychiatry.

* * *

MacISAAC, Sharon

PERSONAL: Born in Scott, Saskatchewan, Canada; daughter of Francis Matthew (a horticulturist) and Regina (Fuchs) MacIsaac. *Education:* University of Saskatchewan, B.A., 1961; University of Toronto, M.A., 1964, Ph.D., 1971. *Politics:* "Varies." *Religion:* Roman Catholic. *Home:* 17 Elgin Ave., Toronto, Ontario, Canada. *Office:* Therafields Environmental Centre, 316 DuPont St., Toronto, Ontario, Canada.

CAREER: Canadian Catholic Conference, Ottawa, Ontario, executive director of Commission on Ecumenism, 1967-68; Humber Community College, Toronto, Ontario, instructor in psychology, 1971-72; McMaster University, Hamilton, Ontario, assistant professor of psychology and religion, 1972-75; Therafields Environmental Centre, Toronto, Ontario, therapist, 1975—.

WRITINGS: Freud and Original Sin, Paulist/Newman, 1974. Contributor to theology journals.

* * *

MACKIE, J(ohn) L(eslie) 1917-

PERSONAL: Born August 25, 1917, in Sydney, Australia; son of Alexander (a university professor) and Annie (Duncan) Mackie; married Joan Meredith, November 7, 1947; children: Alexander, Penelope, Nicola, Hilary, David. *Education:* University of Sydney, B.A. (honors), 1938; Oxford University, B.A. (honors), 1940, M.A., 1945. *Religion:* None. *Home:* 178 Banbury Rd., Oxford OX2 7BT, England. *Office:* University College, Oxford University, Oxford OX1 4BH, England.

CAREER: University of Sydney, Sydney, New South Wales, Australia, lecturer, 1946-51, senior lecturer in philosophy, 1951-54; University of Otago, Dunedin, New Zealand, professor of philosophy, 1955-59; University of Sydney, professor of philosophy, 1959-63; University of York, York, England, professor of philosophy, 1963-67; Oxford University, University College, Oxford, England, fellow and tutor in philosophy, 1967—. *Military service:* British Army, 1942-46; became captain; mentioned in dispatches.

Member: British Society for the Philosophy of Science (president, 1968-69; vice-president, 1969—), Mind Association (honorary treasurer, 1970—), British Academy (fellow).

WRITINGS: Truth, Probability, and Paradox, Oxford University Press, 1973; *The Cement of the Universe*, Oxford University Press, 1974. Contributor to professional journals.

WORK IN PROGRESS: A book on John Locke and the theory of knowledge, tentatively titled *Problems from Locke; Ethics.*

* * *

MACKWORTH, Cecily

PERSONAL: Born in Wales; daughter of Francis Julian (an army officer) and Dorothy (Lascelles) Mackworth; married Leon Donckier de Donceel, October 18, 1936 (died, 1939); married Marquis de Chabannes la Palice, July 11, 1956; children: (first marriage) Pascale. *Education:* Privately educated. *Home:* 21 rue Charles V, Paris 4e, France.

CAREER: Has worked as a literary critic for various French and English magazines, including *Horizon, Twentieth Century,* and *Critique;* has also worked as a correspondent for various publications; author and novelist. *Member:* International Association of Literary Critics, P.E.N., Society of Authors. *Awards, honors:* Darmstadt Award, 1963, for *Guillaume Apollinaire and the Cubist Life.*

WRITINGS: I Came Out of France, Routledge & Kegan Paul, 1942; *A Mirror for French Poetry*, Routledge & Kegan Paul, 1945; *Francois Villon*, Westhouse, 1947; *The Mouth of the Sword* (travel), Routledge & Kegan Paul, 1949; *The Destiny of Isabella Eberhardt*, Routledge & Kegan Paul, 1951; *Springs Green Shadow* (novel), Dutton, 1953; *Guillaume Apollinaire and the Cubist Life*, J. Murray, 1961, Horizon Press, 1962; *English Interludes*, Routledge & Kegan Paul, 1974.

WORK IN PROGRESS: Research on the life of Jules Laforgue.

SIDELIGHTS: Cecily Mackworth writes: "I was born in Wales, brought up in England and married in France, where I have spent my whole adult life. I fell in love with French poets of the late 19th century when I was 18 and have never ceased to study and write about them. I have written one novel, too, and occasional poetry, which is published in French and English reviews. I have also worked sporadically throughout my life as a journalist, chiefly because it has given me a chance to travel—the second passion of my life. I have been in most European and Middle Eastern and North African countries and have learned a little of many languages but am fluent only in French, English, and German."

* * *

MACLEAN, Alistair (Stuart) 1922-
(Ian Stuart)

PERSONAL: Born 1922, in Glasgow, Scotland; married second wife, Mary Marcelle Georgeus (a film production company executive), October 13, 1972. *Education:* Attended University of Glasgow. *Home:* Haslemere, Surrey, England. *Office:* c/o William Collins Sons & Co. Ltd., 14 St. James Place, London SW1, England.

CAREER: Former teacher of English and history in Glasgow; writer, 1955—. *Military service:* Royal Navy. *Member:* Writers' Guild.

WRITINGS—All novels: *H.M.S. Ulysses*, Collins, 1955, Doubleday, 1956, also published in omnibus volume with works by other authors, Books Abridged, 1956; *The Guns of Navarone*, Doubleday, 1957; *South by Java Head*, Doubleday, 1958; *The Secret Ways*, Doubleday, 1959, (published in England as *The Last Frontier*, Collins, 1959); *Night Without End*, Doubleday, 1960, also published in an omnibus volume with works by other authors, Doubleday, 1960; *Fear is the Key*, Doubleday, 1961; *The Golden Rendezvous*, Doubleday, 1962, condensed version, Reader's Digest, 1963; *Lawrence of Arabia* (juvenile), Random House, 1962 (published in England as *All About Lawrence of Arabia*, W. H. Allen, 1962); *Ice Station Zebra*, Doubleday, 1963; *When Eight Bells Toll*, Doubleday, 1966; *Where Eagles Dare*, (Companion Book Club and Readers Book Club selections), Doubleday, 1967; *Force 10 from Navarone*, Doubleday, 1968; *Puppet on a Chain*, Doubleday, 1969; *Caravan to Vaccares*, Doubleday, 1970; *Bear Island*, Doubleday, 1971; *Captain Cook*, Doubleday, 1972; *Alistair MacLean Introduces Scotland*, edited by Alastair M. Dunnett, McGraw-Hill, 1972; *The Way to Dusty Death*, Doubleday, 1973; *Breakheart Pass*, Doubleday, 1974.

Under pseudonym Ian Stuart: *The Snow on the Ben*, Ward, Lock, 1961; *The Black Shrike*, Scribner, 1961; *The Dark Crusader*, Collins, 1961, published under name Alistair MacLean, Collins, 1963; *The Satan Bug*, Scribner, 1962.

Screenplays: "The Guns of Navarone," "Where Eagles Dare," "Deakin," "Caravan to Vaccares," "When Eight Bells Toll," "Puppet on a Chain," "Force 10 from Navarone," "Golden Rendezvous."

SIDELIGHTS: Besides the screenplays written by MacLean, some of his other novels have been brought to the screen, including *Fear is the Key, Ice Station Zebra, The Secret Ways, South by Java Head, The Satan Bug, Bear Island*, and *H.M.S. Ulysses.*

David Depledge wrote: "He (MacLean) has made his name by writing superb and highly filmable adventure novels. . . . Writing, to Alistair MacLean, is a business. His workroom is in the attic, cut off even from his family." Several of MacLean's novels were written originally as screenplays, the novels later being realized from the scripts. Depledge continues: "The script for *Where Eagles Dare* was the first he had ever attempted, but having accepted the challenge of doing something new he quickly became fascinated by the technical demands. . . . He works quickly, completes a film script in one to two months and a novel in less. If he gets behind schedule . . . he just works longer hours." *Avocational interests:* Science and astronomy.

BIOGRAPHICAL/CRITICAL SOURCES: Books and Bookmen, May, 1968; *Life*, November 26, 1971; Carolyn Riley, editor, *Contemporary Literary Criticism*, Volume III, Gale, 1975.*

* * *

MacMILLAN, Donald L(ee) 1940-

PERSONAL: Born December 31, 1940, in Cleveland, Ohio; son of Alexander MacRae (an engineer) and Arline (Marnie) MacMillan; married Dianne Daniels, March 18, 1967; children: Andrew, John, Daniel. *Education:* University of Michigan, student, 1958-59; Western Reserve University (now Case Western Reserve University), B.A., 1962; University of California, Los Angeles, M.A., 1963, Ed.D., 1967. *Home:* 1845 Port Renwick Pl., Newport Beach, Calif. 92660. *Office:* School of Education, University of California, Riverside, Calif. 92502.

CAREER: University of California, Riverside, assistant professor, 1968-70, associate professor, 1970-73, professor of education, 1973—. Research specialist for California Department of Mental Hygiene, 1970-73; research educationist for Pacific-Neuropsychiatric Institute at University of California, Los Angeles, 1973—. Member of advisory committee to deputy commissioner of education for "Project Prime," 1973-74; consultant to Bureau of the Education of the Handicapped of U.S. Office of Education. *Member:* American Association on Mental Deficiency, American Educational Research Association, Council for Exceptional Children, Society for Research in Child Development, California Association of Professors of Special Education (member of board of directors, 1971-72).

WRITINGS: Behavior Modification in Education, Macmillan, 1973; (with R. L. Jones) *Special Education in Transition,* Allyn & Bacon, 1974. Contributor of about fifty articles to professional journals. Associate editor of *Exceptional Children,* 1970-75; consulting editor of *American Journal of Mental Deficiency,* 1971, 1972, 1975; editorial consultant to *Journal of School Psychology,* 1973—.

WORK IN PROGRESS: Mental Retardation and Learning, with R. L. Jones; *Introduction to Mental Retardation; Issues in the Education of Exceptional Children.*

* * *

MADDEN, Betty I(senbarger) 1915-

PERSONAL: Born November 12, 1915, in Chicago, Ill.; daughter of Jerome C. (a college educator) and Florence (Hoover) Isenbarger; married Clifford L. Carroll, March 19, 1938 (divorced, 1960); married Wilbur F. Madden, August 31, 1963 (died, 1965); children: (first marriage) Don Allan (deceased), Dennis Bruce. *Education:* Attended Northwestern University, 1933-35, and American Academy of Art, summers, 1933-37; University of Illinois, B.F.A., 1938. *Home:* 1145 South First, Springfield, Ill. 62704. *Office:* Illinois State Museum, Springfield, Ill. 62706.

CAREER: Free-lance artist and craftsman, 1938-44; Consolidated Book Publishers, Chicago, Ill., artist, 1944-45; Evans, Work & Costa Advertising, Inc., Springfield, Ill., artist, 1955-58; S.A. Barker Co., Springfield, Ill., fashion illustrator and advertising manager, 1958-60; Illinois State Museum, Springfield, technical assistant in art department, 1961-63, curator of art, 1963—. Free-lance artist, 1945-60; member of board of directors of Clayville Folk Arts Guild, 1962-65; judge for art fairs and exhibitions. *Member:* American Association of Museums, Illinois State Historical Society (member of board of directors, 1973-76), Sangamon County Historical Society, Springfield Art Association, Kappa Delta (president of University of Illinois chapter, 1937). *Awards, honors:* Pacesetter Award for contributions to the arts, 1969; non-fiction award from Friends of Literature, 1975, for *Art, Crafts, and Architecture in Early Illinois.*

WRITINGS: Art, Crafts, and Architecture in Early Illinois, University of Illinois Press, 1974. Contributor to *Living Museum, Spinning Wheel,* and *Illinois History.*

WORK IN PROGRESS: Continuing research on art, crafts, and architecture of Illinois.

AVOCATIONAL INTERESTS: Painting, crafts, travel (has studied art and architecture in France, Italy, Spain, England, Ireland).

* * *

MADISON, Thomas A(lvin) 1926-
(Tom Madison, Luke Campbell)

PERSONAL: Born May 3, 1926, in Springfield, Ill.; son of Alvin E. (a banker) and Gladys (Houston) Madison; married Georgie L. Frame (a teacher), February 24, 1953; children: J. Mark, Laird D. *Education:* University of Chicago Theological School, B.D., 1947; University of Illinois, M.A., 1955; University of Wisconsin, completed course work toward Ph.D., 1962. *Politics:* Socialist. *Religion:* Episcopal. *Home:* 1290 Maricopa Dr., Oshkosh, Wis. 54901. *Office:* Department of English, University of Wisconsin, Oshkosh, Wis. 54901.

CAREER: University of Wisconsin, Oshkosh, assistant professor of English, 1962—. Director of Oshkosh Community Players, 1958-65.

WRITINGS: (Under pseudonym Luke Campbell) *Ridge Runner Rhymes,* six volumes, St. Cuthbert's Treasury Press, 1974; (under name Tom Madison) *The Poems of Jesus,* St. Cuthbert's Treasury Press, 1975.

WORK IN PROGRESS: Confucian Couplets.

AVOCATIONAL INTERESTS: Travel in Europe, especially Scotland and Holland.

* * *

MADISON, Tom
See MADISON, Thomas A(lvin)

* * *

MAEDKE, Wilmer O(tto) 1922-

PERSONAL: Surname is pronounced "*med*-key"; born July 9, 1922, in Forestville, Wis.; son of Harvey F. (a farmer) and Amanda (Kasten) Maedke. *Education:* Wisconsin State University-Whitewater, B.Ed., 1949; Northwestern University, M.A., 1951, Ph.D., 1957. *Home:* 1326 Sixth Ave., Arcadia, Calif. 91006. *Office:* Department of Business Education, California State University, 5151 State University Dr., Los Angeles, Calif. 90032.

CAREER: Northwestern University, Evanston, Ill., instructor in business, 1953-54; chairman of department in high school in Chicago, Ill., 1954-55; Northern Illinois University, DeKalb, assistant professor, 1955-57, associate professor, 1957-64, professor of business education, 1964-65; Southern Illinois University, Edwardsville, professor of business education, 1965-69; University of North Dakota, Grand Forks, professor of business education, 1969-72; California State University, Los Angeles, professor of business education, 1972—. *Military service:* U.S. Army, 1946-48; became sergeant. *Member:* National Education Association, National Business Education Association, American Records Management Association, American Council on Consumer Interests, Western Business Education Association, California Business Education Association, Delta Pi Epsilon, Pi Omega Pi.

WRITINGS: (With Mary Robek and Gerald Brown) *Information and Records Management,* Glencoe Press, 1974.

* * *

MAESTRO, Giulio 1942-

PERSONAL: Born May 6, 1942, in New York, N.Y.; son

of Marcello (a writer) and Edna (Ten Eyck) Maestro; married Betsy Crippen (a kindergarten teacher), 1972. *Education:* Cooper Union, B.F.A., 1964; further study in printmaking at Pratt Graphics Center. *Residence:* Madison, Conn.

CAREER: Design Organization, Inc. (advertising design), New York, N.Y., assistant to art director, 1965-66; Warren A. Kass Graphics, Inc. (advertising design), New York, N.Y., assistant art director, 1966-69; free-lance book illustrator, 1969—. *Member:* American Institute of Graphic Arts. *Awards, honors:* Two books have been included in American Institute of Graphic Arts Children's Book Shows, *The Tortoise's Tug of War* in the 1971-72 show and *Three Kittens* in the 1973-74 show; artwork from *The Remarkable Plant in Apartment 4* was exhibited in the Society of Illustrators Show, New York, 1974; *Two Good Friends* was chosen an American Library Association Notable Book, 1974.

WRITINGS—Self-illustrated: *The Tortoise's Tug of War* (animal fable retold), Bradbury, 1971; *The Remarkable Plant in Apartment 4*, Bradbury, 1973; (with wife, Betsy Maestro) *A Wise Monkey Tale*, Crown, 1975.

Illustrator—Picture books: Rudyard Kipling, *The Beginning of the Armadillos*, St. Martin's 1970; Mirra Ginsburg, *What Kind of Bird Is That?*, Crown, 1973; Ginsburg, *Three Kittens* (Junior Literary Guild selection), Crown, 1973; Vicki Kimmel Artis, *Gray Duck Catches a Friend*, Putnam, 1974; Tony Johnston, *Fig Tale*, Putnam, 1974; Judy Delton, *Two Good Friends* (Junior Literary Guild selection), Crown, 1974; *One More and One Less* (Junior Literary Guild selection), Crown, 1974; Harry Milgrom, *Egg-Ventures* (Junior Literary Guild selection), Dutton, 1974; Maria Polushkin, *Who Said Meow?* (Junior Literary Guild selection), Crown, 1975; William R. Gerler, *A Pack of Riddles*, Dutton, 1975.

Illustrator—Readers, math, craft, and other books; Catherine Cutler, *From Petals to Pinecones*, Lothrop, 1969; Cutler, *Creative Shellcraft*, Lothrop, 1971; Elyse Sommer, *The Bread Dough Craft Book*, Lothrop, 1972; Franklyn Branley, *The Beginning of the Earth*, Crowell, 1972; Jo Phillips, *Right Angles: Paper-Folding Geometry*, Crowell, 1972; Mannis Charosh, *Number Ideas Through Pictures*, Crowell, 1973; Sommer, *Designing With Cutouts: The Art of Decoupage*, Lothrop, 1973; Sommer, *Make It With Burlap*, Lothrop, 1973; Roma Gans, *Millions and Millions of Crystals*, Crowell, 1973; Gans, *Oil: The Buried Treasure*, Crowell, 1974; John Trivett, *Building Tables on Tables: A Book About Multiplication*, Crowell, 1974; Carolyn Meyer, *Milk, Butter and Cheese: The Story of Dairy Products*, Morrow, 1974; Sarah Riedman, *Trees Alive*, Lothrop, 1974; Melvin Berger, *The New Air Book*, Crowell, 1974.

SIDELIGHTS: Maestro wrote: "I was born in New York City and lived in Greenwich Village most of my life. My family owned a house on Charlton Street and I attended The Little Red School House from kindergarten through grade six. I started drawing and painting before I even went to school." *Avocational interests:* Reading, painting, gardening, travel.

* * *

MAIS, S(tuart) P(etre) B(rodie) 1885-1975

July 4, 1885—April 21, 1975; British journalist, lecturer, author of fiction and books on travel and English literature. Obituaries: *AB Bookman's Weekly*, July 7, 1975.

MAJOR, Alan P(ercival) 1929-
(Dane John)

PERSONAL: Born May 26, 1929, in Gillingham, Kent, England; son of Percy Edward and Anne Mary (Norton) Major; married Jean Audrey Henthorn, February 14, 1959; children: Stephanie Susan, Caroline Alison. *Education:* Attended Medway College of Arts and Crafts, Rochester, England, 1943-50; City and Guilds of London Certificate for Typography, intermediate, 1948, final, 1950. *Politics:* "Used to be Labour, but due to present government's disinterest in creative and self-employed people, now Tory (Conservative)." *Religion:* Church of England. *Home and office:* 32 Bramley Ave., Canterbury, Kent, England.

CAREER: Printer's typesetter and compositor, Panda Press Ltd., Gillingham, Kent, England, 1943-62, W. & J. Mackay Ltd., Chatham, Kent, 1962-65. Writer. *Military service:* Royal Air Force, Air Ministry Unit, 1950-52. *Member:* Society of Authors.

WRITINGS: Coast, Estuary and Seashore Life, Gifford, 1973; *Collecting World Sea Shells*, Arco, 1974; *Collecting Fossils*, John Bartholomew, 1974; *Collecting and Studying Mushrooms, Toadstools and Fungi*, Arco, 1975. Also author of stories for British Broadcasting Corp. Radio, 1951-65, and also broadcast in Australia and New Zealand. Contributor of numerous articles, occasionally under pseudonym Dane John, to journals.

WORK IN PROGRESS: A textbook, *Let's Find Out about Grass*, for F. Watts; research for books about British and foreign royal and state yachts, figureheads, and nautical antiques.

SIDELIGHTS: Major told *CA*: "Fanatically pro-British, could never live outside native country for any length of time . . . Also fanatical about conservation and preservation so books intended to help readers take an interest in their wild life world." *Avocational interests:* Collecting antiques, studying figureheads, visiting old churches, stamp collecting, walking, cycling, British history and rural life.

* * *

MAKKAI, Adam 1935-

PERSONAL: Born December 16, 1935, in Budapest, Hungary; came to United States, 1957, naturalized citizen, 1963; son of John D. (a history writer) and Rozsa (a novelist; maiden name, Ignacz) Makkai; married Valerie June Becker (a professor of linguistics), June 5, 1966; children: Sylvia. *Education:* University of Budapest, student, 1954-56; Harvard University, B.A. (cum laude), 1958; Yale University, M.A., 1962, Ph.D., 1965. *Politics:* "Would like to see science, ecology and pragmatism bury all ideologies." *Religion:* "Born and raised as Hungarian Reformed, became an anthroposophist." *Home:* 360 MacLaren Lane, Lake Bluff, Ill. 60044. *Office:* Department of Linguistics, University of Illinois at Chicago Circle, P.O.B. 4348, Chicago, Ill. 60680.

CAREER: Iolani College Preparatory Academy, Honolulu, Hawaii, teacher of German, French, Latin, and Russian, 1958-60; Yale University, New Haven, Conn., instructor in Russian, 1962-63; University of Malaya, Kuala Lumpur, visiting assistant professor of linguistics, 1963-64; RAND Corp., Santa Monica, Calif., researcher in computational linguistics, 1964-65; Occidental College, Los Angeles, Calif., assistant professor of English and Russian, 1966-67; California State University at Long Beach, assistant professor of linguistics, 1966-67 (concurrently with post at

Occidental College); University of Illinois at Chicago Circle, assistant professor, 1967-69, associate professor, 1969-74, professor of linguistics, 1974—. University of Hawaii, extension lecturer in Russian, 1958-60, lecturer in scientific German, summer, 1961.

MEMBER: Linguistic Society of America, Modern Language Association of America, Linguistic Association of Canada and the United States/Association de Linguistique du Canada et des Etats-Unis (co-founder), Zoltan Kodaly Hungarian Cultural Society of Chicago (founding president, 1968—). *Awards, honors:* Paderewski Foundation and International Development Foundation travel grant for Southeast Asia, 1963-64; National Science Foundation postdoctoral research grant, 1965-66.

WRITINGS: Szomj es ecet (title means "Thirst and Vinegar"; collected poems in Hungarian, 1954-66), Amerikai Magyar Irok, 1966; *K²=13* (collected poems in Hungarian, 1967-70), Amerikai Magyar Irok, 1971; *Idiom Structure in English*, Humanities, 1973; (editor with David G. Lockwood) *Readings in Stratificational Linguistics*, University of Alabama Press, 1973; *A Dictionary of Space English*, Consolidated Book Publishers, 1973; (translator and editor) *Toward a Theory of Context in Linguistics and Literature*, Humanities, in press; (editor with Thomas Kabdebo and Paul Tabori) *The Poetry of Hungary* (anthology), Humanities, in press; (editor with wife, Valerie Becker Makkai, and Luigi Heilmann) *Linguistics at the Crossroads*, English and Italian editions, Il Mulino (Bologna), in press.

Poems in Hungarian included in two anthologies published in London and one in United States. Translator of poetry from English into Hungarian, Hungarian into English, and from other languages into Hungarian for books and journals. Contributor of articles, essays, reviews, and poems, both in English and Hungarian, to periodicals in United States, France, Germany, and other countries.

Member of editorial board, *Otagu Sip* (Hungarian literary magazine published in New Jersey), 1973—; editor with Valerie Becker Makkai, *Forum* (annual publication of Linguistic Association of Canada and United States), 1974—; managing editor, *Word* (journal of International Linguistic Association), 1974-75.

WORK IN PROGRESS: *Toward an Ecological Dictionary of English*, a book-length study on new methods in lexicography; *Pragmo-Ecological Grammar: PEG*, a collection of essays; *Thirst and Vinegar*, translation of poems first published in Hungarian, 1966; *A Comparative Syntax of the Germanic Modal Auxiliaries*, a monograph; editing *Semiotics of Language and Culture*, papers from a symposium held in Burg Wartenstein, August, 1975.

SIDELIGHTS: Makkai is fluent in German, French, and Russian, in addition to English and Hungarian, and also speaks Italian and Indonesian-Malay. He reads and does research in Dutch and other Germanic and Slavic languages, and has done linguistic work on Latin, Greek, Sanskrit, Gothic, Old Church Slavic, Old and Middle English, Tagalog, Hawaiian, Vietnamese, and Thai.

*   *   *

MALE, David Arthur 1928-

PERSONAL: Born February 29, 1928, in Dovercourt, England. *Education:* Goldsmiths College, teacher's certificate and diploma in drama, 1952; L.R.A.M. [Licentiate of the Royal Academy of Music], in speech and drama, 1956, in mime, 1958; University of Bristol, M.Litt., 1966. *Office:* Department of Drama, Homerton College, Cambridge, England.

CAREER: Teacher of drama in state-supported schools in England, 1952-59; Sittingbourne College of Education, Kent, England, principal lecturer in English and drama and head of department, 1969-75; Homerton College, Cambridge, England, principal lecturer in drama and head of department, 1975—. Visiting lecturer at University of Waterloo and University of Calgary.

WRITINGS: *The Story of the Theatre*, A. & C. Black, 1960; *Approaches to Drama*, Allen & Unwin, 1973; (with Kenneth Pickering and William Horrocks) *Investigating Drama*, Allen & Unwin, 1975.

SIDELIGHTS: Male directs plays in a studio of his own design; his special interest is in drama and theater in education. *Avocational interests:* Sailing.

*   *   *

MALEK, James S(tanley) 1941-

PERSONAL: Born August 11, 1941, in Hampton, Neb.; son of Anton James and Wilhma (Lorensen) Malek. *Education:* American University, student, 1959-60; Earlham College, B.A. (with honors), 1963; University of Chicago, A.M. (with honors), 1966, Ph.D. (with honors), 1968. *Home:* 1420 Ridge Rd., Moscow, Idaho 83843. *Office:* Department of English, University of Idaho, Moscow, Idaho 83843.

CAREER: University of Idaho, Moscow, assistant professor, 1968-70, associate professor, 1970-75, professor of eighteenth-century British literature, 1975—. *Member:* Modern Language Association of America, American Society for Aesthetics, American Society for Eighteenth-Century Studies, Rocky Mountain Modern Language Association. *Awards, honors:* Woodrow Wilson fellowship, 1963-64; National Endowment for the Humanities fellowship for younger humanists, 1971.

WRITINGS: *The Arts Compared: An Aspect of Eighteenth-Century British Aesthetics*, Wayne State University Press, 1974. Contributor to literature journals.

WORK IN PROGRESS: *A Study of Essays on the Nature and Functions of Original Genius in Eighteenth-Century British Criticism.*

AVOCATIONAL INTERESTS: Re-reading E. M. Forster (especially *Howards End*).

*   *   *

MALI, Paul 1926-

PERSONAL: Born July 6, 1926, in Hartford, Conn.; married Mary S. Mammone (a general manager), June 28, 1948; children: Faith L., Dawn S. *Education:* University of Connecticut, B.S., 1953, M.S. (management education), 1962, Ph.D., 1966; Cornell University, M.S. (manpower administration), 1963. *Politics:* Independent. *Religion:* Christian. *Home:* 97 Three Acre Rd., Groton, Conn. 06340. *Office:* Groton Shoppers Mart, Groton, Conn. 06340.

CAREER: Certified management consultant; certified psychological test specialist; diplomate, American Management Association, 1963. Western Electric, New York, N.Y., engineer, 1954-58; General Dynamics, Electric Boat Division, Groton, Conn., director of education, 1960-66; University of Hartford, Hartford, Conn., 1967—, now professor of management; Paul Mali & Associates (management consultants), Groton, Conn., senior associate,

1967—. Trustee of Connecticut Colleges, State of Connecticut. *Member:* Academy of Management, American Management Association, American Society of Training and Development, Tau Beta Pi, Eta Kappa Nu, Phi Delta Kappa.

WRITINGS: The Training and Development of Nuclear Technicians, Franklin Press, 1962; *Future Management for the Smaller Businessman,* University of Hartford Press, 1971; (contributor) *Handbook of Personnel Management,* McGraw, 1971; *Managing by Objectives,* Wiley Interscience, 1972.

WORK IN PROGRESS: Motivation and Productivity.

* * *

MALKIEWICZ, J(an) Kris 1931-

PERSONAL: Born February 22, 1931, in Cracow, Poland; son of Zdzislaw D. M. (a physician) and Jadwiga (Konstancja) Malkiewicz; married Judith Toner (an artist weaver), July 20, 1968. *Education:* Jagellonian University, Cracow, Poland, B.A., 1953, M.A., 1956; Polish State Film School, M.A. *Politics:* Democrat. *Religion:* Catholic. *Home:* 23515 Lyons Ave. #167, Valencia, Calif. 91355. *Office:* California Institute of the Arts, 24700 McBean Pkwy., Valencia, Calif. 91355.

CAREER: Polish State Television, Cracow, Poland, producer, 1965; Irish State Television, Dublin, Ireland, producer and director, 1965-67; The Politechnic, London, England, lecturer in film, 1967-68; California Institute of the Arts, Valencia, Calif., film mentor, 1968—, trustee. Cameraman for Walt Disney Productions. *Awards, honors:* First prize as cameraman from Helsinki Youth Festival, 1962, for film *Szkola bez Tablic.*

WRITINGS: (With Robert E. Rogers) *Cinematography: A Guide for Film Makers and Film Teachers,* Van Nostrand, 1973.

WORK IN PROGRESS: A film based on wartime Poland.

SIDELIGHTS: J. Kris Malkiewicz writes: "I came to film after my studies in the history of art and ethnography. I consider film as a powerful witness to the human condition. In this respect documentary films touch me much deeper than features. At the moment I am working on a film combining the documentary element and the more surreal level of life. These stem from my childhood memories of the wartime Poland."

* * *

MALLINSON, Jeremy (John Crosby) 1937-

PERSONAL: Born March 16, 1937, in Ilkley, Yorkshire, England; son of Harold Crosby and Kay (Parkinson) Mallinson; married Odette Louise Guiton, October 26, 1963; children: Julian Justin Crosby, Sophie Jayne. *Education:* Educated in England. *Home:* Clos Tranquil, Rue de Croquet, St. Aubin, Jersey, Channel Islands. *Agent:* Curtis Brown Ltd., 1 Craven Hill, London W.2, England. *Office:* Jersey Wildlife Preservation Trust, Trinity, Jersey, Channel Islands.

CAREER: Employed with H. Crosby Mallinson's (vintners), Jersey, Channel Islands, 1954-56, Rhodesia & Nyasaland Staff Corps., 1956-58; Jersey Zoological Park, Trinity, Jersey, Channel Islands, keeper, 1959-62; Jersey Wildlife Preservation Trust, Jersey, Channel Islands, deputy director, 1963-72, zoological director, 1972—. *Member:* Royal Geographical Society (fellow), Institute of Biology.

WRITINGS: Okavango Adventure, David & Charles, 1973, Norton, 1974; *Earning Your Living with Animals,* David & Charles, 1975; *Threatened European Mammals,* Macmillan, in press. Contributor to *International Zoo Yearbook* and to zoological journals.

SIDELIGHTS: Mallinson has made expeditions to Southern Rhodesia and Bechuanaland, Bolivia, Brazil, Guiana, Madagascar, Assam, India, and the Zaire River, to collect and study animals.

* * *

MALTZ, Maxwell 1899-1975

March 10, 1899—April 7, 1975; American surgeon, biographer, novelist, playwright, and writer on cybernetics. Obituaries: *New York Times,* April 8, 1975; *AB Bookman's Weekly,* May 12, 1975.

* * *

MALTZ, Stephen 1932-

PERSONAL: Born February 22, 1932, in Los Angeles, Calif.; son of Meyer (a county clerk) and Jennie Maltz; married former wife, Clara Galian, June 2, 1958; married Maureen Foley (a teacher), December 23, 1968; children: Duane, Elizabeth, Aaron. *Education:* Los Angeles State College (now California State University, Los Angeles), B.A., 1958; University of Utah, M.S., 1962; graduate study at University of Hawaii, Adelphi College, Stanford University, and California State University at Hayward. *Politics:* Democrat. *Religion:* Jewish. *Home:* 24667 Second Street, Hayward, Calif. 94541. *Office:* Department of Health, Chabot College, 25555 Hesperian Blvd., Hayward, Calif. 94545.

CAREER: High school teacher of science in Arcadia, Calif., 1957-59, Oahu, Hawaii, 1959-60, Hayward, Calif., 1960-63; Chabot College, Hayward, Calif., instructor in biology and health, 1963—. Chairman, Human Relations Commission at Fremont; program designer and facilitator, KCSM (educational television), 1970-71. *Military service:* Served in U.S. Army. *Member:* American Association for the Advancement of Science, California School Health Association, Northern California Photography Club.

WRITINGS: Critical Issues for College Health (text and workbook), William C. Brown, 1970; *First Aid and Safety for Everyone: Workbook,* William C. Brown, 1971; *First Aid and Safety for Everyone: Textbook,* William C. Brown, 1972; (with Harold Chandler and Vern Zellna) *Health Science,* William C. Brown, 1972. Also author of syllabus for educational television programs.

* * *

MALZBERG, Benjamin 1893-1975

December 2, 1893—April 13, 1975; American statistician and social scientist, writer of books on mental health. Obituaries: *New York Times,* April 14, 1975; *AB Bookman's Weekly,* May 12, 1975. (CA-15/16)

* * *

MANCINI, Pat McNees 1940-

PERSONAL: Born January 30, 1940, in Riverside, Calif.; daughter of Glenn Harold (an ironworker) and Eleanor (a banker; maiden name, McCoskrie) McNees; married Anthony Mancini (a reporter for *New York Post*), April 22, 1967; children: Romana. *Education:* University of California, Los Angeles, B.A., 1961; Stanford University, graduate study. *Home and office:* 325 Riverside Dr., New York, N.Y. 10025. *Agent:* Owen Laster, William Morris Agency, 1350 Avenue of the Americas, New York, N.Y. 10019.

CAREER: Harper & Row, New York, N.Y., assistant editor, 1963-66; Fawcett Publications, New York, N.Y., editor of "Fawcett Premier Books," 1966-70; free-lance editor and writer, 1970—. *Member:* Phi Beta Kappa.

WRITINGS: (Editor) *Contemporary Latin American Short Stories*, Fawcett, 1974. Free-lance editor of books for St. Martin's and for Bureau of Social Science Research.

WORK IN PROGRESS: Editing a collection of contemporary American short stories and a collection of international short stories about city life; research for a book on the handicapped.

* * *

MANGURIAN, David 1938-

PERSONAL: Born July 18, 1938, in Baltimore, Md.; son of George Nishan (an aeronautical engineer) and Margaret (Barton) Mangurian; married Luz Maria Paltan (a biology professor), August 2, 1971; children: Christina Victoria. *Education:* Pomona College, B.A., 1961; Columbia University, M.S., 1966. *Politics:* "I'm for necessary social change." *Home address:* 121 Hubinger St., New Haven, Conn. 06511. *Agent:* Harriet Wasserman, 551 Fifth Ave., New York, N.Y. 10017.

CAREER: Ventura Star-Free Press, Ventura, Calif., reporter, 1963-65; *Oxnard Press-Courier*, Oxnard, Calif., deskman and reporter, summer, 1966; free-lance writer and photographer in Central and South America, 1967-73; WPLG-Television, Miami, Fla., television news reporter, 1973-74; free-lance writer and photographer, 1974—. Associate producer of documentary film, "Enriched Baloney and Homemade Bread," 1970. *Awards, honors:* Pulitzer traveling fellowship, 1966, from Columbia University.

WRITINGS: Lito: The Shoeshine Boy (with own photographs), Four Winds, 1975. Contributor of articles and photographs to magazines and newspapers in the United States, Canada, and England, including *Life, Clipper, Signature, Medical World News*, and *Life en Espanol*.

WORK IN PROGRESS: Photographic stories about life and death in Latin America.

SIDELIGHTS: Mangurian writes: "I have worked as a . . . folk singer and bluegrass musician, aircraft factory worker, peach picker.... Folk music I recorded in Arkansas in 1958 was later issued by Folkways Records as 'Music from the Ozarks.' I recorded an album of bluegrass music with a group including my brother in England, and one track on an album by blues singer Wade Walton for Prestige Records under the pseudonym 'Memphis Mango.'

"I have spent much of my time (now almost half my life) traveling to see how other people live.... "I once traveled with a friend by canoe across the United States, paddling 1,300 miles down rivers from Denver to Memphis in three months. I traveled six years in Mexico, Central and South America. I got to every country except Venezuela and saw many places few tourists ever get to including the Amazon jungle, the Galapagos Islands, and the tops of two live volcanoes. I traveled by airplane, helicopter, train, boat, hydrofoil, bus, truck, car, dugout canoe, horse, burro, and foot. In 1969, after the so-called Soccer War between Honduras and El Salvador, I was jailed twice in El Salvador and finally deported for allegedly being a spy. The Salvadoran government later apologized and invited me back."

* * *

MANHEIM, Jarol B(ruce) 1946-

PERSONAL: Born April 17, 1946, in Cleveland, Ohio; son of Harvey (a salesman) and Norma (Blaugrund) Manheim; married Amy Lowen, September 6, 1969. *Education:* Rice University, B.A., 1968; Northwestern University, M.A., 1969, Ph.D., 1971. *Home:* 709 Circle Dr. N.W., Blacksburg, Va. 24060. *Office:* Department of Political Science, Virginia Polytechnic Institute and State University, Blacksburg, Va. 24061.

CAREER: City College of City University of New York, New York, N.Y., assistant professor of political science, 1971-75; Virginia Polytechnic Institute and State University, Blacksburg, assistant professor of political science, 1975—. *Member:* American Political Science Association, American Academy of Political and Social Science, Southern Political Science Association. *Awards, honors:* Woodrow Wilson fellow, 1970-71.

WRITINGS: (Editor) *Annual Editions Readings in American Government '74/'75*, Dushkin, 1974, *'75/'76*, 1975; *The Politics Within: A Primer in Political Attitudes and Behavior*, Prentice-Hall, 1975; (with Melanie Wallace) *Political Violence in the United States, 1875-1974: A Bibliography*, Garland, 1975; (with Wallace) *Deja Vu: Historical Perspectives on Contemporary Political Issues*, St. Martins, in press. Contributor of articles and reviews to professional journals.

WORK IN PROGRESS: Research on mass media and politics, on political psychology, and on political behavior.

AVOCATIONAL INTERESTS: Guitar, writing folk and country music, travel.

* * *

MANNERS, Alexandra
See RUNDLE, Anne

* * *

MANNERS, Ande Miller 1923(?)-1975

1923(?)—May 17, 1975; American author. Obituaries: *New York Times*, May 19, 1975; *AB Bookman's Weekly*, June 23, 1975.

* * *

MANROSS, William Wilson 1905-

PERSONAL: Born February 21, 1905, in Syracuse, N.Y.; son of William Doane (a clergyman) and Martha Elizabeth (Wilson) Manross; married Catharine Ameilia Wisner, January 26, 1936. *Education:* Hobart College, B.A., 1926; Columbia University, M.A., 1931, Ph.D., 1938; General Theological Seminary, M.Div., 1930, S.T.B., 1931. *Home:* 221 Kathmere Rd., Havertown, Pa. 19083.

CAREER: Ordained clergyman of Episcopal Church, 1929; General Theological Seminary, New York, N.Y., fellow and tutor, 1929-39; Church Historical Society, Philadelphia, Pa., librarian, 1948-56; Philadelphia Divinity School, Philadelphia, Pa., lecturer, 1950-59, professor of church history, 1959-73, professor emeritus, 1973—, librarian, 1956-73. Research fellow at General Theological Seminary, 1960-62. *Member:* American Historical Association, Church Historical Society, American Society of Church

History, American Academy, Historical Society of Pennsylvania. *Awards, honors:* D.D. from Philadelphia Divinity School, 1973.

WRITINGS: The History of the American Episcopal Church, Morehouse-Gorham, 1935, 3rd edition, 1959; *The Episcopal Church in the United States: 1800-1840*, Columbia University Press, 1938; *The Fulham Papers in Lambeth Palace Library*, Clarendon Press, 1965; *The S.F.G. Papers in Lambeth Palace Library*, Clarendon Press, 1974.

WORK IN PROGRESS: A History of American Morals; The Achieving Society.

* * *

MANSELL, Darrel (Lee, Jr.) 1934-

PERSONAL: Born April 9, 1934, in Canton, Ohio; son of Darrel Lee (a newspaper editor and columnist) and Virginia (Shepherd) Mansell. *Education:* Oberlin College, B.A., 1956; Pembroke College, Oxford, graduate study, 1961-62; Yale University, Ph.D., 1963. *Home address:* P.O. Box 699, Hanover, N.H. 03755. *Office:* Department of English, Dartmouth College, Hanover, N.H. 03755.

CAREER: Dartmouth College, Hanover, N.H., instructor, 1962-64, assistant professor, 1964-68, associate professor, 1968-74, professor of English, 1974—. *Member:* Phi Beta Kappa. *Awards, honors:* Fulbright scholar at Oxford University, 1961-62; M.A. from Dartmouth College, 1975.

WRITINGS: The Novels of Jane Austen: An Interpretation, Macmillan, 1973. Contributor to literature and language journals.

WORK IN PROGRESS: Off the King's Road, an autobiography; *Written in Eden: The Meaning of Metaphor.*

AVOCATIONAL INTERESTS: Skiing, tennis, squash.

* * *

MANYAN, Gladys 1911-

PERSONAL: Born October 3, 1911, in Tampa, Fla.; daughter of Krikor G. (a salesman) and Louisa (Asdikian) Nalbandian; married V. George Manyan, January 12, 1936 (deceased); children: David R., George M., Gail L. *Education:* Educated in public schools in Providence, R.I. *Politics:* "Independent middle-road." *Religion:* Christian. *Home:* Pussywillow Farm, West Franklin, N.H. 03235. *Agent:* Max Gartenberg, 331 Madison Ave., New York, N.Y. 10017.

CAREER: Uncas Manufacturing Co., Providence, R.I., secretary, 1929-34; City of Providence, R.I., director of research on free educational, recreational, and vocational opportunities for youth, 1936; *Concord Monitor*, Concord, N.H., assistant to Franklin bureau chief, 1965-68, bureau chief, 1968-74; writer, 1974—.

WRITINGS: The Country Seasons Cookbook, Crown, 1974. Author of "A Domestic View," a column in *Concord Monitor*, 1966—, and "The Country Auctioneer," in *New Hampshire Echoes*, 1971.

SIDELIGHTS: Gladys Manyan writes of the early years of her marriage: "When money was our scarcest commodity, we tried to be as self-sufficient as possible by planting a large vegetable garden, getting laying hens, pigs and lambs for meat and a goat for milk. Since our daughter arrived unexpectedly when our finances were most precarious, I tried various money-making ventures with dubious success. These included raising hybrid worms and squabs in addition to selling eggs. On the side, I designed and made clothes for a college specialty shop in Providence.

AVOCATIONAL INTERESTS: Making her own clothes, making woolen braided rugs, macrame, embroidery, batiking, designing jewelry, singing (performed as a concert singer, 1933).

BIOGRAPHICAL/CRITICAL SOURCES: New Hampshire Sunday News, December 15, 1974; *Laconia Evening Citizen*, January 29, 1975; *Providence Journal*, May 24, 1975.

* * *

MARAN, Stephen P(aul) 1938-

PERSONAL: Born December 25, 1938, in Brooklyn, N.Y.; son of Alexander P. (an accountant) and Clara F. (Schoenfeld) Maran; married Sally Ann Scott (an editor), February 14, 1971; children: Michael Scott. *Education:* Brooklyn College of the City University of New York, B.S., 1959; University of Michigan, M.A., 1961, Ph.D., 1964. *Residence:* Chevy Chase, Md. *Office:* NASA-Goddard Space Flight Center, Greenbelt, Md. 20771.

CAREER: Kitt Peak National Observatory, Tucson, Ariz., astronomer, 1964-69; NASA-Goddard Space Flight Center, Greenbelt, Md., astronomer, 1969—, head of Advanced Systems and Ground Observations Branch, 1971—. Consultant to Westinghouse Research Laboratories, 1966, and to E. H. Plessett Associates, 1967. *Member:* International Astronomical Union, Royal Astronomical Society, American Astronomical Society, American Physical Society, American Geophysical Union, American Association for the Advancement of Science.

WRITINGS: (Editor with A.G.W. Cameron) *Physics of Nonthermal Radio Sources*, U.S. Government Printing Office, 1964; (with John C. Brandt) *New Horizons in Astronomy*, W. H. Freeman, 1972; (editor with Brandt and T. P. Stecher) *The Gum Nebula and Related Problems*, U.S. Government Printing Office, 1973; (editor with W. C. Brandeen) *Possible Relationships Between Solar Activity and Meteorological Phenomena*, U.S. Government Printing Office, 1975; (editor with Brandt) *New Astronomy Reader*, W. H. Freeman, in press. Contributor to *Natural History, Science Year, Scientific American, Smithsonian*, and other periodicals. Editor of *Astrophysical Letters*, 1975—.

WORK IN PROGRESS: Research on optical, infrared, and radio astronomy.

SIDELIGHTS: Maran was manager of "Operation Kohoutek" in 1973-74, and is currently project scientist for orbiting solar observatories.

* * *

MARGOLIN, Malcolm 1940-

PERSONAL: Born October 27, 1940, in Boston, Mass.; son of Max (a businessman) and Rose (Curland) Margolin; married Rina Tice (an artist and teacher), 1965; children: Reuben, Sadie. *Education:* Harvard University, B.A., 1964. *Office:* Heyday Books, P.O. Box 9145, Berkeley, Calif. 94709.

CAREER: Between 1964 and 1973 Margolin worked at a variety of jobs, including park groundsman, gardener, tree planter, trucking and steamshipping company manager, and cab driver; Heyday Books, Berkeley, Calif., owner, 1973—; writer.

WRITINGS: The East Bay Out, Heyday Books, 1974; *The Earth Manual*, Houghton, 1975. Contributor to magazines, including *Living Wilderness, Organic Gardening*, and *Nation*.

WORK IN PROGRESS: Guide to the Unseen Animal, on recognizing animal signs.

SIDELIGHTS: Margolin writes: "Writing books is only part of the process. I also enjoy designing books, setting type, doing the layouts and paste-ups, and working with friends who are artists and calligraphers."

* * *

MARNEY, (Leonard) Carlyle   1916-

PERSONAL: Born July 8, 1916, in Harriman, Tenn.; son of John Leonard and Sarah Victoria (Mays) Marney; married Rita Elizabeth Christopher, June 20, 1940; children: Rita Christopher (Mrs. Thomas Roach), Susan Elizabeth (Mrs. Allan Morgan). *Education:* Carson Newman College, A.B., 1938; Southern Baptist Theological Seminary, Th.M., 1943, Th.D., 1946. *Home address:* Route 3, Box 507-D, Waynesville, N.C. 28786. *Office:* Interpreters' House, P.O. Box 36, Lake Junaluska, N.C. 28745.

CAREER: Ordained to Baptist ministry, 1941; pastor in Austin, Tex., 1948-58, and Charlotte, N.C., 1958-67; Austin Presbyterian Seminary, Austin, Tex., professor of Christian ethics, 1951-57, Westervelt Lecturer, 1961; Interpreters' House, Lake Junaluska, N.C., founder and director of ecumenical center, 1967—. Visiting professor, Divinity School of Duke University, 1972—. Holder of Conquest Chair in Humanities, Virginia Military Institute, 1976; has also held positions as Cunningham Lecturer at Austin College, Willson Lecturer at Texas Tech University and Trinity University, Peyton Lecturer at Southern Methodist University, Wells Lecturer at Texas Christian University, and auxiliary Sprunt Lecturer at Union Theological Seminary, Richmond, Va.; lecturer at Princeton Theological Seminary, six summers, and at Colgate-Rochester University, Boston University, University of Chicago, Drew Seminary, and other institutions. Missioner to Far East Air Forces in Korea, Japan, and at other American bases. Member of executive committee, Charlotte-Mecklenburg Council for Human Relations, 1964; member of National Advisory Commission on Rural Poverty, 1967—. *Member:* World Council of Churches, National Council of Churches (vice-president at large, 1963-66), Baptist World Alliance. *Awards, honors:* Litt.D., Wake Forest College, 1963; D.D., Johnson C. Smith University, 1964, Kalamazoo College, 1967.

WRITINGS—All published by Abingdon, except as noted: *These Things Remain* (collected sermons), 1953; *Faith in Conflict*, 1957; *Dangerous Fathers, Problem Mothers, and Terrible Teens*, 1958; *Beggars in Velvet*, 1960; *Structures of Prejudice*, 1961; *The Recovery of the Person: A Christian Humanism*, 1963; *He Became Like Us: The Words of Identification* (collected sermons), 1964; *The Suffering Servant: A Holy Week Exposition of Isaiah 52:13-53:12* (collected sermons), 1965; *The Carpenter's Son* (collected sermons), 1967; *The Crucible of Redemption* (collected sermons), 1968; *The Coming Faith*, 1970; *Priests to Each Other*, Judson Press, 1974.

Sermons are represented in anthologies, including: *Pastoral Preaching*, edited by Charles Kemp, Bethany, 1963; *Best Sermons* (Protestant edition), edited by Paul Butler, Van Nostrand, 1964; *To God Be the Glory*, Abingdon, 1973. Editor, Religious Book Club, 1965-70. Contributor to theo-

logical journals. Trustee, *Christian Century*, 1960—; member of editorial boards, *Religion in Life*, 1960—, *Theology Today*, 1962—.

* * *

MARQUIS, Arnold

PERSONAL: Born in Racine, Wis.; son of Martin and Anna (Walquist) Marquis; married Ruby Doris Tilleson, 1936; children: Eric Lew (died, 1942), Sandra Lynne, Neil Quinn. *Education:* Attended Central State Teachers College (now University of Wisconsin, Stevens Point), 1925-27. *Home:* 4258 St. Clair Ave., Studio City, Calif. 91604.

CAREER: Worked as reporter or correspondent for *Kenosha News*, Kenosha, Wis., *Racine Journal-News*, Racine, Wis., *Chicago Herald-Examiner*, Chicago, Ill., *Milwaukee Journal*, Milwaukee, Wis., and *Wisconsin News*, Milwaukee; feature writer, Newspaper Enterprise Association syndicate; producer, National Broadcasting Co., 1936-47; writer-director-producer in radio and television.

WRITINGS: A Guide to America's Indians, University of Oklahoma Press, 1974.

Writer of documentary radio series presented on N.B.C.: "Enterprising West" (series of 30), 1938; "Unlimited Horizons" (153), 1939-43; "The Pacific Story" (186), 1943-47; "The Fifth Horseman" (8), 1945; "America's Indians" (4), 1949-50. Author of other radio series and of cultural and educational programs. Author of play, "Transition in India," produced on N.B.C., 1946. Also author, with Don Quinn, of "The Ballad of Will Rogers."

Work represented in anthologies, including *Radio Drama in Action*, edited by Erik Barnouw, Farrar-Rinehart, 1945; *Best One Act Plays of 1947*, edited by Margaret Mayorga, Dodd, 1947. Contributor to newspapers and magazines.

WORK IN PROGRESS: The Indians Are Coming.

SIDELIGHTS: Marquis writes: "The Indian Wars are not over. They're still on, only now they are being fought in the courts. Since 1942 (when I first visited the Indian reservations) my chief interest has been in Indians. Research has taken me on Indian reservations throughout the country."

* * *

MARRIOTT, Alice Lee   1910-

PERSONAL: Born January 8, 1910, in Wilmette, Ill.; daughter of Richard Goulding and Sydney (Cunningham) Marriott. *Education:* Oklahoma City University, B.A. (English and French), 1930; University of Oklahoma, B.A. (anthropology), 1935. *Religion:* Episcopalian. *Agent:* Nannine Joseph, 200 West 54th St., New York, N.Y. 10019. *Office:* Southwest Research Associates, 1836 Northwest 56th St., Oklahoma City, Okla. 73118.

CAREER: Field representative with U.S. Department of Interior Indian Arts and Craft Board, 1938-42, and with American Red Cross in southwest United States, 1942-45; University of Oklahoma, Norman, associate professor of anthropology, 1964-66; Central State University, Edmond, Okla., artist-in-residence, 1968—. Associate director, Southwest Research Associates, 1960—; consultant to Oklahoma Indian Council, 1962—. *Member:* American Anthropological Association (fellow), Writers Guild, Oklahoma Museum Association, Phi Beta Kappa, Sigma Xi. *Awards, honors:* University of Oklahoma Achievement Award, 1952; member of Oklahoma Hall of Fame, 1958; Oklahoma City University Achievement Award, 1968; Key

Award from Theta Sigma Pi, 1969; Oklahoma Literary Hall of Fame, 1972.

WRITINGS: The Ten Grandmothers, University of Oklahoma Press, 1945; (with Carol K. Rachlin) *American Indian Mythology*, Sloane, 1947, reprinted, Crowell, 1968; *Winter-telling Stories* (also see below), Crowell, 1947, reprinted, 1968; *Indians on Horseback* (also see below), Crowell, 1948; *Maria, the Potter of San Halefonso*, University of Oklahoma Press, 1948; *Valley Below*, University of Oklahoma Press, 1949; *These Are the People*, Laboratory of Anthropology (Sante Fe), 1951; *Indians of the Four Corners*, Crowell, 1952; *Greener Fields: Experiences Among the American Indians*, Crowell, 1952; *Hell on Horses and Women*, University of Oklahoma Press, 1953; *Sequoyah: Leader of the Cherokees*, Random House, 1956; *Black Stone Knife*, Crowell, 1957.

First Comers: Indians of America's Dawn, Longmans, Green, 1960; (with Edwin C. McReynolds and Estelle Faulconer) *Oklahoma: Its Past and Its Present*, University of Oklahoma Press, 1961; *Saynday's People* (includes *Winter-telling Stories* and *Indians on Horseback*), University of Nebraska Press, 1963; *Indian Anne: Kiowa Captive*, McKay, 1965; *Kiowa Years: A Study in Culture Impact*, Macmillan, 1968; (with Rachlin) *American Epic: The Story of the American Indian*, Putnam, 1969; (with Rachlin) *Peyote*, Putnam, 1971; (with Rachlin) *Oklahoma: The Forty-sixth Star*, Doubleday, 1972; (with Rachlin) *Plains Indian Mythology*, Crowell, 1975.

Contributor to magazines.

WORK IN PROGRESS: Fur Trade on the Lower Missouri and *White Girl: The Life of a Cheyenne Woman*, both with Carol K. Rachlin.

* * *

MARSH, U(lysses) Grant 1911-

PERSONAL: Born April 11, 1911, in Juliaetta, Idaho; son of U. Grant (a physician) and Gladys E. (Seagrave) Marsh; married Phyllis A. Longhurst, July 30, 1933; children: U. Grant III, Phillip Allen. *Education:* Attended Whitman College, 1929-31, University of Washington, Seattle, 1936-37, Stanford University, B.A., 1938; University of Hawaii, M.B.A., 1960; graduate study at University of Oregon, 1960, and University of Colorado, summer, 1965. *Residence:* Vancouver, Wash. *Office:* Department of Business Administration, Clark College, Vancouver, Wash. 98663.

CAREER: Procter & Gamble, Cincinnati, Ohio, district manager, 1938, manager for Hawaii, 1949-64; Clark College, Vancouver, Wash., professor of business administration, 1965-75, chairman of department, 1970-71; management consultant, 1974—. *Member:* Royal Arch Masons, Knights Templar of the U.S.A., Tau Kappa Epsilon.

WRITINGS: Salesmanship: Modern Principles and Practices, Prentice-Hall, 1972; *Salesmanship: Instructor's Manual*, Prentice-Hall, 1972. Contributor of more than thirty-five articles to *Moonbeams*.

WORK IN PROGRESS: Research on behavioral science material relevant to management and leadership.

* * *

MARSHALL, Joanne
See RUNDLE, Anne

MARSHALL, Kathryn 1951-

PERSONAL: Born July 27, 1951, in Memphis, Tenn.; daughter of Charles William (a mathematics professor) and Ruth (Taylor) Marshall. *Education:* Attended Southern Methodist University, 1969-70; University of Texas, B.A., 1973; University of California, Irvine, M.F.A., 1975. *Home:* 3424A East Coast Highway, Corona del Mar, Calif. 92625. *Agent:* Don Congdon, 22 East 40th St., New York, N.Y. 10016. *Office:* Department of English, University of California, Irvine, Calif. 92664.

CAREER: Lecturer in literature and writing at University of California, Irvine, 1973—.

WRITINGS: My Sister Gone (novel), Harper, 1975.

WORK IN PROGRESS: A second novel about Texas; research on vegetation and geological deposits in West Texas, on literary criticism, on contemporary fiction, and on women's fiction.

SIDELIGHTS: Kathryn Marshall told *CA*: "*My Sister Gone* grew out of a short story which won an undergraduate story contest at the University of Texas in 1972. It is in some sense autobiographical, as are most first novels. In it I attempted to capture the fun and the agony of growing up female in Texas. I also wanted to paint a picture of Texas, specifically East Texas and Dallas, which isn't the picture most Texas writers paint. No caricature, no exaggeration of grotesqueries just to please an East Coast audience." *Avocational interests:* Ballet.

* * *

MARTEL, Jane G. 1926-

PERSONAL: Born June 20, 1926, in Pekin, Ill.; daughter of Paul L. (a school superintendent) and Ruby (Murphy) Bolin; married former husband, Roy P. Grenier, June 26, 1948; married John F. Martel (a Beechcraft dealer), June 10, 1970; children: (first marriage) John, James, Jeanne, Paul. *Education:* Illinois Wesleyan University, A.B., 1948. *Home:* 37 Emerson Rd., Winchester, Mass. 01890. *Office:* Muraco School, Bates Rd., Winchester, Mass. 01890.

CAREER: High school social science teacher in El Paso, Ill., 1948-49; elementary school teacher in Bellwood, Ill., 1949-51; nursery school teacher in Boston, Mass., 1963-67; Muraco School, Winchester, Mass., kindergarten teacher, 1967—.

WRITINGS: Smashed Potatoes, Houghton, 1974.

* * *

MARTIN, Dorothy 1921-

PERSONAL: Born March 19, 1921, in Chisolm, Minn.; daughter of John Cameron and Aimee (Sanborn) McKay; married Alfred Martin (vice-president and dean of education at Moody Bible Institute), October 9, 1945; children: Dorothy (Mrs. Timothy Sumners), John, Sarah. *Education:* Macalester College, A.B., 1943; New York Theological Seminary, M.R.E., 1945. *Politics:* Republican. *Religion:* Evangelical Protestant. *Home:* 1030 North State St., Apt. 13-L, Chicago, Ill. 60610.

CAREER: Writer.

WRITINGS—All published by Moody; all adolescent fiction, unless otherwise indicated: *A New Life for Peggy*, 1957; *Open Doors for Peggy*, 1958; *More Answers for Peggy*, 1959; *A Mystery Solved for Peggy*, 1962; *Hopes Fulfilled for Peggy*, 1963; *Heart's Surrender for Peggy*, 1963; *Wider Horizons for Peggy*, 1964; *A Chapter Closed for Peggy*, 1965; *Etiquette for Everyday Living* (adult), 1969; *Faith at Work for Peggy*, 1970; *Edge of Belonging*, 1970; *No Place to Hide* (adult), 1971; *Light at the Top of the Stairs*, 1974.

Personal Bible-study guides, for Moody: *The Bible*, 1971; *God*, 1972; *The Lord Jesus Christ*, 1973; *The Holy Spirit*, 1974. Contributor to church publications. Editor and proofreader for Moody Press and Moody Correspondence School.

WORK IN PROGRESS: A History of Moody Bible Institute; *Establishing a Family Altar*; a juvenile novel.

* * *

MARTIN, Harold S(heaffer) 1930-

PERSONAL: Born August 7, 1930, in Ephrata, Pa.; son of Noah W. (in floor covering business) and Helen (Sheaffer) Martin; married Priscilla A. Miller, August 31, 1950; children: Stephen, Stanley, Sherwood, Christine, Delphine, Berdene. *Education:* Millersville State College, B.S., 1952; Western Maryland College, M.Ed., 1956; Messiah College, B.A., 1962. *Address:* Route 10, Box 149, York, Pa. 17404.

CAREER: Ordained minister of Church of the Brethren; Spring Grove Area School District, Spring Grove, Pa., junior high school teacher of mathematics, 1952—; Pleasant Hill Church of the Brethren, Spring Grove, Pa., minister, 1952—. *Member:* National Council of Teachers of Mathematics, National Association of Evangelicals, Brethren Revival Fellowship.

WRITINGS: Sermons on Eternal Themes, Carlton, 1971; *Simple Messages on Romans*, Brethren Press, 1974. Editor of *Brethren Revival Fellowship Witness*, 1966—.

WORK IN PROGRESS: Research for a series of messages on the Ten Commandments.

SIDELIGHTS: Martin has travelled in every state of the United States and every inhabited continent in the world. He has also conducted two tours to the Middle East.

* * *

MARTIN, Joy 1922-
(Joy Crandall)

PERSONAL: Born May 13, 1922, in Minneapolis, Minn.; daughter of J. P. (a teacher and electrician) and Hazel (a teacher and artist; maiden name, Small) Martin; married Roderick Palmer Crandall (an architect), March 26, 1946 (separated October 27, 1972); children: Roderick Pendelton, Merrie Diane, Alissa Joy. *Education:* Attended University of Southern California, 1940-43; University of Minnesota, B.S., 1947. *Politics:* Republican. *Religion:* Quaker. *Address:* P.O. Box 60821, Sacramento, Calif. 95860. *Agent:* Carousel, 1718 Lynwood Rd., Champaign, Ill. 61820.

CAREER: Worked as secretary in California and Minnesota, summers, 1940-47; Merrie-Go-Round School, Corte Madera, Calif., owner, 1960-69. Consultant to Four R's Preschool, 1974—; substitute teacher on Oahu, 1974—. *Member:* American Association of University Women, League of Women Voters, Pen Women, Paradise Property Owners Association (secretary, 1964-65).

WRITINGS: (Under name Joy Crandall) *Early to Learn*, Dodd, 1974.

WORK IN PROGRESS: Three children's books, *Grandma's Whisker Box*, *Kim Won't Go to School*, and *The Strange Wind*.

AVOCATIONAL INTERESTS: Swimming, baking, gardening, square dancing, music, philosophy.

* * *

MARTIN, L(eslie) John 1921-

PERSONAL: Born January 5, 1921, in Budapest, Hungary; U.S. citizen; son of Joseph (an accountant) and Elizabeth (Kiss) Martin; married Lois A. Henze (an associate school superintendent), March 22, 1951; children: Keith D., Brian J. *Education:* American University, Cairo, Egypt, B.A., 1947; University of Oregon, graduate study, 1948-49; University of Minnesota, M.A., 1954, Ph.D., 1955. *Politics:* Democrat. *Religion:* Episcopalian. *Home:* 5313 Iroquois Rd., Washington, D.C. 20016. *Office:* College of Journalism, University of Maryland, College Park, Md. 20742.

CAREER: Newspaperman and foreign correspondent in the Near East, 1941-47; University of Minnesota, Minneapolis, assistant director of International Relations Center, 1952-53; University of Nebraska, Lincoln, assistant professor of journalism, 1954-57; *Detroit Free Press*, Detroit, Mich., copy editor, 1957-58; University of Florida, Gainesville, professor of journalism, and director of research and graduate studies in journalism and communication, 1958-61; U.S. Information Agency, Washington, D.C., Chief of Near East and South Asia Division Office of Research, 1961-66, coordinator of overseas research, 1966-67, chief of Program Analysis Division, 1967-69; University of Maryland, College Park, professor of journalism, 1969—. Research associate with legislative council of Nebraska Legislature, summer, 1955; adjunct professor at American University, 1966-67; lecturer at U.S. Veterans Administration hospitals, 1972. *Military service:* British Army, 1944-45.

MEMBER: International Communication Association, Association for Education in Journalism (member of executive committee of International Communication Division, 1973-74), Society for Professional Journalists, American Association for Public Opinion Research. *Awards, honors:* Distinguished service award from Sigma Delta Chi, 1958, for *International Propaganda*.

WRITINGS: International Propaganda, University of Minnesota Press, 1958; (editor) *Propaganda in International Affairs* (annals), American Academy of Political and Social Science, 1971; (editor) *The Role of the Mass Media in American Politics* (annals), American Academy of Political and Social Science, in press.

Contributor to *Encyclopaedia Britannica* and *Worldmark Encyclopedia of the Nations*. Contributor of articles and reviews to *Journalism Quarterly, Gazette, Journalism Educator, Annals of the American Academy of Political and Social Science*, and *Journal of Politics*. Editor of *International Communications Bulletin* and "Foreign Bibliography" of *Journalism Quarterly*, 1955-61; copy editor of *Rochester Democrat and Chronicle*, summers, 1956-57; member of editorial staff of *St. Paul Pioneer-Press*, 1959, and *Louisville Courier-Journal*, 1960.

WORK IN PROGRESS: International Communication, for Wiley.

SIDELIGHTS: Martin writes: "My major interest is in international and cross-cultural communication. I also have a lifelong interest in the Near East, where I grew up."

* * *

MARTIN, Ralph 1942-

PERSONAL: Born December 12, 1942, in New York,

N.Y.; son of Ralph C. (a salesman) and Mary (Murry) Martin; married Anne Chapman; children: John, Mary. *Education:* University of Notre Dame, B.A., 1964; Princeton University, graduate study, 1964. *Home:* 818 Center Dr., Ann Arbor, Mich. 48103. *Office: New Covenant*, P.O. Box 102, Ann Arbor, Mich. 48107.

CAREER: National Secretariat for the Cursillo, Lansing, Mich., member, 1964-70; Word of God (Christian community), Ann Arbor, Mich., coordinator, 1970—. Member of Catholic Charismatic Renewal Service Committee, 1970—; director of International Communication Office of Charismatic Renewal Services, 1972—.

WRITINGS: Unless the Lord Build the House, Ave Maria Press, 1971; *Hungry for God: Practical Help in Personal Prayer*, Doubleday, 1974; *Fire in the Earth*, Word of Life, 1975. Editor of *New Covenant*; contributing editor of *His* (newspaper).

WORK IN PROGRESS: A book on family life; research on restoration within the Christian church, on marriage and family life, and on the work of the Holy Spirit in the world today.

*   *   *

MARTIN, Tony 1942-

PERSONAL: Born February 21, 1942, in Trinidad; son of Claude G. and Vida (Scope) Martin. *Education:* Honourable Society of Gray's Inn, Barrister-at-Law, 1965; University of Hull, B.Sc. (honors), 1968; Michigan State University, M.A., 1970, Ph.D., 1973. *Home:* 6 Norfolk Ter., Apt. 2, Wellesley, Mass. 02181. *Office:* Department of Black Studies, Wellesley College, Wellesley, Mass. 02181.

CAREER: Called to English Bar, 1966, and Trinidad Bar, 1969; Trinidad Public Service, Trinidad, accounts clerk in Water Department, 1961; Office of the Prime Minister, Federal Government of the West Indies, Trinidad, accounts clerk, 1961-62; master of Latin, French, Spanish, English, history, and geography in St. Mary's College, Trinidad, 1962-63; Cipriani Labour College, Trinidad, lecturer in economics and politics, 1968-69; Michigan State University, East Lansing, instructor in history, 1970-71; University of Michigan, Flint, assistant professor of history and coordinator of African-Afro-American studies program, 1971-73; Wellesley College, Wellesley, Mass., associate professor of history and Black studies, 1973—. Visiting associate professor at Brandeis University, fall, 1974, and at University of Minnesota, fall, 1975. *Member:* Association for the Study of Afro-American Life and History, African Heritage Studies Association, Caribbean Studies Association, African Studies Association of the West Indies.

WRITINGS: (Contributor) John Henrik Clarke, editor, *Marcus Garvey and the Vision of Africa*, Random House, 1974; *Race First: The Ideological and Organizational Struggles of Marcus Garvey and the Universal Negro Improvement Association*, Greenwood Press, 1975; *Black American Voluntary Organizations: A Historical Dictionary*, Greenwood Press, in press. Contributor of more than twenty articles and reviews to professional journals, including *Negro History Bulletin, American Historical Review, Journal of Modern African Studies, African Studies Review, Journal of Negro History, Mazungumzo, Race,* and *Journal of Human Relations.* Guest editor of *Pan-African Journal*, 1974.

WORK IN PROGRESS: "Race and the Black Experi-

ence," a series of three one-hour sound recordings, for Behavioral Sciences Tape Library.

*   *   *

MARTINE, James J(ohn) 1937-

PERSONAL: Surname is pronounced Martini; born July 23, 1937, in Philadelphia, Pa.; son of James and Theresa (Deni) Martine; married Patricia E. Breen, May 27, 1961; children: Stephanie Ann, James J., Jr., Andrea Maria. *Education:* Temple University, B.A., 1967; Pennsylvania State University, M.A., 1968, Ph.D., 1971. *Politics:* "I have none." *Religion:* "Practicing Roman Catholic." *Home:* 811 West Henley St., Olean, N.Y. 14760. *Office:* Department of English, St. Bonaventure University, St. Bonaventure, N.Y. 14778.

CAREER: St. Bonaventure University, St. Bonaventure, N.Y., assistant professor, 1971-73, associate professor of English, 1974—, head of graduate program in English, 1973—. *Member:* Modern Language Association of America, American Association of University Professors, North East Modern Language Association, Lambda Iota Tau. *Awards, honors:* St. Bonaventure University research council grants, 1973, 1974.

WRITINGS: Fred Lewis Pattee and American Literature, Pennsylvania State University Press, 1973; (contributor) James Nagel, editor, *Critical Essays on Catch-22*, Dickenson, 1974; (contributor) Jackson J. Benson, editor, *Essays on the Short Stories of Ernest Hemingway*, Duke University Press, 1975; (editor) *A History of American Literature Between the Wars: 1918-1942*, Cooper Square, in press. Contributor of about twenty articles and reviews to *Philadelphia Sunday Bulletin* and to journals. Manuscript reader for Dickenson, 1972—; advisory editor, *Studies in American Fiction*, 1973—.

WORK IN PROGRESS: A book on fathers and sons in American literature.

SIDELIGHTS: Martine considers himself apolitical and religious, which is "a reversal of the social order as we have come to know it." He also feels that "teaching and writing in their ideal application are inextricably intertwined. Not only are they both occasions for people who have something to say, to say it—the one is the perfect release, relief, and complement for the other." *Avocational interests:* Sports, opera.

*   *   *

MARTINETTI, Ronald 1945-

PERSONAL: Born August 13, 1945, in New York, N.Y.; son of Alfred Nathan and Frances B. Martinetti. *Education:* Attended Columbia University. *Residence:* New York, N.Y. *Agent:* Jay Garon, Jay Garon-Brooke Associates, 415 Central Park W., New York, N.Y. 10025.

CAREER: Writer.

WRITINGS: The James Dean Story, Pinnacle Books, 1975. Contributor to *New Leader.* Formerly book critic for *Wall Street Journal.*

WORK IN PROGRESS: A biography of Nathan Leopold, for Morrow.

*   *   *

MARTINEZ, Al 1929-

PERSONAL: Born July 21, 1929; son of Alfred and Mary (Larragoite) Martinez; married Joanne Cinelli (a writer),

July 30, 1949; children: Cindy, Linda, Marty. *Education:* Attended San Francisco State College (now University), 1947-50, University of California, Berkeley, 1952-53, and West Contra Costa Junior College. *Politics:* Liberal; usually Democrat. *Religion:* None. *Home:* 20881 Waveview Dr., Topanga, Calif. 90290. *Agent:* Arthur Pine Associates, Inc., 1780 Broadway, New York, N.Y. 10019. *Office: Los Angeles Times*, Times Mirror Sq., Los Angeles, Calif. 90053.

CAREER: Oakland Tribune, Oakland, Calif., reporter, 1955-72, writer of daily humor column for eight years; *Los Angeles Times*, Los Angeles, Calif., feature writer, 1972—. Writer for MGM-TV, 1975—. *Military service:* U.S. Marine Corps, combat correspondent, 1950-52; became sergeant. *Member:* Writers Guild of America. *Awards, honors:* San Francisco Press award; Union League Club award; California Top Story Award; Associated Press award; Western Conservation award.

WRITINGS: Rising Voices, New American Library, 1974; *Jigsaw John*, J. P. Tarcher, 1975. Contributor of more than one hundred short stories to periodicals. Author of pilot movies for NBC-TV, "They Only Come Out at Night," 1974, and for CBS-TV, "Bronk," 1974.

WORK IN PROGRESS: Three movie pilots for MGM-TV.

SIDELIGHTS: Martinez told *CA* that he is very interested in politics and government.

*   *   *

MARTINO, Bill   1933-

PERSONAL: Born September 23, 1933, in Cherokee, Kans.; son of Frank (a businessman) and Virginia (Stough) Martino; married first wife, Bette Eileen Favero, February 9, 1952 (divorced, 1959; died August 9, 1974); married third wife, 1965 (divorced, 1974); children: (first marriage) Bill. *Education:* Kansas State College of Pittsburg, B.A., 1956, graduate study, 1974; University of Wichita, graduate study, 1958. *Politics:* Anarchism. *Religion:* "All." *Home and office address:* RR1, Box 6, Cherokee, Kans. 66724. *Agent:* Broome, Box 3649, Sarasota, Fla. 33578.

CAREER: Worked as flight test engineer for aircraft companies including Boeing, Lockheed, Cessna, and Ryan, 1956-70; free-lance writer, 1970—. *Military service:* U.S. Navy, 1952-54. *Member:* Kappa Mu Epsilon, Alpha Mu Gamma.

WRITINGS: Songs of the Sand Country, privately printed, 1972; *The Dreamer* (novel), Branden Press, 1975. Contributor of articles and poems to magazines.

WORK IN PROGRESS: A novel, *The Winner*.

SIDELIGHTS: Martino writes: "*The Winner*, the novel that I'm about to finish now, tries to show that man has no regard for things that live. Since 1900 man has managed to kill off completely—forever—75 different species. One per year so far this century. My opinion is that man does not have the right to do this.... I really don't take myself seriously as a writer. I am not very creative. I do not have much imagination. And these are qualities that a writer of fiction certainly *ought* to have. I don't have them and I still want to write so I cheat. I use real people, real places, real experience and try to warp time and space enough and change a few names around so that I won't be sued. I guess I'm actually a reporter who does an inaccurate job of reporting in order to please his own whims and fancies."

MARVIN, Dorothy Betts   1894(?)-1975

1894(?)—April 28, 1975; American lecturer, clubwoman, benefactor, editor, and author of book on investments. Obituaries: *Washington Post*, April 30, 1975.

*   *   *

MASER, Jack D(avid)   1937-

PERSONAL: Born December 15, 1937, in Baltimore, Md.; son of Louis Robert (a physician) and Naomi (Shoben) Maser; married Irma Visser (a teacher), November 19, 1962; children: Andrea Lisa. *Education:* University of Maryland, B.S., 1961; Temple University, M.A., 1965, Ph.D., 1970. *Religion:* None. *Office:* Clinical Research Branch, National Institute of Mental Health, 5600 Fishers Lane, Rockville, Md. 20852.

CAREER: Laboratory of Neurological Sciences, Baltimore, Md., research associate, 1964-65; Tulane University, New Orleans, La., assistant professor, 1969-75, associate professor of psychology, 1975; National Institute of Mental Health, Rockville, Md., executive secretary of Clinical Research Branch, 1975—. *Military service:* U.S. Army, 1961-63. *Member:* Psychonomic Society, American Association for the Advancement of Science, Society for Neuroscience, Eastern Psychological Association, Psi Chi.

WRITINGS: (Contributor) Perry Black, editor, *Drugs and the Brain*, Johns Hopkins Press, 1969; (editor and contributor) *Efferent Organization and the Integration of Behavior*, Academic Press, 1973; (editor with M. E. P. Seligman, and contributor) *Psychopathology: Experimental Models*, W. H. Freeman, in press; (contributor) Kenneth Brizzee and Mark Ordy, editors, *Neurobiology of Ageing*, Plenum, in press. Contributor of about twenty articles to *Psychopharmacologia, Physiology and Behavior*, and other journals. Editorial consultant, *Pharmacology, Biochemistry and Behavior* (journal).

WORK IN PROGRESS: A study on the factual basis of death in literature, completion expected in 1977.

*   *   *

MASON, Clarence (Eugene), Jr.   1904-

PERSONAL: Born November 12, 1904, in Charlotte, N.C.; son of Clarence Eugene (a textile broker) and Blonde McConnell (Capps) Mason; married Lois Jessie McShane (a school principal), August 1, 1928; children: Robert Lee, Elizabeth Ann (Mrs. David H. Givens). *Education:* Wheaton College, Wheaton, Ill., B.A., 1924; Dallas Theological Seminary, Th.B. and Th.M., 1927. *Politics:* Independent. *Home:* 330 Harrison Ave., Glenside, Pa. 19038. *Office:* Department of Bible Exposition, Philadelphia College of Bible, Philadelphia, Pa. 19103.

CAREER: Ordained minister of Baptist Church, 1928; pastor in Philadelphia, Pa., 1927-34, and Atlantic City, N.J., 1934-46; Philadelphia College of Bible, Philadelphia, Pa., teacher, part-time, 1927-46 and full-time, 1946—, Scofield Professor of Bible Exposition, 1969-74, Scofield Professor Emeritus, 1974—, dean, part-time, 1943-46 and full-time, 1946-69, vice-president, 1952-69, director of Bristol Evening Campus, 1974—. Educational consultant to Febias College of Bible, 1928; president of Global Gospel Broadcasts, 1953—; member of board of trustees, Overseas Missionary Fellowship, 1932—. *Wartime service:* Served as chaplaincy secretary of General Association of Baptists, 1942-46. *Member:* Evangelical Theological Society, Society of Biblical Literature. *Awards, honors:* D.D. from Wheaton College, Wheaton, Ill., 1940.

WRITINGS: Prophetic Problems with Alternative Solutions, Moody, 1973. Compiler of syllabi, including *Bible Books* and *Bible Doctrines*, both published by College Print Shop in 1970. Author of pamphlets, "Pearl Harbor Disaster," 1942, "The Adequacy of Christ," 1943. Member of editorial committee of *The Pilgrim Bible*, Oxford University Press, 1950, 1952; *The New Scofield Reference Bible*, Oxford University Press, 1967; *The New Scofield Reference Bible*, French edition, Geneva Bible House, 1975.

WORK IN PROGRESS: Three pamphlets on Bible themes.

SIDELIGHTS: Mason has traveled to Israel, Turkey, Egypt, Greece, the Philippines, and throughout Europe.

* * *

MASSA, Richard W(ayne) 1932-

PERSONAL: Born May 2, 1932, in Carona, Kan.; son of Columbo and Ella (Whitehead) Massa; married Mary Lou Marshall, May 28, 1960 (divorced September 13, 1969); married Teresa Ramirez (a department store buyer), May 17, 1971; children: (first marriage) Tod Randall, Daphne Alyson, Sara Catherine. *Education:* University of Missouri, B.J., 1954, M.A., 1955; graduate study at University of Arkansas, 1964-65. *Home:* 2005 East 24th St., Joplin, Mo. 64801. *Office:* Department of Journalism, Missouri Southern State College, Joplin, Mo. 64801.

CAREER: University of Missouri, Columbia, instructor in journalism, 1955; Mississippi State College for Women, Columbus, instructor in journalism, 1957-58; Oklahoma College of Liberal Arts, Chickasha, assistant professor, 1958-67, associate professor of journalism and English, 1967-69; Northeast Missouri State University, Kirksville, special instructor in journalism, 1970; Missouri Southern State College, Joplin, associate professor of journalism, 1972—. Free-lance writer, 1958—; communications consultant and vice-president of Interpersonal Communications Consultants, Oklahoma City, Okla., 1969-72. *Military service:* U.S. Army, 1955-57. *Member:* National Council of College Publications Advisors.

WRITINGS: (Editor with Leon Cherrington) *Philosophical Man: Selected Readings for Contemporary Man*, McCutchan, 1969; (editor with Cherrington) *Aesthetic Man*, McCutchan, 1969; (with Cherrington, Teresa Ramirez, Irene Mitchell, and others) *Contemporary Man in World Society*, McCutchan, 1969; (editor with Cherrington) *Inquisitive Man: In Quest of His Goals*, McCutchan, 1970. Contributor to newspapers and magazines.

WORK IN PROGRESS: Children's fairy tales for adults; researching, with his wife, a book on the 60's.

AVOCATIONAL INTERESTS: Travel.

* * *

MASTERS, Elaine 1932-

PERSONAL: Born October 6, 1932, in Kansas City, Kan.; daughter of David Shepard and Stella (Ragan) Masters; married Donald Ramon Dull (a communications specialist), April 24, 1951; children: David Ray, Vicki Lorraine (Mrs. John Verburg), Jennifer Anne, Kevin Mark. *Education:* Attended universities, 1949-65; University of Missouri at Kansas City, B.A., 1966. *Religion:* Christian. *Home:* 8604 Jackson Ave., Manassas, Va. 22110.

CAREER: At one time, teacher in private schools in Venezuela, Philippine Islands, Indonesia, and Okinawa; teacher in the public schools of Virginia, 1970-73; volunteer worker at Cornerstone Coffeehouse, a Christian coffeehouse for teens.

WRITINGS: Ali and the Ghost Tiger (juvenile), Westminster Press, 1970. Contributor to *Trail/Camping* and *Camping Guide*. Editor, Cornerstone Coffeehouse newsletter.

WORK IN PROGRESS: The Lord's Coffeehouse.

AVOCATIONAL INTERESTS: Travel, hiking, camping, getting away from it all; studying and writing about birds, flowers, trees, and rocks.

* * *

MATARAZZO, Joseph D(ominic) 1925-

PERSONAL: Born November 12, 1925, in Caiazzo, Italy; son of U.S. citizens, Nicklas and Adeline (Mastroianni) Matarazzo; married Ruth Wood Gadbois (a psychologist), March 26, 1949; children: Harris, Elizabeth, Sara. *Education:* Brown University, B.A., 1946; Northwestern University, M.S., 1950, Ph.D., 1952. *Politics:* Republican. *Religion:* Episcopalian. *Home:* 1934 Southwest Vista Ave., Portland, Ore. 97201. *Office:* Department of Medical Psychology, University of Oregon Health Sciences Center, 3181 Southwest Sam Jackson Park Rd., Portland, Ore. 97201.

CAREER: Washington University School of Medicine, St. Louis, Mo., fellow, 1950-51, instructor, 1951-53, assistant professor of medical psychology, 1953-55; Harvard Medical School, Boston, Mass., research associate in psychiatry, 1955-57; University of Oregon Medical School, Portland, professor of medical psychology and chairman of department, 1957—. Attending psychologist, Barnes Hospital Group, St. Louis, 1952-55; associate psychologist, Massachusetts General Hospital, Boston, 1955-57; chief of psychology service at University of Oregon Medical School Hospital, Doernbecher Memorial Hospital for Children, and University Hospital North, Portland, 1957—. Lecturer at universities in Germany, Soviet Union, Italy, Netherlands, and Japan. Diplomate in clinical psychology, American Board of Professional Psychology. Member of advisory group on host factors in lung cancer, American Cancer Society, 1959-61; member of advisory panel, U.S. Department of Defense, 1966-70. Member of board of directors, Northwest Chapter of World Adoption International Fund, 1964-66, Oregon Zoological Research Center, 1971—, International Council of Psychologists, 1973—, Professional Examination Service, American Public Health Association, 1973—. Regent, Boys and Girls Aid Society of Oregon, 1966—, and Uniformed Services University of the Health Sciences, 1973—. *Military service:* U.S. Naval Reserve, 1943—; active duty, 1943-47; present rank, captain.

MEMBER: World Federation for Mental Health, International Association of Applied Psychology, American Psychological Association (fellow), American Association for the Advancement of Science (fellow), National Association for Mental Health (member of board of directors, 1962-68), American Association of State Psychology Boards (president, 1963-64), Society for Applied Anthropology, Association of American Medical Colleges, International Council of Psychologists, Psychonomic Society, American Psychopathological Association, American Association of University Professors, Western Psychological Association, Oregon Psychological Association, Oregon Mental Health Association (president, 1962-63). *Awards, honors:* Hofheimer Prize (annual research award) of American Psychiatric Association, 1962.

WRITINGS: (Editor with J. M. Shlien and others, and contributor) *Research in Psychotherapy*, Volume III, American Psychological Association, 1968; (editor) *Wechsler's Measurement and Appraisal of Adult Intelligence*, 5th edition (Matarazzo was not associated with earlier editions), Williams & Wilkins, 1972; (with Arthur N. Wiens) *The Interview: Research on Its Anatomy and Structure*, Aldine, 1972.

Contributor: Leon A. Pennington and Irwin A. Berg, editors, *Introduction to Clinical Psychology*, Ronald, 1953, 2nd edition, 1966; Paul A. Hoch and Joseph Zubin, editors, *Psychopathology of Communication*, Grune, 1958; E. A. Rubinstein and M. B. Parloff, editors, *Research in Psychotherapy*, Volume I, American Psychological Association, 1959; Irwin A. Berg and Bernard M. Bass, editors, *Conformity and Deviation*, Harper, 1961; Arthur J. Bachrach, editor, *Experimental Foundations of Clinical Psychology*, Basic Books, 1962; Benjamin B. Wolman, editor, *Handbook of Clinical Psychology*, McGraw, 1965; Leonard Krasner and Leonard P. Ullman, editors, *Research in Behavior Modifications: New Developments and Their Implications*, Holt, 1965; W. A. Hunt, editor, *Learning Mechanisms and Smoking*, Aldine, 1970; Alvin R. Mahrer and Leonard Pearson, editors, *Creative Developments in Psychotherapy*, Volume I, Press of Case Western Reserve University, 1971.

Consulting editor, "Aldine Psychology" series, 1964—; co-editor of "Aldine Psychotherapy Annual," 1972, 1973, 1974; psychology editor, *Stedman's Medical Dictionary*, Williams & Wilkins, 1972—. Contributor of more than seventy articles and reviews to professional journals. Associate editor, *Human Organization*, 1954-66; member of editorial board, *Journal of Clinical Psychology*, 1962— (associate editor, 1975—), *Psychotherapy: Theory, Research and Practice*, 1964-68, *Mental Hygiene*, 1969—, *Journal of Community Psychology*, 1974—, and *Psychiatry Digest*, 1975—; consulting editor, *Contemporary Psychology*, 1962-70; member of panel of editorial reviewers, *Psychological Bulletin*, 1968—.

* * *

MATEJKO, Alexander 1924-

PERSONAL: Born July 21, 1924, in Warsaw, Poland; son of Peter (an engineer) and Maria (a lawyer; maiden name, Wroblewska) Matejko; married Joanna Grzeskowiak (a historian), April 4, 1952; children: Agnieszka. *Education:* Jagiellonian University, M.A. (economics) and M.A. (sociology), 1949; University of Michigan, graduate study, 1957-59; University of Warsaw, Ph.D., 1960, docent in sociology, 1962. *Politics:* "No political activity." *Religion:* Roman Catholic. *Home:* 7623 119th St., Edmonton, Alberta T6G 1W4, Canada. *Office:* Department of Sociology, University of Alberta, Edmonton, Alberta T6G 2E1, Canada.

CAREER: University of Warsaw, Warsaw, Poland, associate professor of sociology, 1959-68; University of Alberta, Edmonton, professor of sociology, 1970—. Visiting professor, University of Leningrad, 1962, University of Moscow, 1962-63, University of North Carolina, 1966, University of Zambia, 1968-69, and Carleton University, 1974-75; guest lecturer at numerous universities and institutions in Europe, United States, and Canada. *Member:* International Sociological Association, Canadian Sociology and Anthropology Association, American Sociological Association, Association of Polish Engineers in Canada, Amnesty International.

WRITINGS: Socjologia zakladu pracy (title means "Sociology of a Work Place"), Wiedza Powszechna, 1961, 2nd edition, 1969; *Sacjologia przemyslu w Stanach Zjednoczonych Ameryki Polnocnej* (title means "Industrial Sociology in the U.S."), PWN (Warsaw), 1962; *Kultura pracy zbiorowej* (title means "Culture of Work"), Wydawnictwo Zwiazkowe, 1962; *Praca i kolezenstwo* (title means "Work and Companionship"), Wiedza Powszechna, 1962; *Postawy zawodowe dziennikarzy na tle systemu spolecznego readkgi* (title means "Professional Attitudes of Journalists within the Social System of a Newsroom"), KOBP (Krakow), 1963; *Spoleczne warunki pracy tworczej* (title means "Social Conditions of Creative Work"), PWN, 1963; *Hutnicy na tle ich srodowiska pracy* (title means "Steelworkers and Their Work Environment"), SIN (Katowice, Poland), 1964; *Czlowiek i technika wspolczesna* (title means "Man and Modern Technology"), Wydawnictwo Zwiazkowe, 1964; *System spoleczny zespolu naukowego* (title means "Social System of Research Teams"), PWN, 1965; *Kierowanie kadrami pracowniczymi* (title means "Personnel Administration"), PWE (Warsaw), 1966; *System spoleczny instytutu* (title means "Social System of Research Institutes"), PWN, 1967; *Socjologia pracy* (title means "Sociology of Work"), PWE, 1968; *System spoleczny katedry* (title means "Social System of College Departments"), PWN, 1969; *Wiez i konflikt w zakladzie pracy* (title means "Integration and Conflict at Work Place"), KIW (Warsaw), 1969; *Socjologia kierownictwa* (title means "Sociology of Management"), PWE, 1969.

Uslovia tworczeskogo truda (title means "Conditions of Creative Work"), Mir (Moscow), 1970; *Sociology of Work and Leisure*, European Centre for Leisure and Education (Prague), 1972; *Social Change and Stratification in Eastern Europe: An Interpretive Analysis of Poland and Her Neighbours*, Praeger, 1974; *Social Dimensions of Industrialism*, Sadhna Prakashan (Meerut, India), 1974; *Utilization of Social Research*, Sadhna Prakashan, in press; *Social Upgrading of Zambians*, Sadhna Prakashan, in press; *Overcoming Alienation in Work*, Sadhna Prakashan, in press.

Contributor: Wanda Litterer and Adam Andrzejewski, editors, *Zaludnierie i uzytkowanie mieszkan w nowych osiedlach* (title means "Population of New Towns and Utilization of Public Housing"), Arkady, 1959; Adam Sarapata, editor, *Socjologiczne problemy przedsiebiorstwa socjalistycznego* (title means "Sociological Problems of the Socialist Enterprises"), PWE, 1966; Adam Podgorecki, editor, *Socjotechnika* (title means "Sociotechnique"), KIW, 1970; S. M. A. Hameed and D. Tullen, editors, *Work and Leisure in Alberta*, University of Alberta, 1971; J. Tunstall, editor, *Media Sociology*, Constable, 1971; K. Krotki and G. Nettler, editors, *Social Science and Social Policy*, Alberta Human Resources Research Council, 1971; Adam Bromke and John W. Strong, editors, *Gierek's Poland*, Praeger, 1973; Robert Dubin, editor, *Handbook of Work, Organization and Societies*, Rand McNally, in press; W. Potichnyj, editor, *Political Problems of Eastern Europe*, Praeger, in press; Zbigniew Fallenbuchl, editor, *Economic Reforms in Eastern Europe*, Praeger, in press.

Contributor to newspapers and journals in his field. Co-editor, *Przeglad Zagadnien Socjalnych*, 1950-51; member of editorial board, *International Journal of Contemporary Sociology*, 1971—, *Canadian Slavonic Papers*, 1971-73.

WORK IN PROGRESS: Dilemmas of Industrial Democracy.

SIDELIGHTS: Matejko is fluent in Polish, Russian, Czech, German, and knows some French.

MATHAY, Francis 1925-

PERSONAL: Born February 24, 1925, in Green Bay, Wis.; son of Edward Joseph and Alice (Derenne) Mathy. *Education:* University of Michigan, B.A., 1947, Ph.D., 1963; St. Louis University, M.A., 1953. *Home and office:* 7 Kioicho, Chiyoda-ku, Tokyo 102, Japan.

CAREER: Entered Society of Jesus (Jesuits), 1947, ordained Roman Catholic priest, 1958; Sophia University, Tokyo, Japan, teacher-missionary, 1953-60, 1963—. *Military service:* U.S. Army, 1943-46; became second lieutenant. *Member:* Comparative Literature Society of Japan.

WRITINGS: (Translator from the Japanese) Endo Shusaku, *The Golden Country*, Tuttle, 1970; (translator from the Japanese) Natsume Soseki, *Mon*, P. Owen, 1972; (translator from the Japanese) Shusaku, *Wonderful Fool*, P. Owen, 1974; *Shiga Naoya* (biography), Twayne, 1974.

* * *

MATHEWS, Donald K(enneth) 1923-

PERSONAL: Born March 28, 1923, in Millerton, N.Y.; married, wife's name, Helen Marie; children: two. *Education:* Cortland State College, B.S., 1946; Springfield College, M.Ed., 1949, D.P.E., 1954; also studied at University of Illinois. *Office:* Exercise Physiology Research Laboratory, Ohio State University, Columbus, Ohio.

CAREER: High school teacher in Sharon Springs, N.Y., 1946-47, and Emmitsburg, Md., 1947-48; University of Illinois, Champaign-Urbana, instructor in physical education, 1949-51; Springfield College, Springfield, Mass., assistant professor of physical education, 1952-54; Washington State University, Pullman, associate professor of physical education, 1955-58; Ohio State University, Columbus, professor of education, 1958—, associate professor of physiology, 1970—, director of Exercise Physiology Research Laboratory, 1958—. *Member:* American Heart Association, American Association for Health, Physical Education and Recreation (member of research council), American Physiological Society, Central Ohio Heart Association (member of board of trustees).

WRITINGS: (With Virginia Shaw and Robert Kruse) *Physical Education for the Handicapped*, Harper, 1961; (with Ralph Stacey and George N. Hoover) *Physiology of Muscular Activity and Exercise*, Ronald, 1963; *Conditioning*, Wadsworth, 1964; (with B. L. Hollering, E. L. Fox, and R. L. Bartels) *Metabolic Energy Sources as Affected by a Seven-Week Program of Interval Training*, Exercise Physiology Research Laboratory, Ohio State University, 1970; (with E. L. Fox) *Physiological Basis for Physical Education and Athletics*, Saunders, 1971, revised edition, in press; *Measurement in Physical Education*, Saunders, 1958, 4th edition, 1973; (with Fox) *Interval Training*, Saunders, 1974; (with Bartels, Fox, and B. S. Harger) *Physiological Responses Following High Volume Interval Training*, Exercise Physiology Research Laboratory, Ohio State University, 1974.

Author of technical reports for U.S. Army. Contributor of about thirty articles to physical education journals, including *Michigan Osteopathic Journal*, *Journal of Applied Physiology*, *Archives of Physical Medicine and Rehabilitation*, *Research Quarterly*, and *Journal of Health, Physical Education and Recreation*.

SIDELIGHTS: Mathews holds a patent for "Golf-Lite," an instrument for improving one's golf swing.

MATSEN, Herbert Stanley 1926-

PERSONAL: Born March 15, 1926, in Portland, Ore.; son of Alfred Martin (a farmer) and Sophia (Larsen) Matsen. *Education:* Washington State College (now University), B.S., 1950; Columbia University, M.A., 1961, Ph.D., 1969. *Home:* 2506 Wheat St., Columbia, S.C. 29205. *Office:* Department of Philosophy, University of South Carolina, Columbia, S.C. 29208.

CAREER: Washington College, Chestertown, Md., instructor in philosophy, 1961-62; Converse College, Spartanburg, S.C., instructor, 1962-65, assistant professor of philosophy, 1966-68; University of South Carolina, Columbia, assistant professor, 1969-72, associate professor of philosophy, 1972—. *Military service:* U.S. Naval Reserve, sonarman, 1943-46. *Member:* Mediaeval Academy of America, Renaissance Society of America, American Philosophical Association, American Association of University Professors, History of Science Society, Southeastern Medieval Association, Phi Beta Kappa, Phi Kappa Phi, Psi Chi. *Awards, honors:* Fulbright fellowship for study in Italy, 1958-60.

WRITINGS: Alessandro Achillini (1463-1512) and His Doctrine of "Universals" and "Transcendentals": A Study in Renaissance "Ockhamism," Bucknell University Press, 1974. Contributor to *Quaderni per la Storia dell' a Universita di Padova*.

WORK IN PROGRESS: A study of "Disputes of Scholars (1487-1524)," held by the University of Bologna, with publication expected to result; research on sources and influences of the philosophy of Alessandro Achillini; research on the University of Bologna in the Middle Ages and during the Renaissance.

SIDELIGHTS: "I am historically oriented in philosophy," Matsen wrote, "and find the modern 'analytic' and 'problem' tendencies apart from historical contexts dissatisfying. My hope is to encourage students to learn languages other than English in order to study primary texts in their original languages, even if not now fashionable."

* * *

MATTHEWS, William Richard 1905-1975

June 25, 1905—June 10, 1975; English-born American educator, medievalist, bibliographer, expert on British, Canadian, and American biography, author of books on dialect and philology, and editor of diaries. Obituaries: *New York Times*, June 14, 1975; *AB Bookman's Weekly*, August 4, 1975.

* * *

MAXWELL, Robert S(idney) 1911-

PERSONAL: Born November 26, 1911, in Newport, Ky.; son of William S. (a clergyman in the Methodist Episcopal Church) and Ida (Bogle) Maxwell; married Sarah M. Minick, July 22, 1945 (died June 1, 1947); married Margaret H. Dunning (a director of Texas welfare), October 26, 1951; children: (second marriage) Elizabeth Gail. *Education:* Kentucky Wesleyan College, B.A., 1934; University of Cincinnati, M.A., 1937; graduate study at University of Kentucky, 1938; University of Wisconsin, Ph.D., 1949. *Politics:* Democratic Party. *Religion:* Episcopal. *Home:* 423 Parker Rd., Nacogdoches, Tex. 75961. *Office:* Department of History, Stephen F. Austin State University, Nacogdoches, Tex. 75961.

CAREER: University of Kentucky, Lexington, assistant

professor of history, 1948-52; Stephen F. Austin State University, Nacogdoches, Tex., assistant professor, 1952-56, associate professor, 1956-62, professor of history, 1962—, head of department, 1969—. Visiting Fulbright professor at University of Southampton, 1960-61. Member of Nacogdoches Historical Commission, 1958—, and Chamber of Commerce-Texas University Bicentennial Commission, 1968—, Historical Survey Committee, 1970—. *Military service:* U.S. Army, Infantry, 1942-46; became captain; received Bronze Star with oak-leaf cluster. *Member:* American Historical Association, Organization of American Historians, Southern Historical Association, Southwestern Society for Social Science, Forest History Society, Forest History Foundation (fellow), Texas Forestry Association, Phi Alpha Theta, Nacogdoches Kiwanis Club. *Awards, honors:* L. R. Bryan, Jr. award from Texas Gulf Coast Historical Association, 1963.

WRITINGS: La Follette and the Rise of the Progressives in Wisconsin, State Historical Society of Wisconsin Press, 1956; *Emanuel L. Philipp: Wisconsin Stalwart*, State Historical Society of Wisconsin Press, 1959; *Whistle in the Piney Woods: Paul Bremond and the Houston, East and West Texas Railway*, Texas Gulf Coast Historical Association, 1963; (editor) *La Follette*, Prentice-Hall, 1969; (with James W. Martin) *A Short History of Forest Conservation in Texas*, School of Forestry, Stephen F. Austin State University, 1970. Contributor to historical journals.

WORK IN PROGRESS: Studies in Lumbering and Conservation in Texas and *The Progressive Spirit*, a study of the Progressive Era (tentative titles).

AVOCATIONAL INTERESTS: Golf, tennis, travel.

* * *

MAY, Dean E(dward) 1944-

PERSONAL: Born October 31, 1944, in Lafayette, Ind.; son of Carl E. (a construction company owner) and Mary-Louise (Miller) May; married Judy Gail Rozwat (a public relations counselor and writer), June 26, 1971. *Education:* Purdue University, B.S., 1967. *Home:* 6015 Downing St., Parlin, N.J. 08859. *Office:* Borden Chemical Co., Montclair, N.J.

CAREER: Quaker Oats Co., Chicago, Ill., commodity buyer, 1967-72; Borden Chemical Co., Montclair, N.J., marketing specialist in Resinite Division, 1972—. Freelance consultant and writer of promotion and marketing brochures and sales plans for hardlines manufacturers. Instructor in skin and scuba diving and underwater photography; lecturer on diving topics. Has produced, directed, filmed, and edited underwater motion pictures. *Member:* Cousteau Society, American Littoral Society, Underwater Explorers Club.

WRITINGS: (With wife, Judy Gail May) *Great Diving-I*, Stackpole, 1974. Also author of motion picture script, "Diving in Rotan," 1973.

WORK IN PROGRESS: A script for an ice diving movie.

SIDELIGHTS: Dean May told *CA:* "My diving experience includes caves, shipwrecks, coral reefs, fresh water springs, and lakes, and even wells.... to research *Great Diving-I*, I personally dove extensively throughout the 24 Eastern and Gulf states of the United States and reported on my findings.... [It] was written to help new divers in an eastern or southern area of the United States enjoy some of the diving I have discovered. I feel the sea is our last frontier and is the life blood of our planet. In my writing

and in my films I hope to make people realize how important the seas are and encourage them to stop polluting our most precious resource." He has traveled to Bermuda, the Bahamas, Jamaica, Grand Cayman, Central America, and throughout the United States on diving trips.

* * *

MAY, Jacques M. 1896-1975

January 27, 1896—June 30, 1975; French-born American physician, nutritionist, medical geographer, international consultant, and author of works on malnutrition and ecology. Obituaries: *New York Times*, July 3, 1975; *Washington Post*, July 3, 1975.

* * *

MAY, Judy Gail 1943-

PERSONAL: Born September 5, 1943, in Chicago, Ill.; daughter of Casimir S. (a management analyst) and Elizabeth (Nesterowicz) Rozwat; married Dean E. May (a marketing specialist and writer), June 26, 1971. *Education:* Attended Loyola University, Chicago, Ill., 1961-62, and Loyola University, Rome, Italy, 1962-63. *Home:* 6015 Downing St., Parlin, N.J. 08859. *Office:* Infoplan International, New York, N.Y.

CAREER: Worked as stage and nightclub singer, dancer, and actress, and taught modeling and dance, prior to 1969; Howard Sigmond & Associates (public relations), Chicago, Ill., creative associate, 1969-71; Kanan, Corbin & Schupak (public relations), New York, N.Y., account executive, 1971-73; Infoplan International (public relations), New York, N.Y., account director, 1973—. Instructor in skin and scuba diving; lecturer on diving topics; underwater photographer. *Member:* Underwater Explorers Club, American Littoral Society.

WRITINGS: Scuba Diver's Guide to Underwater Ventures, Stackpole, 1973; (with husband, Dean E. May) *Great Diving-I*, Stackpole, 1974. Author of weekly column, "TV Reception Tips," syndicated in approximately fifty newspapers, 1975—. Contributor of articles and photographs to *Skin Diver*, *Boy's Life*, *WomenSport*, and other journals.

WORK IN PROGRESS: Research for magazine articles on U.S. scuba diving and on the Caribbean Islands.

SIDELIGHTS: Judy May told *CA* that she wrote *Scuba Diver's Guide to Underwater Ventures* "because of the high drop out rate of new divers who take lessons and then drop out because of 'nothing to do' underwater. I have actually done all the activities described and outlined in the book including going under the ice; diving shipwrecks; fish, shell and coral collecting; and diving caves.... My vocation, avocation, hobby, and delight is the sea, diving, and marine life."

* * *

MAY, Robert E(van) 1943-

PERSONAL: Born July 6, 1943, in Brooklyn, N.Y.; married Donna Jill Powell (a professor), June 10, 1967; children: Heather, Sarah. *Education:* Union College, B.A., 1965; University of Wisconsin, Madison, M.A., 1966, Ph.D., 1969. *Home:* 624 Terry Lane, West Lafayette, Ind. 47906. *Office:* Department of History, Purdue University, West Lafayette, Ind. 47907.

CAREER: Purdue University, West Lafayette, Ind., assistant professor, 1969-74, associate professor of history, 1975—. *Member:* American Historical Association, Organization of American Historians, Southern Historical Association. *Awards, honors:* Ford Foundation fellowship, 1968.

WRITINGS: The Southern Dream of a Caribbean Empire, 1854-1861, Louisiana State University Press, 1973.

WORK IN PROGRESS: A biography, tentatively titled *John A. Quitman and the Rise of Secessionism in Mississippi.*

* * *

MAYER, Ann M(argaret) 1938-

PERSONAL: Born August 5, 1938, in Schenectady, N.Y.; daughter of Harry F. (an electrical engineer) and Mary (Insley) Mayer. *Education:* Mount Holyoke College, B.A. (with distinction), 1960; Harvard University, Ed.M., 1964; State University of New York College at Geneseo, M.L.S., 1975. *Home:* 5 Stenwick Dr., Churchville, N.Y. 14428. *Office:* Fairbanks Road School, 175 Fairbanks Rd., Churchville, N.Y. 14428.

CAREER: Minneapolis-Honeywell, Wellesley Hills, Mass., technical writer, 1960-61; Boston Children's Hospital, Boston, Mass., director of out-patient rheumatic fever clinic, 1961-63; teacher of second grade, Medford, Mass., 1964-65; Churchville-Chili Central Schools, Churchville, N.Y., teacher of second and third grades, 1965—. *Member:* American Library Association, National League of American Pen Women, National Education Association, Save the Children Federation, Friends of the Osborne and Lillian Smith Collections.

WRITINGS—All biographies for children: *Dag Hammarskjold: The Peacemaker,* Creative Educational Society, 1974; *Two Worlds of Beatrix Potter,* Creative Educational Society, 1974; *Sir Frederick Banting: Doctor Against Diabetes,* Creative Educational Society, 1974. Contributor of biographies for children to periodicals, including *Adventure, Highlights for Children,* and *Whenever Whatever.*

SIDELIGHTS: Ann Mayer told *CA:* "I became interested in writing biographies for children when I started teaching elementary school and found a lack of biographies for younger children." *Avocational interests:* Traveling and music.

* * *

MAYHEW, Elizabeth
See BEAR, Joan

* * *

MAYNARD, Alan (Keith) 1944-

PERSONAL: Born December 15, 1944, in Cheshire, England; son of Edward Joseph and Hilda (McCausland) Maynard; married Elizabeth Shanahan (a tutor), June 22, 1968; children: Justin, John, Jane. *Education:* University of Newcastle, B.A. (first class honors), 1967; University of York, B.Phil., 1968. *Religion:* Agnostic. *Home:* 4 Abbotsway, Muncaster, York YO3 9LB, North Yorkshire, England. *Office:* Department of Economics, University of York, Heslington, York YO1 5DD, England.

CAREER: University of Exeter, Devon, England, lecturer in economics, 1968-71; University of York, North Yorkshire, England, lecturer in economics, 1971—. Visiting lecturer at Turin University Institute of European Studies,

spring, 1973; consultant to Organisation for Economic Co-Operation and Development. *Member:* Royal Economic Society, United Kingdom Association for Contemporary European Studies, Institute for Fiscal Studies, Institute for European Health Services Research (fellow), American Economic Association.

WRITINGS: (With M. H. Cooper) *The Price of Air Travel,* Institute of Economic Affairs, 1971; (with D. N. King) *Rates or Prices?,* Institute of Economic Affairs, 1972; *Health Care in the European Community,* University of Pittsburgh Press, 1975. Contributor to journals.

WORK IN PROGRESS: Economics of the Welfare State, completion expected in 1976; research for a book, *Comparative Medical Manpower Planning,* 1976.

AVOCATIONAL INTERESTS: Walking, gardening, cricket, watching football, current affairs, recent history.

* * *

MAYS, James A(rthur) 1939-

PERSONAL: Born May 1, 1939, in Pine Bluff, Ark.; son of Talmadge and Edna (Motley) Mays; married Lovella Geans (a Project Headstart teacher), July 15, 1962; children: James Arthur, Jr., James Earl, James Ornet. *Education:* Agricultural, Mechanical & Normal College (now University of Arkansas at Pine Bluff), B.S. (pre-medicine), 1960; University of Arkansas Medical Center, B.S. (medicine) and M.D., 1965. *Politics:* None. *Religion:* Protestant. *Home:* 19808 Galway Ave., Carson, Calif. 90247. *Office:* Martin Luther King, Jr. General Hospital, 12021 South Wilmington Ave., Los Angeles, Calif. 90059.

CAREER: Intern, Queen of Angels Hospital, Los Angeles, 1965-66; resident in internal medicine, Wadsworth Veterans Administration Hospital, Los Angeles, 1968-70; fellow in cardiology, Long Beach Veterans Administration Hospital and University of California at Irvine, 1970-72; Martin Luther King, Jr. General Hospital, Los Angeles, acting chief of cardiology, 1972—. Assistant professor of medicine, Charles R. Drew Medical School, University of Southern California, 1972—. Co-founder and medical director, United High Blood Pressure Foundation, 1974—; executive secretary, West Coast Medical Management, 1970—; member of board of directors, Cherkey Stroke Program, 1974—. *Military service:* U.S. Army, Medical Corps, 1966-68; served in Vietnam; became captain.

MEMBER: American College of Physicians (fellow), American College of Chest Physicians, American Medical Society, American Heart Association (Los Angeles affiliate; chairman of board of South Central governors, 1974—; member of board of directors, 1974—), Charles R. Drew Medical Society, California Medical Association, Arkansas Medical Society, Los Angeles County Medical Society, Long Beach Medical Society, Urban League (Silver Circle member), National Association for the Advancement of Colored People, Compton Intercultural Society (executive secretary, 1970—). *Awards, honors:* American Medical Association physicians recognition awards, 1973-76, 1974-77; National Association of Media Women Newsmaker Award, 1975.

WRITINGS: Mercy Is King (novel), Crescent, 1975. Contributor to professional journals. Associate editor, *Charles R. Drew Society Newsletter,* 1973-74.

WORK IN PROGRESS: Methods to Make Ethnic Foods Safer; a novel, *Douche;* medical papers on high blood pressure and heart resuscitation.

SIDELIGHTS: Mays told *CA:* "*Mercy Is King* represents a story of Black and white professionals in a manner that has not been expressed in writing, and especially has been neglected by the media. I wrote *Mercy Is King* especially for movie and television presentation for image purposes. I now wait to see if producers, particularly television, have courage to present Blacks in realism other than Super Fly and comedy."

* * *

MAZONOWICZ, Douglas 1920-

PERSONAL: Surname is pronounced Maz-*onn*-o-witch; born June 4, 1920, in Swindon, England; son of James (an engineer) and Lillian (Howcroft) Mazonowicz. *Education:* Swindon College of Art, graduate, 1939. *Home:* 50 West 11th St., New York, N.Y. 10011. *Agent:* Porter, Gould & Dierks, 1236 Sherman Ave., Evanston, Ill. 60202.

CAREER: Artist, lecturer, and writer. Co-director of Gallery of Prehistoric Paintings. *Military service:* British Army, Royal Tank Regiment, 1941-45.

WRITINGS: Voices from the Stone Age, Crowell, 1974; *Secret Art Gallery of the Sahara* (juvenile), Harper, in press. Contributor of articles on prehistoric art and travel to magazines.

SIDELIGHTS: In 1959 Mazonowicz decided to devote himself to the recording and accurate copying of prehistoric paintings in various parts of the world. For nine years he lived and worked in the caverns of Spain and France, making serigraphs (screenprinted editions) of the cave and rock art of prehistoric peoples. He also made three treks to the Central Sahara to record the rock art on the Tassili Plateau. His book relates his adventures and experiences during this entire period.

* * *

McAFEE, Ward M(erner) 1939-

PERSONAL: Surname is pronounced *Mac*-ah-fee; born September 20, 1939, in Salem, Ore.; son of William Arthur (a businessman) and Mary Louise (a salesperson; maiden name, Merner) McAfee; married Lois Root (a newspaper reporter), June 18, 1962; children: John, Elizabeth, Paul. *Education:* Stanford University, B.A., 1961, M.A., 1962, Ph.D., 1965. *Home address:* P.O. Box 1722, Wrightwood, Calif. 92397. *Office:* Department of History, California State College, San Bernardino, Calif. 92407.

CAREER: California State College, San Bernardino, assistant professor, 1965-68, associate professor, 1968-73, professor of history, 1973—, dean of School of Social Sciences, 1971-74.

WRITINGS: California's Railroad Era: 1850-1911, Golden West, 1974. Contributor to *Pacific Historical Review* and *Southern California Quarterly.*

WORK IN PROGRESS: A book of readings on the origins of the Mexican War.

* * *

McANELLY, James R. 1932-

PERSONAL: Born March 16, 1932, in Bloomington, Ill.; son of Clyde T. and Virginia (Jett) McAnelly; married Peggy A. Divine, June 30, 1956; children: Michael L., Robert A. *Education:* University of Colorado, B.S., 1955; Northern Illinois University, M.S., 1963, D.B.A., 1975. *Home:* 235 South Elmwood Dr., Aurora, Ill. 60506. *Office:*

Waubonsee Community College, Route 47 and Harter Rd., Sugar Grove, Ill. 60534.

CAREER: Caterpillar Tractor Co., Montgomery, Ill., expediter, 1959; junior high school teacher in St. Charles, Ill., 1959-63; high school teacher and athletic coach in Aurora, Ill., 1963-67; Waubonsee Community College, Sugar Grove, Ill., professor of business administration, 1967—. Claims adjuster for insurance companies in Illinois, 1955-63. *Member:* National Business Education Association, A.U.A., I.B.E.A. *Awards, honors:* Named all-state football player in Illinois, 1950; named to football Hall of Fame in Mooseheart, Ill., 1972.

WRITINGS: (With Benjamin C. Butcher) *Fundamentals of Retailing*, with study guide, Macmillan, 1973.

WORK IN PROGRESS: Business Mathematics, a textbook; a statement of responsibility for cooperative education in the community college; research on nursing homes; research on business mathematics, using electronic hand calculators.

AVOCATIONAL INTERESTS: Music.

* * *

McBRIDE, William Leon 1938-

PERSONAL: Born January 19, 1938, in New York, N.Y.; son of William J. (a pharmacist) and Irene (a high school teacher; maiden name, Choffin) McBride; married M. Angela Barron (a writer and college teacher), June 12, 1965; children: Catherine Alexandra, Kara Angela. *Education:* Georgetown University, A.B., 1959; University of Lille, graduate study, 1958-60; Yale University, M.A., 1962, Ph.D., 1964. *Home:* 744 Cherokee Ave., Lafayette, Ind. 47905. *Office:* Department of Philosophy, Purdue University, West Lafayette, Ind. 47907.

CAREER: Yale University, New Haven, Conn., instructor, 1964-66, assistant professor, 1966-71, associate professor of philosophy, 1971-73; Purdue University, West Lafayette, Ind., associate professor of philosophy, 1973—. Lecturer at Korcula (Yugoslavia) Summer School, summers, 1971, 1973, and at Northwestern University, summer, 1972. *Member:* Association des Amis de Romain Rolland (secretary of United States chapter, 1963-75), American Association of University Professors, American Civil Liberties Union, American Philosophical Association, American Society for Political and Legal Philosophy, Society for Phenomenology and Existential Philosophy. *Awards, honors:* Fulbright scholar, 1959-60; Woodrow Wilson fellow, 1960-61; Social Science Research Council fellow, 1963-64; Morse fellow at Yale University, 1968-69.

WRITINGS: (Contributor) George A. Schrader, Jr., editor, *Existential Philosophers*, McGraw, 1967; (contributor) Graham Hughes, editor, *Law, Reason and Justice*, New York University Press, 1969; (contributor) James Edie, editor, *New Essays in Phenomenology*, Quadrangle, 1969; (contributor) James R. Pennock and John W. Chapman, editors, *Voluntary Associations*, Atherton, 1969; (contributor) Edie and others, editors, *Patterns of the Life-World*, Northwestern University Press, 1970; *Fundamental Change in Law and Society: Hart and Sartre on Revolution*, Mouton & Co., 1970; (contributor) Hwa-Yol Jung, editor, *Existential Phenomenology and Political Theory*, Regnery, 1972; (contributor) Pennock and Chapman, editors, *Coercion*, Aldine-Atherton, 1972; (contributor) Pennock and Chapman, editors, *The Limits of the Law*, Lieber-Atherton, 1974; *The Philosophy of Marx*, Hutchinson University Library, in press. Contributor to professional journals.

WORK IN PROGRESS: A chapter for *The Living Philosophy of Jean-Paul Sartre*, edited by Paul Schilpp.

AVOCATIONAL INTERESTS: Travel.

* * *

McCAULEY, Carole Spearin 1939-

PERSONAL: Born April 18, 1939, in Great Barrington, Mass.; daughter of Kenneth Waldo and Elizabeth (LaPrise) Spearin; married Arthur Leo McCauley (a technical writer), November 14, 1964. *Education:* Attended University of Montpellier, 1959, and University of Besancon, 1959-60; Antioch College, A.B., 1962; graduate study at New School for Social Research, 1965-66, and at Manhattanville College, 1973-74. *Politics:* "Saddened liberal." *Religion:* "Saddened Catholic." *Home:* 23 Buena Vista Dr., Greenwich, Conn. 06830.

CAREER: Antioch College, Yellow Springs, Ohio, secretary-assistant in extramural department, 1962; Grailville, Loveland, Ohio, staff member, 1962-64; secretary-receptionist at Ann Dunn Real Estate, 1964-65; assistant at Grail Art and Bookshop, 1966-74. *Member:* Grail Movement, New England Small Press Association. *Awards, honors:* *Writer's Digest* short story prize, 1968, for "Monty Montgomery Knorr"; *Analecta* short story prize, 1968, for "Hello to All My Readers."

WRITINGS: (Translator from the French) Pierre Babin, *Crisis of Faith*, Herder, 1963; (translator from the French) Maurice Bellet, *Facing the Unbeliever*, Herder, 1967; (contributor) *Women: Omen*, Connecticut Feminists in the Arts, 1971; (contributor) Richard Kostelanetz, editor, *In Youth*, Ballantine, 1972; *Six Portraits* (computer-assisted fiction), Cantz'sche, 1973; *Computers and Creativity* (nonfiction), Praeger, 1974; (contributor) Diane Kruchkow, editor, *Changes of the Day*, New England Small Press Association, 1975; (contributor) Joe David Bellamy, editor, *The New Fiction: Interviews with Innovative American Writers*, University of Illinois Press, 1975; (contributor) Adele Aldridge, editor, *Spaced Out* (computer prose), Magic Circle, 1975; *Happenthing in Travel On* (fiction with computerized sections), Daughters, Inc., 1975; *Pregnancy after Thirty-five* (medical nonfiction), Dutton, in press. Contributor of articles, poems, and reviews to more than fifty periodicals, including *Partisan Review, North American Review*, and *Our Sunday Visitor*. Associate editor of *Panache*, 1969-74.

WORK IN PROGRESS: Computer-assisted prose for an anthology, *We Hold These Truths to Be Statistical*, completion expected in 1976.

SIDELIGHTS: Carole Spearin McCauley has some of her work in traveling art exhibits, including the Third International Computer Art Festival in New York City in 1975. She also does public speaking on such subjects as computers, the humanities and feminism. *Avocational interests:* Drawing, travel.

* * *

McCLANE, Kenneth Anderson, Jr. 1951-

PERSONAL: Born February 19, 1951, in New York, N.Y.; son of Kenneth Anderson (a physician) and Genevieve (a painter; maiden name, Greene) McClane. *Education:* Cornell University, A.B. (with distinction), 1973, M.A., 1974, graduate study, 1975—. *Politics:* "Believe strongly in non-violence." *Home:* 624 West 147th St., New York, N.Y. 10031.

CAREER: Colby College, Waterville, Me., instructor in English, 1974-75. *Member:* Phi Beta Kappa. *Awards, honors:* Corson Morrison poetry prize, 1973; George Harmon Coxe Award in creative writing, Cornell University, 1973.

WRITINGS: *Out Beyond the Bay*, Ithaca House, 1975. Contributor of poems to *Epoch, Beloit Poetry Journal, Crisis, Abraxis, Vinegard Gazette*, and other journals. Member of editorial staff, *Epoch, Watu*, and *Rainy Day* magazines.

WORK IN PROGRESS: A book of poems, *Moons and Low Times*, completion expected, 1976.

SIDELIGHTS: McClane told *CA*: "Writing poetry is, I guess, my highest and most fragile pleasure. Words, and you learn to love them, seem to bring everything into question: heaven and hell, the monumental and the commonplace—all want the rigors and excitements of language to occasion them. And I guess that is what I am about, the occasion and its occasion, the world and its greater worlds. And there is a lot that is scary in this: the world does not terribly like one's sense of order—she has her own—and the paths to ruination are most clear. I think (and this is most obvious in my longer poems), that I am losing touch with it all, losing sight of the hill for the valley and yet both exist. The images are most distinct, but the meaning is difficult. And it is in these tough places, these difficult ones, that good writing is found. Other areas are most painful."

* * *

McCLAURIN, Irma Pearl 1952-

PERSONAL: Born April 2, 1952, in Chicago, Ill.; daughter of Edward (an unskilled worker) and Bennie Pearl (Portis) McClaurin. *Education:* Grinnell College, B.A., 1973; University of Massachusetts, M.F.A., 1975. *Home:* 50 North Whitney, Amherst, Mass. 01002.

WRITINGS: *Black Chicago* (poems), Amuru Rannick Press, 1971; *Song in the Night* (poems), Pearl Press, 1974; (contributor) Nancy E. James, editor, *I, That Am Ever Stranger*, American Association of University Women, 1974; (contributor) Pinkie G. Lane, editor, *Poems By Blacks*, 3rd edition (McClaurin was not represented in earlier editions), SouthWestern, 1975. Contributor to *Black Ascensions, Drum*, and *Obsidian*.

WORK IN PROGRESS: A narrative poem on Harriet Tubman, "The Deliverer"; a partly autobiographical poem, "Pearl's Song."

SIDELIGHTS: Irma McClaurin told *CA*: "I am a young black woman and it is my experiences as such which guide my pen. I see myself wandering [in] a country which denies my cultural heritage and negates my womanhood. My writing is a constant struggle against the systematic cultural and sexual annihilation of my being.

"As a black I feel I have a duty to speak out of that which I am most familiar with. . . . I believe that it is only when artists of oppressed minorities begin to explore *positive* self images that there is a negative reaction to their art by those who follow the mainstream line of thinking. . . . My emphasis upon blackness in African-American writing expresses a historical struggle: my Blackness is not a reaction to whites, but attempts to establish a balance that is a positive assertion of my African-American culture."

McCLEARY, Eliott H(arold) 1927-

PERSONAL: Born September 12, 1927, near Dixon, Ill.; son of Harold E. (a farmer) and Ruth (Lie Van) McCleary; married Ann Morgan, August 18, 1962; children: Bryan, Heather. *Education:* Beloit College, B.A., 1952. *Residence:* Evanston, Ill.

CAREER: Popular Mechanics, Chicago, Ill., assistant editor, 1952-56; *Rotarian*, Evanston, Ill., assistant editor, 1956-65; *Today's Health*, Chicago, Ill., editor, 1966-69; free-lance writer and editor, 1969—. Editorial consultant to Blue Cross Association, Chicago, Ill., 1969—. Guest lecturer at New Mexico State University, 1973, and Northwestern University, 1974; member of institutional review committee of American Academy of Pediatrics, 1975—. *Member:* Society of Magazine Writers, Midwest Magazine Writers, Omicron Delta Kappa.

WRITINGS: Mexico, Scott, Foresman, 1972; *New Miracles of Childbirth*, McKay, 1974. Contributor to *Reader's Digest, McCall's, Ladies' Home Journal, Family Health, Prism*, and other magazines.

WORK IN PROGRESS: A non-fiction book.

* * *

McCLOSKEY, Donald N(ansen) 1942-

PERSONAL: Born September 11, 1942, in Ann Arbor, Mich.; son of Robert Green (an academician) and Helen (a singer; maiden name, Stueland) McCloskey; married Joanne Comi (a nurse), June 19, 1965; children: Daniel. *Education:* Harvard University, B.A. (magna cum laude), 1964, Ph.D., 1970. *Politics:* "Anarchist, registered Democrat." *Religion:* None. *Home:* 5406 South Kimbark, Chicago, Ill. 60615. *Office:* Department of Economics, University of Chicago, 1126 East 59th St., Chicago, Ill. 60637.

CAREER: University of Chicago, Chicago, Ill., assistant professor, 1968-73, associate professor of economics, 1973—. Visiting assistant professor at Stanford University, 1972. *Member:* American Economic Association, American Economic History Association, Economic History Society (England).

WRITINGS: (Editor) *Essays on a Mature Economy*, Princeton University Press, 1971; *Economic Maturity and Entrepreneurial Decline: British Iron and Steel, 1870-1913*, Harvard University Press, 1973. Contributor to professional journals. Member of editorial board of *Journal of Economic History* and *Explorations in Economic History*.

WORK IN PROGRESS: The Theory of Price: Worked Problems; Open Fields and Enclosures in England, completion expected in 1977.

AVOCATIONAL INTERESTS: Playing the guitar, playing cricket.

* * *

McCLUSKEY, John 1944-

PERSONAL: Born October 25, 1944, in Middletown, Ohio; son of John (a truck driver) and Helen (Harris) McCluskey; married Audrey Louise Thomas (a college instructor), December 24, 1969; children: Malik Douglass, Jerome Patrice. *Education:* Harvard University, B.A. (cum laude), 1966; Stanford University, M.A., 1972. *Home:* 15617 Terrace Rd., East Cleveland, Ohio 44112. *Office:* Department of English, Case Western Reserve University, Cleveland, Ohio 44106.

CAREER: Miles College, Birmingham, Ala., instructor in English, 1967-68; Valparaiso University, Valparaiso, Ind., lecturer in humanities and writer-in-residence, 1968-69; Case Western Reserve University, Cleveland, Ohio, coordinator of Afro-American studies, 1969-70, lecturer in Afro-American studies, 1970-72, assistant professor of American studies, 1972—, assistant professor of English, 1974—. Director of black drama troupes in Birmingham and Cleveland. Member of advisory council of Karamu House Writers Conference, 1970; member of executive board of Bell Neighborhood Center, 1972; member of board of trustees of Goodrich Social Settlement, 1972; member of board of directors of Independent School of East Cleveland. Member of Cleveland planning committee for World Festival of Black Arts (Nigeria), 1974. *Member:* American Association of University Professors.

WRITINGS: Look What They Done to My Song (novel), Random House, 1974; (editor) *Blacks in History*, Volume II (McCluskey was not associated with first volume), New Day Press, 1975.

Work has been anthologized in *What We Must See: Young Black Storytellers*, edited by Orde Coombs, Dodd, 1971; *Ethnic American Short Stories*, edited by Katherine Newman Spring, Simon & Schuster, 1975.

Contributor to *Negro Digest, Black World, Studies in Black Literature, Iowa Review*, and *Journal of Black Studies*. Editor of New Day Press, 1971—, and *Juju* (magazine), 1973—.

WORK IN PROGRESS: Another novel; a series of short stories; research on comparative African and Afro-American fiction.

SIDELIGHTS: McCluskey writes: "As a writer, my commitment is to that level of creative excellence so ably demonstrated by Afro-American artists as diverse as Ralph Ellison, Romare Bearden and Miles Davis. Hoping to avoid any fashionable ambiguity and pedantry, I want my fiction and essays to heighten the appreciation of the complexities of Afro-American literature and life." *Avocational interests:* Playing saxophone and bass clarinet, photography, playing basketball and football (McCluskey also coaches Little League football).

* * *

McCOURT, James 1941-

PERSONAL: Born July 4, 1941, in New York, N.Y.; son of James A. and Catherine (a teacher; maiden name, Moore) McCourt. *Education:* Manhattan College, B.A., 1962; graduate study at New York University, 1962-64, and Yale University, 1964-65. *Residence:* New York, N.Y. *Agent:* Elaine Markson, 44 Greenwich Ave., New York, N.Y.

CAREER: Has been employed as an actor in summer stock, 1962, and as a teacher of communication arts, 1968-69; writer.

WRITINGS: Mawrdew Czgowchwz (fiction), Farrar, Straus, 1974. Also author of "Panache," a play.

WORK IN PROGRESS: Continuing the Mawrdew Czgowchwz saga; work in the theater.

AVOCATIONAL INTERESTS: Singing and directing opera, cooking,travel (Europe from Ireland to Czechoslovakia).

BIOGRAPHICAL/CRITICAL SOURCES: Carolyn Riley, editor, *Contemporary Literary Criticism*, Gale, 1976.

McCREA, Joan Marie Ryan 1922-

PERSONAL: Born January 24, 1922, in Chicago, Ill.; daughter of Alexander Charles (an accountant) and Sophia (Hagan) Ryan; married James Aloysius McCrea (a businessman), January 26, 1947. Education: Indiana University, B.A., 1942; University of California, Riverside, graduate study, 1954-55; University of California, Los Angeles, M.A., 1957, Ph.D., 1965. Office: Department of Economics, University of Texas, Arlington, Tex. 76019.

CAREER: Republic Steel, Chicago, Ill., metallurgical observer, 1942-45; secretary, Veterans Administration, 1945-50; U.S. Air Force, personnel technician, methods analyst, 1950-55; University of California, Riverside, instructor in economics, 1959-61; Hollins College, Hollins, Va., assistant professor of economics, 1961-66; University of Texas, Arlington, professor of economics, 1966—. Member: American Economic Association, Association for Evolutionary Economics, Industrial Relations Research Association, Mensa, Western Economic Association, Texas Association of College Teachers. Awards, honors: Ford Foundation fellowship, 1965, for study at University of Virginia.

WRITINGS: The Reemployment Experience of Workers Displaced in a Plant Shutdown, Bureau of Economic Research, University of Virginia, 1968; Texas Labor Laws, Bureau of Business Research, University of Texas, 1971; Labor Laws in Texas, Bureau of Business Research, University of Texas, 1974. Contributor to Encyclopaedia Britannica and to Community College Social Science Quarterly, Western Social Science Journal, and Boletin de la Biblioteca del Congreso de la Nacion (Argentina).

* * *

McCUTCHEON, Lynn E(llis) 1944-

PERSONAL: Born March 19, 1944, in Wilkinsburg, Pa.; son of Chester Myers and Winona (Smith) McCutcheon; married Mary Elizabeth Mathews, December 30, 1967; children: Lauren. Education: Indiana University of Pennsylvania, B.S., 1967; Auburn University, M.S., 1969. Residence: Falls Church, Va. Office: Department of Psychology, Northern Virginia Community College, Annandale, Va. 22003.

CAREER: Erskine College, Due West, S.C., assistant professor of psychology, 1968-70; Northern Virginia Community College, Annandale, assistant professor of psychology, 1971—.

WRITINGS: Rhythm and Blues, R. W. Beatty, 1971; Psychological Effects of the Crowded Environment, Forefront, 1974. Member of editorial board of Community College Social Science Quarterly, 1974—. Contributor to journals in his field.

WORK IN PROGRESS: A book on social psychology.

* * *

McDANIEL, John N. 1941-

PERSONAL: Born January 30, 1941, in Washington, D.C.; son of Noble A. and Emily (a secretary) McDaniel; married Jean Smart (a secretary), August 26, 1967; children: Scott Noble, Craig Thomas. Education: Hampden-Sydney College, B.A., 1963; Johns Hopkins University, M.A., 1964; Florida State University, Ph.D., 1970. Home: 1802 Bartway Dr., Murfreesboro, Tenn. 37130. Office: Department of English, Middle Tennessee State University, Murfreesboro, Tenn. 37130.

CAREER: McDonogh School, McDonogh, Md., instructor in English, 1964-66; Florida State University, Tallahassee, instructor in English at Study Center in Florence, Italy, 1968-69, instructor in English, 1969-70; Middle Tennessee State University, Murfreesboro, assistant professor, 1970-74, associate professor of English, 1975—. Member: Modern Language Association of America, South Atlantic Modern Language Association, Phi Delta Kappa, Omicron Delta Kappa, Psi Chi, Sigma Upsilon.

WRITINGS: The Fiction of Philip Roth, Haddonfield House, 1974. Contributor to Xavier University Studies, Journal of the Folklore Institute, Bulletin of Bibliography, and Tennessee Folklore Society Bulletin.

WORK IN PROGRESS: Translating Giuseppe Cocchiara's Storia del Folklore in Europa to be published as The History of Folklore in Europe.

AVOCATIONAL INTERESTS: Foreign travel.

* * *

McDERMOTT, Robert A(nthony) 1939-

PERSONAL: Born August 5, 1939, in New York; son of John J. (a mechanic) and Helen (Kelly) McDermott; married Ellen Dineen (a ceramicist), November 26, 1964; children: Darren, Deirdre. Education: Queens College of the City University of New York, B.A., 1962; Emory University, M.A., 1965; Boston University, Ph.D., 1969. Home: 612 Forest Ave., Rye, N.Y. 10580. Office: Department of Philosophy, Baruch College of the City University of New York, 17 Lexington Ave., New York, N.Y. 10010.

CAREER: Manhattanville College, Purchase, N.Y., assistant professor of philosophy, 1964-71; Baruch College of the City University of New York, New York, N.Y., associate professor of philosophy, 1971—, head of department, 1971—. Member: American Academy of Religion (secretary, 1969-72), Society for Asian and Comparative Philosophy (member of executive committee, 1970-72), New York American Academy of Religion (president, 1969-70). Awards, honors: Fulbright grants to India, summer, 1966, and Open University, England, 1975-76.

WRITINGS: (Editor and author of introduction) Radhakrishnan: Selected Writings on Philosophy, Religion, and Culture, Dutton, 1970; (author of introduction and annotated bibliography) Sri Aurobindo, The Mind of Light, Dutton, 1971; (editor and author of introduction) The Essential Aurobindo, Schocken, 1973; (editor with V. S. Naravane) The Spirit of Modern India, Crowell, 1974; (editor and contributor) Six Pillars: Introductions to the Major Works of Sri Aurobindo, Wilson Books, 1974. Contributor to proceedings and to journals in his field. Editor of and contributor to a special issue of Cross Currents, "Sri Aurobindo: His Life, Thought, and Legacy; Integral Yoga, Evolution, and Auroville," 1972. Compiler with Haridas Chaudhuri of Sri Aurobindo Centenary Issue of International Philosophical Quarterly, 1972.

WORK IN PROGRESS: Co-editing Ontology East and West (tentative title); editing Hinduism in America (tentative title); studying the works of W. T. Stace and Rudolph Steiner.

* * *

McDONALD, Kay L(aureen) 1934-

PERSONAL: Born November 8, 1934, in Salem, Ore.; daughter of Harold Eugene (a clerk) and Helen L. (Mykol) Fielding; married Norman L. McDonald (a foam and fiberglass applicator), May 14, 1955; children: Jordana L., Derrick L. *Education:* Educated in public schools in Salem, Ore. *Politics:* "Registered Democrat—vote independent." *Religion:* Protestant. *Home and office:* 4316 Riverside Rd. S., Salem, Ore. 97302.

CAREER: Pacific Northwest Bell (telephone company), Salem, Ore., clerk and switchboard operator, 1952-65; writer, 1965—.

WRITINGS: The Brightwood Expedition (historical novel), Norton, in press.

WORK IN PROGRESS: White Eagle, a historical novel, set to precede events in *The Brightwood Expedition*; *The Vision Is Fulfilled*, a historical novel to complete a trilogy about *The Brightwood Expedition*.

SIDELIGHTS: Kay McDonald writes: "I have always desired to do something artistic. I would have loved to paint, sing, or dance, as I love music, but it seems the only thing I ever did on a continuing basis was write—." *Avocational interests:* The outdoors, hunting, fishing, white-water drifting, hiking, golf, bowling, water-skiing, snow-skiing, horseback riding, writing for television, raising food, travel, gardening, canning and freezing food.

* * *

McDONOUGH, Nancy 1935-

PERSONAL: Surname is pronounced Mc-*Don*-na; born December 30, 1935, in Little Rock, Ark.; daughter of Otis Havis and Ila (Sugg) Nixon; married Russell B. McDonough, Jr.; children: Lee Anne, Russell III. *Education:* Attended Agnes Scott College, 1953-55; Long Beach State College, B.A., 1957. *Religion:* Episcopalian. *Home:* 2 Huntington Rd., Little Rock, Ark. 72207.

CAREER: Writer.

WRITINGS: Garden Sass: A Catalog of Arkansas Folkways, Coward, 1974.

* * *

McELROY, Elam E. 1922-

PERSONAL: Born May 22, 1922, in Texas; son of Emmett H. (a minister) and Gladys (Hicks) McElroy; married Cranis Belford, July 27, 1946; children: Randy, Mark. *Education:* University of Oklahoma, B.S.B.A., 1949, M.B.A., 1950. *Politics:* None. *Religion:* Christian. *Home:* 8910 North Regent Rd., Milwaukee, Wis. 53217. *Office:* Department of Business, Marquette University, 608 North 13th St., Milwaukee, Wis. 53233.

CAREER: Marquette University, Milwaukee, Wis., instructor, 1950-53, assistant professor, 1953-58, associate professor of business statistics, 1958—. Metropolitan Milwaukee Association of Commerce, Economic Research Division, manager, 1953-68, consultant, 1968-70. Consultant to WISN-TV, to Fort Howard Paper Co., and to Citizen's Governmental Research Bureau. Member of Wisconsin Industrial Commission's Ad Hoc Committee on Economic Indicators, Wisconsin Southeastern Regional Planning Commission, Milwaukee Community Welfare Council's Research Advisory Committee, and of Milwaukee Metropolitan Study Commission; member of board of directors of Milwaukee Council on Alcoholism. Appeared on Milwaukee Public Library's television program, "Public Conference." *Military service:* U.S. Coast Guard, 1942-45.

MEMBER: American Statistical Association, American Institute for Decision Sciences, American Association of University Professors, Beta Gamma Sigma.

WRITINGS: Applied Business Statistics: An Elementary Approach, Holden-Day, 1971; *Applied Business Statistics: Answers and Solutions Manual*, Holden-Day, 1971. Writer of research reports; contributor to *Milwaukee Sentinel, Milwaukee Journal*, and to business journals.

WORK IN PROGRESS: Revising *Applied Business Statistics: An Elementary Approach*, completion expected in 1977.

AVOCATIONAL INTERESTS: Gardening, swimming.

* * *

McELWEE, William 1907-

PERSONAL: Born September 13, 1907, in London, England; son of John (Deputy Surgeon-General) and Katherine Phock (Lloyd) McElwee; married Patience Arden Kennington (a novelist), December 20, 1930 (died, 1963); children: Harriet Mary (Mrs. David N. Hall). *Education:* Christ Church, Oxford, B.A. (first class honors), 1930, M.A., 1946. *Politics:* Tory. *Religion:* Church of England. *Home:* 99, Winchester Rd., Micheldever, Hampshire, England. *Agent:* Curtis Brown Ltd., 1, Craven Hill, London W.2, England.

CAREER: University of Vienna, Vienna, Austria, research scholar, 1930-32; University of Liverpool, Liverpool, England, junior lecturer in history, 1932-34; Stowe School, Buckingham, England, tutor and head of history department, 1934-62; Royal Military Academy, Sandhurst, Surrey, England, head of modern subjects department, 1962-67. Guest lecturer, British Army Staff College, 1954-66. *Military service:* British Army, 1940-45; became major; received Military Cross, Normandy, 1944. *Member:* Royal Society of Literature (fellow).

WRITINGS: (Translator and editor with A.J.P. Taylor) Heinrich Friedjung, *The Struggle for Supremacy in Germany*, Macmillan, 1935; *The Reign of Charles V*, Macmillan, 1936; *The House* (novel), Bles, 1938; *The Cure* (novel), Melrose, 1946; *Final Objective* (novel), Melrose, 1948; *History of 2nd Argyll & Sutherland Highlanders, 1943-45*, Thomas Nelson, 1949; *The Murder of Sir Thomas Overbury*, Oxford University Press, 1952; *The Story of England*, Faber, 1952, Roy, 1961, 3rd edition, Praeger, 1973; *England's Precedence, 1603-1688*, Hodder & Stoughton, 1956; *The Wisest Fool in Christendom, James VI & I*, Harcourt, 1958; *Teach Yourself the History of England*, Barnes & Noble, 1958; *Britian's Locust Years, 1918-1940*, Faber, 1962; (translator) Friedrich Duerrenmatt, *An Angel Comes to Babylon*, Grove, 1964; *The Battle of D Day*, Faber, 1965; *The Art of War: Waterloo to Mons* (Military Book Club and Book-of-the-Month Club selections), Indiana University Press, 1975. Contributor to *New Statesman* and *London Sunday Telegraph*.

WORK IN PROGRESS: History of the British Army from King Alfred to the Present Day.

AVOCATIONAL INTERESTS: Travel, fox-hunting.

* * *

McFARLAND, Keith D(onavon) 1940-

PERSONAL: Born June 25, 1940, in Dover, Ohio; son of Carl Raymond (an agent of the Internal Revenue Service) and Gladys (Kughler) McFarland; married Nancy Myers, June 12, 1962; children: Mark Alan, Carolyn Ann, Dianna

Lea. *Education:* Kent State University, B.S., 1962; Ohio State University, M.A., 1963, Ph.D., 1969. *Religion:* Presbyterian. *Home:* 2908 Melmar Park, Commerce, Tex. 75428. *Office:* Department of History, East Texas State University, Commerce, Tex. 75428.

CAREER: East Texas State University, Commerce, assistant professor, 1969-73, associate professor of history, 1974—, assistant dean of College of Liberal and Fine Arts, 1973—. Participant in U.S. State Department diplomat program in politico-military affairs, 1975. *Military service:* U.S. Army, Quartermaster Corps, 1963-65; served in Ryukyu Islands; became first lieutenant. *Member:* American Historical Association, Organization of American Historians, American Military Institute, National Historical Society, Kansas State Historical Society, Rotary International.

WRITINGS: Harry H. Woodring: A Political Biography of F.D.R.'s Controversial Secretary of War, University Press of Kansas, 1975. Contributor to history and education journals.

WORK IN PROGRESS: A Biography of Louis A. Johnson: Truman's Secretary of Defense, 1949-1950; research on problems of the War Department in the 1930's.

SIDELIGHTS: McFarland writes: "I feel that the writing of history has traveled from an earlier extreme of overly detailed biographies to the opposite extreme of covering only events and ignoring the role of the individual. I strive to achieve a balance between the personalities, whose uniqueness is so important in decision making, and the events of the times, a kind of 'man and his times' approach. It is also my contention that history can and should teach guiding principles of administration, management, problem solving, and decision making that can be useful in virtually any kind of human endeavor."

* * *

McGAREY, Gladys T(aylor)   1920-

PERSONAL: Born November 30, 1920, in Fatehgarh, India; daughter of John Carl (a physician and missionary) and Elizabeth (a physician and missionary; maiden name, Siehl) Taylor; married William A. McGarey (a physician), December 18, 1943; children: William Carl, John Paul, Anne Louise, Robert Gordon, Helene Elizabeth, David Lester. *Education:* Muskingum College, B.S., 1941; Women's Medical College, Philadelphia, Pa., M.D., 1946. *Religion:* Presbyterian. *Home:* 5401 East Lafayette Blvd., Phoenix, Ariz. 85018. *Office:* A. R. E. Clinic, Inc., 4018 North 40th St., Phoenix, Ariz. 85018.

CAREER: Deaconess Hospital, Cincinnati, Ohio, intern, 1946; private practice of medicine in Wellsville, Ohio, 1946-55, and Phoenix, Ariz., 1955-70; A. R. E. Clinic, Inc., Phoenix, Ariz., staff physician, 1970—. *Member:* American Medical Association, American Academy of Family Physicians, American Academy of Manipulative Medicine, Acupuncture Association of Physicians and Surgeons, Arizona Medical Association, Maricopa County Medical Society.

WRITINGS: (With husband, William A. McGarey) *There Will Your Heart Be Also* (nonfiction), Prentice-Hall, 1975. Member of editorial board of *International Journal of Psychoenergetic Systems*.

WORK IN PROGRESS: Compiling data on baby care from psychic readings of Edgar Cayce.

McGAREY, William A.   1919-

PERSONAL: Born October 31, 1919, in Wellsville, Ohio; son of Everett Lester (a steelworker) and Anna (Hjerpe) McGarey; married Gladys Taylor (a physician), December 20, 1943; children: William Carl, John Paul, Anne Louise, Robert Gordon, Helene Elizabeth, David Lester. *Education:* College of the Ozarks, B.S., 1944; University of Cincinnati, M.D., 1947. *Religion:* Presbyterian. *Home:* 5401 East Lafayette Blvd., Phoenix, Ariz. 85018. *Office:* A. R. E. Clinic, Inc., 4018 North 40th St., Phoenix, Ariz. 85018.

CAREER: Private practice of medicine in Wellsville, Ohio, 1947-55, and Phoenix, Ariz., 1955-70; A. R. E. Clinic, Inc., Phoenix, Ariz., medical director, 1970—. Guest lecturer at Menninger Foundation; director of Medical Research Division of Edgar Cayce Foundation; director of Academy of Parapsychology and Medicine. *Military service:* U.S. Navy, 1943-46. U.S. Air Force, 1953-55; became captain. U.S. Air National Guard, 1955-61. *Member:* North American Academy of Manipulative Medicine, American Medical Association, American Academy of Family Physicians, National Acupuncture Research Society, Acupuncture Association of Physicians and Surgeons (president), Arizona Medical Society, Maricopa County Medical Society.

WRITINGS: Edgar Cayce and the Palma Christi, A.R.E. Press, 1970; (with Mary Ellen Carter) *Edgar Cayce on Healing*, Paperback Library, 1972; *Acupuncture and Body Energies*, Gabriel Press, 1973; (with wife, Gladys Taylor McGarey) *There Will Your Heart Be Also* (nonfiction), Prentice-Hall, 1975. Editor of *Medical Research Bulletin* of A. R. E. Clinic, 1970—; consulting editor of *International Journal of Psychoenergetic Systems*.

WORK IN PROGRESS: Compiling material for a book on do-it-yourself medicine, stressing the relationship between body, mind, and spirit.

SIDELIGHTS: McGarey writes: "The psychic readings of Edgar Cayce have given my work in holistic medicine a meaning which surpasses the understanding of medicine that I received as teaching in medical school. Perhaps it would be factual to say that my effort in medicine is to help the physician and the layman to understand better that the body has a capability of normal function and that this is a concept that should be and might be understood by every person. Our work touches information from other countries, and we have spent time visiting in other cultures in Europe, India, and Indonesia."

BIOGRAPHICAL/CRITICAL SOURCES: Jess Stearn, *The Sleeping Prophet*, Doubleday, 1967; David St. Clair, *Psychic Healers*, Doubleday, 1974; *Psychic*, February, 1974.

* * *

McGAUGH, James L(afayette)   1931-

PERSONAL: Born December 17, 1931, in Long Beach, Calif.; son of William Rufus (a Methodist minister) and Daphne (Hermes) McGaugh; married Carol J. Becker, March 15, 1952; children: Douglas, Janice, Linda. *Education:* San Jose State College (now University), B.A. (with great distinction), 1953; University of California, Berkeley, Ph.D., 1959. *Politics:* Democrat. *Home:* 2327 Aralia St., Newport Beach, Calif. 92660. *Office:* Department of Psychobiology, University of California, Irvine, Calif. 92664.

CAREER: San Jose State College (now University), assistant professor, 1957-60, associate professor of psychology,

1960-61; University of Oregon, Eugene, associate professor of psychology, 1961-64; University of California, Irvine, associate professor, 1964-66, professor of psychobiology, 1966—, chairman of department, 1964-67, 1971-74, professor in department of psychiatry, 1968—, dean of School of Biological Sciences, 1968-70, vice-chancellor of university for academic affairs, 1975—. Consultant to Veterans Administration, 1964—; member of National Institute of Mental Health review committees in training and research, 1968-72, 1975—.

MEMBER: American Psychological Association (fellow), American Association for the Advancement of Science (fellow), International Brain Research Organization, Psychonomic Society, Society for Neuroscience (member of council, 1974—), Sigma Xi. *Awards, honors:* National Academy of Sciences-National Research Council senior postdoctoral fellow at Instituto Superiore di Sanita, Rome, Italy, 1961-62.

WRITINGS: (With Joseph B. Cooper) *Integrating Principles of Social Psychology*, Schenkman, 1963; (editor with R. E. Whalen and N. M. Weinberger) *Psychobiology: The Biological Bases of Behavior*, W. H. Freeman, 1966; (with H. F. Harlow and R. F. Thompson) *Psychology*, Albion Publishing, 1971; (editor) *Psychobiology: Behavior from a Biological Perspective*, Academic Press, 1971; (editor) *The Chemistry of Mood, Motivation and Memory*, Plenum, 1972; (with Michael J. Herz) *Memory Consolidation*, Albion Publishing, 1972; *Learning and Memory: An Introduction* (selection of chapters from *Psychology*, 1971), Albion Publishing, 1974; (editor with Max Fink and others, and contributor) *Psychobiology of Convulsive Therapy*, V. H. Winston, 1974.

Contributor: Daniel P. Kimble, editor, *The Anatomy of Memory*, Science & Behavior, 1965; D. H. Efron and others, editors, *Psychopharmacology: A Review of Progress*, U.S. Government Printing Office, 1968; Perry Black, editor, *Drugs and the Brain*, Johns Hopkins Press, 1969; Samuel Bogoch, editor, *The Future of the Brain Sciences*, Plenum, 1969; Karl H. Pribram and D. E. Broadbent, editors, *Biology of Memory*, Academic Press, 1970; W. K. Honig and P. H. R. James, editors, *Animal Memory*, Academic Press, 1972; J. Anthony Deutsch, editor, *The Physiological Basis of Memory*, Academic Press, 1973; F. E. Bloom and G. H. Acheson, editors, *Brain, Nerves, and Synapses*, Karger, 1973; Samuel Bogoch, editor, *Biological Diagnosis of Brain Disorders*, Spectrum Publications, 1973; R. D. Myers and R. R. Drucker-Colin, editors, *Neurohumoral Coding of Brain Function*, Plenum, 1974; Gordon H. Bower, editor, *The Psychology of Learning and Motivation*, Volume VIII, Academic Press, 1974; G. Maletta, editor, *A Survey Report on the Aging Nervous System*, U.S. Government Printing Office, in press; D. Deutsch and A. J. Deutsch, editors, *Short Term Memory*, Academic Press, in press; W. H. Gispen and others, editors, *Hormones, Homeostasis, and the Brain*, Elsevier, in press; R. G. Grenell and S. Gabay, editors, *Biological Foundations of Psychiatry*, in press.

Contributor to *Recent Advances on Learning and Retention* and other annual publications, and to *International Encyclopedia of the Social Sciences*, *Enciclopedia della Scienza e della tecnica Mondadori*, and *Encyclopedia of Science and Technology*. Contributor of more than one hundred papers and occasional reviews to scientific journals, *Industrial Research* and *Psychology and Life*.

Associate editor, *Communications in Behavioral Biology*,

1969-71; co-editor, *Advances in Behavioral Biology*, 1971—; editor, *Behavioral Biology*, 1972—; member of editorial advisory board, *Psychopharmacologia*, 1966—, *Agents and Actions*, 1969-73, *Journal of Neurobiology*, 1969—, *International Journal of Psychobiology*, 1971—, *Brain Research*, 1974—, and *Psychopharmacology Communications*, 1975—; consulting editor, *Behavior Research Methods and Instrumentation*, 1969—, and *Journal of Experimental Psychology: Animal Behavior Processes*, 1975—.

SIDELIGHTS: "I am strongly interested in the development of brain research in Latin-American countries," McGaugh writes. "When time allows and the seasons are appropriate, I ski (poorly), play squash and tennis (badly), and travel (to Mexico whenever possible)."

* * *

McGINNIES, W(illiam) G(rovenor) 1899-

PERSONAL: Born August 14, 1899, in Steamboat Springs, Colo.; married Rose Almini, February 14, 1925; children: William J. *Education:* University of Arizona, B.S.A., 1922; University of Chicago, Ph.D., 1932. *Home:* 530 East Cambridge, Tucson, Ariz. 85704. *Office:* Office of Arid Lands Studies, University of Arizona, 1201 East Speedway Blvd., Tucson, Ariz. 85719.

CAREER: U.S. Forest Service, employed in range surveys and research in Missoula, Mont., 1923-26; University of Arizona, Tucson, associate professor of botany, 1926-35, range ecologist, 1927-35, acting head of department of botany, 1933-35; U.S. Department of Agriculture, Soil Conservation Service, Window Rock, Ariz., director of Navajo Indian reservation project, 1935-38; U.S. Forest Service, chief of Division of Range Research at Southwest Forest and Range Experiment Station in Tucson, Ariz., 1938-41; Guayule Emergency Rubber Project, Los Angeles, Calif., and Salinas, Calif., chief of Division of Surveys and Investigations, 1942-44; U.S. Forest Service, director of Rocky Mountain Forest and Range Experiment Station in Fort Collins, Colo., 1945-53, director of Central States Forest Experiment Station in Columbus, Ohio, 1954-60; University of Arizona, professor of dendrochronology, 1960-74, director of Laboratory of Tree-Ring Research, 1960-64, coordinator of arid lands program, 1960-64, director of Office of Arid Lands Studies, 1965-69, research ecologist, 1969-74, project manager of Desert Environments Inventory, 1965-69, site coordinator for Tucson Basin Desert Biome and member of steering committee for U.S. Desert Biome Analysis of Ecosystems for International Biological Program, 1968-69, professor emeritus of dendrochronology, and director emeritus of Office of Arid Lands Studies, 1974—.

MEMBER: Ecological Society of America, Society for Range Management (charter member), Tree-Ring Society, American Association for the Advancement of Science (fellow), Arizona Academy of Science (fellow), Sigma Xi, Alpha Zeta, Gamma Alpha, Phi Kappa Phi, Xi Sigma Pi. *Awards, honors:* Certificate of merit from Southwestern and Rocky Mountain Division of American Association for the Advancement of Science, 1970, for distinguished contributions in the field of arid zone research; citation from Society for Range Management, 1973, for outstanding achievement and service; Distinguished Citizen Award from University of Arizona Alumni Association, 1974.

WRITINGS: (Contributor) *Plant Ecology: Review of Research*, UNESCO, 1955; (contributor) *Arid Zone Re-*

search—*Plant Ecology: Proceedings of the Montpellier Symposium*, UNESCO, 1955; (senior editor, with B. J. Goldman and Patricia Paylore, and contributor) *Deserts of the World: An Appraisal of Research into Their Physical and Biological Enviroments*, University of Arizona Press, 1968; (senior editor, with Goldman) *Arid Lands in Perspective*, University of Arizona Press, 1969; (senior editor, with Goldman and Paylore) *Food, Fiber, and the Arid Lands*, University of Arizona Press, 1971; (contributor) C. M. Mekell, J. P. Blaisdell, and J. R. Goodin, editors, *Wildland Shrubs: Their Biology and Utilization*, U.S. Department of Agriculture, 1972. Contributor to *Aridity and Man*, edited by C. Hodge and P. C. Duisberg, 1963. Contributor of articles on range management, forestry, and ecology to technical journals, including *Ecology*.

WORK IN PROGRESS: The Desert Laboratory of the Carnegie Institution of Washington: History and Achievements.

* * *

McGINNIS, Marilyn 1939-

PERSONAL: Born May 20, 1939, in Bremerton, Wash.; daughter of Richard Clark and Eva (Byam) Heiliger; married George Forsythe McGinnis (an industrial designer for Walt Disney Productions), July 10, 1971; children: Shana Marie. *Education:* Seattle Pacific College, B.A., 1961; Talbot Theological Seminary, M.A., 1967. *Religion:* Protestant. *Home:* 2210 Silver Ridge Ave., Los Angeles, Calif. 90039.

CAREER: Seattle Pacific College, Seattle, Wash., secretary, 1957-63; Baxter-Wyckoff Co., Seattle, Wash., secretary-receptionist, 1963-64; Anaheim Community Church, Anaheim, Calif., director of Christian education, 1965-66; Gospel Light Publications, Glendale, Calif., editorial assistant, 1966-67, assistant editor, 1967-69, associate editor of *Teach* (magazine), 1969-71; Talbot Theological Seminary, La Mirada, Calif., instructor in journalism, 1970—. Director of Christian education at Burke Avenue Chapel, 1961-64. *Member:* Evangelical Press Association. *Awards, honors:* Second place prize for general articles from Evangelical Press Association, 1973, for "I'm Free."

WRITINGS: Single, Revell, 1974. Contributor to *Moody Monthly, Eternity, His, Los Angeles, King's Business, Christianity Today*, and *Teach*.

WORK IN PROGRESS: Research for a Bible study book on Nehemiah.

SIDELIGHTS: Marilyn McGinnis has visited most of the Middle East and the lands of the Bible.

* * *

McGUIRE, Richard L(en) 1940-

PERSONAL: Born June 10, 1940, in Parsons, Kan.; son of H. Richard (an electrician) and Maxine (a hospital aide; maiden name, McEntire) McGuire; married Mary Jeane Starkey, 1961; children: Kevin, David. *Education:* Kansas State University, B.A., 1961, M.A., 1963; Rice University, Ph.D., 1968. *Home:* 125 Westminster, Jacksonville, Ill. 62650. *Office:* Department of English, MacMurray College, Jacksonville, Ill. 62650.

CAREER: University of Southwest Louisiana, Lafayette, instructor in English, 1963-65; University of Washington, Seattle, assistant professor of English, 1968-74; MacMurray College, Jacksonville, Ill., associate professor of English, 1974—.

WRITINGS: Passionate Attention, Norton, 1973.

WORK IN PROGRESS: A study of the ethical problems generated by the plurality of modern concepts of history; a study of the historiographies of the Romantic poets.

* * *

McILHANY, William H(erbert) II 1951-

PERSONAL: Born March 10, 1951, in Roanoke, Va.; son of H. Hoge (an executive and distributor of construction equipment) and Zirleta (Kent) McIlhany; married Mary Lee Merrill (a high school teacher of English), June 29, 1974. *Education:* Washington and Lee University, B.A., 1973. *Politics:* "Libertarian: Non-party affiliated." *Religion:* Anglican Orthodox. *Residence:* Newport Beach, Calif. *Agent:* Sanford J. Greenburger Associates, Inc., 979 3rd Ave., New York, N.Y. 10017.

CAREER: McIlhany Equipment Co., Roanoke, Va., director and counsultant, 1973-75; full-time writer in Newport Beach, Calif., 1973—. Instructor at Santa Ana College, 1974-75. *Member:* International Brotherhood of Magicians (vice-president of Roanoke chapter, 1972-73), Society of American Magicians, Academy of Magical Arts, John Birch Society (leader of Roanoke chapter, 1973-74).

WRITINGS: Klandestine: The Untold Story of Delmar Dennis and His Role in the F.B.I.'s War Against the Ku Klux Klan, Arlington House, 1975; *Nationkill: Not a Civil War at All, Eighty Years of Conspiracy to Destroy the United States*, Western Islands, 1975.

WORK IN PROGRESS: The American Civil Liberties Union on Trial, for Arlington House, completion expected in 1975; *Who Was Diana Vaughan? The Satanic Palladian Rite Controversy, Paris, 1884-1897*; *Diabolical Protector: An Unpleasant View of Oliver Cromwell*; a philosophical novel, *Syllogism*; a biography of a western Virginia mountain doctor as seen through the eyes of his daughter, *On Earth: Almost Heaven, The Story of Doctor Albert Hoge*; a multi-volume world history, starting with the year 1776, from the viewpoint of the John Birch Society, *History of the Master Conspiracy*; a review of patterns in American political assassinations, *Kill the President: The Lincoln-Kennedy Parallels*.

SIDELIGHTS: McIlhany traveled and studied in Russia during the summer of 1969 as part of a course program with the American Institute for Foreign Study. *Avocational interests:* Magic, cinematography, collecting rare books.

* * *

McINTYRE, John A(rmin) 1920-

PERSONAL: Born June 2, 1920, in Seattle, Wash.; son of Harry John (a professor) and Florence (a teacher; maiden name, Armin) McIntyre; married Madeleine Forsman, June 15, 1947; children: John Forsman. *Education:* University of Washington, Seattle, B.S., 1943; Princeton University, M.A., 1948, Ph.D., 1950. *Religion:* Presbyterian. *Home:* 2316 Bristol St., Bryan, Tex. 77801. *Office:* Department of Physics, Texas A & M University, College Station, Tex. 77843.

CAREER: Carnegie Institute of Technology (now Carnegie-Mellon University), Pittsburgh, Pa., instructor in electrical engineering, 1943-44; Westinghouse Electric Corp., Baltimore, Md., radio engineer, 1944-45; Stanford University, Stanford, Calif., research associate, 1950-57; Yale University, New Haven, Conn., assistant professor, 1957-60, associate professor of physics, 1960-63; Texas A

& M University, College Station, professor of physics, 1963—, associate director, Cyclotron Institute, 1965-70. Consultant, Varian Associates, 1955; visiting scientist, National Science Foundation, 1960-66. *Member:* American Association for the Advancement of Science, American Physical Society (fellow), American Association of University Professors, American Scientific Association (member of executive council, 1968-73), Society of Nuclear Medicine, Sigma Xi. *Awards, honors:* Oak Ridge Institute for Nuclear Studies research grant, 1963-66; Welch Foundation grant, 1964-66.

WRITINGS: The Appeal of Christianity to a Scientist, Inter-Varsity Press, 1975.

* * *

McKAY, Douglas R(ich) 1936-

PERSONAL: Born November 12, 1936, in Salt Lake City, Utah; son of Llewelyn R. (a professor) and Alice (a social worker; maiden name, Smith) McKay; married Diane Reid (an interior decorator), December 19, 1962; children: Elizabeth, Stephen. *Education:* University of Utah, B.A., 1962; University of Oregon, M.A., 1964; Michigan State University, Ph.D., 1968. *Home:* 5410 Galena Dr., Colorado Springs, Colo. 80918. *Office:* Department of Foreign Language and Literature, University of Colorado, Colorado Springs, Cragmor Rd., Colorado Springs, Colo. 80907.

CAREER: University of Hawaii, Honolulu, acting assistant professor of Spanish, 1967-68; University of Colorado, Colorado Springs, assistant professor, 1968-72, associate professor of Spanish, 1972—, head of department of foreign language and literature, 1968—. *Member:* Modern Language Association of America, American Association of Teachers of Spanish and Portuguese, Rocky Mountain Modern Language Association. *Awards, honors:* Woodrow Wilson fellowship, 1962.

WRITINGS: Carlos Arniches, Twayne, 1972; (editor) *Misterio y pavor: Trece cuentos* (title means "Mystery and Terror: Thirteen Tales"), Holt, 1974; *Enrique Jardiel Poncela,* Twayne, 1974. Contributor to professional journals. Spanish book review editor of *Modern Language Journal,* 1970—.

WORK IN PROGRESS: A critical-analytical biography of Miguel Mihura for Twayne; a first-year Spanish reader; a novel concerning personal glimpses into treachery and lechery in the academic world.

AVOCATIONAL INTERESTS: Theater, enjoying students and other human beings when they are themselves.

* * *

McKAY, Quinn G(unn) 1926-

PERSONAL: Born October 30, 1926, in Ogden, Utah; son of James Gunn (a farmer and rancher) and Elizabeth Catherine (Peterson) McKay; married Shirley Frame, August 16, 1954; children: Shirene, Cathy, David, Mary Ann, Rebecca. *Education:* Brigham Young University, B.S., 1954; Harvard University, M.B.A., 1956, D.B.A., 1960. *Office:* Skaggs Companies, Inc., P.O. Box 658, Salt Lake City, Utah 84110.

CAREER: Brigham Young University, Provo, Utah, 1960-63, began as assistant professor, became associate professor of business management, director of Master of Business Administration program; University of Pittsburgh, Pittsburgh, Pa., professor of management at Ahmadu Bello University, Zaria, Northern Nigeria, 1963-65; Weber State

College, Ogden, Utah, dean of School of Business and Economics, 1965-69; Texas Christian University, Fort Worth, David L. Tandy Professor of American Enterprise Management, 1969-75; Skaggs Companies, Inc., Salt Lake City, Utah, senior vice-president of Human Resources Development, 1975—. Visiting professor at University of Rangoon, 1956-58, and University of Lausanne, 1971-72. Staff associate of Governmental Affairs Institute, Washington, D.C., 1961-63. Consultant to governmental and private organizations, including Boeing Co., U.S. Steel, and General Electric. *Military service:* U.S. Marine Corps, 1944-47; served in the South Pacific theater.

MEMBER: International Communication Association, American Management Association, Academy of Arts and Science, Academy of Management, Society for Applied Anthropology, Society for International Development.

WRITINGS: (Contributor) Herbert J. Chruden and Arthur W. Sherman, editors, *Readings in Personnel Management,* 2nd edition (McKay was not associated with 1st edition), Southwestern Publishing, 1966; (contributor) Kenneth R. Andrews, editor, *The Effectiveness of University Management Development Programs,* Graduate School of Business Administration, Harvard University, 1966; (contributor) John M. Champion and Francis J. Bridges, editors, *Critical Incidents in Management,* Irwin, 1968; (with Saul Sells) *Overview of Performance Evaluation* (monograph), Institute of Behavioral Science, Texas Christian University, 1970; (with William Tilleman) *Money Matters in Your Marriage,* Deseret, 1971. Contributor to business journals.

* * *

McKAY, Robert B(udge) 1919-

PERSONAL: Born August 11, 1919, in Wichita, Kan.; son of John B. (a businessman) and Ruth G. (Gelsthorpe) McKay; married Kate Warmack (a librarian), November 20, 1954; children: Kathy, Sally. *Education:* University of Kansas, B.S., 1940; Yale University, J.D., 1947. *Home:* 29 Washington Sq. W., New York, N.Y. 10011. *Office:* Aspen Institute for Humanistic Studies, 717 Fifth Ave., New York, N.Y. 10022.

CAREER: Admitted to the Bar of New York State; U.S. Department of Justice, Washington, D.C., attorney, 1947-50; Emory University, Atlanta, Ga., assistant professor, 1950-52, associate professor of law, 1952-53; New York University, School of Law, New York, N.Y., associate professor, 1953-56, professor of law, 1956-67, dean, 1967-75; Aspen Institute of Humanistic Studies, Aspen, Colo., director of Program on Justice, Society and the Individual, 1975—. Chairman of New York State Reapportionment Committee, 1965, Mayor's Rent Control Committee, 1968-69, New York State Special Commission on Attica, 1971-72, Citizens Union, 1971—, and New York City Board of Correction, 1973-74; vice-chairman of National News Council, 1973—; vice-president of Legal Aid Society, 1972—. *Military service:* U.S. Army Air Forces, 1941-46; became captain.

MEMBER: American Bar Association, Association of the Bar of the City of New York (member of executive committee, 1973—), Lawyers Committee for Civil Rights Under Law (member of executive committee, 1972—). *Awards, honors:* Ross Essay Prize from American Bar Association, 1961; Torch of Learning Award from American Friends of Hebrew University, 1972; William Nelson Cromwell Award from New York County Lawyers Association, 1973; D.H.L., Mount Saint Mary College, 1973; D.L., Emory University, 1973.

WRITINGS: Reapportionment, Twentieth Century Fund, 1965, new edition, Simon & Schuster, 1971. Consultant to Time-Life, Inc., 1971.

WORK IN PROGRESS: Study of school desegregation, for Twentieth Century Fund.

* * *

McKEE, Barbara Hastings 1902-

PERSONAL: Born December 31, 1902, in Mineral Hill, N.M.; daughter of Clive (a businessman) and Esther (Eddy) Hastings; married Edwin D. McKee (a geologist), December 31, 1929; children: William D., Barbara (Mrs. John L. Lajoie), Edwin H. *Education:* University of Wisconsin, B.S., 1924. *Religion:* Episcopalian. *Home:* 4845 Redwood Dr., Littleton, Colo. 80123.

CAREER: Craftswoman, author.

WRITINGS: (With husband, Edwin D. McKee) *Havasupai Baskets and Their Makers, 1930-40*, Northland Press, 1974.

* * *

McKEE, Edwin D(inwiddie) 1906-

PERSONAL: Born September 24, 1906, in Washington, D.C.; son of Edwin Jones (a lawyer) and Ethel (Swope) McKee; married Barbara Hastings (a craftswoman), December 31, 1929; children: William D., Barbara (Mrs. John L. Lajoie), Edwin H. *Education:* Cornell University, A.B., 1928; graduate study at University of Arizona, 1930-31, University of California at Berkeley, 1933-34, and Yale University, 1939-40. *Home:* 4845 Redwood Dr., Littleton, Colo. 80123. *Office:* U.S. Geological Survey, Federal Center, Denver, Colo. 80225.

CAREER: Grand Canyon National Park, park naturalist, 1929-40; Museum of Northern Arizona, Flagstaff, assistant director in charge of research, 1941-42, and summers, 1942-53, trustee, 1953—; University of Arizona, Tucson, assistant professor, 1942-47, associate professor, 1947-50, professor of geology, 1950-53, head of department, 1951-53; U.S. Geological Survey, Denver, Colo., chief of Paleotectonic Map Section, 1953-61, research geologist, 1962—. Collaborator, National Park Service, 1941—. Visiting professor of geology, Free University of Berlin, 1963, and Cornell University, 1966; visiting lecturer in the U.S.S.R., as invited guest of the Soviet Academy of Sciences, 1970; visiting lectureships also include Powell Lecturer of American Association for the Advancement of Science, 1950, Gurley Lecturer at Cornell University, 1956, and distinguished lecturer of American Association of Petroleum Geologists, 1957. Participant or director of numerous expeditions, sponsored by Pacific Science Board, Durham University, National Research Council of Brazil, and others; has served as research associate or consultant to Carnegie Institution of Washington, California Institute of Technology, National Aeronautics and Space Administration (NASA), Atomic Energy Commission, and other organizations. Chairman, American Commission on Stratigraphic Nomenclature, 1957; member of advisory panel, Desert Protective Council, 1958—.

MEMBER: International Association for Quaternary Research, International Union of Geological Sciences, American Association of Petroleum Geologists, American Geological Institute, Geological Society of America, Society of Economic Paleontologists and Mineralogists (honorary member; vice-president, 1963-64; president, 1967-68), Grand Canyon Natural History Association (executive secretary, 1937-39), Rocky Mountain Association of Geologists (honorary member), Southwest Monuments Association (chairman of board of directors, 1962-63), Southwest Park and Monument Association (chairman of board of trustees, 1972-73), Arizona Geological Society (president, 1952-53), Tucson Natural History Society (president, 1944), Sigma Xi (president of Arizona chapter, 1950). *Awards, honors:* D.Sc. from Northern Arizona University, 1957; distinguished service award from U.S. Department of the Interior, 1962; group achievement award from National Aeronautics and Space Administration, 1974, in recognition of work on Skylab.

WRITINGS: (With wife, Barbara McKee) *Havasupai Baskets and Their Makers, 1930-40*, Northland Press, 1974.

Contributor: Roderick Peattie, editor, *The Inverted Mountains: Canyons of the West, Arizona-Utah*, Vanguard, 1948; John Imbrie and Norman Newell, editors, *Approaches to Paleoecology*, Wiley, 1964; W. J. Breed and E. C. Roat, editors, *Geology of the Grand Canyon*, Museum of Northern Arizona and Grand Canyon Natural History Association, 1974.

Science editor for film, "In the Beginning," General Petroleum Co., 1954, and director of "John Wesley Powell, Canyon Geologist," for U.S. Geological Survey, 1969. Author of numerous scientific publications. Contributor to proceedings, symposia, yearbooks, and to journals in his field. Member of editorial board, *Palaeogeography, Palaeoclimatology, Palaeoecology*, 1967-69.

WORK IN PROGRESS: Further scientific publications.

* * *

McKINNEY, Donald 1909-

PERSONAL: Born May 31, 1909, in Centerville, Ind.; son of Andrew and Ida (Ebersol) McKinney. *Education:* DePauw University, Rector Scholar, 1932; Keble College, Oxford, graduate study; Ball State University, M.A., 1949. *Address:* P.O. Box 91, Centerville, Ind. 47330.

CAREER: Richmond Palladium-Item, Richmond, Ind., feature writer, 1933-38; Earlham College-Indiana University Extension, Richmond, instructor, 1951-55; Richmond High School, Richmond, Ind., teacher of adult education, 1947-72; full-time writer, 1973—. High school principal, 1945-46. Former member of boards of Historic Centerville, Richmond Zoological Society, Centerville Library, and Family Service Bureau. Volunteer worker for Red Cross, Y.W.C.A., Reid Hospital, and Richmond State Hospital.

WRITINGS: A Crooked Tree (inspirational short stories), Vantage Press, 1973; *Joy Begins with You* (inspirational short stories), Abingdon, 1975. Author of newspaper columns, "Your Garden," in *Richmond Palladium-Item*, 1933-38, and "Maybe I'm Wrong, But—," 1930-35, and "Echoes of Yesterday," 1960-70, both in *Old Trails Echo*. Contributor to *Indianapolis Sunday Star Magazine, Grail*, and religious magazines.

WORK IN PROGRESS: Thanks for the Memory; *Bible Adventures for Boys and Girls*; *The Golden Violin* (for children); three novels, *I Die Each Night, A Man Goes to a Hospital, The Lord Is My Shepherd*.

AVOCATIONAL INTERESTS: Travel.

* * *

McKINNEY, George W(esley), Jr. 1922-

PERSONAL: Born May 27, 1922, in Amigo, W. Va.; son

of George Wesley (a teacher) and Charlotte (a teacher; maiden name, Ashworth) McKinney; married Lucille Christian, September 5, 1941; children: George Wesley III, Mary Christine (Mrs. Robert L. Schweitzer), Ruth Ann (Mrs. Ronald W. Gerbe). *Education:* Berea College, A.B., 1942; University of Virginia, M.A., 1947, Ph.D., 1949. *Home:* 590 Ridgewood Ave., Glen Ridge, N.J. 07028. *Office:* Irving Trust Co., 1 Wall St., New York, N.Y. 10015.

CAREER: Federal Reserve Bank, Richmond, Va., economist, 1948-58, assistant vice-president, 1958-60; Irving Trust Co., New York, N.Y., assistant vice-president, 1960-61, vice-president, 1961-68, senior vice-president, 1968—, head economist in research and planning division, 1973—. *Military service:* U.S. Army, 1942-45; became captain. *Member:* National Association of Business Economists (fellow; president, 1966).

WRITINGS: Federal Reserve Discount Window, Rutgers University Press, 1960; (with W. J. Brown) *Management of Commercial Bank Funds*, American Institute of Banking, 1974.

* * *

McKINNEY, Virginia (Marie) 1940-

PERSONAL: Born July 31, 1940, in Brooklyn, N.Y.; daughter of William Henry (an engineer) and Alma (a dress designer and beautician; maiden name, Vanasse) Field; married George William McKinney (an engineer), May 4, 1958; children: Deborah Ann, Linda Jean, Joyce Marie, Jo Anne, David Scott. *Education:* Attended Farmingdale University, 1971-73. *Office:* J. Mark Press, North Babylon, N.Y.

CAREER: Poet and writer. Assistant editor for J. Mark Press, 1973—. Founder and director of poetry workshop "Friends of the Muse"; producer and performer on "The Poet's Voice," television program for New York Cablevision, 1973; has given readings at the Walt Whitman birthplace, Huntington, N.Y., 1974, and in the New York area. *Member:* Centro Studi e Scambi, American Poetry League.

WRITINGS: Sudden Ripples (poems), J. Mark Press, 1974; *Brandy Moons* (poems), J. Mark Press, 1975. Contributor of about a hundred poems to literary journals, including *Sunburst, Archer, Hyacinth's Biscuits, El Viento, Notable American Poetry, Poetry of the Year*, and *Journal of Contemporary Poets.*

WORK IN PROGRESS: A third book of poems; children's books; *The Elephant's New Shoes, Miss Abigail*, and *Zabir.*

SIDELIGHTS: Virginia McKinney writes: "My main goal right now, is to re-kindle public interest in aesthetic poetry.... In the future I am planning to work with young children and the elderly, creating and re-creating in them their deepest most profound expressions." *Avocational interests:* Breeding and exhibiting St. Bernard dogs, art, gourmet cookery.

* * *

McLEAN, J. Sloan (joint pseudonym)
See GILLETTE, Virginia M(ary)
and WUNSCH, Josephine (McLean)

* * *

McLEISH, Garen
See STINE, Whitney Ward

McLEISH, John 1917-

PERSONAL: Born May 21, 1917, in Glasgow, Scotland; son of John Donald and Mary (King) McLeish; married Stella Nancy Tyrrell, December 16, 1940; children: Kenneth, Martin, Rosemary, Stewart, Richard, David. *Education:* University of Glasgow, B.Sc., 1939, Ed.B., 1947, M.Ed., 1962; University of Leeds, Ph.D., 1963. *Politics:* Liberal Democrat. *Religion:* None. *Residence:* Edmonton, Alberta, Canada. *Office:* University of Alberta, Edmonton, Alberta, Canada.

CAREER: University of Glasgow, Glasgow, Scotland, lecturer in psychology, 1947-49; University of Leeds, Leeds, England, lecturer in criminology, 1949-62; University of Bradford, Bradford, England, professor of behavioral science, 1962-64; Cambridge University, Cambridge Institute of Education, Cambridge, England, research director of education, 1964-69; University of Alberta, Edmonton, Alberta, professor of educational psychology, 1969—. President, Worker's Educational Association, Bradford, 1959-60. *Member:* British Psychological Society, Canadian Educational Researchers Association, American Educational Research Association, British Society for Research in Higher Education, Canadian Society for the Study of Education, Comparative and International Education Society. *Awards, honors:* Human Resources Council grant, University of Alberta, 1969-70; Canada Council awards, 1970-75.

WRITINGS: The Science of Behaviour, Barrie & Rockcliff, 1963; *Evangelical Religion and Popular Education*, Methuen, 1969; *The Theory of Social Change*, Routledge & Kegan Paul, 1970; *Students' Attitudes and College Environments*, Heffer, 1970; (with others) *The Psychology of the Learning Group*, Hutchinson, 1973; *Soviet Psychology*, Methuen, 1975. Also writer of BBC broadcasts on psychological topics.

WORK IN PROGRESS: Psychoanalysis and Group Behavior.

SIDELIGHTS: McLeish told *CA:* "Lifelong interest in foreign civilizations, especially Eastern Europe, combined with a similar commitment to empirical scientific study of human behaviour have been prime motivations. My most recent book *Soviet Psychology* is the product of twenty-five years continuing interest in the problem of understanding the Russian 'mentality'."

* * *

McLURE, Charles E., Jr. 1940-

PERSONAL: Born April 14, 1940, in Sierra Blanca, Tex.; son of Charles E. (a retailer) and Dessie (Evans) McClure; married Patsy Nell Carroll, September 17, 1962. *Education:* Attended University of Texas at El Paso, 1961; Kansas University, B.A., 1962; Princeton University, M.A., 1964, Ph.D., 1966. *Home:* 3634 Merrick, Houston, Tex. 77025. *Office:* Economics Department, Rice University, Houston, Tex. 77001.

CAREER: Rice University, Houston, Tex., assistant professor, 1965-69, associate professor, 1969-72, professor of economics, 1972-73, Allyn R. and Gladys M. Cline Professor of Economics and Finance, 1973—. Honorary research associate, Harvard University, 1967-68; senior staff economist, Council of Economic Advisers, 1969-70; adjunct scholar, American Enterprise Institute, 1972—. Consultant to private and governmental agencies. Visiting lecturer, St. Thomas University, 1968-70; John S. Bugas Visiting Distinguished Lecturer in Economics, University of Wyoming, 1972; visiting professor, Stanford University, 1973. *Member:* International Institute of Public Finance, American Economic Association, National Tax Association, Phi Beta Kappa, Omicron Delta Kappa. *Awards, honors:* Woodrow Wilson fellowship, 1962-63; Ford Foundation fellowship, 1964-65, 1967-68.

WRITINGS: (Contributor) Malcolm Gillis, editor, *Fiscal Reform for Colombia: The Final Report and Staff Papers of the Colombian Commission on Tax Reform*, Harvard Law School, International Tax Program, Part II, 1971; *Fiscal Failure: Lessons of the Sixties*, American Enterprise Institute, 1972; (with Norman B. Ture) *Value Added Tax: Two Views*, American Enterprise Institute, 1972; (contributor) Richard A. Musgrave, editor, *Broad-Based Taxes: New Options and Sources*, Johns Hopkins Press, 1973; (contributor) *La Politica Tributaria como Instrumento del Desarrollo* (title means "Tax Policy as an Instrument of Economic Development"), Organization of American States, 1973; (with others) *A New Look at Inflation*, American Enterprise Institute, 1973; (contributor) *The Impact of Multinational Corporations on Development and On International Relations*, United Nations, 1975. Contributor to journals in his field.

Referee for *Quarterly Journal of Economics, National Tax Journal, Public Finance Quarterly, Public Policy, American Economic Review, Journal of Political Economy, Growth and Change, Journal of Public Economics*, and *Economic Development and Cultural Change*; also, reader, *Quarterly Journal of Economics*; member of editorial advisory board, *National Tax Journal*, 1975-77; member of editorial board, *Public Finance Quarterly*.

WORK IN PROGRESS: Research on tax reform in Colombia, taxation of natural resources, and tax incidence.

AVOCATIONAL INTERESTS: Backpacking, ski touring, canoeing, and similar activities.

* * *

McMILLEN, Howard 1938-

PERSONAL: Born January 7, 1938, in Eureka, Kan.; son of A. E. and Dorothy (a teacher; maiden name, Buffalow) McMillen; married Barbara Jolan (a writer), June 13, 1969. *Education:* Kansas State University, B.A., 1964; University of Iowa, M.F.A., 1970. *Home address:* R.R. 51, Box 248, Terre Haute, Ind. 47805. *Agent:* Peter Shephard, 40 East 49th St., New York, N.Y. 10017. *Office:* Department of English, Indiana State University, Terre Haute, Ind. 47809.

CAREER: Indiana State University, Terre Haute, instructor, 1970-72, assistant professor of creative writing, 1972—, coordinator of creative writing program. *Military service:* U.S. Army, 1958-62.

WRITINGS: The Many Mansions of Sam Peeples (novel), Viking, 1972. Adapted "The Buzzard's Lope," for WMT-Television, 1970. Contributor of articles and stories to *Touchstone, Iowa State Liquor Store*, and *TV Guide*.

WORK IN PROGRESS: A second novel.

* * *

McMORROW, Fred 1925-
(Clark Redfield)

PERSONAL: Born November 29, 1925, in New York, N.Y.; son of Thomas (a writer) and Hedwig (Evers) McMorrow; married Eileen Palmer, June 5, 1953; children: Thomas, Robert, Mary, Fritz. *Education:* Adelphi College (now University), B.A., 1949. *Politics:* Registered Democrat. *Home:* 2 Riverside Ave., Baldwin, N.Y. 11510. *Agent:* Ann Elmo, 52 Vanderbilt Ave., New York, N.Y. 10017. *Office: New York Times*, 229 West 43rd St., New York, N.Y. 10036.

CAREER: Worked as copy editor on daily newspapers in New York, N.Y., including *Long Island Press, Post, Journal-American, Herald Tribune*, and *Daily News*, 1949-71; *New York Times*, New York, N.Y., foreign news copy editor, 1971—. *Military service:* U.S. Army, field artillery radio operator, 1944-46; served in Italy.

WRITINGS: Midolescence: The Dangerous Years, Quadrangle, 1974. Contributor of more than 30 short stories and articles, sometimes under pseudonym Clark Redfield, to magazines and newspapers.

* * *

McNAIL, Eddie Gathings 1905-

PERSONAL: Born November 28, 1905, in Prairie, Miss.; daughter of James Covington (a physician) and Lavinia (Prewett) Gathings; married John Leonard McNail, April 5, 1928; children: Joseph Covington (deceased), Mary Gathings (Mrs. Grover Williams). *Education:* University of Mississippi, B.A., 1927; University of Texas, graduate study, 1945; Agricultural and Industrial University, M.A., 1948. *Home:* 204 West, La Feria, Tex. 78559.

CAREER: La Feria Independent School District, La Feria, Tex., English teacher, 1927-37; Mercedes Independent School District, Mercedes, Tex., English teacher, 1950-60; La Feria Independent School District, English teacher, 1960-69. Member of La Feria Bicentennial Committee, 1974-76. *Member:* Daughters of the American Colonists, Daughters of the American Revolution, Order of the Eastern Star, American Legion Auxiliary, Texas State Teachers Association, Cameron County Historical Survey Society, Rio Grande Valley Poetry Society (president, 1969-71), Cultura Club (president, 1964-65), Rio Grande Valley Federation of Women's Clubs (president, 1973-75), Delta Kappa Gamma (president of Zeta Rho Chapter, 1964-66). *Awards, honors:* Daughters of the American Revolution State Leadership Award, 1974-75, and award for television coverage at state level, 1974-75.

WRITINGS: The Silver Cord (poems), Dorrance, 1971. Also author of *The History and Development of Irrigation in the Lower Rio Grande Valley*.

WORK IN PROGRESS: The Bicentennial History of LaFeria; a book of poetry.

* * *

McNAUGHTON, Arnold 1930-

PERSONAL: Born November 21, 1930, in Hemmingford, Quebec, Canada; son of Earl and Marguerite (Campbell) McNaughton. *Education:* Attended high school in Hemmingford, Quebec. *Politics:* "Confirmed Monarchist, with a smattering of republicanism tossed in." *Religion:* Protestant. *Home address:* R.R. 1, Hemmingford, Quebec J0L 1H0, Canada. *Office:* 5500 Trans-Canada Hwy., Point Claire, Quebec, Canada.

CAREER: Avon Cosmetics Co., Pointe Claire, Quebec, printer. *Member:* Constantian Society.

WRITINGS: (Compiler, with foreword by Lord Mountbatten) *Book of Kings*, Garnstone Press, 1973.

WORK IN PROGRESS: A Guide to Europe's Royal Houses (tentative title).

SIDELIGHTS: McNaughton has personally visited with Queen Elizabeth II of England, Prince Philip, Prince of Wales, Lord Mountbatten, Grand Duchess Olga of Russia, Prince Ranier and Princess Grace of Monaco, King Constantine II and Queen Anne Marie of Greece, King Simeon II and Queen Margarita of Bulgaria, Princess Marie Louise of Bulgaria, Princess Margarita and Prince Gottfried of Hohenlohe-Langenburg, Princess Sophia and Prince George William of Hanover, and other members of royal families. McNaughton's book is a genealogical study of all the descendants of Britain's King George I.

BIOGRAPHICAL/CRITICAL SOURCES: Chatelaine, November, 1964.

* * *

McNAUGHTON, Howard (Douglas) 1945-

PERSONAL: Born May 9, 1945, in Dunedin, New Zealand; son of John Douglas (an auditor) and Olive Violet (McDonald) McNaughton; married Barbara Helen Strang, February, 1966 (separated, 1974); children: Esther Helen, Angus George. *Education:* University of Otago, B.A., 1965, M.A., 1966; University of Canterbury, M.A., 1971, Ph.D., 1975. *Politics:* Stoic. *Religion:* Stoic. *Residence:* Christchurch, New Zealand. *Office:* English Department, University of Canterbury, Christchurch, New Zealand.

CAREER: Shirley Boys' High School, Christchurch, New Zealand, Latin teacher, 1968-71; University of Canterbury, Christchurch, lecturer in English, 1973-74, lecturer in modern drama, 1975—. Free-lance writer. Member of drama advisory board of Queen Elizabeth II Arts Council of New Zealand, 1973—; member of advisory board of Playmarket, 1974—.

WRITINGS: (Editor) *Contemporary New Zealand Plays,* Oxford University Press, 1974; (compiler) *New Zealand Drama: A Bibliographical Guide,* University of Canterbury Publications, 1975. Drama critic, *The Press,* 1968—, and *New Zealand Listener,* 1974—; book review editor, *Act,* 1974—. Contributor of articles to magazines including *Landfall, Islands,* and *Education.*

WORK IN PROGRESS: A critical book on the plays of Bruce Mason, for Oxford University Press; editing and writing the official history of New Zealand theatre, for New Zealand Theatre Federation; editing collections of plays by Bruce Mason and James K. Baxter.

SIDELIGHTS: McNaughton writes that his is a "pre-colonial New Zealand family, descended from a whaler." While an "extremely puritanical upbringing and background" encouraged his study of Latin and Greek "for religious purposes," McNaughton stresses that it is the completion of his classics degree that precipitated his interest in drama and film.

* * *

McNEILL, John Thomas 1885-1975

July 28, 1885—February 5, 1975; Candian-born American educator, Presbyterian minister, church historian, ecumenical theologian, editor, and author of books on Calvinism and various periods of church history. Obituaries: *New York Times,* February 8, 1975; *AB Bookman's Weekly,* February 24, 1975. (*CA*-11/12)

McNITT, Gale 1921-

PERSONAL: Born March 5, 1921, in Logan, Utah; daughter of Julius Levine (a musician and mechanic) and Flora M. (Allen) Jacobsen; married Gordon Ernest McNitt, Jr. (a supervisor in electronic technology), June 3, 1939; children: Geraldine (Mrs. Dan L. Crew), Barbara Ruth (Mrs. Waldemar Mistchenko), Paul Lloyd, Bruce John. *Education:* Attended high school in Salt Lake City, Utah. *Religion:* "My idea of the goodness of God." *Home:* c/o FAA, Fire Island, Alaska 99695.

CAREER: Office worker; poet. *Awards, honors:* Citation from *Cycloflame,* 1973, 1974; Poet of the Year Award from *Poetry of Our Time,* 1973; award from *Notable Poets,* 1974, for "Voice of the Woods."

WRITINGS: Seasoned Stones (poetry), Branden Press, 1975. Poems represented in anthologies, including *Dance of the Muse,* edited by Jeanne Hollyfield, Young Publishing, 1970; *Yearbook of Modern Poetry,* edited by Hollyfield, Young Publishing, 1971; *Lyrics of Love,* edited by Hollyfield, Young Publishing, 1972; *Outstanding Contemporary Poetry,* edited by Dale R. and Arthur R. Moore, Pied Piper Press, 1972; *Outstanding Contemporary Poetry,* edited by Dale. R. and Arthur R. Moore, Pied Piper Press, 1973. Contributor to poetry magazines, including *Haiku Highlights, Encore,* and *Cycloflame.*

SIDELIGHTS: Mrs. McNitt told *CA:* "Each person is at all times expressing an individual idea of their relationship to reality or Truth. Poetry is a channel for the expression of Truth. Poetry will never lie. Each reader will interpret the poem from his own idea of himself as related to Truth. Because of this poetry is a remarkable avenue of communication." *Avocational interests:* Painting in oils, playing the organ.

* * *

McNOWN, John S(tephenson) 1916-

PERSONAL: Born January 15, 1916, in Kansas City, Kan.; son of William C. (an engineer) and Florence (Klahr) McNown; married Miriam Ellis, September 6, 1938 (divorced November 15, 1971); married Eva Fernqvist, July 15, 1973; children: (first marriage) Stephen (deceased), Robert Neville, Cynthia Leigh (Mrs. Michael Maloney), Mark William. *Education:* University of Kansas, B.S., 1936; University of Iowa, M.S., 1937; University of Minnesota, Ph.D., 1942; University of Grenoble, D.es Sc., 1951. *Politics:* Democrat. *Religion:* Congregational. *Home:* 2412 Whitehall Manor, Meadowbrook, Lawrence, Kan. 66044. *Office:* Department of Civil Engineering, University of Kansas, Lawrence, Kan. 66045.

CAREER: Registered professional engineer in Kansas, 1958; University of Minnesota, Minneapolis, instructor in mathematics, 1937-42; University of California, San Diego, research associate in Division of War Research, 1942-43; University of Iowa, Iowa City, assistant professor, 1943-47, associate professor, 1947-52, professor of mechanics and hydraulics, 1952-54; University of Michigan, Ann Arbor, professor of engineering, 1954-57; University of Kansas, Lawrence, professor, 1957-65, Albert P. Learned Professor of Civil Engineering, 1965—, dean of School of Engineering and Architecture, 1957-65, executive director of Center for Research in Engineering Science, 1959-62, director of Engineering Science Division, 1959-62. Lecturer at Colorado Agricultural and Mechanical College, 1949, University of Michigan, 1950, Universities of Lille, Grenoble, Toulouse, and Poitiers, 1951, University of Bogota,

1952, Ecole Polytechnique, 1953, University of Nebraska, 1958, and Purdue University, 1959. Member of board of trustees of University of Kansas Center for Research, 1962—, and of Rocky Mountain Hydraulic Laboratory, 1963-73; member of board of governors at University of Guyana, 1967-72. Consultant or advisor to numerous private and governmental organizations; has served as member or chairman of committees and commissions in the field of education.

MEMBER: Permanent International Association of Navigation Congresses, International Association for Hydraulic Research (member of council, 1955-59), African Studies Association, National Conference of Engineering Education, American Society of Civil Engineers (fellow), American Society of Engineering Education, American Association for the Advancement of Science, American Association of University Professors, American Academy of Mechanics (fellow), Committee on Engineering Education in Middle Africa, Sigma Xi, Theta Tau, Phi Delta Theta, Tau Beta Pi, Phi Kappa Phi, Chi Epsilon. *Awards, honors:* J. C. Stevens Award, 1946, and research program prize, 1949; Fulbright research scholar in France, 1950-51; J. James R. Croes medal from American Society of Civil Engineers, 1955.

WRITINGS: (Contributor) Hunter Rouse, *Engineering Hydraulics*, Wiley, 1950; (contributor) Rouse, editor, *Advanced Mechanics of Fluids*, Wiley, 1959; *Technical Education in Africa*, East African Publishing House, 1970. Contributor of more than sixty articles to English, French, and Portuguese professional and scientific journals.

WORK IN PROGRESS: Research on inland navigation, on technical education, and on third world development.

* * *

McPHERSON, William 1939-

PERSONAL: Born February 9, 1939, in Minot, N.D.; son of James M. (a high school teacher) and Miriam O. (an elementary school teacher) McPherson; married Dorothy Stine (a librarian), September 5, 1959; children: Robert. *Education:* Macalester College, B.A., 1961; Harvard University, M.A., 1963, Ph.D., 1967. *Politics:* Democrat. *Home:* 880 Lake Shore Rd., Lake Oswego, Ore. 97034. *Office:* Department of Sociology, Lewis and Clark College, P.O. Box 100, Portland, Ore. 97219.

CAREER: American University, Washington, D.C., assistant professor of sociology, 1964-66; lecturer in sociology, Boston, Mass., at Northeastern University, 1966-67, and Boston University, 1967; Pomona College, Claremont, Calif., assistant professor of sociology, 1967-72; Lewis and Clark College, Portland, Ore., assistant professor of sociology, 1972—. *Member:* American Sociological Association, Society for the Scientific Study of Religion, Religious Research Association, Association for the Sociology of Religion, American Association of University Professors, Pacific Sociological Association.

WRITINGS: Ideology and Change: Radicalism and Fundamentalism in America, National Press Books, 1973. Contributor to sociology and religious research journals.

WORK IN PROGRESS: Ideology of the Jesus Movement; Ideology and Religion; Religions of Japan.

SIDELIGHTS: McPherson has spent several months in Japan, and is learning Japanese, with the intention of making a comparative analysis of Japanese and American religions.

McRAE, Hamish (Malcolm Donald) 1943-

PERSONAL: Born October 20, 1943, in Barnstaple, England; son of Donald Barrington (a textile agent) and Jasmine (Budd) McRae; married Frances Cairncross (a journalist), September 10, 1971. *Education:* Trinity College, Dublin, B.A. (honors), 1966. *Home:* 6 Canonbury Lane, London N.1, England. *Office: Guardian*, Grays Inn Rd., London W.C.1, England.

CAREER: Liverpool Post (daily newspaper), Liverpool, England, trainee, 1966-67; *Banker* (financial magazine), London, England, editorial assistant, 1967-69, assistant editor, 1969-70, deputy editor, 1970-72; *Euromoney* (financial magazine), London, England, editor, 1972-74; *Guardian* (known in the United States as *Manchester Guardian*; national daily newspaper), London, England, financial editor, 1975—. Radio and television broadcaster in Great Britain. *Awards, honors:* Joint winner, with Frances Cairncross, of Harold Wincott Award for outstanding financial journalist under twenty-eight years old, from Harold Wincott Foundation, 1971, for contributions to *The Banker* and other journals during 1970-71.

WRITINGS: (With wife, Frances Cairncross) *Capital City: London as a Financial Centre*, Methuen, 1973; (with Frances Cairncross) *The Second Great Crash*, Prentice-Hall, 1975. Author of column in *Money Manager*.

WORK IN PROGRESS: A study of London money markets, with a book expected to result.

SIDELIGHTS: McRae writes: "People get frightened because they think they cannot understand finance and economics. What we are trying to do is to demonstrate that economics and financial organizations are very straightforward and easy to understand—and hopefully fun, too!"

* * *

MEADOW, Kathryn Pendleton 1929-

PERSONAL: Born June 12, 1929, in Joplin, Mo.; daughter of Orien A. and Wilma M. (Karnes) Pendleton; married Lloyd Meadow, 1953; children: Lynn, Robert. *Education:* Denison University, B.A., 1951; University of Chicago, M.A., 1952; University of California, Berkeley, Ph.D., 1967. *Home:* 2285 Cedar St., Berkeley, Calif. 94709. *Office:* Mental Health Services for the Deaf, 1474 Fifth Ave., San Francisco, Calif. 94143.

CAREER: Chicago Land Clearance Commission, Chicago, Ill., planning analyst, 1953-55; Merrill-Palmer Institute of Family Life and Human Development, Detroit, Mich., research associate of community studies program, 1960-62; Recreation Department, Greater Cities Project, Oakland, Calif., research director, 1962-63; University of California, Berkeley, lecturer in integrated social science program, 1967-68; University of California, San Francisco, lecturer, 1968-73, associate adjunct professor of sociology, 1973—; Langley Porter Neuropsychiatric Institute, San Francisco, Calif., research specialist, 1968-73, research director of mental health services for the deaf, 1973—. Visiting scholar at University of California, Berkeley, summer, 1968; visiting lecturer at University of Reading, 1968-69, and San Francisco State University, 1973-74; lecturer at National Technical Institute for the Deaf, summer, 1974.

MEMBER: International Society for the Study of Behavioral Development, American Sociological Association, Society for Research in Child Development, Pacific Sociological Association. *Awards, honors:* National Institute of Mental Health fellow, 1968-69; research grants from U.S.

Social and Rehabilitation Service, 1968-71, Department of Health, Education, and Welfare, 1970-75, and Office of Education, 1971-77; Daniel Cloud Award from California State University, Northridge, 1974, for outstanding contributions to research on deafness.

WRITINGS: (With H. S. Schlesinger) *Sound and Sign: Childhood Deafness and Mental Health*, University of California Press, 1972; (contributor) T. J. O'Rourke, editor, *Psycholinguistics and Total Communication: The State of the Art*, American Annals of the Deaf, 1972; (contributor) D. L. Lillie, editor, *Parent Programs in Child Development Centers: First Chance for Children*, University of North Carolina Press, 1972; (contributor) E. P. Trapp and P. Himelstein, editors, *Readings on the Exceptional Child*, Appleton, 1972. Contributor to proceedings; contributor to professional journals including *Exceptional Children, American Annals of the Deaf*, and *Social Forces*. Member of the editorial board of *Journal of Rehabilitation of the Deaf*, 1973.

WORK IN PROGRESS: Co-authoring *A Handbook for Parents and Teachers of Deaf Children*; *Deafness and Child Development*.

* * *

MECKLER, Alan Marshall 1945-

PERSONAL: Born July 25, 1945, in Queens, New York; son of Herman Lewis (a businessman) and Lillian (Brodsky) Meckler; married Ellen Finkelstein, September 10, 1969; children: Naomi Anne, Catherine Sarah. *Education:* Columbia University, B.A., 1967, M.A., 1968, candidate for Ph.D., 1968—. *Religion:* Jewish. *Office address:* Microform Review, P.O. Box 1297, Weston, Conn. 06880.

CAREER: Microform Review, Inc., Weston, Conn., founder and publisher, 1971—. *Military service:* U.S. Army Reserve, 1968-74.

WRITINGS: (Editor with John O'Sullivan) *The Draft and Its Enemies*, University of Illinois Press, 1974; (with James P. Shenton) *U.S. History to 1877*, Learning Systems Co., 1974; (with Shenton) *U.S. History Since 1865*, Learning Systems Co., 1975; (editor with Ruth McMullin) *Oral History Collections*, Bowker, 1975.

WORK IN PROGRESS: A biography of Mary Heaton Vorse.

* * *

MEDEA, Andra 1953-

PERSONAL: Born September 17, 1953, in Chicago, Ill.; daughter of Edward Albert (a machine designer) and Emily Daphne (an organizer; maiden name, Lee) Thomas. *Home address:* c/o Kathleen Thompson, 1137 West Webster, Chicago, Ill. 60614.

CAREER: Writer and instructor in self-defense methods.

WRITINGS: (With Kathleen Thompson) *Against Rape*, Farrar, Straus, 1974.

WORK IN PROGRESS: A novel about Chicago; a book on women and violence; a collection of short stories.

* * *

MEDLEY, Morris L(ee) 1942-

PERSONAL: Born September 16, 1942, in Detroit, Mich.; son of Louis Morris and Katherine (Alvis) Medley; married Janet Anne Gelb, June 6, 1962; children: Cynthia Kay. *Education:* Vincennes University Junior College, A.S.,

1962; Indiana State University, B.S., 1964, M.S., 1966; Purdue University, Ph.D., 1974. *Home:* 610 Monterey Ave., Terre Haute, Ind. 47803. *Office:* Department of Sociology, Indiana State University, Terre Haute, Ind. 47809.

CAREER: High school science teacher in Vincennes, Ind., 1964-67; Indiana State University, Evansville, instructor in sociology, winter, 1967; Vincennes University Junior College, Vincennes, Ind., counselor, summer, 1967; Indiana State University, Evansville, instructor in sociology, 1967-68; Indiana State University, Terre Haute, instructor, 1968-72, assistant professor of sociology, 1973—. *Member:* American Sociological Association, National Council on Family Relations, North Central Sociological Society, Indiana Academy of Social Sciences, Indiana Council on Family Relations, Alpha Kappa Delta.

WRITINGS: (With Sharron L. Timmerman) *An Instructor's Manual to Accompany Scott-McNall's The Sociological Experience*, Little, Brown, 1971; (editor with James E. Conyers) *Sociology for the Seventies*, with instructor's manual, Wiley, 1972; (editor with Arthur F. Kline) *Dating and Marriage: An Interactionist Perspective*, Holbrook, 1973. Contributor of articles and reviews to sociology and education journals.

WORK IN PROGRESS: Research on academic self-concept among Black high school seniors; research on marriage and the college plans of Black high school seniors; studying social class, family structure, academic performance, perceived maternal encouragement, and academic self-concept as determinants of college plans among Black high school graduating seniors.

* * *

MEDLIN, Virgil D(ewain) 1943-

PERSONAL: Born February 21, 1943, in Chickasha, Okla.; son of Virgil O. and Beatrice L. (Fellows) Medlin. *Education:* Oklahoma City University, B.A., 1965, M.A.T., 1967; University of Oklahoma, M.A., 1968, Ph.D., 1974; also studied at Institut zur Erforschung UdSSR (Munich), Oxford University, and University of Paris. *Politics:* Democrat. *Religion:* Methodist. *Home:* 2125 Turner Dr., Midwest City, Okla. 73110. *Office:* Department of History, Oklahoma City University, Oklahoma City, Okla. 73106.

CAREER: Oklahoma City Southwestern College, Oklahoma City, Okla., instructor in history and government, 1966-68, associate dean of arts and sciences and chairman of Social Science Division, both 1968-69; Central State University, Edmond, Okla., instructor in social science, summer, 1969; Oklahoma City University, assistant professor, 1969-73, associate professor of history, 1973—. Special instructor at University of Oklahoma, 1970-71; director of Russian and Soviet studies at Graz Centre (Graz, Austria). Classics programmer at KFNB-FM Radio. *Military service:* U.S. Army Reserve, 1968-69.

MEMBER: American Historical Association, Association for Asian Studies, American Association for the Advancement of Slavic Studies, Southern Historical Association, Southwest Conference on Asian Studies (past member of board of directors), Oklahoma Academy of Sciences (social sciences president, 1975-76). *Awards, honors:* Fulbright grant, 1967-68; French Government fellow, 1967-68.

WRITINGS: (Editor) *The Russian Revolution: Democracy Or Deference?*, Holt, 1974; (translator and editor with Steven L. Parsons) *V. D. Nabokov and the Russian Provi-*

sional Government, 1917, Yale University Press, 1975; *A Bibliography of English Works on Imperial Russia: 1801-1917*, Basil Blackwell, in press. Contributor to history and to Asian and Russian studies journals.

Editor of newsletter of Southwest Conference on Asian Studies, 1973—; member of editorial board of *Russian History/Histoire Russe*, 1974—; managing editor for music and ballet for *Soviet Union/Union sovietique*, 1974—, member of editorial board, 1974—.

WORK IN PROGRESS: Alexander III, for Twayne; *Napoleon*, with Vernon Puryear, Volume I: *Escape to Dictatorship*, Volume II: *Egypt Enters World Politics*, Volume III: *Bonaparte's Round Trip to Syria*.

AVOCATIONAL INTERESTS: Classical music, tennis, sailing.

* * *

MEISS, Millard   1904-1975

March 25, 1904—June 12, 1975; American educator, art historian, connoisseur, curator, editor, and author of books on art. Obituaries: *New York Times*, June 14, 1974; *AB Bookman's Weekly*, September 8, 1975.

* * *

MEISTER, Richard J(ulius)   1938-

PERSONAL: Born September 22, 1938, in Gary, Ind.; son of Edward J. (in insurance) and Lillian (Jones) Meister; married Joan M. Costanza, April 4, 1964; children: Christopher B., Erica Ann, Jonathan R. *Education:* St. Joseph's College, Rensselaer, Ind., B.A., 1960; University of Notre Dame, M.A., 1962, Ph.D., 1967. *Politics:* Democrat. *Religion:* Roman Catholic. *Home:* 1626 Euclid, Flint, Mich. 48503. *Office:* Department of History, University of Michigan—Flint, Flint, Mich. 48503.

CAREER: Xavier University, Cincinnati, Ohio, assistant professor of history, 1965-69; University of Michigan—Flint, assistant professor, 1969-71, associate professor of history, 1971—, chairman of department of urban studies, 1972-73, chairman of department of history, 1973—. *Member:* American Historical Association, Organization of American Historians, American Association of University Professors, Immigration History Society. *Awards, honors:* Danforth associate, 1975-81.

WRITINGS: (Editor) *Black Ghetto: Promised Land or Colony?*, Heath, 1972; (editor) *Race and Ethnicity in Modern America*, Heath, 1974.

WORK IN PROGRESS: Boss and Machine Politics in Twentieth Century America, with Zane Miller and Bruce Stave, for Schenkman; a study of Flint, Michigan; a study of accommodation, acculturation, and assimilation in urban America.

* * *

MELHORN, Charles M(ason)   1918-

PERSONAL: Born July 22, 1918, in Portsmouth, Va.; son of Kent Churchill (a physician) and Jeanne (a pianist; maiden name, Andrews) Melhorn; married Wilberta Leavine, March 14, 1943 (divorced, 1944); married Jacqueline Mullen, August 4, 1944 (divorced, 1966); married Liselotte Kaufmann (a photographer), May 8, 1970. *Education:* University of California, Los Angeles, A.B., 1940; San Diego State College (now University), M.A., 1966; University of California at San Diego, Ph.D., 1973. *Politics:* Republican.

Religion: Episcopalian. *Residence:* Beverly Hills, Calif. 90210.

CAREER: U.S. Navy career officer, 1940-61, holding various assignments, including duty on motor torpedo boat at Guadalcanal, 1942; commanding officer, Torpedo Bombing Squadron 50, Third Fleet, 1945; flight deck officer, USS Leyte, 1947; flag secretary, staff, Commander Carrier Division 4, Sixth Fleet, 1950; operations officer, Airborne Early Warning Squadron 12, Sixth Fleet, 1956; air operations officer, staff, Commander Carrier Division 15, Seventh Fleet, 1959; staff member, North American Air Defense Command, 1961; left service as commander, 1961. Lecturer in history at San Diego State University, 1967. *Awards, honors*—Military: Purple Heart, 1942; Navy Cross, 1945.

WRITINGS: Two-Block Fox: The Rise of the Aircraft Carrier, 1911-1929, Naval Institute Press, 1974.

WORK IN PROGRESS: A novel on the peace-time Navy, *Commodore's Privilege*.

AVOCATIONAL INTERESTS: Mountaineering.

* * *

MELTSNER, Arnold J(erry)   1931-

PERSONAL: Born June 16, 1931, in Los Angeles, Calif.; son of Leonard and Lorraine (Berger) Meltsner; married Ruth Vida, August 16, 1953; children: Laura, Carolyn, Kenneth. *Education:* University of California, Los Angeles, B.A. (with honors), 1956; University of California, Berkeley, M.A., 1966, Ph.D., 1969. *Home:* 8653 Don Carol Dr., El Cerrito, Calif. 94530. *Office:* Graduate School of Public Policy, University of California, Berkeley, Calif. 94720.

CAREER: General Telephone Co., Santa Monica, Calif., engineer, 1956-58; Rand Corp., Santa Monica and Washington, D.C., cost analyst, 1958-63; Research Analysis Corp., McChan, Va., chief of cost analysis, 1963-65; University of California, Berkeley, assistant professor of political science, 1969-71, associate professor, 1971-75, professor of public policy, 1975—, specialist at Center for Planning and Development, 1966-68. Consultant to City of Oakland, Calif., 1966-68, to Bay Area Social Planning Council, 1974-75, and to National Planning Association, 1974-75; member of Advisory committee on income taxation for League of California Cities, 1974, and Bay Area Council on Education for the Public Service, 1974-75. *Military service:* U.S. Air Force, 1950-54. *Member:* American Political Science Association, American Society for Public Administration, Joint Study Group on Resource Association Methodology, American Association for Advancement of Science.

WRITINGS: (Contributor) John P. Crecine, editor, *Financing the Metropolis: Public Policy in Urban Economies*, Sage Publications, 1970; *The Politics of City Revenue*, University of California Press, 1971; (with Gregory W. Kast, John F. Kramer, and Robert T. Nakamura) *Political Feasibility of Reform in School Financing: The Case of California*, Praeger, 1973; (with Frank S. Levy and Aaron Wildavsky) *Urban Outcomes: Schools, Streets, and Libraries*, University of California Press, 1974; (contributor) John Pincus, editor, *School Finance in Transition*, Ballinger, 1974; *Policy Analysts in the Bureaucracy*, University of California Press, in press. Editor of *Policy Analysis*, 1975—; member of the editorial advisory board of *Sage Public Administration Abstracts*, 1975—.

WORK IN PROGRESS: Earthquakes: Public Policy and Response.

AVOCATIONAL INTERESTS: Chinese food, writing detective stories.

* * *

MENVILLE, Douglas 1935-

PERSONAL: Born August 16, 1935, in Baton Rouge, La.; son of Raoul Louis, Jr. (a chemist) and Nevalee (Bradsher) Menville. *Education:* Attended Louisiana State University, 1953-56; University of Southern California, B.A., 1958, M.A., 1959. *Home and office:* 823 North McCadden Pl., Los Angeles, Calif. 90038.

CAREER: Famous Artists Agency (now International Creative Management), Beverly Hills, Calif., librarian and story editor, 1960-62; Film Associates (now B.F.A.; makers of educational films), Los Angeles, Calif., writer, 1962-64; free-lance film writer and editor, 1964-67; Technical Communications, Inc., Los Angeles, Calif., film and manual writer and editor, 1967-69; free-lance film writer and editor, 1969-70; Universal Studios, Studio City, Calif., film editor, 1970-71; Sutherland Learning Associates, Los Angeles, Calif., film editor and writer, 1971-75. *Military service:* U.S. Army National Guard, 1959-65; became sergeant.

WRITINGS: A Historical and Critical Survey of the Science-Fiction Film, Arno, 1975; (editor with Robert Reginald) *Ancestral Voices: An Anthology of Early Science Fiction*, Arno, 1975. Advisory editor of "Science Fiction Reprint Series," 1975, and "Supernatural Reprint Series," 1976, for Arno. Editor of *Forgotten Fantasy*, 1970-71; editor for Newcastle, 1971—.

WORK IN PROGRESS: Contributing to *Science Fiction and Fantasy Literature: A Checklist*, for Gale.

SIDELIGHTS: Menville writes: "... For thirty years now, I have been an avid collector and reader in the fields of science fiction, fantasy, comic art, films and related media. I am continually fascinated by the variety of strange and unusual material that turns up related to these fields, and by the number of 'main-stream' writers, both contemporary and of centuries back, who have been attracted to fantasy and science fiction as vehicles for expressing ideas and concepts they could express nowhere else." *Avocational interests:* Collecting books and related material, listening to classical music, attending films.

* * *

MERTENS, Thomas R(obert) 1930-

PERSONAL: Born May 22, 1930, in Fort Wayne, Ind.; son of Herbert F. and Hulda (Burg) Mertens; married Beatrice Abair (a secretary), April 1, 1953; children: Julia Ann, David Gerhard. *Education:* Ball State University, B.S., 1952; Purdue University, M.S., 1954, Ph.D., 1956; postdoctoral study at Stanford University, 1963-64. *Politics:* Independent. *Religion:* Lutheran. *Home:* 2506 Johnson Rd., Muncie, Ind. 47304. *Office:* Department of Biology, Ball State University, Muncie, Ind. 47306.

CAREER: Ball State University, Muncie, Ind., assistant professor, 1957-62, associate professor, 1962-66, professor of biology, 1966—. *Member:* American Association for the Advancement of Science, Genetics Society of America, American Genetic Association, National Association of Biology Teachers, National Science Teachers Association, Indiana College Biology Teachers (president, 1968-69), Indiana Academy of Science (fellow), Sigma Xi, Sigma Zeta (national president, 1966-67). *Awards, honors:* National

Science Foundation faculty fellow at Stanford University, 1963-64.

WRITINGS: (With J. C. Malayer) *Laboratory Exercises in the Principles of Biology*, Burgess, 1966, 2nd edition, with A. S. Bennett, published as *Laboratory Investigations in the Principles of Biology*, 1968, 3rd edition, 1973; (with S. F. Cooper) *Probability and Chi-Square for Biology Students: A Programmed Text*, Educational Methods, 1969, 2nd edition, 1974; (with E. J. Gardner) *Genetics Laboratory Investigations*, Burgess, 1970, 2nd edition, 1975; (with J. L. Lines) *Principles of Biosystematics*, Educational Methods, 1970; (with Michael Geary) *Animal Development*, Educational Methods, 1970; (with Gary E. Parker) *Life's Basis: Biomolecules*, Wiley, 1973; (editor with S. K. Robinson) *Human Genetics and Social Problems: A Book of Readings*, MSS Information Corp., 1973; (with Rex Reynolds) *The Microscope: A Programmed Text*, Allied Education Council, 1973; (with Thomas Mangum) *Ecology: The Environmental Crisis*, Educational Methods, 1973; (with F. F. Stevenson) *Plant Life Cycles*, Wiley, 1975; (editor) *Human Genetics: Readings on the Implications of Genetic Engineering*, Wiley, 1975; (co-author) *Plant Anatomy*, Wiley, in press. Contributor to proceedings; contributor of reviews and articles to journals in his field.

* * *

MESSER, Ronald Keith 1942-

PERSONAL: Born October 4, 1942, in Pacolet Mills, S.C.; son of Arthur (a merchant) and Sue Evelyn (Dulin) Messer; married Mary Kathryn Porter, November 24, 1965; children: Paula Kay, Natalie Karen, Sue Evelyn, Shara Jeanne. *Education:* Ricks College, A.A., 1966; Idaho State University, B.A., 1968, M.A., 1971. *Politics:* Conservative. *Religion:* Church of Jesus Christ of Latter-day Saints (Mormons). *Home:* 212 North Third E., Rexburg, Idaho 83440. *Agent:* Ruth Cantor, 156 Fifth Ave., Room 1005, New York, N.Y. 10010. *Office:* Department of English, Ricks College, Rexburg, Idaho 83440.

CAREER: Ricks College, Rexburg, Idaho, instructor in English, 1969—. Taught English to Bannock-Shoshoni Indians, 1969.

WRITINGS: Shumway (novel), Thomas Nelson, 1975; *Miracle of Revision* (text), with workbook, Kendall-Hunt, 1975.

WORK IN PROGRESS: A sequel to *Shumway*; an adventure novel; a collection of short stories; children's fantasy stories.

* * *

MESSING, Simon D(avid) 1922-

PERSONAL: Born July 13, 1922, in Frankfurt, Germany; naturalized U.S. citizen in 1943; son of Jacob and Helen (Friedler) Messing; married Denise Ullmo, July 25, 1967; children: Jacqueline. *Education:* City College of New York (now City College of the City University of New York), B.S.S., 1949; University of Pennsylvania, Ph.D., 1957. *Office:* Department of Anthropology, Southern Connecticut State College, New Haven, Conn. 06515.

CAREER: Paine College, Augusta, Ga., assistant professor of social sciences, 1956-58; Hiram College, Hiram, Ohio, associate professor of social sciences, 1958-60; University of South Florida, Tampa, associate professor of anthropology, 1960-64; officer with U.S. Agency for International Development in Ethiopia, 1961-67; Southern Connecticut State College, New Haven, professor of anthropology, 1968—. Lecturer at Bowling Green State University, summer, 1960. Consultant to Pinellas County Public Health Department, 1960-61, and University of Maryland, School of Medicine, Community Pediatrics Center, 1967-68. *Member:* Society for International Development, African Studies Society (fellow), American Anthropological Association (fellow), American Association for the Advancement of Science (fellow), Society for Applied Anthropology (fellow), American Public Health Association, Phi Beta Kappa. *Awards, honors:* Danforth Foundation scholarship, summer, 1959.

WRITINGS: (Contributor) M. K. Opler, editor, *Culture and Mental Health*, Macmillan, 1959; (contributor) Paul Bohannan and G. Dalton, editors, *Markets in Africa*, Northwestern University Press, 1962; *The Target of Health in Ethiopia*, MSS Educational Publishing, 1972. Contributor of articles and reviews to professional journals. Author of television scripts and of handbooks on Middle Eastern countries.

WORK IN PROGRESS: Health Problems in Undeveloped Areas.

* * *

MESTA, Perle 1893(?)-1975

1893(?)—March 16, 1975; American society hostess, former U.S. foreign minister, and author of autobiography. Obituaries: *New York Times*, March 17, 1975; *Current Biography*, May, 1975.

* * *

MESZAROS, Istvan 1930-

PERSONAL: Born December 19, 1930, in Budapest, Hungary; son of Istvan and Ilona (Kocsis) Meszaros; married Donatella Morisi (a teacher), February 15, 1956; children: Laura, Susan, George. *Education:* Attended Eotvos College, 1949-50; Budapest University, B.A. (first class honors), 1953; Friedrich Schiller University, Dr.Phil., 1955. *Politics:* Socialist. *Home:* 16 Graham Ave., Brighton, Sussex BN1 8HA, England. *Office:* Division of Social Science, York University, 4700 Keele St., Toronto, Ontario, Canada.

CAREER: Budapest University, Budapest, Hungary, assistant professor, 1951-55, associate professor of philosophy, 1956; University of Turin, Turin, Italy, assistant professor of philosophy, 1956-59; University of London, London, England, research fellow of Bedford College, 1959-61; St. Andrews University, St. Andrews, Scotland, associate professor of philosophy, 1961-66; Sussex University, Brighton, Sussex, England, associate professor of philosophy, 1966-72; York University, Toronto, Ontario, professor of social science, 1972—. *Member:* International Sociological Association, Societe Europeenne de Culture, Toronto Society for the Study of Social and Political Thought. *Awards, honors:* Attila Jozsef Prize, 1951, for an essay; Issac Deutscher Memorial Prize, 1970, for *Marx's Theory of Alienation.*

WRITINGS: Szatira es valosag: Adalekok a szatira elmeletehez (title means "Satire and Reality: Contributions to the Theory of Satire"), SZKK (Budapest), 1955; *La rivolta degli intellettuali in Ungheria* (title means "Revolt of the Intellectuals in Hungary"), Einaudi (Turin), 1958; *Attila Jozsef e l'arte moderna* (title means "Atilla Jozsef and Modern Art"), Lerici (Milan), 1964; *Marx's Theory of Al-*

ienation, Merlin, 1970, 4th edition, 1975; *The Necessity of Social Control*, Merlin, 1971; (editor and contributor) *Aspects of History and Class Consciousness*, Routledge & Kegan Paul, 1971; *Lukacs' Concept of Dialectic*, Merlin, 1972; *The Philosophy of Jean-Paul Sartre*, Sussex University Press and Chatto & Windus, in press; *Social Structure and Forms of Consciousness*, Merlin, in press. General editor of series, "International Library of Social and Political Thought," Merlin, 1975—.

WORK IN PROGRESS: Beyond Capital: Towards a Theory of Transition.

SIDELIGHTS: Meszaros is competent in Hungarian, Italian, French, German, Spanish. *Avocational interests:* Music and poetry.

* * *

METRAUX, Rhoda 1914-

PERSONAL: Surname is pronounced *Met*-ro; born October 18, 1914, in Brooklyn, N.Y.; daughter of Karl Frederick (a banker) and Anna Marie (Kappelman) Bubendey; married Alfred Metraux, March 5, 1941 (divorced March, 1959); children: Daniel Alfred. *Education:* Vassar College, B.A., 1934; graduate study at Yale University, 1940-41; Columbia University, Ph.D., 1951. *Politics:* Independent Democrat. *Religion:* Episcopalian. *Home:* 211 Central Park West, New York, N.Y. 10024. *Office:* American Museum of Natural History, New York, N.Y.

CAREER: Employed on staff at Oxford University Press, 1936-40; National Research Council, Washington, D.C., member of committee on food habits, 1942-43; Office of Strategic Services, Washington, D.C., member of planning staff, 1943-45; Columbia University, New York, N.Y., researcher in contemporary cultures, 1947-52; American Museum of Natural History, New York, N.Y., assistant director of studies in contemporary cultures, 1952-53; director of Montserrat anthropolitical expedition, 1953-54; Cornell University Medical College, Ithaca, N.Y., research fellow, 1954-57; consultant to Institute of Intercultural Studies, 1957; Image of the Scientist, 1959; American Museum of Natural History, New York, associate director of studies in allopsychic orientation, 1960-65, project director of cultural structure of perceptual communication, 1965-69, research associate, 1970—. Anthropological field work conducted in Haiti, 1941, 1946, 1948-49, in Mexico, 1943, in Argentina, 1946, in Montserrat, 1966, and Iatmul, New Guinea, 1967-68, 1971, 1972.

MEMBER: American Association for the Advancement of Science, American Anthropological Association (fellow), Society of Applied Anthropology, American Ethnological Association, New York Academy of Sciences, Columbia University Seminar Content and Method in the Social Sciences. *Awards, honors:* Social Science Research Council fellow, 1953-54; research grants from National Institute of Mental Health, 1960-65, and National Science Foundation, 1965-69.

WRITINGS: (Co-author) *German National Character: A Study of German Self-Images*, American Museum of Natural History, 1953; (editor with Margaret Mead) *The Study of Culture at a Distance*, University of Chicago Press, 1953; (with Mead) *Themes in French Culture: Preface to a Study of French Community*, Stanford University Press, 1954; (with Mead) *A Way of Seeing*, McCall Books, 1970. Also author, with Theodora M. Abel, of *Culture and Psychotherapy*. Contributor to *Science, New Insights* and other professional journals.

WORK IN PROGRESS: Organization of field research on Iatmul people of Sepik District, New Guinea; research on cultural applications of projective tests, especially Lowenfeld Mosaic Test.

* * *

METRESS, James F(rancis) 1933-

PERSONAL: Born September 25, 1933, in Southampton, N.Y.; son of James F. (a machinist) and Hilda (Gugel) Metress; married Eileen Seitz (a professor of community health education), October 31, 1974. *Education:* University of Notre Dame, B.S., 1955; Columbia University, M.A., 1957; Indiana University, Ph.D., 1971. *Religion:* Roman Catholic. *Home:* 2224 Torrey Hill, Toledo, Ohio 43606. *Office:* Laboratory of Bioanthropology, University of Toledo, Toledo, Ohio 43606.

CAREER: High school teacher of biology and coach in the public schools of Spring Valley, N.Y., 1955-57, and Saginaw and Fennville, Mich., 1957-64; Aquinas College, Grand Rapids, Mich., instructor in biology, 1964-65; Clarion State College, Clarion, Pa., assistant professor, 1966-68, associate professor of anthropology, 1968—; University of Toledo, Toledo, Ohio, associate professor of anthropology, 1969—. *Member:* International Association of Human Biologists, American Association of Physical Anthropologists, American Anthropological Association, Society for the Study of Human Biology, Human Biology Council, Society for the Study of Social Biology, Nutrition Education Society, Society for Medical Anthropology, Nutrition Today Society, Sigma Xi.

WRITINGS: (Editor) *Man in Ecological Perspective*, MSS Educational Publishing, 1971; (editor with C. L. Brace) *Man in Evolutionary Perspective*, Wiley, 1973; (with Thor A. Conway) *A Guide to the Literature on the Dental Anthropology of Post Pleistocene Man* (monograph), Toledo Area Aboriginal Research Club, 1974. Co-editor of *Toledo Area Aboriginal Research Club Bulletin*, 1972-75.

WORK IN PROGRESS: Research on evolution of disease, nutritional ecology, and dental anthropology; a book, *The Biocultural Nature of Man*; a technical manual, *Outline of Human Osteology for Anthropologists.*

AVOCATIONAL INTERESTS: Nature study, horticulture, Irish folk music.

* * *

METZDORF, Robert F(rederic) 1912-1975

July 2, 1912—April 16, 1975; American bibliographer, library curator and archivist, rare book collector and appraiser, publisher, editor, and compiler of bibliographies and catalogues. Obituaries: *New York Times*, March 19, 1975; *AB Bookman's Weekly*, March 31, 1975.

* * *

METZLER, Paul 1914-

PERSONAL: Born June 9, 1914, in Sydney, Australia; son of Paul Gerhardt (a wool buyer) and Beryl (Buss) Metzler; married Iris Louise French, November 1, 1941; children: Judy (Mrs. Richard Lawrence Hargrave), Geoffrey Richard. *Education:* Attended Barker College, Sydney, Australia. *Politics:* Liberal. *Religion:* Church of England. *Home:* Airlie, 98 Buxton St., Canberra, Australian Capital Territory 2600, Australia.

CAREER: Royal Australian Air Force, regular officer,

1938, retiring as group captain. *Member:* Commonwealth Club, Catalina Club.

WRITINGS: Advanced Tennis, Angus & Robertson, 1967, Sterling, 1968, revised edition, 1971; *Tennis Styles and Stylists*, Angus & Robertson, 1969, Macmillan, 1970; *Getting Started in Tennis*, Sterling, 1971; *Tennis Weaknesses and Remedies*, Sterling, 1973; *Tennis Doubles: Tactics and Formations*, Sterling, 1975. Contributor of short stories to magazines.

* * *

MEWS, Siegfried 1933-

PERSONAL: Born September 28, 1933, in Berlin, Germany; son of Ernest and Erna Mews; married Linda Mueller; children: Randolph. *Education:* University of Halle, student, 1953-57; University of Hamburg, Staatsexamen, 1961; Southern Illinois University, M.A., 1963; University of Illinois, Ph.D., 1967. *Home:* 716 Churchill Dr., Chapel Hill, N.C. 27514. *Office:* Department of Germanic Languages and Literatures, 442 Dey Hall, University of North Carolina, Chapel Hill, N.C. 27514.

CAREER: Centre College, Danville, Ky., instructor in German, 1962-63; University of Illinois, Urbana, instructor in German, 1966-67; University of North Carolina, Chapel Hill, assistant professor, 1967-71, associate professor of German, 1971—, editor of *Studies in Germanic Languages and Literatures*, 1968—. *Member:* American Association of Teachers of German, Modern Language Association of America, Heinrich-von Kleist-Gesellschaft, International Brecht Society, American Association of University Professors, American Comparative Literature Association, South Atlantic Modern Language Association, Delta Phi Alpha.

WRITINGS: (Editor) *Studies in German Literature of the Nineteenth and Twentieth Centures: Festschrift for Frederic E. Coenen*, University of North Carolina Press, 1970, 2nd edition, 1972; *Zuckmayer: Der Hauptmann von Koepenick*, Diesterweg, 1972; *Zuckmayer: Des Teufels General*, Diesterweg, 1973; (editor with Herbert Knust and contributor) *Essays on Brecht: Theater and Politics*, University of North Carolina Press, 1974; *Bertolt Brecht: Herr Puntila und sein Knecht Matti*, Diesterweg, in press.

Contributor: Norman H. Binger and A. Wayne Wonderley, editors, *Studies in Nineteenth Century and Early Twentieth Century German Literature: Essays in Honor of Paul K. Whitaker*, Apra Press, 1974; Roger Johnson and others, editors, *Moliere and the Commonwealth of Letters*, University and College Press of Mississippi, in press; Wolfgang Paulsen, editor, *Sterotyp und Wirklichkeit: Der Deutsche in der amerikanischen und der Amerikaner in der deutschen Literatur der Gegenwart*, Francke, in press. Contributor of articles and reviews to language journals. Member of editorial advisory board, *Perspectives on Contemporary Literature*, 1975—.

WORK IN PROGRESS: A book on German playwright Carl Zuckmayer, for Twayne.

* * *

MEYER, Bernard F. 1891(?)-1975

1891(?)—May 8, 1975; American Roman Catholic priest, missionary in China, writer of bilingual dictionary and catechisms. Obituaries: *New York Times*, May 11, 1975; *AB Bookman's Weekly*, June 23, 1975.

MEYER, Fred(erick Robert) 1922-

PERSONAL: Born December 20, 1922, in Oshkosh, Wis.; son of Fred L. (a grocer) and Elizabeth (Voss) Meyer; married Joan Frantz (a potter), October 2, 1951; children: Michael Ryder, Sarah L'Estrange. *Education:* Attended Oshkosh State Teachers College, 1940-42, and University of Wisconsin, 1942-43; Cranbrook Academy of Art, B.F.A., 1947, M.F.A., 1950. *Residence:* Scottsville, N.Y. *Office:* College of Fine and Applied Arts, Rochester Institute of Technology, Rochester, N.Y. 14623.

CAREER: Rochester Institute of Technology, Rochester, N.Y., assistant professor of design, 1950-56, associate professor of design and painting, 1956-67, professor of painting, 1967-75, chairman of graduate programs, 1973—. Four one-man shows, Midtown Galleries, New York, N.Y., 1949, 1951, 1969, 1974. *Military service:* U.S. Naval Reserve, 1943-44. *Member:* American Society of Interior Designers, Midtown Galleries. *Awards, honors:* Ford Foundation fellow, 1955-56.

WRITINGS: Sculpture in Ceramic, Watson-Guptill, 1972. Contributor to *Crafts Horizons*. Author of a film, "Christmas in Venice".

WORK IN PROGRESS: A book on aesthetics.

SIDELIGHTS: Meyer works in bronze in a foundry in Tuscany when not teaching in America; he is also a painter and sculptor.

* * *

MEYER, Jerome Sydney 1895-1975
(S. M. Jennings)

January 14, 1895—February 26, 1975; American editor, and writer of books on science, mathematical games and puzzles. Obituaries: *New York Times*, February 28, 1975; *AB Bookman's Weekly*, March 17, 1975. (*CA-2*)

* * *

MEYER, Joachim-Ernst 1917-

PERSONAL: Born July 2, 1917, in Koenigsberg, Germany; son of Ernst (a psychiatrist) and Kaete (Schmieden) Meyer; married Ruth Thwaites, July 11, 1953; children: Barbara, Marion. *Education:* University of Berlin, M.D., 1940; University of Freiburg, Br. Habilitation, 1952. *Religion:* Lutheran. *Home:* Herzberger Landstrasse 46, Goettingen D 34, Germany. *Office:* Nervenkliniken v. Siebold-Strasse 5, Goettingen D 34, Germany.

CAREER: University of Munich, Nervenklinik, Munich, Germany, psychiatrist, 1954-63; University of Goettingen, Goettingen, Germany, professor of psychiatry, 1963—, chancellor, 1968. Co-chairman of Psychotherapeutic Training Center, Goettingen, 1964—; member of Federal Republic of Germany Commission on the Development of Psychiatry, 1972-75. *Member:* British College of Psychiatrists (corresponding member).

WRITINGS: Die Entfremdungserlebnisse (title means "Experiences of Estrangement"), Thieme, 1959; (editor with Harald Feldmann) *Anorexia nervosa*, Thieme, 1965; (editor with Heinz Ahlenstiehl) *Selbstschilderungen eines Geisteskranken* (title means "Self-Description of a Mental Patient around 1800"), Bayer, 1967; (editor) *Depersonalisation*, Wissenschaftliche Buchgesellschaft, 1968; (editor with Hans Lauter) *Der psychisch Kranke und die Gesellschaft* (title means "The Mentally Ill and Society"), Thieme, 1971; (editor with Kurt P. Kisker, Max Mueller,

and Erik Stroemgren) *Psychiatrie der Gegenwart*, 2nd edition (Meyer was not associated with 1st edition), Springer-Verlag, 1972; *Tod und Neurose*, Vandenhoeck & Ruprecht, 1973, translation by M. Nunberg published as *Death and Neurosis*, International Universities Press, 1974.

WORK IN PROGRESS: Psychopathology in Obesity.

* * *

MEYERS, Carlton R(oy) 1922-

PERSONAL: Born December 16, 1922, in Buffalo, N.Y.; son of Roy E. (a lumber dealer) and Helena (Kiphuth) Meyers; married Eleanor Exner (an elementary school teacher), June 21, 1947; children: Marsha J. (Mrs. Bruce Fishbane), Jo Ellen (Mrs. John Schweichler), Pamela J., Suzanne J. *Education:* Trinity College, Hartford, Conn., student, 1943-44; Springfield College, B.S., 1947; Columbia University, A.M., 1948, Ed.D., 1950. *Religion:* Lutheran. *Home:* 1281 East Robinson St., North Tonawanda, N.Y. 14120. *Office:* Department of Physical Education, State University of New York at Buffalo, 314A Clark Hall, Buffalo, N.Y. 14214.

CAREER: Yale University, New Haven, Conn., assistant professor of physical education, 1949-54; Meyers Lumber Co., Inc., North Tonawanda, N.Y., salesman, 1954-57; State University of New York at Buffalo, assistant professor, 1957-61, associate professor, 1961-66, professor of physical education and of education, 1967—, chairman of department of instruction, 1968-72. Fulbright lecturer in Iran, 1963-64; visiting professor and resident director of exchange program at Didsbury College, 1970-71. *Military service:* U.S. Naval Reserve, active duty, 1943-46; became lieutenant senior grade.

MEMBER: International Council on Health, Physical Education and Recreation, American College of Sports Medicine (fellow), American Alliance for Health, Physical Education and Recreation, American Association of University Professors, American Educational Research Association, National College Physical Education Association for Men, National Council on Measurement in Education, National Education Association, New York State Association for Health, Physical Education and Recreation, Kappa Delta Pi, Phi Delta Kappa.

WRITINGS: Measurement in Physical Education, Ronald, 1962, 2nd edition, 1974; (with W. H. Sanford) *Swimming and Diving Officiating*, National Press, 1963, 3rd edition, 1970; *Essential Statistics for the Physical Education Teacher*, State University of New York at Buffalo, 1967, revised edition, 1973; *Basic Computations for Measurement in Physical Education*, Didsbury College, 1971. Contributor to *Physical Fitness Encyclopedia* and *Encyclopedia of Sport Services and Medicine*. Contributor to education and sports journals. Associate editor of *Research Quarterly*.

AVOCATIONAL INTERESTS: International travel, sailing, water skiing, handball, tennis, jogging.

* * *

MEYERS, Lawrence Stanley 1943-

PERSONAL: Born April 6, 1943, in Brooklyn, N.Y.; son of Mayer (an accountant) and Lillian (Schneider) Meyers; married Ronni Buchalter, September 11, 1966 (divorced September, 1974); married Gail M. Clark, October 28, 1974; children: (first marriage) Erin. *Education:* Brooklyn

College of the City University of New York, B.S., 1964; Adelphi University, Ph.D., 1968. *Home:* 8919 Salmon Falls Dr., Sacramento, Calif. 95826. *Office:* Department of Psychology, California State University, Sacramento, Calif. 95819.

CAREER: Adelphi University, Garden City, N.Y., instructor in psychology, 1966-68; California State University, Sacramento, assistant professor, 1970-74, associate professor of psychology, 1974—. Visiting professor at University of Texas, Austin, 1968-69, and Purdue University, 1969-70. *Member:* American Psychological Association, American Association for the Advancement of Science, Psychonomic Society, Western Psychological Association, Eastern Psychological Association. *Awards, honors:* National Science Foundation fellowship to University of Texas, 1968-69, and Purdue University, 1969-70.

WRITINGS: (With Neal E. Grossen) *Behavioral Research: Theory, Procedure, and Design*, W. H. Freeman, 1974. Contributor to psychological journals, including *Memory and Cognition* and *American Journal of Psychology*.

WORK IN PROGRESS: Two books, *Knowledge, Behavior, and Learning*, completion expected in 1976, and *Philosophy of Science*.

AVOCATIONAL INTERESTS: Ancient civilizations as known through archeological findings and mythological-religious writings.

* * *

MEYNELL, Francis 1891-1975

May 12, 1891—July 10, 1975; British book designer, editor, publisher, poet, and author of autobiography and works on typography. Obituaries: *New York Times*, July 11, 1975. (CA-19/20)

* * *

MEZEY, Robert 1935-

PERSONAL: Surname is pronounced *Mez-ee*; born February 28, 1935, in Philadelphia, Pa.; son of Ralph and Claire (Mandell) Mezey; married Ollie Simpson, July 14, 1963; children: Eve, Naomi, Judah. *Education:* Attended Kenyon College, 1951-53; University of Iowa, B.A., 1959; graduate study at Stanford University, 1960-61. *Politics:* Anarchist. *Religion:* "Indescribable". *Home:* 116 Q St., Salt Lake City, Utah 84103. *Office:* Department of English, Univeristy of Utah, Salt Lake City, Utah 84112.

CAREER: Former probation officer, psychology technician, social worker, and advertising copy writer; Western Reserve University (now Case Western Reserve), Cleveland, Ohio, instructor in English, 1963-64; Franklin and Marshall College, Lancaster, Pa., poet-in-residence, 1965-66; Fresno State College (now California State University), Fresno, Calif., assistant professor of English, 1966-68; University of Utah, Salt Lake City, associate professor of English, 1973—. *Military service:* U.S. Army, 1953-55. *Awards, honors:* Lamont Poetry Award, 1960, for *The Lovemaker*; Ingram-Merrill Foundation grant, 1973.

WRITINGS—All poems: *The Lovemaker*, Cummington, 1961; *White Blossoms*, Cummington, 1965; (editor with Stephen Berg) *Naked Poetry*, Bobbs-Merrill, 1968; *A Book of Dying*, Kayak, 1970; *The Door Standing Open: New and Selected Poems, 1954-1969*, Houghton, 1970; (translator with others, and editor) *Poems from the Hebrew*, Crowell, 1973. Work included in anthologies, including

Where is Vietnam? American Poets Respond, edited by Walter Lowenfels, Doubleday, 1967. Contributor to *New Yorker, Poetry, Stand, Kayak, Paris Review, Partisan Review*, and other journals and magazines.

WORK IN PROGRESS: Translating *Coplas a la muerte de mi tia Daniela* by Manuel Vasquez Montalban; other translations and poems.

AVOCATIONAL INTERESTS: Chess, tennis, any game in sight.

BIOGRAPHICAL/CRITICAL SOURCES: Poetry, December, 1966; *Observer*, September 6, 1970; *American Poetry Review*, fall, 1974.

* * *

MICELI, Frank 1932-

PERSONAL: Born May 22, 1932, in New York, N.Y.; married Frederica Komanoff (a stockbroker), May 28, 1967; children: Drew. *Education:* New York University, B.S., 1957, M.A., 1958, Ph.D., 1969. *Politics:* "Oblique Democratic." *Religion:* Humanist. *Home:* 37 Washington Sq. West, New York, N.Y. 10011. *Office:* Media Department, Jersey City State College, 2039 Kennedy Blvd., Jersey City, N.J. 07305.

CAREER: Jersey City State College, Jersey City, N.J., associate professor and chairman of media department, 1969—. Consultant to Department of the U.S. Virgin Islands, 1967-68; member of the Mayor's Council on Communications, Jersey City, N.J., 1974-75. *Military service:* U.S. Army, 1952-54. *Awards, honors:* Frederick Fell Prize Novel Award, 1969.

WRITINGS: (Contributor) Postman and Weingartner, editors, *Teaching as a Subversive Activity*, Delacorte, 1969; *The Seventh Month* (novel), Fell, 1969; (editor) *Major American Authors: The Modern Short Story*, Holt, 1970; (contributing editor) *The Negro Almanac*, Bellwether, 1971; (contributor) *The Seed Catalogue*, Beacon Press, 1974. Work included in *The Book of Golden Verse*, Golden Eagle Press, 1974. Contributor of reviews and articles to *Education Synopsis, Teachers College Record, Gothic Times*, and *Man*.

WORK IN PROGRESS: Why Education Died.

* * *

MICHAELS, Barbara
See PETERS, Elizabeth

* * *

MICHEL, Pierre 1934-

PERSONAL: Born February 4, 1934, in Belgium; married Christiane Fraiture (a psychology teacher), March 5, 1959; children: Bernard, Pierre-Alain, Anne. *Education:* University of Liege, B.A., 1956, Ph.D., 1968. *Religion:* Roman Catholic. *Home:* Sept Collines, Beaufays 4950, Belgium. *Office:* Center for American Studies, 4 bvd. de l'Empereur, Brussels 1000, Belgium.

CAREER: University of Liege, Liege, Belgium, professor of American literature, 1959—; Center for American Studies, Brussels, Belgium, director, 1965—. Visiting professor at Kent State University, 1971-72, 1974-75. *Military service:* Served 1957-58. *Member:* Societe Belge pour le progres des etudes philologigues, Belgian-Luxembourg American Studies Association (president, 1968-74), Modern Language Association of America. *Awards, honors:* Fulbright Hays fellowship, 1961-63; American Council of Learned Societies research fellow, 1969-70.

WRITINGS: Cozzens: An Annotated Bibliography, Kent State University Press, 1972; *James Gould Cozzens*, Twayne, 1974. Contributor to *English Studies, Revue Internationale de Philosophie*, and *Dutch Quarterly Review of Anglo-American Letters*. Editor of *Revue des Langues Vivantes*, 1973—.

WORK IN PROGRESS: Research on contemporary American fiction.

* * *

MICHMAN, Ronald D(avid) 1931-

PERSONAL: Born October 31, 1931, in Hartford, Conn.; son of Morris and Rose (Garber) Michman; married Ruth Krefting (a teacher), September 5, 1955; children: Laura S., Carol Ann. *Education:* New York University, B.S., 1953, M.A., 1957, Ed.D., 1966. *Home:* 2645 Remington Rd., Utica, N.Y. 13501. *Office:* Division of Business, Syracuse University—Utica, Burrstone Campus, Utica, N.Y. 13502.

CAREER: University of New Hampshire, Durham, assistant professor of marketing, 1960-64; Syracuse University—Utica, Utica, N.Y., assistant professor, 1964-68, associate professor, 1968-74, professor of marketing, 1974—, coordinator of Division of Business, 1965—. *Military service:* U.S. Army, Quartermasters Corps, 1954-56. *Member:* American Marketing Association, American Association of University Professors. *Awards, honors:* Study grant from Foundation for Economic Education, 1967, for research on the ice-cream industry; research grant from American Federation of Teachers, 1971, to study moonlighting teachers.

WRITINGS: (Contributor) John Ryons, J. Donnelly, and I. Ivancevich, editors, *New Dimensions in Retailing: A Decision-Oriented Approach*, Wadsworth, 1970; (contributor) William Moller and David Wileman, editors, *Marketing Channels: A Systems Viewpoint*, Irwin, 1971; (contributor) David L. Kurtz, editor, *Marketing Concepts: Issues and Viewpoints*, General Learning Corp., 1972; *Marketing Channels*, Grid Publishing, 1974; (with Donald W. Jugenheimer) *Strategic Advertising Decisions*, Grid Publishing, in press. Contributor to business journals. Member of editorial board for marketing abstracts of *Journal of Marketing*, 1972-75.

WORK IN PROGRESS: Marketing Channel Strategy, with Taylor Sims and M. Gable, publication by American Marketing Association expected in 1977.

AVOCATIONAL INTERESTS: Swimming, gardening, checkers, old movies.

* * *

MIDLARSKY, Manus I(ssachar) 1937-

PERSONAL: Born January 28, 1937, in New York, N.Y.; son of Max and Rachel (Potechin) Midlarsky; married Elizabeth Steckel (a university professor), January 25, 1961; children: Susan, Miriam. *Education:* City College (now City College of the City University of New York), B.S., 1959; Stevens Institute of Technology, M.S., 1963; Northwestern University, Ph.D., 1969. *Home:* 2100 Dartmouth Ave., Boulder, Colo. 80303. *Office:* Department of Political Science, University of Colorado, Boulder, Colo. 80302.

CAREER: University of Colorado, Boulder, instructor, 1967-68, assistant professor, 1968-71, associate professor, 1971-74, professor of political science, 1974—, project

director of Institute of Behavioral Science, 1973—. *Member:* International Studies Association, American Political Science Association, American Society for Political and Legal Philosophy, Inter-University Seminar on Armed Forces and Society. *Awards, honors:* Ford Foundation fellow in international relations, 1965-66; Council on Research and Creative Work summer research initiation faculty fellow, 1969; National Science Foundation grant, 1973-76.

WRITINGS: On War: Political Violence in the International System, Free Press, 1975. Contributor to journals.

WORK IN PROGRESS: A book on the effects of domestic conflict behavior on the distribution of party seats in parliaments, *Power and Autonomy in the Conflict Process*; a chapter for a book which examines the effects of power and distance on international conflict in the form of crises and interventions.

* * *

MIGDAL, Joel S(amuel) 1945-

PERSONAL: Born April 1, 1945, in Roosevelt, N.J.; son of Benjamin (a storekeeper) and Rebecca (Marshak) Migdal; married R. Marcia Alexander (a developer of curriculum in education), July 4, 1968; children: Ariela. *Education:* Rutgers University, B.A., 1967; Harvard University, M.A., 1968, Ph.D., 1972. *Religion:* Jewish. *Office:* Department of Government, Harvard University, Cambridge, Mass. 02138.

CAREER: Tel-Aviv University, Tel-Aviv, Israel, lecturer in political science, 1972-75; Harvard University, Cambridge, Mass., associate professor of government, 1975—. *Member:* American Political Science Association, Phi Beta Kappa. *Awards, honors:* Woodrow Wilson fellowship, 1967-68.

WRITINGS: Peasants, Politics, and Revolution: Pressures toward Political and Social Change in the Third World, Princeton University Press, 1974. Contributor to international studies journals.

WORK IN PROGRESS: A book on political and social change of Palestinian Arabs in the nineteenth and twentieth centuries.

SIDELIGHTS: Migdal has traveled and studied in Mexico, Spain, Portugal, India, and Israel. *Avocational interests:* Photography.

* * *

MILES, David H(olmes) 1940-

PERSONAL: Born May 25, 1940, in Bangor, Maine; son of E. Kenneth (a German teacher) and Evelyn (Adriance) Miles; married Jennifer Hardy, 1965; children: Julia. *Education:* University of Maine, B.A., 1962; graduate study at University of Freiburg, 1962-63, and University of Mainz, 1963-64; Princeton University, Ph.D., 1968. *Office:* Department of German, University of Virginia, Charlottesville, Va. 22903.

CAREER: University of Massachusetts, Boston, instructor, 1967-68, assistant professor of German, 1968-72; Ohio State University, Columbus, associate professor of German, 1972-75; University of Virginia, Charlottesville, associate professor of German and member of Center for Advanced Study, 1975—. *Member:* Modern Language Association of America, American Association of Teachers of German. *Awards, honors:* Fulbright fellowships, 1962-

63, 1963-64; Alexander von Humboldt fellowship to Freiburg, Germany, 1970-71; Guggenheim fellowship, 1976-77.

WRITINGS: Hofmannsthal's Novel "Andreas": Memory and Self, Princeton University Press, 1972. Contributor to language and literature journals.

WORK IN PROGRESS: Research on theory of literary criticism and Marxist culture criticism.

* * *

MILITELLO, Pietro
See NATALI, Alfred Maxim

* * *

MILLER, David Harry 1938-

PERSONAL: Born August 26, 1938, in Spangler, Pa.; son of George Russell (a laborer) and Gladys (a clerk; maiden name, Patterson) Miller; married Agnes A. Corcoran, April 19, 1963 (divorced January 18, 1972); married Ann Margaret Darks (a museologist), October 9, 1972; children: (second marriage) Gabriel FitzDavid. *Education:* Baldwin-Wallace College, B.A., 1963; Michigan State University, M.A., 1965, Ph.D., 1967. *Religion:* Non-believer. *Home:* 224 Barbour, Norman, Okla. 73069. *Office:* Department of History, 455 West Lindsay, University of Oklahoma, Norman, Okla. 73069.

CAREER: University of Oklahoma, Norman, assistant professor, 1967-71, associate professor of history, 1971—. *Military service:* U.S. Army, Security Agency, 1956-59. *Member:* American Historical Association, Mediaeval Academy of America, American Society of Church History, American Catholic Historical Association, American Philatelic Society. *Awards, honors:* National Endowment for the Humanities fellow, 1968.

WRITINGS: (Editor with William W. Savage, Jr.) Frederick Jackson Turner, *The Indian Fur Trade in Wisconsin*, University of Oklahoma Press, 1975. Contributor of articles and reviews to historical journals.

WORK IN PROGRESS: Research for a book on comparative feudalism.

AVOCATIONAL INTERESTS: Philately.

* * *

MILLER, Donald C(urtis) 1933-

PERSONAL: Born July 15, 1933, in Carthage, S.D.; son of Carl Louis and Elsie (Anderson) Miller; married Sue C. MacKenzie, November 24, 1961 (divorced March, 1974); children: Shari Lynne. *Education:* University of South Dakota, B.A., 1955, M.A., 1960; Columbia University, further graduate study, 1963-64. *Home:* 775 Monroe, Apt. 110, Missoula, Mont. 59801. *Office:* School of Journalism, University of Montana, Missoula, Mont. 59801.

CAREER: Has worked as recording engineer, studio engineer, and remote engineer; KOTA-Radio and Television, Rapid City, S.D., announcer and newsman, summer, 1955; University of South Dakota, Vermillion, instructor in radio, television, and film, 1957-63; KUSD-Radio and Television, Vermillion, S.D., acting production director, 1957-58, film director, 1958-60, program director, 1960-63; WDSE-Television, Duluth, Minn., program director, 1964-66; University of Minnesota, St. Paul, writer and photographer, summer, 1966; University of Montana, Missoula, assistant professor, 1966-71, associate professor of radio news, cinematography, elementary photography, news pho-

tography, and public affairs, 1971—. Director and cinematographer for Vermont Educational Television Series, 1968. *Military service:* U.S. Army, Writers Branch, 1955-57; served in Germany; became first lieutenant. *Member:* Western Montana Ghost Town Preservation Society (president, 1971-74). *Awards, honors:* Columbia Broadcasting System (CBS) news and public affairs fellowship, 1963-64; grant from National Endowment for the Humanities, 1971, to photograph western ghost towns.

WRITINGS: Ghost Towns of Montana, Pruett, 1974. Author of documentary film scripts for U.S. Army. Author, producer, director, editor, and cinematographer for film "Gary Schildt: A Self Portrait," National Endowment for the Arts, 1970. Contributor of about twenty articles to magazines and newspapers.

WORK IN PROGRESS: Research, with photography, on ghost towns of Utah, Arizona, New Mexico, South Dakota, Idaho, and Wyoming, with publication expected to result; research on ghost towns of Washington and Oregon.

SIDELIGHTS: Miller writes: "I research, write, photograph Western ghost towns and mining camps because these 'playthings of the wind' are fast-disappearing. If these remnants aren't captured on film now, we'll lose a significant part of our cultural-historic past."

* * *

MILLER, Marilyn McMeen 1938-

PERSONAL: Born November 6, 1938, in Denver, Colo.; daughter of William Otho (a civil engineer) and Lola Frances (Murphy) McMeen; married Lloyd Clifton Miller, June 1, 1964 (divorced, 1967); children: Simeen Bird. *Education:* Brigham Young University, B.A., 1962, M.A., 1964. *Politics:* "Conservative: 'Even artists should earn their own way.'" *Religion:* Church of Jesus Christ of Latter-day Saints (Mormons). *Home:* 233 South 500 E., Provo, Utah 84601. *Office:* Brigham Young University Press, Provo, Utah 84602.

CAREER: Bureau of Reclamation, Denver, Colo., clerk-typist, 1955-60; teacher of Latin and English in junior high school in Denver, Colo., 1960-61; Brigham Young University, Provo, Utah, instructor in English, 1962-70; Prudential Federal Savings, Provo, Utah, typist, summer, 1971; Brigham Young University Press, Provo, Utah, editor and writer, 1972—. Member of board of directors of Utah Repertory Theater. *Member:* Utah League of Writers (president, 1969), Utah Poetry Society. *Awards, honors:* First prizes from Utah League of Writers, 1969, other prizes, 1969-72; Utah State Fine Arts prizes for unpublished novel, *Rainy*, 1972, and poem "Year of the Rains," 1971, and light verse, 1970.

WRITINGS: Rainflowers (poems; self-illustrated), Art Publishers, 1969; (with John C. Moffitt) *Provo: A Story of People in Motion*, Brigham Young University Press, 1974; *I Have Lost My Heart Again: I Pray I Will Not Lose My Head, Amen* (poems; self-illustrated), Art Publishers (Provo, Utah), 1974. Ghost writer for *Roughing It Easy*, By Dian Thomas, Brigham Young University Press, 1974. Contributor of stories, articles, and poems to magazines, including *Dialogue, Children's Friend, Era, New Era, Ensign*, and *Relief Society*.

WORK IN PROGRESS: Rainy, a Mormon novel; *Touch*, a gothic, science fiction novel; a book of poems on the life of Vontella Kimbell, Mormon woman and cosmetic magnate.

SIDELIGHTS: Marilyn Miller writes: "I am a Mormon writer—immersed in Mormon tradition and local history—who hopes to speak out for the unique contribution of my sub-culture—this isolated religious community of the West which is now participating in an influential world religious movement.... My unpublished novels are all written on Mormon historical subjects: the handcart movement, the settlement of small outlying towns in Utah and Idaho. I have a deep interest in defining the Mormon experience for a modern audience and in creating a literature acceptable to the scrutiny of the most demanding criticism." *Avocational interests:* Art, music (symphony flautist; has made recordings of Middle and Far Eastern music; plays sitar), poetry (has given readings of Uzbeck poet Hamid Alimjan), dramatics (acts with Utah Reportory Theater).

* * *

MILLER, Marshall Lee 1942-

PERSONAL: Born October 18, 1942, in Chattanooga, Tenn.; son of W. Landon (a clergyman) and Katherine (Rankin) Miller; married Marlene Siskin (a journalist), June 21, 1970. *Education:* Harvard University, B.A., 1964; Yale University, J.D., 1970; also studied at Oxford University and University of Heidelberg, 1964-67. *Home:* 7117 Devonshire Rd., Alexandria, Va. 22307. *Office:* Occupational Safety and Health Administration, U.S. Department of Labor, 200 Constitution Ave. N.W., Washington, D.C.

CAREER: Arnold & Porter, Washington, D.C., attorney, 1970-71; U.S. Environmental Protection Agency, Washington, special assistant to the administrator, 1971-73; U.S. Department of Justice, Washington, associate deputy attorney general, 1973-74; Jones, Day, Reavis & Pogue, Washington, attorney, 1974-75; U.S. Department of Labor, Washington, deputy administrator of Occupational Safety and Health Administration, 1974—. Lecturer at Yale University and Government Institute Seminars on the Environment. Member of National Academy of Sciences' advisory panel on government regulation of chemicals in the environment.

WRITINGS: Bulgaria in the Second World War, Stanford University Press, 1975; *Environmental Law Handbook*, Government Institute, 1975.

SIDELIGHTS: Miller writes that his current interests are the "Middle East, military affairs, Balkans, environment, and foreign languages."

* * *

MILLER, Mary Britton 1883-1975
(Isabel Bolton)

August 6, 1883—April 13, 1975; American poet and novelist. Obituaries: *New York Times*, April 14, 1975; *Washington Post*, April 6, 1975. (*CA*-2)

* * *

MILLER, William McElwee 1892-

PERSONAL: Born December 12, 1892, in Middlesboro, Ky.; son of Henry (a minister) and Flora (McElwee) Miller; married Isabelle Haines Nicholson, November 12, 1924; children: William, Flora, Elise (Mrs. David Sprunt), Margaret (Mrs. Alan Weir). *Education:* Washington and Lee University, B.A., 1912, M.A., 1913; Princeton Theological Seminary, B.D., 1919. *Politics:* Democrat. *Home:* 326 West Allen Lane, Philadelphia, Pa. 19119.

CAREER: Ordained minister of Presbyterian Church in the United States, 1916; missionary in Iran, 1919-62. *Member:* Committee of Fellowship of Faith for Muslims, Bible and Medical Missionary Fellowship (member of board, 1965—), Phi Beta Kappa. *Awards, honors:* D.D., Washington and Lee University, 1932.

WRITINGS: (Translator from the Persian) *Al-Babu'l-Hadi 'Ashar* (Shi'ite creed), Royal Asiatic Society, 1928, reprinted, 1958; *A History of the Ancient Church in the Roman and Persian Empires* (in Persian), [Germany], 1931; *Baha'ism: Its Origin, History, and Teachings*, Revell, 1931; (translator with E. E. Elder from the Arabic) *Al-Kitab Al-Aqdas* (*Most Holy Book* of Baha'u'llah), Royal Asiatic Society, 1961; (contributor) Howard F. Vos, editor, *Religions in a Changing World*, Moody, 1959; *Ten Muslims Meet Christ*, Eerdmans, 1969; *Beliefs and Practices of Christians* (in English), Masihi Isha'at Khana (Lahore, Pakistan), 1973; *The Baha'i Faith: Its History and Teachings*, William Carey Library (Pasadena, Calif.), 1974. Also author of *The Way of Evangelism* and *The Way of Salvation*, both printed in Teheran by Inter-Mission Literature Committee, and commentaries on several books of the New Testament, all in Persian. Has also written works in English published by Christian publishing houses in Pakistan, Bangladesh, Indonesia, and other countries.

* * *

MILLGATE, Jane 1937-

PERSONAL: Born June 8, 1937, in Leeds, England; daughter of Maurice and Marie Barr; married Michael Millgate (a professor), February 27, 1960. *Education:* University of Leeds, B.A., 1959, M.A., 1963; University of Kent at Canterbury, Ph.D., 1970. *Home:* 75 Highland Ave., Toronto, Ontario M4W 2A4, Canada. *Office:* Victoria College, University of Toronto, Toronto, Ontario M5S 1K7, Canada.

CAREER: University of Toronto, Victoria College, Toronto, Ontario, instructor, 1964-65, lecturer, 1965-70, assistant professor, 1970-72, associate professor of English, 1972—. *Member:* Modern Language Association of America, Humanities Research Association of Canada.

WRITINGS: Macaulay, Routledge & Kegan Paul, 1973. Contributor to professional journals.

WORK IN PROGRESS: A study of Sir Walter Scott.

* * *

MILLIMAKI, Robert H. 1931-

PERSONAL: Born April 4, 1931, in Gwinn, Mich.; son of William A. (a glass blower) and Bertha S. (Viitata) Millimaki; married Joan Marie (a secretary), September 8, 1950; children: Debra, Karen (Mrs. William Kukla), Robert. *Education:* Attended College of Lake County, 1970-71, and Federal Bureau of Investigation National Academy, 1975. *Politics:* Independent. *Religion:* Agnostic. *Home:* 3151 21st Place, North Chicago, Ill. 60004. *Office:* North Chicago Police Department, 1850 Lewis Ave., North Chicago, Ill. 60064.

CAREER: North Chicago Police Department, North Chicago, Ill., chief of detectives, 1958—. *Military service:* U.S. Air Force, 1951-55. *Member:* International Association of Identification, Author's Guild, Federal Bureau of Investigation Academy Associates.

WRITINGS: Fingerprint Detective, Lippincott, 1973; *Making of a Detective*, Lippincott, in press. Contributor to law enforcement publications and to detective magazines.

WORK IN PROGRESS: A novel, *Deliver Up the Shield.*

AVOCATIONAL INTERESTS: Watercolor painting, guitar.

*   *   *

MILLON, Theodore 1929-

PERSONAL: Born August 18, 1929, in New York, N.Y.; son of Abner (a manufacturer) and Mollie (Gorky) Millon; married Renee Baratz (a social worker and author), August 16, 1952; children: Diane, Carolyn, Andrew, Adrienne. *Education:* City College (now City College of the City University of New York), B.A. and M.A., 1949; University of Connecticut, Ph.D. (psychology), 1953; Yale University, Ph.D. (philosophy), 1954. *Home:* 1320 Lincoln Ave., Highland Park, Ill. 60035. *Office:* University of Illinois Medical School, 912 South Wood St., Chicago, Ill. 60612.

CAREER: Lehigh University, Bethlehem, Pa., 1954-70, began as assistant professor, became professor of psychology; University of Illinois, Medical College, Chicago, professor of psychology and director of division, 1970—. Chairman of research committee and board of directors, Allentown (Pa.) State Hospital, 1955-70; chairman of clinical staff, Lincoln Mental Health Center, 1964-70; senior consultant, Westside Veterans Administration Hospital, Illinois State Psychiatric Institute, and Illinois Institute for Juvenile Research, all 1970—. *Member:* American Psychological Association.

WRITINGS: (Co-author) *Experiments in Psychology,* Edwards Bros., 1953; (editor) *Theories of Psychopathology,* Saunders, 1967; (editor) *Approaches to Personality,* Pitman, 1968; *Modern Psychopathology,* Saunders, 1969; (with Herman I. Diesenhaus) *Research Methods in Psychopathology,* Wiley, 1972; (with wife, Renee Millon) *Abnormal Behavior and Personality: A Biosocial Learning Approach,* with study guide by Theodore Millon and Leila Foster, Saunders, 1974; *Medical Behavioral Science,* Saunders, 1975. Contributor to professional journals. Member of editorial board, *Journal of Abnormal Psychology.*

AVOCATIONAL INTERESTS: Painting, sculpture, composing music.

*   *   *

MILLS, Watson Early 1939-

PERSONAL: Born August 13, 1939, in Martinsville, Va.; son of James Claiborne (a salesman) and Martha (a teacher; maiden name, Watson) Mills; married Joyce Hawkins (a teacher), December 19, 1959; children: Michael Arthur. *Education:* University of Richmond, B.A., 1961; Southern Baptist Seminary, B.D., 1964, Th.M., 1965, Th.D., 1968; University of Louisville, M.A., 1967; Baylor University, Ph.D., 1973; University of North Carolina, postdoctoral study, 1970-71. *Home:* 193 Grove Park Circle, Danville, Va. 24541. *Office:* Department of Religion and Philosophy, Averett College, Danville, Va. 24541.

CAREER: Ordained Baptist clergyman, 1961; pastor of Baptist churches in Virginia, Kentucky, and Indiana, 1961-68; Southern Baptist Seminary, instructor in New Testament Greek, 1964; University of Louisville, Louisville, Ky., lecturer in humanities and philosophy, 1966-68; Averett College, Danville, Va., assistant professor, 1968-70, associate professor of religion and philosophy, 1970—. *Member:* American Academy of Religion, Society of Biblical Literature, Association of Baptist Professors of Religion, Phi Delta Kappa.

WRITINGS: Understanding Speaking in Tongues, Eerdmans, 1972; *Speaking the Truth in Love: A Professor Looks at the Gospel,* Averett College Press, 1972; (editor and contributor) *Speaking in Tongues: Let's Talk About It,* Word Books, 1973; (editor with M. Thomas Starkes, and contributor) *The Lure of the Occult: A Christian Response,* Home Mission Board, 1974; *Speaking in Tongues: A Classified Bibliography,* Society for Pentecostal Studies, 1974. Contributor of more than a hundred fifty articles and reviews to theology journals. Editor of *Perspectives in Religious Studies.*

WORK IN PROGRESS: Editing an anthology of readings in the charismatic movement, specifically speaking in tongues.

AVOCATIONAL INTERESTS: Travel (Japan, Thailand, India, Israel, Europe, Greece), flying (holds private pilot's license).

*   *   *

MILTON, Hilary (Herbert) 1920-

PERSONAL: Born April 2, 1920, in Jasper, Ala.; son of Hilary Herbert and Erline (Moore) Milton; married Patty Sanders (a writer), September 26, 1952; children: Michelle, David Rodgers. *Education:* Attended Alabama Polytechnic Institute (now Auburn University), 1938, and Birmingham-Southern College, 1939-40; University of Alabama, A.B., 1948, M.A., 1949. *Politics:* Independent. *Religion:* Methodist. *Home:* 3540 Oakdale Dr., Birmingham, Ala. 35223. *Office:* Department of English, Samford University, 800 Lakeshore Dr., Birmingham, Ala.

CAREER: University of Alabama, Tuscaloosa, instructor in business writing, 1948-51; U.S. Department of the Air Force, Washington, D.C., civilian educational specialist in Montgomery, Ala., 1951-52, informational specialist in St. Louis, Mo., 1952-55; Department of the Air Force, Washington, D.C., editorial director, 1955-56, speech writer, 1956-62; National Aeronautics & Space Administration (NASA), Washington, D.C., report writer, 1962-70; full-time research and writing, 1970-71; Samford University, Birmingham, Ala., writer-in-residence, 1971—. Special lecturer at George Washington University, 1960. *Military service:* U.S. Army Air Forces, 1942-45.

WRITINGS: Steps to Better Writing, Spartan, 1962; *The Gitaway Box* (novel), Luce, 1968; *The House of God and Minnie May* (novel), Luce, 1969; *The Tipple Bell* (novel), Luce, 1970. Author of writing instruction manuals. Contributor of articles on U.S. space activities to encyclopedias; contributor of articles to educational and government publications.

WORK IN PROGRESS: November's Wheel, a novel; *The Ancient Legend of Dornar Caule,* a novel.

SIDELIGHTS: Milton writes: "I prefer to write about people of the South, many caught in dilemmas not of their own making; I am motivated to write by convictions, not by ideas that are currently 'in'; I believe in people, not movements, and have the utmost faith in the ability of a free people to survive.... I am proud of the fact that I worked as an iron ore miner, a truck driver, a postal clerk, a night watchman, and a life guard during earlier years."
Avocational interests: His family, photography, target shooting, citizens' band radio.

*   *   *

MINCKLER, (Sherwood) Leon 1906-

PERSONAL: Born May 7, 1906, in New Milford, N.Y.;

son of Walter Harmon (a farmer) and Eva (Williams) Minckler; married Althea Singleton, March, 1929 (died, 1946); married Edith Springer, March, 1947; children: (first marriage) Sherwood, Maxine, Christina Minckler Dusenbury; (second marriage) Sandra Minckler Maynard, David. *Education:* State University of New York College of Forestry (now State University of New York College of Environmental Science and Forestry), B.S., 1928, Ph.D., 1936. *Politics:* Democrat. *Religion:* Protestant. *Home:* Coon Hill Rd., Route 3, Skaneateles, N.Y. 13152. *Office:* State University of New York College of Environmental Science and Forestry, Syracuse, N.Y. 13210.

CAREER: U.S. Forest Service, researcher in St. Paul, Minn., 1935-36, research silviculturist in Asheville, N.C., 1936-45, research silviculturist in Bockingham, Va., 1945-46, silviculturist and research forester in Carbondale, Ill., 1946-68; Virginia Polytechnic Institute and State University, Blacksburg, professor of silviculture, 1968-70; State University of New York College of Environmental Science and Forestry, Syracuse, adjunct professor of silviculture, 1970—. Visiting professor at University of Michigan, 1957-58, Southern Illinois University, 1959. *Member:* Society of American Foresters, Ecological Society of America (fellow), American Association for the Advancement of Science, Sierra Club, Illinois Technical Forestry Association.

WRITINGS: Woodland Ecology: Environmental Forestry for the Small Owner, Syracuse University Press, 1975. Contributor of about a hundred thirty articles on silviculture, ecology, and forest management to professional journals.

WORK IN PROGRESS: Environmental Forestry for College Students.

SIDELIGHTS: Minckler is an owner of woodland and has twenty years experience in the application and evaluation of silvicultural and forest management practices on mixed hardwood and oak-hickory experimental forests in the central United States. His expertise lies in eastern forest types. He has recently testified before the U.S. Senate on forestry matters.

* * *

MINDSZENTY, Jozsef Cardinal 1892-1975

March 29, 1892—May 6, 1975; Hungarian Roman Catholic Primate, Archbishop of Esztergom, political exile, author of memoirs. Obituaries: *New York Times,* May 7, 1975; *Washington Post,* May 7, 1975; *Newsweek,* May 19, 1975; *Time,* May 19, 1975; *Current Biography,* June, 1975.

* * *

MINTON, Robert 1918-

PERSONAL: Born July 28, 1918, in Boston, Mass.; son of William Henry (a financier) and Alice (Cronan) Minton; married Helen Lou Sick (a lecturer in French), January 29, 1942; children: Michael Cronan, Helena. *Education:* Princeton University, B.A., 1940; Columbia University, M.S., 1946; Northeastern University, M.A., 1970. *Politics:* Democrat. *Religion:* Episcopalian. *Home and office:* 349 Main St., Concord, Mass. 01742. *Agent:* Max Gartenberg, 331 Madison Ave., New York, N.Y. 10017.

CAREER: Metro-Goldwyn-Mayer (motion picture studios), Culver City, Calif., junior writer, 1940-41; worked in aircraft industry, 1941-42, as high school teacher in Seattle, Wash., 1942-43, and as brewery office manager in Salem, Ore., 1944-45; *New York World Telegram and Sun,* New York, N.Y., reporter, 1946-50; U.S. Government, Paris, France, information officer for Marshall Plan, 1951-53; worked as public relations account executive in New York, N.Y., 1953-56; Radio Free Europe, New York, N.Y., director of public affairs in Munich, Germany, 1956-64; *Braintree Observer,* Braintree, Mass., editor and publisher, 1965-67; Boston University, Boston, Mass., director of public relations, 1968-72; free-lance writer and public relations consultant, 1972—.

MEMBER: Princeton Alumni Association of New England (vice-president). *Awards, honors:* Alternate Pulitzer traveling fellow, 1946; New Look Award from American College Public Relations Association, 1970.

WRITINGS: (With Howard Greene) *Scaling the Ivy Wall,* Abelard-Schuman, 1975; *John Law: The Father of Paper Money,* Association Press, 1975; *Forest Hills: An Illustrated History,* Lippincott, 1975.

Author of "Double Entry," a radio play, 1946, and "Stranglehold," a television play, 1947. Contributor to *Yankee, Boston, Barron's, Colliers, Esquire, Saturday Review, Nation, Coronet, Think, Woman's Day, Cavalier, Boston University Journal,* and *Finance.*

SIDELIGHTS: Minton writes: "[I] began writing in high school, edited my college humor magazine, went to journalism school. The latter and newspaper work created the writing habit, but only late in life has it been possible to devote full time to writing. . . . I was much affected by the Crash of 1929 and probably *John Law* stems from that." *Avocational interests:* Tennis, canoeing, playing the recorder, travel.

* * *

MINTZ, Leigh W(ayne) 1939-

PERSONAL: Born June 12, 1939, in Cleveland, Ohio; son of William Michael (a commercial artist) and Laverne (Bulicek) Mintz; married Carol Sue Jackson, August 4, 1962; children: Kevin Randall, Susan Carol. *Education:* University of Michigan, B.S., 1961, M.S., 1962; University of the Pacific, study in marine biology, summer, 1963; University of California, Berkeley, Ph.D., 1966. *Home:* 5940 Highwood Rd., Castro Valley, Calif. 94546. *Office:* Department of Undergraduate Studies, California State University, Hayward, Calif. 94542.

CAREER: California State University, Hayward, assistant professor, 1965-70, associate professor of earth sciences, 1970—, associate dean of instruction, 1969-70, associate dean of science, 1971-72, dean of undergraduate studies, 1974—. *Member:* Paleontological Society, American Geological Institute, American Association for the Advancement of Science, Geological Society of America, Paleontological Research Institution, Phi Beta Kappa, Phi Kappa Phi, Phi Eta Sigma, Sigma Xi.

WRITINGS: Historical Geology: The Science of a Dynamic Earth (text with teacher's manual), C. E. Merrill, 1972. Author of *Laboratory Manual for Paleontology,* Cal-State Audio-Visual Services, 1970. Contributor to paleontology journals.

WORK IN PROGRESS: Second edition of *Historical Geology; Prehistoric Life of California,* for University of California "Natural History Guide" series; a paleontology textbook.

* * *

MITCHELL, Alan 1922-

PERSONAL: Born November 4, 1922, in Ilford, Essex,

England; son of Alec Duncan (a research chemist) and Marjorie (Fyson) Mitchell; married Marjorie Beryl Clark, October 5, 1946 (divorced, 1961); married Philippa Dunn, February 20, 1962; children: (second marriage) Clio, Julia. *Education:* University of Liverpool, student, 1942-43; Trinity College, Dublin, B.A., 1951, B.A.Ag. (first class honors), 1951. *Politics:* "Socialist, tinged with anarchy and very independent." *Religion:* "Positively nil." *Home:* 1 Jubilee Lane, Boundstone, Farnham, Surrey, England. *Office:* Forestry Commission, Alice Holt Lodge, Wrecclesham, Farnham, Surrey, England.

CAREER: Forestry Commission, Farnham, England, assistant geneticist, 1953-63, silviculturist, 1963-70, dendrologist, 1970—. *Military service:* Royal Navy, 1941-45; became petty officer; served in Far East. *Member:* Royal Forestry Society, Institute of Foresters, British Trust for Ornithology, Royal Horticultural Society, National Trust, Surrey Bird Club, Surrey Naturalists. *Awards, honors:* Veitch Memorial Medal from Royal Horticultural Society, 1966; Victorian Medal of Honor from Royal Horticultural Society, 1971.

WRITINGS: Field Guide to Trees of Britain and Northern Europe, Collins, 1974. Author of fortnightly column, "Nature Notes," in *Farnham Herald*, and of occasional tree items in *The Guardian*. Contributor to *Guinness Book of Records* and to forestry and gardening journals.

WORK IN PROGRESS: Birds of Woods and Gardens; Field Guide to Trees of North America; another bird book; three more tree books.

SIDELIGHTS: Mitchell writes that he has ". . . no faith whatever in mankind's . . . 'leaders' who are contemptible, ignorant hate-mongers ruining the world to make its destruction more and more inevitable. Hopeless really, but I try to arouse interest in the delights of the natural world and show the utter evil of destroying life, people, forests, anything, for absurd temporary vague propaganda like 'the Western way of life' or any other and the lies and tortures excused by such partisan nonsense." *Avocational interests:* Astronomy, traditional jazz, evolution, steam engines, travel, making love, watching children grow, good health, gardening.

* * *

MITCHELL, Henry H(eywood) 1919-

PERSONAL: Born September 10, 1919, in Columbus, Ohio; son of Orlando Washington (a post office letter carrier) and Bertha (Estis) Mitchell; married Ella Parson (a teacher), August 12, 1944; children: Henry H., Jr., Muriel (Mrs. Spurgeon P. Smith), Elizabeth, Kenneth. *Education:* Attended Ohio State University, 1937-38; Lincoln University, B.A. (cum laude), 1941; California State University, Fresno, M.A., 1966; Union Theological Seminary, New York, N.Y., M.Div., 1944; School of Theology at Claremont, Th.D., 1973. *Office:* Southern California School of Theology at Claremont, 1325 North College Ave., Claremont, Calif. 91711.

CAREER: Ordained Baptist minister, 1944; Northern California Baptist Convention, Oakland, Calif., member of executive staff, 1945-59; pastor in Fresno, Calif., 1959-66, and in Santa Monica, Calif., 1966-69; Colgate Rochester Divinity School, Rochester, N.Y., Martin Luther King Professor of Black Church Studies, 1969-74; Ecumenical Center for Black Church Studies, Los Angeles, Calif., director, 1974—. Adjunct professor at Fuller Theological Seminary, 1974—, and at Southern California School of Theology at Claremont, 1974—. Lecturer and consultant in Black Church Studies at Princeton Theological Seminary, Union Theological Seminary, Yale Divinity School, Boston University, Northwestern University, and Pittsburgh Theological Seminary. Member of board of trustees of Berkeley Baptist Divinity School, 1959-70; Northern California Baptist Convention, president, 1961-62, chairman of board, 1963-64; chairman of Fresno Mayor's Bi-Racial Commission, 1963-65; president of Fresno County Economic Opportunity Commission, 1966; chairman of board of World Inquiry School, 1971-72. *Member:* Society for the Study of Black Religion, American Association of University Professors, National Committee of Black Churchmen, Phi Kappa Epsilon, Phi Kappa Phi.

WRITINGS: Black Preaching, Lippincott, 1970; *Black Belief*, Harper, 1975; (contributor) E. L. McCall, editor, *The Black Religious Experience*, Broadman, 1972. Contributor to journals.

WORK IN PROGRESS: Revising *Black Preaching*.

* * *

MITCHELL, Pamela Holsclaw 1940-

PERSONAL: Born June 27, 1940, in Denver, Colo.; daughter of Harold L. and Maurine (Boatman) Holsclaw; married Donald W. Mitchell (a physician), September 17, 1966; children: Robert, Kenneth, Andrew. *Education:* University of Washington, Seattle, B.S.N., 1962; University of California, San Francisco, M.S., 1965. *Politics:* Democrat. *Religion:* Protestant. *Residence:* Seattle, Wash. *Office:* Department of Physiological Nursing, University of Washington, Seattle, Wash. 98195.

CAREER: Massachusetts General Hospital, Boston, staff nurse, 1962-63, head nurse in neurology, 1963-64; Dane County Health Department, Madison, Wis., public health nurse, 1966-67; Emory University, Atlanta, Ga., instructor in nursing, 1967-68; University of Washington, Seattle, assistant professor of nursing, 1971—. *Member:* American Association of University Professors, American Association for the Advancement of Science, American Nurses Association, American Association of Neurosurgical Nurses, Sierra Club, Common Cause, Center for the Study of Democratic Institutions, Washington State Heart Association, Sigma Theta Tau, Alpha Gamma Delta.

WRITINGS: (Contributor) H. C. Moidel and other editors, *Nursing Care of Patients with Medical Surgical Disorders*, McGraw, 1969, 2nd edition, in press; (editor and principal author) *Concepts Basic to Nursing*, McGraw, 1973; (contributor) Judith Bloom, Geraldene Pardee, and Doris Molbo, editors, *The Dynamics of the Problem-Oriented Approach to Patient Care*, Lippincott, in press. Contributor to *Nursing Forum, Nursing Research*, and *Nursing Clinics of North America*.

WORK IN PROGRESS: Second edition of *Concepts Basic to Nursing*; research on the effects of nursing care on intracranial pressure and on increased intracranial pressure; studying problem-oriented patient care.

SIDELIGHTS: Pamela Mitchell writes: "My interest in problems of neurologically-handicapped persons has been maintained since my first staff nursing position and is the focus of my current teaching and research." Her book has been published in Norway, and is scheduled for publication in Mexico.

MITTLEBEELER, Emmet V(aughn) 1915-

PERSONAL: Born August 8, 1915, in Louisville, Ky.; son of Jacob (a coal dealer) and Katherine (a real estate agent; maiden name, Moorman) Mittlebeeler. *Education:* University of Louisville, B.A., 1936, J.D., 1939; University of Chicago, M.A., 1950, Ph.D., 1951. *Politics:* Independent Republican. *Religion:* Protestant. *Home:* 2007 Grasmere Dr., Louisville, Ky. 40205. *Office:* College of Public Affairs, American University, Washington, D.C. 20016.

CAREER: Private practice of law, 1939—; assistant attorney general of the State of Kentucky, 1945-48; University of Louisville, Louisville, Ky., lecturer in history and political science, 1951-53; assistant to Congressman John M. Robsion, Jr. of Kentucky, 1953-54; American University, Washington, D.C., assistant professor, 1954-57, associate professor, 1957-61, professor of government and public administration, 1961—. Member of board of directors, Association for Academic Travel Abroad, 1969—; Fulbright Professor at University College of Rhodesia and Nyasaland (now University of Rhodesia), 1962-63; visiting professor, University of Ife, 1969-70. *Military service:* U.S. Army Air Forces and Counter Intelligence Corps, 1942-45; served in South America, Africa, Middle East, and Central and Western Europe. *Member:* International African Law Association, American Political Science Association, American Association of University Professors, Kentucky Bar Association, Kentucky Historical Society, Pi Sigma Alpha, Phi Alpha Delta, Filson Club.

WRITINGS: (With William Pincus) *Executive Orders and Proclamations: A Study of a Use of Presidential Powers*, Committee on Government Operations, U.S. House of Representatives, 1957; *African Custom and Western Law: The Development of the Rhodesian Criminal Law for Africans*, Africana, 1975. Contributor to journals in his field. Editor of special issue of *Social Science*, 1961.

WORK IN PROGRESS: Research on constitutional right to travel abroad.

SIDELIGHTS: Mittlebeeler, who is competent in German, writes: "I have written on vexillology, the scientific study of flags. It's such a new discipline the word does not even yet appear in dictionaries."

* * *

MOFFITT, William J. 1930-

PERSONAL: Born June 26, 1930, in Chatham, New Brunswick, Canada; son of Winslow B. (a U.S. Customs agent) and Annie (Gallant) Moffitt; married Bonnie S. Moffitt, July 7, 1956 (divorced, 1968); children: Carole Leah (Mrs. Edward Hamm), Jeffrey W., Alan Robert. *Education:* Attended public schools in Calais, Me. *Residence:* Arlington, Va. 22204. *Office:* National Reporting, 2009 North 14th St., Arlington, Va. 22201.

CAREER: U.S. Navy, 1948-62; retiring as yeoman first class; National Reporting, Arlington, Va., court reporter, 1962—. *Member:* Loyal Order of Moose, Elks. *Awards, honors*—Military: Korean Service Medal.

WRITINGS: The Guide to Home Income, G. Banta, 1975.

AVOCATIONAL INTERESTS: Golf, flying private airplanes, working crossword puzzles.

* * *

MOLEY, Richard 1886-1975

September 27, 1886—February 18, 1975; American political scientist, educator, presidental economic advisor, columnist, and author of books on politics and government. Obituaries: *New York Times*, February 19, 1975; *Newsweek*, March 3, 1975; *Time*, March 3, 1975; *AB Bookman's Weekly*, March 17, 1975; *Current Biography*, April, 1975.

* * *

MOLINE, Mary 1932-

PERSONAL: Born May 30, 1932, in Bretz, W.Va.; daughter of John (a stonemason) and Mary (Sbardella) Sommavilla; married Walter Neal Moline (an industry manager), April 5, 1956; children: David Neal, Dawn Ellen. *Education:* Attended West Virginia University, 1950-53, Johns Hopkins University, 1952, and University of California, Los Angeles, 1975. *Home and office:* 6639 Blucher Ave., Van Nuys, Calif. 91406. *Agent:* Donald Shepherd Agency, 1680 Vine St., Hollywood, Calif. 90028.

CAREER: Editor and publisher, *Condenser*, 1965-71; *Car Classics* (magazine), Reseda, Calif., columnist, 1968-72, technical editor, 1971-75; *Ford Life* (magazine), St. Helena, Calif., associate editor, 1971-74; Rumbleseat Press, Van Nuys, Calif., president and publisher, 1972—. Free-lance writer, 1968-75. *Member:* Society of Automotive Historians, American Film Institute.

WRITINGS: Model A Miseries and Cures, Rumbleseat Press, 1972; (compiler) *The Best of Ford* (anthology), Rumbleseat Press, 1973; *Alex Tremulis* (biography), Krause Publications, 1973. Contributor to numerous journals.

WORK IN PROGRESS: A novel, *Bindle Stiff*; research for a Norman Rockwell anthology; "The Vanishing American Hobo," first in a series of teleplays.

SIDELIGHTS: Mary Moline told *CA* that when her husband was restoring a Model A Ford, she became the chief parts chaser and researcher. As a result of her efforts she became quite knowledgeable on restoration and wrote her first book, *Model A Miseries and Cures. Avocational interests:* Refinishing antiques, collecting old dolls, watching airplanes, international travel, ecology.

BIOGRAPHICAL/CRITICAL SOURCES: Restorer, July, 1967, December, 1969; *Car Classics*, March, 1969; *Condenser*, December, 1971.

* * *

MONAHAN, Arthur P(atrick) 1928-

PERSONAL: Born August 17, 1928, in Brantford, Ontario, Canada; son of Arthur Joseph and Grace (Fitzgerald) Monahan; married Margaret Jean Munro (a realtor), September 8, 1953; children: Michael, Paul, Moira, Corinne, Christopher, Valery. *Education:* University of Toronto, B.A., 1949, M.A., 1950, Ph.D., 1953; Pontifical Institute of Mediaeval Studies, M.S.L., 1952. *Religion:* Roman Catholic. *Home:* 15 St. Margaret's Bay Rd., Halifax, Nova Scotia, Canada. *Office:* Department of Philosophy, St. Mary's University, Halifax, Nova Scotia, Canada.

CAREER: Marquette University, Milwaukee, Wis., instructor in philosophy, 1953-54; St. Jerome's College, Kitchener, Ontario, assistant professor of philosophy, 1954-58; Mt. St. Vincent University, Halifax, Nova Scotia, assistant professor of philosophy, 1958-61; St. Mary's University, Halifax, Nova Scotia, associate professor, 1961-70, professor of philosophy, 1970—. *Member:* Canadian Philosophical Association, Canadian Catholic Historical Association (secretary, 1956-61), Canadian Association of University Teachers (member of executive board, 1965-72; treasurer, 1969-71), Mediaeval Academy of America.

WRITINGS: Beginning Philosophy, privately printed, 1963; *On the Confines of Two Worlds*, St. Francis Xavier University Press, 1964; (contributor) Patrick J. Corish, editor, *History of Irish Catholicism*, Gill, 1970; *John of Paris on Royal and Papal Power*, Columbia University Press, 1974.

WORK IN PROGRESS: A book on the notion of popular consent in late medieval thought; a biography of Roger Casement; *Aegidius of Rome on Ecclesiastical Power.*

* * *

MONKHOUSE, Francis John 1914-1975

May 15, 1914—1975; British educator and author of books on geography. Obituaries: *AB Bookman's Weekly*, April 14, 1975. (*CA*-13/14)

* * *

MONROE, Alan D(ouglas) 1944-

PERSONAL: Born October 11, 1944, in Baltimore, Md.; son of Robert Lloyd (a traffic manager) and Florence June (Pavey) Monroe; married Paula S. Conroy, December 28, 1975. *Education:* Butler University, B.A., 1966; Indiana University, Ph.D., 1971. *Office:* Department of Political Science, Illinois State Univeristy, Normal, Ill. 61761.

CAREER: Illinois State University, Normal, assistant professor, 1970-75, associate professor of political science, 1975—. *Member:* American Political Science Association.

WRITINGS: Public Opinion in America, Dodd, 1975.

* * *

MONTANDON, Pat

PERSONAL: Born in Texas; daughter of Charles Clay (a minister) and Myrtle (a minister; maiden name, Taylor) Montandon; married Alfred Spalding Wilsey (chairman of the board of directors of Wilsey-Bennet Co.), May 14, 1969; children: Sean Montandon. *Education:* Attended Oklahoma College for Women, 1948. *Residence:* San Francisco, Calif. *Agent:* Julian Bach, Jr., 3 East 48th St., New York, N.Y. 10017.

CAREER: Joseph Magnin, San Francisco, Calif., store manager, 1960-64; Saks Fifth Avenue, San Francisco, buyer, 1964-65; lecturer on the Soviet Union, safaris, the liberated woman, and other topics, 1966—. Appeared on "Ask the Expert," on KCBS-Radio, 1968, on "Boutique," CBS-Television, 1969, and on "Pat's Prize Movie," ABC-Television, 1966-69. Founder of local Woman's Round Table, 1973. *Member:* United Nations Association of San Francisco.

WRITINGS: How to Be a Party Girl, McGraw, 1968; *The Intruders* (autobiography), Coward, 1975. Author, producer, and director of plays for American Heart Association, 1954-60.

WORK IN PROGRESS: The Search for Prince Charming.

SIDELIGHTS: In 1947, Pat Montandon was one of the first successful heart surgery patients in the world. Since then she has conducted charity work for the American Heart Association and for Charila, a home for girls from Juvenile Hall. She has become a leader in women's rights, especially interested in the right of choice in married women using their maiden names, and has caused legisla-

tion to be passed emphasizing a woman's common law right to her own name.

BIOGRAPHICAL/CRITICAL SOURCES: San Francisco, October, 1973; *Los Angeles Times*, December 30, 1973; *San Francisco Chronicle & Examiner*, February 3, 1974; *Oakland Tribune*, February 3, 1974.

* * *

MOOD, John J(ordan) L(indemann) 1932-

PERSONAL: Born July 29, 1932, in Nocona, Tex.; son of Francis A. (a physician) and Emily (Jordan) Mood; married Ann Hardin, May 1952 (divorced, July, 1971): married Stephanie Lindemann (a financial consultant and poet), May, 1974; children: (first marriage) Mark, Melanie, Marcy, Michelle, Jordan. *Education:* Attended Muskogee Junior College, 1950-51; Southwestern University, B.A., 1953; Southern Methodist University, M.Th., 1956; Drew University, Ph.D., 1969. *Politics:* "Socialist-anarchist." *Religion:* "Ex-polytheist." *Home:* 1721 Donax Ave., San Diego, Calif. 92154.

CAREER: Ordained Methodist minister, 1957; minister in Carbon, Tex., 1955-56, and in Frenchtown, N.J., 1960-63; left ministry, 1969; Oklahoma College of Liberal Arts, Chickasha, minister-director of Wesley Foundation, 1956-57; University of Mississippi, Oxford, minister-director of Wesley Foundation, 1957-58: Oklahoma Department of Public Welfare, Oklahoma City, child welfare worker, 1958-60; Mercer County Community College, Trenton, N.J., instructor in liberal arts, 1963-66; Illinois Wesleyan University, Bloomington, assistant professor of humanities, 1966-68; Ball State University, Muncie, Ind., assistant professor of English, 1968-73. *Awards, honors:* American Council of Learned Societies grant, 1973, for Fifth International James Joyce Symposium in Dublin.

WRITINGS: Rilke on Love and Other Difficulties, Norton, 1975. Contributor of articles, poems, and reviews to journals, including *Western Humanities Review, Encounter, Midwest Quarterly, Village Voice*, and *Chicago Review*. Columnist for *Bucks County Gazette*, 1965-66.

WORK IN PROGRESS: With wife, Stephanie Mood, *In Celebration of Anne Sexton*, completion expected in 1975; an anthology, *Learning to Die: Readings in Death*, 1976; *Toward Orgasmic Consciousness: Essays on Sexualizing Thinking*, 1976; *Rock Music.*

SIDELIGHTS: Mood wrote: "My journey has been from religion to social concerns to philosophy to the arts. My lasting problem is the relation of art to the transformation of everyday life."

AVOCATIONAL INTERESTS: Rock music, contemporary American female poets, television, movies, psychedelic drugs, the ocean, cooking, gardening.

* * *

MOORE, Daniel G(eorge) 1899-

PERSONAL: Born March 5, 1899, in Springfield, Mo.; son of Horace Milton (a railroader) and Minnette (Goode) Moore; married Jean Cobb, January 16, 1948. *Education:* Educated in public schools in Missouri and New Mexico. *Politics:* Republican. *Religion:* Episcopalian. *Home:* 2866 East Copper St., Tucson, Ariz. 85716; (summers) 370 Park Ave., Prescott, Ariz. 86301.

CAREER: Cowboy, 1914-1917, 1919-38; Arizona State Prison, Florence, guard and dog sergeant, 1938-48; Pima

County Sheriff's Office, Tucson, Ariz., deputy sheriff, 1949; Livestock Sanitary Board of Arizona, Tucson, state livestock inspector, 1949-65. *Military service:* U.S. Army, 1917-19; became staff sergeant. *Member:* Society of Southwestern Authors, Arizona Historical Society, Mountain Oyster Club, Tucson Corral of the Westerners.

WRITINGS: Log of a Twentieth Century Cowboy, University of Arizona Press, 1965; *Enter Without Knocking*, University of Arizona Press, 1969; *Shoot Me a Biscuit: Stories of Yesteryear's Roundup Cooks*, University of Arizona Press, 1974.

AVOCATIONAL INTERESTS: Archaeology, art, prison reform, Southwest history.

* * *

MOORE, Donald Joseph 1929-

PERSONAL: Born May 11, 1929, in Flushing, N.Y.; son of Patrick William (a businessman) and Blanche Marie (Staub) Moore. *Education:* St. Peter's College, B.A., 1950; Bellarmine College, Plattsburgh, N.Y., Ph.L., 1954; Woodstock College, Woodstock, Md., S.T.L., 1961; University of Strasbourg, Dr. es Sci. Rel., 1969. *Office:* Department of Theology, Fordham University, Bronx, N.Y. 10458.

CAREER: Entered Society of Jesus (Jesuits), 1950, ordained Roman Catholic priest, 1960; high school teacher of Latin, mathematics, and science in Rochester, N.Y., 1954-57; New York Province of the Society of Jesus, Bronx, N.Y., provincial secretary, 1962-63; Fordham University, Bronx, N.Y., instructor, 1963-67, assistant professor of theology, 1969—, vice-chairman of department, 1969-71, associate director of campus ministry. Professor and member of executive council of Malcolm-King Harlem College Extension of Fordham University, Marymount Manhattan College, and College of Mount St. Vincent.

WRITINGS: Martin Buber: Prophet of Religious Secularism, Jewish Publication Society, 1975. Contributor to *America* and *Religion in Life.*

WORK IN PROGRESS: Theology of Liberation; research on religion and the experience of death and dying.

SIDELIGHTS: Moore writes: "As a theologian and a Catholic priest, I am primarily interested in the interrelation of religion, religious faith, and authentic human living."

* * *

MOORE, Edward M(umford) 1940-

PERSONAL: Born January 19, 1940, in Macon, Ga.; son of Edward M. (an executive) and Adele (Ruan) Moore; married Sally Blackmon, June 5, 1964; children: Edward Alexander, Anna Blackmon. *Education:* University of the South, B.A., 1962; University of Lille, graduate study, 1962-63; Harvard University, M.A., 1964, Ph.D., 1967. *Politics:* Democrat. *Home:* 1708 Third Ave., Grinnell, Iowa 50112. *Office:* Department of English, Grinnell College, Grinnell, Iowa 50112.

CAREER: Grinnell College, Grinnell, Iowa, instructor, 1967-68, assistant professor, 1968-72, associate professor of English, 1972—. *Member:* Modern Language Association of America. *Awards, honors:* Fulbright scholarship at University of Lille, 1962-63; Woodrow Wilson fellowship, 1963-64; National Endowment for the Humanities grant, 1970.

WRITINGS: (Editor) *More Prefaces to Shakespeare by Harley Granville-Barker*, Princeton University Press, 1974.

Contributor to *Shakespeare Quarterly, Sewanee Review*, and *Theatre Survey.*

WORK IN PROGRESS: Research on Shakespeare and on Faulkner.

AVOCATIONAL INTERESTS: Classical music, state and national politics.

* * *

MOORE, John Hammond 1924-

PERSONAL: Born October 20, 1924, in Houlton, Me.; son of Millard W. (a farmer) and Isa (Bubar) Moore. *Education:* Hamilton College, A.B., 1949; University of Virginia, M.A., 1953, Ph.D., 1961. *Home and office:* 321 C St. N.E., Washington, D.C. 20002. *Agent:* Theron Raines, 244 Madison Ave., New York, N.Y. 10016.

CAREER: Bangor Commercial, Bangor, Me., reporter, 1949-50; *Virginia Gazette*, Williamsburg, news editor, 1951-53; McGraw-Hill Book Co., New York, N.Y., associate editor, 1954-58; Winthrop College, Rock Hill, S.C., assistant professor, 1962-63, associate professor of history, 1963-65; Georgia State University, Atlanta, associate professor of history, 1965-68; Macquarie University, Sydney, Australia, senior lecturer, 1968-72. *Military service:* U.S. Navy, 1944-46.

WRITINGS: Before and After: Race Relations at the South, Louisiana State University Press, 1967; *Research Materials in South Carolina: A Guide*, University of South Carolina Press, 1967; *The American Alliance*, Cassell (Melbourne), 1971; *Juhl Letters to 'The Charleston Courier,'* University of Georgia Press, 1974; *The Young Errol: Flynn before Hollywood*, Angus & Robertson, 1975; *Albermarle: Jefferson's County, 1727-1976*, University Press of Virginia, in press. Contributor of about fifty articles to journals.

WORK IN PROGRESS: Three books, *Australians in America, 1870-1970*, for University of Queensland Press; *Distant Friendship: United States and Australia, 1898-1945*; and *Americans in Australia, 1870-1970.*

* * *

MOORE, Robert E(verett) 1914-

PERSONAL: Born March 2, 1914, in Laurel, Neb.; son of Everett Poc (a clothier) and Mary Helen (Tolles) Moore; married Marianne E. Tyler, September 29, 1933 (divorced, December, 1964); married Dolores Althea Gralak, February 13, 1965; children: (first marriage) James W., Charles E., Helen Roberta; (second marriage) Melanie A., Stanley B. *Education:* Stanford University, A.B., 1935; San Francisco State College (now San Francisco State University), M.A., 1965. *Politics:* Democrat. *Religion:* Unitarian-Universalist. *Home:* 5560 Dugan Ave., LaMesa, Calif. 92041. *Office:* Department of English, Grossmont College, El Cajon, Calif. 92020.

CAREER: Moore's Menswear, Santa Fe, N.M., salesman, 1935-41; U.S. Army, career officer in Field Artillery, 1942-62, retiring as lieutenant colonel; Grossmont College, El Cajon, Calif., instructor in English, 1965—. *Member:* American Federation of Teachers, California Community Colleges Faculty Association. *Awards, honors*—Military: Bronze Star Medal.

WRITINGS: The Bright Blue Plymouth Station Wagon (grammar text), Boyd & Fraser, 1972; *So You Want to Be a Writer*, Boyd & Fraser, 1974. Contributor to *English Journal* and *Journal of Reading.*

WORK IN PROGRESS: Nude Descending a Fire Escape, a novel; *Mind Blowers* (tentative title), a case book on literary works which present exotic ethical concepts.

* * *

MOORE, Sally Falk 1924-
PERSONAL: Born 1924, in New York, N.Y.; daughter of Henry Charles (a surgeon) and Mildred (Hymanson) Falk; married Cresap Moore (a professor of history), July 14, 1951; children: two. *Education:* Barnard College, B.A., 1943; Columbia University, LL.B., 1945, Ph.D., 1957. *Home:* 12436 Rochedale Lane, Los Angeles, Calif. 90049. *Office:* Department of Sociology and Anthropology, University of Southern California, Los Angeles, Calif. 90007.

CAREER: Spence, Hotchkiss, Parker & Duryea, New York, N.Y., associate attorney, 1945-46; staff attorney for U.S. Department of War at Nuremburg Trials in Germany, 1946; University of Southern California, Los Angeles, assistant professor, 1963-65, associate professor, 1965-67, 1969-70, professor of anthropology, 1970—, part-time lecturer in Law School, 1970—, chairman of anthropology section, department of sociology and anthropology, 1972—. Research associate, University College, University of East Africa, 1968-69, University of Dar es Salaam, 1973-74; visiting professor, Yale University, 1975-76. Member of board of directors, Social Science Research Council, 1974-76. *Member:* International African Institute, American Anthropological Association (fellow), Royal Anthropological Institute (Great Britain; fellow), Association of Social Anthropologists (United Kingdom), New York State Bar. *Awards, honors:* Postdoctoral research grant, African Studies Center, University of California at Los Angeles, 1967-68; Social Science Research Council grant, 1968-69; National Science Foundation grant, 1972-75; named honorary research fellow, University College, London, 1973-75.

WRITINGS: Power and Property in Inca Peru, Columbia University Press, 1958; (editor and contributor with B. Myerhoff) *Symbol and Politics in Communal Ideology*, Cornell University Press, in press.

Contributor: *A History of the Faculty of Political Science: The Bicentennial History of Columbia University*, Columbia University Press, 1955; J. Middleton, editor, *Myth and Cosmos*, Natural History Press, 1967; L. Nader, editor, *Law in Culture and Society*, Aldine, 1969; B. Siegel, editor, *Biennial Review of Anthropology*, Stanford University Press, 1969; M. Gluckman, editor, *The Allocation of Responsibility*, Manchester University Press, 1972; P. B. Hammond, editor, *Cultural and Social Anthropology: Selected Readings*, Macmillan, 1975; *Ethnographic Survey of Africa*, International African Institute (London), in press. Contributor to *American Anthropologist, Law and Society Review, Africa, Current Anthropology*, and other publications.

WORK IN PROGRESS: Legal Norms and Their Transformations, general essays on law and anthropology, to include both new and reprinted material, for Routledge & Kegan Paul; *Social Facts and Social Fabrications: Essays on Chagga Law*, for International African Institute, London; editing, with B. Myerhoff, a volume of essays, *Secular Ritual*.

* * *

MOORSTEEN, Richard H. 1926(?)-1975
1926(?)—April 11, 1975; American economist, State De-

partment official, expert on foreign affairs, and author of books on economics and foreign policy. Obituaries: *New York Times*, April 14, 1975; *Washington Post*, April 15, 1975.

* * *

MORAMARCO, Fred Stephen 1938-
PERSONAL: Born July 13, 1938, in New York; son of Stephen (a laborer) and Nina (Toriello) Moramarco; married Sheila Sobell (a writer), August 15, 1964; children: Stephen, Nicholas. *Education:* Long Island University, B.A., 1964; University of Utah, M.A., 1966, Ph.D., 1969. *Politics:* Democrat. *Home:* 8015 Rainey St., LaMesa, Calif. 92041. *Office:* School of Literature, San Diego State University, San Diego, Calif. 92182.

CAREER: University of Utah, Salt Lake City, instructor in English, 1968-69; San Diego State University, San Diego, Calif., assistant professor, 1969-71, associate professor of literature, 1971—, director of School of Literature, 1974—. Fulbright lecturer at Universita Cattolica di Sacro Cuore, 1973; lecturer in Italy for U.S. Information Service, 1973. *Member:* Modern Language Association of America, American Studies Association, United Professors of California.

WRITINGS: Edward Dahlberg, Twayne, 1972. Contributor of about thirty articles and reviews to literature journals, including *Western Humanities Review, Tri-Quarterly, American Literature, Mid-Continent American Studies Journal, Mosaic, Paideuma, Nation*, and *Utah Papers in Language and Literature*. Associate editor of *Western Humanities Review*, 1967-70.

WORK IN PROGRESS: Grappling with the Cantos, a study of Ezra Pound's major poem; research on relationships between contemporary painting and poetry.

* * *

MOREHEAD, Joe 1931-
PERSONAL: Born January 30, 1931, in New York, N.Y.; son of Joseph H. and Irma (Gray) Morehead; married Bebe Ann Behnke, September 4, 1966; children: Adam Gray. *Education:* Trinity College, Hartford, Conn., B.A., 1952; Columbia University, M.A., 1955; University of Kentucky, M.L.S., 1964; University of California, Berkeley, Ph.D., 1973. *Office:* School of Library and Information Science, State University of New York at Albany, Albany, N.Y. 12222.

CAREER: Orlando Junior College, Orlando, Fla., instructor in English, 1954-56; U.S. Department of Air Force, education director in London, England, 1957-62; San Francisco Public Library, San Francisco, Calif., documents librarian, 1964-70; State University of New York at Albany, assistant professor of library and information science, 1970—. Library consultant to Mark Hopkins College and New York State Library. *Military service:* U.S. Air Force, 1952-54; became first lieutenant. *Member:* American Library Association, American Academy of Political and Social Science, Government Documents Round Table, New York Library Association, Phi Beta Kappa (charter member of Alpha Alpha chapter).

WRITINGS: (Contributor) Bill Katz, editor, *Magazines for Libraries*, Bowker, 2nd edition (Morehead was not associated with first edition), 1972; (editor) *Albany Municipal Documents: A Directory of Sources* (booklet), School of Library and Information Science, State University of New

York at Albany, 1974; *Introduction to United States Public Documents*, Libraries Unlimited, 1975.

Author of "U.S. Government Documents: A Mazeway Miscellany," a column in *Reference Quarterly*, 1968—. Contributor of about eighty articles and reviews to *Synergy, Bulletin of Bibliography, Reference Quarterly, Journal of Education for Librarianship, College Student Journal, Library Journal, Government Publications Review*, and *American Reference Books Annual*. Member of editorial advisory board of *Index to U.S. Government Periodicals*.

WORK IN PROGRESS: Research on access and use of documents collections in the National Archives.

SIDELIGHTS: Morehead writes: "Without access to the public records of government, democratic policies give way to cynicism and mistrust. My teaching and research are devoted to an explication of government decision-making through the symbolic forms of public documents."

*   *   *

MORENO, Martin
     See SWARTZ, Harry (Felix)

*   *   *

MORGAN, Helen (Gertrude Louise)   1921-

PERSONAL: Born April 11, 1921, in Ilford, Essex, England; daughter of Herbert (a builder) and Sarah Ann (Hotchkiss) Axford; married Tudor Meredydd Morgan, May 15, 1954; children: Sian Margaret, Megan Nansi, Bronwen Delydd Elizabeth. *Education:* Attended Royal Normal College and Academy of Music for the Blind, 1938-42. *Residence:* Carmarthen, Wales. *Office:* c/o Barclays Bank, the Pantiles, Tunbridge Wells, Kent, England.

CAREER: Children's author. *Member:* Society of Authors.

WRITINGS—Children's books: *The Little Old Lady*, Faber, 1961; *Tales of Tigg's Farm*, Faber, 1963; *Meet Mary Kate*, Faber, 1963; *A Mouthful of Magic*, Harrap, 1963; *Two in the Garden*, Brockhampton Press, 1964; *The Tailor, the Sailor and the Small Black Cat*, Thomas Nelson, 1964; *Two in the House*, Brockhampton Press, 1965; *A Dream of Dragons*, Faber, 1965; *Two on the Farm*, Brockhampton Press, 1966; *Satchkin Patchkin*, Faber, 1966, Macrae, 1970; *Two by the Sea*, Brockhampton Press, 1967; *Mary Kate and the Jumble Bear*, Faber, 1967; *Mrs. Pinny and the Blowing Day*, Faber, 1968; *Mrs. Pinny and the Sudden Snow*, Faber, 1969; *Mary Kate and the School Bus*, Faber, 1970, published as *Mary Kate*, Thomas Nelson, 1972; *Mother Farthing's Luck*, Faber, 1971; *Mrs. Pinny and the Salty Sea Day*, Faber, 1972. Contributor to magazines.

WORK IN PROGRESS: Death of a Cat, a detective story; *The Private World of Mrs. Wilmington*, a novel; "A Family House," a television play; *A Little Candle*, a collection of poetry.

*   *   *

MORGAN-GRENVILLE, Gerard (Wyndham)   1931-
     (George Ross)

PERSONAL: Born March 26, 1931, in Sussex, England; son of Robert William (an engineer) and Elizabeth (Renshaw) Morgan-Grenville; married Virginia Peto, April 27, 1955; children: Hugo, Laura, George. *Education:* Eton College, A.A., 1949. *Politics:* Independent. *Religion:* Church of England. *Home and office:* Burgate House, Hascombe, Godalming, Surrey, England.

CAREER: Export manager and sales director, Flexible Drives Ltd., 1953-56; Dexam International, Haslemere, England, director, 1956—, director of office in Paris, France, 1963—, and of Dexam International Holdings in Haslemere, 1969—. Director of Goodwood Metalcraft, 1963—; chairman of National Centre for Alternative Technology. *Military service:* British Army, 1950-53; became captain. *Member:* Society for Environmental Improvement (president).

WRITINGS: Barging into France, David & Charles, 1972; *Barging into Southern France*, David & Charles, 1973; *Holiday Cruising in France*, David & Charles, 1973; *Barging into Burgundy*, David & Charles, 1974; *Cruising the Sahara*, David & Charles, 1974. Contributor to magazines; author of articles on design under pseudonym George Ross.

SIDELIGHTS: Morgan-Grenville writes that his principal interests include ". . . conservation of normal resources, conservation of our architectural heritage, promotion of the concept of greater personal freedom and public responsibility, . . . abolition of non-automated mass-production methods, . . . the suppression of all bureaucracies, . . . discarding needless or hazardous technologies. . . ."

*   *   *

MORREALE, Ben   1924-

PERSONAL: Born April 10, 1924, in New York, N.Y.; son of Marco (a laborer) and Teresa (Melluzzo) Morreale; married Anita Liebowitz (a teacher). *Education:* Brooklyn College (now of the City University of New York), B.A., 1950; Columbia University, graduate study, 1951; University of Paris, D.Phil., 1956. *Home address:* P.O. Box 21, Adamant, Vt. *Office:* Department of History, State University of New York College at Plattsburgh, Plattsburgh, N.Y. 12901.

CAREER: American School, Paris, France, teacher, 1953-55; International Business Machines (IBM), New York, N.Y., historical consultant, 1958; Goddard College, Plainfield, Vt., instructor in history, 1959-62; State University of New York College at Plattsburgh, assistant professor, 1963-65, associate professor, 1965-69, professor of history, 1969—. *Military service:* U.S. Army Air Forces, 1942-45. *Member:* American Historical Association, Society for French Studies, Tom Paine Society.

WRITINGS: The Seventh Saracen (novel), Coward, 1958; *Down and Out in Academia* (nonfiction), Pitman, 1972; *A Few Virtuous Men* (novel), Tundra Books, 1973. Contributor of stories and articles to *Paris Review, Encounter, Antioch Review*, and *Les Annales de la Revolution Francaise*.

WORK IN PROGRESS: A novel of Sicily and America; a book on the relationship between films and history.

SIDELIGHTS: Morreale spent his childhood in Sicily.

*   *   *

MORRELL, David   1943-

PERSONAL: Born April 24, 1943, in Kitchener, Ontario, Canada; son of George Morrell (an Air Force instructor) and Beatrice (Markle) Morrell Bamberger; married Donna Maziarz, 1965; children: Sarie, Matthew. *Education:* University of Waterloo, B.A., 1966; Pennsylvania State University, M.A., 1967, Ph.D., 1970. *Religion:* Roman Catholic. *Agent:* Henry Morrison, Inc., 58 West 10th Ave., New York, N.Y. 10011. *Office:* Department of English, University of Iowa, Iowa City, Iowa 52240.

CAREER: University of Iowa, Iowa City, assistant professor, 1970-74, associate professor of American literature, 1974—. *Awards, honors:* Distinguished recognition award from Friends of American Writers, 1973, for *First Blood.*

WRITINGS—Novels: *First Blood*, M. Evans, 1972; *Testament*, M. Evans, 1975. Contributor to *Ellery Queen's Mystery Magazine, Journal of General Education,* and *Bulletin of the Midwest Modern Language Association.*

WORK IN PROGRESS: John Barth: An Introduction.

SIDELIGHTS: Morrell is a graduate of the National Outdoor Leadership School, a mountain training school in Wyoming.

* * *

MORRIS, Adalaide K(irby)   1942-

PERSONAL: Born July 17, 1942, in Chicago, Ill.; daughter of Davis Greene and Adalaide (Ball) Kirby; married David Brown Morris (a professor), June 26, 1965; children: Ellen Greene. *Education:* Wells College, B.A. (magna cum laude), 1964; University of Minnesota, M.A., 1966, Ph.D., 1971. *Home:* 627 Bradley St., Iowa City, Iowa 52240. *Office:* Department of English, University of Iowa, Iowa City, Iowa 52242.

CAREER: University of Virginia, Charlottesville, lecturer in English, 1971; lived in London, 1971-73; Georgetown University, Washington, D.C., assistant professor of English, 1973-74; University of Iowa, Iowa City, assistant professor of English, 1974—. Member of board of directors of Women's Resource and Action Center. *Member:* Modern Language Association of America, Phi Beta Kappa.

WRITINGS: Wallace Stevens: Imagination and Faith, Princeton University Press, 1974.

WORK IN PROGRESS: Research on modern poetry and poetics, and on feminism and feminist aesthetics.

* * *

MORRIS, Kenneth T(hompson)   1941-

PERSONAL: Born January 11, 1941, in Gary, Ind.; son of Robert W. (an electrician) and Phyllis (a postal clerk; maiden name, Thompson) Morris; married Judy Vance, August 5, 1967 (divorced, 1975); children: Kevin, Lisa. *Education:* Lewis College, B.A., 1963; Bradley University, M.A., 1965; Purdue University, Ph.D., 1968. *Home:* 1509 Granger, Mount Pleasant, Mich. 48858. *Office:* Counseling Center, Central Michigan University, Mount Pleasant, Mich. 48859.

CAREER: Akron University, Akron, Ohio, counselor, 1967-68; Central Michigan University, Mount Pleasant, associate professor of counseling and counselor at Counseling Center, 1968—. Consultant to Michigan Department of Vocational Rehabilitation. *Member:* American Personnel and Guidance Association, American College Personnel Association, American Psychological Association, Association of Specialists in Group Work, Michigan College Counselors Association (executive secretary of executive board, 1971-73).

WRITINGS: (With Kenneth M. Cinnamon) *A Handbook of Verbal Group Exercises*, C. C Thomas, 1975; (with Cinnamon) *A Handbook of Non-Verbal Group Exercises*, C. C Thomas, 1975; (with H. E. Kanitz) *Rational Emotive Psychotherapy*, Houghton, 1975; (editor with Cinnamon) *Controversial Issues in Human Relations Training Groups*, C. C Thomas, 1975.

WORK IN PROGRESS: The Resident Assistants Manual of Intervention Techniques.

AVOCATIONAL INTERESTS: Bridge, pool, golf, crossword puzzles, reading, and "almost all varieties of music."

* * *

MORRIS, Margaret Francine   1938-

PERSONAL: Born June 26, 1938, in Gilmer, Tex.; daughter of Gus S. (an attorney) and Margaret (a teacher; maiden name, Aldredge) Morris. *Education:* University of Texas at Austin, B.A., 1961; East Texas State University, M.S. in L.S., 1964. *Politics:* Independent. *Religion:* Episcopalian. *Residence:* Washington, D.C. *Office:* Library, University of Texas, Arlington, Tex. 76019.

CAREER: Texas State Library, Austin, Tex., bookmobile librarian, 1964; University of Texas at Arlington, assistant reference librarian, 1964-66, head of reference, 1966-72, curator of Special Collections, 1972—, currently on leave for graduate study. *Member:* American Library Association, American Association of University Professors, American Library Association of University Women, Western History Association, Southwest Library Association, Texas Library Association, Texas State Historical Association, Society of Southwest Archivists, Sherlock Holmes Society of London, Red Circle of Washington, Crew of the Barque "Lone Star".

WRITINGS: (Editor) *Essays on the Gilded Age*, University of Texas Press, 1973; (editor with Sandra L. Myres) *Essays on American Foreign Policy*, University of Texas Press, 1974; (editor with Elliott West) *Essays on Urban America*, University of Texas Press, 1975.

WORK IN PROGRESS: Articles for *Baker Street Journal.*

AVOCATIONAL INTERESTS: Reading Sherlock Holmes and medieval literature; collecting comic book titles and author/title combinations; enjoying legal and literary humor; Southwestern bibliography; needlepoint.

* * *

MORRIS, Milton D(onald)   1939-

PERSONAL: Born September 12, 1939, in Trelawny, Jamaica; son of Charles and Olga C. (Lunan) Morris; married to wife Merrillie, August 25, 1964; children: Marcia D., Marlene D. *Education:* Columbia Union College, B.A., 1964; University of Maryland, M.A., 1966, Ph.D., 1970. *Religion:* Seventh-Day Adventist. *Home:* 208 Wedgewood Lane, Carbondale, Ill. 62901. *Office:* Department of Political Science, Southern Illinois University, Carbondale, Ill. 62901.

CAREER: Columbia Union College, Takoma Park, Md., part-time instructor in political science, 1967-70; Southern Illinois University, Carbondale, assistant professor, 1970-73, associate professor of political science, 1973—. Visiting associate professor at Howard University, and public policy fellow at Joint Center for Political Studies, both 1974-75. *Member:* American Political Science Association, National Conference of Black Political Scientists, Midwest Political Science Association.

WRITINGS: *The Politics of Black America: An Annotated Bibliography*, Public Affairs Research Bureau, Southern Illinois University, 1971; (contributor) *Introduction to Black America*, Southern Illinois University Press, 1974; *The Politics of Black America*, Harper, 1975; *The A-95 Review Process: Making It Work for Minority Groups*, Joint Center for Political Studies, Washington, D.C., 1975; *The Housing and Community Development Act of 1974: A Review and Preliminary Evaluation*, Joint Center for Political Studies, Washington, D.C., in press. Contributor to political science and public affairs journals.

WORK IN PROGRESS: *Federal Policy Making for Community Development*; research on community development and the changing face of American federalism; research on the affirmative action dilemma in implementing equal opportunity.

* * *

MORRISON, Denton E(dward) 1932-

PERSONAL: Born in 1932. *Education:* South Dakota State University, B.S., 1954, M.S., 1958; University of Wisconsin, Ph.D., 1962. *Office:* Department of Sociology, Michigan State University, East Lansing, Mich. 48824.

CAREER: University of California, Berkeley, assistant professor of sociology, 1962-64; Michigan State University, East Lansing, assistant professor, 1964-67, associate professor, 1967-71, professor of sociology, 1971— . Researcher at Michigan Agricultural Experiment Station, 1964— .

WRITINGS: (With G. A. Kristjanson) *Personal Adjustment Among Older Persons* (bulletin), Agricultural Experiment Station, South Dakota State University, 1958; (editor with Dale Hathaway, James Shaffer, and Richard Feltner, and contributor) *Michigan Farmers in the Mid-Sixties: A Survey of Their Views of Marketing Problems and Organizations* (bulletin), Agricultural Experiment Station, Michigan State University, 1966; (with Patricia Phillips) *A Silent Minority: A Research Feasibility Probe of Discontent Among the Rural Poor* (pamphlet), Rural Manpower Center, Michigan State University, 1970; (editor) *Farmers' Organizations and Farmers' Movements: Research Needs and a Bibliography of the United States and Canada* (bulletin), Agricultural Experiment Station, Michigan State University, 1970; (editor with Ramon E. Henkel) *The Significance Test Controversy*, Aldine, 1970; *A Directory of Environmental Organizations*, Environmental Resources, 1971; (compiler with Kenneth E. Hornback and W. Keith Warner) *Environment: A Bibliography of Social Science and Related Literature*, U.S. Government Printing Office, 1974; (editor) *Energy: A Bibliography of Social Science and Related Literature*, Garland Publishing, 1975; (editor with Hornback) *Collective Behavior: A Draft Bibliography*, Garland Publishing, in press.

Contributor: James Copp, editor, *Projection Papers: Orientations for Rural Sociological Research and Action*, Rural Sociological Society, 1964; William Burch, Neil Cheek, and Lee Taylor, editors, *Social Behavior, Natural Resources, and the Environment*, Harper, 1972; Robert Evans, editor, *Readings in Social Movements*, Rand McNally, 1973; Zaltman and other editors, *Processes and Phenomena of Social Change*, Wiley, 1973; Evans, editor, *Social Movements*, Rand McNally, 1973; A. Murch, editor, *Environmental Concern*, MSS Educational Publishing, 1974; Marcello Truzzi, editor, *Sociology for Pleasure*, Prentice-Hall, 1974; Arthur Shostak, editor, *Sociology and Personal Life*, Macmillan, in press; Robert B. Smith, editor, *Social Science Methods*, Free Press, in press. Contributor to journals in his field.

WORK IN PROGRESS: *Stratification and Risk Taking: A Further Negative Replication of Cancian's Theory*, with Krishna Kumar, Everett Rogers, and Frederick Fliegel; research on declining resources, discontent, and some imperatives for the future; research on attitude structure of social movement participants; research on the role of public opinion in social movement evolution.

* * *

MORRISON, James L(unsford), Jr. 1923-

PERSONAL: Born December 16, 1923, in Petersburg, Va.; son of James L. and Maria Brander (Wyatt) Morrison; married Jane Carol Brown, June 12, 1947; children: Jane Brander, Anne Phillips (Mrs. Douglas S. Becker), James E. B. *Education:* Virginia Military Institute, B.A., 1947; University of Virginia, M.A., 1960; Columbia University, Ph.D., 1970. *Politics:* Independent. *Religion:* Presbyterian. *Home address:* R.D. 1, Box 137, Thomasville, Pa. 17364. *Office:* Department of History, York College of Pennsylvania, York, Pa. 17405.

CAREER: U.S. Army, career officer in Cavalry and Armor Branches, 1947-71, instructor in history at U.S. Military Academy, 1961-62, assistant professor, 1962-64, associate professor, 1966-71, retiring as colonel; York College of Pennsylvania, York, associate professor of history, 1971— . *Member:* Organization of American Historians, American Military Institute, National Wildlife Federation, American Horse Protective Association, Pennsylvania Historical Association. *Awards, honors*—Military: Legion of Merit, Air Medal, Bronze Star.

WRITINGS: *The Memoirs of Henry Heth*, Greenwood Press, 1974; (editor) *The Presidential Crisis*, York College of Pennsylvania, 1974. Contributor to *Military Affairs* and *Civil War History*.

WORK IN PROGRESS: "Sectionalism versus Nationalism at Antebellum West Point," an article to be included in a Civil War anthology, edited by John Hubbell, for Greenwood Press.

AVOCATIONAL INTERESTS: Horsemanship and riding (owns a horse; played polo at Virginia Military Institute).

BIOGRAPHICAL/CRITICAL SOURCES: *Virginia Military Institute Alumni Review*, spring, 1974.

* * *

MORRISS, James E(dward) 1932-

PERSONAL: Born February 9, 1932, in Oklahoma City, Okla.; son of William Jacob (a farmer) and Anna Ellen Morriss. *Education:* John Brown University, B.A. and B.S., 1952; City University of New York, Graduate School of Education, M.A., 1963; further graduate study at New School for Social Research and New York University, 1968. *Home:* Oak Beach, N.Y. 11702. *Office:* Division Avenue High School, Levittown, N.Y. 11756.

CAREER: High school teacher of life sciences in public schools of Levittown, N.Y., 1958— , presently teaching courses he designed in ecology, human behavior, animal behavior and parapsychology at Division Avenue High School. Member of environmental advisory board, Town of Babylon, N.Y. *Member:* National Audubon Society, American Society for Psychical Research, American Museum of Natural History, New York Zoological Society.

Awards, honors: The Brains of Animals and Man was named one of five best nonfiction books of the year by *School Library Journal*, 1972.

WRITINGS—With Russell Freedman: *How Animals Learn*, Holiday House, 1969; *Animal Instincts*, Holiday House, 1970; *The Brains of Animals and Man* (Junior Literary Guild selection), Holiday House, 1972. Director of research, National Broadcasting Co. television series, "Animal Secrets," 1966-67.

WORK IN PROGRESS: A book for young adults, *Man's Mysterious Mind*; developing a teaching module on parapsychology for the Human Behavior Curriculum Project, possibly funded by National Science Foundation.

SIDELIGHTS: Morriss wrote: "Growing up in the country (Ozark Mountains) gave me a special reverence for nature. To sustain this sacred communion with the out-of-doors I divide my time between a cabin in the wooded hills of New England and my home on an almost deserted stretch of beach on the Atlantic Coast. I find these sanctuaries conducive to writing.... My present focus of attention is on describing the advances being made by scientists in understanding the dimensions of consciousness, and the potential of the human mind."

Morriss has tamed and trained a variety of animals. He and his high school students even taught a pet chicken to play baseball.

* * *

MORSE, Edward Lewis 1942-

PERSONAL: Born January 5, 1942, in Brooklyn, N.Y.; son of Jonah Benjamin (in advertising) and Rebecca (in exporting; maiden name, Freiberg) Morse; married Linda Kasle (a university administrator), August 15, 1965; children: Michael Ari, Molly Rachel. *Education:* Johns Hopkins University, A.B. (with honors), 1963; Johns Hopkins School of Advanced International Studies, M.A. (with distinction), 1966; Princeton University, Ph.D., 1969. *Politics:* Democrat. *Religion:* Jewish. *Office:* Council on Foreign Relations, 58 East 68th St., New York, N.Y. 10021.

CAREER: Princeton University, Woodrow Wilson School of Public and International Affairs, Princeton, N.J., assistant professor of politics and international affairs, 1969-74, associate and member of policy committee of Center for International Studies, 1969-74; Council on Foreign Relations, New York, N.Y., senior research fellow, 1974—. Member of City University of New York Faculty Colloquium on European Communities and Colloquium on Political Economy; Columbia University Seminar on the Atlantic Community; International Institute for Strategic Studies (London); International Political Economy Studies Group (London); Lehrman Institute; member of Atlantic studies committee of Atlantic Council.

MEMBER: International Studies Association, American Political Science Association, Phi Beta Kappa. *Awards, honors:* John Nobel fellowship, 1964-65, and Italian Government fellowship, 1965-66, both for study in Italy; North Atlantic Treaty Organization postdoctoral fellowship, 1971-72, fellowship and travel grant, 1974; international affairs fellowship from Council on Foreign Relations, 1971-72.

WRITINGS: A Comparative Approach to the Study of Foreign Policy: Notes on Theorizing (monograph), Center of International Studies, Princeton University, 1971; *Defense Autonomy in Gaullist France: Welfare Versus Warfare and the Dilemma of Insufficient Resources* (booklet),

General Learning Press, 1972; *Foreign Policy and Interdependence in Gaullist France*, Princeton University Press, 1973; *Modernization and the New Diplomacy*, Free Press, in press.

Contributor: Robert O. Keohane and Joseph S. Nye, Jr., editors, *Transnational Relations and World Politics*, Harvard University Press, 1972; Raymond Tanter and Richard H. Ullman, editors, *Theory and Policy in International Relations*, Princeton University Press, 1972; Wolfram Hanreider, editor, *The United States and Western Europe: Political, Economic, and Strategic Perspectives*, Winthrop, 1974; I. William Zartman, editor, *The Analysis of Negotiation*, Anchor Books, in press; James Rosenau, Kenneth Thompson, and Gavin Boyd, editors, *World Politics*, Free Press, in press.

Contributor of articles and reviews to *World Politics, Journal of International Affairs, International Organization, Mercurio, Revue Francaise de Science Politique, American Political Science Review, Foreign Affairs,* and *World Today.* Associate editor of *World Politics,* 1970-75; member of editorial board of *Sage International Yearbook of Foreign Policy Studies,* 1972—.

WORK IN PROGRESS: Contributions to *Comparative Foreign Economic Policy,* edited by Wilfrid Kohl, *French Foreign Policy after de Gaulle,* edited by Bruce Marshall, and *Economics, Technology, and Foreign Policy,* edited by Robert Bauer.

* * *

MORSE, Roger A(lfred) 1927-

PERSONAL: Born July 5, 1927, in Saugerties, N.Y.; son of Grant D. (a superintendent of schools) and Margery A. (a teacher; maiden name, Saxe) Morse; married Mary Lou Smith, October 6, 1951; children: Joseph G., Susan A., Mary Ann. *Education:* Cornell University, B.S., 1950, M.S., 1953, Ph.D., 1955. *Politics:* Republican. *Home:* 425 Hanshaw Rd., Ithaca, N.Y. 14850. *Agent:* Frieda Fishbein, 353 West 57th St., New York, N.Y. 10019. *Office:* Department of Entomology, Cornell University, Ithaca, N.Y. 14853.

CAREER: State Plant Board of Florida, Gainesville, apiculturist, 1955-57; University of Massachusetts, Field Station, Amherst, assistant professor of horticulture, 1957; Cornell University, Ithaca, N.Y., assistant professor, 1957-64, associate professor, 1964-70, professor of apiculture, 1970—. Guest lecturer at colleges and universities. Former volunteer fire chief, presently volunteer fireman; member of Tompkins County Fair Board; member of Tompkins County Board of Representatives. *Military service:* U.S. Army, 1944-47; became staff sergeant.

MEMBER: International Union for the Study of Social Insects, Entomological Society of America, Bee Research Association, American Association for the Advancement of Science (fellow), Philippine Association of Entomologists, Eastern Apicultural Society, Florida Entomological Society, Sigma Xi, Delta Sigma Rho, Rotary International (Ithaca section). *Awards, honors:* Travel grants from National Science Foundation, 1961, 1965, 1969, and U.S. Army, 1966.

WRITINGS: The Complete Guide to Beekeeping, Dutton, 1972, revised edition, 1974; *Bees and Beekeeping,* Comstock, 1975; (contributor) Eva Crane, editor, *Honey,* Bee Research Association, 1975; (editor) *Pests, Predators, and Diseases of Honey Bees,* Cornell University Press, in press. Contributor of hundreds of articles to conservation, natural history, and beekeeping journals. Research editor of *Gleanings in Bee Culture*, 1959—.

WORK IN PROGRESS: Reproduction in Honey Bees.

SIDELIGHTS: Morse conducted a research study in the Far East in 1966 and 1968; he has made four European tours, and study trips to Brazil in 1972 and the Dominican Republic in 1974. He holds a U.S. patent on a method of making wine from honey. *Avocational interests:* Farming.

* * *

MORTIMER, Penelope (Ruth) 1918-
(Penelope Dimont, Ann Temple)

PERSONAL: Born September 19, 1918, in Rhyl, North Wales; daughter of A. F. G. (a clergyman) and Amy Caroline Fletcher; married Charles Dimont, 1937 (divorced, 1949); married John Clifford Mortimer (playwright and lawyer), 1949 (divorced, 1972); children: (first marriage) Madelon Lee, Caroline, Julia, Deborah; (second marriage) Sally, Jeremy. *Education:* Attended University of London. *Home:* 134 Loudon Rd., London N.W.8, England. *Agent:* Georges Borchardt, 145 East 52nd St., New York, N.Y. 10022; Deborah Rogers, 29 Goodge St., London W.1, England.

CAREER: The Observer, London, England, film critic, 1967-70. Lecturer, New School for Social Research and Boston University, 1975-76. *Member:* Royal Society of Literature (fellow).

WRITINGS—Novels, except as indicated: *A Villa in Summer*, M. Joseph, 1954, Harcourt, 1955; *The Bright Prison*, M. Joseph, 1956, Harcourt, 1957; (with John Clifford Mortimer) *With Love and Lizards* (travel), M. Joseph, 1957; *Daddy's Gone A-Hunting*, M. Joseph, 1958, published as *Cave of Ice*, Harcourt, 1959; *Saturday Lunch With the Brownings* (short stories), Hutchinson, 1960, McGraw, 1961; *The Pumpkin Eater*, Hutchinson, 1962, McGraw, 1963; *My Friend Says It's Bullet-Proof*, Hutchinson, 1967, Random House, 1968; *The Home*, Hutchinson, 1971, Random House, 1972; *Long Distance*, Doubleday, 1974.

Under name Penelope Dimont: *Johanna* (novel), Secker and Warburg, 1947.

Author of television adaptation of Colette's *Ripening Seed*, for British Broadcasting Corp., and other television plays; author of three screenplays, including "Bunny Lake Is Missing," with John Clifford Mortimer, Columbia Pictures, 1965, and "The Apple Tree" (based on John Galsworthy's story of the same name), for Metro-Goldwyn-Mayer. Former columnist, under pseudonym Ann Temple, for *Daily Mail* (London). Regular contributor of short stories to *New Yorker* and of reviews to *Sunday Times* (London) and other newspapers.

WORK IN PROGRESS: About Time, "an aspect of autobiography."

SIDELIGHTS: David Galloway notes in the *Spectator*: "The dry precision and incisive economy of Penelope Mortimer's prose clearly establish her as one of the most outstanding contemporary novelists—not that her methods are in any way inventive or unique, but they are distinctively shaped by an intelligence and compassion which seem continuously to extend the carefully circumscribed horizons of her novels." Doris Grumbach writes: "*Long Distance* rises above a single view to become a multilayered pure pleasure on its own inscrutable terms . . . I predict [it] will

gather friends . . . and remain among the books our grandchildren (if they are still literate and the art of the printed word does not disappear under the fierce light of the raytheon tube) will read."

The Pumpkin Eater was adapted as a film by Harold Pinter; a series of television plays adapted from *Saturday Lunch with the Brownings* is scheduled for production by ATV (Independent Television) in 1976.

BIOGRAPHICAL/CRITICAL SOURCES: Carolyn Riley, editor, *Contemporary Literary Criticism*, Gale, 1976.

* * *

MORTON, Donald E(dward) 1938-

PERSONAL: Born June 22, 1938, in Forest Glade, Tex.; son of Edward Everett (a tailor) and Velma Roberta (Jackson) Morton; married Karen Bedney, August 9, 1970; children: Samantha Jane, Benjamin Wesley. *Education:* Rice University, B.A. (cum laude), 1961; Johns Hopkins University, M.A., 1963, Ph.D., 1972. *Residence:* Syracuse, N.Y. *Office:* Humanities Doctoral Program, 416 Hall of Languages, Syracuse University, Syracuse, N.Y. 13210.

CAREER: Syracuse University, Syracuse, N.Y., lecturer, 1966-71, assistant professor, 1971-74, associate professor of English, 1974—, director of humanities doctoral program, 1974—. *Member:* Modern Language Association of America, College English Association, American Association of University Professors, Northeast Modern Language Association. *Awards, honors:* Younger Humanist Fellowship from National Endowment for the Humanities, 1973-74.

WRITINGS: Vladimir Nabokov, Ungar, 1974. Contributor to scholarly journals.

WORK IN PROGRESS: A book on the literary use of the aphorism in the works of Romantic and Victorian writers; a critical reading of the works of George Meredith, completion expected in 1977; editing an anthology on aphorism as a literary genre, with Gerhard Neumann, and translating articles for the anthology.

* * *

MOSER, Norman Calvin 1931-

PERSONAL: Born October 15, 1931, in Durham, N.C.; son of William M. (a barber; also in real estate) and Myrtle (Jordan) Moser. *Education:* Attended University of Maryland campus in Ulm, Germany, 1955-56, College of the Pacific (now University), 1957; San Francisco State College (now University), B.A., 1961, M.A., 1966; graduate study at University of Washington, 1962, and University of British Columbia, 1963. *Politics:* Independent or Democrat ("Peace & Freedom"). *Religion:* "Informal" Zen Buddhist. *Home:* 1341 Chester Rd., Raleigh, N.C. 27702. *Office:* Illuminations Press, 1007-A North Greensboro St., Carrboro, N.C. 27510.

CAREER: Professional singer, 1950-53, continuing to entertain while in U.S. Air Force Special Services, 1953-56; *Bay Window* (later *Bay Area Arts Review*), San Francisco, Calif., co-publisher and writer, 1957-59; Arthur Little, Inc., San Francisco, research assistant, 1963-64; Illuminations Press, Carrboro, N.C., editor and publisher, 1965—; poet, author. Instructor at University of California at Berkeley, Downtown Extension, San Francisco, 1967-68, and University of Arizona, Tucson, 1969; instructor of informal correspondence course in writing, under auspices of P.E.N., 1975—. Has directed four plays, including "No Exit," at College of the Pacific, and "Dona Engracia's

Wake," at Forge Theatre, Santa Fe, N.M.; actor in plays and films. *Military service:* U.S. Air Force, 1953-56. *Member:* Coordinating Council of Literary Magazines, Committee of Small Magazine Editors and Publishers, Alpha Phi Gamma. *Awards, honors:* Grants from Coordinating Council of Literary Magazines, 1967, 1971, 1974, from P.E.N., 1972, 1974, 1975.

WRITINGS: "Travelin Man" (one-act play), first produced in San Francisco, Calif., at Theatre for the World, 1959; *Jumpsongs*, Gar Press, 1973; *A Shaman's Song Book: Poems, Songs and Tales*, Thorp Springs Press, 1975. Work is included in anthologies: *The Living Underground: Anthology of Contemporary Poetry*, edited by Hugh Fox, Whitston, 1973; *The Living Underground: Anthology of Prose Fiction*, edited by Fox, Whitston, 1975; *New Southern Poets*, edited by Guy Owen and Mary Williams, University of North Carolina Press, 1975.

Theatre and film critic, *Activities* Magazine (Bay area), 1958-59; West Coast columnist, *Off Broadway*, 1961-62, and *East Village Other*, 1966-68; contributing editor, *Grande Ronde Review*, 1972-73; contributing editor, *The Gar*, 1972-73, staff writer, 1973-74. Contributor to about seventy-five magazines and papers, including *Spero, Synapse, Wild Dog, Fiddlehead, December, Hyperion, Second Coming, Ante, Vagabond*, and *Red Clay Reader #5*.

WORK IN PROGRESS: A book of poems, *South by Southwest*, completion expected in 1975; two short novels, *The Arena* and *Ritual of Stone*, 1975; short fiction, *The Bicycle*, 1975; a book-length essay on Zen, poetry, love, and other topics, *Mysticism from the Inside Out*, 1976 or 1977; various plays.

SIDELIGHTS: Moser told *CA:* "I came to my senses (awakened) circa 1955-56 in Ulm, Germany while in U.S.A.F. Two years later was student of writing in Frisco. I see poetry, fiction, etc., as a form of prophecy and myself as a visionary in a shamanistic sense: healer of the Soul, Spirit, whatever, Leader of Rituals. Love hiking, meditation, jazz, theatre, and women. Speak German fluently, can get about in French and Spanish. Been all over Europe, Canada, Mexico, *love* Mexico City, Cuernavaca, etc. Quite fond of Chicanos, Mexicans, Indians, Blacks, etc. In fact, Anglos are the only group I don't get on well with often."

BIOGRAPHICAL/CRITICAL SOURCES: Durham Herald, July 8, 1973, September 9, 1973; *Berkeley Samisdat Review*, fall, 1973; *Ally*, December, 1973.

* * *

MOSES, Gerald Robert 1938-

PERSONAL: Born June 7, 1938, in Chicago, Ill.; son of Gerald Charles (an executive) and Eleanor (Buckley) Moses; married Karen Ann Demes, September 2, 1961; children: Gerald Raymond, Jill Ellen. *Education:* St. Mary-of-the-Lake Seminary, Chicago, Ill., B.S., 1961; Western Michigan University, M.A., 1965; Ohio State University, Ph.D., 1969. *Home:* 907 Pleasant Dr., Ypsilanti, Mich. 48197. *Office:* Department of Special Education, Eastern Michigan University, Ypsilanti, Mich.

CAREER: Certified in speech pathology by American Speech and Hearing Association; Miami University, Oxford, Ohio, member of faculty and director of stuttering program, 1965-67; Eastern Michigan University, Ypsilanti, member of faculty in department of special education, and director of stuttering program, 1969—, affiliated teacher of

military history, 1971-72. Founder and clinical director of Preble County Speech and Hearing Clinic, 1965-67, consultant to Preble County Retarded Children's School; director of workshops on stuttering therapy and speech improvement.

MEMBER: American Speech and Hearing Association, National Association of Hearing and Speech Agencies, American Association of University Professors, American Association for Higher Education, Association of the U.S. Army, Michigan Speech and Hearing Association, Michigan Academy of Research in Speech and Hearing, Ohio Speech and Hearing Association, Sigma Alpha Eta.

WRITINGS: (Editor) *Readings in Speech Disfluency*, MSS Educational Publishing, 1972; (contributor) *A Handbook for Adult Stutterers*, Speech Foundation of America, 1972. Contributor to *Journal of Communication Pathology*. Member of editorial board of *Journal of the College of Education* (of Eastern Michigan University), *Biographic Essays in Speech*, and *Journal of Communication Pathology*.

WORK IN PROGRESS: Communication Therapy for Stutterers, with Kenneth J. Knepflar.

AVOCATIONAL INTERESTS: Playing bridge (junior master of American Contract Bridge League).

* * *

MOSS, Gordon E(rvin) 1937-

PERSONAL: Born April 28, 1937, in Ogden, Utah; son of Ervin R. (a mail clerk) and Norma (Fowers) Moss; married Carolee Ferguson (a free-lance writer), May 11, 1962; children: Michelle, Nicole, Nanette. *Education:* Brigham Young University, B.S., 1963; Rutgers University, M.A., 1967; State University of New York at Buffalo, Ph.D., 1972; also studied at Weber College and University of Utah. *Religion:* Church of Jesus Christ of Latter-day Saints (Mormons). *Residence:* Ann Arbor, Mich. *Office:* Department of Sociology, Eastern Michigan University, Ypsilanti, Mich. 48197.

CAREER: University of Maine, Orono, instructor in sociology and anthropology, 1966-68; Eastern Michigan University, Ypsilanti, assistant professor of sociology, 1971—. Adjunct assistant professor at University of Michigan, 1974. *Member:* American Sociological Association, Society for Epidemiological Research.

WRITINGS: Illness, Immunity, and Social Interaction: The Dynamics of Biosocial Resonation, Wiley, 1973; (with Walter Moss) *Growing Old*, Washington Square Press, 1975; (contributor) George G. Haydu, editor, *Experience Forms: Their Cultural and Individual Place and Function*, Mouton & Co., in press. Contributor of articles to *Journal of the Maine Medical Association* and *International Journal of Psychiatry in Medicine*.

WORK IN PROGRESS: A book examining social behavior and the ecology of the larger environment; research on the irreducible minimum level of social stress; research on social stress among college freshmen and laid-off industrial workers.

SIDELIGHTS: Moss served his mission for the Church of Jesus Christ of Latter-day Saints in the West Central States Mission, 1957-59. He writes: "Most of my concern with social stress grew out of my experiences with everyday people as a Mormon missionary. I felt people were so close to happiness yet missed it for reasons that could be easily corrected, and I wanted to see what I could do. Another source of my interest has been a continuing concern for the relations between the social and physiological growing out of an early religious concern with how the 'spirit' influenced the body. Though I no longer believe in spirits the fascination about the links between social and physical remains." *Avocational interests:* Fishing, camping, skiing, tennis.

* * *

MOULD, George 1894-

PERSONAL: Born November 29, 1894, in Lancashire, England; son of James Diggle (an architect) and Jane Taylor (Rogers) Mould; married Anne Constance Fairlie Colquhoun, August 24, 1922. *Education:* Educated in England. *Politics:* None. *Religion:* Christian. *Home and office:* 3 Fylde Court, Esplanade, Knott End-on-Sea, Lancashire FY6 0BD, England.

CAREER: Radcliffe Times, Radcliffe, Lancashire, England, reporter, 1913; *Bury Times*, Bury, Lancashire, reporter, 1914; Thomas Leng Publications, Manchester, England, sub-editor, 1914-34; *Daily Mail*, London, England, crime reporter, drama critic, and news editor, 1934-40; special writer for *Manchester Evening News* and *Manchester Guardian*, both Manchester, England, 1940-62. Worked as civil servant for Government Information Service. *Military service:* Royal Flying Corps, 1914-19. *Member:* National Union of Journalists (life member), Men's Forum (vice-chairman, 1975—), Civil Service Club, Knott End Men's Fellowship (vice-chairman, 1965—), Manchester Press Club (honorary member). *Awards, honors:* Officer of the Order of the British Empire, 1943; member of Victorian Order, 1952.

WRITINGS: Lancashire's Unknown River, Terrence Dalton, 1970, British Book Centre, 1974; *Manchester Memories: One Man's Memories of Manchester as He Remembers It*, Terence Dalton, 1972, British Book Centre, 1974. Also author of play, "They Build a City," produced in England at Rusholme Repertory Theatre, 1937. Contributor to newspapers.

WORK IN PROGRESS: Desert Island Story.

BIOGRAPHICAL/CRITICAL SOURCES: Manchester Evening Chronicle, June 15, 1960.

* * *

MUDD, Stuart 1893-1975

September 23, 1893—May 6, 1975; American microbiologist, educator, author of books on scientific topics, editor of works on world population and education. Obituaries: *AB Bookman's Weekly*, August 4, 1975. (*CA*-11/12)

* * *

MUELLER, Amelia 1911-

PERSONAL: Born August 27, 1911, in Burrton, Kan.; daughter of Jacob (a farmer) and Elisabeth (Ellenberger) Mueller. *Education:* Attended Bethel College, North Newton, Kan., 1930-32; Emporia State College, B.S., 1942; Colorado State University, M.Ed., 1955; graduate study at Kansas University, summers, 1955, 1961, 1971, Northwestern University, 1957, Ohio State University, 1960, and Wichita State University, summer 1969. *Politics:* Democrat. *Religion:* Mennonite. *Home:* 604 North St., Halstead, Kan. 67056.

CAREER: Rural school teacher of all grades in Harvey

County, Kan., 1932-39; elementary school teacher in Mankato, Kan., 1939-41, Manhattan, Kan., 1942-43, Hutchinson, Kan., 1943-49, and Ansbach, Germany, 1949-50; Hutchinson Public Schools, Hutchinson, Kan., kindergarten teacher, 1950-55, speech clinician, 1955-71, teacher of hard of hearing, 1971—. Day care director for children of migrants, summer, 1946; remedial reading teacher in East Harlem, summer, 1964. *Member:* American Speech and Hearing Association, Council for Exceptional Children, American Association of University Women, National Education Association, Kansas Speech and Hearing Association, Kansas Author's Club. *Awards, honors:* Hymn awards from Mennonite Song Festival Society, 1959, 1965; Kansas Author's Club Awards, 1967-70, for poetry, short stories, and articles.

WRITINGS: There Have to be Six (nonfiction), Herald Press, 1966; *Sissy Kid Brother* (novel), Herald Press, 1975.

* * *

MUELLER, James W(illiam) 1941-

PERSONAL: Born July 20, 1941, in Newark, N.J.; son of William Aloysius (in insurance business) and Anna (Fischer) Mueller; married Sandra Smith, January 22, 1966; children: Sarah Alyssa. *Education:* Rutgers University, A.B., 1963; graduate study at University of Pittsburgh, 1965, and Northwestern University, 1968-69; University of Arizona, M.A., 1971, Ph.D., 1972. *Home:* 28 Oak St., Bridgewater, Mass. 02324. *Office:* Department of Anthropology, Bridgewater State College, Bridgewater, Mass. 02324.

CAREER: Bridgewater State College, Bridgewater, Mass., assistant professor, 1971-75, associate professor of anthropology, 1975—. Fellow in salvage archaeology at Museum of Northern Arizona, 1969-70; has conducted archaeological field work in Arizona, Illinois, and Massachusetts. *Military service:* U.S. Army, 1963-65; became first lieutenant. *Member:* Society for American Archaeology, American Anthropological Association, American Museum of Natural History, Northern Arizona Society of Science and Art, Sigma Xi.

WRITINGS: The Use of Sampling in Archaeological Survey, Society for American Archaeology, 1974; (editor and contributor) *Sampling in Archaeology*, University of Arizona Press, 1975.

WORK IN PROGRESS: Research on economic archaeology.

AVOCATIONAL INTERESTS: Tennis, handball, home landscaping, automobile maintenance, and staghorn ferns.

* * *

MUKHERJEE, Ramkrishna 1919-

PERSONAL: Born October 28, 1919, in Calcutta, India; son of Satindra Nath (an engineer) and Sati Rani (Chatterjee) Mukherjee; married Prabhati Ghosh (a research worker), February, 1952; children: Rila (a daughter). *Education:* Calcutta University, M.Sc., 1941; Cambridge University, Ph.D., 1948. *Religion:* Atheist. *Home:* 17/3 Moore Ave., Calcutta 40, India 700040. *Office:* Indian Statistical Institute, 203 Barrackpore Trunk Rd., Calcutta 35, India.

CAREER: H. M. Social Survey, London, England, chief research officer, 1948-49; Indian Statistical Institute, Calcutta, India, director of field research and specification, 1950-51; London School of Economics and Political Science, London, England, consultant, 1952; Humboldt University, Berlin, Germany, professor of Indian studies, 1953-57; Indian Statistical Institute, research professor, 1957—, additional director of Research and Training School, 1970-72. Consultant, Central Statistical Office, Ankara, Turkey, 1949; member of academic council, Jawaharlal Nehru University, 1965—; member of Council for Social Development, India, 1968-70; scientific adviser, Bielefield University, 1970—; member of executive and general council, National Institute of Community Development, India, 1971—. *Member:* International Sociological Association (member of executive and editorial committee, 1974-78), International Social Science Council, Indian Sociological Society (president, 1973-74), Indian Social Science Association (patron), Indian Council of Social Science Research.

WRITINGS: (With others) *Famine and Rehabilitation of Bengal*, Statistical Publishing Society (Calcutta), 1946; (with others) *Plan for Rehabilitation of Bengal*, Statistical Publishing Society, 1946; *The New Czechoslovakia: An Indian Sociologist Looks at Czechoslovakia Today*, Current Book House (Bombay), 1951; (with C. R. Rao and J. C. Trevor) *The Ancient Inhabitants of Jebel Moya*, Cambridge University Press, 1955; *The Problem of Uganda: A Study in Acculturation*, Akademie Verlag (Berlin), 1956; *The Dynamics of a Rural Society*, Akademie Verlag, 1957; *The Rise and Fall of the East India Company*, Deutscher Verlag den Wissenschaften (Berlin), 1958, Monthly Review Press, 1974; *Six Villages of Bengal: A Socio-economic Survey*, Asiatic Society of Bengal (Calcutta), 1958; *The Sociologist and Social Change in India Today*, Prentice-Hall of India, 1965; (with others) *Data Inventory on Social Sciences: India*, Statistical Publishing Society, 1971; *Social Indicators*, Macmillan, in press; *West Bengal Family Structures: 1946-1966*, Allied Publishers, in press; *Anthropologists' Value-Base*, Calcutta University Press, in press. Contributor: D. V. Glass, editor, *Social Mobility in Britain: A Symposium*, Routledge & Kegan Paul, 1954; R. N. Saksena, editor, *Sociology, Social Research and Social Problems in India*, Asia Publishing House (Bombay), 1961; T. N. Madan & G. Sarana, editors, *Indian Anthropology: Essays in Memory of D. N. Majumdar*, Asia Publishing House, 1962; C. R. Rao, editor, *Contributions to Statistics: Presented to Professor P. C. Mahalanobis on the Occasion of His 70th Birthday*, Statistical Publishing Society and Pergamon, 1963; T. K. N. Unnithan and others, editors, *Towards a Sociology of Culture in India: Essays in Honour of Professor D. P. Mukerji*, Prentice-Hall of India, 1965; Horst Kruger, editor, *New Indology*, Akademie Verlag, 1970; A. R. Desai, editor, *Essays on Modernization of Underdeveloped Societies*, Thacker & Co., 1972; S. P. Varma and Virendra Narain, editors, *Pakistan Political System in Crisis: Emergence of Bangladesh*, South Asia Studies Centre, Rajasthan University, 1972; Kathleen Gough and Hari P. Sharma, editors, *Imperialism and Revolution in South Asia*, Monthly Review Press, 1973; S. Rokkan and S. N. Eisenstadt, editors, *Building States and Nations: Analyses by Region*, Sage Publications, Volume II, 1973; Tadashi Fukutake, editor, *Lecturers on Sociology*, Tokyo University Press, 1974; Rajni Kothari, editor, *State and Nation-Building: A Third World Perspective*, Orient Longman, 1974; Fukutake and K. Morioka, editors, *Sociology and Social Development in Asia*, Tokyo University Press, 1974; M. S. A. Rao, editor, *Urban Sociology in India*, Orient Longman, 1974; Dhirendra Narain, editor, *Explorations in the Family and Other Essays*, Thacker & Co., 1975; (editor with R. Richta) *Science, Technology and*

Society, Sage Publications, in press. Contributor to journals in his field. Member of advisory committee, *Current Sociology*, 1973—.

WORK IN PROGRESS: Research on social science with special reference to India, Asia, Africa; research on conceptualization, methodology, survey research, data-archiving, value-base, family, and population; *What Will It Be?*; *Classification and Inferential Problems in Social Science*; *Family and Planning.*

* * *

MULLER, Edward John 1916-

PERSONAL: Born September 27, 1916, in Minnesota; son of Edward George (a merchant) and Mary (Zamrzla) Muller; married Colette Y. Roche, January 6, 1947; children: Joel Frederick. *Education:* University of Wisconsin—Stout Menomonie, B.S., 1948; University of Georgia, M.A.E., 1973. *Religion:* Baptist. *Home:* 4122 Ashford-Dunwoody Rd., Atlanta, Ga. 30319. *Office:* Department of Architectural Engineering Technology, Southern Technical Institute, Marietta, Ga. 30060.

CAREER: Southern Technical Institute, Marietta, Ga., assistant professor, 1948-56, associate professor, 1956-70, professor of architectural engineering technology, 1970—, head of department of engineering drawing, 1948-69. *Military service:* U.S. Army, Armored Infantry, 1941-46; became staff sergeant; received Purple Heart and Bronze Star. *Member:* American Society of Engineering Education.

WRITINGS: Architectural Drawing and Light Construction, Prentice-Hall, 1967, 2nd edition, in press; *Reading Architectural Working Drawings*, Prentice-Hall, 1970.

AVOCATIONAL INTERESTS: Tennis, oil painting, woodworking, travel (Europe, Polynesia, West Indies).

* * *

MUMFORD, Emily 1920-

PERSONAL: Born December 19, 1920, in Cape Girardeau, Mo.; daughter of Barney Adolph (an attorney) and Dola Gladys (Stolzer) Hamilton; married Robert S. Mumford (a psychiatrist), September 15, 1950 (divorced). *Education:* University of Tulsa, B.A., 1941; Columbia University, M.A., 1959, Ph.D., 1963. *Home:* 360 East 72nd St., New York, N.Y. 10021. *Office:* Downstate Medical Center of State University of New York, 450 Clarkson Ave., Brooklyn, N.Y. 11203.

CAREER: Family Circle (magazine), New York, N.Y., shopping editor, 1950-56; Hunter College of the City University of New York, New York, N.Y., instructor in sociology, 1960-64; New College, Sarasota, Fla., visiting professor of sociology, 1965-66; Mount Sinai School of Medicine, New York, N.Y., assistant professor, 1966-68, associate professor of sociology in psychiatry, 1968-73, research associate in sociology, 1966-73; Lehman College of the City University of New York, New York, N.Y., professor of sociology, 1973—. Associate professor at City University of New York's Graduate Center, 1968-73, professor, 1973—; professor at State University of New York's Downstate Medical Center, 1974—. Guest lecturer at Columbia-Presbyterian School of Nursing and Psychiatric Institute, both 1961-66; member of task force on studies development of United Hospital Fund of New York, 1969-71; evaluator for Second National House Staff Conference of Health Service and Mental Health Administration, 1972.

MEMBER: World Association of Public Opinion Research, World Organization of Social Science in Medicine, American Sociological Association, American Association of Public Opinion Research, American Public Health Association, Eastern Sociological Society. *Awards, honors:* Commonwealth Fund grant, 1968-70, to study internships and residencies; Milbank Memorial Fund travel grant, 1969, to study medical education and the medical care system in the Soviet Union; National Institute of Mental Health grant, 1969-73, to study teaching behavioral sciences in a medical school.

WRITINGS: (With James Skipper, Jr.) *Sociology in Hospital Care*, Harper, 1967; (contributor) Gerald Schoenberg, Helen F. Pettit, and Arthur C. Carr, editors, *Teaching Psychosocial Aspects of Patient Care*, Columbia University Press, 1968; *Interns: From Students to Physicians*, Harvard University Press, 1970; (contributor) Marvin D. Dunnette, editor, *Work and Non-Work in the Year Two Thousand One*, Brooks-Cole, 1973. Contributor of more than twenty-five articles and reviews to medical and sociology journals, including *Medical Dimensions, Psychoanalytic Quarterly, American Journal of Psychiatry, Psychology in the Schools, Mental Health Digest, Current Psychiatric Therapies*, and *Nursing Outlook*.

WORK IN PROGRESS: A study of an emergency room; a study of patients' responses to medical advice; research on medical education.

SIDELIGHTS: Emily Mumford has visited medical schools and hospitals in the Soviet Union, India, Sweden, and Malaysia.

* * *

MUNCH, Theodore W(illiam) 1919-

PERSONAL: Born November 9, 1919, in Columbus, Ohio; son of Paul Ralph and Esther (Boyer) Munch; married Julia MacFarlane (a director of clinical nursing), November 25, 1960. *Education:* Ohio State University, B.S., 1941, B.S.Ed., 1947; Colorado State College, Greeley, M.A.Ed., 1948; Stanford University, Ed.D., 1952. *Politics:* Democrat. *Religion:* Methodist. *Home:* 2125 East Golf Ave., Tempe, Ariz. 85282. *Office:* Department of Physics, Arizona State University, Tempe, Ariz. 85281.

CAREER: Seagram & Sons, Lawrenceburg, Ind., chemist, 1941; high school science instructor in Balboa, Canal Zone, 1948-50; San Francisco State College (now San Francisco State University), San Francisco, Calif., instructor in Science Division and in Education Division, 1952-53; Fullerton Junior College (now California State University at Fullerton), instructor in life science, 1953-54; University of Texas, Austin, assistant professor of science education, 1954-59; Arizona State University, Tempe, associate professor, 1959-63, professor of science education, 1963—. *Military service:* U.S. Army, Infantry, 1941-45; served in European theater; became first lieutenant; received Bronze Star and three battle stars.

MEMBER: National Education Association (life member), National Science Teachers Association, American Association for the Advancement of Science (fellow). *Awards, honors:* National Science Foundation grant, 1963, and faculty fellowship at Michigan State University, 1967-68.

WRITINGS: (With M. Vere Devault) *Horned Lizards*, Steck, 1957; (with Devault) *The Road Runner*, Steck, 1958; (with Devault) *The Armadillo*, Steck, 1958; *What Is a Rocket?*, Benefic, 1958; *What Is a Solar System?*, Benefic,

1959; *What Is Heat?*, Benefic, 1959; *What Is Light?*, Benefic, 1960; *How to Individualize Science Instruction in the Elementary School*, National Science Teachers Association, 1966; (with B. John Syrocki) "Science for a Changing World" series, six texts with separate teacher's manuals, Benefic, 1967; *Man the Engineer: Nature's Copycat*, Westminster, 1974. Programmed instructional materials include "Our Solar System," "How We Forecast the Weather," and "How Scientists Think and Work," all published by Coronet Instructional Films. Contributor to *Rethinking Science Education* (yearbook) and to education journals.

WORK IN PROGRESS: A juvenile suspense novel, *Thunder on Forbidden Mountain*.

SIDELIGHTS: Munch likes to write for young people because "they treat each bit of information as a bright new toy to be delighted in and used." He is co-designer of Flexi-Lab, a portable laboratory designed to facilitate science demonstrations at all grade levels, and designer of a biology table, also manufactured commercially.

AVOCATIONAL INTERESTS: Hiking in mountains, conducting classes in outdoor education, weight-lifting, swimming.

* * *

MUNSON, Charlie E(llis) 1877-

PERSONAL: Born February 11, 1877, in Hope, Tex.; son of Edwin William (a farmer) and Amanda (Dismukes) Munson; married Emma Esther Kerby, September 1, 1909; children: Charles, Jr., Kenneth, Allen, Marion Munson Burnett, Weldon, Virginia Munson White, Earline Munson Grant. *Education:* Educated in one-room schoolhouses in Texas. *Religion:* Methodist. *Home address:* Stevens' Nursing Home, Yoakum, Tex. 77995. *Mailing address:* c/o Kenneth Munson, Rt. 1, Box 229E, San Marcos, Tex.

CAREER: Farmer in Hope, Tex., 1894-1902; chief deputy sheriff in Hallettsville, Tex., 1902-09; farmer in Hope, Tex., 1910-42; Corpus Christi Naval Air Base, Corpus Christi, Tex., security guard, 1942-46; *Corpus Christi Caller-Times*, Corpus Christi, Tex., night watchman, 1946-66. President of Hope (Tex.) School Board, 1920-42.

WRITINGS: Mister Charlie (memoirs), with introduction and epilog by son, Kenneth E. Munson, Madrona, 1975.

SIDELIGHTS: Mister Charlie recalls the days before the turn of the century, stories of cabins and early schools, oxen drives, and a simple life, and the author's career as a sheriff near the turn of the century.

* * *

MURPHY, Buck
See WHITCOMB, Ian

* * *

MURPHY, Grace E. Barstow 1888-1975

1888—May 28, 1975; American naturalist, conservationist, author. Obituaries: *New York Times*, May 30, 1975.

* * *

MURPHY, Hazel
See THURSTON, Hazel (Patricia)

* * *

MURRAY, Rebecca (Jean) 1936-

PERSONAL: Born January 30, 1936, in Raleigh, N.C.;

daughter of Edward (a clerk of the North Carolina Supreme Court) and Fannie B. (Phillips) Murray. *Education:* Meredith College, A.B., 1958; University of North Carolina, M.Ed., 1961; Duke University, Ed.D., 1973. *Office:* Department of Education, Meredith College, Raleigh, N.C. 27611.

CAREER: Elementary and junior high school teacher in the public schools of Charlotte, N.C., 1958-60, and Raleigh, N.C., 1960-69; WRAL-TV, Raleigh, N.C., worked on children's program, 1966-71; Columbia College, Columbia, S.C., instructor, 1971-73, assistant professor of education, 1973-74; Meredith College, Raleigh, N.C., assistant professor of education, 1973—.

MEMBER: Association for Childhood Education International, National Association for the Education of Young Children, National Association of Elementary School Principals, Council for Exceptional Children, Elementary-Kindergarten-Nursery Education, National Society for the Study of Education, American Educational Research Association, National Education Association, National Council of Teachers of English, American Association of University Professors, Southern Association on Children Under Six, North Carolina Association on Children Under Six, North Carolina Association of Educators, Kappa Delta Pi, Delta Kappa Gamma, Phi Delta Kappa.

WRITINGS: History of the Public School Kindergarten in North Carolina, MSS Information Corp., 1974. Contributor to education journals.

SIDELIGHTS: Rebecca Murray wrote: "Too many of us are still teaching our students as if tomorrow will be basically the same as today.... Instead of confining our children's thinking with answers, answers, and more answers, we should be assisting in the release of their potential by pointing out that perhaps the right questions have yet to be asked."

* * *

MUSIKER, Reuben 1931-

PERSONAL: Born January 12, 1931, in Johannesburg, South Africa; son of Julius and Sophia (Joffe) Musiker; married Naomi Measroch, April 9, 1961; children: Judith, Arnon, Carmel. *Education:* University of the Witwatersrand, B.Sc., 1953; University of Capetown, H. Dipl. Lib., 1957; University of Pretoria, M.A., 1968. *Residence:* Johannesburg, South Africa. *Office:* The Library, University of the Witwatersrand, Jan Smuts Ave., Johannesburg, South Africa.

CAREER: Rhodes University, Grahamstown, South Africa, deputy university librarian, 1962-72; University of the Witwatersrand, Johannesburg, South Africa, director of library services, 1973-74, university librarian and professor of librarianship, 1975—. *Member:* South African Library Association (fellow).

WRITINGS: (Compiler) *The Australopithecinae,* University of Capetown Libraries, 1954; *Guide to South African Reference Books,* University of Capetown Libraries, 1958, 5th edition, A. A. Balkema, 1971, supplementary volumes (covering 1970-74), Witwatersrand University Library, 1975; (compiler) *Directory of Libraries in the Eastern Cape,* South African Library Association, 1962; *Guide to Sources of Information in the Humanites,* Potchefstroom University for Higher Christian Education, 1962, *Supplement,* 1965; (compiler) *Directory of Libraries in the Southern Transvaal,* South African Library Association,

1963; *Library Science Literature: A Selective Review,* Volume I: *1965-1969,* Volume II: *1970-1971,* Department of Librarianship, Rhodes University, 1970; *Special Libraries: A General Survey with Particular Reference to South Africa,* Scarecrow, 1970; *South African Bibliography: A Survey of Bibliographies and Bibliographical Work,* Archon, 1970, supplement, Witwatersrand University Library, 1975; *Guide to Cape Offical Publications, 1854-1910,* G. K. Hall, 1975.

* * *

MWANGA
See STARK, Claude Alan

* * *

MYERS, Charles B(ennett) 1939-

PERSONAL: Born June 8, 1939, in Columbia, Pa.; son of J. Charles (a dentist) and Bernice (Seiple) Myers; married Lynn Knisely (a teacher), September 12, 1959; children: Jeffrey A., Mark D., Brian L. *Education:* Pennsylvania State University, B.S. (magna cum laude), 1961; George Peabody College for Teachers, M.A., 1963, Ph.D., 1968; post-doctoral study at Carnegie-Mellon University, 1968. *Home:* 1050 Percy Warner Blvd., Nashville, Tenn. 37205. *Office:* Programs for Educators of Youth, George Peabody College for Teachers, Nashville, Tenn. 37203.

CAREER: Junior high and high school teacher of social studies in the public schools of Harrisburg, Pa., 1961-62, and at Peabody Democratic School, Nashville, Tenn., 1963; Rider College, Trenton, N.J., assistant professor of history and education, 1965-69; Teacher Education Alliance for Metro, Nashville, Tenn., program development specialist, 1970-73; George Peabody College for Teachers, Nashville, Tenn., associate professor of history and social science education, 1965—, director of Programs for Educators of Youth, 1974—. Social science specialist for SPEEDIER Project, 1968-70. Member of board of directors of Social Action Committee of Christians and Jews, Nashville, Tenn., 1972-74. *Member:* National Council for the Social Studies, Association for Supervision and Curriculum Development, Tennessee Education Association, Tennessee Council for the Social Studies (member of executive committee, 1973-74; president, 1974-75), Metropolitan Nashville Council for the Social Studies, Phi Delta Kappa, Kappa Delta Pi, Pi Gamma Mu, Phi Kappa Phi, Phi Alpha Theta.

WRITINGS: (Editor) *New Approaches to Social Studies Instruction,* Rider College Press, 1966; (contributing editor) *Current Innovations in Education: Language Arts, Social Studies, and Teacher Behavior,* SPEEDIER Project, 1969; *Social Studies Innovations: 1968-1969,* SPEEDIER Project, 1969; *Social Studies Pilots 1969-1970,* SPEEDIER Project, 1970; (with Mary C. Durkin and Patricia Hardy) *Teaching Strategies for Developing Children's Thinking: Application of Generalizations, Junior High-Middle School Edition,* Institute for Staff Development, 1970; (with Durkin and Hardy) *Teaching Strategies for Developing Children's Thinking: Feelings, Attitudes, and Values, Junior High-Middle School Edition,* Institute for Staff Development, 1970; (with Durkin and Hardy) *Teaching Strategies for Developing Children's Thinking: Interpretation of Data, Junior High-Middle School Edition,* Institute for Staff Development, 1970; (with Durkin and Hardy) *Teaching Strategies for Developing Children's Thinking: Concept Development, Junior High-Middle School Edi-*

tion, Institute for Staff Development, 1970; *The Environmental Crisis*, Prentice-Hall, 1972; (general editor and contributor) *The Taba Program in Social Science*, Addison-Wesley, 1973-1975. Contributor to education journals.

* * *

NAGERA, Humberto 1927-

PERSONAL: Surname is pronounced Na-her-a; born May 23, 1927, in Havana, Cuba; naturalized British citizen, 1968; son of Evaristo and Emilia (Perez) Nagera; married Gloria Hernandez-Fernandez, September 8, 1952; children: Lisette M., Humberto F., Daniel. *Education:* Maristas School, B.Sc., 1945; University of Havana, M.D., 1952; London Institute of Psychoanalysis, certification as adult psychoanalyst, 1961, as child psychoanalyst, 1962. *Home:* 1421 Crawford Lane, Ann Arbor, Mich. 48105. *Office:* University Hospital, Ann Arbor, Mich. 48104.

CAREER: Licensed to practice medicine in Michigan; private practice of medicine in Havana, Cuba, 1955-58, London, England, 1961-68, and in Ann Arbor, Mich., 1968—. University Hospital, Havana, Cuba, intern, 1950-52, resident in psychiatry, 1952-55; Hampstead Child Therapy Clinic, London, England, research leader and lecturer, 1961-68, training analyst and supervisor, 1964-68; London Institute of Psychoanalysis, London, England, lecturer, 1968; University of Michigan, Ann Arbor, professor of psychiatry and director of Child Analytic Study Program at Children's Psychiatric Hospital, 1968—. Consultant to National Institute for Examination and Diagnosis, Havana, 1954-56, and to Hewitt Research Center, 1972. Visiting professor at University of Chicago, 1967. Michigan Psychoanalytic Institute and Society, lecturer, training analyst, and supervisor, and director of Child Analysis Training Program, 1968—. Member of advisory council of Children's Psychiatric Hospital of University of Michigan, 1968—, and of Princeton Center for Advancement of Psychoanalysis, 1970—. Visiting lecturer at University of Havana, summer, 1956, University of Leiden, 1966-68, University of Oklahoma, 1966, Baltimore Psychoanalytic Society, 1966, 1972, Cleveland Psychoanalytic Society, 1966, 1970, University of Miami, Coral Gables, Fla., 1967, University of Michigan, 1967, University of Utah, 1967, Seattle Psychoanalytic Society, 1967, 1969, 1970, 1971, Michigan Psychoanalytic Society, 1967, Lafayette Clinic, 1968—, University of Cincinnati, 1969, San Francisco Psychoanalytic Society, 1969, 1970, 1971, 1972, Cincinnati Psychoanalytic Society, 1969, St. Louis Psychoanalytic Society, 1970, University of Washington, Seattle, 1970, Philadelphia Psychoanalytic Society, 1971, University of Tulane, 1971, Washington Psychoanalytic Society, 1971, Chicago Psychoanalytic Institute, 1972, Chicago Council of Child Psychiatry, 1972, and Baylor University, 1972.

MEMBER: International Psychoanalytic Association, British Psychoanalytic Society, Cuban Medical Association in Exile, American Association for Child Psychoanalysis, Association for Child Psychoanalysis (councillor, 1971-72), Michigan Psychoanalytic Society.

WRITINGS: La Educacion y el Desarrollo Emocional del Nino (title means "The Education and Emotional Development of Children"), La Prensa Medica Mejicana, 1958, 2nd edition, 1971; *Early Childhood Disturbances, the Infantile Neurosis, and the Adulthood Disturbances; Problems of a Developmental Psychoanalytic Psychology* (monograph), International Universities Press, 1966; *Vincent Van Gogh: A Psychological Study*, International Universities Press,

1967; *On Female Sexuality and the Oedipus Complex*, Jason Aronson, 1975.

"Basic Psychoanalytic Concepts" series, published by Basic Books: *Basic Psychoanalytic Concepts on the Libido Theory*, 1969; *. . . on the Theory of Dreams*, 1969; *. . . on the Theory of Instincts*, 1970; *. . . on Metapsychology Conflicts, Anxiety, and Other Subjects*, 1970. Member of editorial board of *Journal of Child Psychiatry and Human Development*, 1969—, and of *Annals of Adolescent Psychiatry: Clinical and Developmental Aspects*, 1970—.

WORK IN PROGRESS: On Obsessional Neurosis.

* * *

NALL, Hiram Abiff 1950-
   (Sedeka Wadinasi)

PERSONAL: Born October 1, 1950, in West Blocton, Ala.; son of Mitchell Raymond (a clergyman) and Mattie (a cook; maiden name, Johnson) Nall. *Education:* Los Angeles City College, A.A., 1973; California State University, Los Angeles, B.A., 1974; University of California, Los Angeles, M.A., 1975, doctoral candidate, 1975—. *Home:* 4051 Abourne Rd., #B, Los Angeles, Calif. 90008. *Office:* Department of Pan-African Studies, California State University, Los Angeles, 5151 State University Dr., Los Angeles, Calif. 90032.

CAREER: Oscar Mayer and Co., Los Angeles, Calif., green weights scaler, 1969-74; California State University, Los Angeles, lecturer in Pan-African studies, 1974—, editor of *PASS: A Journal of the Black Experience and Pan-African Issues*, 1974—. *Member:* American Folklore Society, National Urban League. *Awards, honors:* International Poetry Association awards, 1974.

WRITINGS: Up From the Dead Level, FAS Publishing, 1974; *When Leilani Wears Yellow*, Thomas Hendricks Publishers, 1975. Intercollegiate correspondent, *Black Collegian*, 1974—. Consulting and contributing editor, *Nommo*, 1974—, and *Osagyefo*, 1974—, and *Journal of Afro-American Studies*, 1975—.

WORK IN PROGRESS: The Historical Development of Black Literature in America: A Folkloristic and Thematic Approach, under pseudonym Sedeka Wadinasi; *The Black Situation in America: Ten Years Since Watts*.

* * *

NAMIR, Mordecai 1897-1975

February 23, 1897—February 22, 1975; Soviet-born Israeli government official, statesman, author of books on economics. Obituaries: *New York Times*, February 23, 1975.

* * *

NARRAMORE, Stanley Bruce 1941-

PERSONAL: Born November 22, 1941, in Phoenix, Ariz.; son of Edward Laurence (a farmer) and Jennie Belle (Waterhouse) Narramore; married Kathleen Margaret Rice, May 28, 1966; children: Richard Dean, Deborah Lea. *Education:* Westmont College, B.A., 1963; Pepperdine University, M.A., 1964; University of Kentucky, Ph.D., 1967. *Religion:* Protestant. *Home:* 2426 Sarondi Grande, Hacienda Heights, Calif. 91745. *Office:* Rosemead Graduate School of Psychology, 1409 North Walnut Grove, Rosemead, Calif. 91770.

CAREER: Child Guidance Service, Lexington, Ky., staff psychologist, 1965-67; Rosemead Counseling Service, Rosemead, Calif., staff psychologist, 1967-70; Rosemead Graduate School of Psychology, Rosemead, Calif., academic dean, 1970—. *Member:* American Psychological Association, Western Association of Christians for Psychological Studies (president, 1975-76), California State Psychological Association, Los Angeles County Psychological Association.

WRITINGS: Help!: I'm a Parent, Zondervan, 1972; *A Guide to Child Rearing*, Zondervan, 1972; *An Ounce of Prevention*, Zondervan, 1973; *Guilt and Freedom*, Vision House, 1974. Co-editor of *Journal of Psychology and·Theology.*

SIDELIGHTS: Narramore writes: "A primary focus of all my writings is the integration of psychological and theological conceptions of personality functioning."

* * *

NATALI, Alfred Maxim 1915-
(Pietro Militello)

PERSONAL: Born March 9, 1915, in Genoa, Italy; came to U.S., 1928; naturalized U.S. citizen, 1939; son of Amilcare (a mechanic) and Victoria Lavinia (a seamstress; maiden name, Daziani) Natali. *Education:* Villanova University, B.A., 1940, M.A., 1943; St. Augustine College, Washington, D.C., graduate study, 1940-44. *Politics:* None. *Home address:* P.O. Box 495, Williamstown, N.J. 08094. *Agent:* Writers Institute, 2 Park Ave., New York, N.Y. 08360. *Office:* Our Lady of Pompeii Church, Vineland, N.J. 08360.

CAREER: Ordained Roman Catholic priest, 1943; assistant priest in Lawrence, Mass., 1944, North Queensland, Australia, 1944-45, pastor in North Queensland, 1945-52, assistant in Staten Island, N.Y., Philadelphia, Pa., and Lawrence, Mass., 1952-62, pastor in Lawrence, Mass., 1962-71, assistant in Vineland, N.J., 1974—. *Member:* American Society of Composers, Authors, and Publishers, Society of Children's Book Writers. *Awards, honors:* Citation from State of Massachusetts, 1968, for religious work abroad and in U.S.

WRITINGS: (Under pseudonym Pietro Militello) *Italians in America*, Franklin Publishing Co., 1973; *Jonathan Scroll*, Dorrance, 1973. Also author of song lyrics. Contributor to magazines and newspapers.

WORK IN PROGRESS: Northeast Downunder, a novel about northeastern part of Australia; translating *The Mask of the World* and *Marconi: His Life and Mystery of His Death.*

SIDELIGHTS: Father Natali has traveled to Australia, Italy, England, Ireland, Ceylon, Aden, Portugal, Spain, and France. He speaks and writes classical Italian and is fluent in the Genoese dialect.

* * *

NATHAN, Richard P(erle) 1935-

PERSONAL: Born November 4, 1935, in Schenectady, N.Y.; son of Sidney Robert and Betty (Green) Nathan; married Mary McNamara, June 5, 1957; children: Robert Joseph, Carol Hewit. *Education:* Brown University, B.A. (magna cum laude), 1957; Harvard University, M.Pub.Admin., 1959, Ph.D., 1966. *Home:* 7503 Cayuga Ave., Bethesda, Md. 20034. *Office:* Brookings Institution, Washington, D.C. 20036.

CAREER: Legislative assistant to Senator Kenneth B.

Keating, 1959-62; director of domestic policy research for Nelson A. Rockefeller, 1963-64; Brookings Institution, Washington, D.C., research associate, 1966-69, U.S. Government, Washington, D.C., assistant director of Office of Management and Budget, 1969-71; U.S. Department of Health, Education, and Welfare, Washington, D.C., deputy under secretary, 1971-72; Brookings Institution, director of study of general revenue sharing, 1972—. Associate director, National Advisory Commission on Civil Disorders, 1967; chairman of Transitions Task Forces on Welfare and Intergovernmental Fiscal Relations, 1968; member of U.S. Government Commission on Organization, 1969—; chairman of Domestic Council Commission on Welfare Reform Planning, 1971—; secretary-treasurer, Manpower Demonstration Research Corporation, 1974—; Visiting Woodrow Wilson Professor at University of Virginia, 1972-73. *Member:* National Academy of Public Administration, Phi Beta Kappa, Theta Delta Chi.

WRITINGS: (Editor with Harvey S. Perloff) *Revenue Sharing and the City*, Johns Hopkins Press, 1968; *Jobs and Civil Rights*, U.S. Commission on Civil Rights, 1969; (contributor) *Fiscal Issues in the Future of Federalism*, Committee for Economic Development, 1968; (with Allen D. Manvel and Susannah E. Calkins) *Monitoring Revenue Sharing*, Brookings Institution, 1974; *The Plot That Failed: Nixon and the Administrative Presidency*, Wiley, 1975.

* * *

NATHANSON, Jerome 1908-1975

1908—March 21, 1975; American philosopher, educator, author of books on philosophical topics. Obituaries: *New York Times*, March 22, 1975; *AB Bookman's Weekly*, April 28, 1975.

* * *

NAUGHTON, John 1933-

PERSONAL: Born May 20, 1933, in West Nanticoke, Pa.; son of John Patrick (a restaurant owner) and Anne Frances (McCormik) Naughton; married Margaret Louise Fox; children: Bruce, Marcia, Lisa, George, Michael, Thomas. *Education:* Cameron State College, A.A., 1952; St. Louis University, B.S., 1954; University of Oklahoma, M.D., 1958, postgraduate cardiovascular traineeship, 1961-64. *Politics:* Independent Democrat. *Religion:* Episcopalian. *Home:* 902 Le Brun, Eggertsville, N.Y. 14226. *Office:* School of Medicine, State University of New York at Buffalo, Buffalo, N.Y. 14214.

CAREER: George Washington University Medical Center, Washington, D.C., intern, 1958-59; University of Oklahoma Health Sciences Center, Oklahoma City, Medical Center, resident, 1959-61, chief resident, 1962-63, School of Medicine, instructor, 1964-66, assistant professor of medicine and physiology, 1966-68; University of Illinois at the Medical Center, Chicago, associate professor of medicine and director of Rehabilitation Center, 1968-70; George Washington University Medical Center, professor of medicine, 1970-75, director of division of rehabilitation medicine, 1970-75, director of regional Rehabilitation and Training Center, 1970-75, director of coordinating Center for National Study in Exercise and Heart Disease, 1972—, acting associate dean for academic affairs, 1972-73, dean for academic affairs, 1973-75; State University of New York at Buffalo, dean of School of Medicine, 1975—. Member, Governing Board of D.C. General Hospital, 1972—, National Heart and Lung Institute Task Force on Cardiac

Rehabilitation, 1973—, and Mayor's Task Force on Out-Patient Care in District of Columbia, 1973—.
MEMBER: American Medical Association, American College of Cardiology (fellow), American College of Physicians (fellow), American Heart Association, American Congress of Physical Medicine and Rehabilitation, American Physiologic Society, American Psychosomatic Society, American Society of Internal Medicine, American College of Sports Physicians (vice-president, 1967-69; president, 1970-71; fellow), American Association of University Professors, New York Academy of Sciences, District of Columbia Medical Society, Washington Heart Association, American Cancer Society of D.C. (member of board of trustees, 1973—). *Awards, honors:* Career Development Award, National Heart Institute, 1966; International Health Research Act fellowships, 1971-74.
WRITINGS: (Editor with H. Hellerstein and I. Mohler) *Exercise Testing and Exercise Training in Coronary Heart Disease*, Academic Press, 1973; (contributor) E. Levine and J. Garrett, *Rehabilitation Practices with the Physically Disabled*, Columbia University Press, 1973.
WORK IN PROGRESS: A textbook on exercise physiology and rehabilitation techniques.

* * *

NEAL, James T(homas)   1936-
   (Thomas N. James)

PERSONAL: Born February 9, 1936, in Detroit, Mich.; son of Herbert R. and Ida (Forster) Neal; married Mary Virginia Klinedinst, July 30, 1960; children: Rebecca, Martha, Ruth, Matthew. *Education:* Michigan State University, B.S., 1957, M.S., 1959; Boston College, graduate study, 1962-63. *Religion:* Episcopal. *Home:* 712 Raton Ave., S.E., Albuquerque, N.M. 87123. *Office:* Air Force Weapons Laboratory, Kirkland Air Force Base, N.M. 87117.
CAREER: Canadian Cliffs Ltd., Port Arthur, Ont., geologist, 1957; Albanel Minerals Ltd., Lake Albanel, Que., geologist, 1957-59; Air Force Cambridge Research Laboratories, Bedford, Mass., project scientist to branch chief, 1960-68; U.S. Air Force Academy, Colorado Springs, Colo., instructor, 1968-69, assistant professor, 1969-72, associate professor of geology, 1972-73; Air Force Weapons Laboratory, Kirkland Air Force Base, N.M., chief of cratering geophysics in Civil Engineering Research Division, 1973—. *Member:* Geological Society of America (fellow), American Quaternary Association (charter member), Sigma Xi. *Awards, honors:* U.S. Air Force Outstanding Research and Development award, 1966; Past President's Award from Colorado Scientific Society, 1970, for an article, "Patterned Ground as Indicators of Environment."
WRITINGS: (Under pseudonym Thomas N. James) *These Beautiful Hills*, Filter Press, 1972; *Playas, Pans, & Saline Flats*, Encyclopaedia Britannica, 1974; *Playas and Dried Lakes*, Dowden, Hutchinson & Ross, 1975. Contributor to journals in his field.
WORK IN PROGRESS: *Famous Volcanoes of the West*; *Gold in Them Thar Lakes*.
AVOCATIONAL INTERESTS: Photography and travel.

* * *

NEEPER, Carolyn   1937-
   (Cary Neeper)

PERSONAl: Born November 7, 1937, in Oakland, Calif.;

daughter of Harold R., Sr. (a building contractor) and Jessie (a teacher and organist; maiden name, Jones) Almond; married Donald A. Neeper (a physicist), December 31, 1958; children: Indra, Tasha, Monte, Shawne. *Education:* Pomona College, B.A. (magna cum laude), 1958; University of Wisconsin, M.S., 1960, Ph.D., 1962. *Politics:* Independent. *Religion:* Unitarian Universalist. *Residence:* Los Alamos, N.M.
CAREER: Research microbiologist; University of Wisconsin, Madison, postdoctoral fellow, 1962-63. *Member:* Science Fiction Writers of America, Los Alamos Recorder Society (president, 1969-71), Phi Beta Kappa, Sigma Xi. *Awards, honors:* Woodrow Wilson fellow, 1958; National Institutes of Health fellow, 1962-63.
WRITINGS: (Under name Cary Neeper) *A Place Beyond Man*, Scribner, 1975. Contributor to journals in her field.
WORK IN PROGRESS: *The Webs of Varok*, completion expected in 1976; *Accept My Love*, 1976; *Mike, Profoundly Retarded*, 1977.
AVOCATIONAL INTERESTS: String bass, recorders, harpsichord, mandolin, music arranging, ice dancing, painting, ceramics, gardening.

* * *

NEEPER, Cary
   See NEEPER, Carolyn

* * *

NEIER, Aryeh   1937-

PERSONAL: Born April 22, 1937, in Berlin, Germany; son of Wolf (a teacher) and Gitla (Bendzinska) Neier; married Yvette Celton (a merchandiser), June 22, 1958; children: David. *Education:* Cornell University, B.S., 1958. *Office:* American Civil Liberties Union, 22 East 40th St., New York, N.Y. 10016.
CAREER: League for Industrial Democracy, New York, N.Y. executive director, 1958-60; associate magazine editor, 1960-63; American Civil Liberties Union, New York, N.Y., staff member, 1963-64, field representative, 1964-70, executive director of New York Civil Liberties Union, 1970—.
WRITINGS: *Dossier: The Secret Files They Keep on You*, Stein & Day, 1975; *Crime and Punishment: A Radical Solution*, Stein & Day, in press. Contributor to magazines, including *Civil Liberties Review* and *Crime and Delinquency*, and to newspapers, including *Village Voice* and *New York Times*.

* * *

NELSON, Amirtharaj   1934-

PERSONAL: Born October 6, 1934, in Tanjore, India; son of William Mangalaraj (a minister) and Grace (Tyyakannu) Nelson; married Kalyani Purushotham, February 8, 1963; children: Joshua, Deepak. *Education:* University of Madras, B.A., 1955; Cliff College, Sheffield, England, graduate study, 1967-68; Asbury Theological Seminary, M.Div., 1971; Fuller Theological Seminary, D.Miss., 1974. *Home:* 9 Govinda Naicken St., Choolai, Madras 600007, India. *Address:* P.O. Box 2950, Pasadena, Calif. 91105.
CAREER: Ordained Methodist minister; Gordon, Woodroofe Leather Manufacturing Co., Madras, India, officer in charge of tanning, 1956-67; California Wesleyan Church, Los Angeles, pastor, 1973—. Honorary president of

Church Growth Fellowship of India. Itinerant preacher and missionary around the world.

WRITINGS: A New Day in Madras (nonfiction), William Carey Library, 1975; (with wife, Kalyani Nelson) *On the Road with Jesus* (autobiographical), Regal Books, in press.

WORK IN PROGRESS: Research on what John Wesley did to catapult the growth of churches around the world, and on the Protestant churches in Bangalore, India; small Christian devotional books.

AVOCATIONAL INTERESTS: Travel, photography, reading, tennis.

* * *

NELSON, Oswald George
See NELSON, Ozzie

* * *

NELSON, Ozzie 1907-1975
(Oswald George Nelson)

March 20, 1907—June 3, 1975; American actor, producer, director, bandleader and musician, lawyer, and author of autobiography. Obituaries: *New York Times*, June 4, 1975; *Washington Post*, June 4, 1975; *Newsweek*, June 16, 1975; *Current Biography*, August, 1975.

* * *

NEMETH, Laszlo 1901-1975

1901—March(?), 1975; Hungarian philosopher, physician, translator, essayist, critic, novelist, and playwright. Obituaries: *Washington Post*, March 8, 1975; *AB Bookman's Weekly*, April 21, 1975.

* * *

NERE, Jacques 1917-

PERSONAL: Born May 8, 1917, in Chambery, France; son of Georges (an electricity expert) and Gabrielle (Alliot) Nere; married Jacqueline Rapin (a teacher), October 9, 1943; children: Marie Bernadette, Jean Jacques. *Education:* Attended Ecole Normale Superieure, 1938-43; Sorbonne, University of Paris, Docteur es Lettres, 1959. *Home:* 122 rue d'Alesia, Paris 14, France.

CAREER: University of Caen, Caen, France, assistant professor of contemporary history, 1954-59; Banque de Paris et des Pays Bas, Paris, France, chief of economic studies, 1960-67; University of Brest, Brest, France, professor of contemporary history, 1967—. *Military service:* Free French Air Force, 1939-40. *Member:* Societe d'Histoire Moderne, Institut des Hautes Etudes de Defense Nationale, Association pour l'Etude des Problemes de l'Europe. *Awards, honors:* Officier des Palmes Academiques, 1967; Chevalier de l'Ordre National du Merite, 1970.

WRITINGS: La Guerre de secession (title means "The War Between the States"), Presses Universitaires de France (Paris), 1961; *Le Boulangisme et la presse* (title means "Boulangism and the Press"), Armand Colin (Paris), 1963; *La Troisieme Republique, 1914-1940* (title means "The Third Republic, 1914-1940"), Armand Colin, 1965, 5th edition, 1972; *La Crise de 1929* (title means "The 1929 Crisis"), Armand Colin, 1968; (with others) *Precis d'Histoire contemporaine* (title means "An Abstract of Contemporary History"), Presses Universitaires de France, 1973; *The Foreign Policy of France, 1914-1945*, Routledge & Kegan Paul, 1975.

WORK IN PROGRESS: Les Crises du franc et le probleme du mur d'Argent, 1924-26 (title means "The Crisis of the Franc and the Problem of the 'Money Wall,' 1924-26").

* * *

NEWMAN, Howard 1911-

PERSONAL: Born December 22, 1911, in New York, N.Y.; son of Samuel (a college professor) and Gussie (Halpern) Newman. *Education:* Attended City College (now City College of the City University of New York), 1929, and Columbia University, 1930. *Religion:* Jewish. *Home:* 205 West 57th St., New York, N.Y. 10019. *Agent:* Al Zuckerman, Writers' House, 305 West 42nd St., New York, N.Y. 10036. *Office:* Howard Newman Public Relations, 250 West 57th St., New York, N.Y. 10019.

CAREER: Office boy for Dwight Deere Wiman Productions, 1929; worked as press agent assistant on theatre productions, including "On Borrowed Time," "The Gay Divorce," and "Kiss Me, Kate," and six Rogers and Hart musicals, c. 1930-46; free-lance film publicist for forty films including "Spellbound," "Spartacus," "The Fall of the Roman Empire," "The Godfather," "Taxi Driver," and "The Exorcist," 1946—; Samuel Bronston Studios, Madrid, Spain, head of publicity, 1961-64; Twentieth Century Fox, New York, N.Y., director of publicity, 1964-67; Paramount, New York, N.Y., director of publicity, 1968-70; Howard Newman Public Relations, New York, N.Y., independent publicist for major film companies on special films, 1970—. *Member:* Motion Picture Academy of Arts and Sciences, Publicists' Guild of America.

WRITINGS: The Exorcist: The Strange Story Behind the Film, Pinnacle Books, 1974.

Plays: (Author of American adaptation) Valentine Katayev, "Squaring the Circle" (three-act), first produced on Broadway at Lyceum Theatre, October, 1936; (with Beatrice Aliott) "Brooklyn Biarritz" (three-act), first produced on Broadway at Royal Theatre, 1941.

WORK IN PROGRESS: Negotiating to translate and adapt American production of French play in 1976.

SIDELIGHTS: Newman has covered two-thirds of the globe on film locations and worked in more than a dozen countries. He has had several one-man and group shows of his paintings. *Avocational interests:* Painting, gardening.

* * *

NEWMAN, William Mark 1943-

PERSONAL: Born February 9, 1943, in Newburgh, N.Y.; son of Thomas L. (a retailer) and Muriel (Delit) Newman; married Susan LeMay Smith (a photo-journalist), 1968; children: Victoria LeMay. *Education:* Syracuse University, B.A., 1965, M.A., 1967; New School for Social Research, Ph.D., 1970. *Home address:* Cowles Rd., R.F.D. 2, Willington, Conn. 06279. *Office:* Department of Sociology, Box U-68, University of Connecticut, Storrs, Conn. 06268.

CAREER: Metropolitan Urban Service Training Facility, New York, N.Y., research associate in sociology and religion, 1967-68; University of Connecticut, Storrs, instructor, 1969-70, assistant professor, 1970-74, associate professor of sociology, 1974—. Member of Windham Regional Planning Agency, 1969-73; chairman of Willington Planning and Zoning Commission, 1972-74. Consultant, National Science Foundation. *Member:* American Sociological Association, American Association of University Professors,

Society for the Scientific Study of Religion, Religious Research Association.

WRITINGS: (Contributor) Deborah I. Offenbacher and C. Poster, editors, *Social Problems and Social Policy*, Appleton, 1970; (editor with Arnold Dashefsky) *Abstracts of Papers*, Society for the Scientific Study of Religion, 1971; *American Pluralism*, Harper, 1974; (editor) *The Social Meanings of Religion*, Rand McNally, 1974; (contributor) Barry Schwartz, editor, *The Changing Face of the Suburbs*, University of Chicago Press, 1975. Contributor to sociological journals. Contributing editor, *Review of Religious Research;* editorial consultant to *American Journal of Sociology, Journal for the Scientific Study of Religion*, and *School Review*.

* * *

NEWMAR, Rima
See WAGMAN, Naomi

* * *

NEWTON, Stu
See WHITCOMB, Ian

* * *

NICOLAEFF, Ariadne 1915-

PERSONAL: Born November 27, 1915, in Odessa, Russia. *Education:* Attended high school in Istanbul, Turkey, and London, England. *Address:* BM-BOX 8855, London WC1V 6XX, England. *Agent:* Robert Freedman and Harold Freedman, Brandt & Brandt, 101 Park Ave., New York, N.Y. 10017; John Cadell Ltd., 64 Highgate High St., London N6 5HX, England.

CAREER: Stage director for provincial repertories, 1943-47; British Broadcasting Corp., London, England, radio producer, 1947-63; now full-time free-lance writer and translator. Director, Vista Plays Ltd. *Member:* Society of Authors, Great Britain-USSR Association, National Book League. *Awards, honors:* Arts Council of Great Britain New Play Scheme awards for "The Third Wife," and the translation of "Abel, Where Is Your Brother?"

WRITINGS: Poems, Bodley Head, 1937; (compiler with Peter Norman) *Russian Readings*, British Broadcasting Corp., 1962; (editor) Dennis Ward, *Starting Russian*, British Broadcasting Corp., 1963; "The Third Wife" (play), produced in London, England at Arts Theatre, 1973.

Translator: Dennis Ward, *Keep Up Your Russian*, British Broadcasting Corp., 1963; Aleksandr Volodin, *Five Evenings*, University of Minnesota Press, 1966; (with Sir John Gielgud) Anton Chekhov, *Ivanov*, Heinemann, 1966; Aleksei Arbuzov, *The Promise*, Oxford University Press, 1967; Arbuzov, *Confession at Night*, Davis-Poynter, 1971; Julius Edliss, "Abel, Where Is Your Brother?" (play), produced in London at Act Inn, 1974; Ivan Turgenev, "A Month in the Country" (five-act comedy), produced in Chichester, England, 1974; Vassily Shkvarkin, "The Other Man's Child" (play), produced in London at The Cockpit, January, 1975; Arbuzov, "Once Upon a Time" (play), produced in Cambridge, England at Arts Theatre, February, 1975. Also translator of Arbuzov's "Evening Light," to be produced by BBC Radio, 1975.

Author of radio talks and contributor of articles to newspapers.

WORK IN PROGRESS: Two plays.

NIK
See LEE, Francis Nigel

* * *

NIMOY, Leonard 1931-

PERSONAL: Born March 26, 1931, in Boston, Mass.; son of Max and Dora (Spinner) Nimoy; married Sandi Zober, February 21, 1954; children: Julie, Adam. *Education:* Studied drama at Boston College, summer, 1949, and at Pasadena Playhouse, Pasadena, Calif., 1949-50. *Politics:* Democrat. *Religion:* Jewish. *Residence:* Los Angeles, Calif. *Agent:* Phyllis Jackson, International Famous Agency, 1301 Avenue of the Americas, New York, N.Y. 10019.

CAREER: Actor in television, films, and theatre; photographer and author. Television roles include Mr. Spock on NBC series, "Star Trek," 1966-68, and Paris on CBS "Mission Impossible" series, 1969-70; has also held roles in numerous other series, such as "Sea Hunt," "Kraft Theatre," "Perry Mason," "Twilight Zone," "Bonanza," and "Profiles in Courage." Actor in about twenty-five stage plays, 1939-75, including "Full Circle," produced on Broadway, 1973, and "The Fourposter," produced in Lincolnshire, Ill., 1975, and in over a dozen films, 1950-75. Director of a "Night Gallery" television episode, and of an Atlanta, Ga. production of "A Streetcar Named Desire"; co-produced Genet's "Deathwatch" for Beverly Pictures, 1966, and produced a television documentary, "If the Mind Is Free," 1971. Operated own drama studio in North Hollywood, 1962-65; teacher, Synanon, Santa Monica, Calif., 1964-65; owner, Adajul Music Publishing Co. *Military service:* U.S. Army, 1954-56. *Member:* American Federation of Television and Radio Artists, Screen Actors Guild, Actors' Equity Association, American Civil Liberties Union.

WRITINGS—Poetry; self-illustrated with photographs: *You and I*, Celestial Arts, 1973; *Will I Think of You*, Celestial Arts, 1974.

Contributor to *Bio-Cosmos*, by James Christian, 1975.

WORK IN PROGRESS: A book on his experiences as Mr. Spock, tentatively titled *I Am Not Spock*, for Celestial Arts.

SIDELIGHTS: Nimoy has made several recordings for Dot, beginning in 1967: "Leonard Nimoy Presents Mr. Spock's Music from Outer Space," "Two Sides of Leonard Nimoy," "The Way I Feel," "The Touch of Leonard Nimoy," and "The New World of Leonard Nimoy." He specializes in black and white photography, much of which has been shown, and does his own processing.

BIOGRAPHICAL/CRITICAL SOURCES: David Gerrold, *The World of Star Trek*, Ballantine, 1973; Stephen E. Whitfield and Gene Roddenberry, *The Making of Star Trek*, Ballantine, 1973.

* * *

NITZSCHE, Jane Chance 1945-

PERSONAL: Born October 26, 1945, in Neosho, Mo.; daughter of Donald William (a U.S. Army lieutenant colonel) and Julia (Mile) Chance; married Dennis Carl Nitzsche, June, 1966 (divorced, March, 1969); children: Therese Chance. *Education:* Purdue University, B.A., 1967; University of Illinois, A.M., 1968, Ph.D., 1971. *Home:* 2332 Albans, Houston, Tex. 77005. *Office:* Department of English, Rice University, Houston, Tex. 77001.

CAREER: University of Saskatchewan, Saskatoon, assistant professor of English 1971-73; Rice University, Houston, Tex., assistant professor of English, 1973—. *Member:* Modern Language Association of America, American Association of University Professors, Mediaeval Academy of America, Mortarboard, Alpha Lambda Delta, Theta Sigma Phi, Delta Rho Kappa.

WRITINGS: *The Genius Figure in Antiquity and the Middle Ages*, Columbia University Press, 1975.

WORK IN PROGRESS: Research on women writers.

* * *

NONET, Philippe 1939-

PERSONAL: Born February 25, 1939, in Liege, Belgium; son of Leon (a physician) and Helene (a physician; maiden name, Reginster) Nonet; married Anne-Marie Wurth, July 26, 1961; children: Michael, Genevieve, Beatrice. *Education:* University of Liege, Docteur en Droit, 1961; University of California, Berkeley, M.A., 1963, Ph.D., 1966. *Home:* 784 Santa Barbara Rd., Berkeley, Calif. 95707. *Office:* Center for the Study of Law and Society, University of California, Berkeley, Calif. 94720.

CAREER: University of California, Berkeley, assistant professor, 1966-70, associate professor of sociology, 1970—, associate research sociologist at Center for the Study of Law and Society, 1970—. Lecturer at University of Louvain, 1966-70; visiting fellow at Nuffield College, Oxford, spring, 1971. *Member:* American Sociological Association, Law and Society Association (trustee), American Society for Political and Legal Philosophy, Amintaphil.

WRITINGS: *Administrative Justice: Advocacy and Change in a Government Agency*, Russell Sage Foundation, 1969; (with Philip Selznick and Howard Vollmer) *Law, Society, and Industrial Justice*, Russell Sage Foundation, 1970. Contributor to *International Encyclopedia of the Social Sciences*.

WORK IN PROGRESS: Research on law, accountability, and responsiveness in the administration of federal programs.

* * *

NORDBY, Vernon James 1945-

PERSONAL: Born April 28, 1945, in St. Paul, Minn.; son of Carl Henry (an upholsterer) and Elizabeth (Braun) Nordby. *Education:* Cabrillo College, R.T.; also studied at C. G. Jung Institute, Univeristy of California, Santa Cruz, and Institute of Dream Research. *Religion:* Lutheran. *Home:* 417 Cliff St., Santa Cruz, Calif. 95060.

CAREER: Realtor, involved in restoration of Victorian homes, 1965—. Sleep and dream researcher at Institute of Dream Research, 1966—; X-ray technologist at department of health of University of California, Santa Cruz, 1969-71; farmer, 1970—. *Member:* American Registry of Radiologic Technologists.

WRITINGS: *Studies of Dreams Reported in the Laboratory and at Home* (monograph), Big Trees Press, 1966; (with Calvin S. Hall) *The Individual and His Dreams*, New American Library, 1971; (with Hall) *A Primer of Jungian Psychology*, Taplinger, 1973; (with Hall) *A Guide to Psychologists and Their Concepts*, W. H. Freeman, 1974.

WORK IN PROGRESS: *A Primer of Existential Psychology*; *Personal Glimpses of Freud and Jung.*

AVOCATIONAL INTERESTS: Restoring antiques and nineteenth-century buildings, preserving historical objects and works of nature, travel (Europe, Polynesia; preferably by sea), art, history, nature.

* * *

NORMAN, Cecilia 1927-

PERSONAL: Born November 7, 1927, in London, England; daughter of Hyman (a clergyman) and Esther (a suffragette; maiden name, Lev) Miller; married Laurie Norman; children: Dilys (Mrs. Thomas Tausz), Barrister, Kerry (all daughters). *Education:* Studied at Regent Polytechnic, 1948-50; Southgate College, teaching diploma, 1968. *Home:* Apple Tree Cottage, South Hill Park, Hampstead, London, England.

CAREER: Writer, 1970—; Inner London Education Authority, London, England, teacher of home economics and cookery, 1970-74; Kilburn Polytechnic, London, visiting lecturer in microwave cookery, 1973—.

WRITINGS: *Microwave Cookery for the Housewife*, Pitman, 1974; *The Heart-Watchers Cookbook*, Hippocrene Books, 1975. Cookery correspondent for *Hornsey Journal*, 1974—. Contributor to *Home Economics Journal.*

WORK IN PROGRESS: *Advanced International Microwave Cookbook*; a series of cookbooks dealing with health.

SIDELIGHTS: Cecilia Norman feels that ". . . increasing tolerance will result in the total emancipation of women. A woman must have career training even if she chooses to stay at home. More marriages fall apart from boredom than adultery." *Avocational interests:* Squash, bowls, skiing.

* * *

NOUVEAU, Arthur
See WHITCOMB, Ian

* * *

NULMAN, Macy 1923-

PERSONAL: Born June 22, 1923, in Newark, N.J.; son of Samuel (a grocer) and Nellie (Feder) Nulman; married Sarah Rosenberg (a teacher), June 17, 1945; children: Judy (Mrs. David Koenigsberg), Efrem. *Education:* Yeshiva University, B.A., 1945. *Religion:* Jewish. *Residence:* Brooklyn, N.Y. *Office:* Cantorial Training Institute, Yeshiva University, Amsterdam Ave. & 186th St., New York, N.Y. 10033.

CAREER: Cantor at Congregation Etz Chaim of Flatbush, Brooklyn, N.Y., 1944-46 and 1947-66, at First Congregation Anshe Sfard, Brooklyn, N.Y., 1946-47; Yeshiva University, Cantorial Council of America, New York, N.Y., instructor of liturgical music and assistant director, 1951-66, executive secretary, 1961-74, director, 1966—. Adjunct assistant professor at Brooklyn College of the City University of New York, 1970-72. Member of executive board of National Jewish Music Council, 1965-75, and National Jewish Welfare Board, 1965-75.

WRITINGS: *Wedding Service*, Bloch Publishing, 1948; *Sabbath Chants*, Yeshiva University, 1958; *Maariv Chants*, Yeshiva University, 1965; *Concise Encyclopedia of Jewish Music*, McGraw, 1975. Contributor to *International Cyclopedia of Music and Musicians*; contributor to journals in his field.

WORK IN PROGRESS: A text for teaching liturgical music; an anthology on the ancient musical instrument shofar.

OAKLEY, Ann 1944-

PERSONAL: Born January 17, 1944, in London, England; daughter of Richard Morris (a university professor) and Kathleen (a social worker; maiden name, Miller) Titmuss; children: two. *Education:* Somerville College, Oxford, M.A. (honors), 1965; Bedford College, London, Ph.D., 1974. *Politics:* Feminist. *Agent:* Deborah Rogers Ltd., 29 Goodge St., London W1, England. *Office:* Social Research Unit, Bedford College, University of London, 51 Harley St., London W1, England.

CAREER: University of London, Bedford College, London, England, research officer in Social Research Unit, 1974—.

WRITINGS: Sex, Gender & Society, Maurice Temple Smith, 1972, Harper, 1973; *The Sociology of Housework,* Martin Robertson, 1974, Pantheon, 1975; *Housewife,* Allen Lane, 1974, published as *Woman's Work: A History of the Housewife,* Pantheon, 1975; (contributor) David Tuckett, editor, *Medical Sociology,* Tavistock, 1975.

WORK IN PROGRESS: Editing, with Juliet Mitchell, *Women and Change;* research into attitudes on childbirth.

*   *   *

OAKMAN, Barbara F(rances) 1931-

PERSONAL: Born April 19, 1931, in San Rafael, Calif.; daughter of Richard M. and Margaret (Gould) Hoen; married James R. Oakman (a teacher), June 18, 1960; children: James R., Stella Margaret, Frances Rosemary. *Education:* San Francisco State College (now University), A.B., 1953, M.A., 1954; graduate study at College of the Holy Names, 1954-59, and University of Arizona, 1975—. *Home:* 7114 East Sylvane Drive, Tucson, Ariz. 85710. *Office:* Pima Community College, 2202 West Anklam Road, Tucson, Ariz. 85709.

CAREER: Reading specialist or consultant with schools in Los Gatos, Fremont, and Pittsburg, Calif., 1954-66; American River College, Sacramento, Calif., reading specialist, 1966-68; Pima Community College, Tucson, Ariz., reading coordinator, 1969—. Consultant to Indian Health Service and to Community Health Medics Program, 1971—. *Member:* International Reading Association, American Association of Junior Colleges, Western College Reading Association, Arizona State Reading Council.

WRITINGS: Countdown to Successful Reading, Appleton, 1971; *Aids to Learning,* U.S. Government Printing Office, 1973. Contributor to professional journals. Member of editorial board, *Newsletter.*

WORK IN PROGRESS: Research on Indian culture and language.

*   *   *

OBEY, Andre 1892-1975

May 8, 1892—1975; French journalist, essayist, short story writer, novelist, and playwright. Obituaries: *AB Bookman's Weekly,* June 2, 1975.

*   *   *

OBOLER, Eli M(artin) 1915-

PERSONAL: Surname is pronounced *Ob*-o-ler; born September 26, 1915, in Chicago, Ill.; son of Leo (an optometrist) and Clara (Obeler) Oboler; married Marcia Lois Wolf (an art teacher), December 25, 1938; children: Leon David, Carol Judy (Mrs. Paul Gustav Tamminen). *Educa-*

tion: University of Chicago, B.A., 1941, graduate study, 1946-49; Columbia University, B.S. in L.S., 1942. *Politics:* Independent. *Religion:* Jewish. *Home:* 1397 Jane St., Pocatello, Idaho 83201. *Office:* Idaho State University Library, Pocatello, Idaho 83209.

CAREER: U.S. War Production Board, Washington, D.C., assistant chief of lend-lease expediting bureau, 1942-43; University of Chicago, Chicago, Ill., head of reserve room, 1946-49, University College, librarian, 1947-49; Idaho State University, Pocatello, librarian, 1949—. Great Books Foundation, consultant, 1947-49, lecturer, 1948-49. Lecturer at Utah State University, summers, 1960, 1966, and University of Washington, Seattle, summer, 1975. National Advisory Committee on Library Training and Research Projects of U.S. Office of Education, member, 1966-69, chairman, 1968-69. Member of Pocatello Chamber of Commerce, 1966-68; member of advisory committee of Pacific Northwest Regional Health Sciences Library, 1968—, and Idaho Health Information Retrieval Center, 1974—; member of board of trustees of Freedom to Read Foundation, 1971-75. Commentator on weekly radio program, "Books and You," on KEYY, 1949-50, on KSEI, 1950—; participant on television program, "You're Invited," on KID, 1959-60, "It Seems to Me," on KBGL, 1965-66, and "Idaho Looks at the World," on KBGL, 1972—. *Military service:* U.S. Army, 1943-46; served in Canal Zone.

MEMBER: American Library Association (councilor, 1954-59), Association of College and Research Libraries (chairman of college section, 1963-64), American Association of University Professors, Pacific Northwest Library Association (honorary life member; president, 1955-56), Idaho State Library Association (president, 1950-53), Idaho Council of State Academic Librarians (chairman, 1968-69, 1973-74), B'nai B'rith (president of Pocatello chapter, 1951-53), Kiwanis (member of local board of directors, 1972-74). *Awards, honors:* American Library Association-H. W. Wilson Co. library periodical award, 1964, for editorship of *PNLA Quarterly;* commendation by Pocatello Mayor's Committee on Employment of Handicapped, 1968; selected as Idaho Librarian of the Year by Idaho Library Association, 1974.

WRITINGS: (Editor) *College and University Library Accreditation Standards: 1957,* Association of College and Research Libraries, 1958; (contributor) Eric Moon, editor, *Book Selection and Censorship in the Sixties,* Bowker, 1969; (contributor) Alan Angoff, editor, *Public Relations for Libraries,* Greenwood Press, 1973; *The Fear of the Word: Censorship and Sex,* Scarecrow, 1974. Contributor of regular column to *Intermountain,* 1952-60, *Idaho State Journal,* 1960-65, *Intermountain Observer,* 1967-73, and *Western Critic,* 1973—. Contributor to proceedings and of more than one hundred thirty articles and reviews to journals. Editor of *Idaho Librarian,* 1950-54, 1957-58, *PNLA Quarterly,* 1958-67, *Temple Topics,* 1969-73; assistant editor, 1953-54, editor, 1961-62, of *Library Periodicals Round Table Newsletter;* member of editorial board of *College and Research Libraries,* 1962-63.

WORK IN PROGRESS: The Parameters of Intellectual Freedom, completion expected in 1976; *The Supreme Court and Censorship,* 1978; *New England Puritans and Censorship,* 1980.

AVOCATIONAL INTERESTS: Philately, classical music.

*   *   *

O'BRIEN, Lawrence Francis 1917-

PERSONAL: Born July 7, 1917, in Springfield, Mass.; son

of Lawrence Francis, Sr. and Myra (Sweeney) O'Brien; married Elva Brassard, 1944; children: Lawrence Francis III. *Education:* Northwestern University, LL.B., 1942. *Politics:* Democrat. *Religion:* Roman Catholic. *Home:* 860 United Nations Plaza, New York, N.Y. 10017. *Office:* 2700 Calvert St. N.W., Washington, D.C. 20008.

CAREER: O'Brien Realty Co., Springfield, Mass., president of board of directors, 1942-52; businessman and president of the board, Western Massachusetts Hotel and Restaurant Health Fund, 1952-58; state director of organization for campaigns of John F. Kennedy for U.S. Senate, Massachusetts, 1952, 1958; public relations consultant in Springfield, Mass., 1958-60; Democratic National Committee, Washington, D.C., national director of organization, and director for Kennedy-Johnson presidential campaign, 1960; White House, Washington, D.C., special assistant to Presidents Kennedy and Johnson for Congressional relations, 1961-65; U.S. Post Office, Washington, D.C., postmaster general, 1965-68; McDonnell & Co. (investment firm), New York, N.Y., president, 1969; Democratic National Committee, chairman, 1970-72; O'Brien Associates (management consulting firm), Washington, D.C., president, 1973-75. *Military service:* U.S. Army, 1943-45.

AWARDS, HONORS: Honorary degrees from Western New England College, 1962, Northeastern University, 1965, Villanova University, 1966, St. Anselm's College, 1966, Loyola University, 1967, and Seton Hall University, 1967; L.H.D. from American International College and Wheeling College, both 1971; LL.D. from Xavier University, 1971.

WRITINGS: The O'Brien Campaign Manual, Democratic National Committee, 1960, 6th edition, 1972; *No Final Victories: A Life in Politics from John F. Kennedy to Watergate*, Doubleday, 1974.

* * *

O'CATHASAIGH, Donal
See CASEY, Daniel J(oseph)

* * *

O'CONNOR, Richard   1915-1975
(Frank Archer, John Burke, Patrick Wayland)

March 10, 1915—February 15, 1975; American actor, newspaper reporter, author of biographies, popular histories, Western sagas, and murder mysteries. Obituaries: *New York Times*, February 21, 1975; *Publishers Weekly*, March 3, 1975; *AB Bookman's Weekly*, March 17, 1975.

* * *

OCTOBER, John
See PORTWAY, Christopher (John)

* * *

O'DONNELL, James Kevin   1951-
(Jim O'Donnell)

PERSONAL: Born May 14, 1951, in Jersey City, N.J.; son of Amos Louis (an electrical engineer) and Vera (a teacher; maiden name, Horan) O'Donnell. *Education:* St. Peter's College, B.A., 1973. *Home:* 822 Pavonia Ave., Jersey City, N.J. 07306.

CAREER: Writer. Teacher of "Rock 'n' Roll for Your Mind," at St. Peter's College, 1975. *Awards, honors:* Most valuable staffer award from *Jersey Journal*, 1969; North

Jersey Press scholarship, 1972; New Jersey Press scholarship, 1972.

WRITINGS—All under name Jim O'Donnell: *The Rock Book*, Pinnacle Books, 1975. Sportswriter for *Jersey Journal*, 1969-70; correspondent for *New York Times*, 1971-72.

WORK IN PROGRESS: A book on the Beatles; a book on Jim Morrison, former lead singer for "The Doors."

* * *

O'DONNELL, Jim
See O'DONNELL, James Kevin

* * *

OENSLAGER, Donald (Mitchell)   1902-1975

March 7, 1902—June 21, 1975; American stage designer, architectural consultant, and author of books on scenery and set designs. Obituaries: *New York Times*, June 23, 1975; *Current Biography*, August, 1975.

* * *

O'FLAHERTY, Louise   1920-

PERSONAL: Born September 27, 1920, on Mikonos, Greece; daughter of Carl (a lawyer) and Helen (Akin) Wilde; married Joseph S. O'Flaherty (an executive), December 15, 1944; children: Joseph, Michael, Mary (Mrs. Darwin Horn). *Education:* Wellesley College, B.A., 1942. *Religion:* Roman Catholic. *Residence:* Rolling Hills, Calif. 90274. *Agent:* Curtis Brown, Ltd., 60 East 56th St., New York, N.Y. 10022.

WRITINGS: House of the Lost Woman (novel), Pyramid, 1974; *A Tear in the Silk* (novel), Pyramid, in press.

WORK IN PROGRESS: A novel, *Come to Gospel Swamp*, completion expected in 1975.

* * *

OGRAM, Ernest W(illiam), Jr.   1928-

PERSONAL: Born June 29, 1928, in Hartford, Conn.; son of Ernest William (a businessman) and Edith (Sickles) Ogram; married Antonia Santangelo, December 26, 1953; children: Robbin VanSyckle. *Education:* American University, B.A., 1950; University of Connecticut, M.A., 1951; University of Illinois, Ph.D., 1957. *Religion:* Presbyterian. *Home:* 2670 Northside Dr., Atlanta, Ga. 30305. *Office:* Department of Economics, Georgia State University, Atlanta, Ga. 30303.

CAREER: Georgia State University, Atlanta, 1958—, member of faculty in economics. President of Georgia Partners of the Americas, 1969-71. *Military service:* U.S. Army, Infantry; became first lieutenant. *Member:* American Economic Association, Academy of International Business. *Awards, honors:* World Trade Council award from Atlanta Chamber of Commerce, 1970.

WRITINGS: (Co-author) *The Manager and the Multinational Enterprise*, Addison-Wesley, 1975. Contributor to proceedings; contributor to economic and business journals. Editor of *Journal of International Business Studies* and *Essays in International Business*.

WORK IN PROGRESS: International Marketing; writing on East-West trade.

AVOCATIONAL INTERESTS: Travel.

OHLES, John Ford 1920-

PERSONAL: Surname rhymes with "holes"; born July 30, 1920, in Nashwauk, Minn.; son of Wilbur Morris (a merchant) and Mildred (Wiltse) Ohles; married Shirley Mae Sorbo, August 7, 1948; children: Frederik, Janet, Margaret, Judith. Education: University of Minnesota, B.S. (with distinction), 1948, M.A., 1952; graduate study at University of Copenhagen, 1952-53, and Harvard University, 1953-54; State University of New York at Buffalo, Ed.D., 1964. Politics: Democrat. Religion: Presbyterian. Home: 1583 Chadwick Dr., Kent, Ohio 44240. Office: Department of Education, Kent State University, Kent, Ohio 44242.

CAREER: High school teacher of social studies in the public schools of Fergus Falls, Minn., 1948-51; State University of New York College, Fredonia, assistant professor, 1957-59, associate professor of education, 1959-60; State University of New York College, Cortland, associate professor of education, 1960-66; Kent State University, Kent, Ohio, associate professor, 1969-70, professor of secondary education, 1970—. Military service: U.S. Naval Reserve, 1942-46; became lieutenant junior grade. Member: American Association for the Advancement of Science, Society of Professors in Education, National Education Association, National Council for the Social Studies, Ohio Academy of Science, Ohio Education Association, Grafton (Vt.) Historical Society, Phi Delta Kappa, Phi Alpha Theta, Psi Chi.

WRITINGS: Introduction to Teaching, Random House, 1970; (editor) Principles and Practice of Teaching: Selected Readings, Random House, 1970; Instructor's Manual for Introduction to Teaching, Random House, 1970. Contributor of over eighty articles to professional journals.

WORK IN PROGRESS: Teaching Adolescents; Educating American Minorities; Bicentennial Directory of Eminent American Educators, completion expected in 1976.

* * *

OHMER, Merlin M(aurice) 1923-

PERSONAL: Born March 15, 1923, in Napoleonville, La.; married Beverly Landwerlin, August 30, 1947; children: Carol Ann (Mrs. Darrel Falterman), Merlin Paul, Susan Stephanie. Education: Tulane University, B.S., 1944, M.S., 1948; University of Pittsburgh, Ph.D., 1954. Politics: Active voter. Religion: Roman Catholic. Home: 106 Acadia Lane, Thibodaux, La. 70301. Office: College of Sciences, Nicholls State University, Thibodaux, La. 70301.

CAREER: University of Southwestern Louisiana, Lafayette, assistant professor, 1948-53, associate professor, 1953-56, professor of mathematics, 1956-66, lecturer and associate director for National Science Foundation Institutes, 1959-66; Nicholls State University, Thibodaux, La., professor of mathematics, 1966—, head of department, 1966-69, dean of College of Sciences, 1969—, director of Cooperative College-School Science Program, 1966-71. Visiting professor at University of Pittsburgh, 1953-54; visiting scientist for Louisiana Academy of Sciences, 1961-67; visiting lecturer for Mathematical Association of America, 1964-73; director of visiting scientist program at Louisiana Academy of Sciences, 1965-67. Chairman of advisory board of Mt. Carmel High School, Lafayette, La., 1962-66, and Louisiana Mathematics Advisory Council, 1968—; member of Thibodaux Mayor's Advisory Committee, 1971—. Military service: U.S. Navy, 1943-46; served in Mediterranean and Pacific theaters; became lieutenant; U.S. Naval Reserve,

1946-70; retired as commander. Member: American Mathematical Society, Mathematical Association of America (vice-president, 1955), National Council of Teachers of Mathematics, National Council of Deans of Arts and Sciences, Louisiana Academy of Sciences, Louisiana Association of Teachers of Mathematics, Louisiana Teachers Association, Rotary Club, Veterans of Foreign Wars.

WRITINGS: (With others) Elementary Contemporary Mathematics, Ginn, 1964, 2nd edition, 1972; (with others) Elementary Contemporary Algebra, Ginn, 1965; The Real Number System, Louisiana State Board of Education, 1965; (with others) College Algebra, Ginn, 1966; (with others) Modern Mathematics for Elementary School Teachers, Ginn, 1966; Elementary Geometry for Teachers, Addison-Wesley, 1969; Mathematics for a Liberal Education, Addison-Wesley, 1971; (with others) K-12 Guidelines, Louisiana State Board of Education, 1971. Also author of State Board of Education career education guidelines. Contributor to professional journals. Author, producer, and teacher of two television programs, "Summing Up the Difference" (sixty-five half-hour programs), and "The Real Number System" (twenty half-hour programs).

* * *

O'KEEFE, Richard R(obert) 1934-

PERSONAL: Born December 24, 1934, in Pittsburgh, Pa.; son of James H. (a clerk) and Marie (Cornelius) O'Keefe. Education: Duquesne University, B.A., 1957; Pennsylvania State University, M.A., 1959; Northwestern University, graduate study, 1963-64. Home: 4770 Schlaff, Dearborn, Mich. 48126. Office: Dearborn Campus, University of Michigan, Dearborn, Mich. 48120.

CAREER: Instructor in English at Kent State University, Kent, Ohio, 1961-62, and Loyola University, Chicago, Ill., 1963-65; Carnegie-Mellon University, Pittsburgh, Pa., instructor, 1965-68, assistant professor, 1968-71, associate professor, 1971-72, lecturer in English, 1972-73; University of Michigan, Dearborn Campus, lecturer in humanities, 1974—. Awards, honors: National Endowment for the Arts authors grant for 1969-70.

WRITINGS: Uccello's Horse (poems), Three Rivers Press, 1972, 2nd edition, 1973. Poems have been included in Cathedral Poets I and American Literary Anthology, Volume III, and published in Antioch Review, Poetry Northwest, Prism International, Chicago Review, and other literary journals.

WORK IN PROGRESS: Two collections of his poems.

* * *

OKLAHOMA PEDDLER
See GILLES, Albert S(imeon), Sr.

* * *

OLORUNSOLA, Victor A. 1939-

PERSONAL: Born March 23, 1939, in Mopa, Nigeria; son of Thomas Bello (a teacher) and Justina Olayemi (Lawani) Olorunsola; married Carol Ann Bradley (an anthropologist), January 30, 1967; children: Adetokunbo, Michael. Education: Friends University, B.A., 1963; Indiana University, M.A., 1964, Ph.D., 1967. Home: 3187 Stelling Dr., Palo Alto, Calif. 94303. Office: Hoover Institution, Stanford University, Stanford, Calif. 94305.

CAREER: California State University, Long Beach, assistant professor of political science, 1967; Iowa State University, Ames, assistant professor, 1967-70, associate professor of political science, 1970—. National fellow of Hoover Institution for the Study of War, Revolution, and Peace, Stanford University, 1974-75. Visiting professor at Ohio University, spring, 1971. *Member:* International Studies Association, National Conference of Black Political Scientists, American Political Science Association, Royal African Society of England, African Studies Association, Midwest Political Science Association. *Awards, honors:* International Development and Research Center grant from Indiana University, 1971-72; Social Science Research Council grant, 1971-72; Ford Foundation faculty research fellowship in political science, sociology and economics, 1971-72.

WRITINGS: (Editor and contributor) *The Politics of Cultural Nationalism in Africa*, Doubleday, 1972; *Societal Reconstruction in Two African States*, NOK Publishers, 1974; (contributor) *African Political Thought*, East African Literature Bureau, 1975. Contributor to symposia and to journals in his field. Associate editor of *Pan-African Journal*, 1975—.

*   *   *

OLTMANS, Willem L(eonard)   1925-

PERSONAL: Born June 10, 1925, in Huizen, Netherlands; son of Ir A. C. (a chemical engineer and lawyer) and Alexandrine (van der Woude) Oltmans. *Education:* Attended Netherlands Institute for Foreign Relations, 1946-48, Yale University, 1948-50. *Home:* 118-09 83rd Ave., Kew Gardens, New York, N.Y. 11415; and Amerbos 205, Amsterdam, Netherlands. *Agent:* Francis Greenburger, 757 Third Ave., New York, N.Y. 10017.

CAREER: Neiuve Rotterdamse Courant Algemeen, Handelsblad, Netherlands, foreign affairs editor, 1952; United Press International, editor in Amsterdam bureau, 1953-55; *De Telegraaf*, Amsterdam, foreign correspondent in Rome, Italy, 1955-56; foreign correspondent in Southeast Asia, based in Jakarta, Indonesia, 1956-58; *Vrij Nederland* (weekly magazine), staff correspondent at United Nations, 1958-68; Nederlanse Omroep Stichting (National Dutch TV), staff correspondent in United States, 1968-72; freelance correspondent and writer, 1972—.

WRITINGS: De Verraders (title means "The Traitors"), P. R. van Amelrooij (Utrecht), 1968; *Grenzen aan de groei*, Bruna (Holland), Volume I, 1973, Volume II, 1974; *On Growth*, Putnam, Volume I, 1974, Volume II, 1975; *Vaderland Getrouwe* (title means "Loyal to the Fatherland"), Bruna, 1974; *Die Grenzen des Wachtums* (title means "Limits to Growth"), Rowohlt Verlag, 1974.

WORK IN PROGRESS: Europe, twenty-five interviews taken in East and West Europe on the future of the European continent, for Bruna; *Aurelio Peccei*, conversations with the chairman of the Club of Rome, for Editions Stock, Paris.

*   *   *

OPPONG, Christine   1940-

PERSONAL: Born March 3, 1940, in Derby, England; daughter of James (a manager of a textile factory) and Mary (Parkinson) Slater; married E. N. W. Oppong (a veterinary surgeon and professor of animal science), December, 1962; children: Kofi (son), Amma Kyerewaa (daughter), Yaa Pokuaa (daughter). *Education:* Cambridge University,

B.A., 1962, Ph.D., 1971; University of Ghana, M.A., 1965. *Office:* Institute of African Studies, University of Ghana, Legon, Accra, Ghana.

CAREER: University of Ghana, Legon, Accra, research fellow at Institute of African Studies, 1965-73, senior research fellow, 1973—. Bye fellow at Girton College, Cambridge, 1968-69; research associate at University of Manchester, spring, 1974. *Member:* International Sociological Association, Ghana Sociological Association, Royal Anthropological Institute (fellow), Association of Anthropologists of the Commonwealth, British Sociological Association, National Council of Family Relations (United States). *Awards, honors:* Leverhulme Scholar, University of Ghana, 1962-64; Ford Foundation travel grant, 1975, to visit family and population study centers in the United States.

WRITINGS: Growing Up in Dagbon, Ghana Publishing, 1973; *Marriage Among a Matrilineal Elite: A Family Study of Ghanaian Senior Civil Servants*, Cambridge University Press, 1974; (editor) *Domestic Rights and Duties in Southern Ghana*, Institute of African Studies, University of Ghana, 1974. General editor of "Legon Family Research Papers," Institute of African Studies, University of Ghana. Contributor to sociology and African studies journals. Assistant editor of *Ghana Journal of Sociology*.

WORK IN PROGRESS: Synthesizing qualitative and quantitative approaches to the study of the family in a rapidly changing social context; research on processes of domestic change among middle-level, educated government employees in Ghana; a study of family size, family planning, and the family system among Ghanaian primary school teachers.

SIDELIGHTS: Christine Oppong's early work focused on conservative and innovative aspects of education and socialization in a traditional kingdom of northern Ghana. She subsequently studied family relations among elite urban-dwellers, members of the Akan ethnic group, which practices matrilineal descent and inheritance. She believes that Ghanaian women have much to teach women elsewhere in terms of economic responsibility and independence, domestic control and personal autonomy. She looks forward to putting together some new materials on Ghanaian women's roles and is working towards this with a group of friends.

*   *   *

ORDWAY, Sally   1939-

PERSONAL: Born January 5, 1939, in Lafayette, Ala.; daughter of Charles B. (a chemist) and Mary (a teacher; maiden name, Tucker) Ordway. *Education:* Hollins College, B.A., 1959; attended Yale Drama School, 1967-68; Hunter College of the City University of New York, M.A., 1970. *Residence:* New York, N.Y.

CAREER: Mitchell Junior College, New London, Conn., instructor in English, 1963-64; New York Film Festival, New York, N.Y., publicist, 1967-75. Has also held numerous theatrical production and secretarial jobs. Member, Actors Studio, 1966-69. *Member:* Dramatists Guild, Authors League of America, Westbeth Playwrights Feminist Collective. *Awards, honors:* American Broadcasting Co. television fellowship in writing for the camera at Yale Drama School, 1967-68.

WRITINGS—Plays: "Free! Free! Free!," first produced in New York at Theatre Genesis, spring, 1965, new full-length version produced in New York at Hunter College Playwrights' Project, Westside Y, spring, 1969; "There's a Wall Between Us, Darling," first produced at Theatre Genesis, spring, 1965, published in *Yale/Theatre*, summer, 1968; "A Desolate Place near a Deep Hole," first produced in New York at Caffe Cino, August, 1965; "A Passage through Bohemia," first produced in Waterford, Conn., at Eugene O'Neill Theatre Center, summer, 1966; "Movie, Movie on the Wall," first produced at Eugene O'Neill Theatre Center, summer, 1968, produced in Los Angeles at New Theatre for Now at Mark Taper Forum, fall, 1968.

"We Agree," first produced in New York at Westbeth Opening, spring, 1970; "Allison," first produced in Stockbridge, Mass., at Music Barn Theatre, summer, 1970; "Crabs," first produced in New York at Assembly Theatre, spring, 1971, produced in London at Almost Free Theatre, fall, 1973; "San Fernando Valley" and "Australia Play," both first produced in New York by New York Theatre Ensemble, fall, 1971; "Family, Family," produced with other plays under title "Up!" in New York at Westbeth Cabaret, spring, 1972, published in *The Scene*, Horizon, 1974; "Playthings" and "The Chinese Caper," both first produced in New York at Theatre for the New City, winter, 1973; "Sex Warfare," produced with other works under title "We Can Feed Everybody Here," in Westbeth, N.Y., January, 1974; "The Hostess," first produced in Westbeth, April, 1975.

Author of screenplay based on novel, *Wait 'til the Sun Shines, Nellie*, for Columbia Pictures, 1969, and of short film, "Street Corner," 1968. "Crabs," "San Fernando Valley," and "Movie, Movie on the Wall," were published in *Scripts* magazine (of the New York Public Theatre), fall, 1971; publishing rights to "Australia Play" and "We Agree" were sold to Breakthrough Press.

WORK IN PROGRESS: A long play, as yet untitled.

AVOCATIONAL INTERESTS: Archaeology, travel.

* * *

ORLICK, Terrance D(ouglas)   1945-

PERSONAL: Born May 21, 1945, in Montreal, Quebec, Canada; son of Emanuel (a small business consultant) and Agnes (Whalen) Orlick; married Catharine Payne (a high school teacher), August 17, 1968. *Education:* Syracuse University, B.A., 1967; College of William and Mary, M.Ed., 1968; University of Alberta, Ph.D., 1972. *Home:* Old Chelsea, Quebec, Quebec JOX 2NO, Canada. *Office:* School of Human Kinetics and Leisure Studies, University of Ottawa, Ottawa, Ontario, Canada.

CAREER: Montclair State College, Montclair, N.J., assistant professor of physical education, 1968-70; University of Western Ontario, London, Ontario, assistant professor of physical education, 1972-73; University of Ottawa, Ottawa, Ontario, associate professor of kinanthropology, 1973—. Consultant to Canadian National Coaching Development Program, 1973—. *Member:* International Society for Sport Psychology, Canadian Sport Psychology Society (member of executive committee, 1973-75).

WRITINGS: (With Cal Botterill) *Every Kid Can Win*, Nelson-Hall, 1975; (contributor) B. S. Rushall, editor, *The Status of Psychomotor Learning and Sport Psychology Research*, Sport Science Association, 1975; (contributor) J. S. Salmela, editor, *The Advanced Study of Gymnastics*, C. C Thomas, in press. Contributor to journals.

WORK IN PROGRESS: A book tentatively titled, *Cooperative Games: Cooperative Lives*, completion expected in 1976; research on alternative sport environments, and on games of acceptance and psycho-social development.

AVOCATIONAL INTERESTS: Travel, outdoor sports, especially cross country ski touring, canoeing.

* * *

ORSO, Kathryn Wickey   1921-

PERSONAL: Born July 19, 1921, in Fargo, N.D.; daughter of Gould (an educator) and Ethel (Basehoar) Wickey; married Paul Michael Orso (a clergyman), May 30, 1944; children: Donald Paul, Carolyn (Mrs. John Bertelsmeyer). *Education:* Wittenberg University, A.B., 1942; Wesley Theological Seminary, M.R.E. (cum laude), 1968; American University, Ed.D., 1971. *Politics:* Republican. *Religion:* Lutheran. *Home:* 6900 Lachlan Circle, Baltimore, Md. 21239. *Office:* Department of Continuing Education, Essex Community College, Baltimore, Md. 21237.

CAREER: Parent educator in public schools of Baltimore, Md., 1970-74; Essex Community College, Baltimore, Md., assistant in continuing education, 1974—. Member of Baltimore Mayor's Professional Advisory Committee, 1972—; secretary of board of directors, Woodbourne Center for Emotionally Disturbed Children, 1973—. *Member:* Religious Education Association, Association for Exceptional Children, League of Women Voters, Citizens Concerned with Juvenile Justice.

WRITINGS: Manual for Christian Parents, Fortress, 1966; *Double Your Fun and Effectiveness Through Team Teaching*, Fortress, 1968; *It's Great to Pray*, Morehouse, 1974; *As We Love and Forgive*, CSS Publishing, 1975; *Parenthood: Commitment in Faith*, Morehouse, 1975.

WORK IN PROGRESS: Religious Education for the Superior Child, completion expected in 1976.

* * *

ORTON, Harold   1898-1975

1898—March 7, 1975; British educator and authority on the study of English dialectology, author of studies in his field. Obituaries: *AB Bookman's Weekly*, April 21, 1975.

* * *

OSBORN, John Jay, Jr.   1945-

PERSONAL: Born August 5, 1945; son of John Jay and Anne (Kidder) Osborn; married Emilie H. S., 1968. *Education:* Harvard University, B.A., 1967, J.D., 1970. *Religion:* Episcopal. *Home:* 4695 Independence Ave., Riverdale, New York, N.Y. 10471.

CAREER: Admitted to Bar of State of New York, 1974; practicing attorney, 1974—.

WRITINGS: The Paper Chase (novel), Houghton, 1971. Contributor to *Yachting*.

WORK IN PROGRESS: A novel for Houghton, publication expected in 1976.

* * *

OSBORNE, Harold W(ayne)   1930-

PERSONAL: Born September 5, 1930, in El Dorado, Ark.; son of Carl C. and Mary Eunice Osborne; married Alice June Williams, February 15, 1953; children: Mike, Van, Hayes. *Education:* Ouachita College, B.A., 1952; Louisiana State University, M.A., 1956, Ph.D., 1959. *Politics:* Democrat. *Religion:* Baptist. *Home:* 2717 Braemar, Waco, Tex. 76710. *Office:* Department of Sociology, Baylor University, Waco, Tex. 76703.

CAREER: U.S. Department of Agriculture, Baton Rouge, La., social science analyst, 1956-58; Baylor University, Waco, Tex., assistant professor, 1958-60, associate professor, 1960-63, professor of sociology, 1963—. Member of board of directors of Goodwill Industries, 1960-62, local Planned Parenthood, 1965-71, and Action Planning Council, 1966-68. *Military service:* U.S. Army, Infantry, 1952-54; became captain. *Member:* American Sociological Association, Population Association of America, American Social Health Association (member of board of directors of Southwest region, 1968—), Southwestern Sociological Association, Southwestern Social Science Association, McLennan County Health Association (member of board of directors, 1966-72).

WRITINGS: (Editor with Bill Franklin) *Research Methods: Issues and Insights*, Wadsworth, 1971. Contributor to sociology journals. Associate editor of *Social Science Quarterly*, 1966-72, member of editorial board, 1972—.

WORK IN PROGRESS: Editing a book of readings on gerontology; a textbook on juvenile delinquency.

*   *   *

OVERTON, Jenny (Margaret Mary) 1942-

PERSONAL: Born January 22, 1942, in Cranleigh, Surrey, England; daughter of John French (a schoolmaster) and Joyce Margaret (Botting) Overton. *Education:* Girton College, Cambridge, B.A. (honors), 1964, M.A., 1966. *Agent:* Raines & Raines, 244 Madison Ave., New York, N.Y. 10016. *Office:* Lutterworth Press, Luke House, Farnham Rd., Guildford, Surrey, England.

CAREER: Cambridge University, Newnham College, Cambridge, England, principal's private secretary, 1966-67; Aluminium Federation, London, England, assistant editor, 1967-69; Macmillan & Co., London, England, book editor, 1970-71; Lutterworth Press, Guildford, Surrey, England, children's book editor, 1971—.

WRITINGS—All juvenile: *Creed Country*, Faber, 1969, Macmillan, 1970; *The Thirteen Days of Christmas*, Faber, 1972, Thomas Nelson, 1974; *The Nightwatch Winter*, Faber, 1973.

*   *   *

OWEN, Bruce M(anning) 1943-

PERSONAL: Born October 13, 1943, in Worcester, Mass.; son of John W. (an executive) and Barbara (Manning) Owen; married Josetta Knopf, June 19, 1965; children: Peter, Bradford. *Education:* Williams College, B.A., 1965; Stanford University, Ph.D., 1970. *Home:* 593 Salvatierra St., Stanford, Calif. 94305. *Office:* Department of Economics, Stanford University, Stanford, Calif. 94305.

CAREER: Double A Products Co., Manchester, Mich., analyst, 1965; Stanford University, Stanford, Calif., acting assistant professor of economics, 1969-70; Executive Office of the President, Office of Telecommunications Policy, Washington, D.C., chief economist, 1971-72; Stanford University, Stanford, Calif., assistant professor of economics, 1973—. Consultant to White House Office of Telecommunications Policy, Department of Justice Antitrust Division, Federal Trade Commission, and RAND Corp.

Member: American Economic Association, Econometric Society. *Awards, honors:* Woodrow Wilson fellow, 1966; economic policy fellow of Brookings Institution, 1970-71; Hoover Institution on War, Revolution, and Peace national fellow, 1974-75.

WRITINGS: (Contributor) R. E. Park, editor, *The Role of Analysis in Regulatory Decision-making: The Case of Cable Television*, Lexington Books, 1973; (with Jack H. Beebe and Willard G. Manning, Jr.) *Television Economics*, Heath, 1974; *Media Structure and Public Policy: Economics and Freedom of Expression*, Ballinger, 1975. Contributor of articles to journals. Author of government reports. Member of advisory board of *Communication Research*, 1973—.

*   *   *

OYLE, Irving 1925-

PERSONAL: Born September 12, 1925, in New York, N.Y.; son of Harry (a grocer) and Ethel (Ackiron) Oyle; married Pearl Ann Adler, February 11, 1951; children: Julie, Frederick, Abby and Ben (twins). *Education:* College of the City of New York (now City College of the City University of New York), B.S., 1947; New York University, graduate study, 1947-49; Philadelphia College of Osteopathic Medicine and Surgery, D.O., 1953. *Politics:* Independent. *Religion:* "Alchemist." *Residence:* West Marin, Calif.

CAREER: Physician and psychiatrist in private practice in New York, N.Y., 1965-70, and in West Marin, Calif., 1970-75. Director, Spencer Church Health Service, 1968-70, and Headlands Healing Service, 1970-75. Lecturer at New York University, 1948-49.

WRITINGS: *Magic, Mysticism & Modern Medicine*, privately printed, 1973, Celestial Arts, 1976; *The Healing Mind*, Celestial Arts, 1975. Contributor to *American Journal of Acupuncture*.

WORK IN PROGRESS: *Time, Space & the Mind*, science fiction story; research into prime cause healing.

SIDELIGHTS: Oyle was a hand puppeteer with the Bread & Puppet Theatre in New York City, 1960-66.

BIOGRAPHICAL/CRITICAL SOURCES: *Marin Independent Journal*, February 15, 1975; *San Francisco Examiner & Chronicle*, March 23, 1975; *Harpers' Weekly*, June, 1975.

*   *   *

PACKARD, Robert G(eorge) 1933-

PERSONAL: Born February 8, 1933, in Minneapolis, Minn.; son of R. W. (a business manager) and C. (Carlson) Packard; married Sally A. Miclot, November 7, 1969; children: Julie, Randy, Tina, Cristy. *Education:* St. Paul Seminary, M.A., 1958; Western Michigan University, M.A., 1969; University of Minnesota, Ph.D., 1971. *Home:* 1010 Vega Dr., Colorado Springs, Colo. 80906. *Office:* Pikes Peak Mental Health Center, 1353 South 8th St., Colorado Springs, Colo. 80906.

CAREER: University of Minnesota, Minneapolis, instructor in psychology, 1971; University of Missouri, St. Louis, assistant professor of education and psychology, 1971-74; Pikes Peak Mental Health Center, Colorado Springs, Colo., director of evaluation and research, 1974—. *Member:* American Psychological Association, American Personnel and Guidance Association, American Association of Colleges for Teacher Education, Association of Teacher Educators, American Civil Liberties Union, American Association of University Professors, Public Citizen.

WRITINGS: (Contributor) W. R. Houston, editor, *Competency-Based Materials Resource Catalogue*, New York State Department of Education, 1973; *Education and Teaching: Twenty-one Performance-Based Units for an Introduction to Education*, C. E. Merrill, 1974; *The Psychology of Learning and Instruction*, C. E. Merrill, 1975. Author of eleven monographs and four programmed texts. Contributor to professional journals. Editorial consultant to *Journal of Applied Behavior Analysis*, 1972—.

WORK IN PROGRESS: Research on methods for evaluating mental health programs.

SIDELIGHTS: Packard is active in child abuse prevention programs and in training programs for foster parents. He and his wife are also foster parents.

* * *

PAKULA, Marion Broome 1926-

PERSONAL: Born January 27, 1926, in Brooklyn, N.Y.; daughter of Sol (a fish merchant) and Tilda (Nanes) Broome; married Robert S. Pakula (an import salesman), January 11, 1948; children: Ross Sloane, Malanie Dale, Scott Ian. *Education:* Attended Brooklyn College (now of the City University of New York), 1942-44; University of Connecticut, B.A., 1946. *Home:* 10 Kensington Dr., Huntington, N.Y. 11743. *Office:* Periphonics Corp., 75 Orville Dr., Bohemia, N.Y. 11716.

CAREER: Book-of-the-Month Club, New York, N.Y., member correspondent, 1946-47; publicity assistant at radio station WNEW, New York, N.Y., 1947-48; Pakula Associates (editorial typing business), New Hyde Park, N.Y., editor, 1957-62, Huntington, N.Y., 1962-74; National Cash Register Co., Hempstead, N.Y., programmer analyst, 1967-70; Mark Computer Systems, Commack, N.Y., documentation manager, 1970-73; Periphonics Corp., Bohemia, N.Y., technical writer, 1973—. Owner of Pakula Plaids, Inc., 1975—. *Member:* Long Island Embroiderers' Guild, Pencraft, Hadassah.

WRITINGS: Needlepoint Plaids, Crown, 1975, *New Ideas for Needlepointers*, Crown, in press.

WORK IN PROGRESS: Annotated Catalog of Needlepoint Books.

* * *

PALMER, Bernard 1914-
(John Runyan)

PERSONAL: Born November, 1914, in Central City, Neb.; son of Ben H. (in monument business) and Stella (Jarvis) Palmer; married June Berger, June 20, 1934 (died September 28, 1939); married Marjorie Matthews (a writer), December 12, 1940; children: James Barrett (deceased), Morris Jay, Bonnie Lou (Mrs. Douglas Young), Janice Kay (Mrs. Edward Fowler). *Education:* Attended Kearney State College, 1933, and Hastings College, 1940. *Politics:* Republican. *Religion:* Protestant—Evangelical Free Church of America. *Home:* 1013 14th Ave., Holdrege, Neb. 68949. *Office:* 421 East Ave., Holdrege, Neb. 68949.

CAREER: Palmer Bros. Monument Co., Holdrege, Neb., stonecutter and shop foreman, 1957-67, vice-president, 1962-74, president, 1974—, chairman of board of directors,

1974—; full-time writer, 1967—. Member of board of directors, Tyndale Foundation, 1963—. *Member:* Gideons International (past president of Nebraska chapter), Kiwanis.

WRITINGS—All published by Moody, except as indicated: *Parson John*, Eerdmans, 1942; *Storm Winds*, Eerdmans, 1942; *Visibility Zero*, Zondervan, 1944; *Dark Are the Shadows*, Zondervan, 1945; *Dangerous Mission*, Zondervan, 1945; *Mission of Mercy*, Hitchcock, 1946; *Goon Walford Fights Back*, Van Kampen, 1946; *Withering Grass*, Van Kampen, 1949.

Radio Stories, Back to the Bible Broadcast, 1950; *Radio Stories #3*, Back to the Bible Broadcast, 1952; *Danny Orlis Stories*, Back to the Bible Broadcast, 1953; *Sky Pilot Gang Busters*, Sky Pilot Press, 1955; *Jungle Jim*, 1956; *Storm on the Muskeg*, 1957; *New Skipper of the Flying Swede*, 1957; (with wife, Marjorie Palmer) *Miracle of the Prairies*, 1958, new edition published as *Beacon on the Prairies*, Briercrest Bible Institute, 1970.

Andy Logan and the Oregon Trail Mystery, 1961; *Mystery of Dungu Re*, 1961; *Tattered Loin Cloth*, 1962; *Adventure in Tanganyika*, 1963; *Yukuma the Brave*, 1963; *The Wind Blows Wild*, 1968; *Sue Riley and the Mysterious Cargo*, 1968; *Across the Deep Valleys*, Nebraska Christian Press, 1969.

My Son, My Son, 1970; *So Restless, So Lonely*, Bethany Fellowship, 1970; *Seek No Tomorrow*, 1971; *Whisper the Robin*, Zondervan, 1972; *God Understands*, 1973; (with Marjorie Palmer) *The Winds of God Are Blowing*, Tyndale, 1973; (with Irene Hanson) *The Wheelbarrow and the Comrade*, 1973; *Amsterdam Rebel*, 1973; (with Fred Eggerichs) *A Bag without Holes*, Bethany Fellowship, 1975; *Frosty Roberts and the Golden Jade Mystery*, 1975; *Silent Thunder*, Bethany Fellowship, 1975; *White Water on the Yukon*, in press.

"Brigade Boys" series: *Brigade Boys and the Flight to Danger*, 1960; *. . . and the Phantom Radio*, 1960; *. . . in the Arctic Wilderness*, 1961; *. . .and the Disappearing Stranger*, 1961; *. . .and the Basketball Mystery*, 1963.

"Career" series: (With Marjorie Palmer) *Student Nurse*, 1960; (with Marjorie Palmer) *Barbara Nichols, Fifth Grade Teacher*, 1960; *Big Season*, 1960; *Mystery of the Musty Ledger*, 1960; *Peggy Archer, Missionary Candidate*, 1961; *Brad Foster, Engineer*, 1962; (with Marjorie Palmer) *Karen Simms, Private Secretary*, 1963; *Randy Warren, First Term Missionary*, 1963; *Cal Henderson, M.D.*, 1963; *Jim Shelton, Radio Engineer*, 1964; (with Marjorie Palmer) *Sandra Emerson, R.N.*, 1966; *Lee Sloan, Missionary Pilot*, 1966; *Dennis Harper, Missionary Journalist*, 1966.

"Danny Orlis" series: *Danny Orlis and the Point Barrow Mystery*, Good News Publishing, 1954; *. . .and the Angle Inlet Mystery*, 1954; *. . .and the Strange Forest Fires*, 1955; *. . .and the Hunters*, 1955; *. . .Goes to School*, 1955; *. . .and the Rocks that Talk*, 1955; *. . .on Superstition Mountain*, 1956; *. . .Makes the Team*, 1956; *. . .Changes Schools*, 1956; *. . .and the Wrecked Plane*, 1956; *. . .and the Big Indian*, 1956; *. . .and the Sacred Cave*, 1957; *. . .*, *Star Back*, 1957; *. . .and the Boy Who Would Not Listen*, 1957; *. . .Plays Hockey*, 1957; *. . .and His Big Chance*, 1958; *. . .and the Contrary Mrs. Forester*, 1958; *. . .and the Man from the Past*, 1959; *. . .*, *Big Brother*, 1959; *. . .on the Valiant*, 1959; *. . . and Marilyn's Great Trial*, 1959.

Danny Orlis and the Mystery of the Sunken Ship, 1960; *. . .and Ron Orlis in the Canadian Wilderness*, 1960; *. . .in*

the Mysterious Zandeland, 1960; . . .and the Time of Testing, 1961; . . ., Bush Pilot, 1961; . . .and Hal's Great Victory, 1962; . . .and the Drug Store Mystery, 1962; . . .and Ron's Call to Service, 1963; . . .and the Headstrong Linda Penner, 1963; . . .and the Ordeal at Camp, 1963; . . .and Linda's Struggle, 1964; . . .and the Ice Fishing Escapade, 1964; . . .and Linda's New Mother, 1965; . . .and Ron in the Mexican Jungle Mystery, 1965; . . .and the Defiant Kent Gilbert, 1965; . . .and Robin's Big Battle, 1965; . . .and the Old Mine Mystery, 1966; . . .and Kent's Encounter with the Law, 1966; . . .and Robin's Rebellion, 1966; . . .and Robin's Big Mistake, 1966; . . .and Jim's Northern Adventure, 1967; . . .and Kent Gilbert's Tragedy, 1967; . . .and the Teen-Age Marriage, 1967; . . . and the Guatemala Adventure, 1967; . . .and Fritz McCloud, High School Star, 1968; . . .and Excitement at the Circle R, 1968; . . .and Jim Morgan's Scholarship, 1968; . . .and Trouble on the Circle R Ranch, 1968; . . .and the Accident that Shook Fairview, 1968; . . .: Bid for Victory, 1969; . . .and the Dry Gulch Mystery, 1969; . . .and Johnny's New Life, 1969.

Danny Orlis and DeeDee's Defiance, 1970; . . .and Dee-Dee's Best Friend, 1970; . . .and the Football Feud, 1971; . . .and the Crisis at Cedarton, 1971; . . .and the Bewildered Runaway, 1971; . . .and the Mexican Kidnapping, 1971; . . .and the Canadian Caper, 1972; . . .and the Alaskan Highway Adventure, 1972; . . .: Forced Down, 1972; . . .and the Live-in Tragedy, 1972; . . .and the Colorado Challenge, 1972; . . .and Doug's Big Disappointment, 1973; . . .and the Ski Slope Emergency, 1973; . . .and the Mystery at Northwest High, 1973; . . .and the Girl Who Dared, 1974; . . .and the Mysterious Intruder, 1974; . . .and the Rock Point Rebel, 1974; . . .and the Model Plane Mystery, 1975.

"Dell Norton" series: The Wild Float Trip, 1958; The Vanishing Mountain Lion, 1958; The Echo Mountain Hermit, 1958; Dell Norton in the Ozarks, 1958; Dell Norton and the Hidden Cave, 1959.

"Felicia Cartwright" series: Felicia Cartwright and the Frantic Search, 1958; . . .and the Missing Sideboard, 1958; . . .and the Green Medallion, 1958; . . .and the Uncut Diamond, 1958; . . .and the Case of the Twisted Key, 1959; . . .and the Case of the Frightened Student, 1959; . . .and the Case of the Lonely Teacher, 1960; . . .and the Case of the Dancing Fire, 1960; . . .and the Case of the Troubled Rancher, 1961; . . .and the Case of the Storm Scarred Mountain, 1961; . . .and the Case of the Hungry Fiddler, 1962; . . .and the Case of the Antique Bookmark, 1963; . . .and the Case of the Lost Puppy, 1965; . . .and the Case of the Knotted Wire, 1966; . . .and the Case of the Honorable Traitor, 1967; . . .and the Case of the Black Phantom, 1968; . . .and the Case of the Lone Ski Boot, 1969; . . .and the Case of the Bad-Eyed Girl, 1970; . . .and the Case of the Pink Poodle, 1970.

"Golden Boy" series: Golden Boy, Van Kampen, 1954; . . .: Outlaw, Van Kampen, 1954; . . .and the Counterfeiters, Scripture Press, 1958.

"Halliway Boys" series: The Halliway Boys on Crusade Island, 1957; . . .and the Disappearing Staircase, 1958; . . .on the Secret Expedition, 1958; . . .on a Dangerous Voyage, 1958; . . .and the Mysterious Treasure Map, 1960; . . .and the Missing Film Mystery, 1960; . . .on Forbidden Mountain, 1962; . . .on a Secret African Safari, 1962.

"Jim Dunlap" series—see "Pat Collins" series, below.

"Little Feather" series, published by Zondervan: Little Feather Goes Hunting, 1946; . . .at Big Bear Lake, 1947;

. . .Rides Herd, 1947; . . .and the Mystery Mine, 1948; . . .at Tonak Bay, 1950; . . .and the Secret Package, 1951; . . .and the River of Grass, 1953.

"Lori Adams" series: Lori Adams and the Old Carter House Mystery, 1969; . . .and the Adopted Rebel, 1971; . . .and the River Boat Mystery, 1971; . . .and the Jungle Search, 1974.

"Mel Webb" series: Mel Webb and the Border Collie, 1964; . . .on the Danger Trail, 1964; . . .and the Stolen Dog Mystery, 1964.

"Mickey Turner" series: The Fire Detectives, 1955; Trapped on Sugar Loaf Mountain, 1955; Mickey Turner and the Phantom Dog, 1955; Mickey Turner, Ranger's Son, 1955.

"Orlis Twins" series: The Orlis Twins and the Secret of the Mountain, 1959; . . .and the High School Gang, 1959; . . .Live for Christ, 1959; . . .and the New Coach, 1960; . . .and Mike's Last Chance, 1960; . . .and Ron's Big Problem, 1961; . . .and Jim Morgan's Ordeal, 1962; . . .and Roxie's Triumph, 1963.

"Pat Collins" series (later revised and issued as "Jim Dunlap" series as noted): Pat Collins and the Peculiar Dr. Brockton, 1957, revised edition published as Jim Dunlap and the Strange Doctor Brockton, 1967; Pat Collins and the Hidden Treasure, 1957; Pat Collins and the Wingless Plane, 1957, reissued as Jim Dunlap and the Wingless Plane, 1968; Pat Collins and the Captive Scientist, 1958; Pat Collins and the Mysterious Orbiting Rocket, 1958, reissued as Jim and the Mysterious Orbiting Rocket, 1968; Pat Collins and the Secret Engine, 1967.

"Pioneer Girls" series; all with Marjorie Palmer: Pioneer Girls and the Mystery of Oak Ridge Manor, 1959; . . .and the Mystery of the Missing Cocker, 1959; . . .and the Strange Adventures on Tomahawk Hill, 1959; . . .at Caribou Flats, 1959; . . .and the Secret of the Jungle, 1962; . . .and the Mysterious Bedouin Cave, 1963; . . .and the Dutch Mill Mystery, 1968.

"Ted and Terri" series: Ted and Terri and the Broken Arrow, 1971; . . .and the Crooked Trapper, 1971; . . .and the Troubled Trumpeter, 1971; . . .and the Stubborn Bully, 1971; . . .and the Secret Captive, 1971.

Under pseudonym John Runyan; "Biff Norris" series: Biff Norris and the Clue of the Lonely Landing Strip, 1962; . . .and the Clue of the Worn Saddle, 1962; . . .and the Clue of the Nervous Stranger, 1962; . . .and the Clue of the Golden Ram, 1962; . . .and the Clue of the Midnight Stage, 1963; . . .and the Clue of the Lavender Mink, 1964; . . .and the Clue of the Gold Ring, 1965; . . .and the Clue of the Angry Fisherman, 1966; . . .and the Clue of the Disappearing Wolf, 1967; . . .and the Clue of the Mysterious Letter, 1968; . . .and the Clue of the Half-Burned Book, 1969.

Under pseudonym John Runyan; "Tom Barnes" series: Tom Barnes and the Substitute Second Baseman, 1964; . . ., Blocking Back, 1966; . . ., Forward, 1968.

Ghost-writer of God is for the Alcoholic, by Jerry Dunn, Moody, 1965. Author of weekly radio series, "Saturday Youth Program," broadcast in United States and abroad by Back to the Bible Broadcast, 1945—. Contributor to screenplay, "My Son, My Son" (based on his book of the same title), and to "Silent Thunder," and an additional film for Ken Anderson Films (Winona Lake, Ind.). Contributor to Christian Life. Member of board of publications, Evangelical Free Church of America, 1965-71, 1971-74.

WORK IN PROGRESS: A book on Redwood Chapel in Castro Valley, Calif., for Victor Books; a biography of evangelists Louie and Phil Palermo, tentatively titled *Atsa Nice*, for Victor Books; *Yoneko*, a story of a Japanese girl's life after an attempted suicide.

AVOCATIONAL INTERESTS: Travel, fishing, boating.

BIOGRAPHICAL/CRITICAL SOURCES: Christian Life, February, 1970.

* * *

PALMER, Dorothy Ann 1935-

PERSONAL: Born May 23, 1935, in Indiana, Pa.; daughter of Bain (a salesman) and Ruth (Russell) Palmer. *Education:* Indiana University of Pennsylvania, B.S., 1957; Miami University, Oxford, Ohio, A.M., 1963; University of Missouri, graduate study, 1964-65. *Politics:* Democrat. *Religion:* Presbyterian. *Home:* 927 Philadelphia St., Indiana, Pa. 15701. *Office:* Department of Political Science, Indiana University of Pennsylvania, Indiana, Pa. 15701.

CAREER: Indiana University of Pennsylvania, Indiana, Pa., assistant professor, 1965-70, associate professor of political science, 1970—. *Member:* American Political Science Association, American Academy of Political and Social Science, Northeast Political Science Association, Midwest Political Science Association, Pennsylvania Political Science Association.

WRITINGS: (With Raymond L. Lee) *America in Crisis: Contemporary Political Dilemmas*, Winthrop Publishing, 1972.

WORK IN PROGRESS: Mass Media and the American Political Process.

* * *

PALMER, Marjorie 1919-

PERSONAL: Born October 2, 1919, in Randolph, Neb.; daughter of Locie Floyd (a farmer) and Maud (Jay) Matthews; married Bernard Palmer (an author), December 12, 1940; children: Morris Jay, Bonnie Lou (Mrs. Douglas Young), Janice Kay (Mrs. Edward Fowler); stepchildren: James Barrett (deceased). *Education:* Attended high school in Wilcox, Neb. *Politics:* Republican. *Religion:* Protestant—Evangelical Free Church of America. *Home:* 1013 14th Ave., Holdrege, Neb. 68949.

CAREER: Author. *Member:* Gideons International (Nebraska chapter; past president of auxiliary).

WRITINGS: (With husband, Bernard Palmer) *Miracle of the Prairies*, Moody, 1958, new edition published as *Beacon on the Prairies*, Briercrest Bible Institute, 1970; (with Ethel Bowman) *The Bride's Book of Ideas*, Tyndale, 1970; (with Bowman) *The Young Mother's Book of Ideas*, Tyndale, 1973; (with Bernard Palmer) *The Winds of God Are Blowing*, Tyndale, 1973.

"Career" series of Moody Press; all with Bernard Palmer: *Student Nurse*, 1960; *Barbara Nichols, Fifth Grade Teacher*, 1960; *Karen Simms, Private Secretary*, 1963; *Sandra Emerson, R.N.*, 1966.

"Pioneer Girls" series of Moody Press; all with Bernard Palmer: *Pioneer Girls and the Mystery of Oak Ridge Manor*, 1959; *...and the Missing Cocker*, 1959; *...and the Strange Adventures on Tomahawk Hill*, 1959; *...at Caribou Flats*, 1959; *...and the Secret of the Jungle*, 1962; *...and the Mysterious Bedouin Cave*, 1963; *...and the Dutch Hill Mystery*, 1968.

WORK IN PROGRESS: Cookbook of Ideas, completion expected in 1975; a complete camping book.

* * *

PALMER, Richard Phillips 1921-

PERSONAL: Born March 10, 1921, in Milwaukee, Wis.; son of Claude Wood (a railroad engineer) and Amy Grace (Phillips) Palmer; married Jocelyn Wold (a school secretary), May 22, 1954; children: Jonathan Wold. *Education:* Attended Business Institute of Milwaukee, 1939-40; Principia College, B.A. (with highest honors), 1949; University of Wisconsin, M.A. (English), 1964, M.A. (library science), 1965, Ph.D., 1970. *Home:* 10 Linden Gardens, Wellesley, Mass. 02181. *Office:* School of Library Science, Simmons College, Boston, Mass. 02115.

CAREER: Burroughs Adding Machine Co., Milwaukee, Wis., clerk, 1940-41; public school teacher in Glen Arbor, Mich., 1941-42; Christian Science practitioner in Milwaukee, Wis., 1949-59; Bresler Galleries, Milwaukee, Wis., salesman, 1959-60; Purtell Real Estate, Milwaukee, Wis., salesman, 1960-62; University of Wisconsin–Milwaukee, acting instructor in English, 1963-64, reference librarian, summer, 1964; Wisconsin Library Commission, Madison, project assistant, autumn, 1964; University of Wisconsin–Madison, visiting lecturer in library science, summer, 1965; Illinois State University, Normal, assistant professor of library science and assistant librarian, 1965-66; University of Michigan, Ann Arbor, lecturer in library science, summer, 1967-68, research associate at Institute of Science and Technology, 1967-68; Community Systems Foundation, Ann Arbor, Mich., research associate, 1968-69; Eastern Michigan University, Ypsilanti, lecturer in library science, spring, 1970; Simmons College, Boston, Mass., assistant professor, 1970-74, associate professor of library science, 1974—. Director of Advanced Institute on Budgeting and Accountability, 1972; vice-chairman of board of trustees of Wayland Public Library, 1974. Director of seminars and workshops; consultant to Foundation for Biblical Research and Preservation of Primitive Christianity. *Military service:* U.S. Naval Reserve, Naval Intelligence, 1942-46.

MEMBER: American Society for Information Science, Association of American Library Schools, New England Technical Services Librarians (member of executive board), New England Library Association, Massachusetts Library Association, Phi Alpha Eta, Sigma Tau Delta (president of University of Wisconsin chapter, 1963-64), Beta Phi Mu (president of University of Michigan chapter, 1967-69). *Awards, honors:* Grants from Emily Hollowell Research Fund, 1972-74.

WRITINGS: User Requirements of a University Library Card Catalog, School of Library Science, University of Michigan, 1970; *Computerizing the Card Catalog in the University Library: A Survey of User Requirements*, Libraries Unlimited, 1972; (contributor) Frank Slater, editor, *Cost Reduction for Special Libraries and Information Centers*, American Society for Information Science, 1973; *Case Studies in Library Computer Systems*, Bowker, 1973; (contributor) Helen J. Waldron and F. Raymond Long, editors, *Innovative Developments in Information Systems: Their Benefits and Costs*, American Society for Information Science, 1974; *Librarianship: Educational Preparation, Financial Aid, Certification in Massachusetts* (booklet), Massachusetts Library Association, 1974. Book reviewer for *American Reference Books Annual*, 1971-73.

WORK IN PROGRESS: Systems Analysis for Library Management; Library Computer Networks.

* * *

PANSHIN, Alexei 1940-

PERSONAL: Born August 14, 1940, in Lansing, Mich.; son of Alexis John (a college professor) and Lucie (Padget) Panshin; married Cory Seidman (a writer), June 4, 1969. *Education:* Attended University of Michigan, 1958-60; Michigan State University, B.A., 1965; University of Chicago, M.A., 1966. *Home address:* R.R. 2, Box 261, Perkasie, Pa. 18944.

CAREER: Brooklyn Public Library, Brooklyn, N.Y., librarian, 1966-67. Writer of science fiction and criticism. Visiting lecturer in science fiction, Cornell University, summer, 1971, 1972. *Military service:* U.S. Army, 1960-62. *Member:* Science Fiction Writers of America. *Awards, honors:* Hugo Award, 25th World Science Fiction Convention, 1967; Nebula Award, Science Fiction Writers of America, 1968, for *Rite of Passage.*

WRITINGS—All fiction, except as indicated: *Rite of Passage*, Ace Books, 1968; *Star Well*, Ace Books, 1968; *The Thurb Revolution*, Ace Books, 1968; *Heinlein in Dimension* (criticism), Advent, 1968; *Masque World*, Ace Books, 1969; *Farewell to Yesterday's Tomorrow* (short stories), Berkley Publishing, 1975; (with wife, Cory Panshin) *Science Fiction in Dimension: A Book of Explorations* (criticism), Advent, in press. Also author, with Cory Panshin, of fiction, "The Son of Black Morca," published in *Fantastic Stories*, April-September, 1973. Editor, Science Fiction Writers of America *Bulletin* and *Forum*, 1968-69.

WORK IN PROGRESS: Two novels, *The Universal Pantograph*, and *The Princess of Palsance*, both with his wife, Cory Panshin; a history of science fiction, *The World Beyond the Hill*, completion expected in 1976.

* * *

PAPENFUSE, Edward C(arl), Jr. 1943-

PERSONAL: Born October 15, 1943, in Toledo, Ohio; son of Edward C. (an engineer) and Ruth (Wilson) Papenfuse; married Sallie Fisher (a teacher), June 19, 1965; children: Eric, David. *Education:* American University, B.A., 1965; University of Colorado, M.A., 1967; Johns Hopkins University, Ph.D., 1973. *Home:* 206 Oakdale Rd., Baltimore, Md. 21210. *Office:* Maryland Hall of Records, P.O. Box 828, Annapolis, Md. 21404.

CAREER: American Historical Review, Washington, D.C., associate editor-bibliographer, 1970-73; Maryland Hall of Records, Annapolis, Md., assistant state archivist, 1973-75, state archivist, 1975—. Lecturer on Maryland archives and history. *Member:* American Historical Association, Society of American Archivists, Organization of American Historians, Association for State and Local History, Maryland Historical Society. *Awards, honors:* National Endowment for the Humanities grant, 1974-76.

WRITINGS: (Compiler with Jack Phillip Greene) *The American Colonies in the Eighteenth Century*, Appleton, 1968; (with Jane W. McWilliams and Carol Tilles) *Directory of Maryland Legislators: 1635-1789*, Maryland Bicentennial Commission, 1974; *Guide to the Microfilm Edition of the Papers of Thomas Sim Lee*, Maryland Historical Society, 1974; (compiler) *Writings on American History*, Volume I, Kraus Reprint, 1974; *In Pursuit of Profit: The Annapolis Merchants in the Era of the American Revolu-*

tion, Johns Hopkins University Press, 1975. Contributor of articles and reviews to professional journals.

WORK IN PROGRESS: History of the Maryland Legislature: 1635-1789, for Maryland Hall of Records, and editing, with Jack Phillip Greene and Charles Mullett, *Magna Charta for America*, for Huntington Library, publication of both expected in 1977.

* * *

PARENT, David J(oseph) 1931-

PERSONAL: Born May 31, 1931, in Hamlin, Me.; son of Patrick D. (a worker) and Yvonne Marie (Violette) Parent; married Ana Maria Ferran (a Spanish teacher), May 2, 1971; children: David Alberto, Michael Joseph. *Education:* Marist College, B.A., 1953; University of Cincinnati, M.A., 1965, Ph.D., 1967. *Home:* 1 Payne Pl., Normal, Ill. 61761. *Office:* Department of German, Illinois State University, Normal, Ill. 61761.

CAREER: College of Mount St. Joseph, Cincinnati, Ohio, instructor in German, 1963-65; Boston College, Boston, Mass., assistant professor of German, 1965-68; Illinois State University, Normal, associate professor of German, 1968—. *Military service:* U.S. Army, 1954-56.

WRITINGS: Werner Bergengruen's Das Buch Rodenstein: A Detailed Study, Mouton & Co., 1974; *Werner Bergengruen's Ungeschriebene Novelle*, Bouvier, 1974; (translator) Michael Landmann, *Philosophical Anthropology*, Westminster, 1974.

WORK IN PROGRESS: Studies in German literature and translations of philosophical works.

* * *

PARHAM, Robert Randall 1943-
(Rand Roberts)

PERSONAL: Born April 21, 1943, in Takoma Park, Md.; son of Orion Lee and LaVon Louise (Marshall) Parham; married Dorothy Ann Van Hook (a teacher), July 31, 1965; children: Misty Dawn, Thomas Orion. *Education:* Belmont College, B.A., 1965; Florida State University, M.S., 1970. *Politics:* Independent. *Religion:* "Unitarian Universalist, I guess." *Home:* 521 South Coit St., Florence, S.C. 29501. *Office:* Department of English, Francis Marion College, Florence, S.C. 29501.

CAREER: Francis Marion College, Florence, S.C., instructor in English, 1970—. Member of South Carolina Arts Commission's poet-in-the-schools program. *Member:* Blue Key. *Awards, honors:* William Gilmore Simms Poetry Prize from South Carolina Poetry Society, 1971, for "Generations and Medallions."

WRITINGS: Sending the Children for Song (poems), Francis Marion Press, 1975. Contributor of more than two hundred stories, poems, and articles to literary publications, sometimes under pseudonym Rand Roberts, including *Southern Humanities Review, Wisconsin Review, Orb, Discourse, Forum, Clod and Pebble, Nimrod, Spirit, Discovery, Spectrum, Patterns, Wind*, and *Twigs.*

WORK IN PROGRESS: The Beast with the Ugly Head, poems; a novel.

SIDELIGHTS: Parham writes: "A writer learns—with a sheet of blank paper before him—that he doesn't have to run from a damned thing . . . that he cannot . . . he's still no better off than Faustus in the eleventh hour . . . but he gets to rewrite the agony until it's right . . . better however than wasting it in a bar, forgetting all in the stupor except the rude resonance left there . . . .not that bars are bad places to begin . . . certainly better than today's churches.''

* * *

PARISH, Peter J(oseph)   1929-

PERSONAL: Born April 24, 1929, in London, England; son of Arthur John (a schoolmaster) and Doris (Nicholls) Parish; married Norma Telfer, September 14, 1957; children: Helen Louise. *Education:* University of London, B.A. (first class honors), 1950; graduate study at Institute of Historical Research, 1952-54, and Bowdoin College, 1954-55. *Religion:* Roman Catholic. *Home:* 5 Glenbank Rd., Lenzie, Glasgow G66 5AG, Scotland. *Agent:* John Farquharson, 15 Red Lion Sq., London WC1R 4QW, England. *Office:* Department of History, University of Glasgow, Glasgow G12 8QQ, Scotland.

CAREER: University of Manchester, Manchester, England, member of library staff, 1955-58; University of Glasgow, Glasgow, Scotland, lecturer, 1958-72, senior lecturer in American history, 1972—. *Military service:* Royal Air Force, 1950-52. *Member:* Historical Association, British Association for American Studies (member of executive committee, 1975—). *Awards, honors:* American Council of Learned Societies fellow in history at Johns Hopkins University, 1963-64.

WRITINGS: The American Civil War, Holmes & Meier, 1975. Contributor to *Nelson's Dictionary of World History* and to history journals.

WORK IN PROGRESS: Research on the American Civil War, and on Daniel Webster, with publication of a study of his political career expected to result.

* * *

PARK, Charles F(rederick), Jr.   1903-

PERSONAL: Born December 18, 1903, in Wilmington, Del.; son of Charles F. and Ida (Morey) Park; married Eula Blair, October 1, 1931; children: Frederick Blair, Allan Morey, Martha. *Education:* New Mexico Institute of Mining and Technology, B.S., 1926; University of Arizona, M.S., 1929; University of Minnesota, Ph.D., 1931. *Politics:* Independent. *Religion:* Protestant. *Home:* 444 Lassen St., Apt. 11, Los Altos, Calif. 94022. *Office:* Department of Applied Earth Sciences, Stanford University, Palo Alto, Calif. 94305.

CAREER: Empire Zinc Co., Hanover, N.M., assistant geologist, 1927-28; University of Minnesota, Minneapolis, instructor in geology, 1929-31; U.S. Geological Survey, Washington, D.C., junior geologist, 1931-34, assistant geologist, 1934-36, associate geologist, 1936-38, geologist, 1938-41, senior geologist, 1941-44, geologist in charge of metals section, 1944-46; Stanford University, Palo Alto, Calif., professor of geology, 1946-65, Donald Steel Professor, 1965-69, professor emeritus, 1969—, dean of School of Mineral Science, 1950-65, dean emeritus, 1969—. Member of board of directors, Homestake Mining Co., Golden Cycle Corp., and Freeman, Cooper & Co. Civilian consultant to U.S. Army Corps of Engineers. *Member:* International Association of Genesis Ore Deposits (president, 1968-72), American Institute of Mining Engineers, Geological Society of America (fellow; councilor, 1962); Society of Economic Geologists (president, 1965), American Mineralogical Society (fellow), Geological Society of Brazil. *Awards, honors:* D.Sc. from New Mexico Institute of Mining and Technology, 1972.

WRITINGS: (With R. A. MacDiarmid) *Ore Deposits*, W. H. Freeman, 1964, 3rd edition, in press; (with Margaret C. Freeman) *Affluence in Jeopardy: Minerals and the Political Economy*, Freeman, Cooper, 1968; (with Freeman) *Earthbound: Minerals, Energy and Man's Future*, Freeman, Cooper, 1975. Contributor to journals in his field.

WORK IN PROGRESS: Mining in History; Ore Localization.

SIDELIGHTS: Park has traveled in Latin America, Africa (north of the Congo River), Australia, Europe, India, Japan, Philippine Islands.

BIOGRAPHICAL/CRITICAL SOURCES: New Yorker, March 23, 1972.

* * *

PARKER, Betty June   1929-

PERSONAL: Born June 3, 1929, in Decatur, Ala.; daughter of Charles (a steelworker) and Jane (Meadows) Persinger; married Franklin Parker (a professor), June 12, 1950. *Education:* Berea College, B.A., 1950; George Peabody College, M.A., 1956. *Home:* 750 Amherst Rd., Morgantown, W.Va. 26505.

CAREER: Ferrum College, Ferrum, Va., instructor in English, 1950-52; Belmont College, Nashville, Tenn., instructor in English, 1955-56; Walkill School, Walkill, N.Y., teacher of English, 1956-57. *Member:* League of Women Voters.

WRITINGS—Editor with husband, Franklin Parker: *American Dissertations on Foreign Education: A Bibliography with Abstracts*, Whitston Publishing, Volume V: *Scandinavia*, 1974, Volume VI: *China*, parts 1 & 2, 1975, Volume VII: *Korea*, in press, Volume VIII: *Mexico*, in press, Volume IX: *Central America*, in press, Volume X: *South America*, in press.

WORK IN PROGRESS: Two books, *British Graduate Theses and Dissertations on Foreign Education: A Bibliography of 910 Entries, with Subject Index*, and *Education in Puerto Rico: A Bibliography of American Doctoral Dissertations with Abstracts*.

* * *

PARKER, Howard J(ohn)   1948-

PERSONAL: Born November 2, 1948, in Preston, England; son of John (a production manager) and Doreen (Taylor) Parker; married Diana Barlow (a teacher), January 4, 1972. *Education:* University of Liverpool, B.A. (first class honors), 1970, M.A., 1974. *Politics:* Socialist. *Religion:* None. *Office:* Department of Sociology, University of Liverpool, Liverpool, England.

CAREER: University of Liverpool, Liverpool, England, lecturer in sociology, 1974—.

WRITINGS: (With K. Roberts and G. White) *The Character Training Industry*, David & Charles, 1974; *View from the Boys: A Sociology of Downtown Adolescents*, David & Charles, 1974. Contributor to local newspapers and radio stations and of articles on youth and adolescent deviancy to periodicals.

WORK IN PROGRESS: Publications from community development projects in Liverpool.

* * *

PARKER, J(ohn) Carlyle   1931-

PERSONAL: Born October 14, 1931, in Ogden, Utah; son

of Levi C. and Marrietta (Parkinson) Parker; married Janet
C. Greene, May 31, 1956; children: Denise, Nathan, Bret.
Education: Brigham Young University, B.A., 1957; University of California, Berkeley, M.L.S., 1958; graduate
study at Humbolt State College, 1959-60. *Politics:* Democrat. *Religion:* Church of Jesus Christ of Latter-day Saints
(Mormon). *Home:* 2115 North Denair Ave., Turlock,
Calif. 95380. *Office:* Library, California State College at
Stanislaus, 800 Monte Vista Ave., Turlock, Calif. 95380.

CAREER: Humboldt State College, Arcata, Calif., librarian, 1958-60; Church College of Hawaii, Laie, assistant and
acting librarian, 1960-63; California State College at Stanislaus, Library, Turlock, head of public services, 1963—,
assistant library director, 1968—. Founder and librarian of
Modesto California Stake Branch Genealogical Library,
1968—. Secretary of Turlock Centennial Foundation
Board, 1971—; president of Turlock Community Concert
Association, 1973-75. *Military service:* U.S. Army, 1953-
55. *Member:* American Library Association, American
Association of University Professors, California Library
Association, Stanislaus County Historical Society. *Awards,
honors:* American Library Association fellowship, 1965.

WRITINGS: (Compiler) *An Annotated Bibliography of the
History of Del Norte and Humboldt Counties*, Humboldt
State College Library, 1960; *Sources of Californiana: From
Padron to Voter Registration*, Genealogical Society (Salt
Lake City), 1969; (editor) *Genealogy in the Central Association of Libraries: A Union List Based on Filby's "American and British Genealogy and Heraldry,"* Library, California State College at Stanislaus, 1974. Contributor of
articles and reviews to library journals.

WORK IN PROGRESS: Editing "Genealogy and Local
History Information Guide Series," and *City and County
Index to the 1850 Census Schedule*, both for Gale.

*   *   *

PARKER, Pat 1944-

PERSONAL: Born January 20, 1944, in Houston, Tex.;
daughter of Ernest N. (a tire retreader) and Marie (a domestic; maiden name, Anderson) Cooks; married Ed Bullins, June 20, 1962 (divorced January 17, 1966); married
Robert F. Parker, January 20, 1966 (divorced). *Education:*
Attended Los Angeles City College and San Francisco
State College (now University). *Politics:* "Black Feminist
Lesbian." *Residence:* Oakland, Calif. *Office:* Women's
Press Collective, 5251 Broadway, Oakland, Calif. 94618.

CAREER: Has worked as proof reader, NCR proof operator, waitress, maid, clerk, and creative writing instructor;
writer. *Member:* Gente.

WRITINGS: Child of Myself, Women's Press Collective,
1972; *Pit Stop*, Women's Press Collective, 1974.

WORK IN PROGRESS: A novel; a book of short stories;
a three-act play.

*   *   *

PARKS, Lloyd Clifford 1922-

PERSONAL: Born January 30, 1922, in Chicago, Ill.; son
of Olin (a farmer) and Alma (Olsen) Parks; married Genevieve Marie Therese Poughon (a teacher of French), June
10, 1950; children: Louis Dominique, Rachel Alma. *Education:* Kenyon College, B.A., 1950; University of Washington, Seattle, M.A., 1953, Ph.D., 1959. *Politics:* Independent. *Home:* 1517 Panhandle, Denton, Tex. 76201. *Office:*
Department of English, North Texas State University,
Denton, Tex. 76203.

CAREER: Cortland State Teachers College, Cortland,
N.Y., assistant professor of English, 1954-58; Ohio State
University, Columbus, assistant professor of English, 1959-
67; North Texas State University, Denton, professor of
English, 1967—. Fulbright lecturer at University of Grenoble, 1963-64, and University of Lille, 1964-65. *Military service:* U.S. Navy, 1942-45. *Member:* Modern Language
Association of America, American Association of University Professors, American Civil Liberties Union, South
Central Modern Language Association. *Awards, honors:*
Fulbright grant to study at Sorbonne, University of Paris,
1950-51.

WRITINGS: (Translator) Stendahl, *The Red and the
Black*, New American Library, 1970. Contributor of articles and poems to literary journals, including *Kenyon Review, Poetry Northwest, South Central Bulletin: Studies by
Members of the South Central Modern Language Association*, and *Botteghe Oscure*.

WORK IN PROGRESS: A book on the influence of
French symbolist poets upon William Butler Yeats.

*   *   *

PARRIS, Judith (Ann) H(eimlich) 1939-

PERSONAL: Born June 5, 1939, in Columbus, Ohio;
daughter of William F. (an advertising executive) and Mary
(Eitel) Heimlich; married Addison Wilson Parris, October
12, 1968 (deceased). *Education:* Smith College, A.B. (cum
laude), 1961; Columbia University, M.A., 1963, Ph.D.,
1967. *Home:* 3105 Northampton St. N.W., Washington,
D.C. 20015. *Office:* Governmental Studies Program,
Brookings Institution, 1775 Massachusetts Ave. N.W.,
Washington, D.C. 20036.

CAREER: Democratic Senatorial Campaign Committee,
Washington, D.C., research assistant, 1960; *Housing and
Urban Affairs Daily*, Washington, D.C., reporter, 1961-62;
press assistant to U.S. Senator George A. Smathers,
Washington, D.C., 1962; Small Business Administration,
Washington, D.C., research assistant in policy planning,
1963-65; Brookings Institution, Washington, D.C., research
assistant in governmental studies program, 1966-68, research associate, 1968—. Professorial lecturer at American
University, 1970. *Member:* American Political Science
Association, Policy Studies Organization, Metropolitan
Washington Political Science Association.

WRITINGS: (With F. A. Cleaveland and others) *Congress and Urban Problems: A Casebook on the Legislative
Process*, Brookings Institution, 1969; (with Wallace S.
Sayre) *Voting for President*, Brookings Institution, 1970;
The Convention Problem, Brookings Institution, 1972;
(with Richard C. Bain) *Convention Decisions and Voting
Records*, Brookings Institution, 2nd edition (Parris was not
associated with original edition), 1973. Contributor to professional journals.

WORK IN PROGRESS: A book on the power of the U.S.
Senate to confirm nominations, for Brookings Institution.

*   *   *

PARSEGIAN, V(ozcan) Lawrence 1908-

PERSONAL: Born May 13, 1908, in Van, Armenia; came
to United States in 1916, naturalized in 1931; son of Sahag
Hovsepian and Lilian (Krikorian) Parsegian; married Varsenig Boyajian, April 17, 1938; children: Vozken Adrian,
Elsa Varsenig. *Education:* Massachusetts Institute of
Technology, B.S., 1933; Washington University, graduate

study, 1935-36; New York University, Ph.D., 1948. *Politics:* Republican (liberal). *Religion:* Armenian Apostolic Church. *Home:* Brunswick Hills, East Rd., Troy, N.Y., 12180. *Office:* Rensselaer Polytechnic Institute, Troy, N.Y. 12181.

CAREER: Industrial research director of various firms, New York, N.Y., 1937-50; director of research of New York Operations Office, Atomic Energy Commission, 1950-54; Rensselaer Polytechnic Institute, Troy, N.Y., dean of School of Engineering, 1954-61, Rensselaer Professor, 1961-73, professor emeritus, 1973—. Ramo lecturer, Harvey Mudd College, 1962; Distinguished Visiting Professor of Education, Brooklyn College of the City University of New York, 1973-74. Academies of Sciences exchange scholar to Soviet Union, 1962. Member, New York Governor's Committee on Nuclear Energy and Radiation, U.S. Chamber of Commerce committees on atomic energy and technology; member of board of directors of philanthropic organizations. Consultant to industrial firms.

MEMBER: American Nuclear Society (former member of board of directors), American Physical Society, American Association for the Advancement of Science, New York Academy of Sciences.

WRITINGS: Industrial Management in the Atomic Age, Addison-Wesley, 1965; (with others) *Introduction to Natural Science,* Academic Press, Part 1, 1968, Part 2, 1971; *The Cybernetic World,* Doubleday, 1972. Contributor of chapters to books and articles to journals.

WORK IN PROGRESS: Research on the integration of science and the humanities, and on religion, science and human progress.

SIDELIGHTS: The Cybernetic World has been translated into German and Japanese.

*   *   *

PASTINE, Maureen (Diane) 1944-

PERSONAL: Born November 21, 1944, in Hays, Kan.; daughter of Gerhard Walter and Ada (Hillman) Hillman: married Jerry Joel Pastine (an electrician), February 5, 1966. *Education:* Fort Hays Kansas State College, A.B., 1967; Kansas State Teachers College, M.L.S., 1970; graduate study at Fort Hays Kansas State College and University of Nebraska at Omaha. *Home:* 811 South 60th St., Omaha, Neb. 68106. *Office:* Reference Department, Gene Eppley Library, University of Nebraska, Omaha, Neb. 68101.

CAREER: High school teacher in Kingman, Kan., 1967-69, Palco, Kan., 1970-71; University of Nebraska at Omaha, Gene Eppley Library, assistant head of reference department, 1971-75, acting chairperson of reference department, 1975—, assistant professor at university, 1974—. *Member:* Nebraska Library Association, Beta Phi Mu.

WRITINGS: (With Sara Lou Williams and Peter Hernon) *Library and Library Related Publications: A Directory of Publishing Opportunities in Journals, Series, and Annuals,* Libraries Unlimited, 1973. Contributor of articles and reviews to professional journals.

WORK IN PROGRESS: Research on academic libraries, educational librarianship, women's studies, and little magazines and underground newspapers.

*   *   *

PATCHEN, Martin 1932-

PERSONAL: Born July 3, 1932; married; children: two.

Education: Columbia University, B.A., 1953; University of North Carolina, M.A., 1954; University of Michigan, Ph.D., 1960. *Home:* 131 Rockland Dr., West Lafayette, Ind. 47906. *Office:* Department of Sociology and Anthropology, Purdue University, West Lafayette, Ind. 47907.

CAREER: University of Michigan, Institute for Social Research, Ann Arbor, lecturer, 1959-64, assistant professor of psychology, 1964-68, study director, 1959-63, senior study director of Survey Research Center, 1963-68; Purdue University, West Lafayette, Ind., associate professor, 1968-72, professor of sociology and anthropology, 1972—. *Member:* American Sociological Association, Society for Study of Social Problems.

WRITINGS: The Choice of Wage Comparisons, Prentice-Hall, 1961; *Some Questionnaire Measures of Employee Motivation and Morale,* Institute for Social Research, University of Michigan, 1965; *Participation, Achievement, and Involvement on the Job,* Prentice-Hall, 1970.

Contributor: J. Brigham and T. Weissbach, editors, *Racial Attitudes in America,* Harper, 1960; D. Porter and P. Applewhite, editors, *Organizational Behavior and Management,* International Textbook Co., 1964; C. Backmen and P. Secord, editors, *Problems in Social Psychology: Selected Readings,* McGraw, 1966; A. T. Steele, editor, *The American People and China,* McGraw, 1966; H. Hymna, editor, *Readings in Reference Group Theory and Research,* Free Press, 1967; M. Wadia, editor, *Management and the Behavioral Sciences,* Allyn & Bacon, 1968; W. Scott and L. Cummings, editors, *Readings in Organizational Behavior and Human Performance,* Dorsey, 1969; C. Smith, editor, *Conflict Resolution: Contributions of the Behavioral Sciences,* University of Notre Dame Press, 1971; D. S. Beach, editor, *Managing People at Work,* Macmillan, 1971; D. Nimno and C. Bonjean, editors, *Political Attitudes and Public Opinion,* McKay, 1972.

Contributor of about twenty articles and reviews to journals. Member of editorial board of *Journal of Applied Social Psychology*; editorial consultant to *Sociometry.*

WORK IN PROGRESS: Research on the amount and nature of interaction between white and black students in eleven Indianapolis high schools.

*   *   *

PATRA, Atul Chandra 1915-

PERSONAL: Born April 14, 1915, in Bankura, West Bengal, India; son of Rakhal Chandra and Suradhuni (Devi) Patra; married Avanti Devi, 1942; children: Amita, Dhimati, Kalyan, Himadri, Samjukta. *Education:* Presidency College, Calcutta, B.A. (honors), 1939; University of Calcutta, M.A., 1942, LL.B., 1944. *Politics:* Democratic Socialist. *Religion:* Hinduism. *Home:* 94 Neeti Bagh, New Delhi 49, India. *Office:* Supreme Court Bar Association, New Delhi, India.

CAREER: Lawyer; senior advocate, Supreme Court of India, New Delhi.

WRITINGS: Administration of Justice Under the East-India Company in Bengal, Bichar and Orissa, Asia Publishing House, 1961; *Essays on the Indian Penal Code,* Indian Law Institute, 1962; *Indian Stamp Act,* Eastern Book Co., 1963; *Laws Governing Craftsmen and Their Crafts from Ancient Days Till Today* (monograph), Office of the Registrar General, Ministry of Home Affairs, 1966; *Indian Contract Act,* Asia Publishing House, Volume I, 1967, Volume II, 1975. Contributor of articles to *Indian Law Institute Journal.*

WORK IN PROGRESS: Law and Its Interpretation in Ancient and Mediaeval India; Indian Constitution in Bengali.

* * *

PATTERSON, Margaret C(leveland) 1923-

PERSONAL: Born April 13, 1923, in Woburn, Mass.; daughter of Alden Milton (a banker) and Ruth (a lawyer; maiden name, Lambert) Cleveland; divorced; children: Barry, James. Education: Sullins Junior College, A.A., 1942; Wellesley College, B.A., 1944; University of Florida, M.Ed., 1965, certificate in library science, 1965, Ph.D., 1970. Religion: Episcopal. Home: 1125 Northwest 109th Dr., Gainesville, Fla. 32601. Office: Department of English, Anderson Hall, University of Florida, Gainesville, Fla. 32601.

CAREER: University of Florida, Gainesville, assistant professor of English, 1970—. Member: American Library Association, Modern Language Association of America, South Atlantic Modern Language Association, Hopkins Society, Phi Kappa Phi, Pi Lambda Theta. Awards, honors: Carnegie Foundation grants, 1972, 1974.

WRITINGS: Literary Research Guide, Gale, 1975. Contributor to journals in her field, including Florida Naturalist, Bulletin of Bibliography, and Walt Whitman Review. Also author of Methodology Manual, Carnegie Program, University of Florida, 1972, 2nd edition, 1974, Creative Writers Bibliography, 1949-72, University of Florida, and three correspondence courses in literature for University of Florida. Member of bibliography committee of MLA International Bibliography, 1972—.

WORK IN PROGRESS: A reference book, Hopkins Handbook, on all the poetry of Gerard Manley Hopkins.

SIDELIGHTS: Margaret Patterson wrote: "The contemporary scene has forced me into a personal—and lonely—crusade against shoddy, careless, lacklustre performance of any kind, whether it be in the mechanics of writing, the quality of literary criticism, the accuracy and efficiency of research procedures, or the zest and wisdom vital to all teaching and learning, work and play. Dedication to excellence is a forgotten shibboleth, but here's one Yankee who will maintain that C is an average grade, that training in writing an essay will produce a better student and a more articulate, knowledgeable citizen than will a million multiple-choice quizzes, and that it is the duty of every teacher and every adult to help the younger generation evaluate themselves honestly and realistically—there can be no growth otherwise."

AVOCATIONAL INTERESTS: Sailing, skiing, golfing, swimming, tennis, bridge, traveling, refinishing antiques, history, art, music, politics, the stock market, any new language.

* * *

PATTERSON, Ward L(amont) 1933-

PERSONAL: Born December 26, 1933, in Killbuck, Ohio; son of Raymond Floyd and Florence May (Crosby) Patterson. Education: Cincinnati Bible Seminary, A.B., 1956, M.A., 1958; Fort Hays Kansas State College, M.S., 1960; University of Melbourne, further graduate study, 1961; Indiana University, doctoral study, 1972—. Religion: Undenominational Christian. Home and office: 4166 Belle Ave., Bloomington, Ind. 47401.

CAREER: Ordained minister of Christian Church, 1958; pastor of churches in Montgomery, Ind., 1955-58, and Hays, Kan., 1958-59; professional artist specializing in archaeological designs from the Middle East, 1965—. Associate instructor in speech at Indiana University, 1972-75; associate minister with Campus Christian Ministry of Indiana University, 1974—. Member: Lambda Iota Tau, Phi Kappa Phi. Awards, honors: Rotary International student exchange fellowship, 1960, for study in Australia.

WRITINGS: Yesterday Today, Standard Publishing, 1974; Struggle, Crisis, and Victory, Standard Publishing, 1975. Creator of "The Adventures of Alan West," an illustrated comic strip for young people. Curriculum writer for Standard Publishing. Contributor to Christian Standard and Seek.

WORK IN PROGRESS: Research on early Egyptian, Persian, Mesopotamian, and Greek art; research on the rhetorical exigencies of the North American Christian Convention.

SIDELIGHTS: Patterson writes: "My interests concern religion, history, archeology, art, and travel. I spent nine years abroad, traveling for seven years on a 1946 motorcycle on which I visited over thirty countries of the Middle and Far East." He has trekked 500 miles into the high Himalayas of Nepal in order to reach Mount Everest, stayed in northern Afghan villages, climbed Mount Ararat, crewed on a yacht in the Mediterranean, worked as an extra in a movie being shot by Twentieth Century-Fox in Tunisia, and made a living as a "grave-robber" in Egypt. He has an extensive collection of rubbings of ancient Middle Eastern bas reliefs.

BIOGRAPHICAL/CRITICAL SOURCES: Rotarian, October, 1972.

* * *

PAVALKO, Ronald M(ichael) 1934-

PERSONAL: Born Sptember 20, 1934, in Youngstown, Ohio; son of Michael (a tile setter) and Mary (Husack) Pavalko; married Linda A. Loye (a nurse), January 15, 1960; children: Fredrick M., Peter E. Education: Attended Arizona State University, 1952-53; University of California at Los Angeles, B.A., 1956, M.A., 1961, Ph.D., 1963. Home: 2310 Delgado Dr., Tallahassee, Fla. 32304. Office: Department of Sociology, Florida State University, Tallahassee, Fla. 32306.

CAREER: Los Angeles State College, Los Angeles, California., assistant professor of sociology, 1963 (part-time); University of Wisconsin, Madison, assistant professor of sociology, 1963-67; Florida State University, Tallahassee, associate professor, 1967-71, professor of sociology, 1971—, head of department 1971-72. Consultant to Bureau of Research, Department of Education, State of Florida, 1970. Military service: U.S. Army, 1956-58. Member: American Sociological Association, American Educational Research Association, Southern Sociological Society, Pacific Sociological Association. Awards, honors: National Institutes of Health, Division of Nursing research grant, 1965-67.

WRITINGS: Sociology of Education: A Book of Readings, F. E. Peacock, 1968; Sociology of Occupations and Professions, F. E. Peacock, 1971; (contributor) W. E. Mann, editor, Canada: A Sociological Profile, Copp Clark, 1971; Sociological Perspectives on Occupations, F. E. Peacock, 1972. Contributor of twenty articles and reviews to sociology journals. Book reviewer for Sociology: Reviews of New Books, 1974—.

WORK IN PROGRESS: Research on assimilation of Slavic immigrant groups and their descendants in the United States.

* * *

PAYNE, Alan
    See JAKES, John W(illiam)

* * *

PAYNE, Eric Francis Jules 1895-

PERSONAL: Born February 17, 1895, in London, England; son of Francis John and Jessie Henrietta Payne; married Eileen Lucy Sutton, February 9, 1932; children: Valerie Frances (Mrs. Jacques Egret). *Education:* Attended Cambridge University. *Politics:* Conservative. *Religion:* Buddhist. *Home:* The Beacon South, Beacon Rd., Crowborough, Sussex, England.

CAREER: British Army, Royal Engineers, stationed in India, retiring in 1948 as a lieutenant colonel. *Member:* Royal Institute of Philosophy, Royal Central Asian Society.

WRITINGS—Translator; all works by Arthur Schopenhauer: *The World as Will and Representation*, Falcon's Wing Press, 1958; *On the Basis of Morality*, Bobbs-Merrill, 1965; *Parerga and Paralipomena*, Clarendon Press, 1974; *On the Fourfold Root*, Open Court, 1974.

* * *

PEACOCK, Mary Reynolds (Bradshaw) 1916-

PERSONAL: Born March 29, 1916, in Walters, Va.; daughter of Thomas Gavin (a physician) and Julia (Reynolds) Bradshaw; married Lucian Allen Peacock (a special agent for Prudential Life Insurance Co.), June 8, 1940; children: Lucian Allen, Jr., Mary Reynolds (Mrs. Frederick Louis Beyer II), Julia Anne. *Education:* University of North Carolina, Greensboro, A.B., 1936; North Carolina State University, M.A., 1970. *Religion:* Methodist. *Home:* 832 Lake Boone Trail, Raleigh, N.C. 27607. *Office:* North Carolina Department of Cultural Resources, 109 East Jones, Raleigh, N.C. 27611.

CAREER: English teacher in public high schools in Wilson, N.C. and in Johnston County, N.C., 1936-40; substitute teacher in public schools in North Carolina, 1960-70; North Carolina Department of Cultural Resources, Raleigh, editorial assistant in Division of Archives and History, 1970—. *Member:* United Methodist Women's Society (vice-president, 1966-68), Wake County Historical Society, Raleigh Woman's Club, Raleigh Music Club, Phi Beta Kappa (Wake County chapter), Phi Kappa Phi.

WRITINGS: (Editor and reviser) George Barton Cutten, *Silversmiths of North Carolina: 1699-1850*, Division of Archives and History, North Carolina Department of Cultural Resources, revised edition (Peacock was not associated with original edition), 1973.

WORK IN PROGRESS: A supplement to *Silversmiths of North Carolina*.

* * *

PEAKE, Miriam Morrison 1901-

PERSONAL: Born March 1, 1901, in Indianapolis, Ind.; daughter of Samuel Andrew (a banker) and Callie Gladys Morrison; married Junius Bew Peake, June 16, 1926 (died January 13, 1969); children: Miraed (Mrs. R. Leigh Smith,

Jr.), Junius W. *Education:* Bryn Mawr College, B.A., 1921. *Politics:* Republican. *Religion:* Episcopalian. *Home:* 167 East 67th St., New York, N.Y. 10021.

CAREER: U.S. Postal Censorship, New York, N.Y., deputy assistant censor, 1942-44; Coats & Clark, Inc., New York, N.Y., designer and and instruction writer, 1945-46; *Today's Woman* (magazine), New York, N.Y., needlework editor, 1946-48, 1950-52; Peerless Fashion Syndicate, New York, N.Y., member of copy and layout staff, 1952-53; Coats & Clark, Inc., designer and instruction writer, 1956-61. Lecturer for New York State Department of Labor. Free-lance editor for magazines. Consultant to yarn and thread companies. *Member:* Authors League of America. *Awards, honors:* Silver Medal of Fine Arts, Cooper Union, 1922.

WRITINGS: Wise Handbook of Knitting and Crocheting, William H. Wise, 1949; (with Marguerite Maddox) *The Complete Book of Curtains, Slipcovers and Upholstery*, Pocket Books, 1963, hardcover edition, Gramercy Press, c. 1970; *One Hundred One Things to Make for Love or Money*, Scholastic Book Services, 1964; *A Job for You*, Scholastic Book Services, 1964; *One Hundred One Glamorous Gifts to Make*, Scholastic Book Services, 1967, hardcover edition, Four Winds, 1968.

SIDELIGHTS: Miriam Peake told *CA* that as a child she attended schools in Germany, Belgium, and Switzerland. She has also traveled in Italy and France.

* * *

PEARLSTEIN, Howard J. 1942-
    (Joshua Rush)

PERSONAL: Born August 25, 1942, in Philadelphia, Pa.; son of Martin (a dentist) and Evelyn (Cramer) Pearlstein; married Mary Susan Clisbee, July, 1964 (divorced, 1966); present wife, Jane Walsh (a visual artist). *Education:* Attended Pennsylvania State University, 1960-63, University of California, Berkeley, 1964, and San Francisco State College (now University), 1965. *Politics:* "Huang Po Anarchist." *Religion:* "Whatever serves." *Agent:* Bob Stricker, 2068 Union St., San Francisco, Calif.

CAREER: TIBET Productions, San Francisco, Calif., creative consultant, 1969-70; *Organ* (magazine), San Francisco, associate editor, 1970-71; Alotovus Production, San Francisco, stage manager and promotion agent, 1972; *City* (magazine), San Francisco, managing editor, writer, and columnist, 1973-74. Media consultant for California Marijuana Initiative, 1972. *Military service:* U.S. Marine Corps Reserve, 1963.

WRITINGS: Mandrake's Book, John Muir, 1974; *A Slice of Colin Wilson*, Best Books, 1975; (editor) *Understanding the Thing They Call Video* (anthology), John Muir, in press. Contributor of poetry to *Cassxeopeia/Ephemeris* and of articles and reviews to *Organ, City, Time Out, San Francisco Magazine, San Francisco Examiner, San Francisco Bay Guardian*, and other periodicals and newspapers.

WORK IN PROGRESS: Hebe, "which could be called a 'detective novel,'" expected publication in 1976; *The Sticky Fingers of God*, a novel extending and developing the theory that insanity is not only a viable alternative method of resolving insoluble situations, but one of the more commonly used methods.

SIDELIGHTS: Pearlstein told *CA:* "My self-appelation, under the heading, *Politics*, as a Huang Po Anarchist refers purely to the fact that I am not in the least concerned with politics, and only minimally with government. My attitudes on that level are toward personal harmony leading to inter-personal harmonies. . . .When forced to have an opinion on such matters, I tend toward visualizing some sort of mu-tated Maoism, a libertarian composite of non-profit-ori-ented activity. I do not believe that such things as food, shelter and communication access are negotiables, and in any way subject to commercial pressures. Include in that category medical care and transportation.

"My primary concern in writing is the way in which mad-nesses and realities blend, from which blending mythical actualization occurs. I am concerned with transmission of vision, regardless of the implications. I do not care to edito-rialize on the vision, and hope that readers of my work will not expect to find that I, personally, exemplify my own ideal. 'Regardless of implications' means that I, too, am subject to finding myself on the negative side of what I feel to be true. It's only fair.

"I pursue the Art, defining Art as that which leaves the reader (viewer, listener, etc.) with more of himself than when he first came in."

* * *

PEARSON, Bill
   See PEARSON, William Harrison

* * *

PEARSON, Carol 1944-

PERSONAL: Born March 21, 1944, in Chicago, Ill.; daughter of John A. (a manufacturer's representative) and Thelma (a teacher; maiden name, Widman) Pearson; mar-ried Robert H. Havemann, August 6, 1966 (divorced, 1972); married David Merkowitz (a newspaper editor), June 8, 1975. *Education:* Rice University, B.A., 1966, M.A., 1969, Ph.D., 1971. *Politics:* "Feminist." *Home:* 1046 Grandview, Boulder, Colo. 80302. *Office:* Woman Studies Program, Hillside Court, #7, University of Colorado, Boulder, Colo. 80302.

CAREER: University of Colorado, Boulder, instructor in literature at Mini-College and in Division of Continuing Education, 1970-72, assistant professor of English, 1972—, director of Woman Studies, 1974—. *Member:* Modern Lan-guage Association of America (member of Women's Cau-cus), College English Association, American Federation of Teachers (member of executive committee, 1975—).

WRITINGS: (Editor with Katherine Pope) *Who Am I This Time?: An Anthology of Female Portraits in British and American Literature*, McGraw, 1976. Contributor to litera-ture journals.

WORK IN PROGRESS: A book, *Thematic Motifs in Fic-tion by Women*; articles on Joseph Heller, Ken Kesey, and Thomas Pynchon.

SIDELIGHTS: Carol Pearson writes: "I was motivated to write *Who Am I This Time* because people must under-stand the myths the society presents for their emulation to be free of negative and limiting sex role conditioning. My primary commitment as a writer and teacher is to freeing minds so that we all can have freer and more joyful lives."

* * *

PEARSON, William Harrison 1922-
   (Bill Pearson)

PERSONAL: Born January 18, 1922, in Greymouth, New Zealand; son of James (a railway clerk) and Agnes Ellen (McLean) Pearson. *Education:* Attended Otago Univer-sity, 1940-41; Dunedin Teachers' College, teacher's certifi-cate, 1941; University of Canterbury, B.A., 1947, M.A., 1948; King's College, London, Ph.D., 1952. *Politics:* So-cialist. *Office:* English Department, University of Auck-land, Auckland, New Zealand.

CAREER: Elementary school teacher in Blackball, N.Z., 1942, in Oxford, N.Z., 1949; substitute teacher in London, England, 1952-53; University of Auckland, Auckland, N.Z., lecturer in English literature, 1954-66; Australian National University, Canberra, senior research fellow, 1967-69; University of Auckland, associate professor of English literature, 1970—. *Military service:* New Zealand Army, 1942-46. *Awards, honors:* Joint winner of *Landfall* Readers' Award for nonfiction, 1960, for essay, "Fretful Sleepers"; New Zealand Prose Award for nonfiction, 1974, for *Fretful Sleepers and Other Essays.*

WRITINGS—Under name Bill Pearson: *Coal Flat* (novel), Angus & Robertson, 1963, revised edition, Longman Paul, 1970; (editor) Frank Sargeson, *Collected Stories, 1935-1963*, Blackwood & Janet Paul, 1964; *Henry Lawson Among Maoris*, Australian National University Press, 1968; (editor) Roderick Finlayson, *Brown Man's Burden and Later Stories*, Auckland University Press, 1973; *Fretful Sleepers and Other Essays*, International Publications Service, 1974. Contributor to journals in his field and to literary magazines.

WORK IN PROGRESS: A study of imaginative writing in English set in the Pacific Islands since 1768.

BIOGRAPHICAL/CRITICAL SOURCES: Joan Stevens, *The New Zealand Novel, 1860-1965*, A. H. Reed, 1966; *Landfall*, December, 1967; H. Winston Rhodes, *New Zea-land Fiction Since 1945*, John McIndoe, 1968.

* * *

PEDERSEN, (Thelma) Jean J(orgensen) 1934-

PERSONAL: Born September 17, 1934, in Salt Lake City, Utah; daughter of Ralph Enoch (a physician and eye spe-cialist) and Margaret Thelma (Turpin) Jorgensen; married Kent Alden Pedersen (an electrical engineer), May 31, 1956; children: Christen Kent, Jennifer Jean. *Education:* Brigham Young University, B.S., 1955; University of Utah, M.S., 1958. *Religion:* Church of Jesus Christ of Latter-day Saints (Mormon). *Home address:* P.O. Box 26, New Almaden, Calif. 95042. *Office:* Department of Mathe-matics, University of Santa Clara, Santa Clara, Calif. 95053.

CAREER: Brigham Young University, Provo, Utah, math-ematics teacher at university high school, 1955-56; high school mathematics teacher in Salt Lake City, Utah, 1958-59; University of Utah, Salt Lake City, instructor in mathe-matics, 1959-65; University of Santa Clara, Santa Clara, Calif., lecturer, 1966-72, assistant professor of mathemat-ics, 1972—. Visiting scientist for National Science Founda-tion, 1963-65. *Member:* Mathematical Association of Amer-ica, National Council of Teachers of Mathematics, Utah Council of Teachers of Mathematics (member of board of directors, 1963-65), California Mathematics Council, Santa Clara Valley Mathematical Association (college chairman, 1972-73; president-elect, 1975), Sigma Xi, Pi Kappa Kappa, Pi Mu Epsilon.

WRITINGS: (With E. Allan Davis) *Essentials of Trigo-nometry*, Prindle, 1969, 2nd edition, James E. Freel & Associates, 1973; (with husband, Kent A. Pedersen) *Geometric Playthings*, Troubador, 1973; (with Davis) *Trigonometry*, Page-Ficklin, 1975. Contributor of about a dozen articles to *Mathematics Teacher, Fibonacci Quarterly, Utah Newsletter, Mathematical Log, Australian Mathematics Teacher,* and *Two Year College Mathematics Journal.*

* * *

PEDRICK, Jean 1922-
(Jean Kefferstan)

PERSONAL: Born August 5, 1922, in Salem, Mass.; daughter of Laurence Davis (a businessman) and Elfrieda (Virchow) Pedrick; married F. J. Kefferstan (a physician), February 8, 1948; children: Laurence, John. *Education:* Wheaton College, Norton, Mass., B.A., 1943. *Home:* 48 Mt. Vernon St., Boston, Mass. 02108.

CAREER: Houghton Mifflin Co., Boston, Mass., secretary and first reader, 1944-47; writer, 1947-68, 1970-72; Northeastern University, Boston, Mass., instructor in poetry at Center for Continuing Education, 1968-70; *Executive Digest*, Boston, Mass., editor, 1972-74; volunteer worker, Alice James Poetry Cooperative, Inc., 1974—. *Member:* New England Poetry Club. *Awards, honors:* Gretchen Warren Award from New England Poetry Club, 1972, for poem, "Making the Skeleton"; Melora Hobbs Pond Award from New England Poetry Club, 1973, for poem, "Intensive Care."

WRITINGS: The Fascination (novel), Houghton, 1947; *Wolf Moon* (poems), Alice James Books, 1974; *Pride and Splendor* (poems), Alice James Books, in press. Staff writer, writing essay features under name Jean Kefferstan, for *Beacon Hill News*, 1967—.

WORK IN PROGRESS: Books of poetry, *Base, Cold Grease*, and *Gaudy Night.*

* * *

PEELE, Stanton 1946-

PERSONAL: Born January 8, 1946, in Philadelphia, Pa.; *Education:* University of Pennsylvania, B.A., 1967; University of Michigan, Ph.D., 1971. *Politics:* "Organized libertarian." *Religion:* None. *Home:* 7 High Rock Way, #2, Allston, Mass. 02134. *Office:* Harvard Business School, Soldiers Field, Boston, Mass. 02163.

CAREER: Harvard University, Business School, Boston, Mass., assistant professor of organizational behavior, 1971—; Fred's Firm, Inc. (consultants), Allston, Mass., president, 1973—. Consultant to Massachusetts Department of Correction. *Awards, honors:* Woodrow Wilson fellow, 1967.

WRITINGS: (With Archie Brodsky) *Love and Addiction* (nonfiction), Taplinger, 1975. Contributor to *Cosmopolitan, Psychology Today, American Political Science Review,* and other journals.

WORK IN PROGRESS: With Archie Brodsky, a book on Hitchcock's films, completion expected in 1976, and a novel.

* * *

PENNINGER' F(rieda) Elaine 1927-

PERSONAL: Born April 11, 1927, in Marion, N.C.; daughter of Fred Hoyle and Lena (Young) Penninger. *Education:* University of North Carolina at Greensboro, A.B.,

1948; Duke University, M.A., 1950, Ph.D., 1961. *Politics:* Democrat. *Religion:* Presbyterian. *Home:* 4312 Kensington Ave., Richmond, Va. 23221. *Office:* Department of English, Westhampton College, University of Richmond, Richmond, Va. 23173.

CAREER: Flora Macdonald College, Red Springs, N.C., assistant professor of English, 1950-51; public school teacher in Barnwell, S.C., 1951-52, and in Brunswick, Ga., 1952-53; University of Tennessee, Knoxville, instructor in English, 1953-56; University of North Carolina, Greensboro, instructor, 1956-58, assistant professor of English, 1960-63; University of Richmond, Westhampton College, Richmond, Va., assistant professor, 1963-66, associate professor, 1966-71, professor of English, 1971—, chairman of department, 1969—.

MEMBER: American Association of University Professors, Modern Language Association of America, Mediaeval Academy of America, Renaissance Society of America, South Atlantic Modern Language Association, Southeastern Renaissance Society, Southeastern Medieval Association (member of council, 1975—), Phi Beta Kappa (vice-president of Epsilon chapter of Virginia, 1974-75; chapter president, 1975-76). *Awards, honors:* Southeastern Institute of Medieval and Renaissance Studies fellow, summers, 1965, 1967, 1969.

WRITINGS: (Editor) *English Drama to 1660, Excluding Shakespeare*, Gale, 1975. Contributor of essays, notes, or poetry to *Journal of American Folklore, North Carolina Folklore, South Atlantic Quarterly,* and *Long View Journal.*

WORK IN PROGRESS: Editing *A Festschrift in Honor of Dr. Marguerite Roberts; William Caxton; Love and Chivalry in the Works of Chaucer.*

* * *

PENNINGTON, Albert Joe 1950-

PERSONAL: Born October 29, 1950; son of Daniel Douglas (a farmer and writer) and Eunice (a librarian, teacher, and writer; maiden name, Randolph) Pennington. *Education:* Attended University of Arkansas. *Religion:* Christian. *Residence:* Fremont, Mo. 63941.

CAREER: Farmer and writer. *Member:* American Rifle Association, American Angus Association, Missouri Cattlemen's Association, Carter County Extension Association (vice-president).

WRITINGS: (With parents, Daniel Douglas Pennington and Eunice Pennington) *Ozark National Scenic Riverways*, privately printed, 1968; *Big Boy: The Story of a Dog*, School of the Ozarks Press, 1970. Contributor to conservation and natural history magazines and local publications.

WORK IN PROGRESS: A historical novel about horse stealing during the turn of the century.

SIDELIGHTS: Pennington sold his first magazine articles when he was fourteen. He is a naturalist and outdoorsman, a conservationist who believes in the "harvesting of wildlife during season and where overproduction exists." *Avocational interests:* Riding and training quarter horses, breeding and training registered treeing walker dogs.

* * *

PENNINGTON, Eunice 1923-

PERSONAL: Born February 16, 1923, in Fremont, Mo.; daughter of Charlie Albert (a farmer) and Hattie (Pritchard)

Randolph; married Daniel Douglas Pennington (a farmer and writer), August 29, 1942; children: Mary Ann (Mrs. Kenneth McDowell), Albert Joe. *Education:* Attended Southeast Missouri State University and Arizona State College (now University); Arkansas State University, B.S.E., 1962; George Peabody College for Teachers, M.S. in L.S., 1968. *Religion:* Christian. *Residence:* Fremont, Mo. 63941. *Office:* Current River Regional Library, Van Buren, Mo. 63965.

CAREER: Teacher in Carter County, Mo., 1952-61, and Shannon County, Mo., 1961-63; Current River Regional Library, Van Buren, Mo., regional librarian, 1963—. Member of Ozark Community Council. *Member:* American Folklore Society, American Library Association, National Ozarks Scenic Riverways Historical Society (past president), Missouri State Historical Society, Missouri Library Association, Carter County Historical Society. *Awards, honors:* Ed.D., Colorado Christian College, 1973.

WRITINGS: History of Carter County, privately printed, 1959; (with husband, Daniel Douglas Pennington, and son, Albert Joe Pennington) *Ozarks National Scenic Riverways,* privately printed, 1968; *History of the Ozarks,* School of the Ozarks Press, 1971; *Perry, the Peg Pig* (juvenile), School of the Ozarks Press, 1971; *Master of the Mountains* (historical novel), School of the Ozarks Press, 1971; *The Ladybird Mystery* (juvenile), School of the Ozarks Press, 1974. Contributor to history and education journals, and to regional publications, including *Grit, Capper's Weekly,* and *Ozark Guide.*

WORK IN PROGRESS: History of Reynolds County, Missouri, completion expected in 1976; a collection of folklore, *Ozark Mountain Folklore,* 1976; a historical novel, *Cordrevia's Mysterious Shadow,* 1976.

SIDELIGHTS: Eunice Pennington writes that she serves a deprived area of the Ozarks, helping to improve the economy there and to preserve the culture of the Ozark people. She has worked for better educational facilities and conservation of natural resources.

BIOGRAPHICAL/CRITICAL SOURCES: Daniel D. March, *History of Missouri,* Volume III, Lewis Historical Publishing, 1967.

*   *   *

PENTECOST, Edward C(lyde)   1917-

PERSONAL: Born March 29, 1917, in Schenectady, N.Y.; son of John C. (a teacher) and Edna (Brundage) Pentecost; married Margaret Atkinson, April 26, 1946; children: Edna Margaret, William Richard, Lois Elizabeth, John Edward. *Education:* Hampden-Sydney College, A.B., 1941; Dallas Theological Seminary, Th.M., 1945; University of Mexico, M.A., 1947; Fuller Theological Seminary, D. Miss., 1974. *Home:* 4012 Swiss Ave., Apt. 103B, Dallas, Tex. 75204. *Office:* Dallas Theological Seminary, 3909 Swiss Ave., Dallas, Tex. 75204.

CAREER: Ordained minister of Evangelical Church, 1964; International Fellowship of Evangelical Students, Chicago, Ill., missionary to Mexico, 1945-62; Philadelphia College of Bible, Philadelphia, Pa., professor of missions, 1962-71, chairman of department, 1965-71; World Vision International, Monrovia, Calif., research coordinator for International Congress on World Evangelization, 1972-74; Dallas Theological Seminary, Dallas, Tex., assistant professor of missions and assistant director of World Missions Research Center, 1974—.

WRITINGS: Reaching the Unreached: An Introductory Study on Developing an Overall Strategy for World Evangelization, William Carey Library, 1974. Contributor to *Evangelical Missions Quarterly, Voice.*

WORK IN PROGRESS: Research on the Evangelical Missions and Church in Japan; *Study Manual on the Pastor, the Local Church and Missions,* in Spanish.

*   *   *

PENUEL, Arnold M(cCoy)   1936-

PERSONAL: Born February 9, 1936, in old Hickory, Tenn.; son of Carmack Sneed (a clergyman) and Mary Elisabeth (McCoy) Penuel; married Carmen Patricia Forbes, August 21, 1965; children: John Forbes, Mary Kathryn, Suzanne Marie. *Education:* Attended Union University, 1954-55, and Belmont College, 1955-56; University of Tennessee, B.A., 1958; University of the Americas, M.A. (magna cum laude), 1963; University of Illinois, Ph.D., 1968. *Politics:* "Eclectic, but mostly democratic candidates." *Religion:* Unitarian-Universalist. *Home:* 115 Patton Ave., Shreveport, La. 71105. *Office:* Department of Foreign Languages, Centenary College of Louisiana, Shreveport, La. 71104.

CAREER: University of Georgia, Athens, assistant professor of Spanish, 1968-72; Centenary College of Louisiana, Shreveport, associate professor of Spanish, 1972—. *Military service:* U.S. Navy, 1959-63; became lieutenant junior grade. *Member:* Modern Language Association of America, American Association of Teachers of Spanish and Portuguese, South Central Modern Language Association.

WRITINGS: Charity in the Novels of Galdos, University of Georgia Press, 1972. Contributor to *Hispania, Anales Galdosianos,* and *Revista de Estudios Hispanicos.*

WORK IN PROGRESS: Research on Galdos' ideas on literary theory.

AVOCATIONAL INTERESTS: Travel, vegetable gardening, listening to music.

*   *   *

PEPPER, William M., Jr.   1903-1975

August 25, 1903—May 15, 1975; American newspaperman, lawyer, and lexicographer, editor and compiler of language dictionaries and books on journalism. Obituaries: *AB Bookman's Weekly,* July 7, 1975.

*   *   *

PERKINS, Agnes (Regan)   1926-

PERSONAL: Born April 28, 1926, in Helena, Mont.; daughter of Thomas P. (a dentist) and Agnes (a librarian; maiden name, Dickerson) Regan; married William David Perkins (a college teacher of English), July 26, 1950; children: Todd, Aaron, Stuart. *Education:* University of Montana, B.A., 1947, M.A., 1949. *Home:* 2565 West Ellsworth Rd., Ann Arbor, Mich. 48104. *Agent:* John Schaffner, 425 East 51st St., New York, N.Y. 10022. *Office:* Eastern Michigan University, 612 E Pray-Harrold Bldg., Ypsilanti, Mich. 48197.

CAREER: Eastern Michigan University, Ypsilanti, assistant professor of English, 1961—. *Member:* American Association of University Professors, Midwest Modern Language Association, Children's Literature Association, National Council of Teachers of English.

WRITINGS: (With Helen Hill) *New Coasts and Strange*

Harbors: Discovering Poems, Crowell, 1974; (contributor) Jared Lobdell, editor, *A Tolkien Compass*, Open Court, 1974.

WORK IN PROGRESS: An annotated, selective bibliography of children's literature, completion expected in 1976; compiling with Helen Hill and Alethea Helbig, *Hunting Dragonflies* (tentative title), poems for children; two anthologies of poems for children.

*   *   *

PERKINS, Al(bert R.) 1905(?)-1975

1905(?)—February 10, 1975; American writer, magazine managing editor, reporter, educator, and author of screenplays. Obituaries: *New York Times*, February 13, 1975.

*   *   *

PERLMUTTER, O(scar) William 1920-1975

PERSONAL: Born July 5, 1920; son of Julius B. and Hermina (Langer) Perlmutter; married Eila Helen Siren (a professor), September 10, 1945; children: William, Charles, Francis Xavier, Josette-Marie, Gregory. *Education:* Studied at Yeshiva University, 1938-42, and University of Wyoming, 1943-44; University of Chicago, M.A., 1949, Ph.D., 1959. *Politics:* Independent. *Religion:* Formerly Jewish; converted to Catholicism, 1975. *Home:* Big Watab Lake, Route 2, St. Joseph, Minn. 56374. *Agent:* Curtis Brown Ltd., 60 East 56th St., New York, N.Y. 10022. *Office:* St. John's University, Collegeville, Minn. 56321.

CAREER: University of Chicago, Chicago, Ill., lecturer in political science, 1948-51; St. Xavier College, Chicago, Ill., instructor, 1948-51, assistant professor, 1951-54, professor of social sciences and chairman of division, 1954-59, vice-president of college, 1956-59; academic adviser from Institute of European Studies at Universities of Vienna, Freiburg, and Paris, 1959-62; University of Minnesota, Minneapolis, visiting professor of political science, 1962-63; University of Santa Clara, Santa Clara, Calif., honors professor, 1963-64; Kent State University, Kent, Ohio, professor of political science and dean of College of Fine and Professional Arts, 1964-66; State University of New York at Albany, professor of political science and dean of College of Arts and Sciences, 1966-72; St. John's University, Collegeville, Minn., professor of government and academic vice-president, 1972-75. Consultant to U.S. Office of Education and U.S. Office of Economic Opportunity. Executive director, New York State Commission to Review Compensation of Judges and Legislators, 1970. *Military service:* U.S. Army and U.S. Army Air Forces, 1942-46; served in European and Pacific theaters; received Air Medal and five battle stars.

MEMBER: American Association of School Administrators, National Education Association, American Political Science Association, American Sociological Association; other academic organizations. *Awards, honors:* Ford Foundation faculty fellow at Yale University, 1952-53; Palmes Academiques (France), 1969.

WRITINGS: (With Jacqueline Jackson) *The Endless Pavement* (Junior Literary Guild selection), Seabury, 1973. Contributor of articles to education and political science journals.

AVOCATIONAL INTERESTS: Camping and outdoor life in Minnesota's north woods and lakes, traveling abroad, "love of languages."

(Died March 5, 1975)

PERLOFF, Marjorie G(abrielle) 1931-

PERSONAL: Born September 28, 1931, in Vienna, Austria; naturalized U.S. citizen in 1945; daughter of Maximillan (a lawyer) and Ilse (an economist; maiden name, Schueller) Mintz; married Joseph K. Perloff (a physician), July 31, 1953; children: Nancy, Carey. *Education:* Attended Oberlin College, 1949-52; Barnard College, A.B., 1953; Catholic University of America, M.A., 1956, Ph.D., 1965. *Religion:* Jewish. *Home:* 6905 Scotforth Rd., Philadelphia, Pa. 19119. *Office:* Department of English, University of Maryland, College Park, Md. 20742.

CAREER: Catholic University of America, Washington, D.C., assistant professor of English, 1965-71; University of Maryland, College Park, associate professor, 1971-73, professor of English, 1973—. *Member:* Modern Language Association of America, American Association of University Professors, Modern Humanities Research Association, Northeast Modern Language Association, South Atlantic Modern Language Association, Phi Beta Kappa.

WRITINGS: Rhyme and Meaning in the Poetry of Yeats, Mouton & Co., 1970; *The Poetic Art of Robert Lowell*, Cornell University Press, 1973; (contributor) Dannie Abse, editor, *Poetry Dimension, No. 2*, Haworth, 1975; *Frank O'Hara: A Critical Introduction*, Braziller, in press. Contributor of more than twenty-five articles and reviews to journals.

WORK IN PROGRESS: A study of the anti-symbolist mode in modern poetry, *Landscapes without Depth: The Rimbaud Tradition in Modern American Poetry*, publication expected in 1977.

AVOCATIONAL INTERESTS: Travel, France.

*   *   *

PERLSTEIN, Gary R(obert) 1940-

PERSONAL: Last syllable of surname is pronounced "steen"; born February 7, 1940, in Bronx, N.Y.; son of Maurice (a businessman) and Eva (Abramowitz) Perlstein; married Judith Ann Wilkinson (a vocational rehabilitation counselor), June 15, 1968. *Education:* Central College, Fayette, Mo., B.A., 1961; University of Missouri, Kansas City, M.A., 1965; Florida State University, Ph.D., 1971. *Religion:* Jewish. *Address:* Administration of Justice Program, Portland State University, P.O. Box 751, Portland, Ore. 97207.

CAREER: Missouri Division of Welfare, Jackson County and Buchanan County, liaison between child welfare unit and juvenile court, 1961-63; Planned Parenthood Association, Kansas City, Mo., social worker, 1963-65; Southwest Missouri State College, Springfield, instructor in sociology, 1965-68; Inter-Agency Law Enforcement Planning Council, Tallahassee, Fla., senior planner for corrections, 1970-71; Portland State University, Portland, Ore., assistant professor of criminology and associate director of Administration of Justice Program, 1971—. Adjunct professor at Florida A&M University, 1969-70. Instructor for Oregon Board on Police Standards and Training, 1972, and for Oregon State Penitentiary, 1972-73. Member of oral examining board for sergeants' examination of Portland Civil Service Commission, 1972, of citizen's advisory council for Portland Women's Community Treatment Center of Oregon Division of Corrections, 1972-75, and of subcommittee on training and education for Portland Office City-County Police Consolidation, 1973-74.

MEMBER: International Association of Chiefs of Police

(associate member), American Correctional Association, Society for the Study of Social Problems, Law and Society Association, Academy of Criminal Justice Sciences, American Society of Criminology, Oregon Corrections Association, Alpha Kappa Delta, Delta Tau Kappa.

WRITINGS: (With Thomas R. Phelps) *Instead of Prison: Community-Based Corrections*, Goodyear Publishing, 1975. Contributor to professional journals.

WORK IN PROGRESS: With Harold J. Vetter, *Theory in Criminology.*

*   *   *

PERRY, Kenneth W(ilbur)   1919-

PERSONAL: Born May 21, 1919, in Lawrenceburg, Ky.; son of Ollie T. and Minnie (Monroe) Perry; married Shirley Kimball (a librarian), September 5, 1942; children: Constance June (Mrs. Linden Warfel). *Education:* Eastern Kentucky University, B.S., 1942; Ohio University, M.S., 1949; University of Illinois, Ph.D., 1953. *Religion:* Protestant. *Home:* 1302 Mitchem Dr., Urbana, Ill. 61801. *Office:* 208 Commerce W., University of Illinois, Urbana, Ill. 61801.

CAREER: Certified public accountant in Illinois; Berea College, Berea, Ky., instructor in business, 1949; University of Kentucky, Lexington, instructor in business, summer, 1949; University of Illinois, Urbana, professor of accountancy, 1950-75, Alexander Grant Professor of Accountancy, 1975—. Professor at Northeastern University, summer, 1966, and at Florida A.&M. University, autumn, 1971-72; Carman Blough Professor of Commerce at University of Virginia, 1975-76. *Military service:* U.S. Army, 1942-46; became major. U.S. Army Reserve, 1946—; present rank, colonel.

MEMBER: American Accounting Association (vice-president, 1963), American Institute of Certified Public Accountants, American Statistical Association, National Association of Accountants (director, 1969-71), Reserve Officers Association, Illinois Society of Certified Public Accountants, Beta Alpha Psi, Beta Gamma Sigma, Delta Sigma Pi, Omicron Delta Kappa.

WRITINGS: (Editor and contributor) *Accountants' Cost Handbook*, Ronald, 2nd edition, 1960; (with Norton M. Bedford and Arthur R. Wyatt) *Advanced Accounting*, Wiley, 1960, 3rd edition, 1971; *Passing the C.P.A. Examination*, Stipes, 1964, 4th edition, 1975; (contributor) *Complete Guide to a Profitable Accounting Practice*, Prentice-Hall, 1965; *Accounting: An Introduction*, McGraw, 1971; (contributor) *C.P.A. Review Manual*, Prentice-Hall, 4th edition, 1973; (contributor) *Accounting Education: Problems and Prospects*, American Accounting Association, 1975.

WORK IN PROGRESS: Intermediate Accounting, with Charles J. Woelfel and John Willingham, for West Publishing; revising *Accounting: An Introduction, Advanced Accounting*, with Norton M. Bedford and Arthur R. Wyatt, and *C.P.A. Review Manual*, with others.

*   *   *

PETERMAN, Ruth   1924-

PERSONAL: Born June 18, 1924, in Hull, N.D.; daughter of Leonard (a teacher and clerk) and Nella (Van Soest) Jellema; married Clinton Alvin Peterman (a superintendent with an insurance company), May 27, 1944; children: Grace (Mrs. Larry Christensen), Elliot, Nella (Mrs. Roderick Hauser), Brian, David. *Education:* Valley City State College, student, 1941-42. *Politics:* Republican. *Religion:* Covenant. *Home:* 3220 33rd Ave. S., Minneapolis, Minn. 55406.

CAREER: Teacher of writing courses in adult education programs in St. Paul, Minn., and Minneapolis, Minn., both 1968—. Instructor at Northwestern College, 1972—, Normandale Community College, 1974—, Minnetonka Center of Arts and Education, 1974—, and University of Minnesota's program of continuing education for women, 1975—. Delegate to Republican State Convention and to State Central Committee, 1972—.

WRITINGS: My World Was Too Small (articles), Tyndale, 1974; *Held for Ransom: The Story of the Kronholm Kidnapping*, Tyndale, 1975. Contributor to over thirty magazines, including *Writer's Digest, Lutheran Standard, Church Administration, Marriage, Living Today, American Legion, Campus Life, Home Life*, and *Scope.*

WORK IN PROGRESS: A book of inspirational articles.

*   *   *

PETERS, Elizabeth   1927-
(Barbara Michaels)

PERSONAL: Born September 29, 1927, in Illinois; daughter of Earl D. and Grace (Tregellas) Gross; children: Elizabeth, Peter. *Education:* University of Chicago, Ph.B., 1945, M.A., 1947, Ph.D., 1950. *Residence:* Potomac, Md. *Agent:* Raines & Raines, 244 Madison Ave., New York, N.Y. 10016.

CAREER: Writer.

WRITINGS—Novels: The Jackals Head, Meredith, 1968; *The Camelot Caper*, Meredith, 1969; *The Dead Sea Cipher*, Dodd, 1970; *The Night of Four Hundred Rabbits*, Dodd, 1971; *The Seventh Sinner*, Dodd, 1972; *Borrower of the Night*, Dodd, 1973; *The Murders of Richard III*, Dodd, 1974; *Crocodile on the Sandbank*, Dodd, 1975.

Under pseudonym Barbara Michaels; novels: *The Master of Blacktower*, Meredith, 1966; *Sons of the Wolf*, Meredith, 1967; *Ammie Come Home*, Meredith, 1968; *Prince of Darkness*, Meredith, 1969; *The Dark on the Other Side*, Dodd, 1970; *The Crying Child*, Dodd, 1971; *Graygallows*, Dodd, 1972; *Witch*, Dodd, 1973; *House of Many Shadows*, Dodd, 1974.

WORK IN PROGRESS: The Ghost in Green Velvet; The Sea King's Daughter, under pseudonym Barbara Michaels.

*   *   *

PETERS, Max S(tone)   1920-

PERSONAL: Born August 23, 1920, in Delaware, Ohio: son of Charles C. and Dixie (May) Peters; married Laurnell Stephens, June 29, 1947; children: Margaret Peters Schmatz, Stephen. *Education:* Pennsylvania State University, B.S., 1942, M.S., 1947, Ph.D., 1951. *Home:* 1965 Vassar Circle, Boulder, Colo. 80303. *Office:* Engineering Center AD 1-1, University of Colorado, Boulder, Colo. 80302.

CAREER: Hercules Powder Co., production supervisor in Virginia and Kansas, 1942-44; George I. Treyz Chemicals Co., Cooks Falls, N.Y., technical plant superintendent, 1947-49; University of Illinois, Urbana, assistant professor, 1951-57, professor of chemical engineering, 1957-62, head of Chemical Engineering Division, 1958-62; University of Colorado, Boulder, professor of chemical engineering, 1962—, dean of College of Engineering and Applied Science, 1962—. Member of board of directors of Commission on Engineering Education, 1967-70; chairman of Colorado Environmental Commission, 1970-72; member of various committees, commissions, and advisory panels of agencies and organizations, including National Science Foundation, National Air Pollution Control Administration, and National Research Council. *Military service:* U.S. Army, Mountain Infantry, 1944-46; became first sergeant; received Silver Star, Bronze Star, and Purple Heart.

Member: American Institute of Chemical Engineers (fellow; director, 1961-64; vice-president, 1967; president, 1968), American Chemical Society, American Society for Engineering Education, American Association of Cost Engineers, Engineers' Council for Professional Development (member of executive board, 1970-75; secretary, 1971—), National Academy of Engineering, Professional Engineers of Colorado (member of board of advisors, 1970), Alpha Chi Sigma, Phi Eta Sigma, Phi Lambda Upsilon, Tau Beta Pi, Sigma Tau, Sigma Xi. *Awards, honors:* George Westinghouse Award, 1959, and Lamme Award, 1973, from American Society for Engineering Education; award of merit from American Association of Cost Engineers, 1969; engineer-of-the-year award from Professional Engineers of Colorado, 1971; Founders Award from American Institute of Chemical Engineers, 1974.

WRITINGS: Elementary Chemical Engineering, McGraw, 1954; (contributor) P. L. Magill, F. R. Holden, and C. Ackley, editors, *Air Pollution Handbook,* McGraw, 1956; *Plant Design and Economics for Chemical Engineers,* McGraw, 1958, 2nd edition, 1968; (contributor) F. Jelen, editor, *Cost and Optimization Engineering,* McGraw, 1970. Contributor to chemical engineering journals. Author of technical reports on chemical engineering.

WORK IN PROGRESS: Catalytic Reduction of Nitrogen Oxides.

* * *

PETERSEN, Carol Otto 1914-

PERSONAL: Born February 23, 1914, in Bucharest, Romania; son of Otto Gustav (a banker) and Therese (Luerman) Petersen; children: Horst Manfred (adopted). *Education:* Attended University of Greifswald, University of Leipsig; University of Berlin, M.A., 1946. *Religion:* Lutheran. *Home:* 1904 Chicago St., Apt. 43, Valpariso, Ind. 46383. *Office address:* Box 178, University St., Valparaiso, Ind. 46383.

CAREER: Teacher in German Gymnasium (high school), 1946-68, Rugby School, Warwickshire, England, 1948, Institut Francais de Berlin, Berlin, Germany, 1949-67; Valparaiso University, Valparaiso, Ind., professor of French and German language and literature, 1968—. French interpreter in Europa Union and Municipality of West Berlin, 1953-63. *Military service:* German Navy, 1941-45; radio operator. *Member:* Hoelderlin-Gesellschaft, Modern Language Association of America. *Awards, honors:* Chevalier des Palmes Academiques de France, 1965.

WRITINGS: Mensch der Stille (title means "Man in a Silent World"), Hanseatische Verlagsanstalt, 1948; *Hans Carossa,* Paedagogischer Verlag, 1950; (contributor) *Christliche Dichter der Gegenwart* (title means "Contemporary Christian Authors"), Wolfgang Rothe Verlag, 1955; (contributor) *Expressionismus: Gestalten einer literarischen Bewegung,* Wolfgang Rothe Verlag, 1957; *Albert Camus,* Colloquium Verlag, 1961, translation by Alexander Gode published under same title, Ungar, 1969; *Max Frisch,* Col-

loquium Verlag Otto Hess, 1966, translation by Charlotte La Rue published under same title, Ungar, 1972; (contributor) *Christliche Dichter im zwanzig Jahrhundert,* Francke Verlag, 1968; (contributor) *Expressionismus als Literatur,* Francke Verlag, 1969; *Andre Gide,* Colloquium Verlag Otto Hess, 1969; *John Steinbeck,* Colloquium Verlag Otto Hess, 1972; *Tennessee Williams,* Colloquium Verlag Otto Hess, 1975. Also author of poetry and lyrics.

* * *

PETERSEN, Peter (Barron) 1932-

PERSONAL: Born October 21, 1932, in Chicago, Ill.; son of Marius K. and Agnes (Barron) Petersen; married Janet E. McKenney (a personnel officer), March 31, 1955; children: John, William, James. *Education:* Long Island Agricultural and Technical Institute, A.B.S., 1952; University of Omaha, B.Sc., 1962; George Washington University, M.B.A., 1967, D.B.A., 1971. *Politics:* "Middle of the road Republican." *Religion:* Methodist. *Home:* 4400 36th St. N., Arlington, Va. 22207. *Office:* Headquarters UNC/USFK/EUSA J-3 (CS/CT), APO San Francisco, 96301.

CAREER: U.S. Army, 1953—; drafted into service as private, presently Infantry colonel commanding combat support coordination team in Korea; has had airborne, troop, and command assignments, including command of Special Forces unit in Vietnam, 1962-63, and battalion commander with Infantry unit in Vietnam, 1968-69. *Member:* American Psychological Association, Academy of Management. *Awards, honors*—Military: Silver Star with oak-leaf cluster; Distinguished Flying Cross; Legion of Merit with oak-leaf cluster; Bronze Star; and other decorations.

WRITINGS: Against the Tide: An Argument in Favor of the American Soldier, Arlington House, 1974. Contributor to *Journal of Applied Psychology, Training and Development Journal,* and other periodicals.

WORK IN PROGRESS: An investigation of the effect and stability of military training; an analysis of the psychological dimensions of a group of soldiers who left the Army and their reasons for leaving.

SIDELIGHTS: In research connected with his master's thesis and doctoral dissertation Petersen sampled the views of more than four thousand soldiers and veterans during a six-year period. *Against the Tide* resulted from his surveys and testing.

* * *

PETERSON, Marilyn Ann 1933-

PERSONAL: Born July 22, 1933, in Holdrege, Neb.; daughter of Claude Francis (a farmer) and Esther (Soderholm) Whitney; married Richard Fay Peterson (a photographer), June 16, 1956. *Education:* Kearney State College, B.A., 1955; University of Northern Colorado, M.A., 1963. *Politics:* Republican. *Religion:* Methodist. *Home:* 1710 Mayfair, Fremont, Neb. 68025. *Office:* Department of English and Journalism, Midland College, Fremont, Neb. 68025.

CAREER: Public school teacher in junior high and high schools, 1955-64; Midland College, Fremont, Neb.; assistant professor, 1964-75, associate professor of English and journalism, 1975—. *Member:* American Association of University Women (president, 1975-77), National Council of College Publications Advisers, American Association of University Professors, National Press Photographers Association, Dodge County Historical Society, Delta Kappa Gamma (president, 1974-76), Pi Delta Epsilon (adviser, 1964-75), Altrusa International (local president, 1973-75).

WRITINGS: The Mimeographed Newspaper, Henington Press, 1972. Author of brochures. Contributor to *School Activities*.

WORK IN PROGRESS: Poems and photographs.

AVOCATIONAL INTERESTS: Bridge, painting, music, reading, unusual ideas, antiques, travel (England, Germany, France, Spain, Africa).

* * *

PETERSON, Susan (Annette) H(arnly)   1925-

PERSONAL: Born July 21, 1925, in McPherson, Kan.; daughter of Paul Whitmore (an educator) and Iva (Curtis) Harnly; married Jack L. Peterson, October 9, 1949 (divorced, 1972); children: Jill Kristin, Jan Sigrid, Taag Paul. *Education:* Monticello College, A.A., 1944; Mills College, A.B. (with honors), 1946; State University of New York College of Ceramics, M.F.A., 1950. *Office:* Department of Art, Hunter College of the City University of New York, 695 Park Ave., New York, N.Y.

CAREER: Public school teacher in Honolulu, Hawaii, 1946-47; Wichita Art Association School, Wichita, Kan., founder and head of ceramics department, 1947-49; high school teacher in Whittier, Calif., 1951-52; Chouinard Art Institute, Los Angeles, Calif., teacher of ceramics and head of department, 1952-56; University of Southern California, Los Angeles, professor of ceramics and fine arts, 1956—, head of department of ceramics of Idyllwild School of Music and the Arts, 1958—. Professor at Hunter College of the City University of New York, 1972—. Director of Clayworks Studio; creator of "Wheels, Kilns, and Clay," a television series, for Public Broadcasting Library. Exhibits stoneware and porcelain in group and one-woman shows; work is represented in major American museums and private collections, and in foreign museums and exhibitions. Consultant and designer for industry.

MEMBER: World Crafts Council, American Crafts Council, National Ceramics Educators Council, American Ceramic Society, Southern California Designer-Craftsmen (director, 1956-61), Phi Beta Kappa. *Awards, honors:* Knight of the Order of the Lion of Finland, 1969, for furthering cultural relations with the United States.

WRITINGS: Wheels, Kilns, and Clay (textbook), Learning Systems Center, University of Southern California Press, 1970; *Shoji Hamada: A Potter's Way and Work*, Kodansha International, 1974, distributed by Harper. Author of fifty-four scripts for "Wheels, Kilns, and Clay," for CBS-KNXT Television, 1950-75. Contributor to craft magazines, including *Craft Horizons*.

WORK IN PROGRESS: A book on Maria, the potter of San Ildefonso; a definitive handbook on ceramics.

SIDELIGHTS: Susan Peterson writes: "I have travelled extensively for twenty years visiting and documenting folk art cultures of the world. My relationship with Shoji Hamada began in 1952 and has continued to widen a circle of east-west understandings. It's a world art I'm interested in historically and presently."

BIOGRAPHICAL/CRITICAL SOURCES: Rose Slivka, *Crafts of the Modern World*, Horizon Press, 1968, revised edition, 1972.

PETESCH, Natalie L(evin) M(aines)

PERSONAL: Born in Detroit, Mich.; daughter of Samuel (a grocer) and Anna (Goldman) Levin; married John Maines, December 21, 1945 (divorced, January, 1959); married Donald Anthony Petesch (a professor of contemporary literature), August 30, 1959; children: (first marriage) Mrs. Christopher Cooper; (second marriage) Nicholas Donald. *Education:* Boston University, B.S., 1955; Brandeis University, M.A., 1956; University of Texas at Austin, Ph.D., 1962. *Home and office:* 6320 Crombie St., Pittsburgh, Pa. 15217. *Agent:* Virginia Barber, 44 Greenwich Ave., New York, N.Y. 10010.

CAREER: University of Texas at Austin, special instructor, 1959-60, instructor in British and American literature, 1963-65; San Francisco State College (now University), San Francisco, Calif., assistant professor of British and American literature, 1961-62; Southwest Texas State College, San Marcos, assistant professor of British and American literature, 1961-62; full-time writer in Pittsburgh, Pa., 1965—. *Awards, honors:* Iowa School of Letters award for short fiction, 1974, for *After the First Death There Is No Other*.

WRITINGS: After the First Death There Is No Other (short story collection), University of Iowa Press, 1974; *The Odyssey of Katinou Kalokovich* (novel), United Sisters, 1974.

Work is represented in anthologies, including *Different Drummers*, edited by Elizabeth Canar and Cecile Vye, Random House, 1973; *Michigan Hot Apples: An Anthology of Michigan Writers*, edited by Gay Rubin, Hot Apples Press, 1973; *Moving to Antarctica*, edited by Margaret Kaminski, Dustbooks, 1975.

WORK IN PROGRESS: A novel that deals with a futuristic society in which all the activities of society are in control of a single multi-national system, *The Grievance Adjuster*; a novel about a colony gathered together in a commune to learn principles of survival for the coming Armageddon, *The Last Chronicle of Eden*; *The Long Hot Summer of Yasha K*, a novel.

AVOCATIONAL INTERESTS: Travel in Latin America, Third World culture, French culture.

* * *

PETRUCCI, Kenneth R(occo)   1947-

PERSONAL: Born July 31, 1947, in Providence, R.I.; son of Rocco (an opera singer) and Filomena Petrucci. *Education:* Rhode Island Junior College, A.A., 1969; Memphis State University, B.F.A., 1972. *Home:* 6 Piedmont St., Providence, R.I. 02909.

CAREER: Poet, writing full-time, 1970—; reads own poetry, and that of others, in New England area and other parts of the United States. Formerly comedian in Providence and Cape Cod, under name Kenney Pipe. *Awards, honors:* Co-winner of World Poems Contest of Illinois, 1970.

WRITINGS: Soul's Eye (poetry), Branden Press, 1975. Poetry anthologized in *The Best in Poetry*, edited by Barbara Fischer, J. Mark Press, 1974. Contributor of poems to *Chicago Tribune, Poet's Guild, Creative Review, Nimrod, Bachaet, Cardinal Quarterly, Bardic Echoes*, and other publications.

WORK IN PROGRESS: Another book of poems, completion expected in 1976.

AVOCATIONAL INTERESTS: Comedy, philosophy, astrology, psychic world, and many facets of the world around us, travel.

*   *   *

PETZOLDT, Paul Kiesow   1908-

PERSONAL: Born January 16, 1908, in Lincoln Township, Union County, Iowa; son of Charles Frederick (a farmer) and Emma Louise (Kiesow) Petzoldt; married Joan Ann Pflugradt, May 1, 1975. *Education:* Attended University of Idaho, 1929-30, University of Wyoming, 1931, University of Utah, 1932, Deanery at Windsor Castle, London, England, 1933, and Louisiana State University, 1934, 1935. *Office:* National Outdoor Leadership School, P.O. Box AA, Lander, Wyo. 82520.

CAREER: Mountaineer. Established mountaineering guide service in Teton Range, Wyo., 1924-55; worked at ranching, Riverton, Wyo., 1955-62; Colorado Outward Bound, Marble, Colo., chief instructor, 1962-64; National Outdoor Leadership School, Lander, Wyo., organizer and director, 1965—. President of Paul Petzoldt Wilderness Equipment. Director of American School of Mountaineering, 1928-55; worked as liaison for lend-lease food in U.S. Department of Agriculture, 1942-43; member of Berlin Control Council, 1945-46; assistant to chief of transportation of Government of Taiwan, 1946-47. Has lectured at universities including Stanford University, University of California, University of Washington, Seattle, University of Idaho, Washington State College, University of Michigan, Michigan State University, Rutgers University, and University of Pennsylvania. *Military service:* U.S. Army, Tenth Mountain Division, originated methods of medical evacuation in mountains with ski troops, 1943-46; served in European theater; became captain. *Member:* Kappa Sigma. *Awards, honors:* Conservation award from U.S. Department of the Interior, 1951, and American Academy of Achievement, 1971.

WRITINGS: The Wilderness Handbook, Norton, 1975.

SIDELIGHTS: Petzoldt climbed the Grand Teton in cowboy boots at age sixteen. He has climbed in the Alps, making a double traverse of the Matterhorn in a single day in 1934, the Sierra Nevada de Santa Marta in South America, 1941, the Wind River Range in Wyoming, the Karakorum of Pakistan, setting a new altitude record for Americans, 1948, and rescued a parachutist from the top of Devil's Tower in Wyoming.

He developed mountaineering voice signals, 1924-28, sliding middle man snow climbing technique, 1925-28, also methods of rhythmatic breathing, pressure breathing, salt and water intake, food consumption, body heat control for endurance, preventing mountain sickness, and adjustment to high altitudes.

Petzoldt still spends time in the mountains, and attempts to climb the Grand Teton every New Year's Day.

*   *   *

PEVSNER, Stella

PERSONAL: Born in Lincoln, Ill.; married; children: four. *Education:* Attended Illinois University. *Home:* Palatine, Ill.

CAREER: Stella Pevsner describes her career: "I was taking art courses that first summer in Chicago when one evening, in an amiable mood, I registered for a course in advertising at Northwestern University to keep a friend company. She went on to become a reporter but I landed a job in advertising. From the lowly assignment of writing ads for a drug chain I advanced to the pots and pans division of a State Street store's ad department. After about a year I managed to land a job in an advertising agency writing high fashion copy, and from then on went to various other agencies and finally to Dana Perfumes, where I was promotion director. After marriage I wrote free-lance articles until, at the suggestion of one of my children, I turned to juvenile novels."

WRITINGS: The Young Brontes (one-act play for young adults), Baker, 1967; *Break a Leg!*, Crown, 1969; *Footsteps on the Stairs*, Crown, 1970; *Call Me Heller, That's My Name*, Seabury, 1973. Writes advertising copy, promotion, publicity, free-lance articles, commercial film strips.

SIDELIGHTS: Mrs. Pevsner writes: One of my children suggested that since I spent so much time at the typewriter (robbing her of my precious company) I might at least write something she could enjoy. I turned to the theatre for inspiration. *Break a Leg!* describes how the participation in a play not only helps a young girl overcome her shyness but also makes her aware of the fact that off-beat kids have something to offer. *Footsteps on the Stairs* deals with the young brother of the first book, his fear, and how he learns to overcome it.

"Once, as a respite, I took a course in collage and found that this art form bears a close relationship to writing. In each . . . a collage or novel . . . the artist/author takes bits of this and that, scraps and dreams and memories and weaves them into a design which is new and strange and yet somehow familiar. . . . While the teacher and mother parts of me try to inject something positive into each book, my main purpose in writing is to entertain. I would like to lead at least some children into the pleasant path of reading with the hope that they will go on and on to other books for the rest of their lives."

*   *   *

PFANNER, Helmut Franz   1933-

PERSONAL: Born November 8, 1933, in Hohenweiler, Vorarlberg, Austria; son of Georg Franz (a customs official) and Luise (Huber) Pfanner; married Rosemary Griffin, March 19, 1959 (divorced, 1964); married Beverly Radcliffe, September 16, 1966; children: (first marriage) Renate; (second marriage) Heidi, Eric, Marta. *Education:* Lehrerbildungsanstalt Feldkirch, teaching certificate, 1952; University of Kansas, graduate study, 1957-58; Stanford University, M.A., 1961, Ph.D., 1965. *Politics:* "As long as there are oppressors and those who are oppressed, always on the side of the oppressed." *Religion:* "catholic (sic)." *Home:* 8 Bartlett Rd., Durham, N.H. 03824. *Office:* Department of German, University of New Hampshire, Durham, N.H. 03824.

CAREER: Landesschulrat, Bregenz, Austria, elementary school teacher, 1952-57, 1958-59; University of Washington, Seattle, instructor in German, 1964-67; University of Virginia, Charlottesville, assistant professor of German, 1967-69; University of New Hampshire, Durham, associate professor of German, 1969—. Teacher of summer German institutes at University of Washington, 1965, University of Scranton, 1966, Lewis & Clark College, 1967, Wells College, 1968, and University of New Hampshire, 1970, 1972, 1974. *Member:* International Association for the Promotion of the World University, International Brecht Society, International Organization for the Study of German Exile Literature, International Oskar Maria Graf Society, American Association of Teachers of German, American Association of University Professors, American Council for the Study of Austrian Literature, Modern Language Association of America. *Awards, honors:* Fulbright scholarship, 1957-58; American Philosophical Society grants, 1969, 1971; Alexander von Humboldt fellowship, 1972-73.

WRITINGS: Hanns Johst: Vom Expressionismus zum Nationalsozialismus (title means "Hanns Johst: From Expressionism to National Socialism"), Mouton & Co., 1970; (editor with Wolfgang Dietz) *Oskar Maria Graf*, Annedore Leber (Munich), 1974; *Oskar Maria Graf (1894-1967)* (exhibition catalogue), University of New Hampshire, 1974; *Oskar Maria Graf. Eine kritische Bibliographie* (title means "Oskar Maria Graf: An Annotated Bibliography"), Francke, in press. Contributor to journals in his field.

WORK IN PROGRESS: Research in German and Austrian literature in exile, especially in the United States.

SIDELIGHTS: Pfanner writes: "The studies of language and of literature are important means for the improvement of life in the modern world. At a point in history where the advancement of science and the polarization of economic growth have brought imminent danger to all mankind, it is essential that the humanistic side of man's endeavors be further developed. Our technological know-how must be combined with better methods of communication between individuals and between nations, and the traditional 'values' of personal industry, professional success and political strength must be brought into harmony with love of leisure, respect for the products of human imagination and tolerance for the convictions of others. In my teaching and writing, I aim at the propagation of these views."

AVOCATIONAL INTERESTS: Hiking, skiing, travelling, being with friends, reading, music, and gardening.

*   *   *

PFEIFFER, C(urtis) Boyd   1937-

PERSONAL: Born August 5, 1937, in Baltimore, Md.; son of Elmer Curt and Vera V. (Boyd) Pfeiffer; married Jacqueline Brown (a secretary), January 23, 1963; children: Debbie, Greg, Jeff. *Education:* Gettysburg College, A.B., 1960; University of Maryland, graduate study, 1960-65. *Home:* 9306 Joey Dr., Ellicott City, Md. 21043. *Office: Washington Post*, Washington, D.C.

CAREER: University of Maryland, School of Medicine, Baltimore, instructor in anatomy, 1961-71; *Baltimore Sunday Sun*, Baltimore, Md., recreation editor, 1970-71; *Washington Post*, Washington, D.C., outdoor editor, 1971—. *Member:* Outdoor Writers Association of America, Mason-Dixon Outdoor Writers Association (member of board of directors, 1975-77), Pennsylvania Outdoor Writers Association (member of board of directors, 1970-75), Virginia Outdoor Writers Association. *Awards, honors:* Mason-Dixon Outdoor Writers Association first place informative writing award, 1971, 1972, 1974, second place conservation award, 1972, first place best outdoor full-length feature award, 1973; National Shooting Sports Foundation award, 1972, for best newspaper column covering National Hunting and Fishing Day; first place editorial award from Recreation Vehicle Industry Association, 1974.

WRITINGS: (With L. James Bashline) *1972 Field and Stream Fishing Guide*, Field and Stream, 1972; *Tackle Craft*, Crown, 1974; *Shad Fishing*, Crown, 1975; *Salt Water Fishing Guide*, Field and Stream, in press. Contributor of columns to *Virginia Camper*, 1973—, *Metro East*

Outdoor News, 1973—, and *Sports Afield*, 1975—. Contributor to more than twenty-six outdoor magazines.

WORK IN PROGRESS: Two more fishing books.

AVOCATIONAL INTERESTS: Photography, hiking, camping.

*   *   *

PHILLIPS, L(ouis) C(hristopher)   1939-

PERSONAL: Born July 16, 1939, in Chester, Pa.; son of Louis O. (an architect) and Maria Phillips; married Jennifer D. Roach, December 19, 1965 (divorced, 1973); children: Blake Vaughn, Jason Louis. *Education:* St. Joseph's College, Philadelphia, Pa., A.B., 1961; University of Notre Dame, M.A., 1962; University of Rome, graduate study, 1963; University of Iowa, M.F.A., 1965. *Home:* 530 Newport Rd., C-9, Xenia, Ohio 45385. *Office:* Department of English, Central State University, Wilberforce, Ohio 45385.

CAREER: Central State University, Wilberforce, Ohio, associate professor of English, 1966—, director of creative writing, 1970—

WRITINGS: The Dream Winners, Exposition, 1967; *Sistine Cartoons* (poetry), Pulse-Finger Press, 1969, 2nd edition, 1971; *Bloodlines* (poetry), Pulse-Finger Press, 1971.

*   *   *

PHILLIPSON, David   1930-

PERSONAL: Born December 26, 1930, in Derby, England; son of Albert Edward (a barber) and Dorothy (Fletcher) Phillipson; married Mary Gray (an occupational therapist), April 10, 1954; children: Claire, Peter, Sue. *Education:* Educated in England. *Politics:* Reactionary. *Religion:* Church of England. *Home:* Felsteads, Coppice Row, Theydon Bois, Essex CM16 7DS, England. *Office:* Her Majesty's Commissioners of Customs & Excises, King's Beam House, London, England.

CAREER: Temporary teacher, Walthamstow Education Committee, Essex, England, and later production assistant, Phoenix House Publications, London, England, 1958; Her Majesty's Commissioners of Customs & Excises, London, assistant preventive officer, 1958-66, preventive officer, 1966-74, higher executive officer, 1974—. *Military service:* Royal Navy, Submarine Service, 1946-57; became chief petty officer.

WRITINGS: Smuggling, David & Charles, 1973.

WORK IN PROGRESS: Boy Seaman, a memoir of initial training in the navy and early sea-service; research for an anthology of international smuggling; a history of Theydon Bois area, for Village Association.

SIDELIGHTS: Phillipson writes: "My all-consuming interest lies in social history—not in great events which shaped the course of mankind . . . but in the minutiae of daily life. . . . Am fascinated by human institutions—armies, navies, religious orders, seats of learning, and their hierarchy, grades and orders. The more ancient, the more estimable . . ." *Avocational interests:* "Alequaffing."

*   *   *

PICKENS, Roy   1939-

PERSONAL: Born August 17, 1939, in Greenville, Ala.; son of Ealon Roy (an automobile dealer) and Wynette (Wilson) Pickens; married Patricia Henderson, August 20,

1957; children: Robert, Sharon. *Education:* Troy State University, student, 1957-59; Auburn University, B.A., 1961, M.S., 1962; University of Mississippi, Ph.D., 1965; University of Minnesota, postdoctoral study, 1965-66. *Home:* 696 East County Road B, Maplewood, Minn. 55117. *Office:* Department of Psychiatry, Box 392 Mayo, University of Minnesota, Minneapolis, Minn. 55455.

CAREER: University of Minnesota, Minneapolis, assistant professor, 1966-70, associate professor, 1970-73, professor of psychiatry, 1973—. Chairman of advisory council on controlled substances, for Minnesota State Board of Pharmacy, 1971—. *Member:* American Association for the Advancement of Science, Behavioral Pharmacology Society, Psychonomic Society, American Psychological Association. *Awards, honors:* Postdoctoral fellowship from U.S. Public Health Service, 1965-66.

WRITINGS: (Editor with Travis I. Thompson and Richard A. Meisch) *Readings in Behavioral Pharmacology,* Appleton, 1970; (with Thompson) *Stimulus Properties of Drugs,* Appleton, 1971. Writer and technical consultant for "Drugs: The Risks Are . . .," a series on KTCA-Television, 1972.

WORK IN PROGRESS: Research on drug abuse and behavioral action of drugs.

* * *

PICKERING, Jerry V(ane) 1931-

PERSONAL: Born October 19, 1931, in Jackson, Mich.; son of Harrison Vane and Gladys (Wood) Pickering; married Eve Yankovich (a university club director), March 7, 1953; children: Jeffrey, James, David. *Education:* Sacramento State College (now California State University, Sacramento), B.A., 1956, M.A., 1959; University of California, Davis, Ph.D., 1972. *Home:* 622 South Pine, Brea, Calif. 92621. *Office:* Theatre Department, California State University, Fullerton, Calif. 92634.

CAREER: California Test Bureau, Monterey, editor, 1960-61; University of California, Davis, editor of campus publications, 1961-68; California State University, Fullerton, assistant professor, 1968-71, associate professor, 1971-75, professor of theatre, 1975—. *Military service:* U.S. Air Force, 1949-53; became staff sergeant. *Member:* American Theatre Association, Medieval Association of the Pacific, Mediaeval Academy of America.

WRITINGS: Readers Theatre, Dickenson, 1975; *A Treasury of Drama: Classical Through Modern,* West Publishing, 1975; *Theatre: A Contemporary Introduction,* West Publishing, 1975. Contributor to journals in his field.

WORK IN PROGRESS: Makers of Theatre; also a murder mystery.

SIDELIGHTS: Pickering writes: "I am profoundly grateful that I was born to a family that stressed the importance of education and that fully supported any educational venture, no matter how unusual or demanding. My wife, thank God, has continued this tradition."

* * *

PICKERING, Stephen 1947-
(Chofetz Chaim ben-Avraham)

PERSONAL: Born August 16, 1947, in Los Angeles, Calif.; son of Raymond Albert and Pansy (Wilson) Pickering; married Sandra Herr (a bookkeeper), July 13, 1974; children: one. *Education:* Attended Bakersfield College;

independent studies in the Talmud and Jewish mysticism, 1969—. *Politics:* "Radical; coupled with Torah." *Religion:* "Jew, bordering on orthodox." *Residence:* Aptos, Calif.

CAREER: Writer.

WRITINGS: (Editor and contributor) *Dylan: A Commemoration,* Book People, 1971; (editor and contributor) *Praxis One,* Book People, 1971; *Bob Dylan: Tour 1974,* Echo Publications, 1973; *Bob Dylan Approximately: A Midrash,* McKay, 1975. Contributor to *Fusion* and *Rolling Stone.* Editor of *Sun Daze* (underground newspaper), 1970-71.

WORK IN PROGRESS: Editing *Aggadah: Studies in Bob Dylan and Torah Judaism; Blood on the Tracks: A Kabbalistic Exegesis of Hope,* on Bob Dylan; editing *Kavvanah: Jewish Quests and Dylaneutics;* "Knockin' on Heaven's Door" and "Billy": A Monograph on Gilluy Shekhinah;* further studies of Bob Dylan.

SIDELIGHTS: Pickering writes: "I first heard Bob Dylan, on tape, in September, 1960; and, since then, have amassed what some consider to be the largest private collection of tapes, photographs, articles concerning Mr. Dylan in existence. It is my firm belief, as a religious Jew, that Dylan is the *most* important poet in Jewish history, and the analogies between his archetypes and those of the kabbalists (primarily in the sixteenth century) and the Chassidim (primarily Chabad Chassidim) are not always coincidental. Kabbalah is the melody of the Torah, that ineluctable liberating sea of bridges between man and the covenant at Sinai. For man, since the flames of Auschwitz forever buried the pseudo-legitimacy of Christianity, chaos has become a particularly dangerous mistress. Bob Dylan, using his Jewish consciousness, offers not an 'answer' to this chaos, but, like Elie Wiesel, a question, an existential demand nurtured from Sinai." Pickering lists Chofetz Chaim ben-Avraham as his Hebrew name.

* * *

PICKLE, Hal B(rittain) 1929-

PERSONAL: Born January 16, 1929, in Ennis, Tex.; son of Oren M. (a barber) and Bessie Mae (Beard) Pickle; married Anna Lucille Toupal, June 24, 1953; children: Debra Lyn, Karen Kay, Eric Brian, Lance Oram. *Education:* North Texas State University, B.B.A., 1959, M.B.A., 1960; University of Arkansas, Ph.D., 1964. *Home:* 4905 Saddle Dr., Austin, Tex. 78759. *Office:* 5425-B Burnet Rd., Austin, Tex. 78756.

CAREER: Southwest Texas State University, San Marcos, associate professor of management, 1962-69; Auburn University, Auburn, Ala., professor of management, 1969-73; Hal B. Pickle (research and consulting), Austin, Tex., president, 1973—. President of Auburn Business Consultants, Inc., 1972—. *Military service:* U.S. Army, Engineers, 1950-52. *Member:* Academy of Management, National Council of Small Business Management Development. *Awards, honors:* National Science Foundation research grant, 1971; Small Business Administration research grant, 1971; Office of Water Resources Research grant, 1971-73.

WRITINGS: Personality and Success: An Evaluation of Personal Characteristics of Successful Small Business Managers, Small Business Administration, 1964; *Introduction to Business: Text and Cases,* Goodyear Publishing, 1972, 2nd edition, 1974; *Introduction to Business: Readings,* Goodyear Publishing, 1972, 2nd edition, 1974; *Introduction to Business: Study Guide,* Goodyear Publishing, 1972, 2nd edition, 1974; *Introduction to Business: Instruc-*

tor's Manual, Goodyear Publishing, 1972, 2nd edition, 1974; *The Impact of Water Pollution Abatement on Competition and Pricing in the Alabama Textile Industry*, Water Resources Research Institute, Auburn University, 1973; *The Impact of Water Pollution Abatement on Competition and Pricing in the Alabama Steel Industry*, Water Resources Research Institute, Auburn University, 1973; *The Economic Benefits of Abating Water Pollution in the Steel, Textile, and Paper Industries in Alabama*, Water Resources Research Institute, Auburn University, 1973. Contributor to journals in his field.

WORK IN PROGRESS: Small Business Management: Text and Cases, with *Study Guide* and *Instructor's Manual*, all for Wiley.

* * *

PIEL, Gerard 1915-

PERSONAL: Born March 1, 1915, in Woodmere, N.Y.; son of William (a brewer) and Loretto (Scott) Piel; married Mary Tapp Bird; married second wife, Eleanor Virden Jackson (a lawyer), June 24, 1955; children: (first marriage) Jonathan Bird, Samuel Bird (deceased); (second marriage) Eleanor Jackson, Jr. *Education:* Harvard University, A.B. (magna cum laude), 1937. *Home:* 320 Central Park W., New York, N.Y. 10025. *Office:* 415 Madison Ave., New York, N.Y. 10017.

CAREER: Time, Inc., New York, N.Y., editorial trainee, 1937-39; *Life* (magazine), New York, N.Y., science editor, 1939-44; Henry J. Kaiser Co. and Associated Companies, Oakland, Calif., assistant to president, 1945-46; *Scientific American* (magazine), New York, N.Y., publisher, 1948—. Overseer of Harvard University; trustee of Radcliffe College, Phillips Academy, American Museum of Natural History, New York University, Foundation for Child Development, and Henry J. Kaiser Family Foundation.

MEMBER: American Philosophical Society, Council on Foreign Relations, American Academy of Arts and Sciences, Institute of Medicine of National Academy of Sciences, Phi Beta Kappa, Sigma Xi. *Awards, honors:* Sc.D., Lawrence College, 1956, Colby College, 1960, University of British Columbia, 1965, Brandeis University, 1965; Litt.D., Rutgers University, 1961, Bates College, 1974; L.H.D., Columbia University, 1962, Williams College, 1966; LL.D., Tuskegee Institute, 1963, University of Bridgeport, 1964, Polytechnic Institute of Brooklyn, 1965, Carnegie-Mellon University, 1968; Kalinga Prize from UNESCO, 1962, Arches of Science Award from Pacific Science Center, Seattle, 1969, and Rosenberger Medal from University of Chicago, 1973, all for contribution to public understanding of science. George K. Polk Award, 1961, for contribution to journalism.

WRITINGS: Science in the Cause of Man, Knopf, 1962; *The Acceleration of History*, Knopf, 1972.

* * *

PIETROFESA, John J(oseph) 1940-

PERSONAL: Born September 12, 1940, in New York, N.Y.; son of Louis J. and Margaret (Proietti) Pietrofesa; married Diana Pinto (a counselor), June 8, 1963; children: John, Paul. *Education:* University of Miami, Coral Gables, Fla., B.Ed., 1961, M.Ed., 1963, Ed.D., 1967. *Home:* 2437 Clawson, Royal Oak, Mich. 48073. *Office:* Department of Counseling and Guidance, Wayne State University, Detroit, Mich. 48202.

CAREER: American University, Fort Benning, Ga., instructor in counseling, 1963-64; counselor for public schools in Dade County, Fla., 1965-67; Wayne State University, Detroit, Mich., assistant professor, 1967-70, professor of counseling, 1970—. *Military service:* U.S. Army, Military Police, 1963-65; became first lieutenant. *Member:* American Psychological Association, American Personnel and Guidance Association, Society for the Scientific Study of Sex, Michigan Personnel and Guidance Association.

WRITINGS: (With William Van Hoose) *Counseling and Guidance in the Twentieth Century*, Houghton, 1970; (with John Vriend) *The School Counselor as a Professional*, F. E. Peacock, 1971; (with Van Hoose and George E. Leonard) *The Authentic Counselor*, Rand McNally, 1971, 6th edition, 1975; (with Van Hoose and Jon Carlson) *Guidance and Counseling in the Elementary School*, Houghton, 1973; (with Roy Giroux) *Career Education*, American Personnel and Guidance Association, 1975; (with Howard Splete) *Career Development*, Grune, 1975; *Student Personnel*, American Personnel and Guidance Association, in press. Contributor of more than a hundred articles to professional journals. Member of board of editors of Michigan Personnel and Guidance Association.

WORK IN PROGRESS: Counseling, publication by Rand McNally expected in 1977.

AVOCATIONAL INTERESTS: Tennis, raquetball.

* * *

PIKE, Charles R.
See HARKNETT, Terry

* * *

PILCHER, Rosamunde 1924-
(Jane Fraser)

PERSONAL: Born September 22, 1924, in Lelant, Cornwall, England; daughter of Charles (a commander in the Royal Navy) and Helen (Harvey) Scott; married Graham Hope Pilcher (a company director), December 7, 1946; children: Fiona, Robin, Philippa, Mark. *Education:* Educated at public schools in England and Wales. *Politics:* Conservative. *Religion:* Church of Scotland. *Home:* Over Pilmore, Invergowrie, by Dundee, Scotland. *Agent:* Curtis Brown, 1 Craven Hill, London W.2, England.

CAREER: Writer. *Military service:* Women's Royal Naval Service, 1942-46.

WRITINGS—All published by Collins, with subsequent publication as indicated: *A Secret to Tell*, 1955; *April*, 1957; *On My Own*, 1965; *Sleeping Tiger*, 1967, St. Martin's, 1974; *Another View*, 1969, St. Martin's 1974; *The End of the Summer*, 1971, St. Martin's, 1975; *Snow in April*, 1972, St. Martin's, 1972; *The Empty House*, 1973, St. Martin's, 1975; *The Day of the Storm*, 1975; *Under Gemini*, in press.

Under pseudonym Jane Fraser; all published by Mills & Boon: *Halfway to the Moon*, 1949; *The Brown Fields*, 1951; *Dangerous Intruder*, 1951; *Young Bar*, 1952; *A Day Like Spring*, 1953; *Dear Tom*, 1954; *Bridge of Corvie*, 1956; *A Family Affair*, 1958; *A Long Way from Home*, 1963; *The Keeper's House*, 1963.

* * *

PINAR, William 1947-

PERSONAL: Born August 27, 1947, in Huntington, W.Va.; son of Frederick Eugene (a mechanical engineer) and Malinda Love (Brooke) Pinar. *Education:* Ohio State University, B.S., 1969, M.A., 1970, Ph.D., 1972. *Office:* College of Education, University of Rochester, Rochester, N.Y. 14627.

CAREER: University of Rochester, Rochester, N.Y., assistant professor of educational theory of the humanities, 1972—. *Member:* Philosophy of Education Society, American Psychological Association, American Educational Research Association, Association of Humanistic Psychology, Association for Transpersonal Psychology, American Educational Studies Association.

WRITINGS: Heightened Consciousness, Cultural Revolution, and Curriculum Theory, McCutchan, 1974; *Curriculum Theorizing: The Reconceptualists,* McCutchan, 1975; *Sanity, Madness, and the School,* Sadhna Prakashan, in press.

WORK IN PROGRESS: The Analysis of Educational Experience, Volume I.

* * *

PINE, William
    See HARKNETT, Terry

* * *

PLACERE, Morris N.
    See GUPTA, S(ushil) (Kumar)

* * *

PLAUGER, P(hillip) J(ames) 1944-

PERSONAL: Surname rhymes with "logger"; born January 13, 1944, in Petersburg, W.Va.; son of James H. and Jessie (Mowery) Plauger; married Lillian A. Rankel (a chemist), November 26, 1971. *Education:* Princeton University, A.B., 1965; Michigan State University, Ph.D., 1969. *Politics:* "Independent, with a small i." *Religion:* None. *Address:* C15 Millstone Apts., Princeton, N.J. 08540. *Office:* Yourdon, Inc., 1133 Ave. of the Americas, New York, N.Y. 10036.

CAREER: Bell Laboratories, Murray Hill, N.J., member of technical staff, 1969-75; Yourdon, Inc. (computer consultants), New York, N.Y., senior staff consultant, 1975—. *Member:* American Physical Society, Association for Computing Machinery, Science Fiction Writers of America. *Awards, honors:* John W. Campbell Award for best new science fiction writer, 1975.

WRITINGS: (With B. W. Kernighan) *The Elements of Programming Style* (textbook), McGraw, 1974; (contributor) Vanda McIntyre and Susan Anderson, editors, *Aurora: Beyond Equality,* Fawcett, 1975. Contributor of short stories and novelettes to *Analog: Science Fact-Science Fiction.*

WORK IN PROGRESS: A science fiction novel, *Fighting Madness*; with B. W. Kernighan, a computer science textbook, *Software Tools*; short stories.

SIDELIGHTS: Plauger told *CA:* "[I] started out as a physicist who liked to play with computers and occasionally write, drifted into 'computer science' and writing, now find myself writing more and more to the exclusion of everything else. Writing science fiction and textbooks is a happy combination for me, since it satisfies sometimes conflicting urges."

PLECK, Joseph H(ealy) 1946-

PERSONAL: Born July 14, 1946, in Evanston, Ill.; son of Joseph H. (a lawyer) and Katherine (Healy) Pleck; married Elizabeth Hafkin (a college professor), June 8, 1968. *Education:* Harvard University, B.A., 1968, M.A., 1971, Ph.D., 1973. *Home:* 1319 Forest Ct., Ann Arbor, Mich. 48104. *Office:* Institute for Social Research, University of Michigan, Ann Arbor, Mich. 48106.

CAREER: University of Michigan, Ann Arbor, lecturer in psychology, 1973—. *Member:* American Psychological Association, Association for Humanistic Psychology, National Council on Family Relations.

WRITINGS: (Editor with Jack Sawyer) *Men and Masculinity,* Prentice-Hall, 1974.

* * *

POAGUE, Leland A(llen) 1948-

PERSONAL: Born December 15, 1948, in San Francisco, Calif.; son of Lloyd Allen (an officer in the U.S. Air Force) and Betty (Prior) Poague; married Susan Aileen Jenson (a weaver), August 24, 1969. *Education:* San Jose State College (now University), B.A., 1970; University of Oregon, Ph.D., 1973. *Office:* Department of English, State University of New York College at Geneseo, Geneseo, N.Y. 14454.

CAREER: State University of New York College at Geneseo, assistant professor of English, 1973—. *Member:* Modern Language Association of America, British Film Institute.

WRITINGS: The Cinema of Frank Capra: An Approach to Film Comedy, A. S. Barnes, 1975. Contributor to *Modern Drama, Journal of Popular Film, Velvet Lighttrap,* and *Journal of Popular Culture.*

WORK IN PROGRESS: Principles of Film Criticism.

SIDELIGHTS: Poague writes: "I'm a Northrop Frye style structuralist. I believe that all literary works—films included—are best understood as constructs in the structure of human culture. Like Dr. Johnson, I believe that knowledge has veto over taste. My vocation, therefore, is the search for knowledge, of films, of literary works, and of the culture they contribute to. For the record, however, my favorite film is John Ford's 'How Green Was My Valley.'"

* * *

POINTER, Michael 1927-

PERSONAL: Born August 18, 1927, in London, England; son of George Sidney and Cicely (Cooper) Pointer; married Mary Isabel Simms, August 2, 1949; children: Isabel (Mrs. Peter Jackson), Martin, Alison, Ruth, Margaret, Rachel. *Home:* 78 Barrowby Rd., Grantham, Lincolnshire NG31 8AF, England.

CAREER: Justice of the Peace, 1964—. *Military service:* Royal Navy, 1945-48. *Member:* Institute of Packaging, Sherlock Holmes Society of London.

WRITINGS: The Public Life of Sherlock Holmes, David & Charles, 1975; *The Sherlock Holmes File,* David & Charles, in press. Contributor of regular column to *Sherlock Holmes Journal,* 1968-74. Contributor to *New York Times, Times, American Film,* and *Plays and Players.*

WORK IN PROGRESS: Charles Dickens on Film; research on the films of Christopher Lee, and on classics on film.

POLETTE, Nancy (Jane) 1930-

PERSONAL: Second syllable of surname is pronounced "leat"; born May 18, 1930, in Richmond Heights, Mo.; daughter of Willard A. (a lawyer) and Alice (Colvin) Mc-Caleb; married Paul L. Polette (an engineering planner), December 23, 1950; children: Pamela (deceased), Paula (Mrs. James Franklin, Jr.), Keith, Marsha. *Education:* William Woods College, A.A., 1950; Washington University, St. Louis, Mo., B.S.Ed., 1962; Southern Illinois University, M.S.Ed., 1968; University of Missouri, graduate study, 1972-73. *Politics:* Democrat. *Religion:* Disciples of Christ. *Home:* 203 San Jose Court, O'Fallon, Mo. 63366. *Agent:* Dorothy Markinko, McIntosh & Otis, 18 East 41st St., New York, N.Y. 10017. *Office:* Pattonville School District, 115 Harding, Maryland Heights, Mo. 63043.

CAREER: Elementary school teacher in Jefferson County, Mo., 1950-51, and in Ritenour, Mo., 1954; Pattonville School District, Maryland Heights, Mo., elementary school teacher, 1955-65, coordinator of elementary school materials, 1965—. Instructor at Southern Illinois University, 1968-72, and at Lindenwood College, 1970—. Lecturer and workshop leader, 1968—; member of board of directors of Leukemia Guild of Missouri, 1959-70, and of Illinois, 1959-70. *Member:* American Library Association, American Association of School Librarians, Missouri Library Association, Suburban Library Association, Missouri Association of School Librarians (vice-president, 1973-74), Missouri State Teachers Association, Chicago Childrens Reading Round Table.

WRITINGS: Basic Library Skills, Milliken Publishing, 1971; *Library Skills for Primary Grades*, Milliken Publishing, 1973; *Developing Methods of Inquiry*, Scarecrow, 1973; *In Service: School Library/ Media Workshops and Conferences*, Scarecrow, 1973; *The Vodka in the Punch and Other Notes from a Library Supervisor*, Shoe String, 1975; (with Marjorie Hamlin) *Reading Guidance in a Media Age*, Scarecrow, 1975; (editor) Helen Saunders, *The Modern School Library*, 2nd edition (Nancy Polette was not associated with earlier edition), Scarecrow, 1975. Contributor to journals; writer of tape and transparencies series for library use; editor of Miller-Brody Newberry Literary Activities Pack Program, 1974-75. Member of book review staff of *School Library Journal*, 1972-73.

WORK IN PROGRESS: A children's book for ages ten to twelve, *Katie Penn*; a book, *E Is for Everybody*; a children's picture book, *Tangles*.

AVOCATIONAL INTERESTS: Theatre, drama.

*   *   *

POLIS, A(lbert) Richard 1937-

PERSONAL: Born March 25, 1937, in Philadelphia, Pa.; son of Louis (a businessman) and Beatrice (Thalheimer) Polis; married Sandra E. Ratner, June 19, 1961; children: Adam Bram, Daniel Lee. *Education:* West Chester State College, B.S., 1959; University of Pennsylvania, M.S., 1965; Temple University, Ed.D., 1974. *Home:* 1917 Palomino Dr., Warrington, Pa. 18976. *Office:* Department of Education and Mathematics, Beaver College, Glenside, Pa. 19038.

CAREER: Teacher of mathematics in public schools of Folsom, Pa., 1960-65, and Arlington, Pa., 1965-66; Camden County College, Blackwood, N.J., assistant professor of mathematics, 1967-68; Beaver College, Glenside, Pa., assistant professor, 1968-75, associate professor of mathe-

matics education, 1975—. *Member:* Mathematical Association of America, National Council of Teachers of Mathematics, American Association of University Professors, Pennsylvania Council of Teachers of Mathematics, Burke County Teachers of Mathematics, Association of Teachers of Mathematics of Philadelphia and Vicinity, Kappa Delta Pi, Phi Delta Kappa. *Awards, honors:* National Science Foundation grant, 1966-67.

WRITINGS: Fundamental Mathematics for Elementary Teachers: A Behavioral Objectives Approach, Harper, 1973.

WORK IN PROGRESS: Fundamental Mathematics, publication by Harper expected about 1977; *Resources for Teaching Mathematics*.

AVOCATIONAL INTERESTS: Writing books for children, music, poetry.

*   *   *

POLK, Judd (Knox) 1913(?)-1975

1913(?)—April 30, 1975; American economist, authority on international finance, and author. Obituaries: *New York Times*, May 1, 1975; *Washington Post*, May 2, 1975.

*   *   *

POLLINGER, Kenneth Joseph 1933-

PERSONAL: Born November 9, 1933, in New York, N.Y.; son of Murray (a hotel manager) and Gladys (Stepp) Pollinger; married Annette C. Haas (a college professor), March 15, 1969; children: Jordan, Erin. *Education:* Attended University of Cincinnati, 1951-56, and Xavier University, 1956-58; Loyola University, Chicago, Ill., Litt.B., 1960; Instituto Libre de Filosofia, Mexico City, Mexico, graduate study, 1963-65; Fordham University, M.A., 1967, Ph.D., 1972. *Politics:* "New Democratic Coalition." *Religion:* "International Interdenominationalist." *Home:* 31 Cobb Ave., White Plains, N.Y. 10606. *Office:* Department of Sociology, University of Bridgeport, Bridgeport, Conn. 06602.

CAREER: General Electric & Bendix Aviation (co-operative), Cincinnati, Ohio, electrical and civil engineer, 1951-56; Jesuit missionary teaching in Arequipa, Peru, 1961-63; University of Bridgeport, Bridgeport, Conn., assistant professor, 1971-75, professor of sociology, 1975—. Adjunct associate professor at Herbert H. Lehman College of the City of University of New York, 1969-72, State University of New York College at Purchase, 1973-75, and College of New Rochelle, 1974-75. District leader of White Plains Democratic Party, 1972-75. *Member:* International Sociological Association, American Sociological Association, Society for the Study of Social Problems, Eastern Sociological Society, New York State Sociological Association, Alpha Kappa Delta.

WRITINGS: (With wife, Annette C. Pollinger) *Community Action and the Poor: Influence versus Social Control in a New York Community*, Praeger, 1972. Contributor to sociology and social science journals.

WORK IN PROGRESS: Innovation among Women: A Case Study of Natural Childbirth, with wife, Annette C. Pollinger; research on statistical analysis in the top three sociology journals, on the teaching of methodology-statistics to undergraduates, and on social action strategies of community organization.

SIDELIGHTS: Pollinger, as a Jesuit missionary, traveled

to Peru and Mexico in pursuit of "deeper insights into Latin American social problems." Disconcerted with the Catholic Church's union with the wealthy, he left the Jesuits and decided to obtain a doctorate in sociology. His concern with the problems of poverty led him to examine one of the twenty-six poverty areas of New York City. The measuring of social control remains one of his key concerns. *Avocational interests:* Participating in sports (especially basketball and jogging), vegetable gardening, travel, working around his house.

* * *

POLLOCK, Bruce   1945-

PERSONAL: Born July 24, 1945, in Brooklyn, N.Y.; son of Joseph and Rose (Prager) Pollock; married Barbara Hoffman (an art teacher, poet, and painter), December 19, 1970. *Education:* City College of the City University of New York, B.A., 1972. *Home:* 162 West 13th St., New York, N.Y. 10011. *Agent:* Jane Rotrosen, 212 East 48th St., New York, N.Y.

CAREER: Free-lance writer in New York, N.Y., 1972—. *Member:* American Society of Composers, Authors and Publishers. *Awards, honors:* Dejur Award for fiction, to permit the writing of *Coney Island Baby*, 1971; Deems Taylor Award, 1973, for articles in *Rock*.

WRITINGS: In Their Own Words: Pop Songwriting, 1955-1974, Macmillan, 1975. Contributor to *New York Times, Village Voice*, and *Saturday Review*. Managing editor of *Rock*, 1972-73; editor of *Contemporary Music*, 1974; associate editor of *Funny Papers*, 1974-75; contributing editor of *Modern Hi-Fi and Music*, 1975.

WORK IN PROGRESS: A novel, *Coney Island Baby; How to Break into Rock and Roll; The Playing of Ping Pong; Trial by Fire: The Ordeal of Being Undiscovered in America;* three hundred song lyrics; 50 collectable articles.

AVOCATIONAL INTERESTS: "Weird Americana," streetgames, sixties, music.

BIOGRAPHICAL/CRITICAL SOURCES: Modern Hi-Fi and Music, July, 1975.

* * *

POMPA, Leon   1933-

PERSONAL: Born February 22, 1933, in Edinburgh, Scotland; son of Dominic Albert (a businessman) and Nancy Pompa; married Juliet Caroline Sich (a teacher of classics), August 9, 1962; children: Nicholas, Antonia. *Education:* University of Edinburgh, M.A. (history; first class honors), 1956, M.A. (philosophy; first class honors), 1961, Ph.D., 1967. *Politics:* Liberal-Socialist. *Religion:* Roman Catholic. *Home:* 84 Great King St., Edinburgh, Scotland. *Office:* Department of Philosophy, University of Edinburgh, George Sq., Edinburgh, Scotland.

CAREER: University of Edinburgh, Edinburgh, Scotland, lecturer in philosophy, 1961—. *Member:* Institute for Cultural Research (fellow), Institute for Comparative Study of History, Philosophy, and the Sciences, Aristotelian Society, Murrayfield Gold Club.

WRITINGS: Vico: A Study of the 'New Science,' Cambridge University Press, 1975. Contributor to philosophical and interdisciplinary journals.

WORK IN PROGRESS: Editing translations of the works of Giambattista Vico; a book on the philosophy of history, completion expected in 1977; a study of metaphysics, the theory of knowledge, the history of philosophy, and the philosophy of history.

SIDELIGHTS: Pompa was trained to be a concert pianist but, when an accident damaged his wrist, he concentrated on academic studies. *Avocational interests:* Music, foreign travel, literature, sports.

* * *

PONTE, Lowell (Alton)   1946-

PERSONAL: Born February 28, 1946, in Redlands, Calif., son of Lloyd Charles (an engineer) and Lula Catherine (Loomis) Ponte; married Ellen Beth Levenson (a television story analyst), June 29, 1975. *Education:* University of Southern California, B.A., 1968, graduate study, 1968-70. *Politics:* Libertarian. *Religion:* Sufi. *Home:* 1224 Tenth St., Santa Monica, Calif. 90401. *Office: Skeptic* Magazine, 812 Anacapa Street, Santa Barbara, Calif. 93101.

CAREER: Hayes & Ponte Promotion & Advertising, Hollywood, Calif., partner, 1965-69; International Research & Technology Corp., Washington, D.C., arms control analyst, 1968-69; KPFK-FM, Los Angeles, Calif., commentator, 1969—; KCET-TV, Los Angeles, commentator, 1970—; *Skeptic* magazine, Santa Barbara, Calif., contributing editor, 1973—. Founder and co-editor, *Nepenthe* magazine, Los Angeles, 1966-68; visiting professor, Experimental College, University of Southern California, Los Angeles, 1967-68; columnist, Los Angeles *Image* and Los Angeles *Free Press*, 1969-71; reporter in Los Angeles, *Human Events* newspaper, Washington, D.C., 1970; writer of column, "Quite Rightly So" for Freedom Newspaper, Inc., 1971, McNaught Syndicate, 1973-74. Member of executive board, Community Action Coordinating Council, Watts, Calif., 1968-71; member of board of directors, Ancient Mediterranean Research Association, Los Angeles, 1973—; coordinator, Institute for Ancient Anthropology, Los Angeles, 1975—. *Member:* U.S. Naval Institute, Modern Language Association of America, American Federation of Television and Radio Artists, Southern California Society for Psychic Research (member of board of directors), Phi Beta Kappa, Phi Kappa Phi.

*WRITINGS—*Published by ABC Press, except as noted: *NATO as a Nuclear Alliance* (monograph), 1968; *Defense Secretary McNamara and the Media* (monograph), 1969; *A New Right Reasoning* (monograph), 1970; *Taxpayer Democracy* (monograph), 1974; *The Cooling: Why the Earth's Climate is Changing and How We Can Survive It*, Prentice-Hall, in press. Contributor to military journals, underground newspapers, and to national magazines.

WORK IN PROGRESS: A book version of *Taxpayer Democracy;* a screenplay based on *The Cooling*, entitled "Thaw."

SIDELIGHTS: Ponte told *CA*: "I've been a radio amateur since 1960 and never ceased to be amazed by how connected we can be here and now in this ether. Do you hear this? Writing is such a connection, and I love it."

* * *

POPIEL, Elda S(taver)   1915-

PERSONAL: Born June 9, 1915, in Scandia, Kan.; daughter of Emil A. and Mae (Johnson) Isaacson; married Allan P. Staver, December 30, 1933 (died, 1948); married Charles Popiel, November 28, 1957 (died, 1975); children: (first marriage) David Allan. *Education:* Research Hospital School of Nursing, diploma, 1935; Avila College, B.S.,

1955; University of Colorado, M.S., 1959. *Home and office:* 3918 East Evans Ave., Denver, Colo. 80210.

CAREER: School nurse in Johnson County, Kan., 1941-56; University of Colorado, School of Nursing, Denver, assistant professor, 1959-62, associate professor, 1962-65, professor of nursing, 1965-74, assistant dean, 1965-74, professor emeritus, 1975—; consultant in continuing education in nursing, 1974—. Head nurse and supervisor of emergency room at University of Kansas Medical Center, summers, 1949-56. *Member:* American Nurses' Association, American College Health Association, Colorado Epilepsy Association, (member of board, 1971; secretary, 1975), Colorado Heart Association, Colorado Nurses' Association (president, 1967), Colorado Mental Health Association, Sigma Theta Tau (life member). *Awards, honors:* Ruth Boynton Award from American College Health Association, 1970.

WRITINGS: Nursing and the Process of Continuing Education, Mosby, 1974; (editor and contributor) *Current Perspectives in Nursing,* Mosby, 1975; (contributor) Janet A. Williamson, *Staff Development,* Contemporary Publishing, 1975; (contributor) *Foundations of Nursing,* 2nd edition, Mosby, 1975. Contributor to professional journals, and other publications.

WORK IN PROGRESS: Second edition of *Nursing and the Process of Continuing Education,* for Mosby; vignettes depicting nursing, 1876-1976, to be developed into a play for the Colorado Centennial.

* * *

PORTER, Margaret Eudine 1905-

PERSONAL: Born June 1, 1905, in Rio Vista, Calif.; daughter of James and Mary Anne (McHugh) Preston; married James Aimsley, June 10, 1942 (died September 11, 1942); married Bernard Harden Porter (an author and publisher), August 27, 1955; children: Carole Aimsley Fohler Kassebaum. *Education:* Attended University of California, Berkeley, 1935, Munson Business College, 1937. *Politics:* Republican. *Religion:* Catholic. *Home and office:* 22 Salmond Rd., Belfast, Me. 04915.

CAREER: U.S. Navy, Sausalito, Calif., member of special services staff, 1938-42; Pacific Gas and Light Co., San Francisco, Calif., member of special services staff, 1944-57; Bern Porter Books, Belfast, Me., director, 1955—; Institute of Advanced Thinking, Belfast, director, 1959—. Correspondent, World Field Research, 1967. Consultant to Small Business Administration, 1968, International Executive Service Corps., 1968. *Member:* Society for International Development.

WRITINGS: (Editor) *Henry: An Anthology of World Poets,* Bern Porter, 1970; *James Joyce and His Times,* Bern Porter, 1973; *Vistiga: Notes on the Life of Janelle Viglini,* Bern Porter, 1975.

WORK IN PROGRESS: Editing two books, *Anthology of American Poets 1930-1960,* and *Poets of the Pacific.*

SIDELIGHTS: Margaret Porter told *CA* that she is concerned with the role of females in poetry, and the problems of small press distribution and author relationships.

* * *

PORTER, Willard H(all) 1920-

PERSONAL: Born September 15, 1920, in Cape May, N.J.; son of Willard H., Jr. and Christine (Fritz) Porter; married Jean Dun (divorced, 1953); married Diana McIntosh (a stock broker), May 5, 1973; children: (first marriage) Podie, Peavey, Weeds. *Education:* Attended University of Arizona, 1940-42. *Politics:* "Does it make any difference?" *Religion:* "Ditto." *Home and office:* 5654 Southeast Harbor Terrace, Stuart, Fla. 33494. *Agent:* August Lenniger, Lenniger Literary Agency, Inc., 11 West 42nd St., New York, N.Y. 10036.

CAREER: Quarter Horse Journal, Amarillo, Tex., editor, 1949-53; *Hoofs and Horns,* Tucson, Ariz., editor and publisher, 1957-65; free-lance writer, 1965—. *Military service:* U.S. Coast Guard, 1942-46.

WRITINGS: Thirteen Flat (nonfiction) A. S. Barnes, 1967; *How to Enjoy the Quarter Horse,* A. S. Barnes, 1973; *Fast Horses and Short Ropes,* A. S. Barnes, 1975. Contributor to newspapers and magazines, including *Argosy, Westways, Popular Mechanics, Saltwater Sportsman, Quarter Horse Journal, Field and Stream, Boating, Sports Afield,* and *Western Livestock Journal.* Columnist for *Western Livestock Journal,* 1973—, and *Cattleman,* 1974—.

AVOCATIONAL INTERESTS: Poker.

* * *

PORTWAY, Christopher (John) 1923-
(John October)

PERSONAL: Born October 30, 1923, in Halstead, Essex, England; son of Cedric and Alice Thelma (Cook) Portway; married Dana Sofrova, May 15, 1947 (divorced December, 1949); married Jaroslava Anna Krupickova (a secretary), April 4, 1957; children: Alice Christine Portway Biddy, Paul Christopher. *Education:* Attended schools in England. *Politics:* Conservative. *Religion:* Church of England. *Home and office:* Jasan, White Ash Green, Halstead, Essex CO9 1PD, England.

CAREER: Tortoise Foundry Co. Ltd., Halstead, Essex, England, sales director, 1947-72; full-time travel writer and novelist, 1972—. Travel consultant. *Military service:* British Army, serving in National Army, 1942-47, in Territorial Army, 1948-64; became captain. *Member:* Institute of Journalists, Guild of Travel Writers, East Anglian Writers, Globetrotters Club (secretary, 1975), World Expeditionary Association, Royal Artillery Association, Royal British Legion, Dorset Regiment Association (secretary, 1952), Colne Valley Railway Preservation Society (secretary, 1974).

WRITINGS: Journey to Dana (autobiographical), Kimber, 1955; *Forbidden Frontier* (autobiographical), Kimber, 1962; *The Pregnant Unicorn* (autobiographical), Terence Dalton, 1969; *All Exits Barred* (novel), R. Hale, 1971, Pinnacle Books, 1974; *Corner Seat: Four European Railway Journeys,* R. Hale, 1972; *Lost Vengeance* (novel), R. Hale, 1973; *Double Circuit* (travel), R. Hale, 1974; *The Tirana Assignment* (novel), R. Hale, 1974, Pinnacle Books, 1975. Contributor (occasionally under pseudonym John October) of short stories and travel articles to magazines and newspapers, including *Daily Telegraph, Daily Express,* and *Times* (all London), *Jewish Chronicle, Country Life, Countryman, Railway Magazine, She, Woman's Own, Railway World, Blackwoods Magazine,* and *Kansas City Times.*

WORK IN PROGRESS: The Anarchy Pedlars, a novel, to be published under pseudonym John October; *Round Trip,* a travel book on the overland route to and from India; *The Road Back,* an autobiographical return to his wartime

P.O.W. escape locations; *The Long Hack*, on the forthcoming "Round the World on Horseback Expedition" (to include the United States), which Portway will accompany on foot; editing English editions of *La Bataille du Calvados*, by Albert Grandais, and *La Gebbia*, by Gino Reale; travel features for *Travel, Holiday*, and other publications in the United States and Britain.

SIDELIGHTS: Portway told *CA*: "Being a keen traveller, particularly to the more off-beat corners of the world, reflects in not only my travel books but in my novels where my plots invariably unwind against a background of some strange country I have recently visited. My favorite vehicle for travel is the train, for on one you are amongst the people of the country. I am also interested in railways in themselves." Portway's factual account, *The Pregnant Unicorn*, is being filmed.

* * *

POTTS, Ralph Bushnell 1901-

PERSONAL: Born October 1, 1901, in Appleton, Wis.; son of George L. (an inventor) and Marh (Bushnell) Potts; married Audrey Norton (divorced); married Lucille Esterbrook, June 29, 1939 (died August, 1973); married Mary Schaumberger, March 7, 1975; children: (first marriage) Ralph, Drusilla, Ruah; (second marriage) Roberta Bushnell Potts. *Education:* Attended Pacific University, 1915-19; University of Oregon, LL.B., 1924. *Politics:* Republican. *Religion:* Episcopalian. *Home:* 7700 Fairway Dr. N.E., Seattle, Wash. 98115. *Office:* 1109 Hoge Bldg., Seattle, Wash. 98104.

CAREER: Admitted to state Bar of Washington, 1924, and to Bar of the U.S. Supreme Court, 1947; attorney in private practice in Seattle, Wash., 1929—. President of Grand Galleria (art gallery); former president of Allied Arts of Seattle; former member of Washington Arts Commission; founder and board member of New Seattle Repertory Theatre; member of board of trustees of Pacific Northwest International Writers Conference. *Member:* American Bar Association, American Legion, Washington State Bar Association, Seattle Bar Association. *Awards, honors:* Seattle Historical Society award, 1956; American Bar Association award, for article later retitled "My Sacred Ballot."

WRITINGS: (With Lowell Stillwell Hawley) *Counsel for the Damned: A Biography of George Francis Vanderveer*, Lippincott, 1953; *Seattle Heritage*, Superior, 1955; *Sir Boss*, Faversham House, 1959; (contributor) Charles L. Wallis, editor, *Our American Heritage*, Harper, 1970; *Come Now the Lawyers*, Washington State Bar Association, 1972. Author of plays: "The Surrender of Chief Joseph" (one-act); "Nevada and a Speck of Dust" (one-act); "The Kingdoms of Storey Wayne." Author of film scripts for Renaissance Productions: "The Specialist" (adaptation of *Come Now the Lawyers*), 1975; "Mr. Bogus," 1975; and "Sir Boss," 1976.

AVOCATIONAL INTERESTS: History, European travel (especially visiting art galleries and museums).

* * *

POWELL, L(awrence) F(itzroy) 1881-1975

1881—July 17, 1975; British librarian, educator, author and editor of books on literature. Obituaries: *AB Bookman's Weekly*, August 4, 1975.

POWELL, Ralph L. 1917-1975

January 31, 1917—May 22, 1975; American educator, consultant and counselor for public affairs, authority on China, and author of books on Chinese political affairs. Obituaries: *Washington Post*, May 26, 1975.

* * *

POWERS, Andy 1896-

PERSONAL: Born May 12, 1896, in Lexington, Tenn.; son of William Clark (a farmer) and Fredonia (Harroll) Powers; married Lena Mae Scott, August 25, 1923; children: Charles Andrew. *Education:* Attended Ardmore Business College, 1932, and University of Oklahoma, 1967-68. *Religion:* Methodist. *Home and office:* 805 Deahl St., Borger, Tex. 79007.

CAREER: Began as salesman with Libby, McNeil & Libby, 1921; worked in dry cleaning and laundry business in Texas and Oklahoma, c. 1922; owner of dry cleaning and laundry plant in Ardmore, Okla., 1923-39; employed by Warren Refining and Chemical Co., 1940-43, field sales manager, 1943-50; jewelry store owner and operator, 1950-62; poet and author. *Military service:* U.S. Army, 1918. *Member:* National Writers Club, Writers Association of the Golden Spread, Masons, Shriners, Eastern Star, American Legion (adjutant), Lions Club.

WRITINGS: Here Lies Our Heart (poems), Adams Press, 1974; *The Arkansas John the Baptist*, Branden Press, 1975.

WORK IN PROGRESS: Buddy, a swampland novel; *El Santo and Pancho Villa*, a novel; *Bits of Heaven*, poems.

* * *

PREBISH, Charles S(tuart) 1944-

PERSONAL: Born October 11, 1944, in Chicago, Ill.; son of Jacob L. (a business executive) and Sydelle (Grossman) Prebish; married Susan Kodicek, August 31, 1968; children: Jared, Robinson. *Education:* Case Western Reserve University, B.A., 1966, M.A., 1967; University of Wisconsin, Ph.D., 1971. *Religion:* Buddhist. *Home:* 454 Douglas Dr., State College, Pa. 16801. *Office:* Department of Religious Studies, Pennsylvania State University, University Park, Pa. 16802.

CAREER: Pennsylvania State University, University Park, assistant professor of religious studies, 1971—. Visiting professor at Naropa Institute, summers, 1974, 1975. *Member:* Association for Asian Studies, American Oriental Society, American Academy of Religion. *Awards, honors:* Ford Foundation summer fellowship, 1969; National Science Foundation research grant, 1972-73.

WRITINGS: (Editor with Jane I. Smith, and contributor) *Introduction to Religions of the East: Reader*, Kendall/Hunt, 1974; *Buddhism: A Modern Perspective*, Pennsylvania State University Press, 1975; *Buddhist Monastic Discipline: The Sanskrit Pratimoksa Sutras of the Mahasamghikas and Mulasarvasti Vadins*, Pennsylvania State University Press, 1975. Contributor to journals.

WORK IN PROGRESS: A monograph, *A Survey of Vinaya Literature*, completion expected in 1976; *Buddhism in America*, 1977.

SIDELIGHTS: Prebish is competent in French, German, Hebrew, Sanskrit, Pali, and Prakrit. *Avocational interests:* Folk music, poetry, houseplants, vegetable gardening.

PREISER, Wolfgang F. E. 1941-

PERSONAL: Born June 26, 1941, in Freiburg, Germany; son of Gerhard F. (a railway executive) and Ursula (von Huelsen) Preiser; married Marie Groenblom, April 8, 1967; children: Johanna M., Andreas F., Nicholas G. *Education:* Vienna Institute of Technology, I.Staatsexam, 1963; University of Karlsruhe, M.S., 1967; Virginia Polytechnic Institute and State University, M.Arch., 1969; Pennsylvania State University, Ph.D., 1973. *Home:* 801 La Sell Dr., Champaign, Ill. 61820. *Office:* Department of Architecture, University of Illinois, Urbana, Ill. 61801.

CAREER: Architect in Europe until 1967; Pennsylvania State University, University Park, member of faculty in department of architecture, 1969-70; Virginia Polytechnic Institute and State University, Blacksburg, member of faculty of College of Architecture, 1970-73; University of Illinois, Urbana-Champaign, member of faculty of department of architecture, 1974—. Research architect for U.S. Army Corps of Engineers, 1973—; visiting lecturer at American and Canadian universities.

MEMBER: Environmental Design Research Association (vice-chairman, 1973—), Association for the Study of Man-Environment Relations, American Association for the Advancement of Science, American Institute of Architects, Phi Kappa Phi. *Awards, honors:* Research grant from Finland's Institute of Technology, 1966; Fulbright grant, 1967.

WRITINGS: (Editor with T. Regan) *Environmental Design Perspectives*, Association for the Study of Man-Environment Relations, 1972; (editor) *Environmental Design Research*, two volumes, D.H.&R., 1973; (contributor) R. Beckman, D. Conway, and A. H. Esser, editors, *International Dictionary of Behavior and Design Research*, Association for the Study of Man-Environment Relations, 1974; (editor) *Programming for Habitability*, University of Illinois Press, 1975; (editor) *Environmental Programming and Design*, D.H.&R., in press. Author of "Environmental Psychology," for German National Broadcasting System. Contributing editor of *Journal of Architectural Research* and *Man-Environment Systems Journal*.

WORK IN PROGRESS: Editing *Environmental Design*, with Steven Parshall, publication by Gale expected in 1978; research on habitability in facility programming for the U.S. Army Corps of Engineers; research on user feedback and satisfaction regarding various building types.

AVOCATIONAL INTERESTS: Tennis, skiing, bridge, international travel.

*   *   *

PREMACK, Ann J(ames) 1929-

PERSONAL: Born January 5, 1929, in Shanghai, China; daughter of Jimmy and Mae Victoria (Parker) James; married David Premack (a professor of psychology), October 26, 1951; children: Ben, Lisa, Timothy. *Education:* University of Minnesota, B.S. (with distinction), 1951. *Home:* 1424 Alameda Padre Serra, Santa Barbara, Calif. 93103.

CAREER: Writer.

WRITINGS: Why Chimps Can Read, Harper, 1975; (contributor) Michael Gazzaniga, editor, *Fundamentals of Psychology*, Academic Press, in press. Contributor to *National Geographic, Scientific American*, and *La Recherche*.

WORK IN PROGRESS: Manic-Depression: One Story, an autobiographical book.

SIDELIGHTS: Ann Premack told *CA:* "My preference is to combine autobiography and science, and I am interested in topics where the two can be joined naturally, without self-consciousness. . . . *Manic-Depression* combines theory and therapy with my own twelve years as a manic-depressive. Later I plan to write about my childhood in China. Started writing at forty and do not plan to stop."

*   *   *

PRENTICE, Ann E(thelynd) 1933-

PERSONAL: Born July 19, 1933, in Cambridgeport, Vt.; daughter of Homer O. (a logger) and Helen (Cooke) Hurlbut; married Paul Prentice (an engineer), 1954; children: David, Melody, Holly, Wayne. *Education:* University of Rochester, B.A., 1954; State University of New York at Albany, M.L.S., 1964; Columbia University, D.L.S., 1972. *Home:* 29 Lawrence Rd., Hyde Park, N.Y. 12538. *Office:* School of Library and Information Science, State University of New York at Albany, Albany, N.Y. 12222.

CAREER: State University of New York at Albany, assistant professor of library science, 1972—. Trustee of Hyde Park Free Library, 1973—, and Mid-Hudson Library System. *Member:* American Library Association, American Management Association, New York Library Association.

WRITINGS: The Public Library Trustee, Scarecrow, 1973; *Suicide*, Scarecrow, 1974; *Public Library Finance*, American Library Association, in press.

AVOCATIONAL INTERESTS: Natural foods (collecting, preparing, and eating), history, historical research.

*   *   *

PRENTING, Theodore O(tto) 1933-

PERSONAL: Born May 23, 1933, in Brooklyn, N.Y.; son of Peter Henry (an engineer) and Mary (Seidel) Prenting; married Bernardine Schlimm, August 25, 1962; children: Peter Joseph, Mary Nell. *Education:* University of Chicago, M.B.A., 1960. *Home:* 2 Alden Rd., Poughkeepsie, N.Y. 12603. *Office:* Department of Business and Economics, Marist College, North Rd., Poughkeepsie, N.Y. 12601.

CAREER: International Business Machines (IBM), Poughkeepsie, N.Y., systems analyst, 1960-63; Illinois Institute of Technology Research Institute, Chicago, manager of operations research and statistics department,1963-68; Marist College, Poughkeepsie, N.Y., assistant professor, 1968-71, associate professor of business and economics, 1971—. *Military service:* U.S. Army, 1953-56. *Member:* American Institute of Industrial Engineers, Institute of Management Sciences, Beta Gamma Sigma.

WRITINGS: (With Nicholas T. Thomopoulos) *Humanism and Technology in Assembly Line Systems*, Spartan Books, 1974. Contributor of about fifteen articles to engineering journals, including *Industrial Engineering, Assembly Engineering, Automation, Mechanical Engineering, Systems and Procedures Journal, Personnel, Purchasing*, and *Management Review*.

WORK IN PROGRESS: Administering and Controlling Plant Assembly Systems; research on the human and technological problems of mass production assembly.

AVOCATIONAL INTERESTS: Music, photography, travel.

PRESCOTT, Kenneth W(ade)   1920-

PERSONAL: Born August 9, 1920, in Jackson, Mich.; son of Edward E. and Harriett (McInerney) Prescott; married Emma-Stina Johnsson, January 13, 1947; children: Kristina Lisen Prescott Bowman, Gertrude Mae. *Education:* Western Michigan College of Education (now Western Michigan University), B.S., 1942; University of Delaware, Ed.M., 1954; University of Michigan, M.A., 1948, Ph.D., 1950. *Home:* 2526 Tanglewood Trail, Austin, Tex. 78703. *Office:* Department of Art, University of Texas, Austin, Tex. 78712.

CAREER: Kansas City Museum, Kansas City, Mo., director, 1954-58; Academy of Natural Sciences, Philadelphia, Pa., managing director, 1958-63; Temple University, School of Graduate Studies, Philadelphia, Pa., adjunct professor, 1961-71; New Jersey State Museum Cultural Center, Trenton, N.J., director, 1963-71; Ford Foundation, New York, N.Y., program officer for visual arts, 1971-74; University of Texas at Austin, professor of art, 1974—, head of department, 1974—. Member of board of directors of Urban League, Kansas City, Mo., 1957-58; chairman of Junior Red Cross, Southeastern Pennsylvania Chapter, 1959-62; member of executive committee of Trenton Symphony, 1963-65; member of White House Conference on Youth, 1971; member of advisory board of U.S. Secretary of the Navy, 1972-75. Consultant to Ford Foundation, Jewish Museum, Kennedy Galleries, and Harry S. Truman Library Museum. *Military service:* U.S. Naval Reserve, served in Southwest Pacific theater, 1942-47, in Korea, 1951-54, recalled intermittently, 1960-70; became captain.

MEMBER: College Art Association of America, National Association of Arts Administration, American Association of Museums, Midwest Museums Conference (president, 1957-58), Northeast Conference of Museums (president, 1961-62), Princeton Club.

WRITINGS: Life History of the Scarlet Tanager, New Jersey State Museum, 1965; (with Gustave von Groswitz) *Domjan the Woodcutter,* River Edge Press, 1966; *The Complete Graphic Works of Ben Shahn,* Quadrangle, 1973. Author of exhibition catalogues on Ben Shahn. Contributor of articles on art, museology, and ornithology to periodicals.

WORK IN PROGRESS: The Complete Sculpture of Dorothea Greenbaum.

AVOCATIONAL INTERESTS: Travel, bird study.

*   *   *

PRESTON, Harry   1923-

PERSONAL: Born September 4, 1923, in Howick, Natal, South Africa; naturalized U.S. citizen, 1956; son of Richard Henry (a chemist) and Lillian Catherine (Walter) Pimm. *Education:* University of Natal, B.A., 1942. *Politics:* "A cesspool I'd rather not discuss." *Religion:* "Truth and honesty." *Home:* 32507 Ortega Highway, Lake Elsinore, Calif. 92330. *Agent:* Jay Caron Associates, 415 Central Park W., 17D, New York, N.Y. 10025.

CAREER: Singer, dancer, actor, and musician in South Africa, 1939-48; Cactus State Radio Network, Big Spring, Tex., program director, 1950-51; Big D Film Studio, Dallas, Tex., writer and director, 1952-55; WFAA-TV, Dallas, Tex., news editor, 1956-58; Metro-Goldwyn-Mayer Studios, Culver City, Calif., editorial analyst, 1959; Jam Handy Organization, Detroit, Mich., writer and director, 1960-62; independent film producer and director in Detroit,

Mich., 1962-67; free-lance film writer and director in Hollywood, Calif., 1967—. *Member:* Dramatists Guild, Authors League of America. *Awards, honors:* Texas Playwrights Contest best play, 1958, for comedy, "Time for Madness"; Best Supporting Actor in Southwest, 1959, for portrayal of Lord Brockhurst in Breck Wall's production of *The Boy Friend.*

WRITINGS: (With Vila Briley) *Housewives Guide to Extra Income,* Books for Better Living, 1972; (with Jeanette Margolin) *Everything a Teenager Wants to Know about Sex and Should,* Books for Better Living, 1973; *Kicking Your Sex Hangups,* Academy, 1973; *Erotic Africa,* Academy, 1973; (with Emil Halley) *The Natural Food Reducing Diet,* Books for Better Living, 1974; *Crucifixion of a Closet Queen,* Academy, 1974; *How to Teach Your Children About Sex,* Books for Better Living, 1974.

Satirical reviews: "Bubblegum," first produced in Cape Town, South Africa, at Hofmeyr Theatre, 1944; "Time for Madness," first produced in Dallas, Tex., at Dallas Institute of Performing Arts, 1958; "You Gotta Be Kidding," first produced in Detroit, Mich., 1965.

Contributor of seven book-length adventure novels serialized in South African newspapers and of more than two hundred short stories to newspapers and magazines. Writer of more than four hundred industrial and documentary filmscripts. Drama critic, *Cape Times,* 1946-48.

WORK IN PROGRESS: A novel, *Amelia;* a nonfiction book, *Conversations in a Curious Country;* a novel based on his experiences writing for television and industrial film production companies, *The Mind Benders;* a humorous account of his teen years touring with the circus and variety shows in South Africa, *I Remember Mau Mau;* a play dealing with contemporary American mores, *Happy New Year.*

SIDELIGHTS: Preston told *CA:* "As an eternal optimist, I find my hopes for harmony between the many races in Africa more idealistic than realistic. This is sad, because the country is one of the most beautiful in the world, and could be a paradise if people could only live together in peace, respecting each other's customs and cultures." Preston began writing at the age of ten, and was first published when he was fourteen. He reports he now writes an average of six hours a day, weekends included. *Avocational interests:* Cooking and gardening.

*   *   *

PRESTON, Ivan L.   1931-

PERSONAL: Born December 18, 1931, in Bryn Mawr, Pa.; son of Albert W. (a civil engineer) and Kathryn (Lautenbacher) Preston; married Roberta Williamson, September 2, 1961; children: Micaela, Julie, Terry Jane. *Education:* College of Wooster, B.A., 1953; Michigan State University, M.A., 1961, Ph.D., 1964. *Religion:* Protestant. *Home:* 4108 Yuma Dr., Madison, Wis. 53711. *Office:* Department of Journalism and Mass Communication, University of Wisconsin, Madison, Wis. 53706.

CAREER: Ketchum, MacLeod & Grove, Inc., Pittsburgh, Pa., advertising account assistant, 1955-57; Carnegie Institute of Technology, Pittsburgh, Pa., editor of News Service, 1957-58; Erwin Wasey, Ruthrauff & Ryan, Pittsburgh, Pa., public relations account executive, 1958-59; Pennsylvania State University, State College, assistant professor of journalism, 1963-68; University of Wisconsin—Madison, associate professor, 1968-74, professor of consumer sciences and journalism, 1974—. Consultant to Federal Trade Commission, on deceptive advertising, 1973—. *Military service:* U.S. Army, personnel specialist, 1953-55, became sergeant. *Member:* Association for Education in Journalism, American Council on Consumer Interests, American Academy of Advertising, Madison Advertising Club. *Awards, honors:* Grant from American Association of Advertising Agencies, 1970-72.

WRITINGS: The Great American Blow-Up: Puffery in Advertising and Selling, University of Wisconsin Press, 1975. Contributor of articles on communication theory, advertising, and consumer affairs to professional journals. Member of editorial board of *Journalism Quarterly, Journal of Advertising Research, Journalism Monographs,* and *Journal of Consumer Affairs.*

WORK IN PROGRESS: A text on consumer education.

SIDELIGHTS: Preston writes: "My interest in writing the above noted book stems from a conviction that the law favors the seller over the consumer, and in my opinion unjustifiably so. I wrote my book in order to correct this imbalance. The area I chose in particular was that of falsities stated by advertisers and sellers which the law declares are legal on the grounds that they are harmless. While I believe the latter claim is possible under certain circumstances, I believe that the law has far over-stated this possibility, and that much deception of consumers, and building of distrust by consumers, has occurred because of this legalized lying. My purpose is to make the advertising process work better by eliminating these problems."

* * *

PRICE, Jimmie
  See WHITE, John I(rwin)

* * *

PRICE, John A(ndrew) 1933-

PERSONAL: Born February 16, 1933, in Merced, Calif.; son of Henry Harrison and Laura (Bucklin) Price; married Caralee Williams, June 10, 1957; children: Michael, Laura, Walter, Kimball. *Education:* University of Utah, B.A., 1959, M.A., 1962; University of Michigan, Ph.D., 1967; also studied at University of Hawaii, summer, 1956. *Religion:* Church of Jesus Christ of Latter-day Saints (Mormon). *Office:* Department of Anthropology, York University, Downsview 463, Ontario, Canada.

CAREER: University of California, Los Angeles, assistant professor of anthropology, 1965-67; San Diego State College (now University), San Diego, Calif., assistant professor of anthropology, 1967-70; York University, Downsview, Ontario, associate professor of anthropology, 1970—. Consultant to Office of Economic Opportunity and Bureau of Indian Affairs. *Military service:* U.S. Army, 1953-55; served in Korea; became sergeant. *Member:* American Anthropological Association (fellow), Society for Applied Anthropology (fellow), American Ethnological Society, Canadian Association of Sociology and Anthropology, Canadian Ethnological Society.

WRITINGS: Washo Economy, Nevada State Museum, 1962; (contributor) G. Devos and H. Wagatsuma, editors, *Japan's Invisible Race,* University of California Press, 1966; (editor) *Modern Approaches to Prehistory,* Simon & Schuster, 1969; *Tijuana: Urbanization in a Border Culture,* University of Notre Dame Press, 1973. Contributor to *Urban Anthropology, Anthropologica, Ethos, Ethnohis-*

tory, Human Organization, Human Relations, New Mexico Quarterly, and *Canadian Review of Sociology and Anthropology.*

WORK IN PROGRESS: Native Studies: New Views on United States and Canadian Indians.

* * *

PRINCE, Gerald (Joseph) 1942-

PERSONAL: Born November 7, 1942, in Alexandria, Egypt; naturalized U.S. citizen in 1964; son of Tully and Marguerite (Bigio) Prince; married Ellen Friedman (a linguist), June 25, 1967. *Education:* Brooklyn College of the City University of New York, B.A., 1963; University of Florida, M.A., 1963; Brown University, Ph.D., 1968. *Home:* 1018 Clinton St., Philadelphia, Pa. 19107. *Office:* Department of Romance Languages, University of Pennsylvania, Philadelphia, Pa. 19174.

CAREER: University of Pennsylvania, Philadelphia, instructor, 1967-68, assistant professor, 1968-73, associate professor of romance languages, 1973—. *Member:* Modern Language Association of America, American Association of Teachers of French, American Association of University Professors.

WRITINGS: Metaphysique et technique dans l'oeuvre romanesque de Sartre (title means "Metaphysics and Technique in Sartre's Fiction"), Droz, 1968; *A Grammar of Stories,* Mouton & Co., 1973. Contributor to *Poetique, Diacritics, Degres, Centrum, French Studies,* and *PMLA.*

WORK IN PROGRESS: Aspects of Narratology, completion expected in 1976; an essay on the diary novel.

* * *

PRISING, Robin 1933-

PERSONAL: Born March 12, 1933, in Vancouver, British Columbia, Canada; adopted son of Frederic William (a tobacco merchant and judge of horse races) and Marie Leslie (a Shakespearean actress) Prising. *Education:* Educated by tutors and in private boarding schools. *Politics:* Pacifist. *Home:* 120 West 71st St., New York, N.Y. 10023.

CAREER: Actor; spent ten years on the stage in the United States and England, acting in plays by Shakespeare, Chekhov, and Shaw; teacher of speech at his own studio, 1967—; Helikon Press, New York, N.Y., editor, 1972—.

WRITINGS: Manila, Goodbye (autobiography), Houghton, 1975.

WORK IN PROGRESS: A sequel to *Manila, Goodbye;* short stories.

SIDELIGHTS: Prising writes: "Until I was twelve years old I lived in Manila during the twilight of the colonialist era; and during World War II I was a civilian prisoner of war of the Japanese. In 1945 I saw the destruction of Manila between the American and Japanese armies. Since that time I have lived in London, Rome, and New York.

"I am a pacifist. Three years in a concentration camp taught me that if I have an enemy it is war itself. And I learned too that soldiers of all sides are the recruits of involuntary obedience, victims of ignorance and nationalism: the last vestige of slavery in modern times. I belong to no political party either of the left or of the right. I believe only in the individual and in the holiness of human life."

PROSTERMAN, Roy L.   1935-

PERSONAL: Born July 13, 1935, in Chicago, Ill.; *Education:* University of Chicago, A.B. (honors), 1954; Harvard University, LL.B. (magna cum laude), 1958. *Home:* 1605 Bellevue Ave., Seattle, Wash. 98122. *Office:* School of Law, University of Washington, Seattle, Wash. 98195.

CAREER: Admitted to Bar of State of Massachusetts of New York, and Washington; Sullivan & Cromwell, New York, N.Y., associate, 1959-65; University of Washington, Seattle, assistant professor, 1965-68, associate professor, 1968-70, professor of law, 1970—. Member of national board of directors of World Without War Council of the United States, 1966—, and World Federalist Education Fund, 1972—; president of World Without War Council of Greater Seattle; member of board of advisors of Center for War/Peace Studies, 1967—. Consultant to Stanford Research Institute, 1967. *Awards, honors:* First Ralph Bunche Award from World Peace Through Law Committee of Seattle King County Bar Association, 1973.

WRITINGS: Surviving to 3000: An Introduction to the Study of Lethal Conflict, Duxbury, 1972; (contributor) *Focus Southeast Asia*, Praeger, 1972. Author of "Crisis Watch" column in *Seattle Post-Intelligence*. Contributor to *Washington Post, Christian Science Monitor, Wall Street Journal, War/Peace Report, Focus, Asian Survey*, and *Foreign Policy.*

WORK IN PROGRESS: A book on the future of foreign aid; with William M. Rose, a book on arms control and disarmament; research on land reform and rural development, on the world food crisis, and on the methods of preventing or resolving large-scale lethal conflict.

SIDELIGHTS: Prosterman told *CA:* "Since 1967, I have done extensive field work on land reform and agricultural development problems, spending some fifty weeks in field work since the summer of 1967 in the Philippines, South Vietnam, Pakistan, India, Indonesia, Taiwan, Japan, Brazil, Colombia, the Dominican Republic, Iran, and the Gaza Strip. . . .I see this work on the roots of rural poverty and inequality as centrally related to my concern with large-scale violence, and with the provision of non-violent methods for processing basic conflict."

*   *   *

PROTOPAPAS, George   1917-

PERSONAL: Born December 9, 1917, in Lowell, Mass. *Education:* Attended University of Paris; University of Maine, M.Ed.; Gregorian University, Rome, Licentiate in Philosophy. *Religion:* Catholic. *Home and office:* Oblate College, 109 Woodland St., Natick, Mass.

CAREER: Ordained Roman Catholic priest; former superior of Oblate seminary, Bucksport, Me.; past rector of St. Joseph's College, Antofagasta, Chile; now doing research on economic development at Oblate College, Natick, Mass.

WRITINGS: Los Cristianos y el Cambio Social en America Latina, Editorial del Pacifico, 1974; *Chile: Allende and After*, Our Sunday Visitor, 1975.

WORK IN PROGRESS: A book, *A Model of Economic Development for Latin America.*

*   *   *

PROWE, Deithelm (Manfred-Hartmut)   1941-

PERSONAL: Surname is pronounced *Proh-*va; born January 4, 1941, in Bonn, Germany; naturalized U.S. citizen; son of Hermann and Hedwig (Buscherbruck) Prowe; married Peggy Epps, March 17, 1968; children: Derek Evan, Freya Tamara. *Education:* Kent State University, B.A. (magna cum laude), 1962; Stanford University, M.A., 1963, Ph.D., 1967; studied at Free University of Berlin, summer, 1964. *Home:* 619 East Ninth St., Northfield, Minn. 55057. *Office:* Department of History, Carleton College, Northfield, Minn. 55057.

CAREER: Carleton College, Northfield, Minn., instructor, 1966-67, assistant professor, 1967-72, associate professor of history, 1972—. Visiting professor at Colorado College, summers, 1968, 1973, director of Institute of Contemporary History, summer, 1970. *Member:* American Historical Association, Conference Group on Central European History. *Awards, honors:* Humboldt fellow at Institut fuer Zeitgeschichte, Munich, Germany, 1975-76.

WRITINGS: Welstadt in Krisen: Berlin, 1949-1958 (title means "City in Crises: Berlin, 1949-58"), Walter de Gruyter, 1973.

WORK IN PROGRESS: Research on post-World War Two German debates on the new socio-economic order in the Western Zones (1945-1949).

*   *   *

PUCKETT, Ruby Parker   1932-

PERSONAL: Born November 26, 1932, in Dora, Ala.; daughter of John Franklin and Ethel V. (Short) Parker; married Larry W. Puckett (a vocational counselor and supervisor), July 2, 1955; children: Laurel Lynn, Hollie Kristina. *Education:* Auburn University, B.S., 1954; graduate study at University of Florida, 1970-73, and at Central Michigan University, 1974-75. *Politics:* Republican. *Religion:* Church of Jesus Christ of Latter-day Saints. *Home:* 3806 Southwest Fourth Pl., Gainesville, Fla. 32607. *Office:* Shands Teaching Hospital and Clinics, University of Florida, Gainesville, Fla. 32610.

CAREER: Veterans Administration Hospital, Houston, Tex., staff dietition, 1955-56; Matty Hersee Hospital, Meridian, Miss., dietition, 1957-58; University of Mississippi, Jackson, Miss., assistant director of dietetics, 1960-61; Fort Sanders Presbyterian Hospital, Knoxville, Tenn., director of dietetics, 1961-63; Waterman Memorial Hospital, Eustis, Fla., director of dietetics, 1963-68; University of Florida, J. Hillis Miller Health Center, Gainesville, director of dietetics, 1968-74, director of Food and Nutrition Services, 1974—. Coordinator of correspondence course for food service supervisors for American Dietetic Association, 1965-70. Lecturer at Meridian Junior College, 1957-58, Sante Fe Community College, 1970-72, and at University of Florida, 1971-72. Member of advisory committee to Florida State Department of Education, 1966-67, and to Sante Fe Junior College, 1968-69. Member of White House Conference on Food, Nutrition and Health, 1969, Florida Conference on Food, Nutrition and Health, 1970, and of North Central Florida Health Planning Council, 1974—. Member of advisory board of Florida Council on Aging, 1974.

MEMBER: International Platform Association, Royal Society of Health (fellow), American Dietetic Association, American Society of Hospital Food Service Administrators, Nutrition Education Society (charter member), Dietetic Internship Council, Field Agency Nutrition (president, 1970), Hospital, Institution, Education Food Service Society (organizer of Florida chapter, 1965; advisor, 1965-

71), Southeastern Hospital Conference for Dietitians (secretary, 1974-75), Florida Dietetic Association (member of executive board, 1965—; president, 1973-74), Gainesville Dietetic Association (president, 1970), Pilot Club (president, 1967), Pi Lambda Theta, Kappa Delta Pi. *Awards, honors:* Named outstanding dietitian in Florida by Florida Dietetic Association, 1972.

WRITINGS: (With others) *Diet Manual: Shands Teaching Hospital and Clinics*, University of Florida, 1971; *Correspondence Course of Study for Food Service Supervisors*, Continuing Education Division, University of Florida, 1972, revised edition, 1974; *Basic Guide to Nutrition and Diet Modification Manual*, University of Florida, 1974; *Preceptor's Guide*, Continuing Education Division, University of Florida, 1974. Author of monographs; contributor to professional journals. Contributor of regular column to *Food Management*, 1975—. Editor of *Orange Blossom*, 1974—.

WORK IN PROGRESS: Food Systems Management, for Cahners, completion expected in 1976; *Purchasing of Food and Supplies*, 1976; with Grace Madden, *Institutional Food Preparation with a Southern Flair*, 1977.

AVOCATIONAL INTERESTS: Gardening, camping, hiking, cooking Creole food, playing games, football.

* * *

PURCELL, Roy E(verett) 1936-

PERSONAL: Born June 25, 1936, in Los Angeles, Calif., son of Clifford Loren and Ella Dean (Mace) Purcell; married Florence Kinsey, February 7, 1959; children: Cyntea, Ramiel, Rischele. *Education:* Utah State University, B.S., 1963, graduate study, 1963-64. *Home and office:* 224 Minor, Henderson, Nev. 89015.

CAREER: Mohave Museum of History and Arts, Kingman, Ariz., director, 1967-70; Southern Nevada Museum, Henderson, Nev., director, 1970-74; poet; artist. Work has been exhibited nationally and is included in many private collections. *Military service:* U.S. Army, Infantry, 1954-56.

WRITINGS—Self-illustrated: *The Wayfarer* (autobiographical), Celestial Arts, 1975; (with Dale Robertson) *The Wells Fargo Legend*, Celestial Arts, 1975. Also author of unpublished works, "The Journey" (etchings and poetry), "The Wayfarers: Songs of Love," "Remnants from Consciousness," "The Mountain," "Journey Images," "Journey into Darkness," "The Long Walk," and "The Eternal Woman."

WORK IN PROGRESS: Journey to Anima, completion expected in 1976.

* * *

PURDOM, P(aul) Walton 1917-

PERSONAL: Born July 23, 1917, in Sparta, Ga.; son of Isaac Walton (founder of Sparks College) and Seaton (Taylor) Purdom; married wife, Bettie M., April 12, 1939; children: Paul Walton, Jr., Anne Elizabeth (Mrs. Lawrence A. Cross), Wayne Miller. *Education:* Georgia Institute of Technology, B.S., 1937; attended Vanderbilt University, 1940; University of Michigan, M.S., 1951; University of Pennsylvania, Master of Governmental Administration, 1958, Ph.D., 1963. *Office:* Department of Civil Engineering, Drexel University, Philadelphia, Pa.

CAREER: Held various engineering posts, including several with state and county health departments and private firms, 1937-43; Tennessee Department of Public Health, Nashville, senior sanitary engineer, 1943-47; Bureau of Health, Knoxville, Tenn., director of Sanitation Division, 1947-52; U.S. Public Health Service, Atlanta, Ga., sanitary engineer in Communicable Disease Center, 1952-53; Philadelphia Department of Public Health, Philadelphia, Pa., director of Division of Environmental Health, 1953-63; Drexel University, Philadelphia, associate professor and associate director, 1963-64, professor and director of environmental engineering and science, 1964-70, professor of environmental engineering, 1970—, director of Center for Urban Research and Environmental Studies, 1970-73, chairman of department of civil engineering, and acting director of Environmental Studies Institute, 1973-75, director of Institute, 1975—.

MEMBER: American Society for Public Administration, Air Pollution Control Association, American Water Works Association, American Academy of Political and Social Science, American Academy of Arts and Sciences, American Public Health Association (president, 1971), American Industrial Hygiene Association, Water Pollution Control Federation, American Association of Professors in Sanitary Engineering, American Society for Engineering Education, Royal Society for Health (honorary fellow), Conference of Local Environmental Health Administrators (secretary, 1950-52; vice-chairman, 1953; chairman, 1954), Pennsylvania Public Health Association (vice-president, 1958; president, 1959), Delta Omega.

WRITINGS: Environmental Health, Academic Press, 1971.

* * *

QUIMBY, George Irving 1913-

PERSONAL: Born May 4, 1913, in Grand Rapids, Mich.; son of George Irving (a bookseller) and Ethelwyn (Sweet) Quimby; married Helen M. Ziehm, October 13, 1940; children: Sedna (Mrs. David Wineland), G. Edward, John E., Robert W. *Education:* University of Michigan, B.A., 1936, M.A., 1937; University of Chicago, graduate study, 1938-39. *Home:* 6001 52nd Ave. N.E., Seattle, Wash. 98115. *Office:* Burke Museum, University of Washington, Seattle, Wash. 98115.

CAREER: Field Museum of Natural History, Chicago, Ill., curator, 1942-65; University of Washington, Seattle, professor of anthropology, 1965—, director of Burke Museum, 1968—. *Member:* American Anthropological Association (fellow), American Association for the Advancement of Science (fellow), Society for American Archaeology (president, 1958), Association of Science Museum Directors (president, 1974), American Association of Museums (member of council, 1971-74), Society for Historical Archaeology (member of board of directors, 1971-74, 1975—).

WRITINGS: (With J. A. Ford) *Tchefuncte Culture*, Society for American Archaeology, 1945; (with Paul S. Martin and Donald Collier) *Indians Before Columbus*, University of Chicago Press, 1947, reprinted, 1975; *Indians of the Western Frontier: Paintings of George Catlin*, Chicago Natural History Museum, 1954; *Indian Life in the Upper Great Lakes*, University of Chicago Press, 1960; *The Dumaw Creek Site*, Field Museum Press, 1966; *Indian Culture and European Trade Goods*, University of Wisconsin Press, 1966; (editor with Richard Casteel) *Maritime Adaptations of the Pacific*, Mouton & Co., 1975.

WORK IN PROGRESS: A book on Edward S. Curtis and motion pictures, with Bill Holm.

QUINCE, Peter Lum
  See RITCHIE, (Harry) Ward

* * *

QUINNEY, Richard 1934-

PERSONAL: Born May 16, 1934, in Wisconsin; son of Floyd and Alice (Holloway) Quinney; married Valerie Yow (a professor of history), 1958; children: Laura, Anne. *Education:* Carroll College, B.S., 1956; Northwestern University, M.S., 1957; University of Wisconsin, Ph.D., 1962. *Office:* Graduate School of the City University of New York, 33 West 42nd St., New York, N.Y.

CAREER: New York University, New York, N.Y., associate professor, 1965-67, professor of sociology, 1967-72, on leave for research and writing at University of North Carolina, 1972-74; Graduate School of the City University of New York, New York, N.Y., professor of sociology, 1974—. *Member:* American Sociological Association.

WRITINGS: The Problem of Crime, Dodd, 1970; *The Social Reality of Crime*, Little, Brown, 1970; *Critique of Legal Order*, Little, Brown, 1974; *Criminal Justice in America*, Little, Brown, 1974; *Criminology*, Little, Brown, 1975.

WORK IN PROGRESS: Crime and the Development of Capitalism.

* * *

QUIRK, James P. 1926-

PERSONAL: Born November 27, 1926, in St. Paul, Minn.; son of William M. (a businessman) and Teresa (McMahon) Quirk; married Shirley Krois (a clerk), June 22, 1949; children: Gail, James, Jr., Janice, Jill, Colleen, Thomas. *Education:* Attended Marquette University, 1944-46; University of Minnesota, B.B.A., 1948, M.A., 1949, Ph.D., 1959. *Politics:* Democrat. *Religion:* None. *Home:* 911 South Oakland, Pasadena, Calif. 91106. *Office:* Division of Humanities, California Institute of Technology, Pasadena, Calif. 91109.

CAREER: Purdue University, Lafayette, Ind., instructor, 1958-60, assistant professor of economics, 1960-63; University of Kansas, Lawrence, associate professor, 1963-66, professor, 1966-68, university professor of economics, 1968-71; California Institute of Technology, Pasadena, professor of economics, 1971—. Consultant to U.S. Senator Alan Cranston. *Military service:* U.S. Navy, 1944-46.

WRITINGS: (With R. Saposnik) *Introduction to General Equilibrium Theory and Welfare Economics*, McGraw, 1968; (editor with Arvid M. Zarley) *Papers in Quantitative Economics*, University of Kansas Press, 1970.

* * *

QUIST, Susan 1944-

PERSONAL: Born September 10, 1944, in Cincinnati, Ohio; divorced; children: one. *Education:* Attended University of Pittsburgh, 1962-63, and University of Cincinnati, 1963-67. *Politics:* "Abolitionist." *Religion:* "Dionysian Buddhist." *Home address:* P.O. Box 335, Cherry Valley, N.Y. 13320.

CAREER: Freeman's Journal, Cooperstown, N.Y., farm editor, 1974; writer, 1974—. Poet in the schools for Pennsylvania Council on the Arts, 1974, and for South Carolina Arts Commission, 1975; chairperson of Cherry Valley Writing Project, 1974. *Member:* Authors Guild of Authors

League of America. *Awards, honors:* P.E.N. grant, 1972; Canaras Award from St. Lawrence University, 1974; grant from Change, Inc., 1974.

WRITINGS: Indecent Exposure (novel), Walker & Co., 1974. Contributor of poems to magazines, including *Oink!, Penumbra, Telephone, Speculum, Thirteenth Moon*, and *Sojourner.* Editor, *Cherry Valley Anthology*, 1975.

WORK IN PROGRESS: Five novels: *Woo Woo, 1985, What I Did on My Summer Vacation, Move It, The Luckiest Girl in the World; Boogie Bible,* a song collection; *Mouth Piece,* a collection of poems; research on the life of Nellie Bly; a stand-up comedy routine.

SIDELIGHTS: Susan Quist writes: ". . . What I am doing . . . is rebelling. Not only against my lot as woman, but against everything well defined, well structured, logical, mechanical. Limited. Plotted . . . What I am after is spontaneity, mystery, reality . . . I've almost made my peace with chaos. The god I know and love is promiscuous, indiscriminate. Also two-faced. Full of contradictions. This is why I'm fond of capitalism. It's so anarchic, in its early stages. But it must be tempered with compassion, some sense of community."

* * *

RABBIE
  See TOWERS, Maxwell

* * *

RABBITT, Thomas 1943-

PERSONAL: Born September 30, 1943, in Boston, Mass.; son of Thomas Francis (a salesman) and Helen Marie (Reardon) Rabbitt. *Education:* Harvard University, A.B., 1966; Johns Hopkins University, M.A., 1968; University of Iowa, M.F.A., 1972. *Home:* 42 Lake Robinwood, Route #1, Coker, Ala. 35452. *Office:* Department of English, University of Alabama, University, Ala. 35486.

CAREER: Fawcett-McDermott, Inc., San Francisco, Calif., advertising account executive and copy writer, 1968-69; elementary school teacher in private school in Menlo Park, Calif., 1969-70; University of Alabama, University, assistant professor of English, and director of creative writing, 1972—. *Member:* Modern Language Association of America, Associated Writing Programs, South Atlantic Modern Language Association. *Awards, honors:* International Poetry Forum award, 1974, for *Exile.*

WRITINGS: Exile (poems), University of Pittsburgh Press, 1975. Contributor of poems to *Nation, Shenandoah, Prairie Schooner, Humanities in the South, Long Island Review, Black Warrior Review,* and other journals.

WORK IN PROGRESS: A book of poems, *Dedications and the Dogs of War,* for University of Pittsburgh Press; poems; a play.

AVOCATIONAL INTERESTS: Horses, dogs, gardening.

* * *

RACHLIN, Carol K(ing) 1919-

PERSONAL: Surname is pronounced Rock-lin; born July 21, 1919, in Newark, N.J.; daughter of Benjamin (a lumberman) and Marjorie (King) Rachlin. *Education:* Chevy Chase Junior College, A.A., 1940; Columbia University, B.S., 1953, graduate study, 1953-55. *Religion:* Hebrew. *Home and office:* 1836 Northwest 56th St., Oklahoma City, Okla. 73118. *Agent:* Nannine Joseph, 200 West 54th St., New York, N.Y. 10019.

CAREER: New Jersey State Museum, Trenton, assistant state archaeologist, 1951-53; Southwest Research Associates, Oklahoma City, Okla., associate director, 1960—; Central State University, Edmund, Okla., permanent artist-in-residence, 1968—. Oklahoma Indian Council, anthropological consultant, 1962—, director of dietary program, 1965-66. Associate professor at University of Oklahoma, 1965-66; special consultant to Philbrook Art Museum, 1965-66.

MEMBER: American Association for the Advancement of Science (fellow), American Anthropological Association (fellow), American Archaeological Association, Authors Guild of Authors League of America, Current Anthropology, Society of Applied Anthropology, American Museum Association, American Ethnological Society, Southwest Literary Review, Oklahoma Folkways Society. *Awards, honors:* Indian Historical Society fellow at Angel Mounds, Evansville, Ind., 1954-58; American Museum of Natural History special research fellow among Woodlands in Iowa, Minnesota, and Wisconsin, 1955-60; American Academy of Arts and Science fellow in Oklahoma, 1961; American Philosophical Society grant among Negro Indians in Oklahoma, 1969-70; key award from Theta Sigma Pi, 1969; Okie Award from Oklahoma Writers Federation, 1971, for *Peyote*.

WRITINGS: (With Alice Marriott) *American Indian Mythology*, Crowell, 1968; (contributor) *The American Indian Today*, Everett/Edwards, 1968; (with Marriott) *American Epic*, Putnam, 1969; (with Marriott) *Oklahoma: The Forty-ninth Star*, Doubleday, 1970; (with Marriott) *Peyote*, Crowell, 1971; (with Marriott) *Plains Indian Mythology*, Crowell, 1975. Contributor to journals of history and anthropology.

WORK IN PROGRESS: With Alice Marriott, *Fur Trade on the Lower Missouri*, for Putnam.

SIDELIGHTS: Carol Rachlin told *CA* that her interest in photography and hand weaving brought her to study pre-Columbian North American Indian textiles. This brought her interest in working with living Indians.

* * *

RACHMAN, David Jay 1928-

PERSONAL: Surname is pronounced Rock-man; born October 9, 1928, in Scranton, Pa.; son of Harry (a salesman) and Mildred (Mendelsohn) Rachman; married Barbara Binik, September 3, 1956; children: Marli, Nancy. *Education:* University of Scranton, B.S., 1950; City College of the City University of New York, M.B.A., 1953; New York University, Ph.D., 1965. *Home:* 3 Hawthorne Terrace, Great Neck, N.Y. 10023. *Office:* Department of Marketing, Bernard Baruch College, City University of New York, New York, N.Y. 10010.

CAREER: City University of New York, Bernard Baruch College, New York, N.Y., assistant professor, 1965-68, associate professor, 1968-73, professor of marketing, 1973—. Research manager of School of Retailing at New York University, 1957—. *Member:* Retail Research Society (member of board of directors, 1970—).

WRITINGS: Retail Strategy and Structure, Prentice-Hall, 1969, revised edition, 1975; (with Houston G. Elam) *Retail Management Cases*, Prentice-Hall, 1969; (editor) *Retail Management Strategy and Selected Readings*, Prentice-Hall, 1970; *Marketing Strategy and Structure*, Prentice-Hall, 1974; *Business Today*, Random House, 1976.

SIDELIGHTS: Rachman told *CA*: "Several years ago, I re-examined a Ford Foundation study of the New York City school system and published an article critical of the Ford research procedures. . . . I received several thousand requests for reprints of this article. I understand the participants in the research project are no longer with the Ford Foundation." *Avocational interests:* Tennis.

* * *

RACHOW, Louis A(ugust) 1927-

PERSONAL: Surname sounds like *Roc*-co; born January 21, 1927, near Shickley, Neb.; son of John Louis (a farmer) and Mable Louise (Dondlinger) Rachow. *Education:* York College, B.S., 1948; Columbia University, M.L.S., 1959. *Office:* 16 Gramercy Park, New York, N.Y. 10003.

CAREER: York College, York, Neb., librarian, 1949-54; Columbia University Law Library, New York, N.Y., serials acquisition assistant, 1957-58; University Club, New York, N.Y., assistant librarian, 1958-62; Walter Hampden Memorial Library at The Players, New York, N.Y., librarian, 1962—. Member of board of advisors of American Theater Co., 1974, Eugene O'Neill Memorial Theater Center Library, 1966, *National Directory for the Performing Arts and Civic Centers*, 1975, and OKC Theater Productions, 1975. *Military service:* U.S. Army, 1954-56; served in Germany. *Member:* American Library Association, American National Theater and Academy, American Society for Theater Research, American Theater Association, Special Libraries Association, Theater Library Association (president, 1967-72), Archons of Colophon, Council of National Library Associations (secretary-treasurer, 1970-71; member of board of directors, 1974—), New York Library Association, New York Library Club (council member, 1973-77), New York Technical Services Librarians.

WRITINGS: Guide to the Performing Arts, 1968, Scarecrow, 1972. Contributor of articles and reviews to professional library and performing arts journals. Assistant editor of *American Notes & Queries*, 1967-71, associate editor, 1971-74; editor of *Broadside: Newsletter of the Theater Library Association*, 1973—.

* * *

RADHAKRISHNAN, C(hakkorayil) 1939-

PERSONAL: Born February 15, 1939, in Calicut, Kerala, India; son of Parappur Madhathil Madhavan (a farmer) and Chakkorayil Janaki (Amma) Nair; married Vatsala Kollathkalam, November 28, 1971; children: Gopal. *Education:* Guruvayurappan College, first class degree, 1960; Government Victoria College, graduate study, 1960-61. *Politics:* None. *Religion:* None. *Home and office:* Chamravattam, Tirur PIN 676102, Kerala, India.

CAREER: Astrophysical Observatory, Kodaikanal, India, scientific assistant, 1961-63; Seismological Office, Poona, India, scientific assistant, 1963-65; *Times of India*, Bombay, sub-editor of "Science Today," 1965-68; *Patriot Daily*, New Delhi, India, assistant editor, 1968-72; writer, 1972—. *Awards, honors:* First prize in novel-writing contest, 1960, from *Mathrubhumi Illustrated Weekly*; Kerala Sahitya Academy Award, 1962.

WRITINGS: Zero (novel), Arnold-Heinemann, 1974. Author of "The Island," a play. Author of works written in Malayalam, including motion picture scripts. Science and literature columnist for *Patriot Daily*; assistant editor of

Link (newsmagazine), 1968-69; editor of *Porul* (literary monthly).

WORK IN PROGRESS: Investigating rediscovery of human freedom through the synthesis of the arts and sciences.

SIDELIGHTS: Radhakrishnan writes: "For what I write, I am indebted to my grandfather, a simple soul, who initiated me into Indian philosophy; my science background; the poverty during early youth which made me discontinue my postgraduate course in applied physics; the river that flows by the village; the sea near and the open (paddy) fields. . . . After a hectic twelve-year period of employment, I have withdrawn myself into this remote corner of the world where I find peace, solace, and the right atmosphere to work, to get lost. I have been a prolific writer in Malayalam; the word I write gives me the feeling I exist."

*   *   *

RADHAKRISHNAN, Sarvepalli   1888-1975

September 5, 1888—April 17, 1975; Indian philosopher, statesman, second president of Republic of India, educator, scholar, orator, and author of books on philosophy and religion. Obituaries: *New York Times*, April 17, 1975; *Washington Post*, April 18, 1975; *Time*, April 28, 1975; *Newsweek*, April 28, 1975; *AB Bookman's Weekly*, May 12, 1975; *Current Biography*, June, 1975. (CA-15/16)

*   *   *

RADKE, Don   1940-

PERSONAL: Born July 19, 1940, in Milwaukee, Wis.; son of Frank and Ottilie (Tucholke) Radke; married Ruth Dusterhoft (an insurance correspondent), August 13, 1960; children: Patricia, Suzanne, Christopher. *Education:* University of Wisconsin—Milwaukee, B.S., 1972. *Politics:* Liberal Republican. *Religion:* Lutheran. *Home:* 508 Greendale St., Lebanon, Wis. 53047. *Office:* E. R. Wagner Manufacturing, 4611 North 32nd St., Milwaukee, Wis. 53209.

CAREER: Ladish Co. (forged metals), Milwaukee, Wis., standards engineer, 1961-66; Milwaukee Gear Co., Milwaukee, Wis., standards engineer, 1966-68; E. R. Wagner Manufacturing (metal stampings), Milwaukee, Wis., industrial engineer, 1968—. *Member:* National Management Association (officer for the Wisconsin council).

WRITINGS: Cheesemaking at Home: The Complete Illustrated Guide, Doubleday, 1974.

*   *   *

RADOM, Matthew   1905-

PERSONAL: Born August 27, 1905, in Poland; son of Daniel (a fresco painter) and Helen (Chmurra) Radom; married Marjorie Roth, May 30, 1946. *Education:* United States Naval Academy, B.S., 1928; New York University, M.A., 1937; Columbia University, Ph.D., 1966. *Politics:* Democrat. *Religion:* Jewish. *Home:* 748 Kingston Rd., Princeton, N.J. 08540. *Office:* Department of Management, University College, Rutgers University, New Brunswick, N.J. 08903.

CAREER: U.S. Navy, 1928-37, 1942-45; served in Pacific theater; became captain; Standard Oil Company of New Jersey, Marine Department, Employee Relations, New York, N.Y., manager, 1937-42, advisor, 1945-61; Rutgers University, University College, New Brunswick, N.J., associate professor, 1961-68, professor of management,

1968—. Chairman of executive committee of United Seamen's Service, 1945-55; member of executive committee of National Training Laboratory, 1955-60. *Member:* International Psychological Association, Industrial Relations Research Association, American Professors for Peace in the Middle East, American Association of University Professors, American Arbitration Association, Columbia University Seminar on Labor. *Awards, honors*—Military: Bronze Star, commendation ribbon, and seventeen battle stars.

WRITINGS: The Social Scientist in American Industry, Rutgers University Press, 1970.

WORK IN PROGRESS: Is There a Decline in the Work Ethic?, completion expected in 1976.

*   *   *

RAE, Walter   1916-

PERSONAL: Born January 21, 1916, in New York, N.Y.; son of John (an artist and juvenile writer) and Helen (Cortelyou) Rae; married Barbara Smith, 1942 (divorced, 1948); married Isabel Boulter, September, 1948; children: Stephen, Rosamond, Jennifer, Walter, Jr. *Education:* Attended New York University, 1960-61. *Home address:* RFD 3, Montpelier, Vt. 05602. *Agent:* John Meyer, 141 East 55th St., New York, N.Y. 10022. *Office:* Vermont State Employees Association, 79 Main St., Montpelier, Vt. 05602.

CAREER: Providence Journal, Providence, R.I., on staff of financial copy desk, 1940-42; American Civil Liberties Union, New York, N.Y., public relations director, 1942-43; free-lance writer, 1943-46; *Newport-Balboa Press*, Newport Beach, Calif., news editor, feature writer, and drama critic, 1946-49; *Los Angeles Times*, Los Angeles, Calif., copy editor, 1949; *American Druggist*, New York, N.Y., news editor, 1950-61; *Journal-News*, Nyack, N.Y., night city editor, 1961-64; *Bergen Evening Record*, Hackensack, N.J., copy editor, 1964-72; free-lance writer, 1972—. Auditor of Middlesex, Vt., 1975—.

WRITINGS: Editing Small Newspapers, M. S. Mill, 1943; *How We Built Our House for Under $10,000*, Yankee, Inc., 1974.

WORK IN PROGRESS: The Meadow, a pastoral piece reflecting love of the land; editing *Chet Grimes, Logger*, an oral history.

SIDELIGHTS: Rae writes: "Writing, for me, is a gruelling affair, a kind of gladiatorial endurance contest to determine who wins—the writer or the blank sheet of paper he does battle with. It took me 40 years of combat to learn to write a coherent English sentence in my native tongue—by doing it doggedly. . . . I really think vanity, mostly, is the artist's slave driver; the fear of failure his chief adversary. What is imperative to the writer's success (however that is conceived) is that the Gladiator learn his limitations. His work is then, mercifully and at last, confined to what he knows and feels."

*   *   *

RAEBURN, John (Hay)   1941-

PERSONAL: Born July 18, 1941, in Indianapolis, Ind.; son of Gordon M. and Katherine (Calwell) Raeburn; married Gillian Kimble, August 18, 1963; children: Daniel, Nicholas. *Education:* Indiana University, A.B., 1963; University of Pennsylvania, Ph.D., 1969. *Home:* 268 St. Matthews Ave., Louisville, Ky. 40207. *Office:* Department of English, University of Louisville, Louisville, Ky. 40208.

CAREER: University of Michigan, Ann Arbor, assistant professor of English and of American culture, 1967-74; University of Iowa, Iowa City, visiting lecturer in American civilization, 1974-75; University of Louisville, Louisville, Ky., associate professor of English, 1975—. *Member:* Modern Language Association of America, American Studies Association, Popular Culture Association.

WRITINGS: (Editor with Richard Glatzer) *Frank Capra: The Man and His Films*, University of Michigan Press, 1975; *Fame Became of Him: Ernest Hemingway as a Culture Hero*, Indiana University Press, in press.

* * *

RAHM, David A. 1931-

PERSONAL: Born May 2, 1931, in Bellevue, Pa.; son of Edward (a mechanical engineer) and Herta (Doenitz) Rahm; married Catherine Jean Kinnier, June 7, 1952 (divorced, 1968); children: Steven Allan, Brian James. *Education:* Pennsylvania State University, B.S., 1956; Harvard University, Ph.D., 1959. *Religion:* Presbyterian. *Office:* Department of Geology, Western Washington State College, Bellingham, Wash. 98225.

CAREER: Western Washington State College, Bellingham, instructor, 1959-60, assistant professor, 1960-63, associate professor, 1963-73, professor of geology, 1973—. *Military service:* U.S. Army, 1953-55. *Member:* International Aerobatic Club, Geological Society of America, National Association of Geology Teachers, Aerobatic Club of America. *Awards, honors:* Named West Coast amateur aerobatic champion by Champion Aircraft Co., 1967.

WRITINGS: (With D. J. Easterbrook) *Landforms of Washington*, Union Printing, 1970; *Reading the Rocks of the American Southwest*, Sierra Club, 1974.

Author of "Slides for Geology" (collection of photographs; with geology study guide), McGraw, 1971. Contributor to geology and aviation journals.

WORK IN PROGRESS: Above the North Cascades: An Illustrated Layman's Guide to a Mountain Range; The Magnificent Peninsula: An Illustrated Layman's Guide to the Olympic Peninsula; From a Point in the Sky: Outstanding Geologic Scenery from the Air.

AVOCATIONAL INTERESTS: Travel, aerial photography, flying (commercial pilot; aerobatic pilot).

* * *

RANDALL, David A(nton) 1905-1975

April 5, 1905—May 25, 1975; American librarian, rare book dealer, educator, and author of books on book-collecting. Obituaries: *AB Bookman's Weekly*, June 16, 1975; *Publishers Weekly*, July 14, 1975.

* * *

RAUCH, Constance 1937-

PERSONAL: Born September 27, 1937, in Frankfurt, Germany; daughter of Hans (a professor) and Senta (an artist; maiden name, Kauffeldt) Weil; married Paul Rauch, February 16, 1957 (divorced, 1974); children: Katharine, Emily. *Education:* Earlham College, B.A., 1958. *Politics:* Independent. *Religion:* Unaffiliated. *Residence:* Yorktown Heights, N.Y. *Agent:* James Brown Associates, Inc., 22 East 60th St., New York, N.Y. 10022. *Office: Reader's Digest*, Pleasantville, N.Y. 10570.

CAREER: McCall Corp., New York, N.Y., promotion assistant, 1958-60; Triangle Publications, New York, N.Y., copy writer, 1960-67; Conde Nast Publications, New York, N.Y., copywriter, 1967-69; *Reader's Digest*, Pleasantville, N.Y., copywriter, 1969—.

WRITINGS: The Landlady (novel), Putnam, 1975.

WORK IN PROGRESS: The Spy on Riverside Drive (tentative title), a novel set in New York City, 1943.

SIDELIGHTS: Constance Rauch writes: "Until the happy day when I can devote all of my time to fiction-writing, I am writing only what Graham Greene referred to as 'entertainments.' I hope to improve my command of the novel form with each effort, so that in time I can set my sights on something more ambitious. Whatever comes, any novel I write will tell a story. I am devoted to the ancient art of the narrative, and feel strongly that you can do anything with it."

* * *

RAW, Isaias 1927-

PERSONAL: Born March 26, 1927, in Sao Paulo, Brazil; son of Azriel Leon (a businessman) and Bertha (Schechtman) Raw; married Zanaide Sirota, October 12, 1952; children: three. *Education:* University of Sao Paulo, M.D., 1950, Ph.D. *Home:* 60 East End Ave., New York, N.Y. 10028. *Office:* City College of the City University of New York, 136 St. and Amsterdam Ave., New York, N.Y. 10031.

CAREER: University of Sao Paulo, Sao Paulo, Brazil, instructor, 1950-53, assistant professor, 1954-57, privat docent, 1957-64, professor of biochemistry and head of department, 1964-69, organizer and dean of experimental Medical School, 1968-69; UNESCO and United Nations Development Program, Jerusalem, Israel, acting head of science education program, 1969-70; Massachusetts Institute of Technology, Cambridge, Mass., research associate of Education Development Center and visiting professor, 1971-73; Harvard University, School of Public Health, Cambridge, Mass., visiting professor, 1973-74; City College of the City University of New York, Center for Biomedical Education, professor of biochemistry and nutrition, 1974—. Visiting professor, University of Indiana, 1957, Hebrew University, 1969-70.

Founder and director of University Press of Sao Paulo, 1960, University Press of Brasilia, 1961, ALECYT, 1973; founder and president of Carlos Chagas Foundation; organized IBECC (now Brazilian Foundation for Science Education Development), 1952; member of board of directors, University of Brasilia Medical School, 1964; advisor to Sao Paulo Minister of Education, 1965; member of task force of education, Alliance of Progress, 1959; consultant to U.S. National Academy of Science, Ford Foundation, OEDC, World Health Organization, National Science Foundation, and Universidad Nacional Autonoma de Mexico.

MEMBER: American Association for the Advancement of Science, American Chemical Society, American Society of Biochemistry, National Science Teachers Association, American Institute of Biological Sciences, Biochemical Society of London, Asociacion Brasileira para o Progresso da Ciencia. *Awards, honors:* Fellowships from New York University, 1952-53, Brazilian National Research Council, 1952, and Rockefeller Foundation, 1957; grants from Rockefeller Foundation, 1952-62, Brazilian National Research Council, 1952-69, Ford Foundation, 1960-69, Fundacao de Amparo a Pesquisa de Sao Paulo, 1960-69, National Institute of Health, 1962.

WRITINGS: (With Walter Colli) *Mapas metabolicos*, University of Sao Paulo, 1960; (with J. Tola Pasquel) *La educacion cientifica en America Latina*, Union Panamericana (Washington, D.C.), 1963; (with Colli) *Fundamentos de bioquimica*, two volumes, Universidade de Brasilia, 1965-66, 2nd edition, Livraria, 1967; (with Colli) *Bioenergetica*, Organization of American States, 1968; (with L. Mennuci) *Mecanismo de Acao de Hormonios*, Edart, 1968; *Organizing Curriculum Evaluation: Procuring Education Research for Decision-Making*, Pan American Federation of Medical Schools (Toronto, Canada), 1972; (with A. Bromley and others) *What People Eat* (textbook with laboratory guide), William Kaufmann, 1975; *Anemia: From Molecules to Disease*, Little, Brown, 1975; *Education Technology Applied to the Learning of Science in Developing Countries*, UNESCO, in press.

WORK IN PROGRESS: Malnutrition: From Molecules to Society; *What People Eat*, Volume II.

* * *

RAWLINS, Jack P. 1946-

PERSONAL: Born December 25, 1946, in Chico, Calif.; son of Jack L. (a rancher) and Elizabeth (Oser) Rawlins; married Claudia Bensel (a biological researcher), March 19, 1968; children: Molly. *Education:* University of California, Berkeley, B.A., 1968; Yale University, M.Phil., 1971, Ph.D., 1972. *Home:* 332 West Frances Willard, Chico, Calif. 95926. *Office:* Department of English, California State University, Chico, Calif. 95926.

CAREER: California State University, Chico, assistant professor of English, 1972—. *Member:* Phi Beta Kappa.

WRITINGS: Thackeray's Novels: A Fiction That Is True, University of California Press, 1974.

WORK IN PROGRESS: A textbook on the history of the English language, with Marie Borroff.

AVOCATIONAL INTERESTS: Fly fishing, softball, photography, woodworking, backpacking, playing the guitar.

* * *

RAY, Deborah 1940-

PERSONAL: Born August 31, 1940, in Philadelphia, Pa.; daughter of Louis X. and Hildegarde (Wimenitz) Cohen; married Christopher Ray (a sculptor), July 8, 1960; children: Karen, Nicole. *Education:* Studied at Philadelphia College of Art, 1958-59, University of Pennsylvania, 1959-61, Pennsylvania Academy of the Fine Arts, 1959-62, and Albert C. Barnes Foundation, 1962-64. *Residence:* Philadelphia, Pa.

CAREER: Artist. Paintings have been shown in six solo exhibitions, mostly in Philadelphia, and in group shows at Philadelphia Art Alliance, Pennsylvania Academy of the Fine Arts, Philadelphia Museum of Arts, Rutgers University, American Institute of Graphic Arts, and elsewhere; represented in collections of Chase Manhattan Bank (graphic mural), Free Library of Philadelphia, University of Minnesota, Library of Congress, Drexel University, and Fidelity Bank. *Member:* Artists Equity Association. *Awards, honors:* Louis Comfort Tiffany Foundation fellowship in painting, 1968; Mabel Rush Homer Award, 1968; Philadelphia Art Directors Award for design and book illustration, 1970; other awards from American Institute of Graphic Arts, 1970, and Woodmere Art Gallery, 1973.

WRITINGS—Reteller for children and illustrator: *The

Fair at Sorochintsi: A Nikolai Gogol Story Retold, Macrae Smith, 1969; *Abdul Abul-Bul Amir and Ivan Skavinsky Skavar*, Macrae Smith, 1969.

Illustrator: Robert Welber, *The Winter Picnic*, Pantheon, 1970; Robert Welber, *Frog, Frog, Frog*, Pantheon, 1971; Robert Welber, *The Train*, Pantheon, 1972; Robert Welber, *Song of the Seasons*, Pantheon, 1973; Robert Welber, *The Winter Wedding*, Pantheon, in press.

SIDELIGHTS: "In illustrating children's books I have found another audience to communicate with. My basic aim is to create a good art for children in books—that children respond to the nuance and look beyond what many adults miss. My first books were in a created or fantasy world. The books I have most recently done must speak directly to the world children are most familiar with in their day to day lives. To create real people they might know from words."

* * *

RAY, Gordon N(orton) 1915-

PERSONAL: Born September 8, 1915, in New York, N.Y.; son of Jess Gordon and Tessie (Norton) Ray. *Education:* Indiana University, A.B., 1936, A.M., 1936; Harvard University, A.M., 1938, Ph.D., 1940. *Home:* 25 Sutton Place South, New York, N.Y. 10022. *Office:* John Simon Guggenheim Memorial Foundation, 90 Park Ave., New York, N.Y. 10016.

CAREER: Harvard University, Cambridge, Mass., instructor in English, 1940-42; Dexter fellow, 1940-41; University of Illinois, Urbana, professor of English, 1946-60, head of department, 1950-57, vice-president and provost, 1957-60; John Simon Guggenheim Memorial Foundation, New York, N.Y., associate secretary general, 1960-61, secretary general, 1961-63, president, 1963—. Professor, New York University, 1962—; summer visiting professor, University of Oregon, 1948; Berg Professor of English and American Literature, New York University, 1952-53; Beckman Professor of English at University of California, Berkeley, summer, 1969. Member of numerous advisory boards of universities and colleges; adviser to Houghton Mifflin Co., 1954-71, Library of Congress, 1965-70, and Soho Bibliographies, 1966—. Member of U.S. Educational Commission in the United Kingdom (establishing the Fulbright program), 1948-49; member of council, Smithsonian Institution, 1968, chairman, 1970—; member of council, Rockefeller University, 1973—; treasurer and member of board of directors, American Council of Learned Societies, 1973—; trustee, Foundation Library Center, 1962-68, Center for Applied Linguistics, 1965-69, Pierpont Morgan Library, 1970—, Rosenbach Foundation, 1972—. *Military service:* U.S. Naval Reserve, 1942-46; served in Pacific theater, 1943-46; became lieutenant senior grade; received seven battle stars.

MEMBER: Royal Society of Literature (fellow), American Antiquarian Society, American Academy of Arts and Sciences (fellow), Modern Language Association of America (managing trustee), American Council on Education, Phi Beta Kappa, Athenaeum Club, Century Club, Grolier Club, Harvard Club. *Awards, honors:* Guggenheim Foundation fellow, 1941-42, 1946, and 1956-57; Rockefeller postservice fellow, 1948-49; Litt.D. from Monmouth College, 1959, Syracuse University, 1961, Duke University, 1965, University of Illinois, 1968, and Northwestern University, 1974; LL.D. from New York University, 1961, Tulane University, 1963, University of California, 1968, Columbia

University, 1969, and University of Southern California, 1974; L.H.D. from Indiana University, 1964.

WRITINGS: (Editor) *The Letters and Private Papers of William Makepeace Thackeray*, four volumes, Harvard University Press, 1945-46; *The Buried Life: A Study of the Relation between Thackeray's Fiction and His Personal History*, Harvard University Press, 1952; *Thackeray*, McGraw, Volume I: *The Uses of Adversity, 1811-1846*, 1955, Volume II: *The Age of Wisdom, 1847-1863*, 1958; (with Leon Edel) *Henry James and H. G. Wells*, University of Illinois Press, 1958; (editor) H. G. Wells, *History of Mr. Polly*, Houghton, 1961; *H. G. Wells and Rebecca West*, Yale University Press, 1974.

Also editor of William Makepeace Thackeray's *Rose and the Ring*, 1947, *History of Henry Esmond*, 1950, and *Contributions to the "Morning Chronicle,"* 1955, and of H. G. Wells' *Desert Daisy*, 1957. Member of editorial board, *Nineteenth Century Fiction*, 1947—, *English Language Notes*, 1964—, *Manuscripta*, c.1967—.

AVOCATIONAL INTERESTS: Book collecting, travel.

* * *

RAYMOND, Lee
See HILL, Mary Raymond

* * *

RAYSIDE, Betty 1931-

PERSONAL: Born November 19, 1931, in Ft. Pierce, Fla.; daughter of William Wemyss and Wanda Lyons (Soper) Pitchford; married Charles E. Rayside, May 12, 1951 (divorced, 1974); children: William Evans, Charles Clayton. *Education:* Attended public schools in Palm Beach, Fla. *Religion:* Presbyterian. *Home:* 1011 Locust St., West Palm Beach, Fla. 33405. *Office:* 7111 Norton Ave., West Palm Beach, Fla. 33405.

CAREER: Whimzies, West Palm Beach, Fla., creator and owner, 1972—. Program director of West Palm Beach Recreation Department, 1966—.

WRITINGS: (With Kathryn Robinette Moyer) *Creating Rug Art with Remnants* (textbook), Crown, 1975. Contributor to journals.

WORK IN PROGRESS: A collection of art work by talented artists and craftsmen using rug remnants.

SIDELIGHTS: Betty Rayside told *CA:* "I became involved in rug art and writing about the craft by making wall pictures for friends. My hobby led to writing articles for magazines . . . and my own manufacturing company."

* * *

READ, Ritchard 1914-

PERSONAL: Born April 17, 1914, in Antwerp, Belgium; son of Gordon (a chief engineer) and Julia (Quistwater) Read; married Elsie Parsons, April 28, 1940; children: Julia (Mrs. John Matthews), Ritchard Walter John. *Education:* Educated in France and England. *Politics:* "Nil." *Religion:* "Nil." *Home:* 43 Holly Ter., Hensingham, Whitehaven, Cumbria CA28 8RF, England.

CAREER: British Army, Medical Corps, 1934-45, leaving service as sergeant; scientific officer for United Kingdom Atomic Energy Authority, 1948-74. *Member:* Marine Biological Association.

WRITINGS: The Living Sea, Penguin, 1974. Contributor to specialized journals.

SIDELIGHTS: Read writes that he is ". . . very much worried about the present lack of concern over the thoughtless pollution of the sea—the cradle of life . . . All politicians should be forced to undergo a comprehensive course in biology . . . I am [presently] studying the rapid disappearance of plankton as well as the lowly and humble barnacle."

* * *

RED BUTTERFLY
See LAURITSEN, John (Phillip)

* * *

REDD, (Newton) Lawrence 1941-

PERSONAL: Born October 18, 1941, in Blytehville, Ark.; son of Andrew (a laborer) and Elsie (a cook; maiden name, McElwee) Redd; married Betty Ann Morrow (an educator), May 24, 1964; children: Ronald, Terri Ann. *Education:* Tennessee State University, B.A., 1964; Michigan State University, M.A., 1971. *Residence:* Lansing, Mich. *Office:* Department of Television and Radio, Michigan State University, 320 Union Bldg., East Lansing, Mich. 48824.

CAREER: WVOL (radio), Nashville, Tenn., disc jockey, 1963-64; high school teacher in the public schools of Grand Rapids, Mich., 1964-69; Michigan State University, WKAR (radio), East Lansing, producer/director, 1970-72; member of department of TV and Radio. Former vice-president of Tawasi Athletic Association, Grand Rapids, Mich.; member of public relations board of Greater Lansing Urban League. *Member:* College of Communication Arts Alumni Association of Michigan State University.

WRITINGS: Rock Is Rhythm and Blues, Michigan State University Press, 1974.

* * *

REDFIELD, Clark
See McMORROW, Fred

* * *

REE, Jonathan 1948-

PERSONAL: Born March 4, 1948, in Bradford, England; son of Harry (a teacher) and Hetty (Vine) Ree. *Education:* University of Sussex, B.A. (first class honors), 1969; Oxford University, B.Phil., 1971, B.Litt., 1973. *Politics:* Socialist. *Religion:* None. *Residence:* Oxford, England. *Agent:* John Wolfers, 3 Regent Sq., London WC1, England. *Office:* Humanities Resource Centre, Middlesex Polytechnic at Hendon, London NW4 4BT, England.

CAREER: Middlesex Polytechnic at Hendon, London, England, lecturer in philosophy, 1972—.

WRITINGS: Descartes, Allen Lane, 1974. Coordinating editor of *Radical Philosophy*.

WORK IN PROGRESS: Research on present histories of philosophy, to show that they systematically misrepresent philosophical theory and practice, and to produce a general account of the nature and importance of historical understanding.

SIDELIGHTS: Ree writes: "My main motivation is hatred of the whole institution of academic philosophy, and more positively, to make philosophy serviceable to socialist movements."

REED, A(lfred) H(amish)   1875-1975(?)

December 30, 1875—1975(?); English-born New Zealand book dealer, founder of publishing firm, the House of Reed, and author of books about New Zealand and its history. Obituaries: *AB Bookman's Weekly*, February 17, 1975. (*CA*-9/10)

*   *   *

REED, John L(incoln)   1938-

PERSONAL: Born February 12, 1938, in Alexandria, Pa.; son of James Clair (a farmer) and Julia (a poet; maiden name, Dueno) Reed; married Sharon Kay Frakes (an artist), June 6, 1964; children: David, Steven, Michelle, Kevin, Shawn. *Education:* Pennsylvania State University, B.A., 1962; Kansas State Teachers' College of Emporia, M.A., 1966; University of Hawaii, M.A., 1973; University of Utah, Ph.D., 1975. *Politics:* Independent. *Religion:* Independent. *Home:* 5041 South 2600 W., Roy, Utah 84067.

CAREER: U.S. Air Force, career officer, 1962-75, leaving service as captain; served in Vietnam, Hawaii, Okinawa, and Utah as munitions staff officer. Lecturer at University of Maryland (Far East Division), 1966-69.

WRITINGS: The Newest Whore of Babylon: The Emergence of Technocracy—A Study in the Mechanization of Man, Branden Press, 1975.

WORK IN PROGRESS: The Religious Suppression of the Social Jesus.

SIDELIGHTS: Reed writes: "I was motivated to write my book on technocracy by abrasive experiences with the technocratic military in Vietnam and at the University of Hawaii. I was stimulated to write the book on Jesus by observing the bureaucratic distortions of organized religion."

*   *   *

REED, Kenneth   1944-

PERSONAL: Born September 19, 1944, in Honey Brook, Pa.; son of Daniel B. (a trucker) and Phebe (Yoder) Reed. *Education:* Eastern Mennonite College, B.A., 1966. *Religion:* "Jesus Freak." *Address:* Box 62-A, Paradise, Pa. 17562.

CAREER: Christian Living (Mennonite family magazine), Scottdale, Pa., assistant editor, 1969-72; author. *Wartime service:* Teacher of English as foreign language in Asahikawa, Japan, as member of PAX (Mennonite organization), 1966-69.

WRITINGS: Mennonite Soldier, Herald Press, 1974; (contributor) *People Pieces* (short stories), Herald Press, 1974. Author of plays, "Joseph Put That Gun Down," 1973, and "Anabaptist," 1975, both first produced in Lancaster, Pa., at Dutch Family Festival. Contributor to journals.

WORK IN PROGRESS: A novel on the theme of faith ("is it real or cooked-up in true believers' heads"), set in the Mennonite-Amish community; an anthology of Amish-Mennonite-Hutterite literature.

SIDELIGHTS: "Although it may be hard for those outside of tight religious communities to understand," Reed wrote, "literary use of profanity, sex scenes, and critical examination of the church and its doctrines are still very emotional issues.

"My aim in writing is not to destroy community or church. It is to tell the truth. The temptation is to veer to the right and do rip-off studies and pieces on ethnic life which will confirm what some tourists or ethnic 'lovers' have always thought of 'the plain people.' Or to veer to the left and do propaganda pieces for the church which confirm what the church and community would perhaps like to think they are like. However, the whole unvarnished truth is a very hot fire that burns up these half-truths."

AVOCATIONAL INTERESTS: Gardening, Pennsylvania Dutch language.

*   *   *

REES, Dilwyn
See DANIEL, Glyn (Edmund)

*   *   *

REESE, Willis L(ivingston) M(esier)   1913-

PERSONAL: Born June 16, 1913, in Bernardsville, N.J.; son of William Willis (a real estate agent) and Augusta (Bliss) Reese; married Frances Stevens, June 26, 1937; children: William W., Frances (Mrs. Antonio Olivieri), John R., George B., Alexander S. *Education:* Yale University, B.A., 1935, LL.B., 1938. *Politics:* Republican. *Religion:* Episcopalian. *Home:* 345 Meadowview Ave., Hewlett, N.Y. 11557. *Office:* Columbia University Law School, 435 West 116th St., New York, N.Y. 10027.

CAREER: Admitted to Bar of State of New York, 1938; law clerk to Judge Thomas Swan, 1938-39; Winthrop, Stimson, Putnam & Roberts (law firm), New York, N.Y., associate, 1939-41; Columbia University, Law School, New York, N.Y., assistant professor, 1946-47, associate professor, 1947-48, professor, 1948-57, Charles Evans Hughes Professor of Law, 1957—, director of Parker School of Foreign and Comparative Law, 1955—. Member of board of directors, New York Legal Aid Society, 1951-71; president of board of trustees, Millbrook School, 1968—; president of Five Towns United Fund, 1959, chairman of board of directors, 1958, 1960; lecturer, Hague Academy of International Law, 1964; U.S. delegate to Hague Conference on Private International Law, 1956, 1960, 1964, 1968, 1972; chairman of Community Action for Legal Services, 1967-70; chairman of New York Law Revision Committee, 1973—. *Military service:* U.S. Army, 1941-46; became captain. *Member:* Institute of International Law (associate member), Hague Academy of International Law, International Law Association, Association for the Study of Comparative Law, Inc. (secretary; member of board of directors), Joint Conference on Legal Education (first vice-president), American Bar Association, American Society of International Law, American Foreign Law Association (president, 1964-67), American Association for the United Nations (president of Five Towns Chapter, 1962-63), American Academy of Political Science (life member), Association of the Bar of City of New York, Phi Beta Kappa, Century Association, Union Club, Rockaway Hunting Club. *Awards, honors:* LL.D., University of Louvain, 1972.

WRITINGS: Reporter Restatement (second): Conflict of Law, American Law Institute, 1971; (with Maurice Rosenberg) *Cases and Materials on Conflict of Laws*, 6th edition (Reese was not associated with earlier editions), Foundation Press, 1971. Member of editorial board of law book department, Little Brown, 1956—.

WORK IN PROGRESS: Ten lectures for 1976 session of Hague Academy of International Law.

REEVES, Thomas Charles 1936-

PERSONAL: Born August 25, 1936, in Tacoma, Wash.; son of Clifford (a laborer) and Dorothy L. (Christ) Reeves; married Kathleen Garrison, February 1, 1958; children: Kirsten, Elizabeth, Margaret. *Education:* Pacific Lutheran University, B.A., 1958; University of Washington, Seattle, M.A., 1961; University of California, Santa Barbara, Ph.D., 1966. *Politics:* Democrat. *Home:* 929 Russet, Racine, Wis. 53405. *Office:* Department of History, University of Wisconsin, Parkside, Wis.

CAREER: Pacific Lutheran University, Tacoma, Wash., instructor in history, 1962-63; University of Colorado, Colorado Springs, assistant professor of history, 1966-70; University of Wisconsin, Parkside, associate professor, 1970-73, professor of history, 1973—. *Military service:* U.S. Marine Corps Reserve, 1954-58. *Member:* American Historical Association, Organization of American Historians. *Awards, honors:* Research grants from El Pomar Investment Co., 1968, 1970, and American Philosophical Society, 1970; Stephen Greene Press award, 1971, for the best article in *Vermont History.*

WRITINGS: Freedom and the Foundation: The Fund for the Republic in the Era of McCarthyism, Knopf, 1969; (editor) *Foundations Under Fire,* Cornell University Press, 1970; (editor) *McCarthyism,* Dryden, 1973; (contributor) Harry J. Sievers, editor, *Six Presidents from the Empire State,* Sleepy Hollow Foundation, 1974; *Gentleman Boss: The Life of Chester Alan Arthur,* Knopf, 1975. Contributor to *Encyclopaedia Britannica;* contributor of articles and book reviews to historical journals.

WORK IN PROGRESS: Cold War Liberals: Americans for Democratic Action, 1947-1960.

AVOCATIONAL INTERESTS: Trumpet playing, history of modern jazz, chess.

* * *

REGELSKI, Thomas A(dam) 1941-

PERSONAL: Born May 4, 1941, in Goshen, N.Y.; son of Adam Thomas (a supermarket executive) and Barbara (Miller) Regelski. *Education:* State University of New York College at Fredonia, B.S., 1962; Columbia University, M.A., 1963; Ohio University, Ph.D., 1970. *Home:* 10021 Patterson Lane, Fredonia, N.Y. 14063. *Office:* Department of Music Education, Mason Hall, State University of New York College at Fredonia, Fredonia, N.Y. 14063.

CAREER: Music teacher in public elementary schools in Bemus Point, N.Y., 1963-66, and Middletown, N.Y., 1965-66; State University of New York College at Fredonia, instructor, 1966-68, associate professor of music and chairman of music education, 1970—. *Member:* Music Educators National Conference, American Society for Aesthetics, Association for Humanistic Psychology, New York State School Music Association, Phi Kappa Phi.

WRITINGS: (With Robert Diamond and Donald Lehr) *A Systems Approach to Music for the Non-Major* (monograph), State University of New York College at Fredonia, 1971; *Principles and Problems of Music Education,* Prentice-Hall, 1975. Author of "Music in the Western World," a programmed independent study course, "Style in Art," a programmed text with audio-visual material, 1971, and "Fundamentals of Music Theory: A Programmed Course," 1973, all for State University of New York College at Fredonia. Contributor to music education and psychology journals.

WORK IN PROGRESS: Practical Approaches to Music Activities for Middle School; Designing and Using Instructional Media in Music Education.

SIDELIGHTS: Regelski writes: "My motivations are simply to improve the quality of arts education. I have been strongly influenced ... by the psychology of Zen and Taoism as propounded by Alan Watts. Most profound of all, however, has been the influence of Abraham Maslow, and his followers in the 'Third Force' of Humanistic Psychology ... In all cases, my interests are to assist young people self-actualize through arts experiences; and training teachers in arts education provides a wide influence." *Avocational interests:* Studying Zen Buddhism and Taoism, photography.

* * *

REGENSTEIN, Lewis 1943-

PERSONAL: Born February 21, 1943, in Washington, D.C.; son of Louis (an attorney and Helen (Moses) Regenstein. *Education:* University of Pennsylvania, B.A., 1965; Emory University, M.A., 1968; also studied at Institute for American Universities, Aix-en-Provence, France. *Religion:* Jewish. *Home and office:* 1765 P St. N.W., Washington, D.C. 20036.

CAREER: Central Intelligence Agency, Washington, D.C., intelligence officer, 1966-71; Fund for Animals, Inc., Washington, D.C., executive vice-president, 1972—.

WRITINGS: The Politics of Extinction: The Shocking Story of the World's Endangered Wildlife, Macmillan, 1975. Contributor to magazines and newspapers, including *Washington Post, New York Times, Los Angeles Times* and *Washington Star.* Wildlife editor of *Environmental Quality.*

WORK IN PROGRESS: An analysis of the history, strengths and weaknesses, administration, and probable future effectiveness of the Endangered Species Act of 1973.

* * *

REGINALD, R(obert) 1948-

PERSONAL: Born February 11, 1948, in Fukuoka, Japan; son of Roy Walter (a U.S. Air Force major) and Betty Jane (Kapel) Burgess. *Education:* Gonzaga University, A.B. (honors), 1969; University of Southern California, M.S. in L.S., 1970. *Politics:* "Monarchist." *Religion:* "Founder, Church of the Holy Toad." *Home and publishing office:* Hill House, 379 Edgerton Dr., San Bernardino, Calif. 92405. *Office:* Periodicals Department, California State College, San Bernardino Library, 5500 State College Pky., San Bernardino, Calif. 92407.

CAREER: California State College, San Bernardino, periodicals librarian, 1970—; *Forgotten Fantasy* (magazine), Hollywood, Calif., associate editor, 1970-71; Newcastle Publishing Co., Inc., Hollywood, editor, 1971—; Borgo Press, San Bernardino, publisher and editor, 1975—. *Member:* Science Fiction Writers of America, Science Fiction Research Association, Fantasy Association, William Morris Society and Kelmscott Fellowship, Society for Creative Anachronism, Mythopoeic Society.

WRITINGS—Editor: Stella Nova: The Contemporary Science Fiction Authors, Unicorn & Son, 1970, published as *Contemporary Science Fiction Authors,* Arno, 1975; (with M. R. Burgess) *Cumulative Paperback Index: 1939-1959,* Gale, 1973; (with Douglas Menville) *Ancestral Voices: An Anthology of Early Science Fiction,* Arno,

1975. Editor of "Forgotten Fantasy Library" series, Newcastle, 1973—; and "Supernatural and Occult Fiction" series, Arno, 1976.

WORK IN PROGRESS: Editing *Cumulative Paperback Index: 1960-1969, Cumulative Paperback Index: 1970-1974*, and a book tentatively entitled *Science Fiction and Fantasy Literature: A Checklist, With Contemporary Science Fiction Authors II*, for Gale; editing two untitled anthologies, for Arno; compiling *The TV Index*; revising *Stokvis' Manual of History*; writing a "Star Trek" parody for publication by Borgo Press.

* * *

REIGER, John F(ranklin) 1943-

PERSONAL: Born June 10, 1943, in Augusta, Ga.; son of Anthony C. (a physician) and Sally (Dance) Reiger; married Andrea Gladys Becker (a registered nurse), December 26, 1970. *Education:* Duke University, B.A., 1965; University of Florida, M.A., 1966; Northwestern University, Ph.D., 1970. *Office address:* Department of History, University of Miami, P.O. Box 248194, Coral Gables, Fla. 33124.

CAREER: University of Miami, Coral Gables, Fla., assistant professor, 1970-75, associate professor of history, 1975—. *Member:* American Historical Association, Organization of American Historians, Forest History Society, Western History Association, Florida Historical Society, Historical Association of Southern Florida, Phi Alpha Theta.

WRITINGS: (Editor) *The Passing of the Great West: Selected Papers of George Bird Grinnell* (National Historical Society book club selection), Winchester Press, 1972; *American Sportsmen and the Origins of Conservation*, Winchester Press, 1975. Contributor of articles to *Florida Historical Quarterly, Tequesta, National Wildlife*, and *Sports Afield.*

SIDELIGHTS: Reiger told *CA:* "I consider myself mainly an 'environmental historian,' one who studies man's past relationship to his natural environment. My second book, *American Sportsmen and the Origins of Conservation*, a scholarly presentation, documents the fact that American sportsmen—those who hunted and fished for recreation rather than commerce or necessity—were the real spearhead of the conservation movement."

* * *

REINCHELD, Bill 1946-

PERSONAL: Born February 10, 1946, in Lancaster, Ohio; son of William A. (a machinist) and Virginia (Smith) Reincheld; married Laren Gail Eisenberg (a teacher), May 26, 1968; children: Nathan Allen. *Education:* Attended Asbury College, 1964-67; Oklahoma City University, B.A., 1968; Asbury Theological Seminary, M.Div., 1971. *Home address:* Route 3, Box 240, Proctorville, Ohio 45669.

CAREER: Ordained minister by United Methodist Church, 1972; pastor of Methodist churches in Martinsville, Ohio, 1969-71, South Webster, Ohio, 1971-74, and Proctorville, Ohio, 1974—.

WRITINGS: Get It Straight (for young people), C.S.S. Publishing, 1974.

* * *

REISS, Stephen (Charles) 1918-

PERSONAL: Surname is pronounced "rice"; born August 7, 1918, in London, England; son of Richard Leopold and Celia (Butts) Reiss; married Elizabeth Gladden, January 17, 1942; children: Nicholas, Bridget. *Education:* Attended Balliol College, Oxford, and Chelsea School of Art. *Home:* 10 Market Cross Pl., Aldeburgh, Suffolk, England.

CAREER: W. E. Duits Ltd. (art dealers), London, England, librarian, 1950-54; Aldeburgh Festival of Music and the Arts, Aldeburgh, Suffolk, England, manager, 1954-71; Fanfare for Europe (national art festival celebrating entry into Common Market), Arts Council, London, director, 1972-73; London Symphony Orchestra, London, administrator, 1973—. Director of Ceylon and Indian Planters' Association Ltd., and New Sylbet Tea Estates Ltd. *Military service:* British Army, Intelligence Officer in Infantry, 1939-45; became captain. *Awards, honors:* Officer of Order of the British Empire, 1973, for service to the arts.

WRITINGS: Aelbert Cuyp, New York Graphic Society, 1975. Author of exhibition catalogs for Aldeburgh Festival of Music and the Arts. Contributor to *Burlington.*

WORK IN PROGRESS: Research on Dutch seventeenth-century painting.

SIDELIGHTS: Reiss writes: "I wished to become a painter but studying painting is almost as satisfying. I write not as a professional but only to communicate discoveries which I think may be useful."

* * *

REMSBERG, Charles A(ndruss) 1936-

PERSONAL: Born March 7, 1936, in Hutchinson, Kan.; son of Harmon Wilson (a physician) and Laura (Andruss) Remsberg; married Bonnie Kohn (a writer and television interviewer), September 14, 1958; children: Jennifer, Richard. *Education:* Northwestern University, B.S.J., 1958, M.S.J. (with distinction), 1959. *Politics:* Independent. *Religion:* Protestant. *Home:* 1521 Kirk St., Evanston, Ill. 60202. *Agent:* Robert Lescher, 155 East 71st St., New York, N.Y. 10021. *Office:* Bylines, Inc., 1521 Kirk St., Evanston, Ill. 60202.

CAREER: Associated Press, Chicago, Ill., reporter and rewriter, 1957-58; *Chicago Sun-Times*, Chicago, Ill., reporter and rewriter, 1959-60; free-lance writer, 1960—. Consultant to U.S. Office of Economic Opportunity, Ford Foundation, U.S. Office of Education, and President's Commission on the Causes and Prevention of Violence. *Member:* International Platform Association, Society of Magazine Writers. *Awards, honors:* Sidney Hillman Award, 1969, for excellence in magazine writing; Penney-Missouri Award, 1974, for excellence in women's interest journalism.

WRITINGS: The New Look of Organized Crime, National Research Bureau, 1962; *Behind the Cotton Curtain: A Study of Mississippi*, Presbyterian National Board of Missions, 1963; (with Daniel Walker) *Rights in Conflict*, Bantam, 1968; (with wife, Bonnie Remsberg, Raymond Mack, and others) *Our Children's Burden*, Random House, 1968; *School without Lunch*, New Community Press, 1969.

Work is represented in anthologies, including: *Treasury of Tips for Writers*, edited by Marvin Weisbord, Writer's Digest, 1965; *America's Troubles: A Case Book on Social Conflict*, edited by Howard E. Freeman and Norman R. Kurtz, Prentice-Hall, 1969; *Smiling Through the Apocalypse*, edited by Harold Hayes, McCall Corp., 1970.

Contributor to educational curricula packages prepared by public school systems, colleges, government agencies, and the Consumer's Union. Contributor of about five hundred articles to national magazines, including *Esquire, Reader's Digest, Good Housekeeping, Saturday Review, Playboy, Reporter, Redbook*, and *Seventeen*.

WORK IN PROGRESS: Baby Doe: An American Woman, for Morrow.

AVOCATIONAL INTERESTS: Badminton, films.

* * *

RESICK, Matthew C(larence) 1916-

PERSONAL: Born February 18, 1916, in South Fork, Pa.; son of Martin (a laborer) and Anna (Mehall) Resick; married Lovina Senseman, August 30, 1941; children: Thomas J., Patricia Ann, Cathy Jo. *Education:* Ashland College, B.A., 1941; Ohio State University, M.A., 1947, Ph.D., 1952. *Politics:* Democrat. *Religion:* Roman Catholic. *Home:* 7702 Diagonal Rd., Kent, Ohio 44240. *Office:* School of Health, Physical Education and Recreation, Kent State University, Kent, Ohio 44242.

CAREER: Kent State University, Kent, Ohio, assistant professor, 1948-52, associate professor, 1952-56, professor of health, physical education and recreation, 1956—, and associate dean of School of Health, Physical Education and Recreation, 1971—. *Military service:* U.S. Army, 1942-46; became major. *Member:* National College Physical Education Association, American Alliance for Health, Physical Education and Recreation (fellow), American School Health Association (fellow), Ohio Association for Health, Physical Education and Recreation. *Awards, honors:* Meritorious award from Ohio Association for Health, Physical Education and Recreation, 1967.

WRITINGS: (With B. Seidel and J. Mason) *Modern Administration of Physical Education*, Addison-Wesley, 1970, revised edition, 1975; *A Case Study Workbook for Modern Administrative Practices in Physical Education and Athletics*, Addison-Wesley, 1970; (with Seidel) *Physical Education: An Overview*, Addison-Wesley, 1972; (with Carl E. Erickson) *Intercollegiate and Interscholastic Athletics for Men and Women*, Addison-Wesley, 1975. Contributor to journals.

AVOCATIONAL INTERESTS: Travel, bridge.

* * *

RETTIG, Edward B(ertram) 1940-

PERSONAL: Born November 8, 1940, in Seattle, Wash.; son of Roy Edward and Mildred (Hegdahl) Rettig; married Elizabeth Cantey (a special education tutor), June 7, 1968; children: Kelli Anne, Jay Austin. *Education:* Princeton University, A.B., 1962; Princeton Theological Seminary, B.D., 1965; graduate study at University of Hamburg, 1965-66; Fuller Theological Seminary, Ph.D., 1974. *Home:* 1380 Lorain Rd., San Marino, Calif. 91108. *Office:* Deacon-Rettig, 4605 Lankershim Blvd., Suite 203, North Hollywood, Calif. 91602.

CAREER: Ordained minister of the Presbyterian Church, 1966; assistant pastor in Bethlehem, Pa., 1966-69; Associates for Behavior Change (consultants, publishers, and distributors in the field of behavior modification), North Hollywood, Calif., partner, 1973—; Deacon-Rettig (psychotherapy and parent-education workshops), North Hollywood, Calif., psychological assistant, 1974—. *Member:* American Psychological Association, California State Psychological Association.

WRITINGS: ABCs for Parents, Associates for Behavior Change, 1973; *ABCs for Teachers*, Associates for Behavioral Change, 1975.

WORK IN PROGRESS: ABCs for Managers, publication expected in 1976.

* * *

RETTIG, Jack L(ouis) 1925-

PERSONAL: Born March 12, 1925, in Louisville, Ky.; son of Adam J. and Clara C. (Rode) Rettig; married June A. Hugger, December 1, 1945; children: Richard H. *Education:* Evansville College, B.S., 1949; San Diego State College (now San Diego State University), M.S., 1956; University of California, Los Angeles, Ph.D., 1961. *Home:* 3155 Northwest McKinley Dr., Corvallis, Ore. 97330. *Office:* Department of Business Administration, Oregon State University, Corvallis, Ore. 97331.

CAREER: United Engineering Corp., Alameda, Calif., marine electrician, 1942-43; Convair, San Diego, Calif., administrator, 1951-58; Oregon State University, Corvallis, assistant professor, 1961-64, associate professor, 1964-67, professor of business administration, 1967—. Fulbright fellow at University of Ghana, 1969-70. *Military service:* U.S. Navy, 1943-46, 1950-51; became lieutenant junior grade. *Member:* American Academy of Management, American Society for Personnel Administration, Pacific Northwest Personnel Management Association, Beta Gamma Sigma, Pi Gamma Mu.

WRITINGS: Career: Exploration and Decision, Prentice-Hall, 1974. Editor of *Northwest Business Management*, 1963-65.

WORK IN PROGRESS: A book on organizational behavior for American Management Association.

* * *

REVAL, Jacques
See LAVER, James

* * *

RHODES, David 1946-

PERSONAL: Born December 6, 1946, in Des Moines, Iowa; son of Luther and Ruth Rhodes. *Education:* Marlboro College, B.A.; University of Iowa, M.F.A. *Residence:* Wisconsin. *Agent:* Lois Wallace, 118 East 61st St., New York, N.Y. 10021.

CAREER: Novelist.

WRITINGS–Novels: *The Last Fair Deal Going Down*, Atlantic, 1972; *The Easter House*, Harper, 1974; *Rock Island Line,* Harper, 1975.

* * *

RHODES, Evan H. 1929-

PERSONAL: Born January 7, 1929, in New York, N.Y.; son of Max and Beatrice (Levine) Rubenstein; married Daphne Bunker, September 7, 1957 (died June 4, 1962). *Education:* Brooklyn College (now Brooklyn College of the City University of New York), B.A., 1952; New York University, M.A., 1960. *Home:* 4 Pinder Lane, Key West, Fla. 33040. *Agent:* Dick Duane, 159 West 53rd St., New York, N.Y. 10019. *Office:* 1 Minetta Lane, New York, N.Y. 10012.

CAREER: Editor, screen reader, advertising copy-writer;

free-lance writer. *Military service:* U.S. Naval Reserve, 1947-51. *Member:* Dramatists Guild, Authors League of America, Alumni Federation of New York University.

WRITINGS: (With Merle Miller) *Only You, Dick Daring! Or, How to Write One Television Script and Make $50,-000,000, A True Life Adventure*, Morrow, 1964; (editor) James Kirkwood, *American Grotesque: An Account of the Clay Shaw-Jim Garrison Affair in the City of New Orleans*, Simon & Schuster, 1970; (editor) James Leo Herlihy, *The Season of the Witch*, Simon & Schuster, 1971; *The Carrion Eaters*, Stein & Day, 1974; *The Prince of Central Park*, Coward, 1975.

WORK IN PROGRESS: A television script, "Open Road"; *Suffer the Little Children*, a historical novel.

SIDELIGHTS: Rhodes writes: "*Dick Daring* concerned itself with the insanities and inequities in the TV industry, *The Carrion Eaters* with sex and survival, and *The Prince of Central Park* is an allegory of modern man's need to return to a simpler, more pastoral and more optimistic view of life. I sculpt as a hobby and have a faltering command of French."

* * *

RICE, C(harles) Duncan 1942-

PERSONAL: Born October 20, 1942, in Aberdeen, Scotland; son of James Inglis (a physician) and Jane Meauras (Scroggie) Rice; married Susan Wunsch (a university dean), July 2, 1967. *Education:* University of Aberdeen, M.A. (first-class honors), 1964; University of Edinburgh, Ph.D., 1969. *Politics:* Melbourne Whig. *Religion:* Deist. *Office:* Office of the Dean, Saybrook College, Yale University, New Haven, Conn. 06520.

CAREER: Henry Fellow at Harvard University, 1965-66; University of Aberdeen, Aberdeen, Scotland, lecturer in history, 1966-70; Yale University, New Haven, Conn., assistant professor, 1969-75, associate professor of history, 1975—, dean of Saybrook College, 1972—. *Member:* British Association of American Studies, American Historical Association, Organization of American Historians. *Awards, honors:* American Council of Learned Societies Fellow at Yale University, 1969-70; Morse Fellow, 1974-75.

WRITINGS: The Rise and Fall of Black Slavery, Harper, 1975. Contributor to *Historical Journal, Journal of American Studies*, and *Northern Scotland*.

WORK IN PROGRESS: Two monographs on Scottish responses to slavery as contributions to study of Scotland's position in the Atlantic world; study of Anglo-American reform movements.

SIDELIGHTS: Rice told *CA:* "[I] have been specially fascinated by the development of the whole Atlantic world, or rather north Atlantic world, as a total civilization. . . . Still retain roots in the northeast of Scotland, where I keep a permanent house. Even from that bastion of stability, [I] cannot avoid the conviction that Western culture is quickly collapsing, and that the academic profession is to blame for this." *Avocational interests:* Squash.

* * *

RICE, Martin P(aul) 1938-

PERSONAL: Born January 4, 1938, in Philadelphia, Pa.; son of David (an engineer) and Vivian (Shaplin) Rice; married Brigette Krusche, May 15, 1964 (divorced, 1974); mar-

ried Kathleen Baker, July 4, 1975; children: David William, Jonas Paul. *Education:* University of Pennsylvania, B.A., 1963; Free University of Berlin, graduate study, 1963-64; Vanderbilt University, M.A., 1969, Ph.D., 1971. *Religion:* Jewish. *Home:* 505 Forest Hills Blvd., Knoxville, Tenn. 37916. *Office:* Department of Russian, University of Tennessee, Knoxville, Tenn. 37916.

CAREER: University of Tennessee, Knoxville, assistant professor, 1971-73, associate professor of Russian, 1973—. *Military service:* U.S. Army, 1958-60. *Member:* American Association for the Advancement of Slavic Studies, American Association of Teachers of Slavic and East European Languages, North American Dostoevsky Society (executive secretary, 1975—), South Atlantic Modern Language Association, South Central Modern Language Association, Southern Conference on Slavic Studies, Southern Comparative Literature Association (president, 1975—). *Awards, honors:* International Research and Exchanges Board exchange student to Union of Soviet Socialist Republics, 1971.

WRITINGS: (Translator from the Russian) Dmitrij Cizevskij, *Comparative History of Slavic Literatures*, Vanderbilt University Press, 1971; *Valery Briusov and the Rise of Russian Symbolism*, Ardis, 1975.

WORK IN PROGRESS: F. M. Dostoevsky: A Bibliography of Non-Slavic Critical Literature, 1900-1974, for University of Tennessee Press.

* * *

RICH, (David) Gibson 1936-

PERSONAL: Born December 19, 1936, in New York, N.Y.; son of Robert Heaton (a municipal bond trader) and Ruth (Ainscough) Rich. *Education:* Attended University of Chicago, 1953-54; University of California, Berkeley, B.A., 1958; graduate study at University of Colorado, 1958-61. *Home address:* Box 2142, Santa Cruz, Calif. 95063.

CAREER: School bus driver, camp counselor, carpenter's helper, construction worker, farm laborer, practical nurse, employment agency counselor, and community development worker; elementary and high school teacher in Santa Cruz, Calif., 1969—. *Member:* Phi Beta Kappa.

WRITINGS: Firegirl (children's picture book), Feminist Press, 1972. Poems anthologized in *Poems Read in the Spirit of Peace and Gladness*, edited by Tove Neville, Peace & Gladness Co-op Press, 1966; *Cannery Row*, edited by Merrie Garoutte, Polygon Press, 1971; *Along with All the Other Once Loved Things*, edited by J. F. Hill, Religious Arts Guild, 1972.

WORK IN PROGRESS: Several children's picture book stories.

SIDELIGHTS: Gibson Rich told *CA:* "I write for all the wrong reasons: to fulfill the early expectations of parents and teachers, to make money, to achieve immortality—and for all the right ones: to tickle the oppressor's foot, to celebrate the sun, tidepools, autumn leaves and other mysteries, and to express my thanks to those pine trees which have waved to me bravely in storms."

* * *

RICH, Joe 1935-

PERSONAL: Born March 12, 1935, in Berlin, Germany; son of Martin Sally (a teacher) and Erna (Kraft) Rich; married Shirlye Lewis, January 12, 1957 (divorced, 1967); married Margaret Daniel, August 19, 1967; children: Renata, Libya, Megan, Catherine. *Education:* University of Melbourne, B.A., 1957. *Politics:* "Bathwater Left." *Religion:* Agnostic. *Home:* 26 Marquis St., Ashburton, Melbourne, Australia. *Office:* School of Humanities and Social Sciences, Royal Melbourne Institute of Technology, Melbourne, Australia.

CAREER: Clerk at Titles Office in Melbourne, and part-time professional actor with Melbourne Radio and Melbourne Union Theatre Repertory Co., 1957-58; teacher at high schools in Victoria, Australia, 1959-63; supply teacher in London, England, 1964; teacher at Cukurova Lisesi, Adana, Turkey, 1964-65; high school teacher in Victoria, 1965-66; Royal Melbourne Institute of Technology, Melbourne, Australia, lecturer in history, 1967—. *Member:* Victorian Historical Association, Australian Historical Association.

WRITINGS: Asia's Modern Century, Longman, 1970; (with J. S. Hagan and others) *Australia and Britain in the Nineteenth Century,* Longman, 1974; *The Australianization of John Bull,* Longman, 1974. Contributor to history and politics journals.

WORK IN PROGRESS: G. W. L. Marshall-Hall and Melbourne Society, 1891-1915, completion expected in 1977.

* * *

RICHARDS, John 1939-

PERSONAL: Born January 2, 1939, in Bournemouth, England; son of Stanley and Bronwen (Masters) Richards; married Rosemary Best, October 30, 1965; children: Paul John. *Education:* University of Durham, B.A., 1960; Ridley Hall, Cambridge, graduate study, 1961-63; Emmanuel College, Cambridge, certificate of education, 1964. *Office:* Canford School, Canford Magna, near Wimborne, Dorset, England.

CAREER: Ordained priest of Church of England, 1965; curate in Fordingbridge, England, 1964-67, Bitterne Park, England, 1967-68, Southbourne, England, 1968-70, and Chesterton, England, 1971-73; Canford School, Canford Magna, England, assistant chaplain, 1973—. Senior research fellow, Queen's College, Birmingham, England, 1970-71. *Military service:* British Army, 1964-68; served as chaplain. *Member:* Institute of Religion and Medicine (life member), Guild of Health (life member), Guild of St. Raphael (life member), St. Luke's Medical Fellowship (associate member), East India Sports and Public Schools' Club (life member).

WRITINGS: But Deliver Us from Evil: An Introduction to the Demonic Dimension in Pastoral Care, Seabury, 1974. Contributor to religious journals.

WORK IN PROGRESS: Research on the Christian ministry of exorcism.

SIDELIGHTS: But Deliver Us from Evil grew out of Richards' involvement as secretary of an Anglican conference on exorcism. He writes: "I wrote it, incidentally, purely because I knew the great need for it, and did it as a matter of duty rather than because I am fascinated with the subject—which I'm not! As a result, while I try to live the life of an ordinary school chaplain and to leave the subject alone, I am regarded as an authority on it, and do a fair amount of speaking to theological students and others, and behind the scenes act as an adviser on clergy training. I am primarily a teacher and trainer and am *not* an exorcist! I

venture into print when films like the "Exorcist" appear or our recent Barnsley-case, and try, by writing and correspondence to clear up misunderstanding."

* * *

RICHARDS, Victor 1918-

PERSONAL: Born June 4, 1918, in Fort Worth, Tex.; son of Jules K. (a teacher) and Minnie (Certin) Richards; married Jennette O'Keefe, June 7, 1941; children: Lane Kress, Victoria Burris, Victor Fredrick, Peter C. *Education:* Stanford University, B.A., 1935, M.D., 1939. *Politics:* Variable. *Religion:* Christian. *Home:* 2714 Broadway, San Francisco, Calif. 94115. *Office:* 3838 California St., San Francisco, Calif. 94118.

CAREER: Private practice of medicine in San Francisco, Calif., 1943—; Stanford University School of Medicine, Stanford, Calif., professor of surgery, 1954-59, head of department, 1954-59, clinical professor of surgery, 1959—; Children's Hospital, San Francisco, Calif., chief of surgery, 1960—; University of California School of Medicine, San Francisco, clinical professor of surgery, 1964—. Commonwealth research fellow at Harvard University, 1950-51. President of Victor Richards, M.D., Inc., 1970—. *Member:* International Society of Surgeons, American Surgical Association, American Thoracic Association, American College of Surgeons, Society of University Surgeons, Pacific Coast Surgical Association, Pan-Pacific Surgical Association, Sigma Xi, Alpha Omega Alpha.

WRITINGS: Surgery for General Practice, Mosby, 1955; *Cancer: The Wayward Cell,* University of California Press, 1972. Editor of *Oncology,* 1967—; member of editorial board of *American Journal of Surgery,* 1953—, *Journal of Continuing Medical Education,* 1970—, and *Journal of Family Practice,* 1972—.

WORK IN PROGRESS: Designing a new audio-visual teaching device for new approaches to visual education.

* * *

RICHARDSON, Charles E(verett) 1928-

PERSONAL: Born December 23, 1928, in Aledo, Ill.; son of Riley F. (a farmer) and Velma P. (Neal) Richardson; married Mary A. Newton (a secretary), December 23, 1947; children: Leigh, Chuck. *Education:* Southern Illinois University, A.B., 1950, M.S., 1951; University of Michigan, M.P.H., 1952; University of California, Los Angeles, Ed.D., 1959. *Politics:* Democrat. *Home:* 1501 Taylor Dr., Carbondale, Ill. 62901. *Office:* School of Medicine, Southern Illinois University, Carbondale, Ill. 62901.

CAREER: Southern Illinois University, Carbondale, assistant professor, 1957-62, associate professor, 1962-68, professor of health, education and medicine, 1968—, assistant provost, 1971-72, associate dean of School of Medicine, 1973—. Visiting professor at University of California, Los Angeles, 1965, and at University of Hawaii, 1968. Consultant to U.S. Department of Health, Education and Welfare, to Job Corps, and to White House Conference on Children and Youth. Member of board of directors of Illinois Heart Association, 1965-68, and of Illinois Public Health Association, 1967-70. *Military service:* U.S. Army, Armored Division Medical Detachment, 1952-53. *Member:* American Public Health Association, American College Health Association, American School Health Association, American Association for Health, Physical Education and Recreation.

WRITINGS: (With D. L. Farnsworth and F. V. Hein) *Perspectives on Living*, Scott, Foresman, 1962; (contributor) *Synthesis of Research in Selected Areas of Health Education*, School Health Education, 1963; (contributor) Dwight W. Allen, editor, *The Teacher's Handbook*, Scott, Foresman, 1971; (with others) *Living: Health, Behavior, and Environment*, Scott, Foresman, 5th edition (Richardson was not associated with earlier editions), 1970, 6th edition, 1975. Contributor to *Teaching about Smoking and Health*, 1964, and to professional journals.

WORK IN PROGRESS: A college health text, completion expected in 1976.

* * *

RICHARDSON, John Adkins 1929-

PERSONAL: Born October 24, 1929, in Gillette, Wyo.; son of John Wesley (an optometrist) and Joyce (a governess; maiden name, Adkins) Richardson; married Charlene Conley, September 5, 1952 (divorced); married Betty Crain (a professor of English), October 8, 1971; children: (first marriage) Christopher, Robin (son). *Education:* Eastern Washington State College, B.A., 1951; Columbia University, M.A., 1952, Ed.D., 1957. *Home:* 802 West High St., Edwardsville, Ill. 62025. *Office:* School of Art and Design, Southern Illinois University, Edwardsville, Ill. 62025.

CAREER: State University of New York College at Geneseo, assistant professor of art, 1957-58; Fresno State College (now California State University, Fresno), assistant professor of art, 1958-59; Southern Illinois University, Edwardsville, assistant professor, 1959-62, associate professor, 1962-69, professor of art, 1969—. *Military service:* U.S. Army, illustrator for Joint Staff Intelligence, 1952-54; served in Pacific theater. *Member:* American Society for Aesthetics, College Art Association of America.

WRITINGS: Modern Art and Scientific Thought, University of Illinois Press, 1971; *Art: The Way It Is*, Abrams, 1974; (contributor) Philip Ritterbush and Martin Green, editors, *Technology as Institutionally Related to Human Values*, Acropolis Books, 1974. Contributor to *Journal of Aesthetics and Art Criticism, British Journal of Aesthetics, Diogenes,* Art Journal, *Journal of Aesthetic Education, School Arts,* and *Art Education.*

WORK IN PROGRESS: A book on American art from 1865 to the present; research on the image of women through history, in terms of the history of ideas.

SIDELIGHTS: Richardson writes: "I have always considered my research and creative activity adjunct to my teaching career. I am always on the lookout for things to drive home the essentials that are fundamental to understanding and this has caused all of my vocations to turn into professional sidelines. In connection with a research project on the relationships between fine arts and vernacular ones I became interested in comic strips; now I'm being offered money to draw and write them. I have a queer feeling of walking downstairs backwards—as if my destiny were already fulfilled."

* * *

RICHARDSON, Nola 1936-

PERSONAL: Born November 12, 1936, in Los Angeles, Calif.; daughter of Oscar and Jessie Mae (Anderson) Smith; divorced, 1969; children: Nolan, Virgil, Anthony, Julie, Dawn. *Education:* Compton Junior College, certificate in management, 1973. *Home:* 10426 Crenshaw Blvd., #1, Inglewood, Calif. 90303. *Office:* Drew Postgraduate Medical School, 12012 Compton Ave., Los Angeles, Calif. 90059.

CAREER: North American Rockwell, Downey, Calif., administrative secretary, 1954-70; Drew Postgraduate Medical School, Los Angeles, Calif., administrative assistant, 1970-73; Central Medical Group, Los Angeles, Calif., executive secretary and supervisor, 1973-74; Drew Postgraduate Medical School, administrative assistant, 1974—. Member of Poetry in the Schools program, 1974-75. Has given poetry readings in colleges and universities.

WRITINGS: When One Loves (poems), Celestial Arts, 1974; *Even in a Maze* (poems), Crescent, 1975. Contributor of poems and medical articles to magazines.

WORK IN PROGRESS: Poet Know Thyself; *Of You*, a poem in book form; *To Share and Care and Then Let Go*, love poems; *Especially in My Dreams*, in poem form.

SIDELIGHTS: Nola Richardson writes: "Writing was stimulated from a need of verbal communication whereby I discovered it was also selftherapy . . . I tend to respond on a hyper-emotional level venting and creating through my writing. I therefore have written on quite a few subjects; such as life in general, sociology, economics, racial and childhood experiences—some relating from a self-therapy aspect in addition to my continued writings of love."

BIOGRAPHICAL/CRITICAL SOURCES: Scoop, June 13, 1974; *George Washington Surveyor*, June 14, 1974; *Los Angeles Times*, July 28, 1974, December 8, 1974; *Orange County Evening News*, September 18, 1974; *The Grapevine*, November, 1974.

* * *

RICHEY, David 1939-
(John Davey, Richard Johnson)

PERSONAL: Born July 22, 1939, in Flint, Mich.; son of Lawrence D. and Helen (Millhouse) Richey; married Carol Warner, August 26, 1961; children: Kimberley, Stacey, David, Jr., Guy. *Education:* Attended high school in Michigan. *Politics:*" "Not active in politics." *Religion:* Protestant. *Home and office:* 2028 West Lake Rd., Clio, Mich. 48420.

CAREER: Full-time free-lance outdoor and travel writer and photographer. Operates a booking agency for travel, fishing, photographic, and hunting trips in Clio, Mich., 1972—. *Military service:* U.S. Naval Reserve, 1956-59.

WRITINGS: (With Jerome Knap) *Getting Hooked on Fishing*, Scribner, 1974; *A Child's Introduction to the Outdoors*, Pagurian Press, 1975. Also author of *The Complete Steelheader*, published by Stackpole Books, and *The Digest Book of Trout Fishing*, published by Digest Books. Contributor of over 650 articles to outdoor magazines, occasionally under pseudonyms, John Davey and Richard Johnson.

WORK IN PROGRESS: Sea Run, with Paul Bernsen; *The Shakespeare Guide to Great Lakes Fishing*; and three additional books.

* * *

RICHTER, Irving 1911-

PERSONAL: Born October 3, 1911, in New York, N.Y.; son of Nathan (a tailor) and Rose (Brenner) Richter; married Betty Jennings, June 1, 1945 (died, 1960); married

Jeanne Dishong (a free-lance voice performer), August 1, 1963; children: Lora (Mrs. Frank Ferguson), Charles, David, James; (stepsons) Bradley, Niles, Lance. *Education:* University of Wisconsin, B.A., 1934; graduate study at Columbia University, 1936, Wayne State University, 1955, 1963 and University of Brussels, 1963-64; Cambridge University, Ph.D., 1974. *Politics:* "Radical." *Religion:* None. *Office:* Department of Urban Studies, Federal City College, 939 E St. N.W., Washington, D.C. 20004.

CAREER: U.S. Federal Emergency Relief Administration, Washington, D.C., senior clerk, 1934-36; Works Progress Administration, Washington, D.C., special assistant and assistant director of transient division, 1936-38; U.S. Department of Labor, Wage and Hour Division, Washington, D.C., 1938-43, junior economist, 1938-39, senior economist in litigation assistance unit, 1940-43; United Automobile, Aerospace, and Agricultural Implement Workers of America, Washington, D.C., research officer, 1943, legislative representative and director of political action, 1943-49; Organization Services, Inc. (services for labor unions), Detroit, Michigan., founder and president, 1949-63; Mount Holyoke College, South Hadley, Mass., visiting lecturer in labor and comparative economic systems, 1966-68; Federal City College, Washington, D.C., associate professor, 1968-75, professor of labor relations and political economy, 1975—. Lecturer at Earlham College, Florida International University, University of Detroit, and University of Aston. Has appeared on radio and television programs.

MEMBER: American Economic Association, American Association of University Professors, Industrial Relations and Research Association, National Capital Labor History Society, Artus.

WRITINGS: Political Purpose in Trade Unions, Allen & Unwin, 1973. Contributor to social science and political science journals, and to newspapers.

WORK IN PROGRESS: Research on Adam Clayton Powell, Jr.; on income policies; on racism; and on the merger of the American Federation of Labor and the Congress of Industrial Organizations.

SIDELIGHTS: Richter has traveled throughout the Caribbean and Europe; he has given lecture tours in the United Kingdom, Czechoslovakia, and Hungary. He writes that he is ". . . especially interested in the Cuban revolution. Have visited there, once before Castro (under Batista) once since Castro won (1961—I was waiting to shake his hand when the telegram announcing the United States' break in relations was handed to him); and plan to visit there again."

BIOGRAPHICAL/CRITICAL SOURCES: Quarterly Review of Economics and Business, spring, 1975.

* * *

RICKETTS, C(arl) E(verett) 1906-

PERSONAL: Born August 19, 1906, in Rockford, Ohio; son of George Ira (a salesman) and Lucinda (Adams) Ricketts; married Helen Regan, March 10, 1930; children: Carl Donald, Patricia Jeanne (Mrs. V. E. Connors), Pauline Carroll (Mrs. J. L. Ralph), Treva Eileen (Mrs. George L. Withers). *Education:* Attended South Dakota School of Mines and Technology, 1954-60. *Politics:* Independent. *Religion:* Protestant. *Address:* Route 4, Box 117A58, Milton-Freewater, Ore. 97862.

CAREER: Has held positions as mining geologist, assayer and researcher, and worked in minerals exploration; presently factory representative for line of two-way radios;

writer. *Military service:* U.S. Army, Cavalry, 1924-27. U.S. Navy, 1950-54; served in Korea; became chief petty officer. *Member:* National Rifle Association, American Legion; also local rifle and pistol clubs.

WRITINGS: El Lobo and Spanish Gold, Madrona, 1973. Contributor to journals. Editor of *Old Prospector's Newsletter*, 1960-65.

WORK IN PROGRESS: A romantic novel containing Mexican Revolutionary history, *Salgado's Gold.*

SIDELIGHTS: Ricketts told *CA:* "Have always been pretty much of an outdoorsman, working as cowhand and bronc stomper, some rodeo work, at one time one of the top saddle makers and designer of Western leather goods in the United States. Always prospected for gold and silver and rare minerals."

* * *

RIDDERBOS, Herman N(icolaas) 1909-

PERSONAL: Born February 13, 1909, in Oosterend, Belgium; son of Jan (a professor of theology) and Gesina (Velthuis) Ridderbos; married Jacoba A.G. Kok, September 18, 1934; children: Geertruy Cornelia, Gezina Roelien, Johanna, Cora. *Education:* Theological Seminary, Kampen, Netherlands, Theol.B., 1931; Free University of Amsterdam, Theol. Dr., 1936. *Politics:* "Anti-Revolutionary Party." *Home:* Fernhoutstrasse 14, Kampen, Netherlands.

CAREER: Minister of Reformed Churches in Eefde, Netherlands, 1934-39, and Rotterdam, Netherlands, 1939-42; Theological Seminary, Kampen, Netherlands, professor of New Testament, 1934-74, named professor emeritus, 1974, Professor extraordinarius, 1975—. *Awards, honors:* Named Knight of Order of the Nederlandse Leeuw, 1959.

WRITINGS: Comment on Galatians, Eerdmans, 1953; *When the Time Had Fully Come*, Eerdmans, 1957; *Paul and Jesus*, Presbyterian Publishing, 1958; *The Coming of the Kingdom*, Presbyterian Publishing, 1962; *Paul: Concept of His Theology*, Eerdmans, 1975. Author of books in Dutch language, including commentaries on Paul's epistles to the *Romans*, 1959, *Colossians*, 1960, and *Pastoral Epistles*, 1967. Editor-in-chief of *Reformed Weekly.*

* * *

RIDRUEJO, Dionisio 1913(?)-1975

1913(?)—June 29, 1975; Spanish politician, orator, poet, and author of books critical of Franco regime. Obituaries: *New York Times*, June 30, 1975.

* * *

RIEWALD, J(acobus) G(erhardus) 1910-

PERSONAL: Born August 15, 1910, in Doesburg, Netherlands; son of Gerhardus Marie (a coppersmith) and Gerritje (Hendriks) Riewald; married Elisabeth Maria Bergefurt, December 31, 1941; children: Lucia (Mrs. W. Mutsaers), Jacobus, Elisabeth (Mrs. P. H. M. van Genugten), Hildebrand. *Education:* University of Michigan, graduate study, 1951; U.S. Office of Education, diploma, 1951; University of Nijmegen, Ph.D., 1953. *Religion:* Roman Catholic. *Home:* "Froonacker," 35 Westerse Drift, Haren (Gr.), Netherlands. *Agent:* Author Aid Associates, 340 East 52nd St., New York, N.Y. 10022. *Office:* Faculty of Arts Building, 2-1 Grote Kruisstraat, University of Groningen, Groningen, Netherlands.

CAREER: Teacher in elementary and secondary schools in

Arnhem, 1929-34, Ede, 1934-41, Doesburg, 1941-46, and Nijmegen, 1946-60; University of Groningen, Groningen, Netherlands, instructor in English, 1960-66, reader in English and American Literature, 1966—. Part-time instructor at Katholieke Leergangen, 1956-63, Gelderse Leergangen, 1959-60, Fryske Akademy, 1963—; examiner in English Language Institute of University of Michigan, 1955-68. *Member:* Dutch Modern Language Association (chairman of English section and member of general committee, 1955-61; vice-chairman, 1958-59), Maatschappij der Nederlandse Letterkunde, Modern Language Association of America, European Association for American Studies, Netherlands-America Institute, Thijmgenootschap, Netherlands Association for American Studies.

WRITINGS: Sir Max Beerbohm, Man and Writer: A Critical Analysis with a Brief Life and a Bibliography, prefatory letter by Max Beerbohm, Nijhoff, 1953, Greene, 1961; (with L. Grooten and T. Zwartkruis) *A Book of English and American Literature,* Paul Brand, Volume I, 1953, 8th edition, 1972, Volume II, 1953, 7th edition, 1970; (with Grooten and Zwartkruis) *The Student's Companion to a Book of English and American Literature,* Paul Brand, Volume I, 1955, 6th edition, 1968, Volume II, 1955, 6th edition, 1970; *Word Study: A Graded English Vocabulary for Dutch Secondary Schools,* Paul Brand, Volume I, 1957, 9th edition, 1975, alternative edition, 1971, revised alternative edition, 1972, Volume II, 1958, 10th edition, 1974, Volume III, 1960, 8th edition, 1975; (with A. J. de Witte, S. G. van der Meer, and J. P. van der Linden) *Moedertaalautomatismen en het Onderwijs in de Levende Talen,* Malmberg, 1960; (compiler) *Max in Verse: Rhymes and Parodies by Max Beerbohm,* Greene, 1963; *Reynier Jansen of Philadelphia, Early American Printer: A Chapter in Seventeenth-Century Nonconformity,* Wolters-Noordhoff, 1970; *Nieuw Engels Woordenboek: De meest voorkomende Engelse woorden en uitdrukkingen in zinsverband,* Paul Brand, 1974; (editor and author of introduction) *The Surprise of Excellence: Modern Essays on Max Beerbohm,* Shoe String, 1974; (with Grooten) *Perspectives in British and American Literature: A Survey for Students,* Paul Brand, 1974.

WORK IN PROGRESS: Compiling *Literary Caricatures by Max Beerbohm: Homer to Huxley; The Critical Reception of American Literature in the Netherlands in the Nineteenth Century: An Annotated Bibliography; Dutch Translations of Nineteenth-Century American Literature; The Latin Correspondence of Willem Sewel, 1653-1720.*

* * *

RIMBERG, John 1929-

PERSONAL: Born March 10, 1929, in New York, N.Y.; son of Adolph J. (a businessman) and Anita (a businesswoman; maiden name, Meyer) Rimberg; married Joella Richardson (a social worker), August 22, 1954; children: Daniel, Alexander, Janet. *Education:* Harvard University, B.A. (cum laude), 1950; Columbia University, M.A., 1952, Ph.D., 1959. *Politics:* Democrat. *Religion:* Jewish. *Home:* 1406 Walnut St., Lumberton, N.C. 28358. *Office:* Department of Sociology and Geography, Pembroke State University, Pembroke, N.C. 28372.

CAREER: Van Sant-Dugdale, Inc. (advertising agency), Baltimore, Md., director of research, 1960-64; Ernest Dichter International Institute for Motivation Research, Croton-on-Hudson, N.Y., assistant to the president, 1965-70; East Carolina University, Greenville, N.C., visiting

associate professor of sociology, 1970-71; Pembroke State University, Pembroke, N.C., professor of sociology and chairman of department of sociology and geography, 1971—, chairman of department of American Indian studies, 1973-74, director of community development program, 1973-74, director of program in minority schools biomedical research support, 1973—, director of project on film of the Lumbee Indians, 1974—, counselor to military personnel, 1974—. *Member:* American Sociological Association, American Association for Public Opinion Research, American Marketing Association (president of Baltimore chapter, 1963-64), Southern Sociological Society, North Carolina Sociological Association, Kiwanis (trustee of Pembroke chapter, 1974—).

WRITINGS: (With Paul Babitsky) *The Soviet Film Industry,* Praeger, 1955; *The Motion Picture in the Soviet Union: 1918-1952,* Arno, 1973. Author of film, "This Is the Soviet Union Today," with Douglas Lanford, 1960.

WORK IN PROGRESS: The Soviet Film Industry: 1953-1964, completion expected in 1976.

* * *

RINKOFF, Barbara Jean (Rich) 1923-1975

January 25, 1923—February 18, 1975; Social worker and author of books for children and young adults. Obituaries: *New York Times,* February 22, 1975; *AB Bookman's Weekly,* March 17, 1975; *Publishers Weekly,* April 28, 1975. (CA-19/20)

* * *

RIOTTE, Louise 1909-

PERSONAL: Born September 25, 1909, in Cloverport, Ky.; daughter of Rudolf (a theater owner) and Louisa (Bauer) Helbach; married Carl de Succa Riotte (a writer and photographer), July 8, 1939; children: Eugene, Madonna (Mrs. Frank Weger). *Education:* Ardmore Business College, graduate, 1928. *Residence:* Charlotte, Vt.

CAREER: Has worked as a secretary, illustrator and photographer; writer. *Member:* National Writers Club, Northern Nut Growers Association.

WRITINGS: Egg Craft, Drake, 1973; *The Complete Guide to Growing Berries and Grapes,* Garden Way Publishing, 1974; *Nuts for the Food Gardener,* Garden Way Publishing, 1975; *Secrets of Companion Planting for Successful Gardening,* Garden Way Publishing, 1975; *Planetary Planting* (Book-of-the-Month Club selection), Simon & Schuster, in press. Contributor of articles to *Organic Gardening, Flower and Garden, Gems and Minerals, Lady's Circle, Popular Archaeology, True West, Golden West, Mobile Home Life, American Astrology,* and other periodicals.

WORK IN PROGRESS: Research for book on domestic animals for food, show and sale.

* * *

RIPLEY, (Sidney) Dillon 1913-

PERSONAL: Born September 20, 1913, in New York, N.Y.; son of Louis Arthur (a businessman and farmer) and Constance Baillie (Rose) Ripley; married Mary Moncrieffe Livingston, August 18, 1949; children: Julie Dillon (Mrs. Robert S. Ridgely), Rosemary Livingston, Sylvia McNeill. *Education:* Yale University, B.A., 1936; Harvard University, Ph.D., 1943. *Religion:* Protestant Episcopal. *Home:*

2324 Massachusetts Ave. N.W., Washington, D.C. 20008. *Agent*: Russell & Volkening, Inc., 551 Fifth Ave., New York, N.Y. 10017. *Office*: Smithsonian Institution, Washington, D.C. 20560.

CAREER: Academy of Natural Sciences of Philadelphia, Philadelphia, Pa., zoological collector, 1936-39; American Museum of Natural History, New York, N.Y., volunteer assistant, 1939-40; Smithsonian Institution, Washington, D.C., assistant curator of birds, 1942; Yale University, New Haven, Conn., lecturer, 1946-52, assistant professor, 1949-55, associate professor of zoology, 1955-61, professor of biology, 1961-64, associate curator of Peabody Museum of Natural History, 1946-52, curator, 1952-64, director, 1959-64; Smithsonian Institution, secretary, 1964—. Leader of expeditions to India and Nepal, 1946-47, Nepal, 1948-49, and Netherlands New Guinea, 1960. Member of board of directors of International Union for the Preservation of Nature, 1964. Trustee of White Memorial Foundation, Conservation Foundation, and Henry Francis du Pont Winterthur Museum; member of board of directors of American Security & Trust Co. and several other institutions. *Wartime service*: Office of Strategic Services, serving overseas as civilian, 1942-45.

MEMBER: National Academy of Sciences, International Council for Bird Preservation (president, 1958—), World Wildlife Fund (chairman of U.S. appeal), American Ornithologists' Union, American Association for the Advancement of Science (fellow), American Association of Museums (vice-president, 1962-66), International Council of Museums (vice-president, 1968-72), Society for the Study of Evolution, American Society of Naturalists, Society of Systematic Zoology, British Ornithologists Union, Cooper Ornithological Society, Wilson Ornithological Society; honorary or corresponding member of ornithological societies in Europe, South Africa, India, and New Zealand; Sigma Xi.

AWARDS, HONORS: Fulbright fellow in Northeast Assam, 1950; Guggenheim, National Science Foundation, and Yale University fellow in Indonesia, 1954; Gold Medal of New York Zoological Society, 1966; Gold Medal of Royal Zoological Society (Belgium), 1970. Honorary M.A., Yale University, 1961; D.H.L. from Marlboro College, 1965, and Williams College, 1972; D.Sc. from George Washington University, 1966, Catholic University of America, 1968, University of Maryland, 1970, Cambridge University, 1974, Brown University, 1975; LL.D. from Dickinson College, 1967, Hofstra University, 1968, Yale University, 1975.

WRITINGS: *Trail of the Money Bird: 30,000 Miles of Adventure With a Naturalist*, Harper, 1942; *Search for the Spiny Babbler: An Adventure in Nepal*, Houghton, 1952; *A Paddling of Ducks* (autobiographical), Harcourt, 1957, reprinted Smithsonian Institution Press, 1969; (with D. S. Rabor) *Notes on a Collection of Birds from Mindoro Island, Philippines*, Peabody Museum of Natural History, Yale University, 1958.

(Compiler with Lynette L. Scribner) *Ornithological Books in the Yale University Library, Including the Library of William Robertson Coe*, Yale University Press, 1961; *A Synopsis of the Birds of India and Pakistan, Together with Those of Nepal, Sikkim, Bhutan and Ceylon*, Bombay Natural History Society, 1961; (with editors of Life) *The Land and Wildlife of Tropical Asia*, Time, Inc., 1964; *A Systematic and Ecological Study of Birds of New Guinea*, Peabody Museum of Natural History, Yale University,

1964; (with Gorman M. Bond) *The Birds of Socotra and Abd-el-Kuri* (booklet), Smithsonian Institution Press, 1966; (with Salim A. Ali) *Handbook of the Birds of India and Pakistan, Together With Those of Nepal, Sikkim, Bhutan and Ceylon*, Oxford University Press, ten Volumes, 1968-74; *The Sacred Grove: Essays on Museums*, Simon & Schuster, 1969.

(With Gorman M. Bond) *Systematic Notes on a Collection of Birds from Kenya* (booklet), *Smithsonian Institution Press, 1971; (with Peter Caws)* The Bankruptcy of Academic Policy, *edited by Philip C. Ritterbush, Acropolis Books, 1972;* The Paradox of the Human Condition, *Tata Foundation and McGraw, 1975.*

Author of prefaces and forewords to books by others, and Peabody Museum of Natural History publications on birds of Western Papuan Islands, Cuba, Angola, India, and elsewhere.

WORK IN PROGRESS: A second edition of *Synopsis of the Birds of India and Pakistan*, for Bombay Natural History Society; *Rails of the World*, Smithsonian Institution Press.

SIDELIGHTS: "Became interested in natural history in school days," Ripley writes. "Also interested in art, archaeology, and foreign affairs." Various of his books have been published in England, Sweden, and Denmark.

*   *   *

RITCHIE, (Harry) Ward 1905-
(Peter Lum Quince)

PERSONAL: Born June 15, 1905, in Los Angeles, Calif.; son of Mossom George (a druggist) and Effie (Palmer) Ritchie; married Janet H. Smith, July 15, 1934 (divorced, 1946); married Marka Skidmore, September 2, 1950; children: (first marriage) Jonathan B., Duncan Ward. *Education*: Attended Stanford University, 1926-27, and University of the South, 1927; Occidental College, A.B., 1928; graduate study at University of Southern California, 1928, and California Institute of Technology, 1942. *Home*: 34 Emerald Bay, Laguna Beach, Calif. 92651.

CAREER: Ward Ritchie Press, Los Angeles, Calif., president, 1932-74. Instructor at Occidental College, 1936-39, and at Scripps College, 1942-46; Foote, Cone & Belding, Los Angeles, Calif., production manager, 1943-50. Member of board of University of California at Los Angeles Library of Arts and Architecture, 1947—, and Friends of Huntington Library, 1960—; president of Library Patrons of Occidental College, 1961-73, and Los Angeles Library Association, 1969-71. *Member*: Association Typographique International, American Institute of Graphic Arts, PEN, Printing Historical Society, Zamorano Club, Roxburghe Club, Rounce and Coffin Club. *Awards, honors*: L.H.D., Occidental College, 1960.

WRITINGS: *John Gutenberg: A Fanciful Story of the Fifteenth Century* (fiction), Ward Ritchie Press, 1940; *Job Printing in California*, G. Dawson, 1955; *William Morris and the Kelmscott Press*, Stanford University Press, 1967; *Modern Fine Printing*, Clark Library, University of California, 1968; *Influences of California Printing*, Clark Library, University of California, 1970; *Bookmen and Their Brothels*, Zamorano, 1970; *The Dohenys of Los Angeles*, Dawson's Book Shop, 1974; *Francois-Louis Schmied: French Painter, Engraver and Printer*, University of Arizona Press, 1975; *Macintyre*, Laguna Verde Imprenta, 1975.

Under pseudonym Peter Lum Quince: *Left-Handed Doctor*, Dent, 1957; *At Doctor Mac's: A Documentary Entertainment*, Dent, 1958. Author of poems privately printed in limited editions: *XV Poems for the Heath Broom*, 1934; *The Year's at the Spring*, 1936; *Fragments of Yesterday*, 1941. Also author of *A Few More for the Powells*, 1949, and *A Summer Sequence*, 1950.

Contributing editor of *Dolphin*.

* * *

RIVEL, Isa De
    See CUEVAS, Clara

* * *

ROACH, Hildred   1937-

PERSONAL: Born March 14, 1937, in Charlotte, N.C.; daughter of Howard (a farmer) and Pearl (Caldwell) Roach. *Education:* Fisk University, B.A., 1957; Yale University, M.M., 1962; also studied at Juilliard School of Music, 1958-59, Oakland University, summer, 1966, and University of Ghana, summer, 1969. *Politics:* Democrat. *Religion:* Protestant. *Home:* 10700 Cavalier Dr., Silver Spring, Md. 20901. *Office:* Department of Music, Federal City College, 916 G St. N.W., Washington, D.C. 20001.

CAREER: Tuskegee Institute, Tuskegee, Ala., instructor in music, 1957-58, 1959-60; Fayetteville State College (now University), Fayetteville, N.C., instructor in music, 1962-66; Howard University, Washington, D.C., assistant professor of music, 1966-67; Virginia State College, Petersburg, assistant professor of music, 1967-68; Federal City College, Washington, D.C., associate professor of piano and history of Afro-American music, 1968—. *Member:* Music Educators National Conference, Black Caucus of Music Educators Association, Afro-American Opportunities Association, National Education Association, National Association for the Advancement of Colored People, Fisk University Alumni Association, Yale University Alumni Association.

WRITINGS: Black American Music: Past and Present, Crescendo, 1973; (with Marva Cooper) *A Resource Guide to Black Music*, Crescendo, in press.

* * *

ROACH, Marilynne K(athleen)   1946-

PERSONAL: Born July 15, 1946, in Cambridge, Mass.; daughter of William Lawrence (a house painter) and Priscilla (Dunbar) Roach. *Education:* Massachusetts College of Art, B.F.A., 1968. *Religion:* Christian. *Residence:* Watertown, Mass. 02172.

CAREER: Mosaic Tile Co., Boston, Mass., designer, 1968-70; free lance writer and illustrator in Watertown, Mass., 1970—.

WRITINGS: The Mouse and the Song, Parents' Magazine Press, 1974. Contributor to *Boston Globe*.

WORK IN PROGRESS: An adaptation of the satirical Roman version of Quintus Horatius Flaccus' city mouse and country mouse, *Two Roman Mice*, for Crowell; research on American folk lore, on the supernatural, on eighteenth-century London, on ancient and local history, on legends of saints, on imaginary countries, on mythology, and on the round of nature.

ROBB, Frank Thomson   1908-

PERSONAL: Born July 19, 1908, in Cape Town, South Africa; son of Frank Thomson (a civil servant) and Mary (Greenshields) Robb; divorced; children: Frank Thomson, Jr. *Education:* Attended high school in Cape Town, South Africa. *Residence:* Cape Peninsula, South Africa. *Office address:* Aquagencies Ltd., Box 202, Rondebosch 7700, South Africa.

CAREER: Law clerk, 1927-32; worked at dam and bridge building and road paving, 1932-38; owner and skipper of fishing boats; operator of a yacht- and ship-broking firm, 1943-64; publisher and writer. *Military service:* South African Artillery, 1939-45; became captain; received Efficiency Decoration, Africa Star, and Italy Star. *Member:* Astronomical Society of South Africa, Royal Cape Yacht Club (life member).

WRITINGS: Master of the Dauntless (novel), Longmans (New York), 1954 (published in England as *Sea Hunters*, Longmans, Green, 1954); *Small Boat Handling in Heavy Weather: A Text*, privately printed, 1969, published as *Handling Small Boats in Heavy Weather*, Adlard Coles, 1970; *Sun-Shot Navigation*, privately printed, 1974; *The Sea Fishermen of the Cape*, Longman, in press. Contributor to newspapers and magazines.

WORK IN PROGRESS: Star-Shot; A Diagram of God; humorous books; an autobiography.

SIDELIGHTS: Robb wrote that he was brought up on the Cape Town docks, and took to the sea as soon as he was able to cast off the painter of a fisherman's dinghy—when the fisherman wasn't looking. "After that came tin canoes, inshore cruisers, and offshore cruisers and racers—a way of life pursued during intervals snatched from earning a living ashore." Of *Sun-Shot Navigation* he says, "a simple form enabling the veriest novice to find his position in mid-ocean. . . . I was tempted to sub-title it *Astro-Navigation for the Mentally Retarded*. . . . The minimum requirement is a sextant. This will enable latitude to be determined. The addition of a watch makes it possible to ascertain longitude as well." Robb's ambition is to acquire a forty-five-foot cruising yacht.

* * *

ROBECK, Mildred C(oen)   1915-

PERSONAL: Born July 29, 1915, in Walum, N.D.; daughter of Archie Blane (a rancher) and Mary Henrietta (Hoffman) Coen; married Martin J. Robeck, Jr. (a teacher), June 2, 1936; children: Martin Jay, Donna Jane (Mrs. Henry D. Thompson), Bruce Wayne. *Education:* Attended University of Wisconsin, 1935-36, and University of Illinois, 1941; University of Washington, Seattle, B.A. (cum laude), 1950, M.Ed., 1954, Ph.D., 1958. *Politics:* Democrat. *Religion:* Congregationalist. *Home:* 320 Ful Vue Dr., Eugene, Ore. 97405. *Office:* College of Education, University of Oregon, Eugene, Ore. 97403.

CAREER: Teacher in public schools in Seattle, Wash., 1946-58; University of California, Santa Barbara, assistant professor of education, 1958-64; California State Department of Education, Sacramento, research consultant, 1964-67; University of Oregon, Eugene, associate professor, 1967-70, professor of education, child development and learning, 1970—. Consultant to Umatilla Indian Tribes; consultant on early childhood education, McGraw-Hill Book Co. *Member:* International Reading Association, American Association for the Advancement of Science,

American Educational Research Association, National Society for the Study of Education, National Association for the Education of Young Children, Phi Beta Kappa, Pi Lambda Theta.

WRITINGS: (With John A. R. Wilson) *Kindergarten Evaluation of Learning Potential*, McGraw, 1967; *Special Class Programs for Intellectually Gifted Minors*, State of California, 1968; (with Wilson and William B. Michael) *Psychological Foundations of Learning and Teaching*, McGraw, 1969, 2nd edition, 1974; (with Wilson) *Psychology of Reading*, Wiley, 1974.

Contributor: William B. Michael, editor, *Teaching for Creative Endeavor*, Indiana University Press, 1968; John A. Wilson, editor, *Diagnosis of Learning Difficulties*, McGraw, 1971; Leo M. Schell and Paul C. Burns, editors, *Remedial Reading: Classroom and Clinic*, Allyn and Bacon, 1972. Contributor to education journals.

WORK IN PROGRESS: Early Learning: Implications for Teaching, publication by McGraw expected in 1977.

SIDELIGHTS: Mildred Robeck writes: "Travel is addictive for me . . . love to observe and photograph children around world. When nearing forty I realized I had conformed to the wishes of my parents for the first twenty years and the needs of my family for the next twenty years. I resolved to take twenty years for me: hence the Ph.D., the university career, the writing and research. The next twenty? Husband, grandchildren, two more books, an autobiography—in that order."

* * *

ROBERTS, Archibald Edward 1915-

PERSONAL: Born March 21, 1915, in Cheboygan, Mich.; son of Archibald Lancaster and Madeline Ruth (Smith) Roberts; married Florence Snure, September 25, 1940 (divorced February, 1950); married Doris Elfriede White, June 23, 1951; children: (first marriage) Michael James, John Douglas; (second marriage) Guy Archer, Charles Lancaster, Christopher Corwin. *Education:* U.S. Army Command and General Staff College, graduate, 1952; attended U.S. Armed Forces Institute, 1953, and University of Maryland, 1958. *Home:* 2218 West Prospect, Fort Collins, Colo. 80521. *Office:* 480 Savings Bldg., Fort Collins, Colo. 80521.

CAREER: U.S. Army, 1939-65; served in Far East and Europe; retired as lieutenant colonel. Information officer in United States, Japan, and Europe, 1950-58; special projects officer in Germany and United States, 1959-61; participated in U.S. Senate Armed Services Committee hearings, 1962. Co-owner and director of Roberts & Roberts Advertising Agency, 1946-49; director of Committee to Restore the Constitution, 1970—. *Member:* Airborne Association, Reserve Officers Association, Sons of the American Revolution, Sons of the American Colonists. *Awards, honors:* Award of merit from American Academy of Public Affairs, 1967; Good Citizenship Medal from Sons of the American Revolution, 1968; medal of merit from American Legion, 1972.

WRITINGS: Rakkasan, Benson Printing Co., 1955; (with others) *Screaming Eagles: 101st Airborne*, Benson Printing Co., 1957; *The Marne Division*, Konrad Triltsch (Wuerzburg, Germany), 1957; *Victory Denied*, Hallberg, 1966; (compiler) *Peace: By the Wonderful People Who Brought You Korea and Viet Nam*, Educators Publications, 1972; *The Republic: Decline & Future Promise*, Betsy Ross Press, 1975. Contributor to magazines.

SIDELIGHTS: In 1962, Roberts was suspended from active duty for a speech on the U.N. he made before the Daughters of the American Revolution which was deemed improper by the secretary of the army. Roberts began legal action and, in 1964, was restored to his former status with back pay and retroactively promoted to his present rank.

* * *

ROBERTS, Dell
See FENDELL, Bob

* * *

ROBERTS, Rand
See PARHAM, Robert Randall

* * *

ROBINSON, Frank M(elvin), Jr. 1928-

PERSONAL: Born April 30, 1928, in Philadelphia, Pa.; son of Frank M. (a plumber) and Margarette (Righter) Robinson; married Patricia T. Fabyan, February 19, 1955 (died, 1961); children: Nancy A., Lynne T. *Education:* Centre College of Kentucky, B.A., 1950; Springfield College, M.Ed., 1955. *Home:* 133 Cliff Ave., Winthrop, Mass. 02152. *Office:* Department of Recreation Education, Northeastern University, 360 Huntington Ave., Boston, Mass. 02115.

CAREER: State of Connecticut Easter Seal Society for Crippled Children and Adults, assistant director of recreation and camping, 1955-56; Cerebral Palsy Association of Western Massachusetts, director of recreation and camping, 1957-58; Recreation and Park Department, Natick, Mass., superintendent, 1958-64; State of Massachusetts Easter Seal Society, director of recreation and camping, 1965-66; Northeastern University, Boston, Mass., assistant professor, 1967-71, associate professor of recreation education, 1972—. Member of executive board of United Community Services of Boston, 1970-74. *Military service:* U.S. Army, 1952-53; served in Europe. *Member:* National Recreation and Park Association (chairman of New England district, 1964-65), Massachusetts Recreation and Park Society (president, 1966-68), Massachusetts Association for Health, Physical Education, and Recreation (vice-president, 1969).

WRITINGS: Therapeutic Recreation, C. C Thomas, 1974. Contributor to *International Encyclopedia on Higher Education* and to journals.

* * *

ROBINSON, Richard 1945-

PERSONAL: Born July 24, 1945, in New Britain, Conn. *Education:* Attended Yale University. *Office address:* P.O. Box 180, Planetarium Station, New York, N.Y. 10027.

CAREER: Journalist. *Member:* Society of American Magicians.

WRITINGS: Electric Rock: Rock Musicians Guide, Pyramid, 1971; *Kung Fu: The Peaceful Way*, Pyramid, 1974; *The Video Primer*, Links Books, 1974.

WORK IN PROGRESS: A book, with television personality Dick Clark.

* * *

ROBINSON, Willard B(ethurem) 1935-

PERSONAL: Born July 26, 1935, in Sheridan, Wyo.; son

of Ralph Roy (a rancher) and Williey (Bethurem) Robinson; married Margaret Ann Heuermann, June 16, 1954; children: Michael Willard, Carolyn Ann. *Education:* Montana State University, B.Arch., 1958; Rice University, M.Arch., 1960. *Home:* 3808 26th St., Lubbock, Tex. 79410. *Office:* Department of Architecture, Texas Tech University, Lubbock, Tex. 79409.

CAREER: Architectural practice with O. Berg, Jr. and Associates, Bozeman, Mont., 1960-63, and in independent practice, Buffalo, Wyo., 1963; Texas Tech University, Lubbock, instructor, 1963-65, assistant professor, 1965-70, associate professor, 1970-75, professor of architecture, 1975—, curator of historical architecture at museum, 1971—. Restoration architect for Ranching Heritage Center, 1971—; technical expert on restoration for Fort Adams, R.I., 1972—. Member of architecture advisory board of Texas Commission on Arts and Humanities; member of board of review for National Register submissions in Texas. *Member:* Society of Architectural Historians (vice-president of Texas chapter, 1971-72; president, 1972-73), American Association of Museums, Texas State Historical Association, Texas Association of Museums.

WRITINGS: Texas Public Buildings of the Nineteenth Century, University of Texas Press, 1974; *Architecture of Defense: Form and Function in American Military Architecture,* University of Illinois Press, in press. Contributor to *Journal of the Society of Architectural Historians, Southwestern Historical Quarterly, Montana: Magazine of Western History,* and *Rhode Island History.*

WORK IN PROGRESS: Seacoast Military Architecture; Texas Federal Architecture.

SIDELIGHTS: Robinson travels extensively, visiting museums and archives. Most of his work concludes with a plea to preserve architectural heritage. He feels that buildings are cultural resources.

* * *

ROBISON, Bonnie 1924-

PERSONAL: Born August 4, 1924, in Mound City, Kan.; daughter of Gilbert L. (a rancher) and Myrtle (Fouts) Bailey; married Richard Robison (an attorney), February 3, 1950; children: Rand, Leslee. *Education:* Attended Woodbury College, 1941-42. *Politics:* Conservative. *Religion:* Protestant. *Home:* 2625 Allenton Ave., Hacienda Heights, Calif. 91745.

CAREER: Has worked as a secretary; licensed real estate agent. *Member:* Hacienda Golf Club, Atlantis Health Club, Reading Is FUNdamental.

WRITINGS: (With others) *Volleyball,* Lippincott, 1972; *Killer: The Outrageous Hawk* (juvenile fiction), Childrens Press, 1974. Contributor to golfing journals and newspapers.

WORK IN PROGRESS: A novel concerned with lobbying in Sacramento; research on overpopulation, abortion, and compulsive birth control; promoting reading in children.

AVOCATIONAL INTERESTS: Golf, volleyball, raquetball, bridge, gardening, and quilting.

* * *

ROCKWOOD, Joyce 1947-

PERSONAL: Born June 1, 1947, in Ames, Iowa; daughter of Frank Bradford (an Episcopalian priest) and Katherine (Graves) Rockwood; married Charles Hudson (a professor

of anthropology), May 28, 1968. *Education:* University of Georgia, A.B. (cum laude), 1969; also studied at University of Wisconsin. *Residence:* Georgia.

CAREER: Writer. *Member:* Authors Guild of Authors League of America, Southern Anthropological Society, Phi Beta Kappa.

WRITINGS: Long Man's Song (novel), Holt, 1975. Contributor to *Appalachian Journal.*

WORK IN PROGRESS: To Spoil the Sun (tentative title), a novel about the earliest European contact on the coast of southeast United States and the smallpox plague among the Indians that resulted.

SIDELIGHTS: Joyce Rockwood writes: "I consider myself an anthropologist as well as a novelist. In my writing I attempt to draw the reader into the drama of other worlds, real worlds where the characters are as human and as moving and as rational as in our own. I write primarily about the American Indians, setting my stories in the cultures of the past, relying heavily on anthropological and historical research in order to recreate the reality that has since been shattered by the European Invasion. Yet I strive above all to entertain. My purpose is not to teach, but to offer a powerful human experience."

* * *

ROEMER, Milton I(rwin) 1916-

PERSONAL: Born in 1916, in Paterson, N.J.; married; children: two. *Education:* Cornell University, B.A., 1936, M.A., 1939; New York University, M.D., 1940; University of Michigan, M.P.H., 1943. *Office:* School of Medicine, University of California, Los Angeles, Calif. 90024.

CAREER: Diplomate of the National Board of Medical Examiners, 1941, and of American Board of Preventive Medicine and Public Health, 1949; Barnert Memorial Hospital, Paterson, N.J., rotating intern, 1940-41; New Jersey State Department of Health, Trenton, medical officer in Venereal Disease Control Division, 1941-42; Yale University, New Haven, Conn., assistant professor, 1949-50; associate professor of public health, 1950-51; World Health Organization, Geneva, Switzerland, chief of social and occupational health section, 1951-53; Saskatchewan Department of Public Health, Regina, director of medical and hospital services, 1953-56; Yeshiva University, Albert Einstein College of Medicine, New York, N.Y., lecturer in medicine, 1956-57; Cornell University, Ithaca, N.Y., associate research professor, 1957-60, research professor of administrative medicine, 1960-62, director of research at Sloan Institute of Hospital Administration, 1957-62; University of California, Los Angeles, professor of public health, 1962—, professor of preventive medicine, 1962—, head of Division of Medical Care Organization, 1962-64, head of Division of Medical and Hospital Administration, 1965-67, head of Division of Health Administration, 1967-70. Member of U.S. National Subcommittee on Medical Care Statistics, Institute of European Health Services Research (fellow), Institute of Medicine (of National Academy of Sciences), California State Health Department committees on medical care for children, seasonal agricultural workers, and hospital utilization, California Center for Health Services Research (member of policy board, 1968-72), Los Angeles Psychiatric Service (member of board of directors), Los Angeles County Committee on Affairs of the Aging. Consultant to state and federal government agencies, and international organizations. *Wartime service:* U.S. Public Health Service, 1943-51; became senior surgeon; assistant to chief medical officer in War Food Administration, 1943-45, associate in medical care administration to chief of the States Relations Division, 1945-47, director of West Virginia Public Health Training Center and Monongalia County Health Department, 1948-49.

MEMBER: International Epidemiological Association, American Public Health Association (fellow; member of governing council, 1967—), American Sociological Association, American College of Preventive Medicine, California Academy of Preventive Medicine (president, 1972—), Phi Beta Kappa, Sigma Xi, Phi Kappa Phi, Alpha Omega Alpha, Delta Omega.

WRITINGS: Social Factors Influencing American Medical Practice, Cornell University, 1939; A System for Quantitative Appraisal of Voluntary Hospitalization Insurance Plans, University of Michigan, 1942; (with F. D. Mott) Rural Health and Medical Care, McGraw, 1948.

A Health Demonstration Area in El Salvador, World Health Organization, 1951; A Health Demonstration Area in Ceylon, World Health Organization, 1951; (with E. A. Wilson) Organized Health Services in a County of the United States, U.S. Government Printing Office, 1952; Medical Care in Relation to Public Health: A Study of Relationships Between Preventive and Curative Health Services Throughout the World, World Health Organization, 1956; (with Max Shain) Hospital Utilization under Insurance, American Hospital Association, 1959; (editor) Henry E. Sigerist on the Sociology of Medicine, M.D. Publications, 1960; Medical Care Administration: Content, Positions, and Training in the United States, Western Branch, American Public Health Association, 1963; Medical Care in Latin America, Pan American Union, 1963; Health Services in the Los Angeles Riot Area, University of California, Los Angeles, 1965; (with Olive Manning) The Rural Health Services Scheme in Malaysia, Office for the Western Pacific, World Health Organization, 1969; The Organization of Medical Care under Social Security: A Study of the Experience of Eight Countries, International Labour Office, 1969.

(Editor with D. M. Du Bois and S. W. Rich) Health Insurance Plans: Studies in Organizational Diversity, School of Public Health, University of California, Los Angeles, 1970; (with J. W. Friedman) Doctors in Hospitals: Medical Staff Organization and Hospital Performance, Johns Hopkins Press, 1971; Evaluation of Community Health Centres, World Health Organization, 1972; (with R. F. Bridgman) Hospital Legislation and Hospital Systems, World Health Organization, 1973; (with R. W. Hetherington, C. E. Hopkins, and others) Health Insurance Effects, School of Public Health, University of Michigan, 1973; Health Care Systems in World Perspective, University of Michigan, in press; Rural Health Services, Mosby, in press; (with R. J. Roemer) Health Manpower in the Changing Australian Health Services Science, U.S. Department of Health, Education and Welfare, in press. Contributor of about two hundred articles on social and organizational aspects of health services to professional journals.

* * *

ROETT, Riordan Joseph Allenby III   1938-

PERSONAL: Born September 10, 1938, in New York, N.Y.; son of Riordan (a lawyer) and Marion (Underwood) Roett. Education: Columbia University, B.A., 1959, M.I.A., 1962, Ph.D., 1968. Religion: Roman Catholic. Home: 4600 Connecticut Ave. N.W., Washington, D.C.

20008. Office: School of Advanced International Studies, Johns Hopkins University, 1740 Massachusetts Ave. N.W., Washington, D.C. 20036.

CAREER: Vanderbilt University, Nashville, Tenn., assistant professor of political science, 1967-73; Johns Hopkins University, School of Advanced International Studies, Washington, D.C., associate professor of political science and director of Latin American studies, 1973—. Member: American Political Science Association, Latin American Studies Association. Awards, honors: Fulbright grant, 1962-63, for study in Brazil; Ford Foundation foreign area fellowship, 1964-66; Social Science Research Council grant, 1972, and New York foreign area fellowship, 1973, both to Latin America.

WRITINGS: (Editor and contributor) Brazil in the Sixties, Vanderbilt University Press, 1972; The Politics of Foreign Aid in the Brazilian Northeast, Vanderbilt University Press, 1972; Brazil: Politics in a Patrimonial Society, Allyn & Bacon, 1973. Contributor to journals, including International Journal of Politics.

SIDELIGHTS: Roett has resided in Latin America for five of the last twelve years.

* * *

ROFF, William R(obert)   1929-

PERSONAL: Born May 2, 1929, in Scotland; son of Robert H. W. (an engineer) and Isabella Mackie (Anderson) Roff. Education: University of New Zealand, B.A., 1957, M.A., 1959; Australian National University, Ph.D., 1965. Office: Southern Asian Institute, Columbia University, New York, N.Y. 10027.

CAREER: Merchant seaman; editor and writer of radio talks and documentaries; Monash University, Melbourne, Australia, lecturer in Southeast Asian history, 1963-65; University of Malaya, Kuala Lumpur, senior lecturer in history, 1966-69; Columbia University, New York, N.Y., associate professor, 1969-73, professor of history, 1973—. Visiting professor at Yale University, fall, 1971; visiting fellow at Institute of Southeast Asian Studies, Singapore, spring, 1972, and Institute of Advanced Studies, Australian National University, summer, 1974. Member: Association for Asian Studies, Royal Asiatic Society (Malaysian Branch), Royal Commonwealth Society. Awards, honors: Guggenheim Foundation fellowship, 1973.

WRITINGS: Guide to Malay Periodicals, 1876-1941, with Details of Known Holdings in Malaya (monograph), Eastern Universities Press, 1961; (editor and author of introduction) Stories of Sir Hugh Clifford, Oxford University Press (Kuala Lumpur), 1966; The Origins of Malay Nationalism, Yale University Press, 1967; Sejarah Surat Khabar Melayu (title means "History of Malay Newspapers"; monograph), Sinaran Press, 1967; (editor and author of introduction) Stories and Sketches by Sir Frank Swettenham, Oxford University Press (Kuala Lumpur), 1967.

(Contributor) P. M. Holt and others, editors, The Cambridge History of Islam, Cambridge University Press, 1970; (with D. J. Steinberg and others) In Search of Southeast Asia: A Modern History, Praeger, 1971; (compiler and author of introduction) Bibliography of Malay and Arabic Periodicals Published in the Straits Settlements and Peninsular Malay States, 1876-1941, Oxford University Press, 1972; (editor and contributor) Kelantan: Religion, Society, and Politics in a Malay State, Oxford University Press (Kuala Lumpur), 1973; (contributor) Dusan Zbavitel, editor, *The Dictionary of Oriental Literature*, Volume II: *South and Southeast Asia*, Basic Books, 1973; (editor and author of introduction) *The Wandering Thoughts of a Dying Man: The Autobiography of Haji Abdul Majid bin Zainuddin of Malaya*, Oxford University Press, in press. Contributor to journals in his field. General editor of "Oxford in Asia Historical Memoirs," 1973—.

WORK IN PROGRESS: Islam in Southeast Asia: A History.

* * *

ROGER, Mae Durham
(Mae Durham)

PERSONAL: Born in Albany, N.Y.; married Edwin Durham, January 29, 1949 (divorced, 1970); married Sidney Roger (a writer, journalist, and teacher), February 27, 1972. *Education:* Russell Sage College, B.A., 1940; State University of New York at Albany, B.L.S., 1941; graduate study at Columbia University, 1942, New School for Social Research, 1943-45, and University of California, Berkeley, 1959-60. *Home:* 55 Hillside Ave., Mill Valley, Calif. 94941. *Office:* School of Librarianship, University of California, Berkeley, Calif. 94720.

CAREER: New York Public Library, New York, N.Y., librarian, 1942-46; San Francisco State College (now University), San Francisco, Calif., librarian, 1947-59; University of California, Berkeley, lecturer in School of Librarianship, 1959—. Lecturer on children's literature in the United States and Europe. *Member:* American Library Association, Women's National Book Association, California Library Association (council member, 1973-75).

WRITINGS: (Under name Mae Durham) *Tit For Tat and Other Latvian Folk Tales*, Harcourt, 1967; *Tobei: A Japanese Folk Tale*, Bradbury, 1974. Contributor to library and education journals.

WORK IN PROGRESS: Fantasy, children's literature, storytelling, and folklore.

* * *

ROGERS, Donald I(rwin) 1918-

PERSONAL: Born November 17, 1918, in New Hartford, Conn.; son of Ernest Eugene (a manufacturer) and Eva McClellan (Driggs) Rogers; married Marjorie Rae Lawson, January 14, 1937; children: Marilyn (Mrs. Yustin Wallrapp), Donald, Mark, David, Nancy. *Education:* Attended Brown University, 1940-41. *Politics:* Independent. *Religion:* None. *Agent:* Evelyn Singer Agency, P.O. Box 163, Briarcliff, N.Y. 10510. *Office:* Hearst Newspapers, 959 Eighth Ave., New York, N.Y. 10019.

CAREER: Worked as reporter, suburban bureau chief, assistant financial editor, editorial writer, and feature writer for *Journal* and *Evening Bulletin*, both Providence, R.I., 1937-48; *Evening Gazette*, Worcester, Mass., acting chief editorial writer, 1948-50; *New York Herald Tribune*, New York, N.Y., business and financial editor, 1950-66; *Sunday Herald*, Bridgeport, Conn., editor and publisher, 1965-66; *Wall Street Transcript*, New York, N.Y., associate publisher, 1966-68; *Fairfield County Courier*, Norwalk, Conn., editor and publisher, 1968-70; American Economic Foundation, New York, N.Y., president and chief executive officer, 1972-75, member of board of trustees, 1974—. Lecturer; appeared on radio and television shows, including "Longines Chronoscope Show," 1954-55, and "Tex & Jinx Show," 1955-56. Member of board of directors, Scripps

Howard Investment Co., 1973—; member of board of trustees, Union Dime Savings Bank, 1959-70. *Military service:* U.S. Army, 1944-45. *Member:* New York Financial Writers Association (member of board of governors, 1953), Douglaston Yacht Squadron (member of board of governors, 1957), Ex-Members of Squadron A, Sigma Delta Chi (president of New York Chapter, 1956). *Awards, honors:* Loeb Newspaper Award from University of Connecticut, 1959, for series of articles, "What Happened to the Boom?"

WRITINGS: Teach Your Wife to Be a Widow, Holt, 1953, reprinted, U.S. News & World Report Books, 1973; *Save It, Invest It & Retire*, Holt, 1956; *Make Your Income Count*, Holt, 1958; *Financial Facts of Life*, Holt, 1959; *The End of Free Enterprise*, Doubleday, 1966; *The Trials of Jimmy Hoffa*, Regnery, 1970; *How to Beat Inflation by Using It*, Arlington, 1970; *The Day the Market Crashed: October 24, 1929*, Arlington, 1972; *How NOT to Buy a Common Stock*, Arlington, 1972; *Since You Went Away*, Arlington, 1973. Also author of textbook, with Harry E. Figgie, Jr., *A Basic Primer for Cost Reduction*. Author of scripts for syndicated radio show, "Your Money and You," 1955-57. Columnist, Herald Tribune Syndicate, 1951—. Contributor to numerous magazines.

WORK IN PROGRESS: The Coming Revolt by the American Middle Class (tentative title), for Dial.

SIDELIGHTS: Rogers writes: "I have always been disturbed that so many Americans do not understand—*really* understand—the functions of the economic system that, despite its flaws and impediments produced the greatest prosperity in mankind's history, bringing benefits to the greatest number. Much of my writing, therefore, is directed toward the simple illumination of what seems to be a complex matter, but actually is not."

* * *

ROGERS, Rolf E(rnst) 1931-

PERSONAL: Surname legally changed to Rogers, 1954; born August 31, 1931, in Stuttgart, Germany, naturalized U.S. citizen; son of Ernst (an engineer) and Philomena (Deinzer) Rosenberger. *Education:* University of Washington, Seattle, M.A., 1968, Ph.D., 1970. *Home:* 9903-104th St., #1907, Edmonton, Alberta, Canada. *Office:* School of Business Administration, University of Alberta, Edmonton, Alberta, Canada.

CAREER: Management consultant (to clients including Boeing Co., Allied Van Lines, and Government of Canada), in Seattle, Wash., 1955-70; University of Alberta, Edmonton, associate professor, 1970-73, professor of management, 1973—. Has appeared on television and radio programs. *Military service:* U.S. Air Force, 1951-55; served in Korea; became staff sergeant. *Member:* Academy of Management, American Sociological Association, Canadian Association of Administrative Science, Beta Gamma Sigma.

WRITINGS: Max Weber's Ideal Type Theory, Philosophical Library, 1969; *The Political Process in Modern Organizations*, Exposition, 1971; *Organizational Theory*, Allyn & Bacon, 1975. Contributor of about twenty articles to *Personnel Journal, Personnel Administration, Journal of Medical Group Management, Journal of Nursing Administration, Journal of Human Resource Management, Sociological Focus*, and *International Journal of Contemporary Sociology*.

WORK IN PROGRESS: Research on organizational and managerial stress.

SIDELIGHTS: Rogers feels that psychiatrists need to be more aware of the role industries and organizations play in producing psychic distress in their employees, particularly psychosomatic disorders. He believes that a new branch of industrial psychiatry should be developed which would go beyond measuring and testing, and develop preventive programs and therapeutic solutions. *Avocational interests:* Chess, classical music, sports cars.

* * *

ROGG, Eleanor H(ertha) Meyer 1942-

PERSONAL: Born December 26, 1942, in New York, N.Y.; daughter of Alfred Karl and Hertha (Troll) Meyer; married Gerald Rogg (an electrical contractor), June 9, 1968. *Education:* Hunter College of the City University of New York, B.A. (magna cum laude), 1963; Columbia University, M.A., 1965; Fordham University, Ph.D., 1970. *Home:* 758 Klondike Ave., Staten Island, N.Y. 10314. *Office:* Department of Sociology, Wagner College, Grymes Hill, Staten Island, N.Y. 10301.

CAREER: City University of New York, New York, N.Y., part-time lecturer in sociology at Hunter College and Herbert H. Lehman College, both 1968; Molloy College for Women, Rockville Centre, N.Y., assistant professor of sociology, 1969-70; Wagner College, Staten Island, N.Y., assistant professor of sociology, 1970—. *Member:* American Sociological Association, Center for Migration Studies, American Immigration and Citizenship Conference, Doctoral Association of New York Educators (member of board of directors and research director), Phi Beta Kappa, Serve to Enrich Retirement by Volunteer Effort (SERVE). *Awards, honors:* Wheatridge Foundation research grant, 1972—.

WRITINGS: The Assimilation of Cuban Exiles: Role of Community and Class, Aberdeen, 1974; (contributor) Leonard Golubchick and Barry Persky, editors, *Urban Social and Educational Issues*, Kendall-Hunt, 1974. Contributor of more than a dozen articles and reviews to professional journals. Book review editor of *International Migration Review*, 1970—.

AVOCATIONAL INTERESTS: Gardening.

* * *

ROMEY, Bill
See ROMEY, William D(owden)

* * *

ROMEY, William D(owden) 1930-
(Bill Romey)

PERSONAL: Born October 26, 1930, in Richmond, Ind.; son of William Minter (in retail furniture business) and Grace (Dowden) Romey; married Lucretia Alice Leonard (a free-lance artist and teacher), July 16, 1955; children: Catherine Louise, Gretchen Elizabeth, William Leonard. *Education:* Indiana University, A.B., 1952; attended University of Paris, Paris, France, 1950-51, 1952-53; University of California, Berkeley, Ph.D., 1962. *Home:* 52 East Main St., Canton, N.Y. 13617. *Office:* St. Lawrence University, Canton, N.Y. 13617.

CAREER: University of California, Berkeley, graduate research engineer in linguistics and geology, 1958-60; Syracuse University, Syracuse, N.Y., assistant professor, 1962-

66, associate professor of geology and science education, 1966-69; executive director of earth science educational program of American Geological Institute, 1969-72; St. Lawrence University, Canton, N.Y., professor of geology and geography and chairman of department, 1971—. Visiting geoscientist, American Geological Institute, 1964-66, 1971; National Academy of Science visitor to U.S.S.R. Academy of Science, 1967. Educational consultant, 1962—. Member of board of directors of Onondaga Nature Centers, Inc., 1966-69. *Military service:* U.S. Naval Reserve, active service, linguist, 1953-57, inactive service, 1957-63; became lieutenant commander.

MEMBER: National Association of Geology Teachers (vice-president, 1971-72; president, 1972-73), Geological Society of America (fellow), Association of American Geographers, American Geophysical Union, Association for Educating Teachers of Science, Natural Science Teachers Association, American Association for the Advancement of Science (fellow), Geological Society of Norway, Phi Beta Kappa, Sigma Xi, Phi Delta Kappa. *Awards, honors:* Woodrow Wilson Foundation fellow, 1959-60, 1961-62; National Science Foundation faculty fellow, University of Oslo Geological Museum, 1967-68.

WRITINGS: (Editor and translator with Paul A. Witherspoon) A. A. Kartsev, *Geochemical Methods of Prospecting for Petroleum and Natural Gas*, University of California Press, 1959; (with J. Kramer, E. Muller, and J. Lewis) *Investigations in Geology*, William C. Brown, 1967; *Inquiry Techniques for Teaching Science*, Prentice-Hall, 1968; *Field Guide to Plutonic and Metamorphic Rocks*, Houghton, 1971; *Risk-Trust-Love: Learning in a Humane Environment*, C. E. Merrill, 1972; (under name Bill Romey) *Consciousness and Creativity: Transcending Science, Humanities, and the Arts*, Ash Lad Press, 1975; *Confluent Education in Science*, Ash Lad Press, 1975. Earth science consultant, *Compton's Encyclopedia*, 1970-71; associate editor, *Journal of College Science Teaching*.

WORK IN PROGRESS: Beginning geology texts; research on small presses and their activities.

SIDELIGHTS: William Romey writes: "I have become interested in open learning environments, humanistic education, and alternative life styles, communication networks, etc. For the past several years I have been trying to express these interests through creating radically innovative programs at the University of Colorado, St. Lawrence University, and through consulting activities in other schools. Recently I have gotten interested in small-press communications and have founded a new small press, the Ash Lad Press. In addition a group of us working to rejuvenate the cultural life of the small town in which we live have opened a small, cooperative fine-arts gallery."

* * *

ROMMETVEIT, Ragnar 1924-

PERSONAL: Born July 11, 1924, in Stord, Norway; son of Rasmus (a civil servant) and Aasa (Loenning) Rommetveit; married Sigrid Larsen (a teacher), July 2, 1949; children: Ragnar, Jr., Stein, Ingrid Aasa. *Education:* University of Oslo, Dr.Philos., 1953. *Residence:* Blommenholm, Norway. *Office:* Department of Psychology, University of Oslo, Blindern, Oslo, Norway.

CAREER: University of Oslo, Blindern, Norway, professor of psychology, 1954—. Visiting professor, University of Minnesota, 1956-57, University of Michigan, 1961, Cornell University, 1964-65; fellow, Center for Advanced

Study in the Behavioral Sciences, 1965-66, Netherlands Institute for Advanced Study, 1972-73. *Member:* Norwegian Academy of Science.

WRITINGS: Social Norms and Roles, Oslo University Press, 1953; *Ego in Modern Psychology*, Oslo University Press, 1958; *Selectivity, Intuition, and Halo Effects in Social Perception*, Oslo University Press, 1960; *Action and Ideation*, Munksgaard, 1960; *Words, Meanings, and Messages*, Academic Press, 1968; (editor with E. A. Carswell) *Social Contexts of Messages*, Academic Press, 1971; *Language Thought and Communication*, Oslo University Press, 1972; *On Message Structure*, Wiley, 1974.

WORK IN PROGRESS: Research on the language and thought of children; relating Piagetian psychology of thought to the theory of language acquisition and communication.

SIDELIGHTS: Rommetveit told *CA* that his most recent work has "aimed at mediation between a continental European and an American tradition of social science." He added, "I am also convinced that further progress in the humanities and social sciences is contingent upon dialogues across encapsulated and narrowly defined sub-disciplines."

*   *   *

RONAN, Georgia
     See CRAMPTON, Georgia Ronan

*   *   *

RONDELL, Florence   1907-

PERSONAL: Born November 22, 1907, in New York, N.Y.; daughter of Alex (a chemist) and Sophia (Berne) Robinson; married Lester Rondell (an artist), January 13, 1930; children: Thomas. *Education:* New York University, B.S., 1929; Columbia University, M.S.S., 1947; Post Graduate Center for Mental Health, certificate in psychoanalysis, 1964. *Politics:* Democrat. *Religion:* None. *Home:* 809 Gretna Green Way, Los Angeles, Calif. 90049.

CAREER: Louise Wise Adoptive Services, New York, N.Y., psychiatric caseworker and supervisor, 1947-50; Community Service Society, Youth Bureau, New York, N.Y., psychiatric caseworker and supervisor, 1950-59; Post Graduate Center for Mental Health, New York, N.Y., psychoanalyst and training supervisor, 1960-72; private practice of psychotherapy in New York, N.Y., 1960-72, and in Los Angeles, 1974—. Lecturer at Columbia University School of Social Work, summer, 1956. *Member:* National Association of Social Workers, American Orthopsychiatric Association (fellow), Professional Society of Post Graduate Center.

WRITINGS: (With Ruth Michaels) *The Adopted Family*, Crown, 1951, revised edition, 1965; (with Anne-Marie Murray) *New Dimensions in Adoption*, Crown, 1975. Contributor to *Journal of Orthopsychiatry*.

SIDELIGHTS: Florence Rodell has traveled around the world, having taken yearly trips for the last twenty-five years.

*   *   *

RONEN, Dov   1933-

PERSONAL: Born September 30, 1933, in Bekescsaba, Hungary; now citizen of Israel; son of Jacob Rubicsek and Lola Schwarcz; married Naomi Ross (a librarian), August 20, 1961; children: David, Mihal, Gili. *Education:* Hebrew

University of Jerusalem, B.A., 1963; Indiana University, M.A., 1965, Ph.D., 1969. *Home:* Rehov Rabbi Binyamin 6, Beit Hakerem, Jerusalem 96306, Israel. *Office:* Department of Political Science, Hebrew University of Jerusalem, Jerusalem, Israel.

CAREER: Purdue University, Lafayette, Ind., assistant professor of political science, 1969-71; Hebrew University, Jerusalem, Israel, lecturer in political science and African studies, 1971—. *Member:* Israeli Political Science Association, American Political Science Association, African Studies Association.

WRITINGS: Dahomey: Between Tradition and Modernity, Cornell University Press, 1975.

WORK IN PROGRESS: Research on the quest for self-determination, its history, and an analysis of prospects for sub-national and supra-national expressions of self-determination.

*   *   *

RONGIONE, Louis Anthony   1912-

PERSONAL: Born August 23, 1912, in Italy; came to United States in 1913; son of Joseph (a chef) and Christina (Celino) Rongione. *Education:* Villanova University, A.B., 1936, B.S. (library science), 1940; Catholic University of America, M.A., 1940. *Home and office:* Villanova University, Villanova, Pa. 19085.

CAREER: Entered Roman Catholic Order of St. Augustine, 1932, ordained priest, 1939; teacher of English, French, religion, Greek, and Latin, and librarian at Roman Catholic high schools in Chicago, Ill., 1940-41, and Staten Island, N.Y., 1941-50; Villanova University, Villanova, Pa., assistant professor of philosophy, 1950-52; Augustinian International College, Rome, Italy, librarian, 1952-53; Villanova University, associate professor of philosophy, 1954-61, professor of education, 1961-68, professor of library science, 1968—, chairman of department, 1968-71, director of library, 1962—, dean of Evening Division, 1952, dean of Graduate and Part-Time Division, 1956-58, dean of Graduate Studies, 1958-62, moderator of campus newspaper and radio station. Prior of St. Mary's Collegiate Seminary, 1969-71, and St. Thomas of Villanova Monastery, 1971—. Member of board of trustees of American Institute for Italian Culture; member of board of advisers of Cabrini College; member of board of governors of Living Authors, 1943-48.

MEMBER: National Educational Association, National Catholic Educational Association, Association for Higher Education, American Library Association, Catholic Library Association (president of New York-New Jersey chapter), Association of College and Research Libraries, Catholic Audio Visual Educators Association (president and member of executive committee), Pennsylvania Library Association, Knights of Columbus. *Awards, honors:* Archbishop's Medal, 1937; Paladin Jewel, 1938; Grand Cross, 1939; Ped.D. from College of Steubenville, 1957.

WRITINGS: The Jubilee Year, Society of St. Paul Press, 1949; *Conferences on the Beatitudes*, Peter Reilly, 1959; *Reform and Rejoice*, Alba, 1974; *Let Your Light Shine*, Exposition Press, 1975.

WORK IN PROGRESS: A book on bibliotherapy; research on St. Augustine; research on the Bible as literature.

AVOCATIONAL INTERESTS: Painting, photography, travel, collecting and telling humorous stories.

RONSHEIM, Sally B(ober)

PERSONAL: Born in New York, N.Y.; daughter of Hymen and Fanny (Newman) Bober; married Julian Ronsheim, September 1, 1940 (died June, 1972); children: Nancy, Jane (Mrs. Eugene Ring), Carol (Mrs. Philip Fox). *Education:* Brooklyn College (now of the City University of New York), B.A., 1940; City University of New York, M.A., 1943; Long Island University, M.S. in L.S., 1962; University of London, certificate of education, 1964; New York University, Ph.D., 1967. *Home:* 39 Windsor Rd., Great Neck, N.Y. *Office:* English Department, C.W. Post Center, Long Island University, Greenvale, N.Y. 11548.

CAREER: High school teacher in New York, N.Y., 1950-60; Long Island University, Greenvale, N.Y., assistant director of Graduate School of Library Science, 1960-62; high school librarian in New Hyde Park, N.Y., 1962-67; Long Island University, C. W. Post Center, adjunct professor, 1962-67, associate professor of English, 1967—, director of freshman composition, 1975—, director of workshops for teachers of English, 1972—. Charter member of board of trustees, Nassau Research Library, 1968—. *Member:* American Association of University Professors (vice-president of C.W. Post Center Chapter, 1971-72, president, 1972-73), National Council of Teachers of English, New York State English Educators (member of board of trustees, 1971-73), Long Island Teachers of English (member of board of directors, 1972-74), Kappa Delta Pi. *Awards, honors:* U.S. Department of Health, Education and Welfare grant, 1965-66.

WRITINGS: (With Jack Ishmole) *New York Portrait: A Literary Look at the Empire State,* Holt, 1964; *Grammatical Terminology: A Combined Traditional and Modern Linguistic Glossary,* Long Island University, 1970. Contributor to journals in her field. Reviewer, ERIC reviews of literature, 1968—.

WORK IN PROGRESS: Autobiography as an Art.

* * *

ROOKMAAKER, Hendrik Roelof 1922-

PERSONAL: Born February 27, 1922; son of Henderik and Dora (Heytink) Rookmaaker; married Anna Maria Huitker, August 1, 1949; children: Henderik R., Leendert C., Maria H. *Education:* University of Amsterdam, Drs., 1952, Dr., 1959. *Religion:* "Christian—orthodox protestant." *Home:* 23 Dr. Guerinweg, Ommeren, Netherlands. *Office:* Free University, Boelelaan, Amsterdam, Netherlands.

CAREER: Trouw (daily newspaper), Amsterdam, Netherlands, art critic, 1948-58; teacher in secondary school, Amsterdam, Netherlands, 1952-58; University of Leyden, Leyden, Netherlands, assistant professor of history of art, 1958-64; Free University, Amsterdam, Netherlands, professor of history of art, 1965—. Lecturer at colleges and universities in the United States and England. Member, programming committee of Dutch Radio NOS, Dutch film censor board, and L'Abri Fellowship Foundation. *Military service:* Dutch Royal Navy, 1939-45. *Member:* International Association of Art Critics, Society for Calvinistic Philosophy.

WRITINGS: Synthetist Art Theories: Genesis and Nature of the Ideas on Art of Gauguin and His Circle, Swets & Zeitlinger, 1959, published as *Gauguin and 19th Century Art Theory,* 1972; *Jazz, Blues, Spirituals* (in Dutch), Zomer & Keuning, 1960; *Kunst en amusement,* J. H. Kok, 1962; *Art and the Public Today,* L'Abri, 1968; *Modern Art and the Death of a Culture,* Inter-Varsity Press, 1970. Contributor of articles to *Philosophia Reformata, Christianity Today,* and other journals.

WORK IN PROGRESS: Research on contemporary problems and modern art, spirituals and gospel songs, rock music, art theory, and the history of painting, particularly since the fifteenth century.

BIOGRAPHICAL/CRITICAL SOURCES: Philosophia Reformata, Volume XXXVI, 1971.

* * *

ROOSEVELT, Felicia Warburg 1927-

PERSONAL: Born October 27, 1927; daughter of Paul F. (a banker) and Jean (Stettheimer) Warburg; married Robert W. Sarnoff, July 7, 1950; married second husband Franklin D. Roosevelt, Jr. (an executive), July 1, 1970 (separated, 1975); children: (first marriage) Serena, Claudia. *Education:* Bennington College, B.A., 1949. *Religion:* Jewish. *Home:* 606 North Bedford Dr., Beverly Hills, Calif. 90210. *Agent:* M. B. Carlton Cole, Waldorf Towers, New York, N.Y.

CAREER: Employed with Museum of Modern Art, New York, N.Y., 1945, and National Broadcasting Co., New York, 1946; Cartier, Inc., New York, N.Y., jewelry designer, 1974. Member of New York Committee to redecorate Blair House in Washington, D.C.; member of board of directors of Project Hope; past member of board of directors of Irvington House and Burlington House; member of advisory board for Bonwit Teller. *Awards, honors:* Award for fund raising for Project Hope.

WRITINGS: Doers and Dowagers, Doubleday, 1975. Contributor to *Harper's Bazaar.*

AVOCATIONAL INTERESTS: Collecting paintings (impressionist and English sporting paintings) and eighteenth-century Chinese export animals and porcelain.

* * *

ROPER, Laura Wood 1911-
(Laura N. Wood)

PERSONAL: Born March 15, 1911, in St. Louis, Mo.; daughter of Benjamin A. (a lawyer) and Edith T. (Smith) Wood; married W. Crosby Roper, Jr. (a lawyer), July 20, 1940; children: Laura E., Crosby Newbold. *Education:* Vassar College, A.B., 1932. *Home:* 3405 O St. N.W., Washington, D.C. 20007.

WRITINGS: FLO: A Biography of Frederick Law Olmstead, Johns Hopkins Press, 1973.

Juveniles; under name Laura N. Wood: *Walter Reed: Doctor in Uniform,* Messner, 1943; *Raymond Detmars: His Exciting Career,* Messner, 1944; *Louis Pasteur,* Messner, 1948.

Contributor to journals.

* * *

ROSA-NIEVES, Cesareo 1901-1974

PERSONAL: Born July 17, 1901, in Juana Diaz, Puerto Rico; son of Cesareo Rosa-Solivan (a merchant) and Evangelina Nieves; married Emilia Perez Carrasquillo (a teacher), September 1, 1928; children: Cesar E. Rosa-Perez. *Education:* University of Puerto Rico, teacher's certificate, 1925, B.A., 1927, M.A., 1936; University of Mexico, Ph.D., 1944. *Religion:* Roman Catholic. *Home and office:* Balboa St. 61, Urb, Cabrera, Rio Piedras, Puerto Rico 00925.

CAREER: Teacher of Spanish language and literature in secondary schools in Humacao, Carolina, and Caguas, all Puerto Rico; University of Puerto Rico, Rio Piedras, instructor, 1936-43, assistant professor, 1943-45, associate professor, 1945-47, professor of Spanish language and literature, 1947 to early 1970's. Has directed conferences in secondary schools, universities, and at the Ateneo de Puerto Rico. Named life secretary of Academy of Arts and Sciences of Puerto Rico, 1969. *Member:* National Education Association, Associacion de Maestros de Puerto Rico, Sociedad de Autores Puertorriquenos, Sodiedad Puertorriquena de Escritores, Masons. *Awards, honors:* Diploma of honor from Institute of Puerto Rican Literature, 1958, for *La Poesia en Puerto Rico*, and 1963, for *Historia panoramica de la literatura puertorriquena*, diploma of honor from Spanish journal *Rumbos*, 1958, for *Los nisperos del alba maduraron*; Gold Medal and diploma of honor from Academy of Arts and Sciences of Puerto Rico, 1967; Gran Premio de Critica Literaria; and other literary prizes.

WRITINGS: Francisco de Ayerra Santa Maria: Poeta puertorriqueno, 1630-1708, Editorial Universitaria, University of Puerto Rico, 1948; (editor and author of introduction and notes) *Aguinaldo lirico de la poesia puertorriquena*, Volume I: 1843-1907, Volume II; 1907-1921, Volume III: 1921-1956, Libreria Campos, 1957, revised edition, Editorial Edil, 1971; *La lampara del faro: Variaciones criticas sobre temas puertorriquenos*, Editorial Club de la Prensa, Volume I, 1957, Volume II, 1960.

Tierra y lamento: Rodeos de contorno para una telurica interpretacion poetica de lo puertorriqueno, Editorial Club de la Prensa, 1958; *La poesia en Puerto Rico* (doctoral thesis, revised and augmented), Editorial Campos, 1958, 3rd edition, Editorial Edil, 1969; (editor with Felix Franco Oppenheimer) *Autologia general del cuento puertorriqueno* (short fiction anthology), two volumes, Editorial Campos, 1959, 2nd edition, Editorial Edil, 1970; *Historia panoramica de la literatura puertorriquena (1589-1959)*, two volumes, Editorial Campos, 1963; *Mi vocacion por el vespero* (short stories), Editorial Rumbos (Barcelona), 1965; *Plumas estelares en las letras de Puerto Rico*, Volume I, Ediciones de la Torre, University of Puerto Rico, 1967, Volume II, [Barcelona], 1972; *Voz folklorica de Puerto Rico*, Troutman Press (Sharon, Conn.), 1967.

Ensayos escogidos, Academy of Arts and Sciences of Puerto Rico, 1970; (with Esther M. Melon) *Biografias puertorriquenas*, Troutman Press, 1970. Also author of *Antologia de decimas cultas de Puerto Rico*, 1971, and *El costumbrismo literario en la prosa de Puerto Rico*, two volumes, 1971.

Poetry: *Siete caminos en luna de suenos*, Biblioteca de Autores Puertorriquenos, 1957; *Los nisperos del alba maduraron*, Editorial Campos, 1959; *Diapason negro*, Editorial Campos, 1960; *Girasol*, Editorial Campos, 1960; *El Plenamar de las garzas de ambar*, Editorail Campos, 1964; *Estrellas y caramelos*, Editorial Partenon (Madrid), 1972. Also author of *Las veredas olvidadas*, 1922; *La feria de las burbujas*, 1930; *Paracaidas*, 1933; *Tu en los pinos*, 1938; *Undumbre*, 1953; *La emocion divertida*, 1967.

Plays: *Roman Baldorioty de Castro* (three-act play in verse), Imprenta Soltero, 1948. Also author of "El huesped del mar," 1945; "Flor de areyto," 1945; "Brazo de oro," 1948; "Pachin Marin," 1948; "Nuestra enemiga la piedra,"

1948; "La otra," 1948; "Campesina en palacio," 1949; "Norka," 1957.

Novels: *El mar bajo de la montana*, Editorial Yaurel, 1963; *La Cancion de los luceros*, Tip. Miguza (Barcelona), 1972; *Los espejos de sal bajo la Luna*, Tip. Miguza, 1972.

Author of critical notes for works by Virgilio Davila; all published by Cordillera, 1963: *Viviendo y amando*, 2nd edition; *Un libro para mis nietos*, 2nd edition; *Aromas del terruno*, 4th edition; *Patria*.

Author of introduction: Jesus Hernandez Ortiz, *Postuma cnacion de mis ayeres intimos*, Cordillera, 1964; Carmen Chiesa de Perez, *La telarana* (novel), Afrodisio Aguado (Madrid), 1969.

Author of booklets, *Apuntes sobre los bailes en Puerto Rico*, 1959, *Consideraciones sobre literatura puertorriquena*, 1963, *Dintorno y contorno*, 1967. Contributor of prose and verse to journals and periodicals, including *El Mundo, Alma Latina, Puerto Rico Ilustrado, Brujula, Prensa, Revista del Instituto de Cultura Puertorriquena*, and *Revista Internacional de Literatura Iberoamericana*. Co-founder, *Noismo*, 1926-27; editor, *Brujula*, 1940.

BIOGRAPHICAL/CRITICAL SOURCES: Patria Figueroa de Cifredo, *Apuntes biograficos en torno a la vida obra de Cesareo Rosa-Nieves*, Editorial Cordillera, 1965; Figueroa, *Nuevo encuentro con la estetica de Rosa-Nieves*, [San Juan], 1969.*

(Died October 3, 1974)

* * *

ROSE, Will(iam Palen) 1889-

PERSONAL: Born March 17, 1889, in Woodstock, N.Y.; son of A. DuBois and Mary (Palen) Rose; married Louise Lamberson, June 14, 1913; children: Jeannette L. (Mrs. Glenn N. Stanford). *Education:* Cornell University, A.B., 1911. *Religion:* Dutch Reformed. *Home:* Holiday Club, Apt. 4b, 815 Ocean Shore Blvd., Ormond Beach, Fla.; and 700 Americana Dr., Apt. 22, Annapolis, Md.

CAREER: Lord & Thomas Advertising Agency, Chicago, Ill., junior clerk, senior clerk, and account supervisor, 1911; *Suburban Life* (magazine), New York, N.Y., advertising salesman, 1911-12; *Erie Evening Herald*, Erie, Pa., advertising manager, 1912-13; *Washington Post*, Washington, D.C., national account supervisor, 1913-14; *Washington Times*, Washington, D.C., automobile editor and retail promotion editor, 1914, assistant advertising manager, 1914-15, circulation manager, 1915-16; Will Rose Newspapers, Pa., owner and publisher, 1916-56; full-time writer, 1956—. Republican candidate for Pennsylvania Senate, 1926; member of Pennsylvania Greater Council, 1931-34; chairman of Young Republican Committee of Crawford County, Pa., 1934-35. Life trustee of Edinboro State College and president of board of trustees; director of Springs National Bank, 1920-31; corporator for Meadville City Hospital, 1940-62, life honorary, 1962—.

MEMBER: Authors League of America, American Academy of Political Science, Pi Delta Epsilon, Sigma Delta Chi, Pi Gamma Mu, Masons, Consistory, Elks, Knights of Pythias. *Awards, honors:* Newspaper service award from Pennsylvania Newspaper Publishers Association and Pennsylvania State University, 1948; Will Rose Hall at Pennsylvania State University was dedicated in honor of Rose, 1966.

WRITINGS: The Vanishing Village, Citadel, 1963, revised edition, Catskill Mountain Books, 1970.

Work has been anthologized in *We Believe in Prayer*, edited by L. W. Brings, Denison, 1958. Author of "Small Town Comment on Big Town Stuff," a column in Will Rose newspapers, 1916-60. Contributor of about thirty stories and articles to popular magazines, including *Reader's Digest*, *Scribner's*, and *Rotarian*.

* * *

ROSEBROCK, Ellen Fletcher 1947-

PERSONAL: Born December 28, 1947; daughter of D. Van (a chemical engineer) and Juanita (Arrowood) Fletcher; married Charles A. Rosebrock (an attorney). *Education:* Pennsylvania State University, B.A.; Emory University, graduate study; Columbia University, M.A. *Home:* 106 Main St., Roslyn, N.Y. 11576. *Office:* South Street Seaport Museum, 16 Fulton St., New York, N.Y. 10038.

CAREER: South Street Seaport Museum, New York, N.Y., editor of museum publications, 1974—. Member of board of trustees and volunteer, Roslyn Landmark Society, 1974—. *Member:* Society of Architectural Historians, National Trust for Historic Preservation.

WRITINGS: (With Robert Pine) *Sag Harbor Past, Present & Future*, Sag Harbor Planning Commission, 1973; *Roslyn Landmark Society: Annual House Tour Guides*, Roslyn Landmark Society, 1973, 1974, 1975; *Walking Around in South Street*, Dover, 1974, 2nd edition, 1976; *Counting-House Days in South Street*, South Street Seaport Museum, 1975; *A Book to Walk With: Historic Roslyn*, Roslyn Bicentennial Commission, 1975. Also author of museum and exhibition catalogs. Contributor to *South Street Reporter*.

WORK IN PROGRESS: Farewell to Old England, an exhibition catalog; research on port cities during the first half of the 19th century.

* * *

ROSEN, George 1920-

PERSONAL: Born February 7, 1920, in Leningrad, Russia; naturalized U.S. citizen, 1931; married Kusum Parekh, August 11, 1956; children: Mark. *Education:* Brooklyn College (now Brooklyn College of the City University of New York), B.A., 1940; Princeton University, M.A., 1942, Ph.D., 1949. *Home:* 641 La Crosse Ave., Wilmette, Ill. 60091. *Office:* Department of Economics, University of Illinois at Chicago Circle, P.O. Box 4348, Chicago, Ill. 60680.

CAREER: Bard College, Annandale-on-Hudson, 1946-50, began as instructor, became assistant professor of economics; U.S. Department of State, Washington, D.C., economist studying Japanese economy, 1951-54; Massachusetts Institute of Technology, Center for International Studies, Cambridge, senior economist working on India project, 1955-59; United Nations, Division of Industrial Development, New York, N.Y., economist, 1959-60; Ford Foundation, New York, N.Y., economist, advising Nepal and West Bengal governments, 1960-62; RAND Corp., Santa Monica, Calif., senior economist, 1962-67; Asian Development Bank, Manila, Philippines, deputy director of department of economic and technical assistance, 1967-69, chief economist, 1969-71; New York University, Center for International Studies, New York, N.Y., senior fellow, 1971-72; University of Illinois at Chicago Circle, Chicago, professor of economics and head of department, 1972—.

Military service: U.S. Army, 1942-45. *Member:* American Economic Association, Royal Economic Society. *Awards, honors:* Ford Foundation grant, 1972.

WRITINGS: Industrial Change in India, Free Press, 1958; *Some Aspects of Industrial Finance in India*, Free Press, 1962; *Democarcy and Economic Change in India*, University of California Press, 1966, revised edition, 1967; *Peasant Society in a Changing Economy*, University of Illinois Press, 1975. Contributor to economic journals and to conference proceedings.

WORK IN PROGRESS: Research towards a theory of economic, social, and political change; study of relationships between developed and developing countries.

SIDELIGHTS: Rosen writes: "I was brought up in the depression of the 1930's and was strongly influenced by Franklin Roosevelt and the New Deal. I have worked and travelled widely in Asia, in all the countries around China. I would like at some time to visit China to see what is happening there."

* * *

ROSEN, Lawrence R(onald) 1938-

PERSONAL: Born January 11, 1938, in Louisville, Ky.; son of Harold (in real estate) and Selma (Schneider) Rosen; married Susan Mann (a teacher), July 20, 1963; children: Stacey Andrea, Shawn Douglas. *Education:* Miami University, Oxford, Ohio, B.S. (cum laude), 1959. *Office:* Lawrence Rosen & Associates, 7008 Springdale Rd., Louisville, Ky. 40222.

CAREER: Investors Continental Services, Geneva, Switzerland, vice-president, 1962-68; Rosen Enterprises, Inc., Louisville, Ky., vice-president and director, 1968—. President of Lawrence Rosen & Associates, 1969—; vice-president of Executive Properties, 1974-75; financial vice-president and director of Omega Ranches, Inc., 1973-74; registered representative of Bache & Co. in Geneva, Switzerland and Louisville, Ky., 1972-73. Director of Australian Fund of Funds, 1969-71; senior foreign adviser to Svenska Internationella Investment Fonden, 1969-71. *Military service:* U.S. Navy, Supply Corps, 1959-62; became lieutenant junior grade. *Member:* Mensa, Phi Beta Kappa, Omicron Delta Kappa, Beta Gamma Sigma, Zeta Beta Tau, Alpha Phi Omega (president), Standard Country Club.

WRITINGS: Go Where the Money Is, Dow Jones-Irwin, 1968, revised edition, 1974; *How to Trade Put and Call Options*, Dow Jones-Irwin, 1974; *Dow Jones-Irwin Guide to Interest* (Investor's Book Club selection), Dow Jones-Irwin, 1974; *When and How to Profit by Buying and Selling Gold*, Dow Jones-Irwin, 1975.

WORK IN PROGRESS: Real Estate Investing; *International Currency Transactions*.

SIDELIGHTS: Rosen has established new investment businesses in Sweden and Australia. While living in Switzerland, he created and operated U.S. brokerage firms in Germany, Italy, Great Britain, France, Turkey, Spain, and the Netherlands. *Avocational interests:* Tennis, skiing, bridge.

BIOGRAPHICAL/CRITICAL SOURCES: Business Week, June 26, 1971.

* * *

ROSENBERG, Harry E. 1932-

PERSONAL: Born June 14, 1932, in California; son of

William R. (a farmer) Eula (Mae) Rosenberg; married Patricia Hengst (a teacher), November 11, 1950; children: Larry, Ann, Robert, Mary. *Education:* Fresno State College (now California State University, Fresno), B.A., 1955, M.A. (with highest honors), 1960; University of Southern California, Ed.D., 1971. *Politics:* Democrat. *Religion:* Episcopalian. *Home:* 2532 Laurel Lane, Visalia, Calif. 93277. *Office:* Visalia Schools, 315 East Acequia, Visalia, Calif. 93277.

CAREER: Visalia Schools, Visalia, Calif., director of special education, 1961—. Lecturer at California State University, Fresno, 1961—, and at University of Southern California, 1969-71. Consultant to California State Department of Education and to U.S. Office of Education. Director of Tulare County Mental Health Services, 1973-75. *Military service:* U.S. Navy, 1952-53. *Member:* Phi Beta Kappa, Phi Delta Kappa, Phi Gamma Mu.

WRITINGS: Classrooms That Work, Dutton, 1974. Contributor to *Psychology Today, London Times, Instructor, Learning,* and *Los Angeles Times.*

WORK IN PROGRESS: A parents' manual.

*　　　*　　　*

ROSENBERG, Judith K(aren) 1945-

PERSONAL: Born December 14, 1945, in Evanston, Ill.; daughter of John Allen (a physician) and Betty (Mills) Campbell; married Kenyon Charles Rosenberg (a professor of library science), April 30, 1971; children: Dana Rebecca. *Education:* Northwestern University, B.S., 1966; Kent State University, M.L.S., 1971. *Home:* 3109 East Edgerton Rd., Silver Lake, Ohio 44224.

CAREER: Akron Public Library, Akron, Ohio, children's librarian, 1968-74. Writer. Member of Weathervane Community Theatre, 1955-69. *Member:* Ohio Library Association, Akron Public Library Staff Association (secretary, 1973-74).

WRITINGS—Editor with husband, Kenyon Charles Rosenberg: *Young People's Literature in Series,* Libraries Unlimited, Volume I: *Fiction Series,* 1972, Volume II: *Non-Fiction and Publishers' Series,* 1973; *Watergate: An Annotated Bibliography,* Libraries Unlimited, 1975. Contributor of reviews to *Library Journal, Akron Beacon Journal,* and *American Reference Books Annual.*

WORK IN PROGRESS: A new edition of *Young People's Literature in Series.*

SIDELIGHTS: Judith Rosenberg told *CA* that *Young People's Literature in Series* "evolved from my own talent for selecting the last book in a series to read first, and working as a children's librarian confirmed the need for a guide in this area.... *Watergate* ... was the obvious result of the proliferation of materials on the subject and the need for easy access to them." *Avocational interests:* Acting, reading, knitting, sewing.

*　　　*　　　*

ROSENBERG, Kenyon Charles 1933-

PERSONAL: Born September 9, 1933, in Chicago, Ill.; son of David (a realtor) and Esther (Friedman) Rosenberg; married Judith Karen Campbell (a writer), April 30, 1971; children: (previous marriage) Lorna Serene, Victoria Lynn; (present marriage) Dana Rebecca. *Education:* Los Angeles City College, A.A., 1957; University of California, Los Angeles, A.B., 1959; University of Southern California,

M.S., 1961; University of Paris, graduate study, 1973—. *Politics:* "Hostile to all existing parties." *Religion:* Jewish. *Home:* 3109 East Edgerton Rd., Silver Lake, Ohio 44224. *Office:* School of Library Science, Kent State University, Kent, Ohio 44242.

CAREER: Los Angeles County Law Library, Los Angeles, Calif., reference librarian, 1955-60; California State Department of Justice, Los Angeles, librarian, 1960-62; Hughes Aircraft Co., Culver City, Calif., head of technical library services, 1962-66; Ampex Corp., Redwood City, Calif., director of technical information services, 1966-68; Kent State University, Kent, Ohio, assistant professor, 1968-72, associate professor of library science, 1972—, associate director of Center for Library Studies, 1972—. Law library consultant to Alaska State Court system, 1962; consultant to Surveyor spacecraft documentation system. *Military service:* U.S. Army, Artillery, 1953-55. *Member:* American Library Association, American Society for Information Science (San Francisco chapter president, 1967-68), Institute of Electrical and Electronics Engineers, American Society for Testing and Materials, American Music Critics Association, Chi Delta Pi, Alpha Mu Gamma.

WRITINGS: (Editor with wife, Judith K. Rosenberg) *Young People's Literature in Series,* Libraries Unlimited, Volume I: *Fiction Series,* 1972, Volume II: *Non-Fiction and Publishers' Series,* 1973; (editor with Judith K. Rosenberg) *Watergate: An Annotated Bibliography,* Libraries Unlimited, 1975; (with John S. Doskey) *The Media Equipment Handbook and Dictionary,* Libraries Unlimited, 1976. Contributor of poems, articles, and reviews to numerous journals. Editor of classical recordings and audiovisual reviews, *Previews,* 1971—; performing arts editor, *American Reference Books Annual,* 1975—; music critic, *B'nai B'rith Messenger,* 1964-66, *Akron Beacon Journal,* 1971.

WORK IN PROGRESS: Research on the gothic elements in the works of Kipling, Hardy, and Wilde; with Dominique Rene De Lerma, an overview of the last 200 years of American music for the Bicentennial, for Libraries Unlimited.

SIDELIGHTS: Kenyon Rosenberg told *CA:* "I believe we are living in the true second renaissance and that we must know as much as possible about the forces shaping our future (the sciences) while simultaneously absorbing as much as possible of the meaningful content of humanity (the arts). Every aspect of education, no matter what the field of endeavor, if education is to be meaningful, must synthesize the sciences and arts in order to provide the student (and the instructor) with the *weltanschauung* necessary not only to survive, but to be creative."

*　　　*　　　*

ROSENBERG, Norman J(ack) 1930-

PERSONAL: Born February 22, 1930, in New York, N.Y.; son of Jacob (a builder) and Rae (Dombrowitz) Rosenberg; married Sarah Zacher (a historian), December 30, 1950; children: Daniel Jonathan, Alyssa Yael. *Education:* Brooklyn College (now of the City University of New York), student, 1947-49; Michigan State University, B.S., 1951; Oklahoma State University, M.S., 1958; Rutgers University, Ph.D., 1961. *Home:* 3950 Pace Blvd., Lincoln, Neb. 68502. *Office:* Agricultural Meteorology Section, 104 Plant Industry, East Campus, University of Nebraska, Lincoln, Neb. 68503.

CAREER: Employed by Government of Israel for soil conservation and irrigation work, 1952-57; University of

Nebraska, Lincoln, assistant professor, 1961-64, associate professor, 1964-67, professor of agricultural meteorology, 1967—. Consultant to U.S. Agency for International Development and National Oceanic and Atmospheric Administration. *Member:* American Meteorological Society, American Society for Agronomy, American Association for the Advancement of Science (fellow). *Awards, honors:* North Atlantic Treaty Organization (NATO) senior fellowship in science, 1968; Centennial Medal from U.S. National Weather Service, 1971.

WRITINGS: Microclimate: The Biological Environment, Wiley, 1974. Contributor of about seventy articles to professional journals. Technical editor of *Climatology-Agronomy Journal.*

WORK IN PROGRESS: A novel based on observations in less developed countries; research to increase crop productivity and reduce water use in agriculture; introducing simple crop improvement methods in less developed countries by modifying the microclimate, the environment in which crops and animals live.

SIDELIGHTS: Rosenberg's consulting work has taken him to Europe, the Near East, Asia, Africa, and South America.

*   *   *

ROSENBERG, Sharon 1942-

PERSONAL: Born December 14, 1942, in New York, N.Y.; daughter of Louis (a salesman) and Mildred (Federbush) Rosenberg. *Education:* Harpur College, student, 1960-63. *Home:* 3917 18th St., San Francisco, Calif. 94114. *Agent:* Oscar Collier, Seligmann & Collier, 280 Madison Ave., New York, N.Y. 10016.

CAREER: Modern dancer in New York, N.Y., 1963-67, working with Martha Graham, Erick Hawkins, and Rod Rodgers, among others; artist and designer with Electric Lotus Co. (designers of environments and multi-media shows), New York, N.Y., 1967; cook in small vegetarian restaurant, and then in macrobiotic restaurant, London, England, 1968-69; designer and seamstress in Formentera and Ibiza, Spain, 1969-70; free-lance work, 1970—, as cook, caterer, costume designer for dance and theater, clothing designer, dancer, seamstress, and model for artist.

WRITINGS: (With Joan Wiener) *The Illustrated Hassle-Free Make Your Own Clothes Book* (for young adults), Straight Arrow, 1971; (With Wiener) *Son of Hassle-Free Sewing: Further Adventures in Homemade Clothes* (for young adults), Straight Arrow, 1972. Magazine columnist with Joan Wiener, writing on sewing in *Rags* and on food in *Sundance.*

WORK IN PROGRESS: A vegetable cookbook; a sewing book for young children.

SIDELIGHTS: Sharon Rosenberg writes: "I must admit the thought of being a writer, much less an author, was about the furthest thing from my mind. My friend, Joan Wiener, who had, herself, already written two or three books, was looking for a new project. . . . She suggested we work together on a sewing book, and I agreed, but didn't actually take it very seriously, until I realized that there was an interested publisher. . . .

"As to how I actually got to the position of knowing enough about sewing to write a book—I have to say simply that I've stood near, watched over the shoulder of, and asked a lot of questions of, some of the most talented and creative people around. I've learned gourmet cooking and

European tailoring this way but mostly I learned about courage. Jump right in, 'cause otherwise you'll never make those mistakes that teach more than the best books. Keep your eyes open, be daring, and mostly work from your heart.''

*   *   *

ROSENBLOOM, Joseph 1928-

PERSONAL: Born June 28, 1928, in New York, N.Y.; son of Jacob and Annie (Heck) Rosenbloom. *Education:* Attended New York University, 1942-44; University of Chicago, M.A., 1949; Rutgers University, M.S.L.S., 1965. *Religion:* Jewish. *Home:* 58 Middagh St., Brooklyn, N.Y. 11201.

CAREER: Einstein Free Public Library, Pompton Lakes, N.J., library director, 1965-67; Piscataway Township Libraries, Piscataway, N.J., library director, 1967-74; Macmillan Publishing Co., New York, N.Y., editorial researcher, 1974—.

WRITINGS: Consumer Complaint Guide, Macmillan, 1972, 4th edition, 1975; *Kits and Plans,* Oliver Press, 1972; *Craft Supplies Supermarket,* Oliver Press, 1973; (with Irving H. Vincent) *Scenes from the New Theatre,* Dell, in press.

WORK IN PROGRESS: Kits and Plans, 2nd edition, for Oliver Press.

*   *   *

ROSENBLUM, Art 1927-

PERSONAL: Born November 14, 1927, in New York, N.Y.; son of Joseph (a businessman) and Sadie (an artist; maiden name, Skoletsky) Rosenblum. *Education:* Attended Hiram College, 1946-47. *Politics:* "Left and right radical." *Religion:* "Jewish, Christian, and non-church." *Home and office:* 5620 Morton St., Philadelphia, Pa. 19144.

CAREER: Has worked in electronics, as mechanic, farmer, translator, inventor, and customs agent for a communal group in Paraguay; Aquarian Research Foundation (scientific and educational non-profit organization concerned with overcoming society's resistance to change), Philadelphia, Pa., director, 1969—. *Member:* International Platform Association.

WRITINGS: Natural Birth Control, Aquarian Research Foundation, 1973; *The Natural Birth Control Book,* Aquarian Research Foundation, 1974; *Unpopular Science,* Running Press, 1974. Editor and contributor to *Aquarian Research Foundation Newsletter.*

SIDELIGHTS: Rosenblum feels that America is "heading for a financial collapse within four years and possibly this summer . . . There have also been threats of revolution, and serious talk of the coming of a chaotic time of disorganized civil war . . . Violence is not caused by the coming of a new age of love and joy. It is not caused by the rapid changes that such a new age requires. The cause of violence is resistance to change . . . If the resistance to change could actually be broken down or overcome, then changes could come at such a rapid rate that much suffering and chaos could be avoided entirely." He believes that such a breakdown of resistance is possible, and that it might be facilitated by the methods of the peace movements and communal living movements with which he has had several years experience.

ROSENBLUM, Leonard A. 1936-

PERSONAL: Born May 18, 1936, in Brooklyn, N.Y.; son of Samuel A. and Mae (Kotkin) Rosenblum; married Marie B. Lopresti, September 8, 1956; children: Gianine Denice, Douglas Smauel. *Education:* Brooklyn College (now Brooklyn College of the City University of New York), B.A., 1956, M.A., 1958; University of Wisconsin, Madison, Ph.D. 1961. *Home:* 900 East 19th St., Brooklyn, N.Y. 11230. *Office:* Department of Psychiatry, Downstate Medical Center, State University of New York, 450 Clarkson Ave., Brooklyn, N.Y. 11203.

CAREER: State University of New York, Downstate Medical Center, Brooklyn, N.Y., professor in department of psychiatry, 1961—. *Member:* International Primatological Society, American Psychological Association, National Institute of Mental Health, Sigma Xi. *Awards, honors:* Research Scientist Award (level II) from National Institute of Mental Health.

WRITINGS: (Editor with R. W. Cooper) *The Squirrel Monkey*, Academic Press, 1968; (editor) *Primate Behavior: Developments in Field and Laboratory Research*, Academic Press, Volume 1, 1970, Volume 11, 1971, Volume III, 1973, Volume IV, 1975; (editor with M. Lewis) *The Effect of the Infant on Its Caregiver*, Wiley, 1974; (editor with Lewis) *The Origins of Fear*, Wiley, 1974; (editor with Lewis) *Peer Relations and Friendship*, Wiley, 1975; (editor with Lewis) *The Origins of Communication*, Wiley, in press. Contributor to journals in his field. Editor, *Brain, Behavior and Evolution, Archives of Sexual Behavior*, consultant reviewer, National Science Foundation and National Institute of Child Health and Human Development.

WORK IN PROGRESS: Research on the establishment of infant bonds to mother in monkeys and the hormonal control and behavioral correlates of sexual behavior in male and female monkeys and its development.

SIDELIGHTS: Rosenblum writes: "I am attempting to learn more about the biological basis of human behavior and its development through the study of non-human primates. Such research, while not providing the answers to man's problems, helps to order the priorities with which we seek to tackle problems at the human level by suggesting the evolutionary background to particular areas of behavioral development."

*   *   *

ROSENTHAL, Douglas E(urico) 1940-

PERSONAL: Born February 12, 1940, in Great Neck, N.Y.; son of Jacob (a business executive) and Louise (an artist; maiden name, Muir) Rosenthal; married Erica Kremen (an attorney), November 12, 1967; children: Benjamin Muir. *Education:* Yale University, B.A. (summa cum laude), 1961, LL.B., 1966, Ph.D., 1970; Balliol College, Oxford, Henry Fellow, 1961-62; Columbia University, M.A., 1963. *Politics:* "I have particularly admired the politics of Adlai Stevenson, Pierre Mendes France and Hugh Gaitskell." *Religion:* Jewish. *Home:* 4530 Connecticut Ave. N.W., Washington, D.C. 20008. *Office:* Antitrust Division, U.S. Department of Justice, Washington, D.C. 20530.

CAREER: Russell Sage Foundation, New York, N.Y., project director, 1968-70; Yale University, New Haven, Conn., assistant instructor in political science, spring, 1970; Fried, Frank, Harris, Shriver & Jacobson, New York, N.Y., associate attorney, 1970-74; U.S. Department of Justice, Washington, D.C., assistant chief of foreign commerce section of Antitrust Division, 1974—. Democratic county committeeman in Nassau, N.Y., 1963-65. *Member:* American Bar Association, New York State Bar Association, Association of the Bar of the City of New York, Phi Beta Kappa. *Awards, honors:* Woodrow Wilson fellow at Columbia University.

WRITINGS: (With Robert Kagan and Debra Quatrone) *Volunteer Attorneys and Legal Services for the Poor: New York's C.L.O. Program*, Russell Sage Foundation, 1971; (contributor) Jay Katz, editor, *Experimentation with Human Beings*, Russell Sage Foundation, 1972; *Lawyer and Client: Who's in Charge?*, Russell Sage Foundation, 1974. Contributor to *Yale Law Journal, Juris Doctor*, and other legal journals.

WORK IN PROGRESS: Research in problems of significance to the United States in international antitrust law; research to help laymen get better legal service and better understand their legal affairs, e.g., draft of a client bill of rights for dealing with lawyers; research on the problems of citizen participation in American democratic society.

SIDELIGHTS: Rosenthal writes: "The principal issue of intellectual importance to me is how can people gain greater and wiser control over their lives without thereby undermining the valuable elements of organized society? A collateral issue is whether the values of decentralization, a high degree of personal autonomy, and the free market are still relevant in today's world." *Avocational interests:* Travel, the theater, good food and wine, reading history and spy stories (Eric Ambler and Graham Greene).

*   *   *

ROSENTHAL, Harry Kenneth 1941-

PERSONAL: Born April 30, 1941, in New York, N.Y.; son of David M. (a textile executive) and Sylvia (Newman) Rosenthal. *Education:* Columbia University, A.B., 1962, Ph.D., 1967; University of California, Los Angeles, M.B.A., 1975. *Home:* 150 East 69th St., #4f, New York, N.Y. 10021.

CAREER: Northern Illinois University, DeKalb, Ill., assistant professor of history, 1967-70; California State University, Los Angeles, assistant professor of history, 1970-74; U.S. State Department, Washington, D.C., attached to German section, 1974—. *Member:* American Association for the Advancement of Slavic Studies. *Awards, honors:* German Academy exchange fellow at University of Heidelberg, 1963-64; grant from U.S. State Department and New York University, 1965, for study at University of Warsaw; Fulbright-Hays award, 1966, for study in Poland; grant from American Council of Learned Societies and Social Science Research Council, 1970-71.

WRITINGS: German and Pole: National Conflict and Modern Myth, Florida State University Press, 1975. Contributor to *Slavic Review, Slavonic and East European Review, Polish Review, Journal of Contemporary History, East Central Europe, European Studies Review*, and *Canadian-American Slavic Studies*.

WORK IN PROGRESS: Research on communism as a system and trade between east and west.

*   *   *

ROSENTHAL, Joel T(homas) 1934-

PERSONAL: Born October 17, 1934, in Chicago, Ill.; son of Hilmar (a social worker) and Dora (Azoff) Rosenthal;

married Naomi Braun (a professor), April 29, 1962; children: Jessica A., Joshua M., Matthew S. *Education:* University of Chicago, B.A., 1954, M.A., 1958, Ph.D., 1963. *Office:* Department of History, State University of New York, Stony Brook, N.Y. 11794.

CAREER: Roosevelt University, Chicago, Ill., assistant professor of history, 1961-64; State University of New York at Stony Brook, assistant professor, 1964-66, associate professor, 1966-73, professor of history, 1973—. Visiting professor at University of Sussex, 1973. *Member:* American Association of University Professors (vice-president of New York State Council, 1969-71). *Awards, honors:* Fulbright fellow in England, 1959-60; Social Science Research Council fellowship, 1965; Huntington Library summer fellow, 1968.

WRITINGS: The Training of an Elite Group: English Bishops in the Fifteenth Century, American Philosophical Society, 1970; *The Purchase of Paradise,* Routledge & Kegan Paul, 1972; *Angels, Angles, and Conquerors,* Knopf, 1973. Contributor of scholarly articles to journals.

WORK IN PROGRESS: Research on medieval social history.

AVOCATIONAL INTERESTS: Travel.

* * *

ROSENTHAL, Renee ?-1975

?—April 29, 1975; French editor and translator. Obituaries: *Publishers Weekly,* June 9, 1975.

* * *

ROSENZWEIG, Norman 1924-

PERSONAL: Born February 28, 1924, in New York, N.Y., son of Jacob Arthur and Edna (Braman) Rosenzweig; married Carol Treleaven, September 20, 1945; children: Elizabeth Ann. *Education:* Attended New York University, 1941-44; Chicago Medical School, M.B., 1947, M.D., 1948; University of Michigan, M.S., 1954. *Home:* 1234 Cedarholm Lane, Bloomfield Hills, Mich. 48013. *Office:* Department of Psychiatry, Sinai Hospital of Detroit, 6767 West Outer Dr., Detroit, Mich. 48235.

CAREER: Jamaica Hospital, Jamaica, N.Y., intern, 1947-48; St. John's Long Island City Hospital, Long Island City, N.Y., intern, 1948; Kings Park State Hospital, New York, N.Y., resident, 1949-51; Veterans Administration Hospital, Battle Creek, Mich., resident, 1951-52; University of Michigan Medical School, Ann Arbor, senior clinical instructor, 1952-53, instructor, 1953-55, assistant professor, 1957-61, lecturer in psychiatry, 1961-63; Sinai Hospital of Detroit, Detroit, Mich., head of department of psychiatry, 1961—; Wayne State University School of Medicine, Detroit, Mich., assistant professor, 1961-68, associate professor, 1968-73, professor of psychiatry, 1973—. Diplomate of American Board of Psychiatry and Neurology, 1954; director, University of Michigan-Ypsilanti State Hospital joint research project in schizophrenia and psychopharmacology, 1957-59. Visiting lecturer at University of Southern California, 1972, University of California at Los Angeles, 1973, Mercy College, 1974, and University of Ottawa, 1974. *Military service:* U.S. Air Force, 1955-57, served in Psychiatric Service; became captain.

MEMBER: American Association for the Advancement of Science, American Association of Directors of Psychiatric Residency Training, American Association of University Professors, American College of Psychiatrists (fellow), American Medical Association, American Psychiatric Association (fellow), British Society of Clinical Psychiatrists, Michigan Psychiatric Society (president, 1975), Michigan State Medical Society (chairman, section on psychiatry, 1974—), New York Academy of Sciences, Pan American Medical Association, Wayne County Medical Society, Beta Lambda Sigma, Tau Kappa Alpha. *Awards, honors:* Certificate from Michigan Society of Psychiatry and Neurology, 1971; Physician's Recognition Award, American Medical Association, 1971, 1975; American Psychiatric Association Rush Gold Medal Award, 1974.

WRITINGS: Community Mental Health Programs in England: An American View, Wayne State University Press, 1975. Contributor of numerous articles to *Journal of Nervous and Mental Disorders, Psychopharmacologia, American Journal of Psychiatry, Mental Health Digest,* and other professional publications.

AVOCATIONAL INTERESTS: Travel, photography, collection of opera and classical music recordings.

* * *

ROSNER, Joseph 1914-

PERSONAL: Born January 6, 1914, in New York, N.Y.; son of Charles and Rose (Kaunitz) Rosner; married Maggy Magerstadt (a book binder), April 17, 1970. *Education:* Educated in public schools of New York City. *Residence:* Fish Creek, Wis. 54212. *Agent:* James O. Brown Associates, Inc., 22 East 60th St., New York, N.Y. 10022.

CAREER: Writer. Second vice-president of Door City Environmental Council, 1974—. *Member:* Authors League.

WRITINGS: All About Psychoanalysis: In Questions and Answers, Crowell-Collier, 1962; *The Hater's Handbook,* Delacorte, 1965; *Public Faces in Private Places* (novel), Delacorte, 1966; *The Story of the Writings,* Behrman, 1970; *The Habits of Command* (novel), Harcourt, 1975. Contributor to *Esquire, Mademoiselle, Pageant,* and other magazines.

* * *

ROSS, Billy I(rvan) 1925-

PERSONAL: Born January 21, 1925, in Murray, Ky.; son of Enoch Herman (a banker) and Mary Emily (Ward) Ross; married Avis Marie Riedlinger, November 26, 1949; children: Randall Irvan. *Education:* Murray State College, student, 1942-43; University of Missouri, B.J., 1948; Eastern New Mexico University, M.A., 1952; Southern Illinois University, Ph.D., 1964. *Home:* 3429 55th St., Lubbock, Tex. 79413. *Office:* Department of Mass Communication, Texas Tech University, Lubbock, Tex. 79409.

CAREER: Assistant manager of movie theaters in Murray, Ky., 1940-42; *Columbia Missourian,* Columbia, Mo., advertising salesman, 1947-48; *High Plains Journal,* Dodge City, Kan., advertising manager, 1948-51; Kentucky Wesleyan College, Owensboro, assistant professor of journalism and director of publicity, 1952-55; University of Houston, Houston, Tex., assistant professor of journalism, 1955-62, faculty business manager of publications, 1955-61; *Daily Egyptian,* Carbondale, Ill., advertising adviser, 1962-64; Texas Tech University, Lubbock, professor of marketing, 1964-70, professor of mass communications and chairman of department, 1970—. Publisher of *Galena Park Reporter,* 1956-60; president of Texas Journalism Education Council, 1972-73. *Military service:* U.S. Army, 1943-46. U.S. Army Reserve, 1946—; present rank, colonel.

MEMBER: American Academy of Advertising (national president, 1960-61), American Advertising Federation (member of board of directors), Advertising Federation of America (member of board of directors), Association for Education in Journalism, American Marketing Association, Reserve Officers Association, Association of the U.S. Army, American Lung Association of Texas (member of board of directors of West Texas chapter), Advertising Association of the West (member of board of directors), Houston Advertising Club (member of board of directors), Lubbock Advertising Federation (president, 1968-69; member of board of directors), Alpha Delta Sigma (national president, 1963-67; chairman of national council, 1967-69), Sigma Delta Chi, Kappa Tau Alpha, Rotary International (Lubbock chapter), Lubbock Chamber of Commerce.

WRITINGS: Advertising Education: Programs in American Four-Year Colleges and Universities, Texas Tech Press, 1965; (with Donald G. Hileman) Toward Professionalism in Advertising, Taylor Publishing, 1969; (contributor of foreword) Leon Quera, Advertising Campaigns, Grid, Inc., 1973; (contributor) Occupational Outlook Handbook, U.S. Department of Labor, 4th edition (Ross was not included in earlier editions), 1974; (with Ralph L. Sellmeyer) School Publications, Allyn & Bacon, 1974. Author, with Hileman, of annual publication, Where Shall I Go to College to Study Advertising?, Advertising Education Publications, c. 1965—. Contributor to professional journals.

WORK IN PROGRESS: Advertising Problems and Cases.

*   *   *

ROSS, George
    See MORGAN-GRENVILLE, Gerard (Wyndham)

*   *   *

ROSS, James S(tiven)   1892-1975

November 4, 1892—1975; British educator and author of books on education and psychology. Obituaries: AB Bookman's Weekly, March 24, 1975.

*   *   *

ROSS, Robert S(amuel)   1940-

PERSONAL: Born May 28, 1940, in Canton, Ohio; son of Joyce W. (a lawyer) and Mildred (Kistler) Ross; married Sharon Hill (a professor), September 15, 1962; children: Andrea, Brian, Jason. Education: Miami University, Oxford, Ohio, B.A., 1962; University of Minnesota, B.S., 1963; University of Colorado, Ph.D., 1968. Home: 767 East Fifth St., Chico, Calif. 95926. Office: Department of Political Science, California State University, Chico, Calif. 95926.

CAREER: California State University, Chico, assistant professor, 1968-70, associate professor of political science, 1971—. Trustee of board of education of Chico Unified School District, 1973-77.

WRITINGS: (Editor with William C. Mitchell, and contributor) Introductory Readings in American Government, Markham, 1971; (editor) Public Choice and Public Policy, Markham, 1971; American National Government, Rand McNally, 1972, 2nd edition, in press. Editor of California State University, Chico, monograph series, 1969—. Associate editor of Western Political Quarterly, 1974—.

ROSS, T(heodore) J(ohn)   1924-

PERSONAL: Born October 3, 1924, in Boston, Mass.; son of Samuel and Rita (Newman) Ross; married Rhoda Pollack, December 25, 1956; children: Richard, Jonathan, Laurence. Education: Clark University, B.A., 1948; Columbia University, M.A., 1949. Home: 2 Woodley Rd., Morristown, N.J. 07960. Office: Department of English, Fairleigh Dickinson University, Madison, N.J. 07940.

CAREER: West Virginia University, Morgantown, instructor in English, 1952-55; Wayne State University, Detroit, Mich., instructor in English, 1956-60; Fairleigh Dickinson University, Madison, N.J., assistant professor, 1960-68, associate professor, 1968-72, professor of English, 1972—. Lecturer at New School for Social Research, summers, 1965—. Lecturer at Morris Museum. Military service: U.S. Army, 1943-46; received Purple Heart. Member: Modern Language Association of America, Northeast Modern Language Association.

WRITINGS: (Contributor) R. Beal and J. Kora, editors, Thought in Prose, 3rd edition (Ross was not associated with earlier editions), Prentice-Hall, 1966; (contributor) Alan Carty, editor, Mass Media and Mass Man, Holt, 1968; (editor) Film and the Liberal Arts, Holt, 1970; (contributor) Julius Bellone, editor, Renaissance of the Film, Collier, 1970; (contributor) Roy Huss, editor, Focus on Blow-Up, Prentice-Hall, 1971; (editor with Huss) Focus on the Horror Film, Prentice-Hall, 1972; (contributor) John Nachbar, editor, Focus on the Western, Prentice-Hall, 1974. Contributor to journals.

WORK IN PROGRESS: Western Approaches: From Hart to Peckinpah, a book on western films; a book on the plays of John Osborne.

AVOCATIONAL INTERESTS: Chess.

*   *   *

ROSS, Timothy A(rrowsmith)   1936-

PERSONAL: Born March 25, 1936, in Des Moines, Iowa; son of William Ernest (a potter) and Julie (Moore) Ross; married Janet Ann Ashton, August 12, 1961; children: Anne, Margaret, David, Sarah. Education: University of Iowa, B.A., 1961, M.A., 1963, Ph.D., 1964. Politics: "Independent with Democratic leanings." Religion: Roman Catholic. Address: P.O. Box 217, State University, Ark. 72467. Office: Division of History, Arkansas State University, State University, Ark. 72467.

CAREER: Arkansas State University, State University, 1965—, began as instructor, became assistant professor, 1969, now associate professor of Chinese history. Military service: U.S. Marine Corps, 1954-57. Member: Association for Asian Studies, American Historical Association, Chinese Language Teachers Association, Phi Beta Kappa.

WRITINGS: Chiang Kuei, Twayne, 1974; (translator from the Chinese) Chiang Kuei, The Whirlwind, Chinese Materials Center (Taiwan), 1974.

WORK IN PROGRESS: Research on and translation of the Taiwan author, Chung Li-ho who lived from 1915 to 1960.

*   *   *

ROTH, David M(orris)   1935-

PERSONAL: Born August 22, 1935, in Philadelphia, Pa.; son of Irwin E. and Delia (Gannon) Roth; married Sandra Kushner (a teacher), December 25, 1957; children: Deborah Anne. *Education:* Brooklyn College (now Brooklyn College of the City University of New York), B.A. (cum laude), 1957; Clark University, M.A., 1958, Ph.D., 1971. *Home:* 178 Foster Dr., Willimantic, Conn. 06226. *Office:* Center for Connecticut Studies, Eastern Connecticut State College, Willimantic, Conn. 06226.

CAREER: Clark University, Worcester, Mass., lecturer in history in Evening College, 1959-60; Brooklyn College of the City University of New York, Brooklyn, N.Y., lecturer in history, 1960-62; Eastern Connecticut State College, Willimantic, instructor, 1962-65, assistant professor, 1965-69, associate professor of history, 1969—, director of Center for Connecticut Studies, 1970—. Historian for Windham Bicentennial Commission, 1974—; historical consultant to American Revolution Bicentennial Commission of Connecticut, 1974-75.

MEMBER: American Association of University Professors (president of Eastern Connecticut State College chapter, 1965-66), American Historical Association, American Association for State and Local History, Noah Webster Foundation, New England Historical Association, Connecticut Historical Society, Association for the Study of Connecticut History (member of board of directors, 1969-71; president, 1973-75), Kappa Delta Pi.

WRITINGS: (Editor with others) Virginia Adams, *Connecticut: The Story of Your State Government,* Pequot Press, 1973; (editor with Arthur E. Soderlind and Rheta A. Clark) *Connecticut Yesterday and Today: A Selected Bibliography for Connecticut Schools,* Connecticut State Department of Education, 1974; *Connecticut's War Governor: Jonathan Trumbull,* Pequot Press, 1974; (with Freeman Meyer) *From Revolution to Constitution: Connecticut, 1763-1818,* Pequot Press, 1975.

Author of filmstrip "The Coming of the Revolution," for American Revolution Bicentennial Commission of Connecticut, 1975. General editor of "Series in Connecticut History," Center for Connecticut Studies, Eastern Connecticut State College, and Pequot Press, 1975. Contributor to *Connecticut League of Historical Societies Bulletin* and *Connecticut Review.* Editor of *Connecticut History* (of Association for the Study of Connecticut History), 1969-75.

* * *

ROTH, Theodore W(illiam) 1916-

PERSONAL: Born February 2, 1916, in Brooklyn, N.Y.; son of Theodore and Pauline C. (Smith) Roth; married Helen Barbara Wildeska, February 20, 1946. *Education:* Bolan Academy for Investigation, Detection, and Criminology, graduate, 1948. *Politics:* None. *Religion:* Roman Catholic. *Residence:* Long Island, N.Y. *Agent:* Julian Bach, Jr., 249 East 48th St., New York, N.Y. 10017. *Office:* 11 West 42nd St., New York, N.Y. 10036.

CAREER: Investigator who searches for missing heirs to estates. Director of Missing Heirs International; major associate of Investigators International, Inc. *Military service:* U.S. Army Air Forces, 1942-46. U.S. Army, agent in Criminal Investigation Division, 1946-48; served in Italy. *Member:* American Association of Criminology (fellow). *Awards, honors:* Named honorary trustee of Police Hall of Fame, 1970; award for patriotism from American Federation of Police, 1973; law degree from American Extension School of Law.

WRITINGS: Is There a Fortune Waiting for You, Citadel, 1975. Author of weekly newspaper columns for publica-

tions including *Midnight*, two years, and *National Insider*, one year. Stories have been run by United Features Syndicate; contributor to *True*, and to newspapers.

* * *

ROTHENBERG, Albert 1930-

PERSONAL: Born June 2, 1930, in New York, N.Y.; son of Gabriel (a businessman) and Rose (Goldberg) Rothenberg; married Elissa Isaacson, September 6, 1953 (divorced, 1969); married Julia C. Johnson (an educator), June 28, 1970; children: (first marriage) Michael, Mora Ruth, Rina Susannah. *Education:* Harvard University, A.B., 1952; Tufts University, M.D., 1956. *Home:* 139 Webb Circle, Monroe, Conn. 06468. *Office:* Health Center, University of Connecticut, Farmington, Conn. 06032.

CAREER: Pennsylvania Hospital, Philadelphia, intern, 1956-57; Yale University, School of Medicine, New Haven, Conn., resident in psychiatry, 1957-60, instructor, 1960-61, 1963-64, assistant professor, 1964-68, associate professor, 1968-74, clinical professor of psychiatry, 1974-75, assistant medical director of Yale Psychiatric Institute, 1964-65, attending psychiatrist at Yale New Haven Medical Center, 1964—; University of Connecticut, Farmington, professor of psychiatry, 1975—. Senior attending physician at Puerto Rico Institute of Psychiatry, 1961-63. Visiting professor at Pennsylvania State University, 1971, Yale University, 1975—. *Military service:* U.S. Army, 1961-63; became captain.

MEMBER: Pan-American Medical Association, American Psychiatric Association (fellow), American Society for Aesthetics, Society for Phenomenology and Existentialism, Royal Society of Health (fellow), Sigma Xi. *Awards, honors:* Research scientist career development program awards from National Institutes of Health, 1964, 1969; Guggenheim fellowship, 1974-75.

WRITINGS: Comprehensive Guide to Creative Writing Programs in American Colleges and Universities, National Council of Teachers of English, 1970; (with B. R. Greenberg) *The Index of Scientific Writings on Creativity: Creative Men and Women,* Archon, 1974; *The Index of Scientific Writings on Creativity: General, 1566-1974,* Archon, 1975; (with C. R. Hausman) *The Creativity Question,* Duke University Press, in press. Contributor to education, philosophy, and medical journals, and to *Saturday Review, Esquire, Comparative Drama,* and *American Poetry Review.* Editorial consultant to *American Journal of Psychiatry, Archives of General Psychiatry,* and *Psychological Reports.*

WORK IN PROGRESS: The Emerging Goddess: The Creative Process in Art, Science, and Other Fields.

SIDELIGHTS: "I study the creative process," Rothenberg wrote, "primarily because of its importance to psychiatry; its applications to concepts of mental health and to the practice of psychotherapy. Also, I love the Arts in all their forms and I have been privileged to glimpse some of their mysteries from the inside (and of creation in science as well)." *Avocational interests:* Tennis, chess, outdoor work around his rural home.

* * *

ROTHSTEIN, Arthur 1915-

PERSONAL: Born July 17, 1915, in New York, N.Y.; son of Isidor and Nettie (Perlstein) Rothstein; married Grace Goodman, July 4, 1947; children: Robert, Ann, Eve,

Daniel. *Education:* Columbia University, B.A., 1935. *Home:* 122 Sutton Manor, New Rochelle, N.Y. 10805. *Office: Parade* Magazine, 733 Third Ave., New York, N.Y. 10017.

CAREER: U.S. Farm Security Administration, Washington, D.C., photographer, 1935-40; *Look* (magazine), New York, N.Y., photographer, 1940-41; U.S. Office of War Information, New York, N.Y., picture editor, 1941-43; *Look,* technical director of photography, 1946-49, director of photography, 1969-71; *Infinity* (magazine), New York, N.Y., editor, 1971-72; *Parade* (magazine), New York, N.Y., associate editor, 1972—. Member of faculty, Columbia University, 1961—; consultant to U.S. Environmental Protection Agency and American Iron and Steel Association. *Military service:* U.S. Army, 1943-46. *Member:* American Society of Magazine Photographers (founding member), Society of Photographers in Communications, National Press Photographers Association, Photographic Administrators (president, 1961-63), Royal Photographic Society (fellow), New York Press Photographers Association, Sigma Delta Chi. *Awards, honors:* Recipient of numerous awards for photography, including an award from National Press Photographers Association, 1967, for career work, and the International Understanding through Photography Award from Photographic Society of America, 1968.

WRITINGS: Photojournalism, Ambassador, 1956, 4th edition, Amphoto, 1974; *Creative Color in Photography,* Chilton, 1963; (with William Saroyan) *Look at Us,* Cowles, 1967; *Color Photography Now,* Chilton, 1970.

WORK IN PROGRESS: Faces and Places; Portfolios.

SIDELIGHTS: Rothstein developed a three dimensional printing technique that was hailed as a major breakthrough in printing technology.

* * *

ROUBINEK, Darrell L(eRoy) 1935-

PERSONAL: Born May 1, 1935, in Narka, Kan.; son of Leonard C. and Hazel (Mitchell) Roubinek; married Jerrianne Thornburgh (a teacher), March 7, 1937; children: Darren Jon. *Education:* Kansas Wesleyan University, B.A., 1957; University of Kansas, M.A., 1962; Oklahoma State University, Ed.D., 1971. *Home:* 7008 Luana, Tucson, Ariz. 85721. *Office:* College of Education, University of Arizona, Tucson, Ariz. 85721.

CAREER: Public elementary school teacher in Olathe, Kans., 1957-60, principal, 1960-67, supervisor, 1967-69; principal of public school in Stillwater, Okla., 1969-71; University of Arizona, Tucson, assistant professor, 1971—. *Member:* National Association for Open Education, Association for Supervision and Curriculum Development, Arizona Association for Supervision and Curriculum Development (member of board of directors, 1975—), Phi Delta Kappa.

WRITINGS: (With Evelyn Carswell) *Open Sesame: A Primer on Open Education,* Goodyear Publishing, 1974. Contributor to journals. Review editor of *Opening Education,* 1974-75.

WORK IN PROGRESS: With Evelyn Carswell, *A Curriculum of Meaningful Relationships,* completion expected in 1976; with Bill Hillman, *Up the Classroom Wall,* 1976.

ROUT, Leslie B(rennan), Jr. 1936-

PERSONAL: Born February 26, 1936, in Chicago, Ill.; son of Leslie B. and Lucille L. (Penn) Rout; married Kathleen Kinsella; children: Deirdre Denise. *Education:* Loyola University, Chicago, Ill., B.A., 1957, M.A., 1961; University of Minnesota, Ph.D., 1966. *Politics:* "Conservative, whatever that means." *Religion:* Roman Catholic. *Home:* 836 Huntington Rd., East Lansing, Mich. 48823. *Office:* Department of History, Michigan State University, 405 Merrill Hall, East Lansing, Mich.

CAREER: Michigan State University, East Lansing, assistant professor, 1967-69, associate professor of history, 1969—. Coordinator of Teacher-Scholar Program of U.S. Department of State, summer, 1967. Producer, director, and performer in WKAR-TV series, "The Blackman in the Americas," 1968-70. *Awards, honors:* Michigan State Council of the Arts creativity award, 1969, for television series, "The Blackman in the Americas"; Ford Foundation grant, 1970; Woodrow Wilson Center for Scholars-Smithsonian Institute grant, 1975-76.

WRITINGS: (Contributor) Ray B. Brown, Richard H. Crowder, and Virgil L. Lokke, editors, *Frontiers of American Culture,* Purdue University Studies, 1968; *Politics of the Chaco Peace Conference: 1935-1939* (monograph), University of Texas Press, 1970; *Which Way Out? An Analysis of the Venezuela-Guayana Boundary Dispute* (monograph), Latin American Studies Center, Michigan State University, 1971; (contributor) Martin L. Kilson and Robert I. Rotberg, editors, *Harvard Studies on the African Diaspora,* Volume I, Harvard University, 1975; *The African Experience in Spanish America,* Cambridge University Press, in press. Contributor to encyclopedias, professional journals, and *Negro Digest.*

SIDELIGHTS: Rout told *CA:* "As a musician, I performed in the orchestras of Claude Thornhill, Woody Herman, Paul Winter, and Lefty Bates between 1961-66. In 1962, as a member of the Paul Winter Sextet, I played in the first jazz concert ever performed in the White House."

* * *

ROUTH, Donald K(ent) 1937-

PERSONAL: Surname rhymes with "youth"; born March 3, 1937, in Oklahoma City, Okla.; son of Ross Holland (a brigadier general in U.S. Army) and Fay (Campbell) Routh; married Marion Wendler (in real estate sales), September 10, 1960; children: Rebecca Ann, Laura Diane. *Education:* University of Oklahoma, B.A. (with distinction), 1962; University of Pittsburgh, M.S., 1965, Ph.D., 1967. *Politics:* Democrat. *Religion:* Unitarian Universalist. *Home:* 314 Brandywine Rd., Chapel Hill, N.C. 27514. *Office:* Department of Psychology, University of North Carolina, Chapel Hill, N.C. 27514.

CAREER: University of Oklahoma, Medical Center, Norman, intern in clinical psychology, 1967; University of Iowa, Iowa City, assistant professor of psychology, 1967-70; Bowling Green State University, Bowling Green, Ohio, associate professor of psychology, 1970-74; University of North Carolina, Chapel Hill, associate professor of psychology, 1971—. *Member:* American Psychological Association, American Association on Mental Deficiency, Society of Pediatric Psychology (president, 1973-74), Phi Beta Kappa, Sigma Xi.

WRITINGS: (Editor) *The Experimental Psychology of Mental Retardation,* Aldine, 1973. Contributor of about fifteen articles to psychology journals, including *Developmental Psychology* and *Journal of Consulting and Clinical*

Psychology. Consulting editor of *Journal of Abnormal Psychology and American Journal of Mental Deficiency.*

WORK IN PROGRESS: Disorders of Activity Level and Attention in Children.

* * *

ROVIN, Ben
   See CLEVENGER, Ernest Allen, Jr.

* * *

RUBIN, Duane R(oger) 1931-

PERSONAL: Born May 11, 1931, in Chicago, Ill.; son of Sanford Louis and Doris (Oakland) Rubin; married Constance L. Harvey, September 14, 1952 (divorced, 1969); children: Sandra (Mrs. Tim Auten), Debra, Susan. *Education:* Attended Northwestern University, 1949, 1950, and La-Sierra College, 1950-53. *Home:* 2290 Stockton St., #414, San Francisco, Calif. 94133. *Office:* Clift Travel Service, 580 Geary St., San Francisco, Calif. 94102.

CAREER: Northwest Orient Airlines, Chicago, Ill., transportation agent, 1953-56; TransWorld Airlines, Chicago, Ill., flight crew scheduler, 1956-59; Riddle Airlines, Miami, Fla., air freight and air charter sales representative, 1959-60; Fleetwood Travel Service, LaGrange, Ill., vice-president and treasurer, 1960-61; Travel Planners, Glendale, Calif., owner, 1961-66; Wright Way Tours, Glendale, general sales manager, 1966-67; Travel Management Corp., San Francisco, Calif., regional sales manager, 1967-68; Travelworld, Inc., New York, N.Y., eastern regional sales manager, 1968-69; free-lance tour manager, 1969-72; Clift Travel Service, San Francisco, Calif., agent and consultant, 1973—. Instructor at International College of Travel, San Francisco, 1974-75; member of board of directors of Glendale Junior Chamber of Commerce, 1963.

WRITINGS—"Customs and Culture" series, published by Celestial Arts: *Japan: Customs and Culture*, 1975; *Hong Kong: . . .*, in press; *Australia/New Zealand: . . .*, in press; *The Hidden Pacific: . . .*, in press. Contributor to travel trade publications.

WORK IN PROGRESS: The Chairman Is Coming, a fictional travel adventure; *Kodama*, a novel; *Two Spoons in a Drawer*, a novel of intrigue on an African safari.

SIDELIGHTS: Rubin once worked as a professional singer in Hollywood, Las Vegas, and Chicago. He has made seventeen trips around the world, forty-four trips to the Orient, six African safaris, and four trips around South America. *Avocational interests:* Music, collecting stamps, art, photography.

* * *

RUBINSTEIN, Hilary 1926-

PERSONAL: Born April 24, 1926, in London, England; son of Harold Frederick (a lawyer) and Lena (Lowy) Rubinstein; married Helge Kitzinger (an author and marriage counsellor), 1955; children: Jonathan, Felicity, Mark, Ben. *Education:* Merton College, Oxford, M.A., 1955. *Home:* 61 Clarendon Rd., London W.11, England. *Agent:* A. P. Watt & Son, 26/28 Bedford Row, London W.C.1, England. *Office:* A. P. Watt & Son, 26/28 Bedford Row, London W.C.1, England.

CAREER: Victor Gollancz Ltd. (publisher), London, England, editor, 1950-54, editorial director, 1954-58, assisting managing director, 1958-63; *Observer,* London, England, special features editor, 1963-64, deputy editor of Sunday magazine, 1964-65; A. P. Watt & Sons (literary agents),

London, England, partner, 1965—. Member of literature panel of Arts Council of Great Britain, 1974—. *Military service:* Royal Air Force, 1944-47.

WRITINGS: Insomniacs of the World, Goodnight: A Bedside Book, Random House, 1974 (published in England as *The Complete Insomniac,* J. Cape, 1974). Contributor to *Observer* (London), *Times* (London), *Guardian, Punch, New Statesman,* and others.

* * *

RUBINSTEIN, Moshe F(ajwel) 1930-

PERSONAL: Born August 13, 1930, in Miechow, Poland; son of Shlomo and Sarah (Rosen) Rubinstein; married Zafrira Gorstein, February 3, 1953; children: Iris, Dorit. *Education:* University of California at Los Angeles, B.S., 1954, M.S., 1957, Ph.D., 1961. *Home:* 10488 Charing Cross Rd., Los Angeles, Calif. 90024. *Office:* 7629 Boelter Hall, School of Engineering, University of California, Los Angeles, Calif. 90024.

CAREER: Murray Erick Associates, Los Angeles, Calif., designer, 1954-56; Victor Gruen Associates, Los Angeles, Calif., structural designer, 1956-61; University of California at Los Angeles, assistant professor, 1961-64, associate professor, 1964-69, professor of engineering, 1969—, head of department, 1969—. Sussman Distinguished Visiting Professor at Technion University, Haifa, Israel, 1967-68. Consultant to Pacific Power and Light Co., 1962, Northrup Corp., 1963, U.S. Army National Aeronautics and Space Administration (NASA) Research Center, 1965, Hughes Space System Division, 1965, U.S. Army Scientific Advisory Committee, 1967-71, Kaiser Aluminum and Chemical Corp., 1969-71, and International Business Machines (IBM), 1971—. *Military service:* Israeli Armed Forces, 1948-50.

MEMBER: American Society of Civil Engineers, American Society for Engineering Education, Seismological Society of America, Tau Beta Pi, Sigma Xi. *Awards, honors:* Western Electric Educational Fund award from American Society for Engineering Education, 1965.

WRITINGS: (With Walter C. Hurty) *Dynamics of Structures,* Prentice-Hall, 1964; *Matrix Computer Analysis of Structures,* Prentice-Hall, 1966; *Structural Systems, Statics, Dynamics, and Stability,* Prentice-Hall, 1970; *Patterns of Problem Solving,* Prentice-Hall, 1975.

WORK IN PROGRESS: Research in problem representation.

* * *

RUDOLPH, Lee (Norman) 1948-

PERSONAL: Born March 28, 1948, in Cleveland, Ohio; son of Norman and Harriet (a teacher; maiden name, Paine) Rudolph. *Education:* Princeton University, A.B., 1969; Massachusetts Institute of Technology, Ph.D., 1974. *Politics:* "Surrealist-anarchist-collectivist." *Religion:* Universal Life Church. *Home:* 3 Belgravia Place, Boston, Mass. 02113. *Office:* Alice James Books, 138 Mount Auburn St., Cambridge, Mass. 02138.

CAREER: Massachusetts Institute of Technology, Artificial Intelligence Laboratory, Cambridge, researcher-writer, 1973; Brown University, Providence, R.I., J. D. Tamarkin Instructor of Mathematics, 1974—. Member and treasurer, Alice James Poetry Cooperative, Inc., 1975—. *Member:* American Mathematical Society, Phi Beta Kappa. *Awards, honors:* Book-of-the-Month Club/College English Association writing fellowship, 1969; Woodrow Wilson fellowship, 1969; National Science Foundation fellowship, 1969-73.

WRITINGS: (With Harold Abelson and Leonard Fellman) *Calculus of Elementary Functions*, Harcourt, Volume 1-AB, 1970; *Curses & Songs & Poems*, Alice James Books, 1974. Poems represented in anthologies, including *Losers Weepers*, edited by George Hitchcock, Kayak Books, 1969; *Let's Eat the Children*, edited by Patricia Cummings and others, Cambridge St. Artists' Cooperative, 1972. Contributor of articles to technical journals and poems to *kayak, Quarterly Review of Literature*, and others.

WORK IN PROGRESS: Several manuscripts-worth of poems to be organized; a long poem, "In the Middle"; research in mathematics.

SIDELIGHTS: Rudolph writes: "Artists must be encouraged to cast off their passivity (as must women, and women artists doubly so), to cease to believe that their job ends when they have delivered a manuscript to an editor's desk (or a painting to a gallery owner). Because it is unpleasant, obnoxious, and perhaps bad for the soul to 'sell oneself' very much (again, especially so for American women), artists do well to organize in collectives and work in them, each for the others. Collectivity may be our salvation." *Avocational interests:* Raising vegetables (organically), cooking them, eating, and guitar.

* * *

RUDOLPH, Lloyd I(rving) 1927-

PERSONAL: Born November 1, 1927, in Chicago, Ill.; son of Charles N. (a lawyer) and Bertha (Margolin) Rudolph; married Susanne Hoeber (a professor of political science at University of Chicago), July 19, 1952; children: Jenny W., Amelia C., Matthew C. J. *Education:* U.S. Military Academy, cadet, 1945-46 (resigned); Harvard University, A.B. (magna cum laude), 1948, M.P.A., 1950, Ph.D., 1956; American University, evening courses, 1948-49. *Home:* 4943 South Woodlawn Ave., Chicago, Ill. 60615. *Office:* Department of Political Science, University of Chicago, 5828 South University Ave., Chicago, Ill. 60637.

CAREER: Experiment in International Living, France, group leader, summers of 1948, 1951; U.S. Government, Washington, D.C., research assistant to executive director of Council of Economic Advisers, Executive Office of the President, 1948-49, administrative assistant in Office of Territories, Department of the Interior, 1949; Harvard University, Cambridge, Mass., instructor, 1957-60, assistant professor of government and Allston Burr Senior Tutor at Dunster House, 1960-64; University of Chicago, Chicago, Ill., associate professor, 1964-72, professor of political science and social sciences in department of political science and in the College, 1972—, chairman of College political science program, 1969-71. Fulbright professor at University of Rajasthan, 1970-71. Consultant to Peace Corps, 1964-65, and to Foreign Service Institute, U.S. Department of State. *Military service:* U.S. Army, cadet, 1945-46, Adjutant General's Corps, 1954-56; became first lieutenant.

MEMBER: American Political Science Association (chairman of Leonard D. White Award committee, 1969), Association for Asian Studies, American Society for Public Administration, Indian Institute of Public Administration, Council on Foreign Relations. *Awards, honors:* Ford Foundation foreign area training fellow in India, 1956-57; Social Science Research Council fellow at Survey Research Center, University of Michigan, summer, 1958; Fulbright senior research scholar in India, 1962-63; American Institute of Indian Studies faculty fellow, 1966-67; grants from American Philosophical Society, 1971-72, American Council of Learned Societies, 1972-73, American Institute of Indian Studies, 1972-76, and National Science Foundation, 1973-74; Guggenheim fellow, 1975-76.

WRITINGS: (With wife, Susanne Hoeber Rudolph) *The Modernity of Tradition: Political Development in India*, University of Chicago Press, 1967; *Education and Politics in India: Studies in Organization, Society and Policy*, Harvard University Press, 1972; (editor with Susanne Hoeber Rudolph and contributor) *The Coordination of Complexity in South Asia*, U.S. Government Printing Office, for Commission on the Organization of the Government for the Conduct of Foreign Policy, 1975.

Contributor: C. J. Friedrich and S. E. Harris, editors, *Public Policy*, Volume IX, Graduate School of Public Administration, Harvard University, 1959; Immanuel Wallerstein, editor, *Social Change: The Colonial Situation*, Wiley, 1966; Willson C. McWilliams, editor, *Garrisons and Government: Politics and the Military in New States*, Chandler Publishing, 1967; Eric Nordlinger, editor, *Politics and Society: Studies in Comparative Sociology*, Prentice-Hall, 1969; Norman Cousins, editor, *Images of Gandhi*, Indian Book Co., 1969; S. P. Varma and Iqbal Narain, editors, *Fourth General Elections in India*, Orient Longmans, 1970; David Apter and Charles Adrian, editors, *Contemporary Analytic Theory*, Prentice-Hall, 1971; M. S. A. Rao, editor, *Urban Sociology in India*, Orient Longmans, 1974.

Articles and portions of books have been included in a number of readers and anthologies, among them *Political Modernization, Modern India, State and Society*, and *The Politics of Developing Nations*. Contributor to *American Political Science Review, Current Anthropology, Illustrated Weekly* (Bombay), *Asian Survey, New York Times Magazine*, and other journals and newspapers.

WORK IN PROGRESS: With Susanne Hoeber Rudolph, *The Diary of Amar Singh*; *Rajput Polity*.

* * *

RUDOLPH, Nancy 1923-

PERSONAL: Born December 26, 1923, in New York, N.Y.; daughter of Morris and Eva (Cohn) Kallman; married Alan Rudolph (a housing consultant), November 26, 1951; children: John, Lucy. *Education:* Attended Cedar Crest College, 1941-43, Artists Workshop, Los Angeles, 1946-47, and Art Students League, New York, N.Y., 1947-49. *Home and office:* 35 West 11th St., New York, N.Y. 10011.

CAREER: Museum of Modern Art, New York, N.Y., secretary and assistant in publicity department, 1947-49; Economic Cooperation Administration, Rome, Italy, press attache, 1949-50; free-lance photographer and writer, 1952—. Photography has been included in group shows of Metropolitan Museum of Art, 1971, and International Exposition of Photography, Hamburg, Germany, 1974, and shown in solo exhibits at Parents' Magazine Gallery, New York, and Menemsha Gallery, Menemsha, Mass., and several other group and solo shows; photographs represented in the Schomburg Collection of New York Public Library. Recreation consultant to schools and cities. *Member:* American Society of Magazine Photographers (member of board of directors, 1974-75), Citizens Committee for Children of New York City (member of board of directors, 1970—), Municipal Art Society, Women's City Club. *Awards, honors:* American Institute of Graphic Arts award of excellence, 1970, for photography in *Play and Playgrounds*.

WRITINGS: (Self-illustrated with photographs) *Work-yards: Playgrounds Planned for Adventure,* Teachers College Press, 1974.

Illustrator: Jeannette Galambos Stone, *Play and Playgrounds,* National Association for the Education of Young Children, 1970.

Contributor of illustrations: *Illustrated Children's Reader,* Chandler Publishing, 1968; *Threshold Program and Materials for Early Learning Centers,* Crowell-Collier, 1969; Arvid Bengsston, *Adventure Playgrounds,* Praeger, 1972; *Found Spaces and Equipment for Children's Centers,* Educational Facilities Laboratories, 1972; Joseph Stone and Joseph Church, *Childhood and Adolescence,* Random House, 1973; Naomi Pile, *Art in Early Childhood Education,* Crowell-Collier, 1973.

Contributor of articles to *Ms.* and *Tuesday,* and photographs to magazines and newspapers, including *L'Arche, Architectural Forum, Christian Science Monitor, Judaica, Cosmopolitan, Harper's Magazine, New York Herald Tribune,* and *New York Times Magazine.*

WORK IN PROGRESS: The Entire Tire Book, completion expected in 1975.

SIDELIGHTS: Mrs. Rudolph Speaks French and Italian. *Avocational Interests:* Skiing, sailing, tennis, listening to music, travel.

BIOGRAPHICAL/CRITICAL SOURCES: Photography Magazine (England), February, 1971.

*   *   *

RUFFINI, (Jacopo) Remo   1942-

PERSONAL: Born May 17, 1942, in La Brigue, Alpes Marittimes, France. son of Dante (an industrialist) and Maddalena (Pettirosso) Ruffini. *Education:* University of Rome, doctorate, 1967. *Home:* 3 Palmer Sq., Princeton, N.J. 08540; and 18 via S. Teodoro, Rome, Italy. *Office:* Department of Physics, Princeton University, Princeton, N.J. 08540.

CAREER: Institute for Advanced Study, Princeton, N.J., member, 1968-70; Princeton University, Princeton, N.J., assistant professor of physics, 1970-74; Institute for Advanced Study, Alfred P. Sloan Fellow, 1974-76. Joseph Henry Lecturer of the American Philosophical Society, 1972—; lecturer for the American Association for the Advancement of Science, 1973-74; director of International School of Relativistic Astrophysics, 1974—; guest lecturer, Soviet Academy of Science, 1974, Kyoto University, 1975. *Member:* European Physical Society, American Physical Society, New York Academy of Science, Sigma Xi. *Awards, honors:* Cressy Morrison Award of New York Academy of Sciences, 1972.

WRITINGS: (With James Bardeen and others) *Black Holes,* Gordon & Breach, 1973; (with Martin Rees and J. A. Wheeler) *Black Holes: Gravitational Waves and Cosmology,* Gordon and Breach, 1974; (with Herbert Gursky) *Neutron Stars, Black Holes and Binary X-Ray Sources,* D. Reidel (Dordrecht, Netherlands), 1975. Contributor of approximately sixty scientific papers to international journals.

WORK IN PROGRESS: Two undergraduate level physics texts.

SIDELIGHTS: Ruffini is competent in Italian, French, Spanish, German, and has traveled to Mexico, the Soviet Union, Japan, the Orient, Australia, and throughout Europe. *Avocational interests:* History, philosophy of science, early civilizations, and prehistoric art.

RUMSCHEIDT, H(ans) Martin   1935-

PERSONAL: Born July 24, 1935, in Leuna, Germany; naturalized Canadian citizen; son of Carl Friedrich (a chemical engineer) and Marie (Oeckinghaus) Rumscheidt; married Barbara Guild, December 28, 1962; children: Peter, Robert, Heidi. *Education:* McGill University, B.A., 1958, B.D., 1961, S.T.M., 1963, Ph.D., 1967; also studied at University of Basel, 1961-62. *Home:* 600 Francklyn St., Halifax, Nova Scotia B3H 3B4, Canada. *Office:* Department of Theological and Historical Studies, Atlantic School of Theology, 640 Francklyn St., Halifax, Nova Scotia B3H 3B5, Canada.

CAREER: Minister of United Church in Enterprise, Ontario, 1965-67; assistant minister of Deer Park United Church in Toronto, Ontario, 1967-70; University of Windsor, Windsor, Ontario, assistant professor of the history of theology, 1970-75; Atlantic School of Theology, Halifax, Nova Scotia, associate professor of historical theology, 1975—. President of Canadian Corp. for Studies in Religion, 1973—. *Member:* Canadian Society for Studies in Religion, Canadian Theological Society (vice-president, 1971-72; president, 1972-73), American Academy of Religion, Gesellschaft fuer Wissenschaftliche Symbolforschung, Gesellschaft fuer evangelische Theologie, Societe Canadienne de Theologie.

WRITINGS: (Editor) Karl Barth, *Fragments Grave and Gay,* Collins, 1971; *Revelation and Theology: The Barth-Harnack Correspondence of 1923,* Cambridge University Press, 1973; (editor) *Footnotes to a Theology: The Karl Barth Colloquium of 1972,* Canadian Corp. for Studies in Religion, 1974. Contributor to journals in his field.

WORK IN PROGRESS: German Theology and Culture of the 1920's.

*   *   *

RUNDLE, Anne
(Marianne Lamont, Alexandra Manners, Joanne Marshall, Jeanne Sanders)

PERSONAL: Born in Berwick-on-Tweed, England; daughter of George Manners (a soldier) and Annie (Sanderson) Lamb; married Edwin Charles Rundle (a civil servant), October 1, 1949; children: Anne M. H. (Mrs. Bruce D. Kelly), James, Iain. *Education:* Attended public schools in Berwick-on-Tweed, England. *Politics:* Conservative. *Religion:* Church of England. *Home and office:* 24 Queen's Dr., Glasgow G42 8DD, Scotland. *Agent:* John McLaughlin, 31 Newington Green, London N16 9PU, England.

CAREER: British Civil Service, Berwick-on-Tweed and Newcastle-on-Tyne, England, civil servant, 1942-50; now full-time writer. *Awards, honors:* Netta Muskett Award of Romantic Novelists Association, 1967, for *The Moon Marriage;* Romantic Novelists Association major awards, 1970, for *Cat on a Broomstick,* and 1971, for *Flower of Silence;* named Daughter of Mark Twain, 1974, in recognition of *Follow a Shadow.*

*WRITINGS—*Under name Anne Rundle: *The Moon Marriage,* Hutchinson, 1967; *Swordlight,* Hutchinson, 1968; *Forest of Fear,* Hutchinson, 1969; *Rakehell,* Hutchinson, 1970; *Dragonscale* (juvenile), Hutchinson, 1969; *Tamlane* (juvenile), Hutchinson, 1970; *Lost Lotus,* R. Hale, 1972; *Amberwood,* R. Hale, 1973, Bantam, 1974; *Heronbrook,* Bantam, 1974; *Judith Lammeter,* R. Hale and Bantam, in press.

Under pseudonym Marianne Lamont: *Dark Changeling,* Hutchinson, 1970, Avon, 1973; *Green Glass Moon,* Hutchinson, 1970; *Bitter Bride Bed,* Hutchinson, 1971.

Under Pseudonym Alexandra Manners: *The Stone Maiden,* Putnam, 1973; *Candles in the Wood,* Putnam, 1974; *The Singing Swans,* Putnam, 1975.

Under pseudonym Joanne Marshall: *Cuckoo at Candlemas,* Jenkins, 1968; *Cat on a Broomstick,* Jenkins, 1969; *The Dreaming Tower,* Jenkins, 1969; *Flower of Silence,* Mills & Boon, 1970, Avon, 1974; *Babylon Was Dust,* Mills & Boon, 1971; *Wild Boar Wood,* Mills & Boon, 1972, Avon, 1973; *The Trellised Walk,* Mills & Boon, 1973; *Sea-Song,* Mills & Boon, 1973; *Follow a Shadow,* Putnam, 1974; *Valley of Tall Chimneys,* Collins, 1975.

Under pseudonym Jeanne Sanders: *Spindrift,* R. Hale, 1974.

WORK IN PROGRESS: An historical novel set in Border Country during the reigh of Elizabeth I, completion expected in 1975; *The Peacock Bed,* a Gothic novel to be issued under pseudonym Alexandra Manners, 1976.

AVOCATIONAL INTERESTS: Painting, reading, walking.

* * *

RUNYAN, John
  See PALMER, Bernard

* * *

RUSH, Joshua
  See PEARLSTEIN, Howard J.

* * *

RUSSELL, James
  See HARKNETT, Terry

* * *

RUSSELL, James E.   1916-1975

1916—May 21, 1975; American authority on education, advocate of liberal education policies, and author of books in his field. Obituaries: *Washington Post,* June 18, 1975.

* * *

RUSSELL, Letty M(andeville)   1929-

PERSONAL: Born September 20, 1929, in Westfield, N.J.; daughter of Ricketson Borden (an engineer) and Miriam (Towl) Russell; married Johannes Christiann Moekendijk (a professor), January 3, 1970. *Education:* Wellesley College, B.A., 1951; Harvard University, S.T.D. (cum laude), 1958; Union Theological Seminary, New York, N.Y., S.T.M., 1967, Th.D. (summa cum laude), 1969. *Politics:* Democrat. *Home:* 99 Claremont Ave., New York, N.Y. 10027. *Office:* 409 Prospect St., New Haven, Conn. 06510.

CAREER: Ordained minister of United Presbyterian Church, 1958; East Harlem Protestant Parish, New York, N.Y., director of Christian education, 1952-55, pastor, 1958-68; Manhattan College, Bronx, N.Y., assistant professor of religious studies, 1969-74; Yale University Divinity School, New Haven, Conn., lecturer, 1973-74, assistant professor of theology, 1974—. Adjunct professor at New York Theological Seminary, 1969—; visiting professor at United Theological College, Bangalore, India, 1972. Member of working committee on studies in evangelism of World Council of Churches, 1962-73, consultant to U.S.

working group on participation of women, 1974-75; religious consultant to national board of Young Women's Christian Association, 1970-73; member of special committee on membership of United Presbyterian Church, U.S.A., 1971-75.

MEMBER: American Association of University Professors, American Academy of Religion (member of the Women's Caucus, 1973—), Professors of Religious Education, Association for Professional Education for Ministry.

WRITINGS: (With Clyde Allison and Daniel C. Little) *The City: God's Gift to the Church,* United Presbyterian Church, 1960; *Christian Education in Mission,* Westminster Press, 1967; *Women's Liberation in a Biblical Perspective* (study guide), National Board of YWCA, 1971; (contributor) John Westerhoff, editor, *Colloquy on Christian Education,* United Church Press, 1972; *Ferment of Freedom,* National Board of YWCA, 1972; *Unfinished Dimensions of the YWCA,* Young Men's Christian Association, 1973; *Human Liberation in a Feminist Perspective: A Theology,* Westminster Press, 1974; (contributor) Alice Hageman, editor, *Sexist Religion and Women in the Church,* Association Press, 1974; (contributor) Thomas McFadden, editor, *Liberation, Revolution and Freedom: Theological Perspectives,* Seabury Press, 1975. Author of *Bible Study Guide,* 1960-68, and *Christian Education Handbook,* 1966, both for East Harlem Protestant Parish. Contributor to theological and church journals.

WORK IN PROGRESS: Researching the relation of feminist theology and black theology, issues in liberation theology, and theology of vocation.

* * *

RUSSELL, O(live) Ruth   1897-

PERSONAL: Born July 9, 1897, in Delta, Ontario, Canada; daughter of William A. and Alice A. (Henderson) Russell. *Education:* University of Toronto, B.A. (honors), 1931; Austro-American Institute, graduate study, summer, 1932; University of Edinburgh, Ph.D., 1935; Columbia University, postdoctoral study, summer, 1941. *Politics:* Liberal. *Religion:* Protestant. *Home:* 3305 Shepherd St., Chevy Chase, Md. 20015.

CAREER: Moulton College, Toronto, Ontario, director of guidance and chairman of department of mathematics, 1935-42; Canadian Department of Veterans Affairs, Ottawa, Ontario, executive assistant to director general of rehabilitation, 1944-47; Winthrop College, Rock Hill, S.C., associate professor of psychology, 1947-49; Western Maryland College, Westminster, professor of psychology and chairman of department, 1949-62. Lecturer at Ontario Department of Education, summer, 1939, and at Johns Hopkins University, summer, 1956. Delegate to Inter-Continental Conference of National Councils of Women, 1946, and to Conference of International Federation of University Women, 1947. Consultant to National Advisory Council of Service Clubs in Canada, 1942-44. *Military service:* Canadian Army, psychologist, 1942-44; became captain.

MEMBER: International Council of Psychologists (fellow; member of board of directors, 1958-60), American Psychological Association (fellow), National Commission for Euthanasia (member of board, 1974—), American Association of University Women.

WRITINGS: Freedom to Die: Moral and Legal Aspects of Euthanasia, Human Sciences Press, 1975. Contributor to *New York Times* and to journals.

WORK IN PROGRESS: Work to encourage euthanasia legislation that would permit death "when the only alternative is useless suffering or a meaningless existence."

AVOCATIONAL INTERESTS: Travel.

* * *

RUSSELL-WOOD, A(nthony) J(ohn) R(ussell) 1939-

PERSONAL: Born October 11, 1939, in Corbridge-on-Tyne, England; son of James (a lecturer) and Ethel Kate (Roberts) Russell-Wood; married Hannelore Schmidt (a forensic pathologist), May 19, 1973; children: Christopher James Owen. *Education:* University of Lisbon, Teacher's Diploma, 1960; Oxford University, B.A. (honors), 1963; M.A. and D.Phil., 1967. *Home:* 31 Wooded Way, Pikesville, Md. 21208. *Office:* Department of History, Johns Hopkins University, Baltimore, Md. 21218.

CAREER: Oxford University, Oxford, England, lecturer in Portuguese language and literature, Faculty of Modern Languages, 1963-64, tutor, 1963-64, 1966-67, research fellow at St. Antony's College, 1967-69; Johns Hopkins University, Baltimore, Md., visiting associate professor, 1971-72, associate professor of history, 1972—, chairman of Alumni College, 1975. Official interpreter for Maryland Commission on Latin American Affairs during Brazilian trade mission, 1974.

MEMBER: Royal Geographical Society (life fellow), Conference on Latin American History, Latin American Studies Association, American Historical Association, Society for Latin American Studies, Anglo-Brazilian Society, Instituto Geografico e Historico of Bahia (corresponding member), Anglo-Brazilian Society, North-American Society for Oceanic History, Friends of Milton S. Eisenhower Library (president, 1974—).

AWARDS, HONORS: Grants for research from Instituto de Alta Cultura, Portugal, 1961, from British Ministry of Education for research in Brazil, 1963-66, from Brazilian Foreign Office for research in archives of Bahia and Rio de Janeiro, 1964-65, from Astor Foundation, 1970; co-winner of Herbert E. Bolton Prize of Conference on Latin American History, 1969, for *Fidalgos and Philanthropists*; commendation for best book on Latin American history by Albert J. Beveridge Award Committee of American Historical Association, 1969, for *Fidalgos and Philanthropists*; Newberry Library fellow, 1974.

WRITINGS: Fidalgos and Philanthropists: The Santa Casa da Misericordia of Bahia, 1550-1755, University of California Press, 1968; *Manuel Francisco Lisboa* (in Portuguese with English summary), Federal University of Minas Gerais, 1968; (contributor) David W. Cohen and Jack P. Greene, editors, *Neither Slave nor Free: The Freedmen of African Descent in the Slave Societies of the New World*, Johns Hopkins Press, 1972; (editor and contributor) *From Colony to Nation: Essays on the Independence of Brazil*, Johns Hopkins Press, 1975; (contributor) Ann Pescatello, editor, *The African in Latin America*, Knopf, 1975. Contributor of articles and reviews to *Comparative Studies in Society and History, Race, Hispanic American Historical Review*, and other journals.

WORK IN PROGRESS: Research on race relations in Portuguese America, with special reference to the free black and mulatto, on comparative government in the colonial Americas, and on relations between Asia and Brazil before 1800.

SIDELIGHTS: Russell-Wood lived in Brazil for a total of about five years before taking up residence in the United States in 1971. He is a former international squash racquets player for Wales, played for Oxford University in that sport, and represented Maryland in the U.S. amateur squash championships in Detroit, 1972. His other sports are karate, surf fishing, tennis, mountain walking, swimming, sailing, and cross country skiing.

* * *

RUUTH, Marianne 1933-

PERSONAL: Born April 28, 1933, in Kumla, Sweden; naturalized U.S. citizen in 1964; daughter of Paul and Maria (Steen) Petersson; married Helge O. Bylund, April, 1955 (divorced, 1957); married Patrick J. Daly (an industrial designer), June 23, 1966; children: Joanne. *Education:* Attended University of Stockholm, 1955-56, Los Angeles City College, 1957-58, and University of California, Los Angeles, 1958-59. *Politics:* "The individual has to come first!" *Home:* 3128 Waverly Dr., Los Angeles, Calif. 90027.

CAREER: Actress in Stockholm, Sweden, 1952-57; freelance writer, 1955—. *Member:* Mensa, Hollywood Foreign Press Association. *Awards, honors:* Bonnier Short Story Award, 1971.

WRITINGS—Fiction: *Droemmen om Hollywood* (title means "The Hollywood Dream"), Bonnier, 1970; *Look to the Blue Horse*, Bouregy, 1973; *Game of Shadows*, Ace Books, 1974; *A Question of Love*, Bouregy, 1975; *Tapestry of Terror*, Ace Books, 1975. Contributor of articles and short stories to journals.

WORK IN PROGRESS: A mystery novel.

SIDELIGHTS: "Why do I write?" Marianne Ruuth wrote to *CA*. "Because it's one way to discover life? Because I don't believe 'ordinary' human beings exist? (How common is the common man?) Because it is exciting to put a few human beings in a certain situation and say 'imagine if . . . .' Because I'd like to learn to understand, analyze, categorize, inform, communicate, create meaning in chaos—all at once? Because I've always wished to be Lewis Carroll? Who knows—and does it matter?"

* * *

RYAN, Charles W(illiam) 1929-

PERSONAL: Born December 14, 1929, in Greenville, Miss.; son of Price Lester (a baker) and Birdie Catherine (Abney) Ryan; married Mary Ann Viel, August 6, 1966 (divorced, 1968); married Elaina Jean Patch (a registered nurse), February 24, 1973; children: (first marriage) Christopher Adrian; (second marriage) Dan Eric. *Education:* University of Chicago, M.A., 1960. *Politics:* Democrat. *Religion:* Roman Catholic. *Home:* 3050 Bostick Ave., Marina, Calif. 93933. *Agent:* Marie Wilkerson, 230 Park Ave., New York, N.Y. 10017.

CAREER: Technical writer and editor in industry, holding positions with Westinghouse, Philco-Ford Corp., and Physics International Co., 1960-72; director of publications, United States Parachute Association, 1973—. Lay missionary teacher in boarding high school, Gaicanjiru, Kenya, 1964. *Military service:* U.S. Navy, 1947-52; U.S. Air Force, 1953-58; became first lieutenant.

WRITINGS: Spelling for Adults, Wiley, 1973; *Writing: A Practical Guide for Business and Industry*, Wiley, 1974; *Sport Parachuting*, Regnery, 1975; *Basic Electricity*, Wiley, in press. Editor of *Parachutist*, 1973—.

AVOCATIONAL INTERESTS: Sport parachuting, travel.

RYAN, John Barry 1933-

PERSONAL: Born April 7, 1933, in Bronx, N.Y.; son of John Michael and Winefred (Barry) Ryan. *Education:* Catholic University of America, A.B., 1955; Manhattan College, M.A., (English) 1961; University of Strasbourg, licentiate in theology, 1969; Institut Catholique de Paris, M.A. (liturgics), 1971, Ph.D., 1973. *Office:* Department of Religious Studies, Manhattan College, Bronx, N.Y. 10471.

CAREER: Member of Roman Catholic Brothers of Christian Schools, 1950—. Elementary school teacher in New York, N.Y., 1955-58; high school teacher in Syracuse, N.Y., 1958-62, and Detroit, Mich., 1962-65; Manhattan College, Bronx, N.Y., lecturer, 1972-73, assistant professor of religious studies, 1973—. Summer professor at St. Mary's College of California, 1973—. *Member:* North American Academy of Liturgy, Catholic Theological Society.

WRITINGS: The Eucharistic Prayer: A Study in Contemporary Liturgy, Paulist/Newman, 1974; *The Eucharistic Prayer: A Study-Text*, U.S. Catholic Conference, 1975. Contributor of articles and reviews to religious publications.

WORK IN PROGRESS: Research on liturgical changes taking place and how to implement them successfully.

SIDELIGHTS: Ryan writes: "My motivation in writing stems from my desire to serve people by submitting cultural phenomena to rational criticism. I have travelled extensively in Western Europe, particularly in France, Ireland, and Germany ... I enjoy working with people from other countries and have an interest in the foreign students at Manhattan College." *Avocational interests:* Photography, travel.

*   *   *

RYAN, Tom 1938-

PERSONAL: Born March 1, 1938; son of William and Ruby (Byrd) Ryan; married Carole Thresa Schneider, August 11, 1962; children: Jill. *Education:* Attended University of Maryland and Lakewood State College, Minnesota. *Politics:* Democrat. *Religion:* Roman Catholic. *Home:* Albany, Minn. 56307. *Agent:* Austin Wahl Agency, 21 East Van Buren St., Chicago, Ill. 60605.

CAREER: Theatre owner and corrections officer; writer. *Military service:* U.S. Air Force. *Member:* Authors Guild. *Awards, honors:* O. Henry Award, 1971.

WRITINGS: Brannigan, Leisure Books, 1974; *The Man from Furnace Creek*, Leisure Books, 1975; *Mark of the Rattler*, Leisure Books, 1975. Contributor to magazines.

WORK IN PROGRESS: Firebrand, a novel; *History of the TV Movies; 12 Gauge Pattern*.

SIDELIGHTS: Ryan is a film historian and collector. He speaks Spanish and French.

*   *   *

SAATY, Thomas L(orie) 1926-

PERSONAL: Born July 18, 1926, in Mosul, Iraq; came to U.S., 1946; son of David M. and Dola (Hayali) Saaty; married Rozann Waldron, December 9, 1964; children: Linda, Michael, Emily, John, Daniel. *Education:* Columbia Union College, B.A., 1948; Catholic University of America, M.S., 1949; Sorbonne, University of Paris, graduate study, 1952-53; Yale University, Ph.D., 1953. *Home:* 224 Almur Lane, Wynnewood, Pa. 19096. *Office:* Wharton

School, University of Pennsylvania, Philadelphia, Pa. 19174.

CAREER: Melpar, Inc., Alexandria, Va., mathematician, 1953-54; Massachusetts Institute of Technology, Cambridge, scientific analyst with Operations Evaluation Group, 1954-57; U.S. Department of the Navy, Washington, D.C., mathematician in Management Office, 1957-58; Office of Naval Research, London, England, mathematician, 1958-59, director of advanced planning of Naval Analysis Group, 1959-61, head of Mathematics Branch, 1961-63; U.S. Arms Control & Disarmament Agency, Washington, D.C., research scientist, 1963-69; University of Pennsylvania, Philadelphia, professor of applied mathematics, 1969—, chairman of Operations Research, 1969-71. Executive director, Conference Board of Math Sciences, 1965-67; visiting lecturer at U.S. Department of Agriculture Graduate School, 1954-69, Catholic University of America, 1960, George Washington University, 1962-65, University of California, Los Angeles, 1963-69, and others; consultant to governmental and private agencies. *Member:* International Institute for Strategic Studies, American Mathematical Society, Mathematical Association of America, Operations Research Society of America, American Association for the Advancement of Science (fellow), World Future Society, Pi Mu Epsilon. *Awards, honors:* Award from Office of Naval Research, 1959, for contributions to the advancement of international scientific cooperation; Lester R. Ford Award from Mathematical Association of America, 1973.

WRITINGS: Mathematical Methods of Operations Research, McGraw, 1959; *Elements of Queueing Theory with Applications*, McGraw, 1961; (with Joseph Bram) *Non-Linear Mathematics*, McGraw, 1964; (editor) *Lectures on Modern Mathematics*, three volumes, Wiley, 1964-65; (with Robert Busacker) *Finite Graphs and Networks*, McGraw, 1965; *Modern Non-Linear Equations*, McGraw, 1967; *Mathematical Models of Arms Control and Disarmament*, Wiley, 1968; (editor with F. J. Weyl) *The Spirit and Use of the Mathematical Sciences*, McGraw, 1969; *Optimization in Integers and Related External Problems*, McGraw, 1970; *Topics on Behavioral Mathematics*, Mathematical Association of America, 1973; (with George Dantzig) *Compact City*, W. H. Freeman, 1973; *Mathematical Models in Physical, Biological and Social Sciences*, American Association for the Advancement of Science, 1975. Contributor to journals in his field. Assistant editor, *Operations Research*, 1958-63, *Naval Research Logistics Quarterly*, 1964—; editor, *Newsletter for the Mathematical Science*, 1965-67.

WORK IN PROGRESS: Research on priorities for energy distribution hierarchies, fuzzy sets, quantitative methods in the social sciences, transport planning for the Sudan, and the construction of a regional energy game.

*   *   *

SABBAH, Hassan i
    See BUTLER, William Huxford

*   *   *

SABERHAGEN, Fred (Thomas) 1930-

PERSONAL: Born May 18, 1930, in Chicago, Ill.; son of Frederick Augustus and Julia (Moynihan) Saberhagen; married Joan Dorothy Spicci, June 29, 1968; children: Jill, Eric, Thomas. *Residence:* Albuquerque, N.M.

CAREER: Writer. *Member:* Science Fiction Writers of America.

WRITINGS: The Golden People, Ace Books, 1964; Water of Thought, Ace Books, 1965; Berserker, Ballantine, 1967; The Broken Lands, Ace Books, 1967; Brother Assassin, Ballantine, 1969; Black Mountains, Ace Books, 1970; Changeling Earth, Daw Books, 1973; Berserker's Planet, Daw Books, 1975; Book of Saberhagen, Daw Books, 1975; The Dracula Tape, Warner Paperback, 1975; Specimens, Popular Library, 1975. Also author of "Love Conquers All," published in Galaxy (magazine), 1974-75.

* * *

SABIN, Katharine Cover 1910-

PERSONAL: Maiden name is pronounced Kove-er, married name is pronounced Say-bin; born April 16, 1910, in Denver, Colo.; daughter of Mark Elbert (a musician and grocer) and Lettie (Skinner) Cover; married Herald John Sabin, October 8, 1936; children: Mark Joseph, Sharon J. Shuman (adopted daughter; Mrs. Willis Gale Sanderson). Education: Attended public schools in Denver, Colo. Politics: "Republicrat." Religion: "Metaphysical," Home: 6361 Celia Vista Dr., San Diego, Calif. 92115. Office: Sabin Publishing Co., 1514 Roosevelt, National City, Calif.

CAREER: Executive sales manager of Sabin Publishing Co., National City, Calif. Formerly executive partner of husband in sales department of Goodyear Tire & Rubber Sales (Fresno, Calif.), and sales department of Capitol Co-Operative Life Insurance Co. (Denver, Colo.). Member: Applied ESP Research Society (founder and president).

WRITINGS: The Cybernetic ESP Breakthrough, Sabin, 1966; ESP and Dream Analysis, Regnery, 1974. Author of "The Associative Card Code," a card reading course published by Sabin. Contributor to Indian Journal of Parapsychology, Fate, Search, and Occult.

WORK IN PROGRESS: Casting the Devil Out of ESP; The Parapsychology of Prayer; ESP in an Ink Blot; Dream Control for ESP; Discovering Cosmic Patterns.

SIDELIGHTS: Katharine Sabin writes: "Previous to my discoveries, predicting the future with a deck of coded cards had been considered too subjective a process for parapsychological laboratory testing . . . Although I am not an expert in cybernetics, probability theory, or neural association theory, I used these principles to evolve sophisticated card codes . . . Many of the messages achieved by my card codes are so objective that even non-psychics can read them . . . Though I had little precognitive ability, I used my card reading methodologies to make outstanding national and international predictions . . . While evolving highly sophisticated card codes I also learned how to upgrade the ESP content of dreams . . ."

* * *

SACHER, Jack, Jr. 1931-

PERSONAL: Born April 26, 1931, in New York, N.Y.; son of Isaac Jacob (a factory manager) and Isabel (an insurance agent; maiden name, Crystal) Sacher; married Josephine Pettit (a singer), 1963; children: Jennifer Ruth, Robert Jacob. Education: Middlebury College, A.B., 1952; Columbia University, M.A., 1956, Ed.D., 1964. Home: 107 Oak Dr., Cedar Grove, N.J. 07009. Office: Department of Music, Montclair State College, Upper Montclair, N.J. 07043.

CAREER: Teacher of music in public schools of Weehawken, N.J., 1958-60; supervisor of music in public schools of North Bergen, N.J., 1960-64; Montclair State College, Upper Montclair, N.J., assistant professor, 1964-68, associate professor, 1969-73, professor of music, 1974—. Freelance choral conductor, 1954—; music director of Society for Choral Music, 1966—, and of Montclair State Opera Workshop, 1968—. Lecturer, Teachers College, Columbia University, 1960-70. Consultant to Metropolitan Opera Guild, 1960—. Military service: U.S. Army, 1952-54; became sergeant. Member: American Musicological Society, American Choral Foundation, American Choral Directors Association, Music Educators National Conference.

WRITINGS: (With F. D. Meyer) The Changing Voice, Augsburg, 1960; (editor and translator from the German) Music A-Z, Grosset, 1963; (with James Eversole) The Art of Sound, Prentice-Hall, 1971, 2nd edition, in press.

WORK IN PROGRESS: History of Orchestral Music, completion expected in 1980.

SIDELIGHTS: Sacher studied opera education in Munich, Germany and London, England, in the spring of 1975. He has conducted the world premiere of Paul Knudson's, "The Actress," at Montclair State College, in May, 1974, and he will conduct the premiere of James Eversole's opera, "Bessy," at Montclair State College, in May, 1976.

* * *

SADLER, Ella Jo 1942-

PERSONAL: Born August 2, 1942, in Quaker, Mo., daughter of George Leonard (a farmer and merchant) and Valle (Hutchings) Barr; married Gerald G. Sadler (an IBM engineer), August 20, 1960; children: Joye Ellen, Clay Gerard, Clint Warren. Education: Attended Flat River Junior College (now Mineral Area Community College), 1960, and Washington University, St. Louis, Mo., 1961. Politics: Republican. Religion: Christian. Home: Christmas Valley Road, P.O. Box 244, Chesterfield, Mo. 63017.

CAREER: National Benevolent Association, St. Louis, Mo., IBM keypunch operator, 1961-65; writer. Piano and organ accompanist for soloists, choirs, and ensembles. Member: American Guild of Organists, St. Louis Christian Business and Professional Women's Club (chairwoman and music coordinator, 1974-75). Awards, honors: Dwight L. Moody Award for Excellence in Christian Literature, 1975, for Murder in the Afternoon.

WRITINGS: Murder in the Afternoon, Zondervan, 1975. Contributor of articles to Christian Review and Christian Standard.

WORK IN PROGRESS: An article and booklet on overcoming fear; a novel.

SIDELIGHTS: Ella Jo Sadler told CA that Murder in the Afternoon was based on her experience as a teenager when her home "was invaded by killers on a spree, and we were all left for dead."

* * *

SAMMARTINO, Peter 1904-

PERSONAL: Born August 15, 1904, in New York, N.Y.; son of Guy and Eva (Amendola) Sammartino; married Sylvia Scaramelli, December 5, 1933. Education: College of the City of New York (now City College of the City University of New York), B.S., 1924; New York University, M.A., 1928, Ph.D., 1931; also attended University of Paris. Politics: Republican. Religion: Roman Catholic. Home: 140 Ridge Rd., Rutherford, N.J. 07070. Office: Office of Chancellor, Fairleigh Dickinson University, Rutherford, N.J.

CAREER: Teacher in public schools in New York, N.Y., and at College of the City of New York (now City College of the City University of New York); Columbia University, New York, N.Y., former head of languages department; Fairleigh Dickinson University, Rutherford, N.J., chancellor and founder, 1942—. Founder and president of International Association of University Presidents, 1942; member of advisory board of the Peace Corps, 1965—; vice-president, New Jersey Constitutional Convention, 1966; president, New York Cultural Center, 1969; member of Board of Foreign Scholarships, 1971—. Delegate to the White House Conference on Education. *Member:* Royal Society of Arts (life fellow), Alpha Phi Delta (former president). *Awards, honors:* Chevalier, Legion of Honor; Officier d'Academie (France); Order of Merit, Republic of Italy; Silver Medal, Sons of the American Revolution; Grand Commander, Order of the Star of Africa (Liberia); Commander, Ordre National (Ivory Coast); Townsend Harris Medal; Gold Medal, University of Bologna; Brotherhood Award, National Conference of Christian and Jews; Distinguished Alumni Award, New York University, 1968; LL.D. from Long Island University and from University of Liberia; Litt.D. from Kyung Hee University, Korea, L.H.D. from Fairleigh Dickinson University.

WRITINGS: (With Edward I. Amateau) *French in Action*, Globe Book Co., 1933; (with Thomas Russo) *Il primo libro*, Crispen, 1936; (with Russo) *Letture Facili*, Crispen, 1937; (with Rene M. Guastalla) *Survey of French Literature*, Longmans, Green, 1937; (with Roy E. Mosher) *Grammaire simple et lectures faciles*, Harper & Brothers, 1938; *Avancons*, Harper & Brothers, 1940; (with Russo) *Il secondo libro*, Harper & Brothers, 1941; (with Ellsworth Tompkins) *Community College in Action*, Fairleigh Dickinson College Press, 1950; *The President of a Small College*, Fairleigh Dickinson College Press, 1954; *Multiple Campuses*, Fairleigh Dickinson University Press, 1964; (editor) *The Private Urban University*, Fairleigh Dickinson University Press, 1966; *The Humanities in the Age of Science*, Fairleigh Dickinson University Press, 1968; *Of Castles and Colleges: Notes toward an Autobiography*, A. S. Barnes, 1972. Also author of *Emile Zola*, and editor of proceedings of Fairleigh Dickinson conferences on higher education and oceanology. Associate editor of *The Clearing House Magazine*, and *Literary Review*.

*   *   *

SAMPSON, Edward C(oolidge) 1920-

PERSONAL: Born December 20, 1920, in Ithaca, N.Y.; son of Martin W. and Julia D. (Pattison) Sampson; married Frances P. Hanford, October 26, 1946 (divorced, 1968); married Cynthia A. Reed (a teacher), December 28, 1968; children: (first marriage) Susan (Mrs. Michael Ives), Edward H. *Education:* Cornell University, B.A., 1942, Ph.D., 1957; Columbia University, M.A., 1948. *Home:* 95 Ford Ave., Oneonta, N.Y. 13820. *Office:* Department of English, State University of New York College at Oneonta, Oneonta, N.Y. 13820.

CAREER: Hofstra University, Hempstead, N.Y., instructor in English, 1946-49; Clarkson College of Technology, Potsdam, N.Y., instructor, 1952-53, assistant professor, 1953-57, associate professor, 1957-61, professor of English, 1961-69; State University of New York College at Oneonta, professor of English, 1969—. Fulbright lecturer at University of Panjab, 1959-60. *Military service:* U.S. Army Air Forces, 1942-46; became captain; received Bronze Star

Medal. *Member:* Modern Language Association of America.

WRITINGS: E. B. White, Twayne, 1974. Contributor of articles and book reviews to journals in his field.

WORK IN PROGRESS: A study of Thomas Hardy and science.

AVOCATIONAL INTERESTS: Art, music, travel, travel literature, the sea.

*   *   *

SANCHEZ-HIDALGO, Efrain Sigisfredo 1918-1974

PERSONAL: Born April 29, 1918, in Moca, Puerto Rico; son of Zenon (a farmer) and Pelegrina (Hidalgo) Sanchez; married Lydia Ayendez (a professor), June 14, 1947; children: Melba Maria, Ivan Gilberto. *Education:* University of Puerto Rico, B.A., 1939; Columbia University, M.A., 1940, Ph.D., 1951. *Religion:* Roman Catholic. *Home:* 152 Mimosa St., Santa Maria, Rio Piedras, Puerto Rico 00927. *Office:* University of Puerto Rico, Rio Piedras, Puerto Rico 00931.

CAREER: University of Puerto Rico, Rio Piedras, instructor, 1940-41, assistant professor, 1948-50, associate professor, 1950-54, professor of education and psychology, 1954-74, founder and director of Guidance and Education Office, 1954-57. Senior training officer, Veterans Administration Center, San Juan, 1946-47; secretary of education, Commonwealth of Puerto Rico, 1957-60; president, Superior Educational Council of Puerto Rico, 1957-60. *Military service:* U.S. Army, Infantry, 1942-46; served in North African and European theatres; became major; received Infantry Combat Badge, Bronze Star Medal. *Member:* American Psychological Association (fellow), P.E.N. (cofounder of Puerto Rico chapter), Puerto Rico Psychological Association (founder; president, 1953-55), Puerto Rico Teachers Association.

WRITINGS: Psicologia Educativa (title means "Educational Psychology"), Editorial Universitaria, 1954, 7th revised edition, 1972; *La Psicologia de la crianza* (title means "The Psychology of Child-Rearing"), Editorial Universitaria, 1962, 3rd edition (with wife, Lydia Sanchez-Hidalgo), 1971; (with Lydia Sanchez-Hidalgo) *La Psicologia de la vejez* (title means "The Psychology of Old Age"), Editorial Universitaria, 1971. Also author of *La Psicologia del Aprendizaje* (title means "The Psychology of Learning"), published in 1974, and of unpublished works, *Hojas de mi arbol* (poems), *La Tortuga negra* (novel), *Impresiones e ideas*. Contributor of more than 140 articles on social, educational, cultural, and psychological subjects to journals and newspapers in Puerto Rico and abroad. Founder, and director, *Pedagogia*, 1953-56; abstractor, *Psychological Abstracts*.

WORK IN PROGRESS: A book on the psychology of women, *La Psicologia de la mujer*, with his wife, Lydia Sanchez-Hidalgo.

(Died April 1, 1974)

*   *   *

**SANDERS, Jeanne
See RUNDLE, Anne**

*   *   *

SANFILIP, Thomas 1952-
PERSONAL: Born June 28, 1952, in Chicago, Ill.; son of

Peter and Frances (Fano) Sanfilip. *Education:* Attended Wright Junior College, 1970-72, and Northern Illinois University, 1972-75. *Home:* 3811 North Pueblo, Chicago, Ill. 60634.

CAREER: Freelance writer in Chicago, Ill., 1973—.

WRITINGS: (Contributor) Kenneth F. Kwint, editor, *Shore Poetry Anthology*, Shore Publishing, 1972; (contributor) Lincoln B. Young, editor, *Lyrics of Love*, Young Publications, 1972; *By the Hours and the Years* (poetry), Branden Press, 1974. Contributor to *Thalassa*, *Towers*, and *Ivory Tower*.

WORK IN PROGRESS: A book of poems, *In Private Singularity*; *In the April Ways*; a book of literary theory and criticism, *The Unific Principle*.

SIDELIGHTS: Sanfilip writes: "My thoughts are largely a product of my own discoveries. I usually am more involved with the process of living than the constant speculation of it, and I find everything I write infused with an uncompromising nature. I anticipate a much more active lifestyle for the future and an exciting, provocative career ahead."

*   *   *

SANTESSON, Hans Stefan   1914(?)-1975

1914(?)—February 21, 1975; Swedish-born American mystery and science fiction magazine and book editor, and author. Obituaries: *New York Times*, February 22, 1975; *Publishers Weekly*, March 10, 1975; *AB Bookman's Weekly*, March 17, 1975.

*   *   *

SARKESIAN, Sam C(harles)   1927-

PERSONAL: Born November 7, 1927, in Chicago, Ill.; son of Charles (a waiter) and Khatoon (Babigian) Sarkesian; married Jeanette Minasian, May 7, 1955; children: Gary Charles, Joye Simone, Guy Samuel. *Education:* Attended Michigan State College (now Michigan State University), 1945; Citadel, B.A., 1951; Syracuse University, graduate study, 1961; Columbia University, M.A., 1962, Ph.D., 1969. *Religion:* Armenian Apostolic. *Home:* 5948 North Hermitage Ave., Chicago, Ill. 60660. *Office:* Department of Political Science, Loyola University, 6525 North Sheridan Rd., Chicago, Ill. 60626.

CAREER: U.S. Army, career officer, 1945-68, assistant professor of political science at U.S. Military Academy (West Point), 1962-66, retiring as lieutenant colonel; DePaul University, Chicago, Ill., assistant professor of political science, 1968-70; Loyola University, Chicago, Ill., associate professor, 1970-74, professor of political science and chairman of department, 1974—. Visiting assistant professor at Northwestern University, summer, 1964, and State University of New York at Buffalo, summer, 1965; lecturer at University of Maryland and in Vietnam, 1967; executive secretary of Inter-University Seminar on the Armed Forces and Society, 1968-72, associate chairman, 1972—; president of Rosehill City Council, 1971-74; member of board of directors of Edgewater Community Council, 1974—.

MEMBER: International Studies Association, American Political Science Association, Midwest Political Science Association, Pi Sigma Alpha, Delta Tau Kappa. *Awards, honors*—Military: Parachutists badge, glider badge, Legion of Merit, Bronze Star with oak leaf cluster. Academic: Russell Sage Foundation grant, 1971; Inter-University Seminar on the Armed Forces and Society travel grant, 1971, for study in Uganda, Kenya, and East Africa; Army Research Institute grant, 1975.

WRITINGS: (Editor) *The Military-Industrial Complex: A Reassessment*, Sage Publications, 1972; *The Professional Army Officer in a Changing Society*, Nelson-Hall, 1975; (with Krishan Nanda) *Power and Politics in American Government*, Alfred Publishing, 1975; (editor) *Revolutionary Guerrilla Warfare*, Precedent, 1975. Co-editor of "Peacekeeping and Revolution," a series on war, Sage Publications. Contributor to *Midwest Journal of Political Science*, *Orbis*, *African Studies Review*, and *Chicago Tribune*. Associate editor of *Armed Forces and Society*.

WORK IN PROGRESS: A textbook on comparative politics, completion expected in 1977; *The New Military Professionalism*, 1978; a monograph on the assessment of African military regimes.

SIDELIGHTS: Sarkesian writes: "My primary concern in writing a book on the Professional Army Officer was to show that the Army officer is, after all, a human being with motivations and expectations similar to most civilians. Too many books on the military assume a stereotyped view of the officer as a man, while focusing on policy matters and grand schemes. What I believe is needed is a 'humanistic' perspective of the Army professional."

*   *   *

SATTERFIELD, Archie   1933-

PERSONAL: Born June 18, 1933, in Howards Ridge, Mo.; son of Homer and Lucile (Howard) Satterfield; married Joyce McLennan, December 28, 1961; children: Cassandra, Erin, Scott, Sarah. *Education:* Attended St. Louis University, 1956-57, University of Missouri, 1957-59; University of Washington, B.A., 1963. *Home:* 2417 Warren Ave. N., Seattle, Wash. 98109. *Office: Seattle Post-Intelligencer*, 5th and Wall, Seattle, Wash. 98111.

CAREER: Seaside Signal, Seaside, Ore., reporter, 1963-64; *Longview Daily News*, Longview, Wash., reporter, 1964-66; *Seattle Times*, Seattle, Wash., reporter and assistant magazine editor, 1966-72; *Seattle Post-Intelligencer*, Seattle, Wash., book review editor, 1972—. *Military service:* U.S. Navy, 1952-56; became petty officer third class. *Member:* Outdoor Writers Association of America, Society of American Travel Writers, Pacific Northwest Writers Conference (vice-president, 1972-73), Lewis & Clark Trail Commission, Seattle Free-Lances (president, 1974-75). *Awards, honors:* State of Washington Governor's Writers Day award, 1970.

WRITINGS: Moods of the Columbia, Superior, 1968; *Alaska Bush Pilots*, Superior, 1969; *Oregon Coast*, Charles H. Belding, 1972; *Washington*, Charles H. Belding, 1973; *California: Coast and Desert*, Charles H. Belding, 1973; *Chilkoot Pass: Then and Now*, Alaska Northwest Publishing, 1973; *Oregon II*, Charles H. Belding, 1974; *Yukon River Guide*, Stackpole, 1975. Contributing editor, *Pacific Search*.

WORK IN PROGRESS: Endless Days, Endless Nights (tentative title), a social history of Yukon Territory, for Lippincott; a history-guide to Lewis & Clark and Oregon Trail books, for Stackpole; compiling an oral history of World War II.

*   *   *

SAUER, Carl (Ortwin)   1889-1975

1889—1975; American geographer, educator, and author of

books on history and geography. Obituaries: *Time*, August 4, 1975.

* * *

SAUNDERS, Keith 1910-

PERSONAL: Born February 21, 1910, in Elizabeth City, N.C.; son of W. O. (an editor) and Columbia (Ballance) Saunders; married Mary Newlin, October 5, 1940; children: Judith Anne Saunders Stephens. *Education:* Attended University of North Carolina, 1927-29. *Politics:* Independent. *Religion:* United Methodist. *Home and office:* 5120 Chevy Chase Pkwy. N.W., Washington, D.C., 20008.

CAREER: The Independent, Elizabeth City, N.C., staff member, 1929-38; *Raleigh Times*, Raleigh, N.C., staff member, 1939-41; *Norfolk Virginian Pilot*, Norfolk, Va., staff member, 1941-43; *Baltimore Evening Sun*, Baltimore, Md., staff member, 1943-46; American Aviation Publications, Washington, D.C., associate editor, 1947-52; *Aviation Daily*, Washington, D.C., managing editor, 1952-59; *Air Travel*, Washington, D.C., executive editor, 1959-68; *Airline Marketing Newsletter*, Washington, D.C., editor, 1968. *Member:* Society of American Travel Wrtiers (director, 1963-65), First Flight Society, National Press Club, Sigma Delta Chi. *Awards, honors:* Trans World Airlines aviation writing award, 1951; man of the year award from Air Line Traffic Association, 1965.

WRITINGS: The Independent Man, privately printed, 1964; *So You Want to Be an Airline Stewardess*, Arco Publishing, 1968; *Guidebook to the Outer Banks of North Carolina*, privately printed, 1974. Contributor to *Encyclopedia Americana Annual* and to *American Way*. Editor of *National Aeronautics*, 1951-61, and *Air Cargo Newsletter*, 1958-68.

WORK IN PROGRESS: A book dealing with the criticisms and controversies surrounding the U.S. national anthem; an annual update of his *Guidebook to the Outer Banks of North Carolina*; another guidebook.

* * *

SAVAGE, William W(oodrow), Jr. 1943-

PERSONAL: Born October 13, 1943, in Richmond, Va.; son of William W. (an educator) and Margaret (Clarke) Savage; married Emily Sue Rubert (a primatologist), April 21, 1970; children: Stephen Shane. *Education:* University of South Carolina, B.A., 1964, M.A., 1966; University of Oklahoma, Ph.D., 1972. *Residence:* Norman, Okla. 73069. *Office:* Department of History, University of Oklahoma, 455 West Lindsey, Room 406, Norman, Okla. 73069.

CAREER: University of South Carolina, Columbia, instructor in history, 1966; University of Oklahoma, Norman, field worker at American Indian Institute, 1967; University of Oklahoma Press, Norman, assistant editor, 1972-75; University of Oklahoma, Norman, assistant professor of history, 1974—. Visiting professor at Iowa State University, 1970, and at University of Oklahoma, 1973-74. *Member:* Organization of American Historians, Western History Association, Omicron Delta Kappa, Phi Alpha Theta, Sigma Delta Chi. *Awards, honors:* Sigma Delta Chi national award, 1964.

WRITINGS: The Cherokee Strip Live Stock Association: Federal Regulation and the Cattleman's Last Frontier, University of Missouri Press, 1973; (editor) *Cowboy Life: Reconstructing an American Myth*, University of Oklahoma Press, 1975; (author of foreword) Grant Foreman,

Indians and Pioneers, University of Oklahoma Press, 1975. Contributor of articles and reviews to historical journals.

WORK IN PROGRESS: Several monographs; editing books; textbooks.

AVOCATIONAL INTERESTS: Philately, musicology.

* * *

SAVOURS, Ann (Margaret) 1927-

PERSONAL: Born November 9, 1927, in Stoke-on-Trent, England; daughter of Edgar Walter (a civil engineer) and Doris Margaret (a teacher and poet; maiden name, Holt) Savours; married Laurence George Samuel Shirley (a postmaster and councillor), November 18, 1961; children: John Alexander, Nicholas Savours. *Education:* Royal Holloway College, University of London, B.A. (honors), 1949; Sorbonne, University of Paris, diplome de civilisation francaise, 1950; graduate study at Burslem School of Art, 1950-51. *Religion:* Anglican. *Home:* Little Bridge Place, Mill Lane, Bridge, Canterbury, Kent CT4 5LG, England. *Agent:* Bruce Hunter, David Higham Associates, 5-8 Lower John St., Golden Sq., London W1R 4HA, England. *Office:* National Maritime Museum, London S.E.10, England.

CAREER: University of Aberdeen, Aberdeen, Scotland, library assistant, 1952-54; Scott Polar Research Institute, Cambridge, England, assistant librarian and curator of manuscripts, 1954-66; National Maritime Museum, London, England, assistant keeper, 1970—. Honorary research fellow at Australian National University, 1960-61. Member of Cambridge Spitsbergen Physiological Expedition, 1955, and Australian National Antarctic Research Expedition, 1960. *Member:* Royal Geographical Society, Hakluyt Society, Society for Nautical Research, National Trust, Society of Archivists, Friends of the Scott Polar Institute.

WRITINGS: Catalogue of MSS of Polar Interest in Australia and New Zealand, Scott Polar Research Institute, 1963; (editor) Edward Wilson, *Diary of 'The Discovery': Expedition to the Antarctic Regions, 1901-1904*, Blandford Press, 1966, Humanities, 1967; (editor) *Scott's Last Voyage: Through the Antarctic Camera of Herbert Ponting*, Sidgwick & Jackson, 1974, Praeger, 1975. Contributor to *Geographical Journal* and *Polar Record*.

WORK IN PROGRESS: Researching John Biscoe's Antarctic voyage of 1830-1833.

AVOCATIONAL INTERESTS: Gardening, travel.

* * *

SAYLES, John Thomas 1950-

PERSONAL: Born September 28, 1950, in Schenectady, N.Y.; son of Donald John (a school administrator) and Mary (a teacher; maiden name, Rausch) Sayles. *Education:* Williams College, B.A., 1972. *Politics:* "Survivalist," *Religion:* "Roman Catholic Atheist." *Residence:* East Boston, Mass.

CAREER: Has been employed as hospital orderly, plastic molder, meat worker, and day laborer; writer.

WRITINGS: Pride of the Bimbos (novel), Little, Brown, 1975.

WORK IN PROGRESS: A novel about the failures of American trade unions and the split-up of the New Left.

SIDELIGHTS: Sayles writes: "I write now because I like to. It's a special way of talking to other people that appeals to me. Writing helps me sort out how I feel about things. A lot of the people I write about don't read books but I hope they'd recognize themselves if they read mine. I am also an actor and am interested in writing and directing movies (other ways to talk with people)."

*   *   *

SCANLAN, Michael 1931-

PERSONAL: Born December 1, 1931, in Far Rockaway, N.Y.; son of Vincent Michael and Marjorie (O'Keefe) Scanlan. Education: Williams College, B.A., 1953; Harvard University, J.D., 1956; graduate study at Catholic University, 1963-64, and Boston University, 1965; Saint Francis Seminary, M.Div., 1975. Home: Holy Spirit Monastery, Steubenville, Ohio 43952. Office: College of Steubenville, Steubenville, Ohio 43952.

CAREER: Admitted to the Bar of New York State, 1956; City of Boston, Boston, Mass., assistant to Boston Public Defender, 1954-56; Roman Catholic priest of Order of St. Francis (T.O.R.), ordained, 1964; College of Steubenville, Steubenville, Ohio, lecturer in theology, 1964-66, acting dean, 1964-66, dean of college, 1966-69, director of general honors program, 1966-69; Saint Francis Major Seminary, Loretto, Pa., religious superior, 1969-73, rector president, 1969-74; College of Steubenville, Steubenville, Ohio, president, 1974—. Vice-chairman of board of trustees of Saint Francis College, Loretto, Pa., 1969-74; member of Pennsylvania Fulbright Committee, 1970; member of board of trustees of Saint Francis Preparatory School, 1969-74; member of national advisory council to Catholic Charismatic Renewal, 1972—. Director of Rumor Control Center, City of Steubenville, 1968-69. Military service: U.S. Air Force, Judge Advocate's staff, 1956-57.

MEMBER: National Catholic Education Association, Eastern Association of Major Seminary Rectors (secretary, 1969), Catholic Education Association of Pennsylvania, New York Bar Association. Awards, honors: Litt.D., College of Steubenville, 1972.

WRITINGS: The Power in Penance, Ave Maria Press, 1972; Inner Healing, Paulist-Newman, 1974. Contributor to religious periodicals.

WORK IN PROGRESS: Christian Authority; Restoration of the Sacraments.

*   *   *

SCANZONI, Letha 1935-

PERSONAL: Born October 9, 1935, in Pittsburgh, Pa.; daughter of James Jackson (a businessman) and Hilda (Koch) Dawson; married John H. Scanzoni (a professor of sociology), July 7, 1956; children: Stephen, David. Education: Attended Eastman School of Music, 1952-54, and Moody Bible Institute, 1954-56; Indiana University, A.B. (with high distinction), 1972. Politics: Democrat. Religion: Presbyterian. Home and office: 2115 Wimbleton Lane, Bloomington, Ind. 47401.

CAREER: Village Missions, Lookingglass, Ore., rural church, music, and youth worker, 1958-61; writer, 1962—. Member: Phi Beta Kappa.

WRITINGS: Youth Looks at Love, Revell, 1964; Why Am I Here? Where Am I Going?, Revell, 1966; Sex and the Single Eye, Zondervan, 1968, published as Why Wait?, Baker Book, 1975; Sex Is a Parent Affair: Sex Education for the Christian Home, Regal Books, 1973; (with Nancy Hardesty) All We're Meant to Be: A Biblical Approach to Women's Liberation, Word Books, 1974; (with husband,

John H. Scanzoni) Men, Women, and Change: A Sociology of Marriage and Family, McGraw, in press. Contributor to church publications and sociology magazines.

SIDELIGHTS: Letha Scanzoni told CA: "As a Christian and a feminist, I am interested in writing about Christianity and social issues—particularly with regard to changes in male-female roles and relationships. I also do quite a bit of travel and speaking on these subjects.... Other areas of interest in my writing and speaking are biblical interpretation, marriage and family, friendship, sex ethics, and sex education. Sociology is of equal interest and is an area in which I try to keep current and plan to do further writing." Avocational interests: Movies, theater, music (trombonist), family activities.

BIOGRAPHICAL/CRITICAL SOURCES: Gladys Hunt, Does Anyone Here Know God?, Zondervan, 1967; Vanguard, March-April, 1975.

*   *   *

SCHAAFSMA, Polly 1935-

PERSONAL: Born October 24, 1935, in Springfield, Vt.; daughter of Raymond Arthur (a machinist) and Mildred (Gafvert) Dix; married Curtis Forrest Schaafsma (an archaeologist), September 28, 1958; children: Scott Hoskinini, Pieter Dix. Education: Mount Holyoke College, B.A., 1957; University of Colorado, M.A., 1962. Home address: Box 776, Arroyo Hondo, N.M. 87513.

CAREER: Museum of New Mexico, Santa Fe, N.M., archaeologist, 1961-63 and 1966; Harvard University, Peabody Museum, Cambridge, Mass., research assistant, 1968-70; School of American Research, Santa Fe, N.M., writer, 1973-75. Member: Taos Art Association (exhibiting artist member).

WRITINGS: Rock Art in the Navajo Reservoir District, Museum of New Mexico, 1963; Early Navaho Rock Paintings and Carvings, Museum of Navaho Ceremonial Art, 1966; The Rock Art of Utah, Harvard University, 1971; Rock Art of New Mexico, New Mexico State Planning Office, 1972; Rock Art in The Cochiti Reservoir District, Museum of New Mexico, 1975. Contributor of articles to El Palacio, American Anthropologist, American Antiquity, and other journals and periodicals.

WORK IN PROGRESS: Southwestern Rock Art, a volume on the rock drawings of the Southwest for the School of American Research, to be published by the University of New Mexico Press.

SIDELIGHTS: Polly Schaafsma told CA: "Until the last decade or so, rock art has been more or less an untapped resource, as an archaeological tool and as a medium of artistic expression which takes countless forms in the prehistoric Southwest.... Concurrent with my interest in Southwestern archaeology is my fascination with the Southwestern landscape (which provides the basis for most of my own art work)." Avocational interests: Horses, travel.

*   *   *

SCHAEFER, John H(arrison) 1937-

PERSONAL: Born June 3, 1937, in Berkeley, Calif.; son of William B. (a college professor) and Helen (Harrison) Schaefer; married Diane Elyse Lazar; children: Michael, John. Education: Attended Deep Springs College; San Francisco State College (now University), B.A., 1966. Home: 2060 Fazzio Court, Walnut Creek, Calif. 94598.

CAREER: Conducts management seminars at University of California, Berkeley; vice-president, Effective Learning Systems Inc. (management consultants), 1967—.

WRITINGS: (With Vincent W. Kafka) Open Management, Peter H. Wyden, 1975. Contributor to Graphic Arts Monthly.

WORK IN PROGRESS: Perceptive Salesmanship; The Practical Guide to the Open Management System.

SIDELIGHTS: Schaefer is concerned with "the development of seminars which enable people to work more effectively with each other in today's environment."

*   *   *

SCHELL, Bunny
    See SCHELL, Rolfe F(inch)

*   *   *

SCHELL, Rolfe F(inch)   1916-
    (Bunny Schell)

PERSONAL: Born November 28, 1916, in Keesville, N.Y.; son of Lindsly B. (a lawyer) and Helen Krum (Finch) Schell; married Elizabeth Blandy, October 18, 1938 (divorced July, 1970); married Lois Wilcox (an illustrator and writer), December 5, 1971; children: (first marriage) Elizabeth B. Schell Sanders, Barbara Schell Ketchum, Lynn Blandy (son). Education: Graduate of Cornell University, 1940, and Rensselaer Polytechnic Institute, 1942. Politics: Republican. Religion: Episcopalian. Home: 175 Bahia Via, Fort Myers Beach, Fla. 33931. Office: 210 Driftwood Lane, Fort Myers Beach, Fla. 33931.

CAREER: Free-lance radio director in New York, N.Y., 1940-44; S. de R. L. Penate (manufacturers of flourescent lighting), Monterrey, Mexico, owner and manager, 1944-50; Rancho del Mar (resort motel), Fort Myers Beach, Fla., owner and manager, 1950-56; free-lance magazine and newspaper writer, 1956-66; Mad Shopper (newspaper), Fort Myers Beach, Fla., owner and editor, 1968-71; free-lance writer and publisher, 1971-75. Research chemist for Esmaltes y Laquers, 1944-50. Member: Explorers Club, Florida Historical Society, Florida Anthropological Society, Rotary International (founder of Fort Myers club; president, 1955-56).

WRITINGS—All published by Island Press: One Thousand Years on Mound Key, 1962; Yank in Yucatan, 1963; Florida's Fascinating Everglades, 1963; DeSoto Didn't Land at Tampa, 1966; (under pseudonym Bunny Schell) Aloysius Alligator (juvenile), 1966; (under pseudonym Bunny Schell) Tigger (juvenile), 1966; Eat, Fast, and Stay Slim, 1967; (with wife, Lois Wilcox Schell) Schell's Guide to Eastern Mexico, 1974, revised edition, 1975; Album Maya, 1974. Contributor of about a hundred articles on science and travel to magazines.

WORK IN PROGRESS: Neola, a historical novel about Florida in 1832; a history of Fort Myers Beach, Fla.

SIDELIGHTS: Schell is fluent in Spanish, Italian, and Latin and speaks some German, French, and Mayan. Avocational interests: Photography, sailing, travel, radio (amateur radio operator).

*   *   *

SCHEUERMAN, Richard D(ean)   1951-

PERSONAL: Born April 18, 1951, in Colfax, Wash.; son of Donovon Clair (a farmer) and Mary Gertrude (Johns) Scheuerman; married Lois Jean Morasch (a receptionist), June 16, 1973. Education: Washington State University, B.A., 1973; Defense Language Institute, diploma in Russian, 1974; Pacific Lutheran University, further graduate study, 1974—. Religion: Lutheran. Home: 400 Tigner Rd., Cashmere, Wash. 98815. Office: Cashmere Public Schools, Cashmere, Wash. 98815.

CAREER: Cashmere Public Schools, Cashmere, Wash., teacher of history, English and Russian, 1974—. Military service: U.S. Air Force, 1973-74. Member: American Historical Society of Germans from Russia, Smithsonian Institute (associate member), Farm House Fraternity, Phi Alpha Theta.

WRITINGS: Pilgrims on the Earth: A German-Russian Chronicle, Ye Galleon Press, 1974.

WORK IN PROGRESS: Revising Pilgrims on the Earth: A German-Russian Chronicle.

*   *   *

SCHILLER, Bradley R(obert)   1943-

PERSONAL: Born September 16, 1943, in San Francisco, Calif.; married. Education: University of California, Berkeley, B.A. (with great distinction), 1965; Harvard University, Ph.D., 1969; also studied at University of Goettinnen, 1963-64. Office: Department of Economics, University of Maryland, College Park, Md.

CAREER: United Nations, New York, N.Y., intern at Secretariat, 1965; political-economic analyst and forecaster in Coordination and Planning Department, Continental Oil Co., 1966; Mobile Oil Co., Genoa, Italy, marketing analyst, 1967; Action for Boston Community Development, Boston, Mass., consultant, 1968; Boston Model City Administration, Boston, Mass., program coordinator, 1968; Social Security Administration, Washington, D.C., economist, 1969-70; Pacific Training and Technical Assistance Corp., Washington, D.C., senior consultant, 1970—; University of Maryland, College Park, assistant professor of economics, 1970—. Visiting lecturer, University of California, Santa Cruz, 1975. Member: Phi Beta Kappa.

WRITINGS: The Economics of Poverty and Discrimination, Prentice-Hall, 1973; (contributor) George V. Furstenberg, editor, Patterns of Racial Discrimination, Heath, 1974; The Economy, Prentice-Hall, 1975. Author of reports for U.S. Department of Labor. Contributor of about a dozen articles to professional journals, including Welfare in Review, Review of Economics and Statistics, Journal of Human Resources, Public Policy, Forensic Quarterly, and Manpower.

WORK IN PROGRESS: Research on relative income mobility in the United States; research on the impact of career paths on income mobility; research on the perpetual poor; research on the impact of private pension plans on worker mobility and current wage rates; research on the impact of manpower training on relative income status.

*   *   *

SCHLERETH, Howard (Hewitt)   1936-

PERSONAL: Surname is pronounced Shh-lare-eth; born July 23, 1936, in Iloilo, Philippines; son of Howard Joseph and Mary Virginia (Hewitt) Schlereth; married Deborah Ann Higgins, January 2, 1962; children: Howard Joseph, David Hewitt. Education: Wesleyan University, Middletown, Conn., B.A., 1958; also studied at University of Munich, 1956-57. Politics: Conservative Republican. Reli-

gion: Episcopalian. *Home:* 92 Hickory Grove Dr., Larchmont, N.Y. 10538. *Agent:* Dominick Abel, 612 North Michigan, Chicago, Ill. 60611. *Office:* McMichael Co., 447 East Post Rd., Mamaroneck, N.Y. 10543.

CAREER: Columbus Dispatch, Columbus, Ohio, reporter, 1960-61; Mobil Oil Corp., Philadelphia, Pa., sales representative in Philadelphia and Allentown, 1963-68; McMichael Co. (yacht brokerage), Mamaroneck, N.Y., broker, 1968—. *Military service:* U.S. Army, 1961-63.

WRITINGS: Commonsense Celestial Navigation, Regnery, 1975; *Commonsense Boat Buying,* Regnery, in press.

WORK IN PROGRESS: The Princess and the Fruit Bat, a Children's book.

AVOCATIONAL INTERESTS: Reading, listening to music (especially opera).

* * *

SCHLESINGER, Stephen C(annon) 1942-

PERSONAL: Born August 17, 1942, in Boston, Mass.; son of Arthur Meier (a professor of history) and Marion (Cannon) Schlesinger. *Education:* Harvard University, A.B. (cum laude), 1964, attended Law School, 1965-68; Cambridge University, certificate of one year study, 1965. *Politics:* Democrat. *Religion:* Unitarian. *Home:* 53 West 71st St., Apt. 3A, New York, N.Y. 10023. *Agent:* Wendy Weil, Julian Bach Literary Agency, 3 East 48th St., New York, N.Y. 10017. *Office: Time* Magazine, Time-Life Bldg., Rockefeller Center, New York, N.Y.

CAREER: Urban Development Corporation, New York, N.Y., special assistant to chief executive officer, 1968-69; *The New Democrat,* New York, N.Y., editor and publisher, 1969-72; free-lance writer, 1973-74; *Time* Magazine, New York, N.Y., writer for "press" section, 1975—. Speechwriter for Senator George McGovern, Democratic Presidential campaign, 1972. *Member:* National Women's Political Caucus, Americans for Democratic Action (member of national board), Newspaper Guild, Harvard Club of New York City.

WRITINGS: The New Reformers, Houghton, 1975. Author of weekly column in *The Boston Globe,* 1974-75. Contributor of articles to periodicals, including *Atlantic Monthly, Nation, Saturday Review,* and *Villiage Voice.*

* * *

SCHMIDT, Nancy Jeanne 1936-

PERSONAL: Born May 17, 1936, in Cincinnati, Ohio; daughter of Leon H. (a medical researcher) and Ida (Genther) Schmidt. *Education:* Oberlin College, B.A., 1958; University of Minnesota, M.A., 1961; Northwestern University, Ph.D., 1965; Indiana University, M.L.S., 1971; also attended University of London, 1956-57. *Residence:* Champaign, Ill. *Office:* African Studies Program, University of Illinois, 1208 West California, Urbana, Ill. 61810.

CAREER: High school teacher in East Islip, N.Y., 1959-60; elementary school teacher in private school in Minneapolis, Minn., 1960-62; National College of Education, Evanston, Ill., instructor in social science, summer, 1964; Wisconsin State University—Stevens Point, assistant professor of anthropology, 1965-66; St. Lawrence University, Canton, N.Y., assistant professor of anthropology, 1966-68; Stanislaus State College, Turlock, Calif., assistant professor of anthropology, 1968-70; Rockford College, Rock-

ford, Ill., associate professor of anthropology, 1971-74; University of Illinois, Urbana-Champaign, visiting associate professor of anthropology and African studies, 1974—. *Member:* African Literature Association, African Studies Association (fellow), American Anthropological Association (fellow), American Association for the Advancement of Science, American Ethnological Society, Council on Anthropology and Education, Current Anthropology (associate), Society for the Anthropology of Visual Communication, Audubon Society (member of board of directors of Sinissippi chapter, 1972-74), Beta Phi Mu.

WRITINGS: (Editor) *Children's Books on Africa and Their Authors: An Annotated Bibliography,* Africana Publishing, 1975. Contributor of about fifty articles and reviews to anthropology journals and other professional publications. Children's and young people's editor of *Africana Library Journal,* 1971-74; book reviewer for *Choice,* 1972—; contributing editor of *Conch Review of Books,* 1973—.

WORK IN PROGRESS: Research on African children's literature, and on African creative writing in English and French.

AVOCATIONAL INTERESTS: Classical music, opera, ballet, modern dance, playing the piano.

* * *

SCHNEIDER, Louis 1915-

PERSONAL: Born March 22, 1915, in Vienna, Austria; came to United States, 1921; naturalized U.S. citizen, 1927; son of Gustave and Frieda (Salz) Schneider; married second wife, Josephine A. Sundine, January 3, 1956; children: David Sancier, Dana Alexandra, Valerie Sundine. *Education:* City College (now City College of the City University of New York), B.A., 1935; Columbia University, M.A., 1938, Ph.D., 1947. *Home:* 4935 Strass Dr., Austin, Tex. 78731. *Office:* 318 Burdine Hall, University of Texas, Austin, Tex. 78712.

CAREER: Labor economist for War Production Board, 1943-45; economist for Office of Price Administration, 1945-47; Colgate University, Hamilton, N.Y., assistant professor of sociology, 1947-49; Purdue University, Lafayette, Ind., associate professor, 1949-54, professor of sociology, 1954-60; University of Illinois, Urbana, professor of sociology, 1960-67, head of department, 1960-64; University of Texas, Austin, professor of sociology, 1967—. Visiting professor of sociology, Dartmouth College, 1959-60. *Member:* American Sociological Association (fellow), Society for the Scientific Study of Religion, Ohio Valley Sociological Society (president, 1959-60), Phi Beta Kappa. *Awards, honors:* Fellowship from Center for Advanced Study in the Behavioral Sciences, Stanford, Calif., 1954-55; fellowship from Center for Advanced Study, University of Illinois, Urbana, 1965-66.

WRITINGS: (With M. B. Ogle and J. W. Wiley) *Power, Order, and the Economy,* Harper, 1954; (with S. M. Dornbusch) *Popular Religion,* University of Chicago Press, 1958; (editor) Carl Menger, *Problems of Economics and Sociology,* University of Illinois Press, 1963; (editor) *Religion, Culture and Society,* Wiley, 1964; (editor) *The Scottish Moralists on Human Nature and Society,* University of Chicago Press, 1967; *Sociological Approach to Religion,* Wiley, 1970; (editor with C. M. Bonjean) *The Idea of Culture in the Social Sciences,* Cambridge University Press, 1973; *The Sociological Way of Looking at the World,* McGraw, 1975; *Classical Theories of Social Change,* General Learning Corp., in press. Contributor of articles to journals in his field, including *Antioch Review, American Journal of Sociology*, and *Journal of the History of the Behavioral Sciences*. Associate editor of *American Sociological Review*, 1958-61, and *Sociological Analysis*, 1967-71; consulting editor of *Journal for the Scientific Study of Religion*, 1967-71.

WORK IN PROGRESS: The Social Thought of the Scottish Enlightenment, completion expected in 1978; editing *Religion and Social Life: A Reader*, for Cambridge University Press.

SIDELIGHTS: Regarding the audience of his work, Schneider comments: "In writing, it has become increasingly important to me to reach sophisticated sectors of non-academic publics." He possesses a strong reading knowledge of German and French. *Avocational interests:* Biological subjects, including entomology.

* * *

SCHNEIDERMAN, L(awrence) J(erome) 1932-

PERSONAL: Born March 24, 1932, in New York, N.Y.; married Barbara Goldman (a pianist), June 10, 1956; children: Rob, Claudia, Heidi, Tanya. *Education:* Yale University, B.A., 1953; Harvard University, M.D., 1957. *Home:* 709 Hoska Dr., Del Mar, Calif. 92014. *Agent:* Ellen Levine, Curtis Brown Ltd., 60 East 56th St., New York, N.Y. 10022. *Office address:* University of California at San Diego, S-004, La Jolla, Calif. 92093.

CAREER: Internship at Boston City Hospital, Boston, Mass., 1957-58, and Strong Memorial Hospital, Rochester, N.Y., 1958-59; National Institutes of Health, Bethesda, Md., clinical associate, 1959-61; University of London, University College and King's College, London, England, honorary research assistant, 1961-62; Stanford University, School of Medicine, Palo Alto, Calif., resident, 1962-64, instructor, 1964-66, assistant professor of medicine, 1966-70; University of California at San Diego, La Jolla, associate professor of medicine and community medicine, 1970—, director of Division of Primary Medical Care, 1970—. Founding member and medical adviser, Linda Vista Health Care Center; consultant and adviser to Ramona Clinic and North County Health Project. *Military service:* U.S. Public Health Services, 1959-61; became lieutenant. *Member:* American College of Physicians (fellow), American Federation for Clinical Research, American Society of Human Genetics, Society of Teachers of Family Medicine, San Diego County Medical Society, Western Society for Clinical Research.

WRITINGS: Sea Nymphs by the Hour (novel), Bobbs-Merrill, 1972.

* * *

SCHOENFELD, Hanns Martin W(alter) 1928-

PERSONAL: Born July 12, 1928, in Leipzig, Germany; came to United States in 1962, naturalized in 1968; son of Alwin (a school principal) and Lisbeth (Kirbach) Schoenfeld; married Margit Frese, August 1956; children: Gabriele Martina (Mrs. Derek S. Robinson) (stepdaughter). *Education:* University of Hamburg, Diplom-Kaufmann, 1952, Dr. rer. pol., 1954; Technical University of Brunswick, Dr. habil., 1966. *Religion:* Lutheran. *home:* 1014 Devonshire Dr., Champaign, Ill. 61820. *Office:* Department of Accountancy, University of Illinois, Champaign-Urbana, 215 Commerce West, Urbana, Ill. 61801.

CAREER: Junior accountant for certified public accounting firm, Hamburg, Germany, 1948-55; University of Hamburg, Hamburg, Germany, research assistant, 1955-56; German Productivity Center, Darmstadt, Germany, business consultant, 1957-62; University of Illinois, Urbana-Champaign, assistant professor, 1962-65, associate professor, 1965-68, professor of accountancy and business administration, 1968—. Lecturer at European management development institutes in Germany, Austria, France, and Switzerland, 1957-62; visiting professor at Technical University of Brunswick, 1966, University of Michigan, 1972, Technical University of Berlin, intermittent, 1965-74, and Free University of Berlin, 1972-73, University of Lodz, 1975. *Military service:* German Army, 1944-46; held prisoner of war, 1945-46.

MEMBER: Academy of International Business, American Accounting Association, American Association of University Professors, Verband der Hochschullehrer fuer Betriebswirtschaft, German Association of Work Study, Verband fuer Arbeitsstudien. *Awards, honors:* Organization for European Economic Cooperation fellowship to University of Illinois, 1956.

WRITINGS: (With W. Sommer) *Management Dictionary*, Walter DeGruyter, Volume I: *English-German*, 1960, 4th edition, 1972, Volume II: *German-English*, 1961, 3rd edition, 1968; *Fuehrungsausbildung im Betrieb* (title means "Management Development within the Firm"), Betriebswirtschaftlicher Verlag Th. Gabler, 1960; *Kostenrechnung* (title means "Cost Accounting"), C. E. Poeschel, 1961, 7th edition, three volumes, 1974-75; *Planung* (title means "Business Planning"), Betriegswirtschaftlicher Verlag Th. Gabler, 1963; *Finanzwesen mit Case Studies* (title means "The Financing Function"), German Productivity Center, 1963; *Grundlagen des Rechnungswesens* (title means "Introduction to Accounting"), C. E. Poeschel, 1964, 2nd edition, 1969; *Die Fuehrungsausbildung im Betrieblichen Funktionsgefuege* (title means "Management Development as a Function of the Firm"), Betriebswirtschaftlicher Verlag Th. Gabler, 1967; (with G. M. Scott and others) *An Introduction to Financial Control and Reporting in Multinational Enterprises*, Bureau of Business Research, University of Texas, 1973; *Cost Terminology and Cost Theory: A Study of Its Development and Present State in Central Europe* (monograph), Center for International Education and Research in Accounting, University of Illinois, 1974. Contributor of over fifty articles to professional journals. Member of editorial board of *Management International Review*, 1970, and *International Journal of Accounting*, 1975.

WORK IN PROGRESS: Research interests include international accounting, management accounting, and management development.

AVOCATIONAL INTERESTS: Music, literature, foreign affairs, travel.

* * *

SCHOENHOLTZ, Larry 1948-

PERSONAL: Born March 18, 1948, in Detroit, Mich.; son of Paul Woodrow (a sign painter) and Martha-Jayne (Oliver) Schoenholtz (an office manager). *Education:* Attended Wayne State University, 1965-73.

CAREER: Michigan Hospital Service (Blue Cross of Michigan), Detroit, Mich., documentation specialist, 1972-73; Gale Research Co., Detroit, printer, 1973-75, sketchwriter, 1975—. *Member:* U.S. Chess Federation, Michigan Chess

Association, American Civil Liberties Union, American Society of Psychical Research.

WRITINGS: New Directions in the I Ching, University Books, 1975.

WORK IN PROGRESS: The Menninger Papers (tentative title), a documentary on the Menninger Foundation studies of consciousness in Himalayan gurus; *Game Essence*, a book of technical studies in chess and roulette, with discussion on the psychology of game motivation generally; "The Second Look Within" (tentative title), a three-part screenplay with musical score.

SIDELIGHTS: Larry Schoenholtz told *CA*: "I'm interested in the lesser-known or little-believed potentials of human awareness, and seek to use both fiction and nonfiction to probe these potentials." *Avocational interests:* Chess, oil painting (has won local competitions in both).

*   *   *

SCHOTT, John R(obert)   1936-

PERSONAL: Born January 30, 1936, in Rochester, N.Y.; son of John (a clergyman) and Ellen (Waite) Schott; married Diane Elizabeth Dempsey, June 19, 1963; children: Jennifer, Jared Reed, Kermit Alexander. *Education:* Haverford College, B.A. (magna cum laude), 1957; Oxford University, graduate study, 1957-59; Harvard University, Ph.D., 1964. *Home:* Main Street, Francestown, N.H. 03043.

CAREER: Wellesley College, Wellesley, Mass., instructor in political science, 1963-65; Agency for International Development, Washington, D.C., member of policy planning staff, 1965-68; Tufts University, Fletcher School of Law and Diplomacy, Medford, Mass., professor of political development, 1968-70; Thunderbird Graduate School, Phoenix, Ariz., senior vice-president, 1970-71; consultant in international affairs, 1971—. Member, Southeast Asia development advisory group, 1967-69; member of planning board, Francestown, N.H., 1969-70, secretary, 1970-75, chairman, bicentennial committee, 1968-72; president, Village Improvement Society, 1969-71, and board of selectmen, 1975—, Francestown, N.H.; president of board of trustees, Spaulding Youth Center, Tilton, N.H. *Member:* American Studies Association (fellow), International Studies Association, American Political Science Association, Harvard Club (Boston). *Awards, honors:* Rotary Foundation fellowship, 1957-58; Coslett Foundation fellowship, 1958-59; Harvard Arts and Sciences fellowship, 1960-61; Fulbright fellowship, 1962-63.

WRITINGS: Frances' Town: A History of Francestown New Hampshire, Town of Francestown, New Hampshire, 1972. Also author of *Kenya Tragedy: The Story of European Colonization in East Africa*, 1964. Contributor to journals including, *Foreign Service Journal, Echoes, New Hampshire Profiles*, and *American Journal of Sociology*.

SIDELIGHTS: Schott has spent time in some thirty-five countries in all major parts of the world, with the exception of the U.S.S.R. and China. *Avocational interests:* Collecting eighteenth century American furniture and early American blown glass.

*   *   *

SCHUETZE, Armin William   1917-

PERSONAL: Born April 25, 1917, in Litchfield, Minn.; son of Martin Paul (a pastor) and Wilhelmina (Albrecht) Schuetze; married Esther Waidelich, September 20, 1941; children: Virginia (Mrs. John Wiederhold), Beth (Mrs. William Gabb), Barbara (Mrs. Carl Otto), Frederick, Kristine (Mrs. Charles Learman), Katherine, John. *Education:* Northwestern College, Watertown, Wis., B.A., 1937; Wisconsin Lutheran Seminary, graduate study, 1937-40; Marquette University, M.A., 1969. *Home:* 11844 North Luther Lane, 65W, Mequon, Wis. 53092. *Office:* Department of Pastoral Theology and Church History, Wisconsin Lutheran Seminary, 11831 North Seminary Dr., Mequon, Wis. 53092.

CAREER: Ordained Lutheran pastor, 1941; Michigan Lutheran Seminary, Saginaw, instructor in Latin, 1940-41; pastor of Lutheran churches in Timber Lake, S.D. and Isabel, S.D., both 1941-43, and in Thiensville, Wis., 1943-48; Northwest Lutheran Academy, Mobridge, S.D., instructor in religion and languages, 1948-56; pastor of Lutheran church in Milwaukee, Wis., 1956-58; Wisconsin Lutheran Seminary, Mequon, professor of church history and pastoral theology, 1958—.

WRITINGS: Guidance from God's Word, Northwestern Publishing, 1967; *Basic Doctrines of the Bible*, Northwestern Publishing, 1969; *Family Life under Christ*, Northwestern Publishing, 1971; *The Shepherd under Christ*, Northwestern Publishing, 1974. Contributor to Lutheran publications. Member of editorial board of *Northwestern Lutheran*; managing editor of *Wisconsin Lutheran Quarterly*.

AVOCATIONAL INTERESTS: Building and repairing antique furniture.

*   *   *

SCHWARTZ, Eleanor Brantley   1937-

PERSONAL: Born January 1, 1937, in Kite, Ga.; daughter of Melvin J. (a businessman) and Hazel (Hill) Brantley; married David J. Schwartz (a professor), June 17, 1967; children: John, Cynthia. *Education:* Attended Mercer University, 1954-55, University of Virginia, 1955, Georgia Southern College, 1956-57; Georgia State University, B.B.A., 1961, M.B.A., 1963, D.B.A., 1969. *Home:* 895 Northboro Dr., Mayfield Village, Ohio 44143. *Office:* Marketing Department, School of Business Administration, Cleveland State University, 1983 Euclid Ave., Cleveland, Ohio 44115.

CAREER: Georgia State University, Atlanta, assistant dean of admissions, 1961-66, assistant professor of business administration, 1966-70; Cleveland State University, Cleveland, Ohio, associate professor of business administration, 1970—. *Member:* American Marketing Association, American Management Association, American Institute of Decision Sciences, Cleveland Sales and Marketing Executives, Business & Professional Women's Club, Sigma Iota Epsilon, Beta Gamma Sigma.

WRITINGS: The Sex Barrier in Business, Bureau of Business and Economic Research, School of Business Administration, Georgia State University, 1971: (with William E. Schlender) *The Redesign of White Motor Corporation*, Intercollegiate Case Clearing House, Harvard University, 1973; (with Schlender) *Jergens, Incorporated*, Intercollegiate Case Clearing House, Harvard University, 1973; (contributor) Francis J. Bridges and Kenneth W. Olm, editors, *Business Policy: Cases, Incidents, and Readings*, Allyn & Bacon, 1974; (with Schlender) *The Acme Company*, Intercollegiate Case Clearing House, Harvard University, 1974; (with Schlender) *Republic Steel Corporation: The J. C. Frisbee, Jr. Advertising Campaign*, Intercollegiate Case Clearing House, Harvard University, 1974; (editor) *Contemporary Readings in Marketing*, Grid, Inc., 1974.

Monographs: *Increasing the Sales Productivity through Innovative Training*, Bureau of Business Research, James J. Nance College of Business, 1973; *Incentives for the Motivation of Sales Personnel*, Bureau of Business Research, James J. Nance College of Business, 1973; *Business Expansion through Franchising: A Look to the 1980's*, Bureau of Business Research, James J. Nance College of Business, 1973; *What You Should Know About Franchising*, two parts, Dartnell Corp., 1974. Contributor of about fifteen articles to business publications, including *Sales Meetings, Retail Directions, Thomas Business Review, Notes and Quotes, Journal of Small Business Management, Office Equipment and Methods, Atlantic Economic Review*, and *Business Report*.

WORK IN PROGRESS: The Woman Executive: A Guide to Professional Development; The Professional Secretary; Selected Marketing Strategies: Design and Execution.

SIDELIGHTS: Eleanor Schwartz has traveled to Puerto Rico, Panama, Kuwait, and Brazil. *Avocational interests:* Painting, piano, poetry, fiction.

* * *

SCHWARZ, Egon 1922-

PERSONAL: Born August 8, 1922, in Vienna, Austria; naturalized U.S. citizen; son of Oscar and Erna (Weissfisch) Schwarz; married Dorothea Klockenbusch, 1950; children: Rudolph Joachim, Caroline Elisabeth, Gabriela Barbara. *Education:* University of Cuenca, B.A., 1950; Ohio State University, M.A., 1951; University of Washington, Seattle, Ph.D., 1954. *Home:* 1036 Oakland, St. Louis, Mo. 63122. *Office:* Department of German, Washington University, St. Louis, Mo. 63130.

CAREER: Instructor in German at Otterbein College, Westerville, Ohio, 1949-51, and University of Washington, Seattle, 1951-54; Harvard University, Cambridge, Mass., instructor, 1954-56, assistant professor of German, 1956-61; Washington University, St. Louis, Mo., associate professor, 1961-62, professor of German, 1963—, Rosa May Distinguished University Professor in the Humanities, 1975—. Visiting professor at University of Hamburg, 1962-63, and University of California, Berkeley, 1964-65. *Member:* American Association of Teachers of German, Modern Language Association of America, Internationale Vereinigung Germanistik. *Awards, honors:* Guggenheim fellow, 1957-58; Fulbright fellow and American Council of Learned Societies fellow, 1962-63; National Endowment for the Humanities fellow, 1970-71.

WRITINGS: Hofmannsthal and Calderon, Harvard University Press, 1962; (editor) *Nation im Widerspruch: Deutsche ueber Deutschland*, C. Wegner (Hamburg), 1963; (editor) *Kurt Tucholsky: Eine Auswahl* (textbook), Norton, 1963; (editor with Matthias Wegner) *Verbannung: Aufzeichnungen deutscher Schriftsteller im Exil*, C. Wegner, 1964; (editor with Hunter Hannum and Edgar Lohner, and contributor) *Festschrift fuer Bernhard Blume*, Vandenhoeck & Ruprecht (Goettingen), 1967; (editor) Joseph von Eichendorff, *Aus dem Leben eines Taugenichts* (an edition with interpretive essays), McGraw, 1969; *Joseph von Eichendorff*, Twayne, 1972; (editor and author of introduction) Josef Popper-Lynkeus, *Das Recht zu leben und die Pflicht zu sterben*, Johnson Reprint, 1972; (editor with Peter Hohendahl and Lindenberger, and contributor) *Essays on Euro-*

pean Literature in Honor of Liselotte Dieckmann, Washington University Press, 1972; *Das Verschluckte Schluchzen: Poesie und Politik bei Rainer Maria Rilke*, Athenaeum Verlag (Frankfurt am Main), 1972; (editor with Peter Hohendahl, and contributor) *Exil und Innere Emigration*, Volume II, Athenaeum Verlag, 1973.

Contributor: Erich Hofacker and Liselotte Diekmann, editors, *Studies in Germanic Languages and Literatures*, Washington University Press, 1963; Willy Schumann, editor, *Einfuehrung in die deutsche Literatur*, Holt, 1964; Robert Spaethling and E. M. Weber, compilers, *A Reader in German Literature*, Oxford University Press, 1969; Arthur R. Evans, editor, *On Four Modern Humanists: Hofmannsthal, Gundolf, Curtius, Kantorowicz*, Princeton University Press, 1970; Reinhold Grimm and Jost Hermand, editors, *Die Sogenannten zwanziger Jahre*, Athenaeum, 1970. Contributor of about thirty articles and more than forty reviews to journals.

WORK IN PROGRESS: Studies on Thomas Mann and fascism, on the reception of Rainer Maria Rilke, and on aristocratic values in bourgeois literature.

SIDELIGHTS: "It took me twenty years," Schwarz writes, "to combine the experiences of my life and my literary interests into a research method that gives expression to both. Having grown up in Austria under the shadows of economic catastrophe and rise of fascism and lived as a migrant worker in Latin America I was entirely a historical creature. But my subsequent academic training was 'new critical,' historical and aesthetic. Most of my professional and intellectual efforts went into reconciling and amalgamating the two."

* * *

SCHWED, Peter 1911-

PERSONAL: Surname is pronounced Shwade; born January 18, 1911, in New York, N.Y.; son of Frederick (a stockbroker) and Bertie (Stiefel) Schwed; married Antonia Holding (an enamelist), March 6, 1947; children: Katharine (Mrs. Eric F. Wood), Peter Gregory, Laura, Roger. *Education:* Attended Princeton University, 1929-31. *Politics:* Democrat. *Religion:* Jewish. *Home:* 151 West 86th St., New York, N.Y. 10024. *Agent:* Scott Meredith Literary Agency, Inc., 580 Fifth Ave., New York, N.Y. 10036. *Office:* Simon & Schuster, Inc., 630 Fifth Ave., New York, N.Y. 10020.

CAREER: Provident Loan Society of New York, New York, N.Y., assistant vice-president, 1932-41; Simon & Schuster, Inc., New York, N.Y., editor, 1945-65, vice-president and executive editor, 1957-62, publisher of trade books, 1966-71, chairman of editorial board, 1972—. Trustee of Lawrenceville School. *Military service:* U.S. Army, Field Artillery, 1942-45; became captain; received Bronze Star and Purple Heart. *Member:* Century Association, Princeton Club of New York.

WRITINGS: (Compiler) *The Cook Charts*, Simon & Schuster, 1949; (editor with Herbert Warren Wind) *Great Stories from the World of Sport*, Simon & Schuster, 1958; (editor with Allison Danzig) *The Fireside Book of Tennis*, Simon & Schuster, 1972; *Sinister Tennis: How to Play Against and with Left-Handers*, Doubleday, 1975; *God Bless Pawnbrokers*, Dodd, 1975. Contributor to *Saturday Review, Tennis*, and *World Tennis*.

SCITHERS, George H(arry) 1929-

PERSONAL: Surname is pronounced Sithers; born May 14, 1929, in Washington, D.C.; son of George Randall (an Army officer) and Ruth (McKelway) Scithers. *Education:* U.S. Military Academy, B.S., 1950; Stanford University, M.S., 1959. *Politics:* Republican. *Home address:* P.O. Box 8243, Philadelphia, Pa. 19101.

CAREER: U.S. Army, career officer, 1946-73, retiring as lieutenant colonel; Philadelphia Department of Public Property, Philadelphia, Pa., electrical engineer, 1973—. Chairman of twenty-first World Science Fiction Convention, 1963. *Member:* Science Fiction Writers of America, Trap Door Spiders, Engineers' Club (Philadelphia). *Awards, honors:* Science fiction achievement award (Hugo), from World Science Fiction Society, 1964, 1967, for *Amra* (magazine).

WRITINGS: (With L. Sprague de Camp) *The Conan Swordbook*, Mirage Press, 1969; (editor with de Camp) *The Conan Grimoire*, Mirage Press, 1972; *To Serve Man: A Cookbook for People*, Owlswick Press, 1975. Editor of *Amra* (magazine), 1959—.

* * *

SCOBEY, Joan 1927-

PERSONAL: Born May 19, 1927, in New York, N.Y.; daughter of Siegfried (a lawyer) and Frieda (a lawyer; maiden name, Loewe) Moisseiff; married Raphael George Scobey (a lawyer), May 3, 1953; children: David, Richard. *Education:* Attended University of Wisconsin, 1945, Cornell University, 1946, and Columbia University, 1947; Smith College, B.A., 1948; graduate study at Alliance Francaise, 1948-49, and Ecole des Beaux Arts, 1948. *Agent:* John Cushman Associates, 25 West 43rd St., New York, N.Y. 10036. *Home and office:* 9 Lenox Pl., Scarsdale, N.Y. 10583.

CAREER: Free-lance writer in Scarsdale, N.Y., 1960—. Creator and writer of "The Children's Corner," WABF radio, 1950-52; writer of program presentations for television, 1959-60; member of executive board and director of public relations and publicity of Art on Tour, 1964-67. Member of board of Scarsdale Parent-Teacher Association, 1963-67, 1970-74. *Member:* Society of Magazine Writers, League of Women Voters (member of board of directors of Scarsdale chapter, 1967-70). *Awards, honors:* *Vogue* Prix de Paris honorable mention, 1948.

WRITINGS: (With L. P. McGrath) *Creative Careers for Women*, Simon & Schuster, 1968; *(with McGrath)* Do-It-All-Yourself Needlepoint, *Simon & Schuster, 1971; (with McGrath)* Celebrity Needlepoint, *Simon & Schuster, 1972;* Needlepoint from Start to Finish, *Lancer Books, 1972;* Rugmaking from Start to Finish, *Lancer Books, 1972; (with Norma Myers)* Gifts from the Kitchen, *Doubleday, 1973; Rugs and Wall Hangings*, Dial, 1974; *(with Myers)* Gifts from Your Garden, *Bobbs-Merrill, 1975; Decorating with Needlepoint*, Meredith, 1975.

Children's books with L. P. McGrath, all published by Simon & Schuster: *What is a Mother*, 1968, *What is a Father*, 1969, *What is a Brother*, 1970, *What is a Sister*, 1970, *What is a Grandmother*, 1970, *What is a Grandfather*, 1970, *What is a Friend*, 1971, *What is a Pet*, 1971.

Contributor to *European Herald Tribune, Mademoiselle, Woman's Day, Coronet, Suburbia Today, Today's Living, This Month, Ford Times, Family Circle, Good Housekeeping, American Home, Reader's Digest, and McCall's.*

Contributing editor of World Scope Encyclopedia, *1960; assistant editor of* Modern Plastics, *1949-52.*

AVOCATIONAL INTERESTS: Travel, reading, tennis, cooking.

* * *

SCOTLAND, Jay
See JAKES, John W(illiam)

* * *

SCOTT, (Henry) Joseph 1917-

PERSONAL: Born September 23, 1917, in New York, N.Y.; son of William Everett (in advertising) and Rose (a writer; maiden name, Riker) Scott; married Lenore Kurtz (an artist), July 22, 1962. *Education:* Attended Antioch College, 1935-37, and Muskingum College, 1938-39; New York University, B.A., 1947; New York Institute of Photography, graduate, 1949; Mergenthaler Linotype School, graduate, 1951; Manhattan School of Printing, graduate, 1953. *Home and office:* 4385 Northwest Malhuer, Portland, Ore. 97229.

CAREER: Arrow Letters Corp. (printing firm), New York, N.Y., president, 1950-64; full-time writer, game developer, and graphic arts consultant, 1964—. Has also worked as magazine and newspaper reporter, editor, and photographer. *Military service:* U.S. Army, Air Corps, 1942-46; became major.

WRITINGS: The Big Fun Book, American Colorprint Corp., 1964; (with Patricia Chapman) *The Celestial Scene: A Horoscope Guide to Turn You On*, Grosset, 1968; *Foretell the Future*, Bantam, 1968; *999 Daily Numbers for 1968, 1969, and 1970: Numerology for You*, Bantam, 1968. Also compiler of horoscope calendars for Hallmark Cards, 1970-73.

With wife, Lenore Scott: *The Shakespeare Game*, Avalon Hill, 1966; *Egyptian Hieroglyphs for Everyone*, Funk, 1968; *Pencil Pushers*, Ace Books, 1973; *Fun and Games with Cards*, Ace Books, 1973; *Puzzles for Everyone*, Ace Books, 1973; *Hieroglyphs for Fun*, Van Nostrand, 1974; *Fun for You*, Ace Books, in press; *Puzzle Book*, Ace Books, in press; *Great Puzzles*, Ace Books, in press.

Contributor of articles to newspapers and magazines.

WORK IN PROGRESS: Games for retail and educational use, puzzle books, research on security and inventory protection for stores, distributors, and manufacturers.

AVOCATIONAL INTERESTS: Travel, photography, theatre.

* * *

SCOTT, Stanley
See FAGERSTROM, Stan

* * *

SCOTTO, Robert M(ichael) 1942-

PERSONAL: Born June 17, 1942, in New York, N.Y.; son of Michael and Marie (Necco) Scotto; married Rosemary Mastrodomencio (a teacher), August 13, 1966. *Education:* Manhattan College, B.A., 1964; Brooklyn College of the City University of New York, M.A., 1965; City University of New York, Ph.D., 1970. *Residence:* New York, N.Y. *Office:* 17 Lexington Ave., New York, N.Y. 10010.

CAREER: St. John's University, Jamaica, N.Y., instructor, 1966-69, assistant professor, 1969-71, associate professor of English, 1971-72; City University of New York, Baruch College, New York, N.Y., assistant professor of English, 1972—. *Member:* Modern Language Association of America, Andiron Club (secretary, 1975-76).

WRITINGS: (Editor) *Joseph Heller's Catch 22: A Critical Edition*, Dell, 1973; (editor and contributor) *The Contemporary American Novel: Essays in Criticism*, Everett Edwards, in press. Contributor to *Journal of Modern Literature, English Literature in Transition, James Joyce Quarterly,* and *Victorian Studies.*

WORK IN PROGRESS: A Reader's Guide to the Contemporary American Novel; a novel about his experiences as a college instructor in New York City, tentatively titled *Home-Going.*

* * *

SEAMAN, L(ewis) C(harles) B(ernard) 1911-

PERSONAL: Born April 18, 1911, in Gravesend, Kent, England; son of Charles Vere (an electrician) and Florence (Morsley) Seaman; married Frances Charlotte Smith, November 4, 1938; children: John Bernard, Richard, Mary. *Education:* Downing College, Cambridge, B.A., 1933, M.A., 1945. *Politics:* "Uncommitted non-rightist." *Religion:* "Christian Agnostic." *Home:* 35 Laleham Ct., Chobham Rd., Woking, Surrey GU21 4AX, England.

CAREER: Tour guide, typist, filing clerk, and internal telephone system salesman; teacher of history in the public schools of London, England, 1939-60, and Woking, England, 1960-71. Lecturer at Polytechnic School of Modern Languages, London, England, 1946-69. Chief examiner in history, University of London, for the general certificate of education at ordinary level, 1960-69, and at advanced level, 1970—. *Military service:* British Army, 1941-45. *Member:* Historical Association, Society of Authors.

WRITINGS: A Short Social History of England, Longmans, Green, 1947; (with C. E. Eckersley) *Pattern of England,* two volumes, Longmans, Green, 1948-49; *From Vienna to Versailles,* Methuen, 1955, Coward, 1956; *Post-Victorian Britain, 1902-1951,* Methuen, 1966; *Life in Britain between the Wars,* Putnam, 1970; *Victorian England,* Methuen, 1973; *Life in Victorian London,* Batsford, 1973; (with I. F. Burton, R. J. Moore, and J. B. Watson) *Multiple Choice Testing in History Examinations,* Chatto & Windus, 1973.

WORK IN PROGRESS: A History of English Life from Anglo-Saxon Times to the 1970's, for Putnam.

AVOCATIONAL INTERESTS: "Getting letters from former pupils about their newly acquired doctorates, listening to Telemann, Ella Fitzgerald, 'The Merry Widow,' and Budd Johnson's version of 'Summertime.'"

* * *

SECOMBE, Harry (Donald) 1921-

PERSONAL: Born September 8, 1921, in Swansea, South Wales; son of Frederick Ernest (a traveling salesman) and Nelly Jane Gladys (Davies) Secombe; married Myra Atherton, February 19, 1948; children: Jennifer, Andrew, David, Katy. *Education:* Educated in Wales. *Religion:* Church of England. *Agent:* Andrew Mann, 32 Wigmore St., London W.1, England. *Office:* 46 St. James's Place, London S.W.1, England.

CAREER: Richard Thomas & Baldwin, Swansea, South

Wales, junior pay clerk, 1939; began show business career as stage comedian in 1946; appeared as a regular on radio programs, "Variety Bandbox," "Welsh Rarebit," and "Educating Archie"; originated and performed on BBC radio series "The Goon Show," with Peter Sellers and Spike Milligan, 1951-56; hosted BBC television series, "Secombe Here," and "The Harry Secombe Show." Has made television guest appearances in England and the United States; has made recordings for Phonogram Records and appeared in stage musicals and films. Member of board of trustees, Variety Artists Benevolent Fund. *Military service:* British Army, 1939-46; served in Europe and North Africa. *Member:* Royal Society of Arts (fellow), Variety Club of Great Britain, Lords Taverners (president, 1967-68), Stars Organization for Spastics (president, 1963-64), London Welsh Association (vice-president, 1968—), Marylebone Cricket Club. *Awards, honors:* named "Show Business Personality of 1959" by Variety Club of Great Britain; Commander of British Empire, 1963.

WRITINGS: Twice Brightly (novel), St. Martin's, 1974; (with Spike Milligan and Peter Sellers) *The Book of the Goons,* St. Martin's, 1975; *Goon to Lunch* (short stories), M. Joseph, 1975. Regular contributor to *Punch.*

WORK IN PROGRESS: Welsh Fargo, a novel for Robson Books.

AVOCATIONAL INTERESTS: Travel, photography, golf, cricket.

* * *

SECONDARI, John H(ermes) 1919-1975

November 1, 1919—February 8, 1975; Italian-born American journalist, executive producer for national television network, and author of novels and documentary films for television. Obituaries: *New York Times,* February 10, 1975; *Washington Post,* February 11, 1975; *AB Bookman's Weekly,* February 24, 1975; *Current Biography,* April, 1975.

* * *

SELIGMANN, Nancy 1948-

PERSONAL: Born May 23, 1948, in New York, N.Y.; daughter of Robert Louis (a photographer) and Rosemarie (a teacher; maiden name, D'Amico) Seligmann; married Michael Paul Linkevich (an engineer), September 17, 1971. *Education:* Western Connecticut State College, B.A., 1970. *Home address:* North St., Litchfield, Conn. 06759. *Agent:* James F. Seligmann, Seligmann & Collier, 280 Madison Ave., New York, N.Y. 10016. *Office:* Regional Educational Service, Litchfield, Conn.

CAREER: U.S. Government, Washington, D.C., Volunteers in Service to America (VISTA) volunteer in Western Monroe County, N.Y., 1971-72; camp counselor for a private school in New Rochelle, N.Y., 1973; New York Child Care Agency, Elmhurst, N.Y., child care worker, 1973-74; Regional Educational Service, Litchfield, Conn., teacher's assistant for hearing impaired-language delayed children, 1975—. *Member:* Historical Society (Litchfield).

WRITINGS: Homesteading in the City: A Survival Manual for Young People Living in Town or Off Campus, Follett, 1975.

WORK IN PROGRESS: Research on school lunch programs, on living in a historical town, on summer camps, and on Argentina, with some publications expected to result.

AVOCATIONAL INTERESTS: Organic gardening, badminton, canoeing.

* * *

SENTNER, David P. 1898-1975

1898—April 22, 1975; American journalist, poet, drama editor, and author. Obituaries: *Washington Post*, April 24, 1975.

* * *

SEPETYS, Jonas 1901-

PERSONAL: Born October 9, 1901, in Kucgalys, Lithuania; came to United States in 1949, naturalized U.S. citizen, 1955; son of Petras (a farmer) and Ursule (Janus) Sepetys; married Meta Veinsreider (a secretary), October 15, 1932; children: George, Ruta Sepetys Tillit. *Education:* Attended army officer school and other military schools in Lithuania; received academic military degree. *Home:* 242 West Savannah, Detroit, Mich. 48203.

CAREER: Former officer in Lithuanian Army; emigrated to Austria, where he worked as a draftsman during World War II; spent four years after the war in refugee camp; came to United States in 1949; employed by Ford Motor Co., Detroit, Mich., as control application engineer, 1952-66.

WRITINGS: A Critique of Relativity, Philosophical Library, 1968: *The Revelation of Humanity*, Philosophical Library, 1974.

WORK IN PROGRESS: The Misconception of Relativity; Comments on Philosophy.

* * *

SEREDY, Kate 1899-1975

November 10, 1899—March 7, 1975; Hungarian-born illustrator and author of children's books. Obituaries: *New York Times*, March 11, 1975; *AB Bookman's Weekly*, March 31, 1975; *Current Biography*, May, 1975. (CA-7/8)

* * *

SERLING, Rod 1924-1975

December 25, 1924—June 28, 1975; American television producer, dramatist, narrator, creator of "Twilight Zone" series, and author of screenplays and short stories on the controversial and the supernatural. Obituaries: *New York Times*, June 29, 1975; *Washington Post*, June 29, 1975; *Newsweek*, July 7, 1975; *Current Biography*, August, 1975.

* * *

SERRA, Diana
See CARY, Peggy-Jean Montgomery

* * *

SETZLER, Frank M(aryl) 1902-1975

September 21, 1902—February 13, 1975; American archaeologist, anthropologist, museum curator, and author of books on North American archaeology. Obituaries: *Washington Post*, February 20, 1975.

* * *

SEYFERT, Carl K(eenan) 1938-

PERSONAL: Born February 12, 1938, in Pecos, Tex.; son of Carl K. (an astronomer) and Muriel (Mussells) Seyfert;

married Karen Morehead, September 6, 1960; children: Lisa, Julie. *Education:* Vanderbilt University, B.A. (magna cum laude), 1960; Stanford University, Ph.D., 1965. *Politics:* Republican. *Religion:* Methodist. *Home:* 385 Countryside Lane, Williamsville, N.Y. 14221. *Office:* Department of Geoscience, State University of New York College at Buffalo, 1300 Elmwood Ave., Buffalo, N.Y. 14222.

CAREER: Queens College of the City University of New York, Flushing, N.Y., assistant professor of geology, 1964-67; State University of New York College at Buffalo, associate professor, 1967-72, professor of geology, 1972—, chairman of department of geoscience, 1969—. *Member:* Geological Society of America, American Association for the Advancement of Science, Phi Beta Kappa, Sigma Xi. *Awards, honors:* Woodrow Wilson fellowship, 1960-61.

WRITINGS: State University of New York Independent Study Course: Physical Geology, State University of New York, 1972; (with Leslie Sirkin) *Earth History and Plate Tectonics*, Harper, 1973.

* * *

SGROI, Peter Philip 1936-

PERSONAL: Surname is pronounced "scroy"; born July 21, 1936, in West Nyack, N.Y.; son of Dominick and Angelina (Caratozzola) Sgroi; married Maryanne Schildwachter, December 30, 1961; children: Mary Jennifer, Peter Anthony. *Education:* Iona College, B.A., 1958; Niagara University, M.A., 1959. *Religion:* Roman Catholic. *Home:* 3 Jill Dr., West Nyack, N.Y. 10994. *Office:* Rye Neck High School, Mamaroneck, N.Y. 10543.

CAREER: Rye Neck High School, Mamaroneck, N.Y., teacher of social studies, 1961—, chairman of department, 1966-71. *Military service:* U.S. National Guard, 1960-66. *Member:* National Education Association, New York State Social Studies Association.

WRITINGS: Purchase of Alaska (monograph), University of Alaska Press, 1970; *The Purchase of Alaska: A Bargain at Two Cents an Acre*, F. Watts, 1975. Contributor to journals.

* * *

SHACKLEFORD, Ruby P(aschall) 1913-

PERSONAL: Born December 17, 1913, in Wilson County, N.C.; daughter of Joshua Walter (a farmer) and Sally (Poole) Paschall; married Richard W. Shackleford (a farmer), December 13, 1938. *Education:* University of North Carolina, Greensboro, A.B., 1933; University of North Carolina, Chapel Hill, M.A., 1950. *Politics:* Democrat. *Religion:* Methodist. *Home address:* Route 5, Box 407, Wilson, N.C. 27893. *Office:* Atlantic Christian College, Wilson, N.C. 27893.

CAREER: High school English teacher in Fremont, N.C., 1935-38, Selma, N.C., 1940-41, Wilson, N.C., 1951-53, and Black Creek, N.C., 1953-61; Atlantic Christian College, Wilson, N.C., assistant professor of English, 1961—. *Member:* National Education Association, American Association of University Professors, North Carolina Association of Education, North Carolina Poetry Society, Sigma Pi Alpha (president of Omicron chapter, 1957-59), Delta Kappa Gamma, Order of the Eastern Star. *Awards, honors:* Awards from North Carolina Poetry Society, 1955, for "Snow," 1970, for "Pattern for a Poem," 1972, for "Sonnet III," and 1975, for "People Do Have Nothing to Say."

WRITINGS: Dreamer's Wine (poems), Exposition, 1957; *Poems and a Visual Diary*, Richmond Polytechnic Institute, 1968; *Poems*, privately printed, 1970; *Poems Four*, privately printed, 1972; *Ascend the Hill* (poems), Windy Row Press, 1974. Contributor to *Elementary English, Clearing House.*

WORK IN PROGRESS: The Bamboo Harp (haiku poems).

AVOCATIONAL INTERESTS: Travel (Germany), painting in oil, water color, and ink, music (singing; playing piano), gardening.

* * *

SHADE, Rose (Marian) 1927-

PERSONAL: Born September 18, 1927, in Los Angeles, Calif.; daughter of Walter Brown (a clergyman) and Harriet (Flanders) Murray; married Hugh Morgan, June 26, 1949 (divorced, 1956); married Roger D. Shade, June 13, 1961 (divorced, 1974); children: (first marriage) Diana Louise. *Education:* Attended University of California, Los Angeles, 1945-47; California State University, Northridge, B.A., 1972, M.A., 1975. *Politics:* Democrat. *Religion:* "Eclectic-Metaphysical." *Residence:* North Hollywood, Calif. *Agent:* Don Shepherd Agency, Taft Bldg., Hollywood, Calif. 90028.

CAREER: California State University, Northridge, research assistant, 1971-73; Headlines, Ink, Studio City, Calif., publicity writer, 1973-75. Worked with various advertising agencies and radio stations in publicity and secretarial positions and wrote verse for Hallmark greeting cards. *Member:* Phi Kappa Phi. *Award, honors:* American Academy of Poets first prize for poetry, 1971.

WRITINGS: (With Eunice Murray) *Marilyn: The Last Months*, Pyramid Publications, 1975. Contributor of short stories and historical articles to *Journal of the West* and other periodicals.

WORK IN PROGRESS: A historical novel and television scripts.

SIDELIGHTS: Rose Shade told *CA* that *Marilyn: The Last Months* "was written to reveal the true circumstances surrounding Marilyn Monroe's death as told by her companion and confidante, Eunice Murray. Her story disputes the murder theory put forth by Norman Mailer and others."

Speaking of her writing, she added that she is interested in incorporating historical research into her creative writing. As a publicity writer she wrote numerous newspaper and magazine features for prominent clients.

* * *

SHAFER, Robert E(ugene) 1925-

PERSONAL: Born March 30, 1925, in Beloit, Wis.; son of James Vaughn (a contractor) and Harriet Ethel (Sewards) Shafer; married Susanne Mueller (a professor of education), June 19, 1953. *Education:* University of Wisconsin, B.S., 1950, M.S., 1953; Columbia University, Ed.D., 1958. *Home:* 3021 Fairway Dr., Tempe, Ariz. 85282. *Office:* Department of English, Arizona State University, Tempe, Ariz. 85281.

CAREER: Public school teacher in Arlington, Va., 1950-53; San Francisco State College (now University), San Francisco, Calif., assistant professor of English, 1955-58; Wayne State University, Detroit, Mich., associate pro-

fessor of English, 1958-62; Columbia University, Teachers College, New York, N.Y., associate professor of English, 1962-66; Arizona State University, Tempe, professor of English, 1966—. Senior researcher at Max-Planck Institute of Education, 1972, and department of educational studies of Oxford University, 1973. *Military service:* U.S. Marine Corps, 1942-46; served in Asiatic Pacific theater.

MEMBER: International Reading Association, Modern Language Association of America, National Council of Teachers of English (vice-president, 1968), English Speaking Union, National Association of Teachers of English, Linguistic Society of America, Arizona Civil Liberties Union, Arizona Four Keys Democratic Club.

WRITINGS: (With Arthur McDonald, John S. Simmons, Karen M. Hess, and Maria Schantz) *Success in Reading*, eight volumes, Silver-Burdett, 1967-72; (with Verlene Bernd) *Personal Values*, Scholastic Book Services, 1975; (with Hess and Lanny Morreau) *Developing Reading Efficiency*, Wiley, 1975. Contributor to education journals.

* * *

SHAFTEL, Oscar 1912-

PERSONAL: Born May 5, 1912, in Brooklyn, N.Y.; son of Maurice B. (a businessman) and Anna (Stoll) Shaftel; married Ruth Marra, February 10, 1945; children: Anthony E., Ann (Mrs. Jonathan Sivitz), Eve. *Education:* City College (now City College of the City University of New York), B.A., 1931; Harvard University, M.A., 1932, Ph.D., 1936. *Residence:* Long Island City, N.Y. *Office:* School of Liberal Studies, Pratt Institute, Brooklyn, N.Y. 11205.

CAREER: Queens College (now of the City University of New York), Flushing, N.Y., tutor, 1937-39, instructor, 1939-48, assistant professor of English, 1948-53; free-lance writer and editor, 1953-65; Pratt Institute, Brooklyn, N.Y., assistant professor, 1965-66, associate professor, 1966-73, professor of humanities, 1973—; Queens College of the City University of New York, adjunct associate professor of Oriental religions, 1973—. *Military service:* U.S. Army Air Forces, 1942-46; became captain.

WRITINGS: An Understanding of the Buddha, Schocken, 1975. Editor for Schocken, 1964—.

WORK IN PROGRESS: Divinity as Projection: A Humanist Approach.

* * *

SHAIN, Henry 1941-

PERSONAL: Born February 9, 1941; son of Harry W. and May (Gelb) Shain; married Jo Ann Webb, May 10, 1975. *Education:* University of California, Berkeley, B.S., 1962; University of San Francisco, J.D., 1965. *Office:* 400 Montgomery St., San Francisco, Calif. 94104.

CAREER: Attorney in San Francisco, Calif., 1965—. Instructor at University of California; film critic. *Member:* American Bar Association, California Bar Association, San Francisco Bar Association.

WRITINGS: Legal First Aid, Crowell, 1975.

* * *

SHAKESBY, Paul S(tewart) 1946-

PERSONAL: Born January 22, 1946, in London, England; son of Stewart Sidney and Elizabeth (Wyatt) Shakesby; married Janice Mary Nagele, December 19, 1970; children: Jennifer Norah. *Education:* Nassau Community College,

A.A., 1969; Hofstra University, B.A., 1971; Temple University, graduate study, 1974—. *Home:* 425 Ellerslie Ave., Ambler, Pa. 19002.

CAREER: Elementary school teacher in London, England, 1971-72, Greenwich, Conn., 1972-73, and in a Montessori school in Philadelphia, Pa., 1973-74; Rockledge Elementary School, Abington, Pa., teacher, 1974-75.

WRITINGS: Child's Work, Running Press, 1974.

WORK IN PROGRESS: Research on early childhood education.

AVOCATIONAL INTERESTS: Travel (Europe, the Caribbean, the Mediterranean, Ireland), music, motorcycles, children's games, chess, athletics.

* * *

SHANNON, John 1943-

PERSONAL: Born November 29, 1943, in Detroit, Mich.; son of Herb (a reporter) and Ruth (Merrick) Shannon; divorced. *Education:* Pomona College, B.A., 1965; University of California, Los Angeles, M.F.A., 1968. *Politics:* "Would like to help overthrow capitalism." *Residence:* Southern California. *Agent:* Wendy Weil, Julian Bach Literary Agency, 3 East 48th St., New York, N.Y. 10017.

CAREER: Has worked as a reporter, television writer, English teacher, and curriculum designer. *Member:* Left History Study Group.

WRITINGS: The Orphan (novel), Saturday Review Press, 1972; *Courage* (novel), Norton, 1975.

WORK IN PROGRESS: Eyes and Ears of the Revolution, a novel; research for a biography and for a historical study.

SIDELIGHTS: Shannon writes that he hopes "... to help bring back into American writing our analytic and intellectual heritage from Europe, which has been squeezed out in this century by the American obsession with·'dramatizing' and by our total immersion in one narrow ideology in the name of 'an end to ideology.' Have been influenced, in quite different ways, by two British writers, Graham Greene and John Berger, as well as by Lukacs, Gramsci, Mao, and Marx. And by a painstaking process of rediscovering the important democratic strands of American history deleted from our texts: history is people, popular movements, struggles, not a litany of dates and laws and other content-less factoids. (Characteristically, I had to live in Europe for some time to begin discovering this.)"

* * *

SHAPP, Charles M(orris) 1906-

PERSONAL: Born February 13, 1906, in New York, N.Y.; son of Morris and Clare (Fox) Shapp; married Martha Segall Glauber (an educator and editor), December 23, 1953; children: Mark, William Glauber (stepson). *Education:* College of the City of New York (now City College of the City University of New York), B.S., 1927, M.S., 1933; New York University, Doctor Juris, 1938. *Religion:* Jewish. *Residence:* Salt Point, N.Y. 12578. *Office:* Pace University, Graduate School of Education, Pace Square, New York, N.Y. 10010.

CAREER: Elementary and junior high school teacher in New York, N.Y., 1928-44; assistant principal of Pershing Junior High School, Brooklyn, N.Y., 1944-46; principal of P.S. 2, Bronx, N.Y., 1946-49; principal of Knowlton Junior High School, Bronx, N.Y., 1949-58; assistant superintendent of New York Public School District 10, 1958-73;

Pace University, Graduate School of Education, New York, N.Y., professor of education, 1974—. Visiting lecturer at colleges and universities including New York University and University of Puerto Rico. Consultant to Job Corps Project, War on Poverty, and to St. Louis Juvenile Delinquency Study. Member of Urban League, East Bronx Youth Board Committee, Yorkville Community Council, and Committee to Keep New York City Clean, and other civic organizations. Member of board of trustees, New Lincoln School. *Military service:* U.S. Army, Medical Corps., 1942-45. *Member:* Association for Supervision and Curriculum Development (member of board of directors; past president New York Division), National Education Association, American Association of School Administrators, Association of Assistant Superintendents, National Conference of Christians and Jews, Kappa Delta Pi.

WRITINGS:–All with wife, Martha Glauber Shapp: *Planning and Organizing Science Programs in Elementary Schools*, Grolier Society, 1958; *Words About Air Travel*, F. Watts, 1969. "Let's Find Out" series, published by F. Watts: *Let's Find Out What's Big and What's Small*, 1959, revised edition, 1975; *... What the Signs Say*, 1959; *... About School*, 1961; *... What Electricity Does*, 1961, revised edition, 1975; *... What's in the Sky*, 1961; *... What's Light and What's Heavy*, 1961, revised edition, 1975; *... About Wheels*, 1962; *...About Water*, 1962; *...About the United Nations*, 1962; *...About Animal Homes*, 1962; *... About Firemen*, 1962; *... About Indians*, 1962; *...About Houses*, 1962; *... About Policemen*, 1962; *... About Winter*, 1963; *...About Summer*, 1963 *...About Spring, 1963; ...About Fall*, 1963; *...About Cowboys*, 1963; *...About Air*, 1963; *... About Christopher Columbus*, 1964; *... About Washington's Birthday*, 1964; *...About Thanksgiving*, 1964; *... About Safety*, 1964; *... About Our Flag*, 1964; *... About the Sun*, 1965, revised edition, 1975; *... About the Moon*, 1965, revised edition, 1975; *... About John Fitzgerald Kennedy*, 1965, revised edition published as *The Picture Life of John Fitzgerald Kennedy*, 1966; *... About Abraham Lincoln*, 1965; *...About Fishes*, 1966; *... About Thomas Alva Edison*, 1966; *... About Birds*, 1967; *...About Daniel Boone*, 1967; *...About New Year's Day*, 1968; *... About Airplanes*, 1968; *... About Animals of Long Ago*, 1968; *...About Snakes*, 1968; (with Sylvia Shepard) *...About Babies*, 1969; *...About Trees*, 1970; *... About Space Travel*, 1971; *... About Jewish Holidays*, 1971; *... About Cavemen*, 1972; *... About Animals of Africa*, 1972.

Also author with wife, of educational filmstrips and teaching guides. Contributor to yearbooks, including *John Dewey Society Yearbook* and *Middle States Council for the Social Studies Yearbook*. Contributor of articles to *High Points, American Weekly, Association for Supervision and Curriculum Development Newsletter, Public Relations Journal*, and other periodicals.

WORK IN PROGRESS: Preparing a series to be entitled "Heroes of Many Lands," introducing to children of our country, the great heroes of other countries.

* * *

SHAPPIRO, Herbert (Arthur) 1899(?)-1975
(Burt Arthur, Herbert Arthur, Arthur Herbert)

1899(?)—March 15, 1975; American playwright, short story writer, author of western novels, editor, newspaperman, advertising agency executive. Obituaries: *New York Times*, March 16, 1975, *AB Bookman's Weekly*, April 21, 1975. (*CA*-21/22)

SHAW, Maxine 1945-

PERSONAL: Born June 4, 1945, in Long Beach, Calif.; daughter of Marion Eugene and Carole Lee (Fuller) Shaw; children: Wamwega Christopher. *Education:* Marquette University, B.A., 1969; University of Massachuetts, graduate study, 1972. *Home:* 103 Browne St., Brookline, Mass. 02146.

CAREER: National Catholic News Service, Washington, D.C., assistant Latin American editor, 1970-71; free-lance news and public relations writer in Boston, Mass. (wrote for Campaign for Human Development), 1971-72; bilingual teacher in public schools in Boston, Mass., 1972—.

WRITINGS: Walking Backwards Down the Keya Coast (poems), privately printed, 1970; *Beautiful Cages* (poems), Stone Soup Poetry, 1974.

WORK IN PROGRESS: A book of translations of the Cuban poet Nicolas Guillen; a book of poems.

SIDELIGHTS: Maxine Shaw has traveled extensively in Spain, Mexico, and South America.

*   *   *

SHAW, Nancy Stoller 1942-

PERSONAL: Born July 16, 1942, in Newport News, Va.; daughter of Morton J. (an engineer) and Ruth (a chemist; maiden name, Klarberg) Stoller; divorced; children: Gwendolyn Ann DuBois. *Education:* Wellesley College, A.B., 1963; Brandeis University, M.A., 1965, Ph.D., 1972. *Residence:* Santa Cruz, Calif. *Office:* Department of Community Studies, University of California, Santa Cruz, Calif. 95064.

CAREER: Emmanuel College, Boston, Mass., instructor in sociology, 1970-73; University of California, Santa Cruz, assistant professor of sociology and community studies, 1973—. Consultant to California State Senate Research Office. *Member:* American Sociological Association, Phi Beta Kappa.

WRITINGS: Forced Labor: Maternity Care in the United States, Pergamon, 1974. Contributor to *Journal of the American Medical Association.*

WORK IN PROGRESS: Behavior Modification; Struggles against Sexism and Racism in Day Care; Women's Health in Prisons.

*   *   *

SHEALY, C(lyde) Norman 1932-

PERSONAL: Born December 4, 1932, in Columbia, S.C.; son of Lemuel and Palma L. (Padget) Shealy; married Mary-Charlotte Bayles, June 13, 1959; children: Brock, Craig, Laurel. *Education:* Duke University, B.Sc., 1952, M.D., 1956. *Home address:* Route 2, LaCrosse, Wis. 54601. *Office:* Pain Rehabilitation Center, S.C., LaCrosse, Wis. 54601.

CAREER: Duke University Hospital, Durham, N.C., medical intern, 1956-57; Barnes Hospital, St. Louis, Mo., assistant resident in surgery, 1957-58; Massachusetts General Hospital, Boston, clinical and research fellow in neurosurgery, 1958-59, assistant resident in neurosurgery, 1959-62, clinical assistant in neurosurgery, 1962-63; Harvard University Medical School, Boston, Mass., teaching fellow in surgery, 1962-63; Western Reserve University (now Case Western Reserve University) School of Medicine, Cleveland, Ohio, senior instructor, 1963-66, assistant professor of neurosurgery, 1966; Gundersen Clinic and Lu-

theran Hospital, LaCrosse, Wis., chief of neurosurgery department, 1966-71; University of Wisconsin Medical School, Madison, assistant clinical professor of neurosurgery, 1967—; University of Minnesota Medical School, Minneapolis, associate professor of neurosurgery, 1970—; Pain Rehabilitation Center, S.C., LaCrosse, Wis., director, 1971—. President of Autogenics Institute Foundation, LaCrosse, 1974—, and Autogenics Institute of America, Inc., LaCrosse, 1974—. Clinical associate, department of psychology, University of Wisconsin-LaCrosse. *Military service:* U.S. Naval Reserve, 1956-63.

MEMBER: American College of Surgeons (fellow), American Medical Association, American Association of Anatomists, American Association for the Study of Headache, International Association for the Study of Pain, Congress of Neurological Surgeons, American Association of Neurological Surgeons, Wisconsin State Medical Society, Wisconsin Heart Association. *Awards, honors:* National Foundation for Infantile Paralysis fellow, 1958-59; Institute of Neurological Disease and Blindness special fellow at Australian National University, 1961.

WRITINGS: Occult Medicine Can Save Your Life, Dial, 1975.

Contributor: David V. Reynolds and Anita E. Sjoberg, editors, *Neurologic Research*, C. C Thomas, 1971; Norman L. Wulfsohn and Anthony Sances, Jr., editors, *The Nervous System and Electric Currents*, Volume II, Plenum, 1971; Guenter B. Risse, editor, *Modern China and Traditional Chinese Medicine*, C. C Thomas, 1973; William S. Fields, editor, *Neural Organization and Its Relevance to Prosthetics*, Intercontinental Medical Book, 1973; John J. Bonica, editor, *Advances in Neurology*, Volume IV, Raven Press, 1974; Robert H. Wilkins, editor, *Clinical Neurosurgery*, Volume XXI, Williams & Wilkins, 1974. Contributor of more than eighty articles to medical journals.

WORK IN PROGRESS: The Pain Game.

AVOCATIONAL INTERESTS: Raising Appaloosa horses, gardening.

*   *   *

SHEEHAN, (James) Vincent 1899-1975

December 5, 1899—March 15, 1975; American journalist, foreign correspondent, world traveller, biographer, novelist, author of political and autobiographical works. Obituaries: *New York Times*, March 17, 1975; *Washington Post*, March 17, 1975; *Time*, March 31, 1975; *Newsweek*, March 31, 1975; *AB Bookman's Weekly*, April 28, 1975; *Current Biography*, May, 1975.

*   *   *

SHEETS, Elva (Darah) 1898-

PERSONAL: Born May 24, 1898, in Huntington County, Ind.; daughter of James and Lottie J. (Bailey) Summers. Children: Mary Cosette, Sumner B. *Education:* Bradley University, graduate, 1919. *Religion:* Methodist. *Home address:* R.R. 4, Box 244, Huntington, Ind. 46750.

CAREER: Writer. *Member:* International Oceanographic Foundation, Smithsonian Associates, Conchologists of America, American Malacological Union, American Museum of Natural History, New Zealand Shell Club, Kepple Bay Shell Club (Australia), Conchology Club of Southern California, Hawaiian Malacological Society.

WRITINGS: The Fascinating World of the Sea, Crown, 1974; *In Pursuit of the Wild Seashell*, Crown, in press.

WORK IN PROGRESS: Glossary of Natural History Terms Explained in Easy English.

SIDELIGHTS: Elva Sheets has spent her entire life on a farm in Indiana. She visited the ocean for the first time at the age of fifty, and developed a continuing interest in the sea and in shells and marine life. She writes: "The timing of the birth of my shell and ocean interest coincided with a radical change in my life. After many years of working hard on a farm and raising a family I suddenly found myself alone at age fifty with my children in homes of their own and my time all my own to use as I pleased . . . To collect the material and information for my totally different project . . . I personally searched all four hemispheres traveling a total distance of seven and two-fifths times around the world."

* * *

SHELLY, (Michael) Bruce   1929-

PERSONAL: Born February 18, 1929, in Reno, Nev.; son of Carl Bunda (a hardware store owner) and Barbara (Bulmer) Shelly; married Nancy Hardgrave, June 14, 1953; children: Scott Lloyd, Anne Katharyn, Reed Carl. *Education:* Attended University of Utah, 1947-48. *Religion:* Religious Scientist. *Home:* 14042 Davana Terrace, Sherman Oaks, Calif. 91423. *Agent:* John Schallert, 450 North Roxbury Dr., Beverly Hills, Calif.

CAREER: Writer for radio program, "Research Report," 1948-50; *Sparks Tribune*, Sparks, Nev., editor, 1950; administrative assistant to Congressman Clifton Young in Washington, D.C., 1953-56; worked in advertising, 1957-72; television and film writer in Sherman Oaks, Calif., 1972—. *Member:* Writers Guild of America, West, National Academy of Television Arts and Sciences.

WRITINGS: My Woman (novel), Merit Books, 1961; *The Miracle of Anne* (nonfiction), Science of Mind, 1974. Contributor of short stories and articles to journals. Author of a series of four audio-books for children, produced by Hoffman Information Systems. Writer of business films and of about one hundred network television scripts, including episodes of "NBC Mystery Movies," "ABC Movie of the Week," "The Rookies," "M*A*S*H," "The Waltons," and "Here's Lucy."

WORK IN PROGRESS: An original screenplay, "The Hazing."

SIDELIGHTS: Shelly told *CA:* "Obviously, I have not concentrated on one particular genre. My fourteen-year-old son recently announced, 'I have been looking at your two books, Dad, and I guess what you are is a pornographer and a religious author.' Put commercial television someplace between those two poles and you see my smorgasbord viewpoint. Maybe one of the reasons I always wanted to be a writer was because it is such a perfect ticket to all the fascinating diversities that make up our world."

* * *

SHEPARD, Jon M(ax)   1939-

PERSONAL: Born July 15, 1939, in Ashland, Ky.; son of Max (a store manager) and Mabel (Martin) Shepard; married Kay Vogel (an administrative assistant), July 16, 1961; children: Jon, Jr.. *Education:* Georgetown College, Georgetown, Ky., B.A., 1961; University of Kentucky, M.A., 1963; Michigan State University, Ph.D., 1968. *Politics:* Independent. *Religion:* Methodist. *Home:* 1433 Lakewood Dr., Lexington, Ky. 40502. *Office:* Department of Sociology, 1563 Patterson Office Tower, University of Kentucky, Lexington, Ky. 40506.

CAREER: University of Kentucky, Lexington, assistant professor of sociology, spring term, 1968; Massachusetts Institute of Technology, Cambridge, research associate, Sloan School of Management, 1968-69; University of Kentucky, assistant professor, 1969-71, associate professor of sociology, 1971—, assistant director of Social Welfare Research Institute, 1970-71, research sociologist of Institute, 1971-73. Consultant to National Science Foundation, Human Relations Resources Research Organization, and to publishers C. E. Merrill and Harper & Row. *Member:* American Sociological Association, Southern Sociological Society.

WRITINGS: Automation and Alienation: A Study of Office and Factory Workers, M.I.T. Press, 1971; (editor) *Organizational Issues in Industrial Society*, Prentice-Hall, 1972; (editor) *Kaleidoscope: Adapted Readings for Introductory Sociology*, Harper, 1973; (editor) *Spectrum on Social Problems: Society, Economy, and Man*, C. E. Merrill, 1973; *Basic Sociology: Structure, Interaction and Change*, Harper, 1974.

Contributor: George L. Wilber, editor, *Anticipating Poverties of the Poor*, Social Welfare Research Institute, University of Kentucky, 1971; George L. Wilber, editor, *Poverty: A New Approach*, University Press of Kentucky, 1974; Ernest Dale, editor, *Management: Theory and Practice*, McGraw, 1975. Contributor of articles and reviews to sociology, industrial relations, and business journals.

WORK IN PROGRESS: With Cyrus S. Stewart, *Sociology and Social Problems*, for Prentice-Hall; with Harwin L. Voss and Neal Garland, *Social Problems*, for Macmillan; with Cyrus S. Stewart, *Delinquent Subcultures and Gangs*, for Free Press.

AVOCATIONAL INTERESTS: Playing golf, other sports as spectator.

* * *

SHEPHARD, Esther   1891-1975

July 29, 1891—February 10, 1975; American educator and author of books for children. Obituaries: *New York Times*, February 13, 1975; *AB Bookman's Weekly*, March 3, 1975. (*CA*-25/28)

* * *

SHEPHERD, Jack   1937-

PERSNAL: Born December 14, 1937, in Summit, N.J.; son of John Edwin (in advertising) and Grace (Anderson) Shepherd; married Kathleen Kessler (a teacher), September 3, 1960; children: Kristen, Caleb. *Education:* Haverford College, B.A., 1960; Columbia University, M.S., 1961. *Home:* 125 West 80th St., New York, N.Y. 10024. *Agent:* Sterling Lord, 660 Madison Ave., New York, N.Y. 10020.

CAREER: Look (magazine), New York, N.Y., senior editor, 1964-69, assistant managing editor, 1969-70, senior editor in charge of special issues, 1970-71; *Newsweek* (magazine), New York, N.Y., associate editor, 1971-72; Carnegie Endowment for International Peace, New York, N.Y., senior associate, 1973-74; free-lance writer, 1974—. *Military service:* U.S. Army Reserve, 1961-62. *Awards, honors:* National Education Award from National Education Association, 1966; National Magazine Award finalist, 1974.

WRITINGS: Quotations from Chairman LBJ, Simon & Schuster, 1968; *The Almanack of Poor Richard Nixon*, World Publishing, 1969; (editor) *Earth Day: The Beginning*, Penguin, 1970; *The Super Summer of Jamie McBride*, Simon & Schuster, 1971; *The Forest Killers*, Weybright, 1975. Also author of television documentary, "Nuclear Power," 1973.

Screenplays: *The Acid Trip*, Guidance Associates, 1969; *Black America's West Africa Heritage*, Guidance Associates, 1970.

Consultant to periodicals, including *New Woman, Single, Saturday Review* (Society).

WORK IN PROGRESS: The Adams Family: Four Generations, 1770-1900; Water: The Last Resource; The Alaskan Pipeline: RIP.

SIDELIGHTS: Shepherd writes: "I am primarily an investigative writer, looking at the new things of the day. I strongly believe in the responsibility of any writer of talent to illuminate society's path, and not trail along as the tailgate. As a writer I have traveled in 46 of the 50 United States on assignments, and throughout Western Europe. I have also been around the world, and covered assignments in the African nations of Ghana, Nigeria, Upper Volta, Kenya, Tanzania and Ethiopia. I speak Swahili, German and Spanish."

BIOGRAPHICAL/CRITICAL SOURCES: Look, August 12, 1969; *Intellectual Digest*, February, 1973, March, 1974.

* * *

SHERMAN, A(lan) Robert 1942-

PERSONAL: Born November 18, 1942, in New York, N.Y.; son of David R. and Goldie (Wax) Sherman; married Llana Helene Tobias, August 14, 1966; children: Jonathan Colbert, Relissa Anne. *Education:* Columbia University, A.B. (with honors), 1964; Yale University, M.S., 1966, Ph.D., 1969. *Office:* Department of Psychology, University of California, Santa Barbara, Calif. 93106.

CAREER: University of California, Santa Barbara, assistant professor, 1969-75, associate professor of psychology, 1975—. Consultant to Dorsey, Brooks-Cole, Goodyear Publishing, and to Santa Barbara County Schools. Santa Barbara Mental Health Association, member of board of directors, 1972—, member of executive committee, 1975—. *Member:* American Association for the Advancement of Science, American Psychological Association, Association for the Advancement of Behavior Therapy, Society for Clinical and Experimental Hypnosis, Western Psychological Association, Phi Beta Kappa, Sigma Xi. *Awards, honors:* University of California faculty research grants, 1969-73, 1974-75, fellowship, summer, 1971; Exxon Education Foundation research grant, 1973-76.

WRITINGS: Behavior Modification: Theory and Practice, Brooks-Cole, 1973. Contributor to journals.

WORK IN PROGRESS: Research on biofeedback and relaxation approaches to self-control of blood pressure; research on principles and procedures of behavioral self-management.

* * *

SHERMAN, Franklin (Eugene) 1928-

PERSONAL: Born August 15, 1928, in New York, N.Y.; son of John Franklin and Helen Seymour (Hazard) Sherman; married Joan Margery Kendall, June 24, 1953;

children: Mark, David, Leslie. *Education:* Muhlenberg College, A.B., 1950; University of Chicago, A.M., 1952, Ph.D., 1961; Lutheran School of Theology at Chicago, M.Div., 1953. *Politics:* Democratic. *Home:* 1455 East 55th Pl., Chicago, Ill. 60637. *Office:* Lutheran School of Theology at Chicago, 1100 East 55th St., Chicago, Ill. 60615.

CAREER: Ordained minister of the Lutheran Church, 1956; pastor in Chicago, Ill., 1956-58; University of Iowa, Iowa City, instructor, 1958-60, assistant professor of theology, 1960-61; Oxford University, Mansfield College, Oxford, England, tutor in religion, 1961-66, dean of Lutheran students, 1961-66; Lutheran School of Theology at Chicago, associate professor, 1966-70, professor of Christian ethics, 1970—, director of graduate studies, 1973—. Visiting lecturer at University of Chicago, 1967-70, and Northwestern University, 1969. *Member:* American Society of Christian Ethics (executive secretary, 1972-76). *Awards, honors:* Honorary M.A. from Oxford University, 1961.

WRITINGS: (Contributor) Harold C. Letts, editor, *Existence Today*, Fortress, 1957; *The Courage to Care: A Study in Christian Social Responsibility*, Fortress, 1959; (contributor) Martin E. Marty, editor, *The Place of Bonhoeffer*, Association Press, 1962; (contributor) Philip J. Hefner, editor, *The Scope of Grace: Essays in Honor of Joseph Sittler*, Fortress, 1964; (contributor) Marty and Dean G. Peerman, editors, *A Handbook of Christian Theologians*, World Publishing Co., 1965; (translator) Paul Althaus, *The Divine Command: A New Perspective on Law and Gospel*, Fortress, 1966; (contributor) Heinrich Foerster, editor, *Reformation Heute*, Lutherisches Verlagshaus, 1967; (editor and contributor) *Christian Hope and the Future of Humanity*, Augsburg, 1969.

The Promise of Heschel, Lippincott, 1970; (editor) *Luther's Works*, Volume XLVII, Fortress, 1971; (contributor) Gail R. Schmidt, editor, *The Meaning of America in a Global Context*, Department for Church and Society, Lutheran Church in America, 1973; (contributor) Paul D. Opsahl and Marc H. Tannenbaum, editors, *Speaking of God Today: Lutherans and Jews in Conversation*, Fortress, 1974; *The Problem of Abortion after the Supreme Court Decision*, Lutheran Church in America, 1974. Editor of Fortress "Facet Books" (social ethics series), 1964—. Contributor to religion journals.

WORK IN PROGRESS: Translating and editing Paul Tillich's *Die sozialistische Entscheidung*, to be published as *The Socialist Decision* by Harper; research on the problem of violence and on the theory of democracy.

* * *

SHERMAN, Lawrence W(illiam) 1949-

PERSONAL: Born October 25, 1949, in Schenectady, N.Y.; son of Donald L. (a Young Men's Christian Association executive) and Margaret (a religious educator; maiden name, Heckman) Sherman; married Eva Fass (a lawyer), October 7, 1973. *Education:* Denison University, B.A. (magna cum laude), 1970; University of Chicago, M.A., 1970; Yale University, M.A., 1974, Ph.D., 1976. *Religion:* Society of Friends (Quaker). *Office:* Department of Sociology, Yale University, 140 Prospect St., New Haven, Conn. 06520.

CAREER: New York City Police Department, New York, N.Y., program research analyst, 1971-72; Kansas City Police Department, Kansas City, Mo., consultant for patrol experiments, 1971-72. Consultant to Baltimore Mayor's Coordinating Council on Criminal Justice, 1972, Police

Foundation on Police Corruption, 1973-74, and National Institute of Law Enforcement, 1974. Lecturer at Marymount Manhattan College, fall, 1971-72, University of Wisconsin, Dayton Police Academy, University of Arizona, and New Jersey State Department of Vocational Rehabilitation. *Wartime service:* Alternate Service, 1970-72.

MEMBER: American Sociological Association, Phi Beta Kappa, Yale Club of New York. *Awards, honors:* New York City Urban fellow, 1970-71; Ford Foundation travel and study grant at Cambridge University, Institute for Criminology, 1972-73.

WRITINGS: (With Catherine H. Milton and Thomas Kelly) *Team Policing: Seven Case Studies*, Police Foundation, 1973; (editor) *Police Corruption: A Sociological Perspective*, Anchor Books, 1974; (contributor) Donald E. J. McNamara and Marc Reidel, editors, *Police: Perspectives, Problems, Prospects*, Praeger, 1975; (contributor) Richard Nelson and Douglas T. Yates, editors, *Innovation and Implementation*, Heath, 1975. Contributor of articles and reviews to *American Sociologist, Criminology, Journal of Police Science and Administration, YMCA Forum, Contemporary Sociology, American Journal of Sociology*, and *New York Journal of Crime and Justice*.

WORK IN PROGRESS: A book of four case studies of reform police chiefs taking over corrupt police departments, *Controlling Police Corruption*, publication expected in 1977.

* * *

SHERWIN, Sterling
See Hagen, John Milton

* * *

SHIARELLA, Robert 1936-

PERSONAL: Born December 16, 1936, in New Kensington, Pa.; son of George Rodger (a banker) and Rose (Sabetta) Shiarella; married Janice Champagne, March 29, 1959 (divorced, 1967); children: John Galt. *Education:* Attended Carnegie Institute of Technology (now Carnegie-Mellon University), 1954-56; Pennsylvania State University, B.A., 1959. *Politics:* Independent. *Religion:* Siddha Yoga. *Home:* 131 West 75th St., No. 4-A, New York, N.Y. 10023. *Agent:* Hyman R. Cohen, 111 West 57th St., New York, N.Y. 10019. *Office:* World Yoga Centre, 265 West 72nd St., New York, N.Y. 10023.

CAREER: National Broadcasting Co., Inc., New York, N.Y., casting coordinator, 1964-65; free-lance writer, 1965-67; *Argosy* (magazine), New York, N.Y., articles editor, 1967-73; *Adventure* and *True Adventure* (magazines), New York, N.Y., editor, 1967-73; World Yoga Centre, New York, N.Y., director, 1973—. Creative consultant, Children's Television Workshop. *Military service:* U.S. Army, 1959-61. *Member:* World Yoga Society International.

WRITINGS: Your Sparkle Cavalcade of Death (novel), Viking, 1974; (contributor) Brother Theodore and Marvin Kaye, compilers, *Brother Theodore's Chamber of Horrors*, Pinnacle Books, 1975. Contributor of more than 100 articles and stories to periodicals; also contributor of reviews to *San Francisco Review of Books*.

WORK IN PROGRESS: A novel, a sequel to *Your Sparkle Cavalcade of Death;* researching and writing on yoga.

SHIEFMAN, Vicky 1942-

PERSONAL: Born June 29, 1942, in Detroit, Mich.; daughter of Saul (in public relations) and Emma (a teacher; maiden name, Goldman) Shiefman. *Education:* University of Chicago, B.A., 1964; New York University, M.A., 1973. *Politics:* Democrat. *Religion:* Jewish. *Residence:* New York, N.Y.

CAREER: Board of Education, New York, N.Y., teacher of pre-kindergarten through second grade classes, 1968—. *Member:* United Federation of Teachers, Society of Children's Book Writers, Authors Guild of Authors League of America, Nu Pi Sigma.

WRITINGS: Mindy (juvenile), Macmillan, 1975. Contributor of articles on education to *Nana, Mademoiselle, Moderator*, and *University of Chicago Maroon*.

WORK IN PROGRESS—For children: *Jenny Ann Birdwell Has Another Mother; Mora of the Mountains*.

* * *

SHIPP, Nelson 1892-

PERSONAL: Born May 12, 1892, in Cordele, Ga.; son of Charles J. and Lillian (Zellner) Shipp; married Mary Effie Shi, December 31, 1912; children: Emily Lillian Shipp Troncone. *Education:* Attended Georgia School of Technology (now Georgia Institute of Technology), 1910, Gordon Military Institute, 1911-1912, Mercer University, fall, 1912, and Georgia Military College. *Home:* 775 Argonne Ave. N.E., Atlanta, Ga. 30308.

CAREER: Canebrake Herald, Uniontown, Ala., editor, 1911; reporter for newspapers in Fulda, Minn., Long Prairie, Minn., and Black River Falls, Wis., 1911; editor and reporter for newspapers in Georgia, 1913-16; *Macon News*, Macon, Ga., state and telegraph editor, 1916-19; *Macon Telegraph*, Macon, chief editorial writer, 1919-24; Stone Mountain Confederate Memorial, Atlanta, Ga., public relations executive and office manager, 1925; executive secretary to U.S. Senator William Harris in Washington, D.C., 1926; public relations executive for William Randolph Hearst interests in Washington, D.C., 1927-28; *Ledger-Enquirer*, Columbus, Ga., news editor, later editor, 1930-40; State Capitol, Atlanta, Ga., ghostwriter and speech writer for five governors and others, and later executive head of Georgia State Department of Commerce, 1943-67; author, 1967—. Instructor in journalism, Mercer University and Wesleyan College. *Member:* Georgia Writers Association; various civic clubs.

WRITINGS: A Vagabond Newsman, Cherokee, 1974. Author of "Wild Fire," a novel, as yet unpublished. Contributor to *Science of Mind* and *Aspire*.

WORK IN PROGRESS: The Battle for Men's Minds, a treatise on the relationship of four Asian religions and Christianity; *Look Upward, Angel*, a book presenting an everyday philosophy of life.

SIDELIGHTS: Shipp told *CA:* "I was born and raised in a frontier, six-gun town in south Georgia; my father was a gunfighter, a duelist of the old South. At the age of nineteen ... I ... wandered around Minnesota, Wisconsin, and across the North as a hobo and vagabond, and several chapters in my book, *A Vagabond Newsman*, recount the dangers I encountered, living in hobo jungles, riding on every part of a train, traveling with a bank robber, and narrowly escaping with my life a number of times."

Speaking of his career, Shipp said, "There were other activities, such as undercover work in Mexico, Texas, and Washington, the last as private investigator in connection with the Teapot Dome national scandal of the 1920's in which I had to leave Washington to escape being the tenth person to die mysteriously...." While with the *Macon Telegraph*, Shipp led the fight against the Ku Klux Klan's illegal activities in Georgia with his editorials.

*   *   *

SHOFNER, Jerrell H(arris) 1929-

PERSONAL: Born January 30, 1929, in Haslet, Tex.; son, of Homer H. (a transportation worker) and Dora Mae (Taylor) Shofner; married Catherine H. Stefonetti, August 27, 1955; children: Charles, Michele. *Education:* Florida State University, B.S., 1960, M.S., 1961, Ph.D., 1963. *Politics:* Democrat. *Address:* Route 2, Box 486A, Longwood, Fla. 32750. *Office:* Department of History, Florida Technological University, Orlando, Fla. 32816.

CAREER: U.S. Air Force, 1946-60, stationed in Japan, 1947-52, Korea, 1952-54, Niagara Falls, N.Y., 1954-56, Alaska, 1956-57, and Valdosta, Ga., 1957-60, retiring as chief master sergeant; Georgia Southern College, Statesboro, assistant professor of history, 1963-64; Texas Woman's University, Denton, assistant professor of history, 1964-67; University of Florida, Gainesville, assistant professor of history, 1967-68; Florida State University, Tallahassee, associate professor of history, 1968-72; Florida Technological University, Orlando, professor of history and chairman of department, 1972—. *Member:* Organization of American Historians, Southern Historical Association, Florida Historical Society (vice-president, 1974-76), Phi Beta Kappa, Phi Kappa Phi. *Awards, honors:* Rembert W. Patrick Book Award from Florida Historical Society, 1974, for *Nor Is It Over Yet: Florida in the Era of Reconstruction, 1865-1877*.

WRITINGS: (Editor and author of introduction) *Sidney Lanier's Florida: Its Climate, Scenery, and History*, University of Florida Facsimile Series, 1973; *Nor Is It Over Yet: Florida in the Era of Reconstruction, 1865-1877*, University of Florida Press, 1974; *Daniel Ladd: Merchant Prince of Frontier Florida*, University of Florida Press, in press. Contributor to professional journals.

WORK IN PROGRESS: A monograph, *Negro Land Tenure in Northeast Florida Following the Civil War*, completion expected in 1977.

*   *   *

SHOFNER, Robert D(ancey) 1933-

PERSONAL: Born November 22, 1933, in Seattle, Wash.; son of Harold T. (a millwright) and Verna (Bilderback) Shofner; married Catherine V. Metzener (a library assistant), July 31, 1950; children: Robert D., Jr. *Education:* University of Puget Sound, B.A. (cum laude), 1961; Yale University, B.D. (cum laude), 1964; Hartford Seminary Foundation, Ph.D. (cum laude), 1972. *Home:* 2212 Stacy Lane, Camarillo, Calif. 93010. *Office:* Department of Religious Studies, California State University, Northridge, Calif. 91324.

CAREER: Ordained minister of United Church of Christ (Congregationalists), 1964; assistant minister of Congregationalist churches in Bethel, Conn., 1961-63, and North Haven, Conn., 1963-64; minister of Congregationalist church in Marlborough, Conn., 1964-67; California State University, Northridge, assistant professor, 1970-74, asso-

ciate professor of religious studies, 1974—, chairman of department, 1972—. *Military service:* U.S. Navy, 1951-54.

MEMBER: American Academy of Religion, American Association of University Professors, Society for the Scientific Study of Religion, Society for Religion in Higher Education, American Philosophical Association, Foundation for Creative Philosophy, Mu Delta Sigma. *Awards, honors:* Danforth Foundation Fellowship, 1961-70.

WRITINGS: Anselm Revisited: A Study of the Role of the Ontological Argument in the Writings of Karl Barth and Charles Hartshorne, E. J. Brill (Leiden, Netherlands), 1974. Contributor to *Scottish Journal of Theology* and *Journal of the American Academy of Religion*.

WORK IN PROGRESS: Research on Karl Barth and the Lutheran tradition; studying Hartshorne's neoclassical metaphysics; research on Torrance's and Nygren's views on scientific theology.

SIDELIGHTS: Shofner writes: "I strive to combine the historical method of research with philosophical-theological analysis ... Barth and Torrance have taught me the importance of thinking seriously about the question of a scientific theology. This is one emphasis in my own work. Another emphasis has to do with the need to develop such a theology in a manner that is constant with the classical Protestant tradition."

*   *   *

SHOWALTER, Elaine 1941-

PERSONAL: Born January 21, 1941, in Cambridge, Mass.; daughter of Paul (a wool merchant) and Violet (Rottenberg) Cottler; married English Showalter, Jr. (a professor of French), June 8, 1963; children: Victoria, Michael. *Education:* Bryn Mawr College, B.A., 1962; Brandeis University, M.A., 1964; University of California, Davis, Ph.D., 1970. *Home:* 119 Snowden Lane, Princeton, N.J. 08540. *Office:* Department of English, Douglass College, Rutgers University, New Brunswick, N.J. 08903.

CAREER: Rutgers University, Douglass College, New Brunswick, N.J., assistant professor, 1970-74, associate professor of English, 1974—. *Member:* Modern Language Association of America, National Organization for Women.

WRITINGS: (Editor) *Women's Liberation and Literature*, Harcourt, 1971; (editor with Carol Ohmann) *Female Studies IV*, KNOW, 1971. Editor of *Women's Studies*, 1972—, and *Signs: Journal of Women, Culture, and Society*, 1975—.

WORK IN PROGRESS: The Female Tradition in the English Novel; *After the Vote* and *Women and Utopia* for Feminist Press.

*   *   *

SHUTE, Alberta V(an Horn) 1906-

PERSONAL: Born November 18, 1906, in Boothbay, Me.; daughter of Simeon Brigham (a marine engineer) and Julia (Dodge) Van Horn; married Donald Shute (a woodsman), February 12, 1943; children: Leon, Sarah (Mrs. Lorne Hale), Daniel. *Education:* Attended Colby College, 1925-26, and Gorham Normal School, 1931-32; University of Maine, Augusta, B.A., 1970. *Politics:* Republican. *Religion:* Protestant. *Home address:* R.F.D. 5, Augusta, Me. 04330.

CAREER: Public school teacher in Boothbay, Me., 1926-

33; taught evening classes and apprentice course at Maine State Library, 1933-38; Maine Department of Health and Welfare, Augusta, account clerk, 1938-45; public school teacher in Augusta, 1943; Manchester School Library, Manchester, Me., librarian, 1962-69; public school teacher in Manchester, 1967-68. *Member:* Woman's Christian Temperance Union, Kennebec Historical Society, Alpha Delta Pi.

WRITINGS—Nonfiction: *A Year and a Day Along Bond Brook*, Living Word Press, 1954; *A Year and a Day in the Park*, Living Word Press, 1956; *A Year and a Day at My Kitchen Window*, Living Word Press, 1965; *A Year and a Day on the Farm*, Balm O'Gilead Press, 1972. Author of "RFD4," a weekly column in *Daily Kennebec Journal*, 1949-58. Contributor to *Boothbay Register, Lewiston Evening Journal* Magazine, and *Portland Evening Express*. Editor of *Star in the East*, 1960—.

WORK IN PROGRESS: Co-editing a bicentennial history of Manchester, Me.; a book about East Boothbay, Me.

AVOCATIONAL INTERESTS: Travel, collecting rocks, bells, and trivets, maps, histories of towns, books, singing in church choirs.

* * *

SICKLES, William Russell 1913-

PERSONAL: Born April 28, 1913, in Springfield, Ohio; son of William Francis (a metalworker) and Grace Mae (Jenkins) Sickles; married Clara Jo Cooper, February 5, 1942; children: Karen Lorna (Mrs. John McNary), Kurt Eugene, Garth Eric. *Education*: Wittenberg University, B.A., 1940; Columbia University, M.A., 1941; University of California, Berkeley, Ph.D., 1955. *Politics*: Independent. *Religion*: "Pagan." *Home*: 5719 Fremont St., Boise, Idaho 83704. *Agent*: Austin Wahl Agency, 21 East Van Buren St., Chicago, Ill. 60605.

CAREER: Cooper Union Institute of Technology, New York, N.Y., director of placement and assistant director of admissions, 1941-42; Veterans Administration, Provo, Utah, chief of center, 1946-50; University of Colorado, Boulder, assistant professor of psychology, 1955-56; Convair, Inc., Fort Worth, Tex., senior design engineer, 1956-57; Johns Hopkins University, Bethesda, Md., senior operations analyst at Operations Research Office, 1957-61; Sylvania Laboratories, Mountain View, Calif., senior engineering specialist, 1961-64; Nortronics, Inc., Anaheim, Calif., chief of systems analysis, 1965-67; Tracor, Inc., San Diego, Calif., senior scientist, 1967; American Institute for Research, Bedford, Mass., senior research scientist, 1967-68; Boise State College, Boise, Idaho, associate professor, 1968-70, professor of psychology, 1970—. *Military service:* U.S. Army, Adjutant General's Office, 1943-46; became first lieutenant. *Member:* American Association for the Advancement of Science, Sigma Xi, Psi Chi, Delta Phi Alpha.

WRITINGS: Herman the Termite (juvenile), Astor-Honor, 1968; *From Tongues of Temple Bells: The Essence of Oriental Philosophy*, A. S. Barnes, 1970. Author of secret technical reports. Contributor to psychology journals.

WORK IN PROGRESS: Psychological Processes: Their Origins in Biophysics and Biochemistry, in several volumes; *Injured Earth*, a novel; *They Hadn't Otter*, a juvenile story; *A Matter of Mind*, non-fiction.

SIEV, Asher 1913-

PERSONAL: Born November 15, 1913, in Jerusalem, Israel; son of Joshua and Anna (Senderov) Siev; married Priscilla Peyser, July 14, 1940; children: Moshe, Yoseph, David. *Education:* Isaac Elchanan Theological Seminary, rabbi, 1937; Yeshiva University, B.A., 1937, D.H.L., 1943. *Home:* 1505 Waring Ave., Bronx, N.Y. 10469. *Office:* Department of Hebrew, Yeshiva University, New York, N.Y. 10033.

CAREER: Ordained rabbi, 1937; rabbi in Bronx, N.Y., 1938-66; Yeshiva University, New York, N.Y., instructor, 1938-58, assistant professor, 1958-62, associate professor, 1963-67, professor of Hebrew literature, 1968—. National leader, Bnei Akiva of America, 1939-41. *Awards, honors:* Rabbi Kook Literary Prize from Tel-Aviv Municipality, Israel, 1972, for *The Responsa of Ramo*.

WRITINGS: Life and Works of Rabbi Moses Isserles, Mosad Harow Kook, 1961; *The Responsa of Ramo*, Yeshiva University Press, 1970; *Life and Times of the Ramo*, Yeshiva University Press, 1972. Editor of *Rabbinical Council of America Manual*, 1949.

WORK IN PROGRESS: The Responsa of Rabbi Joseph Katz.

* * *

SIKES, Walter W(allace) 1925-

PERSONAL: Born June 20, 1925, in Gallatin, Tenn.; son of Walter W. and Ellafrank (Wallace) Sikes; married Evelyn Hisey (a craft shop owner), June 18, 1947; children: Linda, Rebecca, Deborah. *Education:* Oberlin College, A.B., 1949; Purdue University, M.S., 1962, Ph.D., 1964. *Home:* 111 West North College St., Yellow Springs, Ohio 45387.

CAREER: Antioch College, Yellow Springs, Ohio, associate experiential education program director, 1949-52; Morris Bean and Company, Yellow Springs, director of personnel, 1952-60; Purdue University, West Lafayette, Ind., instructor in management, 1961; Kalamazoo College, Kalamazoo, Mich., associate professor of business administration and economics, and director of Career Quarter Program, 1962-63; Antioch College, dean of students, 1963-69; NTL Institute for Applied Behavioral Science, Washington, D.C., director of programs for higher education, 1969-74; Center for Creative Change in Higher Education, Yellow Springs, director, 1974—. Adjunct professor, Wright State University, Union Graduate School, George Washington University; visiting professor, University of Massachusetts, Walden University. Principal investigator of Training Teams for Campus Change, project of National Institute of Mental Health, 1969-74. Consultant to organizations and groups. *Member:* International Association of Applied Social Scientists (charter member), American Psychological Association, American Association for Higher Education, Society for the Psychological Study of Social Ideas, Association for Humanistic Psychology. *Awards, honors:* U.S. Steel Foundation fellow, 1961-62.

WRITINGS: An Analysis of Some Outcomes of Human Relations Training (monograph), Institute for Research in the Behavioral Sciences, Purde University, 1966; (with Lawrence Schlesinger and Charles Seashore) *Renewing Higher Education from Within: A Guide for Campus Change Teams*, Jossey-Bass, 1974. Contributor of articles to journals in his field, including *Journal of Higher Education, Social Change, Advanced Management, Supervisory Management*, and *Hospital Administration*.

SIDELIGHTS: Walter Sikes told *CA*: "My current major interest is humanizing higher education through programs of organizational development and faculty development. I would like to see colleges and universities become more growthful and satisfying places for all of their members."

*　　*　　*

SILL, Sterling Welling 1903-

PERSONAL: Born March 31, 1903, in Layton, Utah; son of Joseph A (a school teacher) and Marietta (Welling) Sill; married Doris Mary Thornley, September 4, 1929; children: John Michael, David S., Carolyn (Mrs. Perry Fitzgerald). *Education:* Attended Utah State University, 1921-22, and University of Utah, 1926-27. *Religion:* Church of Jesus Christ of Latter-day Saints (Mormons). *Home:* 1264 Yale Ave., Salt Lake City, Utah 84105. *Office:* 47 East South Temple St., #223, Salt Lake City, Utah 84111.

CAREER: New York Life Insurance Co., Salt Lake City, Utah, agent, 1927-32, manager of Inter-Mountain Branch Office, 1933-40, inspector of agencies, 1940-68. General authority for Church of Jesus Christ of Latter-day Saints, 1954—. School teacher in Layton, Utah, 1927-29. Chartered life under-writer, 1934. Member of Layton City Council, 1928-32; member of board of regents of University of Utah, 1940-51; vice-president of *Deseret News*, 1952-62. *Member:* American College of Life Underwriters. *Awards, honors:* H.D.L. from University of Utah, 1953; Carnegie Hero Medal, 1959, for helping to save a drowning swimmer.

WRITINGS: Leadership I, Bookcraft, 1958.

Leadership II, *Bookcraft, 1960;* Glory of the Sun, *Bookcraft, 1961;* The Upward Reach, *Bookcraft, 1962;* Law of the Harvest, *Bookcraft, 1963;* The Way of Success, *Bookcraft, 1964;* What Doth It Profit, *Bookcraft, 1964;* The Miracle of Personality, *Bookcraft, 1966;* The Quest for Excellence, *Bookcraft, 1967;* The Power of Believing, *Bookcraft, 1968;* The Three Infinities, *Bookcraft, 1969.*

The Strength of Great Possessions, *Bookcraft, 1970;* Making the Most of Yourself, *Bookcraft, 1971;* The Keys of the Kingdom, *Bookcraft, 1972;* Principles, Promises, and Powers, *Deseret, 1973;* Christmas Sermons, *Deseret, 1973;* The Majesty of Books, *Deseret, 1974;* That Ye Might Have Life, *Deseret, 1974;* The Laws of Success, *Deseret, 1975.*

WORK IN PROGRESS: My Hall of Fame, short biographies of famous people and of the author's chief benefactors; *The Life and Works of William Shakespeare; Your Gallery of Art*, word pictures and personality portraits from literature, including the Bible.

*　　*　　*

SILVER, Alain (Joel) 1947-

PERSONAL: Born December 7, 1947, in Los Angeles, Calif.; son of Elmer I. (a supervisor) and Christiane (Coulon) Silver. *Education:* University of California, Los Angeles, A.B., 1969, M.A., 1973, C.Phil. and Ph.D., both 1975. *Politics:* "Deliberate." *Religion:* "Inactive Roman Catholic." *Home:* 313 South Doheny Dr., Beverly Hills, Calif. 90211.

CAREER: Writer and film maker. *Member:* Film Screening Cooperative (chairman).

WRITINGS: (With James Ursini) *David Lean and His Films*, Leslie Frewin, 1974; *The Samurai Film*, A.S. Barnes, 1975; *The Vampire Film*, A.S. Barnes, 1975. Also

wrote, with Ursini, screenplays, "Bridge," 1967, "Phantom of Delight," 1969, "The Hunting Ground," 1971, and "Harry Tracy," 1973. Contributor to film journals and to *Coast.*

WORK IN PROGRESS: Supernatural Literature and Film (tentative title), for Leslie Frewin; two screenplays; a novel.

SIDELIGHTS: Silver writes that his current interest is on ". . . the relationship of narrative construction in the fiction film to conventions of non-verbal communication," and that his ". . . past writing has mainly dealt with questions of metaphor and genre identity in film." He has most recently completed a series of frame enlargements of "Thieves' Highway" for the library of the Museum of Modern Art and an oral history and filmography of cinematographer James Wong Howe. *Avocational interests:* Photography, design, archery.

*　　*　　*

SILVERMAN, Kenneth 1936-

PERSONAL: Born February 5, 1936, in New York, N.Y.; son of Gustave (a builder) and Bessie (Goldberg) Silverman; married Sharon Medjuck, September 8. 1957; children: Willa, Ethan. *Education:* Columbia University, B.A., 1956, M.A., 1958, Ph.D., 1964. *Home:* 34 Gramercy Park, New York, N.Y. 10003. *Office:* Department of English, New York University, 19 University Place, New York, N.Y. 10003.

CAREER: University of Wyoming, Laramie, instructor in English, 1958-59; New York University, New York, N.Y., associate professor of English, 1964—. *Member:* Modern Language Association of America (chairman of bicentennial committee, 1973-76), Phi Beta Kappa. *Awards, honors:* Bicentennial grant from National Endowment for the Humanities, 1973-75.

WRITINGS: (Editor) *Colonial American Poetry*, Hafner, 1968; *Timothy Dwight*, Twayne, 1969; (editor) *Literature in America: The Founding of a Nation*, Free Press, 1971; (editor) *Selected Letters of Cotton Mather*, Louisiana State University Press, 1971. Contributor to scholarly periodicals in his field. Member of editorial board, *Early American Literature*, 1971-73.

WORK IN PROGRESS: A Cultural History of the American Revolution, a study of the arts in America, 1763-1789, publication expected in 1976.

*　　*　　*

SILVERMAN, Robert A(llan) 1943-

PERSONAL: Born August 15, 1943, in Toronto, Ontario, Canada; son of Sidney and Rose (Gordon) Silverman; married Elaine Goldstein, July 23, 1967; children Jason C., Michael Oren. *Education:* University of Toronto, B.A., 1965; University of Pennsylvania, M.A., 1967, Ph.D., 1971. *Office:* Department of Sociology, University of Alberta, Edmonton, Alberta, Canada.

CAREER: University of Pennsylvania, Philadelphia, instructor in sociology, 1968-71; University of Western Ontario, London, assistant professor of sociology, 1971-75; University of Alberta, Edmonton, associate professor of sociology, 1975—. *Member:* Canadian Sociology and Anthropology Association, Canadian Criminology and Corrections Association, American Sociological Association, American Society of Criminology, American Academy of Political and Social Science, Society for the Study of Social Problems.

WRITINGS: (Editor with Richard Henshel) *Perception in Criminology*, Columbia University Press, 1975; (editor with James J. Teevan, Jr.) *Crime in Canadian Society*, Butterworth & Co., 1975.

WORK IN PROGRESS: Research on victimization and victimology.

* * *

SIMMONS, Otis D(avis) 1928-

PERSONAL: Born April 27, 1928, in Kansas City, Kans.; son of Jessie (with Cudahy Packing Co.) and Nannie (Bell) Simmons; married Wiletta Moore, June 5, 1955; children: Eric Otis. *Education:* University of Kansas, B.M.E., 1956, M.M.E., 1961, Ph.D., 1965. *Politics:* Democrat. *Religion:* Baptist. *Home:* 1406 Deer St., Montgomery, Ala. 36101. *Office:* College of the Arts, Alabama State University, Montgomery, Ala. 36101.

CAREER: Philander Smith College, Little Rock, Ark., director of vocal and choral music, 1956-60; Texas Southern University, Houston, chairman of vocal and choral staff, 1958-62; Southern University, Baton Rouge, La., chairman of vocal staff, 1965-66; Alabama State University, Montgomery, chairman of division of music, 1966-75, dean of College of the Arts, 1975—. *Military service:* U.S. Army, 1949-53; became lieutenant. *Member:* National Association of Teachers of Singing, National Association of Schools of Music, Music Educators National Conference, American Association of University Professors, Phi Delta Kappa, Alpha Phi Alpha, Kappa Kappa Psi, Phi Mu Alpha Sinfonia. *Awards, honors:* Woodrow Wilson fellowship from University of Kansas, 1963.

WRITINGS: Foundation Course in Musicianship, William C. Brown, 1967; *Teaching Music in Urban Schools*, Crescendo, 1975. Contributor of articles to *Music Educators National Conference Journal* and *National Association of Teachers of Singing Bulletin.*

WORK IN PROGRESS: A Beginning Course in Music Theory.

SIDELIGHTS: Simmons tells *CA* he has performed with the Houston Summer Symphony as bass-baritone soloist, as a chorister in the Kansas City Philharmonic Male Chorus for a performance of the Brahms "Alto Rhapsody," and as a principal soloist in the Texas Southern University production of the Mascagni opera, "Calvaleria Rusticana." He adds, "I studied voice with internationally outstanding voice teachers: Endre Kraechmann, who was former leading baritone of the Paris Opera; Frank La Forge, a former vocal coach of Marion Anderson; and Samuel Margolis, vocal coach of Robert Merrill and Jerome Hines of the Metropolitan Opera."

* * *

SIMPICH, Frederick, Jr. 1911-1975

June 2, 1911—May 2, 1975; American businessman and author of books and articles on geography. Obituaries: *Washington Post*, May 9, 1975.

* * *

SINGER, Michael A(lan) 1947-

PERSONAL: Born May 6, 1947, in New York, N.Y.; son of Philip H. (a stock broker) and Margaret (Gervis) Singer. *Education:* University of Florida, B.A., 1969, M.A., 1971. *Religion:* "All." *Address:* Route 2, Box 42, Alachua, Fla.

32615. *Office:* Department of Social Science, Sante Fe Community College, 3000 Northwest 83rd St., Gainesville, Fla. 32601. *Career:* Sante Fe Community College, Gainesville, Fla. instructor in social science, 1973—.

WRITINGS: The Search for Truth (nonfiction), Shanti, 1974; *Three Essays on Universal Law*, Shanti, 1975.

SIDELIGHTS: Singer is very interested in Yoga, and spent a period of intense meditation in a house he built in the woods.

* * *

SINGER, Peter (Albert David) 1946-

PERSONAL: Born July 6, 1946, in Melbourne, Australia; son of Ernest (a businessman) and Cora (a doctor; maiden name, Oppenheim) Singer; married Renata Diamond (a teacher), December 16, 1969; children: Ruth, Lee. *Education:* University of Melbourne, B.A. (honors), 1967, M.A., 1969; University College, Oxford, B.Phil., 1971. *Politics:* Australian Labor Party. *Religion:* None. *Home:* 20 Roseberry St., Hawthorn, Victoria, Australia. *Office:* Department of Philosophy, La Trobe University, Bundoora, Victoria, Australia.

CAREER: Oxford University, University College, Oxford, England, lecturer in philosophy, 1971-73; New York University, New York, N.Y., visiting assistant professor of philosophy, 1973-74; La Trobe University, Bundoora, Victoria, Australia, senior lecturer in philosophy, 1974—.

WRITINGS: Democracy and Disobedience, Clarendon Press, 1973, Oxford University Press (New York), 1974; (editor with Thomas Regan) *Animal Rights and Human Obligations*, Prentice-Hall, 1975; *Animal Liberation*, Random House, 1975. Contributor to *New York Review of Books* and to philosophy journals.

WORK IN PROGRESS: Research in ethics, applied ethics, and bio-ethics; contributing to *Encyclopedia of Bioethics.*

SIDELIGHTS: Singer is a vegetarian.

* * *

SINGLETON, Mary Ann 1934-

PERSONAL: Born March 17, 1934, in Ohio; daughter of Ralph Herbert (a college professor) and Mercedes (editor of Oberlin College alumni magazine; maiden name, Holden) Singleton; divorced; children: Karina Anne Naumer, Helmuth Karl Naumer. *Education:* Oberlin College, B.A., 1956; studied at University of St. Andrews, 1954-55, and Texas Christian University, 1965-66; University of Oregon, Ph.D., 1970. *Residence:* Soquel, Calif. *Agent:* Martha Winston, Curtis Brown Ltd., 60 East 56th St., New York, N.Y. 10022. *Office:* Department of English, Cabrillo College, 6500 Soquel Dr., Aptos, Calif. 95003.

CAREER: Cabrillo College, Aptos, Calif., instructor in literature and writing, 1970—. *Member:* Phi Beta Kappa.

WRITINGS: Life after Marriage: Divorce as a New Beginning, Stein & Day, 1974; *The City and the Veld: The Fiction of Doris Lessing*, Bucknell University Press, in press. Contributor to magazines.

WORK IN PROGRESS: Research on literature by women, with a special emphasis on autobiography.

SIDELIGHTS: Mary Ann Singleton writes: ". . . I am much interested in the problem of personal growth; however, the issue has gone beyond the personal for me. For example, my study of Doris Lessing began with *The*

Golden Notebook, which among other themes deals with the problem of the conventional versus the 'new' woman. I wished to write about Lessing, finally, because I began to see her as the most important novelist writing today, getting to the heart of what prevents human development and causes most of the world's ills: that which stunts the ability to love ... This surely is the crucial issue; every problem we face today falls from that one. In our era, finally, people are looking at it in very realistic and important ways. These are the people and this is the work I find to be important." *Avocational interests:* Hiking, back-packing, skiing.

* * *

SKEHAN, James W(illiam) 1923-

PERSONAL: Born April 25, 1923, in Houlton, Me.; son of James William and Mary Effie (Coffey) Skehan. *Education:* Boston College, A.B., 1946, A.M. (philosophy), 1947; Weston College, Ph.L., 1947, S.T.B., 1954, S.T.L., 1955; Harvard University, A.M. (geology), 1951, Ph.D., 1953. *Office:* Weston Observatory, 319 Concord Rd., Weston, Mass. 02193.

CAREER: Entered Society of Jesus (Jesuits), 1940, ordained Roman Catholic priest, 1954; Boston College, Boston, Mass., assistant professor, 1956-61, associate professor, 1962-68, professor of geology, 1968—, founder of department of geology and first chairman, 1956-68, chairman of department of geology and geophysics, 1968-70, assistant director of Weston Observatory, Weston, Mass., 1956-68, associate director, 1968-72, acting director, 1973-74, director of observatory and director of Boston College Energy Research Center, 1974—. Member of board of directors, General Economics Corp., 1969-71. Chairman of board of overseers, St. Joseph's College, North Windham, Me., 1969—.

MEMBER: Geological Society of America (fellow; chairman of Northeastern Section, 1970-71), Geological Society of London (fellow), International Association for the Geological Study of the Deeper Zones of the Earth's Crust, American Association of Petroleum Geologists, American Geophysical Union, American Geological Institute (secretary-treasurer, 1973), American Institute of Professional Geologists, American Association of Jesuit Scientists (president of Eastern Section, 1962-63), American Association for the Advancement of Science, American Institute of Mining, Metallurgical and Petroleum Engineers, American Society of Civil Engineers, Association of Engineering Geologists (member of executive committee, 1974-75), Mineralogical Society of America, National Association of Geology Teachers (vice-president, 1970-71; president, 1971-72), American Society for Testing and Materials, Seismological Society of America, Society of Exploration Geophysicists, Geological Association of Canada, European Association of Exploration Geophysicists, American Association of University Professors, New England Intercollegiate Geology Conference, Association of Directors of Northeastern Seismological Network, Friends of Northeastern Seismology (secretary, 1974—), and other state and local geological societies; Sigma Xi, Albertus Magnus Guild, Explorers Club (New York), Appalachian Mountain Club.

WRITINGS: (Contributor) *Investigating the Earth*, with teacher's guide and laboratory manual, Houghton, 1967, 4th edition, 1973; (contributor) O. C. Farquhar, editor, *Economic Geology of Massachusetts*, Graduate School, University of Massachusetts (Boston), 1967; (contributor)

E-an Zen, W. S. White, J. B. Hadley, and J. B. Thompson, Jr., editors, *Studies of Appalachian Geology*, Wiley, 1968; (editor with Robert L. Carovillano) *Science and the Future of Man*, M.I.T. Press, 1971; (author of foreword) Frank Byrne, *Earth and Man*, W. C. Brown, 1974. Also author of *Puddingstone, Drumlins, and Ancient Volcanoes: A Field Guide Along Historic Trails of Boston*, for Boston Bicentennial, 1975; compiler of *Centennial Geological Map of Vermont*, Vermont Geological Survey, 1961, and author of geological reports on New England, Eastern United States, Colorado, Nebraska, Kansas, North Atlantic, Pacific Northwest, and Iceland for U.S. Air Force Cambridge Research Laboratories, government agencies, and professional organizations. Contributor to *Annals* of New York Academy of Sciences and professional journals.

WORK IN PROGRESS: Field Guide to the Geology of the Greater Boston Area, a Boston College Bicentennial publication; *Field Guide to the Geology of New England*, for Kendall-Hunt; member of editorial staff preparing *Earth Science Encyclopedia* and author of various sections of the book.

SIDELIGHTS: Skehan's field work has been concentrated in New England and the younger volcanic areas of Iceland and the Pacific Northwest. He was assistant academic director of the Boston College-National Aeronautics and Space Administration expedition to Surtsey and Iceland in 1970.

* * *

SKOLNIK, Peter L(aurence) 1944-

PERSONAL: Born May 26, 1944, in New York, N.Y.; son of Jack (an art director) and Edythe (Savitz) Skolnik; married Sydne Kalet (an executive assistant), April 2, 1966 (divorced June, 1968); married Angela Miller (a literary managing editor), December 26, 1970 (divorced, April, 1975); children: (second marriage) Samantha. *Education:* Harvard University, B.A., 1966; Columbia University, M.F.A., 1968. *Politics:* Liberal. *Residence:* New York, N.Y. *Agent:* Sanford J. Greenburger Associates, Inc., 757 Third Ave., New York, N.Y. 10017.

CAREER: Gil Cates Productions (film and theatrical company), New York, N.Y., associate producer, 1967-70; Newark College of Engineering, Newark, N.J., instructor in theater arts, 1968-69; Drum Company (Off-Broadway), New York, N.Y., director and producer, 1971; Theater by the Sea, Portsmouth, N.H., artistic director, 1972-73; Caliban Productions (independent production company), New York, N.Y., president, 1974—. Executive director of New England Repertory Theater, 1973—. *Member:* Author's Guild, Actor's Studio Directors Unit.

WRITINGS: Jump Rope! (nonfiction), Workman Publishing, 1974; *Passing Fancies, Fancy Passings: A Pictorial History of Fads in America*, Crowell, in press. Also author of screenplay, "Hazard," 1974.

* * *

SLABY, Andrew Edmund 1942-

PERSONAL: Born July 14, 1942, in Milwaukee, Wis.; son of Andrew (a laborer) and Evelyn (Herde) Slaby. *Education:* University of Wisconsin, B.S., 1964, M.S., 1966; Columbia University, M.D., 1968; Yale University, M.P.H., 1972. *Politics:* Democrat. *Religion:* Roman Catholic. *Home:* University Towers, Apt. 4M, 100 York St., New Haven, Conn. 06510. *Office:* Department of Psychiatry, Yale University, 34 Park St., New Haven, Conn. 06510.

CAREER: Boston City Hospital, Boston, Mass., intern, 1968-69; Yale University, New Haven, Conn., resident in psychiatry, 1969-72; National Institute of Mental Health, Washington, D.C., clinical associate, 1972-74; Yale University, New Haven, Conn., assistant professor of psychiatry, 1974—. Diplomate in psychiatry, American Board of Neurology and Psychiatry, 1974; director of Emergency Psychiatric Service, Yale-New Haven Hospital, 1974—; attending psychiatrist, Community Support Service, Connecticut Mental Health Center, 1974—. *Military service:* U.S. Public Health Service, 1972-74; became lieutenant commander.

WRITINGS: (With Julian Lieb and I. I. Lipsitch) *The Crisis Team*, Harper, 1973; (with R. J. Wyatt) *Dementia in the Presenium*, C. C Thomas, 1974; (with M. E. Raymond and Lieb) *The Healing Alliance*, Norton, 1975; (with Lieb) *Integrated Psychiatric Treatment*, Harper, 1975; (with L. R. Tancredi) *Collusion for Conformity*, Jason Aronson, in press; (with Tancredi and Lieb) *Legal Issues in Psychiatric Care*, Harper, in press; (with Lieb and Tancredi) *Emergency Psychiatric Care*, Medical Examination Publishing, in press.

WORK IN PROGRESS: Co-authoring *Social Contracts*, with L. R. Tancredi.

* * *

SLOBODKIN, Louis   1903-1975

February 19, 1903—May 8, 1975; American sculptor, designer, exhibitor and lecturer at museums, and author and illustrator of books for children and other works. Obituaries: *New York Times*, May 9, 1975; *Current Biography*, August, 1975 (*CA*-13/14)

* * *

SMALL, George Raphael   1918-

PERSONAL: Born January 12, 1918, in Syracuse, N.Y.; son of Herman (a salesman) and Lena (Lichtenstein) Small; married Dolores Barbara, March 3, 1945; children: George Edward. *Education:* Woodbury College, B.S., 1949; San Fernando Valley State University, B.A., 1963; California State University, Los Angeles, M.A., 1968. *Home and office:* 970 Newbury Rd., Thousand Oaks, Calif. 91360.

CAREER: Simi Valley School District, Simi, Calif., high school teacher of art and history, 1961—. Professor at Pierce College, 1964—. *Military service:* U.S. Army, 1943-45. *Awards, honors:* Award for oil painting at Los Angeles All-City Show, 1957; award for pastel study at Dominican Fathers Show, 1971.

WRITINGS: Alfredo Ramos Martinez: His Life and Art, F & J Publishing, 1975. Contributor of articles and poems to journals.

WORK IN PROGRESS: A self-illustrated collection of poetry; a novel; a collection of plays for television; a collection of essays on contemporary problems.

SIDELIGHTS: Small is a professional artist who participates regularly in local shows and competitions; he was selected for exhibition in the 1970 All-California Art Competition of the Ventura County Forum of the Arts.

* * *

SMART, James Dick   1906-

PERSONAL: Born March 1, 1906, in Alton, Ontario, Canada; son of John George (a railway agent) and Janet (Dick) Smart; married Christine McKillop, September 24, 1931; children: Margaret Jean (Mrs. R. J. Watson), Mary Eleanor, Janet Ann (Mrs. Paul Young). *Education:* University of Toronto, B.A., 1926, M.A., 1927, Ph.D., 1931; Knox College, Lic. in Theology, 1929; graduate study at University of Marburg and University of Berlin, 1929-30. *Politics:* Liberal. *Religion:* Presbyterian. *Home:* 49 Lambeth Road, Islington, Ontario, Canada.

CAREER: Ordained to ministry of the Presbyterian Church in Canada, 1931. Pastor of churches in Ailsa Craig, Ontario, 1931-34, Galt, Ontario, 1934-41, Peterborough, Ontario, 1941-44; Presbyterian Church in the U.S.A., Board of Christian Education, Philadelphia, Pa., editor-in-chief of curriculum materials, 1944-50; Rosedale Church, Toronto, Ontario, pastor, 1950-57, associate minister, 1970-74; Union Theological Seminary, New York, N.Y., Jessup Foundation Professor of Biblical Interpretation, 1957-71; lecturer at Toronto School of Theology, 1971-76. Lecturer in homiletics and Christian education, Knox College, 1951-57; Carnahan lecturer in Buenos Aires, 1963. *Member:* Society of Biblical Literature and Exigesis, American Theological Society. *Awards, honors:* D.D., Knox College, 1956.

WRITINGS—All published by Westminster Press, except as indicated: *What a Man Can Believe*, 1943; (with David Noel Freedman) *God Has Spoken: An Introduction to the Old Testament for Young People*, 1948; *A Promise to Keep*, 1948; *The Recovery of Humanity*, 1953; *The Teaching Ministry of the Church*, 1954; *The Rebirth of Ministry*, 1960; *Servants of the Word*, 1960; *The Interpretation of Scripture*, 1961; *The Creed in Christian Teaching*, 1962; *The Old Testament in Dialogue With Modern Man*, 1964; (translator) Karl Barth and Eduard Thurneysen, *Revolutionary Theology in the Making: Correspondence 1914-1925*, Epworth, 1964; *History and Theology in Second Isiah*, 1965; *The Divided Mind of Modern Theology: Karl Barth and Rudolph Bultmann, 1908-1933*, 1967; *The ABC's of Christian Faith*, 1968; *The Quiet Revolution: The Radical Impact of Jesus on the Men of His Time*, 1969; (co-editor) *Luther, Erasmus, and the Reformation*, Fordham University Press, 1969; *The Strange Silence of the Bible in the Church: A Study in Hermeneutics*, 1970; *Doorway to a New Age: A Study of Paul's Letter to the Romans*, 1972. Contributor of articles to journals. Associate editor, *Westminster Study Bible*.

WORK IN PROGRESS: Work on the future of Biblical theology.

* * *

SMITH, A. Weston   1900(?)-1975

1900(?)—March 17, 1975; American financial columnist, editor, public relations consultant, and author of books on the stock market and public relations. Obituaries: *New York Times*, March 22, 1975; *AB Bookman's Weekly*, April 7, 1975.

* * *

SMITH, Anna H(ester)   1912-

PERSONAL: Born April 30, 1912, in London, England; daughter of Johannes Jacobus (a professor) and Mabel Florence (Hardy) Smith. *Education:* University of Stellenbosch, M.A., 1933. *Home:* 103 Montevideo 9th St., Killarney, Johannesburg 2001, South Africa. *Office:* Johannesburg Public Library, Market Square, Johannesburg 2001, South Africa.

CAREER: Stellenbosch University Library, Stellenbosch, Cape Province, South Africa, member of staff, 1934-38; Johannesburg Public Library, Johannesburg, South Africa, member of staff, 1938—, city librarian, 1960-75; Africana Museum, Johannesburg, director, 1960-75. Part-time lecturer in librarianship, University of the Witwatersrand beginning, 1958. *Member:* South African Library Association (fellow), Museums Association of Southern Africa, and other professional organizations. *Awards, honors:* Dr. of Laws from University of the Witwatersrand, 1974.

WRITINGS: (Compiler with Jan Ploeger) *Pictorial Atlas of the History of the Union of South Africa*, J. L. van Schaik (Pretoria, South Africa), 1949; (author of notes) *Claudius Water-Colours in the Africana Museum*, Africana Museum, 1952; (editor) *Pictorial History of Johannesburg*, Verry, 1956; (compiler) *Johannesburg Street Names*, Juta, 1971; *South Africa*, Abner Schram, 1971 (published in Amsterdam as *The Spread of Printing: Eastern Hemisphere, South Africa*, Vangendt, 1971).

Compiler of numerous museum and library catalogs, including: *Catalogue of Bantu, Khoisan and Malagasy in the Strange Collection of Africana*, 1942, and *The Language of Stamp Collecting*, 1959, both for Johannesburg Public Library; and *Commemorative Medals of the Z.A.R.*, Africana Museum, 1958. Editor of quarterly, *Africana Notes and News*, 1960—.

WORK IN PROGRESS: A biography of Charles Davidson Bell, completion expected about 1976; editing publications for the City of Johannesburg's 90th birthday in 1976.

* * *

SMITH, Beatrice S(chillinger)

PERSONAL: Born in Madison, Wis.; daugher of Reynold J. and Jeanette (McGowan) Schillinger; married J. Robert Smith; children: Steven Robert, Peter Reynold. *Education:* University of Wisconsin, B.S. *Home address:* Box 116, Westfield, Wis. 53964. *Agent:* Ann Elmo, 52 Vanderbilt Ave., New York, N.Y. 10017.

CAREER: High school teacher of English and art in the United States and South America. *Member:* Council for Wisconsin Writers. *Awards, honors:* Best juvenile by a Wisconsin writer award from Council for Wisconsin Writers, 1974, for *The Road to Galveston*.

WRITINGS—All juveniles: *Proudest Horse on the Prairie*, Lerner, 1972; *The Road to Galveston*, Lerner, 1973; *Don't Mention Moon to Me*, Thomas Nelson, 1974; *Six Mini-Mysteries*, Lerner, 1976. Contributor of articles and short stories to fifty magazines for children and adults.

WORK IN PROGRESS: Suspense fiction for both adults and children; researching the eighteenth century.

* * *

SMITH, David Horton 1939-

PERSONAL: Born May 2, 1939, in Los Angeles, Calif.; son of Paul Roosevelt (a warehouseman) and Helen (Frechem) Smith; married Evelyn Kay Ingram, December 20, 1964 (divorced, 1975); married Barbara Lynn Pankuch MacLaury, 1975; children: (first marriage) Laura G. *Education:* Attended California Institute of Technology, 1956-57; University of Southern California, A.B., 1960; Harvard University, A.M., 1962, Ph.D., 1965. *Politics:* Independent. *Religion:* Unitarian Universalist. *Home:* 242 South St., Medfield, Mass. 02052. *Office:* Department of Sociology, Boston College, Chestnut Hill, Mass. 02167.

CAREER: Harvard University, Cambridge, Mass., lecturer in sociology, 1965-66; University of Southern California, Los Angeles, assistant professor of sociology, 1966-68; Boston College, Chestnut Hill, Mass., associate professor of sociology, 1968—. Director of research, Center for a Voluntary Society, 1970-74; consultant to universities, government agencies, and voluntary organizations; member of board of directors, Voluntary Action Center of Greater Boston, 1974—. *Member:* Association of Voluntary Action Scholars (president, 1971-73; executive officer, 1973—), American Psychological Association (fellow), American Sociological Association (fellow), International Studies Association, World Future Society, Community Development Society, Phi Beta Kappa. *Awards, honors:* Woodrow Wilson honorary fellowship, 1960; National Science Foundation Graduate fellowship, 1960-63.

WRITINGS: (Editor with Richard Reddy and Burt Baldwin) *Voluntary Action Research: 1972*, Heath, 1972; (editor) *Voluntary Action Research: 1973*, Heath, 1973; *Latin American Student Activism*, Heath, 1973; (editor) *Voluntary Action Research: 1974*, Heath, 1974; (with Alex Inkeles) *Becoming Modern*, Harvard University Press, 1974. Regular columnist, *Voluntary Action Leadership*, 1975—. Editor, *Journal of Voluntary Action*, 1971—; consulting editor, *Volunteer Administration*, 1973—.

WORK IN PROGRESS: Leadership and Voluntary Action; The Roots of Voluntary Action; The Prevalence of Voluntary Associations; Community Behavior, with Marc Fried; co-editing *Voluntary Action Research: 1975*; two science fiction books.

SIDELIGHTS: Smith writes: "I have been concerned most broadly with developing a new field of interdisciplinary study and learning—'Voluntary Action Research.' To this end, I have been involved with others in a wide variety of organizational, research, editing and writing activities on voluntary action themes. If successful, this effort will result in an active scholarly-professional field equivalent to such existing fields as 'Urban Studies' or 'International Studies,' with their corresponding bodies of knowledge, centers of research and education, specialized journals and publishing houses, professional meetings, etc." *Avocational interests:* Photography, reading, travel, cinema, cycling, and squash.

* * *

SMITH, Edward W(illiam) 1920-1975

1920—July 28, 1975; American educator, publishing executive, curriculum consultant to government, and author and editor of books in his field. Obituaries: *New York Times*, July 29, 1975.

* * *

SMITH, Frederick Winston Furneaux 1907-1975 (Lord Birkenhead)

December 7, 1907—June 11, 1975; British lord-in-waiting and biographer. Obituaries: *New York Times*, June 12, 1975; *Washington Post*, June 14, 1975.

* * *

SMITH, Nancy Covert 1935-

PERSONAL: Born March 18, 1935, in Bascom, Ohio; daughter of Curtis C. (a machinist) and Mary (Forwalter) Covert; married James Smith, February 27, 1954 (divorced, 1973); married Larry Uno (an associate director of National

Association for Mental Health), 1975; children: (first marriage) Mark, Leanne, Craig, Tammy. *Education:* Attended public schools in Ohio. *Residence:* Alexandria, Va. *Office:* National Association for Mental Health, 1800 Kent St., Arlington, Va. 22209.

CAREER: National Association for Mental Health, Arlington, Va., lecturer, 1973—. *Awards, honors:* Indiana University Writer's Conference non-fiction scholarship, 1970; National Association for Mental Health special award, 1973, for her contribution to public education about mental health through her writing.

WRITINGS: Journey Out of Nowhere (autobiography), Word, Inc., 1973; *Of Pebbles and Pearls* (nonfiction), Word, Inc., 1974; *Josie's Handful of Quietness* (novel), Abingdon, 1975. Contributor to *McCall's, Good Housekeeping, Modern Bride, Jack and Jill, Modern Maturity,* and other journals.

WORK IN PROGRESS: A book on human sexuality and attitudes of marriage for Word, Inc., completion expected in 1976; a juvenile fiction book about Hawaii; an adult fiction about World War II, Abingdon, 1976; and an adult book, *Apple Parings of My Mind,* for Word, Inc.

SIDELIGHTS: Nancy Covert Smith has herself made a successful recovery from mental illness. She has recently lectured in twenty-seven states and ninety cities, giving practical answers to the questions raised by such illness in oneself or a family member. She has appeared on "The Phil Donahue Show." *Avocational interests:* Reading, music.

* * *

SMITH, Nancy Taylor

PERSONAL: Born in Miami, Fla.; daughter of Paul Charles (a lawyer) and Gertrude (Parkhurst) Taylor; married Harris Smith (a salesman), November 7, 1946. *Education:* Sweet Briar College, B.A., 1942. *Politics:* "Independent: Very!" *Religion:* Episcopalian. *Residence:* New Canaan, Conn. 06840. *Agent:* Anita Diamant, 51 East 42nd St., New York, N.Y. 10017.

CAREER: Pan American World Airways, Miami, Fla., flight control clerk, 1943-45. *Member:* Daughters of Founders and Patriots of America, American Recorder Society, Junior League (secretary of local chapter, 1959-61).

WRITINGS: The Golden Fig (novel), Ace Books, 1974. Poems included in *Florida Poets in 1938*, edited by Vivian Yeiser Larramore, Henry Harrison, 1938. Contributor of poems to *Fairfield County*.

WORK IN PROGRESS: A second Gothic novel; an historical novel about witchcraft in seventeenth-century Scotland.

AVOCATIONAL INTERESTS: Church choir, playing the recorder, painting, designing needlepoint, reading.

* * *

SMITH, Paul F. 1919-

PERSONAL: Born December 31, 1919, in Mansfield, Ohio; son of Phillip Fred and Myrtle (Robinson) Smith; married Margaret Peacock, October 30, 1942; children: Terence J., Barbara Jo (Mrs. John Moren). *Education:* University of Chicago, A.B., 1941; Northwestern University, M.A., 1946; American University, Ph.D., 1955. *Home:* 31 Highview Drive, Radnor, Pa. 19087. *Office:* Department of Finance, Dietrech Hall, University of Pennsylvania, Philadelphia, Pa. 19104.

CAREER: Denison University, Granville, Ohio, instructor in economics, 1946-47; Federal Reserve Board, Washington, D.C., economist, 1947-59; University of Pennsylvania, Philadelphia, associate professor, 1959-64, professor of finance, 1964—, chairman of department, 1963-67. Economist, National Bureau of Economic Research, 1960-70. *Military service:* U.S. Navy, 1941-46; became lieutenant commander; received Bronze Star and Purple Heart. *Member:* American Economic Association, American Finance Association.

WRITINGS: Consumer Credit Costs, 1949-1959, Princeton University Press, 1964; *Economics of Financial Institutions and Markets*, Irwin, 1971.

* * *

SMITH, Peter C(harles Horstead) 1940-

PERSONAL: Born October 15, 1940, in North Elmham, Norfolk, England; son of Ernest Gordon and Eileen (Horstead) Smith; married Patricia Ireson, July 27, 1963; children: Paul David, Dawn Tracey. *Education:* Attended Hamonds School. *Home:* 35 St. John's Close, Needingworth, Cambridge PE17 3TT, England.

CAREER: General Post Office, London, England, overseas telegraph officer, 1965-70; W. & J. MacKay Ltd., London, manager of printing sales office, 1970-72; Photo Precision Ltd., St. Ives, Cambridge, England, editor, 1972-74; *Cape Sun*, London, editor and journalist, 1974—. *Member:* Society for Nautical Research, Naval Records Club, Society of East Anglican Authors.

WRITINGS: Destroyer Leader, Kimber, 1968; *Task Force 57*, Kimber, 1969; *Pedestal*, Kimber, 1970; *Hard Lying*, Kimber, 1971, United States Naval Institute, 1972; *Stuka at War*, Ian Allan, 1971, Arco, 1972; *British Battle Cruisers*, Almark, 1971; (with Edwin Walker) *War in the Aegean*, Kimber, 1972; *Heritage of the Sea*, Balfour, 1972; *Royal Navy Ships' Badges*, Balfour, 1973; *Royal Air Force Squadron Badges*, Balfour, 1973; (editor) *Destroyer Action* (anthology), Kimber, 1974; *Per Mare Per Terram*, Balfour, 1974; (with Walker) *Battles of the Malta Striking Forces*, Ian Allan, 1974; (editor) *The Haunted Sea* (anthology), Kimber, 1975; *The Story of the Torpedo Bomber*, Almark, 1975; *Arctic Victory*, Kimber, 1975; *Tel-El-Kebir (1882)*, Almark, in press.

Ghost-writer of publications; all published by Colourmaster, except as indicated: *London's Bridges*, 1972; *Thames Bridges*, 1972; *Britain's Small Railways*, Balfour, 1973; *London's Pageantry*, 1973; *English Market Towns*, 1973; *English Village Greens*, 1974; *Blacksmiths' Shops*, 1974; *Historic Trees*, 1974; *Craft Tools of Yesterday*, 1974; *Castles of Scotland*, Balfour, 1975.

Contributor to *Worship International, Navy International, War Monthly*, and *Mariners Mirror*.

WORK IN PROGRESS: Behind the Black Curtain (short stories).

AVOCATIONAL INTERESTS: Military and naval history, London, science fiction, inner-earth studies.

* * *

SMITH, Roger Montgomery 1915(?)-1975

1915(?)—February 25, 1975; Musician, composer, music teacher, and author. Obituaries: *New York Times*, February 27, 1975; *AB Bookman's Weekly*, March 24, 1975.

SMITH, Steven A(lbert)   1939-

PERSONAL: Born May 12, 1939, in What Cheer, Iowa; son of Irving James (a farmer) and Mary (Emmons) Smith; married Daryl Goldgraben (a dean of students), August 2, 1970; children: David. *Education:* Attended Free University of Berlin, 1959-60; Earlham College, B.A., 1961; Harvard University, M.A., 1964, Ph.D., 1971. *Politics:* Democratic Party. *Religion:* Society of Friends (Quaker). *Home:* 47 Central Ave., Mt. Baldy, Calif. 91759. *Office:* Department of Philosophy, Pitzer Hall, Claremont Men's College, Claremont, Calif. 91711.

CAREER: Claremont Men's College, Claremont, Calif., assistant professor, 1971-75, associate professor of philosophy, 1975—. Vice-president of Mt. Baldy Mutual TV Association, 1973-75; member of board of Mt. Baldy Water Improvement Association, 1974-75. *Member:* American Philosophical Association, American Association of University Professors, Society for Religion in Higher Education, Society for Philosophy of Psychology. *Awards, honors:* Woodrow Wilson fellow, 1961-62; Danforth fellow, 1962-67; National Endowment for the Humanities summer grant, 1972.

WRITINGS: Satisfaction of Interest and the Concept of Morality, Bucknell University Press, 1974. Contributor to *Bucknell Review* and *Southern Journal of Philosophy*.

WORK IN PROGRESS: Research into moral motivation and self-interest; editing text, *Theories of the Good Life.*

*   *   *

SMITH, Steven Phillip   1943-

PERSONAL: Born January 1, 1943, in Minneapolis, Minn.; son of Weldon Hull and Elizabeth (a secretary; maiden name, Sandeen) Smith; married Wendy Benjamin (a psychiatric social worker), June 28, 1970. *Education:* Pasadena City College, A.A., 1962; University of California, Berkeley, A.B., 1968; California State College (now University), Los Angeles, M.A., 1970; University of Massachusetts, M.F.A., 1972. *Home:* 1668 Malcolm Ave., Los Angeles, Calif. 90024. *Agent:* Scott Meredith Literary Agency, Inc., 580 Fifth Ave., New York, N.Y. 10036.

CAREER: Jewish Big Brothers, Los Angeles, Calif., social worker, 1969-70; writer. Lecturer at University of Massachusetts, 1970-72, and University of California, Los Angeles, extension, 1974; private tutoring of junior high school students, 1973—. *Military service:* U.S. Army, 1964-67; received Air Medal, Army Commendation Medal for Valor.

WRITINGS: (Contributor) Basil T. Paquet, editor, *Winning Hearts and Minds* (poems), McGraw, 1972; (contributor) Wayne Karlin, editor, *Free Fire Zone* (short stories), McGraw, 1973; *American Boys* (novel), Putnam, 1975.

WORK IN PROGRESS: A novel about a rural Minnesota town's transformation to a suburb over a period of twenty years.

*   *   *

SMITH, Sydney Goodsir   1915-1975(?)

1915—1975(?); New Zealand-born Scottish journalist, broadcaster, teacher, playwright, and poet. Obituaries: *AB Bookman's Weekly*, February 17, 1975.

*   *   *

SMOLLER, Sanford J(erome)   1937-

PERSONAL: Born February 13, 1937, in Pittsburgh, Pa.; son of Paul (a pharmacist) and Mildred (Rosenthal) Smoller; married Merry Sue Thompson (a municipal television administrator), August 19, 1959; children: Jonathan, Deborah, Pamela. *Education:* Attended Santa Monica City College, 1958-60; University of California, Los Angeles, B.A., 1962; Columbia University, M.A., 1964; University of Wisconsin, Madison, Ph.D., 1972. *Politics* Left. *Home:* 322 Glenway St., Madison, Wis. 53705.

CAREER: Dickinson College, Carlisle, Pa., instructor in English, 1964-67; University of Wisconsin, Madison, extension instructor, 1968, Sheboygan/Wausau, lecturer, 1969, Richland, assistant professor of English, 1969-70, Madison, film coordinator, 1972-74. *Military service:* U.S. Navy, 1955-57. *Member:* Phi Beta Kappa. *Awards, honors:* Woodrow Wilson fellowship, 1962; Danforth teacher grant, 1967.

WRITINGS: (Editor) *The Inner City and the Arts: A Selection of References, 1967-68*, University of Wisconsin Arts Council, 1969; *Adrift Among Geniuses: Robert McAlmon, Writer and Publisher of the Twenties*, Pennsylvania State University Press, 1975. Contributor to *Modern Fiction Studies*.

*   *   *

SNOW, Helen Foster   1907-
(Nym Wales)

PERSONAL: Born September 21, 1907, in Cedar, Utah; daughter of John Moody (a lawyer) and Hannah (a teacher; maiden name, Davis) Foster; married Edgar Snow (an author and foreign correspondent), December 25, 1932 (divorced, 1949; died, 1972). *Education:* Attended University of Utah, 1925-27, and Yenching University and Tsinghua University, both in Peking, 1934-35. *Politics:* Independent. *Religion:* Unitarian-Universalist. *Home and office:* 148 Mungertown Rd., Madison, Conn. 06443. *Agent:* Ellen Levine, Curtis Brown Ltd., 60 East 56th St., New York, N.Y. 10022.

CAREER: String correspondent for Scripps-Canfield League of Newspapers, Seattle, 1931; lived in China, 1931-40, holding positions as book reviewer, 1931-38, and Peking correspondent, 1934-37, for *China Weekly Review*, Shanghai, co-founder and co-editor, with husband Edgar Snow, of magazine *Democracy*, Peking, 1937, and co-founder of Chinese Industrial Cooperatives in Shanghai, 1938; book reviewer for *Saturday Review of Literature*, New York, 1941-49; compiled Nym Wales collection at Stanford University, 1958-61. Certified by Board of Certification of Genealogists, Washington, D.C., 1960. Vice-chairman of board of directors, American Committee in Aid of Chinese Industrial Cooperatives, 1941-51; sponsor, American Committee for Spanish Freedom, 1943; member of board, Committee for a Democratic Far Eastern Policy, 1945-56. Photographs of China have been exhibited at Metropolitan Museum, New York, N.Y., 1972.

MEMBER: National Society of Literature and the Arts, Association for Asian Studies, U.S.-China People's Friendship Association, Committee of Concerned Asian Scholars, Society of Women Geographers, Smithsonian Associates, English-Speaking Union, Natural Food Association, Antiquarian and Landmarks Society, National Genealogical Society, Society of Genealogists (London), Connecticut Society of Genealogists, Madison Conservation Trust, Madison Historical Society, Soil Association (London), Nautical Wheelers Square Dance Club, Semi-Polar Bears Swimming Club (founder), Harbor Rounds Dance Club.

WRITINGS: Women in Modern China, Mouton & Co., 1967.

Under pseudonym Nym Wales: *Inside Red China*, Doubleday, 1939, published as *New China*, Eagle Publishers (Calcutta), 1944, reprinted under original title, Da Capo Press, 1975; *Song of Ariran: The Life Story of an Asian Revolutionary* (autobiography of Kim San, as told to Snow), John Day, 1941, reprinted, Ramparts Press, 1973; *China Builds for Democracy: A Story of Cooperative Industry*, Modern Age Books, 1941, published with foreword by Jawaharlal Nehru, Kitabistan (Allahabad, India), 1942, reprinted, Scholarly Press, 1973; *The Chinese Labor Movement*, John Day, 1945, reprinted, Books for Libraries, 1970; *Fables and Parables for the Mid-Century*, Philosophical Library, 1952; *Red Dust: Autobiographies of Chinese Communists as Told to Nym Wales*, Stanford University Press, 1952, enlarged edition published as *The Chinese Communists*, two books, Greenwood, 1972; *Notes on the Beginnings of the Industrial Cooperatives in China*, Stanford University, 1958, reprinted as *The Beginnings of the Industrial Cooperatives in China*, Scholarly Press, 1972.

Author of books published in Madison, Conn., 1959-61, and reprinted (with "Notes on . . ." deleted from titles, unless otherwise indicated), Scholarly Press, 1973: *Notes on the Chinese Student Movement, 1935-36*; *Notes on the Sian Incident, 1936*; *Notes on Korea and the Life of Kim San*; *My Yenan Notebooks* (reprinted as *An American Experience in Yenan*); *Notes on the Left-Wing Painters and Modern Art in China*.

Historical plays; under name Helen Foster Snow: *The Land beyond the Kuttawoo: The Madison Story*, Gnomen (New Haven, Conn.), 1974; *The Guilford Story, or, Menuncatuck Plantation*, Gnomen, 1974; *The Saybrook Story*, privately printed, 1975.

Contributor: Edgar Snow, editor, *Living China*, John Day, 1936; John Lehmann, editor, *New Writing*, Knopf, 1938; S. H. Fritchman, editor, *Together We Advance*, Beacon Press, 1947; *Readings on China*, George School (Pa.), 1964; John U. Michaelis, editor, *Asia Today* (anthology), School of Education, University of California, 1967.

Poetry is published in *Anthology of Magazine Verse and Year Book of American Poetry*, edited by Alan F. Pater, Paebar, 1938; and *Saturday Review Treasury*, edited by John Haverstick and others, Simon & Schuster, 1957.

Also author of two unpublished works, *Women in Traditional China* (sequel to *Women in Modern China*), and *Totemism: The T'ao-T'ieh and the Chinese Bronzes*. Author of twenty-two books on genealogy, and of song lyrics and music. Photographs appear in *Twentieth Century China*, published by University of Toronto, and *Behind the Great Wall of China, 1870-1970*, by Cornell Capa, Metropolitan Museum of Art (New York), 1972. Contributor to *Encyclopaedia Britannica Junior* and *Encyclopedia of Labor*, and to periodicals, including *Reader's Digest, New Republic, New York Times, Nation, Asia, Pacific Affairs, Ladies' Home Journal*, and *Life and Letters Today* (London).

WORK IN PROGRESS: Return to China, based on her 1972-73 trip; *Mao Country*, based on a trip to Mao Tse-Tung's home province, Hunan; *The Root and the Branch*, an historical novel on the seventeenth-century civil war in England, and the founding of New England.

SIDELIGHTS: Chinese Industrial (or "Gung Ho") Cooperatives, conceived in 1938 by Mrs. Snow, her husband Edgar Snow, and Rewi Alley, became widespread in China, merging into communes in 1959; about fifty thousand of them have been established in India. A Chinese translation of *Inside Red China* is still used in Chinese schools as a record of the country's history during the 1930's. Various of Mrs. Snow's works are translated into Korean and Japanese, as well as Chinese.

Mrs. Snow was a delegate to the American Women's Congress centenary in 1948, and signed calls for various other congresses. She knows Chinese, Spanish, French, and some Italian, and has traveled widely in the Far East, and in Indonesia and Europe.

BIOGRAPHICAL/CRITICAL SOURCES: Sterling North, *Map of the American Literary Renaissance*, Putnam, 1941.

* * *

SNOW, Lois Wheeler 1920-

PERSONAL: Born July 12, 1920, in Stockton, Calif.; daughter of Raymond Joseph and Katherine (Kurtz) Wheeler; married Edgar Snow (an author), May, 1949 (died February 15, 1972); children: Christopher, Sian. *Education:* University of the Pacific, B.A., 1941; studied at Neighborhood Playhouse, New York, N.Y., 1941-43. *Home:* 1262 Eysins, Vaud, Switzerland. *Agent:* Robert Mills, 156 East 52nd St., New York, N.Y. 10022.

CAREER: Actress on Broadway, 1943-59, and on television and radio programs broadcast from New York, N.Y., 1950-59; resident of Switzerland, 1959—; founding member, Actor's Studio, New York; lecturer on topics related to China, in New York, and on national tours, 1972-76; author. *Member:* Amnesty International, Authors Guild, Mark Twain Society, U.S.-China Friendship Association (New York), Society for Anglo-Chinese Understanding (London).

WRITINGS: China on Stage (includes text of three Chinese revolutionary operas), Random House, 1972; *A Death with Dignity: When the Chinese Came* (biographical), Random House, 1975. Contributor to *Le Monde* (Paris), *Saturday Review, New Republic, Vogue*, "*New China*," *Eastern Horizon, National Elementary Principal*, and to Finnish and Italian magazines.

WORK IN PROGRESS: Further articles and lectures on China.

* * *

SNYDER, Guy (Eugene, Jr.) 1951-

PERSONAL: Born May 3, 1951, in Columbus, Ohio; son of Guy Eugene (a salesman) and Rita Clair (Brown) Snyder. *Education:* Wayne State University, B.A., 1973. *Politics:* Independent. *Home:* 19161 Votrobeck Dr., Apt. 101, Detroit, Mich. 48219. *Office:* Contractor Publishing Co., 1629 West Lafayette Blvd., Detroit, Mich. 48216.

CAREER: Contractor Publishing Co., Detroit, Mich., construction reports editor for *Michigan Contractor & Builder*, 1974—. *Member:* Science Fiction Writers of America.

WRITINGS: Testament XXI, DAW Books, 1973.

WORK IN PROGRESS: A novel about Detroit.

SIDELIGHTS: Snyder writes: "I've been a parks and recreation department laborer, a garbageman, and a college student in Detroit. The city has fed and educated me, has always fascinated me, and currently torments me. Detroit, and the county in which it exists, is under seige by powerful forces—in my novel in progress, I will identify and confront them.''

* * *

SOGLOW, Otto 1900-1975

December 23, 1900—April 3, 1975; American cartoonist and illustrator. Obituaries: *New York Times*, April 4, 1975; *Current Biography*, May, 1975.

* * *

SOLEM, (George) Alan 1931-

PERSONAL: Born July 21, 1931, in Chicago, Ill.; son of George Oliver (a physician) and Lillian Taylor (a nurse; maiden name, Kinloch) Solem; married Mary Margaret Conkling, June, 1953 (divorced June, 1956); married Barbara King (an entrepreneur), May 14, 1950; children: (second marriage) Anders Erik, Kirsten Marie. *Education:* Haverford College, B.S. (magna cum laude), 1952; University of Michigan, M.A., 1954, Ph.D., 1956. *Politics:* Independent. *Religion:* None. *Home:* 53 Elizabeth Lane, Barrington, Ill. 60010. *Office:* Field Museum of Natural History, Lake Shore and Roosevelt, Chicago, Ill. 60605.

CAREER: Field Museum of Natural History, Chicago, Ill., curator of invertebrates, 1959—. Lecturer at University of Chicago, 1969—; research associate, Northwestern University, 1969—. Member of board of trustees of Barrington Public Library District, 1970—. *Military service:* U.S. Navy, 1959. *Member:* Malacological Society of London, Conchological Society of Great Britain and Ireland, Unitas Malacologiae Europaea, Deutsches Malakologischen Gesellschaft, American Malacological Union (president, 1969-70), American Association for the Advancement of Science, Ecological Society of America, Society for Systematic Zoology, Malacological Society of Australia, Nederlandese Malacologische Vereniging, Western Society of Malacologists, California Malacozoological Society, Phi Beta Kappa.

WRITINGS: Life along the Seashore (for children), Encyclopaedia Britannica, 1963; *The Shell Makers: Introducing Mollusks*, Wiley, 1974; *Endodontoid Land Snails from Pacific Islands*, Field Museum of Natural History, in press.

Author of more than eighty monographs. Contributor to *Encyclopaedia Britannica*. Consulting editor to *American Malacological Union Bulletin*, 1969—, *Nautilus*, 1972—, *Malacologia*, 1974—.

WORK IN PROGRESS: Studies on non-marine mollusks; a popular book series on scanning electron microscopy; a book on the population and food crisis.

AVOCATIONAL INTERESTS: Travel, photography, reading, collecting primitive art.

* * *

SOLOMON, Goody L(ove)

PERSONAL: Born in New York, N.Y. *Education:* Brooklyn College (now Brooklyn College of the City University of New York), B.A., 1950; New York University, M.A., 1955. *Home:* 1712 Taylor St. N.W., Washington, D.C. 20011.

CAREER: Journalist. U.S. Department of Health, Education, and Welfare, Washington, D.C., executive editor for Office for Consumer Services, 1971-73; New York State Consumer Protection Board, New York, N.Y., consumer education director and producer-moderator of ''The Knowing Consumer,'' a weekly program on the educational television network, 1973; free-lance writer, editor, broadcaster, and consultant, 1973—. Has taught at George Washington University and in high schools in the District of Columbia; has made television and radio appearances.

WRITINGS: The Radical Consumer's Handbook, Ballantine, 1972. Author of syndicated weekly consumer-food column for *Washington Star-News*. Contributor to popular magazines, including *Money, Woman's World, Washingtonian, National Star*, and *Canadian Broadcasting*. Contributing editor of *Modern Textiles*. Editor of *U.S. Consumer*, a biweekly newsletter.

* * *

SOLOMON, Norman 1951-

PERSONAL: Born July 7, 1951, in Washington, D.C.; son of Morris J. (an economist) and Miriam (an economist; maiden name, Abramowitz) Solomon. *Education:* Self-educated. *Politics:* ''Feminist socialism; collective sharing; an end to capitalism and authority culture.'' *Religion:* ''Freedom, justice, and love.'' *Home address:* P.O. Box 42384, Portland, Ore. 97242.

CAREER: Montgomery County Sentinel, Rockville, Md., newspaper reporter, 1968-70; KBOO-FM Radio, Portland, Ore., producer of commentary, 1972—. Student activist associated with Montgomery County Student Alliance, 1968-69; active in anti-war, civil rights, and anti-authoritarian efforts. *Awards, honors:* Third prize for news reporting, 1970, from Maryland-Delaware Press Association.

WRITINGS: No Title (novelette), Out of the Ashes Press, 1971; *In the Belly of the Dinosaurs: Resisting the Death Convention*, Out of the Ashes Press, 1972; *Cockroach* (novel), Out of the Ashes Press, 1974.

Work in anthologized in *How Old Will You Be in 1984?*, edited by Diane Divoky, Avon, 1969; *High School*, edited by Ronald Gross and Paul Osterman, Simon & Schuster, 1970; *The Soft Revolution*, edited by Neil Postman and Charles Weingartner, Delta Books, 1971; *Radical School Reform*, edited by Beatrice Gross and Ronald Gross, Simon & Schuster, 1971; *Generation Rap*, edited by Gene Stanford, Dell, 1971; *Living and Loving in the Americas*, edited by Thomas Carlisle, Angst, in press.

Author of ''The Tragedy of King Lethal'' (adaptation of *King Lear*; first performed as a radio play in Portland, Ore., on KBOO-FM Radio, Portland, Ore., 1972), Out of the Ashes Press, 1971.

Contributor to *Edcentric, WIN, Radical Therapist, San Francisco Good Times*, SunRise, Portland Scribe, Stranger, *and* Fifth Estate. *Member of editorial staff of* Edcentric, *1973-75.*

WORK IN PROGRESS: Now, a novel; *Mind Reader in Washington*, a novel; research on the nature of liberal American repression, the functionings of authoritarian culture, the ageist oppression of children, and robot schooling.

SIDELIGHTS: Solomon writes: ''I feel transfixed with questions of repression and liberation . . . . I want to develop and use my writing abilities to add a voice which people will find joins with their own inner voices; this means also challenging the enshrined 'truths' of those who brandish power—in schools and families, corporate board rooms and political offices, slick media bureaucracies and the Pentagon . . . .

"I grew up in a fairly affluent family. I found that 'comfortable' social positions are based on privilege and immorality as long as the 'comfort' exists with direct connection to the social disadvantages of others . . . At the same time, it is a mistake to believe that the affluent have an ideal life; the personal life of upper class America is a mess, with personal repression the order of the day.

"For so long Americans have deluded themselves into believing that they could cut corners emotionally and get away with it. They can't. We can't. It all comes back. Everything is connected. Sexual repression, economic inequity, imperialism abroad, police-state mentalities all make wreckage of social activities and inner lives. Liberation is essential . . . ."

* * *

SOLOTAROFF, Robert David 1937-

PERSONAL: Born January 2, 1937, in Elizabeth, N.J.; son of Ben (a glass retailer and wholesaler) and Rose (Weiss) Solotaroff; married Sarah Jane Dubsky (an editor and piano teacher), June 23, 1963; children: Jenny, Rachel, Jacob. *Education:* University of Michigan, B.A., 1961; University of Chicago, M.A., 1962, Ph.D., 1969. *Politics:* "Pulpy liberalism lapsing into despondency." *Religion:* Jewish. *Home:* 4028 Colfax Ave. S., Minneapolis, Minn. 55409. *Office:* Department of English, University of Minnesota, Minneapolis, Minn. 55455.

CAREER: University of Chicago, Downtown Center, Chicago, Ill., lecturer in the humanities, 1961-62; Chicago City College, Wright Campus, Chicago, Ill., instructor, 1962-67, assistant professor of the humanities, 1967-69; University of Minnesota, Minneapolis, assistant professor, 1969-73, associate professor of literature, 1973—. Research worker for *Encyclopaedia Britannica*, 1959-60.

WRITINGS: Down Mailer's Way, University of Illinois Press, 1974. Contributor of articles and reviews to *Chicago Review, Nation,* and *Western Humanities Review.*

WORK IN PROGRESS: Research on the creative process, especially concerning Hemingway; research on changing conceptions of the self in contemporary American fiction.

* * *

SOULE, George (Alan) 1930-

PERSONAL: Surname rhymes with "coal"; born March 3, 1930, in Fargo, N.D.; son of George Alan (a lawyer) and Ruth (a teacher; maiden name, Knudsen) Soule; married Carolyn Richards, November 24, 1961; children: Katherine Richards. *Education:* Attended Columbia University, 1949, Kenyon College, 1950; Carleton College, B.A. (magna cum laude), 1951; graduate study, Corpus Christi College, Cambridge, 1952-53, Kansas State College, 1955; Yale University, M.A., 1956, Ph.D., 1960. *Politics:* "Disenchanted Democrat." *Religion:* Episcopalian. *Home:* 313 Nevada St., Northfield, Minn. 55057. *Office:* Department of English, Carleton College, Northfield, Minn. 55057.

CAREER: Carleton College, Northfield, Minn., assistant professor, 1962-66, associate professor, 1966-71, professor of English, 1971—. Member of Northfield Bicentennial Committee. *Military service:* U.S. Army, 1954-55. *Member:* Johnson Society of London, Shakespeare Association of America, Mayflower Society of Minnesota, Johnson Society of Lichfield, Phi Beta Kappa.

WRITINGS: (Editor and contributor) *The Theatre of the Mind*, Prentice-Hall, 1974. Contributor to *Minneapolis Tribune* and *Carleton Miscellany.*

AVOCATIONAL INTERESTS: Travel.

* * *

SOUTHERINGTON, F(rank) R(odney) 1938-

PERSONAL: Born July 26, 1938, in Weymouth, England; son of Frank (in the Royal Air Force) and Muriel (Ashelford) Southerington; married Helene Wikstroem, January 9, 1964 (divorced); married Theresa Anne Koogler (a teacher), August 10, 1972; children: Anna Elisabeth. *Education:* University College, London, B.A., 1961; Magdalen College, Oxford, B.Litt., 1963, D.Phil., 1968. *Home:* 156 North Coalter St., Staunton, Va. 24401. *Office:* Department of English, Mary Baldwin College, Staunton, Va. 24401.

CAREER: University of Uppsala, Uppsala, Sweden, lektor in English, 1962-64; Aabo Akademi, Aabo, Finland, first lektor in English, 1965-68; Mary Baldwin College, Staunton, Va., assistant professor, 1968-72, associate professor of English, 1972—. *Member:* Thomas Hardy Society, Strindberg Society (Stockholm). *Awards, honors:* Aabo Akademi Foundation Medal, 1968.

WRITINGS: Hardy's Vision of Man, Barnes & Noble, 1971; (editor) *Hardy: Jude the Obscure*, Bobbs-Merrill, 1972; (translator) *Strindberg: Three Experimental Plays*, University Press of Virginia, 1975. Author of articles on Thomas Hardy.

WORK IN PROGRESS: Strindberg: A Critical Biography, publication by Chatto & Windus expected in 1977; translations of Strindberg's work.

AVOCATIONAL INTERESTS: Amateur dramatics, music, gardening, Swedish language.

* * *

SPADA, James 1950-

PERSONAL: Born January 23, 1950, in Staten Island, N.Y.; son of Joseph Vincent and Mary (Ruberto) Spada. *Education:* Attended Wagner College, 1968-71, and Hunter College of the City University of New York, 1972-75. *Politics:* "Liberal Democrat, if that means anything." *Religion:* "Discarded." *Home:* 225 West 25th St., New York, N.Y. 10001. *Agent:* Betty Ann Clark, International Creative Management, 1301 Avenue of Americas, New York, N.Y. 10019. *Office: In The Know*, 355 Lexington Ave., New York, N.Y. 10017.

CAREER: New York State Council on the Arts, New York, N.Y., office assistant, 1966, 1969; Wagner College Library, Staten Island, N.Y., assistant librarian in periodicals department, 1969-70; editor and publisher of *EMK: The Edward M. Kennedy Quarterly*, 1969-72; U.S. Senate, Washington, D.C., intern to Senator Edward M. Kennedy, 1970; *In The Know*, New York, N.Y., managing editor, 1975—. *Member:* American Civil Liberties Union, Common Cause.

WRITINGS: Barbra: The First Decade, the Career of Barbra Streisand, Citadel, 1974.

WORK IN PROGRESS: Robert Redford: Films and Career, for Citadel; *Ted Kennedy and the Press*; a novel; a screenplay; short stories.

SIDELIGHTS: "I hope that my future writings will greatly improve on my present efforts," James Spada told *CA*. "Writing is a vocation I find rewarding, educational, rending, draining, fulfilling, hateful, and lovely. My writings will grow as I do." *Avocational interests:* Physical education, sports, drawing, painting, music, photography, antiques, cooking, collecting (books, prints, records, magazines, photos).

*   *   *

SPAIN, David H.   1939-

PERSONAL: Born June 13, 1939, in Columbus, Ohio; son of Norman M. (a salesman) and Ruth A. (Polley) Spain; married Catherine L. Peterson (a teacher), August 10, 1968; children: Andrew D., Ryan G. *Education:* Ohio State University, B.A., 1961, M.A., 1963; Northwestern University, Ph.D., 1969. *Home:* 1237 Federal Ave. E., Seattle, Wash. 98102. *Office:* Department of Anthropology, University of Washington, Seattle, Wash. 98195.

CAREER: University of Washington, Seattle, assistant professor, 1968-75, associate professor of anthropology, 1975—. *Member:* African Studies Association (fellow), American Anthropological Association (fellow), Society for Applied Anthropology (fellow), Current Anthropology (associate).

WRITINGS: (Editor with Mark A. Tessler and William M. O'Barr) *Survey Research in Africa: Its Applications and Limits*, Northwestern University Press, 1973; (with Tessler and O'Barr) *Tradition and Identity in Changing Africa*, Harper, 1973; (with John A. Brim) *Research Design in Anthropology: Paradigms and Pragmatics in the Testing of Hypotheses*, Holt, 1974; (editor) *The Human Experience: Readings in Sociocultural Anthropology*, Dorsey, 1975.

*   *   *

SPECTOR, Ronald (Harvey)   1943-

PERSONAL: Born January 17, 1943, in Pittsburgh, Pa.; son of David D. (a heating contractor) and Ethel (Barsky) Spector; married Dianne Barbara Frank (a social worker), September 27, 1970; children: Daniel Aaron. *Education:* Johns Hopkins University, A.B., 1964; Yale University, M.A., 1966, Ph.D., 1967. *Home:* 1613 Woodbine St., Alexandria, Va. 22302. *Office:* U.S. Army Center of Military History, Washington, D.C. 20315.

CAREER: Yale University, Cambridge, Mass., assistant in instruction in history, 1966-67; University of Maryland, Far East Division, Danang, Vietnam, lecturer in history, 1968-69; Louisiana State University, Baton Rouge, assistant professor of history, 1969-71; U.S. Army Center of Military History, Washington, D.C., historian, 1971—. Lecturer at George Mason University, 1972—. *Military service:* U.S. Marine Corps, 1967-69; served in Vietnam; received Navy Achievement Medal with "V" device. *Member:* International Studies Association, American Historical Association, Society for Historians of American Foreign Relations, Inter-University Seminar on the Armed Forces and Society (fellow).

WRITINGS: Admiral of the New Empire: The Life and Career of George Dewey, Louisiana State University Press, 1974. Contributor to *Dictionary of American History* and *Encyclopedia of Sociology*. Contributor to *American Neptune, Journal of Southeast Asian Studies, Military Affairs, American History Illustrated, Mid-America, Vermont History*, and *Southeast Asia.*

WORK IN PROGRESS: The U.S. Army and Indo-China: 1942-1961, first volume of official history of U.S. Army

activities in Indo-China; *Professors of War: The Naval War College and the Development of the Naval Profession, 1884-1920*, a monograph.

*   *   *

SPENCER, Dale R(ay)   1925-

PERSONAL: Born October 21, 1925, in Pocatello, Idaho; son of Howard and Eleda (Eastman) Spencer; married Joy Hodkins, December 21, 1947; children: Melinda Sue, Jennifer Joy. *Education:* Attended College of Idaho, 1944-45, and University of New Mexico, 1945-46; University of Missouri, Bachelor of Journalism, 1948, M.A., 1955, J.D., 1968. *Home:* 917 La Grange Rd., Columbia, Mo. 65201. *Office:* School of Journalism, University of Missouri, Columbia, Mo.

CAREER: Pocatello Tribune, Pocatello, Idaho, general assignment and sports reporter, 1940-43; E. W. Stephens Publishing Co., Columbia, Mo., sales manager, 1949-50; University of Missouri, Columbia, assistant professor, 1950-63, associate professor, 1963-71, professor of journalism, 1971—; and *Missourian*, Columbia, Mo., assistant managing editor, 1950-73, acting managing editor, 1973-74. Weathercaster, KOMU-TV, 1953-58. *Member:* Society for Professional Journalists (vice-president, 1954, 1955), American Bar Association, Missouri Bar Association, Kappa Tau Alpha, Kappa Alpha Mu.

WRITINGS: Copy Editing I, Lucas Brothers, 1963; *A Handbook of Missouri Statutes and Cases*, Missouri Press Association, 1964; *Copyediting at Missouri*, Lucas Brothers, 1969; *Law for the Newsman*, Lucas Brothers, 1971, 2nd edition, 1973. Contributor to professional magazines. Copy and wire editor, *Buffalo Evening News*, 1952.

WORK IN PROGRESS: Third edition of *Law for the Newsman.*

SIDELIGHTS: Spencer writes: "My writing is an attempt to explain law to journalists and journalism to lawyers."

*   *   *

SPENCER, Michael (Clifford)   1936-

PERSONAL: Born February 3, 1936, in Peterborough, England; son of Stephen Clifford (a clerk) and Elsie (a clerk; maiden name, Cox) Spencer; married Mary King, July 31, 1965; children: Andrew. *Education:* University of Sheffield, B.A. (honors), 1959; Cambridge University, M.A., 1962; Oxford University, D.Phil., 1964. *Politics:* "Left-wing." *Religion:* None. *Home:* 24 Thorpe St., Indooroopilly, Queensland 4068, Australia. *Office:* Department of French, University of Queensland, Brisbane, Queensland 4067, Australia.

CAREER: Cambridge University, Sidney Sussex College, Cambridge, England, fellow in modern languages, 1962-68; University of Adelaide, Adelaide, South Australia, senior lecturer in French, 1969-70; Monash University, Voctoria, Australia, senior lecturer in French and warden of a hall of residence, 1971-73; University of Queensland, Brisbane, Australia, professor of French, 1974—. President of Alliance Francaise (Adelaide), 1970. *Military service:* British Army, 1954-56; became sergeant. *Member:* Australian Universities Language and Literature Association.

WRITINGS: The Art Criticism of Theophile Gautier, Droz, 1969; *Michel Butor*, Twayne, 1974. Contributor of articles and reviews to *Australian Journal of French Studies, Symposium, French Studies, Degres, Raison presente, Music and Letters, Meanjin Quarterly, Modern Language*

Review, and other journals. Member of editorial board of *Australian Journal of French Studies*.

WORK IN PROGRESS: Research on Alain Robbe-Grillet and Charles Fourier; research on *Dans le Labyrinthe*, with publication expected to result.

SIDELIGHTS: Spencer writes: "I came to an academic career more or less by accident, when the British Army and the British Foreign Office discovered simultaneously that I had been a member of the Young Communist League (I had a post waiting for me in the Foreign Office). As it was clear that my career in this direction would not be scintillating, I went to university instead." *Avocational interests:* Travel.

* * *

SPIEGELMAN, J(oseph) Marvin 1926-

PERSONAL: Born May 26, 1926, in Los Angeles, Calif.; son of Irving (a merchant) and Rae (Starr) Spiegelman; married Ryma Silberstein, October 25, 1953; children: Jeffrey Joshua, Tamar. *Education:* University of California, Los Angeles, A.B., 1948, M.A., 1950, Ph.D., 1952; C.G. Jung Institute, analyst's diploma, 1959. *Office:* 4326 Coldwater Canyon, Studio City, Calif. 91604.

CAREER: Private practice in clinical psychology in Beverly Hills, Calif., 1959—, and Studio City, Calif., 1974—. Has taught at University of California, Los Angeles, University of Colorado, University of Southern California, and Hebrew University of Jerusalem. *Military service:* U.S. Naval Reserve, 1944-46. U.S. Merchant Marine, 1944-46; served in Pacific theater, Asian theater, European theater, and Mediterranean theater. U.S. Army, psychologists in Medical Service Corps, 1953-55; became captain. *Member:* International Analytical Psychology Association, American Psychological Association. *Awards, honors:* Fellow of Institute for International Education, 1955-56; Bollingen Foundation fellowship, 1957-59.

WRITINGS: The Tree: Tales in Psychomythology, Phoenix House, 1974.

Contributor to psychology journals. Consulting editor of *Journal of Analytical Psychology, Spring*, and *Revista di Psicologia Analitica*.

WORK IN PROGRESS: The Quest and *The Love*, second and third volumes of a trilogy beginning with *The Tree*; another trilogy, including *The Unhealed Healer, The Failed Artist*, and *The Powerless Magician*.

SIDELIGHTS: Spiegelman writes: "With the term 'psychomythology,' I wish to introduce a new literary genre which bears a familial resemblance to both science-fiction and the historical novel. In these forms, there is a peculiar kind of union of the opposites of fact and fiction. Science fiction starts with current scientific knowledge, makes reasonable extrapolations toward future discoveries, and fuses these with fantasy. Historical novels add romance, conjectured conversation, and embellishment to what is known of recorded events. In both cases, the structure of 'truth' and 'reality' is enriched by imagination, which is psychological truth. Psychomythology stands for a similar union of fact and imagination, but in this field there is a marriage of psychological knowledge with the type of fantasy that reaches the universal, archetypal, mythological level."

* * *

SPIVAK, Mel 1937-

PERSONAL: Born June 1, 1937, in Brooklyn, N.Y.; son of Harry (a laborer) and Pauline (Rogosin) Spivak. *Education:* Attended City College of City University of New York, 1955-57. *Religion:* Jewish. *Home:* B-14, 665 88th St., Brooklyn, N.Y. 11228. *Agent:* George Glay, 663 Fifth Ave., New York, N.Y. 10022.

CAREER: Actor and producer with Seven Arts Center, 1955 and 1958, Dorchester Masquers, 1958-59, Young Men's Hebrew Association, 1959-60; file clerk with various U.S. Government agencies in New York, 1960-68; male maid in San Francisco and department store in Honolulu, 1969-70; hospital porter in Brooklyn, N.Y., 1970—. *Military service:* U.S. Army, 1961-63.

WRITINGS: Underground Mind (poems), Thom Hendricks, 1969; *World Poets: Spring Poets 1971*, Regency Press, 1971; *New Voices in American Poetry: 1972*, Vantage, 1972; *Fantasies* (short stories), Mojave Books, 1972, 2nd edition, 1975. Contributor of articles and poems to *Village Voice, Writer's Digest*, and other journals. Writer of song lyrics.

WORK IN PROGRESS: A novel, *Bindy Becomes a Saint*, completion expected in 1976.

AVOCATIONAL INTERESTS: Travel.

* * *

SPRIGGE, Timothy L(auro) S(quire) 1932-

PERSONAL: Born January 14, 1932, in London, England; son of Cecil Jackson (a journalist) and Katriona (Gordon Brown) Sprigge; married Giglia Gordon (a painter), April 4, 1959; children: Georgina, Lucy, Samuel. *Education:* Gonville & Caius College, Cambridge, B.A. (honors), 1955, M.A. and Ph.D., both 1961. *Religion:* "Spinozist." *Home:* Grey Walls, 16 Avenue, Lewes, Sussex, England. *Office:* School of English and American Studies, University of Sussex, Falmer, Brighton BN1-9QQ, England.

CAREER: University of London, University College, London, England, lecturer in philosophy, 1961-63; University of Sussex, Brighton, England, lecturer, 1963-70, reader in philosophy, 1970—.

WRITINGS: (Editor) *The Correspondence of Jeremy Bentham*, Volumes I and II, Athlone Press (of University of London), 1968; *Facts, Words, and Beliefs*, Routledge & Kegan Paul, 1970; *Santayana: An Examination of His Philosophy*, Routledge & Kegan Paul, 1974. Contributor to philosophy journals, including *Mind, Inquiry*, and *Philosophy*.

WORK IN PROGRESS: Research on panpsychist metaphysics, the logic of relations, and the philosophy of F. H. Bradley.

SIDELIGHTS: Sprigge writes that the ".... main motivation of my writings is to help encourage the philosophical world to return to serious metaphysical enquiry, in which philosophy is concerned with the nature of reality rather than with concepts and language."

BIOGRAPHICAL/CRITICAL SOURCES: Observer Review, February 25, 1968; *Times Literary Supplement*, January 23, 1969.

* * *

SPRING, Ira L(ov) 1918-

PERSONAL: Born December 24, 1918, in Jamestown, N.Y.; son of Elliot B. (an accountant) and Allena (Loomis) Spring; married Patricia Willgress, 1949; children: John, Vicky. *Education:* Attended School of Modern Photography, 1946-47. *Home and office:* 18819 Olympic View Dr., Edmonds, Wash. 98020.

CAREER: Professional photographer in Edmonds, Wash. *Military service:* U.S. Army, 1941-45.

WRITINGS—All with brother, Robert W. Spring: *High Adventure*, Superior, 1952; *Mt. Rainier*, Superior, 1955; (with Byron Fish) *Puget Sound*, Superior, 1955; (with Fish) *Columbia River*, Superior, 1956; (with Fish) *This Is Oregon*, Superior, 1957; (with Fish) *This Is Washington*, Superior, 1958; (with Henry Manning) *High Worlds of the Mountain Climber*, Superior, 1959; (with Fish) *Alaska*, Superior, 1961; *Sigemi, a Japanese Village Girl*, Harcourt, 1965; *Japan*, Thomas Nelson, 1966; *Alaska, Pioneer State*, Thomas Nelson, 1966; *100 Hikes of Western Washington*, Mountaineers, 1966; *Trips & Trails 1*, Mountaineers, 1967; (with E. M. Sterling) *Trips & Trails 2*, Mountaineers, 1968; *Scandinavia*, Thomas Nelson, 1968; *Lars Olaf, a Boy of Norway*, Harcourt, 1968; (with Harvey Edwards) *Leise, a Danish Girl from Dragoer*, Harcourt, 1968; *Northwest Ski Trails*, Mountaineers, 1968; (with Manning) *50 Hikes in Mt. Rainier National Park*, Mountaineers, 1969; (with Janice Krenmayr) *Footloose Around Puget Sound*, Mountaineers, 1969; (with Manning) *North Cascades National Park*, Superior, 1969; (with others) *The Key to Our Environment ... Cool, Clear Water*, Superior, 1970; *Wildflowers of Mt. Rainier and the Cascades*, Mountaineers, 1970; *Alaska Travel Book*, Macmillan, 1970; *Eskimo Boy Today*, Alaska Northwest Publishing Co., 1971; (with Manning) *101 Hikes of the North Cascades*, Mountaineers, 1971; (with Manning) *102 Hikes in the Alpine Lakes, South Cascades, and Olympics*, Mountaineers, 1971; *60 Unbeaten Paths*, Superior, 1972; *Roaming Russia*, Superior, 1973; (with Manning) *Wilderness Trails Northwest*, Touchstone, 1974.

WORK IN PROGRESS: With brother and E. M. Sterling, *The South Cascades*; with brother and Ronald Taylor, *Wildflowers of the Rocky Mountains*; with brother, *Wildlife Encounters*.

SIDELIGHTS: Ira Spring writes: "Bob [his twin brother] and I are not identical. In fact, we don't even have a family resemblance. Our personalities are quite different as well as our interests. We do have one common ground, however, and that is photography. Our differences are probably our strength, for between the two of us, we cover a wide range of subjects." *Avocational interests:* Hiking, mountain climbing, travel.

*　　*　　*

SPRING, Robert W(alton)   1918-

PERSONAL: Born December 24, 1918, in Jamestown, N.Y.; son of Elliot B. (an accountant) and Allena (Loomis) Spring; married Norma Virginia Johnson, 1942; children: Terry Walton, Jacqueline Lee, Tracy Ann. *Education:* Attended Central Washington College of Education, 1937-39, University of Washington, 1939-40, and School of Modern Photography, 1946-47. *Home:* 18961 Marine View Circle S.W., Seattle, Wash. 98166. *Office:* 18819 Olympic View Dr., Edmonds, Wash. 98020.

CAREER: Professional photographer in Edmonds, Wash. *Military service:* U.S. Army, 1941-45.

WRITINGS—All with brother Ira L. Spring: *High Adventure*, Superior, 1952; *Mt. Rainier*, Superior, 1955; (with Byron Fish) *Puget Sound*, Superior, 1955; (with Fish) *Columbia River*, Superior, 1956; (with Fish) *This Is Oregon*,

Superior, 1957; (with Fish) *This Is Washington*, Superior, 1958; (with Harvey Manning) *High Worlds of the Mountain Climber*, Superior, 1959; (with Fish) *Alaska*, Superior, 1961; *Sigemi, a Japanese Village Girl*, Harcourt, 1965; *Japan*, Thomas Nelson, 1966; (with wife, Norma Spring) *Alaska, Pioneer State*, Thomas Nelson, 1966; *100 Hikes of Western Washington*, Mountaineers, 1966; *Trips & Trails 1*, Mountaineers, 1967; (with E. M. Sterling) *Trips & Trails 2*, Mountaineers, 1968; *Scandinavia*, Thomas Nelson, 1968; *Lars Olaf, a Boy of Norway*, Harcourt, 1968; (with Harvey Edwards) *Leise, a Danish Girl from Dragoer*, Harcourt, 1968; *Northwest Ski Trails*, Mountaineers, 1968; (with Manning) *50 Hikes in Mt. Rainier National Park*, Mountaineers, 1969; (with Janice Krenmayr) *Footloose Around Puget Sound*, Mountaineers, 1969; (with Manning) *North Cascades National Park*, Superior, 1969; (with others) *The Key to Our Environment ... Cool, Clear Water*, Superior, 1970; *Wildflowers of Mt. Rainier and the Cascades*, Mountaineers, 1970; (with Norma Spring) *The Complete Alaska Travel Book*, Macmillan, 1970, revised edition, 1975; *Eskimo Boy Today*, Alaska Northwest Publishing Co., 1971; (with Manning) *101 Hikes of the North Cascades*, Mountaineers, 1971; (with Manning) *102 Hikes in the Alpine Lakes, South Cascades, and Olympics*, Mountaineers, 1971; *60 Unbeaten Paths*, Superior, 1972; (with Norma Spring) *Roaming Russia*, Superior, 1973; (with Manning) *Wilderness Trails Northwest*, Touchstone, 1974.

WORK IN PROGRESS: With brother and E. M. Sterling, *The South Cascades*; with brother and Ronald Taylor, *Wildflowers of the Rocky Mountains*; with brother, *Wildlife Encounters*.

*　　*　　*

SPRUCH, Grace Marmor   1926-

PERSONAL: Surname rhymes with "tuck"; born November 19, 1926, in New York, N.Y.; son of Isidor and Mollie Marmor; married Larry Spruch (a professor of physics), January 8, 1950. *Education:* Brooklyn College of the City University of New York, B.A. (magna cum laude), 1947; University of Pennsylvania, M.S., 1949; New York University, Ph.D., 1955. *Home:* 14 East Eighth St., New York, N.Y. 10003. *Office:* Department of Physics, Rutgers University, 101 Warren St., Newark, N.J. 07102.

CAREER: Cooper Union, New York, N.Y., instructor in physics, 1957-58; New York University, New York, N.Y., associate research scientist, 1958-63, 1965-67, research scientist, 1967-68; Rutgers University, Newark, N.J., associate professor, 1969-75, professor of physics, 1975—. Scientific secretary for International Conference on Luminescence, 1961. *Member:* American Physical Society, American Association of University Professors, American Association of University Women, American Civil Liberties Union, Phi Beta Kappa, Sigma Xi, Sigma Pi Sigma, Pi Delta Epsilon. *Awards, honors:* Fellowship from American Association of University Women, 1963-64, for study at Oxford University.

WRITINGS: (Editor with Hartmut Kallmann) *Luminescence of Organic and Inorganic Materials*, Wiley, 1962; (translator from German, with Traude Wess) Robert Jungk, *The Big Machine*, Scribner, 1968; (translator from the French) M. Francon, *Holography*, Academic Press, 1974; (editor and contributor, with husband, Larry Spruch) *The Ubiquitous Atom*, Scribner, 1974. Contributor to *Harper Encyclopedia of Science*. Contributor to technical journals, comic books, and *Saturday Review, Art Forum*, and *Leonardo*.

WORK IN PROGRESS: A book on squirrels; short biographies of scientists involved with society.

AVOCATIONAL INTERESTS: Music, animals, sports, medieval church architecture, travel (lived in Europe for three and a half years).

BIOGRAPHICAL/CRITICAL SOURCES: Newark Star-Ledger, February 17, 1974.

* * *

SQUIRES, Eric
   See BALL, Sylvia Patricia

* * *

SQUIRES, Patricia
   See BALL, Sylvia Patricia

* * *

STABLEFORD, Brian M. 1948-

PERSONAL: Born July 25, 1948, in Shipley, Yorkshire, England; son of William Ernest and Joyce (Wilkinson) Stableford; married Vivien Owen, September 3, 1973. *Education:* University of York, B.A., B.Phil., graduate study. *Home:* 9 Turner's Croft, Heslington, York YO1 5EL, England. *Agent:* Janet Freer, 118 Tottenham Court Rd., London W1P 4HL, England.

CAREER: Writer of speculative fiction. *Member:* Science Fiction Writers of America.

WRITINGS—Novels: *Cradle of the Sun*, Ace Books, 1969; *The Blind Worm*, Ace Books, 1970; *The Days of Glory*, Ace Books, 1971; *In the Kingdom of the Beasts*, Ace Books, 1971; *Day of Wrath*, Ace Books, 1971; *To Challenge Chaos*, DAW Books, 1972; *Halcyon Drift*, DAW Books, 1972; *Rhapsody in Black*, DAW Books, 1973; *Promised Land*, DAW Books, 1974; *The Paradise Game*, DAW Books, 1974; *The Fenris Device*, DAW Books, 1974; *Man in a Cage*, John Day, 1975; *Swan Song*, DAW Books, 1975; *Realms of Tartarus*, Volume I: *The Face of Heaven*, Volume II: *A Vision of Hell*, Volume III: *A Glimpse of Infinity*, Quartet, 1975.

Nonfiction: *Scientific Imagination in Literature* (literary history), Futura, 1975.

WORK IN PROGRESS: Two nonfiction works, *The Mysteries of Modern Science* and *The Sociology of Science Fiction.*

* * *

STACEY, Frank Arthur 1923-

PERSONAL: Born July 26, 1923, in London, England; son of Charles Albert (a business representative) and Edith (a civil servant; maiden name, Read) Stacey; married Margaret Petrie (a professor), May 20, 1945; children: Patricia, Richard, Catherine, Peter, Michael. *Education:* Cambridge University, M.A., 1948; Oxford University, B.Phil., 1950. *Home:* 20 Honeypot Lane, Husbands Bosworth, Leicestershire, England. *Office:* Department of Politics, Nottingham University, Nottingham, England.

CAREER: University of Wales, University College, Swansea, lecturer, 1951-67, senior lecturer in politics, 1967-74; Nottingham University, Nottingham, England, professor of local government, 1974—. Public Administration Committee of Joint University Council, honorary secretary, 1968-71, vice-chairman, 1974—. *Military service:* British Army, Royal Artillery, 1943-46; became captain. *Member:*

Political Studies Association of the United Kingdom, Royal Institute of Public Administration.

WRITINGS: The Government of Modern Britain, Clarendon Press (of Oxford University), 1968; *The British Ombudsman*, Clarendon Press (of Oxford University), 1971, 2nd edition, 1973; *A New Bill of Rights for Britain*, David & Charles, 1973; *British Government, 1966-1974: Eight Years of Reform*, Clarendon Press (of Oxford University), 1975; *Ombudsmen Compared*, Clarendon Press (of Oxford University), in press.

* * *

STAINBACK, Susan Bray 1947-

PERSONAL: Born May 22, 1947, in Baltimore, Md.; daughter of William DeVaughn (an optician) and Cleo (Selig) Bray; married William Clarence Stainback (a university professor), December 16, 1967. *Education:* Radford College, B.S., 1968; University of Virginia, M.Ed., 1971, Ed.D., 1973. *Religion:* Catholic. *Home:* R.R. #1, Denver, Iowa 50622. *Office:* Division of Special Education, University of Northern Iowa, Cedar Falls, Iowa 50613.

CAREER: Albemarle County (Va.) public schools, teacher of intermediate age educable mentally retarded students, 1968-70; held part-time positions as consultative specialist, behavior modification consultant, research assistant, and research associate at various school systems in Virginia, 1971-73; Hope Haven Childrens Hospital, Jacksonville, Fla., educational and behavioral specialist, 1973-74; University of Northern Iowa, Cedar Falls, assistant professor of special education, 1974—. Visiting lecturer in special education, University of Virginia, summer, 1973. *Member:* American Association for the Severely and Profoundly Handicapped, Association for Children with Learning Disabilities, Council for Exceptional Children, American Educational Research Association, National Education Association.

WRITINGS: (With J. S. Payne, R. A. Payne, and husband, William C. Stainback) *Establishing a Token Economy in the Classroom*, C. E. Merrill, 1973; (with William C. Stainback) *Classroom Discipline: A Positive Approach*, C. C Thomas, 1974. Also author, with William C. Stainback, of monograph on background music in the educational setting, 1974. Contributor of numerous articles to professional journals, including *Virginia Journal of Education, Education and Training of the Mentally Retarded, Exceptional Children, Journal of Abnormal Child Psychology*, and *Teacher Educator*. Assistant editor, *Education Review*, 1970-71.

WORK IN PROGRESS: A book on the severely and profoundly handicapped; articles on teacher training for the severely and profoundly retarded.

AVOCATIONAL INTERESTS: Fishing, gardening, animals.

* * *

STAPLETON, Margaret (Lucy) 1903-

PERSONAL: Born March 21, 1903, in Tacoma, Wash.; daughter of Richard Francis (a journalist) and Lucy (McKeone) Stapleton. *Education:* University of Washington, Seattle, B.A. (magna cum laude), 1924, B.S., in L.S., 1926, M.A. (literature), 1937, M.A. (history), 1970; Columbia University, M.S. in L.S., 1934. *Politics:* Democrat. *Home:* 3309 North Union Ave., Tacoma, Wash. 98407.

CAREER: Tacoma Public Library, Tacoma, Wash., reference assistant, 1926-33, 1934-35; University of Idaho, Pocatello, assistant librarian, 1935-36; Detroit Public Library, Detroit, Mich., senior reference assistant, 1937-42, first assistant in Reference Department, 1943-45, chief of Book Selection Division, 1945-46; Tacoma Public Library, Tacoma, Wash., chief of Branch Department, 1946-52, chief of Literature Department, 1952-68. *Member:* American Library Association, American Association of University Women, Mountaineers, Audubon Society, Phi Beta Kappa.

WRITINGS: The Truman and Eisenhower Years: 1945-1960, Scarecrow, 1973; *Sir John Betjeman: A Bibliography of Writings By and About Him*, Scarecrow, 1974. Contributor to *Bulletin of Bibliography and Magazine Notes.*

WORK IN PROGRESS: A bibliography of American history, 1945-1960.

AVOCATIONAL INTERESTS: Outdoor activities, hiking, travel, ecology, wilderness preservation.

* * *

STARBUCK, William H(aynes) 1934-

PERSONAL: Born September 20, 1934, in Portland, Ind.; son of Walter Haynes (a banker) and Julia (a painter; maiden name, Magill) Starbuck; married Sharlene Medler, June 16, 1955; children: Julia Grace, Amelia Hope, Nathaniel Haynes. *Education:* Harvard University, A.B., 1956; Carnegie Institute of Technology (now Carnegie-Mellon University), M.S., 1959, Ph.D., 1964. *Home:* 4167 North Downer, Milwaukee, Wis. 53211. *Office:* School of Business Administration, University of Wisconsin, Milwaukee, Wis. 53201.

CAREER: Purdue University, Lafayette, Ind., instructor in industrial management and economics, 1960-64, assistant professor, 1964-65, associate professor of administrative sciences and economics, 1965-67; Cornell University, Ithaca, N.Y., professor of administration, 1967-71, professor of sociology, 1968-71; International Institute of Management, Berlin, Germany, senior research fellow, 1971-74; University of Wisconsin-Milwaukee, Helfaer Professor of Business Administration, 1974—. Visiting professor at Johns Hopkins University, 1966-67, and London Graduate School of Business Studies, 1970-71. Vice-chairman of College on Organization, Institute of Management Sciences, 1965-68, chairman, 1973-74; member of research advisory committee of U.S. Air Force Personnel Research Laboratory, 1966-69. *Member:* American Association of University Professors, American Psychological Association, American Sociological Association, Institute of Management Sciences, Sigma Xi.

WRITINGS: (Contributor) W. S. Decker, editor, *Emerging Concepts in Marketing*, American Marketing Association, 1963; (contributor) J. G. March, editor, *Handbook of Organizations*, Rand McNally, 1965; (contributor) R. W. Millman and M. P. Hottenstein, editors, *Research Toward the Development of Management Thought*, Academy of Management, 1967; (contributor) Millman and Hottenstein, editors, *Promising Research Directions*, Academy of Management, 1968; *Organizational Growth and Development*, Penguin, 1971; (with J. M. Dutton) *Computer Simulation of Human Behavior*, Wiley, 1971; (contributor) J. W. McGuire, editor, *Contemporary Management: Issues and Viewpoints*, Prentice-Hall, 1974; (contributor) Walter Goldberg, editor, *Simulation Versus Analytical Solutions for Business and Economic Models*, Business Administration Studies, 1974; (contributor) Norbert Szyperski and Erwin Grochla, editors, *Information*

Systems and Organizational Structure, deGruyter, 1975; (contributor) M. D. Dunnette, editor, *Handbook of Industrial and Organizational Psychology*, Rand McNally, 1975.

Contributor to proceedings; contributor to psychological, sociological and business journals. Editor of *Administrative Science Quarterly*, 1968-71; member of editorial board of *Administrative Science Quarterly*, 1966-68, and *Journal of Applied Social Psychology*, 1970—.

WORK IN PROGRESS: Handbook of Organizational Design; research on designing self-designing organizations, and invention and diffusion of computer simulation.

* * *

STARK, Claude Alan 1935-
(Mwanga)

PERSONAL: Born April 27, 1935, in Paris, France; now U.S. citizen; son of Virgil (an engineer) and Judith (Rosenblat) Stark; married Alice May Seitzman (an editor), 1958; children: Victor Lowell, Veda Anne, Roland Bradley, Turiya Ndona. *Education:* Clark University, B.A., 1958; Babson College, M.B.A., 1961; Harvard Divinity School, B.D., 1971; Boston University, Ph.D., 1973. *Politics:* "Supporter of George Wallace." *Home:* 12 Quaker Lane, West Dennis, Mass. 02670. *Office:* Claude Stark & Co., 12 Quaker Lane, West Dennis, Mass. 02670.

CAREER: Ordained minister, 1971; National Shawmut Bank of Boston, Boston, Mass., security analyst, 1961-64; Fidelity Fund of Boston, Boston, Mass., senior security analyst, 1964-66; Export-Import Bank of the United States, Washington, D.C., loan officer, 1966-67; U.S. Senate, Washington, D.C., economic counsel to Select Committee on Small Business and to Sub-Committee on Financing and Investments, 1967; Sodesmir Development Co., Zaire, president and chairman of board, 1969—; Claude Stark & Co. (publishers), West Dennis, Cape Cod, Mass., president, 1974—. Chairman of board of Branden Press, 1973—; member of board of trustees of Institute for Experimental Psychiatry, 1964—; corporator of Cape Cod Conservatory of Music and Art, 1969—.

MEMBER: International Club, American Chamber of Commerce in France, Security Analyst Society, Bankers Club of America, Wallace Patriot's Club, Harvard Club, Downtown Club, Federal City Club. *Awards, honors:* Certificate of merit from U.S. Senate, 1967; appointed chief of Province of Congo Central, Zaire, 1968; designated lieutenant colonel of Alabama State Militia, 1971.

WRITINGS: God of All: Sri Ramakrishna's Approach to Religious Plurality, Claude Stark & Co., 1974; (editor with wife, Alice May Stark) Swami Akhilananda, *Spiritual Practices: Memorial Edition with Reminiscences by His Friends*, Claude Stark & Co., 1974. Contributor to *Journal of Religious Studies.*

WORK IN PROGRESS: Editing books; a sequel to *God of All* called *God in All.*

SIDELIGHTS: Claude Stark describes himself as a disciple of Swami Akhilananda (1894-1962) and of Mama Ndona Santu, of Zaire. "Knowing these two great souls," he writes, "and experiencing their intense love, has motivated and guided my life and activities."

* * *

STARKMAN, Moshe 1906-1975

September 25, 1906—February 2, 1975; American publicity

director, newspaper editor, and author and editor of books on Yiddish poetry and literature. *Obituaries: New York Times*, February 4, 1975.

* * *

STARLING, Thomas
   See HAYTON, Richard Neil

* * *

STATERA, Gianni 1943-

PERSONAL: Born November 27, 1943, in Rome, Italy; son of Vittorio (a journalist) and Vera (Vania) Statera; married Simonetta Lux (an assistant professor), June 30, 1968; children: Daniele. *Education:* University of Rome, Laurea in Filosofia, 1966, Libera Docenza in Sociology, 1971. *Home:* Via Bisagno 28, Rome, Italy, *Office:* Instituto Di Sociologia, Via Toriano 95, Rome, Italy.

CAREER: University of Rome, Rome, Italy, assistant professor of sociology, 1966-69; University of Siena, Siena, Italy, associate professor of sociology, 1970-71; University of Rome, professor of sociology and methodology of social research, 1970—. Visiting professor at University of Connecticut, 1969-70. Consultant to Ministry of Labor, 1966. *Member:* International Sociological Association, Italian Association of Social Sciences, Center for Communication Research, Italian Philosophical Society. *Awards, honors:* Premio Della Cultura (Italian Prize for Culture), 1971.

WRITINGS: Logica, Linguaggio e Sociologia: Studio su O. Neurath e il Neopositivismo (title means "Logic, Language and Sociology: A Study on O. Neurath and Logical Positivism"), Taylor, 1967; *La Conoscenza Sociologica: Aspetti e Problemi* (title means "Sociological Knowledge: Dimensions and Problems"), Carucci, 1968, revised edition, 1970; (editor) Otto Neurath, *Sociologia e Neopositivismo* (title means "Sociology and Neopositivism"), Ubaldini, 1968; (editor) Elihu Katz, and Paul Lazarsfeld, *L'Influenza Personale nelle Comunicazioni di Massa* (title means "Personal Influence: The Part Played by People"), Eri, 1968; (editor) Alfred McClung Lee, *L'Uomo Polivalente* (title means "Multivalent Man"), Utet, 1969; *Societa' e Comunicazioni di Massa* (title means "Society and Mass Communications"), Palumbo, 1972; *Storia di una Utopia: Ascesa e Declino dei Movimenti Studenteschi Europei*, Rizzoli, 1973, translation published as *Death of a Utopia: The Development and Decline of Student Movements in Europe*, Oxford University Press, 1974; *La Conoscenza Sociologica: Problemi e Metodo* (title means "Sociological Knowledge: Problems and Method"), Liguori, 1974; *Analisi Metodologica e Ricerca Sociale* (title means "Methodological Analysis and Social Research"), Elia, 1974. Contributor to sociology journals. Co-editor of *Problemi*, 1974—.

WORK IN PROGRESS: Research on unemployment of Italian graduates; research projects in the sociology of science.

* * *

STAUFFER, Donald Barlow 1930-

PERSONAL: Born September 22, 1930, in East Orange, N.J.; son of Fred B. (a reporter) and Elizabeth (Barlow) Stauffer; married Morag Kennedy (a mental health administrator), September 7, 1957; children: Andrew, Douglas, Margaret. *Education:* Wesleyan University, B.A., 1952; Indiana University, M.A., 1956, Ph.D., 1963. *Politics:*

Democrat. *Home:* 165 Main St., Altamont, N.Y. 12009. *Office:* Department of English, State University of New York, Albany, N.Y. 12222.

CAREER: Williams College, Williamstown, Mass., instructor in English, 1961-64; State University of New York at Albany, assistant professor, 1964-68, associate professor of English, 1968—. *Military service:* U.S. Army, 1953-55. *Member:* Modern Language Association of America, American Association of University Professors, Poe Society.

WRITINGS: (Contributor) Richard Veler, editor, *Papers on Poe*, Chantry Music Press, 1971; *A Short History of American Poetry*, Dutton, 1974. Contributor to *Studies in Short Fiction, Style, Emerson Society Quarterly*, and *Poe Studies*.

WORK IN PROGRESS: Research in contemporary American poetry and on Edgar Allan Poe.

* * *

STEAD, Christian Karlson 1932-

PERSONAL: Surname rhymes with "head"; born October 17, 1932, in Auckland, New Zealand; son of James Walter (an accountant) and Olive (a music teacher; maiden name, Karlson) Stead; married Kathleen Elizabeth Roberts, January 8, 1955; children: Oliver William, Charlotte Mary, Margaret Hermione. *Education:* University of Auckland, B.A., 1953, M.A., 1955; Bristol University, Ph.D., 1959. *Politics:* New Zealand Labour Party. *Religion:* None. *Home:* 37 Tohunga Cres., Auckland 1, New Zealand. *Office:* Department of English, Auckland University, Private Bag, Auckland, New Zealand.

CAREER: University of Auckland, Auckland, New Zealand, lecturer, 1959-61, senior lecturer, 1962-64, associate professor, 1964-68, professor of English, 1968—. Chairman of New Zealand Literary Fund Advisory Committee. *Awards, honors:* Katherine Mansfield Prize, 1960, for a short story; Nuffield travelling fellowship, 1965; Winn-Mansen Menton fellowship, 1972; Jessie McKay Award for Poetry, 1972.

WRITINGS: Whether the Will Is Free (poems), Blackwood, 1964; *The New Poetic: Yeats to Eliot*, Hutchinson, 1964, 2nd edition, 1975, Harper, 1966; (editor) *World's Classics: New Zealand Short Stories*, 2nd series, Stead not associated with earlier series, Oxford University Press, 1966, 3rd edition, 1975; *Smith's Dream* (novel), Longman Paul, 1971; (editor) *Measure for Measure: A Casebook*, Macmillan, 1971, revised edition, 1973; *Crossing the Bar* (poems), Oxford University Press, 1972; *Quesada: Poems 1972-74*, The Shed (Auckland), 1975.

WORK IN PROGRESS: A novel; collecting original short stories in a single volume; essays on New Zealand writers and writing.

BIOGRAPHICAL/CRITICAL SOURCES: Islands, summer, 1972.

* * *

STEINBERG, J(ay) Leonard 1930-

PERSONAL: Born January 20, 1930, in Rio de Janerio, Brazil; came to United States in 1941, naturalized citizen, 1951; son of Isaac Harry and Phyra (Gratz) Steinberg; married Helene Carol Lefkowitz, March 25, 1951; children: Leslie, Diane, Neal. *Education:* Adelphi University, B.A., 1950; Columbia University, M.A., 1951, Ed.D., 1956. *Poli-*

tics: Democrat. *Religion:* Hebrew. *Home:* 268 North Rexford Drive, Beverly Hills, Calif. 90210. *Office:* Division of Counseling and Guidance, California State University, Los Angeles, Calif. 90032.

CAREER: Morningside Mental Hygiene Clinic, New York, N.Y., psychologist, 1952-54; Hofstra University, Hempstead, N.Y., assistant professor of psychology, 1955-56, assistant dean of students, 1954-57; Pasadena Counseling Center, Pasadena, Calif., director, 1957-59; California State University at Los Angeles, assistant professor, 1960-64, associate professor and director of rehabiliation counseling program, 1965-69, professor of counseling, 1969—. Counsultant to Los Angeles Police Department, 1966—, and to Los Angeles schools and social agencies. Member of board of governors of University of Judaism, Los Angeles. Vice-President, Anti Defamation League. *Member:* American Psychology Association; American Association of University Professors, American Personnel and Guidance Association, Los Angeles Personnel and Guidance Association (president, 1968), Phi Delta Kappa, Kappa Delta Pi. *Awards, honors:* Brotherhood Award from National Conference of Christians and Jews, 1973.

WRITINGS: Guide to Careers through the College Curriculum, Robert R. Knapp, 1964; (with Martin Reiser) *A Human Relations Handbook for Police Officers*, C. E. Merrill, 1969; (with Donald W. McEvoy) *The Police and the Behavioral Sciences*, C. C Thomas, 1974; (editor) *The Counselor as an Applied Behavioral Scientist*, MSS Information, 1974. Contributor to books of readings, and to educational journals.

WORK IN PROGRESS: The Counselor as a Psychological Educator; The School Intergroup Relations Specialist.

SIDELIGHTS: Steinberg told *CA:* "Having been born in Brazil, I retain a fluent knowledge of Portuguese and a strong interest in the development of education in that country."

* * *

STEINHART, Carol E(lder) 1935-

PERSONAL: Born March 27, 1935, in Cleveland, Ohio; daughter of Clayton Thomas (an electrical engineer) and Carolyn (Kalkbrenner) Elder; married John S. Steinhart (a physician), December 20, 1958 (separated); children: Gail, Martha, Geoffrey. *Education:* Albion College, A.B. (summa cum laude), 1956; University of Wisconsin, Madison, Ph.D., 1960. *Home:* 104 Lathrop St., Madison, Wis. 53705.

CAREER: National Institute of Mental Health, Bethesda, Md., biologist in Laboratory of General and Comparative Biochemistry, 1961-66, science analyst, 1966-67, and biologist, 1967-70, both in Division of Research Grants, Office for Research Analysis and Evaluation; free-lance science writer and editor in Madison, Wis., 1970—. *Member:* International Society of Plant Morphologists, Botanical Society of America, American Society of Plant Physiologists, American Institute of Biological Sciences, Defenders of Wildlife, Medical Committee for Human Rights, Amateur Chamber Music Players, New York Academy of Sciences, Gordon Setter Club of America, Phi Beta Kappa, Beta Beta Beta, Sigma Xi, Sigma Delta Epsilon.

WRITINGS: (With John S. Steinhart) *A Case Study of the Santa Barbara Oil Spill*, Duxbury Press, 1972; (with Steinhart) *Energy: Sources, Use, and Role in Human Affairs*, Duxbury Press, 1974; (with Steinhart) *The Fires of Cul-*

ture: Energy Yesterday and Tomorrow, Duxbury Press, 1974; (editor and contributor) *Human Ecology*, Duxbury Press, 1975. Contributor to journals in her field.

WORK IN PROGRESS: Two college textbooks, with Donald Job and Kenneth Martlage, *Human Biology*, for Duxbury Press, and *Man's Kinship in Nature*, for W. C. Brown.

AVOCATIONAL INTERESTS: Biking, hiking, playing string quartets, raising dachshunds.

* * *

STELL, Aaron 1911-

PERSONAL: Born March 26, 1911, in Philadelphia, Pa.; son of David (a dress designer) and Diana (an actress) Stell; married second wife, Louise Kellerman, May 27, 1949; children: (first marriage) Linda Stell Taylor; (second marriage) Michael Bender (stepson). *Education:* Attended Otis Art School and Southwestern University. *Home:* 10322 Lorenzo Dr., Los Angeles, Calif. 90064. *Agent:* Ann Elmo Agency, Inc., 52 Vanderbilt Ave., New York, N.Y. 10017.

CAREER: Since childhood, has been employed in motion picture industry, at various times by M.G.M., Twentieth Century Fox, and Columbia Pictures, in earlier years as a child-extra, office messenger, mail boy, laborer, member of prop department, and story reader; later employed in film editorial department, rising from assistant editor, trailer editor, and short editor, to become feature film editor, 1942—. *Member:* American Cinema Editors, Los Angeles Art Association. *Awards, honors:* Honorable mention from American Cinema Editors, 1962, for editing "To Kill a Mockingbird."

WRITINGS: Angel of Satan (suspense novel), Pinnacle, 1974. Editor of *American Cinema Editors Quarterly*, 1954-61.

WORK IN PROGRESS: Riverman, a novel; *Leaves in My Hand*, a novel; "Little Boy Little Burro," a screenplay; "You Gotta Have a Little Luck," a screenplay.

SIDELIGHTS: Stell has edited feature films for the industry's leading directors. His credits include "To Kill a Mockingbird," "Love with a Proper Stranger," "Daisy Clover," "Silent Running," and "Lepke."

Stell is also an artist whose paintings, sculptures in clay and bronze, etchings, silk screens, and lithographs are in several private collections. His sculpture of Martin Luther King, Jr. is at the King Foundation in Georgia.

* * *

STENZEL, Anne K(atherine) 1911-

PERSONAL: Born April 19, 1911, in Breslau, Germany; daughter of Julius (a professor) and Bertha (Mugdan) Stenzel. *Education:* Paedegogische Akademie Altona, Diploma, 1932; Bryn Mawr College, M.A., 1938; graduate study at New York School of Social Work, New School for Social Research, University of Southern California, and University of California, Los Angeles, at various times, 1945-55; University of California, Berkeley, Ph.D., 1963. *Home:* 1500 Oakland Rd. N.E., 303, Cedar Rapids, Iowa 52402. *Office:* Department of Social Work, Mount Mercy College, Cedar Rapids, Iowa 52402.

CAREER: Girl Scout Council, district and camp director in Cleveland, Ohio, 1938-43, executive director in Racine, Wis., 1943-45, and in Richmond, Calif., 1946-50; group worker in settlements in New York, N.Y., 1945-46; Girl Scouts of the United States of America, New York, N.Y., field and training advisor, Pacific Region and National Headquarters, 1950-57; South East Bay Area Girl Scout Council, San Lorenzo, Calif., assistant director and training director, 1958-62; National League for Nursing, San Francisco, Calif., assistant director of Western Office, 1962-64; Young Women's Christian Association (YWCA), New York, N.Y., director of volunteer leadership, 1964-66; Girl Scout Council of Bergen County, Paramus, N.J., director of volunteer personnel and training, 1966-70; Mount Mercy College, Cedar Rapids, Iowa, associate professor of social work, 1970—, head of department, 1970—. Group work consultant in leadership training in Germany for National Social Welfare Assembly and U.S. Department of State, 1951-52; member of the board of directors of Voluntary Action Center, Linn County, 1972-74; member of citizen's advisory committee to Linn County Department of Social Service, 1972—.

MEMBER: National Association of Social Workers (charter member), Academy of Certified Social Workers, American Association of University Professors, Adult Education Association of the U.S.A. *Awards, honors:* Travel grant from the German Federal Republic, 1966.

WRITINGS: (With others) *Volunteer Training and Development: A Manual for Community Groups*, Seabury, 1968; (with others) *Learning by the Case Method*, Seabury, 1970; *Social Training*, Haus Schwalbach, 1972. Contributor to *Adult Leadership* and *Nursing Outlook*.

WORK IN PROGRESS: A revised edition of *Volunteer Training and Development*.

* * *

STEPHENS, Michael D(awson) 1936-

PERSONAL: Born September 24, 1936, in Truro, England; son of Nicholas (a civil servant) and Margaret (Knight) Stephens; married Margaret Heap (a school teacher), September 2, 1961; children: Caroline Susan, David Trethowan, Helen Fiona. *Education:* University of Hull, B.A., 1960; Johns Hopkins University, M.A., 1962; University of Edinburgh, Ph.D., 1965; University of Leicester, M.Ed., 1969. *Home:* 17 Somersby Rd., Mapperley, Nottingham NG3 5QB, England. *Office:* Department of Adult Education, University of Nottingham, Nottingham NG7 2RD, England.

CAREER: University of Liverpool, Liverpool, England, lecturer in education, 1964-69, assistant director of Institute of Extension Studies, 1969-74; University of Nottingham, Nottingham, England, Robert Peers Professor of Education, 1974—. *Military service:* British Army, Light Infantry, 1955-57. *Member:* Royal Geographical Society (fellow).

WRITINGS: (Editor with G. W. Roderick) *Teaching Techniques in Adult Education*, David & Charles, 1971; (with Roderick) *Scientific and Technical Education in Nineteenth-Century England*, David & Charles, 1973; (editor with Roderick) *Universities for a Changing World*, David & Charles, 1975. Editor of "World Education Series," David & Charles, 1972—.

WORK IN PROGRESS: *Nineteenth-Century Scientific and Technical Education; The Regional Commitment of Universities; Dissenting Academies.*

STEPHENS, William M(cLain) 1925-

PERSONAL: Born May 11, 1925, in Chattanooga, Tenn.; son of W. M. and Lela (Brown) Stephens; married Margaret McCurdy, January 5, 1945; children: Don C., Julia Stephens Gustafson, Roger, Melani. *Education:* University of Tennessee, J.D., 1950; University of Miami, Coral Gables, LL.M., 1974. *Religion:* "Loving the one God who is behind *all* religions." *Home:* 1280 Carriage House Lane, Gastonia, N.C. 28052. *Office:* Department of Police Science, Gaston College, Dallas, N.C. 28034.

CAREER: Attorney at law in Chattanooga, Tenn., 1950-53; *Florida Outdoors* (magazine), Sun City and Fort Myers, Fla., editor, 1954-59; *Underwater* (magazine), Homestead, Fla., editor, 1960-62; free-lance writer and photographer, 1962-63; University of Miami, Institute of Marine Science, Coral Gables, Fla., science writer and editor, 1963-66; *Oceanology International* (magazine), Beverly Shores, Ind., editor, 1966-68; Miami Seaquarium, Miami, Fla., director of education, 1968-70; University of Miami, associate director of publications, 1971-74; Gaston College, Dallas, N.C., professor of police science, 1974—. Chairman of Committee on Prison Reform of Concerned Citizens for Justice. *Military service:* U.S. Marine Corps, 1942-45.

MEMBER: International Oceanographic Foundation, American Museum of Natural History, Friends of the Earth, Audubon Society, Smithsonian Institution.

WRITINGS: *Our World Underwater*, Lantern Press, 1962; *Science Beneath the Sea*, Putnam, 1966; *Southern Seashores*, Holiday House, 1968.

For children: *Life in the Open Sea*, McGraw, 1971; *Come with Me to the Edge of the Sea*, Messner, 1972; *A Day in the Life of a Sandy Beach*, McGraw, 1973; *Islands*, Holiday House, 1974; *Life in a Tidepool*, McGraw, 1975.

Children's books, with wife, Peggy Stephens—All published by Holiday House: *Octopus*, 1968; *Sea Horse*, 1969; *Hermit Crab*, 1970; *Sea Turtle*, 1971; *Killer Whale*, 1972; *Flamingo*, 1972.

WORK IN PROGRESS: A novel about a spiritual search in India; a non-fiction book on mysticism.

SIDELIGHTS: Stephens writes: "The Major motivating influence on my life has been the teaching and guidance of a great spiritual master of India, Avatar Meher Baba (1894-1969). Everything else has been secondary."

* * *

STERN, Donald A. 1928(?)-1975

1928(?)—June 20, 1975; American tournament director, and author and editor of books on backgammon and bridge. Obituaries: *New York Times*, June 21, 1975.

* * *

STERN, Edith Mendel 1901-1975

June 24, 1901—February 8, 1975; American editor, lecturer, and author of books on mental health subjects. Obituaries: *Washington Post*, February 13, 1975; *AB Bookman's Weekly*, March 17, 1975.

* * *

STEVENSON, David Lloyd 1910-1975

June 10, 1910—April 28, 1975; American educator, scholar, reviewer, editor, and author of books on Shakespeare. Obituaries: *New York Times*, April 29, 1975. (CA-23/24)

STEVENSON, Vera Kemp 1920-

PERSONAL: Born January 23, 1920, in Flushing, N.Y.; daughter of Archie Reed (a research chemist) and Ruby (Stokesbary) Kemp; married Robert Presley Stevenson, March 15, 1947; children: John Kemp, Peter Day. *Education:* Pennsylvania State University, B.A., 1941; Rutgers University, M.Ed., 1968. *Politics:* Republican. *Religion:* Episcopalian. *Home and office:* 1854 House, Mountainville, Lebanon, N.J. 08833.

CAREER: Secretary, office manager, and personnel executive in business companies, New York, N.Y., 1941-51; teacher in New Jersey public schools, 1962-72; free-lance writer, 1972—. *Member:* Kappa Delta Pi.

WRITINGS: The Illustrated Almanac for Homemakers, Grosset, 1974. Contributor of articles on homemaking to magazines.

WORK IN PROGRESS: Homemaking–Gardening, completion expected in 1977; a mystery novel, completion expected in 1978.

AVOCATIONAL INTERESTS: Flower and vegetable gardening, needlework, furniture refinishing.

*   *   *

STILES, Merritt N. 1899-1975

1899—June 30, 1975; American doctor of medicine, advocate of skiing for the elderly, and author of book on skiing. Obituaries: *New York Times,* July 1, 1975.

*   *   *

STILLMAN, Frances (Jennings) 1910-1975

January 22, 1910—February 3, 1975; American educator, translator of poetry, and author of books of literature. Obituaries: *New York Times,* February 5, 1975. (*CA*-15/16)

*   *   *

STINE, Whitney Ward 1930-
  (Garen McLeish, Jonathon Ward)

PERSONAL: Born March 26, 1930, in Garber, Okla.; son of Raymond Daniel and Hazel (Dell) Whitney. *Education:* Attended Hollywood Professional School, 1946; privately tutored, 1948-49. *Politics:* Republican. *Religion:* Christian Church. *Residence:* North Hollywood, Calif. *Agent:* Reece Halsey Agency, 8733 Sunset Blvd., Hollywood, Calif. 90069; Scott Meredith Agency, 845 Third Ave., New York, N. Y. 10022.

CAREER: Whitney Stine Advertising Agency, Glendale, Calif., proprietor, 1966—. Executive director, Theatre Equipment Dealers Association, 1966-71, and Theatre Equipment Association, 1971-74. *Military service:* U.S. Army, Engineers, 1947-48; became technical sergeant. *Member:* Society of Motion Picture and Television Engineers, Cinemateque de Francaise, Variety Club of Southern California.

WRITINGS: (Contributor) Raymond Friday Locke, editor, *The Human Side of History* (anthology), Hawthorn, 1971; (with commentary by Bette Davis) *Mother Goddam: The Story of the Career of Bette Davis,* Hawthorn, 1974.

Screenplays: "Im Chinarra Yaruh, "produced by Ethnic Dance Films, 1958; "The Evolution of a Theatre," produced by Filbert Co., 1967; "Little Girl with Red Kimono," produced by Ethnic Dance Films, 1970; "Father Kezios," produced by Spero L. Kontos, 1971.

Plays: "The Heretic," produced in Los Angeles by Originals only, 1960.

Also author of novels; under pseudonym Garen McLeish: *Bed and Board,* 1961; under pseudonym Jonathon Ward: *Fury,* 1958, *Love Under Glass,* 1959, and *Cruise for Love,* 1960.

Ghost writer of some thirty books for other writers and Hollywood personalities. Contributor to professional journals and magazines, including *Mankind, Adam, Boxoffice, Film Daily,* and *Knight.* Editor, *Report to Exhibitors* (annual), 1966-73.

*   *   *

STOKES, Daniel M. J. 1950-

PERSONAL: Born December 27, 1950, in Brooklyn, N.Y.; son of Ervin William and Elizabeth (Ray) Stokes. *Politics:* "Poetry." *Religion:* "Poetry." *Home:* 1807 60th St., Brooklyn, N.Y. 11204.

CAREER: Sto-La Gifts, Brooklyn, N.Y., co-owner, 1972-74; *The New York Culture Review,* Brooklyn, editor, 1974—. Has worked as assembler for Rheems Manufacturing Co. (electronics), as commercial fisherman, and as hotel night clerk. *Military service:* U.S. Navy, 1969-71. *Member:* Committee of Small Magazine Editors and Publishers.

WRITINGS: Wired/LSD, New York Culture Review Press, 1974; *The World and Other Places,* [Cambridge, Mass.], 1975. Contributor to magazines, including *Aim, The Lunatic Fringe, Suntemples,* and *Talisman.* Editor of *East River Poetry Pamphlet.*

WORK IN PROGRESS: A book of poetry, *A Water-Face of Death: Selected Works, 1968-74;* a science fiction novel, *Tapa;* "Rotor," a science fiction play.

*   *   *

STONE, Harris B. 1934-

PERSONAL: Born January 18, 1934, in New Haven, Conn.; son of Herman (a lumber company executive) and Stella (Botwinik) Stone; married Joan Phillips (a dancer), 1963. *Education:* Brown University, B.A., 1955; Harvard University, M.Arch., 1959. *Home and office:* 79 Davis, New Haven, Conn.

CAREER: Employed by architectural firms in San Francisco, Calif., and New York, N.Y., 1959-64, and New Haven Redevelopment Agency, New Haven, Conn., 1964-66; self-employed advocate architect and city planner, New Haven, 1966—.

WRITINGS: Workbook of an Unsuccessful Architect (self-illustrated, with handwritten text), Monthly Review Press, 1974.

WORK IN PROGRESS: The Last Building and Other Essays, for Monthly Review Press.

*   *   *

STONE, Thomas H.
  See HARKNETT, Terry

*   *   *

STORER, Doug(las) 1899-

PERSONAL: Born February 23, 1899, in New York, N.Y.; son of John Hudson (a physician) and Catherine (Person) Storer; married Hazel Anderson (a writer-editor),

March 20, 1943. *Education:* Dartmouth College, B.S., 1921. *Home and office:* Amazing But True Inc., 501 Althea Rd., Belleair Estates, Clearwater, Fla. 33516.

CAREER: Began career in advertising in New York, N.Y., 1921; became radio manager and representative for show business personalities, including Perry Como, Bing Crosby, Frank Sinatra, and Jackie Gleason; Ripley's Believe It or Not, New York, N.Y., manager, 1931-49, owner and president, 1949-60; Amazing But True Inc., Clearwater, Fla., owner and president, 1960—. *Member:* Explorers Club, Overseas Press Club, Dartmouth Club, Deke Club.

WRITINGS: Amazing But True Photographs & Stories, Pocket Books, 1960; *Amazing But True Animals*, Fawcett, 1963; *The Most Amazing But True*, Fawcett, 1966; *Stories About the Stamp*, H. Harris, 1968; *Amazing But True People, Places, Things*, Pocket Books, 1973; *Amazing But True Presidents*, Pocket Books, 1975; *Amazing But True Royalty*, Pocket Books, in press; *Amazing But True Mysteries*, Pocket Books, in press. Contributor to newspapers and magazines.

WORK IN PROGRESS: Four books; a radio and television series.

SIDELIGHTS: Storer has designed postage stamps for the governments of Haiti, Colombia, and Turkey.

BIOGRAPHICAL/CRITICAL SOURCES: Floridian (of *St. Petersburg Times*), April 21, 1974.

*   *   *

STOY, R(ichard) H(ugh)   1910-

PERSONAL: Born January 31, 1910, in Wolverhampton, England; son of Hugh Victor Stephen (a company secretary) and Ellen Frances (Channing) Stoy; married Mary Brown Johnston, June 22, 1940; children: Frances Anne, Robert Adrian, Georgina Violet (Mrs. Vincent Guille). *Education:* Gonville and Caius College, Cambridge, B.A., 1931, M.A., 1935, Ph.D., 1935; further study at Lick Observatory of University of California, 1933-35. *Politics:* Liberal. *Religion:* Unitarian Universalist. *Home:* 128 Grange Loan, Edinburgh EH9 2EF, Scotland.

CAREER: Royal Observatory, Cape of Good Hope, South Africa, astronomer, 1935-68; and University of Capetown, Cape Town, South Africa, professor of astronomy, 1958-68; Royal Observatory, Edinburgh, Scotland, astronomer, 1968-75. *Military service:* South African Coastal Defence Force, 1940-43. *Member:* International Astronomical Union (vice-president, 1958-64), Astronomical Society of Southern Africa (president, 1945-46), Royal Society of South Africa (fellow), Royal Astronomical Society of London, Royal Society of Edinburgh (fellow). *Awards, honors:* Commander of the Order of the British Empire, 1957; Gill Medal from Astronomical Society of Southern Africa, 1965.

WRITINGS: (Editor) *Everyman's Astronomy*, St. Martin's, 1975. Contributor to journals in his field.

WORK IN PROGRESS: General astronomical research.

*   *   *

STRANKAY, Sam J.   1905-

PERSONAL: Born April 16, 1905, in Neche, N.D.; son of Julius (a symphony clarinetist) and Louise (Heinz) Strankay; married Myrtle Marie Beaty, December 31, 1941 (died, 1967). *Education:* Attended elementary school in Waldeck, Saskatchewan, Canada. *Politics:* Republican. *Religion:* Episcopalian. *Home:* 2477 West Lincoln, #79, Anaheim, Calif. 92801.

CAREER: Cowherder and farmer until 1930; Kays Beauty Shop, Chicago, Ill., owner, 1930-41; Sam J. Strankay (jeweler), Chicago, Ill., owner, 1944-50; Strankay Jewelers, Bell Gardens, Calif., owner, 1950-59; North American Aviation, Anaheim, Calif., senior technician in inertial navigation, 1959-70; Roberly Jewelers, Anaheim, Calif., diamond consultant, 1970—. Consultant to Hallocks Coins. *Military service:* U.S. Army, General Hospital, 1942-43. *Member:* American Legion (senior vice president, 1934-55; adjutant, 1958-59), Disabled American Veterans (past commander), National Order of Trenchrats, Masons, Eastern Star.

WRITINGS: Selected Poems, privately printed, 1971; *Through a Window in My Garden I Look Far Across a Restless Sea* (poems), Pageant, 1975. Work is represented in *Crown Anthology of Verse*, edited by Edward Uhlan, Carlton, 1938. Editor of *Illinois Watchmaker's Loupe*, 1945-50.

WORK IN PROGRESS: A book of party jokes.

SIDELIGHTS: Strankay was orphaned at an early age. He was forced to find work in farming, commercial fishing, and cowherding until he became a hairstylist in Chicago. *Avocational interests:* Painting portraits and landscapes (has sold more than two hundred items under pseudonym, Stan Kay), collecting coins and stamps.

*   *   *

STRAUS, Robert   1923-

PERSONAL: Born January 9, 1923, in New Haven, Conn.; son of Samuel Hirsh (a teacher) and Alma (Fleischner) Straus; married Ruth Elisabeth Dawson (a teacher), September 8, 1945; children: Robert James, Carol Martin, Margaret Dawson (Mrs. Michael Binion), John William. *Education:* Yale University, B.A., 1943, M.A., 1945, Ph.D., 1947. *Religion:* Unitarian Universalist. *Home:* 511 Ridge Rd., Lexington, Ky. 40503. *Office:* Department of Behavioral Science, College of Medicine, University of Kentucky, Lexington, Ky. 40506.

CAREER: Yale University, New Haven, Conn., staff member, Center of Alcohol Studies, 1945-53, instructor in applied physiology, 1947-48, assistant professor, 1948-51, research associate, 1951-53; State University of New York Upstate Medical Center at Syracuse, assistant professor, 1953-55, associate professor of public health and preventive medicine, 1956; University of Kentucky College of Medicine, Lexington, professor of medical sociology, 1956—, chairman of department of behavioral science, 1959—. Visiting fellow in sociology, Yale University, 1968-69. Staff director of Connecticut Governor's Commission on Health Resources, 1950-51; chairman of Cooperative (United States and Canada) Commission on the Study of Alcoholism, 1961-63, and of National Advisory Committee on Alcoholism, 1966-69. Consultant to National Institute of Mental Health, 1959-70, and to Addiction Research Center, National Institute on Drug Abuse, 1974—. *Military service:* U.S. Army, 1943-44.

MEMBER: American Sociological Association (chairman of section on medical sociology, 1967-68), American Public Health Association (fellow), Association of American Medical Colleges, Society for the Study of Social Problems, Society for Applied Anthropology, Society for Health and Human Values, Association for the Behavioral Sciences and Medical Education (president, 1974), Alcohol and Drug Problems Association of North America, Eastern Sociological Society, Southern Sociological Society, Phi Beta Kappa. *Awards, honors:* Scientific Achievement Award, Kentucky Medical Association, 1966; National Institute of Mental Health research fellow at Yale University, 1968-69.

WRITINGS: Medical Care for Seamen: The Development of Public Health Services in the United States, Yale University Press, 1950; (with Selden D. Bacon) *Alcoholism and Social Stability*, Hillhouse Press (New Haven), 1951; (with Bacon) *Drinking in College*, Yale University Press, 1953, reprinted, Greenwood Press, 1971; *Alcohol and Society* (monograph first published as entire issue of *Psychiatric Annals*, October, 1973), Insight Publishing, 1973; *Escape from Custody: A Study of Alcoholism and of Institutional Dependency as Reflected in the Life Record of a Homeless Man*, Harper, 1974.

Contributor: A. M. Rose, editor, *Mental Health and Mental Disorder*, Norton, 1955; Raymond G. McCarthy, editor, *Drinking and Intoxication*, Yale Center of Alcohol Studies and Free Press, 1959; David J. Pittman and Charles R. Snyder, editors, *Society, Culture and Drinking Patterns*, Wiley, 1962; S. P. Lucia, editor, *Alcohol and Civilization*, McGraw, 1963; M. T. Sussman, editor, *Sociology and Rehabilitation*, American Sociological Association, 1965; Robert K. Merton and Robert A. Nisbet, editors, *Contemporary Social Problems*, 2nd edition (Straus did not contribute to earlier edition), Harcourt, 1966, 3rd edition, 1971; Thomas Weaver and Alvin Magid, editors, *Poverty: New Interdisciplinary Perspectives*, Chandler Publishing, 1969; George L. Maddox, editor, *The Domesticated Drug: Drinking Among Collegians*, College & University Press, 1970; Basil Georgopoulos, editor, *Organization Research on Health Institutions*, Institute for Social Research, University of Michigan, 1972; Karl Schuessler and others, editors, *Social Policy and Sociology*, Academic Press, 1975; W. J. Filstead and others editors, *Alcohol and Alcohol Problems: New Thinking and New Directions*, Ballinger Publishing, in press.

Author or co-author of reports and special studies on public health, alcoholism, and medical education. Contributor of more than fifty articles to annals, yearbooks, and journals. Editor with John A. Clausen, *Medicine and Society*, Annals of the American Academy of Political and Social Science, March, 1963. Associate editor, *Quarterly Journal of Studies on Alcohol*, 1951—, and *Journal of Health and Human Behavior*, 1959-66; member of editorial board, University Press of Kentucky, 1968-72, and *Drugs in Health Care*, 1974—; member of advisory board, *Research Advances in Alcohol and Drug Problems*, 1971—.

* * *

STRUK, Danylo 1940-

PERSONAL: Born April 5, 1940, in Lviv, Ukraine; son of Ostap and Daria (Bukachewska) Struk; married Roma Stefaniw, June 13, 1964 (separated, 1973); children: Boryslava, Ostap, Luka. *Education:* Harvard University, B.A., 1963; University of Alberta, M.A., 1964; University of Toronto, Ph.D., 1970. *Home:* 483 Runnymede Rd., Toronto, Ontario, Canada. *Office:* Slavic Department, University of Toronto, Ontario, Canada.

CAREER: University of Alberta, Edmonton, lecturer, 1964-65; University of Toronto, Toronto, Ontario, assistant professor of Ukrainian, 1967—. President of Knyho-Kliub Books, Inc. *Member:* Canadian Association of Slavists,

American Association for the Advancement of Slavic Studies, American Association of Teachers of Slavic and East European Languages. *Awards, honors:* Woodrow Wilson fellowship, 1963.

WRITINGS: Gamma Sigma (poems), R. Klymasz, 1963; *A Study of Vasyl Stefanyk*, Ukrainian Academic Press, 1973.

WORK IN PROGRESS: Editing a five volume edition of *The Work of Mykola Khvylovy.*

SIDELIGHTS: Struk speaks fluent Russian as well as Ukrainian and reads German, French, and Polish. *Avocational interests:* Theatre and travel.

* * *

STUART, Ian
See MACLEAN, Alistair (Stuart)

* * *

SUKHWAL, Bheru Lal 1929-

PERSONAL: Born June 18, 1929, in Palana Kalan, Udaipur, India; son of Bhuri Lal and Narayani (Bai) Sukhwal; married Lilawati Sharma (a teacher), March 10, 1955; children: Aditya (son), Archan (daughter). *Education:* Agra University, B.A., 1957; University of Rajasthan, B.Ed., 1958, M.A., 1960; University of Oregon, M.A., 1966; University of Oklahoma, Ph.D., 1969. *Home:* 630 West Madison St., Platteville, Wis. 53818. *Office:* Department of Geography, University of Wisconsin, Platteville, Wis. 53818.

CAREER: High school teacher of geography in Saradhna, India, 1954-60, and in Rajasthan, India, 1960-64; University of Oregon, Eugene, map librarian, 1964-66; University of Oklahoma, Norman, map librarian, 1966-69; University of Wisconsin, Platteville, assistant professor, 1969-74, associate professor of geography, 1974—. Representative from State of Ajmer at All India Basic Education Conference, summer, 1956; secretary of Rajasthan District Tournament, 1961.

MEMBER: International Geographic Union, Geographical Society of India (life member), Association of Geography Teachers of India (life member), Association of American Geographers, American Geographic Society (life member), National Council of Geographic Education, Wisconsin Council of Geographic Education, Gamma Theta Upsilon. *Awards, honors:* University of Wisconsin, Platteville, faculty research grant, 1971, to conduct research in India.

WRITINGS: India: A Political Geography, Allied Publishers, 1971; *A Systematic Geographic Bibliography on Bangla Desh* (monograph), Council of Planning Libraries, 1973; *Theses and Dissertations in Geography on South Asia* (monograph), Council of Planning Libraries, 1973; *South Asia: A Systematic Geographic Bibliography*, Scarecrow, 1974. Contributor to journals.

WORK IN PROGRESS: Geo-Political Developments in South Asia Since World War II; research on changing world political patterns, on electoral geography, and on South Asian political geography.

SIDELIGHTS: Sukhwal is competent in Gujarati, Punjabi, and Rajasthani, as well as Hindi and English. *Avocational interests:* Travel.

* * *

SULLIVAN, Francis (Patrick) 1929-

PERSONAL: Born August 29, 1929, in Boston, Mass.; son

of Jeremiah Patrick and Margaret (Spillane) Sullivan. *Education:* Boston College, A.B., 1954, M.A., 1955; studied theology at Weston College, and in Belgium, 1958-66; L'Institut Catholique de Paris, S.T.D., 1970. *Office:* Jesuit School of Theology, 1735 Le Roy Ave., Berkeley, Calif. 94709.

CAREER: Entered Society of Jesus (Jesuits), 1948, ordained Roman Catholic priest, 1961; high school teacher of Latin and English in Portland, Maine, 1955-58; high school teacher of history in Concord, Mass., 1966-70; Loyola University, New Orleans, La., assistant professor, 1970-74, associate professor of religious studies, 1974—. *Member:* American Academy of Religion, Jesuit Institute for the Arts (writer-in-residence, 1971-76).

WRITINGS: Table Talk with the Recent God, Paulist/Newman, 1974. Contributor to theology journals. *New Orleans Review,* poetry editor, 1971-75, poetry reviewer, 1972-75.

WORK IN PROGRESS: Ode to San Francisco, forty poems with forty paintings by Andre Bouler; an extended poem on the life of the Spirit in man; "Oratorio for an Apocalypse," with music by Esther Olin.

SIDELIGHTS: Sullivan told *CA:* "I teach courses on imagination and religious understanding. I am also a student of religious mysticism. My work is an enquiry into the means of relationships in various religions, particularly Western Christianity. I study icons. My next work will be to construct a poetic icon. It derives from my interest in religious relationships."

* * *

SULLIVAN, Ruth Christ 1924-

PERSONAL: Maiden name is pronounced Crist; born April 20, 1924, in Port Arthur, Tex.; daughter of Lawrence A. (a farmer and carpenter) and Ada (Matt) Christ; married William P. Sullivan (a college English professor), December 27, 1952; children: Julie, Christopher, Eva, Lawrence, Joseph, Lydia, Richard. *Education:* Charity Hospital School of Nursing, R.N. (with honors), 1945; Columbia University, B.S., 1951, M.A., 1952. *Religion:* Roman Catholic. *Home:* 101 Richmond St., Huntington, W.Va., 25702. *Office:* National Society for Autistic Children, 306 31st St., Huntington, W.Va. 25702.

CAREER: Industrial nurse, camp nurse, emergency and obstetrics room supervisor, public health nurse, and member of Red Cross Aquatic School faculty in Louisiana, 1947-50; Community Service Society, New York, N.Y., public health nurse, 1953; National Society for Autistic Children, Huntington, W.Va., founding member, representative for northeastern United States, 1965, president, 1968-69, 1969-70, director of National Information and Referral Service, 1970—, honorary member of the board, 1974—. Conducts workshops on autism; co-founder of New York State Society for Autistic Children, 1966, state legislative chairman, 1966-68; member of New York State's Joint Legislative Committee on Mental and Physical Handicaps, 1967; vice-president of state board of West Virginia Association for Mental Health, 1970; chairman of Childhood Mental Illness Committee of West Virginia Association for Mental Health, 1971; member of board of directors of Gannett News Service's Lend-A-Hand, 1974—. Lecturer at University of Missouri, School of Nursing, 1953, College of Saint Rose, 1965-68, Albany Medical Center, Union College, 1967, Marshall University, 1968-75, Ohio State University, 1970-75, Ohio University, 1970, 1974, West Vir-

ginia University, 1970, St. Mary's School of Nursing, 1970—, King's Daughters School of Nursing, 1970-75, Huntington State Hospital, 1970-75, and University of California, Los Angeles, 1973, 1975. *Military service:* U.S. Army Nurse Corps, 1945-47; became first lieutenant.

MEMBER: Delta Kappa Gamma (honorary member). *Awards, honors:* Major Armstrong Award from Armstrong Memorial Research Foundation of Columbia University, 1969, and medical journalism award from American Medical Association, 1970, for WOR New York City radio program on autism; four research grants from Department of Health, Education, and Welfare, Office of Child Development, 1972-75; Special Service Award from National Society for Autistic Children, 1974.

WRITINGS: U.S. Facilities and Programs for Children with Severe Mental Illnesses: A Directory, National Institute of Mental Health, 1974; (contributor) Edward R. Ritvo, editor, *Autism: Diagnosis, Management and Current Research,* Spectrum, in press. Contributor of articles and book reviews to journals in her field, including *Journal of Autism and Childhood Schizophrenia.*

* * *

SUMNER, David (W. K.) 1937-
(Bill Kaiser)

PERSONAL: Born April 17, 1937, in Concord, N.H.; son of William Hobart (an executive) and Jeanette (Swenson) Sumner; married wife, Judith Ann, June 29, 1969; children: Jason Omar, Margaret Anna. *Education:* Yale University, B.A., 1959; Episcopal Theological Seminary, Cambridge, Mass., graduate study, 1961-63; University of Michigan, M.A., 1966. *Politics:* "Situational." *Religion:* "Void." *Home and office address:* P.O. Box 7405, Denver, Colo. 80207.

CAREER: University of Denver, Denver, Colo., instructor in English, 1966-69; *Colorado Magazine,* Denver, Colo., executive editor, 1969-75; free-lance writer, 1975—; photographer. Member-at-large of board of directors, Colorado Open Space Council, 1973—. *Member:* National Audubon Society, Wilderness Society, Sierra Club.

WRITINGS: The Regnery Guide to Ski Touring, Regnery, 1974; *Rocky Mountains,* Graphic Arts Center (Portland, Ore.), 1975. Contributor of articles to *Living Magazine, Sierra Club Bulletin, Backpacker, High Country Living,* and *Colorado Magazine* (under pseudonym Bill Kaiser).

WORK IN PROGRESS: Four books under contract.

* * *

SUN, Ruth Q(uinlan) 1907-

PERSONAL: Born May 16, 1907, in Elmira, N.Y.; daughter of Daniel (an actor) and Margaret Ellen (Doherty) Quinlan; married Norman Sun (a professor of economics), October 30, 1947. *Education:* Elmira College, B.A., 1926; Northwestern University, M.S. (journalism), 1945; University of Southern California, M.A. (Asian studies), 1947; further graduate study at Harvard University, 1950, University of Missouri, 1951-53, and other institutions. *Politics:* Independent. *Home:* 1052 Ollerton Rd., Sherwood Green, Woodbury, N.J. 08096. *Office:* Temple University Press, 617 Carnell Hall, Philadelphia, Pa. 19122.

CAREER: Gannett Newspapers, Elmira, N.Y., reporter, editor, and feature writer, 1936-40; KMBC-Radio, Kansas City, Mo., assistant to director of publicity and promotion,

1947-48; Owen Fields Advertising Agency, writer, 1949-51, chief copy writer, 1951-52; *GP* (magazine of American Academy of General Practice), business and economics editor, 1953-57, manuscript editor, 1958-59; Charles E. Tuttle Publishing Co., Tokyo, Japan, editor, 1959-61; English teacher in Tokyo, Japan, 1960-63 and 1965-67; Blakemore & Mitsuki Law Firm, Tokyo, Japan, editor, 1967-68; Temple University, Philadelphia, Pa., associate editor of *Economic and Business Review*, 1968-70, manuscript editor, 1970—. Coordinator of freshman English courses at International Christian University, 1961-63; lecturer at University of Maryland (Far East Division), 1961-68. Member of board of directors of Kansas City Urban League.

MEMBER: Elmira Club of Chemung County (president, 1939-41), League of Women Voters, Theta Sigma Phi. *Awards, honors:* Chinese cultural scholarship from Ministry of Education of the Chinese National Government, 1946-47, for Chinese studies at University of Southern California; study grant from American Council of Learned Societies, 1950, for study at Harvard University; Fulbright grants for study in Peking, China, 1948-49, Thammasat University, 1956-57, and University of Saigon, 1964-65.

WRITINGS: Style Manual for English, International Christian University (Tokyo), 1962; *Land of Seagull and Fox: Folk Tales of Vietnam*, Weatherhill, 1966; *A China Journey*, Temple University Press, 1973; *The Asian Animal Zodiac: The Yellow Road of the Sun*, Tuttle, 1974. Contributor to magazines, including *GP*, and newspapers.

* * *

SUTTMEIER, Richard Peter 1942-

PERSONAL: Born January 3, 1942, in Richmond Hill, N.Y.; son of Christopher E. and Harriet (Klein) Suttmeier; married Merle Metcalfe (a teacher), February 22, 1963. *Education:* Dartmouth College, A.B., 1963; Indiana University, Ph.D., 1970. *Office:* Department of Political Science, Hamilton College, Clinton, N.Y. 13323.

CAREER: Chinese University of Hong Kong, Chung Chi College, Hong Kong, instructor in general education, 1963-65; National Aeronautics and Space Administration (NASA), Office of International Affairs, Washington, D.C., international affairs specialist, 1969-70; Hamilton College, Clinton, N.Y., assistant professor of political science, 1971—. Visiting fellow at Technology and Development Institute, East-West Center, Honolulu, Hawaii, 1972-73. *Member:* American Political Science Association, Association for Asian Studies, American Society for Public Administration (fellow).

WRITINGS: Research and Revolution: Science Policy and Societal Change in China, Lexington Books, 1974. Contributor to journals in his field.

WORK IN PROGRESS: Research on theories of science, technology, and public policy.

* * *

SWANN, Ingo 1933-

PERSONAL: Born September 14, 1933, in Telluride, Colo.; son of Ingo and Pauline Swann. *Education:* Westminster College, Salt Lake City, Utah, B.A., 1955; studied psychical research with L. Ron Hubbard, New York & Los Angeles, 1969-74. *Home:* 357 Bowery, New York, N.Y. 10003. *Agent:* Ruth Hagy Brod, 15 Park Ave., New York, N.Y.

CAREER: Artist, 1958—. United Nations Secretariat, New York, N.Y., 1958-69; American Society for Psychical Research, New York, N.Y., subject in experimental parapsychology, 1971-74; City College of the City University of New York, New York, N.Y., subject in experimental parapsychology, 1972; Stanford Research Institute, Stanford, Calif., researcher in experimental psi project, 1972-73. Exhibitions of paintings at New York World's Fair of 1964, American Society for Psychical Research, New York, N.Y., 1972, and at various other places. One of Swann's paintings is in the collection of the Erickson Educational Foundation in Baton Rouge, La. *Military service:* U.S. Army, 1955-58.

WRITINGS: To Kiss Earth Good-bye, Hawthorn, 1975; (editor and author of introduction) *Cosmic Art*, Hawthorn, 1975.

WORK IN PROGRESS: A documentary, *Psi-Creativity*; and two novels, *Mega-Psychic* and *Incident at Animosity*.

BIOGRAPHICAL/CRITICAL SOURCES: Psychic, March/April, 1973.

* * *

SWARTZ, Harry (Felix) 1911-
  (Martin Moreno, H. Felix Valcoe)

PERSONAL: Born June 21, 1911, in Detroit, Mich.; son of Isaac and Anne (Srere) Swartz; married Eva Sutton, October 3, 1942; children: Mark Sutton. *Education:* University of Michigan, A.B., 1930, M.D., 1933. *Home:* Apartado 752, Cuernavaca, Morelos, Mexico.

CAREER: Michael Reese Hospital, Chicago, Ill., intern, 1933-35; general practice of medicine in Detroit, Mich., 1935-36; New York University Medical College and Clinics, New York, N.Y., postgraduate work in allergy, 1936-38; private practice in allergy in New York, N.Y., 1938-71; *Investigacion Medica Internacional*, Mexico, editor-in-chief, 1971—. *Military service:* U.S. Army, Medical Corps, chief of allergy department at Tilton General Hospital, Fort Dix, N.J., 1942-46; became major. *Member:* American Medical Association, American Academy of Allergy (fellow), American College of Allergists, American Association of Clinical Immunology and Allergy, American Geriatrics Society, American Association for the Advancement of Science, World Future Society, Royal Society of Health, New York State Medical Society, Medical Society of the County of New York, Phi Beta Kappa, Phi Kappa Phi, Alpha Omega Alpha.

WRITINGS: Allergy: What It Is and What to Do About It, Rutgers University Press, 1949, 2nd revised and enlarged edition, Ungar, 1966; *Your Hay Fever and What to Do About It*, Funk, 1951, revised edition, Ungar, 1962; *The Allergic Child*, Coward, 1954; *Intelligent Layman's Medical Dictionary*, Ungar, 1955, enlarged edition published as *Layman's Medical Dictionary*, Ungar, 1963; *How to Master Your Allergy*, Nelson, 1961, published as *The Allergy Guide Book*, Ungar, 1966; *Your Body* (juvenile), Whitman Publishing, 1962.

Editor of health book series for the lay reader, published by Coward, 1952-53; translator from Spanish to English of biomedical material. Contributor of short stories, under pseudonym H. Felix Valcoe, and articles to medical journals and popular magazines. Scientific director for Ediciones P.L.M., 1971—.

WORK IN PROGRESS: The Mercy Chain of Children, a historical novel about Dr. Xavier Balmis; *The Two Masks of Dr. White*, under pseudonym Martin Moreno.

SIDELIGHTS: Allergy: What It Is and What to Do About It has been published in England, France, Italy, and Brazil.

* * *

SWINGLEHURST, Edmund 1917-

PERSONAL: Born March 14, 1917, in Chile; son of Edward (a banker) and Lydia Jones; married Pamela Search; children: Julian, Mark, Elissa. *Education:* Attended school in Devon, England. *Politics:* None. *Religion:* Christian. *Agent:* David Higham Associates Ltd., 76 Dean St., London W.1, England. *Office:* Thomas Cook, 45 Berkeley St., London W1A1, England.

CAREER: Headmaster of school in Chile, 1939-44; Grant Advertising, Buenos Aires, Argentina, account executive, 1944-46; E. R. Squibb, Buenos Aires, Argentina, publicity manager, 1947-50; artist in Paris, France, 1950-53; Thomas Cook, London, England, public relations representative for Europe, 1953—. *Member:* Press Club, Overseas Press Club.

WRITINGS: (Self-illustrated) *How! The Whole Truth about the Wild West* (humor), Parrish, 1957; (editor) *French Lovers are Lovely* (cartoons), Arco, 1957; (self-illustrated) *All Aboard!* (travel humor) Parrish, 1958; (with Willy Trebich) *The Broken Swastika*, Cooper, 1971; *The Romantic Journey: The Story of Thomas Cook and Victorian Travel*, Pica, 1973; *Victorian Seaside*, Hamlyn, in press.

AVOCATIONAL INTERESTS: Travel, art.

* * *

SWITZER, David Karl 1925-

PERSONAL: Born August 28, 1925, in Beaumont, Tex.; son of Horace S. (a businessman) and Helen (Kone) Switzer; married Shirley Anne Holmes (a mental health clinic therapist), November 3, 1945; children: Rebecca, Eric. *Education:* Southwestern University, Georgetown, Tex., B.A., 1947; Emory University, B.D., 1950; University of Texas, M.A., 1960; Southern California School of Theology, Th.D., 1966. *Religion:* Methodist. *Home:* 6450 Desco Dr., Dallas, Tex. 75225. *Office:* Selecman Hall, Southern Methodist University, Dallas, Tex. 75175.

CAREER: Ordained to Methodist ministry, 1949; minister in Elysian Fields, Tex., 1950-52, Houston, Tex., 1952-56; Humble Oil Co., Houston, training advisor in Employee Relations Department, 1956; Southwestern University, Georgetown, Tex., assistant professor, 1956-59, associate professor of psychology, 1959-65, chaplain, 1956-65; First Methodist Church, Pasadena, Calif., minister of counseling, 1965-67; Southern Methodist University, Dallas, Tex., associate dean of Perkins School of Theology, 1967-71, associate professor of pastoral theology, and counseling chaplain, 1971—. Chairman of Community Council Mental Health Committee, Pasadena, 1966-67; member of board of directors of Houston Committee on Alcoholism, 1954-56, Pasadena Council on Alcoholism, 1965-67, Contact Telephone Ministry, Dallas, 1967-71, Council on Alcoholism, Dallas, 1967—, Dallas County Mental Health Association, 1967-75, Free Medical Clinic, Dallas, 1968-70, Suicide Prevention Center, 1969—, Planned Parenthood, Dallas, 1971-73; member of Houston mayor's advisory committee to Juvenile Delinquency and Crime Commission, 1955-56, Los Angeles Committee on Mental Health and the Clergy, 1965-67, Human Relations Commission, Pasadena, 1966-67, Texas State Advisory Council on Alcoholism, 1973-75.

Military service: U.S. Marine Corps Reserve, Intelligence, active duty, 1943-46, reserve duty, 1946-50; became first lieutenant.

MEMBER: American Association of Pastoral Counselors (fellow), American Psychological Association, Texas Psychological Association, Texas Conference Board of the Ministry, Dallas Psychological Association. *Awards, honors:* Danforth Foundation campus minister's graduate fellowship, 1960-61; Southwestern University distinguished alumni award, 1973.

WRITINGS: (Contributor) Donald G. Zytowski, editor, *Vocational Behavior: A Source Book of Theology and Research*, Holt, 1968; (contributor) Robert M. Toth, David B. Hershenson, and Thomas Hilliard, editors, *The Psychology of Vocational Development: Readings in Theory and Research*, Allyn & Bacon, 1969; *The Dynamics of Grief*, Abingdon, 1970; (contributor) Jeremiah W. Canning, editor, *Values in an Age of Confrontation*, C. E. Merrill, 1970; *The Minister as Crisis Counselor*, Abingdon, 1974 (published in England as *Breaking Point: And How the Christian Ministry Can Help*, Geoffrey Chapman, 1974). Contributor to religion and psychology journals. Member of editorial board, *OMEGA*, 1971—.

* * *

SYLVESTER, Robert McPhierson 1907-1975

February 7, 1907—February 9, 1975; American syndicated newspaper entertainment columnist, drama critic, and author of novels and nonfiction books. Obituaries: *New York Times*, February 10, 1975; *Washington Post*, February 12, 1975; *AB Bookman's Weekly*, February 24, 1975.

* * *

SYPHER, Francis Jacques 1941-

PERSONAL: Born November 4, 1941, in Hackensack, N.J.; son of Francis Jacques (a lawyer) and Mildred (Allen) Sypher; married Eleanor Cole Kramer (an editor), July 11, 1970. *Education:* Columbia University, A.B., 1963, M.A., 1964, Ph.D., 1968. *Residence:* New York, N.Y.

CAREER: State University of New York at Albany, assistant professor of English, 1968-75. *Member:* American Association of University Professors, Modern Language Association of America, Tennyson Society, Research Society for Victorian Periodicals, Friends of Harvard College Library, Art Students League of New York (life member). *Awards, honors:* State University of New York Research Foundation summer stipend, 1973.

WRITINGS: (Editor) Algernon Charles Swinburne, *A Year's Letters*, New York University Press, 1974; (editor) and author of introduction *Undergraduate Papers: An Oxford Journal, 1857-1858, Conducted by A. C. Swinburne, John Nichol, T. H. Green, and Others, A Facsimile Reprint*, Delmar, 1974; (editor and author of introduction) *Pseudo-Martyr by John Donne: A Facsimile Reproduction*, Delmar, 1974. Contributor of articles and reviews to *Harvard Library Bulletin*, *Victorian Poetry*, *Victorian Studies*, and other journals.

WORK IN PROGRESS: Research on the Victorian period, on Greek and Latin literature, and on the literature of the Renaissance.

AVOCATIONAL INTERESTS: Travel and book collecting.

TAETZSCH, Lyn 1941-

PERSONAL: Surname is pronounced "taych"; born September 24, 1941, in East Orange, N.J.; daughter of William Kilpatrick and Ella (Kroupa) Taetzsch; children: Blixy. *Education:* Attended Cooper Union Art School; Rutgers University, B.A. (with honors), 1971. *Home:* 202 Main St., Newfield, N.Y. 14867.

CAREER: Blue Cross-Blue Shield, Newark, N.J., manager and trainer, 1968-70; Holy Cow Leather (leather accessories manufacturer), Newfield, N.Y., owner and president, 1972-74; part-time lecturer on small business management, Ithaca College, Itaca, N.Y., 1974-75, Tompkins-Cortland Community College, Dryden, N.Y., 1975-76. Consultant, Automated Instruction, Inc.

WRITINGS: (With Sandra Z. Taetzsch) *Preschool Games and Activities*, Fearon, 1974; (with Herb Genfan) *How to Start Your Own Craft Business*, Watson-Guptill, 1974; (with Genfan) *Leather Decoration*, Watson-Guptill, 1975; (with Genfan) *Latigo Leather*, Watson-Guptill, 1976; *How to Open and Operate a Retail Store*, Regnery, 1976; *Out of Work: Copying, Growing and Making a Buck*, Regnery, 1976. Contributor to American Society for Training and Development *Training and Development Journal*.

WORK IN PROGRESS: A novel; research for books on flowercraft, paper filigree art, scrap leather, winning at limit poker, and practical accounting for small business.

AVOCATIONAL INTERESTS: Art (Lyn Taetzsch had a one-woman show of her paintings in New York, 1965).

*　　　*　　　*

TAFFY
See LLEWELLYN, D(avid) W(illiam) Alun

*　　　*　　　*

TALAMANTES, Florence Williams 1931-

PERSONAL: Born August 15, 1931, in Alliance, Ohio, daughter of Ernest Martin and Addie (Smith) Williams. married Eduardo Talamantes, March, 1970. *Education:* Mt. Union College, B.A., 1954; University of Cincinnati, M.A., 1956, Ph.D., 1961; Indiana University, graduate study, 1957-58. *Residence:* San Diego, Calif. *Office:* Department of Spanish, San Diego State University, San Diego, Calif. 92115.

CAREER: Teacher of Spanish and English in Windham, Ohio, 1954-55, and in Cincinnati, Ohio, 1956-57; Lake Forest College, Lake Forest, Ill., assistant professor of Spanish, 1961-62; San Diego State University, San Diego, Calif., assistant professor, 1962-67, associate professor of Spanish, 1967—. *Member:* Modern Language Association of American, American Association of Teachers of Spanish and Portuguese, American Federation of Teachers, National Organization for Women, Alpha Mu Gamma, Sigma Delta Pi. *Awards, honors:* San Diego University faculty research grant, 1974.

WRITINGS: Alfonsina Storni: Argentina's Feminist Poet, San Marcos Press, 1975. Also editor, with B. Costa-Amic, of *Don Gonzalo Gonzalez de la Gonzalera*, by Jose Maria -de Pereda, Calle Mesones. *Virginia Woolf Quarterly*, member of editorial board, 1972-74, acting editor, 1973, co-editor, 1975—.

WORK IN PROGRESS: Research on Hispanic elements in the works of Joseph Conrad, in collaboration with Suzanne Henig.

TALBOTT, Robert D(ean) 1928-

PERSONAL: Born February 18, 1928, in Centralia, Ill.; son of James and Gladys (Tresenriter) Talbott; married Alice Milstead, January 27, 1958; children: Lawrence Dean. *Education:* University of Illinois, B.A., 1950, M.A., 1955, Ph.D., 1959. *Home:* 219 Brentwood Dr., Cedar Falls, Iowa 50613. *Office:* Department of History, University of Northern Iowa, Cedar Falls, Iowa 50613.

CAREER: Kansas State Teachers College, Emporia, instructor in Latin American and U.S. history, 1958-59; Valley City State College, Valley City, N.D., associate professor of Latin American and U.S. history, 1959-62; Kearney State College, Kearney, Neb., associate professor of Latin American and U.S. history, 1962-67; University of Northern Iowa, Cedar Falls, assistant professor, 1967-70, associate professor, 1970-74, professor of Latin American history, 1974—. *Military service:* U.S. Army, 1950-52. *Member:* American Historical Association, American Association of University Professors, Latin American Studies Association, Midwest Association of Latin American Studies, Phi Alpha Theta.

WRITINGS: A History of the Chilean Boundaries, Iowa State University Press, 1974. Contributor to history journals.

WORK IN PROGRESS: Research on relations between Chile and Bolivia, the Arica conference, and part of U.S. international relations during the period of World War Two in the Pacific.

AVOCATIONAL INTERESTS: Raising house plants.

*　　　*　　　*

TALLEY-MORRIS, Neva B(ennett) 1909-

PERSONAL: Born August 12, 1909, in Little Rock, Ark.; daughter of John W. (a merchant) and Erma (Rhew) Bennett; married Cecil C. Tally (a lawyer), January 1, 1946 (died November 24, 1948); married Joseph H. Morris (a broker), March 22, 1952 (died December 5, 1974). *Education:* Ouachita Baptist University, B.A. (magna cum laude), 1930; University of Texas, M.Ed., 1938, further study, 1939-41. *Religion:* Baptist. *Home:* 101 North State St., Little Rock, Ark. 72201. *Office:* 722 West Markham, Little Rock, Ark. 72201.

CAREER: Admitted to Bar of State of Arkansas, 1947; private practice of law in Little Rock, Ark., 1947—; high school teacher of business administration in White County, Ark,. 1930-42, principal, 1937-42. *Wartime service:* Ordnance inspector, U.S. Army Services Forces, 1942-45. Chairman of Arkansas Council on Children and Youth, 1952-54.

MEMBER: American Bar Association (member of house of delegates, 1970-74), National Association of Women Lawyers (life member; president, 1956-57), American Academy of Matrimonial Lawyers (fellow; member of board of governors, 1973—), American Association of University Women (life member), American Judicature Society, National Conference of Lawyers and Social Workers (member of executive board, 1962-66), Arkansas Bar Association (member of house of delegates, 1973—), Arkansas Bar Foundation (fellow), Pulaski County Bar Association, Little Rock Association of Women Lawyers (president, 1950-51), North Little Rock Business and Professional Womens Club (president, 1951-52), Delta Kappa Gamma, Phi Alpha Delta. *Awards, honors:* National Association of Women Lawyers annual award, 1962; special award for distinguished service to legal profession from Arkansas Bar Foundation, 1970; Arkansas Association of Women Lawyers achievement award, 1971.

WRITINGS: Family Law Practice and Procedure Handbook, Prentice-Hall, 1973; *Appellate Civil Practice and Procedure Handbook*, Prentice-Hall, 1975. Contributor to legal journals.

* * *

TANZER, Michael David 1935-

PERSONAL: Born July 27, 1935, in New York, N.Y.; married in 1958; children: three. *Education:* Harvard University, A.B. (magna cum laude), 1957, A.M., 1960, Ph.D., 1962. *Office:* Tanzer Economic Associates, Inc., 127 East 59th St., New York, N.Y. 10022.

CAREER: Esso Standard Eastern, Inc., New York, N.Y., economist, 1962-64; Joel Dan Associates (economic and management consultants), New York, N.Y., senior associate, 1964-68; Tanzer Economic Associates, Inc., New York, N.Y., president, 1969—. *Member:* American Economic Association, Phi Beta Kappa. *Awards, honors:* Woodrow Wilson fellowship, 1957-58.

WRITINGS: The Political Economy of International Oil and the Underdeveloped Countries, Beacon Press, 1969; *The Sick Society: An Economic Examination*, Holt, 1971; *The Energy Crisis: World Struggle for Power and Wealth*, Monthly Review Press, 1974. Contributor of about a dozen articles to *Nation, Vista, Social Science, Canadian Dimension, Review of Economics and Statistics, American Economist*, and *New York Times*.

* * *

TAVUCHIS, Nicholas 1934-

PERSONAL: Born November 2, 1934, in New York, N.Y.; son of Constantine and Anthi Tavuchis; married Bess Ternas (a teacher), August 28, 1960; children: Alexander Constantine, Christopher Argery. *Education:* Columbia University, B.A., 1955, M.A., 1961, Ph.D., 1968. *Residence:* Winnipeg, Manitoba, Canada. *Office:* Department of Sociology, University of Manitoba, 317 Isbister, Winnipeg R3T 2N2, Canada.

CAREER: Cornell University, Ithaca, N.Y., 1966-75, began as assistant professor, became associate professor of sociology; University of Manitoba, Winnipeg, associate professor of sociology 1975—. *Military service:* U.S. Army, 1956-58. *Member:* American Sociological Association, American Anthropological Association.

WRITINGS: Pastors and Immigrants, Nifhoff, 1963; *Family and Mobility Among Greek-Americans*, National Centre for Social Research (Athens), 1972; (with William J. Goode) *The Family Through Literature*, McGraw, 1975.

WORK IN PROGRESS: Studies on how young children perceive and learn kinship and on mass media images of kinship.

* * *

TAYLOR, Dalmas A(rnold) 1933-

PERSONAL: Born September 9, 1933, in Detroit, Mich.; son of Robert E. and Phanada (Price) Taylor; married Faye J. Jeffries, May 26, 1961; children Monique, Carla, Courtney. *Education:* Western Reserve University (now Case Western Reserve University), B.A., 1959; Howard University, M.S., 1961; University of Delaware, Ph.D.,

1965. *Home:* 4110 Whispering Lane, Annandale, Va. *Office:* Department of Psychology, University of Maryland, College Park, Md. 20742.

CAREER: National Institutes of Health, Bethesda, Md., psychologist, 1961-62; University of Delaware, Newark, instructor in psychology, 1964; University of Maryland, College Park, lecturer, 1965-70, professor of psychology, 1970—, director of Afro-American Studies Program, 1973-74; Federal City College, Washington, D.C., associate professor of psychology and chairman of department, 1969-70. Research psychologist at National Naval Medical Center, summer, 1963-64, 1965-69; visiting professor at Lincoln University, 1965, and American University, 1968-70. Member of board of directors of Beacon Press, 1971—; member of board of trustees of Northern Virginia Community College, 1973—. *Military service:* U.S. Army, Medical Corps, 1956-58.

MEMBER: American Association for the Advancement of Science, American Psychological Association, Society for the Psychological Study of Social Issues, Society of Experimental Social Psychologists, Eastern Psychological Association, Psi Chi (president of local chapter, 1961-62, 1964-65), Sigma Xi. *Awards, honors:* National Academy of Science postdoctoral fellow, 1965-66.

WRITINGS: Small Groups, Markham, 1971; *A Theory of Social Penetration: The Development of Interpersonal Relationships*, Holt, 1973; (contributor) K. J. Gergen, editor, *Social Psychology*, CRM Books, 1974; (contributor) H. L. Fromkin and J. J. Sherwood, editors, *Integrating the Organization: A Social Psychological Analysis*, Free Press, 1974; (with S. A. Manning) *Psychology: A New Perspective*, Winthrop, 1975; (contributor) B. Seidenberg and A. M. Snadowsky, editors, *Social Psychology: A Textbook*, Macmillan, in press. Contributor to proceedings; contributor of about twenty articles and reviews to professional journals.

WORK IN PROGRESS: Prejudice and Racism; Expectancy Processes.

* * *

TAYLOR, Ethel Stoddard 1895(?)-1975

1895(?)—March 26, 1975; Actress and author of verse and children's stories. Obituaries: *AB Bookman's Weekly*, April 21, 1975.

* * *

TAYLOR, Harry H. 1926-

PERSONAL: Born October 21, 1926, in Mt. Vernon, N.Y. *Education:* George Washington University, B.A., 1951; Columbia University, M.A., 1954; University of Denver, Ph.D., 1961. *Home:* 41 Mann Ave., Muncie, Ind. 47304. *Office:* Department of English, Ball State University, Muncie, Ind. 47306.

CAREER: Member of faculty, University of Puerto Rico, Mayaguez, 1955-58, University of Colorado, Denver, 1959-60; Ball State University, Muncie, Ind., professor of English, and chairman of humanities faculty, 1961—. *Military service:* U.S. Army, Office of Adjutant General, 1945-46. *Awards, honors:* Distinctive mention in Houghton Mifflin's *Best American Short Stories*, 1967, for "The Guards," 1968, for "Will the Wall Come Down," 1969, for "The Cage," 1972, for "Teasing" and "Carolyn"; Pulitzer Prize nomination, 1973, for *The Man Who Tried Out for Tarzan*.

WRITINGS: The Man Who Tried Out for Tarzan (novel),

Louisiana State University Press, 1973; (contributor) Robert Bonazzi, editor, *Extreme Unctions and Other Last Rites: New Departures in American Fiction*, Latitudes Press, 1974. Author of one-act play, "The Nymphs Have Departed." Contributor of short stories, articles and essays to journals, including *Forum, Kansas Magazine, South Dakota Review, Western Humanities Review, Prism International, Pyramid*, and *Epoch*.

* * *

TAYLOR, Joe Gray 1920-

PERSONAL: Born February 14, 1920, in Mason, Tenn.; son of Basil Gray (a carpenter) and Lennie Fee (Shiñault) Taylor; married Helen Eva Friday, April 18, 1945; children: Joe Gray, Jr., Harriette Eva, Edward Coleman. *Education:* Memphis State University, B.S., 1947; Louisiana State University, M.A., 1948, Ph.D., 1951. *Politics:* Democrat. *Religion:* Presbyterian. *Home:* 712 Contour, Lake Charles, La. 70601. *Office:* Department of History, McNeese State University, Ryan St., Lake Charles, La. 70601.

CAREER: Public school teacher in one-room school in Corona, Tenn., 1939-41; Nicholls Junior College (now Nicholls State University), Thibodaux, La., instructor, 1950-52, assistant professor, 1952-53, associate professor of history, 1958-63; Air University, Research Studies Institute, Maxwell Air Force Base, Ala., instructor, 1953-54, assistant professor of military history, 1954-57; Southeastern Louisiana University, Hammond, assistant professor of social science, 1957-58; McNeese State University, Lake Charles, La., professor of history, 1963—, chairman of department, 1968—. Instructor at Memphis State College (now Memphis State University), summer, 1947. *Military service:* U.S. Army Air Forces, bombardier-navigator, 1942-45; became first lieutenant; received Distinguished Flying Cross, Air Medal, three battle stars.

MEMBER: Organization of American Historians, American Association for State and Local History, Southern Historical Association, Red River Valley Historical Association, Louisiana Historical Association (president, 1967), Phi Kappa Phi, Phi Alpha Theta.

WRITINGS: Development of Night Air Operations, 1941-1952, Montgomery, 1953; *Close Air Support in the War Against Japan*, Montgomery, 1954; *Pre-Invasion Air Bombardment: Pacific Theater, 1942-1943*, Montgomery, 1954; *Air Interdiction in China*, Montgomery, 1956; *Air Supply in the Burma Campaigns*, Montgomery, 1957; *Freedom Versus Tyranny*, privately printed, 1962; *Negro Slavery in Louisiana*, Louisiana Historical Association, 1963; *Louisiana: A Student's Guide to Localized History*, Teachers College Press, 1966; (with others) *Rivers and Bayous of Louisiana*, Louisiana Education Research Association, 1968; *Louisiana Reconstructed: 1863-1877*, Louisiana State University Press, 1974. Contributor to professional journals. Editor of *McNeese Review*, 1965-67.

WORK IN PROGRESS: Louisiana: A Bicentennial History, publication expected in 1976.

AVOCATIONAL INTERESTS: Fishing, hunting, bridge, gardening.

* * *

TAYLOR, L(ester) B(arbour), Jr. 1932-

PERSONAL: Born November 9, 1932, in Lynchburg, Va.; son of Lester B. (a salesman) and Ruth (Hanna) Taylor; married Norma Billings, September 6, 1958; children: Cynthia, Chris, Tony. *Education:* Florida State University, B.S., 1955. *Home:* 114 Little John Rd., Williamsburg, Va. 23185.

CAREER: Pan-American Airlines, Kennedy Space Center, Fla., public relations representative, 1957-62; Radio Corporation of America, Kennedy Space Center, Fla., writer and editor, 1963-64; Ling, Temco, Vought (LTV), Kennedy Space Center, Fla., writer and editor, 1964-66; National Aeronautics and Space Administration, Kennedy Space Center, Fla., public information officer, 1966-68; Rockwell International, Pittsburgh, Pa., manager of publications, 1968-74; Dow Badische Co., Williamsburg, Va., public relations director, 1974—. *Military service:* U.S. Army, 1955-57. *Member:* Public Relations Society of America. *Awards, honors:* Special citation from Aviation and Space Writers Association, 1975, for *For All Mankind: America's Space Programs of the Seventies and Beyond.*

WRITINGS: Pieces of Eight: Recovering the Riches of a Lost Spanish Treasure Fleet, Dutton, 1966; *That Others Might Live: The Aerospace Rescue and Recovery Service*, Dutton, 1967; *Liftoff: The Story of America's Spaceport*, Dutton, 1968; *For All Mankind: America's Space Programs of the Seventies and Beyond*, Dutton, 1974. Contributor of more than two hundred articles to national magazines, including *Reader's Digest, Saturday Evening Post, True, Parade, Family Weekly*, and *Popular Science.*

WORK IN PROGRESS: Research for a book on a Spanish treasure fleet from 1622 that sank off Key West, Fla.

SIDELIGHTS: During his years at Kennedy Space Center, Taylor met and interviewed astronauts, space officials, cabinet officers, Senators and Congressmen, and other celebrities. He covered the major space launches, from the days of the first Sputnik to the first manned lunar landing. He feels strongly ". . . that the national space program—low key now—will one day soon be very important to America's and the world's future. Will eventually end poverty, famine, and illiteracy." *Avocational interests:* European and South American travel, golf, poker, California wines, imported cigars.

* * *

TAYLOR, Lloyd C(hamberlain), Jr. 1923-

PERSONAL: Born December 31, 1923, in Richmond, Va.; son of Lloyd Chamberlain (a civil engineer) and Marcia (Estes) Taylor. *Education:* Lehigh University, B.A., 1949, M.A., 1951, Ph.D., 1956. *Politics:* Democrat. *Religion:* Episcopalian. *Home:* 401 Cross St., College Station, Tex. 77840. *Office:* Department of History, Texas A&M University, College Station, Tex. 77843.

CAREER: Texas A&M University, College Station, instructor, 1956-58, assistant professor, 1958-62, associate professor, 1962-69, professor of history, 1969—. *Military service:* U.S. Army, Military Intelligence, 1943-46. *Member:* American Historical Association, American Studies Association. *Awards, honors:* Fund for Organized Research grants, 1960, 1961.

WRITINGS: Margaret Ayer Barnes, Twayne, 1975; *The Medical Profession and Social Reform*, St. Martin's, 1975. Contributor to *Pennsylvania History* and *New York History.*

WORK IN PROGRESS: Isabella Greenway, Bronson Cutting, and Progressivism; Gertrude Vanderbilt Whitney, Juliana Force: Art and Progressivism.

TEMPLE, Ann
　　See MORTIMER, Penelope (Ruth)

* 　 * 　 *

TENISON, Robin Hanbury
　　See HANBURY-TENISON, (Airling) Robin

* 　 * 　 *

TERKEL, (Louis) Studs 1912-

PERSONAL: Born May 16, 1912, in New York, N.Y.; son of Samuel and Anna (Finkel) Terkel; married Ida Goldberg, July 2, 1939; children: Paul. *Education:* University of Chicago, Ph.B., 1932, J.D., 1934. *Home:* 3152 North Pine Grove Ave., Chicago, Ill. 60657. *Office:* WFMT, Inc., 500 North Michigan Ave., Chicago, Ill. 60611.

CAREER: After completing law school, worked as a civil service employee in Washington, D.C., and as a stage actor and movie house manager before turning to radio and television broadcasting; host of interview show "Wax Museum" on radio station WFMT, Chicago, Ill., 1945—. Moderator of television program "Studs' Place," Chicago, Ill., 1950-53. Master of ceremonies at Newport Folk Festival, 1959 and 1960, Ravinia (Ill.) Music Festival, 1959, University of Chicago Folk Festival, 1961, and others; also panel moderator, lecturer, narrator of films, and columnist.

AWARDS, HONORS: Ohio State University award, 1959, and Unesco Prix Italia award, 1962, both for "Wax Museum"; University of Chicago Alumni Association Communicator of the Year award, 1969; National Book Awards nominee, 1975.

WRITINGS: Giants of Jazz, Crowell, 1957; *Division Street: America*, Pantheon, 1967; *Hard Times: An Oral History of the Great Depression*, Pantheon, 1970; *Working: People Talk About What They Do All Day and How They Feel About What They Do*, Pantheon, 1974. Also author of play, "Amazing Grace," first produced in Ann Arbor by the University of Michigan's Professional Theater Program, 1967.

SIDELIGHTS: A *Christian Science Monitor* writer said of Terkel that he practices "a new form of writing 'history,' a special extension of personal journalism in an ever increasingly impersonal world. It is putting the I back in a Them society." Concerning *Hard Times*, L. E. Sissman says: "Most of us have read, and nodded over, a dozen worthy histories of the slump . . . Mr. Terkel, a brilliant radio interviewer, has gone on the road to track down the stories of scores of Americans, a few of them great but most of them ordinary men and women who made and were made by the Depression years. What comes through in their individual stories—and even more strongly in the cumulative effect of all of them—is a sense of solidarity in adversity, of a willingness to reach out to others, of an ability to see others not as households of accreted possessions but as naked human beings."

Geoffrey Wolff comments: "People talk miracles to Terkel. They'll confess anything to him for some reason, but the rarest thing he draws from them is their startling decency. And they talk surprising languages: vital, distinct from one another, rich with curious idioms and odd habits of imagination this country has nurtured."*

* 　 * 　 *

TERMAN, Sibyl 1902(?)-1975

1902(?)—July 23, 1975; American educator and author of books on juvenile reading problems. Obituaries: *New York Times*, July 26, 1975.

* 　 * 　 *

TERRELL, Donna McManus 1908-

PERSONAL: Born June 2, 1908, in Canada. *Education:* Attended Pomona College. *Home:* 121 East Live Oak Ave., San Gabriel, Calif. 91776. *Agent:* A. L. Hart, 419 East 57th St., New York, N.Y. 10022.

CAREER: Researcher-author for historian John Upton Terrell, 1958—.

WRITINGS: Indian Women of the Western Morning, Dial, 1974.

* 　 * 　 *

TERRY, William
　　See HARKNETT, Terry

* 　 * 　 *

TERTIS, Lionel 1876-1975

December 29, 1876—February 22, 1975; British musician, viola soloist, designer of new models of cello, viola, and violin, author of autobiography. Obituaries: *New York Times*, February 25, 1975; *Time*, March 10, 1975.

* 　 * 　 *

TETHER, (Cynthia) Graham 1950-

PERSONAL: Born September 14, 1950, in White Plains, N.Y.; daughter of Willard L. (an investment counselor) and Doris A. (a public health nurse and teacher; maiden name, Bouton) Tether. *Education:* Mount Holyoke College, B.A. (with distinction) and teaching certificate, 1972; New York University, graduate study, 1974—. *Religion:* Protestant. *Home:* 11 DeWitt Ave., Bronxville, N.Y. 10708. *Office:* Harper & Row Publishers, Inc., 10 East 53rd St., New York, N.Y. 10022.

CAREER: First National City Bank, New York, N.Y., research assistant, 1971; News Election Service, New York, N.Y., assistant to payroll manager, 1972; free-lance writer, 1972-73; Harper & Row Publishers, Inc., New York, N.Y., editorial assistant in trade department, 1974—. Assistant concertmistress for All New York State Orchestra; violinist in chamber ensembles. *Member:* Daughters of the American Revolution. *Awards, honors:* Lincoln Center Award for instrumental music, 1968; first prize from Society of Children's Book Writers, 1973, for *King Chub-Chub*.

*WRITINGS—*For children: *Fudge Dream Supreme*, J. Philip O'Hara, 1975. Contributor to national magazines, including *Pencil Puzzle Fun, My Weekly Reader*, and *Friend*.

*WORK IN PROGRESS—*For children: *Danny Dunce; Skunk and Possum*.

* 　 * 　 *

THARPE, Jac Lyndon 1928-

PERSONAL: Born January 7, 1928, in Maynardville, Tenn.; son of Charles Edward (a farmer) and Huella (Butcher) Tharpe; married Dorothy Nace, 1956; children: Cecily, Lindlae. *Education:* University of Tennessee, B.A., 1957, M.A., 1958; Harvard University, Ph.D., 1965. *Home:* 424 Southern Station, Hattiesburg, Miss. 39401.

Office: University Honors Program, University of Southern Mississippi, Hattiesburg, Miss. 39401.

CAREER: University of Tennessee, Knoxville, instructor in English, 1958-61; University of Alaska, Fairbanks, assistant professor of English, 1964-65; Texas Technological College, Lubbock, associate professor of English, 1965-67; Hiram Scott College, Scottsbluff, Neb., professor of English, 1967-70; University of Southern Mississippi, Hattiesburg, professor of English, 1970—, honors professor of English, 19 —. *Awards, honors:* Danforth teacher at Harvard University, 1961-63. *Member:* Phi Kappa Phi, Phi Eta Sigma.

WRITINGS: Nathaniel Hawthorne: Identity and Knowledge, Southern Illinois University Press, 1967; *John Barth: The Comic Sublimity of Paradox*, Southern Illinois University Press, 1974; (editor-in-chief) *Frost: Centennial Essays*, University Press of Mississippi, 1974. Contributor to *Southern Quarterly.*

WORK IN PROGRESS: Textual editor of *Jacksonville: Postmarked 1843-1845; Logos: History of an Idea*; editing *Tennessee Williams: A Reassessment.*

SIDELIGHTS: Tharpe writes: "My major interest is the history of ideas, and I have studied the Greek classical period as much as American culture. I have a strong interest in comparative philology and have studied the structures of many languages, including Gaelic, Roumanian, Polish, Russian, and Japanese . . . I have done a great deal of reading in the literature of the Orient and the Near East as well as in philosophy, the sciences, science fiction, and popular literature . . . I have written many discarded novels and retain an interest in writing satire. Any philosophy of life I may have is expressed in my very personal books on Nathaniel Hawthorne and John Barth." Tharpe reads Spanish, French, German, and Greek.

*   *   *

THIEN-AN, Thich   1926-

PERSONAL: Name originally Doan-Van-An; born September 8, 1926, in Hue, Vietnam; son of Me Van (a Buddhist monk) and Huong Thi (Le) Doan; children: Truth Elan Doan. *Education:* Bao Quoc Institute of Higher Learning, B.A. equiv., 1949; Toyo University, B.A., 1957; Waseda University, M.A., 1959, D.Litt., 1964. *Home:* 928 South New Hampshire Ave., Los Angeles, Calif. 90006. *Office:* College of Oriental Studies, 939 South New Hampshire Ave., Los Angeles, Calif. 90006.

CAREER: Ordained Buddhist monk, 1946; became bishop, 1964, and archbishop, 1974; University of Saigon, Saigon, Vietnam, professor of history and Asian studies, 1962-66, chairman of department, 1964-66; University of California, Los Angeles, visiting professor of Asian languages, 1966-68, professor of Eastern philosophy and Oriental religions at Los Angeles extension, 1968—, instructor in philosophy and religion at various University of California extensions, 1970—; College of Oriental Studies, Los Angeles, founder, president, and dean of instruction, 1973—. Visiting professor, University of Hue, 1963-66; co-founder and dean of faculty of letters & human science, Van Hanh University, 1964-66; chairman of foreign degree evaluation, Education Ministry of Government of Vietnam, 1964-66; chairman of Buddhist education for Unified Buddhist Churches of Vietnam, 1964-66; professor of philosophy, Los Angeles City College, 1968—; founder and president, International Buddhist Meditation Center, 1970—. *Member:* American Oriental Society, Vietnamese Student Association (founder and president, 1960-61).

WRITINGS: Triet-Hoc Zen (title means "Zen Buddhism"), Dong-Phuong (Saigon), Volume I, 1963, Volume II, 1964; *Tu-Tuong Nhat-Ban* (title means "History of Japanese Thought"), Dong-Phuong, 1964; *Giao-Duc Nhat-Ban* (title means "Education in Modern Japan"), Ministry of Education, Government of Vietnam, 1965; *Phat-Giao va Van-Chuong Viet-Nam* (title means "Buddhism and Vietnamese Literature"), Dong-Phuong, 1966; *Buddhism: Awareness in Action* (booklet), College of Oriental Studies, 1973; *Buddhism and Zen in Vietnam*, Tuttle, 1975; *Zen Philosophy, Zen Practice*, Dharma, 1975. Contributor to *Lotus in the West, World Buddhism Journal*, and *American Buddhist.*

WORK IN PROGRESS: Development of Vijnana Thought.

SIDELIGHTS: Thich Thien-An was very active in the Buddhist movement for religious equality in 1963. His father, Thich Tieu-Dieu (religious name), was the first monk in Hue to burn himself to death in protest against South Vietnamese President Ngo Dinh Diem's policy of Buddhist supression. Thien-An speaks Japanese and English and reads French, Chinese, and classical and Buddhist Chinese.

*   *   *

THOMAS, Armstrong   1909(?)-1975

1909(?)—July 19, 1975; American astronomer, historian, educator, actor, and author of works on astronomy and Maryland history. Obituaries: *Washington Post*, July 25, 1975.

*   *   *

THOMAS, Heather Smith   1944-

PERSONAL: Born February 13, 1944, in Kenosha, Wis.; daughter of Don Ian (a minister) and Betty (Moser) Smith; married Lynn Thomas (a rancher), March 5, 1966; children: Michael, Andrea. *Education:* Univeristy of Puget Sound, B.A., 1966. *Politics:* Republican. *Religion:* Methodist. *Address:* Box 215, Salmon, Idaho 83467.

CAREER: Rancher in Salmon, Idaho, 1967—. *Member:* Salmon River Trail Ride Association (secretary, 1974-76).

WRITINGS: A Horse in Your Life: A Guide for the New Owner, A.S. Barnes, 1966; *Your Horse and You*, A.S. Barnes, 1970; *Horses: Their Breeding, Care, and Training*, A.S. Barnes, 1974. Contributor to *Horse and Horseman, Horseman, Horse of Course, Western Livestock Reporter, Quarter Horse Digest, Cattleman, American Horseman*, and other horse and farm periodicals.

WORK IN PROGRESS: A book of ranch stories dealing with livestock anecdotes.

*   *   *

THOMAS, J. C.

PERSONAL: Son of Charles and Marie (Mertz) Thomas. *Education:* University of Wisconsin, Madison, B.A., 1962, M.A., 1964. *Politics:* "Anti." *Religion:* Atheist. *Residence:* Manhattan, N.Y. *Agent:* Maxmilian Becker, 115 East 82nd St., New York, N.Y. 10028.

CAREER: Free-lance writer, and host of television show, "Talking with Thomas." Actor; photographer; musician. *Military service:* U.S. Air Force.

WRITINGS: The Master (novel), Warner, 1970; *Chasin' the Trane: The Music and Mystique of John Coltrane*,

Doubleday, 1975. Contributor to *National Observer, New York Times, Village Voice, Show, Down Beat, Writer's Digest*, and *Publishers Weekly*.

SIDELIGHTS: Thomas told *CA*: "... a writer is still a storyteller; in his or her case, a person with a message that can best be presented in words.... In a sense, I am always writing. Whenever I travel to foreign countries—more than 100 on five continents, so far—I walk the back streets, ride public transportation and eat and drink in the places most favored by the people themselves. Then I write their stories, my story ..."

* * *

THOMAS, J(ames) D(avid)   1910-

PERSONAL: Born July 20, 1910, in Holliday, Tex.; son of William Albert (in clerical work) and Angie Belle (Wisdom) Thomas; married Mary Katherine Payne, February 22, 1931; children Deborah Gayle Thomas Fish (deceased), Hannah Belle (Mrs. Dwayne Kissick), John Paul. *Education:* Attended University of Texas, 1926-28; Abilene Christian College, A.B., 1943; Southern Methodist University, M.A., 1944; University of Chicago, Ph.D., 1957. *Home:* 774 East North 15th St., Abilene, Tex. 79601. *Office address:* Abilene Christian College Station, Box 7768, Abilene, Tex. 79601.

CAREER: Clergyman of Church of Christ, ordained 1937; City of Lubbock, Lubbock, Tex., assistant city manager, 1939-42; minister in Chicago, Ill., 1945-49; Abilene Christian College, Abilene, Tex., associate professor, 1949-57, professor of Bible, 1957—, head of department, 1970—, lectureship director, 1952-70. Publisher, owner, manager, and editor of Biblical Research Press, Abilene, Tex., 1958—. President of corporation board of *Restoration Quarterly*, 1974—. *Member:* American Academy of Religion, Society of Biblical Literature, American Scientific Affiliation, Evangelical Theological Society, American Bible Society (member of advisory council, 1966-67), Southwestern Philosophical Association, Kiwanis Club. *Awards, honors:* Century Book Award from Christian Family Book Club, 1966; Christian journalism award from *Twentieth Century Christian*, 1966.

WRITINGS—All published by Biblical Research Press: We Be Brethren, 1958; *Evolution and Antiquity*, 1961; *Facts and Faith*, Volume I, 1966; *The Spirit and Spirituality*, 1967; *Self Study Guide to Galatians and Romans*, 1971; *Self Study Guide to Corinthians*, 1972; *Heaven's Window*, 1975. Editor, "Great Preachers of Today" and "20th Century Sermons" series for Biblical Research Press. Contributor to *Journal of Biblical Literature*. Member of editorial board of *Restoration Quarterly*, 1957-74; staff writer for *Gospel Advocate* and *Twentieth Century Christian*.

WORK IN PROGRESS: Editing *What Lack We Yet; The Biblical Doctrine of Grace*; volume two of *Facts and Faith*.

SIDELIGHTS: In 1969 Thomas took a four-month world tour visiting missionaries and preaching in thirty countries.

* * *

THOMAS, John Hunter   1928-

PERSONAL: Born March 26, 1928, in Benthen, Germany; son of Roy E. (an engineer) and Lucile (Hunter) Thomas; married Susan E. Davidson, December 3, 1966. *Education:* California Institute of Technology, B.S., 1949; Stanford

University, A.M., 1949, Ph.D., 1959. *Home:* 838 Cedro Way, Stanford, Calif. 94305. *Office:* Department of Biological Science, Stanford University, Stanford, Calif. 94305.

CAREER: Stanford University, Stanford, Calif., holding positions as assistant curator, associate curator, curator, and director of the Dudley Herbarium, 1958—, and associate professor of biological sciences, 1968—. Curator of botany at California Academy of Sciences, 1968—. *Military service:* U.S. Naval Reserve, active duty, 1951-52; became ensign; received Purple Heart. *Member:* American Institute of Biological Science, Botanical Society of America, American Association for the Advancement of Science.

WRITINGS: Flora of the Santa Cruz Mountains of Central California, Stanford University Press, 1961; (with J. L. Wiggins) *A Flora of the Alaskan Arctic Slope*, University of Toronto Press, 1962; (with Dennis Parnell) *Native Shrubs of the Sierra Nevada*, University of California Press, 1974. Editor of *Journal of the California Botanical Society*, 1961-72.

WORK IN PROGRESS: Research on plants of western North America.

* * *

THOMPSON, C(lara) Mildred   1881-1975

1881—February 16, 1975; American historian, educator, university dean, and author of books on American history. Obituaries: *New York Times*, February 17, 1975; *Washington Post*, February 18, 1975.

* * *

THOMPSON, David (Bradford)   1938-

PERSONAL: Born October 16, 1938, in Fitchburg, Mass.; son of Archer Stanley (in insurance) and Irja (in nursing; maiden name, Hackman) Thompson; married Stephanie Closter, 1963 (divorced, 1965); married Grace Maynard Dunes (a teacher and photographer), December 4, 1965; children: (first marriage) Deirdre, Joseph; (second marriage) Damon, Aaron, Lauren. *Education:* Harvard University, A.B., 1960; Cornell University, M.A., 1962, Ph.D., 1968. *Home:* 4528 Northeast 93rd St., Seattle, Wash. 98115.

CAREER: University of California at Los Angeles, acting assistant professor of Latin and humanities, 1964-66; University of New Mexico, Albuquerque, assistant professor of modern and classical languages, 1967-70; University of Washington, Seattle, assistant professor of Romance languages and literature and of comparative literature, 1970-74. *Member:* American Philological Association, American Historical Association, Dante Society of America, Mediaeval Academy of America, Renaissance Society of America. *Awards, honors:* National Endowment for the Humanities fellowship, 1974-75.

WRITINGS: (Editor) *The Idea of Rome*, University of New Mexico Press, 1971; (editor and translator) *Petrarch: A Humanist among Princes*, Harper, 1971; (editor and translator with Alan F. Nagel) *The Three Crowns of Florence*, Harper, 1972; *Dante's Epic Journeys*, Johns Hopkins Press, 1974. Contributor to journals in his field.

WORK IN PROGRESS: Machiavelli's Virtuous Romans; an edition of Verino's *Paradisus*; research on Cristoforo Landino.

AVOCATIONAL INTERESTS: Real estate rehabilitation and investment.

THOMSON, Frank S(elee)   1881-1975

PERSONAL: Born October 20, 1881, in Iowa; son of Lewis Henry and Isabelle (Mitchell) Thomson; married Elsie Margaret Peterson (deceased); children: George H., Edith Margaret Thomson Malcolm. *Education:* Educated in Spearfish, S.D. *Home and office address:* P.O. Box 601, Spearfish, S.D. 57783.

CAREER: Worked as a carpenter building a gold mine mill in Maitland, S.D., 1902-03; contractor for railroad ties in Hill City, S.D., 1903-06; Black Hills National Forest, Custer, S.D. and Sundance, Wyo., forest ranger, 1906-09; farmer and rancher in Spearfish, S.D., 1910-74. Past president of Spearfish Cooperative Creamery. Primary promoter of Thoen Stone as a historical monument and tourist attraction. *Member:* Black Hills Pioneers.

WRITINGS: Last Buffalo in the Black Hills (pamphlet), privately printed, 1968; *The Thoen Stone: A saga of the Black Hills*, Harlo, 1966; *Ninety-Six Years in the Black Hills*, Harlo, 1974. Contributor to western magazines.

SIDELIGHTS: Thomson writes: "The discovery of gold in the Black Hills of South Dakota in 1874 by miners with the Custer expedition is well documented in history, and such characters as Wild Bill Hickok and Calamity Jane have taken their places in books of history and fiction.

"Not until March 1887 did it become known that gold had been discovered in the Hills forty years earlier. This was revealed with the discovery near Spearfish of what is known as the Thoen Stone, found by Louis Thoen, a stone mason. Many of the buildings he built or helped to build still stand and are occupied by businesses."

The message on the stone is: "came to these hills in 1833 seven of us . . . all ded but me Ezra Kind Killed by Ind beyond the high hill got our gold June 1834 . . . Got all of the gold we could carry our ponys all got by the Indians I hav lost my gun and nothing to eat and indians hunting me."

Thomson adds: "When a man through more than ninety years of life personally experiences the thrill of traveling to a new home in a covered wagon, and remembers all of the years, good and bad, from that time until man was walking on the moon, he has something of significance to record and publish."

(Died April 14, 1975)

* * *

THORESEN, Carl E.   1933-

PERSONAL: Born July 22, 1933, in San Francisco, Calif.; son of Trygve and Ruth (Raymond) Thoresen; married Katherine Armstrong; children: Kristen, Trygve, Amy. *Education:* University of California, Berkeley, B.A., 1955; Stanford University, M.A., 1960, Ph.D., 1964. *Home:* 3708 Carlson Circle, Palo Alto, Calif. 94306. *Office:* School of Education, Stanford University, Stanford, Calif. 94305.

CAREER: Stanford University, Stanford, Calif., 1968—, currently professor of education and psychology. Executive director, Learning House, Inc., Palo Alto, Calif. *Member:* American Educational Research Association, American Psychological Association, American Personnel and Guidance Association, American Association for the Advancement of Science. *Awards, honors:* Outstanding Research Award, American Personnel and Guidance Association, 1966, 1968; Guggenheim fellowship, 1973-74.

WRITINGS: (Editor with J. D. Krumboltz) *Behavioral*

Counseling: Case and Techniques, Holt, 1969; (with M. J. Mahoney) *Behavioral Self-Control*, Holt, 1974; (with Mahoney) *Self-Control: Power to the Person*, Brooks/Cole, 1974; (editor with Krumboltz) *Behavioral Counseling Methods*, Holt, 1976; *Let's Get Intensive: Single Case Research*, Prentice-Hall, 1976; *Stop Smoking*, Prentice-Hall, 1976; *Learning How to Sleep Well*, Prentice-Hall, 1976.

WORK IN PROGRESS: Research in self-control in children and adolescents, childhood obesity, insomnia, and stress and tension.

* * *

THORPE, Peter   1932-

PERSONAL: Born May 11, 1932; son of Lloyd and Bee (DuRae) Thorpe; married, 1959 (divorced, 1971); married wife, Peggy (a bookkeeper), December 22, 1971; children: Ann, Paul. *Education:* University of Washington, Seattle, B.A., 1957, M.A., 1961, Ph.D., 1963. *Home:* 49 Benthaven Pl., Boulder, Colo. 80303. *Office:* Department of English, University of Colorado at Denver, Denver, Colo. 80202.

CAREER: U.S. Navy, naval aviator, 1952-56, leaving service with rank of lieutenant; presently English professor at University of Colorado at Denver. *Member:* Samuel Johnson Society of the Northwest.

WRITINGS: Eighteenth-Century English Poetry, Nelson-Hall, 1974. Contributor of poetry to *New Yorker, Lyric, Fiddlehead, Wormwood Review*, and other magazines, and of articles and reviews to journals, including *New England Quarterly, Genre, Northwest Folklore, and Criticism*.

WORK IN PROGRESS: A popular grammar and usage book; a book on the function and value of the humanities; articles on satire for an anthology.

SIDELIGHTS: Thorpe describes himself as "an English professor who wishes he could write a best-seller but knows he can't and so writes about literature instead."

* * *

THORSTAD, David   1941-

PERSONAL: Born October 15, 1941, in Thief River Falls, Minn.; son of Jesse M. (a truck driver) and Hazel (Sorum) Thorstad. *Education:* University of Minnesota, B.A. (magna cum laude), 1963, M.A., 1966, further graduate study, 1967. *Politics:* "Revolutionary socialist." *Religion:* "Atheist; adversary of all religion." *Home:* 316 East 11th St., New York, N.Y. 10003.

CAREER: Young Socialist (magazine), New York, N.Y., staff writer, 1969; *Militant*, New York, N.Y., staff writer and editor of review page, 1970-71; Intercontinental Press, New York, N.Y., staff writer and translator from French, German, Spanish, Norwegian, Swedish, and Danish, 1972-73; Charles Scribner's Sons, New York, N.Y., foreign language textbook editor, 1973-74; writer, 1975—. *Member:* Gay Activists Alliance (New York; president).

WRITINGS: (Translator) Maxime Rodinson, *Israel: A Colonial-Settler State?*, Monad Press, 1973; (with John Lauritsen) *The Early Homosexual Rights Movement (1864-1935)*, Times Change Press, 1974; (with Hugo Blanco, Jean-Pierre Beauvais, Peter Camejo, Gerry Foley, Joseph Hansen, and Dick Roberts) *Disaster in Chile: Allende's Strategy and Why It Failed*, Pathfinder, 1974; (with Lauritsen) *Sexual Morality in Historical Materialist Perspective* (pamphlet), privately printed, 1975. Contributor of articles, poems, and translations to *Boston University Journal* and *Gay Liberator.*

WORK IN PROGRESS: Editing an anthology of materials from the early homosexual rights movement, with John Lauritsen.

SIDELIGHTS: Thorstad writes: "As a Marxist and as a homosexual activist, my main interest at the moment is in developing a theory of homosexual oppression and liberation and in striving to bring about a unity between Marxist theory and practice in the area of sexuality ... this means fighting for a revolutionary approach within the gay liberation movement." Thorstad speaks French, German, Spanish, Norwegian, Swedish, and Danish. *Avocational interests:* Musician (plays oboe, piano, saxophone, trumpet, bass viol, organ), class-struggle politics, cooking.

*   *   *

THURMAN, Kelly   1914-

PERSONAL: Born May 11, 1914, in Lebanon Junction, Ky.; son of Roscoe and Lillie (Coomes) Thurman; married Mary John Rodgers (a librarian), December 22, 1943; children: John Richard, Roger Kelly. *Education:* Western Kentucky University, A.B., 1938; University of Kentucky, M.A., 1945; State University of Iowa, Ph.D., 1950. *Religion:* Baptist. *Home:* 444 Breck Ave., Richmond, Ky. 40475.

CAREER: Public school teacher in Kentucky, 1936-45; Denison University, Granville, Ohio, instructor in English, 1945-46; Auburn University, Auburn, Ala., assistant professor of English, 1948-50; Union University, Jackson, Tenn., professor of English and chairman of department, 1950-58; Stephen F. Austin State College (now University), Nacogdoches, Tex., professor of English, 1958-62; Oklahoma City University, Oklahoma City, professor of English and chairman of department, 1962-66; Eastern Kentucky University, Richmond, professor of English, 1966—, chairman of department, 1967—.

WRITINGS: Semantics, Houghton, 1960; *John Hay as a Man of Letters*, Mojave Books, 1974. Regular contributor to *Oklahoma City Magazine*, 1963-65, including book-length study, "Pulitzer Prize Winning Fiction."

*   *   *

THURSTON, Hazel (Patricia)   1906-
(Hazel Murphy)

PERSONAL: Born August 13, 1906, in Clonmel, Ireland; daughter of Thomas (a brewer) and Mabel (Jorgensen) Murphy; married Perrett Thurston, June 6, 1936 (divorced, 1960); children: Clare (Mrs. William Ratcliffe). *Education:* Attended North Foreland Lodge, Sherfield-on-Loddon, Hampshire, England, 1920-25. *Politics:* Conservative. *Religion:* Church of England. *Home:* 17 Bedford St., Brighton, Sussex, England. *Agent:* Anthony Sheil Associates, 52 Floral St., London W.C. 2, England.

CAREER: Worked with military intelligence, 1940-45; farmed in Ireland, 1946-52; after 1960, held various secretarial posts; assistant story editor, Twentieth Century-Fox, London, England, 1955; free-lance journalist. *Member:* Guild of Travel Writers.

WRITINGS: (Under name Hazel Murphy) *Himself* (novel), Methuen, 1932; (under name Hazel Murphy) *The Travelling People* (novel), Collins, 1934; *The Garlanded Lamb*, Chapman & Hall, 1959; *From Darkest Mum*, Chapman & Hall, 1960; *Our Own Dread Enemy* (novel),

Chapman & Hall, 1961; *Where Is Thy Sting* (novel), Chapman & Hall, 1962; *Let's Look at Ireland* (children's guide), Museum Press, 1965; *The Traveller's Guide to Cyprus*, J. Cape, 1967, revised edition, 1971, Bobbs-Merrill, 1971; *South and South West Ireland* (guide), Charles Letts, 1971; *The Traveller's Guide to Tunisia*, J. Cape, 1973; *Royal Parks for the People*, David & Charles, 1974; *Cat: Man's Fellow Traveller*, Temple Smith, in press. Contributor of travel articles to various British magazines.

WORK IN PROGRESS: The Traveller's Guide to the Balearics, publication by J. Cape expected in 1977; *The Balearics*, for Batsford, 1978.

SIDELIGHTS: Hazel Thurston writes to *CA*: "I travel whenever opportunity occurs and make use of resulting material. I write for subsistence, not pleasure."

*   *   *

TIERNEY, Tom   1928-

PERSONAL: Born October 8, 1928, in Beaumont, Tex.; son of John Taylor (an accountant) and Mary Lou (Gripon) Tierney. *Education:* University of Texas, B.F.A., 1949; attended Pratt Institute, 1953, Art Students League, 1955, School of Visual Arts (N.Y.), 1955. *Politics:* "Not committed." *Religion:* "Not committed." *Home:* Horton Town Hill Rd., Kent Township, N.Y. *Agent:* Lewis Chambers, 102 West 75th St., New York, N.Y. 10023. *Office:* Tom Tierney Studio, 164 West 79th St., New York, N.Y. 10024.

CAREER: Tom Tierney Studio, Inc., New York, N.Y., free-lance fashion illustrator. *Military service:* U.S. Army, 1951-52; became sergeant. *Member:* "None (I am a rabid non-joiner!)"

WRITINGS: Thirty from the Thirties, Prentice-Hall, 1974.

WORK IN PROGRESS: Compiling a history and encyclopedia of American film costume and costume designers, for Prentice-Hall.

SIDELIGHTS: Tom Tierney told *CA*: "My training has all been as a visual artist, painting, sculpture, etc., so most of my interests have been in these areas. Late in life I studied ballet; then singing, which led to a brief career as a night club singer. Throughout, I have always been a film enthusiast—this, coupled with my fashion art career, led to *Thirty from the Thirties*."

*   *   *

TIPTON, James   1942-

PERSONAL: Born January 18, 1942, in Ashland, Ohio; son of J. Robert (a businessman) and Ruth (Burcher) Tipton; married Lynn Ellen Johnson (a teacher), September 5, 1965; children: Jennifer Lynn, James Daniel. *Education:* Purdue University, B.A., 1964, M.A., 1968. *Home:* 7547 North Osborn Rd., Elwell, Mich. 48832. *Office:* Department of English, Alma College, Alma, Mich. 48801.

CAREER: Kalamazoo College, Kalamazoo, Mich., writer-in-residence, 1969-70; Alma College, Alma, Mich., assistant professor of English, 1973—. *Awards, honors:* Grant from National Endowment for the Humanities, 1972, to study ritual in contemporary poetry; first prize from Birmingham, Ala., Festival of the Arts, 1973, for story "Baby Jesus."

WRITINGS: Bittersweet (poems), Cold Mountain Press, 1975.

Work is anthologized in *The Haiku Anthology*, edited by

Cor van den Heuvel, Doubleday, 1974; *Pocket Poems*, edited by Paul B. Janeczko, Washington Square Press, in press; *Heartland II: Poets of the Midwest*, edited by Lucien Stryck, Northern Illinois University Press, in press.

Contributor of poems, stories, translations, and reviews to literary journals and magazines, including *Nation, Esquire, Sumac, South Dakota Review, Carolina Quarterly, Field, Contemporary Poetry, New Orleans Review, Greensboro Review, Works*, and *Southern Humanities Review*.

WORK IN PROGRESS: Editing an anthology of contemporary Michigan poets; a poetry manuscript on the life of Geronimo.

* * *

TISDALE, Celes 1941-

PERSONAL: Born July 31, 1941, in Salters, S.C.; son of Norman (a laborer) and Rachel (McCray) Tisdale; married Ann Parker, June 25, 1966; children: Yvette, Colette, Eric. *Education:* State University of New York College at Buffalo, B.S., 1963, M.S., 1969, doctoral candidate. *Home:* 93 Harvard Place, Buffalo, N.Y. 14209. *Office:* Department of English, Eric Community College, City Campus, Buffalo, N.Y. 14209.

CAREER: Public school teacher of English in Buffalo, N.Y., 1963-68, chairman of department, 1968-69; State University of New York at Buffalo, instructor in English, 1969-72; Erie Community College, City Campus, Buffalo, N.Y., assistant professor of English, 1972—. Buffalo Urban League, director of summer program, 1963-68, and of tutorial services, 1965-68; director of Nia Writers Workshop, 1971—. Teacher of creative writing at Attica State Prison, 1972-75; consultant to New York State Arts Council, 1974. Poet-in-residence, Young Audiences, Inc. *Member:* New York African Studies Association. *Awards, honors:* Speakers award from Valencia College, 1972.

WRITINGS: We Be Poetin', We the People, 1973; *Betcha Ain't: Poems from Attica*, Broadside Press, 1974. Author of "Five Weeks in August" television series for CBS affiliate, 1969. Associate editor of *Obsidian*, 1974—.

WORK IN PROGRESS: Every Wednesday: More Attica Reflections; editing poems by five Black women, *Black Breezes*; a collection of personal poems, *Poem Dance*; *Black Lifesongs*, an original poetry dramatic production.

SIDELIGHTS: Tisdale is a professional actor who wants to become professionally involved in television, especially in the area of news reporting.

* * *

TODD, Hollis N(elson) 1914-

PERSONAL: Born January 28, 1914, in Glenn Falls, N.Y.; married Thelma Larch, June 30, 1936; children: H. Schuyler. *Education:* Cornell University, B.A., 1934, M.Ed., 1935. *Office:* School of Photographic Arts and Sciences, Rochester Institute of Technology, Rochester, N.Y. 14623.

CAREER: School teacher in North Rose, N.Y., 1935-41; science teacher and head of department in public school in Tonawanda, N.Y., 1941-46; Rochester Institute of Technology, Rochester, N.Y., member of faculty, 1946-60, professor of photographic arts and sciences, 1960—, chairman of department of photographic science and instrumentation, 1964-68. Partner of RST Associates (research consultants); director of Photographic Sciences, Inc. *Member:* Society of

Photographic Scientists and Engineers (member of board of directors of Rochester chapter), Society of Motion Picture and Television Engineers, American Association of University Professors.

WRITINGS: Polarized Lights, Bausch & Lomb, 1960; (contributor) C. B. Neblette, editor, *Photography*, Van Nostrand, 6th edition (Todd was not included in earlier editions), 1962; (contributor) F. M. Brown, H. J. Hall, and J. Kosar, editors, *Photographic Systems for Engineers*, Society of Photographic Scientists and Engineers, 1966; (with A. D. Rickmers) *Statistics: An Introduction*, McGraw, 1967; (with R. D. Zakia) *One Hundred One Experiments in Photography*, Morgan & Morgan, 1969; (with Zakia) *Photographic Sensitometry*, Morgan & Morgan, 1969; (with L. D. Stroebel) *The Contemporary Dictionary of Photography*, Morgan & Morgan, 1974; (with Zakia) *Color Primer*, Morgan & Morgan, 1974. Contributor to *Collier's Encyclopedia* and to journals, including *Journal of the Society of Photographic Scientists and Engineers*. Technical editor of *Image Technology*, 1969-73.

WORK IN PROGRESS: A text on visual perception in photography; a text on photographic image evaluation theory and methods; programmed instructional material on photographic science; research on objective and subjective tone reproduction of visual images in monochrome and color.

SIDELIGHTS: Todd writes: "Everything I have done and written in my career was intended to guide students to a rational attitude toward problem-solving in a technological environment. In my field, there are no right answers, except in trivial cases; there are only rational, plausible, defensible ones." *Avocational interests:* Woodcarving, playing the recorder, gardening, carpentry (built a summer home), cooking (making bread).

* * *

TOLLERS, Vincent L(ouis) 1939-

PERSONAL: Born August 23, 1939, in Superior, Wis.; son of Rudolph Floyd (a restaurant owner) and Opal (a restaurant owner; maiden name, Jodell) Tollers; married Martha Miller (a social worker), June 15, 1963; children: Elizabeth Marie, Susan Kathleen. *Education:* University of Wisconsin, Superior, B.A., 1961; University of Colorado, M.A., 1965, Ph.D., 1968. *Religion:* Presbyterian. *Home:* 15 Meadowview Dr., Brockport, N.Y. 14420. *Office:* Department of English, State University of New York, 209 Neff, Brockport, N.Y. 14420.

CAREER: Kansas State Teachers College, Emporia, assistant professor of English, 1968-70; State University of New York at Brockport, assistant professor, 1970-74, associate professor of English, 1974—. *Military service:* U.S. Army, Security Agency, 1961-64. *Member:* Modern Language Association of America. *Awards, honors:* State University of New York research grant, 1971.

WRITINGS: (Editor) *A Bibliography of Matthew Arnold: 1932-1970*, Pennsylvania State University Press, 1974. Contributor to *RQ*, and other publications. Editor of *Literary Research Newsletter*, 1975—.

WORK IN PROGRESS: Books tentatively titled, *The Dynasts, The Bible in Its Literary Milieu: Contemporary Essays*, and *A Beginner's Handbook to Literary Research*.

AVOCATIONAL INTERESTS: Travel, gardening, golf, bridge.

TORRES, Jose Acosta 1925-

PERSONAL: Born December 13, 1925, in Martindale, Tex.; married Patricia Resch (an art teacher), August 15, 1970; children: Gregory, Maruca, Angela. *Education:* Southwest Texas State College (now University), B.S., 1950, M.Ed., 1952; Universidad Interamericana, Ph.D., 1965; further study at Spanish Language Institute (National Defense Education Act), Our Lady of the Lake College, San Antonio, 1963, and at University of Texas at Austin, 1967, 1968. *Religion:* Roman Catholic. *Home:* 800 Cedar Glen, Austin, Tex. 78745. *Office:* Department of Education, St. Edward's University, Austin, Tex. 78704.

CAREER: Elementary school teacher, 1950-58, assistant principal, 1958-60, high school acting assistant principal, 1960-62, coordinator of foreign language department, 1962-65, all in San Antonio, Tex.; San Antonio College, San Antonio, Tex., instructor, 1965-68, assistant professor of Spanish, 1968-70; Southwest Educational Development Laboratory, Austin, Tex., curriculum development specialist, 1970-72; U.S. Office of Education, project coordinator in Crystal City, Tex., 1972-73; St. Edward's University, Austin, Tex., assistant professor of education, 1973—. Coordinator of foreign language department, Fort Sam Houston, 1965-66; consultant to HemisFair '68, to Good Samaritan Center education project, 1969, and to *Compton's Encyclopedia* and *Encyclopaedia Britannica*; vice-president of Intercontinental Translations; initiator and director of community classes in arts and crafts for disadvantaged children and of citizenship classes for Mexican-American adults. *Military service:* U.S. Army, 1944-45; received Purple Heart.

MEMBER: American Association of Teachers of Spanish and Portuguese, Texans for the Educational Advancement of Mexican-Americans , Kappa Pi (past president), Phi Delta Kappa. *Awards, honors:* Certificate of commendation from Spanish Government, 1963, for article on Junipero Serra; certificate of commendation from New Braunfels (Tex.) Kiwanis Club, 1969, for services benefiting youth of the community; Literary Award from Spanish Government, 1969, for HemisFair '68 essay.

WRITINGS: Cachito Mio (title means "My Little One"), Quinto Sol Publications, 1974; *Chicanito Sixty-Nine*, Quinto Sol Publications, 1975. Co-author of textbooks and educational reports published by Southwest Educational Development Laboratory, 1972. *Alamo Messenger* (newspaper), columnist, 1955-58, Spanish-language editor, 1962-64; *La Voz* (newspaper), columnist, 1955-58, editor, 1958-62; editor and co-founder, *Hispanavoz* (newspaper), 1964-66. Contributor of about 300 articles, in Spanish and in English, to various publicatons, including *Texas Outlook* and *El Grito*.

* * *

TOURNEY, Garfield 1927-

PERSONAL: Born Feburary 6, 1927, in Quincy, Ill.; son of Guy and Rose (Werner) Tourney; married Helen W. Wohler, April 4, 1 1950; children: Carolyn Rose, Patricia Ann, Catherine Marie. *Education:* 15 Washington Rd., Grosse Pointe, Mich. 48230. *Office:* 915 East Lafayette, Detroit, Mich. 48207.

CAREER: University of Colorado, School of Medicine, Boulder, instructor in psychiatry, 1952-53; University of Miami, School of Medicine, Coral Gables, Fla., instructor, 1953-54, assistant professor of psychiatry, 1954-55; Wayne State University, School of Medicine, Detroit, Mich., as-sistant professor, 1955-59, associate professor, 1959-65, professor of psychiatry, 1965-67; University of Iowa, College of Medicine, Iowa City, professor of psychiatry, 1967-71; Wayne State University, School of Medicine, professor of psychiatry, 1971—, chairman of department, 1973—. Chief of department of psychiatry, Harper Hospital, 1971—; chief of staff, Lafayette Clinic, 1973—; consultant to Sinai Hospital, Hutzel Hospital, and Bon Secours Hospital. Diplomate, American Board of Psychiatry and Neurology. *Military service:* U.S. Army Reserve, 1948-61; became major.

MEMBER: American Psychiatric Association (fellow), American Medical Association, American College of Psychiatrists, Society of Biological Psychiatry, American Psychopathological Association, American Psychosomatic Society.

WRITINGS: (Editor with Jacques S. Gottlieb, and contributor) *The Lafayette Clinic Studies on Schizophrenia*, Wayne State University Press, 1971.

Contributor: Robert L. Roessler and N. S. Greenfield, editors, *Physiological Correlates of Psychological Disorder*, University of Wisconsin Press, 1962; H. W. Dunham, *Community and Schizophrenia: An Epidemiological Analysis*, Wayne State University Press, 1965; A. J. Enelow editor, *Depression in Medical Practice*, Merck Sharp & Dohme, 1970; Theodore Rothman, editor, *Changing Patterns in Psychiatric Care*, Crown, 1970. Contributor to *Recent Advances in Biological Psychiatry*, 1962, to *Psychotherapy and Behavior Changes 1972*, and about fifty articles to scientific journals.

* * *

TOURVILLE, Elsie A(lma) 1926-

PERSONAL: Born December 4, 1926, in Baltimore, Md.; daughter of Edgar Day and Dorothy (Rhodes) Cannon; married Lloyd W. Tourville (a physical scientist), November 26, 1947. *Education:* Educated in public schools in Belchertown, Mass. *Residence:* Pocomoke City, Md.

CAREER: During years 1944-47, worked packing matches at Diamond Match Co., addressing envelopes at National Scale Co., making notions at Singer Sewing Machine store, and as an advertising department junior secretary, all in Springfield, Mass.; G. & C. Merriam, Springfield, 1951-52, began as typist, worked as editorial assistant for *Webster's New International Dictionary*; Florida State University, Oceanographic Institution, Tallahassee, departmental secretary, 1953-54, writer, 1955.

WRITINGS: Alaska: A Bibliography, 1570-1970, G. K. Hall, 1974.

WORK IN PROGRESS: Indexing selected pre-1800 material about Worcester County, Md.; indexing Worcester County newspapers pre-dating 1900.

SIDELIGHTS: Upon moving to Alaska with her husband in 1955, Mrs. Tourville says that "having been a book collector since childhood . . . it was inevitable that Alaska should crowd itself onto the book shelves." Her random notes and card file became a book. She continues: "Current published works by Alaskan writers are essentially young in orientation and in methods of execution. Records of hunting and fishing action are popular subjects. New histories and ethnological studies have been published in recent years. There are books on a wide range of subjects for children. There seems to have been produced a lesser quantity of poetry, reflective thinking, and literary criticism. . . . There is a strong movement to preserve the oral history of the first peoples of Alaska—the Inupiat (Eskimos) of the northwest and Arctic coasts and of Anaktuvuk Pass, the Aleutian Islanders and the Indians of the Interior and Southeast.''

AVOCATIONAL INTERESTS: Knitting, sewing, cooking, gardening, doing jigsaw and crossword puzzles, composing poetry, camping in Alaska, rockhounding in California, eating in gourmet restaurants, visiting antiquarian bookstores, fishing and boating, reading, enjoying music, art, photographs.

* * *

TOWERS, Maxwell 1909-
(Rabbie)

PERSONAL: Born January 9, 1909, in Glasgow, Scotland; son of John (a stockbroker) and Annie Caroline (Chalmers) Towers; married Elizabeth Torrance Aitchison Moodie, September 19, 1938; children: William Lennox, John Jackson. *Education:* Scottish College of Commerce, received certificate; Glasgow University, diploma in public administration. *Politics:* "Conservative-tinged with Scottish nationalism." *Religion:* Scottish Presbyterian. *Home:* 64 Birmingham Road, Shenstone, Staffordshire, England. *Office:* Institute of Supervisory Management, 22 Bore St., Lichfield, Staffordshire, WS13 6LP, England.

CAREER: Munro, Towers & Stewart, Glasgow, Scotland, stockbrokers' clerk, 1925-29, dealer in stock exchange, 1929-39; Civil Defence First Aid and Rescue Services, Glasgow, staff officer, 1939-45; Clyde Shipbuilder's Association, Glasgow, wage negotiator, 1945-57; Fairfield Shipyard, Govan, Glasgow, industrial relations officer, 1957-59; Scottish Engineering Employers' Association, Glasgow, assistant secretary, 1959-61; West Riding Engineering Employers' Association, Leeds, Yorkshire, England, secretary, 1961-62; R. W. Crabtree & Sons (engineers), Leeds, Yorkshire, personnel manager, 1962-63; Rank Taylor Hobson Engineering & Optical Co., Leeds, Yorkshire, personnel manager, 1963-66; Institute of Supervisory Management, Lichfield, Staffordshire, England, regional training officer, 1966-71, deputy director, 1971-74, director, 1974—. Part-time lecturer at colleges and polytechnics; occasional reader for Management Book Publishers. *Member:* Institute of Personnel Management (associate member), British Institute of Management (associate member), Institute of Supervisory Management, Institute of Advanced Motorists. *Awards, honors:* British National Essay Competition award, 1973, for "Industrial Relations in Britain."

WRITINGS: Role-Playing for Supervisors, Pergamon Press, 1969; *Role-Playing for Managers,* Pergamon Press, 1974. Contributor to *Institute of Supervisory Management Journal.* Formerly author of political, nationalistic, and industrial verse in Scottish dialect under pseudonym Rabbie. Contributor of non-dialect verse to Glasgow newspapers.

WORK IN PROGRESS: A television dramatization of case study from 1974 book; an industrial novel, a thriller with an espionage angle, set in Scotland and England.

AVOCATIONAL INTERESTS: Motoring, literature and drama.

* * *

TOWNLEY, Rod 1942-

PERSONAL: Born June 7, 1942, in Orange, N.J.; son of William Richard (a businessman) and Elise (Fredman) Townley; married Libby Blackman (a reference librarian), April 4, 1970; children: Jesse Blackman. *Education:* Attended Hamilton College, 1960-61, and University of Chicago, 1961-62; Bard College, A.B., 1965; Rutgers University, M.A., 1970, Ph.D., 1972. *Home:* 1911 Pine St., Philadelphia, Pa. 19103.

CAREER: Passaic County Community College, Paterson, N.J., associate professor of world literature, 1972-73; freelance writer in Philadelphia, Pa., 1973—.

WRITINGS: Blue Angels Black Angels (poetry), Bradstreet, 1972; (contributor) Daniel Hoffman, editor, *University and College Poetry Prizes: 1967-1972,* Academy of American Poets, 1974; (contributor) Ray Boxer, editor, *Eleven Young Poets: The Smith Seventeen* (poetry anthology), The Smith, 1975; *The Early Poetry of William Carlos Williams* (criticism), Cornell University Press, 1975; *Summer Street* (chapbook), The Smith, 1975. Regular contributor to *Today,* 1974. Contributor to *Studies in Short Fiction, Philadelphia, TV Guide, Village Voice, Detroit Free Press,* and other publications.

WORK IN PROGRESS: A novel, completion expected in 1975.

SIDELIGHTS: Townley told *CA:* "I'm currently exploring possibilities of polyphony in poetry: poems in which two, three, or more voices proceed down the page side by side, to be read separately or concurrently. The basis of my work is music. I am also exploring ways in which such a poetry might best be performed in public."

* * *

TRAPP, Frank Anderson 1922-

PERSONAL: Born June 13, 1922, in Pittsburgh, Pa.; son of Frank Louis and Mary (Anderson) Trapp. *Education:* Carnegie Institute of Technology (now Carnegie-Mellon University), B.A., 1943; Harvard University, M.A., 1947, Ph.D., 1952. *Home:* 71 Spring St., Amherst, Mass. 01002. *Office:* Department of Fine Arts, Amherst College, Amherst, Mass. 01002.

CAREER: Harvard University, Cambridge, Mass., tutor, 1948-51; Williams College, Williamstown, Mass., instructor, 1951-54, lecturer, 1954-55, assistant professor of fine arts, 1955-56; Amherst College, Amherst, Mass., assistant professor, 1956-58, associate professor, 1958-63, professor of fine arts, 1963—, chairman of department of fine arts, 1963—, director of Mead Art Gallery, 1965—. *Military service:* U.S. Army, 1943-46; served in Pacific theater. *Member:* College Art Association of America, Century Club (New York). *Awards, honors:* Fulbright scholarship, 1949-50; senior fellowship from National Endowment for the Humanities, 1971-72.

WRITINGS: The Attainment of Delacroix, Johns Hopkins Press, 1970. Contributor to scholarly journals.

* * *

TREJO, Arnulfo D(uenes) 1922-

PERSONAL: Born August 15, 1922, in Villa Vicente Guerrero, Durango, Mexico; son of Nicolas F. and Petra (Duenes) Trejo; married Phyllis Bowen, May 21, 1954 (divorced); married Annette Foster Loken, July 1, 1967; children: (first marriage) Rachel, Rebecca, Ruth; stepdaughter: Linda Loken. *Education:* University of Arizona, B.A., 1949; University of the Americas, M.A. (in Spanish language and literature), 1951; Kent State University, M.A.

(in library science), 1953; National University of Mexico, Litt.D. (with honors), 1959. *Home:* 240 East Yvon Dr., Tucson, Ariz. 85704. *Office:* Graduate Library School, University of Arizona, Tucson, Ariz. 85721.

CAREER: National University of Mexico, Mexico City, assistant librarian, 1954-55; University of California at Los Angeles, reference librarian, 1955-59; California State University, Long Beach, assistant librarian, 1959-63; University of California at Los Angeles, assistant professor, 1965-66, associate professor of library science, 1966-68, Latin American bibliographer, 1966-68; University of Arizona, Tucson, associate professor of library science and English, 1970-75, professor of library science, 1975—. Library director of ESAN (graduate school of business administration), Lima, Peru, 1963-65; American Library Association consultant to United States Agency for International Development (USAID), Caracas, Venezuela, 1968-70. Member of board of directors of Tucson Public Library, 1967-68, and City of Tucson Historical Committee, 1972; president of El Tiradito Foundation, 1972-73. *Military service:* U.S. Army, Infantry, 1943-45; served in South Pacific theater; became sergeant; received Philippine Liberation Ribbon, Purple Heart with oak leaf cluster, and Bronze Star Medal.

MEMBER: American Library Association (council member, 1974—), REFORMA (National Organization of Spanish-Speaking Librarians in the United States; president, 1971-74), American Association of University Professors, Seminar on the Acquisition of Latin American Library Materials, Phi Delta Kappa, Beta Phi Mu, Phi Kappa Phi, Sigma Delta Pi. *Awards, honors:* Simon Bolivar Award from Colegio de Biblioteconomos of Venezuela, 1970; El Tiradito Award from El Tiradito Foundation, 1972; annual award from League of Mexican-American Women, 1973.

WRITINGS: Bibliografia Comentada Sobre Administracion de Negocios (title means "Annotated Bibliography on Business Administration"), Addison-Wesley, 1967; *Diccionario Etimologico del Lexico de la Delincuencia* (title means "Etymological Dictionary of the Language of the Underworld"), UTEHA, 1969; (editor) *Directory of Spanish-Speaking/Spanish Surnamed Librarians in the United States*, Bureau of School Services, College of Education, University of Arizona, 1973; *Bibliografia Chicana*, Gale, 1975. Contributor to *Arizona Highways* and *Folklore Americas*.

WORK IN PROGRESS: Editing *The Chicanos: As We See Ourselves*.

* * *

TRENNERT, Robert A., Jr. 1937-

PERSONAL: Born December 15, 1937, in South Gate, Calif.; son of Robert A. and Mabel V. (Chesnut) Trennert; married Linda Griffith, July 31, 1965; children: Robert A. III, Kristina. *Education:* Occidental College, B.A., 1961; Los Angeles State College of Applied Arts and Sciences (now California State University, Los Angeles), M.A., 1963; University of California, Santa Barbara, Ph.D., 1969. *Home:* 2047 East Ellis Dr., Tempe, Ariz. 85282. *Office:* Department of History, Arizona State University, Tempe, Ariz. 85281.

CAREER: Museum of Northern Arizona, Flagstaff, research fellow, 1963-64; Temple University, Philadelphia, Pa., instructor, 1967-69, assistant professor of history, 1969-74; Arizona State University, Tempe, assistant pro-

fessor of history, 1974—. *Member:* Western History Association. *Awards, honors:* Research grants, Temple University, 1970, 1972, 1973, Arizona State University, 1975; James L. Sellers Memorial Award, Nebraska State Historical Society, 1973, for historical article.

WRITINGS: Alternative to Extinction: Federal Indian Policy and the Beginnings of the Reservation System, 1846-1851, Temple University Press, 1975; (contributor) Wilcomb E. Washburn, editor, *The Handbook of American Indians*, Volume IV, Smithsonian Institution, 1976. Contributor of articles and reviews to professional journals, including *Pacific Historical Review, Nebraska History, Ohio History*, and *American West*.

WORK IN PROGRESS: An analysis of a trading company and its impact on Federal Indian policy, *W. G. & G. W. Ewing, Indian Traders: A Company Biography*; articles on American Indians.

* * *

TRENT, May Wong 1939-

PERSONAL: Born May 23, 1939, in Hong Kong; daughter of S. T. (a doctor) and K. L. (Ho) Wong; married Theodore Chang, December 24, 1959 (divorced, 1967); married Peter C. Trent (an investment banker), April 15, 1971; children: (first marriage) Michael, Theodore; (second marriage) Christopher. *Education:* Attended Hong Kong University and Cordon Bleu Cooking School. *Religion:* Anglican. *Home and office:* 430 East 86th St., New York, N.Y. 10028. *Agent:* Toni Mendez, Inc., 140 East 56th St., New York, N.Y. 10022.

CAREER: New York Times and *Baltimore Sun*, Hong Kong, assistant to correspondent, 1967-68; International Research Associates, Hong Kong, marketing research project director, 1968-70; cooking teacher and writer, 1970—. Art gallery member of China Institute; recipe tester for *New York Times*' "Correspondent's Choice," 1974—. *Awards, honors: Eighty Precious Chinese Recipes* was nominated by R. T. French Co. as best cookbook, 1973, and *Oriental Barbecue* was nominated in 1974.

WRITINGS: Eighty Precious Chinese Recipes, Macmillan, 1973; *Oriental Barbecue*, Macmillan, 1974.

WORK IN PROGRESS: Traditional Chinese Recipes for Health, Sex, and Longevity; *Complete One-Dish Chinese Dinners*; *Jasmine*, a story about foreign correspondents covering the Vietnam War.

SIDELIGHTS: May Trent writes that she ". . . began as a chemistry major in college, but discovered the love for experiments and utensils was in fact for cooking in the kitchen, which was just like laboratory work!" She adds that her family is one of the older families in Hong Kong, and that she would someday like to write a novel about Hong Kong. *Avocational interests:* International travel.

* * *

TRESHOW, Michael 1926-

PERSONAL: Born July 14, 1926, in Copenhagen, Denmark; naturalized U.S. citizen; son of Michael and Else (Koefoed) Treshow; married Valora Prentice, June 24, 1951; children: Michael, Paul. *Education:* University of California, Los Angeles, B.S., 1950; University of California, Davis, Ph.D., 1954. *Home:* 1798 Millbrook Rd., Salt Lake City, Utah 84106. *Office:* Department of Biology, University of Utah, Salt Lake City, Utah 84112.

CAREER: University of California, Davis, senior laboratory technician, 1952-53; U.S. Steel Corp., Columbia-Geneva Steel Division, Provo, Utah, plant pathologist, 1953-61; University of Utah, Salt Lake City, assistant professor, 1961-64, associate professor of botany, 1964-67, professor of biology, 1967—. *Military service:* U.S. Naval Reserve, active duty, 1944-46. *Member:* American Phytopathological Society, Mycological Society, American Institute of Biological Sciences, American Association for the Advancement of Science.

WRITINGS: *Common Utah Plants*, Brigham Young University Press, 1966; *Guide to Woody Plants of the Rocky Mountains*, Pruett, 1967; *Environment and Plant Response*, McGraw, 1970; *Whatever Happened to Fresh Air*, University of Utah Press, 1971; *The Human Environment*, McGraw, in press.

WORK IN PROGRESS: *Plants of the Wasatch Region.*

* * *

TRIOLA, Mario F(rank) 1944-

PERSONAL: Born November 27, 1944, in Poughkeepsie, N.Y.; son of Mario C. (a construction worker) and Ellen (Ronson) Triola; married Virginia Greco (a teacher), August 6, 1967; children: Marc, Scott. *Education:* Marist College, B.A., 1966; St. John's University, Jamaica, N.Y., M.A., 1968. *Home:* 30 Robin Hill Dr., Poughkeepsie, N.Y. 12603. *Office:* Department of Mathematics, Dutchess Community College, Pendell Rd., Poughkeepsie, N.Y. 12601.

CAREER: Dutchess Community College, Poughkeepsie, N.Y., instructor, 1968-71, assistant professor, 1971-75, associate professor of mathematics, 1975—. *Member:* Mathematics Association of America, New York State Mathematical Association of Two Year Colleges.

WRITINGS: *Mathematics and the Modern World*, Cummings, 1973; *A Survey of Mathematics*, Cummings, 1975.

WORK IN PROGRESS: *Computer Modeling and Simulations.*

* * *

TRIPLETT, Kenneth E(arl) 1926-

PERSONAL: Born July 16, 1926, in Ohio; son of Myron A (a tire manufacturer) and Ethel (Price) Triplett; married Mary R. Brunner (a registered nurse), July 22, 1949; children: Brian, Bruce. *Education:* Bellevue Hospital School of Nursing, Diploma, 1951; New York University, B.S., 1957, M.A., 1958. *Home address:* Munday-Brohard Rd., Macfarlan, W.Va. 26148. *Office:* Weston State Hospital, River St., Weston, W.Va. 26452.

CAREER: Veterans Administration Hospital, Sunmount, N.Y., staff nurse, 1952-55; Bellevue Hospital, New York, N.Y., instructor, 1955-57, clinical instructor and supervisor, 1957-58; Wilson Research Foundation, New York, N.Y., director of projects, 1964-68; Warren State Hospital, Warren, Pa., director of education, 1968-71; Clarion State College, Oil City, Pa., assistant professor and program director in nursing, 1971-72; Weston State Hospital, Weston, W.Va., nurse educator, 1972—. Publisher, Triplett Enterprises Ltd. *Military service:* U.S. Army, 1962-64; became captain. *Member:* American Nurses' Association, Sigma Theta Tau.

WRITINGS: (With wife, Mary Triplett) *Free Camping in Florida*, Triplett, 1973. Contributor to *Wilson Research*

Foundation Bulletin and *Audience.* Associate editor of *Medical Folio*, 1968.

WORK IN PROGRESS: Poetry; a book on wild edibles; "how to" books and articles on homesteading.

* * *

TRITON, A. N.
See BARCLAY, Oliver R(ainsford)

* * *

TRUITT, Evelyn Mack 1931-

PERSONAL: Born July 2, 1931, in Los Angeles, Calif.; daughter of Everett E. and Celeste (Pratt) Mack; married Edwin A. Truitt, 1950 (divorced, 1958). *Education:* Attended East Los Angeles Junior College, 1949-51, Los Angeles City College, University of California, Los Angeles, and Sawyer School of Business. *Residence:* Los Angeles, Calif. *Office:* Signal Companies, 9665 Wilshire Blvd., Beverly Hills, Calif. 90212.

CAREER: United California Bank, Los Angeles, secretary, 1951-57; Tanner Gray Line Tours, Los Angeles, Calif., group tour coordinator, 1957-60; Signal Companies, Beverly Hills, Calif., executive secretary and corporate officer, 1960—.

WRITINGS: *Who Was Who on Screen*, Bowker, 1974.

WORK IN PROGRESS: Revising *Who Was Who on Screen.*

SIDELIGHTS: Evelyn Mack Truitt writes: "As an avid movie fan turned serious collector of motion picture memorabilia, I have over the years separated the 'publicity' data from the 'factual' data; developed said information into an accurate accumulation of facts. . . ." *Avocational interests:* Films, theater, travel.

* * *

TRUITT, Willis H(arrison) 1936-

PERSONAL: Born August 26, 1936, in Washington, D.C.; son of Willis (a salesman) and Virginia Lee (Harrison) Truitt; married Anne J. Wadleigh (a biologist), April 26, 1964; children: Deborah Jane, Benjamin Harrison. *Education:* George Washington University, A.B., 1961; Boston University, A.M., 1967, Ph.D., 1969; Howard University, graduate study, 1963. *Politics:* Socialist. *Religion:* Atheist. *Home address:* Route 1, Box 317A, Land-o-Lakes, Fla. 33539. *Office:* Department of Philosophy, University of South Florida, Tampa, Fla. 33620.

CAREER: Central Intelligence Agency (CIA), Washington, D.C., information control officer, 1956-59; Georgetown Research Project, Washington, D.C., research analyst, 1961-64; Boston University, Boston, Mass., instructor in humanities, 1965-66; Suffolk Univerity, Boston, Mass., instructor, 1966-67, assistant professor of philosophy and humanities, 1967-68; University of South Florida, Tampa, assistant professor, 1968-71, associate professor, 1971-75, professor of philosophy, 1975—, director of graduate studies, 1970—.

MEMBER: International Max Raphael Society, American Federation of Teachers, American Philosophical Association, American Society for Aesthetics, American Institute for Marxist Studies, American Association of University Professors, British Society of Aesthetics, United Faculty of Florida (vice-president of University of South Florida branch), Florida Education Association, Florida Philosophical Association. *Awards, honors:* National Endowment for the Humanities fellowship, 1973; Florida Endowment for the Humanities grant, 1975.

WRITINGS: (Editor and contributor) *The Black Power Revolt*, Extending Horizons Books, 1968; (editor and contributor) *Social Work and Social Change*, Extending Horizons Books, 1968; (with J. A. Gould) *Political Ideologies: A Philosophical Perspective*, Macmillan, 1973; (with Gould) *Existentialist Philosophy*, Dickenson, 1973; (with T. W. G. Solomons) *Science, Technology, and Freedom*, Houghton, 1974.

Contributor of about twenty-five articles and reviews to scholarly journals, including *Structurist, Journal of Aesthetic Education, Arts and Society, Diogenes, Technology and Culture, British Journal of Aesthetics, Journal of Aesthetics and Art Criticism*, and *Journal of Human Relations*. Humanities and social sciences editor for Extending Horizons Books, 1964-68.

WORK IN PROGRESS: Controversies in Contemporary Aesthetics, Art, and Criticism, with Irving Deer; *Marxist Philosophy*; editing *Marxism and Culture* and *Philosophy and Marxism*, both with R. S. Cohen; contributing to *The Politics of Art*, for Routledge & Kegan Paul; two monographs, *Environmental Aesthetics* and *Ideology and Culture*; editing *Science and Marxism*, with Sheldon Krimsky; research on the following: dialectical development of Zionist ideology, historicism and the growth of science, Forster and Orwell and their opinions of Asia, and meaning, essence, and praxis.

* * *

TUBBS, Stewart L(ee) 1943-

PERSONAL: Born September 6, 1943, in Cleveland, Ohio; son of Edwin B. (an accountant) and Mary (Baker) Tubbs; married Gail Sheahan, August 21, 1965; children: Brian Christian. *Education:* Bowling Green University, B.S.Ed., 1965, M.A., 1966; University of Kansas, Ph.D., 1969. *Residence:* Flint, Mich. *Office:* General Motors Institute, Flint, Mich. 48502.

CAREER: University of Kansas, Lawrence, assistant director of Extension, 1968-69; General Motors Institute, Flint, Mich., assistant professor, 1969-70, associate professor, 1970-74, professor of communication, 1974—. Vice-president of Systems Development Institute; president of Miller Road Farms Association, 1975; consultant to General Motors Corp. *Member:* International Communication Association, American Psychological Association, Speech Communication Association, Central States Speech Association, Michigan Speech Association.

WRITINGS: (Editor) *New Directions in Communication*, International Communication Association, 1972; (with Sylvia Moss) *Human Communication: An Interpersonal Perspective*, Random House, 1974; (with John Baird) *Self-Disclosure and Personal Growth*, C. E. Merrill, in press. Contributor to *Journal of Communication, Today's Education, Journal of Personality and Social Psychology, Speech Monographs, Kansas Speech Journal, Ohio Speech Journal*, and *Michigan Speech Journal*.

WORK IN PROGRESS: Small Group Interaction, publication by Addison-Wesley expected in 1977; *Readings in Human Communication*, for Hayden.

* * *

TUCKMAN, Howard P(aul) 1941-

PERSONAL: Born December 23, 1941, in Brooklyn, N.Y.; son of Louis A. (an attorney) and Beatrice E. (in insurance business) Tuckman; married Barbara Hauben (an economist), December 25, 1965; children: Alec. *Education:* Cornell University, B.S., 1963; University of Wisconsin, M.S., 1967, Ph.D., 1970. *Home:* 2020 Continental Ave., #144, Tallahassee, Fla. 32304. *Office:* Department of Economics, Institute for Social Research, Florida State University, Bellamy Building, Tallahassee, Fla. 32306.

CAREER: Executive Office of the President, Washington, D.C., budget analyst, 1963-65; Technical University of Denmark, Lyngby, research associate, 1967-68; Florida State University, Tallahassee, assistant professor, 1969-72, associate professor of economics, 1972-75. Policy fellow of Brookings Institution, 1975-76. Consultant to National Institute for Education and American Institutes for Research. *Member:* American Economic Association, American Educational Research Association, Southern Economic Association. *Awards, honors:* Ford Foundation fellowship, 1968-70; grant from National Science Foundation and American Council on Education, 1973-75; Rockefeller Foundation grant, 1972-73.

WRITINGS: (Editor with Scott Ford, and contributor) *The Demand for Higher Education*, Heath, 1971; *The Economics of the Rich*, Random House, 1974. Contributor to economics journals. Referee for *Journal of Human Resources*, 1970—; reader for Random House and Praeger.

WORK IN PROGRESS: Salary Determination in Academe; What Is an Article Worth?; The Little Trains That Could; Travel Demand Functions for Florida Tourists; The Structure of Salaries in Academe.

BIOGRAPHICAL/CRITICAL SOURCES: Choice, March, 1973.

* * *

TUGWELL, Franklin 1942-

PERSONAL: Born March 29, 1942, in San Juan, P.R.; married, 1960; children: two sons. *Education:* Columbia University, B.A., 1963, M.A., 1964, Ph.D., 1969. *Home:* 1426 Guadalajara, Claremont, Calif. 91711. *Office:* Department of Government, Pomona College, Claremont, Calif. 91713.

CAREER: Pomona College, Claremont, Calif., instructor, 1968-69, assistant professor, 1970-73, associate professor of government, 1974—, Wig Distinguished Professor, 1971. Guest scholar at Brookings Institution, summer, 1967; visiting professor at Instituto de Estudios Superiores de Administracion (Venezuela), 1973. *Member:* American Political Science Association, Latin American Studies Association, World Future Society, Policy Studies Association, Western Political Science Association. *Awards, honors:* Foreign area postdoctoral award, 1973; research grant from American Philosophical Society, 1973.

WRITINGS: (Contributor) Albert Somit, editor, *Political Science and the Study of the Future*, Dryden, 1973; (editor and contributor) *Search for Alternatives: Public Policy and the Study of the Future*, Winthrop, 1973; *The Politics of Oil in Venezuela*, Stanford University Press, in press. Contributor to *Studies in Comparative International Development, Journal of Inter-American Studies, Analyse et Prevision*, and *Bulletin of the World Future Society*.

WORK IN PROGRESS: Research on Venezuela and U.S. foreign policy, on alternative futures for Venezuelan petroleum, on the role of private sector interest associations and economic policymaking in Latin America and

Venezuela, and on petroleum policy and the political process.

* * *

TUNIS, John R(oberts) 1889-1975

December 7, 1889—February 4, 1975; American sports reporter, broadcaster, and author of sports books for young readers. Obituaries: *AB Bookman's Weekly*, February 24, 1975; *New York Times*, February 26, 1975; *Publishers Weekly*, March 24, 1975.

* * *

TURETZKY, Bertram Jay 1933-

PERSONAL: Born February 14, 1933, in Norwich, Conn.; son of Isadore (a businessman) and Tillie (Feldman) Turetzky; married Nancy Corey (a music teacher), September 6, 1959; children: Gerald Charles, Marc David, Jennifer Glenora. *Education:* Hartt College of Music, B.Music, 1955; New York University, graduate study, 1956-58; University of Hartford, M.Music, 1965. *Politics:* Registered Democrat. *Religion:* Jewish. *Home:* 429 9th St., Del Mar, Calif. 92014. *Office:* Department of Music, University of California at San Diego, La Jolla, Calif. 92037.

CAREER: University of Hartford, West Hartford, Conn., assistant professor of music, 1955-68; University of California at San Diego, 1968—, now professor of music. Member of Hartford Symphony and Hartt Chamber players, 1955-68; artistic consultant to Ars Nova Records; visiting professor of contrabass, University of Connecticut and Wesleyan University. *Member:* International Society of Bassists, American Federation of Musicians, American String Teachers Association.

WRITINGS: (Author of introduction) George Murphy Foster, *Pops Foster: New Orleans Jazzman*, University of California Press, 1971; *The Contemporary Contrabass*, University of California Press, 1974. Author of scripts for television program, "The New World of Sound," for KOGO-TV and University of California at San Diego Extension. Author of musical composition published by McGinnis & Marx. Reader of manuscripts for University of California Press. Contributor to music journals. Associate editor of *Composer* and of *Journal of the International Society of Bassists*.

WORK IN PROGRESS: History of Jazz Bass Playing: A Source Book.

SIDELIGHTS: Turetzky told *CA*: "Much of my writing has been motivated by the notion of communicating with people through music. Some of the aesthetics and techniques need to be articulated, thus, I speak, informally, at my concerts. *But*, it's all about communication. Too many concert artists do their thing, collect their fees, and forget about people! That's all wrong and clearly *one* of the big reasons why America doesn't support the arts *seriously*." Turetzky has made solo and ensemble recordings for Ars Nova, Desto, Nonesuch, and others.

* * *

TURNER, David R(euben) 1915-

PERSONAL: Born December 19, 1915, in New York, N.Y.; son of Charles and Eva (Turner) Moskowitz; married Ann Louise Perkins, April 29, 1946; children: Eve (Mrs. William Watters), Ruth. *Education:* College of the City of New York (now City College of the City University of New York), B.S.S., 1936, M.S., 1937. *Home:* 13 Glen-

gary Rd., Croton-on-Hudson, N.Y. 10520. *Office address:* Arco Production Co., P.O. Box 256, Scarborough, N.Y. 10510.

CAREER: Arco Publishing Co., New York, N.Y., co-founder, vice-president, and editor-in-chief, 1937—. Publishing consultant, Burma Translation Society, 1959, 1960.

WRITINGS—Study guides; all published by Arco: *Jane Austen's Pride and Prejudice*, 1969; *Joseph Conrad's Lord Jim*, 1969; *William Shakespeare's Macbeth*, 1969; *Homer's The Iliad*, 1970; *Charles Dickens' David Copperfield*, 1970.

Also author of editor of over 300 books, all published by Arco, including civil service test manuals, high school and scholastic test handbooks, and career manuals; a partial list including: *Homestudy Course for Civil Service Jobs*, 1965; *Real Estate Assessor-Appraiser-Manager*, 3rd edition, 1969; *Medical College Admission Test*, 1969; *Insurance Agent & Broker Examination*, revised edition, 1970; *Law School Admission Test*, 1970; *Graduate Business Admission Test*, 1971; *Scoring High on College Entrance Tests*, 1973; *U.S. Summer Jobs*, 1974; *College Level Examination Program, General Tests*, 1974; *Tests for Women in the Armed Forces*, 1975; *Practice for the Armed Forces Test*, 1975; *Scholastic Aptitude Tests*, 1975.

Advisor to board of publications of Union of American Hebrew Congregations, 1961-65.

* * *

TYMCHUK, Alexander J(ames) 1942-

PERSONAL: Surname is pronounced Tim-chuck; born October 10, 1942, in Natal, British Columbia; son of George (a mechanic) and Sophie (Sowchey) Tymchuk; married Pauline Beattie (a teacher), July 12, 1963; children: Mark, Christopher. *Education:* Attended Notre Dame College, Nelson, British Columbia, 1960-61, and Victoria College, 1961-62; University of Victoria, B.Ed., 1966, B.A., 1968; University of Western Ontario, M.A., 1968; George Peabody College for Teachers, Ph.D., 1971. *Home:* 3455 Shernoll Pl., Sherman Oaks, Calif. 91403. *Office:* Neuropsychiatric Institute, 760 Westwood Plaza, Los Angeles, Calif. 90024.

CAREER: Elementary teacher in Fernie, British Columbia, 1962-63; Children's Psychiatric Research Institute, London, Ontario, research psychologist, 1967-69; Clover Bottom Hospital and School, Nashville, Tenn., part-time research psychologist, 1969-71; University of California, Los Angeles, assistant professor of psychology in departments of psychology and psychiatry, 1971—. Consultant to Los Angeles County Autism Project. *Member:* Council for Exceptional Children, American Association on Mental Deficiency (member of board, Region II).

WRITINGS: (Contributor) Reginald L. Jones and Donald L. MacMillan, editors, *Special Education in Transition*, Allyn & Bacon, 1972; (editor and contributor) *Psychology of the Exceptional Child: Readings*, Simon & Schuster, 1972; *The Mental Retardation Dictionary*, Western Psychological Services, 1973; *Behavior Modification with Children: A Clinical Training Manual*, C. C Thomas, 1974; (contributor) Jagannath Das and David Baine, editors, *Mental Retardation: A Handbook for Special Educators*, C. C Thomas, in press; John Cull and Richard E. Hardy, editors, *The Problems of Disadvantaged Youth*, C. C Thomas, in press.

Co-author of videotapes, "Parents as Trainers of Their Behavior Problem Children" and "Training an Autistic

Child." Contributor to *Current Psychiatric Therapies* and to journals. Regular reviewer, *American Journal on Mental Deficiency* and *Peabody Journal of Education*, 1970—. Editor, *UCLA-UAF Bibliography on Mental Retardation*, 1971-73.

WORK IN PROGRESS: Parent Handbook on Mental Retardation; a chapter for *Handbook of Learning and Cognition*, Volume III, for publication by Earlbaum; with James Q. Simmons, a book on childhood psychosis and other developmental disabilities.

AVOCATIONAL INTERESTS: History, sculpting, athletics.

* * *

TYRRELL, Bernard (James) 1933-

PERSONAL: Born May 10, 1933, in Yakima, Wash.; son of Ben J. (a service station owner) and Mary (a nurse; maiden name, Koreski) Tyrrell. *Education:* Gonzaga University, B.A., 1957, M.A. (philosophy), 1958; Santa Clara University, M.A. (theology), 1966; Fordham University, Ph.D., 1972. *Politics:* Democrat. *Religion:* Roman Catholic. *Office:* Department of Philosophy and Religious Studies, Gonzaga University, Spokane, Wash. 99202.

CAREER: Entered Roman Catholic order of Society of Jesus (Jesuits), 1951, ordained priest, 1965; Gonzaga University, Spokane, Wash., assistant professor of philosophy and religious studies, 1972-75. Lecturer at Boston College, University of San Francisco, and University of Seattle. *Member:* American Catholic Theological Society, Jesuit Philosophical Association, Northwest Philosophical Society, Phi Beta Kappa.

WRITINGS: (Contributor) Philip McShane, editor, *Language, Truth, and Meaning*, University of Notre Dame Press, 1972; *Bernard Lonergan's Philosophy of God*, University of Notre Dame Press, 1974; (editor) Berpard Lonergan, *A Second Collection*, Westminster, 1974; *Christotherapy: Healing through Enlightenment*, Seabury, 1975. Contributor to *America* and to *Homiletic and Pastoral Review*.

WORK IN PROGRESS: A sequel to *Christotherpay: Healing Through Enlightenment*, dealing with the dynamic relationship between psychology and religion.

* * *

TZANNES, Nicolaos S(tamatios) 1937-

PERSONAL: Surname sounds like "Jonas"; born June 30, 1937, in Patras, Greece; son of Michael and Stavroula Tzannes; married Lita Marie Barker (a registered nurse), June 18, 1960; children: Michael, Marcos, Alexis. *Education:* University of Minnesota, B.E.E., 1960; Syracuse University, M.E.E., 1963; Johns Hopkins University, Ph.D., 1966. *Home address:* Rion, Patras, Greece. *Office:* Information Theory Chair, University of Patras, Patras, Greece.

CAREER: Johns Hopkins University, Baltimore, Md., instructor in electrical engineering, 1964-66; Tufts University, Medford, Mass., assistant professor of electrical engineering, 1966-70; University of Oklahoma, Norman, associate professor of electrical engineering, 1970—. Visiting professor at University of Patras, 1974-75. Consultant to National Aeronautics and Space Administration, 1966-70. *Member:* American Association for the Advancement of Science, Institute of Electrical and Electronics Engineers, Eta Kappa Nu.

WRITINGS: (With Louis Nashelsky) *Logic Circuits*, Electronic Aids Co., 1970; (with Morris Tischler) *Transistor Fundamentals and Circuits*, Electronic Aids Co., 1972; (with brother, Basil Tzannes) *How Good Are You at Backgammon?*, Simon & Schuster, 1974; (with B. Tzannes) *Backgammon Games and Strategies*, A. S. Barnes, 1975. Contributor to engineering journals.

WORK IN PROGRESS: Stochastic Processes and Information Theory in the Study of Sound Patterns, with E. A. Afendras, for Laval University Press.

* * *

UDOFF, Yale M(aurice) 1935-

PERSONAL: Born March 29, 1935, in Brooklyn, N.Y.; son of Julius I. (a businessman) and Martha (Schneider) Udoff. *Education:* Michigan State University, B.A., 1957; Georgetown Law School, law study, 1958-59. *Home:* 1284 Havenhurst Dr., Los Angeles, Calif. 90046. *Agent:* (Theatre) Ellen Neuwald, 905 West End Ave., New York, N.Y. 10025; (Film/TV) Marty Shapiro, Shapiro/Lichtman, 9200 Sunset Blvd., Los Angeles, Calif. 90069.

CAREER: National Broadcasting Co., New York, N.Y., trainee, 1961-62; American Broadcasting Co., New York, N.Y., director of nighttime program development, 1962-66; playwright, television and film writer, 1966—. *Military service:* U.S. Army, 1958-59; became first lieutenant. *Member:* Dramatists Guild, Writers Guild of America. *Awards, honors:* Stanley Drama Award, 1969, for "The Club" and "The Little Gentleman"; Charles MacArthur Playwriting Award (honorable mention), 1974, for "Magritte Skies."

WRITINGS—Plays: *A Gun Play* (full-length; first produced in Hartford, Conn. by Hartford Stage Co., January, 1971; produced Off-Broadway at Cherry Lane Theatre, October, 1971), Samuel French, 1972; "Magritte Skies" (full-length), first produced as staged reading at Eugene O'Neill Theatre Conference, July, 1973; "Shade" (one-act; published in *Mademoiselle*, April, 1972), first produced in Paris, France, December, 1973; "The Academy of Desire" (one-act), first produced in San Francisco, Calif. at American Conservatory Theatre, March, 1974. Also author of plays, "The Little Gentleman" (one-act); "The Club" (one-act); "His Master's Voice" (one-act); "The Rose Critic" (one-act); "Dust to Dust" (one-act); "Fault Line" (full-length). Author of television play, "The Beach House."

Filmscripts: "No One to Blame," 1965; (with Ralph Lev Mailer) "On the Walls of the Subway," 1972; "The Artist Type" (adapted from novel of same name by Brian Glanville), 1973; "Hitchhike," telecast on ABC, 1974; "Stops Along the Way," 1975.

Author of television scripts for "The Survivors" and "Man from U.N.C.L.E."

Play included in anthology, *Best Short Plays 1971*, edited by Stanley Richards, Chilton, 1971.

Contributor of film criticism to *Film Quarterly, Film Comment, 7th Art*, and *Kulchur*.

WORK IN PROGRESS: A full-length play; a screenplay.

BIOGRAPHICAL/CRITICAL SOURCES: New York Times, February 3, 1971.

* * *

UHLINGER, Susan J. 1942-

PERSONAL: Born July 10, 1942, in Sterling, Ill.; daughter

of James R. (a minister) and Gladys I. (Jerrett) Uhlinger. *Education:* Iowa State University, B.S., 1964; University of Massachusetts, M.Ed., 1968. *Home:* 149 Milk Street, Westborough, Mass. 01581. *Office:* Massachusetts 4-H Center, Ashland, Mass. 01721.

CAREER: Berkshire County Extension Service, Pittsfield, Mass., extension home economist, 1964-66; Malden Action, Inc., coordinator of Home Management Project, 1967; Hampden County Extension Service, West Springfield, Mass., extension home economist, 1968-70; University of Massachusetts, Amherst, Mass., state 4-H leader, Nutrition Education Program, 1970-72; Massachusetts 4-H Center, Ashland, Mass., program director, 1972—. *Member:* American Home Economics Association, Massachusetts Home Economics Association.

WRITINGS: (With V. M. Dale) *Resources in Home Economics for the Blind Homemaker* (in print and Braille), Massachusetts Home Economics Association, 1969; *Fish Cookery*, Stephen Greene, 1974. Also writer of "Low Cost Food Series" (eleven articles), for *Holyoke* (Mass.) *Transcript-Telegram.*

*   *   *

UPHAUS, Robert W(alter)   1942-

PERSONAL: Born June 15, 1942, in East Orange, N.J.; son of Walter and Betty (Frank) Uphaus; married Suzanne Henning (a teacher), July 31, 1965; children: Andrew, Todd, Kevin. *Education:* Los Angeles State College, B.A., 1964; University of Washington, Seattle, M.A., 1966, Ph.D., 1969. *Politics:* Independent. *Home:* 205 University Dr., East Lansing, Mich. 48823. *Office:* Department of English, Michigan State University, East Lansing, Mich. 48824.

CAREER: Bellevue Community College, Bellevue, Wash., instructor in English, 1966-68; Michigan State University, East Lansing, assistant professor, 1968-71, associate professor of English, 1972—, director of English/Community College Program, 1974—. Visiting lecturer at University of Leeds, 1971-72. *Member:* Modern Language Association of America, American Society for Eighteenth-Century Studies, Irish American Cultural Institute.

WRITINGS: (Editor) *American Protest in Perspective*, Harper, 1971. Contributor of articles and reviews to professional journals.

WORK IN PROGRESS: A book on the varieties of eighteenth-century prose.

AVOCATIONAL INTERESTS: Tennis, travel.

*   *   *

UPSON, William Hazlett   1891-1975

September 26, 1891—February 5, 1975; American humorist, lecturer, author of short fiction, essays, and other works. Obituaries: *New York Times*, February 8, 1975; *AB Bookman's Weekly*, March 3, 1975. (*CA*-5/6)

*   *   *

UVEZIAN, Sonia

PERSONAL: Born in Beirut, Lebanon; daughter of Hagop (a composer, conductor, and violinist) and Satenig (a singer; maiden name, Kibarian) Uvezian; married David Kaiserman (a concert pianist and university professor). *Education:* Attended Academie des Beaux Arts, Beirut, Lebanon, Ecole Superieur de Musique, Beirut, Columbia

University, and Queens College of the City University of New York; also studied piano privately. *Residence:* New York, N.Y.

CAREER: Concert pianist. Has taught piano at Iowa State University and in New York, N.Y.; has worked as a fashion model in New York, N.Y. *Member:* Armenian Assembly (sponsor).

WRITINGS: The Cuisine of Armenia, Harper, 1974.

WORK IN PROGRESS: Research on foreign cuisine.

SIDELIGHTS: Sonia Uvezian writes: "I wrote *The Cuisine of Armenia* because I had seen no book in English or in any other language that presented the subject properly. It is the first book in the West to include a large number of recipes from Eastern Armenia (in the Caucasus) which had never been published in this country and which were unknown here." *Avocational interests:* Travel, walking, dancing to Bossa Nova, psychology, philosophy, conversation.

*   *   *

VALCOE, H. Felix
See SWARTZ, Harry (Felix)

*   *   *

VALE, Eugene   1916-

PERSONAL: Born April 11, 1916, in Zurich, Switzerland. *Education:* Attended schools in Switzerland. *Home:* 1820 North El Cerrito Pl., Los Angeles, Calif.

CAREER: Novelist, playwright, television and film script writer. *Member:* Academy of Motion Picture Arts and Sciences, Dramatists Guild, Writers Guild of America. *Awards, honors:* Arts of the Theatre Prize, for "Of Shadows Cast by Men"; commendation from City of Los Angeles, 1959, Christopher Gold Medal, Rupert Hughes Award of Authors' Club of Southern California, California Writers Guild Award, Commonwealth Gold Medal for best work of fiction by a California author, 1960, and Annual Book Award of National Secondary Education Board, all for *The Thirteenth Apostle*; nominations for television and film script awards from Writers Guild of America, West, Screen Writers Guild, and Academy of Motion Picture Arts and Sciences.

WRITINGS: The Technique of Screenplay Writing, Crown, 1944, revised and enlarged edition, Grosset, 1972; (contributor) L. G. Yoakem, editor, *TV and Screen Writing*, University of California Press, 1958; *The Thirteenth Apostle* (novel), Scribner, 1959; *Chaos below Heaven* (novel), Doubleday, 1966; *Some State of Affairs* (satire), W. H. Allen, 1972.

Author of plays, "Devils Galore," "The Buffoon," and "Of Shadows Cast by Men." Author of screenplays, "A Global Affair," "Francis of Assisi," "The Second Face," "The Bridge of San Luis Rey," "The Dark Wave," and others for Twentieth Century-Fox, United Artists, and Paramount. Writer of about sixty television dramas, including scripts for Four Star Playhouse, Fireside Theatre, Hallmark Hall of Fame, and Lux Video Theatre. Contributor of short stories, poems, and novelettes to *Esquire* and other periodicals in the United States and Europe.

WORK IN PROGRESS: A novel.

SIDELIGHTS: The original manuscript of *The Thirteenth Apostle* was acquired by the American Literature Collection of University of Southern California.

VALENTE, Michael F(eeney)

PERSONAL: Born in Albany, N.Y.; son of Abel A. (a civil engineer) and Anna (Feeney) Valente. *Education:* Stonehill College, A.B., 1959; University of Notre Dame, M.S., 1961, M.A., 1962; Columbia University, Ph.D., 1968; Yale University, M.S.L., 1974. *Politics:* Non-partisan. *Religion:* Roman Catholic. *Office:* Department of Religious Studies, Seton Hall University, South Orange, N.J. 07079.

CAREER: Manhattanville College, Purchase, N.Y., instructor in religion, 1962-63; Seton Hall University, South Orange, N.J., assistant professor, 1967-70, associate professor of religion, 1970—, head of department, 1968-71. Member of board of consultants to National Committee for Sexual Civil Liberties, 1971—; founder of Institute for the Study of Ethical Issues, president, 1968-73. *Member:* American Association of University Professors, American Academy of Religion, American Society of Christian Ethics, University Club (New York City), Delta Epsilon Sigma. *Awards, honors:* New Jersey Teachers of English author award, 1970, for *Sex: The Radical View of a Catholic Theologian.*

WRITINGS: Sex: The Radical View of a Catholic Theologian, Bruce, 1970. Contributor to *Christian Century* and *American Journal of Jurisprudence.*

WORK IN PROGRESS: Research on the existential dimensions of religious belief, and man's sexual nature as such.

* * *

VALENTINE, William Alexander 1905-

PERSONAL: Born November 1, 1905, in Wilkes-Barre, Pa.; son of William Alfred (a judge) and Mary I. (Shoemaker) Valentine; married Helen Anne MacQueen, June 22, 1938 (died May 14, 1954); married Agnes L. Tomkins (a college teacher), October 22, 1955; children: (first marriage) Nancy Marie (Mrs. Patrick S. Byrne), William Alfred. *Education:* Lafayette College, student, 1923-25; Princeton University, A.B., 1927; Dickinson School of Law, J.D., 1930. *Politics:* Republican. *Religion:* Presbyterian. *Home address:* R.D. 2, Box 325, Dallas, Pa. 18612. *Office address:* Box 325, R.D. 2, Dallas, Pa. 18612.

CAREER: Admitted to Pennsylvania bar, 1933, also bars of Pennsylvania Supreme Court, Pennsylvania Superior Court, and U.S. District Court; in practice of law in Wilkes-Barre, Pa., 1933—. Counsel and director of Commonwealth Telephone Co., 1934—; assistant district attorney of Luzerne County, 1937-41; special deputy attorney general of Pennsylvania, 1947-51. Breeder of registered Jersey cattle, 1940-66; owner and operator of Club Venus (fishing and hunting club in Quebec). Past director of Georgetown Settlement Association.

MEMBER: Association for Research and Enlightenment (of Edgar Cayce Foundation), American Jersey Cattle Club, Pennsylvania-Jersey Cattle Club, Back Mountain Protective Association (founder, 1949), Luzerne County Association of the Deaf, Wilkes-Barre Law and Library Association, DeMolay, Rotary International (past president), Masons, University Club (founder), Sigma Alpha Epsilon, Delta Theta Phi. *Awards, honors:* DeMolay Legion of Honor.

WRITINGS: Subordinate Courts of Pennsylvania, Soney & Sage, 1934; *Dunlap-Hanna Forms*, Part V, Volume III, Bisel, 1973; *ESP at Work*, Franklin Publishing, 1974. Author of *Valentine-Binns Justice*, Bisel, 1966—.

WORK IN PROGRESS: Compiling own comments on philosophical, political, religious, and humorous subjects.

AVOCATIONAL INTERESTS: Farming, composing classical music, playing concert piano, inventing (invented music writing shuttle for Hammond typewriters).

* * *

VAN ABBE, Derek Maurice 1916-

PERSONAL: Born December 28, 1916, in London, England; son of Salomon (an artist) and Hannah (Wolff) Van Abbe; married Nancy Kathleen Good, March, 1943; children: Quentin Philip Mark. *Education:* King's College, Cambridge, M.A., 1938; University of Zurich, graduate study, 1938-39. *Politics:* "Left of centre." *Religion:* "Not noticeable because strongly anti-clerical." *Home:* 19 Parkside, Blackheath, London SE3 7QQ, England. *Agent:* Dorothea Benson, 264 Dacre Park, London S.E.13, England. *Office:* Polytechnic of the South Bank, Francis St., London S.W. 1, England.

CAREER: University of Melbourne, Melbourne, Australia, lecturer in German, 1948-51; University of Adelaide, Adelaide, Australia, reader in German, 1951-59; College of Air Training, Hamble, England, tutor in modern languages, 1959-61; Cambridgeshire College of Art and Technology, Cambridge, England, lecturer in German, 1961-64, head of department of modern languages, 1964-71; Polytechnic of the South Bank, London, England, head of department of modern languages, 1971-74, senior research fellow, 1974—. Foreign and domestic news commentator on state and federal radio stations in Australia, 1951-59. *Military service:* British Army, Infantry, intelligence officer, 1939-45, 1951.

MEMBER: Institute of Linguists (fellow; member of executive council), Audio-Visual Languages Association (founder and first chairman; past member of executive council; honorary president, 1975), British Association for Applied Linguistics (member of executive committee, 1969-71). *Awards, honors:* Ph.D. from University of Melbourne, 1954.

WRITINGS: Renaissance Drama in Germany and Switzerland, Melbourne University Press, 1961; *C. M. Wieland: A Literary Biography*, Harrap, 1961; *Goethe: New Perspectives*, Allen & Unwin, 1974; (with Rene Dirven) *Wild Goose Chase* (novel with linguistic exercises for Belgian children learning English), Plantijn (Antwerp), 1974.

WORK IN PROGRESS: Editing Eckermann's *Gespraeche mit Goethe* (title means "Conversations with Goethe").

* * *

VAN BUREN, James G(eil) 1914-

PERSONAL: Born March 29, 1914; son of Geil and Alice (Dence) Van Buren; married Margaret Ellen Frank (a secretary), November 6, 1934; children: Robert J., Richard F., Lynn Martin. *Education:* Butler University, A.B., 1942; Butler School of Religion (now Christian Theological Seminary), B.D., 1946; Kansas State University, Ph.D., 1967. *Religion:* Christian Church (Disciples of Christ). *Home:* 1444 Laramie St., Manhattan, Kans. 66502. *Office:* Manhattan Christian College, 1407 Anderson Ave., Manhattan, Kans. 66502.

CAREER: Member of the ministry of Christian Church, Disciples of Christ; minister in Clarence, N.Y., 1934-39, in Indiana and Illinois, 1939-46, and in Pittsburgh, Pa., 1946-

60; Manhattan Christian College, Manhattan, Kans., professor of humanities and Christian doctrine, 1960—. President of Camp Christian, Inc., Mill Run, Pa. Member of state board of the Pennsylvania Christian Missionary Society, 1956-59. *Member:* North American Christian Convention (vice-president, 1954; president, 1955), Phi Kappa Phi, Theta Phi. *Awards, honors:* D.D., Milligan College, 1953.

WRITINGS: The Lord of the Early Christians, Manhattan Bible College, 1955; *A Forgotten Scotsman: George MacDonald,* privately printed, 1959; *Ten Thousand Listened,* privately printed, 1959; *Cults Challenge the Church,* Standard Publishing, 1965; *The Search,* Standard Publishing, 1974. Contributor to periodicals in his field, including *Standard Bible Teacher and Leader, The Christian·Standard, Christian Herald,* and *Encounter.*

* * *

VANCE, Barbara Jane 1934-

PERSONAL: Born March 5, 1934, in Salt Lake City, Utah; daughter of Reed (a building subcontractor) and Vidella (Rushton) Vance. *Education:* University of Utah, B.A., 1956; Brigham Young University, M.A., 1959; Stanford University, Ph.D., 1967. *Politics:* Republican Party. *Religion:* Church of Jesus Christ of Latter Day Saints (Mormon). *Home:* 2204 North 200 E, Provo, Utah, 84601. *Office:* Division of Instructional Research, Development, and Evaluation, Brigham Young University, Provo, Utah 84602.

CAREER: Tufts University, Medford, Mass., instructor in early childhood education, 1962-63; San Jose State College (now California State College), San Jose, Calif., lecturer in child development, 1966-67; Fremont Unified School District, Fremont, Calif., director of preschool education, 1966-67; Brigham Young University, Provo, Utah, assistant professor, 1967-70, associate professor of child development and family relations, 1970—; instructional psychologist for university, business, and industry, 1972—. *Member:* National Association for Education of Young Children (national conference chairman, 1969), Society for Research in Child Development, American Educational Research Association, Common Cause, Phi Kappa Phi, Pi Lambda Theta, Mu Phi Epsilon, Utah Valley Symphony Orchestra.

WRITINGS: Teaching the Prekindergarten Child: Instructional Design and Curriculum, Brooks-Cole, 1973; (with Philip E. Allsen and Joyce M. Harrison) *Fitness for Life,* Brigham Young University Press, 1974. Contributor to professional, religious, and lay journals.

WORK IN PROGRESS: Three books for Brooks-Cole: *Child Development: Toward Effective Child Rearing and Instruction,* (with Helen Trickett) *Motivational and Instructional Intervention in Childhood,* and (with others) *Introductory Psychology; Developing Values in the Home,* for Courseware, Inc.

* * *

van der HEYDEN, A(ntonius) A(lphonsus) M(aria) 1922-

PERSONAL: Born June 17, 1922, in Bussum, Netherlands; son of Antonius Johannes Maria and Hermine (Postma) van der Heyden; married Elizabeth Maria Bredius, October 1, 1953; children: Mirjam, Bernadette, Marc, Peter, Hans, Thomas. *Education:* City University of Amsterdam, Doctoraal Letteren en Wijsbegeerte, 1950. *Politics:* Liberal. *Religion:* Roman Catholic. *Home:* Rembrandtlaan 36, Naarden, Netherlands. *Office:* Elsevier Nederland, Amsteldijk 166, Amsterdam, Netherlands.

CAREER: Elsevier Nederland (publishers), Amsterdam, Netherlands, managing director, 1962—.

WRITINGS: (Editor) *Atlas van de antieke wereld,* Elsevier, 1958, English edition, with H. H. Scullard, published as *Atlas of the Classical World,* Thomas Nelson, 1959, abridged edition published as *Shorter Atlas of the Classical World,* 1962; *De wereld van Grieken en Romeinen,* Elsevier, 1968; *The Lore of Amsterdam* (translation of *Kijk op Amsterdam*), Elsevier, 1974; (with Ben Kroon) *Glory of Amsterdam* (translation of *Glorie van Amsterdam*), Funk, 1975; (with J. J. M. Timmers) *Glory of Rome* (translation of *Glorie van Rome*), Funk, 1975.

* * *

VanderMOLEN, Robert 1947-

PERSONAL: Born April 23, 1947, in Grand Rapids, Mich.; son of Robert LaVerne (a teacher) and Marjorie (a teacher; maiden name, Mollo) VanderMolen. *Education:* Michigan State University, B.A., 1971; University of Oregon, M.F.A., 1973. *Home:* 2215 Ducoma Dr., Grand Rapids, Mich. 49504.

CAREER: Foundry worker, sheet metal shop grinder, house painter, carpenter, circus advanceman, ranch hand, book store clerk; State of Michigan Poets-in-Schools Program, lecturer, 1974. *Member:* Associated Writing Programs. *Awards, honors:* R. L. Neuberger Creative Writing Award from State of Oregon, 1973; fellowship to MacDowell Writers' Colony, 1973.

WRITINGS—Poems: Blood Ink, Zeitgeist, 1967; *The Lost Book,* Zeitgeist, 1968; *Variations,* Zeitgeist, 1970; *The Pavilion and Other Poems,* Sumac Press, 1974. Contributor of poetry to periodicals, including *New York Quarterly, Sumac, Dragonfly,* and *Tennessee Poetry Journal.*

WORK IN PROGRESS: A novel, *Richard;* a new collection of poetry.

AVOCATIONAL INTERESTS: Travel, fishing.

* * *

VAN DUSEN, Henry P(itney) 1897-1975

December 11, 1897—February 13, 1975; American clergyman, ecumenist, educator, seminary president, author and editor of books on religion. Obituaries: *New York Times,* February 14, 1975; *Washington Post,* February 15, 1975; *AB Bookman's Weekly,* March 3, 1975; *Current Biography,* April, 1975. (*CA*-3)

* * *

VANOCUR, Edith C. 1924(?)-1975

1924(?)—April 14, 1975; Austrian-born American fashion designer, newspaper columnist, and author of books on cooking. Obituaries: *New York Times,* April 16, 1975; *Washington Post,* April 16, 1975.

* * *

VAN TASSEL, Dennie L(ee) 1939-

PERSONAL: Born July 8, 1939, in South Dakota; son of Rush and Gladys Van Tassel; married Cynthia L. Sokolowski. *Education:* University of Southern California, B.A., 1965; California State College (now University), Los

Angeles, M.A., 1967. *Office:* Computer Center, University of California, Santa Cruz, Calif. 95064.

CAREER: Employed with Statistical Tabulation Corp., 1959-68, San Jose State College (now University), San Jose, Calif., 1968-70; University of California, Santa Cruz, user liaison in Computer Center, 1970—. *Military service:* U.S. Marines, 1957-59. *Member:* Association of Computing Machinery.

WRITINGS: Computer Security Management, Prentice-Hall, 1972; *Program Style, Design, Efficiency, Debugging, Testing*, Prentice-Hall, 1974; *The Compleat Computer*, Science Research Associates, in press.

*   *   *

VAN VORIS, Jacqueline   1922-

PERSONAL: Born November 11, 1922, in Corsicana, Tex.; married William Van Voris (associate professor of English at Smith College), 1949; children: Alice, Richard. *Education:* University of California, Berkeley, A.B., 1948; Smith College, M.A., 1975. *Religion:* Unitarian Universalist. *Home:* 88 Crescent St., Northampton, Mass. 01060. *Office:* Neilson Library, Smith College, Northampton, Mass. 01060.

CAREER: Secretary in Saudi-Arabia, 1948-49; Smith College, Nielson Library, Northampton, Mass., director of Smith Centennial Study, 1970-75. Member of the board of trustees of People's Institute, Northampton, 1960—; appointed by Massachusetts Governor to Board of Library Commissioners, 1974—. *Military service:* U.S. Navy, 1944-46. *Member:* League of Women Voters. *Awards, honors:* National Endowment for the Humanities grant, 1970-75, for oral history project.

WRITINGS: Constance de Markievicz: In the Cause of Ireland, University of Massachusetts Press, 1967, shorter version, for young adults, published as *Constance de Markievicz*, Feminist Press, 1972; *College: A Smith Mosaic*, Smith College Press, 1975.

WORK IN PROGRESS: A book based on the Smith Centennial Study; a book on the WAVES in World War II; co-authoring a biography of Carrie Chapman Catt, with Eleanor Flexner.

*   *   *

VAN WOERKOM, Dorothy (O'Brien)   1924-

PERSONAL: Born June 26, 1924, in Buffalo, N.Y.; daughter of Peter S. (a refinery superintendent) and Helen (Miller) O'Brien; married John W. Van Woerkom (an administrator at Rice University), February 22, 1961. *Education:* Attended Mount Mercy Academy and Bryant and Stratton Business College. *Politics:* "To me the candidate, not the party, matters." *Religion:* Roman Catholic. *Home and office:* 8826 McAvoy Dr., Houston, Tex. 77036.

CAREER: U.S. Army Corps of Engineers, Buffalo, N.Y., secretary, 1943-47; elementary school teacher in the parochial schools of Buffalo, N.Y., 1947-51; U.S. Army Corps of Engineers, Buffalo, N.Y., secretary, 1951-61; free-lance writer, 1968—. *Member:* Association of Childhood Education International, Associated Authors of Children's Literature, Society of Children's Book Writers, American Library Association, Children's Literature Association, National Wilderness Society, National Audubon Society. *Awards, honors: Stepka and the Magic Fire* was named best religious children's book of 1974 by Catholic Press Association.

WRITINGS—Juveniles: *Stepka and the Magic Fire*, Concordia, 1974; *Journeys to Bethlehem*, Concordia, 1974; *The Queen Who Couldn't Bake Gingerbread* (Junior Literary Guild selection), Knopf, 1975; *Becky and the Bear* (Junior Literary Guild selection), Putnam, 1975; *The Dove and the Messiah*, Concordia, 1975; *Sea Frog, City Frog*, Macmillan, in press; *Abu Ali: Three Tales of the Middle East*, Macmillan, in press; *The Rat, the Ox, and the Zodiac*, Crown, in press; *Meat Pies and Sausages*, Morrow, in press; *Let Us Go to Bethlehem!*, Concordia, in press.

Series editor for Concordia's "Beginning Bible Readers," six volumes per year, the first scheduled for 1976 publication. Contributor of book reviews to *Houston Chronicle*; contributor of articles and stories to adult and children's magazines.

WORK IN PROGRESS: A book of poetry, *Wake Up and Listen!*, for Concordia; several folk tales and historical stories for beginning readers.

AVOCATIONAL INTERESTS: Needlework, travel to historic places.

BIOGRAPHICAL/CRITICAL SOURCES: Houston Chronicle, October 14, 1973; *Alvin Sun*, February 20, 1975.

*   *   *

VARAH, Chad   1911-

PERSONAL: Surname is pronounced *Vah*-ruh; born November 12, 1911, in Barton-on-Humber, England; son of William Edward (a canon) and Mary (Atkinson) Varah; married Susan Whanslaw (president of Mothers' Union), January 27, 1940; children: Felicity (Mrs. John Harding), Michael, Andrew, David, Charles. *Education:* Keble College, Oxford, M.A. (honors), 1933; Scholae Cancellarii, G.O.E., 1935. *Politics:* Liberal. *Home:* 39 Walbrook, London EC4N 8BP, England. *Office:* St. Stephen's Church, Walbrook, London EC4N 8BN, England.

CAREER: Ordained Anglican priest, 1935; assistant priest in Lincoln, England, 1935-38, London, England, 1938-40, Barrow-in-Furness, England, 1940-42; vicar in Blackburn, England, 1942-49, London, England, 1949-53; rector of St. Stephen's Church, London, England, 1953—; The Samaritans, London, England, founder, 1953, director of London branch, 1953-74, chairman of Befrienders International (Samaritans Worldwide), 1974—. Fellow of Sion College, London, 1954—. *Member:* Federation Internationale des Services de Secours d'Urgence par Telephone (president, 1964-67), International Association for Suicide Prevention, Oxford Union (life member). *Awards, honors:* Roumanian Patriarchal Cross, 1968; Officer of the Order of the British Empire, 1969; Albert Schweitzer Gold Medal from Johann Wolfgang von Goethe Foundation, 1972; Louis I. Dublin award from American Association of Suicidology, 1974; prebendary of St. Paul's Cathedral, London, 1975.

WRITINGS: (Editor) *After School Hours*, Blackwell, 1931; (editor) *The Samaritans*, Constable, 1965; (editor) *The Samaritans in the Seventies*, Constable, 1973. Contributor to *Forum*, and *Penthouse Forum*. Editor of *Symbol*, 1949-56. Author of British Broadcasting Corporation television drama, "Nobody Understands Miranda", 1972.

WORK IN PROGRESS: A book on sex; three theological works on the doctrine of God, on the doctrine of man, and on the Gospel of Luke.

SIDELIGHTS: Varah told *CA:* "I think an article I wrote in 1952 on a more accepting attitude to sex . . . not only led to the starting of The Samaritans (world's first emergency phone for suicides) but also pioneered what we now call 'The Permissive Society.' Though used pejoratively by Comstockians, this is 'a good thing'—opposite of a repressive, tyrannical society. I want to see censorship (for adults) abolished.... I travel a lot, have done over 100 flights in the last fifteen months.''

BIOGRAPHICAL/CRITICAL SOURCES: Georges Ras, *Ce Soir Je me suicide*, Fayard, 1971; *Observer*, March 11, 1974.

* * *

VARGAS, Julie S. 1938-

PERSONAL: Born April 28, 1938, in Minneapolis, Minn.; daughter of B(urrhus) F(redric) (a behavioral psychologist) and Eva (an art historian; maiden name, Blue) Skinner; married Ernest A. Vargas (an associate professor), June 30, 1962; children: Lisa, Justine. *Education:* Radcliffe College, B.A., 1960; Columbia University, M.A., 1962; University of Pittsburgh, Ph.D., 1969. *Home:* 519 West Park Street, Morgantown, W.Va. 26505. *Office:* Department of Education, West Virginia University, Morgantown, W.Va. 26506.

CAREER: Elementary school teacher in New York, N.Y., 1959-60, and Monroeville, Pa., 1961-62; American Institutes for Research, New York, N.Y., research associate, 1962-63; West Virginia University, Morgantown, associate professor of educational psychology, 1967—. Consultant to Behavioral Engineering of New Jersey, 1968-70; Kennedy Youth Center, 1969-72, and New Century Education Corp., 1972—. *Member:* American Educational Research Association, National Council for Measurement in Education.

WRITINGS: Writing Worthwhile Behavioral Objectives, Harper, 1973. Contributor of articles to *Human Behavior, Early Years*, and *Journal of the American Dietetic Association*.

WORK IN PROGRESS: With husband, Ernest Vargas, *Teaching: An Operant Approach*, for publication by Harper; a beginning reading comprehension series, *Something to Think About*, for New Century Education Corp.

SIDELIGHTS: Julie Vargas told *CA:* ''I'm particularly interested in early childhood education, elementary school education, and in designing programs and materials to teach basic language skills in a format which shows daily progress and which is fun for the learners.''

* * *

VASS, Winifred Kellersberger 1917-

PERSONAL: Born August 30, 1917, in Lusambo, Belgian Congo; daughter of Eugene Roland (a missionary, leprologist, and surgeon) and Edna (Bosche) Kellersberger; married Lachlan C. Vass (a minister), June 16, 1940; children: Edna (Mrs. John Stucky), Julia Lake (Mrs. William Dudley), Elizabeth (Mrs. J. Timothy Guerin), Winifred Walton. *Education:* Agnes Scott College, B.A., 1938; University of Florida, M.A., 1971. *Home:* 3829 McFarlin Blvd., Dallas, Tex. 75205.

CAREER: Presbyterian missionary in Luebo and Kananga, Zaire, 1940-71; National Conference of Christians and Jews, Dallas, Tex., secretary of Dallas Office, 1973-75. Secretary of Highland Park Presbyterian Church, Dallas, Tex., 1975. *Awards, honors:* La Medaille d'Or du merite civigne from Government of Zaire, 1968, for services rendered to the nation for over thirty years.

WRITINGS—All published by J. Leighton Wilson Press (Luebo, Zaire), except as indicated: *Geographie Muinayi* (title means "Fourth Grade Geography"), 1946; *Anu Mu Nsumuinu* (title means "Only in Folktales"), 1951; *Bakaji, Tambulayi!* (title means "Ladies, Quote a Proverb!"), 1958; *Bifuanyikishi Bia Mu Dihungila Dikulukulu* (title means "Old Testament Plays for School Classroom Presentations"), Librairie Evangelique du Congo, 1959; *Mukanda Wetu Wa Nzambi* (title means "Our Bible"), 1960; (with Virginia Pruitt) *A Textbook of the Tshiluba Language*, 1969; *Nsubu Wa Kusambakena* (title means "The Tabernacle), 1970; *Thirty-One Banana Leaves*, John Knox, 1975. Editor, *Lumu Lua Bena Kasai*, 1943-56, and *Tuyaya Kunyi*, 1966-67, advisor, 1967-70.

WORK IN PROGRESS: The Bantu-Speaking Heritage of the United States.

SIDELIGHTS: Winifred Vass writes: "*Bantu-Speaking Heritage*, my next book, is based on all of the Tshiluba vocabulary that I hear here in the United States, which was brought by the slaves and culturally carried over into our nation's life. I have found four categories of these linguistic cultural transferances: place-names, songs and folk-tales, modern United States vocabulary and a major part of the content of the GULLAH language of the Georgia and South Carolina coast and sea islands.''

* * *

VERMES, Geza 1924-

PERSONAL: Born June 22, 1924, in Mako, Hungary; son of Ernest (a journalist) and Theresia (Riesz) Vermes; married Noreen Pamela Hobson (a writer), May 14, 1958. *Education:* Attended University of Budapest, 1945-46; University of Louvain, Lic. in Oriental History, 1952, D. Theol., 1953. *Religion:* Jewish. *Home:* West Wood Cottage, Foxcombe Lane, Boars Hill, Oxford OX1 5DH, England. *Agent:* A. D. Peters, 10 Buckingham St., London W.C.2, England. *Office:* Oriental Institute, University of Oxford, Pusey Lane, Oxford OX1 2LE, England.

CAREER: Centre National de la Recherche Scientifique, Paris, France, researcher, 1955-57; University of Newcastle-Upon-Tyne, Newcastle-Upon-Tyne, England, lecturer, 1957-64, senior lecturer in religious studies, 1964-65; University of Oxford, Oriental Institute, Oxford, England, reader in Jewish studies, 1965—, professorial fellow of Wolfson College, 1965—, chairman of curators, 1971-74. *Member:* World Union of Jewish Studies, Society for Old Testament Studies, British Association for Jewish Studies (president, 1975).

WRITINGS: Les manuscrits du desert de Juda, Desclee, 1953, 2nd edition, 1954, first edition translated and published as *Discovery in the Judean Desert*, Desclee, 1956; *Scripture and Tradition in Judaism*, E. J. Brill, 1961, 2nd edition, 1974; *The Dead Sea Scrolls in English*, Penguin, 1962, revised edition, 1975; *Jesus the Jew*, Collins, 1973, Macmillan, 1974; (reviser with Fergus Millar) Emil Schuerer, *History of the Jewish People*, T. T. Clark, Volume I, 1973, Volume II, in press; *Post Biblical Jewish Studies*, E. J. Brill, 1975. Contributor to Biblical, Semitic, and Jewish academic journals, and to *Jewish Chronicle* and *Times Literary Supplement*. Editor of *Journal of Jewish Studies*, 1971—.

WORK IN PROGRESS: The Gospel of Jesus the Jew.

SIDELIGHTS: Vermes who, unlike his parents, survived the Nazi persecution in Hungary, says he is "fascinated by the history, literature, and religion of Jewish Palestine during the crucial centuries which witnessed the formation of Rabbinic Judaism and the birth of Christianity." He is also concerned with interrelation and historical interaction between Judaism and Christianity. *Avocational interests:* Television, detective novels.

* * *

VESELY, Erik 1905(?)-1970

1905(?)—April 14, 1975; Czechoslovakian-born American educator, study center director, and author of works on Communism. Obituaries: *Washington Post*, April 16, 1975; *New York Times*, April 17, 1975; *AB Bookman's Weekly*, May 12, 1975.

* * *

VICKERY, John B. 1925-

PERSONAL: Born August 20, 1925, in Toronto, Ontario, Canada; son of Stanley (a businessman) and Mona Isabel (Robinson) Vickery; married Olga Alice Westland, August 5, 1950 (died October 4, 1970); children: Anne Elizabeth (Mrs. William H. Floto). *Education:* University of Toronto, B.A., 1947; Colgate University, M.A., 1949; University of Wisconsin, Ph.D., 1955; graduate study at Harvard University, 1951-52. *Home:* 2000 Rincon Ave., Riverside, Calif. 92506. *Office:* Department of English, University of California, Riverside, Calif. 92502.

CAREER: University of Tennessee, Knoxville, instructor in English, 1954-56; Northwestern University, Evanston, Ill., instructor in English, 1956-59; Purdue University, Lafayette, Ind., assistant professor, 1959-64, associate professor of English, 1964-65; University of California, Riverside, associate professor, 1965-72, professor of English, 1972—. *Member:* Modern Language Association of America, American Comparative Literature Association. *Awards, honors:* American Council of Learned Societies fellowship, 1951-52; Guggenheim fellowship, 1974-75.

WRITINGS: (Editor) *Myth and Literature*, University of Nebraska Press, 1966; (editor with J. M. Sellery) *Goethe's "Faust: Part One": Essays in Criticism*, Wadsworth, 1969; (editor with M. J. Friedman) *The Shaken Realist: Essays on Modern Literature*, Louisiana State University Press, 1970; (editor with wife, Olga Westland Vickery) *"Light in August" and the Critical Spectrum*, Wadsworth, 1971; (editor with Sellery) *The Scapegoat: Ritual and Literature*, Houghton, 1971; *Robert Graves and the White Goddess*, University of Nebraska Press, 1972; *The Literary Impact of "The Golden Bough,"* Princeton University Press, 1973.

WORK IN PROGRESS: A study of myth and poetry, particularly late nineteenth and twentieth centuries; research on philosophical fiction in modern English, American, and Continental literature.

* * *

VIGLINI, Janelle (Therese) 1933-

PERSONAL: Born August 18, 1933; daughter of John Potts and Vidella Mae (Pyle) Viglini; married Robert Jones (a chemist), 1953; married Clive Hawthorne (a musician), 1956 (divorced, 1959); children: (second marriage) Mary Janelle. *Education:* Attended University of the Pacific, 1953, and San Francisco Art Institute, 1954; University of San Francisco, B.A., 1969; Institute of Advanced Thinking, LLS, 1973. *Home:* 2860 Golden Gate Ave., San Francisco, Calif. 94118.

CAREER: Teacher of English in San Joaquin, Calif., 1953, in Marin County, Calif., 1972; teacher of poetry, Institute of Advanced Thinking, 1974-75. *Member:* P.E.N. *Awards, honors:* P.E.N. Award Fund grant, 1975.

WRITINGS—Poems: *Saxton's Garter*, Dramatika, 1974; *Dictionary of the Apocalyptic*, Bern Porter, 1974; *The Viglini Letters*, Bern Porter, Volume I, 1975; *The Salvation Merchants*, Bern Porter, 1975; *A.D.*, Bern Porter, 1975.

WORK IN PROGRESS: *P.J.*, a poetic study of Prester John; *Into the Wilderness*, a book of verse; *The Magic Fillmore Fagin; Venus Flytrap.*

* * *

VINACKE, W(illiam) Edgar 1917-

PERSONAL: Born July 26, 1917, in Denver, Colo.; son of Harold M. (a college professor) and Edna (Lewis) Vinacke; married Winifred Ross, February 8, 1947; children: Susan Vinacke Cadby, Alan R., Edna M. *Education:* University of Cincinnati, B.A., 1939; Columbia University, Ph.D., 1942. *Home:* 104 Saratoga Rd., Buffalo, N.Y. 14226. *Office:* Department of Psychology, State University of New York at Buffalo, Buffalo, N.Y. 14226.

CAREER: New York State Psychiatric Institute and Hospital, New York, N.Y., research assistant, 1939-41; research assistant, National Research Council-Civil Aeronautics Administration Committee on Selection and Training of Aviators, 1940-41; technician, supervisor, assistant research analyst, Civil Aeronautics Administration-Works Progress Administration Projects on Selection and Training of Aviators, 1941-44; University of Hawaii, Honolulu, assistant professor, 1946-50, associate professor, 1950-57, professor of psychology, 1957-63; State University of New York at Buffalo, professor of psychology, 1963—. Visiting professor at University of Cincinnati, summer, 1951, and University of Colorado, summers, 1959, 1963; visiting research psychologist at U.S. School of Aviation Medicine, summer, 1956. *Military service:* U.S. Naval Reserve, active duty, 1944-46; became lieutenant junior grade.

MEMBER: International Council of Psychologists, Interamerican Society of Psychology, American Psychological Association (fellow), American Sociological Association, Society for the Psychological Study of Social Issues (fellow), American Association for the Advancement of Science, American Association of University Professors, Psychonomic Society, Society of Experimental Social Psychology (chairman, 1967-69), Eastern Psychological Association, New York Academy of Sciences, Phi Beta Kappa, Sigma Xi. *Awards, honors:* Fellowship from Fund for the Advancement of Education, 1955-56, for study at Princeton University; Guggenheim fellowship, 1959; grants from Office of Naval Research, 1962-68, and U.S. Public Health Service, 1969.

WRITINGS: *The Psychology of Thinking*, McGraw, 1952, 2nd edition, 1974; *The Miniature Social Situation*, University of Hawaii Press, 1954; (contributor) Ernest Harms, editor, *Fundamentals of Psychology: The Psychology of Thinking*, New York Academy of Sciences, 1960; (contributor) T. L. Harris and W. E. Schwahn, editors, *Selected Readings in the Learning Process*, Oxford University Press, 1961; (editor with Warner Wilson and Gerald M. Meredith) *Dimensions of Social Psychology: A Book of Readings*, Scott, Foresman, 1964; *Foundations of Psychology*, Van Nostrand, 1968; (editor) *Readings in General Psychology*, Van Nostrand, 1968; (contributor) P. G. Swingle, editor, *Experiments in Social Psychology*, Academic Press, 1968.

Contributor to *Encyclopedia of the Social Sciences, World Book Encyclopedia*, and *Encyclopaedia Britannica*. Contributor of nearly sixty articles and reviews to journals of the social sciences and education, including *Journal of Personality and Social Psychology, Journal of Gerontology, Developmental Psychology, Psychological Bulletin, Journal of General Psychology, Behavioral Science, Sociometry*, and *American Sociological Review*. Associate editor of *Journal of Conflict Resolution*; editorial consultant, *Sociometry*.

SIDELIGHTS: Vinacke writes: "In recent years I have increasingly turned toward humanistic psychology, with its emphasis on growth, values, constructive and coping behavior, self-actualization, personal experience, and the distinctively human condition. . . . I see humanistic psychology as an important and necessary movement, with vital contributions to make not only in personality theory, but also in research." *Avocational interests:* Reading, music (classical and popular, especially Dixieland), gardening, duplicate bridge.

*   *   *

VINCENT, John J(ames) 1929-

PERSONAL: Born December 29, 1929, in Sunderland, England; son of David and Ethel Beatrice Vincent; married Grace Johnston Stafford, December 4, 1958; children: Christopher John, Helen Faith, James Stafford. *Education:* Richmond College, London, B.D. (first class honors), 1954; Drew University, S.T.M. (summa cum laude), 1955; University of Basel, Dr.Theol. (insigni cum laude), 1960. *Home:* 239 Abbeyfield Rd., Sheffield S4 7AW, England. *Office:* Pitsmoor Study House, 210 Abbeyfield Rd., Sheffield S4 7AZ, England.

CAREER: Clergyman of Methodist Church; minister in Manchester, England, 1956-62, and at Rochdale Mission, 1962-69; Pitsmoor Study House, Urban Theology Unit, Sheffield, England, director, 1970—; Sheffield Inner City Ecumenical Mission, superintendent minister, 1970—. Harris Franklin Rall Lecturer at Garrett Theological Seminary, spring, 1969; visiting professor at Boston University, autumn, 1969, and New York Theological Seminary, spring, 1970.

MEMBER: British Council of Churches (member of Commission on Defence and Disarmament, 1963-65, 1969-74), Studiorum Novi Testamenti Societas, Campaign for Nuclear Disarmament (member of national executive committee, 1957-69), Ashram Community Trust (leader, 1967—), Rochdale Ecumenical Centre (founding member), Pitsmoor Action Group (chairman, 1970—).

WRITINGS: Christ in a Nuclear World, Crux Press, 1962, 2nd edition, 1963; *Christ and Our Stewardship: Six Bible Studies*, Epworth Press, 1963; *Christian Nuclear Perspective*, Epworth Press, 1964; *Christ and Methodism: Towards a New Christianity for a New Age*, Abingdon, 1965, 2nd edition, Epworth Press, 1966; *Here I Stand: The Faith of a Radical*, Epworth Press, 1967; *Secular Christ: A Contemporary Interpretation of Jesus*, Abingdon, 1968; *The Working Christ: Christ's Ministries through His Church in the New Testament and in the Modern City*, Epworth Press, 1968; *The Race Race*, Friendship Press, 1968.

The Jesus Thing, Abingdon, 1973; *Stirrings: Essays Christian and Radical*, Epworth Press, 1975; *The Para Church*, Judson Press, in press; *Disciple and Lord in Mark's Gospel*, Epworth Press, in press. Editor of *New City*.

WORK IN PROGRESS: Dynamics of Christ: A Radical Dogmatics; *Urban Problems and Christian Theology*.

SIDELIGHTS: Vincent wrote that he is "committed to academic writing within the context of personal lifestyle commitment with deprived inner-city communities and small experimental Christian groups."

*   *   *

VOGELGESANG, Sandra Louise 1942-
(Sandy Vogelgesang)

PERSONAL: Born July 27, 1942, in Canton, Ohio; daughter of Glenn Wesley (a lawyer) and Louise (Forry) Vogelgesang. *Education:* Cornell University, B.A., 1964; Fletcher School of Law and Diplomacy, M.A., 1965, M.A.L.D., 1966, Ph.D. (with highest honors), 1971. *Politics:* Independent. *Home:* 3001 Croydon Dr. N.W., Canton, Ohio 44718. *Office:* Policy Planning Staff, U.S. Department of State, Washington, D.C.

CAREER: U.S. Embassy, Helsinki, Finland, youth affairs officer and administrator of U.S. educational exchange program, 1967-69; U.S. Department of State, Washington, D.C., Scandinavian analyst in Bureau of Intelligence and Research, 1971-73, chairperson of Secretary of State's Open Forum Panel and economist in Bureau of Economic and Business Affairs, 1973-74, political economist in Bureau of European Affairs, 1974-75, member of Secretary of State's policy planning staff, 1975—. Fellow of Council on Foreign Relations, 1975-76. *Member:* American Foreign Service Association, Women's Action Organization, Fletcher Alumni Association, Phi Beta Kappa.

WRITINGS—Under name Sandy Vogelgesang *Education in America*, U.S. Information Agency, 1969; *The Long Dark Night of the Soul: The American Intellectual Left and the Vietnam War*, Harper, 1974. Author of essays on European Communism, Hoover Institution Press, 1972-75. Contributor to government and foreign service journals.

Editor of *Current Economic Developments*, 1973-74. Member of editorial board of *Open Forum* and *Foreign Service Journal*.

WORK IN PROGRESS: The Role of Human Rights in U.S. Foreign Policy, for Council on Foreign Relations; research on U.S. diplomacy, domestic politics, and the feminist movement.

SIDELIGHTS: Sandra Vogelgesang writes: "I hope, through my writing and career with the Foreign Service and elsewhere, to help mold constructive New World idealism with Old World *Realpolitik* and remold discredited perceptions of 'national interest.' Related to this general concern about human rights, the achievement of the American Dream, and the evolution of my Vietnam-scarred generation is the issue of equal opportunity for women. I was born too late to pioneer for feminism and too soon to reap its full fruits. Although minds will change too slowly to make feminist or black aspirations easy in our time, there is an anguished exhilaration in the expanding quest."

*   *   *

VOGELGESANG, Sandy
See VOGELGESANG, Sandra Louise

VOGT, Marie Bollinger 1921-

PERSONAL: Born March 9, 1921, in Toledo, Ohio; daughter of Herman John (a physician) and Fannie (Millhaubt) Bollinger; married Theodore Vogt (an attorney), November 29, 1949. Education: University of Toledo, A.B., 1944. Religion: Protestant. Home: 5362 Main St., Sylvania, Ohio 43560. Office: Toledo Ballet School, 3137 West Central Ave., Toledo, Ohio 43606.

CAREER: Toledo Ballet School, Toledo, Ohio, director, 1963—. Founder, artistic director, and chief choreographer of Toledo Ballet; coordinator of International Music Festival; member of Toledo Arts Commission, planning committee for Downtown Toledo Promenade Park, and committee on relations with Toledo, Spain; president of Toledo Bar Association Auxiliary, 1974-75. Member: National Association of Dance Companies, Northeast Regional Ballet Association, Ohioana Library Association. Awards, honors: Scripps-Howard Award for editorial in Campus Collegian, at University of Toledo, 1944.

WRITINGS—All self-illustrated: The Ballet Book, privately printed, 1963; 2nd edition, 1973; The Businessman's Ballet Book, privately printed, 1973; Jill and the Nutcracker Ballet (juvenile), Blair, 1974. Contributor to dance magazines and to Toledo Blade.

SIDELIGHTS: Marie Vogt writes: "The Ballet Book was written as an assist to ballet students in home practice. The Businessman's Ballet Book was written as a 'crash course' for the corporate male who suddenly finds his life style includes the art of ballet either as a pleasure pursuit or as a matter of corporate funding. It was meant for the man who knows much about a good many things but little about others."

* * *

VOLKER, Roy 1924-

PERSONAL: Born December, 1924, in St. Louis, Mo.; son of Clark Ralph (a salesman) and Rhoda Mary (Jackael) Volker; married Margaret Ann Birk, June 18, 1955; children: Deborah, Cindy, Laurie, Angie. Education: Educated in St. Louis, Mo. Religion: Lutheran. Residence: St. Louis, Mo. Agent: James Brown Associates, Inc., 22 East 60th St., New York, N.Y. 10022. Office: Search Electronics, Suite 3, 9953 Lewis & Clark Blvd., St. Louis, Mo. 63136.

CAREER: Professional treasure hunter. Professional boxer, 1947-50; sales manager for Capitol Records, 1955-69; promotion manager for Commercial Music, 1970—; Search Electronics, New York, N.Y., president, 1972—. Military service: U.S. Navy, radioman, 1942-45; served in Atlantic and Pacific theaters; became petty officer second class.

WRITINGS: (With Dick Richmond) Treasure under Your Feet: Adventurers' Handbook of Metal Detecting, Regnery, 1974.

WORK IN PROGRESS: In the Wake of the Golden Galleons, with Dick Richmond, autobiographical material covering their undersea treasure hunting activities.

SIDELIGHTS: Volker writes: "Since my separation from the Navy . . . I have been involved in some form of treasure hunting. . . . It has led to a great appreciation of history, archeology, and of man's romance with the sea."

VOSS, George L. 1922-

PERSONAL: Born July 30, 1922, in Chicago, Ill.; son of Harry A. (a railroad clerk) and Helen (Rennwald) Voss; married Betty Driver (a billing clerk); children: Donna, Linda, Debra, Warren McAlpine, Jerry Wick. Education: Montana State University, B.S., 1951. Religion: Lutheran. Home: 5107 Southwest 19th Dr., Portland, Ore. 97201. Office: Omark Industries, Inc., 2100 Southeast Milport Rd., Portland, Ore. 97222.

CAREER: Cole & Weber (advertising agency), Portland, Ore., copy account representative, 1955-59; Voss Advertising, Portland, Ore., owner, 1959-64; Botsford-Constantine & McCarty (advertising agency), Portland, Ore., creative director, 1964-68; Columbia-Willamette Air Pollution Authority, Portland, Ore., public relations director, 1968-73; now associated with Omark Industries, Inc., Portland, Ore. Military service: U.S. Air Force, pilot; became captain; received Air Medal and Purple Heart. Member: National Rifle Association.

WRITINGS: The Man Who Believed in the Code of the West (novel), St. Martin's, 1975. Associate editor of Timberman.

WORK IN PROGRESS: A Handful of Smoke, a novel.

* * *

VOURNAKIS, John N(icholas) 1939-

PERSONAL: Born December 1, 1939, in Cambridge, Ohio; son of Nicholas J. (a short order cook) and Pota (Andritsakis) Vournakis; married Karen A. Munro (a photographer and artist), September 9, 1961; children: Christopher. Education: Albion College, B.A., 1961; Cornell University, Ph.D., 1968. Politics: "Left-wing-socialist-liberal." Religion: Greek Orthodox. Home: 816 Oakwood, Fayetteville, N.Y. 13066. Office: Department of Biology, Syracuse University, Syracuse, N.Y. 13210.

CAREER: Massachusetts Institute of Technology, Cambridge, Mass., member of staff of Education Research Center, 1969-72; Syracuse University, Syracuse, N.Y., assistant professor of biology, 1973—. Consultant to Massachusetts Institute of Technology and Detroit Institute of Technology Project, 1972-75. Member: Biophysical Society, Society for Developmental Biology. Awards, honors: National Academy of Science postdoctoral fellow, 1968; U.S. Department of Health, Education and Welfare research award, 1975, for messenger ribonucleic acid structure work.

WRITINGS: What People Eat: An Introduction to Food Science, William Kaufmann, 1975. Contributor to journals.

WORK IN PROGRESS: Structure of Messenger Ribonucleic Acid: Biochemical and Biophysical Aspects; Organic Chemistry for Pre-Medical Students; Organic Chemistry for Nursing Students.

* * *

VREULS, Diane

PERSONAL: Born in Chicago, Ill.; daughter of Conrad M. (an engineer) and Jane (Baltic) Vreuls; married Stuart Friebert (a poet and professor), 1960; children: Sarah, Stephen. Education: University of Wisconsin, B.A.; St. Hilda's College, Oxford, B.A. and M.A. Home: 172 Elm St., Oberlin, Ohio 44074. Agent: Harriet Wasserman, Russell & Volkening, 551 Fifth Ave., New York, N.Y. 10017.

CAREER: Writer.

WRITINGS: Instructions (poems), Kayak, 1971; *Are We There Yet?* (novel), Simon & Schuster, 1975; *Sums* (juvenile), Crown, in press. Contributor of short stories to journals.

WORK IN PROGRESS: A second novel.

* * *

WAAGENAAR, Sam 1908-

PERSONAL: Born January 10, 1908, in Amsterdam, Holland; son of Godschalk (a diamond worker) and Duifje (de Jong) Waagenaar. *Education:* Educated in Holland; also studied opera singing in Paris, 1934-39. *Religion:* Jewish. *Home and office:* 85 Via Luigi Bodio, 00191 Rome, Italy. *Agent:* Curtis Brown Ltd., 1 Craven Hill, London W2-3EW, England.

CAREER: Director of public relations in Europe for Metro Goldwyn Mayer, 1930-35; Paris correspondent for Netherlands News Agency, 1935-40; Berlin correspondent for International News Service, 1945-46; free-lance writer, 1946—. Acted in anti-Nazi propaganda films in Hollywood, Calif., 1942; had one-man exhibit of his photographs in Amsterdam, 1960. Worked with Office of War Information, 1943-45. *Member:* Overseas Press Club (New York), Stampa Estera (Rome).

WRITINGS: Asia, with photographs by the author, Suddeutscher Verlag, 1955; *Countries of the Red Sea*, with photographs by the author, Suddeutscher Verlag, 1957; (with Georges Simenon and Heinrich Boell) *Children of the World*, with photographs by the author, Deutsch, 1958; (with Alberto Moravia) *Women of Rome*, with photographs by the author, Deutsch, 1959; *The Little Five*, Bruna, 1960; *Women of Israel*, with photographs by the author, Schocken, 1961; *Mata Hari*, Becht, 1964, Appleton, 1965; *The Pope's Jews*, Open Court, 1974.

Filmscripts for travelogues: "Hong Kong," 1952; "Bangkok," 1952; "Hans Brinker's Return," 1953; "The Miracle of the Midnight Sun," 1953; "Hunting Giants," 1953; "Letter to Five Countries," 1953; "Athens Interlude," 1953.

Also author of television play, "Mata Hari," produced in Stuttgart, Germany, 1965. Author of television documentary, "Ryadh, the Oil Capital of Saudi Arabia," for NBC, 1956. Wrote and narrated Dutch version of "March of Time," 1936-39.

WORK IN PROGRESS: A book on Afghanistan.

SIDELIGHTS: Waagenaar has visited 74 countries and is fluent in English, German, French and Italian, as well as his native tongue, and knows some Spanish.

* * *

WABUN
See JAMES, Marlise Ann

* * *

WADE, Kit
See CARSON, Xanthus

* * *

WADINASI, Sedeka
See NALL, Hiram Abiff

WAGMAN, Naomi 1937-
(Rima Newmar)

PERSONAL: Born March 23, 1937, in Tel-Aviv, Israel; daughter of Samuel and Sonia (Pruss) Wagman; divorced. *Education:* Boston University, B.S., 1958. *Office:* 123 Sewall Ave., Brookline, Mass. 02146.

CAREER: Polaroid Corp., Cambridge, Mass., advertising manager, 1961-63; New York State Council on the Arts, New York, N.Y., manager, 1964-65; Wagman Travel, Brookline, Mass., owner, 1972—. Freelance publicity and public relations agent at Edward A. Finch Co., 1968-71.

WRITINGS: Sun and Daughter Signs, Max Padell, 1974. Contributor under pseudonym Rima Newmar to *Everywoman's Daily Horoscope, Aquarius*, and *Zodiac*.

* * *

WAGNER, Nathaniel N(ed) 1930-

PERSONAL: Born January 31, 1930, in New York; son of Morris W. (a businessman) and Jennie (Silverman) Wagner; married Phyllis Reynolds, July 11, 1954; children: Mark, Joel, Jennifer. *Education:* Long Island University, B.A., 1951; Columbia University, M.A., 1952, Ph.D., 1956. *Home:* 15602 35th Ave. N.E., Seattle, Wash. 98155. *Office:* Department of Psychology, University of Washington, Seattle, Wash. 98195.

CAREER: Supervising psychologist, Astor Home for Children, 1958-62; University of Washington, Seattle, assistant professor, 1962-66, associate professor, 1966-70, professor of psychology, 1970—. *Military service:* U.S. Army, 1953-58. *Member:* American Psychological Association, Washington State Psychological Association.

WRITINGS: (With E. S. Tan) *Psychological Problems and Treatment in Malaysia*, University of Malaya Press, 1971; (with Marsha Haug) *Chicanos: Social and Psychological Perspectives*, Mosby, 1971; (with Stanley Sue) *Asian Americans: Psychological Perspectives*, Science and Behavior Books, 1973; *Perspective on Human Sexuality*, Behavioral Publications, 1974; (with Lee Scheingold) *Sound Sex and the Aging Heart*, Human Sciences Press, 1974.

* * *

WAHLOO, Per 1926-1975

1926—June 23, 1975; Swedish journalist, editor, author of crime novels. Obituaries: *Publishers Weekly*, August 4, 1975.

* * *

WAHLROOS, Sven 1931-

PERSONAL: Born May 6, 1931, in Finland; came to United States, 1950; son of Thure and Inga (Juselius) Wahlroos; married Eva Adam, July 13, 1956; children: Ingalill and Sven-Erik (twins). *Education:* Attended University of Helsinki, 1949-50; Santa Barbara College (now University of California, Santa Barbara), B.A., 1951; University of California, Los Angeles, M.A., 1953, Ph.D., 1954. *Office:* 15243 Vanowen St., Suite 200, Van Nuys, Calif. 91405.

CAREER: Los Angeles Psychiatric Service, Los Angeles, Calif., staff psychologist, 1955-58; Sanford Management Service, Los Angeles, staff psychologist, 1958-60; in private practice, Van Nuys, Calif., 1958—. Diplomate of American Board of Professional Psychology; lecturer in family relations under auspices of Los Angeles County Board of Education. Trustee of Finlandia Foundation.

Member: American Psychological Association, Los Angeles County Psychological Association, San Fernando Valley Psychological Association.

WRITINGS: Family Communication, Macmillan, 1974.

SIDELIGHTS: Sven Wahlroos describes his professional orientation as eclectic and based on an integration of common sense and psychological knowledge. He told *CA* he does not belong to any psychological "school" because he believes in fitting the treatment to the patient and not vice versa. He has traveled extensively both in Europe and in the South Seas, and, among other languages, Wahlroos speaks Tahitian fluently. *Avocational interests:* Sailing, traveling, Polynesian history and culture.

* * *

WALES, Nym
  See SNOW, Helen Foster

* * *

WALKER, Dale L(ee)   1935-

PERSONAL: Born August 3, 1935, in Decatur, Ill.; son of Russell Dale (a career soldier) and Eileen M. (Guysinger) Walker; married Alice McCord, September 30, 1960; children: Dianne, Eric, Christopher, Michael, John. *Education:* University of Texas at El Paso, B.A., 1962. *Politics:* Democrat. *Religion:* Protestant. *Home:* 4569 Skylark Way, El Paso, Tex. 79922. *Office:* University of Texas at El Paso, El Paso, Tex. 79968.

CAREER: KTSM-TV, El Paso, Tex., reporter, 1962-66; University of Texas at El Paso, director of News-Information Office, 1966—. *Military service:* U.S. Navy, 1955-59. *Member:* National Historical Society, Society of WWI Aero Historians, Western Writers of America, El Paso County Historical Society, El Paso Westerner's Corral, Sigma Delta Chi.

WRITINGS: (Author of introductory essay) George Sterling, *Wine of Wizardry*, Pinion Press, 1962; (with Richard O'Connor) *The Lost Revolutionary: A Biography of John Reed*, Harcourt, 1967; *The Fiction of Jack London*, Texas Western Press, 1972; *C. L. Sonnichsen: Grassroots Historian*, Texas Western Press, 1972; *The Alien Worlds of Jack London* (monograph), Wolf House Books, 1973; (editor) Howard A. Craig, *Sunward I've Climbed*, Texas Western Press, 1974; *Jack London, Sherlock Holmes, and Sir Arthur Conan Doyle* (monograph), Alvin S. Fick, 1974; (contributor) W. Burns Taylor and Richard Santelli, editor, *Passing Through*, Santay Publishers, 1974; *Death Was the Black Horse: The Story of Rough Rider, Buckey O'Neill*, Madrona Press, 1975; (editor and author of introduction) *Curious Fragments: Jack London's Tales of Fantasy Fiction*, Kennikat, in press. Contributor to newspapers and magazines.

WORK IN PROGRESS: A biography of American war correspondent, J. A. MacGahan.

SIDELIGHTS: Walker writes: "My principal areas of reading and writing interest are: 1) American and British biographical subjects, 19th century; 2) Victorian era, 1839-1900, military history; 3) Jack London studies."

* * *

WALLACE, Ronald   1945-

PERSONAL: Born February 18, 1945, in Cedar Rapids, Iowa; son of William Edward (a professor of law) and Loretta (Kamprath) Wallace; married Margaret McCreight, August 3, 1968; children: Molly Elizabeth. *Education:* College of Wooster, B.A., 1967; University of Michigan, M.A., 1968, Ph.D., 1971. *Home:* 2216 Chamberlain Ave., Madison, Wis. 53705. *Office:* Department of English, University of Wisconsin, Madison, Wis. 53706.

CAREER: University of Wisconsin-Madison, assistant professor, 1972-75, associate professor of English, 1975—. *Member:* Modern Language Association of America. *Awards, honors:* Avery Hopwood Award, 1970, for poetry; American Council of Learned Societies fellowship, 1975-76.

WRITINGS: Henry James and the Comic Form, University of Michigan Press, 1975. Contributor of poems to *New Yorker, North American Review, Poetry Northwest, Iowa Review, New York Quarterly, Prairie Schooner, Perspective*, and other periodicals.

WORK IN PROGRESS: The Modern Comic Novel; poems, *Making the Best of It*.

AVOCATIONAL INTERESTS: Gardening, bees, bicycling, camping, piano, fishing, Switzerland.

* * *

WALSER, Martin   1927-

PERSONAL: Born March 24, 1926, in Wasserburg, Germany; son of Martin (an innkeeper) and Augusta (Schmid) Walser; married Jehle Kaethe, October 20, 1950; children: Franziska, Katharina, Alissa, Theresia. *Education:* Attended University of Regensburg; University of Tuebingen, Ph.D., 1951. *Religion:* Catholic. *Home:* Hecht 36, Ueberlingen, Germany 777.

CAREER: Writer. *Member:* P.E.N., Deutsche Akademie fuer Sprache und Dichtung, Akademie der Kuenste. *Awards, honors:* Gruppe 47 Preis, 1955; Hermann Hesse Preis, 1957; Gerhart Hauptmann Preis, 1962; Schiller Foerder Preis, 1965; Bodensee Literatur Preis, 1967.

WRITINGS—All first published by Suhrkamp in Germany, except as indicated: *Ein Flugzeug ueber dem Haus und andere Geschichten* (stories; title means "An Airplane Over the Roof and Other Stories"), 1955, 2nd edition, 1966; *Ehen in Philippsburg* (novel), 1957, translation by Eva Figes published as *The Gadarene Clubs*, Longmans, Green, 1960, adaptation of Figes' translation by J. Laughlin published as *Marriage in Philippsburg*, New Directions, 1961; *Halbzeit* (novel; title means "Half-Time"), 1960; *Hoelderlin auf dem Dachboden* (title means "Hoelderlin in the Attic"), 1960; (editor) *Die alternative; oder, Brauchen wir eine neue regierung?* (title means "The Alternative: or, Do We Need a New Government?"), Rowohlt (Hamburg), 1961; *Beschreibung einer Form* (title means "Description of a Form"), C. Hanser (Munich), 1961, 3rd edition, 1968; (editor and author of introduction) *Vorzeichen II: Neun neue deutsche Autoren* (title means "Omens: Nine New German Authors"), 1963; (editor) Franz Kafka, *Er: Prosa*, 1963; *Luegengeschichten* (stories; title means "Lying Stories"), 1965; (author of essay) Jonathan Swift, *Satiren*, Insel-Verlag (Frankfurt), 1965; *Erfahrungen und Leseerfahrungen* (essays; title means "Experiences and Reading Experiences"), 1965, 3rd edition, 1969; *Das Einhorn* (novel), 1966, translation by Barrie Ellis-Jones published as *The Unicorn*, Calder & Boyars, 1971; (with Karl Chargesheimer) *Theater, Theater*, Friedrich (Hanover, Germany), 1967; *Heimatkunde* (essays and addresses; title means "Topography"), 1968; (author of afterword) Ursula Trauberg,

Vorleben, 1968; (with others) *Ueber Ernst Bloch*, 1968; *Hoelderlin zu entsprechen* (address; title means "To Meet Hoelderlin"), K. Thomae (Biberach an der Riss, Germany), 1970; *Fiction* (stories), 1970; *Die Gallistl'sche Krankheit* (novel; title means "Gallistl's Disease"), 1972; *Der Sturz* (novel; title means "The Fall"), 1973; *Wie und wovon handelt Literatur* (essays and addresses; title means "How and On What Does Literature Act"), 1973.

Plays: *Der Abstecher*, 1961, translation by R. Grunberger published as *The Detour* in *The Rabbit [and] The Detour*, J. Calder, 1963; *Eiche und Angora: Eine Deutsche*, *Chronik*, 1962, 3rd edition, 1966, adaptation by R. Ducan published as *The Rabbit* in *The Rabbit [and] The Detour*, J. Calder, 1963; *Ueberlebensgross Herr Knott: Requiem fuer einen Unsterblichen* (title means "More Than Life Size, Mr. Knott"), 1964, 2nd edition, 1969; *Der Schwarze Schwan* (title means "The Black Swan"), 1964; *Der Abstecher [and] Die Zimmerschlacht* (latter title means "Homefront"), 1967; *Ein Kinderspiel* (title means "A Children's Play"), 1970; *Aus dem Wortschatz unserer Kaempfe* (title means "From the Vocabulary of Our Fights"), Verlag Eremiten-Presse (Stierstadt, Germany), 1971; *Gesammelte Stuecke* (collected plays), 1971.

*   *   *

WANSHEL, Jeff(rey Mark) 1947-

PERSONAL: Born August 24, 1947, in White Plains, N.Y.; son of Jerome Nelson (a lawyer) and Sylvia (a real estate agent; maiden name, Greenwald) Wanshel. *Education:* Wesleyan University, B.A. (with high honors in English), 1969; Yale University, graduate study, 1969-70. *Residence:* Larchmont, N.Y. *Agent:* Audrey Wood, International Creative Management, 1301 Avenue of the Americas, New York, N.Y. 10019.

CAREER: Playwright. In residence at William Flanagan Memorial Creative Persons Center, 1971-72; worked with National Theatre of the Deaf, 1972; participant at National Playwrights Conference in Waterford, Conn., 1969, 1971, 1972. *Awards, honors:* Audrey Wood fellowship, 1969-70; Rockefeller Award in Playwriting, 1972-73.

WRITINGS—Plays: *The Disintegration of James Cherry* (first produced by the Repertory Theatre of Lincoln Center, New York, N.Y., 1969), Dramatists Play Service, 1970; "The Rhesus Umbrella," first produced in New Haven, Conn., at Yale Repertory Theatre, 1970; "auto-destruct," first produced in Berkeley, Calif., at Magic Theatre, 1972; "Fog and Mismanagement," first produced in Kingston, R.I., at University of Rhode Island, 1975.

SIDELIGHTS: Wanshel told *CA:* "Spent more than half of 1970-74 period outside the U.S.A., passing through Europe, stopping in Morocco and the Canary Islands, 1970-71; Mexico, 1972; passed through Europe, lived in Greek Islands, passed through Turkey, Iran, Afghanistan, Pakistan, Nepal, lived in India and Ceylon, passed through Burma, Thailand, Malaysia, Singapore, Java, lived in Bali, 1973-74. Finished 'James Cherry' on St. John, U.S. Virgin Islands; finished 'auto-destruct' in Morocco; finished 'Fog and Mismanagement' in Ceylon (Sri Lanka)."

*   *   *

WARD, Colin 1924-

PERSONAL: Born August 14, 1924, in Wanstead, Essex, England; son of Arnold (a teacher) and Ruby (West) Ward; married Harriet Barry (a teacher), September 9, 1966; chil-

dren: Ben; stepsons: Barney Unwin, Tom Unwin. *Education:* Attended Garnett Teachers College, 1964-65. *Politics:* Anarchist. *Religion:* None. *Home:* 19 Schubert Rd., London S.W.15, England. *Agent:* David Higham Associates, 5/8 Lower John St., London W.1, England.

CAREER: Shepheard & Epstein (architects and planners), London, England, senior assistant, 1952-61; Chamberlin, Powell & Bon, London, director of research, 1962-64; Wandsworth Technical College, London, England, lecturer in charge of liberal studies, 1966-71; Town & Country Planning Association (a voluntary organization), London, education officer, 1971—.

WRITINGS: (Contributor) L. I. Krimerman and Lewis Perry, editors, *Patterns of Anarchy*, Doubleday-Anchor, 1966; *Violence* (juvenile), Penguin Education, 1970; (contributor) C. G. Benello and Dimitrios Roussopoulos, editors, *The Case for Participatory Democracy*, Grossman, 1971; *Work* (juvenile), Penguin Education, 1972; *Anarchy in Action*, Harper, 1973; (with Anthony Fyson) *Streetwork: The Exploding School*, Routedge & Kegan Paul, 1973; (editor) *Vandalism*, Van Nostrand, 1973; (contributor) Peter Buckman, editor, *Education Without Schools*, Souvenir Press, 1973; *Utopia* (juvenile), Penguin Books, 1974; (editor) Peter Kropotkin, *Fields, Factories, and Workshops*, Harper, 1974; *Tenants Take Over*, Architectural Press, 1974; *The Child in the City*, Pantheon, in press. Contributor to *Times Educational Supplement*, *New Society*, and architecture journals. Co-editor of *Freedom*, 1947-60; editor of *Anarchy*, 1961-70, and *BEE* (Bulletin of Environmental Education), 1971—; member of editorial board of *Town & Country Planning*, 1971.

WORK IN PROGRESS: Interpreting the Built Environment (research report); *Alternative Architecture*, publication by Pantheon expected in 1977.

*   *   *

WARD, Jonathon
See STINE, Whitney Ward

*   *   *

WARD, Olivia Tucker 1927-

PERSONAL: Born February 16, 1927, in Maryland; daughter of Ira and Margie (Clark) Tucker; married Benjamin Ward (a commissioner of correction), May 30, 1956. *Education:* Maryland State Teachers College, B.S., 1946; New York University, M.A., 1950. *Politics:* Democrat. *Religion:* Presbyterian. *Home:* 216-07, Sawyer Ave., Holliswood, N.Y. 11427. *Office:* Public School 96, 130-01 Rockaway Blvd., South Ozone Park, N.Y. 11420.

CAREER: Teacher in Baltimore, Md. schools, 1946-49; elementary school teacher in New York, N.Y., 1951-66; supervisor of early childhood education in New York City, 1966-74; with Board of Education, New York, N.Y., 1974—. *Member:* National Association for the Advancement of Colored People, Urban League, American Society of Composers, Authors, and Publishers.

WRITINGS: ABC's of Black History, Tandem Press, 1974. Contributor to *Pre-Kindergarten Bulletin*. Author, lyric composer, and singer for "ABC's of Black History" (educational program), 1974.

SIDELIGHTS: Mrs. Ward told *CA* that the program, "ABC's of Black History, is a teaching kit, used in schools throughout the United States—that parts have been used on TV and radio.

WARD, Patricia A(nn) 1940-

PERSONAL: Born August 26, 1940, in Warren, Pa.; daughter of H. Blair (a minister) and Edwinna (Wilson) Ward. *Education:* Eastern Nazarene College, B.A. (summa cum laude), 1962; University of Wisconsin, M.A., 1964, Ph.D., 1968. *Office:* Department of French, Pennsylvania State University, University Park, Pa. 16802.

CAREER: State University of New York at Albany, assistant professor of comparative literature, 1968-72; Pennsylvania State University, University Park, assistant professor, 1972-75, associate professor of French and comparative literature, 1975—. *Member:* American Association of University Professors, Modern Language Association of America, American Comparative Literature Association, American Association of Teachers of French, Conference on Christianity and Literature (treasurer, 1972-74), Evangelical Women's Caucus, Common Cause. *Awards, honors:* Fulbright fellow at University of Paris, 1966-67; State University of New York Research Foundation grant-in-aid, 1971; Pennsylvania State University research initiation grant, 1973-74.

WRITINGS: The Medievalism of Victor Hugo, Pennsylvania State University Press, 1975. Contributor of articles and reviews to periodicals.

WORK IN PROGRESS: Research on the aesthetics of Joseph Joubert, and on the process of comparison in literary studies.

AVOCATIONAL INTERESTS: Travel, music.

* * *

WARE, Emma 1896(?)-1975

1896(?)—May 1, 1975; American educator, biographer, and author. Obituaries: *New York Times,* May 3, 1975.

* * *

WARREN, Roland L(eslie) 1915-

PERSONAL: Born June 24, 1915, in Islip, N.Y.; son of Ruy Waverly and Jenny (Simonds) Warren; married Margaret Hodges (a violin repairer), June 17, 1938; children: Ursula Washburn, David Hardy, Margaret Robin. *Education:* New York University, B.S., 1935; University of Heidelberg, Ph.D., 1937. *Home address:* R.F.D. 2, Farwell Rd., Tyngsboro, Mass. 01879. *Office:* Florence Heller Graduate School for Advanced Studies in Social Welfare, Brandeis University, Waltham, Mass. 02154.

CAREER: Hofstra College (now Hofstra University), Hempstead, N.Y., instructor, 1937-39, assistant professor of social science, 1939-41; Alfred University, Alfred, N.Y., associate professor, 1941-43, professor of sociology, 1945-58; State Charities Aid Association, New York, N.Y., director of Social Research Service, 1958-62; American Friends Service Committee, Philadelphia, Pa., Quaker international affairs representative for Germany, 1962-64; Brandeis University, Waltham, Mass., professor of community theory, 1964—. Member of National Institute of Mental Health's Problems Review Committee, 1969-74, chairman, 1972-74. *Military service:* U.S. Naval Reserve, 1943-45.

MEMBER: International Society for Community Development, American Sociological Association (fellow), Society for the Study of Social Problems, Community Development Society. *Awards, honors:* Guggenheim fellowship, 1956-57, to study voluntary citizen participation in commu-

nity affairs in Stuttgart, Germany; research scientist award from National Institute of Mental Health, 1964-74.

WRITINGS: Studying Your Community, Russell Sage Foundation, 1955; *The Community in America,* Rand McNally, 1963, 2nd edition, 1971; *Social Research Consultation: An Experiment in Health and Welfare Planning,* Russell Sage Foundation, 1963; (editor) *Perspectives on the American Community: A Book of Readings,* Rand McNally, 1966, 2nd edition, 1973; (editor) *Politics and the Ghettos,* Atherton, 1969; *Truth, Love, and Social Change: And Other Essays on Community Change,* Rand McNally, 1971; (with Stephen M. Rose and Ann F. Burgunder) *The Structure of Urban Reform: Community Decision Organizations in Stability and Change,* Heath, 1974.

Contributor: Herman D. Stein and Richard A. Cloward, editors, *Social Perspectives on Behavior: A Reader in Social Science for Social Work and Related Professions,* Free Press, 1958; Terry N. Clark, editor, *Community Structure and Decision Making: Comparative Analyses,* Science Research Associates, 1968; Peter K. Manning, editor, *Research and Theories in Social Deviance,* Lippincott, 1969; Robert Mills French, editor, *The Community: A Comparative Perspective,* F. E. Peacock, 1969; Arthur Dunham, editor, *The New Community Organization,* Crowell, 1969; Ralph M. Kramer and Harry Specht, editors, *Readings in Community Organization,* Prentice-Hall, 1969; Paul White and George Vlasak, editors, *Inter-Organizational Research in Health: Conference Proceedings,* National Center for Health Services Research and Development, Johns Hopkins University, 1970; Lee J. Cary, editor, *Community Development as a Process,* University of Missouri Press, 1970; Robert W. Klenk and Robert M. Ryan, editors, *The Practice of Social Work,* Wadsworth, 1970; Fred M. Cox and other editors, *Strategies of Community Organization,* F. E. Peacock, 1970; *The Social Welfare Forum,* Columbia University Press, 1971; Charles M. Bonjean, Terry N. Clark, and Robert L. Lineberry, editors, *Community Politics: A Behavioral Approach,* Free Press, 1971; R. Serge Denisoff and Richard A. Peterson, editors, *Sounds of Social Change: Studies in Popular Culture,* Rand McNally, 1972; William O'Neill, editor, *Problems and Issues in American Social History,* Burgess, 1972; Melvin B. Brinkerhoff and Phillip R. Kunz, editors, *Complex Organizations and Their Environments,* W. C. Brown, 1972; Matthew Tuite, Robert Chisolm, and Michael Radnor, editors, *Interorganizational Decision-Making,* Aldine, 1972; Sandor Halebsky, editor, *The Sociology of the City,* Scribner, 1973; Bruce Denner and Richard H. Price, editors, *Community Mental Health,* Holt, 1973; Donald N. Rothblatt, editor, *National Policy for Urban and Regional Development,* Heath, 1974; Hans B. C. Spiegel, editor, *Citizen Participation in Urban Development,* National Institute for Applied Behavioral Science, 1974; William C. Sze and June G. Hopps, editors, *Evaluation and Accountability of Human Service Programs,* Schenkman, 1974; Steven A. Waldhorn and Joseph Sneed, editors, *Restructuring the Federal System: Approaches to Accountability in Post-Categorical Programs,* Crane, Russack, in press.

Contributor of more than forty articles to journals of the social sciences, including *Community Development Journal, Social Problems, Social Science Quarterly, Community Mental Health Journal, American Sociological Review,* and *Journal of the American Institute of Planners.* Correspondent for *Community Development Journal International;* member of editorial committee of *Journal of the Community Development Society;* member of editorial board of *Urban Affairs Quarterly*; associate editor of *Journal of Voluntary Action Research.*

WORK IN PROGRESS: Purposive Social Change.

* * *

WASHBURN, O(swell) A(aron)   1914-

PERSONAL: Born February 28, 1914, in Paden, Okla.; son of De Owen (a farmer) and Mabel Pearl (Perry) Washburn; married Eleanor Daggett, October 18, 1938 (divorced, February 28, 1974); married Maria Carlotta Rael (a clothing store owner), September 14, 1974; children: (first marriage) Rochelle Eleanor (Mrs. Joseph D. Genre). *Education:* Attended Adams State College, 1935-36. *Politics:* "Registered Republican: Independent philosophy." *Religion:* "Reared Protestant: now atheist." *Home:* Canones Rd., Chama, N.M. 87520. *Agent:* Broome Agency, Box 3649, Sarasota, Fla. 33578.

CAREER: Rural schoolteacher in New Mexico, 1936-41; forest ranger for U.S. Forest Service in Carson National Forest, N.M., 1941-45; rancher in Chama, N.M., 1945—; free-lance writer in Chama, N.M., 1945—. *Member:* Outdoor Writers of America, New Mexico Outdoor Writers. *Awards, honors:* U.S. Conservation Service conservation essay winner, 1957.

WRITINGS: General Red: The Story of the Hound Who Led the Pack against Bear and Cougar, Jenkins Publishing, 1972; *Highhorse* (novel), Resort Publishing, 1974. Regular outdoor columnist for *Sante Fe New Mexican.* Contributor to *Reader's Digest, Argosy, Saga, Outdoor Life, Field and Stream, National Rifleman, Frontier Times, True West*, and other journals.

WORK IN PROGRESS: A novel, *Enid*; the third in a trilogy of novels set in the Southwest, *How to Live, Love, and Laugh for a Hundred Years or More*; short stories.

SIDELIGHTS: Washburn had a severe back injury in 1953 that was followed by radical spinal fusion. Subsequently he sold the working part of his ranch and built a log house where he could concentrate on writing. To survive in rough times he gathered and peddled bleached bones, junk iron, old batteries, gravel, manure, beans, and fruit. Being a born hunter he trapped coyotes, bobcat, beaver, mink, and skunks. His skill hunting bear and big cats is known all over the world, and he has developed a new breed of trailhound, the Silver Mountain Steel Dust.

* * *

WATSON, Alan D(ouglas)   1942-

PERSONAL: Born May 3, 1942, in Rocky Mount, N.C.; son of Joseph Winstead and Helen (Richardson) Watson; married Margaret Bunn, August 29, 1964; children: Katherine, Jennifer, Westry. *Education:* Duke University, B.A., 1964; East Carolina University, M.A., 1966; University of South Carolina, Ph.D., 1971. *Residence:* Wilmington, N.C. *Office:* Department of History, University of North Carolina, South College Rd., Wilmington, N.C. 28401.

CAREER: University of North Carolina, Wilmington, associate professor of history, 1971—. State of North Carolina Department of Cultural Resources, Raleigh, member of advisory editorial committee for North Carolina Bicentennial, 1974—, member of advisory editorial committee of Divison of Archives and History, 1975-80. *Member:* Organization of American Historians, Southern Historical Association, Historical Society of North Carolina, North Caolina Literary and Historical Association, Association of

Historians in Eastern North Carolina (secretary, 1975-76), Lower Cape Fear Historical Society (member of board of directors, 1975-78). *Awards, honors:* First annual award from North Carolina Society of Sons of the American Revolution, 1975, for periodical article judged best relating to the American Revolution.

WRITINGS: Society in Colonial North Carolina, Division of Archives and History, North Carolina Department of Cultural Resources, 1975. Contributor of articles to *North Carolina Historical Review, South Carolina Historical Magazine, South Atlantic Quarterly, The State*, and *James Sprunt Review.* Editor, *Lower Cape Fear Historical Bulletin.*

WORK IN PROGRESS: A Disparate People: Essays Concerning the Economic and Social History of Colonial North Carolinians; contributions to *Dictionary of North Carolina Biography*, edited by William S. Powell, and *Encyclopedia of Southern History*, edited by David C. Roller and Robert W. Twyman; an investigation of lawlessness and its relation to the coming of the Revolution in North Carolina.

SIDELIGHTS: Watson writes: "Raised in a family atmosphere which stressed the importance of reading and an appreciation of genealogy and history, and living in proximity to land owned over two centuries ago by my forebears, I quickly developed a keen awareness of the past. Collegiate educational opportunities and the approaching bicentennial of the American Revolution further stimulated my interest in history.

"History, to me, is a most fascinating discipline. It is all-encompassing, embracing every conceivable emotion and subject. It is as broad (or as narrow) as the imagination of the writer. It can attempt the exactness of science; it can approach the subjectivity of philosophy. It can serve as a vehicle for change; it can be used to defend the status quo."

Watson further adds: "On the whole, mine is a descriptive history, conservative and appreciative of the past. I would like to enjoy history and be entertained by it. At the same time I would extend the use and appreciation of history to others for their various applications of it. And that is crucial, for so few people care for the past and recognize the values to be derived from it."

* * *

WATSON, Lyall   1939-

PERSONAL: Born April 12, 1939, in Johannesburg, South Africa; son of Douglas (an architect) and Mary (Morkel) Watson. *Education:* University of Witwatersrand, B.S., 1958; University of Natal, M.S., 1959; University of London, Ph.D., 1963. *Politics:* "Absolutely none." *Religion:* "Animist." *Agent:* Murray Pollinger, 11 Long Acre, London WC2E 9LH, England. *Office:* BCM-Biologic, London WC1V 6XX, England.

CAREER: Zoological Garden of Johannesburg, Johannesburg, South Africa, director, 1964-65; British Broadcasting Corp., London, producer of documentary films, 1966-67; expedition leader and researcher in Antarctica, in Amazon River area, in Seychelles, and in Indonesia, 1968-72; Biologic of London (consultants), London, founder and director, 1967—.

WRITINGS: Omnivore, Coward, 1970; *Supernature*, Doubleday, 1973; *The Romeo Error*, Doubleday, 1974. Contributor to Reader's Digest Services' "Living World of

Animals'' series, 1970. Contributor to professional journals.

WORK IN PROGRESS: Research on the building of a bridge between scientific investigation and mystic revelation.

SIDELIGHTS: "Since 1967 I have travelled constantly," Watson wrote, "looking and listening, collecting bits and pieces of apparently useless and unconnected information, stopping every two years to put the fragments together into some sort of meaningful pattern. Never plan ahead, simply follow whichever strange god calls the loudest. Now totally unemployable, but very happy. Enjoy English enormously; speak seven other languages badly."

* * *

WATSTEIN, Esther 1928-

PERSONAL: Born February 8, 1928, in Torrington, Conn.; daughter of Samuel (a merchant) and Celia (a merchant; maiden name, Bresky) Bufferd; married Herbert Watstein, December 27, 1952 (divorced); children: Sarah, Miriam, Rachel. *Education:* Sarah Lawrence College, B.A., 1949. *Religion:* Jewish. *Home address:* Bristol, Conn. 06010.

CAREER: Litchfield Enquirer, Litchfield, Conn., feature writer and reviewer, 1948-53; *Bristol Press,* Bristol, Conn., reviewer, 1953—. Merchandiser for Conde Nast Publishing (of *Glamour* magazine), 1949-51; buyer and advertising representative for Bufferd's Shoe Shop, 1951-54; designer and manufacturer of needlework canvases and kits. *Member:* Embroiderer's Guild of America.

WRITINGS: Pillow Talk, Bantam, 1974; *Design Your Own Needlepoint,* Bantam, 1974; *Needlepoint and Bargello Tricks,* Bantam, 1974.

WORK IN PROGRESS: A needlepoint book, for paperback publication.

AVOCATIONAL INTERESTS: Reading, gardening.

* * *

WATT, Ruth 1919-

PERSONAL: Born February 19, 1919, in Montreal, Quebec, Canada; daughter of William (a moulder) and Julia M. (Duval) McFetridge; married James Watt (a general manager and design engineer), September 28, 1942; children: Trevor James, Mark William, Brant Alexander, Cherie Dell. *Education:* Attended University of Toronto, 1938-39, and Riverside City College, 1962. *Religion:* Church of Religious Science. *Home:* 14960 Sherman Way, #A-106, Van Nuys, Calif. 91405.

CAREER: Canadian National Telegraph, Montreal, Quebec, secretary to general manager, 1943-44; Allied War Supplies, Montreal, Quebec, supervisor, 1944-45; *Hamilton Spectator,* Hamilton, Ontario, reporter, 1946-57; Grinnell's, Toronto, Ontario, purchasing agent, 1947; Civic Advisory Council, Toronto, Ontario, secretary, 1947-50. *Member:* Parent's Group Hearing Society (secretary of Pomona, Calif. branch, 1956-57), California Writers.

WRITINGS: Love Makes the Difference (novel), Bouregy, 1975. Contributor to Sunday school journals.

WORK IN PROGRESS: A book based on travels to Ireland, *Secret of the Veiled Crypt;* a romantic suspense novel with a Scottish background tentatively titled, *When the Piper Plays;* two romantic suspense novels with a Canadian-American border setting based on the War of

1812, and with a Gaspe, Canada setting, especially the Perce Rock area.

AVOCATIONAL INTERESTS: Travel, reading, music, dancing, theater, ballet, watching football, current events, people.

* * *

WATTENBERG, Ben J. 1933-

PERSONAL: Born August 26, 1933, in New York, N.Y.; son of Judah (a lawyer) and Rachel (Gutman) Wattenberg; married Marna Hade, June 24, 1956; children: Ruth Elena, Daniel Eli, Sarah Anita. *Education:* Hobart College, B.A., 1955. *Politics:* Democrat. *Religion:* Jewish. *Home:* 7408 Bybrook Lane, Chevy Chase, Md. 20015. *Agent:* Peter Matson, 22 East 40th St., New York, N.Y. 10016. *Office:* 818 18th St. N.W., Washington D.C. 20006.

CAREER: Speechwriter for President Lyndon B. Johnson, 1966-68; aide to Senator Hubert Humphrey, 1970; aide to Senator Henry Jackson, 1972. Business consultant. *Military service:* U.S. Air Force, 1956-58. *Member:* Federal City Club, Phi Beta Kappa.

WRITINGS: This U.S.A., Doubleday, 1965; (with Richard Scammon) *The Real Majority,* Coward, 1970; *The Birth Dearth and What It Means* (monograph), Family Circle and National Association of Food Chains, 1971; *The Real America,* Doubleday, 1975.

* * *

WAY, Robert E(dward) 1912-
(David Black)

PERSONAL: Born December 19, 1912, in Durban, Natal, South Africa; son of George Curry (a farmer and soldier) and Ethel (Way) Way; married Olwen Garrett (a psychiatric nurse), January 7, 1948; children: Mary (Mrs. Nicholas Andrew), Gregory, Radegunde (Mrs. Michael Smith), James, Gabrielle. *Education:* Emmanuel College, Cambridge, M.A., 19—. *Politics:* "No party affiliations but right wing." *Religion:* Roman Catholic. *Office:* Brettons, Burrough Green, Newmarket, Suffolk, England.

CAREER: Farmer; operator of thoroughbred stud farm, 1936-57; R. E. & G. B. Way, Suffolk, England, antiquarian bookseller, especially of books on horses and field sports, 1957-75. Founder of DeBurgh Basset Hound Pack; former district and county councillor. *Military service:* British Army, served in Finnish International Volunteer Force, Horsed Cavalry, and Mountain Battery (on mules), 1940-43; became second lieutenant. Member of Home Guard. *Member:* Antiquarian Booksellers Association, Burrough Green Cricket Club (president).

WRITINGS: (Author of introduction) Outram Tristram, *Coaching Ways and Coaching Days,* E. P. Publications, 1973; *Garden of the Beloved* (religious allegory), Doubleday, 1975. Contributor to *Horse,* sometimes under pseudonym David Black.

WORK IN PROGRESS: The Pilgrim, a religious allegory; *The Wisdom of the English Mystics; The Life and Times of St. Radegunde: Queen of France.*

SIDELIGHTS: Mr. Way has traveled widely in Europe, Africa, and the United States, but says he is now content to wander over England and Scotland in his motor caravan with his two dogs. He avers he is breeding a mule foal from a thoroughbred mare "on which to continue travels if petrol and money run out."

WAY, Walter L. 1931-

PERSONAL: Born June 27, 1931, in Rochester, N.Y.; son of Kenneth F. (a pharmacist) and Mary T. (Faulkner) Way; married Elizabeth J. Folwell, July 9, 1955; children: Barbara, Jonathan, Jeffrey. *Education:* University of Buffalo, B.S., 1953; State University of New York, Syracuse, M.D., 1957; University of California, M.S. (pharmacology), 1962. *Office:* University of California, S-436, San Francisco, Calif. 94143.

CAREER: University of California, San Francisco, instructor, 1961-62, assistant professor, 1962-68, associate professor, 1968-74, professor of anesthesia and pharmacology, 1974—. *Member:* American Society of Anesthesiologists, American Society for Pharmacology and Experimental Therapeutics, Association of University Anesthetists.

WRITINGS: The Drug Scene, Prentice-Hall, 1970, revised edition, in press. Contributor of articles on drug interaction to scientific journals.

WORK IN PROGRESS: Drug Interactions.

* * *

WAYLAND, Patrick
See O'CONNOR, Richard

* * *

WAYNE, Mary Collier 1913-

PERSONAL: Born May 9, 1913, in South Pasadena, Calif., daughter of Frank Elliot (a horticulturist) and Flora (Robinson) Collier; married Robert Day Wayne (a professor), December 28, 1941; children: William Collier. *Education:* Occidental College, B.A., 1935; Columbia University, M.A., 1939; University of Southern California, M.S. in L.S., 1966. *Politics:* Republican. *Religion:* Congregational. *Home:* 909 Lyndon St., South Pasadena, Calif. 91030. *Office:* South Pasadena Public Library, 1115 El Centro St., South Pasadena, Calif. 91030.

CAREER: Secretary, First Congregational Church, Los Angeles, Calif., 1935-36, and Occidental College, Los Angeles, 1936-38; Furman University, Greenville, S.C., assistant to dean of women and director of student personnel, 1939-42; Occidental College, secretary, 1943-45; South Pasadena Public Library, South Pasadena, Calif., clerk, 1954-66, librarian, 1966-67, assistant city librarian, 1967-72, city librarian, 1972—. Member, alumni board of governors of Occidental College, 1970-73, and board of directors of Library Patrons of Occidental College. *Member:* American Library Association, California Library Association, Public Library Executive Association of Southern California, California Historical Society, Southern California Historical Society.

WRITINGS: (Editor with Helen Raitt) *We Three Came West,* Tofua Press, 1974.

* * *

WECHSLER, Judith Glatzer 1940-

PERSONAL: Born December 28, 1940, in Chicago, Ill.; daughter of Nahum Norbert (a historian, writer, and professor) and Anne (a teacher; maiden name, Stiebel) Glatzer; married Richard Wechsler, September 15, 1963 (divorced, 1969); children: Johanna. *Education:* Brandeis University, B.A., 1962; Columbia University, M.A., 1967; University of California, Los Angeles, Ph.D., 1972. *Reli-*

gion: Jewish. *Home:* 110 Trowbridge St., Cambridge, Mass. 02138. *Office:* Department of Architecture, Massachusetts Institute of Technology, Box 3-309, Cambridge, Mass. 02139.

CAREER: Member of Alwin Nikolais Dance Co., New York, N.Y., 1957; Schocken Books, New York, N.Y., assistant editor, 1963-65; Massachusetts Institute of Technology, Cambridge, Mass., assistant professor, 1970-74, associate professor of art, 1974—. Member of Mark Epstein Mime Co., 1963-64, and Commonplace Theater, 1974—. Lecturer at Brown University, 1970. *Member:* College Art Association.

WRITINGS: (Editor and author of introduction) *Cezanne in Perspective,* Prentice-Hall, 1975; (contributor) Fishbane and Flohr, editors, *Texts and Responses,* Leider, 1975. Contributor to *Artforum, Art News, Aperture,* and *Gazette des Beaux Arts.*

WORK IN PROGRESS: Editing and writing introduction to *Aesthetics in Science;* a study of *Daumier*—on the role of bearing and gesture in nineteenth-century French life, theater, painting, and literature, completion expected in 1976.

SIDELIGHTS: Judith Wechsler has lived in Jerusalem, Paris, and Oxford.

* * *

WECHTER, Nell Wise 1913-

PERSONAL: Born August 6, 1913, in Stumpy Point, N.C.; daughter of Enoch Raymond (a fisherman) and Edith Casey (Best) Wise; married Robert William Wechter (a U.S. Navy officer and teacher), March 12, 1943; children: Marcia Michele (Mrs. Michael Dunlap). *Education:* East Carolina Teachers College, student, 1933; East Carolina College, B.S., 1951, M.A. (elementary education), 1952, further graduate study, 1972; University of North Carolina, Greensboro, M.A. (English and social studies), graduate study, 1958-59, 1962-64. *Politics:* Democrat. *Religion:* Methodist. *Home address:* Stumpy Point, N.C. 27978.

CAREER: Public school teacher in North Carolina, 1933-64; free-lance feature writer for North Carolina newspapers, 1943-68; *Hyde County Herald,* Swan Quarter, N.C., associate editor, 1948-50; College of the Albemarle, Elizabeth City, N.C., teacher of creative writing and English, 1972; writer.

MEMBER: National Education Association, North Carolina Education Association, Outer Banks Woman's Club (honorary member). *Awards, honors:* George Washington Gold Medal from Freedoms Foundation, 1950, for play "All Aboard for Freedom"; first place awards from Guildford Fine Arts Festival, 1955, for essay, and 1956, for poetry; Franklin McNutt Award, 1956, for best essay about teaching the American way of life by a Greensboro teacher; award for best young people's book by a North Carolina author from American Association of University Women, 1957, for *Taffy of Torpedo Junction;* national teacher's medal for North Carolina from Freedoms Foundation, 1958.

WRITINGS: The Romance of Juniper River (novel), Times Printing, 1937; *Taffy of Torpedo Junction* (juvenile fiction), Blair, 1957; *Betsy Dowdy's Ride* (Catholic Children's Book Club selection), Blair, 1960; *Swamp Girl* (juvenile fiction), Blair, 1971; *The Mighty Midgetts of Chicamacomico* (adult fiction), Times Printing, 1974; *Teach's Light* (juvenile fiction), Blair, 1974; *Some Whisper of Our Name* (adult), Times Printing, 1975. Contributor to education journals and to newspapers.

SIDELIGHTS: The Wechters live on Nell Wechter's old home plantation in Stumpy Point where they have built a new cottage facing Pamlico Sound. *Avocational interests:* Sewing, canning and freezing vegetables.

* * *

WEEKS, Thelma E(vans) 1921-

PERSONAL: Born January 15, 1921, in Portland, Ore.; daughter of Harry E. and Clarissa (Marshall) Evans; married Robert L. Weeks (an industrial economist), January 7, 1940; children: Barbara A. (Mrs. William S. Patton), John R. *Education:* San Diego State University, A.B. (with honors), 1962; Stanford University, Ph.D., 1973. *Home address:* P.O. Box 1287, Los Altos, Calif. 94022. *Office:* Center for Cross-Cultural Research, Suite 450, 770 Welch Rd., Palo Alto, Calif. 94304.

CAREER: KUFM-Radio, San Diego, Calif., station manager, 1958-62; Stanford University, Stanford, Calif., writer for project at Institute for Mathematical Studies, 1963-66; Educational Development Corp., Palo Alto, Calif., writer for portions of a series of English composition textbooks for elementary school children, 1966-67; conducted independent linguistic research on the Yakima Indian Reservation, Toppenish, Wash., 1968-74; Center for Cross-Cultural Research, Palo Alto, Calif., director, 1974—. Instructor at University of California, Santa Cruz, autumn, 1974, and University of California, Berkeley, spring, 1974. *Member:* International Linguistics Association, American Anthropological Association (fellow), American Dialect Society, American Educational Research Association, Linguistic Society of America, Modern Language Association of America.

WRITINGS: The Slow Speech Development of a Bright Child, Heath, 1974; (contributor) Dell Hymes, editor, *Language in Culture and Society*, Harper, 2nd edition (Weeks was not associated with original edition), in press. Contributor to journals in her field, and of about one hundred short stories and articles to juvenile publications, including *Jack and Jill* and *Highlights for Children*. Editor of *KUFM Highlights*, 1958-62; editorial assistant for *Journal of Mathematical Psychology* and *Journal of Comparative and Physiological Psychology*, both 1963-66.

WORK IN PROGRESS: A book on the sociolinguistic aspects of child language acquisition; learning the Sahaptin language of the Yakima Indians in Washington, and studying the variety of English spoken among them; studying language problems of Korean children adopted by non-Korean families in the United States.

AVOCATIONAL INTERESTS: Painting, sketching, sculpting, sewing, needlework, gardening.

* * *

WEIGEL, John A(rthur) 1912-

PERSONAL: Born August 17, 1912, in Cleveland, Ohio; son of Edward J. and Maria (Koenigshoff) Weigel. *Education:* Western Reserve University (now Case Western Reserve University), A.B., 1933, M.A., 1937, Ph.D., 1939; Columbia University, M.A., 1951. *Home:* 325 East Vine St., Oxford, Ohio 45056. *Office:* Department of English, Miami University, 226 Upham Hall, Oxford, Ohio 45056.

CAREER: High school teacher of English in public schools in Cleveland, Ohio, 1933-37; Western Reserve University (now Case Western Reserve University), Cleveland, Ohio, lecturer in English, 1937-39; Miami University, Oxford, Ohio, instructor, 1939-45, assistant professor, 1945-48, associate professor, 1948-57, professor of English, 1957—. Lecturer at University of Cincinnati, 1946-52, Indiana University at Earlham College, 1948-52; visiting professor at Columbia University, 1946-47, summers, 1947-50, 1952-53. *Member:* Modern Language Association of America, National Council of Teachers of English, Phi Beta Kappa, Sigma Xi. *Awards, honors:* Ford Foundation fellow, 1952-53.

WRITINGS: Lawrence Durrell, Twayne, 1965; *Colin Wilson*, Twayne, 1975; *B. F. Skinner*, G. K. Hall, in press. Contributor to journals.

WORK IN PROGRESS: Leave Your Dying Alone; a book of verse, *The Sorcerer's Handbook*; a biography of John Barth, completion expected in 1978.

AVOCATIONAL INTERESTS: Art, music.

* * *

WEINER, Bernard 1935-

PERSONAL: Born September 28, 1935, in Chicago, Ill.; son of Julius (a retailer) and Bessie (Mashman) Weiner; married Marijana Benesh (a psychologist), August 28, 1963; children: Mark. *Education:* University of Chicago, B.A., 1955, M.B.A., 1957; University of Michigan, Ph.D., 1963. *Home:* 1272 Holmby, Los Angeles, Calif. 90024. *Office:* Department of Psychology, University of California, Los Angeles, Calif. 90024.

CAREER: University of Minnesota, Minneapolis, assistant professor of psychology, 1963-65; University of California, Los Angeles, assistant professor, 1965-69, associate professor, 1969-74, professor of psychology, 1974—. Guggenheim fellow, Ruhr University, 1970-71. *Military service:* U.S. Army, 1957-59. *Member:* American Psychological Association (fellow), American Educational Research Association.

WRITINGS: Theories of Motivation: From Mechanism to Cognition, Rand McNally, 1972; (with others) *Attribution: Perceiving the Causes of Behavior*, General Learning Press, 1972; (editor) *Achievement Motivation and Attribution Theory*, General Learning Press, 1974; (editor) *Cognitive Views of Human Motivation*, Academic Press, 1975; *Die Wirkung von Erfolg und Misserfolg auf die Leistung* (title means "The Effects of Success and Failure on Achievement Motivation"), Klett Press, 1975.

* * *

WEINGARTEN, Henry

PERSONAL: Born in New York; son of Irving (a construction worker) and Rachel (Carmel) Weingarten. *Education:* New York University, B.S. *Home:* 310 Lexington Ave., New York, N.Y. 10016. *Office:* 127 Madison Ave., New York, N.Y. 10016.

CAREER: National Astrological Society, New York, N.Y., instructor in School of Astrology, 1969—, director, 1969-74, executive secretary, 1974—. Director of ASI Publishers, Inc., 1972—. *Member:* Astrological Society of England.

WRITINGS: New York Astrological Center Manual for Erecting Horoscopes, New York Astrology Center, 1969, 3rd edition, 1974; *The Study of Astrology*, New York Astrology Center, 1969, 4th edition, 1974; *A Modern Introduction to Astrology*, ASI Publishers, 1974; (with Barbara

Somerfield) *The Nixon Years: An Astrological Study*, ASI Publishers, in press.

AVOCATIONAL INTERESTS: International travel.

* * *

WEINLAND, James D(avid) 1894-

PERSONAL: Born June 21, 1894, in Banning, Calif.; son of William H. (a missionary) and Caroline (Yost) Weinland. *Education:* Pomona College, A.B., 1917; Columbia University, M.A., 1922, Ph.D., 1927. *Politics:* "Republican (not very good one)." *Religion:* Protestant. *Home address:* P.O. Box 962, Boulder City, Nev. 89005.

CAREER: New York University, New York, N.Y., 1927-59, began as instructor, became professor of business psychology. *Military service:* U.S. Army, Ambulance Corps, 1917-19. U.S. Aviation Service, 1919-20. *Member:* American Psychological Association.

WRITINGS: General Psychology for Students of Business, Crofts, 1940; (with Margaret Gross) *Personnel Interviewing*, Ronald, 1952; *How to Improve Your Memory*, Harper, 1958; *How to Think Straight*, Littlefield, 1963; *Consciousness, Freedom, and Dignity*, Dorrance, 1974. Contributor to magazines, including *Applied Psychology*.

AVOCATIONAL INTERESTS: Psychology, logic, philosophy.

* * *

WEISS, Margaret R.

PERSONAL: Born in New York, N.Y.; daughter of J. J. (an executive in sales management) and Isabel (Engle) Weiss. *Education:* Barnard College, B.A. (with honors); graduate study at Columbia University. *Office:* c/o *Saturday Review*, 488 Madison Ave., New York, N.Y. 10022.

CAREER: Has held earlier positions as managing editor of *Living for Young Homemakers*, associate editor of *American Mercury*, entertainment editor of *American Magazine*, and contributing editor of *Picture Record Review*; *Saturday Review*, photography editor, 1960—. Instructor in courses and workshops at New York University and Syracuse University; guest lecturer at Fordham University and at Barnard College-N.B.C. Summer Institute. Jurist in numerous national photography competitions; consultant on photographic acquisitions, exhibitions, and purchase awards for universities and galleries. *Member:* Writers Guild of America (charter member), Royal Photographic Society (Great Britain), Phi Beta Kappa, Wig and Pen Club (London; honorary life member). *Awards, honors:* Carpentier fellowship; communications awards from Government of Puerto Rico, 1956, and from Florida Southern University, 1960.

WRITINGS: The TV Writer's Guide, Pellegrini & Cudahy, 1952; (editor and author of introduction) *Ben Shahn, Photographer: An Album from the Thirties*, DeCapo Press, 1973. Writer of articles, scripts, and syndicated columns on the camera arts. Contributor to *Grolier Encyclopedia*.

AVOCATIONAL INTERESTS: Travel abroad, cryptography, ballet, reading, cooking, collecting mosaics and small objects of antiquity.

* * *

WEISSMAN, Stephen R(ichard) 1941-

PERSONAL: Born April 10, 1941, in New York, N.Y.; son of Herman B. (a small businessman) and Beatrice (a secretary; maiden name, Siegel) Weissman; married Nancy Schaff (a social worker), March 10, 1967; children: Daniel. *Education:* Cornell University, B.A. (honors), 1961; Princeton University, graduate study, 1962-63; University of Chicago, A.M., 1965, Ph.D., 1969. *Home:* 19 Grace Ct., Brooklyn, N.Y. 11201. *Office:* Department of Political Science, Jersey City State College, Jersey City, N.J. 07305.

CAREER: New York City Welfare Department, New York, N.Y., caseworker, 1961-62; Fordham University, Bronx, N.Y., instructor, 1966-69, assistant professor of political science (on leave), 1969-71; Jersey City State College, Jersey City, N.J., assistant professor of political science, 1971-72, 1973—. Faculty consultant to New York City Urban Corps Educational Program, 1967. Associate professor at Free University of the Congo, 1969-71; Stanford University Community Development Study, research associate, 1972-73, consultant, 1973—. *Member:* American Political Science Association, Phi Beta Kappa, Phi Kappa Phi.

WRITINGS: American Foreign Policy in the Congo: 1960-1964, Cornell University Press, 1974; (contributor) J. Sneed and S. A. Waldhorn, editors, *Restructuring the Federal System: Approaches to Accountability*, Crane, Russak, 1975. Contributor of articles to *Journal of Modern African Studies, Polity, Nation, New Leader*, and *Commonweal*.

WORK IN PROGRESS: Research on the urban policy system, especially the areas of manpower, housing, education and day care in San Francisco, and on a quantitative and qualitative comparison of the "community controlled" Model Cities manpower system and the Department of Labor's Concentrated Employment Program.

* * *

WELCH, J(oseph) Edmund 1922-

PERSONAL: Born December 4, 1922, in Selma, Ala.; son of William Pressley (a cotton buyer) and Lucile (Burt) Welch; married Edith Crockford (a secretary), March 25, 1945; children: Edmund, Christopher, Richard. *Education:* University of Alabama, student, 1941-43; University of North Carolina, A.B., 1944, M.A.Ed., 1949; Springfield College, M.Ed., 1947; George Peabody College for Teachers, Ed.D., 1962. *Religion:* Episcopalian. *Home:* 1718 Smith Rd., Charleston, W.Va. 25314. *Office:* Department of Physical Education, West Virginia Institute of Technology, Montgomery, W.Va. 25136.

CAREER: Young Men's Christian Association, New York, N.Y., physical director in Vicksburg, Miss., 1948-51, Pensacola, Fla., 1951-54, and Atlanta, Ga., 1954-55; Emory University, Atlanta, Ga., assistant professor of physical education, 1956-63; East Carolina University, Greenville, N.C., associate professor of physical education, 1963-67; West Virginia Institute of Technology, Montgomery, professor of physical education, 1967—. *Military service:* U.S. Marine Corps, 1943-45; became second lieutenant.

MEMBER: North American Society for Sport History, American Association for Health, Physical Education, and Recreation (vice-president of Midwest District, 1973-74), National College Physical Education Association for Men, American Association of University Professors, American College of Sports Medicine, American School Health Association, Canadian Association for Health, Physical Education, and Recreation, Phi Delta Kappa.

WRITINGS: (Editor) *How to Play and Teach Volleyball*,

Association Press, 1960, revised edition, 1969; *Edward Hitchcock, M.D.: Founder of Physical Education in the College Curriculum*, Library, East Carolina College, 1966; *A Physical Education Reader: History and Foundations*, McClain Printing Co., 1975. Editor of *U.S. Volleyball Association Official Volleyball Guide*, published annually by U.S. Volleyball Association, 1959, 1960, 1961. Contributor of about a hundred articles to professional journals.

* * *

WELKER, David 1917-

PERSONAL: Born March 25, 1917, in La Rose, Ill.; son of Harry Linus (a teacher) and Almetta (a teacher; maiden name, Jones) Welker; married Dorothy Bair (a lecturer), May 1, 1937; children: Susan Elizabeth. *Education:* University of Illinois, B.A., 1939, M.A., 1943; University of Minnesota, Ph.D., 1956. *Politics:* Democrat. *Home:* 1301 University Pkwy., Winston-Salem, N.C. 27106. *Office:* Department of Speech, Wake Forest University, Winston-Salem, N.C. 27109.

CAREER: Elementary school teacher in Bradford, Ill., 1939-40, and high school teacher of speech in Bureau Township and Spring Valley, Ill., 1943-46; Illinois Wesleyan University, Bloomington, instructor in speech, 1946-48; University of Minnesota, Minneapolis, instructor in speech, 1948-56; Wisconsin State College, Eau Claire, associate professor of speech, 1956-61; Albion College, Albion, Mich., professor of speech, 1961-69; Wake Forest University, Winston-Salem, N.C., professor of speech, 1969—. Member of the governing board of Minnesota State Art Society, 1955.

WRITINGS: The Educational Theatre Journal: A Ten-Year Index, American Educational Theatre Association, 1959; *Theatrical Set Design: The Basic Techniques*, Allyn & Bacon, 1969; *Theatrical Direction: The Basic Techniques*, Allyn & Bacon, 1972; *Stagecraft: The Basic Techniques*, Allyn & Bacon, in press. Editor, *North Carolina Journal of Speech and Drama*, 1971-73; associate editor, *Southern Speech Communication Journal*, 1975—.

* * *

WENDT, Albert 1939-

PERSONAL: Born October 27, 1939, in Apia, Western Samoa; son of Tuaopepe Alualu (a plumber) and Luisa (Patu) Wendt; married Jenny Whyte; children: Sina, Mele, Michael. *Education:* Attended teacher training college in New Zealand; Victoria University, M.A. (honors), 1964. *Home address:* P.O. Box 131, Apia, Western Samoa. *Agent:* Tim Curnow, Curtis Brown Pty. Ltd., P.O. Box 19, Paddington, Sydney, New South Wales 2021, Australia.

CAREER: Samoa College, Apia, Western Samoa, teacher, 1964-69, principal, 1969-73; University of the South Pacific, Suva, Fiji, senior lecturer in education, 1974, in English, 1975-76. Editor, Mana Publications, 1974—.

WRITINGS—All published by Longman Paul, except as indicated: *Sons for the Return Home* (novel), 1973, International Publications Service, 1974; *Flying-Fox in a Freedom Tree* (stories), 1974; (contributor) Harvey McQueen and Lois Cox, editors, *Ten Modern New Zealand Poets*, 1974; *Inside Us the Dead* (poems), 1975; *Pouliuli* (novel), in press.

Editor; all published by Mana Publications: *Some Modern Poetry from Fiji*, 1974; *Some Modern Poetry from Western Samoa*, 1975; *Some Modern Poetry from the New He-*

brides, 1975; *Some Modern Poetry from the Solomons*, 1975. Contributor of articles, stories, poems, and reviews to literary journals of the islands of the Pacific, including *Landfall*, *Mate*, *Mana*, and *Te Maori*, and to children's publications. Editor of *Samoa Bulletin*, 1967.

WORK IN PROGRESS: A novel, *Leaves of the Banyan Tree*, publication by Longman Paul expected in 1977; editing *Lali: An Anthology of Poetry by Pacific Islanders*, for Longman Paul; editing an anthology of short stories by Pacific Islanders, for Longman Paul.

SIDELIGHTS: Wendt writes: "Up to now, most literature about us [the Pacific Islanders] has been written by outsiders—much of it is superficial and distorted and over-romantic and racist. We now want to examine ourselves and our way of life ourselves ... I'm ... through my work at the University of the South Pacific, trying to encourage other Pacific Islanders (e.g. Fijians, New Hebridians, Tongans, Solomon Islanders, Niueans, Tokelauans, Rotamans, Nauruans, etc.) to write their own literatures and develop their other indigenous art forms."

* * *

WENHAM, John W(illiam) 1913-

PERSONAL: Born December 9, 1913, in Sanderstead, Surrey, England; son of William Knight (an accountant) and Evelyn (Adkins) Wenham; married Grace Isaac, July 28, 1942; children: Gordon, David, Peter, Michael. *Education:* Pembroke College and Ridley Hall, Cambridge, M.A., 1939; University of London, B.D., 1943. *Home:* Chapel Cottage, Allington, near Salisbury, Wiltshire, England.

CAREER: Vicar of Church of England in Durham, England, 1948-53; Tyndale Hall, Bristol, England, vice-principal, 1953-67; tutor, 1967-70; Latimer House, Oxford, England, warden, 1970-73; Cottisford, Oxfordshire, England, assistant rector, 1973-75. *Military service:* Royal Air Force, chaplain, 1943-47. *Member:* Studiorum Novi Testamenti Societas.

WRITINGS: The Elements of New Testament Greek, Cambridge University Press, 1965; *Large Numbers in the Old Testament*, Tyndale, 1967; *The Renewal and Unity of the Church in England*, Society for the Propagation of Christian Knowledge, 1972; *Christ and the Bible*, Inter-Varsity Press, 1972; *The Goodness of God*, Inter-Varsity Press, 1974.

WORK IN PROGRESS: Books on the Old Testament and the New Testament; research on current objections to the truth of the Bible.

SIDELIGHTS: One of Wenham's books has been published in Portuguese. *Avocational interests:* Gardening, tennis, chess.

* * *

WERNER, Emmy Elizabeth 1929-

PERSONAL: Born May 26, 1929, in Eltville, West Germany; daughter of Peter Josef (a businessman) and Liesel (Kunz) Werner. *Education:* Johannes Gutenberg Universitaet, Mainz, Germany, B.A., 1950; University of Nebraska, Lincoln, M.A., 1952, Ph.D., 1955; University of California, Berkeley, graduate study, 1953-54. *Home:* 2330 Haste, #402, Berkeley, Calif. 94704. *Office:* 209 Walker Hall, University of California, Davis, Calif. 95616.

CAREER: University of Minnesota, Minneapolis, assistant

professor and research associate, 1956-59; National Institutes of Health, Bethesda, Md., visiting scientist, 1959-62; University of California, Davis, assistant professor, 1962-65; associate professor, 1965-69, professor of human development, 1969—. Associate child psychologist, University of California, Berkeley, 1965-59. Consultant to UNICEF, and to Department of Health, Education and Welfare, Office of Child Development, and Office of International Activities. *Member:* American Psychological Association, Society for Research in Child Development, Institute of International Education, Psi Chi, Phi Lambda Theta. *Awards, honors:* Elsie Worcester Memorial Award for exceptional accomplishment in the area of special education.

WRITINGS: (Editor) *The Teen-Age Parent: Early Marriage and Childbearing*, University of California Press, 1967; (with J. Bierman and F. French) *The Children of Kauai: A Longitudinal Study from the Prenatal Period to Age Ten*, University of Hawaii Press, 1971; (contributor) Jane S. Jaquette, editor, *Women in Politics*, Wiley Interscience, 1974; (with R. Smith) *Kauai's Children Come of Age*, University of Hawaii Press, in press. Contributor of articles to *Child Development, Developmental Psychology, Journal of Cross-Cultural Psychology, Journal of Social Psychology*, and numerous other psychology journals.

WORK IN PROGRESS: Riders on the Planet Earth: Young Children in the Developing World.

SIDELIGHTS: Emmy Werner told *CA* that her motivation for writing is "to share with others the joys of children, travel, other cultures, the miracle of growth, the plight of those who battle against great biological or environmental risks." She has traveled extensively in Africa, India, Nepal, Indonesia, Thailand, and Israel. In addition to English and German, she speaks French, Spanish, and some Swahili.

* * *

WESLEY, Richard (Errol) 1945-

PERSONAL: Born July 11, 1945, in Newark, N.J.; son of George Richard (a laborer) and Gertrude (Thomas) Wesley; married Valerie Wilson, May 22, 1972; children: Thembi (a daughter). *Education:* Howard University, B.F.A., 1967. *Home:* 57 Chestnut St., East Orange, N.J. 07018. *Office:* Nasaba Artists, Inc., 1860 Broadway, New York, N.Y. 10025.

CAREER: United Airlines, Newark, N.J., passenger service agent, 1967-69; playwright and screenwriter. Member of board of directors, Frank Silvera Writer's Workshop, 1974—. *Member:* Writer's Guild of America, East. *Awards, honors:* Drama Desk Award for Outstanding Playwriting, 1972, for "The Black Terror"; NAACP Image Award, 1974, for "Uptown Saturday Night."

WRITINGS—Plays: "The Black Terror," first produced in New York at the Public Theatre, 1971; "Gettin' It Together," first produced in New York at the Public Theatre, 1972; "Strike Heaven on the Face," first produced in New York at the Bijou Theatre (Showcase), 1973; "Goin' thru Changes," first produced in Waterford, Conn., at the Eugene O'Neill Memorial Theatre Center, 1974, also produced in New York at the Billie Holiday Theatre, 1974; "The Past Is the Past," first produced in Waterford, Conn., at the Eugene O'Neill Memorial Theatre Center, 1974, also produced in New York at the Billie Holiday Theatre, 1974; "The Sirens," first produced in New York at the Manhattan Theatre Club, 1974; "The Mighty Gents," first produced in Waterford, Conn., at the Eugene O'Neill Memorial Theatre Center, 1974.

Screenplays: "Uptown Saturday Night," 1974; "Let's Do It Again," 1975.

The play, "The Black Terror," appears in the anthology, *New Lafayette Theatre Presents*, edited by Ed Bullins, Doubleday, 1973.

SIDELIGHTS: Wesley told *CA*: "Writings inspired primarily by social and political conditions of black people in the United States."

* * *

WEST, Delno C(loyde), Jr. 1936-

PERSONAL: Born April 8, 1936, in Missouri; son of Delno C. (a teacher) and Elsie L. (a teacher) West; married Jean M. Donald, August 31, 1958; children: Douglas, Delisa, Dawn. *Education:* Northeast Missouri State University, B.S.Ed., 1961; University of Denver, M.A., 1962; University of California, Los Angeles, Ph.D., 1970. *Home:* 3120 Walkup, Flagstaff, Ariz. 86001. *Office:* Department of History, Northern Arizona University, P.O. Box 5700, Flagstaff, Ariz.

CAREER: Northern Arizona University, Flagstaff, assistant professor of medieval history, 1969—. Member of board of directors of University Heights Corp. and Arizona Commission for Cultural Exchange with Sonora and Sinaloa. *Military service:* U.S. Army, 1954-57. *Member:* American Historical Association, Mediaeval Academy of America, National Collegiate Honors Council, Rocky Mountain Medieval and Renaissance Association, Kiwanis International.

WRITINGS: Joachim of Fiore in Christian Thought, two volumes, B. Franklin, 1975; (editor with Bert Hall) *Medieval Technology and Science and Society*, University of California Press, 1975; *Early Franciscan Education*, Longman, in press. Contributor to *Archivium Franciscanum Historicum* and *Franciscan Studies*.

AVOCATIONAL INTERESTS: Travel (has led European tours), woodworking, antiques.

* * *

WEST, Don 1928-

PERSONAL: Born April 17, 1928, in Fredonia, Kan.; son of Claude R. (a farmer) and Doris (Pack) West; married Marion E. Shepard, January 18, 1953. *Education:* Attended Montana State University, 1953-54. *Politics:* Democrat. *Address: San Francisco Examiner*, P.O. Box 3100, San Francisco, Calif. 94119.

CAREER: Announcer, newsman, and writer on radio stations in Clifton, Ariz., 1951-52, in Missoula, Mont., 1952-53, in Butte, Mont., 1953-54, and in Mt. Vernon, Wash., 1954-55; *San Diego Independent*, San Diego, Calif., editor, 1958-61; County News Association of San Diego, Riverside and San Jose, Calif., owner, 1962-70; *Perris Progress*, Perris, Calif., publisher, 1965-66; *San Francisco Examiner*, San Francisco, Calif., Peninsular bureau chief, 1970—; KTEH-TV, San Jose, Calif., interview show host, 1972—. *Military service:* U.S. Navy, 1945-49; became second lieutenant. *Member:* San Francisco Newspaper Guild, South Bay Press Club. *Awards, honors:* McQuade Award from Association of Catholic Newsmen, 1971; San Francisco Press Club prize for initiative, 1972.

WRITINGS: Sacrifice Unto Me (nonfiction), Pyramid Publications, 1974; (with Jerry Belcher) *Patty/Tania: The Media Princess Kidnap Case*, Pyramid Publications, 1975.

Contributor to *Prism, California Living, Pageant, Reporter, American Weekly*, and *New York Times*. Editor of *California Gardens*, 1963, and *Santa Clara County Employees*, 1969.

WORK IN PROGRESS: National Health Schemes: A European Perspective; *A Guide for Stringers*, completion expected in 1976; a novel, *Paddy: The Urban Hermit*.

AVOCATIONAL INTERESTS: Travel, poetry, sailing, archaeology.

* * *

WESTSMITH, Kim 1945-

PERSONAL: Born November 1, 1945, in San Angelo, Tex.; daughter of Richard Alan (an ophthalmologist) and Anita (a designer; maiden name, Kollstede) Westsmith; married Robert Sedgwick Chapman, September 2, 1967 (divorced July 14, 1975). *Education:* Radcliffe College, B.A., 1967; Harvard University, M.A.T., 1968. *Home:* 170 Coker Dr., Chapel Hill, N.C. 27514. *Office:* Chapel Hill Schools, Chapel Hill, N.C. 27514.

CAREER: Teacher of English as a second language in public schools in Cambridge, Mass., 1968-71; Chapel Hill Schools, Chapel Hill, N.C., teacher of English as second language, 1973—, library/media specialist, 1974—. Freelance teacher and consultant in sexism courses in North Carolina schools, 1974—.

WRITINGS: The Magic Hat (fiction), Lollipop Power, Inc., 1973.

WORK IN PROGRESS: A short story.

* * *

WETMORE, Ruth Y. 1934-

PERSONAL: Born December 13, 1934, in York, Neb.; daughter of Russell S. (a farmer) and Ruth (Kirkpatrick) Nettleton; married David E. Wetmore (a professor of chemistry), September 1, 1959; children: Jim, Dan. *Education:* Park College, B.A., 1956; University of Kansas, M.A., 1959; additional study at Texas A & M College, 1962, and at St. Andrews Presbyterian College, 1969-71. *Religion:* Presbyterian. *Home:* 811 South Main St., Laurinburg, N.C. 28352. *Office:* Indian Museum of the Carolinas, Laurinburg, N.C. 28352.

CAREER: Secretary to investment banker in Denver, Colo., 1956-57; junior research analyst, Government Research Center, University of Kansas, 1958-59; Indian Museum of the Carolinas, Laurinburg, N.C., cataloguer, 1971-73, assistant curator, 1972-74, curator, 1974—. *Member:* Association of International Philatelic Journalists, American Topical Association, Philatelic Press Club, Oklahoma Anthropological Society, Archaeological Society of North Carolina, D.A.R., P.E.O., Phi Beta Kappa, Pi Sigma Alpha. *Awards, honors:* Bronze medals for literature at ARGENTINA '66, PRAGA '68, and at ANPEX '72; Diploma of Vermeil Medal for literature at EXFICAP '74; Distinguished Topical Philatelist, 1975.

WRITINGS: First on the Land: The North Carolina Indians, Blair, 1975. Author of monographs. Contributor to Philately journals. New issues editor of *Topical Time*, 1971-75.

WORK IN PROGRESS: A report on excavations at Red Springs Mound.

AVOCATIONAL INTERESTS: Horses, stamp collecting.

WETTLAUFER, George 1935-

*PERSONAL:*Born February 27, 1935, in Williamsport, Pa.; married to Nancy (a potter); children: Inge, Kurt. *Education:* State University of New York College at Oswego, B.S. (education); Alfred University, B.S. (ceramic engineering). *Home and office:* 12 East Lake St., Skaneateles, N.Y. 13152.

CAREER: Potter. Formerly engineer for Bendix Corporation and General Electric Corporation. Member of board of directors of *Working Craftsman. Military service:* Served in U.S. armed forces. *Member:* New York State Craftsmen (member of board of directors), Keramos.

WRITINGS: (With wife, Nancy Wettlaufer) *The Craftsman's Survival Manual*, Prentice-Hall, 1974; (with N. Wettlaufer) *Getting into Pots*, Prentice-Hall, in press. Contributor to ceramics journals.

WORK IN PROGRESS: Research on controlling kiln atmospheres.

* * *

WETTLAUFER, Nancy 1939-

PERSONAL: Born June 6, 1939; married George Wettlaufer (a potter); children: Inge, Kurt. *Education:* Wellesley College, B.A., 1961; Yale University, M.A.T., 1962. *Home and office:* 12 East Lake St., Skaneateles, N.Y. 13152.

CAREER: Potter. Formerly teacher of French and German in high schools and at Alfred University, Alfred, N.Y. Chairperson of Skaneateles Conservation Advisory Council. *Awards, honors:* State Fair Award for a piece of pottery.

WRITINGS: (With husband, George Wettlaufer) *The Craftsman's Survival Manual*, Prentice-Hall, 1974; (with G. Wettlaufer) *Getting into Pots*, Prentice-Hall, in press. Contributor to ceramics journals.

AVOCATIONAL INTERESTS: Travel.

* * *

WHALEY, Russell Francis 1934-

PERSONAL: Born October 3, 1934, in Port Jervis, N.Y.; son of Russell Franklin (a chef) and Margaret Mary (Lowery) Whaley; married wife, Kay Elizabeth (divorced, 1969); married Florence L. Eastlund (a college instructor), December, 1970; children: Jenifer, Margaret, Elizabeth. *Education:* State University of New York College at Courtland, B.S., 1956; University of Michigan, M.P.H., 1958; University of Wisconsin, Madison, Ph.D., 1964. *Politics:* Democrat. *Religion:* Deist. *Home:* 315 Center St., Slippery Rock, Pa. 16057. *Office:* Department of Health Science, Slippery Rock State College, Slippery Rock, Pa. 16057.

CAREER: Wisconsin State Board of Health, health educator, 1958-61; University of Wisconsin, instructor in health education, 1961-64; University of British Columbia, Vancouver, assistant professor of continuing education, 1965-66; Oregon State University, Corvallis, associate professor of health education, 1966-69; Slippery Rock State College, Slippery Rock, Pa., chairman of department of health science, 1969—. Consultant, Upstate Medical Center, Syracuse, N.Y., 1968, and Mahoning/Shenanbo Health Education Center, Youngstown, Ohio, 1975. Member of executive committee, Regional Medical Programs, and Comprehensive Health Planning, both western Pennsylvania. *Military service:* U.S. Marine Corps Reserve, 1954-61; became sergeant. *Member:* American Public Health Association, American School Health Association, American Association of Health, Physical Education and Recreation, Society of Public Health Educators, Pennsylvania Association of Health, Physical Education and Recreations, Eta Sigma Gamma, Phi Delta Kappa.

WRITINGS: Health for Happiness, Steck, 1966; (senior author) *Basic Health Science Series*, Lippincott, 1971, revised edition, 1974; *Health Problems of Young Adults*, Holbrook, 1971. Contributor to *Transition Magazine*. Contributing editor, *American Journal of School Health*.

WORK IN PROGRESS: Community Health Education: Theory and Practice, completion expected in 1977; a novel, *The Bugle Bring*, 1980.

* * *

WHEELER, John Archibald 1911-

PERSONAL: Born July 9, 1911, in Jacksonville, Fla.; son of Joseph Lewis (a librarian) and Mabel (a librarian; maiden name, Archibald) Wheeler; married Janette Hegner (a docent), June 10, 1935; children: Letitia (Mrs. Charles W. Ufford, Jr.), James English, Alison (Mrs. Beardsley Ruml II). *Education:* Johns Hopkins University, Ph.D., 1933. *Religion:* Unitarian Universalist. *Home:* 30 Maxwell Lane, Princeton, N.J. 08540. *Office:* Department of Physics, Princeton University, Princeton, N.J. 08540.

CAREER: National Research Council fellow in New York, N.Y., 1933-34, and in Copenhagen, Denmark, 1934-35; University of North Carolina, Chapel Hill, assistant professor of physics, 1935-38; Princeton University, Princeton, N.J., assistant professor, 1938-42, associate professor, 1945-47, professor, 1947-66, Joseph Henry Professor of Physics, 1966—, physicist on Plutonium Project, 1939-42, 1950-53. Physicist on Plutonium Project in Chicago, Ill., 1942, Wilmington, Del., 1943-44, Richland, Wash., 1944-45, and on design of first family of thermonuclear devices in Los Alamos, N.M., 1950-53. Lorentz Professor, University of Leiden, 1956; trustee of Battelle Memorial Institute, 1959—; chairman of Joint Commission of American Physical Society and American Philosophical Society on the History of Theoretical Physics in the Twentieth Century, 1960-72; Fulbright Professor, University of Kyoto, 1962; first visiting fellow at Clare College, Cambridge University, 1964; member of U.S. General Advisory Committee on Arms Control and Disarmament, 1969-72, 1974—; visiting fellow of Merton College, Oxford University, 1974; Battelle Memorial Professor, University of Washington, 1975.

MEMBER: International Astronomical Union, American Physical Society (president, 1966), American Mathematical Society, American Academy of Arts and Sciences, National Academy of Science, American Philosophical Society (vice-president, 1971-73). *Awards, honors:* A. Cressy Morrison Prize, 1947, from New York Academy of Sciences; Guggenheim fellowship, 1949-50; Albert Einstein Prize from Strauss Foundation, 1965; Enrico Fermi Award from Atomic Energy Commission, 1968; Franklin Medal from Franklin Institute, 1971; seven Sc.D. degrees, including one from Yale University, 1974; Karl F. Herzfeld Award from Catholic University of America, 1975; Ph.D. from University of Uppsala, 1975.

WRITINGS: Geometrodynamics, Academic Press, 1962; (with B. K. Harrison, K. S. Thorne, and Masami Wakano) *Gravitation Theory and Gravitational Collapse*, University of Chicago Press, 1965; (with Edwin Taylor) *Spacetime Physics*, W. H. Freeman, 1966; *Einstein's Vision*, Springer Verlag, 1968; (with C. W. Misner and Thorne) *Gravitation*, W. H. Freeman, 1973; (with Martin Rees and Remo Ruffini) *Black Holes, Gravitational Waves, and Cosmology*, Gordon & Breach, 1974.

WORK IN PROGRESS: Research on the question: "Are the laws of physics legislated by the requirement that the universe should have a way to come into being?"

SIDELIGHTS: Wheeler writes: "We will first understand how simple the universe is when we recognize how strange it is." He narrated the television film "The Birth and Death of a Star," Center for Mass Communication, Columbia University, 1973. *Avocational interests:* The sculpture of nature's rocks.

BIOGRAPHICAL/CRITICAL SOURCES: John R. Klauder, editor, *Magic Without Magic: John Archibald Wheeler, A Collection of Essays in Honor of His Sixtieth Birthday*, W. H. Freeman, 1972.

* * *

WHELAN, Elizabeth M(urphy) 1943-

PERSONAL: Born December 4, 1943, in New York, N.Y.; daughter of Joseph F. (an attorney) and Marion (Barrett) Murphy; married Stephen Thomas Whelan (an attorney), April 3, 1971. *Education:* Connecticut College, B.A., 1965; Yale University, M.P.H., 1967; Harvard University, M.S., 1968, Sc.D., 1971. *Home:* 165 West End Ave., #11R, New York, N.Y. 10023. *Agent:* James Brown Associates, 22 East 60th St., New York, N.Y. 10022. *Office:* Demographic Materials, Inc., 165 West End Ave., New York, N.Y.

CAREER: New Haven Health Department, New Haven, Conn., member of staff, 1966-67; Massachusetts Department of Public Health, Boston, epidemiologist/vital statistician, 1968-71; Planned Parenthood-World Population, New York, N.Y., county study coordinator, 1971-72; demographic Materials, Inc., New York, executive director, 1972—. Free-lance medical writer, 1971—. Consultant to Syntex Laboratories, Palo Alto, Calif., to Child Welfare League of America, to Population Council, New York, N.Y., and other organizations. *Member:* American Public Health Association, American Medical Writers Association, Population Association of America.

WRITINGS: Sex and Sensibility: A New Look at Being a Woman, McGraw, 1974; *A Baby?–Maybe: A Guide to Making the Most Fateful Decision of Your Life*, Bobbs-Merrill, 1975; (with father-in-law, Stephen T. Whelan) *Making Sense out of Sex: A New Look at Being a Man*, McGraw, 1975; (with Frederick J. Stare) *Panic in the Pantry: Food Facts and Fallacies*, Atheneum, 1975.

Contributor to *Social Biology, Studies in Family Planning, Journal of Marriage and the Family, Demography, Glamour, Cosmopolitan, Bride, National Review* and other publications. Member of editorial board, *Connecticut College Alumni News*, 1972—.

WORK IN PROGRESS: A general nutrition book, with Fredrick J. Stare, tentatively titled *Eating for Good Health*; a popular treatment of environmental causes of cancer, *The Deadly Cluster* (tentative title).

* * *

WHISENHUNT, Donald W(ayne) 1938-

PERSONAL: Born May 16, 1938, in Meadow, Tex.; son of

William A. and Beulah (Johnson) Whisenhunt; married Betsy Ann Baker, August 27, 1960; children: Donald Wayne, Jr., William Benton. *Education:* McMurry College, B.A., 1960; Eastern New Mexico University, graduate study, 1961-62; Texas Technological College (now Texas Tech University), M.A., 1962, Ph.D., 1966. *Religion:* Methodist. *Home:* 1104 East Libra, Portales, N.M. 88130. *Office:* College of Liberal Arts and Sciences, Eastern New Mexico University, Portales, N.M. 88130.

CAREER: History teacher in public schools in Elida, N.M., 1961-63; Murray State University, Murray, Ky., assistant professor, 1966-68, associate professor of history, 1968-69; Thiel College, Greenville, Pa., associate professor of history and chairman of department, 1969-73; Eastern New Mexico University, Portales, professor of history and dean of College of Liberal Arts and Sciences, 1973—. Visiting professor at Incarnate Word College, summer, 1971, and Allegheny College, summer, 1972. Member of board of directors of Llano Estacado Heritage, Inc., 1974—.

MEMBER: American Historical Association, Organization of American Historians, Popular Culture Association, Western History Association, Southern Historical Association, Red River Valley Historical Association (member of board of directors, 1973—), New Mexico Historical Association, West Texas Historical Association, Mercer County Historical Society (member of board of directors, 1970-73; archivist, 1971-73), Roosevelt County Historical Society, Phi Alpha Theta, Pi Sigma Alpha, Phi Kappa Phi, Pi Delta Epsilon. *Awards, honors:* Research grant from New Jersey Historical Commission, 1970-71, to edit diaries of John Fell; research grant from Lutheran Church in America, 1971-72, to study Texas during the Depression; grant from New Mexico Council on the Humanities, 1974, to present a public conference on water use on the High Plains of Eastern New Mexico; grant from New Mexico Arts Commission, 1974-75, for publication of *Liberal Arts Review.*

WRITINGS: Fort Richardson: Outpost on the Texas Frontier, Texas Western Press, 1968; *Delegate from New Jersey: The Diary of John Fell,* Kennikat, 1973; *Teaching Local History,* Media Workshop, 1974; *The Environment and the American Experience: A Historian Looks at the Ecological Crisis,* Kennikat, 1974; *Elias Boudinot,* New Jersey Historical Commission, in press.

Author of "Point of View," a political column in *Murray Democrat,* 1967, and "Bicentennial Notebook," a column syndicated to fifteen New Mexico newspapers. Contributor of about a hundred articles and reviews to professional journals and to newspapers. Associate editor of *Mercer County History,* 1971-73; editor of *Liberal Arts Review,* 1974—.

WORK IN PROGRESS: Editing *History of Eastern New Mexico University,* by Floyd Golden; *Poetry and the Depression* (tentative title), for Bowling Green Popular Press; preparing a new introduction for *Boy and Girl Tramps of America,* by Thomas Minehan, for University of Washington Press.

* * *

WHITCOMB, Ian 1941-
(Mel Bubb, Buck Murphy, Stu Newton, Arthur Nouveau)

PERSONAL: Born July 10, 1941, in Woking, Surrey, England; son of Patrick (a builder's merchant) and Eileen (Burningham) Whitcomb. *Education:* Trinity College, Dub-

lin, honors degree in modern history and political science, 1965. *Politics:* Apolitical. *Residence:* London, England, and Hollywood, Calif.

CAREER: Writer on music; singer, composer, lyricist, and producer of L.P. albums: "You Turn Me On," Tower, 1965; "Ian Whitcomb's Mod, Mod, Music Hall," Tower, 1966; "Yellow Underground," Tower, 1967; "Sock Me Some Rock," Tower, 1968; "On the Pier," EMI, 1970; "Under the Ragtime Moon," United Artists, 1972; "Hip Horray Neville Chamberlain," Argo, 1974. Producer of album, "Mae West—'Great Balls of Fire'," MGM, 1972; composor of score for "Doo Dah Gang" show, produced in Las Vegas, 1975. Consultant to British Broadcasting Corp. television arts features. Has published articles in *Listener, Los Angeles Times,* and *Let It Rock.*

WRITINGS: After the Ball, Allen Lane, 1972, Simon & Schuster, 1974; *Tin Pan Alley,* Two Continents, 1975.

Scripts: "Tin Pan Alley," for KCET Public Television, 1975; "Chasing Rainbows, for EMI Theater Projects Television, 1975.

WORK IN PROGRESS: Ramona Schmidt: A Tale of Old Los Angeles, publication by Wildwood House expected about 1977.

* * *

WHITE, Irvin L(inwood) 1932-

PERSONAL: Born March 15, 1932, in Hertford, N.C.; son of Irvin Linwood and Katherine (Winslow) White; married Patricia Ann Hathaway, September 12, 1953; children: two. *Education:* Pennsylvania State University, B.A., 1954; University of Arizona, Ph.D., 1967. *Home:* 1320 Westbrooke Ter., Norman, Okla. 73069. *Office:* Science and Public Policy Program, University of Oklahoma, Norman, Okla. 73069.

CAREER: University of Arizona, Tucson, visiting assistant professor of political science, 1967-68; Purdue University, Lafayette, Ind., assistant professor of political science, 1968-70; University of Oklahoma, Norman, associate professor, 1970-74, professor of political science, 1974—, assistant director of Science and Public Policy Program, 1970—. *Military service:* U.S. Navy, 1954-62; became lieutenant. *Member:* International Technology Assessment Association, International Studies Association, American Political Science Association, American Association for the Advancement of Science, American Association of University Professors, Policies Studies Organization, Southwestern Social Sciences Association. *Awards, honors:* National Science Foundation research grants, 1971, 1972; research grant from Council on Environmental Quality, 1973.

WRITINGS: Decision-Making for Space: Law and Politics in Air, Sea, and Outer Space, Purdue University Studies, 1970; *Planning and Organizing for Research: A Guide for Beginners,* Institute of Government Research, University of Arizona, 1970; (compiler with Clifton E. Wilson and John A. Vosburgh, and contributor) *Law and Politics in Outer Space: A Bibliography,* University of Arizona Press, 1972; (contributor) Michael Haas, editor, *International Systems: A Behavioral Approach,* Intext, 1973; (with others) *Energy Under the Oceans: A Technology Assessment of Outer Continental Shelf Oil and Gas Operations,* University of Oklahoma Press, 1973; (with others) *North Sea Oil and Gas: Implications for Future U.S. Development,* University of Oklahoma Press, 1973; (contributor) Walter F.

Scheffer, editor, *Energy Impacts on Public Policy and Administration*, University of Oklahoma Press, 1974; (with others) *Energy Alternatives: A Comparative Analysis*, Government Printing Office, 1975; (contributor) Sherry Arnstein and Alexander Christakis, *Perspectives on Technology Assessment*, Science and Technology Press, 1975. Contributor to proceedings and to professional journals.

WORK IN PROGRESS: A technology assessment of energy resource development in the western United States.

* * *

WHITE, John I(rwin) 1902-
(Whitey Johns, Lone Star Ranger, Lonesome Cowboy, Jimmie Price)

PERSONAL: Born April 12, 1902, in Washington, D.C.; son of Harry Bateman (a high school teacher) and Grace (Brewer) White; married Augusta Postles, October 4, 1930; children: Jonathan, Jennifer (Mrs. Richard H. Fischer). *Education:* University of Maryland, B.A., 1924; graduate study at Columbia University. *Home:* 515 Main St., Apt. 6-B, Chatham, N.J. 07928.

CAREER: Washington Star, Washington, D.C., sports reporter, 1925-26; General Drafting Co., Inc. (map publishers), Convent Station, N.J., travel counselor, 1927-31, touring service manager, 1931-43, production manager, 1943-57, became sales coordinator, 1957, retiring as director and vice-president in 1965. Singer on NBC-Radio, 1926, and WOR-Radio, 1927-30, and for NBC-Radio's "Death Valley Days," 1930-36.

WRITINGS: Git Along, Little Dogies: Songs and Songmakers of the American West, University of Illinois Press, 1975. Contributor of more than forty articles, mostly on the West, to journals and to popular magazines, including *American Heritage, Highlights for Children, American West*, and *American History Illustrated*.

WORK IN PROGRESS: A children's book about sod houses on the Western prairies in the 1880's.

SIDELIGHTS: White made twenty recordings of hillbilly and cowboy songs for American Record Corp., most under pseudonyms Whitey Johns, Jimmie Price, Lone Star Ranger, and Lonesome Cowboy, 1929-31.

BIOGRAPHICAL/CRITICAL SOURCES: Linnell Gentry, *A History and Encyclopedia of Country, Western, and Gospel Music*, Clairmont Corp., 2nd edition (White was not included in first edition), 1969.

* * *

WHITE, Leslie A(lvin) 1900-1975

January 19, 1900—March 31, 1975; American anthropologist, educator, museum administrator, author and editor of books on anthropology. Obituaries: *New York Times*, April 4, 1975; *AB Bookman's Weekly*, April 28, 1975; *Publishers Weekly*, April 28, 1975. (CA-2)

* * *

WHITE, Poppy Cannon 1906(?)-1975

1906(?)—April 1, 1975; South African-born American newspaper columnist, magazine editor, author of cookbooks, poetry, and fiction. Obituaries: *New York Times*, April 2, 1975; *Washington Post*, April 3, 1975; *Newsweek*, April 14, 1975; *AB Bookman's Weekly*, April 28, 1975.

WHITEHOUSE, Roger 1939-

PERSONAL: Born August 23, 1939, in Mansfield, Nottinghamshire, England; son of Tom (an electrical engineer) and Dorothy (Stambridge) Whitehouse. Married Helga Grundhoefer, May 15, 1975. *Education:* Attended Bournemouth School of Art, 1955-57, and Architectural Association School of Architecture, 1957-63; Royal Institute of British Architects, A.R.I.B.A., 1966. *Home:* 33A Christchurch Hill, London NW3 1LA, England. *Agent:* Susan Ann Protter, 156 East 52nd St., New York, N.Y. 10022.

CAREER: Architect in London, England, 1963-67; Columbia University, New York, N.Y., lecturer in design, 1967-68; architect in New York, N.Y., 1969-74; writer, architect, designer, photographer, 1974—. Urban design consultant on Queensborough Bridge area study, 1972. *Member:* Architectural Association, Royal Institute of British Architects (associate member).

WRITINGS: New York: Sunshine and Shadow (photographic history, 1850-1915), Harper, 1974.

WORK IN PROGRESS: A photographic history of London; a book on the disappearing traditional food and drink of the British Isles.

SIDELIGHTS: Whitehouse explained to *CA*: "In the development of the book I did not simply use the old photographs to illustrate a written account of the city's past but as direct archeological evidence in determining that history, resulting, I hope, in a fresh viewpoint." *Avocational interests:* Travel and research into the field of wine and gastronomy.

* * *

WICE, Paul B(ernard) 1942-

PERSONAL: Surname rhymes with "nice"; born April 7, 1942, in Washington, D.C.; son of Israel (a historian) and Helen (Roof) Wice; married Marsha Nye (a professor), September 30, 1967; children: Andrew David. *Education:* Bucknell University, B.A., 1964; American University, M.A., 1966; University of Illinois, Ph.D., 1972. *Home:* 123 Christman Ave., Washington, Pa. 15301. *Office:* Department of Political Science, Washington and Jefferson College, Washington, Pa. 15301.

CAREER: Washington and Jefferson College, Washington, Pa., assistant professor of political science, 1972—. Member of board of directors of Washington County Alcoholism and Drug Abuse Council; member of Volunteers in Probation. *Military service:* U.S. Army, 1966-68; became first lieutenant. *Member:* American Political Science Association, Law and Society Association.

WRITINGS: Freedom for Sale, Heath, 1974; (with Stuart Nagel and Marian Neef) *The Policy Problem of Doing Too Much Or Too Little*, Russell Sage Foundation, 1975. Contributor to sociology and law journals.

WORK IN PROGRESS: Research on a sociological portrait of the criminal lawyer as both public and private defender, completion expected in 1977.

* * *

WICKENS, James F. 1933-

PERSONAL: Born March 22, 1933, in Albany, Calif.; son of James H. (a Pacific Telephone employee) and Margaret (Roworth) Wickens; married Claire Smith, March 22, 1959; children: Timothy, Andrew, Kristina. *Education:* San Mateo Junior College (now College of San Mateo), A.A.,

1952; University of California, Berkeley, B.A., 1954, M.A., 1960; University of Denver, Ph.D., 1964. *Home:* 3349 Hackamore Dr., Hayward, Calif. 94541. *Office:* Chabot College, 25555 Hesperian, Hayward, Calif. 94545.

CAREER: California Polytechnic State University, San Luis Obispo, instructor, 1964-66; Chabot College, Hayward, Calif., instructor, 1966—. *Military service:* U.S. Army, 1954-56.

WRITINGS: Themes in United States History, Glencoe Press, 1970, 2nd edition, 1973; *Highlights of American History*, Rand McNally, 1973; (contributor) John Braeman and others, editors, *The New Deal*, Volume II: *The State and Local Level*, Ohio State University Press, 1975; *Colorado Faces the Great Depression* (series), edited by Frank Friedel, Garland Publishing, in press. Author of U.S. history series on college television channel. Contributor to journals in his field.

* * *

WICKWAR, (William) Hardy 1903-

PERSONAL: Born May 22, 1903, in London, England; son of John W. (a publisher) and Rose Eleanor (Hardy) Wickwar; married Margaret Beauchamp, 1934; children: Vincent B. *Education:* King's College, London, B.A., 1924, M.A., 1927; University of Paris, graduate study, 1927-28. *Home:* 914 Gregg St., Columbia, S.C. 29201. *Office:* Richland Memorial Hospital, 3010 Harden St., Columbia, S.C. 29203.

CAREER: Rockford College, Rockford, Ill., assistant professor of political science, 1938-43; Connecticut College, New London, associate professor of political science, 1943-44; United Nations Relief and Rehabilitation Agency, New York, N.Y., member of staff, 1944-46; Hamilton College, Clinton, N.Y., professor of political science, 1946-48; United Nations Secretariat, New York, N.Y., specialist in comparative social administration and chief of World Food Program section, 1948-65; University of South Carolina, Columbia, professor of political science, 1965-71, professor emeritus, 1971—. Consultant to United Nations in Ivory Coast, 1969, and Togo, 1974; consultant to South Carolina Health Department, Mental Health Department, Corrections Department, and Water Resources Commission, 1967-74, and to U.S. Department of Health, Education, and Welfare, 1969; member of South Carolina Comprehensive Health Planning Council, 1973—; president, Public Service Associates, Inc., 1975—. *Member:* American Society for Public Administration (founder/president of South Carolina chapter, 1973-74), Alliance Francaise de Columbia, S.C. (president, 1972-73). *Awards, honors:* Rockefeller Foundation fellowship, 1927-31, to France, Switzerland, and Germany.

WRITINGS: The Struggle for the Freedom of the Press, Allen & Unwin, 1928; *Baron d'Holbach*, Allen & Unwin, 1935; *The Social Services*, Bodley Head, 1949; *The Modernization of Administration in the Near East*, Khayat, 1963; *The Political Theory of Local Government*, University of South Carolina Press, 1970; *African Probings*, Institute of International Studies, University of South Carolina, 1971.

WORK IN PROGRESS: A book on health-care politics and dynamics.

* * *

WIEDER, Laurance 1946-

PERSONAL: Born June 28, 1946, in New York, N.Y.; son

of Herbert Wieder (a physician) and Gloria (an office manager; maiden name, Cohen) Wieder Sinclair; married Christine Brueckner, November 1, 1969 (divorced February, 1973). *Education:* Columbia University, B.A., 1968; Cornell University, M.A., 1970. *Home:* 171 West 71st St., #9D, New York, N.Y. 10023.

CAREER: Cornell University, Ithaca, N.Y., instructor in English, 1970; University of Colorado, Boulder, associate in English department, 1970-71; Cornell University, lecturer in English, 1971-73; free-lance writer and editor, 1973-74; Harcourt, Brace, Jovanovich, New York, N.Y., assistant to co-publisher, 1974; Winchester Press, New York, N.Y., editor, 1974—. Has given poetry readings on radio and at colleges and universities; part-time ski instructor and professional horse trainer and rider. *Awards, honors:* Ingram Merrill Foundation grant in poetry, 1974-75.

WRITINGS: The Coronet of Tours, Ithaca House, 1972; *No Harm Done*, Ardis, 1975. Contributor to *Paris Review, Poetry, Epoch*, and others.

WORK IN PROGRESS: Opera libretto, book of poems, and collaborative translations of modern Persian dramas.

* * *

WIEMAN, Henry N(elson) 1884-1975

August 19, 1884—June 19, 1975; American theologian, philosopher, educator, and author. Obituaries: *New York Times*, June 21, 1975.

* * *

WILCOX, Herbert 1891-

PERSONAL: Born October 14, 1891, in Elberton, Ga.; son of William Marion (in life insurance) and Martha E. (Tolly) Wilcox; married Irene F. Stilwell (an office manager), April 18, 1918; children: William S. (deceased), Martha M. (Mrs. Eugene C. Chambliss, Jr.). *Education:* Attended Davidson College, 1912-13. *Religion:* Presbyterian. *Home:* 205 South McIntosh, Elberton, Ga. 30635.

CAREER: In cotton buying business, 1916-20; life insurance salesman, 1921-37; *Elberton Star*, Elberton, Ga., bookkeeper, later reporter and feature writer, 1937-66. *Military service:* U.S. Army, 1918-19.

WRITINGS: Georgia Scribe (non-fiction), Cherokee, 1974. Feature writer for *Atlanta Journal-Constitution*'s Sunday magazine.

SIDELIGHTS: Wilcox writes: "... The mayor of Elberton declared May 24, 1974, Herbert Wilcox Day, which I understood after a fashion. School children here have a feeling I was on hand when our county was formed in 1790. For years, much to my pleasure, they have called on me to learn about how things were in my youth."

* * *

WILDE, Daniel U(nderwood) 1937-

PERSONAL: Born December 27, 1937, in Wilmington, Ohio; son of Arthur J. (an engineer) and Dale (Underwood) Wilde. *Education:* University of Illinois, B.S., 1960; Massachusetts Institute of Technology, M.S., 1962, Ph.D., 1966. *Home:* 188 Cedar Swamp Rd., Storrs, Conn. 06268. *Office:* New England Research Application Center, University of Connecticut, Storrs, Conn. 06268.

CAREER: Boston University, Boston, Mass., research instructor in medicine, 1964-66; University of Connecticut, Storrs, assistant professor of business administration, 1966-

72, associate professor of industrial administration, 1969—, New England Research Application Center, associate director, 1967-72, director, 1972—. Consultant to American Society for Metals, 1972—. *Military service:* U.S. Air Force Reserve, 1961—; became first lieutenant. *Member:* Association of Computer Machinery, Institute of Electrical and Electronic Engineers, American Society for Information Science, Association of Information and Dissemination Centers, Tau Beta Pi, Beta Gamma Sigma, Eta Kappa Nu.

WRITINGS: Introduction to Computing: Problem Solving, Algorithms, and Data Structures, Prentice-Hall, 1973; (with R. M. Smith) *Instructor's Manual for Introduction to Computing: Problem Solving, Algorithms, and Data Structures*, Prentice-Hall, 1973. Contributor to proceedings and to journals in his field.

WORK IN PROGRESS: Research on management of large data bases.

* * *

WILDER-SMITH, A(rthur) E(rnest) 1915-

PERSONAL: Born December 22, 1915, in Reading, England; son of Arthur William (a farmer) and Elfrida Minne (Wilder) Smith; married Beate Gottwaldt, September 17, 1950; children: Oliver, Petra, Clive, Einar. *Education:* University of Reading, B.Sc. (general), 1937, B.Sc. (chemistry; with honors), 1938, Ph.D., 1941; Geneva University, P.D., 1955, Dr. es sciences, 1964; Eidgenoessische Technische Hochschule Zuerich, D.Sc., 1964. *Politics:* None. *Religion:* Evangelical (Anglican). *Home and office:* Roggern, Einigen CH 3646, Switzerland.

CAREER: Imperial Chemical Industries, Billingham, England, technical assistant on senior staff, 1940-45; University of London, British Empire Cancer Campaign, London, England, Countess of Lisburne Memorial Fellow in Cancer Research, 1945-49; Geistlich Soehne Ltd. (pharmaceuticals firm), Lucerne, Switzerland, chief of research, 1951-55; University of Geneva, Ecole de Medecine, Geneva, Switzerland, privat docent, 1956-64; University of Illinois, Medical Center, Chicago, professor of pharmacology and member of College of Nursing faculty, 1964-71. Visiting assistant professor, University of Illinois, 1957-58; visiting professor, University of Bergen, 1960-62, Hacetepe University, 1969-71. Consultant to North Atlantic Treaty Organization (NATO) on drug abuse, 1969-74, and to European and U.S. pharmaceutical firms. Lecturer in relationship of science and religion. *Member:* Chemical Society (London), Royal Institute of Chemistry (fellow), Sigma Psi, Rho Chi. *Awards, honors:* Ridley research fellow, 1939-40; University of Illinois, senior class instructor of the year, 1966, 1967, 1968, and 1969, Golden Apple awards, 1966, 1967, and 1969.

WRITINGS: (With wife, Beate Wilder-Smith) *Die Ehe* (title means "Marriage"), Haenssler, 1957; *Warum laesst Gott es zu?*, Haenssler (Stuttgart), English edition published as *Why Does God Allow It? and Other Essays*, Victory Press, 1960; *Herkunft und Zukunft des Menschen: Ein kritischer Ueberblick der dem Darwinismus und Christentum zugrunde liegenden naturwissenschaftlichen und geistlichen Prinzipien*, Brunnen (Basel), 1966, English edition published as *Man's Origin, Man's Destiny: A Critical Survey of the Principles of Evolution and Christianity*, H. Shaw, 1968; *The Drug Users: The Psychopharmacology of Turning On*, H. Shaw, 1969.

Die Erschaffung das Lebens, Haenssler, 1970, English edition published as *The Creation of Life: A Cybernetic Approach to Evolution*, H. Shaw, 1970; *The Paradox of Pain*, H. Shaw, 1971; *Ist das ein Gott der Liebe?* (title means "Is This a God of Love?"), Haenssler, 1971; *Tauferkenntnis und Liebe zu Jesus Christus* (title means "Baptismal Doctrine and Christian Devotion"), Haenssler, 1973; *Gott: Sein oder Nichtsein?*, Haenssler, 1973, English edition published as *God: To Be or Not To Be?*, Haenssler, 1975; *Grundlage zu einer neuen Biologie*, Haenssler, 1974, English edition published as *A Basis for a New Biology*, Haenssler, 1975; *Ursache und Behandlung der Drogenepidemie*, Haenssler, 1974, English edition published as *Causes and Cures of the Drug Epidemic*, 1974; *Ergriffen? Ergreife!* (title means "Won? Then Win!"), Haenssler, 1975. Also author of *Der Mensch im Stress* (title means "Man Under Stress"), Haenssler. Contributor to journals in his field.

WORK IN PROGRESS: Abdication of Scientific Materialism, Universalism: Solution or Problem?, Scientific and Moral Basis for Sex, and *Bertolt Brecht: Influence as Man and Author*, all with wife, Beate Wilder-Smith, all for Haenssler.

* * *

WILDES, Harry Emerson 1890-

PERSONAL: Born April 3, 1890, in Middletown, Del.; son of Albert Adams and Rhoda Catherine (Foster) Wildes; married Helen Jaquette, June 27, 1919 (died June 20, 1958). *Education:* Central High School, Philadelphia, Pa., A.B., 1909; Harvard University, A.B. (cum laude), 1913; University of Pennsylvania, A.M., 1922, Ph.D., 1927. *Home:* 259 South Farragut Ter., Philadelphia, Pa. 19139.

CAREER: Teacher of history and social science in high schools in Philadelphia, 1915-23, 1926-30, 1934-45; *Philadelphia Public Ledger*, Philadelphia, Pa., literary editor, 1930-34; U.S. State Department, Washington, D.C., regional specialist for Japan, working with Office of War Information, 1945-46; Supreme Commander of the Allied Powers in Japan, Tokyo, chief of information management branch at General Headquarters, 1947-50; chief of Division of Political and Social Affairs, 1950-51; International College of the Sacred Heart, Tokyo, Japan, Fulbright lecturer in political science, 1952-53; New School for Social Research, New York, N.Y., lecturer in sociology, 1956-57; Superior State College, Superior, Wis., professor of English, 1957-58. *Awards, honors:* L.H.D. from Temple University, 1944.

WRITINGS: Social Currents in Japan, University of Chicago Press, 1927; *Japan in Crisis*, Macmillan, 1934; *Aliens in the East*, University of Pennsylvania Press, 1937; *Valley Forge*, Macmillan, 1938; *The Delaware*, Farrar & Rinehart, 1940; *Anthony Wayne*, Harcourt, 1941; *Twin Rivers*, Farrar & Rinehart, 1943; *Lonely Midas: Stephen Girard*, Farrar & Rinehart, 1943; *Typhoon in Tokyo*, Macmillan, 1952; *Voice of the Lord: George Fox*, University of Pennsylvania Press, 1964; *William Penn*, Macmillan, 1974.

* * *

WILENSKI, R(eginald) H(oward) 1887-1975

1887—April 19, 1975; Art critic and author of books on modern painting and sculpture. Obituaries: *AB Bookman's Weekly*, May 26, 1975.

* * *

WILLAN, Anne 1938-

PERSONAL: Born January 26, 1938, in Newcastle, England; naturalized U.S. citizen in 1973; daughter of William (a lawyer) and Joyce (Todd) Willan; married Mark Cherniavsky (a banker), June 9, 1966; children: Simon, Emma. *Education:* Cambridge University, M.A., 1959; attended cookery schools in London and Paris, 1960-64. *Home:* 7 Ave. Emile Deschanel, Paris 75007, France. *Agent:* William Kosmas, Kosmas & Messing, 1841 Broadway, New York, N.Y. 10023. *Office:* Ecole de Cuisine La Varenne, 34 Rue St. Dominique, Paris 75007, France.

CAREER: Gourmet, New York, N.Y., member of editorial staff, 1965-66; *Washington Star*, Washington, D.C., food editor, 1966-68; cookery editor and consultant, 1969-74; Ecole de Cuisine La Varenne, Paris, France, director, 1975—.

WRITINGS: Entertaining Menus, Coward, 1974. Editor-in-chief of "Grand Diplome Cooking Course," Grolier, 1970-73.

WORK IN PROGRESS: Great Cooks from Taillevent to Escoffier, an illustrated biographical history.

* * *

WILLERDING, Margaret F(rances) 1919-

PERSONAL: Born April 26, 1919, in St. Louis, Mo.; daughter of Herman J. and Mildred (Icenhower) Willerding. *Education:* Harris Teachers College, A.B., 1940; St. Louis University, M.A., 1943, Ph.D., 1947. *Home:* 10241 Vivera Dr., La Mesa, Calif. 92041. *Office:* Department of Mathematics, San Diego State University, San Diego, Calif. 92115.

CAREER: Washington University, St. Louis, Mo., instructor in mathematics, 1947-48; Harris Teachers College, St. Louis, Mo., assistant professor of mathematics, 1948-56; San Diego State University, San Diego, Calif., associate professor, 1956-62, professor of mathematics, 1962—. Member of the board of directors of Greater San Diego Mathematics Council, 1961-63; consultant to Rogue Valley Ranch School, Central Point, Ore., 1972—. *Member:* National Council of Teachers of Mathematics, American Mathematical Society, Mathematical Association of America, School Science and Mathematics Association, Missouri Mathematics Council (president, 1954-55), California Mathematics Council.

WRITINGS: (With G. D. Bartoo and Jesse Osborn) *Algebra: A Second Course*, Webster, 1954; *Elementary Mathematics*, Wiley, 1966, 3rd edition, 1975; *Mathematics: Patterns and Structure* (workbooks, grades three through eight), Holt, 1966; (with Ruth Hayward) *Mathematics: The Alphabet of Science*, Wiley, 1967, 3rd edition, 1975; *Mathematical Concepts: A Historical Approach*, Prindle, 1967; *A Probability Primer*, Prindle, 1968; *From Fingers to Computers*, Franklin Publications, 1968; *Mathematics Around the Clock*, Franklin Publications, 1968; *Probability: The Science of Chance*, Franklin Publications, 1968; (with Stephen Hoffman) *Modern Intermediate Algebra*, Wiley, 1969, 2nd edition, 1975; *Arithmetic: A First Course in College Mathematics*, Prindle, 1969; *Arithmetic Worktext*, Prindle, 1969.

(With Hoffman) *College Algebra and Trigonometry*, Wiley, 1971, 2nd edition, 1975; (with Hoffman) *College Algebra*, Wiley, 1971, 2nd edition, Prindle, in press; *A First Course in College Mathematics*, Prindle, 1973; *Mathematics Worktext*, Prindle, 1973; *Consumer Mathematics*, Prindle, 1975. Contributor to mathematical journals. Editor of Problem Department of *School Science and Mathematics*, 1954—.

SIDELIGHTS: Mathematics: The Alphabet of Science and *Elementary Mathematics* have had editions in Japanese and Spanish.

* * *

WILLIAMS, Cicely 1907-

PERSONAL: Born February 10, 1907, in Chatham, Kent, England; daughter of Edward Glanville (a bank manager) and Marian (Sheldrake) Kay; married Ronald Ralph Williams (Bishop of Leicester), June 9, 1934. *Education:* Educated in England. *Politics:* Conservative. *Religion:* Church of England. *Home:* Bishop's Lodge, Springfield Rd., Leicester LE2 3BD, England.

CAREER: Free-lance journalist for all media, 1945—. Has appeared on television and radio programs. *Wartime service:* Transport Corps, chauffeuse, 1940-45. *Member:* Ski Club of Great Britain, English-Speaking Union, Alpine Club, Ladies Alpine Club, Swiss Ladies Alpine Club, Rendez-vous Hautes Montagnes.

WRITINGS: Bishop's Wife: But Still Myself (autobiography), Doubleday, 1961; *Zermatt Saga* (nonfiction), Allen & Unwin, 1964; *Dear Abroad* (travel), Allen & Unwin, 1967; *Diary of a Decade* (autobiography), Allen & Unwin, 1970; *Women on the Rope* (nonfiction), Allen & Unwin, 1973. Contributor to journals and newspapers. Member of board of editors of *Ladies Alpine Club Journal*, 1973-75.

AVOCATIONAL INTERESTS: Climbing, skiing, riding, cricket, travel, languages, music.

* * *

WILLIAMS, Edwin B(ucher) 1891-1975

September 20, 1891—April 28, 1975; American lexicographer, educator, university official, author, and editor. Obituaries: *New York Times*, April 29, 1975.

* * *

WILLIAMS, Frances Marion 1919-

PERSONAL: Born November 7, 1919, in Elkton, Ky.; daughter of John Nathan (a merchant) and Frances Marion (Trabue) Williams. *Education:* Transylvania University, A.B., 1942; graduate study at George Peabody College for Teachers, Western Kentucky University, and Austin Peay State University. *Religion:* Disciples of Christ. *Residence:* Elkton, Ky. *Office:* Todd County Central High School Library, Elkton, Ky. 42220.

CAREER: Civilian employee with U.S. Air Force, 1942-50; high school librarian in Elkton, Ky., 1950—. *Member:* National Society of Daughters of the American Revolution, Washington Family Descendants, National Society of Colonial Dames of the Seventeenth Century, National Society of Magna Charta Dames, National Huguenot Society, Huguenot Society of the Founders of Manakin in the Colony of Virginia, National Society of Americans of Royal Descent, Kentucky Education Association, Kentucky Historical Society, Kentucky Association of High School Librarians, Kentucky Heritage Commission, Phi Mu.

WRITINGS: The Story of Todd County, Kentucky: 1820-1970, Parthenon Press, 1972; *A Mother Goose History for Grown-Ups and Children*, Parthenon Press, 1974. Contributor to *Kentucky School Journal*.

WORK IN PROGRESS: Research on fairy tales, in order to work out a means of using them as a teaching device.

WILLIAMS, Hazel Pearson 1914-

PERSONAL: Born January 20, 1914, in Kingsburg, Calif.; daughter of Albert John (a veterinarian) and Nellie E. (Haskell) Kaiser; married Ray McKinley Pearson, June 16, 1935; married Jack Kermit Williams (a publisher), August 22, 1954; children: (first marriage) Charon (Mrs. Robert Wiborg), Gayle (Mrs. Richard Morton II). *Education:* California State College at Los Angeles (now California State University, Los Angeles), B.A., 1966. *Politics:* Republican. *Religion:* Presbyterian. *Home:* 300 West Norman Ave., Arcadia, Calif. 91006. *Agent:* Jack K. Williams, Temple City Blvd., Rosemead, Calif. 91780. *Office:* Hazel Pearson Handicrafts, Rosemead, Calif. 91780.

CAREER: Hazel Pearson Handicrafts, Rosemead, Calif., president and designer, 1945—. *Member:* Hobby Industry Association of America (director), Southern California Hobby Industry Association (director). *Awards, honors:* Award from Craft Division of Hobby Industry Association of America, for contributions to the industry.

WRITINGS: Handicrafts for Fun, Kalmbach, 1969; *Making Things from Discards*, Crown, 1974. Contributor to trade journals. Director of Craft Course Publishers, and consultant in their production of some two hundred craft how-to books.

SIDELIGHTS: Hazel Williams writes that as a result of her travels, she has travel displays for more than thirty countries, for local library use. She began her business at her kitchen table and has expanded to a multi-million-dollar business. *Avocational interests:* Travel.

* * *

WILLIAMS, John D(elane) 1938-

PERSONAL: Born October 26, 1938, in Ordway, Colo.; son of John O. (a truck driver) and Leila (owner of a grocery store; maiden name, Galbraith) Williams; married Concetta DiSipio (a counselor), September 6, 1958; children: Diane V., Brian T. *Education:* Southern Colorado State College, A.A., 1958; University of Northern Colorado, B.A., 1959, M.A., 1960, Ph.D., 1966; University of Oregon, graduate study, 1961-62. *Politics:* Democrat. *Religion:* Roman Catholic. *Home:* 1802 University, Grand Forks, N.D. 58201. *Office:* Center for Teaching, University of North Dakota, Grand Forks, N.D. 58201.

CAREER: Teacher of science and mathematics at junior high school in Oakland, Calif., 1960-61; Western Wyoming Community College, Reliance, instructor in mathematics and statistics, 1962-65; University of North Dakota, Grand Forks, assistant professor, 1966-68, associate professor, 1968-71, professor of educational statistics, 1971—. *Member:* American Educational Research Association, American Statistical Association, American Psychological Association, Phi Delta Kappa.

WRITINGS: (With S. D. Harlow and S. R. Houston) *Action Research for the Classroom Teacher*, Kendall/Hunt, 1969; (editor with Richard G. Landry) *Readings in Multiple Linear Regression and Intermediate Educational Statistics*, MSS Educational Publishing, 1971; *Regression Analysis in Educational Research*, MSS Information Corp., 1974; (contributor) G. I. Lubin, J. F. Magary, and M. K. Paulson, editors, *Piagetian Theory and the Helping Professor*, Publications Department, University of Southern California, 1975. Contributor of more than fifty articles to education, psychology, and statistical journals.

WORK IN PROGRESS: Studies in regression analysis and in the area of Piagetian conservation.

WILLIAMS, Mary C(ameron) 1923-

PERSONAL: Born September 16, 1923, in Albany, N.Y.; daughter of Truman David and Marion (Scudder) Cameron; married D. D. Williams, April 14, 1945 (divorced, 1970); children: Ellen (Mrs. H. L. Leff), Evelyn (Mrs. Mumtaz Durmaz), Carol, John. *Education:* Wellesley College, B.A., 1944; University of North Carolina, Chapel Hill, M.A., 1960, Ph.D., 1970. *Home:* 622 Woodburn Rd., Raleigh, N.C. 27605. *Office:* Department of English, North Carolina State University, Raleigh, N.C. 27607.

CAREER: North Carolina State University, Raleigh, instructor, 1962-70, assistant professor, 1970-74, associate professor of English, 1974—. *Member:* Modern Language Association of America, Renaissance Society, American Association of University Professors, Victorians Institute, League of Women Voters, South Atlantic Modern Language Association, Southeastern Renaissance Conference.

WRITINGS: Unity in Ben Jonson's Early Comedies, University of Salzburg Press, 1972; (editor with Guy Owen) *New Southern Poets*, University of North Carolina Press, 1975. Managing editor of *Southern Poetry Review*, 1970—.

WORK IN PROGRESS: Research on Renaissance drama and on Arthurian legends.

* * *

WILLIAMS, Vergil L(ewis) 1935-

PERSONAL: Born September 29, 1935, in Crosbyton, Tex.; son of Albert Lewis (a farmer) and Neola Bell (Pinkston) Williams; married Vergnel Campbell Smith, June 6, 1957 (divorced February 10, 1968); married Velma Arlene Minor (a home economics teacher), December 23, 1974; children: (first marriage) Delwin Victor; (second marriage) Colleen Jeffries (stepdaughter). *Education:* West Texas State University, B.S., 1966; Southern Illinois University, graduate study, 1966-68; University of Alabama, Ph.D., 1971. *Religion:* Bahai. *Home:* Claymont Apartments, #2B, Tuscaloosa, Ala. 35401. Office: *School of Social Work, P.O. Box 1935, University of Alabama, University, Ala. 35486.*

CAREER: Farmer in Happy, Tex., 1953-60; police patrolman in Amarillo, Tex., 1960-64, patrol sergeant, 1964-66; University of Alabama, Tuscaloosa, assistant professor of criminal justice, 1971—. *Military service:* Texas National Guard, 1953-60. U.S. Army Reserve, Infantry, 1960-66; became captain. *Member:* International Association of Chiefs of Police, American Society of Criminology, National Council on Crime and Delinquency, U.S. Parachute Association, Lambda Alpha Epsilon, Omicron Delta Epsilon.

WRITINGS: (With Mary Fish) *Convicts, Codes, and Contraband: The Prison Life of Men and Women*, Ballinger Publishing, 1974; (contributor) Israel Drapkin and Emilio Viano, editors, *Victimology: A New Focus*, Volume II: *Society's Reaction to Victimization*, Lexington Books, 1974. Contributor of articles and reviews to *Crime and Delinquency, American Journal of Correction, Police Chief, World Order, Midwest Quarterly, Choice, Journal of Correctional Education*, and *Criminal Justice and Behavior: An International Journal of Correctional Psychology*.

WORK IN PROGRESS: Probation and Parole, with Robert T. Sigler; *Dictionary of American Penology*, publication by Greenwood Press expected in 1977; *Smoke It on Down*, a study of sport parachuting, 1977.

SIDELIGHTS: Williams writes: "My research and writing interests often reflect my journey from the sweaty, greasy world of the farm day laborer at the bottom of the lower class to the abstract world of words in the professorial class. Social mobility takes one through a bewildering maze of value systems. Subcultures fascinate me; as does the potential for better human relations due to increased understanding of different belief systems." Avocational interests: Sport parachuting.

* * *

WILLIAMSON, Alan (Bacher) 1944-

PERSONAL: Born January 24, 1944, in Chicago, Ill.; son of George (a professor) and Jehanne (Bacher) Williamson; married Anne Winters (a writer), October 12, 1968. Education: Haverford College, A.B., 1964; Harvard University, M.A., 1965, Ph.D., 1969. Home: 113 Cameron Lane, Charlottesville, Va. 22903. Office: Department of English, University of Virginia, Charlottesville, Va. 22901.

CAREER: University of Virginia, Charlottesville, assistant professor of English, 1969—. Member: American Civil Liberties Union. Awards, honors: Creative writing fellowship from National Endowment for the Arts, 1973-74.

WRITINGS: Pity the Monsters: The Political Vision of Robert Lowell, Yale University Press, 1974. Contributor of poems, articles, and reviews to literary journals, including New Yorker, Poetry, Partisan Review, Shenandoah, New Review, Yale Review, and American Poetry Review.

WORK IN PROGRESS: First Nights Away from Home, a collection of poems; further poems, short stories, and research on contemporary poetry.

SIDELIGHTS: Williamson writes that he is especially interested in psychoanalytic theory in relation to literature. Avocational interests: Travel (Europe).

* * *

WILLIAMSON, Glen 1909-

PERSONAL: Born December 22, 1909, in Masonville, Iowa; son of Andrew Stuart (a farmer) and Rosa Izora (Williams) Williamson; married Corinne Aanas, November 30, 1933; children: Richard, Lorraine (Mrs. Robert Meadows), Anita (Mrs. Gerald Archer), William. Education: Attended Coe College, 1928-29; University of Denver, language study, 1968-69. Home: 5505 Valmont Rd., #297, Boulder, Colo. 80301.

CAREER: Ordained minister of Free Methodist Church, 1944; pastor in Des Moines, Iowa, 1941-45; evangelist in U.S. and Canada, 1945-52; pastor in Des Moines, 1952-56; Free Methodist Church, Winona, Ind., director of international evangelism, 1956-63, director of Rocky Mountain Conference in Denver, Colo., 1963-70; Sermon Builder, Golden, Colo., editor, 1970—. Trustee-at-large, Western Evangelical Seminary, 1968—; vice-president of Church Educational Ministries, 1973—. Awards, honors: D.Litt. from Western Evangelical Seminary, 1947.

WRITINGS: Julia, Giantess in Generosity, Light and Life Press, 1969; Frank and Hazel, the Adamsons of Kibogora, Light and Life Press, 1972; Repair My House, Creation House, 1973; Geneva, Missionary to the Chinese, Light and Life Press, 1974; (with Geneva Sayre) On the Brink, Light and Life Press, 1974. Also author of Born for Such a Day and a film script, "Land Forming for Irrigation." Contributor of short stories to magazines.

WORK IN PROGRESS: History of Missions in Mexico; History of Missions in Japan; a collection of short stories.

SIDELIGHTS: Williamson and his wife lived in Assisi, Italy while doing research for his book, Repair My House, a biographical novel about St. Francis of Assisi.

* * *

WILLIS, Maude
See LOTTMAN, Eileen

* * *

WILLWERTH, James 1943-

PERSONAL: Born June 6, 1943, in Detroit, Mich.; son of H. Victor (a printer) and Margaret (Veenboer) Willwerth; married Irene Kiebert, September 10, 1967 (divorced, 1971); married Ardis Kauer (a teacher), July 28, 1974. Education: Attended College of Marin, 1961-63; University of California, Berkeley, B.A., 1965, M.A., 1966. Politics: Democrat. Religion: Methodist. Home: 79 Monte Vista, Novato, Calif. 94947. Agent: Helen Merrill, 337 West 22nd St., New York, N.Y. 10011.

CAREER: Time (magazine), correspondent in San Francisco, Calif., 1966-67, in New York, N.Y., 1967-70, Saigon, 1970-71, New York, 1971—; free-lance writer. Military service: U.S. Air Force Reserve, active duty, 1968-69; became sergeant. Awards, honors: Sigma Delta Chi award, 1966, for article on Berkeley's "street people."

WRITINGS: Eye in the Last Storm: A Reporter's Journal of One Year in Southeast Asia, Grossman, 1972; Jones: Portrait of a Mugger, M. Evans, 1974; (with Clive Davis) Clive: Inside the Music Business, Morrow, 1975.

WORK IN PROGRESS: A nonfiction work on a New York policeman who went insane on the job.

SIDELIGHTS: Willwerth told CA: "I need to write, which is my way of getting involved with things that interest me—or at least things that I think I should be interested in. I also think that good writing and good journalism perform a public service, so writing is my way of making some kind of contribution."

BIOGRAPHICAL/CRITICAL SOURCES: New York Times Book Review, February 16, 1975.

* * *

WILMOT, William (Wallace) 1943-

PERSONAL: Born May 31, 1943, in Vancouver, Wash.; son of Henry Wallace and Viola Mae Wilmot; married Charney Louise Ziegahn, June 7, 1967; children: Jason Lamar, Carina Louise. Education: University of Wyoming, B.A., 1965; University of Washington, Seattle, M.A., 1967, Ph.D., 1970. Home: 640 Livingston, Missoula, Mont. 59801. Office: Department of Interpersonal Communication, University of Montana, Missoula, Mont. 59801.

CAREER: Central Michigan University, Mount Pleasant, assisant professor of speech communication, 1970-72; University of Montana, Missoula, associate professor of interpersonal communication, 1972—. Member: International Communication Association, Speech Communication Association.

WRITINGS: (With John R. Wenburg) The Personal Communication Process, Wiley, 1973; (editor with Wenburg) Communication Involvement: Personal Perspectives, Wiley, 1974; Dyadic Communication: A Transactional Perspective, Addison-Wesley, 1975. Contributor to Quarterly Journal of Speech and Speech Monographs.

WORK IN PROGRESS: Communication in Conflict, with Joyce Frost; research on classroom communication and dyadic communication.

* * *

WILMS, Barbara 1941-

PERSONAL: Born March 15, 1941, in Chicago, Ill.; daughter of Thomas J. (a banker) and Helen (Fox) Clark; married Wellford Wilms (a researcher), November 28, 1964; children: Thomas, William. *Education:* University of Maine, student, 1958-60; University of Illinois, B.A., 1963. *Politics:* "Coalition." *Home:* 2611 Webster, Berkeley, Calif. 94705. *Office: Landscape*, P.O. Box 7177, Berkeley, Calif. 94707.

CAREER: Berkeley Daily Gazette, Berkeley, Calif., reporter, 1968-73; California Alumni Association, Berkeley, coordinator of public information, 1973-74; presently employed by *Landscape* (magazine), Berkeley, Calif. *Awards, honors:* Distinguished achievement award from Educational Press Association of America.

WRITINGS: Crunchy Bananas and Other Great Recipes Kids Can Cook, Peregrine, 1975. Contributor to *Reader's Digest, College Management, Parents' Magazine*, and *Modern Story*.

WORK IN PROGRESS: Child Rearing Techniques of Adlerian Psychology.

* * *

WILSON, Craig R. 1947-

PERSONAL: Born August 30, 1947, in Johnson City, Tenn.; son of L. Craig (a professor and writer) and Helen (Nunez) Wilson; married Jacqueline M., October 13, 1967 (divorced, 1975); children: Tonya Helen, Craig Leland, Mark Robert. *Education:* Attended University of Delaware and University of Tennessee; University of South Alabama, B.A., 1971. *Home:* 1419 South First Street, Apt. 4, Jacksonville Beach, Fla. 32250. *Office:* 224 Unami Trail Road 2, Newark, Del. 19711.

CAREER: Professional tennis player; photographer; writer. *Member:* U.S. Professional Tennis Association.

WRITINGS: How to Improve Your Tennis Style, Strategy, Analysis, A. S. Barnes, 1974. Writer of column in *Ponte Vedra Recorder*.

WORK IN PROGRESS: Transcendental Tennis, for publication by Barnes; a novel.

* * *

WILSON, Frank L(eondus) 1941-

PERSONAL: Born February 7, 1941, in Los Angeles, Calif.; son of Frank L. II (a contractor) and Ruth Judith (Elieson) Wilson; married Carol Ann West, February 16, 1968; children: Erin Ann, Sara Jean, John Franklin. *Education:* University of California, Los Angeles, B.A., 1964, M.A., 1965, Ph.D., 1969. *Religion:* Church of Jesus Christ of Latter-day Saints (Mormons). *Home:* 148 Dogwood Ct., West Lafayette, Ind. 47906. *Office:* Department of Political Science, Purdue University, West Lafayette, Ind. 47907.

CAREER: University of California, Los Angeles, lecturer in political science, 1969-70; Iowa State University, Ames, assistant professor of political science, 1970-71; Purdue University, West Lafayette, Ind., associate professor of political science, 1971—. *Member:* International Studies Association, American Political Science Association, Con-

ference Group on French Politics and Society, Phi Beta Kappa.

WRITINGS: The French Democratic Left, 1962-1969: Toward a Modern Party System, Stanford University Press, 1971; (with David Roth) *The Comparative Study of Politics: Britain, France, China, the Soviet Union, Mexico, and Nigeria*, Houghton, in press. Contributor to *Comparative Politics, World Politics*, and *Western Political Quarterly*.

* * *

WILSON, Jerry V. 1928-

PERSONAL: Born March 23, 1928, in South Hill, Va.; son of Joe Eric (a mill hand) and Ruth (a mill hand; maiden name, Plyler) Wilson; married Leone Harris, May 5, 1956; children: Brian Jerry, Kevin Harris. *Education:* American University, A.A. *Politics:* Independent. *Religion:* Methodist. *Home:* 4415 Springdale St. N.W., Washington, D.C. 20016.

CAREER: Metropolitan Police Department, Washington, D.C., chief of police, 1969—.

WRITINGS: Police Report: A View of Law Enforcement, Little, Brown, 1975; (with Paul O. Fugua) *Police and the Media*, Little, Brown, in press.

WORK IN PROGRESS: Two books, *The Criminal Justice System*, with Gerald M. Caplan, and *Criminal Investigation*, with Paul Q. Fugua; a report, "The War Against Crime in the District of Columbia, 1956-1976."

* * *

WILSON, Leonard G(ilchrist) 1928-

PERSONAL: Born June 11, 1928, in Ontario, Canada; married Adelia Hans, June 7, 1969. *Education:* University of Toronto, B.A., 1949; University of London, M.Sc., 1955; University of Wisconsin, Ph.D., 1958. *Home:* 797 Goodrich Ave., St. Paul, Minn. 55105. *Office:* Department of the History of Medicine, University of Minnesota, Minneapolis, Minn. 55455.

CAREER: University of California, Berkeley, visiting instructor in history, 1958-59; Cornell University, Ithaca, N.Y., assistant professor of history, 1959-60; Yale University, New Haven, Conn., assistant professor, 1960-65, associate professor of history of medicine, 1965-67; University of Minnesota, Minneapolis, professor of history of medicine, 1967—, head of department. Member of advisory committee for National Institutes of Health and National Science Foundation. *Member:* American Association for the History of Medicine, History of Science Society, American Association for the Advancement of Science, American Historical Association, Society for the History of Technology, Society for the Bibliography of Natural History, Minnesota Academy of Medicine.

WRITINGS: (Editor) *Selected Readings in the History of Physiology*, C. C Thomas, 2nd edition, revised and enlarged, 1966 (1st edition edited by John F. Fulton, 1930); *Sir Charles Lyell's Scientific Journals on the Species Question*, Yale University Press, 1970; *Charles Lyell, the Years to 1841: The Revolution in Geology*, Yale University Press, 1972. Associate editor of *Dictionary of Scientific Biography*; editor of *Journal of the History of Medicine and Allied Sciences*.

WORK IN PROGRESS: A book on Charles Lyell's travels in America between 1841 and 1853.

WILSON, Major L(oyce) 1926-

PERSONAL: Born August 26, 1926, in Arkansas; son of William A. (a farmer) and Lillian (Wall) Wilson; married Donna Sheridan, August 18, 1956; children: Shannon, Morgan. *Education:* Vanderbilt University, B.A., 1950; University of Arkansas, M.A., 1952; University of Kansas, Ph.D., 1964. *Home:* 452 Woodmere Lane, Memphis, Tenn. 38117. *Office:* Department of History, Memphis State University, Memphis, Tenn. 38152.

CAREER: Kansas City Junior College, Kansas City, Mo., instructor in history, 1954-61; Memphis State University, Memphis, Tenn., assistant professor, 1964-66, associate professor, 1966-69, professor of history, 1969—. *Military service:* U.S. Navy, 1944-46. *Member:* Organization of American Historians, Southern Historical Association, Phi Beta Kappa.

WRITINGS: Space, Time, and Freedom: The Quest for Nationality and the Irrepressible Conflict, 1815-1861, Greenwood Press, 1974. Contributor to *Historian, Civil War History, American Quarterly, Journal of Southern History,* and *Church History.*

WORK IN PROGRESS: Research on the idea of progress between 1815 and 1861.

* * *

WILSON, Phillip (John) 1922-

PERSONAL: Born May 12, 1922, in Lower Hutt, New Zealand; son of Robert Dalzell (a postmaster) and Clara (Parsons) Wilson; married June Margaret Honeyfield, December 23, 1946; children: Janet, Andrew, Catherine, Julie. *Education:* Attended Auckland Teachers College, 1940-41; University of New Zealand, M.A., 1948; graduate study at University of Pennsylvania, 1951-52. *Home:* 12 Bank Rd., Wellington 5, New Zealand.

CAREER: Wellington College, Wellington, New Zealand, teacher of English and French, 1947; *New Zealand Listener,* Wellington, New Zealand, journalist, 1947-56; Kaingaroa Forest, New Zealand, firewatcher, 1959-67 (summers); writer. Judge for P. E. N. Young Writers Awards, 1974. *Military service:* New Zealand Army, First Scottish Regiment, 1941, Ninth Heavy Artillery Regiment, 1941-43. Royal New Zealand Air Force, 1943-45; served in South Pacific campaign; became flying officer (navigator). *Member:* P. E. N. (life member). *Awards, honors:* Fulbright scholar at University of Pennsylvania, 1951-52.

WRITINGS: Some Are Lucky (short stories), Denis Glover, 1960; *The Maorilander,* Whitcombe & Tombs, 1961; *Beneath the Thunder* (novel), Robert Hale, 1963; *Pacific Flight* (novel), Robert Hale, 1964; *The Outcasts* (novel), Robert Hale, 1965; *William Satchell* (biography), Twayne, 1968; *New Zealand Jack* (novel), Robert Hale, 1973; (contributor) Alister Taylor and Denis List, editors, *New Zealand Whole Earth Catalogue,* 2nd edition, Alister Taylor, 1975; *Pacific Star* (novel), Robert Hale, in press. Contributor of stories, articles, and reviews to *Islands, Landfall, New Zealand's Heritage,* and *American Quarterly.* Editor of *P. E. N. Gazette,* 1974-75.

WORK IN PROGRESS: The Mongrel Mob, a novel, completion expected in 1977.

SIDELIGHTS: "Novel writing is my life," Wilson told *CA,* "especially novels and stories about the loves, hopes, and conflicts of people in the South Pacific today and the clash of British and Polynesian cultures. My wife's descent from Dicky Barrett, an English whaler of the 1820's, and

Tautara, New Zealand's greatest and most powerful chief of that time, gave me an added insight into our troubled heritage." *Avocational interests:* Films, trout fishing, skiing, planting trees.

* * *

WILSON, Robert L. 1925-

PERSONAL: Born January 19, 1925, in Forty Fort, Pa.; son of Herbert L. and Kathryn C. Wilson; married Betty Berenthien, June 19, 1950; children: Keith Alan, Marian. *Education:* Asbury College, B.A., 1949; Lehigh University, M.A., 1950; Garrett Theological Seminary, B.D., 1955; Northwestern University, Ph.D., 1958. *Home:* 237 Monticello Ave., Durham, N.C. 27707. *Office:* Divinity School, Duke University, Durham, N.C. 27706.

CAREER: Ordained United Methodist clergyman; United Methodist Church, Board of Missions, New York, N.Y., director of research in National Division, 1958-70; Duke University, Durham, N.C., research professor of church and society, 1970—, director of J. M. Ormond Center for Research, Planning, and Development, 1970—. Member of research advisory committee of United Methodist Church. *Military service:* U.S. Navy, 1943-46. *Member:* Religious Research Association.

WRITINGS: (With James H. Davis) *The Church in the Racially Changing Community,* Abingdon, 1966; (with Paul A. Mickey) *Conflict and Resolution,* Abingdon, 1973; (with Ezra E. Jones) *What's Ahead for Old First Church,* Harper, 1974. Contributor of more than eighty articles to journals.

WORK IN PROGRESS: A study of national Protestant church bureaucracy.

* * *

WILT, Fred 1920-

PERSONAL: Born December 14, 1920, in Pendleton, Ind.; married Eleanor Christensen. *Education:* Indiana University, B.S., 1943; Purdue University, M.S., 1960. *Home:* 2525 Kickapoo Dr., Lafayette, Ind. 47905.

CAREER: Federal Bureau of Investigation agent in Indiana. Lecturer in "learning-by-doing" coaching courses in track in England and Canada. Member of U.S. Olympic Track Team in 1948 and 1952. *Military service:* U.S. Navy, 1943-46; became lieutenant.

WRITINGS: How They Train, Track & Field News, 1959, 2nd edition, 1974; *Run-Run-Run,* Track & Field News, 1964; (with Tom Ecker) *Illustrated Guide to Olympic Track and Field Techniques,* Parker Publishing, 1966; *Mechanics Without Tears,* U.S. Track & Field Federation, 1970; *The Jumps: Contemporary Theory, Technique, and Training,* Track & Field News, 1972; *The Throws: Contemporary Theory, Technique, and Training,* Track & Field News, 1974; (with Ecker and Jim Hay) *Olympic Track and Field Techniques,* Parker Publishing, 1974. Editor of *Track Technique,* 1960—.

WORK IN PROGRESS: Women's Track and Field Techniques, for Parker Publishing.

SIDELIGHTS: Wilt has developed himself into one of the top all-around distance racers in the United States. He "advised" Bud Edelen when Edelen was the fastest marathoner the world had known. He insists his interest in the theoretical details of track and field techniques is strictly a hobby.

WILT, Judith 1941-

PERSONAL: Born September 17, 1941, in Pittsburgh, Pa.; daughter of Thomas B. and Katherine Wilt. *Education:* Duquesne University, B.A., 1967; Indiana University, Ph.D., 1972. *Politics:* Democrat. *Religion:* Roman Catholic. *Home:* 2 East Stanworth Dr., Princeton, N.J. 08540. *Office:* Department of English, Princeton University, Princeton, N.J. 08540.

CAREER: Feature and editorial writer for weekly newspapers in Pittsburgh, Pa., 1959-67; Princeton University, Princeton, N.J., assistant professor of English, 1972—. Hospital volunteer worker and adult education teacher.

WRITINGS: The Readable People of George Meredith, Princeton University Press, 1975.

WORK IN PROGRESS: Gothic fiction; popular literature; science fiction; detective and historical romances; feminist literature.

* * *

WINANS, A. D. 1936-

PERSONAL: Born January 12, 1936, in San Francisco, Calif.; son of Allan Davis and Claire Edith (Grierson) Winans. *Education:* City College of San Francisco, A.A., 1960; San Francisco State College (now University), A.B., 1962. *Politics:* Independent. *Religion:* Protestant. *Home:* 118 Laidley St., San Francisco, Calif. 94131. *Agent:* A. L. Fierst, 630 9th Ave., New York, N.Y. *Office address:* P.O. Box 31249, San Francisco, Calif. 94131.

CAREER: Poet. Publisher of Second Coming Press. Office of Naval Intelligence, San Francisco, Calif., special agent, 1965-72; free-lance writer, 1968—; San Francisco Arts Commission Neighborhood Arts Program, San Francisco, editor and writer, 1975—. Member of board of directors, Committee of Small Magazine Editors and Publishers (COSMEP), 1974-76; member of Coordinating Council of Literary Magazines, 1974-76. *Military service:* U.S. Air Force, 1954-58. *Awards, honors:* P.E.N. writing award, 1974; Coordinating Council of Literary Magazines small magazine grant, 1974-75; National Endowment for the Arts small press grant, 1975.

WRITINGS: Carmel Clowns, Atom Mind Publications, 1970; *Crazy John Poems,* Grande Ronde Press, 1972; *Tales of Crazy John,* Second Coming Press, 1975; *Straws of Sanity,* Thorp Springs Press, 1975. Work represented in anthologies. Contributor of poetry, prose, articles, and book reviews to over one hundred-fifty literary and commercial magazines in the United States, Canada, Australia, and New Zealand. Editor of *Second Coming* (magazine).

WORK IN PROGRESS: Screams and Busted Dreams, a collection of prose and short stories dealing with the post-beat generation life of North Beach, completion expected in 1975; *Venus in Pisces,* a collection of love poems, 1975; *After the Blood,* another collection of poems, 1976.

SIDELIGHTS: Winans told *CA:* "I simply believe in writing poetry that people can understand and relate to. . . . I deal with life on the street and people from prisons and all walks of life . . . I am deeply committed to the land and the sea, believing that true peace can only be found within the cosmic particles around us. We are in the end what we make ourselves. There is no substitute for the love of man and the beauty of nature around us. I am committed to social change, however, and my writings clearly reflect that commitment." Winans has given numerous poetry readings in the San Francisco and Bay areas.

WINFREY, John Crawford 1935-

PERSONAL: Born July 2, 1935, in Somerville, Tenn.; son of Arthur Peter and Frances (Crawford) Winfrey; married Barbara Ann Strickland (a business education teacher), July 20, 1957; children: Mae Millicent. *Education:* Davidson College, A.B., 1957; Duke University, Ph.D., 1965. *Politics:* Democrat. *Religion:* Presbyterian. *Home:* 21 University Pl., Lexington, Va. 24450. *Office:* Department of Economics, Washington and Lee University, Lexington, Va. 24450.

CAREER: Washington and Lee University, Lexington, Va., assistant professor, 1965-69, associate professor, 1969-74, professor of economics, 1974—. *Military service:* U.S. Army, 1957-59; became first lieutenant. *Member:* American Economic Association, Southern Economic Association.

WRITINGS: Public Finance: Public Choices and the Public Economy, Harper, 1973.

WORK IN PROGRESS: A study of the philosophical questions of individual and collective relationships especially with regard to economic relationships.

* * *

WING, Jennifer Patai 1942-

PERSONAL: Born February 5, 1942, in Jerusalem, Israel; daughter of Raphael (an anthropologist) and Naomi Tolkowsky (Nir)Patai; married William H. Wing (a physicist), June 10, 1967; children: Benjamin, Jessica. *Education:* Cornell University, B.S., 1963; University of Michigan, M.S., 1964, Ph.D., 1967; University of Arizona, M.D. candidate. *Home:* 2529 Indian Ridge Dr., Tucson, Ariz. 85715. *Office:* College of Medicine, University of Arizona, Tucson, Ariz. 85724.

CAREER: University of Michigan, Ann Arbor, research associate in human genetics, 1967-68; Yale University, New Haven, Conn., research associate in molecular biophysics and biochemistry, 1968-69; Year Book Medical Publishers, Inc., Chicago, Ill., abstractor, 1968-74. Visiting lecturer at Yale University, 1974. *Member:* American Association for the Advancement of Science, American Society for Microbiology, Phi Kappa Phi, Sigma Xi.

WRITINGS: (With father, Raphael Patai) *The Myth of the Jewish Race,* Scribner, 1975. Contributor to professional journals.

* * *

WINKLESS, Nels(on Brock) III 1934-

PERSONAL: Born July 2, 1934, in Milwaukee, Wis.; son of Nelson Brock, Jr. (an advertising copywriter) and Ethel (Withrow) Winkless; married Madge Harvey, November 23, 1955; children: Chantal, Brock, Danielle, Garth. *Education:* College of San Mateo, A.A., 1954; University of California, Berkeley, B.A., 1956. *Residence:* Albuquerque, N.M. *Agent:* John Brockman Associates, Inc., P.O. Box 376, Planetarium Station, New York, N.Y. 10024.

CAREER: Worked as clown, credit manager, office trainee, film production hand, and industrial film writer and director, 1956-60; Communications Contact, Inc., Mountain View, Calif., president, 1960-69; Thomas Bede Foundation, Albuquerque, N.M., research associate, 1969-75, vice-president, 1975—. Director of Microlens, Inc. and Sydnor-Barent, Inc.; lecturer at colleges and for organizations; consultant to All-Indian Pueblo Council, Beckman Microbics, FilmFair, and Walter Landor Associates.

WRITINGS: (With Iben Browning) *Climate and the Affairs of Men*, Harper's Magazine Press, 1975; (with Browning) *Weather, Weapons, and Wisdom*, Harper's Magazine Press, in press. Contributor to trade journals. Editor of *Southwest Correspondent*. Writer and director of industrial films.

SIDELIGHTS: Winkless writes: "As an industrial film writer/director, I inadvertently got into business for myself and learned more than I wanted to about running tough little companies and developing technical projects to the market. My formal technical background is nil, but you can't depend on me not to know what I'm talking about technically, since I have been responsible for both direct laboratory work and communications in a wide variety of scientific matters—from image dissection optics to artificial intelligence. Better, I have worked with some extraordinarily capable people. My knack is for converting trade and technical gibberish into something an outsider can understand and use."

*   *   *

WINN, Ira Jay 1929-

PERSONAL: Born February 15, 1929, in Boston, Mass.; married Arlene Herkus, June 11, 1966; children: Ian Muir. *Education:* University of Illinois, B.A., 1950, M.A., 1952; Boston University, graduate study, 1950-51; University of California, Los Angeles, Ed.D., 1966. *Home:* 1136 Embury St., Pacific Palisades, Calif. 90272. *Office:* Department of Education, California State University, Northridge, Calif. 91324.

CAREER: High school teacher of American government, sociology, history, geography, and English in Los Angeles, Calif., 1955-63; University of California, Los Angeles, program coordinator for Extension and adult education intern, 1963-65; University of California at San Diego, La Jolla, assistant project director at Peace Corps Training Center, 1966; California State University, Northridge, assistant professor, 1966-69, associate professor, 1969-72, professor of environmental education, urban studies, and social science education, 1972—. Educational travel director, 1959-65; educational planning adviser to U.S. Agency for International Development and Brazilian Ministry of Education and Culture, 1967-70. *Awards, honors:* Senior Fulbright scholar in Germany, 1974.

WRITINGS: *Basic Issues in Environment: Studies in Quiet Desperation*, C. E. Merrill, 1972; *Oiling the California Coast: Analysis of Draft Environmental Impact Statement*, U.S. Department of Interior, 1975. Contributor to *Natural History, International Review of Education, Comparative Education Review, Phi Delta Kappan, Nation, Bulletin of the Atomic Scientists, Journal of Environmental Education*, and *Adult Education*.

WORK IN PROGRESS: *Stirrings in the Wilderness*; "Urban Impact: People and the Land," a slide presentation; *Wilderness Dialogue*.

SIDELIGHTS: Winn told *CA*: "I enjoy working in cross-disciplinary situations, such as environmental studies, and other work for which no typical education or university can ever adequately prepare. The challenge is in new directions, and new worlds of thinking, implementing, reflecting, reposing, being—or not being."

*   *   *

WINTER, David G(arrett) 1939-

PERSONAL: Born March 10, 1939, in Grand Rapids, Mich.; son of Garrett E. (a physician) and Wilhelmena T. (Sprick) Winter; married Abigail J. Stewart (a psychologist), June 1, 1974; children: Nicholas J. G. *Education:* Harvard University, A.B., 1960, Ph.D., 1967; St. John's College, Oxford, B.A., 1962, M.A., 1967. *Office:* Department of Psychology, Wesleyan University, Middletown, Conn. 06457.

CAREER: Wesleyan University, Middletown, Conn., assistant professor, 1967-74, associate professor of psychology, 1974—. *Member:* American Psychological Association. *Awards, honors:* Rhodes scholarship, 1960-62, for study in England; Guggenheim fellowship, 1971-72, for study at University of Amsterdam.

WRITINGS: (With D. C. McClelland) *Motivating Economic Achievement*, Free Press, 1969; (contributor) *The Drinking Man*, Free Press, 1972; *The Power Motive*, Free Press, 1973; (contributor of translation, and author of introduction) Otto Rank, *The Don Juan Legend*, Princeton University Press, 1975. Contributor to *Behavioral Science* and *Journal of Personality*.

WORK IN PROGRESS: *Women and Power*; research on motivation.

*   *   *

WINTERBOTHAM, F(rederick) W(illiam) 1897-

PERSONAL: Born April 16, 1897, at Stroud, Gloucestershire, England; son of Frederick (a lawyer) and Florence (Graham) Winterbotham; married Erica Horniman, July 21, 1921 (divorced, 1938); married Joan Petrea Jowitt, December 17, 1947; children: (first marriage) Pamela (Mrs. K. Winterbotham), Jervis Anthony, Susan (Mrs. G. Forrester); (second marriage) Sally Petrea. *Education:* Christ Church, Oxford, B.A., 1920. *Politics:* Conservative. *Religion:* Church of England. *Home:* Frittiscombe, Chillington, Kingsbridge, South Devon TQ7 2JQ, England.

CAREER: Pedigree stock breeder, 1920-29; British Secret Intelligence Service, London, England, chief of Air Department, 1929-45; British Overseas Airways, director of publicity and public relations, political assistant, and chairman, 1945-48; Colonial Development Corp., director of public relations and liason with British Colonial Office, 1948-52; full-time farmer in Kingsbridge, South Devon, England, 1952—. *Military service:* Royal Gloucestershire Hussars, 1915-16; Royal Flying Corps, later Royal Air Force, fighter pilot, 1916-19; became group captain; received Commander of the British Empire, 1943, Legion of Merit, 1945.

WRITINGS: *Secret and Personal* (nonfiction), Kimber & Co., 1969; *The Ultra Secret* (historical), Harper, 1974.

SIDELIGHTS: Winterbotham has "travelled extensively all over the world and personally known characters like Winston Churchill, Hitler, Eisenhower."

*   *   *

WISNESKI, Henry 1940-

PERSONAL: Born September 26, 1940, in East Orange, N.J.; son of Henry Woodrow and Mary (Courter) Wisneski. *Education:* Ohio University, B.F.A., 1962; New York University, graduate study, 1963-66. *Politics:* Democrat. *Religion:* Protestant. *Residence:* New York, N.Y. *Office:* Library and Museum of the Performing Arts, Lincoln Center, New York, N.Y. 10023.

CAREER: *Athens Messenger*, Athens, Ohio, music reviewer, 1960-62; New York Public Library, New York, N.Y., librarian for Toscanini Memorial Archives, 1963-65, Archives of Recorded Sound, 1965-68, and Music Division, 1968-71, member of staff of Dance Collection in Library and Museum of the Performing Arts, 1971—.

WRITINGS: Maria Callas: The Art Behind the Legend, Doubleday, 1975. Translator of librettos for private recordings: "Cendrillon," by Jules Massenet, "Le Prophete," by Giacomo Meyerbeer, "Euryanthe," by Carl Maria von Weber, "La Donna del Lago," by Gioachhino Rossini, "Parisina d'Este," by Gaetano Donizetti, and "La Straniera," by Vincenzo Bellini.

WORK IN PROGRESS: A history of the New York City Opera Company.

AVOCATIONAL INTERESTS: Ballet, opera, European travel, collecting vocal recordings.

* * *

WODEHOUSE, P(elham) G(renville)   1881-1975

October 15, 1881—February 14, 1975; British-born American humorist, novelist, playwright, columnist, critic, and lyricist. Obituaries: *New York Times* February 15, 1975; *Washington Post*, February 16, 1975; *Detroit News*, February 16, 1975; *Time*, February 24, 1975; *Newsweek*, February 24, 1975; *AB Bookman's Weekly*, March 3, 1975; *Current Biography*, April, 1975. (*CA*-45/48; *CLC*-1,2,5)

* * *

WOEHR, Richard (Arthur)   1942-

PERSONAL: Born May 1, 1942, in Portchester, N.Y.; son of Frank (a teacher) and Marie (O'Keefe) Woehr. *Education:* St. Lawrence University, B.A., 1964; Middlebury College, M.A., 1965; University of Virginia, further graduate study, 1965-66; Stanford University, Ph.D., 1971. *Home:* 2100 Divisadero, San Francisco, Calif. 94115. *Office:* Department of Foreign Languages, California State University, Hayward, Calif.

CAREER: College of Notre Dame, Belmont, Calif., assistant professor of Spanish, 1971-74; California State University, Hayward, assistant professor of Spanish, 1974—. *Member:* American Association of Teachers of Spanish and Portuguese, Philological Association of the Pacific Coast, Seminar for Romance Linguistics.

WRITINGS: (With John Barson and Gustavo Valadez) *Espanol esencial,* Holt, 1974. Contributor to *Hispania* and *Language Sciences.*

WORK IN PROGRESS: Research on the syntax of indirect questions in old Spanish.

SIDELIGHTS: Woehr has traveled in the Yucatan Peninsula, Spain, and Portugal.

* * *

WOLCOTT, Patty   1929-

PERSONAL: Born September 26, 1929, in Lowell, Mass.; daughter of John Gilmore and Priscilla (Clapp) Wolcott; married Raoul Berger (a legal historian), April 22, 1967. *Education:* Wheelock College, B.S. in Ed. (with honors), 1952; Columbia University, M.A., 1963. *Religion:* Unitarian Universalist. *Home:* 140 Jennie Dugan Rd., Concord, Mass. 01742.

CAREER: Teacher in public schools in Arlington Co., Va., 1952-55, and Weston, Mass., 1955-56; Houghton Mifflin Co., Boston, Mass., editor of elementary textbooks,

1956-59; Artists & Writers Press, New York, N.Y., editor of children's trade books, 1960-61; teacher of kindergarten in Nassau, Bahamas, 1961-62, and New York, N.Y., 1963-66; assistant to author, Richard Lewis in New York, N.Y., 1966-67; full-time writer, 1969—. Volunteer teacher of creative writing to children in Dorchester, Mass., 1971. *Member:* Kappa Delta Pi.

WRITINGS—Children's books; all published by Addison-Wesley, except as noted: *The Reef of Coral,* Singer-Random House, 1969; *The Cake Story,* 1974; *The Forest Fire,* 1974; *I'm Going to New York to Visit the Queen,* 1974; *The Marvelous Mud Washing Machine,* 1974; *Where Did That Naughty Little Hamster Go?,* 1974; *Beware of a Very Hungry Fox,* 1975; *My Shadow and I,* 1975; *Pickle Pickle Pickle Juice,* 1975; *Super Sam and the Salad Garden,* 1975; *Tunafish Sandwiches,* 1975.

WORK IN PROGRESS: A Fantasy for children, for Addison-Wesley; a book for parents and teachers on the thoughts and feelings of five-year-olds; a nature story book for children 5-8.

SIDELIGHTS: Patty Wolcott writes: "I wrote the first 'Read-by-Myself' books (Addison-Wesley), because as a teacher, I felt most of the published easy-to-read books had too many words for children at the very beginning of their reading lives, and that a means of exciting the interest of these children was essential. My other writing for children, including *The Reef of Coral* mentioned above, is of a different style. There, I attempt to write a story book with lyrical overtones. My interest in children's books was stimulated by Professor Leland Jacobs at Teachers College, with whom I studied children's literature and writing for children, and became aware of the children's book as an art form."

BIOGRAPHICAL/CRITICAL SOURCES: Saturday Review/World, November 30, 1974; *Reading Teacher,* April, 1975; *Learning,* May/June, 1975.

* * *

WOLF, Barbara Herrman   1932-

PERSONAL: Born April 28, 1932, in Rochester, N.Y.; daughter of Roy F. (a physician) and Estelle (Chappel) Herrman; married Jack C. Wolf (a writer and professor). *Education:* Northwestern University, B.S., 1954; State University of New York College at Brockport, M.A. (with honors), 1969. *Home:* 218 Dartmouth St., Rochester, N.Y. 14607. *Office:* Department of Continuing Education, State University of New York College at Brockport, Brockport, N.Y. 14420.

CAREER: Foreign television correspondent in Africa, Middle East, and elsewhere for United Press-Movietone Television, 1958-62; Wolf Gallery, Rochester, N.Y., co-owner, 1963-67; State University of New York College at Brockport, instructor in creative writing, 1970—.

WRITINGS: (Editor with husband, Jack C. Wolf) *Ghosts, Castles, and Victims,* Fawcett, 1974; (with Jack C. Wolf) *Professional Picture Framing for the Amateur,* TAB Books, 1974; (editor with Jack C. Wolf) *Tales of the Occult,* Fawcett, 1975.

WORK IN PROGRESS: Spacemen: Past, Present, and Future.

SIDELIGHTS: Barbara Wolf writes: "My main interest . . . is in relating the actions of past space-oriented peoples to the actions of our current alien visitors in order to understand what ABC's of space travel our astronauts must learn in order to travel successfully in space. As an adjunct to this, I am interested in psychic matters, but only from a serious, intellectual, and scientific standpoint." *Avocational interests:* Painting (work has been shown in Europe, New York, and North Africa), photography.

*   *   *

WOLF, Frank   1940-

PERSONAL: Born December 24, 1940, in New York, N.Y.; son of Arnold (a merchant) and Martha (Vanderlaan) Wolf; married Susan Sternhell (a sociologist), September 11, 1965; children: Joshua Amiel. *Education:* Williams College, B.A. (magna cum laude), 1962; Worcester College, Oxford, B.A., 1964; Columbia University, Ph.D., 1971. *Politics:* Democrat. *Religion:* Jewish. *Home:* 79 Green Village Rd., Madison, N.J. 07940. *Office:* Department of Political Science, Drew University, Madison, N.J. 07940.

CAREER: Drew University, Madison, N.J., instructor, 1967-71, assistant professor, 1971-75, associate professor of political science, 1975—. *Member:* Phi Beta Kappa.

WRITINGS: Television Programming for News and Public Affairs, Praeger, 1972.

*   *   *

WOLF, Frank L(ouis)   1924-

PERSONAL: Born April 18, 1924, in St. Louis, Mo.; son of Louis (an engineer) and Helen (Below) Wolf; married Joy Gifford (a librarian), August 16, 1947; children: Joan (Mrs. Peter P. Bundy), J. Allison, Barbara, Jon. *Education:* Washington University , St. Louis, Mo., B.S., 1944, M.A., 1948; University of Minnesota, Ph.D., 1955. *Office:* Department of Mathematics, Carleton College, Northfield, Minn. 55057.

CAREER: St. Cloud State College, St. Cloud, Minn., instructor in mathematics, 1949-51; Carleton College, Northfield, Minn., instructor, 1952-55, assistant professor, 1955-60, associate professor, 1960-67, professor of mathematics, 1967—. *Military service:* U.S. Army, 1944-46. *Member:* American Association for the Advancement of Science, American Association of University Professors, Mathematical Association of America, Sigma Xi, Pi Mu Epsilon.

WRITINGS: Elements of Probability and Statistics, McGraw, 1963, 2nd edition, 1974; *Number Systems and Their Uses*, Xerox Educational Publishing, 1971.

*   *   *

WOLF, Harvey   1935-

PERSONAL: Born May 5, 1935, in Detroit, Mich.; son of Nathan (in medical electronics) and Rozalind (Schein) Wolf; married June Shaw, February 2, 1962 (divorced August, 1967); children: David Eliot. *Education:* California State University, Los Angeles, B.S., 1958, graduate study at Florida State University, University of California, Los Angeles, California State University at San Fernando and Long Beach, and Long Beach State College; University of Southern California, M.P.A., 1971, D.P.A., 1975. *Politics:* Radical. *Home:* 1414 Pleasant Valley Rd., Fairmont, W.Va. 26554. *Office:* Public Administration Program, West Virginia University, Morgantown, W.Va. 26506.

CAREER: Lockheed Aircraft Corp., Van Nuys, Calif., design draftsman, 1956-58; North American Aviation, Anaheim, Calif., research engineer in Autonetics Division, 1960-61; Hughes Aircraft Co., Culver City, Calif., manager of advanced programs in space operations and logistics, 1961-65, manager of special programs, 1965-69, manager of administrative systems in Data Systems Division, 1969-71; University of Southern California, Los Angeles, lecturer in public administration, 1972-74; West Virginia University, Morgantown, assistant professor of public administration, 1974—. Consultant to National Institutes of Health, Los Angeles Police Department, and Los Angeles International Airport. *Military service:* U.S. Army, operations research analyst and instructor in mathematics, 1959-60.

MEMBER: World Future Society (member of state executive council, 1974-76), American Society for Public Administration, Volunteers for International Technical Assistance, National Organization for Women, American Civil Liberties Union, Rape Information Service (member of board of directors, 1975—).

WRITINGS: (With Masse Bloomfield) *Man in Transition: A Concept of History,* Mojave Books, 1973; (contributor) Ellen Crowley, editor, *Acronyms and Initialisms Dictionary*, Gale, 3rd edition (Wolf was not associated with earlier editions), 1970, 4th edition, 1973. Author of technical reports. Contributor to *Journal of Comparative Cultures.*

WORK IN PROGRESS: Research on the effects of applied research training on future classroom success, on problems of local government in a megalopolis, on legal aid to the poor in civil matters, on the correlation between specific and general consciousness raising, and on the legal/consitutional basis for county governments (a national survey).

SIDELIGHTS: Wolf has patents for connectors held by Hughes Aircraft Co., and for "The City," a game designed to aid in the teaching of urban finance. He writes: "I am concerned with the stagnation and strangulation our organizational forms are creating for the people in the organization and the country. It is my hope to help develop change agents who will effectively destroy the existing organizational forms and replace them with open people-oriented forms. . . . I believe in evolutionary anarchy." *Avocational interests:* Tennis, racket ball, bicycling, science fiction, rare books, backpacking, classical music, live theater.

*   *   *

WOLF, Jack C(lifford)   1922-

PERSONAL: Born May 25, 1922, in Omaha, Neb.; son of Adolph H. and Regina I. (Smith) Wolf; married Barbara Herrman (a writer). *Education:* University of Nebraska at Omaha, student, 1940-43; Creighton University, B.S., 1947; graduate study at University of Grenoble, 1949-50, University of Vienna, 1950, and University of Florence, 1951; State University of New York College at Brockport, M.A. (with honors), 1969; State University of New York at Buffalo, Ph.D., 1972. *Home:* 218 Dartmouth St., Rochester, N.Y. 14607. *Office:* Department of English, State University of New York College at Brockport, Brockport, N.Y.

CAREER: Has held positions as administrative assistant with United States Information Agency, Vienna, Austria; American director for Austrian national radio network; foreign television correspondent for United Press-Movietone Television in Africa and Middle East; currently associate professor of English at State University of New York College at Brockport. Owner of Wolf Art Gallery, Rochester, N.Y., 1963-67; documentary film photographer in Spain and Morocco. *Military service:* U.S. Army, 1943-46. *Member:* Modern Language Association of America.

WRITINGS: *Death Rides a Camel* (novel), Hammond, 1960; *Two Shadows for Death* (novel), Hammond, 1961; *Payoff on Fever Street*, Hammond, 1962; (editor with Gregory Fitz Gerald) *Past, Present and Future Perfect: A Text Anthology of Speculative and Science Fiction*, Fawcett, 1973; (with wife, Barbara H. Wolf) *Ghosts, Castles and Victims: Studies in Gothic Terror*, Fawcett, 1974; (with Barbara H. Wolf) *Professional Picture Framing for the Amateur*, TAB Books, 1974; (with Barbara H. Wolf) *Tales of the Occult*, Fawcett, 1975. Also author of *Hart Crane's Harp of Evil: Orphism in "The Bridge"* and *A Moon for Icarus* (poems). Associate editor, *Modern Language Studies*, 1972-74.

*   *   *

WOLFE, Gene (Rodman) 1931-

PERSONAL: Born May 7, 1931, in Brooklyn, N.Y.; son of Roy Emerson (a salesman) and Mary Olivia (Ayers) Wolfe; married Rosemary Frances Dietsch, November 3, 1956; children: Roy II, Madeleine, Therese, Matthew. *Education:* Attended Texas A & M University, 1949, 1952; University of Houston, B.S.M.E., 1956. *Religion:* Roman Catholic. *Home address:* Box 69, Barrington, Ill. 60010. *Agent:* Virginia Kidd, Box 278, Milford, Pa. 18337.

CAREER: Project engineer with Procter & Gamble, 1956-72; *Plant Engineering* (magazine), Barrington, Ill., senior editor, 1972—. *Military service:* U.S. Army, 1952-54. *Member:* American Institute of Plant Engineers, American Society of Business Press Editors. *Awards, honors:* Nebula Award from Science Fiction Writers of America, 1973, for "The Death of Doctor Island."

WRITINGS: *Operation Ares* (novel), Berkley Publishing, 1970; *The Fifth Head of Cerberus*, Scribner, 1972; *Peace* (novel), Harper, 1975. Work represented in anthologies, including *Best SF: 70*, edited by Harry Harrison and Brian Aldiss, Putnam, 1970; *Nebula Award Stories 9*, edited by Kate Wilhelm, Harper, 1974; *The Best SF of the Year #3*, edited by Terry Carr, Ballantine, 1974; *Best SF: 73*, edited by Harrison and Aldiss, Berkley Publishing/Putnam, 1974. Contributor of short stories to science fiction magazines.

WORK IN PROGRESS: *The Feast of St. Catherine*, a novel.

*   *   *

WOLFF, Jurgen M(ichael) 1948-

PERSONAL: Born April 18, 1948, in Berlin, Germany; son of Erich Otto (a machinist) and Elizabeth (Seydel) Wolff. *Education:* Stanford University, B.A., 1970; California State University, San Francisco (now San Francisco State University), M.A., 1973. *Office address:* P.O. Box 3481, Stanford, Calif. 94305.

CAREER: American Airlines, Tulsa, Okla., public relations representative, 1968-69; American Institutes for Research, Palo Alto, Calif., associate communications specialist, 1970—, audio-visual consultant, 1973-75; Learning Achievement Corp., San Jose, Calif., scriptwriter and story editor for "We the People . . . Read," a television series, 1973-75. *Member:* National Writers Club.

WRITINGS: (With G. B. Jones and others) *Developing Career Guidance Programs*, Educational Properties, Inc., 1974; (with Dewey Lipe) *Slimmanship*, Nelson-Hall, 1975. Contributor to *Gent* and *Entertainer*, and to newspapers.

WORK IN PROGRESS: *The Sixteen Ounce Pint*, a short comic novel; *How Come You're So Fat, Kid?*, a book on weight reduction for parents and children; "New Teacher," a suspense feature film.

SIDELIGHTS: Wolff writes: "My goal is to write in a manner which would do justice to contemporary writers I admire the most. This would require fusing the clarity of thinking and writing of Bertrand Russell, the sense of humor of Kingsley Amis, and the plotting and characterization skills of Graham Greene. Check back with me in twenty years."

*   *   *

WOLSCH, Robert Allen 1925-

PERSONAL: Born November 27, 1925, in New York, N.Y.; son of William (a salesman) and Helen (Mackta) Wolsch; married Lois Ann Cothran (a speech teacher), December 21, 1957; children: William, Jordan, Lisa. *Education:* New York University, B.A., 1949; Columbia University, M.A., 1954, professional diploma, 1956, Ed.D., 1969. *Religion:* "Jewnitarian." *Home:* 19 Homestead Ave., Danbury, Conn. 06810. *Office:* Department of Speech and Theater, Western Connecticut State College, Danbury, Conn. 06814.

CAREER: Krebs Stengel & Co., New York, N.Y., salesman, 1949-55; speech therapist in public schools in Mineola, N.Y., 1955-62, language arts consultant, 1962-67; Urban Job Corps, Brooklyn, N.Y., director of curriculum for TRY Project, 1967; Long Island University, C.W. Post College, Greenvale, N.Y., assistant professor of speech, 1967-69; Western Connecticut State College, Danbury, associate professor, 1969-72, professor of speech and education, 1972—, chairman of department of speech and theater. Director of Speech Associates; member of Young Men's Philanthropic League, 1952-55; chairman of Danbury Cultural Commission, 1974—. *Military service:* U.S. Navy, pharmacist's mate, 1944-46.

MEMBER: American Speech and Hearing Association, National Council of Teachers of English, Speech Communication Association of America, Association for Supervision and Curriculum Development, Connecticut Education Association (president of campus chapter, 1974), Long Island Speech Association (president, 1958).

WRITINGS: *Poetic Composition in the Elementary School: A Handbook for Teachers*, Teachers College Press, 1969; *Poetic Composition through the Grades: A Language Sensitivity Program*, Teachers College Press, 1970. Contributor to *Today's Speech* and *Connecticut Teacher*.

WORK IN PROGRESS: *The Need for a Mobile People's Retirement System*; *Speech Teachers and the Language Arts Program: For Schools of the Future*; *Cooperative Curriculum Development: A Bargain for the Taxpayer*; *The Tragedy of the Reading-Language Arts Program*; *Communication Arts at Western Connecticut State College: A First in Teacher Education*.

SIDELIGHTS: Wolsch writes: "Teachers must hear the sweetness of their own speech and the speech of children before they can help children develop effective listening, speaking, writing, and reading skills. This is too important to be left only to reading teachers.

"I'm struck by the effects of chauvanistic retirement systems on the people of this country. There must be new ways for people to move around and learn and bring new ideas to their new jobs. When people want to grow, they find they lose. Only the people who stay in one place are the winners. There is a terrible loss of freedom here, and we all share the loss in different ways.''

* * *

WOOD, Bruce 1943-

PERSONAL: Born April 22, 1943, in England; son of Leslie A. and Constance (Brew) Wood; married Helen Judith Collinge, September 2, 1967; children: Robert, Eleanor. *Education:* London School of Economics and Political Science, B.Sc., 1964. *Religion:* Anglican. *Home:* 104 Manchester Rd., Bury, Lancashire BL9 0TH, England. *Office:* Department of Government, University of Manchester, Manchester M13 9PL, England.

CAREER: Royal Commission on Local Government in England, Whitehall, London, England, research officer, 1966-68; University of Manchester, Manchester, England, lecturer in government, 1968—.

WRITINGS: (With John P. R., Lord Redcliffe-Maud) *English Local Government Reformed*, Oxford University Press, 1974; (with J. M. Lee) *The Scope of Local Initiative: A Study of Cheshire County Council, 1961-74*, Martin Robertson, 1974; *The Process of Local Government Reform: 1966-74*, Allen & Unwin, in press. Contributor to *Public Administration* and *Political Quarterly.*

AVOCATIONAL INTERESTS: Sports fan, beer-drinker.

* * *

WOOD, James 1889(?)-1975

1889(?)—May 25, 1975; British painter and author. Obituaries: *AB Bookman's Weekly*, August 11-18, 1975.

* * *

WOOD, James L(eslie) 1941-

PERSONAL: Born August 30, 1941, in Oakland, Calif.; son of James L. (a physician) and Maxine E. Wood; married Patricia A. Taylor (a health information director), June 13, 1964; children: Ann M., Jeffrey J. *Education:* University of California, Berkeley, B.A., 1963, M.A. 1966, Ph.D., 1973; also studied at Hastings College of Law, 1963-64. *Residence:* Riverside, Calif. *Office:* Department of Sociology, University of California, Riverside, Calif. 92502.

CAREER: Holy Names College, Oakland, Calif., instructor in sociology, 1971-73; University of California, Riverside, lecturer in sociology, 1973—. Assistant professor of sociology, California State University, San Francisco, summer, 1972. *Member:* American Sociological Association, Pacific Sociological Association.

WRITINGS: (With Willie Thompson) *A Handbook for Block Clubs*, Bay Area Urban Extension, University of California, 1967; *The Sources of American Student Activism*, Lexington-Heath, 1974; *Political Consciousness and Student Activism,* Sage Publications, 1974; *New Left Ideology: Its Dimensions and Development*, Sage Publications, in press; (contributor) David W. Swift, editor, *American Education: A Sociological Survey*, Houghton, in press; (contributor) Alex Inkeles, editor, *Annual Review of Sociology,* Annual Reviews, Inc., in press. Contributor to *Berkeley Journal of Sociology: A Critical Review* and *Human Organization.* Co-editor of *Berkeley Journal of Sociology,* 1969.

WORK IN PROGRESS: Editing *The Politics of the New Working Class.*

BIOGRAPHICAL/CRITICAL SOURCES: Kenneth Keniston, *Radicals and Militants: An Annotated Bibliography of Empirical Research on Campus Unrest*, Lexington-Heath, 1973.

* * *

WOOD, Laura N.
    See ROPER, Laura Wood

* * *

WOOD, Robert S(tephen) 1938-

PERSONAL: Born December 25, 1938, in Idaho Falls, Idaho; son of John Albert (a funeral director) and Blance P. (Jenkins) Wood; married Dixie Leigh Jones, March 30, 1961; children: Jennifer, Rebecca, Amanda. *Education:* Stanford University, B.A., 1961; Harvard University, A.M., 1964, Ph.D., 1968. *Politics:* Independent. *Religion:* Church of Jesus Christ of Latter-day Saints. *Home:* 89 Georgetown Green, Charlottesville, Va. 22901. *Office:* Department of Government, University of Virginia, Charlottesville, Va. 22901.

CAREER: Bentley College, Waltham, Mass., assistant professor of international politics and government, 1965-67; University of Virginia, Charlottesville, assistant professor, 1967-70, associate professor of international politics and government, 1970—. Visiting associate professor, Brigham Young University, summer, 1969; Fulbright visiting professor, Groningen University, 1972; lecturer, University of Tilburg, 1972. Bishop, Church of Jesus Christ of Latter-day Saints. Consultant, John F. Kennedy Institute, Center for International Affairs (University of Tilburg), Netherlands Institute for International Affairs, 1971-72, and Federal Executive Institute. Member of board of directors, Boy Scouts of America. *Member:* International Studies Association, American Political Science Association, Southern Political Science Association, Phi Beta Kappa. *Awards, honors:* Woodrow Wilson fellow, 1961-62; Danforth fellow, 1961-67; American Philosophical Society residence grant, 1971-72.

WRITINGS: The Process of International Organization, Random House, 1971; *France in the World Community*, A. W. Sijthoff, 1973. Contributor of articles to journals in his field, including *American Political Science Review, World Affairs, International Organization*, and *Journal of International Law.*

WORK IN PROGRESS: A book, *Anarchy and Community.*

* * *

WOODBURY, Mildred Fairchild 1894-1975

April 30, 1894—February 9, 1975; American labor economist, social worker, educator, and author of books in her field. Obituaries: *Washington Post*, February 12, 1975; *New York Times*, February 12, 1975.

* * *

WOODFORD, Bruce P(owers) 1919-

PERSONAL: Born September 22, 1919, in Astoria, Ore.; son of Edwin S. and Alice M. (Powers) Woodford; married Xanta Grisogono, November 19, 1955. *Education:* Oregon State College, student, 1938-39; University of Denver, B.A., 1948, M.A., 1949, Ph.D., 1958. *Home:* 140 Mesa Vista, Sante Fe, N.M. 87501. *Office:* Department of English, Purdue University, Lafayette, Ind.

CAREER: University of Colorado, Denver, extension instructor in English, 1949-53; University of Denver, Denver, Colo., assistant director of workshop for writers, 1951-52, editorial assistant of University of Denver Press, 1951-52, librarian, 1954-55; University of Idaho, Moscow, instructor in English, 1955-58; Purdue University, Lafayette, Ind., instructor, 1958-59, assistant professor, 1959-65, associate professor of English, 1965—. *Military service:* U.S. Army, 1942-44; became first lieutenant. *Member:* Modern Language Association of America, American Association of University Professors, American Council of Learned Societies, American Forestry Association, National Wildlife Federation, American Museum of Natural History, Phi Beta Kappa.

WRITINGS: Twenty-One Poems and a Play, Swallow Press, 1958; (self-illustrated) *Love and Other Weathers* (poems), Eastgate Press, 1966; (with A. L. Lazarus, Mills, and Stephanile) *A Suit of Four* (poems), Purdue University Studies, 1973. Contributor of more than sixty short stories and poems to literary magazines, including *Quartet, Talisman, Western Humanities Review, Bitterroot, Nova Media, Sparrow, Renaissance, the goodly co., Encore, South and West*, and *Purdue Miscellany*. Poetry editor of *Quartet*, 1963-70.

WORK IN PROGRESS: A collection of poems on the New Mexico Southwest, *The Adobe Makers*.

AVOCATIONAL INTERESTS: The arts, including crafting furniture and wrought iron, illustrative drawing, lino cuts, wire sculpture.

*   *   *

WOODS, John (Hayden) 1937-

PERSONAL: Born March 16, 1937, in Barrie, Ontario, Canada; son of John Frederick and Gertrude (Hayden) Woods; married Carol Arnold (an educator), June 13, 1957; children: Catherine, Kelly, Michael. *Education:* University of Toronto, B.A., 1958, M.A., 1959; University of Michigan, Ph.D., 1965. *Politics:* "Red Tory." *Religion:* "Retired Catholic." *Home:* 1737 Rockland Ave., Victoria, British Columbia, Canada V8S 1W6. *Office:* Division of Humanities, University of Victoria, Victoria, British Columbia V8W 2Y2, Canada.

CAREER: University of Michigan, Ann Arbor, instructor in philosophy, 1961-62; University of Toronto, Toronto, Ontario, lecturer, 1962-64, assistant professor, 1964-66, associate professor of linguistic studies, 1966-71, associate professor of philosophy, 1966-71; University of Victoria, Victoria, British Columbia, associate professor, 1971-72, professor of philosophy, 1972—, acting chairman of department, 1974-75, associate dean of arts and sciences and dean of humanities, 1975—. Assistant professor at University of Calgary, summer, 1965; associate professor at University of Michigan, summer, 1967; visiting professor at Stanford University, summer, 1971.

MEMBER: Canadian Philosophical Association, Association for Symbolic Logic, Philosophy of Science Association, American Philosophical Association (member of executive committee, 1971-74), Society for Exact Philosophy, Phi Beta Kappa. *Awards, honors:* Canada Council research grants, for research on quantified modal logic at Stanford University, 1968-69, for research on the identity relation at Stanford University, 1971—; named visiting scholar at Stanford University, 1968-69.

WRITINGS: (Editor with L. W. Sumner) *Necessary Truth*, Random House, 1969; (contributor) M. K. Munitz, editor, *Identity and Individuation*, New York University Press, 1971; (contributor) R. S. Peters, editor, *The Philosophy of Education*, Oxford University Press, 1974; *Logic of Fiction: A Philosophical Sounding of Deviant Logics*, Mouton & Co., 1974; *Proof and Truth: Mathematical Logic for Non-Mathematicians*, Peter Martin Associates, 1974. Contributor of about thirty articles to philosophy and language journals. Co-editor of *Proceedings of the Victorial Conference in Formal Ontology*, 1974; editor of *Dialogue: Canadian Philosophical Review*, 1974—.

WORK IN PROGRESS: Identity and Modality, a monograph; research toward a theory of argument, on the relevance of relevant logic, and on the fallacies and informal logic.

SIDELIGHTS: Woods writes: "I have long deplored the Canadian characteristic of cultural self-abasement. Determined that something should be done about it, I have taken the not entirely modest corrective of resisting the temptation and opportunity to be Elsewhere. . . . It is no longer true that the best Canadians are expatriate Canadians, and there is now some reason to think that writers in this country can regularly find their way into print without the corporate intervention of New York, London, Bombay, Caracas, or Tierra del Fuego. Still, Canadians must not exchange vapidity for jingoism. There is precious little gain in being insufferable."

*   *   *

WORELL, Judith 1928-

PERSONAL: Born May 9, 1928, in New York, N.Y.; daughter of Moses and Dorothy Goldfarb; divorced; children: Amy Beth, Beth Ann, Wendy Ellen. *Education:* Queens College (now Queens College of the City University of New York), B.A. (magna cum laude), 1950; Ohio State University, M.A., 1952, Ph.D., 1954. *Home:* 1243 Cross Keys Rd., Lexington, Ky. 40504. *Office:* Department of Educational Psychology and Counseling, College of Education, University of Kentucky, Lexington, Ky. 40506.

CAREER: Oklahoma State University, Stillwater, assistant professor of education, 1960-63; Payne County Mental Health Center, Stillwater, Okla., consultant, 1963; National Defense Education Act Counselor Training Institute, Stillwater, Okla., assistant professor of education, 1963-64; Oklahoma State University, research associate in education, 1964-66; University of Kentucky, Lexington, research associate in psychology, 1966-68, assistant professor, 1968-71, associate professor of educational psychology, 1971—. *Awards, honors:* Elected outstanding woman on University of Kentucky Campus, 1975.

MEMBER: American Association of University Professors, American Women in Psychology, Southeastern Psychological Association, Kentucky Psychological Association, Phi Beta Kappa.

WRITINGS: (With C. M. Nelson) *Managing Instructional Problems*, McGraw, 1974. Contributor to psychology journals. Consulting editor of *Journal of Consulting and Clinical Psychology*.

WORK IN PROGRESS: A book on educational psychology, for McGraw; research on resistance to temptation in children and development of self-control in children; studying the relationship between parent behavior and self-control in children.

SIDELIGHTS: Judith Worell has a particular interest in the psychology of women. She is active in women's liberation activities and women's centers.

*   *   *

WORSTER, Donald E(ugene) 1941-

PERSONAL: Born November 14, 1941, in Needles, Calif.; son of Winfred D. (a bookkeeper) and Bonnie (Ball) Worster; married Beverly Marshall, 1964; children: William Thomas, Catherine Anne. *Education:* University of Kansas, B.A., 1963, M.A., 1964; Yale University, M.Phil., 1970, Ph.D., 1971. *Office:* Department of American Studies, University of Hawaii, 1890 East-West Rd., Honolulu, Hawaii 96822.

CAREER: University of Maine, Orono, instructor in speech and drama, 1964-66; Brandeis University, Waltham, Mass., assistant professor of American studies, 1971-74; University of Hawaii, Honolulu, associate professor of American studies, 1975—. *Member:* American Studies Association, Forest History Society, National Audubon Society, Friends of the Earth, Wilderness Society, Defenders of Wildlife, Western History Association, Sierra Club. *Awards, honors:* Mellon fellow at Aspen Institute for Humanistic Studies, summer, 1974; National Endowment for the Humanities fellowship, 1974-75.

WRITINGS: (Editor) *American Environmentalism: The Formative Period, 1860-1915*, Wiley, 1973.

WORK IN PROGRESS: Nature's Economy: The Roots of Anglo-American Ecological Thought, completion expected in 1975; *Hawaii: An Environmental History.*

SIDELIGHTS: Worster told *CA:* "I am interested in finding ways for myself, family, and others to live on this fragile planet with the least impact, the fullest humanity, and the greatest amount of personal freedom compatible with ecological integrity."

*   *   *

WORTLEY, Ben Atkinson 1907-

PERSONAL: Born November 16, 1907, in Huddersfield, Yorkshire, England; son of John Edward and Mary Cicely (King) Wortley; married Kathleen Mary Prynne, 1935; children: two sons, one daughter. *Education:* University of Leeds, LLB (first class honors), 1928, LLM, 1934. *Home:* 24 Gravel Lane, Wilmslow, Cheshire, England. *Office:* Royal Exchange Bldg., Manchester, 2 Pump Ct., London EC4, England.

CAREER: Solicitor, 1929-46; became barrister, Gray's Inn, 1947; University of London, London School of Economics and Political Science, London, England, assistant in law, 1931-33; University of Manchester, Manchester, England, lecturer in law, 1933-34; University of Birmingham, Birmingham, England, reader in law, 1934-36; University of Manchester, reader in law, 1936-46, professor of jurisprudence and international law, 1946-75. Served in Ministry of Home Security, 1939-43, representative of HM Government at international conferences at Hague, 1951, 1956, 1960, 1964, and at New York, 1955, 1958, sometime member of Lord Chancellor's Committee on Conflict of Laws. Member of board of directors, British Yearbook of International Law, 1946—, Institute for Advanced Legal Studies, 1947—, and International Institute for Unification of Private Law, 1948; visiting professor, Tulane University, 1959. *Military service:* Royal Navy, 1943-46.

MEMBER: Society of Public Teachers of Law (president, 1964-65), Royal Netherlands Academy, Institut de droit international, Hellenic Institute for International and Foreign Law (corresponding member), Belgium Society for Comparative Law (corresponding member), Athenaeum Club (London). *Awards, honors:* LL.D. from University of Manchester, 1940; officer of the Order of the British Empire, 1946; Honorary Docteur from University of Rennes, 1955, University of Strasbourg, 1965; Commendatore (Italy), 1961; named Queen's Counsel, 1969; Hon. D.C.L., University of Durham, 1975.

WRITINGS: Problemes souleves en droit international prive par le legislation sur l'expropriation (title means "Problems Raised in Private International Law by Laws on Expropriation"), Academy of International Law (Hague), 1940; (with Rene David and H. C. Gutteridge) *Introduction a l'etude du droit prive de l'Angleterre* (title means "Introduction to the Study of English Private Law"), Recueil Sirey (Paris), 1948; *The General Principles of Private International Law from the English Standpoint*, Academy of International Law, 1948; *The Interaction of Public and Private International Law Today*, Academy of International Law, 1954; (editor) *The United Nations: The First Ten Years*, Oceana, 1957; *Expropriation in Public International Law*, Cambridge University Press, 1959; *The General Principles of Private International Law*, Academy of International Law, 1959; (editor) Richard O'Sullivan, *The Spirit of the Common Law*, Fowler Wright Books, 1965; *Jurisprudence*, Oceana, 1967; *Les Conditions juridiques des investissements* (title means "Legal Conditions for Investments"), Tribune de Geneve, 1967; (editor) *An Introduction to the Law of the European Economic Community*, Oceana, 1972; (editor) *The Law and the European Economic Community*, University of Manchester Press, 1974.

WORK IN PROGRESS: Contributing articles on international law and legal theory to various festschriften.

*   *   *

WORTON, Stanley N(elson) 1923-

PERSONAL: Born May 27, 1923, in New York, N.Y.; son of Morris L. (a physician) and Estelle (a teacher; maiden name, Levinson) Worton; married Deena L. Cowen (a nursery school head teacher), December 21, 1946; children: Kenneth M., David R. *Education:* New York University, A.B., 1943; University of Bristol, graduate study, 1945; Columbia University, M.A., 1947, Ph.D., 1954. *Politics:* Democrat. *Home:* 22 Cresthill Ave., Clifton, N.J. 07012. *Office:* Department of History, Jersey City State College, Jersey City, N.J. 07305.

CAREER: High school teacher of social studies in New York, N.Y., 1946-50; Columbia University, Teachers College, New York, N.Y., instructor in social sciences, 1950-51; Jersey City State College, Jersey City, N.J., assistant professor, 1951-58, associate professor of social sciences, 1958-63, professor of history, 1963—. Research associate, Regional Planning Association, 1962, 1964, and Rutgers University Urban Studies Center, 1966-68; commissioner of board of trustees, Passaic County Community College, 1971-74; member of school and local history committee of New Jersey Historical Commission, 1973—; member of Hudson County (N.J.) Bicentennial Commission, 1974—; visiting professor, Fairleigh Dickinson University, 1957, Newark State College, 1957-62, University of the Pacific, 1963, and Paterson State College, 1968. *Military service:* U.S. Army, 1943-46. *Member:* American Historical Association, National Council for the Social Studies, American Association of University Professors (chapter president, 1964-66).

WRITINGS: (With others) *New Jersey: Past & Present*, Hayden, 1964; *The Major Works of John Dewey*, Monarch, 1964; *American History*, Monarch, Volume I: *To 1865* and Volume II: *From 1865*, both published in 1965; *Leading Cases of the Constitution*, Monarch, 1966; *The First Americans*, Hayden, 1974; *Freedom of Speech and Press*, Hayden, 1975; *Freedom of Religion*, Hayden, 1975; *Freedom of Assembly and Petition*, Hayden, 1975; *Population*, Hayden, in press.

WORK IN PROGRESS: Law Enforcement and Justice; a teachers' guide on New Jersey's "revolutionary experience" for New Jersey Historical Commission.

AVOCATIONAL INTERESTS: Tennis and bridge.

* * *

WRAGG, E(dward) C(onrad) 1938-

PERSONAL: Born June 26, 1938, in Sheffield, England; son of George William (a florist) and Maria (Brandstetter) Wragg; married Judith King, December 29, 1960; children: Josephine, Caroline, Christopher. *Education:* University of Durham, B.A. (first class honors), 1959, diploma in education, 1960; University of Leicester, M.Ed., 1967; University of Exeter, Ph.D., 1972. *Office:* School of Education, University of Nottingham, Nottingham NG7 2RD, England.

CAREER: Teacher in grammar school in Wakefield, England, 1960-63; teacher of German and head of department in boys' school in Leicester, England, 1964-66; University of Exeter, Exeter, England, lecturer in education, 1966-73; University of Nottingham, Nottingham, England, professor of education, 1973—. *Member:* British Educational Research Association.

WRITINGS: (Author of adaptation) Wolfgang Ecke, *Krimis*, Longmans, 1967; *Life in Germany*, Longmans, 1968; *Teaching Teaching*, David & Charles, 1974; *Classroom Interaction*, Open University, 1975; *Teaching Mixed Ability Groups*, David & Charles, 1975. Editor of teaching series for David & Charles. Contributor to language, education, and medical journals.

WORK IN PROGRESS: Research on teacher education and classroom interaction.

AVOCATIONAL INTERESTS: Travel, reading, sport.

* * *

WRIGHT, H(arry) Norman 1937-

PERSONAL: Born July 25, 1937, in Hollywood, Calif.; son of Harry N. (a salesman) and Amelia (Cornelius) Wright; married Joycelin Archinal, August 22, 1959; children: Sheryl, Matthew. *Education:* Westmont College, B.A., 1959; Fuller Seminary, M.R.E., 1961; Pepperdine University, M.A., 1965. *Religion:* Christian. *Residence:* Long Beach, Calif. *Office:* Biola College, 13800 Biola Ave., La Mirada, Calif. 90639.

CAREER: Licensed marriage and family counselor; Biola College, La Mirada, Calif., professor in marriage and family counseling, 1965—. Christian education consultant, Gospel Light Publications, 1963—. *Member:* National Alliance for Family Life, California Association of Marriage counselors.

WRITINGS: Help! I'm a Camp Counselor, Regal Books, 1967; *Ways to Help Them Learn: Adults*, Regal Books, 1972; *Communication: Key to Your Marriage*, Regal Books, 1974; *The Christian Use of Emotional Power*, Revell, 1974; *The Living Marriage*, Revell, 1975. Contributor to religious publications and to journals in his field.

* * *

WRIGHT, J(ohn) Stafford 1905-

PERSONAL: Born February 15, 1905, in Matlock, Derbyshire, England; son of Walter Herbert (a country gentleman) and Grace (Jackson) Wright; married Sylvia Beatrice Mary Lewis, July 22, 1931; children: Richard Vernon Stafford, Christopher Stafford, John Robert Stafford, Paul Stafford. *Education:* Sidney Sussex College, Cambridge, M.A., 1927. *Politics:* Conservative. *Home:* 14 Byron Pl., Bristol BS8 1JT, England.

CAREER: Ordained clergyman of Church of England, 1928; Tyndale Hall, Bristol, England, tutor, 1930-45, vice-principal, 1930-45; Oak Hill College, London, England, tutor, 1945-51; Tyndale Hall, principal, 1951-69. *Member:* Society for Psychical Research, Victoria Institute, Lundy Field Society. *Awards, honors:* Honorary canon of Bristol Cathedral, 1967—.

WRITINGS: (With W. S. Hooton) *The First Twenty-Five Years of the Bible Churchmen's Missionary Society*, Bible Churchmen's Missionary Society, 1947; *What Is Man?*, Paternoster Press, 1955, revised edition published as *Mind, Man, and the Spirits*, Zondervan, 1971; (with Oswald Sanders) *Some Modern Religions*, Tyndale Press, 1956; (contributor) C. A. Joyce, editor, *My Call to the Ministry*, Marshall, Morgan & Scott, 1968; *Christianity and the Occult*, Scripture Union, 1972; (with Maurice Burrell) *Some Modern Faiths*, Tyndale Press, 1974. Author of monographs on the Old Testament, Zen, and spiritualism. Contributor to *Bible Dictionary* and *Bible Commentaries*.

WORK IN PROGRESS: Who's Who in the Bible.

AVOCATIONAL INTERESTS: Trivia, serendipity, photography.

BIOGRAPHICAL/CRITICAL SOURCES: C. A. Joyce, editor, *My Call to the Ministry*, Marshall, Morgan & Scott, 1968.

* * *

WRIGHT, Muriel H(azel) 1889-1975

1889—February 27, 1975; American historian, author, and editor. Obituaries: *New York Times*, March 1, 1975; *Washington Post*, March 1, 1975.

* * *

WRONE, David R(ogers) 1933-

PERSONAL: Born May 15, 1933, in Clinton, Ill.; son of Harold (a merchant) and Esther (a teacher; maiden name, Matthews) Wrone; married Elaine Ethel Alley (a lecturer in sociology), August 25, 1964; children: Elizabeth Maliha, David Alley. *Education:* University of Illinois, B.A., 1959, M.A., 1960, Ph.D., 1964. *Home address:* Route 5, Box 464, Stevens Point, Wis. 54481. *Office:* Department of History, University of Wisconsin, Stevens Point, Wis. 54481.

CAREER: University of Wisconsin, Stevens Point, assistant professor, 1964-68, associate professor of history, 1968—. *Military service:* U.S. Army, 1954-55. *Member:* American Historical Association, Organization of American Historians, Society of American Hegelians, State Historical Society of Wisconsin, Illinois Historical Society, Illinois Labor Historical Society.

WRITINGS: (Contributor) Clyde C. Walton, editor, *An Illinois Reader,* Northern Illinois University Press, 1970; (editor with Russell S. Nelson, Jr.) *Who's the Savage?: A Documentary History of the Mistreatment of the Native North Americans,* Fawcett, 1973; *The Assassination of John Fitzgerald Kennedy: An Annotated Bibliography,* State Historical Society of Wisconsin, 1973.

Contributor to *Journal of Ethnic Studies, Journalism Quarterly, Journal of the Illinois State Historical Society, Wisconsin Magazine of History, Illinois Libraries,* and *Civil War Times Illustrated.*

WORK IN PROGRESS: A book of essays on war and peace; a book on the history of objective idealism.

*   *   *

WYCKOFF, D(onald) Daryl   1936-

PERSONAL: Born April 28, 1936, in Santa Monica, Calif.; son of Donald K. (a businessman) and Gladys (Hammer) Wyckoff; married Valerie Abdou, August 30, 1958; children: Michele, Abigail. *Education:* Massachusetts Institute of Technology, B.S., 1958; University of Southern California, M.B.A., 1968; Harvard University, D.B.A., 1972. *Office:* Graduate School of Business Administration, Harvard University, Boston, Mass. 02163.

CAREER: Cosmodyne Corp., Torrance, Calif., vice-president, 1959-68; Logistics Systems, Inc., Cambridge, Mass., director, 1969-70; Harvard University, Cambridge, Mass., lecturer, 1972-75, associate professor of business administration, 1975—. Member of board of directors of Victoria Station, Inc. and Lex Transport. *Member:* Transportation Research Forum (vice-president).

WRITINGS: Organizational Formality and Performance in the Motor Carrier Industry, Heath, 1974; (with D. H. Maister) *Owner Operator: Independent Trucker,* Heath, 1975; (with Paul W. Marshall and others) *Operations Management: Text and Cases,* Irwin, 1975.

WORK IN PROGRESS: Railroad Management; Turn Around Management; Transporation Management in the Middle East.

*   *   *

WYNKOOP, Mildred Bangs   1905-

PERSONAL: Surname is pronounced *Wine*-coop; born September 9, 1905, in Seattle, Wash.; daughter of Carl Oliver (a builder) and Mery (Dupertius) Bangs; married Ralph Carl Wynkoop (a clergyman), December 27, 1928. *Education:* Pasadena Nazarene College, A.B., 1931; Western Evangelical Seminary, M.Div., 1948; University of Oregon, M.S., 1952; Northern Baptist Theological Seminary, Th.D., 1955. *Religion:* Protestant. *Residence:* Nashville, Tenn. *Office:* Department of Missiology and Human Services, Trevecca Nazarene College, 333 Murphreesboro, Nashville, Tenn. 37210.

CAREER: Ordained minister in Church of the Nazarene, 1934; minister of churches in Los Angeles, Calif., 1930-34, Coos Bay, Ore., 1934-38, and Portland, Ore., 1944-60; Western Theological Seminary, Portland, Ore., professor of theology, 1955-60, chairman of religion department, 1955-60; Western Evangelical Seminary, Portland, Ore., dean and professor, 1960-62; Japan Nazarene Seminary, Chiba, Japan, president, 1962-66; Trevecca Nazarene Col-

lege, Nashville, Tenn., professor of religion and philosophy, 1966-67, chairman of department of religion and philosophy, 1967-70, chairman of department of missiology and human services, 1970-74. *MEMBER:* International Society for Mission Studies, American Society of Missiology, Society of Biblical Literature, American Society of Church History, American Catholic Historical Society, Wesley Theological Society (president, 1972-74), Wesley Historical Society (England).

WRITINGS: John Wesley: Christian Revolutionary, Beacon Hill Press, 1967; *Foundations of Wesleyan-Arminianism,* Beacon Hill Press, 1968; *Theology of Love,* Beacon Hill Press, 1972; *The Past is Prologue* (history of Trevecca Nazarene College), Trevecca Nazarene College, in press; *The Mirror Image,* Beacon Hill Press, in press. Contributor to *Journal of the Wesley Theological Society* and *Asbury Theological Seminary Journal.*

SIDELIGHTS: Mildred Wynkoop has lived in Europe and in the Orient, and is competent in French, German, Greek, Hebrew, and Spanish. Her books have been translated into Spanish and Japanese. *Avocational interests:* Photography, collecting stamps, history, hiking.

*   *   *

YALE, William   1888(?)-1975

1888(?)—February 26, 1975; American historian, educator, and author. Obituaries: *New York Times,* February 27, 1975.

*   *   *

YANCY, Robert J(ames)   1944-

PERSONAL: Born March 10, 1944, in Tifton, Ga.; son of Preston Martin (a businessman) and Margaret (a public school teacher; maiden name, Robinson) Yancy; married Dorothy Cowser (a college professor), September 8, 1967; children: Yvonne Cowser. *Education:* Morehouse College, B.A. 1964; Atlanta University, M.B.A., 1966; Northwestern University, Ph.D., 1973. *Home:* 2909 Campbellton Rd. S.W., #18-A, Atlanta, Ga. 30311. *Office:* Zebra Corp., 698 Echo St., Atlanta, Ga. 30318.

CAREER: Southern University, Baton Rouge, La., instructor in business administration, 1965-66; Albany State College, Albany, Ga., instructor in business administration, 1966-67; Hampton Institute, Hampton, Va., instructor in business administration, 1967-69; Atlanta University, Atlanta, Ga., assistant professor of business administration, 1971—. President and chairman of board of directors of Zebra Corp. (manufacturers of paints and industrial finishes), 1972—. Research assistant for National Advisory Council on Minority Business; member of committee on community security and enhancement of United Way—Atlanta; consultant to National Task Force on Minority Business Education and Training. *Member:* National Council for Small Business Development, Sales and Marketing Executives of Atlanta.

WRITINGS: Federal Government Policy and Black Business Enterprise, Ballinger, 1974; (contributor) Samuel I. Doctors, editor, *Whatever Happened to Minority Economic Development,* Dryden, 1974.

WORK IN PROGRESS: A longitudinal study of the development of his own minority business venture.

SIDELIGHTS: Yancy writes: "Most Blacks have little to which they can relate in the American business arena. Standard concepts and practices of business and management are unfamiliar to them. Consequently they often experience difficulties understanding and internalizing them. Having shared a common background and experiences with most young Blacks, and having overcome the formidable obstacle of irrelevance ... I feel that I can communicate conventional business administration to young Blacks in a language (and through a medium) with which they can identify and relate.

Recently, my involvement in formal education and training for Blacks in business has been generalized to include informal involvements in minority business development as well as personal involvement in business itself.''

*   *   *

YANG, Linda (Gureasko) 1937-

PERSONAL: Born February 20, 1937, in New York, N.Y.; daughter of Edward M. (a teacher) and Esther (Freden) Gureasko; married John Yang (an architect), May 9, 1960; children: Naomi, David. *Education:* University of Pennsylvania, B.Arch., 1959. *Home:* 505 East 79th St., New York, N.Y. 10021.

CAREER: Architect, author. *Member:* American Horticultural Society, American Rose Society, Nature Conservancy, Audubon Society, Garden Writers Association of America, American Institute of Architects, Architectural League, New York Botanical Garden, Queens Botanical Garden Society, Horticultural Society of New York, Brooklyn Botanic Garden, Friends of Central Park, Sierra Club.

WRITINGS: The Terrace Gardener's Handbook: Raising Plants on a Balcony, Terrace Rooftop, Penthouse, or Patio (American Garden Guild Book Club selection; Literary Guild Book Club alternate selection), Doubleday, 1975. Contributor to periodicals.

*   *   *

YANNELLA, Donald 1934-

PERSONAL: Born May 12, 1934, in New York, N.Y.; son of Donald J. (a senior executive) and Johanna (Meehan) Yannella; married Kathleen Malone, May 23, 1959; children: Susan, Katherine, Donald, Christopher, Clare. *Education:* Fordham University, B.S., 1956, M.A., 1963, Ph.D., 1971. *Home:* 415 Lake Ave., Pitman, N.J. 08071. *Office:* Department of English, Glassboro State College, Glassboro, N.J. 08028.

CAREER: Auburn University, Auburn, Ala., teaching fellow, 1956-57; Westchester Community College, Valhalla, N.Y., assistant professor of English, 1964; Glassboro State College, Glassboro, N.J., assistant professor, 1964-68, associate professor, 1968-71, professor of English, 1971—. Member of National Project on Film and the Humanities Advisory Committee, 1974—. *Military service:* U.S. Army, 1957-58. *Member:* Melville Society (secretary-treasurer, 1975—), American Association of University Professors, Modern Language Association of America, American Studies Association.

WRITINGS: (Editor of reprint) Cornelius Mathews, *Behemoth* (novel), Garrett Press, 1970; (editor of reprint) Mathews, *The Career of Puffer Hopkins and Big Abel and the Little Manhattan* (novel), Garrett Press, 1970; (editor) *Romanticism in American Literature: 1820-1960*, Transcendental, 1973. Contributor of reviews to journals in his field. Editor of *Extracts: The Melville Society Newsletter*, 1973-74.

WORK IN PROGRESS: Ralph Waldo Emerson for Twayne: *Cornelius Mathews* for John Colet Press; *The Diary and Letters of E. A. Duyckinck*; editing with John Roch *American Prose and Criticism to 1820*, for Gale Information Guide Series.

*   *   *

YATES, Frances A(melia) 1899-

PERSONAL: Born November 28, 1899, in Portsmouth, England; daughter of James Alfred (a naval architect) and Hannah (Malpas) Yates. *Education:* University of London, B.A., 1924, M.A., 1926, D.Lit, 1967. *Home:* 5 Coverts Rd., Claygate, Surrey KT10 OJY, England. *Agent:* A. D. Peters & Co., 10 Buckingham St., London WC2N 6BU, England. *Office:* Warburg Institute, Woburn Square, London WC1H OAB, England.

CAREER: Private research, writing, and teaching in London, England, 1926-39; University of London, Warburg Institute, London, England, part-time research assistant, 1941-44, lecturer in Renaissance culture and editor of publications, 1944-56, reader in history of the Renaissance, 1956-67, honorary fellow, 1967—. Honorary fellow, Lady Margaret Hall, Oxford University, 1970—. *Wartime service:* Ambulance attendant in London, England, 1939-41. *Member:* British Academy (fellow), Royal Society of London (fellow), American Academy of Arts and Sciences (honorary foreign member), University Women's Club. *Awards, honors:* Rose Mary Crawshay Prize from British Academy, 1934, for *John Florio: The Life of an Italian in Shakespeare's England;* fellow of the Society of Humanities of Cornell University, 1968; D.Lit., University of Edinburgh, 1969, Oxford University, 1970, University of Exeter, 1971, University of East Anglia, 1971; member of the Order of the British Empire, 1972; Wolfson Prize from Wolfson Foundation, 1973, for historical writing.

WRITINGS: John Florio: The Life of an Italian in Shakespeare's England, Cambridge University Press, 1934, reprinted, Octagon Books, 1968; *A Study of Love's Labour's Lost,* Cambridge University Press, 1936, reprinted, Folcroft Press, 1969; *The French Academies of the Sixteenth Century,* Warburg Institute, University of London, 1947, reprinted, Kraus Reprint, 1968; *The Valois Tapestries,* Warburg Institute, University of London, 1959; *Giordano Bruno and the Hermetic Tradition,* University of Chicago Press, 1964; *The Art of Memory,* University of Chicago Press, 1966; *Theatre of the World,* University of Chicago Press, 1969; *The Rosicrucian Enlightenment,* Routledge & Kegan Paul, 1972; *Astraea: The Imperial Theme,* Routledge & Kegan Paul, 1975; *Shakespeare's Last Plays,* Routledge & Kegan Paul, 1975. Contributor to journals in her field. Editor, *Journal of the Warburg and Courtauld Institutes, 1943–*.

WORK IN PROGRESS: A book on Renaissance philosophy.

AVOCATIONAL INTERESTS: Reading and travel.

BIOGRAPHICAL/CRITICAL SOURCES: Listener, January 18, 1973.

*   *   *

YNGVE, Victor H(use) 1920-

PERSONAL: Surname is pronounced *Ing*-vee; born July 5, 1920, in Niagara Falls, N.Y.; son of Victor (a chemist) and Miriam (Huse) Yngve; married Jean Huber, 1943; children: Marna (Mrs. Stephen Cake), David, Alan. *Education:* Antioch College, B.S., 1943; University of Chicago, S.M., 1950, Ph.D., 1953. *Office:* University of Chicago, Chicago, Ill. 60637.

CAREER: Massachusetts Institute of Technology, Cambridge, researcher on mechanical translation of languages, 1953-65; University of Chicago, Chicago, Ill., professor of library science, linguistics, and behavioral science, 1965—. *Member:* Linguistic Society of America, Association for Computational Linguistics.

WRITINGS: COMIT Programmers' Reference Manual, M.I.T. Press, 1962; *An Introduction to COMIT Programming,* M.I.T. Press, 1962; *Computer Programming with COMIT II,* M.I.T. Press, 1972. Editor of *Mechanical Translation,* 1954-68.

WORK IN PROGRESS: Introduction to Human Linguistics; research in linguistics and psychology, and on how people communicate, including verbal, nonverbal, and written communications and translations.

*   *   *

YOUNG, Alan 1930-

PERSONAL: Born September 30, 1930, in Manchester, England; son of John (an electrical engineer) and Elsie (Armstrong) Young; married Renee Briscoe (a teacher), July 27, 1957; children: Jenny, Jonathan. *Education:* Sheffield City College, certificate in education, 1952; University of Manchester, B.A. (honors), 1955, M.A., 1958, Ph.D., 1974. *Politics:* None. *Religion:* None. *Home:* 43 Ferndown Rd., Manchester M23 9AW, England.

CAREER: English and philosophy teacher in schools in Manchester, England, 1956-62; Didsbury College of Education, Manchester, England, principal lecturer in English studies, 1962-75, head of arts, 1975—. Has lecturer for Workers Educational Association.

WRITINGS: (Contributor) Arthur Pollard and Ralph Willett, editors, *Webster's New World Companion to English and American Literature,* World Publishing, 1973; (editor) Edgeu Rickword, *Essays and Opinions: 1921-1931,* Dufour, 1974. Contributor to literary journals, including *Poetry Nation, Critical Quarterly, English in Education, Times Literary Supplement,* and *Tarasque.*

WORK IN PROGRESS: A book on the response in English literature to Dadaism, surrealism, and neo-Dada, for Manchester University Press; research on the poems and stories of Dylan Thomas.

AVOCATIONAL INTERESTS: Mozart, Manchester United Association Football Club, cricket.

*   *   *

YOUNG, George F(rederick) W(illiam) 1937-

PERSONAL: Born November 13, 1937, in Buffalo, N.Y.; son of George S. (a surgeon) and Esther V. (Hill) Young; married Jacqueline L. Strohm, December 19, 1963; children: G. F. Oakley, G. W. Weber, R. E. Natasha. *Education:* Harvard University, B.A., 1959; University of Freiburg, graduate study, 1959-60; University of Chicago, Ph.D., 1969. *Home:* 6051 South St., Halifax, Nova Scotia B3H 1S9, Canada. *Office:* Department of History, Saint Mary's University, Halifax, Nova Scotia B3H 3C3, Canada.

CAREER: State University of New York at Buffalo, lecturer in history, 1965-69; Saint Mary's University, Halifax, Nova Scotia, assistant professor, 1969-74, associate pro-

fessor of history, 1974—. Instructor at Columbia University, summer, 1971; president of Atlantic Symphony Choir, 1974-75. *Member:* American Historical Association, Society for the History of Discoveries, Canadian Association of Latin American Studies (member of executive council, 1973-76), Royal Canadian College of Organists.

WRITINGS: Miguel Corte-Real and the Dighton Writing-Book, Old Colony Historical Society, 1970; *The Germans in Chile: Immigration and Colonization, 1849-1914,* Center for Migration Studies (New York), 1974. Has composed music for organ and brass. Contributor of articles and reviews to magazines, including *Hispanic American Historical Review, University of Chicago Magazine, Arctic, Terrae Incongitae,* and *Dalhousie Review,* and to foreign journals.

*   *   *

YOUNG, Noel 1922-
(Leon Elder)

PERSONAL: Born December 25, 1922, in San Francisco, Calif.; son of Ralph W. and Gladys (Small) Young; married Margaret Walters, July 14, 1945 (divorced, November, 1965); Judith Purl, August 25, 1966; children: (first marriage) Hilary, Caitilin, Aaron; (second marriage) Molly. *Education:* Pasadena Junior College, A.B.A., 1942; attended Stanford University, 1942-43. *Home:* 41 Mountain Dr., Santa Barbara, Calif. 93103. *Agent:* Buzz Erikson, 223 Via Sevilla, Santa Barbara, Calif. 93109. *Office:* Capra Press, 631 State St., Santa Barbara, Calif. 93101.

CAREER: Pacific Coast Publishing Co., Santa Barbara, Calif., typographer, 1947-49; Noel Young Press, Santa Barbara, Calif., owner and editor, 1949-69; Capra Press, Santa Barbara, Calif., editor and president, 1969—. *Military service:* U.S. Army Air Forces, 1943-46. *Awards, honors:* Short story first prize from Santa Barbara Writers, 1953.

WRITINGS: (Under pseudonym Leon Elder) *Hot Tubs* (nonfiction), Capra, 1973, revised edition, Vintage Books, 1975; (under pseudonym Leon Elder) *Free Beaches* (nonfiction), Capra, 1974; (editor) *Great Hot Springs of the West,* Capra, 1974. Editor of Capra's "Chapbook" series, 1972—.

WORK IN PROGRESS: Research on West Coast fishing ports, and on Santa Barbara architecture from Spanish colonial to modern brutalism; a survey of the growth and development of Santa Barbara.

*   *   *

YOUNG, Perry Deane 1941-

PERSONAL: Born March 27, 1941, in Asheville, N.C.; son of Robert Finley (a farmer) and Rheba Maphry (Tipton) Young. *Education:* University of North Carolina, Chapel Hill, student, 1959-65. *Politics:* None. *Religion:* None. *Agent:* James Brown Associates, 22 East 60th St., New York, N.Y. 10022.

CAREER: Has worked as reporter for newspapers in Durham, Raleigh, Greensboro, and Chapel Hill, N.C., and for *New York Journal-American* and United Press International in New York, N.Y., and Saigon, Vietnam. *Military service:* U.S. Army Reserve, Military Police.

WRITINGS: Two of the Missing: A Reminiscence of Some Friends in the War, Coward, 1975. Contributor to national magazines and newspapers, including *Harper's, Ms., Rolling Stone, Saturday Review, New York Times,* and *Chicago Journalism Review.*

WORK IN PROGRESS: My Mother and Myself: A Story of Love and Shame, a non-fiction memoir of illicit sex and the family structure.

* * *

YOUNG, Stanley (Preston) 1906-1975

February 3, 1906—March 22, 1975; American educator, editor, poet, playwright, literary critic. Obituaries: *New York Times*, March 25, 1975; *AB Bookman's Weekly*, April 28, 1975; *Current Biography*, May, 1975.

* * *

ZAHAVA, Irene 1951-
(Irene Levinson)

PERSONAL: Born April 6, 1951, in New York, N. Y.; daughter of Morton (a teacher) and Eve (a guidance counselor) Levinson. *Education:* Attended Ithaca College, 1968-71; Empire State College, B.A., 1973; current graduate study at Pratt Institute. *Home:* 3363 Sedgwick Ave., Bronx, N. Y. 10463. *Office:* Women's Action Alliance, 370 Lexington Ave., New York, N.Y. 10017.

CAREER: Librarian at Women's Action Alliance, New York, N.Y.

WRITINGS: (Under name Irene Levinson) *Peter Learns to Crochet*, New Seed Press, Feminist Press, 1974.

WORK IN PROGRESS: Two children's books with feminist-orientation.

* * *

ZARNECKI, George 1915-

PERSONAL: Name listed in some sources as Jerzy Zarnecki; born September 12, 1915, in Stara Osota, Poland; son of Zygmunt (a civil engineer) and Julia (Wolszczan) Zarnecki; married Anne Leslie Frith, March 22, 1945; children: John Charles, Julia Mary Zarnecki Hutt. *Education:* Cracow University, M.A., 1938; University of London, Ph.D., 1950. *Home:* 22 Essex Park, London N3 INE, England. *Office:* Courtauld Institute of Art, University of London, 20 Portman Square, London W1H OBE, England.

CAREER: Cracow University, Institute of Art, Cracow, Poland, junior assistant, 1936-39; University of London, London, England, Courtauld Institute of Art, staff member, 1945-49, and Conway Librarian, 1949-59, reader, 1959-63, professor of history of art, 1963—, deputy director of Courtauld Institute of Art, 1961-74. Slade Professor of Fine Arts, Oxford University, 1960-61; member, Institute for Advanced Study, Princeton, N.J., 1966. Member of conservation committee of Council for Places of Worship, 1969—, of Royal Commission on Historical Monuments, 1972—, of Canterbury Cathedral Stained Glass Committee, 1972—, of arts subcommittee of University Grants Committee, 1973—, and of Wells Cathedral Advisory Council, 1974—. Trustee, York Glaziers Trust, 1972—, National Monuments Record, 1973—. *Military service:* Polish Army, 1939-45, served in France and the United Kingdom; prisoner of war in Germany, 1940-42, escaped and interned in Spain, 1942-43; received Polish Cross of Valour and Croix de Guerre, 1940. *Member:* British Academy (fellow), Society of Antiquaries (fellow; vice-president, 1968-72). *Awards, honors:* Commander of the British Empire, 1970.

WRITINGS: Zabytki Wislicy (title means "Monuments of Wislica"), [Poland], 1939; (with K. Estreicher and A. M. Mars) *Cultural Losses of Poland*, [London], 1944; *Polish Art*, Polish Publications Committee (Birkenhead, England), 1945; (with H. D. Molesworth) *Sculpture in England: Medieval*, British Council, 1951; *English Romanesque Sculpture 1066-1140*, A. Tiranti, 1951; *Later English Romanesque Sculpture. 1140-1210*, A. Tiranti, 1953; English Romanesque Lead Sculpture: Lead Fonts of the Twelfth Century, *Philosophical Library, 1957;* The Early Sculpture of Ely Cathedral, *A. Tiranti, 1958.*

(With Denis Grivot) *Gislebertus, sculpteur d'Autun*, Editions Trianon, 1960, translation published as *Gislebertus, Sculptor of Autun*, Orion Press, 1961, revised edition, Trianon Press, 1969; (contributor) *Studies in Western Art*, Volume I: *Romanesque and Gothic Art*, Princeton University Press, 1963; (contributor) Joan Evans, editor, *The Flowering of the Middle Ages*, Thames & Hudson, 1966; *1066 and Architectural Sculpture*, Oxford University Press, 1966; *Romanesque Sculpture at Lincoln Cathedral*, Friends of Lincoln Cathedral, 1968, 2nd edition, 1970. *Romanik*, Belser, 1970, translation published as *Romanesque Art*, Universe Books, 1971; *The Monastic Achievement*, McGraw, 1972; (with J. Betjeman, K. Clark, J. Pope-Hennesy, and A. L. Rowse) *Westminster Abbey*, Weidenfeld & Nicolson, 1972; (contributor) *Festschrift fuer Hans Wentzel*, Beitraege zur Kunst des Mittelalters, 1975. *History of Medieval Art*, Prentice-Hall, in press. Contributor to *Enciclopedia Universale dell'Arte*, *Archaeological Journal*, *Proceedings of the British Academy*, *Journal of The British Archaeological Association*, *Burlington Magazine*, *Listener*, and other publications.

WORK IN PROGRESS: European Sculpture 800-1200, for Pelican "History of Art" series.

* * *

ZEIDENSTEIN, Harvey 1932-

PERSONAL: Surname is pronounced with long "i" sound in first and last syllables; born May 6, 1932, in Chicago, Ill.; son of Sol (a clothier) and Eileen (a store clerk; maiden name, Tzeiger) Zeidenstein; married Evelyn M. Sweet, November 29, 1957; children: Kathryn, Darrow, David. *Education:* Northwestern University, B.S., 1954; University of Chicago, M.A., 1957; New York University, Ph.D., 1965. *Politics:* Democrat—"sometimes with reservations." *Religion:* Agnostic. *Home:* 810 Hester Ave., Normal, Ill. 61761. *Office:* Department of Political Science, Illinois State University, Normal, Ill. 61761.

CAREER: Television continuity writer; high school teacher of political science in the public schools of St. Clair Shores, Mich., 1957-58; Hofstra College (now University), Hempstead, N.Y., instructor, 1960-61; State of Illinois Legislative Council, Springfield, research associate, 1961-65; Illinois State University, Normal, assistant professor, 1965-69, associate professor, 1969-74, professor of political science, 1974—. *Member:* American Political Science Association, Center for the Study of the Presidency, Academy of Political Science, Southern Political Science Association, Midwest Political Science Association.

WRITINGS: Direct Election of the President, Heath, 1973. Contributor to *Journal of Politics* and *International Review of History and Political Science*.

WORK IN PROGRESS: Co-authoring a book analyzing the implications of the War Powers Resolution of 1973.

* * *

ZELIGS, Rose

PERSONAL: Born in Cincinnati, Ohio; daughter of Joseph

(a rabbi) and Betty (Mirkin) Zeligs. *Education:* University of Cincinnati, B.A., 1925, B.E., 1926, M.A., 1932, Ed.D., 1937; further study at University of Chicago, 1934, Claremont College, 1955, 1957, 1958. *Politics:* Independent. *Religion:* Jewish. *Home:* 14284 Dickens St., Sherman Oaks, Calif. 91423. *Office:* 14256 Ventura Blvd., Sherman Oaks, Calif. 91423.

CAREER: Public school teacher in Cincinnati, Ohio, 1926-48; clinical psychologist in private practice in Sherman Oaks, Calif., 1948—. *Member:* American Psychological Association, Western Psychological Association, California State Psychological Association, Los Angeles County Psychological Association, Los Angeles Society of Clinical Psychologists, San Fernando Valley Psychological Association (secretary-treasurer, 1960-62), Tau Kappa Alpha. *Awards, honors:* Numerous awards from Freedoms Foundation for essays.

WRITINGS: Glimpses into Child Life, Morrow, 1942; *Children's Experience with Death,* C. C Thomas, 1974. Contributor to journals in her field. Editor of newsletter of San Fernando Valley Psycholgical Association, 1962-63.

WORK IN PROGRESS: Sudden Infant Death Syndrome; Freedom and Democracy; The Cultural Climate of American Youthlings; Children's Intergroup Attitudes.

* * *

ZELLER, Belle 1903-

PERSONAL: Born April 8, 1903, in New York. *Education:* Hunter College (now of the City University of New York), A.B. (cum laude), 1924; Columbia University, M.A., 1926, Ph.D., 1937. *Home:* 25 Central Park W., New York, N.Y. 10023. *Office:* Department of Political Science, Brooklyn College of the City University of New York, Brooklyn, N.Y. 11210.

CAREER: Hunter College (now of the City University of New York), New York, N.Y., instructor in political science, 1926-30; Brooklyn College of the City University of New York, New York, N.Y., instructor, 1930-37, assistant professor, 1937-44, associate professor, 1944-52, professor of political science, 1952—. Professor at New School for Social Research, 1960-68. President of Professional Staff Congress of the City University of New York, 1973—; member of New York State Commission to Study the Government of New York City, 1953-54; consultant to New York State Constitutional Convention, 1967, and to congressional and state legislative committees. *Member:* American Political Science Association, American Society for Public Administration, National Municipal League, American Association of University Women, American Association of University Professors, National Education Association, American Federation of Teachers, Citizens Union, Phi Beta Kappa. *Awards, honors:* Research grant from Social Science Research Council, 1944-47.

WRITINGS: Pressure Politics in New York, Prentice-Hall, 1937, reprinted, Atheneum, 1967; *Federal Regulation of the Lobbying Act,* American Political Science Association, 1948; (editor and contributor) *American State Legislatures,* Crowell, 1954; *Why Faculties Organize,* Practising Law Institute, 1975.

* * *

ZEMACH, Kaethe 1958-

PERSONAL: Born March 18, 1958, in Boston, Mass.; daughter of Harve (an author of children's books) and Margot (an illustrator of children's books) Zemach. *Education:* Attended schools in England, Denmark, and the United States. *Home:* 2421 Oregon St., Berkeley, Calif. 94705.

CAREER: Artist; writer.

WRITINGS: (With father, Harve Zemach) *The Princess and Froggie* (juvenile; short stories), Farrar, Straus, 1975.

SIDELIGHTS: Kaethe Zemach told *CA* that the stories in *The Princess and Froggie* originated from a simple story structure she devised when telling her youngest sister her first stories.

* * *

ZIEDONIS, Arvids, Jr. 1931-

PERSONAL: Born March 8, 1931, in Daugaupils, Latvia; naturalized U.S. citizen in 1956; son of Arvids (an engineer) and Marija (Kostokevic) Ziedonis; married Zigrida M. Vurlicers, August 23, 1958; children: Douglas, Ruth, Eric. *Education:* Muhlenberg College, A.B., 1955; University of Pennsylvania, graduate study, 1955-58; Lutheran Theological Seminary at Philadelphia, M.Div., 1958, at Gettysburg, S.T.M., 1962; Temple University, Ph.D., 1968. *Politics:* Republican. *Home:* 507 Green Court, Bethlehem, Pa. 18015. *Office:* Department of Languages, Muhlenberg College, Allentown, Pa. 18104.

CAREER: Ordained Lutheran minister, 1958; pastor in Steelton, Pa., 1958-62, and in Bethlehem, Pa., 1962-68; Capitol Area Foreign Language School, Harrisburg, Pa., dean, 1959-62; Muhlenberg College, Allentown, Pa., lecturer, 1962-68, associate professor, 1968-74, professor of Russian, 1974—, director of Russian studies, 1968—. Chaplain of Pennsylvania Exchange Club, 1966-67; secretary of board of Citizen Exchange Corps, 1972—, chairman of Field Institute, 1974—. *Member:* American Latvian Association, Association for the Advancement of Baltic Studies, American Association of University Professors, Modern Language Association of America, American Association of Teachers of Slavic and East European Languages, American Association for the Advancement of Slavic Languages. *Awards, honors:* Ford Foundation research grants, 1970-71.

WRITINGS: The Religious Philosophy of Janis Rainis: Latvian Poet, Latvju Gramata, 1969; (editor) *Problems of Mininations: Baltic Perspectives,* California State University, 1973; (editor) *Baltic Literature and Linguistics,* Ohio State University, 1973; (editor) *Baltic History,* Ohio State University, 1974. Editor of *Proceedings of Second Conference on Baltic Studies,* 1971. Editor of *Journal of Baltic Studies,* 1970—.

WORK IN PROGRESS: A monograph, *A Study of Rudolfs Blaumanis,* completion expected in 1976; studies of the works of Turgenev, of Pasternak, and of Dostoevsky.

SIDELIGHTS: Ziedonis has been group leader of study and cultural exchange visits in the Union of Soviet Socialist Republics.

* * *

ZIEGLER, Arthur P(aul), Jr. 1937-

PERSONAL: Born June 20, 1937, in Pittsburgh, Pa.; son of Arthur P., Sr. and Vinnie (DeWinter) Ziegler. *Education:* University of Pittsburgh, B.A., 1958, M.A., 1959; graduate study, Union Theological Seminary, New York, N.Y., 1959-60, Case Western Reserve University, 1960-61.

Home: 141 Central Sq., Pittsburgh, Pa. 15228. *Office:* 701 Allegheny Sq. W., Pittsburgh, Pa. 15212.

CAREER: Chatham Associates, Inc., Pittsburgh, Pa., managing editor, 1962-64; Van Trump, Ziegler & Shane, Inc., Pittsburgh, Pa., director and publisher, 1964-72; Pittsburgh History and Landmarks Foundation, Pittsburgh, Pa., president, 1964—; Landmarks Planning, Inc., Pittsburgh, Pa., president and director, 1972—. Part-time teacher at Pennsylvania State University, 1960-63; instructor in English, Carnegie-Mellon University, 1961-64. Member of Mayor's Advisory Committee on Housing Relocation, 1967-72; chairman of architectural awards jury of American Institute of Architects, 1971; chairman of Pittsburgh Bicentennial Committee; member of advisory panel of President's Historic Resources Panel; member of boards of directors of Neighborhood Housing Services, Inc., Harmonie Associates, and Pittsburgh Council for the Arts, all 1970, and of Meadowcroft Village, 1972—. *Member:* National Trust for Historic Preservation, Western Pennsylvania Historical Society, Carnegie Society, Pittsburgh Press Club, University Club (Pittsburgh).

WRITINGS: (Co-editor) *A Critical Edition of Lord of the Flies,* Putnam, 1964; (with James D. Van Trump) *1300-1335 Liverpool St.,* Pittsburgh History and Landmarks Foundation, 1965; (with Van Trump) *Landmark Architecture of Allegheny County,* Pittsburgh History and Landmarks Foundation, 1967; *Birmingham,* Pittsburgh History and Landmarks Foundation, 1968; *Cora Street,* Action Housing, 1969; *Historic Preservation in Inner City Areas,* Ober Park Associates, 1971; *Revolving Funds for Historic Preservation,* Ober Park Associates, 1975. Contributor to *Journal of Alleghenies, Pennsylvania Journal of Architecture,* and *Pennsylvania Professional Engineer, Western Humanities Review, London Book Collector, Journal of Housing, Museum News,* and *Historic Preservation.*

* * *

ZIEGLER, Edward K(rusen) 1903-

PERSONAL: Born January 3, 1903, in Royersford, Pa.; son of Harry Horning and Mary (Hunsberger) Ziegler; married Ilda M. Bittinger, January 31, 1924 (died, 1970); married Mary Grace Vivolo (a teacher), November 26, 1970; children: (first marriage) Robert E., Donald M., Ruth Ann (Mrs. Warren W. Baird). *Education:* Elizabethtown Academy and College, B.A. (magna cum laude), 1929; graduate study at Gettysburg Theological Seminary, 1942-43, Chicago Theological Seminary, 1946, and Garrett Biblical Seminary, 1946; Bethany Theological Seminary, B.D., 1947. *Politics:* Democrat. *Address:* Route 1, Box 36, Woodsboro, Md. 21798.

CAREER: Ordained Church of the Brethren minister, 1921; teacher in public schools in Pennsylvania and West Virginia, 1921-24; minister in Johnson City, Tenn., 1929-31, York, Pa., 1940-45, Bridgewater, Va., 1947-51, Roanoke, Va., 1955-61, Oakton, Va., 1961-66, Bakersfield, Calif., 1966-71, and Manassas, Va., 1973-74; missionary in India, 1931-39; Church of the Brethren National Staff, Elgin, Ill., director of evangelism, 1951-55. Lecturer at York Junior College, 1942-45, Bethany Theological Seminary, 1953-55; assistant professor at Manchester College, 1945-47. Church of the Brethren, member of general board, 1947-48, moderator of annual conference, 1959-60; member of World Council of Churches, 1960-66; president of Fairfax County Council of Churches, 1963-66, and of Greater Bakersfield Council of Churches, 1967-70; vice-president of Greater Washington Council of Churches, 1964-66.

MEMBER: National Wildlife Federation, National Geographic Society, Sierra Club American Association of Retired Persons, Common Cause, Kiwanis. *Awards, honors:* D.D., Bethany Theological Seminary, 1950.

WRITINGS: Book of Worship for Village Churches, Agricultural Missions, 1939, 2nd edition, 1941; *Brethren Win Men to Christ,* Brethren Press, 1953; *Rural Preaching,* Revell, 1954; *The Village Pastor,* Agricultural Missions, 1959; *Simple Living,* Brethren Press, 1974. Contributor to journals. Editor of *Brethren Life and Thought,* 1955—. Writer of hymns.

WORK IN PROGRESS: Worship for Families; The Future of Anabaptist or Believers' Churches; Theology for Ecology.

SIDELIGHTS: Book of Worship for Village Churches has had editions in over seventeen languages, including Swahili, Punjab, and Chinese.

Avocational interests: Photography, ornithology, choral music, organ, travel.

* * *

ZILG, Gerard Colby 1945-

PERSONAL: Born December 11, 1945, in Forest Hills, N.Y.; son of Albert Edward (a postal worker) and Veronica (Colby) Zilg; married Sara Schuyler Flounders, January 27, 1968 (divorced, 1975). *Education:* Attended St. John's University, Jamaica, N.Y., 1963-64, Queensborough Community College, 1966, and Delaware Technical College, 1970; State University of New York at Oneonta, B.S., 1970. *Residence:* New York, N.Y. *Agent:* Seligmann & Collier, 280 Madison Ave., New York, N.Y. 10016.

CAREER: Worked as a sheetmetal assembly line worker, stock clerk, taxi driver, short-order cook, and host at New York World's Fair; press secretary for Congressman John Dow in New York, N.Y., 1968; public high school teacher of English and social studies in Wilmington, Del., 1970; full-time writer in New York, N.Y., 1970—.

WRITINGS: Du Pont: Behind the Nylon Curtain, Prentice-Hall, 1974.

WORK IN PROGRESS: A book, *Bonus! The March That Changed America,* on the Bonus Veterans March of 1932, its impact on the fall of Herbert Hoover, and its secret impact on future New Deal legislation, publication expected by McKay; a book on the post-war decline of the Roman Catholic Church, *The Betrayal of Pope John,* for Prentice-Hall; a play; a book of short stories.

AVOCATIONAL INTERESTS: Sketching, painting, vocal music, musical composition, riflery, fishing, boxing, track.

BIOGRAPHICAL/CRITICAL SOURCES: Delaware State News, October 27, 1974, February 24, 1975; *New York Times,* January 21, 1975; *Philadelphia Enquirer,* January 25, 1975.

* * *

ZIMMERMAN, David R(adoff) 1934-

PERSONAL: Born August 10, 1934, in Chicago, Ill.; son of Leo and Sara Zimmerman; married Veva Haupton; children: Jacob, Tobies. *Education:* Brandeis University, A.B. (cum laude), 1955; graduate study at University of Paris, 1955-56. *Home:* 603 West 111th St., New York, N.Y. 10025. *Agent:* Julian Bach, Jr., 3 East 48th St., New York, N.Y. 10017.

CAREER: New York News, New York, N.Y., copy boy, 1956-57; New York Post, New York, N.Y., copy boy and member of news desk staff, 1957-61; free-lance medical book rewriter, 1961-63; New York Academy of Medicine, New York, N.Y., editor, 1963; Medical World News, reporter and senior writer, 1963-69; free-lance writer, 1969—. Part-time instructor at City College of the City University of New York, 1972-73. Member: Society of Magazine Writers (president, 1973-74), National Association of Science Writers. Awards, honors: Award for science writing from Society of Magazine Writers, 1970, for "Death Comes to the Peregrine Falcon"; American Medical Writers Association award for excellence, 1973, for Rh: The Intimate History of a Disease and Its Conquest.

WRITINGS: Rh: The Intimate History of a Disease and Its Conquest, Macmillan, 1973; To Save a Bird in Peril, Coward, 1975. Contributor of feature-length articles to Ladies' Home Journal, New York Times Magazine, Smithsonian, Natural History, and National Wildlife. Contributing editor and author of column "Medicine Today," Ladies' Home Journal, 1967—.

* * *

ZIMMERMAN, Irla Lee 1923-

PERSONAL: Born October 6, 1923, in Madison, Wis.; daughter of William S. (a manufacturer) and Julia (a teacher; maiden name, Murray) Zimmerman; married James L. Oetzel (a flight director), August 10, 1950. Education: University of California at Los Angeles, A.B., 1944, M.A., 1947, Ph.D., 1953. Home: 1732 Kelton Ave., Los Angeles, Calif. 90024. Office: 13006 East Philadelphia St., Whittier, Calif. 90601.

CAREER: Diplomate in clinical psychology, American Board of Professional Psychology, 1958. Private practice in clinical psychology in Whittier, Calif., 1952—. Psychologist at University of California at Los Angeles, 1973—. Member: American Psychological Association (fellow), American Association of Mental Deficiency (fellow), American Association of Orthopsychiatry (fellow).

WRITINGS: (With Alan Glasser) Clinical Interpretation of the Wechsler Intelligence Scale for Children, Grune & Stratton, 1967; (with Violette G. Steiner and Roberta Pond) Preschool Language Scale, C. E. Merrill, 1969; (with James Woo-Sam) Clinical Interpretation of the Wechsler Adult Intelligence Scale, Grune & Stratton, 1973.

* * *

ZOELLNER, Robert 1926-

PERSONAL: Born June 22, 1926, in Denver, Colo.; son of Henry A. and Helen (Husted) Zoellner; divorced; children: Matthew, Jason, Benjamin, Stacey, Evan. Education: Attended University of Oklahoma, 1944-46, and University of Colorado, 1949; Marquette University, B.S., 1952, M.A., 1953; University of Wisconsin, Ph.D., 1960. Home: 107 Briarwood Rd., #1112, Fort Collins, Colo. 80521. Office: Department of English, Colorado State University, Fort Collins, Colo. 80523.

CAREER: University of North Dakota, Grand Forks, instructor in English, 1956-58; Colorado State University, Fort Collins, assistant professor, 1958-64, associate professor, 1964-69, professor of English, 1969—. Military service: U.S. Naval Reserve, 1944-46. Member: Modern Language Association of America, National Council of Teachers of English, Conference on College Composition and Commu-

nication. Awards, honors: National Endowment for the Humanities grant, 1972.

WRITINGS: The Salt-Sea Mastodon: A Reading of Moby-Dick, University of California Press, 1973. Contributor to American Literature, American Quarterly, and other professional journals.

WORK IN PROGRESS: Articles on American authors; a book, Behavioral Humanism: An Essay in Synthesis.

AVOCATIONAL INTERESTS: Hiking, backpacking, skiing, ecology, preservation of environment.

* * *

ZOLBROD, Leon M(ax) 1930-

PERSONAL: Born August 28, 1930, in Pittsburgh, Pa.; naturalized Canadian citizen; son of Herman (a railroad worker) and Caroline (a seamstress; maiden name, Engler) Zolbrod; married Yukiko Oshigami, December 21, 1955 (divorced May 17, 1967); married Fumiko Miura, July 21, 1967; children: (first marriage) Morilun, Aya; (second marriage) Yuichi, Nana, Koji. Education: University of Washington, Seattle, B.A. (magna cum laude), 1955; Columbia University, M.A., 1957, Ph.D., 1963; also studied at Tokyo University, 1959-61, 1964-66, and Kyoto University, 1971-72. Residence: Vancouver, British Columbia, Canada. Office: Department of Asian Studies, University of British Columbia, Vancouver, British Columbia V6T 1W5, Canada.

CAREER: Otaru University of Commerce, Otaru, Japan, instructor in English, 1955-57; University of Kansas, Lawrence, instructor in Japanese, 1961-62; Indiana University, Bloomington, lecturer, 1962-63, assistant professor of Japanese, 1963-66; University of British Columbia, Vancouver, assistant professor, 1966-70, associate professor, 1970-74, professor of Japanese literature, 1974—. Military service: U.S. Army, 1948-52; became sergeant.

MEMBER: International House of Tokyo, Association for Asian Studies, Modern Language Association of America, Canadian Society of Asian Studies, Asiatic Society of Japan, Vancouver Society of Asian Art (member of board of directors, 1969-75), Japan Society of New York, Phi Beta Kappa.

WRITINGS: Takizawa Bakin, Twayne, 1967; Ugetsu Monogatari, Allen & Unwin, 1974. Contributor to Encyclopedia of World Literature in the Twentieth Century and Encyclopaedia Britannica. Contributor of about forty articles to scholarly journals.

WORK IN PROGRESS: Research on haiku poet and painter Yosa Buson.

SIDELIGHTS: Zolbrod writes: "As a youth I was unable to study German to my satisfaction, owing to the wartime circumstances. When, by coincidence, I had a chance to learn Japanese, I was pleased to take advantage of the opportunity. Eventually I became a professor of Japanese, and my main interest in writing is to present the results of my research in such a form that the general reader might become aware of the uniqueness of Japanese civilization."

* * *

ZUNKEL, Charles Edward 1905-

PERSONAL: Born February 26, 1905, in Atwood, Colo.; son of Walter Richard (a blacksmith) and Matilda (Walter) Zunkel; married Cleda Shull, June 12, 1928; children: C. Wayne, Carolyn Marie (Mrs. Robert L. Parker). Educa-

tion: Manchester College, A.B., 1928; Bethany Theological Seminary, M. Div., 1935. *Home:* Timbercrest, Duplex Apt. 23, North Manchester, Ind. 46962.

CAREER: Ordained Church of the Brethren minister, 1924; pastor in Pleasant Hill, Ohio, 1928-32, Danville, Ohio, 1935-39, Lima, Ohio, 1939-44, Wenatchee, Wash., 1944-48; Church of the Brethren General Offices, Elgin, Ill., secretary of Ministry and Home Missions, 1948-58, pastor in Port Republic, Va., 1958-65, and South Bend, Ind., 1965-70; pastor at Akron Church of the Brethren, 1970-76. Church of the Brethren, assistant moderator, 1959-60, moderator, 1960-61. Lecturer at Bridgewater College, Elizabethtown College, Manchester College, McPherson College, LaVerne College, and at Bethany Theological Seminary. Rockingham Council on Human Relations, co-founder, 1963, president, 1963-65; member of board of Indiana Inter-Religious Commission on Human Equality, 1970-75. *Member:* Indiana Council of Churches. *Awards, honors:* St. Joseph Council of Churches leadership citation, 1970.

WRITINGS: (With wife, Cleda Zunkel) *Turn Again to Life*, Brethren Press, 1974. Contributor to *Messenger*.

AVOCATIONAL INTERESTS: Woodworking, antiquing, coin and stamp collecting, collecting precious and semi-precious stones, gardening.

* * *

ZUNKEL, Cleda 1903-

PERSONAL: Born August 15, 1903, in Virden, Ill.; daughter of William Harrison (a farmer and minister) and Clara (Gibson) Shull; married Charles Edward Zunkel (a clergyman), June 12, 1928; children: C. Wayne, Carolyn Marie (Mrs. Robert L. Parker). *Education:* Manchester College, A.B., 1928; also attended Illinois State Normal School, 1922, and Bethany Theological Seminary, Oak Brook, Ill., 1924, 1933. *Religion:* Church of the Brethren. *Home:* Timbercrest, Duplex Apt. #23, North Manchester, Ind. 46962.

CAREER: Public school teacher in Illinois, 1922-24; writer, public speaker. Member of national board of managers of Church Women United; denominational representative to National Council of Churches, 1956-59. *Member:* Chain of Living Poets.

WRITINGS: (With husband, Charles E. Zunkel) *Turn Again to Life* (spiritual), Brethren Press, 1974. Contributor of poems to magazines and newspapers.

WORK IN PROGRESS: Heirloom Altars for Women, devotional meditations; a collection of original poems.

AVOCATIONAL INTERESTS: Reading, walking in nature, refinishing old furniture, handcrafts.

* * *

ZWERDLING, Alex 1932-

PERSONAL: Born June 21, 1932, in Breslau, Germany; naturalized U.S. citizen in 1946; son of Norbert (a designer) and Fanni (Alt) Zwerdling; married Florence Goldberg (a writer), March 23, 1969; children: Antony Daniel. *Education:* Cornell University, B.A,, 1953; University of Munich, graduate study, 1953-54; Princeton University, M.A., 1956, Ph.D., 1960. *Home:* 47 Avis Rd., Berkeley, Calif. 94707. *Office:* Department of English, University of California, Berkeley, Calif. 94720.

CAREER: Swarthmore College, Swarthmore, Pa., in-structor in English, 1957-61; University of California, Berkeley, assistant professor, 1961-67, associate professor, 1967-73, professor of English, 1973—. *Member:* Modern Language Association of America. *Awards, honors:* Fulbright Scholarship to Germany, 1953-54; American Council of Learned Societies fellowship, 1964-65; Center for Advanced Study in the Behavioral Sciences fellowship, 1964-65; National Endowment for the Humanities fellowship, 1973-74.

WRITINGS: Yeats and the Heroic Ideal, New York University Press, 1965; *Orwell and the Left*, Yale University Press, 1974. Contributor to *Sewanee Review, New Review* (London), *PMLA, University of Toronto Quarterly*, and other journals.

WORK IN PROGRESS: A book on the Bloomsbury Group.

* * *

ZWIEBACH, Burton 1933-

PERSONAL: Born September 17, 1933, in New York, N.Y.; son of Harry and Betty (Cohen) Zwiebach; married Sally Bever (a teacher), December 22, 1962; children: Michael, Peter. *Education:* City College (now City College of the City University of New York), B.A., 1954; Columbia University, LL.B., 1957, Ph.D., 1964. *Politics:* "Egalitarian." *Religion:* None. *Home:* 20 Doxey Dr., Glen Cove, N.Y. 11542. *Office:* Department of Political Science, Queens College of the City University of New York, Flushing, N.Y. 11367.

CAREER: Advisory Committee on Practice and Procedure of the New York Legislature, New York, N.Y., research assistant, 1958-60; Queens College of the City University of New York, Flushing, N.Y., associate professor of political science, 1961—. Attorney in New York, N.Y., 1958-59. *Military service:* U.S. Army, 1957, 1961-62. *Member:* American Political Science Association, American Civil Liberties Union.

WRITINGS: Civility and Disobedience, Cambridge University Press, 1975. Contributor of articles and reviews to professional journals.

WORK IN PROGRESS: Constitutional Equality, on the relation between equality and constitutionalism.

SIDELIGHTS: Zwiebach writes: "Like most political philosophers, I want to clarify the moral implications of our political arrangements and traditions. I am particularly interested in calling attention to the way typically modern institutions—such as bureaucracy and the corporation—threaten the attainment of liberty, equality, and democracy."

* * *

ZYSKIND, Harold 1917-

PERSONAL: Born March 3, 1917, in Hurtsboro, Ala.; son of Jacob (a merchant) and Betty (Rubin) Zyskind; married Mascha Lehrer (a realtor), May 5, 1944; children: John. *Education:* University of Chicago, Ph.D., 1964. *Religion:* Jewish. *Home address:* Hill Crescent, Belle Terre, N.Y. 11777. *Office:* Department of Philosophy, State University of New York at Stony Brook, Stony Brook, N.Y. 11790.

CAREER: University of Chicago, Chicago, Ill., 1946-57, began as instructor, became assistant professor of humanities; State University of New York at Stony Brook, 1957—, began as associate professor, now professor of philosophy. *Military service:* U.S. Army, 1941-45; became major. *Member:* American Philosophical Association, Rhetoric Society of America.

WRITINGS: (With Robert Sternfeld) *Voiceless University*, Jossey-Bass, 1970.

WORK IN PROGRESS: Continuing research on philosophy and rhetoric.